**The definitive guide to
the global game**

ALMANACK
OF WORLD
FOOTBALL
2009

Guy Oliver

<u>headline</u>

the-almanack.com

First published in 2008
by HEADLINE PUBLISHING GROUP

1

Front cover photographs: (left) Manchester United celebrate winning the UEFA Champions League after
beating Chelsea on penalties in the final in Moscow - *Action Images/Michael Regan*;
(centre left) Atlético Madrid's Sergio Agüero in action for Argentina - *Sportsphoto Ltd*;
(centre right) Patricio Urrutua lifts the Copa Libertadores after LDU Quito became the first Ecuadorian club to
win the trophy - *Action Images*; (right) Spain's Fernando Torres, scorer of the winning goal in the Euro 2008
final, in action for Liverpool - *Sportsphoto Ltd*

Spine photograph: Spain with the new Henri Delauney trophy after beating Germany 1-0 in the final of
Euro 2008 in Vienna - *Action Images*

Back cover photographs: (left) Karim Benzema in action for Olympique Lyonnais - *Action Images*;
(centre left) Action from the 2007 AFC Champions League final between Japan's Urawa Reds and Sepahan
from Iran - *Action Images*; (centre right) Ghana's Michael Essien in action for Chelsea - *Action Images/Lee
Smith*; (right) Egyptian players hold aloft the Africa Cup of Nations trophy after their 1-0 victory over
Cameroon in the final in Accra - *Action Images*

A CIP catalogue record for this title is available from the British Library

ISBN 978 0 7553 1510 9

Design: Guy Oliver
Design consultant: Peter Ward
Cover design: Head Design Ltd

Printed and bound in Great Britain by Mackays of Chatham PLC,
Chatham, Kent

The data within the Almanack of World Football has been obtained from a variety of sources, official
and unofficial. The Author cannot vouch for the accuracy of the data in all cases.

Headline's policy is to use papers that are natural, renewable and recyclable products and
made from wood grown in sustainable forests. The logging and manufacturing processes
are expected to conform to the environmental regulations of the country of origin.

HEADLINE PUBLISHING GROUP
An Hachette Livre UK Company
338 Euston Road
London NW1 3BH

www.headline.co.uk
www.hachettelivre.co.uk

CONTENTS

PART ONE – FIFA AND WORLD FOOTBALL

PART TWO – THE NATIONS OF THE WORLD

4 CONTENTS

PART THREE – THE
CONTINENTAL CONFEDERATIONS

ASIA

AFRICA

CENTRAL & NORTH AMERICA, THE CARIBBEAN

SOUTH AMERICA

OCEANIA

EUROPE

MISCELLANEOUS

ALPHABETICAL LISTING OF
THE NATIONS OF THE WORLD

As the 208 member associations of FIFA are organised in the Almanack according to their trigram and not alphabetically, the following table provides a quick alphabetical reference to page numbers.

COUNTRY		PAGE	COUNTRY		PAGE
Afghanistan	AFG	57	Bhutan	BHU	136
Albania	ALB	61	Bolivia	BOL	148
Algeria	ALG	65	Bosnia-Herzegovina	BIH	138
American Samoa	ASA	95	Botswana	BOT	152
Andorra	AND	69	Brazil	BRA	156
Angola	ANG	72	British Virgin Islands	VGB	806
Anguilla	AIA	59	Brunei Darussalam	BRU	172
Antigua and Barbuda	ATG	97	Bulgaria	BUL	174
Argentina	ARG	78	Burkina Faso	BFA	129
Armenia	ARM	89	Burma (Myanmar)	MYA	565
Aruba	ARU	93	Burundi	BDI	118
Australia	AUS	99	Cambodia	CAM	178
Austria	AUT	105	Cameroon	CMR	203
Azerbaijan	AZE	109	Canada	CAN	180
Bahamas	BAH	113	Cape Verde Islands	CPV	222
Bahrain	BHR	132	Cayman Islands	CAY	183
Bangladesh	BAN	115	Central African Republic	CTA	232
Barbados	BRB	169	Chad	CHA	188
Belarus	BLR	142	Chile	CHI	190
Belgium	BEL	120	China PR	CHN	195
Belize	BLZ	146	Chinese Taipei (Taiwan)	TPE	758
Benin	BEN	124	Colombia	COL	215
Bermuda	BER	126	Comoros	COM	220

ACKNOWLEDGEMENTS

My thanks to Mark Gleeson and to Michael Church for their invaluable contributions this year. Mark's knowledge of African football is unsurpassed as is Michael's of Asian football and the Almanack is a better publication for their involvement; Thanks to Ricardo Setyon for his Americas input; to Daniel Fein and Tom Lewis for their annual contributions. Tom finds himself in my old job as producer of Futbol Mundial - required viewing if you haven't seen it. Huge thanks once again to Olly Greenleaves for his meticulous statistical input and to Michael Oliver for his help with the text. What a team! Tom Chittick continues his sterling work behind the scenes at the Almanack particularly in his new role as head of web development and a big welcome to Gareth Edwards and Armando Paganelli. A belated thanks also to Julia Bindman; to David Wilson and Lorraine Jerram at Headline and to Rupert Daniels at World Group Media. Thank you all for your wise counsel. The biggest thanks of all to my family. It's a big job writing the Almanack but to move house at the same time has taken a superhuman effort from all of us. My wife Sharyn has even found the time to help on the book. My love to you and to my boys Ally and Archie, to Dorothy and to my Mum and Dad - it's been fantastic having you down the road from us.

Guy Oliver, Thorney Hill, The New Forest, August 2008

PART ONE

FIFA AND
WORLD FOOTBALL

FIFA

Fédération Internationale de Football Association

Sepp Blatter's crusade to protect the interests of national teams worldwide was greatly strengthened when the 2008 FIFA Congress in Sydney overwhelmingly approved his "6+5" concept. This would require clubs to field six players eligible to play for their country's national team. The voting was 155 to 5. Stiff opposition came from the European Union which forbids the restriction of movement on workers within its boundaries. Only 27 of the 208 nations affiliated to FIFA are within the EU, but with the flow of players to the EU greater than ever, the "6+5" concept would be unworkable without its cooperation. The concept was proposed amid growing dissatisfaction with the power wielded by a few elite clubs and leagues. This was epitomised by the reaction to the English Premier League's plan to play a 39th round of games abroad. The move was almost universally condemned – even within the UK – where it was seen as predatory, based on greed, and at the same time undermining other league structures around the world. Blatter argues that "6+5" is not only necessary to enhance the development of young players, but to combat the growing inequality between clubs and national teams. Clubs are also experiencing this same problem between themselves. He believes that the current situation is reducing overall competitiveness and

THE FIFA BIG COUNT OF 2006

	Male	Female		Total
Number of players	238 557 000	25 995 000	Referees and Assistant Referees	843 000
Professionals	113 000		Admin, Coaches, Technical, Medical	4 214 000
Amateurs 18+	15 481 000		Number of clubs	301 000
Youth under 18	21 548 000		Number of teams	1 752 000
Unregistered	226 265 000		Clubs with women's teams	26 000
Total involved in football	264 552 000		Players as % of population	4.13%

making results easier to predict. If the situation is not addressed, Blatter argues, then the very basis on which football has existed since the latter part of the 19th century will be compromised. The EU aside, Blatter's most difficult task may be to persuade armchair supporters worldwide, that a levelling up of standards for the majority of clubs, as a consequence of "6+5", must be for the greater good of the game. FIFA has never traditionally been involved with the organisation of club football but that changed with the introduction of the FIFA Club World Cup in 2000 and its relaunch in 2005. FIFA Congress decided to move the event from its traditional venue in Japan by awarding the hosting of the 2009 and 2010 tournaments to the United Arab Emirates in a bid to increase its profile, although the Japanese were awarded the 2011 and 1012 tournaments. The 2007 FIFA Club World Cup saw a first winner from Europe when Milan beat Boca Juniors 4-2 in the final while other FIFA tournaments played during the year included the FIFA Women's World Cup in China - won by Germany with a 2-0 victory over Brazil in the final - and the FIFA U-17 World Cup in South Korea in which Nigeria beat Spain 3-0 on penalties after a 0-0 draw.

Fédération Internationale de Football Association (FIFA)
FIFA-Strasse 20, PO Box, 8044 Zürich, Switzerland
Tel +41 43 222 7777   Fax +41 43 222 7878
contact@fifa.org
www.fifa.com
President: BLATTER Joseph S.
General Secretary: VALCKE Jérôme   Deputy General Secretary: KATTNER Marksu
Delegate of the President for Special Affairs: CHAMPAGNE Jérôme

FIFA EXECUTIVE COMMITTEE

President: BLATTER Joseph S. SUI

Senior Vice-President: GRONDONA Julio ARG

Vice-President: HAYATOU Issa CMR

Vice-President: CHUNG Mong Joon, Dr KOR

Vice-President: WARNER Jack A. TRI

Vice-President: VILLAR LLONA Angel Maria ESP

Vice-President: PLATINI Michel FRA

Vice-President: TEMARII Reynald TAH

Vice-President: THOMPSON Geoff ENG

ORDINARY MEMBERS OF THE EXECUTIVE COMMITTEE

D'HOOGHE Michel, Dr BEL

TEIXEIRA Ricardo Terra BRA

BIN HAMMAM Mohamed QAT

ERZIK Senes TUR

BLAZER Chuck USA

MAKUDI Worawi THA

LEOZ Nicolás, Dr PAR

KOLOSKOV Viacheslav, Dr RUS

OGURA Junji JPN

CHIBOUB Slim TUN

ADAMU Amos, Dr NGA

LEFKARITIS Marios CYP

ANOUMA Jacques CIV

BECKENBAUER Franz GER

SALGUERO Rafael GUA

General Secretary: VALCKE Jérôme

OTHER FIFA COMMITTEES

	Chairman	Organising Committee for...	Chairman
Emergency Committee	BLATTER Joseph S.	The FIFA World Cup	HAYATOU Issa
Finance Committee	GRONDONA Julio H.	The FIFA Confederations Cup	BLAZER Chuck
Internal Audit Committee	CARRARO Franco, Dr	The Olympic Football Tournaments	HAYATOU Issa
Referees' Committee	VILLAR LLONA Angel Maria	The FIFA U-20 World Cup	WARNER Jack A
Technical & Development Committee	PLATINI Michel	The FIFA U-17 World Cup	WARNER Jack A.
Sports Medical Committee	D'HOOGHE Michel, Dr	Women's Football and FIFA Women's World Cup	MAKUDI Worawi
Players' Status Committee	MAYER-VORFELDER Gerhard	The U-20 and U-17 Women's World Cups	BALZER Chuck
Legal Committee	WILL David H.	Futsal and Beach Soccer Committee	TEIXEIRA Ricardo Terra
Fair Play and Social Responsibility	ERZIK Senes	The FIFA Club World Cup	KOLOSKOV Viacheslav, Dr
Media Committee	MAYER-VORFELDER Gerhard	Associations Committee	KOLOSKOV Viacheslav, Dr
Football Committee	VILLAR LLONA Angel Maria	Marketing and Television Advisory Board	GRONDONA Julio H.
Strategic Studies Committee	BLATTER Joseph S.	Goal Bureau	BIN HAMMAM Mohamed
FIFA Club Task Force	CHIBOUB Slim	FIFA Medical Assessment and Research Centre	D'HOOGHE Michel, Dr
Doping Control Sub-Committee	D'HOOGHE Michel, Dr	Disciplinary Committee	MATHIER Marcel, Me.
Appeal Committee	SALGUERO Rafael	Ethics Committee	COE Sebastian

FIFA TOURNAMENTS

FIFA WORLD CUP

Year	Host Country	Winners	Score	Runners-up	Venue
1930	Uruguay	Uruguay	4-2	Argentina	Centenario, Montevideo
1934	Italy	Italy	2-1	Czechoslovakia	PNF, Rome
1938	France	Italy	4-2	Hungary	Colombes, Paris
1950	Brazil	Uruguay	2-1	Brazil	Maracana, Rio de Janeiro
1954	Switzerland	Germany FR	3-2	Hungary	Wankdorf, Berne
1958	Sweden	Brazil	5-2	Sweden	Råsunda, Stockholm
1962	Chile	Brazil	3-1	Czechoslovakia	Estadio Nacional, Santiago
1966	England	England	4-2	Germany FR	Wembley, London
1970	Mexico	Brazil	4-1	Italy	Azteca, Mexico City
1974	Germany FR	Germany FR	2-1	Netherlands	Olympiastadion, Munich
1978	Argentina	Argentina	3-1	Netherlands	Monumental, Buenos Aires
1982	Spain	Italy	3-1	Germany FR	Bernabeu, Madrid
1986	Mexico	Argentina	3-2	Germany FR	Azteca, Mexico City
1990	Italy	Germany FR	1-0	Argentina	Olimpico, Rome
1994	USA	Brazil	0-0 3-2p	Italy	Rose Bowl, Pasadena
1998	France	France	3-0	Brazil	Stade de France, Paris
2002	Korea Rep/Japan	Brazil	2-0	Germany	International Stadium, Yokohama
2006	Germany	Italy	1-1 5-3p	France	Olympiastadion, Berlin

The FIFA World Cup is the most popular single sports event in the world and ranks alongside the Olympic Games as the focus of sporting attention in the years that the two sporting festivals are held. When FIFA was founded in 1904 it reserved the right to organise a world championship for its members. However, it took more than a quarter of a century for that aim to become reality and it wasn't until the Barcelona Congress of 1929 that a resolution was passed paving the way for the first tournament to be held the following year in Uruguay. The reason the World Cup was such a long time in coming was due to the huge appeal of the Football Tournament of the Olympic Games, the winners of which were regarded as world champions. The Olympic tournament had first been officially organised in 1908 but by the late 1920s there was growing disquiet amongst the members of FIFA that, because of the amateur ethos and the surge of professionalism after 1925, especially within central Europe, the best players were no longer eligible to compete. Although FIFA was responsible for organising the Olympic Football Tournament, the then FIFA President Jules Rimet realised that the best way forward was to organise a separate tournament that was open to anyone. Just 13 teams entered the first tournament, a figure that has risen to over 200 today. It may be the dream of every footballer to take part in the FIFA World Cup but only a very select club of players and nations have won the coveted prize; seven nations and 274 players to be precise. Staged every four years, the finals have been hosted by 15 countries with Mexico, Italy, France and Germany each having been granted the honour twice. For many years the hosting would alternate between the Americas and Europe but in 2002 Asia welcomed the tournament for the first time and in 2010 South Africa will entertain as each continent is given a chance on a rotational basis. Much of the excitement of the FIFA World Cup can also be found in the qualifying tournaments, which in some parts of the world are now spread over nearly three years. The 32 places in the finals are decided on a continental basis with the hosts, but no longer the holders, qualifying automatically. For the 2006 tournament South America had four guaranteed places, Europe 13, Africa five, Asia four and Central and North America three, with the final two places decided via a series of play-offs between all the Confederations bar Europe and Africa. For many just making it to the finals is achievement enough, although for the elite the aim remains winning the Cup itself. Not that the trophy is actually a cup anymore. For the first eight tournaments it was possible to celebrate by drinking champagne from the Jules Rimet trophy, but since 1974 the solid gold trophy is in the form of a globe, held aloft by two athletes at the moment of victory.

FIFA WORLD CUP MEDALS TABLE

	Country	G	S	B	F	SF
1	Brazil	5	2	2	7	7
2	Italy	4	2	1	6	7
3	Germany	3	4	3	7	10
4	Argentina	2	2		4	3
5	Uruguay	2			2	3
6	France	1	1	2	2	5
7	England	1			1	2
8	Czechoslovakia		2		2	2
	Hungary		2		2	2
10	Netherlands		2		2	1
11	Sweden		1	2	1	3
12	Poland			2		1
13	Austria			1		2
	Portugal			1		2
	Yugoslavia			1		2
16	Chile			1		1
	Croatia			1		1
	Turkey			1		1
	USA			1		1
20	Belgium					1
	Bulgaria					1
	Korea Republic					1
	Soviet Union					1
		18	18	19	36	60

This table represents the Gold (winners), Silver (runners-up) and Bronze (3rd place) winners of nations in the FIFA World Cup, along with the number of appearances in the final and semi-finals

FIFA WOMEN'S WORLD CUP

Year	Host Country	Winners	Score	Runners-up	Venue
1991	China PR	USA	2-1	Norway	Tianhe, Guangzhou
1995	Sweden	Norway	2-0	Germany	Råsunda, Stockholm
1999	USA	USA	0-0 5-4p	China PR	Rose Bowl, Pasadena
2003	USA	Germany	2-1	Sweden	Home Depot Centre, Carson
2007	China PR	Germany	2-0	Brazil	Hongkou, Shanghai

With the rapid growth of women's football since the 1970s it was a logical step for FIFA to organise a World Cup for women in 1991 to replace the growing number of unofficial tournaments that were being staged around the world. As early as 1970, 40,000 fans in the Stadio Communale in Turin watched Denmark beat Italy to win the Coppa del Mondo while the following year the Danes won the Mundial 1971 in front of 110,000 fans in Mexico City's Azteca Stadium, beating the hosts in the final of a tournament that had been played to packed stadia throughout. In 1988 FIFA organised the FIFA Women's Invitation Tournament in China PR. Won by Norway, who beat Sweden in the final in Guangzhou, the event was a huge success although it isn't counted as part of the FIFA Women's World Cup record. The first official tournament was held three years later, in 1991, and again hosted by China PR. The winners were the United States, a major player in the popularisation of the women's game thanks to the seven million women involved with football there. Two of the tournaments since then have been held in the USA although the 2003 tournament should have been held in China but was switched to the States due to the SARS outbreak in the Far East. When China did host the tournament again - in 2007 - it was won by Germany, who by beating Brazil in the final, became the most successful nation over the five editions played.

FIFA WOMEN'S WORLD CUP MEDALS TABLE

	Country	G	S	B	F	SF
1	Germany	2	1		3	4
2	USA	2		3	2	5
3	Norway	1	1		2	4
4	Brazil		1	1	1	2
	Sweden		1	1	1	2
6	China PR		1		1	2
7	Canada					1
		5	5	5	10	20

This table represents the Gold (winners), Silver (runners-up) and Bronze (3rd place) winners of nations in the FIFA Women's World Cup, along with the number of appearances in the final and semi-finals

FIFA CLUB WORLD CUP

Year	Host Country	Winners	Score	Runners-up	Venue
2000	Brazil	Corinthians, BRA	0-0 4-3p	Vasco da Gama, BRA	Maracana, Rio de Janeiro
2005	Japan	São Paulo FC, BRA	1-0	Liverpool, ENG	International, Yokohama
2006	Japan	Internacional, BRA	1-0	Barcelona, ESP	International, Yokohama
2007	Japan	Milan, ITA	4-2	Boca Juniors, ARG	International, Yokohama

For many years fans around the world were denied the chance to watch their teams play against clubs from different Confederations and vie for the title of world champions, but since 2000 that has become a reality. European critics railed against FIFA when the FIFA Club World Cup was introduced, citing an overcrowded fixture list, but after taking on their concerns, FIFA announced that from 2005 the tournament would replace the annual Toyota Cup played between the European and South American club champions and that it would be held annually thereafter. By adopting a straight knock-out format, with the European and South American champions joining at the semi-final stage, fixtures have been kept to a minimum. The 2009 and 2010 tournaments will be hosted by the United Arab Emirates before returning to Japan for the two editions after that.

MEN'S OLYMPIC FOOTBALL TOURNAMENT

Year	Host City	Winners	Score	Runners-up	Venue
1896	Athens	No tournament took place			
1900	Paris	Great Britain	4-0	France	Vélodrome Municipal, Paris
1904	St Louis	Canada	4-0	USA	Francis Field, St Louis
1906	Athens	Denmark	9-0	Greece	Podilatodromino, Athens
1908	London	England (as GBR)	2-0	Denmark	White City, London
1912	Stockholm	England (as GBR)	4-2	Denmark	Stockholms Stadion, Stockholm
1916	Berlin	Games cancelled			
1920	Antwerp	Belgium	2-0	Czechoslovakia	Olympisch Stadion, Antwerp
1924	Paris	Uruguay	3-0	Switzerland	Colombes, Paris
1928	Amsterdam	Uruguay	1-1 2-1	Argentina	Olympisch Stadion, Amsterdam
1932	Los Angeles	No football tournament played			
1936	Berlin	Italy	2-1	Austria	Olympiastadion, Berlin
1940	Tokyo/Helsinki	Games cancelled			
1944	London	Games cancelled			
1948	London	Sweden	3-1	Yugoslavia	Wembley, London
1952	Helsinki	Hungary	2-0	Yugoslavia	Olympiastadion, Helsinki
1956	Melbourne	Soviet Union	1-0	Yugoslavia	Melbourne Cricket Ground
1960	Rome	Yugoslavia	3-1	Denmark	Flaminio, Rome
1964	Tokyo	Hungary	2-1	Czechoslovakia	National Stadium, Tokyo
1968	Mexico City	Hungary	4-1	Bulgaria	Azteca, Mexico City
1972	Munich	Poland	2-1	Hungary	Olympiastadion, Munich
1976	Montreal	German DR	3-1	Poland	Olympic Stadium, Montreal
1980	Moscow	Czechoslovakia	1-0	German DR	Centralny, Moscow
1984	Los Angeles	France	2-0	Brazil	Rose Bowl, Pasadena
1988	Seoul	Soviet Union	2-1	Brazil	Olympic Stadium, Seoul
1992	Barcelona	Spain	3-2	Poland	Camp Nou, Barcelona
1996	Atlanta	Nigeria	3-2	Argentina	Sanford Stadium, Athens
2000	Sydney	Cameroon	2-2 5-4p	Spain	Olympic Stadium, Sydney
2004	Athens	Argentina	1-0	Paraguay	Olympic Stadium, Athens

The history of the Men's Olympic Football Tournament can be divided into three broad phases. Before the introduction of the FIFA World Cup in 1930 the winners were lauded as world champions, an honour won twice by Uruguay and England (playing under the banner of Great Britain) and once by Belgium. After 1928 the tournament remained amateur in a world increasingly dominated by professionalism, a situation exploited by countries from the communist bloc who were professionals in all but name. From 1952 until 1980 teams from behind the Iron Curtain walked off with every title, notably the Hungarians, winners in 1952, 1964 and 1968. For the 1984 and 1988 tournaments the amateur restrictions were relaxed with all players who had not taken part in a World Cup eligible to compete, but in 1992 the third major phase began when it became an age-restricted tournament for under-23s although three over-age players were also permitted in the team. Sixteen nations have won Olympic football gold although it is a competition that has been dominated by Europe with only four nations from elsewhere winning the prize. After the legendary triumphs of Uruguay in the 1920s it wasn't until 2004 that another South American team – Argentina – won, and the Olympic title remains the only major title not yet won by Brazil. In 1996 Nigeria broke the duck for Africa and that was followed in Sydney four years later by Cameroon. Four previous winners no longer exist as countries – the Soviet Union, East Germany, Czechoslovakia and Yugoslavia while there is also some confusion as to the inaugural winners. The team representing Great Britain was the famous pre-World War One England amateur team that was so instrumental in spreading the game across Europe, hence the listing as England rather than Great Britain. As with the FIFA World Cup the finalists for the Olympics are decided by continental qualifying competitions which in 2004 resulted in four finalists from Africa and Europe (including hosts Greece), three from Asia, two from South America, two from the rest of the Americas and one from Oceania.

WOMEN'S OLYMPIC FOOTBALL TOURNAMENT

Year	Host City	Winners	Score	Runners-up	Venue
1996	Atlanta	USA	2-1	China	Sanford Stadium, Athens
2000	Sydney	Norway	3-2	USA	Sydney Football Stadium, Sydney
2004	Athens	USA	2-1	Brazil	Karaiskaki, Piraeus

Women's football is a very recent addition to the list of Olympic sports but in conjunction with the FIFA Women's World Cup it now provides the sport with a second championship of world repute, as, unlike the men's Olympic Football Tournament, the full national teams can enter. The 1996 games in Atlanta were the perfect launch pad for the Women's Olympic Football Tournament with the final between the USA and China witnessed by 76,489 in the Sanford Stadium in Athens, Georgia, while the average for all games was 39,362. The United States have remained the dominant force since winning the first final against China, losing to Norway in Sydney and then winning again in 2004 against Brazil. Whereas the participants for the 1996 tournament qualified by finishing among the top eight in the 1995 Women's World Cup, there is now a qualifying tournament run along continental lines.

FIFA CONFEDERATIONS CUP

Year	Host Country	Winners	Score	Runners-up	Venue
1992	Saudi Arabia	Argentina	3-1	Saudi Arabia	King Fahd, Riyadh
1995	Saudi Arabia	Denmark	2-0	Argentina	King Fahd, Riyadh
1997	Saudi Arabia	Brazil	6-0	Australia	King Fahd, Riyadh
1999	Mexico	Mexico	4-3	Brazil	Azteca, Mexico City
2001	Korea/Japan	France	1-0	Japan	International Stadium, Yokohama
2003	France	France	1-0	Cameroon	Stade de France, Paris
2005	Germany	Brazil	4-1	Argentina	Waldstadion, Frankfurt

Conceived in 1992, the Confederations Cup's purpose was to bring together the continental champions from around the world. Initially known as the King Fahd Cup, it was later rebranded the FIFA Confederations Cup in 1997 when it came under FIFA's control. Riyadh in Saudi Arabia staged the first three editions, but from 1999 other countries were give the opportunity to host the tournament in an effort to broaden its appeal and before the 2002 and 2006 FIFA World Cups it was used as a timely trial run in Korea Republic and Japan in 2001 and in Germany in 2005. After drawing criticism from within Europe, especially among the big clubs who complained of fixture overcrowding, FIFA responded by switching the tournament from a two year to a four year cycle. As in 2001 and 2005 it will now be used as a trial run before each FIFA World Cup with the next edition in South Africa in 2009.

FIFA FUTSAL WORLD CHAMPIONSHIP

Year	Host Country	Winners	Score	Runners-up	Venue
1989	Netherlands	Brazil	2-1	Netherlands	Rotterdam
1992	Hong Kong	Brazil	4-1	United States	Hong Kong
1996	Spain	Brazil	6-4	Spain	Barcelona
2000	Guatemala	Spain	4-3	Brazil	Guatemala City
2004	Chinese Taipei	Spain	2-1	Italy	Taipei City

Futsal, the five-a-side indoor version of football, has become an increasingly important part of FIFA's work and since 1989 there have been five FIFA Futsal World Championships. The first three were won by Brazil, the major power in the game, though that position has been challenged by Spain, who have won the past two titles. Via a series of continental qualifiers, most of which double up as continental championships, 16 teams qualify for the finals. Games consist of two periods of 20 minutes and any of seven substitutes may be brought on or taken off throughout the game as many times as desired.

FIFA U–20 WORLD CUP

Year	Host Country	Winners	Score	Runners-up	Final Venue
1977	Tunisia	Soviet Union	2-2 9-8p	Mexico	El Menzah, Tunis
1979	Japan	Argentina	3-1	Soviet Union	National Stadium, Tokyo
1981	Australia	Germany FR	4-0	Qatar	Sydney Cricket Ground
1983	Mexico	Brazil	1-0	Argentina	Azteca, Mexico City
1985	Soviet Union	Brazil	1-0	Spain	Centralny, Moscow
1987	Chile	Yugoslavia	1-1 5-4p	Germany FR	Estadio Nacional, Santiago
1989	Saudi Arabia	Portugal	2-0	Nigeria	King Fahd, Riyadh
1991	Portugal	Portugal	0-0 4-2p	Brazil	Da Luz, Lisbon
1993	Australia	Brazil	2-1	Ghana	Sydney Football Stadium, Sydney
1995	Qatar	Argentina	2-0	Brazil	Khalifa, Doha
1997	Malaysia	Argentina	2-1	Uruguay	Shahalam Stadium, Shah Alam
1999	Nigeria	Spain	4-0	Japan	Surulere, Lagos
2001	Argentina	Argentina	3-0	Ghana	Jose Amalfitani, Buenos Aires
2003	UAE	Brazil	1-0	Spain	Zayed Sports City, Abu Dhabi
2005	Netherlands	Argentina	2-1	Nigeria	Galgenwaard, Utrecht
2007	Canada	Argentina	2-1	Czech Republic	National Soccer Stadium, Toronto

As well as the Football Tournament of the Olympic Games, FIFA now organises four other major age-restricted championships. The longest established of these is the FIFA U-20 World Cup which before 2007 was known as the FIFA World Youth Championship. Since its inception in 1977 in Tunisia, the tournament has been held every two years and countries from all six Confederations have hosted the event at least once. The winners of the FIFA U-20 World Cup have all hailed from either Europe or South America, with Argentina having won six titles and Brazil four. At first, many were sceptical of the value of a youth tournament, especially with the problems associated with over-aged players, but it seems that this issue has died down, largely thanks to the harsh penalties handed out to those caught cheating. The FIFA U-20 World Cup is now seen in most countries as a vital step in the education of the top young footballers, where they can encounter high pressure tournament conditions and different styles of play early in their careers and it is surely no coincidence that countries like Brazil, Argentina and Spain, where support for the tournament is strong, consistently produce young players of a very high calibre. The first tournament, in 1977, was also the first global tournament to take place in Africa, with the Soviet Union beating Mexico 9-8 on penalties in Tunis. Through the years, many great players have graced the tournament, none more so than in 1979 when Diego Maradona lead his team to a title that was celebrated in Argentina almost as much as the FIFA World Cup win the year before. Germany's only title came two years later in Australia, when they beat Qatar, the smallest nation ever to appear in a FIFA final. Then it was the turn of Brazil, who won the 1983 and 1985 tournaments with players such as current national team coach, Dunga, and the 1994 FIFA World Cup winners Cláudio Taffarel, Jorginho and Bebeto. One of the most famous triumphs came in Chile in 1987, when a European team won a FIFA tournament on South American soil for the first and, so far, only time. The triumphant Yugoslav side contained great names such as Zvonimir Boban, Robert Prosinecki and Davor Suker. The next two tournaments, in 1989 and 1991, saw back-to-back wins for Portugal with a group of players that were soon to become known as the 'Golden Generation,' notably Figo, João Pinto, Paulo Sousa and Rui Costa. In the 1990s, Argentina rose to prominence again, winning in 1995, 1997 and 2001 under the guidance of coach Jose Pekerman, and then again in 2005 and 2007 to seal a record six titles. In-between, Spain won a first title in 1999 in Nigeria, the first time a FIFA tournament had been played in sub-Saharan Africa.

FIFA U–17 WOMEN'S WORLD CUP

Year	Host Country	Winners	Score	Runners-up	Final Venue
2008	New Zealand				

The introduction of the FIFA U–17 Women's World Cup completes the line-up of possible FIFA tournaments with the first edition taking place in New Zealand in 2008

FIFA U–17 WORLD CHAMPIONSHIP

Year	Host Country	Winners	Score	Runners-up	Final Venue
1985	China	Nigeria	2-0	Germany FR	Workers' Stadium, Beijing
1987	Canada	Soviet Union	1-1 3-1p	Nigeria	Varsity Stadium, Toronto
1989	Scotland	Saudi Arabia	2-2 5-4p	Scotland	Hampden Park, Glasgow
1991	Italy	Ghana	1-0	Spain	Comunale, Florence
1993	Japan	Nigeria	2-1	Ghana	National Stadium, Tokyo
1995	Ecuador	Ghana	3-2	Brazil	Monumental, Guayaquil
1997	Egypt	Brazil	2-1	Ghana	National Stadium, Cairo
1999	New Zealand	Brazil	0-0 8-7p	Australia	North Harbour, Auckland
2001	Trinidad	France	3-0	Nigeria	Hasely Crawford, Port of Spain
2003	Finland	Brazil	1-0	Spain	Töölö, Helsinki
2005	Peru	Mexico	3-0	Brazil	Estadio Nacional, Lima
2007	Korea Republic	Nigeria	0-0 3-0p	Spain	World Cup Stadium, Seoul

The second of the FIFA age-restricted tournaments to be introduced was the FIFA U-17 World Championship, now known as the FIFA U-17 World Cup. It has been held every two years since 1985 and countries from all six Confederations have hosted the event at least once. Brazil and Nigeria are the most successful nations in the history of the tournament with three titles each. Competition has been much more open than in the U-20 event, with African, Asian and North American sides all challenging the supremacy of the South Americans and Europeans by winning tournaments. Right from the start, Nigeria beat Germany 2-0 in Beijing in the final of the inaugural 1985 tournament to become the first African world champions at any level. The Nigerians reached the final again in Toronto two years later, but were beaten on penalties by the Soviet Union. In the third tournament, Saudi Arabia were the surprise winners, beating Scotland in another final decided on penalties to give Asia its first world championship. By reaching the final, the Scots were the first and so far only host nation to make it that far. African supremacy at this level was then confirmed in Italy in 1991, Japan in 1993 and in Ecuador in 1995, with Ghana appearing in all three finals, winning in 1991 and 1995 and losing to Nigeria in Tokyo in 1993. In the late 1990s, Brazil, rather belatedly, began to flex their muscles with Ronaldinho inspiring his country to its first triumph in the 1997 finals in Egypt - a title successfully defended two years later in New Zealand. France was the first European winner for 14 years when they beat Nigeria in the 2001 final in Trinidad and Tobago, but overall the European record has been poor with only France and Spain reaching the final since the start of the 1990s. Spain's first appearance in the final came in 2003, in Finland, but they were beaten by a Brazil team winning a record third title. In the 2005 final in Peru, Mexico beat Brazil to win a first world championship for the CONCACAF region, the only confederation until then, apart from Oceania, not to have won the trophy.

FIFA U–20 WOMEN'S WORLD CUP

Year	Host Country	Winners	Score	Runners-up	Final Venue
2002	Canada	United States	1-0	Canada	Commonwealth, Edmonton
2004	Thailand	Germany	2-0	China PR	Rajamangala National, Bangkok
2006	Russia	Korea DPR	5-0	China PR	Lokomotiv, Moscow

In 2002, due to the growing interest in women's football, the third of FIFA's youth tournaments was launched, the FIFA U-19 Women's World Championship. After two editions, the tournament was changed to an under 20 contest to bring it in line with the men's event and from the 2008 tournament it will be known as the FIFA U–20 Women's World Cup. The two editions of the U-19 event were played in Canada and Thailand, and the rise in standards has surprised even those involved in the women's game. The USA and Germany have dominated, with the Americans winning the inaugural event and then losing in the semi-finals to Germany in 2004; Germany going on to beat China PR in the final. There were surprise winners of the 2006 tournament, however, when North Korea won their first FIFA title by beating China 5-0 in the final.

FIFA WORLD PLAYER 2007

FIFA WORLD PLAYER 2007

Rank	Player	Club	Nat	1st	x5	2nd	x3	3rd	x1	Total
1	Kaká	Milan	BRA	179	895	42	126	26	26	1047
2	Lionel Messi	Barcelona	ARG	40	200	86	258	46	46	504
3	Cristiano Ronaldo	Manchester United	POR	39	195	58	174	57	57	426
4	Didier Drogba	Chelsea	CIV	20	100	25	75	34	34	209
5	Ronaldinho	Barcelona	BRA	7	35	17	51	23	23	109
6	Steven Gerrard	Liverpool	ENG	2	10	16	48	10	10	68
7	Andrea Pirlo	Milan	ITA	2	10	11	33	14	14	57
8	Thierry Henry	Barcelona	FRA	3	15	8	24	15	15	54
9	Fabio Cannavaro	Real Madrid	ITA	5	25	6	18	4	4	47
10	Gianluigi Buffon	Juventus	ITA	0	0	7	21	10	10	31
11	Franck Ribery	Bayern München	FRA	1	5	7	21	4	4	30
12	Samuel Eto'o	Barcelona	CMR	3	15	3	9	5	5	29
13	Wayne Rooney	Manchester United	ENG	2	10	1	3	9	9	22
14	Miroslav Klose	Bayern München	GER	2	10	2	6	5	5	21
15	Michael Essien	Chelsea	GHA	0	0	5	15	5	5	20
16	Juan Román Riquelme	Boca Juniors	ARG	2	10	1	3	6	6	19
17	Petr Cech	Chelsea	CZE	1	5	2	6	7	7	18
18	Ruud Van Nistelrooij	Real Madrid	ESP	1	5	3	9	4	4	18
19	Frank Lampard	Chelsea	ENG	1	5	1	3	3	3	11
20	Deco	Barcelona	POR	0	0	0	0	9	9	9
21	Juninho	Olympique Lyonnais	BRA	0	0	3	9	0	0	9
22	Gennaro Gattuso	Milan	ITA	0	0	1	3	5	5	8
23	John Terry	Chelsea	ENG	0	0	1	3	3	3	6
24	Patrick Vieira	Internazionale	FRA	0	0	2	6	0	0	6
25	Rafael Marquez	Barcelona	MEX	0	0	1	3	2	2	5
26	Fernando Torres	Liverpool	ESP	0	0	1	3	1	1	4
27	Alessandro Nesta	Milan	ITA	0	0	0	0	2	2	2
28	Carlos Tévez	Manchester United	ARG	0	0	0	0	1	1	1
29	Philipp Lahm	Bayern München	GER	0	0	0	0	0	0	0
30	Lilian Thuram	Barcelona	FRA	0	0	0	0	0	0	0

FIFA WOMEN'S WORLD PLAYER 2007

Rank	Player	Club	Nat	1st	x5	2nd	x3	3rd	x1	Total
1	Marta	Umeå IK	BRA	167	835	44	132	21	21	988
2	Birgit Prinz	1.FFC Frankfurt	GER	44	220	87	261	26	26	507
3	Cristiane	Linköpings FC	BRA	9	45	29	87	18	18	150
4	Kelly Smith	Arsenal	ENG	5	25	19	57	28	28	110
5	Abby Wambach	University of Florida	USA	4	20	14	42	30	30	92
6	Nadine Angerer	Djurgårdens IF Dam	GER	6	30	10	30	23	23	83
7	Kristine Lilly	University of North Carolina	USA	5	25	15	45	12	12	82
8	Daniela	Linköpings FC	BRA	5	25	7	21	26	26	72
9	Renate Lingor	1.FFC Frankfurt	GER	5	25	7	21	16	16	62
10	Ariane Hingst	Djurgårdens IF Dam	GER	6	30	2	6	5	5	41
11	Kerstin Stegemann	SG Wattenscheid 09	GER	4	20	3	9	5	5	34
12	Formiga	Saad EC	BRA	0	0	7	21	11	11	32
13	Han Duan	Dalian	CHN	0	0	3	9	6	6	15
14	Perpetua Nkwocha	Sunnanå SK	NGA	0	0	3	9	6	6	15
15	Li Jie	Beijing	CHN	0	0	4	12	2	2	14
16	Ingvild Stensland	Göteborg FC	NOR	0	0	4	12	2	2	14
17	Ri Un Suk		PRK	1	5	1	3	5	5	13
18	Ragnhild Gulbrandsen	Asker SK	NOR	1	5	0	0	7	7	12
19	Rebecca Smith	Sunnanå SK	NZL	1	5	2	6	0	0	11
20	Adjoa Bayor	Ghatel	GHA	0	0	1	3	5	5	8
21	Lisa de Vanna	AIK Solna	AUS	0	0	1	3	4	4	7
22	Bente Nordby	Djurgårdens IF Dam	NOR	1	5	0	0	2	2	7
23	Christie George	Pelican Stars	NGA	0	0	1	3	2	2	5
24	Cathrine Paaske Sörensen	Brøndby IF	DEN	0	0	1	3	0	0	3
25	Christine Sinclair	Vancouver Whitecaps	CAN	0	0	0	0	2	2	2
26	Ane Stangeland Horpestad	Klepp	NOR	0	0	0	0	0	0	0

Each first placing earns five points • Each second placing earns three points • Each third placing earns one point

FIFA WORLD PLAYER 2007 – HOW THEY VOTED

	Coach	1st	2nd	3rd	Captain	1st	2nd	3rd
AFG	Mohamed Kargar	Kaká	Ronaldo	Henry	Sayed Maqsood	Kaká	Ronaldo	Henry
ALG	Rabah Saadane	Kaká	Buffon	Rooney	Yazid Mansouri	Kaká	Messi	Cech
AND	David Rodrigo	Messi	Kaká	Gerrard	Oscar Sonejee Masand	Kaká	Messi	Drogba
ANG	Luis de Oliveira Gonçalves	Drogba	Kaká	Riquelme	Figueiredo	Drogba	Kaká	Riquelme
ARG	Alfio Basile	no vote	no vote	no vote	Javier Zanetti	Kaká	Buffon	Lampard
ARM	Vardan Minasyan	Ronaldo	Kaká	Messi	Sargis Hovsepyan	Ronaldo	Kaká	Messi
ARU	Marcelo Muñoz	Kaká	Messi	Ronaldo	no vote	no vote	no vote	no vote
ASA	David Brand	Ronaldo	Messi	Kaká	no vote	no vote	no vote	no vote
ATG	Derrick Edwards	Ronaldo	Henry	Ronaldinho	George Dublin	Ronaldo	Ronaldinho	Henry
AUS	Rob Baan	Drogba	Ronaldo	Messi	no vote	no vote	no vote	no vote
AUT	Josef Hickersberger	Kaká	Ronaldo	Riquelme	Andreas Ivanschitz	Kaká	Ribéry	Henry
AZE	Sahin Diniyev	Ronaldo	Messi	Klose	Aslan Karimov	Ronaldo	Messi	Klose
BAH	Neider dos Santos	Kaká	Messi	Ribéry	Happy Hall	Messi	Kaká	Essien
BDI	Adel Amrouche	Kaká	Messi	Ronaldo	Aimé Nzohabonayo	Kaká	Messi	Buffon
BEL	no vote	no vote	no vote	no vote	Timmy Simons	Kaká	Messi	Gerrard
BHR	Milan Macala	Kaká	Ronaldo	Messi	Mohamed Salmeen	Kaká	Messi	Ronaldo
BHU	Khare Basnet	Ronaldo	Ronaldinho	Messi	Pema Chophel	Ronaldinho	Ronaldo	Rooney
BIH	Fuad Muzunovic	Kaká	Ronaldo	Drogba	Zvjezdan Misimovic	Kaká	Ronaldo	Drogba
BLR	Bernd Stange	Kaká	Juninho	Nesta	Alexander Hleb	Kaká	Pirlo	Gattuso
BLZ	Palmeiro Salas	Kaká	Van Nistelrooy	Cannavaro	Harrison Rochez	Messi	Kaká	Márquez
BOL	Erwin Sanchez	Ronaldo	Kaká	Deco	Ronald Baldes	Ronaldo	Kaká	Deco
BRA	Dunga	Pirlo	Drogba	Ronaldo	Lucio	Gerrard	Messi	Klose
BRB	Jerry Sweete	Kaká	Henry	Pirlo	Norman Forde	Gerrard	Cannavarro	Drogba
BUL	Dimitar Penev	Ronaldo	Buffon	Cannavaro	Dimitar Berbatov	Ronaldo	Messi	Messi
CAM	Scott O'Donell	Henry	Messi	Ronaldo	Pok Chan Than	Ronaldo	Gerrard	Riquelme
CAN	Dale Mitchell	Kaká	Messi	Ronaldinho	Kevin McKenna	Kaká	Messi	Ronaldo
CHA	O'Kalah Natoltiga	Kaká	Messi	Torres	Nerembaye Teinkor	Ronaldinho	Messi	Kaká
CHI	Ivo Basay Hatibovic	Messi	Ronaldo	Pirlo	José Marcelo Salas	Kaká	Ribéry	Messi
CHN	Vladimir Petrovic	Kaká	Messi	Drogba	Li Weifeng	Kaká	Gerrard	Eto'o
CIV	Ulrich Stielike	Kaká	Cech	Ribéry	Didier Drogba	Kaká	Pirlo	Cech
CMR	Otto Pfister	Ronaldo	Henry	Kaká	Rigobert Song	Drogba	Essien	Kaká
COD	Joseph Mulamba	Cannavaro	Juninho	Kaká	Gladys Bokese	Messi	Kaká	Van Nistelrooy
COK	Jimmy Katoa	Ronaldo	Buffon	Henry	Tony Jamieson	Pirlo	Drogba	Buffon
COL	Jorge Luis Pinto	Kaká	Pirlo	Messi	Agustin Julio	Ronaldinho	Messi	Buffon
COM	Mohamed Chamité	Henry	Ronaldinho	Drogba	Izzidine Zainoudine	Drogba	Henry	Ronaldinho
CPV	José Rui Aguiar	Ronaldo	Drogba	Kaká	Lito	Ronaldo	Kaká	Ronaldinho
CRC	Hernan Medford	Messi	Kaká	Ronaldo	José Francisco Porras	Messi	Ronaldinho	Ronaldo
CRO	Slaven Bilic	Kaká	Ronaldo	Messi	Niko Kovac	Kaká	Ronaldo	Messi
CUB	Raul Gonzalez Triana	Messi	Kaká	Deco	Yenier Márquez	Messi	Kaká	Deco
CYP	Angelos Anastasiadis	Kaká	Messi	Ronaldo	Yiannis Okkas	Ronaldo	Messi	Kaká
CZE	Karel Brückner	Kaká	Drogba	Pirlo	Tomas Rosicky	Kaká	Gerrard	Ronaldinho
DEN	Morten Olsen	Kaká	Ronaldo	Pirlo	Jon Dahl Tomasson	Pirlo	Drogba	Gattuso
DJI	Mohamed Omar Alt	Drogba	Gerrard	Messi	Miad Charmaké	Messi	Drogba	Pirlo
DMA	Christopher Erickson	Ronaldinho	Kaká	Henry	Colin Bernard	Ronaldinho	Kaká	Ronaldo
DOM	Juan Mojica	Kaká	Messi	Ronaldinho	Kelvin Severino	Kaká	Messi	Tévez
ECU	Luis Fernando Suarez	Kaká	Lampard	Messi	Ivan Hurtado	Ronaldinho	Kaká	Messi
EGY	Hasan Shehata	Kaká	Klose	Drogba	Ahmed Hasan	Kaká	Klose	Drogba
ENG	Steve McClaren	Kaká	Ronaldo	Gattuso	John Terry	Drogba	Messi	Cech
ERI	Haile Tigaber	Messi	Kaká	Ronaldo	Shimangu Yednekatchew	Kaká	Messi	Drogba
ESP	Luis Aragones Suarez	Kaká	Messi	Drogba	Iker Casillas	Van Nistelrooy	Gerrard	Kaká
EST	Viggo Jensen	Kaká	Ronaldo	Messi	Mart Poom	Kaká	Ronaldo	Rooney
FIJ	Juan Carlos Buzzetti	Ronaldo	Kaká	Pirlo	Pita Rabo	Cannavarro	Gerrard	Henry
FIN	Roy Hodgson	Kaká	Gerrard	Ronaldo	Sami Hyypia	Kaká	Gerrard	Nesta
FRA	Raymond Domenech	Drogba	Eto'o	Messi	Patrick Vieira	Kaká	Ronaldo	Messi
FRO	Jogvan Martin Olsen	Ronaldo	Messi	Kaká	Jákup Mikkelsen	Ronaldo	Kaká	Ribéry
GAM	Lamin Sarr	Drogba	Kaká	Rooney	Ousman Koli	Drogba	Essien	Ronaldo
GER	Joachim Löw	Kaká	Messi	Riquelme	Michael Ballack	Kaká	Ronaldo	Drogba
GHA	Claude Le Roy	Kaká	Messi	Ronaldo	Stephen Appiah	Messi	Ronaldo	Essien
GRE	Otto Rehhagel	Klose	Messi	Kaká	Antonios Nikopolidis	Kaká	Drogba	Ronaldo
GUA	Hernan Gomez	Kaká	Messi	Ronaldo	Freddy Thompson	Kaká	Messi	Ronaldinho
HAI	Luis Armelio Garcia	Kaká	Messi	Ronaldo	no vote	no vote	no vote	no vote
HKG	Lai Sun Cheung	Ronaldo	Kaká	Messi	Cheung Sai Ho	Ronaldo	Messi	Kaká
HON	Reinaldo Ruedo Rivera	Messi	Kaká	Ronaldo	Amado Guevara	Kaká	Messi	Ronaldo
HUN	Péter Varhidi	Kaká	Pirlo	Ronaldo	Zoltan Gera	Kaká	Ronaldo	Messi

FIFA WORLD PLAYER 2007 – HOW THEY VOTED

	Coach	1st	2nd	3rd	Captain	1st	2nd	3rd
IND	Robert Houghton	Drogba	Kaká	Ronaldo	Baichung Bhutia	Kaká	Gerrard	Messi
IRL	Stephen Staunton	Messi	Gerrard	Klose	Robert Keane	Messi	Kaká	Pirlo
IRN	no vote	no vote	no vote	no vote	Javad Nekounam	Kaká	Messi	Pirlo
ISL	Eyjolfur Sverrisson	Kaká	Ronaldo	Messi	Eidur Gudjohnsen	Messi	Ronaldo	Kaká
ISR	Dror Kashtani	Kaká	Drogba	Messi	Yossi Benayoun	Kaká	Gerrard	Ronaldo
ITA	Roberto Donadoni	Kaká	Ronaldo	Messi	Fabio Cannavaro	Kaká	Van Nistelrooy	Messi
JAM	Bora Milutinovic	Kaká	Drogba	Márquez	Fabian Taylor	Messi	Kaká	Ronaldo
JOR	Nelo Vingada	Kaká	Messi	Drogba	Faisal Ibrahim	Messi	Eto'o	Ronaldinho
JPN	Ivan Osim	Kaká	Messi	Ronaldo	Yoshikatsu Kawaguchi	Kaká	Messi	Pirlo
KAZ	Arno Pijpers	Kaká	Ronaldo	Messi	Nurbol Zumaskaliyev	Kaká	Messi	Gerrard
KEN	Jacob Mulee	Cannavaro	Drogba	Cech	Robert Mambo	Messi	Ronaldo	Drogba
KGZ	Nematjan Zakirov	Kaká	Ronaldo	Gerrard	Viacheslav Amin	Ribéry	Essien	Lampard
KOR	Cho Young Jung (TD)	Ronaldo	Rooney	Kaká	Lee Woon Jae	Kaká	Ronaldo	Drogba
KSA	Hélio dos Anjos	Kaká	Pirlo	Buffon	Yasser Al-Qahtani	Kaká	Ronaldo	Messi
KUW	Saleh Saleh	Messi	Cannavaro	Ronaldinho	Nohayr Al-Shammari	Messi	Ronaldinho	Buffon
LBY	Fauzi El Benzarti	Kaká	Ronaldinho	Ronaldo	Tarik El Tayib	Kaká	Messi	Ronaldo
LCA	Trevor Anderson	Klose	Gerrard	Kaká	Vernus Abbott	Messi	Márquez	Cannavarro
LIB	Adnan Mekdache	Ronaldo	Kaká	Messi	Faisal Antar	Kaká	Ronaldo	Messi
LIE	Hans-Peter Zaugg	Drogba	Ronaldo	Kaká	Daniel Hasler	Kaká	Cannavarro	Rooney
LTU	Algimantas Liubinskas	Kaká	Ronaldo	Ronaldinho	Tomas Danilevicius	Kaká	Ribéry	Rooney
LUX	Guy Hellers	Kaká	Messi	Pirlo	Sébastien Rémy	Kaká	Drogba	Ronaldo
LVA	Aleksandrs Starkovs	Kaká	Ronaldo	Pirlo	Vitalijs Astafjevs	Kaká	Ronaldo	Ronaldinho
MAC	Kagayama Masanaga	Kaká	Cech	Messi	Lam Ka Koi	Kaká	Cannavarro	Eto'o
MAD	Auguste Raux	Kaká	Buffon	Pirlo	Mamisoa Razafindrakoto	Cannavarro	Drogba	Ribéry
MAR	Henri Michel	Drogba	Messi	Kaká	Talal El Karkouri	Eto'o	Messi	Drogba
MDA	Igor Dobrovolski	Kaká	Drogba	Henry	Radu Rebeja	Kaká	Henry	Drogba
MDV	Jozef Jankech	Ronaldo	Gerrard	Drogba	Assad Abdul Ghani	Messi	Kaká	Gerrard
MEX	Hugo Sanchez Marquez	Kaká	Messi	Drogba	Rafael Marquez Alvarez	Messi	Ronaldinho	Deco
MGL	Ishdorj Otgonbayar	Kaká	Henry	Messi	Donorov Lumbengarav	Kaká	Henry	Messi
MKD	Srecko Katanec	Kaká	Messi	Ronaldo	Goce Sedloski	Messi	Eto'o	Terry
MLT	Dusan Fitzel	Messi	Essien	Kaká	Gilbert Agius	Kaká	Ronaldo	Messi
MNE	Zoran Filipovic	Kaká	Ronaldo	Buffon	Mirko Vucinic	Kaká	Pirlo	Gattuso
MOZ	Martinus Ignatius Nooij	Eto'o	Kaká	Van Nistelrooy	Nasser Amade Carimo	Ronaldo	Messi	Kaká
MRI	YogeshwarChundunang	Kaká	Drogba	Ronaldo	Henri Sperille	Drogba	Ronaldo	Henry
MWI	Eddington Ng'onamo	Kaká	Messi	Ronaldo	Elvis Kafoteka	Kaká	Messi	Ronaldo
MYA	Marcos Falopa	Kaká	Messi	Henry	Soe Myat Min	Kaká	Messi	Ronaldo
NCA	Carlos de Toro	Kaká	Ronaldinho	Van Nistelrooy	Denis Espinoza	Messi	Kaká	Gerrard
NCL	Didier Chambaron	Kaká	Ronaldo	Messi	Pierre Wajoka	Kaká	Ronaldo	Messi
NED	Marco van Basten	Messi	Kaká	Drogba	Edwin van der Sar	Ronaldo	Kaká	Gerrard
NGA	Berti Vogts	Drogba	Ribéry	Messi	Nwankwo Kanu	Ronaldo	Messi	Kaká
NIG	Hamey Amadou	Ronaldo	Ronaldinho	Drogba	Souleymane Sacko	Drogba	Ronaldinho	Henry
NIR	Nigel Worthington	Kaká	Gerrard	Drogba	Aaron Hughes	Kaká	Messi	Gattuso
NOR	Age Hareide	Ronaldo	Messi	Kaká	Martin Andresen	Messi	Ronaldo	Kaká
NZL	Ricki Herbert	Eto'o	Messi	Ronaldo	Tim Brown	Kaká	Messi	Pirlo
PAK	Mohiuddin Akhtar	Ronaldinho	Ronaldo	Drogba	Mohammad Essa	Kaká	Messi	Drogba
PAR	Gerardo Martino	Messi	Ribéry	Riquelme	Denis Caniza	Messi	Ronaldo	Kaká
PER	José del Solar	Riquelme	Messi	Kaká	Claudio Pizarro	Messi	Ronaldinho	Kaká
PHI	José Ariston Caslib	Kaká	Cannavaro	Ronaldinho	Jerome P. Orcullo	Kaká	Cannavaro	Ronaldinho
PLE	Naem Aleswirki	Kaká	Messi	Ronaldinho	Saeb Jendeya	Messi	Kaká	Ronaldinho
PNG	no vote	no vote	no vote	no vote	Richard Daniel	Kaká	Gerrard	Ronaldo
POL	Leo Beenhakker	Ronaldo	Henry	Rooney	Maciej Zurawski	Kaká	Ronaldo	Messi
POR	Luiz Felipe Scolari	Kaká	Messi	Drogba	Nuño Gomes	Kaká	Messi	Drogba
PUR	Garabet Avedissian	Messi	Ronaldo	Kaká	Javier Fiol	Kaká	Messi	Ronaldo
QAT	Jorge Fossati	Kaká	Messi	Lampard	no vote	no vote	no vote	no vote
ROU	Victor Piturca	Messi	Kaká	Ronaldo	Christian Chivu	Messi	Kaká	Ronaldo
RSA	Carlos Alberto Parreira	Kaká	Ronaldinho	Ronaldo	Aaron Mokoena	Ronaldo	Kaká	Cannavarro
RUS	Gus Hiddink	Kaká	Henry	Messi	Andrei Arshavin	Kaká	Ronaldinho	Henry
SCO	Alex McLeish	Kaká	Drogba	Messi	Barry Ferguson	Ronaldo	Messi	Terry
SEN	Henri Kasperczak	Kaká	Henry	Drogba	El Hadji Diouf	Kaká	Ronaldo	Drogba
SEY	Raoul Shungu	Kaká	Messi	Ronaldo	Denis Barbe	Kaká	Messi	Ronaldo
SIN	Radojko Avramovic	Ronaldo	Kaká	Messi	Aide Iskandar	Kaká	Messi	Rooney
SKN	Leonard Taylor	Kaká	Ronaldinho	Drogba	Jevon Francis	Kaká	Ronaldo	Ronaldinho
SLV	Carlos de los Cobos	Kaká	Messi	Deco	Ronald Cerritos	Kaká	Messi	Deco
SMR	Giampaolo Mazza	Kaká	Gattuso	Gerrard	Andy Selva	Kaká	Pirlo	Messi

FIFA WORLD PLAYER 2007 – HOW THEY VOTED

	Coach	1st	2nd	3rd	Captain	1st	2nd	3rd
SOM	Abdi Farah Ali	Kaká	Drogba	Buffon	Omar Abdulkadir	Kaká	Ribéry	Essien
SRB	Javier Clemente	Messi	Torres	Eto'o	Dejan Stankovic	Kaká	Pirlo	Ronaldo
SRI	Jang Jung	Kaká	Drogba	Messi	Chathura Weerasinghe	Drogba	Henry	Cech
STP	Osvaldo Luis Lima	Drogba	Ronaldo	Deco	Denilson	Kaká	Drogba	Deco
SUD	Ahmed Babiker Elfaki	Kaká	Messi	Ronaldo	Hiatham Mustafa	Kaká	Ronaldo	Messi
SUI	Jakob Kuhn	Kaká	Messi	Ronaldo	Ludovic Magnin	Kaká	Messi	Ronaldo
SUR	Kenneth Jaliens	Kaká	Messi	Buffon	Furgill Ong A Fat	Kaká	Messi	Ronaldo
SVK	Jan Kocian	Kaká	Drogba	Cech	Marek Mintal	Kaká	Ronaldo	Cech
SVN	Matjaz Kek	Kaká	Messi	Ronaldinho	Klemen Lavric	Kaká	Ronaldo	Drogba
SWE	Lars Lagerbäck	Kaká	Ronaldo	Messi	Frederik Ljungberg	Messi	Kaká	Drogba
SWZ	Gcina Dlamini	Kaká	Drogba	Messi	Wahdile Mazibuko	Kaká	Ronaldo	Drogba
SYR	Fajer Ibrahim	Messi	Ronaldinho	Ronaldo	Maher Al Sayed	Messi	Ronaldinho	Ronaldo
TAH	Lionel Charbonnier	Kaká	Messi	Ronaldo	Teva Zaveroni	Kaká	Messi	Ronaldo
TCA	Matthew Green	Drogba	Gerrard	Ronaldo	Gavin Glinton	Rooney	Kaká	Pirlo
THA	Chanvit Phalajivin	Kaká	Messi	Ronaldinho	Tawan Sripan	Kaká	Messi	Ronaldinho
TJK	Makhmadjon Khabibulloev	Ronaldo	Ribéry	Kaká	Akmal Kholmatov	Rooney	Ronaldo	Ronaldinho
TPE	Chen Sing An	Kaká	Ronaldo	Messi	Cheng Yuhg Jen	Drogba	Ronaldinho	Henry
TRI	Wim Rijsbergen	Kaká	Messi	Terry	Trent Noel	Kaká	Messi	Essien
TUN	Roger Lemerre	Ronaldo	Essien	Buffon	Jawhar Mnari	Kaká	Drogba	Essien
TUR	Fatih Termin	Kaká	Messi	Henry	Hakan Sükür	Kaká	Messi	Ronaldo
UAE	Bruno Metsu	Ronaldo	Kaká	Drogba	Humaid Fakher Husain	Kaká	Riquelme	Drogba
UGA	Laszlo Csaba	Kaká	Drogba	Klose	Ibrahim Sekagya	Kaká	Drogba	Eto'o
UKR	Oleg Blokhin	Kaká	Terry	Ronaldinho	Andriy Shevchenko	Kaká	Buffon	Ronaldo
URU	Oscar Washington Tabarez	Kaká	Messi	Ronaldo	Diego Lugano	Ronaldo	Drogba	Gerrard
USA	Bob Bradley	Kaká	Messi	Ronaldo	Carlos Bocanegra	Kaká	Drogba	Gerrard
UZB	Rauf Inileyev	Kaká	Buffon	Ronaldo	Maxim Shatskikh	Lampard	Juninho	Eto'o
VEN	Richard Paez	Kaká	Messi	Ronaldo	Luis Vera	Riquelme	Kaká	Ronaldinho
VGB	Vincent Samuel	Ronaldo	Kaká	Ronaldinho	Avondale Williams	Kaká	Ronaldo	Drogba
VIE	Alfred Riedl	Kaká	Van Nistelrooy	Ronaldo	Nguyen Minh Phuong	Kaká	Ronaldo	Van Nistelrooy
VIR	Daryl Rogers	Kaká	Vieira	Messi	Terrence Jones	Cannavarro	Vieira	Buffon
WAL	John Toshack	Cech	Kaká	Messi	no vote	no vote	no vote	no vote
ZAM	Patrick Phiri	Kaká	Ronaldo	Pirlo	Christopher Katongo	Kaká	Ronaldo	Rooney

FIFA WOMEN'S WORLD PLAYER 2007 – HOW THEY VOTED

	Coach	1st	2nd	3rd	Captain	1st	2nd	3rd
AFG	Kargar Swalizada	Prinz	Daniela	Marta	Shamila Khostani	Prinz	Daniela	Marta
ALG	Azzedine Chih	Marta	Lilly	Prinz	Sabrina Delhoum	Daniela	Lilly	Prinz
AND	David Rodrigo	Marta	Wambach	Cristiane	no vote	no vote	no vote	no vote
ANG	André Nzuzi	Marta	Formiga	Prinz	no vote	no vote	no vote	no vote
ARG	José Carlos Borrello	Marta	Smith	Prinz	Eva Gonzalez	Marta	Prinz	Smith
ARM	Mher Mikayelyan	Prinz	Marta	Lingor	Gayane Kostanyan	Prinz	Marta	Lingor
ARU	Gregory Engelbrecht	Marta	Hingst	Prinz	no vote	no vote	no vote	no vote
ASA	Tunoa Lui	Prinz	Marta	Lilly	no vote	no vote	no vote	no vote
ATG	Benjamin Rowan	Marta	Prinz	Lilly	invalid vote	invalid vote	invalid vote	invalid vote
AUS	Tom Sermanni	Prinz	Marta	Wambach	Cheryl Salisbury	Hingst	Marta	Stegemann
AUT	Ernst Weber	Marta	Lingor	Wambach	Sonja Spieler	Marta	Wambach	Prinz
AZE	Shamil Haydarov	Prinz	Cristiane	Lingor	Alfiya Bigbulatova	Prinz	Cristiane	Lingor
BAH	Vandyke Bethel	Marta	Prinz	Lilly	Kelly Simons	Marta	Prinz	Lilly
BEL	Anne Noe	Angerer	Prinz	Marta	Femke Maes	Marta	Prinz	Lingor
BER	Vance Brown	Marta	Angerer	Daniela	Cheyra Bell	Marta	Formiga	Daniela
BHR	Masoud Al-Omairi	Marta	Prinz	Li Jie	Arwa Sami Al Shamlan	Marta	Han Duan	Prinz
BIH	Ismet Bajric	Hingst	Marta	Han Duan	Sabina Pehic	Prinz	Marta	Hingst
BLR	Vladzimir Kasakovski	Smith	Prinz	Marta	Natalia Ryzhevich	Marta	Smith	Prinz
BLZ	Luis Cabrera	Lilly	Marta	Han Duan	no vote	no vote	no vote	no vote
BOL	Óscar Villegas Cámara	Marta	Formiga	Daniela	Karina Soliz	Marta	Cristiane	Daniela
BRA	Jorge Luiz Barcellos	Prinz	Angerer	Wambach	Aline Pelegrino	Gulbrandsen	George	De Vanna
BRB	Edward Smith	Marta	Prinz	Cristiane	Kamillah Burke	Marta	Prinz	Wambach
BUL	Emil Atanassov	Lingor	Prinz	Marta	Diana Petrakieva	Marta	Prinz	Lingor
CAN	Even Pellerud	Marta	Smith	Wambach	Christine Sinclair	Prinz	Smith	Gulbrandsen
CHA	Charlotte Deguidin	Marta	Lingor	George	Gislaine Tagui	Nordby	Smith.R	Bayor
CHI	Marta Tejedor Munuera	Marta	Prinz	Daniela	Maria Barrera Morales	Marta	Prinz	Cristiane
CHN	Marika Domanski-Lyfors	Marta	Prinz	Smith	Zi Jie	Marta	Prinz	Cristiane
CIV	Adélaïde Koudougnon	Marta	Angerer	Prinz	Gnago Jeanne Alexise	Marta	Prinz	Lilly

FIFA WOMEN'S WORLD PLAYER 2007 – HOW THEY VOTED

	Coach	1st	2nd	3rd	Captain	1st	2nd	3rd
CMR	Enow Ngachu	Marta	Prinz	Wambach	Marlyse Ngo	Prinz	Marta	Smith
COD	Muzangi Gauthier	Marta	Prinz	Lilly	Kiuvu Diampagi	Marta	Prinz	Lilly
COK	Tim Jerks	Marta	Cristiane	Lilly	Mii Piri	Marta	Wambach	Cristiane
COL	Jorge Luis Pinto	Daniela	Cristiane	Lilly	no vote	no vote	no vote	no vote
COM	Mohamed Hassane	Marta	Bayor	George	Halifa Hassanati	Smith.R	Marta	Lilly
CRC	Juan Quesada Samuel	Marta	Prinz	Wambach	Monic Malavassi	Marta	Prinz	Lingor
CRO	Damir Ruhek	Marta	Daniela	Lingor	Marina Koljenik	Daniela	Marta	Lingor
CUB	Rufino Sotolongo	Marta	Angerer	Formiga	Liudmila Galindo	Marta	Hingst	Daniela
CYP	Chrysostomos Iakovou	Marta	Prinz	Smith	Mikaella Chaliou	Marta	Prinz	Smith
CZE	Dusan Zovinec	Prinz	Marta	Angerer	Eva Smeralova	Angerer	Prinz	Marta
DEN	Kenneth Heiner-Moller	Marta	Cristiane	Smith	Katrine Pedersen	Marta	Stensland	Smith
DJI	Koureicha Ali Guedi	Marta	Prinz	Smith	Wasira Salem	Prinz	Marta	Smith
DMA	Hypolite Robertson	Marta	Prinz	Lingor	Chrystal Lockhart	Marta	Prinz	Cristiane
DOM	José Luis Elejalde	Marta	Prinz	Lilly	Yohanna Santelise	Marta	Prinz	Lilly
ENG	Hope Powell	Marta	Cristiane	Ri Un Suk	Faye White	Marta	Cristiane	Stensland
EQG	Gary Estupiñan	Marta	Angerer	Prinz	Lorena Aguilar	Prinz	Angerer	Marta
ERI	Ghezai Tesfagabir	Marta	Prinz	Lilly	Ruth Amlesom	Marta	Prinz	Lilly
ESP	Ignacio Queredo Laviña	Prinz	Marta	Lilly	Itziar Gurruchaga	Marta	Prinz	Lingor
EST	Juri Saar	Prinz	Marta	Smith	Elis Meetua	Marta	Smith	Lingor
FIJ	Juan Carlos Buzzetti	Marta	Prinz	Daniela	Asena Ratu	Marta	Prinz	Daniela
FIN	Michael Kälch	Marta	Prinz	Angerer	Tiina Salmen	Marta	Prinz	Wambach
FRA	Bruno Bini	Marta	Angerer	Daniela	Sandrine Soubeyrand	Marta	Wambach	Daniela
FRO	Alvur Hansen	Wambach	Marta	Angerer	Malene Josephsen	Marta	Wambach	Lingor
GAM	Buba Jallow	Angerer	Lilly	Nkwocha	A. Deham	Cristiane	Nkwocha	Bayor
GER	Silvia Neid	Marta	Stensland	Wambach	Birgit Prinz	Marta	Stensland	Wambach
GHA	Isaac Paha	Hingst	Marta	invalid vote	Adjoa Bayor	invalid vote	Lilly	Marta
GRE	Batsilas Dimitris	Marta	Prinz	Daniela	Efi Michailidou	Prinz	Formiga	Gulbrandsen
GUA	Antonio Garcia	Marta	Prinz	Formiga	Maria Rosel	Prinz	Marta	Formiga
GUM	Sang Hoon Kim	invalid vote	invalid vote	invalid vote	Cheri Stewart	Marta	Prinz	Ri Un Suk
HAI	M. Wilner Lamarre	Marta	Cristiane	Prinz	Kensia Marseille	Marta	Cristiane	Nkwocha
HKG	Wai Hoi Ying	Marta	Prinz	Wambach	Ho Wing Kam	Marta	De Vanna	Wambach
HUN	Atilla Vago	Marta	Cristiane	Prinz	Aranka Paraoánu	Marta	Cristiane	Prinz
IRL	Noel King	Angerer	Marta	Smith	Ciara Grant	Marta	Smith	Angerer
IRN	Zhou Xin Feng	Marta	Lingor	Li Jie	Fatemeh Arthangi	Cristiane	Smith	Stegemann
ISL	Siggi Eyjolfsson	Marta	Cristiane	Smith	Asthildur Helgadottir	Marta	Smith	Prinz
ISR	Alon Schraier	Daniela	Wambach	Prinz	Maytal Dayan	Marta	Cristiane	Smith
ITA	Pietro Ghedin	Cristiane	Marta	Lilly	Patrizia Panico	Prinz	Marta	Lilly
JAM	Charles Edwards	Marta	Prinz	Smith	Tanesia Vassell	Marta	Smith	Lilly
JOR	Maher Abu Hantash	Stegemann	Cristiane	Daniela	Naseem Ramounieh	Marta	Prinz	Stegemann
JPN	Hiroshi Ohashi	Marta	Prinz	Cristiane	Hiromi Isozaki	Marta	Smith	Cristiane
KAZ	Boris Yemelin	Marta	Prinz	Han Duan	Natalya Ivanova	Marta	Cristiane	Prinz
KGZ	Gulbara Umatalieva	Marta	Prinz	Ri Un Suk	Svetlana Pokachalova	Marta	Smith	De Vanna
KOR	Ignacio Quereda	Prinz	Marta	Ri Un Suk	Song, Ju Hee	Ri Un Suk	Lilly	Daniela
LBY	Bashir Al Nwesri	Marta	Prinz	De Vanna	Hachem	Prinz	Marta	De Vanna
LCA	Sean Kirton	Marta	Prinz	Daniela	Jamilla Henry	Prinz	Smith.R	Bayor
LTU	Rimantas Viktoravicius	Prinz	Marta	Nordby	Raimonda Kudyte	Prinz	Marta	Gulbrandsen
LUX	Romain Jean	Marta	Wambach	Lingor	Joelle Leuchter	Cristiane	Prinz	Marta
MDA	Boris Bogus	Marta	Cristiane	Wambach	Olga Foma	Marta	Cristiane	Wambach
MDV	Ahmed Nashid	Marta	Cristiane	Angerer	Fadhuna Zahir	Marta	Wambach	Cristiane
MEX	Leonardo Cuellar	Marta	Wambach	Formiga	Monica Canalez	Smith	Marta	Prinz
MKD	Dobrislav Dimovski	Marta	Prinz	Cristiane	Lemana Latifovik	Marta	Cristiane	Angerer
MLI	Aly Diakité	Marta	Angerer	Daniela	Diaty N'Diaye	Marta	Prinz	Cristiane
MLT	Pierre Brincat	Marta	Lingor	Smith	Rebecca D'Agostino	Marta	Angerer	Nordby
MOZ	Hadija Juma Achá	Marta	Prinz	Wambach	Ganoiema Anmendo	Marta	Prinz	Formiga
MWI	Eddington S. NG'onamo	Marta	Angerer	Wambach	Maggie Chombo	Marta	Angerer	Wambach
MYA	U Aye Kyu Gyi	Prinz	Marta	Formiga	San San Maw	Prinz	Marta	Formiga
NAM	Jacqueline Shipanga	Marta	Prinz	Wambach	Stella Williams	Prinz	Marta	Cristiane
NCA	Edward Urroz Cuadra	Marta	Prinz	Wambach	Gretchin Reyes Omaña	Marta	Prinz	Wambach
NCL	Serge Martiningo	Marta	Prinz	Wambach	Elodie Tein-Poawy	Marta	Prinz	Wambach
NED	Vera Pauw	Marta	Prinz	Smith	Marloes de Boer	Prinz	Marta	Smith
NGA	Ntiero Effiom Ntiero	Marta	Stegemann	Daniela	Christie George	Prinz	Marta	Bayor
NIG	Souley Dan Tanine	Lilly	Angerer	Han Duan	Halima Dan Ama	Marta	Lilly	Angerer
NIR	Alfie Wylie	Marta	Smith	Wambach	Stacey Hall	Hingst	Marta	Wambach
NOR	Bjarne Berntsen	Marta	Prinz	Smith	Ane S. Horpestad	Marta	Lingor	Cristiane

FIFA WOMEN'S WORLD PLAYER 2007 – HOW THEY VOTED

	Coach	1st	2nd	3rd	Captain	1st	2nd	3rd
NZL	John Herdman	Marta	Stegemann	Prinz	Rebecca Smith	Marta	Prinz	Stensland
PER	Lizandro Pinedo	Smith	Prinz	Marta	Kiara Ortega	Smith	Marta	Han Duan
PHI	Marlon M. Maro	Prinz	Li Jie	Marta	Marielle M. Benitez	Prinz	Li Jie	Marta
PLE	Waleed Lulu	Hingst	Daniela	Gulbrandsen	Hane Thaljeya	Hingst	Marta	Ri Un Suk
POL	Jan Stepczak	Marta	Prinz	Lilly	Dominika Maciaszczyk	Marta	Prinz	Wambach
POR	Monica Jorge	Marta	Smith	Daniela	Paula Santos	Marta	Lingor	Daniela
PUR	Garabet Avedissian	Marta	Prinz	Cristiane	Patricia Chapa	Marta	Prinz	Cristiane
QAT	Jorge Fossati	Lingor	Nkwocha	Marta	no vote	no vote	no vote	no vote
ROU	Maria Delicoiu	Marta	Prinz	Lilly	Rodica Striblea	Marta	Lilly	Smith
RSA	Augustine Makalakalane	Marta	Prinz	Formiga	Portia Modise	Marta	Prinz	Cristiane
RUS	Yuri Bystritskiy	Prinz	Marta	Smith	Tatiana Skotnikova	Prinz	Cristiane	Smith
SCO	Anna Singeul	Marta	Prinz	Wambach	Julie Fleeting	Marta	Prinz	Smith
SEY	Elsie Erwesta	Marta	Daniela	Prinz	Vesna Cesar	Marta	Prinz	Daniela
SIN	Nathaniel Naplah	Stegemann	Wambach	Marta	Ncor Azean Adam	Marta	Prinz	Angerer
SKN	Lenny Taylor	Marta	Wambach	Daniela	Genecia Bassae	Lilly	Marta	Smith
SLV	Julio Cesar Ramos	Wambach	Prinz	Marta	Jenny Carolina Urias	Wambach	Marta	Formiga
SOM	Hussein Ali Abdulle	Angerer	Daniela	Nkwocha	Leyla Isak	Marta	Han Duan	Bayor
SRB	Perica Kristic	Marta	Prinz	Angerer	Suzana Stanojevic	Marta	Smith	Stegemann
STP	Osvaldo Lima	Marta	Formiga	Nkwocha	Francisca Leal	Cristiane	Smith	Marta
SUI	Béatrice von Siebenthal	Marta	Ri Un Suk	Gulbrandsen	Prisca Steinegger	Daniela	Marta	Stegemann
SUR	Arno Job Berenstein	Marta	Cristiane	Prinz	Malhalie Benjamin	Cristiane	Marta	Prinz
SVK	Frantisek Hrvay	Marta	Daniela	Gulbrandsen	Monika Matysova	Marta	Angerer	Gulbrandsen
SVN	Tanja Lekic	Prinz	Angerer	Daniela	Jadranka Knezevic	Wambach	Smith	Marta
SWE	Thomas Dennerby	Marta	Wambach	Lingor	Victoria Svensson	Marta	Angerer	Formiga
SWZ	Delsile Nxumalo	Marta	Cristiane	Prinz	Xolile Nxumalo	Lilly	Smith	Nkwocha
SYR	Mousa Zoubiah	Marta	Cristiane	Daniela	Randa Muhajer	Marta	Cristiane	Prinz
TAH	Palph Apuarii	Marta	Prinz	Hingst	Angela Tairui	Marta	Prinz	Hingst
TAN	Charles B. Mkwasa	Cristiane	Lilly	Lingor	Sophia Mwasikili	Cristiane	Prinz	Marta
TCA	Matthew Green	Marta	Prinz	Smith	Pekiera Brooks	Marta	Lilly	Smith
THA	Chana Yodprang	Prinz	Cristiane	Daniela	Suphaphon Kaeobaen	Prinz	Cristiane	Daniela
TPE	Lu, Kuei-Hua	Lilly	Li Jie	Angerer	Lao, Hsueh-Hua	Lilly	Li Jie	Angerer
TRI	Jamaal Shabazz	Marta	Cristiane	Smith	Dyanna Russell	Marta	Prinz	Wambach
TUN	Samir Landolsi	Prinz	Smith	Formiga	Haifa Guedri	Prinz	Lingor	Marta
TUR	Hamdi Aslan	Prinz	Smith	Lilly	Dilgih Defterli	Prinz	Stensland	Wambach
UGA	Laszio Csaba	Lingor	Stegemann	Lilly	Majidab Nantanda	Marta	Prinz	Nkwocha
UKR	Anatolii Kutsev	Marta	Wambach	Prinz	Natalia Zinchenko	Marta	Prinz	Sinclair
URU	Fabiana Manzolillo	Marta	Han Duan	Daniela	Alejandra Laborda	Marta	Prinz	Sinclair
USA	Greg Ryan	Marta	Formiga	Cristiane	Kristine Lilly	Lingor	Formiga	Marta
UZB	Abdurahman Yumangulov	Marta	Prinz	Angerer	Kamola Usmanova	Prinz	Marta	Han Duan
VEN	Rolando Bello Sanabria	Lingor	Marta	Daniela	Liria Ferrer	Stegemann	Marta	Prinz
VGB	Samuel Vincent	Marta	Prinz	Smith	Cassandra Gregg	Marta	Prinz	Smith
VIE	Chen Yu Fa	Marta	Prinz	Wambach	Doan Thi Kim Chi	Marta	Prinz	Wambach
VIR	Yohannes Worede	Prinz	P Sörensen	Cristiane	Mackiesh Taylor	Marta	Wambach	Prinz
WAL	Adrian Tucker	Marta	Cristiane	Hingst	Jayne Ludlow	Cristiane	Marta	Hingst
ZAM	George Chikokola	Stegemann	Lilly	Marta	Martha Kapombo	Smith	Nkwocha	Lilly

PAST WINNERS OF THE FIFA WOMEN'S WORLD PLAYER AWARD

WOMEN'S WORLD PLAYER 2001

		Votes
HAMM Mia	USA	154
SUN Wen	CHN	79
MILBRETT Tiffeny	USA	47
PRINZ Birgit	GER	40
FITSCHEN Doris	GER	37
SISSI	BRA	35
LJUNBERG Hanna	SWE	29
WIEGMANN Bettina	GER	17
RIISE Hege	NOR	16
MELLGREN Dagny	NOR	13

WOMEN'S WORLD PLAYER 2002

		Votes
HAMM Mia	USA	161
PRINZ Birgit	GER	96
SUN Wen	CHN	58
MILBRETT Tiffeny	USA	45
PICHON Marinette	FRA	42
SINCLAIR Christine	CAN	38
JONES Steffi	GER	19
RIISE Hege	NOR	17
SISSI	BRA	14
BAI Jie	CHN	13

WOMEN'S WORLD PLAYER 2003

		Votes
PRINZ Birgit	GER	268
HAMM Mia	USA	133
LJUNGBERG Hanna	SWE	84
SVENSSON Victoria	SWE	82
MEINERT Maren	GER	69
WIEGMANN Bettina	GER	49
MOSTROEM Malin	SWE	23
KATIA	BRA	14
LINGOR Renate	GER	14
MARTA	BRA	13

WOMEN'S WORLD PLAYER 2004

		Votes
PRINZ Birgit	GER	376
HAMM Mia	USA	286
MARTA	BRA	281
WAMBACH Abby	USA	126
LILLY Kristine	USA	109
LJUNGBERG Hanna	SWE	109
BOXX Shannon	USA	102
SVENSSON Victoria	SWE	89
LINGOR Renate	GER	89
CRISTIANE	BRA	80

WOMEN'S WORLD PLAYER 2005

		Votes
PRINZ Birgit	GER	513
MARTA	BRA	429
BOXX Shannon	USA	235
LJUNGBERG Hanna	SWE	206
LINGOR Renate	GER	170
DOMINGUEZ Maribel	MEX	115
GULBRANDSEN Solveig	NOR	97
MINNERT Sandra	GER	97
WELSH Christie	USA	78
SMITH Kelly	ENG	60

WOMEN'S WORLD PLAYER 2006

		Votes
MARTA	BRA	475
PRINZ Birgit	GER	388
LINGOR Renate	GER	305
WAMBACH Abby	USA	182
SMITH Kelly	ENG	157
ROTTENBERG Silke	GER	154
HAN Duan	CHN	116
MA Xiaoxu	CHN	99
MOSTROEM Malin	SWE	87
SCHELIN Lotta	SWE	82

PAST WINNERS OF THE FIFA WORLD PLAYER AWARD

FIFA WORLD PLAYER 1991

		Votes
MATTHÄUS Lothar	GER	128
PAPIN Jean-Pierre	FRA	113
LINEKER Gary	ENG	40
PROSINECKI Robert	YUG	38
VAN BASTEN Marco	NED	23
BARESI Franco	ITA	12
ZAMORANO Ivan	CHI	10
BREHME Andreas	GER	9
VIALLI Gianluca	ITA	8
SCIFO Enzo	BEL	7

FIFA WORLD PLAYER 1992

		Votes
VAN BASTEN Marco	NED	151
STOICHKOV Hristo	BUL	88
HÄSSLER Thomas	GER	61
PAPIN Jean-Pierre	FRA	46
LAUDRUP Brian	DEN	44
SCHMEICHEL Peter	DEN	44
BERGKAMP Dennis	NED	29
RIJKAARD Frank	NED	23
PELE Abedi	GHA	10
BARESI Franco	ITA	10

FIFA WORLD PLAYER 1993

		Votes
VAN BASTEN Marco	NED	151
STOICHKOV Hristo	BUL	88
HÄSSLER Thomas	GER	61
PAPIN Jean-Pierre	FRA	46
LAUDRUP Brian	DEN	44
SCHMEICHEL Peter	DEN	44
BERGKAMP Dennis	NED	29
RIJKAARD Frank	NED	23
PELE Abedi	GHA	10
BARESI Franco	ITA	10

FIFA WORLD PLAYER 1994

		Votes
ROMARIO	BRA	346
STOICHKOV Hristo	BUL	100
BAGGIO Roberto	ITA	80
HAGI Georghe	ROU	50
MALDINI Paolo	ITA	40
BEBETO	BRA	16
BERGKAMP Dennis	NED	11
DUNGA Carlos	BRA	9
BARESI Franco	ITA	7
BROLIN Tomas	SWE	7

FIFA WORLD PLAYER 1995

		Votes
WEAH George	LBR	170
MALDINI Paolo	ITA	80
KLINSMANN Jürgen	GER	58
ROMARIO	BRA	50
BAGGIO Roberto	ITA	49
STOICHKOV Hristo	BUL	37
ZAMORANO Ivan	CHI	36
JUNINHO	BRA	28
SAMMER Matthias	GER	23
LAUDRUP Michael	DEN	20

FIFA WORLD PLAYER 1996

		Votes
RONALDO	BRA	329
WEAH George	LBR	140
SHEARER Alan	ENG	123
SAMMER Matthias	GER	109
KLINSMANN Jürgen	GER	54
KANU Nwankwo	NGA	32
MALDINI Paolo	ITA	25
SUKER Davor	CRO	24
BATISTUTA Gabriel	ARG	19
ROMARIO	BRA	13

FIFA WORLD PLAYER 1997

		Votes
RONALDO	BRA	480
ROBERTO CARLOS	BRA	65
BERGKAMP Dennis	NED	62
ZIDANE Zinedine	FRA	62
RAÚL	ESP	51
DEL PIERO Alessandro	ITA	27
SUKER Davor	CRO	20
BATISTUTA Gabriel	ARG	16
SHEARER Alan	ENG	16
LEONARDO	BRA	14

FIFA WORLD PLAYER 1998

		Votes
ZIDANE Zinedine	FRA	518
RONALDO	BRA	164
SUKER Davor	CRO	108
OWEN Michael	ENG	43
BATISTUTA Gabriel	ARG	40
RIVALDO	BRA	37
BERGKAMP Dennis	NED	33
DAVIDS Edgar	NED	26
DESAILLY Marcel	FRA	23
THURAM Lillian	FRA	14

FIFA WORLD PLAYER 1999

		Votes
RIVALDO	BRA	538
BECKHAM David	ENG	194
BATISTUTA Gabriel	ARG	79
ZIDANE Zinedine	FRA	68
VIERI Christian	ITA	39
FIGO Luis	POR	35
SHEVCHENKO Andriy	UKR	34
RAÚL	ESP	31
COLE Andy	ENG	24
YORKE Dwight	TRI	19

FIFA WORLD PLAYER 2000

		Votes
ZIDANE Zinedine	FRA	370
FIGO Luis	POR	329
RIVALDO	BRA	263
BATISTUTA Gabriel	ARG	57
SHEVCHENKO Andriy	UKR	48
BECKHAM David	ENG	41
HENRY Thierry	FRA	35
NESTA Alessandro	ITA	23
KLUIVERT Patrick	NED	22
TOTTI Francesco	ITA	14

FIFA WORLD PLAYER 2001

		Votes
FIGO Luis	POR	250
BECKHAM David	ENG	238
RAÚL	ESP	96
ZIDANE Zinedine	FRA	94
RIVALDO	BRA	92
VERON Juan Sebastian	ARG	71
KAHN Oliver	GER	65
OWEN Michael	ENG	61
SHEVCHENKO Andriy	UKR	46
TOTTI Francesco	ITA	40

FIFA WORLD PLAYER 2002

		Votes
RONALDO	BRA	387
KAHN Oliver	GER	171
ZIDANE Zinedine	FRA	148
ROBERTO CARLOS	BRA	114
RIVALDO	BRA	92
RAÚL	ESP	90
BALLACK Michael	GER	82
BECKHAM David	ENG	51
HENRY Thierry	FRA	38
OWEN Michael	ENG	34

FIFA WORLD PLAYER 2003

		Votes
ZIDANE Zinedine	FRA	264
HENRY Thierry	FRA	186
RONALDO	BRA	176
NEDVED Pavel	CZE	158
ROBERTO CARLOS	BRA	105
VAN NISTELROOY Ruud	NED	86
BECKHAM David	ENG	74
RAÚL	ESP	39
MALDINI Paolo	ITA	37
SHEVCHENKO Andriy	UKR	26

FIFA WORLD PLAYER 2004

		Votes
RONALDINHO	BRA	620
HENRY Thierry	FRA	552
SHEVCHENKO Andriy	UKR	253
NEDVED Pavel	CZE	178
ZIDANE Zinedine	FRA	150
ADRIANO	BRA	98
DECO	POR	96
RONALDO	BRA	96
VAN NISTELROOY Ruud	NED	67
KAKA & ROONEY Wayne		64

FIFA WORLD PLAYER 2005

		Votes
RONALDINHO	BRA	956
LAMPARD Frank	ENG	306
ETO'O Samuel	CMR	190
HENRY Thierry	FRA	172
ADRIANO	BRA	170
SHEVCHENKO Andriy	UKR	153
GERRARD Steven	ENG	131
KAKA	BRA	101
MALDINI Paolo	ITA	76
DROGBA Didier	CIV	65

FIFA WORLD PLAYER 2006

		Votes
CANNAVARO Fabio	ITA	498
ZIDANE Zinedine	FRA	454
RONALDINHO	BRA	380
HENRY Thierry	FRA	317
ETO'O Samuel	CMR	300
DROGBA Didier	CIV	150
KAKA	BRA	139
BUFFON Gianluigi	ITA	118
PIRLO Andrea	ITA	86
RONALDO Cristiano	POR	69

RECORDS OF THE 30 PLAYERS SELECTED FOR THE 2007 AWARD

1 – KAKA

22-04-1982 Brasilia, BRA (1.83/73)

		League			Europe			BRA	
2001	São Paulo	26	7	SA	qf				
2002	São Paulo	20	5	SA	qf			4	1
2003	São Paulo	10	3	SA	-			1	0
03-04	Milan	30	10	SA	1	10	2	CL qf	11	3
04-05	Milan	36	7	SA	2	8	2	CL F	11	4
05-06	Milan	35	14	SA	2	12	5	CL sf	16	4
06-07	Milan	31	8	SA	4	14	10	CL W	9	4
07-08	Milan	30	15	SA	5	8	2	CL r2	7	4

Honours: WC 2002, CC 2005, CWC 2007, CL 2007, Lge 2004
Brazil debut: 31-01-2002 v BOL • 59 caps • 20 goals

2 – LIONEL MESSI

24-06-1987 Rosario, ARG (1.69/67)

		League			Europe			ARG	
04-05	Barcelona	7	1	PD	1	1	0	CL r2		
05-06	Barcelona	17	6	PD	1	6	1	CL W	10	2
06-07	Barcelona	26	14	PD	2	5	1	CL r2	10	3
07-08	Barcelona	27	10	PD	3	9	6	CL sf	10	4

Honours: CL 2006, Lge 2005 2006
Argentina debut: 17-08-2005 v HUN • 58 caps • 21 goals

3 – CRISTIANO RONALDO

5-02-1985 Funchal, POR (1.84/78)

		League			Europe			POR	
02-03	Sporting CP	25	3	SL	3	3	0	CL r1		
03-04	Manchester Utd	29	4	PL	3	5	0	CL r2	13	2
04-05	Manchester Utd	33	5	PL	3	8	0	CL r2	10	7
05-06	Manchester Utd	33	9	PL	2	8	1	CL r1	15	3
06-07	Manchester Utd	34	17	PL	1	11	3	CL sf	8	5
07-08	Manchester Utd	34	31	PL	1	11	8	CL W	12	4

Honours: CL 2008, Lge 2007 2008, Cup 2004, LCup 2006
Portugal debut: 20-08-2003 v KAZ • 46 caps • 17 goals

4 - DIDIER DROGBA

11-03-1978 Abidjan, CIV (1.83/86)

		League			Europe			CIV
98-99	Le Mans	2	0	D2	17			
99-00	Le Mans	30	6	D2	8			
00-01	Le Mans	11	0	D2	14			
01-02	Le Mans	21	5	D2	5			
01-02	Guingamp	11	3	L1	16			
02-03	Guingamp	34	17	L1	7			
03-04	Oly. Marseille	35	18	L1	7	10	6	C/U	F
04-05	Chelsea	26	10	PL	1	9	5	CL	sf
05-06	Chelsea	29	12	PL	1	7	1	CL	r2
06-07	Chelsea	36	20	PL	2	12	6	CL	sf	Total
07-08	Chelsea	19	8	PL	2	10	6	CL	F	50 32

Honours: Lge 2005 2006, Cup 2007, LCup 2005 2007
Côte d'Ivoire debut: 8-09-2002 v RSA

5 - RONALDINHO

21-03-1980 Porto Alegre, BRA (1.80/76)

		League			Sth Am/Europe			BRA
1998	Grêmio	14	1	SA	8	10	1	CL	qf	
1999	Grêmio	17	5	SA	18	5	2	MS GS	10 7
2000	Grêmio	15	8	SA	10	4	1	MS GS	7 1
2001	Grêmio	21	14	SA	5				4 1
01-02	PSG	28	9	L1	4	6	2	UC r3	9 3
02-03	PSG	27	8	L1	11	4	1	UC r3	9 2
03-04	Barcelona	32	15	PD	2	7	4	UC r4	5 2
04-05	Barcelona	35	9	PD	1	7	4	CL r2	16 11
05-06	Barcelona	29	19	PD	1	17	8	CL W	8 0
06-07	Barcelona	32	21	PD	2	8	2	CL r2	7 2
07-08	Barcelona	17	8	PD	3	8	1	CL sf	7 3

Honours: WC 2002, CA 1999, CC 2005; CL 2006 Lge 2005 2006,
Cup 2001; Brazil debut: 26-06-1999 v LVA • 82 caps • 32 goals

6 - STEVEN GERRARD

30-05-1980 Whiston, ENG (1.87/78)

		League			Europe			ENG
97-98	Liverpool	0	0	PL	3				
98-99	Liverpool	12	0	PL	7	1	0	UC r1	
99-00	Liverpool	29	1	PL	4				2 0
00-01	Liverpool	33	7	PL	3	9	2	UC W	3 0
01-02	Liverpool	28	3	PL	2	14	1	CL qf	5 1
02-03	Liverpool	34	5	PL	5	11	0	C/U qf	8 2
03-04	Liverpool	34	4	PL	4	8	2	UC r4	10 1
04-05	Liverpool	30	7	PL	5	10	4	CL W	6 2
05-06	Liverpool	32	10	PL	3	11	6	CL r2	13 3
06-07	Liverpool	36	7	PL	3	12	3	CL F	10 3
07-08	Liverpool	34	11	PL	4	13	6	CL SF	10 1

Honours: CL 2005, UC 2001, Cup 2001 2006, LCup 2001 2003
England debut: 31-05-2000 v UKR • 67 caps • 13 goals

7 - ANDREA PIRLO

19-05-1979 Brescia, ITA (1.77/68)

		League			Europe			ITA
94-95	Brescia	1	0	SA	18				
95-96	Brescia	0	0	SB	16				
96-97	Brescia	17	2	SB	1				
97-98	Brescia	29	4	SA	15				
98-99	Internazionale	18	0	SA	8	7	0	CL qf	
99-00	Reggina	28	6	SA	12				
00-01	Internazionale	4	0	SA	5	3	0	UC r2	
00-01	Brescia	10	0	SA	8				
01-02	Milan	18	2	SA	4	9	0	UC sf	
02-03	Milan	27	9	SA	3	13	0	CL W	4 0
03-04	Milan	32	6	SA	1	11	1	CL qf	7 1
04-05	Milan	30	4	SA	2	12	1	CL F	4 2
05-06	Milan	33	4	SA	3	12	1	CL sf	16 2
06-07	Milan	34	2	SA	4	13	1	CL W	7 0
07-08	Milan	33	3	SA	5	9	2	CL r2	11 3

Honours: WC 2006; CL 2003, Lge 2004, Cup 2003
Italy debut: 7-09-2002 v AZE • 49 caps • 8 goals

8 - THIERRY HENRY

17-08-1977 Paris, FRA (1.87/81)

		League			Europe			FRA
94-95	Monaco	8	3	L1	6				
95-96	Monaco	18	3	L1	3	1	0	UC r1	
96-97	Monaco	36	9	L1	1	9	1	UC sf	
97-98	Monaco	30	4	L1	3	9	7	CL sf	9 3
98-99	Monaco	13	1	L1	4	5	0	UC r3	
98-99	Juventus	16	3	SA	6				2 0
99-00	Arsenal	31	17	PL	2	12	8	C/U F	10 5
00-01	Arsenal	35	17	PL	2	14	4	CL qf	8 2
01-02	Arsenal	33	24	PL	1	11	7	CL r2	9 2
02-03	Arsenal	37	24	PL	2	12	7	CL r2	13 10
03-04	Arsenal	37	30	PL	1	10	5	CL qf	12 5
04-05	Arsenal	32	25	PL	2	8	5	CL r2	7 1
05-06	Arsenal	32	27	PL	4	11	5	CL F	15 8
06-07	Arsenal	17	10	PL	4	7	1	CL r2	7 4
07-08	Barcelona	30	12	PD	3	10	3	CL sf	10 6

Honours: WC 1998, EC 2000, CC 2003; Lge 1997 2002 2004, Cup
2002 2003 • France debut: 11-10-1997 v RSA • 103 caps • 46 goals

9 - FABIO CANNAVARO

13-09-1973 Naples, ITA (1.76/75)

		League			Europe			ITA
92-93	Napoli	2	0	SA	11				
93-94	Napoli	27	0	SA	6				
94-95	Napoli	29	1	SA	7	3	0	UC r3	
95-96	Parma	29	1	SA	6	6	0	CC qf	
96-97	Parma	27	0	SA	2	2	0	UC r1	8 0
97-98	Parma	31	0	SA	6	7	0	CL GS	11 0
98-99	Parma	30	1	SA	4	8	0	UC W	9 0
99-00	Parma	31	2	SA	5	9	1	C/U r4	13 0
00-01	Parma	33	0	SA	4	6	0	UC r4	9 0
01-02	Parma	31	1	SA	10	9	0	C/U r4	11 0
02-03	Internazionale	28	0	SA	2	12	1	CL sf	9 0
03-04	Internazionale	22	2	SA	4	9	0	C/U qf	10 1
04-05	Juventus	38	2	SA	1	9	1	CL qf	5 0
05-06	Juventus	36	4	SA	1	9	0	CL qf	15 0
06-07	Real Madrid	32	0	PD	1	6	0	CL r2	8 0
07-08	Real Madrid	33	0	PD	1	6	0	CL r2	8 0

Honours: WC 2006; UC 1999, Lge 2005 2006 (both withdrawn),
2007 2008; Cup 1999 2002
Italy debut: 22-01-1997 v NIR • 116 caps • 1 goal

10 – GIANLUIGI BUFFON
28-01-1978 Carrara, ITA (1.90/88)

		League			Europe		ITA	
95-96	Parma	9	- SA	5				
96-97	Parma	27	- SA	2	1	- UC r1		
97-98	Parma	32	- SA	6	8	- CL r1	2 -	
98-99	Parma	34	- SA	4	11	- UC W	7 -	
99-00	Parma	32	- SA	5	9	- C/U r4	6 -	
00-01	Parma	34	- SA	4	7	- U r4	5 -	
01-02	Juventus	34	- SA	1	10	- CL r2	10 -	
02-03	Juventus	32	- SA	1	15	- CL F	8 -	
03-04	Juventus	32	- SA	3	6	- CL r2	11 -	
04-05	Juventus	37	- SA	1	11	- CL qf	8 -	
05-06	Juventus	18	- SA	1	4	- CL qf	10 -	
06-07	Juventus	37	- SB	1			8 -	
07-08	Juventu	34	- SA	3			11 -	

Honours: WC 2006; UC 1999; Lge 2002 2003 (2005 2006 withdrawn), Cup 1999 • Italy debut: 29-10-1997 v RUS • 86 caps

11 – FRANCK RIBERY
1-04-1983 Boulogne-sue-Mer, FRA (1.70/62)

		League			Europe		FRA	
01-02	Boulogne	20	5 N	17				
02-03	Olympique Alès	18	1 N	15				
03-04	Stade Brestois	35	3 N	2				
04-05	FC Metz	20	2 L1	16				
04-05	Galatasaray	14	0 SL	2				
05-06	Olymp. Marseille	35	6 L1	5	7	1 UC r4	10 1	
06-07	Olymp. Marseille	25	5 L1	2	3	0 UC r1	8 1	
07-08	Bayern München	28	11 BL	1	11	3 UC sf	12 2	

Honours: Lge 2008; Cup 2005 2008
France debut: 27-05-2006 v MEX • 30 caps • 4 goals

13 – WAYNE ROONEY
24-10-1985 Liverpool, ENG (1.80/76)

		League			Europe		ENG	
02-03	Everton	33	6 PL	7			5 0	
03-04	Everton	34	9 PL	17			12 9	
04-05	Manchester Utd	29	11 PL	3	6	3 CL r2	6 0	
05-06	Manchester Utd	36	16 PL	2	5	1 CL r1	10 2	
06-07	Manchester Utd	35	14 PL	1	12	4 CL sf	5 1	
07-08	Manchester Utd	27	12 PL	1	11	4 CL W	5 2	

Honours: CL 2008, Lge 2007 2008, LCup 2006
England debut: 12-02-2003 v AUS • 43 caps • 14 goals

14 – MIROSLAV KLOSE
9-06-1978 Oppeln/Schlesien, POL (1.82/74)

		League			Europe		GER	
98-99	FC Homburg	18	1 RL	13				
98-99	K'slautern (am)	36	11 RL	14				
99-00	Kaiserslautern	2	0 BL	5				
00-01	Kaiserslautern	29	9 BL	8	12	2 UC sf	4 2	
01-02	Kaiserslautern	31	16 BL	7			15 11	
02-03	Kaiserslautern	32	9 BL	14			10 2	
03-04	Kaiserslautern	26	10 BL	15	2	1 UC r1	11 1	
04-05	Werder Bremen	32	15 BL	3	8	2 CL GS	6 4	
05-06	Werder Bremen	26	25 BL	2	9	4 CL r2	16 9	
06-07	Werder Bremen	31	13 BL	3	13	2 C/U sf	7 4	
07-08	Bayern München	27	10 BL	1	12	5 UC sf	12 8	

Honours: Lge 2008, Cup 2008
Germany debut: 24-03-2001 v ALB • 81 caps • 41 goals

16 – JUAN ROMAN RIQUELME
24-06-1978 Buenos Aires, ARG (1.80/76)

		League			Sth Am/Europe		ARG	
96-97	Boca Juniors	22	4 PD	10/9	2	0 SC r1		
97-98	Boca Juniors	19	0 PD	2/6	6	0 CM qf	1 0	
98-99	Boca Juniors	37	10 PD	1/1	5	0 CM r1	5 0	
99-00	Boca Juniors	24	4 PD	3/7	11	3 CL W		
00-01	Boca Juniors	27	10 PD	1/3	12	3 CL W		
01-02	Boca Juniors	22	10 PD	3/3	4	0 CL qf	1 0	
02-03	Barcelona	30	3 PD	6	11	2 CL r2	3 1	
03-04	Villarreal	33	8 PD	8	12	4 UC sf	2 0	
04-05	Villarreal	35	15 PD	3	9	2 UC qf	12 5	
05-06	Villarreal	25	12 PD	7	14	2 CL sf	12 2	
06-07	Boca Juniors	15	2 PD	2/2	11	8 CL W	6 5	
07-08	Boca Juniors	10	1 PD	1	10	4 CL SF	6 4	

Honours: CL 2000 2001 2007, Lge 1999x2 2001
Argentina debut: 16-11-1997 v COL • 48 caps • 17 goals

12 – SAMUEL ETO'O
10-03-1981 Nkon, CMR (1.80/75)

		League			Europe		CMR	
97-98	Leganés	28	3 D2	13				
98-99	Real Madrid	1	0 PD	2				
98-99	Espanyol	0	0 PD	7				
99-00	Real Madrid	2	0 PD	5	3	0 CL W		
99-00	Mallorca	13	6 PD	10				
00-01	Mallorca	28	11 PD	3				
01-02	Mallorca	30	6 PD	16	9	3 C/U r3		
02-03	Mallorca	30	14 PD	9				
03-04	Mallorca	32	17 PD	11	7	4 UC r4		
04-05	Barcelona	37	24 PD	1	7	4 CL r2		
05-06	Barcelona	34	27 PD	1	11	6 CL W		
06-07	Barcelona	19	11 PD	2	3	1 CL r2	Total	
07-08	Barcelona	18	16 PD	3	7	1 CL sf	80 34	

Honours: CN 2000 2002, Olympic Gold 2000; Lge 2005 2006, Cup 2003 • Cameroon debut: 9-08-1997 v ZAM

15 – MICHAEL ESSIEN
3-12-1982 Accra, GHA (1.80/77)

		League			Europe		GHA	
99-00	Liberty							
00-01	Bastia	12	1 L1	8				
01-02	Bastia	24	4 L1	11				
02-03	Bastia	29	6 L1	12				
03-04	Oly. Lyonnais	34	3 L1	1	8	0 CL qf		
04-05	Oly. Lyonnais	37	4 L1	1	10	5 CL qf		
05-06	Chelsea	31	2 PL	1	6	0 CL r2		
06-07	Chelsea	33	2 PL	2	10	2 CL sf	Total	
07-08	Chelsea	27	6 PL	2	12	0 CL F	41 8	

Honours: Lge 2004 2005 2006, Cup 2007, LCup 2007
Ghana debut: 21-01-2002 v MAR

17 – PETR CECH
20-05-1982 Plzen, CZE (1.96/85)

		League			Europe		CZE	
98-99	Viktoria Plzen	0	- L1	15				
99-00	Chmel	1	- L1	10				
00-01	Chmel	26	- L1	10				
01-02	Sparta Praha	26	- L1	2	12	- CL r2	2 -	
02-03	Stade Rennais	37	- L1	15			10 -	
03-04	Stade Rennais	33	- L1	9			11 -	
04-05	Chelsea	35	- PL	1	12	- CL sf	9 -	
05-06	Chelsea	34	- PL	1	7	- CL r2	12 -	
06-07	Chelsea	20	- PL	2	8	- CL sf	8 -	
07-08	Chelsea	26	- PL	2	9	- CL F	10 -	

Honours: Lge 2005 2006, Cup 2007, LCup 2005 2007
Czech Rep Debut: 12-02-2002 v HUN • 62 caps

18 – RUUD VAN NISTELROOY

1-07-1976 Oss, NED (1.88/80)

	League			Europe			NED	
93-94 Den Bosch	2	0	D2 11					
94-95 Den Bosch	15	3	D2 18					
95-96 Den Bosch	21	2	D2 3					
96-97 Den Bosch	31	12	D2 7					
97-98 Heerenveen	31	13	ED 6					
98-99 PSV Eindhoven	34	31	ED 3	7	6	CL r1	5	1
99-00 PSV Eindhoven	23	29	ED 1	8	3	CL r1	5	0
00-01 PSV Eindhoven	9	2	ED 1				2	3
01-02 Manchester Utd	32	23	ED 3	14	10	CL SF	6	4
02-03 Manchester Utd	34	25	PL 1	11	14	CL qf	7	3
03-04 Manchester Utd	32	20	PL 3	7	4	CL r2	13	7
04-05 Manchester Utd	17	6	PL 3	7	8	CL r2	6	4
05-06 Manchester Utd	35	21	PL 2	8	2	CL r1	10	6
06-07 Real Madrid	37	25	PD 1	7	6	CL r2	0	0
07-08 Real Madrid	24	16	PD 1	7	4	CL r2	10	5

Honours: Lge 2000 2001 2003 2007 2008, Cup 2004, LCup 2006
Netherlands debut: 18-11-1998 v GER • 64 caps • 33 goals

19 – FRANK LAMPARD

21-06-1978 Romford, ENG (1.83/79)

	League			Europe			ENG	
95-96 West Ham Utd	2	0	PL 10					
95-96 Swansea City	9	1	D3 22					
96-97 West Ham Utd	13	0	PL 14					
97-98 West Ham Utd	31	4	PL 8					
98-99 West Ham Utd	38	5	PL 5					
99-00 West Ham Utd	34	7	PL 9	4	1	UC r2	1	0
00-01 West Ham Utd	30	7	PL 15				1	0
01-02 Chelsea	37	5	PL 6	4	1	UC r2	5	0
02-03 Chelsea	38	6	PL 4	2	1	UC r1	4	0
03-04 Chelsea	38	10	PL 2	14	4	CL sf	12	5
04-05 Chelsea	38	13	PL 1	12	4	CL sf	9	3
05-06 Chelsea	35	16	PL 1	8	2	CL r2	13	3
06-07 Chelsea	37	11	PL 2	11	11	CL sf	10	1
07-08 Chelsea	28	10	PL 2	11	4	CL F	6	2

Honours: Lge 2005 2006; Cup 2007, LCup 2005 2007
England debut: 10-10-1999 v BEL • 61 caps • 14 goals

20 – DECO

27-08-1977 São Bernardo do Campo, BRA (1.74/75)

	League			Europe			POR	
1997 Corinthians	0	0	SA 17					
97-98 Alverca	32	13	D2 3					
98-99 Salgueiros	12	2	D1 12					
98-99 Porto	6	0	SL 1					
99-00 Porto	23	1	SL 2	11	3	CL qf		
00-01 Porto	31	6	SL 2	10	0	C/U qf		
01-02 Porto	30	13	SL 3	15	6	CL r2		
02-03 Porto	30	10	SL 1	12	1	UC W	4	1
03-04 Porto	29	2	SL 1	12	2	CL W	15	0
04-05 Barcelona	35	7	PD 1	7	2	CL r2	10	1
05-06 Barcelona	29	3	PD 1	11	2	CL W	10	1
06-07 Barcelona	31	1	PD 2	8	2	CL r2	7	0
07-08 Barcelona	18	1	PD 3	6	0	CL sf	10	1

Honours: CL 2004 2006, UC 2003, Lge 1999 2003 2004 2005 2006, Cup 2000 2001 2003 • Portugal debut: 29-03-2003 v BRA
56 caps • 4 goals

21 – JUNINHO PERNAMBUCO

30-01-1975 Recife, ENG (1.78/72)

	League			Sth Am/Europe			BRA	
1993 Sport Recife	2	0	SA 25					
1994 Sport Recife	22	2	SA 25					
1995 Vasco da Gama	21	3	SA 20					
1996 Vasco da Gama	15	7	SA 18					
1997 Vasco da Gama	18	4	SA 1					
1998 Vasco da Gama	18	3	SA 10					
1999 Vasco da Gama	20	2	SA 6					
2000 Vasco da Gama	22	5	SA 1					
2001 Vasco da Gama	8	0	SA 11					
01-02 Olymp. Lyonnais	29	5	L1 1	4	0	CL GS		
02-03 Olymp. Lyonnais	31	13	L1 1	6	0	CL GS		
03-04 Olymp. Lyonnais	32	10	L1 1	10	5	CL qf		
04-05 Olymp. Lyonnais	32	13	L1 1	9	2	CL qf		
05-06 Olymp. Lyonnais	32	8	L1 1	8	4	CL qf		
06-07 Olymp. Lyonnais	31	10	L1 1	7	1	CL r2		
07-08 Olymp. Lyonnais	32	8	L1 1	8	3	CL r2		

Honours: CC 2005; CL 1998, CMS 2000, Lge 1997 2000 2002 2003 2004 2005 2006 2007 2008, Cup 2008
Brazil debut: 28-03-1999 v KOR • 40 caps • 6 goals

22 – GENNARO GATTUSO

9-01-1978 Corigliano Calabra, ITA (1.77/77)

	League			Europe			ITA	
95-96 Perugia	2	0	SB 3					
96-97 Perugia	8	0	SA 16					
97-98 Rangers	29	3	SPL 2	2	1	CL pr		
98-99 Rangers	4	0	SPL 1	3	1	UC r3		
98-99 Salernitana	25	0	SA 15					
99-00 Milan	22	1	SA 3	5	0	CL GS	2	0
00-01 Milan	24	0	SA 6	10	0	CL r2	4	1
01-02 Milan	32	0	SA 4	10	0	UC sf	9	0
02-03 Milan	25	0	SA 3	14	0	CL W	4	0
03-04 Milan	33	1	SA 1	9	1	CL qf	8	0
04-05 Milan	32	0	SA 2	11	0	CL F	7	0
05-06 Milan	35	3	SA 3	11	0	CL sf	13	0
06-07 Milan	30	1	SA 4	12	0	CL W	6	0
07-08 Milan	31	1	SA 5	8	0	CL r2	7	0

Honours: WC 2006; CL 2003 2007, Lge 2004, Cup 2003
Italy debut: 23-02-2000 v SWE • 60 caps • 1 goal

23 – JOHN TERRY

7-12-1980 Barking, ENG (1.82/74)

	League			Europe			ENG	
98-99 Chelsea	2	0	PL 3	0	0	CW sf		
99-00 Nottm Forest	6	0	D1 14					
99-00 Chelsea	4	0	PL 5	0	0	CL qf		
00-01 Chelsea	22	1	PL 6	0	0	UC r1		
01-02 Chelsea	33	1	PL 6	4	1	UC r2		
02-03 Chelsea	20	3	PL 4	2	1	UC r1	1	0
03-04 Chelsea	33	2	PL 2	11	0	CL sf	10	0
04-05 Chelsea	36	3	PL 1	11	4	CL sf	6	0
05-06 Chelsea	36	4	PL 1	8	0	CL r2	12	1
06-07 Chelsea	28	1	PL 2	10	0	CL sf	10	2
07-08 Chelsea	23	1	PL 2	10	0	CL F	5	1

Honours: Lge 2005 2006, Cup 2007, LCup 2005 2007
England debut: 3-06-2003 v SCG • 44 caps • 4 goals

24 – PATRICK VIEIRA

23-06-1976 Dakar, SEN (1.92/82)

Season	Club	League				Europe				FRA	
93-94	Cannes	5	0	L1	6						
94-95	Cannes	31	2	L1	9	4	1	UC	r2		
95-96	Cannes	13	0	L1	14						
95-96	Milan	2	0	SA	1	2	0	UC	qf		
96-97	Arsenal	31	2	PL	3	1	0	UC	r1	5	0
97-98	Arsenal	33	2	PL	1	2	0	UC	r1	4	0
98-99	Arsenal	34	3	PL	2	3	0	CL	GS	5	0
99-00	Arsenal	30	2	PL	2	14	0	C/U	F	16	0
00-01	Arsenal	30	5	PL	2	12	0	CL	qf	14	2
01-02	Arsenal	36	2	PL	1	11	1	CL	r2	12	1
02-03	Arsenal	24	3	PL	2	12	1	CL	r2	6	1
03-04	Arsenal	29	3	PL	1	6	0	CL	qf	10	0
04-05	Arsenal	32	6	PL	2	6	0	CL	r2	7	0
05-06	Juventus	31	5	SA	1	7	0	CL	qf	15	2
06-07	Internazionale	20	1	SA	1	4	1	CL	r2	7	0
07-08	Internazionale	16	3	SA	1	3	0	CL	r2	4	0

Honours: WC 1998, EC 2000 CC 2001; Lge 1998 2002 2004 (2006 withdrawn) 2007 2008, Cup 1998 2002 2005
France debut: 26-02-1997 v NED • 105 caps • 6 goals

25 – RAFAEL MARQUEZ

13-02-1979 Zamora, MEX (1.80/66)

Season	Club	League				Europe				MEX	
96-97	Atlas	24	2							1	0
97-98	Atlas	20	1							0	0
98-99	Atlas	33	3							12	1
99-00	Monaco	23	3	L1	1	6	0	UC	r4	8	1
00-01	Monaco	15	1	L1	11	4	0	CL	GS	11	1
01-02	Monaco	21	0	L1	15					10	1
02-03	Monaco	30	1	L1	2					4	0
03-04	Barcelona	22	1	PD	2	3	0	UC	r4	6	2
04-05	Barcelona	33	3	PD	1	6	0	CL	r2	8	0
05-06	Barcelona	25	0	PD	1	8	0	CL	W	9	2
06-07	Barcelona	21	1	PD	2	6	0	CL	r2	8	1
07-08	Barcelona	24	2	PD	3	8	0	CL	sf	2	0

Honours: CC 1999, GC 2003; CL 2006, Lge 2000 2005 2006, LCup 2003 • Mexico debut: 5-02-1997 v ECU • 79 caps • 9 goals

26 – FERNANDO TORRES

20-03-1984 Madrid, ESP (1.81/78)

Season	Club	League				Europe				ESP	
00-01	Atlético Madrid	4	1	SD	4						
01-02	Atlético Madrid	36	6	SD	1						
02-03	Atlético Madrid	29	13	PD	12						
03-04	Atlético Madrid	35	20	PD	7					9	1
04-05	Atlético Madrid	38	16	PD	11					10	2
05-06	Atlético Madrid	36	13	PD	10					15	10
06-07	Atlético Madrid	36	14	PD	7					8	1
07-08	Liverpool	33	24	PL	4	11	6	CL	SF	12	3

Honours: EC 2008
Spain debut: 6-09-2003 v POR • 54 caps • 17 goals

27 – ALESSANDRO NESTA

19-03-1976 Rome, ITA (1.87/79)

Season	Club	League				Europe				ITA	
93-94	Lazio	2	0	SA	4						
94-95	Lazio	11	0	SA	2						
95-96	Lazio	23	0	SA	3	3	0	UC	r2		
96-97	Lazio	25	0	SA	4	4	0	UC	r2	5	0
97-98	Lazio	30	0	SA	7	10	1	UC	F	10	0
98-99	Lazio	20	1	SA	2	4	0	CW	W	5	0
99-00	Lazio	28	0	SA	1	10	0	CL	qf	11	0
00-01	Lazio	29	0	SA	3	8	0	CL	r2	7	0
01-02	Lazio	25	0	SA	6	6	0	CL	r1	8	0
02-03	Milan	29	1	SA	3	14	0	CL	W	7	0
03-04	Milan	26	0	SA	1	7	0	CL	qf	9	0
04-05	Milan	29	0	SA	2	12	0	CL	F	5	0
05-06	Milan	30	1	SA	2	10	0	CL	sf	10	0
06-07	Milan	14	0	SA	4	8	0	CL	W	1	0
07-08	Milan	29	1	SA	5	7	0	CL	r2		

Honours: WC 2006; CWC 2007, CL 2003 2007, CW 1999, Lge 2000 2004, Cup 1998 2000 2003; Italy debut: 5-10-1996 v MDA • 78 caps

28 – CARLOS TEVEZ

5-02-1984 Ciudadela, ARG (1.70/74)

Season	Club	League				Sth Am/Europe				ARG	
01-02	Boca Juniors	11	1	PD	2/1	4	1	CL			
02-03	Boca Juniors	32	10	PD	3/1	8	5	CL	W		
03-04	Boca Juniors	23	12	PD	11/1	11	3	CL	F		
04-05	Boca Juniors	9	2	PD	3/10						
2005	Corinthians	29	20	SA	1						
2006	Corinthians	9	5	SA	10	8	4	CL	r2		
06-07	West Ham Utd	26	7	PL	15	2	0	UC	r1		
07-08	Manchester Utd	34	14	PL	1	12	5	CL	W		

Honours: OG 2004; CL 2003 2008, CSA 2004, Lge 2003 2005 2008
Argentina debut: 30-03-2004 v ECU • 40 caps • 7 goals

29 – PHILIPP LAHM

11-11-1983 Munich, GER (1.70/61)

Season	Club	League				Europe				GER	
01-02	B. München AM	27	2	RS	10						
02-03	B. München AM	34	1	RS	4	1	0	CL	GS		
03-04	VfB Stuttgart	31	1	BL	4	7	0	CL	r2	9	1
04-05	VfB Stuttgart	22	1	BL	5	6	1	UC	r3	6	0
05-06	Bayern München	20	0	BL	1	4	0	CL	r2	10	1
06-07	Bayern München	34	1	BL	4	9	0	CL	qf	9	0
07-08	Bayern München	22	0	BL	1	10	1	UC	sf	13	1

Honours: Lge 2006 2008, Cup 2006 2008
Germany debut: 18-02-2004 v CRO • 49 caps • 3 goals

KEY

WC = FIFA World Cup • EC = UEFA European Championship • CC = FIFA Confederations Cup • OG = Olympic gold • CA = Copa America • CN = Africa Cup of Nations • GC = CONCACAF Gold Cup • CL = UEFA Champions League or Copa Libertadores • UC = UEFA Cup • CW = Cup Winners Cup • C/U = UEFA Champions League then the UEFA Cup • CMS = Copa Mercosur • CSA = Copa Sudamericana • LGE = Domestic League championship • CUP = Domestic Cup • LCUP = League Cup • AS = Allsvenskan (Sweden) • BL = Bundesliga (Germany) • B2 = Bundesliga 2 (Germany) • ED = Eredivisie (Netherlands) • L1 = Ligue 1 (France) • PD = Primera Division (Argentina & Spain) • PL = Premier League (England) • RL = Regionalliga • RS = Regionalliga Süd • SA = Serie A (Brazil and Italy) • SB = Serie B (Italy) • SD = Segunda Division • SL = Superliga (Portugal & Turkey) • The first line for each player gives the following information - date and place of birth, nationality, height in meters, weight in kilogrammes • The columns for each table read as follows - season, club, league appearances, league goals, name of the league, final position; continental appearances, continental goals, competition, round reached; international appearances, international goals

2010 FIFA WORLD CUP SOUTH AFRICA

QUALIFYING MATCHES PLAYED IN ASIA

First Round

Sri Lanka	SRI	0	0
Qatar	QAT	1	5
Pakistan	PAK	0	0
Iraq	IRQ	7	0
China PR	CHN	7	4
Myanmar	MYA	0	0
Bahrain	BHR	4	0
Malaysia	MAS	1	0
Oman	OMA	2	2
Nepal	NEP	0	0
Yemen	YEM	Bye	
Thailand	THA	6	7
Macau	MAC	1	1
Mongolia	MGL	1	1
Korea DPR	PRK	4	5
Kyrgyzstan	KGZ	2 0	5p
Jordan	JOR	0 2	6p
Cambodia	CAM	0	1
Turkmenistan	TKM	1	4
Timor-Leste	TLS	2	1
Hong Kong	HKG	3	8
Uzbekistan	UZB	9	2
Chinese Taipei	TPE	0	0
Palestine	PLE	0	0
Singapore	SIN	4	3
Bangladesh	BAN	1	0
Tajikistan	TJK	1	5
Lebanon	LIB	4	2
India	IND	1	2
Vietnam	VIE	0	0
UAE	UAE	1	5
Indonesia	IDN	Bye	
Syria	SYR	3	2
Afghanistan	AFG	0	1

Second Round

Yemen	YEM	1	0
Thailand	THA	1	1
Turkmenistan	TKM	0	3
Hong Kong	HKG	0	0
Singapore	SIN	2	1
Tajikistan	TJK	0	1
Indonesia	IDN	1	0
Syria	SYR	4	7

Third Round Group Stage

Group 1		Pl	W	D	L	F	A	Pts	AUS	QAT	IRQ	CHN
Australia	AUS	6	3	1	2	7	3	10		3-0	1-0	0-1
Qatar	QAT	6	3	1	2	5	6	10	1-3		2-0	0-0
Iraq	IRQ	6	2	1	3	4	6	7	1-0	0-1		1-1
China PR	CHN	6	1	3	2	3	4	6	0-0	0-1	1-2	

Group 2		Pl	W	D	L	F	A	Pts	JPN	BHR	OMA	THA
Japan	JPN	6	4	1	1	12	3	13		1-0	3-0	4-1
Bahrain	BHR	6	3	2	1	7	5	11	1-0		1-1	1-1
Oman	OMA	6	2	2	2	5	7	8	1-1	0-1		2-1
Thailand	THA	6	0	1	5	5	14	1	0-3	2-3	0-1	

Group 3		Pl	W	D	L	F	A	Pts	KOR	PRK	JOR	TKM
Korea Republic	KOR	6	3	3	0	10	3	12		0-0	2-2	4-0
Korea DPR	PRK	6	3	3	0	4	0	12	0-0		2-0	1-0
Jordan	JOR	6	2	1	3	6	6	7	0-1	0-1		2-0
Turkmenistan	TKM	6	0	1	5	1	12	1	1-3	0-0	0-2	

Group 4		Pl	W	D	L	F	A	Pts	KSA	UZB	SIN	LIB
Saudi Arabia	KSA	6	5	0	1	14	5	15		4-0	2-0	4-1
Uzbekistan	UZB	6	5	0	1	15	7	15	3-0		1-0	3-0
Singapore	SIN	6	2	0	4	7	13	6	0-2	3-7		2-0
Lebanon	LIB	6	0	0	6	3	14	0	1-2	0-1	1-2	

Group 5		Pl	W	D	L	F	A	Pts	IRN	UAE	SYR	KUW
Iran	IRN	6	3	3	0	7	2	12		0-0	0-0	2-0
UAE	UAE	6	2	2	2	7	7	8	0-1		1-3	2-0
Syria	SYR	6	2	2	2	7	8	8	0-2	1-1		1-0
Kuwait	KUW	6	1	1	4	8	12	4	2-2	2-3	4-2	

The fourth round consists of two groups
Group 1 – Australia, Japan, Bahrain, Uzbekistan, Qatar
Group 2 – Korea Republic, Iran, Saudi Arabia, Korea DPR, United Arab Emirates
Matches to be played between September 2008 and June 2009. The top two in each group qualify directly for the finals in South Africa. The two third placed teams face each other for the right to play the winner of qualifying in Oceania for a place in the finals

Full match details for every qualifying match on the road to South Africa, from all six qualifying zones, will appear in the next two editions of the *Almanack of World Football*

QUALIFYING MATCHES PLAYED IN AFRICA

Preliminary Round

Madagascar	MAD	6	4
Comoros	COM	2	0

Sierra Leone	SLE	1	0
Guinea-Bissau	GNB	0	0

Djibouti	DJI	1	
Somalia	SOM	0	

First Round Group Stage

Group 1

		Pl	W	D	L	F	A	Pts	CMR	CPV	TAN	MRI
Cameroon	CMR	4	3	1	0	7	1	10		2-0	2-1	
Cape Verde Is	CPV	4	3	0	1	5	3	9			1-0	3-1
Tanzania	TAN	4	0	2	2	2	4	2	0-0			1-1
Mauritius	MRI	4	0	1	3	2	8	1	0-3	0-1		

Group 2

		Pl	W	D	L	F	A	Pts	GUI	KEN	ZIM	NAM
Guinea	GUI	4	2	1	1	6	3	7		0-0		
Kenya	KEN	4	2	1	1	5	2	7	2-0		2-0	4-0
Zimbabwe	ZIM	4	1	2	1	2	2	5		0-0		2-0
Namibia	NAM	4	1	0	3	3	9	3	1-2	2-1		

Group 3

		Pl	W	D	L	F	A	Pts	BEN	ANG	UGA	NIG
Benin	BEN	4	3	0	1	8	4	9			4-1	2-0
Angola	ANG	4	2	1	1	6	4	7	3-0		0-0	
Uganda	UGA	4	2	1	1	5	5	7		3-1		1-0
Niger	NIG	4	0	0	4	1	7	0	0-2	1-2		

Group 4

		Pl	W	D	L	F	A	Pts	NGA	RSA	SLE	EQG
Nigeria	NGA	4	4	0	0	6	0	12		2-0		2-0
South Africa	RSA	4	1	1	2	4	4	4			0-0	4-1
Sierra Leone	SLE	4	1	1	2	1	3	4	0-1	1-0		
Equat. Guinea	EQG	4	1	0	3	3	7	3	0-1		2-0	

Group 5

		Pl	W	D	L	F	A	Pts	GHA	LBY	GAB	LES
Ghana	GHA	4	3	0	1	8	4	9		3-0	2-0	
Libya	LBY	4	3	0	1	6	3	9			1-0	4-0
Gabon	GAB	4	2	0	2	4	3	6	2-0			2-0
Lesotho	LES	4	0	0	4	2	10	0	2-3	0-1		

Group 6

		Pl	W	D	L	F	A	Pts	SEN	ALG	GAM	LBR
Senegal	SEN	4	2	2	0	6	3	8		1-0		3-1
Algeria	ALG	4	2	0	2	4	2	6			1-0	3-0
Gambia	GAM	4	1	2	1	2	2	5	0-0	1-0		
Liberia	LBR	4	0	2	2	4	9	2	2-2		1-1	

First Round Group Stage

Group 7

		Pl	W	D	L	F	A	Pts	CIV	BOT	MOZ	MAD
Côte d'Ivoire	CIV	4	2	2	0	6	1	8		4-0	1-0	
Botswana	BOT	4	1	2	1	3	6	5	1-1			0-0
Mozambique	MOZ	4	1	1	2	5	4	4		1-2		3-0
Madagascar	MAD	4	0	3	1	1	4	3	0-0		1-1	

Group 8

		Pl	W	D	L	F	A	Pts	MAR	RWA	ETH	MTN
Morocco	MAR	4	3	0	1	10	4	9		2-0	3-0	
Rwanda	RWA	4	3	0	1	8	4	9	3-1			3-0
Ethiopia	ETH	4	2	0	2	8	6	6		1-2		6-1
Mauritania	MTN	4	0	0	4	2	14	0	1-4		0-1	

Group 9

		Pl	W	D	L	F	A	Pts	BFA	TUN	BDI	SEY
Burkina Faso	BFA	4	4	0	0	11	4	12			2-0	4-1
Tunisia	TUN	4	3	0	1	6	3	9	1-2		2-1	
Burundi	BDI	4	1	0	3	2	5	3	0-1			1-0
Seychelles	SEY	4	0	0	4	3	10	0	2-3	0-2		

Group 10

		Pl	W	D	L	F	A	Pts	MLI	CGO	CHA	SUD
Mali	MLI	4	3	0	1	11	6	9		4-2		3-0
Congo	CGO	4	2	0	2	6	6	6			2-0	1-0
Chad	CHA	3	1	0	2	3	5	3	1-2	2-1		
Sudan	SUD	3	1	0	2	3	6	3	3-2			

Group 11

		Pl	W	D	L	F	A	Pts	SWZ	ZAM	TOG
Swaziland	SWZ	3	1	1	1	2	2	4		0-0	2-1
Zambia	ZAM	3	1	1	1	1	1	4	1-0		
Togo	TOG	2	1	0	1	2	2	3	1-0		
Eritrea	ERI				Withdrew						

Group 12

		Pl	W	D	L	F	A	Pts	COD	EGY	MWI	DJI
Congo DR	COD	4	3	0	1	13	3	9		1-0		5-1
Egypt	EGY	4	3	0	1	8	2	9	2-1		2-0	
Malawi	MWI	4	2	0	2	9	4	6		1-0		8-1
Djibouti	DJI	4	0	0	4	2	23	0	0-6	0-4		

Tables as of 1/08/2008

The 12 first round group winners qualify for the second round group stage along with the best eight runners-up. This will consist of five groups of four teams with the winners of each qualifying for the finals in South Africa. Following the withdrawl of Eritrea from the first round group stage, and the presence of one group of three teams, the best runners-up will be determined by their record against the first and third placed teams. South Africa are taking part in the qualifiers because the groups are doubling up as the qualifying tournament for the 2010 CAF African Cup of Nations in Angola.

QUALIFYING MATCHES PLAYED IN CENTRAL AMERICA, NORTH AMERICA AND THE CARIBBEAN

First Round				Second Round				Third Round Groups	
Aruba	ARU	0	0						
Antigua and Barbuda	ATG	3	1	Antigua and Barbuda	ATG	3	0		
Cuba	CUB	Bye		Cuba	CUB	4	4		
Guatemala	GUA	Bye		Guatemala	GUA	6	3	**Group 1**	
Turks and Caicos Isl	TCA	2	0	St Lucia	LCA	0	1	Cuba	CUB
St Lucia		1	2					Guatemala	GUA
								Trinidad and Tobago	TRI
Trinidad and Tobago	TRI	Bye		Trinidad and Tobago	TRI	1	2	USA	USA
Bermuda	BER	1	3	Bermuda	BER	2	0		
Cayman Islands	CAY	1	1						
USA	USA			USA	USA	8	1		
Dominica	DMA	1	0	Barbados	BRB	0	0		
Barbados	BRB	1	1						
St Vincent/Grenadines	VIN	Bye		St Vincent/Grenadines	VIN	0	1		
Canada	CAN	Bye		Canada	CAN	3	4		
Honduras	HON	Bye		Honduras	HON	4	2	**Group 2**	
Dominican Republic	DOM	0		Puerto Rico	PUR	0	2	Canada	CAN
Puerto Rico	PUR	1						Honduras	HON
								Jamaica	JAM
Jamaica	JAM	Bye		Jamaica	JAM	7	6	Mexico	MEX
Bahamas	BAH	1	2	Bahamas	BAH	0	0		
British Virgin Islands	VGB	1	2						
Belize	BLZ	3	1						
St Kitts and Nevis	SKN	1	1	Belize	BLZ	0	0		
Mexico	MEX	Bye		Mexico	MEX	2	7		
US Virgin Islands	VIR	0							
Grenada	GRN	10		Grenada	GRN	2	0		
Costa Rica	CRC	Bye		Costa Rica	CRC	2	3		
Panama	PAN	Bye		Panama	PAN	1	1	**Group 3**	
El Salvador	SLV	12	4	El Salvador	SLV	0	3	Costa Rica	CRC
Anguilla	AIA	0	0					El Salvador	SLV
								Haiti	HAI
Haiti	HAI	Bye		Haiti	HAI	0	1	Surinam	SUR
Nicaragua	NCA	0	0	Netherlands Antilles	ANT	0	0		
Netherlands Antilles	ANT	1	2						
Surinam	SUR	7							
Montserrat	MSR	1		Surinam	SUR	1	2		
Guyana	GUY	Bye		Guyana	GUY	0	1		

The top two from each of the third round groups will qualify for the fourth round which will consist of one group of six teams, the top three of which will qualify for the finals in South Africa. The fourth placed team will play-off against the fifth placed team from South America for a further place in the finals

QUALIFYING MATCHES PLAYED IN SOUTH AMERICA

		PL	W	D	L	F	A	PTS	PAR	ARG	COL	CHI	BRA	URU	VEN	ECU	BOL	PER
1	Paraguay	6	4	1	1	13	5	13					2-0	1-0		5-1		
2	Argentina	6	3	2	1	9	3	11			2-0					1-1	3-0	
3	Colombia	6	2	4	0	4	2	10	2-1			0-0		1-0				
4	Chile	6	3	1	2	9	9	10	0-3									2-0
5	Brazil	6	2	3	1	8	4	9	0-0					2-1		5-0		
6	Uruguay	6	2	2	2	15	6	8				2-2			1-1		5-0	6-0
7	Venezuela	6	2	1	3	9	10	7	0-2			2-3					5-3	
8	Ecuador	6	1	2	3	7	13	5			0-0				0-1			5-1
9	Bolivia	6	1	1	4	7	17	4	4-2		0-0	0-2						
10	Peru	6	0	3	3	3	15	3	0-0		1-1		1-1					

The top four teams qualify for the finals in South Africa. The fifth placed team play-offs off against the fourth placed team from the Central American, North American and Caribbean qualifiers

QUALIFYING MATCHES PLAYED IN OCEANIA

First Round Group Stage

Group 1

		Pl	W	D	L	F	A	Pts	NCL	TAH	COK	TVU
Fiji	FIJ	4	3	1	0	25	1	10	1-1	4-0	4-0	16-0
New Caledonia	NCL	4	3	1	0	6	1	10		1-0	3-0	1-0
Tahiti	TAH	4	1	1	2	2	6	4			1-0	1-1
Cook Islands	COK	4	1	0	3	4	9	3				4-1
Tuvalu	TVU	4	0	1	3	2	22	1				

Group 2

		Pl	W	D	L	F	A	Pts	VAN	SAM	TGA	ASA
Solomon Islands	SOL	4	4	0	0	21	1	12	2-0	3-0	4-0	12-1
Vanuatu	VAN	4	3	0	1	23	3	9		4-0	4-1	15-0
Samoa	SAM	4	2	0	2	9	8	6			2-1	7-0
Tonga	TGA	4	1	0	3	6	10	3				4-0
American Samoa	ASA	4	0	0	4	1	38	0				

New Caledonia, Fiji and Vanuatu qualify for round two

Second Round

Group 1

		Pl	W	D	L	F	A	Pts	NZL	NCL	FIJ	VAN
New Zealand	NZL	3	3	0	0	8	2	9				4-1
New Caledonia	NCL	4	2	2	0	11	4	8			4-0	3-0
Fiji	FIJ	3	0	1	2	3	9	1	0-2	3-3		
Vanuatu	VAN	4	0	1	3	3	10	1	1-2	1-1		

Semi–finals

New Caledonia	3
Solomon Islands	2

Vanuatu	0
Fiji	3

Final

New Caledonia	1
Fiji	0

Third place

Vanuatu	2
Solomon Islands	0

The second round group winner will play-off against the fifth placed team in Asia for a place in the finals in South Africa

QUALIFYING MATCHES PLAYED IN EUROPE

Group 1		Group 2		Group 3		Group 4		Group 5	
Portugal	POR	Greece	GRE	Czech Republic	CZE	Germany	GER	Spain	ESP
Sweden	SWE	Israel	ISR	Poland	POL	Russia	RUS	Turkey	TUR
Denmark	DEN	Switzerland	SUI	Northern Ireland	NIR	Finland	FIN	Belgium	BEL
Hungary	HUN	Moldova	MDA	Slovakia	SVK	Wales	WAL	Bosnia-H'govina	BIH
Albania	ALB	Latvia	LVA	Slovenia	SVN	Azerbaijan	AZE	Armenia	ARM
Malta	MLT	Luxembourg	LUX	San Marino	SMR	Liechtenstein	LIE	Estonia	EST

Group 6		Group 7		Group 8		Group 9	
Croatia	CRO	France	FRA	Italy	ITA	Netherlands	NED
England	ENG	Romania	ROU	Bulgaria	BUL	Scotland	SCO
Ukraine	UKR	Serbia	SRB	Republic of Ireland	IRL	Norway	NOR
Belarus	BLR	Lithuania	LTU	Cyprus	CYP	FYR Macedonia	MKD
Kazakhstan	KAZ	Austria	AUT	Georgia	GEO	Iceland	ISL
Andorra	AND	Faroe Islands	FRO	Montenegro	MNE		

The nine group winners qualify for the finals in South Africa while the eight best second placed teams will play-off for the four remaining places

FIFA U–17 WORLD CUP KOREA REPUBLIC 2007

FIFA U-17 WORLD CUP KOREA REPUBLIC 2007

First round groups	Pts	Round of 16		Quarter–finals		Semi–finals		Final	
Group A	Pts								
Peru	7	**Nigeria**	2						
Costa Rica	4	Colombia	1						
Korea Republic	3			**Nigeria**	2				
Togo	2			Argentina	0				
Group B	Pts	Costa Rica	0						
England	7	**Argentina**	2						
Brazil	6					**Nigeria**	3		
Korea DPR	4					Germany	1		
New Zealand	0	**England**	3						
Group C	Pts	Syria	1						
Spain	7			England	1				
Argentina	5			**Germany**	4				
Syria	4	USA	1						
Honduras	0	**Germany**	2						
								Nigeria	0 3p
Group D	Pts							Spain	0 0p
Nigeria	9	**Ghana**	1						
France	4	Brazil	0						
Japan	3			**Ghana**	2				
Haiti	1			Peru	0				
Group E	Pts	Tajikistan	1 4p						
Tunisia	9	**Peru**	1 5p						
USA	3					Ghana	1		
Tajikistan	3					**Spain**	2		
Belgium	3	**France**	3						
Group F	Pts	Tunisia	1						
Germany	7			France	1 4p				
Ghana	6			**Spain**	1 5p			3rd place play-off	
Colombia	4	Korea DPR	0					**Germany**	2
Trinidad & Tob	0	**Spain**	3					Ghana	1

GROUP A		PL	W	D	L	F	A	PTS	CRC	KOR	TOG
1	Peru	3	2	1	0	2	0	7	1-0	1-0	0-0
2	Costa Rica	3	1	1	1	3	2	4		2-0	1-1
3	Korea Republic	3	1	0	2	2	4	3			2-1
4	Togo	3	0	2	1	2	3	2			

GROUP B		PL	W	D	L	F	A	PTS	BRA	PRK	NZL
1	England	3	2	1	0	8	2	7	2-1	1-1	5-0
2	Brazil	3	2	0	1	14	3	6		6-1	7-0
3	Korea DPR	3	1	1	1	3	7	4			1-0
4	New Zealand	3	0	0	3	0	13	0			

GROUP C		PL	W	D	L	F	A	PTS	ARG	SYR	HON
1	Spain	3	2	1	0	7	4	7	1-1	2-1	4-2
2	Argentina	3	1	2	0	5	2	5		0-0	4-1
3	Syria	3	1	1	1	3	2	4			2-0
4	Honduras	3	0	0	3	3	10	0			

GROUP D		PL	W	D	L	F	A	PTS	FRA	JPN	HAI
1	Nigeria	3	3	0	0	9	2	9	2-1	3-0	4-1
2	France	3	1	1	1	4	4	4		2-1	1-1
3	Japan	3	1	0	2	4	6	3			3-1
4	Haiti	3	0	1	2	3	8	1			

GROUP E		PL	W	D	L	F	A	PTS	USA	TJK	BEL
1	Tunisia	3	3	0	0	8	3	9	3-1	1-0	4-2
2	USA	3	1	0	2	6	7	3		3-4	2-0
3	Tajikistan	3	1	0	2	4	5	3			0-1
4	Belgium	3	1	0	2	3	6	3			

GROUP F		PL	W	D	L	F	A	PTS	GHA	COL	TRI
1	Germany	3	2	1	0	11	5	7	3-2	3-3	5-0
2	Ghana	3	2	0	1	8	5	6		2-1	4-1
3	Colombia	3	1	1	1	9	5	4			5-0
4	Trinidad and Tobago	3	0	0	3	1	14	0			

GROUP A

Suwon Stadium, Suwon
18-08-2007, 17:00, 7256, Fagundes BRA

Costa Rica 1

Martinez [81]

Leonel MOREIRA - Roy SMITH, Jordan SMITH, Esteban LUNA, Diego BRENES (Bruno CASTRO 72), David GUZMAN, Jorge CASTRO, Jessy PERALTA, Erick ROJAS, Julio IBARRA (Josue MARTINEZ 80), Daniel VARELA (Marcos URENA 46). Tr: Manuel URENA

Togo 1

Mani [39]

Baba TCHAGOUNI - Awali MAMAH, Kossi SEGBEBIA (Backer ALOENOUVO 65), Sapol MANI, Alex KINVI-BOH, Lalawele ATAKORA (Mohamed ABDOULAYE 84), Alikem SEGBEBIA, James LOEMBE, Koami AYAO•, Papa Koami AWOUNYO, Safiou SAIBOU (Camaldine ABRAW 77). Tr: Paul SAUTER

Suwon Stadium, Suwon
18-08-2007, 20:00, 27 112, Bebek CRO

Korea Republic 0

KIM Seung Gyu - HAN Yong Su•77, LIM Jong Eun, KIM Dong Cheol•, YOON Bitgaram, BAE Chun Suk, CHOI Jin Soo, OH Jae Suk (LEE Yong Joon 64), HAN Kook Young•, KIM Jung Hyung (KIM Ui Beom• 55), BAK Jae Cheol (JU Sung Hwan 46). Tr: PARK Kyung Hoon

Peru 1

Bazalar [29]

Eder HERMOZA - Jersi SOCOLA• (Joseph MUNOZ 46, Nestor DUARTE, Bryan SALAZAR, Reimond MANCO, Carlos BAZALAR, Irven AVILA, Jairo HERNANDEZ, Juan ARCE•, Christian LA TORRE (Cesar RUIZ 65), Gary CORREA (Luis TRUJILLO 61). Tr: Juan Jose ORE

Suwon Stadium, Suwon
21-08-2007, 17:00, 1300, Aguilar SLV

Togo 0

Mensah NSOUHOHO - Sapol MANI, Alex KINVI-BOH, Lalawele ATAKORA, Alikem SEGBEBIA, James LOEMBE, Koami AYAO, Papa Koami AWOUNYO, Camaldine ABRAW (Mohamed ABDOULAYE 73), Safiou SAIBOU (Abdou-Fatawou DODJA 78), Koffi ALOFA 69). Tr: Paul SAUTER

Peru 0

Eder HERMOZA - Joseph MUNOZ, Nestor DUARTE, Bryan SALAZAR, Reimond MANCO, Carlos BAZALAR, Irven AVILA, Luis TRUJILLO (Daniel SANCHEZ 83), Jairo HERNANDEZ•, Juan ARCE, Gary CORREA (Cesar RUIZ 67). Tr: ORE Juan Jose

Suwon Stadium, Suwon
21-08-2007, 20:00, 23 120, Gilewski POL

Costa Rica 2

Urena [85], Peralta [91+]

Leonel MOREIRA - Roy SMITH, Jordan SMITH, Esteban LUNA (Daniel VARELA• 66), Diego BRENES (Josue MARTINEZ 76), David GUZMAN•, Jorge CASTRO, Jessy PERALTA, Bruno CASTRO, Erick ROJAS, Julio IBARRA (Marcos URENA 46). Tr: UR Manuel URENA

Korea Republic 0

KIM Seung Gyu - LIM Jong Eun•, KIM Dong Cheol, CHO Beom Seok, YOON Bitgaram (KIM Ui Beom 67), BAE Chun Suk (LEE Yong Jae 46), CHOI Jin Soo, OH Jae Suk, HAN Kook Young•, JU Sung Hwan• (SEOL Jae Mun 82), JEONG Hyun Yoon. Tr: PARK Kyung Hoon

Ulsan Complex, Ulsan
24-08-2007, 20:00, 22 000, Layec FRA

Korea Republic 2

Seol Jae Mun [45], Yoon Bitgaram [80]

KIM Seung Gyu - HAN Yong Su•, YUN Suk Young, LIM Jong Eun, KIM Dong Cheol, CHO Beom Seok, YOON Bitgaram, CHOI Jin Soo, SEOL Jae Mun (KIM Ui Beom 67), JU Sung Hwan (KIM Jung Hyung 52), JEONG Hyun Yoon (BAE Chun Suk 46). Tr: PARK Kyung Hoon

Togo 1

Atakora [20]

Mensah NSOUHOHO• - Awali MAMAH, Sapol MANI, Alex KINVI-BOH, Lalawele ATAKORA, Alikem SEGBEBIA (Camaldine ABRAW 83), Abdou-Fatawou DODJA (Kossi SEGBEBIA 73), James LOEMBE, Koami AYAO•••71, Papa Koami AWOUNYO, Backer ALOENOUVO• 64). Tr: Paul SAUTER

World Cup Stadium, Jeju
24-08-2007, 20:00, 510, Maillet SEY

Peru 1

Bazalar [89]

Eder HERMOZA - Joseph MUNOZ, Nestor DUARTE, Bryan SALAZAR (Cesar RUIZ 77), Reimond MANCO, Carlos BAZALAR, Irven AVILA, Daniel SANCHEZ (Ernesto SALAZAR 65), Jairo HERNANDEZ•, Juan ARCE (Antony MOLINA 72), Gary CORREA. Tr: Juan Jose ORE

Costa Rica 0

Leonel MOREIRA - Roy SMITH, Jordan SMITH, Diego BRENES, David GUZMAN (Miguel BRENES 65), Jorge CASTRO (Josue MARTINEZ 77), Jessy PERALTA, Bruno CASTRO, Erick ROJAS, Daniel ARIAS (Marcos URENA 46), Daniel VARELA. Tr: Manuel URENA

GROUP B

World Cup Stadium, Jeju
18-08-2007, 14:00, 12 600, Maillet SEY

Korea DPR 1

Rim Chol Min [89]

O Mun Song - RI Hyong Mu, KANG Kuk Chol (JONG Il Ju• 68), KANG Chol Ryong, HAN Kyong Gwang•, MYONG Cha Hyon, RI Sang Chol, AN Il Bom, PAK Kwang Ryong (RIM Chol Min 67), RI Myong Jun (SIM Hyon Jin 57), O Jin Hyok. Tr: AN Ye Gun

England 1

Moses [62]

Alex SMITHIES - Nana OFORI-TWUMASI•, Henri LANSBURY (Daniel GOSLING 84), Krystian PEARCE, Thomas SMITH (Gavin HOYTE 71), Rhys MURPHY, Victor MOSES, Nathan PORRITT (Tristan PLUMMER 73), Michael WOODS, Jordan SPENCE, Jonathan FRANKS. Tr: John PEACOCK

World Cup Stadium, Jeju
18-08-2007, 17:00, 8 500, Gilewski POL

Brazil 7

Fabinho [1], Lazaro [6], Giuliano [33], Fabio [50], Alex [54], Lulinha [60p], Junior [87]

MARCELO – RAFAEL, LAZARO, TIAGO (CHOCO 83), FABIO (BRUNO COLLACO 72), LULINHA, ALEX, DANIEL, TALES, GIULIANO, FABINHO (JUNIOR 79). Tr: Luiz Antonio NIZZO

New Zealand 0

Jacob GLEESON - Anthony HOBBS (Nick CORLISS 68), Mars KEOMAHAVONG, Tim MYERS•, Jacob MATHEWS, Cory CHETTLEBURGH•, Kosta BAR-BAROUSES (MACINTYRE Geoffrey 62), Ben HUNT (Colin MURPHY 73), Fraser COLSON, Chris WOOD, Jason HICKS. Tr: Colin TUAA

World Cup Stadium, Jeju
21-08-2007, 17:00, 2500, Layec FRA

New Zealand 0

Jacob GLEESON - Colin MURPHY, Tim MYERS•, Nick CORLISS, Jacob MATHEWS, Cory CHETTLEBURGH, Kosta BARBAROUSES, Chris WOOD (Geoffrey MACINTYRE 73), Godwin DARKWA, Jason HICKS (Ben HUNT 51), Hamish CHANG (Fraser COLSON• 68). Tr: Colin TUAA

England 5

Welbeck 2 [3 27], Moses 2 [7 30], Chambers [88]

Alex SMITHIES - Nana OFORI-TWUMASI, James REID, Krystian PEARCE (Gavin HOYTE 52), Daniel WELBECK, Victor MOSES (Medi ELITO 71), Daniel GOSLING, Michael WOODS (Tom TAIWO 61), Jordan SPENCE, Tristan PLUMMER, Ashley CHAMBERS. Tr: John PEACOCK

World Cup Stadium, Jeju
21-08-2007, 20:00, 13 500, Irmatov UZB

Brazil 6

Fabio 2 [4 8], Alex [6], Maicon [22], Juliano [47], Choco [90]

MARCELO – RAFAEL, LAZARO, TIAGO (FELLIPE 87), FABIO, MAICON (FABINHO 79), LULINHA (CHOCO 88), ALEX, DANIEL, TALES, GIULIANO. Tr: Luiz Antonio NIZZO

Korea DPR 1

An Il Bom [24]

O Mun Song - RI Hyong Mu•, KANG Kuk Chol (JONG Il Ju 61), KANG Chol Ryong, HAN Kyong Gwang, MYONG Cha Hyon, RI Sang Chol•, AN Il Bom, PAK Kwang Ryong (SIM Hyon Jin 50), RI Myong Jun, O Jin Hyok• (PAK Hyong Jin 74). Tr: AN Ye Gun

Ulsan Complex, Ulsan
24-08-2007, 17:00, 6000, Benquerenca POR

Korea DPR 1

Rim Chol Min [81]

O Mun Song - SIM Hyon Jin, RI Hyong Mu, KANG Kuk Chol, KANG Chol Ryong, MYONG Cha Hyon, JONG Il Ju, RI Sang Chol, AN Il Bom (RIM Chol Min 64), RI Myong Jun (HAN Kyong Gwang 52), O Jin Hyok• (PAK Kwang Ryong 52). Tr: AN Ye Gun

New Zealand 0

Michael O'KEEFFE - Anthony HOBBS (Geoffrey MACINTYRE 56), Colin MURPHY, Nick CORLISS, Jacob MATHEWS, Cory CHETTLEBURGH, Chris WOOD (Kosta BARBAROUSES 46), Tyson BRANDT (Moses PETELO 72), Godwin DARKWA, Jason HICKS, Adam COWEN. Tr: TUAA Colin

Goyang Stadium, Goyang
24-08-2007, 17:00, 9600, Bebek CRO

England 2

Lansbury [45p], Spence [92+]

Alex SMITHIES - Nana OFORI-TWUMASI, Henri LANSBURY•, Krystian PEARCE, Daniel WELBECK (Nathan PORRITT 83), Victor MOSES (Rhys MURPHY 74), Daniel GOSLING, Michael WOODS (Tom TAIWO 69•93+), Jason SPENCE, Gavin HOYTE, Jonathan FRANKS. Tr: PEACOCK John

Brazil 1

Tales [19]

MARCELO – RAFAEL•, LAZARO, FABIO•, FELLIPE•, MAICON (FABINHO 48) (CHOCO 86), LULINHA, ALEX, DANIEL, TALES, GIULIANO. Tr: Luiz Antonio NIZZO

GROUP C

Ulsan Complex, Ulsan
19-08-2007, 16:00, 4800, Breeze AUS

Honduras 2

Martinez [20], Rojas [72]

Marlon LICONA - Gustavo CARIAS● (Julio OCAMPO 66), Angel CASTRO, Fredy ESCOBAR (Orlin PERALTA● 18), Jose FONSECA, Fredy SOSA (Roger ROJAS 58), Christian MARTINEZ, Areal GARAY, Johnny LEVERON, Luis GARRIDO, Alfredo MEJIA●. Tr: Miguel ESCALANTE

Spain 4

Bojan 2 [2 71], Jordi 2 [56 81]

David DE GEA - Alberto MORGADO, David ROCHELA, Ignacio CAMACHO●, XIMO, BOJAN (Daniel AQUINO 79), Fran MERIDA, LUKAS (Isma LOPEZ 46), IAGO (JORDI● 46), SERGIO●, Francisco ATIENZA●. Tr: Juan SANTISTEBAN

Ulsan Complex, Ulsan
22-08-2007, 20:00, 3000, Nishimura JPN

Argentina 4

Meza [45], Mazzola 2 [64 87], Machura [71]

Luis OJEDA● - Mateo MUSACCHIO, Maximiliano OLIVA (Pablo ROLON 38), Damian MARTINEZ (Franco ZUCULINI 71), Fernando MEZA, Eduardo SALVIO, Mariano BITTOLO, Gustavo FERNANDEZ, Santiago FERNANDEZ (Nicolas MAZZOLA 46), Alexis MACHUCA●, Guido PIZARRO. Tr: Miguel Angel TOJO

Honduras 1

Leveron [35p]

Marlon LICONA - Gustavo CARIAS● (Carlos CASTELLANOS 62), Angel CASTRO, Jose FONSECA, Christian MARTINEZ, Roger ROJAS (Fredy SOSA 70), Arael GARAY, Ronald MARTINEZ (Kevin CASTRO 52), Johnny LEVERON● - Luis GARRIDO●, Alfredo MEJIA. Tr: Miguel ESCALANTE

Ulsan Complex, Ulsan
19-08-2007, 19:00, 8100, Layec FRA

Argentina 0

Luis OJEDA – Mateo MUSACCHIO (Damian MARTINEZ 67), Maximiliano OLIVA●, Fernando GODOY, Fernando MEZA, Eduardo SALVIO, Gustavo FERNANDEZ, Santiago FERNANDEZ (Carlos BENITEZ 75), Pablo ROLON (Daniel CARRIZO 62), Alexis MACHUCA, Guido PIZARRO. Tr: Miguel Angel TOJO

Syria 0

Ahmad MADNIA - Mohammed ZBIDA, Abd AL NASR HASAN●, Tamer Haj MOHAMD, Mohamed MIDOU (64), Mohammad ABADI, Ahmmad ALSALIH (Ahmad ALSALIH 50), Oday AL JAFAL (Mohammad ZAYTOUN 89), Alaa AL SHBLI●, Haani AL TAIAR, Ahmad TIT (Ziad AJOUZ 74). Tr: ALJOMAA Mohamad

World Cup Stadium, Jeju
25-08-2007, 16:00, 430, Varman FIJ

Honduras 0

Francisco REYES - Angel CASTRO, Jose FONSECA, Christian MARTINEZ, Roger ROJAS, Arael GARAY (Fredy SOSA 75), Cesear OSEGUERA (Julio OCAMPO 67), Ronald MARTINEZ (Carlos CRUZ 87), Johnny LEVERON, Luis GARRIDO, Alfredo MEJIA. Tr: Miguel ESCALANTE

Syria 2

Al Taiar [22], Alsalih [80]

Ahmad MADNIA - Ahmad ALSALIH●, Mohammed ZBIDA, Abd AL NASR HASAN, Ziad AJOUZ (Mohammad ZAYTOUN 54), Tamer Haj MOHAMD●, Mohammad ABADI, Oday AL JAFAL (Solaiman SOLAIMAN 70), Alaa AL SHBLI, Haani AL TAIAR, Ahmad TIT (Khaled AL BRIJAWI 85). Tr: Mohamad ALJOMAA

Ulsan Complex, Ulsan
22-08-2007, 17:00, 3200, Thomson SCO

Syria 1

Solaiman [70p]

Ahmad MADNIA – Ahmad ALSALIH●, Mohammed ZBIDA●, Abd AL NASR HASAN, Tamer Haj MOHAMD●, Mohamed MIDOU (Ziad AJOUZ 64), Mohammad ABADI● (Mohammad ZAYTOUN 92), Oday AL JAFAL (Solaiman SOLAIMAN 55), Alaa AL SHBLI, Haani AL TAIAR, Ahmed TIT●. Tr: ALJOMAA Mohamad

Spain 2

Merida [56], Aquino [91+]

DE GEA – ALEX●, Alberto MORGADO, David ROCHELA, Ignacio CAMACHO●, BOJAN, Fran MERIDA, Isma LOPEZ (LUKAS 78), SERGIO, JORDI (IAGO 58), (Daniel AQUINO 71), Asier ILLARRAMENDI●. Tr: Juan SANTISTEBAN

Gwangyang Soccer Only Field
25-08-2007, 16:00, 5500, Irmatov UZB

Spain 1

Benitez [32]

David DE GEA - ALEX, David ROCHELA, NACHO (Alberto MORGADO 84), XIMO, David GONZALEZ, LUKAS● (Asier ILLARRAMENDI 77), IAGO, Daniel AQUINO, Francisco ATIENZA, Sergio TEJERA (Isma LOPEZ 46). Tr: Juan SANTISTEBAN

Argentina 1

Aquino [68]

Luis OJEDA - Mateo MUSACCHIO (Fernando GODOY 46), Damien MARTINEZ, Fernando MEZA, Eduardo SALVIO, Mariano BITTOLO, Pablo ROLON (Santiago FERNANDEZ 73), Franco ZUCULINI, Alexis MACHUCA●, Carlos BENITEZ (Nicolas MAZZOLA● 60), Guido PIZARRO. Tr: Miguel Angel TOJO

GROUP D

Gwangyang Soccer Only Field
19-08-2007, 16:00, 8500, Thomson SCO

Nigeria 2

Chrisantus [15], Ibrahim [64]

Laide OKANLAWON - Ganiyu OSENI●, Usman AMODU, Azeez BALOGUN, Kingsley UDOH, King OSANGA, Macauley CHRISANTUS (Saheed FABIYI 37) (Kabiru AKINSOLA 60), Rabiu IBRAHIM, Lukma ABDULKARIM, Mustapha IBRAHIM●, Ademola RAFEAL (Lukman HARUNA 69). Tr: Yemi TELLA

France 1

Saivet [51]

Joris DELLE - Matthieu SAUNIER, Mamadou SAKHO, Said MEHAMHA, Yann MVILA (Vincent ACAPANDIE 86), Damien LE TALLEC (Emmanuel RIVIERE 93+), Thibaut BOURGEOIS, Abdoul CAMARA (Alfred NDIAYE 46), Badis LEBBIHI, Mickael NELSON, Henri SAIVET. Tr: Francois BLAQUART

Gwangyang Soccer Only Field
22-08-2007, 20:00, 4500, Bebek CRO

Japan 0

Ryotaro HIRONAGA – Takashi KANAI, Kimihiro KAI, Shunki TAKAHASHI, Tomotaka OKAMOTO, Yutaka YOSHIDA, Naoki YAMADA, Kota MIZUNUMA (Hiroki KAWANO 75), Takuji YONEMOTO (Yoichiro KAKITANI 55), Manabu SAITO● (Shohei OTSUKA 65), Jin HANATO. Tr: Hiroshi JOFUKU

Nigeria 3

Oseni [21], Chrisantus 2 [31 82]

Oladele AJIBOYE - Ganiyu OSENI (Kabiru AKINSOLA 73), Usman AMODU, Azeez BALOGUN, Kingsley UDOH, King OSANGA (Jimme EGBETA 77), Macauley CHRISANTUS (Sheriff ISA 87), Rabiu IBRAHIM, Yakubu ALFA, Mustapha IBRAHIM, Lukman HARUNA●. Tr: Yemi TELLA

Gwangyang Soccer Only Field
19-08-2007, 19:00, 8500, Varman FIJ

Japan 3

Okamoto [42], Kawano [80], Kakitani [84]

Ryotaro HIRONAGA – Takashi KANAI, Daisuke SUZUKI, Shunki TAKAHASHI, Tomotaka OKAMOTO, Yutaka YOSHIDA, Kohei HATTANDA (Hiroki KAWANO 64), Naoki YAMADA, Kota MIZUNUMA, Shohei OTSUKA (Yoichiro KAKITANI 78), Jin HANATO (Takuji YONEMOTO 87). Tr: Hiroshi JOFUKU

Haiti 1

Guemsly Junior [71]

Dorleans SHELSON - Mechak JEROME, Ismael GREGORY, Peterson DESRIVIERES, Jean Jacques BITIELO●, Fabien VORBE, Saint Cyr WIDNER, Charles HEROLD JUNIOR, Valdo NORMIL (Joseph GERALDY 86), Peterson JOSEPH, Joseph GUEMSLY JUNIOR. Tr: Jean Yves LABAZE

World Cup Stadium, Jeju
25-08-2007, 19:00, 520, Breeze AUS

Nigeria 4

Chrisantus 2 [5 60], Isa 2 [39 41]

Oladele AJIBOYE (Uche OKAFOR 80) - Azeez BALOGUN, Kingsley UDOH, Daniel JOSHUA, Kabiru AKINSOLA, Macauley CHRISANTUS, Mathew EDILE, Yakubu ALFA (Lukman ABDULKARIM 70), Sheriff ISA, Uremu EGBETA, Ademola RAFEAL (Rabiu IBRAHIM 64). Tr: Yemi TELLA

Haiti 1

Joseph [57]

Dorleans SHELSON - Mechak JEROME, Ismael GREGORY●, Peterson DESRIVIERES, Jean Jacques BITIELO, Fabien VORBE●●●63, Saint Cyr WIDNER, Charles HEROLD JUNIOR, Valdo NORMIL (Joseph GERALDY 74), Peterson JOSEPH (Wiselet SAINT LOUIS 90), Joseph GUEMSLY JUNIOR. Tr: Jean Yves LABAZE

Gwangyang Soccer Only Field
22-08-2007, 17:00, 4500, Maillet SEY

Haiti 1

Desrivieres [21p]

Dorleans SHELSON● - Mechak JEROME, Ismael GREGORY●, Peterson DESRIVIERES, Jean Jacques BITIELO, Fabien VORBE (Wiselet SAINT LOUIS 71), Saint Cyr WIDNER●, Charles HEROLD JUNIOR, Valdo NORMIL (Mark LUXAMA 89), Peterson JOSEPH (Joseph GERALDY 75), Joseph GUEMSLY JUNIOR

France 1

Le Tallec [13]

Joris DELLE● - Matthieu SAUNIER, Mamadou SAKHO, Said MEHAMHA, Yann MVILA, Damien LE TALLEC (Emmanuel RIVIERE 46), Thibaut BOURGEOIS (Vincent ACAPANDIE 78), Badis LEBBIHI●●●57, Mickael NELSON, Alfred NDIAYE, Henri SAIVET. Tr: Francois BLAQUART

Goyang Stadium, Goyang City
25-08-2007, 19:00, 11 054, Gilewski POL

France 2

Mehamha [68], Riviere [70]

Abdoulaye KEITA - Frederic DUPLUS●, Matthieu SAUNIER (Martial RIFF 49), Mamadou SAKHO, Said MEHAMHA, Yann MVILA (Damien LE TALLEC 46), Thibaut BOURGEOIS, Mickael NELSON, Alfred NDIAYE, Henri SAIVET, Emmanuel RIVIERE (Abdoul CAMARA 80). Tr: Francois BLAQUART

Japan 1

Kakitani [45]

Ryotaro HIRONAGA - Takashi KANAI, Daisuke SUZUKI, Shunki TAKAHASHI, Tomotaka OKAMOTO, Yutaka YOSHIDA, Yoichiro KAKITANI (Hiroto TANAKA 82), Naoki YAMADA, Kota MIZUNUMA (Manabu SAITO 75), Shohei OTSUKA (Hiroki KAWANO 62), Jin HANATO. Tr: Hiroshi JOFUKU

GROUP E

Changwon Stadium, Changwon
20-08-2007, 17:00, 8230, Nishimura JPN

Belgium 2

Depauw [27], Kis [36]

Jo COPPENS - Dimitri DAESELEIRE, Maxim GEURDEN, Koen HUSTINX•, Koen WEUTS (Rudy NGOMBO 34), Sebastien PHIRI, Nill DEPAUW, Eden HAZARD, Kevin KIS (Guillaume FRANCOIS 72), Kerem ZEVNE (Christian BENTEKE 57), Maurizio AQUINO. Tr: Bob BROWAEYS

Tunisia 4

Boughanmi [20], Ayari [24], Msakni 2 [42 79p]

Atef DIKHILI - IFA Bilel, Meher JABALLAH•, Nour HADHRIA• (Rafik DKHIL 67), Mossaab SASSI (Mohamed KAROUI 57), Sadok ARBI, Khaled AYARI (Mohamed WAZANI 84), Slim MARZOUKI, Majdi MAKHZOUMI, Youssef MSAKNI, Oussama BOUGHANMI•••52. Tr: Maher KANZARI

Changwon Stadium, Changwon
20-08-2007, 20:00, 4570, Coulibaly MLI

Tajikistan 4

Vasiev [32], Shoh'urov [43], Davronov [82], Fatkhuloev [86]

Farrukh BERDIEV - Eradzh RADZHABOV, Farkhod VASIEV, Kurbonali SOBIROV (Nuriddin DAVRONOV 81), Buzurgmekhr YUSUPOV (Manuchehr DZHALILOV 67), Samad SHOHZUKHUROV, Davrondzhon TUKHTASUNOV, Farkhod TOKHIROV (Abdukayum KARABAEV 73), QODIROV Furug, FATKHULOEV• Fatkhullo, QURBONOV Isomiddin. Tr: Pulod KODIROV

USA 3

Bates [9], Garza [48], Schuler [53]

Zac MACMATH - Sheanon WILLIAMS, Mykell BATES, Danny WENZEL•, Kofi SARKODIE, Jared JEFFREY, Bryan DOMINGUEZ (Ellis McLOUGHLIN 85), Abdusalam IBRAHIM (Dane SHEA 71), Billy SCHULER, Greg GARZA (Brandon ZIMMERMAN 79), Alex NIMO. Tr: John HACKWORTH

Changwon Stadium, Changwon
23-08-2007, 17:00, 3115, Buitrago COL

USA 1

Jeffrey [90p]

Zac MACMATH - Sheanon WILLIAMS, Mykell BATES•, Tommy MEYER, Chris KLUTE (Abdusalam IBRAHIM 46), Danny WENZEL, Jared JEFFREY, McLOUGHLIN Ellis (Brendan KING 70), Bryan DOMINGUEZ (Daniel CRUZ 77), Billy SCHULER•, Alex NIMO. Tr: John HACKWORTH

Tunisia 3

Hadhria 2 [8p 45p], Dkhil [94+]

Atef DIKHILI• - Mohamed KAROUI, Bilel IFA, Meher JABALLAH•, Nour HADHRIA, Mossaab SASSI (Rafik DKHIL 52), Sadok ARBI•, Khaled AYARI (Saifeddine BEN AKREMI 79), Slim MARZOUKI, Majdi MAKHZOUMI•, Youssef MSAKNI (Mohamed WAZANI 88). Tr: Maher KANZARI

Changwon Stadium, Changwon
23-08-2007, 20:00, 1400, Varman FIJ

Tajikistan 0

Mirali MURODOV• (Farrukh BERDIEV 47) - Eradzh RADZHABOV•, Farkhod VASIEV, Kurbonali SOBIROV, Buzurgmekhr YUSUPOV (Manuchehr DZHALILOV 59), Samad SHOHZUKHUROV, Davrondzhon TUKHTASUNOV, Abdukayum KARABAEV, Furug QODIROV (Sheroz ABDULLOEV 69), Fatkhullo FATKHULOEV, Isomiddin QURBONOV•. Tr: Pulod KODIROV

Belgium 1

Benteke [92+]

Jo COPPENS - Dimitri DAESELEIRE, Koen HUSTINX, Laurens SPRUYT• (Christian BENTEKE 64), Sebastien PHIRI, Nill DEPAUW, Eden HAZARD, Kevin KIS (Jens DYCK 61), Rudy NGOMBO, Manuel DE CASTRIS, Maurizio AQUINO (Kerem ZEVNE 75). Tr: Bob BROWAEYS

Cheonan Stadium, Cheonan
26-08-2007, 16:00, 14 927, Fagundes BRA

Belgium 0

Jo COPPENS - Dimitri DAESELEIRE, Koen HUSTINX (Maxim GEURDEN 68), Sebastien PHIRI, Nill DEPAUW, Eden HAZARD, Kevin KIS (Guillaume FRANCOIS 46), Rudy NGOMBO, Manuel DE CASTRIS, Maurizio AQUINO (Kerem ZEVNE 62), Christian BENTEKE•36. Tr: Bob BROWAEYS

USA 2

Urso [63], Bates [71]

Josh LAMBO - Sheanon WILLIAMS, Mykell BATES, Tommy MEYER•, Danny WENZEL (Kirk URSO 46), Jared JEFFREY, Ellis McLOUGHLIN, Bily SCHULER•, Brandon ZIMMERMAN• (Abdusalam IBRAHIM 60), Greg GARZA, Alex NIMO (Bryan DOMINGUEZ 93+). Tr: John HACKWORTH

Suwon Stadium, Suwon
26-08-2007, 16:00, 1235, Aguilar SLV

Tunisia 1

Msakni [83]

Habib TOUNSI - Mohamed KAROUI (Majdi MAKHZOUMI 77), Bilel IFA, Mohamed WAZANI, Rafik DKHIL, Ala Eddine ABBES (Khaled AYARI 46), Mossaab SASSI, Slim MARZOUKI, Ahmed MEJRI (Youssef MSAKNI 46), Saifeddine BEN AKREMI, Oussama BOUGHANMI•. Tr: Maher KANZARI

Tajikistan 0

BERDIEV Farrukh - ABDULLOEV Sheroz, RADZHABOV Eradzh, BAKHRIDDINOV Romiz, VASIEV Farkhod, SHOHZUKHUROV Samad (DZHALILOV Manuchehr 60), DAVRONOV Nuriddin, KARABAEV Abdukayum (TUKHTASUNOV Davrondzhon 64), SHARIPOV Umedzhon (SULEIMONOV Shahzod 78), FATKHULOEV Fatkhullo, FUZAYLOV Muzafar. Tr: Pulod KODIROV

GROUP F

Cheonan Stadium, Cheonan
20-08-2007, 17:00, 7741, Benquerenca POR

Colombia 3

Julio [14], Nazarith 2 [66p 88]

Mauricio ACOSTA - Ricardo CHARA, Eduar ZEA, Charles QUINTO, Sebastian VIAFARA, Julian GUILLERMO (Junior ROMERO• 68), Cristian NAZARITH•, James RODRIGUEZ (Santiago TRELLEZ 53), Miguel JULIO, Andres Felipe MOSQUERA•, Edgar PARDO (Ricardo SERNA 53). Tr: Eduardo LARA

Germany 3

Dowidat 2 [34 49], Sukuta-Pasu [39]

Fabian GIEFER• - Jonas STRIFLER, Nils TEIXEIRA, Konstantin RAUSCH (Tony JANTSCHKE 73), Kevin WOLZE•, Richard SUKUTA-PASU, Toni KROOS, Dennis DOWIDAT (Fabian BROGHAMMER 80), Sebastian RUDY•, Mario ERB, Sascha BIGALKE. Tr: Heiko HERRLICH

Cheonan Stadium, Cheonan
20-08-2007, 20:00, 11 521, Fagundes BRA

Trinidad and Tobago 1

Glenroy SAMUEL• - Akeem ADAMS, Leston PAUL•, Aaron MAUND, Stephen KNOX, Daniel JOSEPH (Marcus JOSEPH 78), Robert PRIMUS, Jean Luc ROCHFORD, Chike SULLIVAN, Daneil CYRUS, Micah LEWIS (Stephan CAMPBELL 66). Tr: Anton CORNEAL

Ghana 4

Osei 2 [12 44], Adams [45], Bossman [85]

Joseph ADDO - Paul ADDO•, Daniel OPARE, Francis BOADI, Tetteh NORTEY, Abeiku QUANSAH (Richard MPONG 52), Enoch ADU (Abdul Naza ALHASSAN 77), Sadick ADAMS (Kelvin BOSSMAN 76), Ransford OSEI, Ransford YARTEY, Philip BOAMPONG•. Tr: Sellas TETTEH

Cheonan Stadium, Cheonan
23-08-2007, 17:00, 7516, Aguilar SLV

Ghana 2

Osei [52], Adams [53]

Joseph ADDO - Paul ADDO, Daniel OPARE, Francis BOADI (Abdul Naza ALHASSAN 46), Tetteh NORTEY•, Abeiku QUANSAH, Enoch ADU• (Kelvin BOSSMAN 74), Sadick ADAMS, Ransford OSEI, Ransford YARTEY, Philip BOAMPONG•. Tr: Sellas TETTEH

Germany 2

Bigalke [5], Kroos 2 [12 27]

Fabian GIEFER - Jonas STRIFLER, Nils TEIXEIRA, Konstantin RAUSCH•••83, Kevin WOLZE, Richard SUKUTA-PASU (Alexander ESSWEIN 40) (FUNK Patrick 90), Toni KROOS, Dennis DOWIDAT•, Sebastian RUDY, Mario ERB•, Sascha BIGALKE (Henning SAUERBIER 73). Tr: Heiko HERRLICH

Cheonan Stadium, Cheonan
23-08-2007, 20:00, 13 537, Coulibaly MLI

Trinidad and Tobago 0

Glenroy SAMUEL - Akeem ADAMS (Sheldon BATEAU 70), Leston PAUL, Aaron MAUND (Sean DE SILVA 75), Stephen KNOX, Daniel JOSEPH (Kevin MOLINO 55), Robert PRIMUS, Stephan CAMPBELL, Jean Luc ROCHFORD, Chike SULLIVAN, Daneil CYRUS•. Tr: Anton CORNEAL

Colombia 5

Mosquera 2 [22 63], Trellez [60], Pardo [68], Serna [72]

Mauricio ACOSTA - Ricardo CHARA, Eduar ZEA•, Sebastian VIAFARA, Julian GUILLERMO, Cristian NAZARITH (Edgar PARDO 65), Santiago TRELLEZ (Jose RAMIREZ 78), James RODRIGUEZ (Ricardo SERNA 54), Junior ROMERO, Miguel JULIO, Andres Felipe MOSQUERA•. Tr: Eduardo LARA

Ulsan Complex, Ulsan
26-08-2007, 19:00, 8500, Thomson SCO

Colombia 1

Nazarith [60]

ACOSTA Mauricio - Ricardo CHARA, Eduar ZEA, Sebastian VIAFARA, Julian GUILLERMO, Cristian NAZARITH (Ricardo VILLARRAGA 92+), Santiago TRELLEZ (PARDO Edgar 77), James RODRIGUEZ (Ricardo SERNA 56), Carlos RAMOS, Junior ROMERO, Miguel JULIO. Tr: Eduardo LARA

Ghana 2

Osei [32], Yartey [84]

Joseph ADDO - Daniel OPARE (Abdul Naza ALHASSAN 79), Francis BOADI (Eric OPOKU 74), Tetteh NORTEY, Abeiku QUANSAH, Enoch ADU•, Sadick ADAMS• (Issac DONKOR 91), Ransford OSEI, Ishamel YARTEY, Philip BOAMPONG•, Meisuna ALHASSAN. Tr: Sellas TETTEH

Changwon Stadium, Changwon
26-08-2007, 19:00, 4320, Nishimura JPN

Germany 5

Broghammer [5], Esswein 2 [31 37], Funk [39], Wolze [93+]

Rene VOLLATH - Kai EVERS, Nils TEIXEIRA• (Mario ERB 63), Henning SAUERBIER, Patrick FUNK, Richard SUKUTA-PASU (Alexander ESSWEIN 24), Mehmet EKICI, Matthias HAAS, Tony JANTSCHKE, Fabian BROGHAMMER, Sascha BIGALKE (Kevin WOLZE 46). Tr: Heiko HERRLICH

Trinidad and Tobago 0

Jesse FULLERTON - Sheldon BATEAU•, Akeem ADAMS•, Leston PAUL•, Aaron MAUND (Aubrey DAVID 82), Stephen KNOX, Robert PRIMUS (Ryan O'NEIL• 84), Chike SULLIVAN (Sean DE SILVA 53), Marcus JOSEPH•, Daneil CYRUS, Micah LEWIS. Tr: Anton CORNEAL

2ND ROUND

Gwangyang Soccer Only Field
30-08-2007, 17:00, 4500, Bebek CRO

Nigeria 2
Isa [78], Alfa [83]

Oladele AJIBOYE – Azeez BALOGUN, Kingsley UDOH, King OSANGA (Sheriff ISA 76), Kabiru AKINSOLA● (Lukman ABDULKARIM 89), Macauley CHRISANTUS, Rabiu IBRAHIM (Ganiyu OSENI 55), Matthew EDILE, Yakubu ALFA, Mustapha IBRAHIM, Lukman HARUNA●. Tr: Yemi TELLA

Colombia 1
Trellez [62]

Mauricio ACOSTA – Ricardo CHARA, Eduar ZEA, Sebastian VIAFARA●, Julian GUILLERMO, Cristian NAZARITH, Santiago TRELLEZ (Edgar PARDO 85), Junior ROMERO● (Charles QUINTO 46), Ricardo SERNA (Ricardo VILLARRAGA 71), Miguel JULIO, Andres Felipe MOSQUERA. Tr: Eduardo LARA

Goyang Stadium, Goyang City
30-08-2007, 17:00, 5698, Benquerenca POR

Argentina 2
Sauro 2 [25 41]

Luis OJEDA – Mateo MUSACCHIO, Damian MARTINEZ (Fernando GODOY 61), Fernando MEZA, Eduardo SALVIO (Gustavo FERNANDEZ 64), Mariano BITTOLO, Santiago FERNANDEZ (Pablo ROLON 77), Franco ZUCULINI●, Gaston SAURO, Nicolas MAZZOLA, Guido PIZARRO. Tr: Miguel Angel TOJO

Costa Rica 0

Leonel MOREIRA – Roy SMITH, Jordan SMITH●, Esteban LUNA (Marcos URENA 53), Diego BRENES (Julio IBARRA 73), David GUZMAN, Jorge CASTRO, Jessy PERALTA, Bruno CASTRO (Josue MARTINEZ 46), Erick ROJAS, Daniel VARELA. Tr: Manuel URENA

World Cup Stadium, Jeju
30-08-2007, 20:00, 1650, Buitrago COL

England 3
Lansbury [17p], Pearce [45], Murphy [62]

Alex SMITHIES● – Nana OFORI-TWUMASI, James REID, Henri LANSBURY, Krystian PEARCE●, Daniel WELBECK (Gavin HOYTE 78), Rhys MURPHY (Ashley CHAMBERS 90), Nathan PORRITT (Daniel GOSLING 56), Michael WOODS●, Jordan SPENCE, Jonathan FRANKS. Tr: John PEACOCK

Syria 1
Ajouz [51]

Ahmad MADNIA – Mohammad ZBIDA (Mohammad ZAYTOUN 68), Khaled AL BRIJAWI, Abd AL NASR HASAN, Ziad AJOUZ, Mohammad ABADI, Oday AL JAFAL, Alaa AL SHBLI, Haani AL TAIAR (Mohamed MIDOU 46), Solaiman SOLAIMAN●, Ahmad TIT. Tr: Mohamad ALJOMAA

Cheonan Stadium, Cheonan
30-08-2007, 20:000, 15 069, Thomson SCO

Germany 2
Sukuta-Pasu 2 [65 89]

Rene VOLLATH – Jonas STRIFLER, Nils TEIXEIRA, Konstantin RAUSCH, Kevin WOLZE, Richard SUKUTA-PASU (Alexander ESSWEIN 94), Toni KROOS, Dennis DOWIDAT, Sebastian RUDY, Mario ERB, Sascha BIGALKE (Henning SAUERBIER 91). Tr: Heiko HERRLICH

USA 1
Bates [92+]

Josh LAMBO - Sheanon WILLIAMS●, Mykell BATES, Tommy MEYER, Danny WENZEL● (Daniel CRUZ 83), Jared JEFFREY, Ellis MC LOUGHLIN, Kirk URSO (Bryan DOMINGUEZ 75), Brandon ZIMMERMAN●, Greg GARZA (Abdusalam IBRAHIM 46), Alex NIMO. Tr: John HACKWORTH

Gwangyang Soccer Only Field
29-08-2007, 20:00, 5500, Gilewski POL

Ghana 1
Donkor [51]

Joseph ADDO● – Daniel OPARE, Francis BOADI●●●44, Tetteh NORTEY, Abeiku QUANSAH, Sadick ADAMS● (Abdul Naza ALHASSAN 77), Ransford OSEI, Ishamel YARTEY, Meisuna ALHASSAN, Issac DONKOR (Richard MPONG 91), Eric OPOKU●. Tr: Sellas TETTEH

Brazil 0

MARCELO - RAFAEL (BRUNO COLLACO 59), LAZARO, TIAGO (FABINHO● 83), FABIO, FELLIPE, LULINHA, ALEX, DANIEL, TALES (JUNIOR 54), GIU-LIANO. Tr: Luiz Antonio NIZZO

Suwon Stadium, Suwon
29-08-2007, 20:00, 1150, Breeze AUS

Peru 1 5p
Manco [13]

Eder HERMOZA – Joseph MUNOZ, Nestor DUARTE, Bryan SALAZAR, Reimond MANCO, Carlos BAZALAR, Irven AVILA, Manuel CALDERON, Juan ARCE● (Antony MOLINA 90), Christian LA TORRE (Cesar RUIZ 60), Gary CORREA (Luis TRUJILLO 66). Tr: Juan Jose ORE

Tajikistan 1 4p
Davronov [15]

Farrukh BERDIEV – Sheroz ABDULLOEV●, Eradzh RADZHABOV, Farkhod VASIEV, Kurbonali SOBIROV (Muzafar FUZAYLOV 92+), Manuchehr DZHALILOV●, Nuriddin DAVRONOV (Davrondzhon TUKHTASUNOV 63), Farkhod TOKHIROV, Furug QODIROV, Umedzhon SHARIPOV (Buzurgmekhr YUSUPOV 72), Fatkhullo FATKHULOEV. Tr: Pulod KODIROV

Changwon Stadium, Changwon
29-08-2007, 17:00, 2150, Irmatov UZB

Tunisia 1
Hadhria [49]

Habib TOUNSI● – Mohamed KAROUI●●76, Bilel IFA, Meher JABALLAH, Nour HADHRIA (Majdi MAKHZOUMI 79), Mossaab SASSI, Sadok ARBI, Khaled AYARI (Mohamed WAZANI 97), Slim MAR-ZOUKI, Youssef MSAKNI (Rafik DKHIL 73), Oussama BOUGHANMI. Tr: Maher KANZARI

France 3
Saivet [43], Le Tallec 2 [99 105]

Abdoulaye KEITA - Frederic DUPLUS, Mamadou SAKHO, Said MEHAMHA, Martial RIFF, Damien LE TALLEC (Vincent ACAPANDIE 106), Thibaut BOUR-GEOIS (Herve BAZILE 71), Mickael NELSON, Alfred NDIAYE, Henri SAIVET, Emmanuel RIVIERE (Yann MVILA 91'). Tr: Francois BLAQUART

Ulsan Complex, Ulsan
29-08-2007, 17:00, 8500, Fagundes BRA

Spain 3
Bojan 2 [28 50], Iago [67]

David DE GEA (YELCO 85) – ALEX, Alberto MOR-GADO, David ROCHELA, Ignacio CAMACHO, BOJAN, Fran MERIDA (Asier ILLARRAMENDI 79), Isma LOPEZ, SERGIO●, Daniel AQUINO, JORDI (IAGO 66). Tr: Juan SANTISTEBAN

Korea DPR 0

O Mun Song – SIM Hyon Jin, RI Hyong Mu, KANG Kuk Chol, KANG Chol Ryong, HAN Kyong Gwang, MYONG Cha Hyon, JONG II Ju (RI Myong Jun 31), RI Sang Chol (PAK Yu II 57), AN II Bom●, RIM Chol Min (PAK Kwang Ryong 49). Tr: AN Ye Gun

QUARTER-FINALS

Cheonan Stadium, Cheonan
2-09-2007, 16:00, 14 581, Breeze AUS

Argentina 0

Luis OJEDA - Mateo MUSACCHIO, Fernando MEZA●, Eduardo SALVIO, Mariano BITTOLO (Maximiliano OLIVA 46), Santiago FERNANDEZ, Franco ZUCULINI (Pablo ROLON 68), Alexis MACHUCA, Gaston SAURO, Nicolas MAZZOLA (Carlos BENITEZ 56), Guido PIZARRO. Tr: Miguel Angel TOJO

Nigeria 2
Haruna [33p], Chrisantus [45]

Oladele AJIBOYE - Ganiyu OSENI, Azeez BALOGUN (Daniel JOSHUA 76), Kingsley UDOH, Macauley CHRISANTUS, Rabiu IBRAHIM, Matthew EDILE, Yakubu ALFA, Sheriff ISA (Kabiru AKINSOLA 63), Mustapha IBRAHIM, Lukman HARUNA (King OSANGA 47). Tr: Yemi TELLA

Goyang Stadium, Goyang City
2-09-2007, 19:00, 12 560, Fagundes BRA

England 1
Murphy [65]

Alex SMITHIES – Nana OFORI-TWUMASI, Henri LANSBURY (Medi ELITO 79), Krystian PEARCE●, Rhys MURPHY, Daniel GOSLING, Michael WOODS (Daniel WELBECK 58), Jordan SPENCE, Gavin HOYTE, Tristan PLUMMER (Ashley CHAMBERS 58●88), Jonathan FRANKS. Tr: John PEACOCK

Germany 4
Rudy [50], Sukuta-Pasu [56], Dowidat [74], Kroos [87]

Rene VOLLATH – Jonas STRIFLER, Nils TEIXEIRA, Konstantin RAUSCH, Kevin WOLZE, Richard SUKUTA-PASU (Alexander ESSWEIN 85), Toni KROOS● (Patric FUNK 90), Dennis DOWIDAT●, Sebastian RUDY, Mario ERB, Sascha BIGALKE (Fabian BROGHAMMER 91').Tr: Heiko HERRLICH

Changwon Stadium, Changwon

1-09-2007, 19:00, 7555, Nishimura JPN

Ghana   2

Adams [45], Osei [53]

Joseph ADDO - Paul ADDO (Meisuna ALHASSAN 71), Daniel OPARE∗, Tetteh NORTEY, Enoch ADU, Sadick ADAMS (Kelvin BOSSMAN 80), Ransford OSEI, Ishamel YARTEY (Prince GYIMAH 82), Philip BOAMPONG, Issac DONKOR, Eric OPOKU. Tr: Sellas TETTEH

Peru   0

Eder HERMOZA - Joseph MUNOZ, Nestor DUARTE, Bryan SALAZAR (Ernesto SALAZAR∗ 57), Reimond MANCO, Carlos BAZALAR (Irven AVILA 69), Jairo HERNANDEZ, Juan ZEVALLOS, Cesar RUIZ, Christian LA TORRE, Gary CORREA (Luis TRUJILLO 62). Tr: Juan Jose ORE

World Cup Stadium, Jeju

1-09-2007, 16:00, 2310, Aguilar SLV

France   1 4p

Le Tallec [52]

Abdoulaye KEITA - Frederic DUPLUS, Mamadou SAKHO, Said MEHAMHA (Thibaut BOURGEOIS 75), Yann MVILA∗, Martial RIFF, Damien LE TALLEC, Mickael NELSON, Alfred NDIAYE, Henri SAIVET (Vincent ACAPANDIE 97), Emmanuel RIVIERE (Abdoul CAMARA 78). Tr: Francois BLAQUART

Spain   1 5p

Jordi [72]

David DE GEA - ALEX, Alberto MORGADO (NACHO 42), David ROCHELA, Ignacio CAMACHO, XIMO (JORDI 57), BOJAN, Fran MERIDA, Isma LOPEZ (Daniel AQUINO 57), IAGO, SERGIO. Tr: Juan SANTISTEBAN

SEMI-FINALS

Suwon Stadium, Suwon

6-09-2007, 19:00, 3472, Aguilar SLV

Nigeria   3

Chrisantus [10], Alfa [18], Akinsola [94+]

Oladele AJIBOYE – Ganiyu OSEN (Kabiru AKINSOLA 71), Usman AMODU∗ (Sheriff ISA 46), Kingsley UDOH, Daniel JOSHUA, Macauley CHRISANTUS, Rabiu IBRAHIM, Matthew EDILE, Yakubu ALFA, Mustapha IBRAHIM, Lukman HARUNA (Ademola RAFEAL 16). Tr: Yemi TELLA

Germany   1

Kroos [33]

Rene VOLLATH - Jonas STRIFLER∗ (Kai EVERS 83), Nils TEIXEIRA, Konstantin RAUSCH, Kevin WOLZE, Richard SUKUTA-PASU, Toni KROOS, Dennis DOWIDAT (Alexander ESSWEIN 68), Sebastian RUDY (Fabian BROGHAMMER 83), Mario ERB, Sascha BIGALKE. Tr: Heiko HERRLICH

Ulsan Complex, Ulsan

5-09-2007, 19:00, 9700, Fagundes BRA

Spain   2

Aquino [67], Bojan [116]

David DE GEA - Alberto MORGADO, David ROCHELA, NACHO (ALEX 83), Ignacio CAMACHO∗, BOJAN∗∗∗121, Fran MERIDA∗, Isma LOPEZ (LUKAS 70), IAGO (Asier ILLARRAMENDI 79), SERGIO, Daniel AQUINO. Tr: Juan SANTISTEBAN

Ghana   1

Adams [80]

Joseph ADDO - Paul ADDO, Daniel OPARE, Tetteh NORTEY∗ (Abdul Naza ALHASSAN 100), Enoch ADU, Sadick ADAMS∗ (Kelvin BOSSMAN 106), Ransford OSEI, Ishamel YARTEY, Philip BOAMPONG∗, Issac DONKOR (Abeiku QUANSAH 46), Eric OPOKU∗. Tr: Sellas TETTEH

3RD PLACE PLAY-OFF AND FINAL

World Cup Stadium, Seoul

9-09-2007, 16:00, 22 345, Benquerenca POR

Ghana   1

Osei [67]

Joseph ADDO - Paul ADDO, Daniel OPARE, Francis BOADI (Richard MPONG 87), Tetteh NORTEY, Abeiku QUANSAH, Enoch ADU (Abdul Naza ALHASSAN 62), Ransford OSEI, Ishamel YARTEY∗, Philip BOAMPONG∗, Kelvin BOSSMAN (Issac DONKOR 46). Tr: Sellas TETTEH

Germany   2

Kroos [17], Esswein [92]

Rene VOLLATH - Jonas STRIFLER, Nils TEIXEIRA, Konstantin RAUSCH (Patrick FUNK 95), Kevin WOLZE∗, Richard SUKUTA-PASU (Fabian BROGHAMMER 80), Toni KROOS, Dennis DOWIDAT (Alexander ESSWEIN 82∗∗∗93), Sebastian RUDY∗, Mario ERB, Sascha BIGALKE. Tr: Heiko HERRLICH

Final. World Cup Stadium, Seoul

9-09-2007, 19:00, 36 125, Nishimura JPN

Nigeria   0 3p

Oladele AJIBOYE - Ganiyu OSEN, Kingsley UDOH, Daniel JOSHUA, King OSANGA (Kabiru AKINSOLA 73), Macauley CHRISANTUS, Rabiu IBRAHIM, Matthew EDILE, Yakubu ALFA (Lukman ABDULKARIM∗ 96), Mustapha IBRAHIM, Ademola RAFEAL∗ (Sheriff ISA 46). Tr: Yemi TELLA

Spain   0 0p

David DE GEA - Alberto MORGADO (Asier ILLARRAMENDI 106), David ROCHELA, NACHO (ALEX 67), Ignacio CAMACHO, Fran MERIDA∗, Isma LOPEZ, LUKAS∗ (David GONZALEZ 81), IAGO, SERGIO, Daniel AQUINO. Tr: Juan SANTISTEBAN

**ROUND OF 16 PENALTY SHOOT-OUT JAPAN V CZECH REPUBLIC
CZECH REPUBLIC WON 4-3**

Yasuda ✖; Fenin ✓; Aoki ✓; Kudela ✓; Makino ✓; Suchy ✓;
Morishima ✖; Pekhart ✖; Kashiwagi ✓; Oklestek ✓

**QUARTER-FINAL PENALTY SHOOT-OUT SPAIN V CZECH REPUBLIC
CZECH REPUBLIC WON 4-3**

Mata ✓; Fenin ✓; González ✓; Suchy ✓; Valiente ✖;
Kudela ✓; Javi Garcia ✓; Pekhart ✓; Pique ✖

**FINAL PENALTY SHOOT-OUT NIGERIA V SPAIN
NIGERIA WON 3-0**

Illarramendi ✖; Edile ✓; Merida ✖; Joshua ✓; Iago ✖; Oseni ✓

FIFA WOMEN'S WORLD CUP CHINA PR 2007

FIFA WOMEN'S WORLD CUP CHINA PR 2007

First round groups	Pts	Quarter–finals		Semi–finals		Final	
Germany	7						
England	5	Germany	3				
Japan	4	Korea DPR	0				
Argentina	0						
				Germany	3		
	Pts			Norway	0		
USA	7						
Korea DPR	4	China PR	0				
Sweden	4	Norway	1				
Nigeria	1						
						Germany	2
	Pts					Brazil	0
Norway	7						
Australia	5	USA	3				
Canada	4	England	0				
Ghana	0						
				USA	0		
	Pts			Brazil	4		
Brazil	9					**3rd Place Play-off**	
China PR	6	Australia	2			USA	4
Denmark	3	Brazil	3			Norway	1
New Zealand	0						

		PL	W	D	L	F	A	PTS
1	Germany	3	2	1	0	13	0	7
2	England	3	1	2	0	8	3	5
3	Japan	3	1	1	1	3	4	4
4	Argentina	3	0	0	3	1	18	0

	ENG	JPN	ARG
Germany	0-0	2-0	11-0
England		2-2	6-1
Japan			1-0

Hongkou, Shanghai
10-09-2007, 20:00, 28 098, Ogston AUS, Keen AUS, Ho AUS

GER 11 — 0 ARG

Behringer 2 12 24, Garefrekes 17, Prinz 3 29 46+ 59, Lingor 2 51 91+, Smisek 3 57 70 79

GERMANY

1	Nadine ANGERER	
2	Kerstin STEGEMANN	
6	Linda BRESONIK	
7	Melanie BEHRINGER	68
8	Sandra SMISEK	
9	Birgit PRINZ (C)	
10	Renate LINGOR	
13	Sandra MINNERT	
14	Simone LAUDEHR	74
17	Ariane HINGST	
18	Kerstin GAREFREKES	84
Tr: Silvia NEID		
3	Saskia BARTUSIAK	74
11	Anja MITTAG	84
20	Petra WIMBERSKY	68

ARGENTINA

12	Vanina CORREA	
2	Eva GONZALEZ (C)	
3	Valeria COTELO	
4	Gabriela CHAVEZ	
6	Sabrina BARBITTA	
8	Clarisa HUBER	74
10	Rosana GOMEZ	66
13	Maria QUINONES	
17	Fabiana VALLEJOS	
18	Maria POTASSA	
19	Analia ALMEIDA	53
Tr: Jose Carlos BORRELLO		
7	Ludmila MANICLER	53
15	Florencia MANDRILE	74
20	Mercedes PEREYRA	66

Hongkou, Shanghai
11-09-2007, 20:00, 27 146, Seitz USA, Tovar MEX, Munoz MEX

JPN 2 — 2 ENG

Miyama 2 55 95+

Smith 2 81 83

JAPAN

1	Miho FUKUMOTO	
2	Hiromi ISOZAKI (C)	86
3	Yukari KINGA	46
7	Tomomi MIYAMOTO	71
8	Tomoe SAKAI	
9	Eriko ARAKAWA	
10	Homare SAWA	
15	Azusa IWASHIMIZU	
16	Aya MIYAMA	
18	Shinobu OHNO	
20	Rumi UTSUGI	
Tr: Hiroshi OHASHI		
6	Ayumi HARA	71
13	Kozue ANDO	46
17	Yuki NAGASATO	86

ENGLAND

1	Rachel BROWN	
2	Alex SCOTT	89
3	Casey STONEY	
4	Katie CHAPMAN	
5	Faye WHITE (C)	
6	Mary PHILLIP	
7	Karen CARNEY	
8	Fara WILLIAMS	
9	Eniola ALUKO	74
10	Kelly SMITH	
11	Rachel YANKEY	
Tr: Hope POWELL		
16	Jill SCOTT	74
20	Lindsay JOHNSON	89

Hongkou, Shanghai
14-09-2007, 17:00, 27 730, Damkova CZE, Ndah BEN, Oulhaj MAR

ARG 0 — 1 JPN

Nagasato 91+

ARGENTINA

1	Romina FERRO	
2	Eva GONZALEZ (C)	
4	Gabriela CHAVEZ	
8	Clarisa HUBER	53
13	Maria QUINONES	61
14	Catalina PEREZ	
15	Florencia MANDRILE	
17	Fabiana VALLEJOS	
18	Maria POTASSA	77
19	Analia ALMEIDA	
20	Mercedes PEREYRA	
Tr: Jose Carlos BORRELLO		
7	Ludmila MANICLER	77
10	Emilia MENDIETA	61
16	Andrea OJEDA	53

JAPAN

1	Miho FUKUMOTO	
2	Hiromi ISOZAKI (C)	
4	Kyoko YANO	50
7	Tomomi MIYAMOTO	
8	Tomoe SAKAI	
10	Homare SAWA	
13	Kozue ANDO	79
15	Azusa IWASHIMIZU	
16	Aya MIYAMA	
17	Yuki NAGASATO	
18	Shinobu OHNO	57
Tr: Hiroshi OHASHI		
3	Yukari KINGA	79
9	Eriko ARAKAWA	57
20	Rumi UTSUGI	50

Hongkou, Shanghai
14-09-2007, 20:00, 27 730, Palmqvist SWE, Borg SWE, Steinlund NOR

ENG 0 — 0 GER

ENGLAND

1	Rachel BROWN	
2	Alex SCOTT	
3	Casey STONEY	
4	Katie CHAPMAN	
5	Faye WHITE (C)	
6	Mary PHILLIP	
7	Karen CARNEY	57
8	Fara WILLIAMS	
10	Kelly SMITH	
12	Anita ASANTE	
16	Jill SCOTT	
Tr: Hope POWELL		
11	Rachel YANKEY	57

GERMANY

1	Nadine ANGERER	
2	Kerstin STEGEMANN	
5	Annike KRAHN	
6	Linda BRESONIK	
7	Melanie BEHRINGER	63
8	Sandra SMISEK	
9	Birgit PRINZ (C)	
10	Renate LINGOR	
14	Simone LAUDEHR	
17	Ariane HINGST	
18	Kerstin GAREFREKES	
Tr: Silvia NEID		
19	Fatmire BAJRAMAJ	63

Dragon, Hangzhou
17-09-2007, 20:00, 39 817, Correa COL, Cini ITA, Canales ECU

GER 2 — 0 JPN

Prinz 21, Lingor 87p

GERMANY

1	Nadine ANGERER	
2	Kerstin STEGEMANN	
5	Annike KRAHN	
6	Linda BRESONIK	
7	Melanie BEHRINGER	57
8	Sandra SMISEK	78
9	Birgit PRINZ (C)	
10	Renate LINGOR	
17	Ariane HINGST	
18	Kerstin GAREFREKES	
20	Petra WIMBERSKY	
Tr: Silvia NEID		
16	Martina MUELLER	78
19	Fatmire BAJRAMAJ	57

JAPAN

1	Miho FUKUMOTO		
2	Hiromi ISOZAKI (C)		
3	Yukari KINGA		
5	Miyuki YANAGITA		
6	Ayumi HARA		
8	Tomoe SAKAI		
10	Homare SAWA		
15	Azusa IWASHIMIZU		
16	Aya MIYAMA	46	
17	Yuki NAGASATO	76	
20	Rumi UTSUGI		
Tr: Hiroshi OHASHI			
7	Tomomi MIYAMOTO	76	
9	Eriko ARAKAWA	46	63
18	Shinobu OHNO	63	

Sports Centre, Chengdu
17-09-2007, 20:00, 30 730, Ferreira-James GUY, Mohammed TRI, Jeffery GUY

ENG 6 — 1 ARG

Gonzalez OG 9, Scott 10, Williams 50p, Smith 2 64 77, Exley 90p

Gonzalez 60

ENGLAND

1	Rachel BROWN	
2	Alex SCOTT	68
3	Casey STONEY	
5	Faye WHITE (C)	
6	Mary PHILLIP	
8	Fara WILLIAMS	
9	Eniola ALUKO	80
10	Kelly SMITH	80
11	Rachel YANKEY	
12	Anita ASANTE	
16	Jill SCOTT	
Tr: Hope POWELL		
15	Sue SMITH	68
17	Jodie HANDLEY	80
19	Vicky EXLEY	80

ARGENTINA

1	Romina FERRO	
2	Eva GONZALEZ (C)	
4	Gabriela CHAVEZ	
8	Clarisa HUBER	52
13	Maria QUINONES	76
14	Catalina PEREZ	49
15	Florencia MANDRILE	
17	Fabiana VALLEJOS	
18	Maria POTASSA	
19	Analia ALMEIDA	62
20	Mercedes PEREYRA	
Tr: Jose Carlos BORRELLO		
3	Valeria COTELO	52
9	Natalia GATTI	62
10	Emilia MENDIETA	76

	GROUP B	PL	W	D	L	F	A	PTS		PRK	SWE	NGA
1	USA	3	2	1	0	5	2	7		2-2	2-0	1-0
2	Korea DPR	3	1	1	1	5	4	4			1-2	2-0
3	Sweden	3	1	1	1	3	4	4				1-1
4	Nigeria	3	0	1	2	1	4	1				

Sports Centre, Chengdu
11-09-2007, 17:00, 35 100, Petignat SUI, Lagrange FRA, Vives Solana FRA

USA 2 – 2 PRK

Wambach 50, O'Reilly 69   Kil Son Hui 58, Kim Yong Ae 62

USA					KOREA DPR		
18	Hope SOLO				JON Myong Hui		21
3	Christie RAMPONE				KIM Kyong Hwa		2
4	Cat WHITEHILL				OM Jong Ran		3
7	Shannon BOXX				SONG Jong Sun		5
9	Heather O'REILLY	92	22		HO Sun Hui		7
11	Carli LLOYD				KIL Son Hui		8
13	Kristine LILLY (C)				RI Un Suk		9
14	Stephanie LOPEZ				(C) RI Kum Suk		10
15	Kate MARKGRAF				RI Un Gyong		12
17	Lori CHALUPNY				SONU Kyong Sun		15
20	Abby WAMBACH				KONG Hye Ok		16
	Tr: Greg RYAN				Tr: KIM Kwang Min		
6	Natasha KAI	92		22 90	KIM Yong Ae		17
				90	JONG Pok Sim		19

Sports Centre, Chengdu
11-09-2007, 20:00, 35 100, Niu CHN, Liu CHN, Fu CHN

NGA 1 – 1 SWE

Uwak 82   Svensson 50

NIGERIA					SWEDEN		
1	Precious DEDE				Hedvig LINDAHL		1
4	Perpetua NKWOCHA				Stina SEGERSTROM		3
5	Onome EBI				Hanna MARKLUND		4
8	Ifeanyi CHIEJINE				Caroline SEGER		5
10	Rita CHIKWELU				Sara THUNEBRO		6
11	Chi-Chi IGBO	35	83		Charlotta SCHELIN		8
13	Christie GEORGE (C)		69		Hanna LJUNGBERG		10
14	Faith IKIDI				(C) Victoria SVENSSON		11
15	Maureen MMADU	59			Frida OSTBERG		13
18	Cynthia UWAK				Therese SJOGRAN		15
	Tr: Ntiero EFFIOM				Anna PAULSON		16
2	Efioanwan EKPO	59	69		Tr: Thomas DENNERBY		
7	Stella MBACHU	35	83		Sara JOHANSSON		14
					Linda FORSBERG		20

Sports Centre, Chengdu
14-09-2007, 35 600, Gall HUN, Villa Guttierrez ESP, Cini ITA

SWE 0 – 2 USA

Wambach 2 34p 58

SWEDEN					USA		
1	Hedvig LINDAHL				Hope SOLO		18
3	Stina SEGERSTROM	81			Christie RAMPONE		3
4	Hanna MARKLUND				Cat WHITEHILL		4
5	Caroline SEGER	67			Lindsay TARPLEY		5
8	Charlotta SCHELIN	46			Carli LLOYD		11
10	Hanna LJUNGBERG				Leslie OSBORNE		12
11	Victoria SVENSSON (C)				(C) Kristine LILLY		13
13	Frida OSTBERG				Stephanie LOPEZ		14
15	Therese SJOGRAN	65			Kate MARKGRAF		15
16	Anna PAULSON				Lori CHALUPNY		17
20	Linda FORSBERG				Abby WAMBACH		20
	Tr: Thomas DENNERBY				Tr: Greg RYAN		
9	Therese LUNDIN	81	46		Shannon BOXX	46	7
18	Nilla FISCHER	65	67		Heather O'REILLY	67	9

Sports Centre, Chengdu
14-09-2007, 20:00, 35 600, Ogston AUS, Keen AUS, Ho AUS

PRK 2 – 0 NGA

Kim Kyong Hwa 17, Ri Kum Suk 21

KOREA DPR					NIGERIA		
21	JON Myong Hui				Precious DEDE		1
2	KIM Kyong Hwa	77			Efioanwan EKPO		2
3	OM Jong Ran				Perpetua NKWOCHA		4
5	SONG Jong Sun			30	Onome EBI		5
8	KIL Son Hui				Stella MBACHU		7
9	RI Un Suk			80	Ifeanyi CHIEJINE		8
10	RI Kum Suk (C)			61	Rita CHIKWELU		10
12	RI Un Gyong				(C) Christie GEORGE		13
15	SONU Kyong Sun				Faith IKIDI		14
16	KONG Hye Ok				Ulumma JEROME		16
17	KIM Yong Ae				Cynthia UWAK		18
	Tr: KIM Kwang Min				Tr: Ntiero EFFIOM		
19	JONG Pok Sim	77		80	Chi-Chi IGBO		11
				61	Maureen MMADU		15
				30	Lilian COLE		19

Hongkou, Shanghai
18-09-2007, 20:00, 6100, Oiwa JPN, Yoshizawa JPN, Liu TPE

NGA 0 – 1 USA

Chalupny 1

NIGERIA					USA		
1	Precious DEDE				Hope SOLO		18
2	Efioanwan EKPO	77			Christie RAMPONE		3
4	Perpetua NKWOCHA				Cat WHITEHILL		4
7	Stella MBACHU				Shannon BOXX		7
10	Rita CHIKWELU				Heather O'REILLY		9
11	Chi-Chi IGBO	22	64		Carli LLOYD		11
13	Christie GEORGE	84			Kristine LILLY		13
14	Faith IKIDI				Stephanie LOPEZ		14
16	Ulumma JEROME				Kate MARKGRAF		15
18	Cynthia UWAK	83			Lori CHALUPNY		17
19	Lilian COLE				Abby WAMBACH		20
	Tr: Ntiero EFFIOM				Tr: Greg RYAN		
8	Ifeanyi CHIEJINE	22	84	84	Lindsay TARPLEY		5
9	Ogonna CHUKWUDI	83	77 64	77	Tina ELLERTSON		8
				64	Leslie OSBORNE		12

Olympic, Tianjin
18-09-2007, 20:00, 33 196, Beck GER, Mirt ROU, Draeger GER

PRK 1 – 2 SWE

Ri Un Suk 22   Schelin 2 4 54

KOREA DPR					SWEDEN		
21	JON Myong Hui				Hedvig LINDAHL		1
2	KIM Kyong Hwa	56			Karolina WESTBERG		2
3	OM Jong Ran				Hanna MARKLUND		4
5	SONG Jong Sun				Caroline SEGER		5
8	KIL Son Hui	85			Charlotta SCHELIN		8
9	RI Un Suk			40	Hanna LJUNGBERG		10
10	RI Kum Suk (C)	40			(C) Victoria SVENSSON		11
12	RI Un Gyong				Frida OSTBERG		13
15	SONU Kyong Sun				Therese SJOGRAN		15
16	KONG Hye Ok	69		69	Anna PAULSON		16
17	KIM Yong Ae	60			Nilla FISCHER		18
	Tr: KIM Kwang Min				Tr: Thomas DENNERBY		
6	KIM Ok Sim	85	40 89	40 89	Sara THUNEBRO		6
19	JONG Pok Sim	60	89	89	Therese LUNDIN		9
20	HONG Myong Gum	56	69	69	Sara JOHANSSON		14

GROUP C		PL	W	D	L	F	A	PTS
1	Norway	3	2	1	0	10	4	7
2	Australia	3	1	2	0	7	4	5
3	Canada	3	1	1	1	7	4	4
4	Ghana	3	0	0	3	3	15	0

	AUS	CAN	GHA
	1-1	2-1	7-2
		2-2	4-1
			4-0

Dragon, Hangzhou
12-09-2007, 17:00, 30 752, Correa COL, Canales ECU, Villa Gutierrez ESP

GHA   1   4   AUS

Amankwa [70]

Walsh [15], De Vanna 2 [57 81], Garrick [69]

GHANA				AUSTRALIA	
16	Memunatu SULEMANA			Melissa BARBIERI	1
2	Aminatu IBRAHIM			Kate McSHEA	2
3	Mavis DANSO			Dianne ALAGICH	4
6	Florence OKOE			(C) Cheryl SALISBURY	5
9	Anita AMENUKU	67		Heather GARRIOCK	7
10	Adjoa BAYOR (C)		46	Caitlin MUNOZ	8
12	Olivia AMOAKO			Sarah WALSH	9
13	Yaa AVOE	67	62	Joanne PETERS	10
15	Lydia ANKRAH			Collette McCALLUM	14
18	Anita AMANKWA			Sally SHIPARD	15
21	Memuna DARKU		83	Clare POLKINGHORNE	19
	Tr: Isaac PAHA			Tr: Tom SERMANNI	
17	Hamdya ABASS	67	62	Alicia FERGUSON	3
20	Belinda KANDA	67	46	Lisa DE VANNA	11
			83	Thea SLATYER	13

Dragon, Hangzhou
12-09-2007, 20:00, 30 752, Beck GER, Mirt ROU, Draeger GER

NOR   2   1   CAN

Gulbrandsen [52], Stangeland-Horpestad [81]

Chapman [33]

NORWAY				CANADA	
1	Bente NORDBY			Erin McLEOD	18
2	Ane STANGELAND-H (C)			Kristina KISS	2
3	Gunhild FOLSTAD			Tanya DENNIS	6
4	Ingvild STENSLAND			Diana MATHESON	8
5	Siri NORDBY	46	73	Candace-Marie CHAPMAN	9
7	Trine RONNING			Martina FRANKO	10
8	Solveig GULBRANDSEN			Randee HERMUS	11
10	Melissa WIIK	66		(C) Christine SINCLAIR	12
11	Leni LARSEN KAURIN		46	Melissa TANCREDI	14
16	Ragnhild GULBRANDSEN		83	Kara LANG	15
21	Lene STORLOKKEN	76		Sophie SCHMIDT	19
	Tr: Bjarne BERNTSEN			Tr: Even PELLERUD (NOR)	
6	Camilla HUSE	46		Rhian WILKINSON	7
17	Lene MYKJALAND	66	73	Amy WALSH	15
18	Marie KNUTSEN	76	83	Jodi-Ann ROBINSON	21

Dragon, Hangzhou
15-09-2007, 17:00, 33 835, Petignat SUI, Lagrange FRA, Vives Solana FRA

CAN   4   0   GHA

Sinclair 2 [16 62], Schmidt [55], Franko [77]

CANADA				GHANA	
18	Erin McLEOD			Memunatu SULEMANA	16
2	Kristina KISS			Aminatu IBRAHIM	2
6	Tanya DENNIS			Mavis DANSO	3
8	Diana MATHESON	84		Florence OKOE	6
9	Candace-Marie CHAPMAN		71	(C) Adjoa BAYOR	10
10	Martina FRANKO			Gloria FORIWA	11
11	Randee HERMUS			Olivia AMOAKO	12
12	Christine SINCLAIR (C)		35	Yaa AVOE	13
15	Kara LANG	63		Rumanatu TAHIRU	14
16	Katie THORLAKSON	45		Anita AMANKWA	18
19	Sophie SCHMIDT		77	Memuna DARKU	21
	Tr: Even PELLERUD (NOR)			Tr: Isaac PAHA	
5	Andrea NEIL	84	71	Safia RAHMAN	7
7	Rhian WILKINSON	63	77	Lydia ANKRAH	15
21	Jodi-Ann ROBINSON	45	35	Hamdya ABASS	17

Dragon, Hangzhou
15-09-2007, 20:00, 33 835, Niu CHN, Liu CHN, Fu CHN

AUS   1   1   NOR

De Vanna [83]

Gulbrandsen [5]

AUSTRALIA				NORWAY	
1	Melissa BARBIERI			Bente NORDBY	1
3	Alicia FERGUSON			(C) Ane STANGELAND-H	2
4	Dianne ALAGICH			Gunhild FOLSTAD	3
5	Cheryl SALISBURY (C)			Ingvild STENSLAND	4
7	Heather GARRIOCK			Camilla HUSE	6
12	Kathryn GILL	61		Trine RONNING	7
13	Thea SLATYER		86	Solveig GULBRANDSEN	8
14	Collette McCALLUM		46	Melissa WIIK	10
16	Lauren COLTHORPE	76	74	Leni LARSEN KAURIN	11
17	Danielle SMALL	46		Ragnhild GULBRANDSEN	16
20	Joanne BURGESS			Marie KNUTSEN	18
	Tr: Tom SERMANNI			Tr: Bjarne BERNTSEN	
8	Caitlin MUNOZ	76	74	Guro KNUTSEN	14
9	Sarah WALSH	61	46	Lene MYKJALAND	17
11	Lisa DE VANNA	46	86	Lene STORLOKKEN	21

Dragon, Hangzhou
20-09-2007, 17:00, 29 300, Bennett USA, Lagrange FRA, Vives Solana FRA

NOR   7   2   GHA

Storlokken [4], Gulbrandsen 3 [39 59 62], Stangeland [45p], Herlovsen [56], Klaveness [69]

Bayor [73], Okoe [80p]

NORWAY				GHANA	
1	Bente NORDBY		64	Gladys ENTI	1
2	Ane STANGELAND-H (C)			Aminatu IBRAHIM	2
4	Ingvild STENSLAND			Mavis DANSO	3
5	Siri NORDBY		58	Doreen AWUAH	4
6	Camilla HUSE			Florence OKOE	6
8	Solveig GULBRANDSEN	46	46	Anita AMENUKU	9
11	Leni LARSEN KAURIN	61		(C) Adjoa BAYOR	10
16	Ragnhild GULBRANDSEN			Olivia AMOAKO	12
17	Lene MYKJALAND	46		Yaa AVOE	13
19	Marit FIANE CHRISTENSEN			Rumanatu TAHIRU	14
21	Lene STORLOKKEN			Anita AMANKWA	18
	Tr: Bjarne BERNTSEN			Tr: Isaac PAHA	
3	Isabell HERLOVSEN	46	64	Memunatu SULEMANA	16
15	Madeleine GISKE	46	46	Sheila OKAI	8
20	Lise KLAVENESS	61	58	Memuna DARKU	21

Sports Centre, Chengdu
20-09-2007, 17:00, 29 300, Gaal HUN, Gutierrez ESP, Borg SWE

AUS   2   2   CAN

McCallum [53], Salisbury [92+]

Tancredi [1], Sinclair [85]

AUSTRALIA				CANADA	
1	Melissa BARBIERI		79	Erin McLEOD	18
2	Kate McSHEA			Tanya DENNIS	6
4	Dianne ALAGICH			Rhian WILKINSON	7
5	Cheryl SALISBURY (C)			Diana MATHESON	8
7	Heather GARRIOCK			Candace-Marie CHAPMAN	9
8	Caitlin MUNOZ	62		Martina FRANKO	10
9	Sarah WALSH			Randee HERMUS	11
10	Joanne PETERS	76		Christine SINCLAIR	12
14	Collette McCALLUM		68	Melissa TANCREDI	14
15	Sally SHIPARD		92	Kara LANG	15
16	Lauren COLTHORPE	46		Sophie SCHMIDT	19
	Tr: Tom SERMANNI			Tr: Even PELLERUD (NOR)	
3	Alicia FERGUSON	76	79	Taryn SWIATEK	20
11	Lisa DE VANNA	46	92	Brittany TIMKO	3
20	Joanne BURGESS	62	68	Jodi-Ann ROBINSON	21

GROUP D		PL	W	D	L	F	A	PTS
1	Brazil	3	3	0	0	10	0	9
2	China PR	3	2	0	1	5	6	6
3	Denmark	3	1	0	2	4	4	3
4	New Zealand	3	0	0	3	0	9	0

	CHN	DEN	NZL
	4-0	1-0	5-0
		3-2	2-0
			2-0

Sports Centre, Wuhan
12-09-2007, 17:00, 50 800, Kamnueng THA, Yoshizawa JPN, Liu TPE

NZL 0 5 **BRA**

Daniela [10], Cristiane [54], Marta 2 [74] [93+], Renata Costa [86]

	NEW ZEALAND				BRAZIL	
1	Jenny BINDON				ANDREIA	1
2	Ria PERCIVAL				(C) ALINE	3
4	Katie HOYLE	66			TANIA	4
5	Abby ERCEG				RENATA COSTA	5
6	Rebecca SMITH (C)				DANIELA	7
8	Hayley MOORWOOD				FORMIGA	8
9	Wendi HENDERSON	46	78		MAYCON	9
13	Alexandra RILEY				MARTA	10
15	Maia JACKMAN		84		CRISTIANE	11
16	Emma HUMPHRIES	72			SIMONE	16
19	Emily McCOLL				ESTER	20
	Tr: John HERDMAN (ENG)				Tr: Jorge BARCELLOS	
7	Zoe THOMPSON	72	78		ROSANA	6
17	Rebecca TEGG	46	84		PRETINHA	18
18	Priscilla DUNCAN	66				

Sports Centre, Wuhan
15-09-2007, 17:00, 54 000, Oiwa JPN, Yoshizawa JPN, Kim KOR

DEN 2 0 **NZL**

Pedersen [61], Paaske Sorensen [66]

	DENMARK				NEW ZEALAND	
1	Heidi JOHANSEN				Jenny BINDON	1
2	Mia OLSEN		70		Ria PERCIVAL	2
3	Katrine PEDERSEN (C)				Abby ERCEG	5
4	Gitte ANDERSEN				(C) Rebecca SMITH	6
5	Bettina FALK		87		Hayley MOORWOOD	8
7	Cathrine P-SORENSEN	86	64		Wendi HENDERSON	9
8	Julie RYDAHL BUKH				Marlies OOSTDAM	11
10	Anne D.E. NIELSEN				Alexandra RILEY	13
11	Merete PEDERSEN				Maia JACKMAN	15
13	Johanna RASMUSSEN	72			Priscilla DUNCAN	18
15	Mariann GAJHEDE	46			Emily McCOLL	19
	Tr: Per NIELSEN				Tr: John HERDMAN (ENG)	
9	Maiken PAPE	46	87		Annalie LONGO	10
17	Janne MADSEN	86	70		Emma HUMPHRIES	16
20	Camilla SAND	72	64		Rebecca TEGG	17

Olympic, Tianjin
20-09-2007, 20:00, 56 208, Damkova CZE, Oulhaj MAR, Steinlund NOR

CHN 2 0 **NZL**

Li Jie [57], Xie Caixia [79]

	CHINA PR				NEW ZEALAND	
1	ZHANG Yanru				Jenny BINDON	1
3	LI Jie		73		Ria PERCIVAL	2
4	WANG Kun				Abby ERCEG	5
6	XIE Caixia				(C) Rebecca SMITH	6
7	BI Yan				Hayley MOORWOOD	8
8	PAN Lina	60	62		Wendi HENDERSON	9
9	HAN Duan				Marlies OOSTDAM	11
10	MA Xiaoxu				Alexandra RILEY	13
11	PU Wei (C)				Maia JACKMAN	15
14	ZHANG Ouying	88			Priscilla DUNCAN	18
15	ZHOU Gaoping	65	82		Emily McCOLL	19
	Tr: Marika DOMANSKI-LYFORS (SWE)				Tr: John HERDMAN (ENG)	
16	LIU Yali	65	62		Zoe THOMPSON	7
17	LIU Sa	88	82		Simone FERRARA	14
20	ZHANG Tong	60	73		Merissa SMITH	20

Sports Centre, Wuhan
12-09-2007, 20:00, 50 800, Ferreira-James GUY, Mohammed TRI, Jeffery GUY

CHN 3 2 **DEN**

Li Jie [31], Bi Yan [50], Song Xiaoli [88]

Dot Eggers Nielsen [51], Paaske-Sorensen [87]

	CHINA PR				DENMARK	
18	HAN Wenxia				Heidi JOHANSEN	1
3	LI Jie (C)	93			Mia OLSEN	2
4	WANG Kun				(C) Katrine PEDERSEN	3
6	XIE Caixia				Gitte ANDERSEN	4
7	BI Yan				Bettina FALK	5
8	PAN Lina				Cathrine P-SORENSEN	7
9	HAN Duan				Julie RYDAHL BUKH	8
10	MA Xiaoxu				Maiken PAPE	9
11	PU Wei				Anne D.E. NIELSEN	10
12	QU Feifei	58	75		Johanna RASMUSSEN	13
15	ZHOU Gaoping	68	75		Mariann GAJHEDE	15
	Tr: Marika DOMANSKI-LYFORS (SWE)				Tr: Kenneth HEINER-MOLLER	
5	SONG Xiaoli	58	75		Merete PEDERSEN	11
16	LIU Yali	93	75		Stine DIMUN	12
19	ZHANG Ying	68				

Sports Centre, Wuhan
15-09-2007, 20:00, 54 000, Bennett USA, Tovar MEX, Munoz MEX

BRA 4 0 **CHN**

Marta 2 [42] [70], Cristiane 2 [47] [48]

	BRAZIL				CHINA PR	
1	ANDREIA				HAN Wenxia	18
2	ELAINE				LI Jie	3
3	ALINE (C)				WANG Kun	4
4	TANIA				SONG Xiaoli	5
5	RENATA COSTA		67		XIE Caixia	6
7	DANIELA	79			BI Yan	7
8	FORMIGA	89	52		PAN Lina	8
9	MAYCON				(C) HAN Duan	9
10	MARTA				MA Xiaoxu	10
11	CRISTIANE	85			PU Wei	11
20	ESTER		57		LIU Yali	16
	Tr: Jorge BARCELLOS				Tr: Marika DOMANSKI-LYFORS (SWE)	
6	ROSANA	79	57		ZHOU Gaoping	15
15	KATIA	85	67		LIU Sa	17
16	SIMONE	89	52		ZHANG Tong	20

Dragon, Hangzhou
20-09-2007, 20:00, 43 817, Seitz USA, Tovar MEX, Munoz MEX

BRA 1 0 **DEN**

Pretinha [91+]

	BRAZIL				DENMARK	
1	ANDREIA				Heidi JOHANSEN	1
2	ELAINE				Mia OLSEN	2
4	TANIA				(C) Katrine PEDERSEN	3
7	DANIELA	88			Gitte ANDERSEN	4
8	FORMIGA (C)				Cathrine P-SORENSEN	7
9	MAYCON		65		Julie RYDAHL BUKH	8
10	MARTA				Maiken PAPE	9
11	CRISTIANE	61			Anne D.E. NIELSEN	10
13	MONICA		79		Mariann GAJHEDE	15
16	SIMONE				Christina ORNTOFT	18
20	ESTER		20		Camilla SAND	20
	Tr: Jorge BARCELLOS				Tr: Per NIELSEN	
6	ROSANA	88	79		Merete PEDERSEN	11
18	PRETINHA	61	65		Stine DIMUN	12
			65		Johanna RASMUSSEN	13

QUARTER-FINALS

Sports Centre, Wuhan
22-09-2007, 17:00, 37 200, Ogston AUS, Ho AUS, Keen AUS

GER   3   0   PRK

Garefrekes [44], Lingor [67], Krahn [72]

	GERMANY			KOREA DPR	
1	Nadine ANGERER			JON Myong Hui	21
2	Kerstin STEGEMANN			OM Jong Ran	3
5	Annike KRAHN			SONG Jong Sun	5
6	Linda BRESONIK	77		KIL Son Hui	8
7	Melanie BEHRINGER			RI Un Suk	9
8	Sandra SMISEK	74		(C) RI Kum Suk	10
9	Birgit PRINZ (C)			RI Un Gyong	12
10	Renate LINGOR			SONU Kyong Sun	15
14	Simone LAUDEHR			KONG Hye Ok	16
17	Ariane HINGST		50	KIM Yong Ae	17
18	Kerstin GAREFREKES		74	HONG Myong Gum	20
	Tr: Silvia NEID			Tr: KIM Kwang Min	
13	Sandra MINNERT	77	50	KIM Kyong Hwa	2
16	Martina MUELLER	74	74	JONG Pok Sim	19

Olympic, Tianjin
22-09-2007, 20:00, 29 586, Palmqvist SWE, Borg SWE, Steinlund NOR

USA   3   0   ENG

Wambach [48], Boxx [57], Lilly [60]

	USA			ENGLAND	
18	Hope SOLO			Rachel BROWN	1
3	Christie RAMPONE			Alex SCOTT	2
4	Cat WHITEHILL			Casey STONEY	3
7	Shannon BOXX	82		Katie CHAPMAN	4
9	Heather O'REILLY			(C) Faye WHITE	5
12	Leslie OSBORNE		80	Mary PHILLIP	6
13	Kristine LILLY (C)			Karen CARNEY	7
14	Stephanie LOPEZ		46	Eniola ALUKO	9
15	Kate MARKGRAF			Kelly SMITH	10
17	Lori CHALUPNY			Anita ASANTE	12
20	Abby WAMBACH	86		Jill SCOTT	16
	Tr: Greg RYAN			Tr: Hope POWELL	
6	Natasha KAI	86	46	Rachel YANKEY	11
11	Carli LLOYD	82	80	Lianne SANDERSON	18

Sports Centre, Wuhan
23-09-2007, 17:00, 52 000, Gaal HUN, Villa Gutierrez ESP, Cini ITA

NOR   1   0   CHN

Herlovsen [32]

	NORWAY			CHINA PR	
1	Bente NORDBY			ZHANG Yanru	1
2	Ane STANGELAND-H (C)			LI Jie	3
3	Gunhild FOLSTAD			WANG Kun	4
4	Ingvild STENSLAND		71	XIE Caixia	6
6	Camilla HUSE			(C) BI Yan	7
7	Trine RONNING			PAN Lina	8
8	Solveig GULBRANDSEN	75		HAN Duan	9
9	Isabell HERLOVSEN	93+		MA Xiaoxu	10
11	Leni LARSEN KAURIN	64		PU Wei	11
16	Ragnhild GULBRANDSEN			LIU Yali	16
18	Marie KNUTSEN		75	ZHANG Tong	20
	Tr: Bjarne BERNTSEN			Tr: Marika DOMANSKI-LYFORS (SWE)	
19	Marit FIANE CHRISTENSEN	93+	71	ZHANG Ouying	14
20	Lise KLAVENESS	64	75	LIU Sa	17
21	Lene STORLOKKEN	75			

Olympic, Tianjin
23-09-2007, 20:00, 35 061, Beck GER, Mirt ROU, Draeger GER

BRA   3   2   AUS

Formiga [4], Marta [23p], Cristiane [75]   De Vanna [36], Colthorpe [68]

	BRAZIL			AUSTRALIA	
1	ANDREIA			Melissa BARBIERI	1
2	ELAINE			Dianne ALAGICH	4
3	ALINE (C)		20	(C) Cheryl SALISBURY	5
4	TANIA			Heather GARRIOCK	7
5	RENATA COSTA			Sarah WALSH	9
7	DANIELA		81	Joanne PETERS	10
8	FORMIGA	92+		Lisa DE VANNA	11
9	MAYCON			Thea SLATYER	13
10	MARTA			Collette McCALLUM	14
11	CRISTIANE		78	Sally SHIPARD	15
20	ESTER			Lauren COLTHORPE	16
	Tr: Jorge BARCELLOS			Tr: Tom SERMANNI	
16	SIMONE	92+	20	Kate McSHEA	2
			78	Caitlin MUNOZ	8
			81	Joanne BURGESS	20

SEMI-FINALS

Olympic, Tianjin
26-09-2007, 20:00, 53 819, Damkova CZE, Mirt ROU, Cini ITA

GER   3   0   NOR

Ronning OG [42], Stegemann [72], Mueller [75]

	GERMANY			NORWAY	
1	Nadine ANGERER			Bente NORDBY	1
2	Kerstin STEGEMANN			(C) Ane STANGELAND-H	2
5	Annike KRAHN		48	Gunhild FOLSTAD	3
6	Linda BRESONIK	81		Ingvild STENSLAND	4
7	Melanie BEHRINGER	40		Camilla HUSE	6
8	Sandra SMISEK	65		Trine RONNING	7
9	Birgit PRINZ (C)		56	Solveig GULBRANDSEN	8
10	Renate LINGOR		46	Isabell HERLOVSEN	9
14	Simone LAUDEHR			Leni LARSEN KAURIN	11
17	Ariane HINGST			Ragnhild GULBRANDSEN	16
18	Kerstin GAREFREKES			Marie KNUTSEN	18
	Tr: Silvia NEID			Tr: Bjarne BERNTSEN	
13	Sandra MINNERT	81	48	Siri NORDBY	5
16	Martina MUELLER	65	46	Lise KLAVENESS	20
19	Fatmire BAJRAMAJ	40	56	Lene STORLOKKEN	21

Dragon, Hangzhou
27-09-2007, 20:00, 47 818, Petignat SUI, Vives Solana FRA, Lagrange FRA

USA   0   4   BRA

Osbourne OG [20], Marta 2 [27 79], Cristiane [56]

	USA			BRAZIL	
1	Briana SCURRY			ANDREIA	1
3	Christie RAMPONE			ELAINE	2
4	Cat WHITEHILL			(C) ALINE	3
7	Shannon BOXX	45		TANIA	4
9	Heather O'REILLY	60		RENATA COSTA	5
12	Leslie OSBORNE			DANIELA	7
13	Kristine LILLY (C)			FORMIGA	8
14	Stephanie LOPEZ	46		MAYCON	9
15	Kate MARKGRAF	74		MARTA	10
17	Lori CHALUPNY			CRISTIANE	11
20	Abby WAMBACH			ESTER	20
	Tr: Greg RYAN			Tr: Jorge BARCELLOS	
2	Marian DALMY	74			
8	Tina ELLERTSON	60			
11	Carli LLOYD	46			

THIRD PLACE PLAY-OFF

Hongkou, Shanghai
30-09-2007, 17:00, 32 068, Gaal HUN, Gutierrez ESP, Draeger GER

NOR	1	4	USA

Gulbrandsen [63]

Wambach 2 [30 46], Chalupny [58],
O'Reilly [59]

	NORWAY				USA	
1	Bente NORDBY				Briana SCURRY	1
2	Ane STANGELAND-H (C)				Marian DALMY	2
3	Gunhild FOLSTAD	57		46	Christie RAMPONE	3
4	Ingvild STENSLAND				Cat WHITEHILL	4
6	Camilla HUSE				Heather O'REILLY	9
8	Solveig GULBRANDSEN		59		Aly WAGNER	10
10	Melissa WIIK	78			Leslie OSBORNE	12
16	Ragnhild GULBRANDSEN		89		(C) Kristine LILLY	13
18	Marie KNUTSEN				Stephanie LOPEZ	14
19	Marit FIANE CHRISTENSEN				Lori CHALUPNY	17
21	Lene STORLOKKEN	61			Abby WAMBACH	20
	Tr: Bjarne BERNTSEN				Tr: Greg RYAN	
9	Isabell HERLOVSEN	78	59		Lindsay TARPLEY	5
14	Guro KNUTSEN	61	89		Natasha KAI	6
15	Madeleine GISKE	57	46		Tina ELLERTSON	8

FINAL

Women's World Cup Final	Hongkou, Shanghai	30-09-2007
Kick-off: 20:00		Attendance: 31 000

GER	2	0	BRA

Birgit Prinz [52], Simone Laudehr [86]

		GERMANY			MATCH STATS				BRAZIL		
1	GK	Nadine ANGERER		12	Shots	14			ANDREIA	GK	1
2	DF	Kerstin STEGEMANN		4	Shots on Goal	6		81	ELAINE	DF	2
5	DF	Annike KRAHN		20	Fouls Committed	24		88	(C) ALINE	DF	3
6	MF	Linda BRESONIK		2	Corner Kicks	5			TANIA	DF	4
7	MF	Melanie BEHRINGER	74	0	Offside	1			RENATA COSTA	MF	5
8	FW	Sandra SMISEK	80	43	Possession %	57			DANIELA	MF	7
9	FW	Birgit PRINZ (C)			(C) Captain				FORMIGA	FW	8
10	MF	Renate LINGOR			MATCH OFFICIALS				MAYCON	MF	9
14	MF	Simone LAUDEHR			REFEREE				MARTA	FW	10
17	DF	Ariane HINGST			Tammy OGSTON AUS		63		CRISTIANE	FW	11
18	MF	Kerstin GAREFREKES			ASSISTANTS				ESTER	MF	20
		Tr: Silvia NEID			Maria Isabel TOVAR MEX				Tr: Jorge BARCELLOS		
		Substitutes			Rita MUNOZ MEX				Substitutes		
12	GK	Ursula HOLL			4TH OFFICIAL				BARBARA	GK	12
21	GK	Silke ROTTENBERG			Mayumi OIWA JPN				THAIS	GK	21
3	DF	Saskia BARTUSIAK						63	ROSANA	DF	6
4	DF	Babett PETER							MONICA	DF	13
11	FW	Anja MITTAG							GRAZIELLE	MF	14
13	DF	Sandra MINNERT						88	KATIA	FW	15
15	DF	Sonja FUSS							SIONE	DF	16
16	FW	Martina MUELLER	74						DAIANE	DF	17
19	MF	Fatmire BAJRAMAJ	80					81	PRETINHA	MF	18
20	FW	Petra WIMBERSKY							MICHELE	DF	19

IT WAS AN EVENLY BALANCED MATCH IN TERMS OF CHANCES - BRAZIL MIGHT EVEN HAVE HAD MORE - BUT WE WORKED AS A TEAM, CAME OUT STRONGLY IN THE SECOND HALF AND SCORED AT THE RIGHT TIME. BEFORE THE TOURNAMENT WE ASKED ALL THE PLAYERS TO WORK BACK AND DEFEND AS MUCH AS POSSIBLE. THE END RESULT IS THAT WE HAVE SCORED 21 GOALS TO NIL AT THIS TOURNAMENT

SILVIA NEID

THE GERMANS ONLY HAD A FEW CHANCES BUT THEY TOOK THEIRS WELL. THIS WAS IMPORTANT IN THE SECOND HALF WHEN WE WERE ONE DOWN AND MARTA MISSED SUCH A CRUCIAL PENALTY. BUT IT'S CLEAR THAT MY PLAYERS DID THEIR BEST AND I CAN ONLY SAY THAT I AM VERY SAD WITH THE RESULT. THE PLAYERS ARE EAGER TO WIN AND IT WILL HELP THEM PLAY BETTER IN THE FUTURE.

JORGE BARCELLOS

FIFA CLUB WORLD CUP 2007

FIFA CLUB WORLD CUP JAPAN 2007

Quarter-finals			Semi-finals			Final		
Milan	ITA	Bye						
			Milan	ITA	1			
			Urawa Reds	JPN	0			
Sepahan	IRN	1						
Urawa Reds	JPN	3						
						Milan	ITA	4
						Boca Juniors	ARG	2
Etoile du Sahel	TUN	1						
Pachuca	MEX	0						
			Etoile du Sahel	TUN	0			
			Boca Juniors	ARG	1			
Boca Juniors	ARG	Bye						

Preliminary Round

Sepahan	IRN	1
Waitakere United	NZL	0

Third Place Play-off

Urawa Reds	JPN	2	4p
Etoile du Sahel	TUN	2	2p

PRELIMINARY ROUNDS

National Stadium, Tokyo
7-12-2007, 19:45, 24 788, Rodriguez MEX
Sepahan 3
Emad Mohamed 2 [3 4], Al Hail [47]
Mohammad SAVARI - Ehsan HAJY SAFI*, Hadi AGHILY, Mohsen BENGAR, Jaba MUJIRI - Farshad BAHADORANI, Hadi JAFARI, EMAD MOHAMMED (Kabir BELLO 87) - Mohamad SEYED SALEHI (Ebrahim LOVEINIAN 60) - Abdul Wahab Abu AL HAIL, Mahmoud KARIMI (Hossein KAZEMI* 68). Tr: Luka BONACIC (CRO)
Waitakere United 1
Aghily OG [74]
Simon EADDY - Jonathan PERRY, Matt CUNNEEN, Danny HAY, Darren BAZELEY* - Benjamin TOTORI, Neil SYKES*, Christopher BALE (Jason HAYNE 63), Neil EMBLEN, Graham PEARCE* (Commins MENAPI 85) - Paul SEAMAN (Daniel KOPRIVCIC 91+).
Tr: Christopher MILICICH

National Stadium, Tokyo
9-12-2007, 14:45, 34 934, Shield AUS
Etoile du Sahel 1
Narry [85]
Aymen BALBOULI - Hatem BEJAOUI, Radhouan FALHI, Sabeur BEN FREJ, Saif GHEZAL - Afouan GHARBI*, Mohamed Ali NAFKA, Moussa NARRY, Muri Ola OGUNBIYI - Mahdi BEN DHIFALLAH* (Mohamed SACKO 89), Amine CHERMITI. Tr: Bertrand MARCHAND (FRA)
Pachuca 0
Miguel CALERO - Marvin CABRERA, Leobardo LOPEZ*, Julio MANZUR, Fausto PINTO - Gerardo RODRIGUEZ (Andres CHITIVA 87), Jaime CORREA, Gabriel CABALLERO (Luis REY 91+), Damian ALVAREZ* - Juan Carlos CACHO, Christian GIMENEZ. Tr: Enrique MEZA

Toyota Stadium, Toyota
10-12-2007, 19:30, 33 263, Codjia BEN
Urawa Reds 3
Nagai [32], Washington [54], Aghily OG [70]
Ryota TSUZUKI - Keisuke TSUBOI, Marcus Tulio TANAKA, NENE - Hajime HOSOGAI, Keita SUZUKI, Yuki ABE, Takahito SOMA - Makoto HASEBE (Masayuki OKANO 91+) - Yuichiro NAGAI (Shinji ONO 73), WASHINGTON. Tr: Holger OSIECK (GER)
Sepahan 1
Karimi [80]
Mohammd SAVARI - Ehsan HAJY SAFI, Hadi AGHILY, Mohsen BENGAR, Jaba MUJIRI - Farshad BAHADORANI*, Hadi JAFARI (Saeid BAYAT 46), EMAD MOHAMMED - Mohamad SEYED SALEHI - Abdul Wahab Abu AL HAIL (Ebrahim LOVEINIAN 78), Kabir BELLO (Mahmoud KARIMI 46). Tr: Luka BONACIC (CRO)

SEMI-FINALS

International, Yokohama
13-12-2007, 19:30, 67 005, Larrionda URU
Milan 1
Seedorf [68]
Dida - Massimo ODDO, Alessandro NESTA*, Kakha KALADZE, Marek JANKULOVSKI (Paolo Maldini 80) - Gennaro GATTUSO, Andrea PIRLO, Massimo AMBROSINI - KAKA, Clarence SEEDORF (Cristian BROCCHI 92+) - Alberto GILARDINO (Filippo INZAGHI 63). Tr: Carlo ANCELOTTI
Urawa Reds 0
Ryota TSUZUKI - Keisuke TSUBOI, Marcus Tulio TANAKA (Nobuhisa YAMADA 76), NENE* - Hajime HOSOGAI, Keita SUZUKI, Yuki ABE*, Takahito SOMA (Tadaaki HIRAKAWA 81) - Makoto HASEBE - Yuichiro NAGAI, WASHINGTON. Tr: Holger OSIECK (GER)

National Stadium, Tokyo
12-12-2007, 19:30, 37 255, Larsen DEN
Boca Juniors 1
Cardozo [37]
Mauricio CARANTA - Hugo IBARRA, Jonatan MAIDANA, Gabriel PALETTA, Claudio RODRIGUEZ - Fabian VARGAS**65, Sebastian BATTAGLIA*, Ever BANEGA (Pablo LEDESMA 92+), Neri CARDOZO (Alvaro GONZALEZ 68) - Martin PALERMO*, Rodrigo PALACIO (Mauro BOSELLI 90). Tr: Miguel Angel RUSSO
Etoile du Sahel 0
Aymen BALBOULI - Sabeur BEN FREJ, Saif GHEZAL, Radhouan FALHI, Mehdi MERIAH* - Mejdi TRAOUI (Gilson SILVA 75), Moussa NARRY*, Mohamed Ali NAFKA, Muri Ola OGUNBIYI (Afouan GHARBI* 10) - Mohamed SACKO (Mahdi BEN DHIFALLAH 56), Amine CHERMITI. Tr: Bertrand MARCHAND (FRA)

3RD PLACE PLAY-OFF AND FINAL

3rd Place. International, Yokohama
16-12-2007, 16:00, 53 363, O'Leary NZL
Urawa Reds 2 4p
Frej [5p], Chermiti [75]
Ryota TSUZUKI - Keisuke TSUBOI*, Nobuhisa YAMA-DA, NENE, Hajime HOSOGAI, Keita SUZUKI, Yuki ABE, Takahito SOMA - Makoto HASEBE - Yuichiro NAGAI, WASHINGTON*. Tr: Holger OSIECK (GER)

Etoile du Sahel 2 2p
Washington 2 [35 70]
Aymen BALBOULI (Ahmed JAOUACHI 93+) - Sabeur BEN FREJ*, Saif GHEZAL, Radhouan FALHI, Mehdi MERIAH - Mejdi TRAOUI, Mousa NARRY, Mohamed Ali NAFKA, Mahdi BEN DHIFALLAH* (Bassem BEN NASR 90) - Khaled MELLITI (Gilson SILVA 58), Amine CHERMITI. Tr: Bertrand MARCHAND (FRA)

Final. International, Yokohama
16-12-2007, 19:30, 68 263, Rodriguez MEX
Milan 4
Inzaghi 2 [21 71], Nesta [50], Kaka [61]
Dida - Daniele BONERA, Alessandro NESTA, Kakha KALADZE*77, Paolo MALDINI - Gennaro GATTUSO (EMERSON 65), Andrea PIRLO, Massimo AMBROSINI* - KAKA*, Clarence SEEDORF (Cristian BROCCHI 87) - Filippo INZAGHI (CAFU 76). Tr: Carlo ANCELOTTI

Boca Juniors 2
Palacio [22], Ledesma [85]
Mauricio CARANTA - Hugo IBARRA*, Jonatan MAIDANA, Gabriel PALETTA*, Claudio RODRIGUEZ - Alvaro GONZALEZ (Pablo LEDESMA 67*88), Sebastian BATTAGLIA*, Ever BANEGA, Neri CARDOZO (Leandro GRACIAN 68) - Martin PALERMO, Rodrigo PALACIO. Tr: Miguel Angel RUSSO

FIFA BEACH SOCCER WORLD CUP 2007

FIFA BEACH SOCCER WORLD CUP RIO DE JANEIRO 2007

First round groups

	MEX	RUS	SOL	Pts
Brazil	6-4	2-2	11-2	8
Mexico		2-2	6-3	5
Russia			5-2	3
Solomon Islands				0

	POR	IRN	USA	Pts
Spain	4-2	4-5	8-4	6
Portugal		3-3	6-5	4
Iran			6-7	3
USA				3

	URU	ITA	JPN	Pts
Senegal	5-2	6-5	4-1	9
Uruguay		3-2	3-2	6
Italy			6-3	3
Japan				0

	FRA	ARG	UAE	Pts
Nigeria	3-3	5-3	6-6	7
France		2-2	6-5	5
Argentina			4-2	3
UAE				0

Quarter-finals

Brazil	10
Portugal	7

Senegal	3
France	6

Uruguay	3
Nigeria	1

Spain	4
Mexico	5

Semi-finals

Brazil	6
France	2

Uruguay	2
Mexico	5

Final

Brazil	8
Mexico	2

3rd Place Play-off

Uruguay	2 1p
France	2 0p

Group stage penalty shoot-outs: Mexico 2-1 Russia • Brazil 5-4 Russia • Portugal 1-0 Iran • Nigeria 3-2 France • France 2-1 Argentina • Nigeria 1-0 UAE
Teams winning the shoot-out awarded two points, the losers none • Matches played over three periods of 12 minutes   2/11/2007 - 11/11/2007

FIFA BEACH SOCCER WORLD CUP 2008

FIFA BEACH SOCCER WORLD CUP MARSEILLE 2008

First round groups

	URU	SEN	IRN	Pts
France	4-3	5-5	6-6	5
Uruguay		8-7	6-1	5
Senegal			4-1	5
Iran				0

	ITA	SOL	SLV	Pts
Portugal	5-4	13-4	8-2	8
Italy		7-4	4-1	6
Solomon Islands			6-3	3
El Salvador				0

	RUS	UAE	CMR	Pts
Argentina	5-3	5-2	3-0	9
Russia		5-0	4-0	6
UAE			10-4	3
Cameroon				0

	ESP	MEX	JPN	Pts
Brazil	3-2	7-1	8-1	9
Spain		2-1	6-1	6
Mexico			4-3	3
Japan				0

Quarter-finals

Brazil	6
Russia	4

Uruguay	3
Portugal	6

Spain	2
Argentina	0

France	2
Italy	5

Semi-finals

Brazil	5
Portugal	4

Spain	4 0p
Italy	4 1p

Final

Brazil	5
Italy	3

3rd Place Play-off

Group stage penalty shoot-outs: Senegal 2-1 France • France 2-1 Iran
Teams winning the shoot-out awarded two points, the losers none • Matches played over three periods of 12 minutes   17/07/2008 - 27/07/2008

PART TWO

THE NATIONS OF THE WORLD

AFG – AFGHANISTAN

NATIONAL TEAM RECORD
JULY 10TH 2006 TO JULY 12TH 2010

PL	W	D	L	F	A	%
10	1	3	6	7	22	25

FIFA/COCA-COLA WORLD RANKING

1993	1994	1995	1996	1997	1998	1999	2000	2001	2002	2003	2004	2005	2006	2007
-	-	-	-	-	-	-	-	-	-	196	200	189	180	191

High	
173	07/06

2007–2008											
08/07	09/07	10/07	11/07	12/07	01/08	02/08	03/08	04/08	05/08	06/08	07/08
188	191	190	189	191	190	192	192	196	196	182	181

Low	
204	01/03

Afghanistan's slow but steady progress since emerging from decades in the international wilderness continued throughout 2008 with the national team qualifying for the finals of the AFC Challenge Cup in India. The Klaus Stark-coached side, many of whose players are culled from the lower echelons of German football, recorded a 0-0 draw with Bangladesh before defeating Kyrgyzstan to qualify for the eight-team tournament in India in August 2008. The country's qualification meant Afghanistan were still able to harbour hopes of making it through to the 2011 AFC Asian Cup in Qatar, with the winners of the AFC Challenge Cup earning a berth in the finals.

INTERNATIONAL HONOURS
None

While that didn't happen at the finals in India, where all three matches were losthaving such lofty thoughts at all would have been dismissed out of hand when the Afghans were making their first tentative steps back into the regional game in 2003. Since then, the sport has grown steadily and 2007 even saw the first shoots of organised club football in Kabul with the completion of a 12-team championship. Playing a single round of fixtures, the title was won by Ordu who won 10 of their eleven games and drew the other. Any nationwide tournament remains impossible given the security situation in the country.

THE FIFA BIG COUNT OF 2006

	Male	Female		Total
Number of players	526 441	340	Referees and Assistant Referees	100
Professionals	0		Admin, Coaches, Technical, Medical	45
Amateurs 18+	4928		Number of clubs	224
Youth under 18	13 188		Number of teams	500
Unregistered	4 000		Clubs with women's teams	1
Total players	526 781		Players as % of population	1.70%

Afghanistan Football Federation (AFF)
PO Box 128, Kabul, Afghanistan
Tel +93 75 2023770   Fax +93 75 2023770
aff.kabul@gmail.com   www.aff.com.af
President: KARAMUDDIN Karim   General Secretary: RUSTAMI Mukhtar
Vice-President: MUZAFARI Sayed Zia   Treasurer: TABESH Tawab   Media Officer: MUJAB Nasrat Sayed
Men's Coach: STARK Klaus   Women's Coach: WALI ZADAH Abdul Sabor
AFF formed: 1933   AFC: 1954   FIFA: 1948
Red shirts with white trimmings, Red shorts, Red socks or white shirts with red trimmings, White shorts, White socks

RECENT INTERNATIONALS PLAYED BY AFGHANISTAN

2005	Opponents	Score		Venue	Comp	Scorers	Att	Referee
9-11	Tajikistan	L	0-4	Dushanbe	Fr			
7-12	Maldives	L	1-9	Karachi	SAFr1	Sayed Maqsood [39]		
9-12	Pakistan	L	0-1	Karachi	SAFr1			
11-12	Sri Lanka	W	2-1	Karachi	SAFr1	Hafizullah Qadami [35], Abdul Maroof Gullistani [41]		
2006								
1-04	India	L	0-2	Chittagong	CCr1		2 500	Al Ghatrifi OMA
3-04	Chinese Taipei	D	2-2	Chittagong	CCr1	Hafizullah Qadami 2 [20 23]	2 500	Lee Gi Young KOR
5-04	Philippines	D	1-1	Chittagong	CCr1	Sayed Maqsood [26]	3 000	Mujghef JOR
2007								
8-10	Syria	L	0-3	Damascus	WCq		3 000	Al Ghamdi KSA
26-10	Syria	L	1-2	Dushanbe	WCq	Obaidullah Karimi [15]	2 000	Irmatov UZB
2008								
5-05	Bangladesh	D	0-0	Bishkek	CCq		3 000	Al Senan UAE
7-05	Kyrgyzstan	W	1-0	Bishkek	CCq	Ata Yamrali [38]	7 000	Shaharul MAS
4-06	Sri Lanka	D	2-2	Colombo	SAFr1	Harez Habib 2 [7 49]		
6-06	Bangladesh	D	2-2	Colombo	SAFr1	Ata Yamrali [7], Mustafa Hadid [24]		
8-06	Bhutan	L	1-3	Colombo	SAFr1	Harez Habib [87]		
30-07	India	L	0-1	Hyderabad	CCr1		300	Iemoto JPN
1-08	Turkmenistan	L	0-5	Hyderabad	CCr1		350	Shamsuzzaman
3-08	Tajikistan	L	0-4	Hyderabad	CCr1		150	Vo Minh Tri VIE

SAF = South Asian Football Federation Cup • AC = Asian Cup • CC = AFC Challenge Cup • WC = FIFA World Cup
q = qualifier • r1 = first round group

AFGHANISTAN NATIONAL TEAM RECORDS AND RECORD SEQUENCES

Records			Sequence records				
Victory	2-1	KYR 2003, SRI 2005	Wins	1	2003, 2005	Clean sheets	1	
Defeat	0-11	TKM 2003	Defeats	11	1948-1975	Goals scored	3	1954-59, 1979
Player Caps	n/a		Undefeated	2	2006	Without goal	6	1941-1951
Player Goals	n/a		Without win	28	1941-2003	Goals against	21	1948-1984

AFGHANISTAN 2007 KABUL PREMIER LEAGUE

	Pl	W	D	L	F	A	Pts
Ordu	11	10	1	0	26	2	31
Kabul Bank	11	9	1	1	29	3	28
Hakim Sanayi	11	8	1	2	18	11	25
Javanan Mihan	11	4	5	2	11	10	17
Shiva	11	4	2	5	9	11	14
Shoa	11	3	3	5	16	16	12
Pamir	11	3	3	5	10	14	12
Maiwand	11	2	4	5	10	14	10
Javanan	11	2	4	5	12	27	10
Solh	11	1	6	4	7	14	9
Sarmiyasht	11	1	4	6	7	17	7
Sabavan	11	0	2	9	7	23	2

Started 7/06/2007

RECENT LEAGUE AND CUP RECORD

Championship		Cup
Year	Champions	Winners
2006	Ordu FC	No tournament played
2007	Ordu FC	No tournament played

AFGHANISTAN COUNTRY INFORMATION

Capital	Kabul	Independence	1919 from the UK	GDP per Capita	$700
Population	28 513 677	Status	Islamic Republic of Afghanistan	GNP Ranking	109
Area km²	647 500	Language	Pushtu, Dari	Dialling code	+93
Population density	44 per km²	Literacy rate	36%	Internet code	.af
% in urban areas	20 %	Main religion	Sunni Muslim 80%	GMT + / −	+4.5
Towns/Cities ('000)	Kabul 3 043; Kandahar 391; Mazar-e-Sharif 303; Herat 272; Jalabad 200; Kunduz 161; Ghazni 143; Bamiyan 125; Balkh 114; Baglan 108; Ghardez 103; Khost 96; Maymaneh 79				
Neighbours (km)	Iran 936; Turkmenistan 744; Uzbekistan 137; Tajikistan 1 206; China 76; Pakistan 2 430				
Main stadia	Kabul National Stadium – Kabul 25 000				

AIA – ANGUILLA

NATIONAL TEAM RECORD
JULY 10TH 2006 TO JULY 12TH 2010

PL	W	D	L	F	A	%
5	0	0	5	5	34	0

FIFA/COCA-COLA WORLD RANKING

1993	1994	1995	1996	1997	1998	1999	2000	2001	2002	2003	2004	2005	2006	2007		High	
-	-	-	-	190	197	202	197	194	196	198	197	198	196	198		**189**	06/97

				2007–2008									Low	
08/07	09/07	10/07	11/07	12/07	01/08	02/08	03/08	04/08	05/08	06/08	07/08		**205**	07/06
196	197	197	198	198	198	199	199	202	200	199	199			

Nearly 38,000 fans watched Anguilla's short lived sortie in the 2010 FIFA World Cup qualifiers - almost three times the entire population of the country - but they won't have been very impressed by what they saw with the Anguillans conceding 16 goals in two games. In their defence, they were very unlucky to be drawn against former World Cup finalists El Salvador, who, thanks to their poor recent run of form, found themselves in the first qualifying round. In the first leg in San Salvador, the home side put that record to one side, scoring 12 goals without reply. It signalled the end for Anguilla coach Kerthney Carty who was replaced by the former women's national team coach

INTERNATIONAL HONOURS
None

Colin Johnson, but with many of the players based in the lower reaches of non league football in England, neither was afforded much time to work with the players and the lack of cohesion told in San Salvador. With no suitable stadium to host a match in Anguilla, the return leg at the RFK stadium in Washington was as good as a home tie for the Salvadorians although the Caribbean islanders were able to keep the score down to a more respectable 4-0. Johnson and officials at the football association have been on a mission to find more players with Anguillan roots in the UK and the USA and this may be the only way to avoid heavy defeats in future competitions.

THE FIFA BIG COUNT OF 2006

	Male	Female		Total
Number of players	1 160	437	Referees and Assistant Referees	7
Professionals	10		Admin, Coaches, Technical, Medical	63
Amateurs 18+	230		Number of clubs	11
Youth under 18	662		Number of teams	16
Unregistered	195		Clubs with women's teams	4
Total players	1 597		Players as % of population	11.85%

Anguilla Football Association (AFA)
PO Box 1318, The Valley, Anguilla AI-2640
Tel +1 264 497 7323   Fax +1 264 497 7324
axafa@yahoo.com   www. none
President: GUISHARD Raymond   General Secretary: HUGHES Damien
Vice-President: CARTY Diana   Treasurer: TBD   Media Officer: HUGHES Damien
Men's Coach: JOHNSON Colin   Women's Coach: JOHNSON Colin
AFA formed: 1990   CONCACAF: 1996   FIFA: 1996
Colours: Turquoise & white shirts, Turquoise shorts, Turquoise socks or Orange & blue shirts, Orange shorts, Orange socks

RECENT INTERNATIONALS PLAYED BY ANGUILLA

2002	Opponents	Score		Venue	Comp	Scorers	Att	Referee
6-07	British Virgin Islands	L	1-2	Tortola	Fr			
2003								
No international matches played in 2003								
2004								
19-03	Dominican Republic	D	0-0	Santo Domingo	WCq		400	Mattus CRC
21-03	Dominican Republic	L	0-6	Santo Domingo	WCq		850	Porras CRC
2005								
No international matches played in 2005								
2006								
20-09	Antigua and Barbuda	L	3-5	St John's	CCq	St Hillaire 13, Assent 51, O'Connor 90	300	Wijngaarde SUR
22-09	St Kitts and Nevis	L	1-6	St John's	CCq	O'Connor 22	500	Phillips GRN
24-09	Barbados	L	1-7	St John's	CCq	Connor 48	2 800	Wijngaarde SUR
2007								
No international matches played in 2007								
2008								
6-02	El Salvador	L	0-12	San Salvador	WCq		15 000	Jauregui ANT
26-03	El Salvador	L	0-4	Washington DC	WCq		22 670	Bedeau GRN

Fr = Friendly match • WC = FIFA World Cup • CC = Digicel Caribbean Cup • q = qualifier

ANGUILLA NATIONAL TEAM RECORDS AND RECORD SEQUENCES

Records			Sequence records					
Victory	4-1	MSR 2001	Wins	1		Clean sheets	1	
Defeat	0-14	GUY 1998	Defeats	17	1991-1998	Goals scored	5	2000-2002
Player Caps	n/a		Undefeated	1		Without goal	7	1991-1994
Player Goals	n/a		Without win	18	1991-1998	Goals against	27	1991-2002

RECENT LEAGUE RECORD

Year	Champions
1998	Spartans Interational
1999	Attackers
2000	No tournament played
2001	Roaring Lions
2002	Roaring Lions
2003	Roaring Lions
2004	Spartans International
2005	Roaring Lions
2006	Kicks United
2007	Kicks United
2008	

ANGUILLA COUNTRY INFORMATION

Capital	The Valley	Independence	Overseas territory of the UK	GDP per Capita	$8 600
Population	13 008	Status		GDP Ranking	n/a
Area km²	102	Language	English	Dialling code	+1 264
Population density	128 per km²	Literacy rate	95%	Internet code	.ai
% in urban areas	n/a	Main religion	Christian 88%	GMT + / –	-4
Towns/Cities ('000)	North Side 1; The Valley 1; Stoney Ground 1; The Quarter 1				
Neighbours (km)	Caribbean Sea 61				
Main stadia	Ronald Webster Park Annex – The Valley 1 100				

ALB - ALBANIA

ALBANIA NATIONAL TEAM RECORD
JULY 10TH 2006 TO JULY 12TH 2010

PL	W	D	L	F	A	%
16	4	5	7	18	20	40.6

FIFA/COCA-COLA WORLD RANKING

1993	1994	1995	1996	1997	1998	1999	2000	2001	2002	2003	2004	2005	2006	2007	High	
92	100	91	116	116	106	83	72	96	93	89	86	82	87	80	**62**	08/06

2007-2008												Low	
08/07	09/07	10/07	11/07	12/07	01/08	02/08	03/08	04/08	05/08	06/08	07/08	124	08/97
66	78	70	82	80	80	73	74	76	76	82	100		

With just two wins in their Euro 2008 qualifying campaign - both against minnows Luxembourg - national team coach Oto Baric resigned and was replaced by Dutchman Arie Haan for the 2010 FIFA World Cup qualifiers. The last straw for Baric had been the inept displays in the final two group games which saw a defeat against Belarus at home and a 6-1 thrashing at the hands of Romania in Bucharest - Albania's worst result since losing 9-0 to Spain in December 1990. The turnover of coaches at club level in Albania reached epidemic proportions with 16 changes during the season in the 12-team top division. Despite leading the table at the time, Dinamo fired Agim

INTERNATIONAL HONOURS
Balkan Cup 1946

Canaj in February 2008 after losing to rivals Partizani. His replacement, Ilir Daja, managed to secure the title for Dinamo after they beat Partizani on the last day of the season in a winner-takes-all match. Despite playing most of the second half with nine men Dinamo scored an injury-time winner through Nertil Ferraj to secure their first title since 2002. Reigning champions SK Tirana had a wretched season, finishing outside the top two for the first time since 1993 and they also lost in the Cup Final to Vllaznia, whose coach, Dervish Haxhiosmanovic had been in his job for just two months. Vllaznia's 2-0 triumph was their first Cup success since 1987.

THE FIFA BIG COUNT OF 2006

	Male	Female		Total
Number of players	149 730	15 000	Referees and Assistant Referees	1200
Professionals	550		Admin, Coaches, Technical, Medical	5000
Amateurs 18+	38 800		Number of clubs	440
Youth under 18	14 000		Number of teams	574
Unregistered	34 000		Clubs with women's teams	16
Total players	164 730		Players as % of population	4.60%

The Football Association of Albania (FSHF)
Federata Shqiptare e Futbolit, Rruga Labinoti, Pallati perballe Shkolles, "Gjuhet e Huaja", Tirana, Albania
Tel +355 43 46605   Fax +355 43 46 609
fshf@fshf.org.al   www.fshf.org
President: DUKA Armand   General Secretary: BICI Arben
Vice-President: KASMI Bujar   Treasurer: NURIU Lutfi   Media Officer: KOKONA Tritan
Men's Coach: HAAN Arie   Women's Coach: None
FSHF formed: 1930   UEFA: 1954   FIFA: 1932
Red shirts with black trimming, Black shorts, Red socks or White shirts with red and black trimming, black shorts, White socks

RECENT INTERNATIONALS PLAYED BY ALBANIA

2003	Opponents	Score		Venue	Comp	Scorers	Att	Referee
20-08	Macedonia	L	1-3	Prilep	Fr	Skela [74]	3 000	Mihajlevic SCM
6-09	Georgia	L	0-3	Tbilisi	ECq		18 000	Vollquartz DEN
10-09	Georgia	W	3-1	Tirana	ECq	Hasi [52], Tare [54], Bushi [80]	10 500	Salomir ROM
11-10	Portugal	L	3-5	Lisbon	Fr	Aliaj 2 [13 59], Tare [43]	5 000	Garibian FRA
15-11	Estonia	W	2-0	Tirana	Fr	Aliaj [26], Bushi [81]	5 000	Douros GRE
2004								
18-02	Sweden	W	2-1	Tirana	Fr	Skela [69], Aliaj [75]	15 000	Paparesta ITA
31-03	Iceland	W	2-1	Tirana	Fr	Aliaj [42], Bushi [78]	12 000	Bertini ITA
28-04	Estonia	D	1-1	Tallinn	Fr	Aliaj [51]	1 500	Sipailo LVA
18-08	Cyprus	L	1-2	Nicosia	Fr	Rraklli [64]	200	Kapitanis CYP
4-09	Greece	W	2-1	Tirana	WCq	Murati [2], Aliaj [11]	15 800	Gonzalez ESP
8-09	Georgia	L	0-2	Tbilisi	WCq		20 000	Courtney NIR
9-10	Denmark	L	0-2	Tirana	WCq		14 500	Baskarov RUS
13-10	Kazakhstan	W	1-0	Almaty	WCq	Bushi [61]	12 300	Stuchlik AUT
2005								
9-02	Ukraine	L	0-2	Tirana	WCq		12 000	Bennett ENG
26-03	Turkey	L	0-2	Istanbul	WCq		32 000	Plautz AUT
30-03	Greece	L	0-2	Piraeus	WCq		31 700	Layec FRA
29-05	Poland	L	0-1	Szczecin	Fr		14 000	Weiner GER
4-06	Georgia	W	3-2	Tirana	WCq	Tare 2 [6 56], Skela [33]	BCD	Tudor ROM
8-06	Denmark	L	1-3	Copenhagen	WCq	Bogdani [73]	26 366	Frojdfeldt SWE
17-08	Azerbaijan	W	2-1	Tirana	Fr	Bushi [37], Cana [72]	7 300	
3-09	Kazakhstan	W	2-1	Tirana	WCq	Myrtaj [53], Bogdani [56]	3 000	Slupik POL
8-10	Ukraine	D	2-2	Dnepropetrovsk	WCq	Bogdani 2 [75 83]	24 000	Verbist BEL
12-10	Turkey	L	0-1	Tirana	WCq		8 000	Dauden Ibanez ESP
2006								
1-03	Lithuania	L	1-2	Tirana	Fr	Aliaj [38p]		Pieri ITA
22-03	Georgia	D	0-0	Tirana	Fr			
16-08	San Marino	W	3-0	Serravalle	Fr	Tare [7], Skela [23], Lala [38]		
2-09	Belarus	D	2-2	Minsk	ECq	Skela [7p], Hasi [86]	23 000	Asumaa FIN
6-09	Romania	L	0-2	Tirana	ECq		12 000	Benquerença POR
11-10	Netherlands	L	1-2	Amsterdam	ECq	Curri [67]	40 085	Yefet ISR
2007								
7-02	FYR Macedonia	L	0-1	Tirana	Fr		8 000	Bertini ITA
24-03	Slovenia	D	0-0	Shkoder	ECq		7 000	Attard MLT
28-03	Bulgaria	D	0-0	Sofia	ECq		19 800	Eriksson SWE
2-06	Luxembourg	W	2-0	Tirana	ECq	Kapllani [38], Haxhi [57]	3 000	Silgava GEO
6-06	Luxembourg	W	3-0	Luxembourg	ECq	Skella [25], Kapllani 2 [36 72]	4 325	Malzinskas LTU
22-08	Malta	W	3-0	Tirana	Fr	Salihi [34], Berisha [46], Duro [60]		
12-09	Netherlands	L	0-1	Tirana	ECq		15 000	Riley ENG
13-10	Slovenia	D	0-0	Celje	ECq		3 700	Gomes POR
17-10	Bulgaria	D	1-1	Tirana	ECq	Duro.K [25]	3 000	Stuchlik AUT
17-11	Belarus	L	2-4	Tirana	ECq	Bogdani [43], Kapllani [44]	2 064	Demirlek TUR
21-11	Romania	L	1-6	Bucharest	ECq	Kapllani [64]	23 427	Trivkovic CRO
2008								
27-05	Poland	L	0-1	Reutlingen	Fr		2 200	Kircher GER

Fr = Friendly match • EC = UEFA EURO 2004/2008 • WC = FIFA World Cup • q = qualifier • BCD = behind closed doors

ALBANIA NATIONAL TEAM RECORDS AND RECORD SEQUENCES

Records			Sequence records				
Victory	5-0	VIE 2003	Wins	4	1999-2000	Clean sheets	5	2007
Defeat	0-12	HUN 1950	Defeats	10	1989-1991	Goals scored	7	1973-1980
Player Caps	73	Foto Strakosha	Undefeated	4	Six times	Without goal	6	1987-88, 1990-91
Player Goals	14	Alban Bushi	Without win	25	1985-1991	Goals against	14	1988-1991

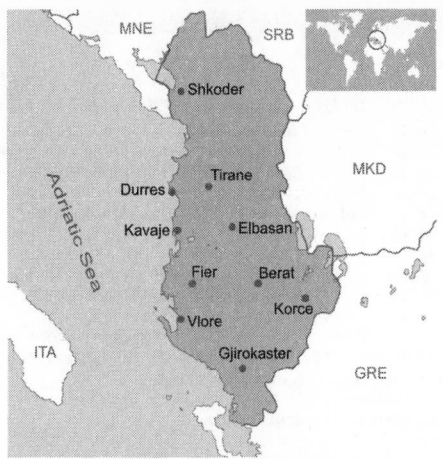

MAJOR CITIES/TOWNS
Population '000

1	Tirana	380
2	Durrës	124
3	Elbasan	102
4	Vlorë	90
5	Shkodër	88
6	Fier	62
7	Korçë	58
8	Berat	47
9	Lushnjë	42
10	Kavajë	29
11	Pogradec	26
12	Laç	25
13	Gjirokastër	23
14	Patos	23
15	Krujë	21
16	Lezhë	19
17	Kuçovë	18
18	Kukës	18
19	Burrel	15
20	Sarandë	15
21	Peshkopi	15
22	Cërrik	14
23	Shijak	14
24	Peqin	7

REPUBLIKA E SHQIPERISE; REPUBLIC OF ALBANIA

Capital	Tirana	Language	Albanian	Independence	1912
Population	3 581 655	Area	28 748 km²	% in cities	37%
GDP per cap	$4 500	Dailling code	+355	Internet	.al	GMT + / -	+1

Density 123 per km²

MEDALS TABLE

		Overall			League			Cup			Europe			City	Stadium	Cap'ty	DoF
		G	S	B	G	S	B	G	S	B	G	S	B				
1	SK Tiranë	35	20	11	23	13	11	12	7					Tirana	Selman Stërmasi	12 500	1920
2	Partizani Tiranë	30	27	8	15	19	8	15	8					Tirana	Qemal Stafa	19 500	1945
3	Dinamo Tiranë	30	14	10	17	9	10	13	5					Tirana	Qemal Stafa	19 500	1950
4	Vllaznia Shkodër	15	16	14	9	10	14	6	6					Shkodër	Loro Borici	16 000	1919
5	Teuta Durrës	4	11	5	1	5	5	3	6					Durrës	Niko Dovana	12 000	1922
6	SK Elbasani	4	2	1	2	1	1	2	1					Elbasan	Ruzhdi Bizhuda	8 000	1923
7	Flamurtari Vlorë	3	14	3	1	6	3	2	8					Vlorë	Flamurtari	8 500	1923
8	Besa Kavajë	1	7	10		1	10	1	6					Kavajë	Besa	8 000	1925
9	Skënderbeu Korçë	1	6	2	1	3	2		3					Korçë	Skënderbeu	8 000	1925
10	Apollonia Fier	1						1						Fier	Loni Papuçiu	6 000	1925
11	Lushnja		3						3					Lushnjë	Roza Haxhiu	12 000	1926
12	Tomori Berat		2			1			1					Berat	Tomori	13 350	1923
13	Albpetrol Patosi		1						1					Patosi	Alush Noga	5 000	1947
	Luftëtari Gjirokastër		1			1								Gjirokastër	Subi Bakiri	8 400	1929
15	Bylis Ballshi			1			1							Bylis	Adush Muça	6 500	1972

RECENT LEAGUE AND CUP RECORD

	Championship						Cup		
Year	Champions	Pts	Runners-up	Pts	Third	Pts	Winners	Score	Runners-up
1995	SK Tirana	44	Teuta Durrës	32	Partizani Tiranë	32	Teuta Durrës	0-0 4-3p	SK Tirana
1996	SK Tirana	55	Teuta Durrës	54	Partizani Tiranë	46	SK Tirana	1-1 4-3p	Flamurtari Vlorë
1997	SK Tirana	46	Vllaznia Shkodër	43	Flamurtari Vlorë	41	Partizani Tiranë	2-2 4-3p	Flamurtari Vlorë
1998	Vllaznia Shkodër	72	SK Tirana	65	Partizani Tiranë	64	Apolonia Fier	1-0	Lushnjë
1999	SK Tirana	61	Vllaznia Shkodër	60	Bylis Ballshi	59	SK Tirana	0-0 3-0p	Vllaznia Shkodër
2000	SK Tirana	52	Tomori Berat	52	Teuta Durrës	49	Teuta Durrës	0-0 5-4p	Lushnjë
2001	Vllaznia Shkodër	56	SK Tirana	54	Dinamo Tiranë	52	SK Tirana	5-0	Teuta Durrës
2002	Dinamo Tiranë	63	SK Tirana	62	Partizani Tiranë	46	SK Tirana	1-0	Dinamo Tiranë
2003	SK Tirana	60	Vllaznia Shkodër	49	Partizani Tiranë	46	Dinamo Tiranë	1-0	Teuta Durrës
2004	SK Tirana	80	Dinamo Tiranë	71	Vllaznia Shkodër	68	Partizani Tiranë	1-0	Dinamo Tiranë
2005	SK Tirana	84	SK Elbasani	79	Dinamo Tiranë	62	Teuta Durrës	0-0 6-5p	SK Tirana
2006	KF Elbasani	72	SK Tirana	62	Dinamo Tiranë	61	SK Tirana	1-0	Vllaznia Shkodër
2007	SK Tirana	72	Teuta Durrës	67	Vllaznia Shkodër	63	Besa Kavajë	3-2	Teuta Durrës
2008	Dinamo Tiranë	70	Partizani Tiranë	65	Besa Kavajë	56	Vllaznia Shkodër	2-0	SK Tirana

ALBANIA 2007–08
KATEGORIA SUPERIORE

	Pl	W	D	L	F	A	Pts	Dinamo	Partizani	Besa	Elbasani	Shkumbini	SK Tirana	Vllaznia	Flamurtari	Teuta	Kastrioti	Besëlidhja	SK. Korçë
Dinamo Tiranë †	33	21	7	5	56	14	70		2-0	2-1	0-0	2-0	0-0	3-1	1-0	0-2	0-0	0-1	6-0
Partizani Tiranë ‡	33	18	11	4	47	22	65	1-0		3-3	0-0	2-1	2-0	0-0	2-1	1-0	2-0	0-0	4-0
Besa Kavajë	33	17	5	11	45	36	56	0-2	2-1		0-1	1-0	1-0	3-0	3-1	2-1	1-0	2-0	0-1
KF Elbasani	33	13	13	7	40	24	52	0-0	0-0	0-0		2-0	3-1	0-0	1-0	1-1	0-0	2-2	1-0
Shkumbini Peqin	33	14	8	11	35	28	50	0-0	0-0	1-1	2-0		1-0	0-2	1-0	4-0	3-2	0-0	1-0
SK Tirana	33	14	7	12	46	36	49	0-0	1-2	1-4	2-0	2-2		2-1	2-0	0-0	5-1	2-0	1-0
Vllaznia Shkodër ‡	33	12	9	12	46	46	45	0-1	0-3	1-1	1-1	2-3	2-1		0-0	3-1	4-1	1-1	2-0
Flamurtari Vlorë	33	10	14	9	35	37	44	1-2	0-0	3-0	1-0	2-1	0-1	2-2		0-0	1-0	2-2	2-2
Teuta Durrës	33	9	8	16	32	45	35	0-1	1-1	1-2	0-1	3-5	0-1	1-1	1-1		0-0	0-3	3-2
Kastrioti Krujë	33	10	5	18	24	43	35	0-3	1-0	0-1	2-1	2-0	0-0	1-0	0-3	1-2		3-1	1-0
Besëlidhja Lezhë	33	9	7	17	31	52	34	0-2	1-0	1-2	2-2	0-1	2-1	0-2	0-2	1-0	2-2		4-2
Skënderbeu Korçë	33	3	2	28	26	80	11	1-2	1-2	1-1	0-1	1-2	1-3	4-2	2-3	1-1	1-4	1-3	

25/08/2007 - 17/05/2008 • † Qualified for the UEFA Champions League • ‡ Qualified for the UEFA Cup
Relegation play-offs: **Teuta** 2-1 Burreli; Kastrioti 0-0 2-4p **Lushnja**
Top scorers: Pero Pejic CRO, Dinamo 13; Vioresin Sinani, Vllaznia 12; Marjus Ngjela, Skënderbeu 10

ALBANIA 2007–08
KATEGORIA E PARE (2)

	Pl	W	D	L	F	A	Pts
Bylis Ballshi	34	23	5	6	70	20	74
Apolonia Fier	34	23	4	7	70	23	73
KS Lushnja	34	22	7	5	57	26	73
Burreli	34	21	4	9	51	26	67
Laçi	34	19	9	6	57	29	65
Ada Velipojë	34	17	6	11	50	37	57
Luftëtari Gjirokastër	34	14	6	14	48	43	48
Skrapari	34	15	3	16	39	39	48
Dajti Kamëz	34	12	8	14	37	29	44
Turbina Cërrik	34	14	2	18	34	48	44
Pogradeci	34	12	7	15	33	33	43
Bilisht Sport	34	13	4	17	37	48	43
Sopoti Librazhd	34	13	4	17	30	42	43
Naftëtari Kuçovë	34	12	4	18	36	51	40
Erzeni Shijak	34	11	6	17	29	42	39
Tomori Berat	34	8	7	19	29	56	31
Gramshi	34	9	2	23	28	58	29
SK Tepelenë	34	2	4	28	23	108	10

15/09/2007 - 18/05/2008

KUPA E SHQIPERISE 2007–08

Round of 16

Vllaznia Shkodër	1	0
Besëlidhja Lezhë	0	0
Luftëtari Gjirokastër	1	0
Besa Kavajë	1	2
Partizani Tiranë	0	5
Skënderbeu Korçë	1	0
Apolonia Fier	0	3
Dinamo Tiranë	1	3
KF Elbasani	0	3
Shkumbini Peqin	2	0
Turbina Cërrik	0	0
Teuta Durrës	0	4
Kastrioti Krujë	1	1
Flamurtari Vlorë	1	0
Laçi *	1	1
SK Tirana	1	3

Quarter–finals

Vllaznia Shkodër	2	5
Besa Kavajë *	2	1
Partizani Tiranë	1	0
Dinamo Tiranë *	3	0
KF Elbasani *	1	2
Teuta Durrës	1	2
Kastrioti Krujë *	0	1
SK Tirana	3	1

Semi–finals

Vllaznia Shkodër *	4	3
Dinamo Tiranë	0	0
KF Elbasani *	0	3
SK Tirana	3	1

Final

Vllaznia Shkodër ‡	2
SK Tirana	0

CUP FINAL
Ruzhuta Bizhuta, Elbasan
27-05-2008, Ref: Rafati

Scorers - Gilman Lika [3],
Xhevair Sukaj [38] for Vllaznia

* Home team in the first leg • ‡ Qualified for the UEFA Cup

ALG – ALGERIA

NATIONAL TEAM RECORD
JULY 10TH 2006 TO JULY 12TH 2010

PL	W	D	L	F	A	%
17	6	3	8	20	22	44.1

FIFA/COCA-COLA WORLD RANKING

1993	1994	1995	1996	1997	1998	1999	2000	2001	2002	2003	2004	2005	2006	2007	High	
35	57	48	49	59	71	86	82	75	68	62	73	80	80	79	**30**	09/93

2007–2008												Low	
08/07	09/07	10/07	11/07	12/07	01/08	02/08	03/08	04/08	05/08	06/08	07/08	**103**	06/08
73	85	89	81	79	76	77	78	101	100	103	93		

Algeria continued its ever increasingly frantic search for a return to the glory days of two decades ago when they were World Cup finalists and African champions. The recall of one of the heroes of that era, Rabah Saadane held out hopes for a marked improvement for the national side, which failed to reach the African Nations Cup finals for a second successive time. Saadane returned in place of the Frenchman Jean-Michel Cavalli, who departed at the end of a disappointing qualifying campaign that saw Algeria miss out on a trip to Ghana. Their woes were highlighted by the ignominy of a 2-1 defeat in the Gambia in their final group match. The two countries were paired

INTERNATIONAL HONOURS
Qualified for the FIFA World Cup™ finals 1982 1986 CAF African Cup of Nations 1990

CAF Youth Cup 1979 All Africa Games 1978 African Champions League Mouloudia Alger 1976, JS Kabylie 1981 1990

again in the qualifiers for the 2010 FIFA World Cup, along with Senegal and Liberia and the Algerians again made a modest start with a defeat in Banjul threatening to derail their hopes of qualifying for the finals. Former national team captain Moussa Saib led JS Kabylie to the league title but blotted his copybook when the club failed to reach the group phase of the African Champions League, eliminated by Cotonsport of Cameroon. The other domestic honour went to JSM Béjaïa who won the first trophy in their history after beating WA Tlemcen in the Cup Final.

THE FIFA BIG COUNT OF 2006

	Male	Female		Total
Number of players	1 719 100	71 100	Referees and Assistant Referees	1 700
Professionals	300		Admin, Coaches, Technical, Medical	22 800
Amateurs 18+	138 800		Number of clubs	2 090
Youth under 18	64 800		Number of teams	2 560
Unregistered	248 300		Clubs with women's teams	0
Total players	1 790 200		Players as % of population	5.44%

Fédération Algérienne de Football (FAF)
Chemin Ahmed Ouaked, Case Postale 39, Dely Brahim, Alger, Algeria
Tel +213 21 372929   Fax +213 21 367266
faffoot@yahoo.fr   www.faf.org.dz
President: HADDADJ Hamid   General Secretary: BOUCHEMLA Mourad
Vice-President: KHELAIFIA Mohamed   Treasurer: MECHRARA Mohamed   Media Officer: HADDADJ Hamid
Men's Coach: SAADANE Rabah   Women's Coach: CHIH Azzedine
FAF formed: 1962   CAF: 1964   FIFA: 1963
Green shirts, White shorts, Green socks or White shirts, Green shorts, White socks

RECENT INTERNATIONALS PLAYED BY ALGERIA

2004	Opponents		Score	Venue	Comp	Scorers	Att	Referee
15-01	Mali	L	0-2	Algiers	Fr		7 000	Zehmoun TUN
25-01	Cameroon	D	1-1	Sousse	CNr1	Zafour 51	20 000	Codjia BEN
29-01	Egypt	W	2-1	Sousse	CNr1	Mamouni 13, Achiou 85	15 000	Hamer LUX
3-02	Zimbabwe	L	1-2	Sousse	CNr1	Achiou 72	10 000	Maillet SEY
8-02	Morocco	L	1-3	Sfax	CNqf	Cherrad 83	20 000	Shelmani LBY
28-04	China PR	L	0-1	Clermont-Ferrand	Fr		1 600	Poulat FRA
30-05	Jordan	D	1-1	Annaba	Fr	Cherrad 60	20 000	Zahmoul TUN
5-06	Angola	D	0-0	Annaba	WCq		55 000	Daami TUN
20-06	Zimbabwe	D	1-1	Harare	WCq	Cherrad 3	65 000	Ntambidila COD
3-07	Nigeria	L	0-1	Abuja	WCq		35 000	Hisseine CHA
17-08	Burkina Faso	D	2-2	Blida	Fr	Tahraoui 33, Arrache 54	15 000	Tahri MAR
5-09	Gabon	L	0-3	Annaba	WCq		51 000	Ndoye SEN
9-10	Rwanda	D	1-1	Kigali	WCq	Bourahli 14	20 000	Abdel Rahmen SUD
17-11	Senegal	L	1-2	Toulon	Fr	Daoud 77	4 000	Bata FRA
2005								
9-02	Burkina Faso	W	3-0	Algiers	Fr	Saifi 2 29 42, Sofiane 72	5 000	Benaissa ALG
27-03	Rwanda	W	1-0	Oran	WCq	Boutabout 48	20 000	Abd El Fatah EGY
5-06	Angola	L	1-2	Luanda	WCq	Boutabout 63	27 000	Hicuburundi BDI
12-06	Mali	L	0-3	Arles	Fr			Derrien FRA
19-06	Zimbabwe	D	2-2	Oran	WCq	Yahia 17, Daoud 48	15 000	Pare BFA
4-09	Nigeria	L	2-5	Oran	WCq	Yacef 48, Boutabout 58	11 000	Shelmani LBY
8-10	Gabon	D	0-0	Port-Gentil	WCq		37 000	Diouf SEN
2006								
28-02	Burkina Faso	D	0-0	Rouen	Fr		2 000	Duhamel FRA
4-06	Sudan	W	1-0	Algiers	Fr	Deham 47		El Harzi TUN
15-08	Gabon	L	0-2	Aix-en-Provence	Fr			Mezouar
3-09	Guinea	D	0-0	Conakry	CNq			Coulibaly MLI
7-10	Gambia	W	1-0	Algiers	CNq	Ziani 75p	48 000	Auda EGY
15-11	Burkina Faso	L	1-2	Aix-en-Provence	Fr	Saifi 88p	700	Falcone FRA
2007								
7-02	Libya	W	2-1	Algiers	Fr	Saifi 62, Meniri 67		El Harzi TUN
24-03	Cape Verde Islands	W	2-0	Algiers	CNq	Daham 60, Meniri 89		Abd El Fatah EGY
2-06	Cape Verde Islands	D	2-2	Praia	CNq	Bougherra 33, Saifi 84		Aboubacar CIV
5-06	Argentina	L	3-4	Barcelona	Fr	Yahia 9, Belhadj 2 42 76		Izquierdo ESP
16-06	Guinea	L	0-2	Algiers	CNq		80 000	Guezzaz MAR
22-08	Brazil	L	0-2	Montpellier	Fr		26 392	Bitton FRA
9-09	Gambia	L	1-2	Banjul	CNq	Saifi 56		Imiere NGA
20-11	Mali	W	3-2	Rouen	Fr	Bouazza 40, Ghilas 73, Belhadj 89		
2008								
26-03	Congo DR	D	1-1	Goussainville	Fr	Ghilas 89p		Rouinsard FRA
31-05	Senegal	L	0-1	Dakar	WCq		50 000	Kotey GHA
6-06	Liberia	W	3-0	Blida	WCq	Djebbour 15, Ziani 2 20 48p	40 000	Lemghambodj MTN
14-06	Gambia	L	0-1	Banjul	WCq		18 000	Coulibaly MLI
20-06	Gambia	W	1-0	Blida	WCq	Yahia 33	25 000	Ndume GAB

Fr = Friendly match • CN = CAF African Cup of Nations • WC = FIFA World Cup • q = qualifier • r1 = first round group • qf = quarter-final

ALGERIA NATIONAL TEAM RECORDS AND RECORD SEQUENCES

Records			Sequence records		
Victory	15-1	YEM 1973	Wins	10	1957-1963	Clean sheets	4	Five times
Defeat	0-5	BFA 1975, GDR 1976	Defeats	5	1974	Goals scored	16	2000-2001
Player Caps	107	Mahieddine Meftah	Undefeated	15	1989-1991	Without goal	5	1989
Player Goals	40	Rabah Madjer	Without win	11	2004	Goals against	9	2000-2001

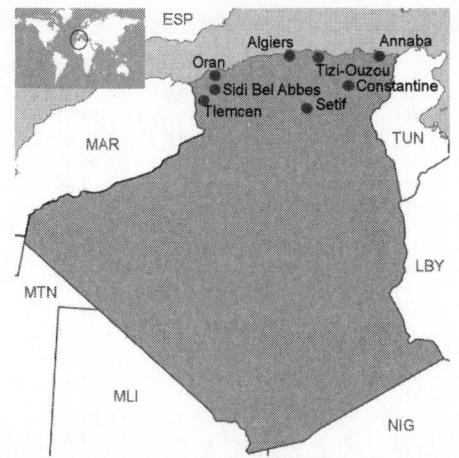

MAJOR CITIES/TOWNS
Population '000

1	Algiers	2 029
2	Oran	642
3	Constantine	446
4	Bab Azwar	295
5	Batna	286
6	Setif	227
7	Djelfa	223
8	Annaba	204
9	Biskra	199
10	Sidi bel Abbès	193
11	Tibissah	186
12	Tiyaret	180
13	El Bouni	177
14	Béjaïa	166
15	Bordj Bou Arreridj	162
16	Blida	162
17	Chlef	157
18	Ouargla	155
19	Tizi-Ouzou	146
20	Béchar	144
21	Saïda	129
22	Tlemcen	120
23	Oum El Bouaghi	104
24	Mascara	87

AL JAZA'IR; PEOPLE'S DEMOCRATIC REPUBLIC OF ALGERIA

Capital	Algiers	Language	Arabic, French, Berber dialects	Independence	1962
Population	32 930 091	Area	2 381 740 km²	Density per km²	
GDP per cap	$6 000	Dailling code	+213	% in cities	56%
			Internet .dz	GMT +/-	+1

MEDALS TABLE

			Overall			League			Cup			Africa			City	Stadium	Cap'ty	DoF
			G	S	B	G	S	B	G	S	G	S	B					
1	JS Kabylie	JSK	24	13	5	14	9	3	4	4	6		2	Tizi-Ouzou	1er Novembre 1954	20 000	1946
2	USM Alger	USMA	12	13	3	5	4	1	7	9			2	Algiers	Omar Hamadi	15 000	1932
3	MC Alger	MCA	13	2	4	6	2	4	6		1			Algiers	5 Juillet	70 000	1921
4	CR Belouizdad	CRB	11	5	3	6	3	2	5	2			1	Algiers	20 Août	20 000	1962
5	ES Sétif	ESS	10	2	5	3	2	4	6		1	1		Sétif	8 Mai 1945	20 000	1958
6	MC Oran	MCO	8	12	4	4	9	3	4	2		1	1	Oran	Ahmed Zabana	50 000	1946
7	USM El Harrach	USMH	3	2		1	2		2					Algiers	1er Novembre	5 000	1931
8	NA Hussein Dey	NAHD	2	8	5	1	4	4	1	3		1	1	Algiers	Mohamed Zioui	3 000	1947
9	WA Tlemcem	WAT	2	3	3			3	2	3				Tlemcen	Birouni	20 000	1962
10	USM Annaba	USMAn	2			1			1					Annaba	19 Mai	70 000	1937
11	MO Constantine	MOC	1	4	2	1	1	2		3				Constantine	Chahid Hamlaoui	45 000	1939
12	RC Kouba	RCK	1	3	2	1	2	2		1				Algiers	Omar Benhaddad	10 000	1945
13	ASO Chlef	ASO	1	2	3		1	3	1	1				Chlef	Mohamed Boumezrag	15 000	1947
14	CS Constantine	CSC	1	2		1	1							Constantine	Chahid Hamlaoui	40 000	1926
15	USM Bel Abbès	USMBA	1		2			2	1					Sidi Bel Abbès	24 Février	45 000	1933
16	US Chaouia	USC	1		1	1		1						Oum El Bouaghi	Hassouna Zerdani	8 000	1936
17	JSM Béjaïa	JSMB	1								1			Béjaïa	L'Unité Maghrébine	20 000	1936

ABBREVIATIONS CR = Chabab Riadhi • CS = Club Sportif • ES = Entente Sportive • GC = Ghali Club • JS = Jeunesse Sportive • MC = Mouloudia Club • MO = Mouloudia Ouloum • NA = Nasr Athletic • USM = Union Sportive Madinet • WA = Widad Athletic

RECENT LEAGUE AND CUP RECORD

	Championship							Cup		
Year	Champions	Pts	Runners-up	Pts	Third	Pts		Winners	Score	Runners-up
1996	USM Algiers	60	MC Oran	58	WA Tlemcen	51		MC Oran	1-0	Ittihad Blida
1997	CS Constantine	56	MC Oran	55	USM Algiers	49		USM Algiers	1-0	CA Batna
1998	USM El Harrach	3-2	USM Algiers					WA Tlemcen	1-0	MC Oran
1999	MC Alger	1-0	JS Kabylie					USM Alger	2-0	JS Kabylie
2000	CR Belouizdad	47	MC Oran	38	MC Constantine	38		MC Ouargla	2-1	WA Tlemcen
2001	CR Belouizdad	62	USM Algiers	55	JS Kabylie	52		USM Alger	1-0	CR Méchria
2002	USM Alger	57	JS Kabylie	52	WA Tlemcen	51		WA Tlemcen	1-0	MC Oran
2003	USM Alger	58	USM Blida	51	NA Hussein Dey	51		USM Alger	2-1	CR Belouizdad
2004	JS Kabylie	61	USM Alger	58	NA Hussein Dey	49		USM Alger	0-0 5-4p	JS Kabylie
2005	USM Alger	67	JS Kabylie	54	MC Alger	49		ASO Chlef	1-0	USM Sétif
2006	JS Kabylie	58	USM Alger	57	ASO Chlef	52		MC Alger	2-1	USM Alger
2007	ES Sétif	54	JS Kabylie	52	JSM Béjaïa	49		MC Alger	1-0	USM Alger
2008	JS Kabylie	59	ASO Chlef	49	ES Sétif	43		JSM Béjaïa	1-1 3-1p	WA Tlemcen

ALGERIA 2007–08

PREMIERE DIVISION

	Pl	W	D	L	F	A	Pts	JSK	ASO	ESS	USMA	USMAn	MCS	MCA	JSMB	ASK	CRB	NAHD	CABBA	USMB	MCO	OMR	WAT
JS Kabylie †	30	18	5	7	45	23	59		1-0	1-0	1-0	1-0	2-0	1-0	4-2	2-1	1-0	3-0	1-0	2-2	2-0	2-0	6-1
ASO Chlef †	30	13	10	7	29	22	49	2-0		1-0	2-0	2-0	0-0	1-0	2-2	2-2	0-0	1-0	1-0	1-0	1-1	2-1	1-0
ES Sétif ‡	30	12	8	10	32	27	43	0-3	3-2		2-1	4-0	0-1	1-0	0-0	0-2	1-1	3-0	0-0	0-0	3-1	0-1	2-1
USM Alger	30	12	6	12	32	27	42	1-0	0-1	1-0		3-1	4-0	0-2	0-0	1-1	2-0	2-1	0-2	2-0	3-2	1-0	0-0
USM Annaba	30	12	6	12	35	37	42	2-2	1-0	0-1	2-0		2-0	3-1	2-0	0-0	2-2	2-2	1-1	2-0	3-0	1-0	2-1
MC Saïda	30	11	9	10	32	38	42	3-2	1-1	2-2	0-2	2-1		0-0	2-0	1-1	2-0	3-2	1-0	2-0	1-1	2-1	1-0
MC Alger	30	9	12	9	26	25	39	0-2	0-1	1-1	1-0	0-1	1-1		2-1	1-0	1-1	3-2	1-0	1-1	1-0	1-1	0-0
JSM Béjaïa ‡	30	9	12	9	36	38	39	2-4	1-0	2-2	0-1	2-1	2-4	2-2		0-0	0-3	1-1	2-1	3-1	2-0	2-1	
AS Khroub	30	10	9	11	26	28	39	2-0	2-0	1-0	0-0	2-0	3-1	1-0	0-0		1-1	1-0	0-0	1-3	1-0	1-0	1-3
CR Bélouizdad	30	8	14	8	21	21	38	0-0	0-0	0-0	1-0	2-1	0-0	0-0	3-1	2-0		0-1	2-0	0-0	1-0	0-1	1-0
NA Hussein Dey	30	10	8	12	34	36	38	0-0	3-1	0-2	1-0	3-3	3-0	1-1	3-1	3-0	2-1		2-1	1-1	0-0	1-2	2-0
CA Bordj Bou Arréridj	30	10	8	12	25	28	38	2-0	0-0	2-0	1-0	1-2	1-0	1-1	0-2	2-1	2-0	1-0		2-1	1-0	2-1	0-0
USM Blida	30	9	10	11	33	34	37	1-1	1-1	2-0	3-2	1-2	2-1	2-3	1-1	1-0	1-1	1-0			2-0	1-1	3-0
MC Oran	30	10	7	13	27	33	37	1-2	1-0	0-2	1-1	1-0	3-0	1-0	2-2	2-0	1-0	2-0	2-1	1-0		2-2	0-0
OMR El Annasser	30	9	9	12	24	29	36	1-0	0-1	1-2	1-1	3-1	0-0	0-2	1-1	1-0	1-1	0-1	0-0	1-2			1-0
WA Tlemcen	30	7	9	14	28	39	30	1-0	1-1	0-1	1-4	1-0	2-1	1-1	0-1	2-1	1-1	0-0	6-2	1-2	1-0	1-1	

23/08/2007 - 26/05/2008 • † Qualified for the CAF Champions League • ‡ Qualified for the CAF Confederation Cup • Top scorer: Nabil Hemani, JSK 16

ALGERIA 2007–08
SECONDE DIVISION (2)

	Pl	W	D	L	F	A	Pts
MC El Eulma	36	21	8	7	57	28	71
MSP Batna	36	23	1	12	55	24	70
USM El Harrach	36	19	11	6	49	20	68
RC Kouba	36	20	8	8	50	26	68
CA Batna	36	18	13	5	46	22	67
MO Constantine	36	15	10	11	42	48	55
ASM Oran	36	15	9	12	50	41	54
Paradou AC	36	14	6	16	43	45	48
USM Sétif	36	14	6	16	38	41	48
CS Constantine	36	12	11	13	36	33	47
USM Bel Abbès	36	13	7	16	31	40	46
MO Béjaïa	36	12	9	15	37	33	45
US Biskra	36	13	6	17	25	39	45
SA Mohamadia	36	13	6	17	31	48	45
OM Arzew	36	12	8	16	42	39	44
NARB Réghaïa	36	13	5	18	31	50	44
UMS Dréan	36	10	5	21	26	60	35
UMS Dréan	36	8	7	21	29	44	31
Bou Saada	36	7	4	25	29	66	25

24/08/2007 - 29/05/2008

COUPE D'ALGERIE 2007–08

Round of 16

JSM Béjaïa *	1 3p
MC Saïda	1 1p
ASO Chlef *	1
MC Oran	3
CR Bélouizdad *	3 4p
USM Blida	3 2p
USM Alger	0 1p
NA Hussein Dey *	2
ESM Koléa *	2
OS Ouenza	0
OMR El Annasser *	0
USM Annaba	1
Paradou AC	3
ASM Oran *	1
ES Souk Ahras *	0
WA Tlemcen	4

Quarter-finals

JSM Béjaïa *	1
MC Oran	0
CR Bélouizdad *	0 1p
NA Hussein Dey	0 3p
ESM Koléa *	
USM Annaba	
Paradou AC *	1 1p
WA Tlemcen	1 4p

Semi-finals

JSM Béjaïa	3
NA Hussein Dey	1
ESM Koléa	1
WA Tlemcen	3

Final

JSM Béjaïa ‡	1 3p
WA Tlemcen	1 1p

CUP FINAL

Tchaker Mustapha, Blida
17-06-2008. Ref: Boumaza

Scorers - Kouider Boukessassa [40] for JSMB; Mokhtar Benmoussa [49] for WAT

* Home team • ‡ Qualified for the CAF Confederation Cup

AND – ANDORRA

NATIONAL TEAM RECORD
JULY 10TH 2006 TO JULY 12TH 2010

PL	W	D	L	F	A	%
16	0	1	15	3	50	3.1

FIFA/COCA-COLA WORLD RANKING

1993	1994	1995	1996	1997	1998	1999	2000	2001	2002	2003	2004	2005	2006	2007
-	-	-	187	185	171	145	145	140	137	147	138	125	164	175

High	
125	12/05

2007–2008											
08/07	09/07	10/07	11/07	12/07	01/08	02/08	03/08	04/08	05/08	06/08	07/08
161	169	173	174	175	175	180	179	181	181	184	183

Low	
188	06/97

With seven straight defeats during the season there was little cheer as far as the national team was concerned although in their final Euro 2008 qualifier Andorra did restrict Russia to a 1-0 victory. The defeat at home to Latvia in March 2008 was their 24th match without a win - a new record for the team beating their run from 1996 to 2000 - and it's hard to see where the next victory will come from, especially in a competitive matches, after they were drawn in a tough 2010 FIFA World Cup qualifying group. Kazakhstan may be their best chance of a win, but the Kazaks are improving and the same can not be said for the Andorrans. In club football, however, there was a major success

INTERNATIONAL HONOURS
None

when Santa Coloma beat Maccabi Tel Aviv 1-0 in first qualifying round of the UEFA Cup. It was the first time an Andorran club had won a game in European club competition, although the Israelis did fight back in the return to win 4-1 on aggregate. It turned out to be a great season for Santa Coloma as they went on to win the Championship, denying Ranger's a hat-trick of titles. They fell just short, however, in their attempt to win the Copa Constitució for the sixth season in a row, losing in the semi-finals to Lusitans on penalties. In the final, Sant Julia then comfortably beat Lusitans 6-1 to win the Cup for the first time - having lost in five of the previous seven finals.

THE FIFA BIG COUNT OF 2006

	Male	Female		Total
Number of players	4 681	356	Referees and Assistant Referees	52
Professionals	0		Admin, Coaches, Technical, Medical	116
Amateurs 18+	804		Number of clubs	26
Youth under 18	1366		Number of teams	34
Unregistered	700		Clubs with women's teams	1
Total players	5 037		Players as % of population	7.07%

Federació Andorrana de Fútbol (FAF)
Avinguda Carlemany 67, 3° pis, Apartado postal 65 AD, Escaldes-Engordany, Principat d'Andorra
Tel +376 805830   Fax +376 862006
administracio@fedanfut.com   www.fedanfut.com
President: AMAT ESCOBAR Francesc   General Secretary: GEA Tomas
Vice-President: MORALES Antonio   Treasurer: GARCIA Josep   Media Officer: GEA Tomas
Men's Coach: RODRIGO David   Women's Coach: RODRIGO David
FAF formed: 1994   UEFA: 1996   FIFA: 1996
Blue shirts with yellow and red trimmings, Blue shorts, Blue socks or Red shirts with yellow and black trimmings, Blue shorts, Blue socks

RECENT INTERNATIONALS PLAYED BY ANDORRA

2002	Opponents		Score	Venue	Comp	Scorers	Att	Referee
21-08	Iceland	L	0-3	Rejkjavik	Fr		2 900	Isaksen FRO
12-10	Belgium	L	0-1	Andorra la Vella	ECq		700	Nalbandyan ARM
16-10	Bulgaria	L	1-2	Sofia	ECq	Lima.A [80]	42 000	Richards WAL
2003								
2-04	Croatia	L	0-2	Varazdin	ECq		8 500	Salomir ROM
30-04	Estonia	L	0-2	Andorra la Vella	ECq		500	Aydin TUR
7-06	Estonia	L	0-2	Tallinn	ECq		3 500	Juhos HUN
11-06	Belgium	L	0-3	Gent	ECq		12 000	Shmolik BLR
13-06	Gabon	L	0-2	Andorra la Vella	Fr			
6-09	Croatia	L	0-3	Andorra la Vella	ECq		800	Liba CZE
10-09	Bulgaria	L	0-3	Andorra la Vella	ECq		1 000	Mikulski POL
2004								
14-04	China PR	D	0-0	Peralada	Fr			
28-05	France	L	0-4	Montpellier	Fr		27 750	Daami TUN
5-06	Spain	L	0-4	Getafe	Fr		14 000	Trefolini ITA
4-09	Finland	L	0-3	Tampere	WCq		7 437	Siric CRO
8-09	Romania	L	1-5	Andorra la Vella	WCq	Pujol [28p]	1 100	Kircher GER
13-10	FYR Macedonia	W	1-0	Andorra la Vella	WCq	Bernaus [60]	350	Podeschi SMR
17-11	Netherlands	L	0-3	Andorra la Vella	WCq		2 000	Yefet ISR
2005								
9-02	FYR Macedonia	D	0-0	Skopje	WCq		5 000	Verbist BEL
26-03	Armenia	L	1-2	Yerevan	WCq	Silva [56]	2 100	Attard MLT
30-03	Czech Republic	L	0-4	Andorra la Vella	WCq		900	Messner AUT
4-06	Czech Republic	L	1-8	Liberec	WCq	Riera [36]	9 520	Dereli TUR
17-08	Romania	L	0-2	Constanta	WCq		8 200	Jakov ISR
3-09	Finland	D	0-0	Andorra la Vella	WCq		860	Ver Eecke BEL
7-09	Netherlands	L	0-4	Eindhoven	WCq		34 000	Hanacsek HUN
12-10	Armenia	L	0-3	Andorra la Vella	WCq		430	Stokes IRL
2006								
16-08	Belarus	L	0-3	Minsk	Fr			
2-09	England	L	0-5	Manchester	ECq		56 290	Brugger AUT
6-09	Israel	L	1-4	Nijmegan	ECq	Fernández [84]	400	Zrnic BIH
7-10	Croatia	L	0-7	Zagreb	ECq		17 618	Zammit MLT
11-10	FYR Macedonia	L	0-3	Andorra la Vella	ECq		300	Silagava GEO
2007								
7-02	Armenia	D	0-0	Andorra la Vella	Fr			
28-03	England	L	0-3	Barcelona	ECq		12 800	Duarte Paixao POR
2-06	Russia	L	0-4	St Petersburg	ECq		21 520	Skjerven NOR
6-06	Israel	L	0-2	Andorra la Vella	ECq		680	Stokes IRL
22-08	Estonia	L	1-2	Tallinn	ECq	Silva [82]	7 500	McCourt NIR
12-09	Croatia	L	0-6	Andorra la Vella	ECq		925	Thual FRA
17-10	FYR Macedonia	L	0-3	Skopje	ECq		17 500	Malzinskas LTU
17-11	Estonia	L	0-2	Andorra la Vella	ECq		700	Collum SCO
21-11	Russia	L	0-1	Andorra la Vella	ECq		780	Hauge NOR
2008								
26-03	Latvia	L	0-3	Andorra la Vella	Fr			Perez ESP
4-06	Azerbaijan	L	1-2	Andorra la Vella	Fr	Lima.I [71]		Gomes POR

Fr = Friendly match • EC = UEFA EURO 2004/2008 • WC = FIFA World Cup • q = qualifier

ANDORRA NATIONAL TEAM RECORDS AND RECORD SEQUENCES

Records				Sequence records			
Victory	2-0	BLR 2000, ALB 2002	Wins	1		Clean sheets	2	2000
Defeat	1-8	CZE 2005	Defeats	11	2002-2003	Goals scored	2	Three times
Player Caps	73	Oscar Sonejee	Undefeated	3	2000	Without goal	11	2003-2004
Player Goals	3	Ildefons Lima	Without win	25	2004-	Goals against	11	2000-02, 2002-03

ANDORRA COUNTRY INFORMATION

Capital	Andorra la Vella	Independence	1278	GDP per Capita	$19 000
Population	69 865	Status	Principality	GNP Ranking	150
Area km²	468	Language	Catalan (official), French	Dialling code	+376
Population density	149 per km²	Literacy rate	99%	Internet code	.ad
% in urban areas	63%	Main religion	Christian 94%	GMT + / –	+1
Towns/Cities ('000)	Andorra la Vella 22; Les Escaldes 13; Encamp 9				
Neighbours (km)	France 56; Spain 63				
Main stadia	Comunal – Andorra la Vella 1 140				

ANDORRA 2007–08

LLIGA ANDORRANA PRIMERA DIVISIO

	Pl	W	D	L	F	A	Pts	S'ta Coloma	Sant Julià	Ranger's	Lusitans	Principat	Inter	Engordany	Benfica
Santa Coloma †	20	14	5	1	69	10	44		1-1 1-1	1-1 2-2	2-0 1-0	5-2	0-0	11-0	7-0
Sant Julià ‡	20	12	5	3	59	19	41	0-1 2-1		1-2 3-0	1-0 2-4	6-0	2-0	4-0	3-0
Ranger's	20	12	4	4	47	30	40	2-2 0-1	1-1 1-4		1-0 3-2	3-2	3-2	4-1	7-0
Lusitans	20	10	1	9	44	29	31	0-1 1-5	1-4 1-1	2-0 2-4		2-0	2-0	8-1	2-0
Principat	20	9	3	8	33	37	30	0-4	2-2	2-5	0-2		0-0 1-1	3-2 4-0	3-0 3-0
Inter Escaldes	20	6	2	12	23	37	20	0-3	0-3	0-2	2-4	0-1 0-1		1-2 4-0	2-0 2-1
Engordany	20	4	1	15	21	79	13	0-11	1-4	2-3	0-5	2-4 0-3	2-1		1-1 1-3
Casa del Benfica	20	2	1	17	13	68	7	0-6	0-10	0-3	1-6	1-3 3-1	1-3 1-2	0-1 1-2	

23/09/2007 - 27/04/2008 • † Qualified for the UEFA Champions League • ‡ Qualified for the UEFA Cup

Relegation play-off:
Engordany 2-3 3-0 Extremenya

ANDORRA 2007–08 SEGONA DIVISIO (2)

	Pl	W	D	L	F	A	Pts
UE Santa Coloma	16	14	2	0	66	11	44
UE Extremenya ‡	16	14	0	2	42	13	42
Encamp	16	9	3	4	38	14	30
Lusitans B	16	7	2	7	39	30	23
Principat B	16	6	0	10	35	39	18
Athlètic Escaldes	16	5	2	9	30	33	17
Ranger's B	16	4	3	9	24	48	15
Sporting Escaldes	16	4	0	12	33	66	12
Inter Escaldes B	16	2	2	12	17	70	8

22/09/2007 - 6/04/2008 • ‡ Qualified for play-off

COPA CONSTITUCIO 2007–08

Quarter–finals		Semi–finals		Final	
Sant Julià	6				
Extremenya	0	Sant Julià	6		
Inter Escaldes	1	Ranger's	1		
Ranger's	2			Sant Julià	6
Santa Coloma				Lusitans	1
Principat		Santa Coloma	1 3p		
Engordany	0	Lusitans	1 4p	24-05-2008	
Lusitans	1				

RECENT LEAGUE AND CUP RECORD

	Championship						Cup		
Year	Champions	Pts	Runners-up	Pts	Third	Pts	Winners	Score	Runners-up
2000	Constelació	64	Santa Coloma	28	Inter d'Escaldes	20	Constelació	6-0	Encamp
2001	Santa Coloma	24	Sant Julià	22	Inter d'Escaldes	12	Santa Coloma	2-0	Sant Julià
2002	Encamp	44	Sant Julià	43	Santa Coloma	42	Lusitans	2-0	Inter d'Escaldes
2003	Santa Coloma	49	Encamp	48	Sant Julià	38	Santa Coloma	5-3	Sant Julià
2004	Santa Coloma	45	Sant Julià	43	Ranger's	34	Santa Coloma	1-0	Sant Julià
2005	Sant Julià	54	Ranger's	51	Santa Coloma	37	Santa Coloma	2-1	Sant Julià
2006	Ranger's	51	Sant Julià	39	Santa Coloma	36	Santa Coloma	1-1 5-3p	Ranger's
2007	Ranger's	53	Santa Coloma	44	Sant Julià	34	Santa Coloma	2-2 2-0p	Sant Julià
2008	Santa Coloma	44	Sant Julià	41	Ranger's	40	Sant Julià	6-1	Lusitans

ANG – ANGOLA

NATIONAL TEAM RECORD
JULY 10TH 2006 TO JULY 12TH 2010

PL	W	D	L	F	A	%
25	10	8	7	39	29	56

FIFA/COCA-COLA WORLD RANKING

1993	1994	1995	1996	1997	1998	1999	2000	2001	2002	2003	2004	2005	2006	2007	High	
102	106	80	70	58	50	52	55	55	76	83	72	61	55		**45**	07/00

	2007–2008											Low	
08/07	09/07	10/07	11/07	12/07	01/08	02/08	03/08	04/08	05/08	06/08	07/08	**124**	06/94

Angola's steady conversion into one of African football's superpowers continued to gather pace after their participation at the 2006 FIFA World Cup finals in Germany. The 'Palancas Negras' set a new benchmark for themselves in getting past the first round group phase at the 2008 African Nations Cup in Ghana, and putting up a gallant fight before bowing out by the odd goal in three to eventual winners Egypt in the quarter-finals. Angola had won their qualifying group with relative ease and look likely to do the same in the 2010 FIFA World Cup preliminaries. Coach Luis Oliveira Goncalves continues to provide the consistency although he has lost influential captain Figuereido

INTERNATIONAL HONOURS
Qualified for the FIFA World Cup™ 2006   CAF Youth Championship 2001   COSAFA Cup 1999 2001 2004

to retirement. In the GiraBola, police team InterClube won a first ever title in a debut coaching season for former Brazilian international Carlos Mozer. But there was little sentiment shown when they started the defence of their title in 2008 with a series of indifferent results and were also eliminated in the African Champions League by Egypt's Zamalek. Mozer was fired, to be replaced by Augusto Inacio, one of several high profile Portuguese coaches now attracted to the country by the growing financial muscle of its top teams. There were also surprise winners in the Cup with Primeiro de Maio, from the city of Benguela, winning their first trophy for 22 years.

THE FIFA BIG COUNT OF 2006

	Male	Female		Total
Number of players	634 090	30 600	Referees and Assistant Referees	259
Professionals	0		Admin, Coaches, Technical, Medical	1 800
Amateurs 18+	5 240		Number of clubs	100
Youth under 18	10 800		Number of teams	500
Unregistered	36 250		Clubs with women's teams	3
Total players	664 690		Players as % of population	5.48

Federaçao Angolana de Futebol (FAF)

Compl. da Cidadela Desportiva, Luanda - 3449, Angola
Tel +244 22 264948   Fax +244 22 260566
sgeral@fafutebol.ebonet.net   www.fafutebol-angola.og.ao
President: FERNANDES Justino Dr   General Secretary: PEREIRA DA SILVA Augusto
Vice-President: MANGUEIRA Antonio   Treasurer: GOMES FURTADO Antonio   Media Officer: MACEDO Arlindo
Men's Coach: DE OLIVEIRA GONCALVES Luis   Women's Coach: NZUZI Andre
FAF formed: 1979   CAF: 1996   FIFA: 1980
Red shirts with black trimmings, Black shorts, Red socks

RECENT INTERNATIONALS PLAYED BY ANGOLA

2006	Opponents	Score		Venue	Comp	Scorers	Att	Referee
11-06	Portugal	L	0-1	Cologne	WCr1		45 000	Larrionda URU
16-06	Mexico	D	0-0	Hanover	WCr1		43 000	Maidin SIN
21-06	Iran	D	1-1	Leipzig	WCr1	Flavio 60	38 000	Shield AUS
3-09	Swaziland	W	2-0	Mbabane	CNq	Gumbi OG 21, Loco 80		Maillet SEY
17-09	Zimbabwe	W	2-1	Harare	CCsf	Gazeta 43, Love 75		Kaoma ZAM
8-10	Kenya	W	3-1	Luanda	CNq	Flavio 2 37 68, Mateus 60		Lwanja MWI
21-10	Zambia	L	0-2	Lusaka	CCf			Raolimanana MAD
18-11	Tanzania	D	1-1	Dar es Salaam	Fr	Manucho 83		
2007								
25-03	Eritrea	W	6-1	Luanda	CNq	Flavio 2 28 69, Mantorras 36p, Ze Kalanga 43, Mendonca 47, Figueiredo 84		Evehe CMR
4-04	Congo	D	0-0	Cabinda	Fr			
2-06	Eritrea	D	1-1	Asmara	CNq	Maurito 62		Marange ZIM
17-06	Swaziland	W	3-0	Luanda	CNq	Figueiredo 18, Love 30, Flavio 57p		
28-07	Lesotho	W	2-0	Gaborone	CCr1	Manucho 40, Santana 83		Disang BOT
29-07	Botswana	D	0-0	Gaborone	CCr1	L 1-3p		
22-08	Congo DR	L	1-3	Kinshasa	Fr	Flavio 33		
8-09	Kenya	L	1-2	Bairobi	CNq	Manucho 35		Katjimune NAM
17-11	Côte d'Ivoire	W	2-1	Melun	Fr	Andre 13, Flavio 39		
20-11	Guinea	L	0-3	Melun	Fr			
2008								
13-01	Egypt	D	3-3	AlvercaDoRibatejo	Fr	Figueiredo 22, Flavio 36, Manucho 47		
16-01	Morocco	L	1-2	Rabat	Fr	Flavio 17		
23-01	South Africa	D	1-1	Tamale	CNr1	Manucho 30		Coulibaly MLI
27-01	Senegal	W	3-1	Tamale	CNr1	Manucho 2 50 67, Flavio 78		Haimoudi ALG
31-01	Tunisia	D	0-0	Tamale	CNr1			Codjia BEN
4-02	Egypt	L	1-2	Kumasi	CNqf	Manucho 27		Nichimura JPN
1-06	Benin	W	3-0	Luanda	WCq	Flavio 62, Job 81, Mendonca 86	6 000	Damon RSA
8-06	Niger	W	2-1	Niamey	WCq	Flavio 30, Yamba Asha 71	23 000	Jedidi TUN
14-06	Uganda	L	1-3	Kampala	WCq	Mantorras 91+	20 000	Mailett SEY
23-06	Uganda	D	0-0	Luanda	WCq		16 000	Mana NGA

Fr = Friendly match • CN = CAF African Cup of Nations • CC = COSAFA Castle Cup • WC = FIFA World Cup
q = qualifier • r1 = first round group • qf = quarter-final • sf = semi-final • f = final

ANGOLA NATIONAL TEAM PLAYERS

	Player		Club	Date of Birth		Player		Club	Date of Birth
1	Lama	GK	Petro Atletico	1 02 1981	12	Nuno	GK	AS Aviacao	25 04 1983
2	Marco Airosa	DF	Fatima POR	6 08 1984	13	Edson	MF	Pacos Ferreira POR	2 03 1980
3	Jamba	DF	AS Aviacao	10 07 1977	14	Mendonca	MF	Estrela Amadora POR	9 10 1982
4	Machado	DF	Anadia POR	24 12 1985	15	Rui Marques	DF	Leeds United ENG	3 09 1977
5	Kali	DF	FC Sion SUI	11 10 1978	16	Flavio	FW	Al Ahli EGY	30 12 1979
6	Yamba Asha	DF	Petro Atletico	31 07 1976	17	Ze Kalanga	MF	Boavista POR	12 10 1983
7	Figueiredo	MF	Osters SWE	28 11 1972	18	Love	FW	Primeiro Agosto	22 09 1979
8	Andre	MF	Kuwait SC	14 05 1978	19	Dede	MF	Pacos Ferreira POR	4 07 1981
9	Mateus	FW	Boavista POR	18 06 1984	20	Loco	DF	Primeiro Agosto	25 12 1984
10	Maurito	MF	Kuwait SC	24 06 1981	21	Delgado	DF	Metz FRA	1 11 1979
11	Gilberto	MF	Al Ahli EGY	21 09 1982	22	Mario	GK	InterClube	1 06 1985
					23	Manucho	FW	Manchester United ENG	7 03 1983

Angola's squad for the 2008 CAF Africa Cup of Nations

ANGOLA NATIONAL TEAM RECORDS AND RECORD SEQUENCES

Records			Sequence records					
Victory	7-1	SWZ 2000	Wins	3	Seven times	Clean sheets	5	2004-2005
Defeat	0-6	POR 1989	Defeats	6	1989-1990	Goals scored	11	2001
Player Caps	80	Akwa	Undefeated	12	2004-2005	Without goal	3	1980-1981
Player Goals	36	Akwa	Without win	13	1980-1982	Goals against	8	1989-90, 1998-91

MAJOR CITIES/TOWNS
Population '000

1	Luanda	2 875
2	Huambo	233
3	Lobito	213
4	Benguela	155
5	Kuito	114
6	Lubango	102
7	Malanje	87
8	Namibe	82
9	Soyo	74
10	Cabinda	67
11	Uíge	60
12	Saurimo	40
13	Sumbe	33
14	Caluquembe	30
15	Caxito	28
16	M'banza-Kongo	25
17	Longonjo	24
18	Caála	21
19	Luena	21
20	N'dalatando	21
21	Lucapa	20
22	N'zeto	19
23	Camacupa	19
24	Cataboia	

REPUBLICA DE ANGOLA; REPUBLIC OF ANGOLA

Capital	Luanda	Language	Portuguese	Independence	1975
Population	12 127 071	Area	1 246 700 km²	Density 9 per km²	% in cities 32
GDP per cap	$1 900	Dailling code	+244	Internet .ao	GMT +/- +1

MEDALS TABLE

		Overall			League			Cup			Africa			City	Stadium	Cap'ty	DoF
		G	S	B	G	S	B	G	S	B	G	S	B				
1	Petro Atlético	21	5	5	13	3	5	8	2					Luanda	Coqueiros	12 000	1980
2	Primeiro de Agosto	13	6	3	9	2	3	4	4					Luanda	Coqueiros	12 000	1977
3	Atlético Sport Aviação	5	7	1	3	5	1	2	2					Luanda	Joaquim Dinis	10 000	1953
4	Primeiro de Maio	5	6		2	4		3	2					Benguela	Municipal	15 000	1955
5	Inter Clube	3	5	4	1	1	4	2	4					Luanda	22 de Junho	10 000	1953
6	Sagrada Esperança	3	3		1	2		2	1					Dundo	Quintalão	3 000	
7	Ferroviário Huila	2	1	1		1		2	1					Lubango	Ferroviario	5 000	
8	Atlético Petróleas Namibe	2						2						Namibe	Joaquim Morais	5 000	
9	Progresso Sambiganza	1						1						Luanda	Campo de São Paulo	4 000	
10	Petro Huambo		2	3	1	3		1						Huambo	Ferrovia	17 000	1955
11	Independente		2	1		1			2					Tombwa	Tombwa	7 000	
12	SL Benfica Luanda		2						2					Luanda	Cidadela	60 000	
13	Nacional Benguela		1	1	1	1								Benguela	Arregaca	8 000	
14	11 de Novembro		1						1					Kuando Kubango			
	Academica Lobito		1			1								Lobito	Electro Clube	3 000	

Atlético Petróleas Namibe were known as Sonangol until 2005

RECENT LEAGUE AND CUP RECORD

	Championship							Cup		
Year	Champions	Pts	Runners-up	Pts	Third	Pts		Winners	Score	Runners-up
1995	Petro Atlético							Atlético Aviação	3-1	Independente
1996	Primeiro de Agosto							Prog. Sambizanga	1-0	Primeiro de Maio
1997	Petro Atlético							Petro Atlético	2-1	Primeiro de Agosto
1998	Primeiro de Agosto	62	Petro Atlético	58	Atlético Aviação	50		Petro Atlético	4-1	Primeiro de Agosto
1999	Primeiro de Agosto	59	Académica Lobito	51	Inter Clube	49		Sagrada Esperança	1-0	Atlético Aviação
2000	Petro Atlético	63	Atlético Aviação	44	Petro Huambo	42		Petro Atlético	1-0	Inter Clube
2001	Petro Atlético	57	Atlético Aviação	50	Petro Huambo	42		Sonangol	3-2	Sporting Cabinda
2002	Atlético Aviação	57	Primeiro de Agosto	53	Petro Atlético	51		Petro Atlético	3-0	Desportivo Huíla
2003	Atlético Aviação	53	Petro Atlético	52	Petro Huambo	46		Inter Clube	1-0	Sagrada Esperança
2004	Atlético Aviação	56	Sagrada Esperança	53	Inter Clube	51		Sonangol	2-0	Primeiro de Agosto
2005	Sagrada Esperança	51	Atlético Aviação	50	Petro Atlético	48		Atlético Aviação	1-0	Inter Clube
2006	Primeiro de Agosto	56	Petro Atlético	46	Inter Clube	44		Primeiro de Agosto	1-1 4-3p	Benfica Luanda
2007	Inter Clube	55	Primeiro de Agosto	54	Petro Atlético	50		Primeiro de Maio	2-1	Benfica Luanda

ANGOLA 2007

CAMPEONATO NACIONAL XXIX GIRABOLA 1° DIVISAO

	PI	W	D	L	F	A	Pts	Inter Clube	1° Agosto	Petro At.	ASA	Sagrada	Petro H'bo	Benfica Lb	Huíla	1° Maio	Benfica Ln	Santos	Acad. Soyo	At. Namibie	Juventude
Inter Clube †	26	16	7	3	32	17	55		0-3	1-0	1-0	1-1	2-1	2-2	0-0	0-0	2-0	2-0	1-0	1-2	2-0
Primeiro de Agosto †	26	16	6	4	41	14	54	0-0		3-4	1-1	2-0	1-2	1-0	2-0	0-0	2-0	4-1	1-0	1-0	3-1
Petro Atlético	26	15	5	6	43	25	50	1-2	1-0		0-0	1-1	3-1	3-1	2-1	4-2	1-0	2-1	2-0	4-1	5-1
Atlético Aviação	26	10	10	6	27	19	40	1-2	0-2	0-0		2-2	1-1	1-0	1-0	0-0	0-2	1-0	0-0	1-0	1-1
Sagrada Esperança	26	10	10	6	37	27	40	1-2	1-1	1-0	2-3		1-0	1-1	1-3	1-0	1-0	2-1	1-0	6-1	3-0
Petro Huambo	26	11	6	9	26	20	39	0-1	1-0	0-1	1-0	2-1		0-0	0-0	2-1	2-0	2-0	2-0	2-0	4-0
Benfica Lubango	26	11	6	9	31	26	39	0-1	1-1	3-2	2-1	2-1	0-1		0-1	3-0	0-2	3-1	1-0	1-0	4-0
Desportivo Huíla	26	10	8	8	26	25	38	2-2	1-1	0-2	1-1	1-1	1-0	0-0		1-0	1-1	2-1	3-2	1-0	2-0
Primeiro de Maio ‡	26	9	9	8	23	23	36	1-2	0-2	1-0	1-1	0-0	1-1	3-1	2-0		1-0	1-0	1-1	1-0	2-0
Benfica Luanda	26	9	8	9	22	21	35	1-1	0-2	1-1	0-2	1-1	3-0	2-1	2-0	0-0		0-1	1-0	2-1	2-0
Santos	26	8	3	15	23	34	27	0-1	0-3	2-0	0-1	1-2	0-0	0-0	2-1	1-0	0-1		2-1	2-1	2-1
Académica Soyo	26	5	8	13	15	29	23	1-0	0-3	1-0	0-4	0-0	1-0	1-2	1-0	1-1	0-0	2-0		2-1	1-1
At. Petróleos Namibe	26	4	4	18	20	41	16	0-1	0-1	2-3	0-3	0-0	1-0	1-2	0-2	2-3	0-0	1-1	1-1		4-0
Juventude do Moxico	26	0	6	20	8	53	6	0-2	0-1	0-0	0-1	1-4	1-1	0-1	0-1	0-1	1-1	1-1	0-4	0-0	

11/02/2007 - 21/10/2007 • † Qualified for CAF Champions League • ‡ Qualified for CAF Confederation Cup
Top scorers: Manucho GONCALVES, Petro Atlético 15

ANGOLA 2007 2° DIVISAO

Zona A	PI	W	D	L	F	A	Pts
Kabuscorp Palanca	12	10	0	2	27	12	30
SC Cabinda	12	9	1	2	18	5	28
Progresso	12	7	1	4	23	14	22
FC Cabinda	11	4	2	5	14	12	14
Belenenses Samba	11	3	3	5	9	10	12
Esperança	11	2	0	9	6	21	6
Dom Afonso Nteka	11	1	1	9	8	31	4

Zona B	PI	W	D	L	F	A	Pts
Onze Bravos Maqui	10	6	3	1	25	6	21
Recreativo Libolo	10	5	3	2	20	7	18
Recreativo Cála	10	4	4	2	23	12	16
Académica Pet. Lobito	10	5	1	4	17	16	16
Leões Tchifuchi	10	1	3	6	3	24	6
Benfica Huambo	10	1	2	7	3	26	5

1/07/2007 - 30/09/2007

TACA NACIONAL 2007

Round of 16		Quarter–finals		Semi–finals		Final	
Primeiro de Maio	1 3p						
Onze Bravos Maqui *	1 0p	Primeiro de Maio	1				
Académica Soyo	0	Juventude do Moxico *	0				
Juventude do Moxico *	1			Primeiro de Maio	1 4p		
Atlético Aviação	0 4p			Primeiro de Agosto	1 3p		
Inter Clube *	0 3p	Atlético Aviação *	0				
Petro Huambo *	0 3p	Primeiro de Agosto	1				
Primeiro de Agosto	0 4p					Primeiro de Maio ‡	2
Petro Atlético *	1					Benfica Luanda	1
Santos	0	Petro Atlético *	1 2p				
Recreativo Libolo	0	Benfica Lubango	1 0p				
Benfica Lubango *	3			Petro Atlético	2 5p		
Sagrada Esperança	1 4p			Benfica Luanda	2 6p		
Desportivo Huíla *	1 2p	Sagrada Esperança *	0 2p				
At. Petróleos Namibe *	0	Benfica Luanda	0 4p				
Benfica Luanda	1						

* Home team • ‡ Qualified for CAF Confederation Cup

CUP FINAL

Estadio Nacional da Cidadela, Luanda
11-11-2007

Scorers - Adolfo 76p, Fita 95 for Maio;
Bena 37 for Benfica

ANT – NETHERLANDS ANTILLES

NATIONAL TEAM RECORD
JULY 10TH 2006 TO JULY 12TH 2010

PL	W	D	L	F	A	%
3	0	1	2	1	7	8.3

FIFA/COCA-COLA WORLD RANKING

1993	1994	1995	1996	1997	1998	1999	2000	2001	2002	2003	2004	2005	2006	2007
128	152	125	142	156	156	167	175	183	177	188	163	168	177	183

High	
98	12/92

	2007–2008										
08/07	09/07	10/07	11/07	12/07	01/08	02/08	03/08	04/08	05/08	06/08	07/08
177	182	183	183	183	179	161	163	150	153	146	149

Low	
188	12/03

The 2010 FIFA World Cup qualifiers are likely to be the last in which the Netherlands Antilles competes under its present structure with Curaçao and Sint Maarten set to follow Aruba and break away from the present status quo. When that happens it is almost certain that Curaçao will once again compete in international football under its own name, as it did from 1924 until 1948. Sint Maarten are likely to follow suit as they are already associate members of CONCACAF and have often taken part in regional tournaments by themselves. The future of Bonaire, Saba and Sint Eustatius is less clear but it could involve them continuing to compete under the banner of the

INTERNATIONAL HONOURS
None

Netherlands Antilles although technically they are to become a direct part of the Netherlands and so will not be independent nations. As it was, the team did themselves proud in the FIFA World Cup qualifiers, knocking out Nicaragua in a first round tie and then giving Caribbean champions Haiti a shock in the next. The Antilles appeared to have done the hard work against Haiti having come away from Port-au-Prince with a well earned draw from the first leg, but experience told in the return as their rivals won 1-0 in Willemstad. In club football, Undeba beat Centro Barber 1-0 in the final of the Curaçao championship to win the title for the second time in three years.

THE FIFA BIG COUNT OF 2006

	Male	Female		Total
Number of players	3 940	280	Referees and Assistant Referees	42
Professionals	0		Admin, Coaches, Technical, Medical	320
Amateurs 18+	780		Number of clubs	40
Youth under 18	980		Number of teams	75
Unregistered	2 400		Clubs with women's teams	1
Total players	4 220		Players as % of population	1.90%

Nederlands Antilliaanse Voetbal Unie (NAVU)
Bonamweg 49, Curaçao
Tel +599 97365040   Fax +599 97365047
navusoccer@interneeds.net   www.navusoccer.org
President: FRANCISCA Rignaal   General Secretary: ISENIA Hubert
Vice-President: BERNABELA Ferdinand   Treasurer: MARIA Nelson   Media Officer: ISENIA Hubert
Men's Coach: LODYEN Leen   Women's Coach: SILICE Etienne
NAVU formed: 1921   CONCACAF: 1961   FIFA: 1932
White shirts with blue trimmings, Blue shorts, Red socks or Blue shirts, White shorts, Blue socks

RECENT INTERNATIONALS PLAYED BY NETHERLANDS ANTILLES

2006	Opponents	Score		Venue	Comp	Scorers	Att	Referee
6-09	Grenada	D	1-1	Willemstad	CCq	Maria [1]		
8-09	Guyana	L	0-5	Willemstad	CCq			
10-09	Surinam	L	0-1	Willemstad	CCq			Suazo DOM
2007								
No international matches played in 2007 before August								
2008								
6-02	Nicaragua	W	1-0	Diriamba	WCq	Jongsma [15]	7 000	Lopez GUA
26-03	Nicaragua	W	2-0	Willemstad	WCq	Loran [42], Zimmerman [81]	9 000	Wijngaarde SUR
21-05	Surinam	W	2-1	Willemstad	Fr	Martha [25], Silberie [53]		
9-06	Venezuela	L	0-1	Willemstad	Fr			
15-06	Haiti	D	0-0	Port-au-Prince	WCq		6 000	Aguilar SLV
22-06	Haiti	L	0-1	Willemstad	WCq		9 000	Brizan TRI
17-07	Trinidad and Tobago	L	0-2	Macoya	Fr			

Fr = Friendly match • CC = Digicel Caribbean Cup • WC = FIFA World Cup • q = qualifier

NETHERLANDS ANTILLES NATIONAL TEAM RECORDS AND RECORD SEQUENCES

Records			Sequence records				
Victory	15-0	PUR 1959	Wins	5	Three times	Clean sheets	3	1961-1962, 1966
Defeat	0-8	NED 1962, MEX 1973	Defeats	6	1973-1980	Goals scored	30	1926-1948
Player Caps	n/a		Undefeated	9	1959-1961	Without goal	4	2008
Player Goals	n/a		Without win	17	1969-1980	Goals against	19	1968-1980

CURACAO 2007-08 FIRST STAGE

	Pl	W	D	L	F	A	Pts
Hubentut Fortuna †	18	10	7	1	26	14	37
Undeba †	18	10	4	4	29	17	34
Centro Barber †	18	10	3	5	28	12	33
Centro Dominguito †	18	10	0	8	43	23	30
VESTA	18	8	5	5	27	22	29
Victory Boys	18	7	5	6	21	20	26
Jong Colombia	18	6	4	8	22	38	22
Jong Holland	18	4	3	11	16	26	15
Sithoc	18	4	1	13	23	35	13
SUBT	18	3	4	11	15	43	13

16/11/2007 - 29/04/2008 • † Qualified for the semi-finals

SECOND STAGE

	Pl	W	D	L	F	A	Pts
Undeba †	3	2	0	1	8	5	6
Centro Barber †	3	2	0	1	4	2	6
Centro Dominguito †	3	2	0	1	2	2	6
Hubentut Fortuna	3	0	0	3	3	8	0

3/05/2008 - 18/05/2008 • † Qualified for the final

FINAL

Stadion Ergilio Hato, Willemstad, 31-05-2008, Att: 6500

Undeba 1-0 Centro Barber

Scorer: Richenel Doran OG

RECENT LEAGUE RECORD CURACAO

Year	Winners	Score	Runners-up
2002	Centro Barber	2-1	SUBT
2003	Centro Barber	1-0	Jong Colombia
2004	Centro Barber	1-0	Victory Boys
2005	Centro Barber	4-1	Victory Boys
2006	Undeba	1-0	Centro Barber
2007	Centro Barber	2-1	Jong Colombia
2008	Undeba	1-0	Centro Barber

RECENT LEAGUE RECORD BONAIRE

Year	Winners	Score	Runners-up
2002	Estrellas	1-0	Real Rincon
2003	Real Rincon	3-0	Juventus
2004	Real Rincon	0-0 1-0	Estrellas
2005	Juventus	1-0	Estrellas
2006	No tournament held		
2007	Vespo	1-0	Real Rincon

RECENT KOPA ANTIANO RECORD

Year	Winners	Score	Runners-up
2002	Centro Barber	1-0	SUBT
2003	Centro Barber	2-1	Jong Colombia
2004	No tournament held		
2005	Centro Barber	2-1	Victory Boys
2006	No tournament held		
2007	Centro Barber	4-2	Jong Colombia

NETHERLANDS ANTILLES COUNTRY INFORMATION

Capital	Willemstad	Independence	Part of the Netherlands with autonomy in internal affairs	GDP per Capita	$11 400
Population	218 126	Status		GNP Ranking	n/a
Area km²	960	Language	Dutch	Dialling code	+599
Population density	227 per km²	Literacy rate	96%	Internet code	.an
% in urban areas	n/a	Main religion	Christian	GMT +/−	-4
Towns/Cities ('000)	Willemstad (Curaçao) 97; Princess Quarter (Sint Maarten) 13; Kraleendijk (Bonaire) 3;				
Neighbours (km)	Netherlands Antilles is a group of Caribbean islands consisting of Bonaire, Curaçao, Saba, Sint Eustatius & Sint Maarten				
Main stadia	Ergilio Hato – Willemstad 15 000; Municipal – Kralendijk 3 000				

ARG – ARGENTINA

NATIONAL TEAM RECORD
JULY 10TH 2006 TO JULY 12TH 2010

PL	W	D	L	F	A	%
23	13	5	5	40	21	67.4

Although Boca Juniors and River Plate remain the best supported and most successful clubs in Argentina, the second half of 2007 saw them take on a supporting role to two of the lesser known clubs in the country - Lanus and Arsenal. In the 2007 Apertura, Lanus won the championship for the first time in their history, thanks largely to the goals of Jose Sand who scored 15 in as many games. They clinched the title with a 1-1 draw against Boca to finish four points ahead of another of the minnows - Tigre. Boca for their part only finished in fourth place while River had a torrid time, finishing way down the table in 14th. At the same time that Lanus were enjoying their brief spell in the limelight, Arsenal, another small club from Buenos Aires, were also re-writing the history books. Having knocked-out River Plate in the semi-finals of the Copa Sudamericana, Arsenal then beat Mexican giants América in the final, thanks to a spirited 3-2 victory in the first leg in the Azteca. Arsenal were formed in the 1950s by the Grondona brothers, one of whom, Julio, is the president of the AFA and a vice-president of FIFA. Based in the neighbourhood of Sarandi in Avellaneda, Arsenal are not even the biggest club on their patch with both Independiente and

INTERNATIONAL HONOURS
FIFA World Cup 1978 1986

Olympic Gold 2004   **FIFA U–20 World Cup** 1979 1995 1997 2001 2005 2007

Copa América 1910 1921 1925 1927 1929 1937 1941 1945 1946 1947 1955 1957 1959 1991 1993

Sudamericana Sub–20 1967 1997 1999 2003   **Sudamericana Sub–17** 1985 2003   **Sudamericana Feminino** 2006

Copa Toyota Libertadores Independiente 1964 1965 1972 1973 1974 1975 1984, Racing Club 1967, Estudiantes 1968 1969 1970, Boca Juniors 1977 1978 2000 2001 2003, Argentinos Juniors 1985, River Plate 1986 1996, Vélez Sarsfield 1994

Racing Club close by. Little surprise then that they were the worst supported club in what was their most successful season. River Plate managed to salvage some pride when they won the Clausura in June 2008, thanks in no small measure to Diego Simeone, who won his second title as a coach following on from his first the previous season with Estudiantes. It was also a personal triumph for the veteran Ariel Ortega who has had to battle with alchohol addiction. In the Copa Libertadores, Boca Juniors were hoping to equal Independiente's record haul of seven titles but they fell just short, losing an epic semi-final against Brazil's Fluminense - the first time in a decade that Boca had been knocked-out by Brazilian opposition. 2007 saw the Argentina national team finish the year at the top of the FIFA/Coca-Cola World Ranking for the first time, but there was cause for concern with a defeat and two draws in consecutive FIFA World Cup qualifiers and rumours of rifts within the Argentine camp, notably between Juan Román Riquelme and Lionel Messi. Despite this, however, Alfio Basile's side remain well placed to qualify for the finals in South Africa.

Asociación del Fútbol Argentino (AFA)
Viamonte 1366/76, Buenos Aires - 1053

Tel +54 11 43717900   Fax +54 11 43754410

gerencia@afa.org.ar   www.afa.org.ar

President: GRONDONA Julio H.   General Secretary: SAVINO Rafael

Vice-President: AGUILAR Jose Maria   Treasurer: PORTELL Carlos   Media Officer: TBD

Men's Coach: BASILE Alfio   Women's Coach: BORRELO Jose Carlos

AFA formed: 1893   CONMEBOL: 1916   FIFA: 1912

Light blue and white striped shirts, Black shorts, White socks or Dark blue shirts, Black shorts, White socks

RECENT INTERNATIONAL MATCHES PLAYED BY ARGENTINA

2006	Opponents	Score	Venue	Comp	Scorers	Att	Referee
10-06	Côte D'Ivoire	W 2-1	Hamburg	WCr1	Crespo [24], Saviola [38]	49 480	De Bleeckere BEL
16-06	Serbia & Montenegro	W 6-0	Gelsenkirchen	WCr1	Rodriguez.M 2 [6 41], Cambiasso [31], Crespo [78], Tevez [84], Messi [88]	52 000	Rosetti ITA
21-06	Netherlands	D 0-0	Frankfurt	WCr1		48 000	Medina Cantalejo ESP
24-06	Mexico	W 2-1	Leipzig	WCr2	Crespo [10], Rodriguez.M [98]	43 000	Busacca SUI
30-06	Germany	D 1-1	Berlin	WCqf	Ayala [49]. L 2-4p	72 000	Michel SVK
3-09	Brazil	L 0-3	London	Fr		59 032	Bennett ENG
11-10	Spain	L 1-2	Murcia	Fr	Bilos [34]	31 000	Duhamel FRA
2007							
7-02	France	W 1-0	Paris	Fr	Saviola [15]	79 862	Skomina SVN
18-04	Chile	D 0-0	Mendoza	Fr		38 000	Vazquez URU
2-06	Switzerland	D 1-1	Basel	Fr	Tevez [49]	29 000	Messina ITA
5-06	Algeria	W 4-3	Barcelona	Fr	Tevez [1], Messi 2 [54 73], Cambiasso [56]		Izquierdo ESP
28-06	USA	W 4-1	Maracaibo	CAr1	Crespo 2 [11 60], Aimar [76], Tevez [84]	34 500	Chandia CHI
2-07	Colombia	W 4-2	Maracaibo	CAr1	Crespo [20p], Riquelme 2 [34 45], Milito.D [91+]	35 000	Simon BRA
5-07	Paraguay	W 1-0	Barquisimeto	CAr1	Mascherano [79]	37 000	Larrionda URU
8-07	Peru	W 4-0	Barquisimeto	CAqf	Riquelme 2 [47 85], Messi [61], Mascherano [75]	37 000	Simon BRA
11-07	Mexico	W 3-0	Puerto Ordaz	CAsf	Heinze [44], Messi [61], Riquelme [66p]	40 000	Chandia CHI
15-07	Brazil	L 0-3	Maracaibo	CAf		42 000	Amarilla PAR
22-08	Norway	L 1-2	Oslo	Fr	Rodriguez.M [84]	23 932	Ceferin SVN
11-09	Australia	W 1-0	Melbourne	Fr	Demichelis [49]	70 000	
13-10	Chile	W 2-0	Buenos Aires	WCq	Riquelme 2 [26 45]	55 000	Vazquez URU
16-10	Venezuela	W 2-0	Maracaibo	WCq	Milito.G [15], Messi [18]	10 600	Simon BRA
17-11	Bolivia	W 3-0	Buenos Aires	WCq	Aguero [41], Riquelme 2 [57 74]	43 308	Rivera PER
20-11	Colombia	L 1-2	Bogota	WCq	Messi [36]	41 700	Larrionda URU
2008							
26-03	Egypt	W 2-0	Cairo	Fr	Aguero [65], Burdisso [84]		Haimoudi ALG
4-06	Mexico	W 4-1	San Diego	Fr	Burdisso [10], Messi [17], Rodriguez.M [29], Aguero [70]	68 498	Navarro CAN
8-06	USA	D 0-0	New York	Fr		78 682	Aguilar SLV
15-06	Ecuador	D 1-1	Buenos Aires	WCq	Palacio [89]	41 167	Ortube BOL
18-06	Brazil	D 0-0	Belo Horizonte	WCq		65 000	Ruiz COL

Fr = Friendly match • KC = Kirin Cup • CA = Copa América • CC = FIFA Confederations Cup • WC = FIFA World Cup
q = qualifier • r1 = 1st round • qf = quarter-final • sf = semi-final • f = final

ARGENTINA NATIONAL TEAM PLAYERS

	Player		Ap	G	Club	Date of Birth		Player		Ap	G	Club	Date of Birth
1	Roberto Abbondanzieri	GK	48	0	Getafe	19 08 1972	14	Javier Mascherano	MF	41	2	Liverpool	8 06 1984
2	Fabricio Coloccini	DF	29	1	Deportivo	22 01 1982	15	Rodrigo Palacio	FW	8	1	Boca Juniors	5 02 1982
3	Jonathan Bottinelli	DF	1	0	San Lorenzo	14 09 1984	16	Sebastián Battaglia	MF	7	0	Boca Juniors	11 08 1980
4	Nicolás Burdisso	DF	23	3	Internazionale	12 04 1981	17	Jonás Gutiérrez	MF	4	0	Mallorca	7 05 1983
5	Fernando Gago	MF	18	0	Real Madrid	10 04 1986	18	Lionel Messi	FW	31	10	Barcelona	24 06 1981
6	Gabriel Heinze	DF	46	2	Real Madrid	19 03 1978		Oscar Ustari	GK	1	0	Getafe	3 07 1986
7	Maxi Rodríguez	MF	27	7	Atlético Madrid	2 01 1981		Martin Demichelis	DF	12	1	Bayern München	20 12 1980
8	Javier Zanetti	DF	122	5	Internazionale	10 08 1973		Pablo Zabaleta	DF	6	0	Espanyol	16 01 1985
9	Julio Cruz	FW	22	3	Internazionale	10 10 1974		Ever Banega	MF	2	0	Valencia	29 06 1988
10	Juan Román Riquelme	MF	46	17	Boca Juniors	24 06 1978		Esteban Cambiasso	MF	40	3	Internazionale	18 08 1980
11	Sergio Agüero	FW	11	4	Atlético Madrid	2 06 1988		José Ernesto Sosa	MF	4	0	Bayern München	19 06 1985
12	Juan Pablo Carrizo	GK	1	0	River Plate	6 05 1984		Juan Sebastián Verón	MF	61	9	Estudiantes	9 03 1975
13	Gonzalo Javier Rodríguez	DF	6	1	Villarreal	22 01 1982		Fernando Cavenaghi	FW	4	0	Bordeaux	21 09 1983
	Argentina's squad for the FIFA World Cup qualifiers in June 2008							Lisandro Lopez	FW	5	0	FC Porto	2 03 1983

ARGENTINA NATIONAL TEAM RECORDS AND RECORD SEQUENCES

Records				Sequence records					
Victory	12-0	ECU 1942		Wins	9	1941-1942	Clean sheets	8	1998
Defeat	1-6	CZE 1958		Defeats	4	1911-1912	Goals scored	42	1942-1954
Player Caps	122	ZANETTI Javier		Undefeated	31	1991-1993	Without goal	8	1989-1990
Player Goals	56	BATISTUTA Gabriel		Without win	10	1989-1990	Goals against	13	1906-1910

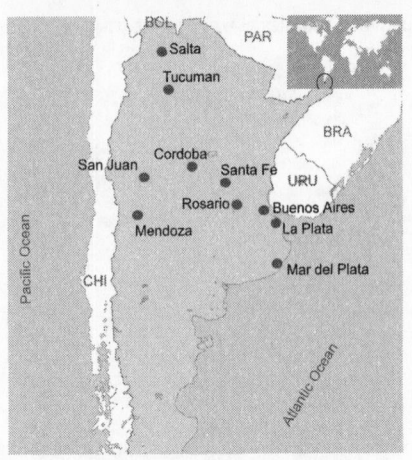

ARGENTINE REPUBLIC; REPUBLICA ARGENTINA

Capital	Buenos Aires	Language	Spanish		Independence	1816
Population	40 301 927	Area	2 766 890 km²	Density 14 per km²	% in cities	88%
GDP per cap	$11 200	Dailling code	+54	Internet .ar	GMT + / -	-3

MAJOR CITIES/TOWNS
Population '000

1	Buenos Aires	11 612
2	Córdoba	1 457
3	Rosario	1 178
4	Mendoza	890
5	Tucumán	803
6	La Plata	699
7	Mar del Plata	558
8	Salta	535
9	Santa Fé	476
10	San Juan	460
11	Resistencia	401
12	Santiago del Estero	368
13	Corrientes	351
14	Posadas	328
15	Jujuy	320
16	Bahía Blanca	278
17	Paraná	269
18	Neuquén	250
19	Tandil	105
20	Rafaela	91
21	Zárate	89
22	Junín	86
23	San Martín	84
24	Tres Arroyos	47

MEDALS TABLE

		Overall G	S	B	League G	S	B	Sth Am G	S	B	City	Stadium	Cap'ty	DoF
1	River Plate	37	34	30	34	30	15	3	4	15	Buenos Aires	Monumental	65 645	1901
2	Boca Juniors	37	25	21	28	21	17	9	4	4	Buenos Aires	La Bombonera	57 395	1905
3	Independiente	25	17	14	16	16	9	9	1	5	Buenos Aires	Doble Visera	52 823	1905
4	Racing Club	18	8	14	16	7	12	2	1	2	Buenos Aires	El Cilindro	64 161	1903
5	San Lorenzo	15	13	21	13	13	15	2		6	Buenos Aires	Nuevo Gasometro	43 480	1908
6	Alumni	10	2		10	2					Buenos Aires			1891-1911
7	Vélez Sarsfield	8	8	10	6	8	8	2		2	Buenos Aires	José Amalfitani	49 540	1910
8	Estudiantes La Plata	8	7	11	5	6	9	3	1	2	La Plata	Luis Jorge Hirsch	20 000	1905
9	Huracán	5	5	8	5	5	7			1	Buenos Aires	Tomás Adolfo Ducó	48 314	1908
10	Rosario Central	5	5	5	4	4	2	1	1	3	Rosario	Gigante de Arroyito	41 654	1889
11	Newell's Old Boys	5	4	3	5	2	3		2		Rosario	El Coloso del Parque	42 000	1903
12	Lomas Athletic Club	5	2	3	5	2	3				Buenos Aires			1891
13	Belgrano Athletic Club	3	3	3	3	3	3				Buenos Aires			1896
14	Argentinos Juniors	3	2	3	2	2	1	1		2	Buenos Aires	Diego Maradona	24 800	1904
15	Lanús	2	4	4	1	3	4	1	1		Buenos Aires	La Fortaleza	46 519	1915
16	Ferro Carril Oeste	2	3	1	2	3	1				Buenos Aires	Ricardo Etcheverry	34 268	1904

RECENT LEAGUE RECORD

	Torneo Clausura					Torneo Apertura				
Year	Champions	Pts	Runners-up	Pts	Third	Pts	Champions	Pts	Runners-up	Pts	Third	Pts
1996	Vélez Sarsfield	40	Gimnasia LP	39	Lanús	34	River Plate	46	Independiente	37	Lanús	37
1997	River Plate	41	Colón Santa Fé	35	Newell's Old Boys	35	River Plate	45	Boca Juniors	44	Rosario Central	35
1998	Vélez Sarsfield	46	Lanús	40	Gimnasia LP	37	Boca Juniors	45	Gimnasia LP	36	Racing Club	33
1999	Boca Juniors	44	River Plate	37	San Lorenzo	36	River Plate	44	Rosario Central	43	Boca Juniors	41
2000	River Plate	42	Independiente	36	Colón Santa Fé	36	Boca Juniors	41	River Plate	37	Gimnasia LP	37
2001	San Lorenzo	47	River Plate	41	Boca Juniors	30	Racing Club	42	River Plate	41	Boca Juniors	33
2002	River Plate	43	Gimnasia LP	37	Boca Juniors	35	Independiente	43	Boca Juniors	40	River Plate	36
2003	River Plate	43	Boca Juniors	39	Vélez Sarsfield	38	Boca Juniors	39	San Lorenzo	36	Banfield	32
2004	River Plate	40	Boca Juniors	36	Talleres Cordoba	35	Newell's Old Boys	36	Vélez Sarsfield	34	River Plate	33
2005	Vélez Sarsfield	39	Banfield	33	Racing Club	32	Boca Juniors	40	Gimnasia LP	37	Vélez Sarsfield	33
2006	Boca Juniors	43	Lanús	35	River Plate	34	Estudiantes LP	44	Boca Juniors	44	River Plate	38
2007	San Lorenzo	45	Boca Juniors	39	Estudiantes LP	37	Lanús	38	Tigre	34	Banfield	32
2008	River Plate	43	Boca Juniors	39	Estudiantes LP	39						

ARGENTINA 2007–08 PRIMERA A APERTURA

	Pl	W	D	L	F	A	Pts
Lanús	19	11	5	3	34	21	38
Tigre	19	10	4	5	28	20	34
Banfield	19	10	2	7	22	21	32
Boca Juniors	19	9	4	6	32	18	31
Argentinos Juniors	19	9	4	6	29	20	31
Estudiantes LP	19	8	6	5	27	19	30
Huracán	19	8	6	5	24	22	30
San Lorenzo	19	8	5	6	29	27	29
Independiente	19	8	4	7	33	23	28
Vélez Sarsfield	19	8	3	8	25	25	27
Newell's Old Boys	19	8	3	8	16	22	27
Arsenal	19	7	5	7	19	24	26
Racing Club	19	7	4	8	23	24	25
River Plate	19	6	5	8	31	33	23
Colón Santa Fe	19	6	4	9	19	22	22
Olimpo Bahía Blanca	19	6	4	9	18	24	22
Gimnasia y Esgrima Jy	19	5	5	9	22	31	20
Gimnasia y Esgrima LP	19	5	4	10	15	27	19
San Martín San Juan	19	5	3	11	18	29	18
Rosario Central	19	2	8	9	21	33	14

3/08/2007 - 9/12/2007
Top scorers: German Denis, Independiente 18; José Sand, Lanús 15; Martín Palermo, Boca 13; Leandro Lazzaro, Tigre 10; Andrés Silvera, San Lorenzo 9; José Luis Vizcarra, Rosario Central 9

ARGENTINA 2007–08 PRIMERA A CLAUSURA

	Pl	W	D	L	F	A	Pts
River Plate	19	13	4	2	29	13	43
Boca Juniors	19	11	6	2	33	15	39
Estudiantes LP	19	11	6	2	29	16	39
San Lorenzo	19	11	2	6	30	21	35
Vélez Sarsfield	19	9	5	5	24	17	32
Independiente	19	8	7	4	25	15	31
Argentinos Juniors	19	9	3	7	23	24	30
Newell's Old Boys	19	8	5	6	21	19	29
Rosario Central	19	7	6	6	26	23	27
Arsenal	19	7	4	8	22	25	25
Colón Santa Fe	19	6	5	8	25	27	23
Banfield	19	6	4	9	36	36	22
Huracán	19	5	7	7	15	17	22
Tigre	19	6	4	9	24	37	22
Olimpo Bahía Blanca	19	6	2	11	21	32	20
Lanús	19	5	3	11	26	39	18
Gimnasia y Esgrima LP	19	4	5	10	19	26	17
San Martín San Juan	19	5	2	12	20	30	17
Gimnasia y Esgrima Jy	19	2	9	8	20	28	15
Racing Club	19	2	9	8	14	22	15

8/02/2008 - 22/06/2008 • Top scorers: Darío Cvitanich, Banfield 13; Martín Palermo, Boca 10; Martín Bravo, San Martín 9; Diego Buonanotte, River 9, Germán Denis, Independiente 9; Santiago Salcedo, Newell's 9; Ruben Ramirez, Colón 8

ARGENTINA 2007–08

PRIMERA A
TORNEO CABLEVISION
APERTURA & CLAUSURA
GILLETTE PRESTOBARA EXCEL

	Pl	W	D	L	F	A	Pts	RA	Boca Juniors	Estudiantes	River Plate	San Lorenzo	Argentinos Jun	Independiente	Vélez Sarsfield	Lanús	Newell's OB	Tigre	Banfield	Hiracán	Arsenal	Colón Santa Fe	Olimpo BB	Rosario Central	Racing Club	Gimnasia LP	Gimnasia Jy	San Martín
Boca Juniors † ‡	38	20	10	8	65	33	70	2.070		1-1	1-0	2-0	4-0	1-1	4-0	1-1	2-1	6-2	1-1	1-0	3-2	1-2	2-0	0-0	2-1	2-1	2-2	1-0
Estudiantes LP ‡	38	19	12	7	56	35	69	1.772	1-0		0-0	1-1	3-0	1-1	1-0	1-0	5-2	2-2	2-1	1-1	1-1	0-0	2-2	3-3	2-1	1-0	1-0	3-2
River Plate † ‡	38	19	9	10	60	46	66	1.746	2-0	4-2		2-0	4-2	1-1	5-0	3-1	3-1	1-0	0-2	1-0	1-0	0-2	2-1	3-3	0-0	4-2	2-0	3-2
San Lorenzo ‡	38	19	7	12	59	48	64	1.693	1-0	3-1	1-1		2-1	0-1	1-0	0-2	2-1	3-2	1-1	2-4	2-1	1-0	3-1	4-3	1-1	4-1	0-1	
Argentinos Juniors‡	38	18	7	13	52	44	61	1.377	3-2	2-1	4-1	2-1		0-1	2-0	3-0	4-0	1-0	2-0	1-1	4-0	2-1	1-0	2-1	1-0	2-0	1-1	0-1
Independiente ‡	38	16	11	11	58	38	59	1.500	2-3	1-2	0-0	1-2	2-0		1-1	5-3	3-0	4-1	3-3	0-1	1-1	3-3	0-1	0-0	3-1	3-0	2-2	
Vélez Sarsfield	38	17	8	13	49	42	59	1.518	1-1	1-0	0-2	2-0	0-0		3-2	1-0	1-1	3-0	1-2	0-0	4-3	3-0	2-1	1-1	3-1	4-2	2-0	
Lanús †	38	16	8	14	60	60	56	1.518	1-3	1-0	0-1	4-3	0-0	1-0	2-1		1-1	2-1	0-5	1-1	2-6	5-1	2-1	0-0	3-3	4-0	2-2	0-0
Newell's Old Boys	38	16	8	14	37	41	56	1.246	1-0	2-1	0-0	1-0	2-0	2-1	2-0	0-0		1-1	1-0	0-1	4-1	1-1	1-0	1-0	0-1	1-0	1-0	2-2
Tigre	38	16	8	14	52	57	56	1.474	1-1	1-1	4-1	1-5	1-0	0-3	0-2	1-4	2-2		1-0	1-2	2-0	0-2	2-0	2-1	3-2	2-1	2-0	3-0
Banfield	38	16	6	16	58	57	54	1.333	0-6	0-3	2-3	1-0	3-2	2-0	1-0	1-2	0-1	3-3		4-3	1-3	3-1	2-1	3-2	3-1	0-0	1-1	5-1
Huracán	38	13	13	12	39	39	52	1.368	0-0	1-1	2-1	1-0	3-2	0-0	1-0	3-1	0-0	1-0		1-1	2-2	3-0	1-1	3-0	0-1	2-1	2-1	
Arsenal ‡	38	14	9	15	41	49	51	1.377	2-1	0-0	2-1	0-1	0-1	3-2	0-0	0-1	1-0	0-4	2-0		2-0	1-0	1-0	0-1	1-0	3-3	2-1	
Colón Santa Fe	38	12	9	17	44	49	45	1.202	1-0	0-2	1-2	0-0	0-1	1-3	0-1	2-1	1-1	1-2	3-2	1-0	3-0		3-0	2-0	1-0	0-0	0-1	1-1
Olimpo B. Blanca	38	12	6	20	39	56	42	1.105	1-1	1-2	4-0	3-2	1-1	3-0	2-3	2-1	0-0	1-1	1-1	3-1	1-0	2-1		1-3	0-2	0-0	2-1	
Rosario Central	38	9	14	15	47	56	41	1.211	1-1	2-2	2-1	1-3	1-1	2-0	2-2	1-4	0-1	4-2	2-1	0-1	3-0	0-0	1-1		3-2	2-2	1-1	3-2
Racing Club	38	9	13	16	37	46	40	1.167	0-3	1-2	1-1	0-1	1-1	0-0	1-0	1-1	2-0	0-0	0-1	1-0	1-0	1-1	2-2			1-1	0-0	1-2
Gimnasia y Esg LP	38	9	9	20	34	53	36	1.272	0-1	1-2	0-2	1-2	0-2	1-0	2-1	1-2	2-0	0-1	1-0	0-1	1-0	1-2	0-4	4-2	2-0		2-1	2-0
Gimnasia y Esgr Jy	38	7	14	17	42	59	35	1.132	1-2	1-0	2-1	2-2	1-1	1-2	0-0	1-0	2-1	0-2	1-0	2-1	0-3	1-1	2-1	4-0		3-1		
San Martín San Juan	38	10	5	23	38	59	35	0.921	0-2	1-0	1-0	1-2	2-0	2-0	3-2	1-2	0-1	1-2	0-1	2-0	1-1	1-2	0-1	0-0	2-1	1-3	2-2	

† Qualified for the Copa Libertadores • ‡ Qualified for the Copa Sudamericana • Apertura results are in the shaded boxes
RA = Relegation average based on the average number of points per game over the past three seasons. Olimpo and San Martín had the lowest and so were relegated automatically. Racing Club and Gimnasia Jujuy had the next lowest and so entered a play-off with Primera B Nacional teams
Relegation play-offs: Belgrano Córdoba 1-1 0-1 Racing Club ; Unión Santa Fe 1-1 0-1 Gimnasia Jujuy • Neither Belgrano nor Unión promoted

ARGENTINA 2007-08

PRIMERA B NACIONAL (2)

	Pl	W	D	L	F	A	Pts
San Martín Tucumán	38	18	12	8	47	28	66
Godoy Cruz	38	19	8	11	54	41	65
Unión Santa Fé	38	15	11	12	52	43	56
Belgrano Córdoba	38	15	11	12	45	41	56
Chacarita Juniors	38	15	11	12	46	45	56
Quilmes	38	14	13	11	43	36	55
Tiro Federal	38	14	12	12	44	36	54
Atlético Rafaela	38	14	11	13	49	44	53
CAI	38	14	9	15	48	52	51
Ferro Carril Oeste	38	13	12	13	40	44	51
Aldosivi	38	13	9	16	52	47	48
Independiente R'davia	38	13	8	17	50	51	47
Talleres Córdoba	38	13	7	18	48	64	46
Almagro §3	38	12	10	16	40	48	43
Instituto Córdoba	38	9	16	13	32	46	43
Defensa y Justicia	38	11	10	17	31	47	43
Platense	38	9	15	14	45	55	42
Almirante Brown §18	38	15	14	9	42	26	41
Sportivo Ben Hur	38	9	11	18	28	46	38
Nueva Chicago §18	38	12	16	10	47	44	34

Results grid (columns: San Martín, Godoy Cruz, Unión SF, Belgrano, Chacarita J, Quilmes, Tiro Federal, At Rafaela, CAI, FC Oeste, Aldosivi, Independ., Talleres, Almagro, Instituto, Defensa y J, Platense, Almirante B, Ben Hur, N Chicago):

	SM	GC	USF	BEL	CHA	QUI	TF	RAF	CAI	FCO	ALD	IND	TAL	ALM	INS	DJ	PLA	AB	BH	NC
San Martín	—	2-1	1-0	2-0	1-1	1-0	0-0	1-1	4-0	1-1	1-0	1-0	3-0	2-0	2-0	1-0	2-2	1-1	2-0	1-1
Godoy Cruz	2-0	—	0-1	1-0	3-2	1-0	0-2	3-2	2-2	2-3	2-2	1-1	3-0	2-0	1-1	3-2	0-1	3-2	0-1	0-2
Unión SF	2-0	0-1	—	1-0	1-1	2-0	1-2	0-1	4-3	2-2	3-1	3-1	2-1	0-0	3-0	1-1	1-1	1-1	1-0	1-0
Belgrano	2-3	3-0	1-1	—	1-0	0-2	1-0	2-0	3-0	0-1	1-1	0-1	0-1	2-0	2-2	3-0	1-1	2-0	0-2	1-1
Chacarita J	2-2	3-2	1-0	1-2	—	0-1	1-2	1-0	2-3	1-1	0-0	1-0	2-1	0-1	1-1	1-0	1-1	3-1		6-2
Quilmes	0-0	0-0	4-3	2-1	2-0	—	0-0	1-0	2-0	0-0	4-3	2-1	0-5	0-2	0-0	1-1	2-0	1-1	1-2	1-3
Tiro Federal	1-0	0-2	1-2	1-1	2-0	1-1	—	1-2	4-0	1-4	0-0	2-1	2-1	4-1	2-0	2-1	1-2	2-2	3-2	1-0
At Rafaela	1-0	1-0	2-1	1-1	2-0	1-1	1-1	—	1-2	4-0	1-0	4-0	2-1	2-1	4-1	2-0	2-1	1-2	2-2	3-2
CAI	0-0	1-0	2-2	1-1	3-0	1-1	1-0	1-2	—	4-2	0-1	2-0	1-1	0-0	0-1	3-1	0-0	3-0	3-0	3-0
FC Oeste	0-1	1-0	1-0	0-0	1-1	1-0	0-0	4-2	1-0	—	4-2	1-1	4-1	0-0	1-0	0-1	2-0	0-0	2-1	1-0
Aldosivi	1-1	2-3	0-0	2-0	0-1	0-1	0-2	0-2	3-3	0-0	—	4-0	4-2	1-0	0-0	3-2	4-2	1-0	0-2	2-2
Independ.	1-0	0-1	3-4	7-0	1-2	1-2	1-0	0-0	3-4	0-0	3-2	—	2-1	0-0	1-0	4-0	0-1	2-1	3-1	1-0
Talleres	1-1	3-2	2-2	0-0	1-2	2-1	1-0	1-2	1-1	1-1	2-1	1-3	—	4-3	2-0	2-0	2-4	2-1	3-1	1-0
Almagro	1-4	3-2	1-0	0-1	0-1	2-1	3-3	2-0	2-0	1-1	1-0	3-2	1-1	—	0-1	0-0	2-0	0-0	3-2	2-2
Instituto	0-1	0-2	1-1	3-1	1-2	0-0	0-0	0-0	3-1	1-0	2-1	3-1	1-0	0-0	—	0-0	0-0	0-0	2-2	1-1
Defensa y J	3-1	1-1	2-3	1-2	1-2	1-1	2-1	2-2	0-2	1-0	1-0	1-0	3-2	2-1		—	0-2	0-1	0-1	1-1
Platense	0-3	1-1	1-2	1-1	4-0	1-1	0-3	2-0	2-1	2-1	1-0	1-1	1-2	3-1	0-1	1-2	—	0-1	0-1	3-3
Almirante B	2-0	0-0	0-0	1-1	0-0	0-1	1-1	3-0	1-0	2-1	1-0	4-0	2-0	3-0	3-2	0-0	3-0	—	3-0	0-0
Ben Hur	0-1	1-2	1-0	1-2	0-0	2-1	1-0	2-0	0-1	2-2	0-0	0-1	1-0	0-2	0-1	0-1	1-0		—	0-2
N Chicago	1-0	1-1	1-0	1-3	1-1	0-0	1-0	1-1	2-1	3-2	1-1	2-1	2-1	1-0	2-0	2-2	1-1	2-0	1-0	—

9/08/2007 - 14/06/2008 • § = points deducted
Top scorers: Leandro Zárate, Unión 21; Cristian Milla, Chacarita Juniors 18; Leandro Armani, Tiro Federal 16; Luis Salmerón, Ferro Carril Oeste 16
Relegation play-off: Racing Córdoba 1-2 1-1 **Talleres Cordoba**; **Los Andes** 1-0 2-0 Nueva Chicago. Los Andes promoted; Nueva Chicago relegated

ARGENTINA 2007-08 PRIMERA DIVISION B METROPOLITANA (3)

	Pl	W	D	L	F	A	Pts
All Boys	40	25	10	5	69	29	85
Deportivo Morón ‡	40	19	13	8	56	39	70
Sportivo Italiano ‡	40	18	15	7	46	32	69
Atlanta ‡	40	19	10	11	56	36	67
Los Andes ‡	40	18	10	12	52	53	64
Comunicaciones ‡	40	16	15	9	53	35	63
Deportivo Armenio ‡	40	15	16	9	53	35	61
Brown Adrogué ‡	40	16	12	12	58	48	60
Sarmiento Junín ‡	40	15	12	13	59	53	57
Estudiantes BA	40	14	12	14	59	52	54
Tristán Suárez	40	14	12	14	53	53	54
Temperley	40	13	13	14	38	35	52
Central Córdoba	40	13	11	16	39	45	50
Flandria	40	11	16	13	41	45	49
Social Español	40	12	10	18	41	59	46
Acassuso	40	11	11	18	48	50	44
Defensores de Belgrano	40	9	16	15	45	61	43
Talleres RE	40	9	16	15	30	46	43
Deportivo Merlo	40	7	15	18	38	55	36
San Telmo ‡	40	9	8	23	43	72	35
Defensores Cambaceres	40	5	11	24	36	80	26

4/08/2007 - 24/05/2008 • ‡ Qualified for the play-offs
Top scorer: Juan Martín, Estudiantes BA 29
Relegation play-off: Barracas Central 2-3 1-0 **San Telmo**

PLAY-OFFS
Quarter-finals: **Los Andes** 3-1 Comunicaciones; Atlanta 0-2 **Dep Armenia**; Dep Morón 2-3 **Sarmiento**; Sp Italiano 1-1 Brown
Semi-finals: Deportivo Armenio 0-0 0-1 **Los Andes**; Sarmiento Junín 0-2 0-1 **Sportivo Italiano**
Final: **Los Andes** 1-1 1-0 Sportivo Italiano

Beneath the top two divisions the AFA operates two different league structures - one for the metropolitan area centered on Buenos Aires and the other for the rest of the country (the interior). There is promotion to the Primera B Nacional from both the metropolitan and interior tournaments

ARGENTINA 2007-08 TORNEO ARGENTINA A FASE FINAL INTERIOR (3)

Group A	Pl	W	D	L	F	A	Pts
Racing Córdoba	6	4	2	0	7	0	14
Sportivo Desamparados	6	3	0	3	4	6	9
Libertad Sunchales	6	1	2	3	6	8	5
Deportivo Santamarina	6	1	2	3	5	8	5

Group B	Pl	W	D	L	F	A	Pts
Atlético Tucumán	6	5	0	1	11	5	15
Cipolletti	6	4	0	2	12	9	12
Talleres Perico	6	2	0	4	6	9	6
Unión de Sunchales	6	1	0	5	11	17	3

4/05/2008 - 8/06/2008 • ‡ Qualified for the final
Top scorer (overall): Claudio Sarría, At. Tucumán 21
Relegation play-off: **Alvarado** 3-1 1-2 La Plata FC
Central Córdoba SdE 4-0 1-1 Luján de Cuyo

PLAY-OFFS
Final: Racing Cordoba 2-1 1-2 2-4p **Atlético Tucumán**
At. Tucumán promoted; Racing qualify to play-off with Talleres

ARGENTINA 2007–08
PRIMERA DIVISION C
METROPOLITANA (4)

	Pl	W	D	L	F	A	Pts
Colegiales	38	22	9	7	59	32	75
Fénix ‡	38	20	10	8	52	33	70
Deportivo Laferrere ‡	38	20	8	10	56	37	68
Luján ‡	38	18	11	9	51	35	65
Barracas Central ‡	38	18	8	12	47	37	62
El Porvenir ‡	38	15	15	8	42	40	60
Argentino Merlo ‡	38	15	13	10	51	40	58
Leandro N. Alem ‡	38	17	7	14	45	34	58
Villa San Carlos ‡	38	15	11	12	38	34	56
San Miguel	38	15	10	13	37	33	55
Sacachispas	38	13	12	13	49	53	51
Sportivo Barracas Bolívar	38	13	10	15	57	52	49
Excursionistas	38	11	11	16	38	49	44
Justo Jose de Urquiza	38	11	10	17	32	48	43
Cañuelas	38	10	12	16	39	45	42
Villa Dálmine	38	7	20	11	30	36	41
General Lamadrid	38	10	10	18	46	64	40
San Martín Burzaco ‡	38	7	13	18	34	53	34
Sportivo Dock Sud	38	8	7	23	35	51	31
Argentino Rosario	38	4	14	20	30	63	26

4/08/2007 - 24/05/2008 • ‡ Qualified for the play-offs
Top scorer: Sebastián Tagliabue, Colegiales 18
Relegation play-off: Berazategui 3-2 0-0 San Martín Burzaco

PLAY-OFFS
Quarter-finals: Barracas Central 1-1 El Porvenir; Fénix 0-0 Villa San Carlos; Luján 6-2 Argentino; Dep Laferrere 4-2 Leandro
Semi-finals: Barracas Central 1-0 2-2 Fénix; Luján 0-1 0-1 Deportivo Laferrera
Final: Barracas Central 1-0 2-1 Deportivo Laferrere

ARGENTINA 2007–08
PRIMERA DIVISION D
METROPOLITANA (5)

	Pl	W	D	L	F	A	Pts
Defensores Unidos	34	22	7	5	73	27	73
Berazategui ‡	34	20	7	7	65	31	67
Argentino Quilmes ‡	34	20	3	11	59	36	63
F.C. Midland ‡	34	19	6	9	55	35	63
Liniers ‡	34	17	9	8	57	39	60
Victoriano Arenas ‡	34	16	7	11	43	40	55
Ituzaingó ‡	34	15	9	10	58	35	54
Atlético Lugano ‡	34	15	8	11	49	44	53
Deportivo Riestra ‡	34	13	13	8	46	34	52
Central Ballester	34	13	11	10	39	35	50
Atlas	34	12	12	10	44	39	48
Juventud Unida	34	11	6	17	49	55	39
Deportivo Paraguayo	34	10	9	15	43	55	39
Claypole	34	8	14	12	38	49	38
F.C. Urquiza	34	8	10	16	49	64	34
Yupanqui	34	4	10	20	33	65	22
Puerto Nuevo	34	4	6	24	36	88	18
Deportivo Muñiz	34	2	7	25	20	87	13

11/08/2007 - 25/05/2008 • ‡ Qualified for the play-offs
Top scorer: Javier Velázquez, Defensores 31

PLAY-OFFS
Quarter-finals: Midland 3-1 Ituzaingó; Argentino 1-1 Lugano; Liniers 3-0 Victoriano; Berazategui 1-0 Riestra
Semi-finals: Midland 1-1 2-0 Argentino; Liniers 0-1 1-3 Berazategui
Final: Midland 2-0 0-2 Berazategui

ARGENTINA 2007–08
TORNEO ARGENTINA B
FASE FINAL INTERIOR (4)

Group A	Pl	W	D	L	F	A	Pts
Central Córdoba SdE ‡	6	4	2	0	9	4	14
Crucero del Norte	6	4	1	1	9	6	13
Central Norte	6	1	1	4	6	9	4
Guaraní Antonio Franco	6	0	2	4	3	8	2

Group B	Pl	W	D	L	F	A	Pts
Patronato Paraná ‡	6	4	1	1	13	3	13
Douglas Haig	6	2	2	2	9	9	8
Sportivo Atenas	6	2	2	2	6	8	8
La Emilia	6	1	1	4	5	12	4

Group C	Pl	W	D	L	F	A	Pts
Deportivo Maipú ‡	6	2	3	1	6	5	9
El Linqueño	6	2	2	2	6	4	8
Deportivo General Roca	6	1	1	4	4	9	4
Sportivo Belgrano SF	6	3	2	1	8	6	2

Group D	Pl	W	D	L	F	A	Pts
Alvarado ‡	6	4	1	1	13	3	13
Deportivo Madryn	6	2	2	2	9	6	8
Racing Olavarría	6	2	1	3	6	10	7
Bella Vista	6	1	2	3	7	16	5

3/05/2008 - 1/06/2008 • ‡ Qualified for the play-offs
Top scorer (overall): Luciano Millares, El Linqueño 22
Relegation play-offs: At. Union MdP 3-1 1-2 Gimnasia Santa Fe; Sportivo Las Parejas 2-1 0-1 Sol de América; Salto Grande 0-0 0-4 At. Trinidad

PLAY-OFFS
Final: Central Córdoba SdE 0-0 0-1 Patronato; Deportivo Maipú 1-1 0-0 5-4p Alvarado
Patronato and Maipú promoted, Central and Alvarado qualify to play-off with Luján de Cuyo and La Plata FC

ARGENTINA 2007–08
TORNEO ARGENTINA B
FASE FINAL INTERIOR (4)

Semi–finals (round six)		Finals (round seven)	
Juan Bartolomé Del Bono	1 3		
Ascensión	1 0	Juan Bartolomé Del Bono	1 2
Sports Club Pergamino	0 0	Sportivo Las Parejas	1 1
Sportivo Las Parejas	3 0		
Huracán C. Rivadavia	4 1		
Independiente Tandil	1 2	Huracán C. Rivadavia	3 3
Atlético Once Tigres	1 1	At. Unión Mar del Plata	4 0
At. Unión Mar del Plata	4 2		
Atlético Concepción	1 2		
Villa San Antoniio	1 0	Atlético Concepción	2 1
Sportivo Ferroviarrio	1 0	Salto Grande	1 0
Salto Grande	1 2		

ARGENTINOS JUNIORS 2007–08

Month	Day	Opponent	Res	Score	Scorers	Att
Aug	4	San Martín	L	0-1		7 000
	12	Boca	W	3-2	Delorte [14], Battión 2 [48 72]	12 000
	17	Gimn'sia LP	W	2-0	Delorte [23], Battión [88]	7 000
	25	Indep'iente	L	0-1		20 000
	29	Huracán	L	2-3	Hauche [1], Cabrera [70]	17 000
Sept	1	Colón	W	2-1	Ortigoza [12p], Chitzoff OG [35]	7 000
	7	Olimpo	D	1-1	Ortigoza [59p]	9 000
	11	Banfield	W	2-0	Pereira [79], Cabrera [84]	8 000
	15	Gimn'sia Jy	D	1-1	Pereira [55]	7 000
	22	Newell's	W	4-0	Hauche [27], Pereira 3 [43 50 64]	10 000
	30	San Lorenzo	L	1-2	Ortigoza [12p]	22 000
Oct	3	River Plate	W	4-1	Hauche [3], Delorte [9], Niell [42], Battión [45]	10 500
	7	Estudiantes	L	0-3		19 000
	20	Racing	W	1-0	Peñalba [60]	11 000
Nov	3	Vélez	L	0-3		15 000
	11	Arsenal	W	4-0	Pereira [43], Delorte [45], Hauche [59]	10 000
	25	Lanús	D	0-0	Peñalba [75]	35 000
Dec	2	Tigre	W	1-0	Barzola [56]	19 000
	7	Rosario C	D	1-1	Pereira [32]	24 000
Feb	9	San Martín	L	0-2		7 000
	17	Boca	L	0-4		40 000
	23	Gimn'sia LP	W	2-0	Mirosevic [60], Pereira [85]	8 500
	1	Indep'iente	L	0-2		18 000
Mar	8	Huracán	D	1-1	Hauche [5]	12 000
	15	Colón	W	1-0	Hauche [15]	16 000
	22	Olimpo	W	1-0	Mercier [11]	15 000
	29	Banfield	L	2-3	Hauche [12], Scotti [92+]	10 000
Apr	6	Gimn'sia Jy	D	1-1	Hauche [63]	9 000
	11	Newell's	L	0-2		27 000
	20	San Lorenzo	W	2-1	Barzola [70], Pérez [90]	15 000
	27	River Plate	L	2-4	Delorte [41], Barzola [57]	18 000
May	3	Estudiantes	W	2-1	Hauche [25], Delorte [50]	12 000
	10	Racing	D	1-1	Ortigoza [2]	20 000
	17	Vélez	W	2-0	Escudero [58], Pereira [86]	18 000
	23	Arsenal	W	1-0	Peñalba [11]	12 000
	30	Lanús	W	3-0	Pereira 2 [20 76], Hauche [23]	8 000
Jun	7	Tigre	L	0-1		16 000
	20	Rosario C	W	2-1	Delorte 2 [44 82]	7 000

ARSENAL 2007–08

Month	Day	Opponent	Res	Score	Scorers	Att
Aug	5	Huracán	D	1-1	Carrera [1]	24 000
	10	Colón	W	2-0	Calderón [21], Ulloa [82]	2 000
	18	Olimpo	L	0-1		12 000
	25	Banfield	L	0-4		6 000
	29	Gimn'sia Jy	L	0-1		10 000
Sept	1	Newell's	W	1-0	Ulloa [24]	3 000
	9	San Lorenzo	W	4-2	Calderón 2 [40p 85], Andrizzi [73], Villar [83]	17 000
	12	River Plate	W	2-1	Matellán [54], Gandolfi [90]	9 000
	15	Estudiantes	D	1-1	Ulloa [92+]	10 000
	23	Racing	L	0-1		7 000
	29	Vélez	D	0-0		13 000
Oct	3	San Martín	D	1-1	San Martín [13]	15 000
	7	Lanús	L	0-1		6 000
	19	Tigre	L	0-2		17 000
Nov	2	Rosario C	W	1-0	Calderón [85]	1 000
	11	Arg Juniors	L	0-4		10 000
	23	Boca	W	2-1	San Martín [21], Gómez [44]	14 000
Dec	9	Indep'iente	W	3-2	Calderón 2 [47 56], Andrizzi [50]	10 000
	‡‡	Gimn'sia LP	D	1-1		
Feb	10	Huracán	W	2-0	Leguizamón [7], Calderón [15]	7 000
	15	Colón	L	0-3		19 000
	24	Olimpo	W	1-0	Biagini [56]	2 000
Mar	2	Banfield	W	3-1	Matellán [22], Biagini [36], Carrera [61]	12 000
	9	Gimn'sia Jy	D	3-3	Leguizamón [1], Gómez [58], Cuenca [93+p]	2 500
	16	Newell's	L	1-4	Calderón [80]	29 000
	21	San Lorenzo	L	0-1		6 000
	30	River Plate	L	0-1		25 000
Apr	5	Estudiantes	D	0-0		10 000
	13	Racing	L	0-1		25 000
	20	Vélez	L	0-2		8 000
	27	San Martín	W	2-1	Leguizamón 2 [60p 85]	1 000
May	2	Lanús	W	6-2	Leguizamón 2 [5 44], Garnier 2 [10 25]	3 500
	9	Tigre	W	1-0	Garnier [51], Biagini [63], Cuenca [71p]	4 000
	17	Rosario C	L	0-3		38 000
	23	Arg Juniors	L	0-1		12 000
Jun	1	Boca	L	1-3	Leguizamón [46]	27 000
	6	Gimn'sia LP	W	1-0	Leguizamón [46]	2 500
	21	Indep'iente	D	1-1	Calderón [33]	15 000

BANFIELD 2007–08

Month	Day	Opponent	Res	Score	Scorers	Att
Aug	3	Estudiantes	L	0-3		11 000
	11	Racing	W	1-0	Civelli [84]	30 000
	18	Vélez	W	1-0	Devaca [31]	13 000
	25	Arsenal	W	4-0	Herner [17], Lucchetti [28], Cvitanich 2 [53 75]	6 000
	28	Lanús	L	1-2	Lucchetti [24p]	18 000
	31	Tigre	L	0-1		22 000
Sept	7	Rosario C	W	3-2	Patiño [85], Pavlovich [93+], Lucchetti [99+]	12 000
	11	Arg Juniors	L	0-2		8 000
	16	Boca	L	0-6		30 000
	22	Gimn'sia LP	W	1-0	Cvitanich [28]	16 000
	29	Indep'iente	W	2-0	Barrales [45], Lucchetti [77]	25 000
Oct	2	Huracán	L	0-1		16 000
	5	Colón	W	3-1	Barrales 3 [14 59 70]	5 000
	20	Olimpo	D	1-1	Lucchetti [40p]	11 000
Nov	2	San Martín	W	1-0	Cvitanich [59]	14 000
	10	Gimn'sia Jy	D	1-1	Cvitanich [72]	8 000
	24	Newell's	L	0-1		20 000
Dec	1	San Lorenzo	W	1-0	Patiño [42]	7 000
	8	River Plate	W	2-0	Cvitanich [4], Lucchetti [64]	12 000
Feb	8	Estudiantes	L	1-2	Cvitanich [58]	23 000
	15	Racing	W	3-1	Cvitanich [40], Lucchetti [67], Pavlovich [90]	10 000
	22	Vélez	L	0-3		15 000
	29	Arsenal	L	1-3	Laso [16], Santana [79]	12 000
Mar	8	Lanús	W	5-0	Laso [21], Cvitanich 2 [37 83], Civelli [46]	20 000
	15	Tigre	D	3-3	Lucchetti [18], Cvitanich [85], Civelli [90]	10 000
	22	Rosario C	L	1-2	Pavlovich [33]	36 000
	29	Arg Juniors	W	3-2	Cvitanich [11], Patiño 2 [61 85]	10 000
Apr	5	Boca	L	0-1	Civelli [16]	35 000
	12	Gimn'sia LP	D	0-0		10 000
	18	Indep'iente	L	0-3		10 000
	25	Huracán	W	4-3	Barrales 2 [18 85], Pavlovich [32], Villarreal [79]	8 000
May	3	Colón	D	2-2	Blazquez OG [23], Cvitanich [88]	15 000
	10	Olimpo	W	2-1	Civelli [4], Barrales [44]	10 000
	16	San Martín	W	5-1	Cvitanich 2 [8 64], Devaca [19], Barrales [49], Patiño [58]	9 000
	24	Gimn'sia Jy	D	1-1	Cvitanich [45], Patiño [58]	6 000
	31	Newell's	L	0-1		5 000
Jun	7	San Lorenzo	L	2-3	Civelli [33], Cvitanich [53]	14 000
	22	River Plate	L	2-3	Cvitanich 2 [41 51p]	25 000

BOCA JUNIORS 2007–08

Month	Day	Opponent	Res	Score	Scorers	Att
Aug	5	Rosario C	D	0-0		35 000
	12	Arg Juniors	L	2-3	Ledesma 2 [13 54p]	12 000
	19	San Martín	W	1-0	Ledesma [21]	30 000
	26	Gimn'sia LP	W	2-1	Palacio [3], Ledesma [90p]	30 000
	29	Indep'iente	W	3-2	Rodriguez OG [16], Palermo [46], Gracián [68]	37 000
	2	Huracán	W	1-0	Ledesma [76p]	45 000
Sept	9	Colón	L	0-1		25 000
	12	Olimpo	W	2-0	Palacio [8], Palermo [41p]	32 000
	16	Banfield	W	6-0	Palermo 4 [6 22 28p 48], Gracian [38]	32 000
	23	Gimn'sia Jy	D	2-2	Boselli [67], Paletta [84], Ledesma [81p]	40 000
	30	Newell's	L	0-1		35 000
Oct	3	San Lorenzo	W	2-0	Palermo [36], Méndez OG [57]	42 000
	7	River Plate	L	0-2		60 000
	21	Estudiantes	D	1-1	Palermo [71]	40 000
	3	Racing	W	3-0	Cardozo [46], Palacio [60], Palermo [94+]	32 000
Nov	11	Vélez	W	4-0	Palermo 2 [14 42], Palacio [73], González [74]	45 000
	25	Arsenal	L	1-2	Bueno [75]	14 000
	28	Tigre	L	1-2	Barzola [56]	30 000
Dec	2	Lanús	D	1-1	Palermo [67]	40 000
Feb	10	Rosario C	D	1-1	Palacio [72]	38 000
	17	Arg Juniors	W	4-0	Palermo [21], Palacio [49], Dátolo [83], Gracián [93+]	18 000
	24	San Martín	W	2-0	Palermo 2 [4 80]	18 000
	2	Gimn'sia LP	W	1-0	Palermo [41]	30 000
Mar	9	Indep'iente	D	1-1	Riquelme [54]	42 000
	16	Huracán	D	0-0		22 000
	23	Colón	W	2-1	Dátolo [6], Gracián [38]	40 000
	30	Olimpo	D	1-1	Gracián [36]	16 000
Apr	5	Banfield	D	1-1	Palermo [58]	35 000
	13	Gimn'sia Jy	W	2-1	Dátolo 2 [59 82]	20 000
	19	Newell's	W	2-1	Palacio [55], Palermo [80]	40 000
	27	San Lorenzo	L	0-1		40 000
	4	River Plate	W	1-0	Battaglia [14]	50 000
May	11	Estudiantes	L	0-1		40 000
	17	Racing	W	2-1	Paletta [73], Noir [94+]	40 000
	25	Vélez	D	1-1	Viatri [85]	30 000
	1	Arsenal	W	3-1	Boselli 3 [58 74 80]	27 000
Jun	8	Lanús	W	3-1	Palermo 2 [45 56p], Palacio [75]	25 000
	22	Tigre	W	6-2	Palacio 2 [6 53], Palermo 2 [30 60], Paletta [40], Chávez [83]	40 000

COLON SANTA FE 2007–08

					Scorers	Att.
Aug	3	Vélez	L	0-1		13 000
	10	Arsenal	L	0-2		2 000
	18	Lanús	W	2-1	Gandín [56], Centurión [75]	18 500
	24	Tigre	W	2-0	Gandín [23], González [36]	20 000
	28	Rosario C	W	2-0	Gandín [12], Romero [21]	16 000
Sept	1	Arg Juniors	L	1-2	Cardetti [93+]	7 000
	9	Boca	W	1-0	Grisales [93+]	25 000
	15	Indep'iente	L	1-3	Rodríguez OG [45]	24 000
	21	Huracán	D	2-2	Romero [5], Gandín [78p]	15 000
	29	San Martín	D	1-1	Gandín [43p]	19 000
Oct	2	Olimpo	W	3-0	Gandín [3], Merlo [41], Quinteros [68]	14 000
	5	Banfield	L	1-3	Rivarola [79]	5 000
	12	Gimn'sia LP	L	0-2		16 000
	20	Gimn'sia Jy	L	0-1		11 500
Nov	3	Newell's	D	1-1	Garcé [49]	22 000
	10	San Lorenzo	D	0-0		15 000
	24	River Plate	W	2-0	Ramírez [44], Grisales [52]	15 000
	30	Estudiantes	L	0-2		15 000
Dc	8	Racing	L	0-1		14 000
Feb	9	Vélez	L	3-4	Aguilar [34], Gandín [83], Capurro [94+]	14 000
	15	Arsenal	W	3-0	Cardetti [60], González 2 [77 91+]	19 000
	22	Lanús	L	1-5	Cardetti [70]	7 000
	1	Tigre	L	1-2	Gandín [54]	15 000
Mar	7	Rosario C	D	0-0		37 000
	15	Arg Juniors	L	0-1		16 000
	23	Boca	L	1-2	González [93+]	40 000
	28	Gimn'sia LP	D	0-0		14 000
Apr	5	Indep'iente	W	3-1	Chitzoff [24], Romero [26], Gandín [46]	17 000
	12	Huracán	W	1-0	Ramírez [92+]	15 000
	20	San Martín	W	2-1	Cardetti [44], Ramírez [49]	14 000
	26	Olimpo	L	1-2	Ramírez [75]	10 000
May	3	Banfield	W	3-2	Prediger [1], Ramírez 2 [49 72]	15 000
	9	Gimn'sia Jy	D	2-2	Ramírez 2 [13 53]	10 000
	16	Newell's	L	1-2	Goux [53]	20 000
	25	San Lorenzo	L	1-2	Ramírez [8]	20 000
	1	River Plate	L	1-2	Gandín [80]	30 000
Jun	8	Estudiantes	D	0-0		30 000
	22	Racing	W	1-0	Rivarola [92+]	35 000

ESTUDIANTES LP 2007–08

					Scorers	Att.
Aug	3	Banfield	W	3-0	Maggiolo [74], OG [82], Verón [94+]	11 000
	12	Gimn'sia Jy	W	1-0	Braña [80]	17 000
	19	Newell's	L	1-2	Badell [48]	28 000
	25	San Lorenzo	D	1-1	Fabianesi [93+]	24 000
	29	River Plate	L	2-4	Benítez 2, Salgueiro [80]	25 000
Sept	2	San Martín	L	0-1		18 000
	9	Racing	W	2-1	Domínguez [50], Desábato [57]	25 000
	12	Vélez	L	0-1		13 000
	15	Arsenal	D	1-1	Benítez [78]	10 000
	23	Lanús	L	0-1		17 000
Oct	28	Tigre	D	2-2	Alayes [82], Maggiolo [90]	24 000
	3	Rosario C	D	2-2	Fabianesi [14p], Lugüercio [45]	17 000
	7	Arg Juniors	W	3-0	Verón 2 [12 90], Maggiolo [72]	19 000
	21	Boca	D	1-1	Piatti [2]	40 000
Nov	4	Gimn'sia LP	W	1-0	Salgueiro [38]	34 000
	11	Indep'iente	W	2-1	Piatti [45], Barroso [58]	28 000
	25	Huracán	D	1-1	Piatti [13]	29 000
	30	Colón	D	2-0	Fernández OG [3], Piatti [44]	15 000
Dc	7	Olimpo	W	2-0	Verón [58], Maggiolo [79]	22 000
Feb	8	Banfield	W	2-1	Maggiolo [1], Piatti [8]	23 000
	16	Gimn'sia Jy	W	2-0	Pérez [11], Lugüercio [50]	8 000
	22	Newell's	W	5-2	Fabianesi [2], Maggiolo [37], Salgueiro [53], Lugüercio [73]	21 000
	1	San Lorenzo	L	1-3	Carrasco [59] ... Piatti 2 [74 81]	20 000
Mar	9	River Plate	D	0-0		33 000
	14	San Martín	W	3-2	Fabianesi [34], Lázzaro 2 [41 43]	20 000
	22	Racing	W	2-0	Galván [58], Lázzaro [61]	30 000
	29	Vélez	W	1-0	Fabianesi [89]	27 000
Apr	5	Arsenal	D	0-0		10 000
	11	Lanús	W	1-0	Verón [86]	14 000
	20	Tigre	D	1-1	Basanta [53]	17 000
	25	Rosario C	W	3-1	Salgueiro [56], Díaz [67], Piatti [71]	20 000
	3	Arg Juniors	L	1-2	Carrasco [73]	12 000
May	11	Boca	W	1-0	Maggiolo [75]	35 000
	17	Gimn'sia LP	W	2-1	Maggiolo 2 [22 70]	40 000
	25	Indep'iente	W	1-0	Verón [51]	32 000
	1	Huracán	D	1-1	Verón [5p]	18 000
Jun	8	Colón	D	0-0		30 000
	22	Olimpo	W	2-1	Lugüercio [2], Maggiolo [63]	14 000

GIMNASIA Y ESGRIMA JUJUY 2007–08

					Scorers	Att.
Aug	12	Estudiantes	L	0-1		17 000
	19	Racing	W	2-1	Carranza [57], Desvaux [65]	10 000
	23	River Plate	D	2-2	Carranza [45], Pieters [60]	20 000
	26	Vélez	L	2-4	Uglessich OG [36], Silva [76]	13 000
	29	Arsenal	W	1-0	Miranda [29]	10 000
Sept	1	Lanús	L	0-2		14 000
	7	Tigre	L	0-2		12 000
	11	Rosario C	D	1-1	Silva [73]	25 000
	15	Arg Juniors	D	1-1	Silva [93+]	7 000
	23	Boca	D	2-2	Miranda [10], Berza [90]	40 000
	29	Gimn'sia LP	W	4-0	Berza [19], Miranda [46], Carranza [68],	9 000
Oct	2	Indep'iente	L	0-3	Quinteros [74]	27 000
	5	Huracán	W	2-0	Goltz OG [9], Miranda [29]	8 000
	20	Colón	W	1-0	Leochbor [85]	11 500
	3	Olimpo	L	0-3		7 000
Nov	10	Banfield	D	1-1	Desaux [50]	8 000
	24	San Martín	L	2-3	Desvaux [42], Silva [55]	10 000
Dc	1	Newell's	L	0-1		7 000
	9	San Lorenzo	L	1-4	Carranza [19]	12 000
Feb	10	River Plate	L	0-2		40 000
	16	Estudiantes	L	0-2		8 000
	23	Racing	D	0-0		20 000
	1	Vélez	D	0-0		8 000
Mar	9	Arsenal	D	3-3	Miranda [15], Carranza [45p], Mateo [80]	2 500
	21	Tigre	L	0-2		10 000
	29	Rosario C	D	1-1	Iuvale [39]	9 000
	6	Arg Juniors	D	1-1	Luna [73]	9 000
Apr	13	Boca	L	1-2	Escalada [84]	20 000
	19	Gimn'sia LP	L	1-2	Arroyo [15]	12 000
	23	Lanús	W	2-0	Carranza [56], Castro [83]	7 000
	26	Indep'iente	L	1-2	Arraya [62]	13 000
May	2	Huracán	L	0-1		7 000
	9	Colón	D	2-2	De Bruno [26], Carranza [27]	10 000
	18	Olimpo	L	0-2		12 000
	24	Banfield	D	1-1	Carranza [27]	6 000
	31	San Martín	W	3-1	Carranza 2 [7 70], Desvaux [65]	7 000
Jun	6	Newell's	D	2-2	Quinteros [38], Carranza [64]	26 000
	22	San Lorenzo	D	2-2	Escalada [13], Luna [87]	11 000

GIMNASIA Y ESGRIMA LA PLATA 2007–08

					Scorers	Att.
Aug	4	Tigre	L	0-1		16 000
	11	Rosario C	D	2-2	Silva [42], Batalla [89]	34 000
	17	Arg Juniors	L	0-2		7 000
	26	Boca	L	1-2	Domínguez [6]	30 000
	29	San Martín	W	2-0	Leguizamón [2], Salvatierra [48]	12 000
Sept	1	Indep'iente	W	1-0	Salvatierra [49]	23 000
	8	Huracán	W	1-0	Escobar [10]	23 000
	15	Olimpo	D	0-0		11 000
	22	Banfield	L	0-1		16 000
	29	Gimn'sia Jy	L	0-4		9 000
Oct	6	San Lorenzo	D	1-1	Piatti [85]	17 000
	12	Colón	W	2-0	Escobar [69], Piatti [88]	16 000
	21	River Plate	L	0-2		18 000
	26	Newell's	W	2-0	Landa [10], Herrera [90]	13 000
Nov	4	Estudiantes	L	0-1		34 000
	9	Racing	L	1-3	Pierguidi [23]	7 000
	24	Vélez	L	1-3	Domínguez [66]	7 000
	28	Lanús	L	0-4		35 000
Dc	2	Arsenal	D	1-1		
Feb	9	Tigre	L	1-2	Piatti [3]	20 000
	16	Rosario C	W	2-0	Civelli 2, Cuevas [73]	17 000
	23	Arg Juniors	L	0-2		8 500
	2	Boca	L	0-1		30 000
Mar	8	San Martín	D	1-1	Piatti [77]	9 000
	15	Indep'iente	L	1-3	Escobar [62]	20 000
	23	Huracán	D	0-0		18 000
	28	Colón	D	0-0		14 000
Apr	6	Olimpo	W	4-2	Alonso 2 [35 69], Domínguez [92+], Salvatierra [95+]	9 000
	12	Banfield	D	0-0		16 000
	19	Gimn'sia Jy	W	2-1	Alonso [26], Domínguez [47]	12 000
	27	Newell's	L	0-1		27 000
May	4	San Lorenzo	L	1-2	Domínguez [30p]	20 000
	11	River Plate	L	2-4	Piatti [26], Neira [40]	22 000
	17	Estudiantes	L	1-2	Domínguez [65]	40 000
	24	Racing	D	1-1	Martirena [86]	20 000
	1	Vélez	W	2-1	Cuevas [17], Martirena [92+]	12 000
Jun	6	Arsenal	L	0-1		2 500
	21	Lanús	L	1-2	Piatti [79]	13 000

HURACAN BUENOS AIRES 2007–08

	Date	Opponent	Res	Score	Scorers	Att
Aug	5	Arsenal	D	1-1	Gómez [6]	24 000
	12	Lanús	D	1-1	Mendoza [42]	15 000
	18	Tigre	D	0-0		30 000
	25	Rosario C	W	1-0	Mendoza [43]	30 000
	29	Arg Juniors	W	3-2	Mendoza [11], Nieto [46], Sánchez [88]	17 000
Sept	2	Boca	L	0-1		45 000
	8	Gimn'sia LP	L	0-1		23 000
	11	Indep'iente	L	0-3		32 000
	15	San Martín	W	2-1	Varaldo [40], Sánchez Prette [64]	17 000
	21	Colón	D	2-2	Mendoza [51], Nieto [72]	15 000
	28	Olimpo	L	1-3	Mendoza [84]	13 000
Oct	2	Banfield	W	1-0	Coyette [66]	16 000
	5	Gimn'sia Jy	L	0-2		8 000
	21	Newell's	W	3-1	Mendoza [40], Schiavi OG [50], Franzoia [71]	10 000
Nov	4	San Lorenzo	D	1-1	Goltz [34]	32 000
	10	River Plate	W	2-1	Sánchez Prette 2 [59] [66]	18 000
	25	Estudiantes	D	1-1	Cellay [67]	29 000
Dec	1	Racing	W	3-0	Cellay [3], Nieto [87], Sánchez Prette [89]	18 000
	9	Vélez	W	2-1	Franzoia 2 [62] [79]	15 000
Feb	10	Arsenal	L	0-2		7 000
	17	Lanús	W	1-0	Sánchez [84]	13 000
	23	Tigre	W	2-1	Franzoia 2 [53] [86]	18 000
	29	Rosario C	D	1-1	Barrientos [8]	20 000
Mar	8	Arg Juniors	D	1-1	Nieto [6]	12 000
	16	Boca	D	0-0		22 000
	23	Gimn'sia LP	D	0-0		18 000
	30	Indep'iente	D	0-0		22 000
Apr	4	San Martín	L	0-2		14 000
	12	Colón	L	0-1		15 000
	18	Olimpo	W	3-0	Franzoia 2 [3] [43], Domínguez [79]	13 000
	25	Banfield	L	3-4	Franzoia [3], Nieto [51], Goltz [90]	8 000
May	2	Gimn'sia Jy	W	1-0	Franzoia [8]	7 000
	11	Newell's	W	1-0	Nieto [43]	27 000
	18	San Lorenzo	D	0-0		20 000
	24	River Plate	L	0-1		28 000
Jun	1	Estudiantes	D	1-1	Nieto [26]	18 000
	7	Racing	L	0-1		30 000
	21	Vélez	L	1-2	Domínguez [92+]	13 000

INDEPENDIENTE 2007–08

	Date	Opponent	Res	Score	Scorers	Att
Aug	4	Lanús	W	5-3	Denis 2 [16] [34], Sosa [45], Montenegro 2 [16] [34]	30 000
	12	Tigre	W	3-0	Sosa [5], Denis 2 [31] [64]	26 000
	17	Rosario C	W	1-0	Denis [78]	26 000
	25	Arg Juniors	W	1-0	Denis [77]	20 000
	29	Boca	L	2-3	Denis [1], Matheu [72]	37 000
Sept	1	Gimn'sia LP	L	0-1		23 000
	8	San Martín	D	2-2	Sosa [45], Montenegro [72]	25 000
	11	Huracán	W	3-0	Sosa [28], Denis 2 [30] [71]	32 000
	15	Colón	W	3-1	Matheu [21], Denis 2 [35] [60]	24 000
	22	Olimpo	W	3-0	Montenegro [14], Denis 2 [18] [65]	45 000
	29	Banfield	L	0-2		25 000
Oct	2	Gimn'sia Jy	W	3-0	Denis 2 [53] [90], Matheu [84]	27 000
	7	Newell's	L	1-2	Montenegro [13]	38 000
	21	San Lorenzo	L	1-2	Denis [36]	35 000
Nov	4	River Plate	D	1-1	Matheu [18]	45 000
	11	Estudiantes	L	1-2	Denis [24]	28 000
	24	Racing	D	0-0		32 000
Dec	2	Vélez	D	1-1	Moreno [81]	19 000
	9	Arsenal	L	2-3	Oyola [34], Denis [52]	10 000
Feb	10	Lanús	L	0-1		25 000
	16	Tigre	W	4-1	OG [22], Montenegro 2 [37] [87], Machín [49]	22 000
	23	Rosario C	L	0-2		38 000
Mar	1	Arg Juniors	W	2-0	Denis [35], Montenegro [80]	18 000
	9	Boca	D	1-1	Caceres OG [7]	42 000
	15	Gimn'sia LP	W	3-1	Montenegro [49], Di Gregorio [54], Denis [57]	20 000
	23	San Martín	L	0-2		14 000
	30	Huracán	D	0-0		22 000
Apr	5	Colón	L	1-3	Denis [80]	17 000
	12	Tigre	W	3-1	Denis 2 [20] [37], Montenegro [32]	12 000
	18	Banfield	W	3-0	Montenegro [4], Denis [55p], Herrón [90p]	17 000
	26	Gimn'sia Jy	W	2-1	Fredes [12], Montenegro [56]	13 000
May	3	Newell's	W	3-0	Denis 2 [32] [37], Montenegro [45]	27 500
	11	San Lorenzo	W	1-0	Rodríguez [46]	40 000
	18	River Plate	D	0-0		40 000
	25	Estudiantes	D	1-1	Denis [86]	32 000
	31	Racing	D	0-0		30 000
Jun	8	Vélez	D	0-0		16 000
	21	Arsenal	D	1-1	Matheu [82]	15 000

LANUS 2007–08

	Date	Opponent	Res	Score	Scorers	Att
Aug	4	Indep'iente	L	3-5	Acosta [15], Salomón [38], Peralta [60]	30 000
	12	Huracán	D	1-1	Valeri [39]	15 000
	18	Colón	L	1-2	Sand [19p]	18 500
	25	Olimpo	W	2-1	Sand [13p], Martínez OG [88]	12 000
	28	Banfield	W	2-1	Sand 2 [35] [45]	18 000
Sept	1	Gimn'sia Jy	W	2-0	Aguirre [24], Valeri [66]	14 000
	8	Newell's	D	0-0	Pelletieri [67]	24 000
	12	San Lorenzo	W	4-3	Sand [34p], Valeri [38], Acosta [43],	15 000
	16	River Plate	L	1-3	Sand [67]	35 000
	23	Estudiantes	W	1-0	Jiménez [92+]	17 000
	30	Racing	D	1-1	Sand [70]	35 000
Oct	3	Vélez	W	2-1	Sand 2 [3] [15p], Coria [50]	7 000
	7	Arsenal	W	1-0	Sand [8]	6 000
	19	San Martín	W	2-0	Valeri [16], Blanco [77]	25 000
Nov	4	Tigre	W	2-1	Sand [16], Fritzler [60]	40 000
	9	Rosario C	W	4-1	Blanco [42], Ribonetto [58], Sand [77],	25 000
	25	Arg Juniors	D	0-0	Valeri [79]	35 000
	28	Gimn'sia LP	W	4-0	Sand 2 [35] [50], Valeri [55], Benítez [86]	35 000
Dec	2	Boca	D	1-1	Sand [38]	40 000
Feb	10	Indep'iente	W	1-0	Gioda OG [50]	25 000
	17	Huracán	L	0-1	Biglieri [82]	13 000
	22	Colón	W	5-1	Valeri 2 [15] [26], Sand [19], Pelletieri [51],	7 000
Mar	1	Olimpo	L	2-3	Gonzalez 2 [27] [54]	13 000
	8	Banfield	L	0-5		20 000
	24	Newell's	D	1-1	Fideleff [24]	9 000
	29	San Lorenzo	L	1-3	Blanco [65]	15 000
Apr	6	River Plate	L	0-1		35 000
	11	Estudiantes	L	0-1		14 000
	19	Racing	D	3-3	Sand 2 [45] [48], Ramírez [89]	15 000
	23	Gimn'sia Jy	L	0-2		7 000
	26	Vélez	L	2-3	Ramírez [5], Cano [13]	10 000
May	2	Arsenal	L	2-3	Sigali [52], Ramírez [54]	3 500
	10	San Martín	W	2-1	Faccioli [91+], Sand [94+]	15 000
	18	Tigre	W	4-1	Sand 2 [13] [45], Fritzler [23], Salomón [54]	15 000
	25	Rosario C	L	0-1		8 000
	30	Arg Juniors	L	0-3		8 000
Jun	8	Boca	L	1-3	Salomón [14]	25 000
	21	Gimn'sia LP	W	2-1	Blanco [32], Sand [49]	13 000

NEWELL'S OLD BOYS 2007–08

	Date	Opponent	Res	Score	Scorers	Att
Aug	5	San Lorenzo	W	1-0	Vangioni [89]	27 000
	19	Estudiantes	W	2-1	Donnet [27], Steinert [80]	28 000
	24	Racing	L	0-2		15 000
	29	Vélez	W	2-0	Da Silva [9], Seri [45]	9 000
Sept	1	Arsenal	L	0-1		3 000
	5	River Plate	L	1-3	Da Silva [68]	17 000
	8	Lanús	D	0-0		24 000
	11	Tigre	D	2-2	Salcedo [20], Schiavi [48]	20 000
	16	Rosario C	L	0-1		38 000
	22	Arg Juniors	L	0-4		10 000
	30	Boca	W	1-0	Salcedo [12]	35 000
Oct	7	Indep'iente	W	2-1	Steinert [9], Salcedo [41]	38 000
	21	Huracán	L	1-3	Schiavi [37p]	10 000
	26	Gimn'sia LP	L	0-2		13 000
Nov	3	Colón	D	1-1	Lucero [89]	22 000
	10	Olimpo	L	0-1		11 000
	24	Banfield	W	1-0	Da Silva [80]	20 000
Dec	1	Gimn'sia Jy	W	1-0	Schiavi [63]	7 000
	8	San Martín	W	1-0	Da Silva [83]	10 000
Feb	8	San Lorenzo	W	2-0	Spolli [52], Salcedo [73]	25 000
	17	River Plate	D	0-0		35 000
	22	Estudiantes	L	2-5	Salcedo [20], Donnet [76]	21 000
	2	Racing	W	1-0	Salcedo [64]	27 000
	8	Vélez	L	0-1		15 000
Mar	16	Arsenal	W	4-1	Da Silva 2 [7] [46], Ferreyra 2 [44] [89]	29 000
	24	Lanús	D	1-1	Dovetta [53]	9 000
	30	Tigre	D	1-1	Schiavi [22p]	28 000
Apr	5	Rosario C	W	1-0	Salcedo [42]	38 000
	11	Arg Juniors	W	2-0	Re [44], Da Silva [49]	27 000
	19	Boca	L	1-2	Salcedo [74]	40 000
	27	Gimn'sia LP	W	1-0	Kletnicki OG [6]	27 000
	3	Indep'iente	L	0-3		27 500
May	11	Huracán	L	0-1		27 000
	16	Colón	D	1-1	Salcedo [54]	20 000
	26	Olimpo	L	0-1		16 000
	31	Banfield	W	1-0	Salcedo [45]	5 000
Jun	6	Gimn'sia Jy	D	2-2	Salcedo 2 [57] [71]	26 000
	21	San Martín	W	1-0	Spolli [78]	16 000

OLIMPO 2007–08

Mon	Date	Opponent	Res	Score	Scorers	Att
Aug	5	Racing	L	0-2		15 000
	11	Vélez	L	0-3		14 000
	18	Arsenal	W	1-0	Torales 47	12 000
	25	Lanús	L	1-2	Gonzáles.S 43	12 000
	28	Tigre	L	0-1		10 000
	31	Rosario C	D	1-1	Lujambio 63	33 000
Sept	7	Arg Juniors	D	1-1	Pinto 46	9 000
	12	Boca	L	0-2		32 000
	15	Gimn'sia LP	D	0-0		11 000
	22	Indep'iente	L	0-3		45 000
	28	Huracán	W	3-1	Lujambio 27, Martínez 59, Olivi 77p	13 000
Oct	2	Colon	L	0-3		14 000
	6	San Martín	W	2-1	Lujambio 84, Olivi 87	10 000
	20	Banfield	D	1-1	González.S 19	11 000
Nov	3	Gimn'sia Jy	W	3-0	González.L 18, Araujo 56, González.S 94+	7 000
	10	Newell's	W	1-0	Morales 92+	11 000
	23	San Lorenzo	L	0-1		10 000
Dec	1	River Plate	W	4-0	Pinto 10, Paez 66, Lujambio 73,	14 000
	7	Estudiantes	L	0-2	González.L 74	22 000
Feb	9	Racing	D	1-1	Paez 34	25 000
	16	Vélez	L	0-2		13 000
	24	Arsenal	L	0-1		2 000
Mar	1	Lanús	W	3-2	Ulloa 2 49 73, Pinto 64	13 000
	8	Tigre	L	0-2		15 000
	14	Rosario C	L	1-3	Lujambio 70	11 000
	22	Arg Juniors	L	0-3		15 000
	30	Boca	D	1-1	Lujambio 80	16 000
Apr	6	Gimn'sia LP	L	2-4	Ulloa 42, Barrado 91+	9 000
	12	Indep'iente	L	1-3	Lujambio 86	12 000
	18	Huracán	L	0-3		13 000
	26	Colon	W	2-1	González.L 10, Lujambio 38	10 000
May	3	San Martín	W	1-0	González.L 45	12 000
	10	Banfield	L	1-2	Lujambio 32	10 000
	18	Gimn'sia Jy	W	2-0	Desvaux OG 88, Olivi 96+	12 000
	26	Newell's	W	1-0	Olivi 59	16 000
Jun	1	San Lorenzo	W	3-2	Barrado 2 48 50, Mancinelli 94+	10 000
	8	River Plate	L	1-2	Lujambio 65	60 000
	22	Estudiantes	L	1-2	Paez 51	14 000

RACING CLUB 2007–08

Mon	Date	Opponent	Res	Score	Scorers	Att
Aug	5	Olimpo	W	2-0	Sava 83, Pellerano 40	15 000
	11	Banfield	L	0-1		30 000
	19	Gimn'sia Jy	L	1-2	Sava 44	10 000
	24	Newell's	W	2-0	Sava 66p, López 89	15 000
	28	San Lorenzo	L	3-4	Torres OG 1, Avalos 21, Pellerano 28	25 000
Sept	2	River Plate	D	1-1	Sava 35p	32 000
	9	Estudiantes	L	1-2	López 66	25 000
	12	San Martín	W	2-0	López 83, Malano 89	20 000
	15	Vélez	W	1-0	Avalos 92+	15 000
	23	Arsenal	W	1-0	Sava 59	7 000
Oct	30	Lanús	D	1-1	Romagnoli 12	35 000
	3	Tigre	L	2-3	Sava 34, Sosa 72	18 000
	6	Rosario C	D	2-2	Sava 2 38 77	20 000
	20	Arg Juniors	L	0-1		11 000
Nov	3	Boca	L	0-3		32 000
	9	Gimn'sia LP	W	3-1	Cejas OG 34, López 2 43 83	7 000
	24	Indep'iente	D	0-0		32 000
Dec	1	Huracán	L	0-3		18 000
	8	Colon	W	1-0	Menghi 2	14 000
Feb	9	Olimpo	D	1-1	Sava 84	25 000
	15	Banfield	L	1-3	Sava 12	10 000
	23	Gimn'sia Jy	D	0-0		20 000
Mar	2	Newell's	L	0-1		27 000
	7	San Lorenzo	L	0-1		26 000
	16	River Plate	D	0-0		50 000
	22	Estudiantes	L	1-2	Fileppi 41, Abandoned 77'	30 000
	28	San Martín	L	1-2	Chatruc 54	0
Apr	4	Vélez	D	1-1	Avalos 57	16 000
	13	Arsenal	W	1-0	Sosa 62	25 000
	19	Lanús	D	3-3	Morales 2 13 44, Faccioli OG 39	15 000
	26	Tigre	D	0-0		20 000
May	4	Rosario C	L	2-3	Raldes OG 43, Sava 87	35 000
	10	Arg Juniors	D	1-1	Sosa 41	20 000
	17	Boca	L	1-2	Navia 14	40 000
	24	Gimn'sia LP	D	1-1	Dominguez OG 3	20 000
	31	Indep'iente	D	0-0		30 000
Jun	7	Huracán	W	1-0	Sava 35	30 000
	22	Colon	L	0-1		35 000

RIVER PLATE 2007–08

Mon	Date	Opponent	Res	Score	Scorers	Att
Aug	19	San Lorenzo	D	1-1	Ortega 57p	21 000
	23	Gimn'sia Jy	D	2-2	Rosales 42, Zárate 72	20 000
	26	San Martín	L	0-1	García 92+	22 000
	29	Estudiantes	W	4-2	Belluschi 7, Ruben 22, Sánchez 81,	25 000
Sept	2	Racing	D	1-1	Lussenhoff 76	32 000
	5	Newell's	W	3-1	Ortega 20p, García 51, Abelairas 74	17 000
	9	Vélez	W	5-0	Rios 23, Belluschi 3 45 61 82, Fernandez 70	35 000
	12	Arsenal	L	1-2	Ruben 23	9 000
	16	Lanús	W	3-1	Belluschi 2 44 77, Sánchez 46	24 000
	23	Tigre	L	1-4	Ruben 66	24 000
	30	Rosario C	D	3-3	Rios 61, Buonanotte 74, García 98+	35 000
Oct	3	Arg Juniors	L	1-4	Ruben 48	10 500
	7	Boca	W	2-0	García 24, Ortega 33p	60 000
	21	Gimn'sia LP	W	2-0	Buonanotte 26, García 81	18 000
Nov	4	Indep'iente	D	1-1	Belluschi 45	45 000
	10	Huracán	L	1-2	Peralta 21	18 000
	24	Colon	L	0-2		15 000
Dec	1	Olimpo	L	0-4		14 000
	8	Banfield	L	0-2		12 000
Feb	10	Gimn'sia Jy	W	2-0	Abelairas 48, Ferrari 56	40 000
	17	Newell's	D	0-0		35 000
	24	San Lorenzo	W	2-0	García 27, Abelairas 53	50 000
Mar	9	Estudiantes	D	0-0		33 000
	16	Racing	D	0-0		50 000
	19	San Martín	W	3-2	Abreu 17, Buonanotte 27, Nasuti 57	35 000
	23	Vélez	W	2-0	Sánchez 8, García 11	28 000
	30	Arsenal	W	1-0	Archubi 34	25 000
Apr	6	Lanús	W	1-0	Buonanotte 68	35 000
	13	Tigre	W	1-0	García 50	20 000
	20	Rosario C	L	1-2	Buonanotte 19	38 000
	27	Arg Juniors	W	4-2	Buonanotte 2 32 49, Abreu 61, García 61	18 000
May	4	Boca	L	0-1		50 000
	11	Gimn'sia LP	W	4-2	Abelairas 2 37 53, Buonanotte 50,	22 000
	18	Indep'iente	D	0-0	Ortega 74	40 000
	24	Huracán	W	1-0	Buonanotte 81	28 000
Jun	1	Colon	W	2-1	Villagra 57, Sánchez 77	30 000
	8	Olimpo	W	2-1	Buonanotte 2 1 78	60 000
	22	Banfield	W	3-2	García 2 70 86, Abelairas 83	25 000

ROSARIO CENTRAL 2007–08

Mon	Date	Opponent	Res	Score	Scorers	Att
Aug	5	Boca	D	0-0		35 000
	11	Gimn'sia LP	D	2-2	Diaz 15, Vizcarra 66	34 000
	17	Indep'iente	L	0-1		26 000
	25	Huracán	L	0-1		30 000
	28	Colon	L	0-3		16 000
	31	Olimpo	D	1-1	Arzuaga 12	33 000
Sept	7	Banfield	L	2-3	Arzuaga 17, Costa 52p	12 000
	11	Gimn'sia Jy	D	1-1	Belloso 50	25 000
	16	Newell's	W	1-0	Arzuaga 73p	38 000
	21	San Lorenzo	W	3-1	Vizcarra 85	30 000
	30	River Plate	D	3-3	García 40, Díaz 48, Raldes 93+	35 000
Oct	3	Estudiantes	D	2-2	Vizcarra 2 73 77	17 000
	6	Racing	D	2-2	Papa 50, Vizcarra 58	20 000
	20	Vélez	D	2-2		25 000
Nov	2	Arsenal	L	0-1		1 000
	9	Lanús	L	1-4	Vizcarra 48	25 000
	23	Tigre	L	1-2	Vizcarra 58	16 000
	30	San Martín	W	3-2	Vizcarra 2 11 83, Borzani 80	24 000
De	7	Arg Juniors	D	1-1	Borzani 48	24 000
Feb	10	Boca	D	1-1	Kily González 84	38 000
	16	Gimn'sia LP	L	0-2		17 000
	23	Indep'iente	W	2-0	Arzuaga 2 10 48	38 000
	29	Huracán	D	1-1	Vizcarra 1	20 000
Mar	7	Colon	D	0-0		37 000
	14	Olimpo	W	3-1	Zelaya 2 35 63, Kily González 86	11 000
	22	Banfield	W	2-1	Zelaya 56, Vizcarra 84	36 000
	29	Gimn'sia Jy	D	1-1	Zelaya 58	9 000
Apr	5	Newell's	L	0-1		38 000
	12	San Lorenzo	L	1-3	Borzani 29	22 000
	19	River Plate	W	2-1	Zelaya 29, Arzuaga 43	38 000
	25	Estudiantes	L	1-3	Vizcarra 65p	38 000
May	4	Racing	W	3-2	Vizcarra 77, Díaz 83, Kily González 90	35 000
	10	Vélez	L	1-2	Paglialunga 86	25 000
	17	Arsenal	W	3-0	Borzani 12, Kily González 22p, Vizcarra 83	8 000
	25	Lanús	D	0-0		8 000
	30	Tigre	W	4-2	Danelón 34, Vizcarra 48, Costa 64,	39 000
Jun	7	San Martín	D	0-0	Arzuaga 76	10 000
	20	Arg Juniors	L	1-2	Díaz 15	7 000

SAN LORENZO 2007–08

Month	Date	Opponent	Res	Score	Scorers	Att
Aug	5	Newell's	L	0-1		27 000
	10	San Martín	W	2-1	Gómez OG [72], Fernández [79]	15 000
	19	River Plate	D	1-1	Silvera [22]	21 000
	25	Estudiantes	D	1-1	Aguirre [41]	24 000
	28	Racing	W	4-3	Silvera 2 [36] [47], Romeo [86] [91+]	25 000
Sept	2	Vélez	L	0-2		27 000
	9	Arsenal	W	4-2	Torres [14], Silvera [42]	17 000
	12	Lanús	L	3-4	Romeo 2 [46] [84], González [75]	13 000
	16	Tigre	W	2-1	Hirsig [20], Silvera [55]	16 000
	21	Rosario C	L	1-3	Silvera [23], Méndez [77], Hirsig [90]	30 000
	30	Arg Juniors	W	2-1	Silvera [4], Ferreyra [75p]	22 000
Oct	3	Boca	L	0-2		42 000
	6	Gimn'sia LP	D	1-1	Ortiz [30]	17 000
	21	Indep'iente	W	2-1	González [27p], Ortiz [66]	35 000
	4	Huracán	D	1-1	Bottinelli [3]	32 000
Nov	10	Colon	D	0-0		15 000
	23	Olimpo	L	0-1	Silvera [86]	10 000
Dec	1	Banfield	L	0-1		7 000
	9	Gimn'sia Jy	W	4-1	Romeo [21], Silvera [52], Ferreyra [75], Hirsig [77]	12000
Feb	8	Newell's	L	0-2		25 000
	16	San Martín	L	0-1		25 000
	24	River Plate	L	0-2		50 000
Mar	1	Estudiantes	W	3-1	González 2 [12] [63], Hirsig [68]	20 000
	7	Racing	W	1-0	Bergessio [72]	26 000
	21	Arsenal	W	1-0	Bergessio [84]	6 000
	29	Lanús	W	3-1	Silvera [2], D'Alessandro 2 [46] [82]	15 000
	6	Tigre	W	5-1	Menseguez 3 [3] [10] [47], Torres [40p], Bilos [61]	22 000
	12	Rosario C	W	3-1	Bergessio [8], Romeo [24], González [58p]	22 000
Apr	20	Arg Juniors	L	1-2	Torres [45p]	15 000
	23	Vélez	W	1-0	Bottinelli [14]	15 000
	27	Boca	W	1-0	Menseguez [2]	40 000
	4	Gimn'sia LP	W	2-1	D'Alessandro [61], Romeo [84]	20 000
May	11	Indep'iente	L	0-1		40 000
	18	Huracán	D	0-0		20 000
	25	Colon	W	2-1	Torres 2 [39] [49p]	20 000
	1	Olimpo	L	2-3	Silvera 2 [45] [67]	10 000
Jun	7	Banfield	W	3-2	Bergessio 3 [17] [24] [73]	14 000
	22	Gimn'sia Jy	D	2-2	Bergessio [9], Romeo [57]	11 000

SAN MARTIN DE SAN JUAN 2007–08

Month	Date	Opponent	Res	Score	Scorers	Att
Aug	4	Arg Juniors	W	1-0	Tonelotto [25]	7 000
	10	San Lorenzo	L	1-2	Tonelotto [70]	15 000
	19	Boca	L	0-1		30 000
	26	River	W	1-0	Brusco [76]	22 000
	29	Gimn'sia LP	L	1-2		12 000
Sept	2	Estudiantes	W	1-0	Tonelotto [58]	18 000
	8	Indep'iente	D	2-2	Herrera 2 [20] [44]	25 000
	12	Racing	L	0-2		20 000
	15	Huracán	L	1-2	Brusco [69p]	17 000
	22	Vélez	W	3-2	Brusco [70p], Tonelotto [93+], Herrera [95+]	16 000
	29	Colon	D	1-1	Brusco [68]	19 000
Oct	3	Arsenal	D	1-1	Roth [88]	15 000
	6	Olimpo	L	1-2	Tonelotto [19]	10 000
	19	Lanús	L	0-2		25 000
	2	Banfield	L	0-1		14 000
Nov	11	Tigre	L	0-3		17 000
	24	Gimn'sia Jy	W	3-2	Tonelotto [15], Frontini [35], Brusco [65]	10 000
	30	Rosario C	L	2-3	Tonelotto 2 [19] [85]	24 000
De	8	Newell's	L	0-1		10 000
Feb	9	Arg Juniors	W	2-0	Bravo [48], Pacheco [62]	7 000
	16	San Lorenzo	W	1-0	Brusco [90]	25 000
	24	Boca	L	0-2		18 000
Mar	8	Gimn'sia LP	D	1-1	Bravo [60]	9 000
	14	Estudiantes	L	2-3	Décima [20], Bravo [58]	20 000
	19	River	L	2-3	Brusco [26], Bravo [62]	35 000
	23	Indep'iente	W	2-0	Bravo [1], Tonelotto [35]	14 000
	28	Racing	W	2-0	Brusco [33p], Bravo [38]	0
	4	Huracán	W	2-0	Pacheco [3], Bravo [86]	14 000
Apr	13	Vélez	L	0-2		15 000
	20	Colon	L	1-2	Frontini [54]	14 000
	27	Arsenal	L	1-2	Bravo [24]	1 000
	3	Olimpo	L	0-1		12 000
May	10	Lanús	L	0-1		15 000
	16	Banfield	L	1-5	Tonelotto [89]	9 000
	23	Tigre	L	1-2	Recalde [11]	14 000
	31	Gimn'sia Jy	L	1-3	Frontini [32]	7 000
Jun	7	Rosario C	D	0-0		10 000
	21	Newell's	L	0-1		16 000

TIGRE 2007–08

Month	Date	Opponent	Res	Score	Scorers	Att
Aug	4	Gimn'sia LP	W	1-0	Galmarini [63]	16 000
	12	Indep'iente	L	0-3		26 000
	18	Huracán	D	0-0		30 000
	24	Colon	L	0-2		20 000
	28	Olimpo	W	1-0	Lazzaro [81]	10 000
	31	Banfield	W	1-0	Lazzaro [16]	22 000
Sept	7	Gimn'sia Jy	W	2-0	Ayala [45], Lazzaro [67]	12 000
	11	Newell's	D	2-2	Lazzaro 2 [3] [82]	20 000
	16	San Lorenzo	L	1-2	Lazzaro [64p]	16 000
	23	River Plate	W	4-1	Martínez [10], Giménez [60], Ayala 2 [62] [84]	22 000
	28	Estudiantes	D	2-2	Ayala [21], Blengio [26]	24 000
Oct	3	Racing	W	3-2	Ayala [60], Lazzaro [61], Suárez [89]	18 000
	3	Vélez	D	1-1	Ereros [19]	16 000
	19	Arsenal	W	2-0	Morel [54], Rusculleda [71]	17 000
	4	Lanús	L	1-2	Lazzaro [33]	40 000
Nov	11	San Martín	W	3-0	Martínez [10], Ayala 2 [15] [49]	17 000
	23	Rosario C	W	2-1	Morel [1], Lazzaro [93+]	16 000
	28	Boca	W	2-1	Lazzaro [71], Morel [76]	30 000
De	2	Arg Juniors	L	0-1		19 000
Feb	9	Gimn'sia Jy	W	2-1	Morel [83], Suárez [87]	20 000
	16	Indep'iente	L	1-4	Ayala [70]	22 000
	23	Huracán	L	0-1	Castaño [70]	18 000
Mar	1	Colon	W	2-1	Martínez [39], Leyes [80]	15 000
	8	Olimpo	W	2-1	Giménez [35], Suárez [89]	15 000
	15	Banfield	D	3-3	Morero [6], Gimén [46], Martínez [80]	15 000
	21	Gimn'sia Jy	W	2-0	Martínez [39], Giménez [85]	10 000
	30	Newell's	L	1-5	Rusculleda [33]	28 000
	6	San Lorenzo	L	1-5	Giménez [21]	22 000
Apr	13	River Plate	L	0-1		20 000
	20	Estudiantes	D	1-1	Galmarini [31]	17 000
	26	Racing	D	0-0		20 000
	4	Vélez	L	0-2		15 000
May	9	Arsenal	L	0-1		4 000
	18	Lanús	L	1-4	Ereros [40]	15 000
	23	San Martín	W	2-1	Pratto [43], Castaño [90]	14 000
	30	Rosario C	W	2-1	Leyes [37], Martínez [50]	39 000
Jun	7	Arg Juniors	W	1-0	Galmarini [12]	16 000
	22	Boca	L	2-6	Martínez 2 [28] [55]	40 000

VELEZ SARSFIELD 2007–08

Month	Date	Opponent	Res	Score	Scorers	Att
Aug	3	Colon	W	1-0	Escudero [51]	13 000
	11	Olimpo	W	3-0	Escudero [7], Zapata [45], Sena [84]	14 000
	18	Banfield	L	0-1		13 000
	26	Gimn'sia Jy	W	4-2	Uglessich [25], Sena 2 [47] [88], Balvorín [81]	13 000
	29	Newell's	L	0-2		9 000
Sept	2	San Lorenzo	W	2-0	Zapata [69], Silva [93+]	27 000
	9	River Plate	L	0-5		35 000
	12	Estudiantes	W	1-0	Balvorín [6]	15 000
	15	Racing	L	0-1		15 000
	22	San Martín	L	2-3	Silva [65], Balvorín [70p]	16 000
	29	Arsenal	D	0-0		13 000
Oct	3	Lanús	L	1-2	Coria [50]	7 000
	6	Tigre	D	1-1	Zapata [45]	16 000
	20	Rosario C	W	2-0	Lima [36], Ríos [94+]	25 000
	5	Arg Juniors	W	3-0	Escudero [22], Ríos [56], Silva [65]	45 000
Nov	1	Boca	L	0-4		45 000
	24	Gimn'sia LP	W	3-1	Lima [25], Cabral [50], Balvorín [91+]	7 000
	2	Indep'iente	D	1-1	Balvorín [67]	19 000
Dec	9	Huracán	L	1-2	Pellerano [74]	15 000
Feb	9	Colon	W	4-3	Balvorín 2 [17] [54], Silva [22], Uglessich [28]	14 000
	16	Olimpo	W	2-0	Balvorín [40], Silva [59]	13 000
	23	Banfield	W	3-0	Sena [44], Silva [49], Balvorín [76]	18 000
Mar	1	Gimn'sia Jy	D	0-0		9 000
	16	Newell's	W	1-0	Ríos [15]	15 000
	23	River Plate	L	0-2		28 000
	29	Estudiantes	L	0-1		27 000
	4	Racing	D	1-1	Coria [74]	15 000
	13	San Martín	W	2-0	Silva 2 [19] [51]	15 000
Apr	20	Arsenal	D	0-0		8 000
	23	San Lorenzo	L	0-1		15 000
	26	Lanús	W	3-2	Ríos [14], Silva [43], Lima [90]	10 000
	4	Tigre	W	2-0	Escudero [65], Silva [80]	15 000
May	10	Rosario C	W	2-1	Cristaldo [61], Escudero [83]	25 000
	17	Arg Juniors	L	0-1		18 000
	25	Boca	D	1-1	Escudero [55]	30 000
	1	Gimn'sia LP	L	1-2	Ponce [4]	12 000
Jun	8	Indep'iente	D	0-0		16 000
	21	Huracán	W	2-1	Cristaldo [2], Ocampo [83]	13 000

ARM – ARMENIA

NATIONAL TEAM RECORD
JULY 10TH 2006 TO JULY 12TH 2010

PL	W	D	L	F	A	%
22	6	7	9	13	22	43.2

FIFA/COCA-COLA WORLD RANKING

1993	1994	1995	1996	1997	1998	1999	2000	2001	2002	2003	2004	2005	2006	2007		High	
-	141	113	106	105	100	85	90	95	107	113	119	108	123	93		79	07/07

2007–2008												Low	
08/07	09/07	10/07	11/07	12/07	01/08	02/08	03/08	04/08	05/08	06/08	07/08	159	07/94
81	87	82	90	93	85	81	83	78	80	78	96		

For a club that was a major power in Soviet times, Ararat Yerevan's ten years without a trophy has been something of a surprise. Their heyday may well have been in the 1970s - they won the double in 1973 along with a further Soviet Cup in 1975 - but unlike other provincial Soviet teams such as Georgia's Dinamo Tbilisi, Ararat have been unable to dominate in their own league since independence, with just one championship to their name. The last of their four Armenian Cup triumphs had been in 1997 but on a rainy Friday night in May 2008, Ararat beat Banants 2-1 in the Cup Final, with a late winner from their naturalised Brazilian striker Marcos Pizelli to secure their first

INTERNATIONAL HONOURS
None

silverware in a decade. There was no change in the status quo in the League, however, with Pyunik winning the 2007 championship - their seventh in-a-row - a testament to the excellent youth set-up which has kept the club at the forefront of football in the country. The national team's Euro 2008 qualifying campaign ended in disappointing fashion with defeat at home to Kazakhstan. Having beaten Poland and held Portugal on home soil, the defeat was all the more surprising but fans will take some solace from the fact that the team finished above fierce rivals Azerbaijan in the standings - although both matches between the two were cancelled by UEFA due to security concerns.

THE FIFA BIG COUNT OF 2006

	Male	Female		Total
Number of players	136 212	15 141	Referees and Assistant Referees	134
Professionals	656		Admin, Coaches, Technical, Medical	4 810
Amateurs 18+	37 228		Number of clubs	80
Youth under 18	2 915		Number of teams	178
Unregistered	37 900		Clubs with women's teams	3
Total players	151 353		Players as % of population	5.09%

Football Federation of Armenia (FFA)
Khanjyan str. 27, Yerevan 375 010, Armenia
Tel +374 1 568 883   Fax +374 1 539 517
ffarm@arminco.com   www.ffa.am
President: HAYRAPETYAN Ruben   General Secretary: MINASYAN Armen
Vice-President: TBD   Treasurer: PAPIKYAN Gevorg   Media Officer: MATEVOSYAN Georgi
Men's Coach: POULSEN Jan   Women's Coach: ADAMYAN Samvel
FFA formed: 1992   UEFA: 1993   FIFA: 1992
Red shirts with white trimmings, Blue shorts, Orange socks or White shirts with blue trimmings, Blue shorts, White socks

RECENT INTERNATIONALS PLAYED BY ARMENIA

2004	Opponents	Score		Venue	Comp	Scorers	Att	Referee
18-08	FYR Macedonia	L	0-3	Skopje	WCq		4 375	Guenov BUL
8-09	Finland	L	0-2	Yerevan	WCq		2 864	Malzinskas LTU
9-10	Finland	L	1-3	Tampere	WCq	Shahgeldyan [32]	7 894	Fandel GER
13-10	Czech Republic	L	0-3	Yerevan	WCq		3 205	Granat POL
17-11	Romania	D	1-1	Yerevan	WCq	Dokhoyan [62]	1 403	De Bleeckere BEL
2005								
18-03	Kuwait	L	1-3	Al Ain	Fr	Mkhitaryan [87p]		Attard MLT
26-03	Andorra	W	2-1	Yerevan	WCq	Ara Hakobyan [30], Khachatryan.R [73]	2 100	Attard MLT
30-03	Netherlands	L	0-2	Eindhoven	WCq		35 000	Trefoloni ITA
4-06	FYR Macedonia	L	1-2	Yerevan	WCq	Manucharyan [55]	2 870	Mikulski POL
8-06	Romania	L	0-3	Constanta	WCq		5 146	Briakos GRE
17-08	Jordan	D	0-0	Amman	Fr			
3-09	Netherlands	L	0-1	Yerevan	WCq		1 747	Dougal SCO
7-09	Czech Republic	L	1-4	Olomouc	WCq	Ara Hakobyan [85]	12 015	Hansson SWE
12-10	Andorra	W	3-0	Andorra la Vella	WCq	OG [40], Aram Hakobyan [52], Ara Hakobyan [62]	430	Stoks IRL
2006								
28-02	Romania	L	0-2	Nicosia	Fr		1 000	Tsacheilidis GRE
1-03	Cyprus	L	0-2	Limassol	Fr			
6-09	Belgium	L	0-1	Yerevan	ECq		4 122	Lehner AUT
7-10	Finland	D	0-0	Yerevan	ECq		2 800	Skomina SVN
11-10	Serbia	L	0-3	Belgrade	ECq		10 987	Kasnaferis GRE
15-11	Finland	L	0-1	Lahti	ECq		9 445	Thomson SCO
2007								
14-01	Panama	D	1-1	Monterey Park	Fr	Ara Hakopyan [p]		
7-02	Andorra	D	0-0	Andorra la Vella	Fr			
28-03	Poland	L	0-1	Kielce	ECq		13 450	Undiano ESP
2-06	Kazakhstan	W	2-1	Almaty	ECq	Arzumanyan [31], Hovsepyan [39p]	17 100	Kralovec CZE
6-06	Poland	W	1-0	Yerevan	ECq	Mkhitaryan [66]	9 800	Balaj ROU
22-08	Portugal	D	1-1	Yerevan	ECq	Arzumanyan [11]	14 935	Larsen DEN
8-09	Cyprus	L	1-3	Larnaca	Fr	Arzumanyan [35]		Trattos CYP
12-09	Malta	W	1-0	Ta'Qali	Fr	Voskanyan [29]		Richmond SCO
13-10	Serbia	D	0-0	Yerevan	ECq		7 150	Johannesson SWE
17-10	Belgium	L	0-3	Brussels	ECq		14 812	Valgeirsson ISL
17-11	Portugal	L	0-1	Leiria	ECq		22 048	Riley ENG
21-11	Kazakhstan	L	0-1	Yerevan	ECq		3 100	Fautrel FRA
2008								
2-02	Malta	W	1-0	Ta'Qali	Fr	Ara Hakopyan [69]		Porisson ISL
4-02	Belarus	W	2-1	Ta'Qali	Fr	Arakelyan [18], Ara Hakopyan [76]		Zammit MLT
6-02	Iceland	L	0-2	Ta'Qali	Fr			Attard MLT
26-03	Kazakhstan	W	1-0	Pernis	Fr	Manucharyan [62]		Vink NED
28-05	Moldova	D	2-2	Tiraspol	Fr	Pizzelli [25], Pachajyan [54]		Ishchenko UKR
1-06	Greece	D	0-0	Offenbach/Main	Fr			

Fr = Friendly match • EC = UEFA EURO 2008 • WC = FIFA World Cup • q = qualifier

ARMENIA NATIONAL TEAM RECORDS AND RECORD SEQUENCES

Records			Sequence records					
Victory	3-0	ALB 1997, AND x2	Wins	2	2004, 2007, 2008	Clean sheets	2	2004, 2007
Defeat	0-7	CHI 1997, GEO 1997	Defeats	5	1995-1996	Goals scored	6	1999-2000
Player Caps	97	Sargis Hovsepyan	Undefeated	3	Four times	Without goal	7	1999
Player Goals	11	Arthur Petrosyan	Without win	10	1996-1997	Goals against	13	1994-1996

REPUBLIC OF ARMENIA; HAYASTANI HANRAPETUT'YUN

Capital	Yerevan	Language	Armenian	Independence	1991
Population	2 976 372	Area km²	29 800	Density 100 per km²	% in cities 69
GDP per cap	$3 500	Dailling code	+374	Internet .am	GMT + / - +4

MEDALS TABLE

		Overall			League			Cup			Europe			City	Stadium	Cap'ty	DoF
		G	S	B	G	S	B	G	S	B	G	S	B				
1	Pyunik Yerevan	13	4		10	1		3	3					Yerevan	Hanrapetakan (Republican)	14 968	1992
2	Ararat Yerevan	6	5	1	1	3	1	5	2					Yerevan	Razdan	48 250	1935
3	Mika Ashtarak	5	2	2		2	2	5						Ashtarak	Vardanank	12 000	1985
4	Shirak Gyumri	3	8	2	3	5	2		3					Gyumri	City Stadium	7 000	1958
5	Tsement Yerevan	3		1	1		1	2						Yerevan			
6	Banants Yerevan	2	6	3		3	3	2	3					Yerevan	Banants	10 000	1992
7	FK Yerevan	1	1	3	1		3		1					Yerevan			1995
8	Araks Ararat	1			1									Ararat			
9	Zvartnots Yerevan		3			1			2					Yerevan			
10	Kotayk Abovyan		2	2			2		2					Abovyan	Kotayk	5 500	1955
11	Kilikia Yerevan		1						1					Yerevan	Razdan	48 250	1992
12	Homenmen Yerevan			1	1									Yerevan			
	Spartak Yerevan			1	1									Yerevan			
14	Gandzasar													Kapan	Lernagorts	3 500	2004
	Lernayin Artsakh													Yerevan	Nayri	6 800	
	Kilikia													Yerevan	Razdan	48 250	
	Ulysses													Yerevan	Hanrapetakan (Republican)	15 000	2004

ARMENIAN CLUBS IN THE SOVIET UNION

		Overall			League			Cup			Europe						
8	Ararat Yerevan	3	4		1	2		2	2								

RECENT LEAGUE AND CUP RECORD

	Championship							Cup		
Year	Champions	Pts	Runners-up	Pts	Third	Pts		Winners	Score	Runners-up
1998	Tsement Ararat	64	Shirak Gyumri	61	FK Yerevan	48		Tsement Ararat	3-1	FK Yerevan
1999	Shirak Gyumri	73	Ararat Yerevan	72	Tsement Ararat	71		Tsement Ararat	3-2	Shirak Yerevan
2000	Araks Ararat	61	Ararat Yerevan	59	Shirak Gyumri	58		Mika Ashtarak	2-1	Zvarnots Yerevan
2001	Pyunik Yerevan	53	Zvarnots Yerevan	48	Spartak Yerevan	48		Mika Ashtarak	1-1 4-3p	Ararat Yerevan
2002	Pyunik Yerevan	59	Shirak Gyumri	51	Banants Yerevan	50		Pyunik Yerevan	2-0	Zvarnots Yerevan
2003	Pyunik Yerevan	74	Banants Yerevan	66	Shirak Gyumri	53		Mika Ashtarak	1-0	Banants Yerevan
2004	Pyunik Yerevan	71	Mika Ashtarak	55	Banants Yerevan	43		Pyunik Yerevan	0-0 6-5p	Banants Yerevan
2005	Pyunik Yerevan	39	Mika Ashtarak	35	Banants Yerevan	33		Mika Ashtarak	2-0	Kilikia Yerevan
2006	Pyunik Yerevan	57	Banants Yerevan	57	Mika Ashtarak	57		Mika Ashtarak	1-0	Pyunik Yerevan
2007	Pyunik Yerevan	57	Banants Yerevan	52	Mika Ashtarak	50		Banants Yerevan	3-1	Ararat Yerevan
2008								Ararat Yerevan	2-1	Banants Yerevan

ARMENIA 2007

PREMIER LEAGUE

	Pl	W	D	L	F	A	Pts	Pyunik	Banants	Mika	Ararat	Gandzasar	Shirak	Ulysses	Kilikia
Pyunik Yerevan †	28	18	3	7	58	22	57		5-1 0-3	1-0 1-0	3-4 4-1	1-0 1-2	1-2 0-2	5-0 3-0	2-0 2-0
Banants Yerevan ‡	28	16	4	8	56	26	52	1-2 2-1		1-1 0-1	1-0 2-0	2-3 3-0	3-0 2-0	2-0 1-2	3-0 2-0
Mika Ashtarak ‡	28	14	8	6	42	24	50	1-2 1-0	1-1 0-2		2-2 4-1	3-2 1-0	3-1 1-1	7-0 1-1	2-1 3-1
Ararat Yerevan	28	15	4	9	49	42	49	0-0 0-6	2-1 0-6	2-0 1-2		1-0 5-4	1-0 4-0	2-0 0-0	5-0 2-1
Gandzasar Kapan	28	11	6	11	35	31	39	0-1 0-0	0-1 3-2	0-2 1-1	1-0 2-1		0-0 4-2	0-0 1-2	2-0 4-0
Shirak Gyumri	28	9	7	12	27	37	34	0-0 1-5	0-0 1-1	1-0 0-0	0-1 0-2	0-0 2-1		3-1 0-1	0-1 2-1
Ulysses Yerevan	28	8	6	14	21	46	30	1-2 0-3	2-3 2-1	0-1 0-0	0-3 2-2	0-2 0-1	0-2 2-0		2-0 1-0
Kilikia Yerevan	28	1	2	25	10	70	5	0-5 0-2	0-3 0-6	1-2 0-2	0-4 1-3	0-0 0-2	1-4 1-3	0-0 1-2	

14/04/2007 - 10/11/2007 • † Qualified for the UEFA Champions League • ‡ Qualified for the UEFA Cup
Kilikia were spared relegation when it was decided to use the second division as a league for reserve teams

ARMENIA 2007
SECOND DIVISION

	Pl	W	D	L	F	A	Pts
Pyunik-2 Yerevan	21	14	2	5	54	19	44
Mika-2 Ashtarak	21	10	9	2	42	23	39
Ararat-2 Yerevan	21	9	7	5	43	26	34
Dinamo Yerevan	21	10	3	8	47	38	33
Banants-2 Yerevan	21	8	4	9	35	38	28
Gandzasar-2 Kapan	21	8	4	9	26	37	28
Shirak-2 Gyumri	21	3	10	8	23	44	19
Patani U–17	21	2	1	18	19	64	7
Bentonit Ijevan				Withdrew after three rounds			

25/04/2007 - 6/10/2007

FFA CUP 2008

First round		Quarter–finals		Semi–finals		Final	
Ararat Yerevan	Bye						
		Ararat Yerevan *	0 2				
Banants-2 Yerevan	1 1	Ulysses Yerevan	1 0				
Ulysses Yerevan *	4 2			Ararat Yerevan	2 3		
Gandzasar Kapan *	3 5			Pyunik Yerevan *	1 0		
Pyunik-2 Yerevan	0 0	Gandzasar Kapan	0 0 1p				
Patani Yerevan	2 0	Pyunik Yerevan *	0 0 4p				
Pyunik Yerevan *	11 4					Ararat Yerevan	2
Mika Ashtarak *	7 4					Banants Yerevan	1
Ararat-2 Yerevan	0 0	Mika Ashtarak *	1 2				
Mika-2 Ashtarak	0 2	Kilikia Yerevan	0 1				
Kilikia Yerevan *	2 3			Mika Ashtarak	1 0		
Shirak Gyumri *	3 0			Banants Yerevan *	3 2		
Shengavit Yerevan	1 1	Shirak Gyumri *	0 1 5p				
		Banants Yerevan	1 0 6p				
Banants Yerevan	Bye						

* Home team in the first leg • ‡ Qualified for the UEFA Cup

CUP FINAL
Arnar, Ijevan
9-05-2008, Att: 2000, Ref: Chagharian

Scorers - Vahagn Minasian [75], Marcos Pizelli [88] for Ararat;
Marko Markov [36] for Banants

ARU – ARUBA

NATIONAL TEAM RECORD
JULY 10TH 2006 TO JULY 12TH 2010

PL	W	D	L	F	A	%
2	0	0	2	0	4	0

FIFA/COCA-COLA WORLD RANKING

1993	1994	1995	1996	1997	1998	1999	2000	2001	2002	2003	2004	2005	2006	2007
165	173	171	181	177	180	191	184	185	189	195	198	200	198	201

High	
160	12/92

2007–2008											
08/07	09/07	10/07	11/07	12/07	01/08	02/08	03/08	04/08	05/08	06/08	07/08
199	200	200	201	201	201	202	202	202	200	199	199

Low	
202	02/08

The national team of Aruba may well find itself at the very bottom of the FIFA/Coca-Cola World Ranking, but sometimes statistics can be misleading and that is surely the case in Aruba. Football on this small Caribbean island may not be the number one sport but it is well organised at club level. The lack of national team matches, and a failure to win any of those played since 2000, is responsible for the poor ranking but Aruba's Argentine coach Marcelo Munoz hopes to change that soon. Munoz, who got the job by researching on the internet, had hoped to get through at least one round of FIFA World Cup qualifying where the prize of a tie against Cuba was on offer. "For us to

INTERNATIONAL HONOURS
None

reach that match would be like a World Cup Final" he stated, but first Aruba had to overcome Antigua and Barbuda. That they failed to do, however, losing the first leg 3-0 at home in Oranjestad and the return 1-0 in St John's. All of the team Munoz fielded against Antigua came from Aruba's Division di Honor, which in the 2007-08 season saw the highest number of aggregate spectators and the fourth different winner in as many seasons. After two group stages, Racing Club beat Britannia in the final to win the title for the first time since 2002. Both Racing and Nacional took part in the 2007 Caribbean Cup but both were eliminated at the first stage.

THE FIFA BIG COUNT OF 2006

	Male	Female		Total
Number of players	9 900	800	Referees and Assistant Referees	26
Professionals	0		Admin, Coaches, Technical, Medical	100
Amateurs 18+	2 400		Number of clubs	60
Youth under 18	3 500		Number of teams	140
Unregistered	1 000		Clubs with women's teams	2
Total players	10 700		Players as % of population	14.88%

Arubaanse Voetbal Bond (AVB)
Avenida Milio J. Croes Z/N, PO Box 376, Oranjestad, Aruba
Tel +297 5829550   Fax +297 5829550
avbaruba@setarnet.aw   www.avbaruba.aw
President: KELLY Rufo   General Secretary: LACLE Egbert
Vice-President: FARO Bernardo   Treasurer: ENGELBRECHT Gregory   Media Officer: CROES Adrian
Men's Coach: MUNOZ Marcelo   Women's Coach: ENGELBRECHT Gregory
AVB formed: 1932   CONCACAF: 1961   FIFA: 1988
Yellow shirts, Blue shorts, Yellow and Blue socks

RECENT INTERNATIONALS PLAYED BY ARUBA

2004	Opponents	Score		Venue	Comp	Scorers	Att	Referee
28-01	Netherlands Antilles	L	1-6	Willemstad	Fr			
28-02	Surinam	L	1-2	Oranjestad	WCq	Escalona.M 89	2 108	Moreno PAN
27-03	Surinam	L	1-8	Paramaribo	WCq	Escalona.M 24	4 000	Prendergast JAM
2005								
No international matches played in 2005								
2006								
No international matches played in 2006								
2007								
No international matches played in 2007								
2008								
6-02	Antigua and Barbuda	L	0-3	Oranjestad	WCq		250	Delgado CUB
26-03	Antigua and Barbuda	L	0-1	St John's	WCq		1 000	Campbell JAM

Fr = Friendly match • CC = Digicel Caribbean Cup • WCq = FIFA World Cup • q = qualifier

ARUBA NATIONAL TEAM RECORDS AND RECORD SEQUENCES

Records			Sequence records					
Victory	4-1	CUB 1953	Wins	1		Clean sheets	1	
Defeat	1-8	SUR 2004	Defeats	12	2000-2008	Goals scored	9	1944-1953
Player Caps	n/a		Undefeated	3	1944-1953	Without goal	5	1991-1992
Player Goals	n/a		Without win	12	1953-1996	Goals against	24	1934-1997

ARUBA 2007-08 DIVISION DI HONOR

	Pl	W	D	L	F	A	Pts
Britannia †	18	11	5	2	44	12	38
La Fama †	18	11	4	3	47	14	37
Racing Club Aruba †	18	9	6	3	68	23	33
Nacional †	18	10	3	5	33	16	33
Dakota	18	9	3	6	25	23	30
Jong Aruba	18	8	1	9	30	35	25
Estrella	18	6	6	6	33	24	24
Riverplate	18	5	6	7	18	27	21
Independiente Caravel	18	2	1	15	13	71	7
Estudiantes	18	1	1	16	17	83	4

28/09/2007 - 27/04/2008 • † Qualified for the semi-finals

SECOND STAGE

	Pl	W	D	L	F	A	Pts
Britannia †	6	4	1	1	10	4	13
Racing Club Aruba †	6	3	2	1	7	4	11
Nacional	6	3	0	3	5	5	9
La Fama	6	0	1	5	3	12	1

8/05/2008 - 1/06/2008 • † Qualified for the final

RECENT LEAGUE AND CUP RECORD

	Championship		
Year	Champions	Score	Runners-up
1998	Estrella	2-1	Dakota
1999	Estrella	2-1	Nacional
2000	Nacional	1-1 1-1 1-0	Dakota
2001	Nacional	3-1 1-0	Racing Club
2002	Racing Club	†	Nacional
2003	Nacional	1-0 2-1	Estrella
2004	No tournament due to season readjustment		
2005	Britannia	2-1 1-0	Racing Club
2006	Estrella	1-0 1-4 2-1	Britannia
2007	Nacional	1-0 0-4 1-0	Racing Club
2008	Racing Club	2-1 2-1	Britannia

† Played on a league basis

FINAL
1st leg. Guillermo Trinidad, Oranjestad, 7-06-2008

Racing Club Aruba 2-1 Britannia

Scorers - Jean Luc Bergen 2 18 47; Jermeen Roberts 32

FINAL
2nd leg. Guillermo Trinidad, Oranjestad, 7-06-2008

Britannia 1-2 **Racing Club Aruba**

Scorers - Jonathan Lake 36; Jean Luc Bergen 55, Juan Santo 71

ARUBA COUNTRY INFORMATION

Capital	Oranjestad	Independence	Part of the Netherlands with	GDP per Capita	$28 000
Population	71 218	Status	autonomy in internal affairs	GNP Ranking	n/a
Area km²	193	Language	Dutch	Dialling code	+297
Population density	369 per km²	Literacy rate	97%	Internet code	.aw
% in urban areas	n/a	Main religion	Christian 90%	GMT +/-	-5
Towns/Cities ('000)	Oranjestad 29; Sint Nicolaas 17; Druif; Santa Cruz; Barcadera;				
Neighbours (km)	Caribbean Sea 68				
Main stadia	Guillermo Trinidad – Oranjestad 5 500				

ASA – AMERICAN SAMOA

NATIONAL TEAM RECORD
JULY 10TH 2006 TO JULY 12TH 2010

PL	W	D	L	F	A	%
4	0	0	4	1	38	0

FIFA/COCA-COLA WORLD RANKING

1993	1994	1995	1996	1997	1998	1999	2000	2001	2002	2003	2004	2005	2006	2007		High	
-	-	-	-	-	193	199	203	201	201	202	204	205	198	201		**192**	10/98

	2007–2008												Low	
08/07	09/07	10/07	11/07	12/07	01/08	02/08	03/08	04/08	05/08	06/08	07/08		**205**	12/05
199	200	200	201	201	201	202	202	202	200	199	199			

In the wake of the national team's 15-0 defeat at the hands of Vanuatu in a 2010 FIFA World Cup qualifier, it might sound strange to say that football is making good progress in American Samoa, but in many respects this does indeed represent progress. It may be some time before the national team wins its first match since 1983 - the year they beat Wallis and Fotuna in what is now regarded as an unofficial international - but with the league reorganised and back in action after a three year break, the game is heading in the right direction. On December 8, 2007, the newly constructed Pago Park staged its first Championship final as Konica Football Club took on Peace Brothers.

INTERNATIONAL HONOURS
None

Tafuna Jets, winners of a seven-a-side tournament in 2006, had topped the eight team group B in the first round which was played over two months. In the semi-finals, however, they lost to Peace brothers who in turn were beaten 4-2 by Konica in the final. The standard among the 16-team league was variable - Aua Old School shipped 61 goals in just seven games - but the fact that the league was played and was well organised was cause for celebration. In time the national teams at all levels are likely to benefit from the new facilities at Pago Park because when you are the lowest ranked nation in the world, the only way is up.

THE FIFA BIG COUNT OF 2006

	Male	Female		Total
Number of players	2 406	842	Referees and Assistant Referees	102
Professionals	0		Admin, Coaches, Technical, Medical	135
Amateurs 18+	810		Number of clubs	27
Youth under 18	1 000		Number of teams	33
Unregistered	410		Clubs with women's teams	6
Total players	3 248		Players as % of population	5.62%

Football Federation American Samoa (FFAS)
Pago Park, PO Box 999413, Pago Pago 96799, American Samoa
Tel +684 6447104   Fax +689 6447102
ffas@blueskynet.as   www.ffas.as
President: GODINET Alex   General Secretary: TAUMUA Tavita
Vice-President: HERRERA Sandra   Treasurer: UHRLE Mina   Media Officer: None
Men's Coach: BRAND David   Women's Coach: LUI Tunoa
ASFA formed: 1984   OFC: 1994   FIFA: 1998
Navy blue shirts, White shorts, Red socks

RECENT INTERNATIONALS PLAYED BY AMERICAN SAMOA

2004	Opponents	Score	Venue	Comp	Scorers	Att	Referee
10-05	Samoa	L 0-4	Apia	WCq		500	Afu SOL
12-05	Vanuatu	L 1-9	Apia	WCq	Natia 39	400	Fox NZL
15-05	Fiji	L 0-11	Apia	WCq		300	Fox NZL
17-05	Papua New Guinea	L 0-10	Apia	WCq		150	Afu SOL
2005							
No international matches played in 2005							
2006							
No international matches played in 2006							
2007							
25-08	Solomon Islands	L 1-12	Apia	WCq	Ott 55p	300	Sosongan PNG
27-08	Samoa	L 0-7	Apia	WCq		2 800	Minan PNG
29-08	Vanuatu	L 0-15	Apia	WCq		200	Hester NZL
1-09	Tonga	L 0-4	Apia	WCq		200	Minan PNG
2008							
No international matches played in 2008 before August							

WC = FIFA World Cup • q = qualifier

AMERICAN SAMOA NATIONAL TEAM RECORDS AND RECORD SEQUENCES

Records				Sequence records			
Victory	3-0 Wallis/Futuna 1983	Wins	1		Clean sheets	1	
Defeat	0-31 AUS 2001	Defeats	32	1983-	Goals scored	3	1983, 1994
Player Caps	n/a	Undefeated	1		Without goal	5	2001-2002
Player Goals	n/a	Without win	32	1983-	Goals against	32	1983-

AMERICAN SAMOA CHAMPIONSHIP 2007

First Round

Pool 1 — Pts
Konica FC 19
Peace Brothers 16
FC SKBC 16
Fagasa CCCAS Youth 13
Manuula Heat 7
Tafuna Jets 2 4
Pago Youth 4
Flame on 1

Pool 2 — Pts
Tafuna Jets 17
Pago Eagles 16
Pansa Mens 13
Utulei Youth 13
Konica Airbase 13
Ilaoa & Toomata 6
Autali Misasa Katolik 3
Aua Old School 0

Semi–finals
Konica FC 4
Pago Eagles 2

Tafuna Jets 0
Peace Brothers 1

Final
Konica FC 4
Peace Brothers 2

RECENT LEAGUE RECORD
Year	Champions
1996	No tournament held
1997	Fat Boys
1998	No tournament held
1999	Konica Machine
2000	PanSa & Wild Wild West
2001	PanSa
2002	PanSa
2003	No tournament held
2004	PanSa
2005	No tournament held
2006	No tournament held
2007	No tournament held
2008	Konica FC

AMERICAN SAMOA COUNTRY INFORMATION

Capital	Pago Pago	Independence	Unincorporated territory of the USA	GDP per Capita	$8 000
Population	57 902	Status		GNP Ranking	n/a
Area km²	199	Language	Samoan	Dialling code	+684
Population density	291 per km²	Literacy rate	97%	Internet code	.as
% in urban areas	n/a	Main religion	Christian	GMT +/–	-10
Towns/Cities ('000)	Tafuna 11; Nu'uuli 5; Pago Pago 4; Leone 4; Faleniu 3; Ili'ili 3				
Neighbours (km)	South Pacific Ocean 116				
Main stadia	Pago Park – Pago Pago				

ATG – ANTIGUA AND BARBUDA

NATIONAL TEAM RECORD
JULY 10TH 2006 TO JULY 12TH 2010

PL	W	D	L	F	A	%
19	9	2	8	32	35	52.6

FIFA/COCA-COLA WORLD RANKING

1993	1994	1995	1996	1997	1998	1999	2000	2001	2002	2003	2004	2005	2006	2007	High	
117	136	137	145	159	137	147	144	157	155	170	153	154	132	151	**109**	10/06

2007–2008												Low	
08/07	09/07	10/07	11/07	12/07	01/08	02/08	03/08	04/08	05/08	06/08	07/08	**170**	01/04
131	131	145	156	151	156	139	140	127	127	124	135		

Antigua may be a cricket stronghold, but football continued to make good progress on and off the field with a crowd of 4,500 turning up at the Sir Vivian Richards Cricket Stadium in St Johns to watch the national team play Cuba in a 2010 FIFA World Cup qualifier. The match was lost but the fans were treated to a great game in which Antigua twice twice took the lead only to lose 4-3, thanks to a late Cuban goal. The return in Havana was also lost, ending Antiguan hopes in the World Cup, but the overall record in the season was positive with five wins in nine games, including a record run of four straight wins. Although the team has a couple of English based pros in

INTERNATIONAL HONOURS
None

Rotherham's Marc Joseph and Millwall's Justin Cochrane, the majority of the side is based in Antigua where the league, although not one of the strongest in the Caribbean, is well organised and provides a good basis for the sport. Antiguan clubs are regular participants in the CFU Club Championship and in 2007 Bassa qualified for the quarter-finals by coming second in their first round group - above Cuba's Pinar del Rio. They were then knocked-out by Trinidad's Joe Public, a defeat which cost them a chance of a place in the newly launched CONCACAF Champions League for the 2008-09 season.

THE FIFA BIG COUNT OF 2006

	Male	Female		Total
Number of players	6 000	600	Referees and Assistant Referees	33
Professionals	0		Admin, Coaches, Technical, Medical	100
Amateurs 18+	1 100		Number of clubs	20
Youth under 18	1 100		Number of teams	60
Unregistered	800		Clubs with women's teams	1
Total players	6 600		Players as % of population	9.55%

Antigua and Barbuda Football Association (ABFA)

Suite 19, Vendors Mall, PO Box 773, St John's, Antigua
Tel +1 268 5626012   Fax +1 268 5626016
abfa@candw.ag   www.antiguafootball.org
President: RICHARDS Mervyn   General Secretary: DERRICK Gordon
Vice-President: GATESWORTH James   Treasurer: GARDNER Dwight   Media Officer: None
Men's Coach: EDWARDS Derrick   Women's Coach: ROWAN Benjamin
ABFA formed: 1928   CONCACAF: 1980   FIFA: 1970
Red shirts with black, yellow and white trimmings, Black shorts, Black socks

RECENT INTERNATIONALS PLAYED BY ANTIGUA AND BARBUDA

2006	Opponents	Score		Venue	Comp	Scorers	Att	Referee
24-02	Guyana	L	1-2	Linden	Fr	Skepples [77]		James GUY
26-02	Guyana	L	1-4	Georgetown	Fr	Julian [76]		Lancaster GUY
27-08	St Vincent/Grenadines	W	1-0	St John's	Fr	Thomas.T [18]		Willett ATG
3-09	Dominica	W	1-0	St John's	Fr	Byers.P [50]		Willett ATG
20-09	Anguilla	W	5-3	St John's	CCq	Byers.P 3 [8p 16 71], Thomas.T [29], Thomas.J [90]	300	Wijngaarde SUR
22-09	Barbados	L	1-3	St John's	CCq	Byers.P [16]	2 500	Frederick VIR
24-09	St Kitts and Nevis	W	2-0	St John's	CCq	Gregory [77]	2 800	Wijngaarde SUR
3-11	Grenada	D	1-1	Kingstown	Fr	Simon.T		
5-11	St Vincent/Grenadines	D	2-2	Kingstown	Fr	Byers.P 2 [8 21p]		
24-11	Guyana	L	0-6	Georgetown	CCq		5 000	
26-11	Dominican Republic	L	0-2	Georgetown	CCq			
28-11	Guadeloupe	L	1-3	Georgetown	CCq	Gregory [45]		Davis TRI
2007								
18-11	St Kitts and Nevis	L	0-3	Basseterre	Fr			
1-12	St Kitts and Nevis	W	2-0	St John's	Fr	Byers.P 2 [63 88]		
2008								
13-01	Barbados	L	2-3	Black Rock	Fr	Byers.P 2 [4 38]		Small BRB
6-02	Aruba	W	3-0	Oranjestad	WCq	Dublin [23], Gregory [27], Sierra OG [40]	250	Delgado CUB
26-03	Aruba	W	1-0	St John's	WCq	Challenger [86]	1 000	Campbell JAM
18-05	St Lucia	W	6-1	St John's	Fr	Skepple 2, Burton 2, Smith.S, Williams.T		
8-06	St Kitts and Nevis	W	2-0	St John's	Fr	Skepple [3], Gregory [87]		
17-06	Cuba	L	3-4	St John's	WCq	Williams.T [9], Skepple [13], Simon.T [80]	4 500	Moreno PAN
22-06	Cuba	L	0-4	Havana	WCq		2 000	Quesada CRC

Fr = Friendly match • CC = Digicel Caribbean Cup • WC = FIFA World Cup • q = qualifier

ANTIGUA AND BARBUDA NATIONAL TEAM RECORDS AND RECORD SEQUENCES

Records			Sequence records					
Victory	8-0	MSR 1994	Wins	4	2008	Clean sheets	3	1992, 1999
Defeat	1-11	TRI 1972	Defeats	7	1972-1984	Goals scored	9	2006
Player Caps	n/a		Undefeated	6	2000	Without goal	3	1990, 2003
Player Goals	n/a		Without win	8	2002-2003	Goals against	12	2000-2001

ANTIGUA AND BARBUDA 2007-08 PREMIER LEAGUE

	Pl	W	D	L	F	A	Pts
Bassa	18	13	3	2	45	12	42
Hoppers	18	12	3	3	41	21	39
Parham	18	9	5	4	29	22	32
Sap	18	8	6	4	29	22	30
Empire	18	7	5	6	28	25	26
Villa Lions	18	6	4	8	17	20	22
Freemansville	18	5	3	10	19	30	18
All Saints United	18	5	3	10	19	35	18
Potters	18	2	6	10	14	36	12
Liberta	18	0	8	10	11	29	8

9/09/2007 - 25/02/2008

RECENT LEAGUE RECORD

Year	Champions	Pts	Runners-up	Pts	Third	Pts
1998	Empire	32	English Harbour	29	Sap	29
1999	Empire		Parham			
2000	Empire	2-0	English Harbour			
2001	Empire	58	Bassa	37	Sap	33
2002	Parham	57	Empire	53	Sap	37
2003	Parham	38	Sap	37	Hoppers	35
2004	Bassa	34	Sap	28	Parham	23
2005	Bassa	43	Hoppers	43	Empire	39
2006	Sap	42	Hoppers	35	Bassa	34
2007	Bassa	48	Sap	32	Hoppers	26
2008	Bassa	42	Hoppers	39	Parham	32

ANTIGUA AND BARBUDA COUNTRY INFORMATION

Capital	St John's	Independence	1981	GDP per Capita	$11 000
Population	68 320	Status	Commonwealth	GNP Ranking	164
Area km²	443	Language	English	Dialling code	+1 268
Population density	154 per km²	Literacy rate	95%	Internet code	.ag
% in urban areas	36%	Main religion	Christian 96%	GMT +/-	-4.5
Towns/Cities ('000)	St John's 25; All Saints 2; Liberta 1; Potters Village 1				
Neighbours (km)	Caribbean Sea & North Atlantic Ocean 153				
Main stadia	Recreation Ground – St John's 18 000; Police Ground – St George's 3 000				

AUS – AUSTRALIA

AUSTRALIA NATIONAL TEAM RECORD
JULY 10TH 2006 TO JULY 12TH 2010

PL	W	D	L	F	A	%
23	10	6	7	29	18	56.5

Following the national team's disappointing showing in their debut appearance at the AFC Asian Cup in the summer of 2007, the Football Federation Australia moved in a new direction with the appointment of Pim Verbeek as head coach. Verbeek, an experienced operator who spent time working in Japan, Korea Republic and the Middle East, was called upon to replace Graham Arnold after the Australian's lack of exposure against Asian opposition was blamed - in part at least - for his side's failure to progress beyond the quarter-finals. The Dutchman, who also worked as assistant to Guus Hiddink when the Koreans reached the semi-finals of the 2002 World Cup finals, successfully steered his side through to the final phase of Asia's qualifying tournament for the 2010 FIFA World Cup finals in South Africa. The Socceroos saw off the challenge of Asian champions Iraq and 2004 Asian Cup finalists China to join Asian Games gold medallists Qatar in the last round, from which four teams are guaranteed places at the World Cup finals. Arnold, meanwhile, took charge of Australia's Olympic squad and successfully qualified his team for the finals of the Beijing Games, after getting the better of Iraq, North Korea and Lebanon. In the A-League, Newcastle Jets won the

INTERNATIONAL HONOURS
Qualified for the FIFA World Cup 1974 2006
Oceania Nations Cup 1980 1996 2000 2004   **Oceania Women's Championship** 1995 1998 2003
Oceania Youth Cup 1978 1982 1985 1987 1988 1990 1994 1996 1998 2001 2003
Oceania U-17 1983 1986 1989 1991 1993 1995 1999 2001 2003
Oceania Champions Cup Adelaide City 1987, South Melbourne 1999, Wollongong Wolves 2001, Sydney FC 2005

Grand Final, defeating Premier champions Central Coast Mariners thanks to a solitary goal from Mark Bridge. Any one of four teams could have claimed top spot in the league ladder going into the final day's play, with Newcastle, Sydney and Queensland Roar also challenging, but it was the Mariners who emerged victorious to earn one of Australia's berths in the 2009 AFC Champions League. That win also took them through to the Major Semi-final, where they defeated second-placed Newcastle to qualify automatically for the Grand Final while the Jets went into a play-off against Queensland, who had downed Sydney in an earlier play-off. The game went into extra-time with Newcastle eventually emerging victorious, setting up a rematch with Central Coast Mariners in the Grand Final, where Gary Van Egmond's team gained their revenge and the championship. Adelaide United, meanwhile, became the first A-League club to progress to the knock-out phase of the AFC Champions League in the second year of participation by Australian clubs. Aurelio Vidmar's team emerged from a qualifying group that featured Chinese Super League champions Changchun Yatai, Vietnam's Binh Duong and Pohang Steelers, to book a spot in the quarter-finals.

Football Federation Australia Limited (FFA)
Level 7, 26 College Street, Locked Bag A4071, Sydney South, NSW 2000 1235, Australia
Tel +61 2 83545555   Fax +61 2 83545590
info@footballaustralia.com.au   www.footballaustralia.com.au
President: LOWY Frank   General Secretary: BUCKLEY Ben
Vice-President: SCHWARTZ Brian   Treasurer: TBD   Media Officers: HODGE Stuart
Men's Coach: VERBEEK Pim   Women's Coach: SERMANNI Tom
FFA formed: 1961   OFC: 1966-72 & 1978-2005   AFC: 2006   FIFA: 1963
Yellow shirts with green trimmings, Green shorts, Yellow socks

RECENT INTERNATIONALS PLAYED BY AUSTRALIA

2005	Opponents	Score		Venue	Comp	Scorers	Att	Referee
3-09	Solomon Islands	W	7-0	Sydney	WCq	Culina [20], Viduka 2 [36 43], Cahill [57], Chipperfield [64], Thompson [68], Emerton [89]	16 000	Mohd Salleh MAS
6-09	Solomon Islands	W	2-1	Honiara	WCq	Thompson 19, Emerton [58]	16 000	Maidin SIN
9-10	Jamaica	W	5-0	London	Fr	Bresciano [2], Thompson [27], Viduka [47], Aloisi [59], Griffiths [84]	6 570	Riley ENG
12-11	Uruguay	L	0-1	Montevideo	WCpo		55 000	Larsen DEN
16-11	Uruguay	W	1-0	Sydney	WCpo	Bresciano [35], W 4-2p	82 698	Medina Cantalejo ESP
2006								
22-02	Bahrain	W	3-1	Manama	ACq	Thompson [53], Skoko [79], Elrich [87p]	2 500	Mohd Salleh MAS
25-05	Greece	W	1-0	Melbourne	Fr	Skoko [16]	95 103	Riley ENG
4-06	Netherlands	D	1-1	Rotterdam	Fr	Cahill [41]	49 000	Dean ENG
7-06	Liechtenstein	W	3-1	Ulm	Fr	Sterjovski [19], Kennedy [74], Aloisi [82]	5 872	Star GER
12-06	Japan	W	3-1	Kaiserslautern	WCr1	Cahill 2 [84 89], Aloisi [92+]	46 000	Abd El Fatah EGY
18-06	Brazil	L	0-2	Munich	WCr1		66 000	Merk GER
22-06	Croatia	D	2-2	Stuttgart	WCr1	Moore [38p], Kewell [79]	52 000	Poll ENG
26-06	Italy	L	0-1	Kaiserslautern	WCr2		46 000	Medina Cantalejo ESP
16-08	Kuwait	W	2-0	Sydney	ACq	Dodd [75], Petrovski [86]	32 000	Huang Junje CHN
6-09	Kuwait	L	0-2	Kuwait City	ACq		8 000	Kamikawa JPN
7-10	Paraguay	D	1-1	Brisbane	Fr	Popovic [88]	47 609	Kashihara JPN
11-10	Bahrain	W	2-0	Sydney	ACq	Aloisi [17], Bresciano [23]	37 000	Al Marzouqi UAE
14-11	Ghana	D	1-1	London	Fr	Aloisi [25p]	14 379	Clattenburg ENG
2007								
6-02	Denmark	L	1-3	London	Fr	Emerton [85]	12 476	Styles ENG
24-03	China PR	W	2-0	Guangzhou	Fr	Holman [8], Bresciano [27]	20 000	Wu Chaojue HKG
2-06	Uruguay	L	1-2	Sydney	Fr	Sterjovski [6]	61 795	Rosetti ITA
30-06	Singapore	W	3-0	Singapore	Fr	Viduka 2 [52 89], Kewell [77]		Iemoto JPN
8-07	Oman	D	1-1	Bangkok	ACr1	Cahill [90]	5 000	Mailett SEY
13-07	Iraq	L	1-3	Bangkok	ACr1	Viduka [47]	7 884	Karim BHR
16-07	Thailand	W	4-0	Bangkok	ACr1	Beauchamp [21], Viduka 2 [80 83], Kewell [90]	46 000	Kwon Jong Chul KOR
21-07	Japan	D	1-1	Hanoi	ACqf	Aloisi [69]	25 000	Al Fadhli KUW
11-09	Argentina	L	0-1	Melbourne	Fr		70 171	Dean ENG
17-11	Nigeria	W	1-0	London	Fr	Carney [52]	11 953	Clattenburg ENG
2008								
6-02	Qatar	W	3-0	Melbourne	WCq	Kennedy [10], Cahill [18], Bresciano [33]	50 969	Mohd Salleh MAS
22-03	Singapore	D	0-0	Singapore	Fr		6 282	Prayoon THA
26-03	China PR	D	0-0	Kunming	WCq		32 000	Al Saeedi UAE
23-05	Ghana	W	1-0	Sydney	Fr	Sterjovski [46]	29 910	Matsuo JPN
1-06	Iraq	W	1-0	Brisbane	WCq	Kewell [47]	48 678	Irmatov UZB
7-06	Iraq	L	0-1	Dubai	WCq		8 000	Matsumura JPN
14-06	Qatar	W	3-1	Doha	WCq	Emerton 2 [17 56], Kewell [75]	12 000	Lee Gi young KOR
22-06	China PR	L	0-1	Sydney	WCq		70 054	Al Ghamdi KSA

Fr = Friendly match • OC = OFC Oceania Nations Cup • CC = FIFA Confederations Cup • AC = AFC Asian Cup • WC = FIFA World Cup
q = qualifier • r1 = first round group • sf = semi-final • f = final

AUSTRALIA NATIONAL TEAM RECORDS AND RECORD SEQUENCES

Records			Sequence records				
Victory	31-0	ASA 2001	Wins	14	1996-1997	Clean sheets	6	2000, 2001
Defeat	0-8	RSA 1955	Defeats	5	1955	Goals scored	31	1924-1954
Player Caps	87	Alex Tobin	Undefeated	20	1996-1997	Without goal	4	Three times
Player Goals	29	Damian Mori	Without win	6	Five times	Goals against	11	1936-1947

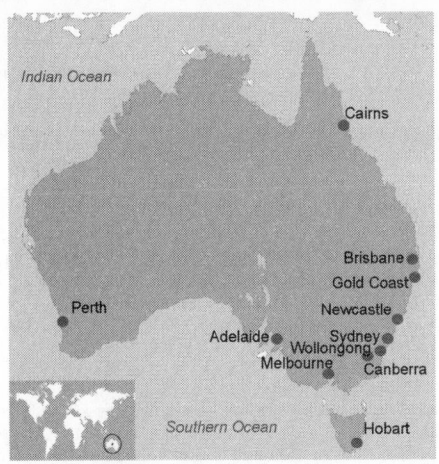

MAJOR CITIES/TOWNS

		Population '000
1	Sydney	4 444
2	Melbourne	3 780
3	Brisbane	1 891
4	Perth	1 472
5	Adelaide	1 076
6	Gold Coast	523
7	Newcastle	500
8	Sunshine Coast	332
9	Canberra	324
10	Wollongong	261
11	Hobart	206
12	Cairns	161
13	Geelong	151
14	Townsville	141
15	Albury	109
16	Shoalhaven	97
17	Toowoomba	93
18	Darwin	93
19	Ballarat	85
20	Bendigo	82
21	Mandurah	79
22	Mackay	77
23	Launceston	73
24	Rockhampton	66

COMMONWEALTH OF AUSTRALIA

Capital	Canberra	Language	English			Independence	1901
Population	20 264 082	Area	7 686 850	Density	2 per km²	% in cities	85%
GDP per cap	$29 000	Dailling code	+61	Internet	.au	GMT +/-	+10

MEDALS TABLE

A-League teams in bold • ST = State Championship

		Overall G	S	B	League G	S	B	Cup G	S	CL G	ST G	City	Stadium	Cap'ty	DoF
1	Sydney City	7	4	1	4	3	1	3	1		5	Sydney	Sydney Athletic Field	15 000	1939
2	South Melbourne	7	3	2	4	2	2	2	1	1	7	Melbourne	Bob Jane Stadium	14 000	1959
3	Adelaide City	7	3		3	2		3	1	1	12	Adelaide	Ram Park	3 000	1946
4	Marconi Stallions	5	6		4	3		1	3			Sydney	Marconi Stadium	11 500	1956
5	Sydney Olympic	4	6		2	4		2	2			Sydney	Belmore Sports Ground	11 500	1957
6	APIA Leichhardt Tigers	4	3		1			3	3		4	Sydney	Lambert Park	7 000	1954
7	Melbourne Knights	3	4		2	3		1	1		1	Melbourne	Somers Street	15 000	1953
8	Wollongong City Wolves	3		1	2		1				1	Wollongong	WIN Stadium	18 500	1980
9	Heidelberg United	2	6	1		2	1	2	4		1	Melbourne	Olympic Village	10 000	1958
10	**Perth Glory**	2	2		2	2						Perth	Members Equity Stadium	18 450	1996
11	**Newcastle Jets**	2	1		1			1	1			Newcastle	Energy Australia Stadium	26 164	2000
	Parramatta Eagles	2	1					2	1			Sydney	Melita Stadium	10 000	1956
13	Brisbane City	2		1		1	2	2				Brisbane	Spencer Park	3 000	1952
14	**Sydney FC**	2			1						1	Sydney	Aussie Stadium	41 159	2004
15	Sydney United	1	4			3		1	1			Sydney	King Tom	12 000	1957
16	St George Saints	1	3	1	1	1	1		2		3	Sydney	St George Stadium	2 500	1957
17	West Adelaide	1	2		1				2		7	Adelaide	Hindmarsh	16 500	1961-99
18	Brunswick	1	1		1				1		7	Melbourne			1948
19	**Melbourne Victory**	1			1							Melbourne	Telstra Dome	53 355	2004
27	**Central Coast Mariners**		2			2						Gosford	Central Coast Stadium	20 059	2004
28	**Adelaide United**		1			1						Adelaide	Hindmarsh Stadium	16 500	2003
29	**Queensland Roar**											Brisbane	Suncorp Stadium	52 579	2005
	Wellington Phoenix											Wellington NZ	Westpac Stadium	34 500	2007

RECENT LEAGUE RECORD

A-League Regular Season							Grand Final		
Year	First	Pts	Second	Pts	Third	Pts	Champions	Score	Runners-up
2006	Adelaide United	43	Sydney FC	36	Central Coast Mar's	32	Sydney FC	1-0	Central Coast Mar's
2007	Melbourne Victory	45	Adelaide United	33	Newcastle Utd Jets	30	Melbourne Victory	6-0	Adelaide United
2008	Central Coast Mar's	34	Newcastle Jets	34	Sydney FC	32	Newcastle Jets	1-0	Central Coast Mar's

AUSTRALIA 2007–08

HYUNDAI A-LEAGUE

	Pl	W	D	L	F	A	Pts	Mariners	Jets	Sydney	Roar	Victory	Adelaide	Glory	Phoenix
Central Coast Mariners †	21	10	4	7	30	25	34		1-1 1-2	4-5	0-1	2-1 2-5	2-0	1-0	3-0 2-0
Newcastle Jets †	21	9	7	5	25	21	34	0-0		0-1	1-1 1-1	2-2	1-0 2-1	1-4 2-1	2-1 2-3
Sydney FC ‡	21	8	8	5	28	24	32	0-1 3-2	1-0 1-0		0-0	0-1 2-2	2-2 0-1	2-4	1-2
Queensland Roar ‡	21	8	7	6	25	21	31	0-1 2-1	0-1	0-1 0-0		1-0 1-2	2-2	3-3	2-1 3-0
Melbourne Victory	21	6	9	6	29	29	27	0-0	0-2 1-3	0-0	2-0		2-2	0-0 2-1	1-1 3-0
Adelaide United	21	6	8	7	31	29	26	2-1 1-2	1-1	1-3	0-1 2-0	1-1 4-1		1-1	4-1
Perth Glory	21	4	8	9	27	34	20	0-1 1-1	0-0	0-0 3-3	1-2 1-4	3-1	0-0 3-2		0-1
Wellington Phoenix	21	5	5	11	25	37	20	1-2	0-1	1-1 0-2	1-1	2-2	2-2 1-2	4-1 3-0	

24/08/2007 - 20/01/2008 • † Qualified for the Major Semi-final • ‡ Qualified for the Minor Semi-final • Top scorer: Joel Griffiths, Jets 12
Central Coast qualified for the AFC Champions League

A-LEAGUE PLAY-OFFS

Minor Semi-final

Sydney FC	0 0
Queensland Roar	0 2

Preliminary Final

Newcastle Jets	3
Queensland Roar	2

Major Semi–Final

Newcastle Jets	2 0
Central Coast Mariners	0 3

Grand Final

Newcastle Jets	1
Central Coast Mariners	0

25/01/2008 - 24/02/2008 • The loser of the Major Semi-final meets the winner of the Minor Semi-final in the Preliminary Final • The winners of the Major Semi-final and the Preliminary Final meet in the Grand Final
Newcastle Jets qualified for the AFC Champions League

GRAND FINAL 2008

Sydney Football Stadium, 24-02-2008, 17:00, 36 354, Ref: Mark Shield

Newcastle Jets	1	Bridge [64]
Central Coast Mariners	0	

Jets - Ante COVIC - Tarek ELRICH, Adam GRIFFITHS•, Jade NORTH, Matt THOMPSON (Jason HOFFMAN 75) - Stuart MUSIALIK, Andrew DURANTE, JIN Hyung Song (DENNI 93+), Adam D'APUZZO - Joel GRIFFITHS•, Mark BRIDGE (James HOLLAND 73).
Tr: Gary VAN EGMOND
Mariners - Danny VUKOVIC•94+ - Tony VIDMAR (Matt SIMON 75), Nigel BOOGAARD•, Alex WILKINSON, John HUTCHINSON - Greg OWENS (Tom PONDELJAK 69), Adam KWASNIK (Andre GUMPRECHT 69), Mile JEDINAK• Alvin CECCOLI - John ALOISI•, Sasho PETROVSKI. Tr: Ian FERGUSON

ADELAIDE UNITED 2007–08

Jul	15	Melbourne	D	1-1	PCgA	Dodd 9	8 000
	20	Perth	D	1-1	PCgA	Cassio 60	3 513
	27	Newcastle	W	4-1	PCgA	Burns 6, Djite 66, Sarkies 80p, Alagich 86	3 800
Aug	5	Queensland	W	3-2	PCsf	Djite 1, Petta 45, Cassio 64	5 221
	12	Perth	W	2-1	PCf	Djite 66, Cassio 83	9 606
	25	Queensland	D	2-2	AL	Burns 8, Djite 47	16 828
Sep	1	Sydney	D	2-2	AL	Alagich 8, Burns 76	14 233
	7	Melbourne	D	1-1	AL	Dodd 83p	12 231
	15	Newcastle	L	0-1	AL		13 267
	22	Wellington	D	2-2	AL	Diego 69, Djite 78	12 127
	30	Cent. Coast	W	2-1	AL	Djite 2 19 88	11 019
Oct	7	Perth	D	0-0	AL		6 252
	12	Melbourne	W	4-1	AL	OG 15, Dodd 2 16 63, Pantelis 91+	13 372
	20	Sydney	W	1-0	AL	Pantelis 52	12 922
	28	Wellington	W	4-1	AL	Giraldi 5, Burns 45, Pantelis 49, Spagnulo 75	11 740
Nov	2	Queensland	L	0-1	AL		10 705
	10	Cent. Coast	L	0-2	AL		11 680
	18	Newcastle	D	1-1	AL	Dodd 76	10 256
	23	Perth	D	1-1	AL	Alagich 40	10 678
	30	Wellington	W	2-1	AL	Agostino 9, Pantelis 79	18 345
Dec	8	Melbourne	D	2-2	AL	Agostino 2 17 49	22 466
	14	Cent. Coast	L	1-2	AL	Agostino 71	11 123
	28	Sydney	L	1-3	AL	Sarkies 19	25 039
Jan	4	Newcastle	L	1-2	AL	Pantelis 41	13 047
	13	Perth	L	2-3	AL	Djite 8, Dodd 59	8 025
	20	Queensland	W	2-0	AL	Djite 17, Pantelis 45	10 803
Mar	12	Pohang	W	2-0	CLgE	Cornthwaite 4, Djite 60	8 436
	19	Changchun	D	0-0	CLgE		10 500
Apr	9	Binh Duong	W	2-1	CLgE	Diego 10, Alagich 78	15 000
	23	Binh Duong	W	4-1	CLgE	Pantelis 56, Dodd 2 58 61, Diego 75	13 802
May	7	Pohang	W	1-0	CLgE	Diego 63	11 805
	21	Changchun	D	0-0	CLgE		20 000

PC = Pre season Cup • AL = Hyundai A-League • CL = AFC Champions
League • gA = Group A • gE = Group E • sf = semi-final • f = final

CENTRAL COAST MARINERS 2007–08

Jul	14	Wellington	W	2-0	PCgB	Wilkinson 3, Kwasnik 31	8 136
	21	Queensland	D	1-1	PCgB	Boogard 6	3 531
	29	Sydney	W	3-0	PCgB	Osman 36, Kwasnik 44, Gumprecht 51	5 735
Aug	4	Perth	L	2-3	PCsf	Mrdja 44, Petrovski 92+	5 967
	12	Queensland	L	1-3	PC3p	Simon 9	3 590
	24	Sydney	W	1-0	AL	Petrovski 7	18 457
	31	Wellington	W	3-0	AL	Mrdja 2 7 34, Kwasnik 13	9 052
Sep	6	Queensland	W	1-0	AL	Kwasnik 55	8 815
	16	Melbourne	D	0-0	AL		27 351
	23	Perth	W	1-0	AL	Petrovski 80	9 274
	30	Adelaide	L	1-2	AL	Petrovski 37	11 019
Oct	7	Newcastle	D	1-1	AL	Pondeljak 61	12 622
	14	Queensland	L	0-1	AL		8 113
	21	Wellington	W	2-1	AL	Heffernan 16, Petrovski 91+	10 562
	28	Sydney	L	2-3	AL	Hutchinson 2 27 56	17 652
Nov	4	Melbourne	W	2-1	AL	Petrovski 82, Pondeljak 88	11 354
	10	Adelaide	W	2-0	AL	Aloisi 2 49p 59	11 680
	18	Perth	W	1-0	AL	Owens 12	7 310
	25	Newcastle	D	0-0	AL		14 169
Dec	9	Queensland	L	1-2	AL	Aloisi 13	16 442
	14	Adelaide	W	2-1	AL	Aloisi 23, Petrovski 49	11 123
	22	Sydney	L	4-5	AL	Jedinak 3, Aloisi 15, Owens 63p, Kwasnik 86	17 514
	31	Melbourne	L	2-5	AL	Jedinak 32, Aloisi 63	18 686
Jan	6	Perth	D	1-1	AL	Hutchinson 38	6 727
	12	Newcastle	L	1-2	AL	Kwasnik 9	19 238
	19	Wellington	W	2-0	AL	Aloisi 52, Kwasnik 94+	9 849
	27	Newcastle	L	0-2	ALsf		22 960
Feb	10	Newcastle	W	3-0	ALsf	Kwasnik 37, Petrovski 2 74 95	19 112
	24	Newcastle	L	0-1	ALf		36 354

PC = Pre season Cup • AL = Hyundai A-League •
gB = Group B • sf = semi-final • 3p = third place play-off • f = final

MELBOURNE VICTORY 2007–08

Jul	15	Adelaide	D	1-1	PCgA	Allsopp 74	8 000
	22	Newcastle	L	0-1	PCgA		8 500
	28	Perth	L	1-2	PCgA	Hernandez 34	2 700
Aug	4	Wellington	L	1-2	PC5p	Dodd 34	
	11	Sydney	L	0-1	PC7p		
	26	Wellington	D	2-2	AL	Muscat 19p, Allsopp 60	14 421
Sep	1	Perth	D	0-0	AL		31 545
	7	Adelaide	D	1-1	AL	Vargas 80	12 231
	16	Cent. Coast	D	0-0	AL		27 351
	21	Newcastle	D	2-2	AL	Thompson 65, Caceres 83	11 179
	28	Queensland	W	2-0	AL	Muscat 68p, Thompson 85	25 622
Oct	6	Sydney	W	1-0	AL	Allsopp 81	18 436
	12	Adelaide	L	1-4	AL	Thompson 45	13 372
	21	Perth	W	2-1	AL	Hernandez 25, Thompson 33	25 598
	26	Newcastle	L	0-2	AL		27 123
Nov	4	Cent. Coast	L	1-2	AL	Hernandez 77	11 354
	10	Sydney	D	0-0	AL		31 884
	16	Queensland	L	0-1	AL		17 207
	24	Wellington	D	1-1	AL	Allsopp 42	20 938
Dec	2	Perth	L	1-3	AL	Caceres 37	8 030
	8	Adelaide	D	2-2	AL	Muscat 71p, Alagich OG 91+	22 466
	16	Newcastle	L	1-3	AL	Hernandez 11	22 626
	31	Cent. Coast	W	5-2	AL	Caceres 4, Allsopp 2 23 61, Thompson 36, Muscat 43p	18 686
Jan	5	Queensland	W	2-1	AL	Allsopp 56, Thompson 63	21 475
	11	Wellington	W	3-0	AL	Hernandez 31, Ward 35, Patafta 88	25 489
	20	Sydney	D	2-2	AL	Milligan OG 46, Allsopp 76	33 458
Mar	12	Chunnam	W	2-0	CLgG	Muscat 28p, Vargas 66	23 000
	19	Chonburi	L	1-3	CLgG	Allsopp 57	10 000
Apr	9	G-Osaka	L	3-4	CLgG	Allsopp 2 4 66, Vargas 41	23 857
	23	G-Osaka	L	0-2	CLgG		8 132
May	7	Chunnam	D	1-1	CLgG	Pondeljak 4	3 000
	21	Chonburi	W	3-1	CLgG	Muscat 56, Thompson 65, Valverde 76	9 558

PC = Pre season Cup • AL = Hyundai A-League • CL = AFC Champions
League • gA = Group A • gG = Group G • 5p = fifth place play-off •
7p = seventh place play-off • sf = semi-final • f = final

NEWCASTLE JETS 2007–08

Jul	14	Perth	L	0-1	PCgA		
	22	Melbourne	W	1-0	PCgA	Wheelhouse 51	8 500
	27	Adelaide	L	1-4	PCgA	Griffiths.J 92+	3 800
Aug	4	Sydney	W	3-2	PC5p	Griffiths.J 2, Tunbridge	2 611
	10	Wellington	D	0-0	PC5p	W 4-2p	
	26	Perth	D	0-0	AL		8 508
Sep	2	Queensland	D	1-1	AL	Griffiths.J 88	13 144
	9	Wellington	W	1-0	AL	Thompson 77	11 478
	15	Adelaide	W	1-0	AL	Bridge 81	13 267
	21	Melbourne	D	2-2	AL	Griffiths.A 4, Musialik 21	11 179
	29	Sydney	L	0-1	AL		13 755
Oct	7	Cent. Coast	D	1-1	AL	Bridge 82	12 622
	14	Wellington	W	2-1	AL	Holland 16, Griffiths.J 40	11 947
	19	Queensland	D	1-1	AL	Griffiths.J 47p	12 326
	26	Melbourne	W	2-0	AL	Griffiths.A 8, Griffiths.J 88	27 123
Nov	3	Sydney	L	0-1	AL		16 433
	9	Perth	L	1-4	AL	Griffiths.J 49	8 112
	18	Adelaide	D	1-1	AL	Griffiths.J 70	10 256
	25	Cent. Coast	D	0-0	AL		14 169
	30	Queensland	W	1-0	AL	Griffiths.J 92+	14 193
Dec	7	Sydney	L	0-1	AL		10 732
	16	Melbourne	W	3-1	AL	Denni 41, Griffiths.J 2 54 75	22 626
	30	Wellington	L	2-3	AL	Bridge 29p, Tunbridge 81	15 107
Jan	4	Adelaide	W	2-1	AL	Griffiths.J 12, Holland 72	13 047
	12	Cent. Coast	W	2-1	AL	Holland 6, Griffiths.J 52	19 238
	18	Perth	W	2-1	AL	Griffiths.J 22, Bridge 64	16 212
	27	Cent. Coast	W	2-0	ALsf	Griffiths.A 22, Griffiths.J 84p	22 960
Feb	10	Cent. Coast	L	0-3	ALsf		19 112
	17	Queensland	W	3-2	ALpf	Thompson 40, Griffiths.J 104p, Elrich 110	16 021
	24	Cent. Coast	W	1-0	ALf	Bridge 64	36 354

PC = Pre season Cup • AL = Hyundai A-League • gA = Group A • 5p = fifth
place play-off • sf = semi-final • f = final

PERTH GLORY 2007–08

Mo	Date	Opponent		Score	Comp	Scorers	Att
Jul	14	Newcastle	W	1-0	PCgA	Harnwell 48	
	20	Adelaide	D	1-1	PCgA	Rukavytsya 53	3 513
	28	Melbourne	W	2-1	PCgA	Rukavytsya 52, Harnwell 70	2 700
Aug	4	Cent. Coast	W	3-2	PCsf	Dragicevic 23, Bertos 57, Tarka 78	5 967
	12	Adelaide	L	1-2	PCf	Bertos 45	9 606
	26	Newcastle	D	0-0	AL		8 508
Sep	1	Melbourne	D	0-0	AL		31 545
	9	Sydney	D	0-0	AL		8 014
	16	Queensland	L	1-2	AL	Harnwell 14	7 203
	23	Cent. Coast	L	0-1	AL		9 274
	30	Wellington	L	1-4	AL	Celeski 10	10 127
Oct	7	Adelaide	D	0-0	AL		6 252
	12	Sydney	D	3-3	AL	Harnwell 52, Robinson 59, Prentice 69	6 876
	21	Melbourne	L	1-2	AL	Harnwell 43	25 598
	27	Queensland	D	3-3	AL	OG 18, Harnwell 43, Coyne 93+	16 715
Nov	2	Wellington	L	0-1	AL		7 105
	9	Newcastle	W	4-1	AL	Durante OG 25, Simpson 51, Rukavytsya 2 63 91+	8 112
	18	Cent. Coast	L	0-1	AL		7 310
	23	Adelaide	D	1-1	AL	Harnwell 69	10 678
Dec	2	Melbourne	W	3-1	AL	Harnwell 18, Rukavytsya 2 27 46	8 030
	7	Wellington	L	0-3	AL		8 039
	15	Sydney	W	4-2	AL	Celeski 3 34 35 77p, Bertos 49	12 402
	30	Queensland	L	1-4	AL	Rizzo 57	9 614
Jan	6	Cent. Coast	D	1-1	AL	Rukavytsya 69	6 727
	13	Adelaide	W	3-2	AL	Robinson 11, Rukavytsya 45, Harnwell 61	8 025
	18	Newcastle	L	1-2	AL	Harnwell 45	16 212

PC = Pre season Cup • AL = Hyundai A-League • gA = Group A •
sf = semi-final • f = final

QUEENSLAND ROAR 2007–08

Mo	Date	Opponent		Score	Comp	Scorers	Att
Jul	14	Sydney	D	0-0	PCgB		4 892
	21	Cent. Coast	D	1-1	PCgB	Lynch 60	3 531
	27	Wellington	W	2-1	PCgB	Lynch 40, Ogenovski 48	
Aug	5	Adelaide	L	2-3	PCsf	Lynch 16, Milicic 73	5 221
	12	Cent. Coast	W	3-1	PC3p	Milicic 30, Marcinho 48, Reinaldo 86	3 590
	25	Adelaide	D	2-2	AL	McKay 45, Ognenovski 76	16 828
Sep	2	Newcastle	D	1-1	AL	Reinaldo 70	13 144
	6	Cent. Coast	L	0-1	AL		8 815
	16	Perth	W	2-1	AL	McCloughan 21, McKay 84	7 203
	22	Sydney	L	0-1	AL		16 582
	28	Melbourne	L	0-2	AL		25 622
Oct	5	Wellington	W	2-1	AL	Zullo 4, Kruse 45	12 458
	14	Cent. Coast	W	1-0	AL	McCloughan 5	8 113
	19	Newcastle	D	1-1	AL	Kruse 1	12 326
	27	Perth	D	3-3	AL	Marcinho 45, Lynch 2 69 86	16 715
Nov	2	Adelaide	W	1-0	AL	Reinaldo 63	10 705
	11	Wellington	W	3-0	AL	Reinaldo 2 66 79, Marcinho 82	13 808
	16	Melbourne	W	1-0	AL	Kruse 10	17 207
	25	Sydney	D	0-0	AL		16 659
	30	Newcastle	L	0-1	AL		14 193
Dec	9	Cent. Coast	W	2-1	AL	Vidmar OG 21, McKay 28	16 442
	14	Wellington	D	1-1	AL	Reinaldo 5	9 384
	30	Perth	W	4-1	AL	Kruse 34, Reinaldo 42, Minniecon 59, McCloughan 74	9 614
Jan	5	Melbourne	L	1-2	AL	Marcinho 73	21 475
	13	Sydney	D	0-0	AL		31 933
	20	Adelaide	L	0-2	AL		10 803
	25	Sydney	D	0-0	ALqf		23 450
Feb	8	Sydney	W	2-0	ALqf	Reinaldo 13, Ognenovski 83p	36 221
	17	Newcastle	L	2-3	ALsf	Reinaldo 2 92+ 118	16 021

PC = Pre season Cup • AL = Hyundai A-League • gB = Group B •
sf = semi-final • 3p = third place play-off

SYDNEY FC 2007–08

Mo	Date	Opponent		Score	Comp	Scorers	Att
Jul	14	Queensland	D	0-0	PCgB		4 892
	22	Wellington	L	0-3	PCgB		6 039
	29	Cent. Coast	L	0-3	PCgB		5 735
Aug	4	Newcastle	L	2-3	PC5p	Zadkovich 79, Talay 83	2 611
	11	Melbourne	W	1-0	PC7p		
	24	Cent. Coast	L	0-1	AL		18 457
Sep	1	Adelaide	D	2-2	AL	Talay 12, Brosque 74	14 233
	9	Perth	D	0-0	AL		8 014
	14	Wellington	L	1-2	AL	Casey 6	11 491
	22	Queensland	W	1-0	AL	Patrick 69	16 582
	29	Newcastle	W	1-0	AL	Brosque 36	13 755
	6	Melbourne	L	0-1	AL		18 436
Oct	12	Perth	D	3-3	AL	Brosque 2 40 93+, Patrick 80	6 876
	20	Adelaide	L	0-1	AL		12 922
	28	Cent. Coast	W	3-2	AL	Brosque 2 16 26, Popovic 31	17 652
Nov	3	Newcastle	W	1-0	AL	Bridges 69	16 433
	10	Melbourne	D	0-0	AL		31 884
	17	Wellington	D	1-1	AL	Talay 93+p	8 062
	25	Queensland	D	0-0	AL		16 659
Dec	7	Newcastle	W	1-0	AL	Corica 92+	10 732
	15	Perth	L	2-4	AL	Corica 50, Bridges 90	12 402
	22	Cent. Coast	W	5-4	AL	Fyfe 33, McFlynn 49, Biddle 71, Santalab 76, Talay 95+p	17 514
	28	Adelaide	W	3-1	AL	Santalab 44, Corica 54, Middleby 66	25 039
Jan	4	Wellington	W	2-0	AL	McFlynn 79, Brosque 83	14 288
	13	Queensland	D	0-0	AL		31 933
	20	Melbourne	D	2-2	AL	Corica 4, Brosque 61	33 458
	25	Queensland	D	0-0	ALqf		23 450
	8	Queensland	L	0-2	ALqf		36 221

PC = Pre season Cup • AL = Hyundai A-League • gB = Group B •
qf = quarter-final • 5p = fifth place play-off • 7p = seventh place play-off

WELLINGTON PHOENIX 2007–08

Mo	Date	Opponent		Score	Comp	Scorers	Att
Jul	14	Cent. Coast	L	0-2	PCgB		8 136
	22	Sydney	W	3-0	PCgB	Smeltz 2 13 89, OG 14	6 039
	27	Queensland	L	1-2	PCgB		
Aug	4	Melbourne	W	2-1	PC5p		
	11	Newcastle	D	0-0	PC5p L 2-4p		
	26	Melbourne	D	2-2	AL	Daniel 79, Smeltz 84	14 421
Sep	31	Cent. Coast	L	0-3	AL		9 052
	9	Newcastle	L	0-1	AL		11 478
	14	Sydney	W	2-1	AL	Felipe 8, Daniel 29p	11 491
	22	Adelaide	D	2-2	AL	Felipe 64, Smeltz 87	12 127
	30	Perth	W	4-1	AL	Aloisi 13, Smeltz 41, Coveny 56, Lochhead 83	10 127
Oct	5	Queensland	L	1-2	AL	Smeltz 95+	12 458
	14	Newcastle	L	0-2	AL	Old 94+	11 947
	21	Cent. Coast	L	1-2	AL	Elrich 24	10 562
	28	Adelaide	L	1-4	AL	Smeltz 3	11 740
Nov	2	Perth	W	1-0	AL	Daniel 51	7 105
	11	Queensland	L	0-3	AL		13 808
	17	Sydney	D	1-1	AL	Aloisi 28	8 062
	24	Melbourne	D	1-1	AL	Lia 58	20 938
	30	Adelaide	L	1-2	AL	Daniel 69p	18 345
Dec	7	Perth	W	3-0	AL	Smeltz 2 29p 71, Felipe 31	8 039
	14	Queensland	D	1-1	AL	Smeltz 25	9 384
	30	Newcastle	W	3-2	AL	Smeltz 16, Ferrante 49, Rees 51	15 107
Jan	4	Sydney	L	0-2	AL		14 288
	11	Melbourne	L	0-3	AL		25 489
	19	Cent. Coast	L	0-2	AL		9 849

PC = Pre season Cup • AL = Hyundai A-League • gB = Group B •
5p = fifth place play-off

AUT – AUSTRIA

NATIONAL TEAM RECORD
JULY 10TH 2006 TO JULY 12TH 2010

PL	W	D	L	F	A	%
25	5	9	11	28	34	38

FIFA/COCA-COLA WORLD RANKING

1993	1994	1995	1996	1997	1998	1999	2000	2001	2002	2003	2004	2005	2006	2007		High	
36	49	39	34	25	22	28	44	56	65	67	83	69	65	94		**17**	05/99

					2007–2008								Low	
08/07	09/07	10/07	11/07	12/07	01/08	02/08	03/08	04/08	05/08	06/08	07/08		**105**	07/08
84	85	88	91	94	90	84	88	102	101	92	105			

Many in Austria expected the national team to crash out of Euro 2008 in embarrassing circumstances, such was the low esteem in which the team was held. One fan even raised a petition asking the team to withdraw from the tournament to avoid the possibility of humiliation. In the event, although Austria did make an exit after the group stages, they left with their heads held high while the country put on a great show for all the fans who came to Austria. Euro 2008 also left a legacy of three first class stadia in the cities of Innsbruck, Salzburg and Klagenfurt which it is hoped will promote the development of domestic football. Salzburg looks best placed to do that

INTERNATIONAL HONOURS
Qualified for the FIFA World Cup 1934 1954 1958 1978 1982 1990 1998 **International Cup** 1932
FIFA Junior Tournament 1950   **UEFA Junior Tournament** 1957   **Mitropa Cup** SK Rapid 1930, First Vienna 1931, FK Austria 1933 1936

with Red Bull Salzburg once again making a strong push for honours, although they failed to defend their League title thanks largely to the extraordinary 7-0 thrashing they suffered at the hands of new champions Rapid in March. It was the heaviest defeat Salzburg coach Giovanni Trapattoni had experienced in his entire career and it meant that Rapid, under coach Peter Pacult, overtook their rivals at the top of the table. In the end Rapid finished six points clear to win only their second title in 12 seasons. The Championship was the only domestic action of the season for the top flight clubs with the Austrian Cup restricted to amateur teams as the country prepared to host Euro 2008.

THE FIFA BIG COUNT OF 2006

	Male	Female		Total
Number of players	912 580	54 701	Referees and Assistant Referees	2 302
Professionals	906		Admin, Coaches, Technical, Medical	390 500
Amateurs 18+	370 828		Number of clubs	2 211
Youth under 18	221 547		Number of teams	9 685
Unregistered	260 000		Clubs with women's teams	100
Total players	967 281		Players as % of population	11.81%

Osterreichischer Fussball-Bund (OFB)
Ernst Happel Stadion, Sektor A/F, Postfach 340, Meiereistrasse 7, Wien 1021, Austria
Tel +43 1 727180   Fax +43 1 7281632
office@oefb.at   www.oefb.at
President: STICKLER Friedrich   General Secretary: LUDWIG Alfred
Vice-President: EHRENBERGER Kurt   Treasurer: TALOS Rudolf   Media Officer: KLINGMUELLER Peter
Men's Coach: BRUCKNER Karel   Women's Coach: WEBER Ernst
OFB formed: 1904   UEFA: 1954   FIFA: 1907
Red shirts, White shorts, Red socks or White shirts, Black shorts, White socks

RECENT INTERNATIONALS PLAYED BY AUSTRIA

2005 Opponents	Score	Venue	Comp	Scorers	Att	Referee
17-08 Scotland	D 2-2	Graz	Fr	Ibertsberger 83, Standfest 87	13 800	Dereli TUR
3-09 Poland	L 2-3	Chorzow	WCq	Linz 2 61 80	40 000	De Santis ITA
7-09 Azerbaijan	D 0-0	Baku	WCq		2 800	Verbist BEL
8-10 England	L 0-1	Manchester	WCq		64 822	Medina Cantalejo ESP
12-10 Northern Ireland	W 2-0	Vienna	WCq	Aufhauser 2 44 90	12 500	Briakos GRE
2006						
1-03 Canada	L 0-2	Vienna	Fr		9 000	Van Egmond NED
23-05 Croatia	L 1-4	Vienna	Fr	Ivanschitz 14	22 000	Fandel GER
16-08 Hungary	L 1-2	Graz	Fr	Kuljic 74	11 000	Havrilla SVK
2-09 Costa Rica	D 2-2	Geneva	Fr	Linz 2 36p 60	300	Circhetta SUI
6-09 Venezuela	L 0-1	Basel	Fr		1 453	Bartolini SUI
6-10 Liechtenstein	W 2-1	Vaduz	Fr	Garics 77, Prager 84	3 750	Rogalla SUI
11-10 Switzerland	W 2-1	Innsbruck	Fr	Linz 24p, Kuljic 36	11 000	Svendsen DEN
15-11 Trinidad and Tobago	W 4-1	Vienna	Fr	Aufhauser 3 14 25 44, Feldhofer 80	13 100	Matejek CZE
2007						
7-02 Malta	D 1-1	Ta'Qali	Fr	Ivanschitz 48	3 000	Bartolini SUI
24-03 Ghana	D 1-1	Graz	Fr	Aufhauser 55	10 608	Verbist BEL
28-03 France	L 0-1	Paris	Fr		68 403	Briakos GRE
30-05 Scotland	L 0-1	Vienna	Fr		13 200	Szabo HUN
2-06 Paraguay	D 0-0	Vienna	Fr		12 700	Bebek CRO
22-08 Czech Republic	D 1-1	Vienna	Fr	Harnik 78	24 500	Mejuto Gonzalez ESP
7-09 Japan	D 0-0	Klagenfurt	Fr	W 4-3p	26 142	Merk GER
11-09 Chile	L 0-2	Vienna	Fr			Granat POL
13-10 Switzerland	L 1-3	Zürich	Fr	Aufhauser 11	22 500	Hamer LUX
17-10 Côte d'Ivoire	W 3-2	Innsbruck	Fr	Kuljic 30p, Ivanschitz 64p, Standfest 74	30 000	Kuipers NED
16-11 England	L 0-1	Vienna	Fr		39 432	Vollquartz DEN
21-11 Tunisia	D 0-0	Vienna	Fr		13 800	Olsiak SVK
2008						
6-02 Germany	L 0-3	Vienna	Fr		48 500	Dondarini ITA
26-03 Netherlands	L 3-4	Vienna	Fr	Ivanschitz 6, Prodl 2 18 35	40 500	Hansson SWE
27-05 Nigeria	D 1-1	Graz	Fr	Kienast 12	15 000	Gumienny BEL
30-05 Malta	W 5-1	Graz	Fr	Aufhauser 8, Linz 2 11 67p, Vastic 77, Harnik 90	14 200	Krajnc SVN
8-06 Croatia	L 0-1	Vienna	ECr1		51 428	Vink NED
12-06 Poland	D 1-1	Vienna	ECr1	Vastic 93+	51 428	Webb ENG
16-06 Germany	L 0-1	Vienna	ECr1		51 428	Mejuto Gonzalez ESP

Fr = Friendly match • EC = UEFA EURO 2008 • WC = FIFA World Cup • q = qualifier • r1 = first round group

AUSTRIA NATIONAL TEAM PLAYERS

	Player		Ap	G	Club	Date of Birth		Player		Ap	G	Club	Date of Birth
1	Alexander Manninger	GK	27	0	Siena	4 06 1977	12	Ronald Gercaliu	DF	12	0	FK Austria Wien	12 02 1986
2	Joachim Standfest	DF	31	2	FK Austria Wien	30 05 1980	13	Markus Katzer	DF	11	0	SK Rapid Wien	11 12 1979
3	Martin Stranzl	DF	48	2	Spartak Moskva	16 06 1980	14	György Garics	MF	14	1	Napoli	8 03 1984
4	Emanuel Pogatetz	DF	30	1	Middlesbrough	16 01 1983	15	Sebastian Prödl	DF	12	2	SK Sturm Graz	21 06 1987
5	Christian Fuchs	MF	18	0	SV Mattersburg	7 04 1986	16	Jürgen Patocka	DF	2	0	SK Rapid Wien	30 07 1977
6	René Aufhauser	MF	54	11	Austria Salzburg	21 06 1976	17	Martin Hiden	DF	50	1	Austria Kärnten	11 03 1973
7	Ivica Vastic	FW	50	14	LASK Linz	29 09 1969	18	Roman Kienast	FW	9	1	Ham-Kam	29 03 1984
8	Christoph Leitgeb	MF	21	0	Austria Salzburg	14 04 1985	19	Jürgen Säumel	MF	14	0	SK Sturm Graz	8 09 1984
9	Roland Linz	FW	34	7	Sporting Braga	9 08 1981	20	Martin Harnik	MF	11	2	Werder Bremen	10 06 1987
10	Andreas Ivanschitz	MF	42	6	Panathinaikos	15 10 1983	21	Jürgen Macho	GK	17	0	AEK Athens	24 08 1977
11	Umit Korkmaz	MF	5	0	SK Rapid Wien	17 09 1985	22	Erwin Hoffer	FW	5	0	SK Rapid Wien	14 04 1987
	Austria's squad for Euro 2008						23	Ramazan Ozcan	GK	0	0	TSG Hoffenheim	28 06 1984

AUSTRIA NATIONAL TEAM RECORDS AND RECORD SEQUENCES

Records			Sequence records					
Victory	9-0	MLT 1977	Wins	7	1933-1934	Clean sheets	5	1931, 1996
Defeat	1-11	ENG 1908	Defeats	6	1946-1947	Goals scored	28	1931-1934
Player Caps	103	Andreas Herzog	Undefeated	14	1931-1932	Without goal	3	
Player Goals	44	Toni Polster	Without win	9	1973-1974, 2007	Goals against	17	1919-22, 1954-56

MAJOR CITIES/TOWNS
Population '000

1	Vienna	1 570
2	Graz	221
3	Linz	179
4	Salzburg	145
5	Innsbruck	112
6	Klagenfurt	90
7	Villach	59
8	Wels	58
9	Sankt Polten	48
10	Dornbirn	43
11	Steyr	39
12	Wiener Neustadt	38
13	Feldkirch	29
14	Bregenz	26
15	Leoben	24
16	Krems	24
17	Kapfenberg	21
18	Modling	20
19	Lustenau	20
20	Reid	11
21	Altach	6
22	Gratkorn	6
23	Mattersburg	6
24	Pasching	6

REPUBLIC OF AUSTRIA; REPUBLIK OESTERREICH

Capital	Vienna/Wien	Language	German	Independence	1918
Population	8 192 880	Area	83 870 km²	% in cities	56%
GDP per cap	$30 000	Dailling code	+43	Internet .at	GMT +/- +1

MEDALS TABLE

		Overall			League			Cup			Europe			City	Stadium	Cap'ty	DoF
		G	S	B	G	S	B	G	S	B	G	S	B				
1	FK Austria Wien	51	27	16	23	17	12	26	9		2	1	4	Vienna	Franz-Horr-Stadion	11 800	1911
2	SK Rapid Wien	47	38	21	32	22	19	14	12		1	4	2	Vienna	Gerhard-Hanappi-Stadion	19 600	1899
3	FC Wacker Tirol	17	11	7	10	5	6	7	6				1	Innsbruck	Tivoli Neu	31 600	1914
4	Admira Wien	13	6	6	8	5	5	5	0		1	1		Vienna	Südstadt		1905-71
5	First Vienna FC	10	12	13	6	6	11	3	6		1		2	Vienna	Hohe Warte	6 000	1894
6	SK Sturm Graz	5	9	4	2	5	4	3	4					Graz	Graz-Liebenau	15 428	1909
7	Grazer AK	5	4	6	1	2	6	4	2					Graz	Graz-Liebenau	15 428	1902
8	Wiener Sport-Club	4	14	5	3	7	5	1	7					Vienna	Sport-Club Platz	8 700	1883
9	RB Austria Salzburg	4	10	1	4	5	1		4			1		Salzburg	Wals-Siezenheim	31 020	1933
10	Wiener AC	4	5	6	1	1	6	3	3			1		Vienna	WAC Platz		1896
11	Wacker Wien	2	8	3	1	7	3	1	1					Vienna	Maidlinger Platz		1908-71
12	Linzer ASK	2	5	4	1	1	4	1	4					Linz	Linzer Stadion	21 328	1908
13	Wiener AF	2	2	3	1	2	3	1						Vienna	Meldenorm Stadion		1912-35
14	FC Linz	1	4	1	1	2	1		2					Linz	Linzer Stadion		1949-97
15	Floridsdorfer AC	1	3	1	1	3	1							Vienna	FAC-Platz		1904

European medals include those won in the Mitropa Cup 1927-1939

RECENT LEAGUE AND CUP RECORD

	Championship						Cup		
Year	Champions	Pts	Runners-up	Pts	Third	Pts	Winners	Score	Runners-up
1995	SV Austria Salzburg	47	SK Sturm Graz	47	SK Rapid Wien	46	SK Rapid Wien	1-0	DSV Leoben
1996	SK Rapid Wien	73	SK Sturm Graz	67	FC Tirol Innsbruck	62	SK Sturm Graz	3-1	Admira-Wacker
1997	SV Austria Salzburg	69	SK Rapid Wien	66	SK Sturm Graz	55	SK Sturm Graz	2-1	First Vienna FC
1998	SK Sturm Graz	81	SK Rapid Wien	62	Grazer AK	61	SV Ried	3-1	SK Sturm Graz
1999	SK Sturm Graz	73	SK Rapid Wien	70	Grazer AK	65	SK Sturm Graz	1-1 4-2	LASK Linz
2000	FC Tirol Innsbruck	74	SV Sturm Graz	74	SK Rapid Wien	66	Grazer AK	2-2 4-3p	SV Austria Salzburg
2001	FC Tirol Innsbruck	68	SK Rapid Wien	60	Grazer AK	57	FC Kärnten	2-1	FC Tirol Innsbruck
2002	FC Tirol Innsbruck	75	SK Sturm Graz	65	Grazer AK	63	Grazer AK	3-2	SK Sturm Graz
2003	FK Austria Wien	70	Grazer AK	57	SV Austria Salzburg	56	FK Austria Wien	3-0	FC Kärnten
2004	Grazer AK	72	FK Austria Wien	71	SV Pasching	63	Grazer AK	3-3 5-4p	FK Austria Wien
2005	SK Rapid Wien	71	Grazer AK	70	FK Austria Wien	69	FK Austria Wien	3-1	SK Rapid Wien
2006	FK Austria Wien	67	RB Austria Salzburg	63	SV Pasching	58	FK Austria Wien	3-0	SV Mattersburg
2007	RB Austria Salzburg	75	SC Ried	56	SV Mattersburg	55	FK Austria Wien	2-1	SV Mattersburg
2008	SK Rapid Wien	69	RB Austria Salzburg	63	FK Austria Wien	58	Not held due to hosting of Euro 2008		

AUSTRIA 2007–08

T-MOBILE BUNDESLIGA

	Pl	W	D	L	F	A	Pts	SK Rapid	RB Salzburg	FK Austria	Sturm Graz	Mattersburg	LASK	Ried	Altach	Kärnten	Wacker
SK Rapid Wien †	36	21	6	9	69	36	69		1-0 1-3	0-0 2-0	1-5 2-1	1-0 3-1	4-4 2-0	4-0 4-0	0-2 3-0	4-0 2-1	3-1 4-1
RB Austria Salzburg †	36	18	9	9	63	42	63	2-1 0-7		0-1 2-0	4-1 3-0	2-1 4-0	2-0 2-0	4-1 4-0	3-0 1-1	3-1 2-0	
FK Austria Wien ‡	36	15	13	8	46	33	58	2-2 0-0	2-2 3-1		1-0 1-2	2-2 0-0	1-1 0-0	2-1 2-0	1-0 1-1	1-0 0-1	6-1 2-1
SK Sturm Graz	36	15	11	10	60	41	56	1-0 0-2	0-0 1-1	2-2 1-2		0-0 2-1	4-0 1-2	5-0 2-0	3-1 6-1	1-3 3-1	3-0 2-0
SV Mattersburg	36	13	14	9	55	43	53	3-2 1-0	1-1 3-2	0-1 1-1	2-2 1-1		0-0 1-0	5-1 1-1	4-1 3-3	5-2 1-0	3-1 2-1
LASK Linz	36	14	11	11	54	47	53	2-0 1-2	4-1 1-1	1-1 2-1	2-2 1-2	0-2 2-1		1-0 1-0	2-0 3-0	1-0 4-0	5-0 3-3
SV Ried	36	10	8	18	38	53	38	0-3 0-1	2-0 1-2	0-1 1-1	5-3 0-0	1-2 0-0	3-0 1-1		3-0 3-1	3-3 0-0	0-0 0-0
SC Rheindorf Altach	36	8	12	16	37	64	36	0-1 2-1	1-1 1-1	0-0 4-0	0-1 2-0	0-0 2-0	2-2 0-0	2-3 3-2		4-1 0-1	2-1 1-1
SK Austria Kärnten	36	8	9	19	26	58	33	1-2 0-2	1-0 0-0	2-1 0-1	0-0 0-2	1-1 1-0	1-4 2-1	0-3 0-0	1-1 1-1		2-0 0-2
FC Wacker Innsbruck	36	6	11	19	32	63	29	1-1 1-1	3-1 1-2	2-0 1-2	0-0 1-0	2-0 5-1	2-2 0-0	0-1 1-0	0-1 1-1	1-1 0-0	

10/07/2007 - 26/04/2008 • † Qualified for the UEFA Champions League • ‡ Qualified for the UEFA Cup
Wacker Tirol changed their name to Wacker Innsbruck • SV Pasching relocated to Klagenfurt and changed their name to SK Austria Kärnten
Top scorers: Alexander Zickler, RB Salzburg 16; Mario Haas, Sturm Graz 14; Ivica Vastic, LASK Linz 13

AUSTRIA 2007–08

RED ZAC ERSTE LIGA (2)

	Pl	W	D	L	F	A	Pts	Kapfenberg	Gratkorn	Austria L	Lustenau	FK Austria	RB Salzburg	Schwans'dt	Leoben	Admira	Kärnten	Parndorf	Bad Aussee
SV Kapfenberg	33	19	9	5	79	45	66		4-1	1-1 3-2	2-1	1-1	1-1 4-0	5-0 2-0	4-2 1-0	4-1	4-1	1-4 4-1	3-1
FC Gratkorn	33	15	10	8	51	35	55	0-2 2-2		3-1	1-1	6-0	1-2 1-3	3-0 1-0	2-0 1-2	3-1 1-0	2-2	2-2 5-0	4-1
SC Austria Lustenau	33	15	9	9	59	45	54	3-2	0-0 2-2		2-2 2-1	1-1 1-2	2-2	3-2	2-0	5-1 1-0	0-4 1	3-2	2-1 3-1
FC Lustenau	33	15	8	10	50	39	53	1-1 3-2	0-1 0-1	1-1		1-1	1-0 2-1	1-0	2-1	3-0 2-1	4-0 0-2	4-1 2-0	4-0
FK Austria Amateure	33	14	8	11	45	44	50	2-2 3-3	0-0 0-2	2-1	0-1 1-0		5-1 1-3	0-1	2-1	2-1	1-0 0-1	2-2	2-1
RB Salzburg Amateure	33	13	7	13	51	52	46	0-2	3-0	2-1 1-1	2-2	2-1		0-1 1-1	2-1 1-0	3-2	2-1	2-2 3-3 0-2	0-0 2-0 0-2
SC Schwanenstadt	33	13	6	14	48	51	45	1-3	0-0	2-3 0-2	2-1 1-1	2-0 0-2	4-2		1-1	1-1 1-0 4-2	2-2	4-1	2-3 3-1
DSV Leoben	33	11	8	14	44	46	41	1-1	2-3	2-0 3-0	2-2 1-1 0-1	2-0 2-0	1-3	1-0 0-1		0-1 2-2	4-0	0-0	0-2 2-2
SKS Admira	33	12	5	16	48	53	41	5-0 1-3	3-0	1-3	4-1	1-3 1-0	3-2 3-2	2-4	2-2		2-0	1-2 1-0 0-2 0	2-0
FC Kärnten	33	11	7	15	37	51	40	0-3 3-1 1-2	1-1	2-1	4-1	0-2 0-1-0	0-0 4-0-0-2	1-0		1-0 2-0		1-0 2-0	2-2
SC/ESV Parndorf	33	10	7	16	45	61	37	1-3	0-0	0-4 2-1	1-1	0-1 0-1 3-0	1-2	1-4 3-1 1-3 1-2	1-1	4-0			2-0 3-0
SV Bad Aussee	33	4	8	21	35	70	20	1-4 1-0 0-0 1	0-1	1-2 0-1 2-1-4	3-2	2-2	2-5	1-2	1-3 1-1	2-3			

31/07/2007 - 16/05/2008 • Top scorers: Rene Gartler, FC Lustenau 21; Andreas Bammer, Schwanenstadt 19; Michael Liendl, Kapfenberg 18

AZE – AZERBAIJAN

NATIONAL TEAM RECORD
JULY 10TH 2006 TO JULY 12TH 2010

PL	W	D	L	F	A	%
23	5	5	13	14	41	32.6

FIFA/COCA-COLA WORLD RANKING

1993	1994	1995	1996	1997	1998	1999	2000	2001	2002	2003	2004	2005	2006	2007	High	
-	147	141	125	123	99	97	115	113	113	119	113	114	125	115	**97**	06/99

2007–2008												Low	
08/07	09/07	10/07	11/07	12/07	01/08	02/08	03/08	04/08	05/08	06/08	07/08	**170**	07/94
107	115	116	118	115	116	122	119	137	137	133	139		

The national team started the season with a win in Takijistan and ended it with a win in Andorra, but in-between it wasn't a happy year with the Azeris finishing bottom of their Euro 2008 qualifying group, four points adrift of the one nation the fans were desperate to finish ahead of - Armenia. Had the matches between the two countries taken place, the outcome may have been different but given the hostility between Azerbaijan and Armenia, UEFA took the unusual decision to simply cancel both matches. In April 2008 the much travelled Berti Vogts was appointed as the new coach of the national team with his principle aim being to avoid the wooden spoon in their 2010 FIFA World

INTERNATIONAL HONOURS
None

Cup qualifying group. In domestic football Olimpik Baku looked to be on course for a first league title after remaining unbeaten for their first 21 matches of the season and conceding just four goals. In their last five matches, however, they drew twice and lost twice and were overtaken on the final day by Inter. The two finished level on points but Inter won their first title having won more matches. Backed by the national bank, Inter then came close to winning the double but with the Cup Final against Khazar heading towards penalties, Osvaldo Junior, Khazar's Brazilian midfielder, scored twice in the last five minutes of extra-time to retain the Cup for his team.

THE FIFA BIG COUNT OF 2006

	Male	Female		Total
Number of players	267 900	38 470	Referees and Assistant Referees	100
Professionals	400		Admin, Coaches, Technical, Medical	12 900
Amateurs 18+	3 150		Number of clubs	80
Youth under 18	14 120		Number of teams	320
Unregistered	82 700		Clubs with women's teams	3
Total players	306 370		Players as % of population	3.85%

Association of Football Federations of Azerbaijan (AFFA)
Nobel prospekti, 2208,, Baku AZ 1025, Azerbaijan
Tel +994 12 908308   Fax +994 12 4908722
info@affa.az   www.affa.az
President: ABDULLAYEV Rovnag   General Secretary: MAMMADOV Elkhan
Vice-President: ALIYEV Rauf   Treasurer: JAFAROV Lativ   Media Officer: HASANOV Natiq
Men's Coach: VOGTS Berti   Women's Coach: HAYDAROV Shamil
AFFA formed: 1992   UEFA: 1994   FIFA: 1994
White shirts, Blue shorts, White socks or Blue shirts, White shorts, Blue socks

RECENT INTERNATIONALS PLAYED BY AZERBAIJAN

2004	Opponents	Score		Venue	Comp	Scorers	Att	Referee
18-08	Jordan	D	1-1	Amman	Fr	Ponomarev [23]	4 000	
4-09	Wales	D	1-1	Baku	WCq	Sadigov [55]	8 000	Trivkovic CRO
8-09	Austria	L	0-2	Vienna	WCq		26 400	Sammut MLT
9-10	Northern Ireland	D	0-0	Baku	WCq		6 460	Hanacsek HUN
13-10	England	L	0-1	Baku	WCq		17 000	Hamer LUX
17-11	Bulgaria	D	0-0	Baku	Fr		10 000	Sipailo LVA
2005								
21-01	Trinidad and Tobago	L	0-1	Port of Spain	Fr		500	
23-01	Trinidad and Tobago	L	0-2	Marabella	Fr		1 000	Gordon TRI
9-02	Moldova	D	0-0	Baku	Fr		3 000	
26-03	Poland	L	0-8	Warsaw	WCq		9 000	Vollquartz DEN
30-03	England	L	0-2	Newcastle	WCq		49 046	Costa POR
29-05	Iran	L	1-2	Tehran	Fr	Gurbanov.G [67]		
4-06	Poland	L	0-3	Baku	WCq		10 458	Undiano Mallenco ESP
17-08	Albania	L	1-2	Tirana	Fr	Tagizade [2]	7 300	
3-09	Northern Ireland	L	0-2	Belfast	WCq		12 000	Stanisic SCG
7-09	Austria	D	0-0	Baku	WCq		2 800	Verbist BEL
12-10	Wales	L	0-2	Cardiff	WCq		32 628	Hansson SWE
2006								
28-02	Ukraine	D	0-0	Baku	Fr			Sipailo LVA
12-04	Turkey	D	1-1	Baku	Fr	Sadygov.RF [64p]		Paniashvili GEO
18-05	Moldova	D	0-0	Chisinau	Fr			
15-08	Ukraine	L	0-6	Kyiv	Fr		6 000	Sukhina RUS
2-09	Serbia	L	0-1	Belgrade	ECq		BCD	Kircher GER
6-09	Kazakhstan	D	1-1	Baku	ECq	Ladaga [16]	8 500	Szabo HUN
7-10	Portugal	L	0-3	Porto	ECq		14 000	Halsey ENG
11-10	Belgium	L	0-3	Brussels	ECq		11 917	Lajuks LVA
2007								
7-02	Uzbekistan	D	0-0	Karshi	Fr			
7-03	Uzbekistan	W	1-0	Shymkent	Fr	Subasic [55]		
9-03	Kazakhstan	L	0-1	Shymkent	Fr			
11-03	Kyrgyzstan	W	1-0	Shymkent	Fr	Dzavadov [17]		
24-03	Poland	L	0-5	Warsaw	ECq		13 000	Jakobsson ISL
28-03	Finland	W	1-0	Baku	ECq	Imamaliev [82]	14 500	Messina ITA
2-06	Poland	L	1-3	Baku	ECq	Subasic [6]	25 800	Kapitanis CYP
6-06	Kazakhstan	D	1-1	Almaty	ECq	Nadyrov [30]	11 800	Toussaint LUX
22-08	Tajikistan	W	3-2	Dushanbe	Fr	Aliyev.S 2 [25 29], Subasic [43]		
12-09	Georgia	D	1-1	Baku	Fr	Subasic [44]	10 000	Kovalenko UZB
13-10	Portugal	L	0-2	Baku	ECq		25 000	Bebek CRO
17-10	Serbia	L	1-6	Baku	ECq	Aliyev.S [26]	3 100	Einwaller AUT
17-11	Finland	L	1-2	Helsinki	ECq	Gurbanov.M [63]	10 325	Hamer LUX
21-11	Belgium	L	0-1	Baku	ECq		7 000	Kenan ISR
2008								
3-02	Kazakhstan	D	0-0	Antalya	Fr			
26-03	Lithuania	L	0-1	Vilnius	Fr		1 500	Satchi MDA
1-06	Bosnia-Herzegovina	L	0-1	Zenica	Fr			
4-06	Andorra	W	2-1	Andorra la Vella	Fr	Ranim [17], Subasic [43]		

Fr = Friendly match • EC = UEFA EURO 2008 • WCq = FIFA World Cup • q = qualifier • BCD = Behind closed doors

AZERBAIJAN NATIONAL TEAM RECORDS AND RECORD SEQUENCES

Records			Sequence records					
Victory	4-0	LIE 1999	Wins	2	1998, 2004	Clean sheets	2	
Defeat	0-10	FRA 1995	Defeats	11	1994-1995	Goals scored	6	2004
Player Caps	78	Aslan Kerimov	Undefeated	4	2002	Without goal	9	1999-2000, 2004-05
Player Goals	12	Gurban Gurbanov	Without win	27	2004-2007	Goals against	19	2002-2004

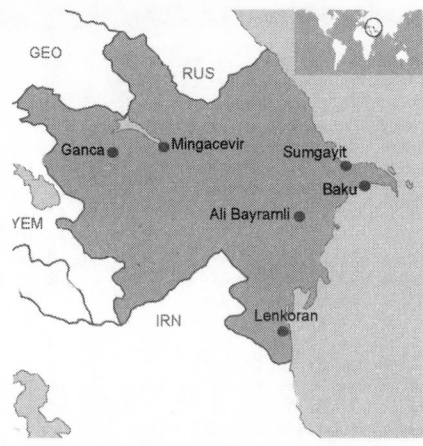

MAJOR CITIES/TOWNS

		Population '000
1	Baku	1856
2	Gäncä	305
3	Sumqayit	293
4	Mingäçevir	96
5	Qaraçuxur	73
6	Ali Bayramli	70
7	Bakikhanov	67
8	Naxçivan	64
9	Säki	62
10	Yevlakh	54
11	Xankändi	52
12	Lenkoran	49
13	Räsulzadä	45
14	Biläcäri	42
15	Mastaga	40
16	Agdam	40
17	Shamkir	35
18	Imisli	31
19	Sabirabad	28
20	Buzovna	24
21	Quba	22
22	Khusar	16
23	Tovuz	12
24	Masali	9

REPUBLIC OF AZERBAIJAN; AZARBAYCAN RESPUBLIKASI

Capital	Baku	Language	Azeri	Independence	1991
Population	7 961 619	Area	86 600 km²	Density	90 per km²	% in cities	56%
GDP per cap	$3 400	Dailling code	+994	Internet	.az	GMT +/-	+5

MEDALS TABLE

		Overall			League			Cup			Europe			City	Stadium	Cap'ty	DoF
		G	S	B	G	S	B	G	S	B	G	S	B				
1	Neftchi Baku	10	3	4	5	2	4	5	1					Baku	Tofik Bakhramov	29 858	1937
2	FK Gança	7	1	2	3	1	2	4						Gança	Sahar	9 300	1959
3	Karabakh Agdam	3	6	1	1	3	1	2	3					Baku	Tofik Ismailov	9 300	1950
4	Khazar Lenkoran	3	2		1	1		2	1					Lenkoran	Rasim Kara	15 000	1975
5	FK Shamkir	2	4	1	2	1	1		3					Shamkir	Sähär	11 500	
6	FK Baku	2		1	1		1	1						Baku	Tofik Bakhramov	29 858	1997
7	Inter Baku	1	2		1				2					Baku	Zabrat	3 000	1995
8	Turan Tovuz	1	1	1	1	1	1							Tovuz	Shehar	5 000	1954
9	Inshaatchi Baku	1						1						Baku			
	Shafa Baku	1						1						Baku	Shafa	7 852	
11	Karvan Yevlakh		2	1		1	1		1					Yevlakh	Yevlakh	5 000	2004
	Khazri Buznova		2	1		1	1		1					Buznova	Genclik	5 000	
13	Khazar Sumqayit		2			2								Sumqayit	Mehdi Huseyinzade	16 000	
	Kur-Nur Mingäçevir		2						2					Mingäçevir	Shehar	16 000	
15	Dinamo Baku		1	1		1	1							Baku	Tofik Bakhramov	29 858	
16	Inshaatchi Sabirabad		1						1					Baku			
	MTK-Araz Imishli		1						1					Imishli	Habio Halilov	8 500	1995
	Olimpik Baku		1						1					Baku	Shafa	7 852	1996

RECENT LEAGUE AND CUP RECORD

	Championship						Cup		
Year	Champions	Pts	Runners-up	Pts	Third	Pts	Winners	Score	Runners-up
1995	Kapaz Gança	42	Turan Tovuz	40	Neftchi Baku	38	Neftchi Baku	1-0	Kur-Nur
1996	Neftchi Baku	36	Khazri Buzovna	33	Kapaz Gança	32	Neftchi Baku	3-0	Karabakh Agdam
1997	Neftchi Baku	74	Karabakh Agdam	71	Khazri Buzovna	66	Kapaz Gança	1-0	Khazri Buzovna
1998	Kapaz Gança	70	Dinamo Baku	54	Shamkir	54	Kapaz Gança	2-0	Karabakh Agdam
1999	Kapaz Gança	58	Karabakh Agdam	54	Dinamo Baku	52	Neftchi Baku	0-0 5-4p	Shamkir
2000	Shamkir	55	Kapaz Gança	44	Neftchi Baku	43	Kapaz Gança	2-1	Karabakh Agdam
2001	Shamkir	51	Neftchi Baku	51	Vilash Masalli	38	Shafa Baku	2-1	Neftchi Baku
2002	Championship abandoned with eight rounds to play						Neftchi Baku	W-0	Shamkir
2003	No championship played						No tournament played		
2004	Neftchi Baku	69	Shamkir	64	Karabakh Agdam	60	Neftchi Baku	1-0	Shamkir
2005	Neftchi Baku	78	Khazar Lenkoran	78	Karvan Yevlakh	76	FK Baku	2-1	Inter Baku
2006	FK Baku	58	Karvan Yevlakh	57	Neftchi Baku	54	Karabakh Agdam	2-1	Karvan Yevlakh
2007	Khazar Lenkoran	56	Neftchi Baku	54	FK Baku	48	Khazar Lenkoran	1-0	MTK-Araz Imishli
2008	Inter Baku	58	Olimpik Baku	58	Neftchi Baku	55	Khazar Lenkoran	2-0	Inter Baku

AZERBAIJAN 2007–08

YUKSAK LIGA (1)

	Pl	W	D	L	F	A	Pts	Inter	Olimpik	Neftchi	Khazar	Karabakh	Khanlar	Simurq	FK Baku	Standard	Masalli	Karvan	Turan	Gen'birligi	Barda
Inter Baku †	26	18	4	4	55	18	58		2-0	0-0	2-2	1-0	4-0	2-0	1-0	1-1	3-0	3-1	3-1	3-0	4-0
Olimpik Baku ‡	26	17	7	2	29	7	58	1-0		0-0	0-0	0-1	2-0	1-0	3-0	1-0	3-1	2-0	3-0	1-0	1-0
Neftchi Baku	26	16	7	3	42	18	55	2-0	0-0		0-1	0-0	2-0	0-0	1-5	3-1	4-0	2-1	1-2	2-0	3-0
Khazar Lenkoran ‡	26	14	10	2	44	16	52	3-1	0-0	0-1		2-0	2-1	2-1	0-0	2-2	4-1	0-0	2-0	5-0	0-0
Karabakh Agdam	26	11	8	7	25	16	41	0-1	0-1	0-0	2-0		2-1	2-2	1-1	1-0	1-1	0-1	0-0	3-1	3-1
FK Khanlar	26	11	3	12	33	36	36	2-1	0-1	2-3	1-1	1-2		1-0	2-0	1-1	1-0	1-1	2-1	2-2	2-0
Simurq Zaqatala	26	9	9	8	31	25	36	3-4	0-0	1-2	1-1	1-0	2-0		0-0	1-0	1-0	0-1	3-0	3-0	3-0
FK Baku	26	8	11	7	35	26	35	0-0	0-1	2-3	2-2	0-0	3-0	1-1		0-1	1-2	3-3	2-2	3-1	0-0
Standard Baku	26	8	8	10	36	26	32	1-2	0-0	1-1	0-1	0-1	0-1	3-0	1-1		4-1	1-2	1-1	3-2	6-0
FK Masalli	26	8	6	12	30	40	30	0-3	1-2	0-2	0-3	1-0	1-0	1-1	2-0	1-1		4-1	3-1	6-0	1-1
Karvan Yevlakh	26	6	5	15	23	36	23	0-3	0-1	0-1	0-1	0-0	1-2	1-1	0-1	1-1	0-1		1-0	1-2	2-0
Turan Tovuz	26	4	6	16	21	49	18	0-4	1-3	0-1	0-4	0-2	4-2	1-2	0-2	0-2	0-0	1-5		2-0	3-0
Genclerbirliyi Sumgayit	26	4	2	20	21	68	14	0-3	0-1	2-6	0-1	0-1	0-6	0-3	0-3	1-5	1-0	3-1	1-1		4-0
ABN Barda	26	2	6	18	12	56	12	1-4	1-1	0-2	0-4	0-3	1-2	1-1	0-4	0-1	1-2	2-0	0-0	2-0	

11/08/2007 - 28/05/2008 • † Qualified for the UEFA Champions League • ‡ Qualified for the UEFA Cup

AZERBAIJAN 2007–08
BIRINCI DASTA (2)

	Pl	W	D	L	F	A	Pts
Bakili Baku	10	3	1	0	5	2	10
Omik Baku	10	2	2	0	5	2	8
NBC Salyan	10	1	1	2	4	5	4
MTK-Araz Imishli	10	1	1	2	3	4	4
ANSAD-Petrol Neftçala	10	1	1	2	3	5	4
Shahdag Khusar	10	1	0	3	3	5	3

20/04/2008 - 25/05/2008

FFA CUP 2007–08

Round of 16			Quarter–finals			Semi–finals			Final		
Khazar Lenkoran	4	5									
Genclerbirliyi S'gayit *	1	0	Khazar Lenkoran	0	2						
ABN Barda *	1	1	Olimpik Baku *	1	0						
Olimpik Baku	1	3				Khazar Lenkoran	3	1			
FK Baku *	3	2				FK Khanlar *	1	1			
Inter-2 Baku	0	0	FK Baku *	1 1 3p							
Simurq Zaqatala	0	2	FK Khanlar	1 1 4p							
FK Khanlar *	1	1							Khazar Lenkoran ‡		2
Neftchi Baku *	3	1							Inter Baku		0
Abseron	0	0	Neftchi Baku *	4	1						
Karvan Yevlakh	0	0	Standard Baku	1	0						
Standard Baku *	2	2				Neftchi Baku *	2	0			
Karabakh Agdam	2	2				Inter Baku	2	1			
Turan Tovuz *	0	1	Karabakh Agdam *	2	0						
FK Masalli *	0	2	Inter Baku	2	1						
Inter Baku	2	3									

CUP FINAL

Baku, 24-05-2008

Scorer - Junior Osvaldo 2 115 118

* Home team in the first leg • ‡ Qualified for the UEFA Cup

BAH – BAHAMAS

NATIONAL TEAM RECORD
JULY 10TH 2006 TO JULY 12TH 2010

PL	W	D	L	F	A	%
10	2	2	6	12	34	30

FIFA/COCA-COLA WORLD RANKING

1993	1994	1995	1996	1997	1998	1999	2000	2001	2002	2003	2004	2005	2006	2007	High	
167	-	-	-	-	-	189	178	184	187	193	192	193	146	174	**1 8**	09/06

2007–2008												Low	
08/07	09/07	10/07	11/07	12/07	01/08	02/08	03/08	04/08	05/08	06/08	07/08	**197**	03/99
149	168	170	171	174	174	179	178	165	164	167	166		

After seven years with Englishman Gary White at the helm of the national team, the Bahamas Football Association decided to change tack and follow the example of Jamaica by looking to Brazil for inspiration. Neider dos Santos, one time coach of Guyana, is the man charged with creating the Bahamas' very own version of the Reggae Boyz after his appointment as coach in March 2007. Known usually as the Baha Boyz, the players of the national team prefer to use the term Rake n'Scrape Boyz in reference to the Bahamas own musical heritage, but it has to be said that it may be some time before the Jamaicans are troubled by this particular mix of Brazil, music

INTERNATIONAL HONOURS
None

and football. In the 2010 FIFA World Cup qualifiers, Bahamas were drawn against the minnows of the British Virgin Islands and were very fortunate to make it through to the next round on away goals, as both drawn games against their opponents were actually played in the Bahamas. Their luck ran out in the next round, however, when they came up against the Jamaicans who, for the time being at least, proved that reggae rules over rake n'scrape with a 13-0 aggregate win. No doubt the FIFA dignitaries will enjoy some of the latter after the Bahamas was chosen to host the 2009 FIFA Congress.

THE FIFA BIG COUNT OF 2006

	Male	Female		Total
Number of players	14 536	3 408	Referees and Assistant Referees	36
Professionals	0		Admin, Coaches, Technical, Medical	230
Amateurs 18+	820		Number of clubs	34
Youth under 18	1 652		Number of teams	111
Unregistered	2 400		Clubs with women's teams	7
Total players	17 944		Players as % of population	5.91%

Bahamas Football Association (BFA)
Plaza on the Way, West Bay Street, PO Box N-8434, Nassau, NP, Bahamas
Tel +1 242 3225897   Fax +1 242 3225898
lehaven@bahamas.net.bs   www.bahamasfootballassoc.com
President: SEALEY Anton   General Secretary: HAVEN Lionel E.
Vice-President: LUNN Fred   Treasurer: HAVEN Lionel E.   Media Officer: HAVEN Lionel E.
Men's Coach: DOS SANTOS Neider   Women's Coach: BETHEL Vandyke
BFA formed: 1967   CONCACAF: 1981   FIFA: 1968
Yellow shirts with sky blue trimmings, Black shorts, Yellow socks

RECENT INTERNATIONAL MATCHES PLAYED BY BAHAMAS

2002	Opponents	Score	Venue	Comp	Scorers	Att	Referee
No international matches played in 2002							
2003							
27-12	Haiti	L 0-6	Miami	Fr			
2004							
26-03	Dominica	D 1-1	Nassau	WCq	Casimir 88	800	Forde BRB
28-03	Dominica	L 1-3	Nassau	WCq	Jean 67	900	Pineda HON
2005							
No international matches played in 2005							
2006							
2-09	Cayman Islands	W 3-1	Havana	CCq	OG 5, Moseley 36, Thompson 86		Stewart JAM
4-09	Cuba	L 0-6	Havana	CCq		100	
6-09	Turks & Caicos Isl	W 3-2	Havana	CCq	Nassies 59, Hall 63, Jean 87	120	Campbell JAM
19-11	Barbados	L 1-2	Bridgetown	CCq	Jean 76p	4 500	
21-11	Bermuda	L 0-4	Bridgetown	CCq			
23-11	St Vincent/Grenadines	L 2-3	Bridgetown	CCq	Christie 55, Moseley 65		
2007							
No international matches played in 2007							
2008							
26-03	British Virgin Islands	D 1-1	Nassau	WCq	St Fleur 47	450	Moreno PAN
30-03	British Virgin Islands	D 2-2	Nassau	WCq	Bethel 41, Mitchell 57	940	Suazo DOM
15-06	Jamaica	L 0-7	Kingston	WCq		20 000	Navarro CAN
18-06	Jamaica	L 0-6	Greenfield-Tr'wny	WCq		10 500	Archundia MEX

Fr = Friendly match • CC = Digicel Caribbean Cup • WC = FIFA World Cup • q = qualifier

BAHAMAS NATIONAL TEAM RECORDS AND RECORD SEQUENCES

Records			Sequence records				
Victory	3-0	TCA 1999	Wins	2	2000	Clean sheets	2	1999
Defeat	0-9	HAI 2000	Defeats	4	1999, 2000-2003	Goals scored	2	2000, 2004
Player Caps	n/a	Lionel Haven	Undefeated	2	1999, 2000, 2007	Without goal	4	2000-2003
Player Goals	n/a	Nesley Jean	Without win	10	2000	Goals against	16	1999

RECENT LEAGUE RECORD

	New Providence Championship						Grand Bahama	New Prov. Cup	National
Year	Champions	Pts	Runners-up	Pts	3rd Place	Pts	Champions	Winners	Winners
2000	Cavalier FC						Abacom United	Cavalier FC	Abacom United
2001	Cavalier FC	42	Gunite Pool Sharks	33	Team Toyota	33	Abacom United	Cavalier FC	Cavalier FC
2002	Bears FC	19	Team Toyota	18	United FC	15	Abacom United	Khaki Superstars	Not played
2003	Bears FC	23	United FC	22	Team Toyota	19	Abacom United	Bears FC	Bears FC
2004	Bears FC	29	United FC	26	Caledonia Celtic	23	Haitian Superstars	Bears FC	Not played
2005	Caledonia Celtic	27	RCA Racing Blue	21	Bears FC	18	Not played		
2006	Caledonia Celtic	29	Bears FC	26	Gunite Pool Sharks	17	Brita Red Bulls	Bears FC	
2007	Bears FC	31	Caledonia Celtic	26	United FC	20	Not played	Bears FC	
2008	Not played								

The National Championship is played between the champions of New Providence and the champions of Grand Bahama

BAHAMAS COUNTRY INFORMATION

Capital	Nassau	Independence	1973	GDP per Capita	$16 700
Population	299 697	Status	Commonwealth	GNP Ranking	117
Area km²	13 940	Language	English	Dialling code	+1 242
Population density	21 per km²	Literacy rate	96%	Internet code	.bs
% in urban areas	87%	Main religion	Christian 94%	GMT +/–	-5
Towns/Cities ('000)	Nassau 227; Freeport 46; Coppers Town 8; Marsh Harbour 5; Freetown 4; High Rock 3				
Neighbours (km)	North Atlantic Ocean 3 542				
Main stadia	Thomas A. Robinson – Nassau 9 100; Grand Bahama – Freeport 3 100				

BAN – BANGLADESH

NATIONAL TEAM RECORD
JULY 10TH 2006 TO JULY 12TH 2010

PL	W	D	L	F	A	%
15	0	5	10	7	32	16.7

FIFA/COCA-COLA WORLD RANKING

1993	1994	1995	1996	1997	1998	1999	2000	2001	2002	2003	2004	2005	2006	2007		High	
116	130	138	136	141	157	130	151	146	159	151	167	160	144	168		**110**	04/96

	2007–2008												Low	
08/07	09/07	10/07	11/07	12/07	01/08	02/08	03/08	04/08	05/08	06/08	07/08		**18**	06/08
176	175	172	173	168	168	171	173	180	180	183	182			

Just two years after finishing as runners-up at the South Asian Football Federation Championship, Bangladesh's fortunes slumped spectacularly during 2008 with the country going on a significant win-less streak that at 17 matches stood at just two less than the national team's all-time record. Draws against minnows Bhutan and Afghanistan plus a defeat at the hands of Sri Lanka saw Bangladesh exit the 2008 edition of the regional competition at the end of the group phase. That failure compounded what had been a disappointing year for the national side after elimination from the 2010 FIFA World Cup qualifiers by Tajikistan along with missing out on qualifying for the

INTERNATIONAL HONOURS
Qualified for AFC Asian Cup Finals 1980   Represented in the Football Tournament of the Asian Games 1978 1982 1986 1990
South Asian Federation Games 1999   South Asian Football Federation Cup 2003

finals of the AFC Challenge Cup in India. Bangladesh picked up just one point in the qualifying round after a 0-0 draw with Afghanistan, a result which was followed by a loss at the hands of Kyrgyzstan. On the domestic scene, the new B-League kicked off its second season in February boasting 12 clubs with Abahani FC defending the title they won in the league's inaugural season. The league is one of the initiatives that came into effect as part of the Asian Football Confederation's Vision Bangladesh programme to which the nation signed up in early 2007.

THE FIFA BIG COUNT OF 2006

	Male	Female		Total
Number of players	6 070 200	210 100	Referees and Assistant Referees	4 304
Professionals	0		Admin, Coaches, Technical, Medical	71 300
Amateurs 18+	98 980		Number of clubs	4 100
Youth under 18	172 320		Number of teams	8 200
Unregistered	5 815 000		Clubs with women's teams	0
Total players	6 280 300		Players as % of population	4.26%

Bangladesh Football Federation (BFF)
BFF House, Motijheel, Dhaka 1000, Bangladesh
Tel +880 2 7161582   Fax +880 2 7160270
bffbd@citechco.net   www.bffonline.com
President: KAZI Mohammed Salahuddin   General Secretary: MANZOOR HOSSAIN O.F.M.
Vice-President: SALAM Abdus Murshedi   Treasurer: ALAM CHOWDHURY Shah   Media Officer: AL FATAH Ahmed Sayed
Men's Coach: TBD   Women's Coach: ABU Yusef
BFF formed: 1972   AFC: 1974   FIFA: 1974
Green with black and red trimmings, Green shorts, Red socks or White shirts with black and red trimmings, White shirts, White socks

RECENT INTERNATIONAL MATCHES PLAYED BY BANGLADESH

2006 Opponents		Score	Venue	Comp	Scorers	Att	Referee
22-02 Uzbekistan	L	0-5	Uzbekistan	ACq		12 000	Ebrahim BHR
1-03 Hong Kong	L	0-1	Dhaka	ACq		1 000	Sarkar IND
1-04 Cambodia	W	2-1	Dhaka	CCr1	Alfaz Ahmed [31], Hasan Ameli [64]	35 000	Tan Hai CHN
3-04 Guam	W	3-0	Dhaka	CCr1	Hasan Ameli [49], Abdul Hossain 2 [83 85]	18 000	U Ein Cho MYA
5-04 Palestine	D	1-1	Dhaka	CCr1	Mahadi Tapu [55]	22 000	Mombini IRN
10-04 Tajikistan	L	1-6	Dhaka	CCqf	Alfaz Ahmed [17]	15 000	AK Nema IRQ
16-08 Qatar	L	1-4	Chittagong	ACq	Mohamad Arman [23]	7 000	Al Yarimi YEM
6-09 Qatar	L	0-3	Doha	ACq		500	Najm LIB
11-10 Uzbekistan	L	0-4	Dhaka	ACq		120	Tan Hai CHN
15-11 Hong Kong	L	0-2	Hong Kong	ACq		1 273	Kim Dong Jin KOR
2007							
18-08 Syria	L	0-2	New Delhi	Fr			
20-08 India	L	0-1	New Delhi	Fr			
22-08 Cambodia	D	1-1	New Delhi	Fr	Abdul Hossain [30]		
24-08 Kyrgyzstan	L	0-3	New Delhi	Fr			
8-10 Tajikistan	D	1-1	Dhaka	WCq	Zumratul Hossain Mithu [50]	700	Al Hilali OMA
28-10 Tajikistan	L	0-5	Dushanbe	WCq		10 000	Chynybekov KGZ
2008							
5-05 Afghanistan	D	0-0	Bishkek	CCq		3 000	Al Senan UAE
9-05 Kyrgyzstan	L	1-2	Bishkek	CCq		5 000	Al Enezi KUW
4-06 Bhutan	D	1-1	Colombo	SAr1	Arup Baidya [26]		
6-06 Afghanistan	D	2-2	Colombo	SAr1	Hasan Ameli [52], Mamunul Islam Mamun [76]		
8-06 Sri Lanka	L	0-1	Colombo	SAr1			

SA = South Asian Football Federation Cup • AC = AFC Asian Cup • CC = AFC Challenge Cup • WCq = FIFA World Cup
q = qualifier • r1 = first round group • sf = semi-final • f = final • GG = Golden Goal

BANGLADESH NATIONAL TEAM RECORDS AND RECORD SEQUENCES

Records			Sequence records		
Victory	8-0	MDV 1985	Wins	4	2003
Defeat	0-9	KOR 1979	Defeats	7	1979-1981
Player Caps	n/a		Undefeated	6	2001-2003
Player Goals	n/a		Without win	19	1973-1979

Clean sheets	3	1984, 1999, 2003
Goals scored	8	1984, 2001-2003
Without goal	5	Three times
Goals against	34	1973-1983

RECENT LEAGUE RECORD

Dhaka League

Year	Champions	Pts	Runners-up	Pts	Third	Pts
1998	Muktijoddha	52	Mohammedan	50	Abahani	42
1999	Mohammedan	40	Abahani	37	Muktijoddha	34
2000	Muktijoddha	40	Abahani	37	Mohammedan	33
2001	Abahani	41	Mohammedan	27	Rahmatganj	18
2002	Mohammedan	33	Abahani	31	Muktijoddha	29
2003	No championship due to a readjustment in the timings of the season					
2004	Brothers Union	40	Sheikh Russell	38	Abahani	33
2005	Brothers Union ‡	39	Mohammedan	39	Abahani	38

† played on a league system • ‡ Play-off in 2005: Brothers Union 1-0 Mohammedan

B.League

Year	Champions	Pts	Runners-up	Pts	Third	Pts
2007	Abahani	47	Mohammedan	40	Muktijoddha	33

National Championship

Winners	Score	Runners-up
Abahani	†	Mohammedan
	Not played	
Mohammedan	0-0 6-5p	Abahani
Muktijoddha	1-1 3-2p	Mohammedan
Brothers Union	0-0 4-2p	Muktijoddha
Mohammedan	2-0	Abahani

BANGLADESH COUNTRY INFORMATION

Capital	Dhaka	Independence	1971	GDP per Capita	$1 900
Population	141 340 476	Status	Republic	GNP Ranking	51
Area km²	144 000	Language	Bengali	Dialling code	+880
Population density	98 per km²	Literacy rate	40%	Internet code	.bd
% in urban areas	18%	Main religion	Muslim 87%	GMT +/–	+6
Towns/Cities ('000)	Dhaka 6 493; Chittagong 3 672; Khulna 1 342; Rajshahi 700; Comilla 389; Tungi 337; Mymensingh 330; Sylhet 326; Rangpur 285; Narsinghdi 281; Barisal 280;				
Neighbours (km)	India 4 053; Burma 193; Bay of Bengal 580				
Main stadia	Bangabandhu – Dkaka 36 000; Sher-e-Bangla Mirpur – Dhaka 30 000				

BDI – BURUNDI

NATIONAL TEAM RECORD
JULY 10TH 2006 TO JULY 12TH 2010

PL	W	D	L	F	A	%
20	7	3	10	18	22	42.5

FIFA/COCA-COLA WORLD RANKING

1993	1994	1995	1996	1997	1998	1999	2000	2001	2002	2003	2004	2005	2006	2007	High	
101	126	146	137	152	141	133	126	139	135	145	152	147	117	109	**96**	08/93

2007–2008												Low	
08/07	09/07	10/07	11/07	12/07	01/08	02/08	03/08	04/08	05/08	06/08	07/08	**160**	07/98
113	110	117	116	109	121	122	123	118	119	119	133		

Burundi finished fourth at the annual East and Central African Senior Challenge Cup in December, scoring a rare win over Kenya along the way. But it was one of few high points for the small central African state, never in serious contention for a place at the 2008 African Nations Cup finals in Ghana, and after just four qualifiers, also out of the running for a 2010 FIFA World Cup berth. Burundi's run at the tournament in Tanzania produced their best results at the regional championships since they reached the final in 2004. They were just as pleased with the goalless draw achieved against African champions Egypt in the 2008 Nations Cup qualifiers, a result in

INTERNATIONAL HONOURS
None

Bujumbura which forced the Pharaohs into the embarrassing position of having to wait until the final round of matches to make sure of qualification. Coach Adel Amrouche, an Algerian with a Belgian passport who had previously worked in the Democratic Republic of Congo, brought more stability to the team, starting with the positive result against Egypt and then continuing the progress with the semifinal spot in Dar-es-Salaam. In club football, Vital'O beat Inter Star 1-0 in the championship final to retain their title but were eliminated in the early stages of the African Champions League by Cameroon's Cotonsport, losing both home and away in their first round tie.

THE FIFA BIG COUNT OF 2006

	Male	Female		Total
Number of players	335 284	17 050	Referees and Assistant Referees	412
Professionals	3		Admin, Coaches, Technical, Medical	9 220
Amateurs 18+	5 612		Number of clubs	165
Youth under 18	6 289		Number of teams	189
Unregistered	17 400		Clubs with women's teams	0
Total players	352 334		Players as % of population	4.36%

Fédération de Football du Burundi (FFB)
Avenue Muyinga, Case postale 3426, Bujumbura, Burundi
Tel +257 79 928762   Fax +257 22 242892
lydiansekera@yahoo.fr   www.none
President: NSEKERA Lydia   General Secretary: MANIRAKIZA Jeremie
Vice-President: SAMUGABO Mustapha   Treasurer: KAZE Diane   Media Officer: None
Men's Coach: AMROUCHE Adel   Women's Coach: None
FFB formed: 1948   CAF: 1972   FIFA: 1972
Red shirts with white trimmings, White shorts, Green socks

RECENT INTERNATIONAL MATCHES PLAYED BY BURUNDI

2006	Opponents		Score	Venue	Comp	Scorers	Att	Referee
2-09	Egypt	L	1-4	Alexandria	CNq	Ndikumana 78p		Haimoudi ALG
8-10	Mauritania	W	3-1	Bujumbura	CNq	Ndikumana 2 2 30, Mbuzumutima 44		Abdelrahman SUD
26-11	Zambia	W	3-2	Addis Abeba	CCr1	Ndizeye 8, Nzohabonayo 17, Ndikumana 46		
29-11	Zanzibar †	D	0-0	Addis Abeba	CCr1			
6-12	Sudan	L	0-1	Addis Abeba	CCqf			
2007								
25-03	Botswana	L	0-1	Gaborone	CNq			Marange ZIM
27-05	Rwanda	L	0-1	Kigali	Fr			
2-06	Botswana	W	1-0	Kigali	CNq	Abdul Ndayishimiye 80		Ssegonga UGA
9-09	Egypt	D	0-0	Bujumbura	CNq			Louzaya CGO
13-10	Mauritania	L	1-2	Nouakchott	CNq	Irambona 85		Aboubacar CIV
10-12	Somalia	W	3-0	Dar es Salaam	CCr1	Nzohabonayo 18, Ndikumana 2 77 82		
12-12	Kenya	W	1-0	Dar es Salaam	CCr1	Mbazumutima 33		
15-12	Tanzania	D	0-0	Dar es Salaam	CCr1			
17-12	Eritrea	W	2-1	Dar es Salaam	CCqf	Mbazumutima 69, Nzohabonayo 81		
19-12	Sudan	L	1-2	Dar es Salaam	CCsf	Nahimana 12		
22-12	Uganda	L	0-2	Dar es Salaam	CC3p			
2008								
6-02	Rwanda	D	0-0	Bujumbura	Fr			
1-06	Seychelles	W	1-0	Bujumbura	WCq	Ndikumana 81	4 000	Imiere NGA
7-06	Burkina Faso	L	0-2	Ouagadougou	WCq		0	Ndume GAB
15-06	Tunisia	L	0-1	Bujumbura	WCq		7 000	Damon RSA
21-06	Tunisia	L	1-2	Rades	WCq	Mbazumutima 45	6 000	Younis EGY

Fr = Friendly match • CN = CAF African Cup of Nations qualifier • CC = CECAFA Cup • WCq = FIFA World Cup
q = qualifier • r1 = 1st round • † Not a full international

BURUNDI NATIONAL TEAM RECORDS AND RECORD SEQUENCES

Records			Sequence records					
Victory	6-2	RWA 1976	Wins	5	1996-1998	Clean sheets	6	1993-1998
Defeat	1-6	CIV 2003	Defeats	4	1999	Goals scored	9	1982-1992
Player Caps	n/a		Undefeated	8	1993-1998	Without goal	4	2006-2007
Player Goals	n/a		Without win	14	2001-2004	Goals against	10	1975-1981

RECENT LEAGUE AND CUP RECORD

Year	Champions	Cup Winners
1996	Fantastique	Vital'O
1997	Maniema	Vital'O
1998	Vital'O	Elite
1999	Vital'O	Vital'O
2000	Vital'O	Atletico Olympique
2001	Prince Louis	
2002	Muzinga	
2003	Championship abandoned	
2004	Atletico Olympique	Bafalo Muramvya
2005	Inter Stars	
2006	Vital'O	
2007	Vital'O	

BURUNDI COUNTRY INFORMATION

Capital	Bujumbura	Independence	1962	GDP per Capita	$600
Population	6 231 221	Status	Republic	GNP Ranking	161
Area km²	27 830	Language	Kirundi/French	Dialling code	+257
Population density	224 per km²	Literacy rate	45%	Internet code	.bi
% in urban areas	8%	Main religion	Muslim 43%	GMT +/–	+2
Towns/Cities ('000)	Bujumbura 330; Muyinga 71; Ruyigi 38; Gitega 23; Ngozi 21; Rutana 20; Bururi 19;				
Neighbours (km)	Rwanda 290, Tanzania 451, Congo DR 233. Burundi also borders Lake Tanganyika				
Main stadia	Prince Louis Rwagasore – Bujumbura 22 000				

BEL – BELGIUM

NATIONAL TEAM RECORD
JULY 10TH 2006 TO JULY 12TH 2010

PL	W	D	L	F	A	%
17	5	3	9	16	25	38.2

FIFA/COCA-COLA WORLD RANKING

1993	1994	1995	1996	1997	1998	1999	2000	2001	2002	2003	2004	2005	2006	2007	High	
25	24	24	42	41	35	33	27	20	17	16	45	55	53	49	**16**	01/03

2007–2008											Low	
08/07	09/07	10/07	11/07	12/07	01/08	02/08	03/08	04/08	05/08	06/08	07/08	**71** 06/07
69	60	54	49	49	49	43	42	48	46	49	46	

It took a quarter of a century, but the long wait for Standard Liège fans eventually came to an end when their team finally got their hands on the championship trophy once again. Standard remained unbeaten until the end of April with their only defeat in the campaign coming in the 32nd round of games - a 2-1 reverse at the hands of Charleroi - by which time they already had the title in the bag. Coached by former national team goalkeeper Michel Preud'homme, Standard boasted one of the youngest squads in the league, epitomised by their 20-year-old captain and Belgian Player of the Year, Steven Defour, although shortly after winning the title Preud'homme resigned to take

INTERNATIONAL HONOURS
Qualified for the FIFA World Cup finals 1930 1934 1938 1954 1970 1982 1986 1990 1994 1998 2002 **Olympic Gold** 1920

over at Gent. Deposed champions Anderlecht beat Gent 3-2 in a dramatic Cup Final in which they twice came from behind. Former Gent players Mbark Boussoufa and Guillaume Gillet scored the decisive goals to secure a first Cup triumph since 1994 for the Brussels club. Overall it was a poor season for Belgian clubs in Europe although having been knocked-out of the Champions League in the third preliminary round, Anderlecht did progress through to the last 16 of the UEFA Cup before losing heavily to Bayern. The national team made very hard work of their Euro 2008 qualifying group, finishing well behind the front pack of Poland, Portugal, Finland and Serbia.

THE FIFA BIG COUNT OF 2006

	Male	Female		Total
Number of players	745 269	71 314	Referees and Assistant Referees	6 898
Professionals	1 399		Admin, Coaches, Technical, Medical	72 747
Amateurs 18+	212 009		Number of clubs	1 869
Youth under 18	208 551		Number of teams	17 960
Unregistered	128 200		Clubs with women's teams	189
Total players	816 583		Players as % of population	7.87%

Union Royale Belge des Sociétés de Football Association / Koninklijke Belgische Voetbalbond (URBSFA/KBVB)
145 Avenue Houba de Strooper, Bruxelles 1020, Belgium
Tel +32 2 4771211   Fax +32 2 4782391
urbsfa.kbvb@footbel.com   www.footbel.com
President: DE KEERSMAECKER Francois   General Secretary: PHILIPS Jean-Marie
Vice-President: COLIN Philippe   Treasurer: LANDSHEERE Germain   Media Officer: CORNU Nicolas
Men's Coach: VANDEREYCKEN Rene   Women's Coach: NOE Anne
URBSFA/KBVB formed: 1895   UEFA: 1954   FIFA: 1904
Red shirts with black trimmings, Red shorts, Red socks or Black shirts with red trimmings, Black shorts, Black socks

RECENT INTERNATIONAL MATCHES PLAYED BY BELGIUM

2004	Opponents	Score		Venue	Comp	Scorers	Att	Referee
18-02	France	L	0-2	Brussels	Fr		43 160	Halsey ENG
31-03	Germany	L	0-3	Cologne	Fr		46 500	Wegereef NED
28-04	Turkey	L	2-3	Brussels	Fr	Sonck [33], Dufer [85]	25 000	Van Egmond NED
29-05	Netherlands	W	1-0	Eindhoven	Fr	Goor [77p]	32 500	Colombo FRA
18-08	Norway	D	2-2	Oslo	Fr	Buffel 2 [25 34]	16 669	Stupik POL
4-09	Lithuania	D	1-1	Charleroi	WCq	Sonck [61]	19 218	Loizou CYP
9-10	Spain	L	0-2	Santander	WCq		17 000	Nielsen DEN
17-11	Serbia & Montenegro	L	0-2	Brussels	WCq		28 350	Frojdfeldt SWE
2005								
9-02	Egypt	L	0-4	Cairo	Fr		5 000	Beltagi EGY
26-03	Bosnia-Herzegovina	W	4-1	Brussels	WCq	Mpenza.E 2 [15 54], Daerden [44], Buffel [77]	36 700	Hrinak SVK
30-03	San Marino	W	2-1	Serravalle	WCq	Simons [18p], Van Buyten [65]	871	Kasnaferis GRE
4-06	Serbia & Montenegro	D	0-0	Belgrade	WCq		16 662	Ivanov.V RUS
17-08	Greece	W	2-0	Brussels	Fr	Mpenza.E [19], Mpenza.M [24]	20 000	Berntsen NOR
3-09	Bosnia-Herzegovina	L	0-1	Zenica	WCq		12 000	Benquerenca POR
7-09	San Marino	W	8-0	Antwerp	WCq	Simons [34p], Daerden 2 [39 67], Buffel [44], Mpenza.M 2 [52 71], Vandenbergh [53], Van Buyten [83]	8 207	Stokes IRL
8-10	Spain	L	0-2	Brussels	WCq		40 300	Michel SVK
12-10	Lithuania	D	1-1	Vilnius	WCq	Garaerts [20]	1 500	Riley ENG
2006								
1-03	Luxembourg	W	2-0	Luxembourg	Fr	Vandenbergh [42], Pieroni [61]. Abandoned 65 mins		Einwaller AUT
11-05	Saudi Arabia	W	2-1	Sittard	Fr	Caluwe [3], Vanden Borre [55]		Bossen NED
20-05	Slovakia	D	1-1	Trnava	Fr	Geraerts [76]	4 174	Kassai HUN
24-05	Turkey	D	3-3	Genk	Fr	OG [28], Sonck [43], Hoefkens [90]	15 000	Stuchlik AUT
16-08	Kazakhstan	D	0-0	Brussels	ECq		15 495	Courtney NIR
6-09	Armenia	W	1-0	Yerevan	ECq	Van Buyten [41]	4 122	Lehner AUT
7-10	Serbia	L	0-1	Belgrade	ECq		16 901	Messina ITA
11-10	Azerbaijan	W	3-0	Brussels	ECq	Simons [24p], Vandenbergh [47], Dembélé [82]	11 917	Lajuks LVA
15-11	Poland	L	0-1	Brussels	ECq		37 928	Dougal SCO
2007								
7-02	Czech Republic	L	0-2	Brussels	Fr		12 000	Granat POL
24-03	Portugal	L	0-4	Lisbon	ECq		47 009	Vassaras GRE
2-06	Portugal	L	1-2	Brussels	ECq	Fellaini [55]	45 383	Hansson SWE
6-06	Finland	L	0-2	Helsinki	ECq		34 818	Riley ENG
22-08	Serbia	W	3-2	Brussels	ECq	Dembélé 2 [10 88], Mirallas [30]	19 202	Hauge NOR
12-09	Kazakhstan	D	2-2	Almaty	ECq	Geraerts [13], Mirallas [24]	18 100	Tudor ROU
13-10	Finland	D	0-0	Brussels	ECq		21 393	Kapitanis CYP
17-10	Armenia	W	3-0	Brussels	ECq	Sonck [63], Dembélé [69], Geraerts [76]	14 812	Valgeirsson ISL
17-11	Poland	L	0-2	Chorzow	ECq		41 450	Larsen DEN
21-11	Azerbaijan	W	1-0	Baku	ECq	Pieroni [52]	7 000	Kenan ISR
2008								
26-03	Morocco	L	1-4	Brussels	Fr	Witsel [50]	24 000	Nijhuis NED
30-05	Italy	L	1-3	Florence	Fr	Sonck [92+]	12 500	Atkinson ENG

Fr = Friendly match • EC = UEFA EURO 2008 • WCq = FIFA World Cup • q = qualifier

BELGIUM NATIONAL TEAM RECORDS AND RECORD SEQUENCES

Records			Sequence records					
Victory	10-1	SMR 2001	Wins	7	1979-1980	Clean sheets	5	1972-1973, 1989
Defeat	2-11	ENG 1909	Defeats	7	1927-1928	Goals scored	21	1937-1945
Player Caps	96	Jan Ceulemans	Undefeated	11	1988-1989	Without goal	5	1999
Player Goals	30	Voorhoof & Van Himst	Without win	13	1933-1935	Goals against	38	1928-1933

KONINKRIJK BELGIE; ROYAUME DE BELGIQUE; KINGDOM OF BELGIUM

Capital	Brussels	Language	Flemish 60%, French 40%	Independence	1830
Population	10 379 067	Area	30 528 km²	Density	339 per km²	% in cities	97%
GDP per cap	$29 100	Dailling code	+32	Internet	.be	GMT + / -	+1

MAJOR CITIES/TOWNS

Population '000

1	Brussels	1 031
2	Antwerp	463
3	Gent	233
4	Charleroi	199
5	Liège	181
6	Brugge	116
	Namur	106
	Leuven	94
7	Mons	91
8	Mechelen	78
	Aalst	77
9	La Louvière	76
	Kortrijk	73
	Oostend	69
10	Tournai	67
11	Genk	63
12	Roeselare	56
13	Mouscron	51
14	Beveren	45
15	Sint-Truiden	38
16	Lokeren	37
17	Waregem	35
18	Lier	33
19	Westerlo	22

MEDALS TABLE

		Overall			League			Cup			Europe			City	Stadium	Cap'ty	DoF
		G	S	B	G	S	B	G	S	B	G	S	B				
1	RSC Anderlecht	41	26	9	29	19	7	9	3		3	4	2	Brussels	Vanden Stock	28 063	1908
2	Club Brugge	23	25	13	13	17	11	10	6			2	2	Brugge	Jan Breydel	29 042	1891
3	Standard Liège	14	20	21	9	10	19	5	9			1	2	Liège	Sclessin	30 035	1898
4	Union St Gilloise	13	8	8	11	8	7	2					1	Brussels	Joseph Marien	8 000	1897
5	Beerschot VAV	9	8	5	7	5		2	1					Antwerp	Kielstadion		1899-1999
6	Racing CB	7	5	3	6	5	3	1						Brussels	Ganzenvijver/Fallon		1891-1973
7	Royal Antwerp	6	14	7	4	12	7	2	1		1			Antwerp	Bosuil	16 649	1880
8	KV Mechelen	6	8	4	4	5	3	1	3		1		1	Mechelen	Scarletstadion	14 145	1904
9	Royal FC Liègeois	6	4	5	5	3	4	1	1		1			Liège	Ans		1892
10	Lierse SK	6	3	2	4	2	2	2	1					Lier	Herman Vanderpoorten	14 538	1906
11	Daring CB	5	5	4	5	4	4		1					Brussels	Edmond Machtens		1895-1973
12	Cercle Brugge	5	3	6	3		6	2	3					Brugge	Jan Breydel	29 268	1899
13	SK Beveren	4	3	1	2			2	3				1	Beveren-Waas	Freethiel	13 290	1934
14	KRC Genk	4	2		2	2		2						Genk	Fenix Stadion (Cristal Arena)	24 738	1988
15	KAA Gent	2	2	6		1	6	2	1					Gent	Jules Ottenstadion	13 265	1898
16	Waterschei Thor	2	1	2			1	2	1				1	Genk	Andre Dumont		1925-1988

RECENT LEAGUE AND CUP RECORD

	Championship						Cup		
Year	Champions	Pts	Runners-up	Pts	Third	Pts	Winners	Score	Runners-up
1995	RSC Anderlecht	52	Standard Liège	51	Club Brugge	49	Club Brugge	3-1	Germinal Ekeren
1996	Club Brugge	81	RSC Anderlecht	71	Germinal Ekeren	53	Club Brugge	2-1	Cercle Brugge
1997	Lierse SK	73	Club Brugge	71	Excelsior Mouscron	61	Germinal Ekeren	4-2	RSC Anderlecht
1998	Club Brugge	84	KRC Genk	66	Germinal Ekeren	58	KRC Genk	4-0	Club Brugge
1999	KRC Genk	73	Club Brugge	71	RSC Anderlecht	70	Lierse SK	3-1	Standard Liège
2000	RSC Anderlecht	75	Club Brugge	67	KAA Gent	63	KRC Genk	4-1	Standard Liège
2001	RSC Anderlecht	83	Club Brugge	78	Standard Liège	60	KVC Westerlo	1-0	KFC Lommelse
2002	KRC Genk	72	Club Brugge	72	RSC Anderlecht	66	Club Brugge	3-1	Excelsior Mouscron
2003	Club Brugge	79	RSC Anderlecht	71	KSC Lokeren	60	La Louvière	3-1	Sint-Truidense
2004	RSC Anderlecht	81	Club Brugge	72	Standard Liège	65	Club Brugge	4-2	KSK Beveren
2005	Club Brugge	79	RSC Anderlecht	76	Standard Liège	70	Germinal Beerschot	2-1	Club Brugge
2006	RSC Anderlecht	70	Standard Liège	65	Club Brugge	64	Zulte Waregem	2-1	Excelsior Mouscron
2007	RSC Anderlecht	77	KRC Genk	72	Standard Liège	64	Club Brugge	1-0	Standard Liège
2008	Standard Liège	77	RSC Anderlecht	70	Club Brugge	67	RSC Anderlecht	3-2	KAA Gent

BELGIUM 2007–08

LIGUE JUPILER

	Pl	W	D	L	F	A	Pts	Standard	Anderlecht	Brugge	Cercle	Beerschot	Gent	Waregem	Charleroi	Westerlo	Genk	Mouscron	Lokeren	Mechelen	Roeselare	Mons	Dender	St Truiden	Brussels
Standard Club Liège †	34	22	11	1	61	19	77		2-0	2-1	4-1	3-1	0-0	3-1	5-1	2-1	3-1	1-0	1-0	2-2	0-0	3-0	2-0	2-1	4-1
RSC Anderlecht †	34	21	7	6	59	31	70	0-0		2-0	3-1	2-0	2-1	2-2	0-1	3-1	1-0	2-1	1-0	1-0	5-0	1-0	3-2	4-1	3-0
Club Brugge ‡	34	20	7	7	45	30	67	1-2	1-0		1-0	3-0	0-0	1-0	0-2	4-0	2-6	1-0	1-1	2-0	1-0	2-0	2-1	3-2	1-0
Cercle Brugge	34	17	9	8	62	33	60	0-0	0-0	1-2		1-1	4-1	2-0	3-1	1-0	5-1	3-0	3-2	2-0	0-0	3-0	0-0	5-1	0-0
Germinal Beerschot	34	16	7	11	46	34	55	1-2	2-0	0-1	3-0		2-2	0-0	1-0	0-2	1-2	3-0	1-1	4-3	2-0	1-0	2-0	2-1	3-0
KAA Gent ‡	34	14	10	10	57	46	52	1-1	2-3	0-0	3-2	2-1		1-1	2-1	1-1	5-0	2-0	4-2	4-1	1-1	2-4	2-0	2-3	1-0
Zulte-Waregem	34	13	8	13	47	54	47	1-4	1-0	2-3	0-3	2-1	2-1		2-2	1-0	2-2	2-1	1-1	2-1	0-3	1-1	2-2	2-1	1-0
RSC Charleroi	34	13	7	14	41	45	46	2-1	0-2	1-1	1-3	0-0	1-2	2-3		1-1	3-1	1-3	1-0	1-0	1-1	1-0	3-1	1-1	1-0
KVC Westerlo	34	12	9	13	43	37	45	1-3	0-2	0-0	1-1	1-2	2-0	1-1	1-0		2-1	0-2	1-2	1-1	6-0	0-0	0-0	2-0	7-2
KRC Genk	34	12	9	13	54	55	45	0-2	1-1	1-2	3-1	1-3	3-3	5-2	1-0	1-0		3-1	2-3	2-1	0-0	2-0	1-2	0-1	2-1
Excelsior Mouscron	34	12	6	16	38	43	42	0-0	1-2	2-0	1-0	1-0	1-4	0-2	3-1	1-2	1-1		2-0	0-1	1-3	2-1	3-1	0-0	1-1
KSC Lokeren	34	9	15	10	32	33	42	0-0	0-0	0-1	1-0	1-0	1-0	1-0	1-1	0-1	1-1	1-1		3-1	3-0	1-0	1-2	2-0	1-0
KV Mechelen	34	10	10	14	45	52	40	0-1	0-1	1-1	0-4	1-2	1-0	2-1	1-0	0-2	2-2	2-1	1-1		4-3	2-2	2-0	2-3	4-0
KSV Roeselare	34	9	11	14	36	55	38	0-4	2-2	1-2	0-1	1-0	0-1	3-2	1-2	0-2	0-0	2-1	1-1	2-2		3-1	4-3	2-0	2-1
RAEC Mons	34	9	6	19	33	59	33	0-0	0-0	2-1	0-2	1-0	2-4	1-2	0-3	2-1	2-4	2-0	2-0	0-3	0-1		0-3	1-0	2-1
Verbroedering Dender	34	7	12	15	37	45	33	1-1	1-2	0-1	0-2	0-0	4-0	3-0	0-0	1-3	1-1	2-0	1-1	1-1	2-2	1-2		0-0	2-1
Sint-Truiden VV	34	6	9	19	32	58	27	0-0	4-3	1-1	0-0	0-3	2-1	2-1	0-3	0-2	1-2	0-2	1-1	0-1	0-1	1-2	1-1		1-1
FC Brussels	34	4	7	23	27	66	19	0-1	2-4	1-3	1-4	1-2	0-2	1-2	1-2	0-1	0-5	0-2	2-0	2-2	0-0	4-1	1-1	2-0	

3/08/2007 - 9/05/2008 • † Qualified for the UEFA Champions League • ‡ Qualified for the UEFA Cup • ‡‡ Relegation play-off
Top scorers: Joseph Akpala, Charleroi 18; Elianiv Barda, Genk 16; Milan Jovanovic, Standard 16; Mbaye Laye, Zulte-Waregem 16; Sanharib Malki, Beerschot 16; Dieumerci Mbokani, Standard 16

BELGIUM 2007–08 TWEEDE CLASSE (2)

	Pl	W	D	L	F	A	Pts
KV Kortrijk	36	23	7	6	73	35	76
AFC Tubize ‡	36	19	9	8	49	29	66
Oud-Heverlee Leuven ‡	36	18	7	11	61	42	61
KVSK United ‡	36	16	12	8	51	36	60
Royal Antwerp ‡	36	16	11	9	64	38	59
Excelsior Virton	36	15	11	10	56	44	56
Lierse SK	36	15	8	13	47	36	53
VW Hamme	36	14	7	15	54	45	49
KSK Beveren	36	14	6	16	48	56	48
KVK Tienen	36	13	9	14	49	51	48
Olympic Charleroi	36	13	7	16	40	53	46
RFC Tournai	36	12	10	14	34	37	46
AS Eupen	36	11	12	13	45	49	45
Red Star Waasland	36	10	13	13	46	47	43
KMSK Deinze	36	10	13	13	44	58	43
KV Oostende	36	11	9	16	44	59	42
UR Namur	36	10	12	14	51	63	42
Union St Gilloise	36	11	7	18	48	61	40
Verbroedering Geel	36	4	4	28	33	98	16

29/08/2007 - 11/05/2008 • ‡ Qualified for play-offs

TWEEDE CLASSE PROMOTION PLAY-OFFS

	Pl	W	D	L	F	A	Pts	Tubize	Antwerp	KVSK	Leuven
AFC Tubize	6	6	0	0	9	1	18		1-0	3-1	2-0
Royal Antwerp	6	4	0	2	10	5	12	0-1		3-1	1-0
KVSK United	6	2	0	4	6	12	6	0-1	1-4		2-1
Oud-Heverlee Leuven	6	0	0	6	2	9	0	0-1	1-2	0-1	

17/05/2008 - 5/06/2008

COUPE DE BELGIQUE 2007–08

Round of 16		Quarter-finals		Semi-finals		Final	
RSC Anderlecht *	2						
Red Star Waasland	0	RSC Anderlecht *	3 1				
Eendracht Aalst	1	Verbroedering Dender	0 1				
Verbroedering Dender*	2			RSC Anderlecht *	1 1		
KSV Roeselare *	2 5p			Germinal Beerschot	0 1		
Olympic Charleroi	2 4p	KSV Roeselare	1 1				
Oud-Heverlee Leuven	2 1p	Germinal Beerschot *	5 1				
Germinal Beerschot *	2 3p					RSC Anderlecht	3
Standard Club Liège *	2					KAA Gent ‡	2
KRC Genk	0	Standard Club Liège	1 4				
Club Brugge	0	Cercle Brugge *	4 0				
Cercle Brugge *	1			Standard Club Liège *	2 0		
KV Kortrijk *	2			KAA Gent	2 4		
Zulte-Waregem	1	KV Kortrijk *	5 0				
RAEC Mons *	0	KAA Gent	1 4				
KAA Gent	1						

CUP FINAL
Brussels
18-05-2008
Scorers - Polak [7], Boussoufa [70], Gillet [72] for Anderlecht; Foley [6], Olufade [33] for Gent

* Home team/home team in 1st leg • ‡ Qualified for the UEFA Cup

BEN – BENIN

NATIONAL TEAM RECORD
JULY 10TH 2006 TO JULY 12TH 2010

PL	W	D	L	F	A	%
19	7	3	9	26	26	44.7

FIFA/COCA-COLA WORLD RANKING

1993	1994	1995	1996	1997	1998	1999	2000	2001	2002	2003	2004	2005	2006	2007	High	
130	143	161	143	137	127	140	148	152	146	121	122	113	114	97	79	08/07

2007–2008											Low	
08/07	09/07	10/07	11/07	12/07	01/08	02/08	03/08	04/08	05/08	06/08	07/08	165 07/96
79	82	84	97	97	94	112	110	103	103	101	99	

Benin returned to the African Nations Cup finals for only the second time but, as was the case in 2004, went home without any points. It was still an achievement to make the elite tournament, however, after qualifying as one of the best placed runners-up. The all-powerful sports minister Ganiou Soglo continued to hold sway over the federation's affairs and decided that locally-born coach Wabi Gomez, who had been in charge for most of the qualifiers, was not sufficiently experienced enough to take the squad to the finals in nearby Ghana. It meant the German Reinard Fabisch came on board with around a month only to prepare his team, his appointment made after

INTERNATIONAL HONOURS
None

several other higher profile candidates had turned down approaches. Fabisch made headlines in Ghana with allegations he had been approached to try and fix the outcome of their matches in Sekondi by a mysterious betting syndicate. On the field, Swedish-based striker Razak Omotoyossi and the Le Mans midfielder Stephan Sessegnon were their leading players with Sessegnon signing for PSG in June 2008 for eight million Euros. Fabisch quit soon after the Nations Cup because of ill health and in June died from cancer. His replacement was appointed only after Benin had begun their 2010 FIFA World Cup qualifying campaign with Michel Dussuyer taking on the job.

THE FIFA BIG COUNT OF 2006

	Male	Female		Total
Number of players	320 600	0	Referees and Assistant Referees	200
Professionals	0		Admin, Coaches, Technical, Medical	1 500
Amateurs 18+	5 000		Number of clubs	110
Youth under 18	2 800		Number of teams	440
Unregistered	33 800		Clubs with women's teams	0
Total players	320 600		Players as % of population	4.08%

Fédération Béninoise de Football (FBF)

Stade René Pleven d'Akpakpa, Case Postale 965, Cotonou 01, Benin
Tel +229 21 330537   Fax +229 21 330537
www.none
President: ANJORIN Moucharafou   General Secretary: DIDAVI Bruno Arthur
Vice-President: AKPLOGAN Firmin   Treasurer: AHOUANVOEBLA Augustin   Media Officer: None
Men's Coach: DUSSUYER Michel   Women's Coach: None
FBF formed: 1962   CAF: 1969   FIFA: 1962
Green shirts with yellow and red trimmings, Yellow shorts, Red socks

RECENT INTERNATIONAL MATCHES PLAYED BY BENIN

2005	Opponents	Score		Venue	Comp	Scorers	Att	Referee
17-08	Sudan	L	0-1	Omdurman	WCq		12 000	Maillet SEY
4-09	Egypt	L	1-4	Cairo	WCq	Sessegnon 60	5 000	Buenkadila COD
23-09	United Arab Emirates	D	0-0	Dubai	Fr			
9-10	Libya	W	1-0	Cotonou	WCq	Chitou 60	1 880	Mususa ZIM
2006								
26-02	Equatorial Guinea	L	0-1	Cotonou	Fr			
29-03	Equatorial Guinea	L	0-2	Bata	Fr			
3-09	Togo	L	1-2	Lome	CNq	Tchomogo 86		Louzaya CGO
8-10	Sierra Leone	W	2-0	Cotonou	CNq	Chitou 22p, Ogunbiyi 82		Sowe GAM
2007								
7-02	Senegal	L	1-2	Rouen	Fr	Omotoyossi 79		Lannoy FRA
22-02	Chad	L	0-1	Cotonou	Fr			
25-03	Mali	D	1-1	Bamako	CNq	Ogunbiyi 44		Doue CIV
3-06	Mali	D	0-0	Cotonou	CNq			
17-06	Togo	W	4-1	Cotonou	CNq	Omotoyossi 2 45 53, Sessegnon 48, Ogonbiyi 58		
21-08	Gabon	D	2-2	Colombes	Fr	Maiga 21, OG 55		
12-10	Sierra Leone	W	2-0	Freetown	CNq			
17-11	UAE	W	1-0	Accra	Fr	Maiga 45		
21-11	Ghana	L	2-4	Accra	Fr	Sessegnon 24p, Omotoyossi 46		
2008								
16-01	Senegal	L	1-2	Ouagadougou	Fr	Oketola 45		
21-01	Mali	L	0-1	Sekondi	CNr1		20 000	Damon RSA
25-01	Côte d'Ivoire	L	1-4	Sekondi	CNr1	Omotoyossi 89		Marange ZIM
29-01	Nigeria	L	0-2	Sekondi	CNr1			Bennaceur TUN
1-06	Angola	L	0-3	Luanda	WCq		6 000	Damon RSA
8-06	Uganda	W	4-1	Cotonou	WCq	Omotoyossi 2 16 87, Tchomogo 21, Sessegnon 70	10 200	Karembe MLI
14-06	Niger	W	2-0	Niamey	WCq	Tchomogo 54, Omotoyossi 70	5 000	Haimoudi ALG
22-06	Niger	W	2-0	Cotonou	WCq	Ahoueya 45	25 000	Niyongabo BDI

Fr = Friendly match • CN = CAF African Cup of Nations • WCq = FIFA World Cup • q = qualifier • r1 = first round group

BENIN NATIONAL TEAM PLAYERS

	Player		Club	Date of Birth		Player		Club	Date of Birth
1	Rachad Chitou	GK	Wikki Tourists	1 01 1980	12	Achille Rouga	MF	Stade Rennais	10 06 1987
2	Djiman Koukou	MF	Soleil	14 11 1980	13	Noel Seka	DF	FC Fyn	9 03 1984
3	Abdul Adenon	DF	Le Mans	27 07 1985	14	Alain Gaspoz	DF	FC Bagnes	16 05 1970
4	Bio Ai Traore	MF	Pantheres	9 06 1985	15	Anicet Adjamossi	DF	Creteil	15 03 1984
5	Damien Chrystosome	DF	Casale	24 05 1982	16	Yoann Djidonou	GK	Red Star	17 06 1985
6	Jonas Oketola	DF	None		17	Stephane Sessegnon	MF	Le Mans	1 06 1984
7	Romauld Boco	DF	Accrington Stanley	8 07 1985	18	Seidath Tchomogo	MF	East Riffa	13 08 1985
8	Razak Omotoyossi	FW	Helsingborg	8 10 1985	19	Jocelyn Ahoueya	MF	FC Sion	19 12 1985
9	Abou Maiga	FW	Creteil		20	Wassiou Oladipikpo	FW	JS Kabylie	17 12 1983
10	Oumar Tchomogo	FW	Portimonense	7 01 1978	21	Sosthene Soglo	FW	Energie	3 07 1986
11	Mouri Ogunbiyi	MF	Etoile du Sahel	5 06 1985	22	Valere Amoussou	GK	Mogas 90	13 03 1987
					23	Abdoulaye Ouzerou	FW	Al Jazeera	24 10 1985

Benin's squad for the 2008 CAF Africa Cup of Nations

BENIN NATIONAL TEAM RECORDS AND RECORD SEQUENCES

Records			Sequence records					
Victory	6-2	CHA 1963	Wins	3	2003, 2008	Clean sheets	3	2003
Defeat	1-10	NGA 1959	Defeats	9	1991-1993	Goals scored	7	1963-1965, 2004
Player Caps	n/a		Undefeated	7	1963-1965	Without goal	5	1988-1990, 1991
Player Goals	n/a		Without win	24	1984-1991	Goals against	14	1963-1969

BENIN 2007
CHAMPIONNAT NATIONAL

	Pl	W	D	L	F	A	Pts
Tonnerre	34	21	8	5	35	10	71
Soleil	34	20	9	5	39	15	69
Buffles	34	20	5	9	43	18	65
Université Nationale	34	19	6	9	30	31	63
Energie	34	18	8	8	59	29	62
Mogas 90	34	16	9	9	45	22	57
AS Oussou Saka	34	16	9	9	36	27	57
Dragons de l'Ouémé	34	13	9	12	26	16	48
Requins de 'Atlantique	34	12	7	15	39	32	43
Jeunesse Pobè	34	11	10	13	22	31	43
Dynamo Parakou	34	10	10	14	22	30	40
Cheminots	34	9	12	13	26	47	39
Panthères	34	9	7	18	14	12	34
Dynamo Abomey	34	8	9	17	27	25	33
Avrankou Omnisport	34	8	9	17	17	62	33
Mambas Noirs	34	8	7	19	26	37	31
Espoir	34	8	5	21	30	52	29
Jeunesse At. Missérété	34	6	3	25	17	57	21

20/01/2007 - 12/08/2007

COUPE DU BENIN 2007

Round of 16		Quarter-finals		Semi-finals		Final	
Université Nationale	2						
Astek	0	Université Nationale	1				
Requins de 'Atlantique	0	Jeunesse Pobè	0				
Jeunesse Pobè	3			Université Nationale	0 4p		
Aspac	2			US Kraké	0 2p		
Dragons de l'Ouémé	0	Aspac	1				
		US Kraké	3				
US Kraké	Bye						
						Université Nationale	2
						AS Oussou Saka	0
				Energie	0		
Energie	0 5p			AS Oussou Saka	2		
Mogas 90	0 3p	Energie	2				
Dynamo Parakou		AS Oussou Saka †	1				
AS Oussou Saka	w-0						

* Home team/home team in 1st leg • † ASOS through as best loser

CUP FINAL
Stade de l'Amite, Kouhounou
15-11-2007

Scorers - Dieudonné Dossou [68p],
Salifou Latifou [72]

RECENT LEAGUE AND CUP RECORD

	Championship						Coupe de l'Independence		
Year	Champions	Pts	Runners-up	Pts	Third	Pts	Winners	Score	Runners-up
2001	No championship held						Buffles Borgou	1-0	Dragons
2002	Dragons	15	Requins	15	Postel	13	Jeunesse Pobe	0-0 1-1 4-3p	Mogas 90
2003	Dragons	21	Buffles Borgou	19	Postel	14	Mogas 90	1-0	Soleil
2004	Championship unfinished						Mogas 90	1-0	Requins
2005	No championship held						No competition		
2006	Mogas 90	34	Dragons	33	Buffles Borgou	32	Dragons	0-0 2-0	Mogas 90
2007	Tonnerre	71	Soleil	69	Buffles Borgou	65	Univ. Nationale	2-0	Oussou Saka

BENIN COUNTRY INFORMATION

Capital	Porto-Novo	Independence	1960	GDP per Capita	$1 100
Population	7 250 033	Status	Republic	GNP Ranking	135
Area km²	112 620	Language	French, Fon, Yoruba	Dialling code	+229
Population density	64 per km²	Literacy rate	40%	Internet code	.bj
% in urban areas	31%	Main religion	Indigenous 50%	GMT + / -	+1
Towns/Cities ('000)	Cotonou 690; Abomey 385; Porto Novo 234; Djougou 202; Parakou 163; Bohicon 125				
Neighbours (km)	Niger 226; Nigeria 773; Togo 644; Burkina Faso 306; Atlantic Ocean (Bight of Benin) 121				
Main stadia	Stade de l'Amitié – Cotonou 35 000; Stade Municipale – Porto Novo 20 000				

BER – BERMUDA

NATIONAL TEAM RECORD
JULY 10TH 2006 TO JULY 12TH 2010

PL	W	D	L	F	A	%
18	8	2	8	30	26	50

FIFA/COCA-COLA WORLD RANKING

1993	1994	1995	1996	1997	1998	1999	2000	2001	2002	2003	2004	2005	2006	2007
84	102	140	167	176	185	163	153	166	172	183	157	161	107	147

High	
78	08/93

2007–2008											
08/07	09/07	10/07	11/07	12/07	01/08	02/08	03/08	04/08	05/08	06/08	07/08
130	135	134	138	147	147	147	146	139	139	139	118

Low	
185	12/98

The Bermuda national team almost caused one of the major upsets of the 2010 FIFA World Cup qualifiers when they very nearly knocked out 2006 finalists Trinidad. In the first leg of the tie, the Gombey Warriors beat Trinidad 2-1 away from home, with John Nusum's brace of goals securing one of Bermuda's finest ever results. A victory over the Trinidadians at home in the return would not only have seen them through to the group stage of qualifying but it would also have set a new national team record of five consecutive wins. Alas, it wasn't to be as the Soca Warriors rediscovered their form and ran out 2-0 winners. In domestic football no team has ever won the quadruple of

INTERNATIONAL HONOURS
None

League, FA Cup, Friendship Trophy and Martonmere Cup but PFC Zebras almost pulled that off during the 2007-08 season. In November they beat Devonshire Cougars on penalties in the final of the Martonmere Cup; they then secured the League title on the final day of the season finishing a point head of North Village Rams and they also claimed the FA Cup in mid-April when they beat Dandy Town Hornets 2-0 in the final. A week before that, however, they had lost 7-3 to North Village in the final of the Friendship Trophy. Zebras did equal one record during the season - their League title was the ninth in their history, matching the number won by Somerset Cricket Club.

THE FIFA BIG COUNT OF 2006

	Male	Female		Total
Number of players	6 205	950	Referees and Assistant Referees	35
Professionals	5		Admin, Coaches, Technical, Medical	220
Amateurs 18+	2 250		Number of clubs	50
Youth under 18	1 600		Number of teams	100
Unregistered	800		Clubs with women's teams	8
Total players	7 155		Players as % of population	10.88

Bermuda Football Association (BFA)
48 Cedar Avenue, PO Box HM 745, Hamilton, Bermuda
Tel +1 441 2952199   Fax +1 441 2950773
bfa@northrock.bm   www.bermudafa.com
President: MUSSENDEN Larry   General Secretary: SABIR David
Vice-President: BLANKENDAL Calvin   Treasurer: GRIFFITH Andrew   Media Officer: None
Men's Coach: THOMPSON Kenny   Women's Coach: BROWN Vance
BFA formed: 1928   CONCACAF: 1966   FIFA: 1966
Blue shirts with red and white trimmings, Blue shorts, Blue socks

RECENT INTERNATIONAL MATCHES PLAYED BY BERMUDA

2004	Opponents	Score	Venue	Comp	Scorers	Att	Referee
29-02	Montserrat	W 13-0	Hamilton	WCq	Ming 3 [5 20 50], Nusum 3 [15 54 60], Smith.K [36], Bean.R 2 [41 52], Steede [43], Wade [77], Simons [83], Burgess [87]	3 000	Kennedy USA
21-03	Montserrat	W 7-0	Plymouth	WCq	Hill [15], Nusum 2 [21 44], Bean.R [39], Smith.K 2 [45 46], Ming [76]	250	Charles DOM
31-03	Nicaragua	W 3-0	Hamilton	Fr	Goater 2 [33 65p], Simons [90]		Crockwell BER
2-04	Nicaragua	W 2-1	Hamilton	Fr	Nusum 2 [47 67]		Raynor BER
28-04	Panama	L 1-4	Panama City	Fr	Ashwood [14]		
30-04	Nicaragua	L 0-2	Diriamba	Fr		800	
2-05	Nicaragua	L 0-2	Esteli	Fr			
13-06	El Salvador	L 1-2	San Salvador	WCq	Nusum [30]	12 000	Campos NCA
20-06	El Salvador	D 2-2	Hamilton	WCq	Burgess [5p], Nusum [21]	4 000	Whittaker CAY
24-11	Cayman Islands	W 2-1	Kingstown	CCq	Smith.K [4], Hill [34]	200	Mathews SKN
26-11	St Vincent/Grenadines	D 3-3	Kingstown	CCq	Smith.K [42], Lowe [82], Ming [90p]		
28-11	British Virgin Islands	L 0-2	Kingstown	CCq		400	Mathews SKN
2005							
25-05	Trinidad and Tobago	L 0-4	Port of Spain	Fr		400	
27-05	Trinidad and Tobago	L 0-1	Marabella	Fr			
2006							
27-09	US Virgin Islands	W 6-0	Charlotte Amalie	CCq	Steede 2 [1 36], Cordington 2 [31 54], Nusum [38], Jennings [90]	150	Small BRB
29-09	Dominican Republic	W 3-1	Charlotte Amalie	CCq	Zuill [25], Cox [48], Steede [53]	300	Martis ANT
19-11	St Vincent/Grenadines	L 0-3	Bridgetown	CCq			
21-11	Bahamas	W 4-0	Bridgetown	CCq	Smith.K 2 [6 28], Barry [17], Steede [87]		
23-11	Barbados	D 1-1	Bridgetown	CCq	Nusum [42]		
2007							
7-01	Haiti	L 0-2	Couva	CCq			Brizan TRI
9-01	Haiti	L 0-3	Couva	CCq			Davis TRI
25-03	Canada	L 0-3	Hamilton	Fr			
14-12	St Kitts and Nevis	L 1-2	Hamilton	Fr	Davis.J [86]		
16-12	St Kitts and Nevis	W 4-2	Hamilton	Fr	Zuill 3 [3 40 83], De Graff [35]		
2008							
16-01	Puerto Rico	L 0-2	Hamilton	Fr			
18-01	Puerto Rico	L 0-1	Hamilton	Fr			Raynor BER
3-02	Cayman Islands	D 1-1	Hamilton	WCq	Burgess [18]	2 000	Navarro CAN
30-03	Cayman Islands	W 3-1	Georgetown	WCq	DeGraff 2 [19 23], Steede [53]	3 200	Marrufo USA
6-06	Barbados	W 2-1	Hamilton	Fr	Shakir [41], Ming [86]		
9-06	Barbados	W 3-0	Hamilton	Fr	Bean 2 [12 18], Nusum [45]		
15-06	Trinidad and Tobago	W 2-1	Macoya	WCq	Nusum 2 [7 38]	4 585	Quesada CRC
22-06	Trinidad and Tobago	L 0-2	Prospect	WCq		5 000	Batres GUA

Fr = Friendly match • CC = Digicel Caribbean Cup • WC = FIFA World Cup • q = qualifier

BERMUDA NATIONAL TEAM RECORDS AND RECORD SEQUENCES

Records			Sequence records					
Victory	13-0	MSR 2004	Wins	4	2004, 2008	Clean sheets	3	2004
Defeat	0-6	DEN 1969, CAN 1983	Defeats	6	1968-1969	Goals scored	17	1990-1992
Player Caps	n/a		Undefeated	7	1990-1991	Without goal	3	2004-2005, 2007
Player Goals	n/a		Without win	10	1964-1969	Goals against	12	1968-1971

BERMUDA COUNTRY INFORMATION

Capital	Hamilton	Independence	British Crown Colony	GDP per Capita	$36 000
Population	64 935	Status		GNP Ranking	n/a
Area km²	53.3	Language	English	Dialling code	+1 441
Population density	1 218 per km²	Literacy rate	99%	Internet code	.bm
% in urban areas	100%	Main religion	Christian	GMT + / −	-4
Towns/Cities ('000)	Hamilton 1; St George 1				
Neighbours (km)	North Atlantic Ocean				
Main stadia	National Stadium – Hamilton 8 500; White Hill – Sandys				

BERMUDA 2007–08

CINGULAR WIRELESS PREMIER DIVISION

	Pl	W	D	L	F	A	Pts	Zebras	Rams	Cougars	Blazers	Hornets	Colts	Trojans	Rangers
PHC Zebras	14	10	2	2	30	12	30		1-1	1-1	1-0	4-0	1-1	7-0	2-1
North Village Rams	14	7	6	1	35	18	29	3-1		2-2	1-1	1-0	3-2	6-1	4-1
Devonshire Cougars	14	6	6	2	32	11	24	1-2	1-2		0-0	4-1	7-0	3-0	3-0
Boulevard Blazers	14	4	4	6	20	21	16	0-4	2-2	2-2		0-3	2-3	3-0	5-1
Dandy Town Hornets	14	4	3	7	18	23	15	2-0	0-1	0-0	1-3		2-2	0-0	5-1
Devonshire Colts	14	4	3	7	22	31	15	1-2	2-1	0-3	1-2	1-2		1-3	2-2
Somerset Trojans	14	3	5	6	13	29	14	1-2	1-1	0-0	1-0	3-0	1-4		1-1
Ireland Rangers	14	2	3	9	16	41	9	0-2	3-7	1-5	1-0	3-2	0-2	1-1	

7/10/2007 - 23/03/2008 • Top scorers: Kwame STEEDE, Cougars 15; Aljame Zuill, Colts 11

FRIENDSHIP TROPHY 2007–08

Semi–finals		Final	
North Village Rams	4		
Devonshire Colts	2		
		North Village Rams	7
		PHC Zebras	3
Devonshire Cougars	1		13-04-2008
PHC Zebras	2		

MARTONMERE CUP 2007

Semi–finals		Final	
PHC Zebras	1		
Somerset Trojans	0		
		PHC Zebras	1 5p
		Devonshire Cougars	1 3p
Dandy Town Hornets	1		11-11-2007
Devonshire Cougars	4		

FA CUP 2007–08

Round of sixteen		Quarter–finals		Semi–finals		Final	
PHC Zebras	0						
North Village Rams	1	PHC Zebras	12				
BAA	0	Key West Rangers	0				
Key West Rangers	2			PHC Zebras	3		
Devonshire Colts	14			Wolves	0		
Pest Control	0	Devonshire Colts	0				
Southampton Rangers	2 0	Wolves	1				
Wolves	2 1					PHC Zebras	2
Boulevard Blazers	2 2					Dandy Town Hornets	0
St Georges Colts	2 0	Boulevard Blazers	3				
Ireland Rangers	2	Young Men Social Club	1				
Young Men Social Club	3			Boulevard Blazers	0 0		
Lobster Pot	4			Dandy Town Hornets	0 1		
Prospect United	3	Lobster Pot	0				
Somerset Eagles	0	Dandy Town Hornets	3				
Dandy Town Hornets	5						

CUP FINAL

National Sports Centre
20-04-2008, Ref: Raynor

Scorers - Kevin Lambe [55], Keston
Lewis [84] for Zebras

RECENT LEAGUE AND CUP RECORD

Championship								FA Cup		
Year	Champions	Pts	Runners-up	Pts	Third	Pts		Winners	Score	Runners-up
1997	Devonshire Colts	41	Vasco da Gama	34	Dandy Town	31		Boulevard Blazers	3-2	Wolves
1998	Vasco da Gama		Dandy Town		Boulevard Blazers			Vasco da Gama	2-1	Devonshire Colts
1999	Vasco da Gama	41	Dandy Town	33	North Village	32		Devonshire Colts	1-0	Dandy Town
2000	PHC Zebras	39	North Village	37	Dandy Town	32		North Village	2-1	Devonshire Colts
2001	Dandy Town	29	North Village	28	Devonshire Colts	26		Devonshire Colts	3-1	North Village
2002	North Village	27	Dandy Town	23	Devonshire Cougars	22		North Village	3-0	Dandy Town
2003	North Village	29	Devonshire Cougars	23	Boulevard Blazers	20		North Village	5-1	Prospect
2004	Dandy Town	31	Devonshire Cougars	30	Boulevard Blazers	25		Dandy Town	3-3 2-1	Devonshire Cougars
2005	Devonshire Cougars	32	Dandy Town	30	PHC Zebras	26		North Village	2-0	Hamilton Parish
2006	North Village	35	Somerset Trojans	28	Dandy Town	28		North Village	4-1	Dandy Town
2007	Devonshire Cougars	30	North Village	28	Boulevard Blazers	25		Devonshire Colts	2-0	Boulevard Blazers
2008	PHC Zebras	30	North Village	29	Devonshire Cougars	24		PHC Zebras	2-0	Dandy Town

BFA – BURKINA FASO

NATIONAL TEAM RECORD
JULY 10TH 2006 TO JULY 12TH 2010

PL	W	D	L	F	A	%
17	6	3	8	21	24	44.1

FIFA/COCA-COLA WORLD RANKING

1993	1994	1995	1996	1997	1998	1999	2000	2001	2002	2003	2004	2005	2006	2007
127	97	101	107	106	75	71	69	78	75	78	84	87	61	113

High	
54	05/07

2007–2008											
08/07	09/07	10/07	11/07	12/07	01/08	02/08	03/08	04/08	05/08	06/08	07/08
77	106	110	113	113	112	109	109	109	108	111	64

Low	
127	12/93

Humiliated in the 2008 African Nations Cup qualifiers, Burkina Faso's national side bounced back in spectacular fashion at the start of the 2010 FIFA World Cup qualifiers. This dramatic swing of fortune for the Burkinabe turned on just 10 minutes of football at the start of June 2008, when they came from a goal down to score twice through Norwegian-based forward Yssouf Kone and win a surprise three points away at heavily fancied Tunisia. Just over six months earlier, 'Les Etalons' had been humiliated 5-1 by Senegal at the conclusion to the qualifiers for the Nations Cup finals in Ghana. They had also been beaten at home by Tanzania and finished bottom of their qualifying

INTERNATIONAL HONOURS
None

group. French coach Didier Notheaux departed after these setbacks to be replaced by Paulo Duarte, a former Uniao Leiria coach in his native Portugal but without any profile on the international circuit. He had little preparation time, and indeed lost his first international in a friendly against lowly ranked Cape Verde islands, but after that Burkina Faso set off on a four match winning streak to set themselves up easily for progress to the final phase of the African World Cup qualifiers. At home, Etoile Filante won their first title for seven seasons, losing just one game all season - against bottom club Boulgou - and then completed by double by beating USO 3-2 in the Cup Final.

THE FIFA BIG COUNT OF 2006

	Male	Female		Total
Number of players	576 800	28 300	Referees and Assistant Referees	700
Professionals	0		Admin, Coaches, Technical, Medical	2 400
Amateurs 18+	13 000		Number of clubs	100
Youth under 18	10 200		Number of teams	850
Unregistered	45 900		Clubs with women's teams	0
Total players	605 100		Players as % of population	4.35

Fédération Burkinabé de Foot-Ball (FBF)
Centre Technique National, Ouaga 2000, Casa Postale 57, Ouagadougou 01, Burkina Faso
Tel +226 50 396864   Fax +226 50 396866
febefoo@fasonet.bf   www.fasofoot.com
President: SAWADOGO Theodore   General Secretary: ZOMBRE Emmanuel
Vice-President: KARA Paulin   Treasurer: NION Phillippe Nere   Media Officer: BARRY Alpha
Men's Coach: DUARTE Paulo   Women's Coach: None
FBF formed: 1960   CAF: 1964   FIFA: 1964
Green shirts with red and white trimmings, Green shorts, Green socks

RECENT INTERNATIONAL MATCHES PLAYED BY BURKINA FASO

2004	Opponents		Score	Venue	Comp	Scorers	Att	Referee
17-08	Algeria	D	2-2	Blida	Fr	Zongo [50p], Ouedraogo.H [67]	15 000	Tahri MAR
4-09	Uganda	W	2-0	Ouagadougou	WCq	Dagano [34], Nikiema [79]	30 000	Lemghambodj MTN
9-10	Cape Verde Islands	L	0-1	Praia	WCq		6 000	Aziaka TOG
17-11	Morocco	L	0-4	Rabat	Fr		5 000	Keita.M MLI
2005								
9-02	Algeria	L	0-3	Algiers	Fr		3 000	Benaissa ALG
20-03	Korea Republic	L	0-1	Dubai	Fr			
26-03	Cape Verde Islands	L	1-2	Ouagadougou	WCq	Dagano [71]	27 500	Evehe CMR
29-05	Togo	L	0-1	Lome	Fr			
5-06	Ghana	L	1-2	Kumasi	WCq	Dagano [30]	11 920	Abd El Fatah EGY
18-06	Congo DR	W	2-0	Ouagadougou	WCq	Panandetiguiri [3], Dagano [68]	25 000	Shelmani LBY
3-09	South Africa	W	3-1	Ouagadougou	WCq	Abdoulaye Cisse 2 [32 47], Kebe [39]	25 000	Codjia BEN
8-10	Uganda	D	2-2	Kampala	WCq	Kebe [15], Rouamba [75]	1 433	Benouza ALG
2006								
28-02	Algeria	D	0-0	Rouen	Fr		2 000	Duhamel FRA
16-08	Morocco	L	0-1	Rabat	Fr			
29-08	Uganda	D	0-0	Kampala	Fr			
2-09	Tanzania	L	1-2	Dar es Salaam	CNq	Abdoulaye Cisse [39]		Ndinya KEN
7-10	Senegal	W	1-0	Ouagadougou	CNq	Yameogo [59p]		Guezzaz MAR
15-11	Algeria	W	2-1	Aix-en-Provence	Fr	Yameogo [60p], Koffi [82]	700	Falcone FRA
2007								
24-03	Mozambique	D	1-1	Ouagadougou	CNq	Pitroipa [26]		Imiere NGA
29-05	Zimbabwe	D	1-1	Masvingo	Fr	Kabore [71]	12 000	
3-06	Mozambique	L	1-3	Maputo	CNq	Sanou [38]		Raolimanana MAD
9-06	Mali	L	0-1	Ouagadougou	Fr			
16-06	Tanzania	L	0-1	Ouagadougou	CNq			Coulibaly MLI
22-08	Mali	L	2-3	Paris	Fr	Sanou, Coulibaly		
8-09	Senegal	L	1-5	Dakar	CNq	Alain Traore [34]		Haimoudi ALG
2008								
24-05	Cape Verde Islands	L	0-1	Alcochete	Fr			
1-06	Tunisia	W	2-1	Rades	WCq	Yssouf Kone 2 [85 87]	15 000	Ambaya LBY
7-06	Burundi	W	2-0	Ouagadougou	WCq	Dagano 2 [23p 44p]		Ndume GAB
14-06	Seychelles	W	3-2	Victoria	WCq	Dagano 3 [25 57 78]	1 000	Seechurn MRI
21-06	Seychelles	W	4-1	Ouagadougou	WCq	Kabore [21], Kere [28], Ouattara [54], Yssouf Kone [89]	12 500	Lamptey GHA

Fr = Friendly match • CN = CAF African Cup of Nations • WC = FIFA World Cup • q = qualifier, r1 = first round group

BURKINA FASO NATIONAL TEAM RECORDS AND RECORD SEQUENCES

Records			Sequence records					
Victory	4-0	MOZ 2003	Wins	6	1988	Clean sheets	6	2003
Defeat	0-7	ALG 1981	Defeats	10	1976-1981	Goals scored	24	1998-2000
Player Caps	n/a		Undefeated	7	1999	Without goal	4	Three times
Player Goals	n/a		Without win	13	1976-82, 1994-96	Goals against	13	1960-1967

BURKINA FASO COUNTRY INFORMATION

Capital	Ouagadougou	Independence	1960	GDP per Capita	$1 100
Population	13 574 820	Status	Republic	GNP Ranking	133
Area km²	274 200	Language	French	Dialling code	+226
Population density	49 per km²	Literacy rate	26%	Internet code	.bf
% in urban areas	27%	Main religion	Muslim 50%	GMT +/−	0
Towns/Cities ('000)	Ouagadougou 1 031; Bobo-Dioulasso 370; Koudougou 86; Banfora 63; Ouahigouya 61				
Neighbours (km)	Mali 1,000; Niger 628; Benin 306; Togo 126; Ghana 549; Côte d'Ivoire 584				
Main stadia	Stade du 4 Août – Ouagadougou 40 000; Stade Municipal – Bobo-Dioulasso 30 000				

BURKINA FASO 2007–08

PREMIERE DIVISION

	Pl	W	D	L	F	A	Pts	EFO	USO	ASFA/Y	RCB	CFO	BPFC	USFA	RCK	USCO	SONABEL	USY	ASFB	Bobo Sport	Boulgou
Etoile Filante †	26	14	11	1	41	13	53		3-1	1-1	2-1	2-1	2-1	1-0	0-0	3-1	1-0	2-0	2-0	0-0	10-0
US Ouagadougou	26	14	7	5	43	15	49	1-1		0-0	1-2	0-0	2-1	0-0	2-0	4-0	2-0	3-0	0-0	4-0	7-1
ASFA/Yennenga	26	13	9	4	32	14	48	0-0	2-0		2-0	1-1	2-1	1-0	1-1	0-0	1-1	2-0	2-0	1-0	3-0
Racing Club B-D	26	13	6	7	34	22	45	2-2	1-0	2-0		3-0	1-1	1-2	1-0	1-0	2-1	1-0	3-1	1-1	
Commune FC	26	11	9	6	28	21	42	0-0	0-0	1-0	0-3		2-0	1-1	1-0	1-1	3-0	2-0	2-1	2-0	
Bouloumpokou FC	26	12	6	8	29	23	42	0-0	0-0	0-1	1-1	2-1		1-0	1-0	1-0	2-1	4-1	2-0	1-0	2-0
US Forces Armées	26	9	8	9	24	20	35	0-1	0-0	1-3	1-0	1-3	2-0		0-0	2-0	1-2	1-1	1-1	1-2	3-0
Rail Club Kadiogo	26	7	11	8	20	20	32	1-1	1-3	2-2	1-0	1-1	0-1	0-1		0-2	0-0	3-1	0-0	2-0	3-0
US Comoé	26	7	9	10	19	24	30	1-2	0-1	1-0	0-0	1-0	2-2	0-0	0-0		2-0	1-1	3-0	0-0	2-1
AS SONABEL	26	6	11	9	23	25	29	1-1	1-3	1-1	0-2	2-2	2-0	0-1	1-1	1-0		4-1	2-0	1-1	2-0
US Yatenga	26	5	10	11	19	37	25	0-0	0-2	1-0	2-1	0-0	1-1	1-1	0-0	1-1	0-0		1-0	0-0	3-0
ASF Bobo-Dioulasso	26	6	6	14	15	30	24	0-3	2-1	0-1	1-0	0-0	0-2	0-1	0-1	0-2	1-0	3-0		2-0	4-2
Bobo Sport	26	3	8	15	17	35	17	0-1	0-1	0-2	1-2	0-1	1-2	0-3	0-1	3-0	0-0	3-1	1-1		2-2
Boulgou	26	3	7	16	13	58	16	1-0	0-4	0-3	2-2	0-1	1-0	1-0	0-1	0-0	0-0	0-2	0-0	1-1	

15/12/2007 - 19/07/2008 • † Qualified for the CAF Champions League • Matches in bold were awarded • SONABEL also relegated as the worst club from Ougadougou • Top scorer: Abdramane Diarra, Etoile Filante 16

COUPE NATIONALE DU FASO 2007–08

Round of 16		Quarter-finals		Semi-finals		Final	
Etoile Filante	3						
Jeunesse Club B-D	1	Etoile Filante	1				
US Forces Armées	1	AS SONABEL	0				
AS SONABEL	2			Etoile Filante	3		
Canon du Sud	0 5p			US Comoé	0		
Saman Boromo	0 4p	Canon du Sud	0				
AS Koupéla	0	US Comoé	2				
US Comoé	2					Etoile Filante	3
Commune FC	4					US Ouagadougou ‡	2
CAS Somgandé	0	Commune FC	1				
Espoir de Colsama	1	ASF Bobo-Dioulasso	0				
ASF Bobo-Dioulasso	2			Commune FC	1		
Bouloumpokou FC	3			US Ouagadougou	2		
CJSK Kombissiri	2	Bouloumpokou FC	0				
Rail Club Kadiogo	0	US Ouagadougou	1				
US Ouagadougou	1						

‡ Qualified for the CAF Confederation Cup

CUP FINAL
Stade 4 août, Ouagadougou
5-08-2008
Scorers -
Eric Dagbeí 3 34 69 81 for EFO;
Felix Kabore 52, Roger Nikiema 94+ for USO

RECENT LEAGUE AND CUP RECORD

	Championship						Cup		
Year	Champions	Pts	Runners-up	Pts	Third	Pts	Winners	Score	Runners-up
1990	Etoile Filante	64	ASFA Yennenga	61	Rail Club Kadiogo	61	Etoile Filante	2-1	ASFA Yennenga
1991	Etoile Filante	60	US Cheminots	52	Rail Club Kadiogo	51	ASFA Yennenga		
1992	Etoile Filante	53	ASFA Yennenga	53	AS Fonctionnaire	49	Etoile Filante	2-1	Rail Club Kadiogo
1993	Etoile Filante	55	Racing Club B-D	54	Rail Club Kadiogo	49	Etoile Filante	2-0	ASF Bobo-Dioulasso
1994	Etoile Filante						Rail Club Kadiogo	1-0	Racing Club B-D
1995	ASFA Yennenga								
1996	Racing Club B-D						Etoile Filante		
1997	Racing Club B-D						ASF Bobo-Dioulasso		
1998	US Forces Armées						ASF Bobo-Dioulasso	0-0 7-6p	US Forces Armées
1999	ASFA Yennenga	53	Etoile Filante	47	US Forces Armées	43	Etoile Filante	3-2	US Forces Armées
2000	US Forces Armées	44	Etoile Filante	41	ASFA Yennenga	39	Etoile Filante	3-1	US Ouagadougou
2001	Etoile Filante	51	ASFA Yennenga	49	US Forces Armées	41	Etoile Filante	3-1	ASF Bobo-Dioulasso
2002	ASFA Yennenga	49	US Forces Armées	44	Etoile Filante	39	US Forces Armées	2-0	ASF Bobo-Dioulasso
2003	ASFA Yennenga	51	US Ouagadougou	47	Etoile Filante	45	Etoile Filante	0-0 5-4p	ASFA Yennenga
2004	ASFA Yennenga	43	US Ouagadougou	40	Etoile Filante	39	ASF Bobo-Dioulasso	0-0 3-2p	US Forces Armées
2005	Rail Club Kadiogo	57	US Ouagadougou	50	US Forces Armées	50	US Ouagadougou	2-0	ASF Bobo-Dioulasso
2006	ASFA Yennenga	53	Rail Club Kadiogo	52	US Ouagadougou	50	Etoile Filante	3-2	Racing Club B-D
2007	Commune FC	49	Etoile Filante	48	US Forces Armées	41	Racing Club B-D	2-1	US Ouagadougou
2008	Etoile Filante	53	US Ouagadougou	49	ASFA Yennenga	48	Etoile Filante	3-2	US Ouagadougou

BHR – BAHRAIN

BAHRAIN NATIONAL TEAM RECORD
JULY 10TH 2006 TO JULY 12TH 2010

PL	W	D	L	F	A	%
32	15	6	11	44	40	58.1

FIFA/COCA-COLA WORLD RANKING

1993	1994	1995	1996	1997	1998	1999	2000	2001	2002	2003	2004	2005	2006	2007
78	73	99	118	121	119	136	138	110	105	64	49	52	97	102

High	
44	09/04

2007–2008											
08/07	09/07	10/07	11/07	12/07	01/08	02/08	03/08	04/08	05/08	06/08	07/08
92	98	96	101	102	100	83	82	71	72	72	72

Low	
1 8	12/00

After a disappointing showing at the AFC Asian Cup finals in South East Asia in the summer of 2007, Bahrain's national team took aim at qualifying for their first-ever FIFA World Cup. The Bahrainis narrowly missed out on a place in Germany in 2006 after losing a play-off against Trinidad, but their attempt to qualify for South Africa was alive and well as the continent's qualifying schedule went into its final phase. Coach Milan Macala masterminded a rare win over three-time Asian champions Japan in the penultimate phase of qualifying as both Bahrain and the Japanese earned places in the final round, where four guaranteed spots in the World Cup finals are

INTERNATIONAL HONOURS
Qualified for the AFC Asian Cup finals 1988 2004 2007   Represented at the Asian Games 1974 1978 1986 1994 2002

available. There was no such success in the qualifying competition for the Beijing Olympics. Bahrain missed out after losing to South Korea. Muharraq continued their dominance of the domestic scene, once again claiming the Bahrain league title by a commanding margin from second-placed Busaiteen while also winning the King's Cup with a 2-0 victory over Al Najma in the final. However, in continental competition the club struggled to match the success of 2006, when they reached the final of the AFC Cup. In the 2007 edition, Muharraq were eliminated at the group stage of Asian football's second-tier club tournament.

THE FIFA BIG COUNT OF 2006

	Male	Female		Total
Number of players	16 828	1 450	Referees and Assistant Referees	90
Professionals	66		Admin, Coaches, Technical, Medical	620
Amateurs 18+	730		Number of clubs	48
Youth under 18	2 800		Number of teams	150
Unregistered	2 400		Clubs with women's teams	4
Total players	18 278		Players as % of population	2.62%

Bahrain Football Association (BFA)
Bahrain National Stadium, PO Box 5464, Manama, Bahrain
Tel +973 17 689569   Fax +973 17 781188
bhrfa@batelco.com.bh   www.bahrainfootball.org
President: AL-KHALIFA Sheik Salman Bin Ibrahim   General Secretary: JASSEM Ahmed Mohammed
Vice-President: AL-KHALIFA Sheik Ali Bin Khalifa   Treasurer: AL NA'AMI Ahmed Abdulla   Media Officer: AL BASHA Ali Abdullah
Men's Coach: MACALA Milan   Women's Coach: AL-OUMAIRY Masoud
BFA formed: 1957   AFC: 1970   FIFA: 1966
Red shirts with white trimmings, Red shorts, Red socks or White shirts with red trimmings, White shorts, White socks

RECENT INTERNATIONAL MATCHES PLAYED BY BAHRAIN

2005	Opponents	Score		Venue	Comp	Scorers	Att	Referee
17-08	Korea DPR	L	2-3	Manama	WCq	Salman Isa [49], Hussain Ali [54]	3 000	Maidin SIN
8-10	Uzbekistan	D	1-1	Tashkent	WCpo	Mohamed.T [17]	55 000	Busacca SUI
12-10	Uzbekistan	D	0-0	Manama	WCpo		25 000	Poll ENG
27-10	Panama	W	5-0	Manama	Fr	Al Dakeel [44], Al Hejeri [82], Abbas [83], Al Marzooki [88], Mubarak [89]		
12-11	Trinidad and Tobago	D	1-1	Port of Spain	WCpo	Salman Issa [72]	24 991	Shield AUS
16-11	Trinidad and Tobago	L	0-1	Manama	WCpo		35 000	Ruiz COL
2006								
30-01	Syria	D	1-1	Manama	Fr	Faouzi Aaish [60]		
16-02	Palestine	L	0-2	Muharraq	Fr			
22-02	Australia	L	1-3	Manama	ACq	Hussain Ali [35]	2 500	Mohd Salleh MAS
1-03	Kuwait	D	0-0	Kuwait City	ACq		16 000	Moradi IRN
9-08	Saudi Arabia	L	0-1	Dammam	Fr			
2-09	Jordan	L	0-2	Manama	Fr			
11-10	Australia	L	0-2	Sydney	ACq		37 000	Al Marzouqi UAE
8-11	Oman	D	1-1	Muscat	Fr	A'ala Hubail [18]		
15-11	Kuwait	W	2-1	Manama	ACq	Talal Yusuf [34], Salman Isa [43]	20 000	Kwon Jong Chul KOR
2007								
12-01	Yemen	W	4-0	Dubai	Fr	Al Marzooki 2 [22 62], Maki Habib [31], Talal Yusuf [45]		
18-01	Saudi Arabia	L	1-2	Abu Dhabi	GCr1	Talal Yusuf [14p]		
21-01	Iraq	D	1-1	Abu Dhabi	GCr1	Al Marzouki [8]		
24-01	Qatar	W	2-1	Abu Dhabi	GCr1	A'ala Hubail 2 [45 91+]		
27-01	Oman	L	0-1	Abu Dhabi	GCr1			
27-06	UAE	D	2-2	Kuala Lumpur	Fr	Sayed Mahmoud Jalal [7], Jaycee John [88]		
30-06	Vietnam	L	3-5	Hanoi	Fr	Abdul Rahman [3], A'ala Hubail [62], Jaycee John [72]		
10-07	Indonesia	L	1-2	Jakarta	ACr1	Sayed Mahmoud Jalal [27]	60 000	Nishimura JPN
15-07	Korea Republic	W	2-1	Jakarta	ACr1	Salman Isa [43], Ismael Abdullatif [85]	9 000	Sun Baojie CHN
18-07	Saudi Arabia	L	0-4	Palembang	ACr1		500	Nishimura JPN
7-09	Jordan	L	1-3	Muharraq	Fr	Al Muqla [58]		
4-10	Singapore	W	3-1	Manama	Fr	Jaycee John 3 [36 60 77]		
16-10	Libya	W	2-0	Muharraq	Fr	Salman Isa 2 [40 70]		
21-10	Malaysia	W	4-1	Manama	WCq	Baba Fatadi [3], Jaycee John [15], Abdul Rahman [55], A'ala Hubail [90p]	4 000	Yang Zhiqiang CHN
28-10	Malaysia	D	0-0	Kuala Lumpur	WCq		2 000	Lee Gi Young KOR
2008								
16-01	Kuwait	W	1-0	Manama	Fr	Baba Fatadi [83]		
23-01	Syria	L	1-2	Manama	Fr	Rashid Jamal [15]		
26-01	Yemen	W	2-1	Manama	Fr	Baba Fatadi [15], Al Wadi OG [83]		
6-02	Oman	W	1-0	Muscat	WCq	A'ala Hubail [14]	28 000	Lee Gi Young KOR
4-03	Qatar	W	2-1	Doha	Fr	Salman Isa [25], Al Hamad OG [66]		
21-03	Iran	W	1-0	Manama	Fr	Mohamed Husain [66]		
26-03	Japan	W	1-0	Manama	WCq	A'ala Hubail [78]	26 000	Shield AUS
28-05	Singapore	W	1-0	Singapore	Fr	Humood Hamad [82]		
2-06	Thailand	W	3-2	Bagkok	WCq	Salman Isa [22], Ismaeel Latif [35], Mohamed Husain [57]	15 000	Sun Baojie CHN
7-06	Thailand	D	1-1	Manama	WCq	Salman Isa [67]	21 000	Basma SYR
14-06	Oman	D	1-1	Manama	WCq	Faouzi Aaish [41]	25 000	Al Fadhli KUW
22-06	Japan	L	0-1	Saitama	WCq		51 180	Irmatov UZB

Fr = Friendly match • AC = AFC Asian Cup • GC = Gulf Cup • WC = FIFA World Cup
q = qualifier • r1 = first round group • qf = quarter-final • sf = semi-final • f = final • 3p = third place play-off • po = play-off

BAHRAIN NATIONAL TEAM RECORDS AND RECORD SEQUENCES

Records			Sequence records					
Victory	6-0	SRI 1991	Wins	7	2008	Clean sheets	5	1988
Defeat	1-10	IRQ 1966	Defeats	9	1974-1975	Goals scored	11	2004
Player Caps	102	Abdulrazzaq	Undefeated	9	2008	Without goal	7	1988-1990
Player Goals	30	A'ala Hubail	Without win	12	1988-1990	Goals against	12	1974-1976

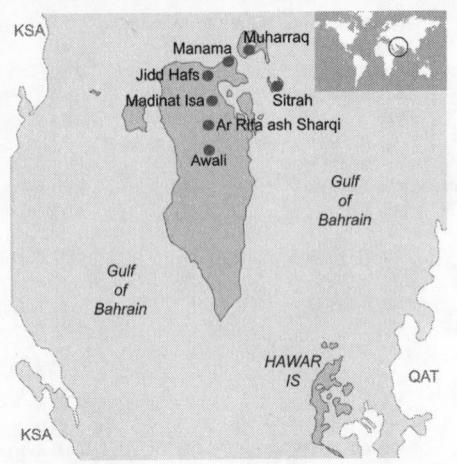

KINGDOM OF BAHRAIN; MAMLAKAT AL BAHRAYN

Capital	Manama	Language	Arabic			Independence	1971
Population	718 306	Area	665 km²	Density	1019 per km²	% in cities	90%
GDP per cap	$16 900	Dailling code	+973	Internet	.bh	GMT + / -	+3

MEDALS TABLE

		Overall			Lge	KC	FAC	CPC	Asia			City	Stadium	Cap'ty	DoF
		G	S	B	G	G			G	S	B				
1	Muharraq	61	2		30	27	1	3		2		Muharraq	Al Muharraq	20 000	1928
2	Riffa	20			9	4	3	4				Riffa	National Stadium	30 000	1953
3	Al Ahli	13			4	8	1					Manama	Al Ahli	15 000	1936
4	Bahrain Club	7			5	2						Manama	National Stadium	30 000	
5	Al Hala	4			1	3						Muharraq			
6	East Riffa	3			1	2						Manama	Al Ahli	15 000	1958
	Al Wahda	3				3									
8	Al Arabi	2			1	1									
	Al Najma	2				2						Manama	Madinat Isa	20 000	1943
10	Al Shabab	1				1						Manama			
	Busaiteen	1					1					Busaiteen			
	Al Nasr	1			1										

RECENT LEAGUE AND CUP RECORD

Championship								King's Cup		
Year	Champions	Pts	Runners-up	Pts	Third	Pts		Winners	Score	Runners-up
1998	West Riffa	45	Muharraq	38	East Riffa	36		West Riffa	2-1	Budaia
1999	Muharraq	39	Al Ahli	30	West Riffa	28		East Riffa	1-0	Al-Hala
2000	West Riffa	4-0	East Riffa					East Riffa	3-1	Qadisiya
2001	Muharraq	52	Besaiteen	45	West Riffa	40		Al Ahli	1-0	Essa Town
2002	Muharraq	46	Al Ahli	46	Riffa	36		Muharraq	0-0 4-2p	Al Ahli
2003	Riffa	40	Muharraq	34	Al Ahli	32		Al Ahli	2-1	Muharraq
2004	Muharraq	48	Riffa	36	Al Ahli	30		Al Shabab	2-1	Busaiteen
2005	Riffa	40	Muharraq	36	Al Ahli	33		Muharraq	1-0	Al Shabab
2006	Muharraq	38	Al Ahli	37	Riffa	33		Al Najma	1-0	Al Ahli
2007	Muharraq	53	Riffa	41	Al Najma	38		Al Najma	2-0	Al Hala
2008	Muharraq	55	Busaiteen	42	Al Ahli	42		Muharraq	2-0	Al Najma

BAHRAIN 2007–08

FIRST DIVISION

	Pl	W	D	L	F	A	Pts	Muharraq	Busaiteen	Al Ahli	Riffa	East Riffa	Manama	Al Najma	Al Ittihad	Al Hala	Al Shabab	Al Hadd	Bahrain
Muharraq †	22	16	4	2	66	14	52		1-0	1-1	0-0	5-1	1-2	1-0	3-0	6-1	3-1	3-0	6-2
Busaiteen	22	13	3	6	45	23	42	4-2		1-0	1-2	3-2	5-2	1-0	1-1	0-0	4-2	1-1	3-2
Al Ahli	22	13	3	6	36	28	42	1-7	1-0		1-0	2-3	2-0	2-0	2-1	1-0	4-2	2-0	0-1
Riffa	22	11	7	4	40	22	40	0-0	1-2	4-3		3-0	0-1	2-2	1-1	7-1	4-1	1-0	2-0
East Riffa	22	9	3	10	28	36	30	0-5	2-1	0-1	2-2		1-2	1-2	0-2	2-0	1-0	0-0	2-1
Manama	22	8	4	10	27	36	28	0-3	0-5	0-0	2-1	3-1		2-1	1-2	1-1	1-2	2-2	2-1
Al Najma	21	7	7	8	33	26	28	0-0	0-2	2-3	0-0	2-1	2-1		2-1	2-2	0-0	0-0	4-0
Al Ittihad	22	6	6	10	26	39	24	0-5	2-1	2-1	1-2	2-2	2-1	3-2		1-2	1-1	0-2	2-2
Al Hala	22	6	4	12	28	50	22	1-4	0-2	1-1	1-3	1-2	1-3	2-1	1-0		2-4	2-0	0-1
Al Shabab	22	5	6	11	30	44	21	0-1	0-7	1-2	1-1	0-1	0-0	1-5	3-0	6-3		0-2	1-1
Al Hadd	22	5	5	12	20	39	20	0-4	2-0	2-3	1-2	0-3	2-1	0-5	2-2	2-3	1-1		0-3
Bahrain Club	22	5	4	13	19	41	19	0-5	0-1	0-3	1-2	0-2	1-0	1-1	2-0	1-3	0-3	0-1	

2/11/2007 - 27/05/2008 • † Qualified for the AFC Cup

KINGS CUP 2007–08

Round of sixteen

Muharraq	4
Bahrain Club	0
Al Shabab	0 0p
Al Ahli	0 3p
Al Hadd	3
Al Tadamun	0
Al Ittifaq	0
Busaiteen	2
Riffa	2
Al Hala	0
Al Ittihad	1
Qalali	2
Malikiya	2
Manama	1
East Riffa	0
Al Najma	2

Quarter-finals

Muharraq	2
Al Ahli	0
Al Hadd	3
Busaiteen	6
Riffa	1
Qalali	0
Malikiya	1
Al Najma	2

Semi-finals

Muharraq	4
Busaiteen	1
Riffa	0
Al Najma	2

Final

Muharraq	2
Al Najma	0

CUP FINAL

24-02-2008

Scorers - Mahmoud Abdulrahman 23, Fouzi Aaish 51 for Muharraq

BHU – BHUTAN

NATIONAL TEAM RECORD
JULY 10TH 2006 TO JULY 12TH 2010

PL	W	D	L	F	A	%
7	1	2	4	7	13	28.6

FIFA/COCA-COLA WORLD RANKING

1993	1994	1995	1996	1997	1998	1999	2000	2001	2002	2003	2004	2005	2006	2007
-	-	-	-	-	-	-	201	202	199	187	187	190	192	198

High	
187	08/06

	2007–2008										
08/07	09/07	10/07	11/07	12/07	01/08	02/08	03/08	04/08	05/08	06/08	07/08
196	197	197	198	198	198	199	199	200	199	196	190

Low	
202	05/01

After struggling to make an impact since being accepted as a full member of FIFA in 2000, 2008 saw Bhutan go close to reaching the final of an international tournament for the first time in their history. The tiny kingdom in the Himalayas had only recorded a handful of wins since their arrival on the international scene, but victory over Afghanistan in the group stages of the South Asian Football Federation Championships played a key role in taking the team into the knockout phase of the competition. Having earlier drawn with Bangladesh before losing to Sri Lanka, the 3-1 victory over the Afghans saw Bhutan finish second in their group and earn a semi-final clash with defend-

INTERNATIONAL HONOURS
None

ing champions and favourites India. Midfielder Kinlay Dorji gave Bhutan an unlikely lead in the semi-final before Sunil Chetri equalised to take the game into extra-time. where a goal in the final minute from Goumangi Moirangthem Singh denied Bhutan the opportunity of a penalty shootout and a potential place in the final. Exposure to international competition for club teams in the AFC President's Cup has helped the national team, and Transport United achieved a notable win in the delayed 2007 tournament, beating Pakistan Army 3-2 in the first round group stage. That was their only win, however, and in 2008 they finishing bottom of their first round group without a win.

THE FIFA BIG COUNT OF 2006

	Male	Female		Total
Number of players	17 100	0	Referees and Assistant Referees	100
Professionals	0		Admin, Coaches, Technical, Medical	100
Amateurs 18+	600		Number of clubs	10
Youth under 18	600		Number of teams	70
Unregistered	2 900		Clubs with women's teams	0
Total players	17 100		Players as % of population	0.75%

Bhutan Football Federation (BFF)
PO Box 365, Thimphu, Bhutan
Tel +975 2 322350   Fax +975 2 321131
bff@druknet.net.bt   www.none
President: WANGCHUK Lyonpo Khandu HE   General Secretary: WANGCHUK Ugyen
Vice-President: DUKPA Sonam   Treasurer: DORJI B.T.   Media Officer: None
Men's Coach: GYOTOKU Koji   Women's Coach: None
BFF formed: 1983   AFC: 1993   FIFA: 2000
Yellow shirts with red trimmings, Yellow shorts, Yellow socks or Red shirts with yellow trimmings, Red shorts, Red socks

RECENT INTERNATIONAL MATCHES PLAYED BY BHUTAN

2003	Opponents	Score			Venue	Comp	Scorers	Att	Referee
6-10	Indonesia	L	0-2		Jeddah	ACq			
8-10	Saudi Arabia	L	0-6		Jeddah	ACq			
10-10	Yemen	L	0-8		Jeddah	ACq			
13-10	Indonesia	L	0-2		Jeddah	ACq			
15-10	Saudi Arabia	L	0-4		Jeddah	ACq			
17-10	Yemen	L	0-4		Jeddah	ACq			
2004									
No international matches played in 2004									
2005									
8-12	Bangladesh	L	0-3		Karachi	SAr1			
10-12	India	L	0-3		Karachi	SAr1			
12-12	Nepal	L	1-3		Karachi	SAr1	Pradhan [47]		
2006									
2-04	Nepal	L	0-2		Chittagong	CCr1		3 500	Gosh BAN
4-04	Sri Lanka	L	0-1		Chittagong	CCr1			Saidov UZB
6-04	Brunei Darussalam	D	0-0		Chittagong	CCr1		2 000	Al Ghatrifi OMA
2007									
No international matches played in 2007 before August									
2008									
13-05	Tajikistan	L	1-3		Barotac	CCq	Pasang Tshering [69]	5 000	Ng Chiu Kok HGK
15-05	Brunei Darussalam	D	1-1		Barotac	CCq	Nawang Dendup [12]	4 000	Mahapab THA
17-05	Philippines	L	0-3		Barotac	CCq		7 000	Saleem MDV
4-06	Bangladesh	D	1-1		Colombo	SAr1	Nima Sanghe [79]		
6-06	Sri Lanka	L	0-2		Colombo	SAr1			
8-06	Afghanistan	W	3-1		Colombo	SAr1	Kinlay Dorji [13], Gyeltshen 2 [31 80]		
11-06	India	L	1-2		Male	SAsf	Kinlay Dorji [18]		

SA = South Asian Football Federation Cup • AC = AFC Asian Cup • CC = AFC Challenge Cup • q = qualifier • r1 = first round group

BHUTAN NATIONAL TEAM RECORDS AND RECORD SEQUENCES

Records			Sequence records					
Victory	6-0	GUM 2003	Wins	1		Clean sheets	2	2003
Defeat	0-20	KUW 2000	Defeats	15	1984-2001	Goals scored	3	2000-2002
Player Caps	n/a		Undefeated	2	2003	Without goal	9	2003-2005
Player Goals	5	WANGYEL DORJI	Without win	18	2003-2008	Goals against	15	1984-2001

RECENT LEAGUE AND CUP RECORD

	Championship	Cup
Year	Champions	Winners
2002	Druk Star	No tournament played
2003	Druk Pol	No tournament played
2004	Transport United	Druk Pol
2005	Transport United	Druk Pol
2006	Transport United	
2007	Transport United	

BHUTAN COUNTRY INFORMATION

Capital	Thimphu	Independence	1949	GDP per Capita	$1 300
Population	2 185 569	Status	Kingdom	GNP Ranking	170
Area km²	47 000	Language	Dzongkha	Dialling code	+975
Population density	46 per km²	Literacy rate	44%	Internet code	.bt
% in urban areas	6%	Main religion	Buddhist 70%	GMT +/-	+6
Towns/Cities ('000)	Thimphu 66; Phuntsholing 65; Punakha 18; Samdrup Jongkhar 14; Geylegphug 7; Jakar 4				
Neighbours (km)	China 470; India 605				
Main stadia	Changlimithang – Thimphu 15 000; PSA Phuntsholing – Phuntsholing 6 000				

BIH – BOSNIA-HERZEGOVINA

NATIONAL TEAM RECORD
JULY 10TH 2006 TO JULY 12TH 2010

PL	W	D	L	F	A	%
17	5	2	10	23	34	35.3

FIFA/COCA-COLA WORLD RANKING

1993	1994	1995	1996	1997	1998	1999	2000	2001	2002	2003	2004	2005	2006	2007	High	
-	-	-	152	99	96	75	78	69	87	59	79	65	59	51	**25**	08/07

				2007–2008								Low	
08/07	09/07	10/07	11/07	12/07	01/08	02/08	03/08	04/08	05/08	06/08	07/08	**17**	09/96
25	39	48	51	51	51	59	60	62	62	67	74		

With four wins in their first seven Euro 2008 qualifying matches, Bosnia harboured genuine aspirations of making it to the finals but those hopes came crashing down around them as the national team embarked on a record run of seven consecutive defeats at the start of the new season. Matters reached their nadir when the former Barcelona player Meho Kodro was sacked as national team coach after refusing to take charge of the team in a match against Iran in May. A fixture against Poland on the same day had been cancelled by the federation against Kodro's wishes, in favour of the game in Iran, a decision which Kodro's assistant Elvir Bolic described as a farce.

INTERNATIONAL HONOURS
None

With open hostility from many quarters against those in charge of football in Bosnia, prospects for the 2010 FIFA World Cup qualifiers appear to be limited. In domestic football, there was little to separate 15 of the 16 teams in the Premijer Liga as once again home advantage played a critical role in deciding which team won the title. Zepec Limorad aside, there were just 13 away wins all season and with remarkably few draws, the points difference between first-time champions Modrica Maksima and relegated Jedinstvo Bihic was just 15. There was also a new name on the Cup as Zrinjski Mostar won the trophy for the first time after beating Sloboda Tuzla on penalties.

THE FIFA BIG COUNT OF 2006

	Male	Female		Total
Number of players	181 640	18 600	Referees and Assistant Referees	1 720
Professionals	430		Admin, Coaches, Technical, Medical	10 100
Amateurs 18+	40 370		Number of clubs	763
Youth under 18	26 570		Number of teams	1 000
Unregistered	36 200		Clubs with women's teams	10
Total players	200 240		Players as % of population	4.45%

Football Federation of Bosnia–Herzegovina (FFBH/NSBiH)

Nogometni/Fudbalski Savez Bosne i Hercegovine, Ferhadija 30, Sarajevo - 71000, Bosnia-Herzegovina
Tel +387 33 276660   Fax +387 33 444332
nsbih@bih.net.ba   www.nfsbih.ba
President: DOMINKOVIC Iljo   General Secretary: BOGDAN Ceko
Vice-President: COLAKOVIC Sulejman   Treasurer: KURES Miodrag   Media Officer: PECIKOZA Slavica
Men's Coach: BLAZEVIC Miroslav   Women's Coach: BAJRIC Ismet
FFBH formed: 1992   UEFA: 1996   FIFA: 1996
White shirts with blue trimmings, Blue shorts, White socks or Blue shirts with white trimmings, White shorts, Blue socks

RECENT INTERNATIONAL MATCHES PLAYED BY BOSNIA–HERZEGOVINA

2004	Opponents	Score		Venue	Comp	Scorers	Att	Referee
18-02	Macedonia FYR	L	0-1	Skopje	Fr		8 000	Vrajkov BUL
31-03	Luxembourg	W	2-1	Luxembourg	Fr	Misimovic [63], Bolic [71]	2 000	Rogalla SUI
28-04	Finland	W	1-0	Zenica	Fr	Misimovic [88]	20 000	Bozinovski MKD
18-08	France	D	1-1	Rennes	Fr	Grlic [37]	26 527	McDonald SCO
8-09	Spain	D	1-1	Zenica	WCq	Bolic [79]	14 380	De Santis ITA
9-10	Serbia & Montenegro	D	0-0	Sarajevo	WCq		22 440	Veissiere FRA
2005								
2-02	Iran	L	1-2	Tehran	Fr	Bolic [17]	15 000	
26-03	Belgium	L	1-4	Brussels	WCq	Bolic [1]	36 700	Hrinak SVK
30-03	Lithuania	D	1-1	Sarajevo	WCq	Misimovic [21]	6 000	Baskakov RUS
4-06	San Marino	W	3-1	Serravalle	WCq	Salihamidzic 2 [17 38], Barbarez [75]	750	Demirlek TUR
8-06	Spain	D	1-1	Valencia	WCq	Misimovic [39]	38 041	Bennett ENG
17-08	Estonia	L	0-1	Tallinn	Fr		4 000	Fojdfeldt SWE
3-09	Belgium	W	1-0	Zenica	WCq	Barbarez [62]	12 000	Benquerenca POR
7-09	Lithuania	W	1-0	Vilnius	WCq	Barbarez [28]	4 000	Kassai HUN
8-10	San Marino	W	3-0	Zenica	WCq	Bolic 3 [46 75 82]	8 500	Hamer LUX
12-10	Serbia & Montenegro	L	0-1	Belgrade	WCq		46 305	Vassaras GRE
2006								
28-02	Japan	D	2-2	Dortmund	Fr	Misimovic [56p], Spahic [67]	10 000	Wack GER
26-05	Korea Republic	L	0-2	Seoul	Fr		64 836	Cheung Yim Yau HKG
31-05	Iran	L	2-5	Tehran	Fr	Misimovic [4], Barbarez [17]		Mohd Salleh MAS
16-08	France	L	1-2	Sarajevo	Fr	Barbarez [16]	35 000	Wack GER
2-09	Malta	W	5-2	Ta'Qali	ECq	Barbarez [4], Hrgovic [10], Bartolovic [46+], Muslimovic [48], Misimovic [51]	2 000	Vejlgaard DEN
6-09	Hungary	L	1-3	Zenica	ECq	Misimovic [64]	11 800	Kapitanis CYP
7-10	Moldova	D	2-2	Chisinau	ECq	Misimovic [62], Grlic [68]	7 114	Piccirillo FRA
11-10	Greece	L	0-4	Zenica	ECq		8 000	Baskakov RUS
2007								
24-03	Norway	W	2-1	Oslo	ECq	Misimovic [18], Muslimovic [33]	16 987	Riley ENG
2-06	Turkey	W	3-2	Sarajevo	ECq	Muslimovic [27], Dzeko [47], Custovic [90]	13 800	Fröjdfeldt SWE
6-06	Malta	W	1-0	Sarajevo	ECq	Muslimovic [6]	15 000	Richards WAL
22-08	Croatia	L	3-5	Sarajevo	Fr	Muslimovic 3 [37 70 77]	8 000	Skomina SVN
8-09	Hungary	L	0-1	Szekesfehervar	ECq		10 773	Trefoloni ITA
12-09	Moldova	L	0-1	Sarajevo	ECq		2 000	Hyytia FIN
13-10	Greece	L	2-3	Athens	ECq	Hrgovic.M [54], Ibisevic [92+]	30 250	Gilewski POL
17-10	Norway	L	0-2	Sarajevo	ECq		1 500	Lannoy FRA
21-11	Turkey	L	0-1	Istanbul	ECq		20 106	Braamhaar NED
2008								
30-01	Japan	L	0-3	Tokyo	Fr		26 971	Kım Euı Soo KOR
26-03	FYR Macedonia	D	2-2	Zenica	Fr	Damjanovic 2 [17 20]		Svilokos CRO
1-06	Azerbaijan	W	1-0	Zenica	Fr	Nokolic [72]		

Fr = Friendly match • EC = UEFA EURO 2008 • WC = FIFA World Cup • q = qualifier

BOSNIA–HERZEGOVINA NATIONAL TEAM RECORDS AND RECORD SEQUENCES

Records			Sequence records					
Victory	5-0	LIE 2001	Wins	3	Four times	Clean sheets	3	2005
Defeat	0-5	ARG 1998	Defeats	7	2007-2008	Goals scored	10	1998-1999
Player Caps	52	Elvir Bolic	Undefeated	4	1997, 2004	Without goal	3	Three times
Player Goals	24	Elvir Bolic	Without win	8	2007-2008	Goals against	11	2005-2007

MAJOR CITIES/TOWNS
Population '000

	City	Population
1	Sarajevo	737
2	Banja Luka	232
3	Zenica	174
4	Tuzla	150
5	Mostar	109
6	Bihac	80
7	Bugojno	43
8	Brcko	39
9	Bijeljina	38
10	Prijedor	37
11	Trebinje	34
12	Travnik	32
13	Doboj	27
14	Cazin	22
15	Velika Kladusa	20
16	Visoko	18
17	Gorazde	17
18	Konjic	16
19	Siroki Brijeg	7
20	Banovici	7
21	Zepce	6
22	Posusje	5
23	Modrica	5
24	Orasje	3

BOSNIA AND HERCEGOVINA; BOSNIA I HERCEGOVINA

Capital	Sarajevo	Language	Bosnian, Croatian, Serbian	Independence	1992
Population	4 498 976	Area	51 129 km^2	Density 78 per km^2	% in cities 49%
GDP per cap	$6 100	Dailling code	+387	Internet .ba	GMT + / - +1

MEDALS TABLE

		Overall			League			Cup			Europe			City	Stadium	Cap'ty	DoF
		G	S	B	G	S	B	G	S	B	G	S	B				
1	Zeljeznicar Sarajevo	6	5	1	3	3		3	2					Sarajevo	Grbavica	15 000	1921
2	FK Sarajevo	5	6	3	1	4	3	4	2					Sarajevo	Olimpijski Kosevo	37 500	1946
3	Celik Zenica	5		1	3		1	2						Zenica	Bilino Polje	16 000	1945
4	NK Siroki Brijeg	3	4	1	2	2	1	1	2					Siroki Brijeg	Pecara	6 000	1948
5	Zrinjski Mostar	2	1	1	1	1	1	1						Mostar	Bijeli brijeg	10 000	1912
6	FK Modrica Maxima	2			1			1						Modrica	Modrica	2 500	1974
7	Brotnjo Citluk	1	1	1	1	1	1							Citluk	Bare	4 800	1955
8	Leotar Trebinje	1	1		1					1				Trebinje	Police	8 500	1925
9	Bosna Visoko	1		2			2	1						Visoko	Luke	3 500	1953
10	NK Orasje	1						1						Orasje	Goal	3 000	1996
11	Sloboda Tuzla		4	1			1		4					Tuzla	Tusanj	7 000	1919
12	Slavija Sarajevo		1	1			1		1					Sarajevo-Lukavica	Slavija Lukavica	5 000	1908
13	Buducnost Banovici		1			1								Banovici	Gradski	5 000	1947
	Borac Banja Luka		1							1				Banja Luka	Gradski	15 000	1926
	Radniki Lukavac		1			1								Lukavac			1923

BOSNIAN CLUBS IN YUGOSLAV FOOTBALL

		Overall			League			Cup			Europe		
7	Velez Mostar	2	5	4				3	4		2	2	
9	FK Sarajevo	2	4		2	2					2		
13	Zeljeznicar Sarajevo	1	2	2	1	1	2		1			1	
14	Borac Banja Luka	1	1					1	1				

RECENT LEAGUE AND CUP RECORD

	Championship						Cup		
Year	Champions	Pts	Runners-up	Pts	Third	Pts	Winners	Score	Runners-up
2001	Zeljeznicar	91	Brotnjo Citluk	84	Sarajevo	81	Zeljeznicar	3-2	Sarajevo
2002	Zeljeznicar	62	Siroki Brijeg	51	Brotnjo Citluk	47	Sarajevo	2-1	Zeljeznicar
2003	Leotar Trebinje	85	Zeljeznicar	82	Sarajevo	69	Zeljeznicar	0-0 2-0	Leotar Trebinje
2004	Siroki Brijeg	61	Zeljeznicar	59	Sarajevo	56	Modrica Maksima	1-1 4-2p	Borac Banja Luka
2005	Zrinjski Mostar	61	Zeljeznicar	51	Siroki Brijeg	45	Sarajevo	1-0 1-1	Siroki Brijeg
2006	Siroki Brijeg	63	Sarajevo	60	Zrinjski Mostar	54	Orasje	0-0 3-0	Siroki Brijeg
2007	Sarajevo	57	Zrinjski Mostar	54	Slavija Sarajevo	53	Siroki Brijeg	1-1 1-0	Slavija Sarajevo
2008	Modrica Maksima	55	Siroki Brijeg	54	Celik Zenica	52	Zrinjski Mostar	1-2 2-1 4-1p	Sloboda Tuzla

BOSNIA-HERZEGOVINA 2007-08

PREMIJER LIGA

	Pl	W	D	L	F	A	Pts	Modrica	Siroki	Celik	Zrinjski	Sarajevo	Sloboda	Zeljeznicar	Velez	Slavija	Laktasi	Posuje	Orasje	Travnik	Leotar	Jedinstvo	Zepce
Modrica Maksima †	30	18	1	11	57	45	55		2-1	2-0	2-1	0-1	3-2	1-0	3-1	1-0	1-0	4-1	4-1	6-1	2-1	3-0	6-2
Siroki Brijeg ‡	30	17	3	10	44	29	54	4-1		0-0	1-0	1-0	2-0	2-1	2-0	3-1	1-0	1-2	1-0	1-0	2-0	2-1	1-0
Celik Zenica	30	16	4	10	38	32	52	3-1	3-2		1-0	1-0	1-0	3-1	2-0	2-0	1-0	3-0	2-0	0-0	2-0	1-0	3-1
Zrinjski Mostar ‡	30	15	4	11	46	27	48	4-0	2-1	3-1		4-0	0-0	1-1	2-0	2-0	2-0	1-0	2-0	1-1	2-1	4-1	2-1
Sarajevo	30	14	6	10	42	29	48	2-4	2-2	3-0	1-0		2-1	0-0	1-0	1-1	2-0	4-1	4-1	1-0	3-0	4-0	3-0
Sloboda Tuzla	30	15	2	13	44	38	47	3-0	3-0	2-0	1-2	1-0		2-1	5-1	2-0	1-0	4-2	1-0	2-0	2-0	1-0	3-0
Zeljeznicar Sarajevo	30	14	3	13	47	35	45	4-1	2-1	3-2	2-1	0-0	4-0		4-0	4-0	1-0	4-2	2-1	1-0	3-0	6-0	1-0
Velez Mostar	30	14	2	14	39	46	44	1-0	1-1	2-0	1-0	2-2	2-0	2-1		4-0	2-0	2-0	3-1	2-1	3-2	2-1	1-0
Slavija Sarajevo	30	14	2	14	39	44	44	1-0	0-2	0-1	2-0	1-0	3-1	3-0	2-1		0-0	2-0	3-2	4-0	4-2	2-1	2-1
Laktasi	30	13	4	13	42	40	43	2-1	2-0	4-0	3-2	1-3	2-0	3-2	3-2	2-1		1-1	5-2	3-1	4-0	2-0	2-0
Posusje	30	13	4	13	42	46	43	1-3	1-0	3-2	1-0	0-0	4-1	3-0	1-0	3-0	1-1		3-1	1-0	0-0	1-0	3-1
Orasje	30	13	3	14	50	45	42	4-0	2-0	3-0	0-0	3-1	2-2	1-0	6-0	2-1	1-0	4-2		2-0	3-0	2-1	2-0
Travnik	30	13	3	14	35	39	42	1-0	1-5	0-0	2-1	1-0	2-1	1-0	2-0	0-0	5-1	2-0	1-0		4-1	2-0	4-1
Leotar Trebinje	30	13	2	15	38	45	41	1-2	1-2	2-0	0-2	2-0	2-0	1-0	2-1	4-3	4-0	1-0	2-0	1-0		4-1	2-0
Jedinstvo Bihac	30	12	4	14	28	43	40	1-1	1-0	1-1	2-1	1-0	2-1	1-0	1-0	3-1	2-0	3-2	0-0	1-0	0-0		2-0
Zepce Limorad	30	2	1	27	25	73	7	1-3	0-3	0-2	1-4	1-3	1-2	3-0	1-3	0-1	1-1	2-3	5-4	2-3	0-2	0-1	

4/08/2007 - 31/05/2008 • † Qualified for the UEFA Champions League • ‡ Qualified for the UEFA Cup

BOSNIA 2007-08 PRVA LIGA NS FBIH (2)

	Pl	W	D	L	F	A	Pts
Zvijezda Gradacac	30	21	6	3	56	11	69
GOSK Gabela	30	16	1	13	43	35	49
Rudar Kakanj	30	14	4	12	44	39	46
Bratstvo Banovici	30	13	6	11	37	31	45
Buducnost Banovici	30	13	5	12	39	30	44
Iskra Bugojno	30	13	5	12	40	33	44
Troglav Livno	30	13	5	12	36	31	44
Napredak Sarajevo	30	13	5	12	36	31	44
Ozren Semizovac	30	13	5	12	38	36	44
Bosna Visoko	30	13	4	13	41	39	43
Drinovci	30	13	4	13	29	36	43
Radnicki Lukavac	30	13	4	13	34	43	43
Igman Konjic	30	11	8	11	38	41	41
Gradina Srebrenik	30	8	5	17	26	49	29
MIS Kresevo	30	7	7	17	28	49	28
Brotnjo Citluk	30	8	2	19	31	62	26

11/08/2007 - 7/06/2008

BOSNIA 2007-08 PRVA LIGA FS RS (2)

	Pl	W	D	L	F	A	Pts
Borac Banja Luka	30	21	4	5	62	29	67
Sloga Doboj	30	16	5	9	60	41	53
Kozara Gradiska	30	14	10	6	44	25	52
Sloboda Novi Grad	30	15	5	10	43	29	50
Famos Vojkovici	30	14	6	10	48	38	48
Sutjeska Foca	30	13	7	10	39	32	46
Ljubic Prnjavor	30	14	4	12	41	35	46
Drina Zvornik	30	12	9	9	43	32	45
Proleter Teslic	30	13	3	14	49	42	42
Drina Visegrad	30	13	2	15	38	48	41
Mladost Gacko	30	11	7	12	23	36	40
Crni Djordje Banja Luka	30	10	8	12	42	47	38
Radnik Bijeljina	30	10	7	13	39	36	37
Borac Samac	30	8	8	14	30	44	32
Rudar Ugljevik	30	5	9	16	22	47	24
Jedinstvo Brcko	30	1	6	23	14	76	9

11/08/2007 - 7/06/2008

KUP BIH 2007-08

Round of sixteen

Zrinjski Mostar	3	1
Slavija Sarajevo	2	0
Bratstvo Gracanica	0	1
Siroki Brijeg	1	3
Laktasi	2	4
Brotnjo Citluk	2	1
Celik Zenica	0	0
Posusje	2	2
Zeljeznicar Sarajevo	3	3
Modrica Maksima	3	2
Velez Mostar	1 1 6p	
Sarajevo	1 1 7p	
Leotar Trebinje	0	2
Travnik *	0	1
Orasje	0	1
Sloboda Tuzla	0	5

Quarter-finals

Zrinjski Mostar *	1 0 3p	
Siroki Brijeg	0 1 2p	
Laktasi	0	1
Posusje *	1	3
Zeljeznicar Sarajevo *	3	2
Sarajevo	1	4
Leotar Trebinje	1	1
Sloboda Tuzla *	6	0

Semi-finals

Zrinjski Mostar *	4	2
Posusje	0	0
Zeljeznicar Sarajevo *	1	0
Sloboda Tuzla	1	1

Final

Zrinjski Mostar ‡	1 2 4p	
Sloboda Tuzla *	2 1 1p	

CUP FINAL

2nd leg. Bijeli brijeg, Mostar, 4-06-2008

Scorers - Ivica Dzidic [3], Davor Landeka [66] for Zrinjski; Damir Tosunovic [48] for Sloboda

* Home team in the 1st leg • ‡ Qualified for the UEFA Cup

BLR – BELARUS

NATIONAL TEAM RECORD
JULY 10TH 2006 TO JULY 12TH 2010

PL	W	D	L	F	A	%
23	8	5	10	35	37	45.7

FIFA/COCA-COLA WORLD RANKING

1993	1994	1995	1996	1997	1998	1999	2000	2001	2002	2003	2004	2005	2006	2007
137	121	88	90	110	104	95	96	85	74	90	69	61	70	60

High	
57	06/08

2007–2008											
08/07	09/07	10/07	11/07	12/07	01/08	02/08	03/08	04/08	05/08	06/08	07/08
69	70	94	60	60	62	62	61	61	60	57	57

Low	
146	12/92

The Belarus national team continued its Jekyll and Hyde existence during a Euro 2008 qualifying competition that saw them finish some distance behind the three front-runners of Romania, the Netherlands and Bulgaria. The 1-0 defeat at home to Luxembourg should haunt the players for years to come - it was only the third time in 88 years that Luxembourg had won a competitive international away from home - and yet the following month Belarus comfortably beat the Dutch in the final match of the campaign. In domestic football, BATE Borisov reinforced their claim as the biggest club in the country when they successfully defended their league title in November 2007 -

INTERNATIONAL HONOURS
None

the first club to do so for over a decade. They also became the first club from the country to make it as far as the third preliminary round of the Champions League. They faced Steaua Bucharest for a place in the group stage, but having held the Romanians to a 2-2 draw at home, they then lost the return. As part of Vladimir Romanov's stable of clubs, MTZ-RIPO might dispute BATE's claim and they reinforced their credentials when they beat Shakhter 2-1 in the Cup Final. Traditional giants Dinamo Minsk, on the other hand, have won just two trophies in the past decade - hence their decision to tempt BATE coach Igor Kryushenko to take over for the 2008 season.

THE FIFA BIG COUNT OF 2006

	Male	Female		Total
Number of players	326 390	47 420	Referees and Assistant Referees	527
Professionals	1 370		Admin, Coaches, Technical, Medical	948
Amateurs 18+	4 530		Number of clubs	155
Youth under 18	18 760		Number of teams	270
Unregistered	113 000		Clubs with women's teams	5
Total players	373 810		Players as % of population	3.63%

Belarus Football Federation (BFF)
Prospekt Pobeditelei 20/3 Minsk 220 020, Belarus
Tel +375 172 545600   Fax +375 172 544483
info@bff.by   www.bff.by
President: NEVYGLAS Gennady   General Secretary: DMITRANITSA Leonid
Vice-President: NOVIKOV Victor   Treasurer: KOLTOVICH Valentina   Media Officer: NOVYSH Siarhei
Men's Coach: STANGE Bernd   Women's Coach: KOSAKOVSKIJ Vladimir
BFF formed: 1989   UEFA: 1993   FIFA: 1992
Red shirts with green trimmings, Green shorts, Red socks or White shirts, White shorts, White socks

RECENT INTERNATIONAL MATCHES PLAYED BY BELARUS

2004	Opponents		Score	Venue	Comp	Scorers	Att	Referee
18-08	Turkey	W	2-1	Denizli	Fr	Hleb.V [67], Kouba [90]	18 000	Mrkovic BIH
8-09	Norway	D	1-1	Oslo	WCq	Kutuzov [77]	25 272	Gomes Costa POR
9-10	Moldova	W	4-0	Minsk	WCq	Omelyanchuk [45], Kutuzov [65], Bulyga [75], Romashchenko.Ma [90]	21 000	Dereli TUR
13-10	Italy	L	3-4	Parma	WCq	Romashchenko 2 [52 88], Bulyga [76]	19 833	Megia Davila ESP
22-11	United Arab Emirates	W	3-2	Dubai	Fr	Shkabara [44], Kovel [60], Kulchy [90]	600	Al Delawar BHR
2005								
9-02	Poland	W	3-1	Warsaw	Fr	Hleb.A [8], Hleb.V [84], Lavrik [92+]	6 000	Zuta LTU
30-03	Slovenia	D	1-1	Celje	WCq	Kulchy [49]	6 450	Al Ghamdi KSA
4-06	Slovenia	D	1-1	Minsk	WCq	Belkevich [18]	29 042	Hansson SWE
8-06	Scotland	D	0-0	Minsk	WCq		28 287	Benquerenca POR
17-08	Lithuania	L	0-1	Vilnius	Fr		2 500	Sipailo LVA
3-09	Moldova	L	0-2	Chisinau	WCq		5 000	Duhamel FRA
7-09	Italy	L	1-4	Minsk	WCq	Kutuzov [4]	30 299	Temmink NED
8-10	Scotland	W	1-0	Glasgow	WCq	Kutuzov [5]	51 105	Szabo HUN
12-10	Norway	L	0-1	Minsk	WCq		13 222	Plautz AUT
12-11	Latvia	W	3-1	Minsk	Fr	Kortyko [26], Kornilenko 2 [52 90]	8 300	Egorov RUS
2006								
28-02	Greece	L	0-1	Limassol	Fr		3 000	Salomir ROU
1-03	Finland	D	2-2	Larnaca	Fr	Kornilenko [34], Shkabara [53]. L 4-5p	120	Krajnic SVN
30-05	Tunisia	L	0-3	Radès/Tunis	Fr			
2-06	Libya	D	1-1	Radès/Tunis	Fr	Shtanyuk [13]. L 1-3p		
16-08	Andorra	W	3-0	Minsk	Fr	Hleb.A [36], Bulyga [77], Kornilenko [85]		
2-09	Albania	D	2-2	Minsk	ECq	Kalachev [2], Romashchenko [24]	23 000	Asumaa FIN
6-09	Netherlands	L	0-3	Eindhoven	ECq		30 089	Webb ENG
7-10	Romania	L	1-3	Bucharest	ECq	Kornilenko [20]	12 000	Undiano ESP
11-10	Slovenia	W	4-2	Minsk	ECq	Kovba [18], Kornilenko 2 [52 60], Korythko [85]	21 150	Kassai HUN
15-11	Estonia	L	1-2	Tallinn	Fr	Hleb.V [63p]	3 000	Hermansen DEN
2007								
7-02	Iran	D	2-2	Tehran	Fr	Hleb.V 2 [53 59]	15 000	Al Fadhli KUW
24-03	Luxembourg	W	2-1	Luxembourg	ECq	Kalachev [25], Kutuzov [54]	2 021	Whitby WAL
2-06	Bulgaria	L	0-2	Minsk	ECq		29 000	Jara CZE
6-06	Bulgaria	L	1-2	Sofia	ECq	Vasilyuk [5p]	10 501	Jakobsson ISL
22-08	Israel	W	2-1	Minsk	Fr	Vasilyuk [2], Romaschenko [90p]	10 000	Malzinskas LTU
8-09	Romania	L	1-3	Minsk	ECq	Romaschenko [20]	19 320	Fröjdfeldt SWE
12-09	Slovenia	L	0-1	Celje	ECq		3 500	Banari MDA
13-10	Luxembourg	L	0-1	Gomel	ECq		14 000	Svendson DEN
17-10	Israel	L	1-2	Tel Aviv	Fr	Romaschenko [68]	4 362	Georgiev BUL
17-11	Albania	W	4-2	Tirana	ECq	Romaschenko 2 [32 63p], Kutuzov 2 [45 54]	2 064	Demirlek TUR
21-11	Netherlands	W	2-1	Minsk	ECq	Bulyga [49], Korythko [65]	11 900	Layec FRA
2008								
2-02	Iceland	W	2-0	Ta'Qali	Fr	Vasilyuk [33], Plaskonny [47]	100	Lautier MLT
4-02	Armenia	L	1-2	Ta'Qali	Fr	Hleb.V [5]	100	Zammit MLT
6-02	Malta	W	1-0	Ta'Qali	Fr	Romaschenko [89]	1 000	Tshagharyan ARM
26-03	Turkey	D	2-2	Minsk	Fr	Kutuzov [35], Hleb.V [64]	12 000	Malzinskas LTU
27-05	Germany	D	2-2	Kaiserslautern	Fr	Bulyga 2 [61 88]	47 258	Ceferin SVN
2-06	Finalnd	D	1-1	Turku	Fr	Shitov [90]	6 474	Skomina SVN

Fr = Friendly match • EC = UEFA EURO 2008 • WC = FIFA World Cup • q = qualifier

BELARUS NATIONAL TEAM RECORDS AND RECORD SEQUENCES

Records			Sequence records				
Victory	5-0	LTU 1998	Wins	6	2004	Clean sheets	3	1998, 2004
Defeat	0-5	AUT 2003	Defeats	8	1997	Goals scored	17	2003-2005
Player Caps	80	Sergei Gurenko	Undefeated	8	2004	Without goal	3	Four times
Player Goals	20	Maxim Romaschenko	Without win	14	1998-2000	Goals against	13	2002-2004

MAJOR CITIES/TOWNS

		Population '000
1	Minsk	1 747
2	Gomel	480
3	Mogilev	366
4	Vitebsk	342
5	Grodno	320
6	Brest	303
7	Bobruisk	220
8	Baranovici	169
9	Borisov	150
10	Pinsk	131
11	Orsja	125
12	Mozyr	112
13	Soligorsk	101
14	Novopolotsk	100
15	Molodechno	98
16	Lida	97
17	Polotsk	81
18	Zhlobin	73
19	Svetlogorsk	70
20	Rechitsa	64
21	Slutsk	62
22	Zhodino	61
23	Slonim	51
24	Kobrin	50

REPUBLIC OF BELARUS; RESPUBLIKA BYELARUS

Capital	Minsk	Language	Belarusian, Russian			Independence	1991
Population	10 293 011	Area	207 600km²	Density	49 per km²	% in cities	71%
GDP per cap	$6 100	Dailling code	+375	Internet	.by	GMT +/-	+2

MEDALS TABLE

		Overall			League			Cup			Europe			City	Stadium	Cap'ty	DoF
		G	S	B	G	S	B	G	S	B	G	S	B				
1	Dinamo Minsk	10	6	2	7	4	2	3	2					Minsk	Dinamo	42 375	1927
2	BATE Borisov	5	7	1	4	4	1	1	3					Borisov	City	5 500	1996
3	Slavija Mozyr	4	4		2	2		2	2					Mozyr	Traktor	17 600	1987
4	Belshina Bobruisk	4	2	2	1	1	2	3	1					Bobruisk	Spartak	3 700	1977
5	Shakhter Soligorsk	2	2	4		1	4	1	2					Soligorsk	Stroitel	5 000	1963
6	FC Gomel	2	2	1	1	1	1	1	1					Gomel	Centralnyi	15 000	1995
7	MTZ-RIPO Minsk	2		1			1	2						Minsk	Traktor	17 600	1947
8	Dinamo-93 Minsk	1	2	2	1	2		1	1					Minsk	Dinamo		1993-98
	Lokomotiv Vitebsk	1	2	2		2	2	1						Vitebsk	Central Sport Komplex	8 350	1960
10	Dnepr-Transmash	1	2		1	1			1					Mogilev	Spartak	6 800	1960
11	Neman Grodno	1	1			1		1						Grodno	Neman	6 300	1964
12	Dinamo Brest	1		1				1	1					Brest	Sportkomplex Brestskiy	10 080	1960
13	Lokomotiv Minsk	1							1					Minsk	Lokomotiv	2 000	2000
	Torpedo Mogilev	1							1					Mogilev	Torpedo	7 000	1974
	Torpedo-SKA Minsk	1							1					Minsk	Torpedo	5 000	1947
	Vedrich Rechitsa	1							1					Rechitsa	Rechitsadrev	5 500	1952

BELARUS CLUBS IN THE SOVIET LEAGUE AND CUP

14	Dynamo Minsk	1	1	3		1	3		1					

RECENT LEAGUE AND CUP RECORD

	Championship								Cup		
Year	Champions	Pts	Runners-up	Pts	Third	Pts		Winners	Score	Runners-up	
1995	Dinamo Minsk	38	MPKC Mozyr	36	Dinamo-93 Minsk	32			-		
1996	MPKC Mozyr	76	Dinamo Minsk	75	Belshina Bobruisk	63		MPKC Mozyr	4-1	Dinamo Minsk	
1997	Dinamo Minsk	70	Belshina Bobruisk	66	Lokomotiv Vitebsk	59		Belshina Bobruisk	2-0	Dinamo-93 Minsk	
1998	Dnepr-Transmash	67	BATE Borisov	58	Belshina Bobruisk	57		Lokomotiv Vitebsk	2-1	Dinamo Minsk	
1999	BATE Borisov	77	Slavija Mozyr	65	FC Gomel	63		Belshina Bobruisk	1-1 4-2p	Slavija Mozyr	
2000	Slavija Mozyr	74	BATE Borisov	64	Dinamo Minsk	62		Slavija Mozyr	2-1	Torpedo-SKA Minsk	
2001	Belshina Bobruisk	56	Dinamo Minsk	53	BATE Borisov	51		Belshina Bobruisk	1-0	Slavija Mozyr	
2002	BATE Borisov	56	Neman Grodno	56	Shakhter Soligorsk	51		FC Gomel	2-0	BATE Borisov	
2003	FC Gomel	74	BATE Borisov	66	Dinamo Minsk	64		Dinamo Minsk	2-0	Lokomotiv Minsk	
2004	Dinamo Minsk	75	BATE Borisov	70	Shakhter Soligorsk	65		Shakhter Soligorsk	1-0	FC Gomel	
2005	Shakhter Soligorsk	63	Dinamo Minsk	50	MTZ-RIPO Minsk	49		MTZ-RIPO Minsk	2-1	BATE Borisov	
2006	BATE Borisov	54	Dinamo Minsk	52	Shakhter Soligorsk	51		BATE Borisov	3-1	Shakhter Soligorsk	
2007	BATE Borisov	56	FC Gomel	44	Shakhter Soligorsk	44		Dinamo Brest	0-0 4-3p	BATE Borisov	
2008								MTZ-RIPO Minsk	2-1	Shakhter Soligorsk	

BELARUS 2007

VYSSHAYA LIGA

	Pl	W	D	L	F	A	Pts	BATE	Gomel	Shakhter	Torpedo	MTZ-RIPO	Neman	Baftan	Dinamo M	Vitebsk	Smorgon	Darida	Dinamo B	Dnepr	Minsk
BATE Borisov †	26	18	2	6	50	25	56		2-0	1-0	3-0	0-3	2-1	4-2	**3-0**	4-1	4-2	4-1	2-1	2-0	1-2
FC Gomel ‡	26	12	8	6	49	28	44	1-3		1-1	1-1	2-2	2-0	3-1	4-4	2-1	1-0	4-0	4-1	4-0	1-0
Shakhter Soligorsk	26	12	8	6	41	27	44	3-4	0-0		0-2	1-1	1-1	3-1	2-2	1-2	3-0	3-1	3-2	2-0	1-1
Torpedo Zhodino	26	11	10	5	28	21	43	0-1	2-1	1-1		1-0	0-0	1-2	2-2	2-0	1-0	4-2	1-0	2-0	2-1
MTZ-RIPO Minsk ‡	26	11	9	6	32	25	42	0-0	1-1	1-3	2-0		1-1	1-0	1-0	0-1	2-2	1-0	2-1	2-3	2-1
Neman Grodno	26	9	9	8	23	22	36	1-0	0-1	2-0	0-1	2-1		3-2	1-1	2-1	0-1	0-3	1-0	0-0	3-1
Naftan Novopolotsk	26	9	9	8	28	30	36	2-2	1-0	0-2	1-1	2-2	1-0		1-0	0-0	0-1	1-1	0-0	1-0	3-0
Dinamo Minsk	26	9	8	9	25	28	35	0-3	1-0	1-0	0-0	0-1	0-0	3-0		0-0	2-1	2-1	0-2	1-0	1-0
FK Vitebsk	26	8	11	7	27	28	35	0-1	0-0	1-2	1-1	0-0	0-0	1-2	1-1		1-0	2-1	3-1	0-2	1-0
FC Smorgon	26	6	8	12	15	29	26	1-0	1-1	0-2	0-0	0-1	0-0	1-1	0-1	1-1		1-1	1-0	1-0	2-1
Darida Mikashevichi	26	7	4	15	27	46	25	1-0	2-7	0-3	1-2	1-1	0-1	0-2	1-0	2-3	1-0		1-1	2-1	0-0
Dinamo Brest	26	6	7	13	23	31	25	2-1	2-1	0-2	0-1	1-0	0-1	0-0	2-2	0-1	4-0	2-1		1-1	0-0
Dnepr Mogilev	26	5	8	13	21	33	23	1-2	2-0	2-3	1-1	2-1	1-3	0-0	1-1	1-2	0-0	0-1	3-1		0-0
FC Minsk	26	4	9	13	18	34	21	0-1	2-6	0-0	0-0	1-2	2-1	1-2	2-2	2-1	1-0	0-2	0-0	0-0	

14/04/2007 - 10/11/2007 • † Qualified for the UEFA Champions League • ‡ Qualified for the UEFA Cup • Match in bold awarded (originally 2-1)

BELARUS 2007
PERSHAYA LIGA (2)

	Pl	W	D	L	F	A	Pts
Savit Mogilev	26	16	5	5	50	21	53
Granit Mikashevichi	26	16	4	6	39	22	52
Lokomotiv Minsk	26	16	4	6	49	21	52
Belshina Bobruisk §3	26	15	7	4	46	26	49
Khimik Svetlogorsk	26	12	8	6	46	31	44
Veras Nesvizh	26	12	4	10	28	25	40
Khvalya Pinsk	26	11	6	9	34	38	39
Dinamo Grodno	26	11	3	12	33	37	36
FC Baranovichi	26	10	5	11	23	28	35
Vedrich-97 Rechitsa	26	9	6	11	29	26	33
FC Polatsak	26	6	5	15	26	49	23
Kommunalnik Slonim	26	5	5	16	22	48	20
FC Moazyr-ZLIN	26	4	6	16	26	44	18
Zorka-BDU Minsk	26	2	4	20	17	58	10

22/04/2007 - 3/11/2007 • § = points deducted

BFF CUP 2007–08

Round of sixteen

- MTZ-RIPO Minsk — w-o
- Kommunalnik Zhlobin
- Dinamo Brest — 0 2
- FC Gomel — 2 1
- Khimik Svetlogorsk — 1 1
- My'kambinat Vitebsk — 0 0
- Veras Nesvizh — 0 0
- BATE Borisov — 1 1
- Dinamo Minsk — 2 0
- Lokomotiv Minsk — 0 1
- FK Vitebsk — 0 0
- Dnepr Mogilev — 1 1
- Darida Mikashevichi — 1 1
- Neman Grodno — 0 0
- FC Minsk — 0 2
- Shakhter Soligorsk — 1 3

Quarter-finals

- MTZ-RIPO Minsk * — 4 0
- FC Gomel — 0 2
- Khimik Svetlogorsk * — 1 0
- BATE Borisov — 3 0
- Dinamo Minsk — 0 0
- Dnepr Mogilev * — 0 1
- Darida Mikashevichi * — 1 0
- Shakhter Soligorsk — 2 1

Semi-finals

- MTZ-RIPO Minsk — 4 2
- BATE Borisov * — 2 1
- Dinamo Minsk — 0 2
- Shakhter Soligorsk * — 1 3

Final

- MTZ-RIPO Minsk ‡ — 2
- Shakhter Soligorsk — 1

CUP FINAL
Dinamo, Minsk
18-05-2008
Scorers - Vyacheslav Hleb [5], Oleg Strakhanovich [83] for MTZ-RIPO; Valeri Stripeikis [81] for Shakhter

* Home team in the 1st leg • ‡ Qualified for the UEFA Cup

BLZ – BELIZE

NATIONAL TEAM RECORD
JULY 10TH 2006 TO JULY 12TH 2010

PL	W	D	L	F	A	%
9	1	1	7	7	21	16.7

FIFA/COCA-COLA WORLD RANKING

1993	1994	1995	1996	1997	1998	1999	2000	2001	2002	2003	2004	2005	2006	2007	High
-	-	173	182	179	186	190	186	167	158	174	181	180	198	201	**157** 05/02

2007–2008												Low
08/07	09/07	10/07	11/07	12/07	01/08	02/08	03/08	04/08	05/08	06/08	07/08	**201** 02/08
199	200	200	201	201	201	176	176	171	171	172	175	

In a sign of the changing times for football in Central America's smallest nation, the national team of Belize played a record number of matches in 2008 and managed to do something it had never managed to do before - pass through a round of FIFA World Cup qualification. Drawn against St Kitts and Nevis, Ian Mork's side stunned the favoured Caribbean islanders with a 3-1 victory in the first leg played in Guatemala City. It was the team's first victory since 2002 and the first-ever in a competitive international. With only three full time pros in the side, including captain and goal-keeper Shane Mood-Orio, who plays his club football with Puntarenas in Costa Rica, there was

INTERNATIONAL HONOURS
None

only ever going to be one outcome in the second round of qualifying that saw the team drawn against Mexico. With a lack of suitable facilities to host the match in Belize, Houston staged the home leg of the tie where 50,137 saw the score restricted to a 2-0 victory for the Mexicans. That was followed by a 7-0 defeat in Monterrey and the challenge is now to maintain the impetus with the continued progress of the championship in Belize the key to ensuring progress. Scorer of two of the goals against St Kitts was young striker Deon McCauley and he helped his club side Defence Force reach the championship final, although they lost over two legs to Hankook Verdes United.

THE FIFA BIG COUNT OF 2006

	Male	Female		Total
Number of players	14 800	3 000	Referees and Assistant Referees	45
Professionals	150		Admin, Coaches, Technical, Medical	625
Amateurs 18+	1 700		Number of clubs	32
Youth under 18	1 300		Number of teams	140
Unregistered	3 650		Clubs with women's teams	10
Total players	17 800		Players as % of population	6.19%

Football Federation of Belize (FFB)
26 Hummingbird Highway, Belmopan, PO Box 1742, Belize City
Tel +501 822 3410   Fax +501 822 3377
belizefootball@gmail.com   www.belizefootball.bz
President: CHIMILIO Bertie Dr   General Secretary: HULSE Marguerite
Vice-President: PECH Bernaldino   Treasurer: BAXTER Matthews   Media Officer: None
Men's Coach: MORK Ian   Women's Coach: GRAY Kent
FFB formed: 1980   CONCACAF: 1986   FIFA: 1986
Red shirts with white and blue trimmings, Red shorts, Red socks

RECENT INTERNATIONAL MATCHES PLAYED BY BELIZE

2005	Opponents	Score		Venue	Comp	Scorers	Att	Referee
19-02	Guatemala	L	0-2	Guatemala City	UCr1		10 000	Quesada CRC
21-02	Honduras	L	0-4	Guatemala City	UCr1		3 000	Campos NCA
23-02	Nicaragua	L	0-1	Guatemala City	UCr1		3 000	Campos NCA
2006								
No international matches played in 2006								
2007								
8-02	El Salvador	L	1-2	San Salvador	UCr1	Benavides [61]		Quesada CRC
10-02	Guatemala	L	0-1	San Salvador	UCr1			Vidal PAN
12-02	Nicaragua	L	2-4	San Salvador	UCr1	McCauley 2 [25 34]		Quesada CRC
2008								
22-01	El Salvador	L	0-1	San Ignacio	Fr			
6-02	St Kitts and Nevis	W	3-1	Guatemala City	WCq	McCauley 2 [7 41], Roches [23]	500	Stennet JAM
26-03	St Kitts and Nevis	D	1-1	Basseterre	WCq	Elroy Smith [39]		Brizan TRI
23-05	Honduras	L	0-2	San Pedro Sula	Fr			
15-06	Mexico	L	0-2	Houston	WCq		50 137	Jauregui ANT
21-06	Mexico	L	0-7	Monterrey	WCq		42 000	Petrescu CAN

UC = UNCAF Cup • WC = FIFA World Cup • q = qualifier

BELIZE NATIONAL TEAM RECORDS AND RECORD SEQUENCES

Records				Sequence records					
Victory	7-1	NCA 2002		Wins	3	2001-2002	Clean sheets	2	2000-2001
Defeat	0-7	CRC 1999		Defeats	9	2004-2008	Goals scored	5	2001-2002
Player Caps	25	Vallan Symms		Undefeated	3	2000-01, 2001-02	Without goal	5	2004-2005
Player Goals	4	Deon McCauley		Without win	12	1995-2000	Goals against	21	2001-

RECENT LEAGUE RECORD

Year	Winners	Score	Runners-up
2005	New Site Erei	0-0 1-1 5-4p	Boca FC
2006	New Site Erei	1-0 2-0	Hankook Verdes Utd
2006	FC Belize	2-1 1-1	Wagiya
2007	FC Belize	1-0 1-0	Conquerors
2008	Hankook Verdes Utd	1-1 1-0	Defence Force

BELIZE 2008 RFG INSURANCE LEAGUE STAGE ONE

	Pl	W	D	L	F	A	Pts
Hankook Verdes Utd ‡	16	7	6	3	26	17	27
FC Belize ‡	16	8	3	5	29	22	27
Wagiya ‡	16	7	5	4	29	24	26
Defence Force ‡	16	6	8	2	18	14	26
San Pedro Dolphins	16	6	6	4	20	18	24
Georgetown Ibayani	16	5	4	7	28	32	19
Sugar Boys Juventus	16	5	2	9	31	32	17
Revolut'ry Conquerors	16	3	6	7	25	32	15
Santel's	16	4	2	10	16	31	14

30/09/2007 - 10/02/2008 • ‡ Qualified for the play-offs

RFG INSURANCE LEAGUE STAGE TWO

	Pl	W	D	L	F	A	Pts
Hankook Verdes Utd ‡	6	4	1	1	8	5	13
Defence Force ‡	6	3	2	1	8	5	11
FC Belize	6	3	1	2	8	5	10
Wagiya	6	0	0	6	4	13	0

17/02/2008 - 30/03/2008 • ‡ Qualified for the final

FINAL

1st leg. MCC Grounds, Belize City 6-04-2008

Belize Defence Force	1-1	Hankook Verdes Utd

Scorers - Deon McCauley [61] for BDF; Daniel Jimenez [11] for HVU

FINAL

2nd leg. Norman Broadster Stadium, San Ignacio, 13-04-2008

Hankook Verdes Utd	1-0	Belize Defence Force

Scorer - Orlando Jimenez [9] for HVU

BELIZE COUNTRY INFORMATION

Capital	Belmopan	Independence	1981	GDP per Capita	$4 900
Population	272 945	Status	Commonwealth	GNP Ranking	159
Area km^2	22 966	Language	English	Dialling code	+501
Population density	11 per km^2	Literacy rate	75%	Internet code	.bz
% in urban areas	47%	Main religion	Christian 77%	GMT +/−	-6
Towns/Cities ('000)	Belize City 61; San Ignacio 16; Orange Walk 15; Belmopan 13; Dangriga 10; Corozal 8				
Neighbours (km)	Mexico 250; Guatemala 266; Caribbean Sea 386				
Main stadia	People's Stadium – Orange Walk 3 000; MCC Grounds – Belize City 2 500				

BOL – BOLIVIA

NATIONAL TEAM RECORD
JULY 10TH 2006 TO JULY 12TH 2010

PL	W	D	L	F	A	%
17	5	5	7	21	8	44.1

FIFA/COCA-COLA WORLD RANKING

1993	1994	1995	1996	1997	1998	1999	2000	2001	2002	2003	2004	2005	2006	2007	High	
58	44	53	39	24	61	61	65	70	92	99	94	96	101	108	18	07/97

2007–2008												Low	
08/07	09/07	10/07	11/07	12/07	01/08	02/08	03/08	04/08	05/08	06/08	07/08	114	08/03
68	90	107	106	108	106	102	99	93	94	90	71		

With the debate raging about FIFA's decision to ban competitive international matches above 2500m above sea-level, it was somewhat ironic that the 2007 Apertura was won by Real Potosí, representing a city which at 4090m claims to be the highest in the world. Not to be left out, San Jose from the city of Ouro at 3710m then claimed the 2007 Clausura. Both are higher than La Paz which stands at 3640m so it seems height really does matter in football. Perhaps Oriente Petrolero and Blooming from the low lying city of Santa Cruz should insist the FIFA ruling is applied to domestic football too in order to bolster their chances of winning honours again. Having said that,

INTERNATIONAL HONOURS
Qualified for the FIFA World Cup finals 1930 1950 1994 Copa América 1963

the internationally acclaimed Tauichi Academy in the city passed a notable landmark when it won its 100th trophy on the international youth tournament circuit. Famous for taking poor kids off the street and giving them an education, along with a chance in football, the academy has produced a number of Bolivian internationals in recent years including current national team coach Erwin Sanchez. With just one win in their first six 2010 FIFA World Cup qualifiers, however, it looks unlikely that Sanchez will lead Bolivia to the World Cup finals in South Africa, even though the altitude ban was lifted in time for the qualifiers to be played in La Paz.

THE FIFA BIG COUNT OF 2006

	Male	Female		Total
Number of players	504 700	74 100	Referees and Assistant Referees	500
Professionals	400		Admin, Coaches, Technical, Medical	2 800
Amateurs 18+	16 400		Number of clubs	890
Youth under 18	33 300		Number of teams	1 100
Unregistered	236 600		Clubs with women's teams	7
Total players	578 800		Players as % of population	6.44%

Federación Boliviana de Fútbol (FBF)
Av. Libertador Bolivar 1168, Cochabamba, Bolivia
Tel +591 4 4244982   Fax +591 4 4282132
fbfcba@hotmail.com
President: CHAVES Carlos   General Secretary: ZAMBRANO Jose Pedro
Vice-President: MENDEZ Mauricio   Treasurer: PACHECO Jorge   Media Officer: SILVER Javier
Men's Coach: SANCHEZ Erwin   Women's Coach: MELGAR Herman
FBF formed: 1925   CONMEBOL: 1926   FIFA: 1926
Green shirts, White shorts, Green socks

RECENT INTERNATIONAL MATCHES PLAYED BY BOLIVIA

2004	Opponents	Score		Venue	Comp	Scorers	Att	Referee
5-09	Brazil	L	1-3	Sao Paulo	WCq	Cristaldo [48]	60 000	Baldassi ARG
9-10	Peru	W	1-0	La Paz	WCq	Botero [56]	23 729	Reinoso ECU
12-10	Uruguay	D	0-0	La Paz	WCq		24 349	Rezende BRA
13-11	Guatemala	L	0-1	Washington DC	Fr		22 000	Prus USA
17-11	Colombia	L	0-1	Barranquilla	WCq		25 000	Torres PAR
2005								
26-03	Argentina	L	1-2	La Paz	WCq	Castillo [49]	25 000	Larrionda URU
29-03	Venezuela	W	3-1	La Paz	WCq	Cichero OG [2], Castillo [25], Vaca [84]	7 908	Lecca PER
4-06	Chile	L	1-3	Santiago	WCq	Castillo [83p]	46 729	Rezende BRA
8-06	Paraguay	L	1-4	Asuncion	WCq	Galindo [30]	5 534	Brand VEN
3-09	Ecuador	L	1-2	La Paz	WCq	Vaca [41]	8 434	Baldassi ARG
9-10	Brazil	D	1-1	La Paz	WCq	Castillo [49]	22 725	Larrionda URU
12-10	Peru	L	1-4	Tacna	WCq	Gutierrez.L [66]	14 774	Sequeira ARG
2006								
15-11	El Salvador	W	5-1	La Paz	Fr	Sossa [29], Arce [33], Sanchez.O [41], Reyes [82], Peña.D [90]	25 000	
2007								
28-03	South Africa	W	1-0	Johannesburg	Fr	Vaca [19]	5 000	Ramocha BOT
26-05	Republic of Ireland	D	1-1	Boston	Fr	Hoyos [14]		
20-06	Paraguay	D	0-0	Santa Cruz	Fr		35 000	Antequera BOL
26-06	Venezuela	D	2-2	San Cristobal	CAr1	Moreno [38], Arce [84]	42 000	Reinoso ECU
30-08	Uruguay	L	0-1	San Cristobal	CAr1		18 000	Toledo USA
3-07	Peru	D	2-2	Merida	CAr1	Moreno [24], Campos [45]	35 000	Chandia CHI
22-08	Ecuador	L	0-1	Quito	Fr		20 000	Parra COL
12-09	Peru	L	0-2	Lima	Fr		15 000	Rivera PER
13-10	Uruguay	L	0-5	Montevideo	WCq		25 200	Selman CHI
17-10	Colombia	D	0-0	La Paz	WCq		19 469	Reinoso ECU
17-11	Argentina	L	0-3	Buenos Aires	WCq		43 308	Rivera PER
20-11	Venezuela	L	3-5	San Cristobal	WCq	Martins 2 [19 78], Arce [27]	18 632	Fagundes BRA
2008								
6-02	Peru	W	2-1	La Paz	Fr	Pedriel [65], Reyes.L [88]		
26-03	Venezuela	W	1-0	Puerto La Cruz	Fr	Cichero OG [79]	16 000	Buitrago COL
15-06	Chile	L	0-2	La Paz	WCq		27 722	Rivera PER
18-06	Paraguay	W	4-2	La Paz	WCq	Botero 2 [23 70], Garcia.R [25], Martins [76]	8 561	Gaciba BRA

Fr = Friendly match • CA = Copa América • WC = FIFA World Cup • q = qualifier • r1 = first round group

BOLIVIA NATIONAL TEAM PLAYERS

	Player		Ap	G	Club	Date of Birth		Player		Ap	G	Club	Date of Birth
1	Sergio Galarza	GK	14	0	Oriente Petrolero	25 08 1975	12	Carlos Arias	GK	3	0	Bolívar	18 02 1980
2	Ronald Gutiérrez	MF	4	0	Bursaspor	2 12 1979	13	Abdón Reyes	DF	1	0	Bolívar	7 11 1981
3	Luis Gutiérrez	DF	2	0	Oriente Petrolero	15 01 1985	14	Miguel Hoyos	DF	17	1	Oriente Petrolero	3 03 1981
4	Lorgio Álvarez	DF	36	1	Cerro Porteño	26 06 1978	15	Santos Amador	DF	2	0	Real Potosí	6 04 1982
5	Leonel Reyes	MF	17	1	Bolívar	19 11 1976	16	Ronald Raldes	DF	41	0	Al-Hilal KSA	20 04 1981
6	Limberg Méndez	DF	4	0	Wilstermann	18 08 1982	17	Juan Carlos Arce	FW	17	3	None	10 04 1985
7	Luis Gatty Ribeiro	DF	32	0	Real Potosí	1 11 1979	18	Marcelo Moreno Martins	FW	6	3	Shakhtar D'netsk	18 06 1987
8	Ronald García	MF	28	1	Aris Thessaloníki	17 12 1980	19	Mauricio Saucedo	MF	3	0	San José	14 08 1985
9	Joaquín Botero	FW	41	14	Bolívar	10 12 1977	20	Jhasmani Campos	MF	6	1	Oriente Petrolero	10 05 1988
10	Joselito Vaca	MF	33	2	Blooming	12 08 1982	21	Didi Torrico	MF	1	0	La Paz FC	18 05 1988
11	Ricardo Pedriel	FW	1	1	Wilstermann	19 01 1987	22	Hugo Suárez	GK	4	0	Real Potosí	7 02 1982
							23	Limburg Gutuérrez	MF	52	4	Oriente Petrolero	19 11 1977

Bolivia's squad for the June 2008 World Cup qualifiers

BOLIVIA NATIONAL TEAM RECORDS AND RECORD SEQUENCES

Records			Sequence records					
Victory	9-2	HAI 2000	Wins	5	1963, 1993, 1998	Clean sheets	3	1998, 1999
Defeat	1-10	BRA 1949	Defeats	9	1926-1930	Goals scored	15	1995-1996
Player Caps	93	Sandy & Cristaldo	Undefeated	9	1997	Without goal	7	1994
Player Goals	16	Victor Ugarte	Without win	19	1945-1948	Goals against	18	1977-1980

MAJOR CITIES/TOWNS

		Population '000
1	Santa Cruz	1 404
2	Cochabamba	932
3	El Alto	872
4	La Paz	817
5	Sucre	232
6	Oruro	210
7	Tarija	165
8	Potosí	143
9	Montero	91
10	Yacuíba	88
11	Trinidad	86
12	Riberalta	76
13	Guayaramerín	36
14	Villazón	30
15	Bermejo	28
16	Cobija	28
17	Camiri	28
18	Llallagua	27
19	San Ignacio	24
20	Warnes	23
21	Tupiza	22
22	San Borja	20
23	Villamontes	19
24	Cotoca	19

REPUBLIC OF BOLIVIA; REPUBLICA DE BOLIVIA

Capital	Sucre; La Paz	Language	Spanish	Independence	1825
Population	8 989 046	Area	1 098 580 km²	% in cities	61%
GDP per cap	$2 400	Dailling code	+591	Density 8 per km² Internet .bo	GMT +/- -4

MEDALS TABLE

		Overall G	S	B	Pro G	S	Nat G	S	LL G	S	Sth Am G	S	B	City	Stadium	Cap'ty	DoF
1	Bolívar	20	9	2	16	6	4	2	12	11		1	2	La Paz	Libertador Bolivar	25 000	1925
2	Jorge Wilstermann	9	7	1	4	5	5	2	12	3			1	Cochabamba	Felix Capriles	35 000	1949
3	The Strongest	7	8		6	6	1	2	18	10				La Paz	Rafael Castellón	15 000	1908
4	Oriente Petrolero	5	11		4	9	1	2	7	3				Santa Cruz	Tahuichi	40 000	1955
5	Blooming	4	2	1	4	2			1	2			1	Santa Cruz	Tahuichi	40 000	1946
6	San José	3	2		2	2	1		9	2				Oruro	Jesus Bermudez	28 000	1942
7	Deportivo Municipal	1	4				1	4	4	3				La Paz	Luis Lastra	10 000	1944
8	Real Potosí	1	4		1	4								Potosí	Mario Guzman	15 000	1941
9	Always Ready	1	2				1	2	2	5				La Paz	Rafael Castellón	15 000	
10	Guabirá	1	2		1		1	1	1	1				Montero	Gilberto Parada	18 000	1962
11	Chaco Petrolero	1	1				1	1	1					La Paz	Hernando Siles	55 000	1942
12	Litoral	1					1		4	1				La Paz	Rafael Castellón	15 000	
13	Universitario	1					1		1	4				La Paz	Hernando Siles	55 000	
14	Aurora		1			1			3	8				Cochabamba	Felix Capriles	35 000	1935
15	31 de Octubre		1					1	1	2				La Paz			
16	Deportivo Chaco		1					1	1					La Paz			
17	La Paz FC		1			1								La Paz	Hernando Siles	55 000	1989
18	Destroyers								2	1				Santa Cruz	Tahuichi	40 000	1948

Pro = the Professional League played since 1977 • Nat = the various national competitions played between 1954 and 1976 • LL = the local leagues played throughout the country until 1976 • The totals for the local leagues are not included in the overall totals

RECENT LEAGUE RECORD

Championship Play-off			
Year	Champions	Score	Runners-up
2000	Jorge Wilsterman	4-1 0-4 2-2 4-3p	Oriente Petrolero
2001	Oriente Petrolero	1-4 4-3 2-0	Bolívar
2002	Bolívar	†	

Torneo Apertura					Torneo Clausura			
Year	Champions	Pts	Runners-up	Pts	Champions	Pts	Runners-up	Pts
2003	The Strongest	46	Bolívar	45	The Strongest	13	Jorge Wilsterman	10
2004	Bolívar	53	Aurora	38	The Strongest	27	Oriente Petrolero	27
2005	Bolívar	44	The Strongest	43	Blooming	19	Bolívar	14
2006	Bolívar	48	Real Potosí	45	Jorge Wilsterman	21	Real Potosí	18
2007	Real Potosí	39	Bolívar	37	San José	18	La Paz FC	18

† Won both stages so no play-off • Clausura 2007 play-off: San José 2-2 1-0 La Paz FC

BOLIVIA 2007

TORNEO APERTURA

	Pl	W	D	L	F	A	Pts	Real Potosí	Bolívar	La Paz FC	Wilstermann	O. Petrolero	Blooming	Strongest	Aurora	San José	Destroyers	Universitario	Marmoré
Real Potosí †	22	12	3	7	46	25	39		6-2	2-0	2-1	4-1	4-0	3-4	3-1	3-1	0-0	3-2	6-0
Bolívar	22	10	4	8	32	37	37	0-3		2-1	1-0	1-1	3-2	1-1	2-1	3-1	1-0	2-3	4-1
La Paz FC	22	10	5	7	31	23	35	1-0	3-1		1-0	0-0	1-0	0-0	2-2	3-2	3-0	3-1	0-1
Jorge Wilstermann	22	10	5	7	29	23	35	1-0	1-0	2-1		1-1	2-0	2-3	1-0	1-1	1-1	0-0	4-0
Oriente Petrolero	22	10	7	5	33	30	34	1-0	**3-0**	0-0	3-1		2-0	4-1	1-0	1-0	1-1	2-2	2-0
Blooming	22	10	1	11	32	35	31	4-2	1-0	2-0	1-2	2-1		2-0	4-3	1-2	1-0	1-0	5-1
The Strongest	22	8	5	9	36	40	31	0-2	1-2	0-4	1-1	3-1	0-3		2-2	0-1	6-2	2-1	5-0
Aurora	22	8	4	10	37	34	28	0-1	1-2	1-0	2-3	1-2	2-0	4-0		2-0	1-1	1-0	4-3
San José	22	8	4	10	36	35	27	1-1	1-1	2-3	0-2	9-2	2-0	**2-2**	2-1		1-0	2-1	3-0
Destroyers	22	7	5	10	28	35	26	2-0	1-2	3-4	2-1	1-0	4-1	1-2	1-1	3-2		1-0	3-2
Universitario Sucre	22	7	4	11	32	32	25	0-0	4-1	1-0	0-1	1-1	2-0	1-3	2-4	3-0	3-0		4-0
Real Marmoré	22	7	3	12	32	55	24	3-1	1-1	1-1	3-1	2-3	2-2	1-0	2-3	2-1	2-1	5-1	

6/03/2007 - 13/06/2007 • † Qualified for the Copa Libertadores • In the matches in bold the points were awarded to Bolivar and the Strongest

BOLIVIA 2007

TORNEO CLAUSURA 1ST STAGE

Serie A	Pl	W	D	L	F	A	Pts	Strongest	Blooming	San José	Universitario	Aurora	Destroyers	La Paz FC	Wilstermann	Marmoré	Real Potosí	Bolívar	O. Petrolero
The Strongest ‡	12	6	3	3	23	14	21		1-0	4-0	4-1	2-2	5-0				2-0		
Blooming ‡	12	6	3	3	14	10	21	0-0		1-1	2-1	3-0	2-1						2-1
San José ‡	12	4	5	3	18	17	17	1-0	1-1		4-1	2-2	3-1	1-1					
Universitario Sucre	12	4	4	3	18	18	15	4-1	1-0	1-1		2-0	4-1			1-1			
Aurora	12	3	5	4	13	17	14	0-0	2-0	0-1	2-1		2-2		1-1				
Destroyers	12	3	2	7	17	26	11	4-1	0-1	4-3	0-0	1-2				3-2			

Serie B	Pl	W	D	L	F	A	Pts	Strongest	Blooming	San José	Universitario	Aurora	Destroyers	La Paz FC	Wilstermann	Marmoré	Real Potosí	Bolívar	O. Petrolero
La Paz FC ‡	12	7	2	3	12	6	23		1-0						0-0	1-0	1-0	1-2	2-1
Jorge Wilstermann ‡	12	5	3	4	19	17	18					2-0		0-2		2-1	2-2	1-3	3-1
Real Marmoré ‡	12	5	2	5	15	13	17						1-0	1-0	1-0		1-1	2-1	4-0
Real Potosí	12	4	4	4	17	14	16			2-1				0-1	2-4	2-0		4-1	2-0
Bolívar	12	4	2	6	16	20	14	2-3						0-2	2-3	2-2	0-0		2-0
Oriente Petrolero	12	4	0	8	10	20	12		1-2					1-0	2-1	1-0	2-1	0-1	

22/07/2007 - 30/09/2007 • ‡ Qualified for the 2nd stage with the group winners taking one bonus point each

TORNEO CLAUSURA 2ND STAGE

	Pl	W	D	L	F	A	Pts	San José	La Paz FC	Blooming	Marmoré	Strongest	Wilstermann
San José	10	5	3	2	16	13	18		2-1	1-1	1-0	1-0	4-2
La Paz FC	10	5	2	3	18	16	18	1-2		2-1	2-2	1-4	2-1
Blooming	10	4	3	3	15	11	15	2-0	2-4		0-0	2-1	5-0
Real Marmoré	10	4	3	3	16	16	15	3-2	1-1	0-1		6-1	2-0
The Strongest	10	3	3	4	16	16	12	1-2	0-0	7-0			3-0
Jorge Wilstermann	10	2	1	7	8	21	7	0-0	0-2	3-1	1-2	1-0	

Clausura playoff
La Paz FC 2-2 0-1 **San Jose** †

1st leg. 9-12-2007, La Paz
Scorers - Daison de Jesus Guale 69, Ronald Gutierrez 79 for La Paz; Alex Da Rosa 19, Lisandro Moyano 92+ for San Jose

2nd leg. 12-12-2007, Oruro
Scorer - Alex Da Rosa 32 for San Jose

† Qualified for the Copa Libertadores

20/10/2007 - 5/12/2007 • Copa Libertadores play-off: Bolívar 1-2 1-2 La Paz. La Paz take the third Copa Libertadores berth with Bolívar and Blooming qualifying for the Copa Sudamericana
Destroyers relegated on overall season record over 2006 and 2007 • Copa Simon Bolivar winners: Guabirá. Guabirá promoted to the top level •
Runners-up, Nacional Potosí, entered a play-off against Aurora: Aurora 3-0 2-2 Nacional Potosí. Aurora remain at the top level.

BOT – BOTSWANA

NATIONAL TEAM RECORD
JULY 10TH 2006 TO JULY 12TH 2010

PL	W	D	L	F	A	%
24	8	7	9	15	21	47.9

FIFA/COCA-COLA WORLD RANKING

1993	1994	1995	1996	1997	1998	1999	2000	2001	2002	2003	2004	2005	2006	2007	High	
140	145	155	161	162	155	165	150	153	136	112	102	101	108	103	**95**	09/07

2007–2008												Low	
08/07	09/07	10/07	11/07	12/07	01/08	02/08	03/08	04/08	05/08	06/08	07/08	**165**	02/00
96	95	101	102	103	101	106	107	113	112	107	112		

For the first time ever, Botswana were in with a chance of qualifying for a major tournament with just a single game left in the 2008 African Nations Cup preliminaries. Beating Egypt away in Cairo in October 2007 was always going to be a long shot, and predictably proved a bridge too far, but the fact the southern African nation were in that situation provided further proof of a dramatic advancement. The Zebras have steadily improved their FIFA ranking and have become a competitive outfit, a fact given further credence when they won a rare away encounter in the 2010 FIFA World Cup qualifiers in June 2008, beating Mozambique 2-1 in Maputo. The result came just

INTERNATIONAL HONOURS
None

a week after coach Colwyn Rowe had been fired, his acrimonious relationship with the media fueling a crescendo of criticism after a goalless draw at home to Madagascar in their opening qualifier. Rowe had to deal with expectations that grew increasingly unrealistic, an ironic victim of his own success and the platform laid by his predecessor Vesselin Jelusic. Stanley Tshoane returned to take over the post and quickly put the ship back on an even keel with the win in Maputo and a point against the Cote d'Ivoire. In club football, Mochudi Centre Chiefs were runaway winners of the Premier League, finishing unbeaten and 23 points clear of second placed Gaborone United.

THE FIFA BIG COUNT OF 2006

	Male	Female		Total
Number of players	93 712	4 920	Referees and Assistant Referees	208
Professionals	12		Admin, Coaches, Technical, Medical	2 370
Amateurs 18+	10 440		Number of clubs	63
Youth under 18	4 000		Number of teams	348
Unregistered	12 180		Clubs with women's teams	0
Total players	98 632		Players as % of population	6.01%

Botswana Football Association (BFA)
PO Box 1396, Gaborone, Botswana
Tel +267 3900279   Fax +267 3900280
bfa@bfa.co.bw
www.bfa.co.bw
President: MAKGALEMELE Philip   General Secretary: KGOTLELE Mooketsi
Vice-President: RAMOTLHWA Segolame   Treasurer: KANDJII David   Media Officer: MOOKI Utlwang Ishmael
Men's Coach: TSHOSANE Stanley   Women's Coach: None
BFA formed: 1970   CAF: 1976   FIFA: 1978
Blue shirts with white and black stripes, Blue shorts, Blue socks

RECENT INTERNATIONAL MATCHES PLAYED BY BOTSWANA

2005	Opponents	Score		Venue	Comp	Scorers	Att	Referee
26-02	Zambia	D	0-0	Gaborone	Fr			
16-03	Zimbabwe	D	1-1	Harare	Fr	Moathiaping [72]	3 000	
26-03	Kenya	L	0-1	Nairobi	WCq		15 000	Buenkadila COD
16-04	Namibia	D	1-1	Windhoek	CCr1	Moathiaping [90]		Sentso LES
17-04	Zimbabwe	L	0-2	Windhoek	CCr1			Mavunza ANG
4-06	Tunisia	L	1-3	Gaborone	WCq	Gabonamong [13]	20 000	Mana NGA
18-06	Malawi	W	3-1	Blantyre	WCq	Molwantwa [10], Selolwane [40], Motlhabankwe [87]	20 000	Evehe CMR
1-07	Congo DR	D	0-0	Gaborone	Fr			
9-08	Angola	D	0-0	Johannesburg	Fr			
10-08	Angola	D	0-0	Johannesburg	Fr			
3-09	Morocco	L	0-1	Rabat	WCq		25 000	Benouza ALG
8-10	Guinea	L	1-2	Gaborone	WCq	Molwantwa [35]	16 800	Sowe GAM
2006								
14-05	Zambia	D	0-0	Gaborone	Fr	W 5-4p		
20-05	Madagascar	W	2-0	Gaborone	CCr1	Moathiaping [66], Mothibane [68]		Colembi ANG
21-05	South Africa	D	0-0	Gaborone	CCr1	W 6-5p		Infante MOZ
6-07	Malawi	L	1-2	Lilongwe	Fr	Moloi.P [38]		
8-07	Malawi	D	0-0	Blantyre	Fr			
5-08	Uganda	D	0-0	Kampala	Fr	L 1-3p		
19-08	Zambia	L	0-1	Lusaka	CCsf			Mnkantjo ZIM
3-09	Mauritania	L	0-4	Nouakchott	CNq			Djaoupe TOG
3-10	Lesotho	W	1-0	Gaborone	Fr	Moathiaping [60]		
7-10	Egypt	D	0-0	Gaborone	CNq			Bennett RSA
15-11	Swaziland	W	1-0	Gaborone	Fr	Ramatihakwane [19]		
2007								
6-02	Namibia	W	1-0	Gaborone	Fr	Moloi.P [60]		
25-03	Burundi	W	1-0	Gaborone	CNq	Siska [64]		Marange ZIM
27-05	Libya	D	0-0	Gaborone	Fr			
3-06	Burundi	L	0-1	Kigali	CNq			Ssegonga UGA
16-06	Mauritania	W	2-1	Gaborone	CNq	Mafoko [19], Selolwane [40]		Gasingwa RWA
21-07	Zambia	D	0-0	Orapa	Fr	W 3-2p		
28-07	Namibia	W	1-0	Gaborone	CCr1	Mogaladi [19]		Lwanja MWI
29-07	Angola	D	0-0	Gaborone	CCr1	W 3-1p		
29-09	South Africa	L	0-1	Pretoria	CCsf			Marange ZIM
13-10	Egypt	L	0-1	Cairo	CNq			Imiere NGA
2008								
16-01	South Africa	L	1-2	Durban	Fr	Moatlhaping [54]		
9-02	Swaziland	W	4-1	Mbabane	Fr	Ramatlhakwane 2 [21] [45], Moatlhaping [54], Moloi [73]		
26-03	Zimbabwe	L	0-1	Gaborone	Fr			
31-05	Madagascar	D	0-0	Gaborone	WCq		11 087	Kaoma ZAM
8-06	Mozambique	W	2-1	Maputo	WCq	Selolwane [30], Mafoko [82]	30 000	Fakudze SWZ
14-06	Côte d'Ivoire	D	1-1	Gaborone	WCq	Selolwane [25]	21 400	Ssegonga UGA
22-06	Côte d'Ivoire	L	0-4	Abidjan	WCq		15 000	Bennaceur TUN
27-07	Mozambique	L	0-2	Secunda	CCqf			Katjimune NAM

Fr = Friendly match • CN = CAF African Cup of Nations • CC = COSAFA Cup • WC = FIFA World Cup
q = qualifier • r1 = first round group • qf = quarter-final • sf = semi-final

BOTSWANA NATIONAL TEAM RECORDS AND RECORD SEQUENCES

Records			Sequence records					
Victory	6-2	SWZ 2002	Wins	4	2001-2002	Clean sheets	6	2006-2007
Defeat	1-8	MWI 1968	Defeats	8	1968-1986	Goals scored	4	Three times
Player Caps	n/a		Undefeated	6	2006-2007	Without goal	6	1990-91, 2002
Player Goals	n/a		Without win	24	1994-1999	Goals against	14	1983-1995

MAJOR CITIES/TOWNS

Population '000

1	Gaborone	240
2	Francistown	94
3	Molepolole	69
4	Selibe Phikwe	56
5	Maun	54
6	Mogoditshane	52
7	Serowe	51
8	Mahalapye	47
9	Kanye	47
10	Mochudi	45
11	Palapye	33
12	Lobatse	31
13	Tlokweng	29
14	Thamaga	22
15	Ramotswa	21
16	Moshupa	21
17	Bobonong	21
18	Letlhakane	20
19	Tonota	19
20	Jwaneng	18
21	Tutume	17
22	Gabane	14
23	Mmadinare	14
24	Ghanzi	13

REPUBLIC OF BOTSWANA

Capital	Gaborone	Language	English, Setswana			Independence	1966
Population	1 842 323	Area	600 370	Density	2 per km²	% in cities	28%
GDP per cap	$9000	Dailling code	+267	Internet	.bw	GMT + / -	+2

MEDALS TABLE

		Overall			Lge	Cup	Africa			City	Stadium	Cap'ty	DoF
		G	S	B	G	G	G	S	B				
1	Township Rollers	14			9	5				Gaborone	National Stadium	22 500	1959
2	Gaborone United	11			5	6				Gaborone	National Stadium	22 500	1967
3	Botswana Defence Force	10			7	3				Gaborone	SSKB Stadium		1978
4	Mogoditshane Fighters	7			4	3				Mogoditshane	Molepolole Stadium	15 000	1925
5	Notwane FC	6			3	3				Gaborone	National Stadium	22 500	1965
6	Extension Gunners	5			3	2				Lobatse	Lobatse Stadium	20 000	
7	Centre Chiefs	2			1	1				Mochudi	Mochudi Stadium	10 000	
	Police XI	2			1	1				Otse	National Stadium	22 500	1977
	TASC (Tati Sporting Club)	2				2				Francistown	Francistown Stadium	27 000	1983
10	Botswana Meat Commission	1				1				Lobatse	Lobatse Stadium	20 000	1969
	ECCO City Greens	1			1					Francistown	Francistown Stadium	27 000	2003
	Nico United	1				1				Selibe-Pikwe	Phikwe Stadium	9 000	
	TAFIC	1				1				Francistown	Leseding Tatitown Grounds	27 000	

RECENT LEAGUE AND CUP RECORD

	Championship							Cup		
Year	Champions	Pts	Runners-up	Pts	Third	Pts		Winners	Score	Runners-up
1999	Mogoditshane	25	Defence Force	21	Centre Chiefs	21		Mogodishane	3-0	Satmos
2000	Mogoditshane	42	Centre Chiefs	40	Defence Force	37		Mogodishane	1-1 5-4p	Gaborone United
2001	Mogoditshane	45	Defence Force	44	Police	43		TASC	2-0	Extension Gunners
2002	Defence Force	47	Mogodishane	38	Centre Chiefs	36		TAFIC	0-0 6-5p	TASC
2003	Mogodishane	2-1	Police					Mogodishane	1-0	Township Rollers
2004	Defence Force		Police		TASC	39		Defence Force	2-1	Mogodishane
2005	Township Rollers	52	Police	51	Centre Chiefs	45		Township Rollers	3-1	Defence Force
2006	Police	66	Defence Force	51	Meat Commission	51		Notwane	2-1	Defence Force
2007	ECCO City Greens	67	Centre Chiefs	62	Defence Force	57		Meat Commission	1-1 6-5p	ECCO City Greens
2008	Centre Chiefs	76	Gaborone United	53	U. Flamengo Santos	48				

BOTSWANA 2007-08

PREMIER LEAGUE

	Pl	W	D	L	F	A	Pts	Centre Chiefs	Gaborone Utd	Santos	Nico Utd	ECCO CG	Police	Gunners	T'ship Rollers	TAFIC	Notwane	Boteti YF	Mogoditshane	BMC	BDF	TASC	Comets
Centre Chiefs †	30	23	7	0	67	21	76		2-1	2-2	1-0	2-2	3-1	1-1	3-0	2-1	2-0	0-0	4-1	1-0	0-0	4-1	1-0
Gaborone United	30	15	8	7	46	41	53	0-4		1-0	1-3	3-2	0-3	3-2	0-1	1-1	0-0	3-0	2-1	1-0	1-1	2-1	0-0
Uniao Flamengo Santos	30	14	6	10	43	34	48	1-2	3-1		0-2	0-1	3-0	1-0	2-1	2-1	2-0	1-0	2-0	0-0	1-1	1-0	4-0
Nico United	30	13	5	12	51	50	44	1-3	2-3	4-2		2-2	0-1	2-0	3-2	2-2	3-2	1-0	0-0	1-0	0-0	1-1	1-2
ECCO City Greens	30	11	8	11	44	44	41	0-3	0-0	1-0	2-4		1-1	1-2	0-0	1-0	0-1	3-1	2-1	3-1	0-0	1-2	3-1
Police	30	11	8	11	37	37	41	0-0	1-2	1-1	2-1	0-2		3-2	1-3	2-3	2-2	0-0	0-0	0-2	0-0	1-2	3-2
Extension Gunners	30	11	7	12	44	37	40	0-2	0-1	1-2	1-0	3-2	0-2		3-1	1-0	1-1	1-2	2-1	1-1	2-1	1-1	0-0
Township Rollers	30	9	13	8	38	32	40	2-2	1-1	2-1	4-1	1-2	0-0	0-0		2-3	1-1	0-0	0-1	2-0	1-1	0-1	3-0
TAFIC	30	11	7	12	37	38	40	0-1	3-3	2-1	2-1	3-1	0-1	2-1	0-1		1-3	1-0	0-0	0-1	1-1	1-0	1-2
Notwane FC	30	9	12	9	44	47	39	1-2	2-2	2-2	5-3	1-1	1-0	3-2	2-2	4-1		2-0	1-2	2-1	1-0	0-0	1-1
Boteti Young Fighters	30	11	6	13	31	36	39	1-0	0-0	1-0	3-1	3-0	0-3	0-3	2-2	4-1	2-0		0-2	0-2	1-0	1-0	3-3
Mogoditshane Fighters	30	11	4	15	36	42	37	2-4	1-2	4-1	1-2	2-1	1-0	1-1	0-1	0-3	3-1	2-3		1-2	1-0	1-2	2-0
Bot. Meat Commission	30	10	6	14	33	34	36	1-2	1-2	1-2	2-3	2-2	2-3	1-2	0-0	1-2	3-0	1-0	1-2		0-0	1-0	2-0
Defence Force	30	8	12	10	25	28	36	1-3	2-1	0-2	3-1	3-2	3-1	1-0	0-0	1-0	1-3	0-0	1-2	0-1		0-2	1-0
TASC	30	9	6	15	37	55	33	1-5	1-3	1-1	2-4	1-3	0-3	0-6	2-2	1-1	3-4	1-3	3-1	2-1	0-2		3-1
Jwaneng Comets	30	3	7	20	28	65	16	1-5	3-5	2-3	1-2	1-3	1-2	1-5	0-3	1-2	2-2	2-0	0-1	1-1	0-0	0-3	

2/09/2007 - 24/05/2008 • † Qualified for the CAF Champions League
Top scorers: Master Masitara, Nico United 18; Jerome JJ Ramatlhakwane, Centre Chiefs 18

BOTSWANA 2007-08 FIRST DIVISION NORTH

	Pl	W	D	L	F	A	Pts
Great North Tigers	22	13	5	4	45	20	44
Miscellaneous Serowe‡	22	13	4	5	46	21	43
FC Satmos	22	13	4	5	40	24	43
Mahalapye Hotspurs	22	11	5	6	33	22	38
Motlakase	22	10	4	8	33	25	34
FC Palapye	22	9	7	6	30	27	34
Stonebreakers	22	9	6	7	30	32	33
BR Highlanders	22	7	8	7	29	28	29
Orapa Bucs	22	6	6	10	28	39	24
Sua Flamingoes	22	6	4	12	22	29	22
Boston FC	22	4	4	14	22	39	16
Red Lions	22	1	3	18	12	64	6

8/09/2007 - 11/05/2008 • ‡ Qualified for the play-offs

BOTSWANA 2007-08 FIRST DIVISION SOUTH

	Pl	W	D	L	F	A	Pts
Naughty Boys	22	12	6	4	24	16	42
Prisons ‡	22	10	9	3	34	22	39
Killer Giants	22	10	9	3	33	22	39
Mochudi Buffaloes	22	9	11	2	33	20	38
Young Strikers	22	10	4	8	36	22	34
Masitaoka	22	8	6	8	27	25	30
Tlokweng United	22	6	9	7	20	26	27
Eastern Tigers	22	6	8	8	20	28	26
Southern Callies	22	5	8	9	17	20	23
Wonder Sporting	22	6	5	11	21	26	23
Gantsi Terrors	22	5	6	11	22	35	21
Blue Diamonds	22	2	5	15	20	45	11

8/09/2007 - 11/05/2008 • ‡ Qualified for the play-offs

COCA-COLA CUP 2007

Round of 16

Bot.Meat Commission*	1	
Security Systems	0	
BR Highlanders	0	
Centre Chiefs *	1	
TASC	2	7p
Naughty Boys *	2	6p
Mochudi Buffaloes	0	
Notwane *	3	
Boteti Young Fighters*	2	
TAFIC	1	
Police *	2	
Gaborone United	4	
Township Rollers *	1	
Stonebreakers	0	
Extension Gunners	0	4p
ECCO City Greens *	0	5p

Quarter-finals

Bot. Meat Commission	0	4p
Centre Chiefs *	0	2p
TASC	1	
Notwane *	3	
Boteti Young Fighters	1	
Gaborone United *	0	
Township Rollers *	2	1p
ECCO City Greens	2	3p

Semi-finals

Bot. Meat Commission	1	5p
Notwane	1	4p
Boteti Young Fighters	0	
ECCO City Greens	3	

Final

Bot.Meat Commission‡	1	6p
ECCO City Greens	1	5p

CUP FINAL

National Stadium, Gaborone
1-09-2007

Scorers - Malepa Bolelang 26 for ECCO; Osengogile Seabi 75 for BMC

* Home Team • ‡ Qualified for the CAF Confederation Cup

BRA – BRAZIL

NATIONAL TEAM RECORD
JULY 10TH 2006 TO JULY 12TH 2010

PL	W	D	L	F	A	%
29	18	7	4	53	21	74.1

It was a strange season in Brazil with a staggering 1252 players transfered to 120 countries abroad, almost half of whom were under the age of 22, and yet the average gate at Serie A matches was a healthy 17,471 - not far behind the league's namesake in Italy where some of the players ended up. São Paulo proved once again that they are the best run club in the country retaining their title and matching the record of five held by Flamengo. Their veteran goalscoring goalkeeper Rogerio Ceni was the star of show, his seven goals from free-kicks and penalties helping to earn him the Most Valuable Player award for the championship. Even São Paulo, however, are not immune from the international market with 18-year old Bayern Munich bound Breno the latest prodigy to leave, having made just a handful of appearances for the club. There was a more sombre mood across the city among fans of Corinthians, one of the most popular clubs in the country, after their team suffered the ignominy of relegation just two seasons after being crowned champions. In contrast, football in Rio experienced something of a revival after a number of seasons in the doldrums. Over 140,000 fans packed into the Maracana for the two games in the Carioca final won by Flamengo,

INTERNATIONAL HONOURS
FIFA World Cup 1958 1962 1970 1994 2002   **FIFA Confederations Cup** 1997 2005
FIFA World Youth Championship 1983 1985 1993 2003   **FIFA U-17 World Championship** 1997 1999 2003
Copa América 1919 1922 1949 1989 1997 1999 2004 2007   **South American Women's Championship** 1991 1995 1998 2003
FIFA Club World Championship Corínthians 2000 São Paulo FC 2005 International 2006
Copa Toyota Libertadores Santos 1962 1963 Cruzeiro 1976 1997 Flamengo 1981 Grêmio 1983 1995
São Paulo 1992 1993 2005 Vasco da Gama 1998 Palmeiras 1999 Internacional 2006

but it was Fluminense who re-lived the glory days of old by reaching the Copa Libertadores final for the first time. Having beaten Argentina's Boca Juniors in an epic semi-final, they were odds on favourites to beat unfancied LDU Quito from Ecuador in the final - even after losing the first leg 4-2 away from home. They did win the second leg 3-1 in a packed Maracana - Thiago Neves scoring the first-ever hat-trick in a final - but he was one of the players who had his spot-kick saved as Fluminense lost on penalties. Football fans in Brazil can usually count on the national team when they are in need of a pick-me-up but despite celebrating the 50th anniversary of the their first World Cup triumph with a 1-0 victory over Sweden in London, coach Carlos Dunga came in for a barrage of criticism, not just because of defeats to Paraguay and Venezuela - their first-ever at the hands of La Vinotinto - but more for the uninspired football played by the team which was comprehensively booted off top spot in the FIFA/Coca-Cola World Ranking.

Confederação Brasileira de Futebol (CBF)
Rua Victor Civita 66, Bloco 1 - Edificio 5 - 5 Andar, Barra da Tijuca, Rio de Janeiro 22.775-040, Brazil
Tel +55 21 35359610   Fax +55 21 35359611
CBF@cbffutebol.com.br   www.cbfnews.com.br
President: TEIXEIRA Ricardo Terra   General Secretary: TEIXEIRA Marco Antonio
Vice-President: BASTOS Jose Sebastiao   Treasurer: OSORIO Antonio   Media Officer: PAIVA Rodrigo
Men's Coach: DUNGA Carlos   Women's Coach: BARCELLOS Jorge
CBF formed: 1914   CONMEBOL: 1916   FIFA: 1923
Yellow shirts with green trimmings, Blue shorts, White socks or Blue shirts with white trimmings, White shorts, White socks

RECENT INTERNATIONAL MATCHES PLAYED BY BRAZIL

2006	Opponents	Score	Venue	Comp	Scorers	Att	Referee
27-06	Ghana	W 3-0	Dortmund	WCr2	Ronaldo [5], Adriano [46+], Ze Roberto [84]	65 000	Michel SVK
1-07	France	L 0-1	Frankfurt	WCqf		48 000	Medina Cantalejo ESP
16-08	Norway	D 1-1	Oslo	Fr	Daniel Carvalho [62]	25 062	Dougai SCO
3-09	Argentina	W 3-0	London	Fr	Elano Blumer 2 [3 67], Kaka [89]	59 032	Bennett ENG
5-09	Wales	W 2-0	London	Fr	Marcelo [61], Vágner Love [74]	22 008	Riley ENG
10-10	Ecuador	W 2-1	Stockholm	Fr	Fred [44], Kaka [75]	34 592	Johannesson SWE
15-11	Switzerland	W 2-1	Basel	Fr	Luisão [23], Kaka [35]	39 000	Merk GER
2007							
6-02	Portugal	L 0-2	London	Fr		59 793	Atkinson ENG
24-03	Chile	W 4-0	Gothenburg	Fr	Ronaldinho 2 [16p 49], Kaka [31], Juan [60]	30 122	Berntsen NOR
27-03	Ghana	W 1-0	Stockholm	Fr	Vágner Love [17]	20 104	Fröjdfeldt SWE
1-06	England	D 1-1	London	Fr	Diego [92+]	88 745	Merk GER
5-06	Turkey	D 0-0	Dortmund	Fr		26 700	Meyer GER
27-06	Mexico	L 0-2	Puerto Ordaz	CAr1		40 000	Pezzotta ARG
1-07	Chile	W 3-0	Maturin	CAr1	Robinho 3 [36p 84 87]	42 000	Torres PAR
4-07	Ecuador	W 1-0	Puerto La Cruz	CAr1	Robinho [56p]	34 000	Pezzotta ARG
7-07	Chile	W 6-1	Puerto La Cruz	CAqf	Juan [16], Baptista [23], Robinho 2 [27 50], Josué [68], Vágner Love [85]	25 000	Larrionda URU
10-07	Uruguay	D 2-2	Maracaibo	CAsf	Maicon [13], Julio Baptista [45]. W 5-4p	40 000	Ruiz COL
15-07	Argentina	W 3-0	Maracaibo	CAf	Julio Baptista [4], Ayala OG [40], Daniel Alves [69]	42 000	Amarilla PAR
22-08	Algeria	W 2-0	Montpellier	Fr	Maicon [62], Ronaldinho [82]	26 392	Biton FRA
9-09	USA	W 4-1	Chicago	Fr	Onyewu OG [33], Lucio [53], Ronaldinho [75], Elano [90p]	43 543	Archundia MEX
12-09	Mexico	W 3-1	Boston	Fr	Kleber [44], Kaka [79], Afonso Alves [87]	67 584	Toledo USA
14-10	Colombia	D 0-0	Bogota	WCq		41 000	Amarilla PAR
17-10	Ecuador	W 5-0	Rio de Janeiro	WCq	Vagner Love [18], Ronaldinho [71], Kaka 2 [76 84], Elano [82]	87 000	Larrionda URU
18-11	Peru	D 1-1	Lima	WCq	Kaka [40]	45 847	Torres PAR
21-11	Uruguay	W 2-1	São Paulo	WCq	Luis Fabiano 2 [44 64]	70 000	Baldassi ARG
2008							
6-02	Republic of Ireland	W 1-0	Dublin	Fr	Robinho [66]	30 000	Rogalla SUI
26-03	Sweden	W 1-0	London	Fr	Pato [72]	60 021	Riley ENG
31-05	Canada	W 3-2	Seattle	Fr	Diego [4], Luis Fabiano [45], Robinho [63]		Stott USA
6-06	Venezuela	L 0-2	Boston	Fr		68 000	Marrufo USA
15-06	Paraguay	L 0-2	Asuncion	WCq		38 000	Larrionda URU
18-06	Argentina	D 0-0	Belo Horizonte	WCq		65 000	Ruiz COL

Fr = Friendly match • CA = Copa America • WC = FIFA World Cup
q = qualifier • r1 = 1st round • r2 = second round • qf = quarter-final • sf = semi-final • f = final

BRAZIL NATIONAL TEAM PLAYERS

	Player		Ap	G	Club	Date of Birth		Player		Ap	G	Club	Date of Birth
1	Júlio César	GK	22	0	Internazionale	3 09 1979	12	Doni	GK	11	0	Roma	22 10 1979
2	Maicon	DF	35	3	Internazionale	26 07 1981	13	Daniel Alves	DF	17	1	Barcelona	6 05 1983
3	Lúcio	DF	69	3	Bayern München	8 05 1978	14	Luisão	DF	25	2	Benfica	13 02 1981
4	Juan	DF	64	4	Roma	1 02 1979	15	Thiago Silva	DF	0	0	Fluminense	22 09 1984
5	Josué	MF	17	2	VfL Wolfsburg	19 07 1979	16	Kléber	DF	11	1	Santos	1 04 1980
6	Gilberto	DF	24	1	Tottenham	25 04 1976	17	Elano	MF	30	4	Manchester City	14 06 1981
7	Júlio Baptista	MF	41	10	Real Madrid	1 10 1981	18	Mineiro	MF	15	0	Hertha Berlin	2 08 1975
8	Gilberto Silva	MF	64	3	Arsenal	7 10 1976	19	Anderson	MF	5	0	Manchester Utd	13 04 1988
9	Luís Fabiano	FW	19	10	Sevilla	8 11 1980	20	Adriano	FW	43	27	São Paulo	17 02 1982
10	Diego	MF	37	7	Werder Bremen	28 02 1985	21	Alexandre Pato	FW	4	1	Milan	2 09 1989
11	Robinho	FW	51	15	Real Madrid	25 01 1984	22	Diego Alves	GK	0	0	UD Almería	24 06 1985

Brazil's squad for the FIFA World Cup qualifiers in June 2008

23	Hernanes	MF	1	0	São Paulo	29 05 1985

BRAZIL NATIONAL TEAM RECORDS AND RECORD SEQUENCES

Records			Sequence records				
Victory	10-1	BOL 1949	Wins	14	1997	Clean sheets	8	1989
Defeat	0-6	URU 1920	Defeats	4	2001	Goals scored	47	1994-1997
Player Caps	156	Cafu	Undefeated	45	1993-1997	Without goal	5	1990
Player Goals	77	Pele	Without win	7	1983-84, 1990-91	Goals against	24	1937-1944

MAJOR CITIES/TOWNS

		Population '000
1	São Paulo	10 059
2	Rio de Janeiro	6 055
3	Salvador	2 762
4	Belo Horizonte	2 399
5	Fortaleza	2 349
6	Brasilia	2 260
7	Curitiba	1 746
8	Manaus	1 642
9	Recife	1 489
10	Belém	1 436
11	Porto Alegre	1 380
12	Guarulhos	1 198
13	Goiânia	1 188
14	Campinas	1 047
15	Nova Iguaçu	1 019
16	Maceió	989
17	São Gonçalo	949
18	São Luis	935
19	Duque de Caxias	829
20	Natal	774
21	Teresina	758
22	São Bernardo	756
23	Campo Grande	745
24	Jaboatão	729

FEDERATIVE REPUBLIC OF BRAZIL; REPUBLICA FEDERATIVA DO BRASIL

Capital Brasilia	Language Portuguese		Independence 1822
Population 188 078 227	Area 8 511 965 km²	Density 21 per km²	% in cities 78%
GDP per cap $7 600	Dailling code +55	Internet .br	GMT + / - -3

MEDALS TABLE

	Overall			Nat		Cup		SL		Sth Am			City	Stadium	Cap'ty	DoF
	G	S	B	G	S	G	S		G	S	B				
1 São Paulo FC	10	10	4	5	5		1	21 17	5	4	4	São Paulo	Morumbi	80 000	1935
2 Cruzeiro	10	8	4	1	3	5	1	34	4	4	4	Belo Horizonte	Mineirão	81 987	1921
3 Santos	10	7	4	2	4	5	2	16 8	3	1	4	Santos	Vila Belmiro	25 120	1912
4 Palmeiras	9	8	2	4	2	3	1	22 23	2	5	2	São Paulo	Parque Antartica	29 650	1914
5 Flamengo	9	7	3	5		2	4	29 25	2	3	3	Rio de Janeiro	Arena Petrobrás	30 000	1895
6 Grêmio	8	5	4	2	1	4	2	34	2	2	4	Porto Alegre	Olímpico	51 081	1903
7 Corinthians	6	5	3	4	3	2	2	25 18			3	São Paulo	Pacaembu	37 180	1910
8 Vasco da Gama	6	4	1	4	2		2	22 21	2		1	Rio de Janeiro	São Januário	35 000	1898
9 Internacional	5	6	3	3	4	1	1	38	1	1	3	Porto Alegre	Beira Rio	58 306	1909
10 Atlético Mineiro	3	4	4	1	3			38	2	1	4	Belo Horizonte	Mineirão	81 987	1908
11 Botafogo	3	4	2	1	2	1	2	17 13	1		2	Rio de Janeiro	Arena Petrobrás	30 000	1904
12 Fluminense	2	3		1		1	2	30 20		1		Rio de Janeiro	Raulino de Oliveira	20 000	1902
13 EC Bahia	2	2		1		1	2	45				Salvador	Fonte Nova	66 080	1931
14 Sport Recife	2	1				1	1	36				Recife	Ilha do Retiro	40 000	1905
15 Guarani	1	2	1	1	2			1			1	Campinas	Brinco de Ouro	30 988	1911
Atlético Paranaense	1	2	1	1	1			20		1	1	Curitiba	Arena da Baixada	32 000	1924

Nat = the national championship played since 1971 • Cup = the Copa do Brasil played between 1959-68 and since 1989 • SL = the state leagues played throughout the country • The totals for the state leagues are not included in the overall totals

RECENT LEAGUE AND CUP RECORD

	National Championship				Cup		
Year	Champions	Score/Runners-up	Runners-up/Third		Winners	Score	Runners-up
1995	Botafogo	2-1 1-1	Santos		Corinthians	2-1 1-0	Grêmio
1996	Grêmio	0-2 2-0	Portuguesa		Cruzeiro	1-1 2-1	Palmeiras
1997	Vasco da Gama	0-0 0-0	Palmeiras		Grêmio	0-0 2-2	Flamengo
1998	Corinthians	2-2 1-1 2-0	Cruzeiro		Palmeiras	0-1 2-0	Cruzeiro
1999	Corinthians	2-3 2-0 0-0	Atlético Mineiro		Juventude	2-1 0-0	Botafogo
2000	Vasco da Gama	1-1 3-1	São Caetano		Cruzeiro	0-0 2-1	São Paulo FC
2001	Atlético Paranaense	4-2 1-0	São Caetano		Grêmio	2-2 3-1	Corinthians
2002	Santos	2-0 3-2	Corinthians		Corinthians	2-1 1-1	Brasiliense
2003	Cruzeiro	100	Santos	87	São Paulo FC	78	Cruzeiro	1-1 3-1	Flamengo
2004	Santos	89	Atlético Paranaense	86	São Paulo FC	82	Santo André	2-2 2-0	Flamengo
2005	Corinthians	81	Internacional	78	Goiás	74	Paulista	2-0 0-0	Fluminense
2006	São Paulo FC	78	Internacional	69	Grêmio	67	Flamengo	2-0 1-0	Vasco da Gama
2007	São Paulo FC	77	Santos	62	Flamengo	61	Fluminense	1-1 1-0	Figueirense
2008								Sport Recife	1-3 2-0	Corinthians

BRAZIL 2007

SERIE A

Team	Pl	W	D	L	F	A	Pts	SPa	San	Fla	Flu	Cru	Grê	Pal	AMG	Bot	Vas	Int	APR	Fig	Spo	Náu	Goi	Cor	Juv	Par	Amé
São Paulo FC †	38	23	8	7	55	19	77	—	2-1	0-0	0-1	1-0	1-0	0-0	0-1	2-2	2-0	1-0	2-0	2-0	3-1	5-0	2-0	0-1	3-1	6-0	3-0
Santos †	38	19	5	14	57	47	62	0-2	—	3-0	2-4	4-1	0-0	1-1	2-2	3-0	1-0	2-1	3-1	3-1	2-0	1-2	3-0	1-1	1-0	2-0	2-3
Flamengo †	38	17	10	11	55	49	61	1-0	1-0	—	0-2	3-1	2-0	2-4	1-0	2-2	1-1	2-2	2-0	4-1	1-1	2-1	3-1	2-1	4-0	1-2	3-1
Fluminense †	38	16	13	9	57	39	61	1-1	3-0	0-1	—	2-2	1-1	0-1	1-1	1-2	1-1	3-0	2-1	1-1	3-0	2-1	3-0	1-1	3-2	0-0	2-0
Cruzeiro †	38	18	6	14	73	58	60	1-2	0-1	3-1	4-2	—	2-0	5-0	4-2	3-2	3-1	3-2	1-1	1-2	2-0	2-2	2-1	0-3	2-3	3-4	2-0
Grêmio ‡	38	17	7	14	44	43	58	0-2	1-0	1-0	2-0	0-2	—	1-1	2-2	3-0	3-1	1-0	1-1	1-2	1-0	4-3	2-1	1-1	3-1	2-0	3-0
Palmeiras ‡	38	16	10	12	48	47	58	0-1	2-2	2-1	1-0	1-3	2-0	—	1-3	1-1	3-2	1-1	0-2	2-1	1-2	2-1	2-0	1-0	0-1	3-0	2-0
Atlético Mineiro ‡	38	15	10	13	63	51	55	0-0	1-2	1-1	3-0	3-4	0-1	1-2	—	1-2	1-0	2-2	1-1	4-1	3-1	2-1	4-1	5-2	4-1	0-0	4-1
Botafogo ‡	38	14	13	11	62	58	55	0-2	1-2	1-1	0-2	4-1	3-0	1-1	2-1	—	4-0	1-1	2-0	1-1	3-1	3-1	0-3	2-3	3-1	3-2	4-2
Vasco da Gama ‡	38	15	9	14	58	47	54	0-2	4-0	1-2	1-1	0-2	4-0	2-2	4-0	2-1	—	1-2	1-0	2-2	3-1	4-1	4-1	2-0	0-1	3-0	2-0
Internacional ‡	38	15	9	14	49	44	54	1-2	1-0	3-0	1-4	1-0	0-2	2-1	1-1	2-3	0-2	—	1-0	2-1	0-0	2-0	1-0	3-0	3-0	1-0	2-0
Atlético Paranaense	38	14	12	12	51	50	54	2-1	0-1	2-0	1-1	2-2	2-0	1-1	0-2	0-1	0-2	1-1	—	1-1	0-0	1-1	0-3	2-2	4-0	2-1	2-0
Figueirense	38	14	11	13	57	56	53	0-0	1-0	4-0	0-2	2-1	1-1	0-1	2-2	1-1	3-3	0-0	3-6	—	0-1	2-0	2-1	2-2	4-1	4-0	3-1
Sport Recife	38	14	9	15	54	55	51	1-2	4-1	2-2	0-2	1-0	2-0	3-1	2-0	3-3	0-0	1-5	3-2	0-0	—	4-1	4-0	2-1	3-0	3-1	2-2
Náutico	38	14	7	17	66	63	49	1-0	1-2	1-0	0-0	1-4	0-2	0-1	0-1	4-1	2-2	1-1	5-0	4-2	2-0	—	0-2	1-0	4-1	4-4	4-0
Goiás	38	13	6	19	49	62	45	0-0	1-0	1-3	5-3	0-0	0-3	1-3	2-1	1-2	3-2	2-1	2-3	2-1	3-2	0-3	—	1-1	3-1	2-0	1-1
Corinthians	38	10	14	14	40	50	44	1-1	2-0	2-2	1-1	0-3	2-1	0-1	0-0	0-1	0-1	1-1	2-2	2-1	1-2	0-3	1-0	—	1-0	0-0	1-0
Juventude	38	11	8	19	43	65	41	2-0	0-2	2-2	0-0	1-0	1-2	1-1	1-2	1-1	2-0	2-0	0-0	1-1	2-1	1-1	2-0	2-2	—	1-2	3-0
Paraná	38	11	8	19	42	64	41	0-1	2-3	0-1	3-1	2-2	3-0	1-0	3-0	0-0	0-0	1-0	2-2	1-2	1-0	2-4	1-0	0-3	1-0	—	0-1
América Natal	38	4	5	29	24	80	17	0-1	1-4	0-1	0-1	1-2	0-3	0-0	0-1	1-0	1-1	1-2	2-1	0-1	1-1	1-5	0-3	1-2	0-3	3-2	—

12/05/2007 - 2/12/2007 • † Qualified for the Copa Libertadores • ‡ Qualified for the Copa Sudamericana
Top scorer: Josiel, Paraná 20; Alberto Acosta, Náutico 19; Kléber Pereira, Santos 16; Dodô, Botafogo 15; Leandro Amaral, Vasco 14

BRAZIL 2007

SERIE B

Team	Pl	W	D	L	F	A	Pts	Cor	Ipa	Por	Vit	For	Mar	Cri	CRB	Bra	SCa	PPr	Gam	Bar	SAn	Ava	Cea	Pau	SCz	Rem	Itu
Coritiba	38	21	6	11	54	41	69	—	1-0	2-0	2-2	1-0	2-3	1-0	2-1	2-1	0-1	2-1	1-1	4-1	2-1	1-0	2-0	3-1	2-0	2-1	2-0
Ipatinga	38	20	7	11	60	41	67	1-0	—	1-0	1-0	1-1	3-2	0-2	4-0	3-0	1-0	3-1	0-0	0-2	2-2	4-1	2-0	2-1	3-0	3-0	5-1
Portuguesa	38	17	12	9	63	46	63	3-1	2-3	—	1-0	1-0	2-0	3-1	1-1	1-0	0-3	2-1	0-6	2-3	0-3	1-0	1-1	2-1	2-2	1-0	3-1
Vitória	38	18	5	15	68	50	59	3-1	4-0	2-3	—	6-0	4-1	0-0	4-1	1-0	3-2	4-0	3-1	2-1	0-1	5-1	2-2	0-1	1-0	1-1	0-0
Fortaleza	38	17	5	16	51	46	56	4-1	0-0	3-1	2-1	—	3-1	2-0	1-2	0-1	0-1	1-1	2-3	2-0	2-0	3-3	1-0	2-1	2-1	3-0	2-0
Marília §6	38	17	8	13	66	61	53	0-2	2-1	1-2	1-2	1-2	—	1-0	2-2	1-2	3-0	3-2	3-1	2-1	4-2	4-3	2-2	2-2	1-0	2-1	4-3
Criciúma	38	15	8	15	51	44	53	3-1	0-1	2-2	2-0	2-0	2-1	—	3-0	1-0	2-2	0-0	0-2	0-2	0-2	0-0	3-0	0-0	1-2	2-0	0-0
CRB	38	15	8	15	54	62	53	1-0	0-0	1-0	4-3	1-2	0-1	2-0	—	3-1	1-0	1-0	1-4	4-1	2-3	1-0	4-1	2-2	3-3	2-5	5-1
Brasiliense	38	14	11	13	57	53	53	0-1	1-0	1-0	1-6	0-1	3-2	2-1	1-1	—	0-0	1-0	0-0	0-0	1-1	3-1	3-2	4-1	3-0	3-2	5-1
São Caetano	38	13	14	12	45	39	53	1-1	0-1	1-2	2-0	1-0	1-1	1-0	4-0	1-0	—	0-1	0-0	1-1	1-0	0-1	3-3	2-0	2-2	3-1	2-2
Ponte Preta	38	13	13	12	58	55	52	1-1	5-1	2-4	0-3	2-0	2-1	2-2	1-2	1-2	2-1	—	1-0	2-2	2-1	0-0	1-1	1-0	2-2	1-1	3-0
Gama	38	14	9	15	53	56	51	1-0	0-2	1-3	1-0	1-1	0-1	2-1	1-0	2-0	0-1	0-1	—	5-3	1-1	4-2	4-2	3-4	2-1	3-1	3-1
Grêmio Barueri	38	14	9	15	57	71	51	0-1	4-2	1-0	3-1	2-1	4-3	2-1	2-3	2-2	0-2	2-1	0-2	—	1-1	0-0	2-1	2-1	5-1	2-1	3-2
Santo André	38	13	12	13	51	50	51	0-0	0-0	2-2	0-2	1-1	1-1	2-3	3-1	3-1	2-1	1-0	2-1	0-1	—	3-0	5-2	1-0	3-0	4-3	3-0
Avaí	38	13	12	13	52	55	51	1-0	1-0	1-1	0-0	2-1	1-0	4-2	4-2	1-2	2-1	1-1	1-0	1-0	1-0	—	2-0	2-0	0-0	2-3	4-0
Ceará	38	13	11	14	58	58	50	2-2	2-0	0-0	0-3	1-1	1-1	1-2	1-2	2-3	4-1	3-0	2-1	1-2	1-0	2-1	—	2-1	3-0	2-1	3-0
Paulista	38	12	9	17	58	61	45	3-2	2-5	2-2	3-0	1-0	0-2	3-1	2-2	0-0	1-2	2-2	1-7	0-3	1-0	1-0	0-0	—	2-2	2-0	2-3
Santa Cruz	38	10	12	16	47	65	42	2-3	2-1	2-2	1-3	1-0	1-0	2-1	4-1	1-0	2-2	1-1	1-1	3-0	0-1	2-2	1-1	1-0	—	4-4	1-0
Remo	38	10	6	22	53	69	36	1-2	1-0	1-0	1-2	3-2	1-3	1-2	1-0	5-1	0-1	0-1	3-3	1-2	1-2	2-2	2-0	3-2	2-1	—	2-0
Ituano	38	8	9	20	41	74	33	0-1	2-2	2-1	3-1	1-0	1-1	1-1	0-1	3-0	2-1	1-1	1-1	0-3	0-0	1-1	2-3	3-1	0-2	2-1	—

11/05/2007 - 24/11/2007 • § = Points deducted • Top scorer: Alessandro, Ipatinga 25

BRAZIL 2007

SERIE C FINAL ROUND

	Pl	W	D	L	F	A	Pts	Bragantino	Bahia	Vila Nova	ABC	CRAC	Atlético GO	Barras	Nacional
Bragantino	14	7	5	2	21	13	26		1-1	1-1	1-0	1-0	3-0	3-1	1-0
Bahia	14	6	6	2	26	18	24	2-2		0-0	3-0	1-0	1-1	2-2	3-0
Vila Nova	14	7	2	5	27	20	23	2-0	2-3		3-0	3-1	1-3	2-1	3-0
ABC	14	7	2	5	20	21	23	2-1	4-3	4-0		2-0	1-1	3-1	1-0
CRAC	14	7	0	7	24	20	21	1-2	4-2	1-2	4-0		1-0	2-1	4-1
Atlético Goiâniense	14	6	3	5	24	17	21	1-1	1-2	3-2	2-0	2-3		6-0	2-0
Barras	14	2	4	8	15	31	10	1-1	0-2	2-1	2-2	1-3	2-1		0-0
Nacional	14	2	2	10	9	26	8	1-3	1-1	1-5	0-1	2-0	0-1	3-1	

13/10/2007 - 1/12/2007 • Serie C consisted of 64 teams divided into 16 groups of four in the first round. The top two from each group qualified for the second round where the 32 teams were divided into eight groups of four. Once again the top two from each group progressed with the third round consisting of four groups of four. The top two from these four groups then qualified for the final round

BRAZIL STATE CHAMPIONSHIPS 2008

State	Winners	Score	Runners-up	State	Winners	Score	Runners-up
Acre	Rio Branco	‡		Paraíba	Campinense	3-0 2-0	Treze
Alagoas	CSA	2-1 2-2	ASA	Paraná	Coritiba		
Amapá				Pernambuco	Sport Recife	‡	
Amazonas	Holanda	0-0 1-0	Fast Clube	Piauí	Barras	1-3 3-0	Picos
Bahia	Vitória	†	EC Bahia	Rio de Janeiro	Flamengo	1-0 3-1	Botafogo
Ceará	Fortaleza	2-0 4-2	ICASA	Rio Grande Nor.	ABC	2-2 2-2	Potiguar
Distrito Federal	Brasiliense	†	Dom Pedro II	Rio Grande Sul	Internacional	0-1 8-1	Juventude
Espírito Santo	Serra	1-2 2-0	Rio Bananal	Rondônia			
Goiás	Itumbiara	1-0 3-0	Goiás	Roraima	Atlético Roraima	5-3 1-1	Progresso
Maranhão	Bacabal	†	Sampaio Corrêa	Santa Catarina	Figueirense	1-0 3-1	Criciúma
Mato Grosso	Mixto	0-0 1-0	União	São Paulo	Palmeiras	1-0 5-0	Ponte Preta
Mato Grosso Sul	Ivinhema	2-1 2-0	Misto	Sergipe	Confiança	†	Sergipe
Minas Gerais	Cruzeiro	5-0 1-0	Atlético Mineiro	Tocantins			
Pará	Remo	1-1 2-1	Aguia				

‡ Won both stages so no final needed. † Played on a league basis

BRAZIL STATE CHAMPIONSHIPS 2008 – SÃO PAULO

CAMPEONATO PAULISTA SERIE A1

	Pl	W	D	L	F	A	Pts	G'tinguetá	Palmeiras	São Paulo	Ponte Preta	Corinthians	Barueri	Santos	Mirassol	Noroeste	Portuguesa	Ituano	Paulista	Bragantino	Marília	São Caetano	Guarani	Juventus	Rio Preto	Sertãozinho	Rio Claro
Guaratinguetá ‡	19	13	1	5	27	14	40		1-2	0-3		2-0	0-1							2-1	1-0	1-0	0-1	3-1		2-0	
Palmeiras ‡	19	12	4	3	36	16	40	0-3			4-1	2-1		2-2			1-0	0-1			3-1	3-1			1-1	3-1	
São Paulo FC ‡	19	11	5	3	31	22	38					0-0	2-1	3-2			2-2		2-1			1-1		3-1	1-0	3-1	3-1
Ponte Preta ‡	19	10	5	4	36	23	35			0-0		0-1		3-2	3-2	1-1	4-2					3-0	4-2	5-2	1-0		
Corinthians	19	9	6	4	24	15	33	2-0	0-1					0-0		1-0		2-0	1-1	3-1		3-0	2-2				1-0
Barueri	19	10	2	7	34	24	32			0-3	2-0	1-1				3-0		3-2		3-1					2-0	3-0	2-0
Santos	19	9	4	6	28	23	31					0-0				2-2	2-1	1-2	2-1	3-2		4-1			2-0	1-1	
Mirassol	19	9	2	8	29	28	29	1-3			1-2			2-1				1-2	2-3			3-1	2-0	2-1			3-1
Noroeste	19	8	5	6	29	23	29	0-1	1-0			3-2		0-1				3-0	0-0	1-1	3-2			4-0			
Portuguesa	19	7	7	5	21	17	29	1-1			2-0			2-3	2-0	0-0			0-0	1-0	1-0	1-0					
Ituano	19	8	2	9	24	32	26	1-2			1-1	1-2		1-0		3-1				2-1		0-0	2-1				3-1
Paulista	19	7	4	8	24	24	25		0-2		1-2	3-0	1-1	4-1		1-1				2-1	1-0		1-1				3-2
Bragantino	19	7	4	8	26	27	25	2-5	0-2	3-1		1-2				3-0		0-2						3-2	3-1	3-1	2-1
Marília	19	7	1	11	21	20	22		0-1	3-2	0-0		1-0		0-1			2-0					4-0	3-1			3-1
São Caetano	19	5	5	9	16	30	20			3-1	1-6	0-1	0-2	2-1		0-2	0-0	1-0						0-3			2-1
Guarani	19	5	4	10	20	31	19				0-1			3-2				2-0	0-2	1-0	0-0				2-0	1-1	1-0
Juventus	19	4	5	10	21	36	17	0-1	0-4			0-0	3-1		1-1	3-2		2-1					2-2			0-1	
Rio Preto	19	4	3	12	16	28	15	0-1				0-1			2-1	0-2	3-3		0-1				2-2			1-0	2-0
Sertãozinho	19	4	3	13	16	30	15						0-2	0-0		1-0	2-0		0-1	0-1			2-0	1-1			3-0
Rio Claro	19	3	4	12	16	32	13	0-3	1-1		1-1		1-1			1-2	1-1	2-0			1-0				2-1		

16/01/2008 - 6/04/2008 • ‡ Qualified for the semi-finals • Semi-finals: São Paulo FC 2-1 0-2 Palmeiras; Ponte Preta 1-0 2-1 Guaratinguetá Final: 1st leg. Moises Lucarelli, Campinas, 27-04-2008, Att: 19 111, Ref: Oliveira. Ponte Preta 0-1 Palmeiras. Scorer - Kléber [20] for Palmeiras Final: 2nd leg. Palestra Italia, São Paulo, 4-05-2008, Att: 27 927, Ref: Cléber. Palmeiras 5-0 Ponte Preta. Scorers - Ricardo Conceição OG [19], Alex Mineiro 3 [33 75 77], Valdivia [72] for Palmeiras. Palmeiras are São Paulo champions

BRAZIL STATE CHAMPIONSHIPS 2008 – RIO DE JANEIRO

TAÇA GUANABARA

Group A	Pl	W	D	L	F	A	Pts
Flamengo †	7	6	0	1	19	7	18
Fluminense †	7	5	2	0	23	8	17
Macaé	7	3	2	2	9	5	11
Boavista	7	3	2	2	11	10	11
Volta Redonda	7	2	1	4	13	14	7
Duque de Caxias	7	2	1	4	12	16	7
Cardoso Moreira	7	2	1	4	9	19	7
América	7	0	1	6	8	25	1

Group B	Pl	W	D	L	F	A	Pts
Botafogo †	7	5	1	1	20	8	16
Vasco da Gama †	7	5	0	2	19	8	15
Madureira	7	4	1	2	15	11	13
Cabofriense	7	3	1	3	13	14	10
Friburgense	7	3	1	3	7	8	10
Resende	7	2	0	5	5	14	6
Mesquita	7	1	3	3	5	14	6
Americano	7	1	1	5	5	12	4

19/01/2008 - 10/02/2008 • † Qualified for the semis

TAÇA RIO

Group A	Pl	W	D	L	F	A	Pts
Fluminense †	7	6	1	1	23	10	19
Flamengo †	7	5	2	1	19	9	17
Boavista	7	3	2	3	15	16	11
Volta Redonda	7	3	1	4	12	16	10
Macaé	7	3	1	4	11	16	10
Duque de Caxias	7	3	0	5	9	15	9
América	7	2	3	3	9	9	9
Cardoso Moreira	7	0	2	6	6	16	2

Group B	Pl	W	D	L	F	A	Pts
Botafogo †	7	7	0	1	23	7	21
Vasco da Gama †	7	5	1	2	20	7	16
Resende	7	3	4	1	22	19	13
Madureira	7	3	1	4	7	12	10
Cabofriense	7	3	2	3	8	8	11
Americano	7	3	0	5	7	14	9
Friburgense	7	2	1	5	10	18	7
Mesquita	7	1	3	4	10	19	6

1/03/2008 - 6/04/2008 • † Qualified for the semis

GUANABARA PLAY-OFFS

Semi–finals		Final	
Flamengo	2		
Vasco da Gama	1	Flamengo	2
Fluminense	0	Botafogo	1
Botafogo	2		

Maracana, Rio de Janeiro, 24-02-2008, Att: 78 830,
Scorers - Ibson 18, Diego Tardelli 45 for Flamengo;
Wellington 27 for Botafogo

TAÇA RIO PLAY-OFFS

Semi–finals		Final	
Botafogo	3		
Flamengo	0	Botafogo	1
Vasco da Gama	1 4p	Fluminense	0
Fluminense	1 5p		

Maracana, Rio de Janeiro, 20-04-2008, Att: 64 785,
Scorer - Renato 38 for Botafogo

CARIOCA FINAL

1st leg. Maracana, Rio de Janeiro, 27-04-2008, Att: 63 413, Ref: Fonseca

Flamengo 1-0 Botafogo

Scorer - Obina 79

CARIOCA FINAL

2nd leg. Maracana, Rio de Janeiro, 4-05-2008, Att: 78 716, Ref: Dos Santos

Botafogo 1-3 Flamengo

Scorers - Lucio 22 for Botafogo; Obina 2 48 92+, Diego Tardelli 81 for Fla

BRAZIL STATE CHAMPIONSHIPS 2008 – RIO DE JANEIRO

CAMPEONATO CARIOCA 2008 RESULTS	Flamengo	Botafogo	Fluminense	Vasco	Madureira	Boavista	Cabofriense	Macaé	Resende	V. Redonda	Friburgense	D. de Caxias	Americano	Mesquita	América	C. Moreira
Flamengo		2-3	1-4		0-0	2-0	2-0	1-0	4-2	2-1	4-1	5-1	3-1	2-0	4-0	4-1
Botafogo			3-1		1-2	1-3	1-1	7-0	2-0	3-0	4-1	4-1	3-0	6-2	1-0	1-0
Fluminense				2-1	4-0	1-1	3-1	2-2	2-2	5-1	5-2	3-2	2-0	4-1	6-1	2-0
Vasco da Gama	2-2	2-3			1-2	4-0	5-1	4-0	5-2	1-2	2-0	2-0	1-0	3-0	2-0	4-1
Madureira									3-4	1-0	1-0	2-1	6-3		0-2	
Boavista					3-2		2-1		3-2	1-1			3-0		2-0	
Cabofriense					2-0			1-0	4-1	2-0	0-2			3-0		
Macaé											3-1	2-0	2-0	4-0	1-0	
Resende					1-0	5-4		2-2					1-0			3-0
Volta Redonda					2-1			0-0	3-3		0-1			3-1		5-1
Friburgense								2-0	2-0			1-2	1-0	1-1	0-2	
Duque de Caxias					2-2	2-1			0-1				1-0			1-2
Americano						2-0		3-2						0-0	1-0	2-2
Mesquita					1-1	1-1			1-0			4-2				2-2
América								0-0	4-4	2-4		2-5		1-1		3-3
Cardoso Moreira					0-1	2-1	1-1	0-3			1-2					

Clubs listed according to overall position • Taça Guanabara results in shaded boxes • Taça Rio results in unshaded boxes

COPA DO BRASIL 2008

First Round

Team	Leg 1	Leg 2	Extra
Sport Recife	2	4	
Imperatriz *	2	1	
Ulbra *	1	0	
Brasiliense	1	1	
Central AC Caruaru *	0	2	
Remo	0	0	
CENE *	0		
Palmeiras	2		
Paraná	0	4	
Trem *	0	0	
Sousa *	1		
Vitória	4		
Chapecoense *	3	0	
Guarani	1	0	
Nacional Patos *	0		
Internacional	4		
Corinthians Maceió *	1	1	4p
Atlético Paranaense	1	1	3p
Aguia Negra *	3	3	
Paranavaí	4	3	
Madureira *	1	1	4p
ABC	1	1	3p
Linhares *	0	0	4p
Juventude	0	0	5p
Criciúma	2	2	
Baraúnas *	2	0	
Bahia	2	2	
ICASA *	3	2	
Bragantino	2	2	
Democrata-GV *	3	1	
Itabaiana *	0	2	
Vasco da Gama	1	3	
Botafogo	3		
Rio Branco *	1		
Jaguaré *	3	0	
River AC Teresina	2	2	
Volta Redonda	2		
Roma Apucarana *	0		
Ulbra Ji-Paraná *	1	1	
Portuguesa	1	3	
Náutico	7		
Atlético Roraima *	1		
Coruripe *	4	1	
Juventus São Paulo	1	5	
Nacional Manaus	3		
Esportivo Guará *	1		
Palmas *	0		
Atlético Mineiro	7		
São Caetano			
Maranhão * ‡			
Tuna Luso *	0	0	
Coritiba	0	6	
Grêmio	1	6	
Grêmio Jaciara *	0	0	
Ituiutaba *	0	2	
Atlético Goiâniense	0	3	
Goiás	4		
Cacerense *	1		
Santa Cruz	1	1	
Fast Clube *	3	0	
Fortaleza	0	4	
America Propriá *	0	0	
Barras *	0		
Corinthians	6		

Second Round

Team	Leg 1	Leg 2	Extra
Sport Recife	2	4	
Brasiliense *	1	1	
Central AC Caruaru *	1		
Palmeiras	5		
Paraná *	1	1	
Vitória	0	2	
Chapecoense *	0		
Internacional	2		
Corinthians Maceió	1	4	
Paranavaí *	0	1	
Madureira *	0		
Juventude	3		
Criciúma	6		
ICASA *	1		
Bragantino *	2	1	
Vasco da Gama	2	2	
Botafogo	1	2	
River AC Teresina *	2	0	
Volta Redonda *	0	0	
Portuguesa	0	2	
Náutico	0	3	
Juventus São Paulo *	2	0	
Nacional Manaus *	2	1	
Atlético Mineiro	2	4	
São Caetano *	1	0	
Coritiba	0	0	
Grêmio	1	2	3p
Atlético Goiâniense *	2	1	4p
Goiás	3		
Fast Clube *	1		
Fortaleza *	1	0	
Corinthians	2	2	

Third Round

Team	Leg 1	Leg 2
Sport Recife	0	4
Palmeiras *	0	1
Paraná *	2	1
Internacional	0	5
Corinthians Maceió *	2	1
Juventude	0	3
Criciúma	0	2
Vasco da Gama *	1	2
Botafogo	1	2
Portuguesa *	1	1
Náutico *	3	0
Atlético Mineiro	2	1
São Caetano *	2	2
Atlético Goiâniense	1	1
Goiás *	3	0
Corinthians	1	4

If the away team wins the first leg by two goals in the first or second round no second leg is played

COPA DO BRASIL 2008

Quarter-finals	Semi-finals	Final

Sport Recife	0	3
Internacional *	1	1

Sport Recife *	2 0 5p
Vasco da Gama	0 2 4p

Corinthians Maceió	1	1
Vasco da Gama *	5	3

Sport Recife †	1	2
Corinthians *	3	0

Botafogo	0	2
Atlético Mineiro *	0	0

Botafogo *	2 1 4p
Corinthians	1 2 5p

COPA DO BRASIL FINAL

1st leg. Morumbi, São Paulo, 4-06-2008, Att: 63 871, Ref: Heber Roberto Lopes

Corinthians	3	Dentinho [18], Herrera [22], Acosta [77]
Sport Recife	1	Enílton [91+]

Corinthians - Felipe - Carlos Alberto, Chicão, William, André Santos - Fabinho, Eduardo Ramos
(Nilton), Alessandro (Fábio Ferreira), Diogo Rincón (Acosta) - Dentinho, Herrera. Tr: Mano Menezes
Sport - Magrão – Luisinho Netto, Igor, Durval, Dutra - Daniel, Sandro Goiano (Everton), Fábio Gomes,
Luciano Henrique (Roger) - Carlinhos Bala, Leandro Machado (Enílton). Tr: Nelsinho Batista

São Caetano	1	1
Corinthians *	2	3

2nd leg. Ilha do Retiro, Recife, 11-06-2008, 33 921, Ref: Alício Pena Júnior

Sport Recife	2	Carlinhos Bala [35], Luciano Henrique [38]
Corinthians	0	

Sport - Magrão – Diogo, Igor, Durval, Dutra – Daniel, Sandro Goiano, Luciano Henrique (Everton),
Kássio (Enílton) - Carlinhos Bala, Leandro Machado (Roger). Tr: Nelsinho Batista
Corinthians - Felipe - Carlos Alberto (Lulinha), Chicão, William, André Santos - Fabinho, Eduardo
Ramos, Alessandro, Diogo Rincón (Acosta) - Dentinho (Wellington Saci), Herrera. Tr: Mano Menezes

† Qualified for the Copa Libertadores
* Home team in the first leg
‡ Maranhão disqualified

AMERICA 2007

Month	Day	Opponent	Res	Score	Scorers
May	13	Vasco	L	0-1	
	19	Santos	W	3-2	Edson Borges 3 42 47 53
	26	Figueirense	L	0-1	
	3	Juventude	L	0-3	
	10	Corinthians	L	1-2	Leandro Sena 24
Jun	17	Sport	D	2-2	Luciano Dias 2 13 32
	24	Fluminense	L	0-1	
	30	Goiás	L	0-3	
	4	Palmeiras	L	0-2	
	6	Paraná	W	1-0	Arlon 56
	14	Inter	L	1-2	Rogelio 5
Jul	18	Atlético MG	L	1-4	Edson Borges 25
	21	Atlético PR	W	2-1	Paulo Isidoro 11, Reinaldo 28
	25	Flamengo	L	1-3	Carlos Eduardo 37
	29	São Paulo	L	0-1	
	1	Botafogo	L	2-4	Paulo Isidoro 2 17 53
	4	Náutico	L	1-5	Carlos Eduardo 64
	9	Grêmio	L	0-3	
Aug	12	Cruzeiro	L	1-2	Carlos Eduardo 41
	19	Vasco	L	0-2	
	26	Santos	L	1-4	Ney Santos 84
	29	Figueirense	L	1-3	Geovane 29
	1	Juventude	L	0-3	
	5	Corinthians	L	0-1	
	9	Sport	D	1-1	Leandro Sena 4
Sep	15	Fluminense	L	0-2	
	22	Goiás	D	1-1	Leandro Sena 85p
	30	Palmeiras	D	0-0	
	4	Paraná	W	3-2	Carlos Eduardo 29, Wesley 2 64 79
	7	Inter	L	0-2	
Oct	13	Atlético MG	L	0-1	
	21	Atlético PR	L	0-1	
	28	Flamengo	L	0-1	
	31	São Paulo	L	0-3	
	4	Botafogo	D	1-1	Geovane 51
Nov	10	Náutico	L	0-4	
	24	Grêmio	L	0-3	
	2	Cruzeiro	L	0-2	

ATLETICO MINEIRO 2007

Month	Day	Opponent	Res	Score	Scorers
May	13	Náutico	W	2-1	Lima 26, Germano 94+
	20	Botafogo	L	1-2	Marcos 71
	26	Corinthians	D	0-0	
	2	Atlético PR	D	1-1	Marcos 66
	10	São Paulo	W	1-0	Henrique 82
Jun	17	Figueirense	W	4-1	Danilinho 15, Eder 18, OG 32, Henrique 70
	24	Cruzeiro	L	2-4	Lima 52, Eder 52
	30	Inter	D	1-1	Eder 39
	5	Flamengo	D	1-1	Coelho 88p
	7	Grêmio	L	0-1	
	4	Sport	L	0-2	
Jul	18	América	W	4-1	Marcinho 2 9 41, Galvão 21, Carijo 84
	21	Vasco	L	0-4	
	26	Fluminense	W	3-0	Coelho 2 36 76, Henrique 58
	29	Paraná	W	3-1	Danilinho 23, Marcos 84, Vanderlei 92+
	1	Santos	L	1-2	Danilinho 71
	5	Juventude	L	1-3	Lucio 85
	8	Goiás	L	2-3	Marcos 55, Vanderlei 82
Aug	12	Palmeiras	L	1-2	Eder 5
	19	Náutico	W	1-0	Coelho 62
	26	Botafogo	L	1-2	Danilinho 29
	29	Corinthians	W	5-2	Vanderlei 2 15p 54, Danilinho 36, Marquinhos 37, Eder 71
	2	Atlético PR	L	0-1	
	5	São Paulo	D	0-0	
Sep	8	Figueirense	L	1-2	Leandro 67
	16	Cruzeiro	L	3-4	Gerson 30, Marinho 2 37 57p
	23	Inter	D	2-2	Leandro 86, Vanderlei 89
	29	Flamengo	L	0-1	
	3	Grêmio	D	2-2	Vinicius 2 45 82
	7	Sport	W	3-1	Eder 39, Eduardo 81, Marinho 87
Oct	13	América	W	1-0	Gerson 82p
	21	Vasco	W	1-0	Marcos 47
	27	Fluminense	D	1-1	Eder 30
	31	Paraná	D	0-0	
	4	Santos	D	2-2	OG 9, Eduardo 77
Nov	11	Juventude	W	4-1	Leandro 20, Thiago 65, Marinho 78p, Eder 90
	28	Goiás	W	4-1	Marinho 2 25 80, Danilinho 76, Eder 90
	2	Palmeiras	W	3-1	Eder 33, Marinho 62, Eduardo 79

ATLETICO PARANAENSE 2007

Month	Day	Opponent	Res	Score	Scorers
May	12	Figueirense	W	6-3	Danilo 10, Pedro Oldoni 2 13 30, Alex 2 55 80, Moreno 84
	19	Inter	W	2-1	OG 18, Alex 87
	27	Santos	L	0-1	
	2	Atlético MG	D	1-1	Alex 86
	10	Goiás	L	0-3	
Jun	17	Fluminense	D	1-1	Denis Marques 10
	24	Palmeiras	W	2-0	Edno 34, Alex 60
	30	Paraná	D	2-2	Alex 17, Alan Bahia 80
	4	Náutico	D	1-1	Pedro Oldoni 52
	7	Botafogo	L	0-2	
	12	Vasco	L	0-1	
Jul	18	Juventude	W	4-0	Alex 8p, Jancarlos 50, Dinei 67, Evandro 72
	21	América	L	1-2	Alex 67
	25	Cruzeiro	W	2-1	Gustavo 21, Pedro Oldoni 78
	28	Grêmio	D	1-1	Marcelo 64
	1	Corinthians	D	2-2	Rodolpho 43, OG 90
	4	Sport	L	2-3	Dinei 23, Marcelo 42
	8	Flamengo	W	2-0	Marcelo 2, Edno 59
Aug	15	São Paulo	L	0-2	
	18	Figueirense	D	1-1	Ramon 17
	25	Inter	L	0-1	
	30	Santos	L	1-3	Antonio Carlos 11
	2	Atlético MG	W	1-0	Ramon 29p
	5	Goiás	W	3-2	Netinho 69, Pedro Oldoni 71, William 80
	9	Fluminense	L	0-2	
Sep	16	Palmeiras	W	2-1	Netinho 39, Pedro Oldoni 82
	23	Paraná	W	2-1	Marcelo Ramos 2 21 32
	29	Náutico	L	0-5	
	3	Botafogo	W	2-0	Jancarlos 16, Michel 36
	7	Vasco	W	1-0	David Ferreira 88
Oct	12	Juventude	D	0-0	
	21	América	W	2-0	David Ferreira 19, Marcelo Ramos 65
	27	Cruzeiro	D	1-1	David Ferreira 80
	31	Grêmio	W	2-0	David Ferreira 49, Michel 81
	4	Corinthians	D	2-2	Danilo 52, Alex 82
Nov	11	Sport	D	0-0	
	25	Flamengo	L	0-2	
	2	São Paulo	W	2-1	Marcelo 12, Antonio Carlos 90

BOTAFOGO 2007

Month	Day	Opponent	Res	Score	Scorers
May	13	Inter	W	3-2	Juninho 33, Andre Lima 2 52 57
	20	Atlético MG	W	2-1	Dodo 17, Lucio 46
	27	Flamengo	D	2-2	Lucio 17, Dodo 89
	2	Grêmio	W	3-0	Juninho 18, Luciano Almeida 79, Dodo 86
	9	Palmeiras	D	1-1	Andre Lima 73
Jun	14	Vasco	W	4-0	Dodo 2 2 57, Juninho 16, Leandro 48
	17	Náutico	W	3-1	Juninho 24, Andre Lima 75, Henrique 78
	30	Fluminense	W	2-1	Dodo 2 52p 77
	4	Goiás	D	1-1	Juninho 74
	7	Atlético PR	W	2-0	Lucio 19, Joilson 66
Jul	14	Santos	L	0-3	
	22	Sport	D	3-3	Andre Lima 3 36 51 93+
	26	Juventude	W	3-1	Andre Lima 2 18 67, Joilson 39
	29	Cruzeiro	L	2-3	Andre Lima 86, Renato Silva 92+
	1	América	W	4-2	Lucio 6, Andre Lima 34, Ze Roberto 2 59 71
	5	Paraná	D	0-0	
	8	São Paulo	L	0-2	
Aug	12	Figueirense	D	1-1	Dodo 49
	15	Corinthians	L	2-3	OG 2, Dodo 78p
	18	Inter	D	1-1	Andre Lima 34
	26	Atlético MG	W	2-1	Tulio 59, Lucio 79
	29	Flamengo	D	1-1	Henrique 58
	2	Grêmio	L	0-3	
	6	Palmeiras	D	1-1	Leandro 75
	9	Náutico	L	1-4	Juninho 2
Sep	16	Corinthians	W	1-0	Dodo 72
	23	Fluminense	L	0-2	
	30	Goiás	L	0-3	
	3	Atlético PR	L	0-2	
	5	Santos	L	0-2	
Oct	14	Vasco	L	1-2	Reinaldo 74
	20	Sport	W	3-1	Lucio 5, Luciano Almeida 49, Dodo 57
	28	Juventude	D	1-1	Dodo 38
	1	Cruzeiro	W	4-1	Dodo 5, Tulio 30, Joilson 42, Juninho 58
	4	América	D	1-1	Lucio 7
Nov	10	Paraná	W	3-2	Dodo 48, Juninho 57, Lucio 67
	25	São Paulo	D	2-2	Lucio 10, Juninho 18
	2	Figueirense	D	1-1	Juninho 66

CORINTHIANS 2007

May	13	Juventude	W	1-0 Finazzi [32]
	20	Cruzeiro	W	3-0 Everton Santos [10], Marcelo 2 [46p 67p]
	26	Atlético MG	D	0-0
Jun	3	Santos	D	1-1 Zelao [21]
	10	América	W	2-1 Marcelo Oliveira [54], Finazzi [75]
	16	Paraná	D	0-0
	30	Palmeiras	L	0-1
	5	Sport	L	1-1 Dinelson [57]
	7	Fluminense	D	1-1 Bruno Bonfim [79]
	14	São Paulo	W	1-1 Zelao [91+]
Jul	18	Inter	L	0-3
	22	Náutico	L	0-3
	25	Figueirense	D	2-2 Wilson [11], Clodoaldo [64]
	29	Flamengo	L	2-2 Clodoaldo [36], Dinelson [63]
	1	Atlético PR	D	2-2 Willian 2 [53 59]
	4	Goiás	W	1-0 Clodoaldo
	9	Vasco	L	0-2
Aug	12	Grêmio	W	2-1 Finazzi [81], Gustavo Nery [83]
	15	Botafogo	W	3-2 Arce [9], Nilton [53], Finazzi [56]
	19	Juventude	D	2-2 Finazzi [1], Gustavo Nery [24]
	25	Cruzeiro	L	0-3
	29	Atlético MG	L	2-5 Finazzi [59p], Clodoaldo [64]
	2	Santos	W	2-0 Nilton [9], Arce [52]
	5	América	W	1-0 Finazzi [11]
Sep	9	Paraná	L	0-1
	16	Botafogo	L	0-1
	23	Palmeiras	L	0-1
	29	Sport	L	1-2 Betao [85]
	3	Fluminense	D	1-1 Zelao [43]
	7	São Paulo	W	1-0 Betao [85]
Oct	13	Inter	D	1-1 Finazzi [86]
	21	Náutico	L	0-1
	28	Figueirense	W	2-1 Finazzi 2 [45 68]
	31	Flamengo	L	1-2 Finazzi [26]
	4	Atlético PR	D	2-2 Betao [3], Finazzi [92+]
Nov	11	Goiás	D	1-1 Fabio Ferreira [35]
	28	Vasco	L	0-1
	2	Grêmio	D	1-1 Clodoaldo [30]

CRUZEIRO 2007

May	12	Fluminense	D	2-2 Nene [28], Gabriel [33]
	20	Corinthians	L	0-3
	27	Paraná	L	3-4 Guilherme 2 [43 74], Romulo [67]
Jun	3	Palmeiras	W	3-1 Araujo [5], Ramires [42], Roni [86]
	10	Juventude	L	2-3 Roni 2 [19 89]
	16	Grêmio	W	2-0 Charles [19], Leandro [72]
	24	Atlético MG	W	4-2 Araujo 2 [15 45], Guilherme [76], Ramires [84]
	30	Vasco	W	3-1 Roni [30p], Wagner [87], Guilherme [91+]
	4	Figueirense	L	1-2 Roni [26]
	7	Santos	L	1-4 Fernandinho [9]
	14	Goiás	W	2-1 Wagner [35], Leandro [79]
Jul	18	Náutico	W	4-1 Roni [12], Wagner [59], Araujo [73], Leandro [85]
	22	São Paulo	L	1-2 Leandro [33]
	25	Atlético PR	D	2-2 Araujo [24], Nene [93+]
	29	Botafogo	W	3-2 Guilherme 2 [46 80], Wagner [76]
	5	Inter	W	3-2 Leandro [27], Roni [52p], Alecsandro [80]
	8	Sport	W	2-0 Alecsandro 2 [65 87]
Aug	12	América	W	2-1 Fernandinho [13], Alecsandro [88]
	19	Fluminense	W	4-2 Alecsandro 3 [4 77 88], Marcelo Moreno [90]
	25	Corinthians	W	3-0 Alecsandro 2 [27 79], Jonathan [62]
	29	Paraná	D	2-2 Wagner [25], Marcelo Moreno [63]
	2	Palmeiras	W	5-0 Marcelo Moreno 2 [25 55], Wagner [39], Thiago [70], Maicossuel [85]
	5	Juventude	L	0-1
Sep	8	Grêmio	W	2-0 Marcelo Moreno 2 [38 65]
	12	Flamengo	L	1-3 Guilherme [82]
	16	Atlético MG	W	4-3 Roni 2 [11 25p], Guilherme 2 [61 77]
	23	Vasco	W	2-0 Ramires [15], Thiago [75]
	30	Figueirense	L	1-2 OG [18]
	3	Santos	L	0-1
	7	Goiás	D	0-0
Oct	12	Náutico	D	2-2 Alecsandro [31], Angelo [35]
	21	São Paulo	L	0-1
	27	Atlético PR	D	1-1 Leandro [40]
	1	Botafogo	L	1-4 Guilherme [20]
Nov	4	Flamengo	W	3-1 Roni 2 [26p 38], Charles [57]
	10	Inter	L	0-1
	25	Sport	L	0-1
	2	América	W	2-0 Leandro [19], Roni [26]

FIGUEIRENSE 2007

May	12	Atlético PR	L	3-6 Chicao [39], Ramon [83], Andre Santos [86]
	20	Palmeiras	L	1-2 Peter [68]
	26	América	W	1-0 Henrique [19]
Jun	2	Goiás	W	2-1 Ramon [79], Fernandes [87]
	10	Flamengo	W	4-0 Jean Carlos [12], Chicao 2 [33 57p], Victor [36]
	17	Atlético MG	L	1-4 Fernandes [62]
	23	Juventude	D	1-1 Victor [28]
	28	São Paulo	D	0-0
	4	Cruzeiro	W	2-1 Otacilio Neto [13], Felipe Santana [52]
	7	Inter	L	1-2 Vinicius [88]
	12	Paraná	W	2-1 Henrique [20], Felipe Santana [23]
Jul	18	Sport	L	0-1
	22	Santos	L	1-3 Victor [55]
	25	Corinthians	D	2-2 Jean Carlos [53], Felipe Santana [68]
	29	Fluminense	D	1-1 OG [42]
	2	Grêmio	W	1-0 Peter [86]
	5	Vasco	D	2-2 Andre Santos [43], Peter [54]
	8	Náutico	L	2-4 Otacilio Neto [48], Peter [86]
Aug	12	Botafogo	L	1-0 Otacilio Neto [76]
	18	Atlético PR	D	1-1 Chicao [57]
	26	Palmeiras	L	1-2 Jean Carlos [64]
	29	América	W	3-1 Jean Carlos [20], Andre Santos [58], Leo [74]
	2	Goiás	L	1-2 Jean Carlos [66]
	5	Flamengo	L	1-4
Sep	8	Atlético MG	W	2-1 Chicao [10], Jean Carlos [17]
	16	Juventude	W	4-1 Leo [43], Otacilio Neto 2 [45 76], Chicao [70p]
	22	São Paulo	L	0-2
	30	Cruzeiro	W	2-1 Andre Santos [43], Peter [92+]
	4	Inter	D	0-0
	7	Paraná	W	4-0 Chicao 2 [18 27], Frontini [71], Andre Santos [85]
Oct	12	Sport	D	0-0
	21	Santos	W	1-0 Ramon [45]
	28	Corinthians	L	1-2 Chicao [42p]
	31	Fluminense	L	0-2
	3	Grêmio	W	2-1 Fernandes [64], Otacilio Neto [85]
Nov	11	Vasco	D	3-3 Chicao [65], Peter [75], Jean Carlos [78]
	28	Náutico	W	2-0 Ruy [73], Otacilio Neto [84]
	2	Botafogo	D	1-1 Jean Carlos [88]

FLAMENGO 2007

May	13	Palmeiras	L	2-4 Claiton [33], Renato Augusto [49]
	20	Goiás	W	3-1 Irineu [17], Juan [53], Leonardo Moura [69]
	27	Botafogo	D	2-2 Leonardo [40], Paulo Sergio [77]
Jun	3	Sport	D	2-2 Renato Abreu 2 [15p 61]
	10	Figueirense	L	0-4
	16	Inter	D	2-2 Ronaldo Angelím [77], Juan [90]
	5	Atlético MG	D	1-1 Leonardo [91+]
	7	São Paulo	D	0-0
	19	Paraná	L	1-2 Leo Medeiros [36]
Jul	22	Grêmio	L	0-1
	25	América	W	3-1 Ronaldo Angelím [18], Jailton [61], Obina [73]
	29	Corinthians	D	2-2 Souza [72], Leo Medeiros [80]
	5	Santos	L	0-3
	8	Atlético PR	L	0-2
	11	Náutico	W	2-1 Fabio Luciano [24], Leonardo Moura [87]
Aug	16	Fluminense	W	1-0 Biancucchi [42]
	19	Palmeiras	L	1-2 Paulo Sergio [15]
	23	Juventude	W	4-0 Souza [28], Obina [79], Biancucchi [87], Juan [92+]
	26	Goiás	W	3-1 Leo Medeiros [37], Juan [56], Ibson [60]
	29	Botafogo	D	1-1 Juan [34]
	1	Sport	D	1-1 Thiago Sales [21]
	5	Figueirense	W	4-1 Carlinhos [27], Obina [62], Ibson [86], PauloSergio [89]
	8	Inter	L	0-3
Sep	12	Cruzeiro	W	3-1 Leonardo Moura [27], Souza [65], Obina [88]
	16	Vasco	D	1-1 Leonardo Moura [45]
	23	Juventude	D	2-2 Leonardo Moura [21], Leonardo [51]
	29	Atlético MG	W	1-0 Christian [75]
	4	São Paulo	W	1-0 Ibson [49]
	7	Fluminense	L	0-2
Oct	13	Paraná	W	1-0 Fabio Luciano [65]
	18	Vasco	W	2-1 Toro [8], Ibson [32p]
	21	Grêmio	W	2-0 Souza [25], Ibson [60]
	28	América	W	1-0 Souza [15]
	31	Corinthians	W	2-1 Ibson [45], Roger Flores [75]
	4	Cruzeiro	L	1-3 Roger Flores [66]
Nov	11	Santos	W	1-0 Souza [75]
	25	Atlético PR	W	2-0 Renato Augusto [49], Juan [61]
	2	Náutico	L	0-1

FLUMINENSE 2007

	Date	Opponent	Res	Score	Scorers
May	12	Cruzeiro	D	2-2	Carlos Alberto 45p, Cicero 78
	20	Grêmio	L	0-2	
	26	Inter	W	3-0	Thiago Neves 36, Rafael 49, Rodrigo 57
Jun	3	Vasco	D	1-1	Rafael 39
	10	Sport	W	3-0	Alex Dias 41, Rodrigo 70, Cicero 86
	17	Atlético PR	D	1-1	Thiago Silva 71
	24	América	W	1-0	Adriano Magrao 1
		Botafogo	L	1-2	Alex Dias 27
	4	Paraná	D	0-0	
Jul	7	Corinthians	D	1-1	Somalia 26
	18	São Paulo	W	1-0	Somalia 53
	22	Goiás	W	3-0	Thiago Neves 2 32 47, Somalia 63
	26	Atlético MG	L	0-3	
	29	Figueirense	D	1-1	Somalia 38p
Aug	1	Náutico	D	0-0	
	5	Palmeiras	L	0-1	
	8	Juventude	D	0-0	
	12	Santos	W	3-0	Luiz Alberto 36, Thiago Neves 2 64 71
	16	Flamengo	L	0-1	
	19	Cruzeiro	L	2-4	Arouca 22, Thiago Neves 69
	25	Grêmio	D	1-1	Thiago Silva 14
	29	Inter	W	4-1	Thiago Silva 35, Thiago Neves 2 45 58, Alex Dias 74
Sep	2	Vasco	D	1-1	Cicero 79
	6	Sport	W	2-0	Cicero 72, Rodrigo 87
	9	Atlético PR	W	2-0	Somalia 2 29 67
	15	América	W	2-0	Alex Dias 58, Thiago Neves 83
	23	Botafogo	W	2-0	Thiago Neves 3, Davi 17
	30	Paraná	L	1-3	Somalia 10
Oct	3	Corinthians	D	1-1	Alex Dias 31
	7	Flamengo	W	2-0	Somalia 1, Thiago Neves 48
	13	São Paulo	D	1-1	Thiago Neves 34p
	20	Goiás	L	3-5	Cicero 35, Thiago Silva 2 51p 64p
	27	Atlético MG	D	1-1	Adriano Magrao 1
	31	Figueirense	W	2-0	Tarta 86, Leo 92+
Nov	3	Náutico	W	2-1	Gabriel 2 43 81
	8	Palmeiras	L	0-1	
	24	Juventude	W	3-2	Arouca 2 25 72, Cicero 87 Arouca 72
	2	Santos	W	4-2	Adriano.M 33, L.Alberto 41, Thiago.N 48,

GOIAS 2007

	Date	Opponent	Res	Score	Scorers
May	12	São Paulo	L	0-2	
	20	Flamengo	L	1-3	Fabricio 72
	27	Juventude	W	3-1	Welliton 2 5 61, Paulo Baier 53
	2	Figueirense	L	1-2	Welliton 36
	10	Atlético PR	W	3-0	Paulo Henrique 23, Welliton 27, Diego 89
Jun	17	Palmeiras	W	3-1	Leonardo 7, Amaral 12, Wendel 83
	24	Náutico	W	2-0	Fabricio 2 55 67p
	30	América	W	3-0	Fabricio 30, Leonardo 51, Welliton 69
	4	Botafogo	D	1-1	Paulo Henrique 5
	7	Sport	W	3-2	Felipe 2 76 92+, Paulo Baier 82
	14	Cruzeiro	L	1-2	Felipe 75
Jul	19	Grêmio	D	0-0	
	22	Fluminense	L	0-3	
	25	Santos	W	1-0	Welliton 66
	28	Vasco	L	1-4	Diego 46
	1	Paraná	W	2-0	Paulo Baier 45p, Andre 66
	4	Corinthians	L	0-1	
	8	Atlético MG	W	3-2	Paulo Baier 2 1 52, Cristiano 79
Aug	12	Inter	L	0-1	
	19	São Paulo	D	0-0	
	26	Flamengo	L	1-3	Paulo Baier 92+
	29	Juventude	D	0-0	
	2	Figueirense	W	2-1	Leonardo 29, Paulo Baier 73
	5	Atlético PR	L	2-3	Paulo Baier 57, Paulo Henrique 85
	9	Palmeiras	L	0-2	
Sep	15	Náutico	L	0-3	
	22	América	D	1-1	Paulo Baier 36
	30	Botafogo	W	3-0	Elson 22, Rinaldo 61, Ernando 66
	3	Sport	L	0-4	
	7	Cruzeiro	L	0-3	
Oct	13	Grêmio	L	1-2	Leonardo 8
	20	Fluminense	W	5-3	Paulo Baier 3 43 56p 82, Andre 45, OG 84
	27	Santos	L	0-3	
	31	Vasco	L	2-3	Harison 8, Wendell 77
	3	Paraná	L	0-1	
Nov	11	Corinthians	D	1-1	Paulo Baier 28
	28	Atlético MG	L	1-4	Harison 29
	2	Inter	W	2-1	Elson 2 31 58

GREMIO 2007

	Date	Opponent	Res	Score	Scorers
May	13	Paraná	L	0-3	
	20	Fluminense	W	2-0	Carlos Eduardo 38, Tuta 73
	27	Sport	W	1-0	OG 2
Jun	2	Botafogo	L	0-3	
	9	Vasco	L	0-4	
	16	Cruzeiro	L	0-2	
	24	Inter	W	2-0	Lucio Cajueiro 7, Diego Souza 65
	30	Santos	D	0-0	
Jul	4	Juventude	W	3-1	Diego Souza 2 12p 51, Willian 67
	7	Atlético MG	W	1-0	Diego Souza 87
	14	Palmeiras	D	1-1	Ramon 28
	19	Goiás	D	0-0	
	22	Flamengo	W	1-0	OG 60
	25	Náutico	W	2-0	Tuta 30, Carlos Eduardo 82
	28	Atlético PR	D	1-1	Tcheco 45
Aug	2	Figueirense	L	0-1	
	5	São Paulo	L	0-2	
	9	América	W	3-0	Tuta 2 6 56, Kelly 88
	12	Corinthians	L	1-2	Carlos Eduardo 36
	18	Paraná	W	1-2	Diego Souza 27, Anderson 37
	25	Fluminense	D	1-1	Patricio 88
	29	Sport	L	0-2	
Sep	2	Botafogo	W	3-0	Tuta 3 66 74 77
	5	Vasco	W	3-1	Bustos 9, Ramon 16, Sandro Goiano 69
	8	Cruzeiro	L	0-2	
	16	Inter	W	1-0	Leo 12
	22	Santos	W	1-0	Marcel 55
	30	Juventude	W	2-1	Jonas 53, Diego Souza 60
Oct	3	Atlético MG	D	2-2	Jonas 44, Marcel 59
	6	Palmeiras	L	0-2	
	13	Goiás	W	2-1	Pereira 26, Tuta 51
	21	Flamengo	L	0-2	
	28	Náutico	W	4-3	Tuta 11, Marcel 2 22 70, Diego Souza 42
	31	Atlético PR	L	0-2	
Nov	3	Figueirense	L	1-2	Saja 40p
	11	São Paulo	L	0-1	
	24	América	W	3-0	Willian 21, Marcel 66, Diego Souza 73
	2	Corinthians	D	1-1	Jonas 2

INTERNACIONAL 2007

	Date	Opponent	Res	Score	Scorers
May	13	Botafogo	L	2-3	Alexandre Pato 14, Christian 69
	19	Atlético PR	L	1-2	Mineiro 31
	26	Fluminense	L	0-3	
Jun	3	Náutico	W	2-0	Iarley 22, Alex Meschini 40
	10	Santos	W	1-0	Alexandre Pato 41
	16	Flamengo	D	2-2	Alex Meschini 65, Adriano Martins 86
	24	Grêmio	L	0-2	
	30	Atlético MG	D	1-1	Adriano Martins 58
Jul	6	São Paulo	L	0-1	
	7	Figueirense	W	2-1	Christian Correa 2 18 59
	14	América	W	2-1	Pinga 54, Christian Correa 80p
	18	Corinthians	W	3-0	Alexandre Pato 2 61p 79, Adriano Martins 89
	21	Juventude	L	0-2	
	25	Paraná	L	0-1	
	29	Sport	W	5-1	Pinga 8, Indio 32, Iarley 44, Alex Meschini 77, Adriano Martins 86
Aug	1	Vasco	L	0-2	
	5	Cruzeiro	L	2-3	Iarley 88, Adriano Martins 90
	9	Palmeiras	D	1-1	Alex Meschini 84
	12	Goiás	W	1-0	Adriano Martins 52
	19	Botafogo	D	1-1	Ceara 2
	25	Atlético PR	W	1-0	Alex Meschini 89p
	29	Fluminense	L	1-4	Mineiro 40
Sep	2	Náutico	D	1-1	Adriano Martins 44
	5	Santos	L	1-2	Adriano Martins 11
	8	Flamengo	W	3-0	Wellington 20, Roger 44, Elder 88
	16	Grêmio	L	0-1	
	23	Atlético MG	D	2-2	Gil 56, Fernandao 62
	30	São Paulo	L	1-2	Sorondo 21
Oct	4	Figueirense	D	0-0	
	7	América	W	2-0	Fernandao 6, Magrao 38
	13	Corinthians	D	1-1	Magrao 56
	21	Juventude	W	3-0	Magrao 24, Fernando 2 31 88
	28	Paraná	L	0-1	
	1	Sport	D	0-0	
Nov	4	Vasco	W	2-1	Fernandao 2 16 77p
	10	Cruzeiro	W	2-1	Alex Meschini 92+
	25	Palmeiras	W	2-1	Fernandao 2 40 81
	2	Goiás	L	1-2	Orozco 14

JUVENTUDE 2007

Month	Date	Opponent		Score	Scorers
May	13	Corinthians	L	0-1	
May	19	Paraná	L	1-2	Da Silva 53
May	27	Goiás	L	1-3	Da Silva 48p
Jun	3	América	W	3-0	Da Silva 28, Barao 70, Andre 80
Jun	10	Cruzeiro	W	3-2	Beto 37, Marcao 40, Eber 81
Jun	17	Santos	L	0-2	
Jun	23	Figueirense	D	1-1	Eber 55
Jun	4	Grêmio	L	1-3	Wescley 74
Jun	7	Vasco	W	2-0	Marcao 76, Renato 89
Jun	12	Náutico	D	1-1	Wescley 55p
Jul	18	Atlético PR	L	0-4	
Jul	21	Inter	W	2-0	Marcao 66, Renato 76
Jul	26	Botafogo	L	1-3	Leonardo Silva 24
Jul	29	Palmeiras	D	1-1	Marcao 33
Jul	2	São Paulo	L	1-3	Luciano 2
Jul	5	Atlético MG	L	1-2	Eber 87
Jul	8	Fluminense	D	0-0	
Aug	11	Sport	L	0-3	
Aug	19	Corinthians	D	2-2	Wescley 15, Fabio Baiano 59
Aug	23	Flamengo	L	0-4	
Aug	26	Paraná	L	1-3	Wescley 31p
Aug	29	Goiás	W	2-0	Renato 4, Tadeu 45
Aug	1	América	W	3-0	Tadeu 73, Bruno 81
Aug	5	Cruzeiro	W	2-0	Tadeu 41
Sep	8	Santos	L	0-1	
Sep	16	Figueirense	L	1-4	Tadeu 45
Sep	23	Flamengo	D	2-2	Vanzini 25, Thiago Cavalcante 59
Sep	30	Grêmio	L	1-2	Bruno 52
Sep	3	Vasco	W	1-0	Fabio Baiano 77
Sep	6	Náutico	L	1-4	Vanzini 60
Oct	12	Atlético PR	D	0-0	
Oct	21	Inter	L	0-3	
Oct	28	Botafogo	D	1-1	Tadeu 46
Oct	1	Palmeiras	W	1-0	Regis 26
Nov	7	São Paulo	W	2-0	Renato 24, OG 66
Nov	11	Atlético MG	L	1-4	Nunes 21
Nov	24	Fluminense	L	2-3	Tiago Cavalcanti 16p, Romano 80
Nov	2	Sport	W	2-1	Tiago Cavalcanti 47, William 59

NAUTICO 2007

Month	Date	Opponent		Score	Scorers
May	13	Atlético MG	L	1-2	Acosta 9
May	20	São Paulo	W	1-0	Acosta 77
May	27	Vasco	D	2-2	Marcel 4p, Cris 60
Jun	4	Inter	L	0-2	
Jun	9	Paraná	D	4-4	Marcel 28, Felipe 47, Acosta 2 81p 84
Jun	17	Botafogo	L	1-3	OG 54
Jun	24	Goiás	L	0-2	
Jun	28	Sport	L	1-4	Hamilton 76
Jun	4	Atlético PR	D	1-1	OG 24
Jun	7	Palmeiras	L	0-1	
Jun	12	Juventude	D	1-1	Sidny 57
Jul	18	Cruzeiro	L	1-4	Tales 1
Jul	22	Corinthians	W	3-0	Ferreira 42, OG 64, Felipe 90
Jul	25	Grêmio	L	0-2	
Jul	28	Santos	W	2-1	Elicarlos 33, Acosta 64
Jul	1	Fluminense	D	0-0	
Jul	4	América	W	5-1	OG33, Radames45, Felipe56, Sidny73, Marcelinho88
Aug	8	Figueirense	W	4-2	Acosta 2 3 39, Tales 43, Felipe 68
Aug	11	Flamengo	L	1-2	Felipe 12
Aug	19	Atlético MG	L	0-1	
Aug	26	São Paulo	L	0-5	
Aug	30	Vasco	L	1-4	Marcelinho 56
Aug	2	Inter	D	1-1	Sidny 68
Aug	6	Paraná	W	4-2	Acosta 6,J.Cesar 62,Geraldo 73,Marcelo86
Sep	9	Botafogo	W	4-1	Acosta 4 29 36 57 89
Sep	15	Goiás	W	3-0	Acosta 2 33p 54, Geraldo 74
Sep	23	Sport	W	2-0	Julio Cesar 2 37 78
Sep	29	Atlético PR	W	5-0	Marcelinho4,Acosta20,Felipe2 31 78,Marcelo90
Sep	3	Palmeiras	L	1-2	Felipe 25
Sep	6	Juventude	W	4-1	Geraldo 2 4p 68, Ferreira 43, Felipe 85
Oct	12	Cruzeiro	D	2-2	Acosta 2 62 77
Oct	21	Corinthians	W	1-0	Geraldo 90p
Oct	28	Grêmio	L	3-4	Onildo 6, Acosta 44, Julio Cesar 46
Oct	31	Santos	L	1-2	Felipe 15
Oct	3	Fluminense	L	1-2	Acosta 84p
Nov	10	América	W	4-0	Julio Cesar 38, Ferreira 2 58 81, Sidny 75
Nov	24	Figueirense	L	0-2	
Nov	2	Flamengo	W	1-0	Sidny 78

PALMEIRAS 2007

Month	Date	Opponent		Score	Scorers
May	13	Flamengo	W	4-2	Edmundo 2 3 78, Osmar 21, Florentin 64
May	20	Figueirense	W	2-0	Valdivia 2 5 23
May	27	São Pulo	D	0-0	
Jun	3	Cruzeiro	L	1-3	Martinez 34
Jun	9	Botafogo	D	1-1	Paulo Sergio 34
Jun	17	Goiás	L	1-3	Caio 75
Jun	24	Atlético PR	L	0-2	
Jun	30	Corinthians	W	1-0	Dininho 45
Jun	4	América	W	2-0	Luis 19, Caio 29
Jun	7	Náutico	W	1-0	Luis Henrique 94+
Jun	14	Grêmio	D	1-1	Luis 71
Jul	19	Santos	D	2-2	Nen 18, Rodrigo Souto 92+
Jul	22	Paraná	L	0-1	
Jul	25	Vasco	W	3-2	Valdivia 35, Nen 81, Leandro 86
Jul	29	Juventude	D	1-1	Luis 75
Jul	1	Sport	L	1-2	Martinez 8
Jul	5	Fluminense	W	1-0	Valdivia 40
Jul	9	Inter	D	1-1	Valdivia 1
Aug	12	Atlético MG	W	2-1	Martinez 2 8 56
Aug	19	Flamengo	W	2-1	Caio 13, Gustavo 52
Aug	26	Figueirense	W	2-1	Valdivia 18, Max 83
Aug	29	São Paulo	L	0-1	
Aug	2	Cruzeiro	L	0-5	
Aug	6	Botafogo	D	1-1	Edmundo 40
Sep	9	Goiás	W	2-0	Francis 31, Caio 51
Sep	16	Atlético PR	L	1-2	Dininho 65
Sep	23	Corinthians	W	1-0	Nen 59
Sep	30	América	D	0-0	
Sep	3	Náutico	W	2-0	Caio 2 63 68
Sep	6	Grêmio	W	2-0	Caio 13, Rodrigao 22
Oct	13	Santos	D	1-1	Caio 34
Oct	20	Paraná	W	3-0	Rodrigao 2 42 72, Valdivia 64
Oct	28	Vasco	D	2-2	Gustavo 10, Rodrigo 34
Oct	1	Juventude	L	0-1	
Nov	4	Sport	L	1-3	Caio 48p
Nov	14	Fluminense	W	1-0	Rodrigao 35
Nov	25	Inter	L	1-2	Rodrigao 91+
Nov	2	Atlético MG	L	1-3	Edmundo 36

PARANA 2007

Month	Date	Opponent		Score	Scorers
May	13	Grêmio	W	3-0	Josiel 2 29 70p, Lima 81
May	19	Juventude	W	2-1	Josiel 60, Adriano 88
May	27	Cruzeiro	W	4-3	Joelson 45, Josiel 2 59 80, Ewerthon 82
Jun	3	São Paulo	L	0-1	
Jun	9	Náutico	D	4-4	Neguette 10, Vandinho 12, Josiel 2 16 58
Jun	16	Corinthians	D	0-0	
Jun	23	Sport	W	1-0	Beto 30
Jun	30	Atlético PR	D	2-2	Josiel 2 11 45
Jun	4	Fluminense	D	0-0	
Jun	6	América	L	0-1	
Jun	12	Figueirense	L	1-2	Josiel 66
Jul	19	Flamengo	W	2-1	Josiel 2 27 29
Jul	22	Palmeiras	W	1-0	Marcio Careca 20
Jul	25	Inter	L	0-1	
Jul	29	Atlético MG	L	1-3	Vinicius Pacheco 82
Jul	1	Goiás	L	0-2	
Jul	5	Botafogo	D	0-0	
Jul	9	Santos	L	0-2	
Aug	12	Vasco	D	0-0	
Aug	18	Grêmio	L	0-2	
Aug	26	Juventude	W	3-1	Beto 4, OG 17, Josiel 47
Aug	29	Cruzeiro	D	2-2	Josiel 2 57 71p
Aug	1	São Paulo	L	0-6	
Aug	6	Náutico	L	2-4	Beto 65, Josiel 78
Sep	9	Corinthians	W	1-0	Josiel 25p
Sep	16	Sport	L	1-3	Jeferson 75
Sep	23	Atlético PR	L	1-2	Neguete 23
Sep	30	Fluminense	W	3-1	Jeferson 25, Batista 41, Vandinho 56
Sep	4	América	L	2-3	Josiel 44, Adriano Bahia 50
Sep	7	Figueirense	L	0-4	
Oct	13	Flamengo	L	0-1	
Oct	20	Palmeiras	L	0-3	
Oct	28	Inter	W	1-0	Josiel 68
Oct	31	Atlético MG	D	0-0	
Oct	3	Goiás	W	1-0	Jumar 81
Nov	10	Botafogo	L	2-3	Josiel 65, Guliano 77
Nov	25	Santos	L	2-3	Jumar 30, Paulo Rodrigues 71
Nov	2	Vasco	L	0-3	

SANTOS 2007

Month	Date	Opponent	Res	Score	Scorers
May	13	Sport	L	1-4	Pedrinho 2
May	19	América	L	2-3	Marcelo 2, Marcos Aurelio 67
May	27	Atlético PR	W	1-0	Rodrigo 17
	3	Corinthians	D	1-1	Marcelo 77
	10	Inter	L	0-1	
Jun	17	Juventude	W	2-0	Cleber Santana 1, Marco Aurelio 31
	24	São Paulo	L	0-2	
	30	Grêmio	D	0-0	
	5	Vasco	L	0-4	
	7	Cruzeiro	W	4-1	Marcos Aurelio 6, Rodrigo 30, Pedrinho 2 45 67
	14	Botafogo	W	3-0	Marcos Aurelio 60, Rodrigo 64, Moraes 90
Jul	19	Palmeiras	D	2-2	Kleber 10, Pedrinho 45
	22	Figueirense	W	3-1	Kleber Pereira 2 32 38, Pedrinho 83
	25	Goiás	L	0-1	
	28	Náutico	L	1-2	Kleber Pereira 88
	1	Atlético MG	W	2-1	Marcos Aurelio 33, Kleber Pereira 59
	5	Flamengo	W	3-0	Pedrinho 21, Marcos Aurelio 32, Kleber 50
	9	Paraná	W	2-0	Marcos Aurelio 43, Kleber Pereira 92+
Aug	12	Fluminense	L	0-3	
	18	Sport	W	2-0	Kleber Pereira 25, Pedrinho 54
	26	América	W	4-1	Petkovic 20, Kleber Pereira 2 25 46, Rodrigo 86
	30	Atlético PR	W	3-1	Domingos 29, Pedrinho 53, Kleber P. 76p
	2	Corinthians	L	0-2	
	5	Inter	W	2-1	Kleber Pereira 27, Kleber 33
	8	Juventude	W	1-0	Renatinho 85
Sep	15	São Paulo	L	1-2	Rodrigo 92+
	22	Grêmio	L	0-1	
	30	Vasco	W	1-0	Rodrigo Souto 21
	3	Cruzeiro	W	1-0	Adailton 94+
	6	Botafogo	W	2-1	Rodrigo 51, Renatinho 89
Oct	13	Palmeiras	D	1-1	Renatinho 58
	21	Figueirense	L	0-1	
	22	Goiás	W	3-0	Pedrinho 47, Rodrigo 74, Vitor Junior 81
	31	Náutico	W	2-1	Kleber Pereira 45, Pedrinho 86
	4	Atlético MG	D	2-2	Kleber Pereira 2 51p 76
Nov	11	Flamengo	L	0-1	
	25	Paraná	W	3-2	Kleber Pereira 3 73 80 83
	2	Fluminense	L	2-4	Rodrigo Souto 32, Alessandro 64

SAO PAULO 2007

Month	Date	Opponent	Res	Score	Scorers
May	12	Goiás	W	2-0	Jorge Wagner 16, Rogerio Ceni 35p
May	20	Náutico	L	0-1	
	27	Palmeiras	D	0-0	
	3	Paraná	W	1-0	Rogerio Ceni 75p
	10	Atlético MG	L	0-1	
Jun	17	Vasco	W	2-0	Borges 2 2 26
	24	Santos	W	2-0	Aloisio 20, Dagoberto 40
	28	Figueirense	D	0-0	
	4	Inter	W	1-0	Rogerio Ceni 57p
	7	Flamengo	D	0-0	
	14	Corinthians	D	1-1	Dagoberto
Jul	18	Fluminense	L	0-1	
	22	Cruzeiro	W	2-1	Breno 54, Hernanes 69
	26	Sport	W	3-1	Leandro 48, Willamis 55, Rogerio Ceni 80
	29	América	W	1-0	Richarlysson 28
	2	Juventude	W	3-1	Miranda 32, Borges 76, Hugo 82
	5	Grêmio	W	2-0	Borges 3, Diego Tardelli 88
	8	Botafogo	W	2-0	Alex Silva 63, Leandro 73
Aug	11	Atlético PR	W	2-0	Jorge Wagner 5, Borges 54
	19	Goiás	D	0-0	
	26	Náutico	W	5-0	Dagoberto 56, Rogerio Ceni 64p, Hugo 2 72 90, Aloisio
	29	Palmeiras	W	1-0	Jorge Wagner 39
	1	Paraná	W	6-0	Aloisio 2 27 67, Dagoberto 2 33 62, Willamis 37, Leandro 78
	5	Atlético MG	D	0-0	
	8	Vasco	W	2-0	Dagoberto 61, Hernanes 92+
Sep	15	Santos	W	2-1	Breno 49, Borges 53
	22	Figueirense	W	2-0	Alex Silva 14, Leandro 29
	30	Inter	W	2-1	OG 73, Borges 77
	4	Flamengo	L	0-1	
	7	Corinthians	L	0-1	
Oct	13	Fluminense	D	1-1	Andre Dias 51
	21	Cruzeiro	W	1-0	Jorge Wagner 69
	28	Sport	W	2-1	Rogerio Ceni 27, Aloisio 62
	31	América	W	3-0	Hernanes 38, Miranda 49, Dagoberto 76
	7	Juventude	L	0-2	
Nov	11	Grêmio	W	1-0	Rogerio Ceni 51p
	25	Botafogo	D	2-2	Aloisio 55, Richarlysson 83
	2	Atlético PR	L	1-2	Alex Silva 83

SPORT RECIFE 2007

Month	Date	Opponent	Res	Score	Scorers
May	13	Santos	W	4-1	Weldon 10, Fernando 36, Durval 40, Washington 90
May	20	Vasco	L	1-3	Luciano Henrique 82
	27	Grêmio	L	0-1	
	3	Flamengo	D	2-2	Washington 34, Fernando 77
	10	Fluminense	L	0-3	
Jun	17	América	D	2-2	Durval 23, Carlinhos 69
	23	Paraná	L	0-1	
	28	Náutico	W	4-1	Durval 4, Carlinhos 2 11 50, Washington 58
	5	Corinthians	W	2-1	Igor 45, Weldon 80
	7	Goiás	L	2-3	Ticao 28, Washington 60
	14	Atlético MG	W	2-0	Diogo 17, Carlinhos 49
Jul	18	Figueirense	W	1-0	Carlinhos 88
	2	Botafogo	D	3-3	Bruno 46, Carlinhos 2 56 77
	26	São Paulo	L	1-3	Weldon 30
	29	Inter	L	1-5	OG 25
	1	Palmeiras	W	2-1	Cesar 29, Da Silva 45
	4	Atlético PR	W	3-2	Anderson 46, Cesar 81, Romerito 88
	8	Cruzeiro	L	0-2	
Aug	11	Juventude	W	3-0	Anderson Aquino 2 10 39, Carlinhos 74
	18	Santos	L	0-2	
	26	Vasco	D	0-0	
	29	Grêmio	W	2-0	Da Silva 43, Carlinhos 75
	1	Flamengo	D	1-1	Da Silva 74p
	6	Fluminense	L	0-1	
Sep	9	América	D	1-1	Carlinhos 63
	16	Paraná	W	3-1	Romerito 47, Da Silva 41, Carlinhos 86
	23	Náutico	L	0-2	
	29	Corinthians	W	2-1	Romerito 2 31 62
	3	Goiás	W	4-0	Junior 5, Adriano 41, Anderson 58, Luisinho 72p
	7	Atlético MG	L	1-3	Romerito 29
Oct	12	Figueirense	D	0-0	
	20	Botafogo	L	1-3	Reginaldo 85
	28	São Paulo	L	1-2	Da Silva 64
	1	Inter	D	0-0	
	4	Palmeiras	W	3-1	Da Silva 25p, Carlinhos 2 56 65
Nov	11	Atlético PR	D	0-0	
	25	Cruzeiro	W	1-0	Adriano 65
	2	Juventude	L	1-2	Gustavo 51

VASCO DA GAMA 2007

Month	Date	Opponent	Res	Score	Scorers
May	13	América	W	1-0	Andre Dias 65
May	20	Sport	W	3-1	Andre Dias 2 3 37, Romario 48p
	27	Náutico	D	2-2	Morais 2 25p 83
	3	Fluminense	D	1-1	Abedi 7
	9	Grêmio	W	4-0	Romario 2 15p 45, Andre Dias 42, Abedi 64
Jun	14	Botafogo	L	0-4	
	17	São Paulo	L	0-2	
	30	Cruzeiro	L	1-3	Martin Garcia 9
	5	Santos	W	4-0	Conca 2 21 70, Wagner Diniz 81, Ernane 87
	7	Juventude	L	0-2	
Jul	12	Atlético PR	W	1-0	Leandro 85
	21	Atlético MG	W	4-0	Martin Garcia 2 51 70, Kardec 87, Conca 90
	25	Palmeiras	L	2-3	Rubens Junior 18, Leandro 21
	28	Goiás	W	4-1	Amaral 41, Vilson 80, Leandro 81, Kardec 86
	1	Inter	W	2-0	Kardec 30, Leandro 37
	5	Figueirense	D	2-2	Julio Santos 35, Leandro 92+
	9	Corinthians	W	2-0	Wagner Diniz 23, Enilton 55
Aug	12	Paraná	D	0-0	
	19	América	W	2-0	Leandro 2 40p 75
	26	Sport	D	0-0	
	30	Náutico	W	4-1	Leandro 20p, Marcelinho 2 74 89, Rubens Junior 86
	2	Fluminense	D	1-1	Conca 37
	5	Grêmio	L	1-3	Kardec 14
Sep	8	São Paulo	L	0-2	
	16	Flamengo	D	1-1	Leandro 10
	23	Cruzeiro	L	0-2	
	30	Santos	L	0-1	
	3	Juventude	L	0-1	
	7	Atlético PR	L	0-1	
Oct	14	Botafogo	W	2-1	Leandro 8, Jorge Luiz 86
	18	Flamengo	L	1-2	Andrade 15
	21	Atlético MG	L	0-1	
	28	Palmeiras	D	2-2	Leandro 23, Conca 40
	31	Goiás	W	3-2	Kardec 2 31 71, Leandro 40
	4	Inter	L	1-2	Leandro Bonfim 91+
Nov	11	Figueirense	D	3-3	Conca 41, Leandro Bonfim 51, Kardec 60
	28	Corinthians	W	1-0	Kardec 65
	2	Paraná	W	3-0	Morais 57, Leandro 2 67 71

BRB – BARBADOS

NATIONAL TEAM RECORD
JULY 10TH 2006 TO JULY 12TH 2010

PL	W	D	L	F	A	%
24	8	8	8	37	36	50

FIFA/COCA-COLA WORLD RANKING

1993	1994	1995	1996	1997	1998	1999	2000	2001	2002	2003	2004	2005	2006	2007		High	
114	107	103	110	113	121	113	104	107	99	124	121	115	98	128		**9**	06/00

2007–2008													Low	
08/07	09/07	10/07	11/07	12/07	01/08	02/08	03/08	04/08	05/08	06/08	07/08		**152**	07/06
119	109	93	124	128	142	133	137	116	117	121	137			

The football association in Barbados has been intent on recruiting English talent with connections to the island to play for the Bajan Braves and their quest continued as they spent time and money targeting some big names like Aston Villa's Marlon Harewood and the talented Tom Soares of Crystal Palace. One player that did take the bait was Wigan's Emmerson Boyce who made his debut for Eyre Sealy's team in the 2010 FIFA World Cup qualifier against Dominica. Have drawn the first leg in Roseau, Boyce helped make sure that there were no shocks in the return with a 1-0 win. That meant a second round tie against America and the challenges that still face football in

INTERNATIONAL HONOURS
None

Barbados were clear for all to see as the Braves were on the receiving end of an 8-0 thrashing. Boyce, missing from the first leg returned, along with captain Paul Ifill, for the second leg in Bridgetown where the scoreline was kept down to a more respectable 1-0 defeat. There are plenty more potential targets for the BFA on which to set their sights but there needs to be a louder, brasher clarion call for players to join the Bajan Braves - as Jamaica have done with the Reggae Boyz or Trinidad with the Soca Warriors - but as one of the more naturally reserved and discreet of the Caribbean peoples, that may not be entirely within character.

THE FIFA BIG COUNT OF 2006

	Male	Female		Total
Number of players	33 590	3 960	Referees and Assistant Referees	86
Professionals	0		Admin, Coaches, Technical, Medical	1240
Amateurs 18+	7 095		Number of clubs	130
Youth under 18	8 505		Number of teams	240
Unregistered	18 710		Clubs with women's teams	4
Total players	37 550		Players as % of population	13.41%

Barbados Football Association (BFA)
Richmond Welches, PO Box 1362, Bridgetown, St Michael, BB 11000, Barbados
Tel +1 246 2281707   Fax +1 246 2286484
bdosfootball@caribsurf.com   www.barbadossoccer.com
President: JONES Ronald   General Secretary: TBD
Vice-President: BARROW Keith   Treasurer: HUNTE Curtis   Media Officer: FONES Ronald
Men's Coach: SEALY Eyre   Women's Coach: SMITH Edward
BFA formed: 1910   CONCACAF: 1968   FIFA: 1968
Royal blue shirts with gold trimmings, Gold shorts, White socks

RECENT INTERNATIONAL MATCHES PLAYED BY BARBADOS

2003	Opponents	Score		Venue	Comp	Scorers	Att	Referee
26-12	Bermuda	W	2-1	Hamilton	Fr	Lovell 2 [39] [43]		Mouchette BER
2004								
1-01	Bermuda	W	4-0	Hamilton	Fr	Parris [6], Riley [51], Goodridge 2 [74] [76]		Raynor BER
11-01	Grenada	W	2-0	Bridgetown	Fr	Forde.N [35], Riley [58]	2 000	Small BRB
18-01	Canada	L	0-1	Bridgetown	Fr			Forde BRB
31-01	Grenada	W	1-0	St George's	Fr	Riley [70]		
15-02	Guyana	L	0-2	Bridgetown	Fr		1 200	Small BRB
12-03	Dominica	W	2-1	Bridgetown	Fr	OG [28], Burrowes [85]	46	
30-05	Northern Ireland	D	1-1	Bridgetown	Fr	Skinner [40]	8 000	Brizan TRI
13-06	St Kitts & Nevis	L	0-2	Bridgetown	WCq		3 700	Alfaro SLV
19-06	St Kitts & Nevis	L	2-3	Basseterre	WCq	Skinner [33], Goodridge [45]	3 500	Pineda HON
2005								
23-01	Guyana	W	3-0	Bridgetown	Fr	Forde.M [41], OG [53], Goodridge [58],		
30-01	St Vincent/Grenadines	W	3-1	Bridgetown	Fr	Riley 2 [47] [82], Goodridge [80]	3 000	
6-02	Antigua & Barbuda	W	3-2	Bridgetown	Fr	Forde.M [10], Stanford [40], Goodridge [57]	4 000	
13-02	Guyana	D	3-3	Bridgetown	Fr	Forde.N [5], Lucas [29], James [56]	6 000	Callender BRB
20-02	Cuba	L	0-3	Bridgetown	CC		5 000	Prendergast JAM
22-02	Jamaica	L	0-1	Bridgetown	CC			Brizan TRI
24-02	Trinidad & Tobago	L	2-3	Bridgetown	CC	Forde.N [32], Lucas [86]	3 000	Prendergast JAM
2006								
2-09	Guyana	L	0-1	Bridgetown	Fr		2 000	Forde BRB
10-09	St Vincent/Grenadines	D	1-1	Bridgetown	Fr	Parris [51]		Small BRB
17-09	Dominica	W	5-0	Roseau	Fr	Lovell 2 [27] [57], Goodridge [42p], Williams [75], Marshall [80]		
20-09	St Kitts and Nevis	D	1-1	St John's	CCq	Ifill [42]	300	Campbell JAM
22-09	Antigua & Barbuda	W	3-1	St John's	CCq	Williams [44], McCammon [58], Lovell [90]	2 500	Frederick VIR
24-09	Anguilla	W	7-1	St John's	CCq	McCammon 3 [35] [44] [76], Ifill 3 [40] [58] [83], Niblett [75]		Campbell JAM
5-11	Grenada	D	2-2	Black Rock	Fr	Parris [28], Goodridge [67p]		
19-11	Bahamas	W	2-1	Bridgetown	CCq	Forde.N [38], Skinner [44]		
21-11	St Vincent/Grenadines	W	3-0	Bridgetown	CCq	James [16], Forde.N [34], Ifill [60p]		
23-11	Bermuda	D	1-1	Bridgetown	CCq	Ifill [4]		
2007								
12-01	Trinidad and Tobago	D	1-1	Port of Spain	CCr1	Harvey [66]		Moreno PAN
15-01	Haiti	L	0-2	Port of Spain	CCr1			Jauregua ANT
17-01	Martinique	L	2-3	Port of Spain	CCr1	Harvey [27], Soares [42]		Jauregua ANT
25-03	Guatemala	D	0-0	Bridgetown	Fr			
2008								
13-01	Antigua & Barbuda	W	3-2	Black Rock	Fr	Vaughan [17], Straker [39], Lynch [63]		
6-02	Dominica	D	1-1	Roseau	WCq	Rashida Williams [43]	4 200	Quesada CRC
13-03	St Vincent/Grenadines	W	2-0	Kingstown	Fr	Stanford [38], Forde.N [87]		
15-03	Grenada	D	1-1	St George's	Fr	Worrell [75]		
26-03	Dominica	W	1-0	Bridgetown	WCq	Stanford [80]	4 150	Batres GUA
11-05	Trinidad and Tobago	L	0-3	Macoya	Fr			
6-06	Bermuda	L	1-2	Hamilton	Fr	Forde.N [44]		
9-06	Bermuda	L	0-3	Hamilton	Fr			
15-06	USA	L	0-8	Carson	WCq		11 500	Rodriguex MEX
22-06	USA	L	0-1	Bridgetown	WCq		2 000	Moreno PAN

Fr = Friendly match • CC = Digicel Caribbean Cup • WC = FIFA World Cup • q = qualifier • r1 = first round group

BARBADOS NATIONAL TEAM RECORDS AND RECORD SEQUENCES

Records			Sequence records					
Victory	7-1	AIA 2006	Wins	3	Five times	Clean sheets	3	1990, 1996
Defeat	0-7	USA 2000	Defeats	5	2000, 2008	Goals scored	10	2006-2007
Player Caps	n/a		Undefeated	10	2006-2007	Without goal	3	Three times
Player Goals	n/a		Without win	10	1976-1988	Goals against	15	2000-01

BARBADOS COUNTRY INFORMATION

Capital	Bridgetown	Independence	1966 from the UK	GDP per Capita	$15 700
Population	278 289	Status	Commonwealth	GNP Ranking	132
Area km²	431	Language	English	Dialling code	+1 246
Population density	645 per km²	Literacy rate	98%	Internet code	.bb
% in urban areas	47%	Main religion	Christian 71%	GMT + / –	-4
Towns/Cities ('000)	Bridgetown 98; Speightstown 3; Oistins 2, Bathsheba 1; Holetown 1; Bulkeley 1; Crane 1				
Neighbours (km)	Barbados is an island bordered by the Caribbean Sea and the Atlantic Ocean				
Main stadia	Waterford National Stadium – Bridgetown 15 000				

FA CUP 2007

Round of 16

Brittons Hill	1
Silver Sands	0
Deacons	0
Youth Milan	4
Beverley Hills	4
Lodge Road	0
Exactly Unified	0
Bar'dos Defence Force	5
Technico	5
Paradise	1
Fairy Valley	0
Benfica	2
Belfield	1
Villa	0
Haynesville	0
Eden Stars	1

Quarter–finals

Brittons Hill	3
Youth Milan	0
Beverley Hills	0
Bar'dos Defence Force	1
Technico	1
Benfica	0
Belfield	0 4p
Eden Stars	0 5p

Semi–finals

Brittons Hill	4
Bar'dos Defence Force	1
Technico	0
Eden Stars	1

Technico beat BDF 2-1 in the third place play-off

Final

Brittons Hill	5
Eden Stars	1

CUP FINAL
19-08-2007
Scorers –
Anthony Cumberbatch 3 [44] [61] [76],
Walton Burrows [66], Travis Coppin [92+]
for Brittons Hill; Andre Pinder [11] for
Eden Stars

RECENT LEAGUE AND CUP RECORD

	Championship						Cup		
Year	Champions	Pts	Runners-up	Pts	Third	Pts	Winners	Score	Runners-up
1997	Notre Dame						Notre Dame	1-0	Paradise
1998	Notre Dame	39	Budg-Buy	38	Bayer Pride		Bayer Pride	1-0	Notre Dame
1999	Notre Dame						Gall Hill	2-1	Paradise
2000	Notre Dame	35	Paradise	31	Youth Milan		Paradise	2-1	Notre Dame
2001	Paradise	43	Youth Milan	41	Notre Dame	35	Notre Dame	1-0	Youth Milan
2002	Notre Dame	44	Paradise	32	Youth Milan	30	Youth Milan	2-1	Notre Dame
2003	Paradise	*	BDF				Paradise	1-0	Weymouth Wales
2004	Notre Dame	52	Beverly Hills	42	Youth Milan	40	Notre Dame	3-2	Silver Sands
2005	Notre Dame	41	BDF	33	Silver Sands	32	Paradise	3-1	BDF
2006	Youth Milan	37	Notre Dame	36	Silver Sands	30	Gall Hill	1-0	Paradise
2007	BDF	34	Gall Hill	32	Brittons Hill	31	Brittons Hill	5-1	Eden Stars

* Paradise beat Barbados Defence Force 4-1 on penalties in the Championship final

BRU – BRUNEI DARUSSALAM

NATIONAL TEAM RECORD
JULY 10TH 2006 TO JULY 12TH 2010

PL	W	D	L	F	A	%
7	1	2	4	7	17	28.6

FIFA/COCA-COLA WORLD RANKING

1993	1994	1995	1996	1997	1998	1999	2000	2001	2002	2003	2004	2005	2006	2007	High
151	165	167	170	178	183	185	193	189	194	194	199	199	175	188	**140** 12/92

2007–2008												Low
08/07	09/07	10/07	11/07	12/07	01/08	02/08	03/08	04/08	05/08	06/08	07/08	199 03/06
171	172	177	187	188	187	189	189	190	190	188	187	

Brunei continue to exist on the periphery of the continental and regional football scene after missing out on a place at the AFC Challenge Cup and failing to enter the qualifying tournament for the 2010 World Cup. The sultanate struggled in their attempt to reach the AFC Challenge Cup finals in India, losing 1-0 against the Philippines before being trounced 4-0 by Tajikistan. Brunei's only points came from another disappointing result, a 1-1 draw with minnows Bhutan. The nation also avoided entering their under-23 team for the regional South East Asian Games football competition, although the full national side has been entered to play in the qualifying tournament

INTERNATIONAL HONOURS
None

for the ASEAN Football Federation Championships in Cambodia. The main focus of the country's footballing energy goes towards the DPMM club, who currently play in the Malaysia Super League and are also entered in the Singapore Cup as a foreign guest participant, although they had a disappointing season by their usually high standards, finishing in 10th place. After a year in hibernation, the Premier League in Brunei kicked-off again in November 2007 with QAF and ABDB Armed Forces dominating the proceedings. The two also met in the final of the recently launched League Cup with QAF winning the trophy after a 4-0 victory.

THE FIFA BIG COUNT OF 2006

	Male	Female		Total
Number of players	7 300	200	Referees and Assistant Referees	33
Professionals	0		Admin, Coaches, Technical, Medical	100
Amateurs 18+	300		Number of clubs	20
Youth under 18	600		Number of teams	40
Unregistered	1 100		Clubs with women's teams	0
Total players	7 500		Players as % of population	1.98%

The Football Association of Brunei Darussalam (BAFA)
Stadium Negara Hassanal Bolkiah, PO Box 2010, Bandar Seri Begawan, BB 4313, Brunei Darussalam
Tel +673 2 382761   Fax +673 2 382760
bruneifasg@yahoo.com   www.bafa.org.bn
President: HUSSAIN YUSSOFF Pehin Dato Haji   General Secretary: MATUSIN MATASAN Pengiran Haji
Vice-President: HASSAN ABAS Pengiran Haji   Treasurer: PANG Jeffery   Media Officer: None
Men's Coach: BUKETA Ranko   Women's Coach: None
BAFA formed: 1959   AFC: 1970   FIFA: 1969
Yellow shirts, Black shorts, Black socks

RECENT INTERNATIONAL MATCHES PLAYED BY BRUNEI DARUSSALAM

2006	Opponents	Score		Venue	Comp	Scorers	Att	Referee
2-04	Sri Lanka	L	0-1	Chittagong	CCr1		2 000	Saidov UZB
4-04	Nepal	W	2-1	Chittagong	CCr1	Safari [47], Sallehuddin [70]	2 500	Al Ghatrifi OMA
6-04	Bhutan	D	0-0	Chittagong	CCr1		2 000	Al Ghatrifi OMA
12-11	Timor Leste	W	3-2	Bacolod	AFq	Adie Mohammed Salleh 2 [11][70], Mardi Bujang [66]		
16-11	Cambodia	D	1-1	Bacolod	AFq	Mardi Bujang [90]		
18-11	Laos	L	1-4	Bacolod	AFq	Riwandi Wahit [20]		
20-11	Philippines	L	1-4	Bacolod	AFq	Kamarul Ariffin Ramlee [81]		
2007								
No international matches played in 2007 before August								
2008								
13-05	Philippines	L	0-1	Iloilo City	CCq		3 500	Saleem MDV
15-05	Bhutan	D	1-1	Barotac	CCq	Muhammad Khayrun Bin Salleh [76]	4 000	Mahapab THA
17-05	Tajikistan	L	0-4	Iloilo City	CCq		450	Al Badwawi UAE

CC = AFC Challenge Cup • AF = ASEAN Championship • q = qualifier • r1 = first round group

BRUNEI DARUSSALAM NATIONAL TEAM RECORDS AND RECORD SEQUENCES

Records			Sequence records					
Victory	2-0	PHI 1980, PHI 1989	Wins	2	1980	Clean sheets	1	
Defeat	0-12	UAE 2001	Defeats	12	1972-80, 1999-01	Goals scored	4	1998-1999, 2006
Player Caps	n/a		Undefeated	4	2006	Without goal	11	1999-2001
Player Goals	n/a		Without win	23	1999-2006	Goals against	26	1982-1987

RECENT LEAGUE AND CUP RECORD

	Championship						FA Cup		
Year	Champions	Pts	Runners-up	Pts	Third	Pts	Winners	Score	Runners-up
2002	DPMM	19	ABDB Armed Forces	16	Kasuka	9	Wijaya	1-0	ABDB Armed Forces
2003	Wijaya	25	DPMM	22	ABDB Armed Forces	21	ABDB Armed Forces	3-0	Kota Ranger
2004	DPMM	52	AH United	42	ABDB Armed Forces	37	DPMM	0-0 3-1p	ABDB Armed Forces
2005	No tournament played						No tournament played		
2006	QAF	41	ABDB Armed Forces	39	AH United	38	AH United	2-2 4-3p	ABDB Armed Forces
2007	No tournament played						No tournament played		

RECENT LEAGUE AND CUP RECORD

	League Cup		
Year	Winners	Score	Runners-up
2006	ABDB Armed Forces	3-2	QAF
2007	No tournament played		
2008	QAF	4-0	ABDB Armed Forces

BRUNEI DARUSSALAM COUNTRY INFORMATION

Capital	Bandar Seri Begawan	Independence	1984 from the UK	GDP per Capita	$18 600
Population	365 251	Status	Sultanate	GNP Ranking	97
Area km²	5 770	Language	Malay	Dialling code	+673
Population density	63 per km²	Literacy rate	90%	Internet code	.bn
% in urban areas	70%	Main religion	Muslim 67%	GMT + / –	+8
Towns/Cities ('000)	Bandar Seri Begawan 64; Kuala Belait 31; Pekan Seria 30; Tutong 19; Bangar 3				
Neighbours (km)	Malaysia 381; South China Sea 161				
Main stadia	Sultan Hassal Bolkiah – Bandar Ser Begawan 30 000				

BUL – BULGARIA

NATIONAL TEAM RECORD
JULY 10TH 2006 TO JULY 12TH 2010

PL	W	D	L	F	A	%
17	11	5	3	27	12	79.4

FIFA/COCA-COLA WORLD RANKING

1993	1994	1995	1996	1997	1998	1999	2000	2001	2002	2003	2004	2005	2006	2007
31	16	17	15	36	49	37	53	51	42	34	37	39	43	18

High	
8	06/95

2007–2008											
08/07	09/07	10/07	11/07	12/07	01/08	02/08	03/08	04/08	05/08	06/08	07/08
29	35	34	18	18	18	19	19	18	18	18	17

Low	
58	08/02

After failing to make it to the finals of Euro 2008, the Bulgarian Football Union once again turned to Plamen Markov, who in his previous stint as national team coach had taken Bulgaria to the finals of Euro 2004 in Portugal. The Bulgarians actually had a very good campaign but had the misfortune to be drawn in the same group as the Netherlands and Romania. They lost just once - a 2-0 defeat in Amsterdam - and they finished third, just a point behind the Dutch. Drawn with Italy and the Republic of Ireland in the 2010 FIFA World Cup qualifiers, Bulgaria have never gone more than two World Cups without qualifying for the finals, but having missed out in 2002 and 2006

INTERNATIONAL HONOURS
European Youth Tournament 1959 1969 1974, **Balkan Cup** 1932 1935 1976

they will have to qualify for South Africa to maintain that record. At home, CSKA Sofia romped home to a 31st championship success leaving Levski in their wake as they went through the season undefeated and conceding just 11 goals. Their celebrations were short-lived, however, when they were banned by UEFA from taking part in the 2008-09 Champions League due to unpaid debts. Their place went to Levski, who, just before the end of the season, had sacked coach Stanimir Stoilov - despite having lead the club to four trophies in four seasons. Litex Lovech were the seasons other winners after they beat Cherno More Varna 1-0 in the Cup Final.

THE FIFA BIG COUNT OF 2006

	Male	Female		Total
Number of players	289 348	37 685	Referees and Assistant Referees	1 411
Professionals	1 060		Admin, Coaches, Technical, Medical	1 160
Amateurs 18+	31 324		Number of clubs	559
Youth under 18	17 389		Number of teams	1 301
Unregistered	90 400		Clubs with women's teams	20
Total players	327 033		Players as % of population	4.43%

Bulgarian Football Union (BFU)
Bulgarski Futbolen Soius, 26 Tzar Ivan Assen II Str., Sofia - 1124, Bulgaria
Tel +359 2 9426253   Fax +359 2 9426200
bfu@bfunion.bg   www.bfunion.bg
President: MIHAILOV Borislav   General Secretary: POPOV Borislav
Vice-President: LECHKOV Yordan   Treasurer: PEEV Todor   Media Officer: KONSTANTINOV Borislav
Men's Coach: MARKOV Plamen   Women's Coach: ATANASSOV Emil
BFU formed: 1923   UEFA: 1954   FIFA: 1924
White shirts with green trimmings, Green shorts, White socks or Red shirts, Green, White

RECENT INTERNATIONAL MATCHES PLAYED BY BULGARIA

2005	Opponents	Score		Venue	Comp	Scorers	Att	Referee
26-03	Sweden	L	0-3	Sofia	WCq		42 530	Fandel GER
30-03	Hungary	D	1-1	Budapest	WCq	Petrov.S [51]	11 586	Wegereef NED
4-06	Croatia	L	1-3	Sofia	WCq	Petrov.M [72]	35 000	Nielsen DEN
17-08	Turkey	W	3-1	Sofia	Fr	Berbatov 2 [24 43], Petrov.M [38]	25 000	Zografos GRE
3-09	Sweden	L	0-3	Stockholm	WCq		35 000	De Bleeckere BEL
7-09	Iceland	W	3-2	Sofia	WCq	Berbatov [21], Iliev.G [69], Petrov.M [86]	18 000	Demirlek TUR
8-10	Hungary	W	2-0	Sofia	WCq	Berbatov [29], Lazarov [55]	4 652	Delevic SCG
12-10	Malta	D	1-1	Ta'Qali	WCq	Yankov [67]	2 844	Godulyan UKR
12-11	Georgia	W	6-2	Sofia	Fr	Yankov 2 [2 28], Berbatov 2 [35 47], Todorov 2 [63 90p]		Karadzic SRB
16-11	Mexico	W	3-0	Phoenix	Fr	Valkanov [4], Bojinov [34], Berbatov [80]	35 526	Hall USA
2006								
1-03	FYR Macedonia	W	1-0	Skopje	Fr	Petrov.M [38]	8 000	
9-05	Japan	W	2-1	Osaka	Fr	Todorov.S [1], Yanev [90]	44 851	Megia Davila ESP
11-05	Scotland	L	1-5	Kobe	Fr	Todorov.Y [26]	5 780	Kamikawa JPN
15-08	Wales	D	0-0	Swansea	Fr		8 200	Attard MLT
2-09	Romania	D	2-2	Constanta	ECq	Petrov.M 2 [82 84]	12 620	Farina ITA
6-09	Slovenia	W	3-0	Sofia	ECq	Bozhinov [58], Petrov.M [72], Telkiyski [81]	14 491	Bo Larsen DEN
7-10	Netherlands	D	1-1	Sofia	ECq	Petrov.M [12]	30 547	Ovrebø NOR
11-10	Luxembourg	W	1-0	Luxembourg	ECq	Tunchev [26]	3 156	Panic BIH
15-11	Slovakia	L	1-3	Zilina	Fr	Karadzinov [80]	4 823	Granat POL
2007								
6-02	Latvia	W	2-0	Larnaca	Fr	Surnins OG [14], Yovov [29]	500	Andronikou CYP
7-02	Cyprus	W	3-0	Nicosia	Fr	Berbatov 2 [44p 87], Georgiev [68]	2 000	Trattou CYP
28-03	Albania	D	0-0	Sofia	ECq		19 800	Eriksson SWE
2-06	Belarus	W	2-0	Minsk	ECq	Berbatov 2 [28 46]	29 000	Jara CZE
6-06	Belarus	W	2-1	Sofia	ECq	Petrov.M [10], Yankov [40]	10 501	Jakobsson ISL
22-08	Wales	L	0-1	Burgas	Fr		15 000	Germanakos GRE
8-09	Netherlands	L	0-2	Amsterdam	ECq		49 500	Cantalejo ESP
12-09	Luxembourg	W	3-0	Sofia	ECq	Berbatov 2 [27 28], Petrov.M [54p]	4 674	Demirlek TUR
17-10	Albania	D	1-1	Tirana	ECq	Berbatov [87]	3 000	Stuchlik AUT
17-11	Romania	W	1-0	Sofia	ECq	Dimitrov.V [6]	6 000	Plautz AUT
21-11	Slovenia	W	2-0	Celje	ECq	Georgiev [82], Berbatov [84]	3 700	Webb ENG
2008								
6-02	Northern Ireland	W	1-0	Belfast	Fr	Evans OG [38]	11 000	McDonald SCO
26-03	Finland	W	2-1	Sofia	Fr	Lazarov [49], Guenchev [90]	2 500	Tudor ROU

Fr = Friendly match • EC = UEFA EURO 2008 • WC = FIFA World Cup • q = qualifier

BULGARIA NATIONAL TEAM PLAYERS

	Player		Ap	G	Club	Date of Birth		Player		Ap	G	Club	Date of Birth
1	Georgi Petkov	GK	11	0	Levski	14 04 1976	14	Stanislav Genchev	MF	1	1	Vaslui	2 03 1981
2	Mihail Venkov	DF	3	0	Litex	28 07 1983	15	Blagoy Georgiev	MF	24	2	MSV Duisburg	21 12 1981
3	Aleksandar Tunchev	DF	14	1	CSKA	3 02 1981	16	Zhivko Milanov	DF	4	0	Levski	15 07 1984
4	Igor Tomasic	DF	8	0	Maccabi Tel Aviv	14 12 1976	17	Martin Petrov	FW	68	16	Manchester City	15 01 1979
5	Valentin Iliev	DF	11	0	Terek Grozny	11 07 1980	18	Georgi Sarmov	MF	1	0	Levski	7 09 1985
6	Stanislav Angelov	MF	16	1	Energie Cottbus	12 04 1978	19	Stiliyan Petrov	MF	72	7	Aston Villa	5 07 1979
7	Velizar Dimitrov	MF	21	2	Metal'h Donetsk	13 04 1979	20	Dimitar Ivankov	GK	47	0	Bursaspor	30 10 1975
8	Valeri Bojinov	FW	21	5	Manchester City	15 02 1986		**Selected others**					
9	Dimitar Berbatov	FW	63	39	Tottenham	30 01 1981		Elin Topuzakov	DF	28	0	Hapoel Tel Aviv	5 02 1977
10	Ivelin Popov	FW	3	0	Litex	26 10 1987		Hristo Yovov	MF	24	5	Apollon Limassol	4 11 1977
11	Zdravko Lazarov	FW	31	3	Shinnik Yaroslavl	20 02 1976		Chavdar Yankov	MF	17	3	Hannover 96	30 01 1984

Bulgaria's squad for the March 2008 international against Finland

	Aleksandar Aleksandrov	MF	9	1	Cherno More	19 01 1975

BULGARIA NATIONAL TEAM RECORDS AND RECORD SEQUENCES

Records				Sequence records				
Victory	7-0	NOR 1957, MLT 1982	Wins	5	1983 & 1987	Clean sheets	4	1963, 2007
Defeat	0-13	ESP 1933	Defeats	7	1924-1927	Goals scored	18	1934-1938
Player Caps	102	Borislav Mikhailov	Undefeated	11	1972-1973	Without goal	4	1984 & 1998
Player Goals	47	Hristo Bonev	Without win	16	1977-1978	Goals against	24	1924-1932

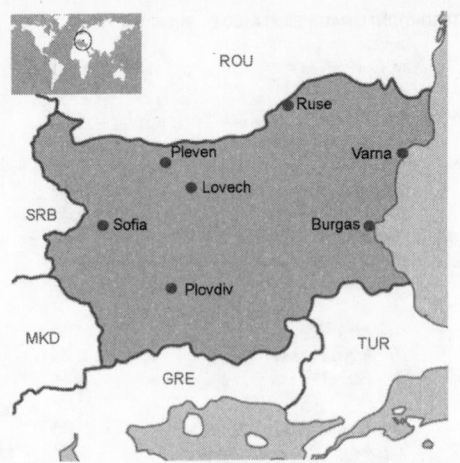

REPUBLIC OF BULGARIA; REPUBLIKA BALGARIYA

Capital	Sofia	Language	Bulgarian			Independence	1908
Population	7 385 367	Area	110 910 km²	Density	67 per km²	% in cities	71%
GDP per cap	$7 600	Dailling code	+359	Internet	.bg	GMT + / -	+2

MEDALS TABLE

		Overall			League			Cup		SAC		Europe			City	Stadium	Cap'ty	DoF
		G	S	B	G	S	B	G	S	G	S	G	S	B				
1	Levski Sofia	54	39	7	25	30	7	13	5	16	4				Sofia	Georgi Asparukhov	29 698	1914
2	CSKA Sofia	54	31	6	31	18	3	10	7	13	6			3	Sofia	Bulgarska Armia	24 000	1948
3	Slavia Sofia	14	11	13	7	9	12	1		6	2			1	Sofia	Slavia	28 000	1913
4	Lokomotiv Sofia	8	9	9	4	6	9	1		3	3				Sofia	Lokomotiv	25 000	1929
5	Litexs Lovech	5	4	2	2	1	2	3	3						Lovech	Lovech	7 000	1921
6	Botev Plovdiv	4	11	11	2	2	11		4	2	5				Plovdiv	Hristo Botev	21 000	1912
7	Cherno More Varna	4	10	2	4	6	2		2		2				Varna	Ticha	12 000	1913
8	Spartak Sofia	3	4			2		2		1	2				Sofia	Rakovski		1907-69
9	Lokomotiv Plovdiv	2	5	4	1	1	4			1	4				Plovdiv	Lokomotiv	20 000	1936
10	Spartak Plovdiv	2	3		1	1				1	2				Plovdiv	9 Septemvri		1947
11	AC 23 Sofia	2			1			1							Sofia	Atletic Park		1923
12	Beroe Stara Zagora	1	4	1	1		1				4				Stara Zagora	Beroe	22 300	1916
	Spartak Varna	1	4	1	1	2	1		1		1				Varna	Spartak	7 500	1918
14	SC Sofia	1	1		1	1									Sofia	Sport Club		1919

SAC = Soviet Army Cup (main cup competition 1946-81)

RECENT LEAGUE AND CUP RECORD

	Championship						Cup		
Year	Champions	Pts	Runners-up	Pts	Third	Pts	Winners	Score	Runners-up
1995	Levski Sofia	79	Lokomotiv Sofia	68	Botev Plovdiv	60	Lokomotiv Sofia	4-2	Botev Plovdiv
1996	Slavia Sofia	67	Levski Sofia	62	Lokomotiv Sofia	58	Slavia Sofia	1-0	Levski Sofia
1997	CSKA Sofia	71	Neftohimik Burgas	67	Slavia Sofia	57	CSKA Sofia	3-1	Levski Sofia
1998	Liteks Lovech	69	Levski Sofia	64	CSKA Sofia	61	Levski Sofia	5-0	CSKA Sofia
1999	Liteks Lovech	73	Levski Sofia	71	Levski Kjustendil	57	CSKA Sofia	1-0	Litex Lovech
2000	Levski Sofia	74	CSKA Sofia	64	Velbazhd	55	Levski Sofia	2-0	Neftohimik Burgas
2001	Levski Sofia	69	CSKA Sofia	62	Velbazhd	57	Litex Lovech	1-0	Velbazhd
2002	Levski Sofia	65	Litex Lovech	55	Lokomotiv Plovdiv	53	Levski Sofia	3-1	CSKA Sofia
2003	CSKA Sofia	66	Levski Sofia	60	Litex Lovech	55	Levski Sofia	2-1	Litex Lovech
2004	Lokomotiv Plovdiv	75	CSKA Sofia	72	CSKA Sofia	65	Litex Lovech	2-2 4-3p	CSKA Sofia
2005	CSKA Sofia	79	Levski Sofia	76	Lokomotiv Plovdiv	58	Levski Sofia	2-1	CSKA Sofia
2006	Levski Sofia	68	CSKA Sofia	65	Litex Lovech	60	CSKA Sofia	3-1	Cherno More Varna
2007	Levski Sofia	77	CSKA Sofia	72	Lokomotiv Sofia	72	Levski Sofia	1-0	Litex Lovech
2008	CSKA Sofia	78	Levski Sofia	62	Lokomotiv Sofia	57	Litex Lovech	1-0	Cherno More Varna

BULGARIA 2007–08

'A' PFG

	Pl	W	D	L	F	A	Pts	CSKA	Levski	Lokomotiv S	Litex	Cherno More	Chernomorets	Slavia	Pirin	Lokomotiv P	Vihren	Spartak	Botev	Belasitsa	Beroe	Vidima	Marek
CSKA Sofia	30	24	6	0	53	11	78		1-1	3-1	0-0	1-0	3-0	2-0	3-0	2-0	1-0	3-2	2-0	2-0	1-0	3-1	4-0
Levski Sofia †	30	19	5	6	56	19	62	0-1		0-1	0-1	4-0	2-1	2-1	4-0	3-1	1-0	3-0	6-2	4-0	1-0	3-0	4-2
Lokomotiv Sofia ‡	30	16	9	5	47	28	57	0-0	0-0		1-2	4-3	4-0	1-2	0-3	2-1	3-2	1-0	2-2	1-0	3-0	2-0	2-0
Litex Lovech ‡	30	16	9	5	51	26	56	1-1	2-1	1-1		1-1	2-1	1-1	1-0	3-1	2-0	1-0	6-0	2-0	1-1	4-1	4-0
Cherno More Varna	30	13	9	8	40	26	48	0-2	0-1	1-1	2-1		2-1	1-0	1-0	2-1	1-0	0-0	2-0	1-1	1-0	7-0	0-0
Chernomorets Burgas	30	13	8	9	40	32	47	1-1	2-1	1-1	2-0	0-1		2-0	1-4	1-0	1-0	1-0	3-1	0-0	2-0	1-0	1-0
Slavia Sofia	30	13	8	9	37	30	47	0-1	0-0	0-0	1-0	3-1	1-1		1-0	1-0	0-0	5-0	4-2	3-1	2-0	2-0	2-1
Pirin Blagoevgrad	30	13	7	10	33	29	46	0-1	1-1	1-3	1-3	1-0	1-0	1-0		1-1	0-0	0-2	1-0	2-1	1-0	3-1	4-0
Lokomotiv Plovdiv	30	12	7	11	37	28	43	0-1	1-0	1-2	1-0	2-1	1-1	1-1	0-0		2-1	1-0	4-0	1-0	2-0	6-1	0-0
Vihren Sandanski	30	9	6	14	26	29	33	1-2	0-1	1-0	2-1	1-1	1-2	1-1	1-1	0-2		0-1	2-0	2-0	2-0	1-1	3-1
Spartak Varna	30	8	7	15	21	34	31	0-2	1-2	0-1	0-0	0-1	1-1	2-1	2-0	2-1	0-1		2-2	1-0	1-0	0-0	2-0
Botev Plovdiv	30	8	6	16	36	54	30	1-3	0-3	2-2	1-2	1-1	0-0	3-0	0-0	1-2	1-0	2-0		2-0	1-0	5-0	4-0
Belasitsa Petrich	30	7	5	18	23	43	26	1-3	0-0	0-1	1-2	1-1	1-6	1-2	0-1	0-0	1-0	2-1	3-1		3-1	1-0	1-0
Beroe Stara Zagora	30	5	6	18	23	39	26	0-1	0-1	1-3	2-2	0-0	2-1	2-2	2-2	0-0	2-0	0-0	3-1	2-1		2-0	1-1
Vidima-Rakovski	30	4	6	20	17	61	18	0-0	1-3	0-0	3-2	0-3	1-1	0-2	1-0	0-3	0-1	1-1	0-1	1-0	3-1		1-0
Marek Dupnitsa	30	5	3	22	16	68	18	1-3	0-4	1-4	0-3	1-4	1-4	1-0	0-2	2-1	0-3	1-0	1-0	1-1	0-1	2-1	

11/08/2007 - 17/05/2008 • † Qualified for the UEFA Champions League • ‡ Qualified for the UEFA Cup
Top scorers: Georgi Hristov, Botev 21; Marcho Dafchev, Lokomotiv Sofia 15; Nei, CSKA 13; Aleksandar Aleksandrov, Cherno More 12

BULGARIA 2007–08 WESTERN 'B' PFG (2)

	Pl	W	D	L	F	A	Pts
Lokomotiv Mezdra	26	20	3	3	56	12	63
Minyor Pernik †	26	14	5	7	45	31	47
Chavdar Etropole	26	14	4	8	39	23	46
Rilski sportist Samokov	26	13	6	7	44	33	45
Belite orli Pleven	26	11	5	10	33	31	38
Sportist Svoge	26	10	6	10	35	30	36
Etar Veliko Tarnovo	26	8	10	8	33	39	34
Montana	26	9	7	10	29	34	34
Spartak Pleven	26	8	8	10	29	40	32
Akademik 1947 Sofia	26	9	5	12	41	43	32
Pirin Gotse Delchev	26	8	7	11	28	33	31
Chavdar Byala Slatina	26	6	7	13	19	34	25
Yantra Gabrovo	26	6	6	14	31	48	24
Velbazhd Kyustendil	26	5	3	18	20	56	18

18/08/2007 - 17/05/2008 • † Play-off
Promotion play-off: Kaliakra 2-2 4-5p Minyor Pernik

BULGARIA 2007–08 EASTERN 'B' PFG (2)

	Pl	W	D	L	F	A	Pts
Sliven 2000	26	19	3	4	63	23	60
Kaliakra Kavarna †	26	16	6	4	49	17	54
Rodopa Smolyan	26	17	2	7	44	18	53
Nesebar	26	16	2	8	43	29	50
Dunav Ruse	26	12	6	8	35	28	42
Maritsa Plovdiv	26	10	5	11	34	41	35
Spartak Plovdiv	26	10	5	11	28	34	35
Naftex Burgas	26	9	7	10	40	35	34
Panayot Volov Shumen	26	9	4	13	23	35	31
Svetkavitsa Targovishte	26	8	4	14	26	46	28
Minyor Radnevo	26	7	5	14	32	50	26
Svilengrad	26	7	4	15	30	43	25
Benkovski Byala	26	6	4	16	26	41	22
Haskovo	26	6	3	17	24	57	21

18/08/2007 - 17/05/2008 • † Play-off

BFU CUP 2007–08

Round of 16		Quarter–finals		Semi–finals		Final	
Litex Lovech *	3						
Vihren Sandanski	0	Litex Lovech *	0 4p				
Chernomorets Burgas	0	Levski Sofia	0 3p				
Levski Sofia	2			Litex Lovech	4		
Lokomotiv Sofia	1			Botev Plovdiv	2		
Spartak Varna	0	Lokomotiv Sofia *	0				
Slavia Sofia *	2	Botev Plovdiv	2				
Botev Plovdiv	4					Litex Lovech ‡	1
Kaliakra Kavarna	2					Cherno More Varna	0
Chavdar Etropole *	0	Kaliakra Kavarna *	3				
Sportist Svoge *	1	Lokomotiv Plovdiv	1				
Lokomotiv Plovdiv	4			Kaliakra Kavarna	1		
Pirin Blagoevgrad *	1			Cherno More Varna	3		
Minyor Pernik	0	Pirin Blagoevgrad	0				
Bansko *	2	Cherno More Varna *	1				
Cherno More Varna	6						

CUP FINAL
Vasil Levski, Sofia
14-05-2008
Scorer - Stanislav Manolev 57 for Litex

* Home team • ‡ Qualified for the UEFA Cup

CAM – CAMBODIA

NATIONAL TEAM RECORD
JULY 10TH 2006 TO JULY 12TH 2010

PL	W	D	L	F	A	%
13	2	3	8	16	34	26.9

FIFA/COCA-COLA WORLD RANKING

1993	1994	1995	1996	1997	1998	1999	2000	2001	2002	2003	2004	2005	2006	2007
-	-	180	186	170	162	168	169	169	176	178	184	188	174	183

High
156 07/98

2007–2008											
08/07	09/07	10/07	11/07	12/07	01/08	02/08	03/08	04/08	05/08	06/08	07/08
173	178	179	183	183	184	186	186	186	186	185	184

Low
188 03/06

After failing to enter the qualifying tournament for the 2006 World Cup in Germany, Cambodia's journey along the road to the 2010 finals was a short one, ending after the first round with defeat at the hands of Turkmenistan over two legs. A narrow 1-0 loss in the first leg in Phnom Penh was followed by a more comprehensive 4-1 reversal in Ashgabat as the Cambodians finished 2007 without a victory to their name. However, the Cambodians did notch up their first win in more than a year-and-a-half in May 2008 with a 3-1 victory over Macau on home soil – thanks to a pair of goals from Nuth Sinoun and a third from Chan Rithy - in the qualifying tournament for the AFC Challenge

INTERNATIONAL HONOURS
None

Cup. The victory was their first since downing Timor Leste in October 2007 in qualifying for the ASEAN Championships but it was not enough to earn a spot in the finals following the 1-0 defeat at the hands of Nepal. The inability to qualify cost Korean coach Yoo Kee-heung his job and he was replaced by Cambodian Prak Sovannara. 2006 club champions Khmera scored an encouraging victory over Chinese Taipei's Tatung in the delayed 2007 AFC Presidents Cup, while 2007 champions Naga Corp could only manage a single point in the 2008 tournament with both failing to progress from the first round group stage.

THE FIFA BIG COUNT OF 2006

	Male	Female		Total
Number of players	229 411	100	Referees and Assistant Referees	70
Professionals	11		Admin, Coaches, Technical, Medical	160
Amateurs 18+	1 600		Number of clubs	65
Youth under 18	3 900		Number of teams	420
Unregistered	6 000		Clubs with women's teams	0
Total players	229 511		Players as % of population	1.65%

Cambodian Football Federation (CFF)
National Football Centre, Road Kabsrov, Sangkat Samrongkrom, Khan Dangkor, Phnom Penh 2327 PPT3, Cambodia
Tel +855 23 364889   Fax +855 23 223537
ffc.cam@gmail.com   www.aseanfootball.org
President: SAO Sokha   General Secretary: OUK Sethycheat
Vice-President: KHEK Ravy   Treasurer: PHUONG-BOPHA Saradeth   Media Officer: None
Men's Coach: SOVANNARA Prak   Women's Coach: None
CFF formed: 1933   AFC: 1957   FIFA: 1953
Blue shirts, Blue shorts, Blue socks

RECENT INTERNATIONAL MATCHES PLAYED BY CAMBODIA

2004	Opponents	Score		Venue	Comp	Scorers	Att	Referee
9-12	Vietnam SR	L	1-9	Ho Chi Minh City	TCr1	Hang Sokunthea 44	8 000	Supian MAS
11-12	Laos	L	1-2	Ho Chi Minh City	TCr1	Hing Darith 27	20 000	Kwon Jong Chul KOR
13-12	Indonesia	L	0-8	Ho Chi Minh City	TCr1		17 000	Sun Baojie CHN
15-12	Singapore	L	0-3	Ho Chi Minh City	TCr1		2 000	Ebrahim BHR
2005								
11-10	Singapore	L	0-2	Phnom Penh	Fr			
2006								
1-04	Bangladesh	L	1-2	Dhaka	CCr1	Chan Rithy 68	35 000	Tan Hai CHN
3-04	Palestine	L	0-4	Dhaka	CCr1		2 500	AK Nema IRQ
6-04	Guam	W	3-0	Dhaka	CCr1	Sok Buntheang 37, Keo Kosal 40, Kouch Sokumpheak 63	500	U Win Cho MYA
14-11	Laos	D	2-2	Bacolod	TCq	Teab Vadhanak 50, Hem Samchay 75		
16-11	Brunei Darussalam	D	1-1	Bacolod	TCq	Samel Nasa 79		
18-11	Philippines	L	0-1	Bacolod	TCq			
20-11	Timor Leste	W	4-1	Bacolod	TCq	Hem Samchay 37, Teab Vadhanak 58, Chan Rithy 2 82 86		
2007								
18-06	Malaysia	L	0-6	Kuala Lumpur	Fr			
17-08	India	L	0-6	New Delhi	Fr			
19-08	Kyrgyzstan	L	3-4	New Delhi	Fr	Hok Sotitya 34, Chan Rithy 40, Chin Chum 43		
22-08	Bangladesh	D	1-1	New Delhi	Fr	Keo Kasal 90		
25-08	Syria	L	1-5	New Delhi	Fr	Teab Vadhanak 69		
11-10	Turkmenistan	L	0-1	Phnom Penh	WCq		3 000	Gosh BAN
28-10	Turkmenistan	L	1-4	Ashgabat	WCq	Samel Nasa 12	5 000	Saidov UZB
2008								
26-05	Nepal	L	0-1	Phnom Penh	CCq		3 000	Torky IRN
28-05	Macau	W	3-1	Phnom Penh	CCq	Nuth Sinoun 2 30 92+, Chan Rithy 67	3 000	Kurbanov TKM

Fr = Friendly match • TC = ASEAN Football Federation Cup/Tiger Cup • CC = AFC Challenge Cup • r1 = first round group

CAMBODIA NATIONAL TEAM RECORDS AND RECORD SEQUENCES

Records			Sequence records				
Victory	11-0	YEM 1966	Wins	1		Clean sheets	1	
Defeat	0-10	IDN 1995	Defeats	10	1995-1997	Goals scored	3	1997
Player Caps	n/a		Undefeated	3	2006	Without goal	5	1996-1997
Player Goals	n/a		Without win	17	1998-2002	Goals against	20	1997-2000

RECENT LEAGUE RECORD

Year	Champions
1997	Body Guards Club
1998	Royal Dolphins
1999	Royal Dolphins
2000	National Police
2001	No tournament played
2002	Samart United
2003	No tournament played
2004	No tournament played
2005	Khemera
2006	Khemera
2007	Naga Corp

CAMBODIA COUNTRY INFORMATION

Capital	Phnom Penh	Independence	1953	GDP per Capita	$1 900
Population	13 363 421	Status	Kingdom	GNP Ranking	127
Area km²	181 040	Language	Khmer	Dialling code	+855
Population density	73 per km²	Literacy rate	66%	Internet code	.kh
% in urban areas	21%	Main religion	Buddhist 95%	GMT +/-	+7
Towns/Cities ('000)	Phnom Penh 1 573; Preah Sihanouk 157; Bat Dambang 150; Siem Reab 148				
Neighbours (km)	Laos 541; Vietnam 1,228; Thailand 803; Gulf of Thailand 443				
Main stadia	National Olympic – Phnom Penh 50 000				

CAN – CANADA

NATIONAL TEAM RECORD
JULY 10TH 2006 TO JULY 12TH 2010

PL	W	D	L	F	A	%
17	7	4	6	28	20	52.9

FIFA/COCA-COLA WORLD RANKING

1993	1994	1995	1996	1997	1998	1999	2000	2001	2002	2003	2004	2005	2006	2007
44	63	65	40	66	101	81	63	92	70	87	90	84	82	55

High	
40	12/96

2007–2008											
08/07	09/07	10/07	11/07	12/07	01/08	02/08	03/08	04/08	05/08	06/08	07/08
53	54	51	55	55	56	58	62	63	62	60	77

Low	
10	03/07

How to find the champions of Canada to take part in the newly created CONCACAF Champions League... That was the challenge facing football officials in a country that has no proper national championship. The solution was relatively easy. Take the only three clubs of any real stature - Toronto FC of the MLS along with the Vancouver Whitecaps and Montreal Impact from the USA A-League and hey presto! The second largest country in the world has the smallest championship on earth! In the end it was Montreal who won the three team round robin to become Canada's first club representatives in international competition for 33 years. Attempts have been made in the past

INTERNATIONAL HONOURS
Qualified for the FIFA World Cup™ 1986 Qualified for the FIFA Women's World Cup 1995 1999 2003 Olympic Gold 1904 (Unofficial)
CONCACAF Gold Cup 2000 CONCACAF Women's Gold Cup 1998 CONCACAF U-20 Championship 1986 1996

to develop a national championship at amateur level with the Canadian Soccer League the latest attempt. Formed in 2006 it consists of clubs in the east of the country and although it wants to expand west, the huge distances involved will always be problematic for anything other than professional clubs. The national team made it safely through to the CONCACAF group stage of the 2010 FIFA World Cup qualifiers after a relatively straight-forward two-leg victory over St Vincent and the Grenadines - Canada's first wins since reaching the semi-finals of the Gold Cup.

THE FIFA BIG COUNT OF 2006

	Male	Female		Total
Number of players	1 800 378	895 334	Referees and Assistant Referees	19 624
Professionals	150		Admin, Coaches, Technical, Medical	170 000
Amateurs 18+	129 725		Number of clubs	7 000
Youth under 18	715837		Number of teams	55 000
Unregistered	800 000		Clubs with women's teams	3 000
Total players	2 695 712		Players as % of population	8.14%

The Canadian Soccer Association (CSA)
Place Soccer Canada, 237 Metcalfe Street, Ottawa, Ontario, K2P 1R2, Canada
Tel +1 613 2377678   Fax +1 613 2371516
info@soccercan.ca   www.canadasoccer.com
President: MAESTRACCI Dominic   General Secretary: MONTOPOLI Peter
Vice-President: MONTAGLIANI Victor   Treasurer: URSINI Vincent   Media Officer: SCOTT Richard
Men's Coach: MITCHELL Dale   Women's Coach: PELLERUD Even
CSA formed: 1912   CONCACAF: 1978   FIFA: 1912-28, 1946
Red shirts with white trimmings, Red shorts, Red socks or White shirts with red trimmings, White shorts, White socks

RECENT INTERNATIONAL MATCHES PLAYED BY CANADA

2003 Opponents	Score	Venue	Comp	Scorers	Att	Referee
11-10 Finland	L 2-3	Tampere	Fr	Radzinski [75], De Rosario [85]	5 350	
15-11 Czech Republic	L 1-5	Teplice	Fr	Radzinski [89]	8 343	Sundell SWE
18-11 Republic of Ireland	L 0-3	Dublin	Fr		23 000	Whitby WAL
2004						
18-01 Barbados	W 1-0	Bridgetown	Fr	Corazzin [10]		Ford BRB
30-05 Wales	L 0-1	Wrexham	Fr		10 805	McKeon IRE
13-06 Belize	W 4-0	Kingston	WCq	Peschisolido [39], Radzinski [55], McKenna [75], Brennan [83]	8 245	Batres GUA
16-06 Belize	W 4-0	Kingston	WCq	Radzinski [45], De Rosario 2 [63 73], Brennan [85]	5 124	Gordon TRI
18-08 Guatemala	L 0-2	Vancouver	WCq		6 725	Sibrian SLV
4-09 Honduras	D 1-1	Edmonton	WCq	De Vos [82]	9 654	Archundia MEX
8-09 Costa Rica	L 0-1	San Jose	WCq		13 000	Ramdhan TRI
9-10 Honduras	D 1-1	San Pedro Sula	WCq	Hutchinson [73]	42 000	Stott USA
13-10 Costa Rica	L 1-3	Vancouver	WCq	De Rosario [12]	4 728	Prendergast JAM
17-11 Guatemala	W 1-0	Guatemala City	WCq	De Rosario [57]	18 000	Rodriguez MEX
2005						
9-02 Northern Ireland	W 1-0	Belfast	Fr	Occean [31]	11 156	Attard MLT
26-03 Portugal	L 1-4	Barcelos	Fr	McKenna [85]	13 000	Ishchenko UKR
2-07 Honduras	L 1-2	Vancouver	Fr	McKenna [70]	4 105	Valenzuela USA
7-07 Costa Rica	L 0-1	Seattle	GCr1		15 831	Prendergast JAM
9-07 USA	L 0-2	Seattle	GCr1		15 109	Brizan TRI
12-07 Cuba	W 2-1	Foxboro	GCr1	Gerba [69], Hutchinson [87]	15 211	Moreno PAN
3-09 Spain	L 1-2	Santander	Fr	Grande [73]	11 978	Colombo FRA
16-11 Luxembourg	W 1-0	Hesperange	Fr	Hume [69]		Gomes Costa POR
2006						
22-01 USA	D 0-0	San Diego	Fr		6 077	Archundia MEX
1-03 Austria	W 2-0	Vienna	Fr	Brennan [65], Reda [71]	9 000	Van Egmond NED
4-09 Jamaica	W 1-0	Montreal	Fr	Friend [41]	6 526	Quesada CRC
8-10 Jamaica	L 1-2	Kingston	Fr	Radzinski [8]	5 000	Brizan TRI
15-11 Hungary	L 0-1	Szekesfehervar	Fr		6 000	Weiner GER
2007						
25-03 Bermuda	W 3-0	Hamilton	Fr	Hutchinson [25], Radzinski [30], Stalteri [44]		
1-06 Venezuela	D 2-2	Maracaibo	Fr	De Rosario [5], Gerba [85]		Lopez COL
6-06 Costa Rica	W 2-1	Miami	GCr1	Deguzman 2 [57 73]	17 420	Wingaarde SUR
9-06 Guadeloupe †	L 1-2	Miami	GCr1	Gerba [35]	22 529	Brizan TRI
11-06 Haiti	W 2-0	Miami	GCr1	De Rosario 2 [32 35p]	15 892	
16-06 Guatemala	W 3-0	Foxboro	GCqf	De Rosario [17], Gerba 2 [33 44]	22 412	Campbell JAM
21-06 USA	L 1-2	Chicago	GCsf	Hume [76]	50 760	Archundia MEX
22-08 Iceland	D 1-1	Reykjavik	Fr	Occean [75]	4 359	Asumaa FIN
12-09 Costa Rica	D 1-1	Toronto	Fr	De Rosario [53]		Marrufo USA
20-11 South Africa	L 0-2	Durban	Fr			Kalyoyo MWI
2008						
26-03 Estonia	L 0-2	Tallinn	Fr		1 600	
31-05 Brazil	L 2-3	Seattle	Fr	Friend [10], De Guzman [56]		Stott USA
4-06 Panama	D 2-2	Sunrise	Fr	Peters [20], Jazic [82]		
15-06 St Vincent/Grenadines	W 3-0	Kingstown	WCq	Nakjima-Farran [29], Gerba 2 [29 89]		Batres GUA
22-06 St Vincent/Grenadines	W 4-1	Montreal	WCq	De Rosario 2 [29 50], Gerba 2 [38 63]	11 500	Aguilar SLV

Fr = Friendly match • GC = CONCACAF Gold Cup • WC = FIFA World Cup • † Not a full international
q = qualifier • r1 = first round group • qf = quarter-final • sf = semi-final

CANADA NATIONAL TEAM RECORDS AND RECORD SEQUENCES

Records			Sequence records				
Victory	7-0	USA 1904	Wins	6	2000	Clean sheets	5	1996
Defeat	0-8	MEX 1993	Defeats	9	1974-1976	Goals scored	10	1980-1983 & 1985
Player Caps	82	Randy Samuel	Undefeated	15	1999-2000	Without goal	5	1986 & 2000
Player Goals	19	Dale Mitchell	Without win	12	1974-1976	Goals against	17	1988-1992

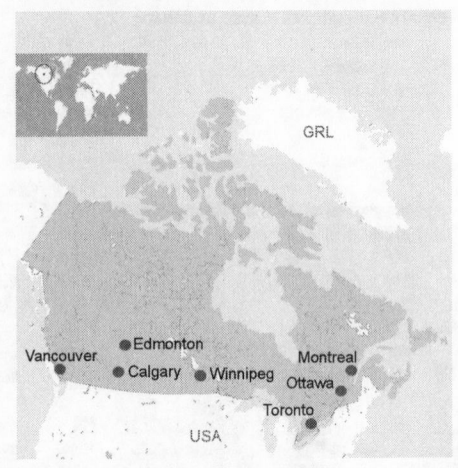

MAJOR CITIES/TOWNS

		Population '000
1	Toronto	4 670
2	Montreal	3 280
3	Vancouver	1 839
4	Calgary	991
5	Ottawa	885
6	Edmonton	831
7	Hamilton	661
8	Quebec	647
9	Winnipeg	632
10	Kitchener	414
11	London	348
12	St Catherines	320
13	Victoria	289
14	Windsor	281
15	Halifax	263
16	Oshawa	251
17	Saskatoon	199
18	Barrie	198
19	Regina	175
20	Abbotsford	157
21	Sherbrooke	129
22	Kelowna	129
23	Trois-Rivières	120
24	Guelph	117

CANADA

Capital	Ottawa	Language	English & French		Independence	1867
Population	33 098 932	Area	9 984 670 km²	Density 3 per km²	% in cities	77%
GDP per cap	$29 800	Dailling code	+1	Internet .ca	GMT + / -	-3.5 / -8

CLUB DIRECTORY

Club	Town/City	Stadium	Capacity	www.	League
Montreal Impact	Montreal	Claude Robillard	14 000	impactmontreal.com	USL A-League
Toronto FC	Toronto	BMO Field	20 000	toronto.fc.mlsnet.com	MLS
Vancouver Whitecaps	Vancouver	Swangard, Burnaby	6 100	whitecapsfc.com	USL A-League

CANADA 2007
CANADIAN SOCCER LEAGUE

National Division	Pl	W	D	L	F	A	Pts
St Catherines Wolves ‡	22	12	6	4	36	19	42
Trois Rivieres Attak ‡	22	10	8	4	48	29	38
North York Astros ‡	22	5	5	12	32	55	20
Windsor Border Stars ‡	22	5	4	13	33	49	19
London City	22	3	2	17	15	82	11

International Division	Pl	W	D	L	F	A	Pts
Serbian White Eagles ‡	22	14	3	5	55	31	45
Toronto Croatia ‡	22	10	11	1	42	16	41
Italia Shooters ‡	22	11	7	4	44	17	39
Canadian Lions ‡	22	6	9	7	40	36	27
Portuguese Supra	22	4	5	13	31	42	17

11/05/2007 - 7/10/2007 • ‡ Qualified for the play-offs

CANADA 2007
CANADIAN SOCCER LEAGUE PLAY-OFFS

Quarter–finals		Semi–finals		Final		
Toronto Croatia	4					
North York Astros	2	**Toronto Croatia**	3			
Canadian Lions	0 9p	St Catherines Wolves	2			
St Catherines Wolves	0 10p			**Toronto Croatia**	4	0
Trois Rivieres Attak	3			Serbian White Eagles	1	0
Italia Shooters	0	Trois Rivieres Attak	1			
Windsor Border Stars	1	**Serbian White Eagles**	2	1st leg. 27-10-2007		
Serbian White Eagles	2			2nd leg. 28-10-2007		

CAY – CAYMAN ISLANDS

NATIONAL TEAM RECORD
JULY 10TH 2006 TO JULY 12TH 2010

PL	W	D	L	F	A	%
5	0	1	4	3	16	10

FIFA/COCA-COLA WORLD RANKING

1993	1994	1995	1996	1997	1998	1999	2000	2001	2002	2003	2004	2005	2006	2007	High	
154	150	131	148	164	153	148	159	165	164	181	176	181	189	192	**127**	11/95

2007–2008												Low	
08/07	09/07	10/07	11/07	12/07	01/08	02/08	03/08	04/08	05/08	06/08	07/08	**192**	12/07
185	188	188	191	192	191	183	183	185	185	188	187		

With more registered businesses than people, the Cayman Islands status as one of the world's largest financial centres should give football in the country the means to punch well above its weight and to that end the football association hired the Jamaican Carl Brown to improve standards in the country. Brown was the assistant to Reggae Boyz coach Rene Simoes at the 1998 World Cup in France and also spent a year working with Sam Allardyce at Bolton Wanderers. His first job was to try and instil some professionalism into a squad based largely around players in the US college system and the immediate results were encouraging. Drawn against the much higher ranked

INTERNATIONAL HONOURS
None

Bermuda in the 2010 FIFA World Cup qualifiers, the Caymans nearly pulled of a shock after coming away from the first leg in Hamilton with a 1-1 draw. Allean Grant's late equaliser ensured a big crowd for the return in George Town but they went home disappointed after the Bermudans raced into a two-goal lead, eventually winning 3-1. The League in the Caymans may not be of a very high standard but it is well run and there are a number of Cup competitions to keep the interest going. Scholars International once again dominated winning the League and CIFA FA Cup double while Roma United won the Digicel League Cup, beating George Town 1-0 in the final.

THE FIFA BIG COUNT OF 2006

	Male	Female		Total
Number of players	3 400	300	Referees and Assistant Referees	100
Professionals	0		Admin, Coaches, Technical, Medical	200
Amateurs 18+	700		Number of clubs	10
Youth under 18	600		Number of teams	50
Unregistered	1 100		Clubs with women's teams	0
Total players	3 700		Players as % of population	8.14%

Cayman Islands Football Association (CIFA)
Truman Bodden Sports Complex, Olympic Way, Off Walkers Road, PO Box 178, GT, Grand Cayman KYI-1104, Cayman Islands
Tel +1 345 9495775   Fax +1 345 9457673
cifa@candw.ky   www.caymanfootball.ky
President: WEBB Jeffrey   General Secretary: BLAKE Bruce
Vice-President: FREDERICK David   Treasurer: WATSON Canover   Media Officer: MILLER Keisha
Men's Coach: BROWN Carl   Women's Coach: CUNHA Thiago
CIFA formed: 1966   CONCACAF: 1993   FIFA: 1992
Red shirts, Blue shorts, White socks or White shirts, White shorts, Red socks

RECENT INTERNATIONAL MATCHES PLAYED BY THE CAYMAN ISLANDS

2004 Opponents	Score	Venue		Scorers	Att.	Referee
22-02 Cuba	L 1-2	Grand Cayman	WCq	Elliot 72	1 789	Sibrian SLV
27-03 Cuba	L 0-3	Havana	WCq		3 500	Rodriguez MEX
24-11 Bermuda	L 1-2	Kingstown	CCq	Berry 48	200	Matthew SKN
26-11 British Virgin Islands	W 1-0	Kingstown	CCq	Whittaker 49		
28-11 St Vincent/Grenadines	L 0-4	Kingstown	CCq		850	Prendergast JAM
2005						
No international matches played in 2005						
2006						
2-09 Bahamas	L 1-3	Havana	CCq	Whittaker 76		Stewart JAM
4-09 Turks & Caicos Isl	L 0-2	Havana	CCq		100	Stennett JAM
6-09 Cuba	L 0-7	Havana	CCq		120	Stewart JAM
2007						
No international matches played in 2007						
2008						
3-02 Bermuda	D 1-1	Hamilton	WCq	Grant 87	2 000	Navarro CAN
30-03 Bermuda	L 1-3	Georgetown	WCq	Forbes 64p	3 200	Marrufo USA

Fr = Friendly match • CC = Digicel Caribbean Cup • WC = FIFA World Cup • q = qualifier

CAYMAN ISLANDS NATIONAL TEAM RECORDS AND RECORD SEQUENCES

Records			Sequence records				
Victory	5-0	VGB 1994	Wins	3	1994	Clean sheets	2	1994, 1995
Defeat	2-9	TRI 1995	Defeats	8	1991-1993	Goals scored	5	1993-94, 2000
Player Caps	n/a		Undefeated	4	1994-1995	Without goal	5	2000
Player Goals	n/a		Without win	9	1991-93, 1995-98	Goals against	10	1991-1993

CAYMAN ISLANDS 2007-08 FOSTERS LEAGUE

	Pl	W	D	L	F	A	Pts
Scholars International	19	15	3	1	53	11	48
Latinos	20	12	6	2	44	20	42
George Town	20	10	4	6	35	24	34
Sunset	19	8	7	4	31	29	31
Future	20	8	5	7	26	26	29
Elite	20	8	3	9	35	38	27
Tigers	20	6	5	9	35	36	23
Roma United	20	6	5	9	29	33	23
East End United	20	4	9	7	24	31	21
Academy	20	4	5	11	21	40	17
Bodden Town	20	0	4	16	17	62	4

3/11/2007 - 28/05/2008

RECENT LEAGUE AND CUP RECORD

Year	Championship Champions	Cup Winners
2005	Western Union	Western Union
2006	Scholars International	Scholars International
2007	Scholars International	Latinos
2008	Scholars International	Scholars International

CIFA FA CUP

Quarter–finals		Semi–finals		Final	
Scholars Int'al	1				
George Town	0	Scholars Int'al	5		
Bodden Town	2	East End Utd	3		
East End Utd	6			Scholars Int'al	1
Latinos	2			Elite	0
Roma Utd	1	Latinos	1 3p		
Sunset	1	Elite	1 4p	North Side, 1-06-2008	
Elite	2			Scorer - David Harding 78	

CIFA DIGICEL CAYMAN CUP

Quarter–finals		Semi–finals		Final	
Roma Utd	3				
Tigers	1	Roma Utd	2 2		
Latinos	0	Elite	0 0		
Elite	1			Roma Utd	1
Scholars Int'al	0 4p			George Town	0
Future	0 3p	Scholars Int'al	1 1	North Side, 10-02-2008	
East End Utd	1	George Town	3 0	Scorer - Wayne Smith 40	
George Town	3				

CAYMAN ISLANDS COUNTRY INFORMATION

Capital	George Town	Independence		GDP per Capita	$35 000
Population	43 103	Status	British Crown Colony	GNP Ranking	n/a
Area km²	262	Language	English	Dialling code	+1 345
Population density	164 per km²	Literacy rate	98%	Internet code	.ky
% in urban areas	%	Main religion	Christian	GMT + / –	-5
Towns/Cities ('000)	George Town 27; West Bay 10; Bodden Town 6; East End 1; North Side 1				
Neighbours (km)	The Cayman Islands consist of three islands in the Caribbean Sea				
Main stadia	Truman Boden – George Town 7 000; ED Bush – West Bay 2 500				

CGO – CONGO

NATIONAL TEAM RECORD
JULY 10TH 2006 TO JULY 12TH 2010

PL	W	D	L	F	A	%
17	7	6	4	22	18	58.8

FIFA/COCA-COLA WORLD RANKING

1993	1994	1995	1996	1997	1998	1999	2000	2001	2002	2003	2004	2005	2006	2007	High
103	114	119	100	101	112	94	86	94	97	108	117	110	89	91	**79** 03/08

				2007–2008								Low
08/07	09/07	10/07	11/07	12/07	01/08	02/08	03/08	04/08	05/08	06/08	07/08	**1 9** 04/96
100	101	99	92	91	89	87	79	92	93	110	100	

Congo are hoping to reap the harvest of the young generation of players, who competed with surprising potential at the 2007 FIFA U-20 World Cup in Canada. Already several of the players have made it through to the national side although the 'Diables Rouge' made a stuttering start to the 2010 FIFA World Cup qualifiers. Congo appointed Ivica Todorov, the Serbian who has previous experience of coaching on the continent, as their new national team coach in March 2008 and unusually provided him with the budget to organise two training camps in France before they embarked on their FIFA World Cup qualifying campaign. While preparations might have been

INTERNATIONAL HONOURS
CAF African Cup of Nations 1972 African Games 1965 African Youth Championship 2007 CAF Champions League CARA Brazzaville 1974

more substantive than usual, results were disappointing with defeats away to Mali and Chad despite influential captain Oscar Ewolo postponing his planned honeymoon. Blackburn Rovers defender Christophe Samba continued his boycott of the side, a result of dissatisfaction with the organisation around the team during their last African Nations Cup qualifiers. Diables Noirs won the championship in November, but hopes of progress past the opening phase of the 2008 African Champions League were quickly stymied by Enyimba of Nigeria in the first round. The other trophy winners were JS Talangaï, who beat CARA Brazzaville in the Cup Final.

THE FIFA BIG COUNT OF 2006

	Male	Female		Total
Number of players	191 600	8 610	Referees and Assistant Referees	504
Professionals	0		Admin, Coaches, Technical, Medical	595
Amateurs 18+	5 410		Number of clubs	90
Youth under 18	3 650		Number of teams	320
Unregistered	35 150		Clubs with women's teams	0
Total players	200 210		Players as % of population	5.41%

Fédération Congolaise de Football (FECOFOOT)
80 Rue Eugene Etienne, Centre Ville Brazzaville, Case postale 11, Brazzaville, Congo
Tel +242 811563   Fax +242 812524
fecofoot@yahoo.fr   www.none
President: IBOVI Antoine   General Secretary: OLANDZOBO Francois Joseph
Vice-President: BAKALA Thomas   Treasurer: NDENGUET Lylian   Media Officer: BAKANDILA Joseph
Men's Coach: TODOROV Ivica   Women's Coach: KAYA Gilbert
FECOFOOT formed: 1962   CAF: 1966   FIFA: 1962
Green shirts, Yellow shorts, Red socks

RECENT INTERNATIONAL MATCHES PLAYED BY CONGO

2003	Opponents	Score		Venue	Comp	Scorers	Att	Referee
12-10	Sierra Leone	W	1-0	Brazzaville	WCq	Mvoubi 89p	4 800	Mana NGA
16-11	Sierra Leone	D	1-1	Freetown	WCq	Nguie 67	20 000	Monteiro Lopez CPV
5-12	Gabon	W	3-2	Brazzaville	CMr1	Ayessa 25, Ndey 56, Beaulia 67		Tchoumba CMR
9-12	Gabon	D	1-1	Brazzaville	CMr1	Ayessa 56		
10-12	Cameroon	L	0-2	Brazzaville	CMsf			Mbera GAB
13-12	Gabon	W	1-0	Brazzaville	CM3p			
2004								
5-06	Senegal	L	0-2	Dakar	WCq		18 000	Benouza ALG
20-06	Liberia	W	3-0	Brazzaville	WCq	Bouanga 52, Mamouna-Ossila 55, Batota 66	25 000	Lemghambodj MTN
4-07	Mali	W	1-0	Brazzaville	WCq	Mamouna-Ossila 30	20 000	Evehe CMR
5-09	Togo	L	0-2	Lome	WCq		20 000	Mbera GAB
10-10	Zambia	L	2-3	Brazzaville	WCq	Bouanga 75, Mamouna-Ossila 81	20 000	Yacoubi TUN
2005								
5-02	Central African Rep.	W	1-0	Libreville	CMr1	Bhebey 10		
8-02	Gabon	L	0-1	Libreville	CMr1			
12-02	Gabon	L	1-2	Libreville	CM3p	Lakou 35		
22-02	Angola	L	0-2	Brazzaville	Fr			
19-03	Gabon	D	0-0	Libreville	Fr			
26-03	Zambia	L	0-2	Chililabombwe	WCq		20 000	Maillet SEY
5-06	Senegal	D	0-0	Brazzaville	WCq		40 000	Damon RSA
19-06	Liberia	W	2-0	Paynesville	WCq	Bhebey 2 3 73	5 000	Sillah GAM
3-09	Mali	L	0-2	Bamako	WCq		10 000	Mbera GAB
8-10	Togo	L	2-3	Brazzaville	WCq	Bouity 26, Mamouna-Ossila 56	20 000	Shelmany LBY
2006								
4-03	Equatorial Guinea	L	1-2	Bata	CMr1			
8-03	Chad	D	0-0	Bata	CMr1			
2-09	South Africa	D	0-0	Joheannesburg	CNq			Aboubacar CIV
8-10	Chad	W	3-1	Brazzaville	CNq	Abdoulaye Bruce 17, Malonga 30, Nguessi 46		Djaoupe TOG
14-11	Mali	L	0-1	La Courneuve	Fr			
2007								
5-03	Equatorial Guinea	W	2-1	N'Djamena	CMr1	Likibi 81, Ngoua 94+		
7-03	Gabon	D	2-2	N'Djamena	CMr1	Lepaye 2 27 44		
12-03	Central African Rep	W	4-1	N'Djamena	CMsf	Lepaye 4, Likibi 2 28 84, Beaulia 47		
16-03	Gabon	W	1-0	N'Djamena	CMf	Papou 59		
25-03	Zambia	D	0-0	Brazzaville	CNq			Coulibaly MLI
4-04	Angola	D	0-0	Cabinda	Fr			
28-05	Congo DR	W	2-1	Brazzaville	Fr	Minga 35, De Bouisson 55p		
2-06	Zambia	L	0-3	Chililabombwe	CNq			Rahman SUD
17-06	South Africa	D	1-1	Pointe-Noire	CNq	Bantsimba 65		Eyene CMR
9-09	Chad	D	1-1	N'Djamena	CNq	Mayembi 6		Pare BFA
2008								
1-06	Mali	L	2-4	Bamoko	WCq	Mouithys 2 5 74	40 000	Bennaceur TUN
8-06	Sudan	W	1-0	Brazzaville	WCq	Endzanga 70	25 000	Mana NGA
14-06	Chad	L	1-2	N'Djamena	WCq	Batota 42	8 000	Doue CIV
22-06	Chad	W	2-0	Brazzaville	WCq	Mouithys 14, Ibara 64	8 000	Diouf SEN

Fr = Friendly match • CN = African Cup of Nations • CM = CEMAC Cup • WC = FIFA World Cup
q = qualifier • r1 = first round group • sf = semi-final • 3p = third place play-off

CONGO NATIONAL TEAM RECORDS AND RECORD SEQUENCES

Records			Sequence records				
Victory	11-0	STP 1976	Wins	5	1983	Clean sheets	4	1983, 1998-1999
Defeat	1-8	MAD 1960	Defeats	5	1968, 1973, 1993	Goals scored	11	1975-1977
Player Caps	n/a		Undefeated	8	1963-1965	Without goal	7	1992-1993
Player Goals	n/a		Without win	9	2001-2002	Goals against	14	1965-1968

CONGO COUNTRY INFORMATION

Capital	Brazzaville	Independence	1960 from France	GDP per Capita	$700
Population	2 998 040	Status	Republic	GNP Ranking	137
Area km²	342 000	Language	French	Dialling code	+242
Population density	8 per km²	Literacy rate	77%	Internet code	.cg
% in urban areas	59%	Main religion	Christian 50%	GMT + / –	+1
Towns/Cities ('000)	Brazzaville 1 115; Pointe-Noire 628; Loubomo 70; Nkayi 70; Loandjili 26; Madingou 22				
Neighbours (km)	Central African Republic 467; Congo DR 2 410; Angola 201; Gabon 1 903; Cameroon 523; Atlantic Ocean 169				
Main stadia	Stade de la Révolution – Brazzaville 50 000				

CONGO 2007 CHAMPIONNAT NATIONALE

Group A	Pl	W	D	L	F	A	Pts
AS Ponténégrin ‡	6	3	3	0	10	1	12
AS Police ‡	6	2	4	0	7	2	10
Club 57	6	2	3	1	11	4	9
Patronage St-Anne	6	2	3	1	5	4	9
Pigeon Vert	6	1	3	2	9	8	6
V. Club Pointe Noir	6	1	3	2	3	9	6
Inter Club Dolise	6	0	1	5	2	19	1

Group A	Pl	W	D	L	F	A	Pts
Diables Noirs ‡	6	5	1	0	11	1	16
St Michel Ouenzé ‡	6	4	1	1	8	2	13
Ajax Ouenzé	6	2	3	1	7	4	9
Etoile du Congo	6	2	3	1	8	7	9
JS Bougainvillées	6	2	0	4	4	6	6
AS Chemimot	6	1	2	3	10	7	5
ASDP Oyo	6	0	0	6	3	24	0

3/11/2007 - 28/05/2008 • ‡ Qualified for the play-offs

PLAY-OFFS

Semi-finals

Diables Noir	2
AS Police	1

St Michel Ouenzé	0	1p
AS Ponténégrin	0	3p

Third place: AS Police 1-0 SMO

Diables Noir	2
AS Ponténégrin	0

Stade Municipal, Pointe-Noir, 22-11-2007
Scorers - Toussaint Mayembi [78], Sidoine Beaullia [87] for Diables Noirs

COUPE DU CONGO 2007

Quarter-finals		Semi-finals		Final	
JS Talangaï	4 1				
AS Cheminot	0 1	**JS Talangaï**	1 1		
Diables Noirs	0 1	Nico-nicoye	0 0		
Nico-nicoye	0 1			**JS Talangaï**	2
Etoile du Congo	1 8			CARA Brazzaville	1
AS Leopard Dolisie	1 0	Etoile du Congo	0 0		
AS Ponténégrin	1 1	**CARA Brazzaville**	2 0	Owando, 14-08-2007	
CARA Brazzaville	2 0			Scorers - Atsono, Onzongo for JS Talangaï; Benchou Ngoma for CARA	

RECENT LEAGUE AND CUP RECORD

	Championship				Cup		
Year	Champions	Score	Runners-up		Winners	Score	Runners-up
1998	Vita Club Mokanda	1-0	Etoile du Congo		Tournament not played		
1999	Vita Club Mokanda				Tournament not played		
2000	Etoile du Congo	†			Etoile du Congo	5-1	Vita Club Mokanda
2001	Etoile du Congo	1-0	La Mancha		AS Police	1-0	Etoile du Congo
2002	AS Police	2-1	Etoile du Congo		Etoile du Congo	2-1	FC Abeilles
2003	St Michel Ouenzé	0-0	La Mancha		Diables Noirs	0-0 3-2p	Vita Club Mokanda
2004	Diables Noirs	2-1	AS Police		Munisport	0-0 3-0p	Vita Club Mokanda
2005	Final abandoned. Neither St Michel nor Diables Noirs awarded title				Diables Noirs	1-1 4-2p	Patronage Sainte Anne
2006	Etoile du Congo	1-0	La Mancha		Etoile du Congo	2-1	JS Talangaï
2007	Diables Noirs	2-0	AS Ponténégrine		JS Talangaï	2-1	CARA Brazzaville

† Played on a league system

CHA – CHAD

NATIONAL TEAM RECORD
JULY 10TH 2006 TO JULY 12TH 2010

PL	W	D	L	F	A	%
14	5	2	7	16	24	42.9

FIFA/COCA-COLA WORLD RANKING

1993	1994	1995	1996	1997	1998	1999	2000	2001	2002	2003	2004	2005	2006	2007
166	175	180	188	184	178	166	163	176	173	152	168	159	142	141

High	
127	07/08

2007–2008											
08/07	09/07	10/07	11/07	12/07	01/08	02/08	03/08	04/08	05/08	06/08	07/08
139	136	142	143	141	140	143	135	145	147	148	127

Low	
190	09/97

A first win in almost four years in a competitive international suggests increased participation on the continental stage is beginning to reap dividends for football in Chad. The 'Sao', as the national team are known in tribute to ancient ancestors, beat Congo 2-1 in Ndjamena in a 2010 FIFA World Cup qualifier, their first win in a qualifying match since they beat Angola 3-1 in October 2003 in the preliminaries for the 2006 FIFA World Cup finals in Germany. There had been glimpses of this potential during the Nations Cup qualifiers for Ghana when they won a surprise away point in Zambia, but Chad still finished bottom of the group. A diplomatic spat with Sudan in May 2008

INTERNATIONAL HONOURS
None

precipitated an unusual decision by FIFA to postpone the FIFA World Cup qualifier between the two neighbours. Sudan had accused Chad of backing a rebel attack on the outskirts of the capital Khartoum and broke off diplomatic relations although they have since been restored. Also off the field, Chad was suspended by FIFA for a brief six week period after government interference in the running of the country's football federation. It cost champions Renaissance the opportunity to play in the 2008 African Champions League, the club being disqualified before their first round tie against TP Mazembe Englebert of the Democratic Republic of Congo.

THE FIFA BIG COUNT OF 2006

	Male	Female		Total
Number of players	408 740	21 010	Referees and Assistant Referees	427
Professionals	0		Admin, Coaches, Technical, Medical	1 855
Amateurs 18+	3 610		Number of clubs	50
Youth under 18	2 140		Number of teams	148
Unregistered	53 000		Clubs with women's teams	0
Total players	429 750		Players as % of population	4.32

Fédération Tchadienne de Football (FTF)
Case postale 886, N'Djamena, Chad
Tel +235 518740   Fax +235 523806
ftfa@intnet.td   www.none
President: MAHAMAT Saleh Issa   General Secretary: RAMADANE Daouda
Vice-President: BANAYE Hisseine   Treasurer: RAMADANE Daouda   Media Officer: ZOUTANE DABA Martin
Men's Coach: NATOLTIGA Okalan   Women's Coach: DEGUIDIN Charlotte
FTF formed: 1962   CAF: 1962   FIFA: 1988
Blue shirts, Yellow shorts, Red socks

RECENT INTERNATIONAL MATCHES PLAYED BY CHAD

2005	Opponents	Score		Venue	Comp	Scorers	Att	Referee
8-02	Equatorial Guinea	D	0-0	Libreville	CMr1			
10-02	Gabon	W	3-2	Libreville	CMsf	Djenet [3], Doumbé [8], Nguembaye [56]		
22-05	Sudan	L	1-4	Khartoum	Fr			
27-05	Sudan	D	1-1	Khartoum	Fr			
2006								
6-03	Equatorial Guinea	D	1-1	Bata	CMr1			
8-03	Congo	D	0-0	Bata	CMr1			
11-03	Cameroon †	L	0-1	Bata	CMsf			
14-03	Gabon	D	2-2	Bata	CM3p	Mahamat [20p], Doumbé [52]		
3-09	Zambia	L	0-2	N'Djamena	CNq			Shelmani LBY
8-10	Congo	L	1-3	Brazzaville	CNq	Missdongarle Betolinga [89]		Djaoupe TOG
2007								
22-02	Benin	W	1-0	Cotonou	Fr	Mahamat [53]		
4-03	Cameroon	W	2-1	N'Djamena	CMr1			
6-03	Central African Rep	W	3-2	N'Djamena	CMr1	Ndouassel [60p], Missdongarle Betolinga [61], Mahamat [89]		
11-03	Gabon	L	1-2	N'Djamena	CMsf	Kedigui [70]		
16-03	Central African Rep	W	1-0	N'Djamena	CM3p	Medego [95]		
24-03	South Africa	L	0-3	N'Djamena	CNq			Aguidissou BEN
2-06	South Africa	L	0-4	Durban	CNq			Gasingwa RWA
16-06	Zambia	D	1-1	Chililabombwe	CNq	Kedigui [13]		Ssegonga UGA
9-09	Congo	D	1-1	N'Djamena	CNq	Djimenam [88]		Pare BFA
2008								
7-06	Mali	L	1-2	N'Djamena	WCq	Kedigui [37]	15 000	Aguidissou BEN
14-06	Congo	W	2-1	N'Djamena	WCq	Kedigui [44p], Syriakata Hassan [48]	8 000	Doue CIV
22-06	Congo	L	0-2	Brazzaville	WCq		8 000	Diouf SEN

Fr = Friendly match • CN = African Cup of Nations • CM = CEMAC Cup • WC = FIFA World Cup
q = qualifier • r1 = first round group • sf = semi-final • 3p = third place play-off • † Not an official international

CHAD NATIONAL TEAM RECORDS AND RECORD SEQUENCES

Records			Sequence records					
Victory	5-0	STP 1976	Wins	3	1999, 2007	Clean sheets	2	1986, 1999
Defeat	2-6	BEN 1963	Defeats	7	1991-1997	Goals scored	6	2006-2007
Player Caps	n/a		Undefeated	4	1984-85, 2005-06	Without goal	5	1992-1997
Player Goals	n/a		Without win	12	1976-86, 1991-99	Goals against	9	1978-86, 1991-98

RECENT LEAGUE RECORD

Year	Champions
1997	Tourbillon
1998	AS Coton Chad
1999	Renaissance
2000	Tourbillon
2001	Tourbillon
2002	No tournament
2003	No tournament
2004	Renaissance
2005	Renaissance
2006	Renaissance
2007	Renaissance

CHAD COUNTRY INFORMATION

Capital	N'Djamena	Independence	1960 from France	GDP per Capita	$1 200
Population	9 538 544	Status	Republic	GNP Ranking	145
Area km²	1 284 000	Language	French, Arabic	Dialling code	+235
Population density	7 per km²	Literacy rate	47%	Internet code	.td
% in urban areas	21%	Main religion	Muslim 51%, Christian 35%	GMT +/−	+1
Towns/Cities ('000)	N'Djamena 721; Moundou 135; Sarh 102; Abeche 74; Kelo 42; Koumra 36; Pala 35				
Neighbours (km)	Libya 1 055; Sudan 1 360; Central African Republic 1 197; Cameroon 1 094; Nigeria 87; Niger 1 175				
Main stadia	Stade National – N'Djamena 30 000				

CHI – CHILE

NATIONAL TEAM RECORD
JULY 10TH 2006 TO JULY 12TH 2010

PL	W	D	L	F	A	%
30	14	7	9	35	36	58.3

FIFA/COCA-COLA WORLD RANKING

1993	1994	1995	1996	1997	1998	1999	2000	2001	2002	2003	2004	2005	2006	2007
55	47	36	26	16	16	23	19	39	84	80	74	64	41	45

High	
6	04/98

2007–2008											
08/07	09/07	10/07	11/07	12/07	01/08	02/08	03/08	04/08	05/08	06/08	07/08
47	47	45	45	45	45	40	39	40	41	47	43

Low	
84	12/02

The appointment of the ex-Argentina coach Marcelo Bielsa to the national team in August 2007 heralded a shift in attitude in Chile that followed significant changes at the football federation. Harold Mayne-Nichols was elected president - the youngest in South America - and quickly made his presence felt when six of the 2007 Copa America squad - including captain Jorge Valdivia - were banned for 20 matches each for breaches of discipline. Bielsa, who lead Argentina to Olympic Gold in 2004, has a reputation as a strict disciplinarian and he was quick to discard nine first team players after losing two of the first four matches in the 2010 FIFA World Cup qualifying campaign.

INTERNATIONAL HONOURS
Qualified for the FIFA World Cup 1930 1950 1962 1966 1974 1982 1998   Copa Libertadores Colo Colo 1991

With two wins in their next two qualifiers, Chile climbed the table and there is genuine optimism that even without the missing players the team can make it to the finals in South Africa. In domestic football, Colo Colo continued to dominate thanks to the presence of another Argentine coach, Claudio Borghi. He led the club to their fourth successive title when they beat Universidad Concepción in the 2007 Clausura final but he then left to take over as coach of Independiente. Colo Colo made it to the 2008 Apertura final but lost to Everton from Viña del Mar who came back from a 2-0 defeat at home to win 3-2 on aggregate and clinch their first title for 32 years.

THE FIFA BIG COUNT OF 2006

	Male	Female		Total
Number of players	2 469 837	138 500	Referees and Assistant Referees	5 204
Professionals	637		Admin, Coaches, Technical, Medical	21 170
Amateurs 18+	138 200		Number of clubs	5 715
Youth under 18	326 500		Number of teams	31 228
Unregistered	2 010 000		Clubs with women's teams	47
Total players	2 608 337		Players as % of population	16.17%

Federación de Fútbol de Chile (FFCH)
Avenida Quilin No. 5635, Comuna Peñalolén, Casilla No. 3733, Central de Casillas, Santiago de Chile, Chile
Tel +56 2 8101800   Fax +56 2 2843510
ffch@anfpchile.cl   www.anfp.cl
President: MAYNE-NICHOLLS Harold   General Secretary: CONTADOR Jorge
Vice-President: JELVEZ Sergio   Treasurer: OLIVARES Claudio   Media Officer: OLMEDO Claudio
Men's Coach: BIELSA Marcelo   Women's Coach: TEJEDOR Marta
FFCH formed: 1895   CONMEBOL: 1916   FIFA: 1913
Red shirts with blue and white trimmings, Blue shorts, White socks or White shirts, White shorts, Blue socks

RECENT INTERNATIONAL MATCHES PLAYED BY CHILE

2005 Opponents	Score		Venue	Comp	Scorers	Att	Referee
30-05 Côte d'Ivoire	D	1-1	Vittel	Fr	Suazo 77p		Lamarre FRA
2-06 Sweden	D	1-1	Stockholm	Fr	Suazo 51	34 735	Stark GER
16-08 Colombia	L	1-2	Santiago	Fr	Suazo 82p	15 000	Larrionda URU
7-10 Peru	W	3-2	Viña del Mar	Fr	Fernandez.M 2 28 49, Navia 70		Vieira URU
11-10 Peru	W	1-0	Tacna	Fr	Navia 24	12 000	Haro ECU
15-11 Paraguay	W	3-2	Viña del Mar	Fr	Ponce 39, Valdivia 50, Figueroa 62p	9 000	Baldassi ARG
2007							
7-02 Venezuela	W	1-0	Maracaibo	Fr	Fernandez.M 43	9 000	Buitrago COL
24-03 Brazil	L	0-4	Gothenburg	Fr		30 122	Berntsen NOR
28-03 Costa Rica	D	1-1	Talca	Fr	Fonseca 60	8 000	Ortube BOL
18-04 Argentina	D	0-0	Mendoza	Fr		38 000	Vazquez URU
9-05 Cuba	W	3-0	Osorno	Fr	Gutierrez.R 5, Rojas.J 27, Flores.L 89	1 800	Cabrera URU
16-05 Cuba	W	2-0	Temuco	Fr	Gutierrez.R 40, Gonzalez.D 71	3 500	Grance PAR
23-05 Haiti	D	0-0	Port-au-Prince	Fr		12 000	Edouard HAI
2-06 Costa Rica	L	0-2	San Jose	Fr		25 000	Glower MEX
5-06 Jamaica	W	1-0	Kingston	Fr	Lorca 19	15 000	Guerrero NCA
27-06 Ecuador	W	3-2	Puerto Ordaz	CAr1	Suazo 2 20 80, Villanueva 86	35 000	Ruiz COL
1-07 Brazil	L	0-3	Maturin	CAr1		42 000	Torres PAR
4-07 Mexico	D	0-0	Puerto La Cruz	CAr1		30 000	Amarilla PAR
7-07 Brazil	L	1-6	Puerto La Cruz	CAqf	Suazo 76	25 000	Larrionda URU
7-09 Switzerland	L	1-2	Vienna	Fr	Sanchez 44	2 500	Stuchlik AUT
11-09 Austria	W	2-0	Vienna	Fr	Droguett 66, Rubio 84	14 500	Granat POL
13-10 Argentina	L	0-2	Buenos Aires	WCq		55 000	Vazquez URU
17-10 Peru	W	2-0	Santiago	WCq	Suazo 11, Fernandez.M 51	58 000	Ruiz COL
18-11 Uruguay	D	2-2	Montevideo	WCq	Salas 2 59 69p	35 000	Pezzotta ARG
21-11 Paraguay	L	0-3	Santiago	WCq		52 320	Ruiz COL
2008							
26-01 Japan	D	0-0	Tokyo	Fr		37 261	Lee Min Hu KOR
30-01 Korea Republic	W	1-0	Seoul	Fr	Fierro 55	15 012	Matsuo JPN
26-03 Israel	L	0-1	Tel Aviv	Fr		24 463	Velasco ESP
4-06 Guatemala	W	2-0	Rancagua	Fr	Sanchez 2 1 35		
7-06 Panama	D	0-0	Valparaiso	Fr			Fagundes BRA
15-06 Bolivia	W	2-0	La Paz	WCq	Medel 2 28 76	27 722	Rivera PER
19-06 Venezuela	W	3-2	Puerto La Cruz	WCq	Suazo 2 54p 92+, Jara 73	38 000	Silvera URU

Fr = Friendly match • CA = Copa América • WC = FIFA World Cup • q = qualifier • r1 = first round group

CHILE NATIONAL TEAM PLAYERS

	Player		Ap	G	Club	Date of Birth		Player		Ap	G	Club	Date of Birth
1	Claudio Bravo	GK	22	0	Real Sociedad	13 04 1983	12	Miguel Pinto	GK	8	0	Univ de Chile	4 05 1983
2	Hugo Droguett	MF	10	1	Morelia	2 09 1982	13	Marco Estrada	MF	4	0	Univ de Chile	28 05 1983
3	Roberto Cereceda	MF	5	0	Colo Colo	10 10 1984	14	Fabián Orellana	FW	0	0	Audax Italiano	27 01 1986
4	Ismael Fuentes	DF	16	0	Chiapas	4 08 1981	15	Jean Beausejour	FW	6	0	O'Higgins	1 06 1984
5	Waldo Ponce	DF	11	1	Vélez Sársfield	12 04 1982	16	Manuel Iturra	MF	26	1	Univ de Chile	2 06 1986
6	Carlos Carmona	MF	1	0	Reggina	21 02 1987	17	Gary Medel	MF	5	2	Univ. Católica	3 08 1987
7	Alexis Sánchez	FW	11	3	Udinese	19 12 1988	18	Gonzalo Jara	DF	12	1	Colo Colo	29 05 1985
8	Daúd Gazale	FW	1	0	Colo Colo	10 08 1984	19	José Pedro Fuenzalida	MF	1	0	O'Higgins	22 02 1985
9	Humberto Suazo	FW	25	10	Monterrey	10 05 1981	20	Osvaldo González	DF	2	0	Univ de Chile	10 08 1984
10	Pedro Morales	MF	6	0	Dinamo Zagreb	25 05 1985	21	Carlos Villanueva	MF	10	1	Blackburn Rov	5 02 1986
11	Mark González	FW	23	3	Real Betis	4 07 1984	22	Cristopher Toselli	GK	0	0	Univ Católica	15 06 1988
							23	Matías Fernández	MF	19	4	Villarreal	15 05 1986

Chile's squad for the June 2008 FIFA World Cup qualifiers

CHILE NATIONAL TEAM RECORDS AND RECORD SEQUENCES

Records			Sequence records					
Victory	7-0	VEN 1979	Wins	5	1950-1952	Clean sheets	8	1983-1985
Defeat	0-7	BRA 1959	Defeats	10	1922-1924	Goals scored	18	1995-1997
Player Caps	84	Leonel Sánchez	Undefeated	10	1995-1996	Without goal	4	Three times
Player Goals	37	Marcelo Salas	Without win	33	1910-1924	Goals against	41	1910-1928

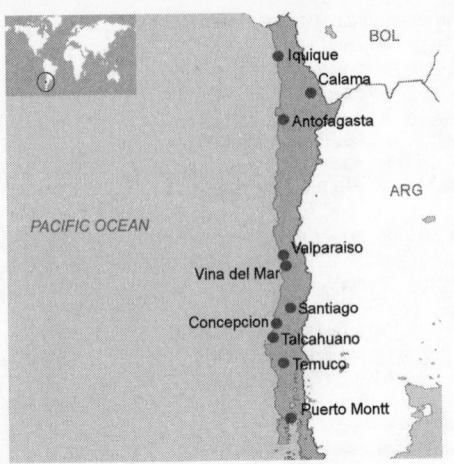

MAJOR CITIES/TOWNS

		Population '000
1	Santiago	4 893
2	Puente Alto	516
3	Antofagasta	314
4	Viña del Mar	297
5	Valparaíso	284
6	Talcahuano	254
7	San Bernardo	252
8	Temuco	239
9	Iquique	231
10	Concepción	216
11	Rancagua	214
12	Talca	198
13	Arica	189
14	Coquimbo	163
15	Puerto Montt	161
16	La Serena	156
17	Chillán	151
18	Calama	145
19	Osorno	136
20	Valdivia	134
21	Quilpué	131
22	Copiapó	130
23	Punta Arenas	117
24	El Salvador	7

REPUBLIC OF CHILE; REPUBLICA DE CHILE

Capital	Santiago	Language	Spanish	Independence	1818
Population	16 134 219	Area	756 950 km²	% in cities	84%
GDP per cap	$9 900	Dailling code	+56	Internet	.cl	GMT +/-	-4

MEDALS TABLE

		Overall			League			Cup			Sth Am			City	Stadium	Cap'ty	DoF
		G	S	B	G	S	B	G	S	B	G	S	B				
1	Colo Colo	38	22	20	27	16	15	10	4		1	2	5	Santiago	Monumental	62 500	1925
2	Universidad de Chile	15	8	16	12	8	13	3					3	Santiago	Nacional	77 000	1911
3	Universidad Catolica	12	23	9	9	15	4	3	7			1	5	Santiago	San Carlos	20 000	1937
4	Cobreloa	9	12	6	8	7	5	1	3		2	1		Calama	Municipal	20 180	1977
5	Union Española	8	10	6	6	7	5	2	2		1	1		Santiago	Santa Laura	25 000	1909
6	Santiago Wanderers	5	5	2	3	3	2	2	2					Valparaíso	Playa Ancha	19 000	1892
7	Audax Italiano	4	10	8	4	8	8		2					Santiago	Municipal La Florida	8 500	1910
8	Palestino	4	4	3	2	3	2	2	1				1	Santiago	La Cisterna	12 000	1920
9	Magallanes	4	4	2	4	4	2							Santiago	Santiago Bueras	8 000	1897
10	Everton	5	2		4	2		1						Viña del Mar	Sausalito	18 037	1909
11	Santiago Morning	1	3	1	1	2	1		1					Santiago	Santiago Bueras	8 000	1936
12	Cobresal	1	2			2		1						El Salvador	El Cobre	20 752	1979
13	Deportes La Serena	1	1	2			2	1	1					La Serena	La Portada	18 000	1955
14	Temuco	1		2	1		2							Temuco	Municipal	28 000	1916
15	Huachipato	1		1	1		1							Talcahuano	Las Higueras	10 000	1947
	Deportes Iquique	1		1				1	1					Iquique	Terra de Campeones	10 000	1978

RECENT LEAGUE AND CUP RECORD (2000–2001)

	Championship							Cup		
Year	Champions	Pts	Runners-up	Pts	Third	Pts		Winners	Score	Runners-up
2000	Universidad de Chile	61	Cobreloa	52	Colo Colo	49		Universidad de Chile	2-1	Santiago Morning
2001	Santiago Wanderers	66	Universidad Católica	60	Universidad de Chile	57		Tournament discontinued		

RECENT LEAGUE RECORD (2002-2006)

	Apertura				Clausura		
Year	Champions	Score	Runners-up		Winners	Score	Runners-up
2002	Universidad Católica	1-1 4-0	Rangers		Colo Colo	2-0 3-2	Universidad Católica
2003	Cobreloa	0-0 4-0	Colo Colo		Cobreloa	2-2 2-1	Colo Colo
2004	Universidad de Chile	0-0 1-1 4-2p	Cobreloa		Cobreloa	3-1 0-0	Unión Española
2005	Unión Española	1-0 3-2	Coquimbo Unido		Universidad Católica	1-0 1-2 5-4p	Universidad de Chile
2006	Colo Colo	2-1 0-1 4-2p	Universidad de Chile		Colo Colo	3-0 3-2	Audax Italiano
2007	Colo Colo	†	Universidad Católica		Colo Colo	1-0 3-0	Universidad Concepción
2008	Everton	0-2 3-0	Colo Colo				

† Played on a league basis with no play-offs

CHILE 2007
PRIMERA DIVISION CLAUSURA

Grupo 1
	Pl	W	D	L	F	A	Pts
Colo Colo †	20	11	6	3	40	21	39
Cobresal †	20	8	8	4	31	23	32
Palestino	20	7	5	8	27	23	26
Deportes La Serena	20	6	4	10	25	33	22
Santiago Wanderers	20	4	5	11	15	43	17

Grupo 2
	Pl	W	D	L	F	A	Pts
Univ. de Concepción †	20	9	8	3	30	19	35
Universidad Católica †	20	10	4	6	33	21	34
Deportes Melipilla	20	7	6	7	32	34	27
Deportes Concepción	20	7	4	9	32	41	25
Unión Española	20	4	5	11	26	36	17

Grupo 3
	Pl	W	D	L	F	A	Pts
Audax Italiano †	20	14	5	1	47	20	47
Universidad de Chile †	20	13	6	1	42	21	45
Cobreloa †	20	8	7	5	35	29	31
Puerto Montt	20	5	6	9	18	22	21
Everton	20	3	4	13	20	36	13

Grupo 4
	Pl	W	D	L	F	A	Pts
O'Higgins †	20	9	7	4	28	23	34
Nublense	20	7	5	8	32	38	26
Antofagasta	20	6	7	7	22	21	25
Huachipato	20	7	4	9	30	36	25
Lota Schwager	20	4	7	9	22	28	19
Coquimbo Unido	20	4	1	15	18	37	13

21/07/2007 - 25/11/2007 • † Qualified for the play-offs
Repechaje: **Cobreloa** 3-1 Nublense

CLAUSURA 2007 PLAY-OFFS

Quarter–finals			Semi–finals		Final		
Colo Colo	5	1					
O'Higgins *	0	1	Colo Colo *	2 1			
Cobresal *	2	1	Univ de Chile	0 0			
Univ de Chile	4	2			Colo Colo	1	3
Audax Italiano	2	1			Univ Concepción*	0	0
Cobreloa *	2	0	Audax Italiano	3 1			
Univ Católica *	5	0	UnivConcepción*	2 3			
Univ Concepción	3	2	* At home in the first leg				

Top scorer: Carlos Villanueva, Audax 20

CLAUSURA 2007 FINAL

1st leg. Municipal, Concepción, 20-12-2007, Att: 32 500, Ref: Pablo Pozo

Univ'dad de Concepción   0
Colo Colo   1   Bizcayzacú [48]

Concepción - Carmelo Vega - Osvaldo González, Fernando Solis, Felipe Muñoz - Pablo González, Roberto Ordenes, Juan José Rivera, Leonel Mena•, Gustavo Lorenzetti - Ricardo Parada, Ricardo Viveros (Emanuel Reinoso 64). Tr: Marcelo Barticciotto
Colo Colo - Cristián Muñoz - Miguel Riffo, Luis Mena, Jorge Carrasco• - Gonzalo Fierro, Rodrigo Meléndez• (Moisés Villarroel 43), Arturo Sanhueza, Roberto Cereceda, Giovanni Hernández, Gustavo Bizcayzacú (Rodolfo Moya 85), Eduardo Rubio (Rodrigo Millar 68). Tr: Claudio Borghi

2nd leg. Monumental, Santiago, 23-12-2007, Att: 45 000, Ref: Enrique Osses

Colo Colo   3   Fierro [18], Bizcayzacú [87], Bieler [90]
Univ'dad de Concepción   0

Colo Colo - Cristián Muñoz - Miguel Riffo•, Luis Mena, David Henríquez (Jorge Carrasco 62); Gonzalo Fierro•, Moisés Villarroel•, Arturo Sanhueza•, Roberto Cereceda•, Giovanni Hernández (Rodrigo Millar 85) - Gustavo Bizcayzacú, Eduardo Rubio• (Claudio Bieler 79). Tr: Claudio Borghi
Concepción - Federico Elduayén - Osvaldo González•, Fernando Solis, Felipe Muñoz; Pablo González, Roberto Ordenes, Juan José Ribera (Manuel Maciel 46), Mauricio Aros•, Gustavo Lorenzetti - Ricardo Parada (Ricardo Viveros 55), Emanuel Reinoso. Tr: Marcelo Barticciotto

CHILE 2007

PRIMERA DIVISION AGGREGATE TABLE

	Pl	W	D	L	F	A	Pts	Audax Italiano	Colo Colo	Univ Católica	Univ de Chile	Cobreloa	Huachipato	Cobresal	O'Higgins	Nublense	Dep Melipilla	Un Concepción	Palestino	Dep La Serena	Dep Conc'ion	Antofagasta	Unión Española	Everton	Puerto Montt	Lota Schwager	Santiago Wand	Coquimbo Un
Audax Italiano ††	40	27	10	3	86	40	91		1-0	1-3	1-1	2-0	1-0	2-1	2-0	5-0	1-1	0-0	2-1	2-1	2-0	0-0	2-0	4-2	1-1	3-2	7-1	2-1
Colo Colo †	40	25	11	4	87	37	86	1-4		2-1	2-1	2-1	1-4	0-4	2-6	2-3	1-4	1-2	2-1	0-4	0-3	0-2	1-2	2-3	0-2	2-3	1-2	1-2-1
Universidad Católica ††	40	24	8	8	69	35	80	1-2	0-1		0-0	2-1	2-0	2-0	4-1	3-0	4-1	1-1	2-0	2-1	2-3	0-0	1-0	1-3	1-3	1-2	0-1	0-3-0
Universidad de Chile	40	19	13	8	62	42	70	2-2	0-0	1-2		0-1	1-1	0-3	0-2	2-1	1-3	0-1	0-3	1-0	0-5	2-2	0-3	2-2	4-1	0-2	1-2	0-2-0
Cobreloa	40	18	12	10	79	52	66	3-3	2-3	2-3	1-1-1		3-1	2-5	0-5	0-1	2-5	1-0	0-3	2-2	0-3	0-7	1-3	2-2	1-2	0-2-1	1-0	5-1
Huachipato	40	19	8	13	65	57	65	1-1	2-2	0-0	2-3	3-0		1-0	0-0	1-1	2-3	2-0	2-1	1-3	0-3	1-2	1-3	0-3	1-2	2-1	0-2	1-1
Cobresal	40	17	13	10	62	44	64	1-3	2-1	1-1	4-1	1-0	2-1		2-0	2-2	0-2	2-1	1-2	1-5	0-1	1-1	0-3	1-1	0-6	0-3	1-3	1-0
O'Higgins	40	17	10	13	58	61	61	1-2	2-1	1-2	1-0	2-2	0-0	1-1		0-1	3-0	4-2	4-1	1-0	1-2	1-3	3-0	2-0	2-1	3-3	3-2	2-1
Nublense	40	15	13	12	63	69	58	3-2	0-2	3-3	1-3	2-2	1-1	1-1	1-1		1-1	2-0	1-0	3-4	2-3	4-0	3-2	3-1	1-2	1-3	2-2	1-2-1
Deportes Melipilla	40	15	10	15	67	68	55	1-3	1-3	2-1	3-2	1-2	4-2	0-2	0-2-0		3-2	1-2	3-3	1-1	1-2	1-3	0-2	1-0	0-3	0-4	0-0	
Univ. de Concepción	40	13	13	14	55	52	52	2-3	0-2	2-4	1-1	1-2	3-3	1-1	2-2	1-1		0-0	2-1	0-0	1-0	0-1	0-2	1-2	0-2	0-3	1-0	0-0
Palestino	40	12	13	15	54	53	49	0-2	0-1	1-1	1-1	1-1	1-1	1-1	1-1	0-1	1-1	1-0-1		3-2	2-0	4-1	1-2	1-0	1-2	2-6	0-3	2-2
Deportes La Serena	40	13	9	18	56	63	48	0-1	1-1	1-2	1-2	4-4	1-1	1-2	1-6	2-2	1-1	0-1-0		2-1	0-2-2	1-1	1-3	0-0	2-2	1-2	2-2	
Deportes Concepción	40	13	9	18	52	75	48	2-1	0-3	0-1	1-0	1-4	4-3	1-3	1-3	1-3	0-2	1-1		1-1	3-2	1-1	0-0-3	3-2	2-1	2-1	2-1	
Antofagasta	40	11	14	15	46	55	47	1-3	1-1	0-0	1-1	2-0	3-1	0-1	1-1	3-1	1-1	3-1	4-3	1		0-1	1-1	1-2	1-5	0-0	0-1	
Unión Española	40	12	9	19	55	61	45	2-2	2-1	3-2	1-1	1-1	2-1	0-1	2-2	2-1	2-0	2-1	1-1	0-1	5-0	0		1-0	4-1	4-0	1-1	1-2
Everton	40	9	12	19	44	63	39	1-2	0-3	1-0	1-3	1-1	3-0	0-2	0-1	2-2	2-2	1-1	1-0	1-1	3-0	1-0-0			1-0	4-2	1-1	3-1
Puerto Montt ‡	40	9	8	23	37	62	35	0-4	0-2	0-1	2-0	0-1	4-0	0-3	0-1	1-1	1-3	2-2	0-3	1-3	1-2	5-1	3		0-1	0-0	0-1	
Lota Schwager	40	6	13	21	50	80	31	1-2	0-1	0-1	1-2	3-1	1-2	0-2	1-1	1-1	4-2	4-3	3-2	2-1	1-1	1-1	2-0	0-0			1-1	1-3
Santiago Wanderers	40	8	9	23	39	76	30	1-2	0-4	1-0	0-2	1-1	0-1	1-1	2-3	0-2	3-2	0-3	1-2-3	2-0	0-0-0	1-0	1-2	1-1	1-5	2		3-1
Coquimbo Unido	40	8	3	29	36	77	27	1-1	0-3	0-2	0-1	2-1	1-3	1-2	1-2	0-1	0-4	0-1	2-3	0-1	3-1	2-1	1-3	0-1	2-0	0-1	0-3	

Matches in the shaded boxes were played in the Apertura • ‡ Relegation play-off • See *Almanack of World Football 2008* for Apertura 2007 details
† Qualified for Copa Libertadores as Apertura/Clausura winners • †† Qualified for Copa Libertadores on season record

CHILE 2007
PRIMERA B (2)

	Pl	W	D	L	F	A	Pts
Provincial Osorno	40	17	13	10	50	41	64
Rangers Talca §3	40	18	12	10	52	36	63
Santiago Morning ‡	40	16	15	9	54	44	63
Deportes Copiapó §5 ‡	40	18	11	11	53	33	60
Unión La Calera	40	16	9	15	49	42	57
San Luis	40	14	13	13	57	54	55
Municipal Iquique	40	12	15	13	33	41	51
Unión San Felipe	40	10	14	16	40	47	44
Curicó Unido	40	11	11	18	34	44	44
Fernández Vial §3	40	13	8	19	31	47	44
	40	10	9	21	31	55	39

24/02/2007 - 25/11/2007 • § = points deducted • ‡ play-off
Top scorer: Mario Núñez, Osorno 19

PROMOTION PLAY-OFFS

	Pl	W	D	L	F	A	Pts	SM	PM	DC
Santiago Morning	4	2	1	1	4	3	7		3-1	1-0
Puerto Montt	4	2	0	2	9	9	6	2-0		3-2
Deportes Copiapó	4	1	1	2	6	7	4	0-0	4-3	

2/12/2007 - 19/12/2007 • Santiago Morning promoted; Puerto Montt relegated

CHILE 2008
PRIMERA DIVISION APERTURA

Grupo 1	Pl	W	D	L	F	A	Pts
Audax Italiano †	19	11	1	7	35	25	34
Everton †	19	10	2	7	34	30	32
Cobresal	19	9	4	6	35	26	31
Huachipato	19	7	6	6	29	29	27
Unión Española	19	7	3	9	20	27	24

Grupo 2	Pl	W	D	L	F	A	Pts
O'Higgins †	19	10	6	3	30	17	36
Universidad de Chile †	19	9	3	7	28	23	30
Santiago Morning	19	9	3	7	35	42	30
Deportes La Serena	19	7	5	7	29	29	26
Palestino	19	7	3	9	28	27	24

Grupo 3	Pl	W	D	L	F	A	Pts
Colo Colo †	19	7	6	6	35	29	27
Cobreloa †	19	6	5	8	25	29	23
Antofagasta	19	4	5	10	16	29	17
Provincial Osorno	19	5	1	13	19	38	16
Deportes Melipilla	19	3	1	15	22	40	10

Grupo 4	Pl	W	D	L	F	A	Pts
Nublense †	19	12	5	2	28	41	41
Universidad Católica †	19	11	3	5	37	36	36
Rangers Talca	19	6	6	7	23	24	24
Univ. de Concepción	19	6	3	10	27	21	21
Deportes Concepción §6	19	7	3	9	33	18	18

25/01/2008 - 4/05/2008 • † Qualified for the play-offs
§ = points deducted
Repechaje: Cobresal 2-2 2-4p Cobreloa

APERTURA 2008 PLAY-OFFS

Quarter–finals		Semi–finals		Final	
Everton *	0 4				
Audax Italiano	3 1	Everton	3 1		
O'Higgins	2 1	Univ de Chile *	1 1		
Univ de Chile *	4 2			Everton	0 3
Nublense	0 2			Colo Colo *	2 0
Cobreloa *	0 1	Nublense	1 1		
Univ Católica	1 1	Colo Colo *	0 2		
Colo Colo *	3 1	* At home in the first leg			

Top scorer: Lucas Barrios (ARG), Colo Colo 19

APERTURA 2008 FINAL
1st leg. Monumental, Santiago, 28-05-2008, Att: 35 000, Ref: Pablo Pozo
Colo Colo	2	Barrios [86], Fierro [92+]
Everton	0	

Colo Colo - Cristián Muñoz - Luis Mena, Jorge Carrasco, Ricardo Rojas•, Domingo Salcedo - Arturo Sanhueza, Rodrigo Meléndez, Gonzalo Fierro•, Daniel González (Gustavo Biscayzacú 69) - Lucas Barrios, Rodolfo Moya. Tr: Fernando Astengo
Everton - Johnny Herrera - Fernando Saavedra, Cristián Oviedo, Adrián Rojas, Mauricio Arias••●58 - Juan Luis González, Marcos Velásquez•, Francisco Sánchez, Jaime Riveros• (Roberto Reyes 81) - Ezequiel Miralles, Cristián Canío•. Tr: Nelson Acosta

2nd leg. Sausalito, Viña del Mar, 3-06-2008, Att: 15 000, Ref: Rubén Selman
Everton	3	Miralles 2 [47 76], Riveros [72]
Colo Colo	0	

Everton - Johnny Herrera - Benjamín Ruiz, Cristián Oviedo, Adrián Rojas, Fernando Saavedra• - Leandro Delgado•, Juan González, Jaime Riveros (Cristián Uribe 88), Cristián Canio - Darío Gigena• (Marco Velásquez 82), Ezequiel Miralles (Francisco Sánchez 92+). Tr: Nelson Acosta
Colo Colo - Cristián Muñoz - Luis Mena (Gustavo Biscayzacú 79), Ricardo Rojas, Jorge Carrasco, José Salcedo (Miguel Riffo 90) - Arturo Sanhueza, Rodrigo Meléndez•, Gonzalo Fierro•, Daniel González (Cristóbal Jorquera 65) - Rodolfo Moya, Lucas Barrios. Tr: Fernando Astengo

CHN – CHINA PR

NATIONAL TEAM RECORD
JULY 10TH 2006 TO JULY 12TH 2010

PL	W	D	L	F	A	%
31	12	10	9	49	32	54.8

Chinese fans have become accustomed to mediocrity and disappointment in recent years, so when the national team was drawn against Australia, Iraq and Qatar in the 2010 FIFA World Cup qualifiers, there weren't many who expected them to progress. The appointment of Vladimir Petrovic, the Serb coach who achieved great success at Dalian Shide, failed to improve matters. While China remain difficult to break down, with veteran Li Weifeng at the back and England-based captain Zheng Zhi in midfield, the absence of a proven goalscorer counted against them. The Chinese lost at home to both Qatar and Australia, scored only three goals in six matches, and their only win, by a single strike in Melbourne, came after elimination was already certain. The successful hosting of the Women's World Cup in September 2007, along with the Beijing Olympics in August 2008, could not have provided a more stark contrast. On the domestic front, there was controversy just weeks before the start of the season, when the owner of Shanghai United, Zhu Jun, bought his more famous city rivals, Shenhua and merged the two under the Shenhua banner. However, his efforts to create a Shanghai superclub brought only mild fixture chaos, as the league kicked off with 15

INTERNATIONAL HONOURS
Qualified for the FIFA World Cup 2002
AFC Asian Women's Championship 1986 1989 1991 1993 1995 1997 1999
Asian U-19 Championship 1985   Asian U-17 Championship 1992 2004
AFC Asian Champions League Liaoning 1990

teams, some last-minute shuffling of players, and an unspectacular fourth-place finish. Shandong Luneng, shorn of the talismanic Zheng Zhi, could not recreate their consistency of recent years - a record 6-1 home defeat to Beijing in mid-August left them with too much to do and they finished third. Beijing Guoan looked like they might take the title to the capital for the first time in the professional era, until a 1-0 home defeat by their main rivals Changchun Yatai lost them the initiative. In the end Changchun, from Jilin province in the far north-east became somewhat unlikely champions. Promoted only in 2006, they relied strongly on imported talent, especially Guillaume Dah Zadi of the Ivory Coast, and Honduran Elvis Scott up front. But they have some good local players, notably young midfielders Du Zhenyu and Wang Dong, both of whom earned national call-ups. At the other end of the table Xiamen Lanshi, who were promoted with Changchun in 2006, finished bottom and promptly folded. Sadly, neither Changchun nor Beijing could make progress in the 2008 AFC Champions League. Beijing traded 1-0 wins with Kashima Antlers, but could not match the Japanese team's firepower against the group minnows while Changchun went through their group unbeaten, but still went out after failing to beat Adelaide United at home.

Football Association of the People's Republic of China (CFA)
Building A, Dong Jiu Da Sha, Xi Zhao Si Street, Chongwen District, Beijing 100061, China PR
Tel +86 10 59291031   Fax +86 10 59290309
info.footballchina@gmail.com   www.fa.org.cn
President: YUAN Weimin   General Secretary: XIE Yalong
Vice-President: XIE Yalong   Treasurer: NAN Yong   Media Officer: CHENG Wei
Men's Coach: TBC   Women's Coach: SHANG Ruihua
CFA formed: 1924   AFC: 1974   FIFA: 1931-58 & 1974
White shirts with red trimmings, White shorts, White socks or Red shirts with white trimmings, Red shorts, Red socks

RECENT INTERNATIONAL MATCHES PLAYED BY CHINA PR

2005	Opponents		Score	Venue	Comp	Scorers	Att	Referee
31-07	Korea Republic	D	1-1	Daejon	EAC	Sun Xiang 52	25 374	Nishimura JPN
3-08	Japan	D	2-2	Daejon	EAC	Li Jinyu 37, Zhang Yonghai 43	1 827	
7-08	Korea DPR	W	2-0	Daegu	EAC	Li Yan 14, Xie Hui 67		
12-10	Germany	L	0-1	Hamburg	Fr		48 734	Batista POR
13-11	Serbia & Montenegro	L	0-2	Nanjing	Fr		30 000	
2006								
12-02	Honduras	L	0-1	Guangzhou	Fr		20 000	Supian MAS
22-02	Palestine	W	2-0	Guangzhou	ACq	Du Wei 23, Li Weifeng 62	16 500	Kwon Jong Chul KOR
1-03	Iraq	L	1-2	Al Ain	ACq	Tao Wei 54	7 700	Al Saeedi UAE
3-06	Switzerland	L	1-4	Zurich	Fr	Dong Fangzhuo 91+	16 000	Stokes IRL
7-06	France	L	1-3	St Etienne	Fr	Zheng Zhi 69p	34 147	Davila ESP
10-08	Thailand	W	4-0	Qinhuangdao	Fr			
16-08	Singapore	W	1-0	Tianjin	ACq	Shao Jiayi 93+p	27 000	Ebrahim BHR
6-09	Singapore	D	0-0	Singapore	ACq		38 824	Shamsuzzaman BAN
11-10	Palestine	W	2-0	Amman	ACq	Mao Jianqing 27, Sun Xiang 64	3 000	Al Fadhli KUW
15-11	Iraq	D	1-1	Changsha	ACq	Han Peng 40		Mohd Salleh MAS
2007								
7-02	Kazakhstan	W	2-1	Suzhou	Fr	Han Peng 30, Li Jinyu 48		
24-03	Australia	L	0-2	Guangzhou	Fr		20 000	Wu Chaojue HKG
27-03	Uzbekistan	W	3-1	Macau	Fr	Han Peng 2 6 41, Karaev OG 65		
16-05	Thailand	L	0-1	Bangkok	Fr			
2-06	USA	L	1-4	San Jose	Fr	Zhang Yaokun 15	20 821	Guajardo MEX
10-07	Malaysia	W	5-1	Kuala Lumpur	ACr1	Han Peng 2 15 55, Shao Jiayi 36, Wang Dong 2 51 93+	20 000	Basma SYR
15-07	Iran	D	2-2	Kuala Lumpur	ACr1	Shao Jiayi 6, Mao Jianqing 33	5 938	Al Ghamdi KSA
18-07	Uzbekistan	L	0-3	Kuala Lumpur	ACr1		2 200	Al Fadhli KUW
21-10	Myanmar	W	7-0	Fushun	WCq	Qu Bo 2 17 79, Du Zhenyu 25, Yang Lin 55, Liu Jian 62, Li Jinyu 74, Li Weifeng 77	21 000	Ebrahim BHR
28-10	Myanmar	W	4-0	Kuala Lumpur	WCq	Wu Weian 13, Liu Jian 14, Zheng Bin 35, Zhang Yaokun 35p	200	Balideh QAT
2008								
10-01	UAE	D	0-0	Dubai	Fr			
20-01	Lebanon	D	0-0	Zhongshan	Fr			
27-01	Syria	W	2-1	Zhongshan	Fr	Qu Bo 64, Zhu Ting 90		
6-02	Iraq	D	1-1	Dubai	WCq	Zheng Zhi 75	11 000	Torky IRN
17-02	Korea Republic	L	2-3	Chongqing	EAC	Zhou Haibin 47, Liu Jian 61	25 000	Torky IRN
20-02	Japan	L	0-1	Chongqing	EAC		38 000	O Tae Song PRK
23-02	Korea DPR	W	3-1	Chongqing	EAC	Zhu Ting 45, Wang Dong 55, Hao Junmin 83	30 500	Torky IRN
15-03	Thailand	D	3-3	Kunming	Fr	Qu Bo 34, Han Peng 67, Zhu Ting 90		
26-03	Australia	D	0-0	Kunming	WCq		32 000	Al Saeedi UAE
16-04	Mexico	L	0-1	Seattle	Fr		56 416	Toledo USA
23-04	El Salvador	D	2-2	Los Angeles	Fr	Xiao Zhanbo 64p, Qu Bo 67		
25-05	Jordan	W	2-0	Kunshan City	Fr	Hao Junming 23p, Li Weifeng 47		
2-06	Qatar	D	0-0	Doha	WCq		9 000	Basma SYR
7-06	Qatar	L	0-1	Tianjin	WCq		50 000	Najm LIB
14-06	Iraq	L	1-2	Tianjin	WCq	Zhou Haibin 33	39 000	Bashir SIN
22-06	Australia	W	1-0	Sydney	WCq	Sun Xiang 11	70 054	Al Ghamdi KSA

Fr = Friendly match • EAC = East Asian Championship • AC = AFC Asian Cup • WC = FIFA World Cup
q = qualifier • r1 = first round group • qf = quarter-final • sf = semi-final • f = final

CHINA PR NATIONAL TEAM RECORDS AND RECORD SEQUENCES

Records				Sequence records				
Victory	19-0	GUM 2000	Wins	10	1919-1930	Clean sheets	8	1998-2000
Defeat	0-5	USA 1992	Defeats	5	1982, 2002	Goals scored	20	1915-1934
Player Caps	141	Li Ming	Undefeated	19	2003-2004	Without goal	5	2002
Player Goals	41	Hao Haidong	Without win	7	1996, 2000-2001	Goals against	9	1934-57, 2006-07

Includes records dating back to the Far-Eastern Games of 1913-1934

PEOPLE'S REPUBLIC OF CHINA; ZHONGHUA RENMIN GONGHEGUO

Capital	Beijing	Language	Mandarin, Cantonese, Shanghaiese	Independence	221 BC
Population	1313973713	Area	9 596 960 km²	% in cities	30%
GDP per cap	$5 000	Dailling code	+86	Internet	.cn	GMT +/−	+8

MEDALS TABLE

		Overall			League			Cup			Asia			City	Stadium	Cap'ty
		G	S	B	G	S	B	G	S	B	G	S	B			
1	Liaoning	11	9	5	8	6	4	2	2		1	1	1	Jinzhou	City	24 000
2	Dalian Shide	11	6	6	8		5	3	4		2	1		Dalian	Jinzhou	31 000
3	Beijing Guoan	9	6	12	5	3	11	4	3				1	Beijing	Fengtai	33 000
4	Shanghai Shenhua	7	12	4	4	10	4	3	2					Shanghai	Hongkou	33 060
5	August 1st (now defunct)	6	6	5	5	6	5							Beijing		
6	Shandong Luneng	6	5	2	2	3	2	4	2					Ji'nan	Provincial	43 700
7	Tianjin Teda	3	6	4	2	5	4	1	1					Tianjin	Teda	36 000
9	Guangdong Hongyuan	1	5	1	1	1	1		4					Guangzhou	Provincial	30 000
10	Shenzhen Shangqingyin (ex Kingway)	1	1	1	1	1							1	Shenzhen	City	33 000
11	Changchun Yatai	1			1									Changchun	Changchun	38 500
	Chongqing Lifan	1						1						Chongqing	Yanghe	58 680
	Qingdao Zhongneng	1						1						Qingdao	Tiantai	60 000
20	Guangzhou Yiyao	3	1		2	1		1						Guangzhou	Yuexiushan	35 000
21	Sichuan Guancheng (now defunct)	1	2			2		1						Chengdu	Sichuan	40 000
23	Shaanxi Baorong (ex Xi'an Chanba)	1	1		1	1								Xi'an	Coca-Cola	30 000
24	Changsha Ginde (ex Shenyang)	1			1									Changsha	He Long	55 000

The table only includes teams that have been active in recent years. Teams such as North East China, who won two championships in the 1950s, have not been included

RECENT LEAGUE AND CUP RECORD

	Championship						FA Cup		
Year	Champions	Pts	Runners-up	Pts	Third	Pts	Winners	Score	Runners-up
1994	Dalian	33	Guangzhou	27	Shanghai Shenhua	26	Tournament not held		
1995	Shanghai Shenhua	46	Beijing	42	Dalian	42	Jinan	2-0	Shanghai Shenhua
1996	Dalian	46	Shanghai Shenhua	39	August 1st	35	Beijing	4-1	Jinan
1997	Dalian	51	Shanghai Shenhua	40	Beijing	34	Beijing	2-1	Shanghai Shenhua
1998	Dalian	62	Shanghai Shenhua	45	Beijing	43	Shanghai Shenhua	2-1 2-1	Liaoning
1999	Shandong	48	Liaoning	47	Sichuan	45	Shandong	2-1 2-1	Dalian
2000	Dalian	56	Shanghai Shenhua	50	Sichuan	44	Chongqing	0-1 4-1	Beijing
2001	Dalian	53	Shanghai Shenhua	48	Liaoning	48	Dalian	1-0 2-1	Beijing
2002	Dalian	57	Shenzhen	52	Beijing	52	Qingdao	1-3 2-0	Liaoning
2003	Shanghai Shenhua	55	Shanghai Int'l	54	Dalian	53	Beijing	3-0	Dalian
2004	Shenzhen	42	Shandong	36	Shanghai Int'l	32	Shandong	2-1	Sichuan
2005	Dalian	65	Shanghai Shenhua	53	Shandong	52	Dalian	1-0	Shandong
2006	Shandong	69	Shanghai Shenhua	52	Beijing Hyundai	49	Shandong	2-0	Dalian Shide
2007	Changchun Yatai	55	Beijing Guoan	54	Shandong	48	Tournament not held		

CHINA PR 2007

CSL (CHINESE SUPER LEAGUE)

	Pl	W	D	L	F	A	Pts	Changchun	Beijing	Shandong	Shanghai	Dalian	Tianjin	Wuhan	Qingdao	Liaoning	Changsha	Zhejiang	Henan	Shaanxi	Shenzhen	Xiamen
Changchun Yatai †	28	16	7	5	48	25	55		0-0	0-0	4-1	1-2	1-0	4-0	1-1	3-2	1-0	1-1	3-1	1-0	4-0	2-1
Beijing Guoan †	28	15	9	4	45	19	54	0-1		1-0	2-3	3-1	2-0	4-1	3-0	3-0	0-0	1-0	0-0	1-1	1-1	4-1
Shandong Luneng T.	28	14	6	8	53	29	48	1-1	1-6		2-1	1-1	2-0	2-0	3-0	5-2	4-2	1-1	1-2	3-0	5-0	4-0
Shanghai Shenhua	28	12	10	6	35	29	46	2-2	0-2	1-0		1-0	3-2	3-1	3-2	1-1	1-1	1-1	1-1	1-1	4-1	1-0
Dalian Shide	28	11	11	6	36	31	44	1-0	1-1	3-2	2-1		2-2	0-0	3-2	0-0	1-3		3-1	1-1	1-1	0-0
Tianjin Teda	28	12	8	8	31	22	44	0-1	1-0	1-0	0-0	0-1		2-0	4-0	1-0	2-0	1-0	0-0	1-0	2-0	2-0
Wuhan Guanggu	28	11	7	10	29	31	40	3-1	0-0	3-2	0-0	1-0	1-1		1-0	0-0	3-0	2-0	2-1	1-0		1-1
Qingdao Zhongneng	28	10	6	12	36	42	36	1-2	3-1	0-4	3-0	1-2	1-0	1-0		2-0	0-1	2-1	2-1	1-1	2-0	2-0
Liaoning	28	9	8	11	26	36	35	1-3	2-3	2-1	1-0	2-1	0-0	1-2	0-0		1-0	0-0	0-0	1-0	1-1	2-1
Changsha Ginde	28	8	10	10	17	24	34	0-0	0-2	0-2	1-1	0-1	1-1	1-0	2-1	1-0		3-2	2-1	0-0	2-0	0-0
Zhejiang Lucheng	28	6	10	12	25	35	28	2-1	0-0	1-3	0-0	1-1	0-1	1-3	1-3	1-1	0-0		2-0	1-0	1-1	2-1
Henan Jianye	28	5	12	11	20	28	27	3-2	1-2	1-1	0-0	2-0	0-0	0-0	3-0	3-1	0-1	0-1		1-1	0-0	2-0
Shaanxi Baorong	28	4	14	10	24	29	26	4-1	0-0	0-0	0-2	2-2	4-2	2-0	1-3	4-1	0-0	2-0	0-0		1-1	1-2
Shenzhen Shangqingyin	28	5	10	13	21	42	25	1-4	0-1	0-1	0-1	0-2	1-1	2-1	2-2	1-2	0-0	1-0	2-0	0-0		1-1
Xiamen Lanshi	28	4	8	16	22	46	20	1-3	1-2	0-2	0-1	2-2	1-2	2-1	2-2	1-3	0-0	2-1	0-0	1-0	1-3	

3/03/2007 - 14/11/2007 • † Qualified for the AFC Champions League • Top scorers: Li Jinyu, Shandong 15; Han Peng, Shandong 13; Elvis Scott (HON), Changchun 12; Guillaume Dah Zadi (CIV), Changchun 10; Jorge Tiago (BRA), Beijing 10

CHINA PR 2007

CHINA LEAGUE (2)

	Pl	W	D	L	F	A	Pts	Guangzhou	Chengdu	Jiangsu	Chongqing	August 1st	Yanbian	Qingdao	Shanghai	Nanjing	Beijing Y	Beijing PS	Harbin	Hohhot
Guangzhou Yiyao	24	19	4	1	65	15	61		0-0	2-1	2-1	3-0	3-1	6-1	4-0	5-1	3-0	4-2	4-0	**7-0**
Chengdu Blades	24	16	7	1	54	14	55	1-2		0-0	1-1	1-1	4-0	3-0	4-2	6-1	2-0	5-1	6-0	**3-0**
Jiangsu Shuntian	24	14	6	4	41	21	48	1-0	1-1		3-2	4-0	3-2	3-0	3-1	1-1	0-1	4-2	1-0	1-0
Chongqing Lifan	24	13	5	6	34	22	44	1-3	0-1	0-0		3-1	4-3	3-2	2-0	1-0	0-0	2-0	1-0	**3-0**
Nanchang August 1st	24	10	6	8	26	26	36	2-1	0-1	2-1	1-0		1-1	0-0	2-0	1-0	0-2	2-1	2-0	2-0
Yanbian	24	9	6	9	36	35	33	0-2	1-2	1-2	1-0	1-1		4-1	1-1	3-2	3-1	3-1	1-1	**3-0**
Qingdao Hailifeng	24	10	3	11	27	36	33	0-1	0-2	1-3	0-1	3-1	1-0		0-0	3-1	1-0	2-1	1-0	2-0
Shanghai Stars	24	7	5	12	26	37	26	0-1	1-3	1-4	1-3	2-0	1-2	2-0		3-1	3-2	1-2	0-0	1-1
Nanjing Yoyo	24	6	6	12	26	39	24	1-4	0-0	2-3	1-2	0-0	1-0	3-2	3-1		2-0	0-1	2-3	**3-0**
Beijing Yanjiesheng	24	6	6	12	21	31	24	2-6	0-2	0-2	1-1	2-1	2-1	0-1	0-0	1-1		1-1	3-1	2-1
Beijing Pat. Students	24	5	7	12	27	40	22	3-3	1-1	0-1	0-0	1-4	1-1	1-2	2-0	0-0	2-0		0-0	**3-0**
Harbin Yiteng	24	4	7	13	18	36	19	1-1	1-3	1-1	0-1	0-1	2-3	1-2	0-1	0-0	1-1	1-0		**3-0**
Hohhot §7	24	1	4	19	8	57	0	**0-3**	1-2	**0-3**	1-1	**0-3**	0-0	**0-3**	**0-3**	0-0	**0-3**	3-1	1-2	

31/03/2007 - 27/10/2007 • Top scorer: Luis Ramirez (HON), Guangzhou 19 • Shanxi Luhu moved to Hohhot • § = points deducted • Matches in bold were awarded

CHINA PR 2007 — YIJIDUI (3)

Northern Group

	Pl	W	D	L	F	A	Pts
Shanghai Dongya †	14	9	3	2	30	12	30
Xinjiang Ticai †	14	8	4	2	27	15	28
Tianjin Dongli †	14	7	3	4	22	15	24
Tianjin Locomotive †	14	7	2	5	21	11	23
Hohhot Binhai	14	4	6	4	19	19	18
Hangzhou Sanchao	14	5	3	6	18	20	18
Zhenjiang Zhong'an	14	3	3	8	12	23	12
Qingdao Liming	14	0	2	12	7	41	2

Southern Group

	Pl	W	D	L	F	A	Pts
Sichuan †	12	8	3	1	22	7	27
Anhui Jiufang †	12	7	2	3	17	11	23
Hunan Xiangtao †	12	4	4	4	8	6	16
Guangxi Tianji †	12	4	4	4	14	14	16
Ningbo Huaao	12	4	3	5	11	14	15
Suzhou Qupushi	12	4	1	7	7	17	13
Guangzhou Rizhiquan	12	2	1	9	11	21	7

5/05/2007 - 29/09/2007 • † Qualified for the play-offs

CHINA PR 2007 — YIJIDUI PLAY-OFFS

Quarter-finals		Semi-finals		Final	
Shanghai	Bye				
		Shanghai	1 2		
Three Gorges U		Anhui	1 1		
Anhui				Shanghai	2
Guangxi				Sichuan	1
Shandong Univ		Guangxi	0 1		
		Sichuan	4 3		
Sichuan	Bye				

Third Place: Anhui 2-1 3-1 Guangxi

Shanghai Dongya, Sichuan and Anhui Jiufang promoted • First round results: Xinjiang Ticai 0-1 0-1 **Guanxi Tianji**; Hunan Xiangtao1-0 0-2 **Shandong University**; Tianjin Dongli 1-0 1-3 **Three Gorges University**; Anhui Jiufang 1-0 1-1 Tianjin L'tive

CIV – COTE D'IVOIRE

NATIONAL TEAM RECORD
JULY 10TH 2006 TO JULY 12TH 2010

PL	W	D	L	F	A	%
26	14	5	7	52	21	63.5

FIFA/COCA-COLA WORLD RANKING

1993	1994	1995	1996	1997	1998	1999	2000	2001	2002	2003	2004	2005	2006	2007
33	25	20	51	52	44	53	51	44	64	70	40	42	18	37

High	
18	01/07

2007–2008											
08/07	09/07	10/07	11/07	12/07	01/08	02/08	03/08	04/08	05/08	06/08	07/08
28	27	32	37	37	38	24	23	22	22	25	28

Low	
75	05/04

Cote d'Ivoire went into the 2008 Africa Nations Cup finals at the start of the year as one of the pre-tournament favourites and quickly set about confirming the pundits' opinions. But the side suffered a spectacular crash in the semifinals against Egypt and ended outside of the medals. Given the star quality of their squad, this was a golden opportunity missed. The team romped through the first round group phase in Ghana despite the tragedy that afflicted their coach Uli Stielike on the eve of the tournament. He had to pull out after the death of his son and was replaced by Olympic team coach Gerard Gili. The qualification of the under-23 team for the Beijing Games - a first for the

INTERNATIONAL HONOURS
Qualified for the FIFA World Cup finals 2006   African Cup of Nations 1992   CAF African Champions League ASEC Mimosas 1998

Ivorians - turned out to be the unexpected highlight of the season. Stielike returned to the helm of the national side in March but only for a single game before being replaced by Vahid Halilhodzic. A combination of injuries and post-season lethargy, however, meant the Elephants made a ponderous, albeit unbeaten, start to the FIFA 2010 World Cup qualifiers. ASEC Abidjan set a new landmark in the African Champions League, reaching the group phase for a ninth time in 12 years - a remarkable record of consistency. But their long standing dominance of Ligue 1 came to an end with regional rivals Africa Sports winning their first title after seven successive championships for ASEC.

THE FIFA BIG COUNT OF 2006

	Male	Female		Total
Number of players	801 700	0	Referees and Assistant Referees	600
Professionals	100		Admin, Coaches, Technical, Medical	3 900
Amateurs 18+	12 100		Number of clubs	220
Youth under 18	11 000		Number of teams	1 320
Unregistered	82 500		Clubs with women's teams	0
Total players	801 700		Players as % of population	4.54%

Fédération Ivoirienne de Football (FIF)
01 Case postale 1202, Abidjan 01, Côte d'Ivoire
Tel +225 21240027   Fax +225 21259552
fifci@aviso.ci   www.fif.ci
President: ANOUMA Jacques   General Secretary: OUATTARA Hego
Vice-President: KESSE Feh Lambert   Treasurer: ABINAN Pascal   Media Officer: None
Men's Coach: HALILHODZIC Vahid   Women's Coach: KOUDOUGNON Adelaide
FIF formed: 1960   CAF: 1960   FIFA: 1960
Orange shirts with white trimmings, White shorts, Green socks

RECENT INTERNATIONAL MATCHES PLAYED BY COTE D'IVOIRE

2006	Opponents	Score		Venue	Comp	Scorers	Att	Referee
10-06	Argentina	L	1-2	Hamburg	WCr1	Drogba 82	49 480	De Bleeckere BEL
16-06	Netherlands	L	1-2	Stuttgart	WCr1	Bakary Kone 38	52 000	Ruiz COL
21-06	Serbia & Montenegro	W	3-2	Munich	WCr1	Dindane 2 37p 67, Kalou 86p	66 000	Rodriguez MEX
16-08	Senegal	L	0-1	Tours	Fr		4 000	Husset FRA
8-10	Gabon	W	5-0	Abidjan	CNq	Kolo Toure 11, Kone 3 23 56 68, Dindane 32		Buenkadila COD
15-11	Sweden	W	1-0	Le Mans	Fr	Drogba 37	3 844	Fautrel FRA
2007								
6-02	Guinea	W	1-0	Rouen	Fr	Drogba 37		
21-03	Mauritius	W	3-0	Bellevue	Fr	Kalou.S 59, Gohouri 2 75 89		
25-03	Madagascar	W	3-0	Antananarivo	CNq	Gohouri 28, Dindane 35, Diane 81		Maillet SEY
3-06	Madagascar	W	5-0	Bouake	CNq	Kalou.S 18, Kone 2 37 82, Yaya Toure 48, Drogba 87		Louzaya CGO
22-08	Egypt	D	0-0	Paris	Fr			
8-09	Gabon	D	0-0	Libreville	CNq			Damon RSA
17-10	Austria	L	2-3	Innsbruck	Fr	Drogba 2 53 89p	30 000	Kuipers NED
17-11	Angola	L	1-2	Melun	Fr	Gilberto OG 63		
21-11	Qatar	W	6-1	Doha	Fr	Diane 2 14 27, Arouna Kone 2 17 88, OG 52, Kalou.S 67		
2008								
12-01	Kuwait	W	2-0	Kuwait City	Fr	Kalou.S 28, Drogba 34		
21-01	Nigeria	W	1-0	Sekondi	CNr1	Kalou.S 66	20 000	Benouza MAR
25-01	Benin	W	4-1	Sekondi	CNr1	Drogba 40, Yaya Toure 44, Keita 52, Dindane 62		Marange ZIM
29-01	Mali	W	3-0	Accra	CNr1	Drogba 9, Zoro 54, Sanogo 85		Maillet SEY
3-02	Guinea	W	5-0	Sekondi	CNqf	Keita 25, Drogba 70, Kalou.S 2 73 81, Bakary Kone 86		Haimoudi ALG
7-02	Egypt	L	1-4	Kumasi	CNsf	Keita 63		Maillet SEY
9-02	Ghana	L	2-4	Kumasi	CN3p	Sanogo 2 24 32		Damon RSA
26-03	Tunisia	L	0-2	Bondoufle	Fr			
22-05	Paraguay	D	1-1	Yokohama	Fr	Kandia Traore 73	5 197	Matsumura JPN
24-05	Japan	L	0-1	Toyota	Fr		40 710	Duarte POR
1-06	Mozambique	W	1-0	Abidjan	WCq	Sekou Cisse 75	20 000	Auda EGY
8-06	Madagascar	D	0-0	Antananarivo	WCq			Labrosse SEY
14-06	Botswana	D	1-1	Gaborone	WCq	Meite 65	21 400	Ssegonga UGA
22-06	Botswana	W	4-0	Abidjan	WCq	Sanogo 16, Zokora 22, Sekou Cisse 2 46 70	15 000	Bennaceur TUN

Fr = Friendly match • CN = African Cup of Nations • WC = FIFA World Cup
q = qualifier • r1 = first round group • qf = quarter-final • sf = semi-final • f = final

COTE D'IVOIRE NATIONAL TEAM PLAYERS

	Player		Club	Date of Birth		Player		Club	Date of Birth
1	Boubacar Barry	GK	Lokeren BEL	30 12 1979	12	Abdoulaye Meite	DF	Bolton Wanderers ENG	6 10 1980
2	Constant Djakpa	DF	Pandurii Targu Jiu ROU	17 10 1986	13	Christian Koffi Ndri	MF	Le Mans FRA	4 06 1983
3	Arthur Boka	DF	VfB Stuttgart GER	2 04 1983	14	Bakary Kone	FW	Nice FRA	17 09 1981
4	Kolo Toure	DF	Arsenal ENG	19 03 1981	15	Aruna Dindane	FW	RC Lens FRA	26 11 1983
5	Didier Zokora	MF	Tottenham ENG	14 12 1980	16	Stephan Loboue	GK	Greuther Furth GER	23 08 1981
6	Steve Gohouri	DF	Bor. M'gladbach GER	8 02 1981	17	Siaka Tiene	MF	St Etienne FRA	22 02 1982
7	Emerse Fae	MF	Reading ENG	24 01 1984	18	Abdelkader Keita	MF	Olympique Lyonnais FRA	6 08 1981
8	Salomon Kalou	FW	Chelsea ENG	5 08 1985	19	Gneri Yaya Toure	MF	Barcelona ESP	13 05 1983
9	Arouna Kone	FW	Sevilla ESP	11 11 1983	20	Boubacar Sanogo	FW	Werder Bremen GER	17 12 1982
10	Gervais Yao Kouassi	FW	Le Mans FRA	27 05 1987	21	Emmanuel Eboue	DF	Arsenal ENG	4 06 1983
11	Didier Drogba	FW	Chelsea ENG	11 03 1978	22	Marc Zoro	DF	Benfica POR	27 12 1983
	Côte d'Ivoire's squad for the 2008 CAF Africa Cup of Nations				23	Tiasse Kone	GK	Africa Sports CIV	11 11 1981

COTE D'IVOIRE NATIONAL TEAM RECORDS AND RECORD SEQUENCES

Records			Sequence records					
Victory	6-0	Four times	Wins	7	1984	Clean sheets	9	1991
Defeat	2-6	GHA 1971	Defeats	6	1977-1979	Goals scored	15	1983-1984
Player Caps	72	Didier Zokora	Undefeated	16	1987-1989	Without goal	3	1985, 1989
Player Goals	33	Didier Drogba	Without win	7	1985	Goals against	11	1980-1983

REPUBLIC OF CÔTE D'IVOIRE; REPUBLIQUE DE CÔTE D'IVOIRE

Capital	Yamoussoukro	Language	French	Independence	1960
Population	17 654 843	Area	322 460 km²	% in cities	44%
GDP per cap	$1 400	Dailling code	+225	Internet .ci	GMT +/- 0

MEDALS TABLE

		Overall			Lge	Cup			Africa			City	Stadium	Cap'ty	DoF
		G	S	B	G	G	S	G	S	B					
1	ASEC Mimosas	38	4	6	22	15	3	1	1	6	Abidjan	Houphouët-Boigny	45 000	1948
2	Africa Sports National	30	10	2	15	13	7	2	3	2	Abidjan	Houphouët-Boigny	45 000	1936
3	Stade d'Abidjan	11	7	1	5	5	7	1		1	Abidjan	Municipal	9 000	1936
4	Stella Club d'Adjamé	6	6		3	2	5	1	1		Abidjan	Parc des Sports	10 000	1936
5	Onze Freres	2			2						Grand-Bassam	Leon Robert	10 000	
6	Sporting Club de Gagnoa	1	7		1		7				Gagnoa	Victor-Biaka-Boda	12 000	
7	ASC Bouaké	1	2			1	2				Bouaké	Bouaké	15 000	
8	SCR Alliance Bouaké	1	1			1	1				Bouaké	Bouaké	15 000	
	Réveil Club de Daloa	1	1			1	1				Daloa	Municipal	4 000	
	Societé Omnisport de l'Armée	1	1			1	1				Abidjan	Robert-Champroux	20 000	
	Issia Wazi FC	1	1			1	1				Gagnoa	Victor-Biaka-Boda	12 000	
12	ASI Abengourou	1				1					Abengourou	Abengourou	12 000	
	CO Bouaflé	1				1					Bouaflé	Bouaflé	4 000	
	ASC Espoir de Man	1				1					Man	Leon Robert	12 000	
	Jeunesse Club d'Abidjan	1				1					Abidjan	Robert-Champroux	20 000	
16	Séwé Sport de San Pedro		2				2				San Pedro	Auguste-Demise	8 000	

RECENT LEAGUE AND CUP RECORD

Championship						Cup		
Year	Champions	Pts	Runners-up	Pts	Third	Pts	Winners	Score	Runners-up
1995	ASEC Mimosas	23	SO Armée	18	Africa Sports	15	ASEC Mimosas	2-0	Stade Abidjan
1996	Africa Sports						SO Armée	0-0 10-9p	Africa Sports
1997	ASEC Mimosas	26	SO Armée	15	Africa Sports	12	ASEC Mimosas	4-0	Africa Sports
1998	ASEC Mimosas	24	FC Man	16	Africa Sports	13	Africa Sports	3-0	Stade Abidjan
1999	Africa Sports	28	ASEC Mimosas	23	Stade Abidjan	16	ASEC Mimosas	5-0	Séwé San Pedro
2000	ASEC Mimosas	21	Sabé Bouna	16	Africa Sports	16	Stade Abidjan	2-1	ASEC Mimosas
2001	ASEC Mimosas	55	Satellite FC	45	Africa Sports	41	Alliance Bouaké	2-0	ASC Bouaké
2002	ASEC Mimosas	22	Jeunesse Abidjan	18	Satellite FC	16	Africa Sports	2-0	Renaissance
2003	ASEC Mimosas	21	Africa Sports	19	Stella Adjamé	15	ASEC Mimosas	1-1 4-2p	Africa Sports
2004	ASEC Mimosas	68	Africa Sport	48	Stella Adjamé	43	CO Bouaflé	2-1	Stade Abidjan
2005	ASEC Mimosas	66	Africa Sport	55	Jeunesse Abidjan	45	ASEC Mimosas	1-0	Séwé San Pedro
2006	ASEC Mimosas	56	Séwé San Pedro	36	Denguélé Odienné	44	Issia Wazi	1-0	SO Armée
2007	Africa Sports	56	ASEC Mimosas	52	Entente Bingerville	38	ASEC Mimosas	3-0	Issia Wazi

COTE D'IVOIRE 2007

LIGUE 1 ORANGE

	Pl	W	D	L	F	A	Pts	Africa Sports	ASEC	Bingerville	Denguélé	Daloa	SOA	Sabé	JCA	Stella	Stade	Issia Wazi	Gagnoa	Séwé	Lagoké
Africa Sports †	26	16	8	2	36	12	56		0-2	1-1	2-1	2-0	0-0	1-0	3-1	0-0	3-0	2-0	2-0	2-0	2-0
ASEC Mimosas †	26	14	10	2	38	17	52	1-0		3-0	1-1	2-1	2-3	1-1	1-1	2-2	1-0	1-0	1-0	2-1	2-0
Entente Bingerville ‡	26	11	5	10	33	28	38	1-2	1-3		2-0	0-1	3-2	1-2	1-1	0-0	2-1	0-0	2-0	2-0	2-0
Denguélé Odienné	26	9	9	8	23	23	36	1-1	0-0	2-2		1-0	1-0	1-0	1-3	0-1	2-1	2-0	2-3	0-3	0-0
Réveil Daloa	26	9	9	8	22	25	36	0-0	0-2	2-1	1-0		0-0	1-0	3-1	0-0	0-0	2-1	1-1	0-1	0-0
SO Armée	26	9	8	9	29	26	35	1-1	1-0	1-2	1-0	1-1		1-1	5-1	0-1	1-2	1-2	0-2	2-0	1-0
Sabé Sports Bouna	26	9	8	9	24	21	35	0-1	1-1	1-0	0-1	2-0	0-2		3-1	0-2	0-0	1-0	4-0	1-2	1-0
Jeunesse Abidjan	26	8	10	8	27	32	34	1-1	1-2	0-2	1-1	0-0	2-0	0-0		2-0	2-1	0-1	1-0	2-1	1-0
Stella Adjamé	26	7	11	8	24	27	32	0-1	1-1	0-3	0-2	1-1	1-2	0-1	1-1		0-1	0-0	2-1	2-1	3-1
Stade Abidjan	26	9	5	12	24	28	32	1-1	0-0	2-1	0-2	4-1	0-2	0-1	2-0	2-0		0-2	3-1	0-1	2-1
Issia Wazi	26	7	10	9	23	28	31	1-4	0-2	2-1	0-0	0-0	0-1	3-1	1-1	2-2	1-0		3-3	0-1	2-1
Sporting Gagnoa	26	6	10	10	28	35	28	0-1	1-1	0-1	1-1	3-1	1-1	1-1	1-1	1-1	2-0	1-1		2-1	0-1
Séwé San Pedro	26	7	7	12	24	31	28	0-2	1-1	2-1	0-0	1-3	2-0	0-0	1-2	1-1	0-1	1-1	1-1		1-1
Lagoké FC	26	2	8	16	13	35	14	0-1	0-3	0-1	0-1	1-2	1-1	1-1	0-0	1-3	1-1	0-0	1-2	2-1	

24/02/2007 - 29/11/2007 • † Qualified for the CAF Champions League • ‡ Qualified for the CAF Confederation Cup

COTE D'IVOIRE 2007
2ÈME DIVISION (2) – ABIDJAN

	Pl	W	D	L	F	A	Pts
USC Bassam	22	17	5	0	34	10	56
Athletic Adjamé	22	12	8	2	32	19	44
RC Koumassi	22	10	7	5	24	16	37
Ecole Yéo Martial	22	9	6	7	21	13	33
Man FC	22	8	8	6	19	16	32
Etoile du Sanwi	22	9	3	10	21	23	30
US Koumassi	22	7	8	7	20	22	29
Oryx Yopougon	22	8	4	10	17	24	28
CO Korhogo	22	4	9	9	18	31	21
FC Adzopé	22	4	6	12	16	34	18
VAC Bouaké	22	3	6	13	9	24	15
Espoir Koumassi	22	1	10	11	8	22	13

2/03/2007 - 22/09/2007

COTE D'IVOIRE 2007
2ÈME DIVISION (2) – INTERIOR

	Pl	W	D	L	F	A	Pts
ASC Ouragahio	22	16	3	3	31	11	51
USF Agnibilékrou	22	13	3	6	33	19	42
FC Hiré	22	12	5	5	27	17	41
ASI Abengourou	22	10	5	7	21	14	35
Lakota	22	9	5	8	27	28	32
US Yamassoukro	22	8	5	9	19	23	29
CO Bouaflé	22	8	3	11	28	29	27
Renaissance Bettié	22	8	3	11	18	26	27
Sacraboutou Bondoukou	22	6	5	11	19	26	23
Ban Danané	22	5	7	10	18	22	22
N'Zi Dimbokro	22	5	7	10	21	36	22
AC Sinfra	22	2	9	11	8	25	15

2/03/2007 - 22/09/2007

Championship Final: **USC Bassam** 2-1 ASC Ouragahio

COUPE NATIONALE 2007

Round of 16

ASEC Mimosas	4	
Séwé San Pedro	0	
Entente Bingerville	0	
Ecole Yéo Martial	1	
Club Domoraud	3	
Satellite FC	0	
Stade Abidjan	2 3p	
Réveil Daloa	2 4p	
Denguélé Odienné	2	
Africa Sports	0	
Mala Yezimala	1	
Sporting Gagnoa	3	
Jeunesse Abidjan	2	
Sacraboutou Bondoukou	0	
Issia Wazi	Bye	

Quarter-finals

ASEC Mimosas	1 4p
Ecole Yéo Martial	1 2p
Club Domoraud	1
Réveil Daloa	2
Denguélé Odienné	2
Sporting Gagnoa	0
Jeunesse Abidjan	0
Issia Wazi	3

Semi-finals

ASEC Mimosas	2
Réveil Daloa	1
Denguélé Odienné	0 8p
Issia Wazi	0 9p

Final

ASEC Mimosas	3
Issia Wazi ‡	0

CUP FINAL

Stade Robert Champroux, Abidjan
30-09-2008

Scorer - Serge Déblé 3 92 110 119

‡ Qualified for the CAF Confederation Cup

CMR – CAMEROON

NATIONAL TEAM RECORD
JULY 10TH 2006 TO JULY 12TH 2010

PL	W	D	L	F	A	%
19	12	3	4	37	18	71.1

FIFA/COCA-COLA WORLD RANKING

1993	1994	1995	1996	1997	1998	1999	2000	2001	2002	2003	2004	2005	2006	2007		High	
23	31	37	56	53	41	58	39	38	16	14	23	23	11	24		11	01/07

					2007–2008							Low	
08/07	09/07	10/07	11/07	12/07	01/08	02/08	03/08	04/08	05/08	06/08	07/08	62	04/97
16	25	23	24	24	25	17	17	17	16	13	13		

The resilience of Cameroon's national team has been one of its trademarks and that showed in abundance at the African Nations Cup finals in Ghana. Despite conceding four goals in their first game, the Indomitable Lions bounced back to reach the final, where they lost to Egypt again. It was a satisfying recovery for a team arguably now in a major state of transition. The likes of Rigobert Song, the only black African footballer to pass 100 international caps, Samuel Eto'o and Geremi Fotso Njitap, remain the backbone of team but the Nations Cup brought to the fore a new generation of stars, including Song's nephew Alexandre, Stephane Mbia and Jean Makoun. Coach

INTERNATIONAL HONOURS

Qualified for the FIFA World Cup finals 1982 1990 1994 1998 2002 African Cup of Nations 1984 1988 2000 2002 African Games 1991 1999 2003
African Youth 1995   African U-17 2003   CAF African Champions League Oryx Doula 1965, Canon Yaounde 1971 1978 1980, Union Douala 1979

Otto Pfister's appointment continues to be the source of a major power battle between the government and the football federation headed by Mohamed Iya. The sports ministry traditionally pays the coach's contract and imposed the 70-year-old German on the team just six weeks before the start of the Nations Cup finals while Iya has striven fruitlessly to manoeuvre Pfister out since. In domestic competition, Cotonsport from the northern town of Garoua won the title for a sixth successive year and they also qualified for the group phase of the African Champions League for the first time, only for their young French coach Denis Lavagne to walk out on them over pay.

THE FIFA BIG COUNT OF 2006

	Male	Female		Total
Number of players	749 576	35 939	Referees and Assistant Referees	2 260
Professionals	540		Admin, Coaches, Technical, Medical	5 516
Amateurs 18+	10 975		Number of clubs	220
Youth under 18	10 110		Number of teams	1 100
Unregistered	45 470		Clubs with women's teams	3
Total players	785 515		Players as % of population	4.53%

Fédération Camerounaise de Football (FECAFOOT)

Avenue du 27 aout 1940, Tsinga-Yaoundé, Case Postale 1116, Yaoundé, Cameroon
Tel +237 22210012   Fax +237 22216662
fecafoot@fecafootonline.com   www.fecafootonline.com
President: IYA Mohammed   General Secretary: TBD
Vice-President: ATANGANA Jean Rene   Treasurer: EPACKA Henri   Media Officer: ABDOURAMAN M.
Men's Coach: PFISTER Otto   Women's Coach: KAMDEM Charles
FECAFOOT formed: 1959   CAF: 1963   FIFA: 1962
Green shirts with yellow trimmings, Red shorts, Yellow socks or Red shirts, Green shorts, Yellow socks

RECENT INTERNATIONAL MATCHES PLAYED BY CAMEROON

2005 Opponents	Score	Venue	Comp	Scorers	Att	Referee
9-02 Senegal	W 1-0	Creteil	Fr	Geremi [87]	8 000	Lhermite FRA
27-03 Sudan	W 2-1	Yaoundé	WCq	Geremi [34], Webo [90]	30 000	Diatta SEN
4-06 Benin	W 4-1	Cotonou	WCq	Rigobert Song [19], Webo [51], Geremi [64], Eto'o [69]	20 000	El Arjoun MAR
19-06 Libya	W 1-0	Yaoundé	WCq	Webo [37]	36 000	Coulibaly MLI
4-09 Côte d'Ivoire	W 3-2	Abidjan	WCq	Webo 3 [30 47 85]	34 500	Daami TUN
8-10 Egypt	D 1-1	Yaounde	WCq	Douala [20]	38 750	Coulibaly MLI
15-11 Morocco	D 0-0	Clairefontaine	Fr			
2006						
21-01 Angola	W 3-1	Cairo	CNr1	Eto'o 3 [21 39 78]	8 000	Guezzaz MAR
25-01 Togo	W 2-0	Cairo	CNr1	Eto'o [68] ,Meyong Ze [86]	3 000	Sowe GAM
29-01 Congo DR	W 2-0	Cairo	CNr1	Geremi [31], Eto'o [33]	5 000	Coulibaly MLI
4-02 Côte d'Ivoire	D 1-1	Cairo	CNqf	Meyong Ze [96], L 11-12p	4 000	Sowe GAM
27-05 Netherlands	L 0-1	Rotterdam	Fr		46 228	Plautz AUT
16-08 Guinea	D 1-1	Rouen	Fr	Webo [90]		Duhamel FRA
3-09 Rwanda	W 3-0	Kigali	CNq	Feutchine [56], Geremi [62], Nguemo [85]		Ssegonga UGA
7-10 Equatorial Guinea	W 3-0	Yaoundé	CNq	Idrissou 2 [72 89], Webo [79]		Daami TUN
2007						
7-02 Togo	D 2-2	Lome	Fr	Boya [65], Ngom Kome [90]		
24-03 Liberia	W 3-1	Yaoundé	CNq	Webo 2 [12 24], Idrissou [85]		Djaoupe TOG
3-06 Liberia	W 2-1	Monrovia	CNq	Mbia [9], Eto'o [54]		Coulibaly MLI
17-06 Rwanda	W 2-1	Garoua	CNq	Idrissou [33], Geremi [48]		Sowe GAM
22-08 Japan	L 0-2	Oita	Fr		37 240	ChoiMyung Yong KOR
9-09 Equatorial Guinea	L 0-1	Malabo	CNq			Sidibe MLI
2008						
22-01 Egypt	L 2-4	Kumasi	CNr1	Eto'o 2 [51 89p]		Sowe GAM
26-01 Zambia	W 5-1	Kumasi	CNr1	Geremi [28], Job 2 [31 82], Emana [43], Eto'o [66p]		Nichimura JPN
30-01 Sudan	W 3-0	Tamale	CNr1	Eto'o 2 [27p 89], Ali Khider OG [33]		Djaoupe TOG
4-02 Tunisia	W 3-2	Tamale	CNqf	Mbia 2 [18 92], Geremi [27]		Coulibaly MLI
7-02 Ghana	W 1-0	Accra	CNsf	Nkong [72]		El Arjoun MAR
10-02 Egypt	L 0-1	Accra	CNf			Codjia BEN
31-05 Cape Verde Islands	W 2-0	Yaoundé	WCq	Rigobert Song 8, Eto'o 57p	20 000	Djaoupe TOG
8-06 Mauritius	W 3-0	Curepipe	WCq	Bikey [11], Eto'o [27], Bebey [87]	2 400	Martins ANG
14-06 Tanzania	D 0-0	Dar es Salaam	WCq		55 000	Codjia BEN
21-06 Tanzania	W 2-1	Yaoundé	WCq	Eto'o 2 [65 89]	25 000	Mendy GAM

Fr = Friendly match • CC = FIFA Confederations Cup • CN = African Cup of Nations • CM = CEMAC Championship • WC = FIFA World Cup
q = qualifier • r1 = 1st round • qf = quarter-final • sf = semi-final • f = final

CAMEROON NATIONAL TEAM PLAYERS

	Player		Club	Date of Birth		Player		Club	Date of Birth
1	Idriss Carlos Kameni	GK	Espanyol ESP	18 02 1984	12	Alain Nkong	MF	Atlante MEX	6 04 1979
2	Augustin Binya	DF	Benfica POR	29 08 1984	13	Landry Nguemo	MF	Nancy FRA	28 11 1985
3	Bill Tchato	DF	Qatar SC QAT	14 05 1975	14	Joel Epalle	MF	VfL Bochum GER	20 02 1978
4	Rigobert Song	DF	Galatasaray TUR	1 07 1976	15	Alexandre Song	MF	Arsenal ENG	9 09 1987
5	Timothee Atouba	DF	Hamburger SV GER	17 02 1982	16	Hamidou Souleymanou	GK	Denizlispor TUR	22 11 1973
6	Benoit Angbwa	DF	Saturn Rameskoye RUS	1 01 1982	17	Mohamadou Idrissou	FW	MSV Duisburg GER	8 03 1980
7	Modeste Mbami	MF	Olymp. Marseille FRA	9 10 1982	18	Bertin Tomou	FW	Excelsior Mouscron BEL	8 08 1978
8	Geremi Fotso Njitap	MF	Newcastle United ENG	20 12 1978	19	Stephane Mbia	MF	Stade Rennais FRA	20 05 1986
9	Samuel Eto'o	FW	Barcelona ESP	10 03 1981	20	Paul Essola	MF	Arsenal Kyiv UKR	13 12 1981
10	Achille Emana	MF	Toulouse FRA	5 06 1982	21	Joseph Desire Job	FW	Nice FRA	1 12 1977
11	Jean Makoun	MF	Lille FRA	29 05 1983	22	Janvier Mbarga	GK	Canon Yaounde CMR	17 01 1985
					23	Andre Bikey	DF	Reading ENG	1 01 1985

Cameroon's squad for the 2008 CAF Africa Cup of Nations

CAMEROON NATIONAL TEAM RECORDS AND RECORD SEQUENCES

Records			Sequence records					
Victory	9-2	SOM 1960	Wins	7	2002	Clean sheets	7	2002
Defeat	1-6	NOR 1990, RUS 1994	Defeats	3	Five times	Goals scored	24	1967-1972
Player Caps	112	Rigobert Song	Undefeated	16	1981-1983	Without goal	4	1981, 2001
Player Goals	33	Mboma & Eto'o	Without win	9	1994-1995	Goals against	11	1969-1972

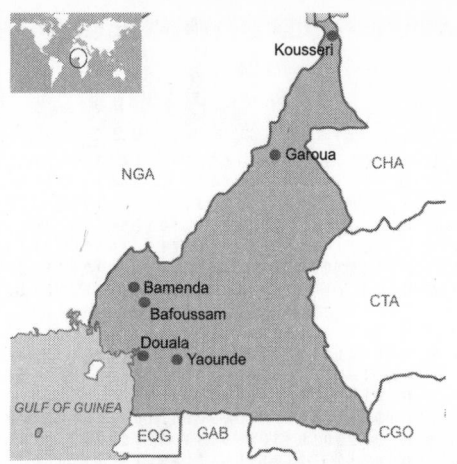

Kousséri

NGA

Garoua

CHA

Bamenda

Bafoussam

CTA

Douala

Yaounde

GULF OF GUINEA

EQG   GAB   CGO

REPUBLIC OF CAMEROON; REPUBLIQUE DU CAMEROUN

Capital	Yaoundé	Language	French, English	Independence	1960
Population	17 340 702	Area	475 440 km²	% in cities	45%
GDP per cap	$1 800	Dailling code	+237	Internet .cm GMT + / - +1	

MEDALS TABLE

		Overall			Lge	Cup		Africa			City	Stadium	Cap'ty	DoF
		G	S	B	G	G	S	G	S	B				
1	Canon Sportif Yaoundé	26	8	4	10	12	5	4	3	4	Yaoundé	Stade Ahmadou Ahidjo	52 000	1930
2	Union Sportive Douala	13	6	1	4	7	6	2		1	Douala	Stade de la Reunification	30 000	1957
3	Cotonsport Garoua	12	2	1	9	3	1		1	1	Garoua	Omnisport Roumdé-Adjia	22 000	1986
4	Tonnerre Kalara Club Yaoundé	11	5	1	5	5	3	1	2	1	Yaoundé	Stade Ahmadou Ahidjo	52 000	1938
5	Oryx Douala	10	1	1	5	4	1	1		1	Douala	Akwa	12 000	
6	Racing Club Bafoussam	5	3		4	1	3				Bafoussam	Municipal de Bamendzi	5 000	
7	Diamant Yaoundé	4	4	1	1	3	4				Yaoundé	Stade Ahmadou Ahidjo	80 000	
8	Caïman Douala	4	3		3	1	3				Douala	Stade de la Reunification	30 000	
9	Lion Club Yaoundé	4				4					Yaoundé	Militaire	20 000	
10	Dynamo Douala	3			3						Douala	Akwa	12 000	
11	Léopards Douala	2	3	1	2		3			1	Douala	Akwa	12 000	
12	Aigle Royal Nkongsamba	2	2		2		2				Nkongsamba	Omnisports	6 000	
13	Fovu Club Baham	2	1		1	1	1				Baham	Stade Municipal	7 000	1978
14	Olympique Mvolyé	2				2					Mvolyé	Mvolyé	11 000	
15	Sable Batié	1	2		1		2				Batié	Batié	5 000	1995
	Unisport Bafang	1	2		1		2				Bafang	Stade Municipal	5 000	
17	Dihep Nkam Yabassi	1	1			1	1				Yabassi	Yabassi	8 000	
18	Kumbo Strikers	1		1		1				1	Kumbo	Municipal	10 000	

RECENT LEAGUE AND CUP RECORD

	Championship						Cup		
Year	Champions	Pts	Runners-up	Pts	Third	Pts	Winners	Score	Runners-up
1995	Racing Bafoussam	52	Léopard Douala	48	Unisport Bafang	48	Canon Yaoundé	1-0	Océan Kribi
1996	Unisport Bafang	56	Cotonsport Garoua	47	Canon Yaoundé	47	Racing Bafoussam	1-0	Stade Banjoun
1997	Cotonsport Garoua	62	Stade Bandjoun	60	Union Douala	55	Union Douala	2-1	Ports FC Douala
1998	Cotonsport Garoua	54	Canon Yaoundé	53	Tonnerre Yaoundé	51	Dynamo Douala	1-0	Canon Yaoundé
1999	Sable Batié	58	Cotonsport Garoua	56	Racing Bafoussam	49	Canon Yaoundé	2-1	Cotonsport Garoua
2000	Fovu Baham	59	Cotonsport Garoua	53	Union Douala	51	Kumbo Strikers	1-0	Unisport Bafang
2001	Cotonsport Garoua	58	Tonnerre Yaoundé	53	Fovu Baham	50	Fovu Baham	3-2	Cintra Yaoundé
2002	Canon Yaoundé	55	Cotonsport Garoua	53	Bamboutos Mbouda	50	Mt Cameroun	2-1	Sable Batié
2003	Cotonsport Garoua	62	Canon Yaoundé	51	PWD Bamenda	51	Cotonsport Garoua	2-1	Sable Batié
2004	Cotonsport Garoua	30	Racing Bafoussam	28	Union Douala	26	Cotonsport Garoua	1-0	Union Douala
2005	Cotonsport Garoua	71	Aigle Royal Menoua	53	Astres Douala	51	Impôts Yaoundé	1-0	Unisport Bafang
2006	Cotonsport Garoua	53	Canon Yaoundé	49	Astres Douala	47	Union Douala	1-0	Fovu Baham
2007	Cotonsport Garoua	75	Union Douala	70	Mount Cameroon	66	Cotonsport Garoua	1-0	Astres Douala
2008	Cotonsport Garoua	58	Canon Yaoundé	51	Union Douala	45			

CAMEROON 2007

DIVISION 1 MTN

	Pl	W	D	L	F	A	Pts	Cotonsport	Union	Mt Cameroon	Fovu	Canon	Astres	Aigle	Lion Ngoma	Tonnerre	Univ Ng'déré	Foudre	Espérance	Sable	Cetef	Sahel	Fédéral	CPSB	Bamboutos
Cotonsport Garoua †	34	22	9	3	55	11	75		1-0	1-1	2-1	1-0	3-1	0-0	3-0	0-0	1-1	4-0	3-0	4-0	2-0	2-0	3-0	9-0	2-1
Union Douala †	34	20	10	4	50	23	70	1-1		2-1	2-2	1-2	2-1	0-0	2-0	3-1	2-0	3-0	1-2	3-0	0-0	3-1	1-0	2-0	**3-0**
Mount Cameroon ‡	34	19	9	6	47	23	66	2-1	0-1		0-0	0-0	1-1	0-0	0-0	3-1	1-1	4-0	1-0	5-0	2-0	2-1	2-1	2-0	
Fovu Baham	34	15	9	10	33	24	54	0-1	0-0	2-4		1-0	1-0	0-1	0-0	1-0	2-1	0-0	1-0	0-2	1-0	1-1	1-0	1-0	0-0
Canon Yaoundé	34	16	6	12	37	26	54	1-0	2-3	0-0	1-1		0-1	2-0	1-0	2-1	*1-0*	1-0	0-0	0-1	2-0	1-0	2-1	3-1	1-0
Les Astres Douala ‡	34	12	15	7	42	34	51	1-0	0-2	0-1	0-2	2-1		1-1	2-1	1-2	1-1	4-0	3-3	1-0	2-1	3-1	3-1	1-1	
Aigle Royal Dschang	34	11	16	7	29	27	49	0-0	1-2	2-2	2-2	0-1	2-2		2-1	1-0	0-0	1-0	1-0	2-1	1-0	2-0	2-2	1-0	
Lion Ngoma	34	12	11	11	26	32	47	0-1	0-0	2-1	0-3	1-1	1-1		1-0	1-0	1-0	1-0	2-1	1-0	2-0	0-0	1-0	1-3	
Tonnerre Kalara	34	11	14	9	28	24	47	0-1	1-1	1-0	1-0	2-0	1-1	2-0	0-0		1-0	1-0	1-1	0-1	2-0	0-0	2-1	0-0	0-1
Université Ngaoundéré	34	13	7	14	40	35	46	1-0	0-1	0-1	0-1	2-2	2-2	4-0	2-0	1-1		2-1	2-1	1-0	1-0	3-1	5-3	2-0	1-0
Foudre Akonolinga	34	11	9	14	32	37	42	1-1	0-0	3-1	1-0	1-2	0-0	0-0	0-2	0-0	1-0		0-0	2-1	4-1	5-1	1-0	2-1	1-2
Espérance Guider	34	11	9	14	23	31	42	0-1	0-1	0-1	1-0	0-0	0-0	3-1	0-0	2-1	0-0		1-2	2-1	1-0	1-0	**3-0**	1-0	
Sable Batie	34	12	6	16	31	37	39	0-0	0-2	1-3	0-3	0-2	0-0	0-0	0-1	0-2	1-0	0-1	2-0		1-2	0-0	1-0	1-0	**3-0**
Cetef Bonabéri	34	9	9	16	35	43	36	0-1	2-2	0-1	0-3	3-0	1-1	0-0	3-0	2-3	2-0	2-0	1-1	2-2		4-1	3-0	2-1	2-0
Sahel Maroua	34	6	13	15	24	43	31	0-1	1-0	1-0	1-1	0-1	1-0	0-1	1-0	1-2	3-0	1-1	1-1	1-1	0-0		1-1	0-0	0-0
Fédéral Noun	34	6	8	20	26	50	23	0-0	2-3	1-2	1-0	1-1	0-1	2-1	0-0	0-0	1-0	3-2	2-0	**0-3**	1-0	1-1		2-0	2-3
CPS Bertoua	34	0	10	24	17	67	7	0-1	1-1	0-1	0-1	0-4	0-2	1-3	0-0	0-0	1-5	1-4	0-1	1-3	0-0	3-3	0-0		1-1
Bamboutos Mbouda	34	12	6	16	31	39	42	**0-3**	3-0	0-1	1-2	2-0	0-1	1-0	1-3	0-0	1-0	0-1	1-0	0-1	1-2	2-1	4-0	2-1	

17/02/2007 - 14/10/2007 • † Qualified for the CAF Champions League • ‡ Qualified for the CAF Confederation Cup • § = points deducted
Bamboutos relegated for attempted match fixing • In the match in italics the points were awarded to Université

CAMEROON 2007 — TOURNOI INTER POULES (2)

Pool A - in Ebolowa	Pl	W	D	L	F	A	Pts
Tiko United	4	3	1	0	5	2	10
Dynamique Ng'déré †	4	2	0	2	3	4	6
Achille FC	4	1	2	1	5	5	5
Yong Sports Academy	4	1	1	2	4	5	4
Diables Rouges	4	1	0	3	4	5	3

6/10/2007 - 20/10/2007 • † Qualified for play-off

Pool B - in Yaoundé	Pl	W	D	L	F	A	Pts
Unisport Bafang	3	1	2	0	3	1	5
Caïman Douala †	3	1	2	0	3	2	5
Pilote Garoua	3	1	0	2	3	4	3
Infinitif Ebolowa	3	0	2	1	2	4	2
US Abong Mbang				Excluded			

7/10/2007 - 21/10/2007 • † Qualified for play-off

Promotion play-off: **Caïman Douala** 3-1 Dynamique Ngaoundéré

CAMEROON 2007–08

DIVISION 1 MTN

	Pl	W	D	L	F	A	Pts	Cotonsport	Canon	Union	Astres	Fovu	Unisport	Tiko	Univ Ng'déré	Aigle	Mt Cameroon	Sable	Foudre	Caïman	Espérance	Tonnerre	Lion Ngoma
Cotonsport Garoua †	30	16	10	4	42	16	58		2-1	2-0	1-2	1-1	2-0	3-0	1-0	1-0	2-0	2-0	0-0	2-0	1-0	5-0	6-0
Canon Yaoundé †	30	15	6	9	30	21	51	0-1		1-0	1-0	2-1	2-0	0-0	1-0	4-2	1-0	3-0	1-1	1-0	1-1	3-1	
Union Douala	30	11	12	7	28	20	45	1-2	0-0		2-0	0-1	0-0	2-1	2-0	2-1	0-0	1-3	3-0	0-0	1-0	3-0	2-1
Les Astres Douala	30	12	8	10	29	27	44	1-1	1-0	1-1		0-1	2-0	0-1	2-0	0-2	1-1	1-2	0-1	3-2	2-2	1-1	1-0
Fovu Baham	30	10	13	7	28	22	43	1-1	2-2	0-0	0-0		0-1	0-0	1-1	1-0	0-0	1-1	2-1	1-0	3-1	1-0	2-0
Unisport Bafang	30	11	8	11	20	18	41	0-0	2-0	0-0	0-1	0-0		2-0	0-0	1-0	2-1	2-1	4-0	1-0	0-1	1-0	0-0
Tiko United	30	11	8	11	34	34	41	4-1	0-2	1-2	2-1	1-1	1-0		3-0	0-1	3-0	2-1	1-0	3-1	0-0	1-1	2-1
Université Ngaoundéré	30	10	10	10	20	23	40	0-0	0-1	1-1	0-1	2-1	1-1	1-1		2-1	2-0	2-0	1-0	0-0	0-0	0-0	1-0
Aigle Royal Dschang	30	10	8	12	20	24	38	3-0	1-0	2-1	0-0	1-0	1-0	0-1	1-1		1-0	1-0	1-1	1-0	1-0	**3-0**	
Mount Cameroon	30	9	11	10	23	28	38	0-0	1-1	0-1	1-1	0-0	1-0	1-0	1-0		0-0	4-0	2-1	2-1	2-1	1-0	
Sable Batie	30	10	7	13	20	27	37	1-1	0-0	0-0	0-2	1-0	1-0	2-0	1-0	1-0	2-0		0-0	0-2	0-0	0-1	1-1
Foudre Akonolinga	30	9	10	11	17	28	37	0-0	1-0	1-2	0-0	0-0	0-1	1-0	1-0	0-1		1-0		2-0	1-0	1-1	
Caïman Douala	30	9	9	12	30	39	36	0-2	1-0	1-1	0-1	2-2	0-0	1-1	1-0	5-0	1-1	2-0	3-1		1-0	2-2	
Espérance Guider	30	8	11	11	24	27	35	0-1	1-0	1-1	0-1	2-1	2-1	2-2	2-1	1-1	1-1	3-1	1-0	0-0		1-0	
Tonnerre Kalara	30	7	10	13	26	30	31	0-1	0-1	0-0	2-2	3-2	0-1	3-0	0-1	3-1	0-1	0-0	4-0	1-1			2-0
Lion Ngoma	30	6	11	13	24	41	29	2-1	0-1	1-0	1-2	2-2	1-1	2-2	1-1	1-1	1-0	2-0	0-0	0-0	1-0	1-3	

8/12/2007 - 6/07/2008 • † Qualified for the CAF Champions League • ‡ Qualified for the Confederation Cup • Matches in bold were awarded

COUPE DE CAMEROUN 2007

First Round

Cotonsport Garoua *	1
Ngaoundéré FC	0
Cetef Bonabéri *	0
Infinitif Ebolowa	1
ACADASPORT	1
Foudre Akonolinga *	0
CPS Bertoua *	0 3p
PWD Bamenda	0 4p
Etoile Sportive Essazok	1
Tonnerre Kalara *	0
Bocki	0
Université Ngaoundéré *	3
Sahel Maroua *	2
Zénith	1
Caïman Douala	0 2p
Mount Cameroon *	2 3p
Sable Batie	0 5p
Union Douala *	0 4p
Espérance Guider *	0
Tiko United	1
Fovu Baham	1 5p
Lion Ngoma *	1 4p
Sanaga	0 2p
Bamboutos Mbouda *	0 4p
Racing Bafoussam	2
Aigle Royal Dschang *	1
Cercle Sportif	0 0p
Fédéral Noun *	0 2p
Canon Yaoundé *	1
Espoir	0
Unisport Bafang	0
Les Astres Douala *	1

Second Round

Cotonsport Garoua	2 3
Infinitif Ebolowa *	0 0
ACADASPORT	0 1
PWD Bamenda *	1 1
Etoile Sportive Essazok *	1 2
Université Ngaoundéré	1 2
Sahel Maroua *	0 0
Mount Cameroon	1 2
Sable Batie	1 0
Tiko United *	0 0
Fovu Baham	0 0
Bamboutos Mbouda *	1 0
Racing Bafoussam	0 2
Fédéral Noun *	0 1
Canon Yaoundé	0 0
Les Astres Douala *	1 0

Quarter-finals

Cotonsport Garoua	1 4
PWD Bamenda *	1 0
Etoile Sportive Essazok	1 1
Mount Cameroon *	2 1
Sable Batie *	0 2
Bamboutos Mbouda	0 1
Racing Bafoussam *	0 1
Les Astres Douala	0 2

Semi-finals

Cotonsport Garoua	3 2
Mount Cameroon *	0 1
Sable Batie	0 0
Les Astres Douala *	0 2

Final

Cotonsport Garoua	1
Les Astres Douala ‡	0

CUP FINAL

Stade Ahmadou Ahidjo, Yaoundé
2-12-2007, Att: 40 000, Ref: Tabopda
Scorer - Kamilou Daouda 72

Cotonsport - Daouda Kassali - Sébastien Ndzana Kana, Makadji Boukar, Ahmadou Ngomna, Kamilou Daouda, Ousmaila Baba, Eric Nijie, Nnouck Minka, Kingue Mpondo, Joel Babanda (Francis Litsingi 23), Valery Noufor. Tr: Denis Lavagne

Astres - Lukong Bongaman - Léopold Bagnack, Ngolo Ndon, Paul Bébé Kingue, Nyamsi Bikima, Mboule Moukoko, Jean Vauclin Bekima, Eric Bassombeng, Otobong Enet Edet (Christian Heumi 44), Jacques Enama Okouda, Aime Mangolo (Paul Ncha 59). Tr: Nicolas Tonye

* Home team in the first leg • ‡ Qualified for the CAF Confederation Cup

COD – CONGO DR

NATIONAL TEAM RECORD
JULY 10TH 2006 TO JULY 12TH 2010

PL	W	D	L	F	A	%
16	6	6	4	26	15	56.3

FIFA/COCA-COLA WORLD RANKING

1993	1994	1995	1996	1997	1998	1999	2000	2001	2002	2003	2004	2005	2006	2007	High	
71	68	68	66	76	62	59	70	77	65	56	78	77	66	74	**51**	09/03

2007–2008												Low	
08/07	09/07	10/07	11/07	12/07	01/08	02/08	03/08	04/08	05/08	06/08	07/08	**85**	04/08
75	77	79	80	74	70	75	77	85	82	77	76		

After qualifying for eight successive African Nations Cup finals, the Democratic Republic of Congo missed out on the 2008 finals after blowing a seemingly safe situation. Instead of what was expected to be a routine home win over Libya in their last qualifier, the Leopards were held to a draw and then discovered Namibia had scored a last minute goal to beat Ethiopia in Addis Abeba to take top place in the group. The failure of the Leopards cost the job of the Belgian coach Henri Depireux, replaced six months later by the well-travelled Frenchman Patrice Neveu. It is noticeable how the focus of Congo's team selection has turned from the almost limitless talent in the provincial

INTERNATIONAL HONOURS
Qualified for the FIFA World Cup finals 1974
African Cup of Nations 1968 1974 CAF Champions League TP Mazembe 1967 1968 AS Vita Club 1973

leagues of the country to the small diaspora of Congolese players in Europe. New selections include goalkeeper Parfait Mandanda, who first appearance came against a France A team that featured his brother Steve in the other goal. At home, TP Mazembe Engelbert easily out-did their traditional rivals from Kinshasa to win the national championship. Mazembe's fortunes have risen recently thanks to the largess of their president Moise Katumbi, whose popularity as the flamboyant benefactor of the south's biggest club led to his election as governor of the mineral-rich Katanga province.

THE FIFA BIG COUNT OF 2006

	Male	Female		Total
Number of players	2 515 600	0	Referees and Assistant Referees	2 900
Professionals	0		Admin, Coaches, Technical, Medical	7 700
Amateurs 18+	55 600		Number of clubs	770
Youth under 18	22 000		Number of teams	3 300
Unregistered	165 000		Clubs with women's teams	0
Total players	2 515 600		Players as % of population	4.01%

Fédération Congolaise de Football-Association (FECOFA)
31 Avenue de la Justice, c/Gombe, Case postale 1284, Kinshasa 1, Congo DR
Tel +243 81 9049788   Fax +243 81 3013527
fecofa_sg@yahoo.fr   www.none
President: SELEMANI Omari   General Secretary: BADI Gregoire
Vice-President: TSHIMANGA Donatien   Treasurer: BONDEMBE Bokanyanga   Media Officer: NZILA Fanan
Men's Coach: NEVEU Patrice   Women's Coach: BONGANYA Poly
FECOFA formed: 1919   CAF: 1973   FIFA: 1962
Blue shirts with yellow trimmings, Blue shorts, Blue socks or Yellow shirts with blue trimmings, Blue shorts, Yellow socks

RECENT INTERNATIONAL MATCHES PLAYED BY CONGO DR

2004	Opponents	Score		Venue	Comp	Scorers	Att	Referee
20-06	Burkina Faso	W	3-2	Kinshasa	WCq	Mbajo [12], Mbala [75], Bageta [88p]	75 000	Djaoupe TOG
3-07	Cape Verde Islands	D	1-1	Praia	WCq	Kaluyitu [1]	3 800	Nahi CIV
18-08	Mali	L	0-3	Paris	Fr			Derrien FRA
5-09	South Africa	W	1-0	Kinshasa	WCq	Kabamba [86]	85 000	Hicuburundi BDI
10-10	Ghana	D	0-0	Kumasi	WCq		30 000	Coulibaly MLI
2005								
8-02	Côte d'Ivoire	D	2-2	Rouen	Fr	Makondele [44], Nonda [92+p]	4 000	Duhamel FRA
27-03	Ghana	D	1-1	Kinshasa	WCq	Nonda [50]	80 000	Sowe GAM
5-06	Uganda	W	4-0	Kinshasa	WCq	Nonda 2 [2 69p], Ilongo [58], Matumona [78]	80 000	Daami TUN
18-06	Burkina Faso	L	0-2	Ouagadougou	WCq		25 000	Shelmani LBY
1-07	Botswana	D	0-0	Gaborone	Fr			
16-08	Guinea	W	3-1	Paris	Fr	Mbala [37], LuaLua [52], Mputu [79]		
4-09	Cape Verde Islands	W	2-1	Kinshasa	WCq	Mubiala [21], Mputu [49]	75 000	Guezzaz MAR
25-09	Zambia	D	2-2	Chililabombwe	Fr	Bokese [54], Matumona [65]		
27-09	Zambia	D	0-0	Lubumbashi	Fr			
8-10	South Africa	D	2-2	Durban	WCq	Mputu [11], Nonda [44]	35 000	Mbera GAB
11-11	Tunisia	D	2-2	Paris	Fr	Mputu [16], Lutula [57]		Garibian FRA
16-11	Libya	L	1-2	Paris	Fr	Mbokane [47]		
11-12	Zambia	D	1-1	Lubumbashi	Fr	OG [28]		
14-12	Zambia	L	1-4	Chingola	Fr	Ilingo [55]		
2006								
9-01	Morocco	L	0-3	Rabat	Fr			
14-01	Senegal	D	0-0	Dakar	Fr			Sowe GAM
21-01	Togo	W	2-0	Cairo	CNr1	Mputu [42], LuaLua [61]	6 000	Daami TUN
25-01	Angola	D	0-0	Cairo	CNr1		2 000	Diatta SEN
29-01	Cameroon	L	0-2	Cairo	CNr1		5 000	Coulibaly MLI
3-02	Egypt	L	1-4	Cairo	CNqf	OG [45]	74 000	Sowe GAM
12-05	Mexico	L	1-2	Mexico City	Fr	Mbokani [51]	75 000	Flores MEX
3-09	Namibia	W	3-2	Kinshasa	CNq	Mbele [32], Kalulika [63], Kinkela [80]		Evehe CMR
7-10	Libya	D	1-1	Tripoli	CNq	Bageta [37]		Pare BFA
9-12	Tanzania	L	0-2	Dar es Salaam	Fr			
2007								
29-04	Ethiopia	W	2-0	Kinshasa	CNq	Mbutu [29], LuaLua [52p]		Bennett RSA
28-05	Congo	L	1-2	Brazzaville	Fr	Nkulukuta [72]		
1-06	Ethiopia	L	0-1	Addis Abeba	CNq			Hicuburundi BDI
16-06	Namibia	D	1-1	Windhoek	CNq	Matumona [25]		Mwanza ZAM
29-07	Madagascar	D	0-0	Antananarivo	Fr			
22-08	Angola	W	3-1	Kinshasa	Fr	Oneseke [6], Yemweni [52], Mputu [90]		
8-09	Libya	D	1-1	Kinshasa	CNq	Nonda [39p]		Djaopupe TOG
2008								
25-03	Gabon	D	0-0	Aubervilliers	Fr			
26-03	Algeria	D	1-1	Nanterre	Fr	Mbokani [25]		
1-06	Egypt	L	1-2	Cairo	WCq	Ilunga [43]	40 000	Seechurn MRI
8-06	Malawi	W	1-0	Kinshasa	WCq	Matumona [76]	35 000	Abdel Gadir SUD
13-06	Djibouti	W	6-0	Djibouti	WCq	Mbokani 2 [24 47], Nonda [30], Matumona 2 [39 51], Mputu [80]	3 000	Disang BOT
22-06	Djibouti	W	5-1	Kinshasa	WCq	Nonda 3 [10 45 52], Tshiolola [60], Mbokani [64]	15 000	Rouaissi MAR

Fr = Friendly match • CN = CAF African Cup of Nations • WC = FIFA World Cup • q = qualifier • r1 = first round group • qf = quarter-final

CONGO DR NATIONAL TEAM RECORDS AND RECORD SEQUENCES

Records			Sequence records					
Victory	10-1	ZAM 1969	Wins	5	1973-1974	Clean sheets	4	Four times
Defeat	0-9	YUG 1974	Defeats	5	2004	Goals scored	38	1976-1985
Player Caps	n/a		Undefeated	12	2002-2004	Without goal	4	1990
Player Goals	19	Shabani Nonda	Without win	9	2005-2006	Goals against	13	1964-1966

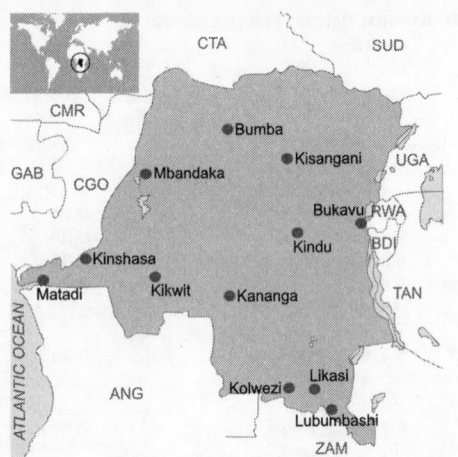

		Population '000
1	Kinshasa	9 166
2	Lubumbashi	1 628
3	Mbuji-Mayi	1 473
4	Kolwezi	932
5	Kisangani	592
6	Boma	508
7	Kananga	507
8	Likasi	496
9	Tshikapa	308
10	Bukavu	240
11	Mwene-Ditu	213
12	Kikwit	200
13	Mbandaka	198
14	Uvira	196
15	Matadi	193
16	Gandajika	176
17	Butembo	176
18	Kalemie	172
19	Goma	161
20	Kindu	151
21	Isiro	137
22	Bandundu	130
23	Gemena	130
24	Ilebo	119

DEMOCRATIC REPUBLIC OF THE CONGO; REPUBLIQUE DEMOCRATIQUE DU CONGO

Capital	Kinshasa	Language	French, Lingala, Kingwana, Kikongo	Independence	1960
Population	65 751 512	Area	2 345 410	Density	24 per km²	% in cities	29%
GDP per cap	$700	Dailling code	+243	Internet	.zr	GMT +/-	+1

MEDALS TABLE

		Overall G	Overall S	Overall B	Lge G	Cup G	Africa G	Africa S	Africa B	City	Stadium	Cap'ty	DoF
1	Daring Club Motema Pembe	23		3	11	11	1		3	Kinshasa	Stade des Martyrs	80 000	1936
2	AS Vita Club	21	1	3	11	9	1	1	3	Kinshasa	Stade des Martyrs	80 000	1935
3	Tout Puissant Mazembe	18	2	2	10	5	3	2	2	Lubumbashi	Stade Municipal	35 000	1932
4	Amicale Sportive Dragons	9	2		4	5		2		Kinshasa	Stade 24 Septembre	24 000	1938
5	FC Saint Eloi Lupopo	8		1	6	2			1	Lubumbashi	Stade de la Victoire		1939
6	AS Kalamu	4				4				Kinshasa			
7	US Bilombe	2			1	1				Bilombe			
	Maniema Union	2				2				Kindu			
9	AC Sodigraf	1	1			1	1						
10	AS Bantous	1			1					Mbuji-Mayi			
	SCOM Mikishi	1			1					Lubumbashi			
	SM Sanga Balende	1			1					Mbuji-Mayi			
	US Tshinkunku	1			1					Kananga			
	CS Cilu	1				1				Lukala			
	US Kenya	1				1				Lubumbashi			
	Lubumbashi Sport	1				1				Lubumbashi			
	AS Vita Kabasha	1				1				Goma			

Motemba Pembe were previously CS Imana • AS Dragons were previously AS Bilima

RECENT LEAGUE AND CUP RECORD

	Championship						Cup		
Year	Champions	Pts	Runners-up	Pts	Third	Pts	Winners	Score	Runners-up
1997	AS Vita Club	†	DC Motema Pembe				AS Dragons	2-1	AS Vita Club
1998	DC Motema Pembe	13	AS Vita Club	8	SM Sanga Balende	6	AS Dragons	1-0	AS Sucrière
1999	DC Motema Pembe		TP Mazembe		AS Vita Club		AS Dragons	3-2	AS Paulino
2000	TP Mazembe	16	SM Sanga Balende	8	AS Vita Club	5	TP Mazembe	2-0	AS St-Luc Kananga
2001	TP Mazembe	†	FC St-Eloi Lupopo				AS Vita Club	3-0	AS Veti Matadi
2002	FC St-Eloi Lupopo	25	TP Mazembe	23	AS Vita Club	18	US Kenya	2-1	SM Sanga Balende
2003	AS Vita Club	27	SC Cilu	18	FC St-Eloi Lupopo	17	DC Motema Pembe	2-0	TP Mazembe
2004	DC Motema Pembe	14	TP Mazembe	11	FC St-Eloi Lupopo	6	CS Cilu Lukala	1-0	AS St Luc Kananga
2005	DC Motema Pembe	19	FC St-Eloi Lupopo	18	TP Mazembe	17	AS Vita Kabasha	1-1 4-2p	CS Cilu Lukala
2006	TP Mazembe	25	FC St-Eloi Lupopo	20	Bukava Dawa	13	DC Motema Pembe	4-1	AS Dragons
2007	TP Mazembe	30	DC Motema Pembe	16	AS Vita Club	13	AS Maniema Union	2-1	FC St-Eloi Lupopo
2008									

† Knock-out format • Tout Puissant Mazembe beat FC Saint-Eloi Lupopo 1-1 3-1 in the 2001 final

CONGO DR 2007
LIGUE NATIONAL DE FOOTBALL XII (LINAFOOT)

Preliminary round

Muungano *	0 1 2p	
AS Maniema Union	1 0 3p	
FC Makila Mabe *	2 1	
CS Imana	0 2	
Singa Mwambe *	1 0	
AS Kabasha Goma	1 2	
TP Molunge *	0 1 3p	
AS Nika Kisangani	1 0 4p	
AS Saint Luc *	2 1	
AS New Soger	4 2	
Mabela a Bana *	1 0	
US Tshinkunku	2 3	

First round

Group 1

	Pl	W	D	L	F	A	Pts	DCMP	ASMU	TPM
DC Motema Pembe	4	3	1	0	11	2	10		4-1	5-0
AS Maniema Union	4	1	2	1	6	7	5	1-1		4-2
TP Molunge	4	0	1	3	2	10	1	0-1	0-0	

Group 2

	Pl	W	D	L	F	A	Pts	ASVC	SCCL	FCMM
AS Vita Club Kinshasa	4	3	0	1	12	2	9		0-1	2-1
SC Cilu Lukala	4	3	0	1	7	4	9	0-3		4-1
FC Makila Mabe	4	0	0	4	2	15	0	0-7	0-2	

Group 3

	Pl	W	D	L	F	A	Pts	ASKG	OCMS	SEL
AS Kabasha Goma	4	2	2	0	2	0	8		0-0	0-0
OC Mbongo Sport	4	1	1	2	1	2	4	0-1		1-0
FC St Eloi Lupopo	4	1	1	2	1	2	4	0-1	1-0	

Group 4

	Pl	W	D	L	F	A	Pts	DCVG	ASNS	ASNK
DC Virunga Goma	4	3	1	0	8	1	10		2-0	3-1
AS New Soger	4	1	2	1	3	3	5	0-0		2-0
AS Nika Kisangani	4	0	1	3	2	9	1	0-3	1-1	

Group 5

	Pl	W	D	L	F	A	Pts	TPM	OCBD	UST
TP Mazembe	4	4	0	0	12	1	12		3-0	3-0
OC Bukavu Dawa	4	2	0	2	5	7	5	1-3		2-0
US Tshinkunku	4	0	0	4	1	10	0	0-3	1-2	

7/01/2007 - 27/02/2007 • * Home team in the first leg • Group winners and best runner-up qualify for the final round • Teams knocked-out in the first round qualify for the Coupe du Congo 2007

CONGO DR 2007
LIGUE NATIONAL DE FOOTBALL XII FINAL ROUND

	Pl	W	D	L	F	A	Pts	Mazembe	Daring Club	Vita Club	Virunga	Cilu Lukala	Kabasha
TP Mazembe †	10	10	0	0	21	3	30		1-0	4-1	2-0	1-0	3-0
DC Motema Pembe †	9	5	1	3	11	6	16	0-2		3-1	0-1	1-0	2-0
AS Vita Club Kinshasa ‡	10	4	1	5	16	15	13	1-2	0-1		2-1	3-1	4-1
DC Virunga Goma	10	3	3	4	7	9	12	0-1	1-1	2-1		0-1	0-0
SC Cilu Lukala	10	1	3	6	3	14	6	0-3	0-3	0-0	1-1		0-0
AS Kabasha Goma	9	1	2	6	4	15	5	1-2	n/p	0-3	0-1	2-0	

15/04/2007 - 16/09/2007 • † Qualified for the CAF Champions League • ‡ Qualified for the CAF Confederation Cup • Match in bold was awarded

CONGO DR 2007
KINSHASA LEAGUE (EPFKIN)

	Pl	W	D	L	F	A	Pts
DC Motema Pembe	14	9	3	2	28	15	30
AS Dragons	14	7	6	1	19	10	27
SC Inter Kinshasa	14	7	5	2	23	12	26
FC Les Stars	14	6	2	6	19	20	20
Olympic Club	14	5	4	5	16	15	19
AS Vita Club Kinshasa	14	5	5	4	16	16	17
AC Bel'Or	14	2	2	10	11	23	8
AS MK Etanchéite	14	3	0	11	12	33	3

2/06/2007 - 17/08/2007 • § = points deducted

CONGO DR 2007
LUBUMBASHI LEAGUE (EUFLU)

	Pl	W	D	L	F	A	Pts
TP Mazembe	11	8	2	1	22	7	26
AS New Soger	11	6	3	2	18	10	21
Saint Eloi Lupopo	11	5	4	2	15	8	19
Lubumbashi Sport	11	6	1	4	17	14	19
JS Lumpas Bazano	11	5	4	2	11	7	19
US Kenya HP	11	4	4	3	12	8	16
CS Don Bosco	11	3	4	4	16	18	13
Scom Mikishi	11	3	4	4	9	11	13
New Vijana Katuba	11	3	3	5	14	17	12
Blessing FC	11	3	1	7	12	17	10
FC Simba	11	3	1	7	7	16	10
CS Imana	11	1	1	9	7	25	4

COUPE DU CONGO 2007

First round

Kinshasa Group A

	Pl	W	D	L	F	A	Pts
AS MK Etanchéite	2	2	0	0	5	0	6
AS Kolo Sport	2	1	0	1	3	2	3
TP Molunge	2	0	0	2	0	6	0

Kinshasa Group B

	Pl	W	D	L	F	A	Pts
FC Makila Mabe	2	2	0	0	4	0	6
AS Ndombe	2	1	0	1	3	1	3
Etoile de Gemena	2	0	0	2	0	6	0

Beni Group A

	Pl	W	D	L	F	A	Pts
AS Maniema Union	2	1	1	0	1	0	4
Capaco	2	1	1	0	1	0	4
AS Nika Kisangani	2	0	1	1	1	3	1
AC Nkoyi	2	0	1	1	1	3	1

Beni Group B

	Pl	W	D	L	F	A	Pts
OC Bukavu Dawa	2	0	2	0	0	0	2
AS Makiso	2	0	2	0	0	0	2
Bande Rouge	2	0	2	0	0	0	2

Lubumbashi Group A

	Pl	W	D	L	F	A	Pts
FC Saint Eloi Lupopo	3	2	1	0	3	0	7
Blessing	3	2	0	1	5	2	6
US Tshinkunku	2	0	1	1	1	2	1
SC Inter-Force	2	0	0	2	0	5	0

Lubumbashi Group B

	Pl	W	D	L	F	A	Pts
AS New Soger	2	2	0	0	5	2	6
Vita Club Mbuji-Mayi	2	0	1	1	2	3	1
OC Mbongo Sport	2	0	1	1	2	4	1

Semi–final groups

Group A

	Pl	W	D	L	F	A	Pts
AS Maniema Union	2	1	1	0	4	1	4
OC Bukavu Dawa	2	0	2	0	1	1	2
AS New Soger	2	0	1	1	2	5	1

Group B

	Pl	W	D	L	F	A	Pts
FC Saint Eloi Lupopo	2	2	0	0	2	0	6
FC Makila Mabe	2	0	1	1	2	3	1
AS MK Etanchéite	2	0	1	1	2	3	1

Final

AS Maniema Union ‡	2
FC Saint Eloi Lupopo	1

CUP FINAL

Stade Patrice Lumumba, Kindu
8-07-2007, Att: 10 000
Scorers - Issa Mateso [45p], Banga
Kalume [70] for Maniema; Sunda [63]
for St Eloi

‡ Qualified for the CAF Confederation Cup

CONGO DR 2008

LIGUE NATIONAL DE FOOTBALL XIII (LINAFOOT) FIRST ROUND GROUPS

Group 1 - Kinshasa

	Pl	W	D	L	F	A	Pts	ASMU	DCMP	FCMM
AS Maniema Union	4	2	2	0	8	3	8		0-0	2-1
DC Motema Pembe	4	2	2	0	7	3	8	2-2		2-0
FC Makila Mabe	4	0	0	4	2	11	0	0-4	1-3	

Group 2 - Matadi

	Pl	W	D	L	F	A	Pts	ASVM	ASVC	TPM
AS Veti Matadi	4	3	1	0	9	0	10		0-0	5-0
AS Vita Club Kinshasa	4	2	1	1	15	1	7	0-1		8-0
TP Molunge	4	0	0	4	0	23	0	0-3	0-7	

Group 3 - Kananga

	Pl	W	D	L	F	A	Pts	ASNS	DCVG	UST
AS New Soger	4	1	3	0	7	5	6		2-2	3-1
DC Virunga Goma	4	1	3	0	5	3	6	1-1		2-0
US Tshinkunku	4	0	2	2	2	6	2	1-1	0-0	

Group 4 - Lubumbashi

	Pl	W	D	L	F	A	Pts	TPM	ASSL	FCMG
TP Mazembe	4	4	0	0	12	1	12		3-0	4-0
AS Saint Luc	4	1	0	3	7	8	3	1-3		0-1
FC Mwangaza Goma	4	1	0	3	2	12	3	0-2	1-6	·

Group 5 - Bukavu

	Pl	W	D	L	F	A	Pts	SCCL	OCBD	VCMM
SC Cilu Lukala	4	2	1	1	3	1	7		1-0	0-1
OC Bukavu Dawa	4	2	0	2	4	5	6	0-2		2-1
Vita Club Mbuji-Mayi	4	1	1	2	3	4	4	0-0	1-2	

Group 6 - Kisangani

	Pl	W	D	L	F	A	Pts	SEL	ASDK	TSM
FC Saint Eloi Lupopo	4	3	1	0	6	1	10		1-0	1-1
AS Dragons Kinshasa	4	2	0	2	6	5	6	0-2		4-2
TS Malekesa	4	0	1	3	3	9	1	0-2	0-2	

10/02/2008 - 2/03/2008 • Group winners and the two best runners-up qualify for the final round • Other clubs qualify for the Coupe du Congo 2008

COK – COOK ISLANDS

NATIONAL TEAM RECORD
JULY 10TH 2006 TO JULY 12TH 2010

PL	W	D	L	F	A	%
3	0	0	3	0	8	0

FIFA/COCA-COLA WORLD RANKING

1993	1994	1995	1996	1997	1998	1999	2000	2001	2002	2003	2004	2005	2006	2007	High	
-	-	-	188	192	173	182	170	179	182	190	190	194	197	200	**169**	07/00

	2007–2008											Low	
08/07	09/07	10/07	11/07	12/07	01/08	02/08	03/08	04/08	05/08	06/08	07/08	**201**	02/08
198	199	199	200	200	200	201	201	200	200	199	199		

The Cook Islands national team came out of hibernation for the South Pacific Games in Samoa in August 2007, making their first appearance for two and a half years in a tournament that doubled up as a 2010 FIFA World Cup qualifying competition. Having lost all ten previous matches since first taking part in the qualifiers for France 98, the 4-1 victory over Tuvalu in their third match in Samoa was met with jubilation, although it will not go down in the record books as a first win for the Cooks Islands in the World Cup. As Tuvalu are only associate members of the Oceania Football Confederation and, crucially, are not members of FIFA, the match does not go down in the record

INTERNATIONAL HONOURS
None

books as a full international. Predictably, the other three ties were lost although there were no heavy defeats for Tim Jerks' side, which meant a first round exit and the dubious distinction of being one of the first teams to be knocked-out of the World Cup - nearly a full three years ahead of the tournament. That was the extent of the Cook Island's senior international excursions for the season after club champions Nikao Sokattack withdrew from a preliminary competition in the 2007-08 O-League. The U–23 team did take part in the qualifiers for the Beijing Olympics but in just five matches they shipped 39 goals to finish comfortably bottom of the Oceania group.

THE FIFA BIG COUNT OF 2006

	Male	Female		Total
Number of players	2 200	0	Referees and Assistant Referees	100
Professionals	0		Admin, Coaches, Technical, Medical	100
Amateurs 18+	800		Number of clubs	40
Youth under 18	1 000		Number of teams	120
Unregistered	200		Clubs with women's teams	2
Total players	2 200		Players as % of population	10.29%

Cook Islands Football Association (CIFA)
Matavera Main Road, PO Box 29, Avarua, Cook Islands
Tel +682 28980   Fax +682 28981
cifa@cisoccer.org.ck   www.none
President: HARMON Lee   General Secretary: PIRI Mii
Vice-President: PARKER Allen   Treasurer: NUMANGA Jake   Media Officer: TBD
Men's Coach: JERKS Tim   Women's Coach: JERKS Tim
CIFA formed: 1971   OFC: 1994   FIFA: 1994
Green shirts with white sleeves, Green shorts, White socks

RECENT INTERNATIONAL MATCHES PLAYED BY COOK ISLANDS

2002	Opponents		Score	Venue	Comp	Scorers	Att	Referee
No international matches played in 2002								
2003								
No international matches played in 2003								
2004								
5-05	Samoa	D	0-0	Auckland	Fr			
10-05	Tahiti	L	0-2	Honiara	WCq		12 000	Singh FIJ
12-05	Solomon Islands	L	0-5	Honiara	WCq		14 000	Fred VAN
15-05	Tonga	L	1-2	Honiara	WCq	Pareanga [59]	15 000	Sosongan PNG
17-05	New Caledonia	L	0-8	Honiara	WCq		400	Singh FIJ
2005								
No international matches played in 2005								
2006								
No international matches played in 2006								
2007								
27-08	Fiji	L	0-4	Apia	WCq		400	Fred VAN
29-08	New Caledonia	L	0-3	Apia	WCq		200	Fox NZL
1-09	Tuvalu *	W	4-1	Apia	WCq	Mateariki 2 [28 69], Le Mouton [88], Tom [93+]	200	Hester NZL
3-09	Tahiti	L	0-1	Apia	WCq		100	Aimaasu SAM

No international matches played in 2008 before August

Fr = Friendly match • WC = FIFA World Cup • q = qualifier

COOK ISLANDS NATIONAL TEAM RECORDS AND RECORD SEQUENCES

Records			Sequence records					
Victory	3-0	ASA 2000	Wins	2	1998, 2000	Clean sheets	1	
Defeat	0-30	TAH 1971	Defeats	6	1971-85, 2000-01	Goals scored	4	1996-1998
Player Caps	n/a		Undefeated	3	1998	Without goal	5	2001-2004
Player Goals	n/a		Without win	11	2000-	Goals against	16	1971-2000

RECENT LEAGUE AND CUP RECORD

	Championship		Cup		
Year	Champions	Winners	Score	Runners-up	
1996	Avatiu FC	Avatiu FC			
1997	Avatiu FC	Avatiu FC			
1998	No Tournament	Teau-o-Tonga			
1999	Tupapa FC	Tupapa FC		Avatiu FC	
1999	Avatiu FC	Avatiu FC	3-1	Tupapa FC	
2000	Nikao Sokattaccк	Avatiu FC	3-1	Nikao Sokattack	
2001	Tupapa FC	Tupapa FC	5-1	Avatiu FC	
2002	Tupapa FC	Nikao Sokattack	3-2	Tupapa FC	
2003	Tupapa FC	Nikao Sokattack	3-1	Tupapa FC	
2004	Nikao Sokattack	Tupapa FC	3-3 3-1p	Nikao Sokattack	
2005	Nikao Sokattack	Nikao Sokattack			
2006	Nikao Sokattack	Takuvaine	0-0 4-1p	Nikao Sokattack	

COOK ISLANDS COUNTRY INFORMATION

Capital	Avarua	Independence	Self-governing in free asso-	GDP per Capita	$5 000
Population	21 200	Status	ciation with New Zealand	GNP Ranking	n/a
Area km²	240	Language	English, Maori	Dialling code	+682
Population density	88 per km²	Literacy rate	95%	Internet code	.ck
% in urban areas	n/a	Main religion	Christian	GMT +/-	-10
Towns/Cities ('000)	Avarua 13; Mangaia; Amuri; Omoka; Atiu; Mauke				
Neighbours (km)	South Pacific Ocean 120				
Main stadia	National Stadium – Avarua 3 000				

COL – COLOMBIA

NATIONAL TEAM RECORD
JULY 10TH 2006 TO JULY 12TH 2010

PL	W	D	L	F	A	%
25	12	7	6	35	27	62

FIFA/COCA-COLA WORLD RANKING

1993	1994	1995	1996	1997	1998	1999	2000	2001	2002	2003	2004	2005	2006	2007	High	
21	17	15	4	10	34	25	15	5	37	39	26	24	34	17	4	05/02

2007–2008											Low	
08/07	09/07	10/07	11/07	12/07	01/08	02/08	03/08	04/08	05/08	06/08	07/08	41	03/04
31	24	25	17	17	17	21	20	19	19	19	23		

The depth of talent being produced in Colombia was illustrated by the fact that, along with Brazil and Argentina, the country has become a major exporter of footballers with Colombian players featuring in 42 leagues around the globe. As with Brazil it doesn't seem to have diminished the popularity of the championship in Colombia, with big crowds watching an exciting and open competition. Since the start of the decade an incredible ten teams have won the twice yearly tournament, the latest being Boyacá Chicó, a small outfit from the city of Tunja who were founded in 2002 in nearby Bogota. They beat 12-times champions América in the final of the 2008 Apertura

INTERNATIONAL HONOURS
Qualified for the FIFA World Cup finals 1962 1990 1994 1998   Copa América 2001   Juventud de América 1987 2005   South America U-17 1993
Copa Toyota Libertadores Atlético Nacional Medellin 1989 Once Caldas 2004

on penalties. A worrying trend has been an increase in the level of spectator violence which prompted the mayors of both Cali and Bogota to threaten to close down the stadia in their cities if the violence continued. After initial scepticism at the appointment of former Cucuta coach Jorge Luis Pintos to the national team, that has slowly disappeared thanks to a series of positive results. Colombia were the only nation unbeaten after the first six matches in the marathon South American 2010 FIFA World Cup qualifying group, having managed to beat Argentina 2-1 in Bogota.

THE FIFA BIG COUNT OF 2006

	Male	Female		Total
Number of players	2 670 029	364 200	Referees and Assistant Referees	2 200
Professionals	929		Admin, Coaches, Technical, Medical	13 600
Amateurs 18+	89 000		Number of clubs	2 750
Youth under 18	166 000		Number of teams	7 700
Unregistered	1 440 000		Clubs with women's teams	23
Total players	3 043 229		Players as % of population	6.98%

Federación Colombiana de Fútbol (COLFUTBOL)
Avenida 32, No. 16-22 Piso 5°, Apdo Aéreo 17602, Bogotá, Colombia
Tel +57 1 2889838   Fax +57 1 2889559
info@colfutbol.org   www.colfutbol.org
President: BEDOYA Luis   General Secretary: SIERRA Celina
Vice-President: JESURUN Ramon   Treasurer: TBD   Media Officer: ROSAS Victor
Men's Coach: PINTO Jorge   Women's Coach: AGUDELO John
COLFUTBOL formed: 1924   CONMEBOL: 1940   FIFA: 1936
Yellow shirts with blue and red trimmings, Blue shorts, Red socks or Blue shirts,

RECENT INTERNATIONAL MATCHES PLAYED BY COLOMBIA

2006 Opponents		Score	Venue	Comp	Scorers	Att	Referee
2-06	Germany	L 0-3	Mönchengladbach	Fr		45 600	Hauge NOR
4-06	Morocco	W 2-0	Barcelona	Fr	Rodallega [41p], Soto [86]	11 000	Segura Garcia ESP
16-08	Chile	W 2-1	Santiago	Fr	Preciado [68], Soto [88]	15 000	Larrionda URU
2007							
7-02	Uruguay	L 1-3	Cucuta	Fr	Rodallega [80]	26 000	Hoyos COL
25-03	Switzerland	W 3-1	Miami	Fr	Perea [5], Viafara [57], Chitiva [85]	16 000	Vaughn USA
28-03	Paraguay	W 2-0	Bogota	Fr	Mosquera [32], Dominguez [86]	32 000	
9-05	Panama	W 4-0	Panama City	Fr	Mendoza [20], Valoyes [58], Rodallega [63], Anchico [67]	4 000	Archundia MEX
3-06	Montenegro	W 1-0	Matsumoto	Fr	Falcao [33]	10 070	Ogiya JPN
5-06	Japan	D 0-0	Saitama	Fr		45 091	Vollquartz DEN
23-06	Ecuador	W 3-1	Barranquilla	Fr	Rodallega [16], Yepes [30], Perea [79]	35 000	Gomes VEN
28-06	Paraguay	L 0-5	Maracaibo	CAr1		30 000	Larrionda URU
2-07	Argentina	L 2-4	Maracaibo	CAr1	Perea [10], Castrillón [76]	35 000	Simon BRA
5-07	USA	W 1-0	Barquisimento	CAr1	Castrillón [15]	37 000	Andarcia VEN
22-08	Mexico	W 1-0	Commerce City	Fr	Castrillon [52]		Stott USA
8-09	Peru	D 2-2	Lima	Fr	Renteria [33], Falcao Garcia [72]	20 000	Carpio ECU
12-09	Paraguay	W 1-0	Bogota	Fr	Renteria [37]	18 000	Buckley PER
14-10	Brazil	D 0-0	Bogota	WCq		41 000	Amarilla PAR
17-10	Bolivia	D 0-0	La Paz	WCq		19 469	Reinoso ECU
17-11	Venezuela	W 1-0	Bogota	WCq	Bustos [82]	28 273	Selman CHI
20-11	Argentina	W 2-1	Bogota	WCq	Bustos [62], Moreno [83]	41 700	Larrionda URU
2008							
6-02	Uruguay	D 2-2	Montevideo	Fr	Perea 2 [23 73]		
26-03	Honduras	L 1-2	Fort Lauderdale	Fr	Renteria [55]		
30-04	Venezuela	W 5-2	Bucaramanga	Fr	Rodallega 2 [1 75], Polo [11], Hernandez [65], Mosquera.LF [84p]	25 000	Carrillo PER
29-05	Republic of Ireland	L 0-1	London	Fr			Clattenburg ENG
3-06	France	L 0-1	Paris	Fr		79 727	Dean ENG
14-06	Peru	D 1-1	Lima	WCq	Rodallega [8]	25 000	Torres PAR
18-06	Ecuador	D 0-0	Quito	WCq		33 588	Baldassi ARG

Fr = Friendly match • CC = FIFA Confederations Cup • GC = CONCACAF Gold Cup • CA = Copa América • WC = FIFA World Cup
q = qualifier • r1 = first round group • qf = quarter-final • sf = semi-final • 3p = third place play-off

COLOMBIA NATIONAL TEAM PLAYERS

	Player		Ap	G	Club	Date of Birth		Player		Ap	G	Club	Date of Birth
1	Agustín Julio	GK	7	0	Santa Fe	25 10 1974	15	Carlos Sánchez	MF			Valenciennes	6 02 1986
2	Walter Jose Moreno	DF	4	0	Atlético Nacional	18 05 1978	16	Freddy Grisales	MF	37	6	Independiente	22 09 1975
3	Pedro Portocarrero	DF			Cúcuta	13 06 1977	17	Dayro Moreno	FW	1	1	Steaua Buc'rest	16 09 1985
4	Julián Estiven Vélez	DF	3	0	Atlético Nacional	9 02 1982	18	Juan Camilo Zúñiga	DF	2	0	Siena	14 12 1985
5	Cristian Zapata	DF	18	0	Udinese	30 09 1986		Aquivaldo Mosquera	DF	17	1	Sevilla	22 06 1981
6	Fabián Andrés Vargas	MF	29	0	Boca Juniors	17 04 1980		Pablo Stifer Armero	DF	4	0	América Cali	2 11 1986
7	Edixon Perea	FW	18	6	Grêmio	20 04 1984		Elvis Gonzalez	DF			Cúcuta	20 02 1982
8	Freddy Guarín	MF	7	0	FC Porto	30 06 1986		Nilson Cortes	MF	1	0	Once Caldas	29 03 1977
9	Radamel Falcao	FW	7	2	River Plate	10 02 1986		Jose Amaya	MF			Maccabi Tel Aviv	16 07 1980
10	Giovanni Hernández	MF	35	5	Atlético Junior	16 06 1976		Juan Carlos Escobar	MF			Krylia Sovetov	30 10 1982
11	Hugo Rodallega	FW	19	6	Necaxa	25 07 1985		Elkin Soto	MF			FSV Mainz 05	4 07 1980
12	Róbinson Zapata	GK	3	0	Steaua Buc'rest	30 09 1978		Nelson Rivas	DF	1	0	Internazionale	25 03 1983
13	Rubén Darío Bustos	DF	10	2	Internacional	28 08 1981		Luis Perea	DF	37	0	Atlético Madrid	30 01 1979
14	Macnelly Torres	MF	9	1	Colo Colo	5 04 1984		Gerardo Bedoya	MF	44	1	Millonarios	26 09 1975
								Wason Renteria	FW	6	3	FC Porto	4 07 1985

Colombia's squad for the June 2008 FIFA World Cup qualifiers

COLOMBIA NATIONAL TEAM RECORDS AND RECORD SEQUENCES

Records			Sequence records					
Victory	5-0	ARG 93, URU 04, PER 05	Wins	7	1988-1989	Clean sheets	6	2001
Defeat	0-9	BRA 1957	Defeats	7	1947-1949	Goals scored	15	1995-1997
Player Caps	111	Carlos Valderrama	Undefeated	27	1992-1994	Without goal	6	2002-2003
Player Goals	31	Adolfo Valencia	Without win	15	1947-1957	Goals against	14	1938-46, 1961-63

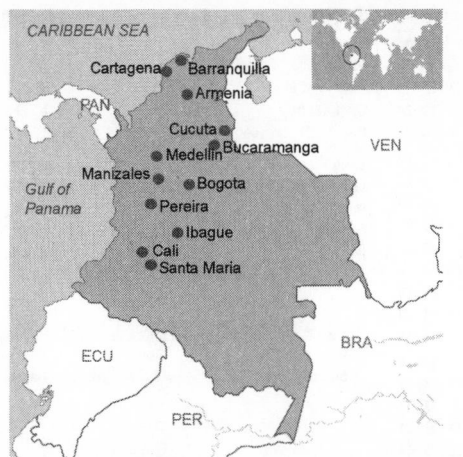

		Population '000
1	Bogotá	7 363
2	Cali	2 498
3	Medellín	2 042
4	Barranquilla	1 429
5	Cartagena	1 001
6	Cúcuta	760
7	Bucaramanga	591
8	Pereira	460
9	Santa Marta	459
10	Ibagué	430
11	Bello	413
12	Pasto	400
13	Neiva	370
14	Manizales	362
15	Soledad	360
16	Villavicencio	338
17	Soacha	332
18	Armenia	326
19	Valledupar	324
20	Itagüí	300
21	Montería	281
22	Sincelejo	275
23	Envigado	172
24	Tuluá	170

REPUBLIC OF COLOMBIA; REPUBLICA DE COLOMBIA

Capital	Bogotá	Language	Spanish			Independence	1810
Population	43 593 035	Area	1 138 910 km²	Density	37 per km²	% in cities	73%
GDP per cap	$6 300	Dailling code	+57	Internet	.co	GMT + / -	-5

MEDALS TABLE

		Overall			League			Sth Am			City	Stadium	Cap'ty	Formed
		G	S	B	G	S	B	G	S	B				
1	Millonarios	14	10	12	13	9	8	1	1	4	Bogotá	El Campin	48 600	1946
2	América Cali	13	11	12	12	7	5	1	4	7	Cali	Pascual Guerrero	45 000	1927
3	Atlético Nacional Medellín	13	11	10	10	9	5	3	2	5	Medellín	Atanasio Girardot	52 700	1942
4	Deportivo Cali	8	15	8	8	12	6		3	2	Cali	Pascual Guerrero	45 000	1908
5	Independiente Santa Fe	6	5	5	6	3	4		2	1	Bogotá	El Campin	48 600	1941
6	Atlético Junior	5	5	3	5	5	2			1	Barranquilla	Metropolitano	58 000	1924
7	Independiente Medellín	4	6	4	4	6	3			1	Medellín	Atanasio Girardot	52 700	1913
8	Once Caldas	3	1	1	2	1	1	1			Manizales	Palogrande	33 000	1930
9	Deportes Tolima	1	4	2	1	4	1			1	Ibagué	Manuel Toro	19 000	1954
10	Deportes Quindío	1	2	1	1	2	1				Armenia	Centenario	29 000	1951
11	Cúcuta Deportivo	1	1	3	1	1	2			1	Cúcuta	General Santander	25 000	1949
12	Deportivo Pasto	1	1		1	1					Pasto	Libertad	14 000	1919
13	Union Magdalena	1		1	1		1				Santa Marta	Eduardo Santos	23 000	1950
14	Boyacá Chico	1			1						Tunja	Independencia	8 500	2002
15	Boca Junior		2	2		2	2				Cali			
16	Atlético Bucaramanga		1	3		1	3				Bucaramanga	Alfonso Lopez	33 000	1949
17	Atlético Huila		1			1					Neiva	Guillermo Alcid	15 000	1990
	Real Cartagena		1			1					Cartagena	Olimpico	14 000	1971
	CD La Equidad		1			1					Bogotá	Metropolitano de Techo	10 000	1982

RECENT LEAGUE AND CUP RECORD

	Championship Play-off/Apertura from 2002				Clausura		
Year	Champions	Score	Runners-up		Winners	Score	Runners-up
1998	Deportivo Cali	4-0 0-0	Once Caldas				
1999	Atlético Nacional	1-1 0-0 4-2p	América Cali				
2000	América Cali	‡	Atlético Junior				
2001	América Cali	1-0 2-0	Independiente Medellín				
2002	América Cali	2-1 1-0	Independiente Medellín		Independiente Medellín	2-0 1-1	Deportivo Pasto
2003	Once Caldas	0-0 1-0	Atlético Junior		Deportes Tolima	2-0 1-3 4-2p	Deportivo Cali
2004	Independiente Medellín	2-1 0-0	Atlético Nacional		Atlético Junior	3-0 2-5 5-4p	Atlético Nacional
2005	Atlético Nacional	0-0 2-0	Independiente Santa Fe		Deportivo Cali	2-0 1-0	Real Cartagena
2006	Deportivo Pasto	1-0 1-1	Deportivo Cali		Cúcuta Deportivo	1-0 1-1	Deportes Tolima
2007	Atlético Nacional	1-0 2-1	Atlético Huila		Atlético Nacional	3-0 0-0	La Equidad Bogota
2008	Boyacá Chico	1-1 1-1 4-2p	América Cali				

Colombia adopted the format of two Championships per year in 2002 • ‡ Final tournament played as a league

COLOMBIA 2007 DIMAYOR TORNEO CLAUSURA

	Pl	W	D	L	F	A	Pts
At. Nacional Medellín †	18	11	5	2	28	12	38
La Equidad Bogotá †	18	10	4	4	27	18	34
América Cali †	18	10	4	4	24	15	34
Deportes Tolima †	18	10	3	5	26	17	33
Cúcuta Deportivo †	18	9	5	4	30	19	32
Deportivo Pasto †	18	8	6	4	28	16	30
Once Caldas †	18	8	5	5	29	22	29
Boyacá Chico †	18	7	6	5	20	18	27
Deportes Quindío	18	8	2	8	29	27	26
Independ. Medellín	18	8	1	9	22	25	25
Millonarios	18	5	5	8	18	28	20
Deportivo Cali	18	3	9	6	18	20	18
Atlético Junior	18	5	3	10	17	28	18
Atlético Bucaramanga	18	5	2	11	20	28	17
Atlético Huila	18	3	8	7	17	27	17
Deportes Pereira	18	3	8	7	15	25	17
Real Cartagena	18	3	5	10	16	25	14
Independ. Santa Fe	18	2	7	9	16	30	13

21/07/2007 - 11/11/2007 • † Qualified for the second stage

TORNEO CLAUSURA SECOND STAGE

Group A	Pl	W	D	L	F	A	Pts	NM	AC	OC	CD
At. Nacional Medellín †	6	3	2	1	8	5	11		2-0	1-0	2-2
América Cali	6	3	1	2	6	6	10	2-1		2-1	1-0
Once Caldas	6	2	1	3	4	5	7	0-0	1-0		1-2
Cúcuta Deportivo	6	1	2	3	6	8	5	1-2	1-1	0-1	

Group B	Pl	W	D	L	F	A	Pts	LE	DP	DT	BC
La Equidad Bogotá †	6	3	3	0	6	3	12		1-0	1-1	1-1
Deportivo Pasto	6	2	2	2	5	3	8	0-1		0-0	0-0
Deportes Tolima	6	1	3	2	6	6	6	1-2	1-2		1-1
Boyacá Chico	6	0	4	2	2	7	4	0-0	0-3	0-2	

24/11/2007 - 12/12/2007 • † Qualified for the final

TORNEO CLAUSURA FINAL

Home team first leg	Score	Home team second leg
La Equidad Bogotá	0-3 0-0	Atlético Nacional Medellín

See *Almanack of World Football 2008* for the 2007 Apertura tables

COLOMBIA 2007 LIGA DIMAYOR REGULAR SEASON RESULTS

PRIMERA A

	América	Bucaramanga	Cali	Cartagena	Chicó	Cúcuta	Huila	Junior	La Equidad	Medellín	Millonarios	Nacional	Once Caldas	Pasto	Perreira	Quindío	Santa Fe	Tolima
América Cali	—	4-2	0-2 0-0	1-0	1-2	1-2	2-1	3-1	1-1	1-1	2-2	1-1	2-2	1-0	2-0	0-0	3-2	1-0
Atlético Bucaramanga	1-0	—	2-0	1-0	2-1	1-2 1-2	5-0	2-1	1-2	0-1	1-0	3-2	0-0	1-0	0-1	3-2	1-1	3-1
Deportivo Cali	2-2 0-1	1-1	—	4-1	2-2	2-1	2-2	4-1	0-1	0-1	2-0	1-1	1-0	4-4	2-1	3-2	1-1	1-2
Real Cartagena	2-2	3-1	0-2	—	1-0	1-0	1-2	1-1	1-0	1-2	2-2	0-0	0-2	1-1	3-3	1-1	0-0	2-1 1-0
Boyacá Chicó	2-1	1-1	1-1	1-1	—	1-0	1-0	2-0	0-0	2-1	1-0	1-2	1-0	0-0	2-0	3-0 1-0	0-1	1-0
Cúcuta Deportivo	2-0	2-0 3-1	1-1	1-0	5-1	—	2-0	2-0	3-1	0-1	2-2	1-1	4-1	2-0	1-0	2-0	4-1	2-1
Atlético Huila	1-1	2-1	1-0	2-0	0-0	2-2	—	1-0	2-0	0-3	1-1	2-2	3-2	2-1	1-0	0-1	0-0	2-3 3-0
Atlético Junior	1-3	0-0	2-1	2-2 4-2	0-0	2-1	3-1	—	2-2	1-2	1-1	2-1	4-2	1-0	0-0	3-2	2-1	1-2
La Equidad Bogotá	1-0	1-1	0-1	2-0	3-1	1-0	2-1	5-0	—	0-1	1-1	3-4	0-0	2-3 0-0	3-3	2-1	1-2	4-1
Indep. Medellín	1-3	1-2	3-3	1-0	0-2	1-1	1-3	3-1	2-1	—	2-1	2-2 1-4	1-0	2-1	1-3	3-4	2-0	2-1
Millonarios	1-2	2-1	1-2	1-0	2-1	1-1	3-0	2-0	1-0	5-1	—	0-1	1-2	0-3	1-0	1-1	4-2 2-2	2-0
At. Nacional Medellín	4-0	1-0	0-2	1-0	3-0	0-1	3-2	0-0	0-0	2-2 1-0	3-0	—	2-0	1-1	2-0	2-1	2-0	1-0
Once Caldas	2-3	1-0	2-2	2-1	1-0	1-0	2-2	1-1	2-1	1-0	2-0	2-2	—	2-3	1-1 2-2	1-0	0-1	0-1
Deportivo Pasto	2-2	2-0	0-0	1-0	1-1	3-0	1-0	1-1	2-0 4-1	1-0	0-1	0-1	3-2	—	1-1	1-2	0-1	2-0
Deportivo Pereira	1-0	1-1	1-0	1-1	0-1	2-2	0-0	0-1	2-2	2-0	1-1	0-2 0-0 3-0	0-1		0-1	2-2	2-0
Deportes Quindío	0-2	1-1	1-1	1-0	1-2 1-5	0-1	1-0	1-0	0-0	0-4	6-1	2-1	1-2	2-0	3-1	—	3-0	1-2
Indep. Santa Fe	2-0	4-1	0-0	1-1	1-0	3-3	1-0	0-0	1-2	2-4 1-2 0-1	0-2	0-4	0-0	2-0	0-0		—	1-1
Deportes Tolima	6-0	3-1	1-1	0-0	2-0	2-0 1-2 3-0	2-1	2-1	4-2	0-0	2-1	3-1	1-2	3-0	1-1	1-2		—

Apertura 2006 results are shown in the shaded boxes • Local rivals play each other four times in the regular season. In this instance the Apertura results are listed first • Real Cartagena had the worst record over three seasons and were relegated. Deportivo Perreira, with the second worst record, entered a play-off against the Primera B runners-up Academica Bogota • Relegation play-off: Academica Bogota 1-1 1-3 Deportivo Pereira

COLOMBIA 2007
PRIMERA B (2) APERTURA

Group A	Pl	W	D	L	F	A	Pts
Envigado †	18	9	4	5	27	15	31
Valledupar †	18	9	3	6	23	19	30
Unión Magdalena †	18	7	8	3	17	13	29
Deportivo Rionegro †	18	8	4	6	25	25	28
Barranquilla FC	18	7	6	5	24	15	27
Atlético Bello	18	6	8	4	25	16	26
Bajo Cauca	18	7	3	8	26	29	24
Córdoba Montería	18	6	4	8	17	18	22
Alianza Petrolera	18	1	3	14	13	51	6

Group B	Pl	W	D	L	F	A	Pts
Bogotá FC †	18	8	6	4	27	19	30
Academia Bogotá †	18	7	8	3	21	14	29
Patriotas Tunja †	18	8	4	6	27	18	28
Centauros Villavicencio†	18	7	5	6	24	24	26
Depor Jamundí	18	6	6	6	15	21	24
Corporación Tuluá	18	6	5	7	15	15	23
Real Santander	18	7	2	9	17	18	23
Girardot FC	18	6	2	10	15	20	20
Expreso Rojo	18	4	5	9	19	27	17

10/02/2007 - 12/05/2007 • † Qualified for the second stage

APERTURA SECOND STAGE

Group A	Pl	W	D	L	F	A	Pts
Envigado †	6	4	2	0	7	2	14
Unión Magdalena	6	3	2	1	9	5	11
Deportivo Rionegro	6	2	2	2	7	5	8
Valledupar	6	0	0	6	3	14	0

Group B	Pl	W	D	L	F	A	Pts
Academia Bogotá †	6	4	2	0	11	1	14
Centauros Villavicencio	6	2	3	1	6	6	9
Patriotas Tunja	6	1	2	3	7	8	5
Bogotá FC	6	1	1	4	4	13	3

16/05/2007 - 2/06/2007 • † Qualified for the final
Final: Academica Bogota 1-1 1-1 3-4p **Envigado**

COLOMBIA 2007
PRIMERA B (2) CLAUSURA

Group A	Pl	W	D	L	F	A	Pts
Bogotá FC †	18	7	8	3	22	14	29
Envigado †	18	6	11	1	16	10	29
Unión Magdalena †	18	8	4	6	23	16	28
Depor Jamundí †	18	8	4	6	19	17	28
Girardot FC	18	5	9	4	14	14	24
Córdoba Montería	18	6	4	8	21	23	22
Atlético Bello	18	4	8	6	18	20	20
Centauros Villavicencio	18	5	5	8	16	22	20
Alianza Petrolera	18	2	6	10	10	25	12

Group B	Pl	W	D	L	F	A	Pts
Deportivo Rionegro †	18	10	5	3	25	14	35
Academia Bogotá †	18	8	4	6	25	16	28
Patriotas Tunja †	18	7	5	6	27	20	26
Valledupar †	18	7	4	7	19	21	25
Expreso Rojo	18	7	4	7	21	18	25
Bajo Cauca	18	5	8	5	21	22	23
Corporación Tuluá	18	5	8	5	21	25	23
Barranquilla FC	18	6	3	9	23	34	21
Real Santander	18	5	2	11	14	24	17

7/07/2007 - 6/10/2007 • † Qualified for the second stage

CLAUSURA SECOND STAGE

Group A	Pl	W	D	L	F	A	Pts
Envigado †	6	3	2	1	8	4	11
Bogotá FC	6	2	3	1	4	4	9
Unión Magdalena	6	0	5	1	3	4	5
Depor Jamundí	6	1	2	3	3	6	5

Group B	Pl	W	D	L	F	A	Pts
Academia Bogotá †	6	4	2	0	12	6	14
Valledupar	6	2	2	2	5	6	8
Deportivo Rionegro	6	1	3	2	5	7	6
Patriotas Tunja	6	1	1	4	7	10	4

13/10/2007 - 3/11/2007 • † Qualified for the final
Final: **Envigado** 2-1 2-1 Academica Bogota

Envigado won both the Apertura and Clausura and were promoted automatically • Academica Bogota qualified for a play-off with Deportivo Perreira

COLOMBIA 2008
DIMAYOR TORNEO APERTURA

	Pl	W	D	L	F	A	Pts
La Equidad Bogotá †	18	10	5	3	25	13	35
Boyacá Chicó †	18	9	5	4	30	19	32
Indep. Santa Fe †	18	9	4	5	25	18	31
Indep. Medellín †	18	8	5	5	26	14	29
Envigado †	18	8	4	6	20	20	28
Deportivo Cali †	18	7	6	5	19	21	27
América Cali †	18	6	8	4	34	28	26
Deportes Quindío †	18	6	7	5	25	22	25
Cúcuta Deportivo	18	7	4	7	20	17	25
Atlético Bucaramanga	18	8	1	9	20	24	25
Millonarios	18	6	6	6	23	23	24
Atlético Junior	18	7	3	8	21	23	24
Atlético Huila	18	5	8	5	25	25	23
At. Nacional Medellín	18	7	1	10	16	19	22
Once Caldas	18	5	4	9	20	28	19
Deportivo Pasto	18	5	4	9	15	24	19
Deportes Pereira	18	5	4	9	21	33	19
Deportes Tolima	18	4	3	11	21	35	15

1/02/2008 - 18/05/2008 • † Qualified for the second stage

TORNEO APERTURA SECOND STAGE

Group A	Pl	W	D	L	F	A	Pts	AC	En	SF	LE
América Cali †	6	4	1	1	11	4	13		2-0	3-0	1-1
Envigado	6	2	2	2	8	9	8	1-3		2-0	1-0
Indep. Santa Fe	6	2	1	3	6	8	7	2-0	2-2		0-1
La Equidad Bogotá	6	1	2	3	4	8	5	0-2	2-2	0-2	

Group B	Pl	W	D	L	F	A	Pts	BC	IM	DQ	DC
Boyacá Chicó †	6	2	4	0	9	7	10		1-1	2-1	2-1
Indep. Medellín	6	2	3	1	10	4	9	1-1		2-0	5-0
Deportes Quindío	6	1	3	2	5	6	6	1-1	0-0		1-1
Deportivo Cali	6	1	2	3	6	13	5	2-2	2-1	0-2	

21/05/2008 - 28/06/2008 • † Qualified for the final

TORNEO APERTURA FINAL

Home team first leg	Score	Home team second leg
América Cali	1-1 1-1 2-4p	**Boyacá Chico**

The results of the 2008 Apertura along with details of the 2008 Clausura will appear in next year's *Almanack of World Football*

COM – COMOROS

NATIONAL TEAM RECORD

JULY 10TH 2006 TO JULY 12TH 2010

PL	W	D	L	F	A	%
8	1	0	7	6	22	12.5

FIFA/COCA-COLA WORLD RANKING

1993	1994	1995	1996	1997	1998	1999	2000	2001	2002	2003	2004	2005	2006	2007		High	
-	-	-	-	-	-	-	-	-	-	-	-	-	207	187		**180**	06/07

	2007–2008											Low	
08/07	09/07	10/07	11/07	12/07	01/08	02/08	03/08	04/08	05/08	06/08	07/08	**207**	12/06
182	184	185	186	187	191	193	195	195	195	194	194		

There was a World Cup debut for Comoros in October 2007 when they played near neighbours Madagascar in one of just three preliminaries in the African zone. The two-legged tie saw the Comoros go down 10-2 on aggregate, but just over six months later there was a substantial improvement as the side participated in a much more competitive fashion in the Cosafa Cup in South Africa. The country has kept up an active brief since joining FIFA in 2005, participating also in the Arab Nations Cup qualifiers and the Indian Ocean Island Games. November's World Cup game against Madagascar was the first official international played at the Moroni stadium, whose

INTERNATIONAL HONOURS

None

artificial turf was installed as part of FIFA's 'Win in Africa with Africa' programme. It also allowed Coin Nord de Mitsamiouli to host their first ever home tie in the CAF Champions League, beating Curepipe Starlight of Mauritius 1-0 in March. They had gone down 2-0 in the first leg of the first round tie and were narrowly eliminated. Previously Comorian clubs had to cede their home leg because the stadium was not sanctioned for the African competitions. At home, Coin Nord beat AJSM 4-2 on penalties after a 3-3 draw in the 2007 Championship final, while Jassem beat Etoile d'Or on penalties in the Cup Final.

THE FIFA BIG COUNT OF 2006

	Male	Female		Total
Number of players	27 100	0	Referees and Assistant Referees	0
Professionals	0		Admin, Coaches, Technical, Medical	100
Amateurs 18+	600		Number of clubs	10
Youth under 18	500		Number of teams	30
Unregistered	0		Clubs with women's teams	0
Total players	27 100		Players as % of population	3.92

Fédération Comorienne de Football (FFC)

Case Postale 798, Moroni, Comoros

Tel +269 733179   Fax +269 733236

dhl@snpt.km   www.none

President: SALIM Tourqui   General Secretary: ABDOU CHAKOUR Mariyatta

Vice-President: ABDELKARIM Abderemane   Treasurer: TBD   Media Officer: None

Men's Coach: CHAMUTE Abderemane Mohamed   Women's Coach: HASSANE Mohamed

FFC formed: 1979   CAF: 1986   FIFA: 2005

Green shirts, Green shorts, Green Socks

RECENT INTERNATIONAL MATCHES PLAYED BY COMOROS

2002 Opponents	Score	Venue	Comp	Scorers	Att	Referee
No international matches played in 2002						
2003						
30-08 Reunion †	L 0-1	Flacq	IOr1		103	Labrosse SEY
2-09 Reunion †	L 0-4	Flacq	IOr1			
4-09 Mauritius †	L 0-5	Curepipe	IOsf		4 500	Labrosse SEY
6-09 Seychelles †	L 0-2	Curepipe	IO3p			
2004						
No international matches played in 2004						
2005						
No international matches played in 2005						
2006						
14-12 Yemen	L 0-2	Sana'a	ARq			
17-12 Djibouti	W 4-2	Sana'a	ARq	Meknesh Bin Daoud [5], Ahmed Seif 2 [33 75], Mohamed Moni [70]		
2007						
14-08 Madagascar	L 0-3	Antananarivo	Fr			
14-10 Madagascar	L 2-6	Antananarivo	WCq	Daoud Midtadi [6], Ibor Bakar [53p]	7 754	Kaoma ZAM
17-11 Madagascar	L 0-4	Moroni	WCq		1 610	Damon RSA
2008						
20-07 Namibia	L 0-3	Secunda	CCr1			
22-07 Malawi	L 0-1	Secunda	CCr1			
24-07 Lesotho	L 0-1	Secunda	CCr1			

IO = Indian Ocean Games • AR = Arab Cup • q = qualifier • r1 = first round group • sf = semi-final • 3p = third place play-off
† Not regarded as a full international because Comoros was not yet a member of FIFA

COMOROS NATIONAL TEAM RECORDS AND RECORD SEQUENCES

Records			Sequence records					
Victory	2-1	REU 1979	Wins	1	1979, 1990	Clean sheets	1	1990
Defeat	1-6	REU 1979	Defeats	10	1990-	Goals scored	3	1979
Player Caps	n/a		Undefeated	1	1979, 1985, 1990	Without goal	8	1993-
Player Goals	n/a		Without win	10	1990	Goals against	10	1990-

Comoros joined FIFA in 2005 and have yet to play an official international. The above data relates to games played in the Indian Ocean Games

RECENT LEAGUE AND CUP RECORD

	Comoros	Grande Comore	Anjouan	Mwali	Cup
Year	Champions	Champions	Champions	Champions	Winners
2003		Volcan Club		Belle Lumière	Coin Nord
2004		Elan Club	Etoile d'Or	Belle Lumière	
2005	Coin Nord	Coin Nord	Chirazienne	Belle Lumière	Volcan Club
2006	AJSM Mutsamudu		AJSM Mutsamudu	Fomboni Club	Chirazienne
2007	Coin Nord	Coin Nord	Ngazi Sports	Fomboni Club	Jassem

COMOROS COUNTRY INFORMATION

Capital	Moroni	Independence	1975 from France	GDP per Capita	$700
Population	671 247	Status	Republic	GNP Ranking	155
Area km²	2 170	Language	Arabic, French, Shikomoro	Dialling code	+269
Population density	309 per km²	Literacy rate	56.5%	Internet code	.km
% in urban areas	34%	Main religion	Muslim 98%	GMT +/-	+3
Towns/Cities ('000)	Moroni 42 (Grande Comore/Njazidja); Mutsamudu 14 (Anjouan/Nzwani); Fomboni 14 (Moheli/Mwali)				
Neighbours (km)	Indian Ocean 340				
Main stadia	Stade de Beaumer, Moroni				

CPV – CAPE VERDE ISLANDS

NATIONAL TEAM RECORD
JULY 10TH 2006 TO JULY 12TH 2010

PL	W	D	L	F	A	%
14	5	5	4	11	15	5.6

FIFA/COCA-COLA WORLD RANKING

1993	1994	1995	1996	1997	1998	1999	2000	2001	2002	2003	2004	2005	2006	2007		High	
147	161	144	155	171	167	177	156	159	154	143	129	118	78	111		**68**	07/07

				2007–2008									Low	

08/07	09/07	10/07	11/07	12/07	01/08	02/08	03/08	04/08	05/08	06/08	07/08		Low	
72	76	112	112	111	110	108	111	107	107	109	85		**182**	04/00

The contrast between the prowess of the Cape Verde Islands and its tiny population continues to be stark as the former Portuguese colony looks to a place in the second phase of the African World Cup qualifiers following two wins over Mauritius and another against Tanzania. Not bad for a country that a decade ago played little international football. The continuing discovery of players from the vast diaspora of people from the west African island archipelago continues unabated. Recently capped internationals have come from communities in Luxembourg, the Netherlands and the USA, to add to talent readily available in Portugal. One of their number, Dutch-born Cecilio

INTERNATIONAL HONOURS
Copa Amilcar Cabral 2000

Lopes, made his debut in a friendly in Luxembourg, becoming arguably the first ever African international that had never been to the continent. It a was situation he remedied a week later when he appeared in the FIFA World Cup qualifier in Cameroon. Striker Dady completed a high profile move to Osasuna in Spain after ending among the top scorers in the Portugese league in 2007 but the Cape Verdians missed out on the talent of Manchester United's Nani, who opted to play for Portugal instead. A locally-based selection reached the final of the Amilcar Cabral Cup in Guinea Bissau, going down 2-1 to Mali's under-23 side in the final.

THE FIFA BIG COUNT OF 2006

	Male	Female		Total
Number of players	33 500	1 600	Referees and Assistant Referees	256
Professionals	0		Admin, Coaches, Technical, Medical	500
Amateurs 18+	7 000		Number of clubs	82
Youth under 18	4 500		Number of teams	180
Unregistered	4 200		Clubs with women's teams	0
Total players	35 100		Players as % of population	8.34%

Federação Caboverdiana de Futebol (FCF)

Praia Cabo Verde, FCF CX, Case postale 234, Praia, Cape Verde Islands
Tel +238 2 611362   Fax +238 2 611362
fcf@cvtelecom.cv   www.fcf.cv
President: SEMEDO Mario   General Secretary: REZENDE Jose João
Vice-President: ALMEIDA Fernando   Treasurer: REZENDE Jose João   Media Officer: None
Men's Coach: DE DEUS Joao   Women's Coach: none
FCF formed: 1982   CAF: 1986   FIFA: 1986
Blue shirts, Blue shorts, Blue socks or White shirts, White shorts, Red socks

RECENT INTERNATIONAL MATCHES PLAYED BY THE CAPE VERDE ISLANDS

2005	Opponents	Score		Venue	Comp	Scorers	Att	Referee
26-03	Burkina Faso	W	2-1	Ouagadougou	WCq	Calo 2 [48] [87]	27 500	Evehe CMR
4-06	South Africa	L	1-2	Praia	WCq	Gomes [77]	6 000	Benouza ALG
18-06	Uganda	L	0-1	Kampala	WCq		5 000	Kidane ERI
17-08	Angola	L	1-2	Lisbon	Fr	Lito [26]		
4-09	Congo DR	L	1-2	Kinshasa	WCq	Cafu [24]	75 000	Guezzaz MAR
8-10	Ghana	L	0-4	Praia	WCq		6 500	Daami TUN
2006								
27-05	Portugal	L	1-4	Evora	Fr	OG [21]		
3-09	Gambia	L	0-2	Bakau	CNq			Pare BFA
7-10	Guinea	W	1-0	Praia	CNq	Lito [52]		Diatta SEN
2007								
24-03	Algeria	L	0-2	Algiers	CNq			Abd El Fatah EGY
2-06	Algeria	D	2-2	Praia	CNq	Marco Soares [58], Hernani [89]		Aboubacar CIV
16-06	Gambia	D	0-0	Praia	CNq			Aguidissou BEN
9-09	Guinea	L	0-4	Conakry	CNq			Trabelsi TUN
3-12	Gambia	D	0-0	Bissau	Fr			
7-12	Guinea-Bissau	D	1-1	Bissau	Fr	Babanco [10]. W 3-2p		
2008								
24-05	Burkina Faso	W	1-0	Alcochete	Fr	Toy Adao		
27-05	Luxembourg	D	1-1	Luxembourg	Fr	Valter [83]	2 051	Radovanovic MNE
31-05	Cameroon	L	0-2	Yaoundé	WCq		20 000	Djaoupe TOG
7-06	Tanzania	W	1-0	Praia	WCq	Babanco [73]	6 000	El Achiri MAR
15-06	Mauritius	W	1-0	Curepipe	WCq	Dady [43p]	1 480	Kaoma ZAM
22-06	Mauritius	W	3-1	Praia	WCq	Dady 2 [45] [58], Marco Soares [78]	2 850	Coulibaly MLI

r = Friendly match • CN = CAF African Cup of Nations • WC = FIFA World Cup
q = qualifier • * Abandoned after 85 minutes when Mauritania were reduced to six players - the result stood

CAPE VERDE ISLANDS NATIONAL TEAM RECORDS AND RECORD SEQUENCES

Records			Sequence records					
Victory	3-0	GNB 81, MTN 03, SWZ 03	Wins	3	2000	Clean sheets	3	2000
Defeat	2-5	SEN 1981	Defeats	7	2005-2006	Goals scored	7	2000
Player Caps	n/a		Undefeated	7	2000	Without goal	5	1985-87, 1998-2000
Player Goals	n/a		Without win	9	1997-2000	Goals against	9	1988-1989

RECENT LEAGUE RECORD

	Championship						Championship Play-off		
Year	Champions	Pts	Runners-up	Pts	Third	Pts	Champions	Score	Runners-up
2001	Onze Unidos	14	Académica do Sal	13	Botafogo	11			
2002	Sporting da Praia	19	Batuque	19	Académica Fogo	16			
2003	Académico do Sal						Académico do Sal	3-1 3-2	FC Ultramarina
2004	Sal-Rei SC						Sal-Rei SC	2-0 1-2	Académica Praia
2005	Derby São Vicente						Derby São Vicente	1-1 4-3	Sporting da Praia
2006	Sporting da Praia						Sporting da Praia	1-0 2-2	Académica do Sal
2007	Sporting da Praia						Sporting da Praia	0-0 1-1	Académica Mindelo
2008									

CAPE VERDE ISLANDS COUNTRY INFORMATION

Capital	Praia	Independence	1975 from Portugal	GDP per Capita	$1 400
Population	415 294	Status	Republic	GNP Ranking	166
Area km²	4 033	Language	Portuguese	Dialling code	+238
Population density	102 per km²	Literacy rate	76%	Internet code	.cv
% in urban areas	54%	Main religion	Christian	GMT +/-	-1
Towns/Cities ('000)	Praia 111; Mindelo 69; Santa Maria 16; Pedra Badejo 9; São Filipe 8; Assomada 7				
Neighbours (km)	Cape Verde consists of a group of 13 islands in the North Atlantic Ocean				
Main stadia	Estadio da Varzea – Praia 8 000; Estadio Municipal Adérito Sena – Midelo 5 000				

CRC – COSTA RICA

NATIONAL TEAM RECORD

JULY 10TH 2006 TO JULY 12TH 2010

PL	W	D	L	F	A	%
26	7	13	6	35	25	51.9

FIFA/COCA-COLA WORLD RANKING

1993	1994	1995	1996	1997	1998	1999	2000	2001	2002	2003	2004	2005	2006	2007		High	
42	65	78	72	51	67	64	60	30	21	17	27	21	68	70		17	05/03

	2007–2008											Low	
08/07	09/07	10/07	11/07	12/07	01/08	02/08	03/08	04/08	05/08	06/08	07/08	9	07/96
52	56	66	69	70	69	71	72	75	77	75	79		

These are worrying times for Central America's most successful nation after the national team went on its longest ever run of matches without a win. Having won a friendly against Chile before the 2007 CONCACAF Gold Cup, the Ticos didn't win again for over a year - 14 matches in total. Hernan Medford's side became noted as draw specialists with 10 of those games ending in a stalemate including a run of six on the trot. Costa Rica finally won again when they beat Grenada in the second leg of a 2010 FIFA World Cup qualifier having predictably drawn the first leg in

INTERNATIONAL HONOURS

Qualified for the FIFA World Cup finals 1990 2002 2006 Central American Championship 1941 1946 1948 1953 1955 1960 1961 1963
UNCAF Championship 1991 1997 1999 2003 2005 CONCACAF U-20 Championship 1954 1960 1988 CONCACAF U-17 Championship 1994
CONCACAF Club Championship LD Alajuelense 1986 2004 Deportivo Saprissa 1993 1995 2005 CS Cartiginés 1995

Grenada. Medford was replaced by Rodrigo Kenton after the victory over Grenada in an effort to try and ensure qualification for a third consecutive World Cup finals. In club football Deportivo Saprissa were once again the team of the year, winning both the Apertura and Clausura in the Costa Rican championship to take the overall title without having to go through an end of season play-off - just as they had done in 2006 and 2007. Saprissa also made it through to the final of the 2008 CONCACAF Champions' Cup where they lost to Mexico's Pachuca.

THE FIFA BIG COUNT OF 2006

	Male	Female		Total
Number of players	1 050 120	34 468	Referees and Assistant Referees	630
Professionals	1 025		Admin, Coaches, Technical, Medical	4 236
Amateurs 18+	17 500		Number of clubs	248
Youth under 18	31 208		Number of teams	1 391
Unregistered	1 005 000		Clubs with women's teams	6
Total players	1 084 588		Players as % of population	26.61%

Federación Costarricense de Fútbol (FEDEFUTBOL)

Costado Norte Estatua, León Cortés, Sabana Este, San José 670-1000, Costa Rica
Tel +506 22221544   Fax +506 22552674
ejecutivo@fedefutbol.com   www.fedefutbol.com
President: LI Eduardo   General Secretary: RAMIREZ ROJAS Joseph
Vice-President: CHACON Miguel   Treasurer: ROJAS ULLOA Rafael Angel   Media Officer: VARGAS Randall
Men's Coach: KENTON Rodrigo   Women's Coach: QUESADA Juan Diego
FEDEFUTBOL formed: 1921   CONMEBOL: 1962   FIFA: 1927
Red shirts, Blue shorts, White socks or White shirts, White shorts, Red socks

RECENT INTERNATIONAL MATCHES PLAYED BY COSTA RICA

2005	Opponents	Score		Venue	Comp	Scorers	Att	Referee
7-07	Canada	W	1-0	Seattle	GCr1	Soto.J [30p]	15 831	Prendergast JAM
9-07	Cuba	W	3-1	Seattle	GCr1	Brenes 2 [61 85p], Soto.J [81p]	15 109	Archundia MEX
12-07	USA	D	0-0	Foxboro	GCr1		15 211	Archundia MEX
16-07	Honduras	L	2-3	Foxboro	GCqf	Bolaños [39], Ruíz [81]	22 108	Archundia MEX
17-08	Mexico	L	0-2	Mexico City	WCq		27 000	Pineda HON
3-09	Panama	W	3-1	Panama City	WCq	Saborio [44], Centeno [51], Gomez [73]	21 000	Stott USA
7-09	Trinidad and Tobago	W	2-0	San Jose	WCq	Saborio [15], Centeno [50]	17 000	Batres GUA
8-10	USA	W	3-0	San Jose	WCq	Wanchope [34], Hernandez.C 2 [60 88]	18 000	Archundia MEX
12-10	Guatemala	L	1-3	Guatemala City	WCq	Myre [60]	23 912	Hall USA
9-11	France	L	2-3	Fort-de-France	Fr	Saborio [14], Fonseca [41]	16 216	Pineda MEX
2006								
11-02	Korea Republic	W	1-0	Oakland	Fr	Saborio [40p]		Vaughn USA
1-03	Iran	L	2-3	Tehran	Fr	Hernandez.C [43], Fonseca [60]	25 000	Al Marzouqi UAE
28-05	Ukraine	L	0-4	Kyiv	Fr		25 000	Ivanov.N RUS
30-05	Czech Republic	L	0-1	Jablonec	Fr		14 500	Bede HUN
9-06	Germany	L	2-4	Munich	WCr1	Wanchope 2 [12 73]	66 000	Elizondo ARG
15-06	Ecuador	L	0-3	Hamburg	WCr1		50 000	Codjia BEN
20-06	Poland	L	1-2	Hanover	WCr1	Gomez [25]	43 000	Maidin SIN
2-09	Austria	D	2-2	Geneva	Fr	Saborio 2 [16p 40]		Circhetta SUI
6-09	Switzerland	L	0-2	Geneva	Fr		12 000	Van Egmond NED
2007								
4-02	Trinidad & Tobago	W	4-0	Alajuela	Fr	Wallace [28], Solis 2 [43 52], Fonseca [57]		Porras CRC
9-02	Honduras	W	3-1	San Salvador	UCr1	Fonseca 2 [4 70], Gonzalez.L [46]		Archundia MEX
13-02	Panama	L	0-1	San Salvador	UCr1			Batres GUA
16-02	El Salvador	W	2-0	San Salvador	UCsf	Wallace [10], Fonseca [12]		Archindia MEX
18-02	Panama	D	1-1	San Salvador	UCf	Bernard [85], W 4-1p		Batres GUA
24-03	New Zealand	W	4-0	San Jose	Fr	Saborio 2 [7 79p], Solis [18], Ruiz [57]	15 000	Rodriguez CRC
28-03	Chile	D	1-1	Talca	Fr	Fonseca [60]	8 000	Ortube BOL
2-06	Chile	W	2-0	San Jose	Fr	Badilla [28], Ruiz [59]	25 000	Glower MEX
6-06	Canada	L	1-2	Miami	GCr1	Centeno [56]	17 420	Wingaarde SUR
9-06	Haiti	D	1-1	Miami	GCr1	Centeno [61]	22 529	Campbell JAM
11-06	Guadeloupe †	W	1-0	Miami	GCr1	Centeno [14]	15 892	Wingaarde SUR
17-06	Mexico	L	0-1	Houston	GCqf		70 092	Vaughn USA
22-08	Peru	D	1-1	San Jose	Fr	Rojas [7]		Mena CRC
9-09	Honduras	D	0-0	East Hartford	Fr	W 3-2p	8 000	Vaughn USA
12-09	Canada	D	1-1	Toronto	Fr	Nunez [48]		Maruffo USA
13-10	El Salvador	D	2-2	San Salvador	Fr	Nunez [25], Castro [36]		Rivera SLV
17-10	Haiti	D	1-1	San Jose	Fr	Centeno [48]		Quesada CRC
21-11	Panama	D	1-1	Panama City	Fr	Nunez [82]		Rodas GUA
2008								
13-01	Sweden	L	0-1	San Jose	Fr		7 000	Batres GUA
30-01	Iran	D	0-0	Tehran	Fr			Al Marzouqi UAE
6-02	Jamaica	D	1-1	Kingston	Fr	Nunez [78]		Brizan TRI
26-03	Peru	L	1-3	Iquitos	Fr	Alpizar [38p]		Buckley PER
14-06	Grenada	D	2-2	St George's	WCq	Alonso [39], Nunez [76]	6 000	Brizan TRI
21-06	Grenada	W	3-0	San Jose	WCq	Saborio [17], Ruiz [32], Azofeifa [90]	16 000	Marrufo USA

Fr = Friendly match • UC = UNCAF Cup • GC = CONCACAF Gold Cup • CA = Copa América • WC = FIFA World Cup
q = qualifier • r1 = first round group • qf = quarter-finals • † not a full international

COSTA RICA NATIONAL TEAM RECORDS AND RECORD SEQUENCES

Records			Sequence records					
Victory	12-0	PUR 1946	Wins	11	1960-1961	Clean sheets	5	1961, 2001-2002
Defeat	0-7	MEX 1975	Defeats	6	2006	Goals scored	28	1935-1946
Player Caps	123	Luis Marín	Undefeated	12	1965	Without goal	4	1980-1983
Player Goals	47	Rolando Fonseca	Without win	14	2007-2008	Goals against	12	Three times

MAJOR CITIES/TOWNS
Population '000

1	San José	343
2	Limón	65
3	San Francisco	63
4	Liberia	50
5	Alajuela	49
6	Paraíso	44
7	Desamparados	40
8	San Isidro	37
9	Puntarenas	36
10	Curridabat	36
11	San Vicente	35
12	San José (Alajuela)	32
13	Purral	31
14	Turrialba	30
15	San Miguel	30
16	Aguacaliente	29
17	San Rafael Abajo	29
18	Mercedes	28
19	Quesada	28
20	San Rafael	28
21	San Pedro	27
22	Cartago	27
23	Heredia	22
24	Guápiles	20

REPUBLIC OF COSTA RICA; REPUBLICA DE COSTA RICA

Capital	San José	Language	Spanish			Independence	1821
Population	4 075 261	Area	51 100 km²	Density	77 per km²	% in cities	50%
GDP per cap	$9100	Dailling code	+506	Internet	.cr	GMT + / -	-6

MEDALS TABLE

		Overall G	S	B	League G	S	B	CON'CAF G	S	B	City	Stadium	Cap'ty	DoF
1	Deportivo Saprissa	29	17	7	26	15	1	3	2	6	San José	Ricardo Saprissa	21 260	1935
2	Liga Deportiva Alajuelense	26	23	13	24	20	9	2	3	4	Alajuela	Alejandro Morera Soto	22 500	1919
3	CS Herediano	21	11	12	21	11	11			1	Heredia	Eladio Rosabal Cordero	8 144	1921
4	CS La Libertad	6	6	4	6	6	4				San José			
5	CS Cartaginés	4	9	7	3	9	7	1			Cartago	Fello Meza	18 000	1906
6	Orión FC	2	7	7	2	7	7							
7	Municipal Puntarenas	1	3	1	1	3	1				Puntarenas			
8	Universidad de Costa Rica	1		3	1		3				San José			
9	CS Uruguay	1			1						Coronado			
10	SG Española		7	5		7	5				Alajuela			
11	Alajuela Junior		2			2					Alajuela			
12	AD Limonense		1			1					Limón	Juan Goban	3 000	1961
	AD Barrio Mexico		1			1								
	AD Pérez Zeledón		1			1					San Isidro	Municipal	5 500	1991
	Puntarenas FC		1			1					Puntarenas	Lito Pérez	8 700	2004
	AD Santos		1			1					Guápiles	Ebal Rodrigues	3 000	

RECENT LEAGUE RECORD

Year	Winners	Score	Runners-up
1995	Deportivo Saprissa	3-1 0-1	Liga Deportiva Alajuelense
1996	Liga Deportiva Alajuelense	3-1 1-1	CS Cartaginés
1997	Liga Deportiva Alajuelense	3-2 1-1	Deportivo Saprissa
1998	Deportivo Saprissa	0-1 2-0	Liga Deportiva Alajuelense
1999	Deportivo Saprissa	†	Liga Deportiva Alajuelense
2000	Liga Deportiva Alajuelense	†	Deportivo Saprissa
2001	Liga Deportiva Alajuelense	0-1 3-0	CS Herediano
2002	Liga Deportiva Alajuelense	2-2 4-0	Santos de Guápiles
2003	Liga Deportiva Alajuelense	†	Deportivo Saprissa
2004	Deportivo Saprissa	1-1 2-1	CS Herediano
2005	Liga Deportiva Alajuelense	3-1 1-0	AD Pérez Zeledón
2006	Deportivo Saprissa	†	Municipal Puntarenas
2007	Deportivo Saprissa	†	Liga Deportiva Alajuelense
2008	Deportivo Saprissa	†	Liga Deportiva Alajuelense

† Won both Apertura and Clausura so automatic champions

COSTA RICA 2007–08
TORNEO APERTURA

Group A	Pl	W	D	L	F	A	Pts
CS Herediano †	16	7	7	2	23	12	28
LD Alajuelense †	16	7	7	2	23	14	28
AD Carmelita †	16	6	6	4	21	20	24
Puntarenas FC	16	5	7	4	19	20	22
San Carlos	16	6	3	7	21	23	21
Universidad Costa Rica	16	3	4	9	19	26	13

Group B	Pl	W	D	L	F	A	Pts
Deportivo Saprissa †	16	9	2	5	22	16	29
Brujas Escazú FC †	16	6	6	4	26	24	24
AD Pérez Zeledón †	16	6	2	8	29	26	20
Municipal Liberia	16	4	5	7	20	24	17
Santos de Guápiles	16	4	5	7	18	24	17
CS Cartaginés	16	4	4	8	18	30	16

28/07/2007 - 25/11/2007 • † Qualified for the play-offs

APERTURA PLAY-OFFS

Quarter–finals		Semi–finals		Final
Dep. Saprissa	Bye			
		Dep. Saprissa	1 1	
Pérez Zeledón *	1 0	LD Alajuelense*	0 1	
LD Alajuelense	2 3			Dep. Saprissa 2 2
Brujas Escazú	0 2			CS Herediano * 0 2
AD Carmelita *	1 0	Brujas Escazú *	0 0	
		CS Herediano	0 1	
CS Herediano	Bye			* at home in the first leg

Final: 1st leg, Heredia, 19-12-2007, scorers - Alonso Solis [40], Celso Borges [46]
2nd leg. San José, 23-12-2007, scorers - Try Bennet [3], José Villalobos [33] for
Saprissa; Marvin Angulo [45], Félix Montoya [95+] for Herediano

COSTA RICA 2007–08
TORNEO CLAUSURA

Group A	Pl	W	D	L	F	A	Pts
Deportivo Saprissa †	16	9	3	4	27	20	30
CS Herediano †	16	5	8	3	20	13	23
Universidad Costa Rica†	16	6	4	6	23	22	22
Puntarenas FC	16	5	7	4	15	19	22
San Carlos	16	5	4	7	16	17	19
AD Carmelita	16	4	3	9	17	29	15

Group B	Pl	W	D	L	F	A	Pts
LD Alajuelense †	16	8	6	2	22	13	30
Brujas Escazú FC †	16	6	4	6	23	23	22
AD Pérez Zeledón †	16	5	7	4	14	14	22
Municipal Liberia	16	5	6	5	22	20	21
CS Cartaginés	16	4	5	7	14	19	17
Santos de Guápiles	16	3	5	8	16	20	14

13/01/2008 - 4/05/2008 • † Qualified for the play-offs

CLAUSURA PLAY-OFFS

Quarter–finals		Semi–finals		Final
Dep. Saprissa	Bye			
		Dep. Saprissa	5 1	
Un. Costa Rica*	2 0	Brujas Escazú *	0 2	
Brujas Escazú	3 1			Dep. Saprissa * 1 1
Pérez Zeledón *	1 2			LD Alajuelense 0 0
CS Herediano	1 1	Pérez Zeledón *	0 3	
		LD Alajuelense	0 5	
LD Alajuelense	Bye			* at home in the first leg

Final: 1st leg, San José, 25-05-2008, scorer -
2nd leg. Alajuela, 1-06-2008, scorer -

COSTA RICA 2007–08
PRIMERA DIVISION CHAMPIONSHIP FINAL
Home team first leg   Score   Home team second leg
Deportivo Saprissa are automatically champions having
won both the Apertura and Clausura

COSTA RICA 2007–08

PRIMERA DIVISION AGGREGATE TABLE	Pl	W	D	L	F	A	Pts	Saprissa	Alajuelense	Herediano	Brujas	Puntarenas	Perez Z'don	San Carlos	Carmelita	Liberia	UCR	Cartaginés	Santos
Deportivo Saprissa	32	18	5	9	49	36	59		0-0	2-0 1-1	2-1 3-1	4-2 2-1	0-1	0-0	4-3	1-0	3-2 1-3	4-0	1-0 2-1
LD Alajuelense	32	15	13	4	45	27	58	0-1		0-1	3-1	1-1 2-0	1-0	2-0 2-0	0-0 2-0	4-1 1-1	2-2	2-0 2-0	1-1
CS Herediano	32	12	15	5	43	25	51	0-2	1-1 0-0		1-1	1-0 0-0	3-0	4-0 1-1	1-1 4-0	2-1	1-0 4-2	1-2	2-1
Brujas Escazú FC	32	12	10	10	49	47	46	2-1	1-1 1-1	2-2		1-2	2-2 1-1	2-0	0-1	2-1 2-1	1-0	1-1 3-1 3-1	2-1
Puntarenas FC	32	10	14	8	34	39	44	4-1 1-0	2-2	0-0 0-2	4-3		0-0	1-1 1-0 1-1	1-1	1-2	0-0 2-1	0-0	1-1
AD Pérez Zeledón	32	11	9	12	43	40	42	0-2	3-0 1-1	0-0	1-1 3-2	2-3		3-1	4-1	2-1 2-2	1-1	4-1 1-0 1-0 1-2	
San Carlos	32	11	7	14	37	40	40	2-0 1-1	1-1	0-0 1-1	1-2	3-0 4-0	2-1		2-0 4-0	2-1	1-2 1-2 2-1 1-1	1-0	
AD Carmelita	32	10	9	13	38	49	39	0-1 2-0	1-3	1-1 0-2	1-2	2-0 1-1	0-1	2-1 2-1		3-3	3-1 1-2	1-0	2-2
Municipal Liberia	32	9	11	12	42	44	38	0-0 2-3	3-1	0-3	2-1 1-0	1-1	3-2 0-0	0-1	1-2		1-1	4-0 2-1 1-1 2-0	
Universidad Costa Rica	32	9	8	15	42	48	35	1-2	1-2 1-2 1-1 1-0	2-0	2-3 1-1	2-1	1-2 4-0 1-1 0-2	1-2		1-1		1-2	
CS Cartaginés	32	8	9	15	32	49	33	2-1 1-3	1-2	2-1	3-0 1-1	0-0	2-1 2-0	1-0	1-3	1-2 1-0	1-2		2-2 1-1
Santos de Guápiles	32	7	10	15	34	44	31	2-1	1-2 0-1	2-2	1-3 1-3	0-1	0-2 2-1	2-1	2-0	0-0 1-1	3-0	1-1	

Clausura matches listed in bold

CRO – CROATIA

NATIONAL TEAM RECORD
JULY 10TH 2006 TO JULY 12TH 2010

PL	W	D	L	F	A	%
24	17	5	2	48	19	81.3

FIFA/COCA-COLA WORLD RANKING

1993	1994	1995	1996	1997	1998	1999	2000	2001	2002	2003	2004	2005	2006	2007
122	62	41	24	19	4	9	18	19	32	20	23	20	15	10

High
01/99

2007–2008											
08/07	09/07	10/07	11/07	12/07	01/08	02/08	03/08	04/08	05/08	06/08	07/08
6	10	10	10	10	10	12	12	13	13	15	7

Low	
125	03/94

To take the lead in their Euro 2008 quarter-final against Turkey with just a minute of extra-time to go, and then to concede a goal two minutes into injury-time was a desperately cruel blow for the Croatian national team and its fans. Coach Slaven Bilic said that the Turkish comeback and Croatia's subsequent penalty shoot-out defeat would haunt him for the rest of his life as his team became the third victims of Turkey's late, late show at Euro 2008. The Croats had been touted as genuine title contenders having taken full points from the group stage, including an impressive 2-1 victory over Germany but they will at least take some satisfaction from their contribution to what

INTERNATIONAL HONOURS
Qualified for the FIFA World Cup finals 1998 2002 2006

was a great tournament. At home it proved to be another superb season for Dinamo Zagreb as they completed a hat-trick of titles, finishing a remarkable 28 points ahead of their closest rivals Slaven Belupo. Dinamo's coach, former national team hero Zvonimir Soldo who was in his first season in club management, also lead his side to a 3-0 aggregate victory in the Cup Final as Dinamo clinched consecutive doubles. Immediately after, however, he resigned, citing disagreements with the club's hierarchy. His predecessor Branko Ivankovic had cited similar reasons when he stood down in January 2008 although he was tempted back following Soldo's departure.

THE FIFA BIG COUNT OF 2006

	Male	Female		Total
Number of players	339 882	22 632	Referees and Assistant Referees	2 380
Professionals	321		Admin, Coaches, Technical, Medical	15 108
Amateurs 18+	42 219		Number of clubs	1 463
Youth under 18	64 495		Number of teams	3 353
Unregistered	232 715		Clubs with women's teams	1
Total players	362 514		Players as % of population	8.07%

Croatian Football Federation (HNS)
Hrvatski nogometni savez, Rusanova 13, Zagreb 10 000, Croatia
Tel +385 1 2361555   Fax +385 1 2441501
info@hns-cff.hr   www.hns-cff.hr
President: MARKOVIC Vlatko   General Secretary: SREBRIC Zorislav
Vice-President: TBC   Treasurer: BAJRIC Ruzica   Media Officer: SUDAC Ivancica
Men's Coach: BILIC Slaven   Women's Coach: RUHEK Damir
HNS formed: 1912   UEFA: 1993   FIFA: 1992
Red and white chequered shirts, White shorts, Blue socks or Blue shirts, Blue shorts, Blue socks

RECENT INTERNATIONAL MATCHES PLAYED BY CROATIA

2006	Opponents	Score		Venue	Comp	Scorers	Att	Referee
13-06	Brazil	L	0-1	Berlin	WCr1		72 000	Archundia MEX
18-06	Japan	D	0-0	Nuremberg	WCr1		41 000	De Bleeckere BEL
22-06	Australia	D	2-2	Stuttgart	WCr1	Srna 2, Kovac.N 56	52 000	Poll ENG
16-08	Italy	W	2-0	Livorno	Fr	Eduardo 27, Modric 43	16 150	Kircher GER
6-09	Russia	D	0-0	Moscow	ECq		27 500	Mejuto Gonzalez ESP
7-10	Andorra	W	7-0	Zagreb	ECq	Petric 4 12 37 48 50, Klasnic 58, Balaban 62, Modric 83	17 618	Zammit MLT
11-10	England	W	2-0	Zagreb	ECq	Eduardo 61, Neville.G OG 69	31 991	Rosetti ENG
15-11	Israel	W	4-3	Tel Aviv	ECq	Srna 35p, Eduardo 3 39 54 72	35 000	Iturralde Gonzalez ESP
2007								
7-02	Norway	W	2-1	Rijeka	Fr	Petric 26, Modric 38	8 000	Kalt FRA
24-03	FYR Macedonia	W	2-1	Zagreb	ECq	Srna 58, Eduardo 88	29 969	Plautz AUT
2-06	Estonia	W	1-0	Tallinn	ECq	Eduardo 32	8 651	Kassai HUN
6-06	Russia	D	0-0	Zagreb	ECq		36 194	Michel SVK
22-08	Bosnia-Herzegovina	W	5-3	Sarajevo	Fr	Eduardo 18, Srna 2 35 74, Kovac.N 2 73 81	8 000	Skomina SVN
8-09	Estonia	W	2-0	Zagreb	ECq	Eduardo 2 39 45	15 102	Laperierre SUI
12-09	Andorra	W	6-0	Andorra la Vella	ECq	Srna 34, Petric 2 38 44, Kranjcar 49, Eduardo 55, Rakitic 64	925	Thual FRA
13-10	Israel	W	1-0	Zagreb	ECq	Eduardo 52	30 084	Stark GER
16-10	Slovakia	W	3-0	Rijeka	Fr	Olic 2 45 69, Vukojevic 48	5 000	Laperriere SUI
17-11	FYR Macedonia	L	0-2	Skopje	ECq		14 500	De Bleeckere BEL
21-11	England	W	3-2	London	ECq	Kranjcar 8, Olic 14, Petric 77	88 017	Fröjdfeldt SWE
2008								
6-02	Netherlands	L	0-3	Split	Fr		28 000	Fernandez ESP
26-03	Scotland	D	1-1	Glasgow	Fr	Kranjcar 10	28 821	Hauge NOR
24-05	Moldova	W	1-0	Rijeka	Fr	Kovac.N 30	7 000	Ceferin SVN
31-05	Hungary	D	1-1	Budapest	Fr	Kovac.N 24	10 000	Ledentu FRA
8-06	Austria	W	1-0	Vienna	ECr1	Modric 4p	51 428	Vink NED
12-06	Germany	W	2-1	Klagenfurt	ECr1	Srna 24, Olic 62	30 461	De Bleeckere BEL
16-06	Poland	W	1-0	Klagenfurt	ECr1	Klasnic 53	30 461	Vassaras GRE
20-06	Turkey	D	1-1	Vienna	ECqf	Klasnic 119	51 428	Rosetti ITA

Fr = Friendly match • EC = UEFA EURO 2008 • WC = FIFA World Cup
q = qualifier • po = play-off • r1 = first round group

CROATIA NATIONAL TEAM PLAYERS

	Player		Ap	G	Club	Date of Birth		Player		Ap	G	Club	Date of Birth
1	Stipe Pletikosa	GK	72	0	Spartak Moskva	8 01 1979	12	Mario Galinovic	GK	2	0	Panathinaikos	15 11 1976
2	Dario Simic	DF	99	3	Milan	12 11 1975	13	Nikola Pokrivac	DF	2	0	AS Monaco	26 11 1985
3	Josip Simunic	DF	65	3	Hertha Berlin	18 02 1978	14	Luka Modric	MF	29	4	Tottenham H	9 09 1985
4	Robert Kovac	DF	77	0	Bor. Dortmund	6 04 1974	15	Dario Knezevic	DF	10	1	Livorno	20 04 1982
5	Vedran Corluka	DF	24	0	Manchester City	5 02 1986	16	Jerko Leko	MF	54	2	AS Monaco	9 04 1980
6	Hrvoje Vejic	DF	3	0	Tom Tomsk	8 06 1977	17	Ivan Klasnic	FW	30	10	Werder Bremen	29 01 1980
7	Ivan Rakitic	MF	11	1	Schalke 04	10 03 1988	18	Ivica Olic	FW	57	10	Hamburger SV	14 09 1979
8	Ognjen Vukojevic	MF	7	1	Dinamo Zagreb	20 12 1983	19	Niko Kranjcar	MF	45	6	Portsmouth	13 08 1984
9	Nikola Kalinic	FW	2	0	Hajduk Split	5 01 1988	20	Igor Budan	FW	6	0	Parma	22 04 1980
10	Niko Kovac	MF	80	13	Austria Salburg	15 10 1971	21	Mladen Petric	FW	27	9	Bor. Bortmund	1 01 1981
11	Darijo Srna	MF	58	16	Sh'tar Donetsk	1 05 1982	22	Danijel Pranjic	MF	15	0	SC Heerenveen	2 12 1981
Croatia's squad for Euro 2008							23	Vedran Runje	GK	5	0	RC Lens	10 02 1976

CROATIA NATIONAL TEAM RECORDS AND RECORD SEQUENCES

Records				Sequence records						
Victory	7-0	AUS 1998		Wins	6	2006-2007		Clean sheets	4	1994, 2002
Defeat	1-5	GER 1941, GER 1942		Defeats	3	2006		Goals scored	21	1996-1998
Player Caps	99	Dario Simic		Undefeated	12	2000-2001		Without goal	3	2005-2006
Player Goals	45	Davor Suker		Without win	6	1999, 2006		Goals against	8	1996-1997

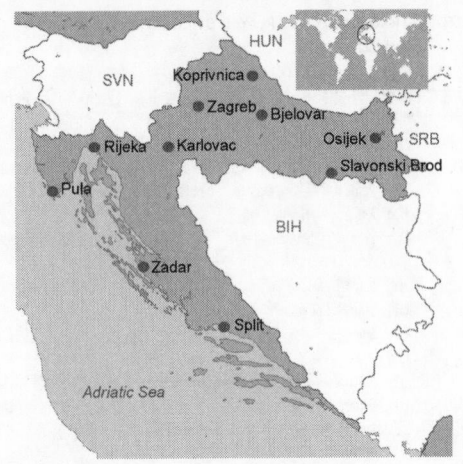

MAJOR CITIES/TOWNS

Population '000

1	Zagreb	702
2	Split	176
3	Rijeka	139
4	Osijek	86
5	Zadar	72
6	Slavonski Brod	61
7	Pula	59
8	Sesvete	56
9	Karlovac	47
10	Varazdin	41
11	Sibenik	37
12	Velika Gorica	35
13	Sisak	35
14	Vinkovci	33
15	Vukovar	29
16	Bjelovar	28
17	Dubrovnik	27
18	Koprivnica	25
19	Dakovo	21
20	Pozega	21
21	Zapresic	17
22	Solin	15
23	Cakovec	15
24	Velika	2

REPUBLIC OF CROATIA; REPUBLIKA HRVATSKA

Capital	Zagreb	Language	Croatian	Independence	1991
Population	4 494 749	Area	56 542 km²	Density	79 per km²	% in cities	64%
GDP per cap	$10 600	Dailling code	+385	Internet	.hr	GMT +/-	+1

MEDALS TABLE

		Overall			League			Cup			Europe			City	Stadium	Cap'ty	DoF
		G	S	B	G	S	B	G	S	B	G	S	B				
1	Dinamo Zagreb	19	7	2	10	3	2	9	4					Zagreb	Maksimir	38 923	1945
2	Hajduk Split	10	11	1	6	8	1	4	3					Split	Poljud	39 941	1911
3	NK Rijeka	2	3	1		2	1	2	1					Rijeka	Kantrida	10 275	1946
4	NK Zagreb	1	3	3	1	2	3		1					Zagreb	Kranjceviceva	12 000	1903
5	Inter Zapresic	1	1			1		1						Zapresic	Inter	8 000	1929
6	NK Osijek	1		6			6	1						Osijek	Gradski Vrt	19 500	1946
7	Varteks Varazdin		5	3			3		5					Varazdin	Varteksa	9 300	1931
8	Slaven Belupo		2			2			1					Koprivnica	Gradski	3 054	1912
9	Cibalia Vinkovici		1						1					Vinkovici	Cibalia	12 000	1947
	NK Pula		1						1					Pula	Gradski	7 000	2003
11	Dragovoljac Zagreb			1			1							Zagreb	Siget	6 000	1975

CROATIAN CLUBS IN YUGOSLAV FOOTBALL

3	Hajduk Split	19	16	11	9	10	10	9	5		1	1	1
4	Dinamo Zagreb	12	20	8	4	12	6	8	8			2	
6	Gradanski Zagreb	5	2	3	5	2	3						
11	Concordia Zagreb	2	1		2	1							
	NK Rijeka	2	1		2	1							

RECENT LEAGUE AND CUP RECORD

	Championship						Cup		
Year	Champions	Pts	Runners-up	Pts	Third	Pts	Winners	Score	Runners-up
1995	Hajduk Split	65	Croatia Zagreb	64	NK Osijek	59	Hajduk Split	3-2 1-0	Croatia Zagreb
1996	Croatia Zagreb	26	Hajduk Split	26	Varteks Varazdin	24	Croatia Zagreb	2-0 1-0	Varteks Varazdin
1997	Croatia Zagreb	81	Hajduk Split	60	Dragovoljac Zagreb	49	Croatia Zagreb	2-1	NK Zagreb
1998	Croatia Zagreb	49	Hajduk Split	36	NK Osijek	32	Croatia Zagreb	1-0 2-1	Varteks Varazdin
1999	Croatia Zagreb	45	NK Rijeka	44	Hajduk Split	39	NK Osijek	2-1	Cibalia Vinkovici
2000	Dinamo Zagreb	75	Hajduk Split	61	NK Osijek	53	Hajduk Split	2-0 0-1	Dinamo Zagreb
2001	Hajduk Split	66	Dinamo Zagreb	65	NK Osijek	57	Dinamo Zagreb	2-0 1-0	Hajduk Split
2002	NK Zagreb	67	Hajduk Split	65	Dinamo Zagreb	59	Dinamo Zagreb	1-1 1-0	Varteks Varazdin
2003	Dinamo Zagreb	78	Hajduk Split	70	Varteks Varazdin	57	Hajduk Spit	1-0 4-0	Uljanik Pula
2004	Hajduk Split	78	Dinamo Zagreb	76	NK Rijeka	42	Dinamo Zagreb	1-1 0-0†	Varteks Varazdin
2005	Hajduk Split	56	Inter Zapresic	54	NK Zagreb	50	Rijeka	2-1 1-0	Hajduk Split
2006	Dinamo Zagreb	76	NK Rijeka	65	Varteks Varazdin	47	Rijeka	4-0 1-5	Varteks Varazdin
2007	Dinamo Zagreb	92	Hajduk Split	72	NK Zagreb	58	Dinamo Zagreb	1-0 1-1	Slaven Belupo
2008	Dinamo Zagreb	79	Slaven Belupo	54	NK Osijek	54	Dinamo Zagreb	3-0 0-0	Hajduk Split

Dinamo Zagreb previously known as HASK Gradjanski and then as Croatia Zagreb • † Dinamo won on away goals

CROATIA 2007–08

PRVA HNL OZUJSKO (1)

Team	Pl	W	D	L	F	A	Pts	Dinamo	Slaven	Osijek	Rijeka	Hajduk	Zagreb	Varteks	Cibalia	Zadar	Sibenik	Inter	Medimurje
Dinamo Zagreb †	33	26	4	3	91	34	82		4-0	1-0 1-0	3-2 1-0	6-1 1-0	6-3	1-2	2-1 4-0	5-1	5-0 5-1	5-0 1-0	3-1
Slaven B. Koprivnica ‡	33	16	6	11	45	29	54	5-2		2-0	1-0 1-1	2-2	1-0 1-0	6-0 2-1	2-2 0-4	2-2 0		1-0	2-0 2-0 4-0
NK Osijek	33	16	6	11	43	34	54	1-3	1-0 1-0		2-2 1-0	0-1	1-1 2-1 0-1 2-0 5-1 2-1	1-0	1-1	1-0	4-0 3-1		
NK Rijeka	33	14	11	8	53	41	53	2-4	1-0	1-1		4-0 1-1 2-1 1-1 1-1 2-2 3-0 2-0 2-0 5-3	2-0	2-1	3-1	5-2			
Hajduk Split ‡	33	14	10	9	57	41	52	1-2 1-1	1-0 2-0	1-0 0-2	1-1		2-1	3-1 2-2 1-2	4-1	2-0 4-1 7-0 7-2			3-3
NK Zagreb	33	11	11	11	51	40	44	1-3 0-0	0-2	0-2	2-2 1-0 2-1			0-0 3-1	4-1 7-2 0-0	3-1	3-0	1-1	6-1
Varteks Varazdin	33	11	7	15	46	53	40	4-3 1-1	1-1	1-2	1-2 1-3 4-0 0-1				2-1	2-0 5-2 3-0 1-1	1-2	2-0 3-2	
Cibalia Vinkovci	33	11	7	15	40	48	40	1-2	3-0	2-0	2-0	0-0 3-1 2-2 1-0 0-1				0-2	3-3 2-0 2-0 1-1	2-0 3-0	
NK Zadar	33	11	7	15	49	61	40	1-2 2-5	1-0	5-1 1-1	0-0	0-0 1-3	1-0	2-0 1-1 1-0			2-2 0-2 3-0 3-1	4-0	
NK Sibenik	33	9	12	12	34	52	39	0-2 0-2 0-2 0-0 1-0 1-0 3-2 0-0	1-0	0-0	4-3	2-0	0-0					1-1 0-0	4-2
Inter Zapresic	33	8	9	16	27	59	33	0-4	1-0 0-0 1-1 1-2 0-1 2-1	0-1	1-1 0-0 0-0 1-0	1-0	2-1	2-2					3-0
Medimurje Cakovec	33	3	6	24	37	81	15	1-1 1-2	2-0	0-1	0-1	1-1 2-2	0-3	4-1	0-1	2-4 2-3	2-2 0-1	2-3 4-0	

20/07/2007 - 10/05/2008 • † Qualified for the UEFA Champions League • ‡ Qualified for the UEFA Cup
Play-off: Inter 2-0 0-0 Hrvatski dragovoljac • Top scorer: Zelimir Terkes, Zadar 21; Radomir Dalovic, Rijeka 18; Nikola Kalinic, Hajduk 17

CROATIA 2007–08 DRUGA HNL (2)

	Pl	W	D	L	F	A	Pts
Croatia Sesvete	30	20	6	4	67	25	66
Hrvatski dragovoljac	30	19	7	4	60	28	64
Istra Pula	30	17	7	6	42	14	58
Pomorac Kostrena	30	14	7	9	42	28	49
Vinogradar Lokosin Dol	30	12	8	10	42	43	44
Slavonac Stari Perkovci	30	14	2	14	44	51	44
Segesta Sisak	30	11	10	9	39	37	43
NK Trogir	30	12	6	12	40	37	42
Moslavina Kutina	30	11	8	11	51	42	41
NK Imotski	30	11	7	12	49	53	40
Mosor Zrnovnica	30	10	8	12	27	42	38
NK Solin	30	10	7	13	46	48	37
Marsonia Slav'ski Brod	30	8	7	15	34	58	31
Kamen Ingrad Velika	30	7	7	16	26	49	28
HNK Vukovar '91	30	6	6	18	29	53	24
NK Belisce	30	3	7	20	23	53	16

18/08/2007 - 11/05/2008

HRVATSKOG NOGOMETNOG KUPA 2007–08

Round of 16

Dinamo Zagreb	3
NK Sibenik *	2
Pomorac Kostrena	0
Slaven B. Koprivnica *	1
Segesta Sisak *	3
NK Rijeka	0
Dakovo *	0
NK Zagreb	7
Varteks Varazdin	1 5p
NK Bjelovar *	1 4p
NK Osijek	1
Cibalia Vinkovci *	2
Inter Zapresic	1
Podravina Ludbreg	0
Croatia Sesvete	0
Hajduk Split *	2

Quarter–finals

Dinamo Zagreb	1 2
Slaven B. Koprivnica *	0 1
Segesta Sisak *	0 2
NK Zagreb	0 3
Varteks Varazdin *	4 2
Cibalia Vinkovci	0 0
Inter Zapresic	1 0
Hajduk Split *	2 4

Semi–finals

Dinamo Zagreb *	3 3
NK Zagreb	1 2
Varteks Varazdin *	1 0
Hajduk Split	1 4

Final

Dinamo Zagreb *	3 0
Hajduk Split ‡	0 0

* Home team/home team in the first leg • ‡ Qualified for the UEFA Cup

CUP FINAL
1st leg. Maksimir, Zagreb, 7-05-2008
Scorers - Josip Tadic [8], Mario Mandzukic 2 [20][88]
2nd leg. Poljud, Split, 14-05-2008

CTA – CENTRAL AFRICAN REPUBLIC

NATIONAL TEAM RECORD
JULY 10TH 2006 TO JULY 12TH 2010

PL	W	D	L	F	A	%
4	0	1	3	3	8	12.5

FIFA/COCA-COLA WORLD RANKING

1993	1994	1995	1996	1997	1998	1999	2000	2001	2002	2003	2004	2005	2006	2007	High
157	174	180	183	188	192	175	176	182	179	177	180	183	179	182	**148** 12/92

2007–2008												Low
08/07	09/07	10/07	11/07	12/07	01/08	02/08	03/08	04/08	05/08	06/08	07/08	**198** 04/08
185	188	188	191	182	181	196	197	198	198	198	198	

It was another year of inactivity for the Central African Republic, one of just a handful of African countries who failed to participate in the preliminaries for the 2010 FIFA World Cup. It was also a third successive time that the 'Fauves de Bas-Oubangui' had not entered a major competition, having also sat out the 2006 and 2008 African Nations Cup qualifiers. Government interference in the running of the football association put at risk its continued membership of FIFA and left the country as one of the blind spots on the African football scene. FIFA installed a normalisation committee to run the affairs of the federation after contested elections in September 2007 and

INTERNATIONAL HONOURS
None

subsequent polls have now installed Patrice-Edouard Ngaïssona as the new leader of the federation. It remains one of the few countries were on the continent where football takes a back seat to another sport, basketball being the major attraction in the former French colony. The Central African Republic last played a full international in March 2007 in the CEMAC Cup, the regional event for countries of the central African customs union. The appointment in June 2008 of former national team coach Jean-Jacques Ombi to take over as technical director at the federation suggests plans are in place for an end to the self-imposed exile.

THE FIFA BIG COUNT OF 2006

	Male	Female		Total
Number of players	183 004	9 400	Referees and Assistant Referees	360
Professionals	4		Admin, Coaches, Technical, Medical	3 250
Amateurs 18+	5 200		Number of clubs	80
Youth under 18	3 200		Number of teams	400
Unregistered	13 000		Clubs with women's teams	60
Total players	192 404		Players as % of population	4.47%

Fédération Centrafricaine de Football (RCA)
Avenue de Martyrs, Case Postale 344, Bangui, Central African Republic
Tel +236 75503118   Fax +236 21615660
fedefoot60@yahoo.fr   www.none
President: NGAISSONA Edouard Patrice   General Secretary: TDB
Vice-President: YANINDJI Celestin   Treasurer: TBD   Media Officer: None
Men's Coach: YANGUERE Francois Cesar   Women's Coach: NGBANGANDIMBO Camille
RCA formed: 1961   CAF: 1965   FIFA: 1963
Blue shirts, White shorts, Blue socks

RECENT INTERNATIONAL MATCHES PLAYED BY THE CENTRAL AFRICAN REPUBLIC

2003	Opponents	Score		Venue	Comp	Scorers	Att	Referee
4-05	Congo	L	1-2	Brazzaville	CNq	Makita 84		
8-06	Congo	D	0-0	Bangui	CNq			Hissene CHA
22-06	Mozambique	L	0-1	Maputo	CNq		15 000	
6-07	Burkina Faso	L	0-3	Bangui	CNq			
7-12	Cameroon	D	2-2	Brazzaville	CMr1	Oroko 10, Sandjo 30		Mbera GAB
9-12	Cameroon	W	1-0	Brazzaville	CMr1	Sandjo 85		Mandioukouta CGO
11-12	Gabon	W	2-0	Brazzaville	CMsf			
13-12	Cameroon	L	2-3	Brazzaville	CMf	Oroko 63, Destin 74		Bansimba CGO
2004								
No international matches played in 2004								
2005								
3-02	Gabon	L	0-4	Libreville	CMr1			
5-02	Congo	L	0-1	Libreville	CMr1			
2006								
6-03	Cameroon	L	0-2	Malabo	CMr1			
8-03	Gabon	D	2-2	Malabo	CMr1			
2007								
6-03	Chad	L	2-3	N'Djamena	CMr1	Hilaire 14, Fiacre 34		
8-03	Cameroon	D	0-0	N'Djamena	CMr1			
12-03	Congo	L	1-4	N'Djamena	CMsf	Romaric 15		
16-03	Chad	L	0-1	N'Djamena	CM3p			
2008								
No international matches played in 2008 before August								

CN = CAF African Cup of Nations • CM = CEMAC Cup
q = qualifier • r1 = first round group • sf = semi-final • 3p = third place play-off • f = final

CENTRAL AFRICAN REPUBLIC NATIONAL TEAM RECORDS AND RECORD SEQUENCES

Records			Sequence records					
Victory	4-0	CHA 1999	Wins	2	1976, 1999, 2003	Clean sheets	2	2003
Defeat	1-7	CMR 1984	Defeats	9	1985-1987	Goals scored	7	1990-1999
Player Caps	n/a		Undefeated	3	2003	Without goal	4	1988-1989
Player Goals	n/a		Without win	16	1976-1987	Goals against	19	1976-1988

RECENT LEAGUE AND CUP RECORD

	League		Cup		
Year	Champions		Winners	Score	Runners-up
1996	Tempête Mocaf				
1997	Tempête Mocaf		USCA de Bangui	2-0	Anges de Fatima
1998	Championship not finished		Anges de Fatima	3-0	AS Petroca
1999	Tempête Mocaf		Olympique Réal		
2000	Olympique Réal		Anges de Fatima	2-1	Olympique Réal
2001	Olympique Réal		Stade Centrafricain	2-1	Tempête Mocaf
2002	Championship annulled				
2003	Tempête Mocaf		Tempête Mocaf	8-0	Ouham Pendé
2004	Olympique Réal		Tempête Mocaf	2-0	SCAF
2005	Anges de Fatima		USCA de Bangui		Lobaye

CENTRAL AFRICAN REPUBLIC COUNTRY INFORMATION

Capital	Bangui	Independence	1960 from France	GDP per Capita	$1100
Population	3 742 482	Status	Republic	GNP Ranking	154
Area km²	622 984	Language	French	Dialling code	+236
Population density	6 per km²	Literacy rate	42%	Internet code	.cf
% in urban areas	39%	Main religion	Christian 50%	GMT +/-	+1
Towns/Cities ('000)	Bangui 684; Carnot 83; Kaga-Bandoro 82; Mbaiki 76; Berbérati 59; Bouar 55; Bouar 55				
Neighbours (km)	Sudan 1 165; Congo DR 1 577; Congo 467; Cameroon 797; Chad 1 197				
Main stadia	Barthelemy Boganda – Bangui 35 000				

CUB – CUBA

NATIONAL TEAM RECORD
JULY 10TH 2006 TO JULY 12TH 2010

PL	W	D	L	F	A	%
22	11	4	7	45	28	59.1

FIFA/COCA-COLA WORLD RANKING

1993	1994	1995	1996	1997	1998	1999	2000	2001	2002	2003	2004	2005	2006	2007
159	175	96	68	88	107	77	77	76	71	75	76	75	46	71

High	
46	12/06

2007–2008											
08/07	09/07	10/07	11/07	12/07	01/08	02/08	03/08	04/08	05/08	06/08	07/08
91	71	64	70	71	71	88	112	110	109	104	78

Low	
175	12/94

The 2007-08 international season saw the Cuban national team take their traditional time-out between major tournaments with just three matches played - all in June 2008. That doesn't mean Cuba are not serious in their attempts to qualify for the 2010 FIFA World Cup - far from it. In January 2008 the federation appointed the experienced German Reinhold Fanz as coach with the mission of making it to the finals. The Leones del Caribe overcame a tricky hurdle in the form of a much improved Antigua and Barbuda to make it through to the group stage of the CONCACAF qualifiers and an enticing first meeting against the USA in World Cup matches since 1949 - with

INTERNATIONAL HONOURS
Qualified for the FIFA World Cup finals 1938
CONCACAF U-17 Championship 1988   Central American and Caribbean Games 1930 1974 1978 1986

the trip to Havana in September 2008 a first for the Americans. Having defected to America during the 2007 Gold Cup, the inspirational Lester More won't be part of the campaign as the political situation in Cuba continued to hamper progress - seven of the U-23 squad jumped ship when playing abroad in 2008. At home, Cienfuegos won their first title for 17 years when they beat Ciudad de La Habana 4-1 on aggregate in the final. 2007 champions Pinar del Rio took part in the CFU Caribbean Championship but were knocked-out in the first round group phase.

THE FIFA BIG COUNT OF 2006

	Male	Female		Total
Number of players	1 045 900	95 925	Referees and Assistant Referees	225
Professionals	100		Admin, Coaches, Technical, Medical	5 030
Amateurs 18+	27 375		Number of clubs	338
Youth under 18	12 650		Number of teams	1 500
Unregistered	1 012 400		Clubs with women's teams	15
Total players	1 141 825		Players as % of population	10.03%

Asociación de Fútbol de Cuba (AFC)

Estadio Pedro Marrero Escuela Nacional de Futbol, Mario Lopez Avenida 41, 44 y 46, Municipio Playa La Habana, Cuba
Tel +53 7 2076440   Fax +53 7 2043563
futbol@inder.co.cu   www.none
President: HERNANDEZ Luis   General Secretary: GARCES Antonio
Vice-President: ARAGON Victor   Treasurer: CAMINO Otto   Media Officer: PEREIRA Jesus
Men's Coach: FRANZ Reinhold   Women's Coach: SOTOLONGO Rufino
AFC formed: 1924   CONCACAF: 1961   FIFA: 1932
Red shirts with white trimmings, Red shorts, Red socks or White shirts, White shorts, White socks

RECENT INTERNATIONAL MATCHES PLAYED BY CUBA

2005	Opponents	Score		Venue	Comp	Scorers	Att	Referee
9-01	Haiti	W	1-0	Port-au-Prince	GCq	Galindo [51]	15 000	Minyetti DOM
16-01	Haiti	D	1-1	Havana	GCq	Marquez [112]		Brizan TRI
20-02	Barbados	W	3-0	Bridgetown	GCq	Moré 2 [24 71], Galindo [90]	7 000	Prendergast JAM
22-02	Trinidad and Tobago	W	2-1	Bridgetown	GCq	Moré 2 [23 48]	2 100	Lancaster GUY
24-02	Jamaica	L	0-1	Bridgetown	GCq		3 000	Brizan TRI
7-07	USA	L	1-4	Seattle	GCr1	Moré [18]	15 831	Pineda HON
9-07	Costa Rica	L	1-3	Seattle	GCr1	Galindo [72]	15 109	Archundia MEX
12-07	Canada	L	1-2	Foxboro	GCr1	Cervantes [90]	15 211	Moreno PAN
2006								
2-09	Turks & Caicos Isl	W	6-0	Havana	CCq	Alonso [4], Arencibia [18], Alcantara 3 [20 58 71], Ocaña [83]		Campbell JAM
4-09	Bahamas	W	6-0	Havana	CCq	Alcantara 3 [22 50 64], Colome [30], Ocaña [40], Martinez [42]	100	Prendergast JAM
6-09	Cayman Islands	W	7-0	Havana	CCq	Alcantara [5], Ocaña 2 [10 34], Martinez 2 [45 58], Colome [83], Muñoz [85]	120	Campbell JAM
17-10	Haiti	D	0-0	Port-au-Prince	Fr			
19-10	Haiti	W	1-0	Cap Haitien	Fr	Villaurrutia [8p]		
8-11	Haiti	W	2-1	Fort-de-France	CCq	Marquez [21], Moré [79]		
10-11	Suriname	W	3-1	Fort-de-France	CCq	Alvarez 2 [4 26], Colome [41]		
12-11	Martinique	D	0-0	Fort-de-France	CCq			
2007								
14-01	Guadeloupe	L	1-2	Marabella	CCr1	Alonso [69]		Brizan TRI
16-01	St Vincent/Grenadines	W	3-0	Marabella	CCr1	Moré 2 [27 59], Duarte [90]		
18-01	Guyana	D	0-0	Marabella	CCr1			Moreno PAN
20-01	Trinidad and Tobago	L	1-3	Port of Spain	CCsf	Duarte [75]		Campbell JAM
23-01	Guadeloupe	W	2-1	Port of Spain	CC3p	Cervantes 2 [24 48]		Brizan TRI
24-03	Venezuela	L	1-3	Merida	Fr	Alcantara [47]	12 000	Andarcia VEN
9-05	Chile	L	0-3	Osorno	Fr		1 800	Cabrera VEN
16-05	Chile	L	0-2	Temuco	Fr		3 500	Grance PAR
8-06	Mexico	L	1-2	New Jersey	GCr1	Alcantara [22]	20 230	Aguilar SLV
10-06	Panama	D	2-2	New Jersey	GCr1	Colome [29], Alcantara [78]	68 123	
13-06	Honduras	L	0-5	Houston	GCr1		68 417	
2008								
7-06	St Vincent/Grenadines	W	1-0	Havana	Fr			
17-06	Antigua and Barbuda	W	4-3	St John's	WCq	Colome 2 [10 74], Linares [22], Duarte [85]	4 500	Moreno PAN
22-06	Antigua and Barbuda	W	4-0	Havana	WCq	Linares 2 [9 53], Gonsalves OG [45], Marquez [69]	2 000	Quesada CRC

Fr = Friendly match • GC = CONCACAF Gold Cup • WC = FIFA World Cup • q = qualifier • r1 = first round group

CUBA NATIONAL TEAM RECORDS AND RECORD SEQUENCES

Records			Sequence records					
Victory	9-0	PUR 1995	Wins	7	1998-1999	Clean sheets	7	1996
Defeat	0-8	SWE 1938	Defeats	18	1949-1960	Goals scored	12	2003-2005
Player Caps	n/a		Undefeated	11	1981-83, 2004-05	Without goal	4	1957, 1983, 2002
Player Goals	n/a		Without win	20	1949-1960	Goals against	26	1949-1961

CUBA COUNTRY INFORMATION

Capital	Havana	Independence	1902 from Spain	GDP per Capita	$2 900
Population	11 308 764	Status	Republic	GNP Ranking	69
Area km²	110 860	Language	Spanish	Dialling code	+53
Population density	102 per km²	Literacy rate	97%	Internet code	.cu
% in urban areas	76%	Main religion	None	GMT +/-	-5
Towns/Cities ('000)	Havana 2 163; Santiago 555; Camagüey 347; Holguin 319; Guantánamo 272; Santa Clara 250				
Neighbours (km)	North Atlantic Ocean, Caribbean Sea and the Gulf of Mexico 3 735				
Main stadia	Estadio Panamericano – Havana 34 000; Pedro Marrero – Havana 28 000				

CUBA 2007–08

CAMPEONATO NACIONAL

	Pl	W	D	L	F	A	Pts	Ciudad LH	Pinar d. Río	La Habana	Juventud	Villa Clara	Cienfuegos	Matanzas	Industriales	Ciego Avila	Camagüey	Las Tunas	S. Spiritus	Holguín	Guantánamo	Santiago DC	Granma
Occidental Group A																							
Ciudad de La Habana†	30	17	8	5	61	28	59		1-0	2-0	8-0	2-2	1-1	2-0	2-1	3-1	1-1	3-0	3-0	2-0	2-1		7-0
Pinar del Río †	30	14	8	8	50	24	50	1-0		5-0	5-0	1-2	0-0	2-0	7-1	0-1	0-0	2-0	3-1	3-0	0-0	1-0	1-0
La Habana	30	12	7	11	32	37	43	1-2	0-0		1-2	1-2	2-2	1-2	1-0	1-2	0-0	2-1	2-0	2-0	2-1	3-2	0-1
Isla de la Juventud	27	4	2	21	17	53	14	0-1	2-2	2-0		1-2	0-1	2-0	0-1	0-2	0-1	1-0	n/p	1-3	1-2	1-1	0-1
Occidental Group B																							
Villa Clara †	30	22	3	5	72	24	69	3-1	1-0	3-0	2-0		1-2	1-2	7-1	1-0	1-1	4-0	4-1	3-0	2-1	3-1	6-0
Cienfuegos †	30	20	5	5	56	24	65	2-1	2-0	0-0	3-0	1-0		3-2	3-1	2-0	2-1	2-0	7-1	2-2	0-1	2-0	7-1
Matanzas	30	9	7	14	32	39	34	0-2	2-2	1-1	1-0	2-1	0-1		1-0	1-1	0-0	3-1	2-0	3-1	4-0	0-0	0-1
Industriales La Habana	29	5	3	21	25	65	18	0-1	1-3	0-1	2-1	1-3	0-1	1-1		0-2	0-5	0-3	n/p	1-3	0-1	2-4	4-3
Oriental Group C																							
Ciego de Avila †	30	13	10	7	32	28	49	1-1	0-2	0-0	2-0	0-3	3-2	0-0	0-0		2-1	1-1	1-0	2-2	1-0	3-1	1-1
Camagüey †	30	12	10	8	37	32	46	3-3	3-2	0-3	1-0	0-2	1-0	2-0	2-1	1-0		1-3	1-1	0-1	0-1	0-0	2-2
Las Tunas	30	11	9	10	46	42	42	2-2	1-1	2-2	3-1	2-1	2-1	3-0	4-0	1-1	2-2		2-0	1-1	3-1	4-1	1-1
Sancti Spíritus	28	3	6	19	19	55	15	0-2	0-2	0-1	3-1	1-3	1-2	2-1	0-2	1-2	0-2	0-2		1-4	2-1	1-1	0-0
Oriental Group D																							
Holguín †	29	11	8	10	45	46	41	3-1	2-2	0-1	n/p	1-1	0-1	3-2	3-2	0-1	4-1	1-1	2-1		1-0	2-3	2-1
Guantánamo †	30	12	5	13	36	39	41	0-0	1-2	4-1	3-1	1-3	2-1	3-1	2-0	1-2	2-0	0-0	2-2			0-4	2-1
Santiago de Cuba	30	11	7	12	36	34	40	3-3	2-1	0-1	2-0	0-3	0-1	1-0	1-1	0-1	0-1	2-0	0-0	2-0	1-1		1-0
Granma	29	7	8	14	30	56	29	2-2	1-0	1-2	n/p	0-2	1-2	2-1	0-2	1-1	0-2	3-1	2-2	2-2	2-1	0-2	

1/09/2007 - 30/01/2008 • † Qualified for the quarter-finals • Top scorer: Geovanni Ayala, Las Tunas 22

CAMPEONATO NACIONAL PLAY-OFFS

Quarter–finals

Cienfuegos *	1	0
Holguín	0	0
Guantánamo *	0	0
Villa Clara	2	1
Pinar del Río *	2	0
Ciego de Avila	0	0
Camagüey *	0	0
Ciudad de La Habana	0	3

Semi–finals

Cienfuegos *	0	2
Villa Clara	1	1
Pinar del Río *	1	0 11p
Ciudad de La Habana	0	1 12p

* at home in the first leg

Final

Cienfuegos *	2	2
Ciudad de La Habana	0	1

CAMPEONATO NACIONAL FINAL

1st leg. Estadio Luis Pérez Lozano, Cienfuegos, 28-02-2008

Cienfuegos	2-0	Ciudad La Habana

Scorers - Yusvani Caballero OG 36, Yusniel Benítez 44

CAMPEONATO NACIONAL FINAL

2nd leg. Estadio Pedro Marrero, Havana, 1-03-2008

Ciudad La Habana	1-2	**Cienfuegos**

Scorers - Loannys Cartaya 27 for Ciudad La Habana;
Alexei Carrazana 29p, Walberto Carrazana 75 for Cienfuegos

RECENT LEAGUE RECORD

Year	Winners	Score	Runners-up
1996	Villa Clara	2-3 4-0	Cienfuegos
1997	Villa Clara	1-2 2-0	Pinar del Río
1998	Ciudad de la Habana	2-1 1-0	Villa Clara
1999	No championship due to season readjustment		
2000	Pinar del Río	0-1 2-1	Ciudad de La Habana
2001	Ciudad de La Habana	2-1 0-0	Villa Clara
2002	Ciego de Avila	1-0 0-0	Granma Bayamo
2003	Villa Clara	1-0 2-0	Ciudad de La Habana
2003	Ciego de Avila	1-1 2-0	Villa Clara
2004	Villa Clara	0-1 3-0	Pinar del Río
2005	Holguín	‡	Ciudad de La Habana
2006	Pinar del Río	‡	Villa Clara
2008	Cienfuegos	2-0 2-1	Ciudad de La Habana

† Won on away goals • ‡ Played on a league basis

CLUB DIRECTORY

Club	Town/City	Stadium	Lge
Camagüey	Camagüey	Terreno de Futbol de Florida	0
Ciego de Avila	Ciego de Avila	CVD Deportivo	3
Cienfuegos	Cienfuegos		3
Ciudad de La Habana	Havana	Pedro Marrero	6
Granma	Bayamo	Conrado Benitez	0
Holguín	Holguín	Turcio Lima	1
Industriales	Havana	Campo Armada	4
Las Tunas	Victoria de Las Tunas	Ovidio Torres	0
Matanzas	Matanzas	Terreno de Futbol de Colon	0
Pinar del Río	Pinar del Río	La Bombonera	7
Santiago de Cuba	Santiago de Cuba	Antonio Maceo	0
Villa Clara	Santa Clara	Camilo Cienfuegos	10

CYP – CYPRUS

NATIONAL TEAM RECORD
JULY 10TH 2006 TO JULY 12TH 2010

PL	W	D	L	F	A	%
18	6	3	9	23	34	41.7

FIFA/COCA-COLA WORLD RANKING

1993	1994	1995	1996	1997	1998	1999	2000	2001	2002	2003	2004	2005	2006	2007	High	
72	67	73	78	82	78	63	62	79	80	97	108	96	73	66	57	10/07

2007–2008												Low	
08/07	09/07	10/07	11/07	12/07	01/08	02/08	03/08	04/08	05/08	06/08	07/08	11	03/05
82	68	57	65	66	65	66	63	58	58	64	63		

The Cypriot national team proved once again that the recent upturn in their fortunes is no fluke, with a number of good displays in the qualifiers for Euro 2008. Although they finished second from bottom in their group they were just three points behind the Republic of Ireland in third place, a performance that earned coach Angelos Anastasiadis a renewal of his contract. The Cypriots began the season in fine style with four consecutive wins, the first time in the team's 60-year history that it had managed such a feat, although they were followed by predictable losses against both the Czech Republic and Germany. In the championship Anorthosis went all 32 games unbeaten as they

INTERNATIONAL HONOURS
None

secured the title 11 points ahead of defending champions APOEL - one of just two teams in Europe along with CSKA Sofia to go through the season undefeated. Temuri Ketsbaia's team fell just short of winning the double, however, when they lost 2-0 to APOEL in the Cup Final. Anorthosis had the better season of the two in Europe beating Macedonia's Vardar and Romania's Cluj in the UEFA Cup preliminaries before losing heavily to Tottenham in the first round while APOEL lost 3-2 on aggregate to BATE Borisov of Belarus in the first preliminary round of the Champions League - despite having won the first leg 2-0 at home.

THE FIFA BIG COUNT OF 2006

	Male	Female		Total
Number of players	47 768	4 635	Referees and Assistant Referees	200
Professionals	800		Admin, Coaches, Technical, Medical	2 000
Amateurs 18+	10 091		Number of clubs	100
Youth under 18	6 644		Number of teams	328
Unregistered	20 200		Clubs with women's teams	8
Total players	52 403		Players as % of population	6.68%

Cyprus Football Association (CFA)
10 Achaion Street, 2413 Engomi, Nicosia, Cyprus
Tel +357 22 352341   Fax +357 22 590544
info@cfa.com.cy   www.none
President: KOUTSOKOUMNIS Costakis   General Secretary: ECONOMIDES George
Vice-President: LOIZIDES Charis   Treasurer: MARANGOS Spyros   Media Officer: GIORGALIS Kyriakos
Men's Coach: ANASTASIADIS Angelos   Women's Coach: IAKOVOU Pepis
CFA formed: 1934   UEFA: 1962   FIFA: 1948
Blue shirts with white trimmings, White shorts, Blue socks or White shirts with blue trimmings, White shorts, White socks

RECENT INTERNATIONAL MATCHES PLAYED BY CYPRUS

2004	Opponents	Score	Venue	Comp	Scorers	Att	Referee
18-02	Belarus	L 0-2	Achnas	Fr		500	Kailis CYP
19-02	Georgia	W 3-1	Nicosia	Fr	Charalampidis 2 44 55, Ilia 73	200	Kapitanis CYP
21-02	Kazakhstan	W 2-1	Larnaca	Fr	Charalampidis 3, Michail.C 8	300	Lajuks LVA
19-05	Jordan	D 0-0	Nicosia	Fr		2 500	Loizou CYP
18-08	Albania	W 2-1	Nicosia	Fr	Konstantinou.M 2 13p 48	200	Kapitanis CYP
4-09	Republic of Ireland	L 0-3	Dublin	WCq		36 000	Paniashvili GEO
8-09	Israel	L 1-2	Tel Aviv	WCq	Konstantinou.M 59	21 872	Shmolik BLR
9-10	Faroe Islands	D 2-2	Nicosia	WCq	Konstantinou.M 15, Okkas 81	1 400	Gadiyev AZE
13-10	France	L 0-2	Nicosia	WCq		3 319	Larsen DEN
17-11	Israel	L 1-2	Nicosia	WCq	Okkas 45	1 624	Kaldma EST
2005							
8-02	Austria	D 1-1	Limassol	Fr	Charalampidis 90. W 5-4p	300	Hyytia FIN
9-02	Finland	L 1-2	Nicosia	Fr	Michail.C 24	300	Lajuks LVA
26-03	Jordan	W 2-1	Larnaca	Fr	Charalampidis 9, Okkas 28	200	Kapitanis CYP
30-03	Switzerland	L 0-1	Zurich	WCq		16 066	Dougal SCO
13-08	Iraq	W 2-1	Limassol	Fr	Yiasoumi 2 63 79	500	
17-08	Faroe Islands	W 3-0	Toftir	WCq	Konstantinou.M 2 39 77, Krassas 95+	2 720	Johannesson SWE
7-09	Switzerland	L 1-3	Nicosia	WCq	Aloneftis 35	2 561	Ivanov.N RUS
8-10	Republic of Ireland	L 0-1	Nicosia	WCq		13 546	Kassai HUN
12-10	France	L 0-4	Paris	WCq		78 864	Stark GER
16-11	Wales	W 1-0	Limassol	Fr	Michail.C 43p	1 000	Jakov ISR
2006							
28-02	Slovenia	L 0-1	Larnaca	Fr		1 000	Tsacheilidis GRE
1-03	Armenia	W 2-0	Limassol	Fr	Okkas 18, Michail.C 61		
16-08	Romania	L 0-2	Constanta	Fr		10 000	Corpodean ROU
2-09	Slovakia	L 1-6	Bratislava	ECq	Yiasoumis 90	4 723	Orekhov UKR
7-10	Republic of Ireland	W 5-2	Nicosia	ECq	Konstantinou.M 2 10 50p, Garpozis 16, Charalambides 2 60 75	5 000	Batista OR
11-10	Wales	L 1-3	Cardiff	ECq	Okkas 83	20 456	Granat POL
15-11	Germany	D 1-1	Nicosia	ECq	Okkas 43	12 300	Fröjdfeldt SWE
2007							
6-02	Hungary	W 2-1	Limassol	Fr	Yiasoumis 18, Okkas 72	500	Gerasimou CYP
7-02	Bulgaria	L 0-3	Nicosia	Fr		2 000	
24-03	Slovakia	L 1-3	Nicosia	ECq	Aloneftis 43	2 696	Lehner AUT
28-03	Czech Republic	L 0-1	Liberec	ECq		9 310	Bebek CRO
22-08	San Marino	W 1-0	Serravalle	ECq	Okkas 54	552	Janku ALB
8-09	Armenia	W 3-1	Larnaca	Fr	Michael 31, Okkas 42, Constantinou 52		Trattos CYP
12-09	San Marino	W 3-0	Nicosia	ECq	Makridis 15, Aloneftis 2 41 92+	1 000	Kulbakov BLR
13-10	Wales	W 3-1	Nicosia	ECq	Okkas 2 59 68, Charalampidis 79	2 852	Bertolini SUI
17-10	Republic of Ireland	D 1-1	Dublin	ECq	Okkarides 80	54 861	Vuorela FIN
17-11	Germany	L 0-4	Hanover	ECq		45 016	Rasmussen DEN
21-11	Czech Republic	L 0-2	Nicosia	ECq		5 866	Paniashvili GEO
2008							
6-02	Ukraine	D 1-1	Nicosia	Fr	Alonefitis 19p	500	
19-05	Greece	L 0-2	Patras	Fr		16 216	MacDonald SCO

Fr = Friendly match • EC = UEFA EURO 2008 • WC = FIFA World Cup • q = qualifier

CYPRUS NATIONAL TEAM RECORDS AND RECORD SEQUENCES

Records			Sequence records				
Victory	5-0	AND 2000	Wins	4	2007	Clean sheets	2	1992-93, 1994,1996
Defeat	0-12	GER 1969	Defeats	19	1973-1978	Goals scored	7	1997-1998
Player Caps	82	Pittas & Okkas	Undefeated	6	1997-1998	Without goal	6	1975, 1987-1988
Player Goals	24	Michalis Konstantinou	Without win	39	1984-1992	Goals against	36	1973-1981

MAJOR CITIES/TOWNS

Population '000

1	Nicosia	204
2	Limassol	158
3	Larnaca	49
4	Famagusta (T)	45
5	Nicosia (T)	42
6	Paphos	38
7	Girne (T)	29
8	Morphou (T)	15
9	Aradippou	14
10	Paralimni	12
11	Lefka (T)	8
12	Geri	8
13	Ypsonas	7
14	Dali	6
15	Tseri	5
16	Livadia	5
17	Dipkarpaz (T)	5
18	Lapithos (T)	5
19	Dromolaxia	5
20	Xylofagou	5
21	Deryneia	5
22	Ayia Napa	2
23	Achna	2

(T) = in Turkish controlled zone

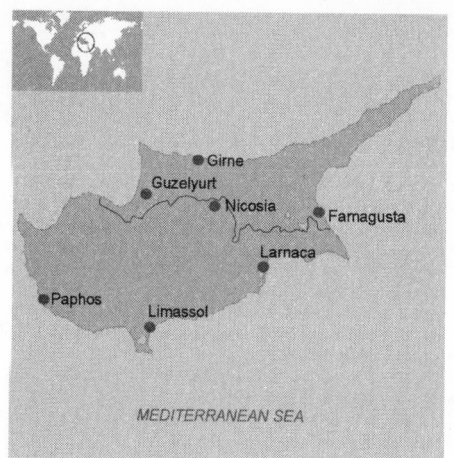

Girne
Guzelyurt
Nicosia
Farnagusta
Larnaca
Paphos
Limassol
MEDITERRANEAN SEA

REPUBLIC OF CYPRUS; KYPRIAKI DIMOKRATIA

Capital	Nicosia	Language	Greek, Turkish, English			Independence	1960
Population	784 301	Area	9 250 km²	Density	83 per km²	% in cities	54%
GDP per cap	$19 200	Dialling code	+357	Internet	.cy	GMT +/-	+2

MEDALS TABLE

		Overall			League			Cup			Europe			City	Stadium	Cap'ty	DoF
		G	S	B	G	S	B	G	S	B	G	S	B				
1	APOEL Nicosia	38	26	15	19	18	15	19	8					Nicosia	Neo GSP/Pancypria	23 400	1926
2	Omonia Nicosia	31	19	8	19	13	8	12	6					Nicosia	Neo GSP/Pancypria	23 400	1948
3	Anorthosis Famagusta	21	16	5	13	10	5	8	6					Larnaca	Andonis Papadopoulos	9 500	1911
4	AEL Limassol	12	6	6	6	1	6	6	5					Limassol	Tsirion	13 152	1930
5	Apollon Limassol	8	10	4	3	4	4	5	6					Limassol	Tsirion	13 152	1954
6	EPA Larnaca	7	9	4	2	6	4	5	3					Larnaca	Neo GSZ/Zenon	13 032	1932-94
7	Olympiakos Nicosia	4	7	2	3	4	2	1	3					Nicosia	Pancypria	23 400	1931
8	Trust AC	4	3		1	2		3	1					Larnaca	Old Gymnastica		1896-44
9	Pezoporikos Larnaca	3	15	14	2	8	14	1	7					Larnaca	Old Gymnastica		1927-94
10	Chetin Kaya	3	4	3	1	1	3	2	3					Nicosia	GSP		1916
11	NEA Salamina	1	2	4			4	1	2					Larnaca	Ammochostos	8 000	1948
12	AEK Larnaca	1	2					1	2					Larnaca	Neo GSZ/Zenon	13 032	1994
13	Union Paralimni (ENP)		5	2		1	2		4					Paralimni	Municipal	8 000	1936
14	Alki Larnaca		5	1			1		5					Larnaca	Zenon	13 032	1948
15	Digenis Morphou		2			1			1					Nicosia	Makarion	20 000	1931
16	Aris Limassol		1	1			1		1					Limassol	Tsirion	13 152	1930
17	Ethnikos Achnas		1						1					Achna	Dasaki	4 000	1968

RECENT LEAGUE AND CUP RECORD

	Championship						Cup		
Year	Champions	Pts	Runners-up	Pts	Third	Pts	Winners	Score	Runners-up
1995	Anorthosis F'gusta	73	Omonia Nicosia	67	NEA Salamina	57	APOEL Nicosia	4-2	Apollon Limassol
1996	APOEL Nicosia	64	Anorthosis F'gusta	55	Omonia Nicosia	53	APOEL Nicosia	2-0	AEK Larnaca
1997	Anorthosis F'gusta	65	Apollon Limassol	52	Omonia Nicosia	46	APOEL Nicosia	2-0	Omonia Nicosia
1998	Anorthosis F'gusta	66	Omonia Nicosia	62	Apollon Limassol	55	Anothosis F'gusta	3-1	Apollon Limassol
1999	Anorthosis F'gusta	67	Omonia Nicosia	67	APOEL Nicosia	59	APOEL Nicosia	2-0	Anorthosis F'gusta
2000	Anorthosis F'gusta	65	Omonia Nicosia	59	APOEL Nicosia	46	Omonia Nicosia	4-2	APOEL Nicosia
2001	Omonia Nicosia	57	Olympiakos	54	AEL Limassol	52	Apollon Limassol	1-0	NEA Salamina
2002	APOEL Nicosia	59	Anorthosis F'gusta	58	AEL Limassol	54	Anorthosis F'gusta	1-0	Ethnikos Achnas
2003	Omonia Nicosia	60	Anorthosis F'gusta	59	APOEL Nicosia	55	Anorthosis F'gusta	0-0 5-3p	AEL Limassol
2004	APOEL Nicosia	65	Omonia Nicosia	62	Apollon Limassol	49	AEK Larnaca	2-1	AEL Limassol
2005	Anorthosis F'gusta	62	APOEL Nicosia	58	Omonia Nicosia	47	Omonia Nicosia	2-0	Digenis Morfu
2006	Apollon Limassol	64	Omonia Nicosia	63	APOEL Nicosia	62	APOEL Nicosia	3-2	AEK Larnaca
2007	APOEL Nicosia	64	Omonia Nicosia	57	Anorthosis F'gusta	53	Anorthosis F'gusta	3-2	Omonia Nicosia
2008	Anorthosis F'gusta	72	APOEL Nicosia	61	Omonia Nicosia	52	APOEL Nicosia	2-0	Anorthosis F'gusta

CYPRUS 2007–08

MARFIN LAIKI A KATEGORIA (1)

Team	Pl	W	D	L	F	A	Pts	Anorthosis	APOEL	Omonia	AEK	Apollon	ENP	Ethnikos	APOP	AEL	Alki	Doxa	Aris	Nea S'mina	Olympiakos
Anorthosis Famagusta†	32	20	12	0	58	19	72		1-0 3-0	2-0 0-0	2-1 3-3	1-1	1-0	5-1	3-1	3-1	1-0	2-1	4-0	5-0	1-0
APOEL Nicosia ‡	32	18	7	7	58	28	61	0-1 1-1		1-0 2-2	1-0 2-1	2-0	0-1	2-1	4-0	2-0	3-0	3-2	3-0	3-1	4-0
Omonia Nicosia ‡	32	14	10	8	42	31	52	1-1 0-0	2-1 1-1-2		3-2 0-0	1-1	0-1	2-1	1-0	1-0	3-0	2-1	0-0	3-0	2-0
AEK Larnaca	32	14	8	10	46	42	50	1-1 2-2	0-3 1-0	1-0 5-3		0-2	1-3	1-0	1-1	2-2	2-0	1-2	1-0	2-2	2-1
Apollon Limassol	32	12	11	9	49	41	47	2-2	0-2	3-3	2-0		3-0 4-1	2-1 0-2	2-0 2-2	4-3	1-0	2-2	2-1	4-1	3-2
ENP Paralimni	32	13	7	12	42	45	46	1-2	1-0	1-3	0-1	2-2 1-0		0-2 1-0-2-4-3	1-1	2-1	0-1	1-0	1-0	1-0	0-1
Ethnikos Achnas	32	13	4	15	44	43	43	0-1	0-2	1-2	0-2	2-1-1-0-1-4-3		2-1-2-2	2-1	1-1	3-1	2-0	5-0	2-1	
APOP	32	11	9	12	47	49	42	0-2	1-1	0-0	0-1	1-0-1-2-1-1-3-4	2-1-1-0			0-1	5-3	3-1	1-0	4-2	3-1
AEL Limassol	32	11	7	14	39	45	40	1-2	1-1	1-1	0-2	0-0	1-4	1-2	0-0		2-0 1-0-2-2-5-1-2-1-0-3-0	1-0	3-1		
Alki Larnaca	32	11	7	14	41	44	40	0-0	0-4	2-1	0-2	1-0	0-1	1-3	3-1	2-0-2-1		1-1-1-0-1-1-4-1-4	4-1	5-0	
Doxa Katokopia	32	10	9	13	43	48	39	1-1	2-2	1-0	3-3	1-0	2-2	2-1	2-2	2-1-1-2-1-0-0-0			2-1-2-0	2-3	2-0
Aris Limassol	32	8	6	18	31	48	30	0-4	1-3	0-2	2-0	0-0	2-2	1-2	2-3	3-1	2-1-0-2-2-5-1-2-1-0-3-0			1-0	3-0
Nea Salamina	26	6	6	14	28	54	24	0-4	1-3	0-2	2-0	0-0	1-3	0-2	2-0	1-1	0-2	1-2	1-0		4-2
Olympiakos Nicosia	26	3	5	18	23	54	14	0-1	2-2	0-1	0-2	2-2	2-2	1-0	1-1	1-2	1-1	2-1	0-1	2-4	

1/09/2007 – 10/05/2008 • † Qualified for the UEFA Champions League • ‡ Qualified for the UEFA Cup
Top scorers: Lukasz Sosin, Anorthosis, 16; David Pereira da Costa, Doxa 16; Constantinos Makrides, APOEL 13

CYPRUS 2007–08 B KATEGORIA (2)

Team	Pl	W	D	L	F	A	Pts
AEP Paphos	26	17	3	6	46	22	54
APEP	26	15	6	5	45	26	51
Atromitos	26	13	7	6	41	23	46
Digenis Morfu	26	14	4	8	44	26	46
Ermis Aradippou	26	11	5	10	51	43	38
Onisilos Sotiras	26	9	11	6	32	23	38
Ayia Napa	26	9	7	10	32	32	34
Omonia Aradippou	26	8	9	9	25	24	33
ASIL	26	8	8	10	20	24	32
THOI Lakatamia	26	8	7	11	28	40	31
MEAP Nisou	26	9	4	13	32	49	31
Anagennisi Yermasoyia	26	8	6	12	21	35	30
Akritas Chloraka	26	5	7	14	22	39	22
Olympos Xylofagou	26	4	4	18	23	56	16

22/09/2007 – 12/04/2008

CYPRUS 2007–08 G KATEGORIA (3)

Team	Pl	W	D	L	F	A	Pts
PAEEK	26	16	4	6	55	38	52
Ethnikos Assias	26	15	6	5	53	24	51
Halkanoras Dhaliou	26	12	10	4	42	30	46
Spartakos Kitiou	26	12	8	6	59	38	44
Frenaros FC 2000	26	12	7	7	48	43	43
Adonis Idaliou	26	12	6	8	59	35	42
AEZ Zakakiou	26	10	6	10	41	33	36
AEK Kouklion	26	9	6	11	37	46	33
Anagennisi Trahoniou	26	8	9	9	43	41	33
Kissos Kissonergas	26	9	5	12	43	54	32
Elpida Xylofagou	26	9	4	13	33	48	31
Anagennisi Ger'soyias	26	6	8	12	29	45	26
ENAD Polis	26	5	5	16	31	62	20
Iraklis Yerolakkou	26	4	2	20	39	75	14

22/09/2007 – 12/04/2008

COCA-COLA CUP 2007–08

Round of 16

APOEL Nicosia *	6	3
Olympos Xylofagou	0	0
ENP Paralimni	0	3
Nea Salamina	1	2
Ethnikos Achnas	1	1
AEP Paphos *	1	0
Olympiakos Nicosia	0	2
Omonia Nicosia *	1	4
Apollon Limassol	3	2
Digenis Morfu *	1	0
AEK Larnaca *	0	1
Ayia Napa	2	1
Aris Limassol	2	1
Ermis Aradippou *	1	1
APOP *	0	0
Anorthosis Famagusta	2	2

Quarter-finals

Group A		Pts
Apollon Limassol		12
Omonia Nicosia		9
Nea Salamina		9
Ethnikos Achnas		2

Group B		Pts
Anorthosis Famagusta		14
APOEL Nicosia		11
Ayia Napa		6
Aris Limassol		3

Semi-finals

APOEL Nicosia	1	2
Omonia Nicosia *	2	0

Apollon Limassol *	1	1
Anorthosis Famagusta	0	4

Final

APOEL Nicosia ‡	2
Anorthosis Famagusta	0

CUP FINAL

17-05-2008

Scorers – Nuno Morais [53], Nenad Mirosavljevic [75]

* Home team in the first leg • ‡ Qualified for the UEFA Cup

CZE – CZECH REPUBLIC

NATIONAL TEAM RECORD
JULY 10TH 2006 TO JULY 12TH 2010

PL	W	D	L	F	A	%
23	13	5	5	42	20	67.4

FIFA/COCA-COLA WORLD RANKING

1993	1994	1995	1996	1997	1998	1999	2000	2001	2002	2003	2004	2005	2006	2007		High	
-	34	14	5	3	8	2	5	14	15	6	4	2	10	6		2	

				2007–2008								Low	
08/07	09/07	10/07	11/07	12/07	01/08	02/08	03/08	04/08	05/08	06/08	07/08	67	03/94
9	11	9	6	6	6	6	6	6	6	6	8		

In the annals of spectacular capitulations, the Czech Republic's 3-2 defeat at the hands of Turkey in their final group match at Euro 2008 will go down as one of the most notable. Leading 2-0 with 75 minutes on the clock, the following fifteen minutes won't be forgotten by the nation in a hurry - especially by the normally reliable goalkeeper Petr Cech who was wholly culpable for the equaliser on 87 minutes. To be fair, the Czechs had never really impressed during the finals but they did have one foot in the quarters before the Turk's dramatic finale. It proved to be the last match in charge for coach Karel Brückner as well as for their giant striker Jan Koller, who finished

INTERNATIONAL HONOURS
Qualified for the FIFA World Cup™ finals 2006   UEFA U-21 Championship 2002

his international career as the all-time leading scorer for the Czech Republic (and Czechoslovakia) with 55 goals in 90 internationals. At home Slavia celebrated the dawn of a new era when they won their first championship for 12 years, winning the title on the final day of the season in what was their first game at their newly constructed Eden Stadium, a facility they hope will give them the ability to compete with fierce rivals Sparta. In Europe Slavia knocked out Ajax to qualify for the group stage of the Champions League for the first time, where they finished third in their group ahead of Steaua, although they will want quickly to forget the 7-0 defeat at the hands of Arsenal.

THE FIFA BIG COUNT OF 2006

	Male	Female		Total
Number of players	976 355	64 002	Referees and Assistant Referees	4 351
Professionals	1 558		Admin, Coaches, Technical, Medical	8 530
Amateurs 18+	435 605		Number of clubs	3 968
Youth under 18	208 451		Number of teams	15 463
Unregistered	103 100		Clubs with women's teams	140
Total players	1 040 357		Players as % of population	10.16

Football Association of Czech Republic (CMFS)
Ceskomoravsky Fotbalovy Svaz, Diskarska 100, PO Box 11, Praha 6 - 16900, Czech Republic
Tel +420 2 33029111   Fax +420 2 33353107
cmfs@fotbal.cz   www.fotbal.cz
President: MOKRY Pavel   General Secretary: REPKA Rudolf
Vice-President: KOSTAL Vlastimil   Treasurer: FISCHER Jiri   Media Officer: TUCEK Lukas
Men's Coach: RADA Petr   Women's Coach: ZOVINEC Dusan
CMFS formed: 1901   UEFA: 1954   FIFA: 1907 & 1994
Red shirts with blue and white trimmings, White shorts, Blue socks or White shirts, White shorts, White socks

RECENT INTERNATIONAL MATCHES PLAYED BY THE CZECH REPUBLIC

2006	Opponents	Score		Venue	Comp	Scorers	Att	Referee
1-03	Turkey	D	2-2	Izmir	Fr	Poborsky [21]p, Stajner [63]	58 000	Meyer GER
26-05	Saudi Arabia	W	2-0	Innsbruck	Fr	Baros [15], Jankulovski [90]p	4 000	Einwaller AUT
30-05	Costa Rica	W	1-0	Jablonec	Fr	Lokvenc [82]	14 500	Bede HUN
3-06	Trinidad and Tobago	W	3-0	Prague	Fr	Koller 2 [6 40], Nedved [22]	15 910	Johansson SWE
12-06	USA	W	3-0	Gelsenkirchen	WCr1	Koller [5], Rosicky 2 [36 76]	52 000	Amarilla PAR
17-06	Ghana	L	0-2	Cologne	WCr1		45 000	Elizondo ARG
22-06	Italy	L	0-2	Hamburg	WCr1		50 000	Archundia MEX
16-08	Serbia	L	1-3	Uherske Hradiste	Fr	Stajner [3]	8 047	Drabek AUT
2-09	Wales	W	2-1	Teplice	ECq	Lafata 2 [76 89]	16 200	Eriksson SWE
6-09	Slovakia	W	3-0	Bratislava	ECq	Sionko 2 [10 21], Koller [57]	27 684	Bennett ENG
7-10	San Marino	W	7-0	Liberec	ECq	Kulic [15], Polak [22], Baros 2 [28 68], Koller 2 [43 52], Jaroléim [49]	9 514	Aliyev AZE
11-10	Republic of Ireland	D	1-1	Dublin	ECq	Koller [64]	35 500	Layec FRA
15-11	Denmark	D	1-1	Prague	Fr	Baros [93+]	6 852	Skomina SVN
2007								
7-02	Belgium	W	2-0	Brussels	Fr	Koller [6], Kulic [74]	12 000	Granat POL
24-03	Germany	L	1-2	Prague	ECq	Baros [77]	17 821	Rosetti ITA
28-03	Cyprus	W	1-0	Liberec	ECq	Kovác [22]	9 310	Bebek CRO
2-06	Wales	D	0-0	Cardiff	ECq		30 174	Allaerts BEL
22-08	Austria	D	1-1	Vienna	Fr	Koller [33]	24 500	Gonzalez ESP
8-09	San Marino	W	3-0	Serravalle	ECq	Rosicky [33], Jankulovski [75], Koller [93+]	3 412	Filipovic SRB
12-09	Republic of Ireland	W	1-0	Prague	ECq	Jankulovski [15]	16 648	Vassaras GRE
17-10	Germany	W	3-0	Munich	ECq	Sionko [2], Matejovski [23], Plasil [63]	66 445	Webb ENG
17-11	Slovakia	W	3-1	Prague	ECq	Grygera [13], Kulic [76], Rosicky [83]	15 651	Asumaa FIN
21-11	Cyprus	W	2-0	Nicosia	ECq	Pudil [11], Koller [74]	5 866	Paniashvili GEO
2008								
6-02	Poland	L	0-2	Larnaca	Fr		1 500	Tryfonos CYP
26-03	Denmark	D	1-1	Herning	Fr	Koller [42]	11 900	Mikulski POL
27-05	Lithuania	W	2-0	Prague	Fr	Koller 2 [39 63]	14 220	Hrinak SVK
30-05	Scotland	W	3-1	Prague	Fr	Sionko 2 [60 90], Kadlec [84]	11 314	Braamhaar NED
7-06	Switzerland	W	1-0	Basel	ECr1	Sverkos [71]	39 730	Rosetti ITA
11-06	Portugal	L	1-3	Geneva	ECr1	Sionko [17]	29 016	Vassaras GRE
15-06	Turkey	L	2-3	Geneva	ECr1	Koller [34], Plasil [62]	29 016	Fröjdfeldt SWE

Fr = Friendly match • EC = UEFA EURO 2008 • WC = FIFA World Cup • q = qualifier • r1 = first round group

CZECH REPUBLIC NATIONAL TEAM PLAYERS

	Player		Ap	G	Club	Date of Birth		Player		Ap	G	Club	Date of Birth
1	Petr Cech	GK	62	0	Chelsea	20 05 1982	12	Zdenek Pospech	DF	8	0	FC København	14 12 1978
2	Zdenek Grygera	DF	56	2	Juventus	14 05 1980	13	Michal Kadlec	DF	7	1	Sparta Praha	13 12 1984
3	Jan Polák	MF	41	6	RSC Anderlecht	14 03 1981	14	David Jarolím	MF	19	1	Hamburger SV	17 05 1979
4	Tomás Galásek	MF	69	1	1.FC Nürnberg	15 01 1973	15	Milan Baros	FW	65	31	Portsmouth	28 10 1981
5	Radoslav Kovác	MF	24	1	Spartak Moskva	27 11 1979	16	Jaromír Blazek	GK	14	0	1.FC Nürnberg	29 12 1972
6	Marek Jankulovski	DF	67	10	Milan	9 05 1977	17	Marek Matejovsky	MF	12	1	Reading	20 12 1981
7	Libor Sionko	FW	33	7	FC København	1 02 1977	18	Tomás Sivok	MF	6	0	Sparta Praha	15 09 1983
8	Martin Fenin	FW	5	0	Eint. Frankfurt	16 04 1987	19	Rudolf Skácel	MF	5	1	Hertha Berlin	17 07 1979
9	Jan Koller	FW	90	55	1.FC Nürnberg	30 03 1973	20	Jaroslav Plasil	MF	40	3	Osasuna	5 01 1982
10	Václav Sverkos	FW	3	1	Banik Ostrava	1 11 1983	21	Tomás Ujfalusi	DF	71	2	Fiorentina	24 03 1978
11	Stanislav Vlcek	FW	13	0	RSC Anderlecht	26 02 1976	22	David Rozehnal	DF	48	0	Lazio	5 07 1980
The Czech Republic squad for Euro 2008							23	Daniel Zitka	GK	1	0	RSC Anderlecht	20 06 1975

CZECH REPUBLIC NATIONAL TEAM RECORDS AND RECORD SEQUENCES

Records			Sequence records		
Victory	8-1	AND 2005	Wins	8	2004-2005
Defeat	0-3	SUI 1994	Defeats	3	2000, 2006
Player Caps	118	Karel Poborsky	Undefeated	20	2002-2004
Player Goals	48	Jan Koller	Without win	3	Five times

Clean sheets	4	Three times
Goals scored	17	2002-2004
Without goal	3	2004
Goals against	8	1999-2000, 2003-04

MAJOR CITIES/TOWNS

Population '000

#	City	Pop.
1	Prague	1 168
2	Brno	363
3	Ostrava	309
4	Plzen	163
5	Olomouc	100
6	Liberec	97
7	Hradec Králové	93
8	Ceske Budejovice	93
9	Usti nad Labem	93
10	Pardubice	87
11	Havirov	84
12	Zlin	77
13	Kladno	69
14	Most	67
15	Karvina	62
16	Frydek-Mistek	59
17	Opava	59
18	Decin	51
19	Teplice	51
20	Prostejov	46
21	Jablonec nad Nisou	44
22	Mladá Boleslav	43
23	Pribram	36
24	Uhersky Hradiste	26

CZECH REPUBLIC; CESKA REPUBLIKA

Capital	Prague (Praha)	Language	Czech
Population	10 235 455	Area	78 866
GDP per cap	$15 700	Dailling code	+420

Density	129 per km²	Independence	1993
		% in cities	65%
Internet	.cz	GMT + / -	+1

CZECH REPUBLIC MEDALS TABLE POST 1993

		Overall			League			Cup			Europe			City	Stadium	Cap'ty	DoF
		G	S	B	G	S	B	G	S	B	G	S	B				
1	Sparta Praha	15	6		10	3		5	3					Prague	AXA Arena (Letná)	20 565	1893
2	Slavia Praha	5	9	2	2	9	2	3						Prague	Stadion Eden	21 000	1893
3	Slovan Liberec	3	2		2			1	2					Liberec	U Nisy	9 900	1958
4	Baník Ostrava	2	2	2	1		2	1	2					Ostrava	Bazaly	17 372	1922
5	Viktoria Zizkov	2	1	2			2	2	1					Prague	Viktoria	4 898	1903
6	FK Jablonec 97	1	2	2			2	1	2					Jablonec nad Nisou	Strelnice	6 246	1945
7	FK Teplice	1	1	1		1	1	1						Teplice	Na Stinadlech	18 221	1945
8	FC Hradec Králové	1						1						Hradec Králové	Vsesportovni	17 000	1905

CLUBS IN CZECHOSLOVAKIAN FOOTBALL 1925–1993

		Overall			League			Cup			Europe		
		G	S	B	G	S	B	G	S	B	G	S	B
1	Sparta Praha	27	21	8	19	16	7	8	5				1
2	Dukla Praha	19	9	5	11	7	3	8	2				2
4	Slavia Praha	9	11	8	9	9	7		2				1
6	Baník Ostrava	6	7	2	3	6	1	3	1				1
10	Bohemians Praha	1	2	12	1	1	11						1

CLUBS IN CZECH FOOTBALL 1896–1946

		Overall			League			Cup		
		G	S	B	G	S	B	G	S	
1	Sparta Praha	25	15		11	3		14	12	
2	Slavia Praha	25	13		10	7		15	6	
3	Viktoria Zizkov	7	4	3	1	2		7	3	

RECENT LEAGUE AND CUP RECORD

	Championship						Cup		
Year	Champions	Pts	Runners-up	Pts	Third	Pts	Winners	Score	Runners-up
1995	Sparta Praha	70	Slavia Praha	64	Boby Brno	54	SK Hradec Kralové	0-0 3-1p	Viktoria Zizkov
1996	Slavia Praha	70	Sigma Olomouc	61	Jablonec nad Nisou	53	Sparta Praha	4-0	Petra Drnovice
1997	Sparta Praha	65	Sigma Olomouc	61	Jablonec nad Nisou	56	Slavia Praha	1-0	Dukla Praha
1998	Sparta Praha	71	Slavia Praha	59	Sigma Olomouc	55	FK Jablonec	2-1	Petra Drnovice
1999	Sparta Praha	60	FK Teplice	55	Slavia Praha	55	Slavia Praha	1-0	Slovan Liberec
2000	Sparta Praha	76	Slavia Praha	68	FK Drnovice	48	Slovan Liberec	2-1	Baník Ratiskovice
2001	Sparta Praha	68	Slavia Praha	52	Sigma Olomouc	52	Viktoria Zizkov	2-1	Sparta Praha
2002	Slovan Liberec	64	Sparta Praha	63	Viktoria Zizkov	63	Slavia Praha	2-1	Sparta Praha
2003	Sparta Praha	65	Slavia Praha	64	Viktoria Zizkov	50	FK Teplice	1-0	FK Jablonec
2004	Baník Ostrava	63	Sparta Praha	58	Sigma Olomouc	55	Sparta Praha	2-1	Baník Ostrava
2005	Sparta Praha	64	Slavia Praha	53	FK Teplice	53	Baník Ostrava	2-1	1.FC Slovácko
2006	Slovan Liberec	59	Mladá Boleslav	54	Slavia Praha	54	Sparta Praha	0-0 4-2p	Baník Ostrava
2007	Sparta Praha	62	Slavia Praha	58	Mladá Boleslav	58	Sparta Praha	2-1	FK Jablonec
2008	Slavia Praha	60	Sparta Praha	57	Baník Ostrava	55	Sparta Praha	0-0 4-3p	Slovan Liberec

CZECH REPUBLIC 2007–08

I. GAMBRINUS LIGA

	Pl	W	D	L	F	A	Pts	Slavia	Sparta	Baník	Brno	Teplice	Slovan	Mladá	Zlin	Plzen	Zizkov	Sigma	Jablonec	Budejovice	Kladno	Bohemians	Most
Slavia Praha †	30	17	9	4	45	24	60		1-1	0-0	1-0	1-0	1-0	1-1	7-1	3-0	0-3	0-0	2-2	1-0	2-0	2-1	2-0
Sparta Praha †	30	17	6	7	53	26	57	0-2		1-2	0-2	1-0	1-0	0-1	2-1	3-1	6-1	1-0	1-0	1-0	4-1	3-1	3-0
Baník Ostrava ‡	30	15	10	5	51	28	55	2-2	0-0		2-1	0-0	3-1	3-3	2-1	2-0	3-0	0-1	3-0	2-0	4-1	2-0	5-2
1.FC Brno	30	16	7	7	43	32	55	2-1	4-2	0-0		2-2	2-0	0-3	0-0	0-1	3-1	1-0	2-1	2-1	0-0	2-0	2-1
FK Teplice	30	16	5	9	40	27	53	3-1	2-1	1-1	0-1		2-0	1-2	2-1	1-0	4-1	1-1	1-0	4-2	1-0	2-0	1-0
Slovan Liberec ‡	30	12	8	10	35	31	44	1-1	4-3	1-1	1-1	4-0		1-2	0-1	2-0	2-2	2-1	2-1	0-0	1-1	0-0	2-1
Mladá Boleslav	30	11	9	10	37	36	42	0-2	1-4	3-1	1-3	1-1	0-2		0-1	3-0	0-1	1-1	1-1	2-1	2-1	2-0	1-1
Tescoma Zlin	30	10	8	12	28	31	38	0-1	0-2	2-2	0-1	1-0	0-1	0-1		3-1	0-0	0-0	0-1	1-0	4-0	0-0	1-1
Viktoria Plzen	30	10	8	12	32	37	38	0-0	0-0	0-4	2-0	0-2	0-1	2-0	1-1		3-1	2-0	2-0	1-1	1-2	2-0	6-2
Viktoria Zizkov	30	10	7	13	35	48	37	1-1	1-4	0-2	3-4	1-2	1-1	1-0	2-0	0-0		2-0	2-0	1-0	1-0	2-1	1-0
Sigma Olomouc	30	8	12	10	20	26	36	1-3	0-0	1-0	1-1	1-0	1-0	0-1	1-0	2-0	0-0		1-1	1-0	1-1	1-1	2-2
FK Jablonec 97	30	8	9	13	24	32	33	0-1	0-2	1-1	2-0	1-0	1-2	1-1	0-3	0-1	3-0	2-0		1-0	1-0	0-0	1-0
Ceské Budejovice	30	8	8	14	27	35	32	1-2	1-1	3-0	0-2	1-0	0-2	2-0	2-2	1-0	1-1	1-1	2-0		0-0	2-0	1-0
SK Kladno	30	6	9	15	31	45	27	0-1	0-1	3-0	1-2	0-2	1-3	0-1	2-2	1-2	3-2	1-0	1-1	5-1		2-1	1-1
Bohemians 1905 Praha	30	5	11	14	24	40	26	2-0	0-0	0-2	3-1	0-2	1-0	1-1	1-2	2-2	2-2	0-0	1-1	0-2	1-1		1-0
Siad Most	30	4	8	18	31	58	20	2-3	0-5	0-2	2-2	2-3	0-1	2-1	0-1	1-1	1-0	1-1	2-1	3-1	2-2	2-4	

5/08/2007 - 17/05/2008 • † Qualified for the UEFA Champions League • ‡ Qualified for the UEFA Cup • Top scorer: Václav Sverkos, Baník 12

CZECH REPUBLIC 2007–08
DRUHA LIGA (2)

	Pl	W	D	L	F	A	Pts
Bohemians Praha	30	15	8	7	46	38	53
Marila Pribram	30	14	10	6	33	18	52
Slezsky Opava	30	15	5	10	46	31	50
Hradec Králové	30	13	11	6	34	24	50
1.FC Slovácko	30	13	9	8	40	27	48
Fulnek	30	12	11	7	36	36	47
Vysocina Jihlava	30	11	10	9	42	35	43
1.HFK Olomouc	30	11	8	11	33	38	41
Baník Sokolov	30	9	13	8	26	24	40
Trinec	30	10	6	14	26	39	36
Vitkovice	30	10	6	14	35	41	36
MFK Usti nad Labem	30	9	7	14	35	44	34
Zenit Cáslav	30	8	9	13	37	44	33
Dukla Praha	30	9	6	15	36	44	33
Hlucin	30	7	9	14	26	35	30
Sparta Krc	30	4	12	14	27	40	21

3/08/2007 - 5/06/2008

POHAR CMFS 2007–08

Round of 16
- Sparta Praha * 2
- Bohemians 1905 0
- Chomutov * 0
- 1.HFK Olomouc 3
- Viktoria Zizkov 1
- SK Lísen * 0
- Viktoria Plzen 0
- Bohemians Praha * 2
- 1.FC Brno 2
- Ceské Budejovice * 0
- Fotbal F-M * 1
- FK Jablonec 97 2
- Trinec * 2
- Mladá Boleslav 1
- Fulnek * 1 3p
- Slovan Liberec 1 4p

Quarter-finals
- Sparta Praha 2 3
- 1.HFK Olomouc * 1 1
- Viktoria Zizkov * 1 0
- Bohemians Praha 1 0
- 1.FC Brno 3 2
- FK Jablonec 97 * 0 1
- Trinec * 0 2
- Slovan Liberec 3 2

Semi-finals
- Sparta Praha 1 1
- Bohemians Praha * 0 0
- 1.FC Brno * 2 1
- Slovan Liberec 2 2

Final
- Sparta Praha 0 4p
- Slovan Liberec ‡ 0 3p

CUP FINAL
Rosického, Prague
13-05-2008

* Home team/home team in the first leg • ‡ Qualified for the UEFA Cup

DEN – DENMARK

NATIONAL TEAM RECORD
JULY 10TH 2006 TO JULY 12TH 2010

PL	W	D	L	F	A	%
22	11	6	5	40	23	63.6

FIFA/COCA-COLA WORLD RANKING

1993	1994	1995	1996	1997	1998	1999	2000	2001	2002	2003	2004	2005	2006	2007	High
6	14	9	6	8	19	11	22	18	12	13	14	13	21	31	05/97

					2007–2008							Low	
08/07	09/07	10/07	11/07	12/07	01/08	02/08	03/08	04/08	05/08	06/08	07/08	6	07/08
30	28	29	31	31	31	33	33	33	33	33	36		

Denmark's failure to qualify for the finals of Euro 2008 came as no surprise at the end of a campaign in which they forfeited a home match against Sweden and were forced to play three qualifiers away from Copenhagen in Aarhus. They finished behind Northern Ireland in fourth place to miss the finals for the first time since 1980. Long-serving coach Morten Olsen now has the tough task of ensuring the Danes don't miss out on a hat-trick of tournaments by qualifying for the 2010 FIFA World Cup from a group containing both Sweden and Portugal. At home there were surprise winners of the Superliga when provincial outfit AaB Aalborg from the north-west of the country

INTERNATIONAL HONOURS
Qualified for the FIFA World Cup™ finals 1986 1998 2002 Qualified for the FIFA Women's World Cup finals 1991 1995 1999
UEFA European Championship 1992

took the title out of Copenhagen for the first time since 2000. Coached by the Swede Erik Hamren, AaB were consistently better than their big spending rivals from the capital, finishing the campaign well ahead of FC Midtjylland and defending champions FC København, who suffered a disastrous run of form after the spring break. Brøndby, the capital's other major club, rescued a miserable season when they beat Esbjerg FB in a thrilling Cup Final. Twice they took the lead and twice they were pegged back, only for Martin Retov to win the tie six minutes from time.

THE FIFA BIG COUNT OF 2006

	Male	Female		Total
Number of players	420 258	91 075	Referees and Assistant Referees	2 992
Professionals	852		Admin, Coaches, Technical, Medical	54 000
Amateurs 18+	111 757		Number of clubs	1 615
Youth under 18	188 724		Number of teams	17 365
Unregistered	100 000		Clubs with women's teams	768
Total players	511 333		Players as % of population	9.38%

Dansk Boldspil-Union (DBU)
DBU Allé 1, Brøndby 2605, Denmark
Tel +45 43 262222   Fax +45 43 262245
dbu@dbu.dk   www.dbu.dk
President: HANSEN Allan   General Secretary: HANSEN Jim
Vice-President: MOLLER Jesper   Treasurer: MOGENSEN Torben   Media Officer: BERENDT Lars
Men's Coach: OLSEN Morten   Women's Coach: HEINER-MOLLER Kenneth
DBU formed: 1889   UEFA: 1954   FIFA: 1904
Red shirts with white trimmings, White shorts, Red socks or White shirts with red trimmings, Red shorts, White socks

RECENT INTERNATIONAL MATCHES PLAYED BY DENMARK

2006	Opponents	Score		Venue	Comp	Scorers	Att	Referee
26-01	Singapore	W	2-1	Singapore	Fr	Bech 2 [58 67]	10 392	Srinivasan IND
29-01	Hong Kong	W	3-0	Hong Kong	Fr	Berg [19], Augustinussen [39], Due [51]	16 841	Iemoto JPN
1-02	Korea Republic	W	3-1	Hong Kong	Fr	Jacobsen [43], Bech [65], Silberbauer [88]	13 971	Fong Yau Fat HKG
1-03	Israel	W	2-0	Tel Aviv	Fr	Perez [3], Skoubo [18]	15 762	Sippel GER
27-05	Paraguay	D	1-1	Aarhus	Fr	Tomasson [51]	20 047	Bennett ENG
31-05	France	L	0-2	Lens	Fr		39 000	Kelly IRL
16-08	Poland	W	2-0	Odense	Fr	Bendtner [33], Rommedahl [63]	11 088	Asumaa FIN
1-09	Portugal	W	4-2	Copenhagen	Fr	Tomasson [14], Kahlenberg [21], Jorgensen [77], Bendtner [92+]	13 186	Kelly IRL
6-09	Iceland	W	2-0	Reykjavík	ECq	Rommedahl [5], Tomasson [33]	10 007	Ivanov.N RUS
7-10	Northern Ireland	D	0-0	Copenhagen	ECq		41 482	Plautz AUT
11-10	Liechtenstein	W	4-0	Vaduz	ECq	Jensen.D [29], Gravgaard [32], Tomasson 2 [51 64]	2 665	Richards WAL
15-11	Czech Republic	D	1-1	Prague	Fr	Løvenkrands [28]	6 852	Skomina SVN
2007								
6-02	Australia	W	3-1	London	Fr	Tomasson 2 [4 37], Jensen.D [27]	12 476	Styles END
24-03	Spain	L	1-2	Madrid	ECq	Gravgaard [49]	73 575	Busacca SUI
28-03	Germany	W	1-0	Duisberg	Fr	Bendtner [81]	31 500	Webb ENG
2-06	Sweden	D	3-3	Copenhagen	ECq	Agger [34], Tomasson [62], Andreason [75]. Abandoned after 89 minutes. Match awarded 3-0 to Sweden	42 083	Fandel GER
6-06	Latvia	W	2-0	Riga	ECq	Rommedahl 2 [15 17]	7 500	Trefoloni ITA
22-08	Republic of Ireland	L	0-4	Aarhus	Fr		30 000	Einwaller AUT
8-09	Sweden	D	0-0	Stockholm	ECq		33 082	De Bleeckere BEL
12-09	Liechtenstein	W	4-0	Aarhus	ECq	Nordstrand 2 [3 36], Laursen.M [12], Tomasson [18]	20 005	Clattenburg ENG
13-10	Spain	L	1-3	Aarhus	ECq	Tomasson [87]	19 849	Michel SVK
17-10	Latvia	W	3-1	Copenhagen	ECq	Tomasson [7p], Laursen.U [27], Rommedahl [90]	19 004	Cakir TUR
17-11	Northern Ireland	L	1-2	Belfast	ECq	Bendtner [51]	12 997	Vink NED
21-11	Iceland	W	3-0	Copenhagen	ECq	Bendtner [34], Tomasson [44], Kahlenberg [59]	15 393	Benquerenca POR
2008								
6-02	Slovenia	W	2-1	Nova Gorica	Fr	Tomasson [30p], Bendtner [62]	1 700	Kinhofer GER
26-03	Czech Republic	D	1-1	Herning	Fr	Bendtner [25]	11 900	Mikulski POL
29-05	Netherlands	D	1-1	Eindhoven	Fr	Poulsen [56]	35 000	Chapron FRA
1-06	Poland	D	1-1	Chorzow	Fr	Vingaard [29]	40 000	Kalt FRA

Fr = Friendly match • EC = UEFA EURO 2008 • WC = FIFA World Cup • q = qualifier • r1 = first round group • qf = quarter-final

DENMARK NATIONAL TEAM PLAYERS

Player		Ap	G	Club	Date of Birth	Player		Ap	G	Club	Date of Birth
Jesper Christiansen	GK	9	0	FC København	24 04 1978	Thomas Augustinussen	MF	1	0	AaB Aalborg	20 03 1981
Stephan Andersen	GK	1	0	Brøndby IF	26 11 1981	Thomas Kahlenberg	MF	24	2	Auxerre	20 03 1983
Thomas Sørensen	GK	73	0	None	12 06 1976	Thomas Kristensen	MF	2	0	FC København	17 04 1983
Anders M. Christensen	DF	2	0	Odense Boldklub	26 07 1977	William Kvist	MF	6	0	FC København	24 02 1985
Lars Jacobsen	DF	15	0	None	20 09 1979	Dennis Rommedahl	FW	78	16	Ajax	22 07 1978
Magnus Troest	DF	0	0	Parma	5 06 1987	Dennis Sørensen	FW	5	0	Energie Cottbus	24 05 1981
Per Krøldrup	DF	22	0	Fiorentina	31 07 1979	Martin Jørgensen	FW	85	12	Fiorentina	6 10 1975
Thomas Rasmussen	DF	6	0	Brøndby IF	16 04 1977	Morten Nordstrand	FW	4	2	FC København	8 06 1983
Christian Poulsen	MF	56	3	Juventus	28 02 1980	Nicklas Bendtner	FW	18	7	Arsenal	16 01 1988
Kenneth Perez	MF	24	2	Ajax	29 08 1974	**Selected others**					
Martin Retov	MF	3	0	Hansa Rostock	5 05 1980	Martin Laursen	DF	49	2	Aston Villa	26 07 1977
Martin Vingaard	MF	2	1	Esbjerg FB	20 03 1985	Daniel Jensen	MF	36	2	Werder Bremen	25 06 1979
Mikkel Beckmann	MF	2	0	Lyngby Boldklub	24 10 1983	Leon Andreason	MF	10	1	Fulham	23 04 1983
Denmark's squad for the June 2008 match against Poland						Jon Dahl Tomasson	FW	99	51	Feyenoord	29 08 1976

DENMARK NATIONAL TEAM RECORDS AND RECORD SEQUENCES

Records				Sequence records			
Victory	17-1	FRA 1908	Wins	11	1912-1916	Clean sheets	4	1993, 1995
Defeat	0-8	GER 1937	Defeats	7	1970-1971	Goals scored	26	1942-1948
Player Caps	129	Peter Schmeichel	Undefeated	12	1992-93, 2005-06	Without goal	7	1970-1971
Player Goals	52	Poul "Tist" Nielsen	Without win	14	1969-1971	Goals against	21	1939-1946

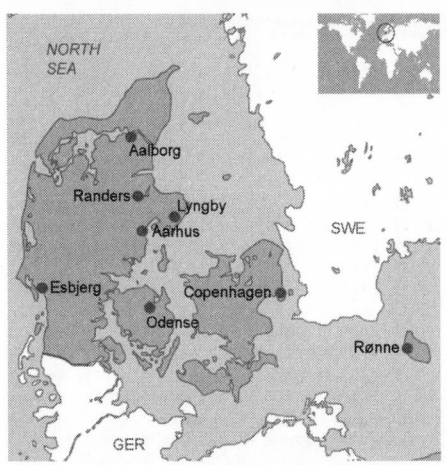

MAJOR CITIES/TOWNS
Population '000

1	Copenhagen	1 093
2	Aarhus	230
3	Odense	146
4	Aalborg	123
5	Esbjerg	71
6	Kolding	56
7	Randers	55
8	Vejle	52
9	Horsens	50
10	Roskilde	44
11	Greve Strand	41
12	Næstved	41
13	Silkeborg	39
14	Hørsholm	37
15	Fredericia	37
16	Helsingør	35
17	Viborg	34
18	Køge	34
19	Herning	30
20	Holbæk	24
21	Fredrikshavn	23
22	Nykøbing	16
23	Ikast	14
24	Farum	11

KINGDOM OF DENMARK; KONGERIGET DANMARK

Capital Copenhagen	Language Danish		Independence 950
Population 5 468 120	Area 43 094 km^2	Density 125 per km^2	% in cities 85
GDP per cap $31 100	Dailling code +45	Internet .dk	GMT +/- +1

MEDALS TABLE

		Overall			League			Cup		Europe			City	Stadium	Cap'ty	DoF
		G	S	B	G	S	B	G	S	G	S	B				
1	KB København	16	19	8	15	15	8	1	4				Copenhagen	Parken		1876-1992
2	Brøndby IF	16	11	3	10	9	2	6	2		1		Copenhagen	Brøndby	29 000	1964
3	AGF Aarhus	14	8	11	5	5	11	9	3				Aarhus	Aarhus Idrætspark	21 000	1880
4	B 93 København	11	5	9	10	5	9	1					Copenhagen	Østerbro	7 000	1893
5	Vejle BK	11	4	2	5	3	2	6	1				Vejle	Vejle	15 000	1891
6	Akademisk København	10	14	11	9	11	11	1	3				Copenhagen	Gladsaxe	13 200	1889
7	B 1903 København	9	10	8	7	8	8	2	2				Copenhagen	Gentofte		1903-1992
8	FC Københvn	9	6	2	6	3	2	3	3				Copenhagen	Parken	42 305	1992
9	Frem København	8	15	9	6	12	9	2	3				Copenhagen	Valby Idrætspark	12 000	1886
10	OB Odense	8	4	5	3	3	5	5	1				Odense	Odense	15 633	1887
11	Esbjerg FB	7	9	2	5	3	2	2	6				Esbjerg	Esbjerg Idrætspark	13 282	1924
12	AaB Aalborg	5	7	3	3		3	2	7				Aalborg	Aalborg	16 000	1885
13	Lyngby BK	5	5	3	2	3	3	3	2				Lyngby	Lyngby	12 000	1921
14	B 1909 Odense	4	1	1	2		1	2	1				Odense	Atletikstadion	8 000	1909-2006
	Hvidovre IF	4	1	1	3	1	1	1					Copenhagen	Hvidovre	15 000	1925
16	Randers FC	4	1			1		4					Randers	Essex Park	12 000	2002

RECENT LEAGUE AND CUP RECORD

	Championship						Cup		
Year	Champions	Pts	Runners-up	Pts	Third	Pts	Winners	Score	Runners-up
1995	AaB Aalborg	31	Brøndby IF	29	Silkeborg IF	24	FC København	5-0	Akademisk
1996	Brøndby IF	67	AGF Aarhus	66	OB Odense	60	AGF Aarhus	2-0	Brøndby IF
1997	Brøndby IF	68	Vejle BK	54	AGF Aarhus	52	FC København	2-0	Ikast FS
1998	Brøndby IF	76	Silkeborg IF	63	FC København	61	Brøndby IF	4-1	FC København
1999	AaB Aalborg	64	Brøndby IF	61	Akademisk	56	Akademisk	2-1	AaB Aalborg
2000	Herfølge BK	56	Brøndby IF	54	Akademisk	52	Viborg FF	1-0	AaB Aalborg
2001	FC København	63	Brøndby IF	58	Silkeborg IF	56	Silkeborg IF	4-1	Akademisk
2002	Brøndby IF	69	FC København	69	FC Midtjylland	57	OB Odense	2-1	FC København
2003	FC København	61	Brøndby IF	56	Farum BK	51	Brøndby IF	3-0	FC Midtjylland
2004	FC København	68	Brøndby IF	67	Esbjerg FB	62	FC København	1-0	AaB Aalborg
2005	Brøndby IF	69	FC København	57	FC Midtjylland	57	Brøndby IF	3-2	FC Midtjylland
2006	FC København	73	Brøndby IF	67	OB Odense	58	Randers FC	1-0	Esbjerg FB
2007	FC København	76	FC Midtjylland	63	AaB Aalborg	61	OB Odense	2-1	FC København
2008	AaB Aalborg	71	FC Midtjylland	62	FC København	57	Brøndby IF	3-2	Esbjerg FB

DENMARK 2007–08

SAS LIGAEN

	Pl	W	D	L	F	A	Pts	AaB	Midtjylland	København	OB	Horsens	Randers	Esbjerg	Brøndby	Nordsjælland	AGF	Viborg	Lyngby
AaB Aalborg †	33	22	5	6	60	38	71		1-0	1-1	0-0 2-3	2-0	1-0	3-0	2-0	3-0 2-0	2-1 3-1	2-0 3-1	3-2 2-0 5-3
FC Midtjylland ‡	33	18	8	7	53	36	62	2-1 2-0		2-2 2-1 3-1	1-1	3-2 2-1	2-2	5-0 1-1	1-0	2-0 3-2 1-0		2-1	
FC København	33	17	9	7	51	29	57	4-0	0-0 0-2		2-1	1-0 1-0 1-0 0-0 1-5	2-2 1-1	1-1	1-1		3-1 3-0	2-0 3-1	
OB Odense	33	12	16	5	46	27	52	1-1	0-1	0-0 0-0		3-3 2-0	0-0	1-1 1-1	0-0	3-0 1-1	2-0	4-0 1-0	1-1 1-1
AC Horsens	33	14	10	9	47	43	52	1-1 1-2 2-1 1-1	3-2	2-2			1-0 1-0 4-3 3-1	4-2 1-3	2-0	0-0	1-1	2-1	
Randers FC	33	13	8	12	41	33	47	5-0 1-0	3-0	2-1	0-0 0-2	0-0		1-0	2-1	1-1 2-1 0-1 4-1	2-0 0-2	2-2	2-2
Esbjerg FB	33	13	6	14	59	54	45	1-2 1-1 2-0 3-2	2-1	2-0 3-2	2-1	0-0	1-3 1-3 3-2	2-1		1-0 3-2	1-2 2-2 0-1	2-1	2-1
Brøndby IF ‡	33	11	10	12	44	44	43	0-1	2-1	0-1 2-1 1-1 0-2	3-0	1-1 3-1	2-1			2-2 3-0 0-1 2-1	1-1	3-0 3-0	
FC Nordsjælland	33	11	10	12	47	51	43	1-2	1-1 0-3 1-0 1-2	3-3	0-0 1-2	2-1	3-1 3-2	1-0			3-2	4-0 5-3 0-1 0-0	
AGF Aarhus	33	7	8	18	33	51	29	3-5	2-0	0-1 0-2 0-2 0-2 1-2 1-2	0-0	0-1	1-1 1-2 3-3			0-0		0-3 1	
Viborg FF	33	5	5	23	29	68	20	0-1	1-1	2-3	0-2	1-1 3-0	0-1	0-5 0-4 1-0 3-0 0-1	6-1 3-2	2-3	2-0 0-2		2-1 3-2
Lyngby BK	33	3	9	21	33	69	18	3-4 0-2 1-2 1-2	1-4	0-3	0-0 4-1 0-3 0-0 1-6	1-3	2-2	0-0	1-3	2-0			

18/07/2007 - 24/05/2008 • † Qualified for the UEFA Champions League • ‡ Qualified for the UEFA Cup
Top scorers: Jeppe Curth, AaB 17; Martin Bernburg, Nordsjælland 14; Peter Graulund, AGF 13; Henrik Hansen, Horsens 13

DENMARK 2007–08
VIASAT SPORT DIVISION (2)

	Pl	W	D	L	F	A	Pts
Vejle BK	30	25	3	2	80	24	78
SønderjyskE	30	17	10	3	55	32	61
Silkeborg IF	30	16	9	5	60	33	57
Herfølge BK	30	15	6	9	55	43	51
FC Fredericia	30	12	8	10	49	36	44
Akademisk Boldclub	30	11	8	11	38	36	41
Kolding FC	30	11	7	12	53	47	40
Næstved BK	30	11	7	12	36	39	40
Hvidovre IF	30	10	7	13	31	33	37
Skive IK	30	10	4	16	36	52	34
Frem København	30	12	3	15	46	54	33
Lolland-Falster All'cen	30	8	9	13	28	41	33
Køge BK	30	8	9	13	36	51	33
Hellerup IK	30	8	7	15	36	56	31
Aarhus Fremad	30	7	7	16	22	43	28
Ølstykke	30	4	6	20	20	61	18

4/08/2007 - 8/06/2008

DBU LANDSPOKAL 2007–08

Round of 16		Quarter–finals		Semi–finals		Final	
Brøndby IF	1						
OB Odense *	0	Brøndby IF *	2				
SønderjyskE *	0	Randers FC	1				
Randers FC	2			Brøndby IF *	3 2		
Vejle BK *	0 5p			FC Midtjylland	0 0		
AaB Aalborg	0 4p	Vejle BK *	1				
AGF Aarhus *	0	FC Midtjylland	2				
FC Midtjylland	1					Brøndby IF ‡	3
FC København	4					Esbjerg FB	2
Varde IF *	0	FC København	2				
Kolding FC	2	Næstved IF *	0				
Næstved IF *	5			FC København *	0 2		
Skive IK	2			Esbjerg FB	1 2		
Greve *	0	Skive IK *	0				
Herfølge BK *	0	Esbjerg FB	4				
Esbjerg FB	1						

* Home team/home team in the first leg • ‡ Qualified for the UEFA Cup

CUP FINAL
Parken, Copenhagen, 1-05-2008, Att: 33 154
Scorers - Samuel Holmén [15], Max von Schlebrügge [68], Martin Retov [84] for Brøndby; Søren Rieks 2 [61 75] for Esbjerg

DJI – DJIBOUTI

NATIONAL TEAM RECORD
JULY 10TH 2006 TO JULY 12TH 2010

PL	W	D	L	F	A	%
13	1	0	12	8	60	7.7

FIFA/COCA-COLA WORLD RANKING

1993	1994	1995	1996	1997	1998	1999	2000	2001	2002	2003	2004	2005	2006	2007	High	
-	169	177	185	189	191	195	189	193	195	197	201	200	198	173	**169**	12/94

2007–2008												Low	
08/07	09/07	10/07	11/07	12/07	01/08	02/08	03/08	04/08	05/08	06/08	07/08	**201**	12/04
199	200	200	175	173	173	176	176	179	179	180	186		

Delirium greeted a first ever win at full international level for Djibouti in November 2007, when a late goal from Hussein Yassin secured a 1-0 victory over Somalia. To add to the achievement was the prestige of it having been achieved in the FIFA World Cup qualifiers, advancing Djibouti into the league phase of the preliminaries against the likes of African Nations Cup holders Egypt and former continental champions the Congo DR. The win came in Djibouti's 24th international since joining FIFA in 1994. They had previously lost all but two encounters, draws achieved in 2000 against the Congo DR and Somalia. Victory over the Somalis also ended a run of 14 straight defeats

INTERNATIONAL HONOURS
None

although subsequent participation in the East and Central African Senior Challenge Cup in Tanzania and four FIFA World Cup qualifiers in June put some perspective back into their ability. They conceded 19 goals in three games at December's regional championship in Dar-es-Salaam and in the FIFA World Cup group matches a further 23 in four games as the rigour of top flight competition took its toll on the limited resources of the Red Sea republic. Victory in the Super Cup at the start of the new season in November proved the catalyst for Societe Immobiliere Djibouti to go on and win the championship while perennial rivals CDE Djibouti were National Cup winners.

THE FIFA BIG COUNT OF 2006

	Male	Female		Total
Number of players	34 480	1 840	Referees and Assistant Referees	75
Professionals	0		Admin, Coaches, Technical, Medical	405
Amateurs 18+	1 800		Number of clubs	6
Youth under 18	720		Number of teams	84
Unregistered	2 800		Clubs with women's teams	2
Total players	36 320		Players as % of population	7.47%

Fédération Djiboutienne de Football (FDF)
Centre Technique National, Case postale 2694, Djibouti
Tel +253 353599   Fax +253 353588
fdf-1979@yahoo.fr   www.none
President: HOUSSEIN Fadoul   General Secretary: KAMIL ALI Ali
Vice-President: YONIS Mohamed Yacin   Treasurer: HASSAN Ziad Moussa   Media Officer: None
Men's Coach: ABAR Mohamed   Women's Coach: GUEDI Koureicha
FDF formed: 1979   CAF: 1986   FIFA: 1994
Green shirts, White shorts, Blue socks

RECENT INTERNATIONAL MATCHES PLAYED BY DJIBOUTI

2005	Opponents	Score		Venue	Comp	Scorers	Att	Referee
27-11	Somalia	L	1-2	Kigali	CCr1	Abdoul Rahman Okishi		
30-11	Uganda	L	1-6	Kigali	CCr1	Abdirahman Okieh		
3-12	Ethiopia	L	0-6	Kigali	CCr1			
5-12	Sudan	L	0-4	Kigali	CCr1			
2006								
26-11	Malawi	L	0-3	Addis Abeba	CCr1			
28-11	Ethiopia	L	0-4	Addis Abeba	CCr1			
1-12	Tanzania	L	0-3	Addis Abeba	CCr1			
17-12	Comoros	L	2-4	Sana'a	ARq	Khaliff Hassan [45], Abdoul Rahman Okishi [92+]		
20-12	Yemen	L	1-4	Sana'a	ARq	Abdoul Rahman Okishi [7]		
2007								
16-11	Somalia	W	1-0	Djibouti	WCq	Hussein Yassin [84]	10 000	Abdel Rahman SUD
9-12	Uganda	L	0-7	Dar es Salaam	CCr1			
11-12	Eritrea	L	2-3	Dar es Salaam	CCr1	Ahmed Daher [45], Salim Kadar [84]		
13-12	Rwanda	L	0-9	Dar es Salaam	CCr1			
2008								
31-05	Malawi	L	1-8	Blantyre	WCq	Ahmed Daher [23]	35 000	Katjimune NAM
6-06	Egypt	L	0-4	Djibouti	WCq		6 000	Eyob ERI
13-06	Congo DR	L	0-6	Djibouti	WCq		3 000	Disang BOT
22-06	Congo DR	L	1-5	Kinshasa	WCq	Moussa Hirir [85]	15 000	Rouaissi MAR

CC = CECAFA Cup • AR = Arab Cup • q = qualifier • r1 = First round group

DJIBOUTI NATIONAL TEAM RECORDS AND RECORD SEQUENCES

Records			Sequence records					
Victory	4-1	YEM 1988	Wins	1		Clean sheets	1	
Defeat	1-10	UGA 2001	Defeats	14	2000-2006	Goals scored	6	1998-2000
Player Caps	n/a		Undefeated	1		Without goal	5	2005-2006
Player Goals	n/a		Without win	23	1994-2006	Goals against	20	1983-2000

RECENT LEAGUE AND CUP RECORD

	League	Cup		
Year	Champions	Winners	Score	Runners-up
1996	Force Nationale de Police	Balbala		
1997	Force Nationale de Police	Force Nationale de Police		
1998	Force Nationale de Police	Force Nationale de Police		
1999	Force Nationale de Police	Balbala		
2000	CDE Djibouti			
2001	Force Nationale de Police	Chemin de Fer		
2002	AS Borreh	Jeunesse Espoir		Chemin de Fer
2003	Gendarmerie Nationale	AS Borreh	1-1 5-4p	AS Ali-Sabieh
2004	Gendarmerie Nationale	Chemin de Fer	6-2	AS Borreh
2005	CDE Djibouti	Poste de Djibouti	2-0	AS Port
2006	Société Immobiliere Djibouti	AS Ali Sabieh	3-0	Gendarmerie Nationale
2007	CDE Djibouti	Société Immobiliere Djibouti	1-1 4-3p	CDE Djibouti
2008	Société Immobiliere Djibouti	CDE Djibouti	1-1 4-3p	Guelleh Batal

Poste de Djibouti renamed Société Immobiliere Djibouti in 2005

DJIBOUTI COUNTRY INFORMATION

Capital	Djibouti	Independence	1977 from France	GDP per Capita	$1 300
Population	768 200	Status	Republic	GNP Ranking	167
Area km²	23 000	Language	Arabic, French	Dialling code	+253
Population density	20 per km²	Literacy rate	49%	Internet code	.dj
% in urban areas	83%	Main religion	Muslim 94%	GMT +/–	+3
Towns/Cities ('000)	Djibouti 623; Ali Sabieh 40; Tadjoura 22; Obock 17; Dikhil 12				
Neighbours (km)	Somalia 58; Ethiopia 349; Eritrea 109; Red Sea & Gulf of Aden 314				
Main stadia	Stade du Ville – Djibouti 10 000				

DMA – DOMINICA

NATIONAL TEAM RECORD
JULY 10TH 2006 TO JULY 12TH 2010

PL	W	D	L	F	A	%
4	0	1	3	1	8	12.5

FIFA/COCA-COLA WORLD RANKING

1993	1994	1995	1996	1997	1998	1999	2000	2001	2002	2003	2004	2005	2006	2007	High	
-	-	158	138	139	133	149	152	161	174	185	165	172	181	189	**129**	7/98

2007–2008												Low	
08/07	09/07	10/07	11/07	12/07	01/08	02/08	03/08	04/08	05/08	06/08	07/08	**191**	04/08
184	186	187	189	189	188	182	181	191	191	191	191		

After 17 months of inactivity, the Dominican national team came out of hibernation to take part in the 2010 FIFA World Cup preliminaries and were drawn against Barbados, against whom they weren't expected to progress. In the first match, at home at Windsor Park in Roseau, Dominica did manage to hold their neighbours to a 1-1 draw with the scorer of the goal that day, debutant Richard Pacquette. He had been part of the Havant & Waterlooville team that gained nationwide notoriety in England for giving Liverpool such a scare in the fourth round of the FA Cup. Although his team lost 5-2, they twice took the lead with Pacquette opening the scoring after just seven minutes and

INTERNATIONAL HONOURS
None

were given a standing ovation on the final whistle by the Liverpool fans. With both of his parents born in Dominica, Pacquette was called up by national team coach Christopher Erickson for the World Cup qualifiers, although it was another English based international, Wigan's Emmerson Boyce, making his debut for Barbados in the return, who helped end Dominica's World Cup campaign after a 1-0 victory in Bridgetown. Domestic football in Dominica was severely disrupted by problems within the football association which led at one point to all 16 clubs in the championship being suspended by the DFA.

THE FIFA BIG COUNT OF 2006

	Male	Female		Total
Number of players	3 900	600	Referees and Assistant Referees	39
Professionals	0		Admin, Coaches, Technical, Medical	100
Amateurs 18+	500		Number of clubs	20
Youth under 18	700		Number of teams	20
Unregistered	600		Clubs with women's teams	1
Total players	4 500		Players as % of population	6.53%

Dominica Football Association (DFA)
Patrick John Football House, Bath Estate, PO Box 372, Roseau, Dominica
Tel +1 767 4487577   Fax +1 767 4487587
domfootball@cwdom.dm   www.none
President: JOHN Patrick   General Secretary: CELAIRE Clifford
Vice-President: LEBLANC Ericson   Treasurer: WHITE Philip   Media Officer: GEORGE Gerald
Men's Coach: ERICKSON Christopher   Women's Coach: ROBERTSON Hypolite
DFA formed: 1970   CONMEBOL: 1994   FIFA: 1994
Emerald shirts, Black shorts, Green socks

RECENT INTERNATIONAL MATCHES PLAYED BY DOMINICA

2004	Opponents		Score	Venue	Comp	Scorers	Att	Referee
28-01	British Virgin Islands	W	1-0	Tortola	Fr	Cuffy [34]		Matthew SKN
31-01	US Virgin Islands	W	5-0	St Thomas	Fr	OG [12], Marshall [42], Dangler [68], Casimir [87], George [90]		Matthew SKN
1-02	British Virgin Islands	W	2-1	Tortola	Fr	Marshall [44], Peters [70]		Charles DMA
12-03	Barbados	L	1-2	Bridgetown	Fr	Peters [88]	46	
26-03	Bahamas	D	1-1	Nassau	WCq	Casimir [88]	800	Forde BRB
28-03	Bahamas	W	3-1	Nassau	WCq	Casimir 2 [39 86], Peters [85]	900	Pineda HON
19-06	Mexico	L	0-10	San Antonio, USA	WCq		36 451	Callender BRB
27-06	Mexico	L	0-8	Aguascalientes	WCq		17 000	Stott USA
10-11	Martinique †	L	1-5	Fort de France	CCq	Peltier [42]		Arthur LCA
12-11	Guadeloupe †	L	0-7	Rivière-Pilote	CCq			Arthur LCA
14-11	French Guyana †	L	0-4	Fort de France	CCq		5 800	Fenus LCA
2005								
30-09	Guyana	L	0-3	Linden	Fr			Lancaster GUY
2-10	Guyana	L	0-3	Georgetown	Fr			Kia SUR
2006								
3-09	Antigua and Barbuda	L	0-1	St John's	Fr			Willett ATG
17-09	Barbados	L	0-5	Roseau	Fr			
20-09	Martinique †	L	0-4	Abymes	CCq		1 000	Fanus LCA
22-09	Guadeloupe †	L	0-1	Abymes	CCq		1 100	Willett ATG
24-09	Saint Martin †	D	0-0	Abymes	CCq			
2007								
No international matches played in 2007								
2008								
6-02	Barbados	D	1-1	Roseau	WCq	Pacquette [21]	4 200	Quesada CRC
26-03	Barbados	L	0-1	Bridgetown	WCq		4 150	Batres GUA

Fr = Friendly match • CC = Digicel Caribbean Cup • WC = FIFA World Cup • q = qualifier • † Not a full international

DOMINICA NATIONAL TEAM RECORDS AND RECORD SEQUENCES

Records			Sequence records					
Victory	6-1	VGB 1997	Wins	3	1997, 1999, 2004	Clean sheets	2	1997 2004
Defeat	0-10	MEX 2004	Defeats	6	2004-2006	Goals scored	8	1999-2000
Player Caps	n/a		Undefeated	4	1998	Without goal	6	2004-2006
Player Goals	n/a		Without win	8	2001-2002	Goals against	17	1997-1999

RECENT LEAGUE AND CUP RECORD

	Championship						Cup		
Year	Champions	Pts	Runners-up	Pts	Third	Pts	Winners	Score	Runners-up
2000	Harlem United	13	Dublanc Strikers	13					
2001	Harlem United	22	Dublanc Strikers	22	South East	19			
2002	St Joseph	12	ACS Zebians	12	Harlem Bombers	10	South East	1-0	Antilles Kensbro
2003	Harlem United	†	ACS Zebians				Harlem United		
2004	Harlem United						Harlem United	3-0	ACS Zebians
2005	Dublanc Strikers	31	Pointe Michel	29	South East	29	South East	2-0	Harlem United
2006	Harlem United	29	River Bombers	28					
2007	Sagicor South East	31	Fone Shack Bombers	29					
2008									

† Harlem United beat Zebians in the final

DOMINICA COUNTRY INFORMATION

Capital	Roseau	Independence	1978 from the UK	GDP per Capita	$5 400
Population	69 278	Status	Republic/Commonwealth	GNP Ranking	181
Area km²	754	Language	English	Dialling code	+1767
Population density	91 per km²	Literacy rate	94%	Internet code	.dm
% in urban areas	69%	Main religion	Christian 92%	GMT +/–	-4
Towns/Cities ('000)	Roseau 16; Berekua 3; Portsmouth 3; Marigot 2; Atkinson 2; La Plaine 2; Mahaut 2				
Neighbours (km)	Caribbean Sea and the North Atlantic 148				
Main stadia	Windsor Park – Roseau 6 000				

DOM – DOMINICAN REPUBLIC

NATIONAL TEAM RECORD
JULY 10TH 2006 TO JULY 12TH 2010

PL	W	D	L	F	A	%
10	2	0	8	12	21	20

FIFA/COCA-COLA WORLD RANKING

1993	1994	1995	1996	1997	1998	1999	2000	2001	2002	2003	2004	2005	2006	2007		High
153	164	159	130	144	152	155	157	160	149	171	170	174	136	166		**116** 05/96

2007–2008												Low
08/07	09/07	10/07	11/07	12/07	01/08	02/08	03/08	04/08	05/08	06/08	07/08	**186** 07/06
140	139	148	147	166	164	166	166	178	178	179	177	

The Dominican Republic continued its inexorable slide down the FIFA/Coca-Cola World Ranking after yet another year in which football barely managed to be noticed. The national team did at least enter the 2010 FIFA World Cup qualifiers but the contrast between the Dominican Republic and their opponents that day, another baseball obsessed Caribbean neighbour in Puerto Rico, was marked. The Puerto Rican federation has used club side Puerto Rico Islanders, who play in America's A-League, to foster a small but vociferous band of football supporters in the country, 8,000 of whom turned up for the World Cup clash in Bayamon. The Dominican Republic had even

INTERNATIONAL HONOURS
None

forfeited the right to play a home leg against the Puerto Ricans, ostensibly due to the lack of suitable facilities, although the cynics might point to a distinct lack of interest, and they were duly knocked-out after a 1-0 defeat. With no dedicated national championship to foster development in the country, it is hard to see how the fortunes of the national team can ever follow the lead of Puerto Rico and to a greater extent Cuba and become the power in the region that its large population merits. The eight team Liga Mayor was played in 2007, returning after a year's break for its fourth edition six years after its launch in 2001, and it was won by the rather inaptly named Barcelona.

THE FIFA BIG COUNT OF 2006

	Male	Female		Total
Number of players	417 804	83 200	Referees and Assistant Referees	1 420
Professionals	4		Admin, Coaches, Technical, Medical	190
Amateurs 18+	35 000		Number of clubs	250
Youth under 18	12 000		Number of teams	600
Unregistered	106 000		Clubs with women's teams	100
Total players	501 004		Players as % of population	5.46%

Federación Dominicana de Fútbol (FEDOFUTBOL)
Centro Olimpico Juan Pablo Duarte, Ensanche Miraflores, Apartado postal 1953, Santo Domingo, Dominican Republic
Tel +1 809 5426923   Fax +1 809 3812734
fedofutbol.f@codetel.net.do   www.fedofutbol.org
President: GUZMAN Osiris   General Secretary: MIRANDA Angel
Vice-President: QUISPE MENDOZA Fortunato   Treasurer: LEDESMA Felix   Media Officer: SANCHEZ Angel
Men's Coach: CRNOKRAK Ljubomir   Women's Coach: ELEJALDE Jose
FEDOFUTBOL formed: 1953   CONCACAF: 1964   FIFA: 1958
Navy blue shirts, White shorts, Red socks

RECENT INTERNATIONAL MATCHES PLAYED BY THE DOMINICAN REPUBLIC

2004	Opponents	Score		Venue	Comp	Scorers	Att	Referee
19-03	Anguilla	D	0-0	Santo Domingo	WCq		400	Mattus CRC
21-03	Anguilla	W	6-0	Santo Domingo	WCq	Zapata [15], Severino 2 [38 61], Contrera 2 [57 90], Casquez [77]	850	Porras CRC
27-04	Netherlands Antilles	L	1-3	Willemstad	Fr	Zapata [9]		Faneijte ANT
13-06	Trinidad and Tobago	L	0-2	Santo Domingo	WCq		2 500	Moreno PAN
20-06	Trinidad and Tobago	L	0-4	Marabella	WCq		5 500	Pinas SUR
2005								
No international matches played in 2005								
2006								
15-09	Haiti	L	1-3	Saint-Marc	Fr	Perez.M [22]		
17-09	Haiti	L	1-2	Port-au-Prince	Fr	Perez.M [30p]		
29-09	Bermuda	L	1-3	Charlotte Amalie	CCq	Faña [85]	300	Martis ANT
1-10	US Virgin Islands	W	6-1	Charlotte Amalie	CCq	Corporan [14], Faña 4 [25 55 82 89], Rodriguez.K [87]	250	Davis TRI
24-11	Guadeloupe	L	0-3	Georgetown	CCq		5 000	
26-11	Antigua and Barbuda	W	2-0	Georgetown	CCq	Severino [70p], Batista [81]	5 000	
28-11	Guyana	L	0-4	Georgetown	CCq		4 000	
2007								
No international matches played in 2007 before August								
2008								
27-02	Haiti	L	1-2	San Cristobal	Fr			
28-02	Haiti	L	0-2	San Cristobal	Fr			
26-03	Puerto Rico	L	0-1	Bayamon	WCq		8 000	Morales MEX

Fr = Friendly match • CC = Digicel Caribbean Cup • WC = FIFA World Cup • q = qualifier

DOMINICAN REPUBLIC NATIONAL TEAM RECORDS AND RECORD SEQUENCES

Records			Sequence records				
Victory	6-0	AIA 2004	Wins	4	1999-2000	Clean sheets	3	1999-2000
Defeat	0-8	HAI 1967, TRI 1996	Defeats	6	2004-2006	Goals scored	5	1987-91, 1991-93
Player Caps	n/a		Undefeated	4	1999-2000	Without goal	3	Three times
Player Goals	n/a		Without win	16	1987-1992	Goals against	15	1991-1996

RECENT LEAGUE RECORD

Championship

Year	Champions
1997	San Cristóbal
1998	No tournament played
1999	FC Don Bosco
2000	No tournament played
2001	CD Pantoja
2002	Baninter Jarabacoa
2003	Baninter Jarabacoa
2004	No tournament played
2005	Deportivo Pantoja
2006	No tournament played
2007	Barcelona

DOMINICAN REPUBLIC 2007 LIGA MAYOR (IV)

	Pl	W	D	L	F	A	Pts
Barcelona	20	13	3	4	41	22	42
Deportivo Pantoja	20	12	3	5	28	14	39
Moca	20	10	6	4	41	22	36
Jaracoba	20	9	4	7	29	21	31
San Cristobal	20	7	5	8	32	26	26
Casa de España	20	6	4	10	23	44	22
Montellano	20	4	6	10	16	25	18
La Romana	20	3	1	16	20	56	10

6/05/2007 - 30/09/2007

DOMINICAN REPUBLIC COUNTRY INFORMATION

Capital	Santo Domingo	Independence	1865	GDP per Capita	$6 000
Population	8 833 634	Status	Republic	GNP Ranking	67
Area km²	48 730	Language	Spanish	Dialling code	+1 809
Population density	181 per km²	Literacy rate	84%	Internet code	.do
% in urban areas	65%	Main religion	Christian 95%	GMT +/−	-4
Towns/Cities ('000)	Santo Domingo 2 240; Santiago 505; La Romana 171; San Pedro de Macorís 152; Puerto Plata 135				
Neighbours (km)	Haiti 360; Atlantic Ocean & Caribbean Sea 1 288				
Main stadia	Olimpico – Santo Domingo 35 000; Quisqueya – Santo Domingo 30 000				

ECU – ECUADOR

NATIONAL TEAM RECORD
JULY 10TH 2006 TO JULY 12TH 2010

PL	W	D	L	F	A	%
23	6	5	12	32	40	36.9

FIFA/COCA-COLA WORLD RANKING

1993	1994	1995	1996	1997	1998	1999	2000	2001	2002	2003	2004	2005	2006	2007	High	
48	55	55	33	28	63	65	54	37	31	37	39	37	30	56	**24**	03/07

2007–2008												Low	
08/07	09/07	10/07	11/07	12/07	01/08	02/08	03/08	04/08	05/08	06/08	07/08	**76**	06/95
55	57	59	56	56	52	57	54	55	55	59	60		

It has been quite a decade for football in Ecuador with qualification for two World Cup final tournaments but the icing on the cake must surely be LDU Quito's historic triumph in the 2008 Copa Libertadores. It was the first time an Ecuadorian club had won South America's top honour and was wildly celebrated in the streets of the capital when the team returned home from Rio de Janeiro. The image of captain Patricio Urrutua lifting the trophy in the Maracana having beaten Fluminense in the final, is likely to become an iconic image for football in Ecuador and although LDU may not have been magnificent on their way to the title - they needed two penalties

INTERNATIONAL HONOURS
Qualified for the FIFA World Cup finals 2002 2006   Copa Libertadores LDU Quto 2008

shoot-outs and won just two games in the the knockout stage - the team were welcomed as heroes. None more so than 37-year old goalkeeper Jose Francisco 'Pancho' Cevallas - twice on the losing side with rivals Barcelona in the 1990s - who saved three penalties in the shoot-out. Unbelievably for a club with an annual budget of just six million dollars, LDU will now be joining Manchester United in Tokyo for the FIFA Club World Cup. LDU's heroics somewhat overshadowed another game played in the Maracana 11 months earlier that had seen the Ecuador U-17 team win the Panamerican Games title - Ecuador's first international honour.

THE FIFA BIG COUNT OF 2006

	Male	Female		Total
Number of players	918 800	110 855	Referees and Assistant Referees	405
Professionals	700		Admin, Coaches, Technical, Medical	4 050
Amateurs 18+	12 855		Number of clubs	199
Youth under 18	9 800		Number of teams	416
Unregistered	811 800		Clubs with women's teams	2
Total players	1 029 655		Players as % of population	7.60%

Federación Ecuatoriana de Fútbol (FEF)
Avenida las Aguas y Calle, Alianza, PO Box 09-01-7447, Guayaquil 593, Ecuador
Tel +593 42 880610   Fax +593 42 880615
fef@gye.satnet.net   www.ecuafutbol.org
President: CHIRIBOGA Luis   General Secretary: ACOSTA Francisco
Vice-President: VILLACIS Carlos   Treasurer: MORA Hugo   Media Officer: MESTANZA Victor
Men's Coach: VIZUETE Sixto   Women's Coach: ESTUPINAN Garis
FEF formed: 1925   CONMEBOL: 1930   FIFA: 1926
Yellow shirts with blue and red trimmings, Blue shorts, Red socks

RECENT INTERNATIONAL MATCHES PLAYED BY ECUADOR

2006 Opponents	Score	Venue	Comp	Scorers	Att	Referee
25-01 Honduras	W 1-0	Guayaquil	Fr	Caicedo [67]	10 000	Ramos ECU
1-03 Netherlands	L 0-1	Amsterdam	Fr		35 000	Benquerenca POR
30-03 Japan	L 0-1	Oita	Fr		36 507	Maidin ECU
24-05 Colombia	D 1-1	East Rutherford	Fr	Castillo [51]	52 425	Vaughn USA
28-05 FYR Macedonia	L 1-2	Madrid	Fr	Tenorio.C [25]	4 000	
9-06 Poland	W 2-0	Gelsenkirchen	WCr1	Tenorio.C [24]	52 000	Kamikawa JPN
15-06 Costa Rica	W 3-0	Hamburg	WCr1	Tenorio.C [8], Delgado [54], Kaviedes [92+]	50 000	Codjia BEN
20-06 Germany	L 0-3	Berlin	WCr1		72 000	Ivanov.V RUS
25-06 England	L 0-1	Stuttgart	WCr2		52 000	De Bleeckere BEL
6-09 Peru	D 1-1	New Jersey	Fr	Benitez.C [14]	20 000	
10-10 Brazil	L 1-2	Stockholm	Fr	Borja [23]	34 592	Johannesson SWE
2007						
18-01 Sweden	W 2-1	Cuenca	Fr	Vaca [16], Tenorio [25]	20 000	Carrillo PER
21-01 Sweden	D 1-1	Quito	Fr	Zura [82]	18 000	Garay PER
25-03 USA	L 1-3	Tampa	Fr	Caicedo [11]	31 547	Petrescu CAN
28-03 Mexico	L 2-4	Oakland	Fr	Tenorio.C [44], Espinoza OG [57]	47 416	Toledo USA
23-05 Republic of Ireland	D 1-1	New Jersey	Fr	Benitez.C [13]	20 823	
3-06 Peru	L 1-2	Madrid	Fr	Tenorio.C [10p]	25 000	Puerta ESP
6-06 Peru	W 2-0	Barcelona	Fr	Benitez.C [85], De la Cruz [94+]	20 000	Crespo ESP
27-06 Chile	L 2-3	Puerto Ordaz	CAr1	Valencia [16], Benítez [23]	35 000	Ruiz COL
1-07 Mexico	L 1-2	Maturin	CAr1	Méndez [84]	42 000	Ortube BOL
4-07 Brazil	L 0-1	Puerto La Cruz	CAr1		34 000	Pezzotta ARG
22-08 Bolivia	W 1-0	Quito	Fr	Urrutia [34p]	20 000	Parra COL
8-09 El Salvador	W 5-1	Quito	Fr	Lara [13], Benitez 2 [29 49], Caicedo.F [45], Urrutia [53p]		Carillo PER
12-09 Honduras	L 1-2	San Pedro Sula	Fr	Guagua [89]	25 000	Batres GUA
13-10 Venezuela	L 0-1	Quito	WCq		29 644	Ortube BOL
17-10 Brazil	L 0-5	Rio de Janeiro	WCq		87 000	Larrionda URU
17-11 Paraguay	L 1-5	Asuncion	WCq	Kaviedes [80]	25 433	Lopes BRA
21-11 Peru	W 5-1	Quito	WCq	Ayovi.W 2 [10 48], Kaviedes [24], Mendez 2 [44 62]	28 557	Chandia CHI
2008						
26-03 Haiti	W 3-1	Latacunga	Fr	Castillo 45, Ayovi.W 58, Tenorio.C 60p	10 000	
27-05 France	L 0-2	Grenoble	Fr		20 000	Allaerts BEL
15-06 Argentina	D 1-1	Buenos Aires	WCq	Urrutia [69]	41 167	Ortube BOL
18-06 Colombia	D 0-0	Quito	WCq		33 588	Baldassi ARG

Fr = Friendly match • CA = Copa América • WC = FIFA World Cup • q = qualifier • r1 = first round group

ECUADOR NATIONAL TEAM PLAYERS

	Player		Ap	G	Club	Date of Birth		Player		Ap	G	Club	Date of Birth
1	Jose Cevallos	GK	78	0	LDU Quito	17 04 1971	12	Marcelo Elizaga	GK	5	0	Emelec	19 04 1972
2	Carlos Castro	DF			Barcelona SC	24 09 1978	13	Isaac Mina	DF	0	0	Deportivo Quito	
3	Ivan Hurtado	DF	146	5	Barcelona SC	16 08 1974	14	Segundo Castillo	MF	28	1	Crvena Zvezda	15 05 1982
4	Ulises de la Cruz	DF	90	5	Reading	8 02 1974	15	Walter Ayoví	MF			El Nacional	11 08 1979
5	Omar de Jesus	DF	5	0	El Nacional	29 02 1974	16	Antonio Valencia	MF	29	4	Wigan Athletic	4 08 1985
6	Paul Ambrosi	DF	29	0	LDU Quito	14 10 1980	17	Giovanny Espinoza	DF	98	6	Cruzeiro	12 04 1977
7	David Quiróz	MF			Barcelona SC	8 09 1982	18	Joffre Guerrón	FW	3	1	Getafe	28 04 1985
8	Patricio Urrutia	MF			LDU Quito	15 10 1978	19	Máximo Banguera	GK	1	0	Espoli	16 12 1985
9	Carlos Tenorio	FW	43	9	Al-Sadd QAT	14 05 1979	20	Jairo Campos	DF			LDU Quito	9 07 1984
10	Luís Bolaños	MF	3	0	LDU Quito	3 03 1985	21	Edison Mendez	MF	83	19	PSV Eindhoven	16 03 1979
11	Cristian Benítez	FW			Santos Laguna	1 05 1986	22	Luis Saritama	MF	15	0	Deportivo Quito	20 10 1983
Ecuador's squad for the June 2008 FIFA World Cup qualifiers							23	Felipe Caicedo	FW	15	2	Manchester City	5 09 1988

ECUADOR NATIONAL TEAM RECORDS AND RECORD SEQUENCES

Records			Sequence records					
Victory	6-0	PER 1975	Wins	6	1996	Clean sheets	3	Five times
Defeat	0-12	ARG 1942	Defeats	18	1938-1945	Goals scored	16	1991-1993
Player Caps	146	HURTADO Iván	Undefeated	8	1996, 2000-2001	Without goal	5	1985-1987
Player Goals	31	DELGADO Augustin	Without win	34	1938-1949	Goals against	28	1953-1963

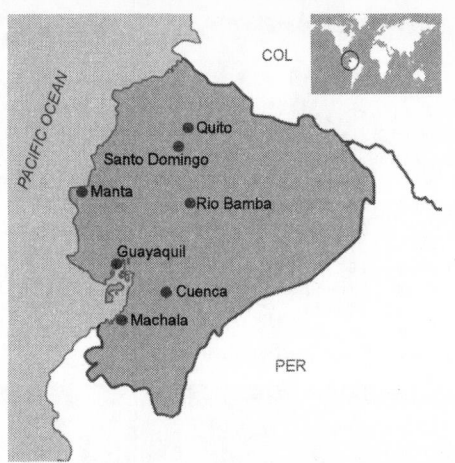

REPUBLIC OF ECUADOR; REPUBLICA DEL ECUADOR

Capital	Quito	Language	Spanish			Independence	1822
Population	13 547 510	Area	283 560 km²	Density	46 per km²	% in cities	58%
GDP per cap	$3300	Dailling code	+593	Internet	.ec	GMT +/-	-5

MAJOR CITIES/TOWNS
Population '000

1	Guayaquil	1 952
2	Quito	1 399
3	Cuenca	276
4	Santo Domingo	200
5	Machala	198
6	Manta	183
7	Portoviejo	170
8	Eloy Alfaro	167
9	Ambato	154
10	Riobamba	124
11	Quevedo	119
12	Loja	117
13	Milagro	110
14	Ibarra	108
15	Esmeraldas	95
16	Babahoyo	76
17	La Libertad	75
18	El Carmen	66
19	Daule	52
20	Latacunga	51
21	Velasco Ibarra	50
22	Ventanas	48
23	Tulcán	47
24	Salinas	45

MEDALS TABLE

		Overall			League			Sth Am			City	Stadium	Cap'ty	DoF
		G	S	B	G	S	B	G	S	B				
1	El Nacional	15	7	7	15	7	4			3	Quito	Olimpico Atahualpa	40 948	1964
2	Barcelona	13	13	10	13	11	5		2	5	Guayaquil	Monumental	59 283	1925
3	Emelec	10	11	12	10	10	10		1	2	Guayaquil	George Capwell	18 222	1929
4	Liga Deportiva Universitaria (LDU)	9	3	9	8	3	6	1		3	Quito	Casa Blanca	41 596	1930
5	Deportivo Quito	2	3	3	2	3	3				Quito	Olimpico Atahualpa	40 948	1940
6	Deportivo Cuenca	1	4		1	4					Cuenca	Alejandro Aguilar	18 830	1971
7	Olmedo	1	1	2	1	1	2				Riobamba	Olimpico Riobamba	18 936	1919
8	Everest	1		1	1		1				Guayaquil			1931
9	Universidad Católica		2	2		2	2				Quito	Olimpico Atahualpa	40 948	1961
10	América Quito		2	1		2	1				Quito			1939
	9 de Octubre		2	1		2	1				Guayaquil			1926
	Tecnico Universitario		2	1		2	1				Ambato	Bellavista	20 000	1971
13	Filanbanco		1	1		1	1				Guayaquil			1979-91
	Patria Guayaquil		1	1		1	1				Guayaquil			
15	Espoli			1			1				Quito	Guillermo Albornoz		1986
	Valdez			1			1				Milagro			1991

RECENT LEAGUE RECORD

	Championship						Championship Play-off		
Year	Champions	Pts	Runners-up	Pts	Third	Pts	Champions	Score	Runners-up
1995	Barcelona						Barcelona	2-0 1-0	Espoli
1996	El Nacional						El Nacional	2-1 2-0	Emelec
1997	Barcelona	19	Deportivo Quito	19	Emelec	15			
1998	LDU Quito						LDU Quito	0-1 7-0	Emelec
1999	El Nacional	20	LDU Quito	19	Emelec	18			
2000	Olmedo	23	El Nacional	20	Emelec	20			
2001	Emelec	22	El Nacional	21	Olmedo	20			
2002	Emelec	20	Barcelona	19	El Nacional	18			
2003	LDU Quito	26	Barcelona	23	El Nacional	20			
2004	Deportivo Cuenca	19.5	Olmedo	19	LDU Quito	18			
2005	LDU Quito						LDU Quito	0-1 3-0	Barcelona
2005	El Nacional	25	Deportivo Cuenca	20	LDU Quito	17			
2006	El Nacional	19	Emelec	17	LDU Quito	16			
2007	LDU Quito	27	Deportivo Cuenca	20	Olmedo	19			

ECUADOR 2007

SERIE A — TORNEO APERTURA

	Pl	W	D	L	F	A	Pts	Olmedo	Cuenca	LDU Quito	Azogues	Nacional	Dep Quito	Barcelona	Imbabura	Macará	Emelec
Olmedo †	18	11	4	3	27	15	37		0-3	1-0	2-1	2-1	2-0	4-1	2-1	2-1	3-1
Deportivo Cuenca †	18	10	2	6	26	19	32	1-0		0-0	3-1	0-2	2-0	1-0	4-0	2-1	1-0
LDU Quito †	18	8	4	6	36	26	28	1-3	4-0		2-0	3-3	1-1	2-1	4-1	2-1	1-0
Deportivo Azogues	18	8	4	6	26	26	28	0-0	0-2	2-1		2-1	1-0	3-1	1-1	3-1	1-2
El Nacional	18	8	3	7	37	27	27	1-2	2-1	3-1	4-1		3-1	3-1	0-1	3-0	4-2
Deportivo Quito	18	5	6	7	21	26	21	1-1	2-1	2-2	0-1	2-2		0-0	2-3	1-0	2-0
Barcelona	18	5	5	8	19	28	20	1-0	1-1	2-1	2-2	1-0	3-1		1-2	1-2	0-0
Imbabura	18	5	5	8	21	33	20	0-2	1-2	1-6	1-1	0-0	1-2	1-2		2-2	2-1
Macará	18	5	3	10	25	31	18	0-0	2-1	1-2	2-4	3-2	2-3	4-0	0-2		3-1
Emelec	18	4	6	8	23	30	18	1-1	3-1	4-3	1-2	4-3	1-1	1-1	1-1	0-0	

10/02/2007 - 13/06/2007 • † Qualified for the Liguilla final • ‡ Qualified for the Copa Sudamericana

SERIE A — TORNEO CLAUSURA

	Pl	W	D	L	F	A	Pts	LDU Quito	Nacional	Dep Quito	Emelec	Azogues	Barcelona	Olmedo	Macará	Cuenca	Imbabura
LDU Quito †	18	10	3	5	28	11	33		2-1	2-0	3-0	0-1	2-0	0-0	2-0	2-1	5-0
El Nacional †	18	9	5	4	24	18	32	0-2		0-0	2-1	2-0	2-1	0-0	3-1	1-1	2-0
Deportivo Quito †	18	9	2	7	22	15	29	1-0	1-2		2-0	4-0	0-0	2-1	4-0	0-1	
Emelec	18	8	2	8	23	21	26	2-0	1-0	2-1		2-0	1-2	2-0	3-0	4-0	2-2
Deportivo Azogues	18	7	3	8	20	25	24	1-1	2-3	1-0	1-0		1-2	0-2	0-1	1-0	2-3
Barcelona	18	7	3	8	19	25	24	0-3	1-2	1-0	0-1	1-1		2-0	1-1	2-1	2-1
Olmedo	18	5	7	6	13	15	22	1-0	0-1	1-2	3-0	2-0	2-0		0-0	2-1	0-0
Macará	18	5	6	7	21	25	21	1-3	1-1	0-1	2-0	3-2	2-2	1-1		1-1	1-0
Deportivo Cuenca	18	5	4	9	22	25	19	0-0	2-0	2-3	2-1	3-0	0-2	4-0	0-1		3-0
Imbabura	18	4	7	7	18	30	19	2-1	2-2	0-1	1-1	2-2	1-0	1-1	1-4	1-1	

13/07/2007 - 7/10/2007 • † Qualified for the Liguilla final. As LDU Quito had already qualified from the Apertura, the sixth place went to Deportivo Azogues due to their overall record in both the Apertura and Clausura • ‡ Qualified for the Copa Sudamericana • Imbabura relegated

SERIE A — LIGUILLA FINAL (1)

	Pl	W	D	L	F	A	Pts	LDU Quito	Cuenca	Olmedo	Azogues	Nacional	Deportivo
LDU Quito † §4	10	7	2	1	13	4	27		1-1	1-0	2-0	2-0	1-0
Deportivo Cuenca §2	10	4	6	0	12	5	20	0-0		0-0	1-0	3-1	2-1
Olmedo §3	10	4	4	2	9	5	19	2-0	0-0		1-0	1-1	1-0
Deportivo Azogues	10	4	2	4	8	8	14	0-1	1-1	1-0		2-1	1-0
El Nacional §2	10	1	3	6	10	18	8	0-2	1-1	2-2	0-2		3-1
Deportivo Quito §1	10	1	1	8	6	18	5	1-3	0-3	0-2	1-1	2-1	

19/10/2007 - 16/12/2007 • † Qualified for the Copa Libertadores • § = Bonus points from the first two stages
Top scorers: Juan Carlos Ferreyra, Cuenca 17; Luis Miguel Escalada, LDU 16; Cristian Lara, LDU 16; Daniel Neculman 16; Pablo Palacios, Deportivo Quito 15; Ivan Kaviedes, Nacional 14; Pedro Guzman, Olmedo 13

ECUADOR 2007 — SERIE B APERTURA/CLAUSURA

	Pl	W	D	L	F	A	Pts
Universidad Católica †	36	19	8	9	59	42	65
Espoli †	36	18	8	10	58	32	62
Aucas †	36	18	8	10	54	40	62
LDU Portoviejo †	36	16	7	13	54	54	55
Manta †	36	14	10	12	47	50	52
Técnico Universitario †	36	15	5	16	48	41	50
Municipal Cañar	36	14	5	17	48	41	47
Brasilia	36	10	11	15	43	67	41
LDU de Loja	36	9	6	21	36	50	33
Delfín	36	8	9	19	38	68	33

10/02/2007 - 14/10/2007 • † Qualified for the Liguilla finals

ECUADOR 2007 — SERIE B LIGUILLA FINAL (2)

	Pl	W	D	L	F	A	Pts
Universidad Católica §5	10	5	3	2	21	12	23
Espoli §2	10	4	5	1	11	7	19
Técnico Universitario §2	10	2	7	1	13	9	15
Aucas §3	10	2	3	5	10	14	12
LDU Portoviejo	10	3	3	4	9	15	12
Manta	10	2	3	5	8	15	9

20/10/2007 - 8/12/2007 • § = Bonus points from the first two stages • The first round was played in two stages with Universidad Católica winning the Apertura and Aucas winning the Clausura

EGY – EGYPT

NATIONAL TEAM RECORD
JULY 10TH 2006 TO JULY 12TH 2010

PL	W	D	L	F	A	%
28	16	8	4	46	22	71.4

Although they were holders, Egypt flew quietly under the radar in defence of their CAF Africa Cup of Nations title, and stunned even themselves when they won the trophy again. The Pharaohs, dismissed by pundits before the tournament as traditionally ineffective in the bustle of west Africa, picked up momentum with each passing game and in the end were worthy winners of the 2008 tournament in Ghana. In so doing, they extended their record run of titles to six, became only the third team successfully to defend their crown and again imposed the dominance of Egyptian football on the rest of the continent. Egypt beat Cameroon 1-0 in the final with Mohamed Aboutrika, who scored the winning goal, again proving the hero as he has been so many times before. Midfielder Hosni Abd Rabou was named the tournament's best player with his midfield prowess and some crucial goals. The team started with a dramatic 4-2 win over Cameroon in their opening game at the tournament but looked most lethal in demolishing Cote d'Ivoire in the semi-finals and should have won the final by a bigger margin The success of Egypt has been built on the backbone of Cairo giants Al Ahly, who are also record-holding champions at continental club level.

INTERNATIONAL HONOURS
Qualified for the FIFA World Cup finals 1934 1990
CAF African Cup of Nations 1957 1959 1986 1998 2006 2008   **African Games** 1987 1991
CAF African Youth Championship 1981 1991 2003 **CAF African U-17 Championship** 1997
CAF African Champions League Ismaili 1969, Al Ahly 1982 1987 2001 2005 2006, Zamalek 1984 1986 1993 1996 2002

But they were surprisingly denied a sixth CAF Champions League title in November when Etoile du Sahel of Tunisia stunned them in their own backyard. Al Ahly had been on course to become the first club to win three successive Champions League titles, particularly after forcing a goalless draw away in the first leg but were then beaten 3-1 at home. It led to chaotic scenes of bitter disappointment including the stoning of coach Manuel Jose with an assortment of missiles as he went up to pick up a consolation medal. The all-conquering Portuguese-born coach went instantly from hero to zero but a contrite crowd assembled in their thousands just days later to beg him to stay in the job. Jose led Al Ahly to another conformable championship win, this time by 17 points from second placed Ismaily. Consolation for arch rivals Zamalek came in the form of victory in the Egypt Cup, where Al Ahly had suffered a surprising first round defeat. A goal five minutes from the end by Amr Zaki handed Zamalek a 2-1 win over ENPPI in the final, the last game in charge for Dutch coach Ruud Krol. Reiner Hollmann, who took Al Ahly to a string of league titles more than a decade ago, has since replaced him as Zamalek look to stop Al Ahly from winning a fifth consecutive title in the 2008-09 season.

Egyptian Football Association (EFA)
5 Gabalaya Street, Gezira, El Borg Post Office, Cairo, Egypt
Tel +20 2 7351793   Fax +20 2 7367817
efa_football@hotmail.com   www.efa.com.eg
President: ZAHER Samir   General Secretary: HOSNY Salah
Vice-President: SHOUBEIR Ahmed   Treasurer: ABDEL HAMID SHAHIN Ahmed Shaker   Media Officer: SHALABY Medhat
Men's Coach: SHEHATA Hassan   Women's Coach: None
EFA formed: 1921   CAF: 1957   FIFA: 1923
Red shirts with white trimmings, White shorts, White socks

RECENT INTERNATIONAL MATCHES PLAYED BY EGYPT

2006	Opponents		Score	Venue	Comp	Scorers	Att	Referee
10-02	Côte d'Ivoire	D	0-0	Cairo	CNf	W 4-2p	74 000	Daami TUN
3-06	Spain	L	0-2	Elche	Fr		38 000	Farina ITA
16-08	Uruguay	L	0-2	Alexandria	Fr		10 000	Benouza ALG
2-09	Burundi	W	4-1	Alexandria	CNq	Zidan [5], Hosni Abd Rabou [29], Aboutraika [39], Ahmed Hassan [53p]		Haimoudi ALG
7-10	Botswana	D	0-0	Gaborone	CNq			Bennett RSA
15-11	South Africa	W	1-0	London	Fr	Emad Moteab [3]	2 000	Styles ENG
2007								
7-02	Sweden	W	2-0	Cairo	Fr	Amr Zaki [44], Ahmed Fathi [87]	40 000	Abdalla LBY
25-03	Mauritania	W	3-0	Cairo	CNq	Zidan [20], Sidibe OG [23], Ghali [66]		Benouza ALG
3-06	Mauritania	D	1-1	Nouakchott	CNq	Ahmed Hassan [10]		Sowe GAM
12-06	Kuwait	D	1-1	Kuwait City	Fr	Abd El Razak [56]		
22-08	Côte d'Ivoire	D	0-0	Paris	Fr			
9-09	Burundi	D	0-0	Bujumbura	CNq			Louzaya CGO
13-10	Botswana	W	1-0	Cairo	CNq	Mohamed Fadl [78]		Imiere NGA
17-10	Japan	L	1-4	Osaka	Fr	Mohamed Fadl [78]	41 901	Gilewski POL
21-11	Libya	D	0-0	Port Said	Fr			
25-11	Saudi Arabia	W	2-1	Cairo	Fr	Ghali [39], Emad Moteab [45]		
2008								
5-01	Namibia	W	3-0	Aswam	Fr	Amr Zaki 2 [53 88], Ahmed Hassan [77]		
10-01	Mali	W	1-0	Abu Dhabi	Fr	Hosni Abd Rabou [41p]		
13-01	Angola	D	3-3	AlvercadoRibatejo	Fr	Emad Moteab 3 [5 23 61]		
22-01	Cameroon	W	4-2	Kumasi	CNr1	Hosni Abd Rabou 2 [14p 82], Zidan 2 [17 44]		Sowe GAM
26-01	Sudan	W	3-0	Kumasi	CNr1	Hosni Abd Rabou [29p], Aboutrtika 2 [77 83]		Codjia BEN
30-01	Zambia	D	1-1	Kumasi	CNr1	Amr Zaki [15]		Coulibaly MLI
4-02	Angola	W	2-1	Kumasi	CNqf	Hosni Abd Rabou [23p], Amr Zaki [38]		Nichimura JPN
7-02	Côte d'Ivoire	W	4-1	Kumasi	CNsf	Ahmed Fathi [12], Amr Zaki 2 [62 67], Aboutrika [89]		Maillet SEY
10-02	Cameroon	W	1-0	Accra	CNf	Aboutrika [77]		Codjia BEN
26-03	Argentina	L	0-2	Cairo	Fr			Haimoudi ALG
1-06	Congo DR	W	2-1	Cairo	WCq	Amr Zaki [68], Ahmed Abdelmalk [80]	40 000	Seechurn MRI
6-06	Djibouti	W	4-0	Djibouti	WCq	Amr Zaki [40], Hosni Abd Rabou [46p], Ahmed Hassan [53], Ahmed Abdelmalk [64]	6 000	Eyob ERI
14-06	Malawi	L	0-1	Blantyre	WCq		40 000	Keita GUI
22-06	Malawi	W	2-0	Cairo	WCq	Emad Moteab 2 [17 50]		Diatta SEN

Fr = Friendly match • CN = CAF African Cup of Nations • WC = FIFA World Cup
q = qualifier • r1 = first round group • qf = quarter-final • sf = semi-final • f = final

EGYPT NATIONAL TEAM PLAYERS

	Player		Ap	G	Club	Date of Birth		Player		Ap	G	Club	Date of Birth
1	Essam Al Hadari	GK	98	0	Al Ahli	15 01 1973	12	Omar Gamal	MF	13	0	Ismaili	6 09 1982
2	Mahmoud Fathallah	DF	14	0	ENPPI	13 02 1982	13	Tarek El Sayed	DF	47	4	Zamalek	9 10 1978
3	Ahmed Al Muhammadi	DF	12	0	ENPPI	9 09 1987	14	Sayed Moawad	DF	30	2	Ismaili	25 05 1979
4	Ibrahim Said	DF	52	2	Ankaragucu	16 10 1979	15	Ahmed Shaaban	MF	2	0	Petrojet	10 10 1978
5	Shady Mohamed	DF	25	1	Al Ahli	29 11 1977	16	Mohamed Abdemoncef	GK	11	0	Zamalek	6 02 1977
6	Hani Said	DF	45	0	Ismaili	22 04 1980	17	Ahmed Hassan	MF	134	22	Anderlecht	2 05 1975
7	Ahmed Fathi	DF	47	2	Al Ahli	10 11 1984	18	Mohamed Fadl	FW	3	2	Ismaili	12 08 1980
8	Hosni Abd Rabou	MF	44	6	Ismaili	1 11 1984	19	Amr Zaki	FW	44	25	Zamalek	1 04 1983
9	Mohamed Zidan	FW	16	6	Hamburger SV	11 12 1981	20	Wael Gomaa	DF	63	0	Al Siliya QAT	3 08 1975
10	Emad Moteab	FW	44	20	Al Ahli	20 02 1983	21	Hassan Mostafa	MF	26	2	Al Wahda KSA	20 11 1979
11	Mohamed Shawky	MF	48	3	Middllesboro	5 10 1981	22	Mohamed Aboutrika	MF	52	14	Al Ahli	7 11 1978
							23	Mohamed Sobhi	GK	0	0	Ismaili	30 08 1981

Egypt's squad for the 2008 CAF Africa Cup of Nations

EGYPT NATIONAL TEAM RECORDS AND RECORD SEQUENCES

Records			Sequence records					
Victory	15-0	LAO 1963	Wins	9	2003-2004	Clean sheets	10	1989
Defeat	3-11	ITA 1928	Defeats	4	1990	Goals scored	22	1963-1964
Player Caps	170	Hossam Hassan	Undefeated	15	1963-64, 2000-01	Without goal	4	1985, 1990
Player Goals	69	Hossam Hassan	Without win	9	1981-1983	Goals against	13	1972-1973

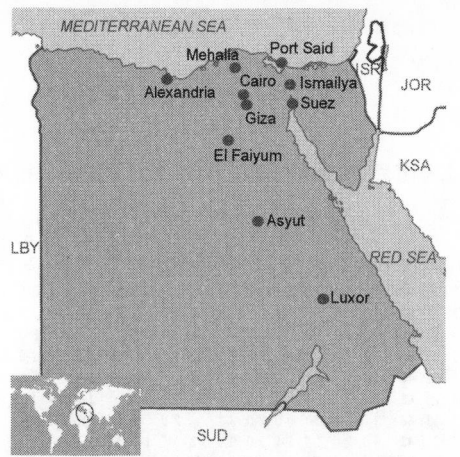

ARAB REPUBLIC OF EGYPT; JUMHURIYAT MISR AL ARABIYAH

Capital	Cairo	Language	Arabic			Independence	1936
Population	76 117 421	Area	1 001 450 km²	Density	76 per km²	% in cities	45%
GDP per cap	$4000	Dailling code	+20	Internet	.eg	GMT +/-	+2

MAJOR CITIES/TOWNS

Population '000

1	Cairo	7 933
2	Alexandria	4 368
3	Giza	2 491
4	Shubra	1 019
5	Port Said	554
6	Suez	506
7	Assiout	438
8	Mehalla Al Kubra	437
9	Luxor	437
10	Mansoura	431
11	Tanta	411
12	El Faiyum	316
13	Ismailya	291
14	El Zagazig	288
15	Kafr el Dauwar	275
16	Qena	251
17	Aswan	245
18	Menia	232
19	Damanhoor	231
20	Sohag	218
21	Beni Suef	193
22	Shebin El Kom	189
23	Edfo	188
24	Talkha	175

MEDALS TABLE

		Overall			League			Cup			Africa			City	Stadium	Cap'ty	DoF
		G	S	B	G	S	B	G	S	B	G	S	B				
1	Al Ahly	77	21	4	33	10	2	35	9		9	2	2	Cairo	Cairo Stadium	74 100	1907
2	Zamalek	38	39	10	11	28	6	21	10		6	1	4	Cairo	Cairo Stadium	74 100	1911
3	Al Tersana	7	8	7	1	4	7	6	4					Cairo	Mit Okba	15 000	1920
4	Mokawloon	7	3	2	1		1	3	3		3		1	Cairo	Osman Ahmed Osman	60 000	1962
5	Ismaily	6	11	18	3	5	14	2	4		1	2	4	Ismailya	Ismailiya Stadium	16 500	1920
6	Al Ittihad	6	4	3		2		6	4				1	Alexandria	Alexandria Stadium	20 000	1914
7	Olympic	3	3	1	1		1	2	3								1905
8	Al Masry	1	9	7		5		1	9				2	Port Said	Port Said Stadium	22 000	1920
9	Ghazl Al Mehalla	1	7	6	1		5		6		1	1		Al Mehalla	Al Mehalla	20 000	1946
10	Suez	1	3	1		1		1	3								
11	ENPPI	1	2	1	1	1		1	1					Cairo	Osman Ahmed Osman	60 000	1985
12	Al Teram	1						1									
13	Sekka		6						6					Cairo			
14	Mansoura		1	2		1			1			1					
15	Aswan		1						1								
	Baladeyet Mehalla		1						1								
	Shroeders		1						1								
18	Haras Al Hedod (ex Sawahel)			1		1								Alexandria	Haras Al Hedod	22 000	1950

RECENT LEAGUE AND CUP RECORD

	Championship						Cup		
Year	Champions	Pts	Runners-up	Pts	Third	Pts	Winners	Score	Runners-up
1995	Al Ahly	58	Zamalek	56	Ismaili	43	Mokawloon	2-0	Ghazl Al Mehalla
1996	Al Ahly	70	Zamalek	66	Ismaili	52	Al Ahly	3-1	Mansoura
1997	Al Ahly	69	Zamalek	60	Mansoura	49	Ismaily	1-0	Al Ahly
1998	Al Ahly	68	Zamalek	62	Mokawloon	54	Al Masry	4-3	Mokawloon
1999	Al Ahly	68	Zamalek	41	Ismaily	40	Zamalek	3-1	Ismaily
2000	Al Ahly	60	Ismaily	54	Zamalek	52	Ismaily	4-0	Mokawloon
2001	Zamalek	65	Al Ahly	57	Al Masry	46	Al Ahly	2-0	Ghazl Al Mehalla
2002	Ismaily	66	Al Ahly	64	Zamalek	53	Zamalek	1-0	Baladeyet Mehalla
2003	Zamalek	67	Al Ahly	66	Ismaily	46	Al Ahly	1-1 4-3p	Ismaily
2004	Zamalek	68	Al Ahly	59	Ismaily	51	Mokawloon	2-1	Al Ahly
2005	Al Ahly	74	ENPPI	43	Sawahel	39	ENPPI	1-0	Ittihad
2006	Al Ahly	72	Zamalek	58	ENPPI	46	Al Ahly	3-0	Zamalek
2007	Al Ahly	73	Zamalek	68	Ismaily	67	Al Ahly	4-3	Zamalek
2008	Al Ahly	70	Ismaily	53	Zamalek	53	Zamalek	2-1	ENPPI

EGYPT 2007–08

PREMIER LEAGUE

	Pl	W	D	L	F	A	Pts	Al Ahly	Ismaily	Zamalek	Al Jaish	Petrojet	Haras	ENPPI	Ghazl	Al Masry	Ittihad	Al Tersana	Mokawloon	Itesalat	Aluminium	Baladiyyat	Suez C'nt
Al Ahly †	30	21	7	2	47	22	70		1-1	2-0	0-0	2-0	2-0	4-3	3-2	1-0	0-2	1-0	0-0	1-1	3-0	1-0	1-0
Ismaily †	30	14	11	5	47	27	53	1-1		1-0	4-2	0-1	1-0	2-0	2-1	2-0	4-4	3-0	1-0	2-0	1-1	0-0	3-0
Zamalek ‡	30	16	5	9	45	30	53	0-1	0-1		2-1	1-3	1-0	1-0	3-1	1-2	2-0	1-0	1-0	3-0	5-1	1-0	1-1
Al Jaish ‡	30	14	9	7	33	22	51	0-1	1-0	2-1		0-0	2-1	1-2	3-1	1-0	2-1	0-0	1-1	1-0	2-0	1-0	0-1
Petrojet	30	13	7	10	51	38	46	1-3	2-2	1-0	2-1		2-3	3-1	2-2	4-2	0-1	4-0	1-0	2-0	3-0	3-2	1-1
Haras Al Hedod	30	11	13	6	38	26	46	1-2	1-1	1-1	0-0	2-2		2-0	1-1	0-0	0-0	1-1	0-0	1-1	3-0	2-0	1-1
ENPPI	30	12	10	8	42	33	46	3-0	1-1	0-1	0-0	2-0	3-2		2-0	0-0	2-1	3-1	2-1	0-1	1-0	3-0	2-0
Ghazl Al Mehalla	30	12	7	11	45	37	43	0-1	2-0	1-2	1-1	3-0	0-1	3-2		1-0	3-0	1-1	0-0	1-1	4-2	2-0	4-0
Al Masry	30	7	13	10	29	32	34	2-2	2-1	**0-2**	1-1	2-1	0-0	2-2	3-1		2-2	1-0	1-1	3-1	1-1	0-1	2-0
Ittihad	30	7	12	11	32	39	33	0-2	1-1	1-1	2-1	0-0	0-2	0-0	1-2	1-1		1-1	1-2	1-0	5-0	0-2	1-0
Al Tersana	30	8	8	14	30	40	32	0-1	0-0	0-3	1-2	3-1	1-3	2-3	2-1	1-0	1-1		2-1	3-0	1-0	4-1	1-1
Mokawloon	30	6	13	11	34	38	31	1-4	3-1	1-1	0-2	2-2	0-2	1-1	1-2	0-0	2-2	1-1		0-1	2-2	2-3	3-1
Itesalat	30	8	7	15	25	46	31	1-2	1-4	3-2	0-3	1-0	0-2	1-1	2-2	1-1	2-0	0-2	0-4		0-1	1-1	3-2
Aluminium	30	7	9	14	29	50	30	1-2	1-1	2-2	0-1	1-0	1-2	0-1	1-0	2-1	2-0	2-0	2-2	1-0		2-2	2-2
Baladiyyat Al Mehalla	30	5	10	15	23	40	25	0-0	0-2	1-2	0-0	1-2	2-2	1-1	0-2	0-0	1-1	1-0	0-1	0-1	0-2	2-0	1-1
Suez Cement	30	5	7	18	27	57	22	2-3	1-4	3-4	0-1	0-8	1-2	1-1	0-1	1-0	1-2	2-1	1-2	0-1	1-0	2-1	

13/08/2007 - 22/05/2008 • † Qualified for the CAF Champions League • ‡ Qualified for the CAF Confederation Cup
Top scorers: Alaa Ibrahim, Petrojet 15; Ahmed Hassan Farag, Ghazl 12; Mohamed Fadl, Ismaily 10

CUP 2007–08

Round of 16

Zamalek *	2
Maleyat Kafr Al Zayyat	0
Al Masry	0
Suez Cement *	3
Petrojet *	3
Ismaily	0
Itesalat	2 1p
Haras Al Hedod *	2 3p
Mokawloon	4 4p
Al Jaish *	4 3p
Military Production *	0
Aluminium	5
Ittihad	1
Al Tersana *	0
Assiout Petrol	0
ENPPI *	2

Quarter–finals

Zamalek *	4
Suez Cement	1
Petrojet	0
Haras Al Hedod *	1
Mokawloon	4
Aluminium *	1
Ittihad	0
ENPPI *	1

Semi–finals

Zamalek	2
Haras Al Hedod	1
Mokawloon	2
ENPPI	3

Final

Zamalek	2
ENPPI	1

CUP FINAL
25-05-2008

Scorers - Osama Hassan [34]p, Amr Zaki [80] for Zamalek; Mohamed Younis [64] for ENPPI

* Home team

ENG – ENGLAND

NATIONAL TEAM RECORD
JULY 10TH 2006 TO JULY 12TH 2010

PL	W	D	L	F	A	%
22	12	4	6	39	14	63.6

The split personality of English football was never more marked than during a season in which the national team failed to qualify for the finals of the European Championship, but which also saw an all-English Champions League final. As far as the national team was concerned, rarely has its stock fallen so low. Steve McLaren's brief tenure as coach ended in disaster with a defeat at Wembley by Croatia, which ensured that England missed out on the European Championship finals for the first time since 1984. For his replacement, the FA once again looked abroad appointing the Italian Fabio Capello. It was a bold move but whether Capello can reinvigorate the national team set-up remains to be seen. His claims that the national team's troubles are down to the lack of a winning mentality when playing for England seemed to be borne out by the outstanding success of English clubs in the Champions League. Both finalists - Manchester United and Chelsea - played with a central core of English players and of the English quartet in the competition, only Arsenal - with almost no English players - failed to reach the semi-finals; this despite playing some of the best football of the tournament, especially in their victory over Milan in the first knock-out round. In

INTERNATIONAL HONOURS
FIFA World Cup 1966   **Olympic Gold** 1908 1912
Qualified for the FIFA World Cup 1950 1954 1958 1962 1966 1970 1982 1986 1990 1998 2002 2006
European U-21 Championship 1982 1984   **European Junior Championship** 1948 1963 1964 1971 1972 1973 1975 1980 1993
UEFA Champions League Manchester United 1968 1999 2008 Liverpool 1977 1978 1981 1984 2005 Nottingham Forest 1979 1980 Aston Villa 1982

an epic final in Moscow that was decided on penalties, Manchester United won their third European Cup consigning Chelsea to their third runners-up spot of the season. Ten days earlier, on the final day of the league season, United had clinched their 17th championship, pipping Chelsea to the post by two points. Having sensationally parted company with coach Jose Mourinho early on in the season, it proved to be a turbulent and ultimately unsuccessful campaign for his replacement, Avram Grant. With Tottenham beating Chelsea in the League Cup final - a first trophy in England for coach Juande Ramos - the Cups provided a welcome relief from the dominance of the big four - none more so than in the FA Cup where Portsmouth won the trophy for the first time since 1939, beating Cardiff City of the second division 1-0 in the final. For many it was the story of the season. There was no question as to the most absurd episode of the season - the Premier League's bizarre plan to play a 39th league game abroad, a move that was seen by most as predatory and which did no favours for England's bid to host the 2018 World Cup. The hope is that Manchester United's triumphant season, lit up by the 42 goals of Cristiano Ronaldo and a 10th league title for Ryan Giggs, will have restored the image of English club football abroad.

The Football Association (The FA)
25 Soho Square, London W1D 4FA, United Kingdom
Tel +44 20 77454545   Fax +44 20 77454546
communique@thefa.com   www.TheFA.com
President: TRIESMAN Lord   General Secretary: BARWICK Brian
Vice-President: BRIGHT Barry   Treasurer: WILLIAMS Steve   Media Officer: BEVINGTON Adrian
Men's Coach: CAPELLO Fabio   Women's Coach: POWELL Hope
The FA formed: 1863   UEFA: 1954   FIFA: 1905-20 & 1945
White shirts with red trimmings, Navy blue shorts, White socks or Red shirts with white trimmings, White shorts, Red socks

RECENT INTERNATIONAL MATCHES PLAYED BY ENGLAND

2006	Opponents	Score		Venue	Comp	Scorers	Att	Referee
10-06	Paraguay	W	1-0	Frankfurt	WCr1	Gamarra OG [3]	48 000	Rodriguez MEX
15-06	Trinidad and Tobago	W	2-0	Nuremburg	WCr1	Crouch [83], Gerrard [91+]	41 000	Kamikawa JPN
20-06	Sweden	D	2-2	Cologne	WCr1	Cole.J [34], Gerrard [85]	45 000	Busacca SUI
25-06	Ecuador	W	1-0	Stuttgart	WCr2	Beckham [60]	52 000	De Bleeckere BEL
1-07	Portugal	D	0-0	Gelsenkirchen	WCqf	L 1-3p	52 000	Elizondo ARG
16-08	Greece	W	4-0	Manchester	Fr	Terry [14], Lampard [30], Crouch 2 [36 42]	45 864	Stark GER
2-09	Andorra	W	5-0	Manchester	ECq	Crouch 2 [5 67], Gerrard [13], Defoe 2 [38 47]	56 290	Brugger AUT
6-09	Macedonia	W	1-0	Skopje	ECq	Crouch [46]	16 500	Layec FRA
7-10	Macedonia	D	0-0	Manchester	ECq		72 062	Merk GER
11-10	Croatia	L	0-2	Zagreb	ECq		38 000	Rosetti ITA
15-11	Netherlands	D	1-1	Amsterdam	Fr	Rooney [37]	44 000	Michel SVK
2007								
7-02	Spain	L	0-1	Manchester	Fr		58 247	Weiner GER
24-03	Israel	D	0-0	Tel Aviv	ECq		38 000	Ovrebo NOR
28-03	Andorra	W	3-0	Barcelona	ECq	Gerrard 2 [54 76], Nugent [92+]	12 800	Paixao POR
1-06	Brazil	D	1-1	London	Fr	Terry [68]	88 745	Merk GER
6-06	Estonia	W	3-0	Tallinn	ECq	Cole.J [37], Crouch [54], Owen [62]	11 000	Gilewski POL
22-08	Germany	L	1-2	London	Fr	Lampard [9]	86 133	Busacca SUI
8-09	Israel	W	3-0	London	ECq	Wright-Phillips [20], Owen [49], Richards [66]	85 372	Vink NED
12-09	Russia	W	3-0	London	ECq	Owen 2 [7 31], Ferdinand [84]	86 106	Hansson SWE
13-10	Estonia	W	3-0	London	ECq	Wright-Phillips [11], Rooney [32], Rahm OG [33]	86 655	Vollquartz DEN
17-10	Russia	L	1-2	Moscow	ECq	Rooney [29]		Medina ESP
16-11	Austria	W	1-0	Vienna	Fr	Crouch [44]	39 432	Vollquartz DEN
21-11	Croatia	L	2-3	London	ECq	Lampard [56p], Crouch [65]	88 091	Frojdfeldt SWE
2008								
6-02	Switzerland	W	2-1	London	Fr	Jenas [40], Wright-Phillips [62]	86 857	Brych GER
26-03	France	L	0-1	Paris	Fr		78 500	Meyer GER
28-05	USA	W	2-0	London	Fr	Terry [38], Gerrard [59]	71 233	Vassaras GRE
1-06	Trinidad and Tobago	W	3-0	Port of Spain	Fr	Barry [12], Defoe 2 [15 49]	25 001	Wijngaarde SUR

Fr = Friendly • EC = UEFA EURO 2008 • WC = FIFA World Cup • q = qualifier • r1 = first round group • r2 - first knock-out round • qf = quarter-final

ENGLAND NATIONAL TEAM PLAYERS

	Player		Ap	G	Club	Date of Birth		Player		Ap	G	Club	Date of Birth
1	David JAMES	GK	39	0	Portsmouth	1 08 1970	15	Stephen WARNOCK	DF	1	0	Blackburn Rov	12 12 1981
2	Wes BROWN	DF	17	0	Manchester Utd	13 10 1979	16	Jonathan WOODGATE	DF	7	0	Tottenham H.	22 01 1980
3	Ashley COLE	DF	64	0	Chelsea	20 12 1980	17	David BENTLEY	MF	6	0	Blackburn Rov	27 08 1984
4	Owen HARGREAVES	MF	42	0	Manchester Utd	20 01 1981	18	Phil JAGIELKA	DF	1	0	Everton	17 08 1982
5	Rio FERDINAND	DF	68	2	Manchester Utd	7 11 1978	19	David WHEATER	DF	0	0	Middlesbrough	14 02 1987
6	John TERRY	DF	44	4	Chelsea	7 12 1980	20	Tom HUDDLESTONE	MF	0	0	Tottenham H	28 12 1986
7	David BECKHAM	MF	102	17	LA Galaxy	2 05 1975	21	Gareth BARRY	MF	20	1	Aston Villa	23 02 1981
8	Frank LAMPARD	MF	61	14	Chelsea	20 06 1978	22	Joe COLE	MF	50	7	Chelsea	8 11 1981
9	Jermain DEFOE	FW	28	5	Portsmouth	7 10 1982	23	Stewart DOWNING	MF	18	0	Middlesbrough	22 07 1984
10	Steven GERRARD	MF	67	13	Liverpool	30 05 1980	24	Ashley YOUNG	FW	3	0	Aston Villa	9 07 1985
11	Wayne ROONEY	FW	43	14	Manchester Utd	24 10 1985	25	Peter CROUCH	FW	28	14	Liverpool	30 01 1981
12	Joe HART	GK	0	0	Manchester City	19 04 1987	26	Dean ASHTON	FW	1	0	West Ham Utd	24 11 1983
13	Glen JOHNSON	DF	8	0	Portsmouth	23 08 1984	27	Theo WALCOTT	FW	2	0	Arsenal	16 03 1989
14	Wayne BRIDGE	DF	30	1	Chelsea	5 08 1980	28	Gabriel AGBONLAHOR	FW	0	0	Aston Villa	13 10 1986

England's squad for the USA international

29	Joe Lewis	GK	0	0	Peterborough U	6 10 1987

ENGLAND NATIONAL TEAM RECORDS AND RECORD SEQUENCES

Records			Sequence records					
Victory	13-0	IRL 1882	Wins	10	1908-1909	Clean sheets	7	1908-1909
Defeat	1-7	HUN 1954	Defeats	3	Six times	Goals scored	52	1884-1902
Player Caps	125	SHILTON Peter	Undefeated	20	1890-1896	Without goal	4	1981
Player Goals	49	CHARLTON Bobby	Without win	7	1958	Goals against	13	1873-81, 1959-60

The England Amateur team beat France 15-0 in 1906. The FA do not regard it as a full international although the match is part of the official French records • The England Amateurs won a world record 17 consecutive matches from 1906 to 1909 • Vivian Woodward scored a combined 73 goals for the England team and the England amateur team

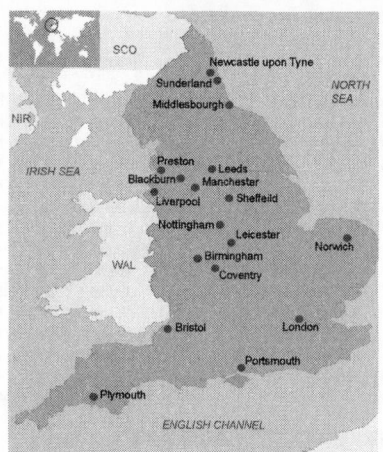

ENGLAND (PART OF THE UNITED KINGDOM)

Capital	London	Language	English		Independence	n/a
Population	49 138 831	Area	130 439 km²	Density	380 per km²	% in cities	89%
GDP per cap	$29 600	Dialling code	+44	Internet	.uk	GMT +/-	0

MAJOR CITIES/TOWNS
Population '000

1	London	7 172
2	West Midlands	2 555
3	Greater Manchester	2 482
4	West Yorkshire	2 079
5	Merseyside	1 362
6	South Yorkshire	1 266
7	Tyne & Wear	1 075
8	Bristol	380
9	Leicester	279
10	Nottingham	266
11	Hull	243
12	Stoke-on-Trent	240
13	Plymouth	240
14	Derby	221
15	Southampton	217
16	Portsmouth	186
17	Luton	184
18	Reading	143
19	Blackpool	142
20	Blackburn	137
21	Middlesbrough	134
22	Preston	129
23	Norwich	121
24	Ipswich	117

West Midlands consists of Birmingham (977), Coventry (300), Dudley (305), Sandwell (West Bromwich) (282), Solihull (199), Walsall (253) and Wolverhampton (236) • **Greater Manchester** consists of Bolton (261), Bury (180), Manchester (392), Oldham (217), Rochdale (205), Salford (216), Stockport (284), Tameside (213), Trafford (210) and Wigan (301) • **West Yorkshire** consists of Bradford (467), Calderdale (192), Kirklees (Huddersfield) (388), Leeds (715) and Wakefield (315) • **Merseyside** consists of Knowsley (150), Liverpool (439), St Helens (176), Sefton (282) and Wirral (312) • **South Yorkshire** consists of Barnsley (218), Doncaster (286), Rotherham (248) and Sheffield (513) • **Tyne & Wear** consists of Gateshead (191), Newcastle upon Tyne (259), North Tyneside (191), South Tyneside (152) and Sunderland (280)

MEDALS TABLE

	Overall			League			Cup			LC			Europe			Stadium	Cap'ty	DoF
	G	S	B	G	S	B	G	S	B	G	S	B	G	S	B			
1 Liverpool	40	23	23	18	11	7	7	6	9	7	3	3	8	3	4	Anfield	45 362	1892
2 Manchester United	34	24	27	17	13	6	11	7	7	2	4	4	4		9	Old Trafford	76 212	1878
3 Arsenal	27	23	21	13	8	6	10	7	8	2	4	7	2	4		The Emirates	60 000	1886
4 Aston Villa	20	15	16	7	10	2	7	3	9	5	2	5	1			Villa Park	42 551	1874
5 Tottenham Hotspur	17	8	26	2	4	9	8	1	8	4	2	6	3	1	3	White Hart Lane	36 237	1882
6 Everton	15	16	20	9	7	7	5	7	11		2	2	1			Goodison Park	40 394	1878
7 Chelsea	13	10	23	3	3	4	4	4	9	4	2	4	2	1	6	Stamford Bridge	42 294	1905
8 Newcastle United	11	10	8	4	2	4	6	7	3	1				1	1	St James' Park	52 387	1881
9 Blackburn Rovers	10	3	17	3	1	3	6	2	10	1		4				Ewood Park	31 154	1875
10 Wolverhampton Wanderers	9	10	14	3	5	6	4	4	6	2		1		1	1	Molineux	29 277	1877
11 Manchester City	9	8	4	2	3	3	4	4	2	2	1	2	1		1	City of Manchester	47 500	1887
12 Nottingham Forest	9	5	14	1	2	4	2	1	9	4	2		2		1	City Ground	30 602	1865
13 Sunderland	8	8	18	6	5	8	2	2	8		1	2				Stadium of Light	49 000	1879
14 Sheffield Wednesday	8	5	19	4	1	7	3	3	10	1	1	2				Hillsborough	39 812	1867
15 Leeds United	7	12	13	3	5	2	1	3	4	1	1	3	2	3	4	Elland Road	39 460	1919
16 West Bromwich Albion	7	9	12	1	2	1	5	5	10	1	2	1				The Hawthorns	28 000	1878
17 Sheffield United	5	4	8	1	2		4	2	7			1				Bramall Lane	30 864	1889
18 The Wanderers	5						5											
19 Preston North End	4	11	5	2	6	2	2	5	3							Deepdale	20 600	1881
20 Huddersfield Town	4	7	6	3	3	3	1	4	2			1				The Galpharm	24 590	1908
21 Bolton Wanderers	4	5	11			3	4	3	6		2	2				The Reebok	28 101	1874
22 West Ham United	4	5	9			1	3	2	2		2	5	1	1	1	Upton Park	35 303	1895
23 Portsmouth	4	2	3	2		1	2	2	2							Fratton Park	20 328	1898
24 Leicester City	3	7	5		1	1		4	4	3	2					The Walkers	32 312	1884
25 Derby County	3	6	15	2	3	4	1	3	9			1			1	Pride Park	33 597	1884
26 Burnley	3	4	13	2	2	5	1	2	5			3				Turf Moor	22 610	1882
27 Ipswich Town	3	2	8	1	2	3	1		2			3	1			Portman Road	30 311	1878

RECENT LEAGUE AND CUP RECORD

Year	Champions	Pts	Runners-up	Pts	Third	Pts	Winners	Score	Runners-up
			Championship					Cup	
1993	Manchester United	84	Aston Villa	74	Norwich City	72	Arsenal	1-1-2-1	Sheffield Wed'day
1994	Manchester United	92	Blackburn Rovers	84	Newcastle United	77	Manchester United	4-0	Chelsea
1995	Blackburn Rovers	89	Manchester United	88	Nottingham Forest	77	Everton	1-0	Manchester United
1996	Manchester United	82	Newcastle United	78	Liverpool	71	Manchester United	1-0	Liverpool
1997	Manchester United	75	Newcastle United	68	Arsenal	68	Chelsea	2-0	Middlesbrough
1998	Arsenal	78	Manchester United	77	Liverpool	65	Arsenal	2-0	Newcastle United
1999	Manchester United	79	Arsenal	78	Chelsea	75	Manchester United	2-0	Newcastle United
2000	Manchester United	91	Arsenal	73	Leeds United	69	Chelsea	1-0	Aston Villa
2001	Manchester United	80	Arsenal	70	Liverpool	69	Liverpool	2-1	Arsenal
2002	Arsenal	87	Liverpool	80	Manchester United	77	Arsenal	2-0	Chelsea
2003	Manchester United	83	Arsenal	78	Newcastle United	69	Arsenal	1-0	Southampton
2004	Arsenal	90	Chelsea	79	Manchester United	75	Manchester United	3-0	Millwall
2005	Chelsea	95	Arsenal	83	Manchester United	77	Arsenal	0-0 5-4p	Manchester United
2006	Chelsea	91	Manchester United	83	Liverpool	82	Liverpool	3-3 3-1p	West Ham United
2007	Manchester United	89	Chelsea	83	Liverpool	68	Chelsea	1-0	Manchester United
2008	Manchester United	87	Chelsea	85	Arsenal	83	Portsmouth	1-0	Cardiff City

LEAGUE CUP FINALS

Year	Winners	Score	Runners-up
1995	Liverpool	2-1	Bolton Wanderers
1996	Aston Villa	3-0	Leeds United
1997	Leicester City	1-1 1-0	Middlesbrough
1998	Chelsea	2-0	Middlesbrough
1999	Tottenham Hotspur	1-0	Leicester City
2000	Leicester City	2-1	Tranmere Rovers
2001	Liverpool	1-1 5-4p	Birmingham City
2002	Blackburn Rovers	2-1	Tottenham Hotspur
2003	Liverpool	2-0	Manchester United
2004	Middlesbrough	2-1	Bolton Wanderers
2005	Chelsea	3-2	Liverpool
2006	Manchester United	4-0	Wigan Athletic
2007	Chelsea	2-1	Arsenal
2008	Tottenham Hotspur	2-1	Chelsea

ENGLAND 2007–08

BARCLAYS PREMIER LEAGUE

	Pl	W	D	L	F	A	Pts	Man Utd	Chelsea	Arsenal	Liverpool	Everton	Aston Villa	Blackburn	Portsmouth	Man City	West Ham	Tottenham	Newcastle	Midd'boro	Wigan	Sunderland	Bolton	Fulham	Readig	B'ham City	Derby
Manchester United †	38	27	6	5	80	22	87		2-0	2-1	3-0	2-1	4-0	2-0	2-0	1-2	4-1	1-0	6-0	4-1	4-0	1-0	2-0	2-0	0-0	1-0	4-1
Chelsea †	38	25	10	3	65	26	85	2-1		2-1	0-0	1-1	4-4	0-0	1-0	6-0	1-0	2-0	2-1	1-0	1-1	2-0	1-1	0-0	1-0	3-2	6-1
Arsenal †	38	24	11	3	74	31	83	2-2	1-0		1-1	1-0	1-1	2-0	3-1	1-0	2-0	2-1	3-0	1-1	2-0	3-2	2-2	2-1	2-0	1-1	5-0
Liverpool †	38	21	13	4	67	28	76	0-1	1-1	1-1		1-0	2-2	3-1	4-1	1-0	4-0	2-2	3-0	3-2	1-1	3-0	4-0	2-0	2-1	0-0	6-0
Everton ‡	38	19	8	11	55	33	65	0-1	0-1	1-4	1-2		2-2	1-1	3-1	1-0	1-1	0-0	3-1	2-0	2-1	7-1	2-0	3-0	1-0	3-1	1-0
Aston Villa	38	16	12	10	71	51	60	1-4	2-0	1-2	1-2	2-0		1-1	3-1	1-1	0-2	1-4	1-1	0-2	0-1	4-4	2-1	3-1	5-1	2-0
Blackburn Rovers	38	15	13	10	50	48	58	1-1	0-1	1-1	0-0	0-0	0-4		0-1	1-0	0-1	1-1	3-1	1-1	3-1	1-0	4-1	1-1	4-2	2-1	3-1
Portsmouth ‡	38	16	9	13	48	40	57	1-1	1-1	0-0	0-0	0-0	2-0	0-1		0-0	0-0	0-1	0-0	0-1	2-0	1-0	3-1	0-1	7-4	4-2	3-1
Manchester City	38	15	10	13	45	53	55	1-0	0-2	1-3	0-0	0-2	1-0	2-2	3-1		1-1	2-1	3-1	3-1	0-0	1-0	4-2	2-3	2-1	1-0	1-0
West Ham United	38	13	10	15	42	50	49	2-1	0-4	0-1	1-0	0-2	2-2	1-0	1-0	0-2		1-1	2-2	3-0	1-1	2-1	1-1	2-1	1-1	1-1	2-1
Tottenham Hotspur ‡	38	11	13	14	66	61	46	1-1	4-4	1-3	0-2	1-3	4-4	1-2	2-0	2-1	4-0		1-4	1-1	4-0	2-0	1-1	5-1	6-4	2-3	4-0
Newcastle United	38	11	10	17	45	65	43	1-5	0-2	1-1	0-3	3-2	0-0	0-1	1-4	0-2	3-1	3-1		1-1	1-0	2-0	0-0	2-0	3-0	2-1	2-2
Middlesbrough	38	10	12	16	43	53	42	2-2	0-2	2-1	1-1	0-2	0-3	1-2	2-0	8-1	1-2	1-1	2-2		1-0	2-2	0-1	1-0	0-1	2-0	1-0
Wigan Athletic	38	10	10	18	34	51	40	0-2	0-2	0-0	0-0	1-1	2-1	1-2	5-3	0-2	1-1	1-0	1-1	0-1	1-0		3-0	1-0	1-0	1-0	0-0	2-0	2-0
Sunderland	38	11	6	21	36	59	39	0-4	0-1	0-1	0-2	0-1	1-1	2-0	1-2	2-1	1-0	1-1	3-2	2-0		3-1	1-1	2-1	2-1	1-0
Bolton Wanderers	38	9	10	19	36	54	37	1-0	0-1	2-3	1-3	1-2	1-1	1-2	0-1	0-0	1-0	1-1	1-3	0-0	4-1	2-0		0-0	3-0	3-0	1-0
Fulham	38	8	12	18	38	60	36	0-3	1-2	0-3	0-2	1-0	2-1	2-2	0-2	3-3	0-1	3-3	0-1	1-2	1-1	1-3	2-1		3-1	2-0	0-0
Reading	38	10	6	22	41	66	36	0-1	0-1	1-3	3-1	1-0	2-0	0-3	0-1	2-1	1-1	2-1	1-2	1-2	1-0	2-0		2-1	1-0
Birmingham City	38	8	11	19	46	62	35	0-1	0-1	1-2	2-2	1-1	1-2	4-1	0-2	3-1	0-1	4-1	1-1	3-0	3-2	2-2	1-0	1-1	1-1		1-1
Derby County	38	1	8	29	20	89	11	0-1	0-2	2-6	1-2	0-2	0-6	1-2	2-2	1-1	0-5	0-3	1-0	0-1	0-1	0-0	1-1	2-2	0-4	1-2	

11/08/2007 - 11/05/2008 • † Qualified for the UEFA Champions League • ‡ Qualified for the UEFA Cup

Top scorers: Ronaldo, Man Utd 31; Emmanuel Adebayor, Arsenal 24; Fernando Torres, Liverpool 24; Roque Santa Cruz, Blackburn 19; Dimitar Berbatov, Tottenham 15; Robbie Keane, Tottenham 15; Benjani, Portsmouth/Man City 15; Yakubu, Everton 15; Carlos Tévez, Man Utd 14

ENGLAND 2007–08

COCA-COLA FOOTBALL LEAGUE CHAMPIONSHIP (2)

	Pl	W	D	L	F	A	Pts
West Bromwich Alb	46	23	12	11	88	55	81
Stoke City	46	21	16	9	69	55	79
Hull City ‡	46	21	12	13	65	47	75
Bristol City ‡	46	20	14	12	54	53	74
Crystal Palace ‡	46	18	17	11	58	42	71
Watford ‡	46	18	16	12	62	56	70
Wolverhampton W	46	18	16	12	53	48	70
Ipswich Town	46	18	15	13	65	56	69
Sheffield United	46	17	15	14	56	51	66
Plymouth Argyle	46	17	13	16	60	50	64
Charlton Athletic	46	17	13	16	63	58	64
Cardiff City	46	16	16	14	59	55	64
Burnley	46	16	14	16	60	67	62
Queens Park Rang's	46	14	16	16	60	66	58
Preston North End	46	15	11	20	50	56	56
Sheffield Wed'day	46	14	13	19	54	55	55
Norwich City	46	15	10	21	49	59	55
Barnsley	46	14	13	19	52	65	55
Blackpool	46	12	18	16	59	64	54
Southampton	46	13	15	18	56	72	54
Coventry City	46	14	11	21	52	64	53
Leicester City	46	12	16	18	42	45	52
Scunthorpe United	46	11	13	22	46	69	46
Colchester United	46	7	17	22	62	86	38

11/08/2007 - 4/05/2008 • ‡ Qualified for the play-offs • Top scorers: Sylvan Ebanks-Blake, Wolves 23; James Beattie, Sheff Utd 22; Kevin Phillips, WBA 22; Play-off semi-finals: Crystal Palace 1-2 1-2 **Bristol City**; Watford 0-2 1-4 **Hull City**
Play-off final: **Hull City** 1-0 Bristol City (Wembley, 24-05-2008, Att: 86 703. Scorer - Windass [38])

ENGLAND 2007–08

COCA-COLA FOOTBALL LEAGUE ONE (3)

	Pl	W	D	L	F	A	Pts
Swansea City	46	27	11	8	82	42	92
Nottingham Forest	46	22	16	8	64	32	82
Doncaster Rovers ‡	46	23	11	12	65	41	80
Carlisle United ‡	46	23	11	12	64	46	80
Leeds United ‡ §15	46	27	10	9	72	38	76
Southend United ‡	46	22	10	14	70	55	76
Brighton & Hove Alb	46	19	12	15	58	50	69
Oldham Athletic	46	18	13	15	58	46	67
Northampton Town	46	17	15	14	60	55	66
Huddersfield Town	46	20	6	20	50	62	66
Tranmere Rovers	46	18	11	17	52	47	65
Walsall	46	16	16	14	52	46	64
Swindon Town	46	16	13	17	63	56	61
Leyton Orient	46	16	12	18	49	63	60
Hartlepool	46	15	9	22	63	66	54
Bristol Rovers	46	12	17	17	45	53	53
Millwall	46	14	10	22	45	60	52
Yeovil Town	46	14	12	20	38	59	52
Cheltenham Town	46	13	12	21	42	64	51
Crewe Alexandra	46	12	14	20	47	65	50
Bournemouth §10	46	17	7	22	62	72	48
Gillingham	46	11	13	22	44	73	46
Port Vale	46	9	11	26	47	81	38
Luton Town §10	46	11	10	25	43	63	33

11/08/2007 - 3/05/2008 • ‡ Qualified for the play-offs • § = points deducted • Top scorers: Jason Scotland, Swansea 24; Jermaine Beckford, Leeds 20; Play-off semi-finals: Southend 0-0 1-5 **Doncaster**; **Leeds** 1-2 2-0 Carlisle
Play-off final: **Doncaster** 1-0 Leeds (Wembley, 25-05-2008. Att: 75 132. Scorer - Hayter [48])

ENGLAND 2007–08

COCA-COLA FOOTBALL LEAGUE TWO (4)

	Pl	W	D	L	F	A	Pts
Milton Keynes Dons	46	29	10	7	82	37	97
Peterborough Utd	46	28	8	10	84	43	92
Hereford United	46	26	10	10	72	41	88
Stockport County ‡	46	24	10	12	72	54	82
Rochdale ‡	46	23	11	12	77	54	80
Darlington ‡	46	22	12	12	67	40	78
Wycombe Wand's ‡	46	22	12	12	56	42	78
Chesterfield	46	19	12	15	76	56	69
Rotherham United	46	21	11	14	62	58	64
Bradford City	46	17	11	18	63	61	62
Morecambe	46	16	12	18	63	61	60
Barnet	46	16	12	18	56	63	60
Bury	46	16	11	19	58	61	59
Brentford	46	17	8	21	52	70	59
Lincoln City	46	18	4	24	61	77	58
Grimsby Town	46	15	10	21	55	66	55
Accrington Stanley	46	16	3	27	49	83	51
Shrewsbury Town	46	12	14	20	56	65	50
Macclesfield Town	46	11	17	18	47	64	50
Dagenham & Red.	46	13	10	23	49	70	49
Notts County	46	10	18	18	37	53	48
Chester City	46	12	11	23	51	68	47
Mansfield Town	46	11	9	26	48	68	42
Wrexham	46	10	10	26	38	70	40

11/08/2007 - 3/05/2008 • ‡ Qualified for the play-offs • Top scorers: Aaron McLean, Peterborough 29; Scott McGleish, Wycombe 26
Play-off semi-finals: Wycombe 1-1 0-1 **Stockport**; Darlington 2-1 1-2 4-5p **Rochdale**
Play-off final: Stockport 3-2 Rochdale (Wembley, 26-05-2008, Att: 35 715. Scorers - Stanton OG [34], Pilkington [49], Dickinson [67] for Stockport; McArdle [24], Rundle [77] for Rochdale)

ENGLAND 2007–08

BLUE SQUARE PREMIER (5)

	Pl	W	D	L	F	A	Pts
Aldershot	46	31	8	7	82	48	101
Cambridge United ‡	46	25	11	10	68	41	86
Torquay United ‡	46	26	8	12	83	57	86
Exeter City ‡	46	22	17	7	83	58	83
Burton Albion	46	23	12	11	79	56	81
Stevenage Borough	46	24	7	15	82	55	79
Histon	46	20	12	14	76	67	72
Forest Green	46	19	14	13	76	59	71
Oxford United	46	20	11	15	56	48	71
Grays Athletic	46	19	13	14	58	47	70
Ebbsfleet United	46	19	12	15	65	61	69
Salisbury City	46	18	14	14	70	60	68
Kidderminster Har's	46	19	10	17	74	57	67
York City	46	17	11	18	71	74	62
Crawley Town §6	46	19	9	18	73	67	60
Rushden & D'monds	46	15	14	17	55	55	59
Woking	46	12	17	17	53	61	53
Weymouth	46	11	13	22	53	73	46
Northwich Victoria	46	11	11	24	52	78	44
Halifax Town §10	46	12	16	18	61	70	42
Altrincham	46	9	14	23	56	82	41
Farsley Celtic	46	10	9	27	48	86	39
Stafford Rangers	46	5	10	31	42	99	25
Droylsden	46	5	9	32	46	103	24

11/08/2007 - 26/04/2008 • ‡ Qualified for the play-offs • § = points deducted • Top scorers: Fleetwood, Forest Green 27; Morison, Stevenage 22
Play-off semi-finals: **Exeter City** 1-2 4-1 Torquay United; Burton Albion 2-2 1-2 **Cambridge United**
Play-off final: Exeter City 1-0 Cambridge United (Wembley, 18-05-2008, Att: 42 511. Scorer - Edwards [22])

ENGLAND 2007–08 BLUE SQUARE NORTH (6)

	Pl	W	D	L	F	A	Pts
Kettering Town	42	30	7	5	93	34	97
AFC Telford ‡	42	24	8	10	70	43	80
Stalybridge Celtic ‡	42	25	4	13	88	51	79
Southport ‡	42	22	11	9	77	50	77
Barrow ‡	42	21	13	8	70	39	76
Harrogate Town	42	21	11	10	55	41	74
Nuneaton Borough	42	19	14	9	58	40	71
Burscough	42	19	8	15	62	58	65
Hyde United	42	20	3	19	84	66	63
Boston United	42	17	8	17	65	57	59
Gainsborough Tr'ty	42	15	12	15	62	65	57
Worcester City	42	14	12	16	48	68	54
Redditch United	42	15	8	19	41	58	53
Workington	42	13	11	18	52	56	50
Tamworth	42	13	11	18	53	59	50
Alfreton Town	42	12	11	19	49	54	47
Solihull Moors	42	12	11	19	56	76	47
Blyth Spartans	42	12	10	20	52	62	46
Hinckley	42	11	12	19	48	69	45
Hucknall Town	42	11	6	25	53	75	39
Vauxhall Motors	42	7	7	28	42	100	28
Leigh RMI	42	6	8	28	36	87	26

11/08/2007 - 26/04/2008 • ‡ Qualified for the play-offs
Play-off semis: Telford 0-2 0-2 **Barrow**;
Stalybridge 2-1 0-1 5-3p Southport
Play-off final: Barrow 1-0 Stalybridge

ENGLAND 2007–08 BLUE SQUARE SOUTH (6)

	Pl	W	D	L	F	A	Pts
Lewes	42	27	8	7	81	39	89
Eastbourne Boro ‡	42	23	11	8	83	38	80
Hampton & Rich'd ‡	42	21	14	7	87	49	77
Fisher Athletic ‡	42	22	5	15	65	61	71
Braintree Town ‡	42	19	12	11	52	42	69
Eastleigh	42	19	10	13	76	62	67
Havant & Wat'ville	42	19	10	13	59	53	67
Bath City	42	17	15	10	59	36	66
Newport County	42	18	12	12	64	49	66
Bishops Stortford	42	18	10	14	72	60	64
Bromley	42	19	7	16	77	66	64
Thurrock	42	18	9	15	63	64	63
Hayes & Yeading	42	14	13	15	68	72	55
Cambridge City	42	14	10	18	71	72	52
Basingstoke Town	42	12	14	16	54	75	50
Welling United	42	13	7	22	41	64	46
Maidenhead United	42	11	12	19	56	59	45
Bognor Regis Town	42	10	12	20	48	68	42
St Albans City	42	10	12	20	43	69	42
Weston-Super-Mare	42	9	10	23	52	85	37
Dorchester Town	42	8	10	24	36	70	34
Sutton United	42	5	9	28	32	86	24

11/08/2007 - 26/04/2008 • ‡ Qualified for the play-offs
Play-off semis: Eastbourne Borough 2-0 3-0 Braintree;
Fisher Athletic 1-1 0-0 2-4p **Hampton & Richmond**
Play-off final: Eastbourne Boro 2-0 Hampton & Richmond

ENGLAND 2007–08 RYMAN PREMIER (7)

	Pl	W	D	L	F	A	Pts
Chelmsford City	42	26	9	7	84	39	87
Staines Town ‡	42	22	12	8	85	54	78
AFC Wimbledon ‡	42	22	9	11	81	47	75
AFC Hornchurch ‡	42	20	10	12	68	44	70
Ramsgate ‡	42	19	11	12	67	53	68
Ashford Town	42	20	6	16	79	65	66
Hendon	42	18	11	13	79	67	65
Tonbridge Angels	42	17	12	13	77	57	63
Margate	42	17	11	14	71	68	62
Billericay Town	42	16	12	14	60	50	60
Horsham	42	18	5	19	63	63	59
Heybridge Swifts	42	14	13	15	64	64	55
Wealdstone	42	15	9	18	68	75	54
Hastings United	42	15	8	19	58	67	53
Harlow Town	42	13	13	16	56	52	52
Harrow Borough	42	15	7	20	61	74	52
Maidstone United	42	16	4	22	56	79	52
Carshalton Ath	42	14	8	20	52	65	50
Boreham Wood	42	15	5	22	56	73	50
East Thurrock Utd	42	14	9	19	48	67	50
Folkestone Inv'ta	42	13	10	19	49	70	49
Leyton	42	4	4	34	35	123	16

18/08/2007 - 26/04/2008 • ‡ Play-offs
Play-off semis: Wimbledon 3-1 Hornchurch;
Staines 2-1 Ramsgate
Play-off final: Staines 1-2 **Wimbledon**

ENGLAND 2007–08 BRITISH GAS PREMIER (7)

	Pl	W	D	L	F	A	Pts
Kings Lynn	42	24	13	5	91	36	85
Team Bath ‡	42	25	8	9	71	41	83
Halesowen T ‡	42	22	13	7	80	46	79
Chippenham T ‡	42	20	13	9	73	44	73
Bashley ‡	42	19	12	11	60	46	69
Gloucester City	42	19	11	12	81	50	68
Hemel Hempstead	42	19	11	12	67	50	68
Brackley Town	42	16	12	14	57	53	60
Banbury United	42	14	16	12	55	57	58
Yate Town	42	16	10	16	71	76	58
Clevedon Town	42	13	18	11	49	46	57
Swindon S'marine	42	14	12	16	51	67	54
Merthyr Tydfil	42	13	14	15	65	70	53
Mangotsfield Utd	42	12	16	14	38	42	52
Rugby Town	42	13	12	17	55	66	51
Corby Town	42	14	8	20	60	67	50
Tiverton Town	42	13	11	18	45	60	50
Hitchin Town	42	12	11	19	46	61	47
Bedford Town	42	12	9	21	54	73	45
Bromsgrove Rov	42	10	12	20	46	67	42
Cirencester Town	42	8	8	26	44	80	32
Cheshunt	42	5	8	29	42	103	23

18/08/2007 - 26/04/2008 • ‡ Play-offs
Play-off semis: Team Bath 4-1 Bashley;
Halesowen 2-1 Chippenham
Play-off final: Team Bath 2-1 Halesowen

ENGLAND 2007–08 UNIBOND PREMIER (7)

	Pl	W	D	L	F	A	Pts
Fleetwood Town	40	28	7	5	81	39	91
Witton Albion ‡	40	27	8	5	84	28	89
Gateshead ‡	40	26	7	7	93	42	85
Eastwood Town ‡	40	20	9	11	61	45	69
Buxton ‡	40	20	8	12	60	50	68
Guiseley	40	19	10	11	65	43	67
Marine	40	19	4	17	70	65	61
Hednesford Town	40	15	8	17	62	65	53
Worksop Town	40	13	12	15	59	62	51
Ashton United	40	11	15	14	63	73	48
Kendal Town	40	12	11	17	61	70	47
Whitby Town	40	13	7	20	68	75	46
Prescot Cables	40	13	8	19	48	62	46
Frickley Athletic	40	11	13	16	50	68	46
North Ferriby Utd	40	13	7	20	53	76	46
Matlock Town	40	12	9	19	55	68	45
Ilkeston Town	40	10	14	16	64	72	44
Ossett Town	40	12	8	20	48	60	44
Leek Town	40	11	11	18	54	68	44
Stamford	40	11	10	19	59	86	43
Lincoln United	40	7	8	25	44	85	29

18/08/2007 - 26/04/2008 • ‡ Play-offs
Play-off semis: Gateshead 4-0 Eastwood;
Witton 1-1 5-6p **Buxton**
Play-off final: Gateshead 2-0 Buxton

FA CUP (SPONSORED BY E.ON) 2007–08

Third Round			Fourth Round		Fifth Round	
Portsmouth	1					
Ipswich Town *	0		Portsmouth *	2		
Hull City	2		Plymouth Argyle	1		
Plymouth Argyle *	3				Portsmouth	1
Derby County *	2 1 4p				Preston North End *	0
Sheffield Wednesday	2 1 2p		Derby County *	1		
Scunthorpe United	0		Preston North End	4		
Preston North End *	1					
Arsenal	2					
Burnley *	0		Arsenal *	3		
Stoke City *	0 1		Newcastle United	0		
Newcastle United	0 4				Arsenal	0
Tottenham Hotspur *	2 1				Manchester United *	4
Reading	2 0		Tottenham Hotspur	1		
Aston Villa *	0		Manchester United *	3		
Manchester United	2					
Bristol Rovers	2 0 5p		Bristol Rovers	1		
Fulham *	2 0 3p		Barnet *	0		
Swindon Town *	1 1 0p				Bristol Rovers *	1
Barnet	1 1 2p				Southampton	0
Bury	1 2					
Norwich City *	1 1		Bury	0		
Leicester City	0		Southampton *	2		
Southampton *	2					
Coventry City	4					
Blackburn Rovers *	1		Coventry City *	2		
Walsall *	0 1		Millwall	1		
Millwall	0 2				Coventry City *	0
Peterborough United	3				West Bromwich Albion	5
Colchester United *	1		Peterborough United *	0		
Charlton Athletic *	1 2 3p		West Bromwich Albion	3		
West Bromwich Albion	1 2 4p					
Barnsley *	2					
Blackpool	1		Barnsley	1		
Dagenham & Redbridge	2		Southend United *	0		
Southend United *	5				Barnsley	2
Havant & Waterlooville	1 4				Liverpool *	1
Swansea City *	1 2		Havant & Waterlooville	2		
Luton Town *	1 0		Liverpool *	5		
Liverpool	1 5					
Huddersfield Town *	2					
Birmingham City	1		Huddersfield Town	1		
Everton *	0		Oldham Athletic *	0		
Oldham Athletic	1				Huddersfield Town	1
Wigan Athletic	3				Chelsea *	3
Sunderland *	0		Wigan Athletic *	1		
Queens Park Rangers	0		Chelsea	2		
Chelsea *	1					
Middlesbrough	2					
Bristol City *	1		Middlesbrough	2		
Brighton & Hove Albion *	1		Mansfield Town *	0		
Mansfield Town	2				Middlesbrough	0 1
Manchester City	0 1				Sheffield United *	0 0
West Ham United *	0 0		Manchester City	1		
Bolton Wanderers *	0		Sheffield United *	2		
Sheffield United	1					
Wolverhampton Wanderers *	2					
Cambridge United	1		Wolverhampton Wanderers	4		
Crystal Palace	0		Watford *	1		
Watford *	2				Wolverhampton Wanderers	0
Hereford United	2 1				Cardiff City *	2
Tranmere Rovers *	2 0		Hereford United *	1		
Chasetown *	1		Cardiff City	2		
Cardiff City	3					

* Home team

FA CUP (SPONSORED BY E.ON) 2007–08

Quarter–finals **Semi–finals** **Final**

| Portsmouth | 1 |
| Manchester United * | 0 |

| Portsmouth | 1 |
| West Bromwich Albion | 0 |

| Bristol Rovers * | 1 |
| **West Bromwich Albion** | 5 |

| Portsmouth | 1 |
| Cardiff City | 0 |

| **Barnsley** * | 0 |
| Chelsea | 1 |

| Barnsley | 0 |
| **Cardiff City** | 1 |

FA CUP FINAL 2008

Wembley Stadium, London, 17-05-2008, 15:00, Att 89 874, Ref: Dean

| Portsmouth | 1 | Kanu |
| Cardiff City | 0 | |

| Middlesbrough * | 0 |
| **Cardiff City** | 2 |

Portsmouth - David James - Glen Johnson, Sol Campbell, Sylvain Distin, Hermann Hreidarsson●, John Utaka (David Nugent 69), Miguel Pedro Mendes (Papa Bouba Diop 78), Lassana Diarra●, Sulley Muntari, Niko Kranjcar●, Nwankwo Kanu (Milan Baros 87). Tr: Harry Redknapp
Cardiff - Peter Enckelman - Kevin McNaughton, Roger Johnson, Glenn Loovens, Tony Capaldi, Joe Ledley, Gavin Rae (Trevor Sinclair 86), Stephen McPhail, Peter Whittingham (Aaron Ramsey 61), Paul Parry, Jimmy Floyd Hasselbaink (Steven Thompson 70). Tr: David Jones

‡ Qualified for the UEFA Cup
Semi-finals played at Wembley Stadium, London

CARLING LEAGUE CUP 2007–08

Second Round		Third Round		Fourth Round	
Tottenham Hotspur	Bye				
		Tottenham Hotspur *	2		
Northampton Town	0	Middlesbrough	0		
Middlesbrough *	2			Tottenham Hotspur *	2
Southend United *	2			Blackpool	0
Watford	0	Southend United	1		
Derby County *	2 6p	Blackpool *	2		
Blackpool	2 7p				
Bolton Wanderers	Bye				
		Bolton Wanderers	2		
Shrewsbury Town *	0	Fulham *	1		
Fulham	1			Bolton Wanderers *	0
Norwich City	1 4p			Manchester City	1
Rochdale *	1 3p	Norwich City	0		
Bristol City *	1	Manchester City *	1		
Manchester City	2				
Blackburn Rovers	Bye				
		Blackburn Rovers *	3		
Hereford United	1	Birmingham City	0		
Birmingham City *	2			Blackburn Rovers	2
Burnley *	3			Portsmouth *	1
Oldham Athletic	0	Burnley *	0		
Leeds United	0	Portsmouth	1		
Portsmouth *	3				
Sheffield United	3				
Milton Keynes Dons *	2	Sheffield United *	5		
Wolverhampton Wanderers *	1	Morecambe	0		
Morecambe	3			Sheffield United *	0
Newcastle United *	2			Arsenal	3
Barnsley	0	Newcastle United	0		
		Arsenal *	2		
Arsenal	Bye				
Everton	Bye				
		Everton	3		
Hartlepool United	1	Sheffield Wednesday *	0		
Sheffield Wednesday *	2			Everton	1
Charlton Athletic *	4			Luton Town *	0
Stockport County	3	Charlton Athletic	1		
Sunderland	0	Luton Town *	3		
Luton Town *	3				
Coventry City	2				
Carlisle United *	0	Coventry City	2		
		Manchester United *	0		
Manchester United	Bye				
Plymouth Argyle *	2			Coventry City *	1
Doncaster Rovers	0	Plymouth Argyle	0	West Ham United	2
Bristol Rovers *	1	West Ham United *	1		
West Ham United	2				
Liverpool	Bye				
		Liverpool	4		
Swansea City *	0	Reading *	2		
Reading	1			Liverpool *	2
West Bromwich Albion	2			Cardiff City	1
Peterborough United *	0	West Bromwich Albion *	2		
Leyton Orient	0	Cardiff City	4		
Cardiff City *	1				
Leicester City	3				
Nottingham Forest *	2	Leicester City	1		
Wrexham *	0	Aston Villa *	0		
Aston Villa	5			Leicester City	3
Hull City	1			Chelsea *	4
Wigan Athletic *	0	Hull City *	0		
		Chelsea	4		
Chelsea	Bye				

* Home team/Home team in the first leg

CARLING LEAGUE CUP 2007–08

Quarter–finals		Semi–finals			Final	

Tottenham Hotspur	2
Manchester City *	0

Tottenham Hotspur	1	5
Arsenal *	1	1

Blackburn Rovers *	2
Arsenal	3

Tottenham Hotspur ‡	2
Chelsea	1

Everton	2
West Ham United *	1

Everton	1	0
Chelsea *	2	1

Liverpool	0
Chelsea *	2

CARLING LEAGUE CUP FINAL 2008

Wembley Stadium, London, 24-02-2008, Att: 87 660, Ref: Mark Halsey

Tottenham Hotspur	2	Berbatov [70], Woodgate [94]
Chelsea	1	Drogba [39]

Tottenham - Paul Robinson - Alan Hutton, Jonathan Woodgate, Ledley King, Pascal Chimbonda (Tom Huddlestone 61) - Aaron Lennon•, Jermaine Jenas•, Didier Zokora•, Steed Malbranque (Teemu Tainio• 75) - Dimitar Berbatov, Robbie Keane (Younes Kaboul 102). Tr: Juande Ramos
Chelsea - Petr Cech - Juliano Belletti, Ricardo Carvalho•, John Terry, Wayne Bridge - Shaun Wright-Phillips (Salomon Kalou 72), Michael Essien (Michael Ballack 88), Frank Lampard, John Obi Mikel• (Joe Cole 98) - Nicolas Anelka, Didier Drogba. Tr: Avram Grant

‡ Qualified for the UEFA Cup

JOHNSTONE'S PAINT FOOTBALL LEAGUE TROPHY 2007-08

Second Round

Milton Keynes Dons *	3
Peterborough United	1
Bristol Rovers *	0
Bournemouth	1
Dagenham & Redbridge	1
Leyton Orient *	0
Luton Town	3
Gillingham *	4
Brighton & Hove Albion *	2
Barnet	1
Swindon Town *	1
Cheltenham Town	3
Yeovil Town	0 4p
Hereford United *	0 2p
Wycombe Wanderers	0
Swansea City *	2
Morecambe *	2 4p
Port Vale	2 2p
Lincoln City *	2
Hartlepool United	5
Leeds United	1
Darlington *	0
Rochdale *	1
Bury	3
Stockport County	1
Macclesfield Town *	0
Chester City	2
Carlisle United *	4
Doncaster Rovers *	3
Oldham Athletic	0
Rotherham United *	1 2p
Grimsby Town	1 4p

Third Round

Milton Keynes Dons	2
Bournemouth *	0
Dagenham & Redbridge	0
Gillingham *	4
Brighton & Hove Albion *	4
Cheltenham Town	1
Yeovil Town	0
Swansea City *	1
Morecambe	1 4p
Hartlepool United *	1 2p
Leeds United *	1
Bury	2
Stockport County	3
Carlisle United *	0
Doncaster Rovers	2 4p
Grimsby Town *	2 5p

Quarter-finals (regional semi-finals)

Milton Keynes Dons	1 5p
Gillingham *	1 4p
Brighton & Hove Albion	0
Swansea City *	1
Morecambe *	2
Bury	0
Stockport County *	1
Grimsby Town	2

Semi-finals (regional finals)

Milton Keynes Dons	1 0 5p
Swansea City *	0 1 4p
Morecambe *	0 0
Grimsby Town	1 0

Final

Milton Keynes Dons	2
Grimsby Town	0

* Home team/home team in the first leg

TROPHY FINAL

Wembley, London
30-03-2008, Att: 56 618. Ref: Joslin
Scorers - Andrews 74, O'Hanlon 81

MK Dons - Gueret - Stirling, O'Hanlon, Swailes, Lewington, Andrews, Navarro, Dyer, Cameron (Baldock 90), Johnson (Wright 77), Gallen (Wilbraham 77). Tr: Paul Ince

Grimsby - Barnes - Clarke, Atkinson, Fenton, Newey, Hegarty, Hunt (Toner 79), Bolland, Boshell, Till (Jones 61), North (Bore 46).
Tr: Alan Buckley

ARSENAL 2007-08

	Date	Opponent	Res	Score	Comp	Scorers	Att
Aug	12	Fulham	W	2-1	PL	Van Persie 84p, Hleb 90	60 093
	15	Sparta P'ha	W	2-0	CLp3	Fabregas 72, Hleb 92+	19 586
	19	Blackburn	D	1-1	PL	Van Persie 18	24 917
	25	Man City	W	1-0	PL	Fabregas 80	60 114
	29	Sparta P'ha	W	3-0	CLp3	Rosicky 7, Fabregas 88, Eduardo 89	58 462
Sep	2	Portsmouth	W	3-1	PL	Adebayor 7p, Fabregas 34, Rosicky 58	60 114
	15	Tottenham	W	3-1	PL	Adebayor 2 65 90, Fabregas 80	36 053
	19	Sevilla	W	3-0	CLgH	Fabregas 27, Van Persie 59, Eduardo 92+	59 992
	22	Derby	W	5-0	PL	Diaby 9, Adebayor 3 25 49p 78, Fabregas 69	60 122
	25	Newcastle	W	2-0	LCr3	Bendtner 83, Denilson 89	60 004
	29	West Ham	W	1-0	PL	Van Persie 12	34 966
Oct	2	Steaua B'st	W	1-0	CLgH	Van Persie 76	12 807
	7	Sunderland	W	3-2	PL	Van Persie 2 7 80, Senderos 13	60 098
	20	Bolton	W	2-0	PL	Toure 67, Rosicky 80	59 442
	23	Slavia P'ha	W	7-0	CLgH	Fabregas 2 5 58, Walcott 2 41 55, OG 24, Hleb 51, Bendtner 89	59 621
	28	Liverpool	D	1-1	PL	Fabregas 79	44 122
	31	Sheff Utd	W	3-0	LCr4	Eduardo 2 8 50, Denilson 69	16 971
Nov	3	Man Utd	D	2-2	PL	Fabregas 47, Gallas 90	60 161
	7	Slavia P'ha	D	0-0	CLgH		18 000
	10	Reading	W	3-1	PL	Flamini 44, Adebayor 52, Hleb 19	24 024
	24	Wigan	W	2-0	PL	Gallas 83, Rosicky 85	60 126
	27	Sevilla	L	1-3	CLgA	Eduardo 11	35 529
Dec	1	Aston Villa	W	2-1	PL	Flamini 23, Adebayor 35	42 018
	5	Newcastle	D	1-1	PL	Adebayor 3	50 305
	9	Midd'boro	L	1-2	PL	Rosicky 90	26 428
	12	Steaua B'st	W	2-1	CLgH	Diaby 8, Bendtner 42	59 786
	16	Chelsea	W	1-0	PL	Gallas 45	60 139
	18	Blackburn	W	3-2	LCqf	Diaby 6, Eduardo 2 29 104	16 207
	22	Tottenham	W	2-1	PL	Adebayor 47, Bendtner 75	60 087
	26	Portsmouth	D	0-0	PL		20 556
	29	Everton	W	4-1	PL	Eduardo 2 46 58, Adebayor 78, Rosicky 90	39 443
Jan	1	West Ham	W	2-0	PL	Eduardo 1, Adebayor 18	60 102
	6	Burnley	W	2-0	FAr3	Eduardo 8, Bendtner 74	16 709
	9	Tottenham	D	1-1	LCsf	Walcott 79	53 136
	12	B'ham City	D	1-1	PL	Adebayor 20p	60 037
	19	Fulham	W	3-0	PL	Adebayor 2 19 38, Rosicky 81	25 297
	22	Tottenham	L	1-5	LCsf	Adebayor 70	35 979
	26	Newcastle	W		FAr4	Adebayor 2 50 82, Butt OG 88	60 064
	29	Newcastle	W	3-0	PL	Adebayor 40, Flamini 72, Fabregas 79	60 127
Feb	2	Man City	W	3-1	PL	Adebayor 2 9 88, Eduardo 25	46 426
	11	Blackburn	W	2-0	PL	Senderos 4, Adebayor 90	60 049
	16	Man Utd	L	0-4	FAr5		75 550
	20	Milan	D	0-0	CLr2		60 082
	23	B'ham City	D	2-2	PL	Walcott 2 49 55	27 195
Mar	1	Aston Villa	D	1-1	PL	Bendtner 90	60 097
	4	Milan	W	2-0	CLr2	Fabregas 84, Adebayor 92+	81 879
	9	Wigan	D	0-0	PL		19 676
	15	Midd'boro	D	1-1	PL	Toure 86	60 084
	23	Chelsea	L	1-2	PL	Sagna	41 824
	29	Bolton	W	3-2	PL	Gallas 63, Van Persie 69p, Samuel OG 90	22 431
Apr	2	Liverpool	D	1-1	CLqf	Adebayor 23	60 041
	5	Liverpool	D	1-1	PL	Bendtner 54	60 111
	8	Liverpool	L	2-4	CLqf	Diaby 13, Adebayor 84	41 985
	13	Man Utd	L	1-2	PL	Adebayor 48	75 985
	19	Reading	W	2-0	PL	Adebayor 30, Gilberto 38	60 109
	28	Derby	W	6-2	PL	Bendtner 25, Van Persie 39, Adebayor 3 59 80 90, Walcott 37	33 003
May	4	Everton	W	1-0	PL	Bendtner 77	60 123
	11	Sunderland	W	1-0	PL	Walcott 24	47 802

PL = FA Premier League (Barclays Premier League) • CL = UEFA Champions League • FA = FA Cup • LC = Carling League Cup
p3 = third preliminary round • gH = Group F • r2 = second round • r3 = third round • r4 = fourth round • r5 = fifth round • qf = quarter-final • sf = semi-final

ASTON VILLA 2007-08

	Date	Opponent	Res	Score	Scorers	Att
Aug	11	Liverpool	L	1-2	Barry 84p	42 640
	18	Newcastle	D	0-0		51 049
	25	Fulham	W	2-1	Knight OG 50, Maloney 90	36 638
Sept	2	Chelsea	W	2-0	Knight 46, Agbonlahor 88	37 714
	16	Man City	L	0-1		38 363
	23	Everton	W	2-0	Carew 13, Agbonlahor	38 237
Oct	1	Tottenham	D	4-4	Laursen 2 22 33, Agbonlahor 40, Gardner 59	36 094
	6	West Ham	W	1-0	Gardner 23	40 842
	20	Man Utd	L	1-4	Agbonlahor 13	42 640
	28	Bolton	D	1-1	Moore 57	18 413
Nov	3	Derby	W	2-0	Laursen 57, Young 61	40 938
	11	B'ham City	W	2-1	Ridgewell OG 10, Agbonlahor 86	26 539
	24	Midd'boro	W	3-0	Carew 45, Mellberg 48, Agbonlahor 58	23 900
	28	Blackburn	W	4-0	Carew 29, Barry 53p, Young 81, Harewood 89	20 254
Dec	1	Arsenal	L	1-2	Gardner 14	42 018
	8	Portsmouth	L	1-3	Barry 72p	35 790
	15	Sunderland	D	1-1	Maloney 73	43 248
	22	Man City	D	1-1	Carew 14	41 455
	26	Chelsea	D	4-4	Maloney 2 14 44, Laursen 72, Barry 92+	41 686
	29	Wigan	W	2-1	Davies 55, Agbonlahor 70	18 806
Jan	1	Tottenham	W	2-1	Mellberg 41, Laursen 85	41 609
	12	Reading	W	3-1	Carew 2 22 88, Laursen 55	38 288
	21	Liverpool	D	2-2	Harewood 69, Aurelio OG 72	42 590
	26	Blackburn	D	1-1	Young 73	39 602
Feb	3	Fulham	L	1-2	Hughes OG 69	24 760
	9	Newcastle	W	4-1	Bouma 48, Carew 3 51 72 90p	42 640
	24	Reading	W	2-1	Young 45, Harewood 83	23 889
Mar	4	Arsenal	D	1-1	Senderos OG 27	60 097
	12	Midd'boro	D	1-1	Barry 74p	39 874
	15	Portsmouth	L	0-2		20 388
	22	Sunderland	L	0-1		42 640
	29	Man Utd	L	0-4		75 932
Apr	5	Bolton	W	4-0	Barry 2 9 60, Agbonlahor 56, Harewood 85	37 773
	12	Derby	W	6-0	Young 25, Carew 26, Petrov 36, Barry 58, Agbonlahor 76, Harewood 90	33 036
	20	B'ham City	W	5-1	Young 2 28 63, Carew 2 42 53, Agbonlahor 78	42 584
	27	Everton	D	2-2	Agbonlahor 80, Carew 86	37 936
May	3	Wigan	L	0-2		42 640
	11	West Ham	D	2-2	Young 14, Barry 58	34 969

BIRMINGHAM CITY 2007-08

	Date	Opponent	Res	Score	Scorers	Att
Aug	12	Chelsea	L	2-3	Forssell 15, Kapo 36	41 590
	15	Sunderland	D	2-2	McShane OG 28, O'Connor 82	24 898
	18	West Ham	L	0-1		24 961
	25	Derby	W	2-1	Jerome 2 1 63	31 117
Sept	1	Midd'bro	L	0-2		22 920
	15	Bolton	W	1-0	Kapo 37	28 124
	22	Liverpool	D	0-0		44 215
	29	Man Utd	L	0-1		26 526
Oct	7	Blackburn	L	1-2	Jerome 68	19 316
	20	Man City	L	0-1		45 688
	27	Wigan	W	3-2	Kapo 2 26p 81, Ridgewell 67	27 661
Nov	3	Everton	L	1-3	Kapo 80	35 115
	11	Aston Villa	L	1-2	Forssell 62	26 539
	24	Portsmouth	L	0-2		22 089
Dec	2	Tottenham	W	3-2	McSheffrey 24p, Jerome 62, Larsson 92+	35 635
	8	Newcastle	L	1-2	Jerome 9	49 948
	15	Reading	D	1-1	Forssell 4	27 300
	22	Bolton	L	0-3		19 111
	26	Midd'boro	W	3-0	OG 22, Forssell 45, McSheffrey 94+p	24 094
	29	Fulham	D	1-1	Larsson 55	28 923
Jan	1	Man Utd	L	0-1		75 459
	12	Arsenal	D	1-1	O'Connor 48	60 037
	19	Chelsea	L	0-1		26 567
	29	Sunderland	L	0-2		37 674
Feb	2	Derby	D	1-1	Larsson 68	25 924
	9	West Ham	D	1-1	McFadden 16p	34 884
	23	Arsenal	D	2-2	McFadden 2 28 90p	27 195
Mar	1	Tottenham	W	4-1	Forssell 3 58 81, Larsson 55	26 055
	12	Portsmouth	L	2-4	Muamba 10, Larsson 40	20 138
	17	Newcastle	D	1-1	McFadden 33	25 777
	22	Reading	L	1-2	Zarate 64	24 085
	29	Man City	W	3-1	Zarate 2 40 54, McSheffrey 77p	22 962
Apr	5	Wigan	L	0-2		17 926
	12	Everton	D	1-1	Zarate 83	25 923
	20	Aston Villa	L	1-5	Forssell 67	42 584
	26	Liverpool	D	2-2	Forssell 34, Larsson 55	29 252
May	3	Fulham	L	0-2		25 308
	11	Blackburn	W	4-1	Murphy 31, Jerome 2 73 89, Muamba 90	26 668

BLACKBURN ROVERS 2007–08

	Date	Opponent		Score	Scorers	Att
Aug	11	Midd'boro	W	2-1	Santa Cruz 63, Derbyshire 79	25 058
	19	Arsenal	D	1-1	Dunn 72	24 917
	25	Everton	D	1-1	Santa Cruz 15	33 850
	2	Man City	W	1-0	McCarthy 13	26 881
Sept	15	Chelsea	D	0-0		41 062
	23	Portsmouth	L	0-1		19 506
	29	Sunderland	W	2-1	Bentley 53, Santa Cruz 55	41 252
	7	B'ham City	W	2-1	Bentley 15, McCarthy 56p	19 316
Oct	20	Reading	W	4-2	McCarthy 2 18 82p, S. Cruz 22, Kerimoglu 32	19 425
	28	Tottenham	W	2-1	McCarthy 60, Samba 93+	36 086
Nov	3	Liverpool	D	0-0		30 033
	11	Man Utd	L	0-2		75 710
	25	Fulham	D	2-2	Emerton 57, Warnock 79	22 826
	28	Aston Villa	L	0-4		20 254
Dec	1	Newcastle	W	3-1	Bentley 2 54 67, Kerimoglu 93+	27 477
	9	West Ham	L	0-1		20 870
	15	Wigan	L	3-5	Santa Cruz 3 45 50 61	16 489
	23	Chelsea	L	0-1		23 966
	27	Man City	D	2-2	Santa Cruz 2 28 84	42 112
	30	Derby	W	2-1	Santa Cruz 39, Bentley 42	30 048
	2	Sunderland	W	1-0	McCarthy 57p	23 212
Jan	13	Bolton	W	2-1	Samba 53, Roberts 90	18 315
	19	Midd'boro	L	0-1	Derbyshire 75	21 687
	26	Aston Villa	D	1-1	Santa Cruz 67	39 602
	2	Everton	D	0-0		27 946
Feb	11	Arsenal	L	0-2		60 049
	24	Bolton	W	4-1	McCarthy 2 25p 67p, Bentley 71, Pedersen 94+	23 995
Mar	1	Newcastle	W	1-0	Derbyshire 90	50 796
	8	Fulham	D	1-1	Pedersen 59	20 362
	15	West Ham	L	1-2	Santa Cruz 19	34 006
	22	Wigan	W	3-1	Santa Cruz 2 12 63, Roberts 45	23 541
	29	Reading	D	0-0		23 374
Apr	5	Tottenham	D	1-1	Pedersen 30	24 592
	13	Liverpool	L	1-3	Santa Cruz 92+	43 283
	19	Man Utd	L	0-1	Santa Cruz 21	30 316
	27	Portsmouth	W	1-0	Santa Cruz 74	18 722
May	3	Derby	W	3-1	Santa Cruz 2 45 77, Roberts 47	26 110
	11	B'ham City	L	1-4	Pedersen 48	26 668

BOLTON WANDERERS 2007–08

	Date	Opponent		Score	Scorers	Att
Aug	11	Newcastle	L	1-3	Anelka 50	25 414
	19	Fulham	L	1-2	Helguson 12	21 102
	18	Portsmouth	L	1-3	Anelka 12	17 108
	25	Reading	W	3-0	Speed 32, Anelka 55, Braaten 91+	20 023
	1	Everton	L	1-2	Anelka 55	22 064
Sept	5	B'ham City	L	0-1		28 124
	23	Tottenham	D	1-1	Campo 39	20 308
	29	Derby	D	1-1	Anelka 39	31 305
	7	Chelsea	L	0-1		20 059
Oct	20	Arsenal	L	0-2		59 442
	28	Aston Villa	D	1-1	Anelka 22	18 413
	4	West Ham	D	1-1	Nolan 93+	33 867
Nov	11	Midd'boro	D	0-0		17 634
	24	Man Utd	W	1-0	Anelka 11	25 028
	2	Liverpool	L	0-4		43 270
Dec	9	Wigan	W	4-1	OG 3, Nolan 37, Davies 70, Anelka 89	20 309
	15	Man City	L	2-4	Diouf 31, Nolan 40	40 506
	22	B'ham City	W	3-0	Diouf 72, Anelka 2 78 93+	19 111
	26	Everton	L	0-2		38 918
	29	Sunderland	L	1-3	Diouf 41	42 058
Jan	2	Derby	W	1-0	Giannakopoulos 91+	17 014
	13	Blackburn	L	1-2	Nolan 42	18 315
	19	Newcastle	D	0-0		52 250
	29	Fulham	D	0-0		17 732
Feb	2	Reading	W	2-0	Nolan 33, Helguson 58	21 893
	9	Portsmouth	L	0-1		18 544
	24	Blackburn	L	1-4	Davies 50	23 995
	2	Liverpool	L	1-3	Cohen 79	24 004
Mar	16	Wigan	L	0-1		17 055
	19	Man Utd	L	0-2		75 476
	22	Man City	D	0-0		22 633
	29	Arsenal	L	2-3	Taylor 2 14 43	22 431
	5	Aston Villa	L	0-4		37 773
Apr	12	West Ham	W	1-0	Davies 47	23 043
	19	Midd'boro	W	1-0	McCann 61	25 037
	26	Tottenham	D	1-1	Giannakopoulos 46	36 176
May	3	Sunderland	W	2-0	Diouf 42, Murphy OG 83	25 053
	11	Chelsea	D	1-1	Taylor 93+	41 755

CHELSEA 2007–08

	Date	Opponent		Score	Comp	Scorers	Att
Aug	5	Man Utd	D	1-1	CS	Malouda 44. L 0-3p	80 731
	12	B'ham City	W	3-2	PL	Pizarro 14, Malouda 30, Essien 49	41 590
	15	Reading	W	2-1	PL	Lampard 47, Drogba 50	24 031
	19	Liverpool	D	1-1	PL	Lampard 61	43 924
	25	Portsmouth	W	1-0	PL	Lampard 30	41 501
	2	Aston Villa	L	0-2	PL		37 714
Sept	15	Blackburn	D	0-0	PL		41 062
	18	Rosenborg	D	1-1	CLgB	Shevchenko 63	24 973
	23	Man Utd	L	0-2	PL		75 663
	26	Hull City	W	4-0	LCr3	Sinclair 37, Kalou 2 48 81, Sidwell 52	23 543
	29	Fulham	D	0-0	PL		41 837
	3	Valencia	W	2-1	CLgB	Cole.J 21, Drogba 71	34 935
	7	Bolton	W	1-0	PL	Kalou 60	20 059
Oct	20	Midd'boro	W	2-0	PL	Drogba 7, Alex 56	27 699
	24	Schalke	W	2-0	CLgB	Malouda 4, Drogba 47	40 910
	27	Man City	W	6-0	PL	Essien 17, Drogba 2 30 55, Cole.J 60, Kalou 75, Shevchenko 90	41 832
	31	Leicester	W	4-3	LCr4	Lampard 3 20 29 92+, Shevchenko 87	40 037
Nov	3	Wigan	W	2-0	PL	Lampard 10, Belletti 17	19 011
	6	Schalke	D	0-0	CLgB		53 951
	11	Everton	D	1-1	PL	Drogba 70	41 683
	24	Derby	W	2-0	PL	Kalou 16, W-Phillips 72	32 789
	28	Rosenborg	W	4-0	CLgB	Drogba 2 8 20, Alex 40, Cole.J 73	21 582
Dec	1	West Ham	W	1-0	PL	Cole.J 75	41 830
	8	Sunderland	W	2-0	PL	Shevchenko 22, Lampard 74	41 707
	12	Valencia	D	0-0	CLgB		41 139
	16	Arsenal	L	0-1	PL		60 139
	19	Liverpool	W	2-0	LCqf	Lampard 59, Shevchenko 91+	41 366
	23	Blackburn	W	1-0	PL	Cole.J 21	23 966
	26	Aston Villa	D	4-4	PL	Shevchenko 2 45 49, Alex 65, Ballack 87	41 686
	29	Newcastle	W	2-1	PL	Essien 28, Kalou 86	41 751
Jan	1	Fulham	W	2-1	PL	Kalou 53, Ballack 61p	25 357
	5	QPR	W	1-0	FAr3	Camp OG 27	41 289
	8	Everton	W	2-1	LCsf	W-Phillips 26, Lescott OG 93+	41 178
	12	Tottenham	W	2-0	PL	Belletti 18, W-Phillips 80	41 777
	16	B'ham City	W	1-0	PL	Pizarro 78	26 567
	23	Everton	L	0-1	LCsf	Cole.J 69	37 086
	26	Wigan	W	2-1	FAr4	Anelka 52, W-Phillips 81	14 166
	30	Reading	W	1-0	PL	Ballack 31	41 171
	2	Portsmouth	D	1-1	PL	Anelka 54	20 488
Feb	10	Liverpool	D	0-0	PL		41 788
	16	Hudd'field	W	3-1	FAr5	Lampard 2 17 59, Kalou 69	41 324
	19	Olympiacos	D	0-0	CLr2		31 302
	24	Tottenham	L	1-2	LCf	Drogba 39	87 660
Mar	1	West Ham	W	4-0	PL	Lampard 16p, Cole.J 19, Ballack 21, Cole.A 63	34 969
	5	Olympiacos	W	3-0	CLr2	Ballack 5, Lampard 25, Kalou 48	37 721
	8	Barnsley	L	0-1	FAqf		22 410
	12	Derby	W	6-1	PL	Lampard 4 27p 56 65 71, Kalou 42, Cole.J 63	39 447
	15	Sunderland	W	1-0	PL	Terry 9	44 679
	19	Tottenham	D	4-4	PL	Drogba 3, Essien 19, Cole.J 2 51 79	36 178
	23	Arsenal	W	2-1	PL	Drogba 2 74 80	41 824
	30	Midd'boro	W	1-0	PL	Carvalho 4	39 993
Apr	2	Fenerbahçe	L	1-2	CLqf	Deivid OG 13	49 055
	5	Man City	W	2-0	PL	Dunne OG 6, Kalou 52	42 594
	8	Fenerbahçe	W	2-0	CLqf	Ballack 4, Lampard 87	38 369
	14	Wigan	D	1-1	PL	Essien 54	40 487
	19	Everton	W	1-0	PL	Lescott 78	37 112
	22	Liverpool	D	1-1	CLsf	Riise OG 94+	42 180
	26	Man Utd	W	2-1	PL	Ballack 2 45 86	41 828
	30	Liverpool	W	3-2	CLsf	Drogba 2 33 105, Lampard 98p	38 900
May	5	Newcastle	W	2-0	PL	Ballack 59, Malouda 82	52 305
	11	Bolton	D	1-1	PL	Shevchenko 62	41 755
	21	Man Utd	D	1-1	CLf	Lampard 45	67 310

CS = Community Shield • PL = FA Premier League (Barclays Premier League) • CL = UEFA Champions League • FA = FA Cup • LC = Carling League Cup • gB = Group B • r2 = second round • r3 = third round • r4 = fourth round • r5 = fifth round • qf = quarter-final • sf = semi-final • f = final

DERBY COUNTY 2007–08

Month	Date	Opponent	Res	Score	Scorers	Att
Aug	11	Portsmouth	D	2-2	Oakley 5, Todd 84	32 176
	15	Man City	L	0-1		43 620
	18	Tottenham	L	0-4		35 600
	25	B'ham City	L	1-2	Oakley 51	31 117
Sept	1	Liverpool	L	0-6		44 076
	17	Newcastle	W	1-0	Miller 39	33 016
	22	Arsenal	L	0-5		60 122
	29	Bolton	D	1-1	Miller 19	31 503
Oct	7	Reading	L	0-1		23 091
	20	Fulham	D	0-0		22 576
	28	Everton	L	0-2		33 048
Nov	3	Aston Villa	L	0-2		40 938
	10	West Ham	L	0-5		32 440
	24	Chelsea	L	0-2		32 789
Dec	1	Sunderland	L	0-1		42 380
	8	Man Utd	L	1-4	Howard 76	75 725
	15	Midd'boro	L	0-1		32 676
	23	Newcastle	D	2-2	Barnes 6, Miller 52	51 386
	26	Liverpool	L	1-2	McEveley 67	33 029
	30	Blackburn	L	1-2	Oakley 27	30 048
Jan	2	Bolton	L	0-1		17 014
	12	Wigan	L	0-1		31 658
	19	Portsmouth	L	1-3	Nyatanga 4	19 401
	30	Man City	D	1-1	Sun OG 46	31 368
Feb	2	B'ham City	D	1-1	Villa 89	25 924
	9	Tottenham	L	0-3		33 058
	23	Wigan	L	0-2		20 176
Mar	1	Sunderland	D	0-0		33 058
	12	Chelsea	L	1-6	Jones 73	39 447
	15	Man Utd	L	0-1		33 072
	22	Midd'boro	L	0-1		25 649
	29	Fulham	D	2-2	Villa 2 10 80	33 034
Apr	6	Everton	L	0-1		36 017
	12	Aston Villa	L	0-6		33 036
	19	West Ham	L	1-2	Mears 65	34 612
	28	Arsenal	L	2-6	McEveley 31, Earnshaw 77	33 003
May	3	Blackburn	L	1-3	Miller 19	26 110
	11	Reading	L	0-4		33 087

EVERTON 2007–08

Month	Date	Opponent	Res	Score	Scorers	Att
Aug	11	Wigan	W	2-1	Osman 25, Anichebe 74	39 220
	14	Tottenham	W	3-1	Lescott 2, Osman 36, Stubbs 45	35 716
	18	Reading	L	0-1		22 813
	25	Blackburn	D	1-1	McFadden 77	33 850
Sept	1	Bolton	W	2-0	Yakubu 10, Lescott 89	22 064
	15	Man Utd	L	0-1		39 364
	23	Aston Villa	L	0-2		38 235
	30	Midd'boro	W	2-0	Lescott 6, Pienaar 57	31 885
Oct	7	Newcastle	L	2-3	Johnson 52, Given OG 90	50 152
	20	Liverpool	L	1-2	Hyypia OG 37	40 049
	28	Derby	W	2-0	Arteta 25, Yakubu 62	33 048
Nov	3	B'ham City	W	3-1	Yakubu 9, Carsley 90, Vaughan 90	35 155
	11	Chelsea	D	1-1	Cahill 89	41 683
	24	Sunderland	W	7-1	Yakubu 2 11 72, Cahill 2 16 61, Pienaar 42, Johnson 79, Osman 84	38 594
Dec	1	Portsmouth	D	0-0		20 102
	8	Fulham	W	3-0	Yakubu 3 50 60 78	32 743
	15	West Ham	W	2-0	Yakubu 45, Johnson 90	34 430
	23	Man Utd	L	1-2	Cahill 26	75 749
	26	Bolton	W	2-0	Neville 50, Cahill 69	38 918
	29	Arsenal	L	1-4	Cahill 18	39 443
Jan	1	Midd'boro	W	2-0	Johnson 66, McFadden 71	27 028
	12	Man City	W	1-0	Lescott 30	38 474
	20	Wigan	W	2-1	Johnson 38, Lescott 41	18 820
	30	Tottenham	D	0-0		35 840
Feb	2	Blackburn	D	0-0		27 946
	9	Reading	W	1-0	Jagielka 61	36 582
	25	Man City	W	2-0	Yakubu 29, Lescott 37	41 728
Mar	2	Portsmouth	W	3-1	Yakubu 2 1 80, Cahill 72	33 938
	9	Sunderland	W	1-0	Johnson 54	42 595
	16	Fulham	L	0-1		25 262
	22	West Ham	D	1-1	Yakubu 7	37 430
	30	Liverpool	L	0-1		44 295
Apr	6	Derby	W	1-0	Osman 55	36 017
	12	B'ham City	D	1-1	Lescott 77	25 923
	17	Chelsea	L	0-1		37 112
	27	Aston Villa	D	2-2	Neville 55, Yobo 83	37 936
May	4	Arsenal	L	0-1		60 123
	11	Newcastle	W	3-1	Yakubu 2 28 82p, Lescott 70	39 592

FULHAM 2007–08

Month	Date	Opponent	Res	Score	Scorers	Att
Aug	12	Arsenal	L	1-2	Healy 1	60 093
	15	Bolton	W	2-1	Healy 23, Smertin 26	21 102
	18	Midd'boro	L	1-2	McBride 16	20 948
	25	Aston Villa	L	1-2	Dempsey 6	36 638
Sept	1	Tottenham	D	3-3	Dempsey 42, Smertin 77, Kamara 90	24 007
	15	Wigan	D	1-1	Dempsey 11	16 975
	22	Man City	D	3-3	Davies 13, Bouazza 48, Murphy 75	24 674
	29	Chelsea	D	0-0		41 147
Oct	7	Portsmouth	L	0-2		20 774
	20	Derby	D	0-0		22 576
	27	Sunderland	D	1-1	Davies 32	39 392
Nov	3	Reading	W	3-1	Davies 18, Dempsey 72, Healy 91+	22 086
	10	Liverpool	L	0-2		43 057
	25	Blackburn	D	2-2	Murphy 51, Kamara 63	22 826
Dec	3	Man Utd	L	0-2		75 055
	8	Everton	L	0-3		32 743
	15	Newcastle	L	0-1		24 959
	22	Wigan	D	1-1	Dempsey 78	20 820
	26	Tottenham	L	1-5	Dempsey 60	36 077
	29	B'ham City	D	1-1	Bocanegra 8	28 923
Jan	1	Chelsea	L	1-2	Murphy 10	25 357
	12	West Ham	L	1-2	Davies 8	34 947
	19	Arsenal	L	0-3		25 297
	29	Bolton	D	0-0		17 732
Feb	2	Aston Villa	W	2-1	Davies 73, Bullard 86	24 760
	9	Midd'boro	L	0-1		26 885
	23	West Ham	L	0-1		25 280
Mar	1	Man Utd	L	0-3		25 314
	8	Blackburn	D	1-1	Bullard 89	20 362
	16	Everton	W	1-0	McBride 67	25 262
	22	Newcastle	L	0-2		52 293
	29	Derby	D	2-2	Kamara 24, Leacock OG 78	33 034
Apr	5	Sunderland	L	1-3	Healy 74	25 053
	12	Reading	W	2-0	McBride 24, Nevland 92+	24 112
	19	Liverpool	L	0-2		25 311
	26	Man City	W	3-2	Kamara 2 70 92+, Murphy 79	44 504
May	3	B'ham City	W	2-0	McBride 52, Nevland 87	25 380
	11	Portsmouth	W	1-0	Murphy 76	20 532

MANCHESTER CITY 2007–08

Month	Date	Opponent	Res	Score	Scorers	Att
Aug	11	West Ham	W	2-0	Bianchi 18, Geovanni 87	34 921
	15	Derby	W	1-0	Johnson 43	43 620
	19	Man Utd	W	1-0	Geovanni 31	44 955
	25	Arsenal	L	0-1		60 114
Sept	2	Blackburn	L	0-1		26 881
	16	Aston Villa	W	1-0	Johnson 48	38 363
	22	Fulham	D	3-3	Petrov 2 36 60, Mpenza 50	24 674
	29	Newcastle	W	3-1	Petrov 37, Mpenza 47, Elano 87	40 606
Oct	7	Midd'boro	W	3-1	Riggott OG 10, Elano 2 33 63	40 438
	20	B'ham City	W	1-0	Elano 36	45 688
	27	Chelsea	L	0-6		41 832
Nov	5	Sunderland	W	1-0	Ireland 66	40 038
	11	Portsmouth	D	0-0		19 529
	24	Reading	W	2-1	Petrov 11, Ireland 90	43 813
Dec	1	Wigan	D	1-1	Geovanni 1	18 614
	9	Tottenham	L	1-2	Bianchi 60	35 646
	15	Bolton	W	4-2	Bianchi 7, OG 48, Vassell 77, Etuhu 90	40 506
	22	Aston Villa	D	1-1	Bianchi 11	41 455
	27	Blackburn	D	2-2	Vassell 27, Nelson OG 30	42 112
	30	Liverpool	D	0-0		47 321
Jan	2	Newcastle	W	2-0	Elano 38, Fernandes 76	50 956
	12	Everton	L	0-1		38 474
	19	West Ham	D	1-1	Vassell 16	39 042
	29	Derby	D	1-1	Sturridge 63	31 368
Feb	2	Arsenal	L	1-3	Fernandes 27	46 426
	10	Man Utd	W	2-1	Vassell 24, Benjani 45	75 970
	25	Everton	L	0-2		41 728
Mar	1	Wigan	D	0-0		38 261
	8	Reading	L	0-2		24 062
	16	Tottenham	W	2-1	Ireland 59, Onuoha 71	40 180
	22	Bolton	D	0-0		22 633
	29	B'ham City	L	1-3	Elano 59p	22 962
Apr	5	Chelsea	L	0-2		42 594
	12	Sunderland	W	2-1	Elano 79p, Vassell 87	46 797
	20	Portsmouth	W	3-1	Vassell 11, Petrov 13, Benjani 74	40 205
	26	Fulham	L	2-3	Ireland 10, Benjani 21	43 634
May	4	Liverpool	L	0-1		43 074
	11	Midd'boro	L	1-8	Elano 87	27 613

LIVERPOOL 2007–08

Mth	Date	Opponent	Res	Comp	Scorers	Att
Aug	11	Aston Villa	W 2-1	PL	Laursen OG 30, Gerrard 87	42 640
	15	Toulouse	W 1-0	CLp3	Voronin 43	30 380
	19	Chelsea	D 1-1	PL	Torres 16	43 924
	25	Sunderland	W 2-0	PL	Sissoko 37, Voronin 87	45 645
	28	Toulouse	W 4-0	CLp3	Crouch 2 19, Hyypia 49, Kuyt 2 87 91+	43 118
Sep	1	Derby	W 6-0	PL	Alonso 2 26 69, Babel 45, Torres 2 56 77, Voronin 76	44 076
	15	Portsmouth	D 0-0	PL		20 388
	18	FC Porto	D 1-1	CLgA	Kuyt 17	41 208
	22	B'ham City	D 0-0	PL		44 215
	25	Reading	W 4-2	LCr3	Benayoun 23, Torres 3 50 72 86	23 563
	29	Wigan	W 1-0	PL	Benayoun 75	24 311
Oct	3	Marseille	L 0-1	CLgA		41 355
	7	Tottenham	D 2-2	PL	Voronin 12, Torres 90	43 986
	20	Everton	W 2-1	PL	Kuyt 2 54 90	40 049
	24	Besiktas	L 1-2	CLgA	Gerrard 85	25 837
	28	Arsenal	D 1-1	PL	Gerrard 7	44 122
	31	Cardiff City	W 2-1	LCr4	El Zhar 48, Gerrard 66	41 780
Nov	3	Blackburn	D 0-0	PL		30 043
	6	Besiktas	W 8-0	CLgA	Crouch 2 19 89, Benayoun 3 32 53 56, Gerrard 69, Babel 2 78 81	41 143
	10	Fulham	W 2-0	PL	Torres 81, Gerrard 85p	43 073
	24	Newcastle	W 3-0	PL	Gerrard 27, Kuyt 46, Babel 66	52 307
	28	FC Porto	W 4-1	CLgA	Torres 2 19 78, Gerrard 84p, Crouch 87	41 095
Dec	2	Bolton	W 4-0	PL	Hyypia 17, Torres 45, Gerrard 56, Babel 28	43 270
	8	Reading	L 1-3	PL	Gerrard 28	24 022
	11	Marseille	W 4-0	CLgA	Gerrard 4, Torres 11, Kuyt 48, Babel 91+	53 097
	16	Man Utd	L 0-1	PL		44 459
	19	Chelsea	L 0-2	LCqf		41 366
	22	Portsmouth	W 4-1	PL	Benayoun 13, OG 16, Torres 2 66 85	43 071
	26	Derby	W 2-1	PL	Torres 11, Gerrard 90	33 029
	30	Man City	D 0-0	PL		47 321
Jan	2	Wigan	D 1-1	PL	Torres 49	42 308
	6	Luton	D 1-1	FAr3	Crouch 73	10 226
	12	Midd'boro	D 1-1	PL	Torres 71	33 035
	15	Luton	W 5-0	FAr3	Babel 45, Gerrard 3 51 63 71, Hyypia 56	41 446
	21	Aston Villa	D 2-2	PL	Benayoun 19, Crouch 88	42 590
	26	Havant & W	W 5-2	FAr4	Lucas 26, Benayoun 3 43 55 58, Crouch 89	42 566
	30	West Ham	L 0-1	PL		34 977
Feb	2	Sunderland	W 3-0	PL	Crouch 57, Torres 69, Gerrard 89	43 244
	6	Chelsea	D 0-0	PL		41 788
	16	Barnsley	L 1-2	FAr5	Kuyt 31	42 449
	19	Inter	W 2-0	CLr2	Kuyt 85, Gerrard 90	41 999
	23	Midd'boro	W 3-2	PL	Torres 3 28 29 61	43 612
Mar	2	Bolton	W 3-1	PL	OG 10, Babel 60, Aurelio 75	24 004
	5	West Ham	W 4-0	PL	Torres 3 7 60 80, Gerrard 82	42 954
	8	Newcastle	W 3-0	PL	Pennant 43, Torres 45, Gerrard 50	44 031
	11	Inter	W 1-0	CLr2	Torres 64	78 923
	16	Reading	W 2-1	PL	Mascherano 19, Torres 48	43 524
	23	Man Utd	L 0-3	PL		76 000
	30	Everton	W 1-0	PL	Torres 7	44 295
Apr	2	Arsenal	D 1-1	CLqf	Kuyt 26	60 041
	5	Arsenal	D 1-1	PL	Crouch 41	60 111
	8	Arsenal	W 4-2	CLqf	Hyypia 30, Torres 69, Gerrard 85p, Babel 92+	41 985
	13	Blackburn	W 3-1	PL	Gerrard 60, Torres 82, Voronin 90	43 283
	19	Fulham	W 2-0	PL	Pennant 17, Crouch 70	25 311
	22	Chelsea	D 1-1	CLsf	Kuyt 43	42 180
	26	B'ham City	D 2-2	PL	Crouch 63, Jaidi OG 75	29 252
	30	Chelsea	L 2-3	CLsf	Torres 64, Babel 117	38 900
May	4	Man City	W 1-0	PL	Torres 58	43 074
	11	Tottenham	W 2-0	PL	Voronin 69, Torres 74	36 063

PL = FA Premier League (Barclays Premier League) • CL = UEFA Champions League • FA = FA Cup • LC = Carling League Cup gA = Group A • r2 = second round • r3 = third round • r4 = fourth round • r5 = fifth round • qf = quarter-final • sf = semi-final

MANCHESTER UNITED 2007–08

Mth	Date	Opponent	Res	Comp	Scorers	Att
Aug	5	Chelsea	D 1-1	CS	Giggs 35, W 3-0p	80 731
	12	Reading	D 0-0	PL		75 655
	15	Portsmouth	D 1-1	PL	Scholes 15	20 510
	19	Man City	L 0-1	PL		44 955
	26	Tottenham	W 1-0	PL	Nani 68	75 696
Sep	1	Sunderland	W 1-0	PL	Saha 71	75 648
	15	Everton	W 1-0	PL	Vidic 83	39 364
	19	Sporting CL	W 1-0	CLgF	Ronaldo 62	41 510
	23	Chelsea	W 2-0	PL	Tévez 45, Saha 89	75 633
	26	Coventry	L 0-2	LCr3		74 055
	29	B'ham City	W 1-0	PL	Ronaldo 51	26 526
Oct	2	Roma	W 1-0	CLgF	Rooney 70	73 652
	6	Wigan	W 4-0	PL	Tévez 54, Ronaldo 2 59 76, Rooney 82	75 300
	20	Aston Villa	W 4-1	PL	Rooney 2 36 44, Ferdinand 45, Giggs 75	42 640
	23	Dy'mo Kyiv	W 4-2	CLgF	Ferdinand 10, Rooney 18, Ronaldo 2 41 68p	42 000
	27	Midd'boro	W 4-1	PL	Nani 3, Rooney 33, Tévez 2 55 85	75 720
Nov	3	Arsenal	D 2-2	PL	Rooney 45, Ronaldo 82	60 161
	7	Dy'mo Kyiv	W 4-0	CLgF	Piqué 31, Tévez 37, Rooney 76, Ronaldo 88	75 017
	11	Blackburn	W 2-0	PL	Ronaldo 2 34 35	75 710
	24	Bolton	L 0-1	PL		25 028
	27	Sporting CL	W 2-1	CLgF	Tévez 61, Ronaldo 92+	74 162
Dec	3	Fulham	W 2-0	PL	Ronaldo 2 10 58	75 055
	8	Derby	W 4-1	PL	Giggs 40, Tévez 2 45 60, Ronaldo 90	75 725
	12	Roma	D 1-1	CLgF	Piqué 34	29 490
	16	Liverpool	W 1-0	PL	Tévez 43	44 459
	23	Everton	W 2-1	PL	Ronaldo 2 22 88p	75 749
	26	Sunderland	W 4-0	PL	Rooney 19, Saha 2 29 85p, Ronaldo 45	47 360
	29	West Ham	L 1-2	PL	Ronaldo 14	34 966
Jan	1	B'ham City	W 1-0	PL	Tévez 25	75 459
	5	Aston Villa	W 2-0	FAr3	Ronaldo 80, Rooney 88	33 630
	12	Newcastle	W 6-0	PL	Rooney 77, Ronaldo 3 49 70 88, Tévez 2 55 90, Ferdinand 85	75 965
	19	Reading	W 2-0	PL	Rooney 77, Ronaldo 90	24 135
	27	Tottenham	W 3-1	FAr4	Tévez 37, Ronaldo 2 68p 87	75 369
	30	Portsmouth	W 2-0	PL	Ronaldo 2 10 13	75 415
Feb	2	Tottenham	D 1-1	PL	Tévez 90	36 075
	10	Man City	L 1-2	PL	Carrick 90	75 970
	16	Arsenal	W 4-0	FAr5	Rooney 15, Fletcher 2 19 73, Nani 37	75 550
	19	Lyon	D 1-1	CLr2	Tévez 87	39 219
	23	Newcastle	W 5-1	PL	Rooney 2 25 80, Ronaldo 2 45 56, Saha 90	52 291
Mar	1	Fulham	W 3-0	PL	Hargreaves 15, Park 44, OG 72	25 314
	4	Lyon	W 1-0	CLr2	Ronaldo 41	75 520
	8	Portsmouth	L 0-1	FAqf		75 463
	15	Derby	W 1-0	PL	Ronaldo 76	33 072
	19	Bolton	W 2-0	PL	Ronaldo 2 9 20	75 476
	23	Liverpool	W 3-0	PL	Brown 34, Ronaldo 79, Nani 81	76 000
	29	Aston Villa	W 4-0	PL	Ronaldo 17, Tévez 33, Rooney 2 53 70	75 932
Apr	1	Roma	W 2-0	CLqf	Ronaldo 39, Rooney 66	60 931
	6	Midd'boro	D 2-2	PL	Ronaldo 10, Rooney 74	33 952
	9	Roma	W 1-0	CLqf	Tévez 70	74 423
	19	Arsenal	W 2-1	PL	Ronaldo 54p, Hargreaves 72	75 985
	23	Barcelona	D 0-0	CLsf		95 949
	26	Chelsea	L 1-2	PL	Rooney 57	41 828
	29	Barcelona	W 1-0	CLsf	Scholes 14	75 061
May	3	West Ham	W 4-1	PL	Ronaldo 2 3 24, Tévez 26, Carrick 59	76 013
	11	Wigan	W 2-0	PL	Ronaldo 33p, Giggs 80	25 133
	21	Chelsea	D 1-1	CLf	Ronaldo 26, W 6-5p	67 310

CS = Community Shield • PL = FA Premier League (Barclays Premier League) • CL = UEFA Champions League • FA = FA Cup • LC = Carling League Cup • gF = Group F • r2 = second round • r3 = third round • r4 = fourth round • r5 = fifth round • qf = quarter-final • sf = semi-final • f = final

MIDDLESBROUGH 2007–08

Month	Date	Opponent	Res	Score	Scorers	Att
Aug	11	Blackburn	L	1-2	Downing 30	25 058
Aug	15	Wigan	L	0-1		14 007
Aug	18	Fulham	W	2-1	Mido 55, Cattermole 88	20 948
Aug	26	Newcastle	D	2-2	Mido 28, Arca 80	28 875
Sept	1	B'ham City	W	2-0	Wheater 12, Downing 37	22 920
Sept	15	West Ham	L	0-3		34 351
Sept	22	Sunderland	D	2-2	Arca 15, Downing 67	30 675
Sept	30	Everton	L	0-2		31 855
Oct	7	Man City	L	1-3	Hutchinson 89	40 438
Oct	20	Chelsea	L	0-2		27 699
Oct	27	Man Utd	L	1-4	Aliadiere 6	75 720
Nov	3	Tottenham	D	1-1	Young 52	25 625
Nov	11	Bolton	D	0-0		17 624
Nov	24	Aston Villa	L	0-3		23 900
Dec	1	Reading	D	1-1	Sanli 83	22 262
Dec	9	Arsenal	W	2-1	Downing 4p, Sanli 74	26 428
Dec	15	Derby	W	1-0	Sanli 38	32 676
Dec	22	West Ham	L	1-2	Wheater 40	26 007
Dec	26	B'ham City	L	0-3		24 094
Dec	29	Portsmouth	W	1-0	Sanli 20	20 089
Jan	1	Everton	L	0-2		27 028
Jan	12	Liverpool	D	1-1	Boateng 26	33 035
Jan	19	Blackburn	D	1-1	Wheater 13	21 687
Jan	29	Wigan	W	1-0	Aliadiere 19	22 963
Feb	3	Newcastle	D	1-1	Huth 87	51 105
Feb	9	Fulham	W	1-0	Aliadiere 11	26 885
Feb	23	Liverpool	L	2-3	Sanli 9, Downing 83	43 612
Mar	1	Reading	L	0-1		23 273
Mar	12	Aston Villa	D	1-1	Downing 23	39 874
Mar	15	Arsenal	D	1-1	Aliadiere 25	60 084
Mar	22	Derby	W	1-0	Sanli 32	25 649
Mar	30	Chelsea	L	0-1		39 993
Apr	6	Man Utd	D	2-2	Alves 2 35 56	33 952
Apr	12	Tottenham	D	1-1	Downing 69	36 092
Apr	19	Bolton	L	0-1		25 037
Apr	26	Sunderland	L	2-3	Sanli 4, Alves 73	45 059
May	3	Portsmouth	W	2-0	Riggott 40, Sanli 53	24 828
May	11	Man City	W	8-1	Downing 2 16p 58, Alves 3 37 60 90, Johnson 70, Rochemback 80, Aliadiere 85	27 613

NEWCASTLE UNITED 2007–08

Month	Date	Opponent	Res	Score	Scorers	Att
Aug	11	Bolton	W	3-1	N'Zogbia 11, Martins 2 21 27	25 414
Aug	18	Aston Villa	D	0-0		51 049
Aug	26	Midd'boro	D	2-2	N'Zogbia 22, Viduka 77	28 875
Sept	1	Wigan	W	1-0	Owen 87	50 461
Sept	17	Derby	L	0-1		33 016
Sept	23	West Ham	W	3-1	Viduka 2 2 41, N'Zogbia 76	50 104
Sept	29	Man City	L	1-3	Martins 29	40 606
Oct	7	Everton	W	3-2	Butt 42, Emre 86, Owen 90	50 152
Oct	22	Tottenham	W	3-1	Martins 45, Cacapa 51, Milner 73	51 411
Oct	27	Reading	L	1-2	Duberry OG 76	24 119
Nov	3	Portsmouth	L	1-4	Campbell OG 16	51 490
Nov	10	Sunderland	D	1-1	Milner 65	47 701
Nov	24	Liverpool	L	0-3		52 307
Dec	1	Blackburn	L	1-3	Martins 47	27 477
Dec	5	Arsenal	D	1-1	Taylor 60	50 305
Dec	8	B'ham City	W	2-1	Martins 37p, Beye 90	49 948
Dec	15	Fulham	W	1-0	Barton 92+	24 959
Dec	23	Derby	D	2-2	Viduka 2 27 87	51 386
Dec	26	Wigan	L	0-1		20 304
Dec	29	Chelsea	L	1-2	Butt 56	41 751
Jan	2	Man City	L	0-2		50 956
Jan	12	Man Utd	L	0-6		75 965
Jan	19	Bolton	D	0-0		52 250
Jan	29	Arsenal	L	0-3		60 127
Feb	3	Midd'boro	D	1-1	Owen 60	51 105
Feb	9	Aston Villa	L	1-4	Owen 4	42 640
Feb	23	Man Utd	L	1-5	Faye 79	52 291
Mar	1	Blackburn	L	0-1		50 796
Mar	8	Liverpool	L	0-3		44 031
Mar	17	B'ham City	D	1-1	Owen 56	25 777
Mar	22	Fulham	W	2-0	Viduka 6, Owen 83	52 293
Mar	30	Tottenham	W	4-1	Butt 45, Geremi 52, Owen 65, Martins 83	36 067
Apr	5	Reading	W	3-0	Martins 18, Owen 43, Viduka 58	52 179
Apr	12	Portsmouth	D	0-0		20 507
Apr	20	Sunderland	W	2-0	Owen 2 4 45p	52 305
Apr	26	West Ham	D	2-2	Martins 42, Geremi 45	34 980
May	5	Chelsea	L	0-2		52 305
May	11	Everton	L	1-3	Owen 47p	39 592

PORTSMOUTH 2007–08

Month	Date	Opponent	Res	Score	Comp	Scorers	Att
Aug	11	Derby	D	2-2	PL	Benjani 27, Utaka 82	32 176
Aug	15	Man Utd	D	1-1	PL	Benjani 53	20 510
Aug	18	Bolton	W	3-1	PL	Kanu 15, Utaka 30, Taylor 87p	17 108
Aug	25	Chelsea	L	0-1	PL		41 501
Aug	28	Leeds	W	3-0	LCr2	Pamarot 2 43 81, Nugent 85	8 502
Sept	2	Arsenal	L	1-3	PL	Kanu 60	60 114
Sept	15	Liverpool	D	0-0	PL		20 388
Sept	23	Blackburn	W	1-0	PL	Kanu 24	19 506
Sept	25	Burnley	W	1-0	LCr3	Nugent 69	8 202
Sept	29	Reading	W	7-4	PL	Benjani 3 6 37 70, Hreidarsson 55, Kranjcar 74, Davis 80, Muntari 90p	20 102
Oct	7	Fulham	W	2-0	PL	Benjani 49, Hreidarsson 52	20 774
Oct	20	Wigan	W	2-0	PL	Benjani 81, Johnson 85	17 695
Oct	27	West Ham	D	0-0	PL		20 525
Oct	31	Blackburn	L	1-2	LCr4	Kanu 90	11 788
Nov	3	Newcastle	W	4-1	PL	Pamarot 8, Benjani 9, Utaka 11, Kranjcar 76	51 490
Nov	11	Man City	D	0-0	PL		19 529
Nov	24	B'ham City	W	2-0	PL	Muntari 33, Kranjcar 82	22 089
Dec	1	Everton	D	0-0	PL		20 102
Dec	8	Aston Villa	W	3-1	PL	Gardner OG 10, Muntari 2 39 60	35 790
Dec	15	Tottenham	L	0-1	PL		20 520
Dec	22	Liverpool	L	1-4	PL	Benjani 56	43 071
Dec	26	Arsenal	D	0-0	PL		20 556
Dec	29	Midd'boro	L	0-1	PL		20 089
Jan	1	Reading	W	2-0	PL	Campbell 8, Utaka 66	24 084
Jan	5	Ipswich	W	1-0	FAr3	Nugent 50	23 436
Jan	13	Sunderland	L	0-2	PL		37 369
Jan	19	Derby	W	3-1	PL	Benjani 3 38 42 54	19 401
Jan	26	Plymouth	W	2-1	FAr4	Diarra 34, Kranjcar 44	19 512
Jan	30	Man Utd	L	0-2	PL		75 415
Feb	2	Chelsea	D	1-1	PL	Defoe 64	20 488
Feb	9	Bolton	W	1-0	PL	Diarra 80	18 544
Feb	17	Preston NE	W	1-0	FAr5	Carter OG 90	11 840
Feb	23	Sunderland	W	1-0	PL	Defoe 69p	20 139
Mar	2	Everton	L	1-3	PL	Defoe 37	33 938
Mar	8	Man Utd	W	1-0	FAqf	Muntari 77p	75 463
Mar	12	B'ham City	W	4-2	PL	Defoe 2 6p 8, Hreidarsson 48, Kanu 90	20 138
Mar	15	Aston Villa	W	2-0	PL	Defoe 11, Reo-Coker OG 38	20 388
Mar	22	Tottenham	L	0-2	PL		35 998
Mar	29	Wigan	W	2-0	PL	Defoe 2 31 90	18 623
Apr	5	West Brom	W	1-0	FAsf	Kanu 53	83 584
Apr	8	West Ham	W	1-0	PL	Kranjcar 61	33 629
Apr	12	Newcastle	D	0-0	PL		20 507
Apr	20	Man City	L	1-3	PL	Utaka 24	40 205
Apr	27	Blackburn	L	0-1	PL		18 722
May	3	Midd'boro	L	0-2	PL		24 828
May	11	Fulham	L	0-1	PL		20 532
May	17	Cardiff	W	1-0	FAf	Kanu 37	89 874

PL = FA Premier League (Barclays Premier League) • FA = FA Cup • LC = Carling League Cup • r2 = second round • r3 = third round • r4 = fourth round • r5 = fifth round • qf = quarter-final • sf = semi-final • f = final

READING 2007–08

Month	Date	Opponent	Res	Score	Scorers	Att
Aug	12	Man Utd	D	0-0		75 655
	15	Chelsea	L	1-2	Bikey 30	24 031
	18	Everton	W	1-0	Hunt 44	22 813
	25	Bolton	L	0-3		20 023
Sept	1	West Ham	L	0-3		23 533
	15	Sunderland	L	1-2	Kitson 85	39 272
	22	Wigan	W	2-1	Kitson 29, Harper 90	21 379
	29	Portsmouth	L	4-7	Rosenior 44, Kitson 48, Long 79, OG 90	20 102
Oct	7	Derby	W	1-0	Doyle 63	23 091
	20	Blackburn	L	2-4	Doyle 2 80 90	19 425
	27	Newcastle	W	2-1	Kitson 53, Long 84	24 119
Nov	3	Fulham	L	1-3	Doyle 54	22 086
	12	Arsenal	L	1-3	Shorey 87	24 024
	24	Man City	L	1-2	Harper 43	43 813
Dec	1	Midd'boro	D	1-1	Kitson 54	22 262
	8	Liverpool	W	3-1	Hunt 16p, Doyle 59, Harper 67	24 022
	15	B'ham City	D	1-1	Hunt 51p	27 300
	22	Sunderland	W	2-1	Ingimarsson 69, Hunt 90	24 082
	26	West Ham	D	1-1	Kitson 60	34 277
	29	Tottenham	L	4-6	Cisse 16, Ingimarsson 53, Kitson 2 69 74	36 178
Jan	1	Portsmouth	L	0-2		24 084
	12	Aston Villa	L	1-3	Harper 90	38 288
	19	Man Utd	L	0-2		24 135
	30	Chelsea	L	0-1		41 171
Feb	2	Bolton	L	0-2		21 893
	9	Everton	L	0-1		36 582
	24	Aston Villa	L	1-2	Shorey 90	23 889
Mar	1	Midd'boro	W	1-0	Harper 91+	23 273
	8	Man City	L	1-2	Long 61, Kitson 87	24 062
	15	Liverpool	L	1-2	Matejovsky 5	43 524
	22	B'ham City	W	2-1	Bikey 2 31 79	24 085
	29	Blackburn	D	0-0		23 374
Apr	5	Newcastle	L	0-3		52 179
	12	Fulham	L	0-2		24 112
	19	Arsenal	L	0-2		60 109
	26	Wigan	D	0-0		19 043
May	3	Tottenham	L	0-1		24 125
	11	Derby	W	4-0	Harper 15, Kitson 61, Doyle 69, Lita 90	

SUNDERLAND 2007–08

Month	Date	Opponent	Res	Score	Scorers	Att
Aug	11	Tottenham	W	1-0	Chopra 90	43 967
	15	B'ham City	D	2-2	Chopra 74, John 90	24 898
	18	Wigan	L	0-3		18 639
	25	Liverpool	L	0-2		45 645
Sept	1	Man Utd	L	0-1		75 648
	15	Reading	W	2-1	Jones 28, Wallace 46	39 272
	22	Midd'boro	D	2-2	Leadbitter 1, Miller 88	30 675
	29	Blackburn	L	1-2	Leadbitter 89	41 252
Oct	7	Arsenal	L	2-3	Wallace 24, Jones 47	60 098
	21	West Ham	D	1-1	Jones 51	34 913
	27	Fulham	L	1-3	Jones 85	39 392
Nov	5	Man City	L	0-1		40 038
	10	Newcastle	D	1-1	Higginbotham 51	47 701
	24	Everton	L	1-7	Yorke 45	38 594
Dec	1	Derby	W	1-0	Stokes 90	42 380
	8	Chelsea	L	0-1		41 707
	15	Aston Villa	D	1-1	Higginbotham 9	43 248
	22	Reading	L	1-2	Chopra 81p	24 082
	26	Man Utd	L	0-4		47 360
	29	Bolton	W	3-1	Richardson 12, Jones 31, Murphy 90	42 058
Jan	2	Blackburn	L	0-1		23 212
	12	Portsmouth	W	2-0	Richardson 2 32 43	37 369
	19	Tottenham	L	0-2		36 010
	29	B'ham City	W	2-0	Murphy 14, Prica 65	37 674
Feb	2	Liverpool	L	0-3		43 244
	9	Wigan	W	2-0	Etuhu 41, Murphy 74	43 600
	23	Portsmouth	L	0-1		20 139
Mar	1	Derby	D	0-0		33 058
	9	Everton	L	0-1		42 595
	15	Chelsea	L	0-1		44 679
	22	Aston Villa	W	1-0	Chopra 82	42 640
	29	West Ham	W	2-1	Jones 28, Reid 90	45 690
Apr	5	Fulham	W	3-1	Collins 44, Chopra 53, Jones 75	25 053
	12	Man City	L	1-2	Whitehead 81	46 797
	20	Newcastle	L	0-2		52 305
	26	Midd'boro	W	3-2	Higginbotham 5, Chopra 45, Pogatetz OG 90	45 059
May	3	Bolton	L	0-2		25 053
	11	Arsenal	L	0-1		47 802

TOTTENHAM HOTSPUR 2007–08

Month	Date	Opponent	Res	Score	Comp	Scorers	Att
Aug	11	Sunderland	L	0-1	PL		43 967
	14	Everton	L	1-3	PL	Gardner 26	35 716
	18	Derby	W	4-0	PL	Malbranque 2 1 6, Jenas 13, Bent 79	35 600
	26	Man Utd	L	0-1	PL		75 696
Sept	1	Fulham	D	3-3	PL	Kaboul 10, Berbatov 28, Bale 60	24 007
	15	Arsenal	L	1-3	PL	Bale 14	36 053
	20	Anorthosis	W	6-1	UCr1	Kaboul 5, Dawson 39, Keane 42, Bent 43, Defoe 2 65 91+	35 780
	23	Bolton	D	1-1	PL	Keane 33	20 308
	26	Midd'boro	W	2-0	LCr3	Bale 72, Huddlestone 75	32 280
Oct	1	Aston Villa	D	4-4	PL	Berbatov 19, Chimbonda 69, Keane 82p, Kaboul 90	36 094
	4	Anorthosis	D	1-1	UCr1	Keane 78	7 800
	7	Liverpool	D	2-2	PL	Keane 2 44 46	43 986
	22	Newcastle	L	1-3	PL	Keane 56	51 411
	25	Getafe	L	1-2	UCgG	Defoe 19	26 122
	28	Blackburn	L	1-2	PL	Keane 48p	36 086
	31	Blackpool	W	2-0	LCr4	Keane 18, Chimbonda 58	32 196
Nov	3	Midd'boro	D	1-1	PL	Bent 34	25 625
	8	Hapoel TA	W	2-0	UCgG	Keane 26, Berbatov 31	9 722
	11	Wigan	W	4-0	PL	Jenas 2 12 25, Lennon 34, Bent 71	35 504
	25	West Ham	D	1-1	PL	Dawson 66	34 966
	29	Aalborg	W	3-2	UCgG	Berbatov 46, Malbranque 51, Bent 66	29 758
Dec	2	B'ham City	L	2-3	PL	Keane 2 49p 52	35 635
	6	Anderlecht	D	1-1	UCgG	Berbatov 71p	19 753
	9	Man City	W	2-1	PL	Chimbonda 44, Defoe 82	35 646
	15	Portsmouth	W	1-0	PL	Berbatov 80	20 520
	18	Man City	W	2-0	LCqf	Defoe 5, Malbranque 82	38 564
	22	Arsenal	L	1-2	PL	Berbatov 65	60 087
	26	Fulham	W	5-1	PL	Keane 2 26 61, Huddlestone 2 45 70, Defoe 90	36 077
	29	Reading	W	6-4	PL	Berbatov 4 6 52 72 82, Malbranque 75, Defoe 78	36 118
Jan	1	Aston Villa	L	1-2	PL	Defoe 79	41 609
	5	Reading	D	2-2	FAr3	Keane 2 27 49p	35 243
	9	Arsenal	D	1-1	LCsf	Jenas 37	53 136
	12	Chelsea	L	0-2	PL		41 777
	15	Reading	W	1-0	FAr3	Keane 14	22 130
	19	Sunderland	W	2-0	PL	Lennon 2, Keane 90	36 070
	22	Arsenal	W	5-1	LCsf	Jenas 3, Bendtner OG 27, Keane 48, Lennon 60, Malbranque 90	35 979
	27	Man Utd	L	1-3	FAr4	Keane 23	75 369
	30	Everton	D	0-0	PL		35 840
Feb	2	Man Utd	D	1-1	PL	Berbatov 20	36 075
	9	Derby	W	3-0	PL	Keane 67, Kaboul 80, Berbatov 90p	33 058
	14	Slavia	W	2-1	UCr2	Berbatov 4, Keane 30	11 134
	21	Slavia	D	1-1	UCr2	O'Hara 7	34 224
	24	Chelsea	W	2-1	LCf	Berbatov 70, Woodgate 94	87 660
Mar	1	B'ham City	L	1-4	PL	Jenas 90	26 055
	6	PSV	L	0-1	UCr3		33 259
	9	West Ham	W	4-0	PL	Berbatov 2 8 10, Gilberto 85, Bent 90	36 062
	12	PSV	W	1-0	UCr3	Berbatov 81. L 5-6p	33 050
	16	Man City	L	1-2			40 188
	19	Chelsea	D	4-4	PL	Woodgate 11, Berbatov 60, Huddlestone 74, Keane 88	36 178
	22	Portsmouth	W	2-0	PL	Bent 80, O'Hara 81	35 998
	30	Newcastle	L	1-4	PL	Bent 25	36 067
Apr	5	Blackburn	D	1-1	PL	Berbatov 6	24 592
	13	Midd'boro	D	1-1	PL	Grounds OG 27	36 092
	19	Wigan	D	1-1	PL	Berbatov 5	18 673
	26	Bolton	D	1-1	PL	Malbranque 51	36 176
May	3	Reading	W	1-0	PL	Keane 15	24 125
	11	Liverpool	L	0-2	PL		36 063

PL = FA Premier League (Barclays Premier League) • UC = UEFA Cup • FA = FA Cup • LC = Carling League Cup • gF = Group F • r2 = second round • r3 = third round • r4 = fourth round • qf = quarter-final • sf = semi-final • f = final

WEST HAM UNITED 2007–08

	Date	Opponent	Res	Score	Scorers	Att
Aug	11	Man City	L	0-2		34 921
	18	B'ham City	W	1-0	Noble 70p	24 961
	25	Wigan	D	1-1	Bowyer 81	33 793
Sept	1	Reading	W	3-0	Bellamy 6, Etherington 2 49 94+	23 533
	15	Midd'boro	W	3-0	Bowyer 46, Young OG 51, Ashton 62	34 351
	23	Newcastle	L	1-3	Ashton 32	50 104
	29	Arsenal	L	0-1		34 966
Oct	6	Aston Villa	L	0-1		40 842
	21	Sunderland	W	3-1	Cole 9, Gordon OG 78, Bellamy 92+	34 913
	27	Portsmouth	D	0-0		20 525
Nov	4	Bolton	D	1-1	McCartney 20	33 867
	10	Derby	W	5-0	Bowyer 2 42 59, Etherington 51, Lewis OG 55, Solano 69	32 440
	25	Tottenham	D	1-1	Cole 20	34 966
Dec	1	Chelsea	L	0-1		41 830
	9	Blackburn	W	1-0	Ashton 52	20 870
	15	Everton	L	0-2		34 430
	22	Midd'boro	W	2-1	Ashton 44, Parker 90	26 007
	26	Reading	D	1-1	Solano 42	34 277
	29	Man Utd	W	2-1	Ferdinand 77, Upson 82	34 966
Jan	1	Arsenal	L	0-2		60 102
	12	Fulham	W	2-1	Ashton 28, Ferdinand 69	34 947
	20	Man City	D	1-1	Cole 8	39 042
	30	Liverpool	W	1-0	Noble 94+	34 977
Feb	2	Wigan	L	0-1		20 525
	9	B'ham City	D	1-1	Ljungberg 7	34 884
	23	Fulham	W	1-0	Solano 87	25 280
Mar	1	Chelsea	L	0-4		34 969
	5	Liverpool	L	0-4		42 954
	9	Tottenham	L	0-4		36 062
	15	Blackburn	W	2-1	Ashton 39, Sears 81	34 006
	22	Everton	D	1-1	Ashton 68	37 430
	29	Sunderland	L	1-2	Ljungberg 18	45 690
Apr	8	Portsmouth	L	0-1		33 629
	12	Bolton	L	0-1		23 043
	19	Derby	W	2-1	Zamora 20, Cole 77	34 612
	26	Newcastle	D	2-2	Noble 10, Ashton 23	34 980
May	3	Man Utd	L	1-4	Ashton 28	76 013
	11	Aston Villa	D	2-2	Solano 8, Ashton 88	34 969

WIGAN ATHLETIC 2007–08

	Date	Opponent	Res	Score	Scorers	Att
Aug	1	Everton	L	1-2	Sibierski 80	39 220
	15	Midd'boro	W	1-0	Sibierski 55	14 007
	18	Sunderland	W	3-0	Heskey 19, Landzaat 62p, Sibierski 69p	18 639
	25	West Ham	D	1-1	Scharner 78	33 793
Sept	1	Newcastle	L	0-1		50 461
	15	Fulham	D	1-1	Koumas 80p	16 973
	22	Reading	L	1-2	Bent 50	21 379
	29	Liverpool	L	0-1		24 311
Oct	6	Man Utd	L	0-4		75 300
	20	Portsmouth	L	0-2		17 695
	27	B'ham City	L	2-3	Bent 2 23 59	27 661
Nov	3	Chelsea	L	0-2		19 011
	11	Tottenham	L	0-4		35 504
	24	Arsenal	L	0-2		60 126
Dec	1	Man City	D	1-1	Scharner 25	18 614
	9	Bolton	L	1-4	Landzaat 14	20 309
	15	Blackburn	W	5-3	Landzaat 10, Bent 3 12 66 81, Scharner 37	16 489
	22	Fulham	D	1-1	Bent 70	20 820
	26	Newcastle	W	1-0	Taylor 65	20 304
	29	Aston Villa	L	1-2	Bramble 28	18 806
Jan	2	Liverpool	D	1-1	Bramble 80	42 308
	12	Derby	W	1-0	Sibierski 82	31 658
	20	Everton	L	1-2	Jagielka OG 53	18 820
	29	Midd'boro	L	0-1		22 963
Feb	2	West Ham	W	1-0	Kilbane 45	20 525
	9	Sunderland	L	0-2		43 600
	23	Derby	W	2-0	Scharner 60, Valencia 84	20 176
Mar	1	Man City	D	0-0		38 261
	9	Arsenal	D	0-0		19 676
	16	Bolton	W	1-0	Heskey 34	17 055
	22	Blackburn	L	1-3	King 17p	23 541
	29	Portsmouth	L	0-2		18 623
Apr	5	B'ham City	W	2-0	Taylor 2 15 55	17 926
	14	Chelsea	D	1-1	Heskey 92+	40 487
	19	Tottenham	D	1-1	Heskey 12	18 673
	26	Reading	D	0-0		19 043
May	3	Aston Villa	W	2-0	Valencia 2 52 63	42 640
	11	Man Utd	L	0-2		25 133

EQG – EQUATORIAL GUINEA

NATIONAL TEAM RECORD
JULY 10TH 2006 TO JULY 12TH 2010

PL	W	D	L	F	A	%
13	4	3	6	12	18	42.3

FIFA/COCA-COLA WORLD RANKING

1993	1994	1995	1996	1997	1998	1999	2000	2001	2002	2003	2004	2005	2006	2007
-	-	-	-	-	195	188	187	190	192	160	171	171	109	85

High	
64	03/08

2007–2008											
08/07	09/07	10/07	11/07	12/07	01/08	02/08	03/08	04/08	05/08	06/08	07/08
105	72	72	74	85	84	78	64	72	73	74	84

Low	
195	12/98

Equatorial Guinea is the closest any national team comes to being a modern club side, not from the perspective of the frequency of games played but rather the multi-cultural make up of the team. Despite FIFA edicts tightening up on the granting of instant nationality to footballers offered the opportunity to play international football for countries other than their own, Equatorial Guinea have assembled a national side with players of Brazilian, Cameroon, Liberian and Senegalese heritage. This is on top of a growing number of players from the diaspora who have made themselves available for the team, the most notable being Javier Balboa. Spanish-born to parents

INTERNATIONAL HONOURS
CEMAC Cup 2006

from Equatorial Guinea, Balboa played in the UEFA Champions League for Real Madrid last season and has made a pre-season move to Portuguese giants Benfica. Equatorial Guinea's Brazilian coach Jordan de Freitas steered the team through the closing stages of the 2008 CAF African Cup of Nations qualifiers where they scored arguably their biggest win to date - a 1-0 home triumph over Cameroon. In the FIFA World Cup qualifiers they suffered three defeats in four matches in June 2008 leaving them with little chance of progressing to the second phase of the African preliminaries for the 2010 finals in South Africa.

THE FIFA BIG COUNT OF 2006

	Male	Female		Total
Number of players	25 240	350	Referees and Assistant Referees	50
Professionals	230		Admin, Coaches, Technical, Medical	65
Amateurs 18+	1 400		Number of clubs	18
Youth under 18	600		Number of teams	48
Unregistered	3 300		Clubs with women's teams	4
Total players	25 590		Players as % of population	4.74%

Federación Ecuatoguineana de Fútbol (FEGUIFUT)
Apartado de correo numero 1017, Malabo, Equatorial Guinea
Tel +240 9 1874   Fax +240 9 6565
bonmanga@orange.gq   www.feguifut.net
President: MANGA OBIANG Bonifacio   General Secretary: ETUGU NAMATUE Esteban
Vice-President: ESONO EDJO Melchior   Treasurer: MANUEL Nsi Nguema   Media Officer: BORABOFA Clemente
Men's Coach: DE FREITAS Jordan   Women's Coach: MANGUE NGA Sebastian
FEGUIFUT formed: 1960   CAF: 1986   FIFA: 1986
Red shirts, Red shorts, Red socks

RECENT INTERNATIONAL MATCHES PLAYED BY EQUATORIAL GUINEA

2005	Opponents	Score		Venue	Comp	Scorers	Att	Referee
5-02	Cameroon †	L	0-3	Libreville	CMrl			
8-02	Chad	D	0-0	Libreville	CMrl			
2006								
26-02	Benin	W	1-0	Cotonou	Fr	Daniel Sahino [9]		
4-03	Congo	W	2-1	Bata	CMrl			
6-03	Chad	D	1-1	Bata	CMrl			
11-03	Gabon	D	0-0	Bata	CMsf	W 4-2p		
14-03	Cameroon †	D	1-1	Bata	CMf	W 4-2p		
29-03	Benin	W	2-0	Bata	Fr	Ivan Zarandona [18], Armando Justice [44]		
3-09	Liberia	W	2-1	Malabo	CNq	Juan Epitie [24], Rodolfo Bodipo [88]		Agbenyega GHA
7-10	Cameroon	L	0-3	Yaounde	CNq			Daami TUN
2007								
5-03	Congo	L	1-2	N'Djamena	CMrl	Desire Pierre [18]		
9-03	Gabon	D	1-1	N'Djamena	CMrl	Ibrahima Toure [44p]		
25-03	Rwanda	W	3-1	Malabo	CNq	Andre Moreira [29], Juvenal Edjogo [75], Juan Epitie [81]		Louzaya CGO
2-06	Rwanda	L	0-2	Kigali	CNq			Auda EGY
17-06	Liberia	D	0-0	Monrovia	CNq			Diouf SEN
9-09	Cameroon	W	1-0	Malabo	CNq	Juvenal Edjogo [39]		Sidibe MLI
21-11	Niger	D	1-1	Malabo	Fr			
2008								
1-06	Sierra Leone	W	2-0	Malabo	WCq	Falcao Carolino [47], Juan Epitie [57]	13 000	Codjia BEN
7-06	South Africa	L	1-4	Atteridgeville	WCq	Juvenal Edjogo [78p]	10 000	Diouf SEN
15-06	Nigeria	L	0-1	Malabo	WCq		15 200	Mendy GAM
21-06	Nigeria	L	0-2	Abuja	WCq		20 000	Ambaya LBY

Fr = Friendly match • CN = CAF African Cup of Nations • CM = CEMAC Cup • WC = FIFA World Cup
q = qualifier • r1 = first round group • sf = semi-final • f = final • † Not a full international

EQUATORIAL GUINEA NATIONAL TEAM RECORDS AND RECORD SEQUENCES

Records			Sequence records					
Victory	4-2	CAR 1999	Wins	2	2003, 2006x2	Clean sheets	2	2005-2006
Defeat	0-6	CGO 1990	Defeats	9	1999-2003	Goals scored	3	2006, 2007
Player Caps	n/a		Undefeated	7	2005-2006	Without goal	2	Five times
Player Goals	n/a		Without win	22	1984-1999	Goals against	22	1988-2003

RECENT LEAGUE AND CUP RECORD

Year	Champions	Cup Winners
1997	Deportivo Mongomo	Union Vesper
1998	CD Ela Nguema	Union Vesper
1999	FC Akonangui	CD Unidad
2000	CD Ela Nguema	CD Unidad
2001	FC Akonangui	Atlético Malabo
2002	CD Ela Nguema	FC Akonangui
2003	Atlético Malabo	Deportivo Mongomo
2004	Renacimiento	CD Ela Nguema
2005	Renacimiento	
2006	Renacimiento	
2007	Renacimiento	FC Akonangui

EQUATORIAL GUINEA COUNTRY INFORMATION

Capital	Malabo	Independence	1968 from Spain	GDP per Capita	$2 700
Population	523 051	Status	Republic	GNP Ranking	175
Area km²	28 051	Language	Spanish	Dialling code	+240
Population density	18 per km²	Literacy rate	80%	Internet code	.gq
% in urban areas	42%	Main religion	Christian	GMT +/−	+1
Towns/Cities ('000)	Malabo 101; Bata 82; Ebebiyin 13; Mbini 12; Luba 7				
Neighbours (km)	Cameroon 189; Gabon 350; Bight of Biafra 296. Malabo is on the island of Bioko in the Atlantic				
Main stadia	Internacional – Malabo 6 000				

ERI – ERITREA

NATIONAL TEAM RECORD
JULY 10TH 2006 TO JULY 12TH 2010

PL	W	D	L	F	A	%
8	3	3	2	8	13	56.2

FIFA/COCA-COLA WORLD RANKING

1993	1994	1995	1996	1997	1998	1999	2000	2001	2002	2003	2004	2005	2006	2007
-	-	-	-	-	189	169	158	171	157	155	169	169	140	132

High	
121	08/07

2007–2008											
08/07	09/07	10/07	11/07	12/07	01/08	02/08	03/08	04/08	05/08	06/08	07/08
121	128	123	126	132	134	131	133	133	132	130	142

Low	
189	12/98

Eritrea withdrew from the 2010 FIFA World Cup qualifiers and also pulled their clubs out of African club competition in a major setback for football in the small Red Sea state. Eritrea were drawn to compete against Swaziland, Togo and Zambia in the qualifiers for the 2010 finals in South Africa but told FIFA financial constraints necessitated their withdrawal. Al Tahrir also pulled out of a dream tie against Egyptian giants Al Ahly in the CAF Champions League. Ironically, the club had traveled to Kenya for their scheduled first round match against Tusker FC but it was cancelled after FIFA suspended the Kenya federation, handing the Eritrean side a walkover to round two. But

INTERNATIONAL HONOURS
None

they then failed to take up the opportunity to play the former African champions. While economic reasons were given, there is a consensus that the Eritrea government was fearful of losing more high profile players to political defections. Six players absconded from the national team and asked for asylum in Angola in 2007 after a CAF Africa Cup of Nations qualifier in Luanda. Eritrea did compete at the 2007 East and Central African Senior Challenge tournament in Tanzania and with some success. After beating both Djibouti and Uganda in the first round group stage they qualified for the quarter-finals where they lost to Burundi.

THE FIFA BIG COUNT OF 2006

	Male	Female		Total
Number of players	307 799	73 419	Referees and Assistant Referees	239
Professionals	0		Admin, Coaches, Technical, Medical	1 314
Amateurs 18+	6 524		Number of clubs	24
Youth under 18	21		Number of teams	258
Unregistered	694		Clubs with women's teams	2
Total players	381 218		Players as % of population	7.96%

Eritrean National Football Federation (ENFF)
Sematat Avenue 29-31, PO Box 3665, Asmara, Eritrea
Tel +291 1 120335   Fax +291 1 126821
enff@tse.com.er   www.none
President: GEBREYESUS Tesfaye   General Secretary: GHIDEY Mekonnen
Vice-President: MELLES Kidane   Treasurer: GUISH Tuccu   Media Officer: NEGA Woldegiorgis
Men's Coach: TBD   Women's Coach: TESFAGABIR Ghezai
ENFF formed: 1996   CAF: 1998   FIFA: 1998
Blue shirts, Red shorts, Green socks

RECENT INTERNATIONAL MATCHES PLAYED BY ERITREA

2005	Opponents	Score	Venue	Comp	Scorers	Att	Referee
28-11	Zanzibar †	L 0-3	Kigali	CCr1			
30-11	Rwanda	L 2-3	Kigali	CCr1	Suleiman Muhamoul 2		
2-12	Burundi	D 0-0	Kigali	CCr1			
4-12	Tanzania	L 0-1	Kigali	CCr1			
2006							
2-09	Kenya	W 2-1	Nairobi	CNq	Origi OG 15, Shimangus Yednekatchew 67		Lwanja MWI
7-10	Swaziland	D 0-0	Asmara	CNq			Gasingwa RWA
2007							
7-01	Yemen	L 1-4	Sana'a	Fr			
25-03	Angola	L 1-6	Luanda	CNq	Misgina Besirat 73		Evehe CMR
21-05	Sudan	W 1-0	Asmara	Fr	Shimangus Yednekatchew 46		
26-05	Sudan	D 1-1	Asmara	Fr			
2-06	Angola	D 1-1	Asmara	CNq	Hamiday Abdelkadir 15		Marange ZIM
16-06	Kenya	W 1-0	Asmara	CNq	Berhane Arega 80		Abdelrahman SUD
9-09	Swaziland	D 0-0	Manzini	CNq			Ssegonga UGA
30-11	Sudan	L 0-1	Omdurman	Fr			
3-12	Sudan	L 0-1	Omdurman	Fr			
9-12	Rwanda	L 1-2	Dar es Salaam	CCr1	Berhane Arega 38		
11-12	Djibouti	W 3-2	Dar es Salaam	CCr1	Berhane Arega 6, Shimangus Yednekatchew 42, Binam Fissehaye 68		
14-12	Uganda	W 3-2	Dar es Salaam	CCr1	Elmon Yeamekibron 2 53 64, Samuel Ghebrehine 82		
17-12	Burundi	L 1-2	Dar es Salaam	CCqf	Berhane Arega 20		
2008							

No international matches played in 2008 before August

CN = CAF African Cup of Nations • CC = CECAFA Cup • WC = FIFA World Cup • q = qualifier • r1 = first round group • † Not a full international

ERITREA NATIONAL TEAM RECORDS AND RECORD SEQUENCES

Records			Sequence records					
Victory	2-0	KEN 1994	Wins	2	1994	Clean sheets	3	1994
Defeat	1-6	ANG 2007	Defeats	3	Three times	Goals scored	6	2007
Player Caps	n/a		Undefeated	4	2007	Without goal	6	1999-2000
Player Goals	n/a		Without win	10	2000-2002	Goals against	9	2001-2003

RECENT LEAGUE AND CUP RECORD

Year	Champions	Cup Winners
1998	Red Sea FC Asmara	Hintsa Asmara
1999	Red Sea FC Asmara	
2000	Red Sea FC Asmara	
2001	Hintsa Asmara	
2002	Red Sea FC Asmara	
2003	Anseba Sports Club Keren	
2004	Adulis Club Asmara	
2005	Red Sea FC Asmara	
2006	Adulis Club Asmara	
2007	Al Tahir	

ERITREA COUNTRY INFORMATION

Capital	Asmara	Independence	1993	GDP per Capita	$700
Population	4 447 307	Status	Transitional	GNP Ranking	162
Area km²	121 320	Language	Tigrinya, Arabic	Dialling code	+291
Population density	36 per km²	Literacy rate	80%	Internet code	.er
% in urban areas	17%	Main religion	Christian, Muslim	GMT +/−	+3
Towns/Cities ('000)	Asmara 563; Assab 78; Keren 58; Mitsiwa 39; Addi Ugri 17; Barentu 15; Addi Keyih 13				
Neighbours (km)	Djibouti 109; Ethiopia 912; Sudan 605; Red Sea 2 234				
Main stadia	ChicChero – Asmara 12 000				

ESP – SPAIN

NATIONAL TEAM RECORD
JULY 10TH 2006 TO JULY 12TH 2010

PL	W	D	L	F	A	%
28	21	4	3	46	16	82.1

It's not often that the Primera División in Spain is cast in a supporting role to the national team, but by winning Euro 2008, Luis Aragones and his team have written a new chapter in the history of the game in a country where the club versus country debate has always been won hands down by the clubs. There may not have been the same public outpouring of joy in Barcelona and Bilbao as there was in Madrid but this was a team backed by the whole nation and that's what made the triumph special and unique - along with, of course, the exhilarating brand of fast attacking technical football that the Spanish showcased at the finals. Team spirit was the key to the success - Aragones left out Raul so as not to disturb the balance - but this was a triumph based on years of hard work and success at youth tournaments, where Spain has few equals. In 22 matches played from the start of 2007, to the victory over Germany in Vienna, the Spanish won 19 times, with the other three matches drawn - a sensational record that also earned them the top spot in the FIFA/Coca-Cola World Ranking for the first time. Spain must surely now be regarded as the top football nation in the world, although the Primera División is now facing some stiff competition as it seeks to

INTERNATIONAL HONOURS
Olympic Gold 1992   UEFA European Championship 1964 2008
Qualified for the FIFA World Cup finals 1934 1950 1962 1966 1978 1982 (hosts) 1986 1990 1994 1998 2002 2006
FIFA World Youth Championship 1999   FIFA Junior Tournament 1952 1954
UEFA U-21 Championship 1986 1998 UEFA U-19 Championship 1995 2002 2004 2006 UEFA U-17 Championship 1986 1988 1991 1997 1999 2001
UEFA Champions League Real Madrid 1956 1957 1958 1959 1960 1966 1998 2000 2002 Barcelona 1992 2006

maintain its superiority, especially from the Premier League in England. The title was won by an often pedestrian Real Madrid team who gave their rivals enough chances to catch them, opportunities that Barcelona especially, failed to seize. The title was a triumph for new coach Bernd Schuster as his team eventually finished 10 points clear of surprise package Villarreal and a massive 20 points ahead of Barcelona. It proved to be a wretched season for Barcelona with Ronaldinho, so often their inspiration in the past, a shadow of his former self. They did make it to the semi-finals of the Champions League before losing to Manchester United but that wasn't enough for coach Frank Rijkaard to save his job and he was replaced by Josep Guardiola at the end of the season having delivered two league titles and the European Cup during five often thrilling years at the club. In the Champions League, both Real Madrid and Sevilla failed to get past the first knock-out round and with Valencia finishing bottom of their group, it was a very ordinary season for Spanish clubs in Europe. There was some relief in an otherwise dire season for Valencia, however, when they won the Copa del Rey, beating Getafe 3-1 in the final.

Real Federación Española de Fútbol (RFEF)
Ramon y Cajal s/n, Apartado postale 385, Las Rozas 28230, Madrid, Spain
Tel +34 91 4959800   Fax +34 91 4959801
rfef@rfef.es   www.rfef.es
President: VILLAR LLONA Angel Maria   General Secretary: PEREZ Jorge
Vice-President: PADRON Juan   Treasurer: LARREA Juan   Media Officer: ANTORANZ Paloma
Men's Coach: DEL BOSQUE Vicente   Women's Coach: QUEREDA Ignacio
RFEF formed: 1913   UEFA: 1954   FIFA: 1904
Red shirts with yellow trimmings, Blue shorts, Blue socks or White shirts with red trimmings, White shorts, White socks

RECENT INTERNATIONAL MATCHES PLAYED BY SPAIN

2006	Opponents	Score	Venue	Comp	Scorers	Att	Referee
14-06	Ukraine	W 4-0	Leipzig	WCr1	Xabi Alonso [13], Villa 2 [17 48p], Fernando Torres [81]	43 000	Busacca SUI
19-06	Tunisia	W 3-1	Stuttgart	WCr1	Raúl [71], Fernando Torres 2 [76 91+]	52 000	Simon BRA
23-06	Saudi Arabia	W 1-0	Kaiserslautern	WCr1	Juanito [36]	46 000	Codjia BEN
27-06	France	L 1-3	Hanover	WCr2	Villa [28p]	43 000	Rosetti ITA
15-08	Iceland	D 0-0	Reykjavik	Fr		12 327	Stokes IRL
2-09	Liechtenstein	W 4-0	Badajoz	ECq	Torres [20], Villa 2 [45 62], Luis Garcia [56]	13 876	Bozinovski MKD
6-09	Northern Ireland	L 2-3	Belfast	ECq	Xavi [14], Villa [52]	13 885	De Bleeckere BEL
7-10	Sweden	L 0-2	Stockholm	ECq		41 482	Bennett ENG
11-10	Argentina	W 2-1	Murcia	Fr	Xavi [33], Villa [64p]	31 000	Duhamel FRA
15-11	Romania	L 0-1	Cadiz	Fr		15 000	Messina ITA
2007							
7-02	England	W 1-0	Manchester	Fr	Iniesta [63]	58 247	Weiner GER
24-03	Denmark	W 2-1	Madrid	ECq	Morientes [34], Villa [46+]	73 575	Busacca SUI
28-03	Iceland	W 1-0	Palma	ECq	Iniesta [81]	18 326	Duhamel FRA
2-06	Latvia	W 2-0	Riga	ECq	Villa [45], Xavi [60]	10 000	Thomson SCO
6-06	Liechtenstein	W 2-0	Vaduz	ECq	Villa 2 [8 14]	5 739	Ivanov.N RUS
22-08	Greece	W 3-2	Thessaloniki	Fr	Marchena [37], Silva 2 [66 90]	15 000	Lannoy FRA
8-09	Iceland	D 1-1	Reykjavik	ECq	Iniesta [86]	9 483	Stark GER
12-09	Latvia	W 2-0	Oviedo	ECq	Xavi [13], Torres [85]	22 560	Yefet ISR
13-10	Denmark	W 3-1	Aarhus	ECq	Tamudo [14], Sergio Ramos [40], Riera [89]	19 849	Michel SVK
17-10	Finland	D 0-0	Helsinki	Fr		8 000	Bre FRA
17-11	Sweden	W 3-0	Madrid	ECq	Capdevila [14], Iniesta [39], Sergio Ramos [65]	67 055	Rosetti ITA
21-11	Northern Ireland	W 1-0	Las Palmas	ECq	Xavi [52]	30 339	Fandel GER
2008							
6-02	France	W 1-0	Malaga	Fr	Capdevila [80]	35 000	Asumaa FIN
26-03	Italy	W 1-0	Elche	Fr	Villa [78]	38 000	Stuchlik AUT
31-05	Peru	W 2-1	Huelva	Fr	Villa [38], Capdevila [90]	17 500	Meckarovski MKD
4-06	USA	W 1-0	Santander	Fr	Xavi [79]	14 232	Jareci ALB
10-06	Russia	W 4-1	Innsbruck	ECr1	Villa 3 [20 44 75], Fabregas [93+]	30 772	Plautz AUT
14-06	Sweden	W 2-1	Innsbruck	ECr1	Torres [15], Villa [92+]	30 772	Vink NED
18-06	Greece	W 2-1	Salzburg	ECr1	De la Red [61], Güiza [88]	30 883	Webb ENG
22-06	Italy	D 0-0	Vienna	ECqf	W 4-2p	48 000	Fandel GER
26-06	Russia	W 3-0	Vienna	ECsf	Xavi [6], Güiza [73], Silva [82]	51 428	De Bleeckere BEL
29-06	Germany	W 1-0	Vienna	ECf	Torres [33]	51 428	Rosetti ITA

Fr = Friendly match • EC = UEFA EURO 2008 • WC = FIFA World Cup
q = qualifier • r1 = first round group • r2 = second round • qf = quarter-final • sf = semi-final • f = final

SPAIN NATIONAL TEAM PLAYERS

	Player		Ap	G	Club	Date of Birth		Player		Ap	G	Club	Date of Birth
1	Iker Casillas	GK	82	0	Real Madrid	20 05 1981	12	Santi Cazorla	MF	7	0	Villarreal	13 12 1984
2	Raúl Albiol	DF	6	0	Valencia	4 09 1985	13	Andrés Palop	GK	0	0	Sevilla	22 10 1973
3	Fernando Navarro	DF	2	0	RCD Mallorca	25 06 1982	14	Xabi Alonso	MF	47	1	Liverpool	25 11 1981
4	Carlos Marchena	DF	47	2	Valencia	31 07 1979	15	Sergio Ramos	DF	39	4	Real Madrid	30 03 1986
5	Carles Puyol	DF	66	1	Barcelona	13 04 1978	16	Sergio García	FW	2	0	Real Zaragoza	9 06 1983
6	Andrés Iniesta	MF	29	4	Barcelona	11 05 1984	17	Daniel Güiza	FW	8	2	RCD Mallorca	17 08 1980
7	David Villa	FW	35	18	Valencia	3 12 1981	18	Alvaro Arbeloa	DF	3	0	Liverpool	17 01 1983
8	Xavi Hernández	MF	63	8	Barcelona	25 01 1980	19	Marcos Senna	MF	16	0	Villarreal	17 07 1976
9	Fernando Torres	FW	54	17	Liverpool	20 03 1984	20	Juanito	DF	24	2	Real Betis	23 07 1976
10	Cesc Fábregas	MF	32	1	Arsenal	4 05 1987	21	David Silva	FW	19	3	Valencia	8 01 1986
11	Joan Capdevila	DF	23	3	Villarreal	3 02 1978	22	Rubén de la Red	MF	3	1	Getafe	5 06 1985
	Spain's squad for Euro 2008						23	Pepe Reina	GK	10	0	Liverpool	31 08 1982

SPAIN NATIONAL TEAM RECORDS AND RECORD SEQUENCES

Records			Sequence records		
Victory	13-0	BUL 1933	Wins	9	1924-27, 2007-08	Clean sheets	7	1992
Defeat	1-7	ITA 1928, ENG 1931	Defeats	3	Five times	Goals scored	20	1947-1951
Player Caps	126	Andoni Zubizarreta	Undefeated	30	1994-1997	Without goal	3	1985, 1992
Player Goals	44	Raúl	Without win	10	1980	Goals against	11	1952 1955

MAJOR CITIES/TOWNS

		Population '000
1	Madrid	6 097
2	Barcelona	4 853
3	Valencia	1 759
4	Sevilla	1 293
5	Bilbao	1 132
6	Málaga	851
7	Las Palmas	684
8	Zaragoza	683
9	Murcia	626
10	Palma	481
11	Granada	467
12	Alicante	460
13	Oviedo	432
14	Tenerife	427
15	Vigo	407
16	Donostia †	400
17	Cádiz	398
18	Valladolid	379
19	La Coruña	375
20	Pamplona	300
21	Gijón	283
22	Vitoria	227
23	Santander	183
24	Huelva	144

KINGDOM OF SPAIN; REINO DE ESPANA

Capital	Madrid	Language	Spanish, Catalan, Galician, Basque	Independence	1492
Population	40 397 842	Area	504 782 km²	Density 79 per km²	% in cities 76%
GDP per cap	$22 000	Dailling code	+34	Internet .es	GMT +/- +1

The population totals for the Spanish cities above are for the metroplitan areas where relevant. † Official name is Donostia-San Sebastián

MEDALS TABLE

		Overall			League			Cup		Europe			City	Stadium	Cap'ty	DoF
		G	S	B	G	S	B	G	S	G	S	B				
1	Real Madrid	59	41	17	31	17	7	17	19	11	5	10	Madrid	Santiago Bernabeu	80 000	1902
2	Barcelona	51	37	21	18	22	12	24	8	9	6	9	Barcelona	Camp Nou	98 260	1899
3	Athletic Bilbao	31	19	10	8	7	10	23	11		1		Bilbao	San Mamés	39 750	1898
4	Atlético Madrid	19	19	19	9	8	12	9	8	1	3	7	Madrid	Vicente Calderón	54 851	1903
5	Valencia	17	18	7	6	6	7	7	9	4	3		Valencia	Mestalla	55 000	1919
6	Real Zaragoza	8	7	6		1	4	6	5	2	1	2	Zaragoza	La Romareda	34 596	1932
7	Sevilla	7	6	3	1	4	3	4	2	2			Sevilla	Sánchez Pizjuán	43 000	1905
8	Real Sociedad	4	7	3	2	3	2	2	4			1	San Sebastián	Anoeta	32 082	1909
9	RCD Espanyol	4	7	4			4	4	5		2		Barcelona	Olímpic de Montjuïc	55 000	1900
10	Deportivo La Coruña	3	5	6	1	5	4	2				2	La Coruña	Riazor	34 178	1906
11	Real Betis Balompié	3	2	2	1		2	2	2				Sevilla	Ruiz de Lopera	52 500	1907
12	Real Union Irún	3	1					3	1				Irún	Gal	5 000	1915
13	RCD Mallorca	1	3	2		2	1	1	2		1		Palma	Son Moix	24 142	1916
14	Arenas Guecho Bilbao	1	3	1		1	1	1	3				Bilbao	Gobela	1 200	1909
15	Racing Irún	1					1						Irún			1908-15

RECENT LEAGUE AND CUP RECORD

	Championship							Cup		
Year	Champions	Pts	Runners-up	Pts	Third	Pts		Winners	Score	Runners-up
1995	Real Madrid	55	Deportivo	51	Real Betis	46		Deportivo	2-1	Valencia
1996	Atlético Madrid	87	Valencia	83	Barcelona	80		Atlético Madrid	1-0	Barcelona
1997	Real Madrid	92	Barcelona	90	Deportivo	77		Barcelona	3-2	Real Betis
1998	Barcelona	74	Athletic Bilbao	65	Real Sociedad	63		Barcelona	1-1 4-3p	Mallorca
1999	Barcelona	79	Real Madrid	68	Mallorca	66		Valencia	3-0	Atlético Madrid
2000	Deportivo	69	Barcelona	64	Valencia	64		Espanyol	2-1	Atlético Madrid
2001	Real Madrid	80	Deportivo	73	Mallorca	71		Real Zaragoza	3-1	Celta Vigo
2002	Valencia	75	Deportivo	68	Real Madrid	66		Deportivo	2-1	Real Madrid
2003	Real Madrid	78	Real Sociedad	76	Deportivo	72		Mallorca	3-0	Recreativo Huelva
2004	Valencia	77	Barcelona	72	Deportivo	71		Real Zaragoza	3-2	Real Madrid
2005	Barcelona	84	Real Madrid	80	Villarreal	65		Real Betis	2-1	Osasuna
2006	Barcelona	82	Real Madrid	70	Valencia	69		Espanyol	4-1	Real Zaragoza
2007	Real Madrid	76	Barcelona	76	Sevilla	71		Sevilla	1-0	Getafe
2008	Real Madrid	87	Villarreal	77	Barcelona	67		Valencia	3-1	Getafe

SPAIN 2007–08

PRIMERA DIVISION

	Pl	W	D	L	F	A	Pts	Real Madrid	Villarreal	Barcelona	Atlético	Sevilla	Racing	Mallorca	Almería	Deportivo	Valencia	Athletic	Espanyol	Betis	Getafe	Valladolid	Recreativo	Osasuna	Zaragoza	Real Murcia	Levante
Real Madrid †	38	27	4	7	84	36	87		3-2	4-1	2-1	3-1	3-1	4-3	3-1	3-1	2-3	3-0	2-1	2-0	0-1	7-0	2-0	2-0	2-0	1-0	5-2
Villarreal †	38	24	5	9	63	40	77	0-5		3-1	3-0	3-2	0-0	1-1	1-1	4-3	3-0	1-0	2-0	0-1	2-0	2-0	1-1	0-0	2-0	2-0	4-0
Barcelona †	38	19	10	9	76	43	67	0-1	1-2		3-0	2-1	1-0	2-3	2-0	2-1	6-0	3-1	0-0	3-0	0-0	4-1	3-0	1-0	4-1	4-0	5-1
Atlético Madrid †	38	19	7	12	66	47	64	0-2	3-4	4-2		4-3	4-0	1-1	6-3	1-0	1-0	1-2	1-2	1-3	1-0	4-3	3-0	2-0	4-0	1-1	3-0
Sevilla ‡	38	20	4	14	75	49	64	2-0	2-0	1-1	1-2		4-1	1-2	1-4	0-1	3-0	4-1	2-3	3-0	4-1	2-0	4-1	2-1	5-0	3-1	2-1
Racing Santander ‡	38	17	9	12	42	41	60	0-2	0-2	0-0	0-2	0-3		3-1	1-0	1-3	1-0	1-0	1-3	0-2	0-2	0-2	1-0	2-3	2-3	1-0	
RCD Mallorca	38	15	14	9	69	54	59	1-1	0-1	0-2	1-0	2-3	3-1		0-0	1-0	0-2	0-0	2-2	1-1	4-2	4-2	7-1	2-1	3-2	1-1	3-0
Almería	38	14	10	14	42	45	52	1-0	1-0	2-2	0-0	1-0	0-1	1-1		1-0	1-2	1-1	1-0	1-1	0-2	1-0	0-2	2-0	0-1	1-0	2-1
Deportivo La Coruña	38	15	7	16	46	47	52	1-0	0-2	2-0	0-3	2-1	0-1	1-1	0-3		2-4	3-0	2-0	1-0	1-1	3-1	0-2	1-2	1-1	3-1	1-0
Valencia ‡	38	15	6	17	48	62	51	1-5	0-3	0-3	3-1	1-2	1-2	0-3	0-1	2-2		0-3	1-2	3-1	2-1	2-1	1-1	3-0	1-0	3-0	0-0
Athletic Bilbao	38	13	11	14	40	43	50	0-1	1-2	1-1	0-2	2-0	0-0	1-2	1-1	2-2	5-1		1-0	0-0	1-0	2-0	2-0	0-1	1-1	1-1	1-0
RCD Espanyol	38	13	9	16	43	53	48	2-1	3-0	1-1	0-2	2-4	0-3	2-1	1-3	1-0	2-0	2-1		1-2	1-0	0-1	1-1	0-3	2-1	4-0	0-1
Real Betis	38	12	11	15	45	51	47	2-1	0-1	3-2	0-2	0-2	1-1	3-0	3-1	0-1	1-2	1-2	2-2		3-2	1-1	1-1	0-3	2-1	4-0	0-1
Getafe	38	12	11	15	44	48	47	0-1	1-3	2-0	1-1	3-2	2-1	3-3	4-2	0-0	0-0	2-0	0-1	1-1		0-3	1-1	0-2	0-2	0-2	2-1
Real Valladolid	38	11	12	15	42	57	45	1-1	2-0	1-1	1-1	0-2	1-1	1-0	1-1	0-2	2-0	2-0	2-0	1-0	0-0		3-1	0-0	2-1	1-4	1-0
Recreativo Huelva	38	11	11	16	40	60	44	2-3	0-2	2-2	0-0	1-2	0-0	0-2	1-1	3-2	0-1	1-1	2-1	1-1	1-3	1-1		1-0	2-1	4-2	2-0
Osasuna	38	12	7	19	37	44	43	1-2	3-2	0-0	3-1	1-1	0-2	3-1	2-1	0-1	0-0	2-0	1-2	0-1	0-2	2-2	0-1		1-0	2-1	4-1
Real Zaragoza	38	10	12	16	50	61	42	2-2	4-1	1-2	2-1	2-0	1-1	2-1	1-0	2-2	1-0	3-3	0-3	1-1	2-3	3-0	2-1			3-1	3-0
Real Murcia	38	7	9	22	36	65	30	1-1	0-1	3-5	1-1	0-0	2-1	1-4	0-1	0-2	1-0	1-2	4-0	0-0	0-3	1-1	0-2	0-2			2-3
Levante	38	7	5	26	33	75	26	0-2	1-2	1-4	0-1	0-2	1-1	2-2	3-0	0-1	1-5	1-2	1-1	4-3	3-1	0-3	0-2	2-1	2-1	0-0	

25/08/2007 - 18/05/2008 • † Qualified for the UEFA Champions League • ‡ Qualified for the UEFA Cup
Top scorers: Dani Güiza, Mallorca 27; Luis Fabiano, Sevilla 24; Sergio Agüero, Atlético Madrid 19; David Villa, Valencia 18; Nihat Kahveci, Villarreal 18; Raúl, Real Madrid; Ricardo Oliveira, Zaragoza 17; Samuel Eto'o, Barcelona 16; Diego Forlan, Atlético 16; Frédéric Kanoute, Sevilla 16; Ruud Van Nistelrooij, Real Madrid 16

SPAIN 2007–08

SEGUNDA DIVISION A (2)

	Pl	W	D	L	F	A	Pts
Numancia	42	22	11	9	59	38	77
Málaga	42	20	12	10	58	42	72
Sporting Gijón	42	20	12	10	61	40	72
Real Sociedad	42	18	14	10	55	39	68
Castellón	42	16	13	13	42	37	61
Hércules	42	14	16	12	66	55	58
Salamanca	42	13	18	11	52	44	57
Las Palmas	42	15	12	15	51	55	57
Sevilla Atlético	42	14	14	14	43	48	56
Elche	42	14	12	16	44	50	54
Tenerife	42	12	17	13	51	57	53
Albacete	42	13	13	16	37	40	52
Eibar	42	14	10	18	42	51	52
Gimnàstic Tarragona	42	12	16	14	49	51	52
Xerez	42	12	16	14	47	56	52
Celta Vigo	42	13	13	16	56	55	52
Deportivo Alavés	42	12	15	15	41	47	51
Córdoba	42	11	17	14	50	56	50
Racing Ferrol	42	12	14	16	46	51	50
Cádiz	42	12	13	17	40	47	49
Granada 74	42	10	15	17	45	59	45
Polideportivo Ejido	42	11	11	20	37	54	44

25/08/2007 - 15/06/2008 • Top scorers: Yordi, Xerez 20; Nino, Tenerife 19; José Juan Luque, Granada 17; Iñigo Diaz de Cerio, Sociedad 16

SPAIN 2007–08

SEGUNDA DIVISION B (3) GRUPO 1

	Pl	W	D	L	F	A	Pts	Vallecano	Pontevedra	Fuerteventura	Deportivo B	Castilla	Universidad	Lugo	Celta B	Pájara Playas	Atlético B	Vecindario	Leganés	Lanzarote	Alcorcón	Marino	Santa Brigida	Ourense	Fuenlabrada	SS Reyes	San Isidro
Rayo Vallecano ‡	38	20	10	8	66	31	70		1-0	2-1	0-1	1-0	1-0	2-2	4-1	0-1	5-0	3-1	2-0	0-0	3-2	3-0	2-0	5-0	3-1	4-0	3-1
Pontevedra ‡	38	18	13	7	52	29	67	1-0		1-0	0-0	2-0	1-1	1-1	2-0	3-1	1-0	0-0	2-0	1-2	0-1	0-0	3-0	1-1	1-1	3-1	3-0
Fuerteventura ‡	38	18	9	11	50	45	63	0-3	0-0		2-1	1-2	1-0	2-0	2-2	2-3	2-2	0-0	2-1	1-0	2-1	1-3	1-1	1-1	1-1	1-1	0-2
Deportivo La Coruña B	38	17	11	10	46	33	62	3-1	1-1	3-2		1-0	1-1	1-2	1-1	1-0	1-1	2-0	3-1	1-2	0-1	0-0	1-0	4-2	1-1	1-0	3-1
Real Madrid Castilla	38	17	10	11	60	42	61	0-1	2-2	1-1	2-1		4-0	1-2	2-2	2-0	2-1	1-2	3-1	2-1	3-1	2-2	1-0	4-0	4-2	0-0	1-0
Universidad LPCG	38	16	13	9	45	32	61	0-0	2-0	0-1	1-0	1-0		3-0	0-2	2-1	4-0	1-0	3-2	2-0	0-0	3-0	3-1	1-1	4-1	2-0	2-2
Lugo	38	17	9	12	51	49	60	2-1	1-0	0-1	3-1	1-4	3-1		3-2	0-0	1-1	4-1	2-0	2-0	1-0	2-0	2-2	1-0	0-1	2-0	3-3
Celta B	38	16	8	14	56	50	56	3-2	0-2	1-1	3-1	3-1	1-1	2-1		1-0	5-1	1-1	2-4	1-1	1-0	3-0	3-1	1-0	2-0	3-0	2-0
Pájara Playas Jandía	38	14	11	13	36	41	53	2-5	1-1	1-1	1-3	1-1	0-0	2-0	1-0		1-1	1-0	2-1	1-0	0-2	1-1	2-1	2-0	1-0	2-1	0-0
Atlético Madrid B	38	12	16	10	49	55	52	3-2	1-1	2-3	0-2	1-1	1-0	3-1	3-2	1-1		1-0	0-0	0-0	2-0	2-2	3-1	2-2	1-1	0-0	3-1
Vecindario	38	15	6	17	52	44	51	1-1	1-3	0-2	0-3	2-0	1-6	0-3	0-2	0-4	0-0		1-0	4-1	1-0	5-1	0-3	2-1	2-0	2-0	2-3
Leganés	38	13	12	13	43	44	51	0-0	3-2	3-1	0-0	0-0	0-0	1-0	1-0	0-1	0-3	2-1		1-2	3-1	1-1	1-1	1-1	3-1	2-0	3-1
Lanzarote	38	13	11	14	43	46	50	1-1	1-3	0-1	0-0	3-1	2-0	1-2	2-0	1-2	3-3	1-1	1-0		1-0	2-1	1-1	0-1	1-1	1-1	3-1
Alcorcón	38	13	9	16	38	39	48	0-0	1-1	1-0	0-0	1-1	0-0	1-0	1-2	1-0	0-1	1-2	3-0	2-2	1-2		2-1	1-0	1-0	0-2	1-2
Marino	38	12	10	16	31	42	46	0-2	0-1	0-1	1-0	0-1	0-1	1-0	0-1	2-1	0-1	1-0	1-1	0-1	2-1	0-3		2-0	2-0	1-0	0-0
Villa Santa Brigida †	38	11	13	14	39	45	46	0-0	1-2	0-1	0-2	2-1	1-1	1-1	1-2	0-1	1-1	1-0	0-0	3-1	0-3	2-1		1-1	2-1	0-0	1-1
Ourense	38	11	13	14	36	46	46	0-1	1-0	3-1	0-1	1-2	2-2	0-1	1-1	1-0	0-0	1-1	3-2	1-0	0-0	0-0	0-0		1-0	3-1	3-1
Fuenlabrada	38	6	15	17	29	48	33	2-0	2-4	3-0	0-0	0-2	0-0	1-1	0-1	1-0	1-1	0-0	0-1	0-2	1-1	1-1	0-2	1-1		0-1	0-1
San Sebastian Reyes	38	7	10	21	23	50	31	0-0	1-2	0-3	0-1	1-0	0-1	0-2	1-2	0-2	1-0	1-2	1-1	1-2	1-0	1-2	0-2	1-1	4-1		
San Isidro	38	6	7	25	41	75	25	2-2	1-2	2-4	1-4	0-3	3-1	2-3	1-3	2-2	0-1	0-3	0-1	1-2	3-2	0-1	1-2	2-0	0-1	0-1	

26/08/2007 - 18/05/2008 • ‡ Qualified for promotion play-offs • † Relegation play-off

SPAIN 2007–08

SEGUNDA DIVISION B (3) GRUPO 2

	Pl	W	D	L	F	A	Pts	Ponferradina	Huesca	Zamora	Barakaldo	Real Unión	Conquense	Lemona	Guadalajara	Guijuelo	Sestao River	Cultural	Sociedad B	CD Logroñes	Valladolid B	Bilbao Ath.	Osasuna B	Logroñes CF	Burgos	Palencia	Peña Sport
Ponferradina ‡	38	18	13	7	52	28	67		0-0	0-0	2-3	2-1	3-2	0-0	1-2	4-0	2-1	4-1	0-0	2-1	2-0	5-0	2-1	3-0	0-1	2-1	2-1
Huesca ‡	38	18	13	7	45	27	67	0-0		1-1	2-1	2-1	4-2	0-3	0-1	3-1	2-1	3-1	5-1	0-0	0-0	4-2	1-0	1-0	1-0	1-0	2-1
Zamora ‡	38	17	12	9	43	38	63	1-1	1-0		3-2	0-0	2-0	1-1	2-1	2-3	1-1	2-1	2-1	1-1	1-2	1-0	2-0	1-1	1-0	2-0	3-1
Barakaldo ‡	38	18	9	11	45	34	63	1-0	1-0	1-3		2-1	1-1	0-0	3-1	3-2	2-0	1-1	0-1	2-1	1-1	1-1	2-2	3-0	1-0	2-0	1-0
Real Unión Irún	38	17	11	10	48	34	62	0-0	0-0	2-0	2-0		2-1	1-1	3-0	1-0	0-2	1-2	3-1	1-1	0-1	1-0	1-0	3-1	3-1	3-0	1-0
Conquense	38	17	10	11	54	44	61	1-1	1-0	1-0	0-3	2-1		2-1	3-1	1-0	2-1	0-0	3-3	1-0	0-0	5-0	2-1	1-2	2-0	3-1	2-0
Lemona	38	17	9	12	42	34	60	1-0	1-0	2-1	1-2	2-0	3-0		1-0	2-1	1-0	1-1	0-0	2-1	0-2	1-0	2-1	2-2	0-2	1-1	2-1
Guadalajara	38	17	7	14	45	49	58	0-0	0-1	0-1	3-2	2-0	1-1	3-2		1-0	1-0	2-2	1-2	1-3	1-0	2-3	0-4	0-0	2-1	2-0	3-1
Guijuelo	38	16	9	13	42	41	57	2-0	1-1	0-0	2-0	0-1	1-1	1-0	0-0		0-1	1-0	2-2	2-0	0-0	0-3	2-0		0-1	2-0	2-1
Sestao River	38	15	10	13	34	26	55	1-2	0-0	3-0	0-0	1-2	1-0	0-2	2-0	3-		0-1	0-1	2-0	1-0	1-0	0-0	1-2	1-0	1-0	3-0
Cultural Leonesa	38	14	10	14	49	44	52	0-1	1-3	4-0	1-1	1-2	0-1	0-1	2-0	3-2	1-1		3-0	3-2	2-1	0-0	0-0	0-2	3-1	3-0	
Real Sociedad B	38	12	14	12	40	38	50	0-1	0-0	0-0	0-0	0-2	1-2	1-0	2-0	5-0	0-1	3-2		3-0	2-1	1-1	0-0	2-2	1-1	1-0	1-0
CD Logroñes	38	11	14	13	40	46	47	1-1	0-2	0-0	0-2	3-1	1-0		0-1	0-1	0-3	3-1	0-		1-0	1-0	0-0	1-1	0-0	2-1	
Real Valladolid B	38	11	11	16	37	48	44	3-3	3-0	1-2	2-0	2-1	1-3	1-0	2-1	0-3	1-1	1-1	0-0	1-0		2-0	0-0	2-4	0-3	0-2	1-0
Bilbao Athletic	38	11	9	18	40	50	42	0-0	1-1	2-1	0-1	1-1	2-2	2-0	1-2	0-0	0-0	0-0	1-2	0-3	2-2		0-1		2-0	2-2	2-1
Osasuna B †	38	9	13	16	25	37	40	1-1	1-3	0-1	0-0	0-0	0-1	1-1	0-1	2-0	0-3	1-0	1-0	1-3	1-1	1-2		0-0	1-0	1-2	0-0
Logroñes CF	38	8	16	14	37	40	40	1-0	0-0	3-0	0-1	1-1	1-2	1-2	3-1		0-0	0-1	0-2	0-0	3-1		0-0		0-0	1-0	1-2
Burgos	38	9	13	16	30	39	40	0-2	0-0	2-1	1-0	0-0	0-1	1-1	1-0	2-1	1-2	0-1	1-0	2-0	0-0	0-0	3-2	1-3		4-2	
Palencia	38	9	13	16	30	46	39	0-1	0-0	0-1	1-0	1-0	2-2	2-1	1-2	0-1	1-0	0-0	3-2	1-3	1-0	1-0	1-0	0-1	1-1		2-2
Peña Sport	38	5	8	25	31	66	23	0-2	0-1	1-1	0-2	0-2	2-3	1-0	0-2	1-1	0-2	1-2	1-0		1-2	3-2	1-2	3-3	2-4	1-0	

26/08/2007 - 18/05/2008 • ‡ Qualified for promotion play-offs • † Relegation play-off

FIFA/COCA-COLA WORLD RANKING FOR SPAIN

1993	1994	1995	1996	1997	1998	1999	2000	2001	2002	2003	2004	2005	2006	2007		High	
5	2	4	8	11	15	4	7	7	3	3	5	5	12	4		1	07/08

2007–2008												Low	
08/07	09/07	10/07	11/07	12/07	01/08	02/08	03/08	04/08	05/08	06/08	07/08	25	03/98
8	7	6	4	4	4	4	4	4	4	4	1		

SPAIN 2007-08

SEGUNDA DIVISION B (3) — GRUPO 3

Team	Pl	W	D	L	F	A	Pts	Gir	Ali	Gav	Ben	Ori	Ont	Eiv	Alc	Bad	VlB	Gra	Den	Lle	Sab	Ter	Vll	Cas	EsB	LHo	LvB
Girona ‡	38	20	12	6	61	28	72		0-1	0-0	4-1	0-3	3-1	1-1	2-0	2-0	0-1	2-0	4-0	3-0	0-2	3-1	2-1	1-1	4-2	1-0	3-0
Alicante ‡	38	16	16	6	52	21	64	0-2		2-1	3-0	0-1	2-0	0-1	1-1	1-1	0-1	1-1	2-2	2-0	5-0	4-0	2-0	2-0	3-0	5-0	0-0
Gavá ‡	38	16	15	7	46	33	63	0-0	1-1		1-0	1-0	2-0	0-0	1-1	1-0	0-2	1-1	2-2	3-0	2-0	2-0	3-1	2-1	1-0	2-0	
Benidorm ‡	38	16	11	11	43	39	59	1-1	0-0	1-0		2-1	2-2	3-0	0-0	1-3	2-0	2-1	3-1	1-0	0-0	2-1	0-1	5-1	1-0	0-1	
Orihuela	38	13	17	8	51	32	56	0-0	1-1	1-1	3-1		4-0	6-0	1-0	0-1	2-2	1-1	0-1	0-2	1-1	2-1	3-0	2-0	2-2	0-1	3-2
Ontinyent	38	16	8	14	46	46	56	0-0	1-0	1-0	2-1	2-0		1-2	1-1	2-1	1-2	1-1	0-0	1-3	0-0	2-1	2-0	1-2	1-0	2-2	
Eivissa	38	12	17	9	43	42	53	1-0	0-1	4-0	1-1	0-0	1-2		2-2	1-0	0-2	2-2	1-0	0-0	1-1	1-1	4-0	3-0	1-1	3-0	2-1
Alcoyano	38	11	18	9	38	31	51	3-1	1-1	0-0	0-1	1-1	0-1	0-0		1-0	0-1	1-1	1-0	2-0	0-0	3-0	3-0	3-0	3-1	1-1	
Badalona	38	11	17	10	38	40	50	2-2	0-0	2-4	0-0	1-1	2-1	0-0	0-0		0-0	2-1	2-1	1-1	2-1	1-0	0-1	2-2	1-4	1-0	0-0
Villarreal B	38	13	10	15	37	38	49	0-1	0-3	0-0	0-2	0-0	2-1	3-0	2-0	1-1		2-0	0-1	2-1	3-1	1-3	1-0	0-2	1-1	0-1	0-1
Atlético Gramanet	38	12	13	12	42	47	49	1-1	0-0	2-1	2-0	2-2	1-3	0-2	2-1	3-2	1-3		2-0	1-2	0-2	0-0	1-0	2-1	3-2	2-2	1-0
Denia	38	11	15	12	34	36	48	1-3	0-0	0-0	3-0	1-1	0-1	2-1	0-0	1-0	0-0	1-0		3-0	1-1	0-1	0-2	2-2	1-1	1-0	
Lleida	38	11	15	12	38	44	48	0-1	1-1	1-1	0-1	2-2	3-3	3-2	1-0	0-1	2-1	1-0	1-1		1-1	0-1	0-0	2-1	1-0	1-2	1-1
Sabadell	38	10	18	10	39	47	48	0-5	1-1	1-1	2-0	1-3	2-1	1-0	0-0	1-1	2-2	1-0	1-1		1-1	0-1	0-0	2-1	3-0	0-0	
Terrassa	38	11	13	14	44	46	46	1-1	1-2	3-0	2-1	0-0	2-3	1-2	1-1	4-1	1-0	1-1	1-2	2-4		2-0	1-0	2-0	0-0	2-1	
Villajoyosa †	38	11	12	14	31	36	45	1-2	3-1	0-2	1-0	0-0	2-0	0-1	1-1	1-0	0-0	3-1	0-0	2-0	-		1-1	4-0	2-0	0-0	
Castelldefels	38	11	11	16	41	54	44	1-1	0-1	2-2	0-1	0-0	3-2	1-1	0-3	1-1	3-2	2-0	1-2	1-2	0-2	1-3	2-1		1-0	0-2	3-0
Espanyol B	38	8	15	15	45	59	39	0-2	1-1	1-1	1-1	2-2	2-0	1-1	0-1	2-0	1-1	1-1	2-2	3-1	1-1	1-1	0-0	3-2		3-1	2-2
L'Hospitalet	38	8	11	19	21	47	35	0-2	0-0	1-2	1-1	0-1	1-0	0-0	3-1	0-2	1-0	0-1	0-0	1-2	0-0	0-4	0-2	0-2	1-0		1-0
Levante B	38	4	12	22	33	57	24	1-2	0-2	2-3	1-2	1-4	0-1	3-1	1-2	2-3	1-3	0-0	1-2	1-1	1-2	1-3	0-0	1-1	3-0	1-1	

26/08/2007 - 18/05/2008 • ‡ Qualified for promotion play-offs • † Relegation play-off

SPAIN 2007-08

SEGUNDA DIVISION B (3) — GRUPO 4

Team	Pl	W	D	L	F	A	Pts	Eci	Lin	Ceu	Mer	Gra	Agu	Mel	Car	RJa	Luc	Lor	BeB	Pue	Por	Mar	Baz	Maz	Alc	Tal	Alg
Ecija ‡	38	21	9	8	54	29	72		3-0	0-1	2-1	1-0	0-2	1-0	2-0	1-1	1-1	1-0	0-2	0-2	1-0	2-1	1-1	1-1	4-0	4-0	1-1
Linares ‡	38	20	7	11	61	43	67	2-1		1-0	3-0	0-1	4-2	0-0	1-3	0-3	0-2	0-1	0-2	3-1	2-2	2-1	1-1	4-1	1-3	1-1	3-1
Ceuta ‡	38	18	12	8	48	30	66	2-0	2-1		4-3	2-2	2-1	1-1	0-2	1-0	1-0	0-2	0-1	3-0	4-1	0-0	1-0	3-0	1-0	1-0	1-1
Mérida ‡	38	19	7	12	59	47	64	4-2	4-0	0-1		2-1	1-0	2-1	3-0	2-0	1-1	0-0	1-2	2-1	3-0	0-1	2-1	4-2	0-1	2-2	0-0
Granada	38	16	15	7	52	36	63	1-1	3-1	1-0	4-2		0-0	0-0	0-0	1-0	1-2	1-0	0-0	0-2	4-1	2-1	1-1	1-0	2-2	6-2	1-0
Aguilas	38	16	10	12	50	38	58	1-3	1-0	2-0	0-1	1-1		2-0	1-3	1-2	2-0	1-0	0-2	2-2	0-1	0-0	1-1	5-3	1-0	3-1	2-1
Melilla	38	15	13	10	47	36	58	1-2	1-1	1-1	6-0	1-0	2-1		0-0	1-2	3-2	1-2	1-1	0-1	2-1	1-0	0-0	2-1	1-1	2-0	0-0
Cartagena	38	15	12	11	42	33	57	0-2	3-1	0-0	3-3	1-1	2-1	1-2		2-0	2-1	3-1	1-2	0-0	1-0	0-1	1-1	2-0	0-0	2-3	3-0
Real Jaén	38	16	8	14	30	28	56	1-1	2-1	0-0	0-2	1-2	2-2	2-0	2-0		1-0	1-0	1-0	0-0	2-0	1-0	1-0	1-0	1-0	1-0	1-0
Lucena	38	13	13	12	40	34	52	0-2	0-2	1-1	3-0	0-2	0-0	0-0	0-0	1-1		1-1	5-0	0-1	2-0	2-4	1-0	1-1	0-2	2-0	3-1
Lorca Deportiva	38	13	10	15	38	40	49	2-1	0-1	0-3	0-0	1-2	0-0	2-3	1-0	0-0	1-1		2-1	3-1	1-0	1-2	0-2	0-0	2-0	0-0	1-2
Real Betis B	38	14	7	17	39	42	49	0-0	0-4	2-0	0-1	2-2	0-1	3-0	0-1	1-0	0-0	0-1		2-1	4-0	2-0	0-0	3-0	3-1	0-1	0-2
Puertollano	38	12	11	15	36	42	47	1-0	1-1	1-1	1-2	2-2	1-1	1-3	0-2	0-1	0-0	0-1	0-1		3-0	2-0	2-2	0-1	0-0	1-0	1-0
Racing Portuense	38	11	13	14	34	46	46	0-2	1-2	2-0	1-2	2-2	0-0	0-0	0-0	1-1	0-2	2-1	1-1	1-1		1-0	1-1	3-0	1-0	2-0	2-1
Marbella	38	12	10	16	29	42	46	1-1	1-2	0-0	1-0	0-2	0-0	0-2	0-1	1-0	0-0	0-3	2-1	1-3	1-0		2-1	3-2	1-0	0-0	3-1
Baza †	38	9	16	13	36	44	43	0-1	1-2	1-1	2-4	3-3	0-1	1-4	0-0	1-0	0-0	0-3	2-1	0-1	0-0	0-0		0-0	2-1	1-0	2-0
Mazarrón	38	11	9	18	37	55	42	2-1	0-0	1-3	0-3	1-0	0-3	0-2	2-0	0-1	1-0	2-1	2-1	1-3	1-2	0-0	1-1		0-0	3-0	4-2
Alcalá	38	10	10	11	17	32	43	41	1-0	1-1	1-3	0-0	1-0	1-2	1-1	0-0	0-0	1-0	2-2	4-1	2-0	0-2	2-0	0-1	1-1		1-2	2-0
Talavera	38	8	11	19	37	62	35	0-2	0-2	2-4	0-1	0-0	1-4	0-0	2-1	0-2	1-0	1-2	4-0	1-1	2-1	1-2	0-1	2-1	2-3		3-1
Algeciras	38	4	10	24	31	62	22	0-1	1-1	0-3	0-2	0-1	0-2	2-3	0-2	1-0	0-0	1-0	1-0	1-1	2-2	2-3	0-1	2-2	2-2	2-2	

26/08/2007 - 18/05/2008 • ‡ Qualified for promotion play-offs • † Relegation play-off

SEGUNDA DIVISION B (3) PLAY-OFFS

Grupo A • Semi-finals: Benidorm 1-1 0-1 **Rayo Vallecano**; **Zamora** 1-1 2-1 Linares • Final: Zamora 0-1 1-1 **Rayo Vallecano**

Grupo B • Semi-finals: Fuerteventura 0-0 0-3 **Alicante**; Mérida 1-2 **Ponferradina** • Final: **Alicante** 2-0 0-1 Ponferradina

Grupo C • Semi-finals: Gavá 2-2 1-1 **Huesca**; Deportivo B 1-0 0-3 **Ecija** • Final: **Huesca** 2-0 1-1 Ecija

Grupo D • Semi-finals: Barakaldo 0-0 0-2 **Girona**; **Ceuta** 1-1 2-1 Pontevedra • Final: Ceuta 0-0 0-1 **Girona**

Relegation play-offs: Baza 0-0 0-0 3-1p Villa Santa Brigida; Osasuna B 1-1 1-0 Villajoyosa • Villa Santa Brigida and Villajoyosa relegated

COPA DEL REY 2007-08

Third Round		Fourth Round			Round of Sixteen		
		Valencia	2	3			
L'Hospitalet	1	Real Unión Irún	1	0			
Real Unión Irún *	2				Valencia	2	2
Elche *	2				Real Betis *	1	1
Eibar	1	Elche	1	0			
		Real Betis	1	3			
		Real Valladolid *	1	3			
		Real Murcia	1	2			
					Real Valladolid	0	1
Granada 74	3				Atlético Madrid *	0	1
Cádiz *	2	Granada 74 *	1	1			
		Atlético Madrid	2	1			
		Villarreal	4	2			
		Las Palmas *	2	1			
Las Palmas	Bye				Villarreal	0	2
Xerez	2				Recreativo Huelva *	1	0
Albacete *	0	Xerez *	0	1			
		Recreativo Huelva	1	1			
		Sevilla	1	4			
Portuense	1	Denia *	1	3			
Denia *	3				Sevilla *	1	0
Alcoyano *	1 5p				Barcelona	1	0
Rayo Vallecano	1 3p	Alcoyano *	0	2			
		Barcelona	3	2			
		Racing Santander	0	2			
Tenerife *	1	Málaga *	0	0			
Málaga	2				Racing Santander	1	4
Pontevedra *	2				Real Zaragoza *	1	2
Puertollano	0	Pontevedra *	1	1			
		Real Zaragoza	0	3			
		RCD Espanyol *	1	2			
		Deportivo La Coruña	1	1			
					RCD Espanyol	1 1 3p	
Hércules *	2				Athletic Bilbao *	1 1 4p	
Alaves	1	Hércules *	2	0			
		Athletic Bilbao	2	2			
		RCD Mallorca	0	4			
		Osasuna *	2	0			
					RCD Mallorca *	2	1
Alicante	2				Real Madrid	1	0
Talavera *	0	Alicante *	1	1			
		Real Madrid	1	2			
		Levante *	2	1			
		Almeria	1	1			
					Levante	0	0
Burgos *	2				Getafe *	3	1
Ponferradina	0	Burgos *	0	1			
		Getafe	1	4			

* Home team/home team in the first leg

COPA DEL REY 2007-08

Quarter–finals	Semi–finals	Final

Valencia * 1 2
Atlético Madrid 0 3

Valencia 1 3
Barcelona * 1 2

Villarreal * 0 0
Barcelona 0 1

Valencia ‡ 3
Getafe 1

Racing Santander * 2 3
Athletic Bilbao 0 3

Racing Santander 1 1
Getafe * 3 1

RCD Mallorca 0 2
Getafe * 1 1

COPA DEL REY FINAL 2008

Estadio Vicente Calderón, Madrid, 16-04-2008, Att: 55 000, Ref: Undiano Mallenco

Valencia 3 Mata [4], Alexis [11], Morientes [84]
Getafe 1 Granero [45p]

Valencia - Timo Hildebrand - Miguel•, Raúl Albiol (Marco Caneira 57), Alexis•, Emiliano Moretti (Edu 67) - Angel Arizmendi, Rubén Baraja•, Carlos Marchena - Juan Mata• - David Silva•, David Villa (Fernando Morientes• 74). Tr: Ronald Koeman
Getafe - Oscar Ustari - David Cortes, Manuel Tena (Braulio 76), Daniel 'Cata' Diaz•, Lucas Licht• - Cosmin Contra (Pablo Hernandez 55), Javi Casquero• (Fabio Celestini 64•89), Rubén De La Red, Esteban Granero• - Manu del Moral, Juan Albin. Tr: Michael Laudrup

‡ Qualified for the UEFA Cup

ALMERIA 2007–08

Month	Date	Opponent	Result	Scorers	Att.
Sept	26	Deportivo	W 3-0	Negredo 18, Soriano 33, Crusat 50	20 000
	2	Valencia	L 1-2	Negredo 63	17 523
	15	Real Madrid	L 1-3	Uche 72	73 000
	23	Mallorca	D 1-1	Mane 33	14 271
	26	Murcia	W 1-0	Felipe Melo 41	24 250
	30	Racing	L 0-1		14 944
Oct	7	Ath. Bilbao	D 1-1	Felipe Melo 62	37 000
	21	Osasuna	W 2-0	Felipe Melo 51p, Negredo 69	13 148
	28	Barcelona	L 0-2		79 253
	31	Zaragoza	D 0-0		13 964
Nov	4	Levante	L 0-3		12 950
	11	At. Madrid	D 0-0		17 286
	25	Villarreal	D 1-1	Negredo 53	15 000
Dec	1	Sevilla	W 1-0	Acasiete 86	17 248
	9	Valladolid	W 1-0	Negredo 75	14 320
	16	Betis	L 1-3	Negredo 9p	40 000
	22	Getafe	L 0-2		13 476
Jan	6	Recreativo	D 1-1	Mane 19	13 198
	13	Espanyol	W 1-0	Uche 86	13 373
	20	Deportivo	W 1-0	Pulido 87	14 766
	27	Valencia	W 1-0	Felipe Melo 20	40 000
Feb	2	Real Madrid	W 2-0	Juanito 16, Negredo 47p	21 300
	10	Mallorca	D 0-0		15 000
	17	Murcia	W 1-0	Negredo 42	13 576
	24	Racing	L 0-1		18 624
Mar	2	Ath. Bilbao	D 1-1	Negredo 59p	14 161
	9	Osasuna	L 1-2	Corona 20	15 849
	16	Barcelona	D 2-2	Pulido 33, Uche 87	18 605
	23	Zaragoza	L 1-2	Negredo 89	30 000
	30	Levante	W 2-1	Soriano 2, Felipe Melo 35	21 477
Apr	6	At. Madrid	L 3-6	Felipe Melo 10, Jose Ortiz 17, Negredo 36	54 000
	13	Villarreal	L 1-2	Acasiete 84	14 330
	19	Sevilla	W 4-1	OG 24, Negredo 2 46 65, Juan Ortiz 62	23 000
	27	Valladolid	L 0-1		21 600
May	4	Betis	D 1-1	Pulido 47	14 575
	7	Getafe	L 2-4	Crusat 3, Paunovic 11	10 000
	11	Recreativo	L 0-2		14 324
	18	Espanyol	W 3-1	Felipe Melo 44, Crusat 53, Paunovic 90	9 400

ATHLETIC BILBAO 2007–08

Month	Date	Opponent	Result	Scorers	Att.
Sept	26	Osasuna	D 0-0		40 000
	2	Barcelona	L 1-3	Susaeta 70	76 817
	15	Zaragoza	D 1-1	Susaeta 8	40 000
	23	Levante	W 2-1	Aduritz 2 8 73	13 884
	26	At. Madrid	L 0-2		39 000
	30	Villarreal	L 0-1		18 000
Oct	7	Almeria	D 1-1	Etxeberria 31	37 000
	21	Valladolid	W 2-1	Aduritz 2 8 31	18 000
	27	Betis	D 0-0		36 000
	31	Getafe	L 0-2		11 000
Nov	4	Recreativo	W 2-0	Etxeberria 2 51 61	36 000
	11	Espanyol	L 1-2	Gabilondo 2	24 800
	25	Deportivo	D 2-2	OG 23, David Lopez 54	35 000
Dec	2	Valencia	W 3-0	Yeste 33, Llorente 2 61 90	42 000
	8	Real Madrid	L 0-1		40 000
	16	Mallorca	D 0-0		21 000
	23	Murcia	D 1-1	Koikili 45	36 000
Jan	6	Racing	L 0-1		17 124
	12	Sevilla	W 2-0	Yeste 28, Susaeta 68	35 000
	20	Osasuna	L 0-2		18 695
	27	Barcelona	D 1-1	Thuram OG 79	40 000
Feb	3	Zaragoza	L 0-1		28 000
	10	Levante	W 1-0	Llorente 55	34 000
	17	At. Madrid	W 2-1	Susaeta 39, Llorente 45	35 000
	24	Villarreal	L 1-2	Llorente 4	35 000
Mar	2	Almeria	D 1-1	Llorente 72	14 161
	9	Valladolid	W 2-0	Gabilondo 2 5 68	32 000
	15	Betis	W 2-1	Yeste 8, Lopez 65p	40 000
	23	Getafe	W 1-0	Etxeberria 28	32 000
	30	Recreativo	D 1-1	Aduritz 81	17 000
Apr	6	Espanyol	W 1-0	Garmendia 13	35 000
	13	Deportivo	L 0-3		18 000
	20	Valencia	W 5-1	Javi Martinez 20, Llorente 2 50 67, Iraola 86, Aduritz 90	33 000
	27	Real Madrid	L 0-3		79 500
May	4	Mallorca	W 1-0	Llorente 8	38 000
	7	Murcia	W 2-1	Llorente 31, Gabilondo 83	14 051
	11	Racing	D 0-0		36 000
	18	Sevilla	L 1-3	Aduritz 3p	35 000

ATLETICO MADRID 2007–08

Month	Date	Opponent	Result	Scorers	Att.
Sept	25	Real Madrid	L 1-2	Aguero 1	78 000
	2	Mallorca	D 1-1	Pernia 77	40 000
	16	Murcia	D 1-1	Aguero 14	32 000
	23	Racing	W 4-0	R.Garcia 11, Aguero 69, Forlan 76, Simão 86	45 000
	26	Ath. Bilbao	W 2-0	Aguero 13, Forlan 77	39 000
	30	Osasuna	W 2-0	R.Garcia 37, Aguero 81	48 000
Oct	7	Barcelona	L 0-3		89 976
	21	Zaragoza	W 4-0	L.Garcia 10, Forlan 34, Rodriguez 2 64 90p	48 000
	28	Levante	W 1-0	Forlan 27	16 281
	31	Sevilla	W 4-3	Maniche 2, Aguero 16, Rodriguez 69, Jurado 89	50 000
Nov	4	Villarreal	L 3-4	Pablo Ibanez 9, Simão 24, Aguero 61	53 000
	11	Almeria	D 0-0		17 286
	25	Valladolid	W 4-3	Maniche 3, Rodriguez 2 49 56, OG 90	40 000
Dec	2	Betis	W 2-0	Forlan 33, R.Garcia 90	36 000
	9	Getafe	W 1-0	Forlan 19	50 000
	16	Recreativo	D 0-0		19 000
	23	Espanyol	L 1-2	Simão 37	45 000
Jan	6	Deportivo	W 3-0	Forlan 39, Aguero 52, Jurado 64	9 000
	13	Valencia	W 1-0	Aguero 27	54 000
	20	Real Madrid	L 0-2		54 800
	27	Mallorca	L 0-1		18 000
Feb	3	Murcia	D 1-1	L.Garcia 62	35 000
	10	Racing	W 2-0	Forlan 2 55 73	20 224
	17	Ath. Bilbao	L 1-2	Antonio Lopez 5	35 000
	24	Osasuna	L 1-3	Forlan 26	17 384
Mar	2	Barcelona	W 4-2	Aguero 2 36 71, Rodriguez 42, Forlan 61p	54 851
	9	Zaragoza	L 1-2	Simão 26	33 000
	16	Levante	W 3-0	Simão 25, Forlan 2 39 55	35 000
	22	Sevilla	W 2-1	Rodriguez 18, Aguero 57	40 000
	29	Villarreal	L 0-3		24 000
Apr	6	Almeria	W 6-3	Antonio Lopez 2, Forlan 5p, Simão 2 34 45, Aguero 2 53 69	54 000
	13	Valladolid	D 1-1	Rodriguez 69	17 000
	19	Betis	L 1-3	Aguero 25	30 000
	27	Getafe	D 1-1	Aguero 39	13 000
May	3	Recreativo	W 3-0	Nacho Camacho 2 23 74, Aguero 54	24 000
	8	Espanyol	W 2-0	Aguero 27, Forlan 30	12 150
	11	Deportivo	W 1-0	Forlan 45	53 000
	18	Valencia	L 1-3	Aguero 77	15 000

REAL BETIS 2007–08

Month	Date	Opponent	Result	Scorers	Att.
Sept	26	Recreativo	D 1-1	Nano 39	19 000
	2	Espanyol	D 2-2	Fernando 84, Rafael Sobis 85	35 000
	16	Deportivo	L 0-1		10 000
	23	Valencia	L 1-2	Rafael Sobis 86	35 000
	27	Real Madrid	L 0-2		75 000
	30	Mallorca	W 3-0	Xisco 58, Rafael Sobis 77, Edu 90	35 000
Oct	7	Murcia	D 0-0		26 140
	21	Racing	D 1-1	Xisco 62	34 000
	27	Ath. Bilbao	D 0-0		36 000
	31	Osasuna	L 0-3		35 000
Nov	4	Barcelona	L 0-3		73 704
	11	Zaragoza	W 2-1	Pavone 2 80 90	40 000
	25	Levante	L 3-4	Arzu 9, Edu 25p, Pavone 52	13 981
Dec	2	At. Madrid	L 0-2		36 000
	9	Villarreal	W 1-0	Capi 8	21 000
	16	Almeria	W 3-1	Edu 27p, Pavone 50 82	40 000
	23	Valladolid	D 0-0		15 500
Jan	6	Sevilla	L 0-3		45 000
	13	Getafe	W 3-2	Pavone 3, Edu 33, OG 59	30 000
	20	Recreativo	D 1-1	Edu 56	40 000
	27	Espanyol	W 2-1	Rivera 45, Edu 90	30 200
Feb	3	Deportivo	L 0-1		35 000
	10	Valencia	L 1-3	Edu 47	40 000
	17	Real Madrid	L 2-3	Edu 32, Pavone 36	45 000
	24	Mallorca	D 1-1	Edu 69	16 000
Mar	2	Murcia	W 4-0	OG 15, Edu 41, Pavone 57, Rafael Sobis 57p	17 000
	9	Racing	L 0-3		17 000
	16	Ath. Bilbao	L 1-2	Gonzalez 35	40 000
	22	Osasuna	W 1-0	Gonzalez 53	13 672
	30	Barcelona	W 3-2	Edu 2 63 78, Juanito 76	48 000
Apr	6	Zaragoza	W 3-0	Gonzalez 2 8 16, Pavone 63	34 500
	13	Levante	L 0-1		35 000
	19	At. Madrid	W 3-1	Juande 15, Xisco 48, Capi 65	30 000
	27	Villarreal	L 0-1		35 000
May	4	Almeria	D 1-1	Odonkor 44	14 575
	7	Valladolid	D 1-1	Gonzalez 51p	35 000
	11	Sevilla	L 0-2		45 000
	18	Getafe	D 1-1	Nano 69	7 000

BARCELONA 2007–08

	Date	Opponent	Res		Comp	Scorers	Att
Sep	26	Racing	D	0-0	PD		24 000
	2	Ath. Bilbao	W	3-1	PD	Ronaldinho 2 [8] [35p], Toure [72]	76 817
	16	Osasuna	D	0-0	PD		17 933
	19	Lyon	W	3-0	ClgE	Clerc OG [21], Messi [82], Henry [91+]	78 698
	22	Sevilla	W	2-1	PD	Messi 2 [73] [80p]	77 399
	26	Zaragoza	W	4-1	PD	Messi 2 [5] [11], Iniesta [22], Marquez [45]	70 676
Oct	7	Levante	W	4-1	PD	Henry 3 [17] [24] [49], Messi [51]	20 229
	2	Stuttgart	W	2-0	ClgE	Puyol [53], Messi [67]	49 725
	7	At. Madrid	W	3-0	PD	Deco [14], Messi [18], Xavi [89]	89 976
	20	Villarreal	L	1-3	PD	Bojan [24]	22 000
	23	Rangers	D	0-0	ClgE		49 957
	28	Almeria	D	2-0	PD	Henry [38], Messi [80p]	79 253
Nov	1	Valladolid	D	1-1	PD	Ronaldinho [42]	26 000
	4	Betis	W	3-0	PD	Henry [32], Ronaldinho 2 [52] [90]	73 704
	7	Rangers	W	2-0	ClgE	Henry [6], Messi [43]	82 887
	10	Getafe	L	0-2	PD		14 000
	3	Alcoyano	W	3-0	CRr4	Henry [25], Gudjohnsen [89p], Bojan [94+]	
	24	Recreativo	W	3-0	PD	Milito [64], Bojan [66], Messi [81p]	66 385
	27	Lyon	D	2-2	ClgE	Iniesta [3], Messi [58p]	36 500
Dec	1	Espanyol	D	1-1	PD	Iniesta [5]	37 286
	9	Deportivo	W	2-1	PD	Ronaldinho [41p], Xavi [71]	57 579
	12	Stuttgart	W	3-1	ClgE	Giovanni [36], Eto'o [57], Ronaldinho [67]	52 761
	15	Valencia	W	3-0	PD	Eto'o 2 [12] [26], Gudjohnsen [61]	45 000
	23	Real Madrid	L	0-1	PD		98 248
	3	Alcoyano	D	2-2	CRr4	Ezquerro 2 [2] [10]	30 504
	5	Mallorca	W	2-0	PD	Marquez [62], Eto'o [90]	19 000
	9	Sevilla	D	1-1	CRr5	Henry [24]	45 000
Jan	12	Murcia	W	4-0	PD	Gudjohnsen [27], Bojan [52], Eto'o 2 [76] [87]	61 443
	15	Sevilla	D	0-0	CRr5		75 917
	20	Racing	W	1-0	PD	Henry [31]	60 039
	24	Villarreal	D	0-0	CRqf		20 000
	27	Ath. Bilbao	L	0-1	PD		40 000
	31	Villarreal	W	1-0	CRqf	Henry [41]	64 424
	3	Osasuna	W	1-0	PD	Xavi [87]	56 221
Feb	9	Sevilla	D	1-1	PD	Xavi [75]	45 500
	16	Zaragoza	W	2-1	PD	Henry [33], Ronaldinho [82]	34 596
	20	Celtic	W	3-2	CLr2	Messi 2 [18] [79], Henry [52]	58 426
	24	Levante	W	5-1	PD	Xavi [14], Messi [44], Eto'o 3 [56] [62] [87]	71 979
	27	Valencia	D	1-1	CRsf	Xavi [94+]	74 378
	1	At. Madrid	L	2-4	PD	Ronaldinho [30], Eto'o [74]	54 851
Mar	4	Celtic	W	1-0	CLr2	Xavi [3]	75 326
	1	Valencia	L	1-2	PD	Xavi [67]	52 827
	16	Almeria	D	2-2	PD	Bojan [17], Eto'o [58]	18 605
	20	Valencia	L	2-3	CRsf	Henry [71], Eto'o [80]	50 000
	23	Valladolid	W	4-1	PD	Eto'o [23], Iniesta [46], Bojan 2 [61] [83]	56 737
	29	Betis	L	2-3	PD	Bojan [13], Eto'o [15]	48 000
	1	Schalke	W	1-0	CLqf	Bojan [12]	53 951
	6	Getafe	D	0-0	PL		59 523
	9	Schalke	W	1-0	CLqf	Toure [43]	72 113
Apr	12	Recreativo	D	2-2	PL	Eto'o 2 [1] [46]	20 096
	19	Espanyol	D	0-0	PL		75 451
	23	Man Utd	D	0-0	CLsf		95 949
	26	Deportivo	L	0-2	PL		34 600
	29	Man Utd	L	0-1	CLsf		75 061
	4	Valencia	W	6-0	PL	Messi [5p], Xavi [8], Henry 2 [14] [58], Bojan 2 [72] [79]	54 905
May	7	Real Madrid	L	1-4	PL	Henry [87]	80 354
	11	Mallorca	L	2-3	PL	Henry [17], Eto'o [56]	39 928
	17	Murcia	W	5-3	PL	Eto'o [23], Henry [26], Giovanni 3 [32] [53] [67]	18 535

PD = Primera División • CL = UEFA Champions League • CR = Copa del Rey • gE = Group E • r2 = second round • r4 = fourth round • r5 = fifth round • qf = quarter-final • sf = semi-final

DEPORTIVO LA CORUNA 2007–08

	Date	Opponent	Res		Scorers	Att
Sep	26	Almeria	L	0-3		20 000
	2	Valladolid	D	2-2	Taborda [53], Riki [78]	20 000
	16	Betis	W	1-0	Guardado [7]	10 000
	23	Getafe	D	0-0		8 000
	26	Recreativo	L	0-2		13 000
	30	Espanyol	L	0-1		21 650
	7	Sevilla	W	1-0	Riki [73]	38 000
Oct	21	Valencia	L	2-4	Xisco [28], Bodipo [88]	15 000
	28	Real Madrid	L	1-3	Xisco [2]	69 000
	31	Mallorca	D	1-1	Guardado [41p]	14 000
	4	Murcia	W	2-0	Xisco [55], Guardado [71]	25 000
Nov	11	Racing	L	0-1		21 000
	25	Ath. Bilbao	D	2-2	Riki [63], Taborda [89]	35 000
	2	Osasuna	L	1-2	Ruben Castro [83]	10 000
Dec	9	Barcelona	L	1-2	Cristian [3]	57 579
	16	Zaragoza	D	1-1	Coloccini [52]	22 000
	23	Levante	W	1-0	Sergio [85p]	12 000
	6	At. Madrid	L	0-3		9 000
	13	Villarreal	L	3-4	Sergio [26p], Pablo Amo [57], Guardado [90]	18 000
Jan	20	Almeria	L	0-1		14 766
	27	Valladolid	W	3-1	Lopo [7], Xisco [46], Guardado [71]	16 000
	2	Betis	W	1-0	Pablo Amo [35]	35 000
	9	Getafe	D	1-1	Mario OG [43]	16 000
Feb	17	Recreativo	L	2-3	Verdu [8p], Riki [80]	15 000
	24	Espanyol	W	2-0	Coloccini [17], Lafita [23]	23 000
	2	Sevilla	W	2-1	Wilhelmsson [35p], Lafita [65]	27 000
	9	Valencia	D	2-2	Sergio [38], Lafita [45]	40 000
Mar	15	Real Madrid	W	1-0	Pepe OG [57]	34 600
	22	Mallorca	L	0-1		14 000
	30	Murcia	W	3-1	Xisco 3 [24] [47] [50]	15 000
	6	Racing	W	3-1	Xisco 2 [2] [42], Coloccini [24]	20 131
Apr	13	Ath. Bilbao	W	3-0	Coloccini [30], Sergio [64p], Luis Felipe [78]	18 000
	20	Osasuna	W	1-0	Sergio [64p]	18 122
	26	Barcelona	W	2-0	Juan Rodriguez [54], Pablo Amo [76]	34 600
	3	Zaragoza	L	0-1		30 000
May	7	Levante	W	1-0	Riki [87]	15 000
	11	At. Madrid	L	0-1		53 000
	18	Villarreal	L	0-2		17 000

ESPANYOL 2007–08

	Date	Opponent	Res		Scorers	Att
Sept	26	Valladolid	L	0-1		16 225
	2	Betis	D	2-2	Luis Garcia 2 [33] [41]	12 000
	16	Getafe	W	1-0	Jonathan [87]	18 750
	22	Recreativo	L	1-2	Riera [4]	18 500
	25	Sevilla	W	3-2	Angel [29], Luis Garcia [54], Tamudo [88]	40 000
	30	Deportivo	W	1-0	Tamudo [45]	21 650
Oct	6	Valencia	W	2-1	Riera [19], Luis Garcia [80]	45 000
	21	Real Madrid	W	2-1	Riera [1], Tamudo [53]	36 250
	27	Mallorca	D	2-2	OG [20], Tamudo [26]	18 000
	1	Murcia	D	0-0		14 150
Nov	4	Racing	D	1-1	Tamudo [90p]	16 848
	11	Ath. Bilbao	W	2-1	Tamudo [39], OG [89]	24 800
	25	Osasuna	W	2-1	Angel [30], Valdo [32]	16 004
	2	Barcelona	D	1-1	Smiljanic [68]	37 286
Dec	9	Zaragoza	D	3-3	Tamudo [7], Valdo [10], Zabaleta [14]	28 000
	15	Levante	W	1-0	Jarque [8]	10 900
	23	At. Madrid	W	2-1	Tamudo [53], Luis Garcia [85]	45 000
	6	Villarreal	W	2-1	Tamudo 2 [8] [36], Valdo [13]	14 100
Jan	13	Almeria	L	0-1		13 373
	20	Valladolid	L	1-2	Marc Torrejon [58]	16 500
	27	Betis	L	1-2	Luis Garcia [51]	30 200
	3	Getafe	W	1-0	Jonathan [17]	6 000
Feb	10	Recreativo	L	1-2	Ewerthon [39]	22 650
	16	Sevilla	L	2-4	Luis Garcia [41], Corominas [76]	21 910
	24	Deportivo	L	0-2		23 000
	1	Valencia	W	2-0	Luis Garcia 2 [4] [52p]	18 100
	9	Real Madrid	L	1-2	Valdo [29]	65 000
Mar	16	Mallorca	W	2-1	Luis Garcia 2 [58p] [89]	20 600
	22	Murcia	L	0-4		20 000
	30	Racing	L	0-3		22 100
	6	Ath. Bilbao	L	0-1		35 000
Apr	13	Osasuna	L	0-1		21 150
	19	Barcelona	D	0-0		75 451
	27	Zaragoza	D	1-1	Riera [59]	25 150
	4	Levante	D	1-1	Luis Garcia [90p]	7 882
May	7	At. Madrid	L	0-2		12 150
	11	Villarreal	L	0-2		22 500
	18	Almeria	L	1-3	Luis Garcia [58]	9 400

GETAFE 2007–08

Sept	25	Sevilla	L	1-4	Pablo [2] — 45 000
	2	Recreativo	D	1-1	Del Moral [90] — 12 000
	16	Espanyol	L	0-1	18 750
	23	Deportivo	D	0-0	8 000
	26	Valencia	L	1-2	Braulio [76] — 45 000
	30	Real Madrid	L	0-1	14 000
Oct	7	Mallorca	L	2-4	Sousa 2 [1 47] — 15 000
	21	Murcia	W	2-0	Kepa [54], Javi Casquero [59] — 13 000
	28	Racing	L	0-2	16 695
	31	Ath. Bilbao	W	2-0	Javi Casquero [8], Uche [29] — 11 000
Nov	4	Osasuna	W	2-0	Pablo [80p], Granero [81] — 16 124
	10	Barcelona	L	2-0	Del Moral [27], Albin [90] — 14 000
	25	Zaragoza	D	1-1	Sousa [64] — 26 000
Dec	2	Levante	W	2-1	Braulio 2 [60 89] — 12 000
	9	At. Madrid	L	0-1	50 000
	16	Villarreal	L	1-3	Kepa [85] — 16 000
	22	Almería	W	2-0	Licht [37], De la Red [85] — 13 476
Jan	6	Valladolid	L	0-3	9 000
	13	Betis	L	2-3	De la Red [61p], Del Moral [77] — 30 000
	19	Sevilla	W	3-2	Javi Casquero [32], Albin [58], Contra [90] — 13 000
	27	Recreativo	W	3-1	Albin [1], Granero [43], Del Moral [90] — 15 609
Feb	3	Espanyol	L	0-1	6 000
	9	Deportivo	D	1-1	Uche [68] — 16 000
	17	Valencia	D	0-0	8 000
	24	Real Madrid	W	1-0	Uche [68] — 78 000
Mar	2	Mallorca	D	3-3	Mario Cotelo [2], Albin [11], Ramis OG [59] — 13 000
	9	Murcia	W	3-0	Pablo [55], Albin [83], Javi Casquero [87] — 23 000
	16	Racing	W	2-1	Uche [66], Gavilan [76] — 10 000
	23	Ath. Bilbao	L	0-1	32 000
	30	Osasuna	L	0-2	10 500
Apr	6	Barcelona	D	0-0	59 523
	13	Zaragoza	D	0-0	10 000
	20	Levante	L	1-3	De la Red [59p] — 10 743
	27	At. Madrid	D	1-1	Albin [13] — 13 000
May	4	Villarreal	L	0-2	22 000
	7	Almería	W	4-2	Albin [32], Del Moral 2 [62 68], Granero [74p] — 10 000
	11	Valladolid	D	0-0	20 700
	18	Betis	D	1-1	Del Moral [5] — 7 000

LEVANTE 2007–08

Sept	26	Mallorca	L	0-3	21 000
	1	Murcia	D	0-0	12 000
	16	Racing	L	0-1	15 323
	23	Ath. Bilbao	L	1-2	Rigano [77] — 13 884
	26	Osasuna	L	1-4	Ettien [34] — 15 405
	29	Barcelona	L	1-4	Viqueira [72] — 20 229
Oct	7	Zaragoza	L	0-3	29 000
	20	Sevilla	L	0-2	12 276
	28	At. Madrid	L	0-1	16 281
	31	Villarreal	L	0-3	18 000
Nov	4	Almería	W	3-0	Rigano 3 [1 15 34] — 12 950
	11	Valladolid	L	0-1	15 420
	25	Betis	W	4-3	Tommasi [38], Riga 2 [41 49], Javi Fuego [81] — 13 981
Dec	2	Getafe	L	1-2	Riga [14] — 12 000
	9	Recreativo	L	0-2	12 918
	15	Espanyol	L	0-1	10 900
	23	Deportivo	L	0-1	12 000
Jan	6	Valencia	D	0-0	35 000
	13	Real Madrid	L	0-2	13 000
	20	Mallorca	D	2-2	Geijo [19], Alvaro [88] — 10 880
	27	Murcia	W	3-2	Alvaro [72], Riga [81p], Pedro Leon [89] — 22 750
	3	Racing	D	1-1	Riga [57] — 10 548
Feb	10	Ath. Bilbao	L	0-1	34 000
	17	Osasuna	W	2-1	Alvaro [54], Geijo [58] — 8 457
	24	Barcelona	L	1-5	Riga Mustapha [41p] — 71 979
Mar	2	Zaragoza	W	2-1	Geijo [19], Riga Mustapha [61] — 14 640
	9	Sevilla	L	1-2	Riga Mustapha [4] — 38 000
	16	At. Madrid	L	0-3	35 000
	23	Villarreal	L	1-2	Miguel Angel [64] — 11 938
	30	Almería	L	1-2	Iborra [90] — 21 500
Apr	6	Valladolid	L	0-3	10 864
	13	Betis	W	1-0	Pedro Leon [52] — 35 000
	20	Getafe	W	3-1	Juanma [41], Berson [44], Pedro Leon [53] — 10 743
	27	Recreativo	L	0-2	16 500
May	4	Espanyol	D	1-1	Juanma [77] — 7 882
	7	Deportivo	L	0-1	15 000
	11	Valencia	L	1-5	Serrano [32] — 13 418
	18	Real Madrid	L	2-5	Geijo 2 [52 63] — 80 300

RCD MALLORCA 2007–08

Sept	26	Levante	W	3-0	Ibagaza 2 [24p 71], Guiza [56] — 21 000
	2	At. Madrid	D	1-1	Guiza [18] — 40 000
	16	Villarreal	L	0-1	17 000
	23	Almería	D	1-1	Guiza [78] — 14 271
	26	Valladolid	W	4-2	Nunes [48], Arango 2 [50 87], Victor [83] — 13 200
	30	Betis	L	0-3	35 000
Oct	7	Getafe	W	4-2	Ibagaza 2 [53p], Arango 2 [70 78], Ramis [90] — 15 000
	21	Recreativo	W	2-0	Guiza [1], Tuni [78] — 18 000
	27	Espanyol	D	2-2	Arango [2], Guiza [69] — 18 000
	31	Deportivo	D	1-1	Guiza [11] — 14 000
Nov	3	Valencia	L	0-2	18 000
	11	Real Madrid	L	3-4	Borja Valero 2 [13 36], Guiza [57] — 78 000
	24	Sevilla	W	2-1	Ibagaza [16], Varela [38] — 39 000
Dec	2	Murcia	D	1-1	Webo [68] — 21 000
	9	Racing	L	1-3	Webo [11] — 16 160
	16	Ath. Bilbao	D	0-0	21 000
	23	Osasuna	L	1-3	Guiza [49] — 15 551
Jan	5	Barcelona	L	0-2	19 000
	13	Zaragoza	D	2-2	Varela [17], Guiza [61] — 28 000
	20	Levante	D	2-2	Guiza 2 [30 77] — 10 880
	27	At. Madrid	W	1-0	Arango [20] — 18 000
Feb	3	Villarreal	D	1-1	Basinas [38p] — 18 000
	10	Almería	D	0-0	22 000
	17	Valladolid	D	1-1	Ibagaza [78p] — 16 408
	24	Betis	D	1-1	Varela [55] — 16 000
Mar	2	Getafe	D	3-3	Guiza [14], Arango [76], Ramis [81] — 13 000
	9	Recreativo	W	7-1	Arango 3 [17 47 52], Guiza 2 [21 31], Borja Valero 2 [37 41] — 14 000
	16	Espanyol	L	1-2	Guiza [13] — 20 600
	22	Deportivo	W	1-0	Arango [21] — 14 000
	30	Valencia	W	3-0	Guiza 2 [12 58], Ramis [20] — 40 000
Apr	5	Real Madrid	D	1-1	Borja Valero [72] — 20 000
	13	Sevilla	L	2-3	Guiza [48] Webo [89] — 16 000
	20	Murcia	W	4-1	Guiza 3 [9 47 86], Arango [19] — 21 012
	27	Racing	W	3-1	Nunes [48], Trejo [82], Guiza [89] — 15 000
May	4	Ath. Bilbao	W	2-1	Guiza 2 [3 72] — 38 000
	7	Osasuna	W	2-1	Guiza [32], Trejo [90] — 16 000
	11	Barcelona	W	3-2	Borja Valero [67], Webo [70], Guiza [90] — 39 298
	18	Zaragoza	W	3-2	Guiza [17], Webo [66], Castro [90] — 17 000

REAL MURCIA 2007–08

Sept	25	Zaragoza	W	2-1	Mejia [16], Fernando [68] — 22 000
	1	Levante	D	0-0	12 000
	16	At. Madrid	D	1-1	Gallardo [80] — 32 000
	23	Villarreal	L	0-2	15 000
	26	Almería	L	0-1	24 250
	30	Valladolid	W	4-1	De Lucas [27], Fernando Baiano [75], Ivan Alonso [80], Abel [87] — 14 521
Oct	7	Betis	D	0-0	26 140
	21	Getafe	L	0-2	13 000
	28	Recreativo	W	1-0	Regueiro [46] — 23 390
Nov	1	Espanyol	D	0-0	11 150
	4	Deportivo	L	0-2	25 000
	10	Valencia	L	0-3	40 000
	24	Real Madrid	D	1-1	De Lucas [48] — 30 929
Dec	2	Mallorca	D	1-1	Inigo [23] — 21 000
	9	Sevilla	L	1-3	Fernando Baiano [65] — 39 000
	16	Racing	W	2-1	Goitom [56], Fernando Baiano [83p] — 22 950
	23	Ath. Bilbao	D	1-1	Fernando Baiano [54p] — 36 000
Jan	6	Osasuna	W	2-0	Goitom [72], Abel [90p] — 25 000
	12	Barcelona	L	0-4	61 443
	20	Zaragoza	L	1-3	Ivan Alonso [90] — 32 000
	27	Levante	L	2-3	Ivan Alonso [45], Rosinei [88] — 22 750
	3	At. Madrid	D	1-1	Jofre [51p] — 35 000
Feb	9	Villarreal	L	0-1	23 150
	17	Almería	L	0-1	13 500
	24	Valladolid	L	1-4	18 334
Mar	2	Betis	L	0-4	40 000
	9	Getafe	L	0-3	23 000
	15	Recreativo	L	2-4	De Lucas [15], Ivan Alonso [74p] — 15 453
	23	Espanyol	W	4-0	Ivan Alonso 2 [35p 46], Abel [62p], Richi [84] — 20 000
	30	Deportivo	L	1-3	De Lucas [3] — 15 000
Apr	6	Valencia	W	1-0	Ivan Alonso [34] — 24 541
	13	Real Madrid	L	0-1	76 000
	20	Mallorca	L	1-4	21 012
	26	Sevilla	D	0-0	20 000
May	4	Racing	L	2-3	Aquino [13], Ivan Alonso [28] — 17 915
	7	Ath. Bilbao	L	1-2	Ivan Alonso [17] — 14 051
	11	Osasuna	L	1-2	Abel [90] — 18 037
	18	Barcelona	L	3-5	Otxoa [16], Ivan Alonso [82p], Abel [86] — 18 535

OSASUNA 2007–08

	Date	Opponent	Res	Score	Scorers	Att
Sept	26	Ath. Bilbao	D	0-0		40 000
	16	Barcelona	D	0-0		17 933
	23	Zaragoza	L	1-2	Juanfran 24	30 000
	26	Levante	W	4-1	Pandiani 2 32 52, Juanfran 57, Javi 77	15 405
	30	At. Madrid	L	0-2		48 000
Oct	7	Villarreal	W	3-2	OG 22, Dady 35, Javi 79	16 648
	21	Almería	L	0-2		14 000
	28	Valladolid	D	2-2	Dady 2 72 78	16 307
	31	Betis	W	3-0	Crutxaga 42, Dady 52, Vela 55	35 000
Nov	4	Getafe	L	0-2		16 124
	11	Recreativo	L	0-1		15 000
	25	Espanyol	L	1-2	Portillo 75	16 004
Dec	2	Deportivo	W	2-1	Plasil 46, Dady 88	10 000
	5	Sevilla	D	1-1	Plasil 18	17 253
	8	Valencia	D	0-0		16 984
	16	Real Madrid	L	0-2		75 000
	23	Mallorca	W	3-1	Hector Font 9, Plasil 47, Hugo Viana 90	15 551
Jan	6	Murcia	L	0-2		25 000
	13	Racing	L	0-2		16 023
	20	Ath. Bilbao	W	2-0	Dady 67, Vela 68	18 695
	26	Sevilla	L	1-2	Kike Sola 69	42 000
Feb	3	Barcelona	L	0-1		56 221
	10	Zaragoza	W	1-0	Plasil 45	17 243
	17	Levante	L	1-2	Monreal 20	8 457
	24	At. Madrid	W	3-1	Kike Sola 1, Vela 5, Hector Font 75	17 384
Mar	2	Villarreal	D	0-0		17 000
	9	Almería	W	2-1	Kike Sola 6, Crutxaga 29	15 849
	16	Valladolid	D	0-0		16 000
	23	Betis	L	0-1		13 672
	30	Getafe	W	2-0	Miguel Flano 40, Punal 68p	10 500
Apr	5	Recreativo	L	0-1		18 493
	13	Espanyol	W	1-0	Astudillo 30	21 150
	20	Deportivo	L	0-1		18 122
	27	Valencia	L	0-3		50 000
May	4	Real Madrid	L	1-2	Punal 82	18 815
	7	Mallorca	L	1-2	Portillo 74	16 000
	11	Murcia	W	2-1	Dady 1, Juanfran 53	18 037
	18	Racing	L	0-1		22 000

RACING SANTANDER 2007–08

	Date	Opponent	Res	Score	Scorers	Att
Sept	26	Barcelona	D	0-0		24 000
	1	Zaragoza	D	1-1	Serrano 55	33 000
	16	Levante	W	1-0	Munitis 27	15 323
	23	At. Madrid	L	0-4		45 000
	26	Villarreal	L	0-2		15 036
	30	Almería	W	1-0	Garay 6	14 944
Oct	7	Valladolid	W	2-0	Smolarek 52, Tchite 90	14 554
	21	Betis	D	1-1	Jorge Lopez 86	34 000
	28	Getafe	W	2-0	Serrano 40, Jorge Lopez 74	16 695
	31	Recreativo	D	0-0		16 000
Nov	4	Espanyol	D	1-1	Tchite 54p	16 848
	11	Deportivo	W	1-0	Tchite 68	21 000
	25	Valencia	W	1-0	Jorge Lopez 70	17 555
Dec	1	Real Madrid	L	1-3	Munitis 73	79 500
	9	Mallorca	W	3-1	Jorge Lopez 18, Duscher 29, Munitis 83	16 160
	16	Murcia	L	1-2	Smolarek 62	22 950
	22	Sevilla	L	1-4	Garay 49	45 000
Jan	8	Ath. Bilbao	W	1-0	Tchite 43	17 124
	13	Osasuna	W	2-0	Colsa 81, Pablo Alvarez 83	16 023
	20	Barcelona	L	0-1		60 039
	27	Zaragoza	D	2-2	Bolado 3, Tchite 90	18 363
Feb	3	Levante	D	1-1	Duscher 74p	10 548
	10	At. Madrid	L	0-2		20 224
	17	Villarreal	D	0-0		18 000
	24	Almería	W	1-0	Tchite 61	18 624
Mar	2	Valladolid	W	1-0	Duscher 86	19 179
	9	Betis	W	2-0	Duscher 49, Garay 58	17 000
	16	Getafe	L	1-2	Smolarek 54	10 000
	23	Recreativo	W	2-0	Ortemo 80, Smolarek 90	13 991
	30	Espanyol	W	3-0	Serrano 15, Munitis 24, Bolado 90	22 100
Apr	6	Deportivo	L	1-3	Jorge Lopez 36	20 131
	12	Valencia	W	2-1	Colsa 60, Tchite 83	50 000
	20	Real Madrid	L	0-2		20 000
	27	Mallorca	L	1-3	Duscher 85	17 555
May	4	Murcia	W	3-2	De Coz OG 36, Jorge Lopez 45, Munitis 58	17 915
	7	Sevilla	L	0-3		19 497
	11	Ath. Bilbao	D	0-0		36 000
	18	Osasuna	W	1-0	Bolado 84	22 000

REAL MADRID 2007–08

	Date	Opponent	Res	Score	Comp	Scorers	Att
Aug	11	Sevilla	L	0-1	SC		45 000
	19	Sevilla	L	3-5	SC	Drenthe 24, Cannavaro 44, Sergio Ramos 79	69 000
	25	At. Madrid	W	2-1	PD	Raul 15, Sneijder 80	78 000
	2	Villarreal	W	5-0	PD	Raul 38, Sneijder 2 48 73, V.Nistelrooij 50, Guti 80	23 000
Sep	15	Almería	W	3-1	PD	Saviola 36, Sneijder 68, Higuain 87	73 000
	18	W. Bremen	W	2-1	CLgC		63 500
	23	Valladolid	D	1-1	PD	Saviola 87	22 000
	27	Betis	W	2-0	PD	Raul 66, Baptista 84	75 000
	30	Getafe	W	1-0	PD	Ramos 65	14 000
Oct	3	Lazio	D	2-2	CLgC		52 400
	7	Recreativo	W	2-0	PD	V.Nistelrooij 73, Higuain 90	75 000
	20	Espanyol	L	1-2	PD	Ramos 90	36 250
	24	Olympiacos	W	4-2	CLgC		64 477
	28	Deportivo	W	3-1	PD	V.Nistelrooij 8p, Raul 79, Robinho 85	69 000
	31	Valencia	W	5-1	PD	Raul 1, V.Nistelrooij 2 25 37, Ramos 30, Robinho 65	49 500
Nov	3	Sevilla	L	0-2	PD		45 500
	6	Olympiacos	D	0-0	CLgC		30 549
	11	Mallorca	W	4-3	PD	Robinho 2 11 16, Raul 62, V.Nistelrooij 72	78 000
	24	Murcia	D	1-1	PD	Robinho 8	30 929
	28	W. Bremen	L	2-3	CLgC		36 350
Dec	1	Racing	W	3-1	PD	Raul 2 5 70, Sneijder 10	79 500
	8	Ath. Bilbao	W	1-0	PD	V.Nistelrooij 55	40 000
	12	Lazio	W	3-1	CLgC		70 559
	16	Osasuna	W	2-0	PD	V.Nistelrooij 16, Sneijder 76	75 000
	19	Alicante	D	1-1	CRr4	Balboa 90	20 000
	23	Barcelona	W	1-0	PD	Baptista 35	98 248
Jan	2	Alicante	W	2-1	CRr4	Robben 31, Guti 92	35 000
	6	Zaragoza	W	2-0	PD	V.Nistelrooij 65, Robinho 76	74 000
	10	Mallorca	L	1-2	CRr5	Higuain 24	19 000
	13	Levante	W	2-0	PD	V.Nistelrooij 2 76p 88	13 000
	16	Mallorca	L	0-1	CRr5		68 000
	20	At. Madrid	W	2-0	PD	Raul 1, V.Nistelrooij 42	54 800
	27	Villarreal	W	3-2	PD	Robinho 2 9 53, Sneijder 77	78 000
Feb	3	Almería	L	0-2	PD		21 300
	10	Valladolid	W	7-0	PD	Baptista 8, Raul 2 30 38, Robben 32, Guti 2 43 61, Drenthe 79	79 300
	16	Betis	L	1-2	PD	Drenthe 5	45 000
	19	Roma	L	1-2	CLr2	Raul 8	56 231
	24	Getafe	L	0-1	PD		78 000
Mar	1	Recreativo	W	3-2	PD	Raul 27, Robinho 2 73 89	20 096
	5	Roma	L	1-2	CLr2	Raul 75	71 569
	8	Espanyol	W	2-1	PD	Higuain 42, Raul 72p	65 000
	16	Deportivo	L	0-1	PD		34 600
	23	Valencia	L	2-3	PD	Raul 2 34 55	75 000
	30	Sevilla	W	3-1	PD	Heinze 7, Raul 39, Higuain 65	79 000
Apr	5	Mallorca	D	1-1	PD	Sneijder 43	20 000
	13	Murcia	W	1-0	PD	Sneijder 59	76 000
	20	Racing	W	2-0	PD	Raul 14, Higuain 90	20 000
	27	Ath. Bilbao	W	3-0	PD	Saviola 13, Robben 74, Higuain 76	79 500
	4	Osasuna	W	2-1	PD	Robben 87, Higuain 89	18 815
May	7	Barcelona	W	4-1	PD	Raul 13, Robben 21, Higuain 63, V.Nistelrooij 78p	80 354
	11	Zaragoza	D	2-2	PD	V.Nistelrooij 26, Robinho 77	33 000
	18	Levante	W	5-2	PD	V.Nistelrooij 2 22 40, Sergio Ramos 2 77 77, Sneijder 54	80 300

SC = Supercopa • PD = Primera División • CL = UEFA Champions League • CR = Copa del Rey • gC = Group C • r2 = second round • r4 = fourth round • r5 = fifth round • Shaded matches are played at home

RECREATIVO HUELVA 2007–08

Month	Date	Opponent	Res	Score	Scorers	Att
Sept	26	Betis	D	1-1	Sinama-Pongolle [25]	19 000
	2	Getafe	D	1-1	Sinama-Pongolle [85]	12 000
	16	Sevilla	L	1-4	Aitor [54]	45 000
	22	Espanyol	W	2-1	Javi Guerrero 2 [53][60]	18 500
	26	Deportivo	W	2-0	Carlos Martins [13], Javi Guerrero [47]	13 000
	30	Valencia	L	0-1		16 000
Oct	7	Real Madrid	L	0-2		75 000
	21	Mallorca	D	0-0		18 000
	28	Murcia	L	0-1		23 390
	31	Racing	D	0-0		16 000
Nov	4	Ath. Bilbao	L	0-2		36 000
	11	Osasuna	W	1-0	Carlos Martins [69]	15 000
	24	Barcelona	L	0-3		66 385
Dec	2	Zaragoza	W	2-1	Carlos Martins 2 [25][41]	15 687
	9	Levante	W	2-0	Camunas [38], Jesus [54]	12 918
	16	At. Madrid	D	0-0		19 000
	23	Villarreal	D	1-1	Camunas [37]	16 000
Jan	6	Almería	W	1-0	Sinama-Pongolle [13]	13 198
	13	Valladolid	L	1-3	Camunas [43]	14 900
	20	Betis	D	1-1	Javi Guerrero [58]	40 000
	27	Getafe	L	1-3	Camunas [15]	15 609
Feb	3	Sevilla	L	1-2	Beto [88]	20 000
	10	Espanyol	W	2-1	Sinama-Pongolle 2 [17][25]	22 650
	17	Deportivo	W	3-2	Beto [52], Sinama-Pongolle [56], Caceres [56]	15 000
	24	Valencia	D	1-1	Carlos Martins [51]	40 000
Mar	1	Real Madrid	L	2-3	Caceres [17], Carlos Martins [90]	20 096
	9	Mallorca	L	1-7	Ruben [39]	14 000
	15	Murcia	W	4-2	Sinama-Pongolle 2 [19][70], Ruben [58], Marcos Garcia [85]	15 453
	23	Racing	L	0-2		13 991
	30	Ath. Bilbao	D	1-1	Amorebieta OG [13]	17 000
Apr	5	Osasuna	W	1-0	Sinama-Pongolle [37]	18 493
	12	Barcelona	D	2-2	Ruben 2 [40][70]	20 096
	19	Zaragoza	L	0-3		33 000
	27	Levante	W	2-0	Ersen Martin [9], Camunas [41]	16 500
May	3	At. Madrid	L	0-3		35 000
	7	Villarreal	L	0-2		17 757
	11	Almería	W	2-0	Jesus [24], Sinama-Pongolle [43]	14 324
	18	Valladolid	L	0-1	Javi Guerrero [90]	20 096

REAL VALLADOLID 2007–08

Month	Date	Opponent	Res	Score	Scorers	Att
Sept	26	Espanyol	W	1-0	Llorente [54]	16 225
	2	Deportivo	D	2-2	Garcia Calvo [45], Sisi [72]	20 000
	15	Valencia	L	1-2	Ngom Kome [10]	40 000
	23	Real Madrid	D	1-1	Pedro Lopez [70]	22 000
	26	Mallorca	L	2-4	Ogbeche [6], Victor [26]	13 200
	30	Murcia	L	1-4	Llorente [48]	14 521
Oct	7	Racing	L	0-2		14 554
	21	Ath. Bilbao	L	1-2	Victor [69p]	16 000
	28	Osasuna	D	2-2	Alvaro Rubio [35], Jonathan Sesma [52]	16 307
Nov	1	Barcelona	D	1-1	Llorente [16]	26 000
	4	Zaragoza	W	3-2	Victor 2 [28][30], Alvaro Rubio [32]	31 000
	11	Levante	W	1-0	Jonathan Sesma [63]	15 420
	25	At. Madrid	L	3-4	Victor [40], Sisi [48], Llorente [54]	40 000
Dec	2	Villarreal	W	2-0	Llorente [18], Victor [56]	16 885
	9	Almería	L	0-1		14 320
	16	Sevilla	D	0-0		17 667
	23	Betis	D	0-0		15 500
Jan	6	Getafe	W	3-0	Vivar Dorado 2 [53][75], Alvaro Rubio [67]	9 000
	13	Recreativo	W	3-0	Llorente 3 [7][22][87]	14 900
	20	Espanyol	W	2-1	Llorente 2 [1][33]	16 500
	2	Deportivo	L	1-3	Victor [82]	16 000
Feb	3	Valencia	L	0-2		16 300
	10	Real Madrid	L	0-7		79 300
	17	Mallorca	D	1-1	Llorente [37]	16 408
	24	Murcia	W	1-0	Llorente [41]	18 334
Mar	2	Racing	L	0-1		19 179
	9	Ath. Bilbao	L	0-2		32 000
	16	Osasuna	D	0-0		16 000
	23	Barcelona	L	1-4	Jonathan Sesma [30p]	56 737
	30	Zaragoza	W	2-1	Victor [53], Llorente [75]	15 300
Apr	6	Levante	W	3-0	Llorente [23], Victor [59], Borja [87]	10 864
	13	At. Madrid	D	1-1	Ogbeche [90]	17 000
	20	Villarreal	L	0-2		20 000
	27	Almería	W	1-0	Jonathan Sesma [90]	21 600
May	4	Sevilla	L	0-2		38 000
	7	Betis	D	1-1	Victor [63]	35 000
	11	Getafe	D	0-0		20 700
	18	Recreativo	D	1-1	Llorente [40]	20 096

SEVILLA 2007–08

Month	Date	Opponent	Res	Score	Comp	Scorers	Att
Aug	11	Real Madrid	W	1-0	SC	Luis Fabiano [28p]	45 000
	15	AEK Athens	W	2-0	CLp3	Luis Fabiano [48], Kanoute [68]	34 852
	19	Real Madrid	W	5-3	SC	Renato 2 [17][27], Kanoute 3 [37p][82][90]	69 000
	25	Getafe	W	4-1	PD	Jesus Navas [45], Luis Fabiano [66], Kanoute [69], Kerzhakov [81]	45 000
	31	Milan	L	1-3	ESC	Renato [13]	20 000
Sep	3	AEK Athens	W	4-1	CLp3	Luis Fabiano 2 [31p][45], Keita [40], Kerzhakov [53]	37 777
	16	Recreativo	W	4-1	PD	Kerzhakov 2 [11][74], Kanoute 2 [30][53]	45 000
	19	Arsenal	L	0-3	CLgH		59 992
	22	Barcelona	L	1-2	PD	Kanoute [90]	77 399
	25	Espanyol	L	2-3	PD	OG [60], Kone [68]	40 000
	29	Zaragoza	L	0-2	PD		30 000
Oct	2	Slavia P'ha	W	4-2	CLgH	Kanoute [8], Luis Fabiano [27], Escude [58], Arouna Kone [68]	24 202
	7	Deportivo	L	0-1	PD		38 000
	20	Levante	W	2-0	PD	Luis Fabiano 2 [6][13p]	12 276
	23	Steaua	W	2-1	CLgH	Kanoute [5], Luis Fabiano [17]	28 945
	28	Valencia	W	3-0	PD	Kanoute [10], Poulsen [73], Luis Fabiano [86]	45 000
	31	At. Madrid	L	3-4	PD	Luis Fabiano 2 [14][90], OG [44]	50 000
Nov	3	Real Madrid	W	2-0	PD	Keita [19], Luis Fabiano [21]	45 500
	7	Steaua	W	2-0	CLgH	Renato 2 [25][65]	7 984
	11	Villarreal	L	2-3	PD	Kanoute [35], Luis Fabiano [50]	20 000
	13	Denia	D	1-1	CRr4	Chevanton [75]	4 000
	24	Mallorca	L	1-2	PD	Kanoute [49]	39 000
	27	Arsenal	W	3-1	CLgH	Keita [24], Luis Fabiano [34], Kanoute [89p]	35 529
Dec	1	Almería	L	0-1	PD		17 248
	5	Osasuna	D	1-1	PD	Jesus Navas [46]	17 253
	9	Murcia	W	3-1	PD	Luis Fabiano 2 [4][90], Maresca [58p]	39 000
	12	Slavia	W	3-0	CLgH	Luis Fabiano [66], Kanoute [69], Daniel Alves [87]	11 689
	16	Valladolid	D	0-0	PD		17 667
	22	Racing	W	4-1	PD	Kanoute [26], Chevanton [66], Jesus Navas [84], Adriano Correia [90]	45 000
Jan	2	Denia	W	4-3	CRr4	Luis Fabiano [15], Fazio [28], Chevanton [89], Kanoute [91p]	15 000
	6	Betis	W	3-0	PD	Luis Fabiano 2 [26][42], Daniel Alves [64]	45 000
	9	Barcelona	D	1-1	CRr5	Diego Capel [44]	45 000
	12	Ath. Bilbao	L	0-2	PD		35 000
	15	Barcelona	D	0-0	CRr5		75 917
	19	Getafe	L	2-3	PD	Luis Fabiano [16], Dragutinovic [89]	13 000
	26	Osasuna	W	2-1	PD	Poulsen [55], Luis Fabiano [90p]	42 000
Feb	3	Recreativo	W	2-1	PD	Luis Fabiano 2 [45][83]	20 000
	9	Barcelona	D	1-1	PD	Diego Capel [34]	45 500
	16	Espanyol	W	4-2	PD	Luis Fabiano [6], Kanoute [11], Poulsen [74], Diego Capel [78]	21 910
	20	Fenerbahçe	L	2-3	CLr2	Edu OG [23], Escude [66]	46 210
	23	Zaragoza	W	5-0	PD	Luis Fabiano 2 [19][24], Ayala OG [43], Diogo OG [49], Keita [67]	25 000
Mar	1	Deportivo	L	1-2	PD	Kanoute [25]	27 000
	4	Fenerbahçe	W	3-2	CLr2	Daniel Alves 2, Keita [9], Kanoute [41]	38 626
	9	Levante	W	2-1	PD	Keita [27], Luis Fabiano [47]	38 000
	15	Valencia	W	2-1	PD	Luis Fabiano 2 [10][21]	35 000
	22	At. Madrid	L	1-2	PD	Diego Capel [48]	40 000
	30	Real Madrid	L	1-3	PD	Kanoute [37]	79 000
Apr	6	Villarreal	W	2-0	PD	Luis Fabiano [19p], Kanoute [87]	40 000
	13	Mallorca	W	3-2	PD	Renato [43], Kanoute [67], Daniel Alves [77]	16 000
	19	Almería	L	1-4	PD	Kanoute [72]	23 000
	26	Murcia	D	0-0	PD		20 000
May	4	Valladolid	W	2-0	PD	Renato 2 [11][41]	38 000
	7	Racing	W	3-0	PD	Fazio 2 [29][65], Moraton OG [90]	19 497
	11	Betis	W	2-0	PD	Luis Fabiano [32], Fazio [51]	45 000
	18	Ath. Bilbao	D	3-1	PD	Kanoute 2 [40][80], Keita [78]	35 000

SC = Supercopa • ESC = UEFA Super Cup • PD = Primera División •
CL = UEFA Champions League • CDR = Copa del Rey • gH = Group H •
r2 = second round • r4 = fourth round • r5 = fifth round

VALENCIA 2007–08

Month	Date	Opponent	Res	Score	Comp	Scorers	Att
Aug	14	IF Elfsborg	W	3-0	CLp3	Vicente 14, Silva 58, Morientes 70	46 320
	26	Villarreal	L	0-3			45 000
	29	IF Elfsborg	W	2-1	CLp3	Helguera 4, Villa 90	13 148
	2	Almería	W	2-1	PD	Morientes 46, Moretti 80	17 523
Sep	15	Valladolid	W	2-1	PD	Morientes 23, Silva 89	40 000
	18	Schalke	W	1-0	CLgB	Villa 63	53 951
	23	Betis	W	2-1	PD	Miguel 68, Joaquin 82	35 000
	26	Getafe	W	2-1	PD	Silva 16, Villa 32	45 000
	30	Recreativo	W	1-0	PD	Villa 6	16 000
Oct	3	Chelsea	L	1-2	CLgB	Villa 9	34 935
	6	Espanyol	L	1-2	PD	Baraja 5	45 000
	20	Deportivo	W	4-2	PD	Joaquin 9p, Baraja 13, Morientes 2 38 73	15 000
	24	Rosenborg	L	0-2	CLgB		21 119
	28	Sevilla	L	0-3	PD		45 000
	31	Real Madrid	L	1-5	PD	Angulo 59	49 500
Nov	3	Mallorca	W	2-0	PD	Morientes 2 45 61	18 000
	6	Rosenborg	L	0-2	CLgB		29 725
	10	Murcia	W	3-0	PD	Ivan Helguera 12, Villa 2 26 51	40 000
	25	Racing	L	0-1	PD		17 555
	28	Schalke	D	0-0	CLgB		29 232
Dec	2	Ath. Bilbao	L	0-3	PD		42 000
	8	Osasuna	D	0-0	PD		16 984
	11	Chelsea	D	0-0	CLgB		41 139
	15	Barcelona	L	0-3	PD		45 000
	19	Real Unión	W	2-1	CRr4	Zigic 2 60 70	3 500
	23	Zaragoza	D	2-2	PD	Zigic 76, Silva 82	28 000
Jan	2	Real Unión	W	3-0	CRr4	Zigic 65, Joaquín 2 78 90	7 000
	6	Levante	D	0-0	PD		35 000
	9	Betis	W	2-1	CRr5	Joaquín 2 4 11	15 000
	13	At. Madrid	L	0-1	PD		54 000
	16	Betis	W	2-1	CRr5	Zigic 9, Vicente 68	15 000
	19	Villarreal	L	0-3	PD		19 000
	23	At. Madrid	W	1-0	CRqf	Silva 32	44 000
	27	Almería	L	0-1	PD		40 000
	30	At. Madrid	L	2-3	CRqf	Cleeber 28p, Mata 35	40 000
Feb	3	Valladolid	W	2-0	PD	Mata 59, Villa 71	16 300
	10	Betis	W	3-1	PD	Villa 2 16 89, Silva 28	40 000
	17	Getafe	D	0-0	PD		8 000
	23	Recreativo	D	1-1	PD	Mata 38	40 000
	2	Barcelona	D	1-1	CRsf	Villa 70	74 378
Mar	1	Espanyol	L	0-2	PD		18 100
	9	Deportivo	D	2-2	PD	Mata 17, Villa 24	40 000
	15	Sevilla	L	1-2	PD	Albiol 89	35 000
	19	Barcelona	W	3-2	CRsf	Baraja 17, Mata 2 44 72	50 000
	23	Real Madrid	W	3-2	PD	Villa 2 33 66p, Arizmendi 88	75 000
	30	Mallorca	L	0-3	PD		40 000
Apr	6	Murcia	L	0-1	PD		24 541
	12	Racing	L	1-2	PD	Villa 65p	50 000
	16	Getafe	W	3-1	CRf	Mata 4, Alexis 11, Morientes 84	55 000
	20	Ath. Bilbao	L	1-5	PD	Villa 76	33 000
	27	Osasuna	W	3-0	PD	Villa 19, Mata 51, Joaquin 82	20 000
	4	Barcelona	L	0-6	PD		54 905
	7	Zaragoza	W	1-0	PD	Silva 20	45 000
May	11	Levante	W	5-1	PD	Villa 3 14 30 67, Mata 35, Angulo 66	13 418
	18	At. Madrid	W	3-1	PD	Seitaridis OG 11, Villa 2 41 56	15 000

PD = Primera División • CL = UEFA Champions League • CR = Copa del Rey
gB = Group B •r4 = fourth round • r5 = fifth round • qf = quarter-final
• sf = semi-final • f = final

VILLARREAL 2007–08

Month	Date	Opponent	Res	Score	Scorers	Att
	26	Valencia	W	3-0	Tomasson 15, Rossi 62p, Cazoria 72	45 000
	2	Real Madrid	L	0-5		23 000
Sept	16	Mallorca	W	1-0	Nihat 82	17 000
	23	Murcia	W	2-0	Rossi 2 85 90	15 000
	26	Racing	W	2-0	Nihat 39, Rossi 77	15 036
	30	Ath. Bilbao	W	1-0	Fuentes 62	18 000
Oct	7	Osasuna	L	2-3	Rossi 20, Godin 37	16 648
	20	Barcelona	W	3-1	Santi Cazorla 2, Marcos Senna 2 13 34p	22 000
	28	Zaragoza	L	1-4	Pires 81	32 000
	31	Levante	W	3-0	Franco 4, Rossi 16p, Cygan 38	18 000
Nov	4	At. Madrid	W	4-3	Rossi 30, Fuentes 41, Nihat 2 69 89	53 000
	11	Sevilla	W	3-2	Franco 2 31 68, Fernandez 86p	20 000
	25	Almería	D	1-1	Nihat 14	15 000
Dec	2	Valladolid	L	0-2		16 885
	9	Betis	L	0-1		21 000
	16	Getafe	W	3-1	Nihat 2 15 78, Santi Cazorla 83	16 000
	23	Recreativo	D	1-1	Nihat 39	16 000
Jan	5	Espanyol	L	0-3		14 100
	13	Deportivo	W	4-3	Rossi 30p, Nihat 2 64 67, Tomasson 79p	18 000
	19	Valencia	W	3-0	Pires 5, Capdevila 63, Nihat 70	19 000
	27	Real Madrid	L	2-3	Rossi 16, Capdevila 76	78 000
Feb	3	Mallorca	D	1-1	Rossi 26p	18 000
	9	Murcia	W	1-0	Franco 90	23 150
	17	Racing	D	0-0		18 000
	24	Ath. Bilbao	W	2-1	Franco 65, Capdevila 82	35 000
Mar	2	Osasuna	D	0-0		17 000
	9	Barcelona	W	2-1	Marcos Senna 31p, Tomasson 81	52 827
	16	Zaragoza	W	2-0	Nihat 10, Rossi 64p	18 000
	23	Levante	W	2-1	Fernandez 27, Franco 82	11 938
	29	At. Madrid	W	3-0	Santi Cazorla 39, Nihat 2 43 66	24 000
Apr	6	Sevilla	L	0-2		40 000
	13	Almería	L	0-1		17 000
	20	Valladolid	W	2-0	Nihat 16, Santi Cazorla 46	20 000
	27	Betis	W	1-0	Senna 15	35 000
May	4	Getafe	W	2-0	Nihat 2 37 44	22 000
	7	Recreativo	W	2-0	Nihat 54, Franco 82	17 757
	11	Espanyol	W	2-0	Javi Venta 31, Pires 45	22 500
	18	Deportivo	W	2-0	Fernandez 34, Franco 90	17 000

REAL ZARAGOZA 2007–08

Month	Date	Opponent	Res	Score	Scorers	Att
	25	Murcia	L	1-2	Ricardo Oliveira 29	22 000
	1	Racing	D	1-1	Ricardo Oliveira 75	33 000
Sept	15	Ath. Bilbao	D	1-1	Milito 15	40 000
	23	Osasuna	W	2-1	Matuzalem 17, Milito 70	30 000
	26	Barcelona	L	1-4	Zapater 9	70 676
	29	Sevilla	W	2-0	A'Alessandro 52, Sergio Garcia 86	30 000
Oct	7	Levante	W	3-0	Sergio Garcia 64, Ricardo Oliveira 2 72 82	29 000
	21	At. Madrid	L	0-4		48 000
	28	Villarreal	W	4-1	Ricardo Oliveira 37, Oscar 49, Milito 66p, Sergio Garcia 78	32 000
	31	Almería	W	1-0	Milito 78p	13 964
Nov	4	Valladolid	L	2-3	Ricardo Oliveira 13, Milito 89	31 000
	11	Betis	L	1-2	D'Alessandro 34	40 000
	25	Getafe	D	1-1	D'Alessandro 85	26 000
Dec	2	Recreativo	L	1-2	Milito 21	15 687
	9	Espanyol	D	3-3	Milito 5, Ricardo Oliveira 2 85 89	28 000
	16	Deportivo	D	1-1	Milito 16	22 000
	22	Valencia	D	2-2	Milito 18p, OG 30	28 000
	6	Real Madrid	L	0-2		74 000
Jan	13	Mallorca	D	2-2	Milito 2 23 36	28 000
	20	Murcia	W	3-1	Ricardo Oliveira 33, Milito 2 61 81	32 000
	27	Racing	D	2-2	Milito 60, Celades 83	18 363
	3	Ath. Bilbao	W	1-0	Ricardo Oliveira 27	28 000
Feb	10	Osasuna	L	0-1		17 243
	16	Barcelona	L	1-2	Ricardo Oliveira 52	34 596
	23	Sevilla	L	0-5		25 000
	2	Levante	L	1-2	Oscar 66	14 640
	8	At. Madrid	W	2-1	Pablo Ibañez OG 34, Milito 73p	33 000
Mar	16	Villarreal	L	0-2		18 000
	23	Almería	D	1-1	Ricardo Oliveira 68	30 000
	30	Valladolid	L	1-2	Zapater 29	15 300
	6	Betis	L	0-3		34 500
Apr	13	Getafe	D	0-0		10 000
	19	Recreativo	W	3-0	Sergio Garcia 1, Ricardo Oliveira 2 20 77	33 000
	27	Espanyol	D	1-1	Ricardo Oliveira 84	25 150
	3	Deportivo	W	1-0	Ayala 90	30 000
May	7	Valencia	L	0-1		45 000
	11	Real Madrid	D	2-2	Ricardo Oliveira 19, Sergio 86	33 000
	18	Mallorca	L	2-3	Ricardo Oliveira 2 56 90	17 000

EST – ESTONIA

NATIONAL TEAM RECORD
JULY 10TH 2006 TO JULY 12TH 2010

PL	W	D	L	F	A	%
24	5	3	16	14	38	27.1

FIFA/COCA-COLA WORLD RANKING

1993	1994	1995	1996	1997	1998	1999	2000	2001	2002	2003	2004	2005	2006	2007		High	
109	119	129	102	100	90	70	67	83	60	68	81	76	106	124		**60**	12/02

	2007–2008												Low	
08/07	09/07	10/07	11/07	12/07	01/08	02/08	03/08	04/08	05/08	06/08	07/08		**135**	02/96
125	127	130	128	124	124	125	129	119	115	121	120			

The top four clubs in the Meistriliiga - Levadia, Flora, TVMK and Trans Narva - once again dominated the championship, losing just four matches between them against the other six teams, as Levadia successfully defended their title; this despite a 19-match unbeaten run at the end of the season by Flora. Three of those defeats were against Maag Tammeka, perhaps the only team capable of mounting a serious challenge to the elite, and in their first season Maag made it to the 2008 Cup Final. There, however, they lost to a Flora side that won the trophy for the first time in ten years. Martin Reim had played a key part in their 1998 triumph and once again he was the

INTERNATIONAL HONOURS
Baltic Cup 1929 1931 1938

inspiration, the day before his 37th birthday. In a sign of the growing profile of football in Estonia the clubs signed their first TV deal since independence, a deal which will see regular broadcasts of the Meistriliiga on local television. Having led Levadia to their title, Tarmo Rüütli was appointed national team coach in November 2007 but he faces an uphill task in a 2010 FIFA World Cup qualifying group in which Estonia are comfortably the lowest ranked nation. In their Euro 2008 qualifying group, Estonia at least had Andorra ranked beneath them and true to form they won both matches to finish the group on seven points, having also managed a draw away to Macedonia.

THE FIFA BIG COUNT OF 2006

	Male	Female		Total
Number of players	49 725	7 299	Referees and Assistant Referees	182
Professionals	140		Admin, Coaches, Technical, Medical	480
Amateurs 18+	3 922		Number of clubs	138
Youth under 18	5 042		Number of teams	671
Unregistered	15 700		Clubs with women's teams	14
Total players	57 024		Players as % of population	4.31%

Estonian Football Association (EFA)
Eesti Jalgpalli Liit, A.Le Coq Arena, Asula 4c, Tallinn 11312, Estonia
Tel +372 6 279960   Fax +372 6 279969
efa@jalgpall.ee   www.jalgpall.ee
President: POHLAK Aivar   General Secretary: SIREL Tonu
Vice-President: SEDIN Pjotr   Treasurer: HOBEMAEGI Andri   Media Officer: UIBOLEHT Mihkel
Men's Coach: RUUTLI Tarmo   Women's Coach: LILLEVERE Aivar
EFA formed: 1921   UEFA: 1992   FIFA: 1923-43 & 1992
Blue shirts with white trimmings, Black shorts, White socks or White shirts with black trimmings, Black shorts, Blue socks

RECENT INTERNATIONAL MATCHES PLAYED BY ESTONIA

2005	Opponents	Score		Venue	Comp	Scorers	Att	Referee
3-09	Latvia	W	2-1	Tallinn	WCq	Oper [11], Smirnov [71]	8 970	Undiano Mallenco ESP
8-10	Slovakia	L	0-1	Bratislava	WCq		12 800	Allaerts BEL
12-10	Luxembourg	W	2-0	Luxembourg	WCq	Oper 2 [7 78]	2 010	Dereli TUR
12-11	Finland	D	2-2	Helsinki	Fr	Kruglov [62p], Lindpere [85]	1 900	Gilewski POL
16-11	Poland	L	1-3	Ostrowiec	Fr	Teever [68]	8 500	Hyytia FIN
2006								
1-03	Northern Ireland	L	0-1	Belfast	Fr		13 600	Vink NED
28-05	Turkey	D	1-1	Hamburg	Fr	Neemelo [87]	6 000	Weiner GER
31-05	New Zealand	D	1-1	Tallinn	Fr	Klavan [3]	3 500	Rasmussen DEN
16-08	FYR Macedonia	L	0-1	Tallinn	ECq		7 500	Jakbsson ISL
2-09	Israel	L	0-1	Tallinn	ECq		7 800	Verbist BEL
11-10	Russia	L	0-2	St Petersburg	ECq		21 517	Braamhaar NED
15-11	Belarus	W	2-1	Tallinn	Fr	Oper 2 [17 66]	3 000	Hermansen DEN
2007								
3-02	Poland	L	0-4	Jerez	Fr		100	Ruiz-Herrera ESP
7-02	Slovenia	L	0-1	Domzale	Fr		3 000	Ledentu FRA
24-03	Russia	L	0-2	Tallinn	ECq		8 212	Ceferin SVN
28-03	Israel	L	0-4	Tel Aviv	ECq		21 000	Cüneyt Cakir TUR
2-06	Croatia	L	0-1	Tallinn	ECq		8 651	Kassai HUN
6-06	England	L	0-3	Tallinn	ECq		9 635	Gilewski POL
22-08	Andorra	W	2-1	Tallinn	ECq	Piiroja [34], Zelinski [92+]	7 500	McCourt NIR
8-09	Croatia	L	0-2	Zagreb	ECq		15 102	Laperriere SUI
12-09	FYR Macedonia	D	1-1	Skopje	ECq	Piiroja [17]	5 000	Trattou CYP
13-10	England	L	0-3	London	ECq		86 655	Vollquartz DEN
17-10	Montenegro	L	0-1	Tallinn	Fr		2 000	Fröjdfeldt SWE
9-11	Saudi Arabia	L	0-2	Jeddah	Fr		2 500	Al Shehri KSA
17-11	Andorra	W	2-0	Andorra la Vella	ECq	Oper [31], Lindpere [60]	700	Collum SCO
21-11	Uzbekistan	D	0-0	Tashkent	Fr		3 000	Irmatov UZB
2008								
27-02	Poland	L	0-2	Wronki	Fr		4 500	Todorov BUL
26-03	Canada	W	2-0	Tallinn	Fr	Stalteri OG [59], Zahovaiko [90]	1 600	Zuta LTU
27-05	Georgia	D	1-1	Tallinn	Fr	Kink [64p]	2 500	Vejlgaard DEN
30-05	Latvia	L	0-1	Riga	BC		4 500	Zuta LTU
31-05	Lithuania	L	0-1	Jurmala	BC		1 300	Lajuks LVA
4-06	Faroe Islands	W	4-3	Tallinn	Fr	Zahovaiko 2 [9 14], Kink [28], Novikov [75]	2 300	Stalhammar SWE

Fr = Friendly match • EC = UEFA EURO 2008 • BC = Baltic Cup • WC = FIFA World Cup • q = qualifier

ESTONIA NATIONAL TEAM PLAYERS

	Player		Ap	G	Club	Date of Birth		Player		Ap	G	Club	Date of Birth
1	Mart Poom	GK	118	0	Watford	3 02 1972	14	Konstantin Vassiljev	MF	9	0	Nafta Lendava	16 08 1984
2	Igor Morozov	DF	2	0	Levadia	27 05 1989	15	Tarmo Kink	MF	23	2	Levadia	6 10 1985
3	Andrei Stepanov	DF	78	1	Khimki	16 03 1979	16	Mihkel Aksalu	GK	3	0	Flora	7 11 1984
6	Aleksandr Dmitrijev	MF	34	0	Hønefoss BK	18 02 1982	17	Enar Jääger	DF	53	0	Aalesunds FK	18 11 1984
7	Ats Purje	MF	8	0	Inter Turku	3 08 1985	20	Andrei Sidorenkov	DF	10	0	Flora	12 02 1984
8	Jevgeni Novikov	MF	13	2	FK Riga	28 06 1980	22	Martin Vunk	MF	6	0	Flora	21 08 1984
9	Vladimir Voskoboinikov	FW	7	0	Torpedo	2 02 1983	24	Kristen Viikmäe	MF	106	14	Jönköpings Södra	10 02 1979
10	Sander Puri	MF	3	0	Levadia	7 05 1988	27	Vjatšeslav Zahovaiko	FW	37	7	Flora	29 12 1981
11	Aivar Anniste	MF	43	3	TVMK	18 02 1980		**Selected others**					
12	Artur Kotenko	GK	15	0	Sandnes Ulf	20 08 1981		Raio Piiroja	DF	75	6	Fredrikstad FK	11 07 1979
13	Urmas Rooba	DF	70	1	TPS Turku	8 07 1978		Sergei Terehhov	MF	94	5	TVMK	18 04 1975

Estonia's squad for the June 2008 friendly against the Faroe Islands — Andres Oper — FW 108 33 Roda JC 7 11 1977

ESTONIA NATIONAL TEAM RECORDS AND RECORD SEQUENCES

Records			Sequence records		
Victory	6-0	LTU 1928	Wins	3	2000
Defeat	2-10	FIN 1922	Defeats	13	1994-1995
Player Caps	156	REIM Martin	Undefeated	6	Three times
Player Goals	33	OPER Andreas	Without win	34	1993-1996
			Clean sheets	3	1999, 2000, 2003
			Goals scored	13	1928-30, 1999-00
			Without goal	11	1994-1995
			Goals against	19	1934-1937

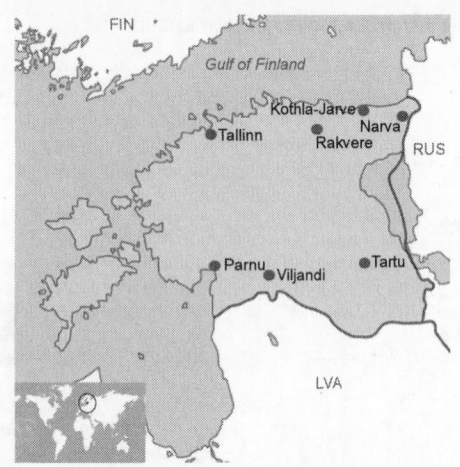

MAJOR CITIES/TOWNS

		Population '000
1	Tallinn	390
2	Tartu	100
3	Narva	66
4	Kohtla-Järve	45
5	Pärnu	43
6	Viljandi	20
7	Maardu	16
8	Rakvere	16
9	Sillamäe	16
10	Kuressaare	14
11	Voru	14
12	Valga	13
13	Haapsalu	11
14	Jõhvi	11
15	Paide	9
16	Keila	9
17	Kivioli	6
18	Polva	6
19	Tapa	6
20	Jogeva	6
21	Türi	6
22	Elva	5
23	Rapla	5
24	Saue	5

REPUBLIC OF ESTONIA; EESTI VABARIIK

Capital	Tallinn	Language	Estonian, Russian			Independence	1991
Population	1 324 333	Area	45 226 km²	Density	3 per km²	% in cities	73%
GDP per cap	$12 300	Dailling code	+372	Internet	.ee	GMT + / -	+2

MEDALS TABLE

		Overall			League			Cup			Europe			City	Stadium	Cap'ty	DoF
		G	S	B	G	S	B	G	S	B	G	S	B				
1	Flora Tallinn	10	8	3	7	5	3	3	3					Tallinn	A. Le Coq Arena	9 300	1990
2	Levadia Tallinn	10	3	2	5	2	2	5	1					Tallinn	Kadriorg Staadion	4 700	1999
3	TVMK Tallinn	3	5	4	1	3	4	2	2					Tallinn	Kadriorg Staadion	4 700	1951
4	Lantana Tallinn	3	4	5	2	1	5	1	3					Tallinn			1994-99
5	Norma Tallinn	3	2		2	1		1	1					Tallinn			1990-97
6	Tallinna Sadam	2	2	1		2	1	2						Tallinn			1991-99
7	Trans Narva	1	3	2		1	2	1	2					Narva	Kreenholmi Staadion	3 000	1979
8	Tulevik Viljandi		3			1			2					Viljandi	Linnastaadion	2 506	1992
9	EP Jõhvi		2			1			1					Jõhvi	Kaevur	2 000	1974
10	Maag Tammeka Tartu	1				1								Tartu	Tamme Stadion	700	2006
11	Ajax Lasnamäe													Lasnamäe	Ajax	500	1993
	Vaprus Pärnu													Pärnu	Pärnu Kalevi Staadion	1 900	1999
	Warrior Valga													Valga	Valga Keskstaadion	2 500	1997

RECENT LEAGUE AND CUP RECORD

	Championship						Cup		
Year	Champions	Pts	Runners-up	Pts	Third	Pts	Winners	Score	Runners-up
1995	Flora Tallinn	41	Lantana-Marlekor	40	Trans Narva	26	Flora Tallinn	2-0	Lantana-Marlekor
1996	Lantana Tallinn	37	Flora Tallinn	31	Tevalte-Marlekor	31	Tallinna Sadam	2-0	EP Jõhvi
1997	Lantana Tallinn	41	Flora Tallinn	38	Tallinna Sadam	24	Tallinna Sadam	3-2	Lantana Tallinn
1998	Flora Tallinn	42	Tallinna Sadam	32	Lantana Tallinn	25	Flora Tallinn	3-2	Lantana Tallinn
1998	Flora Tallinn	35	Tallinna Sadam	34	Lantana Tallinn	25			
1999	Levadia Maardu	73	Tulevik Viljandi	53	Flora Tallinn	47	Levadia Maardu	3-2	Tulevik Viljandi
2000	Levadia Maardu	74	Flora Tallinn	55	TVMK Tallinn	48	Levadia Maardu	2-0	Tulevik Viljandi
2001	Flora Tallinn	68	TVMK Tallinn	56	Levadia Maardu	55	Trans Narva	1-0	Flora Tallinn
2002	Flora Tallinn	64	Levadia Maardu	62	TVMK Tallinn	53	Levadia Tallinn	2-0	Levadia Maardu
2003	Flora Tallinn	76	TVMK Tallinn	65	Levadia Maardu	49	TVMK Tallinn	2-2 4-1p	Flora Tallinn
2004	Levadia Tallinn	69	TVMK Tallinn	63	Flora Tallinn	58	Levadia Tallinn	3-0	TVMK Tallinn
2005	TVMK Tallinn	95	Levadia Tallinn	89	Trans Narva	75	Levadia Tallinn	1-0	TVMK Tallinn
2006	Levadia Tallinn	94	Trans Narva	83	Flora Tallinn	82	TVMK Tallinn	1-0	Flora Tallinn
2007	Levadia Tallinn	91	Flora Tallinn	83	TVMK Tallinn	79	Levadia Tallinn	3-0	Trans Narva
2008							Flora Tallinn	3-1	Maag Tammeka

ESTONIA 2007

MEISTRILIIGA

	Pl	W	D	L	F	A	Pts	Levadia	Flora	TVMK	Trans Narva	Maag T'ka	Kalev	Tulevik	Vaprus	Kuressaare	Ajax
Levadia Tallinn †	36	29	4	3	126	20	91		2-1 1-1	2-0 1-0	2-0 1-2	2-2 4-0	4-2 8-0	4-0 5-0	4-1 5-0	4-0 4-0	5-0 7-1
Flora Tallinn ‡	36	26	5	5	108	30	83	1-2 3-2		2-2 2-0	0-2 0-0	3-0 3-1	4-2 4-1	4-0 5-0	7-0 8-1	5-0 5-1	11-0 10-0
TVMK Tallinn ‡	36	25	4	7	116	36	79	1-1 2-6	6-0 1-2		2-2 1-0	2-0 2-0	5-0 5-0	3-1 5-1	9-0 6-3	4-0 5-1	7-1 9-0
Trans Narva	36	25	3	8	89	28	78	0-0 0-3	3-1 0-3	3-1 4-0		0-1 2-3	0-1 2-0	5-1 7-0	2-0 2-1	3-1 5-0	2-0 6-1
Maag Tammeka Tartu	36	18	8	10	54	40	62	1-3 0-3	0-0 0-0	1-3 0-1	0-2 2-1		1-1 4-1	1-1 3-1	2-0 3-0	4-1 1-0	2-0 5-1
Kalev Tallinn	36	13	4	19	44	77	43	1-0 0-4	0-1 1-3	1-2 1-3	0-2 1-5	0-2 2-2		2-1 1-1	0-2 2-1	2-1 2-1	5-0 1-0
Tulevik Viljandi	36	11	4	21	43	80	37	0-4 0-6	1-2 0-3	1-1 0-1	0-2 1-4	0-1 0-0	2-1 1-2		0-1 4-1	0-1 3-2	2-0 4-1
Vaprus Pärnu	36	8	1	27	35	96	25	0-5 0-2	0-3 0-1	0-2 0-5	0-3 1-3	0-1 0-4	0-1 1-2	2-3 0-3		0-0 2-0	1-0 2-0
FC Kuressaare	36	5	3	28	25	94	18	0-5 0-3	0-1 1-3	0-2 0-6	0-5 0-3	0-2 1-1	1-3 2-0	0-1 0-2	3-0 0-3		2-2 0-1
Ajax Lasnanäe	36	1	2	33	14	153	5	0-10 1-2	0-2 0-4	0-6 0-2	0-4 1-3	0-2 0-2	1-4 1-1	0-5 0-3	0-5 1-7	1-4 1-2	

10/03/2007 - 13/11/2007 • † Qualified for the UEFA Champions League • ‡ Qualified for the UEFA Cup
Relegation play-off: **Nomme Kalju** 0-1 2-1 FC Kuressaare
Top scorers: Dmitri Lipartov, Trans Narva 30; Indrek Zelinski, Levadia 24; Tiit Tikenberg, Kalev 20; Maksim Gruznov, Trans Narva 18; Jarmo Ahjupera, Flora 17; Tarmo Kink, Levadia 16

ESTONIA 2007
ESILIIGA (2)

	Pl	W	D	L	F	A	Pts
Levadia Tallinn II	36	27	5	4	95	20	86
Flora Tallinn II	36	24	6	6	97	33	78
Kalev Sillamäe	36	20	9	7	67	40	69
TVMK Tallinn II	36	15	8	13	81	68	53
Maag Tammeka Tartu II	36	14	11	11	51	39	53
Nomme Kalju	36	13	9	14	69	69	48
Warrior Valga	36	13	5	18	72	73	44
Tulevik Viljandi II	36	9	7	20	37	84	35
Välk 494 Tartu	36	7	8	21	49	93	29
FC Elva	36	3	2	31	17	116	11

11/03/2007 - 11/11/2007
Second teams of the major clubs ineligible for promotion

EFA CUP 2007–08

Round of sixteen		Quarter–finals		Semi–finals		Final	
Flora Tallinn *	6						
Tabasalu Palliklubi	0	Flora Tallinn	4				
Ganvix Türi	0	Maag Tammeka II *	1				
Maag Tammeka II *	4			Flora Tallinn *	1 4p		
Trans Narva *	9			Levadia Tallinn	1 1p		
Esteve Maardu	1	Trans Narva	1				
Maag Tammeka III	1	Levadia Tallinn *	3				
Levadia Tallinn *	4					Flora Tallinn ‡	3
Flora Tallinn II	8					Maag Tammeka Tartu	1
FC Elva	1	Flora Tallinn II	3				
Trans Narva II	0	Kalev Tallinn *	1				
Kalev Tallinn *	1			Flora Tallinn II *	0		
Santos Tartu *	3			Maag Tammeka Tartu	3		
Viljandi Tulevik II	1	Santos Tartu *	0				
TVMK Tallinn *	1	Maag Tammeka Tartu	3				
Maag Tammeka Tartu	3						

* Home team • ‡ Qualified for the UEFA Cup

CUP FINAL
Kadriorg, Tallinn
13-05-2008, Att: 500
Scorers -
Sander Post [1], Juha Hakola 2 [47p 64] for Flora; Artur Ossipov [72p] for Maag Tammeka

ETH – ETHIOPIA

NATIONAL TEAM RECORD
JULY 10TH 2006 TO JULY 12TH 2010

PL	W	D	L	F	A	%
18	9	1	8	22	18	52.8

FIFA/COCA-COLA WORLD RANKING

1993	1994	1995	1996	1997	1998	1999	2000	2001	2002	2003	2004	2005	2006	2007		High	
96	115	105	108	126	145	142	133	155	138	130	151	112	92	105		85	12/92

2007–2008													Low	
08/07	09/07	10/07	11/07	12/07	01/08	02/08	03/08	04/08	05/08	06/08	07/08		155	12/01
92	113	108	108	105	90	86	87	88	89	131	108			

Squabbling politicians and administrators have caused a crisis in Ethiopian football, overshadowing events on the field and threatening the immediate future of the game in the country. In late July 2008 FIFA moved to suspend the country again for interference in the running of the affairs of the football association, threatening the national team's continued participation in the 2010 FIFA World Cup qualifiers. Although Ethiopia had lost their opening two matches, including a surprise 3-1 home defeat at the hands of Rwanda, they had bounced back with double victories over Mauritania to restore their chances of progress to the second group stage. The mixed results saw Ethiopia tumble

INTERNATIONAL HONOURS
CAF African Cup of Nations 1962   **CECAFA Cup** 1987 2001 2004 2005

some 40 places in the FIFA/Coca-Cola World Ranking, to outside the world's top 100. The squabble comes over the position at the head of the federation of Ashebir Woldegiorgis, who had been unconstitutionally removed from the post by the government. A dispute between the Premier League clubs and the federation also dominated the agenda. It delayed the start of the season and limited the amount of football played. A total of 16 teams will get the 2008/2009 season underway. On the field, Abraham Teklehaimanot was appointed national team coach, replacing Swenet Bishaw who went to work in Yemen, where many Ethiopian players and coaches go for more lucrative earnings.

THE FIFA BIG COUNT OF 2006

	Male	Female		Total
Number of players	3 309 020	165 225	Referees and Assistant Referees	10 100
Professionals	20		Admin, Coaches, Technical, Medical	300 500
Amateurs 18+	21 225		Number of clubs	1 000
Youth under 18	35 000		Number of teams	3 000
Unregistered	520 000		Clubs with women's teams	4
Total players	3 474 245		Players as % of population	4.65%

Ethiopian Football Federation (EFF)
Cherchel Road, PO Box 8214, Addis Abeba, Ethiopia
Tel +251 0911 208486   Fax +251 111 569701
ethiokaz@ethionet.et   www.none
President: WOLDEGIORGIS Ashebir Dr   General Secretary: EJIGU Ashenafi
Vice-President: BEKELE Horpdfa   Treasurer: YADEITA Abu   Media Officer: None
Men's Coach: TEKLEHAYMANOT Abraham   Women's Coach: MELESE Shale
EFF formed: 1943   CAF: 1957   FIFA: 1953
Green shirts, Yellow shorts, Red socks

RECENT INTERNATIONAL MATCHES PLAYED BY ETHIOPIA

2005	Opponents	Score		Venue	Comp	Scorers	Att	Referee
10-12	Rwanda	W	1-0	Kigali	CCf	Andualem Negussie 59		
2006								
17-07	Yemen	W	1-0	Addis Abeba	Fr	Andre Lomani 72		
11-08	Kenya	W	1-0	Addis Abeba	Fr			
13-08	Kenya	W	1-0	Addis Abeba	Fr			
3-09	Libya	W	1-0	Addis Abeba	CNq	Dawit Mebratu 15		Abd El Fatah EGY
7-10	Namibia	L	0-1	Katutura	CNq			Moeketsi LES
25-11	Tanzania	L	1-2	Addis Abeba	CCr1	Binyam Assefa 24		
28-11	Djibouti	W	4-0	Addis Abeba	CCr1	Dawit Mebratu 27p, Tesfaye Tafese 45, Behailu Demeke 57p, Bizuneh Worku 64		
1-12	Malawi	W	1-0	Addis Abeba	CCr1	Dawit Mebratu 42		
5-12	Zambia	L	0-1	Addis Abeba	CCqf			
2007								
29-04	Congo DR	L	0-2	Kinshasa	CNq			Bennett RSA
1-06	Congo DR	W	1-0	Addis Abeba	CNq	Salhadin Said 30		Hicuburundi BDI
17-06	Libya	L	1-3	Tripoli	CNq	Fikru Tefera 58		Saadallah TUN
8-09	Namibia	L	2-3	Addis Abeba	CNq	Birhanu Bogale 44, Salhadin Said 66		Auda EGY
15-12	Sudan	D	0-0	Arusha	Fr			
2008								
31-05	Morocco	L	0-3	Casablanca	WCq		5 000	Diatta SEN
8-06	Rwanda	L	1-2	Addis Abeba	WCq	Tesfaye Tafese 44	18 000	Ndinya KEN
13-06	Mauritania	W	1-0	Nouakchott	WCq	Salhadin Said 93+	5 000	Ambaya LBY
22-06	Mauritania	W	6-1	Addis Abeba	WCq	Fikru Tefera 2 38p 89, Andualem Negussie 2 55 63, Mohamed Mesud 83, Girma Adane 90	13 000	Lwanja MWI

Fr = Friendly match • CN = CAF African Cup of Nations • CC = CECAFA Cup • WC = FIFA World Cup
q = qualifier • r1 = first round group • sf = semi-final • f = final • † Not an official International

ETHIOPIA NATIONAL TEAM RECORDS AND RECORD SEQUENCES

Records			Sequence records					
Victory	8-1	DJI 1983	Wins	9	2005-2006	Clean sheets	6	2005-2006
Defeat	0-13	IRQ 1992	Defeats	4	Five times	Goals scored	10	1995-97, 2000-02
Player Caps	n/a		Undefeated	11	1984-88, 2005-06	Without goal	5	1995
Player Goals	n/a		Without win	9	1996-1999	Goals against	18	1956-1962

RECENT LEAGUE AND CUP RECORD

	Championship							Cup		
Year	Champions	Pts	Runners-up	Pts	Third	Pts		Winners	Score	Runners-up
2000	St George	46	EEPCO Mebrat Hail	39	Ethiopian Coffee	38		Ethiopian Coffee	2-1	Awassa City
2001	EEPCO Mebrat Hail	59	St George	49	Ethiopian Coffee	48		EEPCO Mebrat Hail	2-1	Guna Trading
2002	St George	61	Ethiopian Coffee	50	EEPCO Mebrat Hail	45		Medhin	6-3p	EEPCO Mebrat Hail
2003	St George	56	Arba Minch Textile	55	Ethiopian Coffee	44		Ethiopian Coffee	2-0	EEPCO Mebrat Hail
2004	Awassa City	48	Ethiopian Coffee	46	Trans Ethiopia	45		Banks	1-0	Ethiopian Coffee
2005	St George	64	Trans Ethiopia	46	Awassa City	44		Awassa City	2-2 wop	Muger Cement
2006	St George	56	Ethiopian Coffee	52	EEPCO Mebrat Hail			Mekelakeya	1-0	Ethiopian Coffee
2007	Awassa City awarded the title after 12 clubs withdrew							Harar Bira		
2008	St George	62	Adama City	53	Awassa City	48		Not held		

ETHIOPIA COUNTRY INFORMATION

Capital	Addis Abeba	Independence	Occupied by Italy 1936-41	GDP per Capita	$700
Population	67 851 281	Status	Republic	GNP Ranking	103
Area km²	1 127 127	Language	Amharic	Dialling code	+251
Population density	60 per km²	Literacy rate	42%	Internet code	.et
% in urban areas	13%	Main religion	Muslim 45%, Christian 40%	GMT +/−	+3
Towns/Cities ('000)	Addis Abeba 2 757; Dire Dawa 252; Nazret 214; Bahir Dar 168; Gondar 153; Mek'ele 151; Dese 136; Awassa 133; Jimma 128; Debre Zeyit 104; Kembolcha 93; Harer 90				
Neighbours (km)	Eritrea 912; Djibouti 349; Somalia 1 600; Kenya 861; Sudan 1 606				
Main stadia	Addis Abeba Stadium – Addis Abeba 35 000; Awassa Kenema – Awassa 25 000				

FIJ – FIJI

NATIONAL TEAM RECORD
JULY 10TH 2006 TO JULY 12TH 2010

PL	W	D	L	F	A	%
9	4	2	3	31	11	55.6

FIFA/COCA-COLA WORLD RANKING

1993	1994	1995	1996	1997	1998	1999	2000	2001	2002	2003	2004	2005	2006	2007
107	120	139	157	146	124	135	141	123	140	149	135	135	150	131

High **94** 07/94

	2007–2008										
08/07	09/07	10/07	11/07	12/07	01/08	02/08	03/08	04/08	05/08	06/08	07/08
170	119	127	133	131	131	130	132	134	133	144	148

Low **170** 08/07

It was a busy sporting year for Fiji with the focus primarily on the fortunes of the rugby union team at the World Cup in France where they came within a whisker of beating eventual winners South Africa in the quarter-finals. The previous month, amid much less fanfare, the national football team reached the final of the South Pacific Games, a tournament which acted as Oceania's first round of qualifying for the 2010 FIFA World Cup. Fiji started their campaign with a rugby-like score against Tuvalu, winning 16-0, and they easily qualified for the semi-finals. By beating Vanuatu there, the Fijians ensured that they qualified for the main Oceania group, but they failed to retain their South

INTERNATIONAL HONOURS
Melanesian Cup 1988 1989 1992 1998 2000 South Pacific Games 1991 2003

Pacific Games crown when they lost heavily to New Caledonia in the final. In club football Ba finished bottom of their group in the 2007-08 OFC O-League and they also saw their winning streak at home come to an end when they finished third in the National League in December 2007. They finished nine points behind Labasa - champions for the first time since 1991 - bringing to an end their six year reign. Ba did win the Inter-District Competition in the same month, beating Nadi 2-1 in the final, while in June 2008 Nauva won the first major trophy of the year when they beat Labasa in the final of the FA Cup.

THE FIFA BIG COUNT OF 2006

	Male	Female		Total
Number of players	46 338	3 350	Referees and Assistant Referees	117
Professionals	0		Admin, Coaches, Technical, Medical	2 929
Amateurs 18+	11 188		Number of clubs	400
Youth under 18	17 300		Number of teams	2 000
Unregistered	8 200		Clubs with women's teams	10
Total players	49 688		Players as % of population	5.48%

Fiji Football Association (FFA)
73 Knolly Street, PO Box 2514, Suva, Fiji
Tel +679 3300453   Fax +679 3304642
bobkumar@fijifootball.com.fj   www.fijifootball.com
President: SAHU KHAN Muhammad   General Secretary: KUMAR Bob Sant
Vice-President: KEWAL Hari   Treasurer: TBD   Media Officer: None
Men's Coach: BUZZETTI Juan   Women's Coach: FAROUK Janeman
FFA formed: 1938   OFC: 1966   FIFA: 1963
White shirts, Black shorts, Black socks

RECENT INTERNATIONAL MATCHES PLAYED BY FIJI

2004	Opponents	Score		Venue	Comp	Scorers	Att	Referee
29-05	Tahiti	D	0-0	Adelaide	WCq		3 000	Farina ITA
31-05	Vanuatu	W	1-0	Adelaide	WCq	Veresa Toma [73]	500	Ariiotima TAH
2-06	Australia	L	1-6	Adelaide	WCq	Gataurua [19]	2 200	Iturralde Gonzalez ESP
4-06	Solomon Islands	L	1-2	Adelaide	WCq	Veresa Toma [21]	1 500	Attison VAN
6-06	New Zealand	L	0-2	Adelaide	WCq		300	Larsen DEN
2005								
12-08	India	W	1-0	Lautoka	Fr	Esala Masi [14p]	10 000	Fox NZL
14-08	India	W	2-1	Suva	Fr	Luke Vidovi [25], Esala Masi [61]	11 000	O'Leary NZL
2006								
No international matches played in 2006								
2007								
25-08	Tuvalu †	W	16-0	Apia	WCq	Krishna 3 [6 14 22], Rabo 3 [11 34 45], Baleitoga [17], Tiwa 2 [28 30], Vakatalesau 6 [42 46 65 73 82 89], Finau [68p]	200	Aimaasu SAM
27-08	Cook Islands	W	4-0	Apia	WCq	Vakatalesau [19], Waqa [40], Bukalidi [63], Kainihewe [82]	400	Fred VAN
1-09	Tahiti	W	4-0	Apia	WCq	Waqa [17], Baleitoga [38], Vakatalesau 2 [49 73]	200	Fox NZL
3-09	New Caledonia	D	1-1	Apia	WCq	Kainihewe [56]	1 000	Fred VAN
5-09	Vanuatu	W	3-0	Apia	WCq	Baleitoga [44], Vakatalesau [69p], Krishna [70]	600	Hester NZL
7-09	New Caledonia	L	0-1	Apia	WCq		400	Hester NZL
17-10	New Zealand	L	0-2	Lautoka	WCq		6 000	Marrufo USA
17-11	New Caledonia	D	3-3	Ba	WCq	Nawau [3], Vakatalesau 2 [28 87]	1 500	O'Leary NZL
21-11	New Caledonia	L	0-4	Noumea	WCq		0	Breeze AUS
2008								
No international matches played in 2008 before August								

OC = Oceania Nations Cup • SP = South Pacific Games • WC = FIFA World Cup
q = qualifier • r1 = first round group • sf = semi-final • f = final • † Not a full international

FIJI NATIONAL TEAM RECORDS AND RECORD SEQUENCES

Records			Sequence records					
Victory	15-1	GUM 1991, COK 1971	Wins	6	2003-2004	Clean sheets	4	1992, 1989-90
Defeat	0-13	NZL 1981	Defeats	8	1985-1986	Goals scored	15	1985-1989
Player Caps	n/a		Undefeated	13	1989-1991	Without goal	5	1985
Player Goals	n/a		Without win	12	1983-1988	Goals against	13	1983-1988

RECENT LEAGUE AND CUP RECORD

	League	Inter-District Competition			Battle of the Giants			FA Cup		
Year	Winners	Winners	Score	Finalist	Winners	Score	Finalist	Winners	Score	Finalist
1997	Suva	Ba	2-0	Nadi	Labasa	1-0	Nadi	Labasa	0-0	Ba
1998	Nadi	Nadi	3-1	Lautoka	Ba	1-0	Nadi	Ba	3-0	Nadi
1999	Ba	Nadi	1-0	Ba	Ba	1-0	Tavua	Labasa	2-1	Lautoka
2000	Nadi	Ba	1-0	Nadi	Ba	2-0	Labasa	Lautoka	2-0	Nadroga
2001	Ba	Rewa	1-0	Ba	Ba	2-0	Lautoka	Nadroga	1-1 7-6p	Labasa
2002	Ba	Nadi	1-1 4-2p	Rewa	Nadroga	2-1	Labasa	Lautoka	1-1 3-2p	Nasinu
2003	Ba	Ba	1-0	Nadi	Rewa	1-0	Ba	Navua	1-0	Rewa
2004	Ba	Ba	3-0	Rewa	Rewa	2-0	Nadi	Ba	2-0	Suva
2005	Ba	Lautoka	2-0	Ba	Navua	1-0	Rewa	Ba	1-0	Nadi
2006	Ba	Ba	3-0	Suva	Ba	2-1	Suva	Ba	3-0	Labasa
2007	Labasa	Ba	2-1	Nadi	Ba	2-1	Nadi	Ba	1-0	Labasa
2008								Navua	1-0	Labasa

FIJI COUNTRY INFORMATION

Capital	Suva	Independence	1970 from the UK	GDP per Capita	$5 800
Population	880 874	Status	Republic	GNP Ranking	141
Area km²	18 270	Language	English, Fijian	Dialling code	+679
Population density	48 per km²	Literacy rate	93%	Internet code	.fj
% in urban areas	41%	Main religion	Christian 52%, Hindu 38%	GMT +/−	+12
Towns/Cities ('000)	Suva 199; Nadi 53; Lautoka 49; Labasa 33; Nausori 32; Lami 21; Ba 20; Sigatoka 12				
Neighbours (km)	Fiji consists of two large islands, Viti Levu and Vanua Levu, along with 880 islets in the South Pacific				
Main stadia	National Stadium – Suva 5 000; Govind Park – Ba 4 000; Churchill Park – Lautoka 2 000				

FIN – FINLAND

NATIONAL TEAM RECORD
JULY 10TH 2006 TO JULY 12TH 2010

PL	W	D	L	F	A	%
20	6	8	6	17	16	50

FIFA/COCA-COLA WORLD RANKING

1993	1994	1995	1996	1997	1998	1999	2000	2001	2002	2003	2004	2005	2006	2007	High	
45	38	44	79	60	55	56	59	46	43	40	43	46	52	36	**33**	03/07

	2007–2008											Low	
08/07	09/07	10/07	11/07	12/07	01/08	02/08	03/08	04/08	05/08	06/08	07/08	**79**	12/96
38	44	44	36	36	37	37	35	35	34	36	44		

Although unsuccessful in attempting to qualify for Euro 2008, the national team regained some of the ground it had lost in recent seasons. With just two defeats in the campaign, Finland played a large part in determining the outcome of the group, finishing just four points behind winners Poland. Much of the credit went to experienced coach Roy Hodgson who organised the team well defensively, although there was criticism of the lack of firepower up front with five of the 14 matches finishing 0-0. Hodgson moved on in November 2007 and was replaced by another Englishman, Stuart Baxter in preparation for the 2010 FIFA World Cup qualifiers. In the

INTERNATIONAL HONOURS
None

Veikkausliiga, Tampere United with Ari Hjelm at the helm, successfully defended their title, while a penalty shoot-out victory over Honka Espoo in the Cup Final saw them secure a first double - just nine years on from their formation following the merger of Ilves and TPV. Tampere had also came close to becoming the first Finnish side to qualify for the group stage of the Champions League, but having beaten Levski Sofia, they then lost 5-0 on aggregate to their more experienced Scandinavian rivals Rosenborg of Norway in the third preliminary round. Tampere then fell just short of making it to the group stage of the UEFA Cup, losing 4-3 on aggregate to Bordeaux.

THE FIFA BIG COUNT OF 2006

	Male	Female		Total
Number of players	304 398	58 251	Referees and Assistant Referees	2 655
Professionals	360		Admin, Coaches, Technical, Medical	14 300
Amateurs 18+	26 555		Number of clubs	990
Youth under 18	101 334		Number of teams	4 258
Unregistered	120 000		Clubs with women's teams	270
Total players	362 469		Players as % of population	6.93%

Suomen Palloliitto (SPL/FBF)
Urheilukatu 5, PO Box 191, Helsinki 00251, Finland
Tel +358 9 742151   Fax +358 9 74215200
firstname.lastname@palloliitto.fi   www.palloliitto.fi
President: HAMALAINEN Pekka   General Secretary: HOLOPAINEN Teuvo
Vice-President: LEHTOLA Markku   Treasurer: HOLOPAINEN Teuvo   Media Officer: TERAVA Sami
Men's Coach: BAXTER Stuart   Women's Coach: KALD Michael
SPL/FBF formed: 1907   UEFA: 1954   FIFA: 1908
White shirts with blue trimmings, Blue shorts, White socks or Blue shirts with white trimmings, White shorts, Red socks

RECENT INTERNATIONAL MATCHES PLAYED BY FINLAND

2005	Opponents	Score		Venue	Comp	Scorers	Att	Referee
17-08	FYR Macedonia	W	3-0	Skopje	WCq	Eremenko 2 8 45, Roiha 87	6 800	Messias ENG
3-09	Andorra	D	0-0	Andorra la Vella	WCq		860	Van Eecke BEL
7-09	FYR Macedonia	W	5-1	Tampere	WCq	Forssell 3 10 12 61, Tihinen 41, Eremenko 54	6 467	Jakobsson ISL
8-10	Romania	L	0-1	Helsinki	WCq		11 500	Guenov BUL
12-10	Czech Republic	L	0-3	Helsinki	WCq		11 234	Mejuto Gonzalez ESP
12-11	Estonia	D	2-2	Helsinki	Fr	Sjolund 7, Arkivuo 59	1 900	Gilewski POL
2006								
21-01	Saudi Arabia	D	1-1	Riyadh	Fr	Roiha 87	3 000	Al Anzi KUW
25-01	Korea Republic	L	0-1	Riyadh	Fr		800	Al Jerman KSA
18-02	Japan	L	0-2	Shizuoka	Fr		40 702	Lee Gi Young KOR
28-02	Kazakhstan	D	0-0	Larnaca	Fr	L 1-3p	100	Trattos CYP
1-03	Belarus	D	2-2	Larnaca	Fr	Riihilahti 82, Forssell 90. W 5-4p	120	Krajnic SVN
25-05	Sweden	D	0-0	Gothenburg	Fr		25 754	Gilewski POL
16-08	Northern Ireland	L	1-2	Helsinki	Fr	Väyrynen 74	12 500	Svendsen DEN
2-09	Poland	W	3-1	Bydgoszcz	ECq	Litmanen 2 54 76p, Väyrynen 84	13 000	Duhamel FRA
6-09	Portugal	D	1-1	Helsinki	ECq	Johansson 22	38 010	Plautz AUT
7-10	Armenia	D	0-0	Yerevan	ECq		2 800	Skomina SVN
11-10	Kazakhstan	W	2-0	Almaty	ECq	Litmanen 27, Hyypiä 65	17 863	Briakos GRE
15-11	Armenia	W	1-0	Helsinki	ECq	Nurmela 10	9 445	Thomson SCO
2007								
28-03	Azerbaijan	L	0-1	Baku	ECq		14 500	Messina ITA
2-06	Serbia	L	0-2	Helsinki	ECq		33 615	Mejuto Gonzalez ESP
6-06	Belgium	W	2-0	Helsinki	ECq	Johansson 27, Eremenko Jr 71	34 818	Riley ENG
22-08	Kazakhstan	W	2-1	Tampere	ECq	Eremenko Jr 13, Tainio 61	13 047	Kassai HUN
8-09	Serbia	D	0-0	Belgrade	ECq		10 530	Braamhaar NED
12-09	Poland	D	0-0	Helsinki	ECq		34 088	Fandel GER
13-10	Belgium	D	0-0	Brussels	ECq		21 393	Kapitanis CYP
17-10	Spain	D	0-0	Helsinki	Fr		8 000	Bre FRA
17-11	Azerbaijan	W	2-1	Helsinki	ECq	Forssell 79, Kuqi 86	10 325	Hamer LUX
21-11	Portugal	D	0-0	Porto	ECq		49 000	Michel SVK
2008								
6-02	Greece	L	1-2	Nicosia	Fr	Litmanen 66	500	Kailis CYP
26-03	Bulgaria	L	1-2	Sofia	Fr	Litmanen 22p	2 500	Tudor ROU
29-05	Turkey	L	0-2	Duisburg	Fr			Kinhofer GER
2-06	Belarus	D	1-1	Helsinki	Fr	Kallio 90	6 474	Skomina SVN

Fr = Friendly match • EC = UEFA EURO 2008 • WC = FIFA World Cup • q = qualifier

FINLAND NATIONAL TEAM PLAYERS

Player		Ap	G	Club	Date of Birth	Player		Ap	G	Club	Date of Birth
Peter Enckelman	GK	11	0	Cardiff City	10 03 1977	Alexei Eremenko jr	MF	35	12	Saturn	24 03 1983
Niki Mäenpää	GK	1	0	FC Den Bosch	23 01 1985	Roman Eremenko	MF	9	0	Udinese	19 03 1987
Otto Fredrikson	GK	1	0	Lillestrøm SK	30 11 1981	Markus Heikkinen	MF	36	0	SK Rapid Wien	13 10 1978
Veli Lampi	DF	8	0	FC Zürich	18 07 1984	Mika Väyrynen	MF	36	2	PSV Eindhoven	28 11 1981
Toni Kuivasto	DF	72	1	Djurgårdens IF	31 12 1975	Teemu Tainio	MF	43	6	Tottenham H	27 11 1979
Ari Nyman	DF	18	0	FC Thun	7 02 1984	Tim Sparv	MF	0	0	VPS Vaasa	20 02 1987
Juha Pasoja	DF	15	0	Ham-Kam	16 11 1976	Kasper Hämäläinen	MF	0	0	TPS Turku	8 08 1986
Niklas Moisander	DF	1	0	FC Zwolle	29 09 1985	Mikael Forssell	FW	55	17	Birmingham City	15 03 1981
Toni Kallio	DF	38	2	Fulham	9 08 1978	Jonatan Johansson	FW	89	14	Malmö FF	16 08 1975
Jukka Sauso	DF	5	0	HJK Helsinki	20 06 1982	Jari Litmanen	FW	114	30	Fulham	20 01 1971
Joonas Kolkka	MF	86	11	NAC Breda	28 09 1974	Berat Sadik	FW	2	0	Arminia Bielefeld	14 09 1986

Finland's squad for the friendlies against Turkey & Belarus in May 2008

FINLAND NATIONAL TEAM RECORDS AND RECORD SEQUENCES

Records			Sequence records					
Victory	10-2	EST 1922	Wins	4	2005	Clean sheets	3	1924, 1993
Defeat	0-13	GER 1940	Defeats	14	1967-1969	Goals scored	14	1925-1927
Player Caps	114	LITMANEN Jari	Undefeated	10	2001-2002	Without goal	5	1937, 1971-1972
Player Goals	30	LITMANEN Jari	Without win	27	1939-1949	Goals against	44	1936-1949

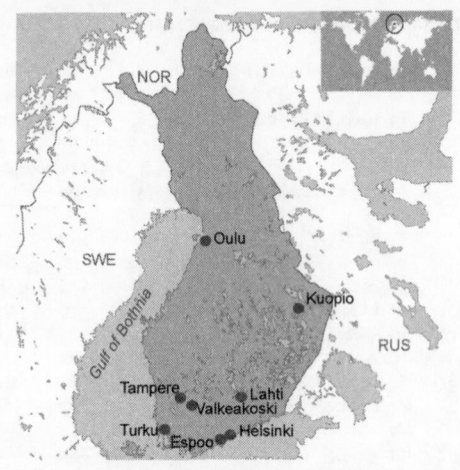

REPUBLIC OF FINLAND; SUOMEN TASAVALTA

Capital	Helsinki	Language	Finnish		Independence	1917
Population	5 231 372	Area	338 145 km²	Density 15 per km²	% in cities	63%
GDP per cap	$27 000	Dailling code	+358	Internet .fi	GMT +/-	+2

MAJOR CITIES/TOWNS
Population '000

	City	Population
1	Helsinki	558
2	Espoo	235
3	Tampere	204
4	Vantaa	192
5	Turku	176
6	Oulu	131
7	Lahti	99
8	Kuopio	89
9	Jyväskylä	87
10	Pori	77
11	Lappeenranta	59
12	Vaasa	57
13	Kotka	54
14	Joensuu	54
15	Porvoo	48
16	Hämeenlinna	47
17	Mikkeli	46
18	Hyvinkää	43
19	Kokkola	35
20	Rovaniemi	34
21	Kouvola	30
22	Valkeakoski	20
23	Pietarsaari	19
24	Anjalankoski	16

MEDALS TABLE

		Overall			League			Cup			Europe			City	Stadium	Cap'ty	DoF
		G	S	B	G	S	B	G	S	B	G	S	B				
1	HJK Helsinki	30	17	11	21	13	11	9	4					Helsinki	Finnair Stadion	10 770	1907
2	Haka Valkeakoski	21	10	10	9	7	10	12	3					Valkeakoski	Tehtaan kenttä	6 400	1934
3	TPS Turku	10	17	7	8	12	7	2	5					Turku	Veritas Stadion	9 000	1922
4	Reipas Lahti	10	9	3	3	6	3	7	3					Lahti			1891
5	HPS Helsinki	10	7	2	9	6	2	1	1					Helsinki			1917
6	Tampere United	8	3	3	5	1	3	3	2					Tampere	Ratina Stadion	16 850	1998
7	HIFK Helsinki	7	8	4	7	7	4		1					Helsinki			1897
8	KuPS Kuopio	7	8	1	5	8	1	2						Kuopio	Magnum Arena	2 700	1923
9	FC Lahti	7	8		5	4		2	4					Lahti	Lahden Stadion	14 500	1996
10	KTP Kotka	6	3	2	2		2	4	3					Kotka			1927-2001
11	MyPa-47	4	5	3	1	5	3	3						Anjalankoski	Jalkapallokenttä	4 067	1947
12	Abo IFK Turku	4	5	1	3	5	1	1						Turku			1908
13	Kronshagen IF Helsinki	4	2	3	4	1	3				1			Helsinki			1908
14	IFK Vaasa	3	2	2	3	2	2							Vaasa			1900
15	VPS Vaasa	2	6	1	2	5	1		1					Vaasa	Hietalahti	4 300	1924

RECENT LEAGUE AND CUP RECORD

	Championship						Cup		
Year	Champions	Pts	Runners-up	Pts	Third	Pts	Winners	Score	Runners-up
1995	Haka Valkeakoski	59	MyPa-47	53	HJK Helsinki	52	MyPa-47	1-0	FC Jazz Pori
1996	FC Jazz Pori	47	MyPa-47	45	TPS Turku	44	HJK Helsinki	0-0 4-3p	TPS Turku
1997	HJK Helsinki	58	VPS Vaasa	48	FinnPa Helsinki	39	Haka Valkeakoski	2-1	TPS Turku
1998	Haka Valkeakoski	48	VPS Vaasa	45	PK-35 Helsinki	44	HJK Helsinki	3-2	PK-35 Helsinki
1999	Haka Valkeakoski	67	HJK Helsinki	65	MyPa-47	47	Jokerit Helsinki	2-1	FF Jaro Pietarsaari
2000	Haka Valkeakoski	66	Jokerit Helsinki	62	MyPa-47	61	HJK Helsinki	1-0	KTP Kotka
2001	Tampere United	68	HJK Helsinki	67	MyPa-47	62	Atlantis Helsinki	1-0	Tampere United
2002	HJK Helsinki	65	MyPa-47	60	Haka Valkeakoski	52	Haka Valkeakoski	4-1	FC Lahti
2003	HJK Helsinki	57	Haka Valkeakoski	53	Tampere United	47	HJK Helsinki	2-1	Allianssi Vantaa
2004	Haka Valkeakoski	59	Allianssi Vantaa	48	Tampere United	47	MyPa-47	2-1	Hämeenlinna
2005	MyPa-47	56	HJK Helsinki	52	Tampere United	51	Haka Valkeakoski	4-1	TPS Turku
2006	Tampere United	59	HJK Helsinki	45	Haka Valkeakoski	44	HJK Helsinki	1-0	KPV Kokkola
2007	Tampere United	54	Haka Valkeakoski	46	TPS Turku	43	Tampere United	3-3 3-1p	Honka Espoo

FINLAND 2007

VEIKKAUSLIIGA (1)

	Pl	W	D	L	F	A	Pts	TamU	Haka	TPS	Honka	MyPa	IFK	HJK	Lahti	Inter	VPS	Jaro	KooTeePee	Viikingit	AC Oulu
Tampere United †	26	16	6	4	45	27	54		2-1	3-0	0-2	1-1	2-1	2-1	1-0	2-1	2-2	2-1	2-1	1-0	4-1
Haka Valkeakoski ‡	26	13	7	6	39	23	46	1-1		2-1	1-1	0-0	1-2	3-3	1-2	1-0	1-0	4-0	3-0	1-0	2-0
TPS Turku	26	13	4	9	43	33	43	1-3	2-1		1-3	1-0	0-0	0-1	3-1	1-0	5-1	1-1	3-2	5-0	4-0
Honka Espoo ‡	26	10	11	5	34	25	41	1-2	0-2	2-0		2-1	2-0	0-0	0-0	1-2	1-0	2-2	0-0	1-1	2-0
MyPa-47 Anjalankoski	26	11	7	8	29	26	40	4-1	0-3	0-2	1-0		0-0	0-0	1-0	1-3	0-1	2-0	1-0	1-1	3-2
IFK Mariehamn	26	9	10	7	31	30	37	1-0	0-1	0-3	0-0	0-2		0-0	0-0	2-0	1-3	1-1	3-2	4-2	0-0
HJK Helsinki	26	7	13	6	31	25	34	0-2	2-1	3-0	0-1	5-0	2-2		0-2	2-0	0-0	2-2	1-1	1-1	0-0
FC Lahti	26	9	6	11	38	34	33	0-2	1-1	2-3	2-2	0-1	4-1	3-1		2-2	6-0	1-4	2-0	0-2	2-1
Inter Turku	26	9	6	11	32	28	33	1-1	3-1	1-1	1-1	1-2	0-2	1-1	0-1		5-0	5-2	1-0	0-1	1-0
VPS Vaasa	26	7	11	8	26	35	32	1-1	0-0	0-0	1-0	1-3	2-1	1-0	0-0			1-2	1-0	1-1	5-0
Jaro Pietarsaari	26	7	7	12	30	41	28	0-2	1-2	2-0	1-2	0-3	1-1	0-0	3-0	1-0	0-1		0-0	2-0	0-1
KooTeePee Kotka	26	7	5	14	27	38	26	0-3	1-2	4-2	1-2	1-0	1-2	1-3	2-2	0-2	1-1	2-1		1-0	3-0
Viikingit Helsinki	26	5	8	13	25	44	23	3-3	0-2	0-1	3-2	1-4	2-2	1-1	0-4	0-2	1-0	1-2	0-1		3-1
AC Oulu	26	5	7	14	28	49	22	2-0	1-1	1-3	3-3	1-1	0-3	0-1	2-1	2-0	3-3	5-1	1-2	1-1	

21/04/2007 - 27/10/2007 • † Qualified for the UEFA Champions League • ‡ Qualified for the UEFA Cup • Top scorer: Rafael Pires Vieira, Lahti 14

FINLAND 2007

YKKONEN (2)

	Pl	W	D	L	F	A	Pts	KuPS	RoPS	JJK	Hämeenlin'a	TP-47	VIFK	Atlantis	PK-35	JIPPO	KPV	TPV	GBK	PP-70	Klubi-04
KuPS Kuopio	26	16	8	2	44	17	56		0-1	4-1	1-1	1-0	4-0	3-2	2-1	1-1	5-0	1-0	2-1	4-1	1-1
RoPS Rovaniemi	26	16	3	4	44	23	55	0-0		2-1	1-0	2-0	0-0	2-0	2-2	2-1	2-0	0-0	3-2	2-0	3-1
JJK Jyväskylä	26	11	8	7	45	30	41	4-0	1-1		1-2	0-1	2-2	2-0	0-2	0-0	3-0	2-2	5-1	1-1	
FC Hämeenlinna	26	11	8	7	37	27	41	1-1	3-2	1-3		0-1	1-1	2-1	0-0	2-0	1-1	3-0	4-0	0-1	3-1
TP-47 Tornio	26	10	7	9	36	29	37	0-1	2-1	1-3	1-2		0-1	2-2	1-0	1-2	0-0	5-0	3-0	2-0	0-1
VIFK Vaasa	26	9	9	8	31	35	36	0-4	0-3	0-2	1-0	2-2		0-1	4-2	2-0	3-0	0-1	0-2	3-3	2-2
Atlantis Helsinki	26	9	7	10	33	32	34	0-1	1-2	2-0	2-2	1-2	1-2		2-0	1-0	1-2	3-0	2-0	1-3	2-1
PK-35 Helsinki	26	8	9	9	36	33	33	0-0	3-2	1-1	0-0	1-1	2-0	1-2		4-1	2-0	1-1	1-2	1-1	1-1
JIPPO Joensuu	26	8	8	10	32	37	32	0-1	2-3	1-1	0-2	2-2	2-2	1-1	3-1		2-1	0-3	0-1	2-1	1-1
KPV Kokkola	26	8	7	11	27	46	31	0-3	2-4	1-3	3-2	2-1	0-0	0-0	1-4	0-3		2-2	1-0	1-2	3-2
TPV Tampere	26	8	6	12	24	37	30	1-1	1-2	1-1	3-0	1-3	0-1	0-0	1-0	0-1	0-1		2-1	2-0	3-1
GBK Kokkola	26	7	6	13	28	38	27	1-1	0-0	0-3	0-0	2-3	0-0	0-1	1-4	0-0	3-4	4-0		2-1	2-0
PP-70 Tampere	26	6	7	13	31	44	25	0-1	0-0	1-2	1-3	0-0	1-2	3-3	4-1	2-2	0-1	2-0	0-2		2-1
Klubi-04 Helsinki	26	2	9	15	25	45	15	0-1	1-2	1-2	1-2	2-2	0-3	1-1	0-1	1-3	1-1	1-2	1-0	1-1	

28/04/2007 - 20/10/2007 • Play-off: RoPS 1-0 1-1 Viikingit

SUOMEN CUP 2007

Round of 16		Quarter–finals		Semi–finals		Final	
Tampere United	4						
JIPPO Joensuu *	1	Tampere United *	0 4p				
Haka Valkeakoski	0	AC Oulu	0 3p				
AC Oulu *	2			Tampere United *	2		
FC Lahti	3			GBK Kokkola	0		
PP-70 Tampere *	1	FC Lahti	0 3p				
City Stars	0	GBK Kokkola *	0 5p				
GBK Kokkola *	1					Tampere United	3 3p
HJK Helsinki *	8					Honka Espoo ‡	3 1p
SoVo	1	HJK Helsinki	4				
MyPa-47 Anjalankoski	0	JJK Jyväskylä *	0				
JJK Jyväskylä *	2			HJK Helsinki *	0		
Inter Turku *	2			Honka Espoo	1		
HIFK Soccer	0	Inter Turku	2 2p				
FC Kuusankoski	0	Honka Espoo *	2 4p				
Honka Espoo *	4						

CUP FINAL

Finnair Stadium, Helsinki
11-11-2007, Att: 1457, Ref: Hätilä
Goals - Miki Sipiläinen 90, Antti Hynynen 95, Henri Myntti 101 for TamU; Jami Puustinen 60, Ville Jalasto 114, Janne Saarinen 116 for Honka

* Home team • ‡ Qualified for the UEFA Cup

FRA – FRANCE

NATIONAL TEAM RECORD
JULY 10TH 2006 TO JULY 12TH 2010

PL	W	D	L	F	A	%
11	9	0	2	19	4	81.8

At the finals of Euro 2008 the French national team lost two matches on the trot for the first time since 1993 when they were beaten 4-1 by the Dutch and then 2-0 by the Italians, defeats that saw Les Bleus make an unexpected exit after the first round. Although it was the toughest group of all at the finals, few expected the French to fail to qualify for the quarter-finals - let alone finish bottom of their group. Coach Raymond Domenech pointed the finger of blame at himself saying that he had put too much pressure on his players but the calls for him to resign seemed harsh given his achievement in taking the French to the World Cup final in 2006. Nevertheless, France were deeply unimpressive at the finals, especially in central midfield, starting their campaign with a tepid 0-0 draw against Romania. In Domenech's defence, the Dutch were quite brilliant in the second match while against Italy, their poor display could perhaps be mitigated by Franck Ribery's early cruciate ligament injury and Eric Abidal's sending-off soon after. At home Ligue 1 maintained its position as one of the leading competitions in world football with average crowds of 21,817 - the fourth highest behind the Bundesliga, the Premier League and La Liga - and for the

INTERNATIONAL HONOURS
FIFA World Cup 1998   UEFA European Championship 1984 2000

Qualified for the FIFA World Cup finals 1930 1934 1938 1954 1958 1966 1978 1982 1986 1998 2002 2006

FIFA Junior Tournament 1949   FIFA U-17 World Championship 2001

UEFA U-21 Championship 1988 UEFA U-19 Championship 1983 1996 1997 2000 UEFA U-17 Championship 2004

UEFA Champions League Olympique Marseille 1993

first time in four seasons, Lyon had some real competition on their hands with Bordeaux taking them to the final day before they clinched a seventh consecutive championship. Goalkeeper Grégory Coupet, midfielder Juninho and forward Sidney Govou have been part of all seven triumphs but for coach Alain Perrin it was a first. He also achieved something that his title winning predecessors, Jacques Santini, Paul Le Guen and Gérard Houllier couldn't manage - win the Coupe de France. Lyon's 1-0 extra-time victory over PSG at the Stade de France in the 2008 final was Lyon's first Cup triumph since 1973 and it was only the second time that any French club has won the double since start of 1990s. Perrin's achievement wasn't enough, however, for him to keep his job and he was sacked shortly after the end of the season with the hierarchy at Lyon critical of the style of his double winning team. Time will tell if this was a triumphant end to an era or if the Lyon bandwagon will carry on rolling to an eighth title. PSG just missed out on a cup double having earlier beaten Lens in the League Cup final. Remarkably both clubs were involved in a relegation dog-fight which Lens lost, dropping out of the top division along with Strasbourg and Metz.

Fédération Française de Football (FFF)
87, Boulevard de Grenelle, Paris 75738, France
Tel +33 1 44317300   Fax +33 1 44317373
webmaster@fff.fr   www.fff.fr
President: ESCALETTES Jean-Pierre   General Secretary: LAMBERT Jacques
Vice-President: THIRIEZ Frederic   Treasurer: DESUMER Bernard   Media Officer: LE GUILLARD Yann
Men's Coach: DOMENECH Raymond   Women's Coach: BINI Bruno
FFF formed: 1919   UEFA: 1954   FIFA: 1904
Blue shirts with white trimmings, White shorts, Red socks or White shirts with blue trimmings, Blue shorts, Red socks

RECENT INTERNATIONAL MATCHES PLAYED BY FRANCE

2006	Opponents	Score		Venue	Comp	Scorers	Att	Referee
13-06	Switzerland	D	0-0	Stuttgart	WCr1		52 000	Ivanov RUS
18-06	Korea Republic	D	1-1	Leipzig	WCr1	Henry [9]	43 000	Archundia MEX
23-06	Togo	W	2-0	Cologne	WCr1	Vieira [55], Henry [61]	45 000	Larrionda URU
27-06	Spain	W	3-1	Hanover	WCr2	Ribery [41], Vieira [83], Zidane [92+]	43 000	Rosetti ITA
1-07	Brazil	W	1-0	Frankfurt	WCqf	Henry [57]	48 000	Medina Cantalejo ESP
5-07	Portugal	W	1-0	Munich	WCsf	Zidane [33p]	66 000	Larrionda URU
9-07	Italy	D	1-1	Berlin	WCf	Zidane [7p], L 3-5p	69 000	Elizondo ARG
16-08	Bosnia-Herzegovina	W	2-1	Sarajevo	Fr	Gallas [41], Faubert [90]	35 000	Wack GER
2-09	Georgia	W	3-0	Tbilisi	ECq	Malouda [7], Saha [16], Asatiani OG [47]	54 000	Wegereef NED
6-09	Italy	W	3-1	Paris	ECq	Govou 2 [2 55], Henry [18]	78 831	Fandel GER
7-10	Scotland	L	0-1	Glasgow	ECq		50 456	Busacca SUI
11-10	Faroe Islands	W	5-0	Sochaux	ECq	Saha [1], Henry [22], Anelka [77], Trezeguet 2 [78 84]	19 314	Corpodean ROU
15-11	Greece	W	1-0	Paris	Fr	Henry [27]	63 680	Wack GER/Wezel GER
2007								
7-02	Argentina	L	0-1	Paris	Fr		79 862	Skomina SVN
24-03	Lithuania	W	1-0	Kaunas	ECq	Anelka [73]	8 740	Webb ENG
28-03	Austria	W	1-0	Paris	Fr	Benzema [53]	65 000	Briakos GRE
2-06	Ukraine	W	2-0	Paris	ECq	Ribery [57], Anelka [71]	79 000	Medina Cantalejo ESP
6-06	Georgia	W	1-0	Auxerre	ECq	Nasri [33]	19 345	Batista POR
22-08	Slovakia	W	1-0	Trnava	Fr	Henry [39]	13 064	Egorov RUS
8-09	Italy	D	0-0	Milan	ECq		81 200	Michel SVK
12-09	Scotland	L	0-1	Paris	ECq		43 342	Plautz AUT
13-10	Faroe Islands	W	6-0	Tórshavn	ECq	Anelka [6], Henry [8], Benzema 2 [50 81], Rothen [66], Arfa [94+]	1 980	Rossi SMR
17-10	Lithuania	W	2-0	Nantes	ECq	Henry 2 [80 81]	36 650	Kassai HUN
16-11	Morocco	D	2-2	Paris	Fr	Govou [15], Nasri [75]	78 000	Bossen NED
21-11	Ukraine	D	2-2	Kyiv	ECq	Henry [20], Govou [34]	7 800	Ovrebø NOR
2008								
6-02	Spain	L	0-1	Malaga	Fr		35 000	Asumaa FIN
26-03	England	W	1-0	Paris	Fr	Ribery [32p]	78 500	Meyer GER
27-05	Ecuador	W	2-0	Grenoble	Fr	Gomis 2 [60 86]	20 000	Allaerts BEL
31-05	Paraguay	D	0-0	Toulouse	Fr		33 418	Proenca POR
3-06	Colombia	W	1-0	Paris	Fr	Ribery [25p]	79 727	Dean ENG
9-06	Romania	D	0-0	Zürich	ECr1		30 585	Mejuto Gonzalez ESP
13-06	Netherlands	L	1-4	Berne	ECr1	Henry [71]	30 777	Fandel GER
17-06	Italy	L	0-2	Zürich	ECr1		30 585	Michel SVK

Fr = Friendly match • EC = UEFA EURO 2008 • WC = FIFA World Cup
q = qualifier • r1 = first round group • r2 = second round • qf = quarter-final • sf = semi-final • f = final

FRANCE NATIONAL TEAM PLAYERS

	Player	Ap	G	Club	Date of Birth		Player	Ap	G	Club	Date of Birth
1	Steve Mandanda	GK	1	0	Olymp. Marseille 28 03 1985	12	Thierry Henry	FW	102 45	Barcelona	17 08 1977
2	Jean-Alain Boumsong	DF	24	1	Olymp. Lyonnais 14 12 1979	13	Patrice Evra	DF	13 0	Manchester Utd	15 05 1981
3	Eric Abidal	DF	37	0	Barcelona	11 09 1979	14	François Clerc	DF	13 0	Olymp. Lyonnais	18 04 1983
4	Patrick Vieira	MF	105	6	Internazionale	23 06 1976	15	Lilian Thuram	DF	142 2	Barcelona	1 01 1972
5	William Gallas	DF	65	2	Arsenal	17 08 1977	16	Sébastien Frey	GK	2 0	Fiorentina	18 03 1980
6	Claude Makelele	MF	71	0	Chelsea	18 02 1973	17	Sébastien Squillaci	DF	13 0	Olymp. Lyonnais	11 08 1980
7	Florent Malouda	MF	41	3	Chelsea	13 06 1980	18	Bafetimbi Gomis	FW	4 2	AS Saint-Etienne	6 08 1985
8	Nicolas Anelka	FW	51	11	Chelsea	14 03 1979	19	Willy Sagnol	DF	58 0	Bayern München	18 03 1977
9	Karim Benzema	FW	13	3	Olymp. Lyonnais	19 12 1987	20	Jérémy Toulalan	MF	16 0	Olymp. Lyonnais	10 09 1983
10	Sidney Govou	FW	34	7	Olymp. Lyonnais	27 07 1979	21	Lassana Diarra	MF	13 0	Portsmouth	10 03 1985
11	Samir Nasri	MF	12	2	Olymp. Marseille	26 06 1987	22	Franck Ribéry	MF	30 4	Bayern München	7 04 1983
The French squad for Euro 2008						23	Grégory Coupet	GK	34 0	Olymp. Lyonnais	31 12 1972

FRANCE NATIONAL TEAM RECORDS AND RECORD SEQUENCES

Records			Sequence records					
Victory	10-0	AZE 1995	Wins	14	2003-2004	Clean sheets	11	2003-2004
Defeat	1-17	DEN 1908	Defeats	12	1908-1911	Goals scored	17	1999-2000
Player Caps	142	THURAM Lilian	Undefeated	30	1994-1996	Without goal	4	1924-1925, 1986
Player Goals	45	HENRY Thierry	Without win	15	1908-1911	Goals against	24	1905-1912

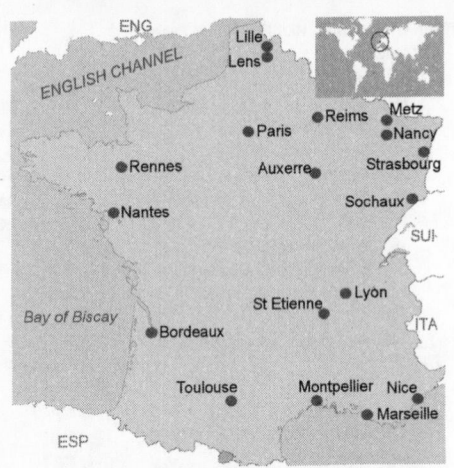

MAJOR CITIES/TOWNS

		Population '000
1	Paris	2 143
2	Marseille	791
3	Lyon	479
4	Toulouse	445
5	Nice	336
6	Nantes	278
7	Strasbourg	277
8	Montpellier	255
9	Lille	240
10	Bordeaux	236
11	Rennes	209
12	Reims	198
13	Le Havre	183
14	Saint-Etienne	173
15	Angers	172
16	Toulon	169
17	Grenoble	159
18	Nîmes	151
19	Le Mans	142
20	Metz	123
21	Nancy	105
22	Cannes	70
23	Troyes	60
24	Lens	38

FRENCH REPUBLIC; REPUBLIQUE FRANCAISE

Capital	Paris	Language	French		Unified state	486
Population	60 876136	Area	547 030 km²	Density	110 per km²	% in cities	73%
GDP per cap	$27 600	Dailling code	+33	Internet	.fr	GMT + / –	+1

MEDALS TABLE

		Overall			League			Cup			LC		Europe			Stadium	Cap'ty	DoF
		G	S	B	G	S	B	G	S	B	G	S	G	S	B			
1	Olympique Marseille	19	19	7	8	8	5	10	8				1	3	2	Stade Velodrome	60 013	1899
2	AS Saint-Etienne	16	7	3	10	3	2	6	3					1	1	Geoffroy-Guichard	35 616	1920
3	AS Monaco	13	11	14	7	5	10	5	3	1	1			2	4	Stade Louis II	18 521	1924
4	Paris Saint-Germain	13	11	6	2	6	3	7	3	3	1	1	1	1	3	Parc des Princes	48 527	1970
5	Olympique Lyonnais	12	6	5	7	2	4	4	3	1	1				1	Stade Gerland	41 044	1950
6	FC Nantes Atlantique	11	13	4	8	7	2	3	5			1			2	Stade Beaujoire	38 373	1943
7	Girondins Bordeaux	10	18	6	5	9	4	3	6	2	2		1	2		Chaban-Delmas	34 198	1881
8	Lille OSC	8	11	3	3	7	3	5	4							Métropole	18 086	1944
9	Stade de Reims	8	6	4	6	3	4	2	1					2		Auguste-Delaune	7 000	1931
10	OGC Nice	7	5		4	3		3	1	1						Stade du Ray	18 696	1904
11	Racing Club Paris	6	4	5	1	2	5	5	2							Colombes	7 000	1897
12	Racing Club Strasbourg	6	4	3	1	1	3	3	3	2						Stade de la Meinau	29 000	1906
13	FC Sochaux-Montbéliard	5	7	5	2	3	4	2	3	1	1				1	Stade Bonal	20 005	1930
14	AJ Auxerre	5	1	5	1		4	4	1						1	Abbé-Deschamps	23 493	1905
15	Red Star 93 Paris	5	1					5	1							Stade de Marville	10 003	1897
16	FC Sète	4	4	1	2		1	2	4							Louis-Michel	1 200	1914
17	FC Metz	3	3	1		1	1	2	1	1	1					Saint-Symphorien	26 304	1932
18	Racing Club Lens	2	8	3	1	4	2		3	1	1				1	Félix-Bollaert	41 233	1906

RECENT LEAGUE AND CUP RECORD

	Championship							Cup		
Year	Champions	Pts	Runners-up	Pts	Third	Pts		Winners	Score	Runners-up
1995	FC Nantes	79	Olympique Lyonnais	69	Paris St-Germain	67		Paris St-Germain	1-0	RC Strasbourg
1996	AJ Auxerre	72	Paris St-Germain	68	AS Monaco	68		AJ Auxerre	2-1	Nimes Olympique
1997	AS Monaco	79	Paris St-Germain	67	FC Nantes	64		OGC Nice	1-1 4-3p	Guingamp
1998	Racing Club Lens	68	FC Metz	68	AS Monaco	59		Paris St-Germain	2-1	Racing Club Lens
1999	Girondins Bordeaux	72	Olympique Marseille	71	Olympique Lyonnais	63		FC Nantes	1-0	CS Sedan Ardennes
2000	AS Monaco	65	Paris St-Germain	58	Olympique Lyonnais	56		FC Nantes	2-1	Calais
2001	FC Nantes	68	Olympique Lyonnais	64	Lille OSC	59		RC Strasbourg	0-0 5-4p	Amiens SC
2002	Olympique Lyonnais	66	Racing Club Lens	64	AJ Auxerre	59		FC Lorient	1-0	SC Bastia
2003	Olympique Lyonnais	68	AS Monaco	67	Olympique Marseille	65		AJ Auxerre	2-1	Paris St-Germain
2004	Olympique Lyonnais	79	Paris St-Germain	76	AS Monaco	75		Paris St-Germain	1-0	Châteauroux
2005	Olympique Lyonnais	79	Lille OSC	67	AS Monaco	63		AJ Auxerre	2-1	CS Sedan
2006	Olympique Lyonnais	84	Girondins Bordeaux	69	Lille OSC	62		Paris St-Germain	2-1	Olympique Marseille
2007	Olympique Lyonnais	81	Olympique Marseille	64	Toulouse FC	58		Sochaux	2-2 5-4p	Olympique Marseille
2008	Olympique Lyonnais	79	Girondins Bordeaux	75	Olympique Marseille	62		Olympique Lyonnais	1-0	Paris St-Germain

FRANCE 2007-08

LIGUE 1 ORANGE

Team	Pl	W	D	L	F	A	Pts
Olympique Lyonnais †	38	24	7	7	74	37	79
Girondins Bordeaux	38	22	9	7	65	38	75
Olympique Marseille	38	17	11	10	58	45	62
AS Nancy-Lorraine	38	15	15	8	44	30	60
AS Saint-Etienne	38	16	10	12	47	34	58
Stade Rennais	38	16	10	12	47	44	58
Lille OSC	38	13	18	7	45	32	57
OGC Nice	38	13	16	9	35	30	55
Le Mans UC 72	38	14	11	13	46	49	53
FC Lorient	38	12	16	10	32	35	52
SM Caen	38	13	12	13	48	53	51
AS Monaco	38	13	8	17	40	48	47
Valenciennes FC	38	12	9	17	42	40	45
Sochaux-Montbéliard	38	10	14	14	34	43	44
AJ Auxerre	38	12	8	18	33	52	44
Paris Saint-Germain	38	10	13	15	37	45	43
Toulouse FC	38	9	15	14	36	42	42
Racing Club Lens	38	9	13	16	43	52	40
RC Strasbourg	38	9	8	21	34	55	35
FC Metz	38	5	9	24	28	64	24

Results grid (home team in rows):

	Lyon	Bordeaux	Marseille	Nancy	St-Etienne	Rennes	Lille	Nice	Le Mans	Lorient	Caen	Monaco	Val'ciennes	Sochaux	Auxerre	PSG	Toulouse	Lens	Strasbourg	Metz
Lyon		4-2	1-2	1-0	1-0	1-1	1-1	0-0	3-2	2-0	2-2	3-1	2-0	4-1	2-0	4-2	3-2	3-0	5-0	2-0
Bordeaux	1-3		2-2	2-1	1-0	3-0	0-0	0-0	1-2	2-2	2-1	2-1	2-1	2-0	4-1	3-0	4-3	1-0	3-0	3-0
Marseille	3-1	1-2		2-2	2-0	0-0	1-3	0-2	1-0	0-0	6-1	2-0	3-1	0-1	2-1	2-1	1-2	1-0	4-3	3-1
Nancy	1-1	1-0	1-1		2-0	2-3	2-0	2-1	1-1	2-0	1-0	2-0	0-0	1-1	4-1	1-0	1-0	2-1	3-0	2-1
St-Etienne	1-1	0-0	1-0	4-0		2-0	0-0	0-0	4-1	1-0	3-0	4-0	3-1	1-0	0-0	0-0	0-2	0-0	2-0	2-0
Rennes	0-2	0-2	3-1	0-2	1-0		2-2	1-1	3-0	2-0	1-2	0-1	1-0	0-1	2-2	2-0	2-1	3-1	3-0	2-0
Lille	0-1	1-1	1-1	2-1	3-0	3-1		1-1	3-1	0-0	5-0	0-1	3-0	1-1	0-2	1-2	0-0	3-2	2-1	1-1
Nice	0-0	1-0	1-2	1-0	3-0	1-1	0-0		0-0	1-2	3-1	0-2	1-0	0-0	1-2	2-1	1-1	1-0	1-0	3-1
Le Mans	1-0	1-1	2-0	0-2	1-3	2-1	1-1	1-2		0-0	1-1	1-0	2-0	0-2	3-0	0-2	1-1	3-2	0-1	1-0
Lorient	2-1	1-0	1-2	0-0	1-1	0-1	1-1	0-0	0-0		0-0	2-1	1-3	2-1	1-1	1-0	0-1	0-2	1-0	1-0
Caen	1-0	5-0	1-2	0-0	1-3	2-2	1-1	0-3	2-0			4-1	1-0	2-0	3-0	0-2	1-4	2-0	1-2	
Monaco	0-3	0-6	2-3	1-3	1-1	1-2	0-0	1-3	1-1	0-0			0-0	1-0	3-0	1-2	0-2	2-0	3-0	2-0
Valenciennes	1-2	3-1	2-1	1-1	2-0	3-0	0-0	1-2	1-2	3-0	3-0	1-0		3-1	3-0	0-0	3-1	1-2	2-0	0-0
Sochaux	1-2	0-1	2-1	1-1	1-1	0-0	1-1	1-0	1-3	1-1	1-0	3-1	1-0		1-1	1-2	0-1	0-2	0-0	0-0
Auxerre	1-3	0-2	2-0	0-0	1-3	0-2	0-1	2-0	3-0	5-3	1-0	1-0	2-0	0-1		0-1	1-0	0-1	1-0	
PSG	2-3	0-2	1-1	0-0	1-1	1-3	1-1	2-3	0-0	1-3	0-1	1-1	1-0	0-3	1-0		1-2	3-0	1-0	3-0
Toulouse	1-0	0-1	0-0	1-1	0-2	0-0	1-0	1-1	1-1	0-0	1-0	0-2	1-1	2-2	2-0	1-1		1-1	1-3	0-0
Lens	3-0	2-2	3-3	1-0	3-2	1-2	1-2	0-0	1-3	1-1	1-0	0-0	0-3	2-2	0-0	0-1	1-1		2-1	1-1
Strasbourg	1-2	1-1	0-0	0-1	0-0	3-0	3-0	0-1	0-1	0-1	1-4	0-2	0-0	2-3	3-1	1-2	2-0	1-2		2-3
Metz	1-5	0-1	1-2	0-0	1-1	1-1	1-2	1-2	4-3	1-2	2-1	1-4	2-1	1-2	0-1	0-0	0-2	1-2	1-2	

4/08/2007 - 17/05/2008 • † Qualified for the UEFA Champions League • ‡ Qualified for the UEFA Cup
Top scorers: Karim Benzema, Lyon 20; Mamadou Niang, Marseille 18; Bafetimbi Gomis, St-Etienne 16; Djibril Cisse, Marseille 16; Fernando Cavenaghi, Bordeaux 15; Bakari Kone, Nice 14; Rafik Saifi, Lorient 14; Steve Savidan, Valenciennes 13; Tulio De Melo, Le Mans 13

FRANCE 2007-08

LIGUE 2 ORANGE

Team	Pl	W	D	L	F	A	Pts
Le Havre AC	38	22	12	4	66	30	78
FC Nantes	38	19	13	6	58	34	70
Grenoble Foot 38	38	17	12	9	44	30	63
CS Sedan Ardennes	38	15	13	10	46	40	58
Clermont Foot	38	14	15	9	50	41	57
ES Troyes FC	38	15	12	11	46	44	57
Stade Brestois	38	15	12	11	38	38	57
Montpellier-Hérault	38	14	12	12	43	32	54
AC Ajaccio	38	14	12	12	37	41	54
SC Angers	38	13	14	11	39	35	53
SC Bastia	38	14	9	15	45	46	49
En Avant Guingamp	38	11	15	12	41	37	48
Stade de Reims	38	12	10	16	44	52	46
Amiens SFC	38	12	12	15	49	51	45
LB Châteauroux	38	11	12	15	34	42	45
US Boulogne-sur-mer	38	12	7	19	37	54	43
Dijon FCO	38	9	15	14	32	51	42
Chamois Niortais	38	11	8	19	38	48	41
Libourne St-Seurin	38	7	11	20	41	62	32
FC Gueugnon	38	5	12	21	39	59	27

Results grid (home team in rows):

	Le Havre	Nantes	Grenoble	Sedan	Clermont	Troyes	Brest	Montpellier	Ajaccio	Angers	Bastia	Guingamp	Reims	Amiens	Chât'roux	Boulogne	Dijon	Niort	Libourne	Gueugnon
Le Havre		1-0	0-0	0-0	1-0	0-0	1-1	0-0	2-0	3-2	6-0	2-1	2-0	2-2	2-0	2-0	1-0	1-1	1-1	4-1
Nantes	0-1		1-0	2-1	2-2	2-0	3-0	1-1	2-1	1-1	2-0	1-1	1-5	0-3	1-2	1-3	0-2	1-1	2-2	2-0
Grenoble	0-2	0-3		0-0	2-0	2-0	3-1	2-0	0-0	0-0	1-0	0-0	2-0	1-2	2-0	3-1	1-0	3-1		
Sedan	2-1	1-2	2-1		2-2	0-1	2-0	3-1	2-1	2-2	0-0	1-0	2-1	1-1	2-1	1-1	0-1	1-0	1-0	3-1
Clermont	1-0	2-1	0-0	2-1		1-2	1-0	3-2	2-0	2-0	2-3	3-3	4-1	4-2	0-0	0-0	3-0	1-0	1-1	1-0
Troyes	4-1	0-2	2-2	0-1	1-2		3-2	1-0	1-2	2-2	1-0	4-2	1-0	2-0	2-2	3-0	1-1	2-0	2-2	
Brest	0-2	1-2	1-0	1-1	1-1	0-0		1-0	0-1	1-0	3-1	1-1	1-1	1-0	2-1	3-0	4-2	0-1	4-2	2-1
Montpellier	0-0	0-0	1-0	2-3	3-0	2-1			1-0	1-0	2-1	0-0	0-0	2-0	0-3	0-1	1-0	5-0	0-0	
Ajaccio	0-3	2-1	2-1	2-1	3-1	1-0	1-1	2-1		1-1	1-3	1-1	0-0	1-0	0-0	2-1	1-1	2-1	2-3	2-0
Angers	1-2	0-0	0-2	1-2	1-3	1-1	1-0				1-2	1-1	2-0	3-0	2-0	0-1	0-1	1-1	1-0	2-1
Bastia	0-2	0-1	0-0	3-1	0-0	1-0	4-0	1-0	1-0	1-0		0-1	1-2	1-0	2-3	4-0	0-0	2-2	2-1	1-0
Guingamp	1-0	0-1	1-2	2-1	0-0	5-0	1-0	0-2	1-1	1-0	0-1		2-1	1-0	2-2	4-2	0-0	0-0	1-0	1-1
Reims	3-3	3-3	3-4	3-1	0-0	0-1	0-0	2-1	0-0	0-1	1-2	3-2		0-0	2-0	4-1	0-1	3-1	2-1	2-1
Amiens	1-3	2-1	1-2	2-1	0-0	0-0	1-1	1-1	4-0	2-0	1-3	1-1	1-0		1-2	2-1	2-2	0-2	1-0	4-4
Châteauroux	0-0	1-2	1-1	5-1	0-1	1-3	1-2	1-0	0-0	0-2	1-1	0-0	0-1	1-0		1-0	2-0	1-0	2-1	
Boulogne	0-3	4-0	0-1	0-1	1-2	1-2	2-0	0-0	1-0	2-0	0-2	0-0	1-2	1-3			0-1	1-0	0-0	
Dijon	2-3	0-0	0-1	1-3	1-2	2-2	0-2	1-1	1-3	2-1	1-0	2-2	1-0	0-0	0-2			1-3	3-1	2-1
Niort	0-3	0-1	2-1	0-1	1-0	0-0	0-1	2-0	2-0	0-1	1-3	1-3	0-1	1-3	2-1	1-2	1-3		2-1	2-2
Libourne	3-1	2-3	1-2	0-1	1-0	0-0	0-1	3-1	2-1	1-2	4-2	1-1	2-1	1-2	5-1	0-2	2-0	0-2		2-0
Gueugnon	3-4	1-1	1-2	3-1	1-1	1-1	0-1	1-2	0-2	2-2	1-0	1-0	1-3	2-1	3-1	0-1	3-1	0-1	3-1	

27/07/2007 - 16/05/2008 • Top scorers: Guillaume Hoarau, Le Havre 28; Gregory Thil, Boulogne 16; Cédric Fauré, Reims 16; Titi Buengo, Amiens 14

FRANCE 2007–08

NATIONAL (3)

	Pl	W	D	L	F	A	Pts
Vannes Olympique	38	20	9	9	47	31	69
Tours FC	38	18	11	9	53	31	65
Nîmes Olympique	38	17	12	9	51	40	63
AS Cherbourg	38	17	10	11	47	37	61
Stade Lavallois	38	14	16	8	51	31	58
FC Sète 34	38	14	14	10	39	29	56
US Créteil-Lusitanos	38	12	15	11	47	35	51
AC Arlésien	38	12	15	11	37	36	51
AS Beauvais Oise	38	13	12	13	44	44	51
Paris FC	38	12	14	12	52	53	50
Entente SSG	38	15	5	18	46	52	50
FC Istres	38	13	11	14	40	42	50
Rodez Aveyron	38	14	6	18	42	49	48
AS Cannes §3	38	12	14	12	41	49	47
Calais RUFC	38	11	14	13	39	41	47
Louhans-Cuiseaux 71	38	12	9	17	40	61	45
FC Pau	38	12	5	21	39	61	41
Villemomble Sports	38	9	14	15	29	38	41
FC Martigues	38	9	13	16	40	48	40
SO Romorantinais	38	8	13	17	31	47	37

Results grid (home team in rows; columns: Vannes, Tours, Nîmes, Cherbourg, Laval, Sète, Créteil, Arles, Beauvais, Paris, Entente, Istres, Rodez, Cannes, Calais, Louhans, Pau, Villem'ble, Martigues, Romorantin):

	Van	Tou	Nîm	Che	Lav	Sèt	Cré	Arl	Bea	Par	Ent	Ist	Rod	Can	Cal	Lou	Pau	Vil	Mar	Rom
Vannes		0-1	2-0	1-0	1-1	1-0	1-1	2-0	3-0	0-0	1-0	3-1	1-0	1-0	0-1	3-1	2-1	0-0	0-1	1-0
Tours	2-2		1-1	4-2	1-0	3-0	2-1	1-2	2-1	3-3	3-0	0-1	1-0	4-0	1-1	4-1	0-1	3-0	3-0	0-1
Nîmes	1-0	0-0		2-2	3-1	0-1	1-1	2-1	3-1	2-0	2-0	2-1	2-1	2-1	2-1	4-2	2-0	1-0	0-0	1-1
Cherbourg	0-1	0-0	2-1		2-0	1-1	4-2	0-0	2-1	1-0	1-1	3-0	1-0	3-0	1-2	1-0	2-1	2-0	2-1	0-1
Lavallois	3-0	0-0	1-1	1-0		1-1	1-1	3-0	4-3	1-0	1-1	1-2	4-0	3-0	0-0	3-0	2-1	3-2	2-2	4-2
Sète	3-0	1-1	1-3	1-0	0-0		0-1	1-0	1-1	1-0	4-0	4-2	5-0	1-2	0-0	1-0	1-2	0-0	1-1	1-0
Créteil	0-1	0-1	2-0	0-1	1-1	0-0		3-0	1-0	1-2	2-0	1-2	0-2	3-0	0-1	6-0	1-3	1-1	1-1	0-0
Arlésien	2-2	2-0	1-1	1-0	0-0	0-0	1-1		1-0	1-1	0-0	0-2	1-0	0-1	1-0	2-0	3-0	2-1	1-0	2-1
Beauvais	0-4	2-1	3-0	1-1	0-0	0-0	1-1	1-1		2-1	3-0	0-2	3-0	1-1	3-1	0-2	2-0	2-2	2-0	2-1
Paris	0-0	1-0	4-3	3-2	0-0	0-1	2-2	1-2	1-2		1-2	1-0	2-3	0-0	0-1	0-3	1-2	2-1	2-3	1-0
Entente	1-3	0-1	2-0	0-1	0-3	2-1	1-1	4-2	2-0	1-3		1-0	1-2	1-2	3-2	0-1	3-0	2-1	2-1	2-1
Istres	2-2	0-0	0-1	1-1	2-1	0-2	0-0	0-0	0-0	2-2	3-2		1-0	0-2	0-0	1-2	0-2	0-1	0-1	1-2
Rodez	0-1	2-0	1-1	4-2	1-0	2-1	0-1	1-1	2-1	1-0	0-1	1-0		3-1	0-1	0-2	1-2	2-2	0-0	3-0
Cannes	0-1	1-2	0-2	1-1	0-3	1-2	0-0	1-1	1-0	2-1	0-2	0-3	1-1		1-0	3-1	5-0	0-0	4-4	0-0
Calais	0-2	1-2	0-2	1-1	0-3	1-2	0-0	1-1	1-0	2-1	0-2	0-0	2-1	0-0		3-1	5-0	0-0	4-4	0-0
Louhans	2-1	0-2	1-0	1-2	0-1	1-0	2-2	1-0	0-0	0-1	1-4	1-1	1-5	1-1	3-2		2-2	1-2	3-1	1-2
Pau	0-0	1-0	4-3	3-2	0-0	0-1	0-1	2-2	1-2	1-2	1-0	2-3	0-0	0-0	0-1	0-1		2-1	2-3	1-0
Villemomble	0-0	1-0	4-3	3-2	0-0	0-0	0-0	0-2	1-0	1-2	2-2	1-1	2-1	0-0	0-0	0-1	0-1		0-0	1-0
Martigues	1-2	1-0	2-1	0-2	0-0	0-0	0-2	1-0	1-2	2-5	0-2	2-0	0-2	2-1	2-1	0-1	0-1	3-0		3-0
Romorantin	0-0	1-1	1-1	0-2	0-1	0-1	1-0	1-1	1-3	1-0	1-0	0-2	3-3	2-2	0-0	2-3	1-3	0-0		

3/08/2007 - 16/05/2008 • § = Points deducted • Top scorers: Youssef Adnane, Cherbourg 19; Hamado Ouédraogo, Beauvais 18; Dantas, Entente 17

FRANCE 2007–08 CFA GROUPE A (4)

	Pl	W	D	L	F	A	Pts
Pacy-sur-Eure	34	18	8	8	51	31	96
Rouen	34	17	9	8	43	26	94
Quevilly	34	16	8	10	49	38	90
Dunkerque	34	16	7	11	55	42	89
Lille B	34	13	13	8	48	37	86
Racing CF 92	34	15	4	15	42	45	83
Caen B	34	12	12	10	41	41	82
Vitré	34	14	6	14	37	47	82
La Vitréenne	34	10	17	7	29	28	81
Guingamp B	34	12	10	12	46	38	80
Compiègne	34	9	19	6	39	42	80
Lens B	34	12	9	13	47	48	79
Rennes B	34	12	8	14	40	39	78
Le Havre B	34	11	9	14	43	41	76
Plabennec	34	10	10	14	30	44	74
Lesquin	34	10	9	15	43	46	73
Wasquehal	34	9	8	17	32	43	69
Valenciennes B	34	3	8	23	29	68	51

3/08/2007 - 24/05/2008 • Four points for a win, two for a draw and one for a defeat

FRANCE 2007–08 CFA GROUPE B (4)

	Pl	W	D	L	F	A	Pts
Croix-de-Savoie	34	22	8	4	52	17	108
Besançon	34	19	11	4	61	20	102
Vesoul	34	17	10	7	61	42	95
Sochaux B	34	17	9	8	65	45	94
Saint Priest	34	13	14	7	50	38	87
Lyon B	34	12	13	9	45	32	83
Montceau	34	13	9	12	36	33	82
Auxerre B	34	12	9	13	52	48	79
Strasbourg B	34	11	12	11	42	43	79
Red Star 93	34	10	10	14	38	40	74
Metz B	34	10	9	15	39	46	73
Jura Sud	34	8	14	12	31	37	72
Raon-l'Etape	34	10	7	17	37	61	71
Mulhouse	34	10	8	16	31	55	71
Nancy B	34	6	16	12	28	36	68
Epinal	34	6	16	12	33	49	68
Belfort	34	7	11	16	30	50	66
Epernay	34	6	8	20	25	64	60

3/08/2007 - 24/05/2008 • Four points for a win, two for a draw and one for a defeat

FRANCE 2007-08
CFA GROUPE C (4)

	Pl	W	D	L	F	A	Pts
Cassis-Camoux	34	21	6	7	49	31	103
Gap	34	17	12	5	58	28	97
GFCO Ajaccio	34	15	12	7	37	32	91
Monaco B	34	14	10	10	47	33	86
Marignane	34	14	9	11	41	32	85
Albi	34	12	14	8	45	32	84
St-Etienne B	34	13	8	13	33	35	81
Toulon	34	13	7	14	36	36	80
Hyères	34	10	16	8	33	26	80
Fréjus	34	14	4	16	41	43	80
CA Bastia	34	11	11	12	35	48	78
Luzenac	34	11	10	13	49	51	77
Balma	34	10	9	15	34	44	73
Montpellier B	34	10	9	15	33	43	73
Nice B	34	8	13	13	36	41	71
Andrézieux	34	9	14	11	31	33	69
Toulouse B	34	5	14	15	31	49	63
Manosque	34	8	4	22	33	65	62

3/08/2007 - 24/05/2008 • Four points for a win, two for a draw and one for a defeat

FRANCE 2007-08
CFA GROUPE D (4)

	Pl	W	D	L	F	A	Pts
Bordeaux B	34	18	9	7	56	28	97
Bayonne	34	15	13	6	47	30	92
Fontenay-le-Comte	34	13	15	6	40	33	88
Moulins	34	14	11	9	44	34	87
Orléans	34	11	17	6	44	35	84
Le Mans B	34	14	8	12	55	49	84
Paris St-Germain B	34	12	12	10	28	26	82
Anglet Genêts	34	13	9	12	42	37	82
St-Geneviève	34	13	7	14	43	50	80
Châtellerault	34	12	9	13	45	52	78
Yzeure	34	11	11	12	38	46	78
Montluçon	34	9	15	10	44	37	76
Stade Bordelais	34	9	14	11	40	48	75
Sénart-Moissy	34	9	11	14	43	54	72
Aurillac	34	8	11	15	34	46	69
Nantes B	34	8	11	15	27	41	68
Sables-d'Olonne	34	8	10	16	29	45	68
Poissy	34	7	11	16	40	48	66

3/08/2007 - 24/05/2008 • Four points for a win, two for a draw and one for a defeat

COUPE DE FRANCE 2007-08

Round of 64		Round of 32		Round of 16	
Olympique Lyonnais	4				
US Créteil-Lusitanos *	0	Olympique Lyonnais	1		
Raon l'Etape	1 3p	Croix-de-Savoie *	0		
Croix-de-Savoie *	1 4p			Olympique Lyonnais *	2
Montpellier-Hérault *	1			Sochaux-Montbéliard	1
ES Troyes FC	0	Montpellier-Hérault	1 3p		
Maubeuge *	0	Sochaux-Montbéliard *	1 4p		
Sochaux-Montbéliard	2				
FC Lorient *	2				
Valenciennes FC	1	FC Lorient *	0 3p		
FC Martigues *	0	Stade Rennais	0 1p		
Stade Rennais	3			FC Lorient *	0
RC Strasbourg	0 5p			FC Metz	1
Rouen *	0 4p	RC Strasbourg *	0		
Vesoul *	1	FC Metz	3		
FC Metz	6				
Girondins Bordeaux	3				
Quevilly *	1	Girondins Bordeaux *	1		
Selongey *	2	Le Mans UC 72	0		
Le Mans UC 72	3			Girondins Bordeaux *	2
Lyon-Duchère *	3			Lille OSC	0
Luzenac	2	Lyon-Duchère *	0		
Avion *	0	Lille OSC	1		
Lille OSC	3				
SC Angers *	2				
Vannes Olympique	0	SC Angers *	3		
Le Havre AC	1	OGC Nice	1		
OGC Nice *	2			SC Angers	0
FC Nantes	3			CS Sedan Ardennes *	2
Montluçon *	0	FC Nantes	0 2p		
SM Caen	2	CS Sedan Ardennes *	0 4p		
CS Sedan Ardennes *	3				
Amiens SFC *	2				
En Avant Guingamp	1	Amiens SFC *	1		
Fréjus	0	GFCO Ajaccio	0		
GFCO Ajaccio *	1			Amiens SFC *	1 4p
Chamois Niortais	1			AC Arlésien	1 2p
Racing Club Lens *	0	Chamois Niortais	0 7p		
Marignane *	1 2p	AC Arlésien *	0 6p		
AC Arlésien	1 3p				
Tours FC	3				
Saint Omer *	0	Tours FC	2		
SO Romorantinais *	1	US Boulogne-sur-mer *	1		
US Boulogne-sur-mer	2			Tours FC	1
Paris FC	2			Dijon FCO *	3
Toulouse FC *	1	Paris FC *	0 5p		
Avranches *	0	Dijon FCO	0 6p		
Dijon FCO	2				
Carquefou *	1				
FC Gueugnon	0	Carquefou *	2		
Stade de Reims	1	AS Nancy-Lorraine	1		
AS Nancy-Lorraine *	2			Carquefou *	1
AS Monaco	3			Olympique Marseille	0
Stade Brestois *	1	AS Monaco	1		
AS Beauvais Oise *	0	Olympique Marseille *	3		
Olympique Marseille	2				
SC Bastia	5				
Viry-Châtillon *	2	SC Bastia *	3		
AS Saint-Etienne	2	AJ Auxerre	0		
AJ Auxerre	3			SC Bastia	1
Le Poiré-sur-Vie *	4			Paris Saint-Germain *	2
Coulaines	1	Le Poiré-sur-Vie *	1		
Epinal *	0	Paris Saint-Germain	3		
Paris Saint-Germain	2				

* Home team

COUPE DE FRANCE 2007-08

Quarter–finals	Semi–finals	Final

Olympique Lyonnais *   1
FC Metz   0

Olympique Lyonnais *   1
CS Sedan Ardennes   0

Girondins Bordeaux *   0 3p
CS Sedan Ardennes   0 4p

Olympique Lyonnais   1
Paris Saint-Germain   0

Amiens SFC *   1
Dijon FCO   0

Amiens SFC *   0
Paris Saint-Germain   1

COUPE DE FRANCE FINAL 2008

Stade de France, Paris, 24-05-2008, 21:00, Att: 79 204, Ref: Philippe Kalt

Olympique Lyonnais   1   Govou [103]
Paris Saint-Germain   0

Carquefou *   0
Paris Saint-Germain   1

Lyon - Grégory Coupet - Anthony Reveillère, Jérémy Toulalan•, Jean-Alain Boumsong, Sébastien Squillaci•, Kim Källström (Mathieu Bodmer 67), Sidney Govou (Clerc 117), Juninho, Fred (Kader Keita• 72), Karim Benzema, Fabio Grosso.
Tr: Alain Perrin
PSG - Jérôme Alonzo - Ceara, Sylvain Armand, Zoumana Camara•, Grégory Bourillon (Souza 104), Mario Yepes, Jérôme Rothen, Jérémy Clément, Pauleta (Péguy Luyindula 79), Clément Chantôme• (Bernard Mendy• 82), Amara Diané.
Tr: Paul Le Guen

‡ Qualified for the UEFA Cup

COUPE DE LA LIGUE 2007-08

Third Round		Fourth Round		Quarter-finals		Semi-finals		Final	
Paris Saint-Germain	3	Paris Saint-Germain *	2	Paris Saint-Germain	4	Paris Saint-Germain *	3	Paris Saint-Germain ‡	2
FC Lorient *	0	Montpellier-Hérault	0	Valenciennes	0	AJ Auxerre	2	Racing Club Lens	1
Stade Brestois *	1								
Montpellier-Hérault	2								
Stade Rennais	1	Stade Rennais *	0						
Clermont-Foot *	0	Valenciennes	2						
Sochaux-Montbelliard	1								
Valenciennes *	2								
Olympique Marseille	Bye	Olympique Marseille *	2 5p	Olympique Marseille	0				
Girondins Bordeaux *	1	FC Metz	2 4p	AJ Auxerre	1				
FC Metz	2								
OGC Nice	1	OGC Nice	2						
ES Troyes FC *	0	AJ Auxerre *	6						
AS Saint-Etienne	0								
AJ Auxerre *	1								
Le Mans	1	Le Mans	3	Le Mans	1	Le Mans *	4		
Stade Lavallois *	0	Chamois Niortais *	0	Olympique Lyonnais	0	Racing Club Lens	5		
Le Havre AC	2								
Chamois Niortais *	3								
SM Caen	2 4p	SM Caen *	1						
Toulouse FC *	2 2p	Olympique Lyonnais	3						
Olympique Lyonnais	Bye								
Nancy-Lorraine *	3	Nancy-Lorraine *	1	Nancy-Lorraine	0				
Boulogne-sur-mer	0	Amiens SFC	0	Racing Club Lens	3				
RC Strasbourg *	0								
Amiens SFC	2								
AS Monaco	3	AS Monaco *	1						
FC Nantes *	2	Racing Club Lens	2						
Lille OSC	0								
Racing Club Lens *	1								

* Home team • Ligue 1 clubs enter in the third round • ‡ Qualified for the UEFA Cup

COUPE DE LA LIGUE FINAL

Stade de France, St-Denis, Paris
29-03-2008. Att: 78 741 Ref: Duhamel

Scorers - Pauleta 19, Mendy 93+p for PSG; Carriere 51 for Lens

PSG - Landreau - Ceara, Sakho, Camara, Armand, Bourillon, Chantome» (Mendy 64), Clement, Rothen, Pauleta (c) (Luyindula 66), Diane. Tr: Paul Le Guen

Lens - Le Crom - Hilton» (c), Coulibaly, Belhadj, Laurenti», Mangane, Carriere, Kovacevic, Maoulida (Demont 84), Remy (Monterrubio 13), Monnet-Paquet (Dindane 68). Tr: Jean-Pierre Papin

AJ AUXERRE 2007–08

	Date	Opp	Res	Score	Scorers	Att
Aug	5	Lyon	L	0-2		35 537
	11	Bordeaux	L	0-2		11 512
	15	Strasbourg	L	0-3		20 030
	18	Caen	W	1-0	Maoulida 35	7 439
	25	Nancy	L	1-4	Lejeune 60	18 132
	29	Rennes	L	0-2		7 896
Sept	1	Toulouse	L	0-2		14 795
	15	Nice	W	2-0	Lejeune 5, Niculae 93+	7 817
	22	Marseille	W	2-0	Niculae 2 18 25	18 736
Oct	6	Lens	L	0-2		31 139
	20	Lorient	W	5-3	Niculae 2 55 82, Jelen 3 73 75 91+	8 157
	27	St Etienne	D	0-0		30 448
Nov	3	Lille	L	0-1		8 856
	10	Sochaux	D	1-1	Kahlenberg 8p	18 442
	25	Le Mans	W	3-0	Chafni 35, Niculae 81, Jelen 87	7 222
Dec	1	Metz	W	1-0	Kahlenberg 54	10 281
	9	Paris SG	L	0-1		11 015
	15	Val'ciennes	L	0-3		13 057
	22	Monaco	W	1-0	Traore 68	8 952
Jan	12	Bordeaux	L	1-4	Niculae 2	21 223
	19	Strasbourg	D	1-1	Niculae 5	6 553
	23	Caen	D	0-0		19 613
	26	Nancy	D	0-0		6 548
Feb	9	Rennes	W	2-1	Oliech 2 45 89	22 733
	16	Toulouse	W	1-0	Niculae 51	9 106
	23	Nice	W	2-1	Niculae 67, Chafni 70	10 114
Mar	1	Marseille	L	1-2	Pedretti 88	53 100
	8	Lens	D	0-0		10 591
	15	Lorient	D	1-1	Jaures 71p	12 881
	22	St Etienne	L	1-3	Benalouane OG 6	13 137
	30	Lille	W	2-0	Oliech 42, Niculae 57	16 017
Apr	5	Sochaux	L	0-1		10 282
	12	Le Mans	L	0-3		12 339
	19	Metz	D	0-0		8 620
	26	Paris SG	L	1-3	Mignot 78	37 671
May	3	Val'ciennes	W	2-0	Lejeune 17, Jelen 92+	19 000
	10	Monaco	L	0-3		9 839
	17	Lyon	L	1-3	Thomas 77	19 799

SM CAEN 2007–08

	Date	Opp	Res	Score	Scorers	Att
Aug	4	Nice	W	1-0	Compan 82	19 045
	11	Nancy	L	0-1		17 545
	18	Auxerre	L	0-1		7 439
	25	Marseille	L	1-2	Samson 92+	20 790
Sept	1	Sochaux	D	2-2	Eluchans 33, Proment 66	18 099
	15	St Etienne	L	0-3		25 638
	22	Metz	L	1-2	Gouffran 9	17 883
	30	Toulouse	W	3-2	Compan 12, Nivet 55	17 119
Oct	6	Lorient	D	0-0		10 215
	20	Lille	W	1-0	Tafforeau OG 60	18 275
	27	Monaco	D	0-0		8 986
Nov	4	Le Mans	W	3-2	Gouffran 2 33 65, Eluchans 58	20 286
	10	Val'ciennes	L	0-3		12 449
	24	Bordeaux	W	5-0	Gouffran 10, Sorbon 29, Grandin 74p, Eluchans 84, Gomis 87	20 047
	28	Lens	D	1-1	Sorbon 87	36 409
Dec	1	Paris SG	W	1-0	Florentin 76	37 148
	8	Lyon	W	1-0	Gouffran 18	20 664
	15	Rennes	W	2-1	Deroin 63p, Eluchans 78	26 081
	22	Strasbourg	W	2-0	Eluchans 40, Hengbart 79p	20 391
Jan	12	Nancy	D	0-0		20 327
	19	Toulouse	D	1-1	Deroin 69	13 938
	23	Auxerre	D	0-0		19 613
Feb	26	Marseille	L	1-6	Toudic 2	48 481
	10	Lens	L	1-4	Lemaitre 69	20 289
	16	Sochaux	D	1-1	Gouffran 55	11 378
	23	St Etienne	L	1-3	Compan 63	20 713
Mar	1	Metz	L	1-2	Jemaa 79	10 767
	8	Lorient	D	0-0		18 493
	15	Lille	L	0-5		13 668
	22	Monaco	W	4-1	Hengbart 2 62p, Sorbon 76, Gouffran 86, Jemaa 93+	20 082
	30	Le Mans	D	1-1	Gouffran 14.	11 091
Apr	5	Val'ciennes	W	1-0	Jemaa 21	19 477
	13	Bordeaux	L	1-2	Sorbon 89	27 686
	19	Paris SG	W	3-0	Deroin 52, Lemaitre 75, Gouffran 89	20 933
	26	Lyon	D	2-2	Eluchans 38, Compan 44	39 068
May	3	Rennes	D	2-2	Compan 54, Nivet 87	20 624
	10	Strasbourg	W	4-1	Toudic 2 6 84, OG 12, Gouffran 31	17 311
	17	Nice	L	1-3	Toudic 44	11 540

GIRONDINS BORDEAUX 2007–08

	Date	Opp	Res	Score	Comp	Scorers	Att
Aug	4	Lens	W	1-0	L1	Bellion 30	30 667
	11	Auxerre	W	2-0	L1	Wendel 2 45 52	11 512
	15	Le Mans	L	1-2	L1	Bellion 14	30 438
	18	St Etienne	D	0-0	L1		32 630
	25	Lorient	D	2-2	L1	Bellion 2 11 68	23 392
	29	Metz	W	1-0	L1	Diarra 62	14 169
Sept	1	Monaco	W	2-1	L1	Camakh 61, Wendel 74	23 390
	15	Lille	D	1-1	L1	Bellion 40	13 770
	20	Tampere	W	3-2	UCr1		5 719
	23	Paris SG	W	2-0	L1	Micoud 10, Bellion 47	37 108
	26	Metz	L	1-2	LCr3	Obertan 3	2 467
Oct	4	Tampere	D	1-1	UCr1		8 445
	7	Lyon	L	1-3	L1	Jussië 85	31 919
	20	Strasbourg	D	1-1	L1	Bellion 62	18 865
	25	Galatasaray	W	2-1	UCgH	Cavenaghi 53, Chamakh 64	10 883
	27	Val'ciennes	W	2-1	L1	Jussië 37p, Bellion 45	18 521
Nov	3	Nancy	L	0-1	L1		19 686
	8	FK Austria	W	2-1	UCgH	Chamakh 45, Wendel 88p	20 300
	11	Rennes	W	3-0	L1	Bellion 2 18 49, Obertan 82	21 759
	24	Caen	L	0-5	L1		20 047
Dec	2	Toulouse	W	4-3	L1	Wendel 3 7 39 86, Diarra 33	21 928
	6	Helsingborg	W	2-1	UCgH	Chamakh 12, Jussië 69	9 357
	9	Nice	D	1-1	L1	Micoud 18	11 988
	16	Marseille	D	2-2	L1	Chamakh 33, Jussië 70	32 286
	19	Panionios	W	3-2	UCgH	Cavenaghi 39, Tremoulinas 75, Moimbe 87	4 239
	22	Sochaux	W	1-0	L1	Jussië 85	12 646
	5	Quevilly	W	3-1	CFr9	Micoud 2 56 93+, Cavenaghi 80	4 706
Jan	12	Auxerre	W	4-1	L1	Cavenaghi 2 13 52, Planus 40, Bellion 92+	21 223
	19	Le Mans	W	2-1	L1	Cavenaghi 14, Fernando 22	10 656
	24	St Etienne	W	1-0	L1	Cavenaghi 56	23 990
	27	Lorient	L	0-1	L1		11 182
	2	Le Mans	W	1-0	CFr10	Wendel 15	9 361
	9	Metz	W	3-0	L1	Cavenaghi 2 25p 72, Diarra 88	19 673
	13	Anderlecht	L	1-2	UCr2	Jussië 69p	15 173
Feb	17	Monaco	W	6-0	L1	Cavenaghi 2 51 64, Micoud 2 60 87, Chamakh 81, Obertan 91+	10 018
	21	Anderlecht	D	1-1	UCr2	Cavenaghi 71	17 985
	24	Lille	D	0-0	L1		21 761
	2	Paris SG	W	3-0	L1	Wendel 3 33 49 51	30 309
Mar	9	Lyon	L	2-4	L1	Wendel 35, Cavenaghi 60p	40 381
	16	Strasbourg	W	3-0	L1	Henrique 2 28 42, Cavenaghi 74	19 474
	19	Lille	W	2-0	CFr11	Fernando 95, Bellion 115	8521
	22	Val'ciennes	L	1-3	L1	Wendel 14	13 657
	29	Nancy	W	2-1	L1	Cavenaghi 2 53 82p	24 308
Apr	5	Rennes	W	2-1	L1	Diarra 18, Fernando 83	28 124
	13	Caen	W	2-1	L1	Cavenaghi 2 52 76p	27 686
	16	Sedan	D	0-0	CFqf	L 3-4p	11 442
	20	Toulouse	W	1-0	L1	Micoud 93+	27 247
	26	Nice	D	0-0	L1		29 097
May	3	Marseille	W	2-1	L1	Wendel 80, Ducasse 91+	55 778
	10	Sochaux	W	2-0	L1	Fernando 45, Chamakh 59	32 487
	17	Lens	D	2-2	L1	Cavenaghi 65, Bellion 82	40 068

L1 = Ligue 1 Orange • UC = UEFA Cup • LC = Coupe de la Ligue •
CF = Coupe de France • gH = Group H • r1 = first round • r3 = third
round • r9 = ninth round • r10 = 10th round • r11 = 11th round •
qf = quarter-final • sf = semi-final • f = final

LE MANS UC 72 2007-08

Month	Day	Opponent	Res	Score	Scorers	Att
	5	Metz	W	1-0	Basa 27	9 831
Aug	11	Sochaux	W	3-1	De Melo 3 30p 51 61	14 033
	15	Bordeaux	W	2-1	De Melo 48, Grafite 72	30 438
	18	Lille	D	1-1	Grafite 58	10 724
	25	Monaco	L	1-3	Matsui 31	11 033
	29	Paris SG	L	0-2		13 072
Sept	1	Lyon	L	2-3	Sessegnon 2 43 55	35 042
	15	Val'ciennes	W	2-0	Sessegnon 41, De Melo 48	9 570
	22	Strasbourg	W	1-0	Romaric 37	17 971
Oct	6	Nice	W	2-0	De Melo 31, Matsui 61	9 604
	20	Rennes	L	0-3		23 349
	28	Toulouse	D	1-1	Sessegnon 61	9 841
Nov	4	Caen	L	2-3	Basa 46, De Melo 72	20 286
	10	St Etienne	W	3-2	De Melo 2 19p 70p, Romaric 43	12 434
	25	Auxerre	L	0-3		7 222
Dec	1	Nancy	W	2-1	Yebda 59, Gervinho 79	9 938
	8	Lens	W	3-1	De Melo 23, Gervinho 50, Le Tallec 89	29 083
	15	Lorient	D	0-0		10 095
	22	Marseille	L	0-1		48 886
Jan	12	Sochaux	L	0-2		9 714
	19	Bordeaux	L	1-2	Douillard 36	10 656
	23	Lille	L	1-3	Yebda 86	10 990
	26	Monaco	W	1-0	Matsui 22	9 417
Feb	9	Paris SG	D	0-0		39 970
	16	Lyon	W	1-0	De Melo 71	14 015
	23	Val'ciennes	W	2-1	Basa 1, Le Tallec 15	12 684
Mar	1	Strasbourg	L	0-1		9 101
	8	Nice	D	0-0		9 713
	15	Rennes	D	1-1	De Melo 49	10 329
	22	Toulouse	D	1-1	Yebda 28	17 259
	30	Caen	D	1-1	Basa 33	11 091
Apr	5	St Etienne	L	1-4	Le Tallec 31	30 006
	12	Auxerre	W	3-0	Samassa 25, Le Tallec 59, Sessegnon 72	12 339
	19	Nancy	D	1-1	Le Tallec 51	18 672
	26	Lens	W	3-2	Matsui 2 20 25, Basa 49	12 125
	3	Lorient	D	0-0		13 947
May	10	Marseille	D	0-0		16 361
	17	Metz	L	3-4	De Melo 51, Coutadeur 65, Baal 85	12 263

RACING CLUB LENS 2007-08

Month	Day	Opponent	Res	Score	Scorers	Att
	4	Bordeaux	L	0-1		30 667
Aug	12	Paris SG	D	0-0		38 836
	19	Val'ciennes	D	0-0		37 194
	25	Strasbourg	L	1-2	Keita 71	24 668
	2	Nice	L	0-1		10 858
Sept	15	Nancy	W	1-0	Dindane 69p	32 774
	22	Toulouse	D	1-1	Monterrubio 38	15 034
	29	Lyon	L	0-3		38 420
Oct	6	Auxerre	W	2-0	Pieroni 24p, Mangane 78	31 139
	21	Marseille	L	0-1		49 245
	28	Rennes	L	1-2	Monterrubio 49	30 441
Nov	4	St Etienne	W	3-2	Coulibaly 63, Demont 65, Dindane 85	33 877
	10	Metz	W	2-1	Monterrubio 56, Khiter 87	12 268
	24	Lorient	D	1-1	Pieroni 19	30 126
	28	Caen	D	1-1	Dindane 79	36 409
Dec	1	Sochaux	W	2-0	Dindane 21, Monterrubio 59	13 950
	8	Le Mans	L	1-3	Dindane 45	29 083
	15	Monaco	L	0-2		14 578
	22	Paris SG	L	0-3		35 658
Jan	20	Lyon	W	3-0	Maoulida 55, Bisevac 69, Mangane 89	32 734
	23	Val'ciennes	W	2-1	Hilton 44, Monnet-Paquet 64	14 824
	26	Strasbourg	D	2-2	Monterrubio 2 5p 82	31 326
	10	Caen	W	4-1	Maoulida 1, Mangane 33, Remy 66, OG 76	20 289
Feb	16	Nice	D	0-0		31 799
	23	Nancy	L	1-2	Mangane 41	17 951
	1	Toulouse	D	1-1	Remy 8	30 786
	8	Auxerre	D	0-0		10 591
Mar	11	Lille	L	1-2	Hilton 86	36 533
	16	Marseille	D	3-3	Maoulida 56, Mangane 66, Remy 74	40 477
	23	Rennes	L	1-3	Maoulida 33	24 411
	5	Metz	D	1-1	Monterrubio 34p	35 952
Apr	9	St Etienne	L	0-2		33 973
	12	Lorient	L	0-1		13 279
	19	Sochaux	W	3-2	Coulibaly 6, Dindane 2 51 70	39 478
	26	Le Mans	L	2-3	Dindane 34, Monnet-Paquet 84	12 125
	3	Monaco	D	0-0		39 399
May	10	Lille	L	1-2	Monterrubio 69p	17 670
	17	Bordeaux	D	2-2	Monterrubio 68p, Maoulida 83	40 068

LILLE OSC 2007-08

Month	Day	Opponent	Res	Score	Scorers	Att
	4	Lorient	D	0-0		14 215
Aug	12	Metz	W	2-1	Bastos 22, Maric 88	15 591
	15	Sochaux	D	1-1	Dumont 27	12 029
	18	Le Mans	D	1-1	Fauvergue 35	10 724
	26	Paris SG	D	1-1	Makoun 43	31 634
	29	Monaco	L	0-1		13 849
Sept	1	Rennes	D	2-2	Franquart 20, Bastos 77	23 934
	15	Bordeaux	D	1-1	Cabaye 3	13 770
	23	Lyon	D	1-1	Bastos 17	32 658
Oct	6	Val'ciennes	W	3-0	Kluivert 5p, Lichtsteiner 44, Plestan 66	13 739
	20	Caen	D	0-0		18 275
	27	Strasbourg	L	0-3		12 147
Nov	3	Auxerre	W	1-0	Grichting OG 76	8 856
	10	Nice	D	1-1	Fauvergue 13	12 286
	24	Nancy	L	0-2		18 029
Dec	1	Marseille	D	1-1	Kluivert 27	17 618
	8	Toulouse	L	0-1		16 584
	15	St Etienne	W	3-0	Lichtsteiner 20, Plestan 32, Cabaye 49p	11 808
	12	Metz	D	1-1	Cabaye 94+	12 602
Jan	19	Sochaux	D	1-1	Obraniak 52	15 862
	23	Le Mans	W	3-1	Mirallas 16, Obraniak 40, Cabaye 52	10 990
	26	Paris SG	D	0-0		14 887
Feb	9	Monaco	D	0-0		7 679
	16	Rennes	W	3-1	Kluivert 2 43p 53, Bastos 56	13 396
	24	Bordeaux	D	0-0		21 761
	1	Lyon	L	0-1		77 840
	8	Val'ciennes	D	0-0		13 955
Mar	11	Lens	W	2-1	Bastos 17, Beria 83	36 533
	15	Caen	W	5-0	Lichtsteiner 2 34 91+, Cabaye 2 44 62p, Frau 87	13 668
	22	Strasbourg	W	1-0	Mavuba 85	16 400
	30	Auxerre	L	0-2		16 017
Apr	5	Nice	D	0-0		9 861
	12	Nancy	W	2-1	Bastos 16p, Mirallas 39	12 242
	20	Marseille	W	3-1	Mirallas 2 37 40, Makoun 67	51 674
	26	Toulouse	W	3-2	Mirallas 2 30 42, Bastos 40p	16 759
	4	St Etienne	D	0-0		33 223
May	10	Lens	W	2-1	Cabaye 43, Frau 66	17 670
	17	Lorient	D	1-1	Bastos 55	12 939

FC LORIENT 2007-08

Month	Day	Opponent	Res	Score	Scorers	Att
	4	Lille	D	0-0		14 215
Aug	11	Monaco	W	2-1	Saifi 2 14 30	11 981
	15	Paris SG	W	3-1	Vahirua 2 69 74, Saifi 92+p	32 227
	18	Lyon	W	3-1	Vahirua 2 14 66	14 612
	25	Bordeaux	D	2-2	Saifi 15, Namouchi 89	23 392
	28	Val'ciennes	L	1-3	Marchal 43	12 588
Sept	1	Strasbourg	D	0-0		20 260
	16	Rennes	L	0-1		13 674
	22	Nancy	L	0-2		18 151
Oct	6	Caen	D	0-0		10 215
	20	Auxerre	L	3-5	Saifi 2 6 58, Bourhani 93+	8 157
	27	Nice	D	0-0		10 868
Nov	3	Marseille	D	0-0		51 864
	11	Toulouse	W	1-0	Abriel 51	9 575
	24	Lens	D	1-1	Vahirua 12	30 126
Dec	1	St Etienne	D	1-1	Saifi 75	11 838
	8	Sochaux	W	2-1	Vahirua 1, Le Pen 48	11 280
	15	Le Mans	D	0-0		10 095
	22	Metz	W	2-0	Saifi 58, Marin 89	12 677
	12	Monaco	L	0-1		7 434
Jan	19	Paris SG	W	1-0	Bourillon OG 19	12 385
	23	Lyon	L	0-2		37 780
	27	Bordeaux	W	1-0	Jallet 77p	11 182
Feb	9	Val'ciennes	L	0-3		12 667
	16	Strasbourg	W	1-0	Le Pen 45	12 153
	23	Rennes	L	0-2		24 633
	1	Nancy	D	0-0		10 275
	8	Caen	D	0-0		18 493
Mar	11	Lens	D	1-1	Saifi 74	12 881
	22	Nice	W	2-1	Vahirua 10, Saifi 71	9 878
	30	Marseille	L	1-2	Saifi 43p	15 436
Apr	5	Toulouse	D	0-0		20 585
	12	Lens	W	1-0	Saifi 85	13 279
	19	St Etienne	L	0-1		33 751
	26	Sochaux	D	1-1	Jouffre 44	17 361
	3	Le Mans	D	0-0		13 947
May	10	Metz	W	2-1	Saifi 45, Abriel 66	0
	17	Lille	D	1-1	Saifi 43	12 939

OLYMPIQUE LYONNAIS 2007–08

Month	Date	Opponent	Res	Score	Comp	Scorers	Att
Jul	28	Sochaux	W	2-1	SC	Govou [21], Cris [43]	30 413
	5	Auxerre	W	2-0	L1	Baros [33], Benzema [70]	35 537
	11	Toulouse	L	0-1	L1		24 980
Aug	18	Lorient	L	1-2	L1	Benzema [32]	14 612
	26	St Etienne	W	1-0	L1	Benzema [54]	38 438
	29	Sochaux	W	2-1	L1	Benzema [20], Bodmer [57]	15 744
	1	Le Mans	W	3-2	L1	Govou [71], Benzema [76], Baros [78]	35 042
	15	Metz	W	5-1	L1	Benzema 3 [4,36,38], Ben Arfa [58], Juninho [86]	21 988
Sep	19	Barcelona	L	0-3	CLgE		78 698
	23	Lille	D	1-1	L1	Govou [58]	32 658
	29	Lens	W	3-0	L1	Santos [42], Källström [81], Benzema [90]	38 420
	2	Rangers	L	0-3	CLgE		38 076
	7	Bordeaux	W	3-1	L1	Anderson [5], Benzema [23], Källström [59]	31 919
Oct	20	Monaco	W	3-1	L1	Juninho [12p], Reveillere [18], Benzema [50]	36 254
	23	Stuttgart	W	2-0	CLgE	Santos [56], Benzema [79]	51 000
	28	Paris SG	W	3-2	L1	Ben Arfa 2 [40,43], Govou [84]	39 787
	31	Caen	W	3-1	LCr4	Keita [14], Bodmer [76], Benzema [89]	16 336
	3	Val'ciennes	W	2-0	L1	Juninho [40], Govou [87]	38 631
	7	Stuttgart	W	4-2	CLgE	Ben Arfa 2 [6,37], Källström [15], Juninho [93+]	38 215
Nov	11	Marseille	L	1-2	L1	Juninho [7]	38 811
	24	Rennes	W	2-0	L1	Juninho [5p], Ben Arfa [18]	28 596
	27	Barcelona	D	2-2	CLgE	Juninho 2 [7,80p]	36 500
	2	Strasbourg	W	5-0	L1	Källström 2 [13,80p], Juninho [19], Benzema [64], Clerc [78]	34 595
Dec	8	Caen	L	0-1	L1		20 664
	12	Rangers	W	3-0	CLgE	Govou [16], Benzema 2 [85,88]	50 260
	15	Nice	D	0-0	L1		37 280
	22	Nancy	D	1-1	L1	Baros [80]	19 898
	6	Créteil	W	4-0	CFr9	Benzema 3 [15,38,80p], Juninho [44]	10 488
	12	Toulouse	W	3-2	L1	Ben Arfa [17], Juninho [56], Benzema [66]	36 587
Jan	16	Le Mans	L	0-1	LCqf		7 934
	20	Lens	L	0-3	L1		32 734
	23	Lorient	W	2-0	L1	Ben Arfa [29], Benzema [74]	37 780
	27	St Etienne	D	1-1	L1	Benzema [92+]	31 537
	3	Croix Savoie	W	1-0	CFr10	Fred [80]	6 000
	9	Sochaux	W	4-1	L1	Bodmer 2 [2,76], Govou [91+], Benzema [94+]	35 904
Feb	16	Le Mans	L	0-1	L1		14 015
	20	Man Utd	D	1-1	CLr2	Benzema [54]	39 219
	23	Metz	W	2-0	L1	Fred 2 [10,69]	37 281
	1	Lille	W	1-0	L1	Fred [32]	77 840
	4	Man Utd	L	0-1	CLr2		75 520
	9	Bordeaux	W	4-2	L1	Bodmer 2 [12,24], Benzema [50], Keita [93+]	40 381
Mar	15	Monaco	W	3-0	L1	Keita 2 [21,38], Fred [35]	12 321
	18	Sochaux	W	2-1	CFr11	Benzema 2 [56,91]	20 012
	23	Paris SG	W	4-2	L1	Fred 2 [8,36], Govou [65], Juninho [73]	37 895
	30	Val'ciennes	W	2-1	L1	Keita [8], Govou [65]	15 313
	6	Marseille	L	1-3	L1	Cana OG [45]	56 271
	12	Rennes	D	1-1	L1	Cris [15]	33 900
Apr	15	Metz	W	1-0	CFqf	Benzema [39]	27 015
	19	Strasbourg	W	2-1	L1	Bodmer [62], Grosso [68]	26 006
	26	Caen	D	2-2	L1	Benzema 2 [34,54]	39 068
	3	Nice	D	0-0	L1		14 206
	6	Sedan	W	1-0	CFsf	Benzema [39]	33 057
May	10	Nancy	W	1-0	L1	Macaluso OG [63]	38 190
	17	Auxerre	W	3-1	L1	Benzema [1], Fred [10], Källström [53]	19 799
	24	Paris SG	W	1-0	CFf	Govou [103]	79 204

SC = Trophée des Champions • L1 = Ligue 1 Orange • CL = UEFA Champions League • LC = Coupe de la Ligue • CF = Coupe de France • gE = Group E • r2 = second round • r4 = fourth round • r9 = ninth round • r10 = 10th round • r11 = 11th round • qf = quarter-final • sf = semi-final • f = final

OLYMPIQUE MARSEILLE 2007–08

Month	Date	Opponent	Res	Score	Comp	Scorers	Att
	4	Strasbourg	D	0-0	L1		26 397
	11	Rennes	D	0-0	L1		55 896
Aug	15	Val'ciennes	L	1-2	L1	Ziani [57]	16 028
	19	Nancy	D	2-2	L1	Niang [22], Cissé [50]	55 732
	25	Caen	W	2-1	L1	Rodriguez [43], Niang [54]	20 790
	29	Nice	L	0-2	L1		55 490
	2	Paris SG	D	1-1	L1	Cissé [10]	43 419
	15	Toulouse	L	1-2	L1	Zubar [91+]	53 650
Sep	18	Besiktas	W	2-0	CLgA	Rodriguez [76], Cissé [91+]	35 676
	22	Auxerre	L	0-2	L1		18 736
	3	Liverpool	W	1-0	CLgA	Valbuena [77]	41 355
	6	St Etienne	L	0-1	L1		32 004
	21	Lens	W	1-0	L1	Zenden [74]	49 245
Oct	24	Porto	D	1-1	CLgA	Niang [69]	46 458
	27	Sochaux	L	1-2	L1	Niang [9]	19 957
	30	Metz	D	2-2	LCr4	Niang [94], Cissé [105], W 5-4p	21 389
	3	Lorient	D	0-0	L1		51 864
	6	Porto	L	1-2	CLgA	Niang [47]	42 217
Nov	11	Lyon	W	2-1	L1	Niang 2 [10p,43]	38 811
	24	Metz	W	3-1	L1	Zenden [29], Niang 2 [36,69]	48 035
	28	Besiktas	L	1-2	CLgA	Taiwo [65]	19 448
	1	Lille	D	1-1	L1	Niang [31]	17 618
	8	Monaco	W	2-0	L1	Rodriguez [52], Cana [69]	50 510
Dec	11	Liverpool	L	0-4	CLgA		53 097
	16	Bordeaux	D	2-2	L1	Niang [2], Cheyrou [27]	32 286
	22	Le Mans	W	1-0	L1	Niang [14]	48 886
	5	Beauvais	W	2-0	CFr9	Cana [23], Cissé [32]	10 465
	13	Rennes	L	1-3	L1	Cissé [16]	29 278
	8	Auxerre	L	0-1	LCqf		13 006
Jan	19	Val'ciennes	W	3-1	L1	Cissé 2 [28,74], Rodriguez [51]	48 152
	23	Nancy	D	1-1	L1	Nasri [85]	19 901
	26	Caen	W	6-1	L1	Cissé 3 [28,55,57], Valbuena 2 [41,44], Nasri [81]	48 481
	3	Monaco	W	3-1	CFr10	Valbuena [7], Grandin [10], Cissé [62]	25 000
	10	Nice	W	2-0	L1	Niang [24], Cissé [77]	15 884
Feb	13	Sp. Moskva	W	3-0	UCr2	Cheyrou [52], Taiwo [68], Niang [79]	31 790
	17	Paris SG	W	2-1	L1	Taiwo [36], Niang [45]	56 106
	21	Sp. Moskva	L	0-2	UCr2		18 000
	24	Toulouse	D	0-0	L1		34 490
	1	Auxerre	W	2-1	L1	Cana [7], Cissé [22]	53 100
	6	Zenit St.P	W	3-1	UCr3	Cissé 2 [37,55], Niang [48]	24 300
	9	St Etienne	W	2-0	L1	Valbuena [59], Taiwo [66]	53 565
Mar	12	Zenit St.P	L	0-2	UCr3		20 400
	16	Lens	D	3-3	L1	Nasri [25], Cheyrou [29], Cissé [89]	40 477
	19	Carquefou	L	0-1	CFr11		37 000
	22	Sochaux	L	0-1	L1		51 435
	30	Lorient	W	2-1	L1	Akale [53], Niang [81]	15 436
	6	Lyon	W	3-1	L1	Cissé [25], Niang 2 [27,53]	56 271
Apr	12	Metz	W	2-1	L1	Cissé [14], Nasri [57]	25 694
	20	Lille	L	1-3	L1	Niang [13]	51 674
	27	Monaco	W	3-2	L1	Nasri [28], Taiwo [61], Cissé [82]	17 351
	3	Bordeaux	L	1-2	L1	Niang [45]	55 778
May	10	Le Mans	D	0-0	L1		16 361
	17	Strasbourg	W	4-3	L1	Niang [6], Cissé 2 [45,78], Nasri [45]	55 543

L1 = Ligue 1 Orange • CL = UEFA Champions League • UC = UEFA Cup • LC = Coupe de la Ligue • CF = Coupe de France • gA = Group A • r2 = second round • r3 = third round • r4 = fourth round • r9 = ninth round • r10 = 10th round • r11 = 11th round • qf = quarter-final

FC METZ 2007–08

Mon	Day	Opponent	Res	Score	Scorers	Att
Aug	5	Le Mans	L	0-1		9 831
	12	Lille	L	1-2	N'Diaye [83]	15 591
	15	Monaco	L	0-2		11 392
	18	Paris SG	D	0-0		19 018
	25	Rennes	L	0-2		24 078
	29	Bordeaux	L	0-1		14 169
Sept	1	Val'ciennes	D	0-0		14 105
	15	Lyon	L	1-5	Gueye [46]	21 988
	22	Caen	W	2-1	N'Diaye [37], Gygax [66]	17 883
Oct	6	Strasbourg	L	1-2	Francois [63]	15 140
	20	Nice	L	1-3	Barbosa [68]	9 525
	27	Nancy	D	0-0		19 585
Nov	4	Toulouse	D	0-0		16 546
	10	Lens	L	1-2	Aguirre [70]	12 268
	24	Marseille	L	1-3	Gueye [87]	48 035
Dec	1	Auxerre	L	0-1		10 281
	8	St Etienne	L	0-2		22 585
	15	Sochaux	L	1-2	Pjanic [88p]	10 370
	22	Lorient	L	0-2		12 677
Jan	12	Lille	D	1-1	Gygax [24]	12 602
	19	Monaco	L	1-4	Aguirre [54]	12 197
	23	Paris SG	L	0-3		38 362
	26	Rennes	D	1-1	N'Diaye [80]	9 823
Feb	9	Bordeaux	L	0-3		19 673
	16	Val'ciennes	W	2-1	Gueye [51], Martinez OG [66]	10 185
	23	Lyon	L	0-2		37 281
Mar	1	Caen	L	2-1	Diop [35], Gueye [83p]	10 767
	8	Strasbourg	W	3-2	Gueye [56], Barbosa [76], N'Diaye [88]	18 545
	15	Nice	L	1-2	Pjanic [47p]	10 683
	22	Nancy	L	1-2	Bessat [87]	18 768
	30	Toulouse	L	0-2		8 960
Apr	5	Lens	D	1-1	N'Diaye [90]	35 952
	12	Marseille	L	1-2	Barbosa [3]	25 694
	19	Auxerre	D	0-0		8 620
	26	St Etienne	L	0-1		11 520
May	3	Sochaux	D	0-0		17 680
	10	Lorient	L	1-2	Gueye [33]	0
	17	Le Mans	W	4-3	Barbosa [4], Pjanic [13], Gueye [34], Bessat [84]	12 263

AS MONACO 2007–08

Mon	Day	Opponent	Res	Score	Scorers	Att
Aug	4	St Etienne	D	1-1	Piquionne [44]	17 134
	11	Lorient	L	1-2	Gakpe [66]	11 981
	15	Metz	W	2-0	Modesto [31], Piquionne [85]	11 392
	18	Sochaux	W	3-0	Koller 2 [1 89], Menez [57]	14 091
	25	Le Mans	W	3-1	Cufre [48p], Menez [50], Piquionne [64]	11 033
	29	Lille	L	1-0	Piquionne [21]	13 849
Sept	1	Bordeaux	L	1-2	Nene [89]	23 390
	16	Paris SG	L	1-2	Menez [85]	12 694
	22	Val'ciennes	D	0-1		14 225
Oct	5	Nancy	L	1-3	Koller [74]	8 851
	20	Lyon	L	1-3	Monsoreau [42]	36 254
	27	Caen	D	0-0		8 986
Nov	3	Rennes	W	1-0	Piquionne [46]	27 754
	10	Strasbourg	W	3-0	Gakpe [43], Nene 2 [62 90]	9 448
	24	Toulouse	D	0-0		15 434
Dec	1	Nice	D	1-1	Koller [86]	15 394
	8	Marseille	L	0-2		50 510
	15	Lens	W	2-0	Menez 2 [52 82]	14 578
	22	Auxerre	L	0-1		8 952
Jan	12	Lorient	W	1-0	Sambou [91+]	7 434
	19	Metz	W	4-1	Menez 2 [30 62], Piquionne [31], Gakpe [84]	12 197
	23	Sochaux	W	1-0	Piquionne [78]	7 093
	26	Le Mans	L	0-1		9 417
Feb	9	Lille	D	0-0		7 679
	17	Bordeaux	L	0-6		10 018
	23	Paris SG	D	1-1	Almiron [72]	38 652
Mar	1	Val'ciennes	D	0-0		7 912
	8	Nancy	L	0-2		18 541
	15	Lyon	L	0-3		12 321
	22	Caen	L	1-4	Sambou [6]	20 082
	31	Rennes	L	1-2	Sambou [37]	7 164
Apr	5	Strasbourg	W	2-0	Nene [66], Fabio Santos [83]	19 106
	12	Toulouse	D	0-0		9 499
	19	Nice	W	2-0	Meriem [35], Almiron [90]	13 455
	27	Marseille	L	2-3	Gonzalez [56], Leko [63]	17 351
May	3	Lens	D	0-0		39 399
	10	Auxerre	W	3-0	Bakar [48], Nene [75], Meriem [82]	9 839
	17	St Etienne	L	0-4		34 237

AS NANCY LORRAINE 2007–08

Mon	Day	Opponent	Res	Score	Scorers	Att
Aug	4	Rennes	W	2-0	Fortune [38], Hadji [41]	23 601
	11	Caen	W	1-0	Kim [7]	17 545
	16	Nice	W	2-1	Puygrenier [51], Berenguer [66]	18 389
	19	Marseille	D	2-2	Gavanon [64p], Hadji [80]	55 732
	25	Auxerre	W	4-1	Malonga [36], Kim [38], Biancalani [48], Fortune [55]	18 132
Sept	1	St Etienne	W	2-0	Kim [12], Fortune [85]	19 332
	15	Lens	L	0-1		32 774
	22	Lorient	W	2-0	Hadji 2 [81 87]	18 151
Oct	5	Monaco	W	3-1	Kim 2 [32 47], Dia [38]	8 851
	21	Sochaux	D	1-1	Kim [26]	18 689
	27	Metz	D	0-0		19 585
Nov	3	Bordeaux	W	1-0	Malonga [29]	19 686
	9	Paris SG	D	0-0		36 495
	24	Lille	W	2-0	Puygrenier [67], Brison [77]	18 029
Dec	1	Le Mans	L	1-2	Gavanon [9p]	9 938
	5	Nancy	L	1-3	Malonga [90]	16 519
	8	Val'ciennes	D	0-0		17 712
	16	Strasbourg	D	0-0		19 087
	22	Lyon	D	1-1	Malonga [86]	19 898
Jan	12	Caen	D	0-0		20 327
	20	Nice	L	0-1		11 813
	23	Marseille	D	1-1	Brison [48]	19 901
	26	Auxerre	D	0-0		6 548
Feb	9	Toulouse	W	1-0	Puygrenier [93+p]	18 151
	16	St Etienne	L	0-4		26 629
	23	Lens	D	2-1	Berenguer [73], Hadji [76]	17 951
Mar	1	Lorient	D	0-0		10 275
	8	Monaco	W	2-0	Modesto OG [6], Hadji [19]	18 541
	15	Sochaux	D	1-1	Zerka [82]	16 487
	22	Metz	W	2-1	Hadji [51], Zerka [88]	18 768
	29	Bordeaux	L	1-2	Zerka [29]	24 308
Apr	6	Paris SG	W	1-0	Fortune [67]	19 474
	12	Lille	L	1-2	Luiz [45]	12 242
	19	Le Mans	D	1-1	Fortune [68]	18 672
	27	Val'ciennes	D	1-1	Berebguer [10]	13 972
May	3	Strasbourg	W	3-0	Berenguer [38], Fortune [45], Zerka [58]	19 507
	10	Lyon	L	0-1		38 190
	17	Rennes	L	2-3	Malonga [7], Luiz [55]	19 563

OGC NICE 2007–08

Mon	Day	Opponent	Res	Score	Scorers	Att
Aug	4	Caen	L	0-1		19 405
	11	Strasbourg	W	1-0	Hognon [86]	11 815
	16	Nancy	L	1-2	Bamogo [61p]	18 389
	19	Rennes	D	1-1	Kone [26]	10 858
	25	Toulouse	D	1-1	Ederson [41]	9 969
	29	Marseille	W	2-0	Hognon [50], Hellebuyck [88]	55 490
Sept	2	Lens	W	2-0	Kone [52]	10 858
	15	Auxerre	L	0-2		7 817
	22	St Etienne	W	3-0	Kone 2 [7 19], Hellebuyck [83]	11 252
Oct	6	Le Mans	L	0-2		9 604
	20	Metz	W	3-1	Kone 2 [11 58p], Kante [65]	9 525
	27	Lorient	D	0-0		10 868
Nov	3	Sochaux	D	0-0		10 221
	10	Lille	D	1-1	Plestan OG [42]	12 286
	25	Paris SG	L	1-2	Laslandes [8], Kone [37]	11 776
Dec	1	Monaco	D	1-1	Laslandes [92+]	15 394
	9	Bordeaux	D	1-1	Kone [13]	11 988
	15	Lyon	D	0-0		37 280
	22	Val'ciennes	W	1-0	Hellebuyck [43]	9 640
Jan	12	Strasbourg	W	1-0	Ederson [53]	15 047
	20	Nancy	W	1-0	Hellebuyck [69]	11 813
	23	Rennes	D	1-1	Modeste [51]	23 241
	26	Toulouse	D	1-1	Ederson [89]	15 792
Feb	9	Marseille	L	0-2		15 884
	16	Lens	D	0-0		31 799
	23	Auxerre	L	1-2	Kone [46]	10 114
Mar	2	St Etienne	D	0-0		28 037
	8	Le Mans	D	0-0		9 713
	15	Metz	W	2-1	Bamogo [41], Ederson [53p]	10 683
	22	Lorient	L	1-2	Kone [51]	9 878
	30	Sochaux	W	1-0		19 303
Apr	5	Lille	D	0-0		9 861
	13	Paris SG	W	3-2	Kone 2 [36 83], Ederson [86]	35 918
	19	Monaco	L	0-2		13 455
	26	Bordeaux	D	0-0		29 097
May	3	Lyon	D	0-0		14 206
	10	Val'ciennes	W	2-1	Ederson [49], Kone [57]	14 546
	17	Caen	W	3-1	Hellebuyck [25], Ederson [57p], Kone [84]	11 540

PARIS SAINT-GERMAIN 2007–08

Aug	4	Sochaux	D	0-0	L1		37 400
	12	Lens	D	0-0	L1		38 836
	15	Lorient	L	1-3	L1	Pauleta [36]	32 227
	18	Metz	D	0-0	L1		19 018
	26	Lille	D	1-1	L1	Frau [87]	31 634
	29	Le Mans	W	2-0	L1	Armand [37], Diane [54]	13 072
Sep	2	Marseille	D	1-1	L1	Luyindula [20]	43 419
	16	Monaco	W	2-1	L1	Armand [40], Diane [53]	12 694
	23	Bordeaux	L	0-2	L1		37 108
	26	Lorient	W	3-0	LCr3	Ngog 2 [22 43], Pauleta [85]	8 189
Oct	6	Rennes	L	1-3	L1	Ceara [57]	35 436
	20	Val'ciennes	D	0-0	L1		15 037
	28	Lyon	L	2-3	L1	Pauleta 2 [61 92+]	39 787
	31	Montpellier	W	2-0	LCr4	Pauleta 2 [6 93+]	24 097
Nov	3	Strasbourg	W	2-1	L1	Rodrigo OG [7], Arnaud [19]	25 770
	10	Nancy	D	0-0	L1		36 495
	25	Nice	L	1-2	L1	Ngog [31]	11 776
Dec	1	Caen	L	0-1	L1		37 148
	9	Auxerre	W	1-0	L1	Luyindula [50]	11 015
	15	Toulouse	L	1-2	L1	Pauleta [91+p]	34 095
	23	St Etienne	W	1-0	L1	Luyindula [51]	31 219
	5	Epinal	W	2-0	CFr9	Chantome [23], Armand [30]	6 098
	13	Lens	W	3-0	L1	Pauleta [58], Diane 2 [65 67]	35 658
Jan	16	Val'ciennes	W	4-0	LCqf	Pauleta [1], Diane 2 [54 61], Rothen [67]	18 771
	19	Lorient	L	0-1	L1		12 385
	23	Metz	W	3-0	L1	Luyindula [5], Rothen [35], Diane [55]	38 362
	26	Lille	D	0-0	L1		14 887
Feb	2	Le Poire SV	W	3-1	CFr10	Mendy [52], Diane 2 [74 76]	28 114
	9	Le Mans	D	0-0	L1		39 970
	17	Marseille	L	1-2	L1	Rothen [29p]	56 106
	23	Monaco	D	1-1	L1	Diane [42]	38 652
	26	Auxerre	W	3-2	LCsf	Yepes [31], Pauleta [43], Mendy [79]	32 198
Mar	2	Bordeaux	L	0-3	L1		30 309
	8	Rennes	L	0-2	L1		27 523
	15	Val'ciennes	D	1-1	L1	Pauleta [82]	32 368
	18	Bastia	W	2-1	CFrl1	Arnaud 2 [18 66]	
	23	Lyon	L	2-4	L1	Camara [45], Rothen [52]	37 895
	29	Lens	W	2-1	LCf	Pauleta [19], Mendy [93+p]	78 741
Apr	2	Strasbourg	W	1-0	L1	Diane [73]	33 288
	6	Nancy	L	0-1	L1		19 474
	13	Nice	L	2-3	L1	Luyindula [50], Pauleta [76]	35 918
	16	Carquefou	W	1-0	CFqf	Pauleta [77]	
	19	Caen	L	0-3	L1		20 933
	26	Auxerre	W	3-1	L1	Pauleta [3], Diane 2 [13 86]	37 671
May	3	Toulouse	D	1-1	L1	Mendy [63]	31 642
	6	Amiens	W	1-0	CFsf	Boli [78]	11 937
	10	St Etienne	D	1-1	L1	Clement [60]	45 353
	17	Sochaux	W	2-1	L1	Diane 2 [23 83]	19 873
	24	Lyon	L	0-1	CFf		79 204

L1 = Ligue 1 Orange • LC = Coupe de la Ligue • CF = Coupe de France • r3 = third round • r4 = fourth round • r9 = ninth round • r10 = 10th round • r11 = 11th round • qf = quarter-final • sf = semi-final • f = final

LEAGUE CUP FINALS

Year	Winners	Score	Runners-up
1995	Paris St-Germain	2-0	SC Bastia
1996	FC Metz	0-0 5-4p	Olympique Lyonnais
1997	RC Strasbourg	0-0 6-5p	Girondins Bordeaux
1998	Paris St-Germain	2-2 4-2p	Girondins Bordeaux
1999	RC Lens	1-0	FC Metz
2000	Gueugnon	2-0	Paris St-Germain
2001	Olympique Lyonnais	2-1	AS Monaco
2002	Girondins Bordeaux	3-0	FC Lorient
2003	AS Monaco	4-1	FC Sochaux
2004	FC Sochaux	1-1 5-4p	FC Nantes
2005	RC Strasbourg	2-1	SM Caen
2006	AS Nancy-Lorraine	2-1	OGC Nice
2007	Girondins Bordeaux	1-0	Olympique Lyonnais
2008	Paris St-Germain	2-1	RC Lens

STADE RENNAIS 2007–08

Aug	4	Nancy	L	0-2			23 601
	11	Marseille	L	0-0			55 896
	15	St Etienne	W	1-0		Hansson [3]	28 316
	19	Nice	D	1-1		Briand [85]	10 858
	25	Metz	W	2-0		Thomert 2 [45 55]	24 078
	29	Auxerre	W	2-0		Mbia [17], Briand [35]	7 896
Sept	1	Lille	D	2-2		Leroy [48], Didot [55]	23 934
	16	Lorient	W	1-0		Didot [35]	13 674
	23	Sochaux	L	0-2			22 589
	6	Paris SG	W	3-1		Leroy [19], Briand [74], Wiltord [84]	35 436
Oct	20	Le Mans	W	3-0		Pagis [11], Wiltord [53], Esteban [92+]	23 349
	28	Lens	W	2-1		Wiltord [57], Leroy [77]	30 441
	3	Monaco	L	0-1			27 754
Nov	11	Bordeaux	L	0-3			21 759
	24	Lyon	L	0-2			28 596
	2	Val'ciennes	L	0-3			12 161
Dec	8	Strasbourg	L	0-3			18 389
	15	Caen	L	1-2		Pagis [88]	26 081
	23	Toulouse	D	0-0			20 718
	13	Marseille	W	3-1		Pagis [39], Wiltord 2 [82 88]	29 278
Jan	19	St Etienne	L	0-2			21 666
	23	Nice	D	1-1		Briand [50]	23 241
	26	Metz	D	1-1		Thomert [28]	9 823
	9	Auxerre	L	1-2		Pagis [50]	22 733
Feb	16	Lille	L	1-3		Pagis [89]	13 396
	23	Lorient	W	2-0		Briand [43], Leroy [64]	24 633
	1	Sochaux	D	0-0			14 564
	8	Paris SG	W	2-0		Sakho OG [44], Briand [51]	27 523
Mar	15	Le Mans	D	1-1		Thomert [39]	10 329
	23	Rennes	W	3-1		Leroy [12], Pagis [43], Thomert [54]	24 411
	31	Monaco	W	2-1		Hansson [19], Pagis [92+]	7 164
	5	Bordeaux	L	0-2			28 124
	12	Lyon	D	1-1		Mbia [92+]	39 900
	19	Val'ciennes	W	1-0		Wiltord [77]	26 532
	26	Strasbourg	W	3-0		Pagis 2 [33 45], Lemoine [35]	24 318
	3	Caen	D	2-2		Leroy [31], Briand [93+]	20 624
May	10	Toulouse	W	2-1		Pagis [54], Mensah [73]	28 078
	17	Nancy	W	3-2		Mbia [32], Pagis 2 [48 58]	19 563

AS SAINT-ETIENNE 2007–08

Aug	4	Monaco	D	1-1		Feindouno [48p]	17 134
	11	Val'ciennes	W	3-1		Gomis [19], Feindouno 2 [70 91+]	30 143
	15	Rennes	L	0-1			28 316
	18	Bordeaux	D	0-0			32 630
	26	Lyon	L	0-1			38 438
	29	Strasbourg	W	2-0		Ilan [36p], Abdessadki OG [69]	25 694
Sept	1	Nancy	L	0-2			19 332
	15	Caen	W	3-0		Ilan 2 [9 21], Gomis [49]	25 638
	22	Nice	L	0-3			11 252
	6	Marseille	W	1-0		Dernis [93+]	32 004
Oct	20	Toulouse	W	2-0		Gomis 2 [29 37]	20 108
	27	Auxerre	D	0-0			30 448
	4	Lens	L	2-3		Gigliotti [17], Landrin [22]	33 877
Nov	10	Le Mans	L	2-3		Varrault [21], Gigliotti [42p]	12 434
	24	Sochaux	W	1-0		Ilan [82]	26 015
	1	Lorient	D	1-1		Gomis [59]	11 838
Dec	8	Metz	W	2-0		Bassong OG [64], Feindouno [94+]	22 585
	15	Lille	L	0-3			11 808
	23	Paris SG	L	0-1			31 219
	12	Val'ciennes	L	0-2			13 516
Jan	19	Rennes	W	2-0		Dernis [13], Gomis [84]	21 666
	24	Bordeaux	L	0-1			23 990
	27	Lyon	D	1-1		Gomis [45]	31 537
	9	Strasbourg	L	0-3			16 766
Feb	16	Nancy	W	4-0		Perrin [17], Gomis 2 [42 72], Feindouno [70p]	26 629
	23	Caen	W	3-1		Dernis 2 [19 36], Gomis [27]	20 714
	2	Nice	D	0-0			28 037
Mar	9	Marseille	L	0-2			53 565
	15	Toulouse	D	0-0			25 991
	22	Auxerre	W	3-1		Landrin [64], Ilan [70], Feindouno [82]	13 137
	5	Le Mans	W	4-1		Dernis 2 [43 64], Gomis [59], Feindouno [87]	30 006
	9	Lens	W	2-0		Gomis 2 [13 15]	33 973
Apr	12	Sochaux	D	1-1		Ilan [8]	19 921
	19	Lorient	W	1-0		Jallet OG [51]	33 751
	26	Metz	W	1-0		Gomis [48]	11 520
	4	Lille	D	0-0			33 223
May	10	Paris SG	D	1-1		Perrin [44]	45 353
	17	Monaco	W	4-0		Gomis 2 [4 7], Dernis [33], Feindouno [81]	34 237

FC SOCHAUX MONTBELIARD 2007–08

Aug	4	Paris SG	D	0-0	37 400
	11	Le Mans	L	1-3	Birsa [18]	14 033
	15	Lille	D	1-1	Dalmat [45]	12 029
	18	Monaco	L	0-3		14 091
	25	Val'ciennes	L	1-3	Quercia [6]	13 566
	29	Lyon	L	1-2	Birsa [22p]	15 744
Sept	1	Caen	D	2-2	N'daw [60], Birsa [72p]	18 099
	15	Strasbourg	D	0-0		16 067
	23	Rennes	W	2-0	Dalmat [37], Isabey [58]	22 589
Oct	7	Toulouse	L	0-1		12 783
	21	Nancy	D	1-1	Erding [56]	18 689
	27	Marseille	W	2-1	Zubar OG [31], Bonnart OG [51]	19 957
Nov	3	Nice	D	0-0		10 221
	10	Auxerre	D	1-1	Pitau [91+]	18 442
	24	St Etienne	L	0-1		26 015
Dec	1	Lens	L	0-2		13 950
	8	Lorient	L	1-2	Erding [81]	11 280
	15	Metz	W	2-1	Erding [11], Dalmat [83p]	10 370
	22	Bordeaux	L	0-1		12 646
Jan	12	Le Mans	W	2-0	Erding [45], Isabey [53]	9 714
	19	Lille	D	1-1	Erding [38]	15 862
	23	Monaco	L	0-1		7 093
	26	Val'ciennes	W	1-0	Brechet [23]	12 518
Feb	9	Lyon	L	1-4	Pancrate [52]	35 904
	16	Caen	D	1-1	Maurice-Belay [40]	11 378
	23	Strasbourg	W	2-0	Isabey [14], Erding [36]	17 084
Mar	1	Rennes	D	0-0		14 564
	8	Toulouse	W	2-1	Erding 2 [6 21]	19 100
	15	Nancy	D	1-1	Erding [55]	16 487
	22	Marseille	W	1-0	N'daw [3]	51 435
	30	Nice	W	1-0	Pitau [88]	19 303
Apr	5	Auxerre	W	1-0	Perquis [44]	10 282
	12	St Etienne	D	1-1	Grax [68]	19 921
	19	Lens	L	2-3	Erding [49], Brechet [79]	39 478
	26	Lorient	D	1-1	Erding [80]	17 361
May	3	Metz	D	0-0		17 680
	10	Bordeaux	L	0-2		32 487
	17	Paris SG	L	1-2	N'Daw [74]	19 873

RACING CLUB STRASBOURG 2007–08

Aug	4	Marseille	D	0-0		26 397
	11	Nice	L	0-1		11 815
	15	Auxerre	W	3-0	Renteria 2 [24 66], Gameiro [90]	20 030
	18	Toulouse	W	3-1	Mouloungui [20], Fanchone [54], Gameiro [71]	16 263
	25	Lens	W	2-1	Renteria [56], Cohade [64]	24 668
	29	St Etienne	L	0-2		25 694
Sept	1	Lorient	D	0-0		20 260
	15	Sochaux	D	0-0		16 087
	22	Le Mans	L	0-1		17 971
Oct	6	Metz	W	2-1	Mouloungui [43], Renteria [52]	15 140
	20	Bordeaux	D	1-1	Gameiro [15]	18 865
	27	Lille	W	3-0	Mouloungui [36], Rodrigo [41], Johansen [68]	12 147
Nov	3	Paris SG	L	1-2	Renteria [50]	25 770
	10	Monaco	L	0-3		9 448
	24	Val'ciennes	D	0-0		15 889
Dec	2	Lyon	L	0-5		34 595
	8	Rennes	W	3-0	Santos 2 [9 87], Renteria [66]	18 389
	16	Nancy	D	0-0		19 087
	22	Caen	L	0-2		20 391
Jan	12	Nice	L	0-1		15 047
	19	Auxerre	D	1-1	Fanchone [85]	6 553
	23	Toulouse	W	2-0	Gameiro [22], Cohade [90]	15 034
	26	Lens	D	2-2	Renteria [4], Santos [76]	31 326
Feb	9	St Etienne	W	3-0	Cohade [38p], Santos [85], Mulenga [91+]	16 766
	16	Lorient	L	0-1		12 153
	23	Sochaux	L	0-2		17 084
Mar	1	Le Mans	W	1-0	Renteria [22]	9 101
	8	Metz	L	2-3	Diop OG [37], Santos [83p]	18 545
	16	Bordeaux	L	0-3		19 474
	22	Lille	L	0-1		16 400
Apr	2	Paris SG	L	0-1		33 288
	5	Monaco	L	0-2		19 106
	12	Val'ciennes	L	0-2		14 276
	19	Lyon	L	1-2	Renteria [21]	26 006
	26	Rennes	L	0-3		24 318
May	3	Nancy	L	0-3		19 507
	10	Caen	L	1-4	Gameiro [23]	17 311
	17	Marseille	L	3-4	Fanchone [10], Gameiro [19], Zenke [72]	55 543

TOULOUSE FC 2007–08

Aug	4	Val'ciennes	L	1-3	Dieuze [11]	12 153
	11	Lyon	W	1-0	Elmander [90]	24 980
	18	Strasbourg	L	1-3	Gignac [35]	16 263
	25	Nice	D	1-1	Gignac [88]	9 969
Sept	1	Auxerre	W	2-0	Elmander [67], Sissoko [91+]	14 795
	15	Marseille	W	2-1	Emana [1], Elmander [37]	53 650
	22	Lens	D	1-1	Bergougnoux [23]	15 034
	30	Caen	L	1-2	Emana [93+]	17 119
Oct	7	Sochaux	W	1-0	Emana [74]	12 783
	20	St Etienne	L	0-2		20 108
	28	Le Mans	D	1-1	Dieuze [82]	9 841
Nov	4	Metz	D	0-0		16 546
	11	Lorient	L	0-1		9 575
	24	Monaco	D	0-0		15 434
Dec	2	Bordeaux	L	3-4	Elmander 3 [62p 72 76]	21 928
	5	Nancy	D	1-1	Elmander [18]	16 519
	8	Lille	W	1-0	Elmander [69]	16 584
	15	Paris SG	W	2-1	Elmander 2 [42 49]	34 095
	23	Rennes	D	0-0		20 718
Jan	12	Lyon	L	2-3	Reveillere OG [9], Fabinho [93+]	36 587
	19	Caen	D	1-1	Dieuze [35]	13 938
	23	Strasbourg	L	0-2		15 034
	26	Nice	D	1-1	Arribage [34]	15 792
Feb	9	Nancy	L	0-1		18 151
	16	Auxerre	L	0-1		9 106
	24	Marseille	D	0-0		34 490
Mar	1	Lens	D	1-1	Emana [74]	30 786
	8	Sochaux	L	1-2	Emana [83]	19 100
	15	St Etienne	D	0-0		25 991
	22	Le Mans	D	1-1	Geder OG [61]	17 259
	30	Metz	W	2-0	Emana 2 [80 82]	8 960
Apr	5	Lorient	D	0-0		20 585
	12	Monaco	W	2-0	Batlles [4], Elmander [47]	9 499
	20	Bordeaux	L	0-1		27 247
	26	Lille	L	2-3	Dieuze [25], Mansare [62]	16 759
May	3	Paris SG	D	1-1	Fofana [87]	31 642
	10	Rennes	L	1-2	Sirieix [11]	28 078
	17	Val'ciennes	W	2-1	Mathieu [3], Sirieix [75]	26 391

VALENCIENNES FC 2007–08

Aug	4	Toulouse	W	3-1	Audel 3 [5 30 57]	12 153
	11	St Etienne	L	1-3	Audel [88]	30 143
	15	Marseille	W	2-1	Savidan 2 [62 87]	16 028
	19	Lens	D	0-0		37 194
	25	Sochaux	W	3-1	Bezzaz [11], Chelle [45], Savidan [75]	13 566
	28	Lorient	W	3-1	Pujol 2 [27 39], Roudet [88]	12 588
Sept	1	Metz	D	0-0		14 105
	15	Le Mans	L	0-2		9 570
	22	Monaco	W	1-0	Audel [11]	14 225
Oct	6	Lille	L	0-3		13 739
	20	Paris SG	D	0-0		15 037
	27	Bordeaux	L	1-2	Diawara OG [34]	18 521
Nov	3	Lyon	L	0-2		38 631
	10	Caen	W	3-0	Sebo 2 [16 43], Savidan [61]	12 449
	24	Strasbourg	D	0-0		15 889
Dec	2	Rennes	W	3-0	Savidan [12], Pujol 2 [65 75]	12 161
	8	Nancy	D	0-0		17 712
	15	Auxerre	W	3-0	Savidan [12p], Chelle [30], Audel [80]	13 057
	22	Nice	L	0-1		9 640
Jan	12	St Etienne	W	2-0	Doumeng [9], Pujol [88]	13 516
	19	Marseille	L	1-3	Audel [82]	48 152
	23	Lens	L	1-2	Savidan [34]	14 824
	26	Sochaux	L	0-1		12 518
Feb	9	Lorient	W	3-0	Savidan [40], Roudet [56], Sebo [86]	12 667
	16	Metz	L	1-2	Belmadi [42]	10 185
	23	Le Mans	L	1-2	Savidan [45]	12 684
Mar	1	Monaco	D	0-0		7 912
	8	Lille	D	0-0		13 955
	15	Paris SG	D	1-1	Ceara OG [52]	32 368
	22	Bordeaux	W	3-1	Roudet [10], Sebo [64], Savidan [78]	13 657
	30	Lyon	L	1-2	Chelle [27]	15 313
Apr	5	Caen	L	0-1		19 477
	12	Strasbourg	W	2-0	Savidan 2 [26 43]	14 276
	19	Rennes	L	0-1		26 532
	27	Nancy	D	1-1	Audel [50]	13 972
May	3	Auxerre	L	0-2		19 000
	10	Nice	L	1-2	Savidan [89p]	14 546
	17	Toulouse	L	1-2	Audel [38]	26 391

FRO – FAROE ISLANDS

NATIONAL TEAM RECORD
JULY 10TH 2006 TO JULY 12TH 2010

PL	W	D	L	F	A	%
14	0	0	14	7	50	0

FIFA/COCA-COLA WORLD RANKING

1993	1994	1995	1996	1997	1998	1999	2000	2001	2002	2003	2004	2005	2006	2007	High	
115	133	120	135	117	125	112	117	117	114	126	131	132	181	194	**94**	12/92

2007–2008												Low	
08/07	09/07	10/07	11/07	12/07	01/08	02/08	03/08	04/08	05/08	06/08	07/08	**195**	07/08
190	193	194	195	194	193	195	193	194	194	193	195		

It was a season of firsts in the Faroes with both the Championship and the Cup having new names inscribed on the trophies. In August 2007 EB/Streymur claimed their first trophy when they beat HB Tórshavn in an exciting Cup Final. Having scored three times in the first 21 minutes, EB looked to be cruising, maintaining their advantage until 13 minutes from time, but then HB staged a determined late comeback scoring three times in just eight minutes. Thankfully for EB fans, Hungarian Karoly Potemkin scored a fourth goal for their side and they held on to win 4-3. With their sights then set on winning the double, EB came up just short in the league, finishing second

INTERNATIONAL HONOURS
None

behind NSI Runavík. Although NSI had twice won the Cup before, this was their first Championship and was won on their 50th anniversary. In European club competition there was the usual tale of first round defeats but national team defender Jón Rói Jacobsen did win the Championship with AaB Aalborg in Denmark - only the third Faroese player to do so after Jákup Mikkelsen and Todi Jónnson. He and the national team, however, continued to suffer at the hands of their European rivals as they failed to win a point in their Euro 2008 campaign. A 2-0 defeat by Estonia in June 2008 was their 22nd loss in succession - just 14 off San Marino's European record.

THE FIFA BIG COUNT OF 2006

	Male	Female		Total
Number of players	6 290	1 804	Referees and Assistant Referees	60
Professionals	0		Admin, Coaches, Technical, Medical	990
Amateurs 18+	1 654		Number of clubs	23
Youth under 18	4 040		Number of teams	303
Unregistered	2 000		Clubs with women's teams	17
Total players	8 094		Players as % of population	17.13%

The Faroe Islands' Football Association (FSF)
Gundadalur, PO Box 3028, Tórshavn 110, Faroe Islands
Tel +298 351979   Fax +298 319079
fsf@football.fo   www.football.fo
President: STORUSTOVU Hogni   General Secretary: MIKLADAL Isak
Vice-President: A LIDARENDA Niklas   Treasurer: TBD   Media Officer: MIKLADAL Isak
Men's Coach: OLSEN Jogvan   Women's Coach: HANSEN Alvur
FSF formed: 1979   UEFA: 1988   FIFA: 1988
White shirts with blue trimmings, Blue shorts, White socks or Blue shirts with white trimmings, White shorts, White socks

RECENT INTERNATIONAL MATCHES PLAYED BY THE FAROE ISLANDS

2003	Opponents	Score		Venue	Comp	Scorers	Att	Referee
20-08	Iceland	L	1-2	Toftir	ECq	Rógvi Jacobsen [65]	3 416	Iturralde Gonzalez ESP
6-09	Scotland	L	1-3	Glasgow	ECq	Johnsson.J [35]	40 901	Ceferin SVN
10-09	Lithuania	L	1-3	Toftir	ECq	Olsen [43]	2 175	Trivkovic CRO
2004								
21-02	Poland	L	0-6	San Fernando	Fr		100	Cascales ESP
1-06	Netherlands	L	0-3	Lausanne	Fr		3 200	Leuba SUI
18-08	Malta	W	3-2	Toftir	Fr	Borg [20], Petersen.J [35], Benjaminsen [77]	1 932	Laursen DEN
4-09	Switzerland	L	0-6	Basel	WCq		11 880	Tudor ROU
8-09	France	L	0-2	Tórshavn	WCq		5 917	Thomson SCO
9-10	Cyprus	D	2-2	Nicosia	WCq	Jorgensen.CB [21], Rógvi Jacobsen [43]	1 400	Gadiyev AZE
13-10	Ireland Republic	L	0-2	Dublin	WCq		36 000	Lajuks LVA
2005								
4-06	Switzerland	L	1-3	Toftir	WCq	Rógvi Jacobsen [70]	2 047	Gumienny BEL
8-06	Ireland Republic	L	0-2	Tórshavn	WCq		5 180	Guenov BUL
17-08	Cyprus	L	0-3	Toftir	WCq		2 720	Johannesson SWE
3-09	France	L	0-3	Lens	WCq		40 126	Jara CZE
7-09	Israel	L	0-2	Tórshavn	WCq		2 240	Vink NED
8-10	Israel	L	1-2	Tel Aviv	WCq	Samuelsen [93+]	31 857	Brugger AUT
2006								
14-05	Poland	L	0-4	Wronki	Fr		4 000	Prus USA
16-08	Georgia	L	0-6	Toftir	ECq		2 114	Ross NIR
2-09	Scotland	L	0-6	Glasgow	ECq		50 059	Egorov RUS
7-10	Lithuania	L	0-1	Tórshavn	ECq		1 982	Buttimer IRL
11-10	France	L	0-5	Sochaux	ECq		19 314	Corpodean ROU
2007								
24-03	Ukraine	L	0-2	Toftir	ECq		717	Skomina SVN
28-03	Georgia	L	1-3	Tbilisi	ECq	Rógvi Jacobsen [57]	12 000	Saliy KAZ
2-06	Italy	L	1-2	Tórshavn	ECq	Rógvi Jacobsen [77]	5 800	Malek POL
6-06	Scotland	L	0-2	Toftir	ECq		4 100	Kasnaferis GRE
12-09	Lithuania	L	1-2	Kaunas	ECq	Rógvi Jacobsen [93+]	5 500	Georgiev BUL
13-10	France	L	0-6	Tórshavn	ECq		1 980	Rossi SMR
17-10	Ukraine	L	0-5	Kyiv	ECq		5 000	Jakov ISR
21-11	Italy	L	1-3	Modena	ECq	Rógvi Jacobsen [83]	16 142	Meyer GER
2008								
16-03	Iceland	L	0-3	Kopavogur	Fr		400	Skjerven NOR
4-06	Estonia	L	3-4	Tallinn	Fr	Holst 2 [63 66], Olsen [70]		

Fr = Friendly match • EC = UEFA EURO 2004/2008 • WC = FIFA World Cup • q = qualifier

FAROE ISLANDS NATIONAL TEAM RECORDS AND RECORD SEQUENCES

Records			Sequence records				
Victory	3-0	SMR 1995	Wins	2	1997, 2002, 2003	Clean sheets	1	
Defeat	0-9	ISL 1985	Defeats	22	2004-	Goals scored	5	1986
Player Caps	83	Oli Johannesen	Undefeated	3	2002	Without goal	7	1991-1992
Player Goals	10	Rógvi Jacobsen	Without win	26	1990-1995	Goals against	33	2002-2007

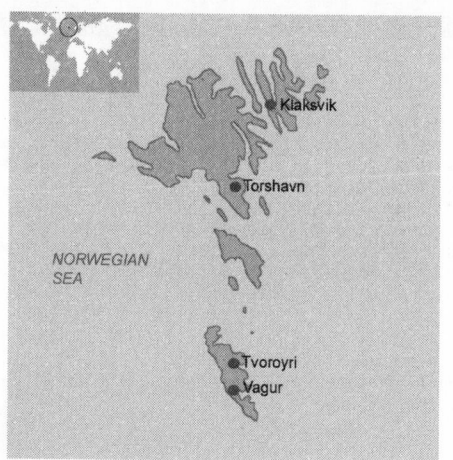

MAJOR CITIES/TOWNS

		Population
1	Tórshavn	13 392
2	Klaksvík	4 618
3	Hoyvík	2 817
4	Argir	1 898
5	Fuglafjarð	1 659
6	Vágur	1 627
7	Vestmanna	1 298
8	Tvøroyri	1 237
9	Sørvag	1 123
10	Kollafjarð	1 076
11	Kollafjørður	1 064
12	Miðvágur	1 063
13	Leirvík	1 011
14	Strendur	867
15	Toftir	867
16	Saltangará	811
17	Sandavágur	805
18	Hvalba	677
19	Eiði	667
20	Skáli	630
21	Sandur	621
22	Norðragøta	582
23	Runavik	511
24	Skopun	450

FAROE ISLANDS; FOROYAR

Capital Tórshavn	Language Faroese, Danish		Independence n/a
Population 47 246	Area 1 399 km²	Density 33 per km²	% in cities n/a
GDP per cap $22 000	Dailling code +298	Internet .fo	GMT + / - 0

MEDALS TABLE

		Overall			League			Cup			Europe			City	Stadium	Cap'ty	DoF
		G	S	B	G	S	B	G	S	G	S	B					
1	HB Tórshavn	45	24	4	19	13	4	26	11					Tórshavn	Gundadalur	6 000	1904
2	KI Klaksvík	22	10	8	17	2	8	5	8					Klaksvik	Klaksvik	4 000	1904
3	B'36 Tórshavn	13	13	5	8	4	5	5	9					Tórshavn	Gundadalur	6 000	1936
4	TB Tvøroyri	12	10		7	5		5	5					Tvøroyri	Sevmyri	3 000	1892
5	GI Gøtu	12	6	4	6	3	4	6	3					Gøtu	Serpugerdi	3 000	1926
6	NSI Runavík	3	5		1	1		2	4					Runavik	Runavik	2 000	1957
7	B'68 Toftir	3	2	6	3	1	6		1					Toftir	Svangaskard	8 020	1962
8	VB Vágur/Sumba	2	3	2	1		2	1	3					Vágur	Vestri a Eidinum	3 000	2006
9	B'71 Sandur	2	2	1	1		1	1	2					Sandur	Sandur	2 000	1970
10	IF Fuglafjørdur	1	4		1				4					Fuglafjordur	Fuglafjordur	3 000	1946
11	EB/Streymur	1	2			2		1						Oyrabakki	Molini	1 000	1993
12	SI Sørvagur	1			1									Sørvag	Sørvágur	2 000	1905
13	Skála		1	1		1	1							Skali	Skali	1 000	1965
14	LIF Leirvik		1						1					Leirvik	Leirvik	2 000	1928
	Royn Valba		1						1					Valba	Hvalba	2 000	1923
16	MB Midvágur			1		1								Miðvágur	Miðvágur	1 000	1905

RECENT LEAGUE AND CUP RECORD

			Championship						Cup		
Year	Champions	Pts	Runners-up	Pts	Third	Pts		Winners	Score	Runners-up	
1995	GI Gøtu	41	HB Tórshavn	33	B'68 Tórshavn	30		HB Tórshavn	3-1	B'68 Toftir	
1996	GI Gøtu	39	KI Klaksvík	39	HB Tórshavn	32		GI Gøtu	2-2 5-3	HB Tórshavn	
1997	B'36 Tórshavn	48	HB Tórshavn	41	GI Gøtu	35		GI Gøtu	6-0	VB Vágur	
1998	HB Tórshavn	45	KI Klaksvík	38	B'36 Tórshavn	37		HB Tórshavn	2-0	KI Klaksvík	
1999	KI Klaksvík	41	GI Gøtu	39	B'36 Tórshavn	38		KI Klaksvík	3-1	B'36 Tórshavn	
2000	VB Vágur	40	HB Tórshavn	38	B'68 Toftir	31		GI Gøtu	1-0	HB Tórshavn	
2001	B'36 Tórshavn	46	GI Gøtu	42	B'68 Toftir	31		B'36 Tórshavn	1-0	KI Klaksvík	
2002	HB Tórshavn	41	NSI Runavík	36	KI Klaksvík	33		NSI Runavík	2-1	HB Tórshavn	
2003	HB Tórshavn	41	B'36 Tórshavn	37	B'68 Toftir	35		B'36 Tórshavn	3-1	GI Gøtu	
2004	HB Tórshavn	41	B'36 Tórshavn	34	Skála	30		HB Tórshavn	3-1	NSI Runavík	
2005	B'36 Tórshavn	54	Skála	50	HB Tórshavn	50		GI Gøtu	4-1	IF Fuglafyørdur	
2006	HB Tórshavn	55	EB Streymur Eidi	54	B'36 Tórshavn	47		B'36 Tórshavn	2-1	KI Klaksvík	
2007	NSI Runavík	61	EB Streymur Eidi	54	B'36 Tórshavn	52		EB Streymur Eidi	4-3	HB Tórshavn	

FAROE ISLANDS 2007

FORMULADEILDIN

	Pl	W	D	L	F	A	Pts	NSI	EB	B'36	HB	GI	Skála	KI	B'71	AB	VB
NSI Runavík †	27	19	4	4	52	24	61		1-1	3-0 1-1	1-0 3-0	3-1	3-1 1-2	3-1	3-0	2-1 2-1	5-2 3-1
EB/Streymur Eidi ‡	27	17	3	7	58	33	54	1-0 0-1		0-1 4-2	1-2	1-1	3-0 2-0	2-1	2-4	3-0 2-2	4-2 6-1
B'36 Tórshavn	27	15	7	5	47	23	52	1-1	1-0		1-1 0-2	4-0	1-1 1-1	1-0 2-2	0-1	4-1 4-1	2-0 2-0
HB Tórshavn	27	15	4	8	59	34	49	2-0	3-0 0-1	0-2		2-3 4-1	5-2	3-1 1-1	0-3 3-1	4-0	3-1 6-2
GI Gøtu	27	11	5	11	46	53	38	1-2 0-3	0-2 1-4	0-3 0-1	3-2		0-3 5-0	0-1	3-2	1-1	2-2
Skála	27	10	4	13	27	40	34	0-1	2-1	0-2	2-5 1-3	0-1		1-0 0-1	2-0 0-0	0-2 2-0	1-1
KI Klaksvík	27	9	6	12	44	47	33	2-0 2-2	1-2 2-5	1-1	0-2	2-3 0-4	1-0		3-3 3-1	1-0	5-0 6-3
B'71 Sandur	27	9	5	13	39	49	32	0-1 1-3	2-3 1-4	1-2 0-3	2-1	1-1 2-3	0-2	3-3		1-0	0-0
AB Argir	27	4	5	18	30	55	17	0-2	1-2	2-1	2-2 1-2	4-4 1-3	1-3 3-1	1-2 0-1			2-2
VB Vagur/Sumba	27	2	5	20	27	71	11	1-2	1-2	0-4	0-0	0-1 2-3	0-1 0-1	1-0	1-4 2-3	1-0 1-2	

1/04/2007 - 27/10/2007 • † Qualified for the UEFA Champions League • ‡ Qualified for the UEFA Cup
Top scorers: Ahmed Sylla, B'36 18; Arnbjorn Hansen, EB 14; Paul Clapson, KI 14; Christian Lundberg, GI 13; Clayton Soares B'71 12

FAROE ISLANDS 2007
1. DEILD (2)

	Pl	W	D	L	F	A	Pts
B'68 Toftir	27	23	3	1	79	20	72
IF Fuglafjørdur	27	19	4	4	84	22	61
FS Vágar	27	16	3	8	47	39	51
TB Tvøroyri	27	14	4	9	56	30	46
LIF Leirvík	27	14	1	12	67	45	43
NSI Runavík 2	27	9	4	14	49	68	31
HB Tórshavn 2	27	9	2	16	38	61	29
SI Sorvágur	27	8	4	15	40	66	28
KI Klaksvík 2	27	5	2	20	28	70	17
B'36 Tórshavn 2	27	3	3	21	22	89	12

31/03/2007 - 20/10/2007

FAROE ISLANDS 2007
2. DEILD (3)

	Pl	W	D	L	F	A	Pts
B'68 Toftir 2	16	11	2	3	35	21	35
GI Gøtu 2	16	10	2	4	46	32	32
EB/Streymur Eidi 2	16	9	2	5	48	33	29
IF Fuglafjørdur 2	16	8	3	5	42	35	27
FS Vágar 2	16	7	2	7	32	26	23
Fram Tórshavn	16	6	4	6	35	29	22
MB Midvágur	16	5	2	9	24	31	17
Skála 2	16	5	1	10	31	34	16
KI Klaksvík 3	16	1	2	13	20	72	5
B'36 Tórshavn 3	Expelled after 10 rounds						

22/04/2007 - 7/10/2007

FFA CUP 2007

Round of 16
EB/Streymur Eidi	4
B'71 Sandur	1
Undri	1
IF Fuglafjørdur	11
KI Klaksvík	4
GI Gøtu	1
FS Vágar	0
Skála	1
VB Vagur/Sumba	3
LIF Leirvík	1
SI Sorvágur	0
TB Tvøroyri	4
AB Argir	3
B'36 Tórshavn	1
NSI Runavík	1
HB Tórshavn	2

Quarter-finals
EB/Streymur Eidi	4	5p
IF Fuglafjørdur	4	4p
KI Klaksvík	0	5p
Skála	0	6p
VB Vagur/Sumba	3	
TB Tvøroyri	1	
AB Argir	0	
HB Tórshavn	4	

Semi-finals
EB/Streymur Eidi	2	1
Skála	0	0
VB Vagur/Sumba		
HB Tórshavn	3	1

Final
EB/Streymur Eidi ‡	4
HB Tórshavn	3

CUP FINAL
Tórshavn, 15-08-2007, Ref: Rasmussen
Scorers -
Sorin Anghel [3p], Hans Samuelson [6], Arnbjorn Hansen [21], Karoly Potemkin [79] for EB; Pall Joensen [77], Rogvi Jacobsen [80], Vagnur Mortensen [85] for HB

‡ Qualified for the UEFA Cup

First round: FS Vágar 8-1 NIF; TB Tvøroyri 2-0 B'68 Toftir; Undri 3-2 MB Midvágur; LIF Leirvík 3-0 Fram Tórshavn

GAB – GABON

NATIONAL TEAM RECORD
JULY 10TH 2006 TO JULY 12TH 2010

PL	W	D	L	F	A	%
16	6	5	5	19	21	53.1

FIFA/COCA-COLA WORLD RANKING

1993	1994	1995	1996	1997	1998	1999	2000	2001	2002	2003	2004	2005	2006	2007	High
60	64	67	46	63	82	74	89	102	121	111	109	104	95	104	**45** 01/96

2007–2008												Low
08/07	09/07	10/07	11/07	12/07	01/08	02/08	03/08	04/08	05/08	06/08	07/08	**125** 05/03
107	110	109	106	104	103	105	104	98	99	94	74	

Gabon were dealt a cruel hand in being paired with Cote d'Ivoire in the same qualifying group for the 2008 CAF Africa Cup of Nations but are hoping for better fortunes in the FIFA World Cup preliminaries. The 'Azingo Nationale' stood little chance of qualifying for the 2008 finals in Ghana because of the presence of the Ivorians in their group plus the fact there were only three teams participating after the withdrawal of Djibouti - effectively ruling out qualifying as one of the best placed runners-up. For the 2010 FIFA World Cup finals, Gabon were handed a tough pairing again, contesting a place in the final phase of the African zone preliminaries with Ghana and Libya in a

INTERNATIONAL HONOURS
None

group where home form has so far proven to be decisive. Former French international coach Alain Giresse had resigned before the start of the qualifiers but had a change of heart. He was incensed by vitriol directed at him by crowd members after Gabon lost to a Cameroon team in the African Nations Championship, a new tournament for locally based players in which the matches do not count as full internationals. Having seen their hat-trick of league titles ended by FC 105 in 2007, Mangasport got back into their winning ways again by claiming the 2008 championship, although it was a close race, with US Bitam letting the title slip from their grasp at the last.

THE FIFA BIG COUNT OF 2006

	Male	Female		Total
Number of players	69 800	0	Referees and Assistant Referees	100
Professionals	0		Admin, Coaches, Technical, Medical	900
Amateurs 18+	5 500		Number of clubs	60
Youth under 18	2 800		Number of teams	220
Unregistered	5 500		Clubs with women's teams	0
Total players	69 800		Players as % of population	4.90%

Fédération Gabonaise de Football (FGF)
Case postale 181, Libreville, Gabon
Tel +241 774862   Fax +241 564199
www.none
President: ABABE Leon   General Secretary: BOUASSA MOUSSADJI Barthelemy
Vice-President: OSSAMY NDJOUBI Alain   Treasurer: NZE NGUEMA Jean   Media Officer: EPIGA Fernand
Men's Coach: GIRESSE Alain   Women's Coach: OBAME BEKOURE Victor
FGF formed: 1962   CAF: 1967   FIFA: 1963
Green shirts, Blue shorts, White socks or Yellow shirts, Yellow shorts, White socks

RECENT INTERNATIONAL MATCHES PLAYED BY GABON

2003	Opponents	Score		Venue	Comp	Scorers	Att	Referee
15-11	Burundi	W	4-1	Libreville	WCq	Nzigou [2], Mwinyi OG [16], Nguéma 2 [38 80]	15 000	Ndoye SEN
5-12	Congo	L	2-3	Brazzaville	CMr1	Nguéma [40], Edou [63]		Tchoumba CMR
9-12	Congo	D	1-1	Brazzaville	CMr1			
11-12	Central African Rep	L	0-2	Brazzaville	CMsf			
13-12	Congo	L	0-1	Brazzaville	CM3p			
2004								
29-05	Egypt	L	0-2	Cairo	Fr		15 000	Auda EGY
5-06	Zimbabwe	D	1-1	Libreville	WCq	Zue [52]	25 000	Quartey GHA
19-06	Rwanda	L	1-3	Kigali	WCq	Zue [20]	16 325	Abdulkadir TAN
3-07	Angola	D	2-2	Libreville	WCq	Issiemou [44], Zue [49]	20 000	Louzaya CGO
5-09	Algeria	W	3-0	Annaba	WCq	Aubame [56], Akieremy [73], Bito'o [84]	51 000	Ndoye SEN
3-10	Benin	W	2-0	Libreville	Fr	Djissikadie, Nguéma		
9-10	Nigeria	D	1-1	Libreville	WCq	Issiemou [29]	26 000	Yameogo BFA
2005								
3-02	Central African Rep	W	4-0	Libreville	CMr1	Akoué [32p], Nguéma [42], Yinda 2 [52 82]		
8-02	Congo	W	1-0	Libreville	CMr1	Poaty [38]		
10-02	Chad	L	2-3	Libreville	CMsf	Akoué [58p], Mabiala [69]		
12-02	Congo	W	2-1	Libreville	CM3p	Yembi, Akoué		
19-03	Congo	D	0-0	Libreville	Fr			
26-03	Nigeria	L	0-2	Port Harcourt	WCq		16 489	Hicuburundi BDI
5-06	Zimbabwe	L	0-1	Harare	WCq		55 000	Ssegonga UGA
18-06	Rwanda	W	3-0	Libreville	WCq	Djissikadie [10], Londo [55], Zue [60]	10 000	El Arjoun MAR
4-09	Angola	L	0-3	Luanda	WCq			
8-10	Algeria	D	0-0	Port-Gentil	WCq			
2006								
4-03	Cameroon	D	0-0	Malabo	CMr1			
8-03	Central African Rep	D	2-2	Malabo	CMr1	Bito'o [26], Tamboulas OG [58]		
11-03	Equatorial Guinea	D	0-0	Bata	CMsf	L 2-4p		
14-03	Chad	D	2-2	Bata	CM3p	Akiremy 2 [63 73], W 7-6p		
15-08	Algeria	W	2-0	Aix-en-Provence	Fr	Mouloungui [65], Djissikadie [67]		Mezouar
2-09	Madagascar	W	4-0	Libreville	CNq	Antchouet [40], Cousin [67p], Nzigou 2 [70 71]		Diatta SEN
8-10	Côte d'Ivoire	L	0-5	Abidjan	CNq			Buenkadila COD
15-11	Morocco	L	0-6	Rabat	Fr		5 000	Ousmane Sidebe MLI
2007								
7-03	Congo	D	2-2	N'Djamena	CMr1	Ambourouet [52], Akiremy [89]		
9-03	Equatorial Guinea	D	1-1	N'Djamena	CMr1	Akiremy [15]		
11-03	Chad	W	2-1	N'Djamena	CMsf	Akiremy 2 [44 56]		
16-03	Congo	L	0-1	N'Djamena	CMf			
17-06	Madagascar	W	2-0	Antananarivo	CNq	Akiremy [20], Meye [89]		Mlangeni SWZ
21-08	Benin	D	2-2	Paris	Fr	Nzigou [4], Mouloungui [42p]		
8-09	Côte d'Ivoire	D	0-0	Libreville	CNq			Damon RSA
2008								
25-03	Congo DR	D	0-0	Aubervilliers	Fr			
7-06	Libya	L	0-1	Tripoli	WCq		30 000	Chaibou NIG
14-06	Ghana	W	2-0	Libreville	WCq	Meye [45], Nguema [59]	13 000	Benouza ALG
22-06	Ghana	L	0-2	Accra	WCq		29 040	Damon RSA
28-06	Lesotho	W	2-0	Libreville	WCq	Do Marcolino 2 [45 63]	15 000	Mendy GAM

Fr = Friendly match • CN = CAF African Cup of Nations • CM = CEMAC Cup • WC = FIFA World Cup
q = qualifier • r1 = first round group • sf = semi-final • 3p = third place play-off • f = final

GABON NATIONAL TEAM RECORDS AND RECORD SEQUENCES

Records			Sequence records					
Victory	7-0	BEN 1995	Wins	4	1985, 1992	Clean sheets	5	1986-87, 1988
Defeat	0-6	MAR 2006	Defeats	5	1967-1971	Goals scored	14	1998-1999
Player Caps	n/a	François Amégasse	Undefeated	11	1996	Without goal	4	2002
Player Goals	n/a		Without win	20	1977-1984	Goals against	11	1996-1997

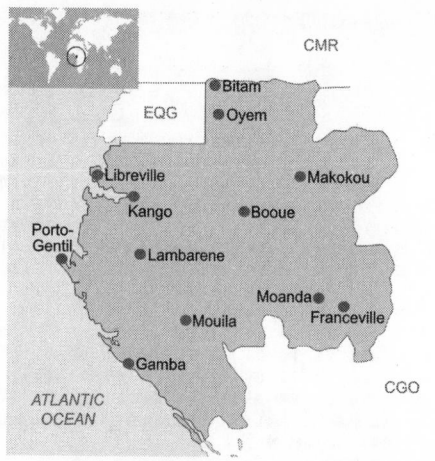

CMR

EQG

Bitam
Oyem

Libreville
Kango
Porto-
Gentil
Lambarene
Mouila
Gamba

Makokou
Booue

Moanda
Franceville

CGO

ATLANTIC
OCEAN

GABONESE REPUBLIC; REPUBLIQUE GABONAISE

Capital	Libreville	Language	French		Independence 1960
Population	1 454 867	Area	267 667 km²	Density 5 per km²	% in cities
GDP per cap	$5500	Dailling code	+241	Internet .ga	GMT + / - +1

MAJOR CITIES/TOWNS
Population '000

1	Libreville	713
2	Port-Gentil	134
3	Masuku	53
4	Oyem	38
5	Moanda	37
6	Mouila	27
7	Lambaréné	25
8	Tchibanga	23
9	Koulamoutou	20
10	Makokou	16
11	Bitam	12
12	Tsogni	12
13	Gamba	12
14	Mounana	10
15	Ntoum	10
16	Nkan	10
17	Lastoursville	10
18	Okandja	8
19	Ndendé	7
20	Booué	7
21	Fougamou	6
22	Ndjolé	6
23	Mbigou	5
24	Mayumba	4

MEDALS TABLE

		Overall			Lge	Cup	Africa			City	Stadium	Cap'ty	DoF
		G	S	B	G	G	G	S	B				
1	FC 105	14			10	4				Libreville	Stade Omar Bongo	40 000	1975
2	Mangasport	11			6	5				Moanda	Stade Henri Sylvoz	4 000	1962
3	AS Sogara	7	1		6	1	1			Port-Gentil			
4	US Mbilianzambi (USM)	7			4	3				Libreville	Augustin Monédan de Sibang	7 000	
5	Mbilinga	6	1		1	5	1			Port-Gentil			
6	Delta Téléstar	3				3				Libreville	Stade Omar Bongo	40 000	
	Vautour Mangoungou	3			2	1				Libreville			
	US Bitam	3			1	2				Bitam	Stade Municipal	5 000	
9	Aigle Royale	2			2					Libreville			
	Olympique Sportif	2			2					Libreville			
	Petrosport	2			1	1				Port-Gentil			
	Stade Mandji	2				2				Port-Gentil	Stade Pierre Divounguy	7 000	1962
	Anges ABC	1			1					Libreville			
	Jeunesse AC (JAC)	1			1					Libreville			
	AS Police	1			1					Libreville			
	AS Solidarité	1			1					Libreville			
	Zalang COC	1			1					Libreville			
	AO Evizo	1				1				Lambaréné			

RECENT LEAGUE AND CUP RECORD

	Championship						Cup		
Year	Champions	Pts	Runners-up	Pts	Third	Pts	Winners	Score	Runners-up
2000	Mangasport	30	AO Evizo	30	FC 105	22	AO Evizo		
2001	FC 105	62	Mangasport	59	TP Akwembé	59	Mangasport	1-0	TP Akwembé
2002	USM Libreville	54	FC 105	49	Mangasport	39	USM Libreville	1-1 4-2p	Jeunesse
2003	US Bitam	45	FC 105	45	Wongosport	37	US Bitam	1-1 4-3p	USM Libreville
2004	Mangasport	32	Téléstar	31	US Bitam	26	FC 105	3-2	Mangasport
2005	Mangasport	23	US Bitam	20	Sogéa	13	Mangasport	2-0	Sogéa
2006	Mangasport	66	FC 105	62	US Bitam	53	Delta Téléstar	3-2	FC 105
2007	FC 105	50	Mangasport	46	Stade Mandji	39	Mangasport	1-0	Sogéa
2008	Mangasport	44	US Bitam	43	FC 105	37			

GABON 2007

CHAMPIONNAT NATIONAL DE D1

	Pl	W	D	L	F	A	Pts	FC 105	Mangasport	Stade	Télestar	USB	Sogéa	USO	CMS	Wongosport	USM	Missiles	Mitzic	Franceville
FC 105 Libreville †	24	15	5	4	32	11	50		1-0	1-0	1-0	2-2	2-0	1-0	2-1	3-0	1-0	3-0	6-1	2-1
Mangasport Moanda ‡	24	13	7	4	31	8	46	2-0		1-1	2-0	2-0	1-0	0-0	3-0	1-0	1-2	3-0	3-0	4-0
AS Stade Mandji	24	11	6	7	25	18	39	0-2	1-0		2-0	0-0	1-0	0-1	1-2	2-2	5-3	1-0	1-0	2-1
Delta Télestar	24	10	6	8	28	22	36	1-0	1-1	0-2		0-0	2-1	1-0	1-3	2-0	3-4	2-2	1-1	3-0
US Bitam §5	24	10	10	4	25	19	35	1-1	0-0	0-0	1-0		0-1	0-0	2-1	1-1	2-2	1-0	1-0	1-2
Sogéa	24	9	6	9	31	20	33	1-0	0-2	0-1	0-1	3-2		5-0	3-0	1-0	*0-1*	0-1	2-1	6-2
US Oyem	23	5	13	5	12	16	28	0-0	0-0	1-1	1-1	0-1	1-0		1-1	1-0	1-0	1-1		0-0
Cercle Mbéri Sportif	24	7	7	10	24	31	28	0-1	0-1	0-3	1-2	1-2	2-2	1-1		3-1	2-1	2-0	1-0	1-0
Wongosport	24	6	8	10	15	24	26	0-1	**0-3**	1-0	*1-0*	1-1	0-0	0-1	0-0		2-0	1-0	2-0	1-1
US Mbilanzambi	24	7	4	13	24	38	25	0-4	0-1	1-2	**0-3**	0-1	0-0	1-1	0-0	2-0		1-0	3-0	2-1
Missile	24	6	6	12	17	27	24	0-0	2-1	1-0	0-1	0-1	1-1	*0-1*	1-0	1-1	0-2		1-2	3-1
AS Mitzic	23	4	7	12	15	31	22	2-0	1-2	2-0	0-0	1-2	1-1	1-1	0-0	0-0	1-0	1-1		0-2
Franceville FC §11	24	6	7	11	24	37	14	0-0	0-0	0-0	**0-3**	1-4	1-4	0-0	3-1	1-1	5-1	1-0	2-0	

26/11/2006 – 5/08/2007 • † Qualified for the CAF Champions League • ‡ Qualified for the CAF Confederation Cup • § = points deducted • Matches in bold were awarded • The scores of the matches in italics are unverified

GABON 2008

CHAMPIONNAT NATIONAL DE D1

	Pl	W	D	L	F	A	Pts	Mangasport	USB	FC 105	Sogéa	Missile	Stade	CMS	USM	Wongosport	USO	ASCM	Télestar
Mangasport †	22	13	5	4	37	16	44		2-1	1-0	2-0	1-1	4-0	2-0	3-0	2-2	5-0		1-0
US Bitam ‡	22	13	4	5	30	16	43	1-1		0-0	1-0	0-1	2-1	2-0	2-0	**3-0**	3-1	2-0	2-0
FC 105	22	10	7	5	30	16	37	1-1	1-2		0-1	1-3	2-0	0-0	1-0	2-1	2-0	4-0	4-0
Sogéa	22	9	6	7	29	26	33	2-2	1-2	3-1		4-2	0-1	3-1	4-2	2-1	1-1	0-1	0-0
Missile	22	8	9	5	29	28	33	0-1	1-1	1-1	2-4		2-1	2-1	0-0	2-1	1-0	3-3	1-1
AS Stade Mandji	22	10	2	10	23	26	32	0-1	2-1	0-1	1-0	1-0		1-2	0-1	0-2	0-0	0-1	2-1
Cercle Mbéri Sportif	22	8	6	8	27	25	30	1-0	2-0	1-3	1-1	0-0	1-2		2-0	3-3	1-0	5-0	1-1
US Mbilanzambi	22	7	4	11	27	31	25	2-3	1-1	1-3	2-0	1-1	1-2	1-0		2-0	2-2	5-2	2-1
Wongosport	22	6	6	10	21	25	24	0-1	0-2	0-0	0-0	1-1	**3-0**	0-0	1-0		0-2	0-0	2-0
US Oyem	22	5	9	8	16	23	24	1-0	0-1	0-0	0-0	1-1	1-2	**0-3**	1-0	1-0		2-1	0-0
ASCM	22	5	5	12	18	40	20	0-1	2-0	0-0	0-1	1-2	1-2	1-0	2-1	1-4	1-1		1-1
Delta Téléstar	22	4	5	13	18	34	17	1-0	0-1	2-1	1-2	2-3	2-4	1-2	1-3	0-2	2-0	1-0	

8/12/2007 – 30/07/2008 • † Qualified for the CAF Champions League • ‡ Qualified for the CAF Confederation Cup • Matches in bold awarded

COUPE DU GABON INTERCLUBS 2007

Round of 16

Mangasport Moanda	1	4p
GBI	1	2p
EPAM	0	
Cercle Mbéri Sportif	1	
Missiles Libreville	2	
AS Stade Mandji	0	
OC Lac Bleu	0	
FC 105 Libreville	1	
Delta Téléstar	2	
Wongosport	0	
Jascam	1	
AS Ogooué-Maritime	2	
Franceville FC	3	
US Bitam	2	
Etoile Filante Poubara	2	
Sogéa FC	3	

Quarter-finals

Mangasport Moanda	3
Cercle Mbéri Sportif	1
Missiles Libreville	0
FC 105 Libreville	1
Delta Téléstar	1
AS Ogooué-Maritime	0
Franceville FC	2
Sogéa FC	3

Semi-finals

Mangasport Moanda	2
FC 105 Libreville	0
Delta Téléstar	0
Sogéa FC	1

Final

| Mangasport Moanda ‡ | 1 |
| Sogéa FC | 0 |

CUP FINAL

Libreville, 5-08-2007

‡ Qualified for the CAF Confederation Cup

GAM – GAMBIA

NATIONAL TEAM RECORD
JULY 10TH 2006 TO JULY 12TH 2010

PL	W	D	L	F	A	%
14	4	5	5	11	14	46.4

FIFA/COCA-COLA WORLD RANKING

1993	1994	1995	1996	1997	1998	1999	2000	2001	2002	2003	2004	2005	2006	2007		High	
125	117	112	128	132	135	151	155	148	143	138	154	164	134	117		**83**	04/08

2007–2008												Low	
08/07	09/07	10/07	11/07	12/07	01/08	02/08	03/08	04/08	05/08	06/08	07/08	**166**	05/06
128	114	112	111	117	111	103	102	83	83	95	91		

Two wins over Algeria in less than a year attests to the new found status of the Gambia as serious contenders on the African football circuit. While the small west African country has yet to qualify for a major event, they are no longer the easy walkover they once were. Gambia's Scorpions beat Algeria, who have twice been FIFA World Cup finalists, in the closing match of the 2008 CAF Africa Cup of Nations qualifiers and then again in June 2008 when they began their campaign for a place at the 2010 FIFA World Cup finals in South Africa. Gambia have appointed Belgian coach Paul Put, banned in his own country for match fixing, and continued to advance their potential on

INTERNATIONAL HONOURS
CAF African U-17 Championship 2005

the back of a growing number of players who have gone to play for clubs in Europe and the Middle East. The latest among them is Omar Koroma, a teenager signed by English Premier League club Manchester City. Put helped the side to a series of good results in their opening FIFA World Cup qualifiers despite having been appointed only days before the first match. Gambia have also benefited from competing at the FIFA U-17 World Cup in Peru in 2005 and the FIFA U-20 World Cup in Canada in 2007, where they advanced past the first round. At home Wallidan won the championship ahead of Samger - their fifth success since the start of the decade.

THE FIFA BIG COUNT OF 2006

	Male	Female		Total
Number of players	67 400	630	Referees and Assistant Referees	100
Professionals	0		Admin, Coaches, Technical, Medical	600
Amateurs 18+	3 080		Number of clubs	50
Youth under 18	1 450		Number of teams	200
Unregistered	2 500		Clubs with women's teams	1
Total players	68 030		Players as % of population	4.14%

Gambia Football Association (GFA)
Independence Stadium, Bakau, PO Box 523, Banjul, The Gambia
Tel +220 4494802   Fax +220 4494802
info@gambiafa.org   www.gambiafa.org
President: KINTEH Seedy   General Secretary: BOJANG Jammeh
Vice-President: TAMBA Lang Tombong   Treasurer: CEESSAY Kemo   Media Officer: JALLOW Bubacarr
Men's Coach: PUT Paul   Women's Coach: CEESAY Kebba
GFA formed: 1952   CAF: 1962   FIFA: 1966
Red shirts, Red shorts, Red socks or Blue shirts, Blue shorts, Blue socks

RECENT INTERNATIONAL MATCHES PLAYED BY GAMBIA

2004	Opponents	Score	Venue	Comp	Scorers	Att	Referee
No international matches played in 2004							
2005							
12-06	Sierra Leone	L 0-1	Freetown	Fr			
2006							
3-09	Cape Verde Islands	W 2-0	Bakau	CNq	Jatto Ceesay [8p], Assan Jatta [89]		Pare BFA
7-10	Algeria	L 0-1	Algiers	CNq			Auda EGY
2007							
8-01	Saudi Arabia	L 0-3	Dammam	Fr			
7-02	Luxembourg	L 1-2	Hesperange	Fr	Mustapha Jarjue [15]	520	Circhetta SUI
24-03	Guinea	L 0-2	Bakau	CNq			Kotey GHA
3-06	Guinea	D 2-2	Conakry	CNq	Edrissa Sonko [53], Pa Modou Jagne [85]		Djaoupe TOG
16-06	Cape Verde Islands	D 0-0	Praia	CNq			Aguidissou BEN
9-09	Algeria	W 2-1	Bakau	CNq	Assan Jatta [71], Mathew Mendy [88]		Imiere NGA
3-12	Cape Verde	D 0-0	Bissau	Fr			
23-12	Sierra Leone	W 2-1	Bakau	Fr	Ebrima Sillah [2], Ebrima Sohna [51]		
2008							
1-06	Liberia	D 1-1	Monrovia	WCq	Mustapha Jarjue [17]	35 000	Keita GUI
8-06	Senegal	D 0-0	Banjul	WCq		24 500	Ncobo RSA
14-06	Algeria	W 1-0	Banjul	WCq	Mustapha Jarjue [19p]	18 000	Coulibaly MLI
20-06	Algeria	L 0-1	Blida	WCq		25 000	Ndume GAB

Fr = Friendly match • CN = CAF African Cup of Nations • WC = FIFA World Cup • q = qualifier

GAMBIA NATIONAL TEAM RECORDS AND RECORD SEQUENCES

Records			Sequence records				
Victory	6-0	LES 2002	Wins	3	2002	Clean sheets	3	1991, 2002
Defeat	0-8	GUI 1972	Defeats	9	1968-1977	Goals scored	7	1962-1971
Player Caps	n/a	Ebou sillah	Undefeated	4	Four times	Without goal	7	1998-2000
Player Goals	n/a	Attor Gomez	Without win	17	1997-2001	Goals against	16	1962-1979

RECENT LEAGUE AND CUP RECORD

Championship		Cup		
Year	Champions	Winners	Score	Runners-up
1997	Real Banjul	Real Banjul	1-0	Banjul Hawks
1998	Real Banjul	Wallidan	1-1 4-3p	Ports Authority
1999	Ports Authority	Wallidan	1-1 4-3p	Mass Sosseh
2000	Real Banjul	Steve Biko	1-1 4-2p	Wallidan
2001	Wallidan	Wallidan	3-0	Blackpool
2002	Wallidan	Wallidan	1-0	Real Banjul
2003	Armed Forces	Wallidan	1-0	Banjul Hawks
2004	Wallidan	Wallidan	1-1 9-8p	Armed Forces
2005	Wallidan	Bakau United	4-1	Wallidan
2006	Ports Authority	Hawks	3-0	Steve Biko
2007	Real Banjul	Ports Authority	1-0	Hawks
2008	Wallidan			

GAMBIA 2008 GFA LEAGUE 1ST DIVISION

	Pl	W	D	L	F	A	Pts
Wallidan	22	10	9	3	25	15	39
Samger	22	10	7	5	22	16	37
Hawks	22	9	9	4	22	16	36
Real Banjul	22	6	13	3	14	9	31
Armed Forces	22	6	11	5	16	14	29
Sait Matty	22	7	6	9	19	17	27
GAMTEL	22	6	9	7	15	20	27
Steve Biko	22	4	14	4	11	11	26
Sea View	22	6	7	9	13	18	25
Bakau United	22	4	11	7	10	13	23
Ports Authority	22	2	14	6	10	15	20
Interior	22	2	10	10	9	22	16

24/02/2008 - 13/07/2008

GAMBIA COUNTRY INFORMATION

Capital	Banjul	Independence	1965 from the UK	GDP per Capita	$1 700
Population	1 546 848	Status	Republic	GNP Ranking	172
Area km²	11 300	Language	English	Dialling code	+220
Population density	136 per km²	Literacy rate	33%	Internet code	.gm
% in urban areas	26%	Main religion	Muslim 90%	GMT +/–	0
Towns/Cities ('000)	Serekunda 218; Brikama 101; Bakau 47; Farafenni 36; Banjul 34; Lamin 16; Sukuta 15				
Neighbours (km)	Senegal 740; Atlantic Ocean 80				
Main stadia	Independence Stadium – Bakau 20 000; Brikama – Banjul 15 000				

GEO – GEORGIA

NATIONAL TEAM RECORD
JULY 10TH 2006 TO JULY 12TH 2010

PL	W	D	L	F	A	%
22	6	4	12	25	33	36.4

FIFA/COCA-COLA WORLD RANKING

1993	1994	1995	1996	1997	1998	1999	2000	2001	2002	2003	2004	2005	2006	2007	High
-	92	79	95	69	52	66	66	58	90	93	104	104	94	77	**42** 09/98

					2007–2008							Low
08/07	09/07	10/07	11/07	12/07	01/08	02/08	03/08	04/08	05/08	06/08	07/08	**156** 04/94
103	104	71	77	77	76	80	76	81	81	80	89	

It was back to winning ways for Dinamo Tbilisi after two trophyless seasons when they comprehensively won the Championship 10 points clear of local rivals WIT Georgia. Dusan Uhrin's side won 23 of their 26 matches in a season that was temporarily suspended due to the state of emergency announced in November following anti-government protests. Dinamo's poor record in the Cup continued, however. Having won six in succession in the 1990's, they have now won just two of the past 11 tournaments and for the third year running it was Ameri Tbilisi and FC Zestafoni who contested the final. Hoping for a hat-trick, Ameri supporters were left disappointed after a 2-

INTERNATIONAL HONOURS
None

1 defeat gave Zestafoni their first trophy - just four years after they were founded as the works team of a metal factory in the town. There were no great adventures in European club competition with 2007 champions Olimpi losing to Kazakstan champions Astana in the first preliminary round of the Champions League, while Dinamo suffered an 8-0 aggregate defeat at the hands of Rapid Wien in the UEFA Cup. The national team's Euro 2008 campaign had never really got going and it ended with defeat at home to Lithuania and a sixth place finish in the seven team group - above only the Faroe Islands. Coach Klaus Toppmöller was soon on his way, resigning in April 2008.

THE FIFA BIG COUNT OF 2006

	Male	Female		Total
Number of players	200 246	21 940	Referees and Assistant Referees	123
Professionals	1 279		Admin, Coaches, Technical, Medical	1 110
Amateurs 18+	1 137		Number of clubs	202
Youth under 18	23 990		Number of teams	522
Unregistered	122 400		Clubs with women's teams	7
Total players	222 186		Players as % of population	4.77%

Georgian Football Federation (GFF)
76a Chavchavadze Avenue, Tbilisi 0162, Georgia
Tel +995 32 912610   Fax +995 32 915995
gff@gff.ge   www.gff.ge
President: AKHALKATSI Nodar   General Secretary: UGULAVA Ucha
Vice-President: KAVTARADZE Gogi   Treasurer: CHKHIKVADZE Nargiza   Media Officer: TZONBILADZE Alexander
Men's Coach: TBD   Women's Coach: JAPARIDZE Maia
GFF formed: 1990   UEFA: 1992   FIFA: 1992
White shirts with red trimmings, White shorts, White socks or Red shirts with white trimmings, Red shorts, Red socks

RECENT INTERNATIONAL MATCHES PLAYED BY GEORGIA

2004 Opponents	Score	Venue	Comp	Scorers	Att	Referee
18-08 Moldova	L 0-1	Tiraspol	Fr		8 000	Godulyan UKR
4-09 Turkey	D 1-1	Trabzon	WCq	Asatiani [85]	10 169	Medina Cantalejpo ESP
8-09 Albania	W 2-0	Tbilisi	WCq	Iashvili [15], Demetradze [90+1]	20 000	Courtney NIR
13-10 Ukraine	L 0-2	Lviv	WCq		28 000	Stark GER
17-11 Denmark	D 2-2	Tbilisi	WCq	Demetradze [33], Asatiani [76]	20 000	Ceferin SVN
2005						
9-02 Lithuania	W 1-0	Tbilisi	Fr	Ashvetia [57]	1 000	Gadiyev AZE
26-03 Greece	L 1-3	Tbilisi	WCq	Asatiani [22]	23 000	Rosetti ITA
30-03 Turkey	L 2-5	Tbilisi	WCq	Amisulashvili [13], Iashvili [40]	10 000	Hauge NOR
4-06 Albania	L 2-3	Tirana	WCq	Burduli [85], Kobiashvili [94+]	BCD	Tudor ROU
17-08 Kazakhstan	W 2-1	Almaty	WCq	Demetradze 2 [50 82]	9 000	Havrilla SVK
3-09 Ukraine	D 1-1	Tbilisi	WCq	Gakhokidze [89]	BCD	Ovrebo NOR
7-09 Denmark	L 1-6	Copenhagen	WCq	Demetradze [37]	27 177	Bozinovski MKD
8-10 Kazakhstan	D 0-0	Tbilisi	WCq		BCD	Hytia FIN
12-10 Greece	L 0-1	Athens	WCq		28 186	Trefoloni ITA
12-11 Bulgaria	L 2-6	Sofia	Fr	Jakobia [83], Gogua [90]		
16-11 Jordan	W 3-2	Tbilisi	Fr	Demetradze 2 [3 64], Arveladze.S [73]		
2006						
27-02 Moldova	L 1-5	Ta'Qali	Fr	Tskitishvili [18p]	330	Casha MLT
1-03 Malta	W 2-0	Ta'Qali	Fr	Martsvaladze [8], Kankava [18]	1 100	Banari MDV
22-03 Albania	D 0-0	Tirana	Fr			Dondarini ITA
27-05 New Zealand	L 1-3	Altenkirchen	Fr	Arveladze.S [41]	1 000	
31-05 Paraguay	L 0-1	Dornbirn	Fr		2 000	Gangle AUT
16-08 Faroe Islands	W 6-0	Toftir	ECq	Mujiri [16], Iashvili [18], Arveladze 3 [37 62 82], Kobiashvili [51p]	2 114	Ross NIR
2-09 France	L 0-3	Tbilisi	ECq		54 000	Wegereef NED
6-09 Ukraine	L 2-3	Kyiv	ECq	Arveladze [38], Demetradze [61]	35 000	Jara CZE
7-10 Germany	L 0-2	Rostock	Fr		28 000	Lehner AUT
11-10 Italy	L 1-3	Tbilisi	ECq	Shashiashvili [26]	48 000	Riley ENG
15-11 Uruguay	W 2-0	Tbilisi	Fr	Kobiashvili 2 [38p 60]	12 000	Godulyan UKR
2007						
7-02 Turkey	W 1-0	Tbilisi	Fr	Siradze [76]	53 000	Lajuks LVA
24-03 Scotland	L 1-2	Glasgow	ECq	Arveladze [41]	52 063	Vollquartz DEN
28-03 Faroe Islands	W 3-1	Tbilisi	ECq	Siradze 26, Iashvili 2 [46+ 92+]	12 000	Saliy KAZ
2-06 Lithuania	L 0-1	Kaunas	ECq		6 400	Circhetta SUI
6-06 France	L 0-1	Auxerre	ECq		19 345	Batista POR
22-08 Luxembourg	D 0-0	Luxembourg	Fr		1 123	Weatherall NIR
8-09 Ukraine	D 1-1	Tbilisi	ECq	Siradze [89]	24 000	Hamer LUX
12-09 Azerbaijan	D 1-1	Baku	Fr	Tatanashvili [48]	10 000	Kovalenko UZB
13-10 Italy	L 0-2	Genoa	ECq		23 057	Davila ESP
17-10 Scotland	W 2-0	Tbilisi	ECq	Mchedlidze [16], Siradze [64]	29 377	Kircher GER
16-11 Qatar	W 2-1	Doha	Fr	Kankava [46], Salukvadze [64]		Al Ghabbaz BAH
21-11 Lithuania	L 0-2	Tbilisi	ECq		21 300	Stavrev MKD
2008						
6-02 Latvia	L 1-3	Tbilisi	Fr	Kaladze [46]	6 000	Shmolik BKR
26-03 Northern Ireland	L 1-4	Belfast	Fr	Healy OG [55]	15 000	Wilmes LUX
27-05 Estonia	D 1-1	Tallinn	Fr	Kenia [82]	2 500	Vejlgaard DEN
31-05 Portugal	L 0-2	Viseu	Fr		8 500	Meir ISR

Fr = Friendly match • EC = UEFA EURO 2008 • WC = FIFA World Cup • q = qualifier • BCD = Behind closed doors

GEORGIA NATIONAL TEAM RECORDS AND RECORD SEQUENCES

Records			Sequence records			
Victory	7-0	ARM 1997	Wins	5	1997-1998	Clean sheets	3	1997
Defeat	0-5	ROM 1996	Defeats	7	2003-2004	Goals scored	10	2001-2002
Player Caps	71	Levan Kobiashvili	Undefeated	8	1997-1998	Without goal	3	Four times
Player Goals	21	Shota Arveladze	Without win	8	1999, 2003-2004	Goals against	11	1998-1999

MAJOR CITIES/TOWNS

		Population '000
1	Tbilisi	1 026
2	Kutaisi	173
3	Batumi	115
4	Rustavi	105
5	Sukhumi	79
6	Zugdidi	75
7	Poti	45
8	Gori	44
9	Samtredia	28
10	Senaki	27
11	Khashuri	27
12	Zestafoni	23
13	Telavi	19
14	Tkvarcheli	18
15	Marneuli	17
16	Kobuleti	17
17	Ozurgeti	17
18	Tskaltubo	16
19	Akhaltsikhe	16
20	Ochamchira	15
21	Kaspi	14
22	Borjomi	13
23	Tkibuli	12
24	Gali	11

GEORGIA; SAKARTVELO

Capital	Tbilisi	Language	Geirgian, Russian, Armenian, Azeri	Independence	1991
Population	4 661 473	Area	69 700 km^2	Density 67 per km^2	% in cities 58%
GDP per cap	$2500	Dailling code	+995	Internet .ge	GMT + / - +4

MEDALS TABLE

		Overall			League			Cup			Europe			City	Stadium	Cap'ty	DoF
		G	S	B	G	S	B	G	S	B	G	S	B				
1	Dinamo Tbilisi	21	2	5	13	1	5	8	1					Tbilisi	Boris Paichadze	20 500	1925
2	Torpedo Kutaisi	5	6	2	3	3	2	2	3					Kutaisi	Torpedo	19 400	1949
3	Lokomotivi Tbilisi	3	3	1		2	1	3	1					Tbilisi	Lokomotivi	24 500	1936
4	Ameri Tbilisi	2	1	1			1	2	1					Tbilisi	Ameri	1 000	2003
5	Dinamo Batumi	1	5	1		1	1	1	4					Batumi	Central	19 600	1923
6	WIT Georgia	1	3	1	1	3	1							Tbilisi	Mtskheta Central	2 000	1968
	FC Zestafoni	1	3	1			1	1	3					Zestafoni	Central	5 000	2004
8	Sioni Bolnisi	1	2		1	1			1					Bolnisi	Temur Stapania	3 000	1936
	Guria Lanchkhuti	1	2			2		1						Lanchkhuti	Central	22 000	1952
10	Olimpi Rustavi	1		1	1		1							Rustavi	Poladi	6 000	1991
11	Tskhumi Sukhumi		3			1			2					Sukhumi			
12	Kolkheti-1913		2	3		2	3							Poti	Phazisi	6 000	1913
13	Gorda Rustavi		1	2			2		1					Rustavi	Poladi	6 000	1948

GEORGIAN CLUBS IN THE SOVIET UNION

| 6 | Dinamo Tbilisi | 4 | 11 | 13 | 2 | 5 | 13 | 2 | 6 | | 1 | | 1 | | | | |

RECENT LEAGUE AND CUP RECORD

	Championship						Cup		
Year	Champions	Pts	Runners-up	Pts	Third	Pts	Winners	Score	Runners-up
1995	Dinamo Tbilisi	78	Samtredia	74	Kolkheti 1913 Poti	63	Dinamo Tbilisi	1-0	Dinamo Batumi
1996	Dinamo Tbilisi	79	Margveti Zestafoni	68	Kolkheti 1913 Poti	68	Dinamo Tbilisi	1-0	Dinamo Batumi
1997	Dinamo Tbilisi	81	Kolkheti 1913 Poti	64	Dinamo Batumi	62	Dinamo Tbilisi	1-0	Dinamo Batumi
1998	Dinamo Tbilisi	71	Dinamo Batumi	61	Kolkheti 1913 Poti	57	Dinamo Batumi	2-1	Dinamo Tbilisi
1999	Dinamo Tbilisi	77	Torpedo Kutaisi	67	Lokomotivi Tbilisi	64	Torpedo Kutaisi	0-0 4-2p	Samgurali
2000	Torpedo Kutaisi	46	WIT Georgia Tbilisi	41	Dinamo Tbilisi	41	Lokomotivi Tbilisi	0-0 4-2p	Torpedo Kutaisi
2001	Torpedo Kutaisi	44	Lokomotivi Tbilisi	41	Dinamo Tbilisi	38	Torpedo Kutaisi	0-0 4-3p	Lokomotivi Tbilisi
2002	Torpedo Kutaisi	48	Lokomotivi Tbilisi	47	Dinamo Tbilisi	44	Lokomotivi Tbilisi	2-0	Torpedo Kutaisi
2003	Dinamo Tbilisi	48	Torpedo Kutaisi	46	WIT Georgia Tbilisi	41	Dinamo Tbilisi	3-1	Sioni Bolnisi
2004	WIT Georgia Tbilisi	41	Sioni Bolnisi	41	Dinamo Tbilisi	40	Dinamo Tbilisi	2-1	Torpedo Kutaisi
2005	Dinamo Tbilisi	75	Torpedo Kutaisi	70	FC Tbilisi	69	Lokomotivi Tbilisi	2-0	FC Zestafoni
2006	Sioni Bolnisi	73	WIT Georgia Tbilisi	68	Dinamo Tbilisi	64	Ameri Tbilisi	2-2 4-3p	FC Zestafoni
2007	Olimpi Rustavi	63	Dinamo Tbilisi	62	Ameri Tbilisi	57	Ameri Tbilisi	1-0	FC Zestafoni
2008	Dinamo Tbilisi	70	WIT Georgia Tbilisi	60	FC Zestafoni	59	FC Zestafoni	2-1	Ameri Tbilisi

GEORGIA 2007–08

UMAGLESI LIGA

	PI	W	D	L	F	A	Pts	Dinamo	WIT Georgia	Zestafoni	Olimpi	Ameri	Meskheti	Mglebi	Sioni	Borjomi	Lokomotivi	Spartaki	Merani	Batumi	Dila Gori
Dinamo Tbilisi †	26	23	1	2	67	18	70		0-1	2-0	0-0	2-1	5-1	1-0	3-0	4-2	6-5	2-1	3-0	7-0	5-0
WIT Georgia Tbilisi ‡	26	19	3	4	45	14	60	0-0		2-1	2-0	0-1	3-0	2-1	4-0	1-2	1-0	1-0	3-0	4-1	2-0
FC Zestafoni ‡	26	18	5	3	56	16	59	0-1	1-1		2-1	3-1	4-1	2-0	3-1	1-0	5-0	2-0	6-1	4-0	5-0
Olimpi Rustavi	26	16	4	6	26	16	52	0-2	0-1	0-3		1-0	0-0	2-1	1-0	1-0	1-0	1-0	2-0	1-0	1-0
Ameri Tbilisi	26	15	3	8	48	27	48	0-2	0-3	1-2	2-1		0-0	5-0	2-0	3-2	1-1	2-0	7-0	4-1	3-2
Meskheti Akhaltsikhe	26	11	6	9	29	30	39	0-2	2-0	0-2	0-0	1-2		1-0	2-2	2-0	0-0	0-0	2-1	3-2	2-0
Mglebi Zugdidi	26	10	3	13	27	33	33	1-2	0-3	0-0	0-2	0-1	1-0		1-0	4-2	0-0	2-1	1-0	1-0	5-0
Sioni Bolnisi	26	9	5	12	34	35	32	1-2	3-1	0-2	1-2	0-0	1-0	3-1		0-1	0-3	1-1	5-0	1-0	5-1
FC Borjomi	26	9	4	13	32	39	31	1-2	1-2	0-2	0-0	3-0	2-0	4-3	2-5		2-1	2-1	1-0	1-2	3-2
Lokomotivi Tbilisi	26	7	6	13	27	35	27	1-2	0-1	1-1	0-1	2-1	2-3	0-1	1-0	1-0		2-2	0-2	4-1	1-0
Spartaki Tskhinvali	26	5	8	13	15	28	23	0-3	0-0	2-2	0-2	0-1	0-2	0-0	0-2	0-0	0-2		1-0	0-1	3-0
Merani Tbilisi	26	6	1	19	15	54	19	0-2	0-3	0-1	0-1	1-5	0-4	0-1	1-1	1-0	0-1	0-1		2-1	1-0
Dinamo Batumi	26	4	4	18	16	51	16	1-4	0-3	0-0	0-1	0-3	1-2	2-0	1-1	1-1	1-0	0-1	0-2		1-2
Dila Gori	26	1	5	20	12	53	8	0-2	0-1	1-2	1-1	0-2	0-1	1-3	0-1	0-0	1-0	0-0	2-3	1-0	

10/08/2007 - 20/05/2008 • † Qualified for the UEFA Champions League • ‡ Qualified for the UEFA Cup • Matches in bold were awarded
Play-off: Spartaki Tskhinvali 1-0 FC Gagra. Spartaki remain in the Umaglesi Liga • Top scorer: Mikheil Khutsishvili, Dinamo Tbilisi 16

GEORGIA 2007–08 PIRVELI LIGA (2) EAST

	PI	W	D	L	F	A	Pts
FC Gagra	27	16	6	5	59	36	54
Dinamo-2 Tbilisi	27	14	7	6	41	24	49
WIT Georgia-2 Tbilisi	27	14	6	7	41	21	48
Meshakre Agara	27	13	9	5	34	22	48
Chikhura Sachkhere	27	12	7	8	40	37	43
Olimpi-2 Rustavi	27	9	8	10	35	41	35
Kakheti Telavi	27	10	4	13	38	41	34
Ameri-2 Tbilisi	27	9	2	16	42	44	29
Olimpiki Tbilisi	27	7	4	16	38	52	25
Merani-2 Tbilisi	27	1	7	19	20	70	10

19/08/2007 - 16/05/2008

GEORGIA 2007–08 PIRVELI LIGA (2) EAST

	PI	W	D	L	F	A	Pts
Magaroeli Chiatura	27	21	4	2	56	17	69
Meshakhte Tqibuli	27	14	2	11	39	41	44
Merani Martvili	27	13	5	9	36	25	44
FC Zestafoni-2	27	12	4	11	39	28	40
Kolkheti Poti	27	11	7	9	36	33	40
Torpedo Kutaisi	27	11	6	10	38	31	39
Kolkheti Khobi	27	10	8	9	35	27	38
FC Samtredia	27	9	5	13	35	51	32
Universiteti Kutaisi	27	9	3	15	24	29	30
Fazisi Racha	27	2	2	23	17	73	8

18/08/2007 - 16/05/2008

Pirveli Liga Championship
Magharoeli Chiatura   2-2 4-1p   FC Gagra

GEORGIAN CUP 2007–08

Group Stage

Group A	Pts
Ameri Tbilisi	15
Spartaki Tskhinvali	12
Meskheti Akhaltsikhe	9
Torpedo Kutaisi	0

Group B	Pts
Dinamo Tbilisi	13
Magaroeli Chiatura	11
WIT Georgia Tbilisi	10
Lokomotivi Tbilisi	0

Group C	Pts
FC Borjomi	12
Olimpi Rustavi	10
Dinamo Batumi	7
Merani Tbilisi	5

Group D	Pts
FC Zestafoni	13
Dila Gori	11
Mglebi Zugdidi	10
Kakheti Telavi	0

Quarter–finals

FC Zestafoni	1	1
Olimpi Rustavi *	0	0

Spartaki Tskhinvali *	0	1
Dinamo Tbilisi	0	2

FC Borjomi	2	3
Dila Gori *	3	1

Magaroeli Chiatura *	1	0
Ameri Tbilisi	2	4

Semi–finals

FC Zestafoni	1	1
Dinamo Tbilisi *	1	0

FC Borjomi	1	1
Ameri Tbilisi *	4	1

Final

FC Zestafoni ‡	2
Ameri Tbilisi	1

CUP FINAL

16-05-2008

Scorers - Roin Oniani [57], Beka Gotsiridze [62] for Zestafoni; Dmitri Tatanashvili [80] for Ameri

* Home team in the first leg • ‡ Qualified for the UEFA Cup

GER – GERMANY

NATIONAL TEAM RECORD
JULY 10TH 2006 TO JULY 12TH 2010

PL	W	D	L	F	A	%
11	9	1	1	37	6	86.3

The changes in German football set in motion by Jurgen Klinsmann when he was appointed national team boss in 2004, gathered pace at Euro 2008 when his successor Joachim Löw took the team to the final of a tournament in which no-one had really expected them to do well. With Michael Ballack as perhaps the only true world class player, this German team may not bear close scrutiny with the great teams of the past, but where the national team has succeeded - at both the World Cup and at Euro 2008 - is in connecting with the nation as a whole, beyond the normal football supporter. 500,000 fans watched the final against Spain in the 'Fan Mile' in Berlin, and 300,000 turned out the following day to welcome the team home, despite their 1-0 defeat. Löw may have been disappointed but he admitted that Germany had been beaten by the better team. He also said that the team had had 'a lot of fun' during the tournament. If ever a phrase signalled a sea change in attitude! It showed in their football too, with 10 goals scored in four victories, the best of which was perhaps the 3-2 quarter-final win over Portugal, one of the pre-tournament favourites. With a stronger defence, the Germans could perhaps start to think about a first international title

INTERNATIONAL HONOURS

FIFA World Cup 1954 1974 1990   **FIFA Women's World Cup** 2003 2007

Olympic Gold 1976 (GDR)   **FIFA World Youth Championship** 1981   **FIFA Women's U-19 Championship** 2004

UEFA European Championship 1972 1980 1996   **UEFA Women's European Championship** 1989 1991 1995 1997 2001 2005

UEFA U-19 Championship 1981 1986 (GDR)   **UEFA U-17 Championship** 1984 1992   **UEFA Women's U-19 Championship** 2000 2001 2002 2006

UEFA Champions League Bayern München 1974 1975 1976 2001, Hamburger SV 1983, Borussia Dortmund 1997

since 1996. Klinsmann has even been tempted out of retirement with Bayern Munich hoping he will have a similar talismanic effect on club football in Germany. The Bundesliga may be the best supported league in the world but it has lagged behind Spain and England in attracting the best players and in the search for international honours and it will be in the Champions League that Bayern will look to Klinsmann for success. Having missed on the 2007-08 tournament, Bayern made sure of qualification by winning both the Bundesliga and the DFB Cup - their fifth double since the start of the decade. The twin signings of the Italian Luca Toni, who finished as top scorer in the Bundesliga, and the Frenchman Franck Ribery, were the key to their success. Toni was also the top scorer in the UEFA Cup as Bayern just missed out on their first European final since 2001 after losing to Zenit St Petersburg in the semi-finals. Schalke also had a good European campaign, qualifying for the knock-out rounds for the first time where they beat Porto before going down to Barcelona in the quarter-finals. There was misery for fans in Nuremberg, however, when a year after winning the DFB Cup, 1.FC Nürnberg were relegated.

Deutscher Fussball-Bund (DFB)
Otto-Fleck-Schneise 6, Postfach 71 02 65, Frankfurt 60528, Germany
Tel +49 69 67880   Fax +49 69 6788266
info@dfb.de   www.dfb.de
President: ZWANZIGER Theo   General Secretary: NIERSBACH Wolfgang
Vice-President: KORFMACHER Hermann   Treasurer: SCHMIDT Horst R.   Media Officer: STENGER Harald
Men's Coach: LOEW Joachim   Women's Coach: NEID Silvia
DFB formed: 1900   UEFA: 1954   FIFA: 1904
White shirts with black trimmings, Black shorts, White socks or Red shirts with black trimmings, White shorts, White socks

RECENT INTERNATIONAL MATCHES PLAYED BY GERMANY

2006	Opponents	Score		Venue	Comp	Scorers	Att	Referee
16-08	Sweden	W	3-0	Gelsenkirchen	Fr	Schneider [4], Klose 2 [8 44]	53 000	Farina ITA
2-09	Republic of Ireland	W	1-0	Stuttgart	ECq	Podolski [57]	53 198	Medina Cantalejo ESP
6-09	San Marino	W	13-0	Serravalle	ECq	Podolski 4 [11 43 64 72], Schweinstiger 2 [28 47], Klose 2 [30 46+], Ballack [35], Hitzlsperger 2 [66 73], Friedrich.M [87], Schneider [90p]	5 090	Dereli TUR
7-10	Georgia	W	2-0	Rostock	Fr	Schweinsteiger [24], Ballack [67]	28 000	Lehner AUT
11-10	Slovakia	W	4-1	Bratislava	ECq	Podolski 2 [13 72], Ballack [25], Schweinsteiger [36]	27 580	Hauge NOR
15-11	Cyprus	D	1-1	Nicosia	ECq	Ballack [16]	12 300	Fröjdfeldt SWE
2007								
7-02	Switzerland	W	3-1	Dusseldorf	Fr	Kuranyi [7], Gomez [30], Frings [66]	51 333	Bossen NED
24-03	Czech Republic	W	2-1	Prague	ECq	Kuranyi 2 [42 62]	17 821	Rosetti ITA
28-03	Denmark	L	0-1	Duisburg	Fr		31 500	Webb ENG
2-06	San Marino	W	6-0	Nuremberg	ECq	Kuranyi [45], Jansen [52], Frings [56p], Gómez 2 [63 65], Fritz [67]	43 967	Asumaa FIN
6-06	Slovakia	W	2-1	Hamburg	ECq	Durica OG [10], Hitzlsperger [43]	51 600	Benquerença POR
22-08	England	W	2-1	London	Fr	Kuranyi [26], Pander [40]	86 133	Busacca SUI
8-09	Wales	W	2-0	Cardiff	ECq	Klose 2 [6 60]	27 889	Mejuto Gonzalez ESP
12-09	Romania	W	3-1	Cologne	Fr	Schneider [42], Odonkor [65], Podolski [82]	44 500	Rizzoli ITA
13-10	Republic of Ireland	D	0-0	Dublin	ECq		67 495	Hansson SWE
17-10	Czech Republic	L	0-3	Munich	ECq		66 445	Webb ENG
17-11	Cyprus	W	4-0	Hanover	ECq	Fritz [2], Klose [20], Podolski [53], Hitzlsperger [82]	45 016	Rasmussen DEN
21-11	Wales	D	0-0	Frankfurt	ECq		49 262	Balaj ROU
2008								
6-02	Austria	W	3-0	Vienna	Fr	Hitzlsperger [53], Klose [63], Gomez [80]	48 500	Dondarini ITA
26-03	Switzerland	W	4-0	Basel	Fr	Klose [23], Gomez 2 [61 67], Podolski [89]	38 500	Braamhaar NED
27-05	Belarus	D	2-2	Kaiserslautern	Fr	Klose [10], Korytko OG [20]	47 258	Ceferin SVN
31-05	Serbia	W	2-1	Gelsenkirchen	Fr	Neuville [74], Ballack [82]	53 951	Fautrel FRA
8-06	Poland	W	2-0	Klagenfurt	ECr1	Podolski 2 [20 72]	30 461	Ovrebø NOR
12-06	Croatia	L	1-2	Klagenfurt	ECr1	Podolski [79]	30 461	De Bleeckere BEL
16-06	Austria	W	1-0	Vienna	ECr1	Ballack [49]	51 428	Mejuto Gonzalez ESP
19-06	Portugal	W	3-2	Basel	ECqf	Schweinsteiger [22], Klose [26], Ballack [61]	39 374	Fröjdfeldt SWE
25-06	Turkey	W	3-2	Basel	ECsf	Schweinsteiger [26], Klose [79], Lahm [90]	39 378	Busacca SUI
29-06	Spain	L	0-1	Vienna	ECf		51 425	Rosetti ITA

Fr = Friendly match • EC = UEFA EURO 2008 • WC = FIFA World Cup
q = qualifier • r1 = first round group • qf = quarter-final • sf = semi-final • f = final

GERMANY NATIONAL TEAM PLAYERS

	Player		Ap	G	Club	Date of Birth		Player		Ap	G	Club	Date of Birth
1	Jens Lehmann	GK	61	0	Arsenal	10 11 1969	12	Robert Enke	GK	1	0	Hannover 96	24 08 1977
2	Marcell Jansen	DF	27	1	Bayern München	4 11 1985	13	Michael Ballack	MF	87	38	Chelsea	26 09 1976
3	Arne Friedrich	DF	61	0	Hertha Berlin	29 05 1979	14	Piotr Trochowski	MF	12	0	Hamburger SV	22 03 1984
4	Clemens Fritz	DF	18	2	Werder Bremen	7 12 1980	15	Thomas Hitzlsperger	MF	38	5	VfB Stuttgart	5 04 1982
5	Heiko Westermann	DF	3	0	Schalke 04	14 08 1983	16	Philipp Lahm	DF	47	3	Bayern München	11 11 1983
6	Simon Rolfes	MF	12	0	B. Leverkusen	21 01 1982	17	Per Mertesacker	DF	49	1	Werder Bremen	29 09 1984
7	Bastian Schweinsteiger	MF	56	15	Bayern München	1 08 1984	18	Tim Borowski	MF	33	2	Werder Bremen	2 05 1980
8	Torsten Frings	MF	77	10	Werder Bremen	22 11 1976	19	David Odonkor	FW	16	1	Real Betis	21 02 1984
9	Mario Gómez	FW	14	6	VfB Stuttgart	10 07 1985	20	Lukas Podolski	FW	54	28	Bayern München	4 06 1985
10	Oliver Neuville	FW	69	10	Bor. M'gladbach	1 05 1973	21	Christoph Metzelder	DF	47	0	Real Madrid	5 11 1980
11	Miroslav Klose	FW	81	41	Bayern München	9 06 1978	22	Kevin Kuranyi	FW	50	19	Schalke 04	2 03 1982
							23	René Adler	GK	0	0	B. Leverkusen	15 01 1985

Germany's squad for Euro 2008

GERMANY NATIONAL TEAM RECORDS AND RECORD SEQUENCES

Records			Sequence records					
Victory	16-0	RUS 1912	Wins	12	1979-1980	Clean sheets	6	1966
Defeat	0-9	ENG 1909	Defeats	7	1912-1913	Goals scored	33	1940-1952
Player Caps	150	Lothar Matthäus	Undefeated	23	1978-1980	Without goal	3	1985
Player Goals	68	Gerd Müller	Without win	10	1912-1920	Goals against	15	1910-1912

FEDERAL REPUBLIC OF GERMANY; BUNDESREPUBLIK DEUTSCHLAND

Capital	Berlin	Language	German			Independence	1871
Population	82 422 299	Area	357 021 km²	Density	230 per km²	% in cities	85%
GDP per cap	$27 600	Dailling code	+49	Internet	.de	GMT +/-	+1

The major metropolitan areas are: Rhein-Ruhr 11 805; Berlin 4 025; Hamburg 3 279; Rhein-Mann 3 123; Stuttgart 2 344; München 2 324

MAJOR CITIES/TOWNS

		Population '000
1	Berlin	3 370
2	Hamburg	1 748
3	Munich/München	1 281
4	Cologne/Köln	958
5	Frankfurt	642
6	Essen	598
7	Stuttgart	590
8	Dortmund	585
9	Düsseldorf	573
10	Bremen	548
11	Hanover	513
12	Leipzig	504
13	Duisburg	500
14	Nuremberg	493
15	Dresden	492
16	Bochum	382
17	Bielefeld	337
18	Bonn	317
19	Karlsruhe	285
20	Aachen	280
21	Gelsenkirchen	265
22	Mönchengladbach	260
23	Leverkusen	164
24	Wolfsburg	123

MEDALS TABLE

		Overall			League			Cup			Europe			City	Stadium	Cap'ty	DoF
		G	S	B	G	S	B	G	S	B	G	S	B				
1	Bayern München	41	12	15	21	7	4	14	2		6	3	11	Munich	Allianz-Arena	69 901	1900
2	1.FC Nürnberg	14	5	1	9	3		5	2				1	Nuremburg	Frankenstadion	46 780	1900
3	Schalke 04	12	16	4	7	9	2	4	7		1		2	Gelsenkirchen	Veltins Arena	61 524	1904
4	Hamburger SV	11	15	4	6	8	2	3	4		2	3	2	Hamburg	HSH Nordbank Arena	55 000	1887
5	Werder Bremen	10	10	9	4	7	5	5	3		1		4	Bremen	Weserstadion	42 466	1899
6	Borussia Dortmund	10	8	8	6	4	5	2	2		2	2	3	Dortmund	Signal Iduna Park	80 700	1909
	B. Mönchengladbach	10	7	8	5	2	5	3	2		2	3	3	Mönchengladbach	Borussia-Park	54 019	1900
8	VfB Stuttgart	9	9	5	6	4	3	3	3			2	2	Stuttgart	Gottlieb-Daimler	55 875	1893
9	1.FC Köln	7	15	9	3	8	2	4	6		1		7	Cologne	Rhein Energy Stadion	50 997	1948
10	1.FC Kaiserslautern	6	9	4	4	4	2	2	5				2	Kaiserslautern	Fritz-Walter-Stadion	48 500	1900
11	Eintracht Frankfurt	6	4	7	1	1	5	4	2		1	1	2	Frankfurt	Commerzbank-Arena	51 052	1899
12	Lokomotive Leipzig (VfB)	4	2		3	2		1						Leipzig	Bruno-Plache-Stadion	15 600	1893
13	Dresdner SC	4	1		2	1		2						Dresden	Heinz-Steyer-Stadion	24 000	1898-1950
14	Fortuna Düsseldorf	3	7	2	1	1	2	2	5		1			Düsseldorf	LTU Arena	51 500	1895
15	Karlsruher SC	3	3	1	1	1		2	2				1	Karlsruhe	Wildparstadion	33 800	1894
16	TSV München 1860	3	3		1	2		2					1	Munich	Allianz-Arena	69 901	1860
17	SpVgg Fürth	3	1		3	1								Fürth	Playmobil Stadion	15 500	1903
18	Hannover 96	3			2			1						Hanover	AWD Arena	49 000	1896
19	Hertha BSC Berlin	2	7	5	2	5	4		2				1	Berlin	Olympiastadion	74 400	1892
20	Bayer 04 Leverkusen	2	6	4		4	3	1	1		1	1	1	Leverkusen	BayArena	22 500	1904

RECENT LEAGUE AND CUP RECORD

	Championship						Cup		
Year	Champions	Pts	Runners-up	Pts	Third	Pts	Winners	Score	Runners-up
1998	1.FC Kaiserslautern	68	Bayern München	66	Bayer Leverkusen	55	Bayern München	2-1	MSV Duisberg
1999	Bayern München	78	Bayer Leverkusen	63	Hertha BSC Berlin	62	Werder Bremen	1-1 5-4p	Bayern München
2000	Bayern München	73	Bayer Leverkusen	73	Hamburger SV	59	Bayern München	3-0	Werder Bremen
2001	Bayern München	63	Schalke 04	62	Borussia Dortmund	58	Schalke 04	2-0	1.FC Union Berlin
2002	Borussia Dortmund	70	Bayer Leverkusen	69	Bayern München	68	Schalke 04	4-2	Bayer Leverkusen
2003	Bayern München	75	VfB Stuttgart	59	Borussia Dortmund	58	Bayern München	3-1	1.FC Kaiserslautern
2004	Werder Bremen	74	Bayern München	68	Bayer Leverkusen	65	Werder Bremen	3-2	Alemannia Aachen
2005	Bayern München	77	Schalke 04	63	Werder Bremen	59	Bayern München	2-1	Schalke 04
2006	Bayern München	75	Werder Bremen	70	Hamburger SV	68	Bayern München	1-0	Eintracht Frankfurt
2007	VfB Stuttgart	70	Schalke 04	68	Werder Bremen	66	1.FC Nürnberg	3-2	VfB Stuttgart
2008	Bayern München	76	Werder Bremen	66	Schalke 04	64	Bayern München	2-1	Borussia Dortmund

GERMANY 2007–08

1. BUNDESLIGA

1. BUNDESLIGA	Pl	W	D	L	F	A	Pts	Bayern	Werder Bremen	Schalke 04	Hamburger SV	VfL Wolfsburg	VfB Stuttgart	Leverkusen	Hannover 96	Eint. Frankfurt	Hertha Berlin	Karlsruher SC	VfL Bochum	Bor. Dortmund	Energie Cottbus	Arm Bielefeld	1.FC Nürnberg	Hansa Rostock	MSV Duisburg
Bayern München †	34	22	10	2	68	21	76		1-1	1-1	1-1	2-1	4-1	2-1	3-0	0-0	4-1	2-0	3-1	5-0	5-0	2-0	3-0	3-0	0-0
Werder Bremen †	34	20	6	8	75	45	66	0-4		5-1	2-1	0-1	4-1	5-2	6-1	2-1	3-2	4-0	1-2	2-0	2-0	8-1	2-0	1-0	1-2
Schalke 04 †	34	18	10	6	55	32	64	0-1	1-1		1-1	1-2	4-1	1-1	1-1	1-0	1-0	0-2	1-0	4-1	5-0	3-0	2-1	1-0	2-1
Hamburger SV ‡	34	14	12	8	47	26	54	1-1	0-1	0-1		2-2	4-1	1-0	1-1	4-1	2-1	7-0	3-0	1-0	0-0	1-1	1-0	2-0	0-1
VfL Wolfsburg ‡	34	15	9	10	58	46	54	0-0	1-1	1-1	1-1		4-0	1-2	3-2	2-2	0-0	1-2	0-1	4-0	3-0	1-3	3-1	1-0	2-1
VfB Stuttgart	34	16	4	14	57	57	52	3-1	6-3	2-2	1-0	3-1		1-0	0-2	4-1	1-3	3-1	1-0	1-2	3-0	2-2	3-0	4-1	1-0
Bayer Leverkusen	34	15	6	13	57	40	51	0-1	0-1	1-0	1-1	2-2	3-0		2-0	0-2	1-2	3-0	2-0	2-2	0-0	4-0	4-1	3-0	4-1
Hannover 96	34	13	10	11	54	56	49	0-3	4-3	2-3	0-1	2-2	0-0	0-3		2-1	2-2	2-2	3-2	2-1	4-0	2-2	2-1	3-0	2-1
Eintracht Frankfurt	34	12	10	12	43	50	46	1-3	1-0	2-2	2-1	2-3	1-4	2-1	0-0		1-0	0-1	1-1	1-1	2-1	2-1	1-3	1-0	4-2
Hertha BSC Berlin ‡	34	12	8	14	39	44	44	0-0	1-2	1-2	0-0	2-1	3-1	0-3	1-0	0-3		3-1	2-0	3-2	0-0	1-0	1-0	1-3	2-0
Karlsruher SC	34	11	10	13	38	53	43	1-4	3-3	0-0	1-1	3-2	1-0	2-2	1-2	0-1	2-1		1-3	3-1	1-1	0-0	2-0	1-2	1-0
VfL Bochum	34	10	11	13	48	54	41	1-2	2-2	0-3	2-1	5-3	1-1	2-0	2-1	0-0	1-1	2-2		3-3	3-3	3-0	3-3	1-2	1-1
Borussia Dortmund ‡	34	10	10	14	50	62	40	0-0	3-0	2-3	0-3	2-4	3-2	2-1	1-3	1-1	1-1	2-1			3-0	6-1	0-0	1-0	1-3
Energie Cottbus	34	9	9	16	35	56	36	2-0	0-2	1-0	2-0	1-2	0-1	2-3	5-1	2-2	2-1	2-0	1-2	0-2		1-2	1-1	2-1	1-2
Arminia Bielefeld	34	8	10	16	35	60	34	0-1	1-1	0-2	0-1	0-1	2-0	1-0	0-2	2-2	2-0	1-0	2-0	2-2	1-1		3-1	4-2	0-2
1.FC Nürnberg	34	7	10	17	35	51	31	1-1	0-1	0-2	0-0	1-0	0-1	1-2	2-2	5-1	2-1	0-2	1-1	0-1	1-2	2-2		1-1	2-0
Hansa Rostock	34	8	6	20	30	52	30	1-2	1-2	1-1	1-3	0-1	2-1	1-2	0-3	1-0	0-0	0-0	2-0	0-1	3-2	1-1	1-2		2-0
MSV Duisburg	34	8	5	21	36	55	29	2-3	1-3	0-2	0-1	1-3	2-3	3-2	1-1	0-1	1-2	0-1	0-2	3-3	0-1	3-0	1-0	1-0	

10/08/2007 - 17/05/2008 • † Qualified for the UEFA Champions League • ‡ Qualified for the UEFA Cup
Top scorers: Luca Toni, Bayern 24; Mario Gomez, Stuttgart 19; Kevin Kuranyi, Schalke 15; Ivica Olic, Hamburg 14; Markus Rosenberg, Werder 14; Theofanis Gekas, Leverkusen 13; Mladen Petric, Dortmund 13; Marko Pantelic, Hertha 13; Stanislav Sestak, Bochum 13; Diego, Werder 13

GERMANY 2007–08

2. BUNDESLIGA (2)

2. BUNDESLIGA (2)	Pl	W	D	L	F	A	Pts	Gladbach	Hoffenheim	1.FC Köln	1.FSV Mainz	SC Freiburg	Greuther Fürth	Alemannia	Wehen	St Pauli	TuS Koblenz	TSV 1860	VfL Osnabrück	Kaiserslautern	FC Augsburg	Kick. Offenbach	Erzgebirge Aue	SC Paderborn	Carl Zeiss Jena
Bor. Mönchengladbach	34	18	12	4	71	38	66		0-0	2-2	0-1	2-3	3-0	2-1	3-0	1-0	1-0	2-2	2-1	1-1	4-2	3-0	2-0	1-1	2-1
TSG Hoffenheim	34	17	9	8	60	40	60	4-2		0-2	1-0	2-0	5-0	1-2	2-3	1-1	3-1	0-3	3-1	1-0	2-0	2-2	1-0	1-0	5-0
1.FC Köln	34	17	9	8	62	44	60	1-1	3-1		2-0	1-3	0-0	0-1	2-1	1-1	1-0	0-0	2-1	3-0	4-1	3-2	2-1	4-3	
1.FSV Mainz	34	16	10	8	62	36	58	4-1	1-1	1-0		1-1	1-2	0-5	5-1	4-1	3-0	4-1	2-1	1-1	1-0	1-0	4-1	6-1	2-2
SC Freiburg	34	15	10	9	49	44	55	1-3	3-2	1-0	1-1		3-2	1-0	0-2	2-0	4-2	2-2	1-1	1-0	1-0	0-1	1-0	2-0	
SpVgg Greuther Fürth	34	14	10	10	53	47	52	1-3	4-1	2-2	3-0	1-1		2-0	1-1	2-1	0-1	3-1	6-3	0-1	3-2	2-1	0-0	1-1	2-2
Alemannia Aachen	34	14	9	11	49	44	51	1-1	2-2	3-2	0-3	2-0	2-5		2-3	2-2	1-3	0-0	3-0	2-1	3-0	4-0	1-0	3-1	2-2
SV Wehen	34	11	11	12	47	53	44	1-1	0-2	4-3	1-3	2-2	1-3	3-0		1-3	0-2	0-0	1-0	0-2	2-1	3-1	1-3	1-1	5-1
FC St Pauli	34	11	9	14	47	53	42	0-3	3-1	0-2	1-0	5-0	1-1	0-2	1-2		1-0	0-0	2-1	3-4	2-0	3-1	4-2	2-1	2-2
TuS Koblenz	34	12	11	11	46	47	41	0-5	2-2	1-2	1-1	3-2	3-0	0-0	2-0	1-1		3-1	1-0	2-2	2-1	1-1	2-2	0-0	2-0
TSV 1860 München	34	9	14	11	42	45	41	0-0	0-1	1-1	1-1	0-3	0-0	2-1	2-1	2-2			1-3	1-0	3-3	5-0	0-0		1-2
VfL Osnabrück	34	10	10	14	43	54	40	2-2	0-3	2-1	0-0	2-0	2-2	0-2	3-1	2-0	3-0			2-0	0-2	2-0	2-1	0-1	1-1
1.FC Kaiserslautern	34	9	12	13	37	37	39	1-1	0-2	3-0	0-0	0-0	2-1	0-2	0-2	2-3	1-2	3-0			2-0	1-1	2-0	2-1	0-0
FC Augsburg	34	10	8	16	39	51	38	0-2	2-2	1-3	2-1	1-1	3-0	1-0	5-1	1-0	2-6	2-0	0-0			1-1	1-1	0-1	1-1
Kickers Offenbach	34	9	11	14	38	60	38	1-7	1-1	1-3	2-0	0-0	1-2	1-0	0-4	1-1	2-0	3-3	0-0	1-0			3-2	2-1	2-1
Erzgebirge Aue	34	7	11	16	49	57	32	2-3	2-2	3-3	3-3	2-2	1-1	2-1	3-0	0-0	0-0	1-1	3-1	0-3	0-1			6-0	5-0
SC Paderborn	34	6	13	15	33	54	31	2-3	0-2	2-2	1-1	3-2	1-0	0-1	1-1	4-3	2-1	3-1	1-3	0-0	1-1	0-2	0-1		2-2
Carl Zeiss Jena	34	6	11	17	45	68	29	2-2	0-1	1-3	1-2	1-2	1-0	2-3	2-2	0-1	1-2	0-2	1-1	2-2	1-2	2-0	2-1	3-0	

10/08/2007 - 18/05/2008 • Top scorers: Milivoje Novakovic, Köln 20; Rob Friend, Mönchengladbach 18; Patrick Helmes, Köln 17; Félix Borja, Mainz 16; Thomas Reichenberger, Osnabrück 16; Oliver Neuville, Mönchengladbach 15

GERMANY 2007-08

REGIONALLIGA NORD (3)

Team	Pl	W	D	L	F	A	Pts	Ahlen	Oberh.	D'dorf	Union	Brem-2	Wupp.	Erfurt	Dresden	Emden	B'schw.	Magdeb.	Essen	Dort-2	Cott-2	Babels.	Lübeck	Hamb-2	Verl	Wolfs-2
Rot-Weiss Ahlen	36	19	10	7	73	41	67		1-3	5-1	3-1	4-2	2-5	1-2	1-2	2-0	0-1	3-1	2-0	1-1	1-0	3-0	3-0	3-0	4-1	1-1
Rot-Weiß Oberhausen	36	19	9	8	64	32	66	0-0		2-2	3-0	1-2	0-1	0-0	0-1	3-2	2-0	2-1	1-0	3-1	0-0	3-2	3-0	5-1	4-2	5-0
Fortuna Düsseldorf	36	19	7	10	49	29	64	1-1	3-0		0-1	2-0	2-0	2-0	1-2	0-2	1-1	0-2	0-0	4-0	3-0	2-0	0-1	1-0	3-0	3-0
1.FC Union Berlin	36	17	9	10	67	49	60	4-4	0-3	0-1		2-0	1-1	1-1	4-2	1-0	2-2	1-2	2-2	2-1	0-1	1-1	4-3	2-1	0-0	4-0
Werder Bremen-2	36	18	5	13	52	44	59	0-0	3-2	2-0	1-0		2-1	1-2	2-1	1-1	3-0	0-4	3-1	3-1	0-0	3-2	2-0	0-1	1-0	7-2
Wuppertaler SV	36	17	7	12	60	50	58	0-4	2-0	0-1	4-3	0-2		3-0	1-1	0-0	1-1	1-2	2-2	1-1	4-3	4-0	2-1	0-2	1-0	7-2
Rot-Weiß Erfurt	36	15	11	10	70	46	56	6-3	1-2	0-4	2-0	3-1	5-1		2-2	3-0	2-2	4-1	4-0	0-0	0-1	1-1	1-1	3-1	3-0	5-0
1.FC Dynamo Dresden	36	15	10	11	45	39	55	1-3	0-2	0-0	0-1	0-2	3-0	2-2		2-1	1-1	1-0	1-0	0-0	1-0	3-2	0-0	4-1	2-0	3-0
BSV Kickers Emden	36	16	6	14	43	39	54	1-0	2-0	1-2	1-0	2-1	1-2	1-0	2-1		0-1	1-0	0-0	4-1	1-0	3-1	0-2	3-2	2-0	1-2
Eint. Braunschweig	36	13	14	9	55	50	53	0-2	2-1	1-1	3-5	0-0	1-4	3-2	3-2	0-1		1-1	2-1	2-0	5-0	1-3	3-3	2-1	3-2	3-1
1.FC Magdeburg	36	14	11	11	39	37	53	2-2	0-0	1-0	1-1	1-1	2-0	3-3	1-0	1-3	1-1		0-1	2-1	1-1	1-1	3-0	2-0	2-0	2-0
Rot-Weiss Essen	36	14	9	13	42	36	51	0-2	1-4	0-0	0-3	3-0	1-0	3-2	1-1	0-1	0-0	2-0		0-0	0-1	1-2	0-1	2-1	2-0	3-0
Borussia Dortmund-2	36	12	12	12	35	37	48	0-2	0-0	0-1	1-1	1-1	1-1	2-0	3-2	1-0	0-1	0-0			2-0	1-0	3-1	1-0	1-2	
Energie Cottbus-2	36	12	8	16	31	44	44	1-1	0-0	0-1	0-2	1-0	0-1	2-1	1-1	4-2	3-2	2-1	1-2	0-3		0-1	1-1	2-0	0-1	0-0
SV Babelsberg 03	36	8	10	18	33	53	34	1-3	1-4	3-0	0-3	1-2	1-0	1-1	0-1	1-1	1-2	0-0	1-3	0-0	0-1		1-0	1-3	0-1	3-2
VfB Lübeck	36	9	7	20	32	58	34	0-2	0-0	3-1	3-7	3-0	0-2	0-3	1-0	2-1	0-0	1-1	2-0	4-0	1-1	1-0		3-1	0-3	0-1
Hamburger SV-2	36	8	9	19	36	58	33	1-1	0-0	0-3	0-2	0-2	2-3	2-1	2-0	0-0	1-1	0-0	0-3	0-0	2-0	0-3	1-1		1-1	3-0
SC Verl	36	9	5	22	32	55	32	2-2	1-2	1-2	2-3	0-3	0-3	0-1	1-1	0-0	0-2	0-1	1-0	1-0	0-1	1-3	1-0	0-2		5-1
VfL Wolfsburg-2	36	5	7	24	20	81	22	0-1	0-4	0-1	0-3	1-0	1-2	0-3	0-2	0-0	3-2	0-1	0-3	0-1	1-1	0-0	0-4	2-2	0-3	

27/07/2007 - 31/05/2008

Note: From the start of the 2008-09 season there will be a new 3. Liga consisting of the four relegated teams from the 2.Bundesliga and the teams placed from third to tenth in the Regionalliga Nord and Regionalliga Süd. The new fourth tier of German football will now consist of the Regionalliga Nord, the Regionalliga Süd and the Regionalliga West

GERMANY 2007-08

REGIONALLIGA SUD (3)

Team	Pl	W	D	L	F	A	Pts	Frankf.	Ingol.	Stutt-2	Aalen	Sandh.	Unterh.	Burgh.	Bayern-2	Regensb.	St'g.Kick	Siegen	Reutl.	1860-2	Kassel	Elversb.	Karls-2	Pfull.	Oggersh.
FSV Frankfurt	34	17	11	6	57	31	62		3-1	1-1	2-0	0-2	1-0	1-1	2-2	1-3	0-0	1-1	2-2	1-2	0-0	2-0	1-1	3-2	2-0
FC Ingolstadt 04	34	18	8	8	50	36	62	0-5		3-1	2-1	0-0	2-0	1-1	1-0	0-1	2-3	2-2	2-0	2-1	3-0	1-1	1-1	2-0	2-1
VfB Stuttgart-2	34	17	8	9	52	30	59	1-1	0-1		2-3	4-0	2-3	1-1	1-0	1-2	1-0	2-2	0-1	1-2	1-0	2-0	2-1	2-0	2-0
VfR Aalen	34	16	9	9	64	45	57	1-0	4-0	1-2		3-1	0-0	2-2	1-1	2-5	1-0	2-1	5-1	2-0	1-2	2-1	2-0	2-2	5-0
SV Sandhausen	34	17	6	11	48	38	57	0-3	0-3	1-0	3-0		1-0	3-0	3-3	1-0	2-2	1-0	0-1	1-0	3-2	1-2	1-0	2-0	3-0
SpVgg Unterhaching	34	15	9	10	55	44	54	1-4	3-0	1-1	2-2	3-2		1-1	0-0	1-0	2-0	1-1	2-0	2-2	5-3	4-1	4-0	2-1	3-0
Wacker Burghausen	34	12	13	9	36	37	49	0-1	1-0	1-1	1-4	1-0	2-0		3-1	1-0	1-2	1-0	0-0	3-1	3-1	0-0	1-0	1-0	1-0
Bayern München-2	34	12	11	11	53	42	47	2-1	1-1	1-3	0-1	3-1	2-4	1-1		3-1	0-1	3-1	0-0	1-0	4-0	1-1	3-1	2-1	7-0
SSV Jahn Regensburg	34	14	5	15	40	48	47	0-2	1-3	0-3	1-1	2-1	2-1	1-2	2-0		1-1	0-1	3-1	0-2	1-0	0-0	2-2	1-4	1-0
Stuttgarter Kickers	34	11	12	11	38	35	45	1-1	0-1	1-1	5-1	1-2	2-0	1-1	0-1	1-3		1-1	1-1	1-2	0-2	0-0	2-0	2-0	1-0
Sportfreunde Siegen	34	10	15	9	35	37	45	0-1	0-1	0-2	1-1	1-2	3-1	1-0	1-1	1-3	1-1		2-1	1-0	1-1	0-0	1-1	1-0	4-2
SSV Reutlingen	34	10	14	10	45	46	44	0-1	2-0	0-2	1-1	3-1	2-2	1-1	2-1	2-0	3-1	1-1		1-4	0-0	4-0	1-1	0-4	3-1
TSV 1860 München-2	34	12	6	16	40	44	42	1-5	0-2	0-1	3-0	0-2	0-1	5-0	3-2	0-1	1-0	3-0	2-2		2-2	0-0	2-1	1-0	0-1
KSV Hessen Kassel	34	8	14	12	51	57	38	1-1	1-1	1-1	1-3	0-3	2-2	1-1	2-3	4-0	1-1	0-0	3-3	4-0		3-0	4-0	3-1	1-1
SV Elversberg	34	10	8	16	35	52	38	1-2	1-5	2-0	1-3	0-4	2-0	1-0	3-0	0-2	0-2	0-0	1-0	2-0	1-1		1-2	0-1	2-0
Karlsruher SC-2	34	8	13	13	33	45	37	1-3	1-1	0-5	1-1	1-1	0-1	0-1	0-0	2-1	0-0	2-1	6-1	3-1	1-1	1-1		1-1	1-0
SC Pfullendorf	34	8	10	16	33	41	34	2-0	0-3	0-1	1-0	0-0	2-1	1-1	0-0	1-1	1-2	0-0	1-1	0-1	1-0	5-2	3-1		3-2
FSV Oggersheim	34	2	6	26	17	74	12	1-3	0-1	0-2	0-6	0-0	1-2	0-2	0-4	1-2	1-2	0-1	3-3	1-1	1-0	0-4	0-1	0-0	

27/07/2007 - 31/05/2008

DFB POKAL 2007–08

First Round			Second Round		Third Round	
Bayern München	1	4p				
Wacker Burghausen *	1	3p	Bayern München *	3		
VfL Osnabruuck *	0		Borussia Mönchengladbach	1		
Borussia Mönchengladbach	1				Bayern München	5
Hertha BSC Berlin	3				Wuppertaler SV *	2
SpVgg Unterhaching *	0		Hertha BSC Berlin	0		
Erzgebirge Aue *	1	3p	Wuppertaler SV *	2		
Wuppertaler SV *	1	4p				
Alemannia Aachen	3					
1.FC Normannia Gmünd *	0		Alemannia Aachen *	3		
Dynamo Dresden *	0		VfL Bochum	2		
VfL Bochum	1				Alemannia Aachen *	2
FSV Mainz 05	6				TSV München 1860	3
Wormatia Worms *	1		FSV Mainz 05	1		
SC Verl *	0		TSV München 1860 *	2		
TSV München 1860	3					
Hamburger SV	5					
Holstein Kiel *	0		Hamburger SV *	3		
FC 08 Villingen *	1		SC Freiburg	1		
SC Freiburg	3				Hamburger SV	3
1.FC Kaiserslautern	4				Rot-Weiss Essen *	0
SV Wilhelmshaven *	0		1.FC Kaiserslautern	1		
Energie Cottbus	2	5p	Rot-Weiss Essen *	2		
Rot-Weiss Essen *	2	6p				
Schalke 04	9					
Eintracht Trier *	0		Schalke 04 *	2		
Rot-Weiß Ahlen *	1		Hannover 96	0		
Hannover 96	3				Schalke 04	1 3p
Karlsruher SC	2				VfL Wolfsburg *	1 5p
TSG Neustrelitz *	0		Karlsruher SC *	0		
Würzburger FV *	0		VfL Wolfsburg	1		
VfL Wolfsburg	4					
Carl Zeiss Jena	3					
1.FC Gera 03 *	0		Carl Zeiss Jena *	2 5p		
Victoria Hamburg *	0		1.FC Nürnberg	2 4p		
1.FC Nürnberg	6				Carl Zeiss Jena *	2
TuS Koblenz	3				Arminia Bielefeld	1
TSV Havelse *	0		TuS Koblenz *	1		
SV Seligenporten *	0		Arminia Bielefeld	2		
Arminia Bielefeld	2					
Werder Bremen II *	4					
1.FC Köln	2		Werder Bremen II *	2 4p		
Bayer Leverkusen	0		St Pauli	2 2p		
St Pauli *	1				Werder Bremen II *	2
SC Paderborn	1				VfB Stuttgart	3
Bayer Leverkusen II *	0		SC Paderborn	2		
Wehen Wiesbaden *	1		VfB Stuttgart *	3		
VfB Stuttgart	2					
TSG Hoffenheim *	4					
FC Augsburg	2		TSG Hoffenheim *	2		
SV Darmstadt 98 *	1		SpVgg Greuther Fürth	1		
SpVgg Greuther Fürth	3				TSG Hoffenheim *	2
Kickers Offenbach	4				Hansa Rostock	1
SV Sandhausen *	0		Kickers Offenbach	0		
Rot-Weiß Hasborn *	0		Hansa Rostock *	6		
Hansa Rostock	8					
Werder Bremen	1					
Eintracht Braunschweig *	0		Werder Bremen *	4		
Babelsberg 03	0		MSV Duisburg	0		
MSV Duisburg	4				Werder Bremen	1
Eintracht Frankfurt	4				Borussia Dortmund *	2
1.FC Union Berlin *	1		Eintracht Frankfurt	1		
1.FC Magdeburg *	1		Borussia Dortmund *	2		
Borussia Dortmund	4					

DFB POKAL 2007-08

Quarter-finals		Semi-finals		Final	

Bayern München * — 1
TSV München 1860 — 0

Bayern München * — 2
VfL Wolfsburg — 0

Hamburger SV — 1
VfL Wolfsburg * — 2

Bayern München — 2
Borussia Dortmund ‡ — 1

Carl Zeiss Jena — 2 5p
VfB Stuttgart * — 2 4p

Carl Zeiss Jena — 0
Borussia Dortmund * — 3

DFB POKAL FINAL 2008
Olympiastadion, Berlin, 19-04-2008, 20:00, Att: 74 244, Ref: Knut Kircher

Bayern München 2 Toni 2 [11] [103]
Borussia Dortmund 1 Petric [92+]

TSG Hoffenheim — 1
Borussia Dortmund * — 3

Bayern - Oliver Kahn (c) - Christian Lell, Lucio, Martin Demichelis, Philipp Lahm - Bastian Schweinsteiger (Willy Sagnol 86), Mark Van Bommel, Ze Roberto∗ (Andreas Ottl 113), Franck Ribery - Miroslav Klose (Lukas Podolski 69), Luca Toni∗. Tr: Ottmar Hitzfeld
Dortmund - Marc Ziegler - Antonio Rukavina∗ (Delron Buckley 79), Christian Wörns (c), Robert Kovac∗, Dede - Jakub Blaszczykowski∗∗109, Sebastian Kehl (Nelson Haedo Valdez 86), Florian Kringe - Tinga∗ - Alexander Frei∗ (Diego Klimowicz 71), Mladen Petric∗. Tr: Thomas Doll

* Home team • ‡ Qualified for the UEFA Cup

ARMINIA BIELEFELD 2007–08

	Date	Opponent	Res	Score	Scorers	Att
Aug	11	Wolfsburg	W	3-1	Wichniarek 38, Eigler 49, Kirch 81	20 921
	18	E Frankfurt	D	2-2	Kuchera 68, Wichniarek 80	21 200
	25	Hertha B	W	2-0	Masmanidis 51, Wichniarek 90	20 300
Sept	1	Duisburg	L	0-3		21 100
	15	H Rostock	W	4-2	OG 31, Eigler 2 50 55, Wichniarek 59	20 600
	22	Schalke	L	0-3		61 482
	26	Hannover	L	0-2		21 800
	29	W Bremen	L	1-8	Wichniarek 37	40 120
Oct	6	Hamburg	L	0-1		22 800
	21	Karlsruher	D	0-0		27 361
	27	E Cottbus	D	1-1	Kamper 77	17 600
Nov	3	Leverkusen	L	0-4		22 500
	11	Nürnberg	W	3-1	Kauf 63, Wichniarek 76, Zuma 90	18 000
	24	Bochum	L	0-3		20 478
Dec	2	Bayern M	L	0-3		23 800
	7	B Dortmund	L	1-6	Kirch 81	78 500
	15	Stuttgart	W	2-0	Kamper 79, Wichniarek 90	20 600
	2	Wolfsburg	L	0-1		18 100
Feb	8	E Frankfurt	L	1-2	Wichniarek 74	43 300
	16	Hertha B	L	0-1		32 031
	23	Duisburg	L	0-2		19 200
Mar	1	H Rostock	D	1-1	Eigler 84	14 000
	8	Schalke	L	0-2		26 100
	15	Hannover	D	2-2	Mijatovic 15, Eigler 38	35 104
	23	W Bremen	D	1-1	Kirch 14	25 800
	29	Hamburg	D	1-1	Bollmann 72	56 398
Apr	5	Karlsruher	W	1-0	Kampantais 90	19 600
	12	E Cottbus	L	0-1		16 103
	16	Leverkusen	W	1-0	Mijatovic 50	19 400
	26	Nürnberg	D	2-2	Wichniarek 47, Bollmann 59	46 300
May	3	Bochum	W	1-0	Mijatovic 70, Kamper 90	23 800
	7	Bayern M	L	0-2		69 000
	10	B Dortmund	D	2-2	Marx 24p, Wichniarek 34	27 400
	17	Stuttgart	D	2-2	Tesche 10, Eigler 87	55 500

BAYERN MUNCHEN 2007–08

	Date	Opponent	Res	Score	Comp	Scorers	Att
Jul	21	W Bremen	W	4-1	LCqf	Schweinsteiger 24, Altintop 27, Ribery 2 35 54p	51 300
	25	Stuttgart	W	2-0	LCsf	Ribery 8, Wagner 66	45 500
	28	Schalke	W	1-0	LCf	Klose 29	43 500
Aug	6	Burghausen	D	1-1	DPr1	W 4-3p. Klose 79	11 582
	11	H Rostock	W	3-0	BL	Toni 14, Klose 2 66 85	69 000
	18	W Bremen	W	4-0	BL	Ribery 31p, Toni 51, Altintop 79, Ottl 87	42 100
	25	Hannover	W	3-0	BL	Toni 28, Van Bommel 69, Altintop 86	69 000
Sept	2	Hamburg	D	1-1	BL	Klose 70	57 000
	15	Schalke	D	1-1	BL	Klose 54	69 000
	20	Belenenses	W	1-0	UCr1	Toni 34	64 000
	22	Karlsruher	W	4-1	BL	Toni 5, Klose 20, Altintop 49, Ze Roberto 75	30 702
	26	E Cottbus	W	5-0	BL	Klose 3 59 75 89, Demichelis 63, Toni 69	69 000
	29	Leverkusen	W	1-0	BL	Toni 40	22 500
Oct	4	Belenenses	W	2-0	UCr1	Toni 59, Altintop 76	6 603
	7	Nürnberg	W	3-0	BL	Toni 2 31 81, Ze Roberto 40	69 000
	20	Bochum	W	2-1	BL	Ribery 35, Schweinsteiger 78	31 328
	25	Cr Zvezda	W	3-2	UCgF	Klose 2 20 86, Kroos 94+	30 944
	28	Dortmund	D	0-0	BL		80 708
	31	M'gladbach	W	3-1	DPr2	Toni 2 47 57, Klose 83	69 000
Nov	3	E Frankfurt	D	0-0	BL		69 000
	8	Bolton	D	2-2	UCgF	Podolski 2 30 49	66 000
	10	Stuttgart	L	1-3	BL	Toni 86	55 600
	24	Wolfsburg	W	2-1	BL	Klose 35, Ribery 50	69 000
	29	Braga	D	1-1	UCgF	Klose 47	8 416
Dec	2	A Bielefeld	W	1-0	BL	Ribery 22	23 800
	8	Duisburg	D	0-0	BL		69 000
	15	Hertha B	D	0-0	BL		74 220
Jan	19	Aris	W	6-0	UCgF	Toni 4 25 38 64 66, Lell 78, Lahm 81	64 000
	29	Wuppertaler	W	5-2	DPr3	Klose 2 14 27, Van Buyten 50, Toni 53, Altintop 78	61 482
Feb	1	H Rostock	W	2-1	BL	Ribery 11, Toni 43	29 000
	10	W Bremen	D	1-1	BL	Ze Roberto 32	69 000
	14	Aberdeen	D	2-2	UCr2	Klose 29, Altintop 55	20 040
	17	Hannover	W	3-0	BL	Toni 3 58 64 82	49 000
	21	Aberdeen	W	5-1	UCr2	Lucio 12, Van Buyten 36, Podolski 2 71 77, Van Bommel 85	66 000
	24	Hamburg	D	1-1	BL	Ze Roberto 66	69 000
	27	TSV 1860	W	1-0	DPqf	Ribery 120p	69 000
Mar	1	Schalke	W	1-0	BL	Klose 14	61 482
	6	Anderlecht	W	5-0	UCr3	Altintop 9, Toni 45, Podolski 57, Klose 67, Ribery 86	21 845
	8	Karlsruher	W	2-0	BL	Toni 41, Ribery 64	69 000
	12	Anderlecht	L	1-2	UCr3	Lucio 9	63 000
	15	E Cottbus	L	0-2	BL		22 743
	19	Wolfsburg	W	2-0	DPsf	Ribery 60, Klose 66	62 000
	22	Leverkusen	W	2-1	BL	Toni 2 17 59	69 000
	29	Nürnberg	D	1-1	BL	Podolski 81	46 500
Apr	3	Getafe	D	1-1	UCqf	Toni 26	62 000
	6	Bochum	W	3-1	BL	Lucio 31, Ribery 74p, Lell 88	69 000
	10	Getafe	D	3-3	UCqf	Ribery 89, Toni 2 115 120	14 225
	13	Dortmund	W	5-0	BL	Podolski 3, Ze Roberto 8, Toni 2 18 22, Ottl 67	69 000
	16	E Frankfurt	W	3-1	BL	Van Buyten 60, Toni 2 74 85	51 500
	19	Dortmund	W	2-1	DPf	Toni 2 11 103	74 244
	24	Zenit	D	1-1	UCsf	Ribery 18	66 000
	27	Stuttgart	W	4-1	BL	Toni 8, Van Bommel 55, Ribery 2 75 76	69 000
May	1	Zenit	L	0-4	UCsf		21 500
	4	Wolfsburg	D	0-0	BL		30 000
	7	A Bielefeld	W	2-0	BL	Ribery 26, Podolski 47	69 000
	10	Duisburg	W	3-2	BL	Ottl 3, Podolski 2 18 20	31 500
	17	Hertha B	W	4-1	BL	Toni 3 4 27 61, Ribery 32	69 000

LC = DFL League Cup • BL = Bundesliga • DP = DFB Pokal • UC = UEFA Cup • gF = Group F • r1 = first round • r2 = second round • r3 = third round • qf = quarter-final • sf = semi-final • f = final

BAYER LEVERKUSEN 2007–08

	Date	Opponent	Res	Score	Scorers	Att
Aug	11	E Cottbus	D	0-0		22 500
	19	Hamburg	L	0-1		52 700
	25	Karlsruher	W	3-0	OG 19, Friedrich.M 27, Gekas 35	22 000
	31	Schalke	D	1-1	Gekas 53	61 482
Sept	15	Bochum	W	2-0	Haggui 62, Friedrich.M 87	22 500
	23	Hannover	W	3-0	Kießling 44, Vidal 68, Gekas 74p	32 161
	26	Nürnberg	W	2-1	Kießling 40, Barnetta 76	40 458
	29	Bayern M	L	0-1		22 500
Oct	7	E Frankfurt	L	1-2	OG 72	47 600
	20	B Dortmund	D	2-2	Gekas 52, Kießling 86	22 500
	27	Stuttgart	L	0-1		51 000
Nov	3	A Bielefeld	W	4-0	Barbarez 2 9 80, Gekas 2 29 33	22 500
	10	Wolfsburg	W	2-1	Barnetta 36, Kießling 52	20 298
	24	Duisburg	W	4-1	Barbarez 47, Rolfes 66, Freier 75p, Gekas 81	22 500
Dec	1	Hertha B	W	3-0	Ramelow 31, Barnetta 50, Barbarez 90	40 527
	9	H Rostock	W	3-0	Rolfes 4, Freier 55p, Gekas 73	21 000
	15	W Bremen	L	2-5	Barnetta 6, Kießling 76	39 308
Feb	2	E Cottbus	W	3-2	Rolfes 2 59 86p, Bulykin 69	13 000
	9	Hamburg	D	1-1	Friedrich.M 60	22 500
	16	Karlsruher	W	2-0	Rolfes 6, Kießling 58	28 470
	23	Schalke	W	1-0	Friedrich.M 85	22 500
Mar	2	Bochum	L	0-1		23 781
	9	Hannover	W	2-0	Gekas 30, Barnetta 39	22 500
	16	Nürnberg	W	4-1	Haggui 6, OG 56, Gekas 59, Kießling 82	22 500
	22	Bayern M	L	0-2		69 000
	29	E Frankfurt	L	0-2		22 500
Apr	6	B Dortmund	L	1-2	Kießling 51	69 400
	13	Stuttgart	W	3-0	Rolfes 2 41 70, Kießling 45	22 500
	16	A Bielefeld	L	0-1		19 400
	27	Wolfsburg	D	2-2	Gekas 33, Ricardo Costa OG 73	21 000
May	4	Duisburg	L	2-3	Sinkiewicz 18, Barnetta 74	25 275
	7	Hertha B	L	0-2		22 500
	10	H Rostock	W	2-1	Rolfes 40p, Castro 58p	22 000
	17	W Bremen	L	0-1		22 500

VFL BOCHUM 2007–08

Aug	11	W Bremen	D	2-2	Sestak [47], Bechmann [49]	29 037
	19	E Cottbus	W	2-1	Bechmann 2 [14 42]	16 382
	24	Hamburg	W	2-1	Sestak [45], Imhof [83]	30 549
Sept	1	Hannover	L	2-3	Bechmann [44], Maltritz [65p]	30 794
	15	Leverkusen	L	0-2		22 500
	21	E Frankfurt	D	0-0		25 536
	26	Stuttgart	L	0-1		34 000
Oct	8	Nürnberg	D	3-3	Sestak 2 [43 66], Mieciel [62]	18 615
	5	B Dortmund	L	1-2	Mieciel [35]	72 200
	20	Bayern M	L	1-2	Grote [11]	31 328
	27	Hertha B	L	0-2		34 580
Nov	4	Wolfsburg	W	5-3	Sestak 2 [4 44], Maltritz [20p], Fuchs [42], Epalle [63]	20 940
	9	Duisburg	W	2-0	Imhof [29], Bechmann [84]	24 259
	24	A Bielefeld	W	3-0	Mieciel 2 [12 15], Dabrowski [55]	20 478
Dec	1	Schalke	L	0-1		61 482
	8	Karlsruher	D	2-2	Sestak 2 [18 59]	20 784
	16	H Rostock	L	0-2		15 000
Feb	3	W Bremen	W	2-1	Auer [68], Yahia [84]	37 149
	9	E Cottbus	D	3-3	Ipsa OG [7], Sestak [42], Auer [68]	22 075
	17	Hamburg	L	0-3		50 069
	22	Hannover	W	2-1	Cherundolo OG [30], Auer [52]	19 902
Mar	2	Leverkusen	W	2-0	Zdebel [66], Dabrowski [88]	23 781
	8	E Frankfurt	D	1-1	Azaouagh [67]	46 700
	15	Stuttgart	D	1-1	Dabrowski [20]	25 086
	22	Nürnberg	D	1-1	Sestak [5]	43 547
	29	B Dortmund	D	3-3	Dabrowski [4], Auer 2 [9 42]	31 328
Apr	6	Bayern M	L	1-3	Azaouagh [4]	69 000
	12	Hertha B	D	1-1	Yahia [42]	20 883
	15	Wolfsburg	W	1-0	Sestak [88]	18 101
	26	Duisburg	L	1-2	Sestak [84]	24 334
May	3	A Bielefeld	L	0-2		23 800
	6	Schalke	L	0-3		31 328
	10	Karlsruher	W	3-1	Azaouagh [45], Dabrowski [48], Sestak [50]	27 920
	17	H Rostock	L	1-2	Mavraj [39]	18 883

BORUSSIA DORTMUND 2007–08

Aug	12	Duisburg	L	1-3	Kringe [86]	75 700
	18	Schalke	L	1-4	Valdez [66]	61 482
	25	E Cottbus	W	3-0	Kringe [44], Klimowicz 2 [70 84]	64 100
Sept	1	H Rostock	W	1-0	Federico [76]	26 000
	14	W Bremen	W	3-0	Petric 2 [22 32], Klimowicz [29]	79 030
	22	Hertha B	L	2-3	Petric 2 [31 88]	52 237
	25	Hamburg	L	0-3		72 300
	29	Karlsruher	L	1-3	Wörns [41]	29 290
Oct	5	Bochum	W	2-1	Tinga 2 [54], Federico [70]	72 200
	20	Leverkusen	D	2-2	Petric 2 [41 54]	22 500
	28	Bayern M	D	0-0		80 708
Nov	3	Hannover	L	1-2	Kringe [79]	45 087
	10	E Frankfurt	D	1-1	Kringe [80]	75 300
	1	Stuttgart	W	2-1	Valdez [11], Petric [79]	55 000
Dec	7	A Bielefeld	W	6-1	Tinga [13], OG [19], Petric [47], Valdez [55p], Kringe [61], Federico [67]	78 500
	15	Wolfsburg	L	0-4		30 000
Feb	2	Duisburg	D	3-3	Kehl [51], Klimowicz 2 [68 90]	29 120
	10	Schalke	L	2-3	Federico [21], Petric [50]	80 708
	16	E Cottbus	W	2-0	Petric 2 [8 84]	17 842
	23	H Rostock	W	1-0	Klimowicz [67]	70 700
	1	W Bremen	L	0-2		42 100
Mar	7	Hertha B	D	1-1	Kehl [45]	69 400
	15	Hamburg	L	0-1		57 000
	22	Karlsruher	D	1-1	Petric [24]	74 300
	29	Bochum	D	3-3	Kehl [37], Petric [39], Tinga [66]	31 328
Apr	6	Leverkusen	W	2-1	Frei [87], Dede [90]	69 400
	13	Bayern M	L	0-5		69 000
	16	Hannover	L	1-3	Frei [65]	61 400
	25	E Frankfurt	D	1-1	Blaszczykowski [51]	51 500
May	2	Nürnberg	D	0-0		70 500
	6	Stuttgart	W	3-2	Tinga [35], Frei 2 [59 79]	64 400
	10	A Bielefeld	D	2-2	Buckley [28], Fernandez OG [83]	27 400
	17	Wolfsburg	L	2-4	Frei 2 [25 69]	74 023

MSV DUISBURG 2007–08

Aug	12	B Dortmund	W	3-1	Ishiaku 2 [8 64], Tararache [62p]	75 700
	18	Wolfsburg	L	1-3	Lavric [88]	23 050
	25	Stuttgart	L	0-1		45 000
Sept	1	A Bielefeld	W	3-0	Maicon [64], Ishiaku 2 [68 70]	21 100
	16	Hertha B	L	1-2	Lavric [78]	25 070
	22	H Rostock	L	0-2		13 000
	25	Schalke	L	0-2		31 500
	30	Hannover	L	1-2	Ishiaku [20]	28 775
Oct	6	W Bremen	L	1-3	Ailton [15]	31 006
	19	E Cottbus	W	2-1	Schlicke [7], Grlic [74]	14 853
	28	Hamburg	L	0-1		30 160
Nov	4	Karlsruher	L	0-1		27 714
	9	Bochum	L	0-2		24 259
	24	Leverkusen	L	1-4	Mokhtari [10]	22 500
Dec	2	Nürnberg	W	1-0	Grlic [72]	20 313
	8	Bayern M	D	0-0		69 000
	16	E Frankfurt	L	0-1		26 557
Feb	2	B Dortmund	D	3-3	Filipescu [18], Willi [30], Tararache [59p]	29 120
	9	Wolfsburg	L	1-2	Niculescu [26]	18 755
	16	Stuttgart	L	2-3	Niculescu [49], Ishiaku [57]	21 562
	23	A Bielefeld	W	2-0	Schröter [8], Ishiaku [48]	19 200
	29	Hertha B	L	0-2		32 382
Mar	8	H Rostock	D	1-1	Grlic [7]	20 206
	14	Schalke	L	1-2	Georgiew [21]	61 482
	22	Hannover	D	1-1	Lamey [77]	20 747
	29	W Bremen	W	2-1	Grlic [32], Ishiaku [42]	39 615
Apr	4	E Cottbus	L	0-1		24 016
	12	Hamburg	W	1-0	Grlic [54]	54 218
	16	Karlsruher	L	0-1		20 255
	26	Bochum	D	1-1	Niculescu [26]	24 334
May	4	Leverkusen	W	3-2	Ishiaku 2 [14 36], Georgiew [90]	25 275
	7	Nürnberg	L	0-2		44 300
	10	Bayern M	L	2-3	Tararache [48], Daun [54]	31 500
	17	E Frankfurt	L	2-4	Niculescu [59], Daun [86]	49 500

EINTRACHT FRANKFURT 2007–08

Aug	11	Hertha B	W	1-0	Amanatidis [31]	45 900
	18	A Bielefeld	D	2-2	Meier [87], Russ [89]	21 200
	26	H Rostock	W	1-0	Meier [3]	44 400
Sept	1	W Bremen	L	1-2	Thurk [85]	40 983
	15	Hamburg	W	2-1	Meier 2 [8 87]	51 500
	21	Bochum	D	0-0		25 536
	26	Karlsruher	L	0-1		48 500
Oct	30	E Cottbus	D	2-2	Amanatidis 2 [49 79p]	14 290
	7	Leverkusen	W	2-1	Kyrgiakos 2 [54 79]	47 600
	20	Nürnberg	L	1-5	Takahara [12]	45 050
	26	Hannover	D	0-0		44 700
Nov	3	Bayern M	D	0-0		69 000
	10	B Dortmund	D	1-1	Amanatidis [55]	75 300
	24	Stuttgart	L	1-4	Köhler [41]	51 500
Dec	1	Wolfsburg	D	2-2	Chris [35], Fink [52]	20 656
	8	Schalke	D	2-2	Toski [49], Amanatidis [82]	51 500
	16	Duisburg	W	1-0	Amanatidis [40]	26 557
Feb	2	Hertha B	W	3-0	Fenin 3 [39 60 90]	35 930
	8	A Bielefeld	W	2-1	Amanatidis [37], Fenin [47]	43 300
	16	H Rostock	L	0-1		15 500
	23	W Bremen	W	1-0	Amanatidis [56]	51 500
	2	Hamburg	L	1-4	Kyrgiakos [70]	53 787
Mar	8	Bochum	D	1-1	Toski [49]	46 700
	15	Karlsruher	W	1-0	Fink [25]	29 348
	20	E Cottbus	W	2-1	Caio [59], Russ [65]	45 100
	29	Leverkusen	W	2-0	Kießling OG [24], Mantzios [90]	22 500
Apr	5	Nürnberg	L	1-3	Fink [3]	51 500
	12	Hannover	L	1-2	Russ [28]	38 104
	16	Bayern M	L	1-3	Köhler [29]	51 500
	25	B Dortmund	D	1-1	Köhler [46]	51 500
May	3	Stuttgart	L	1-4	Amanatidis [63]	55 500
	7	Wolfsburg	L	2-3	Amanatidis [22p], Weissenberger [62]	45 300
	10	Schalke	L	0-1		61 482
	17	Duisburg	W	4-2	Amanatidis [13], Fenin 2 [15 38], Heller [78]	49 500

ENERGIE COTTBUS 2007–08

Month	Day	Opponent	Res	Score	Scorers	Att
Aug	11	Leverkusen	D	0-0		22 500
	19	Bochum	L	1-2	Skela 49	16 382
	25	B Dortmund	L	0-3		64 100
Sept	1	Nürnberg	D	1-1	Sörensen 15p	15 089
	15	Stuttgart	L	0-3		41 000
	22	Wolfsburg	L	1-2	Sörensen 31	15 269
	26	Bayern M	L	0-5		69 000
	30	E Frankfurt	D	2-2	Rangelow 2 8 18	14 290
Oct	6	Hertha B	D	0-0		48 719
	19	Duisburg	L	1-2	Rost.T 66	14 853
	27	A Bielefeld	D	1-1	Sörensen 90	17 600
Nov	2	Schalke	W	1-0	Bassila 46	17 012
	10	H Rostock	L	2-3	Da Silva 58, Skela 90	20 000
	24	W Bremen	L	0-2		14 685
Dec	1	Karlsruher	W	2-0	Angelow 62, Rangelow 75	10 914
	8	Hamburg	D	0-0		56 132
	14	Hannover	W	5-1	Bassila 11, Sörensen 30, Rangelow 2 44 70, Ziebig 65	14 026
Feb	2	Leverkusen	L	2-3	Papadopoulos 14, Bassila 77	13 000
	9	Bochum	D	3-3	Papadopoulos 45, Skela 69, Jelic 79	22 075
	16	B Dortmund	L	0-2		17 842
	24	Nürnberg	D	1-1	Sörensen 59	40 900
Mar	8	Wolfsburg	L	0-3		21 460
	11	Stuttgart	L	0-1		13 150
	15	Bayern M	W	2-0	Jelic 2 18 38	22 743
	20	E Frankfurt	L	1-2	Rost 48	45 100
	30	Hertha B	W	2-1	Skela 2 41 63p	20 746
Apr	4	Duisburg	W	1-0	Skela 4	24 016
	12	A Bielefeld	W	1-0	Skela 51p	16 103
	15	Schalke	L	0-5		60 018
	26	H Rostock	W	2-1	Rost 81, Rangelow 90	21 357
May	3	W Bremen	L	0-2		39 687
	6	Karlsruher	D	1-1	Rivic 60	28 000
	10	Hamburg	W	2-0	Rivic 29, Sörensen 83	22 746
	17	Hannover	L	0-4		46 632

HAMBURGER SV 2007–08

Month	Day	Opponent	Res	Score	Scorers	Att
Aug	11	Hannover	W	1-0	Benjamin 23	49 000
	19	Leverkusen	W	1-0	Van der Vaart 64p	52 700
	24	Bochum	L	1-2	Van der Vaart 86p	30 549
Sept	2	Bayern M	D	1-1	Zidan 87	57 000
	15	E Frankfurt	L	1-2	Van der Vaart 82p	51 500
	22	Nürnberg	W	1-0	Van der Vaart 53	52 365
	25	B Dortmund	W	3-0	Guerrero 7, Van der Vaart 42, Olic 64	72 300
	29	Wolfsburg	D	2-2	Reinhardt.B 17, Van der Vaart 70	54 055
Oct	6	A Bielefeld	W	1-0	Van der Vaart 49	22 800
	20	Stuttgart	W	4-1	Olic 3 7 22 34, Mathijsen 60	57 000
	28	Duisburg	W	1-0	Kompany 37	30 160
Nov	3	Hertha B	W	2-1	Guerrero 4, Reinhardt.B 81	56 493
	10	Schalke	D	1-1	Olic 35	61 482
	25	H Rostock	W	2-0	Van der Vaart 19, Olic 61	57 000
Dec	1	W Bremen	L	1-2	Van der Vaart 61	42 100
	8	E Cottbus	D	0-0		56 132
	15	Karlsruher	D	1-1	Olic 90	30 300
	2	Hannover	D	1-1	Olic 70	57 000
Feb	9	Leverkusen	D	1-1	Van der Vaart 28	22 500
	2	Bochum	W	3-0	Olic 40, Jarolim 2 64 71	50 069
	24	Bayern M	D	1-1	Olic 60	69 000
	2	E Frankfurt	W	4-1	Guerrero 2 5 79, De Jong 57, Zidan 83	53 787
	9	Nürnberg	D	0-0		44 900
Mar	15	B Dortmund	W	1-0	Guerrero 63	57 000
	22	Wolfsburg	D	1-1	Reinhardt 14	30 000
	29	A Bielefeld	D	1-1	Guerrero 82	56 398
Apr	5	Stuttgart	L	0-1		55 000
	12	Duisburg	L	0-1		54 218
	15	Hertha B	D	0-0		40 289
	26	Schalke	L	0-1		57 000
May	3	H Rostock	W	3-1	Olic 2 18 51, Van der Vaart 27	28 000
	7	W Bremen	L	0-1		57 000
	10	E Cottbus	L	0-2		22 746
	17	Karlsruher	W	7-0	Van der Vaart 23p, Guerrero 3 34 43 49, Trochowski 57, Olic 2 78 89	56 037

HANNOVER 96 2007–08

Month	Day	Opponent	Res	Score	Scorers	Att
Aug	11	Hamburg	L	0-1		49 000
	17	Karlsruher	W	2-1	Hanke 55, Balitsch 75	27 800
	25	Bayern M	L	0-3		69 000
Sept	1	Bochum	W	3-2	Hanke 12, Rosenthal 36, Hashemian 71	30 794
	15	Nürnberg	D	2-2	Hanke 2 12 39	39 710
	23	Leverkusen	L	0-3		32 161
	26	A Bielefeld	W	2-0	Huszti 54p, Pinto 85	21 800
	30	Duisburg	W	2-0	Schulz 2 7 63	28 775
Oct	6	Stuttgart	W	2-0	Huszti 2 8p 52	49 000
	21	Wolfsburg	D	2-2	Pinto 28, Tarnat 35	37 812
	26	E Frankfurt	D	0-0		44 700
Nov	3	B Dortmund	W	2-0	Huszti 54p, Schulz 73	45 087
	10	Hertha B	L	0-1		34 213
	24	Schalke	L	2-3	Huszti 2 17p 53	49 000
	30	H Rostock	W	3-0	Fahrenhorst 84, Hanke 86, Stajner 87	17 000
Dec	8	W Bremen	W	4-3	Hanke 3 12 21 77, OG 20	49 000
	14	E Cottbus	L	1-5	Kleine 68	14 026
	2	Hamburg	D	1-1	Huszti 40p	57 000
Feb	9	Karlsruher	D	2-2	Balitsch 45, Rosenthal 87	40 112
	17	Bayern M	L	0-3		69 000
	22	Bochum	L	1-2	Hanke 47	19 902
Mar	1	Nürnberg	W	2-1	Bruggink 29, Huszti 65	31 282
	9	Leverkusen	L	0-2		22 500
	15	A Bielefeld	D	2-2	Bruggink 16, Stajner 56	35 104
	22	Duisburg	D	1-1	Stajner 42	20 747
	30	Stuttgart	D	0-0		45 176
Apr	5	Wolfsburg	L	2-3	Bruggink 27, Steiner 79	29 322
	12	E Frankfurt	W	2-0	Pinto 35, Schultz.C 89	38 104
	16	B Dortmund	W	3-1	Bruggink 37, Fahrenhorst 41, Huszti 79	61 400
	26	Hertha B	D	2-2	Hanke 19, Stajner 26	41 473
May	3	Schalke	D	1-1	Bruggink 8	61 482
	6	H Rostock	W	3-0	Balitsch 19, Rosenthal 2 47 87	35 453
	10	W Bremen	L	1-6	Huszti 90	42 100
	17	E Cottbus	W	4-2	Bruggink 23, Stajner 45, Vinicius 60, Balitsch 90	46 632

HANSA ROSTOCK 2007–08

Month	Day	Opponent	Res	Score	Scorers	Att
Aug	11	Bayern M	L	0-3		69 000
	18	Nürnberg	L	1-2	Orestes 63	25 000
	26	E Frankfurt	L	0-1		44 400
Sept	1	B Dortmund	L	0-1		26 000
	15	A Bielefeld	L	2-4	Kern 47, Bülow 62	20 600
	22	Duisburg	W	2-0	Hähnge 34, Kern 53p	13 000
	23	Hertha B	W	3-1	Rahn 40, Hähnge 54, Dorn 74	48 670
	29	Stuttgart	W	2-1	Rathgeb 16, Orestes 18	19 000
Oct	6	Wolfsburg	L	0-1		26 127
	20	Schalke	D	1-1	Stein 56	29 000
	27	Karlsruher	D	0-0		14 000
Nov	3	W Bremen	L	0-1		41 738
	10	E Cottbus	W	3-2	Kern 3 18 59 74	20 000
	25	Hamburg	L	0-2		57 000
Dec	30	Hannover	L	0-3		17 000
	9	Leverkusen	L	0-3		21 000
	16	Bochum	W	2-0	Bülow 7, Hähnge 43	15 000
Feb	1	Bayern M	L	1-2	Kern 52	29 000
	9	Nürnberg	D	1-1	Rahn 28	36 470
	16	E Frankfurt	W	1-0	Rahn 76	15 500
	23	B Dortmund	L	0-1		70 700
Mar	1	A Bielefeld	D	1-1	Bartels 86	14 000
	8	Duisburg	D	1-1	Agali 20	20 206
	15	Hertha B	D	0-0		22 500
	22	Stuttgart	L	1-4	Gomez OG 56	48 000
	28	Wolfsburg	L	0-1		15 000
Apr	5	Schalke	L	0-1		61 482
	12	Karlsruher	W	2-1	Bartels 2 30 84	27 714
	15	W Bremen	L	1-2	Hähnge 76	22 000
	26	E Cottbus	L	1-2	Cetkovic 16	21 357
	3	Hamburg	L	1-3	Mathijsen OG 76	28 000
May	6	Hannover	L	0-3		35 453
	10	Leverkusen	L	1-2	Menga 67	22 000
	17	Bochum	W	2-1	Kern 40, Bartels 78	18 883

HERTHA BERLIN 2007–08

	Date	Opponent	Res	Score	Scorers	Att.
Aug	11	E Frankfurt	L	0-1		45 900
	18	Stuttgart	W	3-1	Chahed 51p, Fathi 65, Okoronkwo 80	46 000
	25	A Bielefeld	L	0-2		20 300
Sept	1	Wolfsburg	W	2-1	Pantelic 38, Okoronkwo 88	42 075
	16	Duisburg	W	2-1	Pantelic 2 61 70	25 070
	22	B Dortmund	W	3-2	Pantelic 43, Lucio 54, Okoronkwo 76	52 237
	25	H Rostock	L	1-3	Pantelic 2	48 670
	28	Schalke	L	0-1		60 511
Oct	6	E Cottbus	D	0-0		48 719
	20	W Bremen	L	2-3	Gilberto 61, Okoronkwo 90	40 278
	27	Bochum	W	2-0	OG 26, Pantelic 35	34 580
Nov	3	Hamburg	L	1-2	Ebert 59	56 493
	10	Hannover	W	1-0	Andre Lima 87	34 213
	23	Karlsruher	L	1-2	Pantelic 35	29 217
Dec	1	Leverkusen	L	0-3		40 527
	9	Nürnberg	L	1-2	Lustenberger 65	41 490
	15	Bayern M	D	0-0		74 220
	2	E Frankfurt	L	0-3		35 930
Feb	9	Stuttgart	W	3-1	Pantelic 2 7 45, Raffael 49	50 000
	16	A Bielefeld	W	1-0	Raffael 90	32 031
	23	Wolfsburg	D	0-0		23 659
	29	Duisburg	W	2-0	Raffael 35, Pantelic 37	32 382
Mar	7	B Dortmund	D	1-1	Pantelic 50	69 400
	15	H Rostock	D	0-0		22 500
	23	Schalke	L	1-2	Chahed 67p	54 179
	30	E Cottbus	L	1-2	Mineiro 21	20 746
Apr	5	W Bremen	L	1-2	Andre Lima 10	59 728
	12	Bochum	D	1-1	Skacel 28	20 833
	15	Hamburg	D	0-0		40 289
	26	Hannover	D	2-2	Chahed 55p, Piszczek 66	41 473
May	3	Karlsruher	W	3-1	Kacar 25, Pantelic 31, Skacel 87	49 595
	7	Leverkusen	W	2-1	Pantelic 26, Chahed 68p	22 500
	10	Nürnberg	W	1-0	Raffael 74	47 072
	17	Bayern M	L	1-4	Domowtschiski 84	69 000

KARLSRUHE 2007–08

	Date	Opponent	Res	Score	Scorers	Att.
Aug	12	Nürnberg	W	2-0	Hajnal 2 44 74	45 419
	17	Hannover	L	1-2	Franz 37	27 800
	25	Leverkusen	L	0-3		22 000
Sept	2	Stuttgart	L	1-0	Hajnal 54	29 949
	16	Wolfsburg	W	2-1	Eggimann 62, Eichner 79	21 673
	23	Bayern M	L	1-4	Porcello 52	30 702
	26	E Frankfurt	W	1-0	Franz 51	48 500
	29	B Dortmund	W	3-1	Porcello 25, Eggimann 64, Freis 75	29 290
Oct	6	Schalke	W	2-0	Timm 2 68 83	61 482
	21	A Bielefeld	D	0-0		27 361
	27	H Rostock	D	0-0		14 000
Nov	4	Duisburg	W	1-0	Eggimann 29	27 714
	10	W Bremen	L	0-4		39 699
	23	Hertha B	W	2-1	Hajnal 56, Freis 66	29 217
Dec	1	E Cottbus	L	0-2		10 914
	8	Bochum	D	2-2	Hajnal 24, Freis 56	20 784
	15	Hamburg	D	1-1	Timm 46	30 300
	2	Nürnberg	W	2-0	Eichner 66, Kennedy 74	29 670
Feb	9	Hannover	D	2-2	Kennedy 61, Hajnal 64	40 112
	16	Leverkusen	D	2-2	Freis 60, Kennedy 78	28 470
	23	Stuttgart	L	1-3	Hajnal 81	55 000
	1	Wolfsburg	W	3-1	Eggimann 23, Kennedy 73, Iaschwili 90	27 871
	8	Bayern M	L	0-2		69 000
Mar	15	E Frankfurt	L	0-1		29 348
	22	B Dortmund	D	1-1	Freis 63	74 300
	29	Schalke	D	0-0		29 477
Apr	5	A Bielefeld	L	0-1		19 600
	12	H Rostock	L	1-2	Freis 70	27 714
	16	Duisburg	W	1-0	Hajnal 81	20 255
	26	W Bremen	D	3-3	Freis 2 15 59, Kapllani 66	29 470
May	3	Hertha B	L	1-3	Kapllani 53	49 595
	6	E Cottbus	D	1-1	Hajnal 65	28 000
	10	Bochum	L	1-3	Eggimann 88	27 920
	17	Hamburg	L	0-7		56 037

1.FC NURNBERG 2007–08

	Date	Opponent	Res	Score	Scorers	Att.
Aug	12	Karlsruher	L	0-2		45 419
	18	H Rostock	W	2-1	Galasek 16, Kluge 26	25 000
	25	W Bremen	L	0-1		45 200
Sept	1	E Cottbus	D	1-1	Wolf.A 85	15 089
	15	Hannover	D	2-2	Misimovic 60, Mintal 89	39 710
	22	Hamburg	L	0-1		52 365
	26	Leverkusen	L	1-2	Mintal 73p	40 458
	29	Bochum	D	3-3	Kluge 2 40 60, Misimovic 81	18 615
	7	Bayern M	L	0-3		69 000
Oct	20	E Frankfurt	W	5-1	Charisteas 20, Mintal 2 50 64, Misimovic 54p, Kennedy 82	45 050
	27	Wolfsburg	L	1-3	Misimovic 54p	19 798
Nov	3	Stuttgart	L	0-1		45 565
	11	A Bielefeld	L	1-3	Wolf.A 43	18 000
	25	B Dortmund	W	2-0	Galasek 10, Charisteas 90	41 020
Dec	2	Duisburg	L	0-1		20 313
	9	Hertha B	W	2-1	Charisteas 5, Misimovic 39	41 490
	15	Schalke	L	1-2	Charisteas 55	61 482
	2	Karlsruher	L	0-2		29 670
Feb	9	H Rostock	D	1-1	Koller 19	36 470
	16	W Bremen	L	0-2		37 073
	24	E Cottbus	D	1-1	Engelhardt 58	40 900
	1	Hannover	L	1-2	Misimovic 52	31 282
Mar	9	Hamburg	D	0-0		44 900
	16	Leverkusen	L	1-4	Misimovic 12	22 500
	22	Bochum	D	1-1	Misimovic 9	43 547
	29	Bayern M	D	1-1	Misimovic 44	46 500
Apr	5	E Frankfurt	W	3-1	Charisteas 18, Vittek 49, Misimovic 83	51 500
	16	Stuttgart	L	0-3		45 000
	20	Wolfsburg	W	1-0	Koller 79	45 100
	26	A Bielefeld	D	2-2	Mintal 29, Saenko 38	46 300
May	2	B Dortmund	D	0-0		70 500
	7	Duisburg	W	2-0	Charisteas 9, Pinola 32	44 300
	10	Hertha B	L	0-1		47 072
	17	Schalke	L	0-2		47 000

VFB STUTTGART 2007–08

	Date	Opponent	Res	Score	Scorers	Att.
Aug	10	Schalke	D	2-2	Khedira 53, Pardo 67p	55 000
	18	Hertha B	L	1-3	Hitzlsperger 15	46 000
	25	Duisburg	W	1-0	Gomez 35	45 000
Sept	2	Karlsruher	L	0-1		29 949
	15	E Cottbus	W	3-0	Cacau 53, Ewerthon 78, Gomez 83	41 000
	22	W Bremen	L	1-4	Gomez 13	39 282
	26	Bochum	W	1-0	Hilbert 50	34 000
	29	H Rostock	L	1-2	Gomez 73	19 000
Oct	6	Hannover	L	0-2		49 000
	20	Hamburg	L	1-4	Tasci 73	57 000
	27	Leverkusen	W	1-0	Beck 72	51 000
Nov	3	Nürnberg	W	1-0	Gomez 24	45 565
	10	Bayern M	W	3-1	Gomez 2 10 42, Bastürk 30	55 600
	24	E Frankfurt	W	4-1	Hilbert 45, Marica 48, Hitzlsperger 57, Cacau 90	51 500
Dec	1	B Dortmund	L	1-2	Meira 35	55 000
	8	Wolfsburg	W	3-1	Marica 26, Cacau 48, Hitzlsperger 86	53 000
	15	A Bielefeld	L	0-2		20 600
Feb	3	Schalke	L	1-4	Da Silva 61	61 482
	9	Hertha B	L	1-3	Gomez 41	50 000
	16	Duisburg	W	3-2	Gomez 2 16 41, Hitzlsperger 90	21 562
	23	Karlsruher	W	3-1	Gomez 5, Hilbert 25, Cacau 88	55 000
	8	W Bremen	W	6-3	Gomez 3 20 43 65, Cacau 2 66 87, OG 84	55 000
Mar	11	E Cottbus	W	1-0	Meira 30	13 150
	15	Bochum	D	1-1	Hitzlsperger 47	25 086
	22	H Rostock	W	4-1	Pardo 52p, Cacau 54, Gomez 87, Bastürk 90	48 000
	30	Hannover	D	0-0		45 176
Apr	5	Hamburg	W	1-0	Hilbert 20	55 000
	13	Leverkusen	L	2-0		45 000
	16	Nürnberg	W	3-0	Cacau 4, Da Silva 13, Meira 32	45 000
	27	Bayern M	L	1-4	Da Silva 19	69 000
May	4	E Frankfurt	W	4-1	Bastürk 2 3 18, Gomez 6, Cacau 47	55 500
	6	B Dortmund	L	2-3	Gomez 2 55 83	64 400
	10	Wolfsburg	L	0-4		28 001
	17	A Bielefeld	D	2-2	Gomez 75p, Fisher.M 85	55 500

FC SCHALKE 04 2007–08

Month	Date	Opponent	Res	Score	Scorers	Attendance
Aug	10	Stuttgart	D	2-2	Kobiashvili 25, Rakitic 76	55 000
	18	B Dortmund	W	4-1	Bordon 11, Pander 31, Asamoah 59, Kuranyi 78	61 482
	26	Wolfsburg	D	1-1	Halil Altintop 86	29 798
	31	Leverkusen	D	1-1	Kuranyi 45	61 482
Sept	15	Bayern M	D	1-1	Rakitic 36	69 000
	22	A Bielefeld	W	3-0	Kuranyi 24, Asamoah 54, Rafinha 65p	61 482
	25	Duisburg	W	2-0	Halil Altintop 2, Kuranyi 75	31 500
	28	Hertha B	W	1-0	Rafinha 44p	60 511
Oct	6	Karlsruher	L	0-2		61 482
	20	H Rostock	D	1-1	Asamoah 33	29 000
	27	W Bremen	D	1-1	Grossmüller 14	61 482
Nov	2	E Cottbus	L	0-1		17 012
	10	Hamburg	D	1-1	Krstajic 12	61 482
	24	Hannover	W	3-2	Kuranyi 2 41 50, Halil Altintop 61	49 000
Dec	1	Bochum	W	1-0	Bordon 32	61 482
	8	E Frankfurt	D	2-2	Westermann 2 77 89	51 500
	15	Nürnberg	W	2-1	Asamoah 14, OG 35	61 482
Feb	3	Stuttgart	W	4-1	Kuranyi 2 32 52, Westermann 76, Ze Roberto II 90	61 482
	10	B Dortmund	W	2-0	Asamoah 19, Amedick OG 30, Ernst 82	80 708
	15	Wolfsburg	L	1-2	Sanchez 65	60 387
	23	Leverkusen	L	0-1		22 500
Mar	1	Bayern M	L	0-1		61 482
	8	A Bielefeld	W	2-0	Varela 24, Halil Altintop 74	26 100
	12	Duisburg	W	2-1	Kuranyi 60, Westermann 74	61 482
	23	Hertha B	W	1-0	Asamoah 12, Jones 23	54 179
	29	Karlsruher	D	0-0		29 477
Apr	5	H Rostock	W	1-0	Halil Altintop 52	61 482
	12	W Bremen	L	1-5	Kuranyi 42	42 100
	15	E Cottbus	W	5-0	Da Silva OG 31, Kuranyi 4 37 41 59 80	60 018
	26	Hamburg	W	1-0	Kuranyi 2	57 000
May	3	Hannover	D	1-1	Halil Altintop 40	61 482
	6	Bochum	W	3-0	Asamoah 34, Rakitic 67, Bordon 85	31 328
	10	E Frankfurt	W	2-0	Krstajic 65	61 482
	17	Nürnberg	W	2-0	Bordon 2 19 61	47 000

WERDER BREMEN 2007–08

Month	Date	Opponent	Res	Score	Scorers	Attendance
Aug	11	Bochum	D	2-2	Diego 39p, Sanogo 45	29 037
	18	Bayern M	L	0-4		42 100
	25	Nürnberg	W	1-0	Harnik 69	45 200
Sept	1	E Frankfurt	W	2-1	Sanogo 35, Pasanen 79	40 983
	14	B Dortmund	L	0-3		79 030
	22	Stuttgart	W	4-1	Almeida 2 3 4, Sanogo 15, Diego 89	39 282
	25	Wolfsburg	D	1-1	Diego 48	25 533
	29	A Bielefeld	W	8-1	Niemayer 17, Almeida 2 35 88, Sanogo 2 41 44, Mertesacker 59, Rosenberg 66, Diego 85	40 120
Oct	6	Duisburg	W	3-1	Jensen 7, Sanogo 56, Andreason 87	31 006
	20	Hertha B	W	3-2	Almeida 57, Rosenberg 62, Andreason 74	40 278
	27	Schalke	D	1-1	Naldo 34	61 482
Nov	3	H Rostock	W	1-0	Almeida 39	41 738
	10	Karlsruher	W	4-0	Diego 2 25 45, Almeida 66, Naldo 76	39 669
	24	E Cottbus	W	2-0	Diego 63p, Mosquerra 83	14 685
Dec	1	Hamburg	W	2-1	Sanogo 15, Pasanen 64	42 100
	8	Hannover	L	3-4	Rosenberg 2 10 54, Diego 41p	49 000
	15	Leverkusen	W	5-2	Klasnic 2 30 63, Diego 50, Fritz 57, Rosenberg 70	39 308
Feb	3	Bochum	L	2-4	Jensen 44	37 149
	10	Bayern M	D	1-1	Diego 6	69 000
	16	Nürnberg	W	2-0	Rosenberg 30, Klasnic 81	37 073
	23	E Frankfurt	L	0-1		51 500
Mar	1	B Dortmund	W	2-0	Rosenberg 2 45 63	42 100
	8	Stuttgart	L	3-6	Almeida 9, Boenisch 60, Rosenberg 77	55 000
	16	Wolfsburg	L	0-1		39 831
	23	A Bielefeld	D	1-1	Diego 70p	25 800
	29	Duisburg	L	1-2	Diego 58	39 615
Apr	5	Hertha B	W	2-1	Rosenberg 1, Borowski 73	59 728
	12	Schalke	W	5-1	Baumann 19, Sanogo 32, Rosenberg 59, Klasnic 2 76 89	42 100
	15	H Rostock	W	2-1	Frings 57, Klasnic 82	22 000
	26	Karlsruher	D	3-3	Diego 23, Ozil 29, Sanogo 86	29 470
May	3	E Cottbus	W	2-0	Rosenberg 67, Almeida 79	39 687
	7	Hamburg	W	1-0	Almeida 50	57 000
	10	Hannover	W	6-1	Almeida 14, Naldo 27, Borowski 73, Klasnic 80, Rosenberg 82, Hunt 87	42 100
	17	Leverkusen	W	1-0	Rosenberg 80	22 500

VFL WOLFSBURG 2007–08

Month	Date	Opponent	Res	Score	Scorers	Attendance
Aug	11	A Bielefeld	L	1-3	Radu 84	20 921
	18	Duisburg	W	3-1	Marcelinho 41, Madlung 52, Radu 72	23 050
	26	Schalke	D	1-1	Krzynowek 36	29 798
Sept	1	Hertha B	L	1-2	Dejagah 61	42 075
	16	Karlsruher	L	1-2	Krzynowek 21	21 673
	22	E Cottbus	W	2-1	Dzeko 22, Krzynowek 83	15 269
	25	W Bremen	D	1-1	Josue 65	25 533
	29	Hamburg	D	2-2	Grafite 57p, Dejagah 88	54 055
Oct	6	H Rostock	W	1-0	Dzeko 89	26 127
	21	Hannover	D	2-2	Marcelinho 21, Dejagah 29	37 812
	27	Nürnberg	W	3-1	OG 30, Grafite 34, Dejagah 67	19 798
Nov	4	Bochum	L	3-5	Schäfer.M 50, Grafite 2 56 73	20 940
	11	Leverkusen	L	1-2	OG 70	20 298
	24	Bayern M	L	1-2	Dejagah 72	69 000
Dec	1	E Frankfurt	D	2-2	Gentner 6, Dzeko 48	20 656
	8	Stuttgart	L	1-3	Dzeko 51	53 000
	15	B Dortmund	W	4-0	Schäfer.M 8, Ricardo Costa 11, Gentner 59, Dzeko 78	30 000
Feb	2	A Bielefeld	W	1-0	Grafite 27	18 100
	9	Duisburg	W	2-1	Schäfer.M 36, Grafite 54	18 755
	15	Schalke	W	2-1	Grafite 2 73 84p	60 387
	23	Hertha B	D	0-0		23 659
Mar	1	Karlsruher	L	1-3	Schäfer.M 28	27 871
	8	E Cottbus	W	3-0	Gentner 17, Marcelinho 2 20 76	21 460
	16	W Bremen	W	1-0	Grafite 50	39 831
	22	Hamburg	D	1-1	Ljuboja 52	30 000
	28	H Rostock	W	1-0	Krzynowek 90	15 000
Apr	5	Hannover	W	3-2	Dejagah 2 20 71, Marcelinho 29	29 322
	15	Bochum	L	0-1		18 101
	20	Nürnberg	L	0-1		45 100
	27	Leverkusen	D	2-2	Dzeko 13, Hasebe 43	21 000
May	4	Bayern M	D	0-0		30 000
	7	E Frankfurt	W	3-2	Grafite 4, Schäfer.M 28, Dzeko 79	45 300
	10	Stuttgart	W	4-0	Marcelinho 16, Dzeko 22, Ricardo Costa 55, Dejagah 75	28 001
	17	B Dortmund	W	4-2	Riether 3, Marcelinho 6, Schäfer.M 62, Grafite 76	74 023

GHA – GHANA

NATIONAL TEAM RECORD
JULY 10TH 2006 TO JULY 12TH 2010

PL	W	D	L	F	A	%
24	15	3	6	41	25	68.8

Ghana hosted arguably one of the most exciting CAF Africa Cup of Nations tournaments in January 2008 but there proved to be no fairy tale ending for the host nation. The Black Stars got to the semifinals but, afflicted by injury and suspension, lost to Cameroon, although they did provide fans with a thrilling consolation win over neighbours Cote d'Ivoire in the third place play-off. There had been major investment in both infrastructure and in the team with the finals part of the celebrations marking the 50th anniversary of independence from the British, an event precipitating Africa's fabled 'winds of change'. But the fairytale home win always looked a tall order given the lack of an established star striker in the team, a situation exacerbated early on in the tournament when their best forward Asamoah Gyan suffered injury. Inspirational captain Stephen Appiah had already been ruled out of the entire tournament after a serious knee injury picked up while playing for his Turkish club Fenerbahce. The burden of expectation also rode hard on the Ghana team but the turning point was arguably the dismissal of captain John Mensah in the quarter-final against Nigeria. His absence in the semi-final against Cameroon forced Michael

INTERNATIONAL HONOURS
FIFA World U-17 Championship 1991 1995

Qualified for the FIFA World Cup 2006   Qualified for the FIFA Women's World Cup 1999 2003

CAF African Cup of Nations 1963 1965 1978 1982

CAF African Youth Championship 1993 1999   CAF African U-17 Championship 1995 1999

CAF Champions League Asante Kotoko 1970 1983 Hearts of Oak 2000

Essien to play in defence and the effectiveness of the Chelsea man was lost against a physical opponent, who won 1-0. Ghana's French coach Claude LeRoy departed after the tournament but not as he initially promised because he did not win the trophy but rather when new contract terms did not suit him. A search for a replacement was started too late for the beginning of the FIFA World Cup qualifiers, leaving Sellas Tetteh to temporarily take charge of wins over Lesotho, Libya and Gabon and a solitary defeat away in Libreville. At under-23 level, Ghana missed out on the Beijing Olympics failing to beat Nigeria at home in their vital qualifier in November 2007. At under-17 level, though, the country reached the semifinals of the FIFA U-17 World Cup in South Korea, losing in extra time to Spain. Asante Kotoko were easy league winners at the end of the 2007-08 Premier League campaign, deposing perennial rivals Hearts of Oak. Hearts had suffered an ignominious first round defeat in the 2008 CAF Champions League, beaten by FC 105 Libreville of Gabon. AshantiGold, the country's other representatives in Africa's top club competition, lasted one round longer before falling 3-0 on aggregate to JS Kabylie of Algeria.

Ghana Football Association (GFA)
General Secretariat, South East Ridge, PO Box AN 19338, Accra, Ghana
Tel +233 21 910170   Fax +233 21 668590
info@ghanafa.org   www.ghanafa.org
President: NYANTAKYI Kwesi   General Secretary: NSIAH Kofi
Vice-President: PAPPOE Frederick   Treasurer: TBD   Media Officer: RANSFORD Abbey
Men's Coach: TETTEH Sellas   Women's Coach: GAMEL Mumuni
GFA formed: 1957   CAF: 1958   FIFA: 1958
Yellow shirts with black trimmings, Yellow shorts, Yellow socks

RECENT INTERNATIONAL MATCHES PLAYED BY GHANA

2006	Opponents	Score		Venue	Comp	Scorers	Att	Referee
1-03	Mexico	L	0-1	Frisco	Fr		19 513	Hall USA
26-05	Turkey	D	1-1	Bochum	Fr	Amoah 60	9 738	Meier GER
29-05	Jamaica	W	4-1	Leicester	Fr	Muntari 5, OG 19, Appiah 66, Amoah 68	11 163	Halsey ENG
4-06	Korea Republic	W	3-1	Edinburgh	Fr	Gyan 37p, Muntari 63, Essien 81	15 000	McDonald SCO
12-06	Italy	L	0-2	Hanover	WCr1		43 000	Simon BRA
17-06	Czech Republic	W	2-0	Cologne	WCr1	Gyan 2, Muntari 82	45 000	Elizondo ARG
22-06	USA	W	2-1	Nuremberg	WCr1	Draman 22, Appiah 47+p	41 000	Merk GER
27-06	Brazil	L	0-3	Dortmund	WCr2		65 000	Michel SVK
15-08	Togo	W	2-0	London	Fr	Pimpong 75, Tachie-Mensah 85		Dean ENG
4-10	Japan	W	1-0	Yokohama	Fr	Dramani 73	52 437	Yu Byung Seob KOR
8-10	Korea Republic	W	3-1	Seoul	Fr	Gyan 2 48 83, Essien 58	36 515	Takayama JPN
14-11	Australia	D	1-1	London	Fr	Agogo 74	14 379	Clattenburg ENG
2007								
6-02	Nigeria	W	4-1	London	Fr	Kingston 50, Muntari 53, Agogo 60, Frimpong 74		
24-03	Austria	D	1-1	Graz	Fr	Muntari 87	10 608	Verbist BEL
27-03	Brazil	L	0-1	Stockholm	Fr		20 104	Fröjdfeldt SWE
21-08	Senegal	D	1-1	London	Fr	Gyan 43	2 788	D'Urso ENG
8-09	Morocco	W	2-0	Rouen	Fr	Agogo 47, Barusso 67		
11-09	Saudi Arabia	L	0-5	Riyadh	Fr			
18-11	Togo	W	2-0	Accra	Fr	Gyan.B 58, Kingston 76		
21-11	Benin	W	4-2	Accra	Fr	Agogo 47, Kingston 2 71 85, Appiah 83		
2008								
20-01	Guinea	W	2-1	Accra	CNr1	Gyan.A 55p, Muntari 89		Maillet SEY
24-01	Namibia	W	1-0	Accra	CNr1	Agogo 41		Bennaceur TUN
28-01	Morocco	W	2-0	Accra	CNr1	Essien 26, Muntari 44		Sowe GAM
3-02	Nigeria	W	2-1	Accra	CNqf	Essien 44, Agogo 82		Benouza ALG
7-02	Cameroon	L	0-1	Accra	CNsf			El Arjoune MAR
9-02	Côte d'Ivoire	W	4-2	Kumasi	CN3p	Muntari 10, Owusu-Abeyie 70, Agogo 80, Dramani 84		Damon RSA
26-03	Mexico	L	1-2	London	Fr	Essien 54		Styles ENG
23-05	Australia	L	0-1	Sydney	Fr		29 910	Matsuo JPN
1-06	Libya	W	3-0	Kumasi	WCq	Tagoe 17, Agogo 54, Kingston 64	27 908	Maillet SEY
8-06	Lesotho	W	3-2	Bloemfontein	WCq	Kingston 15, Agogo 2 41 63	8 000	Gasingwa RWA
14-06	Gabon	L	0-2	Libreville	WCq		13 000	Benouza ALG
22-06	Gabon	W	2-1	Accra	WCq	Tagoe 31, Muntari 75	29 040	Damon RSA

Fr = Friendly match • CN = CAF African Cup of Nations • WC = FIFA World Cup
q = qualifier • r1 = first round group • r2 = second round •qf = quarter-final • sf = semi-final • 3p = third place play-off

GHANA NATIONAL TEAM PLAYERS

	Player		Club	Date of Birth		Player		Club	Date of Birth
1	Sammy Adjei	GK	Ashdod	1 09 1980	12	Dede Ayew	MF	Olymp. Marseille	17 12 1989
2	Hans Sarpei	DF	Bayer Leverkusen	28 6 1976	13	Baffour Gyan	FW	Saturn Rameskoye	2 07 1980
3	Asamoah Gyan	FW	Udinese	22 11 1985	14	Bernard Yao Kumodzi	MF	Panionios	21 03 1985
4	John Paintsil	DF	West Ham United	15 06 1981	15	Ahmed Barusso	MF	Roma	26 12 1984
5	John Mensah (C)	DF	Stade Rennais	29 11 1982	16	Fatau Dauda	GK	AshantiGold	6 04 1985
6	Anthony Annan	MF	IK Start	21 07 1986	17	Nana Kwasi Asare	DF	Excelsior Moeskroen	11 07 1986
7	Laryea Kingston	MF	Hearts	7 11 1980	18	Eric Addo	MF	PSV Eindhoven	12 11 1978
8	Michael Essien	MF	Chelsea	3 12 1982	19	Shilla Illiasu	DF	Saturn Rameskoye	20 06 1983
9	Junior Agogo	FW	Nottingham Forest	1 08 1979	20	Quincy Owusu Abeyie	FW	Celta Vigo	15 04 1986
10	Kwadwo Asamoah	FW	Liberty Pros	9 12 1988	21	Harrison Afful	DF	Asante Kotoko	24 07 1986
11	Sulley Muntari	MF	Portsmouth	17 08 1984	22	Richard Kingson	GK	Birmingham City	13 07 1975
					23	Haminu Dramani	MF	Lokomotiv Moskva	1 04 1986

Ghana's squad for the 2008 CAF Africa Cup of Nations

GHANA NATIONAL TEAM RECORDS AND RECORD SEQUENCES

Records			Sequence records			
Victory	9-1	NIG 1969	Wins	8	1965-1967	Clean sheets	6	1990-1991
Defeat	2-8	BRA 1996	Defeats	6	1996	Goals scored	29	1963-1967
Player Caps	72	Abedi Pele	Undefeated	21	1981-1983	Without goal	5	1985
Player Goals	33	Abedi Pele	Without win	9	1994-1997	Goals against	15	1967-1968

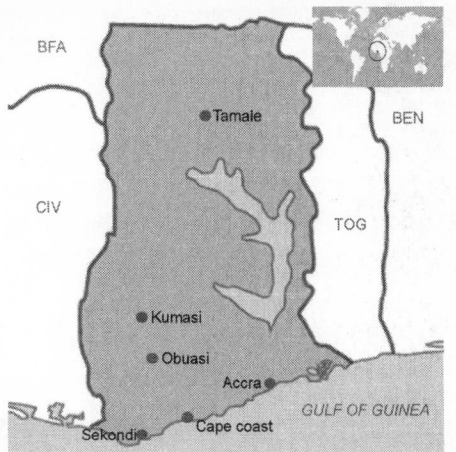

MAJOR CITIES/TOWNS

		Population '000
1	Accra	3 554
2	Kumasi	1 604
3	Tamale	390
4	Takoradi	260
5	Cape Coast	154
6	Sekondi	149
7	Obuasi	147
8	Koforidua	99
9	Wa	83
10	Techiman	75
11	Sunyani	73
12	Ho	73
13	Bawku	59
14	Bolgatanga	56
15	Lashibi	54
16	Tafo	53
17	Swedru	52
18	Ejura	49
19	Berekum	49
20	Aflao	48
21	Nkawkaw	48
22	Oduponkpehe	48
23	Winneba	45
24	Oda	45

REPUBLIC OF GHANA

Capital	Accra	Language English	Independence 1957
Population 22 409 572	Area 239 460 km²	Density 86 per km²	% in cities 36%
GDP per cap $2200	Dailling code +233	Internet .gh	GMT +/- 0

The Accra metropolitan area includes Accra 2 096; Ashiaman 228; Tema 161; Teshie 154; Madina 112; Nungua 75; Tema New Town 74; Dome 56; Lashibi 54; Gbawe 52; Taifa 48 and Adenta East 39

MEDALS TABLE

		Overall			League			Cup			Africa			City	Stadium	Cap'ty	DoF
		G	S	B	G	S	B	G	S	B	G	S	B				
1	Asante Kotoko	30	22	6	20	13	3	8	2		2	7	3	Kumasi	Kumasi Sports Stadium	51 500	1935
2	Hearts of Oak	29	17	7	18	11	5	9	4		2	2	2	Accra	Ohene Djan	35 000	1911
3	Great Olympics	5	3	6	2	2	5	3	1				1	Accra	Accra Sports Stadium	40 000	1954
4	Real Republicans	5		1		1		4					1	Accra			1962-66
5	Ashanti Gold	4	5	3	3	3	3	1	1			1		Obuasi	Len Clay	30 000	1978
6	Eleven Wise	2	5	3	1	3	3	1	2					Sekondi	Gyandu Park	15 000	1919
7	Sekondi Hasaacas	2	4	2	1	3	1	1	1			1		Sekondi	Gyandu Park	15 000	1931
8	Cape Coast Dwarfs	2	3	4	1	1	4	1	2					Cape Coast	Sudu Park	10 000	1968
9	Cornerstones	1	7			4		1	3					Kumasi	Kumasi Sports Stadium	51 500	1931
10	Okwahu United	1	3	2	1	2		1	2					Nkawkaw	Nkawkaw Sports Stadium	15 000	
11	Ghapoha Tema	1	1					1	1					Tema	Tema Sports Stadium	10 000	
12	Voradep Ho	1						1						Ho	Ho Sports Stadium	8 000	
13	Real Tamale United		5	3		2	3				3			Tamale	Kaladan Park	10 000	1976
14	Brong-Ahofu United		2	3		1	3		1					Sunyani	Coronation Park	10 000	
15	Bofoakwa Tano		2	2		1	2		1					Sunyani	Coronation Park	10 000	

RECENT LEAGUE AND CUP RECORD

	Championship						Cup		
Year	Champions	Pts	Runners-up	Pts	Third	Pts	Winners	Score	Runners-up
1995	Goldfields Obuasi	33	Real Tamale United	36	Asante Kotoko	33	Great Olympics		Hearts of Oak
1996	Goldfields Obuasi	51	Asante Kotoko	50	Okwahu United	46	Hearts of Oak	1-0	Ghapoha Tema
1997	Hearts of Oak	54	Real Tamale United	51	Goldfields Obuasi	48	Ghapoha Tema	1-0	Okwahu United
1998	Hearts of Oak	52	Asante Kotoko	48	Great Olympics	39	Asante Kotoko	1-0	Real Tamale United
1999	Hearts of Oak	62	Cape Coast Dwarfs	53	Real Tamale United	52	Hearts of Oak	3-1	Great Olympics
2000	Hearts of Oak	57	Goldfields Obuasi	53	King Faisal Babies	46	Hearts of Oak	2-0	Okwahu United
2001	Hearts of Oak	64	Asante Kotoko	55	Goldfields Obuasi	45	Asante Kotoko	1-0	King Faisal Babies
2002	Hearts of Oak	78	Asante Kotoko	73	Liberty Professionals	48	Ghana FA Cup not played since 2001		
2003	Asante Kotoko	75	Hearts of Oak	66	King Faisal Babies	54			
2004	Hearts of Oak	1-0	Asante Kotoko						
2005	Asante Kotoko	63	Hearts of Oak	56	King Faisal Babies	50			
2006	Season readjustment								
2007	Hearts of Oak	58	AshantiGold	53	Asante Kotoko	51			
2008	Asante Kotoko	69	Heart of Lions	53	Arsenal Berekum	46			

GHANA 2007–08

ONE TOUCH PREMIER LEAGUE

	Pl	W	D	L	F	A	Pts	Asante Kotoko	Heart of Lions	Arsenal	Liberty Pros	AshantiGold	King Faisal	All Stars	Hearts of Oak	Tema Youth	Kessben	RTU	All Blacks	Hasaacas	Real Sportive	Zaytuna	Olympics
Asante Kotoko	30	21	6	3	53	18	69		3-2	2-0	1-0	2-0	2-1	1-0	3-3	2-0	2-0	2-0	3-0	2-1	2-1	2-1	5-0
Heart of Lions	30	16	5	9	40	28	53	1-2		4-2	1-1	1-0	1-0	1-0	2-0	2-0	1-0	1-0	2-1	0-2	2-0	2-1	4-0
Arsenal Berekum	30	13	7	10	32	29	46	0-0	2-0		2-0	1-0	2-1	0-0	2-0	0-0	1-1	1-0	1-0	1-0	2-1	3-0	2-1
Liberty Professionals	30	13	6	11	48	36	45	1-1	0-0	1-0		2-0	4-0	3-1	1-2	2-0	1-1	6-2	1-2	2-0	3-1	2-1	3-1
AshantiGold	30	11	9	10	34	26	42	1-0	1-2	2-2	0-0		0-0	2-0	1-0	1-2	2-0	0-0	4-0	2-1	3-1	3-0	3-1
King Faisal Babies	30	9	14	7	36	29	41	0-0	2-2	2-0	3-1	0-0		2-1	2-0	2-2	0-1	2-1	1-1	2-0	3-1	2-2	4-2
All Stars	30	12	5	13	27	30	41	0-2	3-0	1-0	0-1	0-0	1-0		1-0	1-0	1-0	1-0	2-1	1-0	0-0	0-1	2-1
Hearts of Oak	30	10	10	10	31	31	40	0-0	1-1	2-2	1-0	1-1	0-0	3-0		1-1	2-0	0-0	2-1	2-0	3-2	1-0	0-0
Tema Youth	30	10	10	10	30	35	40	0-2	0-1	2-1	2-1	2-0	0-0	0-3	3-2		1-2	1-0	2-0	1-0	1-1	1-0	1-1
Kessben	30	10	8	12	29	33	38	0-1	1-1	0-1	1-2	1-1	0-0	2-1	1-0	3-1		1-0	1-1	2-0	2-0	2-0	3-0
Real Tamale United	30	12	5	13	31	40	38	1-0	0-4	3-1	4-3	3-1	0-0	0-2	2-0	2-2	2-0		2-1	1-1	1-0	2-1	2-1
Gamba All Blacks	30	11	5	14	30	40	38	1-3	1-0	0-1	1-0	1-0	1-0	1-1	0-1	1-0	1-1	2-0		2-1	3-0	2-0	0-0
Hasaacas Sekondi	30	10	7	13	44	41	37	2-2	1-0	2-1	2-2	0-0	2-2	4-1	3-2	1-1	4-1	**3-0**	5-1		2-1	2-1	0-0
Real Sportive Tema	30	9	6	15	36	47	33	0-3	3-1	2-0	2-1	2-1	1-1	2-1	0-0	0-1	3-0	2-0	1-2	4-3		**0-3**	2-0
Zaytuna	30	9	6	15	32	43	33	0-3	1-0	1-0	3-1	1-2	1-1	1-0	2-1	2-2	1-1	1-2	3-2	2-1	2-2		0-1
Great Olympics	30	5	9	16	23	50	24	2-0	0-1	1-1	1-3	0-3	0-3	2-2	0-1	1-1	2-1	0-1	2-0	2-1	1-1	0-0	

2/07/2007 - 6/07/2008 • † Qualified for the CAF Champions League • ‡ Qualified for the Confederation Cup • Matches in bold awarded
§ = points deducted • Top scorer: Eric Bekoe, Asante Kotoko

GNB – GUINEA-BISSAU

NATIONAL TEAM RECORD
JULY 10TH 2006 TO JULY 12TH 2010

PL	W	D	L	F	A	%
4	1	2	1	3	2	50

FIFA/COCA-COLA WORLD RANKING

1993	1994	1995	1996	1997	1998	1999	2000	2001	2002	2003	2004	2005	2006	2007	High	
131	122	118	133	148	165	173	177	174	183	186	190	186	191	171	115	07/94

	2007–2008											Low	
08/07	09/07	10/07	11/07	12/07	01/08	02/08	03/08	04/08	05/08	06/08	07/08	193	03/07
188	191	190	181	171	171	174	174	176	175	176	174		

After a year without any international activity, football in the impoverished former Portuguese colony burst into a sudden flourish of activity at the end of 2007. Entry into the FIFA World Cup qualifiers saw Guinea-Bissau drawn to play a two-legged preliminary round tie against Sierra Leone, a result of their lowly status in the FIFA/Coca-Cola World Ranking. With Baciro Conde returning to the helm of the national side for the matches, the team belied its lowly status to push Sierra Leone close in a tie that saw just one goal decide the outcome in favour of the Leone Stars. That left Guinea-Bissau eliminated from the 2010 FIFA World Cup qualifiers before they had

INTERNATIONAL HONOURS
None

virtually started, and before the draw had been held for the preliminaries in Durban that November. But the west African country then immediately played host to the 19th Amilcar Cabral Cup, a tournament whose status is being threatened by the failure of its more prominent protagonists to bring full international teams to the competition. For the hosts, failure to reach the final ended hopes of a first ever triumph in a competition but they did beat Sierra Leone in a first round group match before losing to the Cape Verde Islands in the semi-finals. Mali's under-23 side then beat Cape Verde in Bissau to claim the title.

THE FIFA BIG COUNT OF 2006

	Male	Female		Total
Number of players	71 900	0	Referees and Assistant Referees	100
Professionals	0		Admin, Coaches, Technical, Medical	300
Amateurs 18+	1 100		Number of clubs	40
Youth under 18	1 200		Number of teams	110
Unregistered	7 500		Clubs with women's teams	0
Total players	71 900		Players as % of population	4.99%

Federação de Futebol da Guiné-Bissau (FFGB)
Alto Bandim (Nova Sede), Case Postale 375, Bissau 1035, Guinea-Bissau
Tel +245 201918   Fax +245 211414
federacaofutebol@hotmail.com   www.none
President: LOBATO Jose   General Secretary: CASSAMA Infali
Vice-President: CANDIDO Carvalho   Treasurer: DAVYES Lolita Francisca Maria   Media Officer: TCHAGO Jorge
Men's Coach: CANDE Baciro   Women's Coach: KEITA Sidico
FFGB formed: 1974   CAF: 1986   FIFA: 1986
Red shirts, Green shorts, Red socks

RECENT INTERNATIONAL MATCHES PLAYED BY GUINEA-BISSAU

2002	Opponents	Score	Venue	Comp	Scorers	Att	Referee
No international matches played after June 2002							
2003							
10-10	Mali	L 1-2	Bissau	WCq	Dionisio Fernandes 50	22 000	Sowe GAM
14-11	Mali	L 0-2	Bamako	WCq		13 251	Seydou MTN
2004							
No International matches played in 2004							
2005							
18-11	Guinea	D 2-2	Conakry	ACr1	Manuel Fernandes 2 35p 49		
20-11	Sierra Leone	D 1-1	Conakry	ACr1	Agostino Soares 62		
25-11	Senegal †	D 1-1	Conakry	ACsf			
27-11	Mali †	L 0-1	Conakry	AC3p			
2006							
No international matches played in 2006							
2007							
17-10	Sierra Leone	L 0-1	Freetown	WCq		25 000	Mana NGA
17-11	Sierra Leone	D 0-0	Bissau	WCq		12 000	Lamptey GHA
2-12	Sierra Leone	W 2-0	Bissau	ACr1	Emiliano 8, Suleimane 49		
7-12	Cape Verde	D 1-1	Bissau	ACsf	Adilson 7. L 2-3p		
2008							
No international matches played in 2008 before August							

AC = Amilcar Cabral Cup • WC = FIFA World Cup
q = qualifier • r1 = first round group • sf = semi-final • 3p = third place play-off • † Not a full international

GUINEA-BISSAU NATIONAL TEAM RECORDS AND RECORD SEQUENCES

Records			Sequence records					
Victory	7-2	BEN 2001	Wins	3	1990-1991	Clean sheets	5	1987-1988
Defeat	1-6	MLI 1997	Defeats	5	1980-1981	Goals scored	6	1989-1991
Player Caps	n/a		Undefeated	11	1987-1989	Without goal	3	1985, 1997-2000
Player Goals	n/a		Without win	8	1979-1981	Goals against	13	1994-1997

RECENT LEAGUE AND CUP RECORD

	Championship						Cup		
Year	Champions	Pts	Runners-up	Pts	Third	Pts	Winners	Score	Runners-up
1997	Sporting Bissau						No tournament		
1998	Sporting Bissau						No tournament		
1999	No competition held						No tournament		
2000	Sporting Bissau	38	Benfica	36	União Bissau	36	Portas Bissau	2-1	Mavegro FC
2001	No competition held						No tournament		
2002	Sporting Bissau	39	Portas Bissau	37	União Bissau	32	Mavegro FC	3-1	Sporting Bafatá
2003	União Bissau	47	Sporting Bissau	44	Sporting Bafatá	43	Tournament not finished		
2004	Sporting Bissau	39	Benfica	28	Mavegro FC	28	Mavegro FC	1-0	Sporting Bissau
2005	Sporting Bissau	45	Atlético Bissorã	38	Mavegro FC	37	Sporting Bissau	4-2	Atlético Bissorã
2006	Os Balantas	50	Mavegro FC	47	Desportivo Mansabá	33	Portas Bissau	2-1	Benfica
2007	Sporting Bissau	47	Os Balantas	46					
2008									

GUINEA-BISSAU COUNTRY INFORMATION

Capital	Bissau	Independence	1973 from Portugal	GDP per Capita	$800
Population	1 388 363	Status	Republic	GNP Ranking	184
Area km²	36 120	Language	Portuguese	Dialling code	+245
Population density	38 per km²	Literacy rate	34%	Internet code	.gw
% in urban areas	22%	Main religion	Indigenous 50%, Muslim 45%	GMT + / –	0
Towns/Cities ('000)	Bissau 388; Bafatá 22; Gabú 14; Bissorã 12; Bolama 10; Cacheu 10; Bubaque 9				
Neighbours (km)	Senegal 338; Guinea 386; Atlantic Ocean 350				
Main stadia	24 de Setembro – Bissau 20 000; Lino Correia – Bissau 12 000				

GRE – GREECE

NATIONAL TEAM RECORD
JULY 10TH 2006 TO JULY 12TH 2010

PL	W	D	L	F	A	%
24	13	2	9	37	30	58.3

FIFA/COCA-COLA WORLD RANKING

1993	1994	1995	1996	1997	1998	1999	2000	2001	2002	2003	2004	2005	2006	2007	High	
34	28	34	35	42	53	34	42	57	48	30	18	16	16	11	8	04/08

2007–2008											Low	
08/07	09/07	10/07	11/07	12/07	01/08	02/08	03/08	04/08	05/08	06/08	07/08	66	09/98
14	15	14	11	11	11	10	10	8	8	8	18		

Greece came to the finals of Euro 2008 on the back of a fine qualifying campaign that saw them finish comfortably on top of their qualifying group, while in the run up they established a new record for the national team of seven consecutive wins. Lightning, however, never strikes twice and no-one, not even the Greeks themselves, believed that they would retain the European title they won so surprisingly four years previously in Portugal. That lack of belief may help explain their lacklustre performances in the finals as they went home without even a point. With hindsight it proved to be one of the toughest groups with both Spain and Russia reaching the semi-finals and

INTERNATIONAL HONOURS
UEFA European Championship 2004   Qualified for the FIFA World Cup 1994

the Greek federation vowed to stick with coach Otto Rehhagel in the quest to qualify for their first World Cup finals since 1994. In the Superleague, Olympiacos retained their title by the narrowest of margins, finishing two points ahead of AEK, but had Apollon not fielded the ineligible Roman Wallner in their 1-0 victory over Olympiacos, AEK would have been champions. That 1-0 defeat was overturned and Olympiacos were awarded a 3-0 victory and three crucial points that won them the title. There was no consolation of a Champions League place for AEK either after they finished behind Panathinakos in a play-off to determine the second Greek representative. Hard luck indeed.

THE FIFA BIG COUNT OF 2006

	Male	Female		Total
Number of players	705 164	55 457	Referees and Assistant Referees	3 230
Professionals	1 818		Admin, Coaches, Technical, Medical	10 100
Amateurs 18+	268 570		Number of clubs	5 571
Youth under 18	86 779		Number of teams	5 899
Unregistered	145 400		Clubs with women's teams	197
Total players	760 621		Players as % of population	7.12%

Hellenic Football Federation (HFF)
137 Singrou Avenue, 3rd Floor, Athens 17121, Greece
Tel +30 210 9306000   Fax +30 210 9359666
epo@epo.gr   www.epo.gr
President: GAGATSIS Vassilis   General Secretary: ECONOMIDES Ioannis Dr
Vice-President: VARDINOGIANNIS Ioannis   Treasurer: GIRTZIKIS George   Media Officer: TSAPIDIS Michael
Men's Coach: REHHAGEL Otto   Women's Coach: BATSILAS Dimitrios
HFF formed: 1926   UEFA: 1954   FIFA: 1927
Blue shirts with white trimmings, Blue shorts, Blue socks or White shirts with blue trimmings, White shirts, White socks

RECENT INTERNATIONAL MATCHES PLAYED BY GREECE

2006	Opponents	Score	Venue	Comp	Scorers	Att	Referee
21-01	Korea Republic	D 1-1	Riyadh	Fr	Zagorakis [10]		Al Shehri KSA
25-01	Saudi Arabia	D 1-1	Riyadh	Fr	Zagorakis [59p]	2 900	Mohammoud BHR
28-02	Belarus	W 1-0	Limassol	Fr	Samaras [15]	3 000	Salomir ROU
1-03	Kazakhstan	W 2-0	Nicosia	Fr	Samaras [68], Giannakopoulos [90]	2 000	Kailis CYP
25-05	Australia	L 0-1	Melbourne	Fr		95 103	Riley ENG
16-08	England	L 0-4	Manchester	Fr		45 864	Stark GER
2-09	Moldova	W 1-0	Chisinau	ECq	Liberopoulos [77]	10 500	Trefoloni ITA
7-10	Norway	W 1-0	Piraeus	ECq	Katsouranis [33]	21 189	Michel SVK
11-10	Bosnia-Hercegovina	W 4-0	Zenica	ECq	Charisteas [8p], Patsatzoglou [82], Samaras [85], Katsouranis [94+]	8 000	Baskakov RUS
15-11	France	L 0-1	Paris	Fr		63 680	Wack GER/Wezel GER
2007							
6-02	Korea Republic	L 0-1	London	Fr		9 242	Dean ENG
24-03	Turkey	L 1-4	Piraeus	ECq	Kyrgiakos [5]	31 405	Stark GER
28-03	Malta	W 1-0	Ta'Qali	ECq	Basinas [66p]	8 700	Garcia POR
2-06	Hungary	W 2-0	Irákleio	ECq	Gekas [16], Seitaridis [29]	17 244	Larsen DEN
6-06	Moldova	W 2-1	Irákleio	ECq	Charisteas [30], Liberopoulos [95+]	22 000	Wegereef NED
22-08	Spain	L 2-3	Thessaloníki	Fr	Gekas [17], Katsouranis [43]	15 000	Lannoy FRA
12-09	Norway	D 2-2	Oslo	ECq	Kyrgiakos 2 [7 30]	24 080	Busacca SUI
13-10	Bosnia-Hercegovina	W 3-2	Athens	ECq	Charisteas [10], Gekas [58], Liberopoulos [73]	30 250	Gilewski POL
17-10	Turkey	W 1-0	Istanbul	ECq	Amanatidis [79]	22 818	Mejuto Gonzalez ESP
17-11	Malta	W 5-0	Athens	ECq	Gekas 3 [32 72 74], Basinas [54], Amanatidis [61]	31 332	Kaldma EST
21-11	Hungary	W 2-1	Budapest	ECq	Vanczák OG [22], Basinas [59p]	32 300	Styles ENG
2008							
6-02	Finland	W 2-1	Nicosia	Fr	Charisteas [67], Katsouranis [72]	500	Kailis CYP
26-03	Portugal	W 3-2	Dusseldorf	Fr	Karagounis 2 [33 59]	25 000	Kirchen GER
19-05	Cyprus	W 2-0	Patras	Fr	Ninis [5], Katsouranis [58p]	16 216	MacDonald SCO
24-05	Hungary	L 2-3	Budapest	Fr	Amanatidis [45], Katsouranis [93+]	7 000	Blom NED
1-06	Armenia	D 0-0	Offenbach/Main	Fr			
10-06	Sweden	L 0-2	Salzburg	ECr1		31 063	Busacca SUI
14-06	Russia	L 0-1	Salzburg	ECr1		31 063	Rosetti ENG
18-06	Spain	L 1-2	Salzburg	ECr1	Charisteas [42]	30 883	Webb ENG

Fr = Friendly match • EC = UEFA EURO 2008 • WC = FIFA World Cup • q = qualifier • r1 = First round group

GREECE NATIONAL TEAM PLAYERS

	Player		Ap	G	Club	Date of Birth		Player		Ap	G	Club	Date of Birth
1	Antonis Nikopolidis	GK	90	0	Olympiacos	14 01 1971	12	Kostas Chalkias	GK	15	0	Aris Thessaloniki	30 05 1974
2	Giourkas Seitaridis	DF	58	1	Atlético Madrid	4 06 1981	13	Alexandros Tzorvas	GK	0	0	OFI Crete	12 08 1982
3	Christos Patsatzoglou	DF	30	1	Olympiacos	19 03 1979	14	Dimitris Salpingidis	FW	21	1	Panathinaikos	18 08 1981
4	Nikos Spiropoulos	DF	6	0	Panathinaikos	10 10 1983	15	Vassilis Torosidis	DF	15	0	Olympiacos	10 06 1985
5	Traianos Dellas	DF	45	1	AEK Athens	31 01 1976	16	Sotiris Kyrgiakos	DF	41	4	Eint. Frankfurt	23 07 1979
6	Angelos Basinas	MF	91	7	RCD Mallorca	3 01 1976	17	Fanis Gekas	FW	29	6	Bay. Leverkusen	23 05 1980
7	Giorgos Samaras	FW	19	3	Celtic	21 02 1985	18	Giannis Goumas	DF	45	0	Panathinaikos	24 05 1975
8	Stelios Giannakopoulos	MF	77	12	Bolton Wand's	12 07 1974	19	Paraskevas Antzas	DF	26	0	Olympiacos	18 08 1976
9	Angelos Charisteas	FW	68	19	1.FC Nürnberg	9 02 1980	20	Giannis Amanatidis	FW	29	3	Eint. Frankfurt	3 12 1981
10	Giorgos Karagounis	MF	76	6	Panathinaikos	6 03 1977	21	Kostas Katsouranis	MF	52	6	Benfica	21 06 1979
11	Loukas Vintra	DF	19	0	Panathinaikos	5 02 1981	22	Alexandros Tziolis	MF	9	0	Panathinaikos	13 02 1985
							23	Nikos Liberopoulos	FW	60	13	AEK Athens	4 08 1975

The Greek Squad for Euro 2008

GREECE NATIONAL TEAM RECORDS AND RECORD SEQUENCES

Records				Sequence records			
Victory	8-0	SYR 1949	Wins	7	2007-2008	Clean sheets	4	Five times
Defeat	1-11	HUN 1938	Defeats	10	1931-1933	Goals scored	17	1934-1949
Player Caps	120	Theodoros Zagorakis	Undefeated	15	2002-2004	Without goal	6	2005
Player Goals	29	Nikos Anastopoulos	Without win	12	1954-1960	Goals against	21	1957-1964

HELLENIC REPUBLIC; ELLINIKI DHIMOKRATIA

Capital	Athens	Language	Greek			Independence	1829
Population	10 688 058	Area	131 940 km²	Density	80 per km²	% in cities	65%
GDP per cap	$20 000	Dailling code	+30	Internet	.gr	GMT + / -	+2

The Athens metropolitan population figure includes: Piraeus 170; Peristéri 137; Kallithéa 106; Níkaia 95; Glifáda 92; Akharnaí 86; Néa Smírni 76; Egaleo 71 • The Thessaloníki metropolitan figure includes: Kalamariá 93

MEDALS TABLE

		Overall			League			Cup		Europe			City	Stadium	Cap'ty	DoF
		G	S	B	G	S	B	G	S	G	S	B				
1	Olympiacos	59	27	10	36	16	10	23	11				Piraeus	Karaiskaki	33 500	1925
2	Panathinaikos	35	30	18	19	19	16	16	10		1	2	Athens	Apostolos Nikolaidis	16 620	1908
3	AEK	23	25	15	11	19	14	12	6			1	Athens	Olympic Stadium	72 000	1924
4	PAOK	6	16	8	2	4	8	4	12				Thessaloníki	Toumba	28 701	1926
5	Aris	4	10	8	3	3	8	1	7				Thessaloníki	Harilaou	18 308	1914
6	Panionios	2	6	3		2	3	2	4				Athens	Nea Smyrni	11 700	1890
7	Larissa	3	3		1	1		2	2				Larissa	Alkazar	13 108	1964
8	Iraklis	1	7	2		3	2	1	4				Thessaloníki	Kaftanzoglio	28 028	1908
9	OFI Crete	1	2	2		1	2	1	1				Irákleio	Pankritio	33 240	1925
10	Ethnikos	1	2			2		1					Piraeus	Georgios Kamaras	14 200	1925
11	Kastoria	1					1						Kastoria	Kastoria	8 000	1963
12	Apollon Smyrnis		3	5		2	5		1				Athens	Georgios Kamaras	14 200	1891
13	Doxa Dramas		3						3				Drama	Doxa Dramas	7 000	1918
14	Athinaikos		1						1				Athens	Vyrona	4 340	1917
	Ionikos		1						1				Piraeus	Neapolis Public	7 026	1965
	Pierikos Kateríni		1						1				Kateríni			1961
17	Atromitos-Chalkidona			1			1						Peristéri	Peristeri	8 939	1923

RECENT LEAGUE AND CUP RECORD

	Championship						Cup		
Year	Champions	Pts	Runners-up	Pts	Third	Pts	Winners	Score	Runners-up
1996	Panathinaikos	83	AEK	81	Olympiacos	65	AEK	7-1	Apollon
1997	Olympiacos	84	AEK	72	OFI Crete	66	AEK	0-0 5-3p	Panathinaikos
1998	Olympiacos	88	Panathinaikos	85	AEK	74	Panionios	1-0	Panathinaikos
1999	Olympiacos	85	AEK	75	Panathinaikos	74	Olympiacos	2-0	Panathinaikos
2000	Olympiacos	92	Panathinaikos	88	AEK	66	AEK	2-0	Ionikos
2001	Olympiacos	78	Panathinaikos	66	AEK	61	PAOK	4-2	Olympiacos
2002	Olympiacos	58	AEK	58	Panathinaikos	55	AEK	2-1	Olympiacos
2003	Olympiacos	70	Panathinaikos	70	AEK	68	PAOK	1-0	Aris
2004	Panathinaikos	77	Olympiacos	75	PAOK	60	Panathinaikos	3-1	Olympiacos
2005	Olympiacos	65	Panathinaikos	64	AEK	62	Olympiacos	3-0	Aris
2006	Olympiacos	70	AEK	67	Panathinaikos	67	Olympiacos	3-0	AEK
2007	Olympiacos	71	AEK	62	Panathinaikos	54	Larisa	2-1	Panathinaikos
2008	Olympiacos	70	AEK	68	Panathinaikos	66	Olympiacos	2-0	Aris

GREECE 2007-08

SUPERLEAGUE

	Pl	W	D	L	F	A	Pts	Olympiacos	AEK	Pan'naikos	Aris	Panionios	Larisa	Asteras	Xánthi	PAOK	Iraklis	Levadiakos	OFI	Ergotelis	Atromitos	Veria	Apollon
Olympiacos †	30	21	7	2	58	23	70		1-0	1-1	1-0	4-1	2-1	1-1	2-1	2-1	3-1	4-0	6-2	1-0	2-0	1-0	1-0
AEK Athens ‡	30	22	2	6	65	17	68	4-0		1-1	1-1	2-3	1-0	2-0	3-0	2-0	1-2	3-0	4-0	3-1	2-0	5-1	4-0
Panathinaikos †	30	20	6	4	44	18	66	0-0	2-1		1-0	2-1	2-0	2-0	0-0	2-0	1-1	1-0	3-1	1-0	2-0	1-0	1-0
Aris Thessaloníki ‡	30	14	8	8	33	20	50	1-1	0-1	0-1		0-0	1-1	2-0	2-0	3-1	2-2	1-0	2-0	2-0	2-0	1-0	2-2
Panionios	30	13	6	11	39	42	45	0-4	0-3	1-0	0-3		3-1	4-1	3-2	0-0	1-1	2-0	1-3	2-1	2-1	2-2	2-1
Larisa	30	11	12	7	35	30	45	0-0	1-0	2-2	1-0	1-0		1-1	0-0	4-3	1-0	3-3	5-1	3-2	2-0	1-1	2-1
Asteras Tripolis	30	11	11	8	28	24	44	1-0	2-1	1-0	0-0	1-0	0-1		0-0	2-0	0-0	1-2	1-1	1-1	1-0	2-0	1-1
Xánthi	30	10	6	14	33	39	36	1-4	0-1	3-2	0-2	1-2	1-1	2-0		1-0	0-3	4-1	1-0	1-0	0-1	2-0	6-1
PAOK Thessaloníki	30	10	5	15	29	35	35	1-1	0-4	0-1	3-0	3-1	1-0	0-1	0-1		3-0	1-0	2-2	1-0	1-0	2-0	4-1
Iraklis Thesaloníki	30	8	11	11	28	34	35	1-2	0-1	0-1	1-1	1-0	1-1	0-0	1-1	1-0		1-0	1-0	0-1	1-1	1-1	5-2
Levadiakos	30	10	3	17	31	51	33	1-3	0-4	0-4	2-0	1-0	0-1	0-0	2-1	2-0	3-0		0-3	0-0	2-1	5-3	2-0
OFI Crete	30	9	5	16	39	49	32	0-1	1-4	4-1	0-1	1-2	0-0	0-3	2-0	2-0	1-2				4-1	0-1	3-2
Ergotelis	30	7	9	14	28	42	30	3-3	1-4	0-3	1-1	1-1	0-0	3-2	2-0	1-0	2-1	1-1			0-0	2-0	2-2
Atromitos	30	8	5	17	23	36	29	1-3	0-1	0-1	1-2	0-2	2-0	0-2	2-3	0-0	1-1	2-1	1-0	1-2		1-0	3-0
Veria	30	5	8	17	21	44	23	0-1	0-1	0-2	1-0	1-1	1-0	1-0	1-1	1-0	1-2	3-1	2-1	1-1	1-1		0-2
Apollon Kalamarias §1	30	5	8	17	27	57	22	0-3	0-1	1-3	0-0	0-2	1-1	2-2	1-0	0-2	1-1	2-0	1-1	2-1	0-2	1-0	

1/09/2007 - 20/04/2008 • † Qualified for the UEFA Champions League • ‡ Qualified for the UEFA Cup • § = points deducted • Match in bold was awarded after Apollon used an ineligible player. Apollon had won the original match 1-0 • Top scorer: Ismael Blanco, AEK 19

CHAMPIONS LEAGUE PLAY-OFF

	Pl	W	D	L	F	A	Pts	Pa	AA	AT	Pa
Panathinaikos §7	6	4	2	0	14	5	21		4-1	3-1	3-0
AEK Athens §8	6	2	2	2	10	11	16	1-1		1-0	5-0
Aris Thessaloníki §2	6	1	2	3	9	9	7	1-1	4-0		3-3
Panionios	6	1	2	3	7	15	5	1-2	2-2	1-0	

23/04/2008 - 14/05/2008 • § = bonus points • Panathinaikos qualified for the Champions League, AEK and Aris for the UEFA Cup

GREECE 2007-08 BETA ETHNIK (2)

	Pl	W	D	L	F	A	Pts
Panserraikos	34	19	10	5	48	20	67
Thrasivoulos	34	18	7	9	44	27	61
Panthrakikos	34	17	10	7	44	31	60
PAS Giannina	34	16	9	9	54	38	57
Ionikos	34	15	9	10	37	28	54
Kallithea	34	15	7	12	40	35	52
Kérkira	34	13	11	10	39	33	50
Agrotikos Asteras	34	14	5	15	44	47	47
Ethnikos Piraeus	34	11	12	11	32	36	45
Ilisiakos	34	13	4	17	31	38	43
Kalamata	34	11	9	14	30	33	42
Ethnikos Asteras	34	10	11	13	32	37	41
Pierikos Katerini	34	10	14	10	28	33	41
Olympiacos Volos	34	9	12	13	33	38	39
Kastoria	34	10	9	15	26	41	39
Egaleo	34	10	9	15	28	34	39
Chaidari	34	8	14	12	30	31	38
Agios Dimitrios	34	2	8	24	22	62	14

22/09/2007 - 2/06/2008

HELLENIC CUP 2007-08

Round of 16

Olympiacos *	4
Panathinaikos	0
Panionios	0
Iraklis Thessaloníki *	1
Larisa	2
Apollon Kalamarias *	1
PAS Preveza	0
Thrasivoulos *	3
Atromitos	1
Asteras Tripolis *	0
Agrotikos Asteras *	1 0
OFI Crete	1 5
Xánthi *	2
AEK Athens	0
Ethnikos Katerini *	0
Aris Thessaloníki	3

Quarter-finals

Olympiacos *	2 2
Iraklis Thessaloníki	0 2
Larisa	0 1
Thrasivoulos *	1 3
Atromitos *	3 1
OFI Crete	1 2
Xánthi *	0 0
Aris Thessaloníki	0 1

Semi-finals

Olympiacos	3 3
Thrasivoulos *	2 1
Atromitos	0 1
Aris Thessaloníki *	1 2

Final

Olympiacos	2
Aris Thessaloníki ‡	0

* Home team/home team in the first leg • ‡ Qualified for the UEFA Cup

CUP FINAL
Kaftanzoglio, Thessaloníki
17-05-2008, Ref: Kasnaferis

Scorers - Kovacevic 33, Zewlakow 53 for Olympiacos

GRN – GRENADA

NATIONAL TEAM RECORD

JULY 10TH 2006 TO JULY 12TH 2010

PL	W	D	L	F	A	%
14	4	5	5	24	21	46.4

FIFA/COCA-COLA WORLD RANKING

1993	1994	1995	1996	1997	1998	1999	2000	2001	2002	2003	2004	2005	2006	2007	High
143	142	141	127	111	117	121	143	133	131	154	144	151	163	176	105 08/97

				2007–2008								Low
08/07	09/07	10/07	11/07	12/07	01/08	02/08	03/08	04/08	05/08	06/08	07/08	176 01/08
156	162	165	170	176	176	168	157	142	143	143	139	

With Jason Roberts of Blackburn Rovers and Shalrie Joseph of New England Revolution spearheading their 2010 FIFA World Cup campaign, the Spice Boyz of Grenada more than held their own in the three qualifying matches played, especially against Costa Rica. Grenada started their campaign with a resounding 10-0 thrashing of minnows US Virgin Islands at the National Stadium in St George's, a match in which midfielder Ricky Charles - a veteran in his fourth World Cup qualifying campaign - outshone his more illustrious team mates by scoring four goals. The real test came in Grenada's next match, against 2006 finalists Costa Rica and the Spice Boyz nearly

INTERNATIONAL HONOURS
None

caused a huge upset, racing into a 2-0 lead through Patrick Modeste and Roberts. There was disappointment for the huge crowd of 6,000 at the National stadium, however, with the Central Americans fighting back to force a draw through a late goal. Grenada's chance was gone and in the return in San Jose, Costa Rica ran out comfortable 3-0 winners. At home ASOMS Paradise regained the league title they lost in 2006, losing just one match and finishing 11 points ahead of second placed Carib Hurricane, while the end of season 2007 GFA Cup Final was won by Fontenoy United who beat St John's Sports on penalties after a 1-1 draw.

THE FIFA BIG COUNT OF 2006

	Male	Female		Total
Number of players	705 164	55 457	Referees and Assistant Referees	3 230
Professionals	1 818		Admin, Coaches, Technical, Medical	10 100
Amateurs 18+	268 570		Number of clubs	5 571
Youth under 18	86 779		Number of teams	5 899
Unregistered	145 400		Clubs with women's teams	197
Total players	760 621		Players as % of population	7.12%

Grenada Football Association (GFA)

Deco Building, PO Box 326, St George's, Grenada
Tel +1 473 4409903   Fax +1 473 4409973
gfa@spiceisle.com   www.grenadafootball.com
President: FOLKES Ashley Ram   General Secretary: DANIEL Victor
Vice-President: DANIEL Victor   Treasurer: DANIEL Victor   Media Officer: BASCOMBE Michael
Men's Coach: WILSON Norris   Women's Coach: JULES Dean
GFA formed: 1924   CONCACAF: 1969   FIFA: 1978
Green and yellow striped shirts, Red shorts, Yellow socks

RECENT INTERNATIONAL MATCHES PLAYED BY GRENADA

2004	Opponents	Score		Venue	Comp	Scorers	Att	Referee
12-12	St Vincent/Grenadines	L	1-3	Kingstown	CCq	Rennie [59]		Fanus LCA
19-12	St Vincent/Grenadines	L	0-1	St George's	CCq			Small BRB
2005								
23-01	Barbados	L	0-3	Bridgetown	Fr			
2006								
6-09	Netherlands Antilles	D	1-1	Willemstad	CCq	Rennie [52]		
8-09	Surinam	L	0-1	Willemstad	CCq			
10-09	Guyana	L	0-1	Willemstad	CCq			Angela ARU
1-11	St Vincent/Grenadines	L	1-4	Kingstown	Fr			
3-11	Antigua and Barbuda	D	1-1	Kingstown	Fr			
5-11	Barbados	D	2-2	Black Rock	Fr	Redhead 2 [7 45]		
2007								
No international matches played in 2007 before August								
2008								
20-01	Guyana	W	2-1	Georgetown	Fr	Langiagne [42], Dennis [70]		Persaud GUY
10-02	St Vincent/Grenadines	W	2-1	Kingstown	Fr	Rennie [13], Langiagne [61]		
15-03	Barbados	D	1-1	St George's	Fr	Rennie [43]		
26-03	US Virgin Islands	W	10-0	St George's	WCq	Roberts 2 [3 8], Charles 4 [9 43 65 87], Rennie [22], Langiagne [57], Bubb [82], Ferguson OG [89]	3 000	James GUY
27-04	Trinidad and Tobago	L	0-2	Macoya	Fr			
10-06	Jamaica	W	2-1	St George's	Fr	Joseph [68], Roberts [76]		
14-06	Costa Rica	D	2-2	St George's	WCq	Modeste [18], Roberts [23]	6 000	Brizan TRI
21-06	Costa Rica	L	0-3	San Jose	WCq		16 000	Marrufo USA

Fr = Friendly match • CC = Digicel Caribbean Cup • WC = FIFA World Cup • q = qualifier

GRENADA NATIONAL TEAM RECORDS AND RECORD SEQUENCES

Records			Sequence records		
Victory	14-1	AIA 1998	Wins	3	1996	Clean sheets	2	1989, 1994
Defeat	0-7	TRI 1999	Defeats	5	2002-2004	Goals scored	15	2001-2002
Player Caps	n/a		Undefeated	5	1997, 2004	Without goal	3	1990
Player Goals	n/a		Without win	10	1990-1994	Goals against	17	1996-1999

RECENT LEAGUE AND CUP RECORD

	Championship				
Year	Champions	Pts	Runners-up	Pts	Third	Pts
1998	Fontenoy United	3-2	Saint Andrews FL			
1999	Cable Vision SAFL	30	Fontenoy United	28	GBSS	27
2000	GBSS	29	Saint John's Sports	27	Fontenoy United	20
2001	GBSS	34	Hurricane FC	22	Saint Andrews FL	22
2002	Queens Park Rangers					
2003	Hurricane FC	45	Paradise	39	Fontenoy United	31
2004	Abandoned due to Hurricane Ivan					
2005	ASOMS Paradise	37	Fontenoy United	36	Hurricane	35
2006	Hurricane FC	38	Queens Park Rang's	37	Hard Rock	34
2007	ASOMS Paradise	47	Hurricane FC	36	Queens Park Rang's	33

GRENADA 2007 PREMIER DIVISION

	Pl	W	D	L	F	A	Pts
ASOMS Paradise	18	15	2	1	42	18	47
Carib Hurricane	18	11	3	4	38	14	36
Queens Park Rangers	18	10	3	5	38	31	33
Grenada Boys SS	18	6	8	4	21	23	26
South Stars	18	7	4	7	25	29	25
Eagles Super Strikers	18	4	7	7	24	33	19
Fontenoy United	18	4	6	8	24	26	18
Chantimelle	18	4	5	9	24	29	17
Hard Rock	18	4	4	10	30	42	16
Police	18	1	6	11	16	37	9

17/06/2007 - 21/10/2007

GRENADA COUNTRY INFORMATION

Capital	Saint George's	Independence	1974 from the UK	GDP per Capita	$5 500
Population	89 357	Status	Commonwealth	GNP Ranking	174
Area km²	344	Language	English	Dialling code	+1 473
Population density	259 per km²	Literacy rate	98%	Internet code	.gd
% in urban areas	37%	Main religion	Christian	GMT +/–	-4
Towns/Cities ('000)	Saint George's 4; Gouyave 3; Grenville 2; Victoria 2				
Neighbours (km)	Atlantic Ocean and the Caribbean Sea 121				
Main stadia	National Stadium – Saint George's 9 000				

GUA – GUATEMALA

NATIONAL TEAM RECORD
JULY 10TH 2006 TO JULY 12TH 2010

PL	W	D	L	F	A	%
26	8	6	12	25	28	42.3

FIFA/COCA-COLA WORLD RANKING

1993	1994	1995	1996	1997	1998	1999	2000	2001	2002	2003	2004	2005	2006	2007	High	
120	149	145	105	83	73	73	56	67	78	77	71	56	105	106	**50**	08/06

2007–2008												Low	
08/07	09/07	10/07	11/07	12/07	01/08	02/08	03/08	04/08	05/08	06/08	07/08	163	11/95
80	88	100	104	106	105	94	95	95	91	89	104		

Desperate to seal the steady rise of football in Guatemala with a place at the 2010 FIFA World Cup finals in South Africa, the federation took the bold decision to remove the well respected Colombian Hernan Dario Gomez from his position as national team coach and replace him with El Primitivo - Ramon Maradiaga. The Honduran had been in charge of Guatemala during their fine run in the 2006 qualifiers where they came close to a place in the finals in Germany and he started off the 2010 campaign by steering his side to a comfortable 9-1 aggregate win over St Lucia in a preliminary round tie. That qualified the Guatemalans to a tricky second round group involving,

INTERNATIONAL HONOURS
CONCACAF Championship 1967 UNCAF Championship 2001 CONCACAF Club Championship Municipal 1974, Comunicaciones 1978

Cuba, Trinidad and the USA with two to go through to the final group stage. The launch of the CONCACAF Champions League should have a beneficial impact on football in Guatemala with the Apertura and Clausura winners qualifying for the tournament and the winners of a play-off between the two claiming a guaranteed place in the group stage each year. That place went to Municipal for the inaugural tournament after they beat Deportivo Jalapa in the play-off. Jalapa had surprised everyone by winning the 2007-08 Apertura, their first league title, while Municipal beat traditional rivals Communicaciones in the Clausura final to claim their 26th league title.

THE FIFA BIG COUNT OF 2006

	Male	Female		Total
Number of players	1 847 811	158 838	Referees and Assistant Referees	373
Professionals	600		Admin, Coaches, Technical, Medical	5 030
Amateurs 18+	60 008		Number of clubs	138
Youth under 18	93 709		Number of teams	225
Unregistered	1 805 000		Clubs with women's teams	1
Total players	2 006 649		Players as % of population	16.32%

Federación Nacional de Fútbol de Guatemala (FNFG)
2a. Calle 15-57, Zona 15, Boulevard Vista Hermosa, Guatemala City 01015, Guatemala
Tel +502 24227777   Fax +502 24227780
info@fedefutguate.com   www.fedefutguate.com
President: ARROYO Oscar   General Secretary: MONGE Carlos Eduardo
Vice-President: TBD   Treasurer: DE TORREBIARTE Adela   Media Officer: None
Men's Coach: MARADIAGA Ramon   Women's Coach: GARCIA Antonio
FNFG formed: 1919   CONCACAF: 1961   FIFA: 1946
Blue shirts, White shorts, Blue socks

RECENT INTERNATIONAL MATCHES PLAYED BY GUATEMALA

2005	Opponents	Score		Venue	Comp	Scorers	Att	Referee
26-03	Trinidad and Tobago	W	5-1	Guatemala City	WCq	Ramirez [17], Ruiz 2 [30 38], Pezzarossi 2 [78 87]	22 506	Stott USA
30-03	USA	L	0-2	Birmingham	WCq		31 624	Ramdhan TRI
20-04	Jamaica	L	0-1	Atlanta	Fr		7 000	Prus USA
27-04	Brazil	L	0-3	Sao Paulo	Fr		38 000	Vazquez URU
4-06	Mexico	L	0-2	Guatemala City	WCq		26 723	Hall USA
8-06	Costa Rica	L	2-3	San Jose	WCq	Villatoro [74], Rodriguez [77]	BCD	Archundia MEX
8-07	Jamaica	L	3-4	Carson	GCr1	Ruiz 3 [11p 48+ 87]	27 000	Hall USA
10-07	Mexico	L	0-4	Los Angeles	GCr1		30 710	Ruiz COL
13-07	South Africa	D	1-1	Houston	GCr1	Romero [37]	45 311	Stott USA
17-08	Panama	W	2-1	Guatemala City	WCq	Baloy OG [70], Romero [93+]	24 000	Sibrian SLV
3-09	Trinidad and Tobago	L	2-3	Port of Spain	WCq	Andrews OG [3], Romero [61]	15 000	Archundia MEX
7-09	USA	D	0-0	Guatemala City	WCq		27 000	Rodriguez MEX
1-10	Jamaica	L	1-2	Fort Lauderdale	Fr			
8-10	Mexico	L	2-5	San Luis Potosi	WCq	Ruiz [1], Poniciano [53]	30 000	Prendergast JAM
12-10	Costa Rica	W	3-1	Guatemala City	WCq	Poniciano [2], Garcia [16], Ruiz [30]	23 912	Hall USA
2006								
19-02	USA	L	0-4	Frisco	Fr		14 453	Navarro CAN
16-08	Haiti	D	1-1	Miami	Fr	Rodriguez.M [58]	15 000	
6-09	Panama	L	1-2	Guatemala City	Fr	Sandoval [80]		
7-10	Honduras	L	2-3	Fort Lauderdale	Fr	Pezzarossi [27], Avila [32]	19 173	Vaughn USA
10-10	Honduras	L	1-2	Atlanta	Fr	Ruiz [69p]		Prus USA
15-11	Venezuela	L	1-2	Caracas	Fr	Martinez [73]	9 000	Andarcia VEN
2007								
8-02	Nicaragua	W	1-0	San Salvador	UCr1	Quiñónez [29]		Pineda HON
10-02	Belize	W	1-0	San Salvador	UCr1	Cabrera [8]		Vidal PAN
12-02	El Salvador	D	0-0	San Salvador	UCr1			Archundia MEX
16-02	Panama	L	0-2	San Salvador	UCsf			Arredondo MEX
18-02	El Salvador	W	1-0	San Salvador	UC3p	Albizuris [81]		Quesada CRC
25-03	Barbados	D	0-0	Bridgetown	Fr			
28-03	USA	D	0-0	Frisco	Fr		10 932	Archundia MEX
7-06	USA	L	0-1	Los Angeles	GCr1		21 344	Pineda NON
9-06	El Salvador	W	1-0	Los Angeles	GCr1	Contreras [68]	27 000	Jauregui ANT
12-06	Trinidad and Tobago	D	1-1	Foxboro	GCr1	Ruiz [84]	26 523	Pineda HON
16-06	Canada	L	0-3	Foxboro	GCqf		22 412	
22-08	Panama	L	1-2	Panama City	Fr	Montepeque [23]		Rodriguez CRC
17-10	Mexico	W	3-2	Los Angeles	Fr	Gomez.R [55], Avila 2 [64 73]	42 350	Salazar USA
17-11	Honduras	L	0-1	Miami	Fr			Stott USA
21-11	Jamaica	L	0-2	Kingston	Fr			Whittaker CAY
2008								
23-04	Haiti	W	1-0	Guatemala City	Fr	Rodriguez.M [59]		
30-05	El Salvador	D	0-0	Washington DC	Fr		38 759	
1-06	Panama	L	0-1	Fort Lauderdale	Fr			
4-06	Chile	L	0-2	Rancagua	Fr			
14-06	St Lucia	W	6-0	Guatemala City	WCq	Rodrigiez.M [5], Ruiz 4 [36 40 58 93+], Trigueros [91+]	24 600	Archundia MEX
21-06	St Lucia	W	3-1	Los Angeles	WCq	Romero 2 [24 43], Trigueros [86]	12 000	Wijngaarde SUR

Fr = Friendly match • UC = UNCAF Cup • GC = CONCACAF Gold Cup • WC = FIFA World Cup
q = qualifier • r1 = first round group • qf = quarter-final • sf = semi-final • 3p = third place play-off • BCD = Behind closed doors

GUATEMALA NATIONAL TEAM RECORDS AND RECORD SEQUENCES

Records			Sequence records					
Victory	9-0	HON 1921	Wins	6	1967	Clean sheets	4	1984-1985
Defeat	1-9	CRC 1955	Defeats	7	2005	Goals scored	16	1957-1965
Player Caps	103	Victor Hugo Monzón	Undefeated	13	1996-1997	Without goal	8	1989-1991
Player Goals	39	Carlos Ruiz	Without win	14	1989-1991	Goals against	13	1953-1961

REPUBLIC OF GUATEMALA; REPUBLICA DE GUATEMALA

Capital	Guatemala City	Language	Spanish			Independence	1821
Population	12 293 545	Area	108 890 km²	Density	131 per km²	% in cities	41%
GDP per cap	$4100	Dailling code	+502	Internet	.gt	GMT + / -	-6

The Guatemala City metropolitan area includes: Guatemala City 1 024; Mixco 540; Villa Nueva 499; San Juan Sacatepéquez 200; Petapa 189; Villa Canales 174; Chinaulta 112; Santa Caterina Pinula 91, Amatitlán 80; San Pedro Ayampuc 65; San José Pinula 63; Fraijanes 37 and Palencia 22

MEDALS TABLE

		Overall			League			Cup			Cent Am			City	Stadium	Cap'ty	DoF
		G	S	B	G	S	B	G	S	B	G	S	B				
1	Deportivo Municipal	34	16	7	26	13	6	7	2		1	1	1	Guatemala City	Mateo Flores	30 000	1936
2	Comunicaciones	26	21	10	21	19	7	4			1	2	3	Guatemala City	Mateo Flores	30 000	1949
3	Aurora	10	9	6	8	8	5	2	1				1	Guatemala City	Del Ej		1945
4	Xelajú	5	5	2	4	3	1	1	2				1	Quetzaltenango	Mario Camposeco	11 000	1928
5	Deportivo Jalapa	4	1		1			3	1					Jalapa	Las Flores	10 000	1973
6	Suchitepéquez	3	6	2	1	5	1	2	1				1	Mazatenango	Carlos Salazar Hijo	12 000	1960
7	Tip Nac	3	1		3	1								Guatemala City			1924
8	Cobán Imperial	1	6	2	1	3	2		3					Cobán	Verapáz	15 000	1924
9	Juventud Retalteca	1	3	2		2	2	1	1					Retalhuleu	Oscar Monterroso Izaguirre	8 000	
10	IRCA	1		2			2	1									
11	Hospicio	1		1			1	1									
	Amatitlan	1		1			1	1						Amatitlán	Municipal	12 000	
13	Deportivo Marquense		2			2								San Marcos	Marquesa de la Ensenada	10 000	1958
14	Universidad		1	4		1	4							Guatemala City	Campo de Marte		1922
15	Antigua		1	1		1	1							Antigua	Pensativo	9 000	

RECENT LEAGUE AND CUP RECORD

Championship/Clausura from 2000				Apertura				Cup			
Year	Winners	Score	Runners-up	Winners	Score	Runners-up		Winners	Score	Runners-up	
1996	Xelajú MC	1-0 1-1	Comunicaciones					Municipal	1-1 1-0	Xelajú MC	
1997	Comunicaciones	2-0 3-1	Aurora					Amatitlan	1-1 4-3	Municipal	
1998	Comunicaciones	†						Suchitepéquez	3-1	Cobán Imperial	
1999	Comunicaciones	†		Comunicaciones	1-1 2-1	Municipal		Municipal		Aurora	
2000	Municipal	0-1 2-0	Comunicaciones	Municipal	0-0 1-1	Comunicaciones		No tournament			
2001	Comunicaciones	4-0 2-3	Antigua GFC	Municipal	3-0 0-3	Cobán Imperial		No tournament			
2002	Municipal	1-2 2-0	Comunicaciones	Comunicaciones	2-1 1-1	Municipal		Deportivo Jalapa	5-2	Cobán Imperial	
2003	Comunicaciones	0-0 3-2	Cobán Imperial	Municipal	3-2 0-0	Comunicaciones		Municipal	2-1 1-0	Cobán Imperial	
2004	Cobán Imperial	3-2 2-2	Municipal	Municipal	5-1 4-1	Comunicaciones		Municipal	1-0 4-2	Deportivo Jalapa	
2005	Municipal	1-0 4-2	Suchitepéquez	Municipal	0-0 2-0	Comunicaciones		Deportivo Jalapa	3-0 0-2	Xelajú MC	
2006	Municipal	2-0 2-1	Marquense	Municipal	0-0 1-1	Comunicaciones		Deportivo Jalapa	1-1 1-0	Municipal	
2007	Xelajú	0-1 4-1	Marquénse	Deportivo Jalapa	1-1 0-0	Suchitepéquez		No tournament			
2008	Municipal	3-1 1-2	Comunicaciones					No tournament			

† Automatic champions as winners of both the regular season and the play-offs

GUATEMALA 2007-08

TORNEO APERTURA

	Pl	W	D	L	F	A	Pts	Municipal	Jalapa	Com'ciones	Xelajú	Such'quez	Zacapa	Marquense	Malacateco	Heredia	Petapa
Municipal †	18	8	7	3	31	18	31		2-4	1-0	5-0	3-3	3-3	6-1	1-0	2-0	0-0
Deportivo Jalapa †	18	7	7	4	32	26	28	0-0		2-1	2-1	2-2	1-1	3-1	2-0	3-0	2-2
Comunicaciones †	18	7	6	5	27	18	27	1-1	1-0		1-0	2-0	3-3	1-1	2-1	3-2	5-0
Xelajú †	18	7	4	7	14	22	25	1-0	2-1	0-0		0-0	1-0	2-1	1-0	1-0	2-1
Suchitepéquez †	18	6	6	6	32	27	24	1-2	3-1	2-2	2-0		7-1	2-1	1-2	2-1	2-0
Deportivo Zacapa †	18	6	6	6	31	31	24	0-1	5-3	1-1	1-0	4-1		3-1	1-0	3-1	2-2
Deportivo Marquense	18	6	6	6	21	27	24	1-0	1-1	1-0	1-1	2-1	1-0		2-0	1-1	2-1
Malacateco	18	6	2	10	16	22	20	1-2	1-1	1-0	3-1	2-1	2-1	1-1		1-0	0-1
Deportivo Heredia	18	5	4	9	22	26	19	0-0	3-4	1-0	3-1	1-1	2-1	2-0	3-0		2-2
Petapa	18	3	10	5	20	29	19	2-2	0-0	1-4	1-1	1-1	1-1	2-2	2-1	1-0	

28/07/2007 - 25/11/2007 • † Qualified for the play-offs • Top two receive a bye to the semi-finals

APERTURA PLAY-OFFS

Quarter–finals		Semi–finals		Final	
		Deportivo Jalapa	0 2		
Deportivo Zacapa *	1 1 0p	Comunicaciones *	1 0		
Communicaciones	1 1 3p			**Deportivo Jalapa ‡**	1 0
				Suchitepéquez *	1 0
		Municipal	0 1	1st leg. 13-12-2007	
Xelajú	1 1	**Suchitepéquez ***	1 1	2nd leg. 15-12-2007	
Suchitepéquez *	3 0				

* Home team in first leg • ‡ Won on away goals

GUATEMALA 2007-08

TORNEO CLAUSURA

	Pl	W	D	L	F	A	Pts	Com'ciones	Municipal	Petapa	Xelajú	Such'quez	Marquense	Zacapa	Jalapa	Heredia	Malacateco
Comunicaciones †	18	10	5	3	36	18	35		1-1	3-0	1-1	3-1	1-2	2-2	1-1	6-0	1-0
Municipal †	18	10	5	3	34	16	35	1-1		0-1	2-0	3-1	1-1	1-0	6-0	1-0	3-1
Petapa †	18	9	3	6	22	21	30	0-2	0-3		4-3	1-1	1-2	3-2	1-0	1-0	3-0
Xelajú †	18	5	3	10	16	16	25	0-3	0-0	1-0		1-1	0-0	0-0	2-1	1-0	2-0
Suchitepéquez †	18	6	7	5	21	25	25	2-1	5-4	2-1	1-1		1-0	2-1	0-0	2-2	1-0
Deportivo Marquense †	18	6	6	6	24	19	24	4-2	1-1	0-1	1-1	2-0		5-1	1-2	3-2	0-0
Deportivo Zacapa	18	5	6	7	23	27	21	1-2	2-3	0-0	2-2	2-0	1-0		2-0	2-1	3-2
Deportivo Jalapa	18	5	6	7	17	22	21	0-1	1-0	1-2	0-0	2-0	1-1	2-0		2-2	2-0
Deportivo Heredia	18	2	7	9	18	29	13	2-4	0-2	1-1	0-0	1-1	1-0	1-1	1-1		4-0
Malacateco	18	3	3	12	10	28	12	0-1	1-2	0-2	0-1	0-0	2-1	1-1	2-1	1-0	

12/01/2008 - 4/05/2008 • † Qualified for the play-offs • Top two receive a bye to the semi-finals • Malacateco were relegated due to having the worst overall season record • Zacapa and Heredia entered a relegation play-off: Coatepeque 1-0 1-3 **Zacapa**; **Universidad** 3-2 2-3 4-3p Heredia

CLAUSURA PLAY-OFFS

Quarter–finals		Semi–finals		Final	
		Municipal	0 3		
Petapa	0 2	Petapa *	1 0		
Deportivo Marquense*	1 0			**Municipal ***	3 1
Xelajú	0 1			Comunicaciones	1 2
Suchitepéquez *	2 0	Suchitepéquez *	0 2	1st leg. 22-05-2008	
		Comunicaciones	2 1	2nd leg. 25-05-2008	

* Home team in first leg

GUI – GUINEA

NATIONAL TEAM RECORD
JULY 10TH 2006 TO JULY 12TH 2010

PL	W	D	L	F	A	%
21	8	6	7	32	25	52.4

FIFA/COCA-COLA WORLD RANKING

1993	1994	1995	1996	1997	1998	1999	2000	2001	2002	2003	2004	2005	2006	2007	High	
63	66	63	73	65	79	91	80	108	120	101	86	79	23	33	22	01/07

2007–2008											Low	
08/07	09/07	10/07	11/07	12/07	01/08	02/08	03/08	04/08	05/08	06/08	07/08	123 05/03
42	30	31	33	33	33	47	48	41	40	41	39	

Guinea reached the quarter-finals of the CAF Africa Cup of Nations once again but proved how heavily dependent they are on the form of their captain Pascal Feindouno. One of African football's top players, he has been the creative and attacking heart of the Syli Nationale for close on a decade but a needless red card earned at the tournament in Ghana saw him suspended for the rest of the finals. Guinea had the tournament begun by almost upsetting hosts Ghana and then easily beating Morocco. But without Feindouno, they looked rudderless and predictably went out of the event, heavily beaten by Cote d'Ivoire in the last eight. It was expected that the result would be spell the

INTERNATIONAL HONOURS
Copa Amilcar Cabral 1981 1982 1987 1988 2005   CAF Champions League Hafia Conakry 1972 1975 1977

end of tenure of veteran French coach Robert Nouzaret, but he signed a contract extension before the start of the 2010 FIFA World Cup qualifiers in June 2008. Guinea got that campaign off to a slow start with a single point from their first two matches but a double triumph over Namibia restored their chances of advancing to the last phase with Feindouno scoring in both games. In club football Kaloum Stars won the league and cup double in 2007 but with the era of dominance that clubs from Guinea once enjoyed in African club competition now decades ago, Kaloum predictably lost to ASEC Abidjan at the first hurdle in the 2008 CAF Champions League.

THE FIFA BIG COUNT OF 2006

	Male	Female		Total
Number of players	406 600	3 500	Referees and Assistant Referees	433
Professionals	0		Admin, Coaches, Technical, Medical	2 400
Amateurs 18+	10 100		Number of clubs	150
Youth under 18	8 000		Number of teams	700
Unregistered	90 000		Clubs with women's teams	0
Total players	410 100		Players as % of population	4.23%

Fédération Guinéenne de Football (FGF)
PO Box 3645, Conakry, Guinea
Tel +224 20 455878   Fax +224 20 455879
guineefoot59@yahoo.fr   www.none
President: BANGOURA Aboubacar Bruno   General Secretary: CAMARA Fode Capi
Vice-President: CONTE Sory   Treasurer: DIALLO Mamadou   Media Officer: None
Men's Coach: NOUZARET Robert   Women's Coach: CAMARA Fabert
FGF formed: 1960   CAF: 1962   FIFA: 1962
Red shirts, Yellow shorts, Green socks

RECENT INTERNATIONAL MATCHES PLAYED BY GUINEA

2005	Opponents		Score	Venue	Comp	Scorers	Att	Referee
18-11	Guinea-Bissau	D	2-2	Conakry	ACr1	Soumah [7], Camara.O [75]		
22-11	Sierra Leone	W	1-0	Conakry	ACr1	Diawara [19]		
25-11	Mali	D	0-0	Conakry	ACsf	W 6-5p		
27-11	Senegal †	W	1-0	Conakry	ACf	Barujakis [5]	30 000	
2006								
7-01	Togo	W	1-0	Viry-Chatillon	Fr	Ousmane Bangoura [65p]	2 500	Piccirillo FRA
22-01	South Africa	W	2-0	Alexandria	CNr1	Sambegou Bangoura [76], Ousmane Bangoura [87]	10 000	Benouza ALG
26-01	Zambia	W	2-1	Alexandria	CNr1	Feindouno 2 [74p 90]	24 000	Imeire NGA
30-01	Tunisia	W	3-0	Alexandria	CNr1	Ousmane Bangoura [16], Feindouno [69], Diawara [90]	18 000	Maidin SIN
3-02	Senegal	L	2-3	Alexandria	CNqf	Diawara [24], Feindouno [95+]	17 000	Codjia BEN
16-08	Cameroon	D	1-1	Rouen	Fr	Mansare [70p]		Duhamel FRA
3-09	Algeria	D	0-0	Conakry	CNq			Coulibaly MLI
7-10	Cape Verde Islands	L	0-1	Praia	CNq			Diatta SEN
2007								
6-02	Côte d'Ivoire	L	0-1	Rouen	Fr			
24-03	Gambia	W	2-0	Bakau	CNq	Diawara [57], Feindouno [69]		Kotey GHA
3-06	Gambia	D	2-2	Conakry	CNq	Jabi [9], Mansare [55]		Djaoupe TOG
16-06	Algeria	W	2-0	Algiers	CNq	Mansare [44], Feindouno [85]		Guezzaz MAR
22-08	Tunisia	D	1-1	Rades	Fr	Diawara [45]		
9-09	Cape Verde Islands	W	4-0	Conakry	CNq	Feindouno [19p], Mohamed Cisse [32], Ibrahima Camara [37], Ismael Bangoura [44]		Trabelsi TUN
14-10	Senegal	L	1-3	Rouen	Fr	Mansare [44]		
20-11	Angola	L	0-3	Melun	Fr			
2008								
11-01	Sudan	W	6-0	Estepona	Fr	Youla 4, Ismael Bangoura, Correa		
20-01	Ghana	L	1-2	Accra	CNr1	Kalabane [65]		Maillet SEY
24-01	Morocco	W	3-2	Accra	CNr1	Feindouno 2 [11 63p], Ismael Bangoura [60]		Damon RSA
28-01	Namibia	D	1-1	Sekondi	CNr1	Youla [62]		Ssegonga UGA
3-02	Côte d'Ivoire	L	0-5	Sekondi	CNqf			Haimoudi ALG
25-03	Togo	W	2-0	Paris	Fr	Doumbouya 2 [80 90]		
1-06	Zimbabwe	D	0-0	Conakry	WCq		12 000	Haimoudi ALG
7-06	Kenya	L	0-2	Nairobi	WCq		35 000	Eyene CMR
14-06	Namibia	W	2-1	Windhoek	WCq	Ismael Bangoura [22], Feindouno [45]	5 000	Imiere NGA
22-06	Namibia	W	4-0	Conakry	WCq	Feindouno [23], Ismael Bangoura 3 [27 55 60]	15 000	Monteiro Lopez CPV

Fr = Friendly match • CN = CAF African Cup of Nations • AC = Amilcar Cabral Cup • WC = FIFA World Cup
q = qualifier • r1 = first round group • sf = semi-final • f = final • † = not a full international

GUINEA NATIONAL TEAM PLAYERS

	Player		Club	Date of Birth		Player		Club	Date of Birth
1	Naby Diarso	GK	Satellite FC	1 01 1977	12	Alseny Camara	DF	Rodez FRA	4 11 1986
2	Pascal Feindouno (C)	MF	St Etienne FRA	27 02 1981	13	Mohamed Sacko	MF	Etoile du Sahel TUN	5 08 1988
3	Ibrahima Camara	DF	Le Mans FRA	1 01 1985	14	Naby Soumah	MF	CS Sfaxien TUN	4 08 1985
4	Mohamed Cisse	MF	Bursaspor TUR	10 02 1982	15	Oumar Kalabane	DF	Manisaspor TUR	8 04 1981
5	Dianbobo Balde	DF	Celtic SCO	21 07 1975	16	Kemoko Camara	GK	None	5 04 1975
6	Kamil Zayatte	DF	BSC Young Boys SUI	7 03 1985	17	Mohamed Alimou Diallo	DF	Sivasspor TUR	2 12 1984
7	Fode Mansare	FW	Toulouse FRA	3 09 1981	18	Samuel Johnson	MF	Ismaili EGY	25 01 1984
8	Kanfory Sylla	MF	Sivaspor TUR	7 06 1980	19	Karamoko Cisse	FW	Verona ITA	14 11 1988
9	Victor Correa	FW	Cherbourg FRA	12 01 1985	20	Habib Jean Balde	DF	Stade de Reims FRA	8 02 1985
10	Ismael Bangoura	FW	Dynamo Kyiv UKR	2 01 1985	21	Daouda Jabi	DF	Trabonzspor TUR	10 04 1981
11	Souleymane Youla	FW	Lille FRA	29 11 1981	22	Naby Yattara	GK	RACS Couillet BEL	12 01 1984
					23	Mamadou Dioulde Bah	DF	RC Strasbourg FRA	25 04 1988

Guinea's squad for the 2008 CAF Africa Cup of Nations

GUINEA NATIONAL TEAM RECORDS AND RECORD SEQUENCES

Records			Sequence records					
Victory	14-0	MTN 1972	Wins	7	1972-1973	Clean sheets	7	1986-1987
Defeat	2-6	GHA 1975	Defeats	4	1984, 1998-1999	Goals scored	29	1973-1977
Player Caps	n/a		Undefeated	13	1980-1981	Without goal	6	1991
Player Goals	n/a		Without win	14	1983-1984	Goals against	14	1967-1969

MAJOR CITIES/TOWNS

		Population '000
1	Conakry	2 064
2	Nzérékoré	138
3	Kindia	122
4	Kankan	117
5	Kamsar	100
6	Kissidougou	46
7	Labé	44
8	Macenta	43
9	Siguiri	43
10	Mamou	41
11	Télimélé	30
12	Tougué	25
13	Pita	19
14	Boké	15
15	Kouroussa	14
16	Beyla	13
17	Koundara	13
18	Dabola	12
19	Dalaba	12
20	Tondon	12
21	Forécariah	12
22	Dubréka	10
23	Mandiana	10
24	Koubia	9

REPUBLIC OF GUINEA; REPUBLIQUE DE GUINEE

Capital	Conakry	Language	French			Independence	1958
Population	9 690 222	Area	245 857 km²	Density	37 per km²	% in cities	30%
GDP per cap	$2100	Dailling code	+224	Internet	.gn	GMT +/-	0

MEDALS TABLE

		Overall			L	C	Africa			
		G	S	B	G	G	G	S	B	City
1	Hafia Conakry	18	2		12	3	3	2		Conakry
2	Kaloum Star	18	1	2	12	6		1	2	Conakry
3	Horoya Conakry	14		2	9	4	1		2	Conakry
4	ASFAG Conakry	4			1	3				Conakry
5	Conakry II Kakimbo	3		1	3				1	Conakry
6	Fello Star Labé	3			1	2				Labé
	Satellite Conakry	3			2	1				Conakry
8	Olympique Kakandé	2				2				Boké
9	Etoile du Guinée	1				1				Conakry
	Mankona	1				1				

RECENT LEAGUE AND CUP RECORD

	Championship				Cup		
Year	Champions	Score	Runners-up		Winners	Score	Runners-up
2000	Hafia Conakry	†			Fello Stars Labé	2-1	Horoya Conakry
2001	Horoya Conakry	3-1	Satellite Conakry		Kaloum Star		
2002	Satellite Conakry	3-2	Kaloum Star		Hafia Conakry	5-3	Satellite Conakry
2003	ASFAG Conakry	†			Etoile de Guinée		Etoile de Coléah
2004	No championship played				Fello Star Labé	2-2 5-4p	CIK Kamsar
2005	Satellite Conakry	†	Fello Star Labé		Kaloum Star	0-0 5-4p	Gangan Kindia
2006	Fello Star Labé	†	Kaloum Star		Satellite Conakry	1-0	CIK Kamsar
2007	Kaloum Star	†	Fello Star Labé		Kaloum Star	1-0	Satellite Conakry

† Championship played on a league system

COUPE NATIONALE 2007

Quarter–finals		Semi–finals		Final	
Kaloum Star	1				
Hafia Conakry	0	Kaloum Star	1		
Bafing Mamou	1	Milo Kankan	0		
Milo Kankan	2			Kaloum Star	1
Athlético Coléah	1			Satellite Conakry	0
COK Boké	0	Athlético Coléah	1	Stade du 28 Septembre, Conakry	
Niandan Kissidougou	0	Satellite Conakry	3	28-11-2007	
Satellite Conakry	1			Scorer - Abdoul Karim Keita 3	

GUM – GUAM

NATIONAL TEAM RECORD
JULY 10TH 2006 TO JULY 12TH 2010

PL	W	D	L	F	A	%
6	0	0	6	7	48	0

FIFA/COCA-COLA WORLD RANKING

1993	1994	1995	1996	1997	1998	1999	2000	2001	2002	2003	2004	2005	2006	2007	High	
-	-	-	188	191	198	199	200	201	201	2005	204	198	201		182	08/96

2007–2008												Low	
08/07	09/07	10/07	11/07	12/07	01/08	02/08	03/08	04/08	05/08	06/08	07/08	205	12/04
199	200	200	201	201	201	202	202	202	200	199	199		

As the smallest member of the Asian Football Confederation, the footballers of the Pacific island of Guam have struggled in the face of some of the world's largest nations. However, despite what would appear to be insurmountable challenges on a continual basis, Guam continue to make the effort to gain as much international experience and exposure as possible, even if that brings with it regular heavy defeats. The island, which is an unincorporated territory of the United States and home to just over 150,000 people, didn't enter the 2010 FIFA World Cup thanks to huge defeats in past attempts but they did enter the preliminary rounds of the AFC Challenge Cup - a tournament

INTERNATIONAL HONOURS
None

reserved for the weakest nations on the continent - but was incapable of progressing to the finals in India. After holding Sri Lanka goalless in the opening 45 minutes of their first game, Guam lost 5-1 while a goal from Zachary Pangelinan gave his side a surprise lead against Chinese Taipei before slipping to a 4-1 defeat. Pangelinan struck again in Guam's next game, but his goal was little more than academic as Pakistan handed Norio Tsukitate's side a 9-2 hammering to leave them languishing at the bottom of the qualifying group. At home, the five team national championship was won by Quality Distributors, three points ahead of their biggest rivals Guam Shipyard.

THE FIFA BIG COUNT OF 2006

	Male	Female		Total
Number of players	4 172	1 288	Referees and Assistant Referees	21
Professionals	0		Admin, Coaches, Technical, Medical	135
Amateurs 18+	457		Number of clubs	13
Youth under 18	1 943		Number of teams	195
Unregistered	675		Clubs with women's teams	7
Total players	5 460		Players as % of population	3.19%

Guam Football Association (GFA)
PO Box 5093, Hagatna, Guam 96932
Tel +1 671 6374321   Fax +1 671 6374323
info@guamfootball.com   www.guamfootball.com
President: LAI Richard   General Secretary: SAN GIL Valentino
Vice-President: ARTERO Pascual   Treasurer: LAI George   Media Officer: CEPEDA Joseph
Men's Coach: TSUKITATE Norio   Women's Coach: KIM Sang Hoon
GFA formed: 1975   AFC: 1996   FIFA: 1996
Blue shirts, White shorts, Blue socks

RECENT INTERNATIONAL MATCHES PLAYED BY GUAM

2003	Opponents		Score	Venue	Comp	Scorers	Att	Referee
23-04	Bhutan	L	0-6	Thimphu	ACq			
25-04	Mongolia	L	0-5	Thimphu	ACq			
2004								
No international matches played in 2004								
2005								
5-03	Chinese Taipei	L	0-9	Taipei	EACq			
7-03	Hong Kong	L	0-15	Taipei	EACq			
9-03	Mongolia	L	1-4	Taipei	EACq	Pangelinan 69		
11-03	Korea DPR	L	0-21	Taipei	EACq			
2006								
1-04	Palestine	L	0-11	Dhaka	CCr1		3 000	AK Nema IRQ
3-04	Bangladesh	L	0-3	Dhaka	CCr1		18 000	U Win Cho MYA
6-04	Cambodia	L	0-3	Dhaka	CCr1		500	U Win Cho MYA
2007								
25-03	Northern Marianas †	W	3-2	Saipan	EACq	Jamison 9, Pangelinan 2 65 78		
1-04	Northern Marianas †	W	9-0	Hagatna	EACq	Pangelinan 5 6 21 42 54 61, Mendoza 56, Merfalen 57, Jamison 85, Calvo 90	1 324	
17-06	Chinese Taipei	L	0-10	Macau	EACq		10	Wan Daxue CHN
21-06	Hong Kong	L	1-15	Macau	EACq	Mendiola 33	300	Matsuo JPN
23-06	Mongolia	L	2-5	Macau	EACq	Pangelinan 2, Mendiola 8	100	Wan Daxue CHN
2008								
2-04	Sri Lanka	L	1-5	Taipei	CCq	Mendiola 62	300	Kovalenko UZB
4-04	Chinese Taipei	L	1-4	Taipei	CCq	Pangelinan 17	850	Win Cho MYA
6-04	Pakistan	L	2-9	Taipei	CCq	Pangelinan 74, Iltaf OG 80	200	Auda Lazim IRQ

EAC = East Asian Championship • AC = AFC Asian Cup • CC = AFC Challenge Cup
q = qualifier • r1 = first round group • † Not an official international

GUAM NATIONAL TEAM RECORDS AND RECORD SEQUENCES

Records			Sequence records				
Victory	-	Yet to win a match	Wins	0		Clean sheets	0	
Defeat	0-21	PRK 2005	Defeats	40	1975-	Goals scored	5	2007
Player Caps	n/a		Undefeated	0		Without goal	15	1996-2005
Player Goals	n/a		Without win	40	1975-	Goals against	32	1975-2006

RECENT LEAGUE AND CUP RECORD

	Championship				
Year	Champions	Pts	Runners-up	Pts	Third	Pts
2002	Guam Shipyard					
2003	Guam Shipyard					
2004	Under-18					
2005	Guam Shipyard					
2006	Guam Shipyard					
2007	Quality Distributors	19	Guam Shipyard	16	U–19 Nat Team	14
2008	Quality Distributors	45	Guam Shipyard	42	Paintco Strykers	26

GUAM 2007-08 BUDWEISER DIVISION ONE

	Pl	W	D	L	F	A	Pts
Quality Distributors	20	14	3	3	81	27	**45**
Guam Shipyard	20	13	3	4	60	33	**42**
Paintco Strykers	20	8	2	10	54	66	**26**
IT&E Crushers	20	7	3	10	52	64	**24**
No Ka Oi	20	2	1	17	55	112	7

30/09/2007 - 6/04/2008

GUAM COUNTRY INFORMATION

Capital	Hagatna	Independence	Unincorporated territory of the USA	GDP per Capita	$21 000
Population	166 090	Status		GNP Ranking	n/a
Area km²	549	Language	English	Dialling code	+1 671
Population density	302 per km²	Literacy rate	99%	Internet code	.GU
% in urban areas	n/a	Main religion	Christian 99%	GMT +/-	+10
Towns/Cities ('000)	Tamuning 11; Mangilao 8; Yigo 8; Astumbo 5; Barrigada 4; Agat 4; Ordot 4				
Neighbours (km)	North Pacific Ocean 125				
Main stadia	Wettengel Rugby Field – Hagatna				

GUY – GUYANA

NATIONAL TEAM RECORD
JULY 10TH 2006 TO JULY 12TH 2010

PL	W	D	L	F	A	%
17	11	2	4	39	16	70.6

FIFA/COCA-COLA WORLD RANKING

1993	1994	1995	1996	1997	1998	1999	2000	2001	2002	2003	2004	2005	2006	2007		High	
136	154	162	153	168	161	171	183	178	169	182	182	167	100	128		**90**	08/07

				2007–2008								Low	
08/07	09/07	10/07	11/07	12/07	01/08	02/08	03/08	04/08	05/08	06/08	07/08	**185**	02/04
90	103	92	93	128	129	132	113	111	110	108	122		

Rarely had hopes been as high for the Guyana national team, as they prepared to do battle in the 2010 FIFA World Cup qualifiers. In recognition of the great progress that has been made in the country, the Guyanese were seeded through to the second round of qualifying in the CONCACAF zone, A single two-legged tie against neighbours Surinam was all that stood between Jamal Shabazz's side and a place in the group stage. Despite losing the first leg 1-0 away in Paramaribo a huge crowd turned out to watch the return with the cricket authorities making the newly constructed Providence Stadium - built for the 2007 Cricket World Cup - available to the foot-

INTERNATIONAL HONOURS
None

ballers for the first time. The near capacity crowd went home disappointed, however, after a 2-1 defeat saw Guyana's dreams crushed at the first hurdle. The optimism before the Surinam defeat had been based an a fine run of form that had seen the team rise from 185th in the FIFA/Coca-Cola World Ranking in 2004 to a high of 90 in August 2007. One structural problem remains in Guyana - the lack of a national league. With the domestic season a mishmash of regional leagues and cup tournaments, top players like Nigel Codrington at Caledonia are forced to move to neighbouring Trinidad for a higher standard of club football.

THE FIFA BIG COUNT OF 2006

	Male	Female		Total
Number of players	43 000	7 740	Referees and Assistant Referees	95
Professionals	0		Admin, Coaches, Technical, Medical	650
Amateurs 18+	3 240		Number of clubs	90
Youth under 18	4 600		Number of teams	270
Unregistered	12 800		Clubs with women's teams	8
Total players	50 740		Players as % of population	6.61%

Guyana Football Federation (GFF)
Lot 17 Dadanawa Street, Section K, Campbellville, PO Box 10727, Georgetown, Guyana
Tel +592 2 278758   Fax +592 2 252096
gff@networksgy.com   www.guyanaff.com
President: KLASS Colin   General Secretary: ADONIS Noel
Vice-President: CALLENDER Winston   Treasurer: HENRY Aubrey   Media Officer: GRANGER Frederick
Men's Coach: SHABAZZ Jamaal   Women's Coach: SHABAZZ Jamaal
GFF formed: 1902   CONCACAF: 1969   FIFA: 1968
Green shirts, Green shorts, Yellow socks

RECENT INTERNATIONAL MATCHES PLAYED BY GUYANA

2002	Opponents	Score	Venue	Comp	Scorers	Att	Referee
28-07	Netherlands Antilles	W 2-1	Georgetown	CCq	Cole [6], Forbes [56]		
11-08	Netherlands Antilles	L 0-1	Willemstad	CCq	L 2-3p		Villar-Polo ARU
2003							
No international matches played in 2003							
2004							
15-02	Barbados	W 2-0	Bridgetown	Fr	Hernandez [59], Richardson [86]	1 200	Small BRB
28-02	Grenada	L 0-5	St George's	WCq		7 000	Archundia MEX
2-03	Trinidad and Tobago	L 0-1	Tunapuna	Fr			Randham TRI
14-03	Grenada	L 1-3	Blairmont	WCq	Harris [29]	1 200	Quesada Cordero CRC
2005							
13-02	Barbados	D 3-3	Bridgetown	Fr	Richardson [21], Cadogan [36], Abrams [71]	6 000	Callender BRB
30-09	Dominica	W 3-0	Linden	Fr	Abrams [10], Parks [60], Manning [81]		Lancaster GUY
2-10	Dominica	W 3-0	Georgetown	Fr	McKinnon 2 [19 42], Codrington [85]		Kia SUR
2006							
24-02	Antigua and Barbuda	W 2-1	Linden	Fr	Abrams [3], Codrington [61]		James GUY
26-02	Antigua and Barbuda	W 4-1	Linden	Fr	Pollard [34], Abrams [37], Beveney 2 [40 66]		Lancaster GUY
28-07	St Lucia	W 3-2	Linden	Fr	Jerome [5], Hernandez [29], McKinnon [91+]		Lancaster GUY
30-07	St Lucia	W 2-0	Georgetown	Fr	Pollard [74], Codrington [80p]		James GUY
2-09	Barbados	W 1-0	Bridgetown	Fr	Jerome [44p]	2 000	Forde BRB
6-09	Surinam	W 5-0	Willemstad	CCq	Richardson [4], Codrington 2 [15 73], Jerome [42], Abrams [89]		
8-09	Netherlands Antilles	W 5-0	Willemstad	CCq	Richardson [35], Codrington [58], Bishop [65], Abrams [84], Jerome [89]		
10-09	Grenada	W 1-0	Willemstad	CCq	Bishop [46]		Angela ARU
24-11	Antigua and Barbuda	W 6-0	Georgetown	CCq	Richardson 2 [3 12], Jerome 2 [35 54], Codrington [75], McKinnon [77]	5 000	
26-11	Guadeloupe	W 3-2	Georgetown	CCq	Codrington 2 [22 66], Richardson [24]	5 000	
28-11	Dominican Republic	W 4-0	Georgetown	CCq	Richardson [45], Jerome [49], Codrington [57p], Hercules [79]		
2007							
14-01	St Vincent/Grenadines	L 0-2	Marabella	CCr1			
16-01	Guadeloupe	W 4-3	Marabella	CCr1	Codrington 3 [23p 60 81], Lowe [66]		
18-01	Cuba	D 0-0	Marabella	CCr1			
2008							
13-01	St Vincent/Grenadines	W 1-0	Blairmont	Fr	Richardson [11]		
20-01	Grenada	L 1-2	Georgetown	Fr	Beveney [45]		
27-01	St Vincent/Grenadines	D 2-2	Kingstown	Fr	Mannings [56], Abrams [68]		
16-06	Surinam	L 0-1	Paramaribo	WCq		3 000	Guerrero NCA
22-06	Surinam	L 1-2	Georgetown	WCq	Codrington [85]	12 000	Campbell JAM

Fr = Friendly match • GC = CONCACAF Gold Cup • WC = FIFA World Cup • q = qualifier

GUYANA NATIONAL TEAM RECORDS AND RECORD SEQUENCES

Records			Sequence records				
Victory	14-0	AIA 1998	Wins	13	2005-2006	Clean sheets	6	2005-2006
Defeat	0-9	MEX 1987	Defeats	8	1987-1990	Goals scored	15	2004-2006
Player Caps	n/a		Undefeated	14	2005-2006	Without goal	7	1987-1990
Player Goals	n/a		Without win	10	1987-1990	Goals against	13	1992-1996

GUYANA COUNTRY INFORMATION

Capital	Georgetown	Independence	1966 from the UK	GDP per Capita	$4 000
Population	705 803	Status	Republic within Commonwealth	GNP Ranking	163
Area km²	214 970	Language	English	Dialling code	+592
Population density	3 per km²	Literacy rate	98%	Internet code	.gy
% in urban areas	36%	Main religion	Christian 50%, Hindu 35%	GMT +/ –	-4
Towns/Cities ('000)	Georgetown 235; Linden 44; New Amsterdam 35; Corriverton 12; Bartica 11				
Neighbours (km)	Surinam 600; Brazil 1 119; Venezuela 743; Caribbean Sea 459				
Main stadia	Georgetown Football Stadium – Georgetown 2 000				

FRUTA FESTIVAL 2007

First round		Quarter–finals		Semi–finals		Final	
Guyana Defence Force	2 5p						
Santos	2 4p	Guyana Defence Force	2				
Pele	1	Monedderlust	1				
Monedderlust	4			Guyana Defence Force	3		
Western Tigers	3			Pouderoyen	1		
Rosignol United	1	Western Tigers	1 3p				
Flamingoes	1	Pouderoyen	1 4p				
Pouderoyen	5					Guyana Defence Force	1 6p
BV/Triumph United	1					Alpha United	1 5p
Fruta Conquerors	0	BV/Triumph United	4				
Silver Shattas	2 2p	Georgetown FC	3				
Georgetown FC	2 3p			BV/Triumph United	1		
Camptown	1			Alpha United	2		
Mocha Champs	0	Camptown	0				
Uprising	2	Alpha United	1				
Alpha United	5						

CUP FINAL
9-12-2007

Third place: BV/Triumph Utd 3-1 Pouderoyen

KASHIF & SHANGHAI CUP 2007-08

First round		Quarter–finals		Semi–finals		Final	
Alpha United	2						
Pouderoyen	0	Alpha United	2				
Silver Shattas	1	Western Tigers	0				
Western Tigers	4			Alpha United	3		
Amelia's Ward	2			Pele	0		
Santos	0	Amelia's Ward	1				
Buxton Stars	2 2p	Pele	2				
Pele	2 3p					Alpha United	1
Winners Connection	2					Topp XX	0
RUSAL	1	Winners Connection	2 5p				
BV/Triumph United	1	Fruta Conquerors	2 4p				
Fruta Conquerors	2			Winners Connection	0		
Netrockers	3			Topp XX	2		
Camptown	2	Netrockers	1				
Monedderlust	0	Topp XX	3				
Topp XX	4						

CUP FINAL

Mackenzie Sports Club, Linden
1-01-2008

Anthony Abrams [5]

CARIB/DIGICEL SWEET 16 KNOCK-OUT CUP 20008

First round		Quarter–finals		Semi–finals		Final	
Camptown	8						
Black Stallion	0	Camptown	3				
Uprising	1	BV/Triumph United	2				
BV/Triumph United	2			Camptown	2		
Buxton Stars	2			Plaisance	0		
Golden Stars	1	Buxton Stars	1 3p				
Mahaica	1	Plaisance	1 5p				
Plaisance	3					Camptown	2
Western Tigers	4					Guyana Defence Force	0
Alpha United	2	Western Tigers	1				
Pele	1	Victoria Kings	0				
Victoria Kings	2			Western Tigers	0		
Ann's Grove	1			Guyana Defence Force	1		
Santos	0	Ann's Grove	0				
Fruta Conquerors	1	Guyana Defence Force	1				
Guyana Defence Force	4						

CUP FINAL

26-05-2008

Third place: Western Tigers 2-1 Plaisance

HAI – HAITI

NATIONAL TEAM RECORD
JULY 10TH 2006 TO JULY 12TH 2010

PL	W	D	L	F	A	%
39	17	11	11	54	33	57.7

FIFA/COCA-COLA WORLD RANKING

1993	1994	1995	1996	1997	1998	1999	2000	2001	2002	2003	2004	2005	2006	2007	High	
145	132	153	114	125	109	99	84	82	72	96	95	98	102	69	**66**	11/07

2007–2008													Low	
08/07	09/07	10/07	11/07	12/07	01/08	02/08	03/08	04/08	05/08	06/08	07/08		**155**	04/96
88	83	68	66	69	73	100	97	106	113	113	119			

In their attempt to qualify for the FIFA World Cup for the first time since their historic appearance in the 1974 finals, Caribbean champions Haiti surprisingly turned to the untested 34-year-old Wagneau Eloi when appointing a new national team coach in April 2008. Eloi came to the job with a reputation as one the the best footballers ever to come out of Haiti, having won championship medals with both Lens and Monaco in France. Although inexperienced he has displayed a burning desire to improve the fortunes of football in his homeland, something that the more experienced foreigners interested in the job perhaps lacked. Eloi's first task was to negotiate a preliminary

INTERNATIONAL HONOURS
Qualified for the FIFA World Cup finals 1974

CCCF Championship 1957   CFU Caribbean Championship 2007   CONCACAF Champions Cup Racing Club 1963 Violette 1984

round tie against the Netherlands Antilles and he very nearly came badly unstuck after the Antilles forced a 1-1 draw in the first leg in Port-au-Prince. It took an own goal 12 minutes from time in the return to see Haiti safely through to perhaps the least tough of the three second round groups. Conditions for the players at home in Haiti do, however, remain far from ideal with many understandably keen to leave at the first opportunity, although the political situation in the country has stabilised sufficiently for the local league to run relatively unhindered.

THE FIFA BIG COUNT OF 2006

	Male	Female		Total
Number of players	376 278	75 446	Referees and Assistant Referees	234
Professionals	100		Admin, Coaches, Technical, Medical	2 090
Amateurs 18+	7 664		Number of clubs	310
Youth under 18	15 844		Number of teams	1 200
Unregistered	83 300		Clubs with women's teams	30
Total players	451 724		Players as % of population	5.44%

Fédération Haïtienne de Football (FHF)
128 Avenue Christiophe, Case postale 2258, Port-au-Prince, Haiti
Tel +509 2440115   Fax +509 2440117
jbyves@yahoo.com   www.haitifoot.com
President: JEAN-BART Yves   General Secretary: DESIR Lionel
Vice-President: JEAN MARIE Georges   Treasurer: BERTIN Eddy   Media Officer: CHARLES M. Louis
Men's Coach: ELOI Wagneau   Women's Coach: LAMARRE Wilnea
FHF formed: 1904   CONCACAF: 1961   FIFA: 1933
Blue shirts, Red shorts, Blue socks

RECENT INTERNATIONAL MATCHES PLAYED BY HAITI

2006	Opponents	Score		Venue	Comp	Scorers	Att	Referee
16-08	Guatemala	D	1-1	Miami	Fr	Dorcelus 60	15 000	
15-09	Dominican Republic	W	3-1	Saint-Marc	Fr	Francois 13, Saint-Cyr 66, Cadet 92+		
17-09	Dominican Republic	W	2-1	Port-au-Prince	Fr	Fritzson 26, Saint-Jean 79p		
27-09	St Vincent/Grenadines	W	4-0	Kingston	CCq	Mayard 18, Fritzson 54, Jean-Jacques 79, Gracien 90	3 000	Forde BRB
29-09	St Lucia	W	7-1	Kingston	CCq	Jamil 2 4 13, Fritzson 2 17 83, Chéry 42, Neol 64, Mayard 81	3 000	Callendar BRB
1-10	Jamaica	L	0-2	Kingston	CCq		3 000	Brizan TRI
17-10	Cuba	D	0-0	Port-au-Prince	Fr			
19-10	Cuba	L	0-1	Cap-Haitien	Fr			
8-11	Cuba	L	1-2	Fort-de-France	CCq	Fritzson 88		
10-11	Martinique	L	0-1	Fort-de-France	CCq			
12-11	Surinam	D	1-1	Fort-de-France	CCq	Jamil 78p		
2007								
7-01	Bermuda	W	2-0	Couva	CCq	Cadet 9, Lormera 72		Brizan TRI
9-01	Bermuda	W	3-0	Couva	CCq	Cadet 2 25 90, Boucicaut 63		Davis TRI
12-01	Martinique	W	1-0	Port of Spain	CCr1	Brunel 12		
15-01	Barbados	W	2-0	Port of Spain	CCr1	Boucicaut 55, Lormera 91+		
17-01	Trinidad and Tobago	L	1-3	Port of Spain	CCr1	Brunel 54		
20-01	Guadeloupe †	W	3-1	Port of Spain	CCsf	Cadet 56, Brunel 65, Fritzson 76		
23-01	Trinidad and Tobago	W	2-1	Port of Spain	CCf	Boucicaut 23, Brunel 52		Moreno PAN
24-03	Panama	W	3-0	Miami	Fr	Cadet 28, Brunel 53, Saint-Jean 86	12 000	
17-04	El Salvador	W	1-0	San Salvador	Fr	Noncent 92+		
19-04	Honduras	W	3-1	La Ceiba	Fr	Boucicaut 40, Cadet 69, Germain 77		Soriano HON
23-05	Chile	D	0-0	Port-au-Prince	Fr			
28-05	Trinidad and Tobago	L	0-1	Port of Spain	Fr			
30-05	St Vincent/Grenadines	W	3-0	Port of Spain	Fr	Alcenat 2 38 59, Pierre-Louis 67		
6-06	Guadeloupe †	D	1-1	Miami	GCr1	Chery 35p	17 420	Vaughn USA
9-06	Costa Rica	D	1-1	Miami	GCr1	Boucicaut 71	22 529	Campbell JAM
11-06	Canada	L	0-2	Miami	GCr1		15 892	
17-10	Costa Rica	D	1-1	San Jose	Fr	Alcenat 66		Quesada CRC
2008								
26-01	El Salvador	D	0-0	Port au Prince	Fr			
29-01	El Salvador	D	0-0	Saint Marc	Fr			
3-02	Venezuela	L	0-1	Maturin	Fr		20 000	Soto VEN
6-02	Venezuela	D	1-1	Puerto La Cruz	Fr	Brunel 12	30 000	Perluzzo VEN
27-02	Dominican Republic	W	2-1	San Cristobal	Fr			
28-02	Dominican Republic	W	2-0	San Cristobal	Fr			
26-03	Ecuador	L	1-3	Latacunga	Fr	Davison 4	9 000	
23-04	Guatemala	L	0-1	Guatemala City	Fr			
7-06	Honduras	L	1-3	La Ceiba	Fr	Germain 77		
15-06	Netherlands Antilles	D	0-0	Port au Prince	WCq		6 000	Aguilar SLV
22-06	Netherlands Antilles	W	1-0	Willemstad	WCq	Martha OG 78	9 000	Brizan TRI

Fr = Friendly match • CC = Digicel Caribbean Cup • GC = CONCACAF Gold Cup • WC = FIFA World Cup
q = qualifier • r1 = first round group stage • sf = semi-final • f = final • † Not a full international

HAITI NATIONAL TEAM RECORDS AND RECORD SEQUENCES

Records			Sequence records					
Victory	12-1	VIR 2001	Wins	8	1979	Clean sheets	5	1997-1998
Defeat	1-9	BRA 1959	Defeats	6	1974-75, 1984-89	Goals scored	12	1997-1999
Player Caps	n/a		Undefeated	18	1977-1980	Without goal	6	1973-1974
Player Goals	n/a		Without win	12	1973-1975	Goals against	9	1974-1975

HAITI COUNTRY INFORMATION

Capital	Port-au-Prince	Independence	1804 from France	GDP per Capita	$1 600
Population	7 656 166	Status	Republic	GNP Ranking	122
Area km²	27 750	Language	French	Dialling code	+509
Population density	275 per km²	Literacy rate	52%	Internet code	.ht
% in urban areas	32%	Main religion	Christian 96%	GMT + / –	-5
Towns/Cities ('000)	Port-au-Prince 1 234; Carrefour 439; Delmas 377; Cap-Haïtien 134; Pétionville 108				
Neighbours (km)	Dominican Republic 360; Atlantic Ocean & Caribbean Sea 1 771				
Main stadia	Stade Sylvio Cator – Port-au-Prince 10 500; Park St Victor – Cap-Haïtien 7 500				

HAITI 2007 DIVISION 1 OUVERTURE

	Pl	W	D	L	F	A	Pts
Baltimore St Marc	15	9	5	1	19	7	32
Cavaly Léogâne	15	6	8	1	14	5	26
AS Mirebalais	15	6	6	3	12	7	24
Zénith Cap Haïtien	15	6	5	4	16	15	23
Violette AC	15	5	7	3	13	7	22
Tempête St Marc	15	5	7	3	14	13	22
AS Capoise	15	5	7	3	12	12	22
AS Carrefour	15	5	6	4	15	14	21
Don Bosco	15	6	3	6	14	14	21
Racing Gônaïves	15	5	6	4	11	13	21
Victory FC	15	5	5	5	15	11	20
Aigle Noir	15	5	4	6	13	11	19
Racing Club Haïtien	15	4	5	6	11	14	17
AS Rive Artibonitienne	15	3	3	9	9	19	12
Roulado Gônaïves	15	2	4	9	13	21	10
AS Grand Goâve	15	0	5	10	5	23	5

24/02/2007 - 13/05/2007

HAITI 2007 DIVISION 1 FERMATURE

	Pl	W	D	L	F	A	Pts
Cavaly Léogâne	15	8	5	2	15	9	29
AS Capoise	15	6	6	3	23	7	24
AS Carrefour	15	5	9	1	14	6	24
Victory FC	15	6	6	3	18	12	24
Baltimore St Marc	15	6	5	4	20	7	23
Don Bosco	15	5	8	2	12	7	23
Zénith Cap Haïtien	15	6	4	5	21	18	22
Tempête St Marc	15	5	7	3	9	7	22
Aigle Noir	15	6	3	6	15	12	21
Violette AC	15	6	3	6	13	10	21
Racing Club Haïtien	15	5	6	4	11	8	21
Racing Gônaïves	15	5	4	6	7	12	19
AS Mirebalais	15	3	8	4	11	11	17
Roulado Gônaïves	15	3	2	10	12	23	11
AS Rive Artibonitienne	15	2	3	10	6	29	9
AS Grand Goâve	15	2	3	10	8	37	9

22/08/2007 - 28/11/2007

HAITI 2007 DIVISION 1 OVERALL

	Pl	W	D	L	F	A	Pts
Baltimore St Marc †	30	15	10	5	39	14	55
Cavaly Léogâne †	30	14	13	3	29	14	55
AS Capoise †	30	11	13	6	35	19	46
AS Carrefour †	30	10	15	5	29	20	45
Tempête St Marc †	30	10	14	6	23	20	44
Don Bosco †	30	11	11	8	26	21	44
Victory FC †	30	11	11	8	33	23	44
Zénith Cap Haïtien †	30	12	9	9	37	33	42
AS Mirebalais	30	9	14	7	23	18	41
Violette AC	30	11	10	9	26	17	40
Aigle Noir	30	11	7	12	28	23	40
Racing Gônaïves	30	10	10	10	18	25	40
Racing Club Haïtien	30	9	11	10	22	22	38
Roulado Gônaïves	30	5	6	19	25	44	21
AS Rive Artibonitienne	30	5	6	19	15	48	21
AS Grand Goâve	30	2	8	20	13	60	14

4/11/2005 - 26/11/2006 • † Qualified for Super Huit play-offs

HAITI 2007 SUPER HUIT PLAY-OFFS

Quarter-finals	Semi-finals	Final
Tempête *		Parc Levelt, Saint Marc
Carrefour	Tempête *	23-12-2007
Victory *	Cavaly	
Cavaly		
Don Bosco *		Tempête 3
Capoise	Don Bosco	Zénith 0
Baltimore	Zénith *	Scorers - Eliphène
Zénith *	* Home team in the first leg	Cadet 2 [6] [85], Thompson Amius [87]

HAITI 2008 DIVISION 1 OUVERTURE

	Pl	W	D	L	F	A	Pts
Tempête St Marc	13	7	6	0	13	3	27
AS Mirebalais	13	7	2	4	11	11	23
Baltimore St Marc	13	6	4	3	14	5	22
Don Bosco	13	6	3	4	13	11	21
Violette AC	13	6	2	5	14	11	20
Cavaly Léogâne	13	4	6	3	10	4	18
Valencia Léogâne	13	5	3	5	7	8	18
Racing Gônaïves	13	4	5	4	10	12	17
Victory FC	13	3	7	3	7	6	16
Aigle Noir	13	4	3	6	11	17	16
AS Capoise	13	3	5	5	9	9	14
JS Capoise	13	3	4	6	5	10	13
Zénith Cap Haïtien	13	3	3	7	9	17	12
AS Carrefour	13	1	5	7	4	13	8

16/02/2008 - 18/05/2008

HKG – HONG KONG

NATIONAL TEAM RECORD
JULY 10TH 2006 TO JULY 12TH 2010

PL	W	D	L	F	A	%
14	5	4	5	34	19	50

FIFA/COCA-COLA WORLD RANKING

1993	1994	1995	1996	1997	1998	1999	2000	2001	2002	2003	2004	2005	2006	2007	High	
112	98	111	124	129	136	122	123	137	150	142	133	117	117	125	**90**	02/96

2007–2008												Low	
08/07	09/07	10/07	11/07	12/07	01/08	02/08	03/08	04/08	05/08	06/08	07/08	**154**	02/03
126	134	135	129	125	125	126	125	124	125	117	120		

Thanks to their low FIFA/Coca-Cola World Ranking, the Hong Kong national team had to play two rounds of 2010 FIFA World Cup qualifying in order to get through to the Asian group stage but after beating Timor-Leste in the first round, including an 8-1 home win, Hong Kong found themselves paired with Turkmenistan who beat them 3-0 on aggregate. It has now been over two decades since that famous World Cup win away to China, and it seems impossible to imagine such glory ever returning. Domestically, the season belonged to South China once more, although they were taken to the very last game by Citizen. They relied heavily on their Brazilian strike force of

INTERNATIONAL HONOURS
None

Detinho and Maxwell, with the former, plucked from the Portuguese lower leagues, finishing as the league's top scorer with 19 goals. South China also won the League Cup while Citizen made do with the FA Cup. The other trophy winners were Eastern in the Senior Shield, a welcome return for a club that had achieved great success in the early 90s. Eastern had spent a decade in the lower leagues before a timely sponsorship deal led the Hong Kong FA to invite them into the top flight at the start of the season. South China and Kitchee represented Hong Kong in the AFC Cup, but neither was able to negotiate their way past the group phase.

THE FIFA BIG COUNT OF 2006

	Male	Female		Total
Number of players	139 960	9 996	Referees and Assistant Referees	149
Professionals	211		Admin, Coaches, Technical, Medical	910
Amateurs 18+	2 203		Number of clubs	82
Youth under 18	1 762		Number of teams	582
Unregistered	50 780		Clubs with women's teams	2
Total players	149 956		Players as % of population	2.16%

The Hong Kong Football Association Ltd (HKFA)
55 Fat Kwong Street, Homantin, Kowloon, Hong Kong
Tel +852 27129122   Fax +852 27604303
hkfa@hkfa.com   www.hkfa.com
President: FOK Timothy Tsun Ting   General Secretary: KY LEUNG Sunny
Vice-President: LEUNG Brian Hung Tak   Treasurer: LI Sonny   Media Officer: TBD
Men's Coach: LAI Sun Cheung   Women's Coach: YING Wai Hoi
HKFA formed: 1914   AFC: 1954   FIFA: 1954
Red shirts, Red shorts, Red socks

RECENT INTERNATIONAL MATCHES PLAYED BY HONG KONG

2004	Opponents	Score		Venue	Comp	Scorers	Att	Referee
18-02	Malaysia	W	3-1	Kuantan	WCq	Ng Wai Chiu [17], Chu Siu Kei [84], Kwok Yue Hung [93+]	12 000	Nagalingham SIN
31-03	China PR	L	0-1	Hong Kong	WCq		9 000	Rungklay THA
9-06	Kuwait	L	0-4	Kuwait City	WCq		9 000	Najm LIB
8-09	Kuwait	L	0-2	Hong Kong	WCq		1 500	Busurmankulov KGZ
13-10	Malaysia	W	2-0	Hong Kong	WCq	Chu Siu Kei [5], Wong Chun Yue [51]	2 425	Ahamd Rakhil MAS
17-11	China PR	L	0-7	Guangzhou	WCq		20 300	Lee Jong Kuk KOR
30-11	Singapore	D	0-0	Singapore	Fr	W 6-5p	3 359	
2-12	Myanmar	D	2-2	Singapore	Fr	Feng Ji Zhi, Law Chun Bong	2 000	
2005								
9-02	Brazil	L	1-7	Hong Kong	Fr	Lee Sze Ming [85]	23 425	Zhou Weixin CHN
5-03	Mongolia	W	6-0	Taipei	EACq	Chu Siu Kei [30p], Law Chun Bong [48], Wong Chun Yue [50], Lam Ka Wai [73], Chan Yiu Lun 2 [92 93]		
7-03	Guam	W	15-0	Taipei	EACq	Chan Wai Ho [1], Chan Siu Ki 7 [8 18 28 30 35 42 87], Chan Yiu Lun 2 [16 31], Wong Chun Yue 3 [24 43 45], Chu Siu Kei [67], Poon Man Tik [89]		
11-03	Chinese Taipei	W	5-0	Taipei	EACq	Chan Yiu Lun 2 [7 45], Lam Ka Wai [20], Poon Yiu Cheuk [58p], Cheung Sai Ho [60]		
13-03	Korea DPR	L	0-2	Taipei	EACq			
29-05	Macao	W	8-1	Hong Kong	Fr	Chan Siu Ki 3, Lee Chi Ho, Lam Ka Wei, Leung Sze Chung, Cheng Lai Hin		
2006								
29-01	Denmark	L	0-3	Hong Kong	Fr		16 841	Iemoto JPN
1-02	Croatia	L	0-4	Hong Kong	Fr		13 971	Iemoto JPN
15-02	Singapore	D	1-1	Hong Kong	Fr	Ambassa Guy [65]	610	Ong Kim Heng MAS
18-02	India	D	2-2	Hong Kong	Fr	Ambassa Guy [3], Law Chun Bong [17]	3 672	Jae Yong Bae KOR
22-02	Qatar	L	0-3	Hong Kong	ACq		1 806	Nishimura JPN
1-03	Bangladesh	W	1-0	Dhaka	ACq	Chan Siu Ki [82]	1 000	Sarkar IND
3-06	Macao	D	0-0	Macao	Fr			
12-08	Singapore	L	1-2	Hong Kong	Fr	Lee Sze Ming [68]		
16-08	Uzbekistan	D	2-2	Tashkent	ACq	Sham Kwok Keung 2 [66 87]	15 000	Shaban KUW
6-09	Uzbekistan	D	0-0	Hong Kong	ACq		7 608	Lee Gi Young KOR
11-10	Qatar	L	0-2	Doha	ACq		1 000	Kousa SYR
15-11	Bangladesh	W	2-0	Hong Kong	ACq	Ambassa Guy 2 [43 74p]	1 273	Kim Dong Jin KOR
2007								
1-06	Indonesia	L	0-3	Jakarta	Fr			
10-06	Macau	W	2-1	Hong Kong	Fr	Chan Siu Ki 2 [24 66]		
19-06	Chinese Taipei	D	1-1	Macau	EACq	Lo Chi Kwan [56]	200	Kim Eui Soo KOR
21-06	Guam	W	15-1	Macau	EACq	Chan Siu Ki 5 [5 21 36 42 51], Lo Kwan Yee 2 [8 41], Poon Yiu Cheuk [22], Cheng Siu Wai [31], Lo Chi Kwan [38], Cordeiro [56], OG [69], Law Chun Pong [73], Ambassa Guy [76], Luk Koon Pong [86]	300	Matsuo JPN
24-06	Korea DPR	L	0-1	Macau	EACq		300	Ogiya JPN
21-10	Timor-Leste	W	3-2	Gianyar	WCq	Cheng Siu Wai 2 [25 50], Esteves OG [35]	1 500	Shaharul MAS
28-10	Timor-Leste	W	8-1	Hong Kong	WCq	Lo Kwan Yee [3], Chan Siu Ki 3 [6 79 87], Cheung Sai Ho [50], Cheng Siu Wai 2 [68 71], Lam Ka Wai [84]	1 542	Torky IRN
10-11	Turkmenistan	D	0-0	Hong Kong	WCq		2 823	Mujghef JOR
18-11	Turkmenistan	L	0-3	Ashgabat	WCq		30 000	Al Hilali OMA
2008								
No international matches played in 2008 before August								

Fr = Friendly match • EAC = East Asian Championship • AC = AFC Asian Cup • WC = FIFA World Cup • q = qualifier

HONG KONG NATIONAL TEAM RECORDS AND RECORD SEQUENCES

Records			Sequence records				
Victory	15-0	GUM 2005	Wins	7	1985	Clean sheets	4	2003
Defeat	0-7	CHN 1980 2004	Defeats	9	1977-1979	Goals scored	24	1949-1958
Player Caps	n/a		Undefeated	10	1984-1985	Without goal	7	1988-1989
Player Goals	n/a		Without win	13	1967-1968	Goals against	23	1992-1995

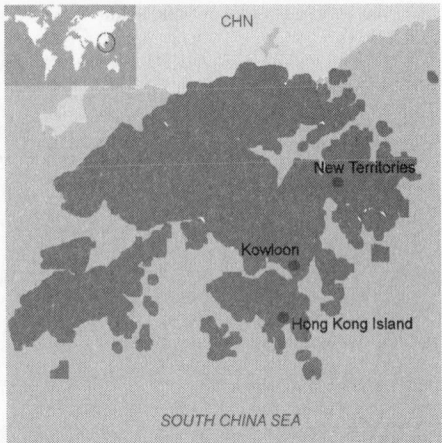

MAJOR CITIES/TOWNS

		Population '000
1	Sha Tin, NT	628
2	Eastern, HKI	616
3	Kwun Tong, Kowloon	562
4	Tuen Mun, NT	488
5	Kwai Tsing, NT	477
6	Yuen Long, NT	449
7	Wong Tai Sin, Kowloon	444
8	Kowloon City	381
9	Sham Shui Po, Kowloon	353
10	Sai Kung, NT	327
11	Tai Po, NT	310
12	North, NT	298
13	Southern, HKI	290
14	Yau Tsim Mong, Kowloon	282
15	Tsuen Wan, NT	275
16	Central & Western, HKI	261
17	Wan Chai, HKI	167
18	Islands, NT	86

NT = New Territories
HKI = Hong Kong Island

HONG KONG SPECIAL ADMINISTRATIVE REGION; XIANGGANG TEBIE XINGZHENGQU

Capital	Victoria	Language	Cantonese, English	Independence	n/a
Population	6 980 412	Area	1 092 km²	% in cities	100%
GDP per cap	$28 800	Dailling code	+852	Internet .hn	GMT + / - +8

MEDALS TABLE

		Overall		Lge		FAC		Shield		VC		LC		Asia		DoF
		G	S	G	B	G	B	G	B	G	B	G	B	G	S	
1	South China	68	37	29	15	9	4	20	10	8	7			2	1	1910
2	Seiko	29	8	9	3	6	1	8	2	6	2					1970-86
3	Eastern	16	10	4	3	3	1	7	2	2	4					
4	Happy Valley	15	38	6	16	2	5	5	9	1	3	1	5			1950
5	Kitchee	10	11	3	5		1	5	4			2	1			1931
6	Sun Hei	10	7	3	2	3	1	1	3			3	1			1986
7	Rangers	9	8	1		2	3	4	2	2	2		1			1958
	Sing Tao	9	8	1	4		1	6	2	2	1					1940-99
9	Instant-Dict (Double Flower)	6	11	2	2	3	2		4	1	3					
10	Bulova	5	4		2	2	1	1	1	2	1					1977-85
11	Kowloon Motor Bus Co.	3	9	2	5			1	4							1947-81
12	Lai Sun	3	4			1	2		1	2	1					
13	Jardines	3	1	1	1			1		1						
	Yuen Long	3	1	1		1		1	1							1959
15	Ernest Borel	2	1			1	1		1							1990-93
16	Caroline Hill	1	3	1						1	2					
17	Orient & Yee Hope Union	1	1			1	1	1								
	Citizen	1	1	1	1											

Lge = League • FAC = FA Cup • Shield = Senior Shield • VC = Viceroy Cup • LC = League Cup

RECENT LEAGUE AND CUP RECORD

	League			FA Cup			Senior Shield		
Year	Champions	Score	Runners-up	Winners	Score	Runners-up	Winners	Score	Runners-up
2001	Happy Valley	1-0	Instant-Dict	Instant-Dict	2-1	South China	O & YH Union	1-0	Instant-Dict
2002	Sun Hei	†	Happy Valley	South China	1-0	Sun Hei	South China	3-2	Sun Hei
2003	Happy Valley	†	Sun Hei	Sun Hei	2-1	Buler Rangers	South China	2-1	Happy Valley
2004	Sun Hei	†	Kitchee	Happy Valley	3-1	Kitchee	Happy Valley	3-0	Sun Hei
2005	Sun Hei	†	Happy Valley	Sun Hei	2-1	Happy Valley	Sun Hei	4-2	Happy Valley
2006	Happy Valley	†	Sun Hei	Sun Hei	1-0	Happy Valley	Kitchee	3-0	Happy Valley
2007	South China	†	Kitchee	South China	2-1	Happy Valley	South China	2-1	Sun Hei
2008	South China	†	Citizen	Citizen	2-0	Tai Po	Eastern	3-1	Kitchee

† Played on a league basis - in 2002 the Championship reverted to a single stage round robin format

HONG KONG 2007–08

COOLPOINT VENTILATION FIRST DIVISION

	Pl	W	D	L	F	A	Pts	South China	Citizen	Tai Po	H Valley	Sun Hei	Kitchee	Eastern	Lanwa	Workable	Rangers
South China †	18	11	3	4	51	17	36		0-0	6-1	0-2	4-1	1-2	2-0	4-1	6-1	0-0
Citizen †	18	10	4	4	31	22	34	2-1		2-1	0-3	0-1	2-1	2-2	0-0	4-1	3-2
Tai Po	18	7	6	5	36	37	27	2-1	2-3		4-3	2-2	3-3	3-1	2-4	2-1	2-0
Happy Valley	18	5	9	4	25	22	24	1-1	0-2	1-1		2-3	0-0	3-3	0-0	0-0	1-1
Sun Hei	18	5	8	5	26	23	23	1-2	3-2	1-2	0-1		2-2	1-1	0-1	0-0	1-1
Kitchee	18	5	7	6	30	33	22	0-5	0-1	2-1	3-3	1-1		2-2	2-3	0-1	3-1
Eastern	18	4	8	6	25	28	20	0-2	4-2	2-3	1-2	0-2	1-1		0-0	0-0	4-3
Lanwa	18	4	8	6	25	31	20	1-3	1-1	1-1	3-2	1-1	2-4	0-2		1-1	2-2
Workable	18	3	6	9	14	34	15	1-4	0-1	2-2	0-1	1-6	1-3	0-2	3-2		1-0
Rangers	18	2	9	7	19	35	15	1-9	0-4	2-2	0-0	0-0	3-1	0-0	3-2	0-0	

2/09/2007 - 27/04/2008 • † Qualified for the AFC Cup • Top scorer: Detinho, South China 19, Giovane, Sun Hei 12, Maxwell, South China 11

HONG KONG 2007–08 SECOND DIVISION

	Pl	W	D	L	F	A	Pts
Mutual	18	14	3	1	60	20	45
HKFC	18	13	2	3	87	24	41
Fukien	18	8	3	7	36	39	27
Tung Po	18	6	7	5	23	27	25
Double Flower	18	7	3	8	24	34	24
Kwai Tsing	18	6	5	7	23	27	23
EU Tai Chung	18	5	4	9	28	38	19
Kwok Keung	18	5	4	9	18	42	19
Lucky Mile	18	4	6	8	27	37	18
New Fair Kui Tan	18	1	5	12	15	53	8

8/09/2007 - 16/03/2008

SENIOR SHIELD 2007–08

Quarter-finals

Eastern	3
Citizen	1
Sun Hei	0
Happy Valley	3
South China	4
Rangers	0
Lanwa	0
Kitchee	5

Prelim round: Rangers 2-0 Workable
Prelim round: Happey Valley 2-1 Tai Po

Semi-finals

Eastern	1
Happy Valley	0
South China	1
Kitchee	2

Final

Eastern	3
Kitchee	1

CUP FINAL
23-12-2007

FA CUP 2007–08

Quarter-finals

Citizen	1 7p
Kitchee	1 6p
Happy Valley	1
Eastern	2
South China	1
Sun Hei	0
Rangers	0
Tai Po	2

Prelim round: Eastern 1-0 Workable
Prelim round: Sun Hei 2-0 Lanwa

Semi-finals

Citizen	1
Eastern	0
South China	1
Tai Po	2

Final

Citizen	2
Tai Po	0

CUP FINAL
18-05-2008
Scorers - Zhi Zhao Chen [14], Padiha OG [85]

LEAGUE CUP 2007–08

Round of 16

Group A	Pts	Ki	Wo	HV	TP
South China	9	2-1	0-1	4-2	3-1
Kitchee	7		1-0	3-3	4-0
Workable	7			0-0	1-1
Happy Valley	5				1-0
Tai Po	1				

Group B	Pts	Ea	Ra	Ci	La
Sun Hei	8	1-1	1-1	2-0	3-0
Eastern	6		2-1	0-0	1-1
Rangers	5			1-1	3-0
Citizen	3				1-1
Lanwa	2				

Semi-finals

South China	1
Eastern	0
Sun Hei	0
Kitchee	2

Final

South China	4
Kitchee	2

CUP FINAL
24-03-2008
Scorers - Li Haiqiang [50], Detinho 3 [59] [64] [87p] for South China; Liu Quankun [17], Wilfred Bamnjo [84] for Kitchee

HON – HONDURAS

NATIONAL TEAM RECORD
JULY 10TH 2006 TO JULY 12TH 2010

PL	W	D	L	F	A	%
28	17	5	6	57	28	69.6

FIFA/COCA-COLA WORLD RANKING

1993	1994	1995	1996	1997	1998	1999	2000	2001	2002	2003	2004	2005	2006	2007		High	
40	53	49	45	73	91	69	46	27	40	49	59	41	56	53		**20**	09/01

2007–2008												Low	
08/07	09/07	10/07	11/07	12/07	01/08	02/08	03/08	04/08	05/08	06/08	07/08	**95**	11/98
57	59	55	54	53	54	50	43	38	36	37	48		

Rarely before has the stock of Honduran football been so high and there was real belief within the country before the 2010 FIFA World Cup qualifiers got underway that a first appearance at the finals since 1982 was a possibility. Coach Reinaldo Rueda has at his disposal a growing number of players making a big name for themselves in Europe, none more so than David Suazo who in the summer of 2007 was at the centre of a battle between the two Milan clubs to sign him from Cagliari, with Inter emerging victorious. Others include Wilson Palacios who was rated as one of the top 10 signings of the season by an English newspaper after impressing at Wigan. In the World

INTERNATIONAL HONOURS
Qualified for the FIFA World Cup finals 1982 UNCAF Cup 1993 1995 CONCACAF Club Championship Olimpia 1972 1988

Cup qualifiers Honduras were drawn in a tough group alongside Canada, Mexico and Jamaica after beating Puerto Rico in a preliminary match. Standards in club football in Honduras look set to improve with the launch of the CONCACAF Champions League. Honduras will be represented in the inaugural tournament by Apertura winners Marathon and Clausura winners Olimpia, with the latter claiming an automatic berth in the group stage after winning a play-off. Absent will be Motagua who in December 2007 were crowned Central American champions before going on to lose to eventual winners Pachuca in the quarter-finals of the last CONCACAF Champions Cup.

THE FIFA BIG COUNT OF 2006

	Male	Female		Total
Number of players	360 800	59 800	Referees and Assistant Referees	1 100
Professionals	100		Admin, Coaches, Technical, Medical	5 700
Amateurs 18+	27 700		Number of clubs	220
Youth under 18	32 800		Number of teams	1 100
Unregistered	79 300		Clubs with women's teams	7
Total players	420 600		Players as % of population	5.74%

Federación Nacional Autónoma de Fútbol de Honduras (FENAFUTH)
Colonia Florencia Norte, Edificio Plaza América, Ave. Roble, 1 y 2 Nivel, Tegucigalpa, Honduras
Tel +504 2311436   Fax +504 2398826
fenafuth@fenafuth.com   www.fenafuth.net
President: CALLEJAS Rafael   General Secretary: HAWIT BANEGAS Alfredo
Vice-President: ATALA Javier   Treasurer: WILLIAMS Vicente   Media Officer: BANEGAS Martin
Men's Coach: RUEDA Reinaldo   Women's Coach: GUITIERREZ ALVAREZ Cesar Efrain
FENAFUTH formed: 1951   CONCACAF: 1961   FIFA: 1951
Blue shirts, Blue shorts, Blue socks

RECENT INTERNATIONAL MATCHES PLAYED BY HONDURAS

2006	Opponents	Score		Venue	Comp	Scorers	Att	Referee
25-01	Ecuador	L	0-1	Guayaquil	Fr		10 000	Ramos ECU
12-02	China PR	W	1-0	Guangzhou	Fr	Oliva [54]	20 000	Supian MAS
16-08	Venezuela	D	0-0	Maracay	Fr		9 000	Brandt VEN
6-09	El Salvador	W	2-0	Tegucigalpa	Fr	Bernardez [32], Palacios [81]	7 000	Zelaya HON
7-10	Guatemala	W	3-2	Fort Lauderdale	Fr	Núñez [52p], De Leon [69], Suazo [87p]	19 173	Vaughn USA
10-10	Guatemala	W	2-1	Atlanta	Fr	Figueroa [4], Martinez.W [49]	7 000	Prus USA
2007								
9-02	Costa Rica	L	1-3	San Salvador	UCr1	Martinez.E [59]		Archundia MEX
11-02	Panama	D	1-1	San Salvador	UCr1	Guardia OG [25]		Aguilar SLV
15-02	Nicaragua	W	9-1	San Salvador	UC5p	Martinez.J [4], Velásquez 4 [6 27 38 39p], Martinez.S 3 [69 81 86], Mejía [77]		Aguilar SLV
24-03	El Salvador	W	2-0	Fort Lauderdale	Fr	Oliva 2 [25 66]	17 095	Marrufo USA
27-03	El Salvador	W	2-0	Cary	Fr	Martinez.J 2 [1 57]	8 365	
19-04	Haiti	L	1-3	La Ceiba	Fr	Pavon [6p]		Soriano HON
25-05	Venezuela	L	1-2	Merida	Fr	Pavon [44]	42 000	Gomez VEN
2-06	Trinidad and Tobago	W	3-1	San Pedro Sula	Fr	Izaguirre [49], Guevara [52p], Costly [84]	1 907	Soriano HON
8-06	Panama	L	2-3	New Jersey	GCr1	Guevara [40], Costly [90]	20 230	Navarro CAN
10-06	Mexico	W	2-1	New Jersey	GCr1	Costly 2 [60 90]	68 123	
13-06	Cuba	W	5-0	Houston	GCr1	Pavon 4 [3 12 43 53], Guevara [90]	68 417	
17-06	Guadeloupe	L	1-2	Houston	GCqf	Pavon [71]	70 092	Navarro CAN
22-08	El Salvador	L	0-2	San Salvador	Fr			Bonilla SLV
9-09	Costa Rica	D	0-0	East Hartford	Fr	L 2-3p	8 000	Vaugh USA
12-09	Ecuador	W	2-1	San Pedro Sula	Fr	De Leon [76], Suazo [82]	25 000	Batres GUA
14-10	Panama	W	1-0	Tegucigalpa	Fr	Martinez.W [54]	23 139	Zelaya HON
17-11	Guatemala	W	1-0	Miami	Fr	Martinez.W [19]		Stott USA
2008								
6-02	Paraguay	W	2-0	San Pedro Sula	Fr	Guevara [47p], Costly [54]	5 000	Rodriguez CRC
26-03	Colombia	W	2-1	Fort Lauderdale	Fr	Suazo [31], Thomas [63]		
23-05	Belize	W	2-0	San Pedro Sula	Fr	Bernardez [3p], Welcome [12]		
30-05	Venezuela	D	1-1	Fort Lauderdale	Fr	Mendoza [2]	10 000	Wiemckowski USA
4-06	Puerto Rico	W	4-0	San Pedro Sula	WCq	De Leon [25], Palacios [51], Suazo 2 [52 92+]	20 000	Campbell JAM
7-06	Haiti	W	3-1	La Ceiba	Fr	Martinez.W [21p], Suazo [67], Guevara [73p]		
14-06	Puerto Rico	D	2-2	Bayamon	WCq	Suazo [22], Palacios [52]	5 000	Lopez GUA

Fr = Friendly match • UC = UNCAF Cup • GC = CONCACAF Gold Cup • WC = FIFA World Cup
q = qualifier • r1 = first round group • qf = quarter-final • 5p = fifth place play-off • sf = semi-final • f = final

HONDURAS NATIONAL TEAM PLAYERS

	Player		Ap	G	Club	Date of Birth		Player		Ap	G	Club	Date of Birth
1	John Hoore	GK	4	0	Victoria	30 10 1981	11	Miguel Castillo	MF	3	0	Motagua	1 12 1986
2	Osman Chávez	DF	5	0	Platense	29 7 1984	12	Iván Guerrero	MF	73	4	DC United	30 11 1977
3	Maynor Figueroa	DF	53	2	Wigan Athletic	2 5 1983	13	Carlo Costly	FW	16	5	GKS Belchatów	17 7 1982
4	Mario Beata	DF	12	0	Marathón	17 10 1974	14	Oscar Bonieck Garcia	DF	31	0	PSG	4 9 1984
5	Víctor Bernárdez	DF	29	2	Motagua	14 5 1982	15	Walter Martínez	FW	14	5	Beijing Guoan	28 3 1982
6	Sergio Mendoza	DF	39	1	Olimpia	23 5 1981	16	Allan Lalin	FW	3	0	Real España	5 1 1981
7	Amado Guevara	MF	109	23	Toronto FC	2 5 1976	17	Danilo Turcios	MF	61	7	Olimpia	8 5 1978
8	Wilson Palacios	MF	52	4	Wigan Athletic	29 7 1984	18	Noel Valladares	GK	48	0	Olimpia	3 5 1977
9	David Suazo	FW	38	14	Internazionale	5 11 1979	19	Emilio Izaguirre	DF	20	1	Motagua	5 10 1986
10	Julio Cesar de Leon	MF	65	11	Parma	13 9 1983	20	Kevin Hernández	GK	2	0	Bella Vista	21 12 1985

The Honduras squad for the June 2008 World Cup qualifiers

HONDURAS NATIONAL TEAM RECORDS AND RECORD SEQUENCES

Records			Sequence records					
Victory	10-0	NCA 1946	Wins	6	Three times	Clean sheets	6	1992
Defeat	1-10	GUA 1921	Defeats	6	1963-1965	Goals scored	15	2006-2007
Player Caps	109	Amado Guevara	Undefeated	14	1991-1992	Without goal	5	1988
Player Goals	46	Carlos Pavon	Without win	14	1987-1991	Goals against	13	1993-1995

REPUBLIC OF HONDURAS; REPUBLICA DE HONDURAS

Capital	Tegucigalpa	Language	Spanish			Independence	1821
Population	7 326 496	Area	112 090 km²	Density	60 per km²	% in cities	44%
GDP per cap	$2 600	Dailling code	+504	Internet	.hn	GMT + / -	-6

MAJOR CITIES/TOWNS
Population '000

1	Tegucigalpa	1 765
2	San Pedro Sula	735
3	La Ceiba	138
4	El Progreso	106
5	Choluteca	78
6	Comayagua	61
7	Puerto Cortés	50
8	Danli	46
9	Siguatepeque	45
10	Juticalpa	35
11	Catacamas	35
12	Villanueva	33
13	Tocoa	33
14	Tela	29
15	Santa Rosa Copán	28
16	Olanchito	27
17	San Lorenzo	23
18	Cofradía	21
19	El Paraíso	19
20	La Paz	18
21	Potrerillos	16
22	Yoro	16
23	Santa Bárbara	15
24	La Entrada	15

MEDALS TABLE

		Overall			Lge			Cent Am			City	Stadium	Cap'ty	DoF
		G	S	B	G	S	B	G	S	B				
1	Olimpia	23	16	1	21	14		2	2	1	Tegucigalpa	Tiburcio Carias Andino	35 000	1912
2	Motagua	11	8		11	8					Tegucigalpa	Tiburcio Carias Andino	35 000	1928
3	Real España	9	8	1	9	8				1	San Pedro Sula	Francisco Morazán	20 000	1929
4	Marathón	6	11	1	6	11				1	San Pedro Sula	Olímpico Metropolitano	40 000	1925
5	Platense	2	3		2	3					Puerto Cortés	Excelsior	10 000	1960
	Vida	2	3		2	3					La Ceiba	Nilmo Edwards	15 000	1940
7	Victoria	1	1		1	1					La Ceiba	Nilmo Edwards	15 000	1935
8	Universidad National - UNAH		3			2		1			Choluteca	Fausto Flores Lagos	5 000	1965
9	Atlético Morazán		1			1								
10	Atlético Olanchano										Catacamas	Rubén Guifarro	5 000	1988
	Hispano										Comayagua	Carlos Miranda	10 000	1945

RECENT LEAGUE RECORD

	Championship/Torneo Clausura from 1998			Torneo Apertura		
Year	Champions	Score	Runners-up	Champions	Score	Runners-up
1995	Victoria	0-0 1-1	Olimpia			
1996	Olimpia	3-0 0-0	Real España			
1997	Olimpia	1-1 3-0	Platense	Motagua	3-0 2-1	Real España
1998	Motagua	0-0 1-0	Olimpia	Olimpia	0-0 1-0	Real España
1999	Season readjustment			Motagua	0-0 0-0 6-5p	Olimpia
2000	Motagua	1-1 1-1 3-2p	Olimpia	Olimpia	1-0 1-1	Platense
2001	Platense	1-0 1-1	Olimpia	Motagua	0-1 3-2	Marathón
2002	Marathón	4-1 0-1	Olimpia	Olimpia	1-1 2-1	Platense
2003	Marathón	1-0 3-1	Motagua	Real España	2-2 2-0	Olimpia
2004	Olimpia	1-1 1-0	Marathón	Marathón	3-2 2-1	Olimpia
2005	Olimpia	1-1 2-1	Marathón	Olimpia	1-2 2-0	Marathón
2006	Olimpia	3-3 1-0	Victoria Ceiba	Motagua	1-1 3-1	Olimpia
2007	Real España	1-2 3-1	Marathón	Marathón	0-0 2-0	Motagua
2008	Olimpia	1-1 1-0	Marathón			

HONDURAS 2007-08

TORNEO APERTURA

	Pl	W	D	L	F	A	Pts	Marathón	Motagua	Victoria	Olimpia	Savio	España	Hispano	Vida	Platense	Olanchano
Marathón †	18	10	5	3	27	16	35		1-0	0-1	1-1	2-2	2-0	3-0	1-0	1-0	1-0
Motagua †	18	9	5	4	28	19	32	4-1		1-0	0-0	1-0	2-4	1-1	2-0	3-1	2-0
Victoria †	18	7	10	1	22	12	31	2-2	2-2		2-1	0-0	2-0	2-2	1-1	1-1	4-0
Olimpia †	18	6	9	3	19	13	27	1-1	1-2	0-0		1-0	1-0	2-0	2-1	3-1	1-1
Deportivo Savio	18	5	7	6	14	15	22	1-0	1-1	1-1	1-0		1-1	0-2	1-1	2-0	0-1
Real España	18	6	4	8	22	25	22	0-1	1-2	1-2	1-3	1-0		1-0	1-1	2-3	3-1
Hispano	18	5	6	7	19	22	21	2-2	2-1	0-0	0-0	2-1	0-1		2-3	1-2	2-0
Vida	18	4	8	6	18	22	20	1-4	0-0	0-1	1-1	0-0	2-2	1-0		1-0	4-1
Platense	18	3	6	9	17	28	15	1-3	3-2	0-0	0-0	0-1	2-2	1-2	0-0		0-0
Atlético Olanchano	18	3	4	11	15	29	13	0-1	1-2	0-1	1-1	1-2	0-1	1-1	3-1	4-2	

11/08/2007 - 25/11/2007 • † Qualified for the play-offs

APERTURA PLAY-OFFS

Semi–finals			Final		
Marathón	0	2			
Olimpia *	1	1	Marathón	0	2
Victoria *	1	0	Motagua *	0	0
Motagua	1	2			

* Home team in the first leg

HONDURAS 2007-08

TORNEO CLAUSURA

	Pl	W	D	L	F	A	Pts	Olimpia	Marathón	España	Motagua	Hispano	Victoria	Olanchano	Platense	Savio	Vida
Olimpia †	18	9	6	3	28	13	33		1-0	3-0	0-1	5-0	1-0	0-0	2-1	1-1	2-0
Marathón †	18	9	3	6	30	23	30	0-2		0-1	2-1	5-2	2-0	2-1	2-2	2-1	3-1
Real España †	18	8	4	6	26	22	28	2-0	2-3		2-1	0-0	2-1	1-0	2-1	4-1	3-1
Motagua †	18	8	3	7	23	19	27	2-1	3-3	2-1		2-0	1-1	2-0	3-1	2-0	2-0
Hispano	18	7	5	6	24	25	26	1-1	0-1	1-1	2-0		2-0	2-0	2-2	3-1	1-0
Victoria	18	6	6	6	17	17	24	2-2	0-0	1-1	2-0	1-2		1-0	1-0	0-0	0-1
Atlético Olanchano	18	6	3	9	19	25	21	0-2	0-2	3-2	1-0	3-2	1-2		1-0	3-2	3-0
Platense	18	5	5	8	18	24	20	0-2	3-2	0-0	1-0	0-2	0-0	3-1		3-0	0-0
Deportivo Savio	18	4	7	7	18	24	19	1-1	1-0	2-1	0-0	1-0	1-2	0-0	4-0		1-1
Vida	18	4	6	8	18	18	18	2-2	2-1	2-1	2-1	2-2	1-3	2-2	0-1	1-1	

12/01/2008 - 3/05/2008 • † Qualified for the play-offs

CLAUSURA PLAY-OFFS

Semi–finals			Final		
Olimpia	4	3			
Motagua *	1	1	Olimpia	1	1
Real España *	1	4	Marathón *	1	0
Marathón	3	2			

* Home team in the first leg

AGGREGATE RELEGATION TABLE

	Pl	W	D	L	F	A	Pts
Marathón	36	19	8	9	57	39	65
Olimpia	36	15	15	6	47	26	60
Motagua	36	17	8	11	51	38	59
Victoria	36	13	16	7	39	29	55
Real España	36	14	8	14	48	47	50
Hispano	36	12	11	13	43	47	47
Deportivo Savio	36	9	14	13	32	39	41
Vida	36	8	14	14	36	51	38
Platense	36	8	11	17	35	52	35
Atlético Olanchano	36	9	7	20	34	54	34

HUN – HUNGARY

NATIONAL TEAM RECORD
JULY 10TH 2006 TO JULY 12TH 2010

PL	W	D	L	F	A	%
22	10	2	10	26	31	50

FIFA/COCA-COLA WORLD RANKING

1993	1994	1995	1996	1997	1998	1999	2000	2001	2002	2003	2004	2005	2006	2007	High	
50	61	62	75	77	46	45	47	66	56	72	64	74	62	50	**36**	12/92

					2007–2008							Low	
08/07	09/07	10/07	11/07	12/07	01/08	02/08	03/08	04/08	05/08	06/08	07/08	**87**	07/96
65	55	48	52	50	50	52	51	56	57	52	52		

Despite some encouraginging signs - notably the victories over the reigning world champions Italy and European champions Greece during the course of the season - it will take a superhuman effort for the Hungarian national team to qualify for their first World Cup since 1986, with Denmark, Sweden and Portugal all standing in the way of a trip to South Africa. New coach Erwin Koeman got off to a promising start with the 3-2 victory over Greece in his first match in charge but in competitive internationals the Hungarians haven't beaten a nation of any significant status since a 1-0 victory over Sweden in the qualifiers for Euro 96 - an astonishing record for a team that was

INTERNATIONAL HONOURS
Qualified for the FIFA World Cup finals 1934 1938 1954 1958 1962 1966 1978 1982 1986   **Olympic Gold** 1952 1964 1968

once so powerful. In domestic football, Debrecen came agonisingly close to a fourth consecutive title but finished two points behind champions MTK. Andras Herczeg's team did, however, win the Hungarian Cup - and in some style - scoring 38 goals in the process. Their 7-0 thrashing of Honved was the biggest score in a final since the 1930s. There was no escape from their exile in the second division for Hungary's most successful team Ferencvaros after they failed to win promotion for the second year running. In April 2008 the club was sold to Kevin McCabe's growing stable of clubs which includes Sheffield United in England and Chengdu Blades in China.

THE FIFA BIG COUNT OF 2006

	Male	Female		Total
Number of players	477 368	49 958	Referees and Assistant Referees	3 615
Professionals	468		Admin, Coaches, Technical, Medical	7 150
Amateurs 18+	61 208		Number of clubs	2 748
Youth under 18	63 744		Number of teams	4 631
Unregistered	203 100		Clubs with women's teams	30
Total players	527 326		Players as % of population	5.28%

Hungarian Football Federation (MLSZ)
Magyar Labdarúgó Szövetség, Koerberek-Tovaros, Kanai u. 314/24.hrsz, Budapest 1112, Hungary

Tel +36 1 5779500   Fax +36 1 5779503

mlsz@mlsz.hu   www.mlsz.hu

President: KISTELEKI Istvan   General Secretary: OKROS Andras

Vice-President: TBD   Treasurer: TBD   Media Officer: DINNYES Marton

Men's Coach: KOEMAN Erwin   Women's Coach: VAGO Attila

MLSZ formed: 1901   UEFA: 1954   FIFA: 1906

Red shirts with white trimmings, White shirts, Green socks or White shirts with red trimmings, White shorts, White socks

RECENT INTERNATIONAL MATCHES PLAYED BY HUNGARY

2004	Opponents	Score		Venue	Comp	Scorers	Att	Referee
18-08	Scotland	W	3-0	Glasgow	Fr	Huszti 2 [45p 53], Marshall OG [73]	15 933	Duhamel FRA
4-09	Croatia	L	0-3	Zagreb	WCq		20 853	Riley ENG
8-09	Iceland	W	3-2	Budapest	WCq	Gera [62], Torghelle [75], Szabics [79]	5 461	Ovrebo NOR
9-10	Sweden	L	0-3	Stockholm	WCq		32 288	Dougal SCO
17-11	Malta	W	2-0	Ta'Qali	WCq	Gera [39], Kovacs.P [93]+	14 500	Asumaa FIN
30-11	Slovakia	L	0-1	Bangkok	Fr		750	Veerapool THA
2-12	Estonia	W	5-0	Bangkok	Fr	Rosa [12], Waltner [14], Kerekes [19], Rajczi [24], Pollak [63]	800	Tongkhan THA
2005								
2-02	Saudi Arabia	D	0-0	Istanbul	Fr		100	Dereli TUR
9-02	Wales	L	0-2	Cardiff	Fr		16 672	Richmond SCO
30-03	Bulgaria	D	1-1	Budapest	WCq	Rajczi [90]	11 586	Wegereef NED
31-05	France	L	1-2	Metz	Fr	Kerekes [78]	26 000	Allaerts BEL
4-06	Iceland	W	3-2	Reykjavik	WCq	Gera 2 [45p 56p], Huszti 73	4 613	Cardoso Batista POR
17-08	Argentina	L	1-2	Budapest	Fr	Torghelle [29]	27 000	Merk GER
3-09	Malta	W	4-0	Budapest	WCq	Torghelle 34, OG 55, Takacs 64, Rajczi 85	5 900	Godulyan UKR
7-09	Sweden	L	0-1	Budapest	WCq		20 161	Farina ITA
8-10	Bulgaria	L	0-2	Sofia	WCq		4 652	Delevic SCG
12-10	Croatia	D	0-0	Budapest	WCq		6 979	Larsen DEN
16-11	Greece	L	1-2	Piraeus	Fr	Kenesei [77]	12 500	Vink NED
14-12	Mexico	L	0-2	Phoenix	Fr		32 466	Valenzuela USA
18-12	Antigua and Barbuda	W	3-0	Fort Lauderdale	Fr	Vadocz [10], Feczesin 2 [32 80]	250	Rutty USA
2006								
24-05	New Zealand	W	2-0	Budapest	Fr	Huszti [48], Szabics [81]	5 000	Hrinak SVK
30-05	England	L	1-3	Manchester	Fr	Dardai [55]	56 323	Vink NED
16-08	Austria	W	2-1	Graz	Fr	Gera [11], Horvath [37]	12 000	Havrilla SVK
2-09	Norway	L	1-4	Budapest	ECq	Gera [90p]	12 283	Braamhaar NED
6-09	Bosnia-Herzegovina	W	3-1	Zenica	ECq	Huszti [36p], Gera [46], Dárdai [49]	11 800	Kapitanis CYP
7-10	Turkey	L	0-1	Budapest	ECq		6 800	Hamer LUX
11-10	Malta	L	1-2	Ta'Qali	ECq	Torghelle [19]	3 600	Ver Eecke BEL
15-11	Canada	W	1-0	Székesfehérvár	Fr	Priskin [36]	6 000	Weiner GER
2007								
6-02	Cyprus	L	1-2	Limassol	Fr	Priskin [88]	500	Gerasimou CYP
7-02	Latvia	W	2-0	Limassol	Fr	Priskin 2 [31 53]	400	Kailisz CYP
28-03	Moldova	W	2-0	Budapest	ECq	Priskin [9], Gera [63]	6 150	Ingvarsson SWE
2-06	Greece	L	0-2	Irákleio	ECq		17 244	Larsen DEN
6-06	Norway	L	0-4	Oslo	ECq		19 198	Iturralde Gonzalez ESP
22-08	Italy	W	3-1	Budapest	Fr	Juhasz [61], Gera [66p], Feczesin [77]	30 000	Mejuto Gonzalez ESP
8-09	Bosnia-Herzegovina	W	1-0	Székesfehérvár	ECq	Gera [39p]	10 773	Trefoloni ITA
12-09	Turkey	L	0-3	Istanbul	ECq		28 020	Dougal SCO
13-10	Malta	W	2-0	Budapest	ECq	Feczesin [34], Tőzsér [78]	7 633	Nalbandyan ARM
17-10	Poland	W	1-0	Lodz	Fr	Hajnal [80p]	6 000	Circhetta SUI
17-11	Moldova	L	0-3	Chisinau	ECq		6 483	Královec CZE
21-11	Greece	L	1-2	Budapest	ECq	Buzsáky [7]	32 300	Styles ENG
2008								
6-02	Slovakia	D	1-1	Limassol	Fr	Gera [54]	100	Trattu CYP
26-03	Slovenia	L	0-1	Zalaegerszeg	Fr		7 000	Messner AUT
24-05	Greece	W	3-2	Budapest	Fr	Dzsudzsak [46], Juhasz [59], Vadocz [63]	7 000	Blom NED
31-05	Croatia	D	1-1	Budapest	Fr	Kovac.N OG [45]	10 000	Ledentu FRA

Fr = Friendly match • EC = UEFA EURO 2008 • WC = FIFA World Cup • q = qualifier

HUNGARY NATIONAL TEAM RECORDS AND RECORD SEQUENCES

Records			Sequence records				
Victory	13-1	FRA 1927	Wins	11	1951-1952	Clean sheets	4	Five times
Defeat	0-7	ENG 1908, GER 1941	Defeats	6	1978	Goals scored	74	1949-1957
Player Caps	101	József Bozsik	Undefeated	30	1950-1954	Without goal	4	1993
Player Goals	84	Ferenc Puskás	Without win	12	1994	Goals against	19	Three times

MAJOR CITIES/TOWNS

Population '000

1	Budapest	2 571
2	Debrecen	203
3	Miskolc	177
4	Szeged	159
5	Pécs	155
6	Györ	128
7	Nyíregyháza	116
8	Kecskemét	105
9	Székesfehérvár	103
10	Szombathely	79
11	Szolnok	75
12	Tatabánya	71
13	Kaposvár	66
14	Békéscsaba	65
15	Zalaegerszeg	60
16	Veszprém	59
17	Eger	55
18	Sopron	55
19	Dunaújváros	53
20	Hódmezővásárhely	47
21	Salgótarján	43
22	Cegléd	40
23	Ozd	38
24	Pápa	32

REPUBLIC OF HUNGARY; MAGYAR KOZTARSASAG

Capital Budapest	Language Hungarian		Unification 1001
Population 9 981 334	Area 93 030 km²	Density 107 per km²	% in cities 65%
GDP per cap $13 900	Dailling code +36	Internet .hu	GMT +/- +1

MEDALS TABLE

		Overall			League			Cup		Europe			City	Stadium	Cap'ty	DoF
		G	S	B	G	S	B	G	S	B	G	S	B				
1	Ferencvárosi TC	49	45	22	28	34	20	20	9	1	2	2	Budapest	Ullöi út	18 100	1899
2	MTK Hungária FC	35	23	16	23	20	15	12	2		1	1	Budapest	Hidegkuti Nandor	7 702	1888
3	Ujpest FC	28	27	20	20	20	18	8	6		1	2	Budapest	Szusza Ferenc	13 501	1885
4	Budapest-Honvéd FC	19	22	5	13	12	5	6	10				Budapest	Bozsik József	13 500	1909
5	Vasas SC	10	5	14	6	2	13	4	3		1		Budapest	Illovsky Rudolf	18 000	1911
6	Györi ETO FC	7	4	5	3	2	4	4	2		1		Györ	Stadion ETO	22 000	1904
7	Debreceni VSC	6	3	3	3	1	3	3	2				Debrecen	Oláh Gábor út	10 200	1902
8	Csepel SC	4	2		4	2							Budapest	Béke téri	10 000	1912
9	Diósgyöri VTK	2	3	1			1	2	3				Miskolc	DVTK	17 000	1910
10	Budapest TC	2	2	3	2	1	3		1				Budapest	Fehér út		1885
11	Dunakanyar-Vac FC	1	5		1	2			3				Vác	Városi	12 000	1899
12	Videoton FC Fehérvár	1	4	3		1	3	1	2		1		Székesfehérvár	Sóstói	19 000	1941
13	Pécsi MFC	1	3	1		1	1	1	2				Pécs	PMFC	7 160	1973
14	Dunaferr	1	1		1	1							Dunaújváros	Dunaferr	11 600	1951
	Nagyváradi AC	1	1		1	1							Oradea - ROU	Varosi		1911

RECENT LEAGUE AND CUP RECORD

	Championship						Cup		
Year	Champions	Pts	Runners-up	Pts	Third	Pts	Winners	Score	Runners-up
1995	Ferencvárosi TC	59	Ujpesti TE	52	Debreceni VSC	49	Ferencvárosi TC	2-0 3-4	Vac FC
1996	Ferencvárosi TC	66	BVSC	61	Ujpesti TE	48	Kispest-Honvéd	0-1 2-0	BVSC
1997	MTK-Hungária	85	Ujpesti TE	76	Ferencvárosi TC	74	MTK-Hungária	6-0 2-0	BVSC
1998	Ujpesti TE	73	Ferencvárosi TC	67	Vasas SC	64	MTK-Hungária	1-0	Ujpesti TE
1999	MTK-Hungária	83	Ferencvárosi TC	64	Ujpesti TE	63	Debreceni VSC	2-0	LFC Tatabánya
2000	Dunaferr FC	79	MTK-Hungária	63	Vasas SC	61	MTK-Hungária	3-1	Vasas SC
2001	Ferencvárosi TC	48	Dunaferr FC	46	Vasas SC	40	Debreceni VSC	5-2	Videoton Fehérvar
2002	Zalaegerszegi TE	71	Ferencvárosi TC	69	MTK-Hungária	59	Ujpesti TE	2-1	Haladás
2003	MTK-Hungária	66	Ferencvárosi TC	64	Debreceni VSC	53	Ferencvárosi TC	2-1	Debreceni VSC
2004	Ferencvárosi TC	57	Ujpesti TE	56	Debreceni VSC	56	Ferencvárosi TC	3-1	Honvéd FC
2005	Debreceni VSC	62	Ferencvárosi TC	56	MTK-Hungária	56	Mátav FC Sopron	5-1	Ferencvárosi TC
2006	Debreceni VSC	68	Ujpesti TE	65	Fehérvár FC	64	Fehérvár	2-2 6-5p	Vasas SC
2007	Debreceni VSC	69	MTK-Hungária	61	Zalaegerszegi TE	55	Honvéd FC	2-2 3-1p	Debreceni VSC
2008	MTK-Hungária	66	Debreceni VSC	64	Györi ETO	58	Debreceni VSC	7-0 2-1	Honvéd FC

HUNGARY 2007-08

SOPRONI LIGA NB I

	Pl	W	D	L	F	A	Pts	MTK	Debrecen	Gyor	Ujpest	Fehérvár	Kaposvár	ZTE	Honvéd	Vasas	Nyíregyházi	Paksi	REAC	Diósgyör	Siófok	Tatabánya	Sopron
MTK-Hungária †	30	20	6	4	67	23	66		3-2	2-2	0-0	2-0	3-2	4-1	1-2	2-0	0-2	1-1	3-0	3-0	1-1	5-1	3-0
Debreceni VSC ‡	30	19	7	4	67	29	64	0-2		2-0	3-1	3-0	4-0	3-2	1-0	4-1	2-0	1-1	4-0	2-0	3-0	4-1	3-0
Györi ETO ‡	30	16	10	4	64	35	58	1-0	3-0		4-2	4-1	1-1	3-2	2-2	5-0	2-1	3-3	2-1	4-1	5-1	2-1	3-0
Ujpesti TE	30	16	7	7	58	40	55	1-3	1-1	1-3		1-0	0-2	1-1	1-0	1-0	1-1	3-1	4-4	3-0	2-2	3-0	3-0
FC Fehérvár	30	17	3	10	48	32	54	1-0	0-0	1-0	1-2		1-1	2-0	0-0	2-1	5-2	3-0	2-1	1-0	3-1	7-0	3-0
Kaposvári Rákóczi	30	14	9	7	48	38	51	0-3	2-2	1-1	0-3	1-0		0-2	1-0	1-1	1-0	2-1	3-0	4-3	1-1	4-2	3-0
Zalaegerszegi TE	30	13	7	10	55	39	46	0-1	1-2	0-0	4-1	1-3	2-1		2-1	0-0	3-3	3-1	3-3	2-0	4-1	4-1	3-0
Honvéd ‡	30	12	7	11	45	36	43	0-2	3-1	2-2	1-4	5-1	0-1	2-1		0-0	0-1	2-1	1-1	1-1	0-1	4-1	3-0
Vasas SC	30	12	5	13	41	45	41	0-2	1-1	1-0	1-2	0-0	2-1	3-0			2-1	1-2	2-0	2-1	2-1	5-0	3-0
Nyíregyházi	30	11	7	12	34	37	40	0-3	0-3	1-1	0-1	1-2	1-2	1-0	0-2	3-1		3-2	2-1	0-0	0-0	3-1	3-0
Paksi SE	30	9	10	11	51	51	37	1-4	2-2	2-1	2-0	2-1	1-1	0-3	0-3	3-0	3-0		0-2	1-1	2-2	6-0	3-0
Rákospalotai EAC	30	7	9	14	42	60	30	0-3	0-4	2-2	1-0	2-1	1-1	1-2	0-3	2-2	2-0	2-1			4-2	5-5	3-2
Diósgyöri VTK	30	5	13	12	43	63	28	1-1	1-1	0-1	2-4	1-0	0-2	1-1	1-2	0-1	1-3	1-1	1-0			4-0	3-0
Bodajk FC Siófok	30	6	9	15	33	46	27	2-2	1-2	1-3	1-4	2-0	2-1	1-1	2-2	0-0	4-5	3-3	0-1	0-3			2-2	3-0
Tatabánya FC	30	2	4	24	34	93	10	1-3	1-2	1-3	2-3	1-3	2-6	0-2	4-3	0-1	0-2	2-4	1-1	2-2	2-2		3-0
FC Sopron §11	30	2	5	23	10	73	0	0-3	0-3	0-3	0-3	0-3	0-3	0-3	0-3	0-3	0-3	0-3	0-3	0-3	0-3	0-3	

20/07/2007 - 2/06/2008 • † Qualified for the UEFA Champions League • ‡ Qualified for the UEFA Cup • § = Points deducted

HUNGARY 2007-08 NB II NYUGATI (WEST)

	Pl	W	D	L	F	A	Pts
Szombathelyi Haladás	30	21	8	1	68	19	71
Felcsút SE	30	20	6	4	61	25	66
Gyirmót SE	30	17	7	6	66	38	58
Pápa TFC	30	15	11	4	40	26	56
Integrál-DAC Györ	30	15	4	11	56	43	49
Pécsi MFC	30	14	6	10	46	34	48
Kozármisleny SE	30	8	16	6	31	29	40
Budaörsi SC	30	9	12	9	47	44	39
Dunaújvárosi Kohász	30	11	5	14	39	47	38
Barcsi FC	30	10	7	13	38	43	37
Kaposvölgye-Nagyberki	30	8	10	12	45	44	34
FC Ajka	30	8	9	13	52	52	33
ESMTK	30	8	5	17	36	60	29
Komlói Bányász SK	30	6	8	16	28	64	26
Soroksári SC	30	3	8	19	22	50	17
Mosonmagyaróvári TE§2	30	3	6	21	18	75	13

11/08/2007 - 31/05/2008 • § = Points deducted

HUNGARY 2007-08 NB II KELETI (EAST)

	Pl	W	D	L	F	A	Pts
Kecskeméti TE	30	24	3	3	74	23	75
Szolnoki MAV	30	20	3	7	52	29	63
Ferencvárosi TC	30	18	8	4	63	35	62
Makói FC	30	13	11	6	52	34	50
Vác Ujbuda LTC	30	13	6	11	57	45	45
Vecsési FC	30	12	9	9	43	42	45
Kazincbarcika SC	30	11	11	8	43	41	44
Bocsi KSC	30	11	9	10	47	42	42
Jászberény	30	9	9	12	28	36	36
Ceglédi VSE	30	10	5	15	33	53	35
Baktalóránrgáza VSE	30	8	10	12	31	43	34
Tököl KSK	30	9	5	16	28	52	32
Békéscsabai Elore FC	30	8	5	17	43	49	29
Orosháza FC	30	7	8	15	41	56	29
Tuzsér SE	30	6	5	19	29	59	23
Mezökövesd-Zsóry SE	30	4	7	19	26	51	19

11/08/2007 - 1/06/2008

MAGYAR KUPA 2007-08

Round of 16			Quarter-finals			Semi-finals			Final		
Debreceni VSC	5	6									
Kaposvölgye-N'berki *	2	2	Debreceni VSC	1	3						
Györi ETO *	1	2	FC Fehérvár *	2	1						
FC Fehérvár	1	3				Debreceni VSC	4	6			
Vasas SC	3	3				Integrál-DAC Györ *	1	0			
Putnok VSE *	1	1	Vasas SC	1	1						
Szekszeardi UFC *	0	0	Integrál-DAC Györ *	0	2						
Integrál-DAC Györ	4	7							Debreceni VSC ‡	7	2
Kaposvári Rákóczi	2	2							Honvéd *	0	1
Ferencvárosi TC *	2	1	Kaposvári Rákóczi	4	3						
Nyíregyház	0	1	Gyirmót SE *	2	0						
Gyirmót SE *	2	0				Kaposvári Rákóczi	0	1			
Kazincbarcika SC *	3	1				Honvéd *	4	2			
Diósgyöri VTK	1	1	Kazincbarcika SC *	2	2						
FC Sopron	1	0	Honvéd	2	4						
Honvéd *	2	3									

CUP FINAL
1st leg. 28-05-2008
2nd leg. 4-06-2008

* Home team in the first leg • ‡ Qualified for the UEFA Cup

IDN – INDONESIA

INDONESIA NATIONAL TEAM RECORD
JULY 10TH 2006 TO JULY 12TH 2010

PL	W	D	L	F	A	%
19	7	5	7	21	26	50

FIFA/COCA-COLA WORLD RANKING

1993	1994	1995	1996	1997	1998	1999	2000	2001	2002	2003	2004	2005	2006	2007	High	
106	134	130	119	91	87	90	97	87	110	91	91	109	153	133	**76**	09/98

2007–2008												Low	
08/07	09/07	10/07	11/07	12/07	01/08	02/08	03/08	04/08	05/08	06/08	07/08	**153**	12/06
129	126	125	134	133	132	128	130	132	131	129	132		

After the relatively successful showing when they co-hosted the AFC Asian Cup in the summer of 2007, Indonesia's footballing fortunes slumped in the intervening months, costing coach Ivan Kolev his job. The Bulgarian saw his side handed a humiliating 11-1 aggregate defeat by Syria in the 2010 FIFA World Cup qualifiers and elimination at the first hurdle. He was replaced by local coach Benny Dollo as Indonesia started to prepare for their latest assault on the Asean Football Championship title, which the nation is due to co-host at the end of 2008. Indonesia's showing at the regional South East Asian Games did little to raise hopes after the nation's under-23 squad was

INTERNATIONAL HONOURS
AFC Youth Championship 1961

eliminated from the competition at the group phase. Sriwijaya Palembang completed the league and cup double, defeating PSMS Medan in the Liga Indonesia play-off before downing Persipura in the final of the cup. For the 2008 season, the structure of the domestic league has been completely overhauled under pressure from the Asian Football Confederation with the top flight streamlined to feature 18 teams in a straightforward league format. Previously, two divisions of anywhere up to 20 teams battled for four places each in the championship playoffs, where the successful teams met in a centralised tournament to determine the league champions.

THE FIFA BIG COUNT OF 2006

	Male	Female		Total
Number of players	7 094 260	0	Referees and Assistant Referees	669
Professionals	800		Admin, Coaches, Technical, Medical	400
Amateurs 18+	2 560		Number of clubs	73
Youth under 18	62 600		Number of teams	73
Unregistered	6 982 300		Clubs with women's teams	10
Total players	7 094 260		Players as % of population	2.89%

Football Association of Indonesia (PSSI)

Gelora Bung Karno, Pintu X-XI, Senayan, PO Box 2305, Jakarta 10023, Indonesia
Tel +62 21 5704762   Fax +62 21 5734386
pssi@pssi-football.com   www.pssi-football.com
President: TBD   General Secretary: BESOES Nugraha
Vice-President: NIRWAN Bakire   Treasurer: YANDHU Hamka   Media Officer: MAFIRON
Men's Coach: DOLO Benny   Women's Coach: none
PSSI formed: 1930   AFC: 1954   FIFA: 1952
Red shirts with white trimmings, White shirts, Red socks

RECENT INTERNATIONAL MATCHES PLAYED BY INDONESIA

2004	Opponents	Score		Venue	Comp	Scorers	Att	Referee
12-02	Jordan	L	1-2	Amman	Fr	Bambang Pamungkas [15]		
18-02	Saudi Arabia	L	0-3	Riyadh	WCq		1 000	Al Ghafary JOR
17-03	Malaysia	D	0-0	Johor Bahru	Fr		8 000	Kim Heng MAS
31-03	Turkmenistan	L	1-3	Ashgabat	WCq	Budi Sunarsono [30]	5 000	Sahib Shakir IRQ
3-06	India	D	1-1	Jakarta	Fr	Ponyaro [33]		
9-06	Sri Lanka	W	1-0	Jakarta	WCq	Elie Aiboy [30]	30 000	Nesar BAN
18-07	Qatar	W	2-1	Beijing	ACr1	Budi Sunarsono [26], Ponaryo [48]	5 000	Moradi IRN
21-07	China PR	L	0-5	Beijing	ACr1			Najm LIB
25-07	Bahrain	L	1-3	Jinan	ACr1	Elie Aiboy [75]	20 000	Codjia BEN
4-09	Singapore	L	0-2	Singapore	Fr			
8-09	Sri Lanka	D	2-2	Colombo	WCq	Jaya [8], Sofyan [51]	4 000	Marshoud JOR
12-10	Saudi Arabia	L	1-3	Jakarta	WCq	Jaya [50]	30 000	Mohd Salleh MAS
17-11	Turkmenistan	W	3-1	Jakarta	WCq	Jaya 3 [20 47 59]	15 000	Shaban KUW
7-12	Laos	W	6-0	Ho Chi Minh City	TCr1	Boas [26], Jaya 2 [29 34], OG [53], Aiboy [60], Kurniawan [87]		Rungklay THA
9-12	Singapore	D	0-0	Ho Chi Minh City	TCr1		4 000	Kwong Jong Chul KOR
11-12	Vietnam	W	3-0	Hanoi	TCr1	Lessy [18], Boas [21], Jaya [45]	40 000	Ebrahim BHR
13-12	Cambodia	W	8-0	Hanoi	TCr1	Jaya 3 [9 48 57], Aiboy 2 [30 55], Kurniawan 2 [72 74], Ortisan [82]	17 000	Sun Baojie CHN
28-12	Malaysia	L	1-2	Jakarta	TCsf	Kurniawan [7]	100 000	Irmatov UZB
2005								
3-01	Malaysia	W	4-1	Kuala Lumpur	TCsf	Kurniawan [59], Yulianto [74], Jaya [77], Boas [84]	70 000	Kunsuta THA
8-01	Singapore	L	1-3	Jakarta	TCf	Mahyadi [90+3]	120 000	Kwong Jong Chul KOR
16-01	Singapore	L	1-2	Singapore	TCf	Elie Aiboy [76]	55 000	Al Ghamdi KSA
29-03	Australia	L	0-3	Perth	Fr		14 000	Yamanishi JPN
2006								
23-08	Malaysia	D	1-1	Kuala Lumpur	Fr	Bambang Pamungkas [16]	20 000	Zhang Lei CHN
25-08	Myanmar	D	0-0	Kuala Lumpur	Fr			Shahrul MAS
27-08	Thailand	W	1-0	Kuala Lumpur	Fr	Baya Sutha [26]	8 000	Lee Jong Kuk KOR
29-08	Myanmar	L	1-2	Kuala Lumpur	Fr	Zaenal Arif [87]	30 000	Shahrul MAS
2007								
13-01	Laos	W	3-1	Singapore	TCr1	Atep 2 [51 75], Saktiawan Sinaga [67]		
15-01	Vietnam	D	1-1	Singapore	TCr1	Saktiawan Sinaga [90]	4 500	Shahbuddin
17-01	Singapore	D	2-2	Singapore	TCr1	Ilham Jaya Kesuma [27], Zaenal Arif [56]	13 819	Sananwai THA
1-06	Hong Kong	W	3-0	Jakarta	Fr	Bambang Pamungkas [16], OG [62], Zaenal Arif [78p]		
3-06	Singapore	L	0-1	Jakarta	Fr			
21-06	Jamaica	W	2-1	Jakarta	Fr	Bambang Pamungkas 2 [58 90]		
24-06	Oman	L	0-1	Jakarta	Fr			
10-07	Bahrain	W	2-1	Jakarta	ACr1	Budi Sunarsono [14], Bambang Pamungkas [64]	60 000	Nishimura JPN
14-07	Saudi Arabia	L	1-2	Jakarta	ACr1	Elie Aiboy [17]	87 000	Al Badwawi UAE
18-07	Korea Republic	L	0-1	Jakarta	ACr1		87 000	Shield AUS
9-11	Syria	L	1-4	Jakarta	WCq	Budi Sunarsoni [39]	35 000	Torky IRN
18-11	Syria	L	0-7	Damascus	WCq		5 000	Sun Baojie CHN
2008								
25-04	Yemen	W	1-0	Bandung	Fr	Bambang Pamungkas [30]		
6-06	Malaysia	D	1-1	Surabaya	Fr	Bambang Pamungkas [25p]		
11-06	Vietnam	W	1-0	Surabaya	Fr	Bambang Pamungkas [12p]		

Fr = Friendly match • TC = ASEAN Tiger Cup/ASEAN Football Federation Championship • AC = AFC Asian Cup • WC = FIFA World Cup
q = qualifier • r1 = first round group • sf = semi-final • f = final

INDONESIA NATIONAL TEAM RECORDS AND RECORD SEQUENCES

Records			Sequence records					
Victory	12-0	PHI 1972	Wins	10	1968-1969	Clean sheets	4	1987, 2004
Defeat	0-9	DEN 1974	Defeats	7	1996	Goals scored	24	1967-1969
Player Caps	60	Kurniawan Dwi Yulianto	Undefeated	10	Three times	Without goal	5	Three times
Player Goals	33	Kurniawan Dwi Yulianto	Without win	18	1985-1986	Goals against	19	1985-1986

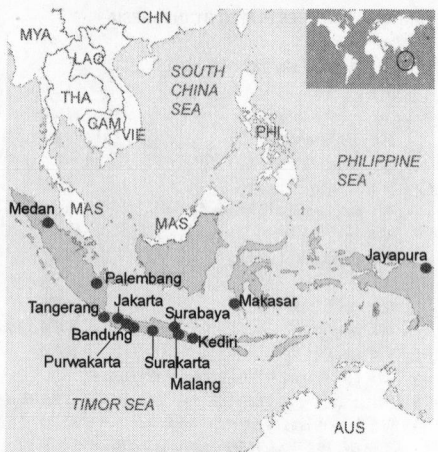

REPUBLIC OF INDONESIA; REPUBLIK INDONESIA

Capital	Jakarta	Language	Bahasa Indonesia			Independence	1945	
Population	245 452 739	Area	1 919 440 km²	Density	124 per km²	% in cities	35%	
GDP per cap	$3200	Dailling code	+62	Internet	.id	GMT +/-	+7	

MEDALS TABLE

		Overall			Lge		Cup		Asia			City	Stadium	Cap'ty	DoF
		G	S	B	G	S	G	S	G	S	B				
1	Persija Jakarta	11	6		11	5	1					Jakarta	Lebak Bulus	12 000	1928
2	Persis Solo	8	1		8	1						Solo	Manahan	15 000	1923
3	Persebaya Surabaya	7	11		7	11						Surabaya	Gelora	30 000	1927
4	Tiga Berlian	7	1	1	4	1	3				1	Palembang			
5	Persib Bandung	6	8		6	8						Bandung	Siliwangi	20 000	1933
	PSM Makasar	6	8		6	8						Makassar	Mattoangin	30 000	1915
7	PSMS Medan	6	7		6	7						Medan	Teladan	15 000	1930
8	Pelita Jaya	3	5		3	2	3					Purwakarta	Punawarman	10 000	1980
9	Mitra Kukar	3	2		3	1	1					Tenggarong	Rondong Demang	20 000	2003
10	Arema Malang	3	1		1		2	1				Malang	Gajayana	20 000	1982
11	Persipura Jayapura	2	3		2	1	2					Jayapura	Mandala	15 000	1950
12	Arseto	2	1		2	1	1					Solo			
	PSIS Semarang	2	1		2	1						Semarang	Jatidiri	21 000	1932
14	Persik Kediri	2			2							Kediri	Brawijaya	10 000	1950
	Sriwijaya Palembang	2			1		1					Palembang	Jakabaring	40 000	2004
16	PSIM Yogyakarta	1	5		1	5						Yogyakarta	Mandala Krida	25 000	
17	Petrokimia / Gresik United	1	1		1	1						Gresik	Tri Dharma	25 000	1986

RECENT LEAGUE RECORD

	Championship				Cup		
Year	Champions	Score	Runners-up		Champions	Score	Runners-up
1995	Persib	1-0	Petrokimia Putra		No Cup competition		
1996	Bandung Raya	2-0	PSM		No Cup competition		
1997	Persebaya	3-1	Bandung Raya		No Cup competition		
1998	Season not finished due to political unrest				No Cup competition		
1999	PSIS	1-0	Persebaya		No Cup competition		
2000	PSM	3-2	Pupuk Kaltim		No Cup competition		
2001	Persija	3-2	PSM		No Cup competition		
2002	Petrokimia Putra	2-1	Persita		No Cup competition		
2003	Persik	†	PSM		No Cup competition		
2004	Persebaya	†	PSM		No Cup competition		
2005	Persipura	3-2	Persija		Arema Malang	4-3	Persija
2006	Persik	1-0	PSIS Semarang		Arema Malang	2-0	Persipura
2007	Sriwijaya Palemban	3-1	PSMS Medan		Sriwijaya Palemban	1-1 3-0p	Persipura

† Championship played on a league system

INDONESIA 2007
LIGA INDONESIA DIVISI UTAMA WILAYA BARAT (WEST)

	Pl	W	D	L	F	A	Pts
Sriwijaya Palembang †	34	20	6	8	59	31	66
Persija Jakarta †	34	18	7	9	55	40	61
PSMS Medan †	34	17	7	10	44	28	58
Persik Kediri †	34	17	5	12	61	51	56
Persib Bandung	34	15	9	10	45	29	54
Persela Lamongan	34	15	9	10	41	34	54
Persitara Jakarta Utara	34	15	8	11	39	33	53
Pelita Jaya Purwakarta	34	15	7	12	43	30	52
Persita Tangerang	34	13	11	10	33	36	50
PSIS Semarang	34	13	10	11	44	34	49
Persikabo Bogor	34	12	12	10	46	38	48
PSS Sleman	34	12	10	12	42	43	46
Persema Malang	34	12	9	13	35	46	45
PSDS Lubuk Pakam	34	12	8	14	39	40	44
Persikota Tangerang	34	6	12	16	26	41	30
Semen Padang	34	7	6	21	21	44	27
Persiraja Banda Aceh	34	6	8	20	18	59	26
PSSB Bireuen	34	6	6	22	26	60	24

10/02/2007 - 30/12/2007 • † Qualified for the play-offs
The top nine clubs qualify for the new 2008 Liga Super

INDONESIA 2007
LIGA INDONESIA DIVISI UTAMA WILAYA TIMUR (EAST)

	Pl	W	D	L	F	A	Pts
Persipura Jayapura †	34	19	7	8	54	24	64
Persiwa Wamena †	34	18	5	11	56	30	59
Delta Putra Sidoarjo †	34	17	8	9	47	30	59
Arema Malang †	34	15	12	7	45	28	57
PSM Makassar	34	17	6	11	43	33	57
Persiter Ternate	34	17	6	11	33	28	57
Persiba Balikpapan	34	16	7	11	48	35	55
Persmin Minahasa	34	14	11	9	43	34	53
Persijap Jepara	34	15	7	12	38	36	52
Persibom Kotamobagu	34	13	7	14	41	47	46
Persis Solo	34	12	7	15	43	43	43
Persma Manado	34	10	11	13	32	50	41
PKT Bontang	34	10	9	15	33	42	39
Persebaya Surabaya	34	11	6	17	36	50	39
PSIM Yogyakarta	34	8	8	18	30	45	32
Persekabpas Pasuran	34	8	8	18	34	52	32
Perseman Manokwari	34	8	8	18	28	55	32
Persegi Bali	34	6	11	17	24	46	29

10/02/2007 - 30/12/2007 • † Qualified for the play-offs
The top nine clubs qualify for the new 2008 Liga Super

SUPERLIGA BABAK 8 BESAR

West	Pl	W	D	L	F	A	Pts	PM	AM	PW
Sriwijaya †	3	1	2	0	4	2	5	2-2	2-0	0-0
PSMS Medan †	3	1	1	1	4	4	4		0-1	2-1
Arema Malang	3	1	1	1	3	4	4	2-2		
Persiwa Wamena	3	0	2	1	3	4	2			

East	Pl	W	D	L	F	A	Pts	PJ	PK	DP
Persipura	3	2	1	0	8	1	7	0-0	4-1	4-0
Persija Jakarta	3	1	2	0	3	2	5		2-2	1-0
Persik Kediri	3	1	1	1	4	6	4			1-0
Delta Putra	3	0	0	3	0	6	0			

16/01/2008 - 26/01/2008 • † Qualified for the semi-finals

PLAY-OFFS

Semi-finals

Sriwijaya	1
Persija Jakarta	0

Finals

Sriwijaya	3
PSMS Medan	1

Persipura Jayapura	0	4p
PSMS Medan	0	5p

LIGA INDONESIA FINAL

Jalak Haruput, Soreang, Kabupaten Bandung
10-02-2008, Att: BCD, Ref: Purwanto

Sriwijaya Palembang   3   Richard [15], Gumbs [107], Rahan [114]
PSMS Medan   1   Lomel [69]

Sriwijaya - Ferry Rotinsulu - Charis Yulianto, Renato Elias, Slamet Riyadi, Isnan Ali - Toni Sucipto, Zah Rahan, Wijay, Benben Berlian - Anoure Obiora Richard, Keith Kayamba Gumbs. Tr: Rahmad Darmawan
PSMS - Markus Horison - Murphy Kumonple, Usep Munandar, Rommy Dias Putra (Andreas Formento 31) - Supardi, Masperi Kasim, Mbom Mbom Julien, Legimin Raharjo, Gustavo Chena - Saktiawan Sinaga, James Koko Lomel. Tr: Freddy Mulli

Top scorers: Cristian Gonzalez, Persik 32; Beto, Persipura 20; Julio Lopez, PSIS 20; Sunday Seah, Persiwa 19; James Lomell, PSMS 18

INDONESIA 2007
LIGA INDONESIA DIVISI SATU (2) CHAMPIONSHIP PLAY-OFFS

Semi-finals

Persibo Bojonegoro	2
PSP Padang	1

Mitra Kukar	1	2p
Persikad Depok	1	4p

Finals

Persibo Bojonegoro	1
Persikad Depok	0

For the 2008 season the top tier of football in Indonesia will be the Liga Super for which the top nine clubs in the two Divisi Utama groups from 2007 will qualify. The second tier of Indonesian club football in 2008 will be called the Divisi Utama and the teams placed from 10 to 18 in both top tier groups in 2007, along with the top four in each of the four groups in the 2007 second tier, will qualify for the new Divisi Utama. The new third tier of Indonesian football will be the Divisi Satu.

PIALA INDONESIA 2007

Second Round

Sriwijaya Palembang	0	4
PSSB Bireuen *	0	0
Persiba Balikpapan *	2	0
Perseman Manokwari	1	1
Gresik United	0	3
Persibo Bojonegoro *	1	1
Semen Padang	1	0
PSMS Medan *	1	2
Persita Tangerang *	2	0
PSDS Deli Serdang	0	1
Persipasi Bekasi	0	0
Persis Solo *	0	1
Persijap Jepara *	0	0 4p
Persib Bandung	0	0 3p
PSS Sleman *	0	0
Pelita Jaya Purwakarta	3	1
Persija Jakarta *	1	1
PSIS Semarang	0	1
Persiwa Wamena	1	2
PSM Makassar *	3	1
PKT Bontang *	0	2
Persipon Pontianak	0	1
Persebaya Surabaya *	1	0
Delta Putra Sidoarjo	1	0
Persekabpas Pasuran *	1	0
Arema Malang	0	0
PSBL Langsa	1	1
PSAP Sigli *	3	0
Persemalra Tual	1	2
Mitra Kukar *	3	0
Persidafon Dafonsoro *	0	0
Persipura Jayapura	0	2

Round of 16

Sriwijaya Palembang	2	
Perseman Manokwari *	1	
Gresik United	0	0
PSMS Medan *	4	1
Persita Tangerang	0	2
Persis Solo *	0	1
Persijap Jepara *	1	1
Pelita Jaya Purwakarta	0	3
Persija Jakarta *	2	0
PSM Makassar	0	1
PKT Bontang *	1	1
Delta Putra Sidoarjo	3	3
Persekabpas Pasuran	2	3
PSAP Sigli *	2	2
Persemalra Tual	0	1
Persipura Jayapura *	4	1

Quarter-finals

Sriwijaya Palembang *	0	4
PSMS Medan *	2	0
Persita Tangerang *	1	0
Pelita Jaya Purwakarta	0	2
Persija Jakarta	1	2
Delta Putra Sidoarjo *	1	0
Persekabpas Pasuran *	2	0
Persipura Jayapura	2	3

Semi-finals

Sriwijaya Palembang	0 6p
Pelita Jaya Purwakarta	0 5p
Persija Jakarta	2
Persipura Jayapura	3

Final

Sriwijaya Palembang	1 3p
Persipura Jayapura	1 0p

PIALA INDONESIA FINAL

Utama Gelora Bung Karno, Senayan
13-01-2008, Ref: Napitupulu
Scorers - Keith Gumbs 73 for Sriwijaya;
Ernest Jeremiah 6 for Persipura
Sriwijaya - Ferry Rotinsulu - Christian Warobay,
Renato Eliyas, Amrizal, Isnan Ali (Dian
Fachrudin 98) - Slamet Riyadi, Zah Rahan,
Anoure Obiora Richard, Benben Berlian (Toni
Sucipto 114), Wijay - Keith Kayamba Gumbs.
Tr: Rahmad Darmawan
Persipura - Jendry Pitoy - Ricardo Salampessy,
Jack Komboy, Bio Paulin Pierre - Victor Igbonefo,
Eduard Ivakdalam, Heru Nerly (David Da Rocca
59), Paulo Rumere, Stevi Bonsapia (Imanuel
Wanggai 38) (Murzal Usman 82) - Alberto
Goncalves, Ernest Jeremiah. Tr: Akram Shah

* Home team in the first leg ● Third place play-off: Persija Jakarta 2-1 Pelita Jaya Purwakarta

IND – INDIA

NATIONAL TEAM RECORD
JULY 10TH 2006 TO JULY 12TH 2010

PL	W	D	L	F	A	%
23	12	4	7	38	32	60.9

FIFA/COCA-COLA WORLD RANKING

1993	1994	1995	1996	1997	1998	1999	2000	2001	2002	2003	2004	2005	2006	2007	High	
100	109	121	120	112	110	106	122	121	127	127	132	127	157	143	**94**	02/96

	2007–2008											Low	
08/07	09/07	10/07	11/07	12/07	01/08	02/08	03/08	04/08	05/08	06/08	07/08	**165**	05/07
151	145	145	145	143	144	145	148	154	151	153	153		

India's status as South Asia's leading nation came under question at the South Asian Football Federation Championship in 2008 when the Bob Houghton-coached team finished second-best behind surprise winners Maldives. Injured pride was restored, however, when they performed well at the prestigious AFC Challenge Cup in August 2008, a tournament for the second tier nations in Asian football. India hosted the tournament in the city of Hyderabad and after beating Afghanistan, Turkmenistan and Myanmar reached a final against Tajikistan that had to be postponed due to severe storms in the city. On the domestic scene, the new I-League was inaugurated to replace the

INTERNATIONAL HONOURS
Asian Games 1951 1962 South Asian Federation Games 1985 1987 1995 South Asian Football Federation Cup 1995

National Football League with 10 teams competing for the title. Despite the changes, Dempo Sports Club continued to dominate, winning the championship just as they had done in the final season of the NFL, finishing ahead of Churchill Brothers on goal difference. The I-League has been extended to 12 teams for the 2009 season and the prize on offer to the winners will be a place in the AFC Champions League as the AFC tries to encourage the development of club football in India. In the 2008 AFC Cup Dempo progressed to the knockout phase after finishing as runners-up in their group behind Muharraq of Bahrain.

THE FIFA BIG COUNT OF 2006

	Male	Female		Total
Number of players	19 020 900	1 567 000	Referees and Assistant Referees	17 640
Professionals	400		Admin, Coaches, Technical, Medical	21 000
Amateurs 18+	71 000		Number of clubs	6 500
Youth under 18	313 500		Number of teams	12 000
Unregistered	2 212 000		Clubs with women's teams	40
Total players	20 587 900		Players as % of population	1.88%

All India Football Federation (AIFF)
Football House, Sector 19, Phase 1 Dwarka, New Dehli 110075, India
Tel +91 11 28041430   Fax +91 11 28041434
gsaiff@gmail.com   www.the-aiff.com
President: DASMUNSI Priya Ranjan   General Secretary: COLACO Alberto
Vice-President: PATEL Praful   Treasurer: SALGAOCAR Shivanand   Media Officer: BMR Mehta
Men's Coach: HOUGHTON Bob   Women's Coach: SINGH Harjinder
AIFF formed: 1937   AFC: 1954   FIFA: 1948
Sky blue shirts, Navy blue shorts, Sky blue and navy blue socks

RECENT INTERNATIONAL MATCHES PLAYED BY INDIA

2005	Opponents	Score		Venue	Comp	Scorers	Att	Referee
12-06	Pakistan	D	1-1	Quetta	Fr	Chetri [65]	20 000	Khan PAK
16-06	Pakistan	W	1-0	Peshawar	Fr	Abdul Hakim [67]	15 000	Imtiaz PAK
18-06	Pakistan	L	0-3	Lahore	Fr			Asif PAK
12-08	Fiji	L	0-1	Lautoka	Fr		10 000	Fox NZL
14-08	Fiji	L	1-2	Suva	Fr	Singh.I [10]	11 000	O'Leary NZL
8-12	Nepal	W	2-1	Karachi	SAr1	Mehtab Hossain 2 [6 28]		
10-12	Bhutan	W	3-0	Karachi	SAr1	Bhutia [45], Gawli [51], Abdul Hakim [64]		
12-12	Bangladesh	D	1-1	Karachi	SAr1	Lawrence [17]		
14-12	Maldives	W	1-0	Karachi	SAsf	Shivananju [38]		
17-12	Bangladesh	W	2-0	Karachi	SAf	Din Wadoo [33], Bhutia [81]		
2006								
18-02	Hong Kong	D	2-2	Hong Kong	Fr	Nabi [61], Bhutia [68p]	3 672	Jae Yong Bae
22-02	Japan	L	0-6	Yokohama	ACq		38 025	Huang CHN
1-03	Yemen	L	0-3	New Dehli	ACq		8 000	Torky IRN
1-04	Afghanistan	W	2-0	Chittagong	CCr1	Pariyar 2 [35 60]	2 500	Al Ghatrifi OMA
3-04	Philippines	D	1-1	Chittagong	CCr1	Pariyar [8]	2 000	Mughef JOR
5-04	Chinese Taipei	D	0-0	Chittagong	CCr1		2 000	Gosh BAN
9-04	Nepal	L	0-3	Chittagong	CCqf		3 000	Gosh BAN
16-08	Saudi Arabia	L	0-3	Calcutta	ACq		10 000	Tongkhan THA
6-09	Saudi Arabia	L	1-7	Jeddah	ACq	Nanjangud [22]	3 000	Al Saeedi UAE
11-10	Japan	L	0-3	Bangalore	ACq		5 000	Chan Siu Kee HKG
15-11	Yemen	L	1-2	Sana'a	ACq	Pradeep [54]	5 500	Marshoud JOR
2007								
17-08	Cambodia	W	6-0	New Delhi	Fr	Pradeep [16], Bhutia [45], Dias 2 [73 90], Chetri 2 [73 90]		
20-08	Bangladesh	W	1-0	New Delhi	Fr	Bhutia [5]		
23-08	Syria	L	2-3	New Delhi	Fr	Chetri [13], Ajayan [81]		
26-08	Kyrgyzstan	W	3-0	New Delhi	Fr	Bhutia [39], Chetri [60], Yadav OG [93+]		
29-08	Syria	W	1-0	New Delhi	Fr	Pradeep [44]		
8-10	Lebanon	L	1-4	Sidon	WCq	Chetri [30]	500	Al Fadhli KUW
30-10	Lebanon	D	2-2	Goa	WCq	Chetri [29], Dias [92+]	10 000	Mughef JOR
2008								
24-05	Chinese Taipei	W	3-0	Goa	Fr	Pradeep [58], Sunil Chetri 2 [75 89]		Arjunan IND
27-05	Chinese Taipei	D	2-2	Chennai	Fr	Pradeep 2		Suresh IND
3-06	Nepal	W	4-0	Male	SAr1	Pradeep [26], Bhutia [34], Chetri [67], Sushil Singh [67]		
5-06	Pakistan	W	2-1	Male	SAr1	Pradeep [25], Dias [45]		
7-06	Maldives	W	1-0	Male	SAr1	Gouramangi Singh [14]		
11-06	Bhutan	W	2-1	Male	SAsf	Chetri 31, Gouramangi Singh [120]		
14-06	Maldives	L	0-1	Colombo	SAf			
22-07	Malaysia	D	1-1	Hyderabad	Fr	Bhutia [65]		Suresh IND
30-07	Afghanistan	W	1-0	Hyderabad	CCr1	Lawrence [92+]	300	Iemoto JPN
1-08	Tajikistan	D	1-1	Hyderabad	CCr1	Tuchiev OG [61]	350	Shamsuzzaman BAN
3-08	Turkmenistan	W	2-1	Hyderabad	CCr1	Bhutia 2 [54 80]	1 000	Jasim UAE
7-08	Myanmar	W	1-0	Hyderabad	CCsf	Sunil Chetri [82]	1 500	Shamsuzzaman BAN
13-08	Tajikistan			Delhi	CCf			

Fr = Friendly match • SA = South Asian Football Federation Cup • CC - AFC Confederation Cup • AC = AFC Asian Cup • WC = FIFA World Cup
q = qualifier • r1 = first round group • qf = quarter-final • sf = semi-final • f = final

INDIA NATIONAL TEAM RECORDS AND RECORD SEQUENCES

Records			Sequence records					
Victory	7-1	SRI 1963	Wins	7	1962-1964	Clean sheets	4	1966
Defeat	1-11	URS 1955	Defeats	8	1978-1980	Goals scored	21	1958-1961
Player Caps	55	Baichung Bhutia	Undefeated	7	1962-64, 1999	Without goal	6	1984-1985
Player Goals	38	Baichung Bhutia	Without win	11	1986-92, 1993	Goals against	15	1952-58, 1973-76

MAJOR CITIES/TOWNS

		Population '000
1	Mumbai/Bombay	13 073
2	Dehli/Dilli	11 505
3	Bangalore	5 281
4	Calcutta/Kolkata	4 643
5	Madras/Chennai	4 376
6	Ahmadabad	3 819
7	Hyderabad	3 665
8	Surat	3 156
9	Pune	3 153
10	Kanpur	2 975
11	Jaipur	2 926
12	Lakhnau	2 611
13	Nagpur	2 317
14	Indore	1 967
15	Patna	1 722
16	Bhopal	1 686
17	Ludhiana	1 624
18	Thana	1 612
19	Agra	1 521
20	Thiruvan'puram	803
21	Jamshedpur	639
22	Phagwara	102
23	Madgaon	91
24	Panaji	69

REPUBLIC OF INDIA; BHARATIYA GANARAJYA

Capital	New Dehli	Language	Hindi, English, 14 other official languages	Independence	1947
Population	1 095 351 995	Area	3287590 km²	Density	324 per km²	% in cities	27%
GDP per cap	$2900	Dialling code	+91	Internet	.in	GMT +/-	+5.5

MEDALS TABLE

		Overall			League			F Cup		D Cup		St	Asia				City	Stadium	Cap'ty	DOF
		G	S	B	G	S	B	G	S	G	S	S	G	S	B					
1	Mohun Bagan	31	14	2	3	1	1	12	4	16	19	26				1	Calcutta	Saltlake	120 000	1889
2	East Bengal FC	23	20	2	3	3	2	5	7	15	10	31					Calcutta	Saltlake	120 000	1920
3	JCT Mills	8	7	1	1	1	1	2		5	6	9					Phagwara	Guru Gobind Singh	12 000	1971
4	Border Security Force	8	3					1	1	7	2	3					Jalandhar			
5	Salgaocar SC	6	4	2	1	1	2	3	3	2		18					Vasco, Goa	Fatorda, Madgaon	35 000	1955
6	Mahindra United	5	6	2	1		2	2	3	2	3	12					Mumbai	The Cooperage	12 000	1962
7	Mohammedan Sporting	3	6					2	3	1	3	11					Calcutta	Mohammedan	7 000	1892
8	Dempo Sports Club	5	3		3	1		1	2	1		10					Panaji, Goa	Fatorda, Madgaon	35 000	1968
9	Kerala Police	2						2				5					Thiruv'puram			
10	Indian Telephone Ind.	1						1				18					Bangalore	Sree Kanteerawa	30 000	
11	Churchill Brothers SC	1	5	2	4	2				1	1	6					Salcete, Goa	Fatorda, Madgaon	35 000	1988
12	Sporting Clube de Goa		4		1			2		1	1						Goa	Fatorda, Madgaon	35 000	1999
13	Tata Football Academy		1							1							Jamshedpur	JRD Tata Complex	15 000	1983
14	Vasco Sports Club		2			2						6					Vasco, Goa	Tilak Maidan	15 000	1951
15	Air India											4					Mumbai	The Cooperage	12 000	1952

FC = Federation Cup • D Cup = Durand Cup • St = State championship (not included in overall total)

RECENT LEAGUE AND CUP RECORD

National Football League/I-League

Year	Champions	Pts	Runners-up	Pts	Third	Pts
2000	Mohun Bagan	47	Churchill Brothers	41	Salgaocar	39
2001	East Bengal	46	Mohun Bagan	45	Churchill Brothers	36
2002	Mohun Bagan	44	Churchill Brothers	42	Vasco	40
2003	East Bengal	49	Salgaocar	44	Vasco	43
2004	East Bengal	49	Dempo	45	Mahindra United	41
2005	Dempo	47	Sporting Clube Goa	45	East Bengal	43
2006	Mahindra United	36	East Bengal	31	Mohun Bagan	30
2007	Dempo	36	JCT Mills	31	Mahindra United	30
2008	Dempo	36	Churchill Brothers	36	JCT Mills	33

Federation Cup

Winners	Score	Runners-up
	Not played	
Mohun Bagan	2-0	Dempo
	Not played	
Mahindra United	1-0	Mohammedan Sporting
Dempo	2-0	Mohun Bagan
Mahindra United	2-1	Sporting Clube Goa
Mohun Bagan	1-1 3-1p	Sporting Clube Goa
East Bengal	2-1	Mahindra United

INDIA 2008

ONGC I-LEAGUE

	Pl	W	D	L	F	A	Pts	Dempo	Churchill B.	JCT Mills	Mohun B.	Mahindra	East Bengal	Sporting	Air India	Viva Kerala	Salgaocar
Dempo Sports Club †	18	10	6	2	35	13	36		4-1	2-1	2-0	1-1	0-0	4-1	0-0	4-0	3-0
Churchill Brothers	18	11	3	4	40	22	36	0-2		1-0	2-2	4-2	3-2	3-0	3-0	5-0	2-1
JCT Mills	18	9	6	3	31	14	33	0-0	3-0		1-1	0-0	3-0	4-2	2-0	2-0	4-0
Mohun Bagan	18	8	6	4	22	17	30	0-0	2-1	1-2		1-0	1-0	1-1	2-0	1-3	1-0
Mahindra United	18	7	7	4	24	18	28	3-1	1-5	3-1	0-0		2-1	3-0	1-1	0-0	2-2
East Bengal	18	5	4	9	17	23	19	1-0	0-1	1-3	0-2	1-0		1-1	0-0	2-0	3-2
Sporting Clube Goa	18	4	7	7	14	24	19	0-1	1-1	0-0	1-0	0-3	1-0		1-0	3-0	1-1
Air India	18	3	8	7	10	20	17	1-4	0-0	0-0	0-0	0-1	1-0	1-0		1-1	2-1
Viva Kerala	18	3	3	12	13	38	12	1-4	1-3	0-2	0-2	0-2	1-3	0-0	3-2		3-1
Salgaocar SC	18	1	8	9	20	37	11	1-1	1-5	3-3	4-5	0-0	0-0	1-1	1-1	1-0	

24/11/2007 - 23/02/2008 • † Qualified for the AFC Cup • Top scorers: Odafe Okolie, Churchill 22; Eduardo, JCT 14

29TH FEDERATION CUP 2007

First round		Quarter-finals		Semi-finals		Final	
East Bengal	3						
MohammedanSporting	1	East Bengal	3				
Vasco Sports Club	1	JCT Mills	2				
JCT Mills	3			East Bengal	3		
Viva Kerala	2			Mohun Bagan	2		
Air-India	1	Viva Kerala	1				
ONGC Mumbai	1	Mohun Bagan	3				
Mohun Bagan	2					East Bengal ‡	2
Dempo Sports Club	3					Mahindra United	1
Chirag United	0	Dempo Sports Club	2				
Salgaocar SC	1	Churchill Brothers	0				
Churchill Brothers	4			Dempo Sports Club	1 1p		
Sporting Clube Goa	1			Mahindra United	1 3p		
Army XI	0	Sporting Clube Goa	1 4p				
Hindustan Aeronautics	0	Mahindra United	1 5p				
Mahindra United	1	4/09/2007 - 15/09/2007 in Ludhiana, Punjab • ‡ Qualified for AFC Cup					

CUP FINAL

Ludhiana, 15-09-2007

Scorers - Edmilson 2 [36] [44] for East Bengal; Manjit Singh [45] for Mahindra

120TH OSIANS DURAND CUP 2007

First round		Quarter-finals		Semi-finals		Final	
Churchill Brothers	4						
Hindustan Aeronautics	1	Churchill Brothers	6				
Tata Academy	1 0p	C. Railway Mumbai	1				
C. Railway Mumbai	1 3p			Churchill Brothers	3		
Dempo Sports Club	5			Air-India	2		
Indian Air-Force	0	Dempo Sports Club	1				
New Delhi Heroes	1	Air-India	2				
Air-India	3					Churchill Brothers	1
Salgaocar SC	4					Mahindra United	0
Viva Kerala	1	Salgaocar SC	2				
Assam Rifles	0	JCT Mills	1				
JCT Mills	5			Salgaocar SC	0 2p		
Sporting Clube Goa	2			Mahindra United	0 4p		
Army XI	1	Sporting Clube Goa	0 3p				
Border Security Force	0	Mahindra United	0 5p				
Mahindra United	1	30/10/2007 - 7/11/2007 in Ludhiana, Punjab					

CUP FINAL

Dr Ambedkar, New Delhi
7-11-2007, Ref: Bhattacharya

Scorer - Odafe Okolie [11]

IRL – REPUBLIC OF IRELAND

NATIONAL TEAM RECORD
JULY 10TH 2006 TO JULY 12TH 2010

PL	W	D	L	F	A	%
19	6	8	5	25	22	52.6

FIFA/COCA-COLA WORLD RANKING

1993	1994	1995	1996	1997	1998	1999	2000	2001	2002	2003	2004	2005	2006	2007	High	
10	9	28	36	47	56	35	31	17	14	14	12	24	49	35	6	08/93

2007–2008												Low	
08/07	09/07	10/07	11/07	12/07	01/08	02/08	03/08	04/08	05/08	06/08	07/08	57	11/98
37	32	32	35	35	36	36	37	42	41	42	41		

The failure of the national team to qualify for their third major championship in a row saw the FAI turn to experienced Italian coach Giovanni Trapattoni in a bid to revive fortunes. The Republic finished third in their group behind the Czech Republic and Germany but were never really in the hunt and in October 2007 Steve Staunton was replaced by Don Givens who took charge on a temporary basis until Trapattoni finished the season with his club side Salzburg. His first game in charge, a 1-1 draw with Serbia, was followed with a victory over Colombia five days later and Irish fans will be hoping he has the same talismanic effect as Jack Charlton had in the 1980s and 1990s although

INTERNATIONAL HONOURS
Qualified for the FIFA World Cup finals 1990 1994 2002 UEFA U-17 Championship 1998

with six different coaching appointments in eight years Trapattoni has not stuck with many jobs for long. With all bar one of his first squad coming from clubs in English football, Trapattoni, along with his backroom staff of Diego Tardelli and Liam Brady, will be a regular visitor to Premier League games, no doubt meeting up with compatriot Fabio Capello. In local football there was a first title for Drogheda United, following on from their FAI Cup win in 2005. It is hoped that the new FAI League of Ireland, launched in March 2007, will improve standards, but with clubs struggling financially, the flow of players across the Irish Sea is likely to continue unabated.

THE FIFA BIG COUNT OF 2006

	Male	Female		Total
Number of players	390 444	31 200	Referees and Assistant Referees	1 020
Professionals	476		Admin, Coaches, Technical, Medical	6 310
Amateurs 18+	77 870		Number of clubs	5 629
Youth under 18	174 498		Number of teams	15 025
Unregistered	98 800		Clubs with women's teams	199
Total players	421 644		Players as % of population	10.38%

The Football Association of Ireland (FAI)
National Sports Campus, Abbotstown, Dublin 15
Tel +353 1 8999500   Fax +353 1 8999501
info@fai.ie   www.fai.ie
President: BLOOD David   General Secretary: DELANEY John
Vice-President: McCAUL Patrick   Treasurer: MURRAY Edward   Media Officer: McDermott Gerry
Men's Coach: TRAPATTONI Giovanni   Women's Coach: KING Noel
FAI formed: 1921   UEFA: 1954   FIFA: 1923
Green shirts with white trimmings, White shirts, Green socks or White shirts with green trimmings, Green shorts, White socks

RECENT INTERNATIONAL MATCHES PLAYED BY THE REPUBLIC OF IRELAND

2004	Opponents	Score		Venue	Comp	Scorers	Att	Referee
18-08	Bulgaria	D	1-1	Dublin	Fr	Reid [15]	31 887	Brines SCO
4-09	Cyprus	W	3-0	Dublin	WCq	Morrison [33], Reid [38], Keane [54]	36 000	Paniashvili GEO
8-09	Switzerland	D	1-1	Basel	WCq	Morrison [8]	28 000	Vassaras GRE
9-10	France	D	0-0	Paris	WCq		78 863	Dauden Ibanez ESP
13-10	Faroe Islands	W	2-0	Dublin	WCq	Keane 2 [14p 32]	36 000	Lajuks LVA
16-11	Croatia	W	1-0	Dublin	Fr	Keane [24]	33 200	Orrason ISL
2005								
9-02	Portugal	W	1-0	Dublin	Fr	O'Brien [21]	44 100	Messias ENG
26-03	Israel	D	1-1	Tel Aviv	WCq	Morrison [43]	32 150	Ivanov.V RUS
29-03	China PR	W	1-0	Dublin	Fr	Morrison [82]	35 222	Casha MLT
4-06	Israel	D	2-2	Dublin	WCq	Harte [5], Keane [11]	36 000	Vassaras GRE
8-06	Faroe Islands	W	2-0	Torshavn	WCq	Harte [51p], Kilbane [59]	5 180	Guenov BUL
17-08	Italy	L	1-2	Dublin	Fr	Reid.A [32]	44 000	Gomes Costa POR
7-09	France	L	0-1	Dublin	WCq		36 000	Fandel GER
8-10	Cyprus	W	1-0	Nicosia	WCq	Elliott [6]	13 546	Kassai HUN
12-10	Switzerland	D	0-0	Dublin	WCq		35 944	Merk GER
2006								
1-03	Sweden	W	3-0	Dublin	Fr	Duff [36], Keane [48], Miller [71]	44 109	Ledentu FRA
24-05	Chile	L	0-1	Dublin	Fr		41 200	Ingvarsson SWE
16-08	Netherlands	L	0-4	Dublin	Fr		42 400	Ovrebo NOR
2-09	Germany	L	0-1	Stuttgart	ECq		53 198	Medina Cantalejo ESP
7-10	Cyprus	L	2-5	Nicosia	ECq	Ireland [8], Dunne [44]	5 000	Batista POR
11-10	Czech Republic	D	1-1	Dublin	ECq	Kilbane [62]	35 500	Layec FRA
15-11	San Marino	W	5-0	Dublin	ECq	Reid [7], Doyle [24], Keane 3 [31 58p 85]	34 018	Isaksen FRO
2007								
7-02	San Marino	W	2-1	Serravalle	ECq	Kilbane [49], Ireland [94+]	3 294	Rasmussen DEN
24-03	Wales	W	1-0	Dublin	ECq	Ireland [39]	73 000	Hauge NOR
28-03	Slovakia	W	1-0	Dublin	ECq	Doyle [13]	71 257	Baskakov RUS
23-05	Ecuador	D	1-1	New Jersey	Fr	Doyle [44]	20 823	
26-05	Bolivia	D	1-1	Foxboro	Fr	Long [13]	13 156	
22-08	Denmark	W	4-0	Aarhus	Fr	Keane 2 [29 40], Long 2 [54 66]	30 000	Einwaller AUT
8-09	Slovakia	D	2-2	Bratislava	ECq	Ireland [7], Doyle [57]	12 360	Farina ITA
12-09	Czech Republic	L	0-1	Prague	ECq		16 648	Vassaras GRE
13-10	Germany	D	0-0	Dublin	ECq		67 495	Hansson SWE
17-10	Cyprus	D	1-1	Dublin	ECq	Finnan [92+]	54 861	Vuorela FIN
17-11	Wales	D	2-2	Cardiff	ECq	Keane [31], Doyle [60]	24 619	Oriekhov UKR
2008								
6-02	Brazil	L	0-1	Dublin	Fr		30 000	Rogalla SUI
24-05	Serbia	D	1-1	Dublin	Fr	Keogh [90]	42 500	Evans WAL
29-05	Colombia	W	1-0	London	Fr	Keane [3]	18 612	Clattenburg ENG

Fr = Friendly match • EC = UEFA EURO 2008 • WC = FIFA World Cup • q = qualifier

REPUBLIC OF IRELAND NATIONAL TEAM RECORDS AND RECORD SEQUENCES

Records			Sequence records					
Victory	8-0	MLT 1983	Wins	8	1987-1988	Clean sheets	5	1989, 1996-1997
Defeat	0-7	BRA 1982	Defeats	5	Six times	Goals scored	17	1954-59, 2000-01
Player Caps	102	Steve Staunton	Undefeated	17	1989-1990	Without goal	5	1995-1996
Player Goals	33	Robbie Keane	Without win	20	1968-1971	Goals against	35	1966-1973

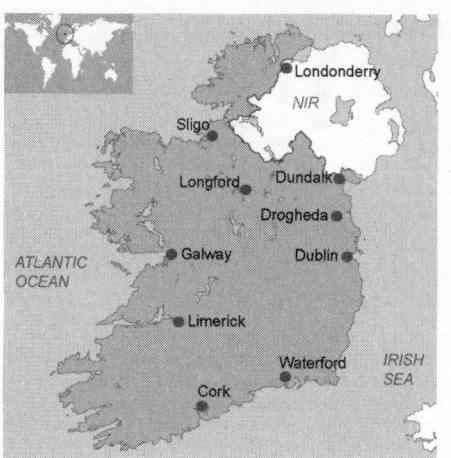

MAJOR CITIES/TOWNS

		Population '000
1	Dublin	1 036
2	Cork	190
3	Limerick	92
4	Galway	73
5	Waterford	48
6	Drogheda	35
7	Dundalk	34
8	Bray	33
9	Navan	28
10	Ennis	26
11	Tralee	23
12	Naas	22
13	Kilkenny	22
14	Carlow	21
15	Sligo	20
16	Newbridge	20
17	Celbridge	19
18	Mullingar	18
19	Letterkenny	18
20	Wexford	18
21	Clonmel	17
22	Athlone	15
23	Longford	7
24	Ballybofey	4

IRELAND; EIRE

Capital	Dublin	Language	English, Irish (Gaelic or Gaeilge)	Independence	1921
Population	4 062 235	Area	70 280 km²	Density	56 per km²	% in cities	58%
GDP per cap	$29 600	Dailling code	+353	Internet	.ie	GMT +/-	0

MEDALS TABLE

		Overall			League			Cup		LC			Europe				Stadium	Cap'ty	DoF
		G	S	B	G	S	B	G	B	G	B	G	S	B						
1	Shamrock Rovers	40	26	12	15	13	12	24	8	1	5				Dublin	Tolka Park	9 681	1901
2	Shelbourne	21	24	11	13	11	11	7	10	1	3				Dublin	Tolka Park	9 681	1895
3	Dundalk	21	19	6	9	10	6	8	5	4	4				Dundalk	Oriel Park	11 000	1903
4	Bohemians	17	23	14	9	13	14	6	7	2	3				Dublin	Dalymount Park	8 200	1890
5	Derry City	14	9	1	2	4	1	4	3	8	2				Londonderry	Brandywell	7 700	1928
6	Cork Athletic	12	8	2	7	2	2	5	6						Cork	Ballinlough Road		1912-57
7	St. Patrick's Athletic	11	12	2	7	3	2	2	7	2	2				Dublin	Richmond Park	5 500	1929
8	Waterford United	10	11	8	6	4	8	2	7	2					Waterford	RSC	8 200	1930
9	Drumcondra	10	9	4	5	5	4	5	4						Dublin	Tolka Park		1924-72
10	Cork City	7	9	4	2	5	4	2	3	3	1				Cork	Turner's Cross	8 000	1984
11	Limerick	7	6	3	2	2	3	2	3	3	1				Limerick	Hogan Park	10 000	1937
12	Athlone Town	6	3	3	2	1	3	1		3	2				Athlone	Lissywoollen	6 000	1887
13	Sligo Rovers	5	10	5	2	2	5	2	5	1	3				Sligo	Showgrounds	5 500	1928
14	St. James' Gate	4	3		2	1		2	2						Dublin	Iveagh Grounds		1913
15	Drogheda United	3	3	4	1	1	4	1	2	1					Drogheda	United Park	5 400	1919
16	Cork Hibernians	3	3	3	1	1	3	2	2						Cork	Flower Lodge		1957-76
17	Galway United	3	3	1		1	1	1	1	2	1				Galway	Terryland Park	3 000	1937
18	Longford Town	3	3					2	2	1	1				Longford	Flancare Park	6 000	1924

RECENT LEAGUE AND CUP RECORD

	Championship						Cup		
Year	Champions	Pts	Runners-up	Pts	Third	Pts	Winners	Score	Runners-up
1996	St Patrick's Ath	67	Bohemians	62	Sligo Rovers	55	Shelbourne	1-1 2-1	St Patrick's Ath
1997	Derry City	67	Bohemians	57	Shelbourne	54	Shelbourne	2-0	Derry City
1998	St Patrick's Ath	68	Shelbourne	67	Cork City	53	Cork City	0-0 1-0	Shelbourne
1999	St Patrick's Ath	73	Cork City	70	Shelbourne	47	Bray Wanderers	0-0 2-2 2-1	Finn Harps
2000	Shelbourne	69	Cork City	58	Bohemians	57	Shelbourne	0-0 1-0	Bohemians
2001	Bohemians	62	Shelbourne	60	Cork City	56	Bohemians	1-0	Longford Town
2002	Shelbourne	63	Shamrock Rovers	57	St Patrick's Ath	53	Dundalk	2-1	Bohemians
2003	Bohemians	54	Shelbourne	49	Shamrock Rovers	43	Derry City	1-0	Shamrock Rovers
2003	Shelbourne	69	Bohemians	64	Cork City	53	Longford Town	2-0	St Patrick's Ath
2004	Shelbourne	68	Cork City	65	Bohemians	60	Longford Town	2-1	Waterford United
2005	Cork City	74	Derry City	72	Shelbourne	67	Drogheda United	2-0	Cork City
2006	Shelbourne	62	Derry City	62	Drogheda United	58	Derry City	4-3	St Patrick's Ath
2007	Drogheda United	68	St Patrick's Ath	61	Bohemians	58	Cork City	1-0	Longford Town

REPUBLIC OF IRELAND 2007

EIRCOM LEAGUE OF IRELAND PREMIER DIVISION

	Pl	W	D	L	F	A	Pts	Drogheda	St Patrick's	Bohemians	Cork City	Shamrock	Sligo Rov	Derry City	Galway Utd	Bray Wand	UCD	Waterford U	Longford T
Drogheda United	33	19	11	3	48	24	68		2-0	1-0	2-2 2-1	0-2	3-0 1-0	2-1 1-0	2-2	4-1 1-1	3-2 0-1	3-0	1-1
St Patrick's Athletic	33	18	7	8	54	29	61	1-0 0-0		0-0 0-1	1-1	2-1 5-0	3-1	2-1	1-2	3-1 4-2	1-1	3-0 4-1	4-2
Bohemians	33	16	10	7	35	17	58	0-0 1-1	2-1		2-1	2-1 0-2	1-0 3-0	0-0	1-1 2-0	2-0	0-0 2-0	1-0	5-0 0-0
Cork City	33	15	10	8	44	32	55	0-0	1-0 0-1	2-1 0-1		0-0	1-0	1-2	1-1	0-0 0-0	2-2 4-1	2-0	2-0 3-2
Shamrock Rovers	33	14	9	10	36	26	51	1-2 0-2	0-0	0-0	2-0		1-0 0-0	1-1	1-0 4-0	1-0	2-0	2-0 0-0	0-2 0-0
Sligo Rovers	33	12	5	16	34	45	41	0-2	0-4 2-3	2-1	4-1 0-1	2-0		0-2 0-0	1-1	3-0	1-0 2-1	1-1	2-1
Derry City	33	8	13	12	30	31	37	0-1	0-1 1-0	0-0	1-2 1-4	1-2 1-0	1-0 1-1		4-1	0-0	1-0 3-0	0-1	1-1
Galway United	33	7	14	12	28	35	35	2-3 1-0	1-0 1-1	1-2	0-1	1-2	2-0	0-2 2-1		1-1	1-2	1-1 2-1	3-1
Bray Wanderers	33	8	10	15	30	48	34	1-2	0-0	1-0 0-3	1-1	1-0	2-3	0-2 0-2	1-1		0-1 1-1	2-1	2-1 1-3
University College	33	7	10	16	31	44	31	0-1	2-2 0-3	1-0	0-1	1-2 0-2	0-4	0-2	1-1	2-2		3-0 2-1	2-0 1-1
Waterford United	33	7	9	17	23	47	30	1-1 1-1	2-1	0-1 0-0	0-0 0-3	0-2	1-2	0-1 2-1	1-0 0-0	1-2	0-0		2-1
Longford Town §7	33	9	9	16	34	49	29	0-1	1-2 1-2	2-1	3-0	1-2	0-3	0-1 1-1 0-0	3-1	0-3	1-1 1-0	1-0	

9/03/2007 - 9/11/2007 • † Qualified for the UEFA Champions League • ‡ Qualified for the UEFA Cup • § = points deducted
Play-offs: **Finn Harps** 2-0 Dundalk • **Finn Harps** 3-0 3-3 Waterford United. Finn Harps promoted; Waterford United relegated
Top scorers: Dave Mooney, Longford 19; Mark Quigley, St Patrick's Athletic 15; Roy O'Donovan, Cork City 14; Tadhg Purcell, Shamrock Rovers 12

REPUBLIC OF IRELAND 2007 FIRST DIVISION

	Pl	W	D	L	F	A	Pts
Cobh Ramblers	36	22	11	3	57	17	77
Finn Harps ‡	36	23	7	6	61	20	76
Dundalk ‡	36	19	9	8	56	30	66
Limerick	36	14	11	11	46	41	53
Shelbourne	36	11	10	15	46	46	43
Athlone Town	36	11	8	17	40	55	41
Kildare County	36	9	12	15	48	62	39
Monaghan United	36	9	11	16	38	52	38
Wexford Youths	36	7	10	19	32	55	31
Kilkenny City	36	5	11	20	33	79	26

8/03/2007 - 10/11/2007 • ‡ Promotion play-offs

IRELAND LEAGUE CUP 2007

Quarter-finals		Semi-finals		Final	
Derry City	2				
Cobh Ramblers*	1	**Derry City** *	3		
Finn Harps	1	Univ. College	0		
Univ. College *	2			**Derry City**	1
Shamrock Rov *	1			Bohemians	0
Athlone Town	0	Shamrock Rov	0		
Cork City	2	**Bohemians** *	1	9-10-2007	
Bohemians *	3		* Home team	Scorer - McHugh [97]	

FA OF IRELAND CUP 2007

Round of 16		Quarter–finals		Semi–finals		Final	
Cork City *	5						
Kilkenny City	1	**Cork City**	1 4				
Sligo Rovers	1 2 3p	Waterford United *	1 0				
Waterford United *	1 2 4p			**Cork City**	2		
St Patrick's Athletic	2			Bohemians *	0		
Bray Wanderers *	1	St Patrick's Athletic *	1				
Malahide United *	0	**Bohemians**	2			**Cork City** ‡	1
Bohemians	1					Longford Town	0
University College	2						
Dundalk *	1	**University College**	1			CUP FINAL	
Finn Harps *	0	Derry City *	0				
Derry City	1			University College *	0	RDS, Dublin	
Limerick *	1 1			**Longford Town**	1	2-12-2007, Att: 10 000, Ref: McKeon	
Douglas Hall	1 0	Limerick	1				
Fanad United	0	**Longford Town** *	3			Scorer - Denis Behan [60]	
Longford Town *	2			* Home team • ‡ Qualified for the UEFA Cup			

IRN – IRAN

NATIONAL TEAM RECORD
JULY 10TH 2006 TO JULY 12TH 2010

PL	W	D	L	F	A	%
31	17	12	2	45	18	74.2

FIFA/COCA-COLA WORLD RANKING

1993	1994	1995	1996	1997	1998	1999	2000	2001	2002	2003	2004	2005	2006	2007	High	
59	75	108	83	46	27	49	37	29	33	28	20	19	38	41	15	07/05

2007–2008												Low	
08/07	09/07	10/07	11/07	12/07	01/08	02/08	03/08	04/08	05/08	06/08	07/08	122	05/96
44	40	38	40	41	41	39	41	51	51	48	37		

Following on from the disappointing showing at the 2007 AFC Asian Cup, a protracted and very public attempt to hire Spaniard Javier Clemente as national team coach ended with both parties failing to agree terms. The Iran Football Federation then took the surprise step of appointing former international striker Ali Daei as national team boss. Daei had steered club side Saipa to the Iran Pro League title the previous season and chose to combine both positions as he sought to take the club to the knockout phase of the AFC Champions League - an objective he achieved before

INTERNATIONAL HONOURS
Qualified for the FIFA World Cup finals 1978 1998 2006   AFC Asian Cup 1968 1972 1976   Asian Games 1974 1990 1998 2002
AFC Asian U-19 Championship 1973 1974 1975 1976   AFC Champions League Esteghlal 1970 1991

standing down to concentrate on working with the national team. Iran's path to the final phase of qualifying for the 2010 FIFA World Cup was anything but straightforward, and it was only in the final stages of the campaign that their results came close to reflecting the team's potential. On the club scene, Sepahan became the first Iranian club to reach the final of the AFC Champions League where they lost to Japan's Urawa Reds. At home Pirouzi won the league title for the first time since 2002 under the guidance of USA based coach Afshin Gotbi, while their arch-rivals Esteghlal claimed the Hazfi Cup as both clubs qualified for the 2009 AFC Champions League.

THE FIFA BIG COUNT OF 2006

	Male	Female		Total
Number of players	1 696 548	109 996	Referees and Assistant Referees	7 300
Professionals	560		Admin, Coaches, Technical, Medical	18 500
Amateurs 18+	286 800		Number of clubs	100
Youth under 18	158 496		Number of teams	270
Unregistered	345 900		Clubs with women's teams	20
Total players	1 806 544		Players as % of population	2.63%

IR Iran Football Federation (IRIFF)
No. 2/2 Third St., Seoul Ave., 19958-73591 Tehran, Iran
Tel +98 21 88213308   Fax +98 21 88053605
www.ffiri.ir
President: KAFASHIAN Ali   General Secretary: MOHAMMAD NABI Mehdi
Vice-President: TAJ Mehdi   Treasurer: KAHAZAEI Mohammad Taghi   Media Officer: HOSSEINI Amir Hossein
Men's Coach: DAEI Ali   Women's Coach: MOZAFAR Shahrzad
IRIFF formed: 1920   AFC: 1958   FIFA: 1945
White shirts with green timmings, White shorts, White socks

RECENT INTERNATIONAL MATCHES PLAYED BY IRAN

2005	Opponents	Score	Venue	Comp	Scorers	Att	Referee
17-08	Japan	L 1-2	Yokohama	WCq	Daei [79]	66 098	Shaban KUW
24-08	Libya	W 4-0	Tehran	Fr	Alavi [7], Nekounam 2 [41 90], Daei [56]	15 000	Delawar BHR
12-10	Korea Republic	L 0-2	Seoul	Fr		61 457	Al Ghamdi KSA
13-11	Togo	W 2-0	Tehran	Fr	Daei [11p], Hashemian [58p]		
2006							
22-02	Chinese Taipei	W 4-0	Tehran	ACq	Timotian [35], Madanchi 2 [47 60], Daei [82]	5 000	AK Nema IRQ
1-03	Costa Rica	W 3-2	Tehran	Fr	Karimi [9], Daei [16], Hashemian [34]	25 000	Marzouqi UAE
28-05	Croatia	D 2-2	Osijek	Fr	Karimi [21], Borhani [81]	19 000	Siric CRO
31-05	Bosnia-Herzegovina	W 5-2	Tehran	Fr	Madanchi [25], Rezaei [45], Hashemian [45], Enayati [88], Khatibi [90]	40 000	Mohd Salleh MAS
11-06	Mexico	L 1-3	Nuremburg	WCr1	Golmohammadi [36]	41 000	Rosetti ITA
17-06	Portugal	L 0-2	Frankfurt	WCr1		48 000	Poulat FRA
21-06	Angola	D 1-1	Leipzig	WCr1	Bakhtiarizadeh [75]	38 000	Shield AUS
8-08	UAE	W 1-0	Tehran	Fr	Enayati [5]	4 000	
16-08	Syria	D 1-1	Tehran	ACq	Nekounam [72]	40 000	Irmatov UZB
2-09	Korea Republic	D 1-1	Seoul	ACq	Hashemian [93+]	63 113	Breeze AUS
6-09	Syria	W 2-0	Damascus	ACq	Nosrati [27], Nekounam [55]	10 000	Matsumura JPN
4-10	Iraq	W 2-0	Amman	Fr	Rezaei [25], Rajabzadeh [70]	5 000	
6-10	Jordan	D 0-0	Amman	Fr		500	Al Blooshi QAT
11-10	Chinese Taipei	W 2-0	Taipei	ACq	Karimi 2 [11 58]	2 000	Shamsuzzaman BAN
15-11	Korea Republic	W 2-0	Tehran	ACq	Enayati [48], Badamaki [91+]	30 000	Ebrahim BHR
2007							
12-01	UAE	W 2-0	Abu Dhabi	Fr	Khatibi [45p], Sadeghi [90]	9 000	Omar UAE
7-02	Belarus	D 2-2	Tehran	Fr	Khatibi [5], Rajabzadeh [88]	15 000	Al Fadhli KUW
24-03	Qatar	W 1-0	Doha	Fr	Vahedi-Nikbakht [7]	5 000	Al Khabbaz BHR
2-06	Mexico	L 0-4	San Luis Potosi	Fr		30 000	Silvera URU
16-06	Iraq	D 0-0	Amman	WAr1		5 000	Abbas SYR
20-06	Palestine	W 2-0	Amman	WAr1	Midavoodi [56], Rajabzadeh [85]	2 000	Abu Loum JOR
22-06	Jordan	W 1-0	Amman	WAsf	Rajabzadeh [32]	5 000	Won Lon Soon KOR
24-06	Iraq	W 2-1	Amman	WAf	Badamaki [9], Beikzadeh [21]	8 000	Ghandour LIB
2-07	Jamaica	W 8-1	Tehran	Fr	Nekounam 2 [1 17], Madanchi 2 [2 45], Hashemian [35], Khatibi 2 [81 88], Enayati [90]	15 000	Mombini IRN
11-07	Uzbekistan	W 2-1	Kuala Lumpur	ACr1	Hosseini [55], Kazemeyan [78]	1 863	Al Fadhli KUW
15-07	China PR	D 2-2	Kuala Lumpur	ACr1	Zandi [45], Nekounam [73]	5 938	Al Ghamdi KSA
18-07	Malaysia	W 2-0	Kuala Lumpur	ACr1	Nekounam [29p], Teymourian [77]	4 520	Basma SYR
22-07	Korea Republic	D 0-0	Kuala Lumpur	ACqf	L 2-4p	8 629	Al Badwawi UAE
2008							
10-01	Qatar	D 0-0	Doha	Fr			
30-01	Costa Rica	D 0-0	Tehran	Fr			
6-02	Syria	D 0-0	Tehran	WCq		45 000	Bashir SIN
21-03	Bahrain	L 0-1	Manama	Fr			
26-03	Kuwait	D 2-2	Kuwait City	WCq	Vahedi [2], Hosseini [5]	15 000	Breeze AUS
25-05	Zambia	W 3-2	Tehran	Fr	Nekounam [13p], Rezaie [35], Aghili [88p]	50 000	
2-06	UAE	D 0-0	Tehran	WCq		50 000	Lee Gi Young KOR
7-06	UAE	W 1-0	Al Ain	WCq	Zandi [7]	9 000	Nishimura JPN
14-06	Syria	W 2-0	Damascus	WCq	Rezaie [65], Khalili [93+]	25 000	Tongkhan THA
22-06	Kuwait	W 2-0	Tehran	WCq	Nekounam [16], Rezaie [92+]	20 000	Sun Baojie CHN

Fr = Friendly match • WA = West Asian Federation Championship • AC = AFC Asian Cup • WC = FIFA World Cup
q = qualifier • r1 = first round group • sf = semi-final • f = final

IRAN NATIONAL TEAM RECORDS AND RECORD SEQUENCES

Records			Sequence records				
Victory	19-0	GUM 2000	Wins	8	1974, 1996	Clean sheets	7	1977
Defeat	1-6	TUR 1950	Defeats	3	1989-1990	Goals scored	20	2000-2001
Player Caps	149	Ali Daei	Undefeated	15	1996-1997	Without goal	5	2007-2008
Player Goals	109	Ali Daei	Without win	10	1997	Goals against	9	1959-1963

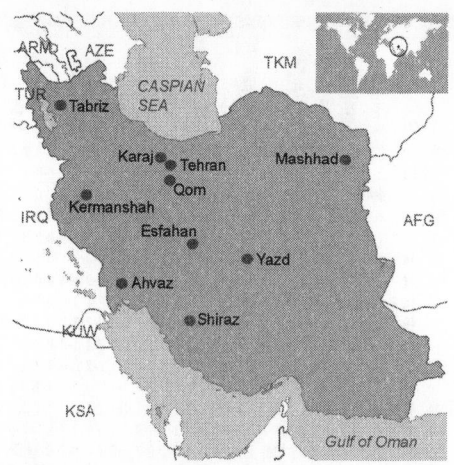

ISLAMIC REPUBLIC OF IRAN; JOMHURI-YE ESLAMI-YE IRAN

Capital	Tehran	Language	Persian, Turkic, Kurdish	Formation	1502
Population	68 688 433	Area	1648 000 km²	Density	42 per km²	% in cities	59%
GDP per cap	$7000	Dailling code	+98	Internet	.ir	GMT + / -	+3.5

The figure for the Tehran metropolitan area also includes: Karaj 1 602; Eslamshahr 324; Qods 303; Qarchak 277; Nazarabad 250; Varamin 197

MEDALS TABLE

		Overall			League			Cup			Asia			City	Stadium	Cap'ty	DoF
		G	S	B	G	S	B	G	S	B	G	S	B				
1	Esteghlal (ex Taj)	13	9	5	6	4	2	5	3		2	2	3	Tehran	Azadi	110 000	1945
2	Pirouzi (aka Persopolis)	13	3	5	9	1	2	3	1		1	1	3	Tehran	Azadi	110 000	1963
3	Pas	6	3		5	3				1				Tehran	Dastgerdi	15 000	1963-07
4	Sepahan Esfahan	4	2	2	1	1	2	3				1		Esfahan	Naghsh e Jahan	50 000	1967
5	Saipa Karaj	4		2	3		2	1						Karaj	Enghelab	30 000	1989
6	Malavan Anzali	3	3					3	3					Bandar Anzali	Takhti	20 000	1969
7	Bahman Karaj	1	4			2		1	2					Karaj	Dr Shariati	20 000	1994
8	Fajr-Sepasi Shiraz	1	2	1			1	1	2					Shiraz	Hafezieh	20 000	1988
	Zob-Ahan Esfahan	1	2	1		1	1	1	1					Esfahan	Fooladshahr	25 000	1969
10	Saba Battery	1	1	1		1	1	1						Tehran	Derakshan	12 000	2002
	Bargh Shiraz	1	1					1	1					Shiraz	Hafezieh	20 000	1946
12	Foolad Ahvaz	1		2	1		2							Ahvaz	Takhti	30 000	1986
13	Shahin Ahvaz	1						1						Ahvaz	Takhti	30 000	

RECENT LEAGUE AND CUP RECORD

	Championship						Cup		
Year	Champions	Pts	Runners-up	Pts	Third	Pts	Winners	Score	Runners-up
1995	Pirouzi						Bahman	0-1 2-0	TraktorSazi
1996	Pirouzi	57	Bahman	51	Esteghlal	51	Esteghlal	3-1 2-0	Bargh
1997	Pirouzi	59	Bahman	53	Sepahan	50	Bargh	1-1 3-0p	Bahman
1998	Esteghlal	58	Pas	52	Zob Ahan	45	No tournament held		
1999	Pirouzi	65	Esteghlal	53	Sepahan	53	Pirouzi	2-1	Esteghlal
2000	Pirouzi	54	Esteghlal	47	Fajr Sepasi	44	Esteghlal	3-1	Bahman
2001	Esteghlal	50	Pirouzi	46	Saipa	33	Fajr Sepasi	1-0 2-1	Zob Ahan
2002	Pirouzi	49	Esteghlal	48	Foolad	45	Esteghlal	2-1 2-2	Fajr Sepasi
2003	Sepahan	52	Pas	45	Pirouzi	44	Zob Ahan	2-2 2-2 6-5p	Fajr Sepasi
2004	Pas	53	Esteghlal	51	Foolad	47	Sepahan	3-2 2-0	Esteghlal
2005	Foolad	64	Zob Ahan	58	Esteghlal	58	Saba Battery	1-1 2-2 4-2p	AbooMoslem
2006	Esteghlal	59	Pas	58	Saipa	52	Sepahan	1-1 1-1 4-2p	Pirouzi
2007	Saipa	56	Esteghlal Ahvaz	54	Pirouzi	53	Sepahan	1-0 3-0	Saba Battery
2008	Pirouzi	59	Sepahan	58	Saba Battery	52	Esteghlal	0-1 3-0	Pegah Gilan

IRAN 2007–08

IRAN PRO LEAGUE

	Pl	W	D	L	F	A	Pts	Pirouzi	Sepahan	Saba Battery	AbooMoslem	Hamedan	Zob Ahan	Bargh	Esteghlal A	Paykan	Mes	Saipa	Rah Ahan	Esteghlal T	Sepasi	Pegah	Malavan	Sanat-Naft	Shirin-Faraz
Pirouzi † §6	34	18	11	5	55	34	59		2-1	2-2	3-3	1-1	2-1	1-1	3-2	2-1	1-0	1-0	0-0	1-1	3-3	2-0	2-0	1-0	5-0
Sepahan §3	34	17	10	7	53	38	58	2-1		2-2	2-1	0-0	2-2	4-0	2-1	1-1	1-1	0-1	2-2	2-1	0-0	3-1	3-2	1-0	1-0
Saba Battery	34	13	13	8	41	37	52	1-4	0-1		0-1	1-0	1-0	2-2	2-2	1-1	0-1	2-1	2-0	0-0	0-0	3-1	3-1	2-2	
AbooMoslem	34	14	8	12	37	37	50	1-0	3-1	1-0		0-0	3-2	2-1	1-1	3-1	2-1	2-1	0-1	2-0	3-1	0-3	2-1	2-1	1-0
Pas Hamedan	34	11	16	7	36	28	49	1-2	3-1	0-1	3-0		1-1	3-0	1-1	3-2	1-0	1-3	3-2	1-1	0-0	3-1	1-1	1-0	0-0
Zob Ahan	34	11	15	8	39	32	48	2-0	1-0	2-1	2-1	0-0		2-1	4-2	1-0	0-0	0-0	2-0	0-1	0-0	2-2	0-0	2-1	0-1
Bargh	34	11	14	9	43	47	47	0-1	3-3	1-1	1-0	1-1	0-0		1-1	1-1	2-1	2-0	1-0	1-0	0-0	1-0	0-2	3-2	1-0
Esteghlal Ahvaz	34	13	13	10	61	51	46	4-1	3-2	4-1	1-0	2-2	1-1	2-0		1-2	2-2	1-2	2-3	1-2	4-1	3-2	0-0	0-0	3-1
Paykan	34	12	10	12	41	42	46	1-2	1-2	0-1	0-0	2-1	2-0	4-2	2-0		1-1	0-1	2-2	3-2	0-3	1-1	0-1	0-0	2-1
Mes	34	11	12	11	36	34	45	0-0	1-1	0-1	1-1	2-0	1-1	1-3	2-1	2-3		2-1	2-1	1-0	0-0	2-1	1-0	0-1	1-2
Saipa	34	12	9	13	33	35	45	0-1	1-0	1-1	0-1	1-1	0-1	1-1	0-1	1-2	0-0		2-2	0-0	1-2	1-2	2-1	0-2	4-2
Rah Ahan	34	11	11	12	45	40	44	2-1	0-1	2-1	2-0	0-0	2-1	2-2	2-2	5-0	3-1	1-0		0-3	1-1	0-1	2-1	1-1	3-0
Esteghlal Tehran	34	11	10	13	44	44	43	1-1	0-1	1-1	1-1	0-1	1-2	4-2	3-2	1-2	1-1	2-2		1-1	1-4	2-0	2-3	2-1	
Moghavemat Sepasi	34	9	15	10	37	41	42	0-2	0-2	3-1	2-1	1-1	1-4	0-1	2-2	1-1	1-3	1-1	0-1	1-2		2-0	2-1	2-0	2-2
Pegah Gilan	34	9	11	14	26	35	38	1-0	0-2	1-0	0-0	0-0	1-0	2-2	1-1	0-1	0-0	0-0	0-1	0-1			0-0	0-0	0-0
Malavan	34	8	12	14	32	41	36	1-1	1-2	1-1	2-0	1-0	1-1	1-1	0-2	0-1	2-0	1-2	2-1	2-1	1-1			0-0	2-2
Sanat-Naft	34	9	8	17	37	46	35	2-3	2-2	2-3	2-0	1-2	1-1	1-3	2-3	2-1	1-2	2-0	0-2	2-1	1-1	0-1	1-2		2-1
Shirin-Faraz	34	3	12	19	25	59	21	0-0	2-3	1-1	0-2	0-1	1-1	2-2	0-3	0-3	0-3	1-1	1-1	1-3	0-1	0-2	2-1	0-0	

16/08/2007 - 17/05/2008 • † Qualified for the AFC Champions League • § = points deducted

IRAN 2007–08 AZADEGAN LEAGUE GROUP A (2)

	Pl	W	D	L	F	A	Pts
Steel Azin Tehran †	22	11	5	6	41	28	38
Payam Mashhad †	22	11	5	6	29	21	38
Niroye Zamini Tehran	22	10	7	5	26	19	37
Gol Gohar Sirjan	22	8	7	7	25	24	31
Teraktor-Sazi Tabriz	22	7	10	5	23	19	31
Sorkh-Pushan Tehran	22	7	10	5	19	20	31
Shahrdari Bandar Abbas	22	7	8	7	26	21	29
Damash Tehran	22	7	7	8	24	26	28
Moghavemat Shiraz	22	7	7	8	23	26	28
Kaveh Zanjan	22	6	8	8	18	18	26
Shamoushak Noshahr	22	7	4	11	19	28	25
Shahin Ahvaz	22	4	2	16	20	44	14

16/08/2007 - 12/06/2008 • † Qualified for the play-offs

IRAN 2007–08 AZADEGAN LEAGUE GROUP B (2)

	Pl	W	D	L	F	A	Pts
Foolad Ahvaz †	22	13	5	4	33	15	44
Sepahan Novin †	22	11	7	4	28	18	40
Tarbyat Badani Yazd	22	11	4	7	36	29	37
Mes Rafsanjan	22	9	7	6	34	26	34
Nassaji	22	10	4	8	27	30	34
Shahrdari Tabriz	22	7	6	9	20	23	27
Etka Tehran	22	6	8	8	28	34	26
Shahin Bushehr	22	6	7	9	22	24	25
Kousar Tehran	22	5	10	7	21	25	25
Sanaye Arak	22	6	5	11	19	24	23
Mashin-Sazi Tabriz	22	3	12	7	15	25	21
Homa Tehran	22	4	7	11	17	27	19

16/08/2007 - 12/06/2008 • † Qualified for the play-offs

Promotion play-offs: Sepahan Novin 0-0 2-1 Steel Azin; Payam Masshad 0-0 1-1 Foolad Ahvaz • Sepahin Novin and Payam Masshad promoted

JAAM HAZFI 2007–08

Round of 16

- Esteghlal Tehran — 1 3p
- Zob Ahan Esfahan * — 1 1p
- Steel Azin Tehran — 2 0p
- Rahahan Tehran * — 2 3p
- Pas Hamedan * — 3
- Pirouzi — 0
- Esteghlal Ahvaz — 4 3p
- Foolad Ahvaz * — 4 4p
- Bargh Shiraz * — 1
- Paykan Tehran — 0
- Saba Battery — 2 3p
- Shahin Bushehr * — 2 4p
- Sepahan Esfahan * — 2
- Moghavemat Sepasi — 1
- Sanaye Arak * — 0
- Pegah Gilan — 1

Quarter-finals

- Esteghlal Tehran * — 2 5p
- Rahahan Tehran — 2 3p
- Pas Hamedan * — 1 3p
- Foolad Ahvaz — 1 4p
- Bargh Shiraz * — 2
- Shahin Bushehr — 0
- Sepahan Esfahan * — 2
- Pegah Gilan — 4

Semi-finals

- Esteghlal Tehran — 1 3p
- Foolad Ahvaz — 1 1p
- Bargh Shiraz — 1
- Pegah Gilan — 2

Final

- Esteghlal Tehran — 0 3
- Pegah Gilan — 1 0

CUP FINAL

1st leg. Sardar-e-Jangal, 9-06-2008
Scorer - Akvsenti Gilauri 40 for Pegah
2nd leg. Azadi, Tehran, 16-06-2008
Scorers - Mehdi Amirabadi 14,
Mojtaba Jabbari 99, Arash Borhani 99
for Esteghlal

* Home team

IRQ – IRAQ

NATIONAL TEAM RECORD
JULY 10TH 2006 TO JULY 12TH 2010

PL	W	D	L	F	A	%
40	15	13	12	49	37	53.8

FIFA/COCA-COLA WORLD RANKING

1993	1994	1995	1996	1997	1998	1999	2000	2001	2002	2003	2004	2005	2006	2007	High	
65	88	110	98	68	94	78	79	72	53	43	44	54	83	68	39	10/04

2007–2008												Low	
08/07	09/07	10/07	11/07	12/07	01/08	02/08	03/08	04/08	05/08	06/08	07/08	139	07/96
64	65	69	70	68	67	69	68	70	70	73	58		

After their astonishing against-the-odds victory at the 2007 AFC Asian Cup, Iraq suffered a major hangover which left the country's hopes of a World Cup appearance in tatters. Jorvan Vieira was deemed surplus to requirements after guiding the team to their first-ever Asian title, and he was replaced with former Norway manager Egil Olsen. Olsen lasted just six games and was replaced after a 1-1 draw with China in World Cup qualifying by former Asian Coach of the Year Adnan Hamed, in his fifth stint as head coach of the national side. He made a valiant attempt to arrest the team's slide and by the last round of matches the Iraqis stood on the verge of progressing to the

INTERNATIONAL HONOURS
Qualified for the FIFA World Cup finals 1986   AFC Asian Cup 2007
Asian Games 1982   AFC Youth Championship 1975 1977 1978 1988 2000   Gulf Cup 1979 1984 1988

final phase of qualifying. Victory over Australia in Dubai, where the Iraqis were forced to play their qualifiers as a result of the ongoing security problems at home, was followed by an away win against the Chinese which meant Iraq needed to defeat Qatar to progress. But a narrow 1-0 defeat against their Arab neighbours saw Qatar qualify at the expense of the Iraqis. Iraq's participants in the AFC Champions League also had disappointing showings in 2008, with champions Arbil and Al Quwa Al Jawiya both exiting the competition at the group phase.

THE FIFA BIG COUNT OF 2006

	Male	Female		Total
Number of players	500 100	39 900	Referees and Assistant Referees	600
Professionals	0		Admin, Coaches, Technical, Medical	2 300
Amateurs 18+	6 600		Number of clubs	110
Youth under 18	7 900		Number of teams	170
Unregistered	100 000		Clubs with women's teams	0
Total players	540 000		Players as % of population	2.02%

Iraqi Football Association (IFA)
Al Shaab Stadium, PO Box 484, Baghdad, Iraq
Tel +964 1 7743652   Fax +964 1 5372021
iraqfed1948@yahoo.com   www.iraqfootball.org
President: HUSSAIN Mohammed Saeed   General Secretary: AHMED A. Ibrahim
Vice-President: HUMOUD Najih   Treasurer: ABDUL KHALIQ Masounel Ahmed   Media Officer: WALID Tabra
Men's Coach: TBD   Women's Coach: AL MUMIN Husam Dr.
IFA formed: 1948   AFC: 1971   FIFA: 1950
White shirts, White shorts, White socks

RECENT INTERNATIONAL MATCHES PLAYED BY IRAQ

2006	Opponents		Score	Venue	Comp	Scorers	Att	Referee
15-03	Saudi Arabia	D	2-2	Jeddah	Fr	Mohammed Nassir [40], Haidar Abdul Amir [92+]		Al Hamdan KSA
15-07	Syria	W	3-1	Damascus	Fr	Emad Mohammed [33], Younis Mahmoud 2 [45 82p]		
21-07	Jordan	L	1-2	Amman	Fr	Younis Mahmoud [53]		
25-07	Syria	W	2-1	Damascus	Fr	Emad Mohammed [34], Saleh Sadir [60]		
9-08	Jordan	W	1-0	Amman	Fr	Younis Mahmoud [12]		
17-08	Palestine	W	3-0	Amman	ACq	Younis Mahmoud 2 [59 61], Mohammad Nasser [90]	5 000	Basma SYR
6-09	Palestine	D	2-2	Al Ain	ACq	Saleh Sadir [70], Hawar Taher [75]	1 000	Mujghef JOR
4-10	Iran	L	0-2	Amman	Fr			
11-10	Singapore	W	4-2	Al Ain	ACq	Younis Mahmoud 2 [35 68], Mahdi Kareem [60], Hawar Mohammed [93+]	3 000	Mamedov TKM
15-11	China PR	D	1-1	Changsha	ACq	Alwan Ahmad [65]		Mohd Salleh MAS
2007								
18-01	Qatar	W	1-0	Abu Dhabi	GCr1	Hawar Mohammed [40]		
21-01	Bahrain	D	1-1	Abu Dhabi	GCr1	Hawar Mohammed [11]		
24-01	Saudi Arabia	L	0-1	Abu Dhabi	GCr1			
8-06	Jordan	D	1-1	Amman	Fr	Ahmed Menajed [25]		
12-06	Jordan	D	0-0	Amman	Fr			
16-06	Iran	D	0-0	Amman	WAr1			
18-06	Palestine	W	1-0	Amman	WAr1	Hawar Mohammed [86]		
22-06	Syria	W	3-0	Amman	WAsf	Younis Mahmoud [10p], Ahmad Manajid [42], Saleh Sadir [85]		
24-06	Iran	L	1-2	Amman	WAf	Saleh Sadir [86p]		
29-06	Korea Republic	L	0-3	Jeju	Fr		32 642	Tojo JPN
2-07	Uzbekistan	L	0-2	Paju	Fr			
7-07	Thailand	D	1-1	Bangkok	ACr1	Younis Mahmoud [32]	30 000	Kwon Jong Chul
13-07	Australia	W	3-1	Bangkok	ACr1	Nashat Akram [22], Hawar Mohammed [60], Karrar Jassim [86]	7 884	Karim BHR
16-07	Oman	D	0-0	Bangkok	ACr1		500	Maillet SEY
21-07	Vietnam	W	2-0	Bangkok	ACqf	Younis Mahmoud 2 [2 65]	9 720	Nishimura JPN
25-07	Korea Republic	D	0-0	Kuala Lumpur	ACsf	W 4-3p	12 500	Al Fadhli KUW
29-07	Saudi Arabia	W	1-0	Jakarta	ACf	Younis Mahmoud [73]	60 000	Shield AUS
16-10	Qatar	L	2-3	Doha	Fr	Ahmed Saleh [20], Emad Mohamed [79]		
22-10	Pakistan	W	7-0	Lahore	WCq	Nashat Akram [17], Mahdi Kareem 4 [23 49 88 89], Jasim Al Hamd [70], Emad Mohammed [83]	2 500	Chynybekov KGZ
28-10	Pakistan	D	0-0	Damascus	WCq		8 000	Al Fadhli KUW
2008								
24-01	Jordan	D	1-1	Dubai	Fr	Ahmad Manajid [19]		
31-01	UAE	W	1-0	Abu Dhabi	Fr	Hawar Mohammed [25]		
6-02	China PR	D	1-1	Dubai	WCq	Hawar Mohammed [51]	11 000	Torky IRN
21-03	Kuwait	D	0-0	Kuwait City	Fr			
26-03	Qatar	L	0-2	Doha	WCq		13 000	Nishimura JPN
17-05	Syria	L	1-2	Damascus	Fr	Mahdi Kareem [67]		
25-05	Thailand	L	1-2	Bangkok	Fr	Nashat Akram [88]		
1-06	Australia	L	0-1	Brisbane	WCq		48 678	Irmatov UZB
7-06	Australia	W	1-0	Dubai	WCq	Emad Mohammed [27]	8 000	Matsumura JPN
14-06	China PR	W	2-1	Tianjin	WCq	Emad Mohammed [41], Nashrat Akram [65]	39 000	Bashir SIN
22-06	Qatar	L	0-1	Dubai	WCq		10 000	Al Badwawi UAE

Fr = Friendly • WA = West Asian Federation Championship • AC = AFC Asian Cup • GC = Gulf Cup • WC = FIFA World Cup
q = qualifier • r1 = first round group • qf = quarter-final • sf = semi-final • f = final

IRAQ NATIONAL TEAM RECORDS AND RECORD SEQUENCES

Records				Sequence records				
Victory	10-1	BHR 1966	Wins	8	1985	Clean sheets	5	Four times
Defeat	1-7	TUR 1959	Defeats	5	1967-1969	Goals scored	21	1993-1996
Player Caps	126	Hussein Saeed	Undefeated	17	1982-84, 1988-89	Without goal	3	2003-2004
Player Goals	63	Hussein Saeed	Without win	9	1967-1971	Goals against	22	2004-2005

REPUBLIC OF IRAQ; AL JUMHURIYAH AL IRAQIYAH

Capital	Baghdad	Language	Arabic, Kurdish			Independence	1932
Population	26 783 383	Area	437 072 km²	Density	58 per km²	% in cities	75%
GDP per cap	$1500	Dailling code	+964	Internet	.iq	GMT + / -	+3

MEDALS TABLE

		Overall			League			Cup			Asia			City	Stadium	Cap'ty	DoF
		G	S	B	G	S	B	G	S	G	S	B					
1	Al Zawra'a	25	7	1	11	5	1	14	1		1		Baghdad	Al Zawra'a Stadium	10 000	1969
2	Al Quwa Al Jawia	11	12	7	6	9	7	5	3				Baghdad	Al Quwa Al Jawia Stadium	10 000	1931
3	Al Talaba	7	13	4	5	6	4	2	6		1		Baghdad	Al Talaba Stadium	10 000	1977
4	Al Karkh (ex Rasheed)	5	3	1	3	2	1	2			1		Baghdad	Al Karkh Stadium	6 000	1963
5	Al Jaish	3	6		1	2		2	4				Baghdad	Al Jaish Stadium	6 000	1974
6	Al Shurta	2	9	8	2	3	8		5		1		Baghdad	Al Kashafa Stadium	12 000	1938
7	Al Mina'a	1	1	1	1	1	1						Basra	Al Mina'a Stadium	10 000	1931
8	Al Sina'a	1		2				2	1				Baghdad	Al Sina'a Stadium	6 000	1974
9	Arbil FC	1			1								Arbil	Franso Hariri	40 000	1958
	Salah al Deen	1			1								Tikrit			
11	Al Shabab		3	1		1			3				Baghdad			
12	Najaf FC		2	1	2	1							Najaf	Al Najaf Stadium	12 000	1961

RECENT LEAGUE AND CUP RECORD

	Championship						Cup		
Year	Champions	Pts	Runners-up	Pts	Third	Pts	Winners	Score	Runners-up
1995	Al Zawra'a	120	Al Quwa Al Jawia	107	Al Najaf	107	Al Zawra'a	3-0	Al Jaish
1996	Al Zawra'a	55	Al Najaf	38	Al Shurta	37	Al Zawra'a	2-1	Al Shurta
1997	Al Quwa Al Jawia	69	Al Zawra'a	67	Al Talaba	60	Al Quwa Al Jawia	1-1 8-7p	Al Shurta
1998	Al Shurta	73	Al Quwa Al Jawia	71	Al Zawra'a	70	Al Zawra'a	1-1 4-3p	Al Quwa Al Jawia
1999	Al Zawra'a	57	Al Talaba	53	Al Quwa Al Jawia	47	Al Zawra'a	1-0	Al Talaba
2000	Al Zawra'a	114	Al Quwa Al Jawia	110	Al Shurta	110	Al Zawra'a	0-0 4-3p	Al Quwa Al Jawia
2001	Al Zawra'a	70	Al Quwa Al Jawia	62	Al Shurta	60	No tournament held		
2002	Al Talaba	91	Al Quwa Al Jawia	85	Al Shurta	80	Al Talaba	1-0	Al Shurta
2003	Championship abandoned						Al Talaba	1-0	Al Shurta
2004	Championship abandoned						No tournament held		
2005	Al Quwa Al Jawia	2-0	Al Mina'a				No tournament held		
2006	Al Zawra'a	†	Al Quwa Al Jawia				No tournament held		
2007	Arbil	1-0	Al Quwa Al Jawia				No tournament held		
2008							No tournament held		

† Won 4-3 on penalties after a 0-0 draw

IRAQ 2007-08
FIRST ROUND GROUP 1 SOUTH

	Pl	W	D	L	F	A	Pts
Karbala †	16	12	2	2	27	12	38
Al Najaf †	16	9	5	2	23	9	32
Al Mina'a †	16	8	6	2	19	10	30
Nafir Al Janob	16	5	6	5	16	14	21
Maysan Umara	16	4	7	5	16	17	19
Kufa	16	4	5	7	13	15	17
Samawa	16	3	7	6	11	18	16
Furat	16	4	2	10	17	33	14
Shatra Dhi Qar	16	2	2	12	12	26	8

26/11/2007 - 29/04/2008 • † Qualified for the next round

IRAQ 2007-08
FIRST ROUND GROUP 2 NORTH

	Pl	W	D	L	F	A	Pts
Arbil †	14	9	4	1	21	5	31
Duhok †	14	9	3	2	16	6	30
Pires Duhok †	14	6	4	4	20	16	22
Kirkuk	14	6	3	5	18	17	21
Sulamaniya	14	4	7	3	16	17	19
Samara'a	14	3	5	6	10	16	14
Sirwan Sulamaniya	14	2	4	8	9	14	10
Zakho Duhok	14	0	4	10	5	24	4

26/11/2007 - 1/05/2008 • † Qualified for the next round

IRAQ 2007-08
FIRST ROUND GROUP 3 CENTRAL

	Pl	W	D	L	F	A	Pts
Al Shurta †	22	13	8	1	40	14	47
Al Quwa Al Jawiya †	21	13	4	4	39	13	43
Kahrabaa †	22	10	8	4	30	10	38
Al Zawra'a †	22	10	7	5	24	12	37
Al Talaba	22	9	9	4	25	17	36
Al Sina'a	22	9	8	5	24	16	35
Bareed	22	8	6	8	25	29	30
Al Nafit	22	6	9	7	18	24	27
Ramadi	22	5	6	11	26	42	21
Al Jaish	22	3	6	13	14	39	15
Al Shula	21	3	4	14	14	41	13
Al Adala	22	3	3	16	11	33	12

26/11/2007 - 3/05/2008 • † Qualified for the next round

The end of season play-offs were held in July and August 2008 and will be included in next year's Almanack of World Football

ISL – ICELAND

NATIONAL TEAM RECORD
JULY 10TH 2006 TO JULY 12TH 2010

PL	W	D	L	F	A	%
20	5	4	11	18	33	35

FIFA/COCA-COLA WORLD RANKING

1993	1994	1995	1996	1997	1998	1999	2000	2001	2002	2003	2004	2005	2006	2007	High	
47	39	50	60	72	64	43	50	52	58	58	93	94	93	90	37	09/94

2007–2008												Low	
08/07	09/07	10/07	11/07	12/07	01/08	02/08	03/08	04/08	05/08	06/08	07/08	117	08/07
117	80	79	89	90	87	89	89	86	85	85	98		

FH Hafnarfjördur, the most successful club in Iceland in the current decade, were denied a fourth straight title when they lost at home to Valur, one of the traditional giants, in the penultimate round of fixtures in the 2007 championship. That gave Valur a point lead going into their final match which they won to secure their first title since 1987. Incredibly, FH had led the league standings for 60 rounds of games up until that defeat - a run stretching back to July 19, 2004 - but there was some compensation the following week when they beat second division Fjölnir 2-1 in the Cup Final thanks to a brace of goals by Matthias Gudmundsson. Crucial to FH's recent dominance has

INTERNATIONAL HONOURS
None

been coach Olafur Johannesson and after a wretched Euro 2008 qualifying campaign he was the natural replacement for Eyjólfur Sverrisson who stepped down as national team coach. With just two wins in the Euro 2008 qualifiers - both against Northern Ireland - Iceland finished sixth in their group, just a point ahead of Liechtenstein and although their decline in fortunes has more to do with rising standards among other teams, there was no disguising the disappointment. Team captain Eidur Gudjohnsen did reach one landmark of note, his two goals against Latvia in October 2007 taking him past past Rikhardur Jónsson's record of 17 international goals.

THE FIFA BIG COUNT OF 2006

	Male	Female		Total
Number of players	25 108	7 300	Referees and Assistant Referees	1 044
Professionals	408		Admin, Coaches, Technical, Medical	750
Amateurs 18+	5 100		Number of clubs	97
Youth under 18	16 000		Number of teams	870
Unregistered	5 100		Clubs with women's teams	48
Total players	32 408		Players as % of population	10.82%

Knattspyrnusamband Islands (KSI)
The Football Association of Iceland, Laugardal, Reykjavík 104, Iceland
Tel +354 5102900   Fax +354 5689793.
ksi@ksi.is   www.ksi.is
President: THORNSTEINSSON Geir   General Secretary: HAKONARSON Thorir
Vice-President: GEORGSSON Ludvik   Treasurer: SIVERTSEN Gudrun Inga   Media Officer: SAMARASON Omar
Men's Coach: JOHANNESSON Olafur   Women's Coach: EYJOLFSSON Siggi
KSI formed: 1947.   UEFA: 1954   FIFA: 1947
Blue shirts with red and white trimmings, Blue shorts, Blue socks or White shirts with blue trimmings, Blue shirts, White socks

RECENT INTERNATIONAL MATCHES PLAYED BY ICELAND

2004 Opponents	Score	Venue	Comp	Scorers	Att	Referee
31-03 Albania	L 1-2	Tirana	Fr	Gudjónsson.Th 66	12 000	Bertini ITA
28-04 Latvia	D 0-0	Riga	Fr		6 500	Shmolik BLR
30-05 Japan	L 2-3	Manchester	Fr	Helguson 2 5 50	1 500	Riley ENG
5-06 England	L 1-6	Manchester	Fr	Helguson 42	43 500	Wegereef NED
18-08 Italy	W 2-0	Reykjavík	Fr	Gudjohnsen.E 17, Einarsson 19	20 204	Frojdfeldt SWE
4-09 Bulgaria	L 1-3	Reykjavík	WCq	Gudjohnsen.E 51p	5 014	Hamer LUX
8-09 Hungary	L 2-3	Budapest	WCq	Gudjohnsen.E 39, Sigurdsson.I 78	5 461	Ovrebo NOR
9-10 Malta	D 0-0	Ta'Qali	WCq		1 130	Corpodean ROU
13-10 Sweden	L 1-4	Reykjavík	WCq	Gudjohnsen.E 66	7 037	Busacca SUI
2005						
26-03 Croatia	L 0-4	Zagreb	WCq		17 912	Damon RSA
30-03 Italy	D 0-0	Padova	Fr		16 697	Hamer LUX
4-06 Hungary	L 2-3	Reykjavík	WCq	Gudjohnsen.E 17, Sigurdsson.K 68	4 613	Cardoso Batista POR
8-06 Malta	W 4-1	Reykjavík	WCq	Thorvaldsson.G 27, Gudjohnsen.E 33 Gudmundsson.T 74, Gunnarsson.V 84	4 887	Skomina SVN
17-08 South Africa	W 4-1	Reykjavík	Fr	Steinsson 25, Vidarsson 42, Helguson 67, Gunnarsson.V 73		
3-09 Croatia	L 1-3	Reykjavík	WCq	Gudjohnsen.E 24	5 520	Stark GER
7-09 Bulgaria	L 2-3	Sofia	WCq	Steinsson 9, Hreidarsson 16	18 000	Demirlek TUR
7-10 Poland	L 2-3	Warsaw	Fr	Sigurdsson.K 15, Sigurdsson.H 39	7 500	Sukhina RUS
12-10 Sweden	L 1-3	Stockholm	WCq	Arnason 11	33 716	Ivanov.V RUS
2006						
28-02 Trinidad and Tobago	L 0-2	London	Fr		7 890	
15-08 Spain	D 0-0	Reykjavík	Fr		12 327	Stokes IRL
2-09 Northern Ireland	W 3-0	Belfast	ECq	Thorvaldsson 13, Hreidarsson 20, Gudjohnsen.E 37	13 522	Skjerven NOR
6-09 Denmark	L 0-2	Reykjavík	ECq		10 007	Ivanov.N RUS
7-10 Latvia	L 0-4	Riga	ECq		6 800	Kelly IRL
11-10 Sweden	L 1-2	Reykjavík	ECq	Vidarsson 6	8 725	Gilewski POL
2007						
28-03 Spain	L 0-1	Palma	ECq		18 326	Duhamel FRA
2-06 Liechtenstein	D 1-1	Reykjavík	ECq	Gunnarsson.B 27	5 139	Kaldma EST
6-06 Sweden	L 0-5	Stockholm	ECq		33 358	Hamer LUX
22-08 Canada	D 1-1	Reykjavík	Fr	Thorvaldsson 65	4 359	Asumaa FIN
8-09 Spain	D 1-1	Reykjavík	ECq	Hallfredsson 40	9 483	Stark GER
12-09 Northern Ireland	W 2-1	Reykjavík	ECq	Armann Bjornsson 6, OG 91+	7 727	Baskakov RUS
13-10 Latvia	L 2-4	Reykjavík	ECq	Gudjohnsen 2 4 52	5 865	Dean ENG
17-10 Liechtenstein	L 0-3	Vaduz	ECq		2 589	Zografos GRE
21-11 Denmark	L 0-3	Copenhagen	ECq		15 393	Benquerenca POR
2008						
2-02 Belarus	L 0-2	Ta'Qali	Fr			
4-02 Malta	L 0-1	Ta'Qali	Fr			
6-02 Armenia	W 2-0	Ta'Qali	Fr	Gudmundsson 45, Thorvaldsson 72		Attard MLT
16-03 Faroe Islands	W 3-0	Kopavogur	Fr	Saevarsson.J 45, OG 72, Gudmundsson 80	400	Skjerven NOR
26-03 Slovakia	W 2-1	Zilina	Fr	Thorvaldsson 71, Gudjohnsen 82	4 120	Lehner AUT
28-05 Wales	L 0-1	Reykjavík	Fr		5 322	McCourt NIR

Fr = Friendly match • EC = UEFA EURO 2008 • WC = FIFA World Cup • q = qualifier

ICELAND NATIONAL TEAM RECORDS AND RECORD SEQUENCES

Records			Sequence records					
Victory	9-0	FRO 1985	Wins	4	2000	Clean sheets	3	1984
Defeat	2-14	DEN 1967	Defeats	10	1978-1980	Goals scored	7	Three times
Player Caps	104	Rúnar Kristinsson	Undefeated	11	1998-1999	Without goal	6	1977-1978
Player Goals	20	Eidur Gudjohnsen	Without win	17	1977-1980	Goals against	19	1978-1981

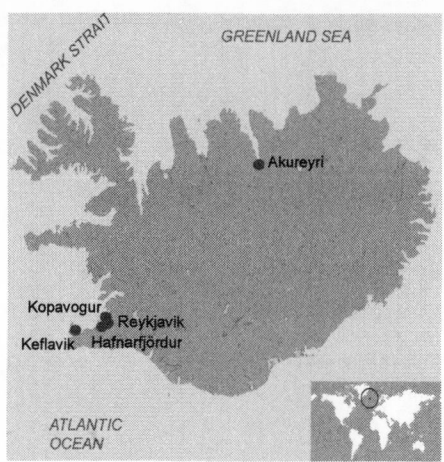

GREENLAND SEA

Kopavogur Reykjavik
Keflavik Hafnarfjördur

Akureyri

ATLANTIC
OCEAN

MAJOR CITIES/TOWNS
Population '000

1	Reykjaveik	115
2	Kópavogur	26
3	Hafnarfjörðor	23
4	Akureyri	17
5	Garðabær	9
6	Keflavík	7
7	Mosfellsbær	7
8	Selfoss	5
9	Akranes	5
10	Seltjarnarnes	4
11	Vestmannæyjar	4
12	Njarðvík	2
13	Sauðárkrókur	2
14	Grindavík	2
15	Isafjörður	2
16	Alftanes	2
17	Húsavík	2
18	Egilsstaðir	2
19	Hveragerði	1
20	Borgarnes	1
21	Höfn	1
22	Garður	1
23	Neskaupstaður	1
24	Sandgerði	1

REPUBLIC OF ICELAND; LYDVELDID ISLAND

Capital Reykjavík	Language Icelandic		Independence 1918		
Population 299 388	Area 103 000 km²	Density 3 per km²	% in cities 92%		
GDP per cap $30 900	Dailling code +354	Internet .is	GMT + / - 0		

MEDALS TABLE

	Overall G S B	League G S B	Cup G S	Europe G S B	City	Stadium	Cap'ty	DoF
1 KR Reykjavík	34 30 12	24 26 12	10 4		Reykjavík	KR-Völlur	2 781	1899
2 Valur	29 20 18	20 17 18	9 3		Reykjavík	Hlidarendi	4 590	1911
3 IA Akranes	27 21 13	18 12 13	9 9		Akranes	Akranesvöllur	2 780	1946
4 Fram	25 26 15	18 17 15	7 9		Reykjavík	Laugardalsvöllur	7 176	1908
5 Keflavík IF	8 7 7	4 2 7	4 5		Keflavík	Keflavíkurvöllur	4 957	1929
6 IBV Vestmannæyjar	7 12 7	3 6 7	4 6		Vestmannæyjar	Hásteinsvöllur	2 384	1945
7 Víkingur	6 8 8	5 7 8	1 1		Reykjavík	Víkin	1 249	1908
8 FH Hafnarfjördur	4 8 1	3 5 1	1 3		Hafnarfjördur	Kaplakrikavöllur	6 738	1929
9 Fylkir	2 2	2	2		Reykjavík	Fylkisvöllur	2 872	1967
10 KA Akureyri	1 3	1	3		Akureyri	Akureyrarvöllur	2 000	1928
11 IBA Akureyri	1 4	4 1			Akureyri	Akureyrarvöllur	2 000	1928
12 Leiftur	1 3	3	1		Olafsfjördur	Olafsfjördurvöllur	1 000	1931
13 Grindavík	1 2	2	1		Grindavík	Grindavíkurvöllur	1 750	1935
14 Breiðablik Kópavogur	1 1	1	1		Kópavogur	Kópavogsvöllur	5 501	1950
15 Vídir Gardur	1		1		Gardi	Gardsvöllur	1 500	1936
16 Fjölnir	1		1		Reykjavík	Fjölnisvöllur	1 000	1988
17 Thór Akureyri	2	2			Akureyri	Akureyrarvöllur	2 000	1915
Thróttur					Reykjavík	Valbjarnarvöllur	2 500	1949

RECENT LEAGUE AND CUP RECORD

	Championship						Cup		
Year	Champions	Pts	Runners-up	Pts	Third	Pts	Winners	Score	Runners-up
1995	IA Akranes	49	KR Reykjavík	35	IBV Vestmannæyjar	31	KR Reykjavík	2-1	Fram Reykjavík
1996	IA Akranes	40	KR Reykjavík	37	Leiftur	29	IA Akranes	2-1	IBV Vestmannæyjar
1997	IBV Vestmannæyjar	40	IA Akranes	35	Leiftur	30	Keflavík	1-1 0-0 5-4p	IBV Vestmannæyjar
1998	IBV Vestmannæyjar	38	KR Reykjavík	33	IA Akranes	30	IBV Vestmannæyjar	2-0	Leiftur
1999	KR Reykjavík	45	IBV Vestmannæyjar	38	Leiftur	26	KR Reykjavík	3-1	IA Akranes
2000	KR Reykjavík	37	Fylkir Reykjavík	35	Grindavík	30	IA Akranes	2-1	IBV Vestmannæyjar
2001	IA Akranes	36	IBV Vestmannæyjar	36	FH Hafnarfjördur	32	Fylkir Reykjavík	2-2 5-4p	KA Akureyri
2002	KR Reykjavík	36	Fylkir Reykjavík	34	Grindavík	29	Fylkir Reykjavík	3-1	Fram Reykjavík
2003	KR Reykjavík	33	FH Hafnarfjördur	33	IA Akranes	30	IA Akranes	1-0	FH Hafnarfjördur
2004	FH Hafnarfjördur	37	IBV Vestmannæyjar	31	IA Akranes	31	Keflavík	3-0	KA Akureyri
2005	FH Hafnarfjördur	48	Valur Reykjavik	32	IA Akranes	32	Valur Reykjavík	1-0	Fram Reykjavík
2006	FH Hafnarfjördur	36	KR Reykjavík	30	Valur Reykjavík	29	Keflavík	2-0	KR Reykjavík
2007	Valur Reykjavík	38	FH Hafnarfjördur	37	IA Akranes	30	FH Hafnarfjördur	2-1	Fjölnir Reykjavík

ICELAND 2007

URVALSDEILD (1)

	Pl	W	D	L	F	A	Pts	Valur	FH	IA	Fylkir	Breiðablik	Keflavík	Fram	KR	HK	Vikingur
Valur Reykjavík †	18	11	5	2	41	20	38		4-1	2-2	2-4	2-2	2-2	1-1	2-1	1-0	3-1
FH Hafnarfjördur	18	11	4	3	42	26	37	0-2		1-1	0-0	2-1	3-2	3-3	5-1	4-0	4-1
IA Akranes	18	8	6	4	34	27	30	2-1	2-3		0-2	2-1	2-1	2-2	3-1	4-1	1-0
Fylkir Reykjavík	18	8	5	5	23	18	29	1-2	1-2	2-2		0-3	4-0	1-1	0-0	1-0	1-0
Breiðablik	18	5	9	4	29	20	24	0-0	4-3	3-0	0-1		2-2	2-2	1-1	3-0	1-1
Keflavík	18	5	6	7	26	32	21	1-3	1-2	3-3	1-0	0-3		2-1	1-1	3-0	0-0
Fram Reykjavík	18	3	7	8	25	31	16	0-2	0-2	2-4	3-1	1-0	2-2		1-1	3-0	0-2
KR Reykjavík	18	3	7	8	17	30	16	0-3	0-2	1-1	1-1	1-1	1-2	2-1		3-2	1-2
HK Kópavogur	18	4	4	10	17	35	16	1-4	2-2	1-0	1-2	1-1	2-1	2-1	2-0		2-2
Vikingur Reykjavík	18	3	5	10	15	30	14	1-5	1-3	0-3	0-1	1-1	1-2	2-1	0-1	0-0	

12/05/2007 - 29/09/2007 • † Qualified for the UEFA Champions League • ‡ Qualified for the UEFA Cup
Top scorers: Jonas Gardarsson, Fram 13; Helgi Sigurdsson, Valur 12

ICELAND 2007 1.DEILD (2)

	Pl	W	D	L	F	A	Pts
Grindavík	22	15	2	5	47	21	47
Thróttur Reykjavík	22	15	2	5	47	24	47
Fjölnir Reykjavík	22	14	3	5	61	29	45
IBV Vestmannæyjar	22	13	5	4	42	23	44
Fjarðabyggð	22	11	4	7	23	17	37
Leiknir Reykjavík	22	6	7	9	22	27	25
Thór Akureyri	22	6	6	10	33	40	24
Njarðvík	22	5	8	9	25	32	23
Stjarnan Garðabær	22	5	5	12	39	44	20
Vikingur Olafsvík	22	5	5	12	22	33	20
KA Akureyri	22	5	4	13	14	45	19
Reynir Sandgerði	22	3	7	12	22	62	16

13/05/2007 - 28/09/2007

ICELAND 2007 2.DEILD (3)

	Pl	W	D	L	F	A	Pts
Haukar Hafnarfjördur	18	12	6	0	46	16	42
Selfoss	18	11	3	4	39	17	36
KS/Leiftur Siglufjörður	18	10	6	2	36	17	36
IR Reykjavík	18	8	8	2	40	19	32
Afturelding Mosfellsbær	18	8	2	8	26	23	26
Höttur Egilsstaðir	18	7	2	9	25	28	23
Völsungur Húsavík	18	7	2	9	22	26	23
IH Hafnarfjördur	18	3	4	11	23	38	13
Magni Grenivík	18	3	2	13	15	44	11
Sindri Hofn	18	3	1	14	20	64	10

13/05/2007 - 15/09/2007

BIKARKEPPNI 2007

Round of 16
FH Hafnarfjördur — 3
IBV Vestmannæyjar * — 0
KR Reykjavík * — 1 0p
Valur Reykjavík — 1 3p
Keflavík — 1
Thróttur Reykjavík * — 0
HK Kópavogur — 1
Breiðablik * — 3
Fylkir Reykjavík — 4
Thór Akureyri * — 1
Vikingur Reykjavík — 1
IA Akranes * — 2
Haukar Hafnarfjördur * — 2 4p
Fram Reykjavík — 2 3p
Fjarðabyggð * — 3
Fjölnir Reykjavík — 4

Quarter–finals
FH Hafnarfjördur — 1
Valur Reykjavík * — 0
Keflavík — 3
Breiðablik * — 1
Fylkir Reykjavík * — 3
IA Akranes — 1
Haukar Hafnarfjördur — 3
Fjölnir Reykjavík * — 4

Semi–finals
FH Hafnarfjördur — 3
Breiðablik — 1
Fylkir Reykjavík — 1
Fjölnir Reykjavík — 2
Semis played at Laugardalsvøllur

Final
FH Hafnarfjördur — 2
Fjölnir Reykjavík — 1

* Home team • ‡ Qualified for the UEFA Cup

CUP FINAL
Laugardalsvollur, Reykjavik
6-10-2007, Att: 3739, Ref: Markusson
Scorers - Matthias
Gudmundsson 2 [17] [105] for FH;
Gunnar Gudmundsson [86p] for Fjölnir

ISR – ISRAEL

NATIONAL TEAM RECORD
JULY 10TH 2006 TO JULY 12TH 2010

PL	W	D	L	F	A	%
18	10	4	4	27	17	66.7

FIFA/COCA-COLA WORLD RANKING

1993	1994	1995	1996	1997	1998	1999	2000	2001	2002	2003	2004	2005	2006	2007	High	
57	42	42	52	61	43	26	41	49	46	51	48	44	44	26	**20**	04/08

	2007–2008										Low	
08/07	09/07	10/07	11/07	12/07	01/08	02/08	03/08	04/08	05/08	06/08	07/08	**71**	09/93
33	33	37	26	26	26	23	22	20	20	22	21		

May 17, 2008 is a date the Gaydamak family will remember for a long time. Not only did Beitar Jerusalem clinch a first-ever double for owner Arkady Gaydamak, but his son Alexandre saw his team Portsmouth win the FA Cup in England. A 3-0 win over closest rivals Maccabi Netanya secured a second Championship in a row for Beitar with three games to go. Four days previously, Beitar had won their first State Cup since 1989 thanks to a penalty shoot-out win against Hapoel Tel Aviv. The final had finished goalless and went to sudden death in the penalties with keeper Tvrtko Kale making the crucial save from Reueven Oved. Israeli clubs continued to attract players

INTERNATIONAL HONOURS
Qualified for the FIFA World Cup finals 1970 **AFC Asian Cup** 1964 **AFC Champions League** Hapoel Tel Aviv 1967 Maccabi Tel Aviv 1969 1971

from abroad, but they have yet to be of a calibre that has driven success in European club football, with Beitar failing to get beyond FC København in the second preliminary round of the UEFA Champions League, while Hapoel Tel Aviv finished bottom of their UEFA Cup group. The national team had an eventful Euro 2008 qualifying campaign, finishing fourth behind Croatia, Russia and England but just a solitary point separated them from eventual semi-finalists Russia in second place. Former national team coach Avram Grant had an eventful season after taking over as coach of Chelsea from Jose Mourinho, leading the club to the final of the UEFA Champions League.

THE FIFA BIG COUNT OF 2006

	Male	Female		Total
Number of players	251 516	32 350	Referees and Assistant Referees	1 350
Professionals	1 360		Admin, Coaches, Technical, Medical	10 800
Amateurs 18+	8 423		Number of clubs	280
Youth under 18	33 883		Number of teams	1 400
Unregistered	77 000		Clubs with women's teams	10
Total players	283 866		Players as % of population	4.47%

The Israel Football Association (IFA)
Ramat-Gan Stadium, 299 Aba Hilell Street, Ramat Gan 52134, Israel
Tel +972 3 6171500   Fax +972 3 5702044
r.dori@israel-football.org.il   www.israel-football.org.il
President: LUZON Avi   General Secretary: SHILO Ori
Vice-President: TBD   Treasurer: LIEBER Meir   Media Officer: LEBANONY Gil
Men's Coach: KASHTAN Dror   Women's Coach: SCHRAIER Alon
IFA formed: 1928 & 1948   UEFA: 1992 (AFC 1956-1976)   FIFA: 1929
Blue shirts with white trimmings, White shorts, Blue socks or White shirts with blue trimmings, Blue shorts, White socks

RECENT INTERNATIONAL MATCHES PLAYED BY ISRAEL

2003	Opponents	Score		Venue	Comp	Scorers	Att	Referee
20-08	Russia	W	2-1	Moscow	Fr	Nimni [52], Balili [82]	5 000	Ishchenko UKR
6-09	Slovenia	L	1-3	Ljubljana	ECq	Revivo [69]	8 000	Fandel GER
10-09	Malta	D	2-2	Antalya	ECq	Revivo [16], Abuksis [78]	300	Blareau BEL
11-10	France	L	0-3	Paris	ECq		57 900	Bolognino ITA
2004								
18-02	Azerbaijan	W	6-0	Tel Aviv	Fr	Arbeitman 3 [9 65 69], Tal [24p], Katan 2 [45 61]	13 250	Gomes Paraty POR
30-03	Lithuania	W	2-1	Tel Aviv	Fr	Balili [34], Badeer [64]	9 872	Dougal SCO
28-04	Moldova	D	1-1	Tel Aviv	Fr	Covalenco OG [31]	4 500	Corpodean ROU
27-05	Georgia	W	1-0	Tbilisi	Fr	Badeer [33]	22 000	Oriekhov UKR
18-08	Croatia	L	0-1	Zagreb	Fr		10 000	Granat POL
4-09	France	D	0-0	Paris	WCq		43 527	Temmink NED
8-09	Cyprus	W	2-1	Tel Aviv	WCq	Benayoun [64], Badeer [75]	21 872	Shmolik BLR
9-10	Switzerland	D	2-2	Tel Aviv	WCq	Benayoun 2 [9 48]	37 976	Shield AUS
17-11	Cyprus	W	2-1	Nicosia	WCq	Keisi [17], Nimni [86]	1 624	Kaldma EST
2005								
9-02	Croatia	D	3-3	Jerusalem	Fr	Balili [38], Benayoun [74], Golan [84]	4 000	Kailis CYP
26-03	Republic of Ireland	D	1-1	Tel Aviv	WCq	Souan [90]	32 150	Ivanov.V RUS
30-03	France	D	1-1	Tel Aviv	WCq	Badeer [83]	32 150	Merk GER
4-06	Republic of Ireland	D	2-2	Dublin	WCq	Yemiel [39], Nimni [46+]	36 000	Vassaras GRE
15-08	Ukraine	D	0-0	Kyiv	Fr	W 5-3p		Mikullski POL
17-08	Poland	L	2-3	Kyiv	Fr	Badir [35], Katan [47]	2 000	Karadzic SCG
3-09	Switzerland	D	1-1	Basel	WCq	Keisi [20]	30 000	Rosetti ITA
7-09	Faroe Islands	W	2-0	Tórshavn	WCq	Nimni [54], Katan [79]	2 240	VINK NED
8-10	Faroe Islands	W	2-1	Tel Aviv	WCq	Benayoun [1], Zaudberg [91+]	31 857	Brugger AUT
2006								
1-03	Denmark	L	0-2	Tel Aviv	Fr		15 762	Sippel GER
15-08	Slovenia	D	1-1	Celje	Fr	Benayoun [81]	3 000	Kralovec CZE
2-09	Estonia	W	1-0	Tallinn	ECq	Colautti [8]	7 800	Verbist BEL
6-09	Andorra	W	4-1	Nijmegan	ECq	Benayoun [9], Ben Shushan [11], Gershon [43p], Tamuz [69]	400	Zrnic BIH
7-10	Russia	D	1-1	Moscow	ECq	Ben Shushan [84]	22 000	Meyer GER
15-11	Croatia	L	3-4	Tel Aviv	ECq	Colautti 2 [8 89], Benayoun [68]	35 000	Iturralde Gonzalez ESP
2007								
7-02	Ukraine	D	1-1	Tel Aviv	Fr	Badeer [38]	12 000	S. Rodriguez ESP
24-03	England	D	0-0	Tel Aviv	ECq		38 000	Ovrebø NOR
28-03	Estonia	W	4-0	Tel Aviv	ECq	Idan Tal [19], Colautti [29], Sahar 2 [77 80]	21 000	Cüneyt Cakir TUR
2-06	FYR Macedonia	W	2-1	Skopje	ECq	Itzhaki [11], Colautti [44]	12 000	Kircher GER
6-06	Andorra	W	2-0	Andorra-La-Vella	ECq	Tamuz [37], Colautti [53]	680	Stokes IRL
22-08	Belarus	L	1-2	Minsk	Fr	Gershon [29p]	10 000	Malzhinskas LTU
8-09	England	L	0-3	London	ECq		85 372	Vink NED
13-10	Croatia	L	0-1	Zagreb	ECq		30 084	Stark GER
17-10	Belarus	W	2-1	Tel Aviv	Fr	Bruchian [37], Alberman [72]	4 362	Georgiev BUL
17-11	Russia	W	2-1	Tel Aviv	ECq	Barda [10], Golan [92+]	29 787	Farina ITA
21-11	FYR Macedonia	W	1-0	Tel Aviv	ECq	Barda [35]	2 736	Mikulski POL
2008								
6-02	Romania	W	1-0	Tel Aviv	Fr	Golan [25]	8 000	Duarte Gomez POR
26-03	Chile	W	1-0	Tel Aviv	Fr	Benayoun [30]	24 463	Velasco ESP

Fr = Friendly match • EC = UEFA EURO 2004/2008 • WC = FIFA World Cup • q = qualifier

ISRAEL NATIONAL TEAM RECORDS AND RECORD SEQUENCES

Records			Sequence records		
Victory	9-0	TPE 1988	Wins	7	1973-1974	Clean sheets	4	Four times
Defeat	1-7	EGY 1934, GER 2002	Defeats	8	1950-1956	Goals scored	9	1968-69, 2000-01
Player Caps	95	Arik Benado	Undefeated	12	1971-1973	Without goal	5	1964-1965
Player Goals	26	Mordechai Spiegler	Without win	22	1985-1988	Goals against	22	1934-1958

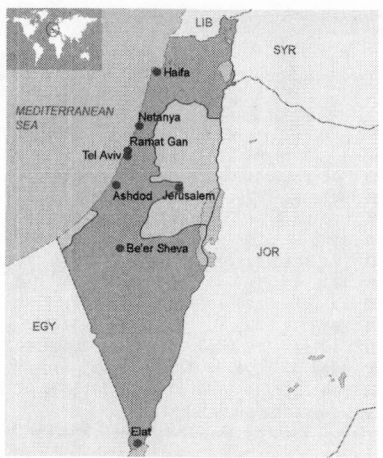

STATE OF ISRAEL; MEDINAT YISRA'EL

Capital	Jerusalem	Language	Hebrew, Arabic, English	Independence	1948
Population	6 352 117	Area	20 770 km²	Density 298 per km²	% in cities 91%
GDP per cap	$19 800	Dailling code	+972	Internet .il	GMT + / - +2

MAJOR CITIES/TOWNS

Population '000

1	Jerusalem	743
2	Tel Aviv-Jaffa	388
3	Haifa	265
4	Rishon Letzion	228
5	Ashdod	214
6	Be'er Sheva	190
7	Petah Tikva	182
8	Netanya	176
9	Holon	165
10	Ben Beraq	148
11	Ramat Gan	128
12	Bat Yam	126
13	Ashkelon	108
14	Rehoboth	106
15	Hertzelia	83
16	Kfar Saba	82
17	Bet Shemesh	78
18	Hadera	77
19	Ra'anana	73
20	Lod	67
21	Nazerat	67
22	Ramla	64
23	Nahariyya	52
24	Qiryat Atta	49

MEDALS TABLE

		Overall G S B			League G S B			Cup G S		Asia/Euro G S B			City	Stadium	Cap'ty	DoF
1	Maccabi Tel Aviv	42	20	7	18	9	7	22	11	2			Tel Aviv	Bloomfield	15 400	1906
2	Hapoel Tel Aviv	24	19	6	11	10	6	12	8	1	1		Tel Aviv	Bloomfield	15 400	1928
3	Maccabi Haifa	15	12	5	10	5	5	5	7				Haifa	Kiryat Eli'ezer	17 000	1913
4	Beitar Jerusalem	12	9	4	6	6	4	6	3				Jerusalem	Teddy Maicha	18 500	1939
5	Hapoel Petach Tikva	8	15	4	6	9	4	2	6				Petach Tikva	Petach Tikva	8 000	1935
6	Maccabi Netanya	6	6	4	5	4	4	1	2				Netanya	Maccabi Netanya	6 500	1942
7	Hapoel Haifa	4	7	8	1	2	8	3	5				Haifa	Kiryat Eli'ezer	17 000	1921
8	Hakoah Ramat Gan	4	1	1	2		1	2	1				Ramat Gan	Winter	8 000	1961
9	Hapoel Kfar Saba	4			1		3						Kfar Saba	Levita	4 500	1936
10	Bnei Yehuda Tel Aviv	3	6	2	1	3	2	2	3				Tel Aviv	Shchonat H'atikva	8 000	1935
11	Hapoel Beer Sheva	3	2	5	2		5	1	2				Beer Sheva	Artur Vasermil	13 000	1949
12	Maccabi Petach Tikva	2	5	1		3	1	2	2				Petach Tikva	Petach Tikva	8 000	1912
13	Beitar Tel Aviv	2	2	1		1		2	2				Tel Aviv	Bloomfield	15 400	1934-2000
14	British Police	2			1			1								
15	Hapoel Ramat Gan	2			1			1					Ramat Gan	HaMakhtesh	5 500	1927

RECENT LEAGUE AND CUP RECORD

	Championship						Cup		
Year	Champions	Pts	Runners-up	Pts	Third	Pts	Winners	Score	Runners-up
1995	Maccabi Tel Aviv	63	Maccabi Haifa	58	Hapoel Beer Sheva	50	Maccabi Haifa	2-0	Hapoel Haifa
1996	Maccabi Tel Aviv	74	Maccabi Haifa	66	Beitar Jerusalem	64	Maccabi Tel Aviv	4-1	Hapoel Ironi RL
1997	Beitar Jerusalem	69	Hapoel Petah Tikva	60	Hapoel Beer Sheva	60	Hapoel Beer Sheva	1-0	Maccabi Tel Aviv
1998	Beitar Jerusalem	69	Hapoel Tel Aviv	68	Hapoel Haifa	60	Maccabi Haifa	2-0	Hapoel Jerusalem
1999	Hapoel Haifa	71	Maccabi Tel Aviv	63	Maccabi Haifa	60	Hapoel Tel Aviv	1-1 3-1p	Beitar Jerusalem
2000	Hapoel Tel Aviv	85	Maccabi Haifa	76	Hapoel Petah Tikva	74	Hapoel Tel Aviv	2-2 4-2p	Beitar Jerusalem
2001	Maccabi Haifa	82	Hapoel Tel Aviv	75	Hapoel Haifa	71	Maccabi Tel Aviv	3-0	Maccabi Petah Tikva
2002	Maccabi Haifa	75	Hapoel Tel Aviv	67	Maccabi Tel Aviv	57	Maccabi Tel Aviv	0-0 5-4p	Maccabi Haifa
2003	Maccabi Tel Aviv	69	Maccabi Haifa	69	Hapoel Tel Aviv	67	Hapoel Ramat Gan	1-1 5-4p	Hapoel Beer Sheva
2004	Maccabi Haifa	63	Maccabi Tel Aviv	57	Hapoel Petah Tikva	56	Hapoel Bnei Sakhnin	4-1	Hapoel Haifa
2005	Maccabi Haifa	71	Maccabi Petah Tikva	60	Ashdod	50	Maccabi Tel Aviv	2-2 5-3p	Maccabi Herzliya
2006	Maccabi Haifa	75	Hapoel Tel Aviv	59	Beitar Jerusalem	58	Hapoel Tel Aviv	1-0	Bnei Yehuda
2007	Beitar Jerusalem	67	Maccabi Netanya	54	Maccabi Tel Aviv	54	Hapoel Tel Aviv	1-1 5-4p	Hapoel Ashkelon
2008	Beitar Jerusalem	67	Maccabi Netanya	58	Ironi Kiriat Shmona	56	Beitar Jerusalem	0-0 5-4p	Hapoel Tel Aviv

ISRAEL 2007–08
LIGAT HA'AL

	Pl	W	D	L	F	A	Pts	Beitar	Mac Netanya	Ironi	Hapoel BS	Mac Haifa	Mac Tel Aviv	Hapoel TA	Ashdod	Bnei Yehuda	Maccabi PT	H Kfar Saba	Mac Herzliya
Beitar Jerusalem †	33	20	7	6	61	23	67		2-0	3-0	0-0	0-1	1-2	1-0	2-0	1-1	1-0	5-0	4-0
Maccabi Netanya ‡	33	16	10	7	40	24	58	0-1		0-0	1-2	1-2	2-1	0-2	1-0	0-0	3-0	3-1	0-0
Ironi Kiriat Shmona	33	15	11	7	43	34	56	0-3	3-2		0-0	0-1	1-1	1-0	3-2	1-2	2-1	2-1	2-2
Hapoel Bnei Sakhnin	33	15	10	8	35	29	55	2-2	0-0	1-1		0-0	1-1	1-0	3-2	1-0	0-1	3-0	1-2
Maccabi Haifa	33	13	8	12	38	27	47	0-0	0-1	0-2	1-0		3-1	3-3	2-0	3-0	2-0	1-0	3-0
Maccabi Tel Aviv	33	11	8	14	43	43	41	0-0	0-2	0-0	2-2	2-1		0-0	3-1	0-3	1-3	1-1	3-1
Hapoel Tel Aviv ‡	33	12	5	16	35	40	41	1-2	3-1	0-1	0-1	2-0	0-1		2-0	1-1	1-0	0-2	1-0
MS Ashdod	33	11	6	16	36	52	39	1-2	1-0	1-6	0-0	2-0	3-1	1-0		2-0	0-0	1-1	2-1
Bnei Yehuda Tel Aviv	33	11	5	17	31	43	38	0-3	1-2	1-1	3-0	0-3	0-4	1-0	1-1		2-3	3-2	2-0
Maccabi Petah Tikva	33	10	7	16	28	39	37	1-2	0-0	0-1	3-1	2-0	0-4	1-1	3-2	2-1		0-1	1-0
Hapoel Kfar Saba	33	9	10	14	37	54	37	1-1	0-4	1-2	2-3	1-3	0-0	0-3	1-0	0-3	2-3		3-3
Maccabi Hertzelia	33	7	9	17	32	51	30	1-1	1-2	0-2	1-3	0-1	0-2	0-1	1-3	1-0	2-3	1-1	

18/08/2007 - 1/06/2008 • † Qualified for the UEFA Champions League • ‡ Qualified for the UEFA Cup

Top scorers: Samuel Yeboah, Hapoel Kfar Saba 15; Rômulo, Beitar 12; Yannick Kamanan, Maccabi Tel Aviv 12; Moshe Biton, Bnei Yehuda 12

ISRAEL 2007–08
LIGA LEUMIT (2)

	Pl	W	D	L	F	A	Pts
Hakoah Ramat Gan	33	16	9	8	41	30	57
Hapoel Petah Tikva	33	16	6	11	40	27	54
Hapoel Haifa	33	15	7	11	36	29	52
Hapoel Be'er Sheva	33	14	9	10	31	18	51
Bnei Lod	33	14	7	12	41	42	49
Hapoel Ramat Gan	33	13	9	11	33	38	48
Hapoel Ranana	33	11	13	9	34	31	46
Ironi Ramat Hasharon	33	11	10	12	33	37	43
Maccabi Akhi Nazareth	33	10	11	12	37	39	41
Hapoel Acre	33	9	10	14	29	32	37
Ironi Rishon Letzion	33	7	16	10	31	38	37
Hapoel Upper Nazareth	33	5	7	21	28	53	22

17/08/2007 - 23/05/2008

ISRAEL 2007–08
LIGA ARTZIT (3)

	Pl	W	D	L	F	A	Pts
Hapoel Jerusalem	33	20	10	3	49	19	70
MI Kiriat Ata	33	19	4	10	41	28	61
Hapoel Bnei Jadida	33	14	8	11	39	29	50
Hapoel Ashkelon §2	33	12	14	7	36	32	48
Maccabi Kfar Kana §1	33	13	10	10	32	30	48
Hapoel Bnei Timra §3	33	14	8	11	37	30	47
Sektzia Nes Tziona	33	10	14	9	32	22	44
Hapoel Marmorek	33	12	8	13	34	35	44
Beitar/Shimshon TA	33	12	7	14	36	35	43
Maccabi Tirat Carmel	33	10	6	17	27	46	36
Maccabi HaShikma	33	8	7	18	42	57	31
Hapoel Kfar Shelem	33	4	4	25	26	68	16

31/08/2007 - 17/05/2008 • § = points deducted

STATE CUP 2007–08

Round of 16

Beitar Jerusalem	3
Maccabi A. Nazareth *	0
Ironi Rishon Letzion *	4
Hapoel Kfar Saba	5
Hakoah Ramat Gan *	0 5p
Hapoel Ramat Gan	0 3p
Maccabi Haifa	0
Maccabi Netanya *	1
Beitar/Shimshon TA *	2
Hapoel Petah Tikva	0
MI Kiriat Ata	1
Ironi Kiriat Shmona *	2
Bnei Yehuda Tel Aviv *	1
Ironi Ramat Hasharon	0
Hapoel Be'er Sheva *	0
Hapoel Tel Aviv	1

Quarter-finals

Beitar Jerusalem *	3
Hapoel Kfar Saba	2
Hakoah Ramat Gan *	1 1p
Maccabi Netanya	1 4p
Beitar/Shimshon TA	2
Ironi Kiriat Shmona *	1
Bnei Yehuda Tel Aviv	0
Hapoel Tel Aviv *	2

Semi-finals

Beitar Jerusalem	1
Maccabi Netanya	0
Beitar/Shimshon TA	1 7p
Hapoel Tel Aviv	1 8p

Final

Beitar Jerusalem	0 5p
Hapoel Tel Aviv ‡	0 4p

CUP FINAL
Tel Aviv, 13-05-2008

* Home team • ‡ Qualified for the UEFA Cup

ITA – ITALY

NATIONAL TEAM RECORD
JULY 10TH 2006 TO JULY 12TH 2010

PL	W	D	L	F	A	%
23	13	5	5	35	23	67.4

Two years on from their triumph in the final of the 2006 FIFA World Cup, the Italian federation once again turned to Marcelo Lippi, their victorious coach that day, following a mediocre display at Euro 2008. At the finals the Italians may have been without their inspirational captain Fabio Cannavaro, who damaged ankle ligaments just before the tournament, but against the Dutch in their opening game they were comprehensibly outplayed in a 3-0 defeat. Had it not been for the outstanding Gianluigi Buffon, the Italians would have been one of the first teams on the plane home. Once again he proved his credentials as perhaps the best goalkeepers in the world by saving a late penalty from Romania's Adrian Mutu in the next match which kept the Italians in the tournament. That left a winner-takes-all final group match against the French, where Italy played their best game of the tournament, salvaging some pride with a 2-0 win to set up a quarter-final against Spain. The Italians have a reputation for often scraping through the group stage at major tournaments and then going on to better things, but not this time. Against the Spanish the midfield was largely devoid of ideas as they played for penalties - which they then lost - and it was this lack of

INTERNATIONAL HONOURS
FIFA World Cup 1934 1938 1982 2006

Olympic Gold 1936

International Cup 1930 1935   **UEFA European Championship** 1968   **UEFA Junior Tournament** 1958 1966

UEFA U-21 Championship 1992 1994 1996 2000 2004   **UEFA U-19 Championship** 2003   **UEFA U-17 Championship** 1982 1987

UEFA Champions League Milan 1963 1969 1989 1990 1994 2003 2007, Internazionale 1964 1965, Juventus 1985 1996

ambition which cost Donadoni his job. At home, Inter and Roma once again filled the top two places in both Serie A and the Coppa Italia as for the first time in three seasons the outcome of the League was decided solely by events on the pitch. Inter secured a hat-trick of titles and then promptly replaced coach Roberto Mancini with Jose Mourinho. Once again they had built up a substantial lead, remaining unbeaten until early March, but Roma made a determined bid to catch them, only to fall short by three points. For the fourth year in a row the two also met in the Coppa Italia final, with Roma winning the Cup for a record equalling ninth time thanks to a 2-1 win in their own Stadio Olimpico. Milan's failure to qualify for the Champions League made the headlines at the end of the season as did Parma's relegation - the end of a glorious era for the club - but once again the season was marked by violence, notably the death of a Lazio fan in a motorway service station. The overall sense of gloom was added to by the below par performances of Italian clubs in Europe with the exception of Roma, who reached the Champions League quarter-finals, and of Fiorentina who lost on penalties to Rangers in the semi-final of the UEFA Cup.

Federazione Italiana Giuoco Calcio (FIGC)
Via Gregorio Allegri 14, Roma 00198, Italy
Tel +39 06 84912500   Fax +39 06 84912526
international@figc.it   www.figc.it
President: ABETE Giancarlo   General Secretary: DI SEBASTIANO Antonio
Vice-President: GUSSONI Cesare   Treasurer: TBD   Media Officer: VALENTINI Antonio
Men's Coach: LIPPI Marcello   Women's Coach: GHEDIN Pietro
FIGC formed: 1898   UEFA: 1954   FIFA: 1905
Blue shirts with white trimmings, White shorts, Blue socks or White shirts with blue trimmings, Blue shorts, White socks

RECENT INTERNATIONAL MATCHES PLAYED BY ITALY

2006	Opponents	Score		Venue	Comp	Scorers	Att	Referee
12-06	Ghana	W	2-0	Hannover	WCr1	Pirlo [40], Iaquinta [83]	43 000	Simon BRA
17-06	USA	D	1-1	Kaiserslautern	WCr1	Gilardino [22]	46 000	Larrionda URU
22-06	Czech Republic	W	2-0	Hamburg	WCr1	Materazzi [26], Inzaghi [87]	50 000	Archundia MEX
26-06	Australia	W	1-0	Kaiserslautern	WCr2	Totti [95+p]	46 000	Medina Cantalejo ESP
30-06	Ukraine	W	3-0	Hamburg	WCqf	Zambrotta [6], Toni 2 [59 69]	50 000	De Bleeckere BEL
4-07	Germany	W	2-0	Dortmund	WCsf	Grosso [119], Del Piero [121+]	65 000	Archundia MEX
9-07	France	D	1-1	Berlin	WCf	Materazzi [19], W 5-3p	69 000	Elizondo ARG
16-08	Croatia	L	0-2	Livorno	Fr		16 150	Kircher GER
2-09	Lithuania	D	1-1	Naples	ECq	Inzaghi [30]	43 440	Hansson SWE
6-09	France	L	1-3	Paris	ECq	Gilardino [20]	78 831	Fandel GER
7-10	Ukraine	W	2-0	Rome	ECq	Oddo [71p], Toni [79]	49 149	Vassaras GRE
11-10	Georgia	W	3-1	Tbilisi	ECq	De Rossi [18], Camoranesi [63], Perrotta [71]	48 000	Riley ENG
15-11	Turkey	D	1-1	Bergamo	Fr	Di Natale [39]	24 386	Busacca SUI
2007								
28-03	Scotland	W	2-0	Bari	ECq	Toni 2 [12 70]	37 600	De Bleeckere BEL
2-06	Faroe Islands	W	2-1	Torshavn	ECq	Inzaghi 2 [12 48]	5 800	Malek POL
6-06	Lithuania	W	2-0	Kaunas	ECq	Quagliarella 2 [31 45]	7 800	Vink NED
22-08	Hungary	L	1-3	Budapest	Fr	Di Natale [49]	30 000	Mejuto Ganzalez ESP
8-09	France	D	0-0	Milan	ECq		81 200	Michel SVK
12-09	Ukraine	W	2-1	Kyiv	ECq	Di Natale 2 [41 77]	41 500	Webb ENG
13-10	Georgia	W	2-0	Genoa	ECq	Pirlo [44], Grosso [84]	23 057	Davila ESP
17-10	South Africa	W	2-0	Siena	Fr	Lucarelli 2 [82 90]	7 219	Weiner GER
17-11	Scotland	W	2-1	Glasgow	ECq	Toni [2], Panucci [91+]	51 301	Mejuto Gonzalez ESP
21-11	Faroe Islands	W	3-1	Modena	ECq	Benjaminsen OG [11], Toni [36], Chiellini [41]	16 142	Meyer GER
2008								
6-02	Portugal	W	3-1	Zürich	Fr	Toni [45], Pirlo [51], Quagliarella [79]	30 500	Kever SUI
26-03	Spain	L	0-1	Elche	Fr		38 000	Stuchlik AUT
30-05	Belgium	W	3-1	Florence	Fr	Di Natale 2 [9 39], Camoranesi [49]	12 500	Atkinson ENG
9-06	Netherlands	L	0-3	Berne	ECr1		30 777	Fröjdfeldt SWE
13-06	Romania	D	1-1	Zürich	ECr1	Panucci [56]	30 585	Ovrebø NOR
17-06	France	W	2-0	Zürich	ECr1	Pirlo [25p], De Rossi [62]	30 585	Michel SVK
22-06	Spain	D	0-0	Vienna	ECqf	L 2-4p	51 178	Fandel GER

Fr = Friendly match • EC = UEFA EURO 2008 • WC = FIFA World Cup
q = qualifier • r1 = first round group • r2 = second round • qf = quarter-finals • sf = semi-finals • f = final

ITALY NATIONAL TEAM PLAYERS

	Player		Ap	G	Club	Date of Birth		Player		Ap	G	Club	Date of Birth
1	Gianluigi Buffon	GK	86	0	Juventus	28 01 1978	12	Marco Borriello	FW	3	0	Genoa	18 06 1982
2	Christian Panucci	DF	57	4	Roma	12 04 1973	13	Massimo Ambrosini	MF	35	0	Milan	29 05 1977
3	Fabio Grosso	DF	35	3	Olymp Lyonnais	28 11 1977	14	Marco Amelia	GK	6	0	Livorno	2 04 1982
4	Giorgio Chiellini	DF	13	1	Juventus	14 08 1984	15	Fabio Quagliarella	FW	9	3	Sampdoria	31 01 1983
5	Alessandro Gamberini	DF	2	0	Fiorentina	27 08 1981	16	Mauro Camoranesi	MF	39	4	Juventus	4 10 1976
6	Andrea Barzagli	DF	23	0	Palermo	8 05 1981	17	Morgan De Sanctis	GK	0	0	Sevilla	26 03 1977
7	Alessandro Del Piero	FW	89	27	Juventus	9 11 1974	18	Antonio Cassano	FW	15	3	Sampdoria	12 07 1982
8	Gennaro Gattuso	MF	60	1	Milan	9 01 1978	19	Gianluca Zambrotta	DF	75	2	Barcelona	19 02 1977
9	Luca Toni	FW	38	15	Bayern München	26 05 1977	20	Simone Perrotta	MF	43	2	Roma	17 09 1977
10	Daniele De Rossi	MF	36	5	Roma	24 07 1983	21	Andrea Pirlo	MF	49	8	Milan	19 05 1979
11	Antonio Di Natale	FW	20	7	Udinese	13 10 1977	22	Alberto Aquilani	MF	7	0	Roma	7 07 1984
							23	Marco Materazzi	DF	41	2	Internazionale	19 08 1973

The Italian squad for Euro 2008

ITALY NATIONAL TEAM RECORDS AND RECORD SEQUENCES

Records			Sequence records					
Victory	9-0	USA 1948	Wins	9	1938-1939	Clean sheets	12	1972-1974
Defeat	1-7	HUN 1924	Defeats	3	Three times	Goals scored	43	1931-1937
Player Caps	126	Paolo Maldini	Undefeated	30	1935-1939	Without goal	3	Three times
Player Goals	35	Luigi Riva	Without win	8	1958-1959	Goals against	19	1927-1930

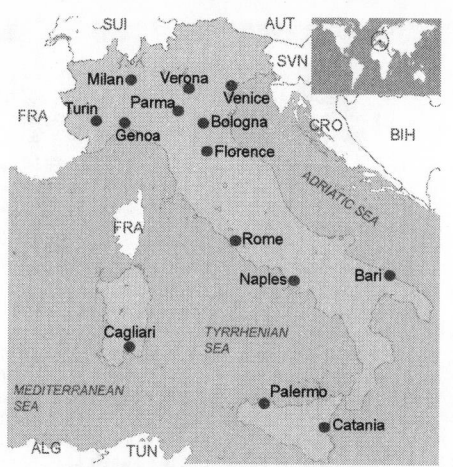

ITALIAN REPUBLIC; REPUBBLICA ITALIANA

Capital	Rome	Language	Italian	Formation	1870
Population	58 133 509	Area	301 230 km²	Density	193 per km²	% in cities	67%
GDP per cap	$26 700	Dailling code	+39	Internet	.it	GMT +/-	+1

MEDALS TABLE

		Overall			League			Cup		Europe			City	Stadium	Cap'ty	DoF
		G	S	B	G	S	B	G	S	G	S	B				
1	Juventus	42	31	19	27	19	13	9	4	6	8	6	Turin	Stadio delle Alpi	69 041	1897
2	Milan	31	24	20	17	13	16	5	6	9	5	4	Milan	Giuseppe Meazza (San Siro)	85 700	1899
3	Internazionale	26	22	22	16	13	14	5	6	5	3	8	Milan	Giuseppe Meazza (San Siro)	85 700	1908
4	Roma	13	18	7	3	10	5	9	6	1	2	2	Rome	Stadio Olimpico	82 307	1927
5	Torino	13	17	7	8	9	6	5	7		1	1	Turin	Stadio delle Alpi	69 041	1906
6	Genoa 1893	10	5	2	9	4	1	1	1			1	Genoa	Luigi Ferraris	40 117	1893
7	Fiorentina	9	11	7	2	5	5	6	3	1	3	2	Florence	Artemio Franchi	44 781	1926
8	Bologna	9	4	5	7	4	3	2				2	Bologna	Renato Dall'Ara	39 444	1909
9	Lazio	7	8	5	2	6	4	4	1	1	1	1	Rome	Stadio Olimpico	82 307	1900
10	Pro Vercelli	7	1		7	1							Vercelli	Silvio Piola	6 165	1892
11	Napoli	6	8	7	2	4	6	3	4	1		1	Naples	San Paolo	78 210	1904
12	Sampdoria	6	5	4	1	1	3	4	2	1	2	1	Genoa	Luigi Ferraris	40 117	1946
13	Parma	6	4	3		1	2	3	2	3	1	1	Parma	Ennio Tardini	28 783	1913
14	Hellas-Verona	1	3		1				3				Verona	Marc'Antonio Bentegodi	42 160	1903
15	Atalanta	1	2	1				1	2			1	Bergamo	Atleti Azzurri d'Italia	28 430	1907
	Venezia	1	2	1	1	1		1	1				Venice	Pierluigi Penzo	9 977	1907
	Vicenza	1	2	1		2			1			1	Vicenza	Romeo Menti	17 163	1902
18	Cagliari	1	1	1	1	1						1	Cagliari	Sant'Elia	24 000	1920

RECENT LEAGUE AND CUP RECORD

	Championship							Cup		
Year	Champions	Pts	Runners-up	Pts	Third	Pts		Winners	Score	Runners-up
1996	Milan	73	Juventus	65	Lazio	59		Fiorentina	1-0 2-0	Atalanta
1997	Juventus	65	Parma	64	Internazionale	59		Vicenza	0-1 3-0	Napoli
1998	Juventus	74	Internazionale	69	Udinese	64		Lazio	0-1 3-1	Milan
1999	Milan	70	Lazio	69	Fiorentina	56		Parma	1-1 2-2	Fiorentina
2000	Lazio	72	Juventus	71	Milan	61		Lazio	2-1 0-0	Internazionale
2001	Roma	75	Juventus	73	Lazio	69		Fiorentina	1-0 1-1	Parma
2002	Juventus	71	Roma	70	Internazionale	69		Parma	1-2 1-0	Juventus
2003	Juventus	72	Internazionale	65	Milan	61		Milan	4-1 2-2	Roma
2004	Milan	82	Roma	71	Juventus	69		Lazio	2-0 2-2	Juventus
2005	Juventus	86	Milan	79	Internazionale	72		Internazionale	2-0 1-0	Roma
2006	Internazionale	76	Roma	69	Milan	58		Internazionale	1-1 3-1	Roma
2007	Internazionale	97	Roma	75	Lazio	62		Roma	6-2 1-2	Internazionale
2008	Internazionale	85	Roma	82	Juventus	72		Roma	2-1	Internazionale

Juventus were stripped of the titles they won in 2005 and 2006

ITALY 2007–08

SERIE A

	Pl	W	D	L	F	A	Pts	Inter	Roma	Juventus	Fiorentina	Milan	Sampdoria	Udinese	Napoli	Atalanta	Genoa	Palermo	Lazio	Siena	Cagliari	Torino	Reggina	Catania	Empoli	Parma	Livorno
Internazionale †	38	25	10	3	69	26	85	—	1-1	1-2	2-0	2-1	3-0	1-1	2-1	2-1	4-1	2-1	3-0	2-2	2-1	4-0	2-0	2-0	1-0	3-2	2-0
Roma †	38	24	10	4	72	37	82	1-4	—	2-2	1-0	2-1	2-0	2-1	4-4	2-1	3-2	1-0	3-2	3-0	2-0	4-1	2-0	2-0	2-1	4-0	1-1
Juventus †	38	20	12	6	72	37	72	1-1	1-0	—	2-3	3-2	0-0	1-0	1-0	1-0	5-0	5-2	2-0	1-1	0-0	4-0	1-1	3-0	3-0	5-1	
Fiorentina †	38	19	9	10	55	39	66	0-2	2-1	1-1	—	0-1	2-2	1-2	0-2	3-1	1-1	0-0	3-0	5-1	2-1	2-0	2-1	3-1	3-1	1-0	
Milan ‡	38	18	10	10	66	38	64	2-1	0-1	0-0	1-1	—	1-2	4-1	5-2	2-2	2-1	1-1	1-0	3-1	0-0	5-1	1-0	1-0	1-1	1-1	
Sampdoria ‡	38	17	9	12	56	46	60	1-1	0-3	3-3	2-2	0-5	—	3-0	2-0	3-0	0-0	3-0	0-0	1-0	1-1	2-2	3-0	3-1	3-0	3-0	2-0
Udinese ‡	38	16	9	13	48	53	57	0-0	1-3	1-2	3-1	0-1	3-2	—	0-5	2-0	3-5	1-1	2-2	0-0	2-1	2-1	2-2	2-1	2-2	2-1	2-0
Napoli	38	14	8	16	50	53	50	1-0	0-2	3-1	2-0	3-1	2-0	3-1	—	2-0	1-2	1-0	2-2	0-0	2-1	1-1	1-2	1-1	1-1	2-0	1-1
Atalanta	38	12	12	14	52	56	48	0-2	1-2	0-4	2-2	2-1	4-1	0-0	5-1	—	2-0	1-3	2-1	2-2	2-2	2-2	2-2	2-0	0-4	1-2	0-3-2
Genoa	38	13	9	16	44	52	48	1-1	0-1	0-2	0-0	0-3	0-1	3-2	2-0	2-1	—	3-3	0-2	1-3	2-0	3-0	2-0	2-1	0-1	1-0	1-1
Palermo	38	12	11	15	47	57	47	0-0	0-2	3-2	2-0	2-1	0-2	1-1	2-1	0-0	2-3	—	2-2	2-3	2-1	1-1	1-1	1-0	2-0	1-1	1-0
Lazio	38	11	13	14	47	51	46	1-1	1-3	2-0	3-1	1-5	2-1	0-1	2-1	2-1	3-0	1-2	—	1-3	1-2	2-1	2-0	0-0	0-1	0-2-0	
Siena	38	9	17	12	40	45	44	2-3	3-0	1-0	1-1	1-2	1-1	1-1	1-1	1-0	1-1	0-1	2-1	—	1-0	0-0	0-0	1-1	3-0	2-0	2-3
Cagliari	38	11	9	18	40	56	42	0-2	1-2	3-2	1-1	2-0	3-0	1-2	1-1	0-2	1-0	0-1	0-1	1-0	—	3-0	2-2	1-1	2-0	1-1	0-0
Torino	38	8	16	14	36	49	40	0-1	0-0	0-1	0-1	0-1	1-0	0-1	2-1	1-0	1-1	3-1	0-0	1-1	2-0	—	2-1	1-1	0-1	4-4	1-2
Reggina	38	9	13	16	37	56	40	0-1	0-2	1-0	0-0	1-0	1-0	1-3	1-1	1-2	0-0	0-1	4-0	2-0	1-3	—	3-1	2-2	1-1	1-3	
Catania	38	8	13	17	33	45	37	0-2	1-1	1-0	1-1	1-1	1-2	0-2	0-3	0-1	2-0	3-0	1-2	1-2	1-2	1-2	1-2	—	1-0	0-0	1-0
Empoli	38	9	9	20	29	52	36	0-2	2-2	0-0	0-2	1-3	0-2	0-1	0-0	0-1	1-1	3-1	1-0	0-2	4-1	0-0	1-1	2-0	—	1-1	2-1
Parma	38	7	13	18	42	62	34	0-2	0-3	2-2	1-2	0-0	1-2	2-0	1-2	2-3	1-0	2-1	2-2	2-2	1-1	2-0	3-0	2-2	1-0	—	3-2
Livorno	38	6	12	20	35	60	30	2-2	1-1	1-3	0-3	1-4	3-1	0-0	1-2	0-1	1-1	2-4	0-1	0-1	1-1	1-0	1-0	1-0	0-1	1-1	—

25/08/2007 - 18/05/2008 • † Qualified for the UEFA Champions League • ‡ Qualified for the UEFA Cup
Top scorers: Alessandro Del Piero, Juventus 21; David Trezeguet, Juventus 20; Marco Borriello, Genoa 19; Antonio Di Natale, Udinese 17; Zlatan Ibrahimovic, Inter 17; Adrian Mutu, Fiorentina 17; Amauri, Palermo 15; Kaká, Milan 15; Goran Pandev, Lazio 14; Tommaso Rocchi, Lazio 14; Francesco Totti, Roma 14; Julio Cruz, Inter 13; Massimo Maccarone, Siena 13

ITALY 2007–08

SERIE B

	Pl	W	D	L	F	A	Pts	Chievo	Bologna	Lecce	Albinoleffe	Brescia	Pisa	Rimini	Ascoli	Mantova	Frosinone	Bari	Triestina	Grosseto	Messina	Piacenza	Modena	Vicenza	Treviso	Avellino	Ravenna	Spezia	Cesena
Chievo Verona	42	24	13	5	77	43	85	—	1-1	3-0	1-3	0-2	2-2	2-3	1-2	3-2	0-2	2-3	0-2	4-0	4-1	1-0	0-0	2-1	1-0	3-0	3-2	5-0	3-1
Bologna	42	24	12	6	58	29	84	4-0	—	1-0	1-0	2-2	1-0	0-0	0-0	3-0	2-1	1-1	2-0	1-0	3-0	1-2	4-1	1-0	1-0	3-1	2-1	3-2	2-1
Lecce ‡	42	23	14	5	70	29	83	3-0	0-0	—	3-0	1-2	1-0	0-3	0-1	2-0	1-0	3-1	0-1	0-1	0-1	0-0	2-0	3-3	1-3	1-2	2-0	3-0	
Albinoleffe ‡	42	23	9	10	67	48	78	0-2	1-0	0-4	—	2-3	2-3	0-4	0-2	0-2	0-4	1-5	1-2	1-1	0-2	1-0	3-1	0-0	3-3	3-3	1-3	2-1	0
Brescia ‡	42	20	12	10	59	40	72	0-2	2-0	0-0	1-2	—	1-0	2-0	0-4	0-3	2-2	0-0	4-1	4-1	3-1	2-0	2-0	0-2	0-0	0-3	0-2	1-1	0-3-0
Pisa ‡	42	19	14	9	61	44	71	1-1	1-0	0-1	1-2	0-0	—	3-0	0-2	2-1	1-1	1-2	1-4	3-2	0-3	1-1	3-3	1-2	0-0	0-1	0-1	1-0	3-0
Rimini	42	20	9	13	68	46	69	0-0	1-2	2-3	0-0	0-1	1-1	—	3-0	1-1	1-1	2-1	4-3	2-0	3-0	0-0	1-1	0-5	1-2	1-2	3-4	4-2	4-1
Ascoli	42	16	14	12	64	49	62	1-2	2-2	2-1	3-2	0-1	1-0	0-0	—	1-3	2-0	2-0	3-1	3-5	1-4	1-1	1-1	0-2	1-3	1-5	0-1	0-5	2-2
Mantova	42	16	12	14	56	49	60	1-0	0-1	1-0	0-1	1-1	0-1	0-1	0-1	—	3-2	1-2	0-0	4-0	0-1	0-3	2-2	3-2	1-1	1-0	1-3	1-4	1
Frosinone	42	15	11	16	63	67	56	1-2	0-0	1-2	2-2	0-0	1-5	3-2	3-2	1-1	—	4-1	0-1	4-1	4-4	0-2	2-2	4-0	0-1	0-2	1-2	4-2	2-1 0-0
Bari	42	13	16	13	50	55	55	2-3	1-0	0-4	0-0	1-0	1-0	2-1	1-1	2-0	3-1	—	2-0	0-0	0-1	1-0	1-0	0-4	2-2	1-0	0-0		
Triestina	42	13	12	17	55	67	51	1-1	1-3	1-2	4-1	0-1	1-0	1-1	1-0	1-1	2-1	—		4-0	1-1	1-1	3-1	5-1	0-1	2-2	4-3	0-2	1
Grosseto	42	10	19	13	47	54	49	1-1	3-0	1-1	2-2	0-1	2-0	2-1	1-1	1-0	1-1	2-1	2-2	—	0-0	2-1	0-2	2-1	1-1	2-1	2-3	0-0	0
Messina	42	13	10	19	38	62	49	2-3	2-1	1-3	2-1	2-1	1-2	1-0	1-0	0-0	0-1	2-1	2-1	1-1	—	2-0	3-3	0-2	2-0	1-0	2-1	0-1	0-1 0
Piacenza	42	13	8	21	43	59	47	1-3	0-1	1-0	1-3	2-4	4-2	2-1	2-0	1-4	3-1	2-1	1-1	3-0	1-2	—	1-2	1-0	0-0	2-0	1-0	1-0	0
Modena	42	10	16	16	57	65	46	1-2	1-2	1-2	2-3	0-3	0-0	0-2	2-1	2-2	2-2	3-0	1-2	3-0	1-0	2-0	—	1-1	1-1	1-0	1-2	2-2	1-1
Vicenza	42	10	15	17	43	60	45	1-3	0-1	1-3	1-1	1-1	1-3	3-2	1-1	0-0	2-1	2-3	2-2	0-0	3-1	0-1	1-2	—	0-0	2-1	1-0	0-1	0
Treviso	42	11	12	19	41	52	45	0-1	0-2	0-0	0-1	3-0	2-3	0-2	2-1	2-2	2-1	1-2	2-0	2-1	6-2	1-0	1-1	1-3	—	1-0	1-1	1-1	2-1
Avellino	42	8	12	22	42	64	36	1-1	1-0	0-2	0-0	1-3	1-2	1-0	2-0	1-0	1-3	2-2	2-0	3-1	2-0	1-1	1-3	0-1	1-1	—	3-2	2-3	3-1
Ravenna	42	8	11	23	48	75	35	1-1	1-1	1-3	0-2	0-0	1-4	0-1	2-1	5-2	0-2	1-2	2-2	1-1	0-1	0-1	1-0	1-1	0-0	1-1	—	2-0	0
Spezia §1	42	6	16	20	45	66	33	0-1	0-2	1-1	0-2	1-4	0-1	0-0	1-3	0-1	1-0	1-2	2-2	0-1	2-2	1-1	5-2	2-2	2-0			—	1-0
Cesena	42	5	17	20	37	66	32	1-1	0-0	0-1	0-3	1-1	1-2	1-2	1-1	1-3	0-0	0-1	1-0	0-1	0-2	2-2	1-3	3-3	1-1	0-1	1-1	1-1	—

25/08/2007 - 1/06/2008 • § = points deducted • ‡ = promotion play-off • Top scorers: Denis Godeas, Mantova 28; Pablo Granoche, Triestina 24
Play-off semis: Pisa 0-1 1-2 Lecce; Brescia 1-0 1-2 Albinoleffe
Play-off final: Albinoleffe 0-1 1-1 Lecce

ITALY 2007-08
SERIE C1 GROUP A

	Pl	W	D	L	F	A	Pts
Sassuolo	34	19	6	9	46	32	63
Cremonese ‡	34	16	12	6	50	36	60
Cittadella ‡	34	15	13	6	52	34	58
Foligno ‡	34	15	12	7	38	30	57
Foggia ‡	34	15	11	8	47	34	56
Padova	34	14	13	7	57	37	55
Legnano	34	13	9	12	42	34	48
Monza	34	11	13	10	38	35	46
Novara	34	12	10	12	44	52	46
Cavese	34	11	11	12	44	44	44
Pro Sesto	34	11	10	13	42	45	43
Venezia §1	34	13	5	16	38	41	43
Ternana	34	11	8	15	34	40	41
Pro Patria ‡	34	7	17	10	33	35	38
Paganese ‡	34	7	11	16	26	41	32
Lecco ‡	34	8	8	18	30	48	32
Hellas Verona ‡	34	7	10	17	24	41	31
Manfredonia	34	8	7	19	24	50	31

25/08/2007 - 4/05/2008 • ‡ Entered play-offs

SERIE C1 GROUP A PROMOTION PLAY-OFFS

Semi–finals

Cittadella	0 2
Foligno *	1 0
Foggia *	0 1
Cremonese	0 1

Final

Cittadella *	0 3
Cremonese	1 1

* Home team in the first leg • Pisa promoted along with champions Grosseto

SERIE C1 GROUP A RELEGATION PLAY-OFFS

Verona 1-0 1-1 Pro Patria

Lecco 1-0 0-2 **Paganese**

Pro Patria and Lecco relegated along with Manfredonia

SERIE C1 SUPERCUP

Sassuolo 0-1 1-0 5-4p Salernitana

ITALY 2007-08
SERIE C1 GROUP B

	Pl	W	D	L	F	A	Pts
Salernitana	34	16	14	4	43	25	62
Ancona ‡	34	15	12	7	43	26	57
Taranto ‡	34	14	13	7	47	31	55
Crotone ‡	34	14	13	7	45	30	55
Perugia ‡	34	15	8	11	35	34	53
Pescara §1	34	15	9	10	47	36	53
Arezzo	34	13	14	7	42	32	53
Lucchese	34	12	15	7	36	30	51
Gallipoli	34	12	10	12	51	44	46
Sorrento	34	10	14	10	29	30	44
Potenza	34	10	10	14	34	38	40
Sambenedettese	34	9	13	12	32	39	40
Massese	34	9	13	12	34	43	40
Pistoiese ‡	34	7	13	14	27	38	34
Juve Stabia ‡	34	7	12	15	34	42	33
Lanciano §10 ‡	34	9	15	10	30	34	32
Sangiovannese ‡	34	6	11	17	24	48	29
Martina §1	34	4	9	21	25	58	20

25/08/2007 - 4/05/2008 • ‡ Entered play-offs
§ Points deducted

SERIE C1 GROUP B PROMOTION PLAY-OFFS

Semi–finals

Ancona	1 2
Perugia *	3 0
Crotone *	3 0
Taranto	2 2

Final

Ancona	0 2
Taranto *	0 1

* Home team in the first leg • Ancona promoted along with champions Salernitana

SERIE C1 GROUP B RELEGATION PLAY-OFFS

Sangiovannese 0-3 0-1 **Pistoiese**

Lanciano 0-1 0-0 **Juve Stabia**

Lanciano and Sangiovannese relegated along with Martina

COPPA ITALIA 2007–08

Second Round | **Third Round** | **Round of 16**

		Roma	1 4
		Torino *	3 0
Rimini *	3		
Treviso	1	Rimini	2
		Torino *	3
		Cagliari *	2
		Siena	1
			Cagliari *	1 0
			Sampdoria	0 4
		Udinese *	0 1
		Palermo	0 0
Bari *	2		
Vicenza	0	Bari	0
		Udinese *	3
		Catania	0 4p
Bologna *	1 3p	Triestina *	0 2p
Triestina	1 4p		
			Milan *	1 1
			Catania	2 1
			Lazio *	2 1
			Napoli	1 1
		Livorno	1 3p
Pisa	1	Napoli *	1 4p
Napoli *	3		
Ascoli *	3		
Genoa	2	Ascoli *	2
		Atalanta	1
			Ascoli *	1 0
			Fiorentina	1 2
			Juventus	1 5
			Empoli *	2 3
		Parma *	1
		Juventus	3
		Reggina *	3
Ravenna *	1	Piacenza	2
Piacenza	2		
			Reggina *	1 0
			Internazionale	4 3

The 2008 Coppa Italia was restricted to the 42 clubs playing in Serie A and Serie B

COPPA ITALIA 2007–08

Quarter–finals   **Semi–finals**   **Final**

Roma	1	1
Sampdoria *	1	0

Roma *	1	1
Catania	0	1

Udinese *	3	1
Catania	2	2

Roma		2
Internazionale		1

Lazio *	2	2
Fiorentina	1	1

Lazio	0	0
Internazionale *	0	0

Juventus	2	2
Internazionale *	2	3

COPPA ITALIA FINAL 2008

Stadio Olimpico, Rome, 24-05-2008, 20:45, Att: 50 000, Ref: Emidio Morganti

Roma	2	Mexès [36], Perrotta [54]
Internazionale	1	Pélé [60]

Roma - Doni - Marco Cassetti, Philippe Mexès, Juan, Max Tonetto - Ludovic Giuly (Cicinho 66), Daniele De Rossi, David Pizarro, Alberto Aquilani (Christian Panucci 90) - Simone Perrotta* (Matteo Brighi 72), Mirko Vucinic*. Tr: Luciano Spalletti
Inter - Francesco Toldo* - Maicon, Cristian Chivu, Nicolas Burdisso*, Maxwell - Javier Zanetti (Hernán Crespo 90), Patrick Vieira*, Dejan Stankovic (Pélé* 46), César (Luis Jimenez 62) - David Suazo, Mario Balotelli. Tr: Roberto Mancini

* Home team in the first leg

ATALANTA 2007–08

Month	Date	Opponent	Res	Score	Scorers	Att
Sept	26	Reggina	D	1-1	Doni 85p	12 963
	2	Parma	W	2-0	Zampagna 21p, Carozzieri 65	10 141
	16	Fiorentina	D	2-2	Doni 51, Zampagna 86	28 383
	23	Lazio	W	2-1	Langella 43, Zampagna 95+	10 861
	26	Siena	D	1-1	Doni 61p	8 377
	30	Sampdoria	L	0-3		21 000
Oct	6	Udinese	D	0-0		11 377
	21	Torino	D	2-2	Ferreira Pinto 45, Doni 67p	10 962
	28	Empoli	W	1-0	Doni 75	5 616
	31	Cagliari	D	2-2	Capelli 50, Doni 80	10 152
Nov	4	Catania	W	2-1	Langella 2 57 59	16 101
	24	Inter	L	1-2	Floccari 39	43 190
Dec	2	Napoli	W	5-1	Floccari 6, Langella 21, Doni 36, Carozzieri 47, Ferreira Pinto 74	6 388
	9	Juventus	L	0-1		20 132
	16	Palermo	L	1-3	Amauri OG 62	5 452
	23	Livorno	D	1-1	Tissone 33	7 719
Jan	13	Roma	L	1-2	Ferreira Pinto 17	7 662
	19	Genoa	L	1-2	Doni 67p	23 743
	23	Milan	L	1-2	Langella 42, Tissone 68	12 500
	27	Reggina	D	2-2	Rivalta 18, Langella 46	12 584
Feb	3	Parma	W	3-2	Pellegrino 18, Bellini 55, Floccari 68	13 089
	9	Fiorentina	D	2-2	Muslimovic 2 30 92+	10 822
	17	Lazio	L	0-3		19 003
	3	Siena	D	2-2	Floccari 2 42 45	9 226
	27	Sampdoria	W	4-1	Doni 2 13 31, Floccari 36, Capelli 53	10 244
Mar	2	Udinese	L	0-2		13 245
	9	Torino	L	0-1		18 208
	16	Empoli	W	4-1	Langella 19, Doni 27, Padoin 2 80 85	9 220
	19	Cagliari	L	0-1		15 000
	2	Catania	D	0-0		9 414
	30	Milan	W	2-1	Floccari 32, Langella 42	50 356
Apr	6	Inter	L	0-2		19 081
	13	Napoli	L	0-2		38 688
	20	Juventus	L	0-4		21 323
	27	Palermo	D	0-0		23 288
May	4	Livorno	W	3-2	Doni 57, Ferreira Pinto 60, Padoin 89	8 999
	11	Roma	L	1-2	Bellini 89	36 416
	18	Genoa	W	2-0	Floccari 32, Marconi 93+	10 925

CAGLIARI 2007–08

Month	Date	Opponent	Res	Score	Scorers	Att
Sept	26	Napoli	W	2-0	Matri 49, Foggia 59	39 026
	2	Juventus	L	2-3	Foggia 2 56p 81p	23 000
	16	Parma	D	1-1	Matri 40	12 853
	23	Palermo	L	0-1		8 000
	26	Lazio	L	1-3	Acquafresca 69	17 652
	30	Siena	W	1-0	Foggia 7p	10 000
Oct	7	Genoa	L	0-2		23 319
	21	Catania	D	1-1	Matri 46	8 000
	27	Torino	L	0-2		18 226
	31	Atalanta	D	2-2	Fini 39p, Matri 70	10 152
Nov	4	Sampdoria	L	0-3		10 000
	25	Milan	L	1-2	Acquafresca 4	15 000
Dec	2	Livorno	D	0-0		10 000
	5	Roma	L	0-2		32 019
	9	Empoli	L	1-4	Conti 82	5 200
	16	Inter	L	0-2		8 000
	23	Fiorentina	L	1-5	Fini 5	26 076
Jan	13	Udinese	L	0-1		7 100
	20	Reggina	L	0-2		10 122
	27	Napoli	W	2-1	Matri 95+, Conti 97+	11 000
	3	Juventus	D	1-1	Bianco 55	19 412
Feb	10	Parma	D	1-1	Jeda 34	12 135
	17	Palermo	L	1-2	Cavani OG 52	21 829
	24	Lazio	W	1-0	Matri 88	12 126
	2	Siena	L	0-1		8 913
	2	Genoa	W	2-1	Acquafresca 29, Rubinho OG 45	13 000
	9	Catania	L	1-2	Conti 22	30 643
Mar	16	Torino	W	3-0	Jeda 11, Acquafresca 2 22p 57	10 560
	19	Atalanta	W	1-0	Acquafresca 18p	15 000
	22	Sampdoria	D	1-1	Foggia 41	19 877
	29	Roma	D	1-1	Ferrari OG 3	25 140
	5	Milan	L	1-3	Conti 49	52 422
Apr	13	Livorno	W	2-1	Acquafresca 2 10 54	13 941
	20	Empoli	W	2-0	Acquafresca 9, Fini 64	12 000
	27	Inter	L	1-2	Biondini 91+	56 676
	4	Fiorentina	W	2-1	Jeda 20, Conti 51	12 000
May	11	Udinese	W	2-0	Acquafresca 48, Cossu 55	16 689
	18	Reggina	D	2-2	Larrevey 18, Bianco 81	20 124

CATANIA 2007–08

Month	Date	Opponent	Res	Score	Scorers	Att
Sept	26	Parma	D	2-2	Moromoto 12, Baiocco 44	12 579
	2	Genoa	D	0-0		15 987
	16	Inter	L	0-2		41 720
	23	Fiorentina	L	0-1		16 782
	26	Empoli	W	1-0	Martinez 50	15 887
	30	Milan	D	1-1	Martinez 25	49 835
Oct	7	Livorno	W	1-0	Sardo 20	16 313
	21	Cagliari	D	1-1	Tedesco 11	8 000
	28	Sampdoria	W	2-0	Mascara 1, Martinez 43	16 276
	3	Siena	D	1-1	Vargas 89	7 898
Nov	4	Atalanta	L	1-2	Spinesi 82	16 101
	11	Torino	D	1-1	Martinez 63	18 597
	25	Napoli	L	0-2		31 344
Dec	2	Palermo	W	3-1	Mascara 29, Spinesi 41p, Martinez 89	17 400
	8	Lazio	L	0-2		17 391
	15	Udinese	W	2-0	Mascara 2 7 87	16 551
	23	Reggina	L	1-3	Vargas 91+	11 925
Jan	12	Juventus	D	1-1	Spinesi 15	21 148
	20	Roma	L	0-2		33 378
	27	Parma	D	0-0		16 287
	3	Genoa	L	1-2	Bovo OG 59	22 935
	10	Inter	L	0-2		20 356
Feb	17	Fiorentina	L	1-2	Vargas 60	26 648
	24	Empoli	L	0-2		5 712
	27	Milan	D	1-1	Spinesi 63	21 000
	2	Livorno	L	0-1		9 759
	9	Cagliari	W	2-1	Silvestri 44, Canini OG 48	30 643
Mar	16	Sampdoria	L	1-3	Stovini 73	19 409
	19	Siena	D	0-0		16 655
	22	Atalanta	D	0-0		9 414
	30	Torino	W	1-0	Spinesi 3	16 955
	6	Napoli	W	3-0	Colucci 4, Spinesi 16, Vargas 48	14 246
Apr	12	Palermo	L	0-1		24 847
	20	Lazio	W	1-0	Spinesi 34p	16 000
	27	Udinese	L	1-2	Vargas 34	13 958
	4	Reggina	L	1-2	Martinez 94+	18 177
May	11	Juventus	D	1-1	Martinez 49	20 638
	18	Roma	D	1-1	Martinez 85	21 148

EMPOLI 2007–08

Month	Date	Opponent	Res	Score	Scorers	Att
Sept	26	Fiorentina	L	1-3	Saudati 95+	31 280
	2	Inter	L	0-2		16 326
	15	Lazio	D	0-0		19 460
	23	Napoli	D	0-0		11 985
	26	Catania	L	0-1		15 887
	30	Palermo	W	3-0	Pozzi 52, Giovinco 87, Vannucchi 96+p	6 002
Oct	7	Siena	L	0-3		8 189
	21	Milan	W	1-0	Saudati 55	50 991
	28	Atalanta	L	0-1		5 616
	31	Juventus	L	0-3		19 075
Nov	4	Roma	D	2-2	Vannucchi 68, Giovinco 93+	7 499
	10	Sampdoria	L	0-3		19 327
	25	Torino	D	0-0		5 579
Dec	2	Parma	L	0-1		12 736
	9	Cagliari	W	4-1	Pozzi 4 2 10 50 64	5 200
	16	Genoa	D	1-1	Giovinco 45	6 483
	23	Udinese	D	2-2	Raggi 50, Marzoratti 93	13 104
	12	Reggina	D	1-1	Saudati 5p	5 349
Jan	20	Livorno	L	0-1		8 428
	27	Fiorentina	L	0-2		10 873
	3	Inter	L	0-1		43 946
	10	Lazio	W	1-0	Vannucchi 7	10 268
Feb	17	Napoli	W	3-1	Pozzi 2 21 65, Budel 81	50 175
	24	Catania	W	2-0	Giovinco 36, Budel 78	5 712
	27	Palermo	L	0-2		22 897
	2	Siena	L	0-2		6 139
	9	Milan	L	1-3	Busce 23	9 532
Mar	16	Atalanta	L	1-4	Vannucchi 83	9 220
	19	Juventus	D	0-0		8 719
	22	Roma	L	1-2	Giovinco 50	31 392
	30	Sampdoria	L	0-2		7 066
	6	Torino	W	1-0	Vannucchi 88	18 750
Apr	13	Parma	D	1-1	Giovinco 30	5 938
	20	Cagliari	L	0-2		12 000
	27	Genoa	W	1-0	Abate 15	23 885
	4	Udinese	L	0-1		7 257
May	11	Reggina	L	0-2		23 248
	18	Livorno	W	2-1	Busce 10, Saudati 56	6 858

GENOA 2007-08

Month	Date	Opponent	Res	Score	Scorers	Att
Sept	26	Milan	L	0-3		23 533
	2	Catania	D	0-0		15 987
	16	Livorno	D	1-1	Borriello 58	23 569
	23	Sampdoria	D	0-0		33 060
	26	Udinese	W	3-2	Borriello 3 21 47 74p	22 253
	30	Napoli	W	2-1	Cannavaro OG 12 Sculli 89	0
Oct	7	Cagliari	W	2-0	Borriello 59, Di Vaio 73	23 319
	21	Juventus	L	0-1		21 414
	28	Fiorentina	D	0-0		24 876
	31	Inter	L	1-4	Konko 73	47 230
Nov	4	Palermo	D	3-3	Leon 2 59 66, Borriello 82	23 595
	11	Reggina	L	0-2		10 312
	24	Roma	L	0-1		24 106
Dec	2	Torino	D	1-1	Borriello 47	18 404
	9	Siena	L	1-3	Figueroa 89	22 697
	16	Empoli	D	1-1	Masiello 87	6 483
	22	Parma	W	1-0	Borriello 43p	22 914
Jan	13	Lazio	W	2-1	Borriello 2 51p 55	18 964
	19	Atalanta	W	2-1	Borriello 73, Figueroa 84	23 743
	27	Milan	L	0-2		49 028
Feb	3	Catania	W	2-1	Danilo 13, Borriello 71p	22 935
	10	Livorno	D	1-1	Di Vaio 83	9 445
	17	Sampdoria	L	0-1		37 508
	24	Udinese	W	5-3	Leon 8, Sculli 43, Borriello 3 55 78 85	13 640
	27	Napoli	W	2-0	Sculli 41, Borriello 75p	26 417
Mar	2	Cagliari	L	1-2	Lucarelli 15	13 000
	9	Juventus	L	0-2		28 151
	16	Fiorentina	L	1-3	Masiero 83	28 728
	19	Inter	D	1-1	Borriello 85	27 624
	22	Palermo	W	3-2	Figueroa 29, Milanetto 50, Konko 62	23 260
	30	Napoli	W	2-0	Borriello 59, Rossi 93+	23 349
Apr	5	Roma	L	2-3	Rossi 58, Leon 59	36 366
	13	Torino	W	3-0	Di Vaio 51, Borriello 61, Sculli 69	25 751
	20	Siena	W	1-0	Konko 24	12 228
		Empoli	L	0-1		23 885
May	4	Parma	L	0-1		17 693
	11	Lazio	L	0-2		25 077
	18	Atalanta	L	0-2		10 925

INTERNAZIONALE 2007-08

Month	Date	Opponent	Res	Score	Comp	Scorers	Att
Aug	18	Roma	L	0-1	SC		55 000
	26	Udinese	D	1-1	SA	Stankovic 9	42 797
	1	Empoli	W	2-0	SA	Ibrahimovic 2 14 83	16 326
	16	Catania	W	2-0	SA	Crespo 15, Cesar 79	41 720
	19	Fenerbahçe	L	0-1	CLgG		44 212
Sep	23	Livorno	D	2-2	SA	Ibrahimovic 2 35 72p	11 922
	26	Sampdoria	W	3-0	SA	Ibrahimovic 2 24 49, Figo 58	42 013
	29	Roma	W	4-1	SA	Ibrahimovic 29p, Crespo 57, Cruz 60, Cordoba 68	51 150
	2	PSV	W	2-0	CLgG	Ibrahimovic 2 15p 31	34 238
	6	Napoli	W	2-1	SA	Cruz 2 20 36	46 536
	20	Reggina	W	1-0	SA	Adriano 18	16 965
Nov	23	CSKA M'kva	W	2-1	CLgG	Crespo 52, Samuel 80	24 000
	28	Palermo	D	0-0	SA		33 972
	31	Genoa	W	4-1	SA	Cordoba 8, Cambiasso 50, Suazo 74, Cruz 86p	47 230
	4	Juventus	D	1-1	SA	Cruz 41	22 722
	7	CSKA M'kva	W	4-2	CLgG	Ibrahimovic 2 32 75, Cambiasso 2 34 67	17 495
	24	Atalanta	W	2-1	SA	Suazo 10, Cruz 30	43 190
	27	Fenerbahçe	W	3-0	CLgG	Cruz 55, Ibrahimovic 66, Jiménez 92+	24 736
	2	Fiorentina	W	2-0	SA	Jimenez 10, Cruz 45	42 449
	5	Lazio	W	3-0	SA	Ibrahimovic 22p, Maicon 33, Suazo 56	44 667
Dec	9	Torino	W	4-0	SA	Ibrahimovic 38p, Cruz 50, Jimenez 52, Cordoba 75	46 148
	12	PSV	W	1-0	CLgG	Cruz 64	35 000
	16	Cagliari	W	2-0	SA	Cruz 57, Suazo 79	8 000
	19	Reggina	W	4-1	ICr4	Crespo 14, Balotelli 2 29 86, Solari 62	1 564
	23	Milan	W	2-1	SA	Cruz 36, Cambiasso 63	78 675
	13	Siena	W	3-2	SA	Ibrahimovic 2 26p 52, Cambiasso 45	14 682
	17	Reggina	W	4-0	ICr4	Crespo 33, OG 45, Cesar 91+	4 391
Jan	20	Parma	W	3-2	SA	Cambiasso 30, Ibrahimovic 2 91+p 96+	43 413
	23	Juventus	D	2-2	ICqf	Cruz 2 53 74	29 329
	27	Udinese	D	0-0	SA		21 913
	30	Juventus	W	3-2	ICqf	Balotelli 2 10 53, Cruz 39p	20 616
	3	Empoli	W	1-0	SA	Ibrahimovic 34p	43 413
	10	Catania	W	2-0	SA	Cambiasso 64, Suazo 67	20 356
Feb	16	Livorno	W	2-0	SA	Suazo 2 14 18	45 276
	19	Liverpool	L	0-2	CLr2		41 999
	24	Sampdoria	D	1-1	SA	Crespo 76	26 306
	27	Roma	D	1-1	SA	Zanetti 88	48 717
	2	Napoli	L	0-1	SA		53 818
	8	Reggina	W	2-0	SA	Ibrahimovic 14p, Burdisso 34	64 575
	11	Liverpool	L	0-1	CLr2		78 923
Mar	16	Palermo	W	2-1	SA	Vieira 5, Jimenez 36	49 360
	19	Genoa	D	1-1	SA	Suazo 11	27 624
	22	Juventus	L	1-2	SA	Maniche 83	58 049
	29	Lazio	D	1-1	SA	Crespo 17	32 802
	6	Atalanta	W	2-0	SA	Vieira 21, Balotelli 74	19 081
	13	Fiorentina	W	2-0	SA	Cambiasso 55, Balotelli 62	53 483
Apr	16	Lazio	D	0-0	ICsf		11 016
	20	Torino	W	1-0	SA	Cruz 30	21 865
	27	Cagliari	W	2-1	SA	Cruz 22, Materazzi 82	56 676
	4	Milan	L	1-2	SA	Cruz 76	81 766
	7	Lazio	W	2-0	ICsf	Pele 53, Cruz 87	43 732
May	11	Siena	D	2-2	SA	Vieira 11, Balotelli 45	76 633
	18	Parma	W	2-0	SA	Ibrahimovic 2 61 79	25 149
	1	Lazio	L	1-2	ICf	Pele 62	50 000

SC = Supercoppa Italia • SA = Serie A • CL = UEFA Champions League • IC = Coppa Italia • gG = group G • r2 = second round • r4 = fourth round • qf = quarter-final • sf = semi-final • f = final

FIORENTINA 2007-08

Month	Date	Opponent	Res	Score	Scorers	Att
Sept	26	Empoli	W	3-1	Pazzini 56, Mutu 63, Montolivio 70	31 280
	2	Milan	D	1-1	Mutu 56	61 559
	16	Atalanta	D	2-2	Rivalta OG 25, Vieri 74	28 383
	23	Catania	W	1-0	Mutu 4	16 782
	26	Roma	D	2-2	Gamberini 24, Mutu 79p	36 056
	29	Livorno	W	3-0	Osvaldo 2 45 67, Santana 69	10 415
Oct	7	Juventus	D	1-1	Mutu 89p	40 077
	21	Siena	W	3-0	Pazzini 15, Mutu 31, Vieri 71	28 307
	28	Genoa	D	0-0		24 876
	31	Napoli	W	1-0	Vieri 62	32 568
Nov	3	Lazio	W	1-0	Pazzini 19	19 165
	11	Udinese	L	1-2	Pazzini 28	27 882
	25	Reggina	D	0-0		10 375
	2	Inter	L	0-2		42 449
Dec	8	Palermo	L	0-2		21 823
	16	Sampdoria	D	2-2	Mutu 39, Donadel 57	22 161
	23	Cagliari	W	5-1	Montolivio 3, Mutu 2 42 45p, Santana 2 47 79	26 076
Jan	2	Parma	W	2-1	Mutu 2 43 66p	14 663
	19	Torino	W	2-1	Vieri 45p, Mutu 76p	27 992
	27	Empoli	W	2-0	Mutu 85, Pazzini 94+	10 873
	3	Milan	L	0-1		38 977
Feb	9	Atalanta	D	2-2	Pazzini 29, Semioli 60	10 822
	17	Catania	W	2-1	Kuzmanovic 40, Mutu 70	26 648
	24	Roma	L	0-1		34 254
	27	Livorno	W	1-0	N'Diaye 58	26 291
Mar	2	Juventus	W	3-2	Gobbi 18, N'Diaye 76, Osvaldo 93+	20 993
	9	Siena	L	0-1		12 785
	16	Genoa	W	3-1	Santana 19, Mutu 30, Pazzini 56	28 728
	19	Napoli	L	0-2		42 661
	22	Lazio	W	1-0	Pazzini 77	26 579
	30	Udinese	L	1-3	Vieri 62	15 374
Apr	6	Reggina	W	2-0	Pazzini 23, Mutu 94+	27 321
	13	Inter	L	0-2		53 483
	19	Palermo	W	1-0	Donadel 5	28 827
	27	Sampdoria	D	2-2	Vieri 78, Mutu 85p	36 627
May	4	Cagliari	L	1-2	Santana 53	12 000
	11	Parma	W	3-1	Santana 38, Montolivio 63, Osvaldo 86	36 289
	18	Torino	W	1-0	Osvaldo 76	23 771

JUVENTUS 2007–08

	Date	Opponent	Res	Score	Scorers	Att
Sept	25	Livorno	W	5-1	Trezeguet 3 29 87 90, Iaquinta 2 71p 86	21 414
	2	Cagliari	W	3-2	Trezeguet 54, Del Piero 77, Chiellini 92+	23 000
	16	Udinese	L	0-1		20 414
	23	Roma	D	2-2	Trezeguet 17, Iaquinta 88	62 241
	26	Reggina	W	4-0	Legrottaglie 48, Salihamidzic 50, Trezeguet 75, Palladino 92+	19 050
	30	Torino	W	1-0	Trezeguet 94+	23 974
Oct	7	Fiorentina	D	1-1	Iaquinta 23	40 077
	21	Genoa	W	1-0	Del Piero 36	21 414
	27	Napoli	L	1-3	Del Piero 46	56 022
	31	Empoli	W	3-0	Trezeguet 3 51p 63 70	19 075
Nov	4	Inter	D	1-1	Camoranesi 77	22 722
	11	Parma	D	2-2	Legrottaglie 75, Iaquinta 81	22 278
	25	Palermo	W	5-0	Trezeguet 29, Iaquinta 41, Marchionni 75, Del Piero 2 71 94+p	20 036
Dec	1	Milan	D	0-0		76 145
	9	Atalanta	W	1-0	Nedved 86	20 132
	15	Lazio	W	3-2	Trezeguet 29, Del Piero 2 48 71	24 098
	23	Siena	W	2-0	Salihamidzic 32, Trezeguet 59	20 421
Jan	12	Catania	L	1-1	Del Piero 93p	21 148
	20	Sampdoria	D	0-0		22 379
	27	Livorno	W	3-1	Trezeguet 2 30 63, Del Piero 49	14 630
Feb	3	Cagliari	D	1-1	Nedved 56	19 412
	9	Udinese	W	2-1	Camoranesi 60, Iaquinta 75	25 152
	16	Roma	W	1-0	Del Piero 45	21 139
	23	Reggina	L	1-2	Del Piero 72	21 884
	26	Torino	D	0-0		22 636
Mar	2	Fiorentina	L	2-3	Sissoko 29, Camoranesi 57	20 993
	9	Genoa	W	2-0	Grygera 25, Trezeguet 32	28 151
	16	Napoli	W	1-0	Iaquinta 88	21 095
	19	Empoli	D	0-0		8 719
	22	Inter	W	2-1	Camoranesi 49, Trezeguet 63	58 049
Apr	6	Palermo	L	2-3	Del Piero 2 52 71	34 271
	12	Milan	W	3-2	Del Piero 12, Salihamidzic 2 45 80	21 605
	16	Parma	W	3-0	Trezeguet 16, Palladino 30, OG 78	21 403
	20	Atalanta	W	4-0	Legrottaglie 1, Del Piero 3 6 34 65	21 323
	27	Lazio	W	5-2	Chiellini 2 15 88, Camoranesi 20, Del Piero 32, Trezeguet 33	20 588
May	4	Siena	L	0-1		15 419
	11	Catania	D	1-1	Del Piero 89	20 638
	17	Sampdoria	D	3-3	Del Piero 2 7 65p, Trezeguet 16p	26 954

LIVORNO 2007–08

	Date	Opponent	Res	Score	Scorers	Att
Sept	25	Juventus	L	1-5	Loviso 95+	21 414
	2	Palermo	L	2-4	Rossini 54, Grandoni 74	8 475
	16	Genoa	D	1-1	Tavano 53p	23 569
	23	Inter	D	2-2	De Vezze 1, Loviso 63p	11 922
	26	Napoli	L	0-1		37 163
	29	Fiorentina	L	0-3		10 415
Oct	7	Catania	L	0-1		16 313
	21	Lazio	L	0-1		8 018
	28	Parma	L	2-3	Tavano 2 23 50p	11 890
	31	Reggina	W	3-1	Pulzetti 34, Valdez OG 78, Rossini 90	10 157
Nov	4	Udinese	D	0-0		7 773
	11	Siena	W	3-2	Tavano 17, Bergvold 31, Knezevic 42	8 532
	25	Sampdoria	L	1-2	Knezevic 9, Tavano 2 10 89	7 675
Dec	2	Cagliari	D	0-0		10 000
	9	Roma	D	1-1	Diego Tristan 6	5 500
	23	Atalanta	D	1-1	Galante 26	7 719
Jan	13	Torino	W	2-1	Tavano 2 21 50	17 515
	20	Empoli	W	1-0	Tavano 51p	8 428
	27	Juventus	L	1-3	Bogdani 79	14 630
Feb	2	Palermo	L	0-1		23 033
	10	Genoa	D	1-1	Tavano 15	9 445
	13	Milan	D	1-1	Pulzetti 50	47 382
	16	Inter	L	0-2		45 276
	24	Napoli	L	1-2	Diamanti 74	8 495
	27	Fiorentina	L	0-1		26 291
Mar	2	Catania	W	1-0	Diamanti 62	9 759
	9	Lazio	L	0-2		19 110
	16	Parma	D	1-1	Vidigal 41	11 008
	19	Reggina	D	1-1	Bogdani 61	9 027
	22	Udinese	L	0-2		12 594
	30	Siena	D	0-0		10 207
Apr	6	Sampdoria	L	0-2		21 426
	13	Cagliari	L	1-2	Galante 2	13 941
	19	Roma	L	1-1	Diamanti 83	34 061
	27	Milan	L	1-4	Knezevic 73	14 504
May	4	Atalanta	L	2-3	Rossini 64, Pavan 81	8 999
	11	Torino	L	0-1		8 813
	18	Empoli	L	1-2	Diamanti 84	6 858

LAZIO 2007–08

	Date	Opponent	Res	Score	Comp	Scorers	Att
Aug	14	D Bucharest	D	1-1	CLp3	Mutarelli 54	35 172
	25	Torino	D	2-2	SA	Pandev 56, Rocchi 61	21 495
	28	D Bucharest	W	3-1	CLp3	Rocchi 2 47p 66, Pandev 53	40 164
Sep	2	Sampdoria	D	0-0	SA		20 564
	15	Empoli	D	0-0	SA		19 460
	18	Olympiacos	D	1-1	CLgC	Zauri 77	BCD
	23	Atalanta	L	1-2	SA	Mutarelli 69	10 861
	26	Cagliari	W	3-1	SA	Rocchi 2 48 83, Pandev 60	17 652
	30	Reggina	D	1-1	SA	Kolarov 73	10 169
Oct	3	Real Madrid	D	2-2	CLgC	Pandev 2 32 75	52 400
	7	Milan	L	1-5	SA	Mauri 23	26 364
	21	Livorno	W	1-0	SA	Pandev 49	8 018
	24	W. Bremen	L	1-2	CLgC	Manfredini 82	36 587
	28	Udinese	L	0-1	SA		17 536
	31	Roma	L	2-3	SA	Rocchi 11, Ledesma 70	54 860
Nov	3	Fiorentina	L	0-1	SA		19 165
	6	W. Bremen	W	2-1	CLgC	Rocchi 2 57 68	28 236
	25	Parma	W	1-0	SA	Firmani 91+	17 289
	28	Olympiacos	L	1-2	CLgC	Pandev 30	39 996
Dec	2	Siena	D	1-1	SA	Pandev 23	9 186
	5	Inter	L	0-3	SA		44 667
	8	Catania	W	2-0	SA	Rocchi 8, Pandev 89	17 391
	11	Real Madrid	L	1-3	CLgC	Pandev 80	70 559
	15	Juventus	L	2-3	SA	Pandev 2 36 94+	24 098
	19	Napoli	W	2-1	ICr4	De Silvestri 67, Baronio 72	5 056
	23	Palermo	D	2-2	SA	Firmani 95, Tare 81	24 148
Jan	13	Genoa	L	1-2	SA	Mauri 26	18 964
	17	Napoli	D	1-1	ICr4	Tare 57	29 564
	20	Napoli	D	2-2	SA	Ledesma 25, Pandev 31	34 480
	24	Fiorentina	W	2-1	ICqf	Kolarov 21, Behrami 22	9 948
	27	Torino	D	0-0	SA		17 653
	30	Fiorentina	W	2-1	ICqf	Kolarov 34, Rocchi 62	10 457
Feb	3	Sampdoria	W	2-1	SA	Mauri 37, Rocchi 77	18 683
	10	Empoli	L	0-1	SA		10 268
	17	Atalanta	W	3-0	SA	Rocchi 2 26p 88p, Pandev 56	19 003
	24	Cagliari	L	0-1	SA		12 126
	27	Reggina	W	1-0	SA	Bianchi 45p	17 663
Mar	1	Milan	D	1-1	SA	Bianchi 54	52 016
	9	Livorno	W	2-0	SA	Rocchi 15, Pandev 25	19 110
	15	Udinese	D	2-2	SA	Rocchi 12, Ledesma 80	13 084
	19	Roma	W	3-2	SA	Pandev 43, Rocchi 58p, Behrami 93+	49 284
Apr	22	Fiorentina	L	0-1	SA		26 579
	29	Inter	D	1-1	SA	Rocchi 59	32 802
	6	Parma	D	2-2	SA	Pandev 35, Bianchi 38	13 370
	13	Siena	D	1-1	SA	Mutarelli 45	18 996
	16	Inter	D	0-0	ICsf		11 016
	20	Catania	L	0-1	SA		16 000
	27	Juventus	L	2-5	SA	Bianchi 55, Siviglia 62	20 588
May	4	Palermo	L	1-2	SA	Pandev 25p	20 786
	7	Inter	L	0-2	ICsf		43 732
	11	Genoa	W	2-0	SA	Pandev 31, Rocchi 45	25 077
	18	Napoli	W	2-1	SA	Rocchi 14, Firmani 71	14 891

SA = Serie A • CL = UEFA Champions League • IC = Coppa Italia •
p3 = third preliminary round • gC = group C • r4 = fourth round •
qf = quarter-final • sf = semi-final • f = final • BCD = behind closed doors

MILAN 2007–08

Month	Day	Opponent	Res	Score	Comp	Scorers	Attendance
Aug	26	Genoa	W	3-0	SA	Ambrosini 21, Kaka 2 44 45p	23 533
	31	Sevilla	W	3-1	ESC	Inzaghi 54, Jankulovski 61, Kaka 86	20 000
Sep	3	Fiorentina	D	1-1	SA	Kaka 27p	61 559
	15	Siena	D	1-1	SA	Nesta 91+	14 084
	18	Benfica	W	2-1	CLgD	Pirlo 9, Inzaghi 24	38 358
	22	Parma	D	1-1	SA	Seedorf 44	51 026
	26	Palermo	L	1-2	SA	Seedorf 10	30 761
	30	Catania	D	1-1	SA	Kaka 48p	49 835
Oct	3	Celtic	L	1-2	CLgD	Kaka 68p	58 462
	7	Lazio	W	5-1	SA	Ambrosini 16, Kaka 2 33p 52, Gilardino 2 70 79	26 364
	21	Empoli	L	0-1	SA		50 991
	24	Shakhtar	W	4-1	CLgD	Gilardino 2 6 14, Seedorf 2 62 69	36 850
	28	Roma	L	0-1	SA		60 205
	31	Sampdoria	W	5-0	SA	Kaka 47, Gilardino 2 53 62, Gourcuff 76, Seedorf 81	22 095
Nov	3	Torino	D	0-0	SA		54 980
	6	Shakhtar	W	3-0	CLgD	Inzaghi 2 66 93+, Kaka 72	25 700
	25	Cagliari	W	2-1	SA	Gilardino 61, Pirlo 86	15 000
	28	Benfica	D	1-1	CLgD	Pirlo 15	46 034
Dec	1	Juventus	D	0-0	SA		76 145
	4	Celtic	W	1-0	CLgD	Inzaghi 70	38 409
	13	Urawa Reds	W	1-0	CWsf	Seedorf 68	67 005
	16	Boca J	W	4-2	CWf	Inzaghi 2 21 71, Nesta 50, Kaka 61	68 263
	20	Catania	L	1-2	ICr4	Paloschi 59	4 156
	23	Inter	L	1-2	SA	Pirlo 18	78 675
Jan	13	Napoli	W	5-2	SA	Ronaldo 2 15 46, Seedorf 31, Kaka 68, Pato 74	70 085
	16	Catania	D	1-1	ICr4	Paloschi 70	20 021
	20	Sampdoria	W	1-0	SA	Gilardino 92+	24 574
	23	Atalanta	L	1-2	SA	Gattuso 16	12 500
	27	Genoa	W	2-0	SA	Pato 2 69 82	49 028
	30	Reggina	W	1-0	SA	Gilardino 18	17 426
Feb	3	Fiorentina	W	1-0	SA	Pato 77	38 977
	10	Siena	W	1-0	SA	Paloschi 63	51 552
	13	Livorno	W	1-0	SA	Pirlo 61p	47 382
	16	Parma	D	0-0	SA		19 361
	20	Arsenal	D	0-0	CLr2		60 082
	24	Palermo	W	2-1	SA	Ambrosini 25, Inzaghi 92+	50 643
	27	Catania	D	1-1	SA	Pato 55	21 000
Mar	1	Lazio	D	1-1	SA	Bianchi 54	52 016
	4	Arsenal	L	0-2	CLr2		81 879
	9	Empoli	W	3-1	SA	Pato 19, Ambrosini 86, Kaka 89	9 532
	15	Roma	L	1-2	SA	Kaka 56	48 447
	19	Sampdoria	L	1-2	SA	Paloschi 71	52 477
	22	Torino	W	1-0	SA	Pato 66	21 009
	30	Atalanta	L	1-2	SA	Maldini 85	50 990
Apr	5	Cagliari	W	3-1	SA	Kaka 8, Inzaghi 2 31 70	52 422
	12	Juventus	L	2-3	SA	Inzaghi 2 14 31	21 605
	20	Reggina	W	5-1	SA	Kaka 3 8p 34p 68, Inzaghi 73, Pato 88	55 274
	27	Livorno	W	4-1	SA	Inzaghi 3 22 52 60, Seedorf 71	14 504
May	4	Inter	W	2-1	SA	Inzaghi 51, Kaka 56	81 766
	11	Napoli	L	1-3	SA	Seedorf 96+	55 874
	18	Udinese	W	4-1	SA	Pato 48, Inzaghi 59, Cafu 79, Seedorf 65	820

ESC = European Super Cup • SA = Serie A • CL = UEFA Champions League • CW = FIFA Club World Cup • CI = Coppa Italia • gD = group D • r2 = second round • r4 = fourth round • sf = semi-final • f = final

NAPOLI 2007–08

Month	Day	Opponent	Res	Score	Scorers	Attendance
	26	Cagliari	L	0-2		39 026
	2	Udinese	W	5-0	Zalayetta 2 16 70, Domizzi 41, Lavezzi 65, Sosa 81	16 197
Sept	16	Sampdoria	W	2-0	Zalayeta 43, Hamsik 76	43 490
	23	Empoli	D	0-0		11 985
	26	Livorno	W	1-0	Sosa 85	37 163
	30	Genoa	L	1-2	Domizzi 52p	0
	6	Inter	L	1-2	Sosa 84	46 536
Oct	20	Roma	D	4-4	Lavezzi 2, Hamsik 46, Gargano 64, Zalayeta 84	27 313
	27	Juventus	W	3-1	Gargano 49, Domizzi 2 62p 69p	56 022
	31	Fiorentina	L	0-1		32 568
Nov	4	Reggina	D	1-1	Lavezzi 90	34 940
	10	Palermo	L	1-2	Bogliacino 54	25 138
	25	Catania	W	2-0	Zalayeta 2 43 65	31 344
	1	Atalanta	L	1-5	Sosa 60	6 388
Dec	9	Parma	W	1-0	Zalayeta 17	35 349
	16	Siena	D	1-1	Bogliacino 64	10 686
	23	Torino	D	1-1	Hamsik 76	40 795
	13	Milan	L	2-5	Sosa 28, Domizzi 38p	70 085
Jan	20	Lazio	D	2-2	Hamsik 2 5 94+	34 480
	27	Cagliari	L	1-2	Hamsik 12	11 000
	2	Udinese	W	3-1	OG 3, Lavezzi 2 74 75	36 034
	10	Sampdoria	L	0-2		19 592
Feb	17	Empoli	L	1-3	Mannini 37	50 175
	24	Livorno	W	2-1	Calaio 2 58 94+	8 495
	27	Genoa	L	0-2		26 417
	2	Inter	W	1-0	Zalayeta 3	53 818
	9	Roma	L	0-2		59 272
	16	Juventus	L	0-1		21 095
Mar	19	Fiorentina	W	2-0	Lavezzi 2 23 31	42 661
	22	Reggina	D	1-1	Sosa 76	12 383
	30	Palermo	W	1-0	Hamsik 94+	49 341
	6	Catania	L	0-3		14 246
Apr	13	Atalanta	W	2-0	Hamsik 62, Lavezzi 64	38 688
	20	Parma	W	2-1	Domizzi 45, Bogliacino 74	17 996
	27	Siena	D	0-0		39 086
	4	Torino	L	1-2	Contini 54	21 112
May	11	Milan	W	3-1	Hamsik 35, Domizzi 68p, Garics 94+	55 874
	18	Lazio	L	1-2	Domizzi 83	14 891

PALERMO 2007–08

Month	Day	Opponent	Res	Score	Scorers	Attendance
	26	Roma	L	0-2		32 202
	2	Livorno	W	4-2	Rinaudo 9, Miccoli 2 22 37, Amauri 41	8 475
	16	Torino	D	1-1	Simplicio 4	25 987
Sept	23	Cagliari	W	1-0	Zaccardo 14	8 000
	26	Milan	W	2-1	Diana 73, Miccoli 95+	30 761
	30	Empoli	L	1-3	Cavani 39	6 002
	7	Reggina	D	1-1	Amauri 95+	22 845
Oct	21	Udinese	D	1-1	Amauri 17	13 404
	28	Inter	D	0-0		33 972
	31	Parma	D	1-1	Amauri 87p	22 680
	4	Genoa	D	3-3	Cavani 8, Brienza 76, Amauri 92+	23 595
Nov	10	Napoli	W	2-1	Tedesco 2 57 67	25 138
	25	Juventus	L	0-5		20 036
	2	Catania	L	1-3	Caserta 63	17 400
Dec	8	Fiorentina	W	2-0	Miccoli 13, Simplicio 80	21 823
	16	Atalanta	W	3-1	Cavani 13, OG 35, Amauri 53	5 452
	23	Lazio	D	2-2	Simplicio 34, Amauri 46	24 148
Jan	3	Sampdoria	L	0-3		29 574
	20	Siena	L	2-3	Amauri 4, Miccoli 76p	22 542
	26	Roma	L	0-1		32 618
	3	Livorno	W	1-0	Miccoli 77	23 033
	10	Torino	L	1-3	Amauri 36	17 914
Feb	17	Cagliari	W	2-1	Cavani 23, Jankovic 45	21 829
	24	Milan	L	1-2	Bresciano 9	50 643
	27	Empoli	W	2-0	Simplicio 9, Rinaudo 38	22 897
	2	Reggina	D	0-0		10 316
	8	Udinese	D	1-1	Simplicio 32	24 833
Mar	16	Inter	L	1-2	Materazzi OG 25	49 360
	19	Parma	L	1-2	Cavani 68	12 599
	22	Genoa	L	2-3	Amauri 2 24p 94+	23 260
	30	Napoli	L	0-1		49 341
	6	Juventus	W	3-2	Amauri 2 11 45, Casani 89	34 271
Apr	12	Catania	W	1-0	Miccoli 85	24 847
	19	Fiorentina	L	0-1		28 827
	27	Atalanta	D	0-0		23 288
	4	Lazio	W	2-1	Amauri 2 82 94+	20 786
May	11	Sampdoria	L	0-2		23 929
	18	Siena	D	2-2	Jankovic 23, Miccoli 30	9 339

PARMA 2007–08

	Opponent		Score	Scorers	Att.
Sept	26 Catania	D	2-2	Pisanu 28, Rossi 43	12 579
	2 Atalanta	L	0-2		10 141
	16 Cagliari	D	1-1	Corradi 72	12 853
	22 Milan	D	1-1	Pisanu 73	51 026
	26 Torino	W	2-0	Reginaldo 62, Corradi 64	12 932
	30 Udinese	L	1-2	Corradi 72	12 704
Oct	7 Roma	L	0-3		16 922
	21 Sampdoria	L	0-3		20 038
	28 Livorno	W	3-2	Morrone 10, Paci 54, Morfeo 74	11 890
	31 Palermo	D	1-1	Morrone 3	22 680
Nov	4 Siena	D	2-2	Corradi 23, Matteini 79	12 262
	11 Juventus	D	2-2	Gasbarroni 43p, Pisanu 57	22 278
	25 Lazio	L	0-1		17 289
Dec	2 Empoli	W	1-0	Paci 21	12 736
	9 Napoli	L	0-1		35 349
	16 Reggina	W	3-0	Corradi 26, Pisanu 49, Paci 66	12 171
	22 Genoa	L	0-1		22 914
Jan	13 Fiorentina	L	1-2	Coly 69	14 663
	20 Inter	L	2-3	Cigarini 40, Gasbarroni 68	43 413
	27 Catania	D	0-0		16 287
Feb	3 Atalanta	L	2-3	Lucarelli 39, Gasbarroni 94+p	13 089
	10 Cagliari	D	1-1	Reginaldo 35	12 135
	16 Milan	D	0-0		19 361
	23 Torino	D	4-4	Gasbarroni 2 29 32, Morrone 42, Budan 43	17 999
	27 Udinese	W	2-0	Lucarelli 78, Cigarini 87p	11 999
Mar	1 Roma	L	0-4		31 788
	9 Sampdoria	L	1-2	Budan 67	16 328
	16 Livorno	D	1-1	Reginaldo 60	11 008
	19 Palermo	W	2-1	Budan 2 52 91+p	12 599
	22 Siena	L	0-2		9 342
Apr	6 Lazio	D	2-2	Budan 17, Paci 43	13 370
	13 Empoli	D	1-1	Lucarelli 7	5 938
	16 Juventus	L	0-3		21 405
	20 Napoli	L	1-2	Budan 23p	17 996
	27 Reggina	L	1-2	Cigarini 25p	16 117
May	4 Genoa	W	1-0	Lucarelli 58	17 693
	11 Fiorentina	L	1-3	Budan 11	36 289
	18 Inter	L	0-2		25 149

REGGINA 2007–08

	Opponent		Score	Scorers	Att.
Sept	26 Atalanta	D	1-1	Amoruso 78	12 963
	2 Torino	D	2-2	Amoruso 31, Cozza 90	12 403
	16 Roma	L	0-2		14 030
	22 Udinese	L	0-2		12 782
	26 Juventus	L	0-4		19 050
	30 Lazio	D	1-1	Cozza 8	10 169
Oct	7 Palermo	D	1-1	Amoruso 89	22 845
	20 Inter	L	0-1		16 965
	28 Siena	D	0-0		8 435
	31 Livorno	L	1-3	Amoruso 37	10 157
Nov	4 Napoli	D	1-1	Vigiani 53	34 940
	11 Genoa	W	2-0	Amoruso 31, Joelson 80	10 312
	25 Fiorentina	D	0-0		10 375
Dec	1 Sampdoria	L	0-3		19 059
	16 Parma	L	0-3		12 171
	23 Catania	W	3-1	Vigiani 3 34 79 94+	11 925
Jan	12 Empoli	D	1-1	Ceravolo 2	5 349
	20 Cagliari	W	2-0	Brienza 66, Cozza 80	10 122
	27 Atalanta	D	2-2	Vigiani 61, Barreto 67	12 584
	30 Milan	L	0-1		17 426
Feb	3 Torino	L	1-3	Amoruso 59	10 300
	9 Roma	L	0-2		31 635
	17 Udinese	L	1-3	Modesto 76	9 917
	23 Juventus	L	3-1	Brienza 32, Amoruso 93+p	21 884
	27 Lazio	L	0-1		17 663
Mar	2 Palermo	D	0-0		10 316
	8 Inter	L	0-2		64 575
	16 Siena	W	4-0	Brienza 2 9 29, Cozza 19, Missroli 68	10 300
	19 Livorno	D	1-1	Brienza 33	9 027
	22 Napoli	D	1-1	Brienza 95+	12 383
	30 Genoa	L	0-2		23 349
Apr	6 Fiorentina	L	0-2		27 321
	13 Sampdoria	W	1-0	Brienza 35	11 082
	20 Milan	L	1-5	Barreto 40	55 274
	27 Parma	W	2-1	Cozza 2 56 65	16 117
May	4 Catania	W	2-1	Amoruso 2 41 92+p	18 177
	11 Empoli	W	2-0	Barreto 69, Amoruso 79	23 248
	18 Cagliari	D	2-2	Brienza 2 55 86p	20 124

ROMA 2007–08

	Opponent		Score	Comp	Scorers	Att.
Aug	18 Inter	W	1-0	SC	De Rossi 78p	55 000
	26 Palermo	W	2-0	SA	Mexes 4, Aquilani 27	32 202
Sept	2 Siena	W	3-0	SA	Aquilani 17, Giuly 82, Totti 89	44 037
	16 Reggina	W	2-0	SA	Juan 51, Totti 85	14 030
	19 Dy'mo Kyiv	W	2-0	CLgF	Perrotta 9, Totti 70	35 508
	23 Juventus	D	2-2	SA	Totti 2 30 36	62 241
	26 Fiorentina	D	2-2	SA	Mancini 19, Giuly 36	36 056
	29 Inter	L	1-4	SA	Perrotta 53	51 150
Oct	2 Man Utd	L	0-1	CLgF		73 652
	7 Parma	W	3-0	SA	Totti 2 82, Mancini 21	16 922
	20 Napoli	D	4-4	SA	Totti 30p, Perrotta 42, De Rossi 52, Pizarro 80	27 313
	23 Sporting CL	W	2-1	CLgF	Juan 15, Vucinic 70	26 893
	28 Milan	W	1-0	SA	Vucinic 72	60 205
	31 Lazio	W	3-2	SA	Vucinic 18, Mancini 42, Perrotta 56	54 860
Nov	4 Empoli	D	2-2	SA	Giuly 13, Brighi 32	7 499
	7 Sporting CL	D	2-2	CLgF	Cassetti 4, Polga OG 90	32 273
	24 Genoa	W	1-0	SA	Panucci 90	24 106
	27 Dy'mo Kyiv	W	4-1	CLgF	Panucci 4, Giuly 32, Vucinic 2 36 78	19 700
	2 Udinese	W	2-1	SA	Juan 11, Taddei 27	32 323
Dec	5 Cagliari	W	2-0	SA	Taddei 2 28 36	32 019
	9 Livorno	D	1-1	SA	De Rossi 5	5 500
	12 Man Utd	D	1-1	CLgF	Mancini 71	29 490
	16 Torino	D	0-0	SA		18 501
	19 Torino	L	1-3	ICr4	Mancini 46	5 462
	22 Sampdoria	W	2-0	SA	Totti 2 18p 91+	31 726
Jan	13 Atalanta	W	2-1	SA	Totti 38, Mancini 44	7 662
	16 Torino	W	4-0	ICr4	Mancini 62, Totti 2 64 75p, Giuly 92+	21 034
	20 Catania	W	2-0	SA	Giuly 8, De Rossi 57p	33 378
	23 Sampdoria	D	1-1	ICqf	Vucinic 70	12 062
	26 Palermo	W	1-0	SA	Mancini 59	32 618
	29 Sampdoria	W	1-0	ICqf	Mancini 62	24 715
Feb	3 Siena	L	0-3	SA		10 158
	9 Reggina	W	2-0	SA	Panucci 21, Mancini 76	31 635
	12 Juventus	L	0-1	SA		21 139
	19 Real Madrid	W	2-1	CLr2	Pizarro 24, Mancini 58	56 231
	24 Fiorentina	W	1-0	SA	Cicinho 54	34 254
	27 Inter	D	1-1	SA	Totti 38	48 717
Mar	1 Parma	W	4-0	SA	Aquilani 27, OG 51, Totti 80, Vucinic 95+	31 788
	5 Real Madrid	W	2-1	CLr2	Taddei 73, Vucinic 92+	71 569
	9 Napoli	W	2-0	SA	Perrotta 2, Totti 51p	59 272
	16 Milan	W	2-1	SA	Giuly 81, Vucinic 85	48 447
	19 Lazio	L	2-3	SA	Taddei 31, Perrotta 62	49 284
	22 Empoli	W	2-1	SA	Tonetto 36, Panucci 63	31 392
	29 Cagliari	D	1-1	SA	Totti 45	25 140
Apr	1 Man Utd	L	0-2	CLqf		60 931
	5 Genoa	W	3-2	SA	Taddei 14, Vucinic 17, De Rossi 80p	36 366
	9 Man Utd	L	0-1	CLqf		74 423
	13 Udinese	W	3-1	SA	Vucinic 64, Taddei 70, Giuly 91+	20 405
	16 Catania	W	1-0	ICsf	Totti 47	15 084
	19 Livorno	D	1-1	SA	Vucinic 54	34 061
	27 Torino	W	4-1	SA	Pizarro 18p, Vucinic 20, Mancini 2 26 32	34 001
May	4 Sampdoria	W	3-0	SA	Panucci 75, Pizarro 79, Cicinho 85	24 311
	6 Catania	D	1-1	ICsf	Aquilani 26p	15 229
	11 Atalanta	W	2-0	SA	Panucci 23, De Rossi 67	36 416
	18 Catania	D	1-1	SA	Vucinic 8	21 148
	24 Inter	W	2-1	ICf	Mexes 36, Perrotta 55	50 000

SC = Supercoppa Italia • SA = Serie A • CL = UEFA Champions League • IC = Coppa Italia • gF = group F • r2 = second round • r4 = fourth round • qf = quarter-final • sf = semi-final • f = final

SAMPDORIA 2007–08

	Date	Opponent	Res	Score	Scorers	Att
Sept	26	Siena	W	2-1	Bellucci 34, Montella 84	10 768
	2	Lazio	D	0-0		20 564
	16	Napoli	L	0-2		43 490
	23	Genoa	D	0-0		33 060
	26	Inter	L	0-3		42 013
	30	Atalanta	W	3-0	Bellucci 4, Sammarco 57, Cassano 83	21 000
Oct	7	Torino	L	0-1		16 401
	21	Parma	W	3-0	Montella 25, Bellucci 2 46 58	20 038
	28	Catania	L	0-2		16 276
	31	Milan	L	0-5		22 095
Nov	4	Cagliari	W	3-0	Volpi 33, Caracciolo 39, Maggio 45	10 000
	10	Empoli	W	3-0	OG 5, Montella 40, Sammarco 95+	19 327
	25	Livorno	L	1-3	Bellucci 80	7 675
Dec	1	Reggina	W	3-0	Bellucci 2 4 76, Sammarco 55	19 059
	9	Udinese	L	2-3	Bellucci 32p, Maggio 40	13 406
	16	Fiorentina	D	2-2	Gastaldello 18, Cassano 69	22 161
	22	Roma	L	0-2		31 726
Jan	13	Palermo	W	3-0	Bellucci 20, Sammarco 45, Cassano 77	29 574
	20	Juventus	D	0-0		22 379
	26	Siena	W	1-0	Cassano 44	19 562
Feb	3	Lazio	L	1-2	Cassano 45	18 683
	10	Napoli	W	2-0	Delvecchio 76, Franceschini 81	19 592
	17	Genoa	W	1-0	Maggio 87	37 508
	24	Inter	D	1-1	Cassano 65	26 306
	27	Atalanta	L	1-4	Volpi 3	10 244
Mar	2	Torino	D	2-2	Sala 45, Cassano 52	19 032
	9	Parma	W	2-1	Maggio 12, Bonazzoli 57	16 328
	16	Catania	W	3-1	Palombo 68, Accardi 76, Bellucci 86	19 409
	19	Milan	W	2-1	Maggio 12, Delvecchio 25	52 477
	22	Cagliari	D	1-1	Franceschini 92+	19 877
	30	Empoli	W	2-0	Sammarco 6, Marzoratti OG 16	7 066
Apr	6	Livorno	W	2-0	Maggio 67, Bonazzoli 89	21 426
	13	Reggina	L	0-1		11 082
	20	Udinese	W	3-0	Cassano 24, Bellucci 2 44 55	25 181
	27	Fiorentina	D	2-2	Maggio 63, Gastaldello 94+	36 627
May	4	Roma	L	0-3		24 311
	11	Palermo	W	2-0	Cassano 61, Maggio 76	23 929
	17	Juventus	D	3-3	Cassano 22, Maggio 39, Montella 80	26 954

SIENA 2007–08

	Date	Opponent	Res	Score	Scorers	Att
Sept	26	Sampdoria	L	1-2	Corvia 65	10 768
	2	Roma	L	0-3		44 037
	16	Milan	D	1-1	Maccarone 24	14 085
	23	Torino	D	1-1	Maccarone 53	18 086
	26	Atalanta	D	1-1	Loria 31	8 377
	30	Cagliari	L	0-1		10 000
Oct	7	Empoli	W	3-0	Maccarone 65p, Locatelli 79, Galloppa 82	8 819
	21	Fiorentina	L	0-3		28 307
	28	Reggina	D	0-0		8 435
	31	Catania	D	1-1	De Ceglie 80	7 898
Nov	4	Parma	D	2-2	De Ceglie 33, Galloppa 90	12 262
	11	Livorno	L	2-3	Maccarone 18, Loria 93+	8 532
	25	Udinese	L	0-2		12 989
Dec	2	Lazio	D	1-1	Maccarone 32	9 186
	9	Genoa	W	3-1	Frick 2 11 24, Loria 20	22 697
	16	Napoli	D	1-1	Bogliacino 64	10 686
	23	Juventus	L	0-2		20 421
Jan	13	Inter	L	2-3	Cordoba OG 31, Forestieri 94+	14 682
	20	Palermo	W	3-2	Locatelli 5, Maccarone 11, Loria 78	22 542
	26	Sampdoria	L	0-1		19 562
Feb	3	Roma	W	3-0	Vergassola 11, OG 42, Frick 83	10 158
	10	Milan	L	0-1		51 552
	17	Torino	D	0-0		8 913
	24	Atalanta	D	2-2	Bertotto 32, Locatelli 40	9 226
	27	Cagliari	W	1-0	Maccarone 88	8 913
Mar	2	Empoli	W	2-0	Portanova 33, Rigano 96+	6 139
	9	Fiorentina	W	1-0	Maccarone 80	12 785
	16	Reggina	L	0-4		10 300
	19	Catania	D	0-0		16 655
	22	Parma	W	2-0	Maccarone 2 87p 91+	9 342
	30	Livorno	D	0-0		10 207
Apr	6	Udinese	D	1-1	Kharja 69	8 652
	13	Lazio	D	1-1	Loria 88	18 996
	20	Genoa	L	0-1		12 228
	27	Napoli	D	0-0		39 086
May	4	Juventus	W	1-0	Kharja 7	15 419
	11	Inter	D	2-2	Maccarone 31, Kharja 69	76 633
	18	Palermo	D	2-2	Maccarone 2 2 58	9 339

TORINO 2007–08

	Date	Opponent	Res	Score	Scorers	Att
Sept	25	Lazio	D	2-2	Rosina 34, Vailatti 68	21 495
	2	Reggina	D	2-2	Rosina 45, Ventola 58	12 403
	16	Palermo	D	1-1	Recoba 54	25 987
	23	Siena	D	1-1	Delafiore 24	18 086
	2	Parma	L	0-2		12 932
	30	Juventus	L	0-1		23 974
Oct	7	Sampdoria	W	1-0	Corini 88	16 401
	21	Atalanta	D	2-2	Ventola 75, Motta 87	10 962
	27	Cagliari	W	2-0	Rosina 71, OG 85	18 226
	3	Udinese	L	1-2	Ventola 62	13 117
Nov	3	Milan	D	0-0		54 980
	11	Catania	D	1-1	Malonga 15	18 597
	25	Empoli	D	0-0		5 579
Dec	2	Genoa	D	1-1	Lanna 55	18 404
	9	Inter	L	0-4		46 148
	16	Roma	D	0-0		18 501
	23	Napoli	D	1-1	Rosina 36p	40 795
Jan	13	Livorno	L	1-2	Bottone 78	17 515
	19	Fiorentina	L	1-2	Grella 57	27 992
	27	Lazio	D	0-0		17 653
Feb	3	Reggina	W	3-1	Rosina 2 23p 66p, Stellone 35	10 300
	10	Palermo	W	3-1	Diana 60, Di Michele 2 71 81	17 914
	24	Parma	D	4-4	Stellone 2 11 69, Natali 45, Di Michele 82	17 999
	26	Juventus	D	0-0		22 636
Mar	2	Sampdoria	D	2-2	Comotto 18, Di Michele 50p	19 032
	9	Atalanta	W	1-0	Barone 36	18 208
	16	Cagliari	L	0-3		10 560
	19	Udinese	L	0-1		17 559
	22	Milan	L	0-1		21 009
	30	Catania	W	2-1	Diana 4, Di Michele 62	16 955
Apr	6	Empoli	L	0-1		18 750
	13	Genoa	L	0-3		25 751
	20	Inter	L	0-1		21 865
	27	Roma	L	1-4	Ventola 50	34 001
May	4	Napoli	W	2-1	Rosina 27p, Di Michele 56	21 112
	11	Livorno	W	1-0	Rosina 41	8 813
	18	Fiorentina	L	0-1		23 771

UDINESE 2007–08

	Date	Opponent	Res	Score	Scorers	Att
Sept	26	Inter	D	1-1	Cordoba OG 92+	42 797
	2	Napoli	L	0-5		16 197
	16	Juventus	W	1-0	Di Natale 47	20 414
	22	Reggina	W	2-0	Di Natale 2 5 62	12 782
	26	Genoa	L	2-3	Gyan 51, Mesto 76	22 253
	30	Parma	W	2-1	Quagliarella 78, Zapata 95+	12 704
Oct	6	Atalanta	D	0-0		11 377
	21	Palermo	D	1-1	Gyan 65	13 404
	28	Lazio	W	1-0	Gyan 79	17 536
	31	Torino	W	2-1	Floro Flores 25, Inler 52	13 117
Nov	4	Livorno	D	0-0		7 773
	11	Fiorentina	W	2-1	Quagliarella 23, Di Natale 63	27 882
	25	Siena	W	2-0	Quagliarella 43, Di Natale 80	12 989
Dec	2	Roma	L	1-2	Quagliarella 12	32 323
	9	Sampdoria	W	3-2	Di Natale 23, Quagliarella 2 70 86	13 406
	15	Catania	L	0-2		16 551
	23	Empoli	D	2-2	Dossena 22, Di Natale 85	13 104
Jan	13	Cagliari	W	1-0	Quagliarella 32	7 100
	20	Milan	L	0-1		24 574
	27	Inter	D	0-0		21 913
Feb	2	Napoli	L	1-3	Pepe 9	36 034
	10	Juventus	L	1-2	Dossena 6	25 152
	19	Reggina	W	3-1	Pepe 8, Di Natale 2 63 95+	9 917
	24	Genoa	L	3-5	Di Natale 2 27p 39p, Floro Flores 74	13 640
	27	Parma	L	0-2		11 999
Mar	2	Atalanta	W	2-0	Quagliarella 30, Di Natale 32	13 245
	8	Palermo	D	1-1	Felipe 64	24 833
	15	Lazio	D	2-2	Ferronetti 56, Di Natale 86	13 084
	19	Torino	W	1-0	Pepe 25	17 559
	22	Livorno	W	2-0	Quagliarella 19, Di Natale 47	12 594
	30	Fiorentina	W	3-1	Inler 13, Di Natale 72, Quagliarella 76	15 374
Apr	6	Siena	D	1-1	Floro Flores 77	8 652
	13	Roma	L	1-3	Di Natale 52	20 405
	20	Sampdoria	L	0-3		25 181
	27	Catania	W	2-1	Di Natale 5, Quagliarella 38	13 958
May	4	Empoli	W	1-0	Quagliarella 17	7 257
	11	Cagliari	L	0-2		16 689
	18	Milan	L	1-4	Mesto 32	65 829

JAM – JAMAICA

NATIONAL TEAM RECORD
JULY 10TH 2006 TO JULY 12TH 2010

PL	W	D	L	F	A	%
22	9	5	8	43	29	52.3

FIFA/COCA-COLA WORLD RANKING

1993	1994	1995	1996	1997	1998	1999	2000	2001	2002	2003	2004	2005	2006	2007	High	
80	96	56	32	39	33	41	48	53	51	46	49	42	57	97	27	08/98

				2007–2008								Low	
08/07	09/07	10/07	11/07	12/07	01/08	02/08	03/08	04/08	05/08	06/08	07/08	105	05/08
95	96	103	98	97	98	90	103	103	105	98	94		

The return of Rene Simoes - the 'Magic Man' - to his former post as Jamaican national team coach considerably brightened the mood in the country as the Reggae Boyz set off on their journey to qualify for the 2010 FIFA World Cup finals in South Africa. But Simoes will have to evoke the same team spirit that saw them qualify for the finals in France in 1998 during his previous six year stint in the job if they are to have a chance, having been drawn alongside Mexico, Honduras and Canada in arguably the toughest of the three CONCACAF groups. The Jamaicans had breezed past the Bahamas in a preliminary round with a team of mainly overseas-based players which included

INTERNATIONAL HONOURS
Qualified for the FIFA World Cup finals 1998 **Caribbean Cup** 1991 1998 2005

Wigan's Marlon King. His ban for indiscipline imposed by the federation in 2006 was overturned by the returning president Horace Burrell. It is hoped that more home-based players will make their way into the squad with the introduction of the CONCACAF Champions League potentially bringing big benefits to clubs in Jamaica. Three clubs from the Caribbean will enter the tournament every year with Caribbean champions Harbour View qualifying for the inaugural competition. Portmore United will be looking to make it through to the following tournament after they won the 2008 championship ahead of Tivoli Gardens, who also lost in the Cup Final to Waterhouse.

THE FIFA BIG COUNT OF 2006

	Male	Female		Total
Number of players	144 884	23 610	Referees and Assistant Referees	312
Professionals	270		Admin, Coaches, Technical, Medical	4 725
Amateurs 18+	11 974		Number of clubs	270
Youth under 18	13 060		Number of teams	900
Unregistered	47 900		Clubs with women's teams	4
Total players	168 494		Players as % of population	6.11%

Jamaica Football Federation (JFF)
20 St Lucia Crescent, Kingston 5, Jamaica
Tel +1 876 9298036   Fax +1 876 9290438
jamff@hotmail.com   www.jamaicafootballfederation.com
President: BURRELL Horace   General Secretary: REID Horace
Vice-President: SPENCER Dale   Treasurer: SINCLAIR Garfield   Media Officer: WILLIAMS Gareth
Men's Coach: SIMOES Rene   Women's Coach: EDWARDS Carlos
JFF formed: 1910   CONCACAF: 1961   FIFA: 1962
Gold shirts, Black shorts, Gold socks

RECENT INTERNATIONAL MATCHES PLAYED BY JAMAICA

2004	Opponents	Score		Venue	Comp	Scorers	Att	Referee
12-12	St Lucia	D	1-1	Vieux Fort	CCq	Priestly [42]		Jeanvillier MTQ
19-12	St Lucia	W	2-1	Kingston	CCq	Dean [1], Hue [67]	2 500	Gutierrez CUB
2005								
20-02	Trinidad and Tobago	W	2-1	Bridgetown	CC	Shelton [13], Williams.A [35]	5 000	Callender BRB
22-02	Barbados	W	1-0	Bridgetown	CC	Williams.A [8]	2 100	Brizan TRI
24-02	Cuba	W	1-0	Bridgetown	CC	Shelton [48]	3 000	Brizan TRI
20-04	Guatemala	W	1-0	Atlanta	Fr	Shelton [14]	7 000	Prus USA
4-06	Honduras	D	0-0	Atlanta	Fr		6 500	Valenzuela USA
8-07	Guatemala	W	4-3	Carson	GCr1	Shelton [3], Fuller [5], Williams.A [46+p], Hue [57]	27 000	Hall USA
10-07	South Africa	D	3-3	Los Angeles	GCr1	Hue [35], Stewart [43], Bennett [80]	30 710	Stott USA
13-07	Mexico	L	0-1	Houston	GCr1		45 311	Quesada CRC
16-07	USA	L	1-3	Foxboro	GCqf	Fuller [88]	22 108	Batres GUA
1-10	Guatemala	W	2-1	Fort Lauderdale	Fr	Shelton [41], Crawford [70]	6 000	Rutty USA
9-10	Australia	L	0-5	London	Fr		6 570	Riley ENG
2006								
11-04	USA	D	1-1	Carey	Fr	Bennett [4]	8 093	Gasso MEX
29-05	Ghana	L	1-4	Leicester	Fr	Euell [58]	12 000	Halsey ENG
3-06	England	L	0-6	Manchester	Fr		70 373	Plautz AUT
4-09	Canada	L	0-1	Montreal	Fr		6 526	Quesada CRC
27-09	St Lucia	W	4-0	Kingston	CCq	Smith.W [3], Lemey 2 [22 36], Phillips [31]	4 000	Tamayo CUB
29-09	St Vincent/Grenadines	L	1-2	Kingston	CCq	Dean [72]	3 000	Brizan TRI
1-10	Haiti	W	2-0	Kingston	CCq	Smith.W [9], Dawkins [31]	3 000	Tamayo CUB
8-10	Canada	W	2-1	Kingston	Fr	Shelton [35], Phillips [38]	5 000	Brizan TRI
15-11	Peru	D	1-1	Kingston	Fr	Hue [78p]		
2007								
22-03	Switzerland	L	0-2	Fort Lauderdale	Fr		3 254	Prus USA
26-03	Panama	D	1-1	Kingston	Fr	Shelton [45]	16 554	Brizan TRI
5-06	Chile	L	0-1	Kingston	Fr		15 000	Guerrero NCA
21-06	Indonesia	L	1-2	Jakarta	Fr	Wolfe [72]		
24-06	Vietnam	L	0-3	Hanoi	Fr			
28-06	Malaysia	W	2-0	Kuala Lumpur	Fr	Harvey [44], Wolfe [45]		
2-07	Iran	L	1-8	Tehran	Fr	Taylor [83]		
18-11	El Salvador	W	3-0	Kingston	Fr	Austin [33], Gardner 2 [37 81]	15 000	Whittaker CAY
21-11	Guatemala	W	2-0	Kingston	Fr	Fuller [10], Dalley [21]		Whittaker CAY
2008								
6-02	Costa Rica	D	1-1	Kingston	Fr	Marshall [88]	30 000	Brizan TRI
26-03	Trinidad and Tobago	D	2-2	Kingston	Fr	King [32], Marshall [38]	19 000	Whittaker CAY
3-06	St Vincent/Grenadines	W	5-1	Kingston	Fr	Phillips [17], King 2 [27p 40], Burton [73], Gardner [87]		Whittaker CAY
7-06	Trinidad and Tobago	D	1-1	Macoya	Fr	Shelton [90p]		Small BRB
10-06	Grenada	L	1-2	St George's	Fr	Fuller [20]		
15-06	Bahamas	W	7-0	Kingston	WCq	Gardner [17], Phillips [23], King [34], Shelton 2 [51 66], Goodison [75], Daley [89]	20 000	Navarro CAN
18-06	Bahamas	W	6-0	Greenfield	WCq	Burton 2 [29 55], Shelton 3 [35 37p 42], Marshall [39]	10 500	Archundia MEX

Fr = Friendly match • CC = Digicel Caribbean Cup • GC = CONCACAF Gold Cup • WC = FIFA World Cup
q = qualifier • r1 = first round group • qf = quarter-final • † Not a full international

JAMAICA NATIONAL TEAM RECORDS AND RECORD SEQUENCES

Records			Sequence records				
Victory	12-0	BVI 1994	Wins	7	2000	Clean sheets	5	Three times
Defeat	0-9	CRC 1999	Defeats	7	1967-68, 2001-02	Goals scored	19	1997
Player Caps	107	Durrant Brown	Undefeated	23	1997-1998	Without goal	7	2000
Player Goals	24	Theodore Whitmore	Without win	12	1975-79, 1988-90	Goals against	23	1966-1969

JAMAICA COUNTRY INFORMATION

Capital	Kingston	Independence	1962 from the UK	GDP per Capita	$3 900
Population	2 713 130	Status	Commonweath	GNP Ranking	100
Area km²	10 991	Language	English	Dialling code	+1 876
Population density	247 per km²	Literacy rate	87%	Internet code	.jm
% in urban areas	54%	Main religion	Christian 61%	GMT + / –	-4
Towns/Cities ('000)	Kingston 584; Spanish Town 145; Portmore 102; Montego Bay 83; Mandeville 47				
Neighbours (km)	Caribbean Sea 1 022				
Main stadia	Independence Park – Kingston 35 000; Harbour View – Kingston 7 000				

JAMAICA 2007–08

WRAY AND NEPHEW PREMIER LEAGUE

	Pl	W	D	L	F	A	Pts	Portmore U	Tivoli G'ns	Boys' Town	Harbour V	Waterhouse	Sporting	Village Utd	Arnett G'ns	St George's	Reno	Seba Utd	August T
Portmore United	38	21	12	5	56	25	75		3-0	1-0 0-0	0-2 0-0	1-0 1-3	0-1 3-1	2-0	0-0 1-0	1-2 0-1	2-0	3-1	2-1 1-0 3-1 3-1
Tivoli Gardens	38	20	6	12	50	41	66	1-0 2-4		1-0 1-2	2-1 2-0	1-0 2-1	2-0 0-1	1-0	1-0	3-2 3-1	2-0 3-1	2-0	1-1 2-0
Boys' Town	38	14	16	8	38	32	58	0-0 1-2	0-0 2-1		2-1 1-1	1-4 2-4	1-0 0-1	1-3	0-0 2-0 0-0	1-0	0-0	1-1 2-0	1-1
Harbour View	38	11	18	9	42	37	51	0-1 1-1	1-0 0-0	0-0 0-0		3-2 1-0	2-2 3-0	3-0 1-2	1-1	0-0 0-2	1-0	4-2	1-0
Waterhouse	38	10	17	11	44	49	47	1-0 1-1	2-0 3-4	1-1 1-0	1-1 1-1		1-0 2-2	0-2	2-1	1-1 1-2	1-2	1-1	3-1 1-1
Sporting Central Acad.	38	10	15	13	43	51	45	0-2 1-2	2-0 0-0	0-3 0-2	2-0 3-1	1-1 1-3		0-0 0-0 0-0 4	1-0	4-3 5-2	2-1 2-2	1-2	
Village United	38	11	13	14	41	41	46	1-2 0-0	2-2 3-0	3-0	1-1 1-2	0-0 0-2	0-2		2-1 0-0	2-0 2-0	0-0 0-0	2-0 0-2	1-0
Arnett Gardens	38	9	19	10	35	33	46	1-1	1-0 0-1	0-1	1-1 0-0	0-1 1-1	1-1	2-2 1-1 1-3		2-1 1-0	0-0 1-1	0-1 1-2 1-2	2-2
St George's	38	11	11	16	39	42	44	3-1	1-0	3-0 1-0	2-0	0-1	3-1 0-1 2-1 0-0 2-2			1-1 1-1	1-2 0-1	2-1 1-1	1-1
Reno	38	9	16	13	42	51	43	1-2 0-2	1-3	0-0 1-2	1-2 2-1	1-1	0-0	1-0 3-2	3-1 0-0	2-1 3-1		1-4 3-0	1-0 2-2
Seba United	38	10	12	16	43	52	42	0-0	1-2 1-2	0-1	2-0 0-0	4-3 1-0	2-2	3-2 0-2	1-1 2-2	2-0 0-1	2-0		2-0 3-1
August Town	38	9	11	18	39	58	38	0-5	2-1	1-2 0-1	1-2 2-2	1-1	0-0 1-0	3-2 4-3	1-1 1-0	1-0 1-1	1-1 0-1	3-3 0-0	

30/09/2007 - 11/05/2008 • Match in bold awarded

JFF CITY OF KINGSTON CHAMPIONS CUP 2007–08

Round of 16		Quarter-finals		Semi-finals		Final	
Waterhouse	3						
Albany *	0	Waterhouse *	1				
Sandy Bay	0	August Town	0				
August Town *	8			Waterhouse	4		
Humble Lions *	2			Village United	2		
Duhaney Park	1	Humble Lions *	1				
St George's *	2	Village United	4				
Village United	4					Waterhouse	2
Granville	5					Tivoli Gardens	0
Bath SC *	1	Granville *	1 5p				
Boys' Town	1	Portmore United	1 4p				
Portmore United *	2			Granville	0		
Harbour View *	2			Tivoli Gardens	7		
Arnett Gardens	1	Harbour View	0				
Barbican *	1	Tivoli Gardens *	1				
Tivoli Gardens	2						

* Home team in the first leg • Semis played at Edward Seaga, Kingston

CUP FINAL

Harbour View Ministadium, Kingston
13-05-2008, Ref: Campbell

Scorers - Roberto Fletcher [32], Kenardo Forbes [89]

RECENT LEAGUE AND CUP RECORD

	Championship				Cup		
Year	Champions	Score	Runners-up		Winners	Score	Runners-up
2000	Harbour View	0-0 2-1	Waterhouse		Hazard United	1-0	Wadadah
2001	Arnett Gardens	2-1 2-1	Waterhouse		Harbour View	3-0	Wadadah
2002	Arnett Gardens	1-1 2-1	Hazard United		Harbour View	2-1	Rivoli United
2003	Hazard United	1-1 3-2	Arnett Gardens		Hazard United	1-0	Harbour View
2004	Tivoli Gardens	4-1 1-2	Harbour View		Waterhouse	2-1	Village United
2005	Portmore United	1-1 1-0	Tivoli Gardens		Portmore United	3-1	Harbour View
2006	Waterhouse	†	Harbour View		Tivoli Gardens	3-2	Portmore United
2007	Harbour View	†	Portmore United		Portmore United	1-1 4-3p	Boys' Town
2008	Portmore United	†	Tivoli Gardens		Waterhouse	2-0	Tivoli Gardens

† Played on a League basis • Hazard United now known as Portmore United

JOR – JORDAN

NATIONAL TEAM RECORD
JULY 10TH 2006 TO JULY 12TH 2010

PL	W	D	L	F	A	%
31	13	6	12	42	30	51.6

FIFA/COCA-COLA WORLD RANKING

1993	1994	1995	1996	1997	1998	1999	2000	2001	2002	2003	2004	2005	2006	2007		High	
87	113	143	146	124	126	115	105	99	77	47	40	86	95	120		37	08/04

	2007–2008											Low	
08/07	09/07	10/07	11/07	12/07	01/08	02/08	03/08	04/08	05/08	06/08	07/08	152	07/96
99	99	111	122	120	112	111	106	105	104	100	114		

Jordan's attempts to follow up their impressive showing at the 2004 Asian Cup - when they were surprise quarter-finals and took defending champions Japan to a penalty shootout - continue to flounder as the nation missed out on a place in the final phase of Asia's qualifying tournament for the 2010 FIFA World Cup. Indeed they only just survived a preliminary round tie against Kyrgyzstan after winning a penalty shoot-out. Coached by former Saudi Arabia boss Eduardo Vingada, the Jordanians were eliminated from the first round group stage after a series of inconsistent performances, allowing Korea Republic and Korea DPR to advance at their expense. Despite the

INTERNATIONAL HONOURS
AFC Cup Al Faysali 2005 2006 Shabab Al Ordun 2007

continued disappointments at national team level, Jordanian clubs have dominated the AFC Cup over the last three years. Shahab Al Ordun claimed the title with victory over compatriots - and two-time defending champions - Al Faisaly in the 2007 final to extend the nation's run of success to three years. However, there was a sharp contrast in the fortunes for Jordanian sides in the 2008 edition of the competition, with neither of the participants - Shabab Al Ordun and Al Wihdat - qualifying for the knockout phase. Al Wihdat did at least claim the domestic title, successfully defending their crown ahead of Al Faisaly, who in turn beat Shabab Al Ordun in the Cup Final.

THE FIFA BIG COUNT OF 2006

	Male	Female		Total
Number of players	112 856	8 335	Referees and Assistant Referees	161
Professionals	21		Admin, Coaches, Technical, Medical	6 070
Amateurs 18+	3 637		Number of clubs	93
Youth under 18	1 163		Number of teams	146
Unregistered	40 250		Clubs with women's teams	9
Total players	121 191		Players as % of population	2.05%

Jordan Football Associatiom (JFA)
Al-Hussein Youth City, PO Box 962024, Amman 11196, Jordan
Tel +962 6 5657662   Fax +962 6 565 7660
info@jfa.com.jo   www.jfa.com.jo
President: HRH Prince Ali AL-HUSSEIN   General Secretary: AL DAOUD Mohammad
Vice-President: AL-HADID Nidal   Treasurer: AL DAOUD Jamal   Media Officer: ABU EATA Akram
Men's Coach: VINGADA Nelo   Women's Coach: HANTASH Maher
JFA formed: 1949   AFC: 1970   FIFA: 191958
White shirts with red trimmings, White shorts, White socks or Red shirts with with trimmings, Red shorts, Red socks

RECENT INTERNATIONAL MATCHES PLAYED BY JORDAN

2005	Opponents		Score	Venue	Comp	Scorers	Att	Referee
28-01	Norway	D	0-0	Amman	Fr		8 000	Al Shoufi SYR
26-03	Cyprus	L	1-2	Larnaca	Fr	Ahmet [85]		
8-06	Iraq	L	0-1	Amman	Fr			
17-08	Armenia	D	0-0	Amman	Fr			
16-11	Georgia	L	2-3	Amman	Fr	Salimi [35], Saedi [59]		
2006								
17-01	Côte d'Ivoire	L	0-2	Abu Dhabi	Fr			
23-01	Sweden	D	0-0	Abu Dhabi	Fr			
1-02	Thailand	D	0-0	Ayutthaya	Fr			
7-02	Kuwait	L	1-2	Kuwait City	Fr	Abdulfattah		
14-02	Kazakhstan	W	2-0	Amman	Fr	Ali [13], Aqel [53]		
22-02	Pakistan	W	3-0	Amman	ACq	Aqel [30p], Shelbaieh [38], Al Shagran [41]		Basma SYR
1-03	Oman	L	0-3	Wattayah	ACq		11 000	Irmatov UZB
21-07	Iraq	W	2-1	Amman	Fr	Saleem Mansour [36], Rafat Ali [41]		
30-07	Syria	W	3-0	Amman	Fr	Rafat Ali 3		
9-08	Iraq	L	0-1	Amman	Fr			
16-08	UAE	L	1-2	Amman	ACq	Rafat Ali [88]	18 000	Al Hamdan KSA
2-09	Bahrain	W	2-0	Manama	Fr	Saleem Mansour [5], Siraj Al Tall [61]		
6-09	UAE	D	0-0	Dubai	ACq		9 000	Al Fadhli KUW
6-10	Iran	D	0-0	Amman	Fr			
11-10	Pakistan	W	3-0	Lahore	ACq	Al Maharmeh [16], Rafat Ali [37], Khaled Saed [85]	4 000	Orzuev TJK
8-11	Saudi Arabia	L	1-2	Riyadh	Fr	Hassouneh Qasem [31]		
15-11	Oman	W	3-0	Amman	ACq	Amer Deeb [80], Rafat Ali [83], Al Shiekh [87]	3 000	Najm LIB
2007								
8-06	Iraq	D	1-1	Amman	Fr	Awad Ragheb [10]		
12-06	Iraq	D	0-0	Amman	Fr			
18-06	Syria	L	0-1	Amman	WAr1			
20-06	Lebanon	W	3-0	Amman	WAr1	Awad Ragheb [28], Al Maltaah [53], Al Saify [58]		
22-06	Iran	L	0-2	Amman	WAr1			
7-09	Bahrain	W	3-1	Al Muharraq	Fr	Abdullah Deeb 2 [24 55], Al Maharmeh [94+]		
18-10	Kyrgyzstan	L	0-2	Bishkek	WCq		18 000	Sarkar IND
28-10	Kyrgyzstan	W	2-0	Amman	WCq	Shelbaieh [33], Aqel [51p]. W 6-5p	12 000	Ebrahim BHR
11-12	Oman	W	3-0	Muscat	Fr	Al Saify [1], Al Nawatear 2 [79 90]		
2008								
24-01	Iraq	D	1-1	Dubai	Fr	Shelbaieh [60]		
28-01	Lebanon	W	4-1	Amman	Fr	Awad Ragheb [27], Shelbaieh [78], Amer Deeb [80], Rafat Ali [87]		
31-01	Singapore	W	2-1	Al Zarqa	Fr	Albzour [32], Awad Ragheb [94+]		
6-02	Korea DPR	L	0-1	Amman	WCq		16 000	Shamsuzzaman BAN
16-03	Qatar	L	1-2	Doha	Fr	Al Saify [45]		
22-03	Uzbekistan	L	1-4	Tashkent	Fr	Ala Matalka [11]		
26-03	Turkmenistan	W	2-0	Ashgabat	WCq	Albzzor [34], Bawab [84]	20 000	Tongkhan THA
25-05	China PR	L	0-2	Kunshan City	Fr			
31-05	Korea Republic	D	2-2	Seoul	WCq	Hasan Mahmoud 2 [73 81]	50 000	Shield AUS
7-06	Korea Republic	L	0-1	Amman	WCq		8 000	Moradi IRN
14-06	Korea DPR	L	0-2	Pyongyang	WCq		28 000	Najm LIB
22-06	Turkmenistan	W	2-0	Amman	WCq	Hasan Mahmoud 2 [66 67]	150	Williams AUS

Fr = Friendly match • WA = West Asian Federation Championship • AC = AFC Asian Cup • WC = FIFA World Cup
q = qualifier • r1 = first round group

JORDAN NATIONAL TEAM RECORDS AND RECORD SEQUENCES

Records			Sequence records					
Victory	6-0	TPE 2001	Wins	5	1992, 2003-2004	Clean sheets	4	1988, 2004
Defeat	0-6	SYR, ALG, CHN	Defeats	6	Three times	Goals scored	9	1992
Player Caps	n/a		Undefeated	14	2004	Without goal	7	1996-1997
Player Goals	n/a		Without win	13	1957-1966	Goals against	13	1992-1993

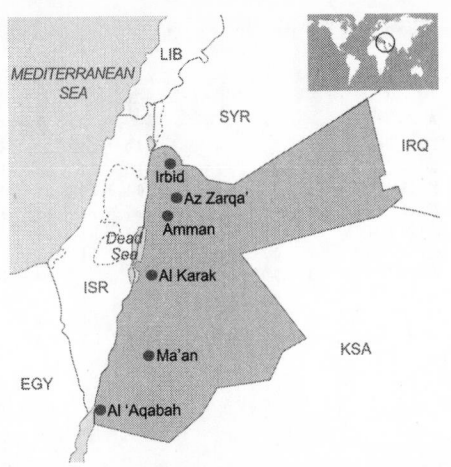

HASHEMITE KINGDOM OF JORDAN; AL MAMLAKAH AL URDUNIYAH AL HASHIMIYA

Capital	Amman	Language	Arabic	Independence	1946
Population	6 198 677	Area	92 300 km²	Density 61 per km²	% in cities 71%
GDP per cap	$4 300	Dailling code	+962	Internet .jo	GMT + / - +2

MEDALS TABLE

	Overall G S B	Lge G	Cup G S	Shield G S	Asia G S B	City	Stadium	Cap'ty	DoF
1 Al Faysali	53 11	30	16 5	5 5	2 1	Amman	Amman International	25 000	1932
2 Al Wihdat	22 10 2	10	6 4	6 6	2	Amman	Amman International	25 000	1956
3 Al Ramtha	9 10	2	2 9	5 1		Irbid	Al Hassan	15 000	1966
4 Al Ahli	8 1	8	1			Amman			
5 Al Jazeera	6 2	3	1 1	2 1		Amman			
6 Shabab Al Ordun	5 1	1	2 1	1	1	Amman	Amman International	25 000	2002
7 Al Hussein	3 12		5	3 7		Irbid	Al Hassan	15 000	1964
8 Amman	3 1	1		2 1		Amman			
9 Al Arabi	1		1			Irbid			
Kfarsoum	1			1					
Al Yarmouk	1			1					
Jordan	1	1							
13 Shabab Al Hussein	3		1	2		Amman	King Abdullah	18 000	1954
14 Al Buq'aa	2		1	1		Amman	Al Quwaysimah	15 000	1968
15 Al Jalil	1			1					
Al Qadisiya	1			1					

RECENT LEAGUE AND CUP RECORD

	Championship							Cup		
Year	Champions	Pts	Runners-up	Pts	Third	Pts		Winners	Score	Runners-up
1997	Al Wihdat	41	Al Faysali	41	Al Ramtha	29		Al Wihdat	2-1	Al Ramtha
1997	Al Wihdat	47	Al Faysali	46	Al Hussein	30		No tournament due to season readjustment		
1998	Al Wihdat	34	Al Faysali	33	Al Ramtha	19		Al Faysali	2-1	Al Wihdat
1999	Al Faysali	57	Al Wihdat	49	Al Ramtha	48		Al Faysali	0-0 5-4p	Al Wihdat
2000	Al Faysali	52	Al Wihdat	44	Al Ahly	34		Al Wihdat	2-0	Al Faysali
2001	Al Faysali	48	Al Wihdat	44	Al Hussein	31		Al Faysali	2-0	Al Hussein
2002	No championship due to season readjustment							No tournament due to season readjustment		
2003	Al Faysali	48	Al Wihdat	45	Al Hussein	35		Al Faysali	2-0	Al Hussein
2004	Al Faysali	9	Al Hussein	4	Al Wihdat	4		Al Faysali	3-1	Al Hussein
2005	Al Wihdat	50	Al Hussein	36	Al Faysali	31		Al Faysali	3-0	Shabab Al Hussein
2006	Shabab Al Ordon	42	Al Faysali	40	Al Wahdat	35		Shabab Al Ordon	2-1	Al Faysali
2007	Al Wihdat	44	Al Faysali	36	Al Buq'aa	34		Shabab Al Ordon	2-0	Al Faysali
2008	Al Wihdat	47	Al Faysali	42	Shabab Al Ordon	29		Al Faysali	3-1	Shabab Al Ordon

JORDAN 2007–08

FIRST DIVISION

	Pl	W	D	L	F	A	Pts	Wahdat	Faysali	Shabab O	Hussein	Buq'aa	Arabi	Jazeera	Shabab H	Ramtha	Ahli
Al Wihdat ‡	18	15	2	1	47	12	47		1-0	5-2	4-0	1-0	7-0	2-1	2-0	5-2	5-2
Al Faysali	18	13	3	2	40	16	42	0-0		3-3	1-2	2-1	1-0	3-1	3-0	1-0	2-1
Shabab Al Ordon	18	7	8	3	27	15	29	0-1	1-1		0-0	1-1	0-1	0-0	2-0	1-1	3-0
Al Hussein	18	8	5	5	25	25	29	2-1	0-4	0-2		2-2	1-1	1-0	2-1	3-0	4-2
Al Buq'aa	18	6	7	5	28	23	25	0-1	1-2	0-0	3-1		5-3	2-2	0-0	1-2	3-1
Al Arabi	18	4	6	8	23	41	18	1-4	2-4	0-3	2-2	0-1		2-1	1-0	1-0	1-1
Al Jazeera	18	2	10	6	25	27	16	1-1	1-3	0-0	0-0	3-3	4-1		2-4	1-1	5-1
Shabab Al Hussein	18	4	4	10	21	36	16	0-1	1-7	0-3	1-0	0-2	4-4	2-2		5-2	3-1
Al Ramtha	18	2	6	10	18	34	12	0-2	1-2	2-3	1-3	1-2	3-3	1-1	0-0		1-0
Al Ahli	18	1	5	12	13	38	8	1-4	0-1	0-3	0-2	1-1	0-0	0-0	2-0	0-0	

30/08/2007 – 11/04/2008 • ‡ Qualified for the AFC Cup

JORDAN 2007–08 SECOND DIVISION (2)

	Pl	W	D	L	F	A	Pts
Al Yarmouk	11	9	2	0	34	6	29
Al Ittihad Al Ramtha	11	6	5	0	20	7	23
Kfarsoum	11	5	4	2	19	13	19
Ain Karem	11	6	1	4	22	20	19
Al Badiah Al Wosta	11	4	3	4	15	13	15
That Ras	11	5	0	6	20	19	15
Al Karmel	11	4	3	4	23	24	15
Al Sareeh	11	4	2	5	17	21	14
Sahab	11	3	3	5	13	16	12
Al Salt	11	2	4	5	16	16	10
Mansheyat B. Hasan	11	2	2	7	16	26	8
Al Rsaifa	11	1	1	9	7	41	4

SHIELD CUP 2007

Round of 16

Group A	Pts
Al Wihdat	12
Al Buq'aa	7
Al Hussein	5
Shabab Al H.	2
Al Ramtha	1

Group B	Pts
Shabab Al O.	9
Al Jazeera	9
Al Faysali	6
Al Arabi	6
Al Ahli	3

Semi-finals

Shabab Ordun	4
Al Buq'aa	2

Al Wihdat	2 3p
Al Jazeera	2 5p

Final

Shabab Ordun	0 4p
Al Jazeera	0 3p

CUP FINAL

11-08-2007

JFA CUP 2007–08

First Round		Quarter-finals		Semi-finals		Final	
Al Faysali	1						
Shabab Al Hussein	0	Al Faysali *	1				
Al Yarmouk	1	Al Buq'aa	0				
Al Buq'aa	4			Al Faysali	2		
Al Jazeera	2			Al Wihdat *	0		
Ain Karem	0	Al Jazeera	0				
Kfarsoum	0	Al Wihdat *	1				
Al Wihdat	6					Al Faysali ‡	3
Al Ahli	1					Shabab Al Ordon	1
Al Arabi	0	Al Ahli *	3				
Qouqazy	0	Al Ramtha	0				
Al Ramtha	2			Al Ahli *	1		
Al Hussein	4			Shabab Al Ordon	3		
Al Jalil	0	Al Hussein	2				
Al Ittihad Al Ramtha	1	Shabab Al Ordon *	3				
Shabab Al Ordon	2						

* Home team • ‡ Qualified for the AFC Cup

CUP FINAL

Amman, 6-05-2008

Scorers - Moayad Abushek 21, Isam Al Mbaydin 58, Hassouneh Sheikh Qassem 60 for Faysali; Mohanad Maharmeh 48 for Shabab

JPN – JAPAN

NATIONAL TEAM RECORD
JULY 10TH 2006 TO JULY 12TH 2010

PL	W	D	L	F	A	%
33	18	10	5	54	20	69.7

Despite the failure of the national team to retain their AFC Asian Cup title in mid-2007, it proved to be yet another encouraging year for football in Japan. Average gates in the J.League were at a very healthy average of 19,081 per match; Urawa Reds became the first Japanese team to win the AFC Champions League since the tournament was relaunched in 2002; and to cap it all there was a very dramatic race for the J.League title which went right down to the final game. Kashima had a terrible start to the season and didn't win at home until over two months in, but they finished off with a run of nine consecutive victories to leapfrog Urawa on the final day thanks to a 3-0 win over Shimizu. In the previous round they had beaten Urawa 1-0 in Saitama, but the Reds would have still won the championship had they beaten Yokohama FC in their last fixture. Despite not having won for 20 matches and rooted firmly to the bottom of the table in their first J.League season, Yokohama pulled off a stunning surprise by winning 1-0 and denying Urawa the title. A month later Kashima completed the double after beating already relegated Sanfrecce Hiroshima 2-0 in the Emperor's Cup final on New Year's day - a incredible turn around in the season for coach Oswaldo

INTERNATIONAL HONOURS
Qualified for the FIFA World Cup 1998 2002 2006
Qualified for the FIFA Women's World Cup 1991 1995 1999 2003
Asian Cup 1992 2000 2004
AFC U-16 Championship 1994
AFC Champions League Furukawa 1987, Jubilo Iwata 1999

Oliveira. For Urawa, just one victory in their last nine games in all matches may have cost them dearly in domestic competition, but the one game that they did win, was perhaps the most important of them all - the AFC Champions League final against Sepahan. Having drawn the first leg 0-0 away in Iran, they became the first Japanese club to win Asia's top club honour since Jubilo Iwata in 1999 when goals from Yuichiro Nagai and Yuki Abe secured the title for Asia's best supported and most passionately followed club. Japan's quest to qualify for their fourth consecutive appearance at the FIFA World Cup finals was rocked when coach Ivica Osim suffered a stroke in November 2007. Osim was replaced by former Yokohama Marinos coach Takeshi Okada whose immediate task was to make it through a first round qualifying group containing Bahrain, Oman and Thailand. Despite two unsuccessful visits to the Middle-East which saw a draw against Oman and a defeat at the hands of Bahrain, Japan qualified for the final group stage in Asia at the top of the group. Paired with Australia, Bahrain, Uzbekistan and Qatar, the Japanese will be hoping for a top two finish and direct qualification for the finals in South Africa.

Japan Football Association (JFA)
JFA House, Football Ave., Bunkyo-ku, Tokyo 113-8311, Japan
Tel +81 3 38302004   Fax +81 3 38302005
www.jfa.or.jp
President: INUKAI Motoaki   General Secretary: TASHIMA Kohzo
Vice-President: OGURA Jinji   Treasurer: SAITO Koji   Media Officer: KUNJI Matsuda
Men's Coach: OKADA Takeshi   Women's Coach: SASAKI Norio
JFA formed: 1921   AFC: 1954   FIFA: 1929-46 & 1950
Blue shirts with white trimmings, White shorts, Blue socks

RECENT INTERNATIONAL MATCHES PLAYED BY JAPAN

2006	Opponents	Score	Venue	Comp	Scorers	Att	Referee
16-08	Yemen	W 2-0	Niigata	ACq	Abe [70], Sato [91+]	40 913	Lee Gi Young KOR
3-09	Saudi Arabia	L 0-1	Jeddah	ACq		15 000	Maidin SIN
6-09	Yemen	W 1-0	Sana'a	ACq	Ganaha [91+]	7 000	Al Ghatrifi OMA
4-10	Ghana	L 0-1	Yokohama	Fr		52 437	Yu Byung Seob KOR
11-10	India	W 3-0	Bangalore	ACq	Bando 2 [22 43], Nakamura.K [81]	5 000	Chan Siu Kee HKG
15-11	Saudi Arabia	W 3-1	Sapporo	ACq	Tanaka.TM [20], Ganaha 2 [29 50]	40 965	Shield AUS
2007							
24-03	Peru	W 2-0	Yokohama	Fr	Maki [19], Takahara [54]	60 400	Nardi AUS
1-06	Montenegro	W 2-0	Shizuoka	KC	Nakazawa [23], Takahara [38]	28 635	Svendsen DEN
5-06	Colombia	D 0-0	Saitama	KC		45 091	Vollquartz DEN
9-07	Qatar	D 1-1	Hanoi	ACr1	Takahara [60]	5 000	Breeze AUS
13-07	UAE	W 3-1	Hanoi	ACr1	Takahara 2 [22 27], Nakamura.S [42p]	5 000	Tongkhan THA
16-07	Vietnam	W 4-1	Hanoi	ACr1	Maki 2 [12 59], Nakamura.S [52]	40 000	Breeze AUS
21-07	Australia	D 1-1	Hanoi	ACqf	Takahara [72], W 4-3p	25 000	Al Fadhli KUW
25-07	Saudi Arabia	L 2-3	Hanoi	ACsf	Nakazawa [37], Abe [53]	10 000	Breeze AUS
28-07	Korea Republic	D 0-0	Palembang	AC3p	L 5-6p	10 000	Al Badwawi UAE
22-08	Cameroon	W 2-0	Oita	Fr	Tanaka.TM [25], Yamase [89]	37 240	Choi Myung Yong KOR
7-09	Austria	D 0-0	Klagenfurt	Fr	L 3-4p	26 142	Merk GER
11-09	Switzerland	W 4-3	Klagenfurt	Fr	Nakamura.S 2 [53p 78p], Maki [68], Yano [90]	19 500	Messner AUT
17-10	Egypt	W 4-1	Osaka	Fr	Okubo 2 [21 42], Maeda [53], Kaji [68]	41 901	Gilewski POL
2008							
26-01	Chile	D 0-0	Tokyo	Fr		37 261	Lee Min Hu KOR
30-01	Bosnia/Herzegovina	W 3-0	Tokyo	Fr	Nakazawa [68], Yamase 2 [83 89]	26 971	Kim Eui Soo
6-02	Thailand	W 4-1	Saitama	WCq	Endo [21], Okubo [54], Nakazawa [66], Maki [91+]	35 130	Al Ghamdi KSA
17-02	Korea DPR	D 1-1	Chongqing	EAF	Maeda [69]	15 000	Choi Myung Yong KOR
20-02	China PR	W 1-0	Chongqing	EAF	Yamase [17]	38 000	O Tae Song PRK
23-02	Korea Republic	D 1-1	Chongqing	EAF	Yamase [68]	29 000	Tan Hai CHN
26-03	Bahrain	L 0-1	Manama	WCq		26 000	Shield AUS
24-05	Côte d'Ivoire	L 0-1	Toyota	Fr	Tamada [21]	40 710	Duarte POR
27-05	Paraguay	D 0-0	Saitama	Fr		27 998	Costa POR
2-06	Oman	W 3-0	Yokohama	WCq	Nakazawa [10], Okubo [22], Nakamura.S [49]	46 764	Bashir SIN
7-06	Oman	D 1-1	Muscat	WCq	Endo [53p]	6 500	Mohd Salleh MAS
14-06	Thailand	W 3-0	Bangkok	WCq	Tanaka.MT [23], Nakazawa [38], Nakamura.K [88]	25 000	Al Badwawi UAE
22-06	Bahrain	W 1-0	Saitama	WCq	Uchida [90]	51 180	Irmatov UZB

Fr = Friendly match • KC = Kirin Cup • EAF - East Asian Federation Cup • AC = AFC Asian Cup • WC = FIFA World Cup
q = qualifier • r1 = first round group • qf = quarter-final • sf = semi-final • 3p = third place play-off • BCD = behind closed doors

JAPAN NATIONAL TEAM PLAYERS

	Player		Ap	G	Club	Date of Birth		Player		Ap	G	Club	Date of Birth
1	Yoshikatsu Kawaguchi	GK	114	0	Jubilo Iwata	15 08 1975	12	Seiichiro Maki	FW	33	8	JEF Utd	7 08 1980
2	Yuji Nakazawa	DF	78	15	Yoko. F-Marinos	25 02 1978	13	Keita Suzuki	MF	28	0	Urawa Reds	21 04 1981
3	Yuichi Komano	DF	38	0	Jubilo Iwata	25 06 1981	14	Kengo Nakamura	MF	25	2	Kawasaki F'tale	31 10 1980
4	Marcos Tulio Tanaka	DF	15	3	Urawa Reds	24 04 1981	15	Michihiro Yasuda	DF	5	0	Shimizu S-Pulse	20 12 1987
5	Yasuyuki Konno	MF	24	0	FC Tokyo	25 07 1981	16	Kisho Yano	FW	12	1	Albirex Niigata	5 04 1984
6	Atsuto Uchida	DF	9	2	Kashima Antlers	27 03 1988	17	Keisuke Honda	MF	1	0	VVV Venlo	13 06 1986
7	Yasuhito Endo	MF	70	6	Gamba Osaka	28 01 1980	18	Seigo Narazaki	GK	59	0	Nagoya G. Eight	15 04 1976
8	Koji Yamase	MF	11	5	Yoko. F-Marinos	22 09 1981		Kazumichi Takagi	DF	0	0	Shimizu S-Pulse	21 11 1980
9	Hisato Sato	FW	20	3	San. Hiroshima	12 03 1982		Shuhei Terada	DF	1	0	Kawasaki F'tale	23 06 1975
10	Shunsuke NAKAMURA	MF	78	21	Celtic	24 06 1978		Yoshito Okubo	FW	29	4	Vissel Kobe	9 06 1982
11	Keiji Tamada	FW	47	10	Nagoya G. Eight	11 04 1980		Daisuke Matsui	MF	11	1	St-Etienne	11 05 1981
								Makoto Hasebe	MF	11	0	VfL Wolfsburg	18 01 1984

Japan's squad for the June 2008 World Cup qualifiers

JAPAN NATIONAL TEAM RECORDS AND RECORD SEQUENCES

Records			Sequence records					
Victory	15-0	PHI 1966	Wins	8	Four times	Clean sheets	7	2003-2004
Defeat	2-15	PHI 1917	Defeats	9	1917-1927	Goals scored	14	1966-1968
Player Caps	123	Masami Ihara	Undefeated	12	2000, 2004	Without goal	6	1988, 1989-1990
Player Goals	82	Kunishige Kamamoto	Without win	11	1976-1977	Goals against	31	1960-1966

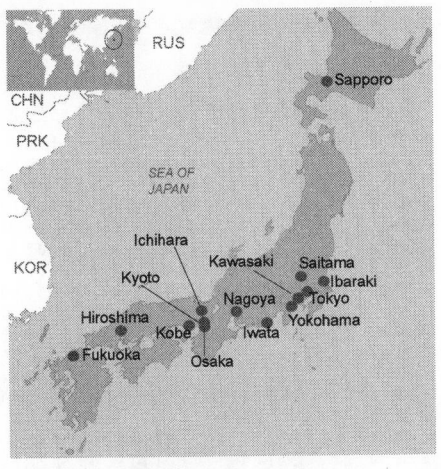

MAJOR CITIES/TOWNS

		Population '000
1	Tokyo	8 403
2	Yokohama	3 632
3	Osaka	2 588
4	Nagoya	2 197
5	Sapporo	1 908
6	Kobe	1 541
7	Kyoto	1 456
8	Fukuoka	1 412
9	Kawasaki	1 328
10	Hiroshima	1 150
11	Saitama	1 100
12	Sendai	1 050
13	Kitakyushu	991
14	Chiba	932
15	Sakai	778
16	Shizuoka	699
17	Niigata	506
18	Oita	453
19	Toyota	366
20	Kashiwa	345
21	Ichihara	286
22	Ibaraki	264
23	Hiratsuka	260
24	Kashima	67

JAPAN; NIPPON-KOKU

Capital	Tokyo	Language	Japanese	Formation	1600
Population	127 463 611	Area	377835 km²	Density	337 per km²	% in cities	78%
GDP per cap	$28 000	Dailling code	+81	Internet	.jp	GMT + / -	+9

The populations for the major metropolitan areas are: Tokyo 37 037; Osaka-Kobe-Kyoto 17 536; Nagoya 8 833; Fukuoka-Kitakyushu 4 288

MEDALS TABLE

	Overall			League			Cup		LC	Asia			City	Previously	Stadium	Cap'ty	DoF
	G	S	B	G	S	B	G	S		G	S	B					
1 Tokyo Verdy 1969	19	7	1	7	4		5	3	6	1		1	Tokyo	Yomiuri	Ajinomoto	50 000	1969
2 Yokohama F-Marinos	17	7	1	5	5		6	1	4	2	1	1	Yokohama	Nissan	International	72 370	1972
3 Urawa Reds	15	12	5	5	9	5	6	3	3	1			Saitama	Mitsubishi	Saitama 2002	63 700	1950
4 Kashima Antlers	11	4	4	5	2	1	3	2	3			1	Ibaraki	Sumitomo	Kashima	39 026	1947
5 JEF United	11	3	4	2	1	4	4	2	5	1			Ichihara	Furukawa	Ichihara	16 933	1946
6 Cerezo Osaka	9	12	1	4	4	1	3	8	2				Osaka	Yanmar	Nagai	50 000	1957
7 Sanfrecce Hiroshima	8	12	2	5	2	1	3	10				1	Hiroshima	Toyo Kogyo	Big Arch	50 000	1938
8 Jubilo Iwata	8	6	3	4	2	3	2	2	1	1	2		Iwata	Yamaha	Yamaha	16 893	1970
9 Shonan Bellmare	7	5	3	3	1	3	3	4		1			Hiratsuka	Fujita	Hiratsuka	18 500	1968
10 Kashiwa Reysol	5	3	5	1	1	5	2	2	2				Kashiwa	Hitachi	Hitachi Kashiwa	15 900	1940
11 Shimizu S-Pulse	3	4	1		1		1	3	1	1		1	Shimizu		Nihondaira	20 339	1991
12 Nippon Kokan	3	4		3		1	1	2									
13 Yokohama Flugels	3	2	3	1	2		2			1		1	Yokohama	All Nippon			
14 Gamba Osaka	3	1	2	1		2	1	1	1				Osaka	Matsushita	Expo'70	23 000	1980
15 Nagoya Grampus Eight	2	2			1		2					1	Nagoya	Toyota	Mizuho-ku	17 000	

RECENT LEAGUE AND CUP RECORD

National Championship					Cup		
Year	Champions	Score/Runners-up	Runners-up/Third		Winners	Score	Runners-up
1995	Yokohama Marinos	1-0 1-0	Verdy Kawasaki		Nagoya G'pus Eight	3-0	S'frecce Hiroshima
1996	Kashima Antlers	‡	Nagoya Grampus Eight		Verdy Kawasaki	3-0	S'frecce Hiroshima
1997	Jubilo Iwata	3-2 1-0	Kashima Antlers		Kashima Antlers	3-0	Yokohama Flugels
1998	Kashima Antlers	2-1 2-1	Jubilo Iwata		Yokohama Flugels	2-1	Shimizu S-Pulse
1999	Jubilo Iwata	2-1 1-2 4-2p	Shimizu S-Pulse		Nagoya G'pus Eight	2-0	S'frecce Hiroshima
2000	Kashima Antlers	0-0 3-0	Yokohama F-Marinos		Kashima Antlers	3-2	Shimizu S-Pulse
2001	Kashima Antlers	2-2 1-0	Jubilo Iwata		Shimizu S-Pulse	3-2	Cerezo Osaka
2002	Jubilo Iwata	†			Kyoto Purple Sanga	2-1	Kashima Antlers
2003	Yokohama F-Marinos	†			Jubilo Iwata	1-0	Cerezo Osaka
2004	Yokohama F-1Marinos	1-0 0-1 4-2p	Urawa Reds		Tokyo Verdy 1969	2-1	Jubilo Iwata

Year	Champions		Runners-up		Third		Winners	Score	Runners-up
2005	Gamba Osaka	60	Urawa Reds	59	Kashima Antlers	59	Urawa Reds	2-1	Shimizu S-Pulse
2006	Urawa Reds	72	Kawasaki Frontale	67	Gamba Osaka	66	Urawa Reds	1-0	Gamba Osaka
2007	Kashima Antlers	72	Urawa Reds	70	Gamba Osaka	67	Kashima Antlers	2-0	S'frecce Hiroshima

† Both stages won by the same team so no play-off was required • ‡ Played on a single stage league system with no play-off

JAPAN 2007

J.LEAGUE DIVISION 1

Team	Pl	W	D	L	F	A	Pts	Kashima	Urawa	Gamba	Shimizu	Kawasaki	Albirex	Marinos	Kashiwa	Jubilo	Vissel	Nagoya	FC Tokyo	JEF United	Oita	Omiya	Sanfrecce	Ventforet	Yokohama
Kashima Antlers ‡	34	22	6	6	60	36	72		0-1	0-1	3-0	4-1	3-1	1-1	1-0	2-1	3-2	2-1	1-2	3-1	3-0	0-0	5-1	2-0	2-1
Urawa Reds	34	20	10	4	55	28	70	0-1		1-1	0-0	1-2	1-0	1-1	1-1	2-1	0-0	3-2	1-1	2-1	0-1	4-1	2-0	2-1	
Gamba Osaka	34	19	10	5	71	37	67	5-1	0-1		1-1	2-2	3-1	0-2	2-1	5-2	1-1	3-1	6-2	2-0	1-0	1-0	3-0	5-0	2-1
Shimizu S-Pulse	34	18	7	9	53	36	61	1-2	0-1	3-1		3-1	3-1	1-0	2-1	1-0	3-0	1-3	2-2	2-0	2-2	3-1	2-0	1-0	
Kawasaki Frontale	34	14	12	8	66	48	54	1-0	1-1	4-1	2-1		4-3	1-2	0-0	2-3	2-1	1-1	5-2	1-1	2-2	1-1	3-0	1-1	6-0
Albirex Niigata	34	15	6	13	48	47	51	1-1	2-2	2-1	0-2	2-0		0-6	1-2	1-3	4-0	2-1	0-1	0-2	1-0	2-1	3-1	3-1	
Yokohama F-Marinos	34	14	8	12	54	35	50	2-3	0-1	0-0	0-2	2-1	1-0		0-2	4-1	1-4	0-2	0-1	1-0	5-0	0-2	2-2	1-0	8-1
Kashiwa Reysol	34	14	8	12	43	36	50	0-1	0-2	1-2	1-3	4-0	0-0	1-0		4-0	1-3	2-0	2-0	1-0	2-0	0-0	2-1	1-1	1-1
Jubilo Iwata	34	15	4	15	54	55	49	1-3	0-2	1-1	0-1	1-3	2-4	1-0	4-0		2-3	1-0	5-2	1-0	2-1	0-0	4-2	2-1	3-0
Vissel Kobe	34	13	8	13	58	48	47	1-1	1-2	2-2	1-0	1-1	0-1	0-0	2-1	4-0		5-0	0-1	2-1	1-3	0-0	3-2	4-1	3-0
Nagoya Grampus Eight	34	13	6	15	43	45	45	3-0	1-2	1-4	1-2	2-2	2-0	0-3	2-0	0-0	2-0		0-1	2-0	1-2	5-0	2-3	1-1	0-0
FC Tokyo	34	14	3	17	49	58	45	1-2	0-2	1-1	2-0	0-7	1-3	2-1	0-1	0-1	3-1	0-1		4-1	1-2	1-2	2-4	2-1	1-0
JEF United Chiba	34	12	6	16	51	56	42	3-3	2-4	1-6	1-3	1-2	2-3	1-1	3-2	4-2	0-2	3-2			6-0	1-0	1-3	3-2	4-0
Oita Trinita	34	12	5	17	42	60	41	2-2	2-2	0-4	3-4	2-0	1-0	0-3	2-1	1-0	2-0	1-3	0-0	0-1		3-1	1-2	4-1	2-0
Omiya Ardija	34	8	11	15	24	40	35	1-2	1-1	0-3	1-2	1-1	2-1	0-0	1-0	2-1	1-2	1-3	1-0	0-2	1-2		1-0	1-2	1-0
Sanfrecce Hiroshima	34	8	8	18	44	71	32	0-1	2-4	2-2	2-1	1-1	0-0	1-3	1-1	0-1	1-1	1-3	0-5	2-2	2-0	2-1		2-2	0-2
Ventforet Kofu	34	7	6	21	33	65	27	0-1	1-4	1-2	0-0	1-3	0-1	1-1	3-2	1-6	4-3	0-2	0-1	0-1	2-0	0-0	2-1		1-0
Yokohama FC	34	4	4	26	19	66	16	0-1	1-0	1-1	1-1	0-0	0-2	1-0	2-4	1-2	0-3	1-2	0-2	0-1	2-1	0-1	1-2	0-2	

3/03/2007 - 1/12/2007 • ‡ Qualified for the AFC Champions League • Relegation play-off: **Kyoto Sanga** 2-1 0-0 Sanfrecce Hiroshima
Top scorers: Juninho, Kawasaki 22; Bare, Gamba 20; Edmilson, Albirex 19; Ueslei, Sanfrecce 17; Washington, Urawa 16; Leandro, Vissel 15; Marquinhos, Kashima 14; Hideo Oshima, Marinos 14; Yoshito Okubo, Kobe 14; Cho Jae Jin, Shimizu 13; Frode Johnsen, Nagoya 13

JAPAN 2007

J.LEAGUE DIVISION 2

Team	Pl	W	D	L	F	A	Pts
Consadole Sapporo	48	27	10	11	66	45	91
Tokyo Verdy 1969	48	26	11	11	90	57	89
Kyoto Sanga †	48	24	14	10	80	59	86
Vegalta Sendai	48	24	11	13	72	54	83
Cerezo Osaka	48	24	8	16	72	55	80
Shonan Bellmare	48	23	8	17	72	55	77
Avispa Fukuoka	48	22	7	19	77	61	73
Sagan Tosu	48	21	9	18	63	66	72
Montedio Yamagata	48	15	13	20	46	56	58
Ehime FC	48	12	9	27	39	66	45
Thespa Kusatsu	48	7	21	20	42	71	42
Mito Hollyhock	48	8	10	30	32	70	34
Tokushima Vortis	48	6	15	27	31	67	33

3/03/2007 - 1/12/2007 • † Qualified for play-off • No clubs relegated • Promotion play-off: **Kyoto Sanga** 2-1 0-0 Sanfrecce Hiroshima
Top scorers: Hulk, Verdy 37; Alex, Avispa 26; Paulinho, Kyoto 24; Yoshihito Fujita, Sagan 24; Tatsuya Furuhashi, Cerezo 18

JAPAN 2007

9TH JAPAN FOOTBALL LEAGUE (JFL) (3)

	Pl	W	D	L	F	A	Pts	Sagawa Ex	Rosso	Gifu	Alo's	Honda	YKK	Yokogawa	Tochigi	JEF United	Ryutsu KU	Sony	Sagawa P	TDK	Gainare	Mitsubishi	Kariya	Ryukyu	Arte
Sagawa Express	34	26	5	3	81	31	83		1-0	2-1	4-0	1-1	2-4	4-3	1-0	1-1	4-0	3-0	1-0	1-0	2-0	3-1	3-2	4-0	2-1
Rosso Kumamoto	34	21	6	7	65	34	69	1-1		0-1	2-0	1-1	1-2	3-2	1-0	0-1	2-1	1-1	6-3	3-0	3-2	1-1	1-0	6-0	1-0
FC Gifu	34	17	9	8	45	31	60	1-3	1-1		0-0	0-1	3-3	1-1	0-2	1-2	3-0	3-2	1-3	1-0	4-2	1-0	1-0	1-0	2-0
Alo's Hokuriku	34	16	11	7	50	35	59	2-2	2-1	0-0		1-2	2-1	1-0	1-0	3-3	3-1	1-0	1-0	2-2	0-0	0-1	1-0	2-0	7-0
Honda FC	34	16	10	8	61	42	58	2-2	2-4	0-1	2-2		3-0	3-0	2-2	4-2	0-6	2-2	4-1	4-1	1-1	2-0	1-3	4-0	2-2
YKK AP	34	16	7	11	60	53	55	0-3	1-2	0-0	1-3	1-0		5-1	2-2	2-2	0-1	6-1	4-1	0-3	1-1	4-2	4-3	4-0	2-1
Yokogawa Musashino	34	16	6	12	50	44	54	0-3	2-3	1-1	1-0	1-0	2-0		0-2	2-0	3-2	5-0	2-1	4-1	2-0	1-3	1-1	1-2	1-0
Tochigi SC	34	14	10	10	43	29	52	0-1	0-2	0-1	1-1	0-3	2-0	1-0		1-1	1-1	0-0	1-2	0-0	2-2	5-0	2-1	1-0	4-0
JEF United Reserves	34	14	10	10	50	45	52	0-5	0-1	1-2	2-3	2-2	1-1	0-0	0-2		0-0	3-1	2-1	3-2	2-1	1-0	2-0	1-0	2-1
Ryutsu Keizai Univ.	34	15	5	14	58	49	50	4-1	1-4	2-1	1-1	1-1	3-0	3-1	2-3	1-0		4-1	0-3	0-1	4-2	0-1	1-0	1-0	3-1
Sony Sendai	34	13	5	16	46	59	44	2-4	1-3	1-3	3-0	1-0	0-1	2-3	0-1	0-1	2-0		2-3	1-3	1-0	2-0	2-1	4-1	2-0
Sagawa Printing	34	13	4	17	45	57	43	1-3	0-1	0-0	0-3	0-2	2-2	0-2	2-2	0-2	0-3	1-2		1-0	2-4	2-1	0-1	3-1	2-0
TDK SC	34	11	9	14	49	47	42	0-1	2-2	0-0	2-2	0-2	0-1	1-1	1-1	2-1	1-0	2-3	1-2		1-2	2-0	5-2	2-2	2-0
Gainare Tottori	34	10	9	15	42	51	39	0-3	3-1	0-3	2-1	0-1	3-1	2-2	0-2	1-1	1-0	1-1	1-2	1-1		0-1	1-1	3-1	2-1
Mitsubishi Mizushima	34	11	2	21	36	53	35	2-1	1-0	2-3	1-2	1-2	0-1	0-1	1-0	2-1	1-4	0-1	1-1	0-1	0-2		3-1	3-4	4-0
FC Kariya	34	8	4	22	36	59	28	0-2	0-1	2-1	0-1	1-3	1-2	0-1	0-2	0-3	3-2	1-2	0-3	3-0	1-0	1-0		2-2	0-0
FC Ryukyu	34	7	6	21	38	82	27	1-3	0-4	0-1	0-2	2-1	2-3	0-0	1-0	3-3	3-3	2-2	0-1	0-8	1-2	2-1	3-4		3-1
Arte Takasaki	34	1	4	29	17	71	7	1-4	1-2	0-2	0-0	0-1	0-1	0-1	0-1	0-4	1-3	0-1	1-2	1-2	1-0	1-3	1-1	1-2	

18/03/2007 - 2/12/2007 • Sagawa Express ineligible for promotion • Alo's Hokuriku and YKK AP have merged for the 2008 season as Kataller Toyama • Fagiano Okayama, New Wave Kitakyushu and MIO Biwako Kusatsu promoted from the regional leagues

J.LEAGUE YAMAZAKI NABISCO CUP 2007

Group Stage		Quarter–finals		Semi–finals		Final	
Group A	Pts						
Sanfrecce Hiroshima	12						
Gamba Osaka	10						
JEF United Chiba	9	Gamba Osaka	1				
Vissel Kobe	4	Urawa Reds *	1				
Group B	Pts			Gamba Osaka *	1 2		
Yokohama F.Marinos	8			Kashima Antlers	0 3		
Shimizu S-Pulse	8	Sanfrecce Hiroshima *	1				
Kashiwa Reysol	8	Kashima Antlers	0				
Omiya Ardija	8					Gamba Osaka	1
Group C	Pts					Kawasaki Frontale	0
FC Tokyo	10	Yokohama F.Marinos *	0				
Yokohama FC	9	FC Tokyo	1				
Oita Trinita	9			Yokohama F.Marinos *	1 2		
Jubilo Iwata	7			Kawasaki Frontale	2 4		
Group D	Pts	Ventforet Kofu *	3				
Kashima Antlers	12	Kawasaki Frontale	2				
Ventforet Kofu	10						
Albirex Niigata	9						
Nagoya G'pus Eight	2						

CUP FINAL

National Stadium, Tokyo
3-11-2007, Att: 41 569
Ref: Toshimitsu Yoshida
Scorer - Yasuda [55]

Urawa Reds and Kawasaki Frontale qualified directly for the knock-out stage due to AFC Champions League commitments * Home team in the first leg

Gamba - Yosuke FUJIGAYA• - Akira KAJI, SIDICLEI•, Satoshi YAMAGUCHI, Michihiro YASUDA - Tomokazu MYOJIN, Hideo HASHIMOTO, Yasuhito ENDO•, Takahiro FUTAGAWA - BARE (Ryuji BANDO 89), MAGNO ALVES. Tr: Akira NISHINO

Kawasaki - Eiji KAWASHIMA - Yoshinobu MINOWA, Hideki SAHARA• (Takahiro KAWAMURA 74), Hiroki ITO - Yusuke MORI, Kengo NAKAMURA, Hiroyuki TANIGUCHI, Shuhei TERADA, Masahiro OHASHI (Satoshi KUKINO 63) - CHONG Tese (Masaru KUROTSU 78), JUNINHO. Tr: Takashi SEKIZUKA

EMPEROR'S CUP 2007

Third Round		Fourth Round		Fifth Round	
		Kashima Antlers	2		
		Mito Hollyhock	0		
Zwiegen Kanazawa	0			**Kashima Antlers**	2
Mito Hollyhock	1			Ventforet Kofu	1
Tokushima Voltis	2				
FC Gifu	0	Tokushima Voltis	1		
		Ventforet Kofu	3		
		Nagoya Grampus Eight	3		
		TheSpa Kusatsu	1		
Alo's Hokuriku	0 4p			Nagoya Grampus Eight	0
TheSpa Kusatsu	0 5p			**Honda FC**	2
		Kashiwa Reysol	2		
Tokyo Verdy 1969	0	**Honda FC**	3		
Honda FC	1				
Ehime FC	1				
Okinawa Kariyushi FC	0	**Ehime FC**	2		
		Urawa Reds	0		
				Ehime FC	2
				Yokohama FC	1
		Omiya Ardija	0		
		Yokohama FC	2		
		Vissel Kobe	2		
		Avispa Fukuoka	0		
Tochigi SC	0			Vissel Kobe	0
Avispa Fukuoka	4			**Kawasaki Frontale**	3
Cerezo Osaka	4				
Honda Lock	2	Cerezo Osaka			
		Kawasaki Frontale			
		Gamba Osaka	2 5p		
		Montedio Yamagata	2 3p		
Kaoku Taiiku University	0			**Gamba Osaka**	3
Montedio Yamagata	3			Oita Trinita	1
		JEF United Chiba	1		
		Oita Trinita	3		
		Yokohama F-Marinos	4		
		Sagawa Kyubin SC	1		
Banditonce Kobe	0			Yokohama F-Marinos	3
Sagawa Kyubin SC	4			**Shimizu S-Pulse**	5
Meiji University	1				
Kyoto Sanga FC	0	Meiji University	3 4p		
		Shimizu S-Pulse	3 5p		
		FC Tokyo	2		
		TDK SC	1		
Consadole Sapporo	1 9p			**FC Tokyo**	2
TDK SC	1 10p			Sagan Tosu	1
		Albirex Niigata	2		
Tsukuba University	0	**Sagan Tosu**	3		
Sagan Tosu	1				
		Jubilo Iwata	6		
		Juntendo University	1		
Vegalta Sendai	1			Jubilo Iwata	0
Juntendo University	2			**Sanfrecce Hiroshima**	2
Shonan Bellmare	3				
V-Varen Nagasaki	0	Shonan Bellmare	0		
		Sanfrecce Hiroshima	3		

J.2 clubs join in the third round • J.League clubs join in the fourth round • * Home team

EMPEROR'S CUP 2007

Quarter–finals	Semi–finals	Final

Kashima Antlers	1
Honda FC	0

Kashima Antlers †	1
Kawasaki Frontale	0

Ehime FC	0
Kawasaki Frontale	2

Kashima Antlers	2
Sanfrecce Hiroshima	0

Gamba Osaka	1
Shimizu S-Pulse	0

Gamba Osaka	1
Sanfrecce Hiroshima ††	3

FC Tokyo	0
Sanfrecce Hiroshima	2

† Played at Kokuritsu, Tokyo
†† Played at Ecopa Stadium, Shizuoka
‡ Qualified for the AFC Champions League

87TH EMPEROR'S CUP FINAL 2007

National Stadium (Kokuritsu Kyogijo), Tokyo, 1-01-2008, Att: 46 357

Kashima Antlers	2	Atsuto Achida [8], Danilo [89]
Sanfrecce Hiroshima	0	

Kashima - Hitoshi SOGAHATA - Atsuto UCHIDA, Daiki IWAMASA, Go OIWA, Toru ARAIBA - Takeshi AOKI, Mitsuo OGASAWARA, Masashi MOTOYAMA, Takuya NOZAWA (DANILO (80) - MARQUINHOS (Masaki CHUGO 86), Yuzo TASHIRO (Atsushi YANAGISAWA 89). Tr: OSWALDO OLIVEIRA
Sanfrecce - Takashi SHIMODA - Tomoaki MAKINO, Ilian STOYANOV, Kohei MORITA - Yuichi KOMANO, Kazuyuki MORISAKI, Kota HATTORI, Koji MORISAKI, Yojiro TAKAHAGI (Issei TAKAYANAGI 83) - Hisato SATO, Ryuichi HIRASHIGE (RI Han Jae 77). Tr: Mihailo PETROVIC

ALBIREX NIIGATA 2007

Mon	Date	Opponent		Score	Scorers	Att
Mar	3	Oita	D	1-1	Yano [53]	20 039
	11	Urawa	D	2-2	Kawahara [88], Tanaka [89]	40 524
	18	Nagoya	L	0-2		11 620
	31	Kawasaki	W	2-0	Yano [73], Edmilson [87]	31 500
Apr	7	FC Tokyo	W	3-1	Sakamoto [21], Richardes [52], Edmilson [55]	21 092
	14	G-Osaka	W	2-1	Silvinho [44], Yano [82]	32 686
	21	Hiroshima	D	0-0		8 326
	28	YF-Marinos	L	0-6		41 283
May	3	Kashiwa	D	0-0		13 481
	6	Kofu	W	3-1	Edmilson 2 [58 76], Fukai [89]	39 507
	12	Shimizu-SP	L	1-3	Edmilson [88]	12 197
	19	Kashima	D	1-1	Fukai [15]	38 268
	27	J-Iwata	W	4-2	Edmilson 2 [3 80], Yano [52], Richardes [73]	11 734
	9	Kobe	W	3-1	Richardes 2 [36 53], Edmilson [67]	38 667
Jun	16	Omiya	L	1-2	Chiyotanda [72]	16 795
	20	Yokohama	W	3-1	Uchida [14], Edmilson 2 [27 41]	36 182
	23	JEF Utd	W	2-1	Yano [49], Uchida [80]	15 069
	30	Hiroshima	W	2-1	Richardes 2 [40 58]	40 858
Aug	11	G-Osaka	L	1-3	Richardes [87]	18 112
	15	Nagoya	W	4-0	Homma [11], Yano [34], Edmilson 2 [48 79]	42 015
	19	Kobe	W	1-0	Richardes [12]	9 116
	26	Shimizu-SP	L	0-2		39 912
	29	Kofu	W	1-0	Sakamoto [25]	9 038
Sep	1	JEF Utd	L	0-1		40 488
	16	Kashiwa	L	1-2	Homma [2]	40 574
	22	Kashima	L	1-3	Yano [3]	14 812
	30	Urawa	L	0-1		47 755
Oct	6	Omiya	W	1-0	Edmilson [89]	38 507
	20	Kawasaki	L	3-4	Edmilson [25], Chiyotanda [56], Richardes [65]	14 440
	27	J-Iwata	D	1-1	Edmilson [37]	34 446
Nov	10	FC Tokyo	W	2-1	Edmilson 2 [60 83]	37 851
	10	Yokohama	W	2-0	Edmilson 2 [85 89]	7 751
	24	YF-Marinos	L	0-1		24 956
	1	Oita	L	0-2		37 430

GAMBA OSAKA 2007

Mon	Date	Opponent		Score	Scorers	Att
Mar	3	Omiya	W	1-0	Bare [88]	18 355
	11	Kashima	W	1-0	Magno Alves [66]	18 406
	17	Hiroshima	W	3-0	Futagawa [13], Endo [51], Bare [62]	14 123
	31	Kofu	W	2-1	Bando [73], Magno Alves [83]	13 064
Apr	7	Kawasaki	D	2-2	Myojin [38], Yamaguchi [83]	18 587
	14	Niigata	L	1-2	Endo [43]	32 686
	22	J-Iwata	W	5-2	Bare 2 [7 23], Sidiclei [14], Hashimoto [80], Futagawa [86]	14 495
	28	Oita	W	4-0	Yamaguchi [5], Magno Alves 2 [7 77], Bando [71]	20 806
May	3	Kobe	D	2-2	Endo [16], Bare [64]	22 236
	6	Shimizu-SP	D	1-1	Ienaga [66]	18 223
	13	Urawa	D	1-1	Bare [17]	55 258
	19	Kashiwa	W	2-1	Bare [23], Futagawa [38]	13 765
	26	JEF Utd	W	2-1	Myojin [67], Endo [89]	14 405
	9	Yokohama	W	3-1	Hashimoto [35], Endo [79]	19 752
	16	Nagoya	W	3-1	Bare 2 [63 84], Sidiclei [75]	20 473
Jun	20	YF-Marinos	D	0-0		13 956
	23	FC Tokyo	W	6-2	Futagawa [34], Magno Alves 2 [49 83], Hashimoto [53], Bando 2 [73 79]	15 640
	30	Omiya	W	3-0	Ienaga [63], Futagawa [79], Magno Alves [88]	10 049
	11	Niigata	W	3-1	OG [48], Bare [58], Kaji [78]	18 112
	15	Urawa	L	0-1		20 982
Aug	18	Yokohama	D	1-1	Endo [67]	8 426
	25	Kawasaki	L	1-4	Magno Alves [28]	19 789
	29	Kashima	W	5-1	Bare 2 [11 34], Endo [23], Bando 2 [47 73]	16 152
	1	Nagoya	W	4-1	Bare 3 [14 48 72], Bando [70]	18 425
Sep	16	YF-Marinos	L	0-2		19 419
	23	J-Iwata	L	1-2	Bare [89]	15 797
	29	Oita	W	1-0	Bare [89]	12 163
	6	Kashiwa	W	2-1	Bando [64], Endo [68]	10 640
Oct	21	Kofu	W	5-0	Terada 2 [4 73], Magno Alves [10], Futagawa [38], Maeda [84]	16 071
	27	Shimizu-SP	L	1-3	Yajima [12], Fernandinho [51], Cho [62]	15 898
	10	JEF Utd	W	2-0	Bare 2 [58 61]	20 044
Nov	18	FC Tokyo	D	1-1	Magno Alves [44]	30 157
	24	Kobe	D	1-1	Bando [40]	20 109
	1	Hiroshima	D	2-2	Bare [27], Futagawa [80]	14 173

JEF UNITED CHIBA 2007

Mon	Date	Opponent		Score	Scorers	Att
Mar	4	Nagoya	L	0-2		18 410
	10	Shimizu-SP	L	1-3	Stoyanov [83]	15 373
	17	Kashima	D	3-3	Hanyu [24], Mizuno [27], Djordjevic [46]	14 814
	31	J-Iwata	L	0-1		12 379
Apr	8	Yokohama	W	4-0	Mizuno [27], Maki [65], Hanyu [70], Yamagishi [73]	15 584
	14	Kobe	L	1-2	Djordjevic [86]	10 983
	21	Omiya	W	1-0	Kudo [59]	9 481
	29	Kawasaki	D	1-1	Mizuno [81]	21 804
	3	Urawa	D	1-1	Mizumoto [49]	57 440
May	6	Kashiwa	D	1-1	Yamagishi [71]	11 969
	12	FC Tokyo	L	1-4	Sato [68]	21 821
	19	Hiroshima	L	1-3	Mizuno [66]	10 983
	26	G-Osaka	L	1-2	Arai [22]	14 405
Jun	9	YF-Marinos	L	0-1		23 028
	17	Kofu	W	3-2	Maki 2 [15 38], Hanyu [70]	13 229
	20	Oita	W	1-0	Yamagishi [73]	15 508
	23	Niigata	L	1-2	Hanyu [86]	15 069
	30	Yokohama	W	1-0	Yamagishi [9]	43 117
	11	Kawasaki	L	1-3	Hanyu [33]	16 070
Aug	15	Kashima	L	1-3	OG [19]	19 600
	18	J-Iwata	W	3-2	Maki [37], Sato [83], Arai [86]	16 718
	25	Kashiwa	L	0-1		10 801
Sep	29	Oita	W	6-0	Sato [37], Yamagishi [65], Mizuno 2 [83 89], Kudo [87], Aoki [89]	10 447
	1	Niigata	W	1-0	Arai [73]	40 488
	15	Kobe	W	4-2	Mizuno 2 [19 56], OG [36], Aoki [68]	13 272
	22	Omiya	W	1-0	Saito [32]	8 449
	30	FC Tokyo	W	3-2	Arai [9], Kudo [30], Mizuno [60]	15 346
Oct	6	Kofu	W	1-0	Aoki [89]	14 037
	20	Urawa	L	2-4	Reinaldo [54], Hanyu [77]	16 756
	27	Hiroshima	D	2-2	Arai [49], Yamagishi [89]	9 680
	10	G-Osaka	L	0-2		20 044
Nov	10	YF-Marinos	L	2-3	Reinaldo [67], Kudo [79]	15 678
	24	Shimizu-SP	D	2-2	Maki [3], Djordjevic [64]	18 577
	1	Nagoya	L	0-2		15 341

JUBILO IWATA 2007

Mon	Date	Opponent		Score	Scorers	Att
Mar	4	Kashiwa	L	0-4		10 960
	10	Oita	W	2-1	Nishi [68], Fabricio [82]	11 452
	18	FC Tokyo	W	1-0	Suzuki [82]	27 046
	31	JEF Utd	W	1-0	Cullen [6]	12 379
Apr	7	Urawa	L	1-2	Cullen [32]	45 025
	14	YF-Marinos	W	1-0	Naruoka [54]	11 864
	22	G-Osaka	L	2-5	Murai 2 [69 78]	14 495
	28	Hiroshima	W	4-2	Cullen 2 [4 68], Oi [38], Naruoka [86]	10 131
	3	Shimizu-SP	L	1-2	Nakayama [22]	20 318
May	6	Nagoya	W	1-0	Cullen [62]	23 142
	12	Kashima	L	1-2	Hayashi [89]	13 259
	20	Kobe	L	2-3	Cullen [28], Naruoka [37]	12 149
	27	Niigata	L	2-4	Marquinhos [17], Kaga [36]	11 734
Jun	10	Kofu	W	6-1	Maeda 2 [17 77], Ota 2 [21 73], Kikuchi [51], Fabricio [63]	11 389
	16	Yokohama	W	2-1	Naruoka [23], Maeda [49]	13 605
	20	Omiya	D	0-0		9 292
	23	Kawasaki	W	3-2	Maeda 2 [3 53], Naruoka [48]	16 614
	30	Urawa	L	0-2		35 072
	11	Kobe	L	0-4		12 624
Aug	15	FC Tokyo	W	5-2	Ota [20], Marquinhos [64], Ueda [68], Maruoka [72], Maeda [84]	14 854
	18	JEF Utd	L	2-3	Nishi [24], Chano [54]	16 718
	25	Kofu	W	2-1	Naruoka [44], Maeda [56]	12 757
Sep	1	YF-Marinos	L	1-4	Kaga [11]	10 828
	1	Shimizu-SP	L	0-1		33 678
	15	Omiya	W	2-0	Ueda [71], Ota [85]	8 432
	23	G-Osaka	D	1-1	Cullen [39]	15 797
	29	Kawasaki	W	3-0	Maeda 2 [31 43], Chano [86]	10 752
Oct	6	Hiroshima	W	1-0	Naruoka [83]	9 363
	20	Kashima	L	1-3	Tanaka [87]	25 961
	27	Niigata	D	1-1	Maeda [20]	34 446
Nov	3	Nagoya	D	0-0		17 529
	18	Kawasaki	L	1-3	Maeda [62]	13 172
	24	Oita	L	0-1		23 381
	1	Kashiwa	W	4-0	Maeda [40], Hayashi [46], Ueda [61], Inuzuka [75]	13 923

KASHIMA ANTLERS 2007

Mo	Day	Opponent	Res	Score	Comp	Scorers	Att
Mar	3	Kawasaki	L	0-1	JL		20 295
	11	G-Osaka	L	0-1	JL		18 406
	17	JEF Utd	D	3-3	JL	Marquinhos 2 23 55, Chugo 40	14 814
	21	Niigata	L	1-3	JCgD	Marquinhos 27	33 481
	25	Niigata	W	2-1	JCgD	Yanagisawa 2 8 66	7 359
	31	Kobe	D	1-1	JL	Fabao 44	10 518
Apr	4	Kofu	L	0-1	JCgD		4 376
	7	Omiya	D	0-0	JL		10 234
	11	Nagoya	W	2-1	JCgD	Masuda 21, Marquinhos 29	4 138
	14	Yokohama	W	1-0	JL	Yanagisawa 25	19 367
	21	Shimizu-SP	W	2-1	JL	Yanagisawa 2 32 46	12 738
	29	Urawa	L	0-1	JL		36 146
May	3	FC Tokyo	W	2-1	JL	Chugo 59, Masuda 82	30 436
	6	YF-Marinos	D	1-1	JL	Chugo 52	13 344
	9	Nagoya	W	4-1	JCgD	Oiwa 49, Tashiro 2 54 65, Motoyama 62	3 858
	12	J-Iwata	W	2-1	JL	Chugo 13, Marquinhos 76	13 259
	19	Niigata	D	1-1	JL	Iwamasa 4	38 268
	23	Kofu	W	3-0	JCgD	Tashiro 2 36 60, Motoyama 65	8 844
	26	Kofu	W	2-0	JL	Iwamasa 28, Sasaki 76	10 081
	9	Oita	D	2-2	JL	Koroki 65, Iwamasa 81	21 804
Jun	16	Hiroshima	W	5-1	JL	Motoyama 15, Marquinhos 50, Iwamasa 72, Tashiro 85, Koroki 89	10 524
	20	Kashiwa	W	1-0	JL	Marquinhos 89	10 273
	24	Nagoya	W	2-1	JL	Masuda 65, Marquinhos 70	14 317
	30	FC Tokyo	L	1-2	JL	Marquinhos 21	15 712
Jul	8	Hiroshima	L	0-1	JCqf		7 086
	15	Hiroshima	W	3-1	JCqf	Marquinhos 2 15 40, Nozawa 47	8 647
	12	Kofu	W	1-0	JL	Nozawa 34	14 316
Aug	15	JEF Utd	W	3-1	JL	Araiba 25, Ogasawara 2 31 85	19 600
	19	Omiya	W	2-1	JL	Marquinhos 32, Masuda 89	13 889
	25	Yokohama	W	2-1	JL	Yanagisawa 1, Koroki 82	15 957
	29	G-Osaka	L	1-5	JL	Fabao 69	16 152
Sep	1	Kawasaki	W	4-1	JL	Nozawa 30, Ogasawara 37, Marquinhos 84, Koroki 85	14 856
	15	Nagoya	L	0-3	JL		13 949
	22	Niigata	W	2-1	JL	Tashiro 2 11 33, Nozawa 59	14 812
	30	Hiroshima	W	1-0	JL	Marquinhos 65	13 492
	6	Kobe	W	3-2	JL	Koroki 2 16 29, Tashiro 49	10 503
Oct	10	G-Osaka	L	0-1	JCsf		8 157
	13	G-Osaka	W	3-2	JCsf	Motoyama 2 41 44, Ogasawara 51	16 291
	20	J-Iwata	W	3-1	JL	Marquinhos 58, Iwamasa 62, Yanagisawa 89	25 961
	27	Oita	W	2-1	JL	Iwamasa 31, Tashiro 2 54 80	8 036
Nov	4	Mito H'hock	W	2-0	ECr4		7 005
	10	YF-Marinos	W	3-2	JL	Nozawa 24, Marquinhos 2 48 52	21 109
	18	Kashiwa	W	1-0	JL	Funayama 42	18 887
	24	Urawa	W	1-0	JL	Nozawa 66	62 123
Dec	1	Shimizu-SP	W	3-0	JL	Ogasawara 20, Motoyama 48, Marquinhos 59	31 384
	8	Kofu	W	2-1	ECr5	Tashiro 29, Yanagisawa 109	6 558
	22	Honda	W	1-0	ECqf	Yanagisawa 110	8 537
	29	Kashiwa	W	1-0	ECsf	Motoyama 72	22 457
	1	Hiroshima	W	2-0	ECf	Achida 8, Danilo 89	46 357

JL = J.League • JC = J.League Yamazaki Nabisco Cup • EC = Emperor's Cup • gD = Group D • r4 = fourth round • r5 = fifth round • qf = quarter-final • sf = semi-final • f = final

KASHIWA REYSOL 2007

Mo	Day	Opponent	Res	Score	Scorers	Att
Mar	4	J-Iwata	W	4-0	Franca 2 24 63, Suganuma 2 57 73	10 960
	10	Hiroshima	D	1-1	Suganuma 37	12 891
	17	Shimizu-SP	W	1-0	Ri 66	11 460
	31	FC Tokyo	W	2-0	Suganuma 34, Koga 49	10 793
Apr	7	YF-Marinos	W	2-0	Suzuki 8, Sato 89	18 960
	15	Urawa	L	0-2		35 013
	21	Kofu	L	2-3	Kurakawa 33, Ri 78	11 437
	28	Nagoya	W	2-0	Ri 25, Suganuma 40	11 077
	3	Niigata	D	0-0		13 481
	6	JEF Utd	D	1-1	Yazawa 50	11 969
May	12	Oita	W	2-0	Franca 8, Lee 11	9 374
	19	G-Osaka	L	1-2	Lee 44	13 765
	26	Kobe	L	1-2	Doumbia 67	9 173
	9	Omiya	D	0-0		12 730
Jun	20	Kashima	L	0-1		10 273
	23	Yokohama	W	4-2	Lee 2 38 44, Sato 43, Doumbia 86	7 232
	30	Shimizu-SP	L	1-3	Doumbia 68	11 489
	1	Urawa	D	1-1	Koga 69	47 359
	15	Hiroshima	W	2-0	Franca 44, Ota 56	10 636
	18	FC Tokyo	W	1-0	Franca 52	25 373
	25	JEF Utd	W	1-0	Franca 78	10 801
	29	Omiya	D	1-1	Lee 10	6 149
	2	YF-Marinos	W	1-0	OG 1	23 569
Aug	16	Niigata	W	2-1	Lee 59, Yamane 71	40 574
	23	Kawasaki	W	4-0	Lee 48, Suganuma 51, Ota 72, Alceu 76	10 648
	29	Nagoya	L	0-2		7 553
	6	G-Osaka	L	1-2	Franca 51	10 640
	20	Oita	L	1-2	Franca 49	14 671
	27	Kobe	L	1-3	Ota 44	8 947
Nov	10	Yokohama	D	1-1	Kitajima 75	8 990
	18	Kashima	L	0-1		18 887
	24	Kofu	W	2-1	Kondo 20, Suzuki 84	11 021
	1	J-Iwata	L	0-4		13 923

KAWASAKI FRONTALE 2007

Mo	Day	Opponent	Res	Score	Scorers	Att
Mar	3	Kashima	W	1-0	Magnum 21	20 295
	11	Kobe	D	1-1	Murakami 47	14 664
	17	Yokohama	W	6-0	Juninho 2 14 48, Murakami 23, Magnum 44, Kurotsu 2 69 80	18 621
	31	Niigata	L	0-2		31 500
Apr	7	G-Osaka	D	2-2	Taniguchi 13, Magnum 41	18 587
	15	Shimizu-SP	W	2-1	Kurotsu 61, Juninho 63	21 208
	21	Urawa	W	2-1	Ganaha 50, Magnum 56	50 531
	29	JEF Utd	D	1-1	Chong 66	21 804
	3	YF-Marinos	L	1-2	Magnum 77	33 498
May	6	FC Tokyo	W	5-2	Ohashi 2 2 43, Kurotsu 11, Murakami 44, Juninho 68	14 983
	13	Kofu	W	3-1	Juninho 10, Magnum 26, Mori 56	12 686
	19	Oita	L	0-2		15 371
	27	Omiya	D	1-1	Ohashi 64	14 033
	2	Nagoya	D	2-2	Juninho 22, Chong 67	21 190
	16	Kashiwa	D	0-0		15 244
Jun	20	Hiroshima	D	1-1	Juninho 12	6 037
	23	J-Iwata	L	2-3	Juninho 20, Nakamura 58	16 614
	30	Kobe	W	2-1	Murakami 9, Juninho 89	17 299
	11	JEF Utd	W	3-1	Juninho 3 67 74 88	16 070
	15	YF-Marinos	L	1-2	Chong 85	18 095
Aug	18	Shimizu-SP	L	1-3	Chong 57	19 073
	25	G-Osaka	W	4-1	Chong 2 2 51, Juninho 2 46 48	19 789
	29	Nagoya	D	1-1	Juninho 89	13 185
	1	Kashima	L	1-4	Juninho 50	14 856
Sep	15	Oita	D	2-2	Ohashi 86, Igawa 89	15 535
	23	Kashiwa	L	0-4		10 648
	30	Kofu	D	1-1	Taniguchi 89	13 438
	7	Yokohama	W	1-0	Juninho 26	14 208
Oct	20	Niigata	W	4-3	Nakamura 2 20 89, Kukino 38, Juninho 39	14 440
	28	FC Tokyo	W	7-0	Chong 3 25 29 42, Minowa 40, Magnum 74, Terada 79, Juninho 85	30 494
	11	Urawa	D	1-1	Yabu 10	23 355
Nov	18	J-Iwata	W	3-1	Juninho 2 20 77, Chong 41	13 172
	24	Hiroshima	W	3-0	Chong 15, Juninho 45, Nakamura 47	16 813
	1	Omiya	D	1-1	Chong 21	12 958

NAGOYA GRAMPUS EIGHT 2007

	Date	Opponent	Res	Score	Scorers	Att
Mar	4	JEF Utd	W	2-0	Kim 76, Honda 89	18 410
	10	Kofu	W	2-0	Kim 50, Tamada 79	11 791
	18	Niigata	W	2-0	Johnsen 33, Kim 69	11 620
Apr	1	Yokohama	W	2-1	Sugimoto 64, Yamaguchi 66	10 225
	7	Hiroshima	L	2-3	Yamaguchi 22, Masukawa 62	16 825
	14	Omiya	L	0-1		6 584
	21	Kobe	W	2-0	Johnsen 40, Sugimoto 41	10 363
	28	Kashima	L	0-2		11 077
May	3	Oita	L	1-2	Johnsen 53	14 146
	6	J-Iwata	L	0-1		23 142
	12	YF-Marinos	W	2-0	Sugimoto 11, Katayama 75	19 074
	19	Urawa	L	1-2	Johnsen 35	34 347
	26	FC Tokyo	W	1-0	Johnsen 32	22 679
Jun	9	Kawasaki	D	2-2	Fujita 1, Johnsen 65	21 190
	16	G-Osaka	L	1-3	Masukawa 7	20 473
	20	Shimizu-SP	L	1-2	Tsuda 73	9 416
	24	Kashima	L	1-2	Johnsen 71	14 317
	30	Kofu	D	1-1	Johnsen 29	10 264
Aug	12	Hiroshima	W	3-1	Johnsen 2 35 66, Sugimoto 88	12 595
	15	Niigata	L	0-4		42 015
	18	YF-Marinos	L	0-3		15 703
	25	Omiya	W	5-0	Tamada 21, Fujita 37, Tsuda 44, Sugimoto 2 50 62	10 804
	29	Kawasaki	D	1-1	Tamada 37	13 185
Sep	1	G-Osaka	L	1-2	Sugimoto 86	18 425
	15	Kashima	W	3-0	Honda 2 18 24, Tamada 79	13 949
	22	Kobe	L	0-5		7 793
	29	Kashiwa	W	2-0	Kim 22, Ogawa 54	7 553
Oct	6	Shimizu-SP	L	0-3		14 831
	21	FC Tokyo	L	0-1		18 025
	28	Urawa	D	0-0		52 314
Nov	10	J-Iwata	D	0-0		17 529
	18	Oita	W	3-1	Johnsen 3 15 67 82	27 811
	24	Yokohama	D	0-0		16 370
	1	JEF Utd	W	2-0	Ogawa 63, Tamada 67	15 341

OITA TRINITA 2007

	Date	Opponent	Res	Score	Scorers	Att
Mar	3	Niigata	D	1-1	Fukaya 83	20 039
	10	J-Iwata	L	1-2	Takahashi 76	11 452
	17	Omiya	W	3-1	Miki 47, Matsuhashi.S 65, Takamatsu 69	16 870
	1	Urawa	D	2-2	Takamatsu 11, Fukaya 89	27 163
Apr	8	Shimizu-SP	L	0-2		13 225
	15	FC Tokyo	D	0-0		17 431
	22	YF-Marinos	L	0-5		17 219
	28	G-Osaka	L	0-4		20 806
May	3	Nagoya	W	2-1	Augusto 29, Matsuhashi.M 78	14 146
	6	Hiroshima	L	1-2	Kanazaki 65	20 224
	12	Kashima	L			9 374
	19	Kawasaki	W	2-0	Augusto 26, Serginho 49	15 371
	26	Niigata	L	1-2	Matsuhashi.S 78	4 935
Jun	9	Kashima	D	2-2	Takahashi 2 69 89	21 804
	16	Kobe	W	3-1	Takahashi 2 1 68, Umesaki 40	13 966
	20	JEF Utd	L	0-1		15 508
	23	Kofu	L	0-2		11 298
	30	YF-Marinos	L	0-3		20 315
Aug	11	FC Tokyo	W	2-1	Takamatsu 48, Takahashi 57	20 689
	15	Shimizu-SP	L	3-4	Takamatsu 11, Fujita 34, Kanazaki 86	20 391
	18	Hiroshima	L	0-2		10 402
	25	Kobe	W	2-0	Takahashi 2 21 52	17 910
	29	JEF Utd	L	0-6		10 447
Sep	2	Kofu	W	4-1	Takahashi 23, Umesaki 27, Takamatsu 73, Suzuki 86	14 830
	15	Kawasaki	D	2-2	Edmilson 66, Nishiyama 89	15 535
	22	Yokohama	W	2-0	Takamatsu 31, Yamazaki 42	21 371
	29	G-Osaka	L	0-1		12 163
Oct	7	Urawa	L	1-2	Fujita 60	18 511
	20	Kashiwa	W	2-1	Takahashi 30, Takahashi 64	14 671
	27	Kashima	L	0-3		8 036
Nov	11	Omiya	W	2-1	Fukaya 26, Maeda 88	14 752
	18	Nagoya	L	1-3	Takamatsu 56	27 811
	24	J-Iwata	W	1-0	Suzuki 15	23 381
	1	Niigata	W	2-0	Morishige 9, Suzuki 20	37 430

OMIYA ARDIJA 2007

	Date	Opponent	Res	Score	Scorers	Att
Mar	3	G-Osaka	L	0-1		18 355
	10	FC Tokyo	L	0-2		17 023
	17	Oita	L	1-3	Yoshihara 76	16 870
	31	Shimizu-SP	L	1-2	Morita 86	7 737
Apr	7	Kashima	D	0-0		10 234
	14	Nagoya	W	1-0	Salles 26	6 584
	21	JEF Utd	L	0-1		9 481
	28	Kofu	L	1-2	Fujimoto 56	6 628
May	3	Hiroshima	L	1-2	Kobayashi.Y 40	13 220
	6	Urawa	D	1-1	Kobayashi.Y 38	33 162
	13	Kobe	D	0-0		7 769
	19	Yokohama	W	1-0	Tomita 83	9 466
	27	Kawasaki	D	1-1	Wakabayashi 89	14 033
Jun	9	Kashiwa	D	0-0		12 730
	16	Niigata	W	2-1	Yoshihara 68, Wakabayashi 88	16 795
	20	J-Iwata	D	0-0		9 292
	24	YF-Marinos	D	0-0		10 051
	30	G-Osaka	L	0-3		10 049
Aug	11	Shimizu-SP	D	2-2	Kobayashi.D 5, Yoshihara 18	15 047
	15	Kobe	L	1-3	Yoshihara 20	6 440
	19	Kashima	L	1-2	Denis Marques 27	13 889
	25	Nagoya	L	0-5		10 804
	29	Kashiwa	D	1-1	Denis Marques 30	6 149
Sep	1	Urawa	W	1-0	Morita 60	49 810
	15	J-Iwata	L	0-2		8 432
	22	JEF Utd	L	0-1		8 449
	29	YF-Marinos	W	2-0	Hirano 62, Yoshihara 73	12 923
Oct	8	Niigata	L	0-1		38 507
	20	Hiroshima	W	1-0	Wakabayashi 81	11 038
	27	Yokohama	W	1-0	Kobayashi.D 39	4 114
	11	Oita	L	1-2	Kobayashi.Y 3	14 752
Nov	18	Kofu	D	0-0		15 151
	24	FC Tokyo	W	2-1	Fujimoto 49, Leandro 89	20 749
	1	Kawasaki	D	1-1	Saito 89	12 958

SANFRECCE HIROSHIMA 2007

	Date	Opponent	Res	Score	Scorers	Att
Mar	3	FC Tokyo	W	4-2	Sato 2 13 18, Ueslei 2 27 52	25 257
	10	Kashiwa	D	1-1	Toda 87	12 891
	17	G-Osaka	L	0-3		14 123
	31	YF-Marinos	L	1-3	Ueslei 9	9 337
Apr	7	Nagoya	W	3-2	Ueslei 2 24 77, Sato 72	16 825
	14	Kofu	D	2-2	Sato 17, Ueslei 45	7 181
	21	Niigata	D	0-0		8 326
	28	J-Iwata	L	2-4	Sato 46, Ueslei 81	10 131
May	3	Omiya	W	2-1	Sato 42, Komano 89	13 220
	6	Oita	W	2-1	Sato 34, Ueslei 82	20 224
	12	Yokohama	L	0-2		13 636
	19	JEF Utd	W	3-1	Ueslei 3 6 23 36	10 983
	26	Shimizu-SP	W	2-1	Toda 74, Kashiwagi 78	10 514
Jun	16	Kashima	L	1-5	Kashiwagi 33	10 524
	20	Kawasaki	D	1-1	Ueslei 41	6 037
	23	Kobe	L	2-3	Kashiwagi 21, Ueslei 68	10 362
	30	Niigata	L	1-2	Sato 55	40 858
	1	Urawa	L	1-4	Sato 54	38 682
Aug	12	Nagoya	L	1-3	OG 42	12 595
	15	Kobe	L	0-2		10 636
	18	Oita	W	2-0	Hattori 29, Ueslei 71	10 402
	26	YF-Marinos	D	2-2	Koji Morisaki 12, Kashiwagi 36	19 007
	29	FC Tokyo	L	0-5		7 122
Sep	1	Yokohama	W	2-1	Ueslei 2 54 79	6 341
	15	Urawa	L	2-4	Ueslei 40, Koji Morisaki 82	22 675
	22	Kofu	L	1-2	Hattori 21	11 606
	30	Kashima	L	0-1		13 492
Oct	6	J-Iwata	L	0-1		9 363
	20	Omiya	L	0-1		11 038
	27	JEF Utd	D	2-2	Sato 31, Komano 65	9 680
Nov	11	Shimizu-SP	L	1-3	Kashiwagi 27	16 508
	18	Kobe	D	1-1	Sato 47	13 555
	24	Kawasaki	L	0-3		16 813
	1	G-Osaka	D	2-2	Sato 7, Makino 89	14 173
Dec	5	Kyoto	L	1-2	Hirashige 88	12 637
	8	Kyoto	D	0-0		23 162

SHIMIZU S–PULSE 2007

Mo	Date	Opponent	Res	Score	Scorers	Att
Mar	3	Kobe	W	1-0	Aoyama [6]	18 333
	10	JEF Utd	W	3-1	Cho [16], Edamura [19], Ito [20]	15 373
	17	Kashiwa	L	0-1		11 460
	31	Omiya	W	2-1	Edamura [35], Fernandinho [44]	7 737
Apr	8	Oita	W	2-0	Ichikawa [62], Cho [65]	13 225
	15	Kawasaki	L	1-2	Okazaki [32]	21 208
	21	Kashima	L	1-2	Ichikawa [39]	12 738
	28	Yokohama	D	1-1	Fernandinho [28]	15 008
May	3	J-Iwata	W	2-1	Cho 2 [18 40]	20 318
	6	G-Osaka	D	1-1	Fernandinho [73]	18 223
	12	Niigata	W	3-1	Okazaki [4], Fujimoto 2 [44 73]	12 197
	19	Kofu	D	0-0		12 422
	26	Hiroshima	L	1-2	Cho [65]	10 514
Jun	6	FC Tokyo	L	1-3	Hyodo [43]	15 322
	16	YF-Marinos	L	0-1	Okazaki [63]	15 078
	20	Nagoya	W	2-1	Hyodo [22], Yajima [42]	9 416
	23	Urawa	L	0-1		20 300
	30	Kashima	W	3-1	Okazaki 2 [23 53], Fujimoto [33]	11 489
Aug	11	Omiya	D	2-2	Cho [10], Fernandinho [53]	15 047
	15	Oita	W	4-3	Fernandinho 2 [35 68], Ichikawa [44], Yajima [53]	20 391
	18	Kawasaki	L	2-5	Fujimoto [32], Fernandinho [35], Yajima [58]	19 073
	26	Niigata	W	2-0	Iwashita [62], Cho [78]	39 912
	29	Yokohama	W	1-0	Cho [70]	14 167
Sep	1	J-Iwata	W	1-0	Cho [89]	33 678
	15	Kofu	W	2-0	Yajima [63], Edamura [89]	18 108
	23	FC Tokyo	L	0-2		30 363
	29	Kobe	L	0-1		9 097
Oct	6	Nagoya	W	3-0	Cho 3 [28 49 77]	14 831
	20	YF-Marinos	W	2-0	Yajima 2 [54 68]	25 082
	27	G-Osaka	W	3-1	Yajima [12], Fernandinho [51], Cho [62]	15 898
Nov	1	Hiroshima	W	3-1	Ichikawa [28], Fujimoto [66], Fernandinho [82]	16 508
	18	Urawa	D	0-0		56 368
	24	JEF Utd	D	2-2	Fujimoto 2 [10 20]	18 577
	1	Kashima	L	0-3		31 384

FC TOKYO 2007

Mo	Date	Opponent	Res	Score	Scorers	Att
Mar	3	Hiroshima	L	2-4	Lucas 2 [49 61]	25 257
	10	Omiya	W	2-0	Konno [27], Fukunishi [57]	17 023
	18	J-Iwata	L	0-1		27 046
	31	Kashiwa	L	0-2		10 793
Apr	7	Niigata	L	1-3	OG [61]	21 092
	15	Oita	D	0-0		17 431
	21	Yokohama	W	1-0	Konno [46]	22 168
	28	Kobe	D	0-0		9 213
May	3	Kashima	L	1-2	Wanchope [57]	30 436
	6	Kawasaki	L	2-5	Lucas [75], Ishikawa [86]	14 983
	12	JEF Utd	W	4-1	Lucas [26], Wanchope [45], Rychely [48], Fukunishi [69]	21 821
	20	YF-Marinos	W	1-0	Fukunishi [69]	25 811
	26	Nagoya	L	0-1		22 679
Jun	10	Shimizu-SP	W	3-1	Suzuki 2 [26 46], Baba [72]	15 322
	17	Urawa	L	0-2		38 439
	20	Kofu	W	2-1	Suzuki [30], Lucas [59]	17 264
	23	G-Osaka	L	2-6	Fukunishi [10], Suzuki [15]	15 640
	30	Kashima	W	2-1	Lucas [47], Suzuki [56]	15 712
Aug	11	Oita	L	1-2	Fukunishi [3]	20 689
	15	J-Iwata	L	2-5	Hirayama [89], Akamine [89]	14 854
	18	Kashiwa	L	0-1		25 373
	25	Urawa	L	2-3	Akamine [32], Konno [69]	46 951
	29	Hiroshima	W	5-0	Kajiyama [18], Akamine [54], Fukunishi [88], Hirayama 2 [87 89]	7 122
Sep	1	Kobe	W	3-1	Konno [44], Lucas 2 [68 81]	23 968
	15	Yokohama	W	2-0	Fukunishi [34], Hirayama [89]	13 835
	23	Shimizu-SP	W	2-0	OG [31], Akamine [32]	30 363
	30	JEF Utd	L	2-3	Konno [68], Lucas [77]	15 346
Oct	6	YF-Marinos	W	2-1	Hirayama [66], Ishikawa [84]	21 939
	21	Nagoya	W	1-0	Lucas [57]	18 025
	28	Kawasaki	L	0-7		30 494
Nov	10	Niigata	L	1-2	Ishikawa [42]	37 851
	18	G-Osaka	D	1-1	Lucas [76]	30 157
	24	Omiya	L	1-2	Ishikawa [47]	20 749
	1	Kofu	W	1-0	Lucas [87]	14 777

URAWA REDS 2007

Mo	Date	Opponent	Res	Score	Comp	Scorers	Att
Mar	24	Gamba	L	0-4	SC		35 307
	3	Yokohama	W	2-1	JL	OG [25], Nagai [85]	57 188
	7	Persik	W	3-0	CLgE	Yamada [12], Nagai [45], Ono [76]	31 303
	11	Niigata	D	2-2	JL	Nagai [30], Washington [64]	40 524
	17	Kofu	W	2-0	JL	Washington 2 [57 69]	39 494
Apr	21	Sydney	D	2-2	CLgE	Ponte [30], Nagai [54]	21 010
	1	Oita	D	2-2	JL	Abe 2 [30 35]	27 163
	7	J-Iwata	W	2-1	JL	Washington [39], Ponte [79]	45 025
	11	Shanghai	W	1-0	CLgE	Abe [42]	28 828
Apr	15	Kashiwa	W	1-0	JL	Washington [26], Ono [38]	35 013
	21	Kawasaki	L	1-2	JL	Horinouchi [64]	50 531
	25	Shanghai	D	0-0	CLgE		10 000
	29	Kashima	W	1-0	JL	Ponte [56]	36 146
	3	JEF Utd	D	1-1	JL	Washington [27]	57 440
	6	Omiya	D	1-1	JL	Washington [73]	33 162
	9	Persik	D	3-3	CLgE	Ono [9p], Ponte [50], Abe [62]	
May	13	G-Osaka	W	2-0	JL	Washington [76]	55 258
	19	Nagoya	W	2-1	JL	Nene [27], Washington [84]	34 347
	23	Sydney	D	0-0	CLgE		44 993
	27	YF-Marinos	D	1-1	JL	Nene [66]	51 829
	17	FC Tokyo	W	2-0	JL	Tanaka.T [3], OG [65]	38 439
	20	Kobe	W	2-0	JL	Tanaka.MT [38], Ponte [44]	16 709
	23	Shimizu-SP	W	1-0	JL	Abe [24]	20 300
	30	J-Iwata	W	2-0	JL	Ono 2 [1 28]	35 072
Jul	7	G-Osaka	D	1-1	JCqf	Ono [12]	44 609
	14	G-Osaka	L	2-5	JCqf	Nagai [17], Hosogai [63]	14 213
	1	Hiroshima	W	4-1	JL	Tanaka.MT [64], Ponte [75], Tanaka.T [78], Washington [83]	38 682
	11	Kashiwa	D	1-1	JL	Tanaka.MT [60]	47 359
Aug	8	G-Osaka	W	1-0	JL	Nagai [62]	20 982
	18	Kofu	W	4-1	JL	Tanaka.T 2 [6 63], Nagai [39], Suzuki [42]	36 756
	25	FC Tokyo	W	3-2	JL	Tanaka.T [36], Horinouchi [39], Ponte [50]	46 951
	29	Kobe	W	1-0	JL	Tanaka.T 2 [49 74]	20 067
	1	Omiya	L	0-1	JL		49 810
Sep	15	Hiroshima	W	4-2	JL	Tanaka.T [12], Hasebe [23], Nagai [37], Washington [84]	22 675
	19	Jeonbuk	W	2-1	CLqf	Hasebe [4], Tanaka.T [58]	33 103
	22	YF-Marinos	W	1-0	JL	Nagai [65]	48 166
	26	Jeonbuk	W	2-0	CLqf	Tanaka.T [4], Ponte [66]	31 000
	30	Niigata	W	1-0	JL	Ponte [87]	47 755
Oct	2	Seongnam	D	2-2	CLsf	Tanaka.T [53], Ponte [66p]	17 000
	7	Oita	W	2-1	JL	Tanaka.T 2 [4 68]	18 511
	20	JEF Utd	W	4-2	JL	Washington 2 [28 38], Ponte [49], Tanaka.T [89]	16 756
	24	Seongnam	D	2-2	CLsf	Washington [21], Hasebe [73], W 5-4p	51 651
	27	Nagoya	D	0-0	JL		52 314
Nov	3	Sepahan	D	1-1	CLf	Ponte [45]	25 000
	11	Kawasaki	D	1-1	JL	Washington [32]	23 355
	14	Sepahan	W	2-0	CLf	Nagai [22], Abe [71]	59 034
	18	Shimizu-SP	D	0-0	JL		56 368
	24	Kashima	L	0-1	JL		62 123
	28	Ehime	L	0-2	ECr4		12 247
Dec	1	Yokohama	L	0-1	JL		46 697
	10	Sepahan	W	3-1	CWqf	Nagai [32], Washington [54], OG [70]	33 263
	13	Milan	L	0-1	CWsf		67 005
	16	Etoile Sahel	W	2-2	CW3p	Washington 2 [35 70], W 4-2p	53 363

SC = Xerox Super Cup • JL = J.League • CL = AFC Champions League •
JC = J.League Yamazaki Nabisco Cup • EC = Emperor's Cup •
CW = FIFA Club World Cup
gE = Group E • r4 = fourth round • qf = quarter-final • sf = semi-final
• 3p = third place play-off • f = final

VENTFORET KOFU 2007

Month	Date	Opponent	Result	Scorers	Att
Mar	3	YF-Marinos	L 0-1		24 466
	10	Nagoya	L 0-2		11 791
	17	Urawa	L 0-2		39 494
	31	G-Osaka	L 1-2	Alberto 37	13 064
Apr	7	Kobe	W 4-3	Fujita 5, Shigehara 2 71 75, Hosaka 89	8 373
	14	Hiroshima	D 2-2	Shigehara 2 39 64	7 181
	21	Kashiwa	W 3-2	Ishihara 38, Hosaka 2 84 86	11 437
	28	Omiya	W 2-1	Sudo 36, Hayashi 60	6 628
May	3	Yokohama	W 1-0	Masushima 63	16 279
	6	Niigata	L 1-3	Shigehara 11	39 507
	13	Kawasaki	L 1-3	Masushima 3	12 686
	19	Shimizu-SP	D 0-0		12 422
	26	Kashima	L 0-2		10 081
Jun	10	J-Iwata	L 1-2	Masushima 84	11 389
	17	JEF Utd	L 2-3	Ishihara 2 25 50	13 229
	20	FC Tokyo	L 1-2	Shigehara 66	17 264
	23	Oita	W 2-0	Ishihara 22, Kuno 89	11 298
	30	Nagoya	D 1-1	Sudo 68	14 316
Aug	12	Kashima	L 0-1		
	15	Yokohama	W 2-0	Sudo 2 11 85	5 606
	18	Urawa	L 1-4	Ishihara 46	36 756
	25	J-Iwata	L 1-2	Akimoto 68	12 757
	29	Niigata	L 0-1		9 038
Sep	2	Oita	L 1-4	Radoncic 9	14 830
	15	Shimizu-SP	L 0-2		18 108
	22	Hiroshima	W 2-1	Masushima 56, Alberto 89	11 606
	30	Kawasaki	D 1-1	Fujita 12	13 438
Oct	6	JEF Utd	L 1-3		14 037
	21	G-Osaka	L 0-5		16 071
	27	YF-Marinos	D 1-1	Alberto 38	9 056
Nov	10	Kobe	L 1-4	Akimoto 25	11 236
	18	Omiya	D 0-0		15 151
	24	Kashiwa	L 1-2	Akimoto 65	11 021
	1	FC Tokyo	L 0-1		14 777

VISSEL KOBE 2007

Month	Date	Opponent	Result	Scorers	Att
Mar	3	Shimizu	L 0-1		18 333
	10	Kawasaki	D 1-1	Leandro 61	14 664
	17	YF-Marinos	W 4-1	Okubo 2 38 87, Leandro 2 65 81	16 657
	31	Kashima	D 1-1	Okubo 44	10 518
Apr	7	Kofu	L 3-4	Kondo 2 44 44, Tanaka 48	8 373
	14	JEF Utd	W 2-1	Okubo 13, Kondo 47	10 983
	21	Nagoya	L 0-2		10 363
	28	FC Tokyo	D 0-0		9 213
May	3	G-Osaka	D 2-2	Okubo 17, Komoto 56	22 236
	6	Yokohama	W 3-0	Park 2 33 89, Okubo 44	4 458
	13	Omiya	D 0-0		7 769
	20	J-Iwata	W 3-2	Kondo 10, Leandro 2 14 76	12 149
	26	Kashiwa	W 2-1	Okubo 2 13 72	9 173
Jun	9	Niigata	L 1-3	Leandro 19	38 667
	16	Oita	L 1-3	Leandro 89	13 966
	20	Urawa	L 0-2		16 709
	23	Hiroshima	W 3-2	Botti 48, Park 82, Okubo 89	10 362
	30	Kawasaki	W 1-0	Kondo 14	17 299
	11	J-Iwata	W 4-0	Leandro 2 21 73, Park 69, Okubo 88	12 624
	18	Omiya	W 3-1	Leandro 2 30 73, Okubo 88	6 440
Aug	19	Niigata	L 0-1		9 116
	25	Oita	L 0-2		17 910
	29	Urawa	L 1-2	Kurihara 79	20 067
	1	FC Tokyo	L 1-3	Komoto 27	23 968
Sep	15	JEF Utd	L 2-4	Kitamoto 59, Ishibitsu 81	13 272
	22	Nagoya	W 5-0	Kurihara 5, Okubo 2 38 71, OG 2 83 88	7 793
	29	Shimizu-SP	W 1-0	Okubo 19	9 097
	6	Kashima	L 2-3	Kondo 6, Kitamoto 89	10 503
Oct	20	Yokohama	W 3-0	Koga 2 9 63, Tanaka 83	12 318
	27	Kashiwa	W 3-1	Gabriel 73, Leandro 2 75 80	8 947
	10	Kofu	W 4-1	Leandro 7, Koga 48, Kurihara 61, OG 68	11 236
Nov	18	Hiroshima	D 1-1	Leandro 65	13 555
	24	G-Osaka	D 1-1	Mogi 89	20 109
	1	YF-Marinos	D 0-0		20 687

YOKOHAMA F.MARINOS 2007

Month	Date	Opponent	Result	Scorers	Att
Mar	3	Kofu	W 1-0	Yamase.K 5	24 466
	10	Yokohama	L 0-1		13 737
	17	Kobe	L 1-4	Ueno 42	16 657
	31	Hiroshima	W 3-1	Oshima 2 10 51, Yamase.K 46	9 337
Apr	7	Kashiwa	L 0-2		18 960
	14	J-Iwata	L 0-1		11 864
	22	Oita	W 5-0	Yamase.Y 11, Sakata 2 41 54, Kawai 58, Yamase.K 88	17 219
	28	Niigata	W 6-0	Yamase.Y 37, Yamase.K 38, Yoshida 47, Sakata 2 51 56, Oshima 69	41 283
May	3	Kawasaki	W 2-1	Oshima 4, Yamase.K 66	33 498
	6	Kashima	D 1-1	Yoshida 21	13 344
	12	Nagoya	L 0-1		19 074
	20	FC Tokyo	L 0-1		25 811
	27	Urawa	W 1-0	Yamase.K 50	51 829
Jun	9	JEF Utd	W 1-0	Yoshida 68	23 028
	16	Shimizu-SP	D 1-0	OG 87	15 078
	20	G-Osaka	D 0-0		13 956
	24	Omiya	L 0-1		10 051
	30	Oita	W 3-0	Kawai 35, Nakazawa 68, Yamase.K 83	20 315
Aug	11	Yokohama	W 8-1	Oshima 4 30 65 72 88, Sakata 44, Yamase.K 2 51 74, Yamase.Y 62	53 916
	15	Kawasaki	D 3-3	Oshima 36, Yamase 62	18 095
	18	Nagoya	W 3-0	Matsuda 55, OG 63, Sakata 82	15 703
	26	Hiroshima	D 2-2	Oshima 19, Tanaka.H 71	19 007
	29	J-Iwata	W 4-1	Oshima 43, Shimizu 55, Yamase.K 58, Sakata 71	10 828
Sep	2	Kashiwa	L 0-1		23 569
	16	G-Osaka	W 2-0	Sakata 2 61 63	19 419
	22	Urawa	L 0-1		48 166
	29	Omiya	L 0-2		12 923
Oct	6	FC Tokyo	L 1-2	Yamase.Y 47	21 939
	20	Shimizu SP	L 0-2		25 082
	27	Kofu	D 1-1	Oshima 20	9 056
Nov	10	Kashima	L 2-3	Oshima 2, Sakata 80	21 109
	18	JEF Utd	W 3-2	Nakazawa 20, Oshima 80, Tanaka.H 84	15 678
	24	Niigata	W 1-0	Kawai 82	24 956
	1	Kobe	D 0-0		20 687

YOKOHAMA FC 2007

Month	Date	Opponent	Result	Scorers	Att
Mar	3	Urawa	L 1-2	Kubo 44	57 188
	10	YF-Marinos	W 1-0	Hayakawa 7	13 737
	17	Kawasaki	L 0-6		18 621
Apr	1	Nagoya	L 1-2	Namba 52	10 225
	8	JEF Utd	L 0-4		15 584
	14	Kashiwa	L 0-1		19 367
	21	FC Tokyo	L 0-1		22 168
	28	Shimizu-SP	D 1-1	OG 75	15 008
May	3	Kofu	L 0-1		16 279
	6	Kobe	L 0-3		4 458
	12	Hiroshima	W 2-0	Namba 23, Miura 42	13 636
	19	Omiya	L 0-1		9 466
	26	Oita	W 2-1	Miura 21, Uchida 73	4 935
Jun	9	G-Osaka	L 1-2	Hiramoto 89	19 752
	16	J-Iwata	L 1-2	Hiramoto 5	13 605
	20	Niigata	L 1-3	Oku 81	36 182
	23	Kashiwa	L 2-4	Yamada 58, Namba 83	7 232
	30	JEF Utd	L 0-1		43 117
Aug	11	YF-Marinos	L 1-8	Hiramoto 82	53 916
	15	Kofu	L 0-2		5 606
	18	G-Osaka	D 1-1	Wada 69	8 426
	25	Kashima	L 1-2	Nejime 69	15 957
	29	Shimizu-SP	L 0-1		14 167
Sep	1	Hiroshima	L 1-2	Miura 69	6 341
	15	FC Tokyo	L 0-2		13 835
	22	Oita	L 0-2		21 371
	29	J-Iwata	L 0-3		10 752
Oct	7	Kawasaki	L 0-1		14 208
	20	Kobe	L 0-3		12 318
	27	Omiya	L 0-1		4 114
Nov	10	Kashiwa	D 1-1	Nejime 83	8 990
	18	Niigata	L 0-2		7 751
	24	Nagoya	D 0-0		16 370
	1	Urawa	W 1-0	Nejime 17	46 697

KAZ – KAZAKHSTAN

NATIONAL TEAM RECORD
JULY 10TH 2006 TO JULY 12TH 2010

PL	W	D	L	F	A	%
27	4	9	14	20	40	31.5

FIFA/COCA-COLA WORLD RANKING

1993	1994	1995	1996	1997	1998	1999	2000	2001	2002	2003	2004	2005	2006	2007	High	
-	153	163	156	107	102	123	120	98	117	136	147	137	135	112	**98**	12/01

	2007-2008											Low	
08/07	09/07	10/07	11/07	12/07	01/08	02/08	03/08	04/08	05/08	06/08	07/08	**166**	05/96
115	120	122	110	112	108	110	105	122	122	125	124		

The pace of Kazakhstan's integration into European football has surprised many and the results at both international and club level have been encouraging. The 6-0 thrashing at the hands of Russia in May 2008 show how much more is to be done but in the qualifiers for Euro 2008, Kazakhstan finished above both Armenia and Azerbaijan. Coach Arno Pijpers has had his contract extended to the end of the 2010 FIFA World Cup qualifiers and with the league reduced to 14 teams and thanks to an earlier start to the season, he has been given more preparation time with the team. However, given their tough World Cup qualifying group - containing Croatia, England and Ukraine - it

INTERNATIONAL HONOURS
None

doesn't promise to be the easiest of campaigns. Kazak clubs are also beginning to find their feet in European competition with Aktobe beating Austria's Mattersburg at home in the 2007-08 UEFA Cup. At home, Aktobe went on to regain the Superliga title which they had lost to Astana in 2006 with their captain and Kazak footballer of the year Samat Smakov winning his fourth title - each with a different club. Aktobe finished eight points clear of coach Vladimir Mukanov's previous side Tobol. Tobol did, however, knock Aktobe out of the Cup and they then went on to win the tournament, beating Ordabasy 2-1 in the final to claim their first trophy.

THE FIFA BIG COUNT OF 2006

	Male	Female		Total
Number of players	437 820	72 600	Referees and Assistant Referees	210
Professionals	1 450		Admin, Coaches, Technical, Medical	2 950
Amateurs 18+	5 250		Number of clubs	43
Youth under 18	20 500		Number of teams	300
Unregistered	79 600		Clubs with women's teams	2
Total players	510 420		Players as % of population	3.35%

Football Federation of Kazakhstan (FSK)
Satpayev Street 29/3, Almaty 480 072, Kazakhstan
Tel +7 71 72 924492   Fax +7 3272 921885
kfo@mail.online.kz   www.fsk.kz
President: DZHAKSYBEKOV Adilbek   General Secretary: KHAMITZANOV Sayan
Vice-President: BAISHAKOV Seilda   Treasurer: TBD   Media Officer: KAMASHEV Timur
Men's Coach: PIJPERS Arno   Women's Coach: JAMANTAYEV Aitpay
FSK formed: 1914   AFC: 1994-2002, UEFA: 2002   FIFA: 1994
Blue shirts with yellow trimmings, Blue shorts, Yellow socks or Yellow shirts with blue trimmings, Yellow shorts, Blue socks

RECENT INTERNATIONAL MATCHES PLAYED BY KAZAKHSTAN

2004	Opponents		Score	Venue	Comp	Scorers	Att	Referee
13-10	Albania	L	0-1	Almaty	WCq		12 300	Stuchlik AUT
17-11	Greece	L	1-3	Piraeus	WCq	Baltiyev [88]	31 838	Kostadinov BUL
2005								
29-01	Japan	L	0-4	Yokohama	Fr		46 941	
26-03	Denmark	L	0-3	Copenhagen	WCq		20 980	Gilewski POL
4-06	Ukraine	L	0-2	Kyiv	WCq		45 000	Lehner AUT
8-06	Turkey	L	0-6	Almaty	WCq		20 000	Kassai HUN
17-08	Georgia	L	1-2	Almaty	WCq	Kenzhekhanov [23]	9 000	Havrilla SVK
3-09	Albania	L	1-2	Tirana	WCq	Nizovtsev [62]	3 000	Slupik POL
7-09	Greece	L	1-2	Almaty	WCq	Zhalmagambetov [53]	18 000	Tudor ROU
8-10	Georgia	D	0-0	Tbilisi	WCq		BCD	Hyytia FIN
12-10	Denmark	L	1-2	Almaty	WCq	Kuchma [86]	8 050	Trivkovic CRO
2006								
14-02	Jordan	D	0-0	Amman	Fr			
28-02	Finland	D	0-0	Larnaca	Fr	W 3-1p		
1-03	Greece	L	0-2	Nicosia	Fr		2 000	Kailis CYP
2-07	Tajikistan	W	4-1	Almaty	Fr	Zhumaskaliev [22], Familtsev [40], Kuchma [63], Tleshev [90]		
5-07	Kyrgyzstan	W	1-0	Almaty	Fr	Baltiev [20p]		
16-08	Belgium	D	0-0	Brussels	ECq		15 495	Courtney NIR
6-09	Azerbaijan	D	1-1	Baku	ECq	Byakov [36]	8 500	Szabó HUN
7-10	Poland	L	0-1	Almaty	ECq		22 000	Trivkovic CRO
11-10	Finland	L	0-2	Almaty	ECq		17 863	Briakos GRE
15-11	Portugal	L	0-3	Coimbra	ECq		29 500	Rogalla SUI
24-12	Singapore	D	0-0	Bangkok	Fr			
26-12	Vietnam	L	1-2	Bangkok	Fr	Finonchenko [57]		
28-12	Thailand	D	2-2	Bangkok	Fr	Rodionov [66], Ashirbekov [70]		
2007								
7-02	China PR	L	1-2	Suzhou	Fr	Suyumagambetov [14]		
7-03	Kyrgyzstan	W	2-0	Shymkent	Fr	Byakov [3], Chichulin [68]		
9-03	Azerbaijan	W	1-0	Shymkent	Fr	Finonchenko [80]		
11-03	Uzbekistan	D	1-1	Shymkent	Fr	Suyumagambetov [13]		
24-03	Serbia	W	2-1	Almaty	ECq	Ashirbekov [47], Zhumaskaliyev [61]	19 600	Hrinák SVK
2-06	Armenia	L	1-2	Almaty	ECq	Baltiev [86p]	17 100	Kralovec CZE
6-06	Azerbaijan	D	1-1	Almaty	ECq	Baltiev [53]	11 800	Toussaint LUX
22-08	Finland	L	1-2	Tampere	ECq	Byakov [23]	13 047	Kassai HUN
8-09	Tajikistan	D	1-1	Almaty	Fr	Nurdauletov [54]		
12-09	Belgium	D	2-2	Almaty	ECq	Byakov [39], Smakov [77p]	18 100	Tudor ROU
13-10	Poland	L	1-3	Warsaw	ECq	Byakov [20]	11 040	Berntsen NOR
17-10	Portugal	L	1-2	Almaty	ECq	Byakov [93+]	25 057	Wegeref NED
21-11	Armenia	W	1-0	Yerevan	ECq	Ostapenko [64]	3 100	Fautrel FRA
24-11	Serbia	L	0-1	Belgrade	ECq		500	Vasaras GRE
2008								
3-02	Azerbaijan	D	0-0	Antalya	Fr			
6-02	Moldova	L	0-1	Antalya	Fr		300	Lehner AUT
26-03	Armenia	L	0-1	Pernis	Fr			Vink NED
23-05	Russia	L	0-6	Moscow	Fr		10 000	
27-05	Montenegro	L	0-3	Podgorica	Fr		9 000	Tusin LUX

Fr = Friendly match • EC = UEFA EURO 2008 • WC = FIFA World Cup • q = qualifier • BCD = behind closed doors

KAZAKHSTAN NATIONAL TEAM RECORDS AND RECORD SEQUENCES

Records			Sequence records					
Victory	7-0	PAK 1997	Wins	4	1997	Clean sheets	3	1994-1995
Defeat	0-6	TUR 2005	Defeats	13	2004-2005	Goals scored	15	2006-2007
Player Caps	64	Ruslan Baltiev	Undefeated	7	2001-2003	Without goal	6	2007-2008
Player Goals	12	Viktor Zubarev	Without win	29	2001-2006	Goals against	22	2002-2006

MAJOR CITIES/TOWNS

Population '000

1	Almaty	1 227
2	Shymkent	420
3	Karagandy	404
4	Taraz	366
5	Astana	356
6	Pavlodar	330
7	Oskemen	320
8	Semey	291
9	Aktobe	264
10	Uralsk	235
11	Kostanay	231
12	Petropavl	194
13	Temirtau	169
14	Akmechet	169
15	Aktau	167
16	Atyrau	147
17	Ekibastuz	145
18	Kokshetau	123
19	Rudni	117
20	Taldykorgan	107
21	Zhezkazgan	104
22	Turkistan	100
23	Balkhash	81
24	Sarkand	76

REPUBLIC OF KAZAKHSTAN; QAZAQSTAN RESPUBLIKASY

Capital	Astana	Language	Kazakh, Russian	Independence	1991
Population	15 233 244	Area	2 717 300 km²	% in cities	60%
GDP per cap	$6300	Dailling code	+7	Internet .kz	GMT +/- +4

MEDALS TABLE

		Overall			League			Cup			Asia/Eur			City	Stadium	Cap'ty	DoF
		G	S	B	G	S	B	G	S	B	G	S	B				
1	Kairat Almaty	7	2	3	2		3	5	2					Almaty	Almaty Centralny	26 400	1952
2	Irtysh Pavlodar	6	5	3	5	3	3	1	2					Pavlodar	Centralny	12 000	1965
3	FK Astana (Ex Zhenis)	6	2	1	3		1	3	2					Astana	Kazhimukan Munaitpasov	12 343	1964
4	FK Semey	4		1	3		1	1						Semey	Spartak	11 000	
5	FK Taraz	2	4		1	2		1	2					Taraz	Centralny	12 000	1961
6	FK Aktobe	2	2		2	1			1					Aktobe	Centralny	13 200	1967
7	Tobol Kostanay	1	4	3		3	3	1	1					Kostanay	Centralny	5 800	1967
8	Vostock Oskemen	1	2					1	2					Oskemen	Vostock	12 000	1963
9	Kaisar Kyzylorda	1	1					1	1					Kyzylorda	Gany Muratbayeva	7 000	1968
10	FK Almaty	1						1						Almaty	Almaty Centralny	26 400	2003
	Dostyk Almaty	1						1						Almaty			
12	Yesil-Bogatyr Petropavl		3	1		2	1		1					Petropavl	Avangard	12 000	1968
13	Ordabasy Shymkent		3			1			2					Shymkent	Munaytpasova	30 000	1998
14	FK Atyrau		2			2								Atyrau	Munayshy	9 000	1980
	Ekibastuzetc		2			2								Ekibastuz	Shakhtyor	6 300	1979

RECENT LEAGUE AND CUP RECORD

	Championship						Cup		
Year	Champions	Pts	Runners-up	Pts	Third	Pts	Winners	Score	Runners-up
1995	Yelimay Semey	67	Taraz Zhambul	62	Shakhter Karagandy	60	Yelimay Semipal'sk	1-0	Ordabasy Shymkent
1996	Taraz Zhambul	76	Irtysh Pavlodar	74	Yelimay Semey	74	Kairat Almaty	2-0	Vostock Oskemen
1997	Irtysh Pavlodar	56	FC Taraz	56	Kairat Almaty	53	Not played due to season readjustment		
1998	Yelimay Semey	63	Batyr Ekibastuz	59	Irtysh Pavlodar	57	Irtysh Pavlodar	2-1	Kaysar Kzyl-Orda
1999	Irtysh Pavlodar	76	Yesil Petropavlovsk	72	Kairat Almaty	64	Kaysar Kzyl-Orda	1-1 2-0p	Vostock Oskemen
2000	Zhenis Astana	74	Yesil Petropavlovsk	74	Irtysh Pavlodar	60	Kairat Almaty	5-0	Yesil Petropavlovsk
2001							Zhenis Astana	1-1 5-4p	Irtysh Pavlodar
2001	Zhenis Astana	81	FK Atyrau	70	Yesil Petropavlovsk	69	Kairat Almaty	3-1	Zhenis Astana
2002	Irtysh Pavlodar	71	FK Atyrau	63	Tobol Kostanay	52	Zhenis Astana	1-0	Irtysh Pavlodar
2003	Irtysh Pavlodar	78	Tobol Kostanay	76	Zhenis Astana	64	Kairat Almaty	3-1	Tobol Kostanai
2004	Kairat Almaty	83	Irtysh Pavlodar	79	Tobol Kostanay	77	FC Taraz	1-0	Kairat Almaty
2005	Aktobe Lento	70	Tobol Kostanay	69	Kairat Almaty	62	Zhenis Astana	2-1	Kairat Almaty
2006	FK Astana	64	FK Aktobe	60	Tobol Kostanay	56	FK Almaty	3-1	FK Astana
2007	FK Aktobe	72	Tobol Kostanay	64	Shakhter Karagandy	58	Tobol Kostanay	3-0	Ordabasy Shymkent

Irtysh beat Taraz 1-0 in a play-off in 1997 • Zhenis beat Petropavlovsk 2-0 in a play-off in 2000 • Two cup competitions were held in 2001

KAZAKHSTAN 2007

SUPERLIGA ALMA TV

	Pl	W	D	L	F	A	Pts	Aktobe	Tobol	Shakhter	Irtysh	Zhetysu	Almaty	Astana	Vostock	Ordabasy	Yesil	Kaisar	Ekib'tuzetc	Atyrau	Kairat	Okzhetpes	Taraz
FK Aktobe †	30	22	6	2	55	12	72		1-0	0-0	1-0	2-0	2-0	2-0	1-0	2-1	2-1	5-0	3-1	1-0	2-0	2-1	5-0
Tobol Kostanay ‡	30	19	7	4	60	20	64	0-0		4-2	1-0	0-0	4-2	2-0	7-0	3-0	1-0	2-0	1-0	1-0	10-1	10-1	2-0
Shakhter Karagandy	30	17	7	6	45	23	58	0-0	3-1		2-1	3-1	1-1	2-1	1-1	0-0	5-1	2-0	2-0	2-1	1-0	3-1	2-0
Irtysh Pavlodar	30	16	4	10	34	27	52	2-1	1-1	2-0		3-2	1-0	1-0	3-1	1-0	2-0	1-0	1-1	2-0	2-0	0-1	2-1
Zhetysu Taldykorgan	30	13	7	10	33	32	46	0-3	1-2	1-0	3-0		1-2	2-0	1-0	1-1	0-1	1-1	3-2	2-1	0-0	2-1	1-0
FK Almaty	30	13	5	12	35	32	44	0-1	2-1	1-1	3-1	1-3		0-0	2-1	1-1	1-0	2-0	0-0	1-0	2-0	4-0	4-0
FK Astana	30	11	8	11	34	25	41	1-2	4-1	3-0	0-0	1-1	0-1		1-1	1-0	1-1	1-0	3-1	1-0	5-0	2-0	2-0
Vostock Oskemen	30	12	5	13	30	38	41	2-1	1-2	1-0	1-0	0-2	1-2	2-0		1-2	2-2	0-1	3-2	1-0	1-0	1-0	0-0
Ordabasy Shymkent	30	9	11	10	28	29	38	0-0	0-0	0-2	2-1	3-0	4-0	0-0	0-0		0-1	1-0	1-0	3-0	2-1	0-1	2-1
Yesil-Bogatyr Petropavl	30	8	13	9	24	28	37	1-1	0-0	0-1	0-0	1-1	1-0	2-0	0-1	0-0		1-0	1-1	0-0	2-0	1-1	2-1
Kaisar Kyzylorda	30	10	7	13	27	37	37	0-0	1-1	1-0	3-1	0-1	1-0	2-1	0-4	3-1	0-0		3-2	1-1	2-1	2-2	2-0
Ekibastuzetc	30	8	8	14	28	38	32	1-3	0-1	0-0	1-0	2-0	1-0	0-0	3-1	1-1	1-1	1-0		1-0	1-3	2-0	2-0
FK Atyrau	30	8	6	16	29	39	30	1-2	0-4	0-5	1-2	1-1	1-0	3-2	2-0	0-0	0-2	4-0	1-1		3-0	3-0	3-0
Kairat Almaty	30	9	3	18	23	43	30	0-2	0-2	0-2	0-1	1-0	3-1	0-2	0-2	3-0	2-1	2-1	1-0	3-1		2-4	0-0
Okzhetpes Kokshetau	30	8	5	17	26	56	29	0-6	0-0	1-2	1-0	0-0	0-1	1-3	1-0	1-0	3-1	2-1	0-0	1-0	1-2		3-2
FK Taraz	30	3	6	21	18	50	15	0-2	1-3	0-1	0-1	0-1	1-2	0-2	3-0	2-2	0-0	0-3	3-1	0-0	0-0	3-0	

31/03/2007 - 30/11/2007 • † Qualified for the UEFA Champions League • ‡ Qualified for the UEFA Cup
Top scorers:

KAZAKHSTAN 2007 CONFERENCE NORTH-EAST (2)

	Pl	W	D	L	F	A	Pts
Energetik Pavlodar †	26	24	0	2	62	10	72
Kazakmis Satpayev †	26	22	3	1	67	14	69
Aksu Stepnogorsk	26	18	4	4	65	25	59
Avangard Petropavl	26	13	5	8	35	34	44
Karasay Sarbazdari	26	12	3	11	47	39	39
Irtysh-2 Pavlodar	26	12	2	12	50	42	38
Asbest Jitikara	26	10	5	11	34	42	35
Bolat Temirtau	26	9	5	12	30	33	32
FK Semey	26	7	8	11	29	49	29
Shakhter-Yunost	26	6	6	14	25	38	24
Tobol-2 Kostanay	26	5	8	13	32	49	23
Vostock-2 Oskemen	26	5	5	16	25	61	20
Rahat Astana	26	4	6	16	25	56	18
Batyr Ekibastuz	26	0	10	16	8	42	10

1/05/2007 - 22/10/2007 • † Qualified for the play-offs

KAZAKHSTAN 2007 CONFERENCE SOUTH-WEST (2)

	Pl	W	D	L	F	A	Pts
MegaSport Almaty †	22	21	1	0	89	10	64
Zhayik Uralsk †	22	18	2	2	57	14	56
Kaspiy Aktau	22	13	4	5	46	23	43
Aktobe-Zhas	22	11	4	7	38	32	37
Zhetysu-2 Taldykorgan	22	8	5	9	32	46	29
Gornyak Khromtau	22	7	6	9	31	39	27
Ordabasy-2 Shymkent	22	7	2	13	38	58	23
Cesna Almaty	22	6	5	11	33	30	23
Kaisar-Jas Kyzylorda	22	6	5	11	25	38	23
Zhambil Taraz	22	4	6	12	22	38	18
Zhastar Uralsk	22	5	1	16	21	70	16
Munayli Atyrau	22	4	3	15	27	61	15

1/05/2007 - 22/10/2007 • † Qualified for the play-offs

FOOTBALL CUP OF KAZAKHSTAN 2007

Second round

Tobol Kostanay	4
FK Taraz *	1
Zhetysu Taldykorgan	0
FK Aktobe *	4
Shakhter Karagandy *	3
FK Atyrau	2
Yesil-B'tyr Petropavl	1
Kaisar Kyzylorda *	2
Ekibastuzetc	2 5p
FK Astana *	2 3p
Irtysh Pavlodar	0
MegaSport Almaty *	1
Kairat Almaty *	2
Okzhetpes Kokshetau	0
Vostock Oskemen	0
Ordabasy Shymkent *	2

Quarter–finals

Tobol Kostanay *	3	0
FK Aktobe	1	0
Shakhter Karagandy	0	1
Kaisar Kyzylorda *	0	1
Ekibastuzetc *	0	2
MegaSport Almaty	0	1
Kairat Almaty *	0	0
Ordabasy Shymkent	1	0

Semi–finals

Tobol Kostanay	2
Kaisar Kyzylorda	1
Ekibastuzetc	1 3p
Ordabasy Shymkent	1 5p

Final

Tobol Kostanay	3
Ordabasy Shymkent	0

CUP FINAL

Centralny, Taraz
29-11-2007

Scorers - Ruslan Baltiev 2, Igor Yurin

* Home team/Home team in first leg • ‡ Qualified for the UEFA Cup

KEN – KENYA

NATIONAL TEAM RECORD
JULY 10TH 2006 TO JULY 12TH 2010

PL	W	D	L	F	A	%
20	6	5	9	19	18	42.5

FIFA/COCA-COLA WORLD RANKING

1993	1994	1995	1996	1997	1998	1999	2000	2001	2002	2003	2004	2005	2006	2007	High
74	83	107	112	89	93	103	108	104	81	72	74	89	127	110	**70** 02/04

2007–2008												Low
08/07	09/07	10/07	11/07	12/07	01/08	02/08	03/08	04/08	05/08	06/08	07/08	**137** 07/07
132	115	97	100	110	119	117	118	120	120	115	92	

Kenya made a great start to their FIFA 2010 World Cup qualifiers having been allowed to compete just a week before when FIFA lifted a long running off-and-on suspension. Squabbles between rival factions purporting to run football in the east African country has left the administration of the game in tatters and also threatened to derail the 'Harambee Stars'. But under inexperienced coach Francis Kimanzi, Kenya have surprised even themselves with a haul of seven points from their opening four group games, which puts them well within a chance of progressing to the next phase. Another FIFA suspension had been lifted before the annual East and Central African Senior

INTERNATIONAL HONOURS
Gossage Cup 1926 1931 1941 1942 1944 1946 1953 1958 1959 1960 1961 1966 **Challenge Cup** 1967 1971 **CECAFA Cup** 1975 1981 1982 1983 2002
CECAFA Club Championship Luo Union 1976 1977, AFC Leopards 1979 1982 1983 1984 1997, Gor Mahia 1985, Tusker 1988 1989 2000 2001

Challenge Cup in December 2007 but Kenya looked jaded by all the political wrangling and only recorded a single win against minnows Somalia. Club football has also been devastated by the long-standing wrangle, which FIFA has found difficult to sort out despite several high profile interventions. A unified league went ahead in 2007 and was won by Tusker, just ahead of Mathare United, but Tusker's subsequent participation in the 2008 CAF Champions League was cancelled by the latest suspension, later lifted but by then it was too late to take part.

THE FIFA BIG COUNT OF 2006

	Male	Female		Total
Number of players	1 952 326	88 776	Referees and Assistant Referees	3 700
Professionals	55		Admin, Coaches, Technical, Medical	48 310
Amateurs 18+	25 906		Number of clubs	690
Youth under 18	49 141		Number of teams	3 450
Unregistered	1 003 000		Clubs with women's teams	21
Total players	2 041 102		Players as % of population	5.88%

Kenya Football Federation (KFF)
KFF Complex Centre, next to Moi Sports Complex, Kasarani 26434, Nairobi 00504, Kenya
Tel +254 20 2012194   Fax +254 20 2010798
kffkenya@kff.co.ke   www.kff.co.ke
President: HATIMY Mohammed   General Secretary: OBINGO Sammy
Vice-President: KASUVE Titus Mutuku   Treasurer: TBD   Media Officer: None
Men's Coach: KIMANZI Francis   Women's Coach: None
KFF formed: 1960   CAF: 1968   FIFA: 1960
Red shirts with black trimmings, Red shorts, Red socks

RECENT INTERNATIONAL MATCHES PLAYED BY KENYA

2004	Opponents	Score	Venue	Comp	Scorers	Att	Referee
26-01	Mali	L 1-3	Bizerte	CNr1	Mulama [58]	6 000	Tessema ETH
30-01	Senegal	L 0-3	Bizerte	CNr1		13 500	Abd El Fatah EGY
2-02	Burkina Faso	W 3-0	Bizerte	CNr1	Ake [50], Oliech [63], Baraza [83]	4 550	Sowe GAM
7-08	Uganda	D 1-1	Kampala	Fr	Obua [27p]	25 000	
18-08	Uganda	W 4-1	Nairobi	Fr	Baraza 2 [11 33], Sirengo [65], Omondi [85]	5 000	
4-09	Malawi	W 3-2	Nairobi	WCq	Barasa 2 [21 29], Oliech [25]	13 000	Mwanza ZAM
9-10	Botswana	L 1-2	Gaborone	WCq	Oliech [5]	16 500	Colembi ANG
17-11	Guinea	W 2-1	Nairobi	WCq	Oliech [10], Mukenya [61]	16 000	Abd El Fatah EGY
12-12	Sudan	D 2-2	Addis Abeba	CCr1	Simiyu [37], Baraza [73]		
14-12	Somalia	W 1-0	Addis Abeba	CCr1	Baraza [7]		
18-12	Uganda	D 1-1	Addis Abeba	CCr1	Obua [77p]		
22-12	Ethiopia	D 2-2	Addis Abeba	CCsf	Mururi [66], Baraza [85], L 4-5p	50 000	Ssegonga UGA
25-12	Sudan	L 1-2	Addis Abeba	CC3p	Baraza [82]		
2005							
9-02	Morocco	L 1-5	Rabat	WCq	Otieno [93+]	40 000	Tamuni LBY
12-03	Rwanda	D 1-1	Nairobi	Fr	Mkenya [25]		
23-03	Ghana	D 2-2	Nairobi	Fr	Baraza [44], Sunguti [87]		
26-03	Botswana	W 1-0	Nairobi	WCq	Oliech [44]	15 000	Buenkadila COD
5-06	Guinea	L 0-1	Conakry	WCq		21 000	Mbera GAB
18-06	Morocco	D 0-0	Nairobi	WCq		50 000	Diatta SEN
17-08	Tunisia	L 0-1	Rades	WCq		60 000	Evehe CMR
3-09	Tunisia	L 0-2	Nairobi	WCq			Sowe GAM
8-10	Malawi	L 0-3	Blantyre	WCq		12 000	Codjia BEN
2006							
11-08	Ethiopia	L 0-1	Addis Abeba	Fr			
13-08	Ethiopia	L 0-1	Addis Abeba	Fr			
2-09	Eritrea	L 1-2	Nairobi	CNq	Mambo [64]		Lwanja MWI
30-09	Tanzania	D 0-0	Dar es Salaam	Fr			
8-10	Angola	L 1-3	Luanda	CNq	Ambani [81]		Lwanja MWI
2007							
25-03	Swaziland	W 2-0	Nairobi	CNq	Maringa [51], Oboya [75]		Seechurn MRI
27-05	Nigeria	L 0-1	Nairobi	Fr			
3-06	Swaziland	D 0-0	Mbabane	CNq			Katijume NAM
10-06	Rwanda	W 2-0	Nairobi	Fr	Mulinge [10p], Ambani [20]		
16-06	Eritrea	L 0-1	Asmara	CNq			Abdelrahman SUD
8-09	Angola	W 2-1	Nairobi	CNq	Oboya [18], Oliech [87]		Katijume NAM
21-11	Oman	D 2-2	Muscat	Fr	Ochieng 2 [43 62]		
22-11	Oman	D 1-1	Muscat	Fr	Ajwang [39]		
8-12	Tanzania	L 1-2	Dar es Salaam	CCr1	Wanga [45]		
12-12	Burundi	L 0-1	Dar es Salaam	CCr1			
14-12	Somalia	W 2-0	Dar es Salaam	CCr1	Njoroge [40], Wanga [55]		
2008							
31-05	Namibia	L 1-2	Windhoek	WCq	Makacha [40]	6 000	Ssegonga UGA
7-06	Guinea	W 2-0	Nairobi	WCq	Oliech 2 [3 50]	35 000	Eyene CMR
14-06	Zimbabwe	W 2-0	Nairobi	WCq	Maringa [13], Oliech [88]	27 500	Diatta SEN
22-06	Zimbabwe	D 0-0	Harare	WCq		23 000	Kotey GHA

Fr = Friendly match • CN = CAF African Cup of Nations • CC = CECAFA Cup • WC = FIFA World Cup
q = qualifier • r1 = first round group • sf = semi-final • 3p = third place play-off • f = final

KENYA NATIONAL TEAM RECORDS AND RECORD SEQUENCES

Records			Sequence records					
Victory	9-0	TAN 1956	Wins	5	1993	Clean sheets	7	1983
Defeat	0-13	GHA 1965	Defeats	7	1932-1940	Goals scored	16	1931-1948
Player Caps	n/a		Undefeated	10	1997-1998	Without goal	7	2005-2006
Player Goals	n/a		Without win	10	1984-85, 2005-06	Goals against	16	1931-1948

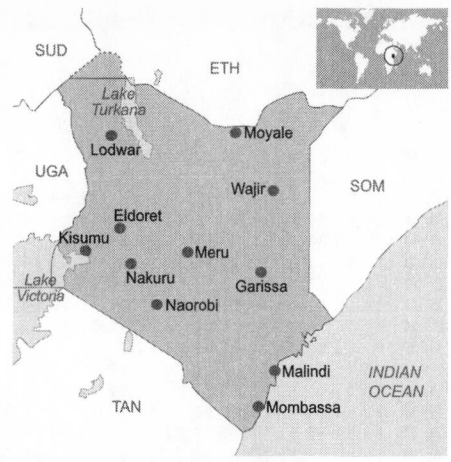

MAJOR CITIES/TOWNS

		Population '000
1	Nairobi	3 038
2	Mombasa	867
3	Nakuru	271
4	Eldoret	239
5	Kisumu	225
6	Ruiru	123
7	Thika	101
8	Kitale	78
9	Malindi	76
10	Kakamega	70
11	Bungoma	66
12	Garissa	56
13	Kilifi	56
14	Mumias	53
15	Meru	50
16	Nyeri	49
17	Busia	49
18	Homa Bay	43
19	Narok	42
20	Naivasha	40
21	Wajir	38
22	Rongai	37
23	Kericho	37
24	Nanyuki	37

REPUBLIC OF KENYA; JAMHURI Y KENYA

Capital	Nairobi	Language	Kiswahili, English	Independence	1963
Population	36 913 721	Area	582 650 km²	Density	55 per km²	% in cities	28%
GDP per cap	$1000	Dailling code	+254	Internet	.ke	GMT +/-	+3

MEDALS TABLE

		Overall			Lge	Cup	Africa			City	Stadium	Cap'ty	DoF
		G	S	B	G	G	G	S	B				
1	Gor Mahia	20	1	1	12	7	1	1	1	Nairobi	Nairobi City Stadium	15 000	1968
2	AFC Leopards	17		2	12	5			2	Nairobi	Nyayo	30 000	1964
3	Tusker (aka Kenya Breweries)	11	1	2	8	3		1	2	Nairobi	Moi International	60 000	1970
4	Luo Union	5			2	3							
5	Ulinzi Stars	3			3					Nakuru	Afraha Stadium	8 200	
6	Nakuru All Stars	2			2								
	Oserian Fastac	2			2								
	Mathare United	2				2				Nairobi	Moi International	60 000	1994
	Mombasa Liverpool	2				2							
	Rivatex	2				2							

RECENT LEAGUE AND CUP RECORD

	Championship							Cup		
Year	Champions	Pts	Runners-up	Pts	Third	Pts		Winners	Score	Runners-up
1996	Kenya Breweries	71	AFC Leopards	65	Eldoret KCC	63		Mumias Sugar	1-0	Reli
1997	Utalii	66	Gor Mahia	64	Mumias Sugar	62		Eldoret KCC	4-1	AFC Leopards
1998	AFC Leopards	69	Mumias Sugar	66	Gor Mahia	60		Mathare United	2-1	Eldoret KCC
1999	Tusker							Mumias Sugar	3-2	Coast Stars
2000	Tusker	6	Oserian Fastac	4	Mumias Sugar	4		Mathare United	2-1	AFC Leopards
2001	Oserian Fastac	88	Mathare United	81	Mumias Sugar	68		AFC Leopards	2-0	Mathare United
2002	Oserian Fastac	†	Nzoia Sugar					Pipeline	1-0	Mumias Sugar
2003	Ulinzi Stars	†	Coast Stars					Chemelil	1-0	AFC Leopards
2004	Ulinzi Stars	†	Tusker					KCB	1-0	Thika United
2005	Ulinzi Stars	†	Tusker					World Hope	2-1	Tusker
2006	Sony Sugar	75	Tusker	74	Thika United	67		Not held		
2007	Tusker	59	Mathare United	56	Sony Sugar	55		Sofapaka	2-0	Homegrown

† Championship play-offs • 2002: Oserian Fastac 2-2 1-0 Nzoia Sugar • 2003: Ulinzi Stars 3-3 4-2p Coast Stars • 2004: Ulinzi Stars 2-2 4-3p Tusker • 2005: Ulinzi Stars 0-0 4-2p Tusker • The original final in 2003 was won by Nzoia Sugar, who beat Tusker 2-1. It was declared void by the KFF after a number of clubs broke away. The 2003 Moi Golden Cup was also disrupted with Utalii beating Gor Mahia 2-1 in an alternative final. The dispute between the KFF, the breakaway clubs and the Kenyan Sports Ministry saw the 2004 season badly affected which lead to the intervention of FIFA and the creation of Stake-holders Transition Committee (STC). Two separate championships had been played but a play-off for all the leading clubs was organised to qualify for CAF competitions

KENYA 2007

UNIFIED LEAGUE

	Pl	W	D	L	F	A	Pts	Tusker	Mathare Utd	Sony Sugar	Red Berets	Sher	Ulinzi	Chemelil	World Hope	Thika Utd	MYSA Youth	Gor Mahia	Agro-Chem'al	Mahakama	KCB	Homegrown	Coast Stars
Tusker FC †	30	16	11	3	43	21	59		0-0	2-1	3-1	3-0	0-0	3-1	3-1	1-1	0-1	0-2	2-1	1-0	1-0	3-2	3-1
Mathare United	30	15	11	4	34	13	56	0-0		2-1	3-0	1-1	1-2	1-1	0-1	1-0	1-1	2-0	2-0	2-1	1-0	1-2	3-0
Sony Sugar	30	14	13	3	35	15	55	1-1	0-0		2-1	1-1	0-0	1-0	1-0	1-1	3-0	3-0	1-0	0-0	0-0	2-1	2-0
Red Berets	30	13	7	10	35	35	46	0-1	0-3	0-1		2-1	1-1	2-1	2-1	1-0	1-1	1-0	0-0	2-0	1-2	1-0	2-2
Sher Agencies	30	12	9	9	34	31	45	2-2	0-0	0-1	1-2		2-0	1-0	2-0	0-0	0-0	2-0	0-0	1-0	2-1	0-2	3-2
Ulinzi Stars	30	11	10	9	31	28	43	2-2	0-0	0-1	0-1	1-0		4-2	1-1	0-0	2-1	1-0	‡	0-2	1-0	0-0	2-0
Chemelil Sugar	30	12	6	12	30	26	42	0-0	1-0	2-1	0-0	0-2	1-0		0-0	0-3	1-0	3-0	0-1	3-0	2-0	4-0	2-0
World Hope FC	30	11	9	10	32	29	42	1-0	1-2	0-1	1-0	1-1	2-3	2-1		1-1	1-2	2-1	1-0	2-0	2-0	1-0	2-1
Thika United	30	8	15	7	24	21	39	0-0	0-0	1-1	1-1	1-1	1-0	0-0	1-0		0-0	3-1	3-3	0-0	1-0	2-0	0-2
Mathare Youth	30	9	7	14	23	33	34	0-2	0-3	0-1	0-2	2-0	1-1	0-1	0-3	0-1		1-2	1-0	1-2	1-0	0-1	2-1
Gor Mahia	30	9	7	14	24	36	34	0-3	1-2	1-1	0-2	2-0	0-2	0-0	0-0	1-0	1-0		1-0	1-3	0-0	4-2	3-0
Agro-Chemical	30	8	9	13	27	28	33	0-0	0-1	0-0	3-1	2-2	3-0	1-0	0-1	2-2	0-2	1-0		2-0	1-0	3-0	0-1
Mahakama	30	8	7	15	28	43	31	0-2	1-1	1-1	0-2	2-1	0-3	0-0	2-1	0-1	1-2	1-0	3-3		0-2	2-1	3-3
Kenya Com'cial Bank	30	7	9	14	30	33	30	2-3	0-1	0-0	3-3	1-2	3-3	1-2	2-1	2-0	1-1	0-0	0-0	4-0		1-1	1-0
Homegrown	30	8	5	17	24	44	29	1-2	0-0	0-5	2-0	1-3	0-1	1-2	1-1	1-0	0-2	0-0	2-0	1-0	0-3		2-0
Coast Stars	30	7	7	16	31	49	28	0-0	0-0	1-1	2-3	1-2	3-1	2-1	1-1	0-0	1-2	1-2	2-1	0-4	3-1	1-0	

16/09/2006 - 17/11/2007 • † Qualified for the CAF Champions League • Matches in bold awarded • ‡ Awarded as a defeat for both sides

KENYA 2007 — NATIONWIDE LEAGUE GROUP A (2)

	Pl	W	D	L	F	A	Pts
Western Stima	34	24	5	5	67	20	77
Panpaper	34	22	10	2	54	17	76
Nairobi Stima	34	19	8	7	46	29	65
Real Kisumu	34	18	10	6	48	27	64
Kenyatta University	34	19	4	11	61	43	61
Eldoret Mahakama	34	17	9	8	55	28	60
Flourspar	34	16	12	6	44	26	60
Power Kericho	34	15	11	8	49	33	56
Oserian	34	15	10	9	37	25	55
Muhoroni Youth	34	15	7	12	38	31	52
Longonot Horticulture	34	14	8	12	28	28	50
St Joseph	34	12	8	14	33	33	44
Green Berets	34	9	15	10	43	37	42
Gachui Black Boots	34	10	4	20	34	66	34
Laikipia Campus	34	10	2	22	47	73	32

21/07/2007 - 16/12/2007

KENYA 2007 — NATIONWIDE LEAGUE GROUP B (2)

	Pl	W	D	L	F	A	Pts
Bandari Mombasa	33	22	8	3	66	13	74
Sofapaka Nairobi	33	21	7	5	71	25	70
Kenya Revenue Auth'y	33	21	5	7	46	21	68
Waterworks	33	18	9	6	54	25	63
Administration Police	33	17	11	5	50	22	62
Bidco United	33	16	10	7	43	29	58
Opera	33	12	11	10	34	27	47
Kawangware	33	11	11	11	30	35	44
Young Peles	33	12	8	13	33	53	44
Kenyatta Hospital	33	11	9	13	35	33	42
Magongo Cosmos	33	13	3	17	48	54	42
Dagoretti Santos	33	10	8	15	27	40	38
Amani Yassets	33	10	5	18	40	55	35
Limuru Olympic	33	9	7	17	33	44	34
Sacramento United	33	9	7	17	34	57	34

14/04/2007 - 25/11/2007

PRESIDENT'S CUP 2007

Second round		Quarter-finals		Semi-finals		Final	
Sofapaka Nairobi	3						
Shabana United	0	Sofapaka Nairobi	4				
Vegpro	1	Kenyatta Hospital	0				
Kenyatta Hospital	5			Sofapaka Nairobi	1		
Sacramento United	w-o			Nakuru Police	0		
		Sacramento	1				
		Nakuru Police	2				
Nakuru Police	w-o					Sofapaka Nairobi	2
Gor Mahia	1					Homegrown Naivasha	0
Lolwe	0	Gor Mahia	0 2				
Thika United		Kenya Revenue A'rity	0 1				
Kenya Revenue A'rity	w-o			Gor Mahia	1		
Green Berets	w-o			Homegrown Naivasha	2		
		Green Berets	0				
		Homegrown Naivasha	1				
Homegrown Naivasha	w-o						

CUP FINAL

Nyayo, Nairobi
1-07-2007
Scorer - James Kiarie 2 [53 61]

* Home team in first leg

KGZ – KYRGYZSTAN

NATIONAL TEAM RECORD
JULY 10TH 2006 TO JULY 12TH 2010

PL	W	D	L	F	A	%
12	4	0	8	12	25	33.3

FIFA/COCA-COLA WORLD RANKING

1993	1994	1995	1996	1997	1998	1999	2000	2001	2002	2003	2004	2005	2006	2007	High	
-	166	172	168	140	151	159	174	164	171	157	150	157	139		**119**	08/06

2007–2008												Low	
08/07	09/07	10/07	11/07	12/07	01/08	02/08	03/08	04/08	05/08	06/08	07/08	**175**	11/03
153	149	133	136	139	138	137	127	131	134	140	145		

Since the dissolution of the Soviet Union and their arrival on the Asian football scene, Kyrgyzstan have struggled to make much of an impact. Inconsistency has been a major problem for the national team, although they almost pulled off a surprise against Jordan in a preliminary round of qualifier for the 2010 FIFA World Cup. A 2-0 win at home in Bishkek set the Kyrgyz side up for a famous win, but a reversal by the same scoreline in Amman saw the game go to penalties with the Jordanians scraping through in sudden-death. Despite that near miss, there was to be little joy for the national team in the AFC Challenge Cup. After reaching the semi-finals in the inaugural

INTERNATIONAL HONOURS
None

competition in 2006, Kyrgyzstan failed to make it to the finals of the 2008 event in India following a surprise defeat in their qualifying group at the hands of Afghanistan. In an attempt to improve the standard of play in Kyrgyzstan, the national association has approached the Asian Football Confederation with a view to participating in the Vision Asia programme. There has, at least, been some success at club level, with league champions Dordoi-Dynamo retaining their AFC President's Cup title in September 2007. In a tournament reserved for countries with the weakest leagues on the continent, Dordoy beat Mahendra Police Club from Nepal 2-1 in the final.

THE FIFA BIG COUNT OF 2006

	Male	Female		Total
Number of players	116 605	7 872	Referees and Assistant Referees	69
Professionals	0		Admin, Coaches, Technical, Medical	1 425
Amateurs 18+	7 985		Number of clubs	100
Youth under 18	460		Number of teams	500
Unregistered	50 500		Clubs with women's teams	0
Total players	124 477		Players as % of population	2.39%

Football Federation of Kyrgyz Republic (FFKR)
Kurenkeeva Street 195, PO Box 1484, Bishkek 720 040, Kyrgyzstan
Tel +996 312 670573   Fax +996 312 670573
media@ffkr.kg   www.ffkr.kg
President: MURALIEV Amangeldi   General Secretary: BERDYBEKOV Klichbek
Vice-President: KUTUEV Omurbek   Treasurer: DJAMANGULOVA Raiham   Media Officer: TOKABAEV Kemel
Men's Coach: PODKORYTOV Boris   Women's Coach: UMATALIEVA Gulbara
FFKR formed: 1992   AFC: 1994   FIFA: 1994
Red shirts, Red shorts, Red socks

RECENT INTERNATIONAL MATCHES PLAYED BY KYRGYZSTAN

2002 Opponents	Score		Venue	Comp	Scorers	Att	Referee
No international matches played in 2002							
2003							
16-03 Afghanistan	L	1-2	Kathmandu	ACq	Gulov 60		
20-03 Nepal	W	2-0	Kathmandu	ACq	Nikov 2 27 47		
29-11 Pakistan	W	2-0	Karachi	WCq	Boldygin 36, Chikishev 59	10 000	Nesar BAN
3-12 Pakistan	W	4-0	Bishkek	WCq	Chikishev 18, Chertkov 28, Boldygin 67, Krasnov 9	12 000	Mamedov TKM
2004							
18-02 Tajikistan	L	1-2	Bishkek	WCq	Berezovsky 12	14 000	Lutfullin UZB
31-03 Syria	D	1-1	Bishkek	WCq	Ishenbaev.A 55	17 000	Bose IND
5-06 Qatar	D	0-0	Doha	Fr			
9-06 Bahrain	L	0-5	Al Muharraq	WCq		2 800	Al Saeedi UAE
8-09 Bahrain	L	1-2	Bishkek	WCq	Kenjisariev 86	10 000	Rungklay THA
13-10 Tajikistan	L	1-2	Dushanbe	WCq	Chikishev 84	11 000	El Enezi KUW
10-11 Kuwait	L	0-3	Kuwait City	Fr			
17-11 Syria	W	1-0	Damascus	WCq	Amin 47	1 000	Tongkhan THA
2005							
No international matches played in 2005							
2006							
2-04 Pakistan	L	0-1	Dhaka	CCr1		2 500	Shamsuzzaman BAN
6-04 Tajikistan	W	1-0	Dhaka	CCr1	Krasnov 22	2 000	AK Nema IRQ
7-04 Macao	W	2-0	Dhaka	CCr1	Ablakimov 35, Ishenbaev.A 58	1 000	Tan Hai CHN
9-04 Palestine	W	1-0	Dhaka	CCqf	Djamshidov 91	150	U Win Cho MYA
13-04 Tajikistan	L	0-2	Dhaka	CCsf		2 000	Tan Hai CHN
5-07 Kazakhstan	L	0-1	Almaty	Fr			
2007							
7-03 Kazakhstan	L	0-2	Shymkent	Fr			
9-03 Uzbekistan	L	0-6	Shymkent	Fr			
11-03 Azerbaijan	L	0-1	Shymkent	Fr			
19-08 Cambodia	W	4-3	New Delhi	Fr	Samsaliev 12, Mamatov 17, Djamshidov 48, Harchenko 65		
21-08 Syria	L	1-4	New Delhi	Fr	OG 13		
24-08 Bangladesh	W	3-0	New Delhi	Fr	Lutfullaev 2 28 54, Djamshidov 57		
26-08 India	L	0-3	New Delhi	Fr			
18-10 Jordan	W	2-0	Bishkek	WCq	Esenkul Uulu 45, Bokoev 76	18 000	Sarkar IND
28-10 Jordan	L	0-2	Amman	WCq	L 5-6p	12 000	Ebrahim BHR
2008							
27-04 Oman	L	0-2	Muscat	Fr			
7-05 Afghanistan	L	0-1	Bishkek	CCq		7 000	Shaharul MAS
9-05 Bangladesh	W	2-1	Bishkek	CCq	Kornilov 83, Sydykov 87	5 000	Al Enezi KUW

Fr = Friendly match • AC = AFC Asian Cup • CC = AFC Challenge Cup • WC = FIFA World Cup
q = qualifier • r1 = first round group • qf = quarter-final • sf = semi-final

KYRGYZSTAN NATIONAL TEAM RECORDS AND RECORD SEQUENCES

Records			Sequence records				
Victory	6-0	MDV 1997	Wins	3	2003, 2006	Clean sheets	3	2003, 2006
Defeat	0-7	IRN 1997	Defeats	8	1999-2001	Goals scored	7	2001-2004
Player Caps	30	SALO Vladimir	Undefeated	3	2003, 2006	Without goal	6	1994-1996
Player Goals	3	Four players	Without win	8	1999-2001	Goals against	8	1991-2001

KYRGYZ REPUBLIC; KYRGYZ RESPUBLIKASY

Capital	Bishkek	Language	Kyrgyz, Russian	Independence	1991
Population	5 284 149	Area	198 500 km²	Density 25 per km²	% in cities 39%
GDP per cap	$1600	Dailling code	+996	Internet .kg	GMT + / - +6

MEDALS TABLE

		Overall			League			Cup		Asia			City	Stadium	Cap'ty	DoF
		G	S	B	G	S	B	G	S	G	S	B				
1	SKA-PVO Bishkek	12	7		4	6		8	1				Bishkek			
2	Dordoy-Dinamo	9	1	3	4		3	3		2	1		Naryn	Spartak	18 000	1988
3	Dunamo Bishkek	3	2		3	1			1				Bishkek			
4	Alga-RIFF Bishkek	2			1			1					Bishkek			
	Kant-Oil	2			2								Kant			
6	Zhashtyk Kara-Su	1	8	5	1	2	5		6				Kara-Su	Tsentralny	6 000	
7	AiK Bishkek	1	2	2		2	2	1					Bishkek			
8	Semetey Kyzyl-Kiya	1	2	1		1	1	1	1				Kyzyl-Kiya			
9	Abdish-Ata Kant	1	2			2		1					Kant	Sportkompleks	3 000	2000
10	Metallurg Kadamjay	1	1		1				1				Kadamjay			
11	Ak-Maral Tokmak	1		1		1		1					Tokmak			

RECENT LEAGUE AND CUP RECORD

	Championship						Cup		
Year	Champions	Pts	Runners-up	Pts	Third	Pts	Winners	Score	Runners-up
1992	Alga Bishkek	38	SKA Sokuluk	32	Alay Osh	27	Alga Bishkek	2-1	Alay Osh
1993	Alga-RIFF Bishkek	61	Spartak Tokmak	55	Alay Osh	53	Alga-RIFF Bishkek	4-0	Alga Bishkek
1994	Kant-Oil Kant	47	Semetey Kyzyl-Kiya	44	Ak-Maral Tokmak	43	Ak-Maral Tokmak	2-1	Alay Osh
1995	Kant-Oil Kant	31	AiK Bishkek	30	Semetey Kyzyl-Kiya	28	Semetey Kyzyl-Kiya	2-0	Dinamo Bishkek
1996	Metallurg Kadamjay	56	AiK Bishkek	56	Alay Osh	45	AiK Bishkek	2-0	Metallurg Kadamjay
1997	Dinamo Bishkek	46	Alga-PVO Bishkek	41	AiK Bishkek	40	Alga-PVO Bishkek	1-0	Alay Osh
1998	Dinamo Bishkek	36	SKA-PVO Bishkek	31	AiK Bishkek	28	SKA-PVO Bishkek	3-0	Alay Osh
1999	Dinamo Bishkek	54	SKA-PVO Bishkek	48	Polyot & Zhashtyk	47	SKA-PVO Bishkek	3-0	Semetey Kyzyl-Kiya
2000	SKA-PVO Bishkek	64	Dinamo Bishkek	52	Polyot Bishkek	48	SKA-PVO Bishkek	2-0	Alay Osh
2001	SKA-PVO Bishkek	66	Zhashtyk Kara-Su	57	Dordoy-Dinamo	53	SKA-PVO Bishkek	1-0	Zhashtyk Kara-Su
2002	SKA-PVO Bishkek	48	Zhashtyk Kara-Su	43	Dordoy-Dinamo	39	SKA-PVO Bishkek	1-0	Zhashtyk Kara-Su
2003	Zhashtyk Kara-Su	36	SKA-PVO Bishkek	31	Dordoy-Dinamo	29	SKA-PVO Bishkek	1-0	Zhashtyk Kara-Su
2004	Dordoy-Dinamo	98	SKA-Shoro Bishkek	93	Zhashtyk Kara-Su	77	Dordoy-Dinamo	1-0	Zhashtyk Kara-Su
2005	Dordoy-Dinamo	60	SKA-Shoro Bishkek	60	Zhashtyk Kara-Su	38	Dordoy-Dinamo	1-0	Zhashtyk Kara-Su
2006	Dordoy-Dinamo	24	Abdish-Ata Kant	24	Zhashtyk Kara-Su	18	Dordoy-Dinamo	4-0	Zhashtyk Kara-Su
2007	Dordoy-Dinamo	76	Abdish-Ata Kant	67	Zhashtyk Kara-Su	55	Abdish-Ata Kant	2-1	Lokomotiv Jalalabad

Play-off in 1996: Metallurg 1-0 AiK (now Guardia) • Play-off in 2005: Dordoy 1-1 4-2p SKA-Shoro • Play-off in 2006: Dordoy 1-0 Abdish-Ata Kant • SKA-Shoro Bishkek previously named Alga Bishkek, Alga-PVO Bishkek then SKA-PVO Bishkek

KYRGYZSTAN 2007

FIRST DIVISION

	Pl	W	D	L	F	A	Pts	Dordoy	Abdish-Ata	Zhashtyk	Lokomotiv	Alay	Neftchi	Sher	A-A-FShM	Kant 77	Aviator
Dordoy-Dinamo †	32	24	4	4	73	4	76		1-0 0-0	3-2 3-0	4-0 3-1	1-0 2-1	1-0	1-1 4-1	4-0 7-0	5-0 3-0	
Abdish-Ata Kant	32	20	7	5	65	5	67	1-1 2-0		3-0 1-1	1-2 2-0	1-0 2-1	0-0	1-0 2-1	6-1 5-1	4-1 5-0	1-0
Zhashtyk Kara-Su	32	16	7	9	58	9	55	1-3 2-1	2-2 0-2		2-1 2-0	3-1 0-1	4-0 1-0	0-1 4-1	2-0 5-0	2-0 1-0	3-2
Lokomotiv Jalalabad	32	16	5	11	36	11	53	0-3 **0-0**	1-2 2-0	2-1 1-1		**0-0 0-0**	0-0 1-2	1-2 1-1	1-0 3-2	1-1 2-0	
Alay Osh	32	16	3	13	48	13	51	2-4 1-0	0-0 0-1	0-1 0-0	1-0 1-2		2-1	0-1 2-1	3-2 4-1	1-0 8-1	0-2
Neftchi Kochkorata	32	12	6	14	36	14	42	0-1	3-2 1-1	1-2 2-1	0-3	2-1		4-1 1-1	5-1 0-1	2-0 1-0	1-1
Sher-Ak Dan Bishkek	32	11	6	15	53	15	39	2-2 0-1	2-0 0-1	4-5 2-2	1-2 3-0	2-1 1-2	2-2 2-3		3-1 4-0	4-0 5-0	0-1
Abdish-Ata-FShM Kant	32	5	3	24	33	24	18	0-5 1-4	1-5 1-4	2-2 2-0	2-2 0-2	1-6 1-2	1-2 0-3	0-2 1-1		0-1 4-1	0-2
Kant 77	32	2	3	27	11	27	9	0-4 1-2	0-6 0-6	0-5 0-2	2-2 0-1	1-5 0-2	0-0 0-1	1-0 1-2	0-3 0-3		
Aviator-AAL Bishkek			Withdrew						2-1	2-1	2-0	2-0	2-0		4-0	6-0	

21/04/2007 - 17/11/2007 • † Qualified for the AFC President's Cup • Both Aviator and Neftchi withdrew. Aviator's matches were annulled while Neftchi's remaining matches were awarded as 0-0 wins to their opponents • Matches in bold were awarded as 0-0 wins for Lokomotiv
Top scorers: Almazbek Mirzaliev, Abdisha-Ata 21; Yevgeniy Boldygin, Zhashtyk 20

KYRGYZSTAN 2007
SECOND DIVISION

	Pl	W	D	L	F	A	Pts
Nashe Pivo Kant	18	16	0	2	64	21	**48**
Pivo-Belovodskoe	18	14	1	3	36	11	**43**
Schastliviy Kant	18	13	1	4	53	20	**40**
Molodezhnaja	18	10	3	5	35	28	**33**
Ysyk-Kol Karakol	18	10	1	7	26	12	**31**
Egrisi-Bereket Bishkek	18	6	3	9	34	35	**21**
Osmolov Kainda	18	3	4	11	24	60	**13**
Shoro-92	18	3	2	13	22	46	**11**
Ala-Too Naryn	18	2	5	11	16	46	**11**
Technolog Talas	18	2	2	14	16	39	**8**

21/04/2007 - 17/11/2007

KYRGYZSTAN CUP 2007

Second round
- **Abdish-Ata Kant** * — 3
- Nashe Pivo Kant — 1
- Bishkek — 0
- **Dordoy-Dinamo** * — 9
- **Kant 77** — 1
- Sher-Ak Dan Bishkek* — 0
- Abdish-Ata-FShM Kant — 2
- **Aviator-AAL Bishkek** * — 5
- **Alay Osh** — 4
- Jalalabad * — 0
- Neftchi Kochkorata — 0
- **AK-Bura Osh** * — 1
- **Zhashtyk Kara-Su** * — w-o
- Batken
- ODYuSSh * — 0
- **Lokomotiv Jalalabad** — 7

Quarter-finals
- **Abdish-Ata Kant** * — 1 1
- Dordoy-Dinamo — 0 0
- Kant 77 * — 0 0
- **Aviator-AAL Bishkek** — 0 6
- **Alay Osh** * — 5 6
- AK-Bura Osh — 1 2
- Zhashtyk Kara-Su * — 2 0
- **Lokomotiv Jalalabad** ‡ — 1 1

Semi-finals
- **Abdish-Ata Kant** — w-o
- Aviator-AAL Bishkek
- Alay Osh * — 1 2
- **Lokomotiv Jalalabad** — 2 2

Final
- **Abdish-Ata Kant** — 2
- Lokomotiv Jalalabad — 1

CUP FINAL
Kant, 31-08-2007

Scorers - Almazbek Mirzaliev 2 [36] [91+] for Abdish-Ata; Shukhrat Yusupov [54] for Lokomotiv

* Home team in first leg • ‡ First leg awarded to Lokomotiv

KOR – KOREA REPUBLIC

NATIONAL TEAM RECORD
JULY 10TH 2006 TO JULY 12TH 2010

PL	W	D	L	F	A	%
27	10	11	6	37	22	57.4

After steering South Korea to third place at the 2007 AFC Asian Cup in South East Asia, Dutchman Pim Verbeek chose to stand down from his position as national team coach after little over a year in the job. The Koreans have not won Asia's premier competition since the second championship in 1960 despite reaching the final on three occasions, most recently in 1988, and this lack of success has been more keenly felt as the tournament grows in stature. Former national team midfielder Huh Jung Moo was called upon to replace Verbeek with the task of qualifying for the FIFA World Cup finals for what would be a record seventh consecutive tournament for an Asian nation. Huh had previously coached the national team from 1998 to 2000 before being replaced by Guus Hiddink in the run up to the 2002 finals. The Koreans had the perfect warm up for their World Cup qualifying campaign by winning the low-key East Asian Championship before progressing to the final phase of Asia's qualifying tournament for South Africa 2010 along with northern neighbours Korea DPR at the expense of Turkmenistan and Jordan. Seongnam Ilhwa Chunma looked set to continue their dominance of the K-League when they finished the 2007 season on top of the standings,

INTERNATIONAL HONOURS
Qualified for the FIFA World Cup finals 1954 1986 1990 1994 1998 2002 2006
AFC Asian Cup 1956 1960 **Asian Games Football Tournament** 1970 (shared) 1978 (shared) 1986 **East Asian Championship** 2003
AFC Youth Championship 1959 1960 1963 1978 1980 1982 1990 1996 1998 2002 2004 **AFC U-17 Championship** 1986 2002
AFC Champions League Daewoo Royals 1986, Ilhwa Chunma 1996, Pohang Steelers 1997 1998, Suwon Samsung Bluewings 2001 2002

but their hopes of retaining the title were to be dashed by great rivals Pohang Steelers in the championship play-offs. Despite only finishing fifth at the end of the regular season, Pohang were crowned champions after edging Gyeongnam on penalties in the first round, downing Ulsan Hyundai Horang-i in the second round and then overturning Suwon Bluewings in the semi-finals. That set up a final against Seongnam and, after a 3-1 win in the first leg, Pohang completed their title-winning heroics with a 1-0 victory in the second leg to claim the championship for the first time since 1992, when they were known as POSCO Atoms. Seongnam's disappointment in the league was matched at continental level when the club was eliminated from the 2007 AFC Champions League at the semi-final stage by Japan's Urawa Reds, who won a close tie 5-4 on penalties before going on to lift the title. A worrying slump in the fortunes of the K-League was highlighted in the 2008 AFC Champions League when, for the first time, no Korean club reached the knockout phase of the competition. The K-League may have been the first professional league in Asia but since it launch in 1986 it has been caught up and even surpassed by the likes of the J.League and even the A-League in Australia, a trend which the Koreans will be keen to reverse.

Korea Football Association (KFA)
1-131 Sinmunno, 2-ga, Jongno-Gu, Seoul 110-062, Korea Republic
Tel +82 2 7377538   Fax +82 2 7352755
kfainfo@kfa.or.kr   www.kfa.or.kr
President: CHUNG Mong Joon Dr   General Secretary: KA Sam Hyun
Vice-President: KIM Jae Han   Treasurer: CHUNG Dong Hwan   Media Officer: LEE Won Jae
Men's Coach: HUH Jung Moo   Women's Coach: AN Ik Soo
KFA formed: 1928   AFC: 1954   FIFA: 1948
Red shirts with blue trimmings, Blue shorts, Red socks

RECENT INTERNATIONAL MATCHES PLAYED BY KOREA REPUBLIC

2006 Opponents		Score	Venue	Comp	Scorers	Att	Referee
13-06 Togo	W	2-1	Frankfurt	WCr1	Lee Chun Soo [54], Ahn Jung Hwan [72]	48 000	Poll ENG
18-06 France	D	1-1	Leipzig	WCr1	Park Ji Sung [81]	43 000	Archundia MEX
23-06 Switzerland	L	0-2	Hannover	WCr1		43 000	Elizondo ARG
16-08 Chinese Taipei	W	3-0	Taipei	ACq	Ahn Jung Hwan [32], Jung Jo Gook [55], Kim Do Heon [81]	1 300	Sarkar IND
2-09 Iran	D	1-1	Seoul	ACq	Seol Ki Hyeon [46]	63 113	Breeze AUS
6-09 Chinese Taipei	W	8-0	Suwon	ACq	Seol Ki Hyeon 2 [4 43], Jung Jo Gook 3 [5 46+ 88], Cho Jae Jin 2 [64 83p], Kim Do Heon [78]	21 053	Arambakade SRI
8-10 Ghana	L	1-3	Seoul	Fr	Kim Dong Hun [63]	36 515	Takayama JPN
11-10 Syria	D	1-1	Seoul	ACq	Cho Jae Jin [9]	24 140	Kunsuta THA
15-11 Iran	L	0-2	Tehran	ACq		30 000	Ebrahim BHR
2007							
6-02 Greece	W	1-0	London	Fr	Lee Chun Soo	9 242	Dean ENG
24-03 Uruguay	L	0-2	Seoul	Fr		42 159	Ogiya JPN
2-06 Netherlands	L	0-2	Seoul	Fr		62 884	Ramachandran MAS
29-06 Iraq	W	3-0	Jeju	Fr	Yeom Ki Hun [5], Lee Chun Soo [34], Lee Keun Ho [40]	32 642	Tojo JPN
5-07 Uzbekistan	W	2-1	Seoul	Fr	Cho Jae Jin 2 [5 19]	21 019	Prayoon THA
11-07 Saudi Arabia	D	1-1	Jakarta	ACr1	Choi Sung Kuk [65]	15 000	Shield AUS
15-07 Bahrain	L	0-1	Jakarta	ACr1		9 000	Sun Baojie CHN
18-07 Indonesia	W	1-0	Jakarta	ACr1	Kim Jung Woo [34]	87 000	Shield AUS
22-07 Iran	D	0-0	Kuala Lumpur	ACqf	W 4-2p	68 629	Al Badwawi UAE
25-07 Iraq	D	0-0	Kuala Lumpur	ACsf	L 3-4p	12 500	Al Fadhli KUW
28-07 Japan	D	0-0	Palembang	AC3p		10 000	Al Badwawi UAE
2008							
30-01 Chile	L	0-1	Seoul	Fr		15 012	Matsuo JPN
6-02 Turkmenistan	W	4-0	Seoul	WCq	Kwak Tae Hee [43], Seol Ki Hyeon 2 [57 85], Park Ji Sung [70]	25 738	Najm LIB
17-02 China PR	W	3-2	Chongqing	EAC	Park Chu Young 2 [43 65], Kwak Tae Hee [92+]	25 000	Torky IRN
20-02 Korea DPR	D	1-1	Chongqing	EAC	Yeom Ki Hun [21]	20 000	Takayama JPN
23-02 Japan	D	1-1	Chongqing	EAC	Yeom Ki Hun [15]	29 000	Tan Hai CHN
26-03 Korea DPR	D	0-0	Shanghai	WCq		20 000	Al Fadhli KUW
31-05 Jordan	D	2-2	Seoul	WCq	Park Ji Sung [39], Park Chu Young [48]	50 000	Shield AUS
7-06 Jordan	W	1-0	Amman	WCq	Park Chu Young [24p]	8 000	Moradi IRN
14-06 Turkmenistan	W	3-1	Ashgabat	WCq	Kim Do Heon 3 [14 81 93+p]	11 000	Takayama JPN
22-06 Korea DPR	D	0-0	Seoul	WCq		48 519	Mohd Salleh MAS

Fr = Friendly match • AC = AFC Asian Cup • EAC = East Asian Championship • WC = FIFA World Cup
q = qualifier • r1 = first round group • qf = quarter-final • sf = semi-final • 3p = third place play-off

KOREA REPUBLIC NATIONAL TEAM PLAYERS

	Player		Ap	G	Club	Date of Birth		Player		Ap	G	Club	Date of Birth
1	KIM Yong Dae	GK	21	0	Gwangju	11 10 1979	12	LEE Young Pyo	MF	96	5	Tottenham H.	23 04 1977
2	OH Beom Seok	DF	14	0	Krylia S. Samara	29 07 1984	13	LEE Chung Yong	MF	1	0	FC Seoul	2 07 1988
3	CHO Won Hee	DF	21	1	Suwon	17 04 1983	14	KANG Min Soo	DF	12	0	Jeonbuk	14 02 1986
4	CHO Yong Hyung	DF	5	0	Jeju United	3 11 1983	15	KIM Chi Woo	DF	11	0	Chunnam	11 11 1983
5	KIM Nam Il	MF	81	0	Vissel Kobe	14 03 1977	16	LEE Jung Soo	DF	2	0	Suwon	8 01 1980
6	KWAK Hee Ju	DF	5	0	Suwon	5 10 1981	17	AHN Jung Hwan	FW	66	17	Busan	27 01 1976
7	PARK Ji Sung	MF	70	8	Manchester Utd	25 02 1981	18	KIM Young Kwang	GK	11	0	Ulsan	28 06 1983
8	KIM Do Heon	MF	49	11	West Brom	14 07 1982	19	CHO Byung Kuk	DF	11	1	Seongnam	1 07 1981
9	KO Ki Gu	FW	3	0	Chunnam	31 07 1980	20	KIM Dong Jin	DF	46	2	Zenit St P'burg	29 01 1982
10	PARK Chu Young	FW	26	9	FC Seoul	10 07 1985	21	OH Jang Eun	MF	8	0	Ulsan	24 07 1985
11	SEOL Ki Hyeon	FW	77	18	Fulham	8 01 1979	22	KIM Jung Woo	MF	34	1	Seongnam	9 05 1982
							23	JUN Sung Ryong	GK	4	0	Seongnam	4 01 1985

South Korea's squad for the June 2008 World Cup qualifiers

KOREA REPUBLIC NATIONAL TEAM RECORDS AND RECORD SEQUENCES

Records				Sequence records					
Victory	16-0	NEP 2003		Wins	11	1975, 1978	Clean sheets	9	1970, 1988-1989
Defeat	0-12	SWE 1948		Defeats	3	Seven times	Goals scored	23	1975-76, 1977-78
Player Caps	136	Hong Myung Bo		Undefeated	28	1977-1978	Without goal	3	Four times
Player Goals	55	Cha Bum Kun		Without win	8	1981-1982	Goals against	11	1948-1953

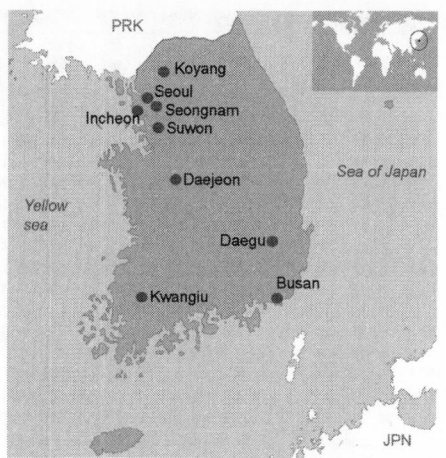

PRK

Koyang
Seoul
Incheon Seongnam
Suwon

Daejeon Sea of Japan

Yellow
sea

Daegu

Kwangiu Busan

JPN

REPUBLIC OF KOREA; TAEHAN-MIN'GUK

Capital	Seoul	Language	Korean		Independence	1945
Population	48 846 823	Area	98 480 km²	Density 493 per km²	% in cities	81%
GDP per cap	$17 800	Dailling code	+82	Internet .kr	GMT + / -	+9

MEDALS TABLE

		Overall			League			Cup			LC			Asia			City	Stadium	Cap'ty	DoF
		G	S	B	G	S	B	G	S	G	S	B	G	S	B				
1	Seongnam Ilhwa Chunma	11	9	1	7	2			2	3	3		1	2	1	Seongnam	Seongnam	27 000	1989
2	Suwon Samsung Bluewings	11	5	3	3	2	3	1	2	5			2	1		Suwon	World Cup	44 047	1996
3	Busan I'Park	9	5	7	4	3	2	1		3	2	4	1		1	Busan	Asiad Main	55 982	1983
4	Pohang Steelers	8	9	4	4	4	3	1	3	1	2	1	2			Pohang	Steel Yard	25 000	1973
5	Ulsan Hyundai Horang-i	6	8	7	3	4	4	1		3	3	1			2	Ulsan	Big Crown	43 550	1983
6	FC Seoul	5	9	1	3	4		1		4	1	1	1			Seoul	World Cup	64 677	1983
7	Jeju United	4	7	4	1	4	4	1		3	2					Seogwipo	World Cup	42 256	1982
8	Jeonbuk Hyundai Motors	4	1	2				3			1	1	1	1		Jeonju	World Cup	42 477	1993
9	Chunnam Dragons	3	5	1		1	1	3	1		2			1		Gwangyang	Gwangyang	14 284	1997
10	Daejeon Citizen	1	1					1		1						Daejeon	World Cup	42 176	1997
11	Gimpo Halleluyah	1			1											Gimpo	Gimpo	10 000	1980
12	Incheon United		1			1										Incheon	Munhak	51 179	2003
	Ulsan Mipo Dockyard		1					1								Ulsan	Mipo	2 500	1988
14	Gyeongnam FC			1								1				Changwon	Changwon	27 085	2005
15	Daegu FC															Daegu	World Cup	68 014	2002
	Gwangju Sangmu Phoenix															Gwangju	Guus Hidink	42 880	1985

NAME CHANGES Ilhwa Chunma → Seongnam Ilhwa Chunma • Daewoo Royals → Pusan Daewoo Royals → Pusan Icons → Busan Icons → Busan I-Park • POSCO Dolphins → POSCO Atoms → Pohang Atoms → Pohang Steelers • Lucky Goldstar → Anyang LG Cheetahs → FC Seoul • Yukong Elephants → Puchong Yukong → Puchong SK → Bucheon SK→ Jeju United • All clubs adopted the revised official Korean spellings in 2000

RECENT LEAGUE AND CUP RECORD

	National Championship				Cup		
Year	Champions	Score/Runners-up	Runners-up/Third		Winners	Score	Runners-up
1998	Suwon Bluewings	1-0 0-0	Ulsan Horang-i		Chunnam Dragons	1-0	Ilhwa Chunma
1999	Suwon Bluewings 59	Bucheon SK 47	Chunnam Dragons 38		Anyang Cheetahs	2-1	Ulsan Horang-i
2000	Anyang Cheetahs	4-1 1-1 (4-2p)	Bucheon SK		Chonbuk Hyundai	2-0	Ilhwa Chunma
2001	Ilhwa Chunma 45	Anyang Cheetahs 43	Suwon Bluewings 41		Daejeon Citizen	1-0	Pohang Steelers
2002	Ilhwa Chunma 49	Ulsan Horang-i 47	Suwon Bluewings 45		Suwon Bluewings	1-0	Pohang Steelers
2003	Ilhwa Chunma 91	Ulsan Horang-i 73	Suwon Bluewings 72		Chonbuk Hyundai	2-2 4-2p	Chunnam Dragons
2004	Suwon Bluewings	0-0 0-0 4-3p	Pohang Steelers		Busan Icons	1-1 4-3p	Bucheon SK
2005	Ulsan Horang-i	5-1 1-2	Incheon United		Chonbuk Hyundai	1-0	Ulsan Dockyard
2006	Ilhwa Chunma	1-0 2-1	Suwon Bluewings		Chunnam Dragons	2-0	Suwon Bluewings
2007	Pohang Steelers	3-1 1-0	Ilhwa Chunma		Chunnam Dragons	3-2 3-1	Pohang Steelers

KOREA REPUBLIC 2007

–LEAGUE OVERALL

	Pl	W	D	L	F	A	Pts	Seongnam	Suwon	Ulsan	Gyeongnam	Pohang	Daejeon	Seoul	Jeonbuk	Incheon	Chunnam	Jeju	Daegu	Busan	Gwangju
Seongnam Ilhwa Chunma †	26	16	7	3	43	18	55		3-1	1-1	1-2	1-1	0-0	0-0	2-1	1-1	1-1	2-0	3-0	2-1	3-1
Suwon Samsung Bluewings ‡	26	15	6	5	36	24	51	2-1		1-2	5-3	1-0	2-1	2-1	2-3	1-0	1-0	3-0	1-1	1-0	0-0
Ulsan Hyundai Horang-i ‡‡	26	12	9	5	34	22	45	0-3	2-0		1-1	0-0	2-1	0-0	2-1	1-0	2-2	2-2	2-1	0-0	4-0
Gyeongnam FC ‡‡	26	13	5	8	41	31	44	0-2	0-0	0-4		1-3	1-2	1-0	1-2	0-0	2-0	3-1	1-0	2-0	1-0
Pohang Steelers ‡‡	26	11	6	9	27	31	39	2-1	0-0	1-0	2-1		1-1	0-0	1-3	3-2	1-0	0-1	1-3	0-1	2-1
Daejeon Citizen ‡‡	26	10	7	9	34	27	37	1-2	1-0	1-3	0-0	3-0		0-0	2-0	0-1	1-1	1-0	4-1	2-2	2-0
FC Seoul	26	8	13	5	23	16	37	0-0	0-1	0-0	0-3	3-0	2-1		1-1	2-1	1-0	1-0	2-0	4-0	0-0
Jeonbuk Hyundai Motors	26	9	9	8	36	32	36	0-2	1-1	0-0	2-3	1-2	0-2	1-1		0-0	1-1	2-1	4-1	1-1	2-1
Incheon United	26	8	9	9	30	32	33	0-2	2-3	1-0	2-1	0-1	3-2	2-2	1-3		2-1	1-1	2-1	2-2	3-2
Chunnam Dragons	26	7	9	10	24	27	30	0-2	0-0	0-1	2-1	1-1	1-2	0-1	1-0	0-0		1-0	3-2	0-0	2-0
Jeju United	26	8	6	12	27	35	30	1-2	0-1	2-1	1-1	2-0	2-3	2-2	2-0	2-2			2-0	1-0	1-1
Daegu FC	26	6	6	14	35	46	24	1-2	1-3	0-1	3-1	1-3	2-2	1-1	1-1	1-1	1-2	2-2		1-1	2-1
Busan I'Park	26	4	8	14	20	39	20	1-3	1-2	0-1	1-4	1-2	1-0	0-0	0-2	0-0	1-3	0-1	1-4		2-1
Gwangju Sangmu Phoenix	26	2	6	18	14	44	12	0-1	1-3	1-2	0-4	0-1	1-0	0-0	0-2	1-1	0-0	0-2	2-1	0-3	

3/03/2007 - 14/10/2007 • † Qualified for the play-off final • ‡ Qualified for the play-off semi-final • ‡‡ Qualified for the play-off first round
First round: Gyeongnam 1-1 3-4p **Pohang**; **Ulsan** 2-0 Daejeon • Second round: **Pohang** 2-1 Ulsan • Semi-final: Suwon 0-1 **Pohang**

–LEAGUE FINAL 2007 1ST LEG

Steelyard, Pohang, 4-11-2007, 20 875

Pohang 3 Park Won Jae 31, Ko Ki Gu 73, Lee Gwang Jae 74
Seongnam 1 Jang Hak Young 91+

–LEAGUE FINAL 2007 2ND LEG

Seongnam Stadium, Seongnam, 11-11-2007, 18 924

Seongnam 0
Pohang 1 Schwenck 43

Pohang Steelers win the 2007 K–League and qualify for the AFC Champions League

KOREA REPUBLIC 2007 — SAMSUNG HAU EN LEAGUE CUP

Group A	Pl	W	D	L	F	A	Pts
Ulsan Hyundai Horang-i †	10	5	4	1	10	4	19
Incheon United †	10	6	1	3	20	15	19
Daegu FC	10	4	1	5	13	16	13
Jeonbuk Hyundai Motors	10	3	3	4	9	10	12
Pohang Steelers	10	2	5	3	8	10	11
Jeju United	10	2	2	6	4	9	8

Group B	Pl	W	D	L	F	A	Pts
FC Seoul	10	6	3	1	17	6	21
Suwon Samsung Bluewings	10	5	2	3	20	12	17
Gwangju Sangmu Phoenix	10	3	3	4	6	12	12
Busan I'Park	10	2	5	3	7	8	11
Daejeon Citizen	10	2	5	3	6	10	11
Gyeongnam FC	10	1	4	5	3	11	7

14/03/2007 - 23/04/2007 • † Qualified for the semi-finals

SAMSUNG HAU EN CUP PLAY-OFFS

Quarter-finals		Semi-finals		Final	
Ulsan	Bye				
		Ulsan	1		
Seongnam	1	Suwon	0		
Suwon	4			Ulsan	2
Incheon	2			Seoul	1
Chunnam	1	Incheon			
		Seoul	1 4p	Seoul World Cup 27-06-2007	
Seoul	Bye				

KOREA REPUBLIC 2007 — N-LEAGUE (2) FIRST STAGE

	Pl	W	D	L	F	A	Pts
Ulsan Mipo Dockyard	11	8	1	2	20	7	25
Gangneung City	11	8	1	2	19	10	25
Incheon Korail	11	7	1	3	16	10	22
Suwon City	11	5	1	5	15	13	16
Daejeon Hydro & Nuclear	11	3	5	3	13	10	14
Goyang Kookmin Bank §10	11	7	2	2	20	8	13
Busan Transportation Corp	11	3	4	4	15	14	13
Icheon Hummel	11	3	3	5	11	13	12
Ansan Halleluyah	11	3	3	5	9	15	12
Seosan Omega	11	2	2	7	11	21	8
Changwon City	11	2	2	7	8	19	8
INGNEX City	11	2	1	8	11	28	7

6/04/2007 - 16/06/2007 • § = points deducted
Ulsan Mipo qualified to meet second stage winners for the title

KOREA REPUBLIC 2007 — N-LEAGUE (2) SECOND STAGE

	Pl	W	D	L	F	A	Pts
Suwon City	11	10	1	0	25	8	31
Ulsan Mipo Dockyard	11	6	4	1	20	11	22
Incheon Korail	11	6	2	3	20	18	20
Gangneung City	11	5	2	4	21	15	17
Busan Transportation Corp	11	4	3	4	16	16	15
Changwon City	11	4	2	5	16	23	14
Ansan Halleluyah	11	3	4	4	16	17	13
Icheon Hummel	11	1	8	2	11	11	11
Goyang Kookmin Bank §10	11	6	2	3	25	12	10
Daejeon Hydro & Nuclear	11	1	4	6	7	17	7
Seosan Omega	11	1	2	8	13	27	5
INGNEX City	11	1	2	8	12	27	5

8/09/2007 - 17/11/2007 • § = points deducted
Championship play-off: Ulsan Mipo Dockyard 3-0 4-1 Suwon City

HANA BANK KOREAN FA CUP 2007

First Round		Second Round	Quarter-finals	Semi-finals	Final
Chunnam Dragons	Bye				
		Chunnam Dragons 1			
Jeonbuk Hyundai Motors	Bye	Jeonbuk Hyundai Motors 0			
Gwangju Sangmu Phoenix	2		**Chunnam Dragons** 0 4p		
Incheon University	1	Gwangju Sangmu Phoenix 1	Ulsan Hyundai Horang-i 0 2p		
Busan Transportation Corp	0	**Ulsan Hyundai Horang-i** 3			
Ulsan Hyundai Horang-i	1			**Chunnam Dragons** 2	
FC Seoul	1 5p			Incheon United 0	
Incheon Korail	1 3p	**FC Seoul** 0 4p			
Seosan Omega	1	Suwon Samsung Bluewings 0 2p	**FC Seoul** 1		
Suwon Samsung Bluewings	4		**Incheon United** 2		
Daegu FC	1 7p				
Gangneung City	1 6p	**Daegu FC** 2			
Daejeon Hydro & Nuclear	0	**Incheon United** 3			**Chunnam Dragons** † 3 3
Incheon United	4				Pohang Steelers 2 1
Jeju United	2				
Ilsan University	0	**Jeju United** 1 5p			
		Seongnam Ilhwa Chunma 1 4p	**Jeju United** 0 5p		
Seongnam Ilhwa Chunma	Bye		Busan I'Park 0 4p		
Daejeon Citizen	2			**Jeju United** 1	
Joongang University	0	Daejeon Citizen 0		**Pohang Steelers** 2	
Icheon Hummel	3	**Busan I'Park** 2			
Busan I'Park	3				
Ulsan Mipo Dockyard	1				
Ansan Hallelujah	0	**Ulsan Mipo Dockyard** 2 4p			
Changwon City	0	Gyeongnam FC 2 2p	**Ulsan Mipo Dockyard** 0		
Gyeongnam FC	2		**Pohang Steelers** 2		
Goyang Kookmin Bank	0 5p				
Suwon City	0 4p	Goyang Kookmin Bank			
Konkuk University	1	**Pohang Steelers**			
Pohang Steelers	4				

CUP FINAL

1st leg. Gwangyang Stadium, Gwangyang
25-11-2007
Scorers – Kim Chi Woo 21, Kim Sung Hyun 81,
Kwak Tae Hee 86 for Chunnam; Tavares 24, Kim
Kwang Suk 50 for Pohang

2nd leg. Steelyard, Pohang
2-12-2007
Scorers – Hwang Jin Sung 47 for Pohang;
Song Jong Hyun 2 34 80, Sandro Hiroshi 84 for
Chunnam

† Qualified for the AFC Champions League

KSA – SAUDI ARABIA

NATIONAL TEAM RECORD
JULY 10TH 2006 TO JULY 12TH 2010

PL	W	D	L	F	A	%
38	28	4	6	77	29	78.9

Helio dos Anjos became the latest Saudi national team coach to exit through what has become a rapidly revolving door, this despite steering the team to the final of the 2007 AFC Asian Cup and to the brink of qualifying for the final group stage of the 2010 FIFA World Cup qualifying competition in Asia. The Brazilian, who took over just weeks before the finals of the Asian Cup, was relieved of his position after leading Saudi to a 2-1 victory over Lebanon in Riyadh in June 2008. With the Saudis in second place in their group following an earlier defeat away to Uzbekistan, Dos Anjos was replaced by former Asian Coach of the Year Nasser Al Johar, who was last seen leading the team to their poor showing at the World Cup finals in Japan in 2002. Al Johar secured the results required - a 2-0 win over Singapore and a 4-0 victory against Uzbekistan - to ensure the Saudis went through to the final phase of qualifying for South Africa as group winners. They have, however, been drawn in the tougher of the two groups and will have to overcome both Iran and South Korea if they are to secure one of the top two spots. Doing so would result in automatic qualification for what would be their fifth consecutive appearance in the finals. Riyadh

INTERNATIONAL HONOURS
Qualified for the FIFA World Cup finals 1994 1998 2002 2006
FIFA U-17 World Championship 1989
AFC Asian Cup 1984 1988 1996   AFC Asian Youth Cup 1986 1992   AFC Asian U-17 1985 1988
AFC Champions League Al Hilal 1992 2000, Al Ittihad 2004 2005

club Al Hilal, meanwhile, won the Saudi league title by the narrowest of margins ahead of bitter rivals Al Ittihad of Jeddah. With the league championship playoffs having been scrapped, Al Hilal claimed their 11th title - and first since 2005 - thanks to their better head-to-head record in the league against Al Ittihad. The two teams went into their clash on the final day of the season in Jeddah knowing that a draw would be enough for Al Ittihad to successfully defend the title. But with a solitary goal from Asian Player of the Year Yasser Al Khahtani, Al Hilal took all three points and, with it, the championship. A 2-0 win over Al Ittifaq also saw Al Hilal win the Crown Prince Cup to claim the league and cup double while Al Shabab downed Al Ittihad 3-1 to win the King's Cup. Al Ittihad's disappointing year continued in the 2008 AFC Champions League, when they missed out on qualifying for the knockout phase of the competition. Al Ittihad – Asian champions in 2004 and 2005 - were surprisingly eliminated by Uzbekistan's Kuruvchi at the end of the group phase, while compatriots Al Ahli were also knocked out in the first round, finishing bottom of their group. As a result, no Saudi side reached the last eight for the first time since the inauguration of the competition back in 2002.

Saudi Arabian Football Federation (SAFF)
Al Mather Quarter, Prince Faisal Bin Fahad Street, PO Box 5844, Riyadh 11432, Saudi Arabia
Tel +966 1 4822240   Fax +966 1 4821215
sa.ff@hotmail.com   www.saff.com.sa
President: HRH Prince Sultan bin Fahad BIN ABDULAZIZ   General Secretary: AL-ABDULHADI Faisal
Vice-President: HRH Prince Nawaf Bin Faisal B.F. BIN ABDULAZIZ   Treasurer: AL-ATHEL Abdullah
Men's Coach: AL JOHAR Nasser   Women's Coach: None
SAFF formed: 1959   AFC: 1972   FIFA: 1959
White shirts with green trimmings, Green shorts, White socks

RECENT INTERNATIONAL MATCHES PLAYED BY SAUDI ARABIA

2006	Opponents	Score		Venue	Comp	Scorers	Att	Referee
14-06	Tunisia	D	2-2	Munich	WCr1	Al Khatani [57], Al Jaber [84]	66 000	Shield AUS
19-06	Ukraine	L	0-4	Hamburg	WCr1		50 000	Poll ENG
23-06	Spain	L	0-1	Kaiserslautern	WCr1		46 000	Codjia BEN
9-08	Bahrain	W	1-0	Dammam	Fr	Al Khatani [16]		
16-08	India	W	3-0	Calcutta	ACq	Sulaimani [2], Al Khatani 2 [18 52]	10 000	Tongkhan THA
27-08	UAE	W	1-0	Jeddah	Fr	Saleh Al Dosari [9]		
3-09	Japan	W	1-0	Jeddah	ACq	Saleh Al Dosari [73]	15 000	Maidin SIN
6-09	India	W	7-1	Jeddah	ACq	Saleh Al Dosari 2 [31 46], Al Mahyani [34], Haidar [57], Al Hagbani [62], Al Suwailh 2 [79 86]	3 000	Al Saeedi UAE
11-10	Yemen	W	5-0	Jeddah	ACq	Saleh Al Dosari [22], Haidar [27], Redha Tukar [66], Al Mahyani 2 [68 92+]	1 500	Nema IRQ
8-11	Jordan	W	2-1	Riyadh	Fr	Al Suwailh 2 [74 90]		
15-11	Japan	L	1-3	Sapporo	ACq	Al Khatani [33p]	40 965	Shield AUS
2007								
8-01	Gambia	W	3-0	Dammam	Fr	Al Montasheri [20], Al Khatani 2 [31 50]		
11-01	Syria	W	2-1	Dammam	Fr	Hagbani [79p], Saleh Al Dosari [88]		
18-01	Bahrain	W	2-1	Abu Dhabi	GCr1	Saleh Al Dosari 2 [25 88]		
21-01	Qatar	D	1-1	Abu Dhabi	GCr1	Malek Maaz [71]		
24-01	Iraq	W	1-0	Abu Dhabi	GCr1	Al Khatani [12p]		
27-01	UAE	L	0-1	Abu Dhabi	GCsf			
24-06	UAE	W	2-0	Singapore	Fr	Al Harthi [49], Malek Maaz [59]		
27-06	Singapore	W	2-1	Singapore	Fr	Abdulrahman Al Khatani [26], Al Jassam [34]		
1-07	Oman	D	1-1	Singapore	Fr	Al Shlhoub [56]. W 3-1p		
4-07	Korea DPR	D	1-1	Singapore	Fr	Malek Maaz [64]		
11-07	Korea Republic	D	1-1	Jakarta	ACr1	Yasser Al Khatani [77p]	15 000	Shield AUS
14-07	Indonesia	W	2-1	Jakarta	ACr1	Yasser Al Khatani [12], Al Harthi [89]	87 000	Al Badwawi UAE
18-07	Bahrain	W	4-0	Palembang	ACr1	Al Mousa [18], Al Khatani.A [45], Al Jassam 2 [68 79]	500	Nishimura JPN
22-07	Uzbekistan	W	2-1	Jakarta	ACqf	Yasser Al Khatani [2], Al Mousa [75]	12 000	Kwon Jong Chul KOR
25-07	Japan	W	3-2	Hanoi	ACsf	Yasser Al Khatani [35], Malek Maaz 2 [47 57]	10 000	Breeze AUS
29-07	Iraq	L	0-1	Jakarta	ACf		60 000	Shield AUS
11-09	Ghana	W	5-0	Riyadh	Fr	Yasser Al Khatani 2 [5 51], Khariri [25], Al Harthi [57p], Redha Tukar [90p]		Al Jarwan KSA
2-11	Namibia	W	1-0	Riyadh	Fr	Al Jassim [14]		Jasim BHR
9-11	Estonia	W	2-0	Jeddah	Fr	Al Jassim [28], Yasser Al Khatani [38]	2 500	Al Shehri KSA
18-11	Libya	L	1-2	Ismailia	Fr	Kariri [9]		Al Hajjar SYR
25-11	Egypt	L	1-2	Cairo	Fr	Yasser Al Khatani [55p]		Al Hajjar SYR
2008								
30-01	Luxembourg	W	2-1	Riyadh	Fr	Abdoh Autef [48p], Yasser Al Khatani [67]	2 000	Al Merdasi KSA
6-02	Singapore	W	2-0	Riyadh	WCq	Yasser Al Khatani [38], Malek Maaz [81]	10 000	Basma SYR
26-03	Uzbekistan	L	0-3	Tashkent	WCq		17 000	Mohd Salleh MAS
24-05	Syria	W	1-0	Riyadh	Fr	Al Mouallad [17]		Al Anazi KUW
27-05	Kuwait	W	2-1	Dammam	Fr	Malek Maaz 2 [50 64]		Al Dosari BHR
2-06	Lebanon	W	4-1	Riyadh	WCq	Yasser Al Khatani 2 [44 90], Osama Hawsawi [62], Redha Tukar [84]	8 000	Al Fadhli KUW
7-06	Lebanon	W	2-1	Riyadh	WCq	Redha Tukar 2 [45 60]	2 000	Tongkhan THA
14-06	Singapore	W	2-0	Singapore	WCq	Abdoh Autef [37], Ahmed Al Fraidi [76]	23 000	Williams AUS
22-06	Uzbekistan	W	4-0	Riyadh	WCq	Abdoh Autef [7], Malek Maaz 2 [37 87], Saad Al Harthi [56]	5 000	Nishimura JPN

Fr = Friendly match • AC = AFC Asian Cup • GC = Gulf Cup • WC = FIFA World Cup
q = qualifier • r1 = first round group • sf = semi-final • f = final

SAUDI ARABIA NATIONAL TEAM RECORDS AND RECORD SEQUENCES

Records				Sequence records			
Victory	8-0	MAC 1993	Wins	11	2001	Clean sheets	9	2001
Defeat	0-13	EGY 1961	Defeats	6	1995	Goals scored	15	2001
Player Caps	181	Mohamed Al-Deayea	Undefeated	19	2003-2004	Without goal	5	1998
Player Goals	67	Majed Abdullah	Without win	10	1988	Goals against	10	1981-1982

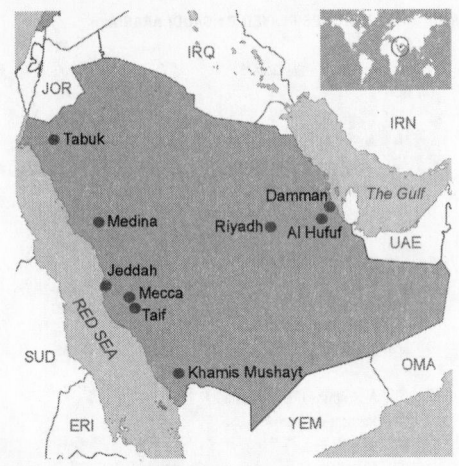

MAJOR CITIES/TOWNS

		Population '000
1	Riyadh	4 453
2	Jeddah	3 002
3	Mecca	1 383
4	Medina	1 004
5	Dammam	819
6	Taif	550
7	Tabuk	484
8	Khamis Mushayt	418
9	Beraida	418
10	Al Hufuf	303
11	Al Mubarraz	302
12	Ha'il	291
13	Najran	283
14	Al Jubayl	270
15	Hafar al Batin	260
16	Abha	229
17	Yanbu	225
18	Al Kharj	215
19	Taqbah	210
20	Khobar	171
21	Ara'ar	155
22	Al Rass	120
23	Saihat	67
24	Al Majma'ah	42

KINGDOM OF SAUDI ARABIA; AL MAMLAKAH AL ARABIYAH AS SUUDIYAH

Capital	Riyadh	Language	Arabic	Formation	1932
Population	27 019 731	Area	1 960 582 km²	Density	13 per km²	% in cities	80%
GDP per cap	$11 800	Dailling code	+966	Internet	.sa	GMT +/-	+3

MEDALS TABLE

		Overall			Lge		Cup		Asia			City	Stadium	Cap'ty	DoF
		G	S	B	G	S	G	S	G	S	B				
1	Al Hilal	24	11		11	2	12	7	1	2		Riyadh	Prince Faisal bin Fahd	27 000	1957
2	Al Ittihad	20	11	2	7	3	10	8	3		2	Jeddah	Prince Abdullah Al Faisal	24 000	1928
3	Al Ahli	15	11		2	4	13	6		1		Jeddah	Prince Sultan bin Fahd	15 000	1937
4	Al Nasr	14	9		6	1	7	6	1	2		Riyadh	Prince Faisal bin Fahd	27 000	1955
5	Al Shabab	9	8		5	2	3	5	1	1		Riyadh	Prince Faisal bin Fahd	27 000	1947
6	Al Ittifaq	4	7		2	1	2	6				Dammam	Prince Mohamed bin Fahd	35 000	1944
7	Al Wahda	2	5				2	5				Mecca	King Abdul Aziz	33 500	1945
8	Al Qadisiya	2	1				1	1	1			Khobar	Prince Saud bin Jalawi	10 000	1967
9	Al Riyadh	1	5			1	1	4				Riyadh	Prince Faisal bin Fahd	27 000	1954
10	Al Ta'ee		1					1				Ha'il	Prince Abdul Aziz bin Musa'ed	10 000	1937

RECENT LEAGUE AND CUP RECORD

	Championship				Cup		
Year	Champions	Score	Runners-up		Winners	Score	Runners-up
1995	Al Nasr	3-1	Al Riyadh		Al Hilal	1-0	Al Riyadh
1996	Al Hilal	2-1	Al Ahli		Al Shabab	3-0	Al Nasr
1997	Al Ittihad	2-0	Al Hilal		Al Ittihad	2-0	Al Ta'ee
1998	Al Hilal	3-2	Al Shabab		Al Ahli	3-2	Al Riyadh
1999	Al Ittihad	1-0	Al Ahli		Al Shabab	1-0	Al Hilal
2000	Al Ittihad	2-1	Al Ahli		Al Hilal	3-0	Al Shabab
2001	Al Ittihad	1-0	Al Nasr		Al Ittihad	3-0	Al Ittifaq
2002	Al Hilal	2-1	Al Ittihad		Al Ahli	2-1	Al Ittihad
2003	Al Ittihad	3-2	Al Ahli		Al Hilal	1-0	Al Ahli
2004	Al Shabab	1-0	Al Ittihad		Al Ittihad	1-0	Al Ahli
2005	Al Hilal	1-0	Al Shabab		Al Hilal	2-1	Al Qadisiya
2006	Al Shabab	3-0	Al Hilal		Al Hilal	1-0	Al Ahli
2007	Al Ittihad	2-1	Al Hilal		Al Ahli	2-1	Al Ittihad
2008	Al Hilal	†	Al Ittihad		Al Hilal	2-0	Al Ittifaq

† Played on a league basis

SAUDI ARABIA 2007-08

SAUDI PREMIER LEAGUE

	Pl	W	D	L	F	A	Pts	Hilal	Ittihad	Shabab	Ittifaq	Nasr	Wahda	Hazm	Ahli	Watani	Najran	Ta'ee	Qadisiya
Al Hilal †	22	14	6	2	36	13	48		0-0	0-0	2-0	1-1	3-1	2-0	1-3	5-0	1-2	2-0	0-0
Al Ittihad	22	14	6	2	40	16	48	0-1		1-1	1-0	4-0	1-1	2-0	1-0	1-1	2-0	5-2	1-0
Al Shabab	22	11	9	2	39	21	42	1-1	3-2		2-1	1-1	2-1	1-2	1-3	6-0	2-2	2-0	2-1
Al Ittifaq	22	10	5	7	34	25	35	1-1	1-2	0-0		1-4	4-1	2-3	1-2	1-1	2-1	2-0	5-1
Al Nasr	22	9	6	7	34	35	33	1-3	1-5	2-2	0-3		1-0	2-1	2-1	2-1	1-1		0-1
Al Wahda	22	8	5	9	29	27	29	0-1	0-1	0-2	1-2	1-1		3-2	1-0	2-1	6-0	1-0	2-1
Al Hazm	22	7	6	9	26	28	27	0-1	1-2	0-0	1-2	1-1	0-1		1-0	1-0	1-1	2-1	2-0
Al Ahli	22	7	5	10	30	31	26	1-2	0-2	1-3	2-2	0-3	1-1	1-1		3-2	4-0	3-1	0-0
Al Watani	22	6	7	9	20	32	25	0-1	0-0	0-1	0-1	1-0	0-0	2-1	3-2		1-1	1-0	2-1
Najran	22	5	6	11	29	44	21	0-2	2-2	1-2	0-1	5-4	3-1	2-2	2-0	0-1		2-2	2-1
Al Ta'ee	22	2	7	13	20	38	13	0-2	1-2	0-0	0-0	1-3	1-1	1-3	0-2	2-2	3-1		0-0
Al Qadisiya	22	2	6	14	17	44	12	2-4	1-3	2-5	0-2	0-2	0-4	1-1	1-1	1-1	1-1	2-1	1-4

23/08/2007 - 13/04/2008 • † Qualified for the AFC Champions League

SAUDI ARABIA 2007-08
FIRST DIVISION (2)

	Pl	W	D	L	F	A	Pts
Al Ra'ed	26	12	9	5	27	15	45
Abha	26	13	6	7	47	37	45
Al Ansar	26	11	10	5	36	28	43
Al Khaleej	26	11	7	8	39	35	40
Al Fat'h	26	10	8	8	29	23	38
Dhemk	26	10	8	8	30	27	38
Sudoos	26	9	7	10	35	30	35
Al Taawun	26	10	5	11	34	35	35
Al Faysali	26	11	2	13	28	33	35
Hajr	26	9	7	10	36	35	34
Ohod	26	10	4	12	30	33	34
Al Riyadh	26	10	4	12	22	30	34
Al Jabalain	26	10	3	13	23	37	33
Faiha'a	26	1	10	15	13	31	13

18/10/2007 - 13/05/2008

THE CUSTODIAN OF THE TWO HOLY MOS UES CHALLENGE CUP 2008

Quarter-finals			Semi-finals			Final		
Al Shabab	6	3						
Al Ahli	1	1	Al Shabab	2	5			
Al Nasr	2	1 5p	Al Hazm	4	0			
Al Hazm	3	0 6p				Al Shabab		3
Al Hilal	0	2				Al Ittihad		1
Al Wahda	0	1	Al Hilal	1	1			
Al Ittifaq	1	1	Al Ittihad	4	2	14-05-2008		
Al Ittihad	1	5	Third Place: Hilal 1-1 3-1p Hazm					

CROWN PRINCE CUP 2007-08

First Round		Quarter-finals		Semi-finals			Final		
Al Hilal *	2								
Al Nasr	0	Al Hilal *	2						
Al Riyadh *	0	Al Hazm	1						
Al Hazm	1			Al Hilal	0	1			
Al Watani	2 5p			Al Shabab *	0	0			
Al Ta'ee *	2 3p	Al Watani *	0						
Dhemk	0	Al Shabab	2						
Al Shabab *	2						Al Hilal		2
Al Ahli *	6						Al Ittifaq		0
Al Jabalain	0	Al Ahli *	3						
Al Wahda *	2	Najran	1						
Najran	3			Al Ahli *	2	1			
Al Ittihad	4			Al Ittifaq	2	2			
Al Qadisiya *	3	Al Ittihad *	1						
Al Rabi'a	0	Al Ittifaq	2						
Al Ittifaq *	5								

CUP FINAL

7-03-2008

Scorers - Yasser Al Khatani [7], Tariq Al Taib [36p]

* Home team in the first leg • ‡ Qualified for the AFC Champions League

KUW – KUWAIT

NATIONAL TEAM RECORD
JULY 10TH 2006 TO JULY 12TH 2010

PL	W	D	L	F	A	%
24	5	7	12	34	35	35.4

FIFA/COCA-COLA WORLD RANKING

1993	1994	1995	1996	1997	1998	1999	2000	2001	2002	2003	2004	2005	2006	2007		High	
64	54	84	62	44	24	82	74	74	83	48	54	72	78	119		24	12/98

	2007–2008												Low	
08/07	09/07	10/07	11/07	12/07	01/08	02/08	03/08	04/08	05/08	06/08	07/08		121	03/08
89	105	115	121	119	115	121	121	116	117	114	116			

With the national team incapable of matching previous heights on the international stage, it is on the continental club scene that Kuwait has been making a more noticeable impact in recent seasons, particularly in the AFC Champions League. Al Qadisiya rekindled memories of their run to the semi-finals in 2006 by once again qualifying for the knockout phase in 2008 when they progressed at the expense of two-time semi-finalists Pakhtakor of Uzbekistan, Qatar's Al Gharafa and Arbil, the Iraqi champions. There was little for the national team to cheer about, however, in a year that saw them win only twice and in which they were unceremoniously dumped out of the 2010

INTERNATIONAL HONOURS
Qualified for the FIFA World Cup finals 1982   Asian Cup 1980   Gulf Cup 1970 1972 1974 1976 1982 1986 1990 1996 1998

FIFA World Cup qualifiers. A friendly win over Lebanon saw the year start in positive fashion but was followed by a run of 10 games without a victory, including World Cup defeats against the United Arab Emirates and Syria as well as a draw with Iran. That run of results ended in Romanian coach Rodion Gacanin being replaced with Mohammed Ibrahim, who had led the national side on a caretaker basis in 2004 and 2005. Ibrahim inspired the team to victory over the Syrians to keep Kuwait's hopes of reaching the final phase of qualifying alive, but successive losses against eventual qualifiers the UAE and Iran saw those chances finally extinguished.

THE FIFA BIG COUNT OF 2006

	Male	Female		Total
Number of players	45 800	0	Referees and Assistant Referees	100
Professionals	0		Admin, Coaches, Technical, Medical	300
Amateurs 18+	1 100		Number of clubs	40
Youth under 18	1 100		Number of teams	110
Unregistered	6 600		Clubs with women's teams	0
Total players	45 800		Players as % of population	1.89%

Kuwait Football Association (KFA)
Udailiya, Block 4, Al-Ittihad Street, PO Box 2029, Safat 13021, Kuwait
Tel +965 2555851   Fax +965 2549955
info@kfa.org.kw   www.kfa.org.kw
President: TBD   General Secretary: AL HABASHI Wael
Vice-President: TBD   Treasurer: TBD   Media Officer: None
Men's Coach: TBD   Women's Coach: None
KFA formed: 1952   AFC: 1962   FIFA: 1962
Blue shirts with white trimmings, Blue shorts, Blue socks

RECENT INTERNATIONAL MATCHES PLAYED BY KUWAIT

2005	Opponents		Score	Venue	Comp	Scorers	Att	Referee
22-01	Norway	D	1-1	Kuwait City	Fr	Bashar 27	200	Shaban KUW
26-01	Syria	W	3-2	Kuwait City	Fr	OG 8, Mussa 70, Al Humaidan 83		
2-02	Korea DPR	D	0-0	Beijing	Fr			
9-02	Korea Republic	L	0-2	Seoul	WCq		53 287	Maidin SIN
12-03	Finland	L	0-1	Kuwait City	Fr		10 000	
18-03	Armenia	W	3-1	Al Ain	Fr	Abdulreda 70, Al Mutwa 79, Al Subaih 90		
25-03	Uzbekistan	W	2-1	Kuwait City	WCq	Bashar 2 7 62	12 000	Sun Baojie CHN
30-03	Saudi Arabia	D	0-0	Kuwait City	WCq		25 000	Moradi IRN
27-05	Egypt	L	0-1	Kuwait City	Fr			
3-06	Saudi Arabia	L	0-3	Riyadh	WCq		72 000	Kamikawa JPN
8-06	Korea Republic	L	0-4	Kuwait City	WCq		15 000	Khanthama THA
29-07	United Arab Emirates	D	1-1	Geneva	Fr	Al Mutawa 43. L 6-7p		
31-07	Qatar	L	0-1	Geneva	Fr			
17-08	Uzbekistan	L	2-3	Tashkent	WCq	Al Mutwa 15, Abdulaziz 30	40 000	Mohd Salleh MAS
26-11	Iraq	D	0-0	Kuwait City	Fr			
2006								
3-02	Singapore	D	2-2	Kuwait City	Fr	Jarragh 8, Al Mutawa 30		
7-02	Jordan	W	2-1	Kuwait City	Fr	Salama 6, Ali 16		
22-02	Lebanon	D	1-1	Beirut	ACq	Al Hamad 25	8 000	Mujghef JOR
1-03	Bahrain	D	0-0	Kuwait City	ACq		16 000	Moradi IRN
16-08	Australia	L	0-2	Sydney	ACq		32 000	Huang Junjie CHN
6-09	Australia	W	2-0	Kuwait City	ACq	Khalaf Al Mutairi 55, Al Mutwa 60	8 000	Kamikawa JPN
11-10	Lithuania	W	1-0	Kuwait City	Fr	Al Hamad 11		Abo QAT
9-11	Chinese Taipei	W	10-0	Al Ain	Fr	Hakem 7, Faraj Laheeb 3 25 35 46, Al Shaikh 27, Al Otaibi 42, Al Rashidi 2 62 85, Al Mutwa 73, Khalaf Al Mutairi 75		
15-11	Bahrain	L	1-2	Manama	ACq	Faraj Laheeb 70	20 000	Kwon Jong Chul KOR
2007								
17-01	Yemen	D	1-1	Abu Dhabi	GCr1	Al Mutwa 73p		
20-01	Oman	L	1-2	Abu Dhabi	GCr1	Al Rashidi 81		
23-01	UAE	L	2-3	Abu Dhabi	GCr1	Al Mutwa 31, Al Hamad 35		
5-06	Portugal	D	1-1	Kuwait City	Fr	Faraj Laheeb 87	10 000	Al Marquozi UAE
12-06	Egypt	D	1-1	Kuwait City	Fr	Bashar 10		
2008								
2-01	Lebanon	W	3-2	Kuwait City	Fr	Ahmed Ajab 3 49 85 92+		
12-01	Côte d'Ivoire	L	0-2	Kuwait City	Fr			
16-01	Bahrain	L	0-1	Manama	Fr			
24-01	Singapore	L	0-2	Muscat	Fr			
30-01	Oman	D	1-1	Muscat	Fr	Ahmed Ajab 93+		
6-02	UAE	L	0-2	Abu Dhabi	WCq		19 000	Irmatov UZB
21-03	Iraq	D	0-0	Kuwait City	Fr			
26-03	Iran	D	2-2	Kuwait City	WCq	Ahmed Ajab 39, Al Rashidi 82	15 000	Breeze AUS
23-05	Qatar	D	1-1	Doha	Fr	Ahmed Ajab 20		
27-05	Saudi Arabia	L	1-2	Dammam	Fr	Ahmed Ajab 55		
2-06	Syria	L	0-1	Damascus	WCq		25 000	Mujghef JOR
8-06	Syria	W	4-2	Kuwait City	WCq	Ahmed Ajab 3 2 19 63, Waleed Jumah 58	10 000	Al Hilali OMA
14-06	UAE	L	2-3	Kuwait City	WCq	Ahmed Ajab 2 52 77	20 000	Mohd Salleh MAS
22-06	Iran	L	0-2	Tehran	WCq		20 000	Sun Baojie CHN

Fr = Friendly match • AC = AFC Asian Cup • GC = Gulf Cup • WC = FIFA World Cup • q = qualifier • r1 = first round group

KUWAIT NATIONAL TEAM RECORDS AND RECORD SEQUENCES

Records			Sequence records					
Victory	20-0	BHU 2000	Wins	7	1974	Clean sheets	7	1988
Defeat	0-8	EGY 1961, POR 2003	Defeats	5	1964-1965	Goals scored	17	1986-1987
Player Caps	134	Bashar Abdullah	Undefeated	21	1985-1987	Without goal	5	1988
Player Goals	75	Bashar Abdullah	Without win	12	1988	Goals against	18	1964-1971

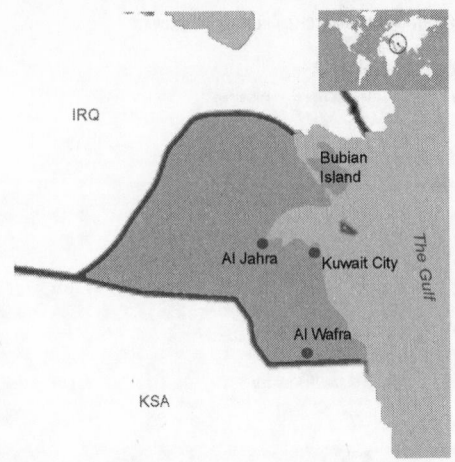

Population '000

	City	Pop.
1	Jaleeb al Shuyukh	177
2	Subbah al Salem	162
3	Salmiya	153
4	Al Qurayn	150
5	Hawalli	97
6	Farwaniya	92
7	Sulaibiah	84
8	Fahaheel	74
9	Tayma	73
10	Al Fardaws	70
11	Al Kuwayt	67
12	Al Qasr	61
13	Ardiya	58
14	Reqa	56
15	Abrak Khitan	50
16	Zahar	44
17	Salwa	42
18	Mangaf	42
19	Doha	42
20	Al Ahmadi	41
21	Sulaibkhat	36
22	Abu Hlaifa	31
23	Kaifan	30
24	Meshref	19

STATE OF KUWAIT; DAWLAT AL KUWAYT

Capital	Kuwait City	Language	Arabic	Independence	1961
Population	2 418 393	Area	17 820 km²	% in cities	97%
GDP per cap	$19 000	Dailling code	+965	Internet	.kw	GMT + / -	+3

All of the towns listed fall within the Al Kuwayt (Kuwait City) metropolitan area

MEDALS TABLE

	Overall G	S	B	League G	S	B	EC G	S	CPC G	S	Asia G	S	B	City	Stadium	Cap'ty	DoF
1 Al Arabi	36	14	3	16	3	3	15	10	5	1				Kuwait City	Sabah Al Salem	22 000	1960
2 Al Qadisiya	28	15	5	11	7	4	12	7	5	1			1	Kuwait City	Mohammed Al Hamad	20 000	1960
3 Al Kuwait	21	13	2	10	3	2	8	7	3	3				Kaifan	Al Kuwait SC	18 000	1960
4 Kazma	11	12	5	4	3	5	6	8	1	1				Kuwait City	Al Sadaqua Walsalam	21 500	1964
5 Salmiya	7	11	5	4	5	5	2	6	1					Salmiya	Thamer	14 000	1964
6 Al Yarmouk	2	2			1		2	1						Meshref	Meshref	12 000	1965
7 Al Jahra	1	2		1				2						Al Jahra			1966
8 Al Fahaheel	1						1							Fahaheel	Al Fahaheel	1 000	1964
9 Al Tadamon		5			1			4						Farwaniya	Al Farwaniya	14 000	1965
10 Al Nasr	1			1										Jaleeb al Shuyukh	Jaleeb al Shuyukh	15 000	1965
Al Sahel	1						1							Abu Hlaifa	Abu Halayfah	2 000	1967
12 Khitan														Abrak Khitan	Abraq Khitan	3 000	1965
Al Shabab														Al Ahmadi	Al Ahmadi	18 000	1963
Sulaibikhat														Kuwait City			1972

RECENT LEAGUE AND CUP RECORD

	Championship						Cup		
Year	Champions	Pts	Runners-up	Pts	Third	Pts	Winners	Score	Runners-up
1996	Kazma	24	Salmiya	22	Al Qadisiya	15	Al Arabi	2-1	Jahra
1997	Al Arabi						Kazma	2-0	Al Qadisiya
1998	Salmiya	64	Kazma	55	Al Qadisiya	50	Kazma	3-1	Al Arabi
1999	Al Qadisiya	1-0	Al Tadamon				Al Arabi	2-1	Al Sahel
2000	Salmiya	23	Al Qadisiya	20	Al Kuwait SC	15	Al Arabi	2-1	Al Tadamon
2001	Al Kuwait SC	28	Salmiya	24	Al Arabi	24	Salmiya	3-1	Kazma
2002	Al Arabi	26	Al Qadisiya	25	Salmiya	23	Al Kuwait SC	1-0	Jahra
2003	Al Qadisiya	28	Al Arabi	26	Kazma	24	Al Qadisiya	2-2 4-1p	Salimiya
2004	Al Qadisiya	2-1	Salmiya				Al Qadisiya	2-0	Al Kuwait SC
2005	Al Qadisiya	9	Al Kuwait SC	8	Al Arabi	6	Al Arabi	1-1 6-5p	Kazma
2006	Al Kuwait SC	66	Al Qadisiya	62	Salmiya	58	Al Arabi	2-2 3-2p	Al Qadisiya
2007	Al Kuwait SC	32	Kazma	32	Salmiya	31	Al Qadisiya	5-0	Salimiya
2008	Al Kuwait SC	35	Al Qadisiya	34	Salmiya	34	Al Arabi	2-1	Salmiya

KUWAIT 2007–08

PREMIER LEAGUE

	Pl	W	D	L	F	A	Pts	Kuwait	Qadisiya	Salmiya	Arabi	Kazma	Tadamon	Nasr	Sahel	Jahra
Al Kuwait SC †	16	11	2	3	25	10	35		1-1	0-1	1-0	1-0	0-0	2-0	2-0	2-0
Al Qadisiya	16	10	4	2	33	11	34	2-3		1-1	1-0	1-2	5-0	1-0	2-1	3-0
Salmiya	16	10	4	2	29	14	34	3-2	1-1		1-3	0-2	1-0	3-1	1-1	3-1
Al Arabi	16	8	3	5	25	18	27	1-2	0-1	0-0		4-2	2-0	0-0	0-1	3-1
Kazma	16	8	3	5	28	18	27	0-2	1-1	0-2	1-2		1-1	1-1	5-0	3-1
Al Tadamon	16	4	4	8	13	26	16	0-2	0-3	0-4	1-1	1-2		3-0	1-0	2-1
Al Nasr	16	4	3	9	16	31	15	1-2	0-6	2-3	1-3	2-4	1-0		3-1	1-1
Al Sahel	16	2	2	12	10	32	8	1-0	0-2	0-1	0-5	0-1	2-3	0-1		2-2
Jahra	16	1	3	12	13	37	6	0-3	1-2	0-5	0-1	0-3	1-1	1-2	3-1	

22/09/2007 - 4/04/2008 • † Qualified for the AFC Champions League

KUWAIT 2007–08 FIRST DIVISION (2)

	Pl	W	D	L	F	A	Pts
Al Shabab	12	4	7	1	12	9	19
Fehayheel	12	5	3	4	13	11	18
Solaybeekhat	12	5	3	4	21	21	18
Khitan	12	3	5	4	17	13	14
Al Yarmouk	12	2	4	6	10	19	9

29/09/2007 - 3/04/2008

CROWN PRINCE CUP 2007–08

First Round

Al Kuwait SC	Bye
Al Nasr	1 1 2 4p
Kazma	2 0 2 5p
Jahra	1 6
Fehayheel	0 4
Al Yarmouk	0 1
Al Tadamon	1 2
Salmiya	1 1
Solaybeekhat	1 0
Al Arabi	Bye
Khitan	1 3
Al Shabab	0 2
Al Sahel	1 1
Al Qadisiya	3 2

Quarter-finals

Al Kuwait SC	1 0
Kazma	1 0
Jahra	0 2
Al Tadamon	1 1
Salmiya	0 1
Al Arabi	0 0
Khitan	1 0
Al Qadisiya	4 3

Semi-finals

Al Kuwait SC	2 3
Al Tadamon	1 2
Salmiya	0 0
Al Qadisiya	2 0

Final

| Al Kuwait SC | 1 |
| Al Qadisiya | 0 |

CUP FINAL
Kuwait City
3-03-2008

EMIR CUP 2007–08

First Round

Al Arabi	5 0
Al Nasr	1 0
Al Shabab	2 1
Al Sahel	2 4
Kazma	1 2
Al Yarmouk	0 0
Al Qadisiya	Bye
Solaybeekhat	5 1
Al Tadamon	0 3
Jahra	1 1
Fehayheel	3 0
Al Kuwait SC	Bye
Khitan	0 0
Salmiya	2 2

Quarter-finals

Al Arabi	2 0
Al Sahel	0 0
Kazma	0 0
Al Qadisiya	1 1
Solaybeekhat	0 5
Fehayheel	0 0
Al Kuwait SC	1 0
Salmiya	1 1

Semi-finals

Al Arabi	0 2 4p
Al Qadisiya	2 0 3p
Solaybeekhat	0 0
Salmiya	1 0

Final replayed after the first match was abandoned at 1-1

† Qualified for the AFC Champions League

Final

| Al Arabi † | 2 |
| Salmiya | 1 |

CUP FINAL
Kuwait City
25-05-2008

LAO – LAOS

NATIONAL TEAM RECORD
JULY 10TH 2006 TO JULY 12TH 2010

PL	W	D	L	F	A	%
9	3	1	5	13	33	38.9

FIFA/COCA-COLA WORLD RANKING

1993	1994	1995	1996	1997	1998	1999	2000	2001	2002	2003	2004	2005	2006	2007
146	160	152	147	143	144	156	165	162	170	167	162	170	151	176

High **134** 09/98

	2007–2008										
08/07	09/07	10/07	11/07	12/07	01/08	02/08	03/08	04/08	05/08	06/08	07/08
165	170	175	175	176	178	185	184	187	187	190	189

Low **190** 06/08

Laos continue to sit on the periphery of the game on the continental and world stage and as a result football within the reclusive South East Asian state has suffered. The national team withdrew from the qualifying rounds of the AFC Challenge Cup, a tournament designed to help countries like Laos improve standards, while the Laos Football Federation did not even enter the team into the draw for the 2010 FIFA World Cup, although with a record of only one win in 14 games in their previous two attempts to qualify for the finals, that came as little surprise. Former France international defender Philippe Mahut took over as head coach in the first half of 2008 and he will take

INTERNATIONAL HONOURS
None

the team into the qualifying rounds of the ASEAN Championships in October, where the Laotians will face Cambodia, the Philippines, Timor-Leste and Brunei for one of two places in the finals. In 2006 they managed to do just that with three wins and a draw against the same opponents maintaining their record of appearing at the final stage every edition of the regional showcase. Laos' capital city Vientiane will host the 2009 edition of the South East Asian Games - which features a keenly contested under-23 football tournament - allowing the country to build a new sporting infrastructure to accommodate as many as 43 sporting events.

THE FIFA BIG COUNT OF 2006

	Male	Female		Total
Number of players	108 550	50	Referees and Assistant Referees	70
Professionals	0		Admin, Coaches, Technical, Medical	350
Amateurs 18+	1 400		Number of clubs	50
Youth under 18	1 200		Number of teams	150
Unregistered	23 000		Clubs with women's teams	0
Total players	108 600		Players as % of population	1.71%

Laos Football Federation (LFF)
Ban Houayhong, Chanthabuly District 3777 , Vientiane 856-21, Laos
Tel +856 21 560821   Fax +856 21 560820
laosff@laotel.com   www.none
President: INTHARA Kasem   General Secretary: XEUNVILAY Soulivanh
Vice-President: SIRIPANYA Boualane   Treasurer: KEOMANY Khammoui   Media Officer: VILAYSAK Sisay
Men's Coach: MAHUT Philippe   Women's Coach: SENGCHANH Viengcavanh
LFF formed: 1951   AFC: 1980   FIFA: 1952
Red shirts, Red shorts, Red socks

RECENT INTERNATIONAL MATCHES PLAYED BY LAOS

2004 Opponents	Score		Venue	Comp	Scorers	Att	Referee
18-02 Jordan	L	0-5	Amman	WCq		5 000	Al Mozahmi OMA
31-03 Iran	L	0-7	Vientiane	WCq		7 000	Yang Mu Sheng TPE
9-06 Qatar	L	0-5	Doha	WCq		500	Abu Armana PAL
8-09 Qatar	L	1-6	Vientiane	WCq	Chanthalome 88	2 900	Napitupulu IDN
13-10 Jordan	L	2-3	Vientiane	WCq	Phaphouvanin 13, Thongphachan 53	3 000	Gosh BAN
17-11 Iran	L	0-7	Tehran	WCq		30 000	Mamedov TKM
7-12 Indonesia	L	0-6	Ho Chi Minh City	TCr1			Mongkol THA
11-12 Cambodia	W	2-1	Hanoi	TCr1	Chalana 2 63 73	20 000	Kwong Jong Chul KOR
13-12 Singapore	L	2-6	Hanoi	TCr1	Phaphouvanin 22, Chalana 72p	17 000	Supian MAS
15-12 Vietnam	L	0-3	Hanoi	TCr1		20 000	Mongkul THA
2005							
No international matches played in 2005							
2006							
12-11 Philippines	W	2-1	Bacolod	TCq	Sisomephone 47, Phaphouvanin 49		
14-11 Cambodia	D	2-2	Bacolod	TCq	Soukhavong 30, Sisomephone 35		
16-11 Timor Leste	W	3-2	Bacolod	TCq	Saysongkham 34, Phothilath 61, Saynakhonevieng 91+		
18-11 Brunei Darussalam	W	4-1	Bacolod	TCq	Saysongkham 6, Phaphouvanin 17, Leupvisay 43, Phothilath 55		
2007							
13-01 Indonesia	L	1-3	Singapore	TCr1	Xaysongkham 13		
15-01 Singapore	L	0-11	Singapore	TCr1		5 224	U Hla Tint MYA
17-01 Vietnam	L	0-9	Singapore	TCr1		1 005	
22-08 Lesotho	L	1-3	Petaling Jaya	Fr	Visay Phaphouvanin		
25-08 Myanmar	L	0-1	Kuala Lumpur	Fr			
2008							
No international matches played in 2008 before August							

TC = Tiger Cup • AC = AFC Asian Cup 2004 • WC = FIFA World Cup • q = qualifier • r1 = first round group

LAOS NATIONAL TEAM RECORDS AND RECORD SEQUENCES

Records			Sequence records					
Victory	4-1	PHI	Wins	3	1993-1995	Clean sheets	3	1995
Defeat	0-12	OMA 2001	Defeats	11	1970-1974	Goals scored	9	1996-1998
Player Caps	n/a		Undefeated	4	1993-1995, 2006	Without goal	8	2000-2001
Player Goals	n/a		Without win	19	1970-1993	Goals against	14	1961-1969

RECENT LEAGUE AND CUP RECORD

Championship		Prime Minister's Cup		
Year	Champions	Winners	Score	Runners-up
2000	Vientiane Municipality			
2001				
2002	MCPTC			
2003	MCPTC	MCPTC	2-1	Army FC
2004	MCPTC	Vientiane FC	2-1	Savannakhet Province
2005	Vientiane FC		Not held	
2006	Vientiane FC	Lao-American College	3-1	Vientiane FC
2007	Lao-American College	MPWT	2-1	Savannakhet Province
2008				

LAOS COUNTRY INFORMATION

Capital	Vientiane	Independence	1953 from France	GDP per Capita	$1 700
Population	6 068 117	Status	Republic	GNP Ranking	143
Area km²	236 800	Language	Lao	Dialling code	+856
Population density	25.5 per km²	Literacy rate	66%	Internet code	.la
% in urban areas	22%	Main religion	Buddhist 60%	GMT +/–	+7
Towns/Cities ('000)	Vientiane 196; Pakxe 88; Savannakhet 66; Luang Prabang 47; Xam Nua 39; Xaignabury 31				
Neighbours (km)	China 423; Vietnam 2 130; Cambodia 541; Thailand 1 754; Burma 235				
Main stadia	National Stadium – Vientiane 18 000				

LBR – LIBERIA

NATIONAL TEAM RECORD
JULY 1OTH 2006 TO JULY 12TH 2010

PL	W	D	L	F	A	%
14	3	3	8	17	28	32.1

FIFA/COCA-COLA WORLD RANKING

1993	1994	1995	1996	1997	1998	1999	2000	2001	2002	2003	2004	2005	2006	2007
123	127	87	94	94	108	105	95	73	88	110	123	135	115	145

High	
66	07/01

				2007–2008							
08/07	09/07	10/07	11/07	12/07	01/08	02/08	03/08	04/08	05/08	06/08	07/08
120	129	143	146	145	144	145	145	138	138	136	139

Low	
146	11/07

Considerably more investment in football has yet to deliver the desired results but Liberia are hoping it will not take long to become competitive again. The Lone Star, the country's national team, were in the past propelled to the CAF Africa Cup of Nations finals and the brink of FIFA World Cup qualification by the magnetism of George Weah. Since his departure, and due to the civil strife in the country, Liberia's national team has survived on a shoe string as scarce resources have been directed elsewhere. But a change of government policy has recently seen more money for the side and the signing of a foreign coach in Antoine Hey. There has also been a budget for friendly warm-

INTERNATIONAL HONOURS
None

up matches outside of the country and training camps in Germany. Yet Liberia's footballers did not produce the desired results in June 2008 at the start of the 2010 FIFA World Cup qualifiers with two defeats and two draws, leaving the Lone Star at the bottom of their group. Elementary mistakes have been largely to blame for the mediocre returns, initially in the goalkeeping department where the recent retirement from international football of Swiss-based goalkeeper Louis Crayton has left a major gap. Meanwhile the country's league - won in 2007 by Invincible Eleven - has become a chaotic affair with threatened rebel breakaways and a myriad of legal actions.

THE FIFA BIG COUNT OF 2006

	Male	Female		Total
Number of players	162 667	600	Referees and Assistant Referees	206
Professionals	27		Admin, Coaches, Technical, Medical	450
Amateurs 18+	6 210		Number of clubs	45
Youth under 18	3 030		Number of teams	125
Unregistered	11 000		Clubs with women's teams	2
Total players	163 267		Players as % of population	5.37%

Liberia Football Association (FLFA)
Antoinette Tubman Stadium (ATS), PO Box 10-1066, Monrovia 1000, Liberia
Tel +231 6513037   Fax +231 227223
gwilliams@liberiafa.com   www.liberiafa.com
President: WESLEY Sombo   General Secretary: WILLIAMS George
Vice-President: BESTMAN Pennoh   Treasurer: KOON Joseph S.   Media Officer: None
Men's Coach: HEY Antoine   Women's Coach: TOGBA Lucretius
FLFA formed: 1936   CAF: 1962   FIFA: 1962
Blue shirts, White shorts, Red socks

RECENT INTERNATIONAL MATCHES PLAYED BY LIBERIA

2004	Opponents		Score	Venue	Comp	Scorers	Att	Referee
6-06	Mali	W	1-0	Monrovia	WCq	Kieh 85	30 000	Codjia BEN
20-06	Congo	L	0-3	Brazzaville	WCq		25 000	Lemghambodj MTN
4-07	Togo	D	0-0	Monrovia	WCq		30 000	Soumah GUI
4-09	Zambia	L	0-1	Lusaka	WCq		30 000	Nchengwa BOT
10-10	Senegal	L	0-3	Monrovia	WCq		26 000	Aboubacar CIV
2005								
26-03	Senegal	L	1-6	Dakar	WCq	Tondo 86	50 000	Shelmani LBY
5-06	Mali	L	1-4	Segou	WCq	Toe 54	11 000	Pare BFA
10-06	Sierra Leone	L	0-2	Freetown	Fr			
19-06	Congo	L	0-2	Paynesville	WCq		5 000	Sillah GAM
4-09	Togo	L	0-3	Lome	WCq		28 000	Abdel Rahman SUD
1-10	Zambia	L	0-5	Monrovia	WCq		0	Evehe CMR
2006								
3-09	Equatorial Guinea	L	1-2	Malabo	CNq	Krangar 35		Agbenyega GHA
8-10	Rwanda	W	3-2	Monrovia	CNq	Doe 27, Makor 68, Williams 76		Olatunde NGA
2007								
24-03	Cameroon	L	1-3	Yaoundé	CNq	Doe 39		Djaoupe TOG
3-06	Cameroon	L	1-2	Monrovia	CNq	Mennoh 65		Coulibaly MLI
17-06	Equatorial Guinea	D	0-0	Monrovia	CNq			Diouf SEN
8-09	Rwanda	L	0-4	Kigali	CNq			Mwanza ZAM
2008								
26-03	Sudan	W	2-0	Omdurman	Fr	Lomell 46, Mennoh 57		
24-04	Oman	L	0-1	Muscat	Fr			
30-04	Sierra Leone	W	3-1	Paynesville	Fr	Krangar 21, Laffor 58, Zortiah 86		
27-05	Libya	L	2-4	Tripoli	Fr	Lomell 56, Zortiah 88		
1-06	Gambia	D	1-1	Monrovia	WCq	Makor 82	35 000	Keita GUI
6-06	Algeria	L	0-3	Blida	WCq		40 000	Lemghambodj MTN
15-06	Senegal	D	2-2	Monrovia	WCq	Williams 74, Makor 85	18 000	Djaoupe TOG
21-06	Senegal	L	1-3	Dakar	WCq	Williams 89	40 000	Chaibou NIG

CN = CAF African Cup of Nations • WC = FIFA World Cup • q = qualifier

LIBERIA NATIONAL TEAM RECORDS AND RECORD SEQUENCES

Records			Sequence records				
Victory	4-0	GAM 1996, MRI 2000	Wins	4	2001	Clean sheets	4	1987-1995
Defeat	2-7	TUN 2001	Defeats	9	2004-2006	Goals scored	8	2001, 2001-02
Player Caps	n/a		Undefeated	11	1994-1995	Without goal	4	Six times
Player Goals	n/a		Without win	17	1971-1980	Goals against	13	1984-1986

RECENT LEAGUE AND CUP RECORD

	Championship	Cup
Year	Champions	Winners
2001	Mighty Barolle	
2002	LPRC Oilers	Mighty Blue Angels
2003	Not finished	
2004	Mighty Barolle	LISCR FC
2005	LPRC Oilers	LPRC Oilers
2006	Mighty Barolle	NPA Anchors
2007	Invincible Eleven	St Joseph Warriors

LIBERIA COUNTRY INFORMATION

Capital	Monrovia	Independence	1847	GDP per Capita	$1 000
Population	3 390 635	Status	Republic	GNP Ranking	171
Area km²	111 370	Language	English	Dialling code	+231
Population density	30 per km²	Literacy rate	57%	Internet code	.lr
% in urban areas	45%	Main religion	Christian & Indigenous 40%	GMT +/-	0
Cities/Towns ('000)	Monrovia 935; Gbarnga 45; Bensonville 33; Harper 33; Buchanan 26; Zwedru 26				
Neighbours (km)	Guinea 563; Côte d'Ivoire 716; Sierra Leone 306; Atlantic Ocean 579				
Main stadia	Samuel Doe Sports Complex – Monrovia 35 000; Antoinette Tubman – Monrovia 10 000				

LBY – LIBYA

NATIONAL TEAM RECORD
JULY 10TH 2006 TO JULY 12TH 2010

PL	W	D	L	F	A	%
26	10	8	8	30	26	53.8

FIFA/COCA-COLA WORLD RANKING

1993	1994	1995	1996	1997	1998	1999	2000	2001	2002	2003	2004	2005	2006	2007	High	
152	167	175	184	147	147	131	116	116	104	83	61	80	99	95	**61**	12/04

2007–2008												Low	
08/07	09/07	10/07	11/07	12/07	01/08	02/08	03/08	04/08	05/08	06/08	07/08	**187**	07/97
87	92	104	95	95	93	85	85	90	90	84	90		

After the breakthrough of qualifying for the 2006 CAF Africa Cup of Nations finals in Egypt, Libya missed out on a trip to the 2008 finals in Ghana. They were competitive throughout the qualifiers but dropped key points away from home, although the 1-1 draw away in Kinshasa against Congo DR in September in their last group match did prove the surprise result of the campaign. The obvious improvement in their performance was also evident in the FIFA World Cup qualifiers, where they began their campaign for a place at the 2010 finals in South Africa with a loss in Ghana but followed it up with three successive victories. It has left the north Africans, whose are coached

INTERNATIONAL HONOURS
None

by the Tunisian Faouzi Benzarti, well placed to advance to the next phase of the African preliminaries. At club level, Al Ittihad reached the semifinal of the 2007 African Champions League in a surprise achievement for a club who have only once before been to the final four of an African club competition. Al Ittihad finished behind Tunisia's Etoile Sahel in their group and pushed the Egyptians giants Al Ahly in the semifinals, eventually exiting only through an own goal. In July 2008, Al Ittihad won a fourth successive league title but hopes of repeat success in the 2007 Champions League came crashing down with a defeat at the hands of TP Mazembe Englebert.

THE FIFA BIG COUNT OF 2006

	Male	Female		Total
Number of players	263 800	0	Referees and Assistant Referees	300
Professionals	0		Admin, Coaches, Technical, Medical	2 100
Amateurs 18+	5 500		Number of clubs	110
Youth under 18	2 800		Number of teams	550
Unregistered	22 000		Clubs with women's teams	0
Total players	263 800		Players as % of population	4.47%

Libyan Football Federation (LFF)
General Sports Federations Building, Sports City, Gorji, PO Box 5137, Tripoli 02, Libya
Tel +218 21 4782009   Fax +218 21 4782006
libyaff@hotmail.com   www.lff.ly.com
President: EL JAAFRI Jamal Saleh   General Secretary: AL SAEDY Ahmed Abdulmagid
Vice-President: EL NAAS Musa Shibani   Treasurer: EL MUGHRBI Abdulmula   Media Officer: EL ASWAD Ali
Men's Coach: BENZARTI Faouzi   Women's Coach: AL NWESRI El Hadi Bashir
LFF formed: 1962   CAF: 1965   FIFA: 1963
Green shirts with white trimmings, Green shorts, Green socks or White shirts with green trimmings, White shorts, White socks

RECENT INTERNATIONAL MATCHES PLAYED BY LIBYA

2005	Opponents	Score		Venue	Comp	Scorers	Att	Referee
27-05	Malawi	D	1-1	Tripoli	Fr			
3-06	Côte d'Ivoire	D	0-0	Tripoli	WCq		45 000	Lim Kee Chong MRI
19-06	Cameroon	L	0-1	Yaoundé	WCq		36 000	Coulibaly MLI
17-08	Nigeria	L	0-1	Tripoli	Fr			
24-08	Iran	L	0-4	Tehran	Fr			
2-09	Sudan	D	0-0	Tripoli	WCq			
9-10	Benin	L	0-1	Cotonou	WCq			
16-11	Congo DR	W	2-1	Paris	Fr	Younus Al Shibani [25], Erwani [76]		
2-12	United Arab Emirates	D	1-1	Sharjah	Fr	Omar Dawood [39]		
2006								
2-01	Qatar	L	0-2	Doha	Fr			
12-01	Tunisia	L	0-1	Radès/Tunis	Fr			
20-01	Egypt	L	0-3	Cairo	CNr1		65 000	Pare BFA
24-01	Côte d'Ivoire	L	1-2	Cairo	CNr1	Khamis [41]	42 000	Maidin SIN
28-01	Morocco	D	0-0	Cairo	CNr1		5 000	Daami TUN
30-05	Uruguay	L	1-2	Rades/Tunis	Fr	Tarek Tayeb [61]		
2-06	Belarus	D	1-1	Rades/Tunis	Fr	Osman [90]. W 3-1p		
5-06	Ukraine	L	0-3	Gossau	Fr		2 500	Wilzhaber SUI
5-08	Sryia	L	1-2	Damascus	Fr	Osman [61]		
16-08	Uganda	W	3-2	Tripoli	Fr	Tarek Tayeb [59], Osman [72], Khaled Hussain [90]		
26-08	Yemen	W	1-0	Sana'a	Fr	Kara [16]		
29-08	Yemen	D	1-1	Sana'a	Fr			
3-09	Ethiopia	L	0-1	Addis Abeba	CNq			AbdelFattah EGY
1-10	Sudan	W	1-0	Tripoli	Fr	El Masli [24]		
8-10	Congo DR	D	1-1	Tripoli	CNq	Khaled Hussain [75]		Pare BFA
15-11	Tunisia	L	0-2	Rades/Tunis	Fr			
2007								
7-02	Algeria	L	1-2	Algiers	Fr	Younus Al Shibani [48]		
20-03	Mauritania	D	0-0	Tripoli	Fr			
25-03	Namibia	W	2-1	Tripoli	CNq	Salem Rewani [12], Tarek Tayeb [66]		Abdelrahman SUD
27-05	Botswana	D	0-0	Gaborone	Fr			
2-06	Namibia	L	0-1	Windhoek	CNq			Ncobo RSA
17-06	Ethiopia	W	3-1	Tripoli	CNq	Ahmed Zuwai 2 [10 47], Salem Rewani [22]		Saadallah TUN
22-08	Sudan	L	0-1	Khartoum	Fr			
8-09	Congo DR	D	1-1	Kinshasa	CNq	Khaled Hussain [51]		Djaoupe TOG
16-10	Bahrain	L	0-2	Al Muharraq	Fr			
18-11	Saudi Arabia	W	2-1	Ismailia	Fr	Osama Al Fazzani [24], Omar Dawood [94+]		
21-11	Egypt	D	0-0	Port Said	Fr			
2008								
26-03	Uganda	D	1-1	Kampala	Fr	Younus Al Shibani [89]		
22-05	Zambia	D	2-2	Tripoli	Fr	Osama Al Fazzani 2 [13 61]		
27-05	Liberia	W	4-1	Tripoli	Fr	Ali Rahuma [4], Omar Dawood [11], Mohamed Al Magrabi [77], Ali Rahuma [82]		
1-06	Ghana	L	0-3	Kumasi	WCq		27 908	Maillet SEY
7-06	Gabon	W	1-0	Tripoli	WCq	Brou OG [5]	30 000	Chaibou NIG
15-06	Lesotho	W	1-0	Bloemfontein	WCq	Ahmed Osman [85]	3 500	Marange ZIM
20-06	Lesotho	W	4-0	Tripoli	WCq	Osama Salah [3], Omar Dawood [50], Younus Al Shibani [68], Hesham Shaban [80]	30 000	Trabelsi TUN

Fr = Friendly match • CN = CAF African Cup of Nations • WC = FIFA World Cup • q = qualifier • r1 = first round

LIBYA NATIONAL TEAM RECORDS AND RECORD SEQUENCES

Records			Sequence records				
Victory	21-0	OMA 1966	Wins	5	2003-04, 2004	Clean sheets	4	1996, 2003-04
Defeat	2-10	EGY 1953	Defeats	5	1953-1960	Goals scored	15	1998-1999
Player Caps	n/a	Tarik El Taib	Undefeated	7	1982-1983	Without goal	6	2005
Player Goals	n/a		Without win	10	2005-2006	Goals against	16	1953-65. 1992-99

LIBYA

Capital	Tripoli	Language	Arabic			Independence	1951
Population	6 036 914	Area	1 759 540 km²	Density	3 per km²	% in cities	86%
GDP per cap	$6400	Dailling code	+218	Internet	.ly	GMT + / -	+1

MEDALS TABLE

		Overall			Lge	Cup	Africa			City	Stadium	Cap'ty	DoF
		G	S	B	G	G	G	S	B				
1	Al Ittihad	20		1	14	6			1	Tripoli	11th June	80 000	1944
2	Al Ahly	19		1	10	9			1	Tripoli	11th June	80 000	1920
3	Al Ahly	9			4	5				Benghazi	28th March	55 000	1950
4	Al Nasr	6		1	1	5			1	Benghazi	28th March	55 000	1954
5	Al Medina	5			3	2				Tripoli	11th June	80 000	1953
6	Al Tahaddy	3			3					Benghazi	28th March	55 000	1954
7	Al Mahalah	2			2					Tripoli			
	Al Shaat	2			1	1				Tripoli	11th June	80 000	1982
9	Al Dahra	1			1					Tripoli			
	Al Olympique	1			1					Az-Zawiyah	Al Olympique	14 000	1947
	Al Hilal	1				1				Benghazi			
	Al Soukour	1				1				Tobruk	Tobruk	2 000	1947
	Al Wahda	1				1				Tripoli	Al Wahda	3 000	1954
	Libya FC	1				1				Tripoli			
	Khaleej Sirt	1				1				Sirt	Sirt	2 000	1963

RECENT LEAGUE AND CUP RECORD

	Championship						Cup		
Year	Champions	Pts	Runners-up	Pts	Third	Pts	Winners	Score	Runners-up
1997	Al Tahaddi Benghazi	54	Al Ahly Tripoli	53	Al Ittihad Tripoli	51	Al Nasr Benghazi	1-1 4-3p	Al Yarmouk
1998	Al Mahalah Tripoli						Al Shaat Tripoli	1-1 4-2p	Al Hilal Benghazi
1999	Al Mahalah Tripoli	30	Al Shat Tripoli	23	Al Hilal Benghazi	21	Al Ittihad Ytipoli	2-0	Al Tahaddi Benghazi
2000	Al Ahly Tripoli	1-0	Al Hilal Benghazi				Al Ahly Tripoli	2-0	Al Shawehly Misurata
2001	Al Medina Tripoli	1-1	Al Tahaddi Benghazi						
2002	Al Ittihad Tripoli	67	Al Nasr Benghazi	67	Al Hilal Benghazi	52			
2003	Al Ittihad Tripoli	65	Al Nasr Benghazi	52	Al Hilal Benghazi	43			
2004	Olympique Az-Zwiyah	57	Al Ittihad Tripoli	52	Al Ahly Tripoli	51	Al Ittihad Tripoli	0-0 8-7p	Al Hilal
2005	Al Ittihad Tripoli	51	Al Uruba	43	Olympique Az-Zwiyah	42	Al Ittihad Tripoli	3-0	Al Akhdar Darnah
2006	Al Ittihad Tripoli	27	Al Ittihad Tripoli	27	Al Akhdar Darnah	10	Al Ahly Tripoli	2-1	Olympique Az-Zwiyah
2007	Al Ittihad Tripoli	55	Al Ahly Tripoli	49	Al Madina Tripoli	43	Al Ittihad Tripoli	1-0	Al Akhdar Darnah
2008	Al Ittihad Tripoli	82	Al Ahly Tripoli	75	Al Ahly Benghazi	55	Khaleej Sart	1-0	Al Madina

Al Medina won the 2001 Championship on penalties after a 1-1 draw

LIBYA 2007–08

FIRST DIVISION

	Pl	W	D	L	F	A	Pts	Ittihad	Ahly Tripoli	Ahly Benghazi	Akhdar	Khaleej	Nasr	Medina	Olympique	Shat	Jazira	Tirsana	Wahda	Tahaddi	Oruba	Soukour	Ngom
Al Ittihad †	30	26	4	0	68	16	82		1-1	2-1	5-2	5-1	1-0	1-1	1-0	2-1	2-1	1-0	1-0	1-0	3-0	3-1	6-0
Al Ahly Tripoli	30	23	6	1	77	28	75	2-2		3-1	4-1	2-0	1-0	2-1	2-1	4-0	3-0	5-2	5-1	3-0	3-1	10-2	1-0
Al Ahly Benghazi	30	15	10	5	44	20	55	0-1	1-1		2-0	5-0	0-0	0-0	1-0	3-0	1-1	2-1	2-1	3-1	4-0	3-0	2-2
Al Akhdar §3	30	15	8	7	48	33	50	0-2	2-2	0-1		2-0	0-0	1-0	2-2	3-0	1-0	2-0	3-0	1-1	1-0	3-0	2-1
Khaleej Sirt	30	11	8	11	34	35	41	0-1	0-1	0-0	1-4		1-1	1-1	1-1	0-1	4-1	4-2	2-2	0-1	3-1	4-0	2-0
Al Nasr §1	30	11	9	10	39	29	41	1-2	1-1	0-0	1-3	0-1		3-1	1-1	2-1	1-1	2-0	1-2	2-0	3-1	5-1	4-1
Al Medina	30	9	13	8	27	26	40	0-1	2-2	1-1	1-1	1-0	0-2		0-1	2-0	0-0	1-0	2-1	1-1	2-2	2-0	1-0
Al Olympique	30	9	12	9	36	34	39	0-0	2-3	2-1	1-1	0-2	0-0	0-0		0-1	1-1	1-1	1-2	3-2	0-3	1-0	5-0
Al Shat	30	11	3	16	34	47	36	0-1	1-2	0-2	3-3	0-0	**2-0**	1-0	2-1		2-1	3-5	1-3	2-3	1-0	3-2	3-0
Al Jazira	30	9	8	13	27	37	35	0-3	0-1	0-2	1-0	2-1	2-1	1-1	1-2	3-1		0-0	1-1	1-0	0-1	2-0	1-0
Al Tirsana	30	8	9	13	32	40	33	0-2	3-4	0-0	0-1	0-1	0-0	2-1	1-1	1-1	1-1		1-0	3-2	0-1	2-0	0-0
Al Wahda	30	6	15	9	38	48	33	1-5	1-2	2-1	0-1	0-2	2-1	1-2	0-1	1-0	2-0	0-0		0-0	1-1	6-1	3-2
Al Tahaddi	30	8	9	13	37	42	33	1-2	1-0	2-2	2-1	0-0	1-3	0-0	1-1	0-1	2-0	0-1	3-3		0-0	3-1	5-1
Al Oruba	30	9	4	17	29	47	31	1-4	1-2	0-1	2-3	1-2	2-1	0-1	1-2	0-2	1-0	0-2	2-1	3-1		2-1	2-1
Al Soukour §1	30	6	3	21	23	69	20	0-4	0-1	0-1	0-0	0-0	0-1	0-1	2-2	1-0	1-3	2-1	2-1	1-0	2-0		1-2
Ngom Ajdabiya	30	3	4	23	25	67	13	1-3	0-2	0-1	1-4	0-1	1-2	1-1	1-3	2-1	1-2	2-3	2-0	2-4	0-0	1-2	

20/09/2007 – 22/07/2008 • † Qualified for the CAF Champions League • Match in bold awarded • § = points deducted

AL FATIH CUP 2007–08

Round of 16
Kaleej Sirt	1	4p	
Al Wahda *	1	3p	
Al Ittihad	0	2p	
Al Akhdar *	0	4p	
Al Ahly Benghazi *	6		
Al Najma	0		
Darnes *	0		
Al Ahly Tripoli †	2		
Al Nasr * †	2		
Al Oruba	0		
Al Tahaddi	0		
Al Hilal *	2		
Ngom Ajdabiya	0	4p	
Al Yarmouk *	0	1p	
Al Olomby	1		
Al Madina *	2		

Quarter-finals
Kaleej Sirt	3
Al Akhdar	2
Al Ahly Benghazi	0 4p
Al Ahly Tripoli	0 5p
Al Nasr	1
Al Hilal	0
Ngom Ajdabiya	0
Al Madina	1

Semi-finals
Kaleej Sirt	5
Al Ahly Tripoli	2
Al Nasr	0
Al Madina	2

Final
Kaleej Sirt	1
Al Madina	0

CUP FINAL
26-07-2008
Scorer - Adress Salem [81]

* Home team • † Awarded • ‡ Qualified for the CAF Confederation Cup

LCA – ST LUCIA

NATIONAL TEAM RECORD
JULY 10TH 2006 TO JULY 12TH 2010

PL	W	D	L	F	A	%
10	1	0	9	8	41	10

FIFA/COCA-COLA WORLD RANKING

1993	1994	1995	1996	1997	1998	1999	2000	2001	2002	2003	2004	2005	2006	2007		High	
139	157	114	134	142	139	152	135	130	112	130	114	128	160	180		**108**	04/03

	2007–2008												Low	
08/07	09/07	10/07	11/07	12/07	01/08	02/08	03/08	04/08	05/08	06/08	07/08		**185**	03/08
158	163	163	177	180	181	184	185	168	168	166	162			

2008 got off to a terrible start for football in St Lucia when the national team suffered an embarrassing defeat at the hands of the Turks and Caicos Islands in the qualifiers for the 2010 FIFA World Cup in South Africa. It was a tie St Lucia were expected to win with ease but the 2-1 defeat in Providenciales gave their opponents a first-ever World Cup win and sent St Lucia plummeting to their lowest position in the FIFA/Coca-Cola World Ranking. Coach Terrence Caroo and his squad of largely home based players were confident that they could overturn the deficit in the return at the National Stadium in Vieux Fort and that's exactly what they did although it took a late

INTERNATIONAL HONOURS
None

goal from Titus Elve to secure a 2-0 win and a place in the next round, where they faced Guatemala. With even the big Caribbean islands like Jamaica and Trinidad struggling to match the standards in Central America, there was only ever going to be one winner of that tie - the Guatemalans winning 9-1 on aggregate - but if standards are to rise in St Lucia the FA will either have to look for players with links to the island in countries like England, or try to give home-based players more international experience at club level by taking part in the Caribbean preliminaries of the newly launched CONCACAF Champions League.

THE FIFA BIG COUNT OF 2006

	Male	Female		Total
Number of players	9 560	1 463	Referees and Assistant Referees	66
Professionals	0		Admin, Coaches, Technical, Medical	324
Amateurs 18+	2 413		Number of clubs	40
Youth under 18	650		Number of teams	125
Unregistered	1 960		Clubs with women's teams	1
Total players	11 023		Players as % of population	6.54%

St Lucia Football Association (SLFA)
La Clery, PO Box 255, Castries, St Lucia
Tel +1 758 4530687   Fax +1 758 4560510
slfa@candw.lc   www.none
President: MATHURIN Patrick   General Secretary: BOXIL Brian
Vice-President: COOPER Lydon   Treasurer: BOXIL Brian   Media Officer: PIERRE Michel
Men's Coach: CAROO Terrence   Women's Coach: KIRTON Sean
SLFA formed: 1979   CONCACAF: 1988   FIFA: 1988
Colours: White with yellow/blue/black stripe, White with yellow/blue/black stripe, White/blue/yellow

RECENT INTERNATIONAL MATCHES PLAYED BY ST LUCIA

2004	Opponents	Score		Venue	Comp	Scorers	Att	Referee
2-06	Grenada	L	0-2	St George's	Fr		2 500	
13-06	Panama	L	0-4	Panama City	WCq		15 000	Phillip GRN
20-06	Panama	L	0-3	Vieux Fort	WCq		400	Gurley VIN
17-10	Grenada	W	3-1	Castries	Fr	Gilbert 3		
2-11	St Kitts and Nevis	D	1-1	Basseterre	CCq	Gilbert 67		Bedeau GRN
4-11	Montserrat	W	3-0	Basseterre	CCq	St Lucia awarded match 3-0		
6-11	Antigua and Barbuda	W	2-1	Basseterre	CCq	Elva 22, Gilbert 27		Bedeau GRN
12-12	Jamaica	D	1-1	Vieux Fort	CCq	Joseph.E 23		Jeanvillier MTQ
19-12	Jamaica	L	1-2	Kingston	CCq	Elva 23	2 500	Gutierrez CUB
2005								
No international matches played in 2005								
2006								
28-07	Guyana	L	2-3	Linden	Fr	Elva 62, Gilbert Levi 70		Lancaster GUY
30-07	Guyana	L	0-2	Georgetown	Fr			James GUY
27-09	Jamaica	L	0-4	Kingston	CCq		4 000	Tamayo CUB
29-09	Haiti	L	1-7	Kingston	CCq	Valcin 90	3 000	Callendar BRB
1-10	St Vincent/Grenadines	L	0-8	Kingston	CCq		3 000	Tamayo CUB
2007								
No international matches played in 2007								
2008								
6-02	Turks and Caicos Isl	L	1-2	Providenciales	WCq	Gilbert 92+	2 200	Whittaker CAY
26-03	Turks and Caicos Isl	W	2-0	Vieux Fort	WCq	McPhee 28, Elva 85	1 200	Forde BRB
18-05	Antigua and Barbuda	L	1-6	St John's	Fr	Bledman 91+		
14-06	Guatemala	L	0-6	Guatemala City	WCq		24 600	Archundia MEX
21-06	Guatemala	L	1-3	Los Angeles	WCq	McPhee 45	12 000	Wijngaarde SUR

Fr = Friendly match • CC = Digicel Caribbean Cup • WC = FIFA World Cup • q = qualifier • † Not a full international

NATIONAL TEAM RECORDS AND RECORD SEQUENCES

Records			Sequence records					
Victory	14-1	VIR 2001	Wins	5	2000	Clean sheets	5	1990-1991
Defeat	0-8	VIN 2006	Defeats	6	2004-2006	Goals scored	14	1999-2000
Player Caps	n/a		Undefeated	7	1982-1983	Without goal	3	2004
Player Goals	n/a		Without win	7	2004-2006	Goals against	12	2001-02

RECENT LEAGUE AND CUP RECORD

	Championship		Cup		
Year	Champions	Winners	Score	Runners-up
2000	Roots Alley Ballers	Rovers United	3-2	Northern United
2001	VSADC	VSADC	2-1	Roots Alley Ballers
2002	VSADC	VSADC	1-1 9-8p	Cimpex Orion
2003	No tournament played	18 Plus	2-1	Pioneers FC
2004	Roots Alley Ballers	Northern United		Rovers United
2005	Northern United	No tournament played		
2006	Canaries	Elite Challengers	1-1 3-2p	Canaries
2007	Anse Chastanet GYSO	Northern United	5-0	Orion
2008				

ST LUCIA COUNTRY INFORMATION

Capital	Castries	Independence	1979 from the UK	GDP per Capita	$5 400
Population	164 213	Status	Parliamentary democracy	GNP Ranking	165
Area km²	616	Language	English	Dialling code	+1758
Population density	266 per km²	Literacy rate	67%	Internet code	.lc
% in urban areas	48%	Main religion	Christian	GMT +/-	-4
Towns/Cities ('000)	Castries 13; Vieux Fort 4; Micoud 3; Dennery 3; Soufrière 3; Gros Islet 2				
Neighbours (km)	Atlantic Ocean & Caribbean Sea 158				
Main stadia	Bones Park – Castries 20 000; National Stadium – Vieux Fort				

LES – LESOTHO

NATIONAL TEAM RECORD
JULY 10TH 2006 TO JULY 12TH 2010

PL	W	D	L	F	A	%
25	5	5	15	21	39	30

FIFA/COCA-COLA WORLD RANKING

1993	1994	1995	1996	1997	1998	1999	2000	2001	2002	2003	2004	2005	2006	2007	High	
138	135	149	162	149	140	154	136	126	132	120	144	145	160	154	120	12/03

2007–2008												Low	
08/07	09/07	10/07	11/07	12/07	01/08	02/08	03/08	04/08	05/08	06/08	07/08	166	03/07
143	153	154	154	154	154	156	156	163	159	150	159		

Lesotho continued to struggle from a lack of playing resources, the disadvantage of a small population evident as the national side was swiftly cast out of the running in the 2010 FIFA World Cup qualifiers. Lesotho were forced to moved their home matches to nearby Bloemfontein in South Africa because of the unsuitability of the ground in Maseru and they lost both 'home' ties to Ghana and Libya in what was difficult start to the tenure of Serbian coach Zavisa Milosaveljvic, a rare foreign appointment at the helm of Likuena (The Crocodiles). There was also further disappointment with an early exit at the Cosafa Senior Challenge tournament in South Africa in July 2008. At club

INTERNATIONAL HONOURS
None

level, a FIFA initiative to professionalise football in the mountain kingdom led to a fundamental rethink by the top division's club chairman. The 'Mohale Declaration', put together at a week-long get away, is to cut the size of the league and make radical changes to basic structures. It remains a constant complaint that the best players are continually poached by teams like Lesotho Correctional Service, Lesotho Police Services or Lesotho Defence Force, because they can offer jobs to footballers in a country where unemployment levels are exceedingly high and players do not earn wages from the game. Little wonder then that LCS were crowned 2008 champions.

THE FIFA BIG COUNT OF 2006

	Male	Female		Total
Number of players	109 900	100	Referees and Assistant Referees	100
Professionals	0		Admin, Coaches, Technical, Medical	2 200
Amateurs 18+	27 200		Number of clubs	110
Youth under 18	2 300		Number of teams	1 000
Unregistered	5 500		Clubs with women's teams	0
Total players	110 000		Players as % of population	5.44%

Lesotho Football Association (FAL)
Old Polo Ground, PO Box 1879, Maseru-100, Lesotho
Tel +266 22311879   Fax +266 22310586
fal@leo.co.ls
President: PHAFANE Salemane   General Secretary: SEMATLANE Mafole
Vice-President: MOSOTHOANE Pitso   Treasurer: TBD   Media Officer: MONNE Tslu
Men's Coach: MILOSAVLJEVIC Zavisa   Women's Coach: MOKHATI Likhetho
LEFA formed: 1932   CAF: 1964   FIFA: 1964
Blue shirts, Green shorts, White socks

RECENT INTERNATIONAL MATCHES PLAYED BY LESOTHO

2007	Opponents	Score		Venue	Comp	Scorers	Att	Referee
25-05	Zimbabwe	D	1-1	Masvingo	Fr	Thulo Ranchobe [58]		
3-06	Niger	L	0-2	Niamey	CNq			Kotey GHA
19-06	Uganda	D	0-0	Maseru	CNq			Mwandike TAN
28-07	Angola	L	0-2	Gaborone	CCr1			Disang BOT
29-07	Namibia	L	2-3	Gaborone	CCr1	Sello Musa 2 [84 87p]		Disang BOT
20-08	Myanmar	L	0-1	Petaling Jaya	Fr			
22-08	Laos	W	3-1	Petaling Jaya	Fr	Refiloe Potse [3], Tefo Maipato [6], Katleho Moleko [23]		
8-09	Nigeria	L	0-2	Warri	Fr			
2008								
10-02	Lesotho	D	2-2	Mbabane	Fr	Bushy Moletsane [33], Thabo Motsweli [87]. W 4-1p		
21-05	Mozambique	W	3-2	Maputo	Fr	Thabane Rankara 2 [23 50], Retselisitswe Molisana [28]		
23-05	Swaziland	D	1-1	Mbabane	Fr	Sello Musa [51]		
8-06	Ghana	L	2-3	Bloemfontein	WCq	Sello Musa [89], Lehlohonolo Seema [90]	8 000	Gasingwa RWA
15-06	Libya	L	0-1	Bloemfontein	WCq		3 500	Marange ZIM
20-06	Libya	L	0-4	Tripoli	WCq		30 000	Trabelsi TUN
28-06	Gabon	L	0-2	Libreville	WCq		15 000	Mendy GAM
20-07	Malawi	L	0-1	Secunda	CCr1			Seechurn MRI
22-07	Namibia	D	1-1	Secunda	CCr1	Thabane Rankara [80]		Seechurn MRI
24-07	Comoros	W	1-0	Secunda	CCr1	Moli Lesesa [50]		Labrosse SEY

Fr = Friendly match • CN = CAF African Cup of Nations • CC = COSAFA Castle Cup • WC = FIFA World Cup • q = qualifier • r1 = first round group

LESOTHO NATIONAL TEAM RECORDS AND RECORD SEQUENCES

Records			Sequence records				
Victory	5-0	SWZ 2006	Wins	3	1979	Clean sheets	3	1992
Defeat	0-7	COD 1993	Defeats	6	1995-1997	Goals scored	6	1992
Player Caps	n/a		Undefeated	7	1992	Without goal	4	2006-2007
Player Goals	n/a		Without win	11	1981-1992	Goals against	12	2000-2001

LESOTHO 2007-08 BUDDIE PREMIER LEAGUE

	Pl	W	D	L	F	A	Pts
LCS Maseru	30	20	7	3	52	20	67
LDF Maseru	30	18	8	4	46	19	62
Matlama	30	16	6	8	48	31	54
Linare	30	16	5	9	42	25	53
LMPS Maseru	30	13	12	5	35	20	51
Lioli	30	13	8	9	43	26	47
Lerotholi Polytechnic	30	8	14	8	32	30	38
Majantja	30	9	11	10	33	32	38
Mphatlalatsane	30	9	9	12	35	44	36
Mazenod Swallows	30	8	9	13	30	38	33
Likhopo	30	8	9	13	25	33	33
Maseru Naughty Boys	30	9	5	16	27	42	32
Joy	30	6	13	11	19	29	31
Roma Rovers	30	7	9	14	29	41	30
Arsenal	30	9	3	18	31	48	30
Qalo	30	4	6	20	22	71	18

1/09/2007 - 29/06/2008

RECENT LEAGUE AND CUP RECORD

Championship		Cup
Year Champions		Winners
2000	LPS Maseru	RLDF Maseru
2001	RLDF Maseru	
2002	LPS Maseru	
2003	Matlama FC Maseru	
2004	RLDF Maseru	
2005	Likhopo Maseru	
2006	Likhopo Maseru	
2007	LCS Maseru	
2008	LCS Maseru	

LESOTHO COUNTRY INFORMATION

Capital	Maseru	Independence	1966 from the UK	GDP per Capita	3 000
Population	1 865 040	Status	Constutional Monarchy	GNP Ranking	153
Area km²	30 355	Language	Sesotho, English	Dialling code	+266
Population density	61 per km²	Literacy rate	84%	Internet code	.ls
% in urban areas	23%	Main religion	Christian 80%	GMT +/−	+2
Towns/Cities ('000)	Maseru 194; Hlotse 46; Mafeteng 40; Maputsoa 31; Teyateyaneng 25; Mohale's Hoek 22				
Neighbours (km)	South Africa 909				
Main stadia	National Stadium – Maseru 20 000				

LIB – LEBANON

NATIONAL TEAM RECORD
JULY 10TH 2006 TO JULY 12TH 2010

PL	W	D	L	F	A	%
20	4	5	11	24	32	32.5

FIFA/COCA-COLA WORLD RANKING

1993	1994	1995	1996	1997	1998	1999	2000	2001	2002	2003	2004	2005	2006	2007
108	129	134	97	90	85	111	110	93	119	115	105	125	126	134

High	
85	12/98

2007–2008											
08/07	09/07	10/07	11/07	12/07	01/08	02/08	03/08	04/08	05/08	06/08	07/08
135	144	138	137	134	133	141	144	148	140	140	150

Low	
161	12/92

In April 2008, a full three years before the finals, Lebanon kicked off their challenge to qualify for the 2011 AFC Asian Cup finals with a comfortable win over the Maldives to guarantee the nation's inclusion in the draw for the qualifying rounds of the competition next year. The Lebanese will be hoping that the political and social situation at home is kinder to them than during the qualifying tournament for the last edition of the continental championship, when the country had to withdraw following Israel's invasion of the southern half of the country in August 2006. If Lebanon are to qualify for the Asian Cup for only the second time in their history, they will have to improve on

INTERNATIONAL HONOURS
None

their showing in the 2010 FIFA World Cup qualifiers. The Lebanese slumped to a series of six defeats against Saudi Arabia, Uzbekistan and Singapore which prompted the Lebanon Football Association to disband the team on the advice of the federation's technical committee. At club level, Al Ahed overtook both of their Beirut rivals Al Ansar and Al Nijmah on the final day of the season, a 2-1 victory over Tadamon enough for them to clinch their first title after Ansar and Nijmeh could only manage to draw against each other. The 2008 FA Cup also produced surprise winners with the little known Al Mabarra beating Safa 2-1 in the final to win their first trophy.

THE FIFA BIG COUNT OF 2006

	Male	Female		Total
Number of players	318 385	100	Referees and Assistant Referees	184
Professionals	50		Admin, Coaches, Technical, Medical	3 311
Amateurs 18+	12 240		Number of clubs	178
Youth under 18	6 130		Number of teams	877
Unregistered	300 000		Clubs with women's teams	0
Total players	318 485		Players as % of population	8.22%

Lebanese Football Association (FLFA)
Verdun Street - Bristol, Radwan Center, PO Box 4732, Beirut, Lebanon
Tel +961 1 745745   Fax +961 1 349529
libanfa@cyberia.net.lb
President: HAYDAR Hachem   General Secretary: ALAMEH Rahif
Vice-President: KAMAR EDDINE Ahmad   Treasurer: AL RABA'A Mahmoud   Media Officer: ALAMEH Rahif
Men's Coach: MEKDACHE Adnan   Women's Coach: SAKRISSIAN Vatche
FLFA formed: 1933   AFC: 1964   FIFA: 1935
Red shirts, White shorts, Red socks

RECENT INTERNATIONAL MATCHES PLAYED BY LEBANON

2004	Opponents	Score		Venue	Comp	Scorers	Att	Referee
8-02	Bahrain	W	2-1	Beirut	Fr	Chahoud 90, Al Jamal 90		
18-02	Korea Republic	L	0-2	Suwon	WCq		22 000	Al Dosari KSA
23-03	Syria	L	0-1	Jounieh	Fr			
31-03	Vietnam	W	2-0	Nam Dinh	WCq	Roda Antar 83, Hamieh 88	25 000	Irmatov UZB
26-05	Bahrain	D	2-2	Beirut	Fr	Ali Atwi 70, Balout 81		
9-06	Maldives	W	3-0	Beirut	WCq	Zein 21, Roda Antar 87, Nasseredine 93+	18 000	Nurilddin Salman IRQ
17-06	Iran	L	0-4	Tehran	WAr1			
19-06	Syria	L	1-3	Tehran	WAr1	Zein 65		
3-07	China PR	L	0-6	Chongqing	Fr			
31-08	Jordan	D	2-2	Amman	Fr			
8-09	Maldives	W	5-2	Male	WCq	Nasseredine 2 4 58, Antar.F 44, Chahoud 63, Roda Antar 75	12 000	Al Ajmi OMA
3-10	Kuwait	L	1-3	Tripoli	Fr	Chahoud 64		
6-10	Kuwait	D	1-1	Beirut	Fr	Chahoud 45		
13-10	Korea Republic	D	1-1	Beirut	WCq	Nasseredine 27	38 000	Irmatov UZB
17-11	Vietnam	D	0-0	Beirut	WCq		1 000	Ebrahim BHR
1-12	Qatar	L	1-4	Doha	Fr	Nasseredine		
2005								
2-02	Bahrain	L	1-2	Doha	Fr	Ali Atwi		
2006								
27-01	Saudi Arabia	W	2-1	Riyadh	Fr	Mohammad Ghaddar 14, Nasseredine 70		
22-02	Kuwait	D	1-1	Beirut	ACq	Nasseredine 67	8 000	Mujghef JOR
21-12	Mauritania	D	0-0	Beirut	ARq			Al Khabbaz BHR
24-12	Somalia	W	4-0	Beirut	ARq	Mohammad Ghaddar 2 4 28, Nasseredine 72, Paul Rustom 83		Hazem Hussain IRQ
27-12	Sudan	D	0-0	Beirut	ARq			
2007								
16-06	Syria	L	0-1	Amman	WAr1			
20-06	Jordan	L	0-3	Amman	WAr1			
23-09	UAE	D	1-1	Dubai	Fr	Mahmoud El Ali 17		
8-10	India	W	4-1	Sidon	WCq	Roda Antar 33, Mohammad Ghaddar 2 62 76, Mahmoud El Ali 63	500	Al Fadhli KUW
30-10	India	D	2-2	Goa	WCq	Mohammad Ghaddar 2 76p 88	10 000	Mujghef JOR
2008								
2-01	Kuwait	L	2-3	Kuwait City	Fr	Mohammad Ghaddar 14p, Mahmoud El Ali 41		
20-01	China PR	D	0-0	Zhongshan	Fr			
28-01	Jordan	L	1-4	Amman	Fr	Tarek El Ali 77		
6-02	Uzbekistan	L	0-1	Beirut	WCq		800	Al Hilali OMA
26-03	Singapore	L	0-2	Singapore	WCq		10 118	Takayama JPN
9-04	Maldives	W	4-0	Beirut	ACq	Mahmoud El Ali 5, Ali Yaacoub 11, Abbas Ali Atwi 13p, Mohammad Ghaddar 40		
23-04	Maldives	W	2-1	Male	ACq	Mohamed Korhani 9, Nasrat Al Jamal 74		
27-05	Qatar	L	1-2	Doha	Fr	Mohammad Ghaddar 20		
2-06	Saudi Arabia	L	1-4	Riyadh	WCq	Mahmoud El Ali 42	8 000	Al Fadhli KUW
7-06	Saudi Arabia	L	1-2	Riyadh	WCq	Mohammad Ghaddar 93+	2 000	Tongkhan THA
14-06	Uzbekistan	L	0-3	Tashkent	WCq		7 000	Breeze AUS
22-06	Singapore	L	1-2	Beirut	WCq	Khaizan OG 62	500	Moradi IRN

Fr = Friendly match • WA = West Asian Federation Cup • AR = Arab Cup • AC = AFC Asian Cup • WC = FIFA World Cup
q = qualifier • r1 = first round group

LEBANON NATIONAL TEAM RECORDS AND RECORD SEQUENCES

Records			Sequence records					
Victory	11-1	PHI 1967	Wins	6	1995-1996	Clean sheets	4	1997, 2002-2003
Defeat	0-8	IRQ 1959	Defeats	5	1979-1985	Goals scored	10	1993-1996
Player Caps	n/a		Undefeated	9	1993-96, 1996-97	Without goal	11	1974-1988
Player Goals	23	Roda Antar	Without win	11	1998	Goals against	11	1997-1998

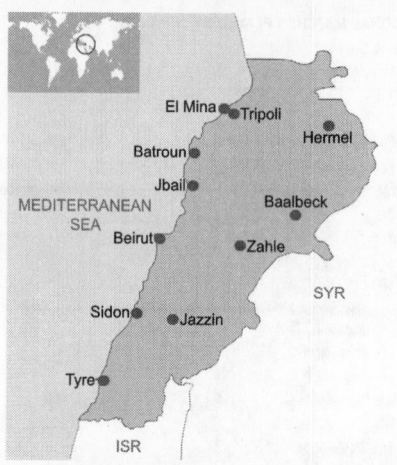

MAJOR CITIES/TOWNS
Population '000

1	Beirut	1 987
2	Tripoli	188
3	Juniyah	98
4	Baalbek	81
5	Sidon (Saida)	57
6	Zahlah	53
7	Kafr Ass	49
8	Alayh	44
9	Jubayl	44
10	Sur (Tyre)	41
11	Nabatiyat	34
12	Riyak	29
13	Talabaya	27
14	Ad Damur	26
15	Al Hirmil	23
16	Ber Al Yaas	23
17	Arsal	16
18	Bint Jubayl	16
19	Amzit	15
20	Batrun	15
21	Amyun	14
22	Jubb Jannin	14
23	Qaqaiyat al Jisr	13
24	Al Insariyah	12

LEBANESE REPUBLIC; AL JUMHURIYAH AL LUBANIYAH

Capital	Beirut	Language	Arabic, French, English, Armenian	Independence	1944
Population	3 925 502	Area	10 400 km²	Density 363 per km²	% in cities 87%
GDP per cap	$4800	Dailling code	+961	Internet .lb	GMT +/- +2

MEDALS TABLE

		Overall		Lge	Cup		Asia			City	Stadium	Cap'ty	DoF
		G	S	B	G	G	S	G	S	B				
1	Al Ansar	24	3		13	11	3				Beirut	Beirut Municipal Stadium	18 000	1925
2	Al Nejmeh	11	6	2	6	5	5	1	2		Beirut	Camille Chamoun Sports City	57 600	1945
3	Homenetmen	10	3		7	3	3				Beirut			1924
4	Al Nahda	9	1		5	4	1							
5	Al Ahed	3	2		1	2	2				Beirut	Beirut Municipal Stadium	18 000	1966
	Racing Club	3	2		3		2				Beirut	Fouad Shehab	5 000	
7	Al Shabiba Mazra	3	1		1	2	1							
	Sika	3	1		3		1							
9	American University	3			3									
10	Al Safa Sporting Club	2	6			2	6				Beirut	Safa Stadium	4 000	
11	Tripoli SC (Prev Olympic Beirut)	2	1		1	1	1				Tripoli	Tripoli Municipal Stadium	18 000	2000
	Helmi Sport	2	1			2	1							
13	Shabab Al Sahel	1	1			1	1				Beirut	Beirut Municipal Stadium	18 000	
	Al Tadamon Sur	1	1			1	1				Tyre	Sur Stadium	6 500	
15	Al Bourj	1				1								
	Al Mabarra	1				1								
17	Homenmen		4				4				Beirut			1921

RECENT LEAGUE AND CUP RECORD

	Championship						Cup		
Year	Champions	Pts	Runners-up	Pts	Third	Pts	Winners	Score	Runners-up
1997	Al Ansar	65	Al Nijmeh	58	Homenetmen	49	Al Nijmeh	2-0	Al Ansar
1998	Al Ansar	63	Al Nijmeh	53	Al Tadamon	43	Al Nijmeh	2-1	Homenmen
1999	Al Ansar	48	Safa	38	Al Tadamon	36	Al Ansar	2-1	Homenmen
2000	Al Njmeh	47	Al Ansar	44	Al Akha 'a-Ahly	33	Shabab Al Sahel	1-1 5-4p	Safa
2001	Championship cancelled due to match fixing scandal						Al Tadamon	2-1	Al Ansar
2002	Al Nijmeh	61	La Sagesse	60	Al Tadamon	59	Al Ansar	2-0	Al Ahed
2003	Olympic Beirut	54	Al Nijmeh	53	Al Ahed	50	Olympic Beirut	3-2	Al Nijmeh
2004	Al Nijmeh	54	Al Ahed	47	Olympic Beirut	35	Al Ahed	2-1	Al Nijmeh
2005	Al Nijmeh	44	Al Ansar	44	Al Ahed	36	Al Ahed	2-1	Olympic Beirut
2006	Al Ansar	47	Al Nijmeh	44	Safa	32	Al Ansar	3-1	Al Hikma
2007	Al Ansar	49	Safa	45	Al Mabarra	39	Al Ansar	3-1	Al Ahed
2008	Al Ahed	49	Al Nijmeh	48	Al Ansar	48	Al Mabarra	2-1	Safa

LEBANON 2007–08

PREMIER LEAGUE

	Pl	W	D	L	F	A	Pts	Ahed	Nijmeh	Ansar	Mabarra	Safa	Sahel	Tripoli	Tadamon	Racing	Hikma	Irshad	Ahli
Al Ahed	22	15	4	3	41	15	49		0-1	0-2	1-0	0-0	1-1	7-1	3-2	1-0	2-1	4-0	0-0
Al Nijmeh	22	15	3	4	49	18	48	1-2		1-3	1-0	2-1	1-0	2-1	2-3	3-2	8-0	2-0	1-1
Al Ansar	22	14	6	2	41	16	48	0-2	1-1		0-0	3-2	2-1	3-1	3-0	3-1	2-0	2-1	4-0
Al Mabarra	22	10	7	5	27	14	37	0-1	2-0	1-1		2-0	1-1		4-2	2-1	0-0	0-0	4-0
Safa	22	10	5	7	31	30	35	0-5	1-1	1-1	0-1		2-0	2-0	1-0	1-0	2-2	2-1	1-2
Shabab Al Sahel	22	7	7	8	28	30	28	1-1	0-5	0-2	2-0	1-2		3-2	3-2	0-0	2-1	1-1	4-1
Tripoli SC	22	6	5	11	26	40	23	3-2	0-1	0-3	1-2	1-2	2-1		1-1	1-1	1-1	2-1	2-2
Al Tadamon Tyre	22	5	6	11	25	35	21	1-2	0-1	0-2	0-0	3-2	2-1	1-0		0-0	0-1	2-2	1-1
Racing Beirut	22	4	8	10	23	28	20	0-2	0-2	2-1	0-2	2-2	1-1	1-2	1-1		1-1	1-0	5-0
Al Hikma	22	4	8	10	20	42	20	1-2	1-8	2-2	0-0	1-2	0-0	1-0	2-1	0-2		1-3	1-1
Al Irshad	22	4	4	14	25	36	16	0-2	0-2	0-1	0-1	2-3	1-3	1-1	2-3	2-1	3-1		0-1
Al Ahli Saida	22	3	7	12	11	43	16	0-1	0-3	0-0	0-3	0-2	0-2	0-1	1-0	1-1	0-2	0-5	

20/10/2007 - 26/06/2008 • † Qualified for AFC Cup

FA CUP 2007–08

Round of 16		Quarter–finals		Semi–finals		Final	
Al Mabarra *	1						
Al Tadamon Sur	0	**Al Mabarra**	1				
Akhaa Alhy	0	Al Ahly Saida *	0				
Al Ahly Saida *	2			**Al Mabarra**	3		
Al Ansar *	4			Irshad	0		
Al Tadamon Beirut	1	Al Ansar *	1 3p				
Homenmen	1	**Irshad**	1 4p				
Irshad *	2					**Al Mabarra**	2
Racing Club Beirut *	1 4p					Safa	1
Al Ahed	1 3p	**Racing Club Beirut**	2				
Al Hikma *	0	Tripoli SC *	1				
Tripoli SC	2			Racing Club Beirut	0		
Shabab Al Sahel	1			**Safa**	1		
Al Nejmeh *	0	Shabab Al Sahel	1 2p				
Nahaza Ber Al Yaas *	1	**Safa** *	1 4p				
Safa	8				* Home team		

CUP FINAL

Sports City, Beirut, 3-07-2008

Scorers - Tarek Al Ali 2 [6] [63] for Mabarra; Ali Ali Saadi [80] for Safa

LIE – LIECHTENSTEIN

NATIONAL TEAM RECORD
JULY 10TH 2006 TO JULY 12TH 2010

PL	W	D	L	F	A	%
17	2	1	14	11	51	14.7

FIFA/COCA-COLA WORLD RANKING

1993	1994	1995	1996	1997	1998	1999	2000	2001	2002	2003	2004	2005	2006	2007	High
160	156	157	154	158	159	125	147	150	147	148	142	122	158	122	**118** 01/08

2007–2008											Low
08/07	09/07	10/07	11/07	12/07	01/08	02/08	03/08	04/08	05/08	06/08	07/08	
133	142	119	123	122	118	118	120	130	130	131	129	**165** 09/98

Seven years after being promoted to the Swiss second division for the first time, Liechtenstein's FC Vaduz finally gained an historic promotion to the Swiss Super League, following two near misses - in 2004 and 2005. Their success was celebrated by a victory ride to Vaduz town hall on a fire engine, but the rise of Vaduz through the Swiss lower leagues to the pinnacle has not been universally welcomed in Switzerland where they are often regarded as outsiders. They will not, for instance, be able to represent Switzerland in European competition. With an average gate of 1,217, Vaduz may not be an immediate threat to the big Swiss clubs but with the world's highest per capita GDP the poten-

INTERNATIONAL HONOURS
None

tial is there for them to become to Swiss football what Monaco are to French football. A key figure in Heinz Hermann's squad, which contained only five players from Liechtenstein, was the Brazilian Gaspar who scored 31 goals, as Vaduz finished a point ahead of Bellinzona in the final standings. Vaduz capped a memorable season by winning their 11th straight Liechtenstein Cup - further increasing their world record for consecutive Cup wins. The Liechtenstein national team further increased the feel-good factor with some sturdy performances in their Euro 2008 qualifiers, finishing their campaign with seven points - which would have been unthinkable a decade ago.

THE FIFA BIG COUNT OF 2006

	Male	Female		Total
Number of players	2 990	325	Referees and Assistant Referees	34
Professionals	10		Admin, Coaches, Technical, Medical	240
Amateurs 18+	795		Number of clubs	7
Youth under 18	1 400		Number of teams	95
Unregistered	310		Clubs with women's teams	3
Total players	3 315		Players as % of population	9.75%

Liechtensteiner Fussballverband (LFV)
Landstrasse 149, Postfach 165, Vaduz 9490, Liechtenstein
Tel +423 2374747   Fax +423 2374748
info@lfv.li   www.lfv.li
President: WALSER Reinhard   General Secretary: OSPELT Roland
Vice-President: HILTI Fredi   Treasurer: GERNER Urs   Media Officer: FROMMELT Judith
Men's Coach: ZAUGG Hanspeter   Women's Coach: None
LFV formed: 1934   UEFA: 1992   FIFA: 1974
Blue shirts with white trimmings, Red shorts, Blue socks or Red shirts with white trimmings, Blue shorts, Red Socks

RECENT INTERNATIONAL MATCHES PLAYED BY LIECHTENSTEIN

2003	Opponents		Score	Venue	Comp	Scorers	Att	Referee
20-08	San Marino	D	2-2	Vaduz	Fr	Frick.M [16], Burgmeier.F [23]	850	Wildhaber SUI
6-09	Turkey	L	0-3	Vaduz	ECq		3 548	Van Egmond NED
10-09	England	L	0-2	Manchester	ECq		64 931	Fisker DEN
11-10	Slovakia	L	0-2	Vaduz	ECq		800	Hyytia FIN
2004								
28-04	San Marino	L	0-1	Serravalle	Fr		700	Sammut MLT
3-06	Greece	L	0-2	Vaduz	Fr		2 000	Petignat SUI
6-06	Switzerland	L	0-1	Zürich	Fr		10 200	Drabek AUT
18-08	Estonia	L	1-2	Vaduz	WCq	D'Elia [49]	912	Bozinovski MKD
3-09	Netherlands	L	0-3	Utrecht	Fr		15 000	Brines SCO
8-09	Slovakia	L	0-7	Bratislava	WCq		5 620	Delevic SCG
9-10	Portugal	D	2-2	Vaduz	WCq	Burgmeier.F [48], Beck.T [76]	3 548	Panic BIH
13-10	Luxembourg	W	4-0	Luxembourg	WCq	Stocklasa.Mt [41], Burgmeier.F 2 [44 85], Frick.M [57p]	3 748	Jara CZE
17-11	Latvia	L	1-3	Vaduz	WCq	Frick.M [32]	1 460	Szabo HUN
2005								
26-03	Russia	L	1-2	Vaduz	WCq	Beck.T [40]	2 400	Bernsten NOR
4-06	Estonia	L	0-2	Tallinn	WCq		3 000	Whitby WAL
8-06	Latvia	L	0-1	Riga	WCq		8 000	Eriksson SWE
17-08	Slovakia	D	0-0	Vaduz	WCq		1 150	Layec FRA
3-09	Russia	L	0-2	Moscow	WCq		18 123	Hyytia FIN
7-09	Luxembourg	W	3-0	Vaduz	WCq	Frick.M [38], Fischer [77], Beck [92+]	2 300	Skomina SVN
8-10	Portugal	L	1-2	Aveiro	WCq	Fischer [32]	29 000	Gilewski POL
12-11	FYR Macedonia	L	1-2	Vaduz	Fr	D'Elia [35]	1 350	Nobs SUI
2006								
2-06	Togo	L	0-1	Vaduz	Fr		2 700	Schorgenhofer AUT
7-06	Australia	L	1-3	Ulm	Fr	OG [8]	5 872	Stark GER
16-08	Switzerland	L	0-3	Vaduz	Fr		4 837	Brugger AUT
2-09	Spain	L	0-4	Badajoz	ECq		13 876	Bozinovski MKD
6-09	Sweden	L	1-3	Gothenburg	ECq	Frick.M [27]	17 735	Banari MDA
6-10	Austria	L	1-2	Vaduz	Fr	Frick.M [69]	3 750	Rogalla SUI
11-10	Denmark	L	0-4	Vaduz	ECq		2 665	Richards WAL
14-11	Wales	L	0-4	Wrexham	Fr		8 752	Wilmes LUX
2007								
24-03	Northern Ireland	L	1-4	Vaduz	ECq	Burgmeier.F [91+]	4 340	Oriekhov UKR
28-03	Latvia	W	1-0	Vaduz	ECq	Frick.M [17]	1 680	Gumienny BEL
2-06	Iceland	D	1-1	Reykjavík	ECq	Rohrer [69]	5 139	Kaldma EST
6-06	Spain	L	0-2	Vaduz	ECq		5 739	Ivanov.N RUS
22-08	Northern Ireland	L	1-3	Belfast	ECq	Frick.M [89]	13 544	Matejek CZE
12-09	Denmark	L	0-4	Aarhus	ECq		20 005	Clattenburg ENG
13-10	Sweden	L	0-3	Vaduz	ECq		4 131	Dondarini ITA
17-10	Iceland	W	3-0	Vaduz	ECq	Frick.M [28], Beck.T 2 [80 82]	2 589	Zografos GRE
17-11	Latvia	L	1-4	Riga	ECq	Zirnis OG [13]	4 800	Moen NOR
2008								
26-03	Malta	L	1-7	Ta'Qali	Fr	Burgmeier [51]		Collum SCO
30-05	Switzerland	L	0-3	St Gallen	Fr		18 000	Thual FRA

Fr = Friendly match • EC = UEFA EURO 2004/2008 • WC = FIFA World Cup • q = qualifier

LIECHTENSTEIN NATIONAL TEAM RECORDS AND RECORD SEQUENCES

Records			Sequence records					
Victory	4-0	LUX 2004	Wins	3	1981-1982	Clean sheets	2	1981-82, 1999
Defeat	1-11	MKD 1996	Defeats	21	1983-1995	Goals scored	4	2004-2005
Player Caps	78	D. Hasler & Mario Frick	Undefeated	3	1981-1982	Without goal	11	1994-96, 2000-02
Player Goals	13	Mario Frick	Without win	29	1984-1998	Goals against	22	1995-1999

MAJOR CITIES/TOWNS

		Population
1	Schaan	5862
2	Vaduz	5299
3	Triesen	4795
4	Balzers	4536
5	Eschen	4088
6	Mauren	3699
7	Triesenberg	2742
8	Ruggell	1899
9	Gamprin	1293
10	Schellenberg	1024
11	Planken	385

PRINCIPALITY OF LIECHTENSTEIN; FUERSTENTUM LIECHTENSTEIN

Capital	Vaduz	Language	German			Formation	1719
Population	33 987	Area	160 km²	Density	208 per km²	% in cities	21%
GDP per cap	$25 000	Dailling code	+423	Internet	.li	GMT + / −	+1

MEDALS TABLE

		Overall			Cup			Europe			Town	Stadium	Cap'ty	DoF
		G	S	B	G	S	B	G	S	B				
1	FC Vaduz	37	12		37	12					Vaduz	Rheinpark Stadion	6 127	1932
2	FC Balzers	11	13		11	13					Balzers	Sportplatz Rheinau Stadion	1 000	1932
3	FC Triesen	8	10		8	10					Triesen	Blumenau Stadion	2 100	1932
4	USV Eschen/Mauren	4	12		4	12					Eschen/Mauren	Sportpark Eschen/Mauren	6 000	1963
5	FC Schaan	3	10		3	10					Schaan	Rheinwiese Stadion	1 000	1949
6	FC Ruggell	5			5						Ruggell	Freizeitpark Widau	1 000	1958
7	FC Triesenberg										Triesenberg	Sportanlage Leitawis Stadion	1 000	1972

LIECHTENSTEINER CUP 2007–08

Second Preliminary round		Quarter–finals		Semi–finals		Final	
FC Vaduz							
		FC Vaduz	5				
FC Balzers-3	0	FC Schaan-2	0				
FC Schaan-2	6			FC Vaduz	9		
FC Balzers-2	2			FC Ruggell	0		
FC Triesenberg	1	FC Balzers-2	0				
		FC Ruggell	1				
FC Ruggell						FC Vaduz ‡	4
USV Eschen/Mauren						FC Balzers	0
		USV Eschen/Mauren	4				
FC Triesen	0	FC Schaan	1				
FC Schaan	4			USV Eschen/Mauren	1		
USV Eschen/Mauren-2				FC Balzers	3		
		USV Eschen/Mauren-2	0				
FC Vaduz-2	0	FC Balzers	8				
FC Balzers	10						

* Home team in the first leg • ‡ Qualified for the UEFA Cup

CUP FINAL

Rheinparkstadion, Vaduz
1-05-2008, Att: 1200, Ref: Johann

Scorers - Tim Grossklaus [27], Gaspar
De Souza 2 [37] [59], Alexandre [81]

LTU – LITHUANIA

NATIONAL TEAM RECORD
JULY 10TH 2006 TO JULY 12TH 2010

PL	W	D	L	F	A	%
22	9	1	12	24	30	43.2

FIFA/COCA-COLA WORLD RANKING

1993	1994	1995	1996	1997	1998	1999	2000	2001	2002	2003	2004	2005	2006	2007	High	
85	59	43	48	45	54	50	85	97	100	101	100	100	69	59	**42**	08/97

2007–2008											Low	
08/07	09/07	10/07	11/07	12/07	01/08	02/08	03/08	04/08	05/08	06/08	07/08	
78	84	90	61	59	61	55	55	48	49	62	59	**118** 09/04

By winning the championship in 2007 - their eighth in nine years - FBK Kaunas became the most successful team in the history of the Lithuanian League, overhauling the seven titles won by Inkaras Kaunas. They then took their total trophy tally to 12 in May 2008 when they beat Vetra Vilnius 2-1 in the Cup Final and capped a memorable few months by knocking-out 2008 UEFA Cup finalists Rangers in a UEFA Champions League preliminary tie. It was a great turn around in fortunes for FBK in international competition having crashed out to Montenegro's Zeta Golubovci the year before. They had also lost in the semi-finals of the expanded 2007 Baltic League to

INTERNATIONAL HONOURS
None

Latvia's Ventspils although compatriots Ekranas fared even worse against their Latvian opponents in the semi-finals, losing 8-3 on aggregate to Liepajas Metalurgs, with the Lithuanian clubs very much second best in the battle for supremacy in the Baltics. In the qualifiers for Euro 2008, Lithuania ended their campaign with a mid-table finish, just one point adrift of 2006 World Cup quarter-finalists Ukraine. Five wins from their 12 games was a good return for coach Algimantas Liubinskas but with France, Romania, Serbia and Austria standing in the way of a place at the 2010 FIFA World Cup finals, anything other than another mid-table finish would be a great achievement.

THE FIFA BIG COUNT OF 2006

	Male	Female		Total
Number of players	119 020	16 854	Referees and Assistant Referees	195
Professionals	340		Admin, Coaches, Technical, Medical	1 370
Amateurs 18+	3 510		Number of clubs	64
Youth under 18	9 764		Number of teams	367
Unregistered	38 100		Clubs with women's teams	1
Total players	135 874		Players as % of population	3.79%

Lithuanian Football Federation (LFF)
Seimyniskiu 15, Vilnius 09312, Lithuania
Tel +370 52638741   Fax +370 52638740
info@futbolas.lt   www.futbolas.lt
President: VARANAVICIUS Liutauras   General Secretary: KVEDARAS Julius
Vice-President: BABRAVICIUS Gintautas   Treasurer: ZYGELIENR Dalia   Media Officer: ZIZAITE Vaiva
Men's Coach: LIUBINSKAS Algimantas   Women's Coach: VIKTORAVICIUS Rimas
LFF formed: 1922   UEFA: 1992   FIFA: 1923-1943 & 1992
Yellow shirts with green trimmings, Green shorts, Yellow socks or Green shirts with yellow trimming, Green shorts, Green socks

RECENT INTERNATIONAL MATCHES PLAYED BY LITHUANIA

2004 Opponents	Score		Venue	Comp	Scorers	Att	Referee
30-03 Israel	L	1-2	Tel Aviv	Fr	OG [43]	9 782	Dougal SCO
28-04 Belarus	L	0-1	Minsk	Fr		8 000	Ivanov RUS
5-06 Portugal	L	1-4	Alcochete	Fr	Vencevicius [74p]	25 000	Wilmes LUX
18-08 Russia	L	3-4	Moscow	Fr	Danilevicius [40], Poskus [83], Barasa [89]	3 500	Mikulski POL
4-09 Belgium	D	1-1	Charleroi	WCq	Jankauskas [73]	19 218	Loizou CYP
8-09 San Marino	W	4-0	Kaunas	WCq	Jankauskas 2 [18 50], Danilevicius [65], Gedgaudas [92+]	4 000	Jareci ALB
13-10 Spain	D	0-0	Vilnius	WCq		9 114	Poulat FRA
17-11 San Marino	W	1-0	Serravalle	WCq	Cesnauskis.D [41]	1 457	Nalbandyan ARM
2005							
9-02 Georgia	L	0-1	Tbilisi	Fr		1 000	Gadiyev AZE
30-03 Bosnia-Herzegovina	D	1-1	Sarajevo	WCq	Stankevicius [60]	6 000	Baskakov RUS
21-05 Latvia	W	2-0	Kaunas	BC	Morinas 2 [25 81]		
4-06 Spain	L	0-1	Valencia	WCq		25 000	Farina ITA
17-08 Belarus	W	1-0	Vilnius	Fr	Cesnauskis.D [45]	2 500	Sipailo LVA
3-09 Serbia & Montenegro	L	0-2	Belgrade	WCq		20 203	Nielsen DEN
7-09 Bosnia-Herzegovina	L	0-1	Vilnius	WCq		4 000	Kassai HUN
8-10 Serbia & Montenegro	L	0-2	Vilnius	WCq		1 500	Wegereef NED
12-10 Belgium	D	1-1	Vilnius	WCq	OG 82	1 500	Riley ENG
2006							
1-03 Albania	W	2-1	Tirana	Fr	Savenas [34], Danilevicius [41]		Pieri ITA
2-05 Poland	W	1-0	Belchatow	Fr	Gedgaudas [14]	3 200	Bozinovski MKD
16-08 Moldova	L	2-3	Chisinau	Fr	Poskus [14], Danilevicius [38]		Godulyan UKR
2-09 Italy	D	1-1	Naples	ECq	Danilevicius [21]	43 440	Hansson SWE
6-09 Scotland	L	1-2	Kaunas	ECq	Miceika [85]	8 000	Hrinák SVK
7-10 Faroe Islands	W	1-0	Tórshavn	ECq	Skerla [89]	1 982	Buttimer IRL
11-10 Kuwait	L	0-1	Kuwait City	Fr			Abo QAT
15-11 Malta	W	4-1	Ta'Qali	Fr	Danilevicius 2 [37 66], Radzinevicius [58], Kavaliauskus [90]		Lawlor WAL
2007							
6-02 Mali	L	1-3	La Courneuve	Fr	Jankauskas [28]		Piccirillo FRA
24-03 France	L	0-1	Kaunas	ECq		8 740	Webb ENG
28-03 Ukraine	L	0-1	Odessa	ECq		33 600	Meyer GER
2-06 Georgia	W	1-0	Kaunas	ECq	Mikoliunas [78]	6 400	Circhetta SUI
6-06 Italy	L	0-2	Kaunas	ECq		7 800	Vink NED
22-08 Turkmenistan	W	2-1	Kaunas	Fr	Danilevicius 2 [42 47]		
8-09 Scotland	L	1-3	Glasgow	ECq	Danilevicius [61p]	52 063	Skomina SVN
12-09 Faroe Islands	W	2-1	Kaunas	ECq	Jankauskas [8], Danilevicius [53]	5 500	Georgiev BUL
17-10 France	L	0-2	Nantes	ECq		36 650	Kassai HUN
17-11 Ukraine	W	2-0	Kaunas	ECq	Savenas [41], Danilevicius [67]	3 000	Malcolm NIR
21-11 Georgia	W	2-0	Tbilisi	ECq	Ksanavicius 2 [52 96+]	21 300	Stavrev MKD
2008							
26-03 Azerbaijan	W	1-0	Vilnius	Fr	Klimavicius [38]	1 500	Satchi MDA
27-05 Czech Republic	L	0-2	Prague	Fr		14 220	Hrinak SVK
31-05 Estonia	W	1-0	Jurmala	BC	Mizigurskis [89]	1 300	Lajuks LVA
1-06 Latvia	L	1-2	Riga	BC	Beniusis [81]	3 300	Kaldma EST
4-06 Russia	L	1-4	Burghausen	Fr	Savenas [24]	2 850	Sippel GER

Fr = Friendly match • EC = UEFA EURO 2008 • BC = Baltic Cup • WC = FIFA World Cup • q = qualifier

LITHUANIA NATIONAL TEAM RECORDS AND RECORD SEQUENCES

Records			Sequence records					
Victory	7-0	EST 1995	Wins	3	1992, 2007-08	Clean sheets	3	2004
Defeat	0-10	EGY 1924	Defeats	10	1936-1938	Goals scored	15	1934-1937
Player Caps	66	Andrius Skerla	Undefeated	5	1935, 1992	Without goal	4	1993, 1997
Player Goals	13	Tomas Danilevicius	Without win	13	1936-1939	Goals against	18	1923-1936

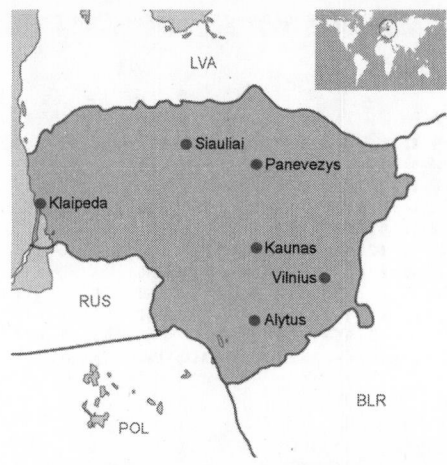

REPUBLIC OF LITHUANIA; LIETUVOS RESPUBLIKA

Capital	Vilnius	Language	Lithuanian, Russian, Polish	Independence	1991
Population	3 585 906	Area	65 200 km²	Density 55 per km²	% in cities 72%
GDP per cap	$11 400	Dailling code	+370	Internet .lt	GMT + / - +2

MEDALS TABLE

		Overall			League			Cup			Europe			City	Stadium	Cap'ty	DoF
		G	S	B	G	S	B	G	S	B	G	S	B				
1	FBK Kaunas	12	3	1	8	1	1	4	2					Kaunas	S. Darius & S. Girenas	7 262	1960
2	Zalgiris Vilnius	8	13	2	3	8	2	5	5					Vilnius	Zalgiris	15 030	1947
3	Ekranas Panevezys	4	6	4	2	3	4	2	3					Panevezys	Aukstaitijos	3 000	1964
4	Kareda Siauliai	4	2		2	2		2						Siauliai	Siauliai	5 000	1954
5	Inkaras Kaunas	3	2	1	2		1	1	2					Kaunas	Inkaras	2 000	1937
6	Atlantas Klaipeda	2	3	3		2	3	2	1					Klaipeda	Klaipeda Central	10 000	1960
7	Sirijus Klaipeda	2	1	1	1		1	1	1					Klaipeda	Zalgiris	15 030	1973
8	Suduva Marijampole	1	2	1		1	1	1	1					Marijampole	Suduvos	4 000	1942
9	Neris Vilnius	1	1		1			1						Vilnius			1966
10	ROMAR Mazeikiai	1		1	1		1							Mazeikiai	Mazeikiai	8 000	1947
11	Vetra Vilnius		3	2			2		3					Vilnius	Vetra	5 300	1996
12	Panerys Vilnius		1	1	1	1								Vilnius	Panerys	2 000	1975-98
13	Tauras Siauliai		1						1					Siauliai			

RECENT LEAGUE AND CUP RECORD

	Championship						Cup		
Year	Champions	Pts	Runners-up	Pts	Third	Pts	Winners	Score	Runners-up
1995	Inkaras Kaunas	36	Zalgiris Vilnius	36	ROMAR Mazeikiai	34	Inkaras Kaunas	2-1	Zalgiris Vilnius
1996	Inkaras Kaunas	56	Kareda Siauliai	52	Zalgiris Vilnius	50	Kareda Siauliai	1-0	Inkaras Kaunas
1997	Kareda Siauliai	64	Zalgiris Vilnius	56	Inkaras Kaunas	53	Zalgiris Vilnius	1-0	Inkaras Kaunas
1998	Kareda Siauliai	79	Zalgiris Vilnius	77	Ekranas Panevezys	68	Ekranas Panevezys	1-0	FBK Kaunas
1999	Zalgiris Vilnius	59	Kareda Siauliai	58	FBK Kaunas	57	Kareda Siauliai	3-0	FBK Kaunas
1999	FBK Kaunas	41	Zalgiris Vilnius	36	Atlantas Klaipeda	33			
2000	FBK Kaunas	86	Zalgiris Vilnius	83	Atlantas Klaipeda	67	Ekranas Panevezys	1-0	Zalgiris Vilnius
2001	FBK Kaunas	85	Atlantas Klaipeda	69	Zalgiris Vilnius	69	Atlantas Klaipeda	1-0	Zalgiris Vilnius
2002	FBK Kaunas	78	Atlantas Klaipeda	67	Ekranas Panevezys	55	FBK Kaunas	3-1	Süduva Marijampole
2003							Atlantas Klaipeda	1-1 3-1p	Vetra Rudiskes
2003	FBK Kaunas	68	Ekranas Panevezys	62	Vetra	47	Zalgiris Vilnius	3-1	Ekranas Panevezys
2004	FBK Kaunas	65	Ekranas Panevezys	62	Atlantas Klaipeda	50	FBK Kaunas	0-0 2-1p	Atlantas Klaipeda
2005	Ekranas Panevezys	92	FBK Kaunas	82	Süduva Marijampole	59	FBK Kaunas	2-0	Vetra Vilnius
2006	FBK Kaunas	88	Ekranas Panevezys	67	Vetra Vilnius	61	Suduva Marijampolé	1-0	Ekranas Panevezys
2007	FBK Kaunas	83	Süduva Marijampole	68	Ekranas Panevezys	66	No tournament due to season readjustment		
2008							FBK Kaunas	2-1	Vetra Vilnius

LITHUANIA 2007

A LYGA

	Pl	W	D	L	F	A	Pts	FBK	Suduva	Ekranas	Zalgiris	Vetra	Atlantas	Vilnius	Siauliai	Silute	Interas
FBK Kaunas †	36	25	8	3	91	26	83		1-1 2-1	1-1 2-1	1-1 1-1	1-2 0-1	4-0 2-1	1-0 6-0	2-1 4-0	4-0 2-0	8-0 3-0
Suduva Marijampole ‡	36	20	8	8	66	34	68	1-1 0-4		1-1 2-1	1-1 1-0	1-0 1-1	1-0 1-0	1-0 7-1	0-2 3-0	4-1 3-0	2-0 5-0
Ekranas Panevezys ‡	36	19	9	8	83	36	66	2-2 1-2	1-1 0-0		4-1 2-0	0-0 2-1	1-2 3-1	0-0 3-1	2-0 3-0	6-1 5-0	6-1 10-0
Zalgiris Vilnius	36	18	10	8	64	34	64	1-0 0-5	1-0 4-1	1-0 4-1		1-0 0-2	1-1 3-0	1-2 3-1	1-1 1-2	2-0 3-0	3-2 7-0
Vetra Vilnius	36	18	7	11	55	30	61	0-1 0-1	0-0 0-1	1-0 1-1	1-1 2-1		2-1 3-1	1-2 5-1	2-1 1-0	3-0 3-1	3-0 3-0
Atlantas Klaipeda	36	13	6	17	54	45	45	1-2 0-2	0-1 1-0	1-1 5-0	1-2 1-3	3-1 1-2		1-2 1-0	0-0 0-0	0-2 2-0	0-0 3-0
FK Vilnius	36	13	6	17	54	63	45	2-2 0-2	3-1 0-3	1-2 1-2	1-1 0-6	0-0 0-1	0-1 0-4		2-1 2-4	4-0 2-0	4-0 9-0
KFK Siauliai	36	13	6	17	47	50	45	0-0 1-3	1-3 2-1	1-2 0-1	0-1 0-0	2-1 2-1	1-3 0-2	**3-0** 1-1		1-0 2-1	4-1 0-2
FK Silute	36	6	4	26	28	86	22	2-5 1-4	1-3 2-4	0-5 0-3	0-0 0-0	0-3 **3-0**	1-1 2-3	0-2 1-0	2-1 1-2		3-0 2-0
Interas Visaginas	36	2	2	32	16	154	8	2-3 1-6	0-7 2-3	0-4 0-6	0-2 0-6	0-2 0-7	0-6 0-7	0-3 0-5	1-4 0-7	1-1 3-0	

7/04/2007 - 10/11/2007 • † Qualified for the UEFA Champions League • ‡ Qualified for the UEFA Cup • Matches in bold awarded

LITHUANIA 2007
LFF 1 LYGA (2)

	Pl	W	D	L	F	A	Pts
Alytis Alytus	27	18	6	3	68	15	60
Rodiklis Kaunas	27	17	6	4	82	25	57
Nevezis Kedainiai	27	15	7	5	48	21	52
Kruoja Pakruojis	27	14	4	9	48	31	46
Lietava Jonava	27	12	6	9	45	30	42
Banga Gargzdai	27	10	10	7	44	15	40
LKKA Teledema Kaunas	27	15	3	9	101	36	48
Kauno Jegeriai	27	11	6	10	51	37	39
Glestum Klaipeda	27	6	6	15	31	68	24
Vilkmerge Ukmerge	27	6	3	18	34	74	21
Tauras ERRA	27	4	3	20	24	144	15
Anyksciai	27	2	4	21	18	98	10

14/04/2007 - 28/10/2007 • Teams split into championship and relegation groups after 22 matches • No teams promoted

LFF TAURE 2007-08

Round of 16		Quarter-finals		Semi-finals		Final	
FBK Kaunas	Bye						
		FBK Kaunas	4				
		Zalgiris Vilnius	2				
Zalgiris Vilnius	Bye			FBK Kaunas	1 5		
Suduva Marijampole	2			Ekranas Panevezys	0 1		
Rodiklis Kaunas	1	Suduva Marijampole	1 3p				
		Ekranas Panevezys	1 4p				
Ekranas Panevezys	Bye					FBK Kaunas	2
KFK Siauliai	5					Vetra Vilnius	1
Interas Visaginas	1	KFK Siauliai	3				
Nevezis Kedainiai	2	Atlantas Klaipeda	2				
Atlantas Klaipeda	5			KFK Siauliai	0 0		
FK Vilnius	3			Vetra Vilnius	1 3		
Kauno Jegeriai	0	FK Vilnius	2				
		Vetra Vilnius	3				
Vetra Vilnius	Bye						

CUP FINAL

17-05-2008

Scorers - Nerijus Radzius 49, Rafael Ledesma 89 for FBK; Darvydas Sernas 25 for Vetra

* Home team in the first leg • ‡ Qualified for the UEFA Cup

LUX – LUXEMBOURG

NATIONAL TEAM RECORD
JULY 10TH 2006 TO JULY 12TH 2010

PL	W	D	L	F	A	%
20	2	4	14	6	30	20

FIFA/COCA-COLA WORLD RANKING

1993	1994	1995	1996	1997	1998	1999	2000	2001	2002	2003	2004	2005	2006	2007		High	
111	128	100	123	138	143	124	139	142	148	153	155	150	186	149		**93**	04/96

2007–2008													Low	
08/07	09/07	10/07	11/07	12/07	01/08	02/08	03/08	04/08	05/08	06/08	07/08		**195**	08/06
174	176	150	152	149	149	154	152	157	157	153	152			

On the face of it, Luxembourg's 1-0 win over Belarus in Gomel in October 2007, doesn't look that remarkable a result, but Fons Leweck's goal that day, scored deep into injury-time at the end of the game, was historic in many ways. This was Luxembourg's first win in a competitive match for 12 years. More remarkable, perhaps, was that it was only the fourth time Luxembourg have won a competitive match away from home - their others being a 6-0 win over Afghanistan at the 1948 Olympics, a 2-1 win over the Dutch in 1963 and a 1-0 win over Malta in 1995. Leweck's goal was one of just two scored in their Euro 2008 qualifiers as Luxembourg finished bottom of their group.

INTERNATIONAL HONOURS
None

The task for Guy Hellers is to try and build on that win and make the same sort of progress that Liechtenstein have made. With a population not far short of half-a-million, it should be within the means of Luxembourg to rise up from the lowest rung of European football. In club football Dudelange proved once again that they have few peers, winning the championship for the fourth straight year and by a huge margin of 21 points over Racing Union. Dudelange won 23 of their 26 league matches but failed to win a hat trick of doubles when they lost to Petange in the quarter-finals of the Cup - which was won by Grevenmacher, who beat Victoria Rosport 4-1 in the final.

THE FIFA BIG COUNT OF 2006

	Male	Female		Total
Number of players	44 626	2 954	Referees and Assistant Referees	264
Professionals	300		Admin, Coaches, Technical, Medical	1 050
Amateurs 18+	15 806		Number of clubs	111
Youth under 18	11 874		Number of teams	746
Unregistered	4 100		Clubs with women's teams	24
Total players	47 580		Players as % of population	10.03%

Fédération Luxembourgeoise de Football (FLF)
PO Box 5, Monderange 3901, Luxembourg
Tel +352 4886651   Fax +352 48866582
flf@football.lu   www.football.lu
President: PHILIPP Paul   General Secretary: WOLFF Joel
Vice-President: SCHAACK Charles   Treasurer: DECKER Erny   Media Officer: DIEDERICH Marc
Men's Coach: HELLERS Guy   Women's Coach: JEAN Romain
FLF formed: 1908   UEFA: 1954   FIFA: 1910
Red shirts with white trimmings, Red shorts, Red socks or White shirts with blue trimmings, White shorts, White socks

RECENT INTERNATIONAL MATCHES PLAYED BY LUXEMBOURG

2004	Opponents	Score		Venue	Comp	Scorers	Att	Referee
31-03	Bosnia-Herzegovina	L	1-2	Luxembourg	Fr	Huss [87]	2 000	Rogalla SUI
28-04	Austria	L	1-4	Innsbruck	Fr	Huss [63]	9 400	Skomina SVN
29-05	Portugal	L	0-3	Agueda	Fr		9 000	Styles ENG
18-08	Slovakia	L	1-3	Bratislava	WCq	Strasser [2]	5 016	Kassai HUN
4-09	Estonia	L	0-4	Tallinn	WCq		3 000	Kelly IRL
8-09	Latvia	L	3-4	Luxembourg	WCq	Braun [11], Leweck [55], Cardoni [62]	2 125	Kasnaferis GRE
9-10	Russia	L	0-4	Luxembourg	WCq		3 670	Braamhaar NED
13-10	Liechtenstein	L	0-4	Luxembourg	WCq		3 478	Jara CZE
17-11	Portugal	L	0-5	Luxembourg	WCq		8 045	Godulyan UKR
2005								
30-03	Latvia	L	0-4	Riga	WCq		8 203	Kovacic CRO
8-06	Slovakia	L	0-4	Luxembourg	WCq		2 108	Styles ENG
3-09	Portugal	L	0-6	Faro-Loule	WCq		25 300	Van Egmond NEd
7-09	Liechtenstein	L	0-3	Vaduz	WCq		2 300	Skomina SVN
8-10	Russia	L	1-5	Moscow	WCq	Reiter [51]	20 000	Tudor ROU
12-10	Estonia	L	0-2	Luxembourg	WCq		2 010	Dereli TUR
16-11	Canada	L	0-1	Hesperange	Fr			Gomes Costa POR
2006								
1-03	Belgium	L	0-2	Luxembourg	Fr	Abandoned after 65 minutes due to snow		Einwaller AUT
27-05	Germany	L	0-7	Freiburg	Fr		23 000	Rogalla SUI
3-06	Portugal	L	0-3	Metz	Fr		19 157	Duhamel FRA
8-06	Ukraine	L	0-3	Luxembourg	Fr			Vervecken BEL
16-08	Turkey	L	0-1	Luxembourg	Fr		3 353	Weiner GER
2-09	Netherlands	L	0-1	Luxembourg	ECq		8 055	Lopes Ferreira POR
6-09	Latvia	D	0-0	Hesperange	Fr		1 755	Bozinovski MKD
7-10	Slovenia	L	0-2	Celje	ECq		3 800	Kailis CYP
11-10	Bulgaria	L	0-1	Luxembourg	ECq		3 156	Panic BIH
15-11	Togo	D	0-0	Luxembourg	Fr		1 417	Richards WAL
2007								
7-02	Gambia	W	2-1	Hesperange	Fr	Joachim [65], Sagramola [83]	520	Circhetta SUI
24-03	Belarus	L	1-2	Luxembourg	ECq	Sagramola [68]	2 021	Whitby WAL
28-03	Romania	L	0-3	Piatra-Neamt	ECq		9 120	Lajuks LVA
2-06	Albania	L	0-2	Tirana	ECq		3 000	Silgava GEO
6-06	Albania	L	0-3	Luxembourg	ECq		4 325	Malzinskas LTU
22-08	Georgia	D	0-0	Luxembourg	Fr		1 123	Weatherall NIR
8-09	Slovenia	L	0-3	Luxembourg	ECq		2 012	Berezka UKR
12-09	Bulgaria	L	0-3	Sofia	ECq		4 674	Demirlek TUR
13-10	Belarus	W	1-0	Gomel	ECq	Fons Leweck [95+]	14 000	Svendsen DEN
17-10	Romania	L	0-2	Luxembourg	ECq		3 584	Brych GER
17-11	Netherlands	L	0-1	Rotterdam	ECq		45 000	Hansson SWE
2008								
30-01	Saudi Arabia	L	1-2	Riyadh	Fr	Peters [87p]	2 000	
26-03	Wales	L	0-2	Luxembourg	Fr		1 879	Kuipers NED
27-05	Cape Verde Islands	D	1-1	Luxembourg	Fr	Fons Leweck [77]	2 051	Radovanovic MNE

Fr = Friendly match • EC = UEFA EURO 2008 • WC = FIFA World Cup • q = qualifier

LUXEMBOURG NATIONAL TEAM RECORDS AND RECORD SEQUENCES

Records			Sequence records				
Victory	6-0	AFG 1948	Wins	3	1939-1943	Clean sheets	3	1995
Defeat	0-12	ITA 'B' 1932	Defeats	34	1980-1985	Goals scored	7	1948-1951
Player Caps	87	Carlo Weis	Undefeated	4	1963	Without goal	11	2005-2006
Player Goals	16	Léon Mart	Without win	83	1995-2006	Goals against	31	1987-95

MAJOR CITIES/TOWNS
Population '000

1	Luxembourg	76
2	Esch-sur-Alzette	28
3	Dudelange	18
4	Schifflange	8
5	Bettembourg	7
6	Pétange	7
7	Ettelbruck	6
8	Diekirch	6
9	Strassen	6
10	Bertrange	5
11	Differdange	5
12	Wiltz	4
13	Bascharage	4
14	Rodange	4
15	Rumelange	4
16	Grevenmacher	4
17	Mondercange	3
18	Niedercorn	3
19	Tétange	2
20	Hesperange	1
21	Eischen	1
22	Frisange	1
23	Walferdange	1
24	Rosport	1

GRAND DUCHY OF LUXEMBOURG; GRAND DUCHE DE LUXEMBOURG

Capital	Luxembourg	Language	Luxembourgish, German, French	Independence	1839
Population	474 413	Area	2 586 km²	Density	179 per km²	% in cities	89%
GDP per cap	$55 100	Dailling code	+352	Internet	.lu	GMT +/-	+1

MEDALS TABLE

		Overall G S B	League G S B	Cup G S B	Europe G S B	City	Stadium	Cap'ty	DoF
1	Jeunesse Esch/Alzette	39 23 15	27 12 15	12 11		Esch-sur-Alzette	Stade de la Frontière	7 500	1907
2	Red Boys Differdange	21 19 14	6 10 14	15 9		Differdange	Thillenberg		1907-2003
3	AC Spora Luxembourg	19 18 10	11 10 10	8 8		Luxembourg	Municipal		1923-2005
4	Union Luxembourg	16 18 12	6 8 12	10 10		Luxembourg	Achille Hammerel		1925-2005
5	Stade Dudeldange	14 13 6	10 6 6	4 7		Dudelange	Alois Mayer		1913-91
6	Avenir Beggen	13 9 3	6 5 3	7 4		Beggen	Henri Dunant	5 500	1915
7	F'91 Dudelange	10 6	7 3	3 3		Dudelange	Jos Nosbaum	5 000	1991
8	Fola Esch/Alzette	8 4	5 7 4	3 1		Esch-sur-Alzette	Emile Mayrisch	3 900	1906
9	Progres Niedercorn	7 8 8	3 5 8	4 3		Niedercorn	Jos Haupert	4 000	1919
10	US Hollerich	5 3 2	5 3 2			Luxembourg	Stade Hollerich		1908-25
11	CS Grevenmacher	5 11 2	1 7 2	4 4		Grevenmacher	Op Flohr	4 500	1909
12	Aris Bonnevoie	4 6 2	3 1 2	1 5		Luxembourg	Camille Polfer		1922-2001
13	US Rumelange	2 5 1	3 1	2 2		Rumelange	Municipal	2 950	1908
14	Sporting Club Luxembourg	2 3 2	2 3 2			Luxembourg	Municipal		1908-23
15	The National Schifflange	2 3	1 2	1 1		Schifflange	Stade National		1912
16	Alliance Dudelange	2 2	1	2 1		Dudelange	Amadeo Barozzi		1916-91
17	Racing Club Luxembourg	2 3	1 3	1		Luxembourg	Municipal		1907-23

RECENT LEAGUE AND CUP RECORD

	Championship						Cup		
Year	Champions	Pts	Runners-up	Pts	Third	Pts	Winners	Score	Runners-up
1995	Jeunesse d'Esch	35	CS Grevenmacher	35	Avenir Beggen	30	CS Grevenmacher	1-1 3-2	Jeunesse d'Esch
1996	Jeunesse d'Esch	48	CS Grevenmacher	47	Union Luxembourg	42	Union Luxembourg	3-1	Jeunesse d'Esch
1997	Jeunesse d'Esch	56	CS Grevenmacher	50	Union Luxembourg	38	Jeunesse d'Esch	2-0	Union Luxembourg
1998	Jeunesse d'Esch	54	Union Luxembourg	53	CS Grevenmacher	43	CS Grevenmacher	2-0	Avenir Beggen
1999	Jeunesse d'Esch	51	F'91 Dudelange	47	Avenir Beggen	45	Jeunesse d'Esch	3-0	FC Mondercange
2000	F'91 Dudelange	57	CS Grevenmacher	46	Jeunesse d'Esch	46	Jeunesse d'Esch	4-1	FC Mondercange
2001	F'91 Dudelange	63	CS Grevenmacher	59	CS Hobscheid	46	Etzella Ettelbruck	5-3	FC Wiltz
2002	F'91 Dudelange	62	CS Grevenmacher	58	Union Luxembourg	47	Avenir Beggen	1-0	F'91 Dudelange
2003	CS Grevenmacher	59	F'91 Dudelange	52	Jeunesse d'Esch	48	CS Grevenmacher	1-0	Etzella Ettelbruck
2004	Jeunesse d'Esch	68	F'91 Dudelange	59	Etzella Ettelbruck	48	F'91 Dudelange	3-1	Etzella Ettelbruck
2005	F'91 Dudelange	70	Etzella Ettelbruck	64	Jeunesse d'Esch	45	CS Petange	5-0	Cebra
2006	F'91 Dudelange	64	Jeunesse d'Esch	53	Etzella Ettelbruck	49	F'91 Dudelange	3-2	Jeunesse d'Esch
2007	F'91 Dudelange	65	Etzella Ettelbruck	52	FC Differdange 03	48	F'91 Dudelange	2-1	UN Käerjéng 97
2008	F'91 Dudelange	71	Racing Union	50	Jeunesse d'Esch	45	CS Grevenmacher	4-1	Victoria Rosport

LUXEMBOURG 2007–08

FORTIS LIGUE – DIVISION NATIONALE

Team	Pl	W	D	L	F	A	Pts	Dudelange	Racing Un	Jeunesse	Etzella	Avenir	Gr'macher	Differdange	Hamm	Swift	Käerjeng	Nieedercorn	Wiltz	Victoria	Pétange
F91 Dudelange †	26	23	2	1	74	12	71		1-1	6-2	7-1	1-0	1-0	2-0	3-0	2-0	1-0	4-1	1-0	3-0	1-0
Racing Union ‡	26	14	8	4	50	28	50	0-2		3-0	3-2	1-4	4-2	0-0	3-0	1-1	2-0	3-1	3-1	4-1	4-0
Jeunesse d'Esch	26	13	6	7	51	39	45	1-1	2-0		2-2	3-0	2-1	2-0	1-1	4-1	2-3	0-0	4-1	2-0	4-1
Etzella Ettelbruck	26	13	5	8	54	48	44	1-3	2-2	5-4		2-2	1-5	2-0	3-0	2-1	0-3	4-2	3-1	1-2	3-1
Avenir Beggen	26	11	4	11	41	38	37	1-0	0-0	1-2	0-2		1-2	1-0	3-1	1-3	2-1	1-2	1-2	4-1	1-1
CS Grevenmacher ‡	26	10	6	10	45	36	36	0-2	1-1	4-2	0-1	2-0		3-2	0-0	1-2	1-0	2-2	2-2	6-0	3-1
FC Differdange 03	26	11	2	13	43	43	35	2-4	3-1	3-0	3-1	2-3	0-3		2-3	2-1	5-0	1-2	4-1	2-1	2-1
RM Hamm Benfica	26	9	5	12	32	48	32	1-5	0-3	0-1	2-1	1-3	2-0	2-3		3-1	2-0	3-1	1-1	2-2	0-2
Swift Hesperange	26	8	7	11	36	44	31	0-2	1-4	1-1	1-5	2-1	1-1	1-2	2-0		0-2	1-0	1-1	0-0	2-2
UN Käerjeng	26	8	6	12	30	40	30	0-4	0-1	0-0	3-3	2-1	2-2	1-2	1-5	1-1		2-1	1-1	3-0	
Progrès Niedercorn	26	7	7	12	31	46	28	1-5	0-1	3-2	0-3	2-1	1-3	1-0	3-0	2-2	1-3		2-2	0-0	0-0
FC Wiltz 71	26	6	7	13	33	48	25	0-2	1-2	0-4	1-3	0-2	1-1	3-0	3-3	2-1	0-1	1-0		3-0	1-0
Victoria Rosport	26	6	6	14	29	56	24	0-7	1-1	0-1	2-3	1-3	3-0	3-2	0-1	1-2	2-1	2-1	2-2		2-1
CS Pétange	26	4	7	15	27	50	19	0-4	2-2	2-2	1-1	1-2	2-1	0-1	1-2	1-3	0-0	1-2	3-2	3-2	

4/08/2007 - 18/05/2008 • † Qualified for the UEFA Champions League • ‡ Qualified for the UEFA Cup
Relegation play-off: FC Wiltz 0-2 **Sporting Steinfort**

LUXEMBOURG 2007–08 — EHRENPROMOTION (2)

Team	Pl	W	D	L	F	A	Pts
US Rumelange	26	21	1	4	62	22	64
Fola Esch/Alzette	26	18	4	4	72	25	58
Sporting Steinfort ‡	26	17	5	4	53	23	56
FC Mondercange	26	15	5	6	76	41	50
Minerva Lintgen	26	13	4	9	48	43	43
Un. Mertet/Wasserbillig	26	11	5	10	55	37	38
Jeunesse Canach	26	9	7	10	30	40	34
FC 72 Erpeldange	26	8	8	10	42	44	33
Sporting Mertzig	26	8	5	13	35	51	29
Atert Bissen	26	8	4	14	51	47	28
FC Cessange	26	8	4	14	41	54	28
FC Mamer 32	26	6	8	12	37	45	26
Blue Boys Muehl'bach	26	7	3	16	31	60	21
CS Obercorn	26	1	2	23	16	117	5

25/08/2007 - 25/05/2008 • ‡ qualified for play-offs
Relegation play-offs: **AS Colmarberg** 3-0 FC Mamer;
US Hostert 1-0 FC Cessange

COUPE DE LUXEMBOURG 2007–08

Round of 16
- CS Grevenmacher 6 / Sporting Betrange * 0
- Racing Union 1 / Jeunesse d'Esch * 5
- Etzella Ettelbruck 3 / Sporting Steinfort * 1
- FC Mamer 32 * 0 / RM Hamm Benfica 4
- CS Pétange 1 3p / U. Mertet/Wasserbillig * 1 1p
- US Sandweiler * 0 / F91 Dudelange 8
- Sporting Mertzig 1 6p / Blue Boys Muehl'bach * 1 5p
- Fola Esch/Alzette * 0 / Victoria Rosport 4

Quarter-finals
- CS Grevenmacher * 3 / Jeunesse d'Esch 0
- Etzella Ettelbruck 0 / RM Hamm Benfica * 6
- CS Pétange 1 / F91 Dudelange * 0
- Sporting Mertzig * 0 / Victoria Rosport 4

Semi-finals
- CS Grevenmacher 1 / RM Hamm Benfica * 0
- CS Pétange 1 4p / Victoria Rosport * 1 5p

Final
- CS Grevenmacher ‡ 4 / Victoria Rosport 1

* Home team • ‡ Qualified for the UEFA Cup

CUP FINAL
Stade Josy Barthel, Luxembourg
24-05-2008

Scorers - Munoz [11], Huss [24], Di Domenico [68], Thimmesch [78] for Grevenmacher; Wagner [81] for Victoria

LVA – LATVIA

NATIONAL TEAM RECORD
JULY 10TH 2006 TO JULY 12TH 2010

PL	W	D	L	F	A	%
21	8	1	12	25	26	40.5

FIFA/COCA-COLA WORLD RANKING

1993	1994	1995	1996	1997	1998	1999	2000	2001	2002	2003	2004	2005	2006	2007	High	
86	69	60	82	75	77	62	92	106	79	51	65	69	90	86	**51**	12/03

2007–2008												Low	
08/07	09/07	10/07	11/07	12/07	01/08	02/08	03/08	04/08	05/08	06/08	07/08	**111**	07/07
110	94	86	88	86	85	72	73	73	75	70	66		

Latvia confirmed its credentials as the strongest of the Baltic nations at football when Liepajas Metalurgs won the Baltic League in November 2007, beating compatriots Ventspils in the final. That was then followed by the national team winning the Baltic Cup the following June. The expanded Baltic League proved to be a happy hunting ground for Latvian clubs with Skonto Riga also qualifying for the quarter-finals after all three clubs had comfortably topped their first round groups without losing a game. That was about as far as international success went, however, with the national team never threatening to repeat their sensational feat of qualifying for Euro 2004.

INTERNATIONAL HONOURS
Baltic Cup 1928 1932 1933 1936 1937 1993 1995 2001 2003 2008

Indeed, Latvia even lost to tiny Liechtenstein in the qualifiers four years on, finishing their group way off the leading pack. At home Ventspils won the 2007 Virsliga after an exciting climax to the season in which they won their last 11 games, conceding just one goal. They clinched the title ahead of a seemingly uncatchable Metalurgs with a 1-0 victory over their rivals in the penultimate round, a victory which also saw them clinch a first double having earlier beaten Olimps Riga in the Cup Final. The finish of the 2008 Cup was brought forward but in the final Ventspils lost on penalties to Daugava, a club formerly known as Ditton, who won their first trophy.

THE FIFA BIG COUNT OF 2006

	Male	Female		Total
Number of players	73 885	11 400	Referees and Assistant Referees	225
Professionals	265		Admin, Coaches, Technical, Medical	430
Amateurs 18+	1 450		Number of clubs	68
Youth under 18	6 550		Number of teams	420
Unregistered	17 900		Clubs with women's teams	29
Total players	85 285		Players as % of population	3.75%

Latvian Football Federation (LFF)

Latvijas Futbola Federacija, Augsiela 1, Riga LV1009, Latvia
Tel +371 67292988   Fax +371 67315604
futbols@lff.lv   www.lff.lv
President: INDRIKSONS Guntis   General Secretary: MEZECKIS Janis
Vice-President: GORKSS Juris   Treasurer: BAHAREVA Nina   Media Officer: HARTMANIS Martins
Men's Coach: STARKOVS Aleksandrs   Women's Coach: BANDOLIS Agris
LFF formed: 1921   UEFA: 1992   FIFA: 1923-43, 1992
Carmine red shirts with white trimmings, Carmine red shorts, Carmine red socks or White shirts, White shorts, White socks

RECENT INTERNATIONAL MATCHES PLAYED BY LATVIA

2004	Opponents		Score	Venue	Comp	Scorers	Att	Referee
9-10	Slovakia	L	1-4	Bratislava	WCq	Verpakovskis [3]	13 025	Farina ITA
13-10	Estonia	D	2-2	Riga	WCq	Astafjevs [65], Laizans [82]	8 500	Meyer GER
17-11	Liechtenstein	W	3-1	Vaduz	WCq	Verpakovskis [7], Zemlinskis [57], Prohorenkovs [89]	1 460	Szabo HUN
1-12	Oman	L	2-3	Manama	Fr	Rimkus [66], Rubins [68]		
3-12	Bahrain	D	2-2	Manama	Fr	Kolesnicenko [22p], Zakresevskis [35]. L 2-4p	2 000	Al Hilali OMA
2005								
8-02	Finland	L	1-2	Nicosia	Fr	Zemlinskis [62p]	102	Kailis CYP
9-02	Austria	D	1-1	Limassol	Fr	Visnakovs [70]. W 5-3p	50	Theodotou CYP
30-03	Luxembourg	W	4-0	Riga	WCq	Bleidelis [32], Laizans [38p], Verpakovskis 2 [73 90]	8 203	Kovacic CRO
21-05	Lithuania	L	0-2	Kaunas	BC			
4-06	Russia	L	0-3	St Pertersburg	WCq		21 575	Poulat FRA
8-06	Liechtenstein	W	1-0	Riga	WCq	Bleidelis [17]	8 000	Eriksson SWE
17-08	Russia	D	1-1	Riga	WCq	Astafjevs [6]	10 000	Poll ENG
3-09	Estonia	L	1-2	Tallinn	WCq	Laizans [90]	8 970	Undiano Mallenco ESP
7-09	Slovakia	D	1-1	Riga	WCq	Laizans [74]	8 800	Plautz AUT
8-10	Japan	D	2-2	Riga	Fr	Rimkus [67], Rubins [89]	6 500	Granatas POL
12-10	Portugal	L	0-3	Porto	WCq		35 000	Frojdfeldt SWE
12-11	Belarus	L	1-3	Minsk	Fr	Visnakovs [24]	8 300	Egorov RUS
24-12	Thailand	D	1-1	Phang Nga	Fr	Solonicins [19]		
26-12	Korea DPR	D	1-1	Phuket	Fr	Karlsons [65]		
30-12	Korea DPR	W	2-1	Phuket	Fr	Karlsons [38], Prohorenkovs [40]		
2006								
28-05	USA	L	0-1	Hartford	Fr		24 636	Dipiero CAN
16-08	Russia	L	0-1	Moscow	Fr		25 600	Gilewski POL
2-09	Sweden	L	0-1	Riga	ECq		7 500	Ceferin SVN
6-09	Luxembourg	D	0-0	Hesperange	Fr			
7-10	Iceland	W	4-0	Riga	ECq	Karlsons.G [14], Verpakovskis 2 [15 25], Visnakovs [52]	6 800	Kelly IRL
11-10	Northern Ireland	L	0-1	Belfast	ECq		13 500	Fleischer GER
2007								
6-02	Bulgaria	L	0-2	Larnaca	Fr		500	Andronikou CYP
7-02	Hungary	L	0-2	Limassol	Fr		400	Kailisz CYP
28-03	Liechtenstein	L	0-1	Vaduz	ECq		1 680	Gumienny BEL
2-06	Spain	L	0-2	Riga	ECq		10 000	Thomson SCO
6-06	Denmark	L	0-2	Riga	ECq		7 500	Trefoloni ITA
22-08	Moldova	L	1-2	Riga	Fr	Astafjevs [31]		
8-09	Northern Ireland	W	1-0	Riga	ECq	Baird OG 69	7 500	Proença POR
12-09	Spain	L	0-2	Oviedo	ECq		22 560	Yefet ISR
13-10	Iceland	W	4-2	Reykjavík	ECq	Klava 27, Laizans 31, Verpakovskis 2 37 46	5 865	Dean ENG
17-10	Denmark	L	1-3	Copenhagen	ECq	Gorkss [80]	19 004	Cakir TUR
17-11	Liechtenstein	W	4-1	Riga	ECq	Karlsons.G [14], Verpakovskis [30], Laizans [63], Visnakovs [87]	4 800	Moen NOR
21-11	Sweden	L	1-2	Stockholm	ECq	Laizans [26]	26 218	Stark GER
2008								
6-02	Georgia	W	3-1	Tbilisi	Fr	Karlsons.G [7], Stepanovs [16], Astafjevs [34]		Shmolik BLR
26-03	Andorra	W	3-0	Andorra la Vella	Fr	Ivanovs [10], Pereplotkins [24], Rimkus [41]		Rubinos Perez ESP
30-05	Estonia	W	1-0	Riga	BC	Laizans [48p]	4 500	Zuta LTU
1-06	Lithuania	W	2-1	Riga	BC	Pereplotkins [57], Alunderis OG [77]	3 300	Kaldma EST

Fr = Friendly match • EC = UEFA EURO 2008 • BC = Baltic Cup • WC = FIFA World Cup
q = qualifier • po = play-off • r1 = first round group

LATVIA NATIONAL TEAM RECORDS AND RECORD SEQUENCES

Records			Sequence records				
Victory	8-1	EST 1942	Wins	4	1936, 2008	Clean sheets	2	
Defeat	0-12	SWE 1927	Defeats	7	2006-2007	Goals scored	10	Three times
Player Caps	144	Vitalijs Astafjevs	Undefeated	6	1937, 1938	Without goal	6	2006-2007
Player Goals	24	Eriks Petersons	Without win	10	1995-1997	Goals against	21	1933-1937

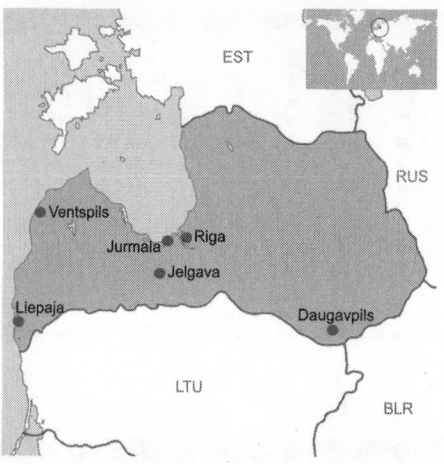

MAJOR CITIES/TOWNS
Population '000

#	City	Pop
1	Riga	733
2	Daugavpils	110
3	Liepaja	83
4	Jelgava	61
5	Jurmala	53
6	Ventspils	42
7	Rezekne	37
8	Jekabspils	26
9	Valmiera	26
10	Ogre	25
11	Tukums	18
12	Cesis	17
13	Salaspils	17
14	Kuldiga	13
15	Olaine	12
16	Saldus	12
17	Talsi	11
18	Dobele	11
19	Kraslava	10
20	Bauska	10
21	Ludza	10
22	Sigulda	10
23	Livani	9
24	Gulbene	9

REPUBLIC OF LATVIA; LATVIJAS REPUBLIKA

Capital Riga	Language Latvian, Russian		Independence 1991
Population 2 274 735	Area 64 589 km^2	Density 35 per km^2	% in cities 73%
GDP per cap $10 200	Dailling code +371	Internet .lv	GMT +/- +2

MEDALS TABLE

		Overall		League			Cup			Europe			City	Stadium	Cap'ty	DoF
		G	S	B	G	S	B	G	S	B	G	S	B				
1	Skonto Riga	21	7	1	14	1	1	7	6					Riga	Stadions Skonto	8 500	1991
2	FK Ventspils	6	4	5	2	3	5	4	1					Ventspils	Olimpiska Centra	3 200	1997
3	Liepajas Metalurgs	2	10	3	1	6	3	1	4					Liepaja	Daugavas Stadions	5 083	1996
4	RAF Jelgava	2	2	2		2	2	2						Jelgava			1988-97
5	Dinaburg Daugavpils	1	3	2		1	2	1	2					Daugavpils	Celtnieka Stadions	4 070	1990
6	Olimpija Riga	1	1		1			1						Riga			1992-95
7	FK Riga	1		1		1	1							Riga	Latvijas Universitates	5 000	1999
8	Daugava Daugavpils	1						1						Daugavpils	Celtnieka Stadions	4 070	1944
9	Daugava Riga		5		3			2						Riga	Daugava Stadions	5 000	1995
10	VEF/DAG/Olimpija/FK		2	3		2		2						Riga/Liepaja			
11	Olimps Riga		1					1						Riga	Stadions Skonto	9 300	2005
12	FK Jurmala													Jurmala	Sloka	1 500	2003
	Venta Kuldiga													Ventspils	Olimpiska Centra	3 200	2004-06
	Blazma Rezekne													Rezekne	Sporta Agenturas	2 500	2007

RECENT LEAGUE AND CUP RECORD

	Championship						Cup		
Year	Champions	Pts	Runners-up	Pts	Third	Pts	Winners	Score	Runners-up
1995	Skonto Riga	78	Vilan-D Daugavpils	51	RAF Jelgava	48	Skonto Riga	3-0	DAG Liepaja
1996	Skonto Riga	73	Daugava Riga	61	Dinaburg Daugavpils	47	RAF Jelgava	2-1	Skonto Riga
1997	Skonto Riga	64	Daugava Riga	43	Dinaburg Daugavpils	42	Skonto Riga	2-1	Dinaburg Daugavpils
1998	Skonto Riga	67	Liepajas Metalurgs	57	FK Ventspils	54	Skonto Riga	1-0	Liepajas Metalurgs
1999	Skonto Riga	69	Liepajas Metalurgs	60	FK Ventspils	56	FK Riga	1-1 6-5p	Skonto Riga
2000	Skonto Riga	75	FK Ventspils	65	Liepajas Metalurgs	55	Skonto Riga	4-1	Liepajas Metalurgs
2001	Skonto Riga	68	FK Ventspils	67	Liepajas Metalurgs	64	Skonto Riga	2-0	Dinaburg Daugavpils
2002	Skonto Riga	73	FK Ventspils	71	Liepajas Metalurgs	51	Skonto Riga	3-0	Liepajas Metalurgs
2003	Skonto Riga	73	Liepajas Metalurgs	68	FK Ventspils	61	FK Ventspils	4-0	Skonto Riga
2004	Skonto Riga	69	Liepajas Metalurgs	66	FK Ventspils	55	FK Ventspils	2-1	Skonto Riga
2005	Liepajas Metalurgs	71	Skonto Riga	58	FK Ventspils	55	FK Ventspils	2-1	Liepajas Metalurgs
2006	FK Ventspils	62	Liepajas Metalurgs	60	Skonto Riga	54	Liepajas Metalurgs	2-1	Skonto Riga
2007	FK Ventspils	60	Liepajas Metalurgs	58	FK Riga	57	FK Ventspils	3-0	Olimps Riga
2008							Daugava D'gavpils	1-1 3-0p	FK Ventspils

LATVIA 2007

VIRSLIGA

	Pl	W	D	L	F	A	Pts	Ventspils	Metalurgs	FK Riga	Skonto	Daugava	Jurmala	Dinaburg	Olimps
FK Ventspils †	28	18	6	4	59	16	60		0-2 1-0	1-0 2-1	2-0 3-1	3-1 1-0	1-1 10-0	4-0 6-0	2-0 4-0
Liepajas Metalurgs ‡	28	18	4	6	42	21	58	2-0 0-2		0-0 2-0	0-2 0-1	3-1 0-0	2-0 3-0	2-1 4-1	1-0 1-0
FK Riga	28	17	6	5	48	28	57	1-0 0-0	3-0 2-0		1-0 2-2	3-2 2-1	2-0 2-1	2-0 3-1	3-2 4-0
Skonto Riga	28	16	7	5	54	27	55	0-0 0-1	0-4 0-0	4-4 3-0		3-1 3-1	2-2 4-0	3-0 2-0	1-0 3-0
Daugava Daugavpils	28	9	6	13	33	38	33	1-1 0-0	1-2 0-1	1-3 2-2	1-3 1-1		1-0 5-0	1-3 1-0	2-0 1-0
FK Jurmala	28	7	5	16	28	51	26	3-1 0-1	3-4 1-1	0-0 2-0	1-2 0-1	1-2 0-1		1-0 3-0	5-0 0-2
Dinaburg Daugavpils	28	6	2	20	23	58	20	2-4 0-3	1-2 0-1	0-2 0-1	2-2 0-4	2-1 0-2	0-0 3-0		1-0 1-2
Olimps Riga	28	2	2	24	15	63	8	1-1 0-5	1-2 0-3	2-3 0-2	1-4 0-3	1-1 0-1	0-2 1-2	0-2 2-3	

7/04/2007 - 4/11/2007 • † Qualified for the UEFA Champions League • ‡ Qualified for the UEFA Cup
No relegation due to the expansion of the Virsliga to 10 clubs for 2008 • Top scorers: Vits Rimkus, Ventspils 20; Andrei Nikolaev, FK Riga 15

LATVIJAS KAUSS 2007

Round of 16		Quarter–finals		Semi–finals		Final	
FK Ventspils	3						
Blazma Rezekne *	1	FK Ventspils *	3				
Vindava Ventspils *	0	Liepajas Metalurgs	0				
Liepajas Metalurgs	1			FK Ventspils	0 4p		
FK Riga	2			Skonto Riga *	0 3p		
Dinamo-Rinuzi/LASD *	0	FK Riga *	1				
Jauniba-Parex Riga *	0	Skonto Riga	3			FK Ventspils	3
Skonto Riga	7					Olimps Riga	0
Daugava Daugavpils	3						
Daugava-90 Riga *	1	Daugava Daugavpils	1				
Varaviksne VOVA *	0	FK Jurmala *	0				
FK Jurmala	5			Daugava Daugavpils *	1		
Dinaburg Daugavpils	6			Olimps Riga	2		
Auda Riga *	1	Dinaburg Daugavpils	1 4p				
Metta/LU Riga *	2	Olimps Riga *	1 5p				
Olimps Riga	3						

* Home teams • ‡ Qualified for the UEFA Cup

CUP FINAL

Skonto, Riga,
30-09-2007, Att: 2800, Ref: Sipailo

Scorers - Vits Rimkus [39], Andrejs
Butriks 2 [58] [70]

LATVIJAS KAUSS 2008

Round of 16		Quarter–finals		Semi–finals		Final	
Daugava Daugavpils	1						
Olimps Riga *	0	Daugava Daugavpils *	2				
Jekabpils SC *	0	Vindava Ventspils	1				
Vindava Ventspils	3			Daugava Daugavpils	2		
Blazma Rezekne *	0 10p			FK Jurmala *	1		
Dinaburg Daugavpils	0 9p	Blazma Rezekne	0				
Metta/LU Riga *	1	FK Jurmala *	3				
FK Jurmala	3					Daugava Daugavpils	1 3p
Skonto Riga	4					FK Ventspils	1 0p
Spartaks Jurmala *	0	Skonto Riga *	2				
Nikars Riga *	0	FK Riga	0				
FK Riga	9			Skonto Riga	1		
Liepajas Metalurgs	13			FK Ventspils *	2		
Viesulis Riga *	0	Liepajas Metalurgs	1				
FK Jelgava *	0	FK Ventspils *	3				
FK Ventspils	2						

* Home teams

CUP FINAL

Skonto, Riga, 15-06-2008
Att: 1800, Ref: Direktorenko

Scorers - Marko Simic [79] for
Daugava; Igors Savcenkovs [43] for
Ventspils

MAC – MACAU

NATIONAL TEAM RECORD
JULY 10TH 2006 TO JULY 12TH 2010

PL	W	D	L	F	A	%
9	0	1	8	9	36	5.6

FIFA/COCA-COLA WORLD RANKING

1993	1994	1995	1996	1997	1998	1999	2000	2001	2002	2003	2004	2005	2006	2007	High	
166	175	180	172	157	174	176	180	180	188	184	188	192	185	190	**156**	09/97

2007–2008												Low	
08/07	09/07	10/07	11/07	12/07	01/08	02/08	03/08	04/08	05/08	06/08	07/08	**196**	07/08
185	188	190	193	190	189	191	191	193	193	195	196		

Macau continued its terrible run of form during the 2007-08 season after losing all four of the international matches played and the team's winless streak now stretches back over five years and 19 matches. Credit to the federation therefore for entering the 2010 FIFA World Cup qualifiers, which some of Macau's Asian counterparts at the wrong end of the FIFA rankings failed to do. Drawn in a preliminary tie against Thailand, there was only ever going to be one outcome and although Macau did score twice over the two legs, they also let in 13. Macau have actually won three World Cup matches in the past after first entering in 1982 - twice against Brunei in 1985 and

INTERNATIONAL HONOURS
None

against Nepal in 1997 - but it is hard to see where a fourth World Cup victory will come from. Even in the 2008 AFC Challenge Cup, a competition designed in order that the less successful nations in Asia could have a competitive platform, Macau lost both games played although by a much closer margin. In a preliminary tournament played in Phonm Penh, new coach Leung Sui Wing from Hong Kong saw his team lose 3-2 to Nepal and then 3-1 to the hosts as Macau slipped to their lowest ever position of 196 in the FIFA/Coca-Cola World Ranking. That was just three places above the worst teams in the world, nine of whom were ranked equal bottom at 199.

THE FIFA BIG COUNT OF 2006

	Male	Female		Total
Number of players	13 423	700	Referees and Assistant Referees	51
Professionals	1		Admin, Coaches, Technical, Medical	703
Amateurs 18+	4 130		Number of clubs	96
Youth under 18	592		Number of teams	120
Unregistered	1 750		Clubs with women's teams	0
Total players	14 123		Players as % of population	3.12%

Macau Football Association (AFM)
Avenida Wai Leong Taipa, University of Science and Technology, Football Field, Block I, Taipa, Macau
Tel +853 28830287   Fax +853 28830409
macaufa@macau.ctm.net   www.macaufa.com
President: CHEUNG Vitor Lup Kwan   General Secretary: CHOI Kam Vai
Vice-President: CHONG Coc Veng   Treasurer: CHIO Kam Vai   Media Officer: None
Men's Coach: LEUNG Sui Wing   Women's Coach: None
AFM formed: 1939   AFC: 1976   FIFA: 1976
Green shirts, Green shorts, Green socks

RECENT INTERNATIONAL MATCHES PLAYED BY MACAU

2003	Opponents		Score	Venue	Comp	Scorers	Att	Referee
23-11	Chinese Taipei	L	0-3	Taipei	WCq		2 000	Napitupulu IDN
29-11	Chinese Taipei	L	1-3	Macau	WCq	Lei Fu Weng [87]	250	Zhou Weixin CHN
2004								
No international matches played in 2004								
2005								
21-05	Hong Kong	L	1-8	Hong Kong	Fr	Chung Koon Kan [86]		
2006								
2-04	Tajikistan	L	0-4	Dhaka	CCr1		2 000	Mombini IRN
6-04	Pakistan	D	2-2	Dhaka	CCr1	Chan Kin Seng 2 [16 52]	1 000	Shamsuzzaman BAN
7-04	Kyrgyzstan	L	0-2	Dhaka	CCr1		1 000	Tan Hai CHN
3-06	Hong Kong	D	0-0	Macau	Fr			
9-08	Chinese Taipei	L	0-1	Macau	Fr			
2007								
10-06	Hong Kong	L	1-2	Hong Kong	Fr	Chan Kin Seng [29]		
17-06	Mongolia	D	0-0	Macau	EAq		300	Matsuo JPN
21-06	Korea DPR	L	1-7	Macau	EAq	Chan Kin Seng [46]	300	Wan Daxue CHN
24-06	Chinese Taipei	L	2-7	Macau	EAq	De Sousa [48], Leong Chong In [78]	200	Kim Eui Soo KOR
8-10	Thailand	L	1-6	Bangkok	WCq	Chan Kin Seng [23]	11 254	Chynybekov KGZ
15-10	Thailand	L	1-7	Macau	WCq	Chan Kin Seng [92+]	500	Recho SYR
2008								
25-05	Nepal	L	2-3	Phnom Penh	CCq	Che Chi Man [29p], Chan Kin Seng [59]	2 000	Vo Minh Tri VIE
28-05	Cambodia	L	1-3	Phnom Penh	CCq	Che Chi Man [55]	3 000	Kurbanov TKM

Fr = Friendly match • EA = East Asian Championship • AC = AFC Asian Cup • CC = AFC Challenge Cup • WC = FIFA World Cup
q = qualifier • r1 = first round group

MACAU NATIONAL TEAM RECORDS AND RECORD SEQUENCES

Records			Sequence records					
Victory	5-1	PHI	Wins	2	1997-1990	Clean sheets	1	Seven times
Defeat	0-10	JPN 1997 (Twice)	Defeats	9	2000-2001	Goals scored	6	2007-
Player Caps	n/a		Undefeated	2	Three times	Without goal	5	1985-1987
Player Goals	n/a		Without win	19	2003-	Goals against	15	1992-1997

MACAU 2008

CAMPEONATO 1° DIVISAO	Pl	W	D	L	F	A	Pts	Monte Carlo	Lam Pak	Hoi Fan	Vong Chiu	Va Luen	Policia	Macau U21	Heng Tai
Monte Carlo	14	12	1	1	51	12	37		5-1	5-0	4-0	6-0	2-1	3-2	7-2
Lam Pak	14	11	2	1	50	14	35	2-2		1-1	5-2	1-0		5-0	6-1
Hoi Fan	14	7	3	4	20	21	24	0-4	0-2		1-0	0-0	1-0	2-4	3-0
Vong Chiu	14	7	2	5	27	28	23	4-3	1-5	2-2		2-2	1-0	2-3	1-0
Va Luen	14	4	3	7	14	28	15	0-3	0-6	0-4	0-1		2-0	2-3	1-0
Policia	14	4	1	9	13	23	13	0-3	1-5	1-2	2-3	1-1		2-0	1-0
Macau U–21	14	4	1	9	20	35	13	0-3	1-2	1-2	1-4	1-5	0-1		1-1
Heng Tai	14	0	1	13	7	41	1	0-1	0-7	1-2	0-4	0-1	1-3	1-3	

1/12/2007 - 27/04/2008

LEAGUE RECORD

Year	Champs
1997	Lam Pak
1998	Lam Pak
1999	Lam Pak
2000	Polícia
2001	Lam Pak
2002	Monte Carlo
2003	Monte Carlo
2004	Monte Carlo
2005	Polícia
2006	Lam Pak
2007	Lam Pak
2008	Monte Carlo

MACAU COUNTRY INFORMATION

Capital	Macau	Status	Special administrative region of China	GDP per Capita	$19 400
Population	445 286			GNP Ranking	n/a
Area km²	25.4 per km²	Language	Portuguese, Cantonese	Dialling code	+853
Population density	17 530	Literacy rate	94%	Internet code	.mo
% in urban areas	100%	Main religion	Buddhist 50%, Christian 15%	GMT +/−	+8
Towns/Cities ('000)	Macao 445				
Neighbours (km)	China 0.34; South China Sea 41				
Main stadia	Campo Desportivo – Macau 15 000				

MAD – MADAGASCAR

NATIONAL TEAM RECORD
JULY 10TH 2006 TO JULY 12TH 2010

PL	W	D	L	F	A	%
20	6	6	8	26	29	45

FIFA/COCA-COLA WORLD RANKING

1993	1994	1995	1996	1997	1998	1999	2000	2001	2002	2003	2004	2005	2006	2007	High	
89	111	132	140	163	150	134	114	122	101	118	147	149	184	149	**74**	12/92

2007–2008												Low	
08/07	09/07	10/07	11/07	12/07	01/08	02/08	03/08	04/08	05/08	06/08	07/08	**188**	11/06
163	164	158	152	149	149	150	149	151	146	135	130		

There was disappointment for Madagascar in their failure to win gold at the Indian Ocean Island Games which they hosted in Antananarivo in August 2007. A goalless draw in the final was followed by a 7-6 penalty shootout win for Reunion as Dimby Rabeariniala missed the vital kick. But it was soon followed by the consolation of an emphatic 10-2 aggregate win over the Comoros Islands in the preliminary round of the 2010 FIFA World Cup qualifiers. The victory was engineered by Franz Gerber, a German coach brought in on a short term contract with the assistance of his country's embassy in the Malagasy capital. He replaced Herve Arsene, who had been in

INTERNATIONAL HONOURS
Indian Ocean Games 1990 1993

charge for most of 2007. Mickael Nivoson took over the reigns for the start of the group phase of the World Cup qualifiers but after three matches was dismissed, replaced by Franck Rajaonarisamba, who was in turn to be replaced by Gerber again. Madagascar almost did not compete in the qualifying group after a brief spell of suspension by FIFA, again because of government interference in the running of the football federation. But the spat between state and the football administrators continued with the secretary of the Malagasy federation barred by the sports ministry from attending the press conference that announced the return of Gerber to the helm of the team.

THE FIFA BIG COUNT OF 2006

	Male	Female		Total
Number of players	787 470	38 950	Referees and Assistant Referees	680
Professionals	0		Admin, Coaches, Technical, Medical	4 108
Amateurs 18+	16 650		Number of clubs	220
Youth under 18	13 700		Number of teams	880
Unregistered	27 000		Clubs with women's teams	0
Total players	826 420		Players as % of population	4.44%

Fédération Malagasy de Football (FMF)
26 rue de Russie, Isoraka, PO Box 4409, Tananarive 101, Madagascar
Tel +261 20 2268374   Fax +261 20 2268373
fmf@blueline.mg   www.none
President: AHMAD   General Secretary: RABIBISOA Anselme
Vice-President: RAZAFINDKIAKA Sylvain   Treasurer: ZAFINANDRO René   Media Officer: RANJALAHY Sylvain
Men's Coach: RAJAONARISAMBA Franck   Women's Coach: ANDRIANTANASASOA Herihaja
FMF formed: 1961   CAF: 19   FIFA: 1962
Red shirts with green trimmings, White shorts, Green socks

RECENT INTERNATIONAL MATCHES PLAYED BY MADAGASCAR

2004	Opponents	Score	Venue	Comp	Scorers	Att	Referee
18-04	Mozambique	L 0-2	Maputo	CCr1		28 000	Damon RSA
2005							
26-02	Mauritius	L 0-2	Curepipe	CCq			Fakude SWZ
23-10	Mauritius	W 2-0	Antananarivo	Fr	Randriamalala [16p], Andriatsima [80]		
2006							
20-05	Botswana	L 0-2	Gaborone	CCr1			Colembi ANG
21-05	Swaziland	L 0-2	Gaborone	CCr1			Malepa BOT
2-09	Gabon	L 0-4	Libreville	CNq			Diatta SEN
2007							
25-03	Côte d'Ivoire	L 0-3	Antananarivo	CNq			Maillet SEY
28-04	Zimbabwe	L 0-1	Maputo	CCr1			Faduco MOZ
29-04	Seychelles	W 5-0	Maputo	CCr1	Voavy 3 [11 14 69], Ramiadamanana [62], Andriatsima [84]		Mpopo LES
3-06	Côte d'Ivoire	L 0-5	Bouaké	CNq			Louzaya CGO
17-06	Gabon	L 0-2	Antananarivo	CNq			Mlangeni SWZ
29-07	Congo DR	D 0-0	Antananarivo	Fr			
14-08	Comoros	W 3-0	Antananarivo	Fr	Voavy 2 [70 89], Ramiadamanana 90		
14-10	Comoros	W 6-2	Antananarivo	WCq	Andriatsima 4 [30 40 49p 57], Rakotomandimby [65], Tsaralaza [79]	7 754	Kaoma ZAM
17-11	Comoros	W 4-0	Moroni	WCq	Nomenjanahary 2 [37 51], Rakotomandimby [61], Robson [73]	1 610	Damon RSA
2008							
9-03	Mauritius	W 2-1	Curepipe	Fr	Rabemananjara 2 [77 81]		
31-05	Botswana	D 0-0	Gaborone	WCq		11 087	Kaoma ZAM
8-06	Côte d'Ivoire	D 0-0	Antananarivo	WCq			Labrosse SEY
15-06	Mozambique	D 1-1	Antananarivo	WCq	Mamihasindrahona [91p]	15 501	Ebrahim RSA
22-06	Mozambique	L 0-3	Maputo	WCq		20 000	Maillet SEY
19-07	Swaziland	D 1-1	Witbank	CCr1	Hubert Robson 65		Nhlapo RSA
21-07	Seychelles	D 1-1	Witbank	CCr1	Tovohery Rabenandrasana 23		Kaoma ZAM
23-07	Mauritius	W 2-1	Witbank	CCr1	Tovohery Rabenandrasana [52], Praxis Rabemananjara [63]		Marange ZIM
30-07	Mozambique	L 1-2	Thulamahashe	CCsf	Praxis Rabemananjara		Marange ZIM
3-08	Zambia	L 0-2	Thulamahashe	CC3p			

Fr = Friendly match • CN = CAF African Cup of Nations • CC = COSAFA Cup • WC = FIFA World Cup
q = qualifier • r1 = first round group • sf = semi-final • 3p = third place play-off

MADAGASCAR NATIONAL TEAM RECORDS AND RECORD SEQUENCES

Records			Sequence records				
Victory	8-1	CGO 1960	Wins	8	1957-1963	Clean sheets	4	1990, 1992-93
Defeat	0-7	MRI 1952	Defeats	8	2001	Goals scored	14	1957-1965
Player Caps	n/a		Undefeated	10	1979-1980	Without goal	6	2001
Player Goals	n/a		Without win	14	2003-2005	Goals against	17	1971-1980

MADAGASCAR COUNTRY INFORMATION

Capital	Antananarivo	Independence	1960 from France	GDP per Capita	$800
Population	17 501 871	Status	Republic	GNP Ranking	119
Area km²	587 040	Language	French, Malagasy	Dialling code	+261
Population density	29 per km²	Literacy rate	68%	Internet code	.mg
% in urban areas	27%	Main religion	Indigenous 52%, Christian 41%	GMT + / –	+3
Towns/Cities ('000)	Antananarivo 1 391; Toamasina 206; Antsirabé 183; Fianarantsoa 167; Mahajanga 155; Toliary 115; Antsiranana 82; Antanifotsy 70; Ambovombe 66; Amparafaravola 51				
Neighbours (km)	Indian Ocean 4 828				
Main stadia	Mahamasina – Antananarivo 22 000				

MADAGASCAR 2007 NATIONAL CHAMPIONSHIP SECOND STAGE

Group A - Toamasina	Pl	W	D	L	F	A	Pts
Adema Antananarivo ‡	4	2	2	0	10	1	8
Ajesaia Antananarivo ‡	4	2	2	0	8	3	8
ASCUM Mahajanga	4	2	0	2	4	4	6
Japan Actuels	4	1	2	1	7	3	5
SC Menabe	4	0	0	4	2	20	0

Group B - Toliara	Pl	W	D	L	F	A	Pts
USCAFOOT ‡	4	2	2	0	6	2	8
Fagnany ‡	4	2	2	0	5	2	8
Voromaherin Alaotra	4	2	1	1	12	5	7
Fomela	4	1	1	2	2	9	4
Mahasolo/AS Andry	4	0	0	4	2	9	0

Group C - Fianarantsoa	Pl	W	D	L	F	A	Pts
Académie Ny Antsika ‡	3	2	1	0	6	0	7
TOP Sport Atsinanana ‡	3	2	1	0	6	4	7
EEF Afoma	3	1	0	2	5	5	3
COSRM21 Ihorombe	3	0	0	3	2	10	0

Group D - Antsiranana	Pl	W	D	L	F	A	Pts
Tiko Vakinankaratra ‡	2	1	0	1	2	2	3
Spoutnik Diana ‡	2	1	0	1	2	2	3
Varatraza Antsohihy	2	1	0	1	1	1	3
Ma-Soci Soma			Withdrew				

12/09/2007 - 15/09/2007 • ‡ Qualified for the third stage

MADAGASCAR 2007 NATIONAL CHAMPIONSHIP THIRD & FOURTH STAGES

Group A - Antananarivo	Pl	W	D	L	F	A	Pts
Ajesaia Antananarivo ‡	3	2	1	0	5	0	7
TOP Sport Atsinanana ‡	3	2	1	0	2	0	7
Fagnany	3	1	0	1	3	4	3
Tiko Vakinankaratra	3	0	0	2	1	7	0

Group B - Toamasina	Pl	W	D	L	F	A	Pts
Adema Antananarivo ‡	3	2	1	0	5	0	7
USCAFOOT ‡	3	2	1	0	4	0	7
Académie Ny Antsika	3	1	0	2	3	4	3
Spoutnik Diana	3	0	0	3	0	8	0

Final Stage - Mahamasina	Pl	W	D	L	F	A	Pts
Ajesaia Antananarivo †	3	2	1	0	9	1	7
Adema Antananarivo	3	2	0	1	6	3	6
USCAFOOT	3	1	1	1	2	2	4
TOP Sport Atsinanana	3	0	0	3	1	12	0

25/09/2007 - 3/11/2007 • ‡ Qualified for the final stage
† Qualified for the CAF Champions League

COUPE DE MADAGASCAR 2007

Round of 16		Quarter–finals		Semi–finals		Final	
Adema Antananarivo	2						
EEF Afoma	1	Adema Antananarivo	2				
Herini Sambava	0	ASCUM Mahajanga	1				
ASCUM Mahajanga	4			Adema Antananarivo	4		
Voromaherin Alaotra	1			COSFA	0		
COSRM21 Ihorombe	0	Voromaherin Alaotra	1				
3FB Ambatondrazaka	1	COSFA	3				
COSFA	4					Adema Antananarivo ‡	1
Ajesaia Antananarivo	2					USCAFOOT	0
FC Fax 2A	0	Ajesaia Antananarivo	4				
Tiko Antsirabe	1	Japan Actuels	0			CUP FINAL	
Japan Actuels	4			Ajesaia Antananarivo	0		
Académie Ny Antsika	1			USCAFOOT	1	Mahamasina, Antananarivo	
Tana AC	0	Académie Ny Antsika	0			25-11-2007	
Fomela Ambalavao	0	USCAFOOT	2				
USCAFOOT	5			‡ Qualified for the CAF Confederation Cup		Scorer - Tsiala Kennedy [1]	

RECENT LEAGUE AND CUP RECORD

	Championship	Cup		
Year	Champions	Winners	Score	Runners-up
1998	DSA Antananarivo	FC Djivan Farafangana	2-0	Fortior Club Mahajanga
1999	Fortior Toamasina	FC Djivan Farafangana	3-0	Akon'Ambatomena
2000	Fortior Toamasina	FC Djivan Farafangana	1-0	FC Jirama Antsirabe
2001	Stade Olympique Antananarivo (SOE)	US Transfoot Toamasina	1-0	Fortior Toamasina
2002	Adema Antananarivo	Fortior Toamasina	3-0	US Transfoot Toamasina
2003	Eco Redipharm Tamatave	Léopards Transfoot	1-0	SOE Antananarivo
2004	USJF/Ravinala	USJF/Ravinala	2-1	USCAFOOT Antananarivo
2005	USCAFOOT Antananarivo	USCAFOOT Antananarivo	2-1	USJF/Ravinala
2006	Adema Antananarivo	Ajesaia Antananarivo	1-0	USCAFOOT Antananarivo
2007	Ajesaia Antananarivo	Adema Antananarivo	1-0	USCAFOOT Antananarivo

MAR – MOROCCO

NATIONAL TEAM RECORD
JULY 10TH 2006 TO JULY 12TH 2010

PL	W	D	L	F	A	%
21	14	3	4	46	18	73.8

FIFA/COCA-COLA WORLD RANKING

1993	1994	1995	1996	1997	1998	1999	2000	2001	2002	2003	2004	2005	2006	2007	High	
30	33	38	27	15	13	24	28	36	35	38	33	36	39	39	10	04/98

	2007–2008											Low	
08/07	09/07	10/07	11/07	12/07	01/08	02/08	03/08	04/08	05/08	06/08	07/08	49	03/08
34	38	42	39	39	39	48	49	46	45	40	37		

For a second successive tournament, Morocco crashed out of the CAF Africa Cup of Nations finals at the first hurdle, failing to make the last eight despite a squad of some potential. Morocco finished third in the Group A at the 2008 finals in Ghana behind the host nation and Guinea. It cost coach Henri Michel his job, barely a handful of months into his second spell with Morocco. The tension between him and the players and the absence of any spark in the side saw officials move swiftly to take a new direction. Roger Lemerre, another taciturn Frenchman who is now a veteran of the African football scene after winning the Nations Cup with Tunisia, was appointed coach, but

INTERNATIONAL HONOURS
Qualified for the FIFA World Cup finals 1970 1986 1994 1998 CAF African Cup of Nations 1976
African Youth Championship 1997 CAF Champions League FAR Rabat 1985, Raja Casablanca 1989 1997 1999, Wydad Casablanca 1992

he only started after Morocco's first four FIFA World Cup qualifiers, in which Fathi Jemal served as caretaker. Morocco amassed nine points in those four games but were handed an eyebrow-raising defeat away against Rwanda in Kigali. At club level, Royal Armed Forces completed a league and cup 'double', first winning the championship with a three-point difference between them and Ittihad Khemisset and then beating Maghreb Fes 1-0 in the Coupe du Trone, after extra time in Rabat. Former international Jawad Ouaddouch grabbed the winner in the 93rd minute.

THE FIFA BIG COUNT OF 2006

	Male	Female		Total
Number of players	1 553 748	74 268	Referees and Assistant Referees	2 007
Professionals	601		Admin, Coaches, Technical, Medical	6 644
Amateurs 18+	40 010		Number of clubs	563
Youth under 18	123 647		Number of teams	2 815
Unregistered	165 000		Clubs with women's teams	36
Total players	1 628 016		Players as % of population	4.90%

Fédération Royale Marocaine de Football (FRMF)
51 Bis Avenue Ibn Sina, Agdal, Case Postale 51, Rabat 10 000, Morocco
Tel +212 37 672706   Fax +212 37 671070
contact@frmf.ma   www.frmf.ma
President: BENSLIMANE Housni   General Secretary: BENCHEIKH Larci
Vice-President: AOUZAL Mohamed   Treasurer: EL AOUFIR Larbi   Media Officer: MOUFID Mohamed
Men's Coach: LEMERRE Roger   Women's Coach: ALAOUI Slimani
FRMF formed: 1955   CAF: 1966   FIFA: 1960
Green shirts with red trimmings, Green shorts, Green socks or Red shirts with green trimmings, Red shorts, Red socks

RECENT INTERNATIONAL MATCHES PLAYED BY MOROCCO

2006 Opponents		Score	Venue	Comp	Scorers	Att	Referee
9-01	Congo DR	W 3-0	Rabat	Fr	Chamakh [32], Aboucherouane [52], Armoumen [67]		
14-01	Zimbabwe	W 1-0	Marrakech	Fr	Armoumen [89]		
17-01	Angola	D 2-2	Marrakech	Fr	Chamakh [6], Youssef Hadji [8]		
21-01	Côte d'Ivoire	L 0-1	Cairo	CNr1		8 000	Damon RSA
24-01	Egypt	D 0-0	Cairo	CNr1		75 000	Codjia BEN
28-01	Libya	D 0-0	Cairo	CNr1		5 000	Daami TUN
23-05	USA	W 1-0	Nashville	Fr	Madihi [90]	26 141	Navarro CAN
28-05	Mali	L 0-1	Paris	Fr			Garibian FRA
4-06	Colombia	L 0-2	Barcelona	Fr		11 000	Segura Garcia ESP
16-08	Burkina Faso	W 1-0	Rabat	Fr	Youssef Hadji [44]		
3-09	Malawi	W 2-0	Rabat	CNq	Chammakh [50], Boussoufa [72]		Codjia BEN
15-11	Gabon	W 6-0	Rabat	Fr	El Moubarki 2 [40 64], Ouaddouch [61], Boukhari [68], Al Mahdoufi [71], Souari [90]	5 000	Sidebe MLI
2007							
7-02	Tunisia	D 1-1	Casablanca	Fr	Chammakh [29]		
25-03	Zimbabwe	D 1-1	Harare	CNq	Youssef Hadji [7]		Damon RSA
2-06	Zimbabwe	W 2-0	Casablanca	CNq	Chamakh [4], Youssef Hadji [26]		Daami TUN
16-06	Malawi	W 1-0	Blantyre	CNq	El Moubarki [10]		Maillet SEY
8-09	Ghana	L 0-2	Rouen	Fr			
17-10	Namibia	W 2-0	Tangiers	Fr	Alloudi [71], El Karkouri [90]		
16-11	France	D 2-2	Paris	Fr	Sektioui [8], Mokhtari [84]	78 000	Bossen NED
21-11	Senegal	W 3-0	Creteil	Fr	Aboucherouane [23], Mokhtari [64], Azmi [73]		Benoit FRA
2008							
12-01	Zambia	W 2-0	Fes	Fr	Sektioui [51p], Alloudi [60]		
16-01	Angola	W 2-1	Rabat	Fr	Chamakh [44], Aboucherouane [51]		
21-01	Namibia	W 5-1	Accra	CNr1	Alloudi 3 [2 5 28], Sektioui [39p], Zerka [74]		Evehe CMR
24-01	Guinea	L 2-3	Accra	CNr1	Aboucherouane [60], Ouaddou [89]		Damon RSA
28-01	Ghana	L 0-2	Accra	CNr1			Sowe GAM
26-03	Belgium	W 4-1	Brussels	Fr			
31-05	Ethiopia	W 3-0	Casablanca	WCq	Benjelloun [4], Aboucherouane [13], Kharja [85]	5 000	Diatta SEN
7-06	Mauritania	W 4-1	Nouakchott	WCq	Sektioui [9], Benjelloun [37], Safri [58], Kharja [79]	9 500	Lamptey GHA
14-06	Rwanda	L 1-3	Kigali	WCq	Safri [78]	12 000	Evehe CMR
21-06	Rwanda	W 2-0	Casablanca	WCq	Safri [12p], El Zhar [49]	2 500	Benouza ALG

Fr = Friendly match • AR = Arab Cup • CN = CAF African Cup of Nations • WC = FIFA World Cup
q = qualifier • r1 = first round group • qf = quarter-final • sf = semi-final • f = final

MOROCCO NATIONAL TEAM PLAYERS

	Player		Club	Date of Birth		Player		Club	Date of Birth
1	Nadir Lamyaghri	GK	Wydad Casablanca	13 02 1976	12	Khalid Fouhami	GK	Raja Casablanca	25 12 1972
2	Michael Chretien	DF	Nancy	10 07 1984	13	Houcine Kharja	MF	Piacenza	9 11 1982
3	Hicham Mahdoufi	DF	Metalist Kharkiv	5 08 1983	14	Abdessamad Chahiri	DF	Difaa El Jadida	17 05 1982
4	Abdeslam Ouaddou	DF	Valenciennes	1 11 1987	15	Youssef Safri	MF	Southampton	13 01 1977
5	Talal El Karkouri	DF	Qatar SC	8 07 1978	16	Youssef Mokhtari	MF	Al Jazeera QAT	5 03 1979
6	El Armine Erbate	DF	Al Dafra UAE	1 01 1981	17	Maroune Chamakh	FW	Girondins Bordeaux	10 01 1984
7	Soufiane Alloudi	MF	Al Ain UAE	1 07 1983	18	Abderrahmane Kabous	MF	CSKA Sofia	24 04 1983
8	Abdelkrim Kissi	MF	EN Paralimni	5 05 1980	19	Jamal Alioui	DF	FC Sion	2 06 1982
9	Bouchaib El Moubarki	FW	Grenoble	12 01 1978	20	Youssef Hadji	FW	Nancy	25 02 1980
10	Tarik Sektioui	MF	FC Porto	13 05 1977	21	Badr El Kaddouri	MF	Dynamo Kyiv	31 01 1981
11	Moncef Zerka	FW	Nancy	30 08 1981	22	Abdelilah Bagui	GK	Maghreb Fes	1 01 1978
	Morocco's squad for the 2008 CAF Africa Cup of Nations				23	Hicham Aboucherouane	FW	Esperance	2 04 1981

MOROCCO NATIONAL TEAM RECORDS AND RECORD SEQUENCES

Records			Sequence records					
Victory	7-0	TOG 1979	Wins	8	1997	Clean sheets	9	1997
Defeat	0-6	HUN 1964	Defeats	4	1994	Goals scored	12	1975-1976
Player Caps	115	NAYBET Noureddine	Undefeated	15	1983-84, 1996-97	Without goal	6	1983
Player Goals	n/a		Without win	7	1988	Goals against	9	1959-1961

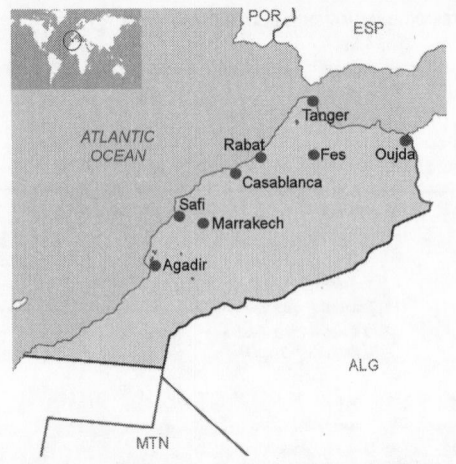

	MAJOR CITIES/TOWNS	
		Population '000
1	Casablanca	3 209
2	Rabat	1 721
3	Fez	1 001
4	Marrakesh	872
5	Agadir	739
6	Tangier	726
7	Meknes	564
8	Oujda	414
9	Kenitra	381
10	Tetouan	337
11	Safi	294
12	Laâyoune	217
13	Mohammedia	196
14	Beni Mellal	172
15	Khouribga	170
16	El Jadida	153
17	Taza	146
18	Nador	135
19	Settat	124
20	Larache	113
21	Ksar El Kebir	111
22	Khemisset	110
23	Guelmim	103
24	Berrechid	102

KINGDOM OF MOROCCO; AL MAMLAKAH AL MAGHRIBIYAH

Capital	Rabat	Language	Arabic, Berber, French			Independence	1956
Population	33 241 259	Area	446 550 km²	Density	72 per km²	% in cities	48%
GDP per cap	$4 000	Dailling code	+212	Internet	.ma	GMT + / -	0

MEDALS TABLE

			Overall			League			Cup			Africa			City	Stadium	Cap'ty	DoF
			G	S	B	G	S	B	G	S	B	G	S	B				
1	FAR Rabat	FAR	24	11	6	12	5	4	10	4		2	2	2	Rabat	Moulay Abdallah	60 000	1957
2	Wydad Casablanca	WAC	22	14	9	11	7	7	9	6		2	1	2	Casablanca	Stade Mohammed V	60 000	1937
3	Raja Casablanca	RCA	18	11	10	8	6	9	6	4		4	1	1	Casablanca	Stade Mohammed V	60 000	1949
4	Kawkab Marrakech	KACM	9	8	3	2	6	3	6	2	1				Marrakech	El Hirati	15 000	1947
5	Maghreb Fès	MAS	6	9	2	4	2	2	2	7					Fès	Complexe Sportif	45 000	1946
6	KAC Kénitra	KAC	5	5	1	4	2	1	1	3					Kénitra	Stade Municipal	15 000	1938
7	Mouloudia Oujda	MCO	5	2	3	1	1	3	4	1					Oujda	Stade d'Honneur	40 000	1946
8	FUS Rabat	FUS	4	3	1		2	1	4	1					Rabat	Ahmed Choude	10 000	1946
9	Olympic Casablanca	OC	3	1		1	1		2						Casablanca	Derejega	15 000	-1995
10	Olympique Khouribga	OCK	2	6	3	1	2	3	1	4					Khouribga	Complexe Al Phosphate	5 000	1923
11	Rennaisance Settat	RSS	2	5	3	1	2	3	1	3					Settat	Stade Municipal	16 000	1946
12	Chabab Mohammedia	SCCM	2	2	1	1		1	1	2					Mohammedia	El Bachir	5 000	1946
13	Hassania Agadir	HUSA	2	2		2				2					Agadir	Al Inbiaâte	15 000	1946
14	COD Meknès	CODM	2	1	1	1		1	1	1					Meknès	Stade d'Honneur	20 000	1962
15	Racing Casablanca	RAC	1	2			2		1						Casablanca	Père Jégo	12 000	

RECENT LEAGUE AND CUP RECORD

	Championship							Cup		
Year	Champions	Pts	Runners-up	Pts	Third	Pts		Winners	Score	Runners-up
1995	COD Meknès	66	Olympic Casablanca	65	Kawkab Marrakech	65		FUS Rabat	2-0	Olympic Khouribga
1996	Raja Casablanca	57	Olympic Khouribga	48	Wydad Casablanca	47		Raja Casablanca	1-0	FAR Rabat
1997	Raja Casablanca	55	Wydad Casablanca	53	Renaissance Settat	53		Wydad Casablanca	1-0	Kawkab Marrakech
1998	Raja Casablanca	67	Kawkab Marrakech	53	Wydad Casablanca	51		Wydad Casablanca	2-1	FAR Rabat
1999	Raja Casablanca	62	Kawkab Marrakech	58	Olympic Khouribga	54		FAR Rabat	1-0	Chabab Mohammedia
2000	Raja Casablanca	59	Wydad Casablanca	54	Maghreb Fès	53		Majd Casablanca	1-1 8-7p	Renaissance Settat
2001	Raja Casablanca	64	FUS Rabat	55	Maghreb Fès	48		Wydad Casablanca	1-0	Maghreb Fès
2002	Hassania Agadir	65	Wydad Casablanca	62	Raja Casablanca	55		Raja Casablanca	2-0	Maghreb Fès
2003	Hassania Agadir	54	Raja Casablanca	52	Wydad Casablanca	52		FAR Rabat	1-0	Wydad Casablanca
2004	Raja Casablanca	56	FAR Rabat	56	AS Salé	51		FAR Rabat	0-0 3-0p	Wydad Casablanca
2005	FAR Rabat	62	Raja Casablanca	60	Wydad Casablanca	50		Raja Casablanca	0-0 5-4p	Olympic Khouribga
2006	Wydad Casablanca	61	FAR Rabat	58	Olympic Khouribga	53		Olympic Khouribga	1-0	Hassania Agadir
2007	Olympic Khouribga	62	FAR Rabat	55	MA Tétouan	54		FAR Rabat	1-1 5-4p	Rachad Bernoussi
2008	FAR Rabat	53	IZ Khemisset	50	Raja Casablanca	48		FAR Rabat	1-0	Maghreb Fès

MOROCCO 2007–08
CHAMPIONNAT DU GNF1

	Pl	W	D	L	F	A	Pts	FAR	IZK	RCA	HUS	DHJ	OCK	WAC	MAT	JSM	OCS	MAS	KACM	KAC	MCO	FUS	CODM
FAR Rabat †	30	14	11	5	36	23	53		1-0	0-0	3-1	0-1	2-1	1-2	3-2	1-1	1-3	2-1	2-1	2-0	1-0	1-0	0-0
IZ Khemisset †	30	14	8	8	34	22	50	1-2		2-1	0-0	2-1	0-0	1-0	2-1	0-1	1-0	1-0	0-0	1-1	2-1	0-1	4-1
Raja Casablanca ‡	30	12	12	6	32	23	48	1-1	0-0		1-0	1-0	0-0	2-0	1-1	3-0	1-1	2-1	1-1	2-2	3-2	1-0	2-0
HUS Agadir	30	11	13	6	23	14	46	0-2	1-0	2-0		1-0	1-1	0-0	1-0	3-1	2-1	0-0	4-0	1-0	1-0	0-0	2-0
Diffa El Jadida	30	12	10	8	29	26	46	1-0	0-3	4-3	1-0		2-2	1-0	0-0	2-1	2-0	1-1	2-1	0-0	2-0	0-0	1-0
Olympique Khouribga	30	10	13	7	32	26	43	2-0	0-0	1-1	0-0	1-1		1-1	1-0	2-0	1-0	2-0	1-1	2-0	2-1	0-0	
Wydad Casablanca	30	10	12	8	28	23	42	0-0	0-2	0-1	1-1	2-1	0-0		0-0	1-1	1-1	1-0	1-1	3-0	4-1	2-1	1-1
MA Tétouan	30	10	12	8	29	19	42	0-0	2-0	0-0	0-0	1-0	2-0	0-1		1-0	1-0	1-2	2-1	1-2	4-0	2-2	2-0
JS Massira	30	8	14	8	27	28	38	0-0	0-1	1-0	1-1	0-0	1-2	1-1	0-0		1-2	1-1	1-0	2-0	0-0	1-1	5-3
Olympique Safi	30	8	12	10	31	31	36	1-1	1-2	0-1	0-0	0-0	2-1	2-1	0-0	2-2		1-0	2-2	2-0	3-1	0-0	2-2
Maghreb Fès ‡	30	9	9	12	27	30	36	0-2	1-2	1-2	0-0	2-1	2-1	0-3	1-1	0-0	1-1		3-1	4-0	1-0	0-0	2-2
Kawkab Marrakech	30	6	15	9	23	31	33	1-1	0-3	1-0	0-0	0-0	0-0	1-0	1-0	0-1	0-0	1-0		2-0	1-2	0-0	1-0
Kénitra AC	30	6	13	11	20	33	31	1-1	0-0	1-0	1-0	1-1	2-1	0-1	0-0	0-1	1-0	0-1	2-2		2-0	0-0	0-0
Mouloudia Oujda	30	8	7	15	29	48	31	2-2	2-1	1-1	0-0	3-1	3-1	2-0	0-3	1-1	3-2	1-0	0-2	1-0		1-1	2-2
FUS Rabat	30	4	14	12	23	30	26	0-1	3-2	0-1	1-0	1-2	1-2	0-0	0-1	0-2	1-2	0-1	1-1	1-1	3-0		2-2
COD Meknès	30	3	15	12	24	40	24	0-3	1-1	0-0	0-1	0-1	3-2	0-1	1-1	0-0	1-0	0-1	0-0	1-1	2-0	2-2	

21/09/2007 – 8/06/2008 • † Qualified for the CAF Champions League • ‡ Qualified for the CAF Confederation Cup

MOROCCO 2007–08
CHAMPIONNAT DU GNF2

	Pl	W	D	L	F	A	Pts
AS Salé	30	14	9	7	41	19	51
Chabab Mohammedia	30	12	13	5	33	22	49
TUS Temara	30	11	14	5	33	20	47
Chabab Houara	30	12	9	9	44	39	45
US Sidi Kacem	30	10	12	8	29	19	42
IR Tanger	30	10	12	8	19	18	42
TAS Casablanca	30	8	17	5	24	22	41
US Mohammedia	30	8	16	6	23	23	40
CAY Berrechid	30	7	17	6	25	20	38
Wafaa Casablanca §4	30	11	8	11	28	28	37
Racing Casablanca	30	9	10	11	18	21	37
CR Hoceima	30	7	15	8	21	21	36
RS Settat	30	7	14	9	24	29	35
Rachad Bernoussi	30	7	13	10	30	31	34
US Touarga	30	7	7	16	25	37	28
Hilal Nador	30	4	6	20	15	63	18

22/09/2007 – 1/06/2008 • § = points deducted

COUPE DU TRONE 2008

Round of 16

FAR Rabat	1	
AS Salé *	0	
Hilal Nador	0	
Kénitra AC *	3	
Diffa El Jadida	2	
HUS Agadir *	1	
UW Sidi Moumen	0	
Olympique Khouribga*	5	
MA Tétouan	1	
US Sidi Kacem *	0	
Kawkab Marrakech	1	
Raja Casablanca *	2	
Chabab Houara *	3	
Wydad Casablanca	1	
Wydad Fès	0	
Maghreb Fès *	1	

Quarter–finals

FAR Rabat	0 10p
Kénitra AC *	0 11p
Diffa El Jadida *	1 4p
Olympique Khouribga	1 5p
MA Tétouan *	1
Raja Casablanca	0
Chabab Houara *	0
Maghreb Fès	1

Semi–finals

FAR Rabat	1
Olympique Khouribga	0
MA Tétouan	1
Maghreb Fès	2

Final

FAR Rabat	1
Maghreb Fès ‡	0

See page 1047 for details of the Coupe du Trone 2007

CUP FINAL

26-07-2008

Scorer - Jawad Ouaddouch 93

Semi-finals played in Marrakech
* Home team • ‡ Qualified for the CAF Confederation Cup

MAS – MALAYSIA

NATIONAL TEAM RECORD
JULY 10TH 2006 TO JULY 12TH 2010

PL	W	D	L	F	A	%
20	4	7	9	26	33	37.5

FIFA/COCA-COLA WORLD RANKING

1993	1994	1995	1996	1997	1998	1999	2000	2001	2002	2003	2004	2005	2006	2007
79	89	106	96	87	113	117	107	111	128	116	120	123	152	159

High	
75	08/93

2007–2008											
08/07	09/07	10/07	11/07	12/07	01/08	02/08	03/08	04/08	05/08	06/08	07/08
156	159	166	159	159	164	165	164	170	169	169	166

Low	
170	04/08

Despite claims that the entire footballing infrastructure of the nation would be overhauled in the aftermath of an abysmal Asian Cup campaign, little has changed for Malaysia as the country struggles to return to its status as one of the leading lights of Asian football. Norizan Bakar stood down as national team coach following the debacle of the Asian Cup – when Malaysia scored just once in three group games on home soil – and was eventually replaced by B. Sathianathan after the under-23 team showed encouraging signs during the 2007 Merdeka Cup tournament. Malaysia's woes continued with their 2010 FIFA World Cup campaign lasting just two games thanks to a 4-1

INTERNATIONAL HONOURS
Southeast Asian Games 1961 1977 1979 1989

aggregate defeat at the hands of Bahrain. The goal now is to re-establish the team at regional level and to aim to reach at least the semi-finals of the ASEAN Championship, as they did in 2006. Kedah, the club with some of the most fanatical fans in the country, retained both the Malaysia Super League title and the Malaysian FA Cup, which along with their 2007 Malaysia Cup success made it an unprecedented five successive titles for the club. Along with Perak, Kedah also reached the quarter-finals of the 2008 AFC Cup, the first time two Malaysian clubs have qualified for the knockout phase of a continental competition in the same season.

THE FIFA BIG COUNT OF 2006

	Male	Female		Total
Number of players	549 300	36 430	Referees and Assistant Referees	1 810
Professionals	600		Admin, Coaches, Technical, Medical	10 000
Amateurs 18+	1 430		Number of clubs	110
Youth under 18	7 300		Number of teams	550
Unregistered	259 800		Clubs with women's teams	0
Total players	585 730		Players as % of population	2.40%

Football Association of Malaysia (FAM)
3rd Floor Wisma FAM, Jalan SS5A/9, Kelana Jaya, Petaling Jaya 47301, Malaysia
Tel +60 3 78733100   Fax +60 3 78757984
gensec@fam.org.my   www.fam.org.my
President: HRH Sultan AHMAD SHAH   General Secretary: BIN AHMAD Azzuddin
Vice-President: HRH Abdullah AHMED SHAH   Treasurer: CHEONG Keap Tai   Media Officer: KHAWARI Ahmad
Men's Coach: BHASKRAN Satiananthan   Women's Coach: SINGH Macky
FAM formed: 1933   AFC: 1954   FIFA: 1956
Yellow shirts with black trimmings, Yellow shorts, Yellow socks

RECENT INTERNATIONAL MATCHES PLAYED BY MALAYSIA

2004	Opponents	Score		Venue	Comp	Scorers	Att	Referee
19-08	Thailand	W	2-1	Bangkok	Fr	Kit Hong [8], Vellu [57]		
8-09	China PR	L	0-1	Penang	WCq		14 000	Karim BHR
13-10	Hong Kong	L	0-2	Hong Kong	WCq		2 425	Ghandour LIB
1-11	Singapore	W	2-1	Singapore	Fr	Bin Jamlus [68], Amri [90]	3 293	Luong The Tai VIE
17-11	Kuwait	L	1-6	Kuwait City	WCq	Mohd [19]	15 000	Lutfullin UZB
8-12	East Timor †	W	5-0	Kuala Lumpur	TCr1	Kit Kong [27], Amri 2 [47 83], Saari [67], Adan [85]	6 000	Lazar SIN
10-12	Philippines	W	4-1	Kuala Lumpur	TCr1	Kit Kong [17], Bin Jamlus 2 [67 77p], Hussein [74]		Napitupulu IDN
12-12	Myanmar	L	0-1	Kuala Lumpur	TCr1		10 000	Hsu Chao Lo TPE
14-12	Thailand	W	2-1	Kuala Lumpur	TCr1	Bin Jamlus 2 [63 65]	10 000	Moradi IRN
28-12	Indonesia	W	2-1	Jakarta	TCsf	Kit Kong 2 [28 47]	100 000	Irmatov UZB
2005								
3-01	Indonesia	L	1-4	Kuala Lumpur	TCsf	Bin Jamlus [26]	70 000	Kunsuta THA
15-01	Myanmar	W	2-1	Singapore	TC3p	Bin Jamlus [15], Nor [56]	2 000	Vo Minh Tri VIE
4-06	Singapore	L	0-2	Singapore	Fr		18 000	Kunsuta THA
8-06	Singapore	L	1-2	Penang	Fr	Ayob [25]	10 000	Napitupulu IDN
2006								
19-02	New Zealand	L	0-1	Christchurch	Fr		10 100	O'Leary NZL
23-02	New Zealand	L	1-2	Albany	Fr	Safee Sali [24]	8 702	Fox NZL
31-05	Singapore	D	0-0	Singapore	Fr	L 4-5p	18 604	Li Yuhong CHN
3-06	Singapore	D	0-0	Paroi	Fr	L 7-8p		
23-08	Indonesia	D	1-1	Kuala Lumpur	Fr	Ridwan OG [77]	20 000	Zhang Lei CHN
25-08	Thailand	W	2-1	Kuala Lumpur	Fr	Indra Putra 2 [39 77]		Lee Jong Kuk KOR
27-08	Myanmar	L	1-2	Kuala Lumpur	Fr	Indra Putra [12p]		Zhang Lei CHN
2007								
12-01	Philippines	W	4-0	Bangkok	TCr1	Hairuddin Omar 2 [9 80], Niaruddin Yusof [16]. OG [69]	5 000	Daud SIN
14-01	Myanmar	D	0-0	Bangkok	TCr1		28 000	Tri Minh Vo VIE
16-01	Thailand	L	0-1	Bangkok	TCr1		25 000	Matsuo JPN
23-01	Singapore	D	1-1	Kuala Lumpur	TCsf	Hardi Jaafar [57]	40 000	Wan Daxue CHN
27-01	Singapore	D	1-1	Singapore	TCsf	Helmi Manan [57]. L 4-5p	55 000	Cheung Yim Yau HKG
24-03	Sri Lanka	W	4-1	Colombo	Fr	Hardi Jaafar [5], Fadzli Saari [12], Azlan Ismail [45], Norhafiz Zamani Misbah [65]		
26-03	Sri Lanka	L	1-2	Colombo	Fr	Kaironnisam Sahabuddin Hussain [16]		Da Silva SRI
18-06	Cambodia	W	6-0	Kuala Lumpur	Fr	Rosdi Talib [23], Mohd Ivan Yusof [47], Hairuddin Omar [58], Helmi Manan 2 [61 88], Aidil Zafuan [90]		
21-06	UAE	L	1-3	Kelana Jaya	Fr	Akmal Rizal Rakhli [88]		
28-06	Jamaica	L	0-2	Kuala Lumpur	Fr			
10-07	China PR	L	1-5	Kuala Lumpur	ACr1	Indra Putra [72]	20 000	Basma SYR
14-07	Uzbekistan	L	0-5	Kuala Lumpur	ACr1		7 137	Abdou QAT
18-07	Iran	L	0-2	Kuala Lumpur	ACr1		4 520	Basma SYR
21-10	Bahrain	L	1-4	Manama	WCq	Bunyamin Umar [45]	4 000	Yang Zhiqiang CHN
28-10	Bahrain	D	0-0	Kuala Lumpur	WCq		2 000	Lee Gi Young KOR
2008								
6-06	Indonesia	D	1-1	Surabaya	Fr	Adan [34]		
22-07	India	D	1-1	Hyderabad	Fr	Indra Putra [75]		

Fr = Friendly match • TC = ASEAN Tiger Cup • AC = AFC Asian Cup • AAG = Afro-Asian Games • WC = FIFA World Cup
q = qualifier • r1 = first round group • sf = semi-final • 3p = third place play-off • † not a full international

MALAYSIA NATIONAL TEAM RECORDS AND RECORD SEQUENCES

Records			Sequence records			
Victory	15-1	PHI 1962	Wins	6	1975, 1989	Clean sheets	5	1979
Defeat	2-8	NZL 1967	Defeats	7	1980-81, 2003-04	Goals scored	14	1999-2000
Player Caps	n/a		Undefeated	10	1961-1962, 1971	Without goal	5	1997-1998
Player Goals	n/a		Without win	12	2003-2004	Goals against	15	1970-1971

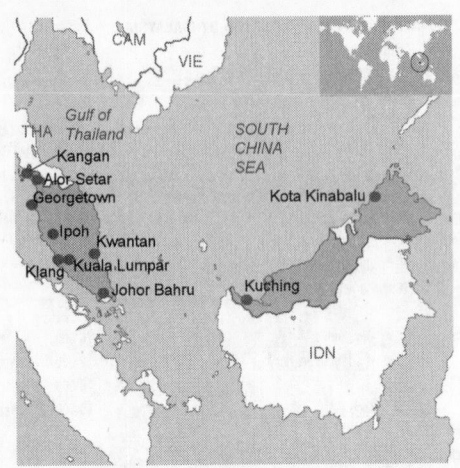

MALAYSIA

Capital	Kuala Lumpur	Language	Malay, English, Chinese		Independence	1963	
Population	24 385 858	Area	329 750 km²	Density	71 per km²	% in cities	54%
GDP per cap	$9 000	Dialling code	+60	Internet	.my	GMT +/−	+8

MEDALS TABLE

		Overall G	Overall S	Overall B	League G	League S	League B	M Cup G	M Cup S	FAC G	FAC S	Asia G	Asia S	Asia B	City	Stadium	Cap'ty	DoF
1	Selangor	40	19		4	2		32	14	4	2		1		Selangor	Shah Alam	80 000	1936
2	FA of Singapore	26	19		2			24	19						Singapore			1892
3	Perak	11	15	3	2	1	3	7	11	2	3				Ipoh	Perak Stadium	40 000	1921
4	Kedah	9	9		3	3		3	6	3					Alor Setar	Darul Aman	40 000	1935
5	Penang	8	13		3	2		4	9	1	2				George Town	Negeri Pulau Pinang	40 000	
6	Pahang	8	7		5	2		2	4	1	1				Kuantan	Darulmakmur	40 000	1959
7	Kuala Lumpur	8	2		2			3	1	3	1				Kuala Lumpur	KLFA Stadium	18 000	1974
8	Johor FA	4	1		1			2	1	1					Johor Bahru	Hassan Yunos	30 000	
9	Perlis	3	4	2	1		2	2	1		3				Kangar	Utama	20 000	
10	Negri Sembilan	3	3	3	1	1	3	1	2	1					Seremban	Abdul Rahman	30 000	
11	Terengganu	2	7			2		1	3	1	2				Kuala Terengganu	Nasiruddin Shah	25 000	1972
12	Sabah	2	6	2	1		2		3	1	3				Kota Kinabalu	Likas	20 000	
13	Sarawak	2	3	1	1	1		1		1	2				Kuching	Sarawak Stadium	40 000	1974
14	Brunei D'salam	1		1		1	1	1							Bandar Seri Beg.			1956
15	Malacca	1			1										Melaka	Bandar Melaka	15 000	
	Selangor MPPJ	1					1								Petaling Jaya	MPPJ	25 000	

RECENT LEAGUE AND CUP RECORD

	Championship						FA Cup		
Year	Champions	Pts	Runners-up	Pts	Third	Pts	Winners	Score	Runners-up
1995	Pahang	65	Selangor	54	Sarawak	54	Sabah	3-1	Pahang
1996	Sabah	58	Kedah	57	Negri Sembilan	57	Kedah	1-0	Sarawak
1997	Sarawak	54	Kedah	50	Sabah	49	Selangor	1-0	Penang
1998	Penang	41	Pahang	40	Brunei	35	Johor	1-0	Sabah
1999	Pahang	34	Penang	31	Negeri Sembilan	29	Kuala Lumpur	0-0 5-3p	Terengganu
2000	Selangor	45	Penang	43	Perak	41	Terengganu	1-1 4-3p	Penang
2001	Penang	50	Terengganu	41	Kelantan	38	Selangor	1-0	Sarawak
2002	Perak	60	Selangor	56	Sabah	47	Penang	1-0	Perak
2003	Perak	47	Kedah	45	Perlis	45	Negeri Sembilan	2-1	Perlis
2004	Pahang	47	Selangor Public Bank	38	Perlis	36	Perak	3-0	Terengganu
2005	Perlis	45	Pahang	35	Perak	30	Selangor	4-2	Perak
2006	Negeri Sembilan	40	Melaka Telekom	33	Perak	30	Pahang	0-0 4-2p	Perlis
2007	Kedah	55	Perak	53	DPMM Brunei	44	Kedah	0-0 4-2p	Perlis
2008	Kedah	56	Negeri Sembilan	48	Johor FC	46	Kedah	3-2	Selangor

MALAYSIA 2007–08

MALAYSIAN SUPER LEAGUE (MSL)

	Pl	W	D	L	F	A	Pts	Kedah	Negeri S	Johor	Selangor	Perak	Terengganu	Perlis	Pahang	PDRM	DPMM	MyTeam	Pinang	Sarawak
Kedah †	24	18	2	4	55	24	56		2-1	2-0	6-2	5-1	2-1	0-0	1-0	4-1	4-1	2-0	4-1	2-0
Negeri Sembilan	24	14	6	4	48	30	48	1-1		2-0	0-2	3-1	1-1	2-0	2-3	3-2	3-2	1-1	2-1	4-0
Johor FC	24	14	4	6	40	27	46	1-3	2-4		3-2	2-0	2-1	1-0	1-0	2-0	0-0	2-1	4-0	3-1
Selangor	24	14	3	7	46	36	45	0-1	0-3	1-1		2-4	0-0	0-1	4-3	4-1	2-1	2-1	2-1	4-1
Perak	24	13	2	9	46	34	41	2-5	0-1	1-2	1-4		2-0	2-0	2-1	5-1	2-0	2-1	3-1	5-0
Terengganu	24	10	7	7	41	31	37	3-1	3-1	1-2	1-1	1-1		1-1	1-2	2-0	2-0	3-1	2-4	4-0
Perlis	24	10	6	8	36	25	36	1-0	2-2	3-1	0-2	2-0	0-1		5-0	4-0	1-1	1-1	2-0	4-1
Pahang	24	8	6	10	26	31	30	1-2	2-2	2-1	1-3	0-1	1-2	1-0		1-0	0-0	1-0	0-0	1-1
PDRM	24	7	3	14	30	52	24	2-1	1-1	1-2	1-2	0-6	4-2	2-3	0-0		2-1	0-2	2-0	3-2
DPMM FC	24	4	10	10	27	34	22	2-0	0-1	0-2	1-2	2-1	1-1	0-0	1-1	2-2		2-3	3-3	5-1
UPB/My Team Melaka	24	6	4	14	30	40	22	0-2	0-2	2-2	0-2	0-1	1-3	4-2	0-2	2-0	0-0		1-2	4-0
Penang	24	4	5	15	30	49	17	2-3	2-3	0-0	4-1	0-2	1-1	1-3	0-2	0-1	1-1	2-4		4-0
Sarawak	24	4	2	18	25	67	14	1-2	2-3	0-4	0-2	1-1	2-4	2-1	2-1	1-4	0-1	4-1	3-0	

18/11/2007 - 3/05/2008 • † Qualified for the AFC Cup

MALAYSIA 2007–08 PREMIER LEAGUE (2)

	Pl	W	D	L	F	A	Pts
Kuala Muda	24	20	1	3	52	27	61
KL Plus FC	24	18	3	3	56	21	57
Kelantan	24	16	5	3	59	30	53
Sabah	24	13	5	6	48	27	44
Johor Pasir Gudang	24	13	4	7	41	26	43
Felda United	24	7	6	11	28	35	27
Proton FC	24	8	3	13	27	45	27
Harimau Muda	24	7	5	12	30	38	26
Melaka	24	8	2	14	29	43	26
Pahang Shahzan Muda	24	7	4	13	28	46	25
Selangor PKNS	24	5	7	12	27	38	22
Kuala Lumpur	24	3	7	14	24	41	16
ATM Lumut	24	4	2	18	29	61	14

17/12/2007 - 3/05/2008

MALAYSIA CUP 2007

Quarter–finals			Semi–finals			Final		
Kedah	6	4						
Melaka	1	0	Kedah	0	2			
Selangor	2	0	Terengganu	0	0			
Terengganu	2	1				Kedah		3
Sabah	0	3				Perak		0
Negeri S'bilan	1	1	Sabah	1	1			
Perlis	2	1	Perak	1	2			
Perak	0	5						

First round played in four groups of four

8-09-2007 Scorers - Mohd Khyril Muhymeen [25], Marlon James 2 [27] [81]

MALAYSIA CUP RECORD

Year	Winners	Score	Runners-up
2000	Perak	2-0	Negeri Sembilan
2001	Terengganu	2-1	Perak
2002	Selangor	1-0	Sabah
2003	Selangor MPPJ	3-0	Sabah
2004	Perlis	1-0	Kedah
2005	Selangor	3-0	Perlis
2006	Perlis	2-1	Negeri Sembilan
2007	Kedah	3-0	Perak

FA CUP 2008

Second Round			Quarter–finals			Semi–finals			Final		
Kedah *	3	2									
Sarawak	0	0	Kedah	4	6						
Proton FC *	3	1	Melaka *	1	2						
Melaka	2	4									
Sabah	1	3				Kedah *	4	2			
PDRM *	2	1	Sabah	1	0	Pahang	1	0			
KL Plus FC	0	0	Pahang *	3	1						
Pahang *	0	2							Kedah		3
Terengganu *	1	4							Selangor		2
Negeri Sembilan	0	1	Terengganu *	3	1						
Kuala Lumpur *	2	1	Felda United	1	1						
Felda United	5	0									
Kuala Muda	0	2				Terengganu	1	1			
Penang *	1	0	Kuala Muda *	1	1	Selangor *	2	1			
Perak *	4	1	Selangor	0	4						
Selangor	4	2									

* Home team/home team in the first leg • † Qualified for the AFC Cup

CUP FINAL

Shah Alam, 21-06-2008, 30 000
Scorers - Mohd Fadly Baharom [1], Mohd Khyril Muhymeen [32], Mohd Syafiq Jamal [50] for Kedah; Mohd Amirulhasi Zainal [13], Frank Seator [71] for Selangor

MDA – MOLDOVA

NATIONAL TEAM RECORD
JULY 10TH 2006 TO JULY 12TH 2010

PL	W	D	L	F	A	%
18	6	4	8	20	27	44.4

FIFA/COCA-COLA WORLD RANKING

1993	1994	1995	1996	1997	1998	1999	2000	2001	2002	2003	2004	2005	2006	2007	High	
-	118	109	117	131	116	93	94	103	111	106	114	107	86	52	**37**	04/08

	2007–2008												Low	
08/07	09/07	10/07	11/07	12/07	01/08	02/08	03/08	04/08	05/08	06/08	07/08		**149**	07/94
106	81	61	53	52	53	49	51	37	38	51	50			

There was little anyone could do to stop the Sheriff juggernaut rolling on as the Tiraspol side cruised to an eighth championship in succession as well as securing their fourth double during the same period. Veteran defender Ion Testemitanu scored the only goal in the Cup Final against Nistru, a goal which meant that Sheriff matched Zimbru Chisinau's total of 12 League and Cup titles since independence. Given the strained political tensions between the two cities, Sheriff's current dominance is viewed with satisfaction by those who want to see Trans-Dniester, of which Tiraspol is the capital, breakaway completely from Moldova. Under Belarussian coach Leonid

INTERNATIONAL HONOURS
None

Kuchuk since 2004, Sheriff have brought in players from as far afield as Burkina Faso, Togo, Argentina and Brazil in an effort to make it through to the UEFA Champions League group stage, but once again those lofty ambitions faltered in the second preliminary round with a 4-0 aggregate defeat at the hands of Besiktas. The national team had a much better time in the second half of their Euro 2008 qualifying campaign, winning three and drawing one of their last four matches and drawn in one of the less fearsome 2010 FIFA World Cup qualifying groups, there has never been a more opportune time for Igor Dobrovolski's team to make a name for itself.

THE FIFA BIG COUNT OF 2006

	Male	Female		Total
Number of players	147 430	21 140	Referees and Assistant Referees	151
Professionals	543		Admin, Coaches, Technical, Medical	560
Amateurs 18+	6 629		Number of clubs	86
Youth under 18	2 603		Number of teams	2 036
Unregistered	66 150		Clubs with women's teams	3
Total players	168 570		Players as % of population	3.77%

Football Association of Moldova (FMF)
Federatia Moldoveneasca de Fotbal, Str. Tricolorului nr. 39, Chisinau MD-2012, Moldova
Tel +373 22 210413   Fax +373 22 210432
fmf@fmf.md   www.fmf.md
President: CEBANU Pavel   General Secretary: CEBOTARI Nicolai
Vice-President: ANGHEL Mihai   Treasurer: SOROCEAN Victor   Media Officer: DAGHI Victor
Men's Coach: DOBROVOLSKY Igor   Women's Coach: BOGUS Boris
FMF formed: 1990   UEFA: 1992   FIFA: 1994
Red shirts, Blue shirts, Red socks or Blue shirts, Red shorts, Blue socks

RECENT INTERNATIONAL MATCHES PLAYED BY MOLDOVA

2003	Opponents	Score		Venue	Comp	Scorers	Att	Referee
20-08	Turkey	L	0-2	Ankara	Fr		15 300	Plautz AUT
10-09	Belarus	W	2-1	Tiraspol	ECq	Dadu [23], Covaliciuc [88]	7 000	Delevic SCG
11-10	Netherlands	L	0-5	Eindhoven	ECq		30 995	Siric CRO
20-11	Luxembourg	W	2-1	Hesperange	Fr	Golban [19], Dadu [90]	623	Duhamel FRA
2004								
14-02	Malta	D	0-0	Ta'Qali	Fr		600	Vialichka BLR
16-02	Belarus	L	0-1	Ta'Qali	Fr		40	Attard MLT
18-02	Estonia	L	0-1	Ta'Qali	Fr		100	Sammut MLT
31-03	Azerbaijan	W	2-1	Chisinau	Fr	Dadu 2 [42p 84]	5 500	Godulyan UKR
28-04	Israel	D	1-1	Tel Aviv	Fr	Rogaciov [71]	4 500	Corpodean ROU
18-08	Georgia	W	1-0	Tiraspol	Fr	Miterev [68]	8 000	Godulyan UKR
4-09	Slovenia	L	0-3	Celje	WCq		3 620	Hyytia FIN
8-09	Italy	L	0-1	Chisinau	WCq		5 200	Benes CZE
9-10	Belarus	L	0-4	Minsk	WCq		21 000	Dereli TUR
13-10	Scotland	D	1-1	Chisinau	WCq	Dadu [28]	7 000	Jakobsson ISL
2005								
9-02	Azerbaijan	D	0-0	Baku	Fr		1 500	
30-03	Norway	D	0-0	Chisinau	WCq		5 000	Meyer GER
4-06	Scotland	L	0-2	Glasgow	WCq		45 317	Braamhaar NED
3-09	Belarus	W	2-0	Chisinau	WCq	Rogaciov 2 [17 49]	5 000	Duhamel FRA
7-09	Slovenia	L	1-2	Chisinau	WCq	Rogaciov [31]	7 200	Baskakov RUS
8-10	Norway	L	0-1	Oslo	WCq		23 409	Bennett RSA
12-10	Italy	L	1-2	Lecce	WCq	Gatcan [76]	28 160	Benquerenca POR
2006								
25-02	Malta	W	2-0	Ta'Qali	Fr	Namasco 46, Bugaev 73	1 125	Silagava GEO
27-02	Georgia	W	5-1	Ta'Qali	Fr	Zislis 2 [5 13], Alexeev [48], Namasco [55p], Golovatenco [72]	330	Casha MLT
18-05	Azerbaijan	D	0-0	Chisinau	Fr			
16-08	Lithuania	W	3-2	Chisinau	Fr	Dadu [15p] Iepureanu [56], Clescenco [87p]		Godulyan UKR
2-09	Greece	L	0-1	Chisinau	ECq		10 500	Trefoloni ITA
6-09	Norway	L	0-2	Oslo	ECq		23 848	Ristoskov BUL
7-10	Bosnia-Herzegovina	D	2-2	Chisinau	ECq	Rogaciov 2 [13 32p]	7 114	Piccirillo FRA
11-10	Turkey	L	0-5	Frankfurt	ECq		BCD	Vollquartz DEN
2007								
7-02	Romania	L	0-2	Bucharest	Fr		8 000	Deaconu ROU
24-03	Malta	D	1-1	Chisinau	ECq	Epureanu [85]	8 033	Aliyev AZE
28-03	Hungary	L	0-2	Budapest	ECq		6 150	Ingvarsson SWE
6-06	Greece	L	1-2	Irákleio	ECq	Frunza [80]	22 000	Wegereef NED
22-08	Latvia	W	2-1	Riga	Fr	Frunza [23], Bordian [53]	4 500	Shandor UKR
8-09	Norway	L	0-1	Chisinau	ECq		10 173	Malek POL
12-09	Bosnia-Herzegovina	W	1-0	Sarajevo	ECq	Bugaev [22]	2 000	Hyytiä FIN
13-10	Turkey	D	1-1	Chisinau	ECq	Frunza [11]	9 815	Atkinson ENG
17-10	Malta	W	3-2	Ta'Qali	ECq	Bugaev [24p], Frunza 2 [31 35]	7 069	Ischenko UKR
17-11	Hungary	W	3-0	Chisinau	ECq	Bugaev 13, Josan 23, Alexeev [86]	6 483	Královec CZE
2008								
6-02	Kazakhstan	W	1-0	Antalya	Fr	Bugaev [13]	300	Lehner AUT
24-05	Croatia	L	0-1	Rijeka	Fr		7 000	Ceferin SVN
28-05	Armenia	D	2-2	Tiraspol	Fr	Arakelyan OG [42], Alexeev [74]	3 653	Ischenko UKR

Fr = Friendly match • EC = UEFA EURO 2004/2008 • WC = FIFA World Cup • q = qualifier

MOLDOVA NATIONAL TEAM RECORDS AND RECORD SEQUENCES

Records			Sequence records					
Victory	5-1	GEO 2006	Wins	3	1994, 2007-08	Clean sheets	2	2000, 2005
Defeat	0-6	SWE 2001	Defeats	9	1996-1998	Goals scored	7	1998-1999
Player Caps	69	Serghei Clescenco	Undefeated	5	2007-2008	Without goal	7	1997-98, 2000-01
Player Goals	11	Serghei Clescenco	Without win	10	1996-98, 2002-03	Goals against	25	1994-1998

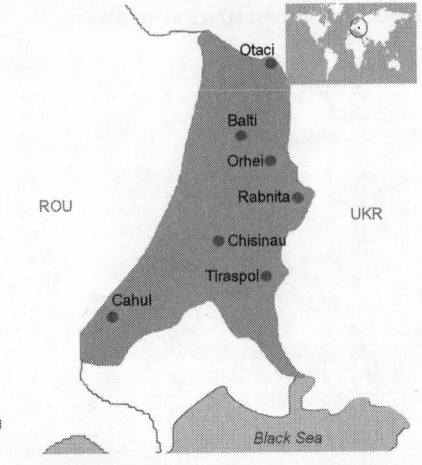

Population '000

1	Chisinau	610
2	Tiraspol	152
3	Balti	109
4	Tighina	103
5	Ribnita	52
6	Ungheni	32
7	Cahul	32
8	Soroca	25
9	Orhei	23
10	Edinet	22
11	Comrat	21
12	Dubasari	21
13	Causeni	21
14	Ocnita	18
15	Ciadir Lunga	18
16	Straseni	18
17	Floresti	16
18	Drochia	15
19	Singerei	14
20	Ialoveni	14
21	Slobozia	14
22	Leova	14
23	Briceni	13
24	Hincesti	13

REPUBLIC OF MOLDOVA; REPUBLICA MOLDOVA

Capital	Chisinau	Language	Moldovan, Russian	Independence	1991
Population	4 466 706	Area	33 843 km²	% in cities	52%
GDP per cap	$1800	Dailling code	+373	Density 131 per km²	Internet .md	GMT + / - +2

MEDALS TABLE

		Overall			League			Cup			Europe			City	Stadium	Cap'ty	DoF
		G	S	B	G	S	B	G	S	B	G	S	B				
1	Zimbru Chisinau	13	7	2	8	5	2	5	2					Chisinau	Baza CSF Zimbru	10 500	1947
2	Sheriff Tiraspol	13	2		8	1		5	1					Tiraspol	Complex Sheriff	14 300	1997
3	Tiligul-Tiras	3	8	3		6	3	3	2					Tiraspol	Municipal	3 525	1938
4	FC Tiraspol	3	3	4	1	1	4	2	2					Tiraspol	Municipal	3 525	1993
5	Nistru Otaci	1	11	3		3	3	1	8					Otaci	Calarasauca	3 000	1953
6	Bugeac Comrat	1			1			1						Comrat	Bugeac		
7	Dacia Chisnau		2	1	1	1			1					Chisinau	Republican	8 100	2000
8	Dinamo Chisinau	1						1						Chisinau			
9	Codru Calarasi			1		1								Calarasi	Codru		
	Moldova Boroseni			1		1								Boroseni			
	Olimpia Balti			1		1								Balti	Municipal	5 000	1984
12	Dinamo Bender													Tighina	Selkovic	1 000	1950
	Iscra-Stali Ribnita													Ribnita	Municipal	3 000	
	Floreni Anenii Noi																
	Politehnica Chisinau													Chisinau	Dinamo	2 900	1964
	Rapid Ghidghici													Ghidghici			

RECENT LEAGUE AND CUP RECORD

	Championship						Cup		
Year	Champions	Pts	Runners-up	Pts	Third	Pts	Winners	Score	Runners-up
1995	Zimbru Chisinau	67	Tiligul Tiraspol	66	Olimpia Balti	57	Tiligul Tiraspol	1-0	Zimbru Chisinau
1996	Zimbru Chisinau	81	Tiligul Tiraspol	74	Constructorul	74	Constructorul	2-1	Tiligul Tiraspol
1997	Constructorul	81	Zimbru Chisinau	70	Tiligul Tiraspol	68	Zimbru Chisinau	0-0 7-6p	Nistru Otaci
1998	Zimbru Chisinau	69	Tiligul Tiraspol	59	Constructorul	54	Zimbru Chisinau	1-0	Constructorul
1999	Zimbru Chisinau	61	Constructorul	51	Tiligul Tiraspol	39	Sheriff Tiraspol	2-1	Constructorul
2000	Zimbru Chisinau	82	Sheriff Tiraspol	81	Constructorul	65	Constructorul	1-0	Zimbru Chisinau
2001	Sheriff Tiraspol	67	Zimbru Chisinau	66	Tiligul Tiraspol	41	Sheriff Tiraspol	0-0 5-4p	Nistru Otaci
2002	Sheriff Tiraspol	67	Nistru Otaci	52	Zimbru Chisinau	46	Sheriff Tiraspol	3-2	Nistru Otaci
2003	Sheriff Tiraspol	60	Zimbru Chisinau	50	Nistru Otaci	42	Zimbru Chisinau	0-0 4-2p	Nistru Otaci
2004	Sheriff Tiraspol	65	Nistru Otaci	57	Zimbru Chisinau	49	Zimbru Chisinau	2-1	Sheriff Tiraspol
2005	Sheriff Tiraspol	70	Nistru Otaci	54	Dacia Chisinau	45	Nistru Otaci	1-0	Dacia Chisinau
2006	Sheriff Tiraspol	71	Zimbru Chisinau	53	FC Tiraspol	37	Sheriff Tiraspol	2-0	Nistru Otaci
2007	Sheriff Tiraspol	92	Zimbru Chisinau	71	Nistru Otaci	57	Zimbru Chisinau	1-0	Nistru Otaci
2008	Sheriff Tiraspol	81	Dacia Chisinau	62	Nistru Otaci	59	Sheriff Tiraspol	1-0	Nistru Otaci

MOLDOVA 2007–08

DIVIZIA NATIONALA

	Pl	W	D	L	F	A	Pts	Sheriff	Dacia	Nistru	Tiraspol	Zimbru	Iscra-Stali	Tiligul-Tiras	Olimpia	Dinamo	CSCA	Politehnica
Sheriff Tiraspol †	30	26	3	1	68	8	81		2-0 2-1	1-0	0-0	0-1 4-2	0-3 6-0	3-0	2-0 1-0	5-0	3-0 7-1	1-0
Dacia Chisinau ‡	30	19	5	6	60	28	62	0-1		2-0 2-4	0-0 0-0	1-5	2-1	2-1 3-0	3-0	5-1 2-0	1-0	3-1 2-0
Nistru Otaci ‡	30	17	8	5	34	17	59	0-0 0-1	0-1		2-1	1-0 2-0	1-0 1-0	0-0	0-0 2-0	3-1	3-0 2-1	0-0
FC Tiraspol	30	16	7	7	36	21	55	0-2 0-2	1-1	1-2 1-0		0-0	0-1 2-0	3-1	2-1 1-0	2-1	1-0 2-0	2-1
Zimbru Chisinau	30	13	13	4	43	21	52	1-1	0-1 3-2	1-1	1-1 0-0		1-0	0-0 3-0	7-0	0-0 3-3	3-1	0-0 0-0
Iscra-Stali Rîbnita	30	9	8	13	23	34	35	0-3	1-3 0-0	1-2	0-0 0-0	0-0		1-0 2-1	2-0	0-1 1-1	1-1	1-0 3-0
Tiligul-Tiras Tiraspol	30	7	8	15	16	36	29	0-1 0-4	0-0	0-1 0-0 0-2 1-1	0-1	0-0			2-1 2-1	3-1	1-0 0-0	1-0
Olimpia Balti	30	7	6	17	24	46	27	0-1	1-4 1-3	0-1	0-2	0-1 1-1 1-0 3-2	1-1			1-0 1-0	4-1	0-1 2-2
Dinamo Bender	30	7	5	18	30	57	26	1-2 0-2	3-7	2-2 1-2 0-3 0-2	1-2	0-0	3-0 1-0	1-3			1-2 2-1	2-0
CSCA-Steaua Chisinau	30	5	3	22	21	55	18	1-4	0-3 2-0	0-1	0-1	0-3 1-3 0-2 2-3	0-1	0-1 1-1	3-0			0-1 1-0
Politehnica Chisinau	30	3	6	21	7	39	15	0-1 0-3	0-2	0-2 0-1 0-2 0-3	0-1		0-0	0-1 1-0	0-0	0-2 0-1	0-2	
Rapid Ghidighici				Withdrew after 16 rounds														

4/07/2007 - 16/05/2008 • † Qualified for the UEFA Champions League • ‡ Qualified for the UEFA Cup
Top scorer: Igor Picusciac, Tiraspol/Sherrif 14; Ngaha Collins, Nistru 13; Alexey Kuchuk, Sheriff 12; Djaba Dvali, Dacia 13

MOLDOVA 2007–08
DIVIZIA A (2)

	Pl	W	D	L	F	A	Pts
Sheriff-2 Tiraspol	32	24	3	5	79	19	75
Besiktas Chisinau	32	21	5	6	73	32	68
Academia Chisinau	32	18	10	4	73	23	64
Petrocub S. Galbena	32	19	6	7	51	27	63
Floreni Anenii Noi	32	15	8	9	63	45	53
Lokomotiva Balti	32	14	8	10	61	57	50
Viitorul Step Soci	32	15	4	13	61	45	49
FC Cahul 2005	32	14	5	13	44	43	47
Gagauziya Comrat	32	13	8	11	43	54	47
Zimbru-2 Chisinau	32	13	5	14	52	39	44
Dinamo-2 Bender	32	10	7	15	46	56	37
Eikomena S. Galbena	32	9	7	16	29	57	34
Intersport	32	8	9	15	32	59	33
Dacia-2 Chisinau	32	7	10	15	36	50	31
Olimpia-2 Balti	32	7	4	21	25	61	25
FCM Ungheni	32	7	4	21	24	81	25
Izvoras 67 Ratus	32	5	3	24	28	72	18
Rapid-2 Ghidighici				Withdrew after 16 rounds			

4/08/2007 - 26/05/2008 • Sheriff ineligible for promotion

CUPA MOLDOVEI 2007–08

Round of sixteen

Sheriff Tiraspol	3
CSCA-Steaua Chisinau *	0
Floreni Anenii Noi *	0 7p
Olimpia Balti	0 8p
Dacia Chisinau *	5
Podis	0
Cricova *	0
FC Tiraspol	2
Zimbru Chisinau	2
Dinamo Bender *	1
Academia Chisinau *	1
Politehnica Chisinau	3
Tiligul-Tiras Tiraspol	4
Gagauziya Comrat	1
Besiktas Chisinau *	0
Nistru Otaci	1

Quarter–finals

Sheriff Tiraspol	2 3
Olimpia Balti *	0 0
Dacia Chisinau	0 0
FC Tiraspol *	1 1
Zimbru Chisinau *	1 2
Politehnica Chisinau	0 1
Tiligul-Tiras Tiraspol	0 0
Nistru Otaci *	1 2

Semi–finals

Sheriff Tiraspol	0 1
FC Tiraspol *	0 0
Zimbru Chisinau	1 2
Nistru Otaci *	2 3

Final

Sheriff Tiraspol	1
Nistru Otaci ‡	0

CUP FINAL

Zimbru, Chisinau
20-05-2008

Scorer - Ivan Testemitanu [49]

* Home team/home team in the first leg • ‡ Qualified for the UEFA Cup

MDV – MALDIVES

NATIONAL TEAM RECORD
JULY 10TH 2006 TO JULY 12TH 2010

PL	W	D	L	F	A	%
10	4	0	6	9	14	40

FIFA/COCA-COLA WORLD RANKING

1993	1994	1995	1996	1997	1998	1999	2000	2001	2002	2003	2004	2005	2006	2007
148	162	169	176	160	166	143	154	147	152	141	139	133	158	151

High	
126	08/06

2007–2008											
08/07	09/07	10/07	11/07	12/07	01/08	02/08	03/08	04/08	05/08	06/08	07/08
158	165	174	149	151	153	155	153	159	160	159	156

Low	
183	09/97

The tiny Indian Ocean archipelago of the Maldives assumed the mantle of South Asia's number one nation with a surprise win over India in the final of the South Asian Football Federation Championship which they co-hosted with Sri Lanka. A solitary goal from Mukhthar Naseer in the final in Colombo earned the Maldives their first-ever international title, but any hopes the Maldives had of qualifying for the 2011 AFC Asian Cup have already evaporated after a pair of defeats at the hands of Lebanon eliminated them from the competition. Head coach Jozef Jankech stood down soon after the SAFF Championship win to take up the position as technical director at ZTS

INTERNATIONAL HONOURS
SAFF Gold Cup 2008

Dubnica in his native Slovakia and has been replaced by Turkish coach Teoman Yamanlar. In club football on the islands, New Radiant denied Victory a hat-trick of national league titles after beating their great rivals in the championship playoffs. Victory had finished on top of the league table at the end of the regular season only to lose 3-1 in the play-off final against New Radiant. There was to be no joy for either team, however, in continental competition as both sides finished bottom of their qualifying groups in the 2008 AFC Cup to miss out on the quarter-finals of the competition.

THE FIFA BIG COUNT OF 2006

	Male	Female		Total
Number of players	18 976	1 310	Referees and Assistant Referees	134
Professionals	120		Admin, Coaches, Technical, Medical	44
Amateurs 18+	3 250		Number of clubs	60
Youth under 18	1 616		Number of teams	367
Unregistered	14 800		Clubs with women's teams	0
Total players	20 286		Players as % of population	5.65%

Football Association of Maldives (FAM)
Ujaalaa Hin'gun, Maafannu, Male 20388, Maldives
Tel +960 3317006   Fax +960 3317005
famaldvs@dhivehinet.net.mv   www.famaldives.gov.mv
President: AZIM Ali   General Secretary: TBD
Vice-President: RASHEED Mohamed   Treasurer: TBD   Media Officer: TBD
Men's Coach: TEOMAN Yamanlar   Women's Coach: NASHID Ahmed
FAM formed: 1982   AFC: 1986   FIFA: 1986
Red shirts, Green shorts, White socks

RECENT INTERNATIONAL MATCHES PLAYED BY THE MALDIVES

2004	Opponents		Score	Venue	Comp	Scorers	Att	Referee
18-02	Vietnam	L	0-4	Hanoi	WCq		25 000	Fong KKG
31-03	Korea Republic	D	0-0	Malé	WCq		12 000	Vidanagamage SRI
31-05	Oman	L	0-3	Muscat	Fr			
3-06	Oman	L	1-4	Muscat	Fr			
9-06	Lebanon	L	0-3	Beirut	WCq		18 000	Nurilddin Salman IRQ
31-08	Oman	L	0-1	Malé	Fr			
3-09	Oman	L	1-2	Malé	Fr	Ali Ashfaq [84]		
8-09	Lebanon	L	2-5	Malé	WCq	Ibrahim Fazeel [79], Ali Umar [88]	12 000	Al Ajmi OMA
13-10	Vietnam	W	3-0	Malé	WCq	Ahmed Thariq [29], Ali Ashfaq 2 [68 85]	10 000	Haq IND
17-11	Korea Republic	L	0-2	Seoul	WCq		64 000	Lazar SIN
18-12	Sri Lanka	D	0-0	Malé	Fr			
2005								
7-12	Afghanistan	W	9-1	Karachi	SAFr1	Ali Umar [11], Ibrahim Fazeel 3 [27 45 69], Ali Ashfaq 2 [32 88], Ahmed Thariq 3 [45 46 86]		
9-12	Sri Lanka	W	2-0	Karachi	SAFr1	Ali Ashfaq [15], Ali Umar [82p]		
11-12	Pakistan	D	0-0	Karachi	SAFr1			
14-12	India	L	0-1	Karachi	SAFsf			
2006								
No international matches played in 2006								
2007								
2-10	Oman	L	0-1	Muscat	Fr			
8-10	Yemen	L	0-3	Sana'a	WCq		3 000	Mansour LIB
28-10	Yemen	L	0-2	Male	WCq		8 900	Sarkar IND
2008								
9-04	Lebanon	L	0-4	Beirut	ACq			
23-04	Lebanon	L	1-2	Male	ACq	Shamveel Qasim [22]		
3-06	Pakistan	W	3-0	Male	SAFr1	Mohamed Shifan [45], Ahmed Thariq [48], Akram OG [90]		
5-06	Nepal	W	4-1	Male	SAFr1	Ismail Mohamed 2 [10 47], Ibrahim Fazeel 2 [51 62]		
7-06	India	L	0-1	Male	SAFr1			
11-06	Sri Lanka	W	1-0	Colombo	SAFsf	Ibrahim Fazeel [70]		
14-06	India	W	1-0	Colombo	SAFf	Mukhtar Naseer [87]		

Fr = Friendly match • SAF = South Asian Football Federation Cup • AC = AFC Asian Cup • WC = FIFA World Cup
q = qualifier • r1 = first round group • sf = semi-final • f = final

MALDIVES NATIONAL TEAM RECORDS AND RECORD SEQUENCES

Records			Sequence records					
Victory	6-0	CAM 2001	Wins	3	1999	Clean sheets	2	1993, 1999, 2003
Defeat	0-17	IRN 1997	Defeats	12	1996-1997	Goals scored	7	1999
Player Caps	n/a		Undefeated	4	2000	Without goal	6	1997, 2005-2008
Player Goals	n/a		Without win	23	1985-1997	Goals against	14	1996-1997

MALDIVES COUNTRY INFORMATION

Capital	Malé	Independence	1965 from the UK	GDP per Capita	$3 900
Population	339 330	Status	Republic	GNP Ranking	168
Area km²	300	Language	Maldivian Dhiveti	Dialling code	+960
Population density	1 131 per km²	Literacy rate	97%	Internet code	.mv
% in urban areas	27%	Main religion	Muslim	GMT +/-	+5
Towns/Cities ('000)	Malé 85; Hithadoo 9; Fuvammulah 8; Kulhudhuffushi 8; Thinadhoo 5; Naifaru 4				
Neighbours (km)	Indian Ocean 644				
Main stadia	Galolhu National Stadium – Male				

MALDIVES 2007

DHIRAAGU DHIVEHI LEAGUE

	Pl	W	D	L	F	A	Pts	Victory	Radiant	Valencia	VB	Vyansa	Maziya	FDV	F'aidhoo
Victory †	12	8	3	1	22	7	27		1-2	1-1	2-0	2-2	1-0	3-0	4-0
New Radiant	12	7	1	4	25	9	22	0-1		0-1	2-0	3-0	0-3	8-0	3-0
Valencia	12	5	5	2	21	11	22	2-2	0-0		0-2	1-3	1-1	5-0	2-0
VB Sports	12	6	1	5	31	9	19	0-1	0-1	1-1		5-1	0-1	6-0	6-0
Vyansa	12	6	1	5	16	28	19	0-2	1-0	1-5	0-8		3-1	2-0	2-1
Maziya SR	12	3	2	7	12	20	11	0-2	2-6	0-2	0-3	0-1		1-1	3-0
FDV	7	1	1	5	4	26	4								3-1
Foakaidhoo EJ	7	0	0	7	2	23	0								

12/07/2007 - 20/08/2007 • Top four qualify for the National Championship play-offs • † Qualified for the AFC Cup

NATIONAL CHAMPIONSHIP PLAY-OFFS 2007

Preliminary round		Major Semi–final		Final	
		New Radiant	2		
		Victory	1		
				New Radiant †	3
				Victory	1
		VB Sports	0		
Valencia	2 6p	**Victory**	1		
VB Sports	2 7p	† Qualified for AFC Cup			

Final: 22-09-2007; Scorers - Assad Abdul Ghanee [22], Shimaz [36], Shamveel Gasim [47] for Radiant; George Rodriguez [65] for Victory

CUP WINNERS CUP 2008

	Pl	W	D	L	F	A	Pts	NR	Vi	Va
New Radiant ‡	4	2	2	0	7	3	8		1-1	2-1
Victory ‡	4	1	2	1	10	4	5	1-1		8-1
Valencia	4	1	0	3	3	13	3	0-3	1-0	

9/02/2008 - 1/03/2008 • ‡ Qualified for the final
Final: 1-03-2008, New Radiant 1-0 Victory; Scorer: Shamveel Qasim [60]

FA CUP 2008

Quarter–finals		Semi–finals		Final	
VB Sports	2				
Vyansa	0	**VB Sports**	1		
Baaz	0	Valencia	0		
Valencia	8			**VB Sports**	1
Victory	2			New Radiant	0
Maziya	1	Victory	0		
Sosun Club	0	**New Radiant**	2		
New Radiant	2	Third place: Victory 3-1 Valencia			

Final: 27-03-2008; Scorer - Adam Lareef [69]

RECENT LEAGUE AND CUP RECORD

National Championship				FA Cup				Cup Winners Cup			
Year	Winners	Score	Runners-up		Winners	Score	Runners-up		Winners	Score	Runners-up
1998	Valencia	1-1 2-0	Victory		New Radiant	1-0	Hurriyya		Valencia	2-0	New Radiant
1999	Valencia	2-1	Hurriyya		Valencia	2-2 2-1	New Radiant		New Radiant	3-1	Victory
2000	Victory				Victory	3-0	Hurriyya		New Radiant		
2001	Victory	2-1	Valencia		New Radiant	1-1 2-0	Valencia		Victory	1-1 5-4p	Valencia
2002	Victory	4-2	Valencia		IFC	2-0	New Radiant		Victory	4-3	Valencia
2003	Victory	2-1	Valencia		IFC	2-0	Valencia		New Radiant	1-1 3-1p	Valencia
2004	New Radiant	1-1 6-5p	Valencia		Valencia	2-0	Victory		Valencia	1-0	IFC
2005	Victory	1-0	New Radiant		New Radiant	2-0	Valencia		Valencia	2-1	Victory
2006	Victory	0-0 3-1p	Valencia		New Radiant	2-0	Valencia		Victory	3-3 2-1p	New Radiant
2007	New Radiant	3-1	Victory		New Radiant	2-0	Valencia		Valencia	3-1	New Radiant
2008					VB Sports (IFC)	1-0	New Radiant		New Radiant	1-0	Victory

MEX – MEXICO

NATIONAL TEAM RECORD
JULY 10TH 2006 TO JULY 12TH 2010

PL	W	D	L	F	A	%
29	17	3	9	57	32	63.8

The appointment of Sven Goran Eriksson as coach of the Mexican national team was greeted with surprise in some football circles there, but by employing a big name coach it signalled the intent of the Mexicans not only to qualify for the 2010 FIFA World Cup finals in South Africa but also to make a big impression at the finals if they get there. El Tri actually got their qualifying campaign underway before Eriksson's arrival, with stand-in coach Ramon Ramirez taking charge of the team for a preliminary round tie against minnows Belize. Mexico had no trouble winning that 9-0 on aggregate but they found themselves drawn in a tricky group containing the skillful Hondurans, a revitalised Jamaica and an unpredictable Canadian side. Few doubt that the Mexicans will make it to South Africa but although coaches from the America's are a common sight in Europe, few make the trip the other way and only by winning and winning with style will Eriksson convince the sceptics in what can be an unforgiving environment. His predecessor for example, the Mexican idol Hugo Sanchez, lost his job after failing to get the U-23 side to the Olympic finals in Beijing. At club level the Mexican championship continued to thrive with Atlante winning the 2007

INTERNATIONAL HONOURS
Qualified for the FIFA World Cup finals 1930 1950 1954 1958 1962 1966 1970 (hosts) 1978 1986 (hosts) 1994 1998 2002 2006

FIFA Confederations Cup 1999   Qualified for the FIFA Women's World Cup finals 1999

North American Championship 1947 1949   CONCACAF Championship 1965 1971   CONCACAF Gold Cup 1993 1996 1998 2003

CONCACAF U-20 1962 1970 1973 1976 1978 1980 1984 1990 1992   CONCACAF U-17 1985 1987 1991 1996

CONCACAF Club Championship Guadalajara 1962 Toluca 1968 2003 Cruz Azul 1969 1970 1971 1996 1997 America 1977 1990 1992 2006
UAG Tecos 1978 UNAM Pumas 1980 1982 1989 Atlante 1983 Puebla 1991 Necaxa 1999 Pachuca 2002 2007

Apertura, played in the second half of the calendar year. Once again "La maldicion del Superlider" - the curse of the Superleader - struck. It is becoming something of a tradition in the Mexican league that the team with the best record in the regular season, in this case Santos Laguna, gets knocked-out in the first round of the play-offs. It happened again in the Clausura with Guadalajara but this time Santos were the beneficiaries, winning their third title after beating Cruz Azul in the final. In international competition Pachuca retained their CONCACAF Champions Cup title after beating Costa Rica's Deportivo Saprissa in the final - their third continental title in just two years having also won the Copa Sudamericana in 2006. At the 2007 FIFA Club World Cup, however, they were knocked-out in the quarter-finals by African champions Etoile du Sahel. In a bid to raise standards in the region and to get Mexican clubs to take continental competition more seriously, CONCACAF announced the launch of their own Champions League in 2008 with four clubs from both Mexico and the USA qualifying for the tournament each year.

Federación Mexicana de Fútbol Asociación, A.C. (FMF)
Colima No. 373, Colonia Roma, Mexico D.F. 06700, Mexico

Tel +52 55 52410166   Fax +52 55 52410191

ddemaria@femexfut.org.mx   www.femexfut.org.mx

President: COMPEAN Justino   General Secretary: DE MARIA Decio

Vice-President: TBD   Treasurer: LEON-PAEZ Luis   Media Officer: KOCHEN Juan Jose

Men's Coach: ERIKSSON Sven Goran   Women's Coach: CUELLAR Leonardo

FMF formed: 1927   CONCACAF: 1961   FIFA: 1929

Green shirts with white trimmings, White shorts, Red socks or White shirts with green trimmings, Green shorts, White socks

RECENT INTERNATIONAL MATCHES PLAYED BY MEXICO

2007	Opponents	Score		Venue	Comp	Scorers	Att	Referee
7-02	USA	L	0-2	Glendale	Fr		62 462	Navarro CAN
28-02	Venezuela	W	3-1	San Diego	Fr	Guardado [25], Arce [34], Blanco [47p]	63 328	Stott USA
25-03	Paraguay	W	2-1	San Nicolas	Fr	Borgetti 2 [79 82]		Pineda HON
28-03	Ecuador	W	4-1	Oakland	Fr	Palencia [1], Márquez [72], Bravo [83], Bautista [87]	47 416	Toledo USA
2-06	Iran	W	4-0	San Luis Potosi	Fr	Borgetti [2], Lozano [27], Fonseca [81], Torrado [84]	30 000	Silvera URU
5-06	Paraguay	L	0-1	Mexico City	Fr		60 000	Larrionda URU
8-06	Cuba	W	2-1	New Jersey	GCr1	Borgetti [37], Castillo [55]	20 230	Aguilar SLV
10-06	Honduras	L	1-2	New Jersey	GCr1	Blanco [29p]	68 123	Quezada CRC
13-06	Panama	W	1-0	Houston	GCr1	Salcido [60]	68 417	Batres GUA
17-06	Costa Rica	W	1-0	Houston	GCqf	Borgetti [97]	70 092	Vaughn USA
21-06	Guadeloupe	W	1-0	Chicago	GCsf	Pardo [70]	50 790	Moreno PAN
24-06	USA	L	1-2	Chicago	GCf	Guardado [44]	60 000	Batres GUA
27-06	Brazil	W	2-0	Puerto Ordaz	CAr1	Castillo [23], Morales [28]	40 000	Pezzotta ARG
1-07	Ecuador	W	2-1	Maturín	CAr1	Méndez [84]	42 000	Ortube BOL
4-07	Chile	D	0-0	Puerto la Cruz	CAr1		30 000	Amarilla PAR
8-07	Paraguay	W	6-0	Maturín	CAqf	Castillo 2 [5p 38], Torrado [27], Arce [79], Blanco [87p], Bravo [91+]	50 000	Pezzotta ARG
11-07	Argentina	L	0-3	Puerto Ordaz	CAsf		40 000	Chandia CHI
14-07	Uruguay	W	3-1	Caracas	CA3p	Blanco [38p], Bravo [68], Guardado [76]	30 000	Reinoso ECU
22-08	Colombia	L	0-1	Commerce City	Fr			Stott USA
12-09	Brazil	L	1-3	Boston	Fr	Cacho [42]	67 584	Toledo USA
14-10	Nigeria	D	2-2	Juarez	Fr	Cacho 2 [54 68p]		Rodas GUA
17-10	Guatemala	L	2-3	Los Angeles	Fr	Vela [31], Villaluz [32]	42 350	Salazar USA
2008								
6-02	USA	D	2-2	Houston	Fr	Magallon 2 [35 47]	70 103	Batres GUA
26-03	Ghana	W	2-1	London	Fr	Salcido [76], Pardo [85p]		Styles ENG
16-04	China PR	W	1-0	Seattle	Fr	Villaluz [14]	56 416	Toledo USA
4-06	Argentina	L	1-4	San Diego	Fr	Naelson [61]	68 498	Navarro CAN
8-06	Peru	W	4-0	Chicago	Fr	Arce 2 [5 28], Guardado [8], Vela [20]		Geiger PER
15-06	Belize	W	2-0	Houston	WCq	Vela [65], Borgetti [92+]	50 137	Jauregui ANT
21-06	Belize	W	7-0	Monterrey	WCq	Vela [8], Borgetti 2 [9 93+], Guardado [33], Arce 2 [45 47], Lennen OG [92+]	42 000	Petrescu CAN

Fr = Friendly match • GC = CONCACAF Gold Cup • CA = Copa America • CC = FIFA Confederations Cup • WC = FIFA World Cup
q = qualifier • r1 = first round group • r2 = second round • qf = quarter-final • sf = semi-final • f = final

MEXICO NATIONAL TEAM PLAYERS

Player		Ap	G	Club	Date of Birth	Player		Ap	G	Club	Date of Birth
Oswaldo Sanchez	GK	91	0	Santos	21 09 1973	Fernando Arce	MF	32	6	Santos	24 04 1980
Guillermo Ochoa	GK	15	0	América	13 07 1985	Gonzalo Pineda	MF	44	1	Guadalajara	19 10 1982
Jonny Magallón	DF	27	2	Guadalajara	21 11 1981	Andrés Guardado	MF	33	5	Deportivo - ESP	28 09 1986
Ricardo Osorio	DF	57	1	VfB Stuttgart	30 03 1980	Zinha	MF	43	6	Toluca	23 05 1976
Carlos Salcido	DF	55	4	PSV Eindhoven	2 04 1980	César Villaluz	FW	9	2	Cruz Azul	18 07 1988
Aarón Galindo	DF	14	0	Eint. Frankfurt	8 05 1982	Sergio Santana	FW	9	4	Guadalajara	10 08 1979
Patricio Araujo	DF	4	0	Guadalajara	30 01 1988	Carlos Vela	FW	7	4	Arsenal	1 03 1989
Héctor Moreno	DF	2	0	AZ Alkmaar	17 01 1988	Edgar Andrade	FW	0	0	Cruz Azul	2 03 1988
Adrián Aldrete	DF	4	0	Morelia	6 02 1988	Jared Borgetti	FW	89	46	Monterrey	14 08 1973
Óscar Rojas	DF	10	0	América	21 08 1981	**Selected other internationals from 2008**					
Julio Domínguez	DF	3	0	Cruz Azul	8 11 1987	Rafael Márquez	DF	80	9	Barcelona	13 02 1979
Gerardo Torrado	MF	83	4	Cruz Azul	30 04 1979	Pavel Pardo	MF	141	8	VfB Stuttgart	26 07 1976
Luis Ernesto Pérez	MF	59	8	Monterrey	12 01 1981	Cuauhtemoc Blanco	MF	97	34	Chicago Fire	17 01 1973
Mexico's squad for the June 2006 World Cup qualifiers against Belize						Omar Bravo	FW	49	13	Deportivo	4 03 1980

MEXICO NATIONAL TEAM RECORDS AND RECORD SEQUENCES

Records			Sequence records					
Victory	11-0	VIN 1992	Wins	8	1947-49, 2004	Clean sheets	6	1965-1966
Defeat	0-8	ENG 1961	Defeats	7	1950-1952	Goals scored	22	1930-1950
Player Caps	179	Claudio Suarez	Undefeated	21	2004-2005	Without goal	5	1975-1976
Player Goals	46	Jared Borgetti	Without win	11	1971	Goals against	12	1957-1960

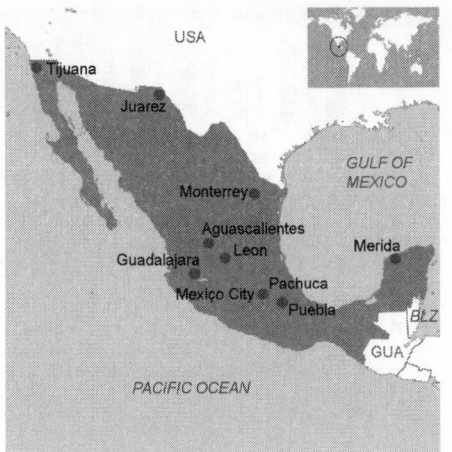

MAJOR CITIES/TOWNS

Population '000

1	Mexico City	8 658
2	Ecatepec	1 884
3	Guadalajara	1 632
4	Juárez	1 496
5	Tijuana	1 482
6	Puebla	1 441
7	Nezahualcóyotl	1 229
8	Léon	1 156
9	Monterrey	1 123
10	Zapopan	1 022
11	Naucalpan	849
12	Guadalupe	747
13	Mérida	740
14	Chihuahua	729
15	Tlalnepantla	713
16	San Luis Potosi	698
17	Aguascalientes	685
18	Querétaro	644
19	Morelia	611
20	Veracruz	581
21	Toluca	535
22	Torreón	532
23	Tuxtla Gutierrez	506
24	Pachuca	344

MEXICO

Capital	Mexico City	Language	Spanish			Independence	1836
Population	107 449 525	Area	1 972 550 km²	Density	53 per km²	% in cities	75%
GDP per cap	$9 000	Dailling code	+52	Internet	.mx	GMT +/-	-6

The whole Mexico City conurbation totals some 22 million people and includes Ecatepec, Nezahualcóyotl, Naucalpan, Tlalnepantla and Toluca, along with others. The Guadalajara conurbation totals just over 4 million and includes Zapopan amongst others

MEDALS TABLE

		Overall			League			Cup			CON'CAF			City	Stadium	Cap'ty	Formed
		G	S	B	G	S	B	G	S	B	G	S	B				
1	Club América	25	13	8	14	10	5	6	3		5		3	Mexico City	Azteca	101 000	1916
2	Real Club España	20	5	4	15	5	4	5									
3	Club Necaxa	15	8	9	7	7	7	7			1	1	2	Aguascalientes	Victoria	20 000	1923
4	Cruz Azul	15	10		8	7		2	2		5	1		Mexico City	Azul	35 161	1927
5	CD Guadalajara	14	16	8	11	9	4	2	5		1	2	4	Guadalajara	Jalisco	56 713	1906
6	CF Pachuca	13	5	6	7	5	5	2			4		1	Pachuca	Hidalgo	25 000	1901
7	CD Toluca	12	8	4	8	5	2	2	1		2	2	2	Toluca	La Bombonera	27 000	1917
8	Asturias	11	4	3	3	4	3	8									
9	Club León	10	10	6	5	5	4	5	4		1	2		León	Estadio León	40 338	1944
10	CF Atlante	9	13	3	5	8	3	3	4		1	1		Mexico City	Azteca	101 000	1916
11	UNAM Pumas	9	8		5	6		1			3	2		Mexico City	Olimpico	63 186	1954
12	Reforma	8	3	2	6	3	2	2									
13	Puebla FC	7	4	3	2	2	3	4	2		1			Puebla	Cuauhtémoc	42 649	1904
14	CF Atlas	5	4	4	1	3	4	4	1					Guadalajara	Jalisco	56 713	1916
15	Tigres UANL	4	4	1	2	3		2	1				1	Monterrey	Universitario	43 000	1960
16	CD Zacatepec	4	3	1	2	1	1	2	2					Zacatepec	Agustin Diaz		
17	UAG Tecos	3	6		1	4		1	2		1			Zapopan	Tres de Marzo	22 988	1971
18	CF Monterrey	3	5	5	2	3	2	1	2				3	Monterrey	Tecnologico	32 662	1945
19	CD Veracruz	3	3	3	2		3	1	3					Veracruz	Luis Pirata Fuente	35 000	1943
20	Santos Laguna	3	2	1	3	2					1			Torreón	Corona	18 050	1983

RECENT LEAGUE RECORD

	Clausura				Apertura		
Year	Champions	Score	Runners-up		Winners	Score	Runners-up
2000	Toluca	2-0 5-1	Santos Laguna		Monarcas Morelia	3-1 0-2 5-4p	Toluca
2001	Santos Laguna	1-2 3-1	Pachuca		Pachuca	2-0 1-1	Tigres UANL
2002	América	0-2 3-0	Necaxa		Toluca	0-1 4-1	Monarcas Morelia
2003	Monterrey	3-1 0-0	Monarcas Morelia		Pachuca	3-1 0-1	Tigres UANL
2004	UNAM Pumas	1-1 0-0 5-4p	Guadalajara		UNAM Pumas	2-1 1-0	Monterrey
2005	América	1-1 6-3	UAG Tecos		Toluca	3-3 3-0	Monterrey
2006	Pachuca	0-0 1-0	San Luis		Guadalajara	1-1 2-1	Toluca
2007	Pachuca	2-1 1-1	América		Atlante	0-0 2-1	UNAM Pumas
2008	Santos	2-1 1-1	Cruz Azul				

MEXICO 2007-08

PRIMERA DIVISION NACIONAL (APERTURA)

Opponent columns (left→right): Tol = Toluca, Pum = Pumas, Pac = Pachuca, Jag = Jaguares, Pue = Puebla, Tec = Tecos, San = Santos, Atl = Atlante, Amé = América, Ver = Veracruz, Mon = Monterrey, Ats = Atlas, Gua = Guadalajara, SLu = San Luis, CAz = Cruz Azul, Mor = Morelia, Nec = Necaxa, Tig = Tigres

Group 1

Team	Pl	W	D	L	F	A	Pts	Tol	Pum	Pac	Jag	Pue	Tec	San	Atl	Amé	Ver	Mon	Ats	Gua	SLu	CAz	Mor	Nec	Tig
Toluca †	17	10	4	3	27	16	34		0-0					2-0	2-3	3-1	2-1			1-0	2-1		2-0	4-0	
Pumas UNAM †	17	6	6	5	32	19	24							2-2	2-0		1-1	8-0		3-2	1-1		1-2		3-0
Pachuca †	17	7	3	7	26	23	24					0-0			0-1		1-2				1-2	4-1	3-1	1-1	
Jaguares	17	3	9	5	22	28	18	0-0	1-2	0-2				2-2		1-1				0-0			2-2	1-1	
Puebla	17	4	5	8	16	24	17		1-2				3-0	0-0	0-0					1-0	0-3			1-1	3-0
UAG Tecos	17	5	2	10	24	38	17	2-3		1-4	2-1					3-1	0-3			3-0			2-3	3-2	

Group 2

Team	Pl	W	D	L	F	A	Pts	Tol	Pum	Pac	Jag	Pue	Tec	San	Atl	Amé	Ver	Mon	Ats	Gua	SLu	CAz	Mor	Nec	Tig
Santos Laguna †	17	11	5	1	40	22	38			3-2					4-1		4-0	2-0		2-1		2-0	3-2		0-0
Atlante †	17	9	6	2	32	19	33	2-0	1-0	1-2		4-0				2-2		2-1			4-3			0-2	
América †	17	7	5	5	26	22	26					6-1		4-1				0-0		2-1	2-1		2-2	1-0	1-1
Veracruz	17	5	3	9	20	35	18					3-0	1-3		3-2	0-2		3-1	2-1		1-4			1-3	2-1
Monterrey	17	3	5	9	18	25	14	1-1		1-0	3-1			2-0		1-1	1-1		0-1			2-3	1-2		
Atlas	17	3	3	11	23	33	12	1-1							0-1	0-1	3-2	2-5			1-2		2-2	1-1	

Group 3

Team	Pl	W	D	L	F	A	Pts	Tol	Pum	Pac	Jag	Pue	Tec	San	Atl	Amé	Ver	Mon	Ats	Gua	SLu	CAz	Mor	Nec	Tig
Guadalajara †	17	9	4	4	28	16	31					5-4		0-0		1-1		3-1	1-0			3-1	1-0	5-1	1-0
San Luis †	17	8	5	4	31	30	29			3-2				0-3		2-2		2-1	2-1			0-0	3-1	2-1	3-2
Cruz Azul †	17	7	4	6	27	22	25	3-1			1-2	1-1				1-2		2-2		2-1	2-0			3-0	1-0
Morelia †	17	6	4	7	20	25	22	0-3				2-0			1-1	2-1	1-1	0-2	1-0		2-1				1-0
Necaxa	17	5	5	7	23	32	20				1-1			1-1	2-1	1-1	2-3	3-2	2-4			1-1			1-0
Tigres UANL	17	4	4	9	16	22	16	0-1		3-2	1-1					4-0		2-3		1-0	3-2		0-0		

3/08/2007 - 11/11/2007 • † Qualified for the play-offs • Repechaje: Pachuca 0-2 0-4 **Cruz Azul**; Morelia 3-0 0-1 **América**

Top scorers (inc play-offs): Alfredo Moreno, San Luis 19; Giancarlo Maldonado, Atlante 18; Daniel Ludeña, Santos 18; Esteban Solari, Pumas 15

APERTURA PLAY-OFFS

Quarter-finals			Semi-finals			Final		
Atlante	1	2						
Cruz Azul *	0	1	Atlante †		0 1			
San Luis *	1	0	Guadalajara*		1 0			
Guadalajara	1	1				**Atlante**		0 2
Santos	2	3				Pumas *		0 1
Morelia *	0	2	Santos		0 4			
Toluca	0	1	**Pumas ***		3 2			
Pumas *	2	1						

* Home team in the first leg • † Qualified on overall season record

APERTURA FINAL

Olimpico, Mexico City, 6-12-2007, Ref: Mauricio Ovalle

Pumas UNAM	0
Atlante	0

Pumas - Sergio Bernal - Fernando Espinoza, Héctor Moreno•, Darío Verón, Efraín Velarde• - Israel Castro, Leandro Augusto•, Pablo Barrera, Rubens Sambueza - Ignacio Scocco, Esteban Solari. Tr: Ricardo Ferretti
Atlante - Federico Vilar - José Daniel Guerrero (Daniel Alcántar 80), Gerardo Omar Castillo, Javier David Muñoz•, Andrés Carevic - Clemente Ovalle•, Alan Miguel Zamora•, José Joel González, David Toledo (Gabriel Pereyra• 54) - Christian Bermúdez (Alain Nkong 90), Giancarlo Maldonado. Tr: José Guadalupe Cruz

Andrés Quintana Roo, Cancún, 9-12-2007, Ref: Armando Téllez

Atlante	2	Maldonado 59, Iñiguez 69
Pumas UNAM	1	Ovalle 85

Atlante - Federico Vilar - José Daniel Guerrero (Arturo Muñoz 46), Gerardo Omar Castillo (Daniel Alcántar 34), Javier David Muñoz, Andrés Carevic - Clemente Ovalle, José Joel González•, David Toledo (Alain Nkong 66), Gabriel Pereyra• - Christian Bermúdez•, Giancarlo Maldonado. Tr: José Guadalupe Cruz
Pumas - Sergio Bernal - Fernando Espinoza, Héctor Moreno•, Darío Verón, Efraín Velarde (Juan Francisco Palencia 88) - Israel Castro•, Leandro Augusto (Jehu Chiapas 76), Pablo Barrera, Rubens Sambueza (Ismael Iñiguez 67) - Ignacio Scocco, Esteban Solari. Tr: Ricardo Ferretti

MEXICO 2007–08

PRIMERA DIVISION NACIONAL (CLAUSURA)

Group 1

Team	Pl	W	D	L	F	A	Pts	Tol	Jag	Pac	Pue	Pum	Tec	San	Mon	Atl	Atn	Ver	Amé	Gua	CrA	SLu	Nec	Tig	Mor
Toluca †	17	7	6	4	23	19	27		1-1	0-2			3-0	1-1	2-1	2-2					1-1			2-0	
Jaguares †	17	7	5	5	23	19	26			0-1		2-0		2-0	1-2	2-1	2-2	1-2					0-0	3-2	
Pachuca †	17	6	4	7	27	25	22		0-1				1-0	1-1	1-0	2-0	1-1				1-4				6-1
Puebla	17	5	6	6	28	25	21	1-2	5-2	1-1		3-3	1-1			2-2						1-2	1-1		4-0
Pumas UNAM	17	5	5	7	21	26	20	0-0	4-1	0-0					1-1	2-1			1-2			2-3	0-3		1-0
UAG Tecos	17	4	5	8	17	29	17				3-2	1-2				3-3	0-0	1-2	1-1	0-2				1-1	2-1

Group 2

Team	Pl	W	D	L	F	A	Pts	Tol	Jag	Pac	Pue	Pum	Tec	San	Mon	Atl	Atn	Ver	Amé	Gua	CrA	SLu	Nec	Tig	Mor
Santos Laguna †	17	8	7	2	36	19	31	2-2	1-3	2-1		4-0			2-0	6-1	3-0						4-1	1-1	
Monterrey †	17	6	6	5	27	22	24				0-0		3-0			1-1		7-2		1-0	3-2			1-1	2-3
Atlas †	17	6	5	6	21	24	23										2-1	2-2	3-1	0-0	2-0		0-1	1-1	3-0
Atlante	17	3	8	6	24	30	17					2-2						1-2	2-3		2-2	1-1	2-3		0-1
Veracruz	17	4	5	8	22	29	17	2-3		0-2	2-4			1-1					4-0	1-2		1-1			0-1
América	17	3	2	12	12	27	11	0-1		1-3	0-0	2-0		0-1	1-0		0-1					1-2			0-1

Group 3

Team	Pl	W	D	L	F	A	Pts	Tol	Jag	Pac	Pue	Pum	Tec	San	Mon	Atl	Atn	Ver	Amé	Gua	CrA	SLu	Nec	Tig	Mor
Guadalajara †	17	9	6	2	32	14	33	1-0			2-1	4-0	3-0	3-2							3-2		2-2		6-0
Cruz Azul †	17	9	4	4	27	17	31				2-0	2-1		1-1			1-0	2-2	0-0			4-0			1-0
San Luis †	17	8	6	3	25	23	30	2-0	0-2	2-1			1-1		3-1	0-0	2-0								1-1
Necaxa	17	5	9	3	18	12	24	1-2		2-2							1-1	0-1	2-0	1-0	2-0	1-1			
Tigres UANL	17	5	4	8	19	28	19			0-3	2-0			1-2			0-3	3-0	0-0	1-0		1-0			2-2
Morelia	17	5	3	9	11	25	18	2-1	1-0	3-2				0-2	0-0	0-1						1-2	0-0		

18/01/2008 - 4/05/2008 • † Qualified for the play-offs • Repechaje: Pachuca 0-1 2-1 **San Luis**; Atlas 1-1 0-0 **Necaxa** (Both San Luis and Necaxa qualify on better season record • Top scorers (inc play-offs): Humberto Suazo, Monterrey 16; Itamar, Jaguares 12; Vicente Vuoso, Santos 11

CLAUSURA PLAY-OFFS

Quarter-finals			Semi-finals			Final		
Santos Laguna	2	1						
Necaxa *	1	1	Santos Laguna	1	1			
Guadalajara	1	4	Monterrey *	1	1			
Monterrey *	4	4				Santos Laguna	2	1
San Luis	1	0				Cruz Azul *	1	1
Toluca *	1	0	San Luis *	0	1			
Jaguares *	1	1	Cruz Azul	1	1			
Cruz Azul	0	2						

* Home team in the first leg • † Qualified on overall season record

CLAUSURA FINAL

Estadio Cruz Azul, Mexico City, 29-05-2008, Ref: Marco Moreno

Cruz Azul	1	Vigneri 16
Santos Laguna	2	Arce 60, Benítez 85

Cruz Azul - Yosgart Gutiérrez - Carlos Bonet, Joaquín Beltrán•, Julio César Domínguez, Nicolás Ignacio Vigneri - Gerardo Torrado•, Christian Riveros, Jaime Lozano, Edgar Andrade• (Edgar Gerardo Lugo 63) - César Villaluz, Pablo Daniel Zeballos (Miguel Sabah 72). Tr: Sergio Markarián
Santos - Oswaldo Sánchez - Jorge Iván Estrada, Rafael Alejandro Figueroa•, Fernando Ortiz, Edgar Eduardo Castillo - Juan Pablo Rodríguez, Walter Jiménez (Francisco Torres 82), Fernando Arce, Daniel Emmanuel Ludueña (Osmar Mares 75) - Christian Benítez (Oribe Peralta 90), Vicente Matías Vuoso. Tr: Daniel Guzmán

Corona en Torreón, Coahuila, 1-06-2008, Ref: Armando Téllez MEX

Santos Laguna	1	Ludueña 16
Cruz Azul	1	Lozano 82

Santos - Oswaldo Sánchez - Jorge Iván Estrada, Rafael Alejandro Figueroa, Fernando Ortiz, Edgar Eduardo Castillo - Juan Pablo Rodríguez, Walter Jiménez (Francisco Torres 54), Fernando Arce, Daniel Emmanuel Ludueña (Osmar Mares 65) - Christian Benítez, Vicente Matías Vuoso (Oribe Peralta 65). Tr: Daniel Guzmán
Cruz Azul - Yosgart Gutiérrez - Carlos Bonet (Jair Garcia 68), Joaquín Beltrán, Julio César Domínguez, Jaime Lozano - Gerardo Torrado••90, Christian Riveros, Edgar Gerardo Lugo (Edgar Andrade 57), César Villaluz - Nicolás Ignacio Vigneri (Pablo Daniel Zeballos 46), Miguel Sabah. Tr: Sergio Markarián

MEXICO 2007–08
PRIMERA A (2) APERTURA

Group 1	Pl	W	D	L	F	A	Pts
León †	17	12	4	1	35	17	40
Dorados †	17	10	5	2	36	18	35
Académicos †	17	8	5	4	20	14	29
Tijuana †	17	7	3	7	22	22	24
Querétaro	17	5	8	4	32	27	23
Real Colima	17	6	4	7	28	29	22
Tapatío Guadalajara	17	6	4	7	25	30	22
UAG Tecos Zapopan	17	4	5	8	19	21	17
Monarcas Morelia	17	3	8	6	24	27	17
Petroleros Salamanca	17	4	5	8	22	31	17
Durango	17	4	4	9	18	27	16
Santos Laguna B	17	3	6	8	22	30	15

Group B	Pl	W	D	L	F	A	Pts
Correcaminos UAT †	17	11	3	3	24	14	36
Lobos BUAP Puebla †	17	9	3	5	24	19	30
Indios Ciudad Juarez †	17	9	3	5	26	22	30
Atlético Mexiquense †	17	8	3	6	29	21	27
Rayados Monterrey	17	6	7	4	18	16	25
Cruz Azul Hidalgo	17	6	7	4	20	20	25
Tampico Madero	17	7	2	8	35	29	23
Tiburones Rojas	17	6	5	6	21	24	23
Tigres B	17	4	7	6	16	21	19
Jaguares Tapachula	17	4	4	9	17	29	16
Pumas Morelos	17	2	8	7	16	22	14
Aguila	17	1	5	11	16	35	8

3/08/2007 - 25/11/2007 • † Qualified for the play-offs

PRIMERA A APERTURA PLAY-OFFS

Quarter–finals		Semi–finals		Final	
Indios *	2 2				
Lobos BUAP	1 2	Indios *	1 1		
Tijuana *	0 0	Léon	0 1		
Léon	1 3			Indios *	3 4
Correcaminos	0 1			Dorados	0 0
Mexiquense *	0 1	Correcaminos	0 0		
Académicos *	1 0	Dorados *	1 0		
Dorados	1 3	* Home team in the first leg			

PRIMERA A PLAY-OFF	Indios	1-0 2-2	Léon	Indios replace Veracruz in the Primera Division

MEXICO 2007–08
PRIMERA A (2) CLAUSURA

Group 1	Pl	W	D	L	F	A	Pts
Dorados †	17	10	5	2	31	14	35
León †	17	9	6	2	45	23	33
Durango †	17	9	4	4	28	23	31
Tijuana †	17	8	3	6	23	16	27
Petroleros Salamanca	17	7	3	7	21	23	24
UAG Tecos Zapopan	17	6	4	7	17	21	22
Tapatío Guadalajara	17	6	3	8	14	21	21
Monarcas Morelia	17	4	6	7	21	25	18
Querétaro	17	4	6	7	23	30	18
Real Colima	17	4	5	8	19	26	17
Académicos	17	4	4	9	18	27	16
Santos Laguna B	17	3	3	11	16	31	12

Group B	Pl	W	D	L	F	A	Pts
Tiburones Rojas †	17	8	6	3	21	18	30
Tampico Madero †	17	8	5	4	23	23	29
Tigres B †	17	7	7	3	22	15	28
Cruz Azul Hidalgo †	17	8	4	5	21	15	28
Indios Ciudad Juarez	17	6	8	3	27	14	26
Lobos BUAP Puebla	17	7	4	6	22	16	25
Pumas Morelos	17	7	4	6	23	26	25
Atlético Mexiquense	17	6	5	6	17	16	23
Correcaminos UAT	17	5	6	6	23	17	21
Rayados Monterrey	17	4	6	7	23	28	18
Aguila	17	5	2	10	14	26	17
Jaguares Tapachula	17	3	3	11	14	32	12

11/01/2008 - 27/04/2008 • † Qualified for the play-offs

PRIMERA A CLAUSURA PLAY-OFFS

Quarter–finals		Semi–finals		Final	
Léon	2 1				
Cruz Azul *	0 1	Léon	0 3		
Tigres B *	0 0	Durango *	0 2		
Durango	0 0			Léon *	2 1
Tiburones	1 4			Dorados	2 0
Tampico *	0 2	Tiburones *	0 0		
Petroleros *	0 1	Dorados *	0 1		
Dorados	0 1	* Home team in the first leg			

MGL – MONGOLIA

NATIONAL TEAM RECORD
JULY 10TH 2006 TO JULY 12TH 2010

PL	W	D	L	F	A	%
5	1	1	3	7	18	30

FIFA/COCA-COLA WORLD RANKING

1993	1994	1995	1996	1997	1998	1999	2000	2001	2002	2003	2004	2005	2006	2007	High	
-	-	-	-	-	196	198	196	187	193	179	185	179	181	178	**173**	07/07

2007–2008												Low	
08/07	09/07	10/07	11/07	12/07	01/08	02/08	03/08	04/08	05/08	06/08	07/08	**200**	02/00
174	176	178	178	178	177	181	181	184	183	187	192		

Mongolia's inauspicious record at international level continued through to the end of 2007 when the remote land-locked nation was eliminated from the 2010 FIFA World Cup at the earliest possible stage. A pair of defeats at the hands of Korea DPR saw the Mongolians knocked out thanks to a 9-2 aggregate scoreline and since that loss in October 2007 the national side has been inactive. The Mongolians were invited to take part in the qualifying tournament for the AFC Challenge Cup but the country's football federation chose not to participate. The harsh conditions in Mongolia - where temperatures in the summer hit over 40 degrees and in the winter can go as

INTERNATIONAL HONOURS
None

low as minus 40 degrees - mean football is confined to being played outdoors from July to September although indoor versions of the game are growing in popularity. Mongolia is part of the FIFA Goal Project, which is seeking to develop the game further in a nation known better for horse riding and, more recently, sumo. In 2007 the Premier League was expanded to a nine team round-robin format played over the course of seven weeks in the summer. Khangarid finished top of the standings but the top four then entered a play-off in which Erchim beat Khangarid in the final to win the title for the first time since 2002.

THE FIFA BIG COUNT OF 2006

	Male	Female		Total
Number of players	51 200	20	Referees and Assistant Referees	30
Professionals	200		Admin, Coaches, Technical, Medical	73
Amateurs 18+	800		Number of clubs	10
Youth under 18	3 020		Number of teams	70
Unregistered	11 000		Clubs with women's teams	0
Total players	51 200		Players as % of population	1.81%

Mongolia Football Federation (MFF)
PO Box 259, Ulaan-Baatar 210646, Mongolia
Tel +976 11 345968   Fax +976 11 345966
ubmaya@yahoo.com   www.none
President: AMARJARGAL Renchinnyam   General Secretary: GANBOLD Buyannemekh
Vice-President: TBD   Treasurer: OYUNTSETSEG Davaa   Media Officer: BAYARTSOGT Ganjuur
Men's Coach: OTGONBAYAR Ishdorj   Women's Coach: TBD
MFF formed: 1959   AFC: 1998   FIFA: 1998
White shirts, Red shorts, White socks

RECENT INTERNATIONAL MATCHES PLAYED BY MONGOLIA

2003	Opponents	Score	Venue	Comp	Scorers	Att	Referee
25-04	Guam	W 5-0	Thimphu	ACq	Batyalat [20], Tugsbayer 3 [26 56 90], Lunmbengaran [61]		
27-04	Bhutan	D 0-0	Thimphu	ACq			
29-11	Maldives	L 0-1	Ulaan-Baatar	WCq		2 000	Yang Zhiqiang CHN
3-12	Maldives	L 0-12	Malé	WCq		9 000	Arambekade SRI
2004							
No international matches played in 2004							
2005							
5-03	Hong Kong	L 0-6	Taipei	EAq			
7-03	Korea DPR	L 0-6	Taipei	EAq			
9-03	Guam	W 4-1	Taipei	EAq	Tugsbayer 2 [31 34], Bayarzorig [46], Buman-Uchral [81]		
13-03	Chinese Taipei	D 0-0	Taipei	EAq			
2006							
No international matches played in 2006							
2007							
17-06	Macau	D 0-0	Macau	EAq		300	Matsuo JPN
19-06	Korea DPR	L 0-7	Macau	EAq		300	Ogiya JPN
23-06	Guam	W 5-2	Macau	EAq	OG [24], Davaa 2 [37 42], Bayasgalan [46], Batchuluun [75]	100	Wan Daxue CHN
21-10	Korea DPR	L 1-4	Ulaan-Baatar	WCq	Selenge [93+]	4 870	Takayama JPN
28-10	Korea DPR	L 1-5	Pyongyang	WCq	Donorov [41]	5 000	Gosh BAN
2008							
No international matches played in 2008 before August							

EA = EAFF East Asian Championship • AC = AFC Asian Cup • WC = FIFA World Cup • q = qualifier

MONGOLIA NATIONAL TEAM RECORDS AND RECORD SEQUENCES

Records			Sequence records					
Victory	5-0	GUM 2003	Wins	1		Clean sheets	2	2003
Defeat	0-15	UZB 1998	Defeats	15	1942-2001	Goals scored	1	
Player Caps	n/a		Undefeated	3	2005-2007	Without goal	5	2001, 2003-2005
Player Goals	n/a		Without win	17	1942-2003	Goals against	13	1998-2003

MONGOLIA 2007

PREMIER LEAGUE

	Pl	W	D	L	F	A	Pts	Khangarid	Erchim	Khor'khon	Cowboys	Khasiin	College	Kharaatsai	Mazaalai	UB United
Khangarid ‡	16	11	3	2	57	23	36		2-0	4-1	2-1	2-1	6-1	4-1	0-0	3-2
Erchim ‡	16	10	3	3	48	14	33	1-1		4-1	2-1	1-0	3-0	3-1	4-0	4-0
Khoromkhon ‡	16	8	2	6	38	31	26	1-5	2-0		0-1	0-4	1-1	5-3	2-0	7-0
Cowboys ‡	16	7	3	6	26	25	24	2-1	0-5	2-1		0-3	3-3	0-0	4-0	1-0
Khasiin Khulguud	16	7	2	7	42	21	23	4-1	1-3	1-2	0-0		2-0	5-2	2-5	14-0
Ulaanbaatar College	16	6	5	5	38	32	23	2-2	1-0	2-2	3-0	1-4		1-1	3-1	6-0
Kharaatsai	16	5	4	7	42	36	19	2-5	1-1	2-3	4-3	2-0	5-1		2-4	8-0
Mazaalai	16	3	4	9	25	43	13	3-8	2-2	1-4	0-1	1-1	1-3	0-0		3-2
UB United	16	2	0	14	16	107	6	1-11	1-15	1-6	1-7	1-0	0-10	1-8	5-4	

1/07/2007 - 21/08/2007 • ‡ Qualified for the play-offs • Top scorer: Enkhtaivan, Khasiin 26
Play-off semi-finals: **Khangarid** 3-3 8-2 Cowboys; **Erchim** 4-0 3-2 Khoromkhon
Play-off final: **Erchim** 1-0 Khangarid. 1-09-2007, Scorer: Garidmagnai [55] • **Erchim are champions**

RECENT RECORD

	Championship
Year	Champions
1997	Delger
1998	Erchim
1999	ITI Bank Bars
2000	Erchim
2001	Khangarid
2002	Erchim
2003	Khangarid
2004	Khangarid
2005	Khoromkhon
2006	Khasiin Khultood
2007	Erchim

MONGOLIA COUNTRY INFORMATION

Capital	Ulaan-Baatar	Independence	1921 from China	GDP per Capita	$1 800
Population	2 751 314	Status	Republic	GNP Ranking	156
Area km²	1 564 116	Language	Khalkha Mongol	Dialling code	+976
Population density	2 per km²	Literacy rate	97%	Internet code	.mn
% in urban areas	61%	Main religion	Buddhist 50%, None 40%	GMT +/–	+8
Towns/Cities ('000)	Ulaan-Baatar 844; Èrdènèt 76; Darhan 72; Cojbalsan 44; Ölgij 30; Sahnsand 28; Ulaangom 28				
Neighbours (km)	China 4 677; Russia 3 543				
Main stadia	National Sports Stadium – Ulaan-Baatar 20 000				

MKD – FYR MACEDONIA

NATIONAL TEAM RECORD
JULY 10TH 2006 TO JULY 12TH 2010

PL	W	D	L	F	A	%
17	5	6	6	17	16	47.1

FIFA/COCA-COLA WORLD RANKING

1993	1994	1995	1996	1997	1998	1999	2000	2001	2002	2003	2004	2005	2006	2007	High	
-	90	94	86	92	59	68	76	89	85	92	92	87	54	58	49	03/07

2007–2008												Low	
08/07	09/07	10/07	11/07	12/07	01/08	02/08	03/08	04/08	05/08	06/08	07/08	147	05/94
67	67	75	59	58	60	61	59	56	56	56	56		

It was never going to be easy for Srecko Katenec and his Macedonian team in a Euro 2008 qualifying group that was just seconds away from producing two of the semi-finalists in Austria and Switzerland. However, a 2-0 victory over group winners Croatia and a 0-0 draw against England in Manchester were the highlights as the Macedonians finished with a respectable 14 points. Having led his native Slovenia to the finals of Euro 2000 and the World Cup finals in 2002, Katanec has his sights set on South Africa with the Netherlands, Scotland, Norway and Iceland standing in the way. It would be a miracle if they make it but three years on from their

INTERNATIONAL HONOURS
None

embarrasing defeat against Andorra, no-one is underestimating them anymore. At club level, Rabotnicki a team from the capital Skopje with their origins in the railways, continued to benefit from the patronage of Trifun Kostovski, the flambouyant businessman and Mayor of Skopje. They won their third title in four years and also won the first league and cup double in the country for eight years after beating Milano Kumanovo 2-0 in the Cup Final. Bizarrely, however, Kostovski and his company Kometal transferred their allegience to city rivals Vardar, buying the club in 2008 and rebuilding the team in the quest for a first championship since 2003.

THE FIFA BIG COUNT OF 2006

	Male	Female		Total
Number of players	82 546	11 350	Referees and Assistant Referees	740
Professionals	356		Admin, Coaches, Technical, Medical	1 125
Amateurs 18+	14 530		Number of clubs	456
Youth under 18	7 760		Number of teams	615
Unregistered	19 000		Clubs with women's teams	16
Total players	93 896		Players as % of population	4.58%

Football Federation of Macedonia (FFM)
8-ma Udarna brigada 31-a, PO Box 84, Skopje 1000, FYR Macedonia
Tel +389 23 222603   Fax +389 23 165448
fsm@fsm.org.mk   www.ffm.com.mk
President: HADZI-RISTESKI Haralampie   General Secretary: KOSTOV Nikola
Vice-President: BEDZETI Redzep   Treasurer: TBD   Media Officer: NIKOLOVSKI Zoran
Men's Coach: KATENEC Srecko   Women's Coach: DIMOVSKI Dobrislav
FFM formed: 1908   UEFA: 1994   FIFA: 1994
Red shirts with white trimmings, Red shorts, Red socks or White shirts with red trimmings, White shorts, White socks

RECENT INTERNATIONAL MATCHES PLAYED BY FYR MACEDONIA

2003 Opponents	Score	Venue	Comp	Scorers	Att	Referee
20-08 Albania	W 3-1	Prilep	Fr	Naumoski [9], Pandev [36], Dimitrovski [77]	3 000	Mihajlevic SCG
6-09 England	L 1-2	Skopje	ECq	Hristov [28]	20 500	De Bleeckere BEL
10-09 Slovakia	D 1-1	Zilina	ECq	Dimitrovski [62]	2 286	Sundell SWE
11-10 Ukraine	D 0-0	Kyiv	Fr		13 000	Orlic MDA
2004						
27-01 China PR	D 0-0	Shanghai	Fr		25 000	Lee Yu CHN
29-01 China PR	L 0-1	Shanghai	Fr		17 500	Zhig Yang CHN
18-02 Bosnia-Herzegovina	W 1-0	Skopje	Fr	Pandev [20]	8 000	Vrajkov BUL
31-03 Ukraine	W 1-0	Skopje	Fr	Stavrevski [26]	16 000	Karagic SCG
28-04 Croatia	L 0-1	Skopje	Fr		15 000	Arzuman TUR
11-06 Estonia	W 4-2	Tallinn	Fr	Sedloski [11], Popov [15], Pandev [31], Grozdanovski [65]	1 500	Fröjfeldt SWE
18-08 Armenia	W 3-0	Skopje	WCq	Pandev [5], Sakiri [37], Sumolikoski [90]	4 375	Guenov BUL
4-09 Romania	L 1-2	Craiova	WCq	Vasoski [70]	14 500	Plautz AUT
9-10 Netherlands	D 2-2	Skopje	WCq	Pandev [45], Stojkov [71]	15 000	Frojdfeldt SWE
13-10 Andorra	L 0-1	Andorra La Vella	WCq		350	Podeschi SMR
17-11 Czech Republic	L 0-2	Skopje	WCq		7 000	Meier SUI
2005						
9-02 Andorra	D 0-0	Skopje	WCq		5 000	Verbist BEL
30-03 Romania	L 1-2	Skopje	WCq	Maznov [31]	15 000	Ovrebo NOR
4-06 Armenia	W 2-1	Yerevan	WCq	Pandev 2 [29p] [47]	2 870	Mikulski POL
8-06 Czech Republic	L 1-6	Teplice	WCq	Pandev [13]	14 150	Dauden Ibanez ESP
17-08 Finland	L 0-3	Skopje	WCq		6 800	Messias ENG
7-09 Finland	L 1-5	Tampere	WCq	Maznov [48]	6 467	Jakobsson ISL
12-10 Netherlands	D 0-0	Amsterdam	WCq		50 000	Farina ITA
12-11 Liechtenstein	W 2-1	Vaduz	Fr	Ilijoski [82], Nuhiji [90]	1 350	Nobs SUI
2006						
1-03 Bulgaria	L 0-1	Skopje	Fr		8 000	
28-05 Ecuador	W 2-1	Madrid	Fr	Maznov [28], Mitreski [73p]	4 000	
4-06 Turkey	W 1-0	Krefeld	Fr	Maznov [82]	7 000	
16-08 Estonia	W 1-0	Tallinn	ECq	Sedloski [73]	7 500	Jakobsson ISL
6-09 England	L 0-1	Skopje	ECq		15 000	Layec FRA
7-10 England	D 0-0	Manchester	ECq		72 060	Merk GER
11-10 Andorra	W 3-0	Andorra la Vella	ECq	Pandev [13], Noveski [16], Naumoski [31]	300	Silagava GEO
15-11 Russia	L 0-2	Skopje	ECq		13 000	Allaerts BEL
2007						
7-02 Albania	W 1-0	Tirana	Fr	Ristic [33]	8 000	Bertini ITA
24-03 Croatia	L 1-2	Zagreb	ECq	Sedloski [38]	29 969	Plautz AUT
2-06 Israel	L 1-2	Skopje	ECq	Stojkov [13]	12 000	Kircher GER
22-08 Nigeria	D 0-0	Skopje	Fr			
8-09 Russia	L 0-3	Moscow	ECq		23 000	Ovrebø NOR
12-09 Estonia	D 1-1	Skopje	ECq	Maznov [30]	5 000	Trattou CYP
17-10 Andorra	W 3-0	Skopje	ECq	Naumoski [30], Sedloski [44], Pandev [59]	17 500	Malzinskas LTU
17-11 Croatia	W 2-0	Skopje	ECq	Maznov [71], Naumoski [83]	14 500	De Bleeckere BEL
21-11 Israel	L 0-1	Tel Aviv	ECq		2 736	Mikulski POL
2008						
6-02 Serbia	D 1-1	Skopje	Fr	Novevski [58]	12 000	
26-03 Bosnia-Herzegovina	D 2-2	Zenica	Fr	Maznov 2 [40] [45]		Svilokos CRO
26-05 Poland	D 1-1	Reutlingen	Fr	Maznov [45]	2 200	Brych GER

Fr = Friendly match • EC = UEFA EURO 2004/2008 • WC = FIFA World Cup • q = qualifier

FYR MACEDONIA NATIONAL TEAM RECORDS AND RECORD SEQUENCES

Records			Sequence records			
Victory	11-1	LIE 1996	Wins	4	1993-1994	Clean sheets	2	
Defeat	1-6	CZE 2005	Defeats	3	Five times	Goals scored	8	2002-2003
Player Caps	84	Goce Sedloski	Undefeated	8	1998	Without goal	4	2001-2002
Player Goals	16	Gjorgji Hristov	Without win	19	2000-2002	Goals against	13	2001-2002

SRB

Kumanovo

BUL

Skopje   Kratovo

Tetovo

Veles

Prilep

Ohrid

Bitola

GRE

ALB

REPUBLIC OF MACEDONIA; REPUBLIKA MAKEDONIJA

Capital	Skopje	Language	Macedonian, Albanian			Independence	1991
Population	2 050 554	Area	25 333 km^2	Density	82 per km^2	% in cities	60%
GDP per cap	$6 700	Dailling code	+389	Internet	.mk	GMT +/-	+1

MEDALS TABLE

		Overall			League			Cup			Europe			City	Stadium	Cap'ty	DoF
		G	S	B	G	S	B	G	S	G	S	B					
1	Vardar Skopje	10	3	3	5	2	3	5	1				Skopje	Gradski	22 000	1947
2	Sloga Jugomagnat	6	7	2	3	2	2	3	5				Skopje	Cair	4 500	1927
3	Sileks Kratovo	5	6		3	5		2	1				Kratovo	Sileks	3 000	1965
4	Pobeda Prilep	3	4	4	2	2	4	1	2				Prilep	Goce Delcev	15 000	1941
5	Rabotnicki Kometal	4	1	1	3	1	1	1					Skopje	Gradski	22 000	1937
6	Pelister Bitola	1	2	1		1		1	2				Bitola	Pod Timbe Kafe	9 000	1945
7	Cementarnica Skopje	1	1	1		1		1	1				Skopje	Cementarnica	2 000	1955
	Makedonija Skopje	1	1	2		1	2	1					Skopje	Gorce Petrov	3 000	1934
9	Baskimi Kumanovo	1						1					Kumanovo	Gradski Arena	7 000	1947
10	Belasica Strumica		2			2							Strumica	Mladost	6 370	1922
	Milano Kumanovo		2			1			1				Kumanovo	Gradski Arena	7 000	1990
12	Madzari Skopje		1						1				Skopje	Boris Trajkovski	2 500	1992
	Napredok Kicevo		1						1				Kicevo	Gradski	5 000	1924
14	Shkendija Tetovo		1						1				Tetovo	Gradski	20 500	1960
15	Balkan Skopje			1		1							Skopje			
	Balkan Stokokomerc			1		1							Skopje			

RECENT LEAGUE AND CUP RECORD

	Championship						Cup		
Year	Champions	Pts	Runners-up	Pts	Third	Pts	Winners	Score	Runners-up
1995	Vardar Skopje	76	Sileks Kratovo	60	Sloga Jugomagnat	58	Vardar Skopje	2-1	Sileks Kratovo
1996	Sileks Kratovo	70	Sloga Jugomagnat	58	Vardar Skopje	57	Sloga Jugomagnat	0-0 5-3p	Vardar Skopje
1997	Sileks Kratovo	62	Pobeda Prilep	54	Sloga Jugomagnat	42	Sileks Kratovo	4-2	Sloga Jugomagnat
1998	Sileks Kratovo	48	Sloga Jugomagnat	43	Makedonija Skopje	42	Vardar Skopje	2-0	Sloga Jugomagnat
1999	Sloga Jugomagnat	60	Sileks Kratovo	57	Pobeda Prilep	53	Vardar Skopje	2-0	Sloga Jugomagnat
2000	Sloga Jugomagnat	61	Pobeda Prilep	52	Rabotnicki Skopje	50	Sloga Jugomagnat	6-0	Pobeda Prilep
2001	Sloga Jugomagnat	63	Vardar Skopje	63	Pobeda Prilep	56	Pelister Bitola	2-1	Sloga Jugomagnat
2002	Vardar Skopje	37	Belasica Strumica	36	Cementarnica	27	Pobeda Prilep	3-1	Cementarnica
2003	Vardar Skopje	72	Belasica Strumica	69	Pobeda Prilep	65	Cementarnica	4-4 3-2p	Sloga Jugomagnat
2004	Pobeda Prilep	71	Sileks Kratovo	66	Vardar Skopje	60	Sloga Jugomagnat	1-0	Napredok Kicevo
2005	Rabotnicki Skopje	78	Vardar Skopje	72	Pobeda Prilep	55	Baskimi Kumanovo	2-1	Madzari Skopje
2006	Rabotnicki Skopje	72	Makedonija Skopje	69	Vardar Skopje	64	Makedonije Skopje	3-2	Shkendija Tetovo
2007	Pobeda Prilep	71	Rabotnicki Skopje	67	Makedonija Skopje	64	Vardar Skopje	2-1	Pobeda Prilep
2008	Rabotnicki Skopje	79	Milano Kumanovo	66	Pelister Bitola	58	Rabotnicki Skopje	2-0	Milano Kumanovo

FYR MACEDONIA 2007–08

PRVA LIGA

	Pl	W	D	L	F	A	Pts	Rabotnicki	Milano	Pelister	Vardar	Renova	Pobeda	Makedonija	Napredok	Sileks	Baskimi	Shkendija	Cement'ca
Rabotnicki Skopje †	33	24	7	2	51	11	**79**		1-0	3-1 1-0	0-0	1-0	3-0 2-0	4-2	3-0 1-0	3-0	4-1 1-0	1-0	2-0 0-0 2-0
Milano Kumanovo ‡	33	21	3	9	74	36	66	1-2		3-0	1-0 9-1	3-0	4-0 2-1 5-0	2-0 2-1 3-0	4-0	4-2 2-1 1-0 4-0			5-1
Pelister Bitola ‡	33	17	7	9	42	27	58	0-0 3-0	3-2		2-1	1-1	1-1 4-0 1-0	1-0 1-1 1-1	1-0	1-0 1-3 3-0 1-0			2-1
Vardar Skopje	33	12	11	10	45	40	47	0-0 1-2	0-0 1-0 1-3			1-0 3-1	0-0	4-1 0-1	5-1 1-0 2-1	6-1	4-1		1-0 1-1
Renova Cepciste	33	13	8	12	34	34	47	0-1	1-2 1-2 1-0 2-1	0-0			2-0	2-1 2-0 2-1 0-0 1-0	1-1	1-1 0-0 1-0 2-0			2-0
Pobeda Prilep	33	12	9	12	48	48	45	0-0 2-0	4-1	2-1	0-0 0-2 0-0 0-1			4-1 2-0	4-1 1-0 1-1	2-1		1-1	4-3 1-1
Makedonija GP Skopje	33	13	5	15	34	42	44	0-0	3-0	0-2	1-1	2-1	2-1	–	1-0 1-0 1-0 0-3	0-3 0-4 1-1	0-1 0-2 0-		
Napredok Kicevo	33	11	9	13	38	49	42	0-2 0-0	2-1	1-1	0-0 5-3	3-1	1-1 4-3	1-0		2-1	2-0 1-0 2-0 4-3		
Sileks Kratovo	33	10	11	12	33	36	41	1-2	0-0 0-1 2-3 2-1	1-1	0-0	3-0	1-0	1-0 1-0 0-0			4-3	1-1	2-0 2-0
Baskimi Kumanovo	33	8	6	19	40	63	30	0-4 1-0	2-2	0-0	1-1 2-0	1-3	3-4 2-0	5-4	4-1 0-2 2-0			1-0	0-2 1-1
Shkendija Tetovo	33	7	5	21	26	57	26	1-2 0-3	1-3	1-0	0-1 1-0	0-2	3-0 1-5	0-0	2-1	0-1 1-2 1-0 4-3			1-0
Cementarnica Skopje	33	5	9	19	24	46	24	0-1	1-2 2-1 0-1	0-1	2-2	1-0 0-3	0-2	0-1	0-0 1-0	1-1	3-0	1-1 1-1	

5/08/2007 - 31/05/2008 • † Qualified for the UEFA Champions League • ‡ Qualified for the UEFA Cup
Relegation play-offs: **Sileks** 2-0 Belasica; **Baskimi** 4-1 Miravci • Top scorer: Ivica Gligorovski, Milano 15

FYR MACEDONIA 2007–08
VTORA LIGA (2)

	Pl	W	D	L	F	A	Pts
Turnovo	32	22	5	5	58	23	**71**
Metalurg Skopje	32	20	7	5	47	24	**67**
Miravci	32	20	5	7	60	22	65
Belasica Strumica	32	16	7	9	49	37	55
Skopje	32	16	6	10	53	44	**54**
Drita Bogovinje	32	13	8	11	47	30	47
Teteks Tetovo	32	14	5	13	32	30	47
Sloga Jugomagnat	32	13	5	14	36	34	44
Ohrid 2004	32	12	5	15	43	53	41
Madzari Solidarnost	32	12	4	15	33	39	40
Nov Milenium Susica	32	10	9	14	41	36	39
Alumina Skopje	32	10	9	13	28	37	39
Vardar Negotino	32	11	6	15	42	58	39
Lokomotiva Skopje	32	12	2	18	40	47	38
Bregalnica Stip	32	9	10	13	36	43	37
Karaorman Struga	32	8	2	22	23	57	**26**
Vlazrimi Kicevo	32	4	5	23	28	82	**17**
Ilinden Skopje					Withdrew after 14 rounds		

4/08/2007 - 1/06/2008

MAKEDONSKI CUP 2007–08

Round of sixteen

Rabotnicki Skopje	0	4
Pelister Bitola *	0	0
Teteks Tetovo *	0	0
Vardar Skopje	3	1
Skopje	1	1
Sileks Kratovo *	0	1
Baskimi Kumanovo *	3	0
Makedonija GP Skopje	4	2
Nov Milenium Susica	3	4
Vardar Negotino *	2	1
Shkendija Tetovo	1	0
Ilinden Skopje *	0	2
Renova Cepciste *	5	1
Napredok Kicevo	1	1
Bregalnica Stip	0	0
Milano Kumanovo *	3	2

Quarter–finals

Rabotnicki Skopje *	2	0
Vardar Skopje	0	1
Skopje	1	0
Makedonija Skopje *	2	0
Nov Milenium Susica *	w-o	
Ilinden Skopje		
Renova Cepciste	0	2
Milano Kumanovo *	2	2

Semi–finals

Rabotnicki Skopje *	0	1
Makedonija GP Skopje	0	1
Nov Milenium Susica	0	1
Milano Kumanovo *	4	2

Final

Rabotnicki Skopje	2
Milano Kumanovo	0

CUP FINAL

Gradski, Skopje
24-05-2008, Att: 5000

Scorer - Nderim Nedzipi 2 [24][42]

* Home team in the first leg • ‡ Qualified for the UEFA Cup

MLI – MALI

NATIONAL TEAM RECORD
JULY 10TH 2006 TO JULY 12TH 2010

PL	W	D	L	F	A	%
21	12	4	5	35	20	61.9

FIFA/COCA-COLA WORLD RANKING

1993	1994	1995	1996	1997	1998	1999	2000	2001	2002	2003	2004	2005	2006	2007	High	
70	52	52	67	80	70	72	98	112	73	54	51	63	36	46	**35**	02/07

2007–2008											Low	
08/07	09/07	10/07	11/07	12/07	01/08	02/08	03/08	04/08	05/08	06/08	07/08	117	10/01
48	49	40	46	46	47	46	45	44	44	46	51		

Mali have suddenly evolved into one of the potential super-powers of African football, thanks to the rich array of talent at their disposal. And after the disappointment of an early exit at the 2008 African Nations Cup finals in Ghana, the west African nation made a positive start to qualification for the 2010 FIFA World Cup finals. Frederic Kanoute was named African Footballer of the Year in February 2008, the first Malian since inaugural winner Salif Keita to have been awarded the distinction. It was tinged with controversy as the Confederation of African Football admitted it had been intended for Didier Drogba but was given to Kanoute instead because he, unlike the Chelsea

INTERNATIONAL HONOURS
None

striker, made the effort of going to the award function held in Togo during the Nations Cup finals. Along with Kanoute, the likes of Seydou Keita, now at Barcelona, and Real Madrid's Mahamadou Diarra make for formidable components of the Mali national side, 'Les Aigles'. Diarra's suspension at a vital juncture of the Nations Cup finals saw Mali fail to make the last eight, ending the tenure of coach Jean Francois Jodar. He has since been replaced by Stephen Keshi, the former Nigeria World Cup captain. In the domestic league Stade Malien continued to dominate, securing a hat-trick of titles while fierce rivals Djoliba beat Bakaridjan 2-0 in the Cup Final.

THE FIFA BIG COUNT OF 2006

	Male	Female		Total
Number of players	1 363 775	27 850	Referees and Assistant Referees	575
Professionals	0		Admin, Coaches, Technical, Medical	5 503
Amateurs 18+	5 100		Number of clubs	140
Youth under 18	9 075		Number of teams	700
Unregistered	1 352 450		Clubs with women's teams	0
Total players	1 391 625		Players as % of population	11.88%

Fédération Malienne de Football (FMF)
Avenue du Mali, Hamdallaye ACI 2000, PO Box 1020, Bamako 12582, Mali
Tel +223 2238844   Fax +223 2224254
malifoot@afribone.net.ml   www.none
President: KEITA Salif   General Secretary: TRAORE Jacouba
Vice-President: KEITA Karounga   Treasurer: TRAORE Brehima   Media Officer: KALOGA Mamadou
Men's Coach: KESHI Stephen   Women's Coach: DIAKITE Aly
FMF formed: 1960   CAF: 1963   FIFA: 1962
Green shirts, Yellow shorts, Red socks

RECENT INTERNATIONAL MATCHES PLAYED BY MALI

2005	Opponents	Score		Venue	Comp	Scorers	Att	Referee
27-03	Togo	L	1-2	Bamako	WCq	Soumaila Coulibaly [12]	45 000	Agbenyega GHA
5-06	Liberia	W	4-1	Liberia	WCq	Dramane Coulibaly 2 [7p 34], Diamoutene [48p], Mahamadou Diarra [75]	11 000	Pare BFA
12-06	Algeria	W	3-0	Arles	Fr	Dramane Coulibaly [33], Dissa 2 [58 79]	2 000	Derrien FRA
17-06	Zambia	L	1-2	Chililabombwe	WCq	Soumaila Coulibaly [73]	29 000	Colembi ANG
3-09	Congo	W	2-0	Bamako	WCq	Demba [48], Momo Sissoko [51]	10 000	Mbera GAB
8-10	Senegal	L	0-3	Dakar	WCq		30 000	Maillet SEY
2006								
28-05	Morocco	W	1-0	Paris	Fr	Kanoute [70]		Garibian FRA
16-08	Tunisia	W	1-0	Narbonne	Fr	Kanoute [39p]		
3-09	Sierra Leone	D	0-0	Freetown	CNq			Mbera GAB
8-10	Togo	W	1-0	Bamako	CNq	Dramane Traore [89]		Benouza ALG
14-11	Congo	W	1-0	La Corneuve	Fr	Kante [90]		
2007								
6-02	Lithuania	W	3-1	La Corneuve	Fr	Tamboura [25], Mahamadou Diarra [31], Mamadou Diallo [43]		Piccirillo FRA
25-03	Benin	D	1-1	Bamako	CNq	Kanoute [53p]		Doue CIV
3-06	Benin	D	0-0	Cotonou	CNq			Guezzaz MAR
9-06	Burkina Faso	W	1-0	Ouagadougou	Fr	Mamadou Diallo [57]		
17-06	Sierra Leone	W	6-0	Bamako	CNq	Djibril Sidibe [20p], Seydou Keita 2 [68 88], Mamadou Diallo [76], Lassana Diallo [90], Bassala Toure [93+]		Lemghambodj MTN
22-08	Burkina Faso	W	3-2	Paris	Fr	Seydou Keita, Mahamadou Diarra, Dramane Traore		
12-10	Togo	W	2-0	Lome	CNq	Kanouté [38], Mamadou Diallo [89]		Abdelfattah EGY
17-11	Senegal	L	2-3	Bondoufle	Fr	Dramane Traore [32], Moussa Traore [32]		
20-11	Algeria	L	2-3	Rouen	Fr	Dramane Traore 2 [42 49p]		
2008								
10-01	Egypt	L	0-1	Abu Dhabi	Fr			
21-01	Benin	W	1-0	Sekondi	CNr1	Kanouté [49p]		Damon RSA
25-01	Nigeria	D	0-0	Sekondi	CNr1			El Arjoun MAR
29-01	Côte d'Ivoire	L	0-3	Accra	CNr1			Maillet SEY
1-06	Congo	W	4-2	Bamoko	WCq	Seydou Keita 2 [1 61], Adama Coulibaly [32], Soumaila Coulibaly [42]	40 000	Bennaceur TUN
7-06	Chad	W	2-1	N'Djamena	WCq	Kanouté 2 [4 22]	15 000	Aguidissou BEN
14-06	Sudan	L	2-3	Khartoum	WCq	Kanouté 2 [63 94+]	15 000	Abdelfattah EGY
22-06	Sudan	W	3-0	Bamoko	WCq	Kanouté 2 [23], Seydou Keita 2 [58 66]	25 000	Doue CIV

Fr = Friendly match • CN = CAF African Cup of Nations • WC = FIFA World Cup
q = qualifier • r1 = first round group • qf = quarter-final • sf = semi-final • 3p = third place play-off

MALI NATIONAL TEAM PLAYERS

	Player		Club	Date of Birth		Player		Club	Date of Birth
1	Mahamadou Sidibe	GK	PAS Giannina	8 10 1978	12	Seydou Keita	MF	Sevilla	13 12 1981
2	Boubacar Sidiki Kone	DF	Maghreb Fes	21 08 1984	13	Mamadou Diallo	FW	Qatar SC	17 04 1982
3	Adama Tamboura	DF	Helsingborg	18 05 1985	14	Drissa Diakite	DF	Nice	18 02 1985
4	Adama Coulibaly	DF	RC Lens	9 10 1980	15	Cedric Kante	DF	Nice	6 08 1979
5	Souleymane Diamoutene	DF	Lecce	30 01 1983	16	Soumbeyla Diakite	GK	Stade Malien	25 08 1984
6	Mahamadou Diarra	MF	Real Madrid	18 06 1981	17	Sammy Traore	DF	Auxerre	25 02 1976
7	Mamady Sidibe	FW	Stoke City	18 12 1979	18	Souleymane Dembele	DF	Djoliba	3 09 1984
8	Bassala Toure	FW	Levadiakos	21 02 1976	19	Frederic Kanoute	FW	Sevilla	2 09 1977
9	Amadou Sidibe	DF	Djoliba	19 02 1986	20	Mohamed Sissoko	MF	Liverpool	22 01 1985
10	Dramane Traore	FW	Lokomotiv Moskva	17 06 1982	21	Mahamadou Dissa	FW	Roeselare	18 05 1979
11	Djibril Sidibe	MF	Chateauroux	23 03 1982	22	Oumar Sissoko	GK	Metz	13 09 1987
	Mali's squad for the 2008 CAF Africa Cup of Nations				23	Moussa Coulibaly	DF	MC Alger	19 05 1981

MALI NATIONAL TEAM RECORDS AND RECORD SEQUENCES

Records			Sequence records					
Victory	6-0	MTN 1975, SLE 2007	Wins	8	2002-2003	Clean sheets	6	2003
Defeat	1-8	KUW 1997	Defeats	5	1997	Goals scored	11	1971-1972
Player Caps	n/a		Undefeated	18	2002-2004	Without goal	4	Three times
Player Goals	n/a		Without win	8	1989-90, 1995-96	Goals against	12	1987-1988

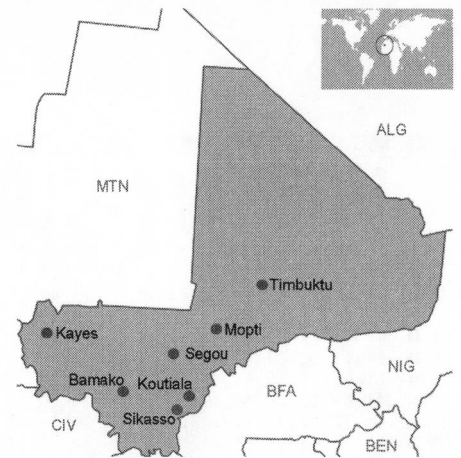

MAJOR CITIES/TOWNS

		Population '000
1	Bamako	1 388
2	Sikasso	154
3	Mopti	112
4	Koutiala	106
5	Kayes	103
6	Ségou	92
7	Nioro	75
8	Markala	59
9	Kolokani	54
10	Kati	43
11	Gao	39
12	Bougouni	37
13	Niono	34
14	Banamba	33
15	Timbuktu	32
16	Bafoulabé	30
17	Nara	30
18	Koulikoro	24
19	San	24
20	Djenné	23
21	Kangaba	17
22	Yorosso	17
23	Kidal	11
24	Diré	10

REPUBLIC OF MALI; REPUBLIQUE DE MALI

Capital	Bamako	Language	French, Bambara		Independence	1960
Population	11 716 829	Area	1 240 000 km²	Density	10 per km²	% in cities 27%
GDP per cap	$900	Dailling code	+223	Internet	.ml	GMT + / - 0

MEDALS TABLE

		Overall			Lge	Cup		Africa				City	Stadium	Cap'ty	DoF
		G	S	B	G	G	S	G	S	B					
1	Djoliba AC	36	10	3	19	17	10			3	Bamako	Complex Sportif Hérémakono	5 000	1960
2	Stade Malien	31	9		15	16	8	1			Bamako	Stade 26 mars	50 000	1960
3	Real Bamako	15	8		6	9	7	1			Bamako	Stade Mobido Keita	35 000	
4	Cercle Olympique	2	1			2	1				Bamako	Stade 26 mars	50 000	1960
5	AS Bamako	1	1			1	1				Bamako	Stade Municipal	5 000	1999
	USFAS Bamako	1	1			1	1				Bamako	Stade Municipal de USFAS	5 000	1965
7	AS Sigui Kayes	1				1					Kayes	Stade Abdoulaye Nakoro Cissoko	15 000	
8	Avenir Ségou		4			4					Ségou			
9	AS Nianan Koulikoro		3			3					Koulikoro	Stade Municipal de Koulikoro	8 000	1979
10	Kayésienne		2			2					Kayes			
11	Africa Sports Gao		1			1					Gao			
	AS Bakaridjan		1			1					Baraouéli			1989
	AS Biton Ségou		1			1					Ségou	Stade Amari Daou	15 000	1960
	Jeunesse Sportive		1			1					Ségou	Stade Amari Daou	15 000	
	Mamahira AC Kati		1			1					Kati			
	AS Mandé Bamako		1			1					Bamako	Stade de Mandé	7 000	
	US Sevaré		1			1					Sevaré			
	AS Tata National		1			1					Sikasso	Stade Omnisports	20 000	
	Tibo Club de Mopti		1			1					Mopti	Stade Taïkiri	6 000	
	Sonni Gao		1			1					Gao			
21	AS Commune II										Bamako	Stade Municipal de Commune II	3 000	
	Baoulé Club										Dioila			
	JS Centre Salif Keita										Bamako	Stade Centre Salif Keita	4 000	1995

RECENT LEAGUE AND CUP RECORD

	Championship						Cup		
Year	Champions	Pts	Runners-up	Pts	Third	Pts	Winners	Score	Runners-up
1999	Djoliba	54	USFAS Bamako	53	Centre Salif Keita		Stade Malien	1-0	Nianan
2000	Stade Malien	52	Djoliba	47	Centre Salif Keita	40	Cercle Olympique	1-0	Stade Malien
2001	Stade Malien	66	Djoliba	54	Cercle Olympique	45	Stade Malien	5-0	Mamahira Kati
2002	Stade Malien	68	Djoliba	61	Centre Salif Keita	54	Cercle Olympique	2-1	Stade Malien
2003	Stade Malien	62	Djoliba	60	Cercle Olympique	53	Djoliba	2-1	Tata National
2004	Djoliba	63	Stade Malien	58	Centre Salif Keita	58	Djoliba	2-0	Nianan
2005	Stade Malien	64	Cercle Olympique	55	Réal Bamako	47	AS Bamako	1-1 5-4p	Djoliba
2006	Stade Malien	62	Djoliba	60	Cercle Olympique	50	Stade Malien	2-1	AS Bamoko
2007	Stade Malien	59	Djoliba	54	Cercle Olympique	54	Djoliba	2-0	AS Bakaridjan

MALI 2007

PREMIERE DIVISION

	Pl	W	D	L	F	A	Pts	Stade Malien	Djoliba	CO Bamako	CSK	ASKO	USFAS	AS Bamako	Bakaridjan	Nianan	Réal	Duguwolofila	Stade Sikasso	Comune II	Sigui Kayes
Stade Malien †	26	17	8	1	52	13	59		0-0	0-1	1-1	1-0	1-1	1-0	3-0	4-0	2-1	3-3	4-0	5-2	0-0
Djoliba ‡	26	15	9	2	46	18	54	1-1		2-1	4-1	1-0	0-0	3-1	3-2	2-0	1-1	0-0	3-0	2-2	4-0
Cercle Olympique	26	17	3	6	41	22	54	0-2	0-4		1-2	1-1	3-1	0-1	2-3	3-0	2-0	3-0	1-0	2-1	5-0
Centre Salif Keita	26	14	7	5	45	24	49	0-2	3-1	1-1		1-2	1-0	1-2	1-2	2-1	2-0	1-1	1-1	7-0	0-1
AS Korofina Bamako	26	9	8	9	23	26	35	0-3	1-0	1-2	0-2		0-0	0-1	3-2	0-0	1-3	1-0	1-1	1-1	3-0
USFAS Bamako	26	7	13	6	23	21	34	1-1	0-3	0-1	2-2	0-1		2-0	1-1	3-1	0-0	1-0	2-1	0-0	2-0
AS Bamako	26	8	10	8	20	22	34	0-1	0-0	1-2	1-1	0-0	1-1		1-0	2-1	1-0	2-3	1-1	0-1	0-0
Bakaridjan Ségou	26	8	7	11	27	35	31	0-6	1-2	1-2	0-1	2-3	1-1	1-1		0-0	3-0	3-2	1-0	1-0	1-0
Nianan Koulikoro	26	7	7	12	17	33	28	1-3	1-1	0-1	0-1	2-0	1-1	0-0	2-1		0-0	**1-2**	2-0	1-1	1-0
Réal Bamako	26	6	9	11	26	34	27	1-1	1-3	0-2	1-1	0-0	1-1	0-1	0-0	4-0		0-3	3-2	1-0	3-0
Duguwolofila Koulikoro	26	6	8	12	25	33	26	0-1	1-3	**1-1**	0-4	2-1	1-0	0-0	0-1	2-0	3-3		**1-0**	1-0	2-1
Stade Sikasso	26	5	7	14	17	34	22	0-2	1-2	0-2	0-1	1-1	0-2	1-0	0-0	2-1	1-0	1-1		3-1	0-1
Comune II Bamako	26	5	7	14	18	38	22	0-2	0-0	0-2	1-4	0-1	0-1	1-2	0-0	0-1	3-1	1-0	0-1		0-0
Sigui Kayes	26	2	9	15	7	34	15	0-2	0-1	1-1	0-1	0-1	0-0	1-1	1-0	0-1	1-2	1-1	0-0	0-1	

6/01/2007 - 30/08/2007 • † Qualified for the CAF Champions League • ‡ Qualified for the CAF Confederation Cup • Matches in bold were awarded as 0-0 wins to Duguwolofila's opponents • Top scorers: Bakary Coulibaly, Stade Malien 16; Aime Koffi, Duguwolofila 13

COUPE DU MALI 2007

Round of 16		Quarter–finals		Semi–finals		Final	
Djoliba	2						
Comune Timbuktu	0	Djoliba	2				
Debo Club Mopti	0	Duguwolofila Koulikoro	0				
Duguwolofila Koulikoro	4			Djoliba	4		
Stade Sikasso	4			Réal Bamako	2		
Atar Club Kidal	0	Stade Sikasso	0				
AS Sahel Gao	1	Réal Bamako	4				
Réal Bamako	2					Djoliba ‡	2
Cercle Olympique	10					Bakaridjan Ségou	0
AS Kafo Kayes	1	Cercle Olympique	1				
Sigui Kayes	0 6p	Etoile Filante Koutiala	0				
Etoile Filante Koutiala	0 7p			Cercle Olympique	1		
Stade Malien	4			Bakaridjan Ségou	2		
CMB Mopti	1	Stade Malien	0				
Fleche Noir	1	Bakaridjan Ségou	2				
Bakaridjan Ségou	4			‡ Qualified for the CAF Confederation Cup			

CUP FINAL

Abdoulaye Sissoko, Kayes
29-07-2007, Ref: Koman Coulibaly

Scorers - Moussa Diallo 52,
Sory Ibrahima Bangoura 81p

MLT – MALTA

NATIONAL TEAM RECORD
JULY 10TH 2006 TO JULY 12TH 2010

PL	W	D	L	F	A	%
22	3	3	16	21	51	27.3

FIFA/COCA-COLA WORLD RANKING

1993	1994	1995	1996	1997	1998	1999	2000	2001	2002	2003	2004	2005	2006	2007	High	
83	78	90	122	133	130	116	119	131	122	129	134	118	119	136	**66**	09/94

	2007–2008											Low	
	08/07	09/07	10/07	11/07	12/07	01/08	02/08	03/08	04/08	05/08	06/08	07/08	**144** 09/06
	115	124	137	139	136	136	134	134	135	135	134	134	

After a seven year wait, Valletta finally got their hands on the championship trophy again thanks in no small part to the club president Victor Scriha. Scriha made his name in football circles at Marsaxlook, one of Malta's peripheral teams whom he bankrolled over an eight year period, eventually winning the championship with them in 2007. Immediately afterwards he moved on to Valletta, arguably the best supported team on the island, and set about professionalising the structures at the club - with immediate results. Valletta fans will be hoping that the championship is the start of a successful new era for the club and that they can add to their tally of 19 titles and close the

INTERNATIONAL HONOURS
None

gap between them and the more successful Sliema Wanderers and Floriana. Birkirkara were the season's other major trophy winners after beating Hamrum Spartans 2-1 in the FA trophy final with Michael Galea scoring a last minute winner. The Maltese national team may not have had the best of times in their Euro 2008 qualifiers, picking up just two points during the campaign, but one of those was against eventual semi-finalists Turkey, who they held to a 2-2 draw in Ta'qali. 2008 did, however, see the national team win two matches, the second of which was a record breaking 7-1 victory over Liechtenstein in which Michael Mifsud scored five goals - another record.

THE FIFA BIG COUNT OF 2006

	Male	Female		Total
Number of players	22 451	2 402	Referees and Assistant Referees	99
Professionals	430		Admin, Coaches, Technical, Medical	2 105
Amateurs 18+	7 000		Number of clubs	51
Youth under 18	2 773		Number of teams	325
Unregistered	3 100		Clubs with women's teams	10
Total players	24 853		Players as % of population	6.21%

Malta Football Association (MFA)
Millenium Stand, Floor 2, National Stadium, Ta'Qali, ATD 400, Malta
Tel +356 21 232581   Fax +356 21 245136
info@mfa.com.mt   www.mfa.com.mt
President: MIFSUD Joseph Dr   General Secretary: GAUCHI Joseph
Vice-President: BARTOLO Carmelo   Treasurer: MANFRE Alex   Media Officer: MUSCAT Mark
Men's Coach: FITZEL Dusan   Women's Coach: BRINCAT Pierre
MFA formed: 1900   UEFA: 1960   FIFA: 1959
Red shirts with white trimmings, White shorts, Red socks or White shirts with red trimmings, Red shorts, White socks

RECENT INTERNATIONAL MATCHES PLAYED BY MALTA

2004	Opponents	Score	Venue	Comp	Scorers	Att	Referee
14-02	Moldova	D 0-0	Ta'Qali	Fr		600	Vialichka BLR
16-02	Estonia	W 5-2	Ta'Qali	Fr	Barbara 2 [12 60], Said [28], Turner [57], Zahra [87]		Orlic MDA
18-02	Belarus	L 0-4	Ta'Qali	Fr			Kaldma EST
31-03	Finland	L 1-2	Ta'Qali	Fr	Mifsud.Mc [90]		Trefoloni ITA
27-05	Germany	L 0-7	Freiburg	Fr		22 000	Stredak SVK
18-08	Faroe Islands	L 2-3	Toftir	Fr	Giglio [50], Mifsud.Mc [65]	1 932	Laursen DEN
4-09	Sweden	L 0-7	Ta'Qali	WCq		4 200	Jakov ISR
9-10	Iceland	D 0-0	Ta'Qali	WCq		1 130	Corpodean ROU
13-10	Bulgaria	L 1-4	Sofia	WCq	Mifsud.Mc [11]	16 800	Richards WAL
17-11	Hungary	L 0-2	Ta'Qali	WCq		14 500	Asumaa FIN
2005							
9-02	Norway	L 0-3	Ta'Qali	Fr		1 000	Malcolm NIR
30-03	Croatia	L 0-3	Zagreb	WCq		15 510	Kapitanis CYP
4-06	Sweden	L 0-6	Gothenburg	WCq		35 593	Ivanov.N RUS
8-06	Iceland	L 1-4	Reykjavik	WCq	Said [58]	4 887	Skomina SVN
17-08	Northern Ireland	D 1-1	Ta'Qali	Fr	Woods [35]	1 850	Riley ENG
3-09	Hungary	L 0-4	Budapest	WCq		5 900	Godulyan UKR
7-09	Croatia	D 1-1	Ta'Qali	WCq	Wellman [74]	916	Briakos GRE
12-10	Bulgaria	D 1-1	Ta'Qali	WCq	Zahra [79]	2 844	Godulyan UKR
2006							
25-02	Moldova	L 0-2	Ta'Qali	Fr		1 125	Silagava GEO
1-03	Georgia	L 0-2	Ta'Qali	Fr		1 100	Banari MDA
4-06	Japan	L 0-1	Dusseldorf	Fr		10 800	Kircher GER
15-08	Slovakia	L 0-3	Bratislava	Fr		2 437	Lajuks LVA
2-09	Bosnia-Herzegovina	L 2-5	Ta'Qali	ECq	Pace [6], Mifsud [85]	2 000	Vejlgaard DEN
6-09	Turkey	L 0-2	Frankfurt	ECq		BCD	Vázquez ESP
11-10	Hungary	W 2-1	Ta'Qali	ECq	Schembri 2 [14 53]	3 600	Ver Eecke BEL
15-11	Lithuania	L 1-4	Paola	Fr	Agius [85]		Lawlor WAL
2007							
7-02	Austria	D 1-1	Ta'Qali	Fr	Agius [8]	3 000	Bartolini SUI
24-03	Moldova	D 1-1	Chisinau	ECq	Mallia [73]	8 033	Aliyev AZE
28-03	Greece	L 0-1	Ta'Qali	ECq		8 700	Garcia POR
2-06	Norway	L 0-4	Oslo	ECq		16 364	Granat POL
6-06	Bosnia-Herzegovina	L 0-1	Sarajevo	ECq		10 500	Richards WAL
22-08	Albania	L 0-3	Tirana	Fr			
8-09	Turkey	D 2-2	Ta'Qali	ECq	Said [41], Schembri [76]	10 500	Messner AUT
12-09	Armenia	L 0-1	Ta'Qali	Fr		2 000	Richmond SCO
13-10	Hungary	L 0-2	Budapest	ECq		7 633	Nalbandyan ARM
17-10	Moldova	L 2-3	Ta'Qali	ECq	Scerri [71], Mifsud [84p]	7 069	Ishchenko UKR
17-11	Greece	L 0-5	Athens	ECq		31 332	Kaldma EST
21-11	Norway	L 1-4	Ta'Qali	ECq	Mifsud [53]	7 000	Baskakov RUS
2008							
2-02	Armenia	L 0-1	Ta'Qali	Fr			
4-02	Iceland	W 1-0	Ta'Qali	Fr	Frendo [18]		
6-02	Belarus	L 0-1	Ta'Qali	Fr			Tshagharyan ARM
26-03	Liechtenstein	W 7-1	Ta'Qali	Fr	Mifsud 5 [2p 17 21p 59 69], Pace [35], Said [86]		Collum SCO
30-05	Austria	L 1-5	Graz	Fr	Mifsud [41]	14 200	Krajnc SVN

Fr = Friendly match • EC = UEFA EURO 2004/2008 • WC = FIFA World Cup • q = qualifier

MALTA NATIONAL TEAM RECORDS AND RECORD SEQUENCES

Records			Sequence records					
Victory	7-1	LIE 2008	Wins	3	1981, 1999-2000	Clean sheets	4	1999-2000
Defeat	1-12	ESP 1983	Defeats	16	1982-1985	Goals scored	7	1991-1992
Player Caps	122	David Carabott	Undefeated	6	2001-2002	Without goal	8	2000-2001
Player Goals	23	Carmel Busuttil	Without win	34	1994-1998	Goals against	29	1996-19999

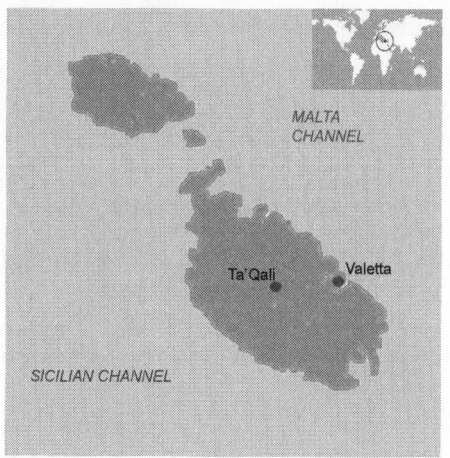

MAJOR CITIES/TOWNS
Population '000

1	Birkirkara	21
2	Qormi	18
3	Mosta	17
4	Zabbar	15
5	Rabat	12
6	San Gwann	12
7	Fgura	11
8	Zejtun	11
9	Zebbug	11
10	Sliema	11
11	Hamrun	10
12	Naxxar	10
13	Attard	9
14	Zurrieq	9
15	Paola	9
16	Tarxien	7
17	Birzebugia	7
18	Siggiewi	7
19	Gzira	7
20	San Pawl il-Bahar	7
21	Msida	6
22	Valletta	6
23	San Giljan	6
24	Marsa	5

REPUBLIC OF MALTA; REPUBBLIKA TA' MALTA

Capital	Valletta	Language	Maltese, English	Independence	1964
Population	400 214	Area	316 km²	Density 1255 per km²	% in cities 89%
GDP per cap	$17 700	Dailling code	+356	Internet .mt	GMT + / - +1

MEDALS TABLE

		Overall			League			Cup			Europe			City	Stadium	Cap'ty	DoF
		G	S	B	G	S	B	G	S	B	G	S	B				
1	Sliema Wanderers	45	50	19	26	31	19	19	19					Sliema	Ta'Qali	17 797	1909
2	Floriana	43	23	13	25	11	13	18	12					Floriana	Ta'Qali	17 797	1894
3	Valletta	30	25	20	19	14	20	11	11					Valletta	Ta'Qali	17 797	1943
4	Hibernians	17	19	9	9	9	9	8	10					Paola	Hibernians Ground	8 000	1922
5	Hamrun Spartans	13	13	13	7	10	13	6	3					Hamrun	Ta'Qali	17 797	1907
6	Birkirkara	6	9	4	2	6	4	4	3					Birkirkara	Infetti	2 500	1950
7	Rabat Ajax	3	2	1	2	1	1	1	1					Rabat	Ta'Qali	17 797	1930
8	St. Georges	1	6	5	1	4	5		2					Cospicua	Ta'Qali	17 797	1890
9	Zurrieq	1	2	2			2	1	2					Zurrieq	Ta'Qali	17 797	1949
10	Melita St. Julians	1	2	1		1	1	1	1					Melita	Ta'Qali	17 797	1906
	Marsaxlokk	1	2	1	1	1	1		1					Marsaxlokk	Ta'Qali	17 797	1949
12	Gzira United	1		1				1	1					Gzira	Ta'Qali	17 797	1950
13	KOMR Militia	1			1												
14	Birkana United		3			1			2								
15	Marsa		2			2								Marsa	Ta'Qali	17 797	1920
16	Msida St Joseph		1	1					1					Msida	Ta'Qali	17 797	1906

RECENT LEAGUE AND CUP RECORD

	Championship						Cup		
Year	Champions	Pts	Runners-up	Pts	Third	Pts	Winners	Score	Runners-up
1995	Hibernians	43	Sliema Wanderers	39	Valletta	37	Valletta	1-0	Hamrun Spartans
1996	Sliema Wanderers	46	Valletta	42	Floriana	37	Valletta	0-0 1-0	Sliema Wanderers
1997	Valletta	67	Birkirkara	60	Floriana	53	Valletta	2-0	Hibernians
1998	Valletta	65	Birkirkara	63	Sliema Wanderers	56	Hibernians	2-1	Valletta
1999	Valletta	70	Birkirkara	68	Sliema Wanderers	47	Valletta	1-0	Birkirkara
2000	Birkirkara	46	Sliema Wanderers	39	Valletta	36	Sliema Wanderers	4-1	Birkirkara
2001	Valletta	46	Sliema Wanderers	40	Birkirkara	36	Valletta	3-0	Birkirkara
2002	Hibernians	43	Sliema Wanderers	36	Birkirkara	31	Birkirkara	1-0	Sliema Wanderers
2003	Sliema Wanderers	42	Birkirkara	37	Valletta	35	Birkirkara	1-0	Sliema Wanderers
2004	Sliema Wanderers	43	Birkirkara	39	Hibernians	35	Sliema Wanderers	2-0	Marsaxlokk
2005	Sliema Wanderers	40	Birkirkara	38	Hibernians	35	Birkirkara	2-1	Msida St Joseph
2006	Birkirkara	42	Sliema Wanderers	37	Marsaxlokk	36	Hibernians	1-0	Floriana
2007	Marsaxlokk	47	Sliema Wanderers	35	Birkirkara	34	Hibernians	1-1 3-0p	Sliema Wanderers
2008	Valletta	40	Marsaxlokk	35	Birkirkara	34	Birkirkara	2-1	Hamrun Spartans

MALTA 2007–08

PREMIER LEAGUE

	Pl	W	D	L	F	A	Pts	Valletta	Marsaxlokk	Birkirkara	Sliema W	Floriana	Hamrun S	Hibernians	Msida SJ	Pietà H	Mqabba
Valletta (18) †	28	17	7	4	58	27	40		7-0 2-1	2-1 2-1	1-2 0-1	2-3 1-0	4-1 4-1	1-1	3-1	3-0	3-1
Marsaxlokk (17) ‡	28	16	3	9	56	40	35	1-1 4-0		3-1 0-2	0-0 4-2	3-2 2-0	0-1 3-1	5-0	5-0	3-1	1-0
Birkirkara (14) ‡	28	13	8	7	46	26	34	0-1 1-1	2-0 2-1		1-1 1-2	3-2 1-1	5-0 4-0	0-2	1-1	2-0	1-0
Sliema Wanderers (16)	28	15	5	8	47	33	34	2-2 0-2	1-0 0-2	1-3 0-1		0-2 1-3	1-1 3-1	2-1	3-0	2-1	4-0
Floriana (14)	28	10	6	12	40	42	22	0-4 0-2	1-4 1-2	0-0 0-2	2-2 0-2		0-1 0-2	1-0	2-3	4-0	4-1
Hamrun Spartans (14)	28	7	7	14	42	60	15	0-0 2-4	7-3 3-4	2-2 0-2	0-3 0-2	2-1 1-2		2-2	1-2	2-3	3-0
Hibernians (13)	24	10	8	6	35	27	26	0-0	1-1	1-1	1-2	1-1	1-1		4-0 3-0	2-0 2-1	2-0 4-2
Msida St Joseph (11)	24	10	4	10	41	46	24	1-1	1-3	0-0	1-4	0-2	0-1	2-0 3-1		7-0 3-1	4-3 4-2
Pietà Hotspurs (8)	24	6	0	18	27	53	11	1-3	0-1	2-1	1-0	1-3	2-5	0-2 1-2	0-1 2-4		5-0 1-0
Mqabba (3)	24	3	2	19	24	62	8	1-2	0-2	1-4	3-2	1-3	1-2	0-1 1-1	2-1 2-2	1-6 2-0	

26/08/2007 – 16/05/2008 • † Qualified for the UEFA Champions League • ‡ Qualified for the UEFA Cup • Points taken forward for the final round in brackets • Top scorer:

MALTA 2007–08 FIRST DIVISION (2)

	Pl	W	D	L	F	A	Pts
Tarxien Rainbows	18	12	3	3	32	17	39
Qormi	18	11	4	3	37	22	37
Mosta	18	11	4	3	34	18	37
Senglea Athletic	18	10	1	7	32	23	31
Dingli Swallows	18	8	3	7	34	27	27
Vittoriosa Stars	18	8	1	9	33	29	25
St George's	18	6	3	9	27	33	21
St Patrick	18	4	4	10	21	27	16
Mellieħa	18	3	4	11	21	43	13
Marsa	18	3	1	14	23	55	10

9/10/2007 – 18/05/2008 • Play-off: Mosta 0-0 3-4p Qormi

MALTA 2007–08 SECOND DIVISION (3)

	Pl	W	D	L	F	A	Pts
San Gwann	22	14	5	3	45	22	47
Rabat Ajax	22	15	2	5	55	25	47
Balzan Youth	22	14	5	3	36	11	47
Melita	22	13	3	6	43	23	42
Birzebbuga St Peter's	22	11	2	9	36	36	35
Lija Athletic	22	8	4	10	25	29	28
Lightenings	22	8	4	10	28	39	28
St Andrews	22	7	5	10	20	26	26
Naxxar Lions	22	7	2	13	17	33	23
Mgarr United	22	5	6	11	23	37	21
Zurrieq §5	22	5	7	10	26	31	17
Sirens	22	1	3	18	11	55	6

21/09/2007 – 11/05/2008 • § = points deducted
Promotion play-off: Balzan 0-3 Rabat Ajax
Relegation play-off: Mgarr United 1-0 Attard

FA TROPHY 2007–08

Round of 16		Quarter-finals		Semi-finals		Final	
Birkirkara	Bye						
		Birkirkara	2				
		Marsaxlokk	1				
Marsaxlokk	Bye			Birkirkara	4		
Hibernians	Bye			Valletta	2		
		Hibernians	1				
Tarxien Rainbows	0	Valletta	2				
Valletta	5					Birkirkara ‡	2
Floriana	3					Hamrun Spartans	1
Senglea Athletic	2	Floriana	2				
		Sliema Wanderers	1				
Sliema Wanderers	Bye			Floriana	2		
Dingli Swallows	1			Hamrun Spartans	4		
Mqabba	0	Dingli Swallows	1				
Pietà Hotspurs	0	Hamrun Spartans	3				
Hamrun Spartans	1						

‡ Qualified for the UEFA Cup

CUP FINAL

Ta'Qali, 25-05-2008

scorers – Michael Galea 2 [58] [90] for Birkirkara; Ryan Fenech [66] for Hamrun

MNE – MONTENEGRO

NATIONAL TEAM RECORD
JULY 10TH 2006 TO JULY 12TH 2010

PL	W	D	L	F	A	%
9	4	1	4	11	12	50

FIFA/COCA-COLA WORLD RANKING

1993	1994	1995	1996	1997	1998	1999	2000	2001	2002	2003	2004	2005	2006	2007	High
-	-	-	-	-	-	-	-	-	-	-	-	-	-	172	142 06/08

2007–2008												Low
08/07	09/07	10/07	11/07	12/07	01/08	02/08	03/08	04/08	05/08	06/08	07/08	199 06/07
199	186	171	172	172	172	175	175	153	150	142	146	

It's an extraordinary testament to the football prowess of the old Yugoslavia that the six new national teams that have emerged from the old republic - soon perhaps to be seven with Kosovo's declaration of independence - have all held their own in the international arena with Montenegro impressing in the handful of matches played since their first in March 2007. Estonia, Norway and Kazakhstan were all beaten in successive internationals during the season as the national team prepared for its competitive debut in the 2010 FIFA World Cup qualifiers. Drawn in a group with world champions Italy, Bulgaria, the Republic of Ireland, Cyprus and Georgia, none of

INTERNATIONAL HONOURS
None

Montenegro's opponents will relish the trip to Podgorica. Roma's Mirko Vucinic is the highest profile player from the country although Fiorentina paid eight million Euros for 18-year old Stevan Jovetic in May 2008 while the 22-year old Simon Vukcevic made a positive impression in his first season at Sporting Lisbon. There was also a modicum of success for Montenegros's club sides when they made their European debuts with Zeta Golubovci knocking out Lithuania's FBK Kaunas in the first preliminary round of the 2007-08 UEFA Champions League. At home the 2008 championship saw a three way tie at the top with the title going to Buducnost on head-to-head records.

THE FIFA BIG COUNT OF 2006

	Male	Female		Total
Number of players	n/a	n/a	Referees and Assistant Referees	n/a
Professionals	n/a		Admin, Coaches, Technical, Medical	n/a
Amateurs 18+	n/a		Number of clubs	n/a
Youth under 18	n/a		Number of teams	n/a
Unregistered	n/a		Clubs with women's teams	n/a
Total players	n/a		Players as % of population	n/a

Football Association of Montenegro (FAM)
Fudbalski savez Crne Gore, Ulica Mirka Banjevica 29, 81000 Podgorica, Montenegro
Tel +382 20 445 600   Fax +382 20 445660
fscgmontenegro@cg.yu   www.fscg.cg.yu
President: SAVICEVIC Dejan   General Secretary: DURDEVAC Momir
Vice-President: LAZOVIC Boro   Treasurer: JANICIC Mirko   Media Officer: RADOVIC Aleksandar
Men's Coach: FILIPOVIC Zoran   Women's Coach: TBD
FAM formed: 1931   UEFA: 2007   FIFA: 2007
Red shirts with gold trimmings, Red shorts, Red socks

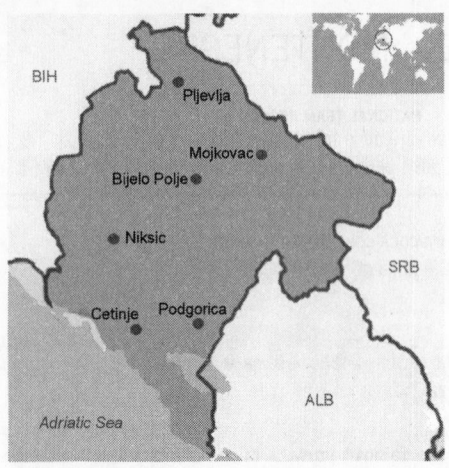

		Population '000
1	Podgorica	163
2	Niksic	67
3	Pljevlja	27
4	Bijelo Polje	15
5	Cetinje	15
6	Bar	13
7	Herceg Novi	12
8	Berane	11
9	Budva	10
10	Ulcinj	10
11	Tivat	9
12	Rozaje	9
13	Dobrota	8
14	Kotor	5
15	Danilovgrad	5
16	Mojkovac	4
17	Igalo	3
18	Plav	3
19	Tuzi	3
20	Bijela	3
21	Burtaisi	3
22	Kolasin	2
23	Zablejak	2
24	Pluzine	1

REPUBLIC OF MONTENEGRO; REPUBLIKA CRNA GORA

Capital	Podgorica	Language	Serbian, Bosnian, Albanian, Croatian	Independence	2006
Population	630 548	Area	14 026 km²	Density 45 per km²	% in cities 57%
GDP per cap	$3800	Dailling code	+381	Internet .me	GMT + / - +1

RECENT INTERNATIONAL MATCHES PLAYED BY MONTENEGRO

2007 Opponents	Score		Venue	Comp	Scorers	Att	Referee
24-03 Hungary	W	2-1	Podgorica	Fr	Vucinic 64p, Burzanovic 82p	11 000	Kranjc SVN
1-06 Japan	L	0-2	Shizuoka	Fr		28 635	Svendsen DEN
3-06 Colombia	L	0-1	Matsumoto	Fr		10 070	Ogiya JPN
22-08 Slovenia	D	1-1	Podgorica	Fr	Vucinic 28p		
12-09 Sweden	L	1-2	Podgorica	Fr	Vucinic 15	9 000	Brugger AUT
17-10 Estonia	W	1-0	Tallinn	Fr	Vucinic 41	2 000	Fröjdfeldt SWE
2008							
26-03 Norway	W	3-1	Podgorica	Fr	Burzanovic 7, Boskovic 37, Djalovic 59	9 000	Stavrev MKD
27-05 Kazakhstan	W	3-0	Podgorica	Fr	Djalovic 2 15 45, Drincic 21	9 000	Tusin LUX
31-05 Romania	L	0-4	Bucharest	Fr		8 000	Tudor ROU

Fr = Friendly match

MONTENEGRO NATIONAL TEAM RECORDS AND RECORD SEQUENCES

Records			Sequence records				
Victory	3-0	KAZ 2008	Wins	3	2007-2008	Clean sheets	1	
Defeat	0-4	ROM 2008	Defeats	2	2007	Goals scored	5	2007-2008
Player Caps	-		Undefeated	3	2007-2008	Without goal	2	2007
Player Goals	4	Mirko Vucinic	Without win	4	2007	Goals against	5	2007

MEDALS TABLE

		Overall			League			Cup			Europe			City	Stadium	Cap'ty	DoF
		G	S	B	G	S	B	G	S	G	S	B					
1	Buducnost Podgorica	1	2		1	1			1				Podgorica	Pod Goricom	18 000	1925
2	Zeta Golubovci	1	1		1	1							Golubovci, Podgorica	Tresnjica	3 000	1927
3	Mogren Budva	1		1		1	1						Budva	Lugovi	4 000	1920
4	Rudar Pljevlja	1						1					Pljevlja	Gradski	7 000	1920
5	Sutjeska Niksic		1					1					Niksic	Gradski	10 800	1927
6	Grbalj Radanovici			1		1							Radanovici, Kotor	u Radanovicima	1 500	1970

RECENT LEAGUE AND CUP RECORD

Championship						Cup		
Year	Champions	Pts	Runners-up	Pts	Third	Pts		Winners	Score	Runners-up
2007	Zeta Golubovci	78	Buducnost Podg'ica	76	Grbalj Radanovici	49	Rudar Pljevlja	2-1	Sutjeska Niksic
2008	Buducnost Podg'ica	66	Zeta Golubovci	66	Mogren Budva	66	Mogren Budva	1-1 6-5p	Buducnost Podg'ica

MONTENEGRO 2007–08

PRVA CRNOGORSKA LIGA

	Pl	W	D	L	F	A	Pts	Buducnost	Zeta	Mogren	Grbalj	Rudar	Lovcen	Decic	Petrovac	Kom	Bokelj	Sutjeska	Mladost
Buducnost Podgorica	33	18	12	3	43	13	66		2-1	1-1 3-0	2-3 0-0	1-1	1-0	2-0 4-0 1-0 3-0	0-0	1-0	2-0 4-0 1-0 2-0
Zeta Golubovci	33	19	9	5	56	28	66	0-0 0-0		1-0	1-0	0-1 2-2 1-0 1-1	2-1	4-1	2-0 4-1 0-1 8-3	1-0	1-0 2-1
Mogren Budva	33	19	9	5	46	21	66	1-1	2-2 2-0		0-3	1-1 2-0 1-0 4-0	2-0	0-1	3-1 4-1 1-0 0-0	1-0	2-1 2-0
Grbalj Radanovici	33	14	13	6	40	25	55	1-1	1-2 0-0 0-2 0-0		1-1	2-0 2-0	3-1	1-1	0-0 3-1 1-0 1-0	1-1	2-1 2-0
Rudar Pljevlja	33	14	10	9	38	26	52	0-1 0-0	1-2	0-0 0-0 1-3		2-0	2-1 2-0 1-0 5-2	3-0	0-0	1-0 2-0 3-1 1-2
Lovcen Cetinje	33	11	10	12	28	30	43	0-1 0-0	1-1	1-0	3-2 1-0 2-1		0-2 0-0	2-2	0-0 1-0	0-0	4-1 0-1 2-0
Decic Tuzi	33	10	8	15	26	37	38	0-1	0-1 1-4 1-1 0-1 0-0 1-0	0-1	1-0		2-1 1-1	2-0	3-1 1-1	1-0	0-0
OFK Petrovac	33	8	12	13	36	46	36	1-1	1-1 2-3 0-2 1-2 4-2 0-2	1-0	1-1 0-1	1-1		1-1	2-4 0-0	1-0	2-1
Kom Podgorica	33	9	9	15	29	49	36	1-0 1-4	2-1	1-3	0-0	2-1 0-0	0-4	0-1 2-0 3-0 1-3		2-0	2-1 1-1 0-0 2-3
Bokelj Kotor	33	8	8	17	24	38	32	0-1 1-0	0-1	0-2	0-2 0-1 1-1 1-0	1-0	0-2	1-2 2-2	0-1	4-1	2-0
Sutjeska Niksic	33	5	11	17	19	44	23	1-1	0-3 0-3 0-0 1-2 0-0 1-1	1-2	1-1	2-0 1-1 0-1 1-1	1-0	0-0		2-1
Mladost Podgorica	33	4	7	22	16	44	19	0-1	1-1	0-2	1-2	0-0	0-1 0-1 0-3 0-1 0-0 1-1	0-2	0-1 1-0 0-0 1-0	

10/08/2007 - 24/05/2008 • † Qualified for the UEFA Champions League • ‡ Qualified for the UEFA Cup
Relegation play-offs: **Sutjeska Niksic** 1-0 0-0 Celik Niksic; Bokelj Kotor 0-0 0-3 **Jedinstvo Bijelo Polje** • Top scorers:

MONTENEGRO 2007–08
II LIGA (2)

	Pl	W	D	L	F	A	Pts
Jezero Plav	33	19	7	7	41	20	64
Celik Niksic ‡	33	18	6	9	48	27	60
Jedinstvo Bijelo Polje ‡	33	17	8	8	47	22	59
FK Berane	33	15	10	8	40	21	55
Ibar Rozaje §1	33	15	5	13	41	36	49
Zabjelo Podgorica	33	12	12	9	40	45	48
Bratstvo Cijevna	33	12	4	17	44	48	40
Crvena stijena §1	33	10	10	13	23	30	39
Arsenal Tivat	33	9	11	13	28	30	38
Otrant Ulcinj	33	9	9	15	39	52	36
Gusinje §1	33	7	10	16	23	45	30
Tekstilac Bijelo Polje	33	6	6	21	20	58	24

12/08/2007 - 25/05/2008 • § = points deducted • ‡ Play-off

KUPA CRNE GORE 2007–08

Round of 16		Quarter-finals		Semi-finals		Final	
Mogren Budva *	1 1						
Sutjeska Niksic	1 0	Mogren Budva *	0 1				
Lovcen Cetinje	0 3	OFK Petrovac	0 0				
OFK Petrovac *	2 1			Mogren Budva	0 1		
Grbalj Radanovici *	7 2			Rudar Pljevlja *	0 0		
OFK Bar	0 0	Grbalj Radanovici	0 0				
Decic Tuzi *	0 0	Rudar Pljevlja *	0 2				
Rudar Pljevlja	1 2					Mogren Budva	1 6p
FK Berane *	1 3					Buducnost Podgorica	1 5p
Ibar Rozaje	0 2	FK Berane *	0 4				
Otrant Ulcinj *	0 2 2p	Arsenal Tivat	0 0				
Arsenal Tivat	2 0 3p			FK Berane *	0 0		
Zeta Golubovci *	1 0			Buducnost Podgorica	0 4		
Mladost Podgorica	0 0	Zeta Golubovci *	0 1				
Kom Podgorica	0 0	Buducnost Podgorica	0 2				
Buducnost Podgorica *	3 3						

* Home team in the first leg • ‡ Qualified for the UEFA Cup

CUP FINAL

Pod Goricom, Podgorica, 7-05-2008,
Att: 8000, Ref: Kaluderovic

Scorers - Ratko Zec [84] for Mogren;
Petar Vukcevic [53] for Buducnost

MOZ – MOZAMBIQUE

NATIONAL TEAM RECORD
JULY 10TH 2006 TO JULY 12TH 2010

PL	W	D	L	F	A	%
18	6	6	6	18	17	50

FIFA/COCA-COLA WORLD RANKING

1993	1994	1995	1996	1997	1998	1999	2000	2001	2002	2003	2004	2005	2006	2007		High	
104	94	76	85	67	80	101	112	128	125	127	126	130	128	75		**66**	11/97

2007–2008													Low	
08/07	09/07	10/07	11/07	12/07	01/08	02/08	03/08	04/08	05/08	06/08	07/08		**134**	09/06
86	74	77	75	75	75	82	84	78	71	90	109			

Mozambique won the award at the 2007 FIFA World Player Gala as the Best Mover in the FIFA/ Coca-Cola World Ranking, moving up 53 places to finish the year in 75th position. It reflected a change in fortunes for a side inspired by the appointment of Dutch coach Mart Nooij who has turned Mozambique into a very organised outfit, even if resources are still on the limited side. The Mambas began a revival of their fortunes during the 2008 CAF Africa Cup of Nations qualifying campaign, but points garnered away in Burkina Faso and Tanzania were not enough to ensure qualification for the finals in Ghana. Nooij almost lost his job after a surprise defeat at home by

INTERNATIONAL HONOURS
None

Botswana in June 2008 in the FIFA World Cup qualifiers but after an emergency meeting, the federation decided to keep him on. With four points from as many games, their chances of making it to the finals in neighbouring South Africa look bleak. In July 2008, Mozambique did reach the final of the regional Cosafa Senior Challenge Cup for the first time, but were beaten 2-1 by South Africa. Costa do Sol completed a League and Cup double with a first Mocambola title since 2001. The Maputo-based club have installed their own artificial turf and have become something of a marketing success story in the southern African region under the acumen of director Rui Tadeu.

THE FIFA BIG COUNT OF 2006

	Male	Female		Total
Number of players	885 600	100	Referees and Assistant Referees	1 000
Professionals	400		Admin, Coaches, Technical, Medical	5 100
Amateurs 18+	19 500		Number of clubs	170
Youth under 18	14 800		Number of teams	850
Unregistered	55 000		Clubs with women's teams	0
Total players	885 700		Players as % of population	4.50%

Federação Moçambicana de Futebol (FMF)
Av. Samora Machel, Número 11, 2 Andar, PO Box 1467, Maputo 1467, Mozambique
Tel +258 21 300366   Fax +258 21 300367
fmfbol@tvcabo.co.mz   www.fmf.org.mz
President: SEDAT Feizal   General Secretary: JOHANE Filipe Lucas
Vice-President: NHANCOLO Luis   Treasurer: NHANCOLO Luis   Media Officer: TBD
Men's Coach: NOOIJ Mart   Women's Coach: MACUACUA Chadreque
FMF formed: 1976   CAF: 1978   FIFA: 1980
Red shirts with black trimmings, Black shorts, Red socks

RECENT INTERNATIONAL MATCHES PLAYED BY MOZAMBIQUE

2004	Opponents	Score		Venue	Comp	Scorers	Att	Referee
11-04	Swaziland	W	2-0	Maputo	Fr	Nando [42], Amilcar [72]		
18-04	Madagascar	W	2-0	Maputo	CCr1	Tico-Tico [64], Fala-Fala [89]	28 000	Damon RSA
26-05	Botswana	D	0-0	Maputo	Fr		2 000	
31-05	Swaziland	D	1-1	Maputo	Fr	Nelinho [43]	5 000	
13-06	Malawi	W	2-0	Maputo	CCqf	Mabedi OG [42], To [62]	30 000	Kaoma ZAM
25-06	Ghana	L	0-1	Maputo	Fr			
19-09	Angola	L	0-1	Maputo	CCsf		50 000	Jovinala MWI
2005								
16-04	Zimbabwe	L	0-3	Windhoek	CCr1			Mufeti NAM
26-06	Lesotho	W	1-0	Maputo	Fr			
28-08	Zimbabwe	D	0-0	Mutare	Fr			
2006								
29-04	Lesotho	D	0-0	Maseru	CCr1	L 4-5p		Jovinala MWI
30-04	Mauritius	D	0-0	Maseru	CCr1			Moeketsi LES
24-06	Swaziland	W	4-0	Maputo	Fr	Macamo [12], Butoana [22], Manoso [60], Massima [79]		
25-06	Malawi	L	1-2	Maputo	Fr	Lomba Da Costa		
2-09	Senegal	L	0-2	Dakar	CNq			Sule NGA
8-10	Tanzania	D	0-0	Maputo	CNq			Kaoma ZAM
2007								
24-03	Burkina Faso	D	1-1	Ouagadougou	CNq	Mano [2]		Imiere NGA
28-04	Seychelles	W	2-0	Maputo	CCr1	Bino 2 [51] [77]		Mpopo LES
29-04	Zimbabwe	D	0-0	Maputo	CCr1	W 5-4p		Seechun MRI
3-06	Burkina Faso	W	3-1	Maputo	CNq	Dario [6p], Tico-Tico 2 [34] [46]		Raolimanana MAD
17-06	Senegal	D	0-0	Maputo	CNq			Seechurn MRI
20-08	Zimbabwe	D	0-0	Beira	Fr	W 3-1p		
8-09	Tanzania	W	1-0	Dar es Salaam	CNq	Tico-Tico [2]		Guezzaz MAR
29-09	Zambia	L	0-3	Atteridgeville	CCsf			Bennett RSA
2008								
13-01	South Africa	L	0-2	Durban	Fr			
21-05	Lesotho	L	2-3	Maputo	Fr	Fanuel [9], Tico-Tico [43]		
1-06	Côte d'Ivoire	L	0-1	Abidjan	WCq		20 000	Auda EGY
8-06	Botswana	L	1-2	Maputo	WCq	Miro [60]	30 000	Faudze SWZ
15-06	Madagascar	D	1-1	Antananarivo	WCq	Dario [33]	15 501	Ebrahim RSA
22-06	Madagascar	W	3-0	Maputo	WCq	Tico-Tico [23], Carlitos [52], Domingues [64]	20 000	Maillett SEY
27-07	Botswana	W	2-0	Secunda	CCqf	Momed Hagi [18], Txuma [89]		Katjimune NAM
30-07	Madagascar	W	2-1	Thulamahashe	CCsf	Tico-Tico [19], Momed Hagi [66]		Marange ZIM

Fr = Friendly match • CN = CAF African Cup of Nations • CC = COSAFA Cup • WC = FIFA World Cup • q = qualifier

MOZAMBIQUE NATIONAL TEAM RECORDS AND RECORD SEQUENCES

Records			Sequence records					
Victory	6-1	LES 1980	Wins	5	1989-1990	Clean sheets	4	Four times
Defeat	0-6	ZIM 1979, ZIM 1980	Defeats	7	1998	Goals scored	15	1980-1982
Player Caps	n/a		Undefeated	7	1995	Without goal	3	1986, 1989, 1991
Player Goals	n/a		Without win	18	1985-1989	Goals against	17	1985-1989

MOZAMBIQUE COUNTRY INFORMATION

Capital	Maputo	Independence	1975 from Portugal	GDP per Capita	$1 200
Population	18 811 731	Status	Republic	GNP Ranking	123
Area km²	801 590	Language	Portuguese, Makhuwa, Tsonga	Dialling code	+258
Population density	23 per km²	Literacy rate	47%	Internet code	.mz
% in urban areas	34%	Main religion	Indigenous 50%, Christian 30%	GMT +/-	+2
Towns/Cities ('000)	Maputo 1 191; Matola 544; Beira 531; Nampula 388; Chomoio 257; Nacala 225; Quelimane 188				
Neighbours (km)	South Africa 491; Swaziland 105; Zimbabwe 1 231; Zambia 419; Malawi 1 569; Tanzania 756; Indian Ocean 2 470				
Main stadia	Estádio da Machava – Maputo 6 000; Estádio do Ferroviário – Beira 7 000				

MOZAMBIQUE 2007

CAMPEONATO NACIONAL DA 1ª DIVISAO

	Pl	W	D	L	F	A	Pts	Costa do Sol	Desportivo	Ferro Nam	Maxaquene	Lichinga	Estrela	Ferro Map	Ferro Beira	Muçulmana	Chingale	Ben Macúti	Académica	Têxtil	Ben Quel
Costa do Sol †	26	16	9	1	37	12	57		0-2	0-0	0-0	1-1	2-0	2-0	0-0	2-2	0-0	2-2	2-1	5-1	1-0
Desportivo Maputo	26	13	9	4	41	17	48	0-0		4-0	4-1	1-2	0-0	2-5	2-3	0-0	3-0	4-0	3-0	2-1	2-1
Ferroviário Nampula	26	11	10	5	19	15	43	0-2	0-0		2-0	2-2	0-0	0-0	2-1	0-0	1-0	1-0	1-0	1-0	1-0
Maxaquene	26	10	11	5	22	16	41	0-1	0-0	0-0		4-2	1-0	2-0	0-0	0-0	1-0	0-0	1-0	2-0	0-3
Lichinga	26	10	8	8	26	25	38	1-2	0-1	0-2	1-1		0-1	0-0	3-1	1-0	2-0	2-0	1-0	1-0	1-0
Estrela Vermelha	26	8	10	8	16	22	34	0-3	1-2	1-3	0-2	2-0		0-0	1-0	0-0	0-1	0-0	1-0	1-0	1-0
Ferroviário Maputo	26	6	16	4	20	16	34	1-2	0-0	0-0	0-0	1-1	1-1		2-2	2-0	2-1	2-0	1-1	0-0	1-0
Ferroviário Beira	26	8	10	8	26	25	34	1-1	1-1	1-0	2-1	1-2	2-0	1-1		0-0	2-0	0-1	1-0	0-0	2-0
Liga Muçulmana	26	7	12	7	20	17	33	0-1	1-1	2-0	0-0	0-0	1-1	0-0	3-1		1-0	1-1	3-0	0-1	2-1
Chingale Tete	26	7	8	11	11	21	29	0-2	0-0	0-0	1-1	0-1	1-1	0-0	1-0	1-0		0-0	1-0	2-1	0-0
Benfica Macúti	26	6	10	10	18	26	28	0-1	0-2	0-1	1-0	1-2	1-2	0-0	1-2	1-0	2-0		1-1	1-1	1-0
Académica Maputo	26	6	7	13	16	25	25	0-1	0-2	0-0	0-1	1-1	3-0	1-0	2-1	1-0	0-1	2-2		2-0	1-0
Têxtil Púnguè	26	4	9	13	14	32	21	0-3	1-1	1-0	0-3	1-0	0-1	1-1	2-2	1-2	1-0	0-0	0-0		0-0
Benfica Quelimane	26	2	7	17	9	26	13	0-1	0-3	0-1	0-0	1-1	0-0	0-1	0-0	1-2	0-1	0-2	0-0	2-1	

31/03/2007 - 18/11/2007 • † Qualified for the CAF Champions League • Top scorer: Tó, Costa do Sol 16

TACA NACIONAL 2007

Round of 16		Quarter–finals		Semi–finals		Final	
Costa do Sol	3						
Académica Maputo	0	Costa do Sol	1				
Club de Gaza	0	Desportivo Maputo	0				
Desportivo Maputo	1			Costa do Sol	2		
Ferroviário Beira	1			Ferroviário Maputo	1		
Benfica Macuti	0	Ferroviário Beira	1				
Vilankulo	0	Ferroviário Maputo	2				
Ferroviário Maputo	2					Costa do Sol	3
Chingale Tete	4					Ferroviário Nampula ‡	0
Textafrica Chimoio	1	Chingale Tete	1				
Sporting Quelimane	1	Desportivo Chimoio	0	Chingale Tete	1		

CUP FINAL

Maxaquene, Maputo
25-11-2007, Ref: Infante

Scorers – Julinho [13p], Tó 2 [57 62]

Round of 16 (cont.)		Quarter–finals (cont.)		Semi–finals (cont.)	
Desportivo Chimoio	2			Chingale Tete	1
Atlético Muçulmano	4			Ferroviário Nampula	2
1° de Maio	0	Atlético Muçulmano	0 5p		
Ferroviário Pemba	p	Ferroviário Nampula	0 6p		
Ferroviário Nampula	p				

‡ Qualified for the CAF Confederation Cup

CLUB DIRECTORY

Club	City/Town	Stadium	Capacity	Lge	Cup
Costa do Sol	Maputo	Costa do Sol	10 000	9	10
Desportivo	Maputo	Desportivo	4 000	5	1
Ferroviário	Beira	Ferroviário	7 000	0	2
Ferroviário	Maputo	Machava	60 000	7	4
Ferroviário	Nampula	Nampula	4 000	1	1
Lichinga	Lichinga	Lichinga	3 000	0	0
Matchedje	Maputo	Costa do Sol	10 000	2	1
Maxaquene	Maputo	Maxaquene	15 000	4	6
Têxtil Púnguè	Beira	Chiveve	5 000	1	0

RECENT LEAGUE AND CUP RECORD

		Championship						Cup		
Year	Champions	Pts	Runners-up	Pts	Third	Pts		Winners	Score	Runners-up
2000	Costa do Sol	51	Ferroviário Maputo	47	Matchadje	38		Costa do Sol	1-0	Matchadje
2001	Costa do Sol	45	Ferroviário Maputo	38	Maxaquene	33		Maxaquene	3-1	Textáfrica Chimoio
2002	Ferroviário Maputo	50	Maxaquene	46	Costa do Sol	43		Costa do Sol	2-0	Académica Maputo
2003	Maxaquene	47	Costa do Sol	43	Desportivo Maputo	40		Ferroviário Nampula	1-1 5-4p	Ferroviário Maputo
2004	Ferroviário Nampula	44	Desportivo Maputo	42	Ferroviário Maputo	35		Ferroviário Maputo	5-1	Textáfrica Chimoio
2005	Ferroviário Maputo	46	Costa do Sol	41	Desportivo Maputo	41		Ferroviário Beira	1-0	Costa do Sol
2006	Desportivo Maputo	47	Ferroviário Maputo	38	Costa do Sol	35		Desportivo Maputo	1-0	Têxtil Púnguè
2007	Costa do Sol	57	Desportivo Maputo	48	Ferroviário Nampula	43		Costa do Sol	3-0	Ferroviário Nampula

MRI – MAURITIUS

NATIONAL TEAM RECORD
JULY 10TH 2006 TO JULY 12TH 2010

PL	W	D	L	F	A	%
18	1	5	12	11	35	19.4

FIFA/COCA-COLA WORLD RANKING

1993	1994	1995	1996	1997	1998	1999	2000	2001	2002	2003	2004	2005	2006	2007
133	146	154	150	151	148	118	118	124	126	123	140	143	138	158

High	
112	12/92

2007–2008											
08/07	09/07	10/07	11/07	12/07	01/08	02/08	03/08	04/08	05/08	06/08	07/08
144	155	153	161	158	164	166	168	174	171	158	163

Low	
174	04/08

Mauritius made a bold move to begin the rebuilding of the national team with a younger generation but they have found the going tough at the top level of the game. Three successive defeats in their 2010 FIFA World Cup qualifying group have left the Indian Ocean island out of contention for a place in the last phase of the African preliminaries for the finals in South Africa. Controversy-attracting coach Ashok Chundusing has turned the focus away from an ageing group of players, who have regularly represented the country over the last decade and gambled on the ability of a new generation. Results have been disappointing, culminating in a shock 7-0 loss to the Seychelles

INTERNATIONAL HONOURS
None

in the Cosafa Senior Challenge tournament in South Africa in July 2008. Chundusing returned after a decade's absence to the helm of the national side, Club M, whose target now is a medal at the next Indian Ocean Island Games in 2011, to be hosted in the Seychelles. Mauritius finished fourth in the 2007 tournament in Madagascar, losing on post-match penalties to the French territory of Mayotte in the bronze medal play-off match. Curepipe Starlight kept up their dominant role in the Premier League and also won the two major cup tournaments to complete the treble, but they lasted only two rounds in the 2008 CAF Champions League.

THE FIFA BIG COUNT OF 2006

	Male	Female		Total
Number of players	73 600	3 200	Referees and Assistant Referees	100
Professionals	0		Admin, Coaches, Technical, Medical	4 400
Amateurs 18+	12 500		Number of clubs	70
Youth under 18	4 600		Number of teams	700
Unregistered	6 700		Clubs with women's teams	0
Total players	76 800		Players as % of population	6.19%

Mauritius Football Association (MFA)
Football House, Trianon, Mauritius
Tel +230 4652200   Fax +230 4547909
mfaho@intnet.mu   www.mauritiusfootball.com
President: JODHA Premlall   General Secretary: VUDDAMALAY Ananda
Vice-President: ELAHEE Mohammed Anwar   Treasurer: BOWUD A.H. Nazir   Media Officer: ARNASSALON Manen
Men's Coach: CHUNDUNSING Ashok   Women's Coach: JULES Alain
MFA formed: 1952   CAF: 1962   FIFA: 1962
Red shirts, Red shorts, Red socks

RECENT INTERNATIONAL MATCHES PLAYED BY MAURITIUS

2003	Opponents	Score		Venue	Comp	Scorers	Att	Referee
11-10	Uganda	L	0-3	Kampala	WCq		6 800	Tangawarima ZIM
16-11	Uganda	W	3-1	Curepipe	WCq	Naboth 37, Mourgine 70, Louis 82	2 465	Maillet SEY
2004								
10-01	South Africa	W	2-0	Curepipe	CCrl	Lekgetho OG 53, Perle 81	5 230	Raolimanana MAD
31-07	Zambia	L	1-3	Lusaka	CCqf	Appou 70		Manuel ZIM
2005								
26-02	Madagascar	W	2-0	Curepipe	CCrl	Appou 44, Louis 48		Fakude SWZ
27-02	South Africa	L	0-1	Curepipe	CCrl			Mnkantjo ZIM
23-10	Madagascar	L	0-2	Antananarivo	Fr			
2006								
29-04	Angola	L	1-5	Maseru	CCrl	Louis 2		Moeketsi LES
30-04	Mozambique	D	0-0	Maseru	CCrl	L 4-5p		Jovinala MWI
26-06	Tanzania	L	1-2	Victoria	Fr	Godon 17		
28-06	Seychelles	L	1-2	Victoria	Fr	Mourgine 90		
3-09	Tunisia	D	0-0	Curepipe	CNq			Ncobo RSA
7-10	Seychelles	L	1-2	Roche Caiman	CNq	Godon 53		Raolimanana MAD
2007								
21-03	Côte d'Ivoire	L	0-3	Bellevue	Fr			
25-03	Sudan	L	1-2	Curepipe	CNq	Naboth 61		Mwanza ZAM
26-05	Swaziland	D	0-0	Mbabane	CCrl	W 6-5p		Labrosse SEY
27-05	South Africa	L	0-2	Mbabane	CCrl			Mufeti NAM
2-06	Sudan	L	0-3	Omdurman	CNq			Lwanja MWI
16-06	Tunisia	L	0-2	Rades/Tunis	CNq			Benouza ALG
14-08	Seychelles	W	3-0	Antananarivo	Fr	Jeannot 2 24 64, Appou 40		
9-09	Seychelles	D	1-1	Curepipe	CNq	Perle 62		Mwandike TAN
2008								
9-03	Madagascar	L	1-2	Curepipe	Fr	Marquette 68		
31-05	Tanzania	D	1-1	Dar es Salaam	WCq	Marquette 39	35 000	Marange ZIM
8-06	Cameroon	L	0-3	Curepipe	WCq		2 400	Martins ANG
15-06	Cape Verde Islands	L	0-1	Curepipe	WCq		1 400	Kaoma ZAM
22-06	Cape Verde Islands	L	1-3	Praia	WCq	Sophie 67	2 850	Coulibaly MLI
19-07	Seychelles	L	0-7	Witbank	CCrl			Kaoma ZAM
21-07	Swaziland	D	1-1	Witbank	CCrl	Marmitte 35		Nhlapo RSA
23-07	Madagascar	L	1-2	Witbank	CCrl	Marquette 34		Marange ZIM

Fr = Friendly match • CN = CAF African Cup of Nations • CC = COSAFA Cup • IO = Indian Ocean Games • WC = FIFA World Cup
q = qualifier • r1 = first round group • qf = quarter-final • sf = semi-final • f = final • † not a full international

MAURITIUS NATIONAL TEAM RECORDS AND RECORD SEQUENCES

Records			Sequence records				
Victory	15-0	REU 1950	Wins	17	1947-1955	Clean sheets	4	1957-1958
Defeat	0-7	EGY 2003	Defeats	6	1974-1975	Goals scored	25	1947-1958
Player Caps	n/a		Undefeated	17	1947-1955	Without goal	6	1994-1995
Player Goals	n/a		Without win	14	2005-2007	Goals against	10	1999-2000

MAURITIUS COUNTRY INFORMATION

Capital	Port Louis	Independence	1968 from the UK	GDP per Capita	$11 400
Population	1 220 481	Status	Republic	GNP Ranking	116
Area km²	2 040	Language	French, English	Dialling code	+230
Population density	598 per km²	Literacy rate	85%	Internet code	.mu
% in urban areas	41%	Main religion	Hindu 52%, Christian 28%	GMT +/–	+4
Towns/Cities ('000)	Port Louis 155; Beau Bassin-Rose Hill 110; Vascoas-Pheinix 107; Curepipe 84; Quatre Bras 80				
Neighbours (km)	Indian Ocean 2 740				
Main stadia	George V Stadium – Curepipe 10 000; Auguste Vollaire – Port Louis				

MAURITIUS 2007–08

BARCLAYS PREMIER LEAGUE

	Pl	W	D	L	F	A	Pts	CSSC	Pamp'sses	ASPL 2000	Savanne	Pet. Riviere	PAS Mates	USBBRH	Etoile	ASVP	Riviere	Bolton City	Olym. Moka
Curepipe Starlight †	20	13	5	2	41	17	44		2-1	1-0	1-2	0-1	1-1	3-0	3-0	2-1	3-2	2-0	3-0
Pamplemousses SC	20	11	4	5	39	15	37	1-1		1-0	2-0	1-0	2-1	1-1	5-0	1-0	1-0	6-1	4-0
AS Port-Louis 2000	20	11	3	6	27	13	36	1-1	1-0		0-1	2-1	1-0	0-1	2-1	3-0	1-2	5-2	
Savanne SC	20	8	4	8	29	25	28	0-2	1-4	1-1		2-0	0-1	0-1	6-0	1-3	1-2	4-0	
Petite Rivière Noire	20	6	9	5	29	27	27	1-1	0-5	0-0	2-3		2-2	1-1	2-0	2-2	1-1	1-1	
Pointe-aux-Sables	20	6	7	7	22	24	25	1-5	1-0	0-2	1-1	2-2		2-1	0-1	0-0	1-1	3-0	3-0
Beau-Basin/Rose Hill	20	5	9	6	21	24	24	1-3	1-1	0-1	1-2	2-2	0-0		4-1	1-1	1-0	0-0	
Etoile de l'Ouest	20	7	2	11	21	40	23	0-3	4-1	0-2	0-1	0-4	2-0	4-1		1-0	1-1	0-0	
AS Vacoas-Phoenix	20	4	8	8	23	23	20	0-1	0-1	1-0	0-0	1-3	1-2	1-1	1-2		3-1	0-0	4-1
AS Rivière Rempart	20	4	8	8	23	29	20	2-2	1-0	0-1	2-2	0-1	1-0	1-3	2-3	1-1		1-1	
Bolton City	20	2	7	11	16	54	13	2-4	0-6	0-4	2-1	1-3	1-4	0-0	2-1	1-7	2-2		4-0
Olympique Moka	Withdrew after 12 rounds							0-15	0-6	0-3	0-2		0-4	0-2				1-2	

5/10/2007 - 20/04/2008 • † Qualified for the CAF Champions League • Top scorer: Westley Marquette, Starlight 14

REPUBLIC CUP 2008

Quarter–finals		Semi–finals		Final	
Curepipe Starlight	2				
Petite Rivière Noire	1	Curepipe Starlight	2		
Pamplemousses SC	1	Savanne SC	1		
Savanne SC	2			Curepipe Starlight	2
Pointe-aux-Sables	3			AS Port-Louis 2000	0
Beau-Basin/Rose Hill	1	Pointe-aux-Sables	0		
Entente B-R/R-M	1	AS Port-Louis 2000	3		
AS Port-Louis 2000	3				

Stade George V, Curepipe, 13-04-2008
Scorers - Westley Marquette 20, Kersley Appou 58

SKYLINE MFA CUP 2007–08

Round of 16		Quarter–finals		Semi–finals		Final	
Curepipe Starlight	3						
Beau-Basin/Rose Hill	1	Curepipe Starlight	3				
AS Quatre-Bornes	0	Bolton City	2				
Bolton City	1			Curepipe Starlight	3		
Pamplemousses SC	8			AS Port-Louis 2000	1		
Entente B-R/R-M	0	Pamplemousses SC	0				
Le Cure Sylvester	0	AS Port-Louis 2000	1				
AS Port-Louis 2000	2					Curepipe Starlight	4
AS Rivière Rempart	2					AS Vacoas-Phoenix	2
Petite Rivière Noire	1	AS Rivière Rempart	5				
US Highlands	2	Sodnac Q-B United	1				
Sodnac Q-B United	3			AS Rivière Rempart	2		
Savanne SC	3			AS Vacoas-Phoenix	3		
Mont Roches Lovelets	0	Savanne SC	1				
US Central Sud	0	AS Vacoas-Phoenix	2				
AS Vacoas-Phoenix	2						

‡ Qualified for the CAF Confederation Cup

CUP FINAL
Stade George V, Curepipe
11-05-2008, Att: 2000, Ref: Roopnah
Scorers - Kersley Appou 39, Chris Perle 66, Nana Kyeremateng 2 102 120 for Starlight; Ishtiak Abdullah 76, Ben Abdullah 80 for ASVP

RECENT LEAGUE AND CUP RECORD

	Championship							Cup		
Year	Champions	Pts	Runners-up	Pts	Third	Pts		Winners	Score	Runners-up
2001	Olympique Moka	57	AS Port Louis 2000	44	US Beau-Basin/RH			US Beau-Basin/RH	2-1	Olympique Moka
2002	AS Port Louis 2000	58	US Beau-Basin/RH	52	Faucon Flacq	40		AS Port Louis 2000	3-0	Olympique Moka
2003	AS Port Louis 2000	26	Faucon Flacq SC	21	US Beau-Basin/RH	21		Savanne SC	1-1 4-2p	AS Port Louis 2000
2004	AS Port Louis 2000	56	Pamplemousses SC	43	Savanne SC	37		Savanne SC	3-2	Faucon Flacq SC
2005	AS Port Louis 2000	31	Savanne SC	26	US Beau-Basin/RH	23		AS Port Louis 2000	2-0	PAS Mates
2006	Pamplemousses SC	28	AS Vacoas-Phoenix	23	Curepipe Starlight	20		Curepipe Starlight	0-0 9-8p	Savanne SC
2007	Curepipe Starlight	54	Pamplemousses SC	42	Savanne SC	41		Petite Rivière Noire	2-0	AS Port Louis 2000
2008	Curepipe Starlight							Curepipe Starlight	4-2	AS Vacoas-Phoenix

MSR – MONTSERRAT

NATIONAL TEAM RECORD
JULY 10TH 2006 TO JULY 12TH 2010

PL	W	D	L	F	A	%
1	0	0	1	1	7	0

FIFA/COCA-COLA WORLD RANKING

1993	1994	1995	1996	1997	1998	1999	2000	2001	2002	2003	2004	2005	2006	2007	High	
-	-	-	-	-	-	201	202	203	203	204	202	202	198	201	**196**	07/06

2007–2008												Low	
08/07	09/07	10/07	11/07	12/07	01/08	02/08	03/08	04/08	05/08	06/08	07/08	**205**	10/04
199	200	200	201	201	201	202	202	202	200	199	199		

Central to Montserrat's continued existence as a footballing nation is a very important computer that sits in the office of the football association in Blakes. On it is a database with the name and address of every player with any sort of connection to the island. "We know pretty much where everyone is!" says national team coach Cecil Lake. Never mind the winning, it's getting enough people to take part that matters for Monserrat on an island where the population is estimated to have fallen to around 5,000 hardy souls who brave the everpresent threat from the Soufriere volcano. And so three years, four months and 22 days after the Montserrat national team last took

INTERNATIONAL HONOURS
None

to the field, they were back in action for a 2010 FIFA World Cup qualifier against Suriname having put together a side from the willing and the able. With the match played over a single leg in neutral Trinidad only 100 fans turned up to witness a 7-1 triumph for the Surinamese. With Aldershot Town's promotion to the Football League in April 2008, Montserrat can even call on a player in the ranks of professional football in England but having missed the match against Suriname, Junior Mendes is likely to have a long wait before the next opportunity to play for Montserrat again. Roll on the qualifiers for the 2014 World Cup in Brazil.

THE FIFA BIG COUNT OF 2006

	Male	Female		Total
Number of players	600	100	Referees and Assistant Referees	6
Professionals	0		Admin, Coaches, Technical, Medical	0
Amateurs 18+	100		Number of clubs	0
Youth under 18	100		Number of teams	10
Unregistered	100		Clubs with women's teams	0
Total players	700		Players as % of population	7.42%

Montserrat Football Association Inc. (MFA)
PO Box 505, Blakes, Montserrat
Tel +1 664 4918744   Fax +1 664 4918801
monfa@candw.ms
President: CASSELL Vincent   General Secretary: TBD
Vice-President: POLLIDORE Clement   Treasurer: TBD   Media Officer: None
Men's Coach: LAKE Cecil   Women's Coach: LAKE Cecil
MFA formed: 1994   CONCACAF: 1996   FIFA: 1996
Green shirts with black and white stripes, Green shorts, Green socks

RECENT INTERNATIONAL MATCHES PLAYED BY MONTSERRAT

2002	Opponents	Score	Venue	Comp	Scorers	Att	Referee
No international matches played in 2002 after June							
2003							
No international matches played in 2003							
2004							
29-02	Bermuda	L 0-13	Hamilton	WCq		3 000	Kennedy USA
21-03	Bermuda	L 0-7	Plymouth	WCq		250	Charles DMA
31-10	St Kitts and Nevis	L 1-6	Basseterre	CCq	Adams [81]		Bedeau GRN
2-11	Antigua and Barbuda	L 4-5	Basseterre	CCq	Tesfaye Bramble [36], Fox [41], Mendes [50], Farrel [61]		Phillip GRN
4-11	St Lucia	L 0-3	Basseterre	CCq	Not played. St Lucia awarded the match 3-0		
2005							
No international matches played in 2005							
2006							
No international matches played in 2006							
2007							
No international matches played in 2007							
2008							
26-03	Surinam	L 1-7	Macoya	WCq	Vladimir Farrell [48]	100	Aguilar SLV

Fr = Friendly match • CC = Digicel Caribbean Cup • WC = FIFA World Cup • q = qualifier

MONTSERRAT NATIONAL TEAM RECORDS AND RECORD SEQUENCES

Records			Sequence records					
Victory	3-2	AIA 1995	Wins	2	1995	Clean sheets	1	1995
Defeat	0-13	BER 2004	Defeats	16	1995-2004	Goals scored	3	1996-99, 2000-01
Player Caps	n/a		Undefeated	2	1995	Without goal	4	2004-2004
Player Goals	n/a		Without win	16	1995-2004	Goals against		

RECENT LEAGUE RECORD

Year	Championship Champions
1996	Royal Montserrat Police Force
1997	Abandoned
1998	Not held
1999	Not Held
2000	Royal Montserrat Police Force
2001	Royal Montserrat Police Force
2002	Not held due to season readjustment
2003	Royal Montserrat Police Force
2004	Ideal SC
2005	Not held
2006	Not held
2007	Not held

MONTSERRAT COUNTRY INFORMATION

Capital	Plymouth	Status	UK Dependent Territory	GDP per Capita	$3 400
Population	9 245			GNP Ranking	n/a
Area km²	102	Language	English	Dialling code	+1 664
Population density	91 per km²	Literacy rate	97%	Internet code	.ms
% in urban areas	n/a	Main religion	Christian	GMT + / –	-4
Towns/Cities	Cork Hill 732; Salem 680; Saints Johns 627; Bransby Point 550; Davy Hill 366; Geralds 314				
Neighbours (km)	Caribbean Sea 40				
Main stadia	Blakes Estate Football Ground – Plymouth				

MTN – MAURITANIA

MAURITANIA NATIONAL TEAM RECORD
JULY 10TH 2006 TO JULY 12TH 2010

PL	W	D	L	F	A	%
14	3	3	8	19	28	32.1

FIFA/COCA-COLA WORLD RANKING

1993	1994	1995	1996	1997	1998	1999	2000	2001	2002	2003	2004	2005	2006	2007	High	
144	137	85	113	135	142	160	161	177	180	165	175	178	133	130	**85**	12/95

2007–2008												Low	
08/07	09/07	10/07	11/07	12/07	01/08	02/08	03/08	04/08	05/08	06/08	07/08	**182**	05/03
136	140	124	130	130	112	113	114	123	123	137	144		

Mauritania had a burst of new-found form in the 2008 African Nations Cup qualifiers, the cause of much excitement in the north African country. Wins over Burundi and Botswana and a combative draw at home against Egypt took the 'Mourabitounes' into unchartered territory at the competitive end of their group. While the country did not qualify for the finals in Ghana, the results held out much hope for the 2010 FIFA World Cup qualifiers. Results were even more remarkable given that before the qualifiers, the national side hadn't played a match for two years. Coaching support from Ali Fergani, a former Algeria coach, certainly helped their cause. At the beginning of 2008, former

INTERNATIONAL HONOURS
None

French international Alain Moizan took over but when Mauritania's bubble burst in the World Cup qualifiers in June 2008, he was hastily shown the door. Mohamed Salem Ould Harouna is now the fourth coach in the space of a year and many of the advances made have been lost. Mauritania is continuing to play with mercenary footballers from France brought in by Noel Tosi when he was coach of the side in 2003. Yohan Langlet, Pascal Gourville and Dominique da Silva were handed instant citizenship when Tosi persuaded them to play and they continue with the Mauritanian team, although recent FIFA edicts have prohibited the practice in the future.

THE FIFA BIG COUNT OF 2006

	Male	Female		Total
Number of players	137 920	0	Referees and Assistant Referees	177
Professionals	0		Admin, Coaches, Technical, Medical	700
Amateurs 18+	3 520		Number of clubs	68
Youth under 18	1 600		Number of teams	250
Unregistered	14 300		Clubs with women's teams	0
Total players	137 920		Players as % of population	4.34%

Fédération de Foot-Ball de la République Islamique de Mauritanie (FFM)
Case postale 566, Nouakchott, Mauritania
Tel +222 5 241860   Fax +222 5 241861
ffrim@mauritel.mr   www.ffrim.com
President: OULD BOUKHREIS Mohemed Salem   General Secretary: OULD MOHAMEDEN Gleiguem
Vice-President: OULD MOHAMED VALL Adallahi   Treasurer: OULD MAOULOUD Cheik   Media Officer: None
Men's Coach: OULD Mohamed   Women's Coach: None
FFM formed: 1961   CAF: 1968   FIFA: 1964
Green shirts with yellow trimmings, Yellow shorts, Green socks

RECENT INTERNATIONAL MATCHES PLAYED BY MAURITANIA

2004 Opponents	Score	Venue	Comp	Scorers	Att	Referee
No international matches played in 2004						
2005						
No international matches played in 2005						
2006						
3-09 Botswana	W 4-0	Nouakchott	CNq	Seydou Mbodji [3], Moussa Karamoko 2 [8 23], Yohan Langlet [83]		Djaoupe TOG
8-10 Burundi	L 1-3	Bujumbura	CNq	Mohamed Benyachou [51]		Abdelrahman SUD
21-12 Lebanon	D 0-0	Beirut	ARr1			Al Jannaz BHR
24-12 Sudan	L 0-2	Beirut	ARr1			Ebel KUW
27-12 Somalia	W 8-2	Beirut	ARr1			
2007						
20-03 Libya	D 0-0	Tripoli	Fr			
25-03 Egypt	L 0-3	Cairo	CNq			Benouza ALG
3-06 Egypt	D 1-1	Nouakchott	CNq	Yohan Langlet [70]		Sowe GAM
16-06 Botswana	L 1-2	Gaborone	CNq	Yohan Langlet [74]		Gasingwa RWA
13-10 Burundi	W 2-1	Nouakchott	CNq	Dominique Da Silva [32], Ahmed Teguedi [47]		Aboubacar CIV
2008						
31-05 Rwanda	L 0-3	Kigali	WCq		12 000	Doue CIV
7-06 Morocco	L 1-4	Nouakchott	WCq	Ahmed Teguedi [82p]	9 500	Lamptey GHA
13-06 Ethiopia	L 0-1	Nouakchott	WCq		5 000	Ambaya EGY
22-06 Ethiopia	L 1-6	Addis Abeba	WCq	Voulani Ely [44]	13 000	Lwanja MWI

Fr = Friendly match • CN = CAF African Cup of Nations • AR = Arab Cup • WC = FIFA World Cup • q = qualifier • r1 = first round group

MAURITANIA NATIONAL TEAM RECORDS AND RECORD SEQUENCES

Records			Sequence records					
Victory	8-2	SOM 2006	Wins	2	Three times	Clean sheets	4	1994-95, 1995-96
Defeat	0-14	GUI 1972	Defeats	11	1976-1979	Goals scored	9	1979-1980
Player Caps	n/a		Undefeated	7	1994-95, 1995-96	Without goal	5	1983-1984
Player Goals	n/a		Without win	34	1995-2003	Goals against	25	1963-1979

RECENT LEAGUE AND CUP RECORD

	Championship	Cup		
Year	Champions	Winners	Score	Runners-up
1997	Not held	ASC Sonalec	2-0	Garde Nationale
1998	Garde Nationale	ASC Sonalec	3-2	SDPA Trarza
1999	SDPA Rosso	ASC Police	2-1	Garde Nationale
2000	ASC Mauritel	Air Mauritanie	4-0	ASC Gendrim
2001	FC Nouadhibou	Garde Nationale		
2002	FC Nouadhibou	No tournament held		
2003	NASR Sebkha	Entente Sebkha	1-0	ACS Ksar
2004	ACS Ksar	FC Nouadhibou	1-0	ACS Ksar
2005	NASR Sebkha	Entente Sebkha	2-1	ASC Socogim
2006	ASC Mauritel	NASR Sebkha	1-0	Trarza Rosso
2007	NASR Sebkha	ASC Mauritel	0-0 4-2p	Garde Nationale
2008	Concorde			

MAURITANIA 2007-08 CHAMPIONNAT NATIONAL

	Pl	W	D	L	F	A	Pts
Concorde	22	15	5	2	26	4	50
ACS Ksar	22	12	6	4	36	14	42
El Ahmedi Sebhka	22	12	4	6	27	18	40
Mauritel	22	9	8	4	23	10	35
NASR Sebkha	22	9	8	5	25	14	35
SNIM Nouadhibou	22	9	6	7	26	21	33
FC Nouadhibou	22	6	11	5	21	22	29
FC Khaïry	22	7	4	11	20	30	25
Garde Nationale	22	5	5	11	17	29	20
Trarza Rosso	22	4	6	10	15	28	18
ASC Police	22	3	6	13	12	32	15
ASC Armée	22	1	7	14	10	36	10

28/12/2007 - 2/08/2008

MAURITANIA COUNTRY INFORMATION

Capital	Nouakchott	Independence	1960 from France	GDP per Capita	$1 800
Population	2 998 563	Status	Republic	GNP Ranking	154
Area km²	1 030 700	Language	Arabic, French, Pulaar	Dialling code	+222
Population density	3 per km²	Literacy rate	47%	Internet code	.mr
% in urban areas	54%	Main religion	Muslim	GMT +/-	0
Towns/Cities ('000)	Nouakchott 709; Nouadhibou 80; Kifah 68; Kayhaydi 51; Zuwarat 44; an-Na'mah 36				
Neighbours (km)	Western Sahara 1 561; Algeria 463; Mali 2 237; Senegal 813; North Atlantic 754				
Main stadia	Stade National – Nouakchott 40 000				

MWI – MALAWI

NATIONAL TEAM RECORD
JULY 10TH 2006 TO JULY 12TH 2010

PL	W	D	L	F	A	%
24	8	3	13	30	28	39.6

FIFA/COCA-COLA WORLD RANKING

1993	1994	1995	1996	1997	1998	1999	2000	2001	2002	2003	2004	2005	2006	2007
67	82	89	88	97	89	114	113	120	95	105	109	106	104	138

High	
53	12/92

2007–2008											
08/07	09/07	10/07	11/07	12/07	01/08	02/08	03/08	04/08	05/08	06/08	07/08
111	121	132	130	138	137	136	138	136	136	126	107

Low	
138	12/07

Malawi had the misfortune to be drawn in the same 2010 FIFA World Cup qualifying group with two past winners of the African Nations Cup, but made a gallant effort in their bid to reach the final phase of the preliminaries in Africa. The return of Kinnah Phiri to the helm of the side led to a change in fortune, including a 1-0 win over reigning continental champions Egypt in Blantyre in June 2008. His predecessor Steven Constantine had resigned in frustration after a series of poor results, although matters looked to be improving with wins in friendly matches in Swaziland and Namibia. The Anglo-Cypriot coach struggled to win over the local media and was constantly under

INTERNATIONAL HONOURS
None

fire, packing up the job shortly before the start of the World Cup qualifiers. Malawi has seen the vast majority of their first choice players head outside of the country to play mostly in South Africa, with a handful in Europe, the most notable being leading striker Esau Kanyenda, who has played in Russia over the last seven seasons. Escom United, the team of the Electricity Supply Corporation based in the economic capital Blantyre, won the Super League for the first time in a close race ahead of city rivals and traditional giants MTL Wanderers. Silver Bullets from the capital Lilongwe finished close behind in third place but beat ESCOM 1-0 in the Cup Final.

THE FIFA BIG COUNT OF 2006

	Male	Female		Total
Number of players	515 600	200	Referees and Assistant Referees	600
Professionals	0		Admin, Coaches, Technical, Medical	1 800
Amateurs 18+	11 400		Number of clubs	70
Youth under 18	8 700		Number of teams	120
Unregistered	29 700		Clubs with women's teams	0
Total players	515 800		Players as % of population	3.96%

Football Association of Malawi (FAM)
Chiwembe Technical Centre, Chiwembe, PO Box 865, Blantyre, Malawi
Tel +265 1 842204   Fax +265 1 842204
gensec@fam.mw   www.fam.mw
President: NYAMILANDU MANDA Walter   General Secretary: NYIRENDA Charles
Vice-President: MKANDAWIRE Moses   Treasurer: TBD   Media Officer: JANGALE Casper
Men's Coach: PHIRI Kinnah   Women's Coach: MBOLEMBOLE Stuart
FAM formed: 1966   CAF: 1968   FIFA: 1967
Red shirts, White shorts, Red socks

RECENT INTERNATIONAL MATCHES PLAYED BY MALAWI

2004	Opponents	Score		Venue	Comp	Scorers	Att	Referee
4-09	Kenya	L	2-3	Nairobi	WCq	Munthali [41], Mabedi [90p]	13 000	Mwanza ZAM
9-10	Tunisia	D	2-2	Blantyre	WCq	Mwafulirwa [19], Chipatala [37]	20 000	Awuye UGA
2005								
27-02	Zimbabwe	W	2-1	Blantyre	Fr	Tambala [45], Phiri.V [51]		
26-03	Tunisia	L	0-7	Tunis	WCq		30 000	Abdel Rahman SUD
27-05	Libya	D	1-1	Tripoli	Fr			
4-06	Morocco	L	1-4	Rabat	WCq	Chipatala [10]	48 000	Buenkadila COD
11-06	Lesotho	W	2-1	Lusaka	CCr1	Chitsulo [54], Zakazaka [73]		Mpanisi ZAM
12-06	Zambia	L	1-2	Lusaka	CCr1	Maduka [55]		Nhlapo RSA
18-06	Botswana	L	1-3	Blantyre	WCq	Mwafulirwa [48]	20 000	Gabonamong BOT
4-09	Guinea	L	1-3	Conakry	WCq	Mkandawire [36]	2 518	Mana NGA
8-10	Kenya	W	3-0	Blantyre	WCq	Zakazaka [6], Mkandawire 2 [49 61]	12 000	Codjia BEN
2006								
24-06	Zimbabwe	D	1-1	Maputo	Fr	Chipatala [6]. W 2-1p		
25-06	Mozambique	W	2-1	Maputo	Fr	Wadabwa [29], Kamwendo		
6-07	Botswana	W	2-1	Lilongwe	Fr	Zakazaka [57], Wadabwa [49]		
8-07	Botswana	D	0-0	Blantyre	Fr	L 2-3p		
22-07	Zambia	L	1-3	Katutura	CCr1	Mkhandawire [16]		Katjimune NAM
23-07	Namibia	L	2-3	Katutura	CCr1	Chavula [19], Chilapondwa [85]		Simisse MRI
3-09	Morocco	L	0-2	Rabat	CNq			Codji BEN
7-10	Zimbabwe	W	1-0	Blantyre	CNq	Chavula [78]		Seechurn MRI
26-11	Djibouti	W	3-0	Addis Abeba	CFr1	Wadabwa [6], Mkhandawire [52], Munthali [82]		
28-11	Tanzania	L	1-2	Addis Abeba	CFr1	Wadabwa [15]		
1-12	Ethiopia	L	0-1	Addis Abeba	CFr1			
6-12	Uganda	D	0-0	Addis Abeba	CFqf	L 2-4p		
2007								
26-05	South Africa	D	0-0	Mbabane	CCr1	L 4-5p		Dlamini SWZ
27-05	Swaziland	L	0-1	Mbabane	CCr1			Labrosse SEY
10-06	Senegal	L	2-3	Blantyre	Fr	Mwafulirwa [75], Mkhandawire [78]		
16-06	Morocco	L	0-1	Blantyre	CNq			Maillet SEY
6-07	Namibia	L	1-2	Blantyre	Fr	Kafoteka [48]		
9-09	Zimbabwe	L	1-3	Bulawayo	CNq	Kanyenda [43]		Hicuburundi BDI
18-11	Swaziland	W	3-0	Manzini	Fr	Mwafulirwa [31], Kanyenda [45], Mkandawire [60]		
2008								
26-03	Namibia	W	3-1	Windhoek	Fr	Nyondo [29], Chirambo [38], Mwakasungula [61]		
25-05	Tanzania	D	1-1	Dar es Salaam	Fr	Kanyenda [56]		
31-05	Djibouti	W	8-1	Blantyre	WCq	Kafoteka [3], Kanyenda 3 [19 46 48], Kamwendo [66], Chavula [73], Ngambi [78], Mkandawire [83]	35 000	Katjimune NAM
8-06	Congo DR	L	0-1	Kinshasa	WCq		35 000	Abdelkadir SUD
14-06	Egypt	W	1-0	Blantyre	WCq	Msowoya [93+]	40 000	Keita GUI
22-06	Egypt	L	0-2	Cairo	WCq			Diatta SEN
20-07	Lesotho	W	1-0	Secunda	CCr1	Msowoya [75]		Rajindraparsad MRI
22-07	Comoros	W	1-0	Secunda	CCr1	Kondowe [62]		Marange ZIM
24-07	Namibia	L	0-1	Secunda	CCr1			Marange ZIM

Fr = Friendly match • CN = CAF African Cup of Nations • CC = COSAFA Cup • CF = CECAFA Cup • WC = FIFA World Cup
q = qualifier • r1 = first round group • qf = quarter-final • sf = semi-final • f = final

MALAWI NATIONAL TEAM RECORDS AND RECORD SEQUENCES

Records			Sequence records					
Victory	8-1	BOT 1968, DJI 2008	Wins	8	1984	Clean sheets	5	1989
Defeat	0-7	ZAM 1969, TUN 2005	Defeats	9	1962-1968	Goals scored	13	1986-1987
Player Caps	n/a		Undefeated	15	1989-1990	Without goal	5	Three times
Player Goals	n/a		Without win	14	1998-2000	Goals against	18	1971-1975

MALAWI COUNTRY INFORMATION

Capital	Lilongwe	Independence	1964 from the UK	GDP per Capita	$600
Population	11 906 855	Status	Republic	GNP Ranking	
Area km²	118 480	Language	English, Chichewa	Dialling code	+265
Population density	100 per km²	Literacy rate	62%	Internet code	.mw
% in urban areas	14%	Main religion	Christian 75%, Muslim 20%	GMT + / −	+2
Towns/Cities ('000)	Lilongwe 647; Blantyre 585; Mzuzu 128; Zomba 81; Kasungu 42; Mangochi 40; Karonga 34				
Neighbours (km)	Mozambique 1 569; Zambia 837; Tanzania 475				
Main stadia	Chichiri – Blantyre 60 000; Chivo – Lilongwe 40 000				

MALAWI 2007

SUPER LEAGUE

Team	Pl	W	D	L	F	A	Pts	Escom Utd	MTL Wand	Silver Str's	Bullets	Red Lions	Moyale	Tigers	Eagle Str's	Blue Eagles	CIVO Utd	Eagle Beaks	Michiru	Nchalo Utd	Dwangwa	Apollo Utd
Escom United	28	18	7	3	45	15	61		2-1	0-0	1-1	2-2	1-0	1-1	2-0	2-0	2-1	1-2	4-0	1-0	2-0	4-0
MTL Wanderers	28	18	6	4	44	16	60	1-1		0-1	1-3	2-1	1-2	1-1	1-0	2-1	1-0	2-0	5-1	3-1	1-0	4-0
Silver Strikers	28	15	11	2	49	17	56	0-0	0-0		2-1	2-3	2-2	2-2	2-0	1-0	0-0	4-1	1-0	2-0	2-0	8-0
Big Bullets	28	13	9	6	42	23	48	0-1	0-0	0-0		1-1	1-1	2-1	2-0	0-0	1-0	3-1	3-1	4-1	3-0	1-0
Red Lions	28	13	9	6	40	25	48	2-1	1-1	1-1	1-0		1-0	1-2	0-2	3-0	0-2	3-0	2-0	2-2	1-0	4-0
Moyale Barracks	28	11	11	6	35	23	44	0-1	0-0	0-3	1-1	0-1		0-1	0-0	2-1	1-0	2-0	7-0	3-0	2-1	3-3
Tigers FC	28	11	11	6	27	24	44	0-0	0-1	2-1	1-5	0-2	0-0		0-0	1-1	1-0	2-0	3-0	2-0	1-0	1-0
Eagle Strikers	28	10	7	11	25	28	37	1-2	0-2	0-2	3-1	2-1	0-1	1-1		0-0	2-0	1-0	0-1	2-1	2-1	4-2
Blue Eagles	28	8	8	12	26	29	32	1-2	0-2	2-0	0-1	1-1	0-0	1-2	1-0		2-0	3-1	0-0	1-1	2-0	1-1
CIVO United	28	7	10	11	19	22	31	1-0	0-1	0-0	0-0	0-0	0-0	0-0	1-0			0-0	1-1	3-0	0-1	2-1
Eagle Beaks	28	9	3	16	29	45	30	0-3	0-1	1-1	2-1	0-2	2-3	4-1	0-0	3-1	1-2		3-0	0-2	1-0	
Michiru Castles	28	6	11	11	21	45	29	1-2	0-3	0-0	2-2	1-1	0-0	0-1	1-0	3-2	2-0			2-2	2-1	1-0
Nchalo United	28	4	8	16	28	51	20	0-4	0-1	1-2	0-2	1-0	1-2	0-2	1-1	2-3	2-2	2-1	1-1		4-1	1-1
Dwangwa United	28	3	5	20	17	45	14	0-2	1-0	0-3	2-7	2-0	0-1	1-2	0-0	3-1	0-1	1-2	1-2	0-0		0-0
Apollo United	28	2	8	18	21	60	14	0-2	1-3	1-2	0-3	2-1	1-0	1-0	1-2	0-3	1-0	1-2	1-1	2-1	1-1	

5/10/2007 - 23/12/2007 • † Qualified for the CAF Champions League • Top scorer: Chiukepo Msowoya, Escom 17

FAM CUP 2007

Quarter–finals

Silver Strikers	0 0 6p
Moyale Barracks	0 0 5p
Red Lions	0
MTL Wanderers	2
Eagle Beaks	1
Tigers Blantyre	0
Cobbe Barracks	0
Escom United	2

Semi–finals

Silver Strikers	1
MTL Wanderers	0
Eagle Beaks	0
Escom United	2

Final

Silver Strikers	1
Escom United	0

Civo Stadium, Lilongwe
14-10-2007, Att: 20 000
Scorer - Atusaye Nyondo 18

RECENT LEAGUE AND CUP RECORD

Year	Champions	Pts	Runners-up	Pts	Third	Pts	Winners	Score	Runners-up
1996	Telecom Wanderers								
1997	Telecom Wanderers								
1998	Telecom Wanderers								
1999	Bata Bullets	62	Telecom Wanderers	60	Red Lions	44	Bata Bullets	3-0	MDC United
2000	Bata Bullets	44	MDC United	41	Silver Strikers	40	Telecom Wanderers	2-1	Bata Bullets
2001	Total Big Bullets	69	MTL Wanderers	66	MDC United	44	Moyale Barracks	1-0	Super ESCOM
2002	Total Big Bullets	62	Silver Strikers	50	MDC United	45	Total Big Bullets	1-0	MTL Wanderers
2003	Bakili Bullets	70	MTL Wanderers	69	MDC United	60	Final between Wanderers and Bullets abandoned		
2004	Bakili Bullets		MTL Wanderers		Silver Strikers		No competition		
2005	Big Bullets	55	MTL Wanderers	54	Silver Strikers	53	ADMARC Tigers	1-1 5-4p	MTL Wanderers
2006	MTL Wanderers	62	Silver Strikers	60	Big Bullets	55	No competition		
2007	Escom United	61	MTL Wanderers	60	Silver Strikers	56	Silver Strikers	1-0	Escom United

Bakili Bullets previously known as Bata Bullets and Total Big Bullets • MTL Wanderers previously known as Limbe Leaf Wanderers and Telecom Wanderers

MYA – MYANMAR

NATIONAL TEAM RECORD
JULY 10TH 2006 TO JULY 12TH 2010

PL	W	D	L	F	A	%
15	6	5	4	15	19	56.7

FIFA/COCA-COLA WORLD RANKING

1993	1994	1995	1996	1997	1998	1999	2000	2001	2002	2003	2004	2005	2006	2007		High	
110	124	115	104	114	115	126	124	151	162	140	144	147	154			**97**	04/96

					2007–2008							Low	
08/07	09/07	10/07	11/07	12/07	01/08	02/08	03/08	04/08	05/08	06/08	07/08	**164**	08/06
152	148	147	156	157	155	157	158	164	163	165	164		

The national team of Myanmar has a long history in international football with its first match dating back to 1951 but extraordinarily the team never entered the World Cup even when they were perhaps the best team in the continent in the 1960s, having won back to back gold medals at the Asian Games of 1966 and 1970. That duck was finally broken when they entered the 2010 FIFA World Cup and were drawn against China in a preliminary round held in late 2007. However, two heavy defeats – a 7-0 loss was followed by a 4-0 reversal – meant the nation's participation ended almost as soon as it had begun. Myanmar's current status as one of the Asian football's also-rans

INTERNATIONAL HONOURS
Asian Games 1966 1970   **SEA Games** 1965 1967 1969 1971   **AFC Youth Championship** 1961 1963 1964 1966 1968 1969 1970

makes for disappointing reading, although many of the problems stem from broader political and social issues at home. Myanmar were admitted by the Asian Football Confederation as one of the automatic qualifiers for the 2008 AFC Challenge Cup where, encouragingly, they made it to the semi-finals before losing to hosts India and they will also be looking to make a positive impact on the ASEAN Championships in the latter part of 2008. Victory in the 2005 edition of the ASEAN Football Federation's Under 20 championship has at least given the national team a pool of talented players to pick from as Myanmar look to regain former glories.

THE FIFA BIG COUNT OF 2006

	Male	Female		Total
Number of players	1 043 159	78 880	Referees and Assistant Referees	830
Professionals	0		Admin, Coaches, Technical, Medical	2 920
Amateurs 18+	104 405		Number of clubs	598
Youth under 18	24 990		Number of teams	4 200
Unregistered	214 380		Clubs with women's teams	7
Total players	1 122 039		Players as % of population	2.37%

Myanmar Football Federation (MFF)

National Football Training Centre, Thuwunna Thingankyun, Township, PO Box 11070, Yangon, Myanmar

Tel +951 500123   Fax +951 527797

zaw@myanmar.com.mm   www.maxmyanmar.co.mm

President: ZAW Zaw   General Secretary: AUNG Tin

Vice-President: NAING Zaw Win   Treasurer: ZAW Than   Media Officer: NAING Tun Tun

Men's Coach: FALOPA Marcos   Women's Coach: U AYE Kyu Gyi

MFF formed: 1947   AFC: 1954   FIFA: 1957

Red shirts, White shorts, Red socks

RECENT INTERNATIONAL MATCHES PLAYED BY MYANMAR

2004	Opponents	Score		Venue	Comp	Scorers	Att	Referee
8-12	Philippines	W	1-0	Kuala Lumpur	TCr1	San Day Thien 92+	1 000	Vo Minh Tri VIE
10-12	Thailand	D	1-1	Kuala Lumpur	TCr1	Zaw Lynn Tun 89		Moradi IRN
12-12	Malaysia	W	1-0	Kuala Lumpur	TCr1	Soe Myat Min 20	10 000	Hsu Chao Lo TPE
16-12	East Timor †	W	3-1	Kuala Lumpur	TCr1	Soe Myat Min 4, San Day Thien 43, Myo Hlaing Win 51	1 000	Hsu Chao Lo TPE
29-12	Singapore	L	3-4	Kuala Lumpur	TCsf	Soe Myat Min 2 34 90, Min Thu 36	12 000	Rungklay THA
2005								
2-01	Singapore	L	2-4	Singapore	TCsf	Soe Myat Min 15, Aung Kyaw Moe 50	30 000	Kamikawa JPN
15-01	Malaysia	L	1-2	Singapore	TC3p	Soe Myat Min 52	2 000	Vo Minh Tri VIE
2006								
23-08	Thailand	D	2-2	Kuala Lumpur	Fr	Si Thu Win 2 35 70	8 000	Heng MAS
25-08	Indonesia	D	0-0	Kuala Lumpur	Fr			Sharul MAS
27-08	Malaysia	W	2-1	Kuala Lumpur	Fr	Kyaw Thu Ra 52, Soe Myat Min 59		Zhang Lei CHN
29-08	Indonesia	W	2-1	Kuala Lumpur	Fr	Kyaw Thu Ra 61, Soe Myat Min 85	30 000	Shahrul MAS
2007								
12-01	Thailand	D	1-1	Bangkok	TCr1	Si Thu Win 25	15 000	Matsuo JPN
14-01	Malaysia	D	0-0	Bangkok	TCr1		28 000	Tri Minh Vo VIE
16-01	Philippines	D	0-0	Bangkok	TCr1		500	Daud SIN
20-08	Lesotho	W	1-0	Petaling Jaya	Fr	Soe Myat Min 49		
25-08	Laos	W	1-0	Kuala Lumpur	Fr	Yan Paing 30		
21-10	China PR	L	0-7	Foshan	WCq		21 000	Ebrahim BHR
28-10	China PR	L	0-4	Kuala Lumpur	WCq		200	Balideh QAT
2008								
31-07	Nepal	W	3-0	Hyderabad	CCr1	Yaza Nyein Thein 66, Myo Min Tun 76, Soe Myat Min 86	150	Jasim UAE
2-08	Sri Lanka	W	3-1	Hyderabad	CCr1	Soe Myat Min 71, Yan Paing 70, Si Thu Win 85	100	Kovalenko UZB
4-08	Korea DPR	L	0-1	Hyderabad	CCr1		100	Shamsuzzaman BAN
7-08	India	L	0-1	Hyderabad	CCsf		1 500	Shamsuzzaman BAN

Fr = Friendly match • TC = Tiger Cup/ASEAN Football Federation Championship • CC = AFC Challenge Cup
q = qualifier • r1 = 1st round • sf = semi-final • 3p = 3rd place play-off • † Not a full international

MYANMAR NATIONAL TEAM RECORDS AND RECORD SEQUENCES

Records			Sequence records					
Victory	9-0	SIN 1969	Wins	8	1971-1972	Clean sheets	7	1966-1967
Defeat	1-9	MAS 1977	Defeats	7	1957-1961	Goals scored	14	1964-1966
Player Caps	n/a		Undefeated	14	1970-1971	Without goal	4	1987-1991
Player Goals	n/a		Without win	9	1987-1993	Goals against	11	2003-2004

MYANMAR RECENT LEAGUE RECORD

Championship		Interstate Championship		
Year	Champions	Winners	Score	Runners-up
2003	Finance & Revenue Yangon	Shan State	2-0	Kayin State
2004	Finance & Revenue Yangon			
2005	Finance & Revenue Yangon			
2006	Finance & Revenue Yangon	Ayerwady	1-1 5-3p	Shan State
2007	Kanbawza			

MYANMAR COUNTRY INFORMATION

Capital	Yangon (Rangoon)	Independence	1948 from the UK	GDP per Capita	$1 800
Population	42 720 196	Status	Republic	GNP Ranking	52
Area km²	678 500	Language	Burmese	Dialling code	+95
Population density	63 per km²	Literacy rate	85%	Internet code	.mm
% in urban areas	29%	Main religion	Buddhist 90%	GMT +/−	+6.5
Towns/Cities ('000)	Yangon 4 477; Mandalay 1 208; Mawlamyine 439; Bago 244; Pathein 237; Monywa 182				
Neighbours (km)	China 2 185; Laos 235; Thailand 1 800; Bangladesh 193; India 1 463; Indian Ocean 1 930				
Main stadia	Bogyoke Aung San – Yangon 40 000; Thuwanna YTC – Yangon 30 000				

NAM – NAMIBIA

NATIONAL TEAM RECORD
JULY 10TH 2006 TO JULY 12TH 2010

PL	W	D	L	F	A	%
31	9	4	18	33	53	35.5

FIFA/COCA-COLA WORLD RANKING

1993	1994	1995	1996	1997	1998	1999	2000	2001	2002	2003	2004	2005	2006	2007		High	
156	123	116	103	86	69	80	87	101	123	144	158	161	116	114		**68**	11/98

2007–2008												Low	
08/07	09/07	10/07	11/07	12/07	01/08	02/08	03/08	04/08	05/08	06/08	07/08	167	07/06
114	108	101	115	114	119	119	122	127	129	116	131		

The 'Brave Warriors' of Namibia produced the most extraordinary last-gasp triumph to book an unexpected place at the 2008 CAF Africa Cup of Nations finals. Namibia were well off the pace for much of the qualifying campaign but the results on the last day fell perfectly with the group's top two contenders, Congo DR and Libya, drawing. It allowed Namibia to sneak first place in the group with a 3-2 away win over Ethiopia in Addis Ababa, the winning goal netted in stoppage time by Muna Katupose, one of a set of twins in the team. It was only the second time Namibia have reached the final tournament and it remains a remarkable achievement for a country with a

INTERNATIONAL HONOURS
None

population of under two million. Predictably, though, their experience in Ghana proved difficult, the side's defensive naivety exposed in the first minute of their first game, en route to a five-goal thrashing from Morocco, although they did manage a draw in their last game with Guinea. Just a month before the finals, coach Ben Bamfuchile had died, which meant Dutch coach Ari Schans had a matter of weeks to prepare. After the Nations Cup finals he had more time but was dismissed in June after a run of poor results in the 2010 FIFA World Cup qualifiers. His short-term replacement is youthful Belgian coach Tom Saintfiet.

THE FIFA BIG COUNT OF 2006

	Male	Female		Total
Number of players	130 960	6 000	Referees and Assistant Referees	230
Professionals	0		Admin, Coaches, Technical, Medical	1 415
Amateurs 18+	6 260		Number of clubs	100
Youth under 18	34 000		Number of teams	250
Unregistered	10 500		Clubs with women's teams	1
Total players	136 960		Players as % of population	6.70%

Namibia Football Association (NFA)
Richard Kamumuka Street, Soccer House, Katutura, PO Box 1345, Windhoek 9000, Namibia
Tel +264 61 265691   Fax +264 61 265693
info@nfa.org.na   www.nfa.org.na
President: MUINJO John   General Secretary: RUKORO Barry
Vice-President: AMUTENYA Korbinian   Treasurer: KAPENDA Cornelius   Media Officer: BEU Kauta
Men's Coach: SAINTFIET Tom   Women's Coach: SHIPANGA Jacqueline
NFA formed: 1990   CAF: 1990   FIFA: 1992
Red shirts, Red shorts, Red socks

RECENT INTERNATIONAL MATCHES PLAYED BY NAMIBIA

2007	Opponents	Score		Venue	Comp	Scorers	Att	Referee
2-06	Libya	W	1-0	Windhoek	CNq	Benjamin [4]		Ncobo RSA
16-06	Congo DR	D	1-1	Windhoek	CNq	Pienaar [38]		Mwanza ZAM
6-07	Malawi	W	2-1	Blantyre	Fr	Katjatenja [23], Bester [65]		
28-07	Botswana	L	0-1	Gaborone	CCr1			Lwanja MWI
29-07	Lesotho	W	3-2	Gaborone	CCr1	Katupose [53], Brendell 2 [67 77]		Disang BOT
8-09	Ethiopia	W	3-2	Addis Abeba	CNq	Bester 2 [64 81], Katupose [89]		Auda EGY
17-10	Morocco	L	0-2	Tanger	Fr			
2-11	Saudi Arabia	L	0-1	Riyadh	Fr			
17-11	Tunisia	L	0-2	Rades	Fr			
2008								
5-01	Egypt	L	0-3	Aswan	Fr			
12-01	Senegal	L	1-3	Dakar	Fr	Brendell [62]		
21-01	Morocco	L	1-5	Accra	CNr1	Brendell [23]		Evehe CMR
24-01	Ghana	L	0-1	Accra	CNr1			Bennaceur TUN
28-01	Guinea	D	1-1	Sekondi	CNr1	Brendell [80]		Ssegonga UGA
26-03	Malawi	L	1-3	Windhoek	Fr	Tuyeni [53]		
31-05	Kenya	W	2-1	Windhoek	WCq	Risser [14], Khaiseb [89]	6 000	Ssegonga UGA
8-06	Zimbabwe	L	0-2	Harare	WCq		27 979	Lwanja MWI
14-06	Guinea	L	1-2	Windhoek	WCq	Bester [42]	5 000	Imiere NGA
22-06	Guinea	L	0-4	Conakry	WCq		15 000	Monteiro Lopes CPV
20-07	Comoros	W	3-0	Secunda	CCr1	Kaimbi [25], Jacobs 2 [43 74]		Labrosse SEY
22-07	Lesotho	D	1-1	Secunda	CCr1	Ngatjizeko [23]		Seechurn MRI
24-07	Malawi	W	1-0	Secunda	CCr1	Kaimbi [50]		Marange ZIM

Fr = Friendly match • CN = CAF African Cup of Nations • CC = COSAFA Cup • WC = FIFA World Cup • q = qualifier • r1 = first round group

NAMIBIA NATIONAL TEAM PLAYERS

	Player		Club	Date of Birth		Player		Club	Date of Birth
1	Athiel Mbaha	GK	Orlando Pirates RSA	5 12 1976	12	Muna Katupose	FW	Oshakati City	22 02 1988
2	Jeremiah Baisako	DF	Ramblers	13 07 1980	13	Michael Pienaar (C)	DF	Ramblers	10 01 1978
3	Hartman Toromba	DF	Black Leopards	2 11 1984	14	Brian Brendell	MF	Civics	7 09 1980
4	Maleagi Ngarizemo	DF	FC Cape Town	20 06 1979	15	Rudolf Bester	FW	Eleven Arrows	19 07 1983
5	Richard Gariseb	DF	Wits University	3 02 1980	16	Abisai Shiningayamwe	GK	Jomo Cosmos	16 05 1982
6	Franklin April	DF	Civics	18 04 1981	17	Quinton Jacobs	MF	Bryne	5 08 1988
7	Collin Benjamin	MF	Hamburger SV	3 08 1978	18	Gottlieb Nakuta	DF	Blue Waters	8 05 1988
8	Oliver Risser	MF	None	17 09 1980	19	Lazarus Kaimbi	FW	Jomo Cosmos	12 08 1988
9	Meraai Swartbooi	FW	Primeiro Agosto	18 03 1984	20	Pineas Jacob	FW	Ramblers	29 10 1985
10	Letu Shatimuene	MF	Primeiro Agosto	2 04 1986	21	Wycliff Kambonde	MF	Jomo Cosmos	10 01 1988
11	Sydney Plaatjies	MF	Jomo Cosmos	25 11 1981	22	Jamunavandu Ngatjizeko	MF	Civics	28 12 1984

Namibia's squad for the 2008 CAF Africa Cup of Nations
23 Ephraim Tjihonge GK Black Leopards 23 05 1986

NAMIBIA NATIONAL TEAM RECORDS AND RECORD SEQUENCES

Records			Sequence records					
Victory	8-2	BEN 2000	Wins	3	1997	Clean sheets	3	1995-1996, 1996
Defeat	2-8	EGY 2001	Defeats	7	2001-03, 2007-08	Goals scored	15	1997-1998
Player Caps	69	Johannes Hindjou	Undefeated	8	1995-1996	Without goal	5	1992-1993, 2001
Player Goals	12	Gervatius Uri Khob	Without win	9	2007-2008	Goals against	25	1997-1998

NAMIBIA COUNTRY INFORMATION

Capital	Windhoek	Independence	1990 from South Africa	GDP per Capita	$7 200
Population	1 954 033	Status	Republic	GNP Ranking	125
Area km²	825 415	Language	English, Afrikaans, Oshivambo	Dialling code	+264
Population density	2 per km²	Literacy rate	84%	Internet code	.na
% in urban areas	37%	Main religion	Christian 80%	GMT +/−	+2
Towns/Cities ('000)	Windhoek 268; Rundu 58; Walvis Bay 52; Oshakati 34; Swakopmund 25; Katima Mulilo 25				
Neighbours (km)	Angola 1 376; Zambia 233; Botswana 1 360; South Africa 967; South Atlantic 1 572				
Main stadia	Independence Stadium – Windhoek 25 000				

NAMIBIA 2007-08

TAFEL LAGER PREMIER LEAGUE

	Pl	W	D	L	F	A	Pts	Pirates	Civics	Ramblers	Black Africa	SK Windhoek	Eleven Arrows	African Stars	Oshakati City	Tigers	Gunners	Blue Waters	Fedics United
Orlando Pirates †	22	11	8	3	35	14	41		1-1	1-1	0-0	0-1	2-1	6-0	2-0	1-1	2-0	1-0	3-0
Civics	22	10	7	5	27	19	37	1-0		3-1	1-0	0-0	1-0	1-1	2-1	2-3	0-0	1-1	1-1
Ramblers	22	9	8	5	35	25	35	2-2	0-2		1-1	2-0	3-0	1-1	3-1	0-1	1-1	4-1	2-0
Black Africa	22	9	7	6	31	28	34	1-2	1-0	0-0		0-1	3-2	2-2	2-4	1-1	3-2	2-0	3-1
SK Windhoek	22	8	10	4	20	17	34	0-2	1-0	2-2	0-2		0-0	2-2	2-1	2-2	0-0	3-1	2-0
Eleven Arrows	22	10	2	10	27	25	32	0-1	1-2	0-2	3-1	1-0		2-1	1-0	1-0	4-0	1-0	2-0
African Stars	22	7	10	5	31	27	31	1-0	2-0	3-1	1-1	0-0	0-2		1-1	1-1	3-1	3-0	3-0
Oshakati City	22	7	7	8	27	30	28	1-1	2-1	1-0	0-2	0-0	2-3	0-0		1-0	1-1	2-2	3-2
United Africa Tigers	22	6	9	7	29	31	27	0-3	0-1	2-3	1-2	2-2	1-1	3-2	1-2		0-0	3-1	3-3
Mighty Gunners	22	3	11	8	20	27	20	1-3	1-2	1-1	4-0	0-0	1-0	1-3	0-0	1-1		0-0	3-0
Blue Waters	22	2	9	11	18	33	15	0-0	2-2	1-2	0-0	0-1	3-1	1-0	0-1	0-1	1-1		3-3
Fedics United	22	3	6	13	26	50	15	2-2	0-3	1-3	2-4	0-1	2-1	2-1	4-3	1-2	2-1	1-1	

28/09/2007 - 12/07/2008 • † Qualified for the CAF Champions League

MTL NFA CUP 2007-08

Round of 16

Civics	1
Orlando Pirates	0
Eleven Brothers	1
Fedics United	6
United Africa Tigers	3
Black Hawks	2
Mighty Gunners	2
Ramblers	9
SK Windhoek	5
Tough Guys	0
Eleven Arrows	0 3p
Black Africa	0 5p
Hotspurs	1
Blue Waters	0
Oshakati City	0
African Stars	2

Quarter-finals

Civics	1
Fedics United	0
United Africa Tigers	0
Ramblers	2
SK Windhoek	1 5p
Black Africa	1 4p
African Stars	2

Semi-finals †

Civics	1 3p
Ramblers	1 2p
SK Windhoek	1
African Stars	2

Semi-finals played in Windhoek
‡ Qualified for the CAF Confederation Cup

Final

Civics ‡	1
African Stars	0

CUP FINAL

Independence Stadium, Windhoek
28-06-2008

Scorer - Floris Diergaart [70]

FNB CUP 2007

Quarter-finals

Ramblers	0 5p
Orlando Pirates	0 4p
African Stars	0 3p
SK Windhoek	0 4p
Eleven Arrows	6
Friends	0
Mighty Gunners	1
Black Africa	3

Semi-finals

Ramblers	2
SK Windhoek	0
Eleven Arrows	0
Black Africa	1

Final

Ramblers	2
Black Africa	0

CLUB DIRECTORY

Club	Town/City	Lge	Cup
African Stars	Windhoek	0	1
Black Africans	Windhoek	5	3
Blue Waters	Walvis Bay	4	1
Chief Santos	Tsumeb	2	4
Civics	Windhoek	3	2
Eleven Arrows	Walvis Bay	1	0
Orlando Pirates	Walvis Bay	2	1
Ramblers	Windhoek	1	1
Tigers	Windhoek	0	2

RECENT LEAGUE AND CUP RECORD

Championship

Year	Champions	Pts	Runners-up	Pts	Third	Pts
2000	Blue Waters	54	Black Africans	45	Nashua Young Ones	40
2001	No Championship due to season readjustment					
2002	Liverpool	57	Blue Waters	56	Chief Santos	56
2003	Chief Santos					
2004	Blue Waters	72	Civics	69	Orlando Pirates	62
2005	Civics	71	Blue Waters	69	Ramblers	61
2006	Civics	53	Ramblers	44	Blue Waters	40
2007	Civics	50	Oshakati City	40	Ramblers	38
2008	Orlando Pirates	41	Civics	37	Ramblers	35

Cup

Winners	Score	Runners-up
Chief Santos	4-2	Life Fighters
Not held due to season readjustment		
Orlando Pirates	2-1	Tigers
Civics	4-2	Tigers
Black Africans	2-0	Life Fighters
Ramblers	2-2 5-4p	Black Africa
Orlando Pirates	1-0	SK Windhoek
African Stars	0-0 5-3p	Orlando Pirates
Civics	1-0	African Stars

NCA – NICARAGUA

NATIONAL TEAM RECORD
JULY 10TH 2006 TO JULY 12TH 2010

PL	W	D	L	F	A	%
6	1	0	5	6	17	16.7

FIFA/COCA-COLA WORLD RANKING

1993	1994	1995	1996	1997	1998	1999	2000	2001	2002	2003	2004	2005	2006	2007	High
155	168	174	179	182	188	193	191	188	186	173	158	152	168	161	**150** 08/93

	2007–2008											Low
08/07	09/07	10/07	11/07	12/07	01/08	02/08	03/08	04/08	05/08	06/08	07/08	**193** 05/01
154	158	161	162	161	158	176	180	182	182	186	185	

For much of the past decade there has been a quiet revolution taking place within football in Nicaragua. With standards rising, symbolised by the construction of the first football only stadium in the capital Managua, there was cautious optimism going into their 2010 FIFA World Cup qualifier against the Netherlands Antilles. In preparation for the tie, coach Mauricio Cruz was able to take the side on an extensive tour of Brazil where a series of friendlies were played against club sides, yet another sign of the growing professionalism within the game. Alas, it was all to no avail. In a packed Estadio Cacique Diriangen in Diriamba, the home fans were hoping to witness a first-

INTERNATIONAL HONOURS
None

ever win for Nicaragua in a World Cup match but Los Pinoleros failed to recover from conceding an early goal and lost 1-0, and that was followed by a 2-0 defeat in the return in Willemstad. Perhaps the most significant event of the year, however, was the launch of the CONCACAF Champions League. Real Esteli qualified for the inaugural edition by winning both the 2007-08 Apertura and Clausura with a preliminary tie against Canada's Montreal Impact standing between them and a place in the group stage. The challenge for the clubs in Nicaragua will be to improve standards to a level where they will be able to make it past that first hurdle.

THE FIFA BIG COUNT OF 2006

	Male	Female		Total
Number of players	408 081	58 950	Referees and Assistant Referees	1 372
Professionals	0		Admin, Coaches, Technical, Medical	4 398
Amateurs 18+	22 050		Number of clubs	1 270
Youth under 18	94 377		Number of teams	4 221
Unregistered	190 354		Clubs with women's teams	11
Total players	467 031		Players as % of population	8.38%

Federación Nicaragüense de Fútbol (FENIFUT)
Hospital Bautista 1, Cuadra abajo, 1 cuadra al Sur y 1/2 cuadra abajo, Managua 976, Nicaragua
Tel +505 2651006   Fax +505 2651006
fenifut1@turbonett.com.ni   www.fenifut.org.ni
President: ROCHA LOPEZ Julio   General Secretary: LECHADO SARAVIA Douglas
Vice-President: LOPEZ SANDERS Rolando   Treasurer: TBD   Media Officer: AVALO Moises
Men's Coach: DE TORRO Carlos   Women's Coach: URROZ Edward
FENIFUT formed: 1931   CONCACAF: 1968   FIFA: 1950
Blue shirts, White shorts, Blue socks

RECENT INTERNATIONAL MATCHES PLAYED BY NICARAGUA

2002	Opponents	Score		Venue	Comp	Scorers	Att	Referee
17-11	Cayman Islands	W	1-0	Grand Cayman	Fr			
2003								
11-02	Honduras	L	0-2	Panama City	UC			Aguilar SLV
13-02	El Salvador	L	0-3	Panama City	UC			Moreno PAN
15-02	Costa Rica	L	0-1	Colon	UC			Aguilar SLV
18-02	Guatemala	L	0-5	Panama City	UC		5 000	Moreno PAN
21-02	Panama	W	1-0	Panama City	UC	Palacios [83]		Aguilar SLV
2004								
31-01	Haiti	D	1-1	West Palm Beach	Fr	Palacios [41]	53	
29-02	Haiti	D	1-1	Esteli	Fr	Calero [58]		
31-03	Bermuda	L	0-3	Hamilton	Fr			Crockwell BER
2-04	Bermuda	L	1-2	Hamilton	Fr	Palacios [72p]		Raynor BER
30-04	Bermuda	W	2-0	Diriamba	Fr	Solorzano [4], Palacios [30]	800	
2-05	Bermuda	W	2-0	Esteli	Fr	Rocha [8], Palacios [46]	4 000	Reyes NCA
4-06	Costa Rica	L	1-5	San Carlos	Fr	Lopez.F [1]	BCD	
13-06	St Vincent/Grenadines	D	2-2	Diriamba	WCq	Palacios [37], Calero [79]	7 500	Delgado CUB
20-06	St Vincent/Grenadines	L	1-4	Kingstown	WCq	Palacios [60]	5 000	Brohim DMA
2005								
19-02	Honduras	L	1-5	Guatemala City	UCr1	Bustos [54]	5 306	Moreno PAN
21-02	Guatemala	L	0-4	Guatemala City	UCr1		8 000	Sibrian SLV
23-02	Belize	W	1-0	Guatemala City	UCr1	Vilchez [85]	3 000	Quesada CRC
2006								
No international matches played in 2006								
2007								
8-02	Guatemala	L	0-1	San Salvador	UCr1			Pineda HON
10-02	El Salvador	L	1-2	San Salvador	UCr1	Wilson [53]		Arredondo MEX
12-02	Belize	W	4-2	San Salvador	UCr1	Palacios 3 [12 20 68], Bustos [28]		Quesada CRC
15-02	Honduras	L	1-9	San Salvador	UC5p	Wilson [31]		Aguilar SLV
2008								
6-02	Netherlands Antilles	L	0-1	Diriamba	WCq		7 000	Lopez GUA
26-03	Netherlands Antilles	L	0-2	Willemstad	WCq		9 000	Wijngaarde SUR

Fr = Friendly match • UC = UNCAF Cup • WC = FIFA World Cup • q = qualifier • BCD = behind closed doors

NICARAGUA NATIONAL TEAM RECORDS AND RECORD SEQUENCES

Records			Sequence records					
Victory	4-2	BLZ 2007	Wins	2	2004	Clean sheets	2	2004
Defeat	1-11	ANT 1950	Defeats	25	1986-2001	Goals scored	7	2004-2005
Player Caps	n/a		Undefeated	3	2003-2004	Without goal	8	1999-2001
Player Goals	n/a		Without win	33	1975-2001	Goals against	55	1966-2002

NICARAGUA COUNTRY INFORMATION

Capital	Managua	Independence	1838 from Spain	GDP per Capita	$2 300
Population	5 359 759	Status	Republic	GNP Ranking	140
Area km²	129 494	Language	Spanish	Dialling code	+505
Population density	41 per km²	Literacy rate	67%	Internet code	.ni
% in urban areas	63%	Main religion	Christian 85%	GMT +/−	-6
Towns/Cities ('000)	Managua 1 140; Léon 150; Chinandega 128; Masaya 123; Granada 92; Estelí 92; Tipitapa 89				
Neighbours (km)	Costa Rica 309; Honduras 922; Caribbean Sea & Pacific Ocean 910				
Main stadia	Estadio Dennis Martinez – Managua 30 000; Cacique Diriangen – Diriamba				

NICARAGUA 2007-08

XXIV CAMPEONATO NACIONAL PRIMERA DIVISION TORNEO APERTURA

	Pl	W	D	L	F	A	Pts	Real Estelí	Diriangén	W Ferreti	Bluefields	Masatepe	Real Madriz	San Marcos	América	Jalapa	Ocotal
Real Estelí †	18	14	3	1	51	19	45		3-3	1-0	1-1	1-0	1-0	2-1	4-1	3-1	10-1
Diriangén †	18	10	7	1	36	19	37	3-2		2-1	1-1	3-1	1-1	0-0	3-0	5-2	2-0
Dep. Walter Ferreti †	18	9	6	3	35	22	33	1-2	1-1		1-0	3-2	4-1	2-2	2-0	5-1	2-1
Deportivo Bluefields †	18	8	5	5	34	24	29	1-3	3-3	1-2		1-0	0-0	2-1	2-0	3-2	5-0
Deportivo Masatepe	18	7	3	8	21	22	24	2-2	0-1	1-1	1-4		3-1	0-1	1-0	3-0	2-1
Real Madriz	18	7	3	8	28	30	24	2-3	0-4	1-1	3-2	0-1		2-0	3-1	3-1	3-0
San Marcos	18	5	6	7	23	36	21	0-4	1-1	3-3	2-4	2-1	1-5		1-0	2-2	0-0
América	18	4	2	12	20	29	14	0-1	2-0	1-3	1-2	1-2	4-1	4-0		2-2	2-0
Deportivo Jalapa	18	3	3	12	21	40	12	2-5	0-1	1-2	2-1	0-1	1-2	1-2	1-0		2-0
Deportivo Ocotal	18	1	6	11	12	40	9	0-3	1-2	1-1	1-1	0-0	2-0	3-4	1-1	0-0	

29/07/2007 - 25/11/2007 • † Qualified for the Apertura play-offs • Top scorers: Ricardo Vega, Estelí 21; César Salandia, Diriangén 15

APERTURA PLAY-OFFS

Semi-finals

Real Estelí	3	3
Deportivo Bluefields	1	0

Dep. Walter Ferreti	1	0
Diriangén	3	1

Finals

Real Estelí	2	0
Diriangén	0	0

NICARAGUA 2007-08

XXIV CAMPEONATO NACIONAL PRIMERA DIVISION TORNEO CLAUSURA STAGE ONE

	Pl	W	D	L	F	A	Pts	Diriangén	Ocotal	W Ferreti	Real Estelí	Real Madriz	Masatepe	Bluefields	América	San Marcos	Jalapa
Diriangén †	18	11	6	1	30	10	39		1-0	2-1	1-1	1-0	0-1	2-2	4-0	3-1	3-0
Deportivo Ocotal †	18	12	2	4	43	12	38	1-1		2-1	1-0	7-0	1-0	3-0	3-0	5-0	3-0
Dep. Walter Ferreti †	18	11	3	4	34	13	36	1-1	2-1		1-0	3-0	2-1	3-0	4-1	2-0	3-0
Real Estelí †	18	10	3	5	37	13	33	0-1	0-3	0-1		2-0	2-0	6-2	0-0	6-2	3-0
Real Madriz	18	6	5	7	16	27	23	0-0	2-1	2-1	0-0		1-0	0-0	2-1	0-0	3-0
Deportivo Masatepe	18	6	3	9	23	24	21	0-2	2-2	1-0	0-2	5-2		2-0	1-2	3-1	3-0
Deportivo Bluefields	18	5	6	7	26	33	21	0-3	1-2	1-1	1-4	2-1	2-2		2-0	4-1	3-0
América	18	6	2	10	19	36	20	1-2	0-5	0-4	0-4	4-0	1-0	0-0		0-2	3-2
San Marcos	18	4	5	9	21	39	17	0-2	1-0	1-1	0-4	0-0	3-1	3-3	1-3		2-2
Deportivo Jalapa	18	0	3	15	7	49	3	1-1	1-3	0-3	0-3	0-3	1-1	0-3	0-3	0-3	

27/01/2008 - 8/06/2008 • † Qualified for the Clausura play-offs

CLAUSURA PLAY-OFFS

Semi-finals

Real Estelí	3	2
Diriangén	0	3

Deportivo Ocotal	0	1
Dep. Walter Ferreti	1	1

Finals

Real Estelí	0	1
Dep. Walter Ferreti	0	0

29-06-2008 & 6-07-2008

CHAMPIONSHIP FINAL

Real Estelí automatically Champions having won both the Apertura and Clausura

RECENT LEAGUE RECORD

Championship/Clausura (2004–2005 only)			
Year	Champions	Score	Runners-up
2000	Diriangén	1-0	Deportivo Walter Ferreti
2001	Deportivo Walter Ferreti	0-0 0-0 5-3p	Diriangén
2002	Deportivo Jalapa	1-1 4-0	Deportivo Walter Ferreti
2003	Real Estelí	0-1 3-0	Diriangén
2004	Real Estelí	1-0 0-0	Diriangén
2005	Diriangén	1-0 0-1 3-2p	Parmalat
2006	Diriangén	2-1 0-1	Real Estelí
2007	Real Estelí	‡	Real Madriz
2008	Real Estelí	‡	Diriangén

Apertura		
Winners	Score	Runners-up
Real Estelí	0-0 1-0	Diriangén
Diriangén	0-0 1-0	Real Estelí

‡ No play-off as Real Estelí won both the Apertura and Clausura

NCL – NEW CALEDONIA

NEW CALEDONIA NATIONAL TEAM RECORD
JULY 10TH 2006 TO JULY 12TH 2010

PL	W	D	L	F	A	%
11	7	3	1	25	12	77.3

FIFA/COCA-COLA WORLD RANKING

1993	1994	1995	1996	1997	1998	1999	2000	2001	2002	2003	2004	2005	2006	2007	High	
-	-	-	-	-	-	-	-	-	-	-	186	187	176	118	**114**	04/08

2007–2008												Low	
08/07	09/07	10/07	11/07	12/07	01/08	02/08	03/08	04/08	05/08	06/08	07/08	**188**	04/06
168	124	120	119	118	117	115	116	114	114	123	126		

New Caledonia established themselves as the major challengers to New Zealand in Oceania with the two 2010 FIFA World Cup qualifiers against the Kiwis in September 2008 proving to be the ultimate test of supremacy in the region. The previous September New Caledonia had won the South Pacific Games when they beat Fiji 1-0 in the final in Apia, a tournament that acted as the first round of World Cup qualifying in Oceania. In the first match of the tournament, Pierre Wajoka had the honour of scoring the first goal in the entire 2010 World Cup tournament. The second round saw New Caledonia face the Fijians, Vanuatu and New Zealand in a round-robin group with

INTERNATIONAL HONOURS
None

Noumea hosting its first ever qualifier - a 4-0 victory over the Fijians. The exploits of the national team were not replicated at club level, however, with 2007 champions JS Baco failing to make it to the group stage of the O–League after losing a preliminary round tie 5-0 at home to Vanuatu's Tafea. AS Magenta earned the right to try their luck in the 2008-09 O-League after they won the four team Super Ligue play-off ahead of AS Mont-Dore, having earlier won the regular stage in Grand Terre. Mont Dore were the other team to win domestic silverware when they beat Lossi 3-0 in the Cup Final to win the trophy for only the second time.

THE FIFA BIG COUNT OF 2006

	Male	Female		Total
Number of players	9 150	650	Referees and Assistant Referees	100
Professionals	0		Admin, Coaches, Technical, Medical	200
Amateurs 18+	2 500		Number of clubs	100
Youth under 18	2 400		Number of teams	250
Unregistered	500		Clubs with women's teams	5
Total players	9 800		Players as % of population	4.47%

Fédération Calédonienne de Football (FCF)
7 bis, rue Suffren Quartier latin, BP 560, Nouméa 99845, New Caledonia
Tel +687 272383   Fax +687 263249
fedcalfoot@canl.nc   www.fedcalfoot.com
President: FOURNIER Claude   General Secretary: SALVATORE Jean-Paul
Vice-President: TAVERGEUX Gilles   Treasurer: ELMOUR Eric   Media Officer: SALVATORE Jean-Paul
Men's Coach: CHAMBARON Didier   Women's Coach: MARTINENGO Serge
FCF formed: 1928   OFC: 19   FIFA: 2004
Grey shirts, Red shorts, Grey socks

RECENT INTERNATIONAL MATCHES PLAYED BY NEW CALEDONIA

2004	Opponents	Score		Venue	Comp	Scorers	Att	Referee
12-05	Tahiti	D	0-0	Honiara	WCq		14 000	Rakaroi FIJ
15-05	Solomon Islands	L	0-2	Honiara	WCq		20 000	Attison VAN
17-05	Cook Islands	W	8-0	Honiara	WCq	Wajoka [3], Hmae.M 5 [20 40 42 52 85], Hmae.J [35], Djamali [25]	400	Singh FIJ
19-05	Tonga	W	8-0	Honiara	WCq	HmaeJ [4], Poatinda 3 [26 42 79], Hmae.M [45], Wajoka 2 [54 58] Kaume [72]	14 000	Fred VAN
2005								
No international matches played in 2005								
2006								
No international matches played in 2006								
2007								
17-07	Vanuatu	W	5-3	Noumea	Fr	Mapou [40], Toto 2 [47 62], Hmae.J [56], Wajoka [69p]		
19-07	Vanuatu	L	0-2	Noumea	Fr			
25-08	Tahiti	W	1-0	Apia	WCq	Wajoka [9p]	400	Hester NZL
27-08	Tuvalu †	W	1-0	Apia	WCq	Kabeu [52]	250	Sogo SOL
29-08	Cook Islands	W	3-0	Apia	WCq	Kabeu 3 [35 51 85]	200	Fox NZL
3-09	Fiji	D	1-1	Apia	WCq	Wajoka [44]	1 000	Fred VAN
5-09	Solomon Islands	W	3-2	Apia	WCq	Kabeu [37], Toto [54], Mercier [94+]	600	Minan PNG
7-09	Fiji	W	1-0	Apia	WCq	Hmae.J [61]	400	Hester NZL
17-11	Fiji	D	3-3	Ba	WCq	Djamali [67], Kaudre [83], Hmae.M [88]	1 500	O'Leary NZL
21-11	Fiji	W	4-0	Noumea	WCq	Wajoka [28p], Hmae.M 2 [30 55], Mapou [59]		Breeze AUS
2008								
14-06	Vanuatu	D	1-1	Port Vila	WCq	Djamali [73]	4 000	Varman FIJ
21-06	Vanuatu	W	3-0	Noumea	WCq	Wajoka [36], Hmae.M [60], Diaike [87]	2 700	Hester NZL

Fr = Friendly match • OC = OFC Oceania Nations Cup • SP = South Pacific Games • WC = FIFA World Cup
q = qualifier • r1 = first round group • sf = semi-final • f = final • † Not a full international

NEW CALEDONIA NATIONAL TEAM RECORDS AND RECORD SEQUENCES

Records			Sequence records		
Victory	18-0	GUM 1991	Wins	6	1964-1966	Clean sheets	4	1987
Defeat	0-8	AUS 1980	Defeats	6	1995-1998	Goals scored	31	1951-1966
Player Caps	n/a		Undefeated	9	1969	Without goal	3	1988
Player Goals	n/a		Without win	6	1995-1998	Goals against	15	1969-1973

RECENT LEAGUE AND CUP RECORD

	Division d'Honneur				National Championship			Cup		
Year	Champions	Pts	Runners-up	Pts	Champions	Score	Runners-up	Winners	Score	Runners-up
1998					AS Poum	4-2	JS Traput Lifou	JS Traput Lifou	1-1 4-3p	CS Nékoué
1999					FC Gaïcha	2-2 4-3p	AS Auteuil	JS Traput Lifou	1-0	AS Auteuil
2000					JS Baco	1-0	JS Traput Lifou	AS Magenta	1-1 4-1p	JS Traput Lifou
2001					JS Baco	1-0	AS Mont-Doré	AS Magenta	4-3	AS Mont-Doré
2002	JS Baco	49	AS Magenta	42	AS Mont-Doré	2-2 4-3p	JS Baco	AS Magenta	5-2	JS Ouvéa
2003	AS Magenta	62	JS Baco	54	AS Magenta	5-3	JS Baco	AS Magenta	1-0	JS Baco
2004	AS Magenta	73	AS Mont-Doré	59	AS Magenta	3-1	AS Mont-Doré	AS Magenta	2-1	AS Mont-Doré
2005	AS Magenta	73	JS Baco	61	AS Magenta	3-2	AS Mont-Doré	AS Magenta	2-1	JS Baco
2006	AS Mont-Doré	49	JS Baco	42	Not played			AS Mont Dore	2-1	JS Baco
2007	AS Lossi	45	AS Magenta	41	JS Baco	League	AS Lössi	AS Lössi	1-0	AS Mont-Doré
2008	AS Magenta	46	JS Baco	45	AS Magenta	League	AS Mont-Doré	AS Mont Dore	3-0	AS Lössi

NEW CALEDONIA COUNTRY INFORMATION

Capital	Nouméa	Status	French overseas territory	GDP per Capita	$15 000
Population	213 679			GNP Ranking	n/a
Area km²	19 060	Language	French	Dialling code	+687
Population density	11 per km²	Literacy rate	91%	Internet code	.nc
% in urban areas	n/a	Main religion	Christian 60%	GMT +/-	+11
Towns/Cities ('000)	Nouméa 93; Mont-Doré 26; Dumbéa 21; Wé 11; Paita 10; Tadine 8; Poindimié 5; Houailu 5				
Neighbours (km)	South Pacific Ocean 2 254				
Main stadia	Nouméa-Daly Magenta – Nouméa				

NED – NETHERLANDS

NATIONAL TEAM RECORD
JULY 10TH 2006 TO JULY 12TH 2010

PL	W	D	L	F	A	%
27	19	4	4	53	18	77.8

For one glorious week at Euro 2008 the Dutch once again looked like world beaters, with Marco Van Basten's side playing spellbinding football as they cast aside both the world champions Italy and World Cup finalists France on the way to topping their first round group. The Netherlands hadn't been entirely convincing in their qualifying campaign, finishing just a point ahead of third placed Bulgaria in a group won by Romania, but on the back of a good run going into the finals, the side clicked into gear with the midfield trio of Wesley Sneijder, Rafael van der Vaart and Arjen Robben pulling the strings to great effect. Against Italy, Sneijder scored the goal of the tournament in a stunning 3-0 victory that left the world champions reeling. It was their first victory over the Italians since the 1978 World Cup finals and they proved it wasn't a one-off by beating France 4-1 in the next match, where once again they used the counter-attack with devastating effect. With the Dutch already through to the knock-out stage, Van Basten decided to field a second string team in the final group match - a 2-0 victory over Romania - but instead of resting the players it seemed to have the opposite effect and against Guus Hiddink's Russia in the quarter-finals the Dutch were

INTERNATIONAL HONOURS
Qualified for the FIFA World Cup finals 1934 1938 1974 1978 1990 1994 1998 2006
UEFA European Championship 1988   **UEFA European U-21 Championship** 2006
UEFA Champions League Feyenoord 1970 Ajax 1971 1972 1973 1995 PSV Eindhoven 1988

never able to get the upper hand, despite a morale boosting equaliser by Ruud van Nistelrooy four minutes before the end of time. In extra-time, however, it was Andrei Arshavin who was the star of the show as the Dutch were knocked-out of a tournament that they could easily have won. It was Van Basten's last match in charge following his decision to take over at Ajax where he will be determined to end the dominance of PSV who won their fourth Eredivisie title on the trot - their seventh since the start of the decade. Despite finishing second, Ajax failed to qualify for the Champions League after losing to Twente Enschede in the end of season play-offs, leaving Van Basten to concentate on the UEFA Cup in his new role and new Twente coach Steve McLaren to enjoy the Champions League. PSV's attempts to win a League and Cup double didn't get very far when they were thrown out of the Cup after playing a second round match against Jong Heerenveen with a suspended player and it was Feyenoord, who hadn't won a trophy since their 2002 UEFA Cup triumph, who won the tournament. They beat Roda 2-0 in the final in their own stadium - a perfect send-off for coach Bert van Marwijk, Van Basten's surprise replacement as the coach of the national team.

Koninklijke Nederlandse Voetbalbond (KNVB)
Woudenbergseweg 56-58, PO Box 515, Am Zeist 3700, Netherlands
Tel +31 343 499201   Fax +31 343 499189
concern@knvb.nl   www.knvb.nl
President: TBD   General Secretary: BEEN Harry
Vice-President: LESTERHUIS Hans   Treasurer: VAN KOUTERIK Jan   Media Officer: JANSMA Kees
Men's Coach: VAN MARWIJK Bert   Women's Coach: PAUW Vera
KNVB formed: 1889   UEFA: 1954   FIFA: 1904
Orange shirts with white trimmings, White shorts, Orange socks or White shirts with orange trimmings, Orange shorts, White socks

RECENT INTERNATIONAL MATCHES PLAYED BY THE NETHERLANDS

2006	Opponents	Score		Venue	Comp	Scorers	Att	Referee
11-06	Serbia & Montenegro	W	1-0	Leipzig	WCr1	Robben [18]	37 216	Merk GER
16-06	Côte d'Ivoire	W	2-1	Stuttgart	WCr1	Van Persie [23], Van Nistelrooij [27]	52 000	Ruiz COL
21-06	Argentina	D	0-0	Frankfurt	WCr1		48 000	Medina Cantalejo ESP
25-06	Portugal	L	0-1	Nuremberg	WCr2		41 000	Ivanov.V RUS
16-08	Republic of Ireland	W	4-0	Dublin	Fr	Huntelaar 2 [24 53], Robben [40], Van Persie [69]	42 400	Ovrebo NOR
2-09	Luxembourg	W	1-0	Luxembourg	ECq	Mathijsen [18]	8 055	Lopes Ferreira POR
6-09	Belarus	W	3-0	Eindhoven	ECq	Van Persie 2 [33 78], Kuyt [92+]	30 089	Webb ENG
7-10	Bulgaria	D	1-1	Sofia	ECq	Van Persie [62]	30 547	Ovrebø NOR
11-10	Albania	W	2-1	Amsterdam	ECq	Van Persie [15], Beqaj OG [42]	40 085	Yefet ISR
15-11	England	D	1-1	Amsterdam	Fr	Van der Vaart [86]	45 090	Michel SVK
2007								
7-02	Russia	W	4-1	Amsterdam	Fr	Babel [68], Sneijder [71], Mathijsen [79], Van der Vaart [89p]	24 589	Clattenburg ENG
24-03	Romania	D	0-0	Rotterdam	ECq		48 000	Merk GER
28-03	Slovenia	W	1-0	Celje	ECq	Van Bronckhorst [86]	10 000	Mejuto Gonzalez ESP
2-06	Korea Republic	W	2-0	Seoul	Fr	Van der Vaart 2 [31p 72]	62 884	Ramachandran MAS
6-06	Thailand	W	3-1	Bangkok	Fr	Van der Vaart [3], Heitinga [42], Hesselink [55]	20 000	Ganesan SIN
22-08	Switzerland	L	1-2	Geneva	Fr	Kuyt [52]	24 000	Duhamel FRA
8-09	Bulgaria	W	2-0	Amsterdam	ECq	Sneijder [22], Van Nistelrooy [58]	49 500	Cantalejo ESP
12-09	Albania	W	1-0	Tirana	ECq	Van Nistelrooy [91+]	15 000	Riley ENG
13-10	Romania	L	0-1	Constanta	ECq		12 595	Vassaras GRE
17-10	Slovenia	W	2-0	Eindhoven	ECq	Sneijder [14], Huntelaar [86]	32 500	Rizzoli ITA
17-11	Luxembourg	W	1-0	Rotterdam	ECq	Koevermans [43]	45 000	Hansson SWE
21-11	Belarus	L	1-2	Minsk	ECq	Van der Vaart [89]	11 900	Layec FRA
2008								
6-02	Croatia	W	3-0	Split	Fr	Heitinga [9], Huntelaar [36], Hesselink [89]	28 000	Muniz ESP
26-03	Austria	W	4-3	Vienna	Fr	Huntelaar 2 [37 87], Heitinga [67], Hesselink [82]	40 500	Hansson SWE
24-05	Ukraine	W	3-0	Rotterdam	Fr	Kuyt [23], Huntelaar [38], Babel [64]	40 000	Circhetta SUI
29-05	Denmark	D	1-1	Eindhoven	Fr	Van Nistelrooy [29]	35 000	Chapron FRA
1-06	Wales	W	2-0	Rotterdam	Fr	Robben [35], Sneijder [54]	48 500	Brych GER
9-06	Italy	W	3-0	Berne	ECr1	Van Nistelrooy [26], Sneijder [31], Van Bronckhorst [79]	30 777	Fröjdfeldt SWE
13-06	France	W	4-1	Berne	ECr1	Kuyt [9], Van Persie [59], Robben [72], Sneijder [92+]	30 777	Fandel GER
17-06	Romania	W	2-0	Berne	ECr1	Huntelaar [54], Van Persie [87]	30 777	Busacca SUI
21-06	Russia	L	1-3	Basel	ECqf	Van Nistelrooy [86]	38 374	Michel SVK

Fr = Friendly match • EC = UEFA EURO 2008 • WC = FIFA World Cup • q = qualifier • r1 = first round group • qf = quarter-final

NETHERLANDS NATIONAL TEAM PLAYERS

	Player	Ap	G	Club	Date of Birth		Player	Ap	G	Club	Date of Birth
1	Edwin van der Sar	GK	128	0	Manchester Utd	29 10 1970	12	Mario Melchiot	DF	22	0	Wigan Athletic	4 11 1976
2	André Ooijer	DF	40	2	Blackburn Rov	11 07 1974	13	Henk Timmer	GK	5	0	Feyenoord	3 12 1971
3	John Heitinga	DF	39	5	Ajax	15 11 1983	14	Wilfred Bouma	DF	35	2	Aston Villa	15 06 1978
4	Joris Mathijsen	DF	35	2	Hamburger SV	5 04 1980	15	Tim de Cler	DF	16	0	Feyenoord	8 11 1978
5	Giovanni v. Bronckhorst	DF	81	5	Feyenoord	5 02 1975	16	Maarten Stekelenburg	GK	12	0	Ajax	22 09 1982
6	Demy de Zeeuw	MF	16	0	AZ Alkmaar	26 05 1983	17	Nigel de Jong	MF	27	0	Hamburger SV	30 11 1984
7	Robin van Persie	FW	28	9	Arsenal	6 08 1983	18	Dirk Kuyt	FW	42	8	Liverpool	22 07 1980
8	Orlando Engelaar	MF	10	0	FC Twente	24 08 1979	19	Klaas Jan Huntelaar	FW	13	8	Ajax	12 08 1983
9	Ruud van Nistelrooy	FW	64	33	Real Madrid	1 07 1976	20	Ibrahim Afellay	MF	8	0	PSV Eindhoven	2 04 1986
10	Wesley Sneijder	MF	48	11	Real Madrid	9 06 1984	21	Khalid Boulahrouz	DF	26	0	Sevilla	28 12 1981
11	Arjen Robben	MF	35	10	Real Madrid	23 01 1984	22	Jan Vennegoor/Hesselink	FW	17	3	Celtic	7 11 1978
						23	Rafael van der Vaart	MF	58	12	Hamburger SV	11 02 1983

The Dutch squad for Euro 2008

NETHERLANDS NATIONAL TEAM RECORDS AND RECORD SEQUENCES

Records			Sequence records				
Victory	9-0	FIN 1912, NOR 1972	Wins	7	1971-72, 2002-03	Clean sheets	6	1987, 2004-05
Defeat	2-12	ENG 1907	Defeats	8	1949-1950	Goals scored	23	1912-1920
Player Caps	128	Edwin van der Sar	Undefeated	17	2001-2003	Without goal	3	1949-50, 1968
Player Goals	40	Patrick Kluivert	Without win	12	1951-1953	Goals against	24	1938-1948

KINGDOM OF THE NETHERLANDS; KONINKRIJK DER NEDERLANDEN

Capital	The Hague	Language	Dutch			Formation	1579	
Population	16 491 461	Area	41 526 km²	Density	393 per km²	% in cities	89%	
GDP per cap	$28 600	Dailling code	+31	Internet	.nl	GMT +/-	+1	

MEDALS TABLE

		Overall			League			Cup		Europe			City	Stadium	Cap'ty	DoF
		G	S	B	G	S	B	G	S	G	S	B				
1	Ajax	51	28	13	29	20	10	16	5	6	3	3	Amsterdam	Amsterdam ArenA	51 859	1900
2	PSV Eindhoven	31	19	16	21	13	12	8	6	2		4	Eindhoven	Philips Stadion	36 500	1913
3	Feyenoord	28	22	16	14	19	12	11	3	3		4	Rotterdam	Feijenoord Stadion -De Kuip	51 180	1908
4	HVV Den Haag	9	3		8			1	3				The Hague			1883
5	Sparta Rotterdam	9	2	5	6		5	3	2				Rotterdam	Sparta - Het Kasteel	11 500	1888
6	HBS Den Haag	5	5		3			2	5				The Hague			1893
7	Willem II Tilburg	5	2	5	3	1	5	2	1				Tilburg	Willem II	14 700	1896
8	Quick Den Haag	5			1			4					The Hague			1896
9	ADO Den Haag	4	6	4	2		4	2	6				The Hague	Zuiderpark	11 000	1905
	Go Ahead Eagles	4	6	4	4	5	4		1				Deventer	Adelaarshorst	6 400	1902
11	AZ Alkmaar	4	4	6	1	2	5	3	1		1	1	Alkmaar	DSB Stadion	17 023	1967
12	FC Utrecht	4	3	2	1	1	2	3	2				Utrecht	Nieuw Galgenwaard	18 500	1970
13	RCH Heemstede	4			2			2					Haarlem			
14	Twente Enschede	3	7	13	1	2	11	2	4		1	2	Enschede	Arke Stadion	13 500	1965
15	Roda JC Kerkrade	3	6		1	2		2	4				Kerkrade	Parkstad Limburg	19 200	1962

RECENT LEAGUE AND CUP RECORD

	Championship						Cup		
Year	Champions	Pts	Runners-up	Pts	Third	Pts	Winners	Score	Runners-up
1995	Ajax	61	Roda JC Kerkrade	54	PSV Eindhoven	47	Feyenoord	2-1	FC Volendam
1996	Ajax	83	PSV Eindhoven	77	Feyenoord	63	PSV Eindhoven	5-2	Sparta Rotterdam
1997	PSV Eindhoven	77	Feyenoord	73	Twente Enschede	65	Roda JC Kerkrade	4-2	SC Heerenveen
1998	Ajax	89	PSV Eindhoven	72	Vitesse Arnhem	70	SC Heerenveen	3-1	Twente Enschede
1999	Feyenoord	80	Willem II Tilburg	65	PSV Eindhoven	61	Ajax	2-0	Fortuna Sittard
2000	PSV Eindhoven	84	SC Heerenveen	68	Feyenoord	64	Roda JC Kerkrade	2-0	NEC Nijmegan
2001	PSV Eindhoven	83	Feyenoord	66	Ajax	61	Twente Enschede	0-0 4-3p	PSV Eindhoven
2002	Ajax	73	PSV Eindhoven	68	Feyenoord	64	Ajax	3-2	FC Utrecht
2003	PSV Eindhoven	84	Ajax	83	Feyenoord	80	FC Utrecht	4-1	Feyenoord
2004	Ajax	80	PSV Eindhoven	74	Feyenoord	68	FC Utrecht	1-0	Twente Enschede
2005	PSV Eindhoven	87	Ajax	77	AZ Alkmaar	64	PSV Eindhoven	4-0	Willem II Tilburg
2006	PSV Eindhoven	84	AZ Alkmaar	74	Feyenoord	71	Ajax	2-1	PSV Eindhoven
2007	PSV Eindhoven	75	Ajax	75	AZ Alkmaar	72	Ajax	1-1 8-7p	AZ Alkmaar
2008	PSV Eindhoven	72	Ajax	69	NAC Breda	63	Feyenoord	2-0	Roda JC Kerkrade

NETHERLANDS 2007–08

EREDIVISIE

	Pl	W	D	L	F	A	Pts	PSV	Ajax	NAC	Twente	Heerenveen	Feyenoord	Groningen	NEC	Roda JC	Utrecht	AZ Alkmaar	Vitesse	Sparta	Heracles	Willem II	Graafschap	VVV Venlo	Excelsior
PSV Eindhoven †	34	21	9	4	65	24	72		0-0	2-0	1-1	1-1	4-0	3-0	5-0	2-4	4-1	1-1	1-0	3-1	2-0	3-0	4-1	3-1	2-1
Ajax ‡	34	20	9	5	94	45	69	0-2		1-3	2-2	4-1	3-0	2-2	0-0	4-2	2-0	6-1	4-1	6-2	5-1	4-1	4-1	6-1	4-0
NAC Breda	34	19	6	9	48	40	63	1-1	2-3		1-0	1-5	3-1	0-3	1-3	0-0	1-0	2-3	1-2	3-0	4-1	1-0	1-0	0-0	2-0
FC Twente Enschede †	34	17	11	6	52	32	62	0-0	2-1	1-1		1-0	2-0	3-1	3-0	0-1	2-2	2-1	4-3	1-2	2-1	2-0	2-0	1-1	1-0
SC Heerenveen	34	18	6	10	88	48	60	2-1	2-4	3-0	1-2		1-1	4-2	2-3	4-3	2-3	4-0	7-0	3-3	9-0	0-0	2-3	5-1	5-0
Feyenoord ‡	34	18	6	10	64	41	60	0-1	2-2	5-0	3-1	2-0		1-1	1-3	3-0	3-1	2-2	1-0	2-0	6-0	2-0	2-0	4-1	1-0
FC Groningen	34	15	6	13	53	54	51	2-1	1-2	1-2	1-0	0-1	3-2		5-1	1-1	0-2	2-1	0-0	1-0	1-2	1-0	0-2	1-0	3-2
NEC Nijmegen ‡	34	14	7	13	49	50	49	0-0	1-1	0-1	2-2	0-1	0-2	5-1		1-1	2-0	5-2	1-0	4-2	3-0	1-0	3-1	2-2	0-1
Roda JC Kerkrade	34	12	11	11	55	55	47	1-1	2-1	0-2	3-1	1-0	1-3	5-1	0-2		1-1	1-1	3-2	2-3	2-1	1-1	1-0	4-1	3-3
FC Utrecht	34	13	7	14	59	55	46	3-1	0-1	0-1	0-1	2-2	0-3	1-0	3-2	3-1		2-2	2-4	7-1	3-1	2-0	2-2	1-4	4-1
AZ Alkmaar	34	11	10	13	48	53	43	0-2	2-3	1-2	0-0	0-1	0-1	2-2	4-0	1-1	2-1		2-1	1-0	1-0	2-0	0-0	4-0	3-0
Vitesse Arnhem	34	12	7	15	46	55	43	0-1	2-2	3-3	2-2	0-1	2-1	1-0	1-2	1-0				3-0	2-0	1-0	0-2	1-3	3-0
Sparta Rotterdam	34	9	7	18	52	76	34	1-4	2-2	0-1	1-1	4-2	3-2	1-3	1-0	4-1	2-1	2-2	1-2		1-1	2-2	6-1	2-0	0-1
Heracles Almelo	34	8	8	18	34	64	32	0-2	0-1	0-1	0-3	2-2	3-3	1-2	0-2	0-0	2-1	2-1	2-2	2-0		1-0	2-0	0-0	2-0
Willem II Tilburg	34	8	7	19	40	49	31	0-1	2-3	0-0	1-3	2-3	3-1	1-2	3-0	1-0	1-4	3-0	4-0	2-2	2-1		1-2	1-2	6-0
De Graafschap ‡‡	34	7	9	18	33	64	30	0-1	1-8	0-1	0-0	0-3	1-3	1-1	1-1	2-1	1-1	2-1	0-3	4-0	0-0	1-2		3-2	1-1
VVV Venlo ‡‡	34	7	8	19	44	76	29	1-1	2-2	1-3	0-2	0-4	0-0	2-5	1-2	3-5	1-2	2-3	2-0	2-0	0-5	1-1	3-0		3-1
Excelsior Rotterdam	34	7	6	21	32	75	27	1-4	2-1	0-3	0-2	2-5	2-1	1-3	2-0	1-2	0-2	1-1	1-2	4-3	1-1	0-0	1-1	2-1	

17/08/2007 - 20/04/2008 • † Qualified for the UEFA Champions League • ‡ Qualified for the UEFA Cup • Teams placed two to five take part in the UEFA Champions League play–offs • Teams placed seven to ten take part in the UEFA Cup play–offs • Feyenoord qualified for the UEFA Cup automatically as Cup winners • ‡‡ Nacompetitie play–off
Top scorers:

UEFA CHAMPIONS LEAGUE PLAY-OFFS

Semi–finals			Finals		
FC Twente Enschede	3	5			
NAC Breda	0	1			
			FC Twente Enschede †	2	0
			Ajax ‡	1	0
SC Heerenveen	1	1			
Ajax	2	3			

† Qualified for the UEFA Champions League • ‡ Qualified for the UEFA Cup
Third place play–off: **SC Heerenveen** 2-0 2-2 NAC Breda
SC Heerenveen qualify for the UEFA Cup; NAC Breda play-off against NEC

UEFA CUP PLAY-OFFS

Semi–finals			Finals		
NEC Nijmegan	1	1			
Roda JC Kerkrade	0	0			
			NEC Nijmegan	1	3
			FC Groningen	0	1
FC Utrecht	2	3			
FC Groningen	2	1			

Third UEFA Cup play–off: **NEC Nijmegan** 6-0 1-0 NAC Breda
NEC Nijmegan qualify for the UEFA Cup

THE FIFA BIG COUNT OF 2006

	Male	Female		Total
Number of players	1 585 604	160 256	Referees and Assistant Referees	6 830
Professionals	1 000		Admin, Coaches, Technical, Medical	4 408
Amateurs 18+	562 260		Number of clubs	3 656
Youth under 18	510 091		Number of teams	55 060
Unregistered	250 000		Clubs with women's teams	1 200
Total players	1 745 860		Players as % of population	10.59%

NETHERLANDS 2007–08

EERSTE DIVISIE

Team	Pl	W	D	L	F	A	Pts	Results (vs Volendam, Waalwijk, Den Bosch, Zwolle, MVV, ADO, Helmond, TOP Oss, Emmen, Go Ahead, Roosendaal, Dordrecht, Omniworld, Stormvogels, Veendam, Fortuna, Cambuur, AGOVV, Eindhoven, Haarlem)
FC Volendam	38	22	11	5	90	46	77	1-1 4-1 2-1 2-1 4-0 3-0 5-1 5-1 1-1 2-0 3-0 2-0 2-2 2-3 3-0 1-2 6-2 1-0
RKC Waalwijk †	38	22	11	5	84	44	77	2-3 — 3-2 2-0 1-0 2-2 2-1 3-0 3-1 7-2 2-0 4-1 1-1 1-2 5-2 2-1 6-3 3-0 1-0 2-0
FC Den Bosch †	38	21	7	10	61	37	70	1-1 1-1 0-0 1-1 0-2 0-2 1-1 1-1 3-1 2-0 2-1 4-1 3-0 4-0 1-1 4-2 3-1 2-0 3-1
FC Zwolle †	38	18	13	7	70	42	67	1-2 0-0 4-1 7-0 2-1 1-1 1-0 1-1 1-1 1-1 1-1 0-3-1 2-3 4-1 5-0 3-3 3-0
MVV Maastricht ††	38	16	12	10	66	50	60	2-0 1-1 2-1 4-1 2-1 0-1 2-2 5-1 0-1 1-1 3-2 0-0 2-1 1-1 4-1 2-2 2-3 4-1 2-0
ADO Den Haag ††	38	16	10	12	58	50	58	0-1 0-1 0-1 3-1 0-3 2-0 5-1 2-2 1-2 0-0 2-1 1-1 3-0 0-0 3-0 1-0 3-0 5-2 2-1
Helmond Sport ††	38	17	7	14	53	52	58	2-1 3-3 0-1 0-2 2-2 2-0 0-1 0-3 3-0 2-0 2-1 2-1 2-1 1-2 1-1 1-2 1-1 1-1 5-0 4-1 1-1
TOP Oss ††	38	15	10	13	58	61	55	0-2 2-2 2-1 2-4 4-1 1-3 1-1 4-4 1-0 3-3 1-1 1-2 1-0 1-2 2-0 3-2 2-0 3-1 4-1
FC Emmen	38	14	11	13	61	74	53	2-2 1-2 0-3 0-1 1-1 1-2 2-1 2-1 3-1 1-2 1-0 0-0 1-1 3-2 1-1 2-0 3-3 2-1 3-0
Go Ahead Eagles †	38	16	3	19	60	64	51	1-2 2-0 2-3 3-1 2-1 1-2 1-2 2-0 6-0 1-2 1-2 1-0 1-2 0-1 2-1 3-1 4-0 1-1 3-3
RBC Roosendaal	38	13	10	15	46	49	49	1-2 0-4 0-1 2-1 1-2 0-1 1-4 0-1 4-0 0-2 1-2 2-1 2-0 4-1 1-0 1-0 2-1 3-0 1-1
FC Dordrecht	38	12	11	15	59	52	47	1-1 0-1 1-0 1-1 1-2 5-0 1-1 1-2 1-5 0-1-0 3-3 1-0 2-2 1-0 2-3 1-1 1-1 1-1
FC Omniworld Almere	38	11	14	13	56	55	47	1-1 2-2 1-0 1-3 1-1 4-0 3-1 4-0 4-1 0-4 2-3 1-0 1-2 0-0 1-1 1-2 5-0 3-1 2-0
Stormvogels/Telstar	38	14	4	20	41	51	46	2-3 2-0 0-1 0-1 0-3 1-2 2-0 1-1 0-1 1-2 2-1 1-4 0-1 2-1 4-1 1-2 4-4 2-0 1-0
BV Veendam §3	38	11	14	13	57	67	44	3-3 0-1 0-3 2-2 0-0 3-3 0-1 0-2 3-1 4-2 0-0 2-1 1-1 2-0 3-1 4-4 5-1 4-1 1-1
Fortuna Sittard	38	10	10	18	48	69	40	1-1 1-0 1-0 3-0 7-2 2-0 0-1 3-3 2-2 0-0 2-5 3-1 0-3 2-0 2-0 5-2 3-0 1-0
Cambuur-Leeuwarden	38	10	9	19	50	68	39	2-1 2-0 0-2 1-1 0-1 2-1 5-1 1-2 0-1 0-2 2-2 1-1 0-0 1-1 1-2 0-1 1-1 1-3
AGOVV Apeldoorn §3	38	12	5	21	66	98	38	3-6 2-6 0-1 0-1 4-1 1-1 3-1 1-4 4-5 2-0 1-3 2-5 1-0 1-5 0-2 3-2 2-2 2-0 4-3
FC Eindhoven	38	8	8	22	49	83	32	2-6 1-4 1-0 1-2 3-1 0-0 3-0 4-2 2-3 2-0 1-2 1-3 2-2 0-0 0-1 1-0 2-1 4-1 2-2
Haarlem	38	5	14	19	39	60	29	2-2 2-2 0-2 1-1 0-0 2-0 0-1 0-0 1-2 0-1 1-1 1-1 2-2 0-1 3-1 1-2 0-1 2-1 3-1

10/08/2007 - 18/04/2008 • † Qualified for Nacompetitie as stage winners • †† Qualified for Nacompetitie on overall record • § = points deducted
Top scorers: Jack Tuyp, Volendam 26; Gunther Thiebaut, MVV 22; Ruud ter Heide, AGOVV 19; Koen van der Biezen, Den Bosch 18

NACOMPETITIE

First round

ADO Den Haag	1 3
Go Ahead Eagles *	1 0

Helmond Sport	2 3
Top Oss *	2 0

Second round

ADO Den Haag *	1 0 8p
VVV Venlo	0 1 9p

MVV Maastricht *	1 0
RKC Waalwijk	0 2

FC Zwolle *	0 2
FC Den Bosch	1 1

Helmond Sport *	2 1
De Graafschap	3 3

Third round

ADO Den Haag *	1 2 2
RKC Waalwijk	1 2 1

FC Zwolle *	1 0
De Graafschap	3 0

ADO Den Haag promoted
VVV Venlo relegated
De Graafschap remain in Eredivisie

* Home team in 1st leg

FIFA/COCA-COLA WORLD RANKING

1993	1994	1995	1996	1997	1998	1999	2000	2001	2002	2003	2004	2005	2006	2007	High	
7	6	6	9	22	11	19	8	8	6	4	6	3	7	9	**2**	11/93

	2007–2008												Low	
08/07	09/07	10/07	11/07	12/07	01/08	02/08	03/08	04/08	05/08	06/08	07/08		
7	5	7	9	9	9	9	9	10	10	10	5	**25**	05/98

KNVB BEKER 2007–08

Second Round			Third Round			Fourth Round		
Feyenoord *	3							
FC Utrecht	0		Feyenoord *	3				
IJsselmeervogels *	1		FC Groningen	1				
FC Groningen	8					Feyenoord	4	
UNA *	1					SV Deurne *	0	
Bennekom	0		UNA	0				
Meerssen	0		SV Deurne *	2				
SV Deurne *	3							
NEC Nijmegan	2							
FC Twente Enschede *	1		NEC Nijmegan	5				
ASWH	0		De Treffers *	1				
De Treffers *	2					NEC Nijmegan *	0	
Go Ahead Eagles	1					FC Zwolle	2	
Helmond Sport *	0		Go Ahead Eagles	0				
ONS Sneek *	2	3p	FC Zwolle *	1				
FC Zwolle	2	4p						
Quick Boys	3							
RBC Roosendaal *	1		Quick Boys	2				
DOTO	0		Groene Ster *	1				
Groene Ster *	1					Quick Boys *	1	3p
ADO Den Haag	0	4p				Jong Heerenveen	1	1p
Be Quick '28 *	0	3p	ADO Den Haag *	1				
PSV Eindhoven †	3		Jong Heerenveen	3				
Jong Heerenveen *	0							
Ajax	2							
Kozakken Boys *	1		Ajax *	3				
Argon *	0		SC Heerenveen	1				
SC Heerenveen	3					Ajax	2	
Sparta Rotterdam	4	4p				NAC Breda *	4	
FC Volendam *	4	2p	Sparta Rotterdam *	2				
Jong Stormvogels/Telstar *	1		NAC Breda	3				
NAC Breda	2							
Heracles Almelo	2							
Stormvogels/Telstar *	1		Heracles Almelo *	3				
Be Quick Groningen *	1		FC Omniworld Almere	0				
FC Omniworld Almere	8					Heracles Almelo *	1	
Fortuna Sittard *	3					FC Den Bosch	0	
FC Emmen	1		Fortuna Sittard *	1				
AFC *	0		FC Den Bosch	3				
FC Den Bosch	4							
RKC Waalwijk *	4							
RBC Roosendaal	3		RKC Waalwijk *	4				
TOP Oss *	1		BV Veendam	0				
BV Veendam	2					RKC Waalwijk *	1	3p
FC Eindhoven *	4					Haarlem	1	5p
Vitesse Arnhem	2		FC Eindhoven *	1				
Willem II Tilburg	1	3p	Haarlem	3				
Haarlem *	1	4p						
FC Dordrecht	2							
WHC *	0		FC Dordrecht	3				
EVV *	1		MVV Maastricht *	1				
MVV Maastricht	3					FC Dordrecht *	4	
HHC Hardenberg	5					AGOVV Apeldoorn	3	
VVSB	2		HHC Hardenberg *	0				
Lisse *	4	4p	AGOVV Apeldoorn	1				
AGOVV Apeldoorn	4	5p						
Excelsior Rotterdam *	3							
VVV Venlo	2		Excelsior Rotterdam	2				
AZ Alkmaar	0		Cambuur-Leeuwarden *	1				
Cambuur-Leeuwarden *	1					Excelsior Rotterdam	0	
De Graafschap	5					Roda JC Kerkrade *	3	
Elinwijk *	1		De Graafschap	2				
Spakenburg *	0		Roda JC Kerkrade *	3				
Roda JC Kerkrade	2							

* Home team • Professional clubs join in the second round • † PSV fielded suspended player

KNVB BEKER 2007–08

Quarter–finals   **Semi–finals**   **Final**

Feyenoord *	2
FC Zwolle	1

Feyenoord *	2
NAC Breda	0

Quick Boys *	0
NAC Breda	3

Feyenoord	2
Roda JC Kerkrade	0

Heracles Almelo	5
Haarlem *	1

Heracles Almelo *	2	3p
Roda JC Kerkrade	2	5p

KNVB BEKER FINAL 2007
De Kuip, Rotterdam, 27-04-2008, 18:00, Att: 45 000, Ref: Jack van Hulten

Feyenoord	2	Landzaat [7], De Guzman [35]
Roda JC Kerkrade	0	

FC Dordrecht *	1
Roda JC Kerkrade	3

Feyenoord - Henk Timmer - Theo Lucius∗, Kevin Hofland (Serginho Greene 46), André Bahia, Tim De Cler - Denny Landzaat∗, Giovanni Van Bronckhorst, Nuri Sahin (Leroy Fer 70) - Jonathan De Guzman, Michael Mols (Roy Makaay 66), Luigi Bruins. Tr: Bert van Marwijk
Roda JC - Bram Castro - Fatih Sonkaya (Frank Van Kouwen 46), Davy De Fauw, Jean-Paul Saeijs, Boldizsár Bodor - Willem Janssen∗, Marcel Meeuwis∗, Cheikh Tioté∗ - Anouar Hadouir (Sekou Cisse 46), Andreas Oper, Lamah. Tr: Raymond Atteveld

NEP – NEPAL

NATIONAL TEAM RECORD
JULY 10TH 2006 TO JULY 12TH 2010

PL	W	D	L	F	A	%
13	5	0	8	14	29	38.5

FIFA/COCA-COLA WORLD RANKING

1993	1994	1995	1996	1997	1998	1999	2000	2001	2002	2003	2004	2005	2006	2007	High	
124	138	147	151	155	176	157	166	156	165	165	177	175	170	186	**124**	12/93

	2007–2008											Low	
08/07	09/07	10/07	11/07	12/07	01/08	02/08	03/08	04/08	05/08	06/08	07/08	**188**	02/08
183	185	186	187	186	186	188	188	183	184	178	177		

Nepal's national team was kept busy at home and abroad with a full schedule of fixtures, despite the political and social upheaval within the nation, which saw the removal of the ruling monarchy. While the start to the domestic league season was delayed as a result, the national side took part in three tournaments. First up in October was a 2010 FIFA World Cup preliminary against Oman which was lost 4-0 on aggregate. Nepal then launched a successful attempt to progress to the finals of the 2008 AFC Challenge Cup with wins over both Macau and Cambodia enough to earn a berth in the finals in India. That proved to be the highlight of the season. There was a mixed

INTERNATIONAL HONOURS
South Asian Games 1984 1993

performance at the South Asian Football Federation Championship, with defeats at the hands of India and the Maldives followed by a 4-1 win over Pakistan. Their trip to Hyderabad in August 2008 for the AFC Challenge Cup finals came to an end after the first round following defeats by both Myanmar and North Korea. There was significant success at club level, however, with Mahendra Police Club reaching the final of the 2007 AFC President's Cup in Pakistan. Their excellent win in the semi-final over Tajikistan's Regar TadAZ, the winners in 2005, saw them take on defending champions Dordoy-Dinamo in the final, but it was a match too far and they lost 2-1.

THE FIFA BIG COUNT OF 2006

	Male	Female		Total
Number of players	477 800	0	Referees and Assistant Referees	200
Professionals	0		Admin, Coaches, Technical, Medical	2 100
Amateurs 18+	6 300		Number of clubs	110
Youth under 18	7 200		Number of teams	440
Unregistered	110 000		Clubs with women's teams	0
Total players	477 800		Players as % of population	1.69%

All-Nepal Football Association (ANFA)

ANFA House, Ward No.4, Bishalnagar, PO Box 12582, Kathmandu, Nepal
Tel +977 1 5201060   Fax +977 1 4424314
anfanepal@gmail.com   www.none
President: THAPA Ganesh   General Secretary: SHRESTHA Narendra
Vice-President: BISTA Mahesh   Treasurer: SHAH Birat Jun   Media Officer: None
Men's Coach: SHRESTHA Birat   Women's Coach: KISHOR K.C.
ANFA formed: 1951   AFC: 1971   FIFA: 1970
Red shirts, Red shorts, Red socks

RECENT INTERNATIONAL MATCHES PLAYED BY NEPAL

2005	Opponents	Score		Venue	Comp	Scorers	Att	Referee
8-12	India	L	1-2	Karachi	SAFr1	Basanta Thapa [35]		
10-12	Bangladesh	L	0-2	Karachi	SAFr1			
12-12	Bhutan	W	3-1	Karachi	SAFr1	Surendra Tamang [10], Basanta Thapa [16], Bijay Gurung [29]		
2006								
2-04	Bhutan	W	2-0	Chittagong	CCr1	Pradeep Maharjan 2 [52 68]	3 500	Gosh BAN
4-04	Brunei Darussalam	L	1-2	Chittagong	CCr1	Tashi Tsering [60]	2 500	Al Ghatrifi OMA
6-04	Sri Lanka	D	1-1	Chittagong	CCr1	Pradeep Maharjan [75p]	2 500	Lee Gi Young KOR
9-04	India	W	3-0	Chittagong	CCqf	Pradeep Maharjan 2 [16 26], Basanta Thapa [28]	3 000	Gosh BAN
12-04	Sri Lanka	D	1-1	Chittagong	CCsf	Basanta Thapa [82]. L 3-5p	2 500	Lee Gi Young KOR
2007								
8-10	Oman	L	0-2	Muscat	WCq		15 000	Al Marzouqi UAE
28-10	Oman	L	0-2	Kathmandu	WCq		10 000	Tongkhan THA
2008								
25-03	Pakistan	W	2-1	Pokhara	Fr	Bharat Khawas [77], Anil Gurung [86]		
27-03	Pakistan	L	0-2	Pokhara	Fr			
20-05	Thailand	L	0-7	Bangkok	Fr			
25-05	Macau	W	3-2	Phnom Penh	CCq	Sandip Rai [43], Ju Manu Rai 2 [57 65]	2 000	Vo Minh Tri VIE
26-05	Cambodia	W	1-0	Phnom Penh	CCq		3 000	Torky IRN
3-06	India	L	0-4	Male	SAFr1			
5-06	Maldives	L	1-4	Male	SAFr1	Vishad Gauchan Thakali [11]		
7-06	Pakistan	W	4-1	Male	SAFr1	Raju Tamang [3], Nirajan Rayajhi [5], Ju Manu Rai 2 [67 87]		
31-07	Myanmar	L	0-3	Hyderabad	CCr1		150	Jassim UAE
2-08	Korea DPR	L	0-1	Hyderabad	CCr1		100	Iemoto JPN
4-08	Sri Lanka	W	3-0	Hyderabad	CCr1	Santosh Shahukhala [14], Ju Manu Rai [55], Anjan [68]	200	Saleem MDV

Fr = Friendly match • SAF = South Asian Football Federation Cup • CC = AFC Challenge Cup • AC = AFC Asian Cup
q = qualifier • r1 = first round group • qf = quarter-final • sf = semi-final

NEPAL NATIONAL TEAM RECORDS AND RECORD SEQUENCES

Records			Sequence records					
Victory	7-0	BHU 1999	Wins	3	1982	Clean sheets	2	Four times
Defeat	0-16	KOR 2003	Defeats	10	1997-1998	Goals scored	6	2005-2006
Player Caps	n/a		Undefeated	3	1982, 1993, 2006	Without goal	13	1987-1989
Player Goals	n/a		Without win	20	1987-93, 1995-98	Goals against	21	1996-1999

RECENT LEAGUE AND CUP RECORD

	Championship	Cup
Year	Champions	Winners
2000	Manang Marsyangdi	
2001	No tournament	
2002	No tournament	Mahendra Police
2003	Manang Marsyangdi	Manang Marsyangdi
2004	Three Star Club	Mahendra Police
2005	Season readjustment	
2006	Manang Marsyangdi	
2007	Mahendra Police Club	
2008	Season delayed	

NEPAL COUNTRY INFORMATION

Capital	Kathmandu	Formation	1769	GDP per Capita	$1 400
Population	27 070 666	Status	Constitutional Monarchy	GNP Ranking	107
Area km²	140 800	Language	Nepali	Dialling code	+977
Population density	19 per km²	Literacy rate	45%	Internet code	.np
% in urban areas	14%	Main religion	Hindu 86%, Buddhism 8%	GMT +/–	5.75
Towns/Cities ('000)	Kathmandu 790; Pokhara 186; Laltipur 183; Biratnagar 183; Birganj 133; Bharatpur 107				
Neighbours (km)	China 1 236; India 1 690				
Main stadia	Dasarath Rangasala – Kathmandu 25 000				

NGA – NIGERIA

NATIONAL TEAM RECORD
JULY 10TH 2006 TO JULY 12TH 2010

PL	W	D	L	F	A	%
22	13	4	5	27	14	68.2

There was a measure of footballing success for Nigeria over the last 12 months but arguably not where they desired it most. The country's under-17 team were crowned world champions again, this time winning the 2007 edition of the FIFA U-17 World Cup in South Korea. The Golden Eaglets beat Spain 3-0 on post-match penalties after a goalless draw in the final. It was a third triumph in the tournament after previous wins in 1985 and 1993, but success was followed by tragedy when the winning coach Yemi Tella died just weeks after the tournament. The under-23 side overcame stout competition from perennial rivals Ghana to qualify for the Beijing Games but at full national team level, the Super Eagles turned in a disappointing performance at the CAF Africa Cup of Nations finals in January 2008. The side needed a favour from Cote d'Ivoire and late goals against Benin to get past the first phase, and were eliminated by hosts Ghana in the quarter-finals despite taking the lead in the match. The failure led to vicious attacks on coach Berti Vogts by a frustrated and parochial home press and the inevitable departure of the German. Shaibu Amodu returned to take over as coach, his ninth different spell in charge of the side over the last

INTERNATIONAL HONOURS

Qualified for the FIFA World Cup finals 1994 1998 2002   Qualified for the FIFA Women's World Cup finals 1991 1995 1999 2003

Olympic Games Gold 1996   FIFA U-17 World Championship 1985 1993

CAF African Cup of Nations 1980 1994   African Women's Championship 1991 1995 1998 2000 2002 2004

African Youth Championship 1983 1985 1987 1989 2005 2007 African U-17 Championship 2001 African Women's U-19 Championship 2002 2004

CAF Champions League Enyimba 2003 2004

decade, and swiftly won four 2010 FIFA World Cup qualifying matches on the trot, ensuring Nigeria became the first country to book their place in the last phase of the African preliminaries for the finals in South Africa. They beat Bafana Bafana in Abuja, won away in Sierra Leone and then followed with a double win home and away over Equatorial Guinea. But Amodu will be mindful of the fact he was also responsible for qualifying the Super Eagles for the 2002 World Cup, only to be fired less than six months before the finals. For the first time Nigeria had an almost complete squad for the qualifiers in what was the off-season, a reflection of the growing competition for places in the national team given the growing talent at top level. Nwankwo Kanu continued his talismanic role, enhanced by the winning goal scored for his English club Portsmouth in the FA Cup final. At home, Kano Pillars won a tightly contested Premier League race by a single point over Heartland, formerly Iwuanyanwu Nationale, for their first-ever title. Ocean Boys followed up their 2006 title success by winning the FA Cup for the first time after beating Gombe United on penalties in the final after the match had finished 2-2.

Nigeria Football Association (NFA)
Plot 2033, Olusegun Obasanjo Way, Zone 7, Wuse Abuja, PO Box 5101 Garki, Abuja, Nigeria
Tel +234 9 5237326   Fax +234 9 5237327
info@nigeriafa.com   www.none
President: ABDULLAHI Sani Lulu   General Secretary: OJO-OBA Bolaji
Vice-President: UCHEGBULAM Amanzee   Treasurer: OJO-OBA Bolaji   Media Officer: OLAJIRE Ademola
Men's Coach: AMODU Shuaibu   Women's Coach: TBD
NFA formed: 1945   CAF: 1959   FIFA: 1959
Green shirts with white trimmings, Green shorts, Green socks

RECENT INTERNATIONAL MATCHES PLAYED BY NIGERIA

2005	Opponents	Score	Venue	Comp	Scorers	Att	Referee
4-09	Algeria	W 5-2	Oran	WCq	Martins 3 20p 88 90, Utaka 42, Obodo 81	11 000	Shelmani LBY
8-10	Zimbabwe	W 5-1	Abuja	WCq	Martins 2 35 75p, Ayila 62, Kanu 80p, Odemwingie 89	45 000	Pare BFA
16-11	Romania	L 0-3	Bucharest	Fr		500	Banari MDA
2006							
23-01	Ghana	W 1-0	Port Said	CNr1	Taiwo 86	20 000	Abd El Fatah EGY
27-01	Zimbabwe	W 2-0	Port Said	CNr1	Obodo 57, Mikel 61	10 000	Coulibaly MLI
31-01	Senegal	W 2-1	Port Said	CNr1	Martins 2 79 88	5 000	Damon RSA
4-02	Tunisia	D 1-1	Port Said	CNqf	Nsofor 6. W 6-5p	15 000	Maillet SEY
7-02	Côte d'Ivoire	L 0-1	Alexandria	CNsf		20 000	Damon RSA
9-02	Senegal	W 1-0	Cairo	CN3p	Lawal 79	11 354	Coulibaly MLI
2-09	Niger	W 2-0	Abuja	CNq	Aiyegbeni 27, Obodo 60		Sowe GAM
8-10	Lesotho	W 1-0	Maseru	CNq	Aiyegbeni 48		Marange ZIM
2007							
6-02	Ghana	L 1-4	London	Fr	Taiwo 65		
24-03	Uganda	W 1-0	Abeokuta	CNq	Kanu 73		Diatta SEN
27-05	Kenya	W 1-0	Niarobi	Fr	Akabueze 38		
2-06	Uganda	L 1-2	Kampala	CNq	Utaka 25		Abdelfattah EGY
17-06	Niger	W 3-1	Niamey	CNq	Kanu 40, Taiwo 74p, Aiyegbeni 89		Pare BFA
22-08	FYR Macedonia	D 0-0	Skopje	Fr			
8-09	Lesotho	W 2-0	Warri	CNq	Makinwa 43, Uche 75		Sowe GAM
14-10	Mexico	D 2-2	Juarez	Fr	Martins 2 31 52		Rodas GUA
17-11	Australia	L 0-1	London	Fr		11 953	Clattenburg ENG
20-11	Switzerland	W 1-0	Zurich	Fr	Taiwo 79	12 700	Bebek CRO
2008							
9-01	Sudan	W 2-0	Estepona	Fr	Uche, Ishiaku		
21-01	Côte d'Ivoire	L 0-1	Sekondi	CNr1			Benouza ALG
25-01	Mali	D 0-0	Sekondi	CNr1			El Arjoune MAR
29-01	Benin	W 2-0	Sekondi	CNr1	Mikel 52, Aiyegbeni 86		Bennaceur TUN
3-02	Ghana	L 1-2	Accra	CNqf	Aiyegbeni 35p		Benouza ALG
27-05	Austria	D 1-1	Graz	Fr	Kalu Uche 19	15 000	Gumienny BEL
1-06	South Africa	W 2-0	Abuja	WCq	Ike Uche 10, Nwaneri 44	50 000	Coulibaly MLI
7-06	Sierra Leone	W 1-0	Freetown	WCq	Yobo 89	25 000	Korti LBR
15-06	Equatorial Guinea	W 1-0	Malabo	WCq	Yobo 5	15 200	Mendy GAM
21-06	Equatorial Guinea	W 2-0	Abuja	WCq	Aiyegbeni 45, Ike Uche 84	20 000	Ambaya LBY

Fr = Friendly match • CN = CAF African Cup of Nations • WC = FIFA World Cup
q = qualifier • r1 = first round group • qf = quarter-final • sf = semi-final • 3p = third place play-off

NIGERIA NATIONAL TEAM PLAYERS

	Player	Club	Date of Birth		Player	Club	Date of Birth
1	Vincent Enyeama	GK Hapoel Tel Aviv	29 08 1982	12	Austin Ejide	GK Bastia	8 04 1984
2	Joseph Yobo	DF Everton	6 09 1980	13	Rabiu Afolabi	DF Sochaux	18 04 1980
3	Taye Taiwo	DF Olymp. Marseille	16 04 1985	14	Seyi Olofinjana	MF Wolves	12 06 1980
4	Nwankwo Kanu	FW Portsmouth	1 08 1976	15	Ike Uche	MF Getafe	5 01 1984
5	Obinna Nwaneri	DF FC Sion	19 03 1982	16	Dickson Etuhu	MF Sunderland	8 06 1982
6	Danny Shittu	DF Watford	2 09 1980	17	Stephen Makinwa	FW Lazio	26 07 1983
7	John Utaka	MF Portsmouth	8 01 1982	18	Obinna Nsofor	MF Chievo Verona	25 03 1987
8	Yakubu Aiyegbeni	FW Everton	22 11 1982	19	Ifeanyi Emeghara	DF Steaua	24 03 1984
9	Obafemi Martins	FW Newcastle	28 10 1984	20	Onyekachi Okonkwo	MF FC Zurich	13 05 1982
10	John Obi Mikel	MF Chelsea	22 04 1987	21	Richard Eromoigbe	MF Levski Sofia	20 06 1984
11	Peter Odemwingie	FW Lokomotiv Moskva	15 07 1981	22	Onyekachi Apam	DF Nice	30 12 1986
				23	Dele Aiyenugba	GK Bnei-Yehuda	20 11 1983

Nigeria's squad for the 2008 CAF Africa Cup of Nations

NIGERIA NATIONAL TEAM RECORDS AND RECORD SEQUENCES

Records			Sequence records				
Victory	8-1	UGA 1991	Wins	5	Four times	Clean sheets	6	1992-1993
Defeat	0-7	GHA 1955	Defeats	5	1963-1964	Goals scored	26	1972-1976
Player Caps	86	Muda Lawal	Undefeated	12	1993-94, 1999-00	Without goal	4	Three times
Player Goals	37	Rashidi Yekini	Without win	9	1985-1987	Goals against	11	1965-1967

FEDERAL REPUBLIC OF NIGERIA

Capital	Abuja	Language	English, Hausa, Yoruba, Igbo	Independence	1960		
Population	135 031 164	Area	923 768 km²	Density	148 per km²	% in cities	39%
GDP per cap	$900	Dailling code	+234	Internet	.ng	GMT + / -	+1

MEDALS TABLE

		Overall G	Overall S	Overall B	Lge G	Cup G	Cup S	Africa G	Africa S	Africa B	City	Stadium	Cap'ty	DoF
1	Shooting Stars	15	4	1	5	8	2	2	2	1	Ibadan	Lekan Salami	18 000	1963
2	Enugu Rangers	11	8	4	5	5	7	1	1	4	Enugu	Nnamdi Azikiwe	25 000	
3	Enyimba	8			5	1		2			Aba	Enyimba International	10 000	1976
4	Lagos Railways	7	1			7	1				Lagos			
5	Heartland (Iwuanyanwu)	6	3	3		5	1		1	3	Owerri	Dan Anyiam	10 000	
6	Bendel Insurance	6	3	2	2	3	2	1	1	2	Benin City	Samuel Ogbemudia	20 000	1973
7	BCC Lions	6	2		1	4	1	1	1		Gboko			
8	Dolphin	6	1		2	4		1			Port Harcourt	Liberation Stadium	25 000	
9	Stationery Stores	5	3	1	1	4	2	1	1		Lagos			1958
10	Julius Berger	4	3		2	2	1	2			Lagos	Kashimawo Abiola	15 000	1972
11	Port Harcourt FC	3	3			3	3				Port Harcourt			
12	Leventis United	3	1		1	2		1			Ibadan	Liberty Stadium	35 000	to 1987
13	Lagos ECN	3				3					Lagos	Onikan	5 000	
14	Abiola Babes	2	2	1		2	2			1	Mashood			to 1989
15	Kano Pillars	2	2		1	1	2				Kano	Sani Abacha	25 000	
16	El Kanemi Warriors	2	1	1		2	1			1	Maiduguri	El Kanemi Stadium	10 000	
17	Lobi Stars	2	1		1	1	1				Makurdi	Aper Aku	15 000	
19	Ocean Boys	2			1	1					Yenagoa	Yenagoa Township	5 000	2002
	Nigerian Ports Authority	2				2					Warri	Warri Township Stadium	20 000	

RECENT LEAGUE AND CUP RECORD

	Championship						Cup		
Year	Champions	Pts	Runners-up	Pts	Third	Pts	Winners	Score	Runners-up
1996	Udoji United	58	Jasper United	58	Sharks	58	Julius Berger	1-0	Katsina United
1997	Eagle Cement	59	Jasper United	58	Shooting Stars	51	BCC Lions	1-0	Katsina United
1998	Shooting Stars	57	Kwara United	53	Enugu Rangers	53	Wikki Tourists	0-0 3-2	Plateau United
1999	Lobi Stars	5	Iwuanyanwu Nat.	5	Plateau United	4	Plateau United	1-0	Iwuanyanwu Nat.
2000	Julius Berger	7	Katsina United	6	Lobi Stars	3	Niger Tornados	1-0	Enugu Rangers
2001	Enyimba	9	Ports Authority	4	Gombe United	3	Dolphin	2-0	El Kanemi Warriors
2002	Enyimba	61	Enugu Rangers	57	Kano Pillars	56	Julius Berger	3-0	Yobe Stars
2003	Enyimba	63	Julius Berger	58	Enugu Rangers	58	Lobi Stars	2-0	Sharks
2004	Dolphin	62	Enyimba	60	Bendel Insurance	56	Dolphin	1-0	Enugu Rangers
2005	Enyimba	72	Enugu Rangers	67	Iwuanyanwu Nat.	65	Enyimba	1-1 6-5p	Lobi Stars
2006	Ocean Boys	7	Nasarawa United	6	Kwara United	2	Dolphin	2-2 4-2p	Bendel Insurance
2007	Enyimba	7	Gombe United	4	Wikki Tourists	3	Dolphin	1-1 3-2p	Enugu Rangers
2008	Kano Pillars	64	Heartland	63	Bayelsa United	63	Ocean Boys	2-2 7-6p	Gombe United

NIGERIA 2007–08

NIGERIAN FOOTBALL LEAGUE

	Pl	W	D	L	F	A	Pts	Kano Pillars	Heartland	Bayelsa United	Sunshine Stars	Niger Tornadoes	Enyimba	Lobi Stars	Enugu Rangers	Wikki Tourists	Gombe United	Zamfara United	Sharks	Ocean Boys	Akwa United	JUTH	Nasarawa Utd	Kwara United	Jigawa G Stars	Prime	Bendel Ins'ance
Kano Pillars †	38	17	13	8	43	28	64		3-0	0-0	2-0	2-0	1-1	2-0	1-0	3-2	1-0	1-0	1-0	3-0	0-0	2-0	1-0	2-0	0-0	1-0	2-0
Heartland †	38	18	9	11	41	25	63	1-1		1-1	1-0	2-1	**0-3**	2-0	1-0	1-0	4-0	3-0	1-0	1-0	3-0	2-0	1-0	1-1	2-0	1-0	**3-0**
Bayelsa United ‡	38	16	15	7	36	22	63	2-0	1-0		2-0	1-1	1-1	1-0	0-0	4-3	1-0	2-0	1-0	1-0	2-0	2-0	1-0	1-0	1-0	2-1	2-0
Sunshine Stars	38	18	7	13	43	28	61	3-0	1-0	3-1		2-0	2-0	1-0	2-1	2-1	1-0	0-0	3-0	2-0	1-0	2-0	3-0	2-0	3-1	2-0	2-0
Niger Tornadoes	38	17	9	12	45	38	60	1-1	2-2	1-0	1-0		2-0	3-1	0-0	2-0	2-0	3-1	0-0	2-1	1-0	2-0	1-0	1-0	1-0		3-1
Enyimba	38	17	8	13	44	32	59	2-2	0-1	1-0	1-0	1-2		1-0	2-2	4-0	3-0	2-1	1-0	2-1	2-0	1-0	1-0	3-2	4-0	3-1	
Lobi Stars	38	17	7	14	46	36	58	0-0	1-1	1-0	2-1	0-0	2-0		1-0	5-0	2-0	**3-0**	1-0	1-1	3-0	2-1	5-2	3-2	1-0	2-0	2-0
Enugu Rangers	38	17	6	15	31	26	57	2-1	2-0	1-1	1-0	2-0	1-0	1-0		1-0	1-0	1-1	1-0	2-0	**3-0**	1-0	2-0	2-1	1-0	4-0	
Wikki Tourists	37	15	8	14	43	42	53	1-1	1-0	1-1	2-0	1-0	3-1	1-0	0-0		2-1	2-1	2-0	1-0	1-0	3-1	n/p	2-0	1-0	2-0	2-0
Gombe United	38	16	4	18	37	42	52	1-0	1-0	1-0	4-2	1-0	1-0	2-0	1-0	2-0		1-1	0-0	3-0	2-0	1-0	2-0	2-0	2-2	4-1	2-0
Zamfara United	38	14	10	14	32	39	52	2-0	1-0	1-0	1-0	3-2	0-0	0-1	1-0	1-0	2-1		2-1	2-0	1-1	2-0	1-0	2-1	0-0	2-2	3-2
Sharks	38	14	8	16	46	42	50	1-2	1-1	2-2	0-0	4-1	1-0	2-1	2-0	2-1	3-1	1-0		1-1	3-0	4-1	3-1	2-0	3-2	0-2	1-0
Ocean Boys ‡	38	14	8	16	31	33	50	1-0	0-0	0-0	2-1	1-1	2-1	2-2	3-0	0-0	1-0	2-0	3-2		2-0	1-0	1-0	2-0	1-3	**3-0**	1-0
Akwa United	38	14	6	18	35	44	48	1-2	1-0	1-1	1-0	2-1	0-0	2-1	2-0	3-1	2-0	0-0	4-1	1-0		1-0	1-1	1-1	1-0	1-0	2-0
JUTH	38	14	6	18	28	42	48	1-0	1-0	0-0	0-0	1-0	0-0	**3-0**	1-0	2-1	1-0	0-0	2-1	1-0	1-0		2-0	2-0	2-1	2-1	1-1
Nasarawa United	37	13	7	17	28	35	46	1-1	1-0	1-0	1-1	2-1	2-0	0-0	0-1	1-0	2-1	4-1	1-1	0-0	2-1	3-2		2-0	2-0	2-0	1-0
Kwara United	38	13	7	18	33	43	46	1-0	0-1	0-0	2-0	3-1	2-1	1-1	1-0	2-1	4-1	1-1	0-0	2-1	3-2	2-1	1-0		2-0	1-0	0-0
Jigawa Golden Stars	38	10	12	16	29	37	42	2-2	1-1	1-1	1-1	3-0	0-1	1-0	2-0	1-1	1-0	1-1	0-0	1-0	0-0	1-0	1-0	1-0		1-0	0-0
Prime	38	11	8	19	21	39	41	1-1	0-0	0-0	0-0	0-0	0-0	1-2	1-0	1-1	2-0	2-0	1-0	1-0	1-0	1-0	1-0	1-0	1-0		1-0
Bendel Insurance	38	9	12	17	26	45	39	1-1	**0-3**	0-0	0-0	0-0	1-0	2-2	2-0	1-1	0-0	0-0	1-0	0-0	3-2	4-1	1-0	3-0	1-0	1-0	

23/09/2007 - 25/05/2008 • † Qualified for the CAF Champions League • ‡ Qualified for the CAF Confederation Cup • Matches in bold awarded

COCA-COLA FA CUP 2007–08

Round of 16	Pts	Quarter–finals		Semi–finals		Final	
Ocean Boys	5						
Nasarawa United	5	**Ocean Boys**	1				
JUTH	2	Bendel Insurance	0				
Gombe Lions	2			**Ocean Boys**	1 3p		
				Enyimba	1 2p		
Lobi Stars	9						
Bendel Insurance	6	Kano Pillars	1			**Ocean Boys**	2 7p
Rising Stars	3	**Enyimba**	2			Gombe United	2 6p
Abia Comets	0						
Bayelsa United	7						
Kano Pillars	5	**Nasarawa United**	1 3p				
Warri Wolves	4	Lobi Stars	1 2p				
El Cruzeiro	1			Nasarawa United	0		
				Gombe United	1		
Enyimba	5						
Gombe United	5	Bayelsa United	1 3p				
El Kanemi Warriors	5	**Gombe United**	1 5p				
Dolphin	0						

CUP FINAL
Aper Aku, Makurdi
6-07-2008
Scorers - Joseph Ochuko 45, Kingsley Akpososo 80 for Ocean Boys; Bala Manu 6, Victor Michael 51 for Gombe

* Home team • Third place: Nasarawa United 1-0 Enyimba

COCA-COLA FA CUP 2007

First National Round

Dolphin	1
Wikki Tourists	0
FC Abuja	0
Akwa United	1
Gabros	1 4p
Mgba	1 2p
Kebbi Links	
Enyimba	2
Idah United	0
Niger Tornadoes	2
Talba	1
El Kanemi Warriors	4
Crown	1 4p
Julius Berger	1 2p
Gombe United	0
Sharks	1
Heartland	
Bussdor	1
Prime	2
Ocean Boys	2
Police	1
Igbino Babes	0
Bendel Insurance	2
Bayelsa United	2
Shooting Stars	1
Yobe Stars	0
Nasarawa United	1
Lobi Stars	1 5p
Mighty Jets Jos	1 4p
Bolowotan	0
Enugu Rangers	1

Second National Round

Team	Pts
Bayelsa United	5
Dolphin	5
Akwa United	5
Gabros	0
Niger Tornadoes	6
Heartland	5
El Kanemi Warriors	4
Crown	1
Bendel Insurance	7
Heartland	4
Prime	4
Ocean Boys	1
Enugu Rangers	5
Enyimba	5
Nasarawa United	4
Lobi Stars	1

Quarter-finals

Dolphin	0 4p
Enyimba	0 2p
Niger Tornadoes	1 3p
Sharks	1 5p
Heartland	1
Bendel Insurance	0
Bayelsa United	0 2p
Enugu Rangers	0 5p

Semi-finals

Dolphin	2 4p
Sharks	2 2p
Heartland	0
Enugu Rangers	1

Final

Dolphin ‡	1 3p
Enugu Rangers	1 2p

CUP FINAL

Teslim Balogun, Lagos
12-08-2007

Scorers - Thankgod Ahameafule 41 for Dolphin; Chinedu Efugh 20p for Rangers

Third Place Play-off

Sharks	0 4p
Heartland	0 3p

‡ Qualified for the CAF Confederation Cup

NIG – NIGER

NATIONAL TEAM RECORD
JULY 10TH 2006 TO JULY 12TH 2010

PL	W	D	L	F	A	%
12	2	2	8	8	20	25

FIFA/COCA-COLA WORLD RANKING

1993	1994	1995	1996	1997	1998	1999	2000	2001	2002	2003	2004	2005	2006	2007	High	
81	70	93	129	150	154	164	182	191	184	164	173	177	147	155	**68**	11/94

	2007–2008											Low	
08/07	09/07	10/07	11/07	12/07	01/08	02/08	03/08	04/08	05/08	06/08	07/08	**196**	08/02
146	152	157	158	155	157	152	150	158	158	170	172		

Four successive defeats in the 2010 FIFA World Cup qualifiers produced another disappointing campaign for Niger, despite the belated employment of a foreign coach to revive the fortunes of their national team, nicknamed 'Mena'. Dan Anghelescu came too late in the campaign in June 2008 to do anything about losing performances against all of their group opponents, Angola, Benin and Uganda. He replaced Hameye Amadou. It effectively condemns Niger to last place in their group, a fate that also befell them in the qualifiers for the 2008 CAF Africa Cup of Nations finals in Ghana. But the growing number of key players moving out to more professional set-ups offers

INTERNATIONAL HONOURS
None

a glimpse of hope for the arid nation on the fringes of the Sahara desert. Their top two goalkeepers play in Cameroon and Nigeria respectively and their top striker Kamilou Daouda is with Cameroon champions Cotonsport. Niger have a dismal record in recent years, never rising higher than 134 in the FIFA/Coca-Cola World Ranking during the past decade having won just a single competitive international over the last five years. That came against Lesotho in the 2008 CAF Africa Cup of Nations preliminaries. Domestic competition was again dominated by Sahel SC, who won back the league title from army club AS FNIS, who were cup winners.

THE FIFA BIG COUNT OF 2006

	Male	Female		Total
Number of players	542 681	30	Referees and Assistant Referees	704
Professionals	20		Admin, Coaches, Technical, Medical	634
Amateurs 18+	6 357		Number of clubs	120
Youth under 18	1 054		Number of teams	1 010
Unregistered	30 000		Clubs with women's teams	0
Total players	542 711		Players as % of population	4.33%

Fédération Nigerienne de Football (FENIFOOT)
Avenue Francois Mitterand, Case postale 10299, Niamey, Niger, Niger
Tel +227 20724575   Fax +227 20725127
fenifoot@gmail.com   www.none
President: DIALLO Amadou   General Secretary: ABDOU Sani
Vice-President: DIAMBEIDOU Oumarou   Treasurer: HASSANE DIABRI Ounteini   Media Officer: IBRAHIM Baderi
Men's Coach: ANGHELESCU Dan   Women's Coach: ACOSTA Frederic
FENIFOOT formed: 1967   CAF: 1967   FIFA: 1967
Orange shirts, White shorts, Green socks

RECENT INTERNATIONAL MATCHES PLAYED BY NIGER

2003	Opponents	Score	Venue	Comp	Scorers	Att	Referee
30-03	Guinea	L 0-2	Conakry	CNq		25 000	Monteiro Duarte CPV
7-06	Guinea	W 1-0	Niamey	CNq	Tankary [69]	50 000	Wellington GHA
22-06	Ethiopia	L 0-2	Addis Abeba	CNq		25 000	
5-07	Liberia	W 1-0	Niamey	CNq	Alhassan [90p]		
11-10	Algeria	L 0-1	Niamey	WCq		20 126	Coulibaly MLI
14-11	Algeria	L 0-6	Algiers	WCq		50 000	El Arjoun MAR
2004							
No international matches played in 2004							
2005							
No international matches played in 2005							
2006							
29-08	Togo	D 1-1	Lomé	Fr	Fankele [90]		
2-09	Nigeria	L 0-2	Abuja	CNq			Sowe GAM
8-10	Uganda	D 0-0	Niamey	CNq			Diouf SEN
2007							
25-03	Lesotho	L 1-3	Maseru	CNq	Kamilou Daouda [41]		Lwanja MWI
3-06	Lesotho	W 2-0	Niamey	CNq	Hamidou Djibo [3], Souleymane Dela Sacko [13]		Kotey GHA
17-06	Nigeria	L 1-3	Niamey	CNq	Kamilou Daouda [68]		Pare BFA
8-09	Uganda	L 1-3	Kampala	CNq	Idrissa Hasseydou [44]		Marange ZIM
21-11	Equatorial Guinea	D 1-1	Malabo	Fr			
2008							
31-05	Uganda	L 0-1	Kampala	WCq		25 000	Evehe CMR
8-06	Angola	L 1-2	Niamey	WCq	Ismael Alassane [3]	23 000	Jedidi TUN
14-06	Benin	L 0-2	Niamey	WCq		5 000	Haimoudi ALG
22-06	Benin	L 0-2	Cotonou	WCq		25 000	Niyongabo BDI

Fr = Friendly match • CN = CAF African Cup of Nations • WC = FIFA World Cup • q = qualifier

NIGER NATIONAL TEAM RECORDS AND RECORD SEQUENCES

Records			Sequence records				
Victory	7-1	MTN 1990	Wins	2	1981	Clean sheets	2	1983
Defeat	1-9	GHA 1969	Defeats	9	1969-1972	Goals scored	5	1994-1995
Player Caps	n/a		Undefeated	4	Three times	Without goal	5	1987-1988
Player Goals	n/a		Without win	23	1963-1976	Goals against	25	1963-1980

RECENT LEAGUE AND CUP RECORD

	Championship		Cup		
Year	Champions	Winners	Score	Runners-up	
1998	Olympic FC Niamey	JS Ténéré Niamey	4-0	Liberté FC Niamey	
1999	Olympic FC Niamey	JS Ténéré Niamey	2-0	Sahel SC Niamey	
2000	JS Ténéré Niamey	JS Ténéré Niamey	3-1	Olympic FC Niamey	
2001	JS Ténéré Niamey	Akokana Agadez	1-1 5-4p	Jangorzo Maradi	
2002	No competition held	Tournament not held			
2003	Sahel SC Niamey	Olympic FC Niamey	4-1	Alkali Nassara Zinder	
2004	Sahel SC Niamey	Sahel SC Niamey	2-1	Akokana Agadez	
2005	AS-FNIS Niamey				
2006	AS-FNIS Niamey	Sahel SC Niamey		AS-FNIS Niamey	
2007	Sahel SC Niamey	AS-FNIS Niamey	3-0	Espoir Zinder	

NIGER COUNTRY INFORMATION

Capital	Niamey	Independence	1960 from France	GDP per Capita	$800
Population	11 360 538	Status	Republic	GNP Ranking	138
Area km²	1 267 000	Language	French, Hausa, Djerma	Dialling code	+227
Population density	9 per km²	Literacy rate	17%	Internet code	.ne
% in urban areas	17%	Main religion	Muslim 80%	GMT +/–	+1
Towns/Cities ('000)	Niamey 774; Zinder 191; Maradi 163; Agadez 88; Arlit 83; Tahoua 80; Dosso 49				
Neighbours (km)	Chad 1 175; Nigeria 1 497; Benin 266; Burkina Faso 628; Mali 821; Algeria 956; Libya 354				
Main stadia	General Seyni Kountche – Niamey 30 000; Municipal – Zinder 10 000; Municipal – Maradi 10 000				

NIR – NORTHERN IRELAND

NATIONAL TEAM RECORD
JULY 10TH 2006 TO JULY 12TH 2010

PL	W	D	L	F	A	%
16	8	3	5	23	17	59.4

FIFA/COCA-COLA WORLD RANKING

1993	1994	1995	1996	1997	1998	1999	2000	2001	2002	2003	2004	2005	2006	2007	High	
39	45	45	64	93	86	84	93	88	103	122	107	103	48	32	**27**	08/07

	2007–2008											Low	
08/07	09/07	10/07	11/07	12/07	01/08	02/08	03/08	04/08	05/08	06/08	07/08	**124**	03/04
27	36	36	32	32	32	34	34	34	34	32	33		

The Irish may not have qualified for Euro 2008 but they put up their best performance in a campaign for a number of years and they did walk off with one prize - or rather David Healy did. The 13 goals he scored during the qualifiers broke the previous record of 12 held by Davor Suker, who's total also included those scored in the finals of Euro 96. In recognition of the feat Healy received a special award from UEFA President Michel Platini before Northern Ireland's match against Georgia. Had the Irish not lost both of their matches against strugglers Iceland, Healy may well have been able to add to his total in the finals. If the Irish are to qualify for their first World

INTERNATIONAL HONOURS
Qualified for the FIFA World Cup finals 1958 1982 1986   British International Championship 1903 1914 1956 1958 1959 1964 1980 1984

Cup finals since 1986, coach Nigel Worthington will need to conjure up the same team spirit that saw victories over the likes of England and Spain under the stewardship of Lawrie Sanchez, and the jury is out as to whether he can deliver that. At club level, the 2008-09 season sees the launch of the new 12-team IFA Premiership with Linfield aiming for a League and Cup double for the fourth year running, having won their third in a row in May 2008 - the first time that any team in the UK has achieved that since Linfield last did it in 1893. They also claimed the League Cup to repeat their treble winning feat of 2006.

THE FIFA BIG COUNT OF 2006

	Male	Female		Total
Number of players	83 220	9 100	Referees and Assistant Referees	553
Professionals	220		Admin, Coaches, Technical, Medical	11 557
Amateurs 18+	22 600		Number of clubs	820
Youth under 18	16 000		Number of teams	1 570
Unregistered	10 500		Clubs with women's teams	9
Total players	92 320		Players as % of population	4.84%

Irish Football Association (IFA)
20 Windsor Avenue, Belfast, BT9 6EG, United Kingdom
Tel +44 28 90669458   Fax +44 28 90667620
enquiries@irishfa.com   www.irishfa.com
President: KENNEDY Raymond   General Secretary: WELLS Howard J C
Vice-President: MARTIN David   Treasurer: JARDINE Neil   Media Officer: HARRISON Sueann
Men's Coach: WORTHINGTON Nigel   Women's Coach: WYLIE Alfie
IFA formed: 1880   UEFA: 1954   FIFA: 1911-20, 1924-28, 1946
Green shirts with blue trimmings, White shorts, Green socks or White shirts with green trimmings, Green shorts, White socks

RECENT INTERNATIONAL MATCHES PLAYED BY NORTHERN IRELAND

2005	Opponents	Score		Venue	Comp	Scorers	Att	Referee
9-02	Canada	L	0-1	Belfast	Fr		11 156	Attard MLT
26-03	England	L	0-4	Manchester	WCq		62 239	Stark GER
30-03	Poland	L	0-1	Warsaw	WCq		13 515	Frojdfeldt SWE
4-06	Germany	L	1-4	Belfast	Fr	Healy 15p	14 000	Richmond SCO
17-08	Malta	D	1-1	Ta'Qali	Fr	Healy 9	1 850	Riley ENG
3-09	Azerbaijan	W	2-0	Belfast	WCq	Elliott 60, Feeney 84	12 000	Stanisic SCG
7-09	England	W	1-0	Belfast	WCq	Healy 73	14 069	Busacca SUI
8-10	Wales	L	2-3	Belfast	WCq	Duff 47, Davis 50	13 451	Bossen NED
12-10	Austria	L	0-2	Vienna	WCq		12 500	Briakos GRE
15-11	Portugal	D	1-1	Belfast	Fr	Feeney 53	20 000	Webb ENG
2006								
1-03	Estonia	W	1-0	Belfast	Fr	Sproule 2	13 600	Vink NED
21-05	Uruguay	L	0-1	New Jersey	Fr		4 152	
26-05	Romania	L	0-2	Chicago	Fr		15 000	Kennedy USA
16-08	Finland	W	2-1	Helsinki	Fr	Healy 32, Lafferty 64	12 500	Svendsen DEN
2-09	Iceland	L	0-3	Belfast	ECq		13 522	Skjerven NOR
6-09	Spain	W	3-2	Belfast	ECq	Healy 3 20 64 80	13 885	De Bleeckere BEL
7-10	Denmark	D	0-0	Copenhagen	ECq		41 482	Plautz AUT
11-10	Latvia	W	1-0	Belfast	ECq	Healy 35	13 500	Fleischer GER
2007								
6-02	Wales	D	0-0	Belfast	Fr		13 500	Richmond SCO
24-03	Liechtenstein	W	4-1	Vaduz	ECq	Healy 3 52 75 83, McCann 92+	4 340	Oriekhov UKR
28-03	Sweden	W	2-1	Belfast	ECq	Healy 2 31 58	13 500	Braamhaar NED
22-08	Liechtenstein	W	3-1	Belfast	ECq	Healy 2 5 35, Lafferty 56	13 544	Matejek CZE
8-09	Latvia	L	0-1	Riga	ECq		7 500	Proença POR
12-09	Iceland	L	1-2	Reykjavík	ECq	Healy 72p	7 727	Baskakov RUS
17-10	Sweden	D	1-1	Stockholm	ECq	Lafferty 72	33 112	Layec FRA
17-11	Denmark	W	2-1	Belfast	ECq	Feeney 62, Healy 80	12 997	Vink NED
21-11	Spain	L	0-1	Las Palmas	ECq		30 339	Fandel GER
2008								
6-02	Bulgaria	L	0-1	Belfast	Fr		11 000	McDonald SCO
26-03	Georgia	W	4-1	Belfast	Fr	Lafferty 2 25 36, Healy 33, Thompson 87	15 000	Wilmes LUX

Fr = Friendly match • EC = UEFA EURO 2008 • WC = FIFA World Cup • q = qualifier

NORTHERN IRELAND NATIONAL TEAM PLAYERS

Player		Ap	G	Club	Date of Birth	Player		Ap	G	Club	Date of Birth
Maik Taylor	GK	67	0	Birmingham C	4 09 1971	Michael O'Connor	MF	1	0	Crewe Alex	6 10 1987
Roy Carroll	GK	19	0	Derby County	30 09 1977	Steven Davis	MF	26	1	Rangers	1 01 1985
Alan Mannus	GK	2	0	Linfield	19 05 1982	Sammy Clingan	MF	13	0	Nottm Forest	13 01 1984
Michael McGovern	GK	0	0	Dundee United	12 07 1984	Chris Brunt	MF	13	0	West Brom	14 12 1984
Jonny Evans	DF	9	0	Sunderland	3 01 1988	Keith Gillespie	MF	80	2	Sheffield United	18 02 1975
George McCartney	DF	23	1	West Ham	29 04 1981	Damien Johnson	MF	47	0	Birmingham C	18 11 1978
Chris Baird	DF	31	0	Fulham	25 02 1982	Stuart Elliott	MF	38	4	Hull City	23 07 1978
Aaron Hughes	DF	58	0	Fulham	8 11 1979	David Healy	FW	63	34	Fulham	5 08 1979
Gareth McAuley	DF	10	0	Leicester City	5 12 1979	Kyle Lafferty	FW	14	5	Rangers	16 09 1987
Stephen Craigan	DF	33	0	Motherwell	29 10 1976	Warren Feeney	FW	24	3	Cardiff City	17 01 1981
Michael Gault	MF	1	0	Linfield	15 04 1983	Martin Paterson	FW	1	0	Burnley	10 05 1987
						Peter Thompson	FW	7	1	Linfield	2 05 1984

Northern Ireland's squad for the March international against Georgia

NORTHERN IRELAND NATIONAL TEAM RECORDS AND RECORD SEQUENCES

Records			Sequence records					
Victory	7-0	WAL 1930	Wins	3	1968, 1984, 2007	Clean sheets	6	1985-1986
Defeat	0-13	ENG 1882	Defeats	11	1884-87, 1959-61	Goals scored	13	1933-1938
Player Caps	119	Pat Jennings	Undefeated	9	1979-80, 1985-86	Without goal	13	2002-2003
Player Goals	34	David Healy	Without win	21	1947-1953	Goals against	46	1882-1897

NORTHERN IRELAND (PART OF THE UNITED KINGDOM)

Capital	Belfast	Language	English			Independence	n/a
Population	1 716 942	Area	14 120 km²	Density	121 per km²	% in cities	89%
GDP per cap	$27 700	Dailling code	+44	Internet	.uk	GMT +/-	0

MAJOR CITIES/TOWNS

Population '000

1	Belfast	274
2	Londonderry	89
3	Lisburn	81
4	Newtonabbey	64
5	Bangor	61
6	Craigavon	60
7	Castlereagh	57
8	Carrickfergus	30
9	Newtonards	30
10	Ballymena	29
11	Newry	27
12	Coleraine	26
13	Portadown	24
14	Omagh	21
15	Antrim	19
16	Larne	18
17	Banbridge	17
18	Enniskillen	14
19	Armagh	14
20	Strabane	14
21	Holywood	13
22	Limavady	13
23	Dungannon	12
24	Cookstown	11

MEDALS TABLE

		Overall			League			Cup		LC		Europe				Stadium	Cap'ty	DoF
		G	S	B	G	S	B	G	B	G	B	G	S	B				
1	Linfield	96	42	14	48	19	14	39	20	9	3				Belfast	Windsor Park	20 332	1886
2	Glentoran	48	48	23	22	24	23	20	19	6	5				Belfast	The Oval	15 000	1882
3	Belfast Celtic	22	8	8	14	4	8	8	4						Belfast	Paradise		1891
4	Lisburn Distillery	18	15	9	6	8	9	12	7						Lisburn	New Grosvenor	8 000	1880
5	Cliftonville	12	17	6	3	5	6	8	10	1	2				Belfast	Solitude	6 000	1879
6	Glenavon	9	21	6	3	10	6	5	10	1	1				Lurgan	Mourneview Park	5 000	1889
7	Portadown	8	16	7	4	9	7	3	6	1	1				Portadown	Shamrock Park	8 000	1924
8	Coleraine	7	18	9	1	9	9	5	6	1	3				Coleraine	The Showgrounds	6 500	1927
9	Crusaders	7	6	3	4	2	3	2	1	1	3				Belfast	Seaview	6 500	1898
10	Ballymena United	6	10	5		2	5	6	8						Ballymena	The Showgrounds	8 000	1928
11	Ards	6	4	8	1	1	8	4	2	1	1				Newtownards	Clandeboye Park	4 000	1902
12	Derry City	4	10	3	1	7	3	3	3						Londonderry			
13	Shelbourne Dublin	3	4	1		1	1	3	3						Dublin			
14	Queen's Island	3	3		1	3		2										
15	Bangor	2	3	2		1	2	1	2	1					Bangor	Clandeboye Park	4 000	1918
16	Bohemians Dublin	1	5					1	5						Dublin			

RECENT LEAGUE AND CUP RECORD

	Championship						Cup		
Year	Champions	Pts	Runners-up	Pts	Third	Pts	Winners	Score	Runners-up
1995	Crusaders	67	Glenavon	60	Portadown	50	Linfield	3-1	Carrick Rangers
1996	Portadown	56	Crusaders	52	Glentoran	46	Glentoran	1-0	Glenavon
1997	Crusaders	46	Coleraine	43	Glentoran	41	Glenavon	1-0	Cliftonville
1998	Cliftonville	68	Linfield	64	Portadown	60	Glentoran	1-0	Glenavon
1999	Glentoran	78	Linfield	70	Crusaders	62	Portadown	w/o	Cliftonville
2000	Linfield	79	Coleraine	61	Glenavon	61	Glentoran	1-0	Portadown
2001	Linfield	75	Glenavon	62	Glentoran	57	Glentoran	1-0	Linfield
2002	Portadown	75	Glentoran	74	Linfield	62	Linfield	2-1	Portadown
2003	Glentoran	90	Portadown	80	Coleraine	73	Coleraine	1-0	Glentoran
2004	Linfield	73	Portadown	70	Lisburn Distillery	55	Glentoran	1-0	Coleraine
2005	Glentoran	74	Linfield	72	Portadown	58	Portadown	5-1	Larne
2006	Linfield	75	Glentoran	63	Portadown	54	Linfield	2-1	Glentoran
2007	Linfield	71	Glentoran	63	Cliftonville	61	Linfield	2-2 3-2p	Dungannon Swifts
2008	Linfield	74	Glentoran	71	Cliftonville	60	Linfield	2-1	Coleraine

NORTHERN IRELAND 2007–08

IRISH PREMIER LEAGUE

	Pl	W	D	L	F	A	Pts	Linfield	Glentoran	Cliftonville	Distillery	Portadown	Ballymena	Crusaders	Newry City	Coleraine	Swifts	Donegal	Glenavon	Larne	Institute	Limavady	Armagh
Linfield †◊	30	23	5	2	71	18	74		0-0	0-0	2-1	1-0	1-0	5-0	5-0	4-0	2-1	2-0	3-2	3-0	1-0	3-0	2-1
Glentoran ‡◊	30	22	5	3	69	24	71	1-0		2-1	2-2	3-1	2-4	3-0	2-1	2-1	1-1	5-1	3-0	1-0	3-0	3-0	1-0
Cliftonville ◊	30	18	6	6	55	32	60	2-2	4-2		2-2	2-1	3-2	0-1	2-0	1-2	2-1	5-1	3-3	1-1	2-0	4-1	2-1
Lisburn Distillery ◊	30	17	7	6	50	28	58	0-0	1-2	1-2		1-0	0-2	1-0	1-0	2-0	1-1	0-1	0-0	2-0	0-0	5-0	1-0
Portadown	30	15	2	13	44	39	47	2-5	0-2	0-2	0-1		2-1	2-0	3-2	1-5	0-1	2-1	0-1	5-1	2-1	2-0	2-1
Ballymena United ◊	30	12	8	10	42	41	44	0-4	0-4	0-1	2-1	2-1		2-2	2-1	2-0	0-0	0-0	0-0	3-0	2-1	3-0	2-1
Crusaders ◊	30	12	7	11	45	47	43	0-3	0-2	1-1	1-3	0-2	3-0		4-1	3-4	1-0	2-0	2-1	4-1	1-0	2-1	1-1
Newry City ◊	30	13	4	13	45	52	43	0-3	0-3	1-0	1-4	2-1	2-2	1-1		0-2	3-0	1-1	2-1	2-2	2-1	3-0	3-0
Coleraine ‡◊	30	11	7	12	41	50	40	1-4	1-4	0-3	1-4	1-1	1-1	3-3	0-1		2-2	3-2	0-1	4-1	2-1	1-0	2-0
Dungannon Swifts ◊	30	9	9	12	38	44	36	4-0	0-0	1-0	0-3	0-3	2-1	1-1	4-6	4-1		0-0	1-4	1-0	0-1	0-2	5-1
Donegal Celtic	30	9	8	13	39	47	35	1-1	3-3	0-2	1-2	0-1	0-2	3-0	2-3	1-1	1-1		2-0	4-3	0-1	3-1	3-0
Glenavon ◊	30	9	3	18	37	51	30	0-2	1-2	1-2	2-3	0-3	1-2	0-4	1-0	1-0	1-2	0-1		2-3	2-0	0-3	5-0
Larne	30	7	4	19	44	71	25	1-5	0-3	1-2	1-2	1-2	2-1	0-2	3-0	1-2	3-3	4-2	3-4		1-2	2-2	0-2
Institute ◊	30	5	8	17	23	41	23	0-1	1-2	1-2	0-2	1-2	1-1	3-1	0-2	0-0	1-0	1-1	2-3	0-1		0-0	1-1
Limavady United	30	6	5	19	26	57	23	0-4	1-0	3-1	1-2	0-2	3-1	1-2	1-3	0-0	1-1	0-1	1-0	2-1	2-3		0-3
Armagh City	30	5	6	19	29	56	21	1-3	0-5	0-1	4-1	1-1	1-2	2-2	1-2	0-1	0-1	1-1	2-0	2-5	1-1	1-0	

22/09/2007 - 26/04/2008 • † Qualified for the UEFA Champions League • ‡ Qualified for the UEFA Cup • ◊ Qualified for new IFA Premiership

NORTHERN IRELAND 2007–08 FIRST DIVISION (2)

	Pl	W	D	L	F	A	Pts
Loughgall	22	15	4	3	42	21	49
Dundela	22	12	3	7	38	28	39
Bangor ◊	22	10	7	5	43	33	37
Ballyclare Comrades	22	10	6	6	28	17	36
Tobermore United	22	10	5	7	41	32	35
Carrick Rangers	22	10	3	9	34	30	33
Banbridge Town	22	10	2	10	38	38	32
Ards	22	8	3	11	32	28	27
Coagh United	22	7	6	9	27	35	27
HW Welders	22	6	8	8	19	27	26
Lurgan Celtic	22	5	3	14	22	44	18
Portstewart	22	1	6	15	19	50	9

22/09/2007 - 6/05/2008

CIS INSURANCE LEAGUE CUP 2007–08

Quarter–finals

Linfield *	5
L'burn Distillery	1

Cliftonville *	1 5p
Newry City	1 6p

Glentoran *	1
D'gannon Swifts	0

Portadown *	3
Crusaders	4

Semi–finals

Linfield *	1 4p
Newry City	1 3p

Glentoran	0
Crusaders *	1

Final

Linfield	3
Crusaders	2

2-02-2008

* Home team • † At The Oval • ‡ At Windsor Park

IRISH CUP 2007–08

Round of 16

Linfield *	3
Bangor	0
Dundela	1 0
Newry City *	1 1
Portadown *	2
Downpatrick	1
Crusaders	0
Cliftonville *	1
Donegal Celtic *	1
Abbey Villa	0
Dungannon Swifts *	0
Glentoran	2
Institute	2 2
Ballyclare Comrades *	2 0
Brantwood	1
Coleraine *	5

Quarter–finals

Linfield	1 4
Newry City *	1 0
Portadown	3
Cliftonville *	4
Donegal Celtic	2
Glentoran *	1
Institute *	0 1
Coleraine	0 5

Semi–finals

Linfield ‡‡	2
Cliftonville	1
Donegal Celtic	1 1
Coleraine †	1 2

Final

Linfield	2
Coleraine ‡	1

CUP FINAL

Windsor Park, Belfast
3-05-2008

‡ Qualified for the UEFA Cup
‡‡ Played at The Oval, Belfast
* Home team • † Both games at the Showgrounds, Ballymena

NOR – NORWAY

NATIONAL TEAM RECORD
JULY 10TH 2006 TO JULY 12TH 2010

PL	W	D	L	F	A	%
19	8	5	6	35	24	55.3

FIFA/COCA-COLA WORLD RANKING

1993	1994	1995	1996	1997	1998	1999	2000	2001	2002	2003	2004	2005	2006	2007		High	
4	8	10	14	13	14	7	14	26	26	42	35	38	50	29		2	10/93

2007–2008													Low	
08/07	09/07	10/07	11/07	12/07	01/08	02/08	03/08	04/08	05/08	06/08	07/08		52	07/06
35	29	21	28	29	29	28	27	28	29	27	31			

The Norwegian national team failed to qualify for their fourth finals in a row when they missed out on Euro 2008. In the past this would have not been unusual but having known relative success in the 1990s, the past decade has been one of gloom for Norwegian fans. Their 2010 FIFA World Cup qualifying group does hold out the possibility of a first appearance at the finals since 1998 with Scotland and the Netherlands standing in the way of Age Hareide's team. A disappointing 2-1 defeat in Oslo at the hands of Turkey in their penultimate group game cost Norway a place in the finals of Euro 2008 as they finished the group in third place just a point behind the Turks. The 2007

INTERNATIONAL HONOURS
Qualified for the FIFA World Cup finals 1938 1994 1998
FIFA Women's World Cup 1995   Women's Olympic Gold 2000   European Women's Championship 1987 1993

domestic season saw two clubs rekindle former glories as traditional giants Rosenborg faltered for the second time in three years. They finished fifth in the Tippeligaen allowing Brann from the port city of Bergen to claim their first league title for 44 years. Less dramatic perhaps was Lillestrøm's 2-0 victory over second division Haugesund in the Cup Final - Canadian striker Olivier Occean's two goals securing Lillestrøm their first trophy since winning the League in 1989. The days of Rosenborg's unrelenting dominance seem to be well and truly over.

THE FIFA BIG COUNT OF 2006

	Male	Female		Total
Number of players	409 007	134 158	Referees and Assistant Referees	2 201
Professionals	1 000		Admin, Coaches, Technical, Medical	5 000
Amateurs 18+	78 207		Number of clubs	1 818
Youth under 18	272 958		Number of teams	19 841
Unregistered	110 000		Clubs with women's teams	1 400
Total players	543 165		Players as % of population	11.78%

Norges Fotballforbund (NFF)
Serviceboks 1, Ullevaal Stadion, Oslo 0840, Norway
Tel +47 21029300   Fax +47 21029301
nff@fotball.no   www.fotball.no
President: KAAFJORD Sondre   General Secretary: ESPELUND Karen
Vice-President: LOE Erik   Treasurer: RIBERG Rune   Media Officer: SOLHEIM Roger
Men's Coach: HAREIDE Age   Women's Coach: BERNTSEN Bjarne
NFF formed: 1902   UEFA: 1954   FIFA: 1908
Red shirts with white and blue trimmings, White shorts, Blue socks or White shirts with blue trimmings, White shorts, White socks

RECENT INTERNATIONAL MATCHES PLAYED BY NORWAY

2005	Opponents	Score		Venue	Comp	Scorers	Att	Referee
17-08	Switzerland	L	0-2	Oslo	Fr		19 623	Vollquartz DEN
3-09	Slovenia	W	3-2	Celje	WCq	Carew [3], Lundekvam [23], Pedersen [92+]	10 055	Medina Cantalejo ESP
7-09	Scotland	L	1-2	Oslo	WCq	Arst [89]	24 904	Hamer LUX
8-10	Moldova	W	1-0	Oslo	WCq	Rushfeldt [50]	23 409	Bennett RSA
12-10	Belarus	W	1-0	Minsk	WCq	Helstad [70]	13 222	Plautz AUT
12-11	Czech Republic	L	0-1	Oslo	WCpo		24 264	Busacca SUI
16-11	Czech Republic	L	0-1	Prague	WCpo		17 464	Poll ENG
2006								
25-01	Mexico	L	1-2	San Francisco	Fr	Vaagen Moen [9]	44 729	Vaughn USA
29-01	USA	L	0-5	Carson	Fr		16 366	Acosta COL
1-03	Senegal	L	1-2	Dakar	Fr	Hagen [41]	45 000	Pare BFA
24-05	Paraguay	D	2-2	Oslo	Fr	Johnsen.F 2 [22 61]	10 227	Olsiak SVK
1-06	Korea Republic	D	0-0	Oslo	Fr		15 487	Verbist BEL
16-08	Brazil	D	1-1	Oslo	Fr	Pedersen [51]	25 062	Dougal SCO
2-09	Hungary	W	4-1	Budapest	ECq	Solskjær 2 [15 54], Strømstad [32], Pedersen [41]	12 283	Braamhaar NED
6-09	Moldova	W	2-0	Oslo	ECq	Strømstad [73], Iversen [79]	23 848	Ristoskov BUL
7-10	Greece	L	0-1	Piraeus	ECq		21 189	Michel SVK
15-11	Serbia	D	1-1	Belgrade	ECq	Carew [22]	15 000	Kasnaferis GRE
2007								
7-02	Croatia	L	1-2	Rijeka	Fr	Moen [86]	8 000	Kalt FRA
24-03	Bosnia-Herzegovina	L	1-2	Oslo	ECq	Carew [50p]	16 987	Riley ENG
28-03	Turkey	D	2-2	Frankfurt	ECq	Brenne [31], Andresen [40]	BCD	Farina ITA
2-06	Malta	W	4-0	Oslo	ECq	Hæsted [31], Helstad [73], Iversen [79], Riise [91+]	16 364	Granat POL
6-06	Hungary	W	4-0	Oslo	ECq	Iversen [22], Braaten [57], Carew 2 [60 78]	19 198	Iturralde Gonzalez ESP
22-08	Argentina	W	2-1	Oslo	Fr	Carew 2 [11p 58]	23 932	Ceferin SVN
8-09	Moldova	W	1-0	Chisinau	ECq	Iversen [48]	10 173	Malek POL
12-09	Greece	D	2-2	Oslo	ECq	Carew [15], Riise [39]	24 080	Busacca SUI
17-10	Bosnia-Herzegovina	W	2-0	Sarajevo	ECq	Hagen [5], Riise.B [74]	1 500	Lannoy FRA
17-11	Turkey	L	1-2	Oslo	ECq	Hagen [12]	23 783	Merk GER
21-11	Malta	W	4-1	Ta'Qali	ECq	Iversen 3 [25 27p 45], Pedersen [75]	7 000	Baskakov RUS
2008								
6-02	Wales	L	0-3	Wrexham	Fr		7 553	McKeon IRL
26-03	Montenegro	L	1-3	Podgorica	Fr	Carew [72]	9 000	Stavrev MKD
28-05	Uruguay	D	2-2	Oslo	Fr	Elyounoussi [55], Riise [84]	12 246	Buttimer IRL

Fr = Friendly match • EC = UEFA EURO 2008 • WC = FIFA World Cup • q = qualifier • po = qualifying play-off

NORWAY NATIONAL TEAM PLAYERS

Player		Ap	G	Club	Date of Birth	Player		Ap	G	Club	Date of Birth
Rune Jarstein	GK	3	0	Rosenborg BK	29 09 1984	Vadim Demidov	MF	1	0	Rosenborg BK	10 10 1986
Håkon Opdal	GK	12	0	SK Brann	11 06 1982	Christian Grindheim	MF	17	0	Heerenveen	17 07 1983
Brede Hangeland	DF	44	0	Fulham	20 06 1981	Per Ciljan Skjelbred	MF	5	0	Rosenborg BK	16 06 1987
Jon Inge Høiland	DF	15	0	Stabæk	20 09 1977	Jan Gunnar Solli	MF	34	1	SK Brann	19 04 1981
Tore Reginiussen	DF	2	0	Tromsø	10 04 1986	Fredrik Strømstad	MF	15	2	Le Mans	20 01 1982
Erik Hagen	DF	28	3	Wigan Athletic	20 07 1975	John Carew	FW	71	21	Aston Villa	5 09 1979
John Arne Riise	DF	71	8	Roma	24 09 1980	Tarik Elyounoussi	FW	1	1	Fredrikstad FK	23 02 1988
Jarl André Storbæk	DF	17	0	Vålerenga IF	21 09 1978	Thorstein Helstad	FW	29	9	SK Brann	28 04 1977
Kjetil Wæhler	DF	3	0	Vålerenga IF	16 03 1976	Daniel Braaten	FW	16	2	Toulouse FC	25 05 1982
Martin Andresen	MF	39	3	Vålerenga IF	2 02 1977	Azar Karadas	FW	10	1	SK Brann	9 08 1981
Eirik Bakke	MF	27	0	SK Brann	13 09 1977	Erik Nevland	FW	6	0	Fulham	10 11 1977
Norway's squad for the May 2008 international against Uruguay						Morten Gamst Pedersen	FW	40	8	Blackburn Rov	8 09 1981

NORWAY NATIONAL TEAM RECORDS AND RECORD SEQUENCES

Records			Sequence records				
Victory	12-0	FIN 1946	Wins	9	1999	Clean sheets	6	Three times
Defeat	0-12	DEN 1917	Defeats	9	1908-1913	Goals scored	21	1929-1933
Player Caps	104	Thorbjørn Svenssen	Undefeated	17	1997-98	Without goal	7	1975-1976
Player Goals	33	Jørgen Juve	Without win	27	1908-18	Goals against	20	1908-1916

MAJOR CITIES/TOWNS

Population '000

	City	Pop
1	Oslo	830
2	Bergen	215
3	Stavanger	176
4	Trondheim	149
5	Drammen	92
6	Skien	85
7	Fredrikstad	70
8	Kristiansand	64
9	Tromsø	53
10	Sarpsborg	50
11	Tønsberg	45
12	Alesund	44
13	Haugesund	40
14	Sandefjord	40
15	Bodø	35
16	Moss	34
17	Arendal	31
18	Hamar	29
19	Horten	24
20	Larvik	23
21	Halden	22
22	Harstad	19
23	Lillehammer	19
24	Molde	18

KINGDOM OF NORWAY; KONGERIKET NORGE

Capital	Oslo	Language	Norwegian	Independence	1905
Population	4 627 926	Area	324 220 km²	% in cities	73%
GDP per cap	$37 800	Dailling code	+47	Internet	.no	GMT +/-	+1

Density	14 per km²		

MEDALS TABLE

		Overall G S B	League G S B	Cup G S B	Europe G S B	City	Stadium	Cap'ty	DoF
1	Rosenborg BK	29 10 1	20 5 1	9 5		Trondheim	Lerkendal	21 166	1917
2	Fredrikstad FK	20 15 1	9 8 1	11 7		Fredrikstad	Nye Fredrikstad Stadion	12 500	1903
3	Viking SK Stavanger	13 7 8	8 2 8	5 5		Stavanger	Viking Stadion	15 300	1899
4	Odd Grenland	12 10	2	12 8		Skien	Odd Stadion	9 008	1894
5	Lillestrøm SK	10 16 3	5 8 3	5 8		Lillestrøm	Aråsen	12 250	1917
6	SFK Lyn Oslo	10 10 4	2 4 4	8 6		Oslo	Ullevaal	25 572	1896
7	SK Brann Bergen	9 12 3	3 5 3	6 7		Bergen	Brann Stadion	17 600	1908
8	FK Skeid Oslo	9 8 1	1 5 1	8 3		Oslo	Bislett	15 400	1915
9	Vålerenga IF	8 4 3	5 2 3	3 2		Oslo	Ullevaal	25 572	1913
10	FK Sarpsborg	6 6 2	2	6 6		Sarpsborg	Sarpsborg	5 500	1903
11	IF Stromsgodset	5 2 3	1 3	4 2		Drammen	Marienlyst	8 500	1907
12	Orn FK Horten	4 4		4 4					
13	Mjøndalen IF	3 7	2	3 5					1910
14	Frigg SK Oslo	3 3		3 3		Oslo			
15	Larvik Turn IF	3 1	3	1		Larvik	Lovisenlund		1906
16	Molde FK	2 7 3	5 3	2 2		Molde	Molde Stadion	11 167	1911
17	FK Bodø-Glimt	2 6	3	2 3		Bodø	Aspmyra	6 100	1916

RECENT LEAGUE AND CUP RECORD

		Championship						Cup		
Year	Champions	Pts	Runners-up	Pts	Third	Pts		Winners	Score	Runners-up
1995	Rosenborg BK	62	Molde FK	47	FK Bodø/Glimt	43		Rosenborg BK	1-1 3-1	SK Brann
1996	Rosenborg BK	59	Lillestrøm	46	Viking SK	43		Tromsø IL	2-1	FK Bodø/Glimt
1997	Rosenborg BK	61	SK Brann	50	Strømsgodset	46		Vålerenga IF	4-2	Strømsgodset
1998	Rosenborg BK	63	Molde FK	54	Stabæk	53		Stabæk	3-1	Rosenborg BK
1999	Rosenborg BK	56	Molde FK	50	SK Brann	49		Rosenborg BK	2-0	SK Brann
2000	Rosenborg BK	54	SK Brann	47	Viking SK	45		Odd Grenland	2-1	Viking SK
2001	Rosenborg BK	57	Lillestrøm	56	Viking SK	49		Viking SK	3-0	Bryne FK
2002	Rosenborg BK	56	Molde FK	50	Lyn Oslo	47		Vålerenga	1-0	Odd Grenland
2003	Rosenborg BK	61	FK Bodø/Glimt	47	Stabæk	42		Rosenborg BK	3-1	FK Bodø/Glimt
2004	Rosenborg BK	48	Vålerenga IF	48	SK Brann	40		SK Brann	4-1	Lyn Oslo
2005	Vålerenga IF	46	IK Start	45	Lyn Oslo	44		Molde FK	4-2	Lillestrøm SK
2006	Rosenborg BK	53	SK Brann	46	Vålerenga IF	44		Fredrikstad FK	3-0	Sandefjord Fotball
2007	SK Brann	54	Stabæk	48	Viking SK	47		Lillestrøm SK	2-0	SK Haugesund

NORWAY 2007

TIPPELIGAEN

	Pl	W	D	L	F	A	Pts	Brann	Stabæk	Viking	Lillestrøm	Rosenborg	Tromsø	Vålerenga	Fredrikstad	Lyn	Strømgodset	Aalesunds	Odd	Start	Sandefjord
SK Brann †	26	17	3	6	59	39	54		3-0	5-2	3-1	3-2	2-1	4-1	2-2	3-1	3-1	2-1	4-0	2-2	1-0
Stabæk Fotball	26	14	6	6	53	35	48	0-1		2-1	3-1	2-1	5-0	2-2	0-2	3-2	3-2	4-2	1-0	1-1	1-1
Viking FK	26	13	6	7	50	40	47	3-1	2-1		1-1	1-1	3-1	2-1	2-2	4-2	3-0	3-0	2-1	2-0	0-0
Lillestrøm SK	26	13	7	6	47	28	44	1-5	1-1	4-1		4-1	0-3	0-1	3-0	3-1	2-0	7-0	1-1	1-0	1-1
Rosenborg BK	26	12	5	9	53	39	41	3-0	3-0	4-2	1-1		4-3	2-0	1-1	3-0	1-2	2-2	4-1	4-1	2-0
Tromsø IL	26	12	4	10	45	44	40	3-0	0-1	2-1	2-1	2-1		1-0	4-1	2-1	2-2	0-2	2-4	1-1	2-1
Vålerenga IF	26	10	6	10	34	34	36	2-0	1-1	1-3	1-3	2-1	2-2		2-0	0-0	0-0	2-1	1-1	3-2	2-0
Fredrikstad FK	26	9	9	8	37	40	36	0-4	1-2	2-0	0-0	4-3	2-1	1-0		3-1	1-1	2-1	1-1	3-0	2-0
FC Lyn Oslo	26	10	4	12	43	46	34	6-0	3-2	2-3	0-4	2-1	4-3	3-1	0-0		1-0	0-0	3-1	4-1	3-0
IF Strømgodset	26	8	6	12	34	47	30	2-4	0-5	1-2	1-1	1-1	1-2	1-2	2-1	1-1		0-4	2-1	3-2	4-0
Aalesunds SK	26	9	3	14	40	56	30	2-1	1-4	0-2	1-3	1-2	2-3	1-0	3-3	3-1	3-2		2-1	2-4	4-1
Odd Grenland	26	8	3	15	33	43	27	0-2	1-5	1-3	0-1	1-2	0-1	1-4	2-0	2-0	0-1	3-0		2-0	4-0
IK Start	26	6	8	12	34	44	26	1-1	1-1	1-1	0-0	2-1	1-1	1-0	3-1	0-1	2-3	1-2	1-2		3-1
Sandefjord Fotball	26	4	4	18	26	53	16	2-3	2-3	4-1	0-2	1-2	2-1	1-3	2-2	3-1	0-1	3-0	0-2	1-3	

9/04/2007 - 3/11/2007 • † Qualified for the UEFA Champions League • ‡ Qualified for the UEFA Cup • Play-off: Odd Grenland 0-1 2-3 **Bodø-Glimt**
Top scorer: Thorsten Helstad, Brann 22; Daniel Nannskog, Stabæk 19; Peter Ijeh, Viking 18; Veigar Páll Gunnarsson, Stabæk 15

NORWAY 2007
ADECCOLIGAEN (2)

	Pl	W	D	L	F	A	Pts
Molde FK	30	22	3	5	62	28	69
Hamarkameratene	30	21	5	4	82	36	68
FK Bodø-Glimt	30	17	4	9	66	39	55
Kongsvinger IL	30	16	5	9	56	42	53
FK Moss	30	15	8	7	46	37	53
Bryne FK	30	14	7	9	57	38	49
Sogndal IL	30	13	5	12	48	44	44
SK Haugesund	30	10	9	11	49	52	39
Notodden FK	30	11	3	16	49	54	36
Hønefoss BK	30	8	11	11	34	52	35
Raufoss	30	10	5	15	37	61	35
Løv-Ham Bergen	30	9	6	15	39	44	33
Sparta Sarpsborg	30	8	8	14	50	52	32
Tromsdalen UIL	30	7	8	15	37	56	29
Skeid Fotball	30	4	8	18	32	60	20
FK Mandalskameratene	30	4	7	19	43	92	19

9/04/2007 - 4/11/2007

NM SAS BRAATHENS CUPEN 2007

Round of 16		Quarter-finals		Semi-finals		Final	
Lillestrøm SK *	1						
Aalesunds SK	0	Lillestrøm SK	1				
FK Bodø-Glimt	0	FC Lyn Oslo *	0				
FC Lyn Oslo *	1			Lillestrøm SK *	2		
IF Strømgodset *	4			Stabæk Fotball	0		
Notodden FK	1	IF Strømgodset *	2				
Tromsø IL	0	Stabæk Fotball	4				
Stabæk Fotball *	3					Lillestrøm SK	2
Odd Grenland	2					SK Haugesund	0
Rosenborg BK *	1	Odd Grenland *	2				
SK Brann	0	Viking FK	1				
Viking FK *	2			Odd Grenland	0		
Nybergsund-Trysil *	3			SK Haugesund *	1		
Vålerenga IF	1	Nybergsund-Trysil	1				
IK Start *	0	SK Haugesund *	6				
SK Haugesund	1						

CUP FINAL
Ullevaal, Oslo
11-11-2007, Att: 24 361, Ref: Staberg

Scorer - Olivier Occean 2 [57 90]

* Home team • ‡ Qualified for the UEFA Cup

NZL – NEW ZEALAND

NATIONAL TEAM RECORD
JULY 10TH 2006 TO JULY 12TH 2010

PL	W	D	L	F	A	%
7	3	2	2	10	13	53.3

FIFA/COCA-COLA WORLD RANKING

1993	1994	1995	1996	1997	1998	1999	2000	2001	2002	2003	2004	2005	2006	2007	High	
77	99	102	132	120	103	100	91	84	49	88	95	120	131	95	47	08/02

2007–2008											Low	
08/07	09/07	10/07	11/07	12/07	01/08	02/08	03/08	04/08	05/08	06/08	07/08	156	09/07
149	156	128	95	95	94	90	91	77	78	88	112		

New Zealand's 2010 FIFA World Cup campaign got off to the perfect start with three consecutive wins in the Oceania group stage, a round robin tournament that also acts as the 2008 Oceania Nations Cup. The winners will qualify for the 2009 Confederations Cup in South Africa but will have to play-off against the 5th placed Asian team to book a place at the World Cup finals, leaving the Kiwis with an uphill struggle to make it to South Africa. With Australia in the final round of Asian qualifying, the possibility of the two facing each other again - or even of both making it to the finals - remained. Waitakere United made an historic first appearance in the FIFA Club World

INTERNATIONAL HONOURS
Qualified for the FIFA World Cup finals 1982   Oceania Nations Cup 1973 1998 2002   Oceania Women's Championship 1983 1991
Oceania Youth Championship 1980 1992   Oceania U-17 Championship 1997

Cup in Japan in December 2007 but they unsurprisingly lost 1-0 to Iran's Sepahan in the preliminary round. Waitakere will be back in the 2008 tournament after retaining their O-League title, although it was a close run thing after they lost 3-1 to Kossa of the Solomon Islands in the first leg of the final in Honiara. They made no mistake in the return, however, winning 5-0. Three weeks earlier Waitakere had broken Auckland City's firm grip on the New Zealand Football Championship, winning the title for the first time after beating Team Wellington 2-0 in the final.

THE FIFA BIG COUNT OF 2006

	Male	Female		Total
Number of players	164 667	34 090	Referees and Assistant Referees	800
Professionals	25		Admin, Coaches, Technical, Medical	19 000
Amateurs 18+	12 067		Number of clubs	325
Youth under 18	79 565		Number of teams	7 524
Unregistered	49 500		Clubs with women's teams	17
Total players	198 757		Players as % of population	4.88%

New Zealand Football (NZF)
North Harbour Stadium, Oteha Valley Road, PO Box 301, 043 Albany, New Zealand
Tel +64 9 4140175   Fax +64 9 4140176
tracy.brady@nzfootball.co.nz   www.nzfootball.co.nz
President: MORRIS John   General Secretary: KEARNS Paula
Vice-President: TBD   Treasurer: TBD   Media Officer: SCOTT Jamie
Men's Coach: HERBERT Ricki   Women's Coach: JONES Allan
NZS formed: 1891   OFC: 1966   FIFA: 1948
White shirts with black trimmings, White shorts, White socks

RECENT INTERNATIONAL MATCHES PLAYED BY NEW ZEALAND

2002	Opponents		Score	Venue	Comp	Scorers	Att	Referee
27-05	Scotland	D	1-1	Edinburgh	Fr	Nelsen [47]	10 016	Ingvarsson SWE
8-06	USA	L	1-2	Richmond	Fr	Coveny [23]	9 116	Liu CAN
18-06	Japan	L	0-3	Paris	CCr1		36 038	Codjia BEN
20-06	Colombia	L	1-3	Lyon	CCr1	De Gregorio [27]	22 811	Batres GUA
22-06	France	L	0-5	Paris	CCr1		36 842	Moradi IRN
12-10	Iran	L	0-3	Tehran	AO		40 000	Kousa SYR
2004								
29-05	Australia	L	0-1	Adelaide	WCq		12 100	Larsen DEN
31-05	Solomon Islands	W	3-0	Adelaide	WCq	Fisher [36], Oughton [81], Lines [90]	217	Iturralde Gonzalez ESP
2-06	Vanuatu	L	2-4	Adelaide	WCq	Coveny 2 [61 75]	356	Farina ITA
4-06	Tahiti	W	10-0	Adelaide	WCq	Coveny 3 [6 38 46+], Fisher 3 [16 22 63], Jones [72] Oughton [74], Nelsen 2 [82 87]	200	Shield AUS
6-06	Fiji	W	2-0	Adelaide	WCq	Bunce [8], Coveny [56]	300	Larsen DEN
2005								
9-06	Australia	L	0-1	London	Fr		9 023	Dean ENG
2006								
19-02	Malaysia	W	1-0	Christchurch	Fr	Old [87]	10 100	O'Leary NZL
23-02	Malaysia	W	2-1	Albany	Fr	Banks [18], Barron [88]	8 702	Fox NZL
25-04	Chile	L	1-4	Rancagua	Fr	Smeltz [14]	8 000	Osorio CHI
27-04	Chile	L	0-1	La Calera	Fr			Acosta CHI
24-05	Hungary	L	0-2	Budapest	Fr		5 000	Hrinak SVK
27-05	Georgia	W	3-1	Altenkirchen	Fr	Coveny 2 [35 53], Killen [37]	1 000	
31-05	Estonia	D	1-1	Tallinn	Fr	Hay [27]	3 000	Rasmussen DEN
4-06	Brazil	L	0-4	Geneva	Fr		32 000	Laperriere SUI
2007								
7-02	Tahiti	D	0-0	Auckland	Fr			Hester NZL
24-03	Costa Rica	L	0-4	San Jose	Fr		15 000	Rodriguez CRC
28-03	Venezuela	L	0-5	Maracaibo	Fr		12 000	
26-05	Wales	D	2-2	Wrexham	Fr	Smeltz 2 [2 24]	7 819	Skjerven DEN
17-10	Fiji	W	2-0	Lautoka	WCq	Vicelich [37], Smeltz [86]	6 000	Marrufo USA
17-11	Vanuatu	W	2-1	Port Vila	WCq	Smeltz [52], Mulligan [93+]	8 000	Minan PNG
21-11	Vanuatu	W	4-1	Wellington	WCq	Mulligan 2 [14 81], Smeltz 2 [29p 34]	2 500	Jacques TAH
2008								

No internationals played in 2008 before August

Fr = Friendly match • OC = OFC Oceania Nations Cup • CC = FIFA Confederations Cup • AO = Asia/Oceania Challenge • WC = FIFA World Cup
q = qualifier • r1 = first round group • sf = semi-final • f = final

NEW ZEALAND NATIONAL TEAM PLAYERS

	Player		Ap	G	Club	Date of Birth		Player		Ap	G	Club	Date of Birth
1	Mark Paston	GK	17	0	Wellington P'nix	13 12 1976	12	James Pritchett	DF	8	0	Auckland City	1 07 1982
2	Jeremy Christie	MF	12	0	Wellington P'nix	22 05 1983	13	Jarrod Smith	FW	10	0	Toronto FC	20 06 1984
3	Tony Lochhead	DF	16	0	Wellington P'nix	12 01 1982	14	Chris James	MF	8	1	Tampere United	4 07 1987
4	David Mulligan	DF	17	3	Unattached	24 03 1982	15	Ben Sigmund	DF	5	0	Wellington P'nix	3 02 1981
5	Andrew Boyens	DF	5	0	RB New York	18 09 1983	16	Duncan Oughton	DF	21	2	Columbus Crew	14 06 1977
6	Ryan Nelson	DF	29	5	Blackburn Rov	18 10 1977	17	Jeff Campbell	MF	19	3	East Coast Bays	25 08 1979
7	Ivan Vicelich	MF	63	7	RKC Waalwijk	3 09 1976	18	Jacob Spoonley	GK	0	0	Miramar Rangers	3 03 1987
8	Tim Brown	MF	14	0	Wellington P'nix	6 03 1981	19	Daniel Ellensohn	FW	1	0	Western Suburbs	9 08 1985
9	Shane Smeltz	FW	19	7	Wellington P'nix	29 09 1981	20	Christian Bouckenooghe	MF	38	3	RS Waasland	7 02 1977
10	Chris Killen	FW	27	15	Celtic	8 10 1981	21	Simon Elliott	MF	54	8	Unattached	10 06 1974
11	Leo Bertos	MF	21	0	Wellington P'nix	20 12 1981	22	Steven Old	DF	17	0	Macarthur Rams	17 02 1986
	New Zealand's squad in June 2008						23	Glen Moss	GK	7	0	Wellington P'nix	19 01 1983

NEW ZEALAND NATIONAL TEAM RECORDS AND RECORD SEQUENCES

Records			Sequence records					
Victory	13-0	FIJ 1981	Wins	9	1951-1954	Clean sheets	10	1981
Defeat	0-10	AUS 1936	Defeats	16	1927-1951	Goals scored	22	1951-1967
Player Caps	71	Vaughan Coveny	Undefeated	11	1981	Without goal	5	1997-1998
Player Goals	30	Vaughan Coveny	Without win	16	1927-1951	Goals against	19	1927-1951

NEW ZEALAND COUNTRY INFORMATION

Capital	Wellington	Independence	1907 from the UK	GDP per Capita	$21 600
Population	3 993 817	Status	Commonnwealth	GNP Ranking	48
Area km²	268 680	Language	English, Maori	Dialling code	+64
Population density	15 per km²	Literacy rate	99%	Internet code	.nz
% in urban areas	86%	Main religion	Christian	GMT +/–	+12
Towns/Cities ('000)	Aukland 417; Manukau 383; Christchurch 364; North Shore 207; Wellington 179; Waitakere 166; Hamilton 152; Dunedin 114; Tauranga 110; Lower Hutt 101; Palmerston North 75; Hastings 61				
Neighbours (km)	South Pacific Ocean 15 134				
Main stadia	Ericsson Stadium – Auckland 50 000; North Harbour Stadium – Albany, Auckland 25 000				

NEW ZEALAND 2007-08

NEW ZEALAND FOOTBALL CHAMPIONSHIP (NZFC)

	Pl	W	D	L	F	A	Pts	Waitakere	Auckland	Wellington	Hawkes Bay	Waikato	Manawatu	Otago	Canterbury
Waitakere United †	21	16	3	2	51	14	51		2-0 1-0	1-2	5-0 2-0	2-0 2-0	3-1	4-0	1-0
Auckland City †	21	16	2	3	44	16	50	1-1		2-0 3-2	2-0	2-0 2-0	4-1 4-1	3-0 2-0	4-1
Team Wellington	21	15	2	4	51	21	47	1-5 0-1	1-1		4-3	2-0 2-0	3-1	1-0 3-1	3-0 2-0
Hawkes Bay United	21	8	5	8	29	33	29	0-1	0-1 2-0	2-2 0-3		0-0 2-2	0-0	3-1 2-1	2-1
Waikato	21	5	5	11	24	34	20	0-1	2-3	1-2	1-1		3-2 4-5	3-1 0-2	3-1 1-1
YoungHeart Manawatu	21	5	2	14	32	57	17	3-2 1-2	1-3	0-8 0-4	1-3 2-3	0-1		6-0	3-2 1-5
Otago United	21	3	4	14	13	43	13	1-1 2-2	0-2	0-5	1-2	0-2	0-0 1-0		0-0 2-0
Canterbury United	21	3	3	15	22	48	12	1-3 1-9	1-2 0-3	0-1	1-3 2-1	1-1	2-3	2-0	

3/11/2007 - 6/04/2008 • Top three qualified for the play-offs • † Qualified for the OFC Champions Cup
Semi-final: Auckland City 3-4 **Team Wellington**; Grand Final: **Waitakere United** 2-0 Team Wellington (Douglas Field, Henderson, 20-04-2008, Att: 2011, Ref: Hester. Scorers - Karl Whalen OG [45], Allan Pearce [66] for Waitakere) • Top scorers: Graham Little, Wellington 12; Gouzalo Nieres, Manawatu 12; Luis Corrales, Wellington 10; Allan Pearce, Waitakere 10; Benjamin Totori, Waitakere 10

CHATHAM CUP 2007

Round of sixteen		Quarter-finals		Semi-finals		Final	
Central United	3 4p						
East Coast Bays	3 3p	Central United *	2				
Metro	2	Eastern Suburbs	1				
Eastern Suburbs	6			Central United *	3		
Hamilton Wanderers	1			North Shore United	1		
Papakura City *	0	Hamilton Wanderers	1				
Manurewa	1	North Shore United *	3				
North Shore United *	2					Central United	0 10p
Caversham	5					Western Suburbs	0 9p
Roslyn Wakari *	2	Caversham *	1				
Western	0	Nomads United	0				
Nomads United *	3			Caversham *	1		
Miramar Rangers *	5			Western Suburbs	3		
Napier City Rovers	0	Miramar Rangers	0				
Wairarapa United	1	Western Suburbs *	1				
Western Suburbs	2						

CUP FINAL

Kiwitea Street, Auckland
2-09-2007, Att: 2000,
Ref: Stoltenkamp

* Home team

RECENT LEAGUE AND CUP RECORD

	Championship				Chatham Cup		
Year	Champions	Score	Runners-up		Winners	Score	Runners-up
1999	Central United	3-1	Dunedin Technical		Dunedin Technical	4-0	Waitakere City
2000	Napier City Rovers	0-0 4-2p	University Mt Wellington		Napier City Rovers	4-1	Central United
2001	Central United	3-2	Miramar Rangers		University Mt Wellington	3-3 5-4p	Central United
2002	Miramar Rangers	3-1	Napier City Rovers		Napier City Rovers	2-0	Tauranga City United
2003	Miramar Rangers	3-2	East Auckland		University Mt Wellington	3-1	Melville United
2004	No tournament held				Miramar Rangers	1-0	Waitakere City
2005	Auckland City	3-2	Waitakere United		Central United	2-1	Palmerston North Marist
2006	Auckland City	3-3 4-3	Canterbury United		Western Suburbs	0-0 3-0p	Eastern Suburbs
2007	Auckland City	3-2	Waitakere United		Central United	0-0 10-9p	Western Suburbs
2008	Waitakere United	2-0	Team Wellington				

OMA – OMAN

NATIONAL TEAM RECORD
JULY 10TH 2006 TO JULY 12TH 2010

PL	W	D	L	F	A	%
40	19	14	7	56	38	65

FIFA/COCA-COLA WORLD RANKING

1993	1994	1995	1996	1997	1998	1999	2000	2001	2002	2003	2004	2005	2006	2007	High	
97	71	98	91	81	58	92	106	91	96	62	56	91	72	84	**50**	08/04

2007–2008												Low	
08/07	09/07	10/07	11/07	12/07	01/08	02/08	03/08	04/08	05/08	06/08	07/08	**117**	07/03
76	79	81	76	84	92	98	86	80	79	81	86		

Since the Oman Football Association parted company with Czech coach Milan Macala in 2007, there has been a revolving door policy with respect to head coaches of the national team - and the form of the side has suffered as a result. Gabriel Calderon was deemed surplus to requirements after Oman failed to progress beyond the first round at the 2007 AFC Asian Cup while his replacement, Julio Cesar Ribas, was also removed from his position after the nation's elimination from the 2010 FIFA World Cup qualifiers. The country's hopes of reaching the World Cup in South Africa for the first time came to an end when they finished third in their group behind Japan and a Bahrain side

INTERNATIONAL HONOURS
AFC U-17 Championship 1996 2000

coached by Macala. Well-travelled Frenchman Claude Le Roy is the latest coach to be handed the task of fulfilling Omani expectations and his first major challenge will be attempting to win the Gulf Cup following successive runners-up finishes in 2004 and 2006. With the success of the national team in recent years, an increasing number of the country's top stars are playing abroad, with goalkeeper Ali Al Habsi the country's highest profile star on the books of English Premier League side Bolton Wanderers. In domestic football Al Urooba won the championship for the first time in six years while Sur beat Muscat on penalties in the Sultan Qaboos Cup Final.

THE FIFA BIG COUNT OF 2006

	Male	Female		Total
Number of players	57 610	0	Referees and Assistant Referees	105
Professionals	0		Admin, Coaches, Technical, Medical	500
Amateurs 18+	3 010		Number of clubs	43
Youth under 18	5 600		Number of teams	129
Unregistered	11 000		Clubs with women's teams	0
Total players	57 610		Players as % of population	1.86%

Oman Football Association (OFA)
Ruwi High Street, PO Box 3462, Ruwi 112, Oman
Tel +968 24 787636   Fax +968 24 787632
omanfa@omantel.net.om   www.none
President: AL-BUSAIDI Sayyid Khalid Hamad Hamoud   General Secretary: AL-KISHRY Taha Suliman
Vice-President: AL-WAHAIBI Sheikh Salim Said   Treasurer: TBD   Media Officer: AL RAWAHI Aiman
Men's Coach: LE ROY Claude   Women's Coach: None
OFA formed: 1978   AFC: 1979   FIFA: 1980
White shirts, White shorts, White socks

RECENT INTERNATIONAL MATCHES PLAYED BY OMAN

2006	Opponents	Score		Venue	Comp	Scorers	Att	Referee
6-02	Singapore	W	1-0	Doha	Fr	Salah [90]		
13-02	Iraq	W	1-0	Wattayah	Fr	Khalifa Ayel [77]	11 000	Shaban KUW
22-02	United Arab Emirates	L	0-1	Dubai	ACq		15 000	Al Ghamdi KSA
1-03	Jordan	W	3-0	Wattayah	ACq	Saleh [7], Sulaiman [18], Al Maghni [54]	11 000	Irmatov UZB
16-08	Pakistan	W	4-1	Quetta	ACq	Bader Mubarak 2 [15p 35], Amad Ali [27], Al Ajmi [90]	4 000	Torky IRN
1-09	Syria	W	3-0	Muscat	Fr	Al Ajmi [41], Al Touqi [59], Sulaiman [65]		
6-09	Pakistan	W	5-0	Muscat	ACq	Amad Ali [7], Fouzi Bashir 2 [36 58], Al Ajmi [47+], Al Touqi [88]	10 000	Nema IRQ
11-10	UAE	W	2-1	Muscat	ACq	Hassan Yousuf [24], Al Ajmi [28]	28 000	Huang Junjie CHN
8-11	Bahrain	D	1-1	Muscat	Fr	Al Touqi [52]		
15-11	Jordan	L	0-3	Amman	ACq		3 000	Najm LIB
2007								
13-01	Qatar	D	1-1	Doha	Fr	Sulaiman [26]		
17-01	UAE	W	2-1	Abu Dhabi	GCr1	Fouzi Bashir [36], Sulaiman [50]		
20-01	Kuwait	W	2-1	Abu Dhabi	GCr1	Sulaiman [8], Hashim Saleh [84]		
23-01	Yemen	W	2-1	Abu Dhabi	GCr1	Al Touqi [1], Al Bufasi [88]		
27-01	Bahrain	W	1-0	Abu Dhabi	GCsf	Al Maimani [54]		
30-01	UAE	L	0-1	Abu Dhabi	GCf			
24-06	Indonesia	W	1-0	Jakarta	Fr	Ahmed Hadid [57]		
28-06	Korea DPR	D	2-2	Singapore	Fr	Ahmed Mubarak [48], Al Ajmi [52]. W 4-3p		
1-07	Saudi Arabia	D	1-1	Singapore	Fr	Fawzi Bashir [56]. W 3-1p		
8-07	Australia	D	1-1	Bangkok	ACr1	Badar Mubarak [32]	5 000	Maillet SEY
12-07	Thailand	L	0-2	Bangkok	ACr1		19 000	LI Gi Young KOR
16-07	Iraq	D	0-0	Bangkok	ACr1		500	Maillet SEY
17-09	Qatar	D	1-1	Doha	Fr	Sulaiman [31]		
2-10	Maldives	W	1-0	Muscat	Fr	Mohamed Mubarak [27]		
8-10	Nepal	W	2-0	Muscat	WCq	Fouzi Bashir [5], Hassan Yousuf [23]	15 000	Al Marzouqi UAE
28-10	Nepal	W	2-0	Kathmandu	WCq	Hashim Saleh [28], Al Hinai [54]	10 000	Tongkhan THA
21-11	Kenya	D	2-2	Muscat	Fr	Al Ajmi [22], Khalifa Ayil [59]		
22-11	Kenya	D	1-1	Muscat	Fr	Al Shamsi [55]		
11-12	Jordan	L	0-3	Muscat	Fr			
16-12	Tajikistan	W	4-2	Muscat	Fr	Taqi 2 [34 51], Imtiaq Ma'athi [67], Al Maghni [89]		
2008								
27-01	Singapore	W	2-0	Muscat	Fr	Sulaiman [6], Hassan Yousuf [8]		
30-01	Kuwait	D	1-1	Muscat	Fr	Khalifa Ayil [26]		
6-02	Bahrain	L	0-1	Muscat	WCq		28 000	Lee Gi Young KOR
19-03	UAE	D	1-1	Muscat	Fr	Talal Khalfan [3]		
26-03	Thailand	W	1-0	Bangkok	WCq	Al Ajmi [1]	40 000	Torky IRN
24-04	Liberia	W	1-0	Muscat	Fr	Al Dhabit [44]		
27-04	Kyrgyzstan	W	2-0	Muscat	Fr	Al Mukhaini [43], Younis Mubarak [70]		
3-05	Yemen	D	0-0	Muscat	Fr			
10-05	Syria	L	1-2	Damascus	Fr	Rafat OG [11]		
18-05	Turkmenistan	W	2-1	Nizwa	Fr	Sulaiman 2 [26 68]		
2-06	Japan	L	0-3	Yokohama	WCq		46 764	Bashir SIN
7-06	Japan	D	1-1	Muscat	WCq	Ahmed Mubarak [12]	6 500	Mohd Salleh MAS
14-06	Bahrain	D	1-1	Manama	WCq	Al Ajmi [72]	25 000	Al Fadhli KUW
22-06	Thailand	W	2-1	Muscat	WCq	Amad Ali 2 [58 84]	3 000	Mujghef JOR

Fr = Friendly match • GC = Gulf Cup • WG = West Asian Games • AC = AFC Asian Cup • WC = FIFA World Cup
q = qualifier • r1 = first round group • sf = semi-final • f = final

OMAN NATIONAL TEAM RECORDS AND RECORD SEQUENCES

Records			Sequence records				
Victory	12-0	LAO 2001	Wins	7	2003	Clean sheets	5	2001
Defeat	0-21	LBY 1966	Defeats	17	1976-1984	Goals scored	11	1994, 2001
Player Caps	n/a		Undefeated	10	2003	Without goal	8	1965-1976
Player Goals	n/a		Without win	29	1965-1984	Goals against	28	1965-1984

SULTANATE OF OMAN; SALTANAT UMAN

Capital	Muscat	Language	Arabic		Independence	1650
Population	3 204 897	Area	212 460 km²	Density 13 per km²	% in cities	13%
GDP per cap	$13 100	Dialling code	+968	Internet .om	GMT + / -	+4

MAJOR CITIES/TOWNS
Population '000

1	Muscat	1 090
2	Salalah	190
3	As-Suwaiq	128
4	Suhar	125
5	Ibri	118
6	Saham	105
7	Barka	100
8	Ar-Rustaq	96
9	Al-Buraymi	91
10	Sur	85
11	Nizwa	84
12	Al-Mudaybi	80
13	Al Musanaah	79
14	Bahla	64
15	Bani Bu Ali	63
16	Al Khaboora	61

The Muscat metroplolitan area consists of:

Seeb	286
Matrah	214
Bawshar	190
Qurayyat	51
Al Amarat	46
Muscat	25

MEDALS TABLE

		Overall			Lge	Cup	Asia			City	Stadium	Cap'ty	DoF
		G	S	B	G	G	G	S	B				
1	Dhofar	16			9	7				Salalah	Al Saada Sport Complex	12 000	
2	Fanja	15			7	8				Fanja			
3	Al Nasr	9			5	4				Salalah	Al Saada Sport Complex	12 000	
4	Al Ahli	6			1	5				Muscat			
5	Sur	5			2	3				Sur	Sur Sports Complex	8 000	1962
6	Al Urooba	5			3	2				Sur	Sur Sports Complex	8 000	1970
7	Muscat (incl Rowi)	4			3	1				Muscat	Sultan Qaboos Sports Complex	39 000	
8	Oman Club	3	1		1	2	1			Muscat	Oman Stadium	5 000	1942
9	Seeb	3				3				Seeb	Seeb Stadium	8 000	1972
10	Al Nahda	1			1					Muscat			
11	Al Tali'aa	1				1							1941

RECENT LEAGUE AND CUP RECORD

	Championship						Cup		
Year	Champions	Pts	Runners-up	Pts	Third	Pts	Winners	Score	Runners-up
2000	Al Urooba	42	Al Nasr	36	Seeb	31	Al Nasr	2-1	Al Urooba
2001	Dhofar	41	Al Urooba	36	Seeb	36	Al Urooba	1-0	Al Nasr
2002	Al Urooba	38	Sur	37	Seeb	30	Al Nasr	2-1	Dhofar
2003	Rowi	65	Dhofar	63	Al Nasr	55	Rowi	2-0	Seeb
2004	Al Nasr	46	Muscat	45	Al Urooba	41	Dhofar	1-0	Muscat
2005	Dhofar	46	Al Urooba	44	Muscat	40	Al Nasr	3-1	Seeb
2006	Muscat	45	Al Nahda	43	Al Tali'aa	43	Dhofar	2-1	Sur
2007	Al Nahda	43	Al Urooba	41	Dhofar	36	Sur	0-0 5-3p	Muscat
2008	Al Urooba	45	Dhofar	38	Khaboora	34			

Muscat were formed by the merger of Rowi and Bustan

OMAN 2007–08

PREMIER LEAGUE

	Pl	W	D	L	F	A	Pts	Al Urooba	Dhofar	Khaboora	Seeb	Al Nasr	Sur	Al Nahda	Muscat	Al Tali'aa	Al Wahda	Oman	Bahla
Al Urooba	22	13	6	3	36	16	45		1-1	1-1	4-0	0-1	0-0	4-1	2-0	1-1	2-0	4-2	0-1
Dhofar	22	10	8	4	32	16	38	2-2		0-1	3-0	1-1	2-0	0-0	0-1	2-1	2-0	3-1	2-0
Khaboora	22	9	7	6	29	20	34	1-2	2-1		0-0	1-1	2-2	0-0	2-0	1-0	2-3	3-0	3-1
Seeb	22	8	9	5	25	20	33	0-1	2-0	1-1		2-0	1-1	0-1	0-0	1-0	1-1	2-0	5-2
Al Nasr	22	8	9	5	19	19	33	0-1	1-1	0-2	0-0		1-0	2-1	1-0	2-1	2-2	0-0	1-0
Sur	22	7	10	5	28	23	31	0-0	0-0	2-1	0-1	1-0		0-0	5-2	0-1	2-1	2-0	2-1
Al Nahda	22	7	7	8	20	20	28	2-0	0-1	1-0	1-1	0-2	1-1		2-0	0-0	3-4	1-0	0-0
Muscat	22	7	6	9	18	27	27	1-4	0-0	2-1	0-1	0-0	1-1	1-0		1-3	1-2	1-1	1-0
Al Tali'aa	22	7	5	10	23	26	26	0-1	1-4	1-0	2-1	0-0	2-2	0-2	2-0		1-0	0-2	4-1
Al Wahda	22	6	7	9	25	34	25	0-1	1-3	1-1	0-3	0-1	1-1	2-1	2-2	0-2		1-1	1-0
Oman Club	22	5	6	11	27	39	21	2-4	0-0	1-2	1-1	4-1	2-4	2-1	0-1	3-2	0-0		4-3
Bahla	22	3	4	15	23	45	13	0-1	1-4	0-2	2-2	2-2	3-2	0-2	0-2	1-1	2-3	3-1	

7/11/2007 - 9/05/2008 • ‡ Qualified for the AFC Cup • Match in bold awarded

SULTAN QABOOS CUP 2007

Round of 16		Quarter-finals		Semi-finals		Final	
Sur *	2 2						
Al Ittihad	0 0	**Sur**	1 2				
Majees	2 0	Khaboora *	1 1				
Khaboora *	2 2			**Sur ***	1 2		
Al Urooba *	1 2			Al Nasr	1 2		
Seeb	0 2	Al Urooba	1 0				
Boshar	0 2	**Al Nasr ***	2 1				
Al Nasr *	4 4					**Sur**	0 5p
Al Nahda *	1 1					Muscat	0 3p
Al Tali'aa	1 0	**Al Nahda ***	1 2				
Saham	2 0	Bahla	1 2			CUP FINAL	
Bahla *	3 0			Al Nahda *	0 0		
Al Wahda *	2 2			**Muscat**	0 2		
Mirbat	2 1	Al Wahda *	1 0			26-11-2007	
Oman Club	0 0	**Muscat**	1 2				
Muscat *	3 3						

* Home team in the first leg • ‡ Qualified for the AFC Cup

PAK – PAKISTAN

NATIONAL TEAM RECORD
JULY 10TH 2006 TO JULY 12TH 2010

PL	W	D	L	F	A	%
14	3	1	10	20	43	25

FIFA/COCA-COLA WORLD RANKING

1993	1994	1995	1996	1997	1998	1999	2000	2001	2002	2003	2004	2005	2006	2007	High
142	158	160	173	153	168	179	190	181	178	168	177	158	164	163	**141** 02/94

2007–2008												Low
08/07	09/07	10/07	11/07	12/07	01/08	02/08	03/08	04/08	05/08	06/08	07/08	**192** 05/01
178	179	181	166	163	163	164	166	161	161	160	169	

In recent years, Pakistan have cast their net into the diaspora in an attempt to boost the nation's lowly standing on the international scene. England-born defender Zesh Rahman became the first player born overseas to feature for Pakistan back in 2005 and since then the Pakistan Football Federation have sought to strengthen the squad further. Adnan Ahmed, who plays his club football for Tranmere Rovers, was the latest to sign up alongside others who feature for clubs at lower league levels in England, Wales and Sweden. To date though, the move has borne little fruit with Pakistan failing to qualify for the finals of the 2008 AFC Challenge Cup in neighbouring India – a

INTERNATIONAL HONOURS
South Asian Federation Games 1989 1991 2004

7-1 thrashing at the hands of Sri Lanka put paid to their hopes. They also lost out in the group phase of the South Asian Football Federation Championship played two months later in the Maldives. Pakistan's 2010 FIFA World Cup qualifying campaign was also cut embarrassingly short, with Asian champions Iraq winning 7-0 in Lahore. Domestically, WAPDA won the domestic title by a single point from defending champions Pakistan Army while Pakistan Navy claimed the National Challenge Cup. However, despite hosting the 2007 AFC President's Cup, Army failed to make the most of the opportunity after finishing bottom of their first round group.

THE FIFA BIG COUNT OF 2006

	Male	Female		Total
Number of players	2 975 400	0	Referees and Assistant Referees	2 500
Professionals	0		Admin, Coaches, Technical, Medical	7 400
Amateurs 18+	40 700		Number of clubs	720
Youth under 18	22 000		Number of teams	2 830
Unregistered	880 000		Clubs with women's teams	0
Total players	2 975 400		Players as % of population	1.79%

Pakistan Football Federation (PFF)
PFF Football House, Opposite Punjab Football Stadium, Ferozepur Road, Lahore, Pakistan
Tel +92 42 9230821   Fax +92 42 9230823
mail@pff.com.pk   www.pff.com.pk
President: SALEH HAYAT Makhdoom Syed   General Secretary: KHAN LODHI Ahmed Yar
Vice-President: ALI SHA Syed Zahir   Treasurer: HAYAT Ali Khan   Media Officer: ALI WAHIDI Syed Akber
Men's Coach: TBD   Women's Coach: None
PFF formed: 1948   AFC: 1954   FIFA: 1948
Green shirts, Green shorts, Green socks

RECENT INTERNATIONAL MATCHES PLAYED BY PAKISTAN

2005	Opponents	Score		Venue	Comp	Scorers	Att	Referee
12-06	India	D	1-1	Quetta	Fr	Muhammad Essa [81]	20 000	Khan PAK
16-06	India	L	0-1	Peshawar	Fr		15 000	Imtiaz PAK
18-06	India	W	3-0	Lahore	Fr	Essa [2], Ahmed Tanveer [45+], Arif Mehmood [46]		Asif PAK
7-12	Sri Lanka	W	1-0	Karachi	SAFr1	Imran Hussain [38]		
9-12	Afghanistan	W	1-0	Karachi	SAFr1	Muhammad Essa [55]		
11-12	Maldives	D	0-0	Karachi	SAFr1			
14-12	Bangladesh	L	0-1	Karachi	SAFsf			
22-12	Bangladesh	D	0-0	Dhaka	ACq			
26-12	Bangladesh	L	0-1	Karachi	ACq			
2006								
18-02	Palestine	L	0-3	Manama	Fr			
22-02	Jordan	L	0-3	Amman	ACq			Basma SYR
1-03	United Arab Emirates	L	1-4	Karachi	ACq	Muhammad Essa [60]	10 000	Tongkhan THA
2-04	Kyrgyzstan	W	1-0	Dhaka	CCr1	Muhammad Essa [59]	2 500	Shamsuzzaman BAN
4-04	Tajikistan	L	0-2	Dhaka	CCr1		5 000	Tan Hai CHN
6-04	Macau	D	2-2	Dhaka	CCr1	Adeel [12], Muhammad Essa [43]	1 000	Shamsuzzaman BAN
16-08	Oman	L	1-4	Quetta	ACq	Muhammad Essa [79p]	4 000	Torky IRN
6-09	Oman	L	0-5	Muscat	ACq		10 000	Nema IRQ
11-10	Jordan	L	0-3	Lahore	ACq		4 000	Orzuev TJK
15-11	UAE	L	2-3	Abu Dhabi	ACq	Naveed Akram [22], Tanveer Ahmed [67]	6 000	Sarkar IND
2007								
22-10	Iraq	L	0-7	Lahore	WCq		2 500	Chynybekov KGZ
28-10	Iraq	D	0-0	Damascus	WCq		8 000	Al Fadhli KUW
2008								
25-03	Nepal	L	1-2	Pokhara	Fr	Muhammad Essa [21]		
27-03	Nepal	W	2-0	Pokhara	Fr	Muhammad Qasim [46], Muhammad Rasool [90]		
2-04	Chinese Taipei	W	2-1	Taipei	CCq	Muhammad Essa [13], Michael Masih [34]	800	Iemoto JPN
4-04	Sri Lanka	L	1-7	Taipei	CCq	Adnan Farooq Ahmed [17]	300	Kovalenko UZB
6-04	Guam	W	9-2	Taipei	CCq	Jamshed Anwar 2 [9 18], Farooq Shah [28], Muhammad Qasim 3 [44 72 82], Ahmed Tanveer [62], Zahid Hameed [65p], Abdul Rehman [85]	200	Auda Lazim IRQ
3-06	Maldives	L	0-3	Male	SAFr1			
5-06	India	L	1-2	Male	SAFr1	Adnan Farooq Ahmed [88]		
7-06	Nepal	L	1-4	Male	SAFr1	Samar Ishaq [54]		

Fr = Friendly match • SA = South Asian Federation Cup • AC = AFC Asian Cup • CC = AFC Challenge Cup • WC = FIFA World Cup
q = qualifier • r1 = first round group • sf = semi-final • 3p = third place play-off

PAKISTAN NATIONAL TEAM RECORDS AND RECORD SEQUENCES

Records			Sequence records					
Victory	9-2	GUM 2008	Wins	3	2003	Clean sheets	5	1952-1953
Defeat	1-9	IRN 1969	Defeats	14	1992-1993	Goals scored	13	1953-1959
Player Caps	n/a		Undefeated	5	1952-1953	Without goal	6	Three times
Player Goals	20	Muhammad Essa	Without win	19	1992-1993	Goals against	21	1965-1981

PAKISTAN COUNTRY INFORMATION

Capital	Islamabad	Independence	1947 from the UK	GDP per Capita	$2 100
Population	159 196 336	Status	Republic	GNP Ranking	44
Area km²	803 940	Language	Punjabi 48%, English	Dialling code	+92
Population density	198 per km²	Literacy rate	45%	Internet code	.pk
% in urban areas	35%	Main religion	Muslim	GMT +/−	+5
Towns/Cities ('000)	Karachi 11 627; Lahore 6 312; Faisalabad 2 507; Rawalpindi 1 743; Multan 1 437; Hyderabad 1 386; Gujranwala 1 384; Peshawar 1 219; Islamabad 756; Quetta 733; Bahawalpur 552				
Neighbours (km)	China 523; India 2 912; Iran 909; Afghanistan 2 430; Arabian Sea 1 046				
Main stadia	Jinnah Sport Stadium – Islamabad 48 200; National Stadium – Karachi 34 228				

PAKISTAN 2007–08

NATIONAL FOOTBALL LEAGUE A DIVISION

	Pl	W	D	L	F	A	Pts	WAPDA	Army	KRL	KPT	NBP	PIA	Navy	KESC	Afghan	HBL	PTV	PMC	Railways	Wohaib
WAPDA †	26	16	10	0	64	23	58		2-1	0-0	2-2	3-0	1-1	2-1	3-0	2-1	6-1	2-2	2-0	4-2	11-1
Pakistan Army	26	17	6	3	41	10	57	0-0		0-0	0-0	1-0	2-1	0-0	1-0	2-0	2-0	6-0	2-0	3-0	1-0
Khan Research Labs	26	15	8	3	45	13	53	1-3	3-2		2-0	4-1	4-1	1-0	0-0	3-0	1-0	4-0	1-0	1-0	4-0
Karachi Port Trust	26	12	8	6	36	24	44	1-2	0-1	0-0		2-3	1-2	0-0	1-0	2-1	2-1	1-0	5-1	7-2	3-2
Nat. Bank of Pakistan	26	11	10	5	36	31	43	2-2	0-4	1-0	0-0		1-1	3-1	2-1	1-1	2-1	2-0	4-1	0-0	2-1
Pakistan Int. Airlines	26	9	12	5	32	23	39	1-1	0-2	0-0	1-1	0-0		0-0	3-1	1-1	2-1	2-0	2-0	4-0	2-0
Pakistan Navy	26	9	11	6	36	26	38	2-3	2-1	0-0	4-0	0-1	2-1		0-0	2-2	1-0	1-1	2-0	2-2	3-0
Karachi Electric SC	26	8	8	10	27	30	32	1-1	0-0	1-0	0-0	0-0	2-1	1-1		2-2	2-1	1-0	2-1	2-0	4-0
Afghan FC	26	5	12	9	23	29	27	1-1	0-1	0-0	0-1	0-0	0-0	2-2	2-0		1-1	0-0	0-0	2-0	3-0
Habib Bank Ltd	26	7	4	15	35	42	25	2-3	1-2	2-4	0-1	1-2	1-1	1-4	2-2	4-0		0-1	6-1	4-2	2-0
Pakistan Television	26	6	5	15	20	45	23	0-3	0-2	0-5	0-2	1-1	0-1	2-3	2-1	1-1	1-2		1-0	2-1	3-0
Punjab Medical Col'ge	26	5	7	14	19	43	22	0-1	1-1	0-0	0-0	2-5	1-1	2-1	2-0	0-2	0-1	2-1		1-1	2-0
Pakistan Railways	26	5	6	15	23	49	21	0-4	0-1	0-4	0-1	1-1	2-1	0-1	2-0	2-0	0-1	1-0	1-1		0-0
Wohaib FC	26	1	5	20	11	60	8	0-0	0-3	2-3	0-3	1-1	0-2	0-0	2-0	1-2	0-0	0-1	1-2	0-3	

1/11/2007 - 30/01/2008 • † Qualified for the AFC Presidents Cup • Top scorers: Arif Mehmood, WAPDA 21; Zulfiqar Ali Shah, WAPDA 18

PAKISTAN NATIONAL CHALLENGE CUP 2008

Round of 16 (Pts)

Team	Pts
Pakistan Navy	9
Khan Research Labs	6
Pakistan Air Force	3
PAK Electron	0
Nat. Bank of Pakistan	6
WAPDA	3
Sui Southern Gas Co.	0
Pakistan TV withdrew	-
Karachi Port Trust	7
Habib Bank Ltd	5
Pakistan Int. Airlines	4
Sindh Govt Press	1
Karachi Electric SC	4
Pak. Public Works Dept	3
Pakistan Steel	1
Pak. Army withdrew	-

Quarter-finals

Pakistan Navy	1
Habib Bank Ltd	0
Pak. Public Works Dept	1
Nat. Bank of Pakistan	3
WAPDA	2
Karachi Electric SC	0
Karachi Port Trust	1
Khan Research Labs	2

Semi-finals

Pakistan Navy	3
Nat. Bank of Pakistan	0
WAPDA	0
Khan Research Labs	2

Final

Pakistan Navy	3
Khan Research Labs	1

CUP FINAL

15-05-2008
Scorers - Sajjad Ahmed 2 [13 69], Asif Mahmood [80] for Navy; Shahid Ahmed [19p] for KRL

Third place: Pakistan National Bank 2-0 WAPDA

RECENT LEAGUE AND CUP RECORD

	Championship			Cup		
Year	Champions	Score	Runners-up	Winners	Score	Runners-up
1997	Allied Bank	0-0 3-0p	Pakistan Int. Airlines	No tournament held		
1998	Pakistan Int. Airlines	1-1 3-1p	Allied Bank	Allied Bank	1-0	Karachi Port Trust
1999	Allied Bank	0-0 4-3p	Pakistan Navy	Allied Bank	1-1 5-4p	Khan Research Labs
2000	Allied Bank	1-0	Habib Bank	Pakistan Army	1-0	Allied Bank
2001	WAPDA	1-1 4-3p	Khan Research Labs	Pakistan Army		Khan Research Labs
2002	No tournament held			Allied Bank	1-1 4-2p	WAPDA
2003	WAPDA	0-0 4-2p	Pakistan Army	Pakistan Telecoms	1-1 ‡	Karachi Port Trust
2004	WAPDA	†	Pakistan Army	No tournament held		
2005	Pakistan Army	†	WAPDA	Pakistan Telecoms	2-1	WAPDA
2006	Season readjustment			No tournament held		
2007	Pakistan Army	†	WAPDA	No tournament held		
2008	WAPDA	†	Pakistan Army	Pakistan Navy	3-1	Khan Research Labs

† Played on a league basis • ‡ Won on the toss of a coin

PAN – PANAMA

NATIONAL TEAM RECORD
JULY 10TH 2006 TO JULY 12TH 2010

PL	W	D	L	F	A	%
28	10	10	8	31	33	53.6

FIFA/COCA-COLA WORLD RANKING

1993	1994	1995	1996	1997	1998	1999	2000	2001	2002	2003	2004	2005	2006	2007	High	
132	140	126	101	119	131	138	121	109	129	125	100	78	81	67	**52**	06/07

2007–2008												Low	
08/07	09/07	10/07	11/07	12/07	01/08	02/08	03/08	04/08	05/08	06/08	07/08	**150**	10/95
71	66	65	66	67	64	63	69	66	67	60	69		

No Central American country has made more progress in recent years than Panama. Thus it was to general dismay that the national team lasted just two matches in the 2010 FIFA World Cup qualifiers, knocked-out by a resurgent El Salvador. 21,000 fans turned up at baseball's Estadio Rod Carew for the first leg in Panama City which the home side won with a goal from Luis Tejada and things looked to be going well in the second leg in Guatemala City when Jose Luis Garces extended their advantage. With just 20 minutes to go and 2-0 up on aggregate Panama had one foot in the group stage, even after the Salvadorians pulled two goals back. With just two minutes left, however,

INTERNATIONAL HONOURS
None

Luis Anaya delivered the killer punch to send the Panamanians crashing out. Coach Alexandre Guimaraes who had taken Costa Rica to the 2006 finals, paid for the failure with his job and was replaced in July 2008 by Englishman Gary Stempel who had built a solid reputation in country, coaching champions San Francisco as well as national youth selections. His first task will be to win the UNCAF Cup which Panama will host in January 2009. The Panamanians adopted the system of two championships a year in 2007 with Apertura champions Tauro and Clausura champions San Francisco both qualifying for the inaugural CONCACAF Champions League.

THE FIFA BIG COUNT OF 2006

	Male	Female		Total
Number of players	176 000	27 400	Referees and Assistant Referees	300
Professionals	300		Admin, Coaches, Technical, Medical	1 700
Amateurs 18+	28 800		Number of clubs	570
Youth under 18	23 200		Number of teams	950
Unregistered	30 800		Clubs with women's teams	18
Total players	203 400		Players as % of population	6.37%

Federación Panameña de Fútbol (FEPAFUT)
Estadio Rommel Fernández, Puerta 24, Ave. Jose Aeustin Araneo, Apartado postal 8-391 Zona 8, Panama
Tel +507 2333896   Fax +507 2330582
fepafut@sinfo.net   www.fepafut.com
President: ALVARADO Ariel   General Secretary: UCROS Eric
Vice-President: ARCE Fernando   Treasurer: POUSA Juan   Media Officer: BOLVARAN Arturo
Men's Coach: STEMPEL Gary   Women's Coach: PEREZ Gaspar
FEPAFUT formed: 1937   CONCACAF: 1961   FIFA: 1938
Red shirts, Red shorts, Red socks

RECENT INTERNATIONAL MATCHES PLAYED BY PANAMA

2005	Opponents	Score		Venue	Comp	Scorers	Att	Referee
6-07	Colombia	W	1-0	Miami	GCr1	Tejada [70]	10 311	Batres GUA
10-07	Trinidad and Tobago	D	2-2	Miami	GCr1	Tejada 2 [24 90]	17 292	Wyngaarde SUR
12-07	Honduras	L	0-1	Miami	GCr1		11 000	Wyngaarde SUR
17-07	South Africa	D	1-1	Houston	GCqf	Jorge Dely Valdes [48] W 5-3p	60 050	Prendergast JAM
21-07	Colombia	W	3-2	New Jersey	GCsf	Phillips 2 [11 72], Jorge Dely Valdes 26	41 721	Sibrian SLV
24-07	USA	D	0-0	New Jersey	GCf	L 1-3p	31 018	Batres GUA
17-08	Guatemala	L	1-2	Guatemala City	WCq	Jorge Dely Valdes [19]	24 000	Sibrian SLV
3-09	Costa Rica	L	1-3	Panama City	WCq	Tejada [90]	21 000	Stott USA
7-09	Mexico	L	0-5	Mexico City	WCq		40 000	Hall USA
8-10	Trinidad and Tobago	L	0-1	Panama City	WCq		1 000	Navarro CAN
12-10	USA	L	0-2	Boston	WCq		2 500	Alcala MEX
27-10	Bahrain	L	0-5	Manama	Fr			
2006								
16-08	Peru	W	2-0	Lima	Fr	Phillips [20], Gomez.G [86]	1 000	Garay PER
6-09	Guatemala	W	2-1	Guatemala City	Fr	Torres [2], Perez.B [32]		
7-10	El Salvador	W	1-0	Panama City	Fr	Tejada [65]		Moreno PAN
11-10	Trinidad & Tobago	L	1-2	Port of Spain	Fr	Canales [44]		
19-11	Peru	L	1-2	Panama City	Fr	Tejada [38p]	2 000	Vidal PAN
29-11	El Salvador	D	0-0	San Salvador	Fr			
2007								
14-01	Armenia	D	1-1	Los Angeles	Fr	Tejada		
31-01	Trinidad & Tobago	W	2-1	Panama City	Fr	Canales [29], Aguilar [82]	5 000	Vidal PAN
11-02	Honduras	D	1-1	San Salvador	UCr1	Rivera [78]		Aguilar SLV
13-02	Costa Rica	W	1-0	San Salvador	UCr1	Blanco [86]		Batres GUA
16-02	Guatemala	W	2-0	San Salvador	UCsf	Phillips [50], Baloy [92+]		Arredondo MEX
18-02	Panama	D	1-1	San Salvador	UCf	Tejada [36], L 1-4p		Batres GUA
24-03	Haiti	L	0-3	Miami	Fr		12 000	
26-03	Jamaica	D	1-1	Kingston	Fr	Garces [3]	16 554	Brizan TRI
9-05	Colombia	L	0-4	Panama City	Fr		4 000	Archundia MEX
8-06	Honduras	W	3-2	New Jersey	GCr1	Rivera 33, Perez.B 42, Garces 82	20 230	Navarro CAN
10-06	Cuba	D	2-2	New Jersey	GCr1	Garces [16], Perez.B [47]	68 123	
13-06	Mexico	L	0-1	Houston	GCr1		68 417	
16-06	USA	L	1-2	Foxboro	GCqf	Perez.B [84]	22 412	Brizan TRI
22-08	Guatemala	W	2-1	Panama City	Fr	Blanco [31], Herrera [52p]		Rodriguez CRC
12-09	Venezuela	D	1-1	Puerto La Cruz	Fr	Escobar [67]	30 000	Buitriago COL
14-10	Honduras	L	0-1	Tegucigalpa	Fr		23 139	Zelaya HON
21-11	Costa Rica	D	1-1	Panama City	Fr	Marin OG [41]		Rodas GUA
2008								
1-06	Guatemala	W	1-0	Fort Lauderdale	Fr	Garces [67]		
4-06	Canada	D	2-2	Sunrise	Fr	Tejada [44p], Garces [48]		
7-06	Chile	D	0-0	Valparaiso	Fr			Fagundes BRA
15-06	El Salvador	W	1-0	Panama City	WCq	Tejada [21]	22 150	Wijngaarde SUR
22-06	El Salvador	L	1-3	San Salvador	WCq	Garces [14]	27 420	Rodriguez MEX

Fr = Friendly match • UC = UNCAF Cup • GC = CONCACAF Gold Cup • WC = FIFA World Cup
q = qualifier • r1 = first round group • qf = quarter-final • sf = semi-final • 3p = third place play-off • f = final

PANAMA NATIONAL TEAM RECORDS AND RECORD SEQUENCES

Records			Sequence records					
Victory	12-0	PUR 1946	Wins	4	2001, 2003	Clean sheets	3	2000
Defeat	0-11	CRC 1938	Defeats	9	1976-1977	Goals scored	11	1946-50, 1974-75
Player Caps	n/a		Undefeated	7	Three times	Without goal	6	1984-1985
Player Goals	n/a		Without win	13	1950-1963	Goals against	17	1975-1979

PANAMA COUNTRY INFORMATION

Capital	Panamá	Independence	1903	GDP per Capita	$6 300
Population	3 000 463	Status	Republic	GNP Ranking	87
Area km²	78 200	Language	Spanish	Dialling code	+507
Population density	38 per km²	Literacy rate	92%	Internet code	.pa
% in urban areas	53%	Main religion	Christian	GMT + / –	-5
Towns/Cities ('000)	Panamá 408; San Miguelito 321; Tocumen 88; David 82; Arraiján 77; Colón 76; Las Cumbres 69				
Neighbours (km)	Colombia 225; Costa Rica 330; Caribbean and North Pacific 2 490				
Main stadia	Rommel Fernandez – Panamá 25 000; Armando Dely Valdez – Colón 3 000				

PANAMA 2007

ANAPROF PRIMERA PROFESIONAL APERTURA

	Pl	W	D	L	F	A	Pts	Tauro	Arabe Un	San Fran'co	Chorrillo	Chepo	At. Chiriquí	Plaza	Sporting	Alianza	Veragüense
Tauro †	18	11	5	2	37	15	38		4-1	1-1	4-2	2-0	3-0	0-1	1-1	4-1	5-0
Arabe Unido †	18	9	3	6	26	20	30	0-0		0-2	1-3	2-1	1-0	3-1	2-0	0-1	6-1
San Francisco †	18	9	2	7	25	17	29	0-1	1-2		0-1	2-0	4-1	0-0	2-0	2-1	4-2
Municipal Chorrillo †	18	8	4	6	29	25	28	1-4	0-1	1-2		4-1	1-0	2-2	0-1	4-2	2-1
Chepo FC	18	8	4	6	27	27	28	0-0	2-1	2-0	0-2		3-1	2-1	0-0	1-0	6-3
Atlético Chiriquí	18	7	4	7	24	23	25	1-2	1-1	1-2	1-1	2-0		3-3	1-0	3-2	2-0
Plaza Amador	18	5	6	7	21	25	21	0-0	0-2	1-0	0-0	2-3	0-2		2-1	1-1	2-3
Sporting San Miguelito	18	5	5	8	17	20	20	3-0	0-0	1-0	3-3	1-2	0-1	2-1		1-2	1-1
Alianza	18	5	2	11	25	36	17	2-3	2-1	2-1	0-1	2-2	0-4	0-2	1-2		5-2
Atlético Veragüense	18	4	3	11	23	46	15	1-3	1-2	0-2	2-1	2-2	0-0	1-2	1-0	2-1	

23/02/2007 - 13/05/2007 • † Qualified for the play-offs • Play-offs: Semi-finals - Chorillo 0-1 1-1 **Tauro**; **San Francisco** 1-1 1-1 3-0p Arabe Unido; Final - **Tauro** 2-0 San Francisco. (Rommel Ferández, Panama City, 28-05-2007, scorers - Alberto Skinner 41, Juan de Dios Pérez 79 for Tauro)
Tauro are the Apertura Champions • Top scorers: Edwin Aguilar, Tauro 14; César Medina, Alianza 12

PANAMA 2007

ANAPROF PRIMERA PROFESIONAL CLAUSURA

	Pl	W	D	L	F	A	Pts	San Fran'co	Arabe Un	Tauro	Chorrillo	At. Chiriquí	Alianza	Chepo	Sporting	Plaza	Veragüense
San Francisco †	18	11	4	3	27	16	37		1-3	0-0	2-0	1-0	2-1	2-0	1-0	3-2	3-2
Arabe Unido †	18	9	5	4	42	27	32	2-3		1-2	1-1	6-3	0-1	3-2	3-2	4-1	4-0
Tauro †	18	8	7	3	38	23	31	3-3	2-2		0-1	1-1	3-2	3-2	3-1	3-0	7-0
Municipal Chorrillo †	18	8	3	7	24	21	27	2-0	2-1	0-1		4-0	1-0	1-2	1-3	2-2	5-2
Atlético Chiriquí	18	6	8	4	21	22	26	0-1	2-2	2-2	4-2		1-0	0-0	1-0	2-0	1-0
Alianza	18	7	3	8	19	20	24	1-0	1-2	1-1	2-0	1-1		1-3	1-0	2-1	0-1
Chepo FC	18	6	5	7	23	21	23	0-3	1-1	3-1	0-1	0-0	0-1		2-3	1-0	2-0
Sporting San Miguelito	18	4	6	8	19	24	18	0-0	0-2	1-1	0-1	1-1	1-1	1-1		1-0	1-2
Plaza Amador	18	4	5	9	24	30	17	0-0	3-3	3-1	1-0	1-2	1-2	0-0	3-4		3-1
Atlético Veragüense	18	3	2	13	10	43	11	0-2	0-2	0-4	0-0	0-1	2-1	0-4	0-0	0-3	

27/07/2007 - 10/11/2007 • † Qualified for the play-offs • Play-offs: Semi-finals - Chorillo 0-1 1-0 3-4p **San Francisco**; Tauro 1-0 1-0-0 **Arabe Unido**; Final - **San Francisco** 0-0 4-2p Arabe Unido. (Estadio Nacional Rod Carew, Panama City, 2-12-2007). San Francisco are the Clausura Champions
No teams relegated • Top scorers: César Medina, Alianza 9; Orlando Rodríguez, Unido Arabe 9; Gabriel Torres, Chepo 9

CLUB DIRECTORY

Club	Town/City	Lge	CL
Alianza		0	0
Deportivo Arabe Unido	Colón	3	0
Atlético Chiriquí	San Cristobal	0	0
Atlético Veragüense	Veraguas	0	0
Colón River	Colón	0	0
El Chorrillo	Balboa	0	0
Plaza Amador	Panama City	5	0
Sporting 89	San Miguelito	0	0
San Francisco	La Chorrera	3	0
Tauro	Panama City	7	0

RECENT LEAGUE RECORD

	Championship		
Year	Winners	Score	Runners-up
2000	Tauro	2-0	Plaza Amador
2001	Panama Viejo	4-3	Tauro
2001	Deportivo Arabe Unido	†	
2002	Plaza Amador	2-0	Deportivo Arabe Unido
2003	Tauro	†	
2004	Deportivo Arabe Unido	†	
2005	Plaza Amador	2-0	San Francisco
2006	San Francisco	2-0	Tauro
2007	Tauro	2-0	San Francisco
2007	San Francisco	0-0 4-2p	Arabe Unido

† Won both Apertura and Clausura so automatic champions

PAR – PARAGUAY

NATIONAL TEAM RECORD
JULY 10TH 2006 TO JULY 12TH 2010

PL	W	D	L	F	A	%
25	7	8	10	30	32	44

FIFA/COCA-COLA WORLD RANKING

1993	1994	1995	1996	1997	1998	1999	2000	2001	2002	2003	2004	2005	2006	2007		High	
61	87	64	38	29	25	17	10	13	18	22	30	30	35	21		**8**	03/01

2007–2008												Low	
08/07	09/07	10/07	11/07	12/07	01/08	02/08	03/08	04/08	05/08	06/08	07/08	**103**	05/95
31	31	26	21	21	21	27	26	26	24	28	25		

Paraguay became the latest nation in the Americas to adopt the system of two championships a year with the traditional play-off between the Apertura and Clausura winners abandoned for the 2008 season. In the 2007 final Libertad confirmed their status as the team of the decade when they beat Sportivo Luqueño 3-1 on aggregate to win their fourth title since 2002. They then made that five after finishing top of the standings in the 2008 Apertura, well clear of second placed Nacional. Libertad have struggled on a continental level, however, as have Paraguayan clubs in general, and

INTERNATIONAL HONOURS
Qualified for the FIFA World Cup finals 1930 1950 1958 1986 1998 2002 2006   Copa America 1953 1979
South America U-23 1992   Juventud de America 1971   South America U-16 2004   Copa Libertadores Olimpia 1979 1990 2002

in the 2008 Copa Libertadores they finished well adrift at the bottom of their group behind eventual finalists LDU Quito and Fluminense. There was much better news for the national team after Gerardo Martino's side won four of their first five matches in the marathon 10-team South American 2010 FIFA World Cup qualifying group. The Argentine has transformed the national team into a much more effective attacking unit and in June 2008 they confirmed their credentials with a 2-0 victory over Brazil. Roque Santa Cruz has revived his career following his transfer to Blackburn in England and he scored one of the goals to defeat the Brazilians.

THE FIFA BIG COUNT OF 2006

	Male	Female		Total
Number of players	886 966	150 469	Referees and Assistant Referees	802
Professionals	590		Admin, Coaches, Technical, Medical	3 200
Amateurs 18+	53 667		Number of clubs	1 696
Youth under 18	29 984		Number of teams	3 500
Unregistered	950 000		Clubs with women's teams	13
Total players	1 037 435		Players as % of population	15.94%

Asociación Paraguaya de Fútbol (APF)
Estadio de los Defensores del Chaco, Calle Mayor Martinez 1393, Asuncion, Paraguay
Tel +595 21 480120   Fax +595 21 480124
apf@telesurf.com.py   www.apf.org.py
President: NAPOUT juan Angel   General Secretary: FILARTIGA Arturo
Vice-President: DAHER Ramon Gonzalez   Treasurer: ACOSTA Federico   Media Officer: ARRUA Gilda
Men's Coach: MARTINO Gerardo   Women's Coach: CABRERA Agustin
APF formed: 1906   CONMEBOL: 1921   FIFA: 1925
Red and white striped shirts, Blue shorts, Blue socks

RECENT INTERNATIONAL MATCHES PLAYED BY PARAGUAY

2006	Opponents	Score		Venue	Comp	Scorers	Att	Referee
1-03	Wales	D	0-0	Cardiff	Fr		12 324	McDonald SCO
29-03	Mexico	L	1-2	Chicago	Fr	Cuevas [2]	46 510	Kennedy USA
24-05	Norway	D	2-2	Oslo	Fr	Gamarra [48], Valdez [54]	10 227	Olsiak SVK
27-05	Denmark	D	1-1	Aarhus	Fr	Cardozo [20]	20 047	Bennett ENG
31-05	Georgia	W	1-0	Dornbirn	Fr	Valdez [40]	2 000	Gangle AUT
10-06	England	L	0-1	Frankfurt	WCr1		48 000	Rodriguez MEX
15-06	Sweden	L	0-1	Berlin	WCr1		72 000	Michel SVK
20-06	Trinidad and Tobago	W	2-0	Kaiserslautern	WCr1	OG [25], Cuevas [86]	46 000	Rosetti ITA
7-10	Australia	D	1-1	Brisbane	Fr	Beauchamp OG [92+]	47 609	Kashihara JPN
15-11	Chile	L	2-3	Viña de Mar	Fr	Jimenez.E [67], Riveros [68]	9 000	Baldassi ARG
2007								
25-03	Mexico	L	1-2	San Nicolas	Fr	Santa Cruz [92+]		Pineda HON
28-03	Colombia	L	0-2	Bogota	Fr		32 000	
2-06	Austria	D	0-0	Vienna	Fr		12 700	Bebek CRO
5-06	Mexico	W	1-0	Mexico City	Fr	Cardozo [88]	60 000	Larrionda URU
20-06	Bolivia	D	0-0	Santa Cruz	Fr		35 000	Antequera BOL
28-06	Colombia	W	5-0	Maracaibo	CAr1	Santa Cruz 3 [30 46 80], Cabañas 2 [84 88]	30 000	Larrionda URU
2-07	USA	W	3-1	Barinas	CAr1	Barreto [29], Cardozo [56], Cabañas [92+]	23 000	Rivera PER
5-07	Argentina	L	0-1	Barquisimeto	CAr1		37 000	Larrionda URU
8-07	Mexico	L	0-6	Maturin	CAqf		50 000	Pezzotta ARG
22-08	Venezuela	D	1-1	Ciudad del Este	Fr	Da Silva.A [24]	5 000	Baldassi ARG
8-09	Venezuela	L	2-3	Puerto Ordaz	Fr	Riveros 2 [38 64]	40 000	Lopez COL
12-09	Colombia	L	0-1	Bogota	Fr		18 000	Buckley PER
13-10	Peru	D	0-0	Lima	WCq		50 000	Simon BRA
17-10	Uruguay	W	1-0	Asuncion	WCq	Valdez [15]	23 200	Baldassi ARG
17-11	Ecuador	W	5-1	Asuncion	WCq	Valdez [9], Riveros 2 [27 88], Santa Cruz [51], Ayala [83]	25 433	Lopes BRA
21-11	Chile	W	3-0	Santiago	WCq	Cabanas [24], Da Silva.P 2 [45 57]	52 320	Ruiz COL
2008								
6-02	Honduras	L	0-2	San Pedro Sula	Fr		5 000	Rodriguez CRC
26-03	South Africa	L	0-3	Atteridgeville	Fr		15 000	
22-05	Côte d'Ivoire	D	1-1	Yokohama	Fr	Bogado [76]	5 197	Matsumura JPN
27-05	Japan	D	0-0	Saitama	Fr		27 998	Costa POR
31-05	France	D	0-0	Toulouse	Fr		33 418	Proença POR
15-06	Brazil	W	2-0	Asuncion	WCq	Santa Cruz [26], Cabanas [49]	38 000	Larrionda URU
18-06	Bolivia	L	2-4	La Paz	WCq	Santa Cruz [66], Valdez [82]	8 561	Gaciba BRA

Fr = Friendly match • CA = Copa América • WC = FIFA World Cup • q = qualifier • r1 = 1st round • qf = quarter-final

PARAGUAY NATIONAL TEAM PLAYERS

	Player		Ap	G	Club	Date of Birth		Player		Ap	G	Club	Date of Birth
1	Aldo Bobadilla	GK	15	0	Indep Medellín	20 04 1976	12	Derlis Gomez	GK	8	0	Nacional	2 11 1972
2	Julio Manzur	DF	23	0	Pachuca	22 06 1981	13	Enrique Vera	DF	4	0	LDU Quito	10 03 1979
3	Claudio Morel Rodriguez	DF	11	0	Boca Juniors	2 02 1978	14	Paulo da Silva	DF	53	3	Toluca	1 02 1980
4	Aureliano Torres	DF	16	1	San Lorenzo	16 06 1982	15	Victor Cáceres	MF	12	0	Libertad	25 03 1985
5	Julio César Cáceres	DF	38	2	Boca Juniors	5 10 1979	16	Cristian Riveros	MF	19	1	Cruz Azul	16 10 1982
6	Caros Bonet	MF	46	1	Cruz Azul	2 10 1977	17	Edgar Gonzales	MF	14	0	Estudiantes LP	10 04 1979
7	Pablo Zeballos	FW	1	0	Cruz Azul	4 03 1986	18	Nelson Valdez	FW	23	7	Bor. Dortmund	28 11 1983
8	Edgar Barreto	MF	34	2	Reggina	15 07 1984	19	Justo Villar	GK	53	0	Real Valladolid	30 06 1977
9	Roque Santa Cruz	FW	61	20	Blackburn Rov	16 08 1981		Darío Verón	DF	17	0	UNAM	26 07 1979
10	Salvador Cabañas	FW	30	5	CF América	5 08 1980		Jorge Núñez	DF	22	1	Cerro Porteño	22 01 1978
11	Oscar Cardozo	FW	15	2	Benfica	20 05 1983		Denis Caniza	DF	84	0	Cruz Azul	29 08 1974

Paraguay's squad for the June 2008 World Cup qualifiers

| | Jonathan Santana | MF | 10 | 0 | VfL Wolfsburg | 19 10 1981 |

PARAGUAY NATIONAL TEAM RECORDS AND RECORD SEQUENCES

Records			Sequence records					
Victory	7-0	BOL 1949	Wins	8	1947-1949	Clean sheets	5	1947-49, 1988
Defeat	0-8	ARG 1926	Defeats	8	1959-1961	Goals scored	15	1958-1960
Player Caps	110	Carlos Gamarra	Undefeated	14	1985-1986	Without goal	4	1981-83, 1993
Player Goals	25	José Cardozo	Without win	20	1959-1962	Goals against	20	1931-1942

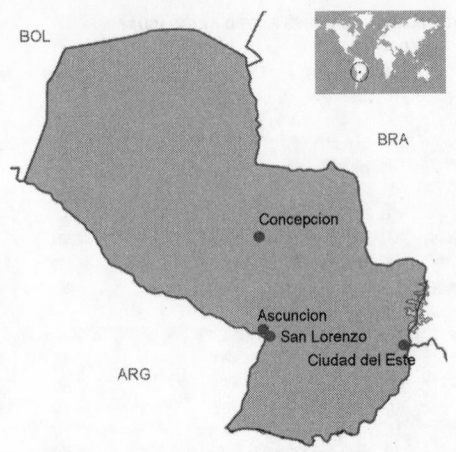

BOL

BRA

Concepcion

Ascuncion
San Lorenzo
Ciudad del Este

ARG

REPUBLIC OF PARAGUAY; REPUBLICA DEL PARAGUAY

Capital	Asunción	Language	Spanish, Guarani	Independence	1811
Population	6 669 086	Area	406 750 km²	% in cities	53%
GDP per cap	$4 700	Dailling code	+595	Internet	.py	GMT +/-	-4

San Lorenzo, Luque, Capiatá, Lambaré, Fernando de la Mora, Limpio, Nemby, Itaguá, San Antonio and Vila Elisa are part of the Greater Asunción metropolitan area which has a population of 1 944 000 • Ciudad del Este, Hernandaríaz, Presidente Franco and Minga Guazú are part of the Foz do Iguaçu metropolitan area which has a population of 713 000

MEDALS TABLE

		Overall			Lge		Sth Am				City	Stadium	Cap'ty	DoF
		G	S	B	G	S	G	S	B					
1	Olimpia	42	23	8	38	19	4	4	8	Asunción	Manuel Ferreira	20 000	1902
2	Cerro Porteño	27	25	5	27	25			5	Asunción	General Pablo Rojas 'La Olla'	25 000	1912
3	Libertad	13	18	2	13	18			2	Asunción	Dr. Nicolás Leoz	16 000	1905
4	Guaraní	9	11	1	9	11			1	Asunción	Rogelio Livieres	10 000	1903
5	Nacional	6	9		6	9				Asunción	Arsenio Erico	4 500	1904
6	Sol de América	2	12		2	12				Vila Elisa	Luis Alfonso Giagni	5 000	1909
7	Sportivo Luqueño	2	4		2	4				Luque	Feliciano Cáceres	24 000	1921
8	Presidente Hayes	1			1					Tacumbu	Kiko Reyes	5 000	1907
9	Atlántida		3			3				Asunción	Flaviano Díaz	1 000	1906
	River Plate		3			3				Asunción	River Plate	5 000	1911
11	12 de Octubre	1			1					Itaugua	Juan Canuto Pettengill	8 000	1914
12	Atlético Colegiales			1					1	Asunción	Luciano Zacarías	4 500	1977
13	3 de Febrero									Ciudad del Este	Antonio Oddone Sarubbi	25 000	1970
	General Caballero									Zeballos Cue	General Caballero	5 000	1918
	2 de Mayo									Pedro Juan Caballero	Monumental Río Parapití	25 000	1935

RECENT LEAGUE RECORD

Year	Championship		
	Winners	Score	Runners-up
1998	Olimpia	2-2 3-1	Cerro Porteño
1999	Olimpia	1-0 3-2	Cerro Porteño
2000	Olimpia	†	Guarani
2001	Cerro Porteño	†	Sportivo Luqueño
2002	Libertad	2-1 4-1	12 de Octubre
2003	Libertad	†	Guarani
2004	Cerro Porteño	†	Libertad
2005	Cerro Porteño	†	Libertad
2006	Libertad	0-0 2-1	Cerro Porteño
2007	Libertad	1-1 2-0	Sportivo Luqueño
2008	Libertad	‡	Nacional

† Won both Apertura and Clausura so automatic champions
‡ Played on a league system

PARAGUAY 2007

DIVISION PROFESIONAL CLAUSURA

	Pl	W	D	L	F	A	Pts	Libertad	Cerro	Olimpia	Sol	Nacional	12 Octubre	Guaraní	Tacuary	Trindense	Luqueño	3 Febrero	2 de Mayo
Libertad † ‡	22	17	4	1	36	14	55		3-2	0-1	3-1	2-1	1-0	2-1	1-0	1-0	3-1	2-1	3-1
Cerro Porteño †	22	15	4	3	52	21	49	0-0		3-1	2-1	1-0	4-1	4-1	5-1	0-0	1-0	2-0	4-0
Olimpia ‡	22	11	5	6	33	23	38	0-0	2-1		1-2	2-3	2-3	1-0	1-1	2-1	5-1	1-2	2-0
Sol de América	22	9	7	6	32	24	34	0-1	2-2	1-2		3-3	1-0	2-1	1-1	0-0	4-2	0-0	6-0
Nacional	22	9	7	6	37	30	34	1-2	1-3	0-0	3-1		0-0	2-2	1-0	1-1	2-1	6-2	1-0
12 de Octubre	22	7	5	10	23	29	26	0-3	2-3	0-3	0-1	0-1		1-0	3-0	0-1	2-1	2-0	2-2
Guaraní	22	6	7	9	24	27	25	0-0	1-4	2-0	0-0	2-1	2-2		1-0	0-1	2-1	1-1	4-0
Tacuary	22	6	7	9	25	29	25	1-1	3-3	0-1	0-2	2-2	1-0	0-1		0-0	4-1	2-0	0-2
Sportivo Trinidense	22	5	9	8	15	18	24	1-2	0-1	0-0	0-0	0-1	1-1	1-2	2-1		1-3	1-0	0-0
Sportivo Luqueño †	22	5	4	13	24	41	19	0-1	2-1	1-2	2-1	2-3	0-0	1-1	0-3	1-0		2-1	1-1
3 de Febrero	22	5	4	13	21	41	19	1-2	0-5	1-1	0-1	1-3	2-2	1-0	2-4	0-2	2-0		2-1
2 de Mayo	22	2	7	13	16	41	13	1-3	0-1	1-3	1-2	2-1	0-1	1-1	0-0	1-1	1-1	1-2	

3/08/2007 - 2/12/2007 • † Qualified for the Copa Libertadores • ‡ Qualified for the Copa Sudamericana • Libertad qualified to meet Apertura champions Sportivo Luqueño for the title • See *Almanack of World Football 2008* for Apertura details
Sportivo Trindense relegated on average over three seasons • Relegation play-off: General Díaz 2-1 2-4 **12 de Octubre**

CHAMPIONSHIP FINAL

1st leg. Feliciano Cáceres, Luque, 9-12-2007. Ref: Carlos Amarilla

Sportivo Luqueño	1	Julio Ortellado [2]
Libertad	1	Omar Pouso [40]

Luqueño - Mario Villasanti - Pablo Aguilar•, Reinaldo Román•, Juan Cardozo - Juan Abente, Luis Alejandro Núñez, Arturo Aquino (Robert Servín 76), Carlos Mereles, Derlis Ortiz (Cristian Hermosilla 61) - Julio Ortellado, Adriano Duarte (Iván Barrios 79)
Libertad - Jorge Bava - Pedro Benítez•, Pedro Sarabia, Edgar Balbuena, Derlis Cardozo• - Omar Pouso, Víctor Caceres•, Osvaldo Martínez, Sergio Aquino (Wilson Pitonni 75), Vladimir Marín - Rodolfo Gamarra• (Nelson Romero 80)

2nd leg. Defensores del Chaco, Asunción, 14-12-2007. Ref: Carlos Torres

Libertad	2	Víctor Cáceres 2 [49] [64]
Sportivo Luqueño	0	

Libertad - Jorge Bava - Pedro Benítez, Pedro Sarabia, Vlaimir Marín (Nelson Romero 81), Edgar Balbuena, Derlis Cardozo - Omar Pouso, Víctor Caceres•, Osvaldo Martínez• (Edgar Robles 75), Sergio Aquino - Roberto Carlos Gamarra•
Luqueño - Mario Villasanti - Pablo Aguilar, Reinaldo Román, Juan Cardozo - Juan Abente, Luis Alejandro Núñez, Arturo Aquino• (Robert Servín 77), Carlos Mereles, Derlis Ortiz (Jorge Sanabria 68) - Julio Ortellado (Adriano Duarte 59), Cristian Hermosilla

PARAGUAY 2007 DIVISION INTERMEDIA (2)

	Pl	W	D	L	F	A	Pts
Silvio Pettirossi	18	9	8	1	27	15	35
General Díaz	18	8	8	2	18	12	32
Rubio Nu	18	8	4	6	22	16	28
Cerro Porteño PF	18	7	5	6	30	31	26
Sportivo Iteño	18	6	6	6	27	24	24
Presidente Hayes	18	6	6	6	17	16	24
Fernando de la Mora	18	5	5	8	21	23	20
General Caballero	18	5	4	9	14	20	19
Martín Lesesma	18	3	8	7	16	23	17
Choré Central	18	5	2	11	14	26	17

21/04/2007 - 26/08/2007

PARAGUAY 2008

DIVISION PROFESIONAL APERTURA

	Pl	W	D	L	F	A	Pts	Libertad	Nacional	Cerro	Guaraní	2 de Mayo	Sol	3 Febrero	Olimpia	Luqueño	Tacuary	12 Octubre	Pettirossi
Libertad	22	18	3	1	53	13	57		1-1	2-0	3-1	3-1	4-0	4-0	1-0	4-3	2-0	1-1	3-0
Nacional	22	14	3	5	44	25	45	1-4		0-3	1-0	2-1	2-1	2-1	4-0	1-3	0-1	3-1	2-0
Cerro Porteño	22	11	5	6	34	26	38	0-2	0-0		1-0	1-0	2-1	2-4	1-0	3-3	0-0	4-3	1-0
Guaraní	22	11	3	8	31	26	36	0-3	2-3	0-2		1-1	3-1	0-1	2-0	2-2	2-0	1-0	1-0
2 de Mayo	22	9	4	9	27	25	31	1-0	0-3	2-1	2-0		2-0	1-2	0-1	2-0	1-2	1-1	3-1
Sol de América	22	8	3	11	40	39	27	0-1	1-3	3-1	1-1	1-2		2-1	2-2	1-3	4-1	2-3	4-0
3 de Febrero	22	8	3	11	32	40	27	0-4	2-2	1-0	1-2	1-3	1-5		3-1	4-2	2-4	4-0	0-0
Olimpia	22	7	5	10	23	32	26	1-2	0-1	1-2	0-2	1-0	0-1	2-1		1-1	2-2	0-0	3-3
Sportivo Luqueño	22	6	7	9	33	44	25	0-1	0-5	0-5	1-3	1-1	2-1	2-1	0-1		1-1	3-2	3-3
Tacuary	22	5	8	9	24	34	23	1-2	2-1	1-1	2-5	1-1	0-2	2-1	1-2	0-0		1-2	1-1
12 de Octubre	22	4	8	10	29	40	20	2-2	1-3	2-2	0-1	2-0	3-3	0-0	1-2	0-3	1-1		3-1
Silvio Pettirossi	22	3	4	15	21	47	13	0-4	1-4	1-2	1-2	0-2	2-4	0-1	2-3	2-0	1-0	2-1	

15/02/2008 - 29/06/2008 • There will be no play-off for the title in 2008

PER – PERU

NATIONAL TEAM RECORD
JULY 10TH 2006 TO JULY 12TH 2010

PL	W	D	L	F	A	%
26	5	8	13	27	49	34.6

FIFA/COCA-COLA WORLD RANKING

1993	1994	1995	1996	1997	1998	1999	2000	2001	2002	2003	2004	2005	2006	2007	High	
73	72	69	54	38	72	42	45	43	82	74	66	66	70	63	**34**	09/97

	2007–2008											Low	
08/07	09/07	10/07	11/07	12/07	01/08	02/08	03/08	04/08	05/08	06/08	07/08	**86**	02/03
54	52	61	63	63	63	67	66	64	61	64	67		

These are desperate times for football in Peru with the national team unable to revive its fortunes no matter who is appointed coach. Julio Cesar Uribe stepped down after the 2007 Copa America and was replaced by Jose del Solar, another ex-national team favourite but the first steps in qualifying for the 2010 FIFA World Cup in South Africa were nothing short of disastrous. The first six matches in the marathon South American group saw three draws at home in Lima but it was the magnitude of the defeats at away from home that were of major concern with the Peruvians losing 5-1 against Ecuador and 6-0 against Uruguay. Left anchored the bottom of the standings

INTERNATIONAL HONOURS
Qualified for the FIFA World Cup finals 1930 1970 1978 1982   Copa America 1939 1975

means a long hard campaign with very little prospect of achieving much, and the general consensus is that the Peruvians have now replaced Venezuela as the whipping boys of the continent. Club football fared no better with all three representatives in the 2008 Copa Libertadores failing to qualify from their group yet again, including 2007 champions Universidad San Martin who claimed their first domestic title in unusual circumstances. Having won the Apertura they should have faced Clausura champions Coronel Bolognesi in the annual play-off, but as neither finished in the top six in the other half of the season, San Martin were named champions due to their overall record.

THE FIFA BIG COUNT OF 2006

	Male	Female		Total
Number of players	1 656 556	235 234	Referees and Assistant Referees	2 663
Professionals	799		Admin, Coaches, Technical, Medical	1 519
Amateurs 18+	70 050		Number of clubs	1 800
Youth under 18	166 140		Number of teams	3 000
Unregistered	835 000		Clubs with women's teams	300
Total players	1 891 790		Players as % of population	6.68%

Federación Peruana de Fútbol (FPF)
Av. Aviación 2085, San Luis, Lima 30, Peru
Tel +51 1 2258236   Fax +51 1 2258240
fepefutbol@fpf.org.pe   www.fpf.com.pe
President: BURGA Manuel Dr   General Secretary: QUINTANA Javier
Vice-President: SILVESTRI Carlos   Treasurer: RAMOS RUIZ Roberto   Media Officer: DEL AGUILA Wilmer
Men's Coach: DEL SOLAR José   Women's Coach: BARBARAN Lizandro
FPF formed: 1922   CONMEBOL: 1926   FIFA: 1926
White shirts with a red sash, White shorts, White socks

RECENT INTERNATIONAL MATCHES PLAYED BY PERU

2005 Opponents		Score	Venue	Comp	Scorers	Att	Referee
17-08 Chile	W	3-1	Tacna	Fr	Vílchez 28, Guerrero 59, Villalta 64		Ortube BOL
3-09 Venezuela	L	1-4	Maracaibo	WCq	Farfan 63	6 000	Rezende BRA
9-10 Argentina	L	0-2	Buenos Aires	WCq		36 977	Torres PAR
12-10 Bolivia	W	4-1	Tacna	WCq	Vassallo 11, Acasiete 38, Farfan 2 45 82	14 774	Sequeira ARG
2006							
10-05 Trinidad and Tobago	D	1-1	Port of Spain	Fr	Vasallo 31	20 000	Prendergast JAM
16-08 Panama	L	0-2	Lima	Fr		1 000	Garay PER
6-09 Ecuador	D	1-1	New Jersey	Fr	Guerrero 76	20 000	
7-10 Chile	L	2-3	Viña del Mar	Fr	Guerrero 8, Pizarro 83		Vieira URU
11-10 Chile	L	0-1	Tacna	Fr		12 000	Haro ECU
15-11 Jamaica	D	1-1	Kingston	Fr	Sanchez.A 64		
19-11 Panama	W	2-1	Panama City	Fr	Mostto 41, Alva 80	2 000	Vidal PAN
2007							
24-03 Japan	L	0-2	Yokohama	Fr		60 400	Nardi AUS
3-06 Ecuador	W	2-1	Madrid	Fr	Farfan 5, De la Cruz OG 51	25 000	Puerta ESP
6-06 Ecuador	L	0-2	Barcelona	Fr		20 000	Crespo ESP
26-06 Uruguay	W	3-0	Merida	CAr1	Villalta 27, Mariño 70, Guerrero 89		Amarilla PAR
30-06 Venezuela	L	0-2	San Cristobal	CAr1			Archundia MEX
3-07 Bolivia	D	2-2	Merida	CAr1	Pizarro 2 34 85		Chandia CHI
8-07 Argentina	L	0-4	Barquisimeto	CAqf			Simon BRA
22-08 Costa Rica	D	1-1	San Jose	Fr	Garcia.P 57		Mena CRC
8-09 Colombia	D	2-2	Lima	Fr	Guerrero 2 49 90	20 000	Carpio ECU
12-09 Bolivia	W	2-0	Lima	Fr	Vargas 15, Guerrero 36	15 000	Rivera PER
13-10 Paraguay	D	0-0	Lima	WCq		50 000	Simon BRA
17-10 Chile	L	0-2	Santiago	WCq		58 000	Ruiz COL
18-11 Brazil	D	1-1	Lima	WCq	Vargas 71	45 847	Torres PAR
21-11 Ecuador	L	1-5	Quito	WCq	Mendoza 86	28 557	Chandia CHI
2008							
6-02 Bolivia	L	1-2	La Paz	Fr	Garcia.P 70		
26-03 Costa Rica	W	3-1	Iquitos	Fr	Rengifo 32, Zambrano 46, Hidalgo 51		Buckley PER
31-05 Spain	L	1-2	Huelva	Fr	Rengifo 74	17 500	Meckarovski MKD
8-06 Mexico	L	0-4	Chicago	Fr			Geiger USA
14-06 Colombia	D	1-1	Lima	WCq	Marino 40	25 000	Torres PAR
17-06 Uruguay	L	0-6	Montevideo	WCq		20 016	Pozo CHI

Fr = Friendly match • CA = Copa América • WC = FIFA World Cup • q = qualifier • r1 = first round group • qf = quarter-final

PERU NATIONAL TEAM PLAYERS

	Player		Club	Date of Birth		Player		Club	Date of Birth
1	Leao Butrón	GK	Un San Martín	6 03 1977	11	Guillermo Salas	DF	Un San Martín	21 10 1974
2	Alberto Rodríguez	DF	SC Braga	31 03 1984	12	George Forsyth	GK	Atalanta	20 06 1982
3	Donny Neyra	MF	Universitario	12 01 1984	13	Amilton Prado	DF	Sporting Cristal	6 05 1979
4	Ernesto Arakaki	DF	Alianza Lima	13 06 1979	14	Hernán Rengifo	FW	Lech Poznan	18 04 1983
5	Martín Hidalgo	DF	Grêmio	15 06 1976	15	Miguel Villalta	DF	Sporting Cristal	16 06 1981
6	Juan Vargas	DF	Fiorentina	5 10 1983	16	Miguel Cevasco	MF	Universitario	27 12 1986
7	Nolberto Solano	MF	free agent	12 12 1974	17	Rinaldo Cruzado	MF	Grasshoppers	21 09 1984
8	Rainer Torres	MF	Universitario	12 01 1980	18	Juan Carlos Mariño	MF	Hércules	2 01 1982
9	José Guerrero	FW	Hamburger SV	1 01 1984	19	Julio César Mesones	MF	AEL Limassol	16 06 1981
10	Miguel Angel Torres	FW	Universitario	17 01 1982					

Peru's squad for the June 2008 World Cup qualifiers

PERU NATIONAL TEAM RECORDS AND RECORD SEQUENCES

Records			Sequence records					
Victory	9-1	ECU 1938	Wins	9	1937-1939	Clean sheets	4	1996
Defeat	0-7	BRA 1997	Defeats	9	1965-1968	Goals scored	12	1937-1941
Player Caps	122	Roberto Palacios	Undefeated	12	1937-1941	Without goal	3	Eight times
Player Goals	26	Teófilo Cubillas	Without win	15	1965-1969	Goals against	16	1959-1965

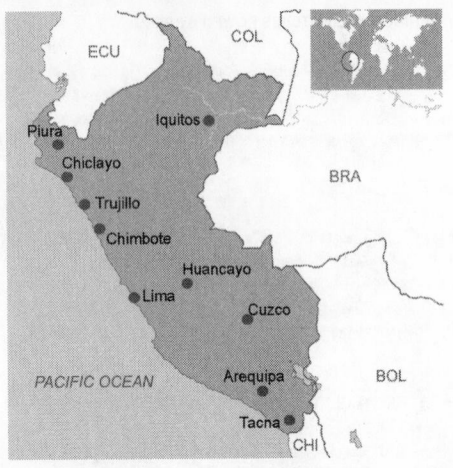

REPUBLIC OF PERU; REPUBLICA DEL PERU

Capital	Lima	Language	Spanish, Quechua			Independence	1821
Population	28 674 757	Area	1 285 220 km²	Density	21 per km²	% in cities	72%
GDP per cap	$5 100	Dailling code	+51	Internet	.pe	GMT + / -	-5

MEDALS TABLE

		Overall			League			Sth Am			City	Stadium	Cap'ty	DoF
		G	S	B	G	S	B	G	S	B				
1	Universitario de Deportes	24	14	18	24	13	14	1		4	Lima	Teodoro Fernández	80 093	1924
2	Alianza Lima	20	17	12	20	17	9			3	Lima	Alejandro Villanueva	35 000	1901
3	Sporting Cristal	15	16	6	15	15	6		1		Lima	San Martín de Porres	18 000	1922
4	Sport Boys	6	7	5	6	7	5				Callao	Miguel Grau	15 000	1927
5	Deportivo Municipal	4	7	6	4	7	6				Lima	Municipal de Chorrillos	15 000	1935
6	Atlético Chalaco	2	5	4	2	5	4				Callao	Telmo Carbajo	8 000	1899
7	Mariscal Sucre	2	2	2	2	2	2				Lima			
8	Unión Huaral	2	1		2	1					Huaral	Julio Lores Colán	6 000	1947
9	Cienciano	1	4			4		1			Cusco	Inca Garcilaso de la Vega	42 056	1901
10	FBC Melgar	1	1	2	1	1	2				Arequipa	Mariano Melgar	20 000	1915
11	Defensor Lima	1		4	1		3			1	Lima			1931
12	Centro Iqueño	1		3	1		3				Chancay			1935-87
13	Colegio San Agustín	1			1						Lima			1982
	Sport Progreso	1			1						Lima			
	Universidad San Martín	1			1						Lima	Estadio Nacional	45 000	2004

RECENT LEAGUE RECORD

	Championship							Championship Play-off		
Year	Champions	Pts	Runners-up	Pts	Third	Pts		Winners	Score	Runners-up
1995	Sporting Cristal	96	Alianza Lima	84	Universitario	84				
1996	Sporting Cristal	69	Alianza Lima	60	Universitario	58				
1997								Alianza Lima	†	
1998								Universitario	2-1 1-2 4-2p	Sporting Cristal
1999								Universitario	3-0 0-1	Alianza Lima
2000								Universitario	†	
2001								Alianza Lima	3-2 0-1 4-2p	Cienciano
2002								Sporting Cristal	‡	
2003								Alianza Lima	2-1	Sporting Cristal
2004								Alianza Lima	0-0 5-4p	Sporting Cristal
2005								Sporting Cristal	1-0	Cienciano
2006								Alianza Lima	0-1 3-1	Cienciano
2007	Univ. San Martin	71	Cienciano	71	Sport Ancash	67				

† Won both Apertura and Clausura so automatic champions • ‡ Apertura champions Universitario forfeited their place in the play-off by failing to finish in the top 4 of the Clausura • In 2007 neither the Apertura or Clausura champions qualified for the championship play-off as they failed to finish in the top six in the other half of the season. The championship was decided on overall standings

PERU 2007

PRIMERA DIVISION CLAUSURA

	Pl	W	D	L	F	A	Pts	Cor Bolognesi	Universitario	Cienciano	Alianza	Sport Ancash	Sport'g Cristal	U San Martin	FBC Melgar	Alianza Atl'co	Total Clean	Dep Municipal	Sport Boys
Coronel Bolognesi	22	10	6	6	28	15	36		0-0	6-2	0-0	2-0	0-1	0-1	2-0	1-0	3-0	1-0	3-1
Universitario	22	9	8	5	27	22	35	1-1		2-1	1-3	1-2	2-1	0-0	2-2	0-0	1-0	2-1	3-1
Cienciano	22	10	4	8	35	28	34	1-0	2-3		3-0	2-1	2-0	4-0	0-0	2-0	3-1	4-0	3-0
Alianza Lima	22	9	7	6	29	25	34	3-2	1-1	1-2		3-0	0-1	0-5	0-0	2-1	2-1	6-0	1-2
Sport Ancash	22	9	6	7	26	27	33	0-0	2-1	1-1	1-1		3-1	1-0	0-2	3-2	1-0	3-1	2-2
Sporting Cristal	22	7	9	6	21	23	30	1-0	1-0	1-0	1-2	2-0		1-1	1-1	1-0	2-2	3-3	1-1
Univer'dad San Martin	22	7	6	9	25	24	27	0-2	0-2	3-1	0-0	2-1	1-1		1-0	3-0	3-0	0-1	1-1
FBC Melgar	22	5	11	6	18	17	26	0-2	0-1	4-1	1-1	0-2	0-0	2-1		0-0	2-2	1-0	2-0
Alianza Atlético	22	6	8	8	17	22	26	0-0	0-0	3-0	0-0	1-1	0-0	2-1	1-0		1-0	1-0	2-1
Total Clean Arequipa	22	7	4	11	22	27	25	1-0	0-1	1-0	2-0	0-1	1-1	2-0	0-0	4-1		4-1	1-0
Deportivo Municipal	22	6	6	10	24	38	24	1-2	3-2	1-1	0-1	2-0	1-0	2-2	0-0	3-2	1-0		2-2
Sport Boys	22	4	11	7	25	29	23	2-2	1-1	0-0	1-2	1-1	3-0	1-0	1-1	0-0	3-0	1-1	

21/07/2007 - 16/12/2007 • Coronel Bolognesi did not qualify to meet Apertura winners Universidad San Martin in the championship decider as they had not finished in the top six in the Apertura. As Apertura winners Universidad San Martin failed to finish in the top six of the Clausura, the title was decided on the overall aggregate standings with no end of season play-off • See *Almanack of World Football 2008* for Apertura details
Top scorers (Apertura and Clausura): Johan Fano, Universitario 19; Richar Estigarribia, Sport Ancash 19

PERU 2007 PRIMERA DIVISION AGGREGATE

	Pl	W	D	L	F	A	Pts
Univer'dad San Martin†	44	20	11	13	69	46	71
Cienciano †	44	20	11	13	67	50	71
Sport Ancash ‡	44	18	13	13	56	49	67
Universitario ‡	44	18	13	13	58	53	67
Alianza Lima	44	18	15	11	60	48	65
Sport Boys	44	13	18	13	58	58	57
Coronel Bolognesi †	44	14	13	17	50	51	55
FBC Melgar	44	13	16	15	50	55	55
Alianza Atlético	44	12	18	14	40	45	54
Sporting Cristal	44	12	16	16	46	58	52
Deportivo Municipal	44	12	12	20	49	68	48
Total Clean Arequipa	44	13	6	25	50	72	45

Universidad San Martin were declared champions with the best overall record • † Qualified for the Copa Libertadores • ‡ Qualified for the Copa Sudamericana

PERU 2007 SEGUNDA DIVISION (2)

	Pl	W	D	L	F	A	Pts
Univ'dad César Vallejo	20	14	3	3	41	12	45
Atlético Mineiro	20	12	7	1	39	10	43
Universidad Técnica	20	11	6	3	25	16	39
Deportivo Aviación	20	10	4	6	28	20	36
Univ'dad San Marcos	20	8	6	6	28	22	30
América Cochahuayco	20	9	3	8	26	21	30
Olímpico Aurora	19	6	6	7	28	25	24
La Peña Sporting	20	6	6	8	19	26	24
Hijos de Acosvinchos	19	4	4	11	13	26	16
Unión Huaral	20	3	2	15	20	49	9
Alfonso Ugarte	20	2	1	17	8	48	7

26/05/2007 - 11/11/2007 • Jose Galvez sat out the season but were promoted after being wrongly relegated in 2006 Copa Peru winners Juan Aurich also promoted

PERU 2008

PRIMERA DIVISION APERTURA

	Pl	W	D	L	F	A	Pts	Universitario	Sport'g Cristal	U San Martin	Cienciano	Cor Bolognesi	Alianza Atl'co	César Vallejo	Juan Aurich	Jose Galvez	FBC Melgar	Alianza	Sport Ancash	Sport Boys	At. Mineiro
Universitario	26	16	7	3	40	21	55		1-0	1-1	3-1	1-0	2-1	0-0	3-1	3-2	2-0	2-1	2-0	5-1	2-1
Sporting Cristal	26	15	4	7	46	32	49	1-2		3-4	1-0	1-1	3-1	3-0	1-1	3-2	2-1	2-2	2-1	5-1	4-1
Univer'dad San Martin	26	11	10	5	40	20	43	1-1	0-1		3-0	0-0	2-0	4-0	1-1	1-1	2-0	5-0	1-0	0-0	4-0
Cienciano	26	12	5	9	37	28	41	4-1	4-0	0-0		1-3	1-0	4-1	3-2	3-0	1-0	3-2	3-0	1-0	1-0
Coronel Bolognesi	26	10	8	8	33	27	38	1-1	0-2	1-2	0-1		1-2	1-1	3-0	1-0	2-1	1-2	1-0	3-0	2-1
Alianza Atlético	26	10	4	12	28	28	34	1-0	1-2	1-1	1-0	1-4		1-3	1-1	3-0	3-0	0-1	3-0	0-0	3-1
Univ'dad César Vallejo	26	9	7	10	26	32	34	0-0	1-1	3-1	1-0	2-0	2-0		2-1	2-0	1-0	2-3	0-1	1-0	2-1
Juan Aurich	26	9	6	11	27	30	33	1-1	1-0	1-0	1-0	2-0	0-2	0-0		0-0	1-0	1-2	3-0	3-0	1-0
Jose Galvez	26	7	9	10	26	32	30	0-1	1-2	0-2	1-0	1-0	0-0	2-2	4-0		2-1	1-1	1-0	3-2	1-0
FBC Melgar	26	7	9	10	18	25	30	0-1	1-0	2-1	1-0	1-1	1-0	1-1	2-1	1-0		1-1	0-2	1-1	1-1
Alianza Lima	26	7	8	11	27	32	29	1-1	1-3	0-1	0-0	0-1	0-1	2-1	0-1	3-0	1-0		1-0	1-1	4-1
Sport Ancash	26	9	2	15	24	36	29	0-1	1-2	1-0	3-3	1-2	2-1	1-0	3-2	0-0	0-2	1-0		4-0	1-0
Sport Boys	26	7	8	11	23	42	27	1-1	1-1	1-2	1-0	1-3	0-1	1-1	0-0	0-0	2-1	1-0	3-2		2-1
Atlético Mineiro	26	6	7	13	26	36	25	0-2	3-1	1-1	2-2	3-1	0-0	0-0	1-0	2-1	0-0	0-0	3-0	3-0	

16/02/2008 - 20/07/2008 • Universitario qualified to meet the winners of the 2008 Clausura in the Championship decider

PHI – PHILIPPINES

NATIONAL TEAM RECORD
JULY 10TH 2006 TO JULY 12TH 2010

PL	W	D	L	F	A	%
11	5	2	4	18	15	54.5

FIFA/COCA-COLA WORLD RANKING

1993	1994	1995	1996	1997	1998	1999	2000	2001	2002	2003	2004	2005	2006	2007	High	
163	171	166	166	175	175	181	179	175	181	189	188	191	171	179	**157**	12/92

	2007–2008										Low	
08/07	09/07	10/07	11/07	12/07	01/08	02/08	03/08	04/08	05/08	06/08	07/08	**195** 10/06
169	170	175	179	179	181	190	190	189	189	170	169	

The Philippines reached the midway point of 2008 with the unlikely record of having not lost any of the three games they played. Indeed, by remaining undefeated in four consecutive matches, the team established a new national record. There was lingering disappointment, however, after the nation missed out on qualifying for the finals of the 2008 AFC Challenge Cup despite the unbeaten run. Victories over Brunei and Bhutan plus a draw with Tajikistan saw them collect seven points on home soil in Iloilio City in the qualifiers for the tournament, but it was Tajikistan who took the place in the finals in India by virtue of a better goal difference. While unfortunate, the results underscore a

INTERNATIONAL HONOURS
Far-Eastern Games 1913

continuing improvement being made in Philippino football, thanks in part to the recruitment of overseas-born players of local heritage. England-based players Christopher Greatwich, Matthew Hartmann, Phil Younghusband, Neil Etheridge and Chad Gould have all earned call ups in the last two years and are playing a major role in allowing the national side to climb from the lowest rungs in the FIFA/Coca-Cola World Ranking. The Philippines' next challenge will be to qualify for the finals of the ASEAN Championships and build on their encouraging performances in the tournament when they last reached the finals in early 2007.

THE FIFA BIG COUNT OF 2006

	Male	Female		Total
Number of players	1 548 746	120 019	Referees and Assistant Referees	167
Professionals	0		Admin, Coaches, Technical, Medical	132
Amateurs 18+	20 910		Number of clubs	75
Youth under 18	8 123		Number of teams	229
Unregistered	340 090		Clubs with women's teams	10
Total players	1 668 765		Players as % of population	1.87%

Philippine Football Federation (PFF)

No 27 Danny Floro, Corner Capt Henry Javiers Sts., Pasig City, Metro Manila 1604, Philippines
Tel +63 2 6871594   Fax +63 2 6871598
philippine_football_federation@yahoo.com   www.philfootball.info
President: MARTINEZ Jose Mari   General Secretary: ARANETA Pablo
Vice-President: ARANETA Pablito   Treasurer: MARTE Antonio   Media Officer: FORMOSO M. Eduardo
Men's Coach: TBD   Women's Coach: MARO Marlon
PFF formed: 1907   AFC: 1954   FIFA: 1930
Blue shirts, Blue shorts, Blue socks or Red shirts, Red shorts, Red socks

RECENT INTERNATIONAL MATCHES PLAYED BY THE PHILIPPINES

2003	Opponents	Score		Venue	Comp	Scorers	Att	Referee
	No international matches played in 2003							
2004								
8-12	Myanmar	L	0-1	Kuala Lumpur	TCr1		1 000	Napitupulu IDN
10-12	Malaysia	L	1-4	Kuala Lumpur	TCr1	Gould 93+		Napitupulu IDN
14-12	Timor-Leste †	W	2-1	Kuala Lumpur	TCr1	Caligdong 2 89 92+	100	Napitupulu IDN
16-12	Thailand	L	1-3	Kuala Lumpur	TCr1	Caligdong 27	300	Lazar SIN
2005								
	No international matches played in 2005							
2006								
26-03	Thailand	L	0-5	Chonburi	Fr			
1-04	Chinese Taipei	L	0-1	Chittagong	CCr1		4 000	Lee Gi Young KOR
3-04	India	D	1-1	Chittagong	CCr1	Valeroso 19	2 000	Mujghef JOR
5-04	Afghanistan	D	1-1	Chittagong	CCr1	Valeroso 59	3 000	Mujghef JOR
12-11	Laos	L	1-2	Bacolod	TCq	Greatwich 62		
14-11	Timor Leste	W	7-0	Bacolod	TCq	Younghusband 4 22 25p 36 69, Greatwich 30, Zerrudo 51, Caligdong 82		
18-11	Cambodia	W	1-0	Bacolod	TCq	Borromeo 81p		
20-11	Brunei Darussalam	W	4-1	Bacolod	TCq	Del Rosario 25, Younghusband 2 59 90, Caligdong 73		
2007								
7-01	Singapore	L	1-4	Singapore	Fr	Younghusband 19p	2 000	
12-01	Malaysia	L	0-4	Bangkok	TCr1		5 000	Daud SIN
14-01	Thailand	L	0-4	Bangkok	TCr1		30 000	
16-01	Myanmar	D	0-0	Bangkok	TCr1		500	Daud SIN
2008								
13-05	Brunei Darussalam	W	1-0	Iloilo City	CCq	Caligdong 28	3 500	Saleem MDV
15-05	Tajikistan	D	0-0	Iloilo City	CCq		4 500	Al Badwawi UAE
17-05	Bhutan	W	3-0	Iloilo City	CCq	Gould 41, Younghusband 43, Pema OG 58	7 000	Saleem MDV

Fr = Friendly match • TC = ASEAN Tiger Cup/ASEAN Football Federation Championship • CC = AFC Challenge Cup
r1 = 1st round • † Not a full international

PHILIPPINES NATIONAL TEAM RECORDS AND RECORD SEQUENCES

Records			Sequence records					
Victory	15-2	JPN 1917	Wins	3	2006	Clean sheets	2	1972, 2006
Defeat	0-15	JPN 1967	Defeats	23	1958-1971	Goals scored	7	2006-2007
Player Caps	n/a		Undefeated	4	2006-2007	Without goal	14	1980-1983
Player Goals	n/a		Without win	39	1977-1991	Goals against	33	1972-1982

RECENT LEAGUE AND CUP RECORD

National Men's Open Championship				ANG Liga			
Year	Champions	Pts	Runners-up		Winners	Score	Runners-up
2003	National Capital Region	4-1	Laguna		San Beda College	1-0	University of Santo Tomas
2004	National Capital Region	0-0 4-3p	Negros Occidental		San Beda College	2-1	University of Santo Tomas
2005	Negros Occidental	2-1	National Capital Region		Saint Benilde	0-0 7-6p	San Beda College
2006							
2007	National Capital Region	2-1	Negros Occidental				
2008							

PHILIPPINES COUNTRY INFORMATION

Capital	Manila	Independence	1946 from the USA	GDP per Capita	$4 600
Population	86 241 697	Status	Republic	GNP Ranking	41
Area km²	300 000	Language	Filipino, English	Dialling code	+63
Population density	274 per km²	Literacy rate	92%	Internet code	.ph
% in urban areas	54%	Main religion	Christian	GMT +/–	+8
Towns/Cities ('000)	Manila 10 443; Davao 1 212; Cebu 758; Antipolo 549; Zamboanga 460; Bacolod 454; Cagayan 445; Dasmariñas 441; Dadiangas 432; Iloilo 387; San Jose del Monte 357				
Neighbours (km)	Philippine Sea & South China Sea 36 289				
Main stadia	José Rizal Memorial Stadium – Manilla 30 000; Pana-ad Stadium – Bacolod 15 000				

PLE – PALESTINE

NATIONAL TEAM RECORD
JULY 10TH 2006 TO JULY 12TH 2010

PL	W	D	L	F	A	%
7	0	1	6	2	17	7.1

FIFA/COCA-COLA WORLD RANKING

1993	1994	1995	1996	1997	1998	1999	2000	2001	2002	2003	2004	2005	2006	2007
-	-	-	-	-	184	170	171	145	151	139	126	137	128	165

High	
115	04/06

						2007–2008						
08/07	09/07	10/07	11/07	12/07	01/08	02/08	03/08	04/08	05/08	06/08	07/08	
142	157	167	167	165	162	162	159	176	175	176	172	

Low	
191	08/99

Political and social instability have made competing at any level immensely difficult for Palestine and the problems associated with travelling in and out the troubled territory brought an early end to the nation's attempts to qualify for the 2010 FIFA World Cup. Palestine kicked off against Singapore in the first leg of their preliminary round meeting with just 75 fans turning up to the stadium in Doha, after the football association was unable to give security guarantees for the match be played on home soil. Singapore won the game 4-0 but there was a bizarre sight in the return when Chinese referee Sun Baojie whistled for the start of the match and then promptly abandoned

INTERNATIONAL HONOURS
None

it as the Palestines hadn't turned up. They had been unable to gain exit visas from the Israeli authorities that would have allowed them to travel to the island state to fulfil their obligations in the return fixture but they hadn't officially informed anyone so their pleas for the match to be rescheduled fell on deaf ears. Palestine's inability to play internationals continued to cause further disruption when the team withdrew from the qualifying tournament for the 2008 AFC Challenge Cup. The Palestinians had been originally drawn to face Nepal, Pakistan and Guam but pulled out of the competition just 10 days before it commenced.

THE FIFA BIG COUNT OF 2006

	Male	Female		Total
Number of players	87 060	5 100	Referees and Assistant Referees	301
Professionals	0		Admin, Coaches, Technical, Medical	494
Amateurs 18+	5 500		Number of clubs	40
Youth under 18	13 200		Number of teams	66
Unregistered	22 100		Clubs with women's teams	0
Total players	92 160		Players as % of population	2.43%

Palestine Football Association (PFA)
PO Box 4373, Ramallah-Al Bireh
Tel +972 2 2959102   Fax +972 2 2959101
info@pfa.ps   www.pfa.com
President: ALRAJOUB Jibril Mahmoud Mohammad   General Secretary: MAKKAWI Sami Hussein
Vice-President: ABU SALIM Ibrahim   Treasurer: ABUHASHIA Omar Mohammad   Media Officer: ABU HASHESH Jamal Khwalda
Men's Coach: SWERKY Naeem   Women's Coach: BARAKAT Abdel Nasser
PFA formed: 1928, 1962   AFC: 1998   FIFA: 1998
White shirts, Black shorts, White socks

RECENT INTERNATIONAL MATCHES PLAYED BY PALESTINE

2004 Opponents	Score	Venue	Comp	Scorers	Att	Referee
18-02 Chinese Taipei	W 8-0	Doha	WCq	Alkord [10], Habaib 2 [20 32], Atura [43], Beshe 2 [52 86], Amar [76], Keshkesh [82]	1 000	Al Yarimi YEM
26-03 Syria	D 1-1	Damascus	Fr			
31-03 Iraq	D 1-1	Doha	WCq	Beshe [72]	500	Al Shoufi SYR
9-06 Uzbekistan	L 0-3	Tashkent	WCq		35 000	Moradi IRN
17-06 Jordan	D 1-1	Tehran	WAr1	Alkord [12]		
19-06 Iraq	L 1-2	Tehran	WAr1	Alkord [40]		
2-09 Bahrain	L 0-1	Al Muharraq	Fr			
8-09 Uzbekistan	L 0-3	Rayyan	WCq		400	Maidin SIN
14-10 Chinese Taipei	W 1-0	Taipei	WCq	Amar [94+]	500	Rasheed MDV
16-11 Iraq	L 1-4	Doha	WCq	Zaatara [71]	500	Al Mutlaq KSA
2005						
1-12 Iraq	L 0-4	Al Rayyan	WGr1			
3-12 Saudi Arabia	L 0-2	Al Rayyan	WGr1			
2006						
7-02 Syria	L 0-3	Damascus	Fr			
16-02 Bahrain	W 2-0	Al Muharraq	Fr	Allam [26], Attal [88]		
18-02 Pakistan	W 3-0	Manama	Fr	Attal 2 [55 75], Salem [85]		
22-02 China PR	L 0-2	Guangzhou	ACq		16 500	Kwon Jong Chul KOR
1-03 Singapore	W 1-0	Amman	ACq	Attal [75]	1 000	Al Hilali OMA
1-04 Guam	W 11-0	Dhaka	CCr1	Keshkesh [6], Attal 6 [14 20 25 32 45 86], Atura [22], Al Amour [39], Al Kord 2 [59 67]	3 000	AK Nema IRQ
3-04 Cambodia	W 4-0	Dhaka	CCr1	Keshkesh [10], Al Sweirki 2 [12 75], Attal [30]	2 500	AK Nema IRQ
5-04 Bangladesh	D 1-1	Dhaka	CCr1	Attal [30]	22 000	Mombini IRN
9-04 Kyrgyzstan	L 0-1	Dhaka	CCqf		150	U Win Cho MYA
17-08 Iraq	L 0-3	Amman	ACq		5 000	Basma SYR
6-09 Iraq	D 2-2	Al Ain	ACq	Amar [13], Al Amour [78]	1 000	Mujghef JOR
11-10 China PR	L 0-2	Amman	ACq		3 000	Al Fadhli KUW
2007						
18-06 Iraq	L 0-1	Amman	WAr1			
20-06 Iran	L 0-2	Amman	WAr1			
8-10 Singapore	L 0-4	Doha	WCq		75	Basma SYR
28-10 Singapore	L 0-3	Singapore	WCq	Awarded to Singapore		Sun Baojie CHN
2008						

No international matches played in 2008 before August

Fr = Friendly match • AC = AFC Asian Cup • WA = West Asian Championship • WC = FIFA World Cup
q = qualifier • r1 = 1st round

PALESTINE NATIONAL TEAM RECORDS AND RECORD SEQUENCES

Records			Sequence records				
Victory	11-0	GUM 2006	Wins	3	2006	Clean sheets	3	1976-1992, 2006
Defeat	1-8	EGY 1953	Defeats	4	2001-02, 2003	Goals scored	8	1953-1965
Player Caps	n/a		Undefeated	4	1999, 2006	Without goal	3	2003
Player Goals	n/a		Without win	14	2001-2003	Goals against	13	2001-2003

The organisation of a Palestinian championship and cup tournament is sporadic and often haphazrad due to the political and geographical difficulties. Champions in the past have included Rafah Services club in 1996, Shabab Al Amari in 1997, Khadamat Rafah in 1998 and Al Aqsa in 2002

PALESTINE COUNTRY INFORMATION

Capital	Ramallah	Independence	1993	GDP per Capita	$600
Population	3 636 195	Status	Republic	GNP Ranking	n/a
Area km²	6 220	Language	Arabic	Dialling code	+972
Population density	584 per km²	Literacy rate	n/a	Internet code	.ps
% in urban areas	n/a	Main religion	Muslim	GMT +/−	+2
Towns/Cities	Ramallah; Nablus; Jericho; Hebron; Gaza; Bethlehem				
Neighbours (km)	For the West Bank and Gaza: Israel 358; Jordan 97; Egypt 11; Mediterranean Sea 40				
Main stadia	None				

PNG – PAPUA NEW GUINEA

NATIONAL TEAM RECORD
JULY 10TH 2006 TO JULY 12TH 2010

PL	W	D	L	F	A	%
1	0	0	1	1	2	0

FIFA/COCA-COLA WORLD RANKING

1993	1994	1995	1996	1997	1998	1999	2000	2001	2002	2003	2004	2005	2006	2007	High
-	-	-	169	167	172	183	192	196	167	172	161	166	178	183	**160** 06/04

	2007–2008											Low
08/07	09/07	10/07	11/07	12/07	01/08	02/08	03/08	04/08	05/08	06/08	07/08	**199** 06/08
180	182	183	183	183	184	186	186	188	188	199	199	

With just one international played in four years, the national team of Papua New Guinea has been one of the least active in the world, and unsurprisingly they find themselves rock bottom of the FIFA/Coca-Cola World Ranking. Despite being among just a handful of countries not to enter the qualifiers for the 2010 FIFA World Cup, Papua New Guinea has embarked on a project to develop club football in order to improve standards for the national team. The establishment of the semi-professional National Soccer League was a key part of those plans. Now in its second season, it was won again by Souths United. They finished top of the first round league table and then won

INTERNATIONAL HONOURS
South Pacific Mini Games 1989

the play-offs, beating Gelle Hills 3-2 in the final with top scorer Kema Jack scoring a hat-trick. It's ironic, however, that since the establishment of the League in 2006, the national team has slipped from 177th in the world rankings and their absence from the South Pacific Games, a tournament which acted as the first round of Oceania's World Cup qualifiers, was surprising given that the women's national team entered. Indeed, the women provided the story of the year when they went on to win the tournament, beating Tonga 3-1 in the final. They then just missed out on a place at the Olympics after losing to New Zealand in a play-off.

THE FIFA BIG COUNT OF 2006

	Male	Female		Total
Number of players	188 900	8 000	Referees and Assistant Referees	1 200
Professionals	0		Admin, Coaches, Technical, Medical	5 200
Amateurs 18+	7 700		Number of clubs	440
Youth under 18	59 200		Number of teams	1 100
Unregistered	57 100		Clubs with women's teams	23
Total players	196 900		Players as % of population	3.47%

Papua New Guinea Football Association (PNGFA)
Lae 411, PO Box 957, Morobe Province, Papua New Guinea
Tel +675 4751398   Fax +675 4751399
pngsoka@datec.net.pg   www.pngfootball.com.pg
President: CHUNG David   General Secretary: DIMIRIT Mileng
Vice-President: DANIELS Seth   Treasurer: SATIMBU Lua   Media Officer: KAMBI Thomas
Men's Coach: GUSAMO Marcos   Women's Coach: TBD
PNGFA formed: 1962   OFC: 1966   FIFA: 1963
Red shirts with yellow trimmings, Black shorts, Yellow socks or Yellow shirts with red trimmings, Red shorts, Yellow socks

RECENT INTERNATIONAL MATCHES PLAYED BY PAPUA NEW GUINEA

2004	Opponents	Score		Venue	Comp	Scorers	Att	Referee
10-05	Vanuatu	D	1-1	Apia	WCq	Wasi [73]	500	Breeze AUS
12-05	Fiji	L	2-4	Apia	WCq	Davani [12], Komboi [44]	400	Diomis AUS
17-05	American Samoa	W	10-0	Apia	WCq	Davani 4 [23 24 40 79], Lepani 3 [26 28 64], Wasi [34] Komboi [37], Lohai [71]	150	Afu SOL
19-05	Samoa	W	4-1	Apia	WCq	Davani [16], Lepani 2 [37 55], Komeng [68]	300	Diomis AUS
2005								
No international matches played in 2005								
2006								
No international matches played in 2006								
2007								
13-07	Solomon Islands	L	1-2	Honiara	Fr	Davani		
2008								
No international matches played in 2008 before August								

Fr = Friendly match • OC = OFC Nations Cup • SP = South Pacific Games • WC = FIFA World Cup • q = qualifier • r1 = first round group

PAPUA NEW GUINEA NATIONAL TEAM RECORDS AND RECORD SEQUENCES

Records			Sequence records				
Victory	10-0	ASA 2004	Wins	4	2002	Clean sheets	2	2002
Defeat	2-11	AUS 1980	Defeats	6	1998-2000	Goals scored	7	2000-2002
Player Caps	n/a		Undefeated	5	1993-97, 2002	Without goal	4	1990-1993
Player Goals	n/a		Without win	10	1985-1986	Goals against	12	1980-1993

PAPUA NEW GUINEA 2007-08 NATIONAL SOCCER LEAGUE

	Pl	W	D	L	F	A	Pts	SU	GH	BK	IR	WH	MB	MF
Souths United †	12	9	2	1	32	13	29		4-0	3-3	1-0	1-0	6-0	5-1
Gelle Hills United †	12	7	3	2	22	15	23	0-3		1-1	2-2	2-0	1-0	5-1
Blue Kumuls Lae †	12	6	3	3	24	15	21	3-0	0-1		2-1	1-2	2-0	6-1
Inspac Rapatona †	12	5	1	6	19	15	16	0-1	2-0	0-3		2-1	3-0	2-3
Welgris Highlanders	12	4	2	6	20	19	14	1-2	1-2	1-1	2-1		1-3	3-3
Madang Besta	12	4	1	7	22	30	13	4-4	1-2	4-0	0-2	1-2		6-5
Madang Fox	12	1	1	10	18	50	4	1-2	0-6	1-2	0-4	0-6	2-3	

10/11/2007 - 9/03/2008 • † Qualified for the play-offs • Top scorer: Kema Jack, Hekari 11

PLAY-OFFS

Semi–finals		Finals	
Souths Utd	3		
Kumuls	1		
		Souths Utd	3
		Gelle Hills	2
Inspac	0		
Gelle Hills	3	22-03-2008	

Third place: Morobe 3-1 Inspac

RECENT LEAGUE AND CUP RECORD

	National Championship			Port Moresby			Lae			Lahi		
Year	Winners	Score	Finalist	Winners	Score	Finalist	Winners	Score	Finalist	Winners	Score	Finalist
2000	Unitech	3-2	Guria	PS United	1-0	Rapatona	Poro SC	1-1 4-3p	Blue Kumuls	Sobou	1-0	Unitech
2001	Sobou	3-1	ICF Univ'sity	ICF Univ'sity	1-0	PS United	Blue Kumuls	2-1	Goro	Unitech	2-0	Sobou
2002	Sobou	1-0	PS United	ICF Univ'sity	3-1	Rapatona	Tarangau	2-0	Poro SC	Sobou	w/o	Unitech
2003	Sobou	1-0	Unitech	Cosmos	2-1	ICF Univ'sity	Blue Kumuls		HC West	Unitech	2-0	Sobou
2004	Sobou	2-0	HC Water	Rapatona	1-0	PS Rutz	HC West	2-1	Tarangau	Sobou	3-0	Bismarck
2005	Sobou	4-2	Cosmos	PS Rutz	2-0	ICF Univ'sity	Blue Kumuls	2-1	HC West	Unitech	4-2	Sobou
2006	ICF Univ'sity	0-0 2-0p	Sobou	ICF Univ'sity	0-0 4-2p	Rapatona	Cosmos	3-2	Poro SC			
2007	Not played			Souths Utd	2-1	ICF Univ'sity	HC West	2-0	Poro SC	Sobou	2-1	Speed Way

PAPUA NEW GUINEA COUNTRY INFORMATION

Capital	Port Moresby	Independence	1975 from Australia	GDP per Capita	$2 200
Population	5 420 280	Status	Constitutional Monarchy	GNP Ranking	131
Area km²	462 840	Language	Melanesian Pidgin, English	Dialling code	+675
Population density	12 per km²	Literacy rate	64%	Internet code	.pg
% in urban areas	16%	Main religion	Christian	GMT +/−	+10
Towns/Cities ('000)	Port Moresby 283; Lae 76; Arawa 40; Mount Hagen 33; Popondetta 28; Madang 27; Kokopo 26				
Neighbours (km)	Indonesia 820; South Pacific Ocean & Coral Sea 5 152				
Main stadia	Hubert Murray – Port Moresby 10 000				

POL – POLAND

NATIONAL TEAM RECORD
JULY 10TH 2006 TO JULY 12TH 2010

PL	W	D	L	F	A	%
29	13	9	7	44	29	60.3

FIFA/COCA-COLA WORLD RANKING

1993	1994	1995	1996	1997	1998	1999	2000	2001	2002	2003	2004	2005	2006	2007		High	
28	29	33	53	48	31	32	43	33	34	25	25	22	24	22		**16**	09/07

2007–2008													Low	
08/07	09/07	10/07	11/07	12/07	01/08	02/08	03/08	04/08	05/08	06/08	07/08		**61**	03/98
20	16	20	23	22	23	20	24	28	27	28	32			

The name Howard Webb will live long in the memory of Poland fans after the English referee awarded Austria a last minute penalty in their crucial Euro 2008 match to deprive the Poles of a win that could have seen them qualify for the quarter-finals. In the event Poland lost their final match against Croatia but by then the wind had gone from their sails, with the team making a first round exit for the second tournament in a row. To add to the sense of gloom, doubts were also being cast about the viability of the Poland/Ukraine joint hosting of the Euro 2012 tournament, although most of the concern raised were directed towards their co-hosts. With six new stadia to be built or

INTERNATIONAL HONOURS
Qualified for the FIFA World Cup Finals 1938 1974 1978 1982 1986 2002 2006

refurbished in Chorzow, Gdansk, Krakow, Poznan, Warsaw and Wroclaw, Euro 2012 represents a great opportunity for domestic football in Poland especially if recent corruption scandals can be put behind them. The football association was certainly taking no prisoners in its attempt to clean up the game with 2007 champions Zaglebie Lubin relegated for their part in the scandal. On the pitch Wisla Krakow returned to winning ways securing their first championship in three years by a hefty margin over Legia Warszawa but the team from the capital denied Maciej Skorza's team the double after beating Wisla in a penalty shoot-out in the Cup Final.

THE FIFA BIG COUNT OF 2006

	Male	Female		Total
Number of players	1 817 819	182 445	Referees and Assistant Referees	11 658
Professionals	1 202		Admin, Coaches, Technical, Medical	60 100
Amateurs 18+	465 854		Number of clubs	5 690
Youth under 18	185 808		Number of teams	13 245
Unregistered	424 300		Clubs with women's teams	201
Total players	2 000 264		Players as % of population	5.19%

Polish Football Association (PZPN)

Polski Zwiazek Pilki Noznej, Miodowa 1, Warsaw 00-080, Poland
Tel +48 22 5512315   Fax +48 22 5512240
pzpn@pzpn.pl   www.pzpn.pl
President: LISTKIEWICZ Michal   General Secretary: KRECINA Zdzislaw
Vice-President: KOLATOR Eugeniusz   Treasurer: BIAKECKA Krystyna   Media Officer: KOCIEBA Michal
Men's Coach: BEENHAKKER Leo   Women's Coach: STEPCZAK Jan
PZPN formed: 1919   UEFA: 1954   FIFA: 1923
White shirts with red trimmings, Red shorts, White socks or Red shirts with white trimmings, Red shorts, Red socks

RECENT INTERNATIONAL MATCHES PLAYED BY POLAND

2006	Opponents	Score		Venue	Comp	Scorers	Att	Referee
9-06	Ecuador	L	0-2	Gelsenkirchen	WCr1		52 000	Kamikawa JPN
14-06	Germany	L	0-1	Dortmund	WCr1		65 000	Medina Cantalejo ESP
20-06	Costa Rica	W	2-1	Hanover	WCr1	Bosacki 2 [33 66]	43 000	Maidin SIN
16-08	Denmark	L	0-2	Odense	Fr		11 008	Asumaa FIN
2-09	Finland	L	1-3	Bydgoszcz	ECq	Gargula [89]	13 000	Duhamel FRA
6-09	Serbia	D	1-1	Warsaw	ECq	Matusiak [30]	4 918	Poll ENG
7-10	Kazakhstan	W	1-0	Almaty	ECq	Smolarek [52]	22 000	Trivkovic CRO
11-10	Portugal	W	1-0	Chorzow	ECq	Smolarek 2 [9 18]	38 199	Stark GER
15-11	Belgium	W	1-0	Brussels	ECq	Matusiak [19]	37 928	Dougal SCO
6-12	UAE	W	5-2	Abu Dhabi	Fr	Grzelak 2 [8 50], Wasilewski [17], Magdon [87], Matusiak [94+]	1 000	Al Hilali OMA
2007								
3-02	Estonia	W	4-0	Jerez	Fr	Dudka [25], Kokoszka [32], Iwanski [70], Golanski [76]	100	Ruiz-Herrera ESP
7-02	Slovakia	D	2-2	Jerez	Fr	Zewlakow [48p], Matusiak [78]	200	Pacheco ESP
24-03	Azerbaijan	W	5-0	Warsaw	ECq	Bak [3], Dudka [6], Lobodzinski [34], Krzynówek [58], Kázmierczak [84]	13 000	Jakobsson ISL
28-03	Armenia	W	1-0	Kielce	ECq	Zurawski [26]	13 450	Undiano Mallenco ESP
2-06	Azerbaijan	W	3-1	Baku	ECq	Smolarek [63], Krzynówek 2 [66 90]	25 800	Kapitanis CYP
6-06	Armenia	L	0-1	Yerevan	ECq		9 800	Balaj ROU
22-08	Russia	D	2-2	Moscow	Fr	Krzynówek [72], Blaszczykowski [77]	15 000	Hrinak SVK
8-09	Portugal	D	2-2	Lisbon	ECq	Lewandowski [44], Krzynówek [88]	48 000	Rosseti ITA
12-09	Finland	D	0-0	Helsinki	ECq		34 088	Fandel GER
13-10	Kazakhstan	W	3-1	Warsaw	ECq	Smolarek 3 [56 65 66]	11 040	Berntsen NOR
17-10	Hungary	L	0-1	Lodz	Fr		6 000	Circhetta SUI
17-11	Belgium	W	2-0	Chorzow	ECq	Smolarek 2 [45 49]	41 450	Larsen DEN
21-11	Serbia	D	2-2	Belgrade	ECq	Murawski [28], Matusiak [46]	3 247	Busacca SUI
2008								
6-02	Czech Republic	W	2-0	Larnaca	Fr	Lobodzinski [6], Lewandowski [29]	1 500	Tryfonos CYP
27-02	Estonia	W	2-0	Wronki	Fr	Matusiak [38], Zahorski [73]	4 500	Todorov BUL
26-03	USA	L	0-3	Krakow	Fr		21 000	Hermansen DEN
26-05	FYR Macedonia	D	1-1	Reutlingen	Fr	Matusiak [84p]	2 200	Brych GER
27-05	Albania	W	1-0	Reutlingen	Fr	Zurawski [3]	2 200	Kircher GER
1-06	Denmark	D	1-1	Chorzow	Fr	Krzynówek [43]	40 000	Kalt FRA
8-06	Germany	L	0-2	Klagenfurt	ECr1		30 461	Ovrebø NOR
12-06	Austria	D	1-1	Vienna	ECr1	Guerreiro [30]	51 428	Webb ENG
16-06	Croatia	L	0-1	Klagenfurt	ECr1		30 461	Vassaras GRE

Fr = Friendly match • EC = UEFA EURO 2008 • WC = FIFA World Cup • q = qualifier • r1 = first round group

POLAND NATIONAL TEAM PLAYERS

	Player	Ap	G	Club	Date of Birth		Player	Ap	G	Club	Date of Birth
1	Artur Boruc	GK	37	0	Celtic	20 02 1980	12	Wojciech Kowalewski	GK	10	0	Steaua Bucuresti	11 05 1977
2	Mariusz Jop	DF	25	0	FK Moskva	3 08 1978	13	Marcin Wasilewski	DF	30	1	RSC Anderlecht	9 06 1980
3	Jakub Wawrzyniak	DF	12	0	Legia Warszawa	7 07 1983	14	Michal Zewlakow	DF	79	2	Olympiacos	22 04 1976
4	Paweł Golański	DF	12	1	Steaua Bucuresti	12 10 1982	15	Michal Pazdan	DF	5	0	Górnik Zabrze	21 09 1987
5	Dariusz Dudka	DF	29	2	Wisla Kraków	9 12 1983	16	Lukasz Piszczek	FW	4	0	Hertha Berlin	3 06 1985
6	Jacek Bak	DF	96	3	FK Austria Wien	24 03 1973	17	Wojciech Lobodzinski	MF	19	2	Wisla Kraków	20 10 1982
7	Euzebiusz Smolarek	MF	34	13	Racing S'tander	9 01 1981	18	Mariusz Lewandowski	MF	50	3	Shakhtar D'netsk	18 05 1979
8	Jacek Krzynówek	MF	82	15	VfL Wolfsburg	15 05 1976	19	Rafal Murawski	MF	11	1	Lech Warszawa	9 10 1981
9	Maciej Zurawski	FW	72	17	Larissa	12 09 1976	20	Roger Guerreiro	MF	5	1	Legia Warszawa	25 05 1982
10	Lukasz Gargula	MF	12	1	GKS Belchatow	25 02 1981	21	Tomasz Zahorski	FW	10	1	Górnik Zabrze	22 11 1984
11	Marek Saganowski	FW	26	3	Southampton	31 10 1978	22	Lukasz Fabianski	GK	8	0	Arsenal	18 04 1985
						23	Adam Kokoszka	DF	8	2	Wisla Kraków	6 10 1986

Poland's squad for Euro 2008

POLAND NATIONAL TEAM RECORDS AND RECORD SEQUENCES

Records				Sequence records			
Victory	9-0	NOR 1963		Wins	7	Four times	Clean sheets	4	1978, 1979, 2003
Defeat	0-8	DEN 1948		Defeats	6	1933-1934	Goals scored	28	1978-1980
Player Caps	100	LATO Grzegorz		Undefeated	13	2000-2001	Without goal	6	1999-2000
Player Goals	48	LUBANSKI Wlodzimeirz		Without win	13	1995-1996	Goals against	17	1957-1960

MAJOR CITIES/TOWNS
Population '000

1	Warsaw	1 618
2	Lódz	756
3	Kraków	752
4	Wroclaw	631
5	Poznan	565
6	Gdánsk	462
7	Szczecin	413
8	Bydgoszcz	362
9	Lublin	362
10	Katowice	311
11	Bialystok	292
12	Gdynia	254
13	Sosnowiec	224
14	Kielce	206
15	Zabrze	190
16	Bytom	186
17	Rzeszow	157
18	Plock	127
19	Chorzów	111
20	Lubin	76
21	Belchatow	62
22	Mielec	60
23	Grod'sk Wielkopolski	14
24	Wronki	11

REPUBLIC OF POLAND; RZECZPOSPOLITA POLSKA

Capital	Warsaw	Language	Polish	Independence	1918
Population	38 518 241	Area	312 685 km²	% in cities	65%
GDP per cap	$11 100	Dailling code	+48	Internet	.pl	GMT + / -	+1

MEDALS TABLE

		Overall			League			Cup			Europe			City	Stadium	Cap'ty	DoF
		G	S	B	G	S	B	G	S	B	G	S	B				
1	Legia Warszawa	21	16	14	8	10	12	13	6				2	Warsaw	Wojska Polskiego	13 628	1916
2	Górnik Zabrze	20	12	7	14	4	7	6	7				1	Zabrze	Ernest Pohl	18 000	1948
3	Wisla Kraków	16	17	9	12	11	9	4	6					Kraków	Stadion Wisly	15 850	1906
4	Ruch Chorzów	16	9	7	13	5	7	3	4					Chorzów	Stadion Ruchu	13 000	1920
5	Lech Poznan	9	1	3	5		3	4	1					Poznan	Stadion Miejski	26 500	1922
6	Widzew Lódz	5	7	4	4	7	3	1					1	Lódz	Stadion Widzewa	9 892	1910
7	Cracovia	5	2		5	2								Kraków	Jana Pawla II	6 500	1906
8	Zaglebie Sosnowiec	4	5	2		4	2	4	1					Sosnowiec	Stadion Ludowy	7 500	1906
9	Pogon Lwow	4	3		4	3								Lvov - UKR	Marshal Rydz-Smigly	10 000	1904-39
	Polonia Warszawa	4	3		2	3		2						Warsaw	Stadion Polonii	7 000	1911
11	GKS Katowice	3	9	4		4	4	3	5					Katowice	Stadion GKS	25 568	1964
12	LKS Lódz	3	2	2	2	1	2	1	1					Lódz	Stadion LKS	25 000	1908
13	Slask Wroclaw	3	2	1	1	2	1	2						Wroclaw	Stadion Slaska	13 000	1947
14	Amica Wronki	3	1	2			2	3	1					Wronki	Stadion Amica	5 296	1992
15	Polonia Bytom	2	7	2	2	4	2					3		Bytom	Edwarda Szymkowiaka	1920	1920
16	Warta Poznan	2	5	6	2	5	6							Poznan	Stadion Warty	4 000	1912
17	Zaglebie Lubin	2	3	1	2	1	1		2					Lubin	Stadion Zaglebia	32 420	1945
18	Stal Mielec	2	2	3	2	1	3		1					Mielec	Stadion Stali Mielec	30 000	1939
19	Groclin Grodzisk	2	2	1		2	1	2						Grodzisk Wielkopolski	Stadion Dyskobolia	7 000	1922

RECENT LEAGUE AND CUP RECORD

Championship							Cup		
Year	Champions	Pts	Runners-up	Pts	Third	Pts	Winners	Score	Runners-up
1996	Widzew Lódz	88	Legia Warszawa	85	Hutnik Kraków	52	Ruch Chorzów	1-0	GKS Belchatów
1997	Widzew Lódz	81	Legia Warszawa	77	Odra Wodzislaw	55	Legia Warszawa	2-0	GKS Katowice
1998	LKS Lódz	66	Polonia Warszawa	63	Wisla Kraków	61	Amica Wronki	5-3	Aluminium Konin
1999	Wisla Kraków	73	Widzew Lódz	56	Legia Warszawa	56	Amica Wronki	1-0	GKS Belchatów
2000	Polonia Warszawa	65	Wisla Kraków	56	Ruch Chorzów	55	Amica Wronki	2-2 3-0	Wisla Kraków
2001	Wisla Kraków	62	Pogon Szczecin	53	Legia Warszawa	50	Polonia Warszawa	2-1 2-2	Górnik Zabrze
2002	Legia Warszawa	42	Wisla Kraków	41	Amica Wronki	36	Wisla Kraków	4-2 4-0	Amica Wronki
2003	Wisla Kraków	68	Groclin Grodzisk	62	GKS Katowice	61	Wisla Kraków	0-1 3-0	Wisla Plock
2004	Wisla Kraków	65	Legia Warszawa	60	Amica Wronki	48	Lech Poznan	2-0 0-1	Legia Warszawa
2005	Wisla Kraków	62	Groclin Grodzisk	51	Legia Warszawa	47	Groclin Grodzisk	2-0 0-1	Zaglebie Lubin
2006	Legia Warszawa	66	Wisla Krakow	64	Zaglebie Lubin	49	Wisla Plock	3-2 3-1	Zaglebie Lubin
2007	Zaglebie Lubin	62	GKS Belchatow	61	Legia Warszawa	52	Groclin Grodzisk	2-0	Korona Kielce
2008	Wisla Kraków	77	Legia Warszawa	63	Groclin Grodzisk	60	Legia Warszawa	0-0 4-3p	Wisla Kraków

POLAND 2007-08

LIGA POLSKA ORANGE EKSTRAKLASA

	Pl	W	D	L	F	A	Pts	Wisla	Legia	Grodzisk	Lech	Zaglebie	Korona	Cracovia	Górnik	Belchatow	Ruch	LKS	Odra	Polonia	Jagiellonia	Widzew	Zaglebie
Wisla Krakow †	30	24	5	1	68	18	77		1-0	3-0	4-2	2-1	4-0	2-1	2-0	2-0	2-0	5-2	0-0	5-0	5-0	1-0	4-0
Legia Warszawa ‡	30	20	3	7	48	17	63	2-1		1-0	0-1	3-0	2-0	1-0	2-0	4-1	2-0	2-1	0-1	3-1	0-0	3-1	5-0
Groclin Dy. Grodzisk	30	18	6	6	52	24	60	0-0	1-0		1-0	2-0	4-0	0-0	3-1	0-0	1-4	2-0	0-0	5-0	3-1	3-0	3-0
Lech Poznan ‡	30	17	6	7	55	32	57	1-2	1-0	2-1		0-0	1-0	3-1	4-1	1-1	6-2	1-2	2-0	1-0	6-1	1-0	4-2
Zaglebie Lubin	30	15	7	8	43	30	52	0-1	0-2	1-2	1-1		1-0	3-1	1-1	1-0	2-1	2-1	3-0	0-0	5-2	2-1	2-1
Korona Kielce	30	15	6	9	38	32	51	1-1	1-0	1-1	1-0	1-4		2-0	3-2	2-2	0-2	2-0	2-0	2-0	4-0	1-1	2-0
Cracovia	30	11	6	13	30	32	39	1-2	0-2	3-1	3-2	1-2	1-1		3-0	0-2	1-0	0-0	3-0	1-1	2-0	1-0	1-0
Górnik Zabrze	30	11	6	13	34	39	39	1-3	0-3	0-0	0-1	0-1	0-3	1-0		2-0	1-0	1-1	1-0	4-0	3-0	1-1	4-2
GKS Belchatow	30	9	11	10	26	32	38	0-0	2-2	0-4	0-3	0-1	2-0	1-1	0-0		2-0	1-0	3-1	0-3	2-0	3-1	2-0
Ruch Chorzów	30	8	10	12	35	41	34	0-3	0-0	1-2	0-2	2-2	1-2	2-0	3-2	1-1		0-0	3-2	2-0	4-0	1-1	1-0
LKS Lodz	30	7	9	14	25	31	30	0-1	0-1	1-2	1-2	2-1	0-1	0-0	0-1	2-0	1-1		0-1	0-0	0-0	2-0	3-0
Odra Wodzislaw Slaski	30	8	5	17	28	47	29	2-2	0-2	2-3	1-2	1-3	1-0	0-1	0-2	1-0	2-0	2-2		0-2	1-3	1-1	1-0
Polonia Bytom	30	7	7	16	22	45	28	1-2	1-2	0-2	2-2	1-0	0-2	1-0	0-1	0-0	1-1	0-1	1-0		0-1	1-1	1-0
Jagiellonia Bialystok	30	7	6	17	27	57	27	1-2	1-2	1-3	4-2	0-0	0-0	0-2	1-1	0-1	1-1	0-1	2-3	2-1		2-1	2-1
Widzew Lodz	30	5	11	14	27	42	26	1-3	0-1	1-0	1-1	1-1	0-2	0-2	0-0	0-0	2-2	0-0	4-3	2-4	2-0		0-1
Zaglebie Sosnowiec	30	4	4	22	19	58	16	1-3	2-1	1-3	0-0	0-3	2-3	1-2	0-2	0-0	0-0	1-3	0-2	1-0	3-1	0-0	

27/07/2007 - 10/05/2008 • † Qualified for the UEFA Champions League • ‡ Qualified for the UEFA Cup • Top scorer: Pawel Brozek, Wisla 23

2007 champions Zaglebie Lubin were relegated as part of the ongoing investigation into match-fixing, as were Widzew and Zaglebie Sosnowiec

Relegation play-off: Jagiellonia Bialystok 0-2 1-2 **Arka Gdynia**
Jagiellonia were spared relegation after Korona were relegated

POLAND 2007-08 II LIGA (2)

	Pl	W	D	L	F	A	Pts
Lechia Gdansk	34	21	6	7	55	34	69
Slask Wroclaw	34	18	10	6	55	30	64
Piast Gliwice	34	17	11	6	45	23	62
Arka Gdynia §5	34	19	10	5	61	30	62
Znicz Pruszkow	34	18	8	8	54	28	62
Podbeskidzie §6	34	19	7	8	53	27	58
Polonia Warszawa	34	14	8	12	45	36	50
Wisla Plock	34	14	8	12	52	51	50
GKS Jastrzebie	34	12	9	13	43	51	45
GKS Katowice	34	11	10	13	38	39	43
Stal Stalowa Wola	34	11	7	16	30	48	40
Motor Lubin	34	10	5	19	33	55	35
Odra Opole	34	8	11	15	28	39	35
Warta Poznan	34	7	11	16	29	45	32
Kmita Zabierzów	34	6	13	15	28	40	31
Tur Turek	34	7	10	17	23	46	31
LKS Lomza	34	8	6	20	32	59	30
Pelikan Lowicz	34	6	10	18	37	60	28

28/07/2007 - 24/05/2008 • § = points deducted

PUCHAR EKSTRAKLASY 2007-08

Quarter-finals		Semi-finals		Final	
Groclin Grodzisk*	2 2				
Odra Wodzislaw	2 1	Groclin Grodzisk*	3 1		
Cracovia	1 0	Górnik Zabrze	0 1		
Górnik Zabrze *	0 2			Groclin Grodzisk	4
Wisla Krakow	1 5			Legia Warszawa	1
Jagiellonia *	1 0	Wisla Krakow	1 0	**CUP FINAL**	
Polonia Bytom *	0 2	Legia Warszawa*	1 1	Grodzisk Wielkopolski 17-05-2008	
Legia Warszawa	2 2	* Home team in first leg			

First round played in four groups of four

PUCHAR POLSKI 2007-08

Round of sixteen		Quarter-finals		Semi-finals		Final	
Legia Warszawa *	1						
LKS Lodz	0	Legia Warszawa *	1 1				
Wisla Plock	1	Lechia Gdansk	0 0				
Lechia Gdansk *	5			Legia Warszawa *	0 1		
Polonia Warszawa *	3			Zaglebie Lubin	0 1		
Korona Kielce	1	Polonia Warszawa	0 2				
Odra Opole *	0	Zaglebie Lubin *	5 3				
Zaglebie Lubin	2					Legia Warszawa ‡	0 4p
Groclin Dy. Grodzisk	3					Wisla Krakow	0 3p
Stal Stalowa Wola *	1	Groclin Dy. Grodzisk *	1 1				
Widzew Lodz	0	Ruch Chorzow	0 1			**CUP FINAL**	
Ruch Chorzów *	1			Groclin Dy. Grodzisk	0 0	Belchatow 13-05-2008	
Arka Gdynia	1			Wisla Krakow *	0 1		
Cracovia *	0	Arka Gdynia *	0 1				
GKS Tychy '71 *	1	Wisla Krakow	0 2				
Wisla Krakow	3						

* Home team/home team in the first leg • ‡ Qualified for the UEFA Cup

POR – PORTUGAL

NATIONAL TEAM RECORD
JULY 10TH 2006 TO JULY 12TH 2010

PL	W	D	L	F	A	%
24	11	7	6	40	26	60.4

With Cristiano Ronaldo emerging as one of the best players in the world following a sensational season with Manchester United, many were predicting that he would end up with a Euro 2008 winners medal to go alongside the UEFA Champions League medal he won with United. That was reckoning without Real Madrid, however, whose public courting of Ronaldo ended up as a major feature of the finals. Whether it distracted Ronaldo is open to debate but the Portuguese star didn't emerge from the tournament with much credit and, more importantly, neither did his team. The finals were Luiz Felipe Scolari's fourth as a national team coach and they were his least successful with Portugal bundled out in the quarter-finals by a much more pedestrian German team. The Portuguese started well enough with victories over Turkey and the Czech Republic. Having qualified for the quarter-finals, Scolari then rested much of the team for the final match - a 2-0 defeat at the hands of hosts Switzerland. As often proves to be the case, his team then lost its momentum and were always chasing the game after going behind early on to the Germans in the quarter-finals. Having agreed to take over at Chelsea, it was Scolari's last match in charge of

INTERNATIONAL HONOURS
Qualified for FIFA World Cup finals 1966 1986 2002 2006
FIFA World Youth Championship 1989 1991
UEFA Youth Tournament 1961   UEFA U-18 Championship 1994 1999   UEFA U-17 Championship 1989 1995 1996 2000 2003
Intercontinental Cup FC Porto 1987 2004   UEFA Champions League Benfica 1961 1962, FC Porto 1987 2004

Portugal after eight years at the helm and he was replaced by Manchester United's Carlos Queiroz. At home the referee-bribery scandal during the 2003–04 season - Apito Dourado (Golden Whistle) - reached a climax with a number of high profile casualties. With the case still going through the courts, the Portuguese federation took action of its own, docking champions Porto six points. Having finished 20 points ahead of Sporting in the table, Porto accepted the punishment in order that the points were taken off in the current season. They were then thrown out of the 2008–09 Champions League by UEFA only to be reprieved on a technicality. Their city neighbours Boavista, champions from as recently as 2001, were relegated for their part in the scandal. Sporting prevented Porto from winning the double when they retained the Portuguese Cup in the Esadio Nacional. The match went to extra-time and was won by substitute Rodrigo Tiuí who scored twice - the second a spectacular overhead kick that will be remembered for a long time by Sporting fans. In Europe, only Porto made it out of their Champions League group but were then knocked-out by Schalke on penalties in the next round. Sporting and Benfica finished third in their groups with Sporting going on to reach the quarter-finals of the UEFA Cup where they lost to Rangers.

Federaçao Portuguesa de Futebol (FPF)
Rua Alexandre Herculano, no.58, Apartado 24013, Lisbon 1250-012, Portugal
Tel +351 21 3252700   Fax +351 21 3252780
secretario_geral@fpf.pt   www.fpf.pt
President: MADAIL Gilberto, Dr   General Secretary: BROU Angelo
Vice-President: LOUREIRO Helio   Treasurer: PACHECO LAMAS Carlos   Media Officers: COSTA Onofre
Men's Coach: QUEIROZ Carlos   Women's Coach: JORGE Monica
FPF formed: 1914   UEFA: 1954   FIFA: 1923
Red shirts with green trimmings, Green shorts, Red socks or White shirts with blue trimmings, Blue shorts, White socks

RECENT INTERNATIONAL MATCHES PLAYED BY PORTUGAL

2006	Opponents	Score	Venue	Comp	Scorers	Att	Referee
11-06	Angola	W 1-0	Cologne	WCr1	Pauleta [4]	45 000	Larrionda URU
17-06	Iran	W 2-0	Frankfurt	WCr1	Deco [63], Ronaldo [80p]	48 000	Poulat FRA
21-06	Mexico	W 2-1	Gelsenkirchen	WCr1	Maniche [6], Simão [24p]	52 000	Michel SVK
25-06	Netherlands	W 1-0	Nuremberg	WCr2	Maniche [23]	41 000	Ivanov.V RUS
1-07	England	D 0-0	Gelsenkirchen	WCqf	W 3-1p	52 000	Elizondo ARG
5-07	France	L 0-1	Munich	WCsf		66 000	Larrionda URU
8-07	Germany	L 1-3	Stuttgart	WC3p	Nuno Gomes [88]	52 000	Kamikawa JPN
1-09	Denmark	L 2-4	Copenhagen	Fr	Ricardo Carvalho [15], Nani [65]	13 186	Kelly IRL
6-09	Finland	D 1-1	Helsinki	ECq	Nuno Gomes [42]	38 010	Plautz AUT
7-10	Azerbaijan	W 3-0	Porto	ECq	Ronaldo 2 [25 63], Ricardo Carvalho [31]	14 000	Halsey ENG
11-10	Poland	L 1-2	Chorzow	ECq	Nuno Gomes [92+]	38 199	Stark GER
15-11	Kazakhstan	W 3-0	Coimbra	ECq	Simão 2 [8 86], Ronaldo [30]	29 500	Rogalla SUI
2007							
6-02	Brazil	W 2-0	London	Fr	Simão [82], Ricardo Carvalho [89]	60 000	Atkinson ENG
24-03	Belgium	W 4-0	Lisbon	ECq	Nuno Gomes [53], Ronaldo 2 [55 75], Quaresma [69]	47 009	Vassaras GRE
28-03	Serbia	D 1-1	Belgrade	ECq	Tiago [5]	46 810	Layec FRA
2-06	Belgium	W 2-1	Brussels	ECq	Nani [43], Postiga [64]	45 383	Hansson SWE
5-06	Kuwait	D 1-1	Kuwait City	Fr	João Tomas [72]	10 000	Al Marzouqi UAE
22-08	Armenia	D 1-1	Yerevan	ECq	Ronaldo [37]	14 935	Larsen DEN
8-09	Poland	D 2-2	Lisbon	ECq	Maniche [50], Ronaldo [73]	48 000	Rosseti ITA
12-09	Serbia	D 1-1	Lisbon	ECq	Simão [11]	48 000	Merk GER
13-10	Azerbaijan	W 2-0	Baku	ECq	Bruno Alves [12], Hugo Almeida [45]	25 000	Bebek CRO
17-10	Kazakhstan	W 2-1	Almaty	ECq	Makukula [84], Ronaldo [91+]	25 057	Wegereef NED
17-11	Armenia	W 1-0	Leiria	ECq	Hugo Almeida [42]	22 048	Riley ENG
21-11	Finland	D 0-0	Porto	ECq		49 000	Michel SVK
2008							
6-02	Italy	L 1-3	Zurich	Fr	Quaresma [77]	30 500	Kever SUI
26-03	Greece	L 1-2	Dusseldorf	Fr	Nuno Gomes [75]	25 000	Kirchen GER
31-05	Georgia	W 2-0	Viseu	Fr	Joao Moutinho [19], Simão [44p]	8 500	Meir ISR
7-06	Turkey	W 2-0	Geneva	ECr1	Pepe [61], Raul Meireles [93+]	29 016	Fandel GER
11-06	Czech Republic	W 3-1	Geneva	ECr1	Deco [8], Ronaldo [63], Quaresma [91+]	29 016	Vassaras GRE
15-06	Switzerland	L 0-2	Basel	ECr1		39 730	Plautz AUT
19-06	Germany	L 2-3	Basel	ECqf	Nuno Gomes [40], Postiga [87]	39 374	Fröjdfeldt SWE

Fr = Friendly match • EC = UEFA EURO 2008 • WC = FIFA World Cup
q = qualifier • r1 = first round group • r2 = second round • qf = quarter-final • sf = semi-final • 3p = third place play-off

PORTUGAL NATIONAL TEAM PLAYERS

	Player	Ap	G	Club	Date of Birth		Player	Ap	G	Club	Date of Birth
1	Ricardo	GK	79	0	Real Betis	11 02 1976	12	Nuno	GK	0	0	FC Porto	25 01 1974
2	Paulo Ferreira	DF	51	0	Chelsea	18 01 1979	13	Miguel	DF	48	1	Valencia	4 01 1980
3	Bruno Alves	DF	12	1	FC Porto	27 11 1981	14	Jorge Ribeiro	DF	9	0	Boavista	9 11 1981
4	Bosingwa	DF	11	0	FC Porto	24 08 1982	15	Pepe	DF	7	1	Real Madrid	26 02 1983
5	Fernando Meira	DF	52	2	VfB Stuttgart	5 06 1978	16	Ricardo Carvalho	DF	46	4	Chelsea	18 05 1978
6	Raul Meireles	MF	12	1	FC Porto	17 03 1983	17	Ricardo Quaresma	FW	23	3	FC Porto	26 09 1983
7	Cristiano Ronaldo	FW	58	21	Manchester Utd	5 02 1985	18	Miguel Veloso	MF	7	0	Sporting CP	11 05 1986
8	Petit	MF	57	4	Benfica	25 09 1976	19	Nani	FW	16	2	Manchester Utd	17 11 1986
9	Hugo Almeida	FW	11	2	Werder Bremen	23 05 1984	20	Deco	MF	56	4	Barcelona	27 08 1977
10	João Moutinho	MF	17	1	Sporting CP	8 09 1986	21	Nuno Gomes	FW	72	29	Benfica	5 07 1976
11	Simão	FW	64	15	Atlético Madrid	31 10 1979	22	Rui Patrício	GK	0	0	Sporting CP	15 02 1988
						23	Hélder Postiga	FW	34	11	Panathinaikos	2 08 1982

The Portuguese squad for Euro 2008

PORTUGAL NATIONAL TEAM RECORDS AND RECORD SEQUENCES

Records			Sequence records				
Victory	8-0	LIE x2, KUW	Wins	9	1966	Clean sheets	8	1998-1999
Defeat	0-10	ENG 1947	Defeats	7	1957-59, 1961-62	Goals scored	16	1966-1967
Player Caps	127	FIGO	Undefeated	19	2005-2006	Without goal	4	1996-1997
Player Goals	47	PAULETA	Without win	13	1949-1953	Goals against	17	1949-1953

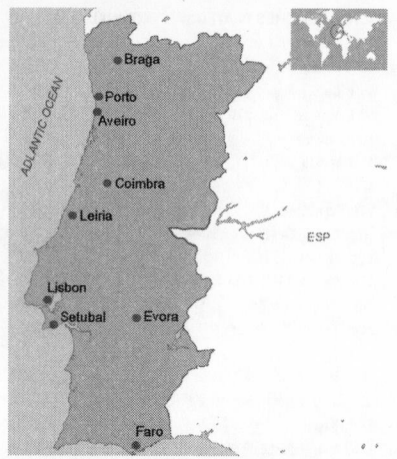

MAJOR CITIES/TOWNS
Population '000

1	Lisbon	498
2	Porto	242
3	Amadora	179
4	Braga	125
5	Setúbal	119
6	Queluz	111
7	Coimbra	108
8	Agualva-Cacém	100
9	Funchal	95
10	Algueirão	81
11	Vila Nova de Gaia	71
12	Loures	66
13	Rio de Mouro	59
14	Corroios	55
15	Aveiro	55
16	Odivelas	54
17	Amora	53
18	Rio Tinto	51
19	Barreiro	50
20	Leiria	47
21	Evora	46
22	Faro	41
23	Guimarães	41
24	Portimão	39

PORTUGUESE REPUBLIC; REPUBLICA PORTUGUESA

Capital	Lisbon	Language	Portuguese	Independence	1640
Population	10 642 836	Area	92 391 km²	% in cities	36%
GDP per cap	$18 000	Dailling code	+351	Internet .pt	GMT +/- 0

MEDALS TABLE

		Overall			League			Cup			Europe			City	Stadium	Cap'ty	DoF
		G	S	B	G	S	B	G	S	B	G	S	B				
1	SL Benfica	60	40	17	31	24	14	27	10		2	6	3	Lisbon	Estádio da Luz	65 647	1904
2	FC Porto	43	39	11	23	24	10	17	14		3	1	1	Porto	Estádio do Dragão	50 948	1893
3	Sporting Clube Portugal	38	35	27	18	18	25	19	16		1	1	2	Lisbon	José Alvalade XXI	52 000	1906
4	OS Belenenses	7	11	14	1	3	14	6	8					Lisbon	Estádio do Restelo	40 000	1919
5	Boavista FC	6	4	2	1	3	1	5	1				1	Porto	Estádio do Bessa	28 263	1903
6	Vitória FC Setúbal	3	9	3		1	3	3	8					Setúbal	Estádio do Bonfim	25 000	1910
7	Académica de Coimbra	1	5			1		1	4					Coimbra	Cidade de Coimbra	30 154	1887
8	Atlético Clube Portugal	1	3	2		2	1	1	3					Lisbon	Estádio Tapadinha	15 000	1942
9	Sporting Clube Braga	1	3					1	3					Braga	Municipal de Braga	30 359	1921
10	CS Marítimo	1	2					1	2					Funchal	Estádio dos Barreiros	14 000	1910
11	SC Olhanense	1	1					1	1					Olhão	José Arcanjo	21 530	1912
	Leixoes SC	1	1					1	1					Matosinhos	Estádio do Mar	25 035	1907
	SC Beira Mar	1	1					1	1					Aveiro	Municipal de Aveiro	31 498	1922
14	CF Estrella Amadora	1						1						Amadora	José Gomes	25 000	1932
15	Vitória SC Guimaraes		4	4				4			4			Guimarães	Afonso Henriques	29 865	1922
16	FC Barreirense		2					2						Barreiro	Manuel de Mello	10 500	1911

RECENT LEAGUE AND CUP RECORD

	Championship							Cup		
Year	Champions	Pts	Runners-up	Pts	Third	Pts		Winners	Score	Runners-up
1995	FC Porto	62	Sporting CP	53	Benfica	49		Sporting CP	2-0	Marítimo
1996	FC Porto	84	Benfica	73	Sporting CP	67		Benfica	3-1	Sporting CP
1997	FC Porto	85	Sporting CP	72	Benfica	58		Boavista	3-2	Benfica
1998	FC Porto	77	Benfica	68	Vitória Guimarães	59		FC Porto	3-1	SC Braga
1999	FC Porto	79	Boavista	71	Benfica	65		Beira-Mar	1-0	Campomaiorense
2000	Sporting CP	77	FC Porto	73	Benfica	69		FC Porto	1-1 2-0	Sporting CP
2001	Boavista	77	FC Porto	76	Sporting CP	62		FC Porto	2-0	Maritimo
2002	Sporting CP	75	Boavista	70	FC Porto	68		Sporting CP	1-0	Leixões
2003	FC Porto	86	Benfica	75	Sporting CP	59		FC Porto	1-0	União Leiria
2004	FC Porto	82	Benfica	74	Sporting CP	73		Benfica	2-1	FC Porto
2005	Benfica	65	FC Porto	62	Sporting CP	61		Vitória Setúbal	2-1	Benfica
2006	FC Porto	79	Sporting CP	72	Benfica	67		FC Porto	1-0	Vitória Setúbal
2007	FC Porto	69	Sporting CP	68	Benfica	67		Sporting CP	1-0	Os Belenenses
2008	FC Porto	69	Sporting CP	55	Vitória Guimarães	53		Sporting CP	2-0	FC Porto

PORTUGAL 2007-08

LIGA SAGRES

	Pl	W	D	L	F	A	Pts	Porto	Sporting	Vitória SC	Benfica	Marítimo	Vitória FC	Braga	Belenenses	Boavista	Nacional	Naval	Académica	Estrela	Leixões	Paços	União
FC Porto † §6	30	24	3	3	60	13	69		1-0	2-0	2-0	1-0	2-0	4-0	1-1	2-0	0-3	1-0	1-0	6-0	3-0	3-0	4-0
Sporting CP †	30	16	7	7	46	28	55	2-0		3-0	1-1	2-1	2-2	2-0	1-0	2-1	4-1	4-1	4-1	2-0	2-0	2-1	1-1
Vitória SC Guimarães †	30	15	8	7	35	31	53	0-5	2-0		1-3	1-0	1-1	1-0	1-0	1-0	1-0	1-0	2-1	4-0	2-1	0-0	2-1
SL Benfica ‡	30	13	13	4	45	21	52	0-1	0-0	0-0		2-1	3-0	1-1	2-0	6-1	0-0	3-0	0-3	3-0	0-0	4-1	2-2
CS Marítimo ‡	30	14	4	12	39	28	46	0-3	1-2	0-1	1-1		0-0	4-1	2-0	2-0	1-0	0-1	2-0	1-1	2-1	3-1	2-0
Vitória FC Setúbal ‡	30	11	12	7	37	33	45	1-2	1-0	0-1	1-1	1-0		3-1	1-1	3-1	1-1	1-2	3-1	0-0	2-0	3-1	2-0
Sporting Braga	30	10	11	9	32	34	41	1-2	3-0	0-0	0-0	2-1	2-3		1-1	0-0	1-0	3-0	2-1	2-1	0-0	2-1	0-1
Os Belenenses §3	30	11	10	9	35	33	40	1-2	1-0	1-1	1-0	1-3	5-0	0-2		2-3	1-1	2-1	0-0	0-0	1-1	1-0	2-1
Boavista	30	8	12	10	32	41	36	0-0	2-0	3-2	0-0	0-2	3-3	0-0	2-4		1-0	2-0	0-0	2-1	0-0	4-3	3-1
CD Nacional	30	9	8	13	23	28	35	1-0	0-0	1-0	0-3	0-2	0-0	0-1	1-2	2-0		2-0	0-3	0-0	1-0	1-2	2-0
Naval 1° de Maio	30	9	7	14	26	45	34	0-2	1-4	1-4	0-2	0-3	0-0	1-1	1-1	1-0	1-1		0-1	1-1	2-1	2-1	1-0
Académica Coimbra	30	6	14	10	31	38	32	0-1	1-1	0-0	1-3	1-0	0-0	3-3	0-0	1-1	1-0	1-1		3-3	1-1	1-0	1-1
Estrela Amadora	30	6	13	11	29	41	31	2-2	0-2	4-1	0-0	1-1	0-1	1-1	0-2	0-0	0-1	3-1	3-1		2-0	1-0	4-2
Leixões	30	4	14	12	27	37	26	1-2	1-1	2-2	1-1	0-1	1-1	3-0	1-2	2-2	1-1	0-1	2-2	0-0		1-0	2-1
Paços de Ferreira	30	6	7	17	31	49	25	0-2	0-1	2-2	1-2	3-1	2-1	0-2	1-2	1-1	1-0	2-2	1-1	2-1	1-1		2-1
União de Leiria §3	30	3	7	20	25	53	13	0-3	4-1	0-1	1-2	1-2	0-2	0-0	1-2	0-0	1-3	0-2	3-1	0-0	1-3	1-1	

17/08/2007 - 11/05/2008 • † Qualified for the UEFA Champions League • ‡ Qualified for the UEFA Cup • § = points deducted • Boavista relegated for their part in the Apito Dourado match-fixing scandal from the 2003-04 season. Porto, Belenenses and União were deducted points
Top scorers: Lisandro Lopez, Porto 24; Oscar Cardozo, Benfica 11; Wesley, Paços de Ferreira 10; Liédson, Sporting CP 10; Roland Linz, Braga 10

PORTUGAL 2007-08

LIGA VITALIS (2)

	Pl	W	D	L	F	A	Pts	Trofense	Rio Ave	Vizela	Gil Vicente	Olhanense	Beira-Mar	Estoril-Praia	Aves	Varzim	Santa Clara	Portimonense	Gondomar	Freamunde	Feirense	Penafiel	Fátima
CD Trofense	30	13	13	4	35	22	52		0-0	0-0	1-0	2-2	1-1	2-0	2-1	1-0	1-1	1-0	1-1	1-2	2-1	1-0	1-0
Rio Ave FC	30	13	12	5	38	26	51	1-1		1-0	1-0	1-1	1-1	1-0	2-1	0-1	1-0	0-0	2-2	3-1	0-1	4-1	1-0
FC Vizela	30	13	11	6	40	22	50	2-2	2-0		2-1	3-1	5-1	0-0	2-0	3-0	0-1	1-1	2-1	3-2	1-0	0-0	1-0
Gil Vicente FC	30	13	11	6	43	34	50	1-1	1-1	1-1		0-0	3-2	3-0	1-4	1-1	2-1	2-1	4-3	1-0	1-0	2-0	3-2
SC Olhanense	30	12	9	9	33	33	45	1-0	0-3	1-0	2-2		0-0	1-2	2-1	2-1	2-2	0-1	0-1	0-1	2-0	3-1	1-1
SC Beira-Mar	30	10	12	8	30	32	42	1-0	1-1	0-3	0-0	2-0		3-2	1-0	1-1	1-2	2-0	1-1	1-1	0-0	1-0	2-1
GD Estoril-Praia	30	11	8	11	41	38	41	1-1	1-2	2-1	2-0	1-2	0-1		2-2	1-0	5-1	1-0	2-0	3-2	0-1	2-2	2-2
Desportivo Aves	30	10	9	11	43	39	39	1-1	0-0	2-1	1-1	1-2	1-1	2-3		2-1	3-1	2-0	1-0	3-0	1-1	2-2	1-0
Varzim SC	30	9	11	10	29	27	38	1-1	0-1	0-0	2-1	0-0	2-0	0-0	2-1		3-1	0-0	2-3	2-0	0-0	0-1	2-0
GD Santa Clara	30	10	7	13	31	50	37	0-4	1-0	1-1	1-4	2-3	1-1	1-1	2-3	1-0		2-1	1-0	2-1	1-0	0-3	0-0
Portimonense SC	30	8	13	9	26	30	37	2-2	2-1	1-1	0-0	2-1	2-1	2-2	0-0	0-4	1-1		1-0	0-2	1-1	1-1	0-0
Gondomar SC	30	8	11	11	37	37	35	1-2	2-3	0-0	1-1	0-1	1-0	1-0	1-1	2-2	4-0	0-0		3-2	2-2	2-0	1-1
SC Freamunde	30	9	8	13	42	49	35	0-2	4-4	1-1	1-2	3-1	0-1	1-3	2-4	1-1	3-1	2-1	0-0		1-1	3-1	2-1
CD Feirense	30	8	9	13	25	27	33	0-1	1-1	1-2	0-1	0-1	0-1	2-1	2-0	3-0	0-1	0-2	2-0	0-1		1-1	2-2
SC Penafiel	30	7	8	15	28	39	29	0-1	0-1	0-2	2-3	0-0	1-0	1-2	2-2	0-0	1-2	1-0	0-2	2-2	0-1		2-0
CD Fátima	30	5	10	15	25	41	25	2-0	1-1	1-0	1-1	0-1	2-2	0-1	2-1	1-2	1-0	0-3	3-2	1-1	0-2	0-3	

18/08/2007 - 11/05/2008

TAÇA DE PORTUGAL 2007-08

Fifth Round

- Sporting CP* — 4
- Lagoa — 0
- UD Oliveirense* — 0
- CS Marítimo — 1

- Sporting Braga — 0
- Estrela Amadora* — 1

- Moreirense — 1
- SC Beira-Mar* — 0

- Atlético Valdevez — Bye

- Paços de Ferreira* — 4
- Abrantes — 0
- CD Feirense — 0
- SL Benfica* — 1

- Vitória FC Setúbal* — 1
- União de Leiria — 0
- CD Nacional — 1
- Vitória SC Guimarães* — 1

- Rio Ave FC* — 2 2p
- SC Olhanense — 2 1p
- Boavista — 1
- Naval 1° de Maio* — 4

- Gil Vicente FC* — 3
- Juventude Evora — 0
- Anadia — 0
- Leixões* — 1

- Sertanense — 1 5p
- SC Penafiel* — 1 4p
- Desportivo Aves — 0
- FC Porto* — 2

Round of sixteen

- Sporting CP* — 2
- CS Marítimo — 1

- Estrela Amadora — Bye

- Moreirense — 3
- Atlético Valdevez* — 0

- Paços de Ferreira — 1
- SL Benfica* — 4

- Vitória FC Setúbal* — 0 4p
- Vitória SC Guimarães — 0 1p

- Rio Ave FC — 1
- Naval 1° de Maio* — 3

- Gil Vicente FC* — 1
- Leixões — 0

- Sertanense* — 0
- FC Porto — 4

Quarter-finals

- Sporting CP* — 1
- Estrela Amadora — 0

- Moreirense — 0
- SL Benfica* — 2

- Vitória FC Setúbal — 2
- Naval 1° de Maio* — 1

- Gil Vicente FC — 0
- FC Porto* — 1

Semi-finals

- Sporting CP* — 5
- SL Benfica — 3

- Vitória FC Setúbal* — 0
- FC Porto — 3

Final

- Sporting CP — 2
- FC Porto — 0

CUP FINAL

Estadio Nacional, Lisbon
18-05-2008, Ref: Benquerença
Scorer - Rodrigo Tiuí 2 110 117
Sporting - Rui Patrício - Anderson Polga, Tonel, Leandro Grimi, Abel79 (Rodrigo Yiuí 90) - Marat Izmailov (Bruno Pereirinha 76), Miguel Veloso, João Moutinho, Romagnoli - Derlei (Gladstone 113), Yannick Djaló. Tr: Paulo Bento
Porto - Nuno - Bruno Alves, Pedro Emanuel, Jorge Fucile, João Paulo71 - Paulo Assunção* (Tarik Sektioui 112), Lucho González*, Mariano González (Lino 79), Raul Meirles* (Kazmierczak 104) - Ricardo Quaresma, Lisandro Lopez. Tr: Jesualdo Ferreira

* Home team

PRK – KOREA DPR

NATIONAL TEAM RECORD
JULY 10TH 2006 TO JULY 12TH 2010

PL	W	D	L	F	A	%
24	11	8	5	42	18	62.5

FIFA/COCA-COLA WORLD RANKING

1993	1994	1995	1996	1997	1998	1999	2000	2001	2002	2003	2004	2005	2006	2007	High	
62	84	117	144	166	158	172	142	136	124	117	95	82	113	115	57	11/93

2007–2008											Low	
08/07	09/07	10/07	11/07	12/07	01/08	02/08	03/08	04/08	05/08	06/08	07/08	181 11/98
127	131	129	117	115	127	120	126	124	125	118	94	

Despite the nation's policy of existing in almost total isolation from the international community, North Korea's football team have become a growing power in Asian football over the last five years. Once again they made it to the final group stage of FIFA World Cup qualifying in Asia - one of just ten Asian nations left in the hunt for a place in the finals in South Africa. In a preliminary round the Koreans comfortably brushed aside Mongolia before being drawn in a group which also featured rivals South Korea. Not surprisingly given that the two countries are still technically at war, political tensions rose in the lead-up to the first game in Pyongyang and, as a result, FIFA

INTERNATIONAL HONOURS
Qualified for the FIFA World Cup finals 1966   Qualified for the FIFA Women's World Cup finals 1999 2003
Asian Games 1978 Asian Women's Championship 2001 2003 Women's Asian Games 2002

ordered the game to be played in Shanghai. Perhaps diplomatically, both games between the two ended in scoreless draws as the pair progressed to the final phase, where they were drawn again to face one another. Given their fine run in the World Cup it was strange to see the North Koreans taking part in the 2008 AFC Challenge Cup in India, a competition reserved for the weaker nations on the continent. After winning their group with three straight victories they then rather surprisingly lost to Tajikistan in the semi-finals.

THE FIFA BIG COUNT OF 2006

	Male	Female		Total
Number of players	436 956	65 956	Referees and Assistant Referees	360
Professionals	0		Admin, Coaches, Technical, Medical	1 498
Amateurs 18+	7 200		Number of clubs	170
Youth under 18	7 712		Number of teams	850
Unregistered	170 000		Clubs with women's teams	69
Total players	502 912		Players as % of population	2.18%

DPR Korea Football Association (PRK)
Kumsongdong, Kwangbok Street, Mangyongdae Dist., PO Box 56, Pyongyang, Korea DPR
Tel +850 2 182228164   Fax +850 2 3814403
noc-kp@co.chesin.com   www.none
President: CHOE Nam Gyun   General Secretary: KIM Jong Su
Vice-President: MUN Jang Hong   Treasurer: TBD   Media Officer: None
Men's Coach: KIM Jong Hun   Women's Coach: KIM Kwang Min
PRK formed: 1945   AFC: 1974   FIFA: 1958
White shirts, White shorts, White socks

RECENT INTERNATIONAL MATCHES PLAYED BY KOREA DPR

2005	Opponents	Score	Venue	Comp	Scorers	Att	Referee
14-08	Korea Republic	L 0-3	Seoul	Fr			
17-08	Bahrain	W 3-2	Manama	WCq	Choe Chol Man [28], Kim Chol Ho [43], An Chol Hyok [89]	3 000	Maidin SIN
26-12	Latvia	D 1-1	Phuket	Fr	An Chol Hyok [26]		
28-12	Thailand	W 2-0	Phuket	Fr	Kim Chol Ho [7], Hong Yong Jo [9]		
30-12	Latvia	L 1-2	Phuket	Fr	Hong Yong Jo [47]		
2006							
No international matches played in 2006							
2007							
19-06	Mongolia	W 7-0	Macau	EAq	Ri Kum Chol 2 [27 43], Jong Tae Se 4 [29 33 34 54], Sin Yong Nam [35]	300	Ogiya JPN
21-06	Macau	W 7-1	Macau	EAq	Ri Kum Chol 2 [5 18], Jong Tae Se 4 [10 12 28 60], Park Chang Il 68	300	Wan Daxue CHN
24-06	Hong Kong	W 1-0	Macau	EAq	Mun In Guk [82]	300	Ogiya JPN
24-06	Singapore	L 1-2	Singapore	Fr	An Chol Hyok [59]		
28-06	Oman	D 2-2	Singapore	Fr	Kang Jin Hyok [20], An Chol Hyok [45p]. L 3-4p		
1-07	UAE	L 0-1	Singapore	Fr			
4-07	Saudi Arabia	D 1-1	Singapore	Fr	Park Nam Chol [84]		
21-10	Mongolia	W 4-1	Ulaan-Baatar	WCq	Pak Chol Min [14], Jong Chol Min 3 [24 32 78]	4 870	Takayama JPN
28-10	Mongolia	W 5-1	Pyongyang	WCq	Pak Chol Min 2 [3 74], Kim Kuk Jin [10], Jong Chol Min [36], Jon Kwang Ik [91+]	5 000	Gosh BAN
24-12	Uzbekistan	D 2-2	Bangkok	Fr	An Chol Hyok [41], Kim Kun Il [91+]		
26-12	Thailand	L 0-1	Bangkok	Fr			
2008							
6-02	Jordan	W 1-0	Amman	WCq	Hong Yong Jo [44]	16 000	Shamsuzzaman BAN
17-02	Japan	D 1-1	Chongqing	EA	Jong Tae Se [5]	15 000	Choi Myung Yong KOR
20-02	Korea Republic	D 1-1	Chongqing	EA	Jong Tae Se [73]	20 000	Takayama JPN
23-02	China PR	L 1-3	Chongqing	EA	Ji Yun Nam [34]	30 500	Torky IRN
26-03	Korea Republic	D 0-0	Shanghai	WCq		20 000	Al Fadhli KUW
2-06	Turkmenistan	D 0-0	Ashgabat	WCq		20 000	Al Ghamdi KSA
7-06	Turkmenistan	W 1-0	Pyongyang	WCq	Choe Kum Chol [72]	25 000	Al Saeedi UAE
14-06	Jordan	W 2-0	Pyongyang	WCq	Hong Yong Jo 2 [44 72]	28 000	Najm LIB
22-06	Korea Republic	D 0-0	Seoul	WCq		48 519	Mohd Salleh MAS
31-07	Sri Lanka	W 3-0	Hyderabad	CCr1	OG [5], Pak Song Chol 2 [9 27]	100	Vo Minh Tri VIE
2-08	Nepal	W 1-0	Hyderabad	CCr1	Pak Song Chol [39]	100	Iemoto JPN
4-08	Myanmar	W 1-0	Hyderabad	CCr1	Ro Hak Su [15]	100	Shamsuzzaman BAN
7-08	Tajikistan	L 0-1	Hyderabad	CCsf		600	Iemoto JPN

Fr = Friendly match • CC = AFC Challenge Cup • EA = East Asian Championship • WC = FIFA World Cup • q = qualifier

KOREA DPR NATIONAL TEAM RECORDS AND RECORD SEQUENCES

Records		Sequence records					
Victory	21-0 GUM 2005	Wins	8	1993	Clean sheets	4	Four times
Defeat	1-6 BUL 1974	Defeats	5	1993	Goals scored	18	1992-1993
Player Caps	n/a	Undefeated	13	1978-1980	Without goal	4	1989-1990
Player Goals	n/a	Without win	15	1993-2000	Goals against	12	1993-2000

KOREA DPR COUNTRY INFORMATION

Capital	Pyongyang	Independence	1945 from Japan	GDP per Capita	$1 400
Population	22 912 177	Status	Communist Republic	GNP Ranking	68
Area km²	120 540	Language	Korean	Dialling code	+850
Population density	190 per km²	Literacy rate	99%	Internet code	.kp
% in urban areas	61%	Main religion	None	GMT +/ –	+9
Towns/Cities ('000)	Pyongyang 2 787; Hamhung 840; Chongjin 689, Nampo 670; Sinuiju 385; Wonsan 355; Phyongsong 323; Sariwon 300; Haeju 271; Kanggye 264; Kimchaek 237; Hyesan 210				
Neighbours (km)	Korea Republic 238; China 1 416; Russia 19; Sea of Japan & Yellow Sea 2 495				
Main stadia	Kim Il-Sung Stadium – Pyongyang 70 000; Yanggakdo – Pyongyang 30 000				

PUR – PUERTO RICO

NATIONAL TEAM RECORD
JULY 10TH 2006 TO JULY 12TH 2010

PL	W	D	L	F	A	%
6	3	2	1	8	8	66.7

FIFA/COCA-COLA WORLD RANKING

1993	1994	1995	1996	1997	1998	1999	2000	2001	2002	2003	2004	2005	2006	2007
105	112	128	149	169	182	186	195	195	198	200	194	195	195	196

High	
97	03/94

2007–2008											
08/07	09/07	10/07	11/07	12/07	01/08	02/08	03/08	04/08	05/08	06/08	07/08
194	195	195	196	196	196	168	168	149	149	149	146

Low	
202	11/04

The Puerto Rico Islanders continued on their mission to change the face of football on this Caribbean island as they enjoyed their most successful season to to date in the 2007 USL First Division - the highest League in the USA after MLS. The Islanders reached the semi-finals of the play-offs before losing to eventual champions Seattle Sounders 3-2 and they also qualified for the inaugural CONCACAF Champions League when, after reaching the semi-finals of the CFU Club Championship, they beat San Juan Jabloteh in a play-off to take one of the three Caribbean places. The upsurge in popularity in football saw the creation of the Puerto Rico Soccer League in May

INTERNATIONAL HONOURS
None

2008, an ambitious plan to develop club football further with five of the eight teams affliated to major club sides abroad including Sevilla, River Plate and Fluminense. At national team level the Puerto Rican federation did the sensible thing after entering the 2010 FIFA World Cup when they appointed the Puerto Rico Islander's coach Colin Clarke as national team manager. With players drawn from his club side, the American college system and from clubs in the new league, Puerto Rica beat the Dominican Republic in Bayamon but then lost to Honduras, their only defeat in the six games played during the first half of 2008.

THE FIFA BIG COUNT OF 2006

	Male	Female		Total
Number of players	187 470	35 200	Referees and Assistant Referees	601
Professionals	45		Admin, Coaches, Technical, Medical	9 016
Amateurs 18+	9 400		Number of clubs	75
Youth under 18	13 700		Number of teams	350
Unregistered	43 900		Clubs with women's teams	2
Total players	222 670		Players as % of population	5.67%

Federación Puertorriquena de Fútbol (FPF)
392 Juan B. Rodriguez, Parque Central Hato Rey, PO Box 360556, San Juan 00936-0556, Puerto Rico
Tel +1 787 7652895   Fax +1 787 7672288
info@fedefutbolpr.com   www.fedefutbolpr.com
President: SERRALTA Joe   General Secretary: GAUTIER Frankie
Vice-President: JIMENEZ Mickey   Treasurer: VILLEGAS Miguel   Media Officer: RAMIREZ Ana
Men's Coach: CLARKE Colin   Women's Coach: AVEDISSIAN Garabet
FPF formed: 1940   CONCACAF: 1962   FIFA: 1960
White shirts with red stripes and blue sleeves, White shorts, White socks

RECENT INTERNATIONAL MATCHES PLAYED BY PUERTO RICO

2005	Opponents	Score		Venue	Comp	Scorers	Att	Referee
No international matches played in 2005								
2006								
No international matches played in 2006								
2007								
No international matches played in 2007								
2008								
16-01	Bermuda	W	2-0	Hamilton	Fr	Taylor Graham [47], Andres Cabrero [67]		
18-01	Bermuda	W	1-0	Hamilton	Fr	Noah Delgado [13]		Raynor BER
26-01	Trinidad and Tobago	D	2-2	Bayamon	Fr	Kupono Low [15], Chris Mesaloudis [33]		
26-03	Dominican Republic	W	1-0	Bayamon	WCq	Petter Villegas [96p]	8 000	Morales MEX
4-06	Honduras	L	0-4	San Pedro Sula	WCq		20 000	Campbell JAM
14-06	Honduras	D	2-2	Bayamon	WCq	Christopher Megaloudis [31], Petter Villegas [41]	5 000	Lopez GUA

GC = CONCACAF Gold Cup • q = qualifier

PUERTO RICO NATIONAL TEAM RECORDS AND RECORD SEQUENCES

Records			Sequence records					
Victory	4-0	CAY 1993	Wins	4	1993	Clean sheets	4	1993
Defeat	0-9	CUB 1995	Defeats	15	1946-1962	Goals scored	6	1988-92, 2004-08
Player Caps	n/a		Undefeated	4	1993, 2008	Without goal	6	1982-1988
Player Goals	n/a		Without win	37	1940-1970	Goals against	26	1949-1970

PUERTO RICO 2007 CAMPEONATO NACIONAL

	Pl	W	D	L	F	A	Pts
Fraigcomar †	10	9	1	0	40	7	28
San Francisco †	10	6	1	3	18	13	19
Atléticos Levittown ‡	10	5	1	4	25	14	16
Huracánes Caguas ‡	10	4	0	6	14	16	12
Tornados Humacao ‡	10	3	2	5	11	35	11
Galaxy San Juan ‡	10	0	1	9	7	30	1

6/05/2007 - 22/07/2007 • † Qualified for the semi-finals
‡ Qualified for the quarter-finals

CAMPEONATO NACIONAL PLAY-OFFS

Quarter–finals		Semi–finals		Final	
		Fraigcomar			
Tornados	0	Huracánes			
Huracánes	**5**			**Fraigcomar**	**2**
				Atléticos	1
		San Francisco	1 4p		
Galaxy	0	**Atléticos**	**1 5p**		
Atléticos	**5**				

RECENT LEAGUE RECORD

	Torneo Nacional	Liga Mayor			Campeonato Nacional		
Year	Champions	Winners	Score	Runners-up	Winners	Score	Runners-up
1998	Académicos Quintana	Islanders San Juan	3-0	Brujos Guayama			
1999	CF Nacional Carolina	Islanders San Juan		Cardenales			
2000	Académicos Quintana	Vaqueros Bayamón	1-0	Gigantes Carolina			
2001	Académicos Quintana	Islanders San Juan	4-3	Brujos Guayama			
2002	Académicos Quintana	Vaqueros Bayamón	3-0	Islanders San Juan			
2003	Discontinued	Sporting Carolina	2-1	Vaqueros Bayamón			
2004		Sporting San Lorenzo	1-0	Huracanes Caguas			
2005		Real Quintana	2-1	Fraigcomar	Fraigcomar	1-0	Huracánes Caguas
2006		Discontinued			Fraigcomar	4-1	Academia Quintana
2007					Fraigcomar	2-1	Atléticos Levittown

PUERTO RICO COUNTRY INFORMATION

Capital	San Juan	Status	Commonwealth associated with the US	GDP per Capita	$16 800
Population	3 897 960			GNP Ranking	n/a
Area km²	9 104	Language	Spanish, English	Dialling code	+1 787
Population density	428 per km²	Literacy rate	94%	Internet code	.pr
% in urban areas	71%	Main religion	Christian	GMT +/−	-5
Towns/Cities ('000)	San Juan 418; Bayamón 203; Carolina 170; Ponce 152; Caguas 86; Guaynabo 81; Mayagüez 76				
Neighbours (km)	Caribbean Sea & North Atlantic 501				
Main stadia	Estadio Sixto Escobar – San Juan 18 000; Country Club – San Juan 2 500				

QAT – QATAR

NATIONAL TEAM RECORD
JULY 10TH 2006 TO JULY 12TH 2010

PL	W	D	L	F	A	%
32	12	9	11	39	37	51.6

FIFA/COCA-COLA WORLD RANKING

1993	1994	1995	1996	1997	1998	1999	2000	2001	2002	2003	2004	2005	2006	2007	High	
54	60	83	69	70	60	107	102	80	62	65	66	95	58	87	51	08/93

	2007–2008											Low	
08/07	09/07	10/07	11/07	12/07	01/08	02/08	03/08	04/08	05/08	06/08	07/08	107	12/99
83	91	84	86	87	88	96	99	83	83	83	80		

With a limited talent pool due to the nation's small population, the Qatari football authorities have turned to naturalised players in an attempt to boost the country's standing in the world game. Controversially, Brazil-born duo Fabio Cesar and Emerson joined the ranks of the national team in early 2008 joining former Uruguayan Sebastian Quintana, and as a result the Jorge Fossati-coached team progressed to the final phase of Asia's 2010 FIFA World Cup qualifiers. However, they did so by the skin of their teeth from a group that contained Australia, Asian champions Iraq and China, with a 1-0 win in their final game over the Iraqis securing their place in the decisive round. Qatar's moves

INTERNATIONAL HONOURS
Gulf Cup 1992 2004

to hire foreign talent for the national team was one of the prime motivators behind FIFA's decision to tighten naturalisation rules after the country also sought to harness young talent through the ASPIRE Academy in Doha. Despite the huge sums of money which have lured leading players to the Q-League in recent years, the country's poor record in the AFC Champions League remains an issue. Neither Al Sadd nor Al Gharafa made much of an impact on the 2008 edition of the competition, with neither team threatening to qualify for the knockout phase of the tournament. Only Al Sadd, in 2005, have reached the last eight since the competition's inception in 2002.

THE FIFA BIG COUNT OF 2006

	Male	Female		Total
Number of players	18 020	136	Referees and Assistant Referees	98
Professionals	0		Admin, Coaches, Technical, Medical	432
Amateurs 18+	2 236		Number of clubs	16
Youth under 18	4 320		Number of teams	160
Unregistered	2 600		Clubs with women's teams	0
Total players	18 156		Players as % of population	2.05%

Qatar Football Association (QFA)
7th Floor, QNOC Building, Cornich, PO Box 5333, Doha, Qatar
Tel +974 4944411   Fax +974 4944414
info@qfa.com.qa   www.qfa.com.qa
President: AL-THANI Shk. Hamad Bin Khalifa   General Secretary: AL-MOHANNADI Saud
Vice-President: TBD   Treasurer: AL BOANAIN Ahmed Abdulaziz   Media Officer: AL SALAT Ali
Men's Coach: FOSSATI Jorge   Women's Coach: None
QFA formed: 1960   AFC: 1972   FIFA: 1970
White shirts, White shorts, White socks

RECENT INTERNATIONAL MATCHES PLAYED BY QATAR

2005	Opponents		Score	Venue	Comp	Scorers	Att	Referee
29-07	Egypt	L	0-5	Geneva	Fr			
31-07	Kuwait	W	1-0	Geneva	Fr	Waleed Jassim [37]		
11-10	Iraq	D	0-0	Doha	Fr			
16-11	Argentina	L	0-3	Doha	Fr			Al Fadhli KUW
2006								
2-01	Libya	W	2-0	Doha	Fr	Adel Lamy 2 [55 61]		
14-02	Tajikistan	W	2-0	Doha	Fr	Sayd Bechir, Waleed Jassim		
22-02	Hong Kong	W	3-0	Hong Kong	ACq	Abdulrahman [11], Sayd Bechir [44], Magid Hassan [95+]	1 806	Nishimura JPN
1-03	Uzbekistan	W	2-1	Doha	ACq	Adel Lamy [45], Ali Naser [49]	7 000	Sun Baoje CHN
16-08	Bangladesh	W	4-1	Dhaka	ACq	Wesam Rizik [7p], Adel Lamy [36], Khalfan Ibrahim 2 [38 74]	7 000	Al Yarimi YEM
6-09	Bangladesh	W	3-0	Doha	ACq	Hussain Yasser [25], Adel Lamy [30], Saad Al Shammari [52]	500	Najm LIB
11-10	Hong Kong	W	2-0	Doha	ACq	Bilal Rajab [43], Hussain Yasser [53]	1 000	Kousa SYR
15-11	Uzbekistan	L	0-2	Tashkent	ACq		14 000	Al Saeedi UAE
2007								
13-01	Oman	D	1-1	Doha	Fr	Majed Mohammed [66]		
18-01	Iraq	L	0-1	Abu Dhabi	GCr1			
21-01	Saudi Arabia	D	1-1	Abu Dhabi	GCr1	Ali Nasser [10]		
24-01	Bahrain	L	1-2	Abu Dhabi	GCr1	Khalfan Ibrahim [19]		
24-03	Iran	L	0-1	Doha	Fr			
25-06	Turkmenistan	W	1-0	Doha	Fr	Waleed Jassim [64]		
2-07	Thailand	L	0-2	Bangkok	Fr			
9-07	Japan	D	1-1	Hanoi	ACr1	Quintana [88]	5 000	Breeze AUS
12-07	Vietnam	D	1-1	Hanoi	ACr1	Quintana [79]	40 000	Moradi IRN
16-07	UAE	L	1-2	Ho Chi Minh City	ACr1	Quintana [42]	3 000	Moradi IRN
17-09	Oman	D	1-1	Doha	Fr	Saad Al Shammari [90]		
16-10	Iraq	W	3-2	Doha	Fr	Sayd Bechir [34], Quintana [70], Saad Al Shammari [83]		
21-10	Sri Lanka	W	1-0	Colombo	WCq	Quintana [69]	6 500	Bashir SIN
28-10	Sri Lanka	W	5-0	Doha	WCq	Quintana 2 [4 75], Sayd Bechir 2 [16 54], Saad Al Shammari [85]	3 000	Al Ghamdi KSA
16-11	Georgia	L	1-2	Doha	Fr	Abdullah Obaid Koni [56]		
21-11	Côte d'Ivoire	L	1-6	Doha	Fr	Mustafa Abdi Abdullah [77]		
2008								
10-01	Iran	D	0-0	Doha	Fr			
13-01	Syria	D	0-0	Damascus	Fr			
6-02	Australia	L	0-3	Melbourne	WCq		50 969	Mohd Salleh MAS
4-03	Bahrain	L	1-2	Doha	Fr	Quintana [8]		
16-03	Jordan	W	2-1	Doha	Fr	Quintana [39], Magid Mohamed Hassan [86]		
26-03	Iraq	W	2-0	Doha	WCq	Montesin 2 [1 62]	13 000	Nishimura JPN
23-05	Kuwait	D	1-1	Doha	Fr	Quintana [35]		
27-05	Lebanon	W	2-1	Doha	Fr	Quintana 2 [45 62]		
2-06	China PR	D	0-0	Doha	WCq		9 000	Basma SYR
7-06	China PR	W	1-0	Tianjin	WCq	Quintana [14]	50 000	Najm LIB
14-06	Australia	L	1-3	Doha	WCq	Al Khalfan [94+]	12 000	Lee Gi Young KOR
22-06	Iraq	W	1-0	Dubai	WCq	Sayd Bechir [76]	10 000	Albadwawi UAE

Fr = Friendly match • AC = AFC Asian Cup • GC = Gulf Cup • WC = FIFA World Cup
q = qualifier • r1 = first round group • sf = semi-final • f = final

QATAR NATIONAL TEAM RECORDS AND RECORD SEQUENCES

Records			Sequence records					
Victory	8-0	AFG 1984, LIB 1985	Wins	7	2006	Clean sheets	7	2003-2004
Defeat	0-9	KUW 1973	Defeats	8	1972-1974	Goals scored	12	1996
Player Caps	n/a		Undefeated	11	2001, 2003-04	Without goal	4	1998, 2003-04
Player Goals	n/a		Without win	11	1970-1974	Goals against	15	1994-1996

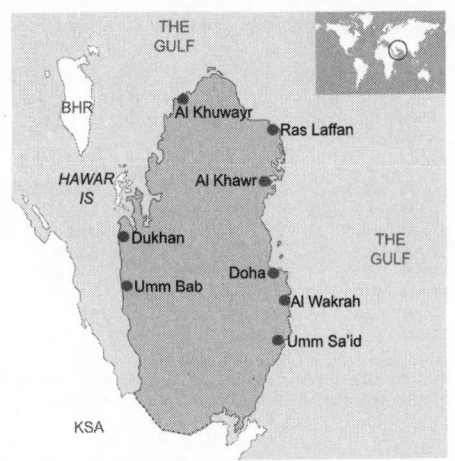

STATE OF QATAR; DAWLAT QATAR

Capital	Doha	Language	Arabic			Independence	1971
Population	907 229	Area	11 437 km²	Density	73 per km²	% in cities	91%
GDP per cap	$21 500	Dailling code	+974	Internet	.qa	GMT +/-	+3

MEDALS TABLE

		Overall		Lg	Cup		CP	QC	Asia				City	Stadium	Cap'ty	DoF
		G S B		G	G S				G S B							
1	Al Sadd	42 6		12	12 6		5	12	1			Doha	Jassim Bin Hamad	18 000	1969
2	Al Arabi	19 4		7	8 3		1	3		1		Doha	Grand Hamad	13 000	1952
3	Al Rayyan	15 8 1		7	3 8		3	2			1	Al Rayyan	Ahmed bin Ali	25 000	
4	Al Gharrafa	14 3		5	5 3		1	3				Doha	Al Gharrafa	25 000	1979
5	Qatar SC	12 3		3	3 3		2	4				Doha	Qatar Sports Club	19 000	1959
6	Al Wakra	7 6		2	6		1	4				Al Wakra	Al Wakra	20 000	1959
7	Al Oruba	5		5											
8	Al Ahli	4 5			4 5							Doha	Al Ahli	20 000	1950
9	Al Maref	3		3											
10	Khor	2 2			2		1	1				Khor	Al Khawr	20 000	1961
11	Al Shamal	1						1				Madinat ash Shamal			1980
12	Al Shabab	1						1							
13	Umm Salal	1						1				Umm Salal			1979

Name changes: Al Ittihad → Al Gharrafa • Al Taawun → Khor • Al Oruba merged with Qatar SC to form Al Esteqlal but renamed to Qatar SC in 1981
Cup = Emir's Cup • CP = Crown Prince Cup • QC = Sheikh Qassim Cup

RECENT LEAGUE AND CUP RECORD

			Championship						Emir's Cup		
Year	Champions	Pts	Runners-up	Pts	Third	Pts			Winners	Score	Runners-up
1997	Al Arabi	34	Al Rayyan	32	Al Ittihad	29			Al Ittihad	1-1 3-2p	Al Rayyan
1998	Al Ittihad	32	Al Rayyan	29	Al Sadd	26			Al Ittihad	4-3	Al Ahli
1999	Al Wakra	39	Al Ittihad	34	Al Sadd	33			Al Rayyan	2-1	Al Ittihad
2000	Al Sadd	38	Al Rayyan	34	Al Arabi	26			Al Sadd	2-0	Al Rayyan
2001	Al Wakra	32	Al Arabi	29	Al Taawun	28			Qatar SC	3-2	Al Sadd
2002	Al Ittihad	41	Qatar SC	29	Al Rayyan	25			Al Ittihad	3-1	Al Sadd
2003	Qatar SC	34	Al Sadd	31	Khor	31			Al Sadd	2-1	Al Ahli
2004	Al Sadd	42	Qatar SC	34	Al Arabi	31			Al Rayyan	3-2	Qatar SC
2005	Al Gharrafa	66	Al Rayyan	52	Khor	48			Al Sadd	0-0 5-4p	Al Wakra
2006	Al Sadd	52	Qatar SC	49	Al Arabi	46			Al Rayyan	1-1 5-3p	Al Gharrafa
2007	Al Sadd	55	Al Gharrafa	43	Umm Salal	39			Al Sadd	0-0 5-4p	Khor
2008	Al Gharrafa	62	Al Sadd	53	Umm Salal	50			Umm Salal	2-2 4-1p	Al Gharrafa

QATAR 2007–08

Q-LEAGUE

	Pl	W	D	L	F	A	Pts	Gharrafa	Sadd	Umm Salal	Qatar	Rayyan	Arabi	Khor	Siliya	Wakra	Shamal
Al Gharrafa †	27	20	2	5	72	35	62		0-4 0-1	2-1 3-4	3-2 0-1	6-0 4-2	1-0 1-1	2-1	3-0	4-1 6-2	2-1
Al Sadd	27	16	5	6	54	38	53	3-3		0-2	1-0 0-4	2-1 4-2	1-3 1-3	3-2 1-0	2-1 2-1	5-2	0-3 2-0
Umm Salal	27	16	2	9	45	36	50	1-3	0-2 2-1		1-0	2-1 1-0	1-1 2-1	0-2	0-0 1-0	3-0 3-1	2-1
Qatar SC	27	14	4	9	53	38	46	0-5	2-2	4-2 1-0		1-1 3-0	2-2	1-3	4-2 1-0	1-1 3-1	3-0
Al Rayyan	27	12	3	12	39	42	39	0-2	0-3	2-1	1-3		2-1	1-1 3-1	1-0 3-0	1-2 2-0	1-1 4-0
Al Arabi	27	8	9	10	37	35	33	0-2	1-1	2-0	0-2 2-3	1-1 1-2		0-0	1-0 1-1	1-0	0-0 2-0
Khor	27	8	4	15	35	48	28	1-3 0-3	1-3	0-4 2-3	2-1 2-0	0-1	1-1 3-2		0-3 4-1	3-3 2-1	1-2 2-1
Al Siliya	27	7	6	14	33	46	27	0-2 0-1	3-3	2-3	1-6	2-0	2-0	2-1		2-2 1-1	1-1 3-0
Al Wakra	27	7	6	14	41	67	27	2-5	1-1 0-4	3-1	3-2	1-4	1-5 3-2	2-0	3-4		2-0 2-1
Shamal	27	5	3	19	27	51	18	2-3 5-3	1-2	0-1 2-4	3-1 0-2	0-3	2-3	1-0	0-1	1-1	

9/09/2007 - 1/04/2008 • † Qualified for AFC Champions League • Top scorer: Clemerson, Al Gharrafa 27
Crown Prince Cup: Semi-finals: **Sadd** 1-0 2-0 Umm Salal; **Gharrafa** 2-1 3-2 Qatar SC • Final: **Sadd** 1-0 Gharrafa (17-04-2008). The Crown Prince Cup is a tournament played at the end of the season between the top four of the league but it is not part of the league season.

SHEIKH QASSIM CUP 2007

Round of 16	Pts	Semi-finals		Final	
Al Gharrafa	7				
Khor	6				
Al Ahli	4				
Maitheer	3	**Al Gharrafa**	0 6p		
Al Rayyan	9	Al Rayyan	0 5p		
Qatar SC	6				
Mseimeer	3			**Al Gharrafa**	4
Al Khritiyat	0			Al Siliya	2
Al Arabi	7				
Al Sadd	6				
Shamal	4				
Markheya	3	Al Arabi	0		
Al Siliya	9	**Al Siliya**	2		
Umm Salal	6				
Shahaniya	3				
Al Wakra	0				

CUP FINAL

Doha Stadium, 31-08-2007
Scorers - Abdelhaq Aarif 2 [35] [66], Younis Mahmoud 2 [103] [112] for Gharrafa; Ahmad Mubarak [10], Abdoulaye Cisse [29] for Siliya

EMIR'S CUP 2007–08

Round of 16		Quarter-finals		Semi-finals		Final	
Umm Salal	Bye						
		Umm Salal	2				
Markheya	0	Al Siliya	1				
Al Siliya	6			**Umm Salal**	3		
Al Rayyan	1 4p			Al Sadd	2		
Al Wakra	1 1p	Al Rayyan	1				
		Al Sadd	3				
Al Sadd	Bye					**Umm Salal** †	2 4p
Qatar SC	Bye					Al Gharrafa	2 1p
		Qatar SC	2				
Al Khritiyat	1	Khor	1				
Khor	6			Qatar SC	1		
Al Arabi	2			**Al Gharrafa**	3		
Mseimeer	0	Al Arabi	3				
		Al Gharrafa	4				
Al Gharrafa	Bye						

† Qualified for AFC Champions League

CUP FINAL

15-05-2008

Maurito 2 [31] [50] for Umm Salal; Mustafa Abidi [15], Younis Mahmoud [56] for Gharrafa

ROU – ROMANIA

NATIONAL TEAM RECORD
JULY 10TH 2006 TO JULY 12TH 2010

PL	W	D	L	F	A	%
23	15	4	4	42	14	73.9

FIFA/COCA-COLA WORLD RANKING

1993	1994	1995	1996	1997	1998	1999	2000	2001	2002	2003	2004	2005	2006	2007		High	
13	11	11	16	7	12	8	13	15	24	27	29	27	19	13		**3**	09/97

					2007–2008								Low	
08/07	09/07	10/07	11/07	12/07	01/08	02/08	03/08	04/08	05/08	06/08	07/08		**35**	08/04
13	12	12	13	13	13	13	13	12	12	12	12			

It was an excellent year for football in Romania with the national team topping their qualifying group for Euro 2008 and although Victor Piturca's men made a first round exit in the finals that was no disgrace after finding themselves in the 'group of death' along with France, Italy and the Netherlands. They earned solid draws against both France and Italy although Adrian Mutu's penalty miss late on against the Italians will haunt him for years to come. Had he scored the Romanians would have been through to the quarter-finals. In another indication of the growing strength of the game in the country, Romanian clubs were awarded a guaranteed berth in the group stage of the

INTERNATIONAL HONOURS
Qualified for the FIFA World Cup finals 1930 1934 1938 1970 1990 1994 1998   UEFA Champions League Steaua Bucuresti 1986

Champions League for the 2008–09 season thanks to past performances in Europe. The beneficiaries of this were surprisingly not Steaua or Dinamo, who both have experience of the group stage, but Caile Ferate Cluj, the team of the national railways, who won the championship for the first time in their 101-year history. A 1-0 victory over cross-town rivals Universitatea on the final day of the season saw them finish a point ahead of Steaua to take the title outside of Bucharest for the first time in 17 years. Three days later Ioan Andone's team then beat Unirea in the Cup final, a goal from Portuguese striker Antonio Semedo securing a first Cup triumph for Cluj - and the double.

THE FIFA BIG COUNT OF 2006

	Male	Female		Total
Number of players	929 488	104 832	Referees and Assistant Referees	4 683
Professionals	1 139		Admin, Coaches, Technical, Medical	16 200
Amateurs 18+	54 158		Number of clubs	2 831
Youth under 18	48 010		Number of teams	4 319
Unregistered	556 700		Clubs with women's teams	1
Total players	1 034 320		Players as % of population	4.64%

Romanian Football Federation (FRF)

Federatia Romana de Fotbal, House of Football, Str. Serg. Serbanica Vasile 12, Bucharest 022186, Romania

Tel +40 21 3250678   Fax +40 21 3250679

frf@frf.ro   www.frf.ro

President: SANDU Mircea   General Secretary: KASSAI Adalbert

Vice-President: DRAGOMIR Dumitru   Treasurer: FILIMON Vasile   Media Officer: ZAHARIA Paul Daniel

Men's Coach: PITURCA Victor   Women's Coach: DELICOIU Maria

FRF formed: 1909   UEFA: 1954   FIFA: 1923

Yellow shirts with red trimmings, Yellow shorts, Yellow socks or White shirts with red trimmings, White shorts, White socks

RECENT INTERNATIONAL MATCHES PLAYED BY ROMANIA

2005	Opponents	Score		Venue	Comp	Scorers	Att	Referee
12-11	Côte d'Ivoire	L	1-2	Le Mans	Fr	Iencsi [52]	5 377	Fautrel FRA
16-11	Nigeria	W	3-0	Bucharest	Fr	Niculae [15], Petre [48], Rosu [90]	500	Banari MDA
2006								
28-02	Armenia	W	2-0	Nicosia	Fr	Maftei [72], Cocis [86]	1 000	Tsacheilidis GRE
1-03	Slovenia	W	2-0	Larnaca	Fr	Mazilu [22], OG [53]	300	Vialichka BLR
23-05	Uruguay	L	0-2	Los Angeles	Fr		10 000	Stott USA
26-05	Northern Ireland	W	2-0	Chicago	Fr	Buga [7], Niculae [11]	15 000	Kennedy USA
27-05	Colombia	D	0-0	Chicago	Fr		15 000	Hall USA
16-08	Cyprus	W	2-0	Constanta	Fr	Dica [4], Mutu [29]	10 000	Corpodean ROU
2-09	Bulgaria	D	2-2	Constanta	ECq	Rosu [40], Marica [44]	12 620	Farina ITA
6-09	Albania	W	2-0	Tirana	ECq	Dica [65], Mutu [75p]	12 000	Benquerença POR
7-10	Belarus	W	3-1	Bucharest	ECq	Mutu [7], Marica [10], Goian [76]	12 000	Undiano Mallenco ESP
15-11	Spain	W	1-0	Cadiz	Fr	Marica [59]	15 000	Messina ITA
2007								
7-02	Moldova	W	2-0	Bucharest	Fr	Mazilu [74], Mutu [87]	8 000	Deaconu ROU
24-03	Netherlands	D	0-0	Rotterdam	ECq		48 000	Merk GER
28-03	Luxembourg	W	3-0	Piatra-Neamt	ECq	Mutu [26], Contra [56], Marica [90]	9 120	Lajuks LVA
2-06	Slovenia	W	2-1	Celje	ECq	Tamas [52], Nicolita [69]	6 500	Dougal SCO
6-06	Slovenia	W	2-0	Timisoara	ECq	Mutu [40], Contra [70]	17 850	Yefet ISR
22-08	Turkey	W	2-0	Bucharest	Fr	Dica [61], Mutu [70]	12 000	Merk GER
8-09	Belarus	W	3-1	Minsk	ECq	Mutu 2 [16 77p], Dica [42]	19 320	Fröjdfeldt SWE
12-09	Germany	L	1-3	Cologne	Fr	Goian [3]	44 500	Rizzoli ITA
13-10	Netherlands	W	1-0	Constanta	ECq	Goian [71]	12 595	Vassaras GRE
17-10	Luxembourg	W	2-0	Luxembourg	ECq	Petre.F [42], Marica [61]	3 584	Brych GER
17-11	Bulgaria	L	0-1	Sofia	ECq		6 000	Plautz AUT
21-11	Albania	W	6-1	Bucharest	ECq	Dica 2 [22 71p], Tamas [53], Niculae.D 2 [62 65], Marica [69p]	23 427	Trivkovic CRO
2008								
6-02	Israel	L	0-1	Tel Aviv	Fr		8 000	Duarte Gomez POR
26-03	Russia	W	3-0	Bucharest	Fr	Marica [45], Niculae.D [60], Niculae.M [75]	10 000	Kenan ISR
31-05	Montenegro	W	4-0	Bucharest	Fr	Mutu [15], Ghionea [49], Dica 2 [55 69]	8 000	Tudor ROU
9-06	France	D	0-0	Zurich	ECr1		30 585	Mejuto Gonzalez ESP
13-06	Italy	D	1-1	Zurich	ECr1	Mutu [55]	30 585	Ovrebø NOR
17-06	Netherlands	L	0-2	Berne	ECr1		30 777	Busacca SUI

Fr = Friendly match • EC = UEFA EURO 2008 • WC = FIFA World Cup • q = qualifier • r1 = first round group

ROMANIA NATIONAL TEAM PLAYERS

	Player		Ap	G	Club	Date of Birth		Player		Ap	G	Club	Date of Birth
1	Bogdan Lobont	GK	66	0	Dinamo Buc'esti	18 01 1978	12	Marius Popa	GK	2	0	Nat'l Bucuresti	31 07 1978
2	Cosmin Contra	DF	66	7	Getafe	15 12 1975	13	Cristian Sapunaru	DF	0	0	Rapid Bucuresti	5 04 1984
3	Razvan Rat	DF	51	1	Shakhtar Donetsk	26 05 1981	14	Sorin Ghionea	DF	11	1	Steaua Bucuresti	11 05 1979
4	Gabriel Tamas	DF	35	2	AJ Auxerre	9 11 1983	15	Dorin Goian	DF	21	3	Steaua Bucuresti	12 12 1980
5	Cristian Chivu	DF	62	3	Internazionale	26 10 1980	16	Banel Nicolita	MF	22	1	Steaua Bucuresti	7 01 1985
6	Mirel Radoi	DF	45	1	Steaua Bucuresti	22 03 1981	17	Cosmin Moti	DF	1	0	Dinamo Buc'esti	3 12 1984
7	Florentin Petre	MF	51	5	CSKA Sofia	15 01 1976	18	Marius Niculae	FW	32	13	Inverness CT	16 05 1981
8	Paul Codrea	MF	36	1	Siena	4 04 1981	19	Adrian Cristea	MF	5	0	Dinamo Buc'esti	30 11 1983
9	Ciprian Marica	FW	24	8	VfB Stuttgart	2 10 1985	20	Nicolae Dica	MF	28	8	Steaua Bucuresti	9 05 1980
10	Adrian Mutu	FW	64	29	Fiorentina	8 01 1979	21	Daniel Niculae	FW	25	5	AJ Auxerre	6 10 1982
11	Razvan Cocis	MF	24	1	Loko'tiv Moskva	19 02 1983	22	Stefan Radu	DF	8	0	Lazio	22 10 1986
	Romania's squad for Euro 2008						23	Eduard Stancioiu	GK	0	0	CFR Cluj	3 03 1981

ROMANIA NATIONAL TEAM RECORDS AND RECORD SEQUENCES

Records			Sequence records					
Victory	9-0	FIN 1973	Wins	8	1996-1997	Clean sheets	5	1996-97, 1999
Defeat	0-9	HUN 1948	Defeats	4	1924-25, 1979	Goals scored	16	1971-1972
Player Caps	134	Dorinel Munteanu	Undefeated	17	1989-1990	Without goal	4	1947-1948
Player Goals	35	Gheorghe Hagi	Without win	20	1968-1971	Goals against	21	1933-1937

MAJOR CITIES/TOWNS
Population '000

1	Bucharest	1 848
2	Iasi	314
3	Cluj-Napoca	314
4	Timisoara	312
5	Craiova	304
6	Constanta	297
7	Galati	290
8	Brasov	270
9	Ploiesti	225
10	Braila	210
11	Oradea	201
12	Bacau	167
13	Arad	166
14	Pitesti	166
15	Sibiu	149
16	Târgu-Mures	144
17	Baia Mare	135
18	Buzau	129
19	Botosani	113
20	Satu Mare	110
21	Piatra Neamt	100
22	Bistrita	80
23	Resita	79
24	Petrosani	43

ROMANIA

Capital	Bucharest	Language	Romanian, Hungarian			Independence	1878
Population	22 276 056	Area	237 500 km²	Density	94 per km²	% in cities	55%
GDP per cap	$7 000	Dailling code	+40	Internet	.ro	GMT + / -	+2

MEDALS TABLE

		Overall			League			Cup		Europe			City	Stadium	Cap'ty	DoF
		G	S	B	G	S	B	G	S	G	S	B				
1	Steaua Bucuresti	45	21	9	23	13	7	21	7	1	1	2	Bucharest	Stadionul Ghencea	27 063	1947
2	Dinamo Bucuresti	31	31	10	19	20	8	12	11			2	Bucharest	Stadionul Dinamo	15 138	1948
3	Rapid Bucuresti	16	19	8	3	14	8	13	5				Bucharest	Stadionul Giulesti	19 100	1923
4	Universitatea Craiova	10	10	8	4	5	7	6	5			1	Craiova	Ion Oblemenco	27 915	1948
5	UT Arad	8	3	1	6	1	1	2	2				Arad	Stadionul UTA	12 000	1945
6	Venus Bucuresti	8	1	1	8	1		1					Bucharest	Venus		1915-49
7	Petrolul Ploiesti	6	4	2	4	3	2	2	1				Ploiesti	Stadionul Ilie Oana	18 000	1924
	Ripensia Timisoara	6	4	2	4	2	2	2	2				Timisoara	Electrica		1928-48
9	Chinezul Timisoara	6	1		6				1				Timisoara	Chinezul		1913-39
10	Politehnica Timisoara	2	5	5			5	2	5				Timisoara	Dan Paltinisanu	32 019	1921
11	FC Arges Pitesti	2	3	4	2	2	4		1				Pitesti	Nicolae Dobrin	15 170	1953
12	FC Bihor Oradea	2	3	1	1	2	1	1	1				Oradea	Municipal	18 000	1902
13	FCM Resita	2	1		1	1		1					Resita	Valea Domanului	12 000	1922
14	CFR 1907 Cluj	2		1	1		1	1					Cluj-Napoca	Dr Constantin Radulescu	14 000	1907
15	Colentina Bucuresti	2			2								Bucharest			
	Olimpia Bucuresti	2			2								Bucharest			
	Prahova Ploiesti	2			2								Ploiesti			

RECENT LEAGUE AND CUP RECORD

	Championship						Cup		
Year	Champions	Pts	Runners-up	Pts	Third	Pts	Winners	Score	Runners-up
1995	Steaua Bucuresti	77	Universit. Craiova	68	Dinamo Bucuresti	65	Petrolul Ploiesti	1-1 5-3p	Rapid Bucuresti
1996	Steaua Bucuresti	71	National Bucuresti	60	Rapid Bucuresti	59	Steaua Bucuresti	3-1	Gloria Bistrita
1997	Steaua Bucuresti	73	National Bucuresti	68	Dinamo Bucuresti	59	Steaua Bucuresti	4-2	National Bucuresti
1998	Steaua Bucuresti	80	Rapid Bucuresti	78	Arges Pitesti	65	Rapid Bucuresti	1-0	Universit. Craiova
1999	Rapid Bucuresti	89	Dinamo Bucuresti	82	Steaua Bucuresti	66	Steaua Bucuresti	2-2 4-2p	Rapid Bucuresti
2000	Dinamo Bucuresti	84	Rapid Bucuresti	72	Ceahlaul P. Neamt	57	Dinamo Bucuresti	2-0	Universit. Craiova
2001	Steaua Bucuresti	60	Dinamo Bucuresti	51	FC Brasov	50	Dinamo Bucuresti	4-2	Rocar Bucuresti
2002	Dinamo Bucuresti	60	National Bucuresti	58	Rapid Bucuresti	50	Rapid Bucuresti	2-1	Dinamo Bucuresti
2003	Rapid Bucuresti	63	Steaua Bucuresti	56	Gloria Bistrita	45	Dinamo Bucuresti	1-0	National Bucuresti
2004	Dinamo Bucuresti	70	Steaua Bucuresti	64	Rapid Bucuresti	55	Dinamo Bucuresti	2-0	Otelul Galati
2005	Steaua Bucuresti	63	Dinamo Bucuresti	62	Rapid Bucuresti	57	Dinamo Bucuresti	1-0	Farul Constanta
2006	Steaua Bucuresti	64	Rapid Bucuresti	59	Dinamo Bucuresti	56	Rapid Bucuresti	1-0	National Bucuresti
2007	Dinamo Bucuresti	77	Steaua Bucuresti	71	CFR 1907 Cluj	69	Rapid Bucuresti	2-0	Politehn. Timisoara
2008	CFR 1907 Cluj	76	Steaua Bucuresti	75	Rapid Bucuresti	61	CFR 1907 Cluj	2-1	Unirea Urziceni

ROMANIA 2007–08

LIGA I BURGER

Team	Pl	W	D	L	F	A	Pts	Cluj	Steaua	Rapid	Dinamo	Unirea	P Timisoara	Vaslui	Otelul	Un. Craiova	Gloria	P. Iasi	Pandurii	Farul	Buzau	Ceahlaul	Dacia	Arad	Un. Cluj
CFR 1907 Cluj †	34	23	7	4	52	22	76		0-0	1-0	1-1	2-0	2-2	1-0	3-1	4-1	1-0	2-1	1-2	2-1	2-0	2-1	1-0	2-0	2-0
Steaua Bucuresti §6 †	34	23	6	5	51	19	69	3-1		0-0	1-0	1-0	1-1	1-0	3-1	1-0	1-0	1-0	0-0	3-0	5-0	2-1	2-0	2-1	4-0
Rapid Bucuresti ‡	34	18	7	9	52	31	61	1-2	0-3		1-2	1-1	0-1	2-1	4-2	2-0	2-2	3-0	1-0	2-0	0-0	5-1	3-0	2-3	1-2
Dinamo Bucuresti ‡	34	17	10	7	55	36	61	1-2	2-1	0-2		1-1	1-1	0-2	6-1	4-4	0-1	2-1	1-2	0-0	2-0	2-1	1-1	3-1	2-1
Unirea Val'm Urziceni‡	34	16	13	5	42	24	61	1-1	1-0	0-1	0-0		4-1	2-0	0-0	2-2	2-0	1-0	1-0	0-0	2-0	2-0	0-2	1-0	3-2
Politehnica Timisoara ‡	34	16	9	9	57	44	57	1-0	2-0	1-1	1-1	0-0		2-1	4-1	1-3	3-1	3-1	3-1	4-1	1-0	3-2	1-2	2-0	3-0
FC Vaslui	34	11	12	11	42	35	47	0-2	0-1	2-4	2-1	1-1	3-0		2-0	2-0	2-0	0-0	1-0	1-1	4-1	0-1	3-0	2-2	0-0
Otelul Galati	34	14	5	15	48	48	46	0-1	0-1	0-1	0-1	3-2	3-1	**0-3**		2-1	2-0	0-0	3-1	2-0	2-3	4-1	3-1	2-1	1-1
Universitatea Craiova	34	12	7	15	42	48	43	1-3	1-2	1-1	1-1	0-1	2-1	2-1	1-1		1-1	2-1	1-0	4-0	3-1	3-2	1-0	0-1	1-1
Gloria Bistrita	34	11	9	14	34	40	42	2-2	1-3	1-2	1-1	2-2	0-0	0-0	2-1	0-1		2-0	3-1	1-0	3-2	0-1	1-0	2-1	2-0
Politehnica Iasi	34	11	8	15	37	41	41	1-0	2-1	0-2	2-5	2-3	2-1	0-1	2-2	2-1	2-0		1-0	1-1	3-0	1-0	1-0	4-1	3-0
Pandurii Târgu Jiu	34	11	7	16	36	43	40	0-1	0-1	1-3	0-1	1-1	1-3	1-1	1-0	2-0	1-3	1-0		0-1	3-0	1-0	0-1	2-1	2-2
Farul Constanta	34	10	10	14	25	38	40	0-2	0-1	0-0	0-1	0-1	1-1	2-0	3-1	1-0	1-1	1-2	0-0		0-0	2-0	1-1	1-0	0-0
Gloria Buzau	34	10	7	17	30	56	37	1-2	1-1	1-0	1-2	0-0	2-1	1-1	0-4	1-0	1-0	1-1	1-3	1-0		4-1	0-1	1-0	3-2
Ceahlaul Piatra Neamt	34	10	6	18	33	46	36	0-0	0-1	1-0	0-3	0-0	2-1	1-1	0-1	1-0	1-0	2-0	1-0	2-1	4-0		1-1	1-1	3-0
Dacia Mioveni	34	7	10	17	26	43	31	0-0	1-2	1-2	1-2	0-3	2-2	2-2	1-0	1-2	0-0	2-1	1-1	2-3	0-0	2-1		0-1	1-0
UTA Arad	34	6	8	20	30	52	26	0-3	1-1	1-0	1-3	1-2	2-3	1-1	0-1	0-1	0-0	3-3	0-1	2-1	0-1	1-0			1-1
Universitatea Cluj §6	34	4	11	19	32	58	17	0-1	2-1	1-2	1-2	0-2	1-2	2-3	2-1	2-0	2-2	1-1	1-1	1-2	1-1	0-0	2-2		

27/07/2007 - 7/05/2008 • † Qualified for the UEFA Champions League • ‡ Qualified for the UEFA Cup • Match in bold awarded • § = points deducted

ROMANIA 2007–08 — LIGA II SERIE 1 (2)

Team	Pl	W	D	L	F	A	Pts
FC Brasov	34	24	6	4	81	23	78
CS Otopeni	34	21	6	7	74	43	69
Petrolul Ploiesti	34	19	7	8	61	31	64
Prefabricate Modelu	34	17	7	10	54	36	58
Concordia Chiajna	34	17	6	11	52	45	57
Forex Brasov	34	15	6	13	36	24	51
Dunarea Giurgiu	34	13	10	11	37	43	49
Delta Tulcea	34	14	6	14	38	37	48
FC Botosani	34	13	8	13	34	41	47
Dinamo Bucuresti-2	34	12	9	13	59	73	45
Progresul Bucuresti	34	12	9	13	38	35	45
Sportul Studentesc	34	10	12	12	37	47	42
FCM Bacau	34	8	14	12	33	37	38
Municipal Campina	34	10	8	16	31	48	38
Intergaz Bucuresti	34	9	7	18	44	52	34
CSM Focsani	34	8	10	16	39	51	34
Dunarea Galati	34	7	7	20	26	66	28
FC Sacele	34	2	12	20	13	55	18

25/08/2007 - 24/05/2008

ROMANIA 2007–08 — LIGA II SERIE 2 (2)

Team	Pl	W	D	L	F	A	Pts
Arges Pitesti	34	25	5	4	77	22	79
Gaz Metan Medias	34	24	1	9	77	43	73
Râmnicu Vâlcea	34	18	7	9	56	39	61
Unirea Alba Iulia	34	18	6	10	56	36	60
Drobeta Turnu Severin	34	17	7	10	46	33	58
Jiul Petrosani §5	34	18	8	8	53	29	57
Muresul Deva	34	14	8	12	39	40	50
FC Târgoviste	34	12	11	11	45	40	47
Liberty Oradea	34	13	8	13	36	33	47
Bihor Oradea	34	13	8	13	32	36	47
Minerul Lupeni	34	10	11	13	41	45	41
Sârmei Câmpia Turzii	34	11	8	15	29	38	41
CFR Timisoara	34	11	6	17	34	45	39
Ariesul Turda	34	10	8	16	35	49	38
FCM Resita	34	9	6	19	38	65	33
Politehnica Timisoara-2	34	9	6	19	27	56	33
FC Caracal	34	6	7	21	34	57	25
Corvinul Hunedoara	34	4	7	23	21	70	19

25/08/2007 - 24/05/2008 • § = points deducted

CUPA ROMANIEI 2007–08

Round of 16

CFR 1907 Cluj	1
Jiul Petrosani	0
Otelul Galati	2 4p
FC Brasov	2 5p
Dinamo Bucuresti	4
Sanatatea Cluj	0
Ceahlaul Piatra Neamt	0
Dacia Mioveni	3
Gloria Buzau	2 5p
Politehnica Timisoara	2 3p
Universitatea Cluj	0
Pandurii Târgu Jiu	2
Rapid Bucuresti	3
Politehnica Iasi	0
Steaua Bucuresti	0
Unirea Val'm Urziceni	2

Quarter-finals

CFR 1907 Cluj	1
FC Brasov	0
Dinamo Bucuresti	0
Dacia Mioveni	1
Gloria Buzau	0 3p
Pandurii Târgu Jiu	0 2p
Rapid Bucuresti	0
Unirea Val'm Urziceni	1

Semi-finals

CFR 1907 Cluj	3
Dacia Mioveni	0
Gloria Buzau	0
Unirea Val'm Urziceni	1

Final

CFR 1907 Cluj	2
Unirea Val'm Urziceni‡	1

CUP FINAL
Ceahlaul, Piatra Neamt
10-05-2008

Scorers - Ruiz 49, Semedo 64 for Cluj; Galamaz 58 for Unirea

‡ Qualified for the UEFA Cup

RSA – SOUTH AFRICA

NATIONAL TEAM RECORD
JULY 10TH 2006 TO JULY 12TH 2010

PL	W	D	L	F	A	%
29	12	8	9	32	21	55.2

The 2010 FIFA World Cup finals are proving both a boon and burden for South Africa as it counts down the days before hosting the tournament. The burden of the event rests heavily on the national team Bafana Bafana, going through yet another slump and mired in a crisis of self-confidence. The side faces the embarrassment of missing out on qualifying for the 2010 Africa Cup of Nations finals in Angola after some poor results in the World Cup preliminaries, in which South Africa are competing because they are also serving as qualifiers for the Nations Cup in Angola. This on the back of the sudden departure of coach Carlos Alberto Parreira, who had been employed from the start of 2007 to build a competitive side for the World Cup finals. The illness of his wife forced Parreira to quit in May 2008, leaving the South African Football Association to look for a replacement. In seeking to keep the consistency of Parreira's work which was beginning to show some bright results - even though South Africa didn't make it past the first round at the 2008 Nations Cup in Ghana - they took up his recommendation of fellow Brazilian Joel Santana, who arrived just weeks before the first Nations Cup/World Cup qualifier in Nigeria. It was baptism of fire made even worse by the absence of star striker Benni McCarthy, with Santana starting his tenure with just a single win and draw in his first four matches and the spectre that South Africa will miss out on the

INTERNATIONAL HONOURS
Qualified for the FIFA World Cup finals 1998 2002
CAF African Cup of Nations 1996   CAF Champions League Orlando Pirates 1995

finals in Angola, having qualified for the last seven tournaments. The flip side of hosting the world's biggest sporting event has been the massive interest generated in the South African league, which is experiencing a commercial boom. The cable channel SuperSport signed a five-year television rights deal with the Premier Soccer League worth nearly 160-million Euros - the seventh biggest deal of its kind worldwide - giving an indication of how buoyant the local market is. Sponsors are fulsome and clubs have newfound purchasing power to buy better players and employ more proficient coaches. Ironically SuperSport United were crowned champions after winning a tight race ahead of the Cape Town clubs Ajax and Santos. There was some reprieve for outgoing champions Mamelodi Sundowns who beat Mpumalanga Black Aces in the Nedbank FA Cup final. Sundowns had started the season by winning the Supa 8 Cup but lost in the final of the League Cup to Kaiser Chiefs in what turned out to be a poor season for the Johannesburg clubs. South African clubs also continued to have problems in continental competition with Sundowns falling at the last hurdle before the Champions League group phase for the second year running, losing 4-3 on aggregate to Al Hilal of Sudan.

South African Football Association (SAFA)
125 Samuel Evans Road, Aeroton, Johannesburg, South Africa
Tel +27 11 4943522   Fax +27 11 4943013
raymond.hack@safa.net   www.safa.net
President: OLIPHANT Molefi   General Secretary: HACK Raymond
Vice-President: KHOZA Irvin   Treasurer: HULYO Gronie   Media Officer: SANYANE Morio
Men's Coach: SANTANA Joel   Women's Coach: MAKALAKALANE Augustine
SAFA formed: 1991   CAF: 1992   FIFA: 1992
White shirts with yellow stripes, White shorts, White socks

RECENT INTERNATIONAL MATCHES PLAYED BY SOUTH AFRICA

2006	Opponents	Score		Venue	Comp	Scorers	Att	Referee
22-01	Guinea	L	0-2	Alexandria	CNr1		10 000	Benouza ALG
26-01	Tunisia	L	0-2	Alexandria	CNr1		10 000	Evehe CMR
30-01	Zambia	L	0-1	Alexandria	CNr1		4 000	Abd El Fatah EGY
10-05	Lesotho	D	0-0	Maseru	Fr		15 000	
20-05	Swaziland	W	1-0	Gaborone	CCr1	Mhlongo [13]		Malepa BOT
21-05	Botswana	D	0-0	Gaborone	CCr1	L 5-6p		Infante MOZ
16-08	Namibia	W	1-0	Katutura	Fr	Mashego [60]		
2-09	Congo	D	0-0	Johannesburg	CNq			Aboubacar CIV
8-10	Zambia	W	1-0	Lusaka	CNq	Mokoena [28]		Maillet SEY
15-11	Egypt	L	0-1	Brentford	Fr		2 000	Styles ENG
2007								
24-03	Chad	W	3-0	N'Djamena	CNq	Moriri [32], Buckley [44], Zuma [78]		Aguidissou BEN
28-03	Bolivia	L	0-1	Johannesburg	Fr		5 000	Ramocha BOT
26-05	Malawi	D	0-0	Mbabane	CCr1	W 5-4p		Dlamini SWZ
27-05	Mauritius	W	2-0	Mbabane	CCr1	Modise 2 [43p 65]		Mufeti NAM
2-06	Chad	W	4-0	Durban	CNq	Morris [13p], Zuma 2 [23 33], Nomvete [70]		Gasingwa RWA
17-06	Congo	D	1-1	Pointe Noire	CNq	Zuma [46]		Eyene CMR
22-08	Scotland	L	0-1	Aberdeen	Fr		13 723	Atkinson ENG
9-09	Zambia	L	1-3	Cape Town	CNq	McCarthy [50]		Evehe CMR
12-09	Uruguay	D	0-0	Johannesburg	Fr			Bwanya ZIM
29-09	Botswana	W	1-0	Atteridgeville	CCsf	Modise [32]		Marange ZIM
17-10	Italy	L	0-2	Sienna	Fr		7 219	Weiner GER
24-10	Zambia	D	0-0	Bloemfontein	CCf	W 4-3p		Andriamiharisoa MAD
17-11	USA	L	0-1	Johannesburg	Fr			Maillet SEY
20-11	Canada	W	2-0	Durban	Fr	Modise 2 [39 44p]		Kalyoto MWI
2008								
13-01	Mozambique	W	2-0	Durban	Fr	Zuma [62], Chabangu [89]		
16-01	Botswana	W	2-1	Durban	Fr	Moon [41], Zuma [81]		
23-01	Angola	D	1-1	Tamale	CNr1	Van Heerden [88]		Coulibaly MLI
27-01	Tunisia	L	1-3	Tamale	CNr1	Mphela [86]		Djaoupe TOG
31-01	Senegal	D	1-1	Kumasi	CNr1	Van Heerden [14]		Kotey GHA
11-03	Zimbabwe	W	2-1	Johannesburg	Fr	Ngcobo [73], Matola OG [93+]		Malepa BOT
26-03	Paraguay	W	3-0	Atteridgeville	Fr	Moriri [31], McCarthy [47], Tshabalala [61]	15 000	
1-06	Nigeria	L	0-2	Abuja	CNq		50 000	Coulibaly MLI
7-06	Equatorial Guinea	W	4-1	Atteridgeville	CNq	Dikgacoi 2 [9 93+], Moriri [33], Fanteni [62]	10 000	Diouf SEN
14-06	Sierra Leone	L	0-1	Freetown	CNq		15 000	Pare BFA
21-06	Sierra Leone	D	0-0	Atteridgeville	CNq		12 000	Evehe CMR

Fr = Friendly match • CN = CAF African Cup of Nations • CC = COSAFA Cup • WC = FIFA World Cup • q = qualifier • r1 = first round group

SOUTH AFRICA NATIONAL TEAM PLAYERS

	Player		Club	Date of Birth		Player		Club	Date of Birth
1	Rowen Fernandez	GK	Arminia Bielefeld GER	28 02 1978	12	Teko Modise	MF	Orlando Pirates	22 12 1982
2	Bevan Fransman	DF	Moroka Swallows	31 10 1983	13	Benson Mhlongo	DF	Mamelodi Sundowns	9 11 1980
3	Tsepo Masilela	DF	Maccabi Haifa ISR	5 01 1985	14	Lerato Chabangu	FW	Mameodi Sundowns	15 08 1985
4	Aaron Mokoena	DF	Blackburn Rovers ENG	25 11 1980	15	Sibusiso Zuma	FW	Arminia Bielefeld GER	23 06 1975
5	Nasief Morris	DF	Panathinaikos GRE	16 04 1981	16	Moeneeb Josephs	GK	Wits University	19 05 1980
6	Lance Davids	MF	Djurgardens SWE	11 04 1983	17	Katlego Mphela	FW	SuperSport United	29 11 1984
7	Tumelo Nhlapo	DF	Bloemfontein Celtic	20 01 1988	18	Excellent Walaza	FW	Orlando Pirates	8 04 1987
8	Siphiwe Tshabalala	MF	Kaizer Chiefs	25 09 1984	19	Bryce Moon	DF	Ajax Cape Town	6 04 1986
9	Surprise Moriri	MF	Mamelodi Sundowns	20 03 1980	20	Brett Evans	DF	Ajax Cape Town	8 03 1982
10	Steven Pienaar	MF	Everton ENG	17 03 1982	21	Thembinkosi Fanteni	FW	Ajax Cape Town	2 02 1984
11	Elrio van Heerden	MF	Club Brugge BEL	11 07 1983	22	Kagisho Dikgacoi	MF	Golden Arrows	24 11 1984
	South Africa's squad for the 2008 CAF Africa Cup of Nations				23	Itumeleng Khune	GK	Kaizer Chiefs	20 06 1987

SOUTH AFRICA NATIONAL TEAM RECORDS AND RECORD SEQUENCES

Records			Sequence records					
Victory	8-0	AUS 1955	Wins	7	1947-50, 1954-92	Clean sheets	7	1997-1997, 2002
Defeat	1-5	AUS 1947	Defeats	3	Five times	Goals scored	12	1947-1950
Player Caps	75	Aaron Mokoena	Undefeated	15	1994-1996	Without goal	4	2006
Player Goals	30	Benni McCarthy	Without win	9	1997-1998, 2005	Goals against	17	2005-2006

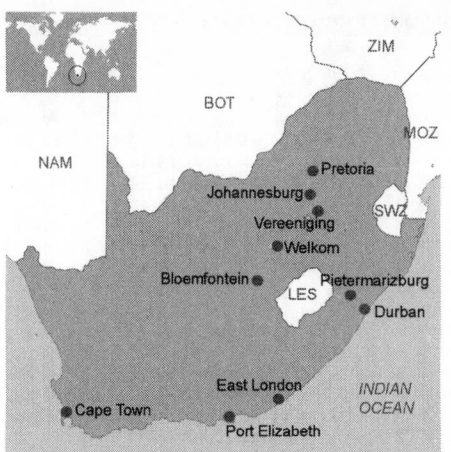

MAJOR CITIES/TOWNS

Population '000

1	Cape Town	3 660
2	Durban	3 368
3	Johannesburg	2 156
4	Soweto	1 839
5	Pretoria	1 757
6	Port Elizabeth	1 017
7	Pietermaritzburg	845
8	Benoni	671
9	Tembisa	577
10	Vereeniging	505
11	Bloemfontein	498
12	Boksburg	489
13	Welkom	483
14	Newcastle	447
15	East London	422
16	Krugersdorp	419
17	Brakpan	347
18	Botshabelo	338
19	Richards Bay	297
20	Witbank	287
21	Verwoerdburg	272
22	Vanderbijlpark	247
23	Uitenhage	242
24	Alberton	215

REPUBLIC OF SOUTH AFRICA

Capital Pretoria	Language Zulu, Xhosa, Afrikaans, Sedepi, English	Independence 1934
Population 43 997 828	Area 1 219 912 km² · Density 35 per km²	% in cities 51%
GDP per cap $10 700	Dialling code +27 · Internet .za	GMT +/- +2

The Johannesburg metropolitan area has a total population of 7 372 000 and includes Johannesburg, Soweto, Pretoria, Benoni, Tembisa, Vereeniging, Boksburg, Krugersdorp, Brakpan, Verwoerdburg, Vanderbijlpark and Alberton

MEDALS TABLE

		Overall			League			Cup		T8		LCup		Africa			City	Stadium	Cap'ty	DoF
		G	S	B	G	S	B	G	S	G	S	G	S	G	S	B				
1	Kaiser Chiefs	46	19	2	10	6	2	12	5	13	5	10	3				Krugersdorp	Amakhosi - 2009	55 000	1970
2	Orlando Pirates	21	18	8	7	4	6	6	7	7	3		4	1		2	Johannesburg	Ellis Park	59 611	1937
3	Mamelodi Sundowns	15	13	3	7	2	3	3	4	2	4	2	2			1	Pretoria	Loftus Versfeld	51 762	1970
4	Moroka Swallows	6	7	1		1	1	4	1	2	3		2				Germiston	Germiston	18 000	1947
5	Jomo Cosmos	5	8	1	1	1		1	4	1	1	2	2			1	Katlehong	Huntersfield	45 000	1983
6	Wits University	5	5	2		2		1	1	2	3	2	1				Johannesburg	Bidvest	5 000	1921
7	SuperSport United	4	7	1	1	2	1	2	1	1	2		2				Pretoria	Loftus Versfeld	51 762	1994
8	Bush Bucks	4	2	1	1	1	1					3	1				Umtata	Independence	25 000	1957
9	Santos	4	1	1		1		2		1		1					Cape Town	Athlone	25 000	1982
10	AmaZulu	2	6	2	1		2	5		1	1						Durban	Princess Magogo	10 000	1932
11	Ajax Cape Town	2	5			2		1	1		1	1	1				Cape Town	Newlands	50 900	1999
12	Arcadia	2	2	1		1				1	2	1					Pretoria			1903
13	Witbank Aces	2	2					1	1	1	1						Witbank	Kwaguqa		1937
14	Cape Town Spurs	2	1		1	1		1									Cape Town	Greenpoint	18 000	1969
15	Bloemfontein Celtic	2	1					1		1							Bloemfontein	Seisa Ramabodu	20 000	1969

RECENT LEAGUE AND CUP RECORD

Championship

Year	Champions	Pts	Runners-up	Pts	Third	Pts
1995	Cape Town Spurs	71	Mamelodi Sundowns	66	Orlando Pirates	60
1996	Not played due to season adjustment					
1997	Manning Rangers	74	Kaiser Chiefs	66	Orlando Pirates	64
1998	Mamelodi Sundowns	68	Kaiser Chiefs	63	Orlando Pirates	57
1999	Mamelodi Sundowns	75	Kaiser Chiefs	75	Orlando Pirates	60
2000	Mamelodi Sundowns	75	Orlando Pirates	60	Kaiser Chiefs	60
2001	Orlando Pirates	61	Kaiser Chiefs	60	Mamelodi Sundowns	59
2002	Santos Cape Town	64	SuperSport United	59	Orlando Pirates	57
2003	Orlando Pirates	61	SuperSport United	55	Wits University	54
2004	Kaiser Chiefs	63	Ajax Cape Town	57	SuperSport United	53
2005	Kaiser Chiefs	62	Orlando Pirates	60	Mamelodi Sundowns	56
2006	Mamelodi Sundowns	57	Orlando Pirates	54	Kaiser Chiefs	50
2007	Mamelodi Sundowns	61	Silver Stars	51	Moroka Swallows	51
2008	SuperSport United	54	Ajax Cape Town	52	Santos	49

Cup

Winners	Score	Runners-up
Cape Town Spurs	3-2	Pretoria City
Orlando Pirates	1-0	Jomo Cosmos
No tournament played		
Mamelodi Sundowns	1-1 1-1 6-5p	Orlando Pirates
SuperSport United	2-1	Kaiser Chiefs
Kaiser Chiefs	1-0	Mamelodi Sundowns
Santos Cape Town	1-0	Mamelodi Sundowns
No tournament played		
Santos Cape Town	2-0	Ajax Cape Town
Moroka Swallows	3-1	Manning Rangers
SuperSport United	1-0	Wits University
Kaiser Chiefs	0-0 5-3p	Orlando Pirates
Ajax Cape Town	2-0	Mamelodi Sundowns
Mamelodi Sundowns	1-0	Black Aces

SOUTH AFRICA 2007–08

ABSA PREMIER SOCCER LEAGUE

	Pl	W	D	L	F	A	Pts	SuperSport	Ajax	Santos	Sundowns	Free State	Chiefs	Swallows	Pirates	Arrows	P. Stars	Celtic	Wits	AmaZulu	Thanda	Leopards	Cosmos
SuperSport United †	30	16	6	8	40	26	54		3-2	0-1	1-3	6-1	0-0	4-2	3-1	2-0	1-1	1-0	0-1	1-0	1-0	3-1	1-1
Ajax Cape Town †	30	14	10	6	44	27	52	0-0		1-1	1-1	0-0	1-1	4-1	2-0	1-1	1-1	3-1	5-2	3-0	3-0	1-0	1-0
Santos ‡	30	12	13	5	36	29	49	0-0	2-1		1-1	2-2	0-0	1-1	2-1	3-1	1-0	1-0	2-1	3-2	0-2	4-0	1-1
Mamelodi Sundowns ‡	30	13	8	9	40	35	47	2-3	2-0	0-0		0-4	1-0	1-3	2-1	1-2	1-2	0-0	2-3	1-2	2-0	1-2	2-2
Free State Stars	30	12	9	9	43	40	45	1-0	1-1	4-1	0-1		0-2	1-3	2-1	3-1	1-0	3-1	2-0	2-2	2-0	2-0	
Kaizer Chiefs	30	10	13	7	32	20	43	0-1	0-1	1-1	0-0	3-0		1-4	1-2	1-0	4-2	0-0	2-0	0-1	1-0	0-1	1-1
Moroka Swallows	30	12	7	11	41	41	43	1-2	2-1	1-4	0-0	3-1	1-3		0-3	1-1	6-2	3-1	0-0	3-2	0-0	1-0	1-3
Orlando Pirates	30	12	6	12	38	30	42	0-1	2-1	1-0	3-1	1-1	2-2	0-1		0-0	0-1	3-0	2-0	4-1	3-1	0-0	0-0
Golden Arrows	30	10	11	9	34	32	41	0-1	2-2	0-1	1-2	2-2	0-1	1-0	2-1		0-1	3-0	2-2	2-1	3-1	1-0	2-0
Platinum Stars	30	10	10	10	28	32	40	0-2	1-1	3-0	0-1	1-3	0-0	1-0	1-1	0-2		1-2	0-0	0-1	2-1	2-0	0-0
Bloemfontein Celtic	30	11	6	13	30	35	39	2-1	1-0	0-1	0-1	1-1	1-1	2-0	0-1	1-1	0-2		2-0	3-2	1-1	2-2	3-1
Wits University	30	10	8	12	28	35	38	2-0	0-1	1-1	1-3	1-3	0-1	1-1	1-3	1-0	0-0	1-2		0-1	1-0	2-1	2-0
AmaZulu	30	9	7	14	27	36	34	2-0	0-1	1-1	1-2	1-1	1-1	0-2	1-0	0-1	0-0	0-1	1-1		1-0	2-0	0-0
Thanda Royal Zulu	30	8	7	15	31	44	31	0-1	1-2	1-1	2-2	2-0	0-2	1-1	2-1	1-1	1-2	0-3	3-2	1-2		2-1	1-0
Black Leopards	30	8	5	17	27	42	29	2-0	1-2	2-0	0-3	1-2	1-0	1-3	2-3	0-0	2-0	0-1	1-0	1-2	3-2		0-0
Jomo Cosmos	30	2	16	12	13	28	22	2-1	0-1	0-0	0-1	0-0	0-0	0-0	0-1	1-1	0-2	0-0	0-0	1-0	2-0	0-2	

15/08/2007 - 18/05/2008 • † Qualified for the CAF Champions League • Top scorers: James Chamanga, Swallows 14; Diyo Sibisi, FS Stars 13;

SOUTH AFRICA 2007–08 NATIONAL FIRST DIVISION (2)

Inland	Pl	W	D	L	F	A	Pts
FC AK	21	10	7	4	21	19	37
Dynamos	21	9	4	8	31	23	31
Winners Park	21	9	4	8	25	24	31
African Warriors	21	8	5	8	20	21	29
Mpuma'ga Black Aces	21	7	7	7	26	23	28
Witbank Spurs	21	6	8	7	21	21	26
Pretoria University	21	6	7	8	23	27	25
Ga-Rankuwa United	21	5	6	10	22	31	21

National First Division Championship: FC AK 1-1 0-2 Maritzburg United
Maritzburg United promoted; AK FC enter play-offs

Play-off semi-finals: Bay United 1-0 1-1 Black Leopards; FC AK 0-0 2-1 Dynamos
Play-off final: Bay United 0-0 1-2 FC AK

Coastal	Pl	W	D	L	F	A	Pts
Maritzburg United	21	14	5	2	31	13	47
Bay United	21	14	3	4	30	10	45
Nathi Lions	21	8	10	3	22	13	34
FC Cape Town	21	6	8	7	24	24	26
Ikapa Sporting	21	5	6	10	25	30	21
Durban Stars	21	5	6	10	19	31	21
Hanover Park	21	5	4	12	22	32	19
Western Province Utd	21	2	8	11	20	40	14

28/09/2007 - 13/04/2008

SAA SUPA 8 CUP 2007

First Round		Semi-finals		Final	
Sundowns	4				
B'fontein Celtic	1	Sundowns	0 5p		
Platinum Stars	1 4p	Jomo Cosmos	0 4p		
Jomo Cosmos	1 5p			Sundowns	1
SuperSport Utd	2			Pirates	0
Swallows	1	SuperSport Utd	1		
Ajax Cape Town	0	Pirates	2	15-09-2007	
Pirates	2			Scorer - Brent Carelse 15	

TELKOM KNOCK-OUT LEAGUE CUP 2007

First Round		Quarter-finals		Semi-finals		Final	
Kaizer Chiefs	2 3p						
Moroka Swallows	2 1p	Kaizer Chiefs	1				
Santos	1	SuperSport United	0				
SuperSport United	2			Kaizer Chiefs	1		
AmaZulu	1			Bloemfontein Celtic	0		
Platinum Stars	0	AmaZulu	0				
Black Leopards	1 4p	Bloemfontein Celtic	1				
Bloemfontein Celtic	1 5p					Kaizer Chiefs	0 3p
Free State Stars	1					Mamelodi Sundowns	0 2p
Ajax Cape Town	0	Free State Stars	1				
Wits University	1	Jomo Cosmos	0				
Jomo Cosmos	2			Free State Stars	1		
Thanda Royal Zulu	1 5p			Mamelodi Sundowns	2		
Orlando Pirates	1 4p	Thanda Royal Zulu	1				
Golden Arrows	0	Mamelodi Sundowns	3				
Mamelodi Sundowns	3						

CUP FINAL

1-12-2007

NEDBANK FA CUP 2007-08

First Round

Mamelodi Sundowns	2
SuperSport United *	1
Ajax Cape Town	0
Kaizer Chiefs *	2
Winners Park	1 5p
Wits University *	1 4p
Durban Stars	0
FC Cape Town *	1
Black Leopards	3
Inspection FC *	0
Bloem'tein Young Tigers	3
Matatiele Professionals *	4
Vasco da Gama	3
Classic *	2
Young Ones	0
AmaZulu *	14
Free State Stars *	1 4p
Platinum Stars	1 3p
Bloemfontein Celtic	2
Ikapa Sporting *	3
Moroka Swallows *	1
African Warriors *	0
Orlando Pirates	2 4p
Santos *	2 5p
Nathi Lions *	0 5p
North West Shining Stars	0
Golden Arrows *	0 3p
Jomo Cosmos	1
FC AK	2 4p
Yebo Yes United *	2 3p
Thanda Royal Zulu	0
Mpumalanga Black Aces *	2

Second Round

Mamelodi Sundowns	1 5p
Kaizer Chiefs *	1 4p
Winners Park	0
FC Cape Town *	1
Black Leopards *	2
Matatiele Professionals	0
Vasco da Gama *	0
AmaZulu	5
Free State Stars *	8
Ikapa Sporting	1
Moroka Swallows *	1
Santos	3
Nathi Lions	0 5p
Jomo Cosmos *	0 3p
FC AK	0
Mpumalanga Black Aces *	1

Quarter-finals

Mamelodi Sundowns	2
FC Cape Town *	0
Black Leopards *	2
AmaZulu	3
Free State Stars *	1
Santos	0
Nathi Lions	0
Mpumalanga Black Aces *	2

Semi-finals

Mamelodi Sundowns ††	1
AmaZulu	0
Free State Stars	0
Mpumalanga Black Aces†	1

Final

Mamelodi Sundowns ‡	1
Mpumalanga Black Aces	0

CUP FINAL

Johannesburg Stadium
24-05-2008, 15:00

Scorer – Lerato Chabangu 87

Sundowns - Batoyi, Mere, Manzini, Johannes, Lekgothoane, Dialdla, Acuna (Carelse 57'), Nyandoro, Chabangu (Ntwgae 90'), Moriri, Ndlovu. Tr: Trott Moloto
Aces - Babale, F Musasa, Rooi, Tihomelang, Gilbert, Mtsweni, Mbatha (Eminike 37'), Dinha, Masondo, Machaka (Mongale 78'), K Musasa. Tr: Kenny Ndlazi

* Home team • † played in Super Stadium, Pretoria • †† played in Olden Park, Potchefstroom • ‡ Qualified for the CAF Cup

RUS – RUSSIA

NATIONAL TEAM RECORD
JULY 10TH 2006 TO JULY 12TH 2010

PL	W	D	L	F	A	%
23	14	3	6	39	24	67.4

FIFA/COCA-COLA WORLD RANKING

1993	1994	1995	1996	1997	1998	1999	2000	2001	2002	2003	2004	2005	2006	2007		High	
14	13	5	7	12	40	18	21	21	23	24	32	34	22	23		3	04/96

	2007–2008											Low	
08/07	09/07	10/07	11/07	12/07	01/08	02/08	03/08	04/08	05/08	06/08	07/08	40	12/98
24	26	16	22	23	24	22	21	25	25	24	11		

Two Dutch coaches dominated the headlines in Russia as Guus Hiddink led the national team to the semi-finals of Euro 2008 while compatriot Dick Advocaat secured a first championship for Zenit St Petersburg since 1984 as well as winning the UEFA Cup. Both teams won many plaudits for the style of their football and central to both was Andrei Arshavin who emerged from the European Championships as one of the players of the tournament. Russia started and ended their campaign by losing to Spain, but in-between they were often majestic, none more so than in the 3-1 victory over the Dutch in the quarter-finals. No-one had expected the Russians to reach the semi-

INTERNATIONAL HONOURS
Qualified for the FIFA World Cup finals 1994 2002 UEFA European Championship 1960 UEFA U-17 Championship 2006 UEFA Women's U-19 2005

finals but the success of Zenit should have given ample warning. Their 2-0 destruction of Rangers in the UEFA Cup final in Manchester brought a second European trophy to Russia in four years - having never won any previously. Backed by Russia's biggest company, Gazprom, Zenit have the financial muscle to now compete with not only the best teams in Russia, but also in Europe, although the title was secured with strong Russian representation in the squad. It was only the second time that the championship had left Moscow since the creation of the Russian League in 1992. CSKA were the other trophy winners when they beat Amkar Perm on penalties in the Cup Final.

THE FIFA BIG COUNT OF 2006

	Male	Female		Total
Number of players	5 105 014	697 522	Referees and Assistant Referees	36 530
Professionals	3 724		Admin, Coaches, Technical, Medical	223 300
Amateurs 18+	582 383		Number of clubs	13 840
Youth under 18	196 170		Number of teams	55 350
Unregistered	1 443 800		Clubs with women's teams	489
Total players	5 802 536		Players as % of population	4.06%

Football Union of Russia (RFU)
House of Football, Ulitsa Narodnaya 7, Moscow 115 172, Russia
Tel +7 495 5401300   Fax +7 501 5401305
rfs@roc.ru   www.rfs.ru
President: MUTKO Vitaliy   General Secretary: TBD
Vice-President: SIMONIAN Nikita   Treasurer: MIRONOVA Svetlana   Media Officer: MALOSOLOV Andrey
Men's Coach: HIDDINK Guus   Women's Coach: SHALIMOV Igor
RFU formed: 1912   UEFA: 1992   FIFA: 1992
White shirts with blue trimmings, White shorts, White socks or Blue shirts with white trimmings, Blue shorts, Blue socks

RECENT INTERNATIONAL MATCHES PLAYED BY RUSSIA

2005	Opponents	Score		Venue	Comp	Scorers	Att	Referee
3-09	Liechtenstein	W	2-0	Moscow	WCq	Kerzhakov 2 [27 66]	18 123	Hyytia FIN
7-09	Portugal	D	0-0	Moscow	WCq		28 800	Merk GER
8-10	Luxembourg	W	5-1	Moscow	WCq	Izmailov [6], Kerzhakov [17], Pavlyuchenko [69], Kirichenko 2 [74 93+]	20 000	Tudor ROU
12-10	Slovakia	D	0-0	Bratislava	WCq		22 317	Rosetti ITA
2006								
1-03	Brazil	L	0-1	Moscow	Fr		19 000	Busacca SUI
27-05	Spain	D	0-0	Albacete	Fr		20 000	Ferreira POR
16-08	Latvia	W	1-0	Moscow	Fr	Pogrebnyak [93+]	25 600	Gilewski POL
6-09	Croatia	D	0-0	Moscow	ECq		27 500	Mejuto Gonzalez ESP
7-10	Israel	D	1-1	Moscow	ECq	Arshavin [5]	22 000	Meyer GER
11-10	Estonia	W	2-0	St Petersburg	ECq	Pogrebnyak [78], Sychev [91+]	21 517	Braamhaar NED
15-11	Macedonia	W	2-0	Skopje	ECq	Bystrov [18], Arshavin [32]	13 000	Allaerts BEL
2007								
7-02	Netherland	L	1-4	Amsterdam	Fr	Bystrov [76]	24 589	Clattenburg ENG
24-03	Estonia	W	2-0	Tallinn	ECq	Kerzhakov.A 2 [66 78]	8 212	Ceferin SVN
2-06	Andorra	W	4-0	St Petersburg	ECq	Kerzhakov.A 3 [8 16 49], Sychev [71]	21 520	Skjerven NOR
6-06	Croatia	D	0-0	Zagreb	ECq		36 194	Michel SVK
22-08	Poland	D	2-2	Moscow	Fr	Sychev [21], Pavlyuchenko [34]	15 000	Hrinak SVK
8-09	Macedonia	W	3-0	Moscow	ECq	Berezutski.V [6], Arshavin [83], Kerzhakov [86]	23 000	Ovrebø NOR
12-09	England	L	0-3	London	ECq		86 106	Hansson SWE
17-10	England	W	2-1	Moscow	ECq	Pavlyuchenko 2 [69p 73]	75 000	Cantalejo ESP
17-11	Israel	L	1-2	Tel Aviv	ECq	Bilyaletdinov [61]	29 787	Farina ITA
21-11	Andorra	W	1-0	Andorra la Vella	ECq	Sychev [38]	780	Hauge NOR
2008								
26-03	Romania	L	0-3	Bucharest	Fr		10 000	Kenan ISR
23-05	Kazakhstan	W	6-0	Moscow	Fr	Pogrebnyak [27p], Bystrov [44], Zyryanov [57], Torbinsky [85], Bilyaletdinov [85p], Sychev [89]	10 000	
28-05	Serbia	W	2-1	Berghausen	Fr	Pogrebnyak [12], Pavlyuchenko [48]		
4-06	Lithuania	W	4-1	Berghausen	Fr	Zyryanov [33], Arshavin [52], Pavlyuchenko [64], Bystrov [80]	2 850	Sippel GER
10-06	Spain	L	1-4	Innsbruck	ECr1	Pavlyuchenko [86]	30 772	Plautz AUT
14-06	Greece	W	1-0	Salzburg	ECr1	Zyryanov [33]	31 063	Rosetti ITA
18-06	Sweden	W	2-0	Innsbruck	ECr1	Pavlyuchenko [24], Arshavin [50]	30 772	De Bleeckere BEL
21-06	Netherlands	W	3-1	Basel	ECqf	Pavlyuchenko [56], Torbinski [112], Arshavin [116]	38 374	Michel SVK
26-06	Spain	L	0-3	Vienna	ECsf		51 428	De Bleeckere BEL

Fr = Friendly match • EC = UEFA EURO 2008 • WC = FIFA World Cup • q = qualifier • r1 = first round group • qf = quarter-final • sf = semi-final

RUSSIA NATIONAL TEAM PLAYERS

	Player		Ap	G	Club	Date of Birth		Player		Ap	G	Club	Date of Birth
1	Igor Akinfeev	GK	25	0	CSKA Moskva	8 04 1986	12	Vladimir Gabulov	GK	5	0	Amkar Perm	19 10 1983
2	Vasili Berezutski	DF	31	1	CSKA Moskva	20 06 1982	13	Oleg Ivanov	MF	0	0	Krylya S. Samara	4 08 1986
3	Renat Yanbaev	MF	2	0	Loko'tiv Moskva	7 04 1984	14	Roman Shirokov	DF	5	0	Zenit St P'sburg	6 07 1981
4	Sergei Ignashevich	DF	41	3	CSKA Moskva	14 07 1979	15	Diniyar Bilyaletdinov	MF	28	2	Loko'tiv Moskva	27 02 1985
5	Aleksei Berezutski	DF	32	0	CSKA Moskva	20 06 1982	16	Vyacheslav Malafeev	GK	16	0	Zenit St P'sburg	4 03 1979
6	Roman Adamov	FW	3	0	FK Moskva	21 06 1982	17	Konstantin Zyryanov	MF	17	3	Zenit St P'sburg	5 10 1977
7	Dmitri Torbinski	MF	14	2	Loko'tiv Moskva	28 04 1984	18	Yuri Zhirkov	MF	24	0	CSKA Moskva	20 08 1983
8	Denis Kolodin	DF	17	0	Dinamo Moskva	11 01 1982	19	Roman Pavlyuchenko	FW	22	9	Spartak Moskva	15 12 1981
9	Ivan Saenko	FW	11	0	1.FC Nürnberg	17 10 1983	20	Igor Semshov	MF	32	0	Dinamo Moskva	6 04 1978
10	Andrei Arshavin	FW	37	13	Zenit St P'sburg	29 05 1981	21	Dmitri Sychev	FW	44	15	Loko'tiv Moskva	26 10 1983
11	Sergei Semak	MF	51	4	Rubin Kazan	27 02 1976	22	Aleksandr Anyukov	DF	37	1	Zenit St P'sburg	28 09 1982
	The Russian squad for Euro 2008						23	Vladimir Bystrov	MF	22	4	Spartak Moskva	31 01 1984

RUSSIA NATIONAL TEAM RECORDS AND RECORD SEQUENCES

Records			Sequence records					
Victory	7-0	SMR 1995	Wins	12	1995-1996	Clean sheets	4	1992-93, 2000
Defeat	0-16	GER 1912	Defeats	6	1998	Goals scored	23	1998-2001
Player Caps	109	Viktor Onopko	Undefeated	17	1995-1996	Without goal	3	Three times
Player Goals	26	Vladimir Beschastnykh	Without win	8	1912-1914, 1998	Goals against	8	Three times

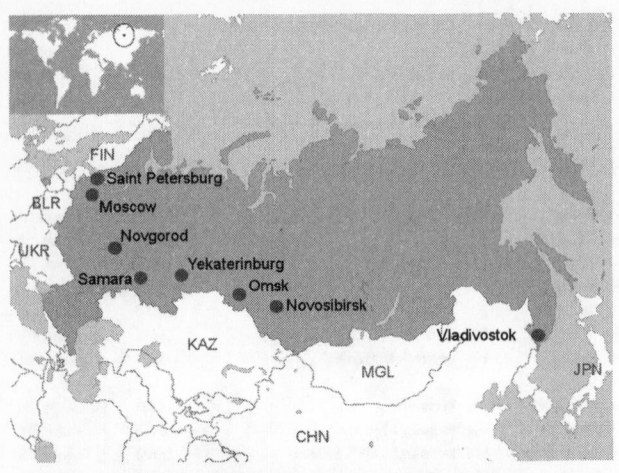

MAJOR CITIES/TOWNS

		Population '000
1	Moscow	10 568
2	Saint Petersburg	3 990
3	Novosibirsk	1 415
4	Yekaterinburg	1 284
5	Nizhny Novgorod	1 266
6	Samara	1 119
7	Omsk	1 126
8	Kazan	1 105
9	Rostov-na-Donu	1 079
10	Chelyabinsk	1 053
11	Ufa	1 027
12	Volgograd	1 010
13	Perm	969
14	Krasnoyarsk	906
15	Saratov	858
16	Voronezh	835
17	Tolyatti	729
18	Krasnodar	652
19	Ulyanovsk	643
20	Izhevsk	630
21	Yaroslavl	602
22	Barnaul	599
23	Irkutsk	582
24	Vladivostock	582

RUSSIAN FEDERATION; ROSSIYSKAYA FEDERATSIYA

Capital	Moscow	Language	Russian			Independence	1991
Population	141 377 752	Area	17 075 200 km²	Density	8 per km²	% in cities	76%
GDP per cap	$8 900	Dailling code	+7	Internet	.ru	GMT +/-	+2/12

MEDALS TABLE

		Overall			League			Cup			Europe			City	Stadium	Cap'ty	DoF
		G	S	B	G	S	B	G	S	G	S	B					
1	Spartak Moskva	12	5	4	9	3	2	3	2			2	Moscow	Luzhniki	84 745	1922
2	CSKA Moskva	8	6	2	3	3	2	4	3	1			Moscow	Dinamo	36 540	1911
3	Lokomotiv Moskva	7	5	6	2	4	4	5	1			2	Moscow	Lokomotiv	30 979	1923
4	Zenit St Petersburg	3	2	1	1	1	1	1	1	1			Saint Petersburg	Petrovski	21 838	1925
5	Dinamo Moskva	1	3	3		1	3	1	2				Moscow	Dinamo	36 540	1923
6	Spartak Vladikavkaz	1	2		1	2							Vladikavkaz	Republican	32 464	1937
7	Topedo Moskva	1		1			1	1					Moscow	Luzhniki	84 745	1924
8	Terek Groznyi	1						1					Groznyi	Tsentralny (Pyatigorsk)	10 300	1946
9	Rotor Volgograd		3	1		2	1		1				Volgograd	Rotor	38 000	1929
10	Krylya Sovetov Samara		1	1			1		1				Samara	Metallurg	35 330	1942

RUSSIAN CLUBS IN SOVIET FOOTBALL

2	Spartak Moskva	22	17	10	12	12	9	10	5			1			
3	Dinamo Moskva	17	11	7	11	11	5	6	5		1	2			
4	CSKA Moskva	12	7	6	7	4	6	5	3						
5	Torpedo Moskva	9	12	6	3	3	6	6	9						
10	Zenit Leningrad	2	3	1	1		1	1	3						

RECENT LEAGUE AND CUP RECORD

	Championship						Cup		
Year	Champions	Pts	Runners-up	Pts	Third	Pts	Winners	Score	Runners-up
1995	Spartak Vladikavkaz	71	Lokomotiv Moskva	65	Spartak Moskva	63	Dinamo Moskva	0-0 8-7p	Rotor Vologrod
1996	Spartak Moskva	72	Alania Vladikavkaz	72	Rotor Volgograd	70	Lokomotiv Moskva	3-2	Spartak Moskva
1997	Spartak Moskva	73	Rotor Volgograd	68	Dinamo Moskva	68	Lokomotiv Moskva	2-0	Dinamo Moskva
1998	Spartak Moskva	59	CSKA Moskva	56	Lokomotiv Moskva	55	Spartak Moskva	1-0	Lokomotiv Moskva
1999	Spartak Moskva	72	Lokomotiv Moskva	65	CSKA Moskva	55	Zenit St Petersburg	3-1	Dynamo Moskva
2000	Spartak Moskva	70	Lokomotiv Moskva	62	Torpedo Moskva	55	Lokomotiv Moskva	3-2	CSKA Moskva
2001	Spartak Moskva	60	Lokomotiv Moskva	56	Zenit St Petersburg	56	Lokomotiv Moskva	2-1	Anzhi Makhachkala
2002	Lokomotiv Moskva	66	CSKA Moskva	56	Spartak Moskva	55	CSKA Moskva	2-0	Zenit St-Peterburg
2003	CSKA Moskva	59	Zenit St Petersburg	56	Rubin Kazan	53	Spartak Moskva	1-0	FK Rostov
2004	Lokomotiv Moskva	61	CSKA Moskva	60	Krylya S. Samara	56	Terek Groznyi	1-0	Krylya S. Samara
2005	CSKA Moskva	62	Spartak Moskva	56	Lokomotiv Moskva	56	CSKA Moskva	1-0	FK Khimki
2006	CSKA Moskva	58	Spartak Moskva	58	Lokomotiv Moskva	53	CSKA Moskva	3-0	Spartak Moskva
2007	Zenit St Petersburg	61	Spartak Moskva	59	CSKA Moskva	53	Lokomotiv Moskva	1-0	FK Moskva
2008							CSKA Moskva	2-2 4-1p	Amkar Perm

RUSSIA 2007

PREMIER LEAGUE

	Pl	W	D	L	F	A	Pts	Zenit	Spartak	CSKA	FK Moskva	Saturn	Dinamo	Lokomotiv	Amkar	Khimki	Rubin	Tom	Spartak N	Krylya	Luch	Kuban	Rostov
Zenit St Petersburg	30	18	7	5	53	33	61		1-3	2-1	1-0	1-1	3-0	1-1	0-0	4-1	2-1	2-1	4-3	1-1	3-1	1-0	2-0
Spartak Moskva	30	17	8	5	50	30	59	3-1		1-1	3-1	2-0	2-1	1-2	0-0	2-0	2-1	3-2	2-2	1-0	2-1	4-0	3-0
CSKA Moskva	30	14	11	5	42	23	53	2-0	1-1		2-0	3-1	0-1	2-0	1-0	0-0	3-1	0-0	2-0	4-2	4-0	0-0	4-0
FK Moskva	30	15	7	8	41	31	52	1-2	2-0	1-0		3-2	4-1	1-2	3-1	0-2	2-1	2-0	1-0	3-1	3-1	2-1	1-0
Saturn Ramenskoe	30	11	12	7	34	28	45	0-1	0-0	2-2	0-0		2-1	1-1	2-0	1-0	1-0	0-0	1-1	1-1	0-1	2-0	1-0
Dinamo Moskva	30	11	8	11	37	35	41	4-2	0-1	1-1	0-0	1-1		2-1	0-0	2-1	0-1	3-1	2-1	1-1	1-0	1-0	3-0
Lokomotiv Moskva	30	11	8	11	39	42	41	0-0	4-3	1-2	1-1	0-2	2-2		0-1	1-0	0-0	3-1	5-2	1-1	2-3	1-2	3-1
Amkar Perm	30	10	11	9	30	27	41	1-1	0-1	1-1	1-1	3-1	1-1	1-0		3-1	2-1	3-3	1-1	4-1	1-0	0-0	3-1
FK Khimki	30	9	10	11	32	33	37	2-2	3-0	1-1	1-3	0-0	1-0	1-2	1-0		0-0	1-1	1-0	4-1	3-0	1-0	1-0
Rubin Kazan	30	10	5	15	31	39	35	1-4	3-1	0-1	1-1	0-1	2-1	3-0	1-0	2-1		1-3	2-1	1-0	3-0	2-2	0-0
Tom Tomsk	30	8	11	11	37	35	35	0-1	1-1	0-1	1-2	1-1	1-0	4-2	0-1	3-1	2-0		2-0	1-2	3-1	2-0	1-1
Spartak Nalchik	30	8	9	13	29	38	33	0-3	1-2	1-1	1-0	1-3	4-1	0-0	0-1	1-1	1-0	1-0		0-0	2-0	1-0	0-0
Krylya Sovetov Samara	30	8	8	14	35	46	32	1-3	0-2	1-0	0-0	0-1	3-2	3-1	1-0	3-0	1-1	1-2			3-0	2-3	0-1
Luch Vladivostock	30	8	8	14	26	39	32	0-1	1-1	4-0	0-1	2-1	0-1	3-0	1-0	1-1	2-0	0-0	2-1	0-0		1-0	1-1
Kuban Krasnodar	30	7	11	12	28	39	32	1-1	0-0	0-1	0-0	4-1	2-2	0-4	0-0	1-1	1-1	0-1	2-1	2-2	3-2		1-1
FK Rostov	30	2	12	16	18	44	18	2-3	1-3	1-1	1-1	1-3	0-0	0-2	2-0	1-1	1-1	2-2	0-1	1-1	1-1	0-1	

10/03/2007 - 11/11/2007 • † Qualified for the UEFA Champions League • ‡ Qualified for the UEFA Cup
Top scorers: Roman Pavlyuchenko, Spartak Moskva 14; Roman Adamov, FK Moskva 14; Jô Alves, CSKA 13; Vágner Love, CSKA 13; Pavel Pogrebnyak, Zenit 11; Dmitriy Sychov, Lokomotiv 11; Andrei Arshavin, Zenit 10; Andrei Karyaka, Saturn 10; Martin Kushev, Amkar 10

RUSSIA 2007

FIRST DIVISION (2)

	Pl	W	D	L	F	A	Pts	Shinnik	Terek	SIBIR	KamAZ	Ural	Torpedo	NoSta	Dinamo B	Salyut	Anzhi	Zvezda	Alania	SKA Energiya	Mashuk	Baltika	Metalurg	SKA Rostov	Avangard	Mordovia	Tekstilshchik	Sodovik	Spartak-MZK
Shinnik Yaroslavl	42	28	8	6	68	30	92		1-1	3-1	2-1	1-0	2-0	1-0	4-0	2-0	2-2	0-2	3-2	3-2	1-0	2-0	5-0	1-0	1-0	2-0	3-0	2-0	2-0
Terek Groznyi	42	28	6	8	69	27	90	0-1		2-0	2-1	1-1	2-0	3-0	2-0	1-0	2-0	1-0	0-2	0-0	2-1	2-0	3-1	3-0	4-2	2-0	1-0	4-0	3-0
SIBIR Novosibirsk	42	25	11	6	80	39	86	3-3	1-0		1-0	0-1	5-3	2-2	2-1	1-1	1-1	0-2	0-1	1-0	1-1	0-1	1-1	0-0	3-0	6-2	5-0	3-2	3-0
KamAZ Chelny	42	23	8	11	67	34	77	0-0	2-1	0-2		2-1	4-0	0-1	5-2	3-0	0-0	3-2	5-0	2-1	4-0	0-0	1-0	3-0	3-1	3-0	2-0	0-0	5-2
Ural Yekaterinburg	42	21	14	7	70	33	77	0-0	4-1	0-0	2-0		3-2	2-2	5-0	3-0	3-0	5-0	0-0	4-0	0-0	1-0	3-0	3-1	1-0	2-0	8-1	1-1	3-0
Torpedo Moskva	42	21	6	15	75	59	69	1-2	1-2	1-3	1-2	1-2		2-1	3-0	2-0	2-1	1-2	3-1	2-0	4-0	3-1	4-0	3-1	3-2	4-0	5-3	1-0	3-0
NoSta Novotroitsk	42	16	16	10	63	40	64	0-1	2-0	0-5	0-0	1-1	0-0		1-1	1-0	3-0	3-0	4-0	1-1	2-2	2-0	2-0	6-0	0-0	3-0	0-1	0-1	3-0
Dinamo Bryansk	42	16	11	15	49	52	59	1-1	1-1	3-0	3-0	4-0	1-1	1-2		2-0	2-0	6-0	0-0	3-0	0-0	1-0	2-2	2-1	1-1	0-0	1-2	2-2	1-0
Salyut Belgorod	42	17	6	19	44	45	57	3-1	0-1	1-2	0-0	2-0	4-1	1-1	0-0		1-0	2-1	4-1	2-2	0-1	1-3	1-2	1-1	1-0	2-1	1-0	1-0	3-0
Anzhi Makhachkala	42	16	9	17	41	44	57	1-0	1-3	0-0	1-2	2-1	3-2	2-2	1-0	2-1		1-1	0-0	2-0	1-1	1-0	1-3	1-3	1-0	1-0	1-0	2-0	5-0
Zvezda Irkutsk	42	16	8	18	60	47	56	0-1	2-0	1-0	1-2	2-2	0-0	0-1	1-0	1-0	1-0		2-0	4-0	0-2	1-1	3-1	1-1	0-1	4-0	0-1	5-0	4-0
Alania Vladikavkaz	42	15	11	16	56	56	56	1-5	2-0	1-0	2-1	0-1	3-1	2-0	3-0	4-0	0-0	0-2		0-0	3-0	3-1	4-3	3-2	2-1	0-0	7-0	5-1	3-0
SKA Khabarovsk	42	14	14	14	50	48	56	0-0	2-1	1-1	1-1	2-3	4-0	0-3	1-2	1-0	1-2	0-2	2-2		2-1	2-1	2-0	1-2	1-0	0-1	2-1	1-0	1-1
Mashuk Pyatigorsk	42	14	13	15	53	55	55	2-1	0-2	2-3	1-2	0-0	2-3	1-1	3-2	0-0	2-0	1-0	3-3	1-1		0-0	3-0	0-0	1-5	2-3	3-0	1-0	3-0
Baltika Kaliningrad	42	14	12	16	53	49	54	1-2	0-1	1-3	0-0	0-0	2-0	1-0	1-2	3-0	1-2	2-2	1-1	2-1	2-2		0-1	3-0	3-2	2-0	2-3	3-0	3-0
Metalurg Novokuznetsk	42	15	8	19	53	70	53	3-1	1-0	3-3	5-0	0-1	3-2	1-0	3-2	0-1	1-3	0-0	1-2	1-0	1-0	3-2		2-0	3-3	2-0	2-3	3-0	3-0
SKA Rostov-na-Donu	42	14	11	17	50	60	53	2-2	0-0	1-1	2-2	1-0	0-2	2-1	1-0	0-1	2-1	2-0	0-0	1-2	2-3	4-1	3-2		4-2	3-4	1-0	1-1	3-0
Avangard Kursk	42	15	6	21	50	55	51	2-2	0-1	0-1	1-0	1-0	2-1	0-0	1-0	0-1	1-0	5-2	0-2	0-1	1-2	1-1	1-0	1-0		2-1	2-2	1-0	1-0
Mordovia Saransk	42	13	4	25	44	88	43	1-3	0-4	2-6	2-0	0-1	2-2	0-3	2-0	2-1	0-2	1-4	3-1	1-0	2-1	1-2	1-2	1-0	3-1		2-1	2-0	2-0
Tekstilshchik Ivanovo	42	10	8	24	38	68	38	1-1	0-4	0-4	0-2	0-0	0-2	0-0	1-0	0-2	0-1	0-1	0-1	0-1	0-1	1-2	1-1	1-0	0-1	0-0		1-2	3-0
Sodovik Sterlitamak	42	8	10	24	32	65	34	0-0	0-2	0-2	0-1	1-1	0-0	1-2	0-0	1-0	2-1	0-2	1-2	0-1	2-3	2-1	3-2	1-2	0-0	1-3	1-0		3-0
Spartak-MZK Ryazan	42	1	4	37	21	122	7	0-3	0-3	1-3	0-3	1-6	1-4	2-2	0-3	2-4	0-3	0-3	1-3	0-3	2-2	1-2	2-2	2-2	4-0	0-3	0-3	0-3	

28/03/2007 - 5/11/2007 • Spartak withdrew after 21 matches. Their remaining 21 matches were awarded as 3-0 victories to their opponents
Top scorers: Dmitriy Akimov, Sibir 34; Mikhail Mysin, Ural 21; Roman Monaryov, Shinnik 20; Stanislav Dubrovin, Alania 19

RUSSIAN CUP 2007-08

Fifth Round

CSKA Moskva	1
Baltika Kaliningrad *	0
Torpedo Moskva *	1
FK Khimki	2
Rubin Kazan	2
FK Lukhovitsy *	1
Shinnik Yaroslavl *	1
Spartak Nalchik	2
Zenit St Petersburg	4
Dinamo Bryansk *	1
Avangard Kursk *	0
Dinamo Moskva	3
FK Rostov	3
SKA Rostov *	0
Salyut-Energiya Belgorod*	0 2p
Tom Tomsk	0 3p
Ural Yekaterinburg *	1
Lokomotiv Moskva	0
Metallurg Novokuznetsk*	1
Kuban Krasnodar	2
Metalurg Krasnoyarsk *	1
Luch Vladivostock	1
SKA Khabarovsk *	1
Saturn Ramenskoe	2
FK Moskva	1 4p
NoSta Novotroitsk *	1 2p
Krylya Sovetov Samara	0
KamAZ Chelny *	1
Terek Groznyi *	1 4p
Spartak	1 3p
Rotor Volgograd *	1
Amkar Perm	4

Sixth Round

CSKA Moskva *	2
FK Khimki	0
Rubin Kazan	2
Spartak Nalchik *	3
Zenit St Petersburg *	9
Dinamo Moskva	3
FK Rostov *	0
Tom Tomsk	1
Ural Yekaterinburg	3
Kuban Krasnodar *	2
Metalurg Krasnoyarsk	1
Saturn Ramenskoe *	2
FK Moskva	1
KamAZ Chelny *	0
Terek Groznyi	1
Amkar Perm *	3

Quarter-finals

CSKA Moskva *	2
Spartak Nalchik	1
Zenit St Petersburg *	0 3p
Tom Tomsk	0 4p
Ural Yekaterinburg *	2
Saturn Ramenskoe	1
FK Moskva	1
Amkar Perm *	2

Semi-finals

CSKA Moskva *	2
Tom Tomsk	1
Ural Yekaterinburg	0
Amkar Perm *	1

Final

CSKA Moskva	2 4p
Amkar Perm	2 1p

CUP FINAL

Lokomotiv Stadium, Moscow
17-05-2008. Att: 24 000. Ref: Sukhina
Scorers – Vágner Love [56], OG [75] for CSKA;
Drincic [57], Dujmovic [64] for Amkar
CSKA – Igor Akinfeyev - Vasiliy Berezutskiy,
Sergei Ignashevich (Elver Rahimic 67),
Aleksei Berezutskii, Deividas Semberas,
Yuriy Zhirkov, Yevgeniy Aldonin (Alan Dzagoyev
61), Dudu Cearense (Dawid Janczyk 87), Miloš
Krasic, Vágner Love, Jô Alves
Amkar – Vladimir Gabulov - Miklós Gaál,
Dmitriy Belorukov, Aleksei Popov, Zahari
Sirakov (Ivan Cherenchikov 70), Ivan Starkov,
Nikola Drincic, Tomislav Dujmovic, Georgi Peyev
(Mikhail Afanasyeu 91+), Martin Kushev,
Predrag Skimic (Nenad Injac 76)

* Home team

RWA – RWANDA

NATIONAL TEAM RECORD
JULY 10TH 2006 TO JULY 12TH 2010

PL	W	D	L	F	A	%
26	11	5	10	39	27	51.9

FIFA/COCA-COLA WORLD RANKING

1993	1994	1995	1996	1997	1998	1999	2000	2001	2002	2003	2004	2005	2006	2007	High	
-	-	168	159	172	107	146	128	144	130	109	99	89	121	99	**87**	07/08

2007–2008												Low	
08/07	09/07	10/07	11/07	12/07	01/08	02/08	03/08	04/08	05/08	06/08	07/08	**178**	07/99
121	118	118	119	99	109	114	115	111	110	106	87		

Rwanda were denied a second title in the East and Central African Senior Challenge Cup after losing on penalties to Sudan in the 2007 final in Dar-es-Salaam. They had come from two goals down to force a 2-2 draw but lost 4-2 on spot kicks. Earlier the Amavubi Stars had been successful in a shootout in the quarter-finals against Zanzibar and had advanced over favourites Uganda in the semi-finals courtesy of an own goal in extra time. It was a successful start for new coach Josip Kuze but he departed for a job in Asia soon after, replaced by fellow Croat Branko Tucak. The turn over of coaches produced few ill effects as Rwanda got off to a storming start in the 2010 FIFA

INTERNATIONAL HONOURS
CECAFA Cup 1999

World Cup qualifiers, winning three successive games, including a convincing home triumph over group favourites Morocco. Football continues to be a major focus for the east African country's government, seeking to rebuild a national identity a decade after the genocide that cost nearly a million lives. Rwanda president Paul Kagame sponsors local tournaments and has also backed regional events under the CECAFA banner. In the 2008 CAF Champions League, APR FC lost to Zamalek of Egypt in the first round and then relinquished their hold on the title after finishing second behind ATRACO in the 2008 championship.

THE FIFA BIG COUNT OF 2006

	Male	Female		Total
Number of players	386 400	0	Referees and Assistant Referees	500
Professionals	0		Admin, Coaches, Technical, Medical	1 500
Amateurs 18+	4 400		Number of clubs	110
Youth under 18	6 500		Number of teams	550
Unregistered	27 500		Clubs with women's teams	0
Total players	386 400		Players as % of population	4.47%

Fédération Rwandaise de Football (FERWAFA)
Case Postale 2000, Kigali, Rwanda
Tel +250 518525   Fax +250 518523
ferwafa@yahoo.fr   www.ferwafa.rw
President: KAZURA Jean-Bosco   General Secretary: KALISA Jules Cesar
Vice-President: NGOGA Martin Charles   Treasurer: ITANGISHAKA Bernard   Media Officer: None
Men's Coach: TUCAK Branko   Women's Coach: BEARD Kyle
FERWAFA formed: 1972   CAF: 1976   FIFA: 1978
Green shirts with red and yellow trimmings, Green shorts, Red socks

RECENT INTERNATIONAL MATCHES PLAYED BY RWANDA

2005	Opponents	Score		Venue	Comp	Scorers	Att	Referee
26-11	Zanzibar †	L	0-1	Kigali	CCr1			
30-11	Eritrea	W	2-1	Kigali	CCr1	Gatete, Lomani 2		
4-12	Burundi	W	2-0	Kigali	CCr1			
6-12	Tanzania	W	3-1	Kigali	CCr1	Gatete 44p, Lomani 2 58 61		
8-12	Uganda	W	1-0	Kigali	CCsf	Karekezi 115		
10-12	Ethiopia	L	0-1	Kigali	CCf			
2006								
26-07	Uganda	D	1-1	Kigali	Fr	Lomani 72		
30-07	Tanzania	L	0-1	Dar es Salaam	Fr			
3-09	Cameroon	L	0-3	Kigali	CNq			Ssegonga UGA
8-10	Liberia	L	2-3	Monrovia	CNq	Karekezi 70, Mulenda 78		Olatunde NGA
27-11	Somalia	W	3-0	Addis Abeba	CCr1	Kayihura 19, Ujeneza 70, Nyonzima 87		
30-11	Uganda	L	0-1	Addis Abeba	CCr1			
3-12	Sudan	D	0-0	Addis Abeba	CCr1			
5-12	Tanzania	W	2-1	Addis Abeba	CCqf	Ujeneza 45, Witakenge 56p		
8-12	Zambia	L	0-1	Addis Abeba	CCsf			
10-12	Uganda	D	0-0	Addis Abeba	CC3p	L 2-4p		
2007								
25-03	Equatorial Guinea	L	1-3	Malabo	CNq	Karekezi 73		Louzaya CGO
27-05	Burundi	W	1-0	Kigali	Fr	Muhayimana 13		
2-06	Equatorial Guinea	W	2-0	Kigali	CNq	Niyonzima 2 55 71		Auda EGY
10-06	Kenya	L	0-2	Nairobi	Fr			
17-06	Cameroon	L	1-2	Garoua	CNq	Gatete 77		Sowe GAM
8-09	Liberia	W	4-0	Kigali	CNq	Bokota 21, Makasi 29, Witakenge 85, Karekezi 89		Mwanza ZAM
9-12	Eritrea	W	2-1	Dar es Salaam	CCr1	Niyonzima 6, Bokota 40		
11-12	Uganda	L	0-2	Dar es Salaam	CCr1			
13-12	Djibouti	W	9-0	Dar es Salaam	CCr1	Karekezi 2 17 84, Abdi OG 25, Bokota 3 36 42 77, Tuyisenge 47, Uzamukunda 54, Ngoma 62		
18-12	Zanzibar †	D	0-0	Dar es Salaam	CCqf			
20-12	Uganda	W	1-0	Dar es Salaam	CCsf	Tuyisenge 118		
22-12	Sudan	D	2-2	Dar es Salaam	CCf	Niyonzima 48, Mulenda 59. L 2-4p		
2008								
6-02	Burundi	D	0-0	Bujumbura	Fr			
31-05	Mauritania	W	3-0	Kigali	WCq	Karekezi 15, Abedi Said 67p, Bokota 72	12 000	Doue CIV
8-06	Ethiopia	W	2-1	Addis Abeba	WCq	Abedi Said 59, Karekezi 82	18 000	Ndinya KEN
14-06	Morocco	W	3-1	Kigali	WCq	Abedi Said 15, Bokota 68, Karekezi 93+	12 000	Evehe CMR
21-06	Morocco	L	0-2	Casablanca	WCq		2 500	Benouza ALG

Fr = Friendly match • CN = CAF African Cup of Nations • CC = CECAFA Cup • WC = FIFA World Cup
q = qualifier • r1 = first round group • sf = semi-final • f = final • † Not a full international

RWANDA NATIONAL TEAM RECORDS AND RECORD SEQUENCES

Records			Sequence records					
Victory	9-0	DJI 2007	Wins	4	2005	Clean sheets	4	1999
Defeat	1-6	COD 1976	Defeats	5	1976-77, 1983-86	Goals scored	14	2000-2001
Player Caps	n/a		Undefeated	10	1998-2000	Without goal	3	1983-1986
Player Goals	n/a		Without win	16	1983-1996	Goals against	11	2003-2004

RWANDA COUNTRY INFORMATION

Capital	Kigali	Independence	1962 from Belgium	GDP per Capita	$1 300
Population	7 954 013	Status	Republic	GNP Ranking	139
Area km²	26 338	Language	Kinyarwanda, English, French	Dialling code	+250
Population density	301 per km²	Literacy rate	70%	Internet code	.rw
% in urban areas	6%	Main religion	Christian	GMT +/–	+2
Towns/Cities ('000)	Kigali 745; Butare 89; Gitarama 87; Ruhengeri 86; Gisenyi 83; Byumba 70; Cyangugu 63				
Neighbours (km)	Tanzania 217; Burundi 290; Congo DR 217; Uganda 169				
Main stadia	Stade Amahoro – Kigali 15 000				

RWANDA 2006-07 CHAMPIONNAT NATIONAL

	Pl	W	D	L	F	A	Pts
APR FC	26	18	5	3	50	12	59
Rayon Sport	26	18	5	3	53	23	59
ATRACO	26	17	5	4	42	14	56
Mukura Victory	26	18	2	6	34	16	56
Kiyovu Sport	26	10	10	6	34	27	40
Kibuye FC	26	9	6	11	26	27	33
Marines FC Gisenyi	26	8	7	11	24	24	31
AS Kigali	26	7	10	9	20	24	31
Etincelles Gisenyi	26	8	6	12	21	32	30
Police FC Kibungo	26	7	8	11	26	33	29
Umuraybo Rwamagana	26	7	7	12	20	30	28
Espoir FC Cyangugu	26	6	5	15	25	41	23
La Jeunesse	26	4	4	18	15	49	16
Zèbres FC Byumba	26	3	4	19	15	53	13

29/12/2006 - 28/08/2007

RWANDA 2007-08 CHAMPIONNAT NATIONAL

	Pl	W	D	L	F	A	Pts
ATRACO	22	18	3	1	38	10	57
APR FC	22	16	5	1	56	10	53
Rayon Sport	22	14	6	2	32	17	48
Kiyovu Sport	22	8	8	6	29	23	32
Mukura Victory	22	9	4	9	31	25	31
AS Kigali	22	5	8	9	18	25	23
Electrogaz	22	5	7	10	25	36	22
Kibuye FC	22	5	7	10	14	30	22
Marines FC Gisenyi	22	4	8	10	20	26	20
Police FC Kibungo	22	4	6	12	22	31	18
Etincelles Gisenyi	22	2	10	10	13	31	16
Military	22	4	4	14	23	57	16

21/11/2007 - 10/08/2008

COUPE AMAHORO 2008

First Round		Quarter–finals		Semi–finals		Final	
APR FC	4						
Espoir FC Cyangugu	0	**APR FC**	2				
Electrogaz	0	Marines FC Gisenyi	0				
Marines FC Gisenyi	1			**APR FC**	4		
Mukura Victory	2			Kiyovu Sport	1		
Etincelles Gisenyi	1	Mukura Victory	0 4p				
Musanze	0 3p	**Kiyovu Sport**	0 5p				
Kiyovu Sport	0 5p					**APR FC**	4
Rayon Sport	2					ATRACO	0
Nyanza	0	**Rayon Sport**	3				
Military		AS Kigali	1				
AS Kigali	w-0			Rayon Sport	1		
Kibuye FC	1 5p			**ATRACO**	2		
Police FC Kibungo	1 4p	Kibuye FC	1				
Union	0	**ATRACO**	3				
ATRACO	11						

CUP FINAL

Nyamirambo, 4-07-2008

Scorers - Ngomairakiza Hegman [20], Elias Ntaganda [30], Elias Nzamukunda 2 [80] [90]

RECENT LEAGUE AND CUP RECORD

	Championship		Cup		
Year	Champions	Winners	Score	Runners-up
1995	APR FC Kigali	Rayon Sports Butare		
1996	APR FC Kigali	APR FC Kigali		
1997	Rayon Sports Butare	Rwanda FC		
1998	Rayon Sports Butare	Rayon Sports Butare	w-0	Kiyovu Sports
1999	APR FC Kigali	APR FC Kigali		
2000	APR FC Kigali	APR FC Kigali		
2001	APR FC Kigali	Citadins	0-0 6-5p	APR FC
2002	Rayon Sports Butare	APR FC Kigali	2-1	Rayon Sports Butare
2003	APR FC Kigali	No tournament held		
2004	Rayon Sports Butare	No tournament held		
2005	APR FC Kigali	Rayon Sports Butare	3-0	Mukura Victory
2006	APR FC Kigali	APR FC Kigali	1-0	ATRACO
2007	APR FC Kigali	APR FC Kigali	2-0	ATRACO
2008	ATRACO	APR FC Kigali	4-0	ATRACO

SAM – SAMOA

NATIONAL TEAM RECORD
JULY 10TH 2006 TO JULY 12TH 2010

PL	W	D	L	F	A	%
4	2	0	2	9	8	50

FIFA/COCA-COLA WORLD RANKING

1993	1994	1995	1996	1997	1998	1999	2000	2001	2002	2003	2004	2005	2006	2007	High	
-	-	-	177	183	164	180	173	172	163	176	179	182	187	146	**146**	12/07

		2007–2008										Low	
08/07	09/07	10/07	11/07	12/07	01/08	02/08	03/08	04/08	05/08	06/08	07/08	**191**	07/07
191	147	149	148	146	146	148	147	151	151	157	157		

Chris Cahill, brother of Everton's Tim Cahill, made his debut for Samoa in August 2007, captaining the national team at the football tournament of the South Pacific Games in Apia, a competition that doubled up as the first round of FIFA World Cup qualifying in Oceania. Drawn in a tough group containing both the Solomon Islands and Vanuatu, Samoa were hoping that home advantage would take them through from the group stage to the semi-finals and at least a third place finish. That would have seen them through to the main Oceania qualifying group, but alas it wasn't to be with Samoa losing comprehensively to both of their Melanesian rivals and finishing

INTERNATIONAL HONOURS
None

the group in third place. There was the consolation of a 7-0 win over America Samoa - a record score for the national team - but this really was a missed opportunity for Samoa to advance and get valuable experience. There are excellent facilities in the country thanks to the FIFA Goal Project; the objective now is to make the best use of them and the development of a proper club structure is a priority given Samoa's continued absence from Oceania's O-League. In the Samoa Soccer Football Federation Champion of Champions final held in December 2007, Cruz Azull beat Strickland Brothers 1-0 while Sinamoga won the title in 2008.

THE FIFA BIG COUNT OF 2006

	Male	Female		Total
Number of players	5 400	300	Referees and Assistant Referees	100
Professionals	0		Admin, Coaches, Technical, Medical	300
Amateurs 18+	1 100		Number of clubs	60
Youth under 18	1 100		Number of teams	220
Unregistered	1 100		Clubs with women's teams	3
Total players	5 700		Players as % of population	3.22%

Samoa Football Soccer Federation (SFSF)

Tuanaimato, PO Box 6172, Apia, Samoa
Tel +685 7783210   Fax +685 22855
www.soccersamoa.ws
President: ROEBECK Tautulu   General Secretary: SOLIA Tilomai
Vice-President: PAPALII Seiuli Poasa   Treasurer: LINO Maiava Visesio   Media Officer: SOLIA Tilomai
Men's Coach: TBD   Women's Coach: TBD
SFSF formed: 1968   OFC: 1984   FIFA: 1986
Blue shirts, Blue shorts, Red socks

RECENT INTERNATIONAL MATCHES PLAYED BY SAMOA

2002	Opponents	Score		Venue	Comp	Scorers	Att	Referee
No international matches played in 2002 after June								
2003								
No international matches played in 2003								
2004								
5-05	Cook Islands	D	0-0	Auckland	Fr			
10-05	American Samoa	W	4-0	Apia	WCq	Bryce [12], Fasavalu 2 [30 53], Michael [66]	500	Afu SOL
15-05	Vanuatu	L	0-3	Apia	WCq		650	Breeze AUS
17-05	Fiji	L	0-4	Apia	WCq		450	Diomis AUS
19-05	Papua New Guinea	L	1-4	Apia	WCq	Michael [69]	300	Diomis AUS
2005								
No international matches played in 2005								
2006								
No international matches played in 2006								
2007								
25-08	Vanuatu	L	0-4	Apia	WCq		300	Jacques TAH
27-08	America Samoa	W	7-0	Apia	WCq	Tumua 2 [24 51], Faaiuaso [29], Cahill 2 [43p 67], Fonotti [61], Michael [76]	2 800	Minan PNG
29-08	Tonga	W	2-1	Apia	WCq	Faaiuaso [45], Taylor [83]	1 850	Sosongan PNG
3-09	Solomon Islands	L	0-3	Apia	WCq		200	Hester NZL
2008								
No international matches played in 2008 before August								

Fr = Friendly match • WC = FIFA World Cup • q = qualifier

SAMOA NATIONAL TEAM RECORDS AND RECORD SEQUENCES

Records			Sequence records					
Victory	7-0	ASA 2007	Wins	3	1998-2000	Clean sheets	2	2002, 2004
Defeat	0-13	TAH 1981	Defeats	8	1979-1981	Goals scored	8	1998-2000
Player Caps	n/a		Undefeated	3	1998-2000	Without goal	4	1983-1988
Player Goals	n/a		Without win	8	1979-1981	Goals against	22	1979-1998

RECENT LEAGUE AND CUP RECORD

	Championship		Cup		
Year	Champions	Winners	Score	Runners-up
1997	Kiwi	Kiwi		Vaivase-tai
1998	Vaivase-tai	Togafuafua		
1999	Moata'a	Moaula		Moata'a
2000	Titavi	Gold Star	4-1	Faatoia
2001	Gold Star Sogi	Strickland Brothers	3-3 5-4p	Moata'a
2002	Strickland Brothers	Vaivase-tai		Hosanna
2003	Strickland Brothers	Strickland Brothers	5-2	Moata'a
2004	Strickland Brothers	Tunaimato Breeze	3-2	Central United
2005	Tunaimato Breeze			
2006	Vaivase-tai			
2007	Cruz Azull			
2008	Sinamoga			

SAMOA COUNTRY INFORMATION

Capital	Apia	Independence	1962 from New Zealand	GDP per Capita	$5 600
Population	177 714	Status	Constitutional Monarchy	GNP Ranking	178
Area km²	2 944	Language	Samoan, English	Dialling code	+685
Population density	60 per km²	Literacy rate	99%	Internet code	.ws
% in urban areas	21%	Main religion	Christian	GMT +/–	-11
Towns/Cities ('000)	Apia 40; Vaitele 5; Faleasiu 3; Vailele 3; Leauvaa 3; Faleula 2; Siusega 2; Malie 2; Fasitoouta 2				
Neighbours (km)	South Pacific Ocean 403				
Main stadia	Toleafoa J.S. Blatter Complex – Apia				

SCO – SCOTLAND

NATIONAL TEAM RECORD
JULY 10TH 2006 TO JULY 12TH 2010

PL	W	D	L	F	A	%
16	10	1	5	25	16	65.6

FIFA/COCA-COLA WORLD RANKING

1993	1994	1995	1996	1997	1998	1999	2000	2001	2002	2003	2004	2005	2006	2007		High	
24	32	26	29	37	38	20	25	50	59	54	86	60	25	14		**13**	10/08

	2007–2008												Low	
08/07	09/07	10/07	11/07	12/07	01/08	02/08	03/08	04/08	05/08	06/08	07/08		**88**	03/05
23	14	13	14	14	14	14	14	15	15	17	16			

Rangers very nearly pulled off an unprecedented quadruple in 2008 but in the end had to settle for a cup double after a fixture overload of 17 games in just under two months finally took its toll. Victory over Dundee United in the League Cup and against surprise finalists Queen of the South in the Scottish Cup couldn't, however, make up for the disappointment of losing in the final of the tournament the club wanted to win most of all - the UEFA Cup. A first European final since 1972 saw Rangers play Zenit St Petersburg, fresh from the Russian close season, who were deserved winners in Manchester with a 2-0 victory. Rangers also lost out in the League to Celtic as the race

INTERNATIONAL HONOURS
Qualified for the FIFA World Cup finals 1954 1958 1974 1978 1982 1986 1990   UEFA Champions League Celtic 1967

for the title went down to a delayed final day. A 1-0 victory against Dundee United was Celtic's 17th win in their final 20 matches, and it secured a championship that had never really looked on the cards for much of the season, and with it their first hat-trick of titles since the early 1970s. Motherwell had their best season since 1995 but it was scarred by the death of their captain Phil O'Donnell who collapsed during the match with Dundee United at the end of December. The national team just missed out on qualification for the finals of Euro 2008 but the task for new coach George Burley is to build on an excellent campaign that has brought self-belief back to the Scots.

THE FIFA BIG COUNT OF 2006

	Male	Female		Total
Number of players	374 075	46 514	Referees and Assistant Referees	2 097
Professionals	4 132		Admin, Coaches, Technical, Medical	8 500
Amateurs 18+	39 234		Number of clubs	6 600
Youth under 18	67 123		Number of teams	8 200
Unregistered	302 500		Clubs with women's teams	127
Total players	420 589		Players as % of population	8.31%

The Scottish Football Association (SFA)
Hampden Park, Glasgow G42 9AY, United Kingdom
Tel +44 141 6166000   Fax +44 141 6166001
info@scottishfa.co.uk   www.scottishfa.co.uk
President: PEAT George   General Secretary: SMITH Gordon
Vice-President: OGILVIE Campbell   Treasurer: TBD   Media Officer: TBD
Men's Coach: BURLEY George   Women's Coach: SIGNEUL Anna
SFA formed: 1873   UEFA: 1954   FIFA: 1910-20, 1924-28, 1946
Dark blue shirts with white trimmings, White shorts, Dark blue socks or yellow shirts with black trimmings, Back shorts, yellow socks

RECENT INTERNATIONAL MATCHES PLAYED BY SCOTLAND

2005	Opponents	Score		Venue	Comp	Scorers	Att	Referee
26-03	Italy	L	0-2	Milan	WCq		45 000	Vassaras GRE
4-06	Moldova	W	2-0	Glasgow	WCq	Dailly 52, McFadden 88	45 317	Braamhaar NED
8-06	Belarus	D	0-0	Minsk	WCq		28 287	Benquerenca POR
17-08	Austria	D	2-2	Graz	Fr	Miller.K 3, O'Connor 39	13 800	Dereli TUR
3-09	Italy	D	1-1	Glasgow	WCq	Miller.K 13	50 185	Michel SVK
7-09	Norway	W	2-1	Oslo	WCq	Miller.K 2 20 30	24 904	Hamer LUX
8-10	Belarus	L	0-1	Glasgow	WCq		51 105	Szabo HUN
12-10	Slovenia	W	3-0	Celje	WCq	Fletcher 4, McFadden 47, Hartley 84	9 100	Temmink NED
12-11	USA	D	1-1	Glasgow	Fr	Webster 37	26 708	Undiano Mallenco ESP
2006								
1-03	Switzerland	L	1-3	Glasgow	Fr	Miller.K 55	20 952	Coue FRA
11-05	Bulgaria	W	5-1	Kobe	Fr	Boyd 2 13 43, McFadden 69, Burke 2 76 88	5 780	Kamikawa JPN
13-05	Japan	D	0-0	Saitama	Fr		56 648	Iturralde Gonzalez ESP
2-09	Faroe Islands	W	6-0	Glasgow	ECq	Fletcher 7, McFadden 10, Boyd 2 24p 38, Miller.K 30p, O'Connor 85	50 059	Egorov RUS
6-09	Lithiania	W	2-1	Kaunas	ECq	Dailly 46, Miller.K 62	8 000	Hrinák SVK
7-10	France	W	1-0	Glasgow	ECq	Caldwell.G 67	50 456	Busacca SUI
11-10	Ukraine	L	0-2	Kyiv	ECq		50 000	Hansson SWE
2007								
24-03	Georgia	W	2-1	Glasgow	ECq	Boyd 11, Beattie 89	52 063	Vollquartz DEN
28-03	Italy	L	0-2	Bari	ECq		37 600	De Bleeckere BEL
30-05	Austria	W	1-0	Vienna	Fr	O'Connor 59	13 200	Szabo HUN
6-06	Faroe Islands	W	2-0	Toftir	ECq	Maloney 31, O'Connor 35	4 100	Kasnaferis GRE
22-08	South Africa	W	1-0	Aberdeen	Fr	Boyd 71	13 723	Atkinson ENG
8-09	Lithiania	W	3-1	Glasgow	ECq	Boyd 31, McManus 77, McFadden 85	52 063	Skomina SVN
12-09	France	W	1-0	Paris	ECq	McFadden 64	43 342	Plautz AUT
13-10	Ukraine	W	3-1	Glasgow	ECq	Miller.K 4, McCulloch 10, McFadden 68	52 063	Vink NED
17-10	Georgia	L	0-2	Tbilisi	ECq		29 377	Kircher GER
17-11	Italy	L	1-2	Glasgow	ECq	Ferguson 65	51 301	Mejuto Gonzalez ESP
2008								
26-03	Croatia	D	1-1	Glasgow	Fr	Miller.K 31	28 821	Hauge NOR
30-05	Czech Republic	L	1-3	Prague	Fr	Clarkson 85	11 314	Braamhaar NED

Fr = Friendly match • EC = UEFA EURO 2008 • WC = FIFA World Cup • q = qualifier

SCOTLAND NATIONAL TEAM PLAYERS

Player		Ap	G	Club	Date of Birth	Player		Ap	G	Club	Date of Birth
Craig Gordon	GK	30	0	Sunderland	31 12 1982	James Morrison	MF	0	0	West Brom	25 05 1986
David Marshall	GK	2	0	Norwich City	5 03 1985	Gavin Rae	MF	12	0	Cardiff City	28 11 1977
Russell Anderson	DF	11	0	Sunderland	25 10 1978	Barry Robson	MF	1	0	Celtic	7 11 1978
Christophe Berra	DF	0	0	Hearts	31 01 1985	Ross McCormack	MF	0	0	Motherwell	18 08 1986
Gary Caldwell	DF	26	2	Celtic	12 04 1982	David Clarkson	FW	0	0	Motherwell	10 09 1985
Christian Dailly	DF	66	6	Rangers	23 10 1973	Shaun Maloney	FW	10	1	Aston Villa	24 01 1983
Stephen McManus	DF	12	1	Celtic	10 09 1982	Kenny Miller	FW	36	11	Derby County	23 12 1979
Kevin McNaughton	DF	3	0	Cardiff City	28 08 1982	**Selected other internationals**					
Gary Naysmith	DF	39	1	Sheffield United	16 11 1978	David Weir	DF	61	1	Rangers	10 05 1970
Darren Fletcher	MF	35	4	Manchester Utd	1 02 1984	Barry Ferguson	MF	43	3	Rangers	2 02 1978
Paul Hartley	MF	18	1	Celtic	19 10 1976	James McFadden	FW	37	13	Birmingham City	14 04 1983
Scotland's squad for the match against the Czech Republic						Kris Boyd	FW	14	7	Rangers	18 08 1983

SCOTLAND NATIONAL TEAM RECORDS AND RECORD SEQUENCES

Records			Sequence records					
Victory	11-0	NIR 1901	Wins	13	1879-1885	Clean sheets	7	1925-27,1996-97
Defeat	0-7	URU 1954	Defeats	5	2002	Goals scored	32	1873-1888
Player Caps	102	Kenny Dalglish	Undefeated	22	1879-1887	Without goal	4	1971
Player Goals	30	Denis Law / Dalglish	Without win	9	1997-1998	Goals against	14	1957-1958

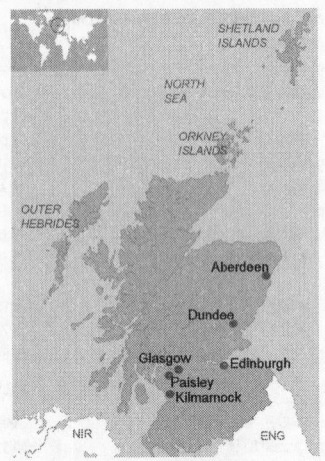

MAJOR CITIES/TOWNS

		Population '000
1	Glasgow	604
2	Edinburgh	441
3	Aberdeen	184
4	Dundee	150
5	East Kilbride	74
6	Paisley	72
7	Livingston	55
8	Cumbernauld	49
9	Hamilton	47
10	Kirkcaldy	46
11	Ayr	45
12	Perth	43
13	Kilmarnock	42
14	Greenock	42
15	Inverness	40
16	Coatbridge	39
17	Dunfermline	39
18	Glenrothes	38
19	Airdrie	35
20	Stirling	33
21	Falkirk	32
22	Clydebank	30
23	Motherwell	29
24	Dumbarton	20

SCOTLAND (PART OF THE UNITED KINGDOM)

Capital	Edinburgh	Language	English	Independence	n/a
Population	5 057 400	Area	77 000 km²	% in cities	89%
GDP per cap	$27 300	Dailling code	+44	Internet	.uk	GMT +/-	0

MEDALS TABLE

	Overall			League			Cup		LC		Europe			Town/City	Stadium	Cap'ty	DoF
	G	S	B	G	S	B	G	S	G	S	G	S	B				
1 Rangers	109	55	19	51	29	17	32	17	25	6	1	3	2	Glasgow	Ibrox	50 444	1873
2 Celtic	90	61	21	42	28	17	34	18	13	13	1	2	4	Glasgow	Celtic Park	60 554	1888
3 Aberdeen	17	28	9	4	13	8	7	8	5	7	1		1	Aberdeen	Pittodrie	21 487	1903
4 Heart of Midlothian	15	22	15	4	14	15	7	6	4	2				Edinburgh	Tynecastle	17 412	1874
5 Queen's Park	10	2					10	2						Glasgow	Hampden Park	52 000	1867
6 Hibernian	9	21	15	4	6	13	2	9	3	6			2	Edinburgh	Easter Road	17 400	1875
7 Dundee	5	11	3	1	4	1	1	4	3	3			2	Dundee	Dens Park	11 760	1893
8 Kilmarnock	4	14	4	1	4	3	3	5		5			1	Kilmarnock	Rugby Park	18 128	1869
9 Dundee United	4	12	8		7		1	7	2	4	1	1		Dundee	Tannadice Park	14 223	1909
10 Motherwell	4	11	7	1	5	7	2	4	1	2				Motherwell	Fir Park	13 742	1886
11 East Fife	4	2	2		2	1	2	3						Methil	Bayview	2 000	1903
12 Third Lanark	3	5	2	1		2	2	4		1				Glasgow	Cathkin Park		1872
13 Dumbarton	3	5		2			1	5						Dumbarton	Strathclyde Homes	2 050	1872
14 St. Mirren	3	4	2		2		3	3		1				Paisley	St Mirren Park	10 866	1877
15 Vale of Leven	3	4					3	4						Alexandria	Millburn Park		1872
16 Clyde	3	3	3		3	3	3	3						Cumbernauld	Broadwood	8 200	1877
17 Dunfermline Athletic	2	6	3		2	2	3						1	Dunfermline	East End Park	12 500	1885

RECENT LEAGUE AND CUP RECORD

	Championship						Cup		
Year	Champions	Pts	Runners-up	Pts	Third	Pts	Winners	Score	Runners-up
1995	Rangers	69	Motherwell	54	Hibernian	53	Celtic	1-0	Airdrieonians
1996	Rangers	87	Celtic	83	Aberdeen	55	Rangers	5-1	Heart of Midlothian
1997	Rangers	80	Celtic	75	Dundee United	60	Kilmarnock	1-0	Falkirk
1998	Celtic	74	Rangers	72	Heart of Midlothian	67	Heart of Midlothian	2-1	Rangers
1999	Rangers	77	Celtic	71	St. Johnstone	57	Rangers	1-0	Celtic
2000	Rangers	90	Celtic	69	Heart of Midlothian	54	Rangers	4-0	Aberdeen
2001	Celtic	97	Rangers	82	Hibernian	66	Celtic	3-0	Hibernian
2002	Celtic	103	Rangers	85	Livingston	58	Rangers	3-2	Celtic
2003	Rangers	97	Celtic	97	Heart of Midlothian	63	Rangers	1-0	Dundee
2004	Celtic	98	Rangers	81	Heart of Midlothian	68	Celtic	3-1	Dunfermline Ath.
2005	Rangers	93	Celtic	92	Hibernian	61	Celtic	1-0	Dundee United
2006	Celtic	85	Heart of Midlothian	65	Rangers	62	Heart of Midlothian	1-1 4-2p	Gretna
2007	Celtic	84	Rangers	72	Aberdeen	65	Celtic	1-0	Dunfermline Ath.
2008	Celtic	89	Rangers	86	Motherwell	60	Rangers	3-2	Queen of the South

SCOTLAND 2007–08

CLYDESDALE BANK PREMIER LEAGUE

	Pl	W	D	L	F	A	Pts	Celtic	Rangers	Motherwell	Aberdeen	Dundee U	Hibs	Falkirk	Hearts	ICT	St Mirren	Kilmarnock	Gretna
Celtic †	38	28	5	5	84	26	89		2-1 3-2	0-0 1-3	0-1 0-3	0-0 0-1	1-2 0-0	4-0	5-0 3-0	5-0 2-1	1-1	0-0 1-0	3-0
Rangers †	38	27	5	6	84	33	86	3-0 1-0		3-1 1-0	3-0 3-1	2-0 3-1	0-3 1-0	1-2	1-7 2-2	0-0 2-1	2-0	2-0 4-0	2-0 4-0 4-2
Motherwell ‡	38	18	6	14	50	46	60	1-4 1-2	1-1 1-1		3-0 2-1	5-3 2-2	2-1 1-0	0-3	0-2 0-1	2-1 3-1	1-1	1-2 1-0	3-0
Aberdeen	38	15	8	15	50	58	53	1-3 1-5	1-2 0-1	2-1 2-1		2-0 2-1	3-1 2-1	1-2	1-1 1-0	1-0 1	4-0 1-1	2-1	2-0 3-0
Dundee United	38	14	10	14	53	47	52	0-2 0-1	2-1 3-3	1-2 0-1	0-3 0-3		0-0 1-1	2-0 0-0	4-1	0-1	2-0 1-1	2-0	1-2
Hibernian	38	14	10	14	49	45	52	3-2 0-2	1-2 0-0	0-1 0-0	2-3 3-3	1-2 2-1		1-1	1-1	1-0 2-0	0-1 2-0	4-1 2-0 4-2	4-2
Falkirk	38	13	10	15	45	49	49	1-4 0-1	1-3 1-3	1-0 0-0	0-0		3-0	1-1 0-2		2-1 2-1	1-0 2-1	0-1 4-0	1-0 0-2 0-0
Heart of Midlothian	38	13	9	16	47	55	48	1-1	4-2 0-4	1-2	4-1	1-3 1-0	0-1 1-0	4-2 0-0		2-3 1-0 0-5	3-2 1-1	0-2 1-1	2-0
Inverness Caley Thistle	38	13	4	21	51	62	43	3-2	0-3 0-1	0-3	1-2 3-4	0-3 1-1	2-0	4-2 0-1	2-1 0-3		1-0 0-0	3-1 0-0	3-0 6-1
St Mirren	38	10	11	17	26	54	41	1-5 0-1	0-3	0-1 3-1	0-1	0-3	2-1	1-5 1-0	1-3 1-2	1-1 1-1		0-0 1-0 1-0 2-0
Kilmarnock	38	10	10	18	39	52	40	1-2	1-2 0-2	0-1	0-1 3-1	2-1 1-2	2-1	0-1 2-1	3-1 0-0	2-2 4-1	0-0 1-0		3-3 1-1
Gretna §10	38	5	8	25	32	83	13	1-2 1-2	1-2	1-2 1-3	1-1	3-2 0-3	0-1	0-4 2-0 1-1	1-0 0-4	1-2 0-0 0-0	1-2 4-2		

4/08/2007 - 22/05/2008 • † Qualified for the UEFA Champions League • ‡ Qualified for the UEFA Cup • Matches in bold are away not home matches
Top scorers: Scott McDonald, Celtic 25; Jan Vennegoor of Hesselink, Celtic 15; Chris Porter, Motherwell 15; Kris Boyd, Rangers 14 • § = points deducted

SCOTLAND 2007–08

IRN-BRU FIRST DIVISION (2)

	Pl	W	D	L	F	A	Pts	Hamilton	Dundee	St J'stone	QofS	D'fermline	Partick	Livingston	Morton	Clyde	Stirling
Hamilton Academical	36	23	7	6	62	27	76		2-0 1-0	1-0 2-0	1-0 1-0	2-1 3-0	2-0 0-0	1-1 3-1	1-0 3-0	0-0 2-0	4-0 0-0
Dundee	36	20	9	7	58	30	69	1-0 1-1		2-1 3-2	2-1 2-3	1-1 0-0	3-0 1-0	4-1 2-0	2-1 2-0	1-2 0-3	3-1 3-0
St Johnstone	36	15	13	8	60	45	58	4-1 2-1	1-1 1-1		2-0 2-1	0-0 1-1	2-1 2-2	5-2 5-2	2-2 3-2	1-1 1-2	2-2 2-1
Queen of the South	36	14	10	12	47	43	52	2-1 2-2	2-1 1-0	3-3 3-1		0-1 1-1	1-2 2-0	1-0 1-0	1-3 0-0	1-1 3-1	2-2 3-1
Dunfermline Athletic	36	13	12	11	36	41	51	0-5 1-0	1-0 0-1	0-0 0-1	2-0 4-0		1-0 1-1	0-4 1-0	1-0 3-0	1-0 3-4	2-1 2-1
Partick Thistle	36	11	12	13	40	39	45	0-3 3-0	1-1 1-0	2-0 2-0	0-0 0-0	1-0 1-1		3-0 2-1	1-0 3-4	4-0 1-1	1-1 1-0
Livingston	36	10	9	17	55	66	39	2-0 1-3	0-2 1-2	2-2 2-1	0-1 0-3	0-1 3-0	4-2 0-0		4-0 6-1	4-2 0-1	4-3 2-1
Greenock Morton	36	9	10	17	40	58	37	0-2 1-3	0-2 1-2	2-2 1-0	0-1 0-3	0-1 3-0	4-2 0-0	2-2 1-1		3-2 1-2	1-1 2-1
Clyde	36	9	10	17	40	59	37	0-2 2-3	1-2 1-1	1-0 1-3	0-0 1-4	2-1 1-2	1-4 2-1	1-2 1-4	2-1 3-2		1-3 3-0
Stirling Albion	36	4	12	20	41	71	24	2-4 0-1	2-2 1-6	0-0 3-1	1-3 0-0	3-0 2-3	1-1 3-3	1-4 0-0	1-2 0-2	1-3 3-0	

4/08/2007 - 26/04/2008 • † Play-off (see second division)

SCOTLAND 2007–08

IRN-BRU SECOND DIVISION (3)

	Pl	W	D	L	F	A	Pts	Ross C'ty	Airdrie	Raith	Alloa	Peterhead	Brechin	Ayr	Q. Park	Cow'beath	Berwick
Ross County	36	22	7	7	78	44	73		1-1 3-2	2-3 2-3	2-6 1-1	0-5 1-1	2-1 0-0	2-0 2-4	1-1 3-2	4-1 3-0	2-1 4-0
Airdrie United †	36	20	6	10	64	34	66	0-1 2-0		0-1 3-0	2-0 1-1	1-1 2-0	2-1 1-2	2-0 0-0	0-2 1-0	3-2 3-1	4-0 4-0 3-0
Raith Rovers	36	19	3	14	60	50	60	0-2 0-1	2-1 1-0		2-1 3-2	2-2 2-5	1-1 1-1	2-3 1-2	0-2 0-1	2-0 3-2	3-1 3-0
Alloa Athletic †	36	16	8	12	57	56	56	3-1 2-0	0-6 1-2	2-1 2-0		2-0 2-0	2-2 0-4	2-1 1-0	2-2 1-0	3-2 3-2	2-1 2-1
Peterhead	36	16	7	13	65	54	55	1-2 1-0	1-1 4-0	1-1 0-1	1-4 2-2		1-2 1-0	3-0 4-1	1-0 1-0	4-2 1-0	4-3 9-2
Brechin City	36	13	13	10	63	48	52	1-2 3-3	4-2 2-1	0-1 3-2	0-0 0-0	2-3 3-1		2-2 5-1	2-1 0-1	1-1 0-1	2-2 5-0
Ayr United	36	13	7	16	51	62	46	1-4 0-2	1-1 1-2	0-3 0-1	2-0 3-1	2-0 3-2	0-3 1-1		2-3 3-1	1-4 1-1	4-0 4-0
Queen's Park	36	13	5	18	48	51	44	3-2 0-1	0-1 0-2	2-5 0-1	1-0 1-1	1-1 1-2	2-0 3-0	2-3 1-1		0-1 2-3	1-0 3-1
Cowdenbeath †	36	10	7	19	47	73	37	2-2 2-4	1-1 0-1	1-0 1-4	1-4 1-1	0-2 0-4	2-0 1-0	2-4 1-0			3-1 1-2
Berwick Rangers	36	3	7	26	40	101	16	0-1 0-4	2-0 2-4	2-1 2-5	0-3 1-2	1-2 2-2	3-3 2-2	1-0 1-1	1-1 1-4	1-1 4-5	

4/08/2007 - 26/04/2008 • † Play-off • Semis: Alloa 2-1 3-5 Clyde; Raith 0-2 2-2 Airdrie • Final: Airdrie 0-1 0-2 Clyde

SCOTLAND 2007–08

IRN-BRU THIRD DIVISION (4)

	Pl	W	D	L	F	A	Pts	East Fife	Stranraer	Montrose	Arbroath	Sten'muir	Elgin	Albion	Dumb'ton	E. Stirling	Forfar
East Fife	36	28	4	4	77	24	88		3-1 2-1	2-0 0-0	0-2 2-1	7-0 0-1	4-0 2-0	4-0 0-0	2-0 2-1	3-1 1-0	3-0 3-0
Stranraer †	36	19	8	9	65	43	65	0-2 0-2		1-0 0-2	1-1 0-3	2-3 3-1	3-3 0-0	3-1 3-0	2-0 2-0	2-1 2-1	3-0 0-1
Montrose †	36	17	8	11	59	36	59	3-1 0-1	2-4 0-2		3-3 5-0	1-0 2-0	0-3 0-1	2-1 0-1	3-1 3-1	2-0 0-1	2-2
Arbroath †	36	14	10	12	54	47	52	2-3 0-1	2-2 0-0	0-0 2-1		2-2 1-0	4-0 2-0	1-0 1-4	1-1 0-0	2-0 0-1	3-4 1-1
Stenhousemuir	36	13	9	14	50	59	48	2-1 0-1	1-4 1-1	0-4 0-0	1-0 0-3		2-3 2-2	0-1 2-2	2-1 1-1	0-3 3-0	4-0 2-0
Elgin City	36	13	8	15	56	68	47	3-2 1-8	1-5 2-6	1-3 2-2	2-0 1-5			3-2 1-1	2-1 2-6	1-0 3-0	2-2 3-1
Albion Rovers	36	9	10	17	51	68	37	1-4 2-2	3-2 1-1	1-3 1-0	5-2 0-2	1-1 3-3	3-4 1-1			2-0 0-1	2-3 2-2 2-1 0-0
Dumbarton	36	9	10	17	31	48	37	1-1 0-3	0-2 0-1	1-3 0-0	1-2 1-1	1-2 1-0	1-0 1-4	2-0 2-0		3-1 1-0	0-0 0-0
East Stirling	36	9	7	20	48	71	34	0-2 0-3	2-1 3-1	3-0 3-1	2-3 0-1	1-3 0-1	1-3 4-0	4-5 3-0	3-2 1-1		2-1 4-1
Forfar Athletic	36	8	9	19	35	62	33	0-2 2-3	1-1 0-3	1-4 1-1	1-3 1-0	0-1 1-2	4-0 0-1	1-0 1-4	3-1 1-1	0-2 1-0	

4/08/2007 - 26/04/2008 • † Play-off • Semis: Arbroath 1-1 2-1 Cowdenbeath; Montrose 1-1 0-3 Stranraer • Final: Arbroath 2-0 0-1 Stranraer

TENNENTS SCOTTISH FA CUP 2007–08

Third Round

Albion Rovers *	1
East Stirlingshire	5
Livingston *	4
Alloa Athletic	0
Arbroath *	0
Cowdenbeath	1
Ayr United	1
Partick Thistle *	2
Berwick Rangers	0
Dumbarton *	2
Clyde *	2
Montrose	0
Ross County *	4
Whitehill Welfare	0
Edinburgh University	0
Cove Rangers *	1
Raith Rovers	5
Threave Rovers *	0
Brechin City *	1 2
East Fife	1 1
Queen's Park	1 2
Airdrie United *	1 4
Stirling Albion	6
Stranraer *	0
Culter *	1
Huntly	3
Morton *	3
Buckie Thistle	2
Linlithgow Rose *	1
Dalbeattie Star	0
Peterhead *	0
Queen of the South	5

Fourth Round

Rangers *	6
East Stirlingshire	0
Inverness Caledonian Thistle	0
Hibernian *	3
Livingston *	2
Cowdenbeath	0
Dunfermline Athletic	1
Partick Thistle *	2
St Mirren *	3
Dumbarton	0
Clyde *	0
Dundee United	1
Ross County	4
Cove Rangers *	2
Raith Rovers	1
St Johnstone *	3
Aberdeen	2 3
Falkirk *	2 1
Brechin City	0 2
Hamilton Academical * †	0 1
Kilmarnock	2
Airdrie United *	0
Stirling Albion	0
Celtic *	3
Dundee	3
Huntly *	1
Heart of Midlothian *	2 0
Motherwell	2 1
Morton *	2 3
Gretna	2 0
Linlithgow Rose	0
Queen of the South *	4

Fifth Round

Rangers	0 1
Hibernian *	0 0
Livingston *	0 1 4p
Partick Thistle	0 1 5p
St Mirren *	0 1
Dundee United	0 0
Ross County *	0
St Johnstone	1
Aberdeen *	1
Hamilton Academical	0
Kilmarnock *	1
Celtic	5
Dundee	2
Motherwell *	1
Morton *	0
Queen of the South	2

* Home team • † Brechin disqualified for fielding two ineligible players

TENNENTS SCOTTISH FA CUP 2007-08

Quarter–finals	Semi–finals	Final

Rangers *   1   2
Partick Thistle   1   0

Rangers   1   4p
St Johnstone   1   3p

St Mirren   1   1
St Johnstone *   1   3

Rangers   3
Queen of the South ‡   2

Aberdeen *   1   1
Celtic   1   0

Aberdeen   3
Queen of the South   4

SCOTTISH FA CUP FINAL 2008

Hampden Park, Glasgow, 24-05-2008, 15:00, Att: 48 821, Ref: Stuart Dougal

Dundee   0
Queen of the South *   2

Rangers   3   Boyd 2 [33][72], Beasley [43]
Queen of the South   2   Tosh [50], Thomson [53]

Top 16 teams from 2006-07 season enter in the fourth round. Clubs positioned 17-32 enter in the third round
Both semi-finals played at Hampden Park
‡ Qualified for the UEFA Cup

Rangers - Neil Alexander - Steven Whittaker, Carlos Cuellar, David Weir, Sasa Papac - DaMarcus Beasley (Steven Davis 76), Barry Ferguson, Kevin Thomson, Lee McCulloch● - Kris Boyd, Jean-Claude Darcheville (John Fleck 86). Tr: Walter Smith
Queen of the South - Jaime MacDonald - Ryan McCann (Scott Robertson 86), Jim Thomson, Andy Aitken , Robert Harris - Paul Burns, Neil MacFarlane, Steve Tosh●, Jaime McQuilken (John Stewart 76) - Stephen Dobbie (John O'Neill 82), Sean O'Connor. Tr: Gordon Chisholm

CIS INSURANCE SCOTTISH LEAGUE CUP 2007-08

Second Round			Third Round		Quarter-finals		Semi-finals		Final	
Rangers	Bye		Rangers	4	Rangers	2	Rangers †	2	Rangers	2 3p
St Mirren *	0		East Fife *	0	Motherwell *	1	Heart of Midlothian	0	Dundee United	2 2p
East Fife	1									
Hibernian	2		Hibernian *	2						
Queen's Park *	1		Motherwell	4						
Raith Rovers	1									
Motherwell *	3									
Celtic	Bye		Celtic	2	Celtic *	0				
Livingston	2 5p		Dundee *	1	Heart of Midlothian	2				
Dundee *	2 6p									
Dunfermline Athletic	Bye		Dunfermline Athletic	1						
Stirling Albion *	0		Heart of Midlothian *	4						
Heart of Midlothian	2									
Aberdeen	Bye		Aberdeen	2	Aberdeen *	4	Aberdeen	1		
St Johnstone	0 4p		Partick Thistle *	0	Inverness CT	1	Dundee United ††	4		
Partick Thistle *	0 5p									
Gretna *	3		Gretna	0						
Cowdenbeath	1		Inverness CT *	3						
Arbroath	1									
Inverness CT *	3									
Hamilton Academical	2		Hamilton Academical *	2	Hamilton Academical	1				
Berwick Rangers *	2		Kilmarnock	0	Dundee United *	3				
Peterhead	0									
Kilmarnock	3									
Falkirk	2		Falkirk *	0						
Montrose *	1		Dundee United	1						
Ross County	1									
Dundee United *	2									

* Home team • † Played at Hampden Park, Glasgow • †† Played at Tynecastle, Edinburgh
Premier League clubs enter in the second round while those in European competition enter in the third round

LEAGUE CUP FINAL

Hampden Park, Glasgow
16-03-2008. Att: 50 019. Ref: Clark

Scorers - Boyd 2 [85] [113] for Rangers;
Hunt [34], De Vries [96] for Dundee United

Rangers - McGregor - Broadfoot, Cuellar, Weir,
Papac (Boyd 61) - Hemdani (Darcheville 45),
Dailly, Burke (Whittaker 116), Ferguson - Davis,
McCulloch. Tr: Walter Smith
Dundee Utd - Zaluska - Kovacevic, Kenneth,
Wilkie, Kalvenes - Buaben (Robertson 97),
Flood, Kerr, Gomis - Hunt (Conway 78), De
Vries. Tr: Craig Levein

ABERDEEN 2007–08

Mon	Date	Opponent		Score	Scorers	Att
Aug	4	Dundee Utd	L	0-1		12 496
	12	Hearts	D	1-1	Nicholson [19]	13 134
	19	Celtic	L	1-3	Brewster [24]	16 232
	25	Hibernian	D	3-3	Brewster 2 [18 37], Smith [57]	15 280
Sept	1	Kilmarnock	W	1-0	Miller [54]	5 814
	15	Motherwell	L	1-2	Smith [65]	10 154
	23	Rangers	L	0-3		49 046
	29	Gretna	W	2-0	Diamond [16], Smith [18]	10 279
Oct	7	St Mirren	W	4-0	Severin 2 [43p 71p], Miller 2 [63 88]	12 841
	21	Inverness	W	2-1	Young [8], Tokely OG [62]	6 023
	28	Falkirk	D	1-1	Severin [47p]	10 399
Nov	3	Dundee Utd	W	2-0	Aluko [45], Miller [91+]	11 964
	11	Hearts	L	1-4	De Visscher [38]	17 122
	24	Celtic	L	0-3		58 000
Dec	2	Hibernian	W	3-1	Miller [33], Clark [47], Young [86]	10 110
	8	Kilmarnock	W	2-1	Nicholson [63p], Miller [75]	10 207
	15	Motherwell	L	0-3		5 326
	23	Rangers	D	1-1	Miller [48]	17 798
	26	Gretna	D	1-1	Lovell [86]	1 730
	29	St Mirren	W	1-0	Lovell [85]	5 025
Jan	2	Inverness	W	1-0	Nicholson [83p]	13 372
	5	Falkirk	D	0-0		5 457
	19	Dundee Utd	L	0-3		8 579
	26	Hearts	L	0-1		14 000
Feb	10	Celtic	L	1-5	Miller [62]	14 651
	17	Hibernian	L	1-3	Diamond [18]	13 825
	24	Kilmarnock	L	1-3	Combe OG [86]	6 113
	27	Motherwell	D	1-1	Diamond [28]	8 240
Mar	1	Rangers	L	1-3	Lovell [28]	50 066
	15	Gretna	W	3-0	Maguire [40], Miller [71p], Nicholson [73]	9 025
	22	St Mirren	D	1-1	Mair [29]	9 779
	29	Inverness	W	4-3	Aluko [7], Nicholson [45], Miller [53], Maguire [93+]	5 655
Apr	7	Falkirk	W	2-1	Maguire 2 [22 82]	11 484
	19	Celtic	L	0-1		55 766
	26	Hibernian	W	2-1	Mackie [63], Miller [70p]	8 387
May	3	Dundee Utd	W	2-1	Foster [30], Touzani [48]	10 312
	10	Motherwell	L	1-2	Aluko [67]	8 574
	22	Rangers	W	2-0	Miller [63], Mackie	17 509

DUNDEE UNITED 2007–08

Mon	Date	Opponent		Score	Scorers	Att
Aug	4	Aberdeen	W	1-0	Robertson [91+]	12 496
	13	Kilmarnock	L	1-2	Hunt [50]	5 557
	18	Hibernian	D	0-0		8 405
	25	Inverness	W	3-0	Dillon [47], Robson 2 [58p 81p]	4 178
Sept	1	Falkirk	W	2-0	Hunt [58], Robson [84]	6 864
	16	St Mirren	W	2-0	Hunt [38], Robertson [68]	6 128
	22	Gretna	L	2-3	Buaben [9], Wilkie [65]	1 624
	29	Celtic	L	0-3		57 006
Oct	6	Motherwell	W	1-0	Dods [78]	6 286
	20	Hearts	W	3-1	Robertson 2 [14 25], Robson [89p]	16 661
	28	Rangers	W	2-1	Wilkie [28], Robson [54p]	12 129
Nov	3	Aberdeen	L	0-2		11 964
	10	Kilmarnock	W	2-0	Hunt [8], Buaben [94+]	6 065
	24	Hibernian	D	2-2	Robertson 2 [66 74]	14 440
Dec	1	Inverness	L	0-1		5 845
	8	Falkirk	L	0-3		4 803
	15	St Mirren	W	3-0	Robertson [49], Hunt [77], Flood [90]	3 490
	22	Gretna	L	1-2	Hunt [29]	6 304
	26	Celtic	L	0-2		12 357
	29	Motherwell	L	3-5	Robertson [36], Hunt 2 [75 92+]	5 227
Jan	2	Hearts	W	4-1	Robson 3 [23 70p 88p], Hunt [84]	12 100
	5	Rangers	L	0-2		48 559
	19	Aberdeen	W	3-0	Hunt [50], Robson 2 [77 84]	8 579
	26	Kilmarnock	W	2-1	Robson [30], Conway [66]	4 803
Feb	9	Hibernian	D	1-1	Hunt [13p]	6 635
	19	Inverness	D	1-1	Buaben [68]	4 087
	23	Falkirk	D	0-0		6 835
	27	St Mirren	D	1-1	Dillon [69]	6 037
Mar	6	Gretna	W	3-0	Kenneth [16], Gomis [51], Robertson [64]	507
	12	Celtic	D	0-0		45 000
	22	Motherwell	W	2-0	Swanson [76], De Vries [89]	6 779
	29	Hearts	L	0-1		16 871
Apr	6	Rangers	D	3-3	Kalvenes [37], Hunt [51], Cuellar OG [65]	11 214
	20	Hibernian	D	1-1	Hunt [60p]	7 404
	26	Motherwell	D	2-2	Craigan OG [45], Wilkie [86]	5 027
May	3	Aberdeen	L	1-2	Swanson [49]	10 312
	10	Rangers	L	1-3	De Vries [76]	50 293
	22	Celtic	L	0-1		13 613

CELTIC 2007–08

Mon	Date	Opponent		Score	Comp	Scorers	Att
Aug	5	Kilmarnock	D	0-0	SPL		60 000
	11	Falkirk	W	4-1	SPL	Milne OG [30], Miller [76], Nakamura [79], Hesselink [81]	6 329
	15	Sp. Moskva	D	1-1	CLp3	Hartley [21]	5 000
	19	Aberdeen	W	3-1	SPL	Donati [61], Miller 2 [85 92+]	16 232
	25	Hearts	W	5-0	SPL	Berra OG [9], Donati [22], Brown [61], Hesselink [63p], Nakamura [79]	57 300
	29	Sp. Moskva	W	1-1	CLp3	McDonald [27]. W 4-3p	57 644
Sept	2	St Mirren	W	5-1	SPL	Brown [22], McDonald [25], Hesselink [53], OG [56], McManus [74]	7 840
	15	Inverness	W	5-0	SPL	Hesselink 2 [15 59], Donati [41], Nakamura [56], McGuire OG [70]	56 020
	18	Sh. Donetsk	L	0-2	CLgD		25 700
	23	Hibernian	L	2-3	SPL	McGeady [26], Caldwell [66]	16 125
	26	Dundee	W	2-1	LCr3	McDonald [27], Hesselink [60]	8 203
	29	Dundee Utd	W	3-0	SPL	McDonald 3 [7 67 72]	57 006
Oct	2	Milan	W	2-1	CLgD	McManus [61], McDonald [89]	58 462
	7	Gretna	W	2-1	SPL	Killen [86], McDonald [91+]	6 011
	20	Rangers	L	0-3	SPL		50 428
	24	Benfica	L	0-1	CLgD		38 512
	27	Motherwell	W	3-0	SPL	McDonald 3 [42 59 88p]	57 633
	31	Hearts	L	0-2	LCqf		21 492
Nov	3	Kilmarnock	W	2-1	SPL	McDonald 2 [34 36]	8 260
	6	Benfica	W	1-0	CLgD	McGeady [45]	58 691
	24	Aberdeen	W	3-0	SPL	Hesselink [14], McGeedy [27], McDonald [49]	58 000
	28	Sh. Donetsk	W	2-1	CLgD	Jarosik [45], Donati [92+]	59 396
Dec	1	Hearts	D	1-1	SPL	McDonald [73]	16 454
	4	Milan	L	0-1	CLgD		38 409
	8	St Mirren	D	1-1	SPL	Riordan [85]	55 747
	11	Falkirk	W	4-0	SPL	McDonald [5p], McGeady 3 [41 67 82]	54 291
	16	Inverness	L	2-3	SPL	Hesselink 2 [24 31]	7 004
	22	Hibernian	D	1-1	SPL	Jarosik [78]	58 016
	26	Dundee Utd	W	2-0	SPL	Hesselink [68], McManus [74]	12 357
	29	Gretna	W	3-0	SPL	McDonald [35], Brown [49], McGeady [89]	57 171
Jan	12	Stirling Alb	W	3-0	FAr4	Hesselink [37], McDonald [70], Nakamura [75]	27 923
	19	Kilmarnock	W	1-0	SPL	Corrigan OG [64]	56 618
	27	Falkirk	W	1-0	SPL	McDonald [48]	6 803
Feb	2	Kilmarnock	W	5-1	FAr5	McDonald 2 [22 70], Caldwell [56], Hesselink [63], Samaras [85]	6 491
	10	Aberdeen	W	5-1	SPL	Nakamura [17], McGeady [34], McDonald 2 [44p 48], Robson [74]	14 651
	16	Hearts	W	3-0	SPL	Hesselink [14], McDonald [51], Hinkel [76]	56 738
	20	Barcelona	L	2-3	CLr2	Hesselink [16], Robson [38]	58 426
	24	St Mirren	W	1-0	SPL	Nakamura [87]	7 213
	27	Inverness	W	2-1	SPL	McDonald [46], Samaras [61]	56 787
Mar	1	Hibernian	W	2-0	SPL	Naylor [64], Samaras [75]	15 735
	4	Barcelona	L	0-1	CLr2		75 326
	9	Aberdeen	D	1-1	FAqf	Hesselink [91+]	10 909
	12	Dundee Utd	D	0-0	SPL		45 000
	18	Aberdeen	L	0-1	FAqf		33 506
	23	Gretna	W	3-0	SPL	McDonald [42], Hesselink [70], Samaras [88]	3 561
	29	Rangers	L	0-1	SPL		50 325
Apr	5	Motherwell	L	0-1	SPL		58 624
	13	Motherwell	W	4-1	SPL	McManus [17], McDonald [30], Hesselink 2 [43 57]	9 771
	16	Rangers	W	2-1	SPL	Nakamura [20], Hesselink [93+]	58 964
	19	Aberdeen	W	1-0	SPL	Samaras [56]	55 766
	27	Rangers	W	3-2	SPL	McDonald 2 [4 43], Robson [70p]	58 662
May	3	Motherwell	W	2-1	SPL	McDonald [62], Samaras [79]	9 158
	11	Hibernian	W	2-0	SPL	McManus [37], McDonald [87]	58 515
	22	Dundee Utd	W	1-0	SPL	Hesselink [72]	13 613

SPL = Premier League • CL = UEFA Champions League • FA = Scottish Cup • LC = League Cup • p3 = third preliminary round • gD = Group D • r2 = second round • r3 = third round • r4 = fourth round • r5 = fifth round • qf = quarter-final

FALKIRK 2007–08

Month	Date	Opponent	Res	Score	Scorers	Att
Aug	4	Gretna	W	4-0	Higdon 2 14 24, Moutinho 66, Latapy 74	2 731
	11	Celtic	L	1-4	Higdon 5	6 329
	18	Rangers	L	2-7	Riera 44, Barrett 72	47 419
	25	St Mirren	L	0-1		5 626
Sept	1	Dundee Utd	L	0-2		6 864
	15	Hibernian	D	1-1	Moutinho 47	6 298
	22	Motherwell	W	1-0	Latapy 74	5 245
	29	Inverness	L	2-4	Milne 28, Arfield 47	4 011
Oct	6	Hearts	L	2-4	Barrett 87, Moutinho 89	15 800
	20	Kilmarnock	D	1-1	Finnigan 2	5 143
	28	Aberdeen	D	1-1	Cregg 68	10 399
Nov	3	Gretna	W	2-0	Barr 41, Barrett 50	4 843
	24	Rangers	L	1-3	Moutinho 62	6 627
Dec	1	St Mirren	W	5-1	Moutinho 2 5 41, Thomson 14, Barrett 82, Finnigan 85	4 133
	8	Dundee Utd	W	3-0	Moutinho 5, Barrett 41, Higdon 66	4 803
	11	Celtic	L	0-4		54 291
	15	Hibernian	D	1-1	Barrett 80	12 391
	22	Motherwell	W	3-0	Higdon 2 49 60, Cregg 65	5 241
	26	Inverness	W	1-0	Aafjes 35	5 265
	29	Hearts	W	2-1	Finnigan 78, Higdon 81	6 614
Jan	2	Kilmarnock	W	1-0	Finnigan 11	5 956
	5	Aberdeen	D	0-0		5 457
	19	Gretna	L	0-2		1 609
	27	Celtic	L	0-1		6 803
Feb	9	Rangers	L	0-2		48 590
	16	St Mirren	W	4-0	Arfield 2 6 58, Cregg 2 61 71	5 803
	23	Dundee Utd	D	0-0		6 835
	27	Hibernian	D	0-0		5 928
Mar	1	Motherwell	D	0-0		5 108
	15	Inverness	W	1-0	Clarke 86	4 012
	22	Hearts	D	0-0		16 682
	29	Kilmarnock	D	0-0		5 134
Apr	7	Aberdeen	L	1-2	Finnigan 49	11 484
	19	Gretna	D	0-0		4 490
	26	St Mirren	L	0-1		3 500
May	5	Hearts	W	2-1	Scobbie 45, Finnigan 52	4 638
	10	Inverness	W	2-1	Higdon 28, Finnigan 68	5 631
	17	Kilmarnock	L	1-2	Moutinho 11	5 475

GRETNA 2007–08

Month	Date	Opponent	Res	Score	Scorers	Att
Aug	4	Falkirk	L	0-4		2 731
	11	Hibernian	L	2-4	Yantorno 17, McMenamin 49	13 795
	18	Hearts	D	1-1	Barr 79	16 407
	25	Motherwell	L	1-2	Osman 18	3 758
Sept	1	Rangers	L	0-4		49 689
	15	Kilmarnock	L	1-2	Skelton 93+	1 516
	22	Dundee Utd	W	3-2	Cowan 2 14 36, Jenkins 86	1 624
	29	Aberdeen	L	0-2		10 279
Oct	7	Celtic	L	1-2	Yantorno 37	6 011
	20	St Mirren	L	0-1		3 646
	27	Inverness	L	0-4		1 020
Nov	3	Falkirk	L	0-2		4 843
	10	Hibernian	L	0-1		2 666
	25	Hearts	D	1-1	Kingston OG 49	1 544
Dec	1	Motherwell	L	0-3		6 431
	15	Kilmarnock	D	3-3	Skelton 5, Grainger 51p, Horwood 57	5 122
	22	Dundee Utd	W	2-1	Deuchar 12, Deverdics 42	6 304
	26	Aberdeen	D	1-1	Jenkins 91+	1 730
	29	Celtic	L	0-3		57 171
Jan	5	Inverness	L	0-3		3 919
	16	Rangers	L	1-2	Deuchar 46	6 137
	19	Falkirk	W	2-0	Deuchar 33, Murray 50	1 609
Feb	9	Hearts	L	0-2		16 138
	13	Hibernian	L	2-4	Skelton 81, Deuchar 88	12 087
	16	Motherwell	L	1-3	McGill 50	2 877
	24	Rangers	L	2-4	Deuchar 2 71 89	48 375
	27	Kilmarnock	W	4-2	Deverdics 27, Meynell 39, Barr 44, Buscher 59	1 545
Mar	6	Dundee Utd	L	0-3		507
	15	Aberdeen	L	0-3		9 025
	23	Celtic	L	0-3		3 561
	29	St Mirren	L	0-2		3 577
Apr	5	Inverness	L	1-2	Barr 80	431
	9	St Mirren	D	0-0		751
	19	Falkirk	D	0-0		4 490
	26	Kilmarnock	D	1-1	Barr 74	4 086
May	3	Inverness	L	1-6	Hogg 27	3 639
	10	St Mirren	D	0-0		3 163
	13	Hearts	W	1-0	Skelton 90	1 090

HEART OF MIDLOTHIAN 2007–08

Month	Date	Opponent	Res	Score	Scorers	Att
Aug	6	Hibernian	L	0-1		16 436
	12	Aberdeen	D	1-1	Stewart 46	13 134
	18	Gretna	D	1-1	Driver 73	16 407
	25	Celtic	L	0-5		57 300
Sept	3	Motherwell	W	2-0	Kingston 24, Velicka 92+	5 081
	15	Rangers	W	4-2	Driver 13, Tall 27, Stewart 66p, Ivaskevicius 70	15 948
	22	Inverness	L	1-2	Black OG 34	4 918
	30	St Mirren	W	3-1	Driver 40, Stewart 56p, Velicka 83	4 233
Oct	6	Falkirk	W	4-2	Ksanavicius 5, Zaliukas 27, Velicka 58, Nade 68	15 800
	20	Dundee Utd	L	1-3	Kingston 95+	16 661
	27	Kilmarnock	L	1-3	Tall 91+	6 373
Nov	4	Hibernian	D	1-1	Nade 46	17 015
	11	Aberdeen	W	4-1	Driver 3, Velicka 14, Tall 54, Nade 62	17 122
	25	Gretna	D	1-1	Kingston 27	1 544
Dec	1	Celtic	D	1-1	Velicka 92+p	16 544
	8	Motherwell	L	1-2	Driver 12	16 663
	15	Rangers	L	1-2	Velicka 56	48 392
	22	Inverness	L	2-3	Berra 62, Velicka 90p	16 202
	26	St Mirren	L	0-1		16 476
	29	Falkirk	L	1-2	Palazuelos 28	6 614
Jan	2	Dundee Utd	L	1-4	Berra 37	12 100
	5	Kilmarnock	D	1-1	Velicka 63	14 346
	19	Hibernian	W	1-0	Velicka 20	17 131
	26	Aberdeen	W	1-0	Nade 55	14 000
Feb	9	Gretna	W	2-0	Velicka 2 3 42p	16 138
	16	Celtic	L	0-3		56 738
	23	Motherwell	W	1-0	Craigan OG 12	5 925
	27	Rangers	L	0-4		16 173
Mar	1	Inverness	W	3-0	Karipidis 22, Elliot 2 33 47	4 489
	15	St Mirren	D	1-1	Mikoliunas 87	4 557
	22	Falkirk	D	0-0		16 682
	29	Dundee Utd	W	1-0	Kingston 27	16 871
Apr	5	Aberdeen	D	0-0		5 901
	19	St Mirren	W	3-2	Jonsson 28, Glen 42, Kingston 81	15 259
	26	Inverness	W	1-0	Glen 80	15 000
May	5	Falkirk	L	1-2	Cesnauskis 77	4 638
	10	Kilmarnock	L	0-2		10 512
	13	Gretna	L	0-1		1 090

HIBERNIAN 2007–08

Month	Date	Opponent	Res	Score	Scorers	Att
Aug	6	Hearts	W	1-0	Kerr 2	16 436
	11	Gretna	W	4-2	Zemmama 2 64 82, Fletcher 66, McCann 90	13 795
	18	Dundee Utd	D	0-0		8 405
	25	Aberdeen	D	3-3	Zemmama 5, Fletcher 70, Shiels 84	15 280
Sept	1	Inverness	W	1-0	Fletcher 2p	13 258
	15	Falkirk	D	1-1	Donaldson 5p	6 298
	23	Celtic	W	3-2	Fletcher 5, Gathuessi 41, Shiels 87	16 125
	29	Kilmarnock	W	4-1	Donaldson 3 12 31p 78p, Antoine-Curier 65	14 500
Oct	6	Rangers	W	1-0	Murphy 61	50 440
	20	Motherwell	L	1-2	Fletcher 31p	7 071
	27	St Mirren	L	0-1		13 884
Nov	4	Hearts	D	1-1	Berra OG 18	17 015
	10	Gretna	W	1-0	Murphy 20	2 666
	24	Dundee Utd	D	2-2	Benjelloun 77, Antoine-Curier 82p	14 440
Dec	2	Aberdeen	L	1-3	Fletcher 24	10 110
	8	Inverness	L	0-2		4 224
	15	Falkirk	D	1-1	Donaldson 21p	12 391
	22	Celtic	D	1-1	Murphy 20	58 016
	26	Kilmarnock	L	1-2	Shiels 90p	6 372
	29	Rangers	L	1-2	Zemmama 88	16 217
Jan	5	St Mirren	L	1-2	Antoine-Curier 89	4 212
	19	Hearts	L	0-1		17 131
Feb	9	Dundee Utd	D	1-1	Rankin 46	6 635
	13	Gretna	W	4-2	Nish 10, Fletcher 3 19 58 92+p	12 087
	17	Aberdeen	W	3-1	Zemmama 49, Shiels 55, Fletcher 94+	13 825
	23	Inverness	W	2-0	Nish 3, Fletcher 5	12 552
	27	Falkirk	W	2-0	Ross OG 12, Rankin 52	5 928
Mar	1	Celtic	L	0-2		15 735
	12	Motherwell	W	1-0	Nish 52	11 692
	15	Kilmarnock	W	2-0	Morais 29, Fletcher 73	12 486
	22	Rangers	L	1-2	Shiels 90	50 111
	29	Motherwell	L	0-1		6 580
Apr	5	St Mirren	W	2-0	Nish 4, Zemmama 5	13 161
	20	Dundee Utd	D	1-1	Shiels 57	7 404
	26	Aberdeen	L	1-2	Shiels 54	8 387
May	4	Rangers	D	0-0		16 872
	11	Celtic	L	0-2		58 515
	22	Motherwell	L	0-2		7 650

INVERNESS CALEDONIAN THISTLE 2007–08

	Opponent	Res	Score	Scorers	Att
Aug	4	Rangers	L	0-3		7 711
	11	Motherwell	L	1-2	Tokely [82]	4 259
	18	St Mirren	L	1-2	Cowie [58]	3 309
	25	Dundee Utd	L	0-3		4 178
Sept	1	Hibernian	L	0-1		13 258
	15	Celtic	L	0-5		56 020
	22	Hearts	W	2-1	Wyness [64], Brewster [92+]	4 918
	29	Falkirk	W	4-2	Wyness 2 [7 54], Duncan [18], Black [32]	4 011
Oct	6	Kilmarnock	D	2-2	Ford OG [22], Cowie [61]	4 456
	21	Aberdeen	L	1-2	Wyness [58]	6 023
	27	Gretna	W	4-0	Wyness 2p, Cowie [31], Wilson [73], McBain [75]	1 020
Nov	3	Rangers	L	0-2		48 898
	10	Motherwell	L	0-3		3 608
	24	St Mirren	W	1-0	Cowie [6]	3 699
Dec	1	Dundee Utd	W	1-0	Black [20]	5 845
	8	Hibernian	W	2-0	Niculae 2 [42 78]	4 224
	16	Celtic	W	3-2	Rankin [42p], Proctor [57], Cowie [61]	7 004
	22	Hearts	W	3-2	Duncan [22], Rankin [53p], Bayne [93+]	16 202
	26	Falkirk	L	0-1		5 265
	29	Kilmarnock	W	3-1	Niculae 2 [42 76], Cowie [52]	4 169
Jan	2	Aberdeen	L	0-1		13 372
	3	Gretna	W	3-0	Niculae 2 [34 43], Rankin [40p]	3 919
	20	Rangers	L	0-3		7 753
	9	St Mirren	D	1-1	Munro [28]	3 609
Feb	16	Dundee Utd	D	1-1	Paatelainen [84]	4 087
	20	Motherwell	L	1-3	Cowie [19]	4 526
	23	Hibernian	L	0-2		12 552
	27	Celtic	L	1-2	Niculae [70]	56 787
Mar	1	Hearts	L	0-3		4 489
	15	Falkirk	L	0-1		4 012
	22	Kilmarnock	L	1-4	Black [14p]	5 100
	29	Aberdeen	L	3-4	Bus OG [21], Duncan [40], McBain [57]	5 655
Apr	5	Gretna	W	2-1	McBain [71], Cowie [73]	431
	19	Kilmarnock	W	3-0	Imrie [10], Lilley OG [71], Niculae [73]	3 420
	26	Hearts	L	0-1		15 000
May	3	Gretna	W	6-1	Imrie [1], McAllister [23], Wilson [51], Cowie [70], Tokely [89], Vigurs [90]	3 639
	10	Falkirk	L	1-2	Wilson [90p]	5 631
	17	St Mirren	D	0-0		3 783

KILMARNOCK 2007–08

	Opponent	Res	Score	Scorers	Att
Aug	5	Celtic	D	0-0		60 000
	13	Dundee Utd	W	2-1	Gibson [79], Nish [87]	5 557
	18	Motherwell	W	2-1	Lilley [60], Dodds [92+]	4 985
	25	Rangers	L	1-2	Invincibile [61]	11 544
Sept	1	Aberdeen	L	0-1		5 814
	15	Gretna	W	2-1	Gibson [4], Jarvis [36]	1 516
	22	St Mirren	D	0-0		5 596
	29	Hibernian	L	1-4	Nish [76]	14 500
Oct	6	Inverness	D	2-2	Koudou [1], Nish [56]	4 456
	20	Falkirk	D	1-1	Wright [10]	5 143
	27	Hearts	W	3-1	Wales [55], Nish [72p], Gibson [77]	6 373
Nov	3	Celtic	L	1-2	Wright [55]	8 260
	10	Dundee Utd	L	0-2		6 065
	24	Motherwell	L	0-1		5 016
Dec	1	Rangers	L	0-2		48 055
	8	Aberdeen	L	1-2	Fernandez [27]	10 207
	15	Gretna	D	3-3	Invincibile [27], Fernandez [53], Nish [73]	5 122
	22	St Mirren	D	0-0		4 216
	26	Hibernian	W	2-1	Nish [36], Taouil [75]	6 372
	29	Inverness	L	1-3	Nish [87p]	4 169
Jan	2	Falkirk	L	0-1		5 956
	5	Hearts	D	1-1	Digiacomo [45]	14 346
	19	Celtic	L	0-1		56 618
	26	Dundee Utd	L	1-2	Wales [83]	4 803
Feb	9	Motherwell	L	0-1		6 618
	17	Rangers	L	0-2		10 546
	24	Aberdeen	W	3-1	Bryson 2 [14 75], Wright [41]	6 113
	27	Gretna	L	2-4	Ford [72], Gibson [83]	1 545
Mar	1	St Mirren	W	1-0	Invincibile [25]	5 352
	15	Hibernian	L	0-2		12 486
	22	Inverness	W	4-1	Wright [38], Bryson 2 [50 56], Flannigan [64]	5 100
	29	Falkirk	D	0-0		5 134
Apr	5	Hearts	D	0-0		5 901
	19	Inverness	L	0-3		3 420
	26	Gretna	D	1-1	Fernandez [57]	4 086
May	3	St Mirren	L	0-1		3 690
	10	Hearts	W	2-0	Murray [74], Di Giacomo [83]	10 512
	11	Falkirk	W	2-1	Taouil [24], Di Giacomo [81]	5 475

RANGERS 2007–08

	Opponent	Res	Comp	Scorers	Att
	31	Zeta	W	2-0 CLp2	Weir [55], Novo [72]	36 145
Aug	4	Inverness	W	3-0 SPL	Ferguson 2 [16 90], Novo [64]	7 711
	7	Zeta	W	1-0 CLp2	Beasley [81]	9 000
	11	St Mirren	W	2-0 SPL	Ferguson [52], Cousin [80]	47 772
	14	Cr. Zvezda	W	1-0 CLp3	Novo [90]	35 364
	18	Falkirk	W	7-2 SPL	Cousin 2 [2 54], Whittaker [34], Boyd [75], Darcheville 2 [88 91+], Broadfoot [93+]	47 419
	25	Kilmarnock	W	2-1 SPL	Beasley [52], Darcheville [76]	11 544
	28	Cr. Zvezda	D	0-0 CLp3		40 104
Sept	1	Gretna	W	4-0 SPL	Boyd [38], Webster [63], Cuellar [81], Collin OG [83]	49 689
	15	Hearts	L	2-4 SPL	Cousin [49p], Beasley [74]	15 948
	19	Stuttgart	W	2-1 CLgE	Adam [62], Darcheville [75p]	49 795
	23	Aberdeen	W	3-0 SPL	McCulloch [46], Naismith [65], Boyd [88]	49 046
	26	East Fife	W	4-0 LCr3	Novo [14], Boyd 2 [35 66p], Cuellar [54]	7 413
	29	Motherwell	D	1-1 SPL	Boyd [67p]	10 009
Oct	2	Lyon	W	3-0 CLgE	McCulloch [23], Cousin [48], Beasley [53]	38 076
	6	Hibernian	L	0-1 SPL		50 440
	20	Celtic	W	3-0 SPL	Novo 2 [28 79p], Ferguson [57]	50 428
	23	Barcelona	D	0-0 CLgE		49 957
	28	Dundee Utd	L	1-2 SPL	Cousin [51p]	12 129
	31	Motherwell	W	2-1 LCqf	Novo [22], Boyd [53]	9 283
Nov	3	Inverness	W	2-0 SPL	Boyd [1], Cuellar [63]	48 898
	6	Barcelona	L	0-2 CLgE		82 887
	24	Falkirk	W	3-1 SPL	Cuellar [20], Darcheville [55], Boyd [93+]	6 627
	27	Stuttgart	L	2-3 CLgE	Adam [27], Ferguson [70]	51 000
Dec	1	Kilmarnock	W	2-0 SPL	Darcheville [4], Whittaker [55]	48 055
	12	Lyon	L	0-3 CLgE		50 260
	15	Hearts	W	2-1 SPL	McCulloch 2 [18 87]	48 392
	23	Aberdeen	D	1-1 SPL	Adam [30]	17 798
	26	Motherwell	W	3-1 SPL	Cousin [42], Porter OG [70], Boyd [93+]	49 823
	29	Hibernian	W	2-1 SPL	Naismith [12], Cousin [59]	16 217
Jan	5	Dundee Utd	W	2-0 SPL	Naismith [9], Ferguson [40]	48 559
	16	Gretna	W	2-1 SPL	Ferguson [45], Cousin [74]	6 137
	20	Inverness	W	1-0 SPL	Darcheville [89]	7 753
	23	East Stirling	W	6-0 FAr4	McCulloch 2 [25 50], Boyd 3 [30 45 62], Hutton [28]	34 024
	26	St Mirren	W	4-0 SPL	Burke [27], Boyd [33], Whittaker 2 [37 81]	49 198
	30	Hearts	W	2-0 LCsf	Ferguson [50], Darcheville [69]	31 989
Feb	3	Hibernian	D	0-0 FAr5		11 513
	9	Falkirk	W	2-0 SPL	Boyd [23], Naismith [89]	48 590
	10	Panath'kos	D	0-0 UCr3		43 203
	17	Kilmarnock	W	2-0 SPL	Cuellar [25], Boyd [63p]	10 546
	21	Panath'kos	D	1-1 UCr3	Novo [81]	14 452
	24	Gretna	W	4-2 SPL	Cousin [13], Naismith [22], Burke [60], Boyd [88]	48 375
	27	Hearts	W	4-0 SPL	Darcheville 2 [25 44], Novo 2 [53 70]	16 173
Mar	1	Aberdeen	W	3-1 SPL	Daily [38], Adam [50], Boyd [83]	50 066
	6	W. Bremen	W	2-0 UCr4	Cousin [45], Davis [48]	42 959
	9	Hibernian	W	1-0 FAr5	Burke [39]	33 837
	13	W. Bremen	L	0-1 UCr4		33 660
	16	Dundee Utd	D	2-2 LCf	Boyd 2 [85 113], W 3-2p	50 019
	19	Partick	D	1-1 FAqf	Boyd [69]	36 724
	22	Hibernian	W	2-1 SPL	Darcheville [40], Novo [79]	50 117
	29	Celtic	W	1-0 SPL	Thomson [45]	50 325
Apr	3	Sporting CL	D	0-0 UCqf		48 923
	6	Dundee Utd	D	3-3 SPL	Weir [44], Novo [58], Boyd [67]	11 214
	10	Sporting CL	W	2-0 UCqf	Darcheville [60], Whittaker [92+]	31 500
	13	Partick	W	2-0 FAqf	Novo [27], Burke [40]	9 909
	16	Celtic	L	1-2 SPL	Novo [55]	58 964
	20	StJohnstone	D	1-1 FAsf	Novo [103p], W 4-3p	26 180
	24	Fiorentina	D	0-0 UCsf		49 199
	27	Celtic	L	2-3 SPL	Weir [17], Cousin [29]	58 662
May	1	Fiorentina	D	0-0 UCsf	W 4-2p	39 130
	4	Hibernian	D	0-0 SPL		16 872
	7	Motherwell	W	1-0 SPL	Ferguson [74]	48 238
	10	Dundee Utd	W	3-1 SPL	Novo 2 [7 18], Darcheville [92+]	50 293
	14	Zenit	L	0-2 UCf		43 878
	17	Motherwell	D	1-1 SPL	Daily [29]	10 445
	19	St Mirren	W	3-0 SPL	Boyd [4], Darcheville 2 [24 69]	7 439
	22	Aberdeen	L	0-2 SPL		17 509
	24	Queen OTS	W	3-2 FAf	Boyd 2 [33 72], Beasley [43]	48 821

SPL = Premier League • CL = UEFA Champions League • FA = Scottish Cup • LC = League Cup • UC = UEFA Cup • p2 = second preliminary round • p3 = third preliminary round • gE = Group E • r3 = third round • r4 = fourth round • r5 = fifth round • qf = quarter-final • sf = semi-final • f = final

MOTHERWELL 2007–08

				Scorers	Att
Aug	4	St Mirren	W	1-0	McGarry [3]	5 257
	11	Inverness	W	2-1	O'Donnell [85], McCormack [91+p]	4 259
	18	Kilmarnock	L	1-2	Clarkson [23]	4 985
	25	Gretna	W	2-1	Lasley [8], Porter [62]	3 758
Sept	3	Hearts	L	0-2		5 081
	15	Aberdeen	W	2-1	Quinn [34], Porter [37]	10 154
	22	Falkirk	L	0-1		5 245
	29	Rangers	D	1-1	Porter [24]	10 009
Oct	6	Dundee Utd	L	0-1		6 286
	20	Hibernian	W	2-1	McCormack 2 [35 37]	7 071
	27	Celtic	L	0-3		57 633
Nov	3	St Mirren	D	1-1		5 123
	10	Inverness	W	3-0	Clarkson 2 [15 53], Smith [87]	3 608
	24	Kilmarnock	W	1-0	O'Donnell [46]	5 016
Dec	1	Gretna	W	3-0	Clarkson 2 [44 74], Porter [61]	6 431
	8	Hearts	W	2-1	Porter [53], Zaliukas OG [67]	16 633
	15	Aberdeen	W	3-0	McCormack 2 [8p 45], McGarry [12]	5 326
	22	Falkirk	L	0-3		5 241
	26	Rangers	L	1-3	Quinn [65]	49 823
	29	Dundee Utd	W	5-3	Hughes [11], Porter [14], McCormack [17], Clarkson 2 [55 56]	5 227
Jan	19	St Mirren	L	1-3	Clarkson [11]	4 291
Feb	9	Kilmarnock	W	1-0	Clarkson [92+]	6 618
	16	Gretna	W	3-1	Porter [25], McCormack 2 [47 90]	2 877
	20	Inverness	W	3-1	Clarkson 2 [7 42], Porter [10]	4 526
	23	Hearts	L	0-1		5 925
	27	Aberdeen	D	1-1	Smith [83]	8 240
Mar	1	Falkirk	D	0-0		5 108
	12	Hibernian	L	0-1		11 692
	22	Dundee Utd	L	0-2		6 779
	29	Hibernian	W	1-0	Clarkson [3]	6 580
Apr	5	Celtic	W	1-0	Lappin [33]	58 624
	13	Celtic	L	1-4	McManus OG [24]	9 771
	26	Dundee Utd	D	2-2	Porter 2 [17 50]	5 027
May	3	Celtic	L	1-2	Porter [60]	9 158
	7	Rangers	L	0-1		48 238
	10	Aberdeen	W	2-1	Smith.D [61], Porter [81]	8 574
	17	Rangers	D	1-1	Porter [50]	10 455
	22	Hibernian	W	2-0	Lappin [4], Murphy [50p]	7 650

ST MIRREN 2007–08

				Scorers	Att
Aug	4	Motherwell	L	0-1		5 257
	11	Rangers	L	0-2		47 772
	18	Inverness	W	2-1	Miranda [19], Corcoran [55]	3 309
	25	Falkirk	W	1-0	Mehmet [90]	5 626
Sept	2	Celtic	L	1-5	Miranda [75]	7 840
	16	Dundee Utd	L	0-2		6 128
	22	Kilmarnock	D	0-0		5 596
	30	Hearts	L	1-3	Corcoran [78]	4 233
Oct	7	Aberdeen	L	0-4		12 841
	20	Gretna	W	1-0	Mehmet [35]	3 646
	27	Hibernian	W	1-0	Mehmet [13]	13 884
Nov	3	Motherwell	D	1-1	Kean [46]	5 123
	24	Inverness	L	0-1		3 699
Dec	1	Falkirk	L	1-5	Mehmet [50]	4 133
	8	Celtic	L	1-1	McGinn [74]	55 747
	15	Dundee Utd	L	0-3		3 490
	22	Kilmarnock	D	0-0		4 216
	26	Hearts	W	1-0	McGinn [17]	16 476
	29	Aberdeen	L	0-1		5 025
Jan	5	Hibernian	W	2-1	Maxwell [4], Mason [43]	4 212
	19	Motherwell	W	3-1	Corcoran [9], Maxwell 2 [38 49]	4 291
	26	Rangers	L	0-4		49 198
Feb	9	Inverness	D	1-1	Mehmet [74]	3 609
	16	Falkirk	L	0-4		5 803
	24	Celtic	L	0-1		7 213
	27	Dundee Utd	D	1-1	Dorman [88]	6 037
Mar	1	Kilmarnock	L	0-1		5 352
	15	Hearts	D	1-1	Hamilton [59]	4 557
	22	Aberdeen	D	1-1	Dorman [10]	9 779
	29	Gretna	W	2-0	Dargo [27], Mehmet [49]	3 577
Apr	5	Hibernian	D	0-0		13 161
	9	Gretna	D	0-0		751
	19	Hearts	L	2-3	McCay [20], Mason [78]	15 259
	26	Falkirk	L	0-1		3 500
May	3	Kilmarnock	W	1-0	Haining [90]	3 690
	10	Gretna	D	0-0		3 163
	17	Inverness	D	0-0		3 783
	19	Rangers	L	0-3		7 439

SEN – SENEGAL

NATIONAL TEAM RECORD
JULY 10TH 2006 TO JULY 12TH 2010

PL	W	D	L	F	A	%
22	12	7	3	40	24	70.4

FIFA/COCA-COLA WORLD RANKING

1993	1994	1995	1996	1997	1998	1999	2000	2001	2002	2003	2004	2005	2006	2007	High	
56	50	47	58	85	95	79	88	65	27	33	31	30	41	38	26	06/04

					2007–2008							Low	
08/07	09/07	10/07	11/07	12/07	01/08	02/08	03/08	04/08	05/08	06/08	07/08	95	12/98
46	40	34	38	38	40	43	44	45	46	43	42		

It has been a tumultuous year for football in Senegal, with a crisis precipitated by a single game at the 2008 CAF Africa Cup of Nations. The 3-1 defeat at the hands of Angola in Ghana set off a sequence of events, which still have to be resolved. It led to the immediate resignation of Henryk Kasperczak, who became the first coach in more than a decade to quit in the middle of the Nations Cup finals and to the dissolution of the football federation. A normalisation committee is now in place and working with FIFA and the country's sports ministry to restoring full autonomy for Senegal soccer. Lamine Ndiaye took over as coach for the last game at the Nations Cup and he kept

INTERNATIONAL HONOURS
Qualified for the FIFA World Cup finals 2002   Copa Amilcar Cabral 1979 1980 1983 1984 1985 1986 1991 2001

his place on a short-term contract. He has since given the team some solidity, vital in the early stages of the 2010 FIFA World Cup qualifiers and Senegal started with a win over Algeria and have gone to the top of their group standings. There has also been a change in attitude from the indiscipline at the Nations Cup finals in Ghana where captain El Hadji Diouf, veteran goalkeeper Tony Sylva and midfielder Ousmane Ndoye were both suspended after being spotted at a night club in Kumasi in breach of a team curfew. At home AS Douanes retained their league in 2007 but again failed to qualify for the group stage of the 2008 CAF Champions League.

THE FIFA BIG COUNT OF 2000

	Male	Female		Male	Female
Registered players	6 593	0	Referees	3 230	0
Non registered players	40 000	0	Officials	2 700	0
Youth players	146 689	0	Total involved	199 212	
Total players	193 282		Number of clubs	82	
Professional players	50	0	Number of teams	12 200	

Fédération Sénégalaise de Football (FSF)
VDN-Ouest-Foire en face du CICES, Case Postale 13021, Dakar, Senegal
Tel +221 33 8692828   Fax +221 33 8200592
fsf@senegalfoot.sn   www.senegalfoot.sn
President: DIAGNA NDIAYE Mamadou   General Secretary: TBD
Vice-President: SECK Saer   Treasurer: TBD   Media Officer: SECK Mbacke
Men's Coach: NDIAYE Lamine   Women's Coach: DIABY Bassouare
FSF formed: 1960   CAF: 1963   FIFA: 1962
White shirts with yellow trimmings, White shorts, White socks or Green shirts with yellow trimmings, Green shorts, Green socks

RECENT INTERNATIONAL MATCHES PLAYED BY SENEGAL

2006 Opponents		Score	Venue	Comp	Scorers	Att	Referee
14-01 Congo DR	D	0-0	Dakar	Fr			
23-01 Zimbabwe	W	2-0	Port Said	CNr1	Henri Camara [60], Issa Ba [80]	15 000	Abdel Rahman SUD
27-01 Ghana	L	0-1	Port Said	CNr1		20 000	El Arjoun MAR
31-01 Nigeria	L	1-2	Port Said	CNr1	Souleymane Camara [59]	5 000	Damon RSA
3-02 Guinea	W	3-2	Alexandria	CNqf	Diop.PB [52], Niang [84], Henri Camara [93+]	17 000	Codjia BEN
7-02 Egypt	L	1-2	Cairo	CNsf	Diomansy Kamara [54]	74 000	Evehe CMR
9-02 Nigeria	L	0-1	Cairo	CN3p		11 354	Coulibaly MLI
1-03 Norway	W	2-1	Dakar	Fr	Moussa N'Diaye [20], Gueye [36]	45 000	Pare BFA
23-05 Korea Republic	D	1-1	Seoul	Fr	Moussa N'Diaye [80]	64 836	
16-08 Côte d'Ivoire	W	1-0	Tours	Fr	Niang [64]	4 000	Husset FRA
2-09 Mozambique	W	2-0	Dakar	CNq	Dario Khan OG [35], Ndaw [61]		Mana NGA
7-10 Burkina Faso	L	0-1	Ouagadougou	CNq			Guezzaz MAR
2007							
7-02 Benin	W	2-1	Rouen	Fr	Demba Toure [9], Papa N'Diaye [64]		Lannoy FRA
24-03 Tanzania	W	4-0	Dakar	CNq	Niang 3 [39 48 62], Diomansy Kamara [46]		Daami TUN
2-06 Tanzania	D	1-1	Mwanza	CNq	Demba Ba [71]		Damon RSA
10-06 Malawi	W	3-2	Blantyre	Fr	OG [22], Demba Toure 2 [44 85]		
17-06 Mozambique	D	0-0	Maputo	CNq			Seechurn MRI
21-08 Ghana	D	1-1	London	Fr	Diouf [72]	2 788	D'Urso ENG
8-09 Burkina Faso	W	5-1	Dakar	CNq	Ndaw [22], Ndoye [72], Henri Camara 2 [74 84], Diouf [89]		Haimoudi ALG
14-10 Guinea	W	3-1	Rouen	Fr	Gueye [20], Niang [43p], Diomansy Kamara [82p]		
17-11 Mali	W	3-2	Bondoufle	Fr	Henri Camara [9], Diomansy Kamara [47], Diatta [55]		
21-11 Morocco	L	0-3	Creteil	Fr			
2008							
12-01 Namibia	W	3-1	Dakar	Fr	Diomansy Kamara 2 [9 73], Henri Camara [83]		
16-01 Benin	W	2-1	Ouagadougou	Fr	Mendy [13], Gueye [82]		
23-01 Tunisia	D	2-2	Tamale	CNr1	Sall [44], Diomansy Kamara [66]		Nichimura JPN
27-01 Angola	L	1-3	Tamale	CNr1	Abdoulaye Faye [20]		Haimoudi ALG
31-01 South Africa	D	1-1	Kumasi	CNr1	Henri Camara [37]		Kotey GHA
31-05 Algeria	W	1-0	Dakar	WCq	Ibrahima Faye [80]	50 000	Kotey GHA
8-06 Gambia	D	0-0	Banjul	WCq		24 500	Ncobo RSA
15-06 Liberia	D	2-2	Monrovia	WCq	Diouf [47], Gueye [55]	18 000	Djaoupe TOG
21-06 Liberia	W	3-1	Dakar	WCq	Sonko [8], Diouf [32], Henri Camara [63]	40 000	Chaibou NIG

Fr = Friendly match • CN = CAF African Cup of Nations • WC = FIFA World Cup • q = qualifier • r1 = first round group • qf = quarter-final

SENEGAL NATIONAL TEAM PLAYERS

	Player		Club	Date of Birth		Player		Club	Date of Birth
1	Tony Sylva	GK	Lille	17 05 1975	12	Moustapha Bayal Sall	MF	St Etienne	30 11 1985
2	Ibrahima Sonko	DF	Reading	22 01 1981	13	Lamine Diatta	DF	None	2 07 1975
3	Guirane Ndaw	DF	Sochaux	24 04 1984	14	Pape Waigo Ndiaye	MF	Genoa	20 01 1984
4	Mohamed Adama Sarr	DF	Standard Liege	23 12 1983	15	Diomansy Kamara	MF	Fulham	8 11 1980
5	Souleymane Diawara	DF	Bordeaux	24 12 1978	16	Cheikh Tidiane Ndiaye	GK	Creteil	15 02 1985
6	Ibrahima Faye	DF	Troyes	22 10 1979	17	Pape Modou Sougou	FW	Uniao Leiria	18 12 1984
7	Henri Camara	FW	West Ham United	10 05 1977	18	Frederic Mendy	MF	Bastia	6 11 1981
8	Mamadou Niang	FW	Olymp. Marseille	13 10 1979	19	Pape Bouba Diop	MF	Portsmouth	28 01 1978
9	Babacar Gueye	MF	Metz	2 03 1986	20	Abdoulaye Diagne Faye	DF	Newcastle United	26 02 1978
10	Ousmane Ndoye	MF	Academica Coimbra	21 03 1978	21	Habib Beye	DF	Newcastle United	19 10 1977
11	El Hadji Diouf	FW	Bolton Wanderers	15 01 1981	22	Pape Malick Ba	MF	Basel	11 11 1980
Senegal's squad for the 2008 CAF Africa Cup of Nations					23	Bouna Coundoul	GK	Colorado Rapids	4 03 1982

SENEGAL NATIONAL TEAM RECORDS AND RECORD SEQUENCES

Records				Sequence records					
Victory	6-0	MTN 1984		Wins	11	1985-1986	Clean sheets	6	1999-2000
Defeat	0-4	Seven times		Defeats	4	1969-1970	Goals scored	14	1999
Player Caps	52	Henri Camara		Undefeated	12	1987-1989	Without goal	7	1987
Player Goals	27	Henri Camara		Without win	12	2000-2001	Goals against	22	1965-1970

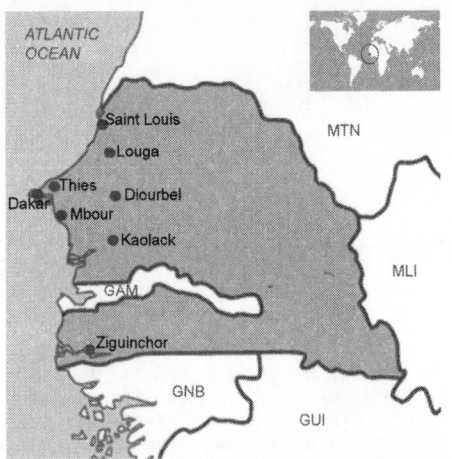

MAJOR CITIES/TOWNS

		Population '000
1	Dakar	2 461
2	Thiès	261
3	Mbour	191
4	Kaolack	179
5	Rufisque	179
6	Saint-Louis	164
7	Ziguinchor	163
8	Diourbel	102
9	Louga	82
10	Tambacounda	77
11	Kolda	62
12	Mbacké	56
13	Tivaouane	53
14	Richard Toll	46
15	Joal-Fadiouth	39
16	Kaffrine	29
17	Dahra	28
18	Bignona	26
19	Fatick	24
20	Velingara	23
21	Bambey	22
22	Nioro	21
23	Sédhiou	20
24	Mékhé	20

REPUBLIC OF SENEGAL; REPUBLIQUE DU SENEGAL

Capital	Dakar	Language	French, Wolof, Pulaar, Jola, Mandinka	Independence	1960
Population	12 521 851	Area	196 190 km²	Density	55 per km²	% in cities	42%
GDP per cap	$1 600	Dailling code	+221	Internet	.sn	GMT +/-	0

MEDALS TABLE

		Overall			Lge	Cup		Africa			City	Stadium	Cap'ty	DoF
		G	S	B	G	G	S	G	S	B				
1	ASC Diaraf	22	6	1	10	12	6			1	Dakar	Stade de Diaraf	10 000	1969
2	Jeanne d'Arc	16	5	3	10	6	4	1		3	Dakar	Stade Leopold Sédar Senghor	60 000	1921
3	AS Douanes	10	2		4	6	2				Dakar	Stade Leopold Sédar Senghor	60 000	
4	US Gorée	7	5	2	3	4	5			2	Gorée, Dakar	Stade Demba Diop	15 000	
5	SUNEOR (ex Sonacos)	5	3		4	1	3				Diourbel	Stade Municipal	5 000	
6	ASC Linguère	4	3			4	3				Saint-Louis	Stade Julton	3 000	1969
7	ASF Police	4	3		1	3	3				Dakar	Stade Municipal de Police	5 000	
8	ASEC Ndiambour	4	2		3	1	2				Louga	Stade ASEC	15 000	
9	Port Autonome	4	1		3	1	1				Dakar	Stade Port Autonome	4 000	
10	ASFA Dakar	3	2		3		2				Dakar	Stade de ASFA	2 000	
11	US Ouakem	3				3					Dakar	Stade Demba Diop	15 000	
12	Olympique Thiès	2	2		2		2				Thiès	Stade Maniang Soumaré	8 000	
13	Espoir Saint-Louis	2			1	1					Saint-Louis	Stade Julton	3 000	
14	Casa Sports	1	1			1	1				Ziginchour	Stade Aline Sitoe Diatta	10 000	
	Saltigues	1	1			1	1				Rufisque	Stade Maniang Soumaré	8 000	

RECENT LEAGUE AND CUP RECORD

	Championship						Cup		
Year	Champions	Pts	Runners-up	Pts	Third	Pts	Winners	Score	Runners-up
1995	ASC Diaraf	2-1	ESO				ASC Diaraf	2-0	AS Douanes
1996	Sonacos	‡	ASC Linguère				US Gorée	1-0	ASC Ndiambour
1997	ASC Douanes	46	Jeanne d'Arc	45	ASC Linguère	43	AS Douanes	3-1	ASC Linguère
1998	ASC Ndiambour	47	ASC Diaraf	46	AS Douanes	39	ASC Yeggo	1-0	US Gorée
1999	Jeanne d'Arc	53	ASC Ndiambour	46	CSS Richard-Toll	43	ASC Ndiambour	1-1 3-0p	Sonacos
2000	ASC Diaraf	37	Port Autoname	36	ASC Ndiambour	35	Port Autonome	4-0	AS Saloum
2001	Jeanne d'Arc	47	ASC Ndiambour	45	US Gorée	44	Sonacos	1-0	US Gorée
2002	Jeanne d'Arc	52	Sonacos	42	ASC Ndiambour	39	AS Douanes	1-1 4-1p	Sonacos
2003	Jeanne d'Arc	51	ASC Diaraf	47	AS Douanes	43	AS Douanes	1-0	ASC Thiès
2004	ASC Diaraf	72	AS Douanes	69	ASC Ndiambour	65	AS Douanes	2-1	ASC Diaraf
2005	Port Autonome	67	ASC Diaraf	54	CSS Richard-Toll	49	AS Douanes	1-0	DUC Dakar
2006	AS Douanes	14	ASC Diaraf	7	US Gorée	6	US Ouakem	1-0	ASC Médiour
2007	AS Douanes	23	AS Saloum	15	Casa-Sport	13	ASC Linguère	1-0	AS Douanes

‡ Sonacos 3-0 0-1 Linguère

SENEGAL 2007

CHAMPIONNAT NATIONAL FINAL STAGE

	Pl	W	D	L	F	A	Pts	Douanes	Saloum	Casa Sport	Xam-Xam	Stade Mbour	US Ouakem
AS Douanes †	10	7	2	1	20	5	23		3-2	2-0	6-1	4-0	0-0
AS Saloum Kaolack †	10	4	3	3	11	7	15	0-0		1-1	2-0	2-0	3-0
Casa Sport ‡	10	3	4	3	8	7	13	2-0	0-0		2-0	1-0	0-0
Xam-Xam	10	4	1	5	11	18	13	0-3	2-0	3-2		1-0	2-0
Stade Mbour	10	3	2	5	5	11	11	0-1	1-0	0-0	1-0		2-2
US Ouakem	10	1	4	5	5	12	7	0-1	0-1	1-0	2-2	0-1	

15/07/2007 - 6/09/2007 • † Qualified for the CAF Champions League • ‡ Qualified for the CAF Confederation Cup

COUPE NATIONALE 2007

Eighth-finals		Quarter–finals		Semi–finals		Final	
ASC Linguère	1						
US Ouakem	0	ASC Linguère	W-0				
US Gorée	†						
ASC Yakaar				ASC Linguère	3		
Thiès FC	1			Espoir Bignona	2		
ASEC Ndiambour	0	Thiès FC	1 4p				
Jeanne d'Arc		Espoir Bignona	1 5p				
Espoir Bignona	W-0					ASC Linguère ‡	1
Stade Mbour	W-0					AS Douanes	0
Renaissance Dakar		Stade Mbour	2				
ASC Diaraf		Modèle Mbao	1				
Modèle Mbao	W-0			Stade Mbour	0		
SUNEOR				AS Douanes	2		
Casa Sports		Suneor	1				
US Rail	0	AS Douanes	2				
AS Douanes	1						

† Both teams disqualified • ‡ Qualified for the CAF Confederation Cup

CUP FINAL

Stade Demba Diop, Dakar
15-09-2007, Att: 7500, Ref: Diouf

Scorer - El Hadji Moustapha Sow [115]

SEY – SEYCHELLES

NATIONAL TEAM RECORD
JULY 10TH 2006 TO JULY 12TH 2010

PL	W	D	L	F	A	%
18	2	3	13	15	39	19.4

FIFA/COCA-COLA WORLD RANKING

1993	1994	1995	1996	1997	1998	1999	2000	2001	2002	2003	2004	2005	2006	2007	High	
157	175	176	175	181	181	192	188	192	185	163	173	176	130	163	**129**	10/06

	2007–2008											Low	
08/07	09/07	10/07	11/07	12/07	01/08	02/08	03/08	04/08	05/08	06/08	07/08	**195**	07/02
147	154	160	165	163	161	163	165	172	175	164	165		

The Seychelles made little progress on the promise they had shown over the preceding 12 months and had a very disappointing start in the 2010 FIFA World Cup qualifiers. Four successive defeats ended any remote hopes Africa's smallest country had of advancing to the second phase of the preliminaries. The islanders had brought Dutch coach Jan Mak in for the brief month long campaign in June 2008, which saw them play Tunisia, Burundi and Burkina Faso. He was, however, on temporary loan from Elfsborg in Sweden and Ulrich Mathiot was brought in for the rest of the qualifying campaign. At the end 2006, the Seychelles' Pirates had climbed some 40

INTERNATIONAL HONOURS
None

places in the FIFA/Coca-Cola World Ranking, on the back of rare wins in competitive qualifiers. But at the end of 2007, after six losses and a solitary draw, they were lower down the rankings again and continue to hover outside the top 150. This followed a disappointing campaign in the 2008 CAF Africa Cup of Nations qualifiers and also in the 2007 Indian Ocean Island Games which Seychelles will host next in 2011. The country's most successful club St Michel United were champions at the end of the 2007 season, a return to the winners' podium after a barren three preceding years and they also secured the double after beating Anse Reunion in the Cup Final.

THE FIFA BIG COUNT OF 2006

	Male	Female		Total
Number of players	5 675	185	Referees and Assistant Referees	70
Professionals	0		Admin, Coaches, Technical, Medical	320
Amateurs 18+	1 225		Number of clubs	20
Youth under 18	835		Number of teams	60
Unregistered	800		Clubs with women's teams	0
Total players	5 860		Players as % of population	7.19%

Seychelles Football Federation (SFF)
Maison Football, Roche Caiman, PO Box 843, Mahe, Seychelles
Tel +248 601160   Fax +248 601163
sff@seychelles.net   www.sff.sc
President: ROCH Henriette   General Secretary: NOURRICE Louis
Vice-President: ADAM Nicholas   Treasurer: MATHIOT Justin   Media Officer: LAURO Gian Carlo
Men's Coach: MATHIOT Ulrich   Women's Coach: ERNESTA Elsie
SFF formed: 1979   CAF: 1986   FIFA: 1986
Red shirts, Red shorts, Red socks

RECENT INTERNATIONAL MATCHES PLAYED BY THE SEYCHELLES

2006 Opponents		Score	Venue	Comp	Scorers	Att	Referee
22-07 Namibia	D	1-1	Katutura	CCr1	Wilnes Brutus [18], W 4-2p		Simisse MRI
23-07 Zambia	L	0-2	Katutura	CCr1			Ngobo RSA
3-09 Sudan	L	0-3	Khartoum	CNq			Kidane ERI
7-10 Mauritius	W	2-1	Roche Caiman	CNq	Wilnes Brutus 2 [23 81]		Raolimanana MAD
2007							
24-03 Tunisia	L	0-3	Victoria	CNq			Ssegonga UGA
28-04 Mozambique	L	0-2	Maputo	CCr1			Mpopo LES
29-04 Madagascar	L	0-5	Maputo	CCr1			Mpopo LES
2-06 Tunisia	L	0-4	Rades/Tunis	CNq			Diatta SEN
16-06 Sudan	L	0-2	Roche Caiman	CNq			Dlamini SWZ
14-08 Mauritius	L	0-3	Antananarivo	Fr			
9-09 Mauritius	D	1-1	Curepipe	CNq	Godfrey Denis [43p]		Mwandike TAN
2008							
1-06 Burundi	L	0-1	Bujumbura	WCq		4 000	Imiere NGA
7-06 Tunisia	L	0-2	Victoria	WCq		2 033	Faduco MOZ
14-06 Burkina Faso	L	2-3	Victoria	WCq	Philip Zialor [47], Don Annacoura [53]	1 000	Seechurn MRI
21-06 Burkina Faso	L	1-4	Ouagadougou	WCq	Bernard St Ange [44]	12 500	Lamptey GHA
19-07 Mauritius	W	7-0	Witbank	CCr1	Colin Laporte [14], Philip Zialor 4 [35 51 59 88], Don Annacoura [66], Trevor Poiret [87]		Kaoma ZAM
21-07 Madagascar	D	1-1	Witbank	CCr1	Godfrey Denis [48]		Kaoma ZAM
23-07 Swaziland	L	0-1	Witbank	CCr1			Katjimune NAM

Fr = Friendly match • CN = CAN African Cup of Nations • IO = Indian Ocean Games • CC = COSAFA Castle Cup • WC = FIFA World Cup
q = qualifier • r1 = first round group

SEYCHELLES NATIONAL TEAM RECORDS AND RECORD SEQUENCES

Records			Sequence records				
Victory	9-0	MDV 1979	Wins	2	2006	Clean sheets	1
Defeat	0-6	MAD 1990	Defeats	11	1992-1996	Goals scored	4	1979-1983
Player Caps	n/a		Undefeated	2	Four times	Without goal	5	2007
Player Goals	n/a		Without win	14	1992-1998	Goals against	17	1990-1998

SEYCHELLES 2007 FIRST DIVISION

	Pl	W	D	L	F	A	Pts
St Michel United	16	11	4	1	35	13	37
Seychelles MB	16	10	2	4	27	16	32
St Louis Suns United	16	9	3	4	31	17	30
Anse Réunion	16	8	2	6	22	16	26
Light Stars	16	7	2	7	21	23	23
La Passe	16	5	4	7	22	22	19
Foresters	16	4	4	8	20	32	16
Northern Dynamo	16	3	4	9	17	31	13
Red Star	16	2	1	13	15	40	7

23/05/2007 - 3/11/2007
Play-off: **Foresters** 1-1 5-3p St Francis

RECENT LEAGUE AND CUP RECORD

	Championship	Cup		
Year	Champions	Winners	Score	Runners-up
1997	St Michel United	St Michel		
1998	Red Star	St Michel United	4-0	Ascot
1999	St Michel United	Red Star	2-1	Sunshine
2000	St Michel United	Sunshine	1-1 4-2p	Red Star
2001	Red Star	St Michel United	2-1	Sunshine
2002	La Passe	Anse Reunion	2-1	Red Star
2003	St Michel United	St Louis	2-1	Light Stars
2004	La Passe	Red Star	1-0	Anse Réunion
2005	La Passe	Seychelles MB	1-0	Anse Réunion
2006	Anse Réunion	St Michel United	2-1	Red Star
2007	St Michel United	St Michel United	1-0	Anse Réunion

SEYCHELLES COUNTRY INFORMATION

Capital	Victoria	Independence	1976 from the UK	GDP per Capita	$7 800
Population	80 832	Status	Republic	GNP Ranking	169
Area km²	455	Language	English, French, Creole	Dialling code	+248
Population density	177 per km²	Literacy rate	58%	Internet code	.sc
% in urban areas	54%	Main religion	Christian	GMT +/−	+4
Towns/Cities	Victoria 26 361				
Neighbours (km)	Indian Ocean 491				
Main stadia	Stade Linité – Victoria 12 000				

SIN – SINGAPORE

NATIONAL TEAM RECORD
JULY 10TH 2006 TO JULY 12TH 2010

PL	W	D	L	F	A	%
35	11	10	14	52	45	45.7

FIFA/COCA-COLA WORLD RANKING

1993	1994	1995	1996	1997	1998	1999	2000	2001	2002	2003	2004	2005	2006	2007	High	
75	95	104	92	103	81	104	101	115	118	106	112	92	111	126	**73**	08/93

2007–2008												Low	
08/07	09/07	10/07	11/07	12/07	01/08	02/08	03/08	04/08	05/08	06/08	07/08	**140**	10/07
134	138	140	130	126	126	129	131	129	128	128	127		

Singapore's standing in Asian football has increased since the nation implemented a policy of coupling naturalised talent with local players, a tactic which has seen the country become South East Asia's number one team. Successive wins in the ASEAN Championship were followed up in 2008 by qualification for the penultimate phase of Asia's qualifying tournament for the 2010 FIFA World Cup. Although Singapore were eliminated from the competition for one of the continent's places in South Africa, the island nation were far from outclassed and picked up wins both home and away against Lebanon. However, defeats against Uzbekistan and Saudi Arabia highlighted the work that

INTERNATIONAL HONOURS
ASEAN Football Federation Championship 1998 2002 2005 2007

still needs to be done by head coach Raddy Avramovic although there were encouraging signs from Singapore's under-23 team with their third-place finish at the South East Asian Games. At club level, S-League sides Home United and Singapore Armed Forces both breezed into the knock-out phase of the AFC Cup, winning their qualifying groups to progress to the quarter-finals. SAF were eliminated at the quarter-final stage of the 2007 competition - as were compatriots Tampines Rovers - but did complete the domestic League and Cup double, finishing one point ahead of Home United in the league and defeating Tampines Rovers in the final of the Singapore Cup.

THE FIFA BIG COUNT OF 2006

	Male	Female		Total
Number of players	188 626	8 377	Referees and Assistant Referees	171
Professionals	233		Admin, Coaches, Technical, Medical	1 345
Amateurs 18+	1 250		Number of clubs	41
Youth under 18	7 300		Number of teams	104
Unregistered	181 000		Clubs with women's teams	13
Total players	197 003		Players as % of population	4.39%

Football Association of Singapore (FAS)
100 Tyrwhitt Road, Jalan Besar Stadium, 01-02, Singapore 207542
Tel +65 63483477   Fax +65 63921194
winstonlee@fas.org.sg   www.fas.org.sg
President: HO Peng Kee   General Secretary: LEE Winston
Vice-President: ZAINUDIN Nordin   Treasurer: PANTHRADIL Samuel   Media Officer: ONG Eric
Men's Coach: AVRAMOVIC Raddy   Women's Coach: NAPLAH Nathaniel
FAS formed: 1892   AFC: 1954   FIFA: 1952
Red shirts with white trimmings, Red shorts, Red socks

RECENT INTERNATIONAL MATCHES PLAYED BY SINGAPORE

2006	Opponents	Score	Venue	Comp	Scorers	Att	Referee
26-01	Denmark	L 1-2	Singapore	Fr	Indra Sahdan Daud [89]	10 392	Srinivasan IND
3-02	Kuwait	D 2-2	Kuwait City	Fr	Khairul Amri [73], Indra Sahdan Daud [90]		
6-02	Oman	L 0-1	Doha	Fr			
15-02	Hong Kong	D 1-1	Hong Kong	Fr	Noh Alam Shah [66p]	610	Heng MAS
22-02	Iraq	W 2-0	Singapore	ACq	Khairul Amri [24], Noh Alam Shah [83]	10 221	Shield AUS
1-03	Palestine	L 0-1	Amman	ACq		1 000	Al Hilali OMA
31-05	Malaysia	D 0-0	Singapore	Fr	W 5-4p	18 604	Li Yuhong CHN
3-06	Malaysia	D 0-0	Paroi	Fr	W 8-7p		
12-08	Hong Kong	W 2-1	Hong Kong	Fr	Noh Alam Shah [19], Dickson [76]		
16-08	China PR	L 0-1	Tianjin	ACq		27 000	Ebrahim BHR
6-09	China PR	D 0-0	Singapore	ACq		38 824	Shamsuzzaman BAN
11-10	Iraq	L 1-2	Al Ain	ACq	Goncalves [9], Khairul Amri [62]	3 000	Mamedov TKM
24-12	Kazakhstan	D 0-0	Bangkok	Fr			
26-12	Thailand	L 0-2	Bangkok	Fr			
28-12	Vietnam	L 2-3	Bangkok	Fr	Bennett [14], Fazrul Shahul [62]		
2007							
7-01	Philippines	W 4-1	Singapore	Fr	Bennet [12], Khairul Amri [26], Indra Sahdan Daud 2 [47 59]		
13-01	Vietnam	D 0-0	Singapore	TCr1		20 000	Sananwai THA
15-01	Laos	W 11-0	Singapore	TCr1	Ridhuan [10], Noh Alam Shah 7 [11 24 61 72 76 88 92+], Shahril Ishak [47], Khairul Amri Kamal [71], Dickson [79]	5 224	U Hla Tint MYA
17-01	Indonesia	D 2-2	Singapore	TCr1	Noh Alam Shah [10p], Indra Sahdan Daud [52]	13 819	Sananwai THA
23-01	Malaysia	D 1-1	Kuala Lumpur	TCsf	Noh Alam Shah [73]	40 000	Wan Daxue CHN
27-01	Malaysia	D 1-1	Singapore	TCsf	Ridhuan [74]. W 5-4p	55 000	Cheung Yim Yau
31-01	Thailand	W 2-1	Singapore	TCf	Noh Alam Shah [17], Fahrudin [90p]	55 000	Ravichandran MAS
4-02	Thailand	D 1-1	Bangkok	TCf	Khairul Amri [81]	30 000	Napitupulu IDN
24-06	Korea DPR	W 2-1	Singapore	Fr	Ridhuan [40], Indra Sahdan Daud [76]		
27-06	Saudi Arabia	L 1-2	Singapore	Fr	Ashrin Shariff [90]		
30-06	Australia	L 0-3	Singapore	Fr			
12-09	UAE	D 1-1	Singapore	Fr	Wilkinson [39]		
4-10	Bahrain	L 1-3	Manama	Fr	Agu Casmir [92+]		
8-10	Palestine	W 4-0	Doha	WCq	Jia Yi Shi 2 [44 53], Wilkinson [73], Noh Alam Shah [86]	75	Basma SYR
28-10	Palestine	W 3-0	Singapore	WCq	Match awarded 3-0		Sun Baojie CHN
9-11	Tajikistan	W 2-0	Singapore	WCq	Duric 2 [23 44]	6 606	Kwon Jong Chul KOR
18-11	Tajikistan	D 1-1	Dushanbe	WCq	Noh Alam Shah [25]	21 500	Shield AUS
2008							
24-01	Kuwait	W 2-0	Muscat	Fr	Fahrudin [61], Duric [72]		
27-01	Oman	L 0-2	Muscat	Fr			
31-01	Jordan	L 1-2	Zarqa	Fr	Fahrudin [76p]		
6-02	Saudi Arabia	L 0-2	Riyadh	WCq		10 000	Basma SYR
22-03	Australia	D 0-0	Singapore	Fr		6 282	Prayoon THA
26-03	Lebanon	W 2-0	Singapore	WCq	Duric [8], Fazrul Shahul [23]	10 118	Takayama JPN
28-05	Bahrain	L 0-1	Singapore	Fr			
2-06	Uzbekistan	L 3-7	Singapore	WCq	Duric [16], Fahrudin [31p], Wilkinson [73]	28 750	Albadwawi UAE
7-06	Uzbekistan	L 0-1	Tashkent	WCq		12 867	Kim Dong Jin KOR
14-06	Saudi Arabia	L 0-2	Singapore	WCq		23 000	Williams AUS
22-06	Lebanon	W 2-1	Beirut	WCq	Dayoub OG [72], Wilkinson [73]	500	Moradi IRN

Fr = Friendly match • AC = AFC Asian Cup • TC = ASEAN Tiger Cup/ASEAN Football Federation Championship • WC = FIFA World Cup
q = qualifier • r1 = first-round group • sf = semi-final • f = final

SINGAPORE NATIONAL TEAM RECORDS AND RECORD SEQUENCES

Records			Sequence records		
Victory	11-0	LAO 2007	Wins	9	2004-2005
Defeat	0-9	MYA 1969	Defeats	9	1977
Player Caps	123	Malik Awab	Undefeated	13	2004-2005
Player Goals	55	Fandi Ahmad	Without win	19	1966-1968
			Clean sheets	4	1985
			Goals scored	14	1993-1995
			Without goal	5	1976-1977
			Goals against	36	1966-1970

SINGAPORE COUNTRY INFORMATION

Capital	Singapore City	Independence	1965 from Malaysia	GDP per Capita	$23 700
Population	4 353 893	Status	Republic	GNP Ranking	38
Area km²	693	Language	Chinese, English, Malay	Dialling code	+65
Population density	6 282 per km²	Literacy rate	92%	Internet code	.sg
% in urban areas	100%	Main religion	Buddhist 54%, Muslim 15%	GMT +/−	+8
Towns/Cities ('000)	Singapore City 3 547				
Neighbours (km)	Strait of Singapore & Johore Strait 193				
Main stadia	Jalan Besar – Singapore 6 000; National Stadium – Singapore 55 000				

SINGAPORE 2007

S.LEAGUE

	Pl	W	D	L	F	A	Pts	SAF	Home Utd	Tampines	Gombak	Lions	Geylang	Woodlands	Albirex	Balestier	Liaoning	Senkang	Reds
S'pore Armed Forces †	33	25	4	4	95	38	79		4-1	1-2 1-1	0-2 2-1	3-1 5-0	3-2	3-1	3-2 1-0	3-1	3-0 3-2	5-3	6-0 6-2
Home United	33	24	6	3	73	35	78	2-0 0-0		3-1 2-0	1-1	1-0 1-2	2-1	4-2	0-0 3-2	3-2	2-1	0-0	5-1 2-1
Tampines Rovers	33	24	5	4	77	32	77	2-0	1-1		1-0 1-1	0-7-1	3-2 2-0	2-2	4-1 3-1	1-2	3-1	4-0	5-1 2-0
Gombak United	33	13	9	11	54	40	48	1-1	0-4 1-1	1-2		2-2 2-1	0-1 1-1	0-2	1-2	2-1 1-0	5-1 5-0	3-0 2-1	6-1
Young Lions	33	13	8	12	45	54	47	2-5	2-4	1-2	2-1		0-0 0-1	0-1 2-0	1-1 0-1	0-3 2-3	2-0-1	4-1	0-0
Geylang United	33	10	9	14	43	44	39	0-2 1-3	0-3 1-2	0-2	1-1	0-1		1-1 1-1	2-1	0-0	3-1 3-0	3-2 4-0	0-1 1-1
Woodlands Wellington §6	33	10	13	10	47	52	37	0-6 1-3	3-2 2-3	2-1 0-2	0-0 1-1	2-2	0-2		2-1	1-1	3-1	1-1	4-0 1-0
Albirex Niigata	33	9	8	16	45	49	35	3-5	1-2	1-2	1-2 2-1	0-1	1-1 1-2	3-2 1-1		1-1 1-1	0-1 2-0	1-3 4-0	1-1
Balestier Khalsa	33	7	8	18	44	63	29	2-4 1-5	1-3 2-3	1-3 1-4	1-3	1-2	2-1 3-4	1-1 2-2	1-2		0-1	0-0 1-1	2-0
Liaoning Guangyuan	33	8	5	20	33	63	29	1-4	1-2 0-2	0-3 2-3	1-0	1-1	2-0	2-0 0-2	0-0	2-3 1-2		0-2 3-3	0-0
Senkang Punggol	33	5	10	18	39	69	25	1-1 0-3	0-1 2-5	0-2 2-4	3-1	3-3 2-2	2-1	2-3 1-1	0-1	1-2	0-1		1-1 1-0
Super Reds	33	3	9	21	24	80	18	0-1	0-3	1-1	3-1 3-1	2-1 3	0-4	1-1	0-5 2-0	2-3 2-1	4-0-0	2-1	

4/03/2007 - 22/11/2007 • † Qualified for the AFC Cup • § = points deducted • Match in bold awarded

SINGAPORE CUP 2007

First round		Quarter–finals		Semi–finals		Final	
S'pore Armed Forces	2						
Geylang United *	0	S'pore Armed Forces	4 5				
Young Lions	1	Gombak United *	2 3				
Gombak United *	2			S'pore Armed Forces	2 5		
Home United *	2			Woodlands Wellington*	1 3		
Super Reds	0	Home United *	0 1				
Liaoning Guangyuan *	3	Woodlands Wellington	1 1				
Woodlands Wellington	4					S'pore Armed Forces	4
Bangkok University	1					Tampines Rovers	3
Albirex Niigata *	0	Bangkok University	3 0				
Chonburi	2	Balestier Khalsa *	1 1				
Balestier Khalsa *	3			Bangkok University	0 1		
Senkang Punggol *	4			Tampines Rovers *	2 0		
Khmer Empire	3	Senkang Punggol	0 2				
DPMM Brunei	0	Tampines Rovers *	3 2				
Tampines Rovers *	1						

* Home Team in the first leg • † Qualified for the AFC Cup

CUP FINAL

25-11-2007

Scorers - Therdsak Chaiman [18], Mustaqim Manzur [26], Aleksandar Duric 2 [62 78] for SAF; Noh Alam Shah [6], Ridhuan Muhamad [23], Peres de Oliveira [39] for Tampines

RECENT LEAGUE AND CUP RECORD

	Championship						Cup		
Year	Champions	Pts	Runners-up	Pts	Third	Pts	Winners	Score	Runners-up
1998	Sing. Armed Forces	46	Tanjong Pagar Utd	46	Geylang United	38	Tanjong Pagar Utd	2-0	Sing. Armed Forces
1999	Home United	51	Sing. Armed Forces	49	Tanjong Pagar Utd	41	Sing. Armed Forces	3-1	Jurong
2000	Sing. Armed Forces	52	Tanjong Pagar Utd	43	Geylang United	41	Home United	1-0	Sing. Armed Forces
2001	Geylang United	76	Sing. Armed Forces	74	Home United	72	Home United	8-0	Geylang United
2002	Sing. Armed Forces	84	Home United	64	Geylang United	59	Tampines Rovers	1-0	Jurong
2003	Home United	85	Geylang United	71	Sing. Armed Forces	69	Home United	2-1	Geylang United
2004	Tampines Rovers	63	Home United	53	Young Lions	47	Tampines Rovers	4-1	Home United
2005	Tampines Rovers	57	Sing. Armed Forces	57	Woodlands Well'ton	50	Home United	3-2	Woodlands Well'ton
2006	Sing. Armed Forces	68	Tampines Rovers	57	Young Lions	52	Tampines Rovers	3-2	Chonburi
2007	Sing. Armed Forces	79	Home United	78	Tampines Rovers	77	Sing. Armed Forces	4-3	Tampines Rovers

SKN – ST KITTS AND NEVIS

NATIONAL TEAM RECORD

JULY 10TH 2006 TO JULY 12TH 2010

PL	W	D	L	F	A	%
10	3	2	5	16	16	40

FIFA/COCA-COLA WORLD RANKING

1993	1994	1995	1996	1997	1998	1999	2000	2001	2002	2003	2004	2005	2006	2007	High	
166	175	150	121	127	132	137	146	129	109	134	118	129	143	160	**108**	07/04

2007–2008												Low	
08/07	09/07	10/07	11/07	12/07	01/08	02/08	03/08	04/08	05/08	06/08	07/08	**176**	11/94
141	146	156	159	160	151	151	150	155	156	156	160		

The heroics of the St Kitts and Nevis national team in the 2006 FIFA World Cup qualifiers now seem a world away as the small Caribbean nation struggles to maintain the high standards it has set itself. The local league provides the basis for the national team, but it is a talent pool that is topped up like other Caribbean islands with pros and semi-pros born and brought up in the UK, the latest of whom to make his debut for the national team was Birmingham City's Aaron Moses-Garvey. The Sugar Boyz best known player, the 23-year old Chivas USA striker Atiba Harris, is St Kitts born and bred but none of the team were prepared for the challenge of Belize in the first round

INTERNATIONAL HONOURS

None

of the 2010 FIFA World Cup qualifiers. Going into the first leg in Guatemala City, St Kitts were the clear favourites but despite taking the lead they suffered a shock 3-1 loss and could manage no more than a draw in the return at home in Basseterre as their campaign came to a premature end. A recall for the veteran Keith Gumbs should perhaps be considered after the striker had a sensational season after his transfer to Sriwijaya in Indonesia. In January 2008 the 35-year old scored the equaliser in their Cup Final win over Persipura and then a month later scored a crucial extra-time goal in the Liga Indonesia final against PSMS Medan to secure the double for Sriwijaya.

THE FIFA BIG COUNT OF 2006

	Male	Female		Total
Number of players	3 100	400	Referees and Assistant Referees	0
Professionals	0		Admin, Coaches, Technical, Medical	100
Amateurs 18+	900		Number of clubs	30
Youth under 18	600		Number of teams	40
Unregistered	600		Clubs with women's teams	1
Total players	3 500		Players as % of population	8.94%

St Kitts and Nevis Football Association (SKNFA)

Warner Park, PO Box 465, Basseterre, St Kitts and Nevis

Tel +1 869 4668502   Fax +1 869 4659033

info@sknfa.com   www.sknfa.com

President: JENKINS Peter   General Secretary: AMORY Spencer Leonard

Vice-President: FRASER Sylvester   Treasurer: AMORY Spencer Leonard   Media Officer: None

Men's Coach: MORRIS Lester   Women's Coach: TAYLOR Lenny

SKNFA formed: 1932   CONCACAF: 1992   FIFA: 1992

Green shirts, Red shorts, Yellow socks

RECENT INTERNATIONAL MATCHES PLAYED BY ST KITTS AND NEVIS

2002	Opponents	Score		Venue	Comp	Scorers	Att	Referee
25-07	Chinese Taipei	W	3-0	Basseterre	Fr			
27-07	Barbados	W	3-0	Basseterre	Fr	Issac, Francis, Gumbs		
28-07	Trinidad and Tobago	W	2-1	Basseterre	Fr	Sargeant [49], Issac [75]	800	
29-10	Antigua and Barbuda	D	1-1	Basseterre	Fr			
13-11	St Lucia	W	2-1	Port of Spain	CCq	Isaac 2 [38 56]		Forde BRB
15-11	Trinidad and Tobago	L	0-2	Port of Spain	CCq		3 500	Faneijte ANT
2003								
29-07	Haiti	W	1-0	Basseterre	Fr	Isaac [3]		Matthew SKN
2-08	Trinidad and Tobago	L	1-2	Basseterre	Fr	Francis [50]		
2004								
1-02	Antigua and Barbuda	L	0-1	St John's	Fr			
18-02	US Virgin Islands	W	4-0	St Thomas	WCq	Huggins [26], Lake 2 [50 64], Isaac [62]	225	Brizan TRI
20-03	British Virgin Islands	W	4-0	Basseterre	Fr			
21-03	Antigua and Barbuda	L	2-3	Basseterre	Fr			
31-03	US Virgin Islands	W	7-0	Basseterre	WCq	Lake 5 [8 38 46 56 77], Isaac 2 [80 90]	800	Recinos SLV
23-05	St Vincent/Grenadines	W	3-2	Basseterre	Fr	Lake [9], Hodge [25], Willock [63]		Matthew SKN
2-06	Northern Ireland	L	0-2	Basseterre	Fr		5 000	Matthew SKN
13-06	Barbados	W	2-0	Bridgetown	WCq	Gumbs [78], Newton [88]	3 700	Alfaro SLV
19-06	Barbados	W	3-2	Basseterre	WCq	Gomez [16], Willock 2 [22 29]	3 500	Pineda HON
4-09	Trinidad and Tobago	L	1-2	Basseterre	WCq	Isaac [40]	2 800	Castillo GUA
10-09	St Vincent/Grenadines	L	0-1	Kingstown	WCq		4 000	Delgado CUB
10-10	Trinidad and Tobago	L	1-5	Marabella	WCq	Gumbs [43p]	7 000	Valenzuela USA
13-10	St Vincent/Grenadines	L	0-3	Basseterre	WCq		500	Whittaker CAY
31-10	Montserrat	W	6-1	Basseterre	CCq	Francis 3 [9 45 86], Connonier [36], Isaac [57], Hodge [83]		Bedeau GRN
2-11	St Lucia	D	1-1	Basseterre	CCq	Francis [14]		Bedeau GRN
4-11	Antigua and Barbuda	W	2-0	Basseterre	CCq	Sargeant [34], Isaac [45]		Phillip GRN
13-11	Mexico	L	0-5	Miami	WCq		18 312	Moreno PAN
17-11	Mexico	L	0-8	Monterrey	WCq		12 000	Stott USA
12-12	Haiti	L	0-1	Fort Lauderdale	CCq		2 500	McNab BAH
15-12	Haiti	L	0-2	Basseterre	CCq		1 000	Bhimull TRI
2005								
No international matches played in 2005								
2006								
20-09	Barbabdos	D	1-1	St John's	CCq	Harris [60]	300	Campbell JAM
22-09	Anguilla	W	6-1	St John's	CCq	Isaac 2 [14 68], Lake 3 [30 46 79], Francis [81]	500	Phillips GRN
24-09	Antigua and Barbuda	L	0-1	St John's	CCq		2 800	Wijngaarde SUR
2007								
18-11	Antigua and Barbuda	W	3-0	Basseterre	Fr	Francis [36], OG [43], Nurse [44]		
1-12	Antigua and Barbuda	L	0-2	St John's	Fr			
14-12	Bermuda	W	2-1	Hamilton	Fr	Francis [25], Lake [38]		
16-12	Bermuda	L	2-4	Hamilton	Fr	Ponteen [44], Charles		
2008								
6-02	Belize	L	1-3	Guatemala City	WCq	Williams [13]	500	Stennet JAM
26-03	Belize	D	1-1	Basseterre	WCq	Mitchum [84]		Brizan TRI
8-06	Antigua and Barbuda	L	0-2	St John's	Fr			

Fr = Friendly match • CC = Digicel Caribbean Cup • WC = FIFA World Cup • q = qualifier

ST KITTS AND NEVIS NATIONAL TEAM RECORDS AND RECORD SEQUENCES

Records			Sequence records					
Victory	9-1	MSR 1994	Wins	4	1996, 2002	Clean sheets	3	1991-1992
Defeat	0-8	MEX 2004	Defeats	4	2004 (Twice)	Goals scored	10	1998-99, 2001
Player Caps	131	Keith Gumbs	Undefeated	10	2001-2002	Without goal	4	2004
Player Goals	47	Keith Gumbs	Without win	5	1996	Goals against	14	1998-2000

ST KITTS AND NEVIS COUNTRY INFORMATION

Capital	Basseterre	Independence	1983 from the UK	GDP per Capita	$8 800
Population	38 836	Status	Constitutional Monarchy	GNP Ranking	177
Area km²	261	Language	English	Dialling code	+1869
Population density	148 per km²	Literacy rate	97%	Internet code	.kn
% in urban areas	42%	Main religion	Christian	GMT + / –	-4
Towns/Cities	Basseterre 12 920; Charlestown 1 538; Saint Paul's 1 483; Sadlers 986; Middle Island 887				
Neighbours (km)	Caribbean Sea 135				
Main stadia	Warner Park – Basseterre 6 000				

ST KITTS 2007–08
PREMIER DIVISION

	Pl	W	D	L	F	A	Pts
Newtown United †	16	12	1	3	36	13	37
Village Superstars †	16	10	3	3	36	15	33
Garden Hotspurs †	16	10	1	5	34	14	31
Washington Archibald†	16	9	4	3	27	13	31
St Pauls United	16	9	4	3	23	12	31
Conaree United	16	6	5	5	18	17	23
St Thomas Strikers	16	2	2	12	10	37	8
St Peters Strikers	16	2	1	13	9	35	7
Mantab United	16	0	3	13	6	43	3

21/10/2007 - 27/04/2008 • † Qualified for play-offs

ST KITTS 2007–08
PREMIER DIVISION SUPER FOUR

	Pl	W	D	L	F	A	Pts
Newtown United †	3	2	1	0	3	0	7
Village Superstars †	3	1	1	1	2	2	4
Garden Hotspurs	3	0	3	0	2	2	3
Washington Archibald	3	0	1	2	1	4	1

4/05/2008 - 11/05/2008 • † Qualified for the final

ST KITTS 2007–08
PREMIER DIVISION FINAL

Champions	Score	Runners-up
Newtown United	0-0 3-2	Village Superstars

RECENT LEAGUE AND CUP RECORD

	Championship				Cup		
Year	Champions	Score	Runners-up		Winners	Score	Runners-up
1998	Newtown United						
1999	St Paul's United	3-0 0-1 4-2	Garden Hotspurs				
2000	No tournament due to season adjustment						
2001	Garden Hotspurs	3-0 0-0 3-4p 1-0	Village Superstars				
2002	Cayon Rockets	0-0 3-2p 3-0	Garden Hotspurs		Cayon Rockets		
2003	Village Superstars	0-1 2-1 0-0 5-4p	Newtown United		Village Superstars	1-0	Newtown United
2004	Newtown United	0-1 1-0 2-0	Village Superstars		Village Superstars	3-1	Cayon Rockets
2005	Village Superstars	1-0 2-1	St Peter's				
2006	Village Superstars	3-1 3-0	St Paul's United				
2007	Newtown United	0-1 4-1 2-0	Village Superstars		Newtown United	0-1 †	Village Superstars
2008	Newtown United	0-0 3-2	Village Superstars				

† Cup awarded to Newtown after Superstars fielded an ineligible player

SLE – SIERRA LEONE

NATIONAL TEAM RECORD
JULY 10TH 2006 TO JULY 12TH 2010

PL	W	D	L	F	A	%
15	2	3	10	5	24	23.3

FIFA/COCA-COLA WORLD RANKING

1993	1994	1995	1996	1997	1998	1999	2000	2001	2002	2003	2004	2005	2006	2007	High	
76	76	58	84	84	111	120	129	138	133	146	160	163	148	156	**51**	01/96

2007–2008												Low	
08/07	09/07	10/07	11/07	12/07	01/08	02/08	03/08	04/08	05/08	06/08	07/08	**172**	09/07
164	172	155	155	156	159	159	161	162	166	163	137		

The fortunes of Sierra Leone have plummeted to such an extent that the national team was among the lowest ranked on the continent in the middle of 2007 and was forced to participate in a two-legged play-off before gaining a spot in the group phase of the FIFA World Cup qualifiers - a marked contrast from a decade previously when they played at the Nations Cup finals. The 'Leone Star' battled to overcome Guinea Bissau in their preliminary round tie in October and November 2007, winning by a slim 1-0 aggregate scoreline. They were also far from convincing at the Amilcar Cabral Cup in Bissau soon after. Following defeats in their first two matches in their

INTERNATIONAL HONOURS
Copa Amilcar Cabral 1993 1995

World Cup qualifying group, Sierra Leone then stunned South Africa by beating them in Freetown and then drawing with them a week later in South Africa. The haul of four points means there is a remote chance of progress to the final round of qualifiers in 2009. The former Inter Milan striker Mohamed Kallon continues to be the pin-up boy of the country's' football and captain of the national team. But he is a shadow of the player who previously competed in Serie A although he is seeking to restore his career at AEK Athens. Former international Ahmed Kanu took over as coach in January 2008 and the results against South Africa have made him something of a local hero.

THE FIFA BIG COUNT OF 2006

	Male	Female		Total
Number of players	247 240	12 390	Referees and Assistant Referees	263
Professionals	0		Admin, Coaches, Technical, Medical	2 200
Amateurs 18+	840		Number of clubs	24
Youth under 18	5 640		Number of teams	196
Unregistered	15 150		Clubs with women's teams	0
Total players	259 630		Players as % of population	4.32%

Sierra Leone Football Association (SLFA)
21 Battery Street, Kingtom, PO Box 672, Freetown, Sierra Leone
Tel +232 22 240071   Fax +232 22 241339
Starssierra@yahoo.com   www.slfa.tk
President: KHADI Nahim   General Secretary: BAH Alimu
Vice-President: BANGURA Bassie   Treasurer: TBD   Media Officer: none
Men's Coach: KANU Ahmed   Women's Coach: MOSES Kargbo
SLFA formed: 1967   CAF: 1967   FIFA: 1967
Green shirts, Green shorts, Green socks

RECENT INTERNATIONAL MATCHES PLAYED BY SIERRA LEONE

2004	Opponents	Score	Venue	Comp	Scorers	Att	Referee
No international matches played in 2004							
2005							
12-06	Gambia	W 1-0	Freetown	Fr	Kpaka 56		
20-11	Guinea-Bissau	D 1-1	Conakry	ACr1	Moustapha Bangoura 49		
22-11	Guinea	L 0-1	Conakry	ACr1			
2006							
3-09	Mali	D 0-0	Freetown	CNq			Mbera GAB
8-10	Benin	L 0-2	Cotonou	CNq			Sowe GAM
2007							
24-03	Togo	L 1-3	Lomé	CNq	Gibrilla Woobay 77		Pare BFA
3-06	Togo	L 0-1	Freetown	CNq			Imiere NGA
17-06	Mali	L 0-6	Bamako	CNq			Lemghambodj MTN
12-10	Benin	L 0-2	Freetown	CNq			Ambaya LBY
17-10	Guinea-Bissau	W 1-0	Freetown	WCq	Kewullay Conteh 17	25 000	Mana NGA
17-11	Guinea-Bissau	D 0-0	Bissau	WCq		12 000	Lamptey GHA
2-12	Guinea-Bissau	L 0-2	Bissau	ACr1			
23-12	Gambia	L 1-2	Bakau	Fr	Alex Sesay 87		
2008							
30-04	Liberia	L 1-3	Paynesville	Fr	Kemokai Kallon 65		
1-06	Equatorial Guinea	L 0-2	Malabo	WCq		13 000	Codjia BEN
7-06	Nigeria	L 0-1	Freetown	WCq		25 000	Korti LBR
14-06	South Africa	W 1-0	Freetown	WCq	Mohammed Kallon 21p	15 000	Pare BFA
21-06	South Africa	D 0-0	Atteridgeville	WCq		12 000	Evehe CMR

Fr = Friendly match • CN = CAF African Cup of Nations • AC = Amilcar Cabral Cup • WC = FIFA World Cup • q = qualifier

SIERRA LEONE NATIONAL TEAM RECORDS AND RECORD SEQUENCES

Records			Sequence records					
Victory	5-1	NIG 1976, NIG 1995	Wins	4	1986	Clean sheets	5	1984, 1991-92
Defeat	0-6	MLI 2007	Defeats	6	1982-83, 1996	Goals scored	11	1985-1987
Player Caps	n/a		Undefeated	14	1991-1993	Without goal	6	1982-83, 1996
Player Goals	n/a		Without win	9	1971-1973	Goals against	19	1976-1983

RECENT LEAGUE AND CUP RECORD

	Championship	Cup
Year	Champions	Winners
1997	East End Lions	
1998	Mighty Blackpool	
1999	East End Lions	
2000	Mighty Blackpool	Mighty Blackpool
2001	Mighty Blackpool	Old Edwardians
2002	No tournament	No tournament
2003	No tournament	
2004	No tournament	
2005	East End Lions	
2006	FC Kallon	
2007	No tournament	FC Kallon
2008	Ports Authority	

SIERRA LEONE COUNTRY INFORMATION

Capital	Freetown	Independence	1961 from UK	GDP per Capita	$500
Population	5 883 889	Status	Republic	GNP Ranking	160
Area km²	71 740	Language	English, Mende, Krio	Dialling code	+232
Population density	82 per km²	Literacy rate	31%	Internet code	.sl
% in urban areas	36%	Main religion	Muslim 60%	GMT +/–	0
Towns/Cities ('000)	Freetown 1 190; Koidu 111; Bo 80; Kenema 70; Makeni 54; Lunsar 21; Waterloo 21				
Neighbours (km)	Guinea 652; Liberia 306; North Atlantic Ocean 402				
Main stadia	National Stadium – Freetown 36 000				

SLV - EL SALVADOR

NATIONAL TEAM RECORD
JULY 10TH 2006 TO JULY 12TH 2010

PL	W	D	L	F	A	%
31	8	8	15	34	40	38.7

FIFA/COCA-COLA WORLD RANKING

1993	1994	1995	1996	1997	1998	1999	2000	2001	2002	2003	2004	2005	2006	2007	High	
66	80	82	65	64	92	96	83	86	94	95	106	124	156	134	**50**	12/92

2007–2008												Low	
08/07	09/07	10/07	11/07	12/07	01/08	02/08	03/08	04/08	05/08	06/08	07/08	**169**	11/06
138	137	141	141	134	135	127	128	126	124	120	117		

Although the El Salvador national team had shown some improvement in the wake of their poor showing in the 2007 CONCACAF Gold Cup and their disasterous run of results leading up to it, an extraordinary 20-minute period during their 2010 FIFA World Cup qualifier against Panama could well signal a sea-change in the fortunes of the side. Such was the lowly status of the team that El Salvador were forced to take part in a first round tie in the CONCACAF qualifiers against tiny Anguilla. That was predictably won 16-0 on aggregate setting up a tie against Panama in a second preliminary round. With just 20 minutes to go in the second leg, El Salvador

INTERNATIONAL HONOURS
Qualified for the FIFA World Cup finals 1970 1982 Central American Championship 1943   Central American and Caribbean Games 1954 2002
CONCACAF Champions Cup   Alianza 1967 Aguila 1976 Deportivo FAS 1979

were 2-0 down on aggregate and heading out of the World Cup but in a fantastic fight back, two goals from Eliseo Quintanilla and a third through Luis Anaya saw the Salvadorians through to the group stage. At home Luis Angel Firpo won both the Apertura and the Clausura and were seeded through to the group stage of the inaugural CONCACAF Champions League, a tournament which it is hoped will help raise standards in the country thanks to the increased exposure of Salvadorian clubs to teams from the USA and Mexico.

THE FIFA BIG COUNT OF 2006

	Male	Female		Total
Number of players	401 040	58 652	Referees and Assistant Referees	315
Professionals	200		Admin, Coaches, Technical, Medical	5 538
Amateurs 18+	21 404		Number of clubs	68
Youth under 18	24 108		Number of teams	2 828
Unregistered	225 900		Clubs with women's teams	2
Total players	459 692		Players as % of population	6.74%

Federacion Salvadorena de Futbol (FESFUT)
Avenida José Matias Delgado, Frente al Centro Español, Colonia Escalón, Zona 10, San Salvador CA 1029, El Salvador
Tel +503 22096200   Fax +503 22637528
rcalvofesfut@org.sv   www.fesfut.org.sv
President: CALVO Rodrigo   General Secretary: MEDINA Jose Rene
Vice-President: TORRES Jose Humberto   Treasurer: DIAZ Mario   Media Officer: LOPEZ Eduardo Alegria
Men's Coach: DE LOS COBOS Carlos   Women's Coach: RAMOS Julio Cesar
FESFUT formed: 1935   CONCACAF: 1961   FIFA: 1938
Blue shirts with white trimmings, Blue shorts, Blue socks

RECENT INTERNATIONAL MATCHES PLAYED BY EL SALVADOR

2004	Opponents	Score		Venue	Comp	Scorers	Att	Referee
3-08	Honduras	L	0-4	San Salvador	Fr			Aguilar Chicas SLV
6-08	Guatemala	L	0-2	Washington DC	Fr		20 000	Valenzuela USA
18-08	Panama	W	2-1	San Salvador	WCq	Velásquez [7], Rodriguez.J [45]	11 400	Navarro CAN
4-09	USA	L	0-2	Boston	WCq		25 266	Brizan TRI
8-09	Jamaica	L	0-3	San Salvador	WCq		25 000	Alcala MEX
9-10	USA	L	0-2	San Salvador	WCq		20 000	Batres GUA
13-10	Jamaica	D	0-0	Kingston	WCq		12 000	Quesada Cordero CRC
17-11	Panama	L	0-3	Panama City	WCq		9 502	Archundia MEX
2005								
19-02	Panama	L	0-1	Guatemala City	UCr1		10 000	Archundia MEX
21-02	Costa Rica	L	1-2	Guatemala City	UCr1	Alas [40]	3 000	Batres GUA
17-08	Paraguay	L	0-3	Ciudad del Este	Fr		12 000	
2006								
6-09	Honduras	L	0-2	Tegucigalpa	Fr		7 000	Zelaya HON
7-10	Panama	L	0-1	Panama City	Fr			Moreno PAN
15-11	Bolivia	L	1-5	La Paz	Fr	Erazo [52]	25 000	
29-11	Panama	D	0-0	San Salvador	Fr			
2007								
8-02	Belize	W	2-1	San Salvador	UCr1	Díaz.J [25], Quintanilla [55]		Quesada CRC
10-02	Nicaragua	W	2-1	San Salvador	UCr1	Quintanilla 2 [16 64p]		Arredondo MEX
12-02	Guatemala	D	0-0	San Salvador	UCr1			Archundia MEX
16-02	Costa Rica	L	0-2	San Salvador	UCsf			Archundia MEX
18-02	Guatemala	L	0-1	San Salvador	UC3p			Quesada CRC
24-03	Honduras	L	0-2	Fort Lauderdale	Fr		17 095	Marrufo USA
27-03	Honduras	L	0-2	Cary	Fr		8 365	
17-04	Haiti	L	0-1	San Salvador	Fr			
7-06	Trinidad and Tobago	W	2-1	Carson	GCr1	Sánchez.R [38], Alas [81]	21 334	Arredondo MEX
9-06	Guatemala	L	0-1	Carson	GCr1		27 000	Jauregui ATG
12-06	USA	L	0-4	Foxboro	GCr1		26 523	Archundia MEX
22-08	Honduras	W	2-0	San Salvador	Fr	Anaya [26], Merino [40]		Bonilla SLV
8-09	Ecuador	L	1-5	Quito	Fr	Quintanilla [36]		Carillo PER
13-10	Costa Rica	D	2-2	San Salvador	Fr	Quintanilla [60], Martin [87]		Rivera SLV
17-10	Trinidad and Tobago	D	0-0	San Salvador	Fr		13 000	Bonilla SLV
18-11	Jamaica	L	0-3	Kingston	Fr		15 000	Whittaker CAY
2008								
22-01	Belize	W	1-0	San Ignacio	Fr	Pacheco [22]		
26-01	Haiti	D	0-0	Port au Prince	Fr			
29-01	Haiti	D	0-0	St Marc	Fr			
6-02	Anguilla	W	12-0	San Salvador	WCq	Martin 2 [5 18], Corrales 5 [31 33 54 65 68], Cerritos 3 [47 77 84], Quintanilla [70], Umana [80]	15 000	Jauregui ANT
19-03	Trinidad and Tobago	L	0-1	Macoya	Fr			
23-03	Venezuela	L	0-1	Puerto Ordaz	Fr			
26-03	Anguilla	W	4-0	Washington DC	WCq	Cerritos [8], Corrales [15], Monteagudo [23], Torres [35]	22 670	Bedeau GRN
23-04	China PR	D	2-2	Los Angeles	Fr	Corrales 2 [39 46]		
30-05	Guatemala	D	0-0	Washington DC	Fr		38 759	
15-06	Panama	L	0-1	Panama City	WCq		22 150	Wijngaarde SUR
22-06	Panama	W	3-1	San Salvador	WCq	Quintanilla 2 [70 81p], Anaya [88]	27 420	Rodriguez MEX

Fr = Friendly match • UC = UNCAF Cup • GC = CONCACAF Gold Cup • WC = FIFA World Cup • q = qualifier

EL SALVADOR NATIONAL TEAM RECORDS AND RECORD SEQUENCES

Records			Sequence records					
Victory	9-0	NCA 1929	Wins	5	1967-1968	Clean sheets	5	1981-1982
Defeat	0-8	MEX 1988	Defeats	7	1989, 2004-06	Goals scored	11	1999-2000
Player Caps	89	Luis Guevara Mora	Undefeated	10	1981-1982	Without goal	6	Three times
Player Goals	41	Jorge González	Without win	12	2004-2006	Goals against	18	1930-1941

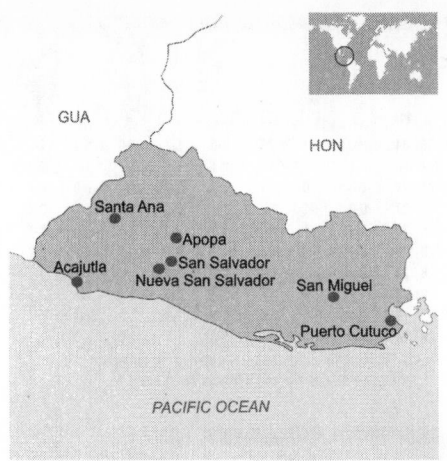

GUA

HON

Santa Ana

●Apopa
Acajutla ●San Salvador
Nueva San Salvador San Miguel

Puerto Cutuco

PACIFIC OCEAN

MAJOR CITIES/TOWNS
Population '000

1	San Salvador	1 912
2	Santa Ana	186
3	San Miguel	171
4	Sonsonate	62
5	Usulután	54
6	Cojutepeque	50
7	San Martín	47
8	Zacatecoluca	41
9	San Vicente	39
10	Quezaltepeque	37
11	Ahuachapán	35
12	Chalchuapa	35
13	La Unión	28
14	Acajutla	27
15	Aguilares	25
16	Izalco	22
17	La Libertad	21
18	San Rafael	21
19	Sensuntepeque	21
20	Metapán	21
21	Ilobasco	20
22	Chalatenango	20
23	Gotera	16
24	Nejapa	6

REPUBLIC OF EL SALVADOR; REPUBLICA DE EL SALVADOR

Capital	San Salvador	Language	Spanish			Independence	1841	
Population	6 948 073	Area	21 040 km²	Density	313 per km²	% in cities	45%	
GDP per cap	$4800	Dailling code	+503	Internet	.sv	GMT + / -	-6	

MEDALS TABLE

		Overall			Lge		Cup		Cent Am				Town/City	Stadium	Cap'ty	DoF
		G	S	B	G	B	G	S	G	S	B					
1	Deportivo FAS	17	17		16	17			1				Santa Ana	Oscar Quiteño	15 000	1947
2	CD Aguila	16	8		14	7	1	1	1				San Miguel	Juan Francisco Barraza	10 000	1926
3	CD Luis Angel Firpo	9	11		9	10		1					Usulután	Sergio Torres	5 000	1923
4	Alianza FC	9	8	2	8	8			1		2		San Salvador	Cuscatlán	40 360	1958
5	CD Atlético Marte	8	1		8					1			San Salvador	Jorge Magico Gonzalez	25 000	1953
6	Once Municipal	3	4		2	4	1						Ahuachapán	Simeón Magaña	5 000	1945
7	Hércules	3			3								San Salvador			
8	Juventud Olimpica	2	3		2	3							San Salvador			
9	CD Dragon	2	2		2	2							San Miguel	Juan Francisco Barraza	10 000	1939
10	CD 33	2			2								San Salvador			
	Quequeisque	2			2								La Libertad			
12	CD Atlético Balboa	1	1		1		1						La Unión	Marcelino Imbers	4 000	1950
	Chacarita Juniors (Chinameca)	1	1		1	1							San Miguel	Municipal		1914
	AD Isidro Metapán	1	1		1	1							Metapán	Jorge El Calero Suárez	5 000	2000
	Libertad FC	1	1										San Salvador			
	San Salvador FC	1	1		1	1							San Salvador	Cuscatlán	40 360	2002
	CD Santiagueño	1	1		1	1							Santiago			
18	CD Platense Municipal	1			1								Zacatecoluca	Antonio Toledo Valle		1951
	CD Vista Hermosa	1			1								Gotera	Luis Amilcar Moreno	2 000	1999

RECENT LEAGUE AND CUP RECORD

Championship/Clausura from 2000					Apertura			
Year	Champions	Score	Runners-up		Winners	Score	Runners-up	
1997	Alianza	0-0 3-2	Luis Angel Firpo					
1998	Luis Angel Firpo	2-0	Deportivo FAS					
1999	Luis Angel Firpo	1-1 5-4p	Deportivo FAS		Aguila	1-0	Municipal Limeño	
2000	Luis Angel Firpo	1-1 10-9p	AD El Tránsito		Aguila	3-2	Municipal Limeño	
2001	Aguila	1-1 2-1	Deportivo FAS		Alianza	2-1	Luis Angel Firpo	
2002	Deportivo FAS	4-0	Alianza		Deportivo FAS	3-1	San Salvador	
2003	San Salvador	3-1	Luis Angel Firpo		Deportivo FAS	2-2 5-3p	Aguila	
2004	Alianza	1-1 3-2p	Deportivo FAS		Deportivo FAS	0-0 4-3p	Atlético Balboa	
2005	Deportivo FAS	3-1	Luis Angel Firpo		Vista Hermosa	2-0	Isidro-Metapán	
2006	Aguila	4-2	Deportivo FAS		Once Municipal	3-1	Deportivo FAS	
2007	Isidro-Metapán	1-0	LA Firpo		Luis Angel Firpo	1-1 5-3p	Deportivo FAS	
2008	Luis Angel Firpo	1-0	Deportivo FAS					

EL SALVADOR 2007-08

PRIMERA DIVISION PROFESIONAL — TORNEO APERTURA

	Pl	W	D	L	F	A	Pts	Ch'tenango	FAS	I-Metapán	LA Firpo	V. Hermosa	Aguila	Alianza	Nejapa	S. Salvador	Municipal
CD Chalatenango †	18	10	4	4	29	16	34		0-1	2-1	2-0	1-1	1-0	5-1	4-2	2-1	2-0
Deportivo FAS †	18	9	3	6	27	21	30	0-1		4-2	2-1	3-0	3-1	1-0	0-1	1-1	2-0
CD Isidro-Metapán †	18	8	5	5	31	24	29	1-0	2-0		1-1	3-0	2-0	0-0	4-2	6-0	1-0
Luis Angel Firpo †	18	7	6	5	23	17	27	0-0	3-1	0-0		2-0	1-1	5-1	2-2	1-0	1-0
Vista Hermosa	18	8	3	7	24	25	27	1-1	2-1	4-2	0-1		0-1	1-0	2-1	2-2	2-0
CD Aguila	18	7	4	7	23	20	25	0-1	3-2	2-2	1-1	1-0		2-1	2-2	3-0	2-0
Alianza	18	6	6	6	26	28	24	2-2	1-1	3-0	2-1	2-2	1-0		3-1	4-2	2-0
Nejapa	18	5	7	6	31	34	22	4-2	1-1	4-1	3-1	2-1	0-4	2-2		2-2	0-0
San Salvador	18	3	6	9	20	35	15	1-0	2-3	2-2	0-2	1-3	2-0	1-1	1-1		2-1
Once Municipal	18	4	2	12	8	22	14	0-3	0-1	0-1	1-0	1-2	1-0	2-0	2-1	0-0	

11/08/2007 - 25/11/2007 • † Qualified for the play-offs • LA Firpo beat Vista Hermosa 3-0 in a play-off for fourth place
Top scorers: William Enrique Reyes, Isidro-Metapán 11; Francisco Jovel Alvarez, Alianza 11; Nicolás Muñoz, Aguila 8

APERTURA PLAY-OFFS

Semi-finals			Finals		
Luis Angel Firpo *	2	0			
CD Chalatenango	0	1	Luis Angel Firpo	1	5p
CD Isidro-Metapán *	0	1	Deportivo FAS	1	3p
Deportivo FAS	0	1	* At home in the first leg		

CHAMPIONSHIP FINAL

Luis Angel Firpo 1-1 5-3p Deportivo FAS
Estadio Cuscatlán, San Salvador, 15-12-2007
Scorers - Patricio Barroche [41] for LA Firpo; Alfredo Pacheco [80] for FAS

EL SALVADOR 2007-08

PRIMERA DIVISION PROFESIONAL — TORNEO CLAUSURA

	Pl	W	D	L	F	A	Pts	LA Firpo	I-Metapán	FAS	V. Hermosa	Ch'tenango	Alianza	Aguila	Nejapa	Municipal	S. Salvador
Luis Angel Firpo †	18	8	8	2	29	15	32		2-1	3-1	3-1	1-1	1-0	2-1	2-4	2-0	5-0
CD Isidro-Metapán †	18	8	8	2	39	27	32	3-2		1-1	3-3	2-1	3-1	2-1	2-0		4-0
Deportivo FAS †	18	8	6	4	26	21	30	1-1	2-2		2-0	3-2	3-2	3-2	1-1	0-0	1-0
Vista Hermosa †	18	6	6	4	20	15	30	0-1	0-0	0-0		2-1	2-0	2-0	3-0	2-2	1-0
CD Chalatenango	18	6	7	5	29	25	25	1-1	1-1	2-1	1-0		1-2	2-2	3-0	1-0	2-2
Alianza	18	5	7	6	20	18	22	1-1	0-0	0-0	4-0	1-2		2-1	0-0	1-1	3-1
CD Aguila	18	5	6	7	25	32	21	1-4	3-3	0-3	1-1	2-1	0-0		2-0	1-1	1-1
Nejapa	18	4	7	7	20	26	19	1-1	2-2	2-2	1-2	1-3	2-1	4-1		1-1	1-1
Once Municipal	18	1	9	8	11	24	12	0-0	2-5	0-1	0-2	1-1	0-0	0-2	1-2		1-0
San Salvador	18	2	6	10	14	30	12	0-0	4-3	2-0	0-1	2-2	0-1	0-1	0-2	1-1	

9/02/2008 - 17/05/2008 • † Qualified for the play-offs • Municipal relegated • Relegation play-off: **Independiente** 1-1 3-1 San Salvador
Top scorer: William Enrique Reyes, Isidro-Metapán 14; Patricio Barroche, LA Firpo 13; Juan Carlos Reyes, Nejapa 9

CLAUSURA PLAY-OFFS

Semi-finals			Finals	
Luis Angel Firpo	0	3		
Vista Hermosa *	1	0	Luis Angel Firpo	1
CD Isidro-Metapán	0	2	Deportivo FAS	0
Deportivo FAS *	3	0	* At home in the first leg	

CHAMPIONSHIP FINAL

Luis Angel Firpo 1-0 Deportivo FAS
Estadio Cuscatlán, San Salvador, 1-06-2008
Scorer - Guillermo Moran [118] for LA Firpo

SMR – SAN MARINO

NATIONAL TEAM RECORD
JULY 10TH 2006 TO JULY 12TH 2010

PL	W	D	L	F	A	%
13	0	0	13	2	60	0

FIFA/COCA-COLA WORLD RANKING

1993	1994	1995	1996	1997	1998	1999	2000	2001	2002	2003	2004	2005	2006	2007	High
121	131	951	165	173	179	150	168	158	160	162	164	155	194	197	**118** 09/03

2007–2008												Low
08/07	09/07	10/07	11/07	12/07	01/08	02/08	03/08	04/08	05/08	06/08	07/08	**200** 05/08
195	196	196	197	197	197	198	198	199	200	199	199	

2007 marked another milestone in the history of football in San Marino when Murata became the first club from the country to take part in the UEFA Champions League. They were drawn against Tampere United in a first round preliminary tie and with the veteran Brazilian Aldair - a World Cup winner in 1994 - and Serie A veteran Massimo Agostini in the team, Murata even managed to take the lead against Tampere in the first leg at home although they eventually lost 4-1 on aggregate. The lure of the Champions League saw Murata make a cheeky bid for both Romario and former racing driver Michael Schumacher to take part in the 2008–09 tournament, having qualified by

INTERNATIONAL HONOURS
None

winning the championship for the third year running. In the final they beat Juvenes/Dogana 1-0, a score they repeated against the same opponents in the Cup Final, a result which ensured they won the double for the second year in a row. San Marino's other representatives in Europe, Libertas, managed a draw against Ireland's Drogheda United before losing the return but there was no such success for the national team which lost its 23rd match in a row when beaten by Slovakia in the final qualifying match for Euro 2008. The campaign saw San Marino drop to the very bottom of the FIFA/Coca-Cola World Ranking, along with the likes of the Cook Islands and Montserrat.

THE FIFA BIG COUNT OF 2006

	Male	Female		Total
Number of players	2 421	415	Referees and Assistant Referees	35
Professionals	0		Admin, Coaches, Technical, Medical	225
Amateurs 18+	763		Number of clubs	16
Youth under 18	823		Number of teams	56
Unregistered	650		Clubs with women's teams	1
Total players	2 836		Players as % of population	9.70%

Federazione Sammarinese Giuoco Calcio (FSGC)
Viale Campo dei Giudei 14, Rep. San Marino 47890
Tel +378 054 9990515   Fax +378 054 9992348
fsgc@omniway.sm   www.fsgc.sm
President: CRESCENTINI Giorgio   General Secretary: CASADEI Luciano
Vice-President: CECCOLI Pier Luigi   Treasurer: GUIDI Joseph   Media Officer: FELICI Elisa
Men's Coach: MAZZA Gianpaolo   Women's Coach: none
FSGC formed: 1931   UEFA: 1988   FIFA: 1988
Light blue shirts with white trimmings, Light blue shorts, Light blue socks or White shirts, White shorts, White socks

RECENT INTERNATIONAL MATCHES PLAYED BY SAN MARINO

2003 Opponents	Score	Venue	Comp	Scorers	Att	Referee
2-04 Poland	L 0-5	Ostrowiec	ECq		8 500	Loizou CYP
30-04 Latvia	L 0-3	Riga	ECq		7 500	Byrne IRE
7-06 Sweden	L 0-6	Serravalle	ECq		2 184	Delevic SCG
11-06 Hungary	L 0-5	Serravalle	ECq		1 410	Clark SCO
20-08 Liechtenstein	D 2-2	Vaduz	Fr	Alex Gasperoni 39, Nicola Ciacci 45	850	Wildhaber SUI
6-09 Sweden	L 0-5	Gothenburg	ECq		31 098	Messner AUT
2004						
28-04 Liechtenstein	W 1-0	Serravalle	Fr	Andy Selva 5	700	Sammut MLT
4-09 Serbia & Montenegro	L 0-3	Serravalle	WCq		1 137	Kholmatov KAZ
8-09 Lithuania	L 0-4	Kaunas	WCq		4 000	Jareci ALB
13-10 Serbia & Montenegro	L 0-5	Belgrade	WCq		4 000	Isaksen FRO
17-11 Lithuania	L 0-1	Serravalle	WCq		1 457	Nalbandyan ARM
2005						
9-02 Spain	L 0-5	Almeria	WCq		12 580	Clark SCO
30-03 Belgium	L 1-2	Serravalle	WCq	Andy Selva 41	871	Kasnaferis GRE
4-06 Bosnia-Herzegovina	L 1-3	Serravalle	WCq	Andy Selva 39	750	Demirlek TUR
7-09 Belgium	L 0-8	Antwerp	WCq		8 207	Stokes IRL
8-10 Bosnia-Herzegovina	L 0-3	Zenica	WCq		8 500	Hamer LUX
12-10 Spain	L 0-6	Serravalle	WCq		3 426	Meyer GER
2006						
16-08 Albania	L 0-3	Serravalle	Fr			
6-09 Germany	L 0-13	Serravalle	ECq		5 090	Dereli TUR
7-10 Czech Republic	L 0-7	Liberec	ECq		9 514	Aliyev AZE
15-11 Republic of Ireland	L 0-5	Dublin	ECq		34 018	Isaksen FRO
2007						
7-02 Republic of Ireland	L 1-2	Serravalle	ECq	Manuel Marani 86	3 294	Rasmussen DEN
28-03 Wales	L 0-3	Cardiff	ECq		18 752	Tchagharyan ARM
2-06 Germany	L 0-6	Nuremberg	ECq		43 967	Asumaa FIN
22-08 Cyprus	L 0-1	Serravalle	ECq		552	Janku ALB
8-09 Czech Republic	L 0-3	Serravalle	ECq		3 412	Filipovic SRB
12-09 Cyprus	L 0-3	Nicosia	ECq		1 000	Kulbakov BLR
13-10 Slovakia	L 0-7	Dubnica n. Vahom	ECq		2 576	Wilmes LUX
17-10 Wales	L 1-2	Serravalle	ECq	Andy Selva 73	1 182	Zammit MLT
21-11 Slovakia	L 0-5	Serravalle	ECq		538	Sipailo LVA
2008						

No international matches played in 2008 before August

Fr = Friendly match • EC = UEFA EURO 2004/2008 • WC = FIFA World Cup • q = qualifier

SAN MARINO NATIONAL TEAM RECORDS AND RECORD SEQUENCES

Records			Sequence records					
Victory	1-0	LIE 2004	Wins	1	2004	Clean sheets	1	1993, 2004
Defeat	0-13	GER 2006	Defeats	36	1993-2001	Goals scored	2	2005
Player Caps	48	Gennari / F.Gasperoni	Undefeated	1	Four times	Without goal	10	1995-1998
Player Goals	7	Andy Selva	Without win	68	1986-2004	Goals against	50	1993-2003

SAN MARINO COUNTRY INFORMATION

Capital	San Marino	Formation	301	GDP per Capita	$34 600
Population	28 503	Status	Republic	GNP Ranking	185
Area km²	61	Language	Italian	Dialling code	+378
Population density	467 per km²	Literacy rate	96%	Internet code	.sm
% in urban areas	94%	Main religion	Christian	GMT +/-	+1
Towns/Cities	Serravalle 9 258; Borgo Maggiore 6 627; San Marino 4 598; Domagnano 2 724; Fiorentino 2 082				
Neighbours (km)	Italy 39				
Main stadia	Stadio Olimpico – Serravalle 2 210				

SAN MARINO 2007–08 CAMPIONATO DILETTANTI GIRONE A

	Pl	W	D	L	F	A	Pts
Tre Penne †	21	13	5	3	51	22	43
Tre Fiori †	21	10	6	5	35	26	36
Juvenes/Dogana †	21	10	6	5	31	18	36
Cailungo	21	10	6	5	37	24	36
Pennarossa	21	7	4	10	33	42	25
Folgore/Falciano	21	6	4	11	21	37	22
Domagnano	21	4	5	12	36	54	17
Fiorentino	21	1	1	19	17	60	4

22/09/2007 - 20/04/2008 • † Qualified for the play-offs

SAN MARINO 2007–08 CAMPIONATO DILETTANTI GIRONE B

	Pl	W	D	L	F	A	Pts
Murata †	20	12	7	1	46	15	43
La Fiorita †	20	12	6	2	39	24	42
Faetano †	20	11	4	5	45	18	37
Virtus	20	9	7	4	34	23	34
Cosmos	20	6	5	9	21	33	23
Libertas	20	5	6	9	27	36	21
San Giovanni	20	1	2	17	15	56	5

21/09/2007 - 19/04/2008 • † Qualified for the play-offs

CAMPIONATO DILETTANTI PLAY-OFFS

First round: **Tre Fiori** 1-0 Faetano; **Juvenes/Dogana** 0-0 4-3p La Fiorita
Second round: **Juvenes/Dogana** 5-1 Tre Penne; **Murata** 2-2 4-1p Tre Fiori
Third round: **Faetano** 2-1 Tre Penne; **Tre Fiori** 1-0 La Fiorita
Fourth round: **Murata** 2-0 Juvenes/Dogana (Murata to final; Juvenes sf)
Fifth round: **Faetano** 2-1 Tre Fiori
Semi-final: **Juvenes/Dogana** 1-0 Faetano

FINAL

Champions	Score	Runners-up
Murata	1-0	Juvenes/Dogana

CLUB DIRECTORY

Club	Lge	Cup
Cailungo	0	1
Cosmos	1	3
Dogana	0	0
Domagnano	4	3
Faetano	3	1
Folgore	3	2
Fiorentino (ex Montevito)	1	0
La Fiorita	2	2
Libertas	1	4
Murata	3	2
Pennarossa	1	2
San Giovanni	0	0
Tre Fiori	4	2
Tre Penne	0	0
Virtus	0	1

COPPA TITANO 2007–08

Quarter-finals		Semi-finals		Final	
Murata	3				
Cosmos	0	**Murata**	2		
Cailungo	1	Faetano	0		
Faetano	2				
Tre Fiori	4			**Murata**	1
Tre Penne	2	Tre Fiori	1 5p	Juvenes/Dogana	0
Libertas	1	**Juvenes/Dogana**	1 6p	Olimpico, Serravalle	
Juvenes/Dogana	2			2-05-2008	
				Scorer - Cristian Protti [20]	

RECENT LEAGUE AND CUP RECORD

	Championship				Cup		
Year	Champions	Score	Runners-up		Winners	Score	Runners-up
1991	Faetano	1-0	Tre Fiori		Libertas	2-0	Faetano
1992	Montevito	4-2	Libertas		Domagnano	1-1 4-2p	Tre Fiori
1993	Tre Fiori	2-0	Domagnano		Faetano	1-0	Libertas
1994	Tre Fiori	2-0	La Fiorita		Faetano	3-1	Folgore
1995	Tre Fiori	1-0	La Fiorita		Cosmos	0-0 3-1p	Faetano
1996	Libertas	4-1	Cosmos		Domagnano	2-0	Cosmos
1997	Folgore Falciano	2-1	La Fiorita		Murata	2-0	Virtus
1998	Folgore Falciano	2-1	Tre Fiori		Faetano	4-1	Cosmos
1999	Faetano	1-0	Folgore Falciano		Cosmos	5-1	Domagnano
2000	Folgore Falciano	3-1	Domagnano		Tre Penne	3-1	Folgore
2001	Cosmos	3-1	Folgore Falciano		Domagnano	1-0	Tre Fiori
2002	Domagnano	1-0	Cailungo		Domagnano	6-1	Cailungo
2003	Domagnano	2-1	Pennarossa		Domagnano	1-0	Pennarossa
2004	Pennarossa	2-2 4-2p	Domanano		Pennarossa	3-0	Domagnano
2005	Domagnano	2-1	Murata		Pennarossa	4-1	Tre Penne
2006	Murata	1-0	Pennarossa		Libertas	4-1	Tre Penne
2007	Murata	4-0	Tre Fiori		Murata	2-1	Libertas
2008	Murata	1-0	Juvenes/Dogana		Murata	1-0	Juvenes/Dogana

SOL – SOLOMON ISLANDS

NATIONAL TEAM RECORD
JULY 10TH 2006 TO JULY 12TH 2010

PL	W	D	L	F	A	%
8	6	0	2	27	8	75

FIFA/COCA-COLA WORLD RANKING

1993	1994	1995	1996	1997	1998	1999	2000	2001	2002	2003	2004	2005	2006	2007	High	
149	163	170	171	130	128	144	130	134	142	156	130	140	160	123	**120**	05/08

	2007–2008											Low	
08/07	09/07	10/07	11/07	12/07	01/08	02/08	03/08	04/08	05/08	06/08	07/08	**177**	08/96
161	121	120	125	123	122	122	123	120	120	127	136		

The failure of the national team to make it to the final round of the 2010 FIFA World Cup qualifiers in Oceania was a huge disappointment for a nation that believed it could get the better of New Zealand and emerge as the top team in the region. Their campaign started well at the football tournament of the South Pacific Games with a 12-1 drubbing of American Samoa. Further wins against Tonga, Vanuatu and Samoa saw the Solomans top their group to qualify for a semi-final clash against their main rivals New Caledonia. They lost that 3-2 to a goal deep into injury-time but still had the chance to qualify for the main Oceania group in the third place

INTERNATIONAL HONOURS
Melanesian Cup 1994

play-off against Vanuatu but a missed Commins Menapi penalty cost them dear as they surprisingly lost 2-0. Proof of the potential of football in the country came in the O-League in which champions Kossa qualified for the final against New Zealand's Waitakere United who boasted the Solomon's top two players - Benjamin Totori and Commins Menapi. A 3-1 victory in the first leg in Honiara saw Kossa within touching distance of the FIFA Club World Cup in Tokyo, but three goals in the last 18 minutes in the return saw them lose 5-0. At home, Koloale emerged as the team of the season, winning both the National Club Championship and the Honiara based DJ League.

THE FIFA BIG COUNT OF 2006

	Male	Female		Total
Number of players	20 880	5 940	Referees and Assistant Referees	160
Professionals	0		Admin, Coaches, Technical, Medical	400
Amateurs 18+	3 000		Number of clubs	200
Youth under 18	5 500		Number of teams	500
Unregistered	15 000		Clubs with women's teams	12
Total players	26 820		Players as % of population	4.85%

Solomon Islands Football Federation (SIFF)
Allan Boso Complex, Ranadi Highway, PO Box 854, Honiara, Solomon Islands
Tel +677 26496   Fax +677 26497
administration@siff.com.sb   www.siff.com.sb
President: ALUFURAI Martin   General Secretary: NGAVA Edward
Vice-President: RIQEO Robert   Treasurer: MAAHANUA Aloysio   Media Officer: PITUVAKA Francis
Men's Coach: ANDRIOLI Ayrton   Women's Coach: INIFIRI Timothy
SIFF formed: 1978   OFC: 1988   FIFA: 1988
Green shirts, Blue shorts, White socks

RECENT INTERNATIONAL MATCHES PLAYED BY THE SOLOMON ISLANDS

2004	Opponents	Score		Venue	Comp	Scorers	Att	Referee
10-05	Tonga	W	6-0	Honiara	WCq	Faarodo 3 [12 30 77], Maemae 2 [62 76], Samani [79]	12 385	Attison VAN
12-05	Cook Islands	W	5-0	Honiara	WCq	Waita [21], Omokirio [27], Samani [45], Maemae [70], Leo [81]	14 000	Fred VAN
15-05	New Caledonia	W	2-0	Honiara	WCq	Omokirio [10], Suri [42]	20 000	Attison VAN
19-05	Tahiti	D	1-1	Honiara	WCq	Suri [80]	18 000	Rakaroi FIJ
29-05	Vanuatu	W	1-0	Adelaide	WCq	Suri [51p]	200	Shield AUS
31-05	New Zealand	L	0-3	Adelaide	WCq		217	Iturralde Gonzalez ESP
2-06	Tahiti	W	4-0	Adelaide	WCq	Faarodo [9], Menapi 2 [14 80], Suri [42]	50	Rakaroi FIJ
4-06	Fiji	W	2-1	Adelaide	WCq	Kakai [16], Houkarawa [82]	1 500	Attison VAN
6-06	Australia	D	2-2	Adelaide	WCq	Menapi 2 [43 75]	1 500	Iturralde Gonzalez ESP
9-10	Australia	L	1-5	Honiara	OCf	Suri [60]	21 000	O'Leary NZL
12-10	Australia	L	0-6	Sydney	OCf		19 208	Rakaroi FIJ
2005								
3-09	Australia	L	0-7	Sydney	WCq		16 000	Mohd Salleh MAS
6-09	Australia	L	1-2	Honiara	WCq	Faarodo [49]	16 000	Maidin SIN
2006								
No international matches played in 2006								
2007								
13-07	Papua New Guinea	W	2-1	Honiara	Fr	Iniga, Maemae		
25-08	American Samoa	W	12-1	Apia	WCq	Totori 2 [12 15], Menapi 4 [20p 41 75 82], Faarodo [43], Waita 2 [58 85], Bebeu [69], Molea [77], Taka [92+]	300	Sosongan PNG
27-08	Tonga	W	4-0	Apia	WCq	Menapi 2 [5 12], Faarodo [51], Maemae [66]	350	Aimaasu SAM
1-09	Vanuatu	W	2-0	Apia	WCq	Bebeu [60], Faarodo [64]	1 000	Jacques TAH
3-09	Samoa	W	3-0	Apia	WCq	Totori 2 [1 37], Maemae [69]	200	Hester NZL
5-09	New Caledonia	L	2-3	Apia	WCq	Faarodo [40], Menapi [47]	600	Minan PNG
7-09	Vanuatu	L	0-2	Apia	WCq		200	Jacques TAH
2008								
No international matchesplayed in 2008 before August								

Fr = Friendly match • OC = OFC Oceania Nations Cup • SP = South Pacific Games • WC = FIFA World Cup
q = qualifier • r1 = first round group • f = final • † Not a full international

SOLOMON ISLANDS NATIONAL TEAM RECORDS AND RECORD SEQUENCES

Records		Sequence records				
Victory	16-0 COK 1995	Wins	5	1994, 2004, 2008	Clean sheets	3	Three times
Defeat	0-8 NCL 1966	Defeats	5	1992-1993	Goals scored	14	2002-2004
Player Caps	n/a	Undefeated	7	2004	Without goal	4	1989-1990
Player Goals	n/a	Without win	9	1963-1975	Goals against	21	1997-2001

RECENT LEAGUE AND CUP RECORD

	National Club Championship		Honiara League		S-League
Year	Winners	Finalist	Winners	Finalist	Champions
2003	Koloale 4-0	Auki Kingz	Koloale †	Marist	Not played
2004	Central Reales w-o	Makuru	Makuru 1-1 4-2p	Marist	Makuru
2005	Not played		Not played		Makuru
2006	Marist 1-0	Koloale	Not played		discontinued
2007	Kossa 4-3	Koloale	Makuru †	Marist	
2008	Koloale 0-0 5-4p	Makuru	Koloale 2-1	Uncles	

† Played on a league basis

SOLOMON ISLANDS COUNTRY INFORMATION

Capital	Honiara	Independence	1978 from the UK	GDP per Capita	$1 700
Population	523 617	Status	Constitutional Monarchy	GNP Ranking	180
Area km²	28 450	Language	Melanesian, English	Dialling code	+677
Population density	18 per km²	Literacy rate	n/a	Internet code	.sb
% in urban areas	17%	Main religion	Christian	GMT +/-	+11
Towns/Cities ('000)	Honiara 56; Gizo 6; Auki 4; Buala 2; Tulagi 1; Kirakira 1				
Neighbours (km)	South Pacific Ocean 5 313				
Main stadia	Lawson Tama Stadium – Honiara 10 000				

SOM – SOMALIA

NATIONAL TEAM RECORD
JULY 10TH 2006 TO JULY 12TH 2010

PL	W	D	L	F	A	%
10	0	0	10	3	31	0

FIFA/COCA-COLA WORLD RANKING

1993	1994	1995	1996	1997	1998	1999	2000	2001	2002	2003	2004	2005	2006	2007		High	
-	159	165	178	187	190	197	194	197	190	191	193	184	193	195		**158**	04/95

		2007–2008											Low	
08/07	09/07	10/07	11/07	12/07	01/08	02/08	03/08	04/08	05/08	06/08	07/08		**199**	04/00
192	194	193	194	195	195	197	196	197	197	197	197			

Somalia continued to astound with their ability to participate in international competition, fulfilling commitments in both the FIFA World Cup and East and Central African Senior Challenge Cup. It has been more than 25 years now since Mogadishu has hosted an international match and facilities are few and far between in the war-ravaged country but Somalia still sent a team to play Djibouti in the World Cup qualifiers and also to Tanzania for the regional tournament. Their 2010 FIFA World Cup qualifying tie against Djibouti was planned for two legs but Somalia, as they have had to do in the recent past, ceded their home tie, playing instead just a single match away in Djibouti,

INTERNATIONAL HONOURS
None

which they lost 1-0. The match winner came close to the end of the game. In the East African championship in Dar-es-Salaam, they lost all three group games - against Burundi, Tanzania and Kenya - but proved competitive in all the encounters. In contrast to the leaky defence they displayed in previous events, the Somalis conceded just four goals in the three matches. But they have now lost 13 successive games and kept up the ignominious record of having won just three matches over the last 30 years. FIFA are still planning to install an artificial pitch in the country as part of the 'Win in Africa with Africa' programme.

THE FIFA BIG COUNT OF 2006

	Male	Female		Total
Number of players	522 433	23 835	Referees and Assistant Referees	1 300
Professionals	3		Admin, Coaches, Technical, Medical	6 030
Amateurs 18+	12 460		Number of clubs	48
Youth under 18	13 450		Number of teams	205
Unregistered	137 400		Clubs with women's teams	8
Total players	546 268		Players as % of population	6/16%

Somali Football Federation (SFF)
DHL Mogadishu, Mogadishu BN 03040, Somalia
Tel +252 1 216199   Fax +252 1 600601
sofofed@hotmail.com   www.somff.com
President: MOHAMUD Nor   General Secretary: ARAB Abdiqani Said
Vice-President: GULED Ali Said   Treasurer: TBD   Media Officer: ISLOW Shafici
Men's Coach: TBD   Women's Coach: HUSSEIN Ali Abdule
SFF formed: 1951   CAF: 1968   FIFA: 1960
Sky blue shirts, Sky blue shorts, White socks

RECENT INTERNATIONAL MATCHES PLAYED BY SOMALIA

2003	Opponents	Score		Venue	Comp	Scorers	Att	Referee
16-11	Ghana	L	0-5	Accra	WCq		19 447	Bebou TOG
19-11	Ghana	L	0-2	Kumasi	WCq		12 000	Chaibou NIG
2004								
12-12	Uganda	L	0-2	Addis Abeba	CCr1			
14-12	Kenya	L	0-1	Addis Abeba	CCr1			
18-12	Sudan	L	0-4	Addis Abeba	CCr1			
2005								
27-11	Djibouti	W	2-1	Kigali	CCr1	Abdul Hakim 28, Mahmoud Sharki 87		
29-11	Sudan	L	1-4	Kigali	CCr1	Abdullahi Sheikh Mohamed 37		
1-12	Uganda	L	0-7	Kigali	CCr1			
5-12	Ethiopia	L	1-4	Kigali	CCr1			
2006								
27-11	Rwanda	L	0-3	Addis Abeba	CCr1			
30-11	Sudan	L	0-3	Addis Abeba	CCr1			
3-12	Uganda	L	0-2	Addis Abeba	CCr1			
21-12	Sudan	L	1-6	Beirut	ARr1	Mohammed Abdulaziz 93+		
24-12	Lebanon	L	0-4	Beirut	ARr1			
27-12	Mauritania	L	2-8	Beirut	ARr1	Abdulaziz Ali 2 26 67		
2007								
16-11	Djibouti	L	0-1	Djibouti	WCq		10 000	Abdul Rahman SUD
10-12	Burundi	L	0-1	Dar es Salaam	CCr1			
12-12	Tanzania	L	0-1	Dar es Salaam	CCr1			
14-12	Kenya	L	0-2	Dar es Salaam	CCr1			
2008								

No international matches played in 2008 before August

Fr = Friendly match • CC = CECAFA Cup • AR = Arab Cup • WC = FIFA World Cup
q = qualifier • r1 = first round group • † Not a full international

SOMALIA NATIONAL TEAM RECORDS AND RECORD SEQUENCES

Records			Sequence records		
Victory	5-2	MTN 1985	Wins	1	
Defeat	2-9	CMR 1960	Defeats	13	2005-
Player Caps	n/a		Undefeated	4	1978-1980
Player Goals	n/a		Without win	17	1995-2002

Clean sheets	1	
Goals scored	4	Six times
Without goal	8	2000-2002
Goals against	19	2003-

RECENT LEAGUE RECORD

Championship

Year	Champions
1999	No tournament
2000	Elman
2001	Elman
2002	Elman
2003	Elman
2004	
2005	
2006	Banaadir Telecom
2007	No tournament

SOMALIA COUNTRY INFORMATION

Capital	Mogadishu	Independence	1960	GDP per Capita	$500
Population	8 304 601	Status	Republic	GNP Ranking	151
Area km²	637 657	Language	Somali	Dialling code	+252
Population density	13 per km²	Literacy rate	37%	Internet code	.so
% in urban areas	26%	Main religion	Muslim	GMT +/-	+3
Towns/Cities ('000)	Mogadishu 2 590; Hargeysa 478; Marka 320; Berbera 242; Kismayo 234; Jamame 185				
Neighbours (km)	Kenya 682; Ethiopia 1 600; Djibouti 58; Gulf of Aden & Indian Ocean 3 025				
Main stadia	Mogadishu Stadium - Mogadishu 35 000				

SRB – SERBIA

NATIONAL TEAM RECORD
JULY 10TH 2006 TO JULY 12TH 2010

PL	W	D	L	F	A	%
21	7	9	5	30	21	54.8

FIFA/COCA-COLA WORLD RANKING

1993	1994	1995	1996	1997	1998	1999	2000	2001	2002	2003	2004	2005	2006	2007
-	-	-	-	-	-	-	-	-	19	41	46	47	33	27

High	
17	07/07

2007–2008											
08/07	09/07	10/07	11/07	12/07	01/08	02/08	03/08	04/08	05/08	06/08	07/08
18	22	27	30	27	27	31	31	31	31	39	35

Low	
47	12/05

It's a very rare thing indeed for a club to go through the season undefeated and still fail to win the championship, but that's exactly what happened to Red Star Belgrade who, after drawing too many of their matches, finished five points behind champions Partizan. Thanks to a defeat by Partizan in the Cup semi-final - their only reverse of the season in domestic competition - they also finished the season trophyless. Having beaten Red Star, Partizan then went on to beat FK Zemun 3-0 in the final to secure their first double for 14 years, a fantastic end to his first season in management for the former Deportivo and Chelsea player Slavisa Jokanovic, having taken over as coach during the

INTERNATIONAL HONOURS
Qualified for the FIFA World Cup finals 2006   UEFA Champions League Crvena Zvezda 1991

winter break. Once again, however, Serb clubs had torrid time in Europe with Red Star losing to Rangers in the third preliminary round of the Champions League and then finishing bottom of their UEFA Cup group. For their part Partizan were thrown out the UEFA Cup after their supporters clashed with riot police during the away match against Bosnia's Zrinjski Mostar. Too many draws in the qualifiers for Euro 2008 meant that the national team were always left chasing Poland and Portugal and the failure to qualify saw the inevitable departure of Javier Clemente at the end of the campaign with the football federation turning to Miroslav Djukic as his replacement.

THE FIFA BIG COUNT OF 2006

	Male	Female		Total
Number of players	400 800	40 882	Referees and Assistant Referees	4 284
Professionals	1 500		Admin, Coaches, Technical, Medical	9 800
Amateurs 18+	43 670		Number of clubs	2 076
Youth under 18	85 412		Number of teams	4 450
Unregistered	134 500		Clubs with women's teams	20
Total players	441 682		Players as % of population	4.70%

Football Association of Serbia (FSS)
Fudbalski savez Srbije, Terazije 35, PO Box 263, Belgrade 11000, Serbia
Tel +381 11 3234253   Fax +381 11 3233433
fsj@beotel.yu   www.fss.org.yu
President: KARADZIC Tomislav   General Secretary: LAKOVIC Zoran
Vice-President: TEOFILOVIC Predrag   Treasurer: BRDARIC Mirjana   Media Officer: BOSKOVIC Aleksandar
Men's Coach: DJUKIC Miroslav   Women's Coach: KRSTIC Perica
FSSCG formed: 1919   UEFA: 1954   FIFA: 1919
Blue shirts with white trimmings, White shorts, Red socks or White shirts with blue trimmings, White shorts, White socks

INTERNATIONAL MATCHES PLAYED BY SERBIA AND MONTENEGRO

2005	Opponents	Score		Venue	Comp	Scorers	Att	Referee
9-02	Bulgaria	D	0-0	Sofia	Fr		3 000	Guenov BUL
30-03	Spain	D	0-0	Belgrade	WCq		48 910	Busacca SUI
4-06	Belgium	D	0-0	Belgrade	WCq		16 662	Ivanov.V RUS
8-06	Italy	D	1-1	Toronto	Fr	Zigic 25	35 000	Depiero CAN
15-08	Poland	L	2-3	Kyiv	Fr	Zigic 32, Vidic 59	2 000	Orekhov UKR
17-08	Ukraine	L	1-2	Kyiv	Fr	Kezman 90		
3-09	Lithuania	W	2-0	Belgrade	WCq	Kezman 18, Ilic 74	20 203	Nielsen DEN
7-09	Spain	D	1-1	Madrid	WCq	Kezman 68	51 491	Poll ENG
8-10	Lithuania	W	2-0	Vilnius	WCq	Kezman 44, Vukic 85	1 500	Wegereef NED
12-10	Bosnia-Herzegovina	W	1-0	Belgrade	WCq	Kezman 7	46 305	Vassaras GRE
13-11	China PR	W	2-0	Nanjing	Fr	Djordjevic 50, Zigic 64	30 000	
16-11	Korea Republic	L	0-2	Seoul	Fr		40 127	
2006								
1-03	Tunisia	W	1-0	Rades/Tunis	Fr	Kezman 11	6 000	Haimoudi ALG
27-05	Uruguay	D	1-1	Belgrade	Fr	Stankovic 17	30 000	Kos SVN
11-06	Netherlands	L	0-1	Leipzig	WCr1		37 216	Merk GER
16-06	Argentina	L	0-6	Gelsenkirchen	WCr1		52 000	Rosetti ITA
21-06	Côte d'Ivoire	L	2-3	Munich	WCr1	Zigic 10, Ilic 20	66 000	Rodriguez MEX

Fr = Friendly match • WC = FIFA World Cup • q = qualifier • r1 = first round group

INTERNATIONAL MATCHES PLAYED BY SERBIA

2006	Opponents	Score		Venue	Comp	Scorers	Att	Referee
16-08	Czech Republic	W	3-1	Uherske Hradiste	Fr	Lazovic 41, Pantelic 54, Trisovic 72	8 047	Drabek AUT
2-09	Azerbaijan	W	1-0	Belgrade	ECq	Zigic 72	BDC	Kircher GER
6-09	Poland	D	1-1	Warsaw	ECq	Lazovic 71	4 918	Poll ENG
7-10	Belgium	W	1-0	Belgrade	ECq	Zigic 54	16 901	Messina ITA
11-10	Armenia	W	3-0	Belgrade	ECq	Stankovic 54p, Lazovic 62, Zigic 92+	10 987	Kasnaferis GRE
15-11	Norway	D	1-1	Belgrade	Fr	Vidic 6	15 000	Kasnaferis GRE
2007								
24-03	Kazakhstan	L	1-2	Almaty	ECq	Zigic 68	19 600	Hrinák SVK
28-03	Portugal	D	1-1	Belgrade	ECq	Jankovic 37	46 810	Layec FRA
2-06	Finland	W	2-0	Helsinki	ECq	Jankovic 3, Jovanovic 86	33 615	Mejuto Gonzalez ESP
22-08	Belgium	L	2-3	Brussels	ECq	Kuzmanovic 2 73 91+	19 202	Hauge NOR
8-09	Finland	D	0-0	Belgrade	ECq		10 530	Braamhaar NED
12-09	Portugal	D	1-1	Lisbon	ECq	Ivanovic 88	48 000	Merk GER
13-10	Armenia	D	0-0	Yerevan	ECq		7 150	Johannesson SWE
17-10	Azerbaijan	W	6-1	Baku	ECq	Tosic.D 4, Zigic 2 17 42, Jankovic 41, Jovanovic 75, Lazovic 81	3 100	Einwaller AUT
21-11	Poland	D	2-2	Belgrade	ECq	Zigic 68, Lazovic 70	3 247	Busacca SUI
24-11	Kazakhstan	W	1-0	Belgrade	ECq	Ostapenko OG 79	500	Vassaras GRE
2008								
6-02	FYR Macedonia	D	1-1	Skopje	Fr	Lazovic 43	12 000	
26-03	Ukraine	L	0-2	Odessa	Fr		8 000	Lajuks LVA
24-05	Republic of Ireland	D	1-1	Dublin	Fr	Pantelic 75	42 500	Evans WAL
28-05	Russia	L	1-2	Burghausen	Fr	Pantelic 40		
31-05	Germany	L	1-2	Gelsenkirchen	Fr	Jankovic 18	53 951	Fautrel FRA

Fr = Friendly match • EC = UEFA EURO 2008 • q = qualifier • BCD = Behind closed doors

SERBIA NATIONAL TEAM RECORDS AND RECORD SEQUENCES

Records			Sequence records					
Victory	10-0	VEN 1972	Wins	10	1978-1980	Clean sheets	7	2004-2005
Defeat	0-7	CZE, URU, CZE	Defeats	6	1931-1932	Goals scored	36	1959-1962
Player Caps	101	Savo Milosevic	Undefeated	16	1996-1998	Without goal	4	1971-72, 1977-78
Player Goals	38	Stjepan Bobek	Without win	7	2002-2003	Goals against	19	1920-1927

REPUBLIC OF SERBIA; REPUBLIKA SRBIJA

Capital	Belgrade	Language	Serbian	Independence	2006
Population	10 150 265	Area	88 361 km²	% in cities	57%
GDP per cap	$2 200	Dailling code	+381	Internet .yu	GMT + / - +1

MEDALS TABLE

		Overall			League			Cup			Europe			City	Stadium	Cap'ty	DoF
		G	S	B	G	S	B	G	S	B	G	S	B				
1	Crvena Zvedza (Red Star)	48	30	12	25	17	8	22	12		1	1	4	Belgrade	Crvena Zvezda	51 328	1945
2	Partizan Beograd	30	24	9	20	16	9	10	7			1		Belgrade	Partizana	30 887	1945
3	OFK Beograd	9	7	6	5	6	5	4	1				1	Belgrade	Omladinski	13 912	1911
4	Vojvodina Novi Sad	2	6	9	2	3	9		3					Novi Sad	Karadorde	12 754	1914
5	Yugoslavia Beograd	2	3	3	2	3	3							Belgrade	Jugoslavija		1919
6	Obilic Beograd	1	3	2	1	1	2		2					Belgrade	Milos Obilic	4 508	1924
7	FK Smederovo	1	1	1			1	1	1					Smederevo	Kraj Stare Zelezare	16 565	1924
8	Zeleznik Beograd	1		1		1	1							Belgrade			
9	Nasa Krila Zemun		2						2					Zemun, Belgrade	Gradski	10 000	1919
	Spartak Subotica		2						2					Subotica	Gradski	25 000	1945
11	FK Radnicki		1	2		2			1					Belgrade	Radnicki		1920
12	FK Bor		1						1					Bor	Gradski		1919
	Trepca Mitrovica		1						1					Kosovska Mitrovica	Kosovska Mitrovica	28 500	1932
	Napredak Krusevac		1						1					Krusevac	Napredak	10 811	1946
	Buducnost Dvor		1						1					Banatski Dvor	Mirko Vucurevic	2 400	
	FK Zemun		1						1					Zemun	Zemun	15 000	1946

RECENT LEAGUE AND CUP RECORD

	Championship						Cup		
Year	Champions	Pts	Runners-up	Pts	Third	Pts	Winners	Score	Runners-up
1995	Crvena Zvezda	42	Partizan Beograd	38	Vojvodina Novi Sad	37	Crvena Zvezda	4-0 0-0	FK Obilic
1996	Partizan Beograd	60	Crvena Zvezda	48	Vojvodina Novi Sad	43	Crvena Zvezda	3-0 3-1	Partizan Beograd
1997	Partizan Beograd	84	Crvena Zvezda	78	Vojvodina Novi Sad	53	Crvena Zvezda	0-0 1-0	Vojvodina Novi Sad
1998	FK Obilic	86	Crvena Zvezda	84	Partizan Beograd	70	Partizan Beograd	0-0 2-0	FK Obilic
1999	Partizan Beograd	66	FK Obilic	64	Crvena Zvezda	51	Crvena Zvezda	4-2	Partizan Beograd
2000	Crvena Zvezda	105	Partizan Beograd	101	FK Obilic	89	Crvena Zvezda	4-0	Napredak Krusevac
2001	Crvena Zvezda	88	Partizan Beograd	86	FK Obilic	63	Partizan Beograd	1-0	Crvena Zvezda
2002	Partizan Beograd	81	Crvena Zvezda	66	Sartid Smederevo	58	Crvena Zvezda	1-0	Sartid Smederevo
2003	Partizan Beograd	89	Crvena Zvezda	70	OFK Beograd	63	Sartid Smederevo	1-0	Crvena Zvezda
2004	Crvena Zvezda	74	Partizan Beograd	63	FK Zeleznik	58	Crvena Zvezda	1-0	Buducnost Dvor
2005	Partizan Beograd	80	Crvena Zvezda	74	Zeta Golubovci	59	Zeleznik Beograd	1-0	Crvena Zvezda
2006	Crvena Zvezda	78	Partizan Beograd	71	Vozdovac Beograd	51	Crvena Zvezda	4-2	OFK Beograd
2007	Crvena Zvezda	74	Partizan Beograd	57	Vojvodina Novi Sad	54	Crvena Zvezda	2-0	Vojvodina Novi Sad
2008	Partizan Beograd	80	Crvena Zvezda	75	Vojvodina Novi Sad	62	Partizan Beograd	3-0	FK Zemun

SERBIA 2007-08 — MERIDIAN SUPERLIGA

	Pl	W	D	L	F	A	Pts	Partizan	Red Star	Vojvodina	Borac	Napredak	Cukaricki	Mladost	Hajduk	OFK	Smederevo	Banat	Bezanija
Partizan Beograd †	33	24	8	1	63	23	80		2-2 1-1	3-3	0-0 1-0	3-1	1-1	4-0 2-0	2-1 1-0	5-1	1-0	4-2 3-1	2-0 2-2
Crvena Zvezda ‡	33	21	12	0	65	22	75	4-1		1-1 5-1	4-0	1-1 5-0	0-0 1-0	2-2	1-1	2-0 1-0	1-0 4-3	2-0	2-0 4-1
Vojvodina Novi Sad ‡	33	18	8	7	53	33	62	0-1 1-1	1-1		1-2 5-0	2-0	0-0	2-1 2-0	1-0 4-1	1-1	2-1	1-0 4-1	3-1 3-2
Borac Cacak ‡	33	12	10	11	29	33	46	0-1	0-0 0-2	2-4		1-0 1-1	1-1 2-1	2-0	2-0 0-0	2-1 1-0	0-0	4-1	2-0
Napredak Krusevac	33	11	8	14	25	33	41	0-2 0-1	0-1	0-1 1-1	0-0		0-2 2-0	0-1	1-0	2-0	1-0 3-1	1-0	0-2 1-0
Cukaricki Stankom	33	10	10	13	31	32	40	0-3 0-1	0-1	1-0 1-3	0-0	0-0		2-0 3-0	1-1 0-1	0-2	2-2	2-1 2-0	0-2 1-0
Mladost Lucani	33	8	14	11	32	41	38	1-4	1-1 0-1	0-1	1-0 2-1	1-1 0-0	2-1		0-0	2-2 3-1	3-2 0-1	1-1	3-0 3-0
Hajduk Kula	33	8	13	12	25	31	37	0-1	0-2 1-1	1-2	0-0	1-1 2-0	2-0	1-1		2-2 0-0	1-0	3-1 0-0	0-0 1-0
OFK Beograd	33	9	9	15	31	45	36	0-1 1-3	0-2	0-0 2-0	2-0	1-1	0-3 1-1	1-1	3-1 1-1		1-2	2-1	1-0
FC Smederevo †	33	10	6	17	33	44	36	1-1 0-1	2-5	1-0 1-2	0-1	1-1	1-0 1-0	0-0	1-0 0-0	0-1		0-1 1-1	2-1
Banat Zrenjanin	33	6	10	17	34	57	28	0-2	2-2 1-2	1-1	2-1 0-1	0-1 0-4	1-3	0-0 2-2	1-2	2-1 1-2	2-3		2-1
Bezanija Novi Beograd §2	33	5	4	24	31	58	17	0-2	0-1	0-1	1-2	2-1 0-1	1-2	0-0 1-0	0-1 1-2	2-2 0-1	0-1 2-6	2-3 3-3	

11/08/2007 - 25/05/2008 • † Qualified for the UEFA Champions League • ‡ Qualified for the UEFA Cup • § = points deducted • † play-offs

SERBIA 2007-08 — II LIGA GRUPA SRBIJA (2)

	Pl	W	D	L	F	A	Pts
Habitpharm Javor	34	18	16	0	38	12	70
Jagodina	34	15	13	6	37	19	58
BSK Borca †	34	17	7	10	38	21	58
Rad Beograd †	34	16	9	9	50	34	57
Vozdovac Beograd †	34	16	9	9	39	27	57
Metalac G. Milanovic †	34	13	10	11	33	26	49
Srem Sremska Mitrovica	34	14	5	15	43	41	47
Mladost Apatin	34	13	8	13	30	31	47
CSK Pivara Celarevo	34	11	13	10	34	29	46
Novi Sad	34	12	10	12	31	30	46
Sevojno	34	11	12	11	34	34	45
Novi Pazar	34	12	9	13	29	39	45
Hajduk Beograd	34	12	8	14	28	33	44
Radnicki Nis †	34	11	10	13	29	31	43
FK Zemun	34	10	12	12	28	40	42
Vlasina Vlasotince	34	9	10	15	35	47	37
Mladenovac	34	7	9	18	28	51	30
Radnicki Pirot	34	1	6	27	16	55	9

18/08/2007 - 24/05/2008 • † play-offs
First round: BSK 0-0 4-3p Metalac; Rad 1-1 3-1p Vozdovac
Semi-finals: BSK 0-0 2-4p Rad
Final: Rad 3-1 1-2 Smederevo

KUP 2007-08

Round of 16
- Partizan Beograd — 3
- Srem Sr'ska Mitrovica* — 0
- Bezanija Novi Beograd
- Sindelic Nis*
- Cukaricki Stankom — 1 5p
- FC Smederevo* — 1 3p
- Napredak Krusevac — 1
- Crvena Zvezda* — 3
- OFK Beograd — 2
- Indija* — 0
- Hajduk Kula* — 0
- Habitpharm Javor — 1
- Banat Zrenjanin — 1
- Radnicki Nis* — 0
- Vlasina Vlasotince — 1 5p
- FK Zemun* — 1 6p

Quarter-finals
- Partizan Beograd* — 5
- Sindelic Nis — 1
- Cukaricki Stankom* — 1 0p
- Crvena Zvezda — 1 3p
- OFK Beograd* — 1 4p
- Habitpharm Javor — 1 3p
- Banat Zrenjanin — 0
- FK Zemun* — 1

Semi-finals
- Partizan Beograd — 3
- Crvena Zvezda — 2
- OFK Beograd — 1 4p
- FK Zemun — 1 5p

Final
- Partizan Beograd — 3
- FK Zemun — 0

CUP FINAL
Partizan, Belgrade
7-05-2008, Att: 17 000, Ref: Krstic
Scorer - Lamine Diarra 3 [12 41 92+]

* Home team

SRI – SRI LANKA

NATIONAL TEAM RECORD
JULY 10TH 2006 TO JULY 12TH 2010

PL	W	D	L	F	A	%
14	5	2	7	23	27	42.9

FIFA/COCA-COLA WORLD RANKING

1993	1994	1995	1996	1997	1998	1999	2000	2001	2002	2003	2004	2005	2006	2007	High	
126	139	135	126	136	134	153	149	143	139	135	140	144	145	167	**122**	08/98

2007–2008												Low	
08/07	09/07	10/07	11/07	12/07	01/08	02/08	03/08	04/08	05/08	06/08	07/08	**170**	02/08
160	166	169	169	167	167	170	168	160	162	162	161		

While Sri Lanka's presence in Asia's 2010 FIFA World Cup qualifying campaign was short-lived, the nation continued to make an impact at regional level. Qatar comfortably disposed of the Indian Ocean islanders from the qualifying tournament for South Africa with a 6-0 aggregate win, but the Sri Lankans put that disappointment behind them by qualifying for the finals of the 2008 AFC Challenge Cup, a competition in which they finished second in 2006. Wins over Guam and Pakistan coupled with a draw against Chinese Taipei earned them a place in the finals in Hyderabad, India, and that was swiftly followed by a run to the semi-finals of the South Asian

INTERNATIONAL HONOURS
None

Football Federation Championship. Despite being held to a surprise draw by Afghanistan, the Sri Lankans notched up wins over Bhutan and Bangladesh to progress to the last four, where they lost to eventual champions the Maldives. In August 2008, at the AFC Challenge Cup finals, however, they failed get past the first round after surprisingly finishing bottom of their group with three successive defeats. Meanwhile, Ratnam underlined their status as Sri Lanka's leading club by successfully defending their national title in November 2007 shortly after reaching the semi-finals of the 2007 AFC President's Cup in Pakistan. There, they lost to eventual winners Dordoi-Dynamo.

THE FIFA BIG COUNT OF 2006

	Male	Female		Total
Number of players	397 000	32 150	Referees and Assistant Referees	390
Professionals	0		Admin, Coaches, Technical, Medical	1 830
Amateurs 18+	23 200		Number of clubs	580
Youth under 18	26 800		Number of teams	1 100
Unregistered	68 000		Clubs with women's teams	3
Total players	429 150		Players as % of population	2.12%

Football Federation of Sri Lanka (FFSL)
100/9 Independence Avenue, Colombo 07, Sri Lanka
Tel +94 11 2686120   Fax +94 11 2682471
ffsl@srilankafootball.com   www.srilankafootball.com
President: SILVEIRA Hurley   General Secretary: MARIKAR Hafiz
Vice-President: WEERASKERA S.   Treasurer: HEWAPANNA Laxman   Media Officer: PERERA Rukmal
Men's Coach: JANG Jung   Women's Coach: DE SILVA Clement
FFSL formed: 1939   AFC: 1958   FIFA: 1950
White shirts, White shorts, White socks

RECENT INTERNATIONAL MATCHES PLAYED BY SRI LANKA

2003	Opponents	Score		Venue	Comp	Scorers	Att	Referee
29-11	Laos	D	0-0	Vientiane	WCq		4 500	Luong The Tai VIE
3-12	Laos	W	3-0	Colombo	WCq	Channa Edribandanage 35, Kasun Weerarathna 59, Hameed 93+	6 000	Saleem MDV
2004								
18-02	Turkmenistan	L	0-2	Ashgabat	WCq		11 000	Al Bannai UAE
31-03	Saudi Arabia	L	0-1	Colombo	WCq		6 000	Chynybekov KGZ
9-06	Indonesia	L	0-1	Jakarta	WCq		30 000	Nesar BAN
8-09	Indonesia	D	2-2	Colombo	WCq	Steinwall 81, Karunaratne 82	4 000	Marshoud JOR
9-10	Turkmenistan	D	2-2	Colombo	WCq	Perera 47, Mudiyanselage 57	4 000	Al Bannai UAE
17-11	Saudi Arabia	L	0-3	Dammam	WCq		2 000	Muflah OMA
18-12	Maldives	D	0-0	Male	Fr			
2005								
7-12	Pakistan	L	0-1	Karachi	SAFr1			
9-12	Maldives	L	0-2	Karachi	SAFr1			
11-12	Afghanistan	L	1-2	Karachi	SAFr1	Karunaratne 85		
2006								
2-04	Brunei Darusalaam	W	1-0	Chittagong	CCr1	Kasun Weerarathna 74	2 000	Saidov UZB
4-04	Bhutan	W	1-0	Chittagong	CCr1	Karu 45		Saidov UZB
6-04	Nepal	D	1-1	Chittagong	CCr1	Izzadeen 19	2 500	Lee Gi Young KOR
8-04	Chinese Taipei	W	3-0	Chittagong	CCqf	Izzadeen 44, Sanjaya 70, Ratnayaka 90	2 500	Al Ghatrifi OMA
12-04	Nepal	D	1-1	Chittagong	CCsf	Kasun Weerarathna 65. W 5-3p	2 500	Lee Gi Young KOR
16-04	Tajikistan	L	0-4	Dhaka	CCf		2 000	Mombini IRN
2007								
24-03	Malaysia	L	1-4	Colombo	Fr	Kasun Weerarathna 75		
26-03	Malaysia	W	2-1	Colombo	Fr	Fazal Fauzan 47, Azmeer Lathif 55		
21-10	Qatar	L	0-1	Colombo	WCq		6 500	Bashir SIN
28-10	Qatar	L	0-5	Doha	WCq		3 000	Al Ghamdi KSA
2008								
2-04	Guam	W	5-1	Taipei	CCq	Channa Edrib'nage 54, Chathura Weerasinghe 2 55 64, Safras Mohamed 82, Kasun Weerarathna 91+	300	Kavalenko UZB
4-04	Pakistan	W	7-1	Taipei	CCq	Chathura Weerasinghe 4 2 7 9 42, Channa Edribandanage 2 13p 82, Fernando 2 72 77	300	Kavalenko UZB
6-04	Chinese Taipei	D	2-2	Taipei	CCq	Chen Po Liang OG 59, Kasun Weerarathna 86	900	Iemoto JPN
4-06	Afghanistan	D	2-2	Colombo	SAFr1	Chathura Weerasinghe 8, Channa Edribandanage 80p		
6-06	Bhutan	W	2-0	Colombo	SAFr1	Chathura Weerasinghe 2 25 39		
8-06	Bangladesh	W	1-0	Colombo	SAFr1	Rawme Mohideen 73		
11-06	Maldives	L	0-1	Colombo	SAFsf			
31-07	Korea DPR	L	0-3	Hyderabad	CCr1		100	Vo Minh Tri VIE
2-08	Myanmar	L	1-3	Hyderabad	CCr1	Kasun Weerarathna 51	100	Kovalenko UZB
4-08	Nepal	L	0-3	Hyderabad	CCr1		200	Saleem MDV

Fr = Friendly match • SAF = South Asian Federation Cup • AC = AFC Asian Cup • CC = AFC Challenge Cup • WC = FIFA World Cup
q = qualifier • r1 = first round group • qf = quarter-final • sf = semi-final • f = final

SRI LANKA NATIONAL TEAM RECORDS AND RECORD SEQUENCES

Records			Sequence records					
Victory	4-0	SIN, NEP, PAK	Wins	3	1996-97, 2002	Clean sheets	2	Five times
Defeat	0-8	IDN 1972, SYR 2003	Defeats	12	1972-79, 1979-84	Goals scored	12	2002-2003
Player Caps	n/a		Undefeated	7	2001-2002	Without goal	10	1991-1993
Player Goals	n/a		Without win	15	1954-72, 1984-93	Goals against	35	1952-1979

SRI LANKA COUNTRY INFORMATION

Capital	Colombo	Independence	1948 from UK	GDP per Capita	$3 700
Population	19 905 165	Status	Republic	GNP Ranking	73
Area km^2	65 610	Language	Sinhala, Tamil, English	Dialling code	+94
Population density	303 per km^2	Literacy rate	92.3%	Internet code	.lk
% in urban areas	22%	Main religion	Buddhist, Hindu	GMT + / −	+5.5
Towns/Cities ('000)	Colombo 648; Dehiwala-Mount Lavinia 215; Jaffna 169; Negombo 137; Chavakachcheri 121; Kotte 118; Kandy 111; Trincomalee 108; Kalmunai 100; Galle 93; Point Pedro 89				
Neighbours (km)	Indian Ocean 1 340				
Main stadia	Sugathadasa Stadium − Colombo 25 000				

SRI LANKA 2007 GROUP A

	Pl	W	D	L	F	A	Pts
Negombo Youth †	10	7	1	2	22	9	22
Ratnam †	10	5	2	3	22	15	17
Army	10	4	2	4	13	14	14
Jupiters	10	3	4	3	13	14	13
Air Force	10	2	4	4	12	14	10
York	10	1	3	6	5	21	6

14/07/2007 - 30/09/2007 • † Qualified for play-offs

SRI LANKA 2007 GROUP B (2)

	Pl	W	D	L	F	A	Pts
New Young †	10	7	2	1	23	11	23
Saunders †	10	7	2	1	14	4	23
Police	10	3	3	4	14	16	12
Blue Star	10	4	0	6	13	15	12
Renown	10	3	1	6	16	16	10
Old Bens	10	1	2	7	6	24	5

14/07/2007 - 30/09/2007 • † Qualified for play-offs

PLAY-OFFS

Semi−finals		Final	
Ratnam	3		
New Young	1	**Ratnam**	2
Negombo Youth	2 4p	Saunders	1
Saunders	2 5p	Sugathadasa, Colombo, 11-11-2007	

CLUB DIRECTORY

Club	Town/City	Lge	Cup
Blue Stars	Kalutara	1	0
Jupiters	Colombo	0	0
Negombo Youth	Negombo	2	1
Old Bens	Colombo	1	1
Pettah United	Colombo	1	0
Ratnam SC	Kotahena	4	4
Renown	Colombo	3	5
Saunders	Colombo	12	6
York	Kandy	0	1

RECENT LEAGUE AND CUP RECORD

Championship		Cup		
Year	Champions	Winners	Score	Runners-up
1999	Saunders	Saunders	3-2	Renown
2000	Ratnam	Ratnam	2-1	Saunders
2001	Saunders	Saunders	4-0	Negombo Youth
2002	Saunders			
2003	Negombo Youth	Renown	1-0	Air Force
2004	Blue Stars	Ratnam	2-2 4-2p	Renown
2005	Saunders	Ratnam	3-1	Saunders
2006	Negombo Youth	Ratnam	2-2 5-3p	Negombo Youth
2007	Ratnam	Negombo Youth	3-0	Saunders
2008	Ratnam			

STP – SAO TOME E PRINCIPE

NATIONAL TEAM RECORD
JULY 10TH 2006 TO JULY 12TH 2010

PL	W	D	L	F	A	%
0	0	0	0	0	0	0

FIFA/COCA-COLA WORLD RANKING

1993	1994	1995	1996	1997	1998	1999	2000	2001	2002	2003	2004	2005	2006	2007	High	
-	-	-	-	-	194	187	181	186	191	192	195	197	198	-	179	08/00

2007–2008												Low	
08/07	09/07	10/07	11/07	12/07	01/08	02/08	03/08	04/08	05/08	06/08	07/08	199	07/07
199	200	200	-	-	-	-	-	-	-	-	-		

São Tome e Principe have now gone almost five years without an international match after failing to enter the qualifiers for the 2010 FIFA World Cup. It was November 2003 when the former Portuguese colony last played a match, losing to Libya in the preliminaries for the 2006 FIFA World Cup. Mario Dende, the president of Santomense federation, blames a lack of resources for the failure to remain competitive internationally. With FIFA beginning the installation of an artificial turf pitch at the National Stadium in the capital in March 2008, the country will soon have reason to rejoin the international ranks. Since becoming members of FIFA more than 20 years ago, São

INTERNATIONAL HONOURS
None

Tome have played just 14 internationals, winning against Equatorial Guinea in the CEMAC Cup and Sierra Leone in the FIFA World Cup qualifiers. One immediate consequence of the lack of internationals matches played is that São Tome were removed from the FIFA/Coca-Cola World Ranking in November 2007, the only member of FIFA not to be included. Ironically their profile is similar to that of the Cape Verde Islands, who have achieved notable success in recent years using players from the sizeable Cape Verde community in Portugal. São Tome also has a number of players on the books of Portuguese clubs who could qualify to play for the national team.

THE FIFA BIG COUNT OF 2006

	Male	Female		Total
Number of players	8 400	0	Referees and Assistant Referees	22
Professionals	0		Admin, Coaches, Technical, Medical	100
Amateurs 18+	600		Number of clubs	10
Youth under 18	200		Number of teams	20
Unregistered	600		Clubs with women's teams	0
Total players	8 400		Players as % of population	4.34%

Federação Santomense de Futebol (FSF)
Rua Ex-João de Deus No QXXIII - 426/26, Casa postale 440, São Tomé, São Tomé e Príncipe
Tel +239 22 6559   Fax +239 22 4231
FSF96STP@gmail.com   www.fsf.st
President: DENDE Manuel   General Secretary: BARROS Ricardino
Vice-President: DA GRACA ANDRADE Celestino   Treasurer: DA GRACA ANDRADE Celestino   Media Officer: none
Men's Coach: LIMA Osvaldo   Women's Coach: LIMA Osvaldo
FSF formed: 1975   CAF: 1986   FIFA: 1986
Green shirts, Yellow shorts, Green socks

RECENT INTERNATIONAL MATCHES PLAYED BY SAO TOME E PRINCIPE

2002	Opponents	Score	Venue	Comp	Scorers	Att	Referee
	No international matches played in 2002 after June						
2003							
11-10	Libya	L 0-1	São Tomé	WCq		4 000	Yameogo JPN
12-11	Equatorial Guinea	L 1-3	Malabo	Fr			
16-11	Libya	L 0-8	Benghazi	WCq		20 000	Guirat TUN
2004							
	No international matches played in 2004						
2005							
	No international matches played in 2005						
2006							
	No international matches played in 2006						
2007							
	No international matches played in 2007						
2008							
	No international matches played in 2008 before August						

Fr = Friendly match • WC = FIFA World Cup • q = qualifier

SAO TOME E PRINCIPE NATIONAL TEAM RECORDS AND RECORD SEQUENCES

Records			Sequence records					
Victory	2-0	EQG 1999, SLE 2000	Wins	2	1999-2000	Clean sheets	2	1999-2000
Defeat	0-11	CGO 1976	Defeats	6	1998-1999	Goals scored	2	1999-2000, 2000
Player Caps	n/a		Undefeated	2	1999-2000	Without goal	3	1999
Player Goals	n/a		Without win	11	1976-1999	Goals against	11	1976-1999

RECENT LEAGUE AND CUP RECORD

	League	Cup			São Tomé	Príncipe
Year	Champions	Winners	Score	Finalist	Champions	Champions
1995	Inter Bom-Bom	Caixão Grande			Inter Bom-Bom	
1996	Caixão Grande	Aliança Nacional				
1997	No Tournament	No Tournament				
1998	Os Operários	Sporting Praia Cruz				
1999	Sporting Praia Cruz	Vitória Riboque	3-2	Os Operários	Sporting Praia Cruz	Os Operários
2000	Inter Bom-Bom	Sporting Praia Cruz	3-1	Caixão Grande	Inter Bom-Bom	GD Sundy
2001	Bairros Unidos	GD Sundy	4-3	Vitória Riboque	Bairros Unidos	GD Sundy
2002	No tournament	No Tournament				
2003	Inter Bom Bom	Os Operários	1-0	UDESCAI	Inter Bom-Bom	1º de Maio
2004	Os Operários	No Tournament			UDESCAI	Os Operários
2005	No Tournament	No Tournament			No Tournament	No Tournament
2006	No Tournament	No Tournament			No Tournament	No Tournament
2007	Sporting Praia Cruz	Virória Riboque		Desportivo Sundy	Sporting Praia Cruz	UDAPB
2008						

SAO TOME E PRINCIPE COUNTRY INFORMATION

Capital	Sao Tomé	Independence	1975 from Portugal	GDP per Capita	$1 200
Population	181 565	Status	Republic	GNP Ranking	190
Area km²	1 001	Language	Portuguese	Dialling code	+239
Population density	185 per km²	Literacy rate	79%	Internet code	.st
% in urban areas	46%	Main religion	Christian	GMT +/−	0
Towns/Cities ('000)	Sao Tomé 62; Santo Amaro 8; Neves 7; Santana 7; Trinidade 7; Sao José dos Agnolares 2				
Neighbours (km)	Atlantic Ocean/Gulf of Guinea 209				
Main stadia	Estadio Nacional 12 de Julho – São Tomé 6 500				

SUD – SUDAN

NATIONAL TEAM RECORD
JULY 10TH 2006 TO JULY 12TH 2010

PL	W	D	L	F	A	%
35	15	8	12	42	42	54.3

FIFA/COCA-COLA WORLD RANKING

1993	1994	1995	1996	1997	1998	1999	2000	2001	2002	2003	2004	2005	2006	2007		High	
119	116	86	74	108	114	132	132	118	106	103	114	92	120	92		**74**	12/96

2007–2008												Low	
08/07	09/07	10/07	11/07	12/07	01/08	02/08	03/08	04/08	05/08	06/08	07/08	137	04/00
117	112	105	105	92	94	107	108	107	106	105	110		

Sudan completed arguably their finest year in 2007 since they won the Nations Cup in 1970, reviving their footballing reputation at both national team and club level. Sudan qualified for the 2008 finals in Ghana, their first appearance in three decades, finishing ahead of Tunisia in their qualifying group. They were less convincing at the finals, however, losing all three matches. The revival of the national team came on the back of strong performances by the country's top two clubs in continental competition. Al Hilal, playing for the first time in the group phase of the CAF Champions League, made it to the semifinals, beating holders Al Ahly of Egypt 3-0 and Tunisia's

INTERNATIONAL HONOURS
CAF African Cup of Nations 1970 CECAFA Cup 1980 2007

highly rated Esperance in the process. The team were propelled by the form of Nigerians Kelechi Osunwa, Yusuf Mohamed and Ndubisi Eze and the defending of Mozambique international Dario Khan. In the meantime, veteran German trainer Otto Pfister took Al Merreikh to the final of the African Confederation Cup, where they lost both legs to Tunisia's CS Sfaxien. Pfister left before the second leg to take over at Cameroon, and was replaced by compatriot Michael Kruger. Al Hilal shaded Al Merreikh for domestic honours as the two continued their fierce domestic rivalry. The two sides supplied all of the players for Sudan's squad at the 2008 CAF Africa Cup of Nations.

THE FIFA BIG COUNT OF 2006

	Male	Female		Total
Number of players	1 567 300	0	Referees and Assistant Referees	1 100
Professionals	0		Admin, Coaches, Technical, Medical	7 700
Amateurs 18+	19 800		Number of clubs	440
Youth under 18	26 500		Number of teams	2 750
Unregistered	88 000		Clubs with women's teams	0
Total players	1 567 300		Players as % of population	3.80%

Sudan Football Association (SFA)
Bladia Street, Khartoum, Sudan
Tel +249 183 773495   Fax +249 183 776633
www.sudanfootball.com
President: SHADDAD Kamal, Dr   General Secretary: MADGI SHAMS Magdi
Vice-President: AL MAAZAL Ahmed   Treasurer: EL KHATEM Mustasim Gaffar Dr   Media Officer: none
Men's Coach: MAZDA Mohamed   Women's Coach: None
SFA formed: 1936   CAF: 1957   FIFA: 1948
Red shirts, White shorts, Black socks

RECENT INTERNATIONAL MATCHES PLAYED BY SUDAN

2006	Opponents	Score		Venue	Comp	Scorers	Att	Referee
6-12	Burundi	W	1-0	Addis Abeba	CCqf	Rtshard Lado [94p]		
8-12	Uganda	D	2-2	Addis Abeba	CCsf	Galag El Dood [3], Alaa Eldin [55]. W 6-5p		
10-12	Zambia	D	0-0	Addis Abeba	CCf	L 10-11p		
21-12	Somalia	W	6-1	Beirut	ARr1	Al Tahir [8], Ali Mohamed 2 [16 18], Haitham Mostafa [21p], Faisal Agab [30], Natali Gemi [55]		
24-12	Mauritania	W	2-0	Beirut	ARr1	Faisal Agab [3], Haitham Tambal [90]		
27-12	Lebanon	D	0-0	Beirut	ARr1			
2007								
25-03	Mauritius	W	2-1	Curepipe	CNq	Faisal Agab 2 [42 77]		Mwanza ZAM
21-05	Eritrea	L	0-1	Asmara	Fr			
26-05	Eritrea	D	1-1	Asmara	Fr	Ahmed Mugahid [10]		
2-06	Mauritius	W	3-0	Omdurman	CNq	Rtshard Lado 2 [25p 65], Faisal Agab [44]		Lwanja MWI
16-06	Seychelles	W	2-0	Roche Caiman	CNq	Faisal Agab [44], Haitham Tambal [61]		Dlamini SWZ
22-08	Libya	W	1-0	Khartoum	Fr	Mohamed Tahir [78]		
9-09	Tunisia	W	3-2	Omdurman	CNq	Babiker Alaledin [26], Faisal Agab [61p], Musa Al Tahir [72]		Codja BEN
30-11	Eritrea	W	1-0	Omdurman	Fr			
3-12	Eritrea	W	1-0	Omdurman	Fr			
13-12	Zanzibar †	D	2-2	Arusha	CCr1	Abdil Ahmed 2 [56 81]		
15-12	Ethiopia	D	0-0	Arusha	CCr1			
17-12	Tanzania	W	2-1	Dar es Salaam	CCqf	Abdelhamid Amari 2 [9 35]		
19-12	Burundi	W	2-1	Dar es Salaam	CCsf	Saifeldin Ali Idris [2], Abdelhamid Amari [45]		
22-12	Rwanda	D	2-2	Dar es Salaam	CCf	Abdelhamid Amari [23], Modather Eltaab [46]. W 4-2p		
2008								
9-01	Nigeria	L	0-2	Estepona	Fr			
11-01	Guinea	L	0-6	Estepona	Fr			
22-01	Zambia	L	0-3	Kumasi	CNr1			Diatta SEN
26-01	Egypt	L	0-3	Kumasi	CNr1			Codja BEN
30-01	Cameroon	L	0-3	Tamale	CNr1			Djaoupe TOG
26-03	Liberia	L	0-2	Omdurman	Fr			
22-05	Yemen	D	1-1	Sana'a	Fr	Haitham Tambal [15]		
8-06	Congo	L	0-1	Brazzaville	WCq		25 000	Mana NGA
14-06	Mali	W	3-2	Khartoum	WCq	Alaeldin Yousif [46], Mohamed Tahir [70], Haytham Kamal [90]	15 000	Abd El Fatah EGY
22-06	Mali	L	0-3	Bamako	WCq		25 000	Doue CIV

Fr = Friendly match • CN = CAF African Cup of Nations • CC = CECAFA Cup • AR = Arab Cup • WC = FIFA World Cup
q = qualifier • r1 = first round group • sf = semi-final • f = final

SUDAN NATIONAL TEAM PLAYERS

	Player		Club	Date of Birth		Player		Club	Date of Birth
1	Akram El Hadi Salem	GK	Al Merreikh	27 02 1987	12	Badreldin El Doud	MF	Al Merreikh	1 04 1981
2	Omar Bakheit	DF	Al Hilal	1 01 1983	13	Mohamed Tahir	MF	Al Hilal	3 12 1984
3	Musa Al Tayeb	DF	Al Merreikh	15 06 1984	14	Mugahid Mohamed	MF	Al Merreikh	14 08 1981
4	Mohamed Ali Khider	DF	Al Hilal	1 01 1985	15	Amir Damar	DF	Al Mereikh	8 12 1979
5	Yousef Alaeldin	MF	Al Hilal	3 01 1982	16	Mahjoub El Moez	GK	Al Hilal	14 08 1983
6	Rtshard Justin Lado	MF	Al Hilal	10 05 1979	17	Faisal Agab	FW	Al Merreikh	24 08 1978
7	Alaeldin Ahmed Gibril	DF	Al Hilal	7 12 1978	18	Khalid Hassan	DF	Al Hilal	27 10 1981
8	Haitham Mostafa	MF	Al Hilal	30 08 1978	19	Ahmed Al Basha	DF	Al Merreikh	2 01 1982
9	Hamouda Bashir	MF	Al Hilal	1 01 1984	20	Abdelhamid Amari	FW	Al Merreikh	20 08 1984
10	Haitham Tambal	FW	Al Merreikh	2 04 1978	21	Bahaeldin Abdallah	GK	Al Merreikh	1 01 1978
11	Alaeldin Babiker	FW	Al Merreikh	6 03 1984	22	Saifeldin Ali Idris	MF	Al Hilal	1 01 1984
					23	Hassan Isaac Korongo	MF	Al Hilal	28 02 1985

Sudan's squad for the 2008 CAF Africa Cup of Nations

SUDAN NATIONAL TEAM RECORDS AND RECORD SEQUENCES

Records			Sequence records					
Victory	15-0	OMA 1965	Wins	6	2007	Clean sheets	5	2003
Defeat	0-8	KOR 1979	Defeats	6	2008	Goals scored	12	1996-1998
Player Caps	n/a		Undefeated	11	2007	Without goal	6	2008
Player Goals	n/a		Without win	9	1980-1982	Goals against	15	1996-1998

SUDAN COUNTRY INFORMATION

Capital	Khartoum	Independence	1956 from Egypt and UK	GDP per Capita	$1 900
Population	39 148 162	Status	Republic	GNP Ranking	83
Area km²	2 505 810	Language	Arabic, English, Nubian	Dialling code	+249
Population density	15 per km²	Literacy rate	61%	Internet code	.sd
% in urban areas	25%	Main religion	Muslim	GMT +/–	+2
Towns/Cities ('000)	Omdurman 2 810; Khartoum 1 974; Khartoum North 1 530; Niyala 499; Port Sudan 459; Kassala 401; El Obeid 393; Kusti 345; Wad Madani 332; Gadaref 322, El Fasher 252				
Neighbours (km)	Eritrea 605; Ethiopia 1 606; Kenya 232; Uganda 435; Congo DR 628; Central African Republic 1 165; Chad 1 360; Libya 383; Egypt 1 273; Red Sea 853				
Main stadia	National Stadium – Khartoum 20 000; El Merreikh – Omdurman 30 000				

SUDAN 2007

PREMIER LEAGUE	Pl	W	D	L	F	A	Pts	Hilal O	Merreikh O	Mawrada	Ahli	Hay Al Arab	Khartoum	Amal	Hilal PS	Ittihad	Jazeerat	Merghani	Merreikh T
Al Hilal Omdurman †	22	21	1	0	70	6	64		1-1	3-0	2-0	3-0	8-1	1-0	4-0	5-0	5-0	4-0	6-1
Al Merreikh Omdurman ‡	22	19	1	2	65	12	58	2-3		1-2	4-1	3-0	5-2	2-0	6-0	1-0	4-0	6-0	5-0
Al Mawrada Omdurman	22	11	6	5	27	17	39	0-1	0-2		0-0	1-0	1-0	3-0	3-0	1-2	0-0	2-1	0-0
Al Ahli Wad Medani	22	10	3	9	30	28	33	0-2	1-3	0-1		2-0	1-0	1-2	2-0	2-2	2-0	2-0	1-0
Hay Al Arab Port Sudan	22	7	7	8	18	21	28	0-2	0-1	0-0	3-0		0-1	2-2	0-0	3-0	1-0	2-1	3-2
Khartoum-3	22	8	3	11	23	34	27	1-2	0-4	2-1	0-1	1-1		3-2	0-0	3-2	0-1	0-1	3-1
Al Amal Atbara	22	5	6	11	22	31	21	0-1	1-3	2-3	1-3	0-1	0-0		2-0	2-1	0-0	1-0	3-0
Al Hilal Port Sudan	22	5	6	11	14	33	21	0-1	0-2	2-3	5-4	0-0	0-1	1-0		1-2	2-0	0-0	0-0
Al Ittihad Wad Medani	22	5	6	11	18	36	21	0-4	0-3	1-1	0-4	1-0	2-0	3-1	0-1		1-1	0-0	0-1
Jazeerat Al-Feel	22	4	8	10	9	35	20	0-6	0-3	0-4	2-0	0-0	1-0	1-0	0-2	1-1		1-1	1-0
Al Merghani Kassala	22	3	8	11	11	30	17	0-2	1-3	0-1	0-0	1-1	0-3	1-1	3-0	1-0	0-0		0-1
Al Merreikh Al Thagher	22	3	7	12	10	34	16	0-4	0-1	0-0	1-3	0-1	0-2	1-1	0-0	0-0	2-0	0-0	

19/02/2007 - 29/11/2007 • † Qualified for the CAF Champions League • ‡ Qualified for the CAF Confederations Cup

SUDAN CUP 2007

Semi–finals

Al Merreikh Omdurman

Al Hilal Omdurman

Final

Al Merreikh Omdurman	1
Al Hilal Omdurman	0

Omdurman, 16-12-2007
Scorer - Endurance Idahor [72]

RECENT LEAGUE AND CUP RECORD

	Championship	Cup		
Year	Champions	Winners	Score	Runners-up
1998	Al Hilal	Al Hilal	2-0	Al Merreikh
1999	Al Hilal	Al Mawrada		
2000	Al Merreikh	Al Hilal	3-0	Al Ahly
2001	Al Merreikh	Al Merreikh	1-0	Al Mawrada
2002	Al Merreikh	Al Hilal	2-0	Al Merreikh
2003	Al Hilal	No competition		
2004	Al Hilal	Al Hilal	0-0 3-2p	Al Merreikh
2005	Al Hilal	Al Merreikh	0-0 4-2p	Al Hilal
2006	Al Hilal	Al Merreikh	2-0	Al Hilal
2007	Al Hilal	Al Merreikh	1-0	Al Hilal

SUI – SWITZERLAND

NATIONAL TEAM RECORD
JULY 10TH 2006 TO JULY 12TH 2010

PL	W	D	L	F	A	%
22	10	1	11	32	29	47.7

FIFA/COCA-COLA WORLD RANKING

1993	1994	1995	1996	1997	1998	1999	2000	2001	2002	2003	2004	2005	2006	2007	High	
12	7	18	47	62	83	47	58	63	44	44	51	35	17	44	**3**	08/93

	2007–2008											Low	
08/07	09/07	10/07	11/07	12/07	01/08	02/08	03/08	04/08	05/08	06/08	07/08	**83**	12/98
45	42	41	44	44	44	41	40	46	48	44	45		

Just five days into Euro 2008 and the hosts Switzerland were out. Never before in European Championship or World Cup history had the hosts lost their first two matches let alone been the first team knocked-out. It was all rather hard on the Swiss who lost captain Alexander Frei to an injury in the opening defeat by the Czech Republic and had to play through a rainstorm in their next game - a grudge match against Turkey. Despite the conditions they managed to take the lead through Hakan Yakin but fell victim to part one of the Turkish late, late show with Arda's deflected winner in injury-time ending Swiss hopes. A meaningless 2-0 victory over an already qualified Portugal brought their

INTERNATIONAL HONOURS
Qualified for the FIFA World Cup finals 1934 1938 1950 1954 1962 1966 1994 2006

tournament to an end along with the managerial career of coach Kobi Kuhn who stepped down and was replaced by Ottmar Hitzfeld. Played very much in the shadows of the upcoming Euro 2008 finals, the Swiss domestic season was dominated by FC Basel, who made up for losing out on the championships by the slightest of margins in the previous two seasons, by winning their fourth title in seven years. Once again there was last day drama with Basel playing their closest rivals Young Boys in the final round. Leading by a single point going into the game, Basel made sure of the title with a 2-0 win, a victory which also secured the double.

THE FIFA BIG COUNT OF 2006

	Male	Female		Total
Number of players	507 900	63 800	Referees and Assistant Referees	4 783
Professionals	550		Admin, Coaches, Technical, Medical	25 300
Amateurs 18+	103 700		Number of clubs	1 412
Youth under 18	127 700		Number of teams	13 005
Unregistered	240 000		Clubs with women's teams	394
Total players	571 700		Players as % of population	7.60%

Schweizerischer Fussball-Verband (SFV/ASF)
Worbstrasse 48, Postfach, Bern 3000, Switzerland
Tel +41 31 9508111   Fax +41 31 9508181
sfv.asf@football.ch   www.football.ch
President: ZLOCZOWER Ralph   General Secretary: GILLIERON Peter
Vice-President: ZUPPINGER Kurt   Treasurer: POMA Giuseppe   Media Officer: BENOIT Pierre
Men's Coach: HITZFELD Ottmar   Women's Coach: VON SIEBENTHAL Beatrice
SFV/ASF formed: 1895   UEFA: 1954   FIFA: 1904
Red shirts with white trimmings, White shorts, Red socks or White shirts with red trimmings, Red shorts, White socks

RECENT INTERNATIONAL MATCHES PLAYED BY SWITZERLAND

2005 Opponents	Score	Venue	Comp	Scorers	Att	Referee
12-11 Turkey	W 2-0	Berne	WCpo	Senderos 41, Behrami 86	31 130	Michel SVK
16-11 Turkey	L 2-4	Istanbul	WCpo	Frei 2p, Streller 84	42 000	De Bleeckere BEL
2006						
1-03 Scotland	W 3-1	Glasgow	Fr	Barnetta 21, Gygax 41, Cabanas 69	20 952	Coue FRA
27-05 Côte d'Ivoire	D 1-1	Basel	Fr	Barnetta 32	20 000	Vuorela FIN
31-05 Italy	D 1-1	Geneva	Fr	Gygax 32	30 000	Sippel GER
3-06 China PR	W 4-1	Zurich	Fr	Frei 2 40 49p, Streller 2 47 73	16 000	Stokes IRL
13-06 France	D 0-0	Stuttgart	WCr1		52 000	Ivanov.V RUS
19-06 Togo	W 2-0	Dortmund	WCr1	Frei 16, Barnetta 88	65 000	Amarilla PAR
23-06 Korea Republic	W 2-0	Hanover	WCr1	Snderos 23, Frei 77	43 000	Elizondo ARG
26-06 Ukraine	D 0-0	Cologne	WCr2	L 0-3p	45 000	Archundia MEX
16-08 Liechtenstein	W 3-0	Vaduz	Fr	Frei 2 11 51p, Margairaz 65	4 837	Brugger AUT
2-09 Venezuela	W 1-0	Basel	Fr	Frei 86	12 500	Hamer LUX
6-09 Costa Rica	W 2-0	Geneva	Fr	Streller 12, Frei 39	12 000	Van Egmond NED
11-10 Austria	L 1-2	Innsbruck	Fr	Streller 70	11 000	Svendsen DEN
15-11 Brazil	L 1-2	Basel	Fr	Maicon OG 71	39 000	Merk GER
2007						
7-02 Germany	L 1-3	Düsseldorf	Fr	Streller 71	51 333	Bossen NED
22-03 Jamaica	W 2-0	Fort Lauderdale	Fr	Streller 7, Inler 12	3 254	Prus USA
25-03 Colombia	L 1-3	Miami	Fr	Frei 39p	16 000	Vaughn USA
2-06 Argentina	D 1-1	Basel	Fr	Streller 64	29 000	Messina ITA
22-08 Netherlands	W 2-1	Geneva	Fr	Barnetta 2 9p 51	24 000	Duhamel FRA
7-09 Chile	W 2-1	Vienna	Fr	Barnetta 13, Streller 55	2 500	Stuchlik AUT
11-09 Japan	L 3-4	Klagenfurt	Fr	Magnin 11, N'Kufo 13p, Djourou 81	19 500	Messner AUT
13-10 Austria	W 3-1	Zurich	Fr	Streller 2 2 55, Hakan Yakin 36	22 500	Hamer LUX
17-10 USA	L 0-1	Basel	Fr		16 500	De Bleeckere BEL
20-11 Nigeria	L 0-1	Zurich	Fr		12 700	Bebek CRO
2008						
6-02 England	L 1-2	London	Fr	Derdiyok 58	86 857	Brych GER
26-03 Germany	L 0-4	Basel	Fr		38 500	Bramhaar NED
24-05 Slovakia	W 2-0	Lugano	Fr	Behrami 56, Frei 63	10 150	Kelly IRL
30-05 Liechtenstein	W 3-0	St Gall	Fr	Frei 2 24 31, Vonlanthen 68	18 000	Thual FRA
7-06 Czech Republic	L 0-1	Basel	ECr1		39 730	Rosetti ITA
11-06 Turkey	L 1-2	Basel	ECr1	Hakan Yakin 32	39 730	Michel SVK
15-06 Portugal	W 2-0	Basel	ECr1	Hakan Yakin 2 71 83p	39 730	Plautz AUT

Fr = Friendly match • EC = UEFA EURO 2008 • WC = FIFA World Cup • q = qualifier • po = play-off

SWITZERLAND NATIONAL TEAM PLAYERS

	Player		Ap	G	Club	Date of Birth		Player		Ap	G	Club	Date of Birth
1	Diego Benaglio	GK	14	0	VfL Wolfsburg	8 09 1983	12	Eren Derdiyok	FW	6	1	FC Basel	12 06 1988
2	Johan Djourou	DF	17	1	Arsenal	18 01 1987	13	Stéphane Grichting	DF	19	0	AJ Auxerre	30 03 1979
3	Ludovic Magnin	DF	53	3	VfB Stuttgart	20 04 1979	14	Daniel Gygax	MF	35	5	FC Metz	28 08 1981
4	Philippe Senderos	DF	31	3	Arsenal	14 02 1985	15	Gelson Fernandes	MF	11	0	Manchester City	2 09 1986
5	Stephan Lichtsteiner	DF	15	0	Lille OSC	16 01 1984	16	Tranquillo Barnetta	MF	35	6	Bay. Leverkusen	22 05 1985
6	Benjamin Huggel	MF	25	0	FC Basel	7 07 1977	17	Christoph Spycher	DF	39	0	Eint. Frankfurt	30 03 1978
7	Ricardo Cabanas	MF	51	4	Grasshoppers	17 01 1979	18	Pascal Zuberbühler	GK	51	0	NeuchâtelXamax	8 01 1971
8	Gökhan Inler	MF	20	1	Udinese	27 06 1984	19	Valon Behrami	MF	19	2	Lazio	19 04 1985
9	Alexander Frei	FW	60	35	Bor. Dortmund	15 07 1979	20	Patrick Müller	DF	81	3	Olymp. Lyonnais	17 12 1976
10	Hakan Yakin	MF	69	18	BSC Young Boys	22 02 1977	21	Eldin Jakupovic	GK	0	0	Lok'tiv Moskva	2 10 1984
11	Marco Streller	FW	29	11	FC Basel	18 06 1981	22	Johan Vonlanthen	MF	33	6	Austria Salzburg	1 02 1986

The Swiss squad for Euro 2008

| | | | | | | 23 | Philipp Degen | DF | 30 | 0 | Bor. Dortmund | 15 02 1983 |

SWITZERLAND NATIONAL TEAM RECORDS AND RECORD SEQUENCES

Records			Sequence records					
Victory	9-0	LTU 1924	Wins	5	1960-1961	Clean sheets	7	2006
Defeat	0-9	ENG 1909, HUN 1911	Defeats	11	1928-1930	Goals scored	22	1921-1924
Player Caps	117	Heinz Hermann	Undefeated	14	2004-2005	Without goal	5	1985
Player Goals	35	Alexander Frei	Without win	16	1928-1930	Goals against	45	1926-1932

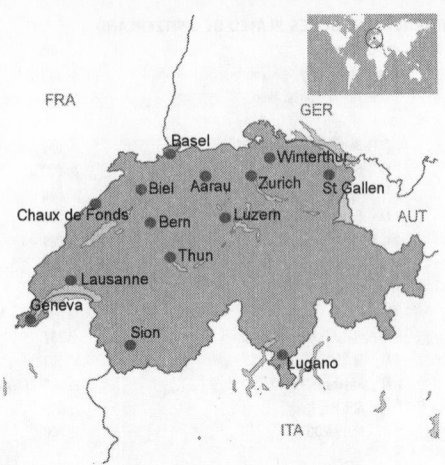

SWITZERLAND; SCHWEIZ; SUISSE; SVIZZERA

Capital	Bern	Language	German, French, Italian	Formation	1291
Population	7 554 661	Area	41 290 km²	Density	180 per km²	% in cities	61%
GDP per cap	$32 700	Dailling code	+41	Internet	.ch	GMT +/-	+1

MAJOR CITIES/TOWNS
Population '000

1	Zürich	1 024
2	Geneva	614
3	Basel	573
4	Bern	119
5	Lausanne	114
6	Winterthur	92
7	Rapperswil	71
8	St Gallen	69
9	Luzern	56
10	Biel	48
11	Thun	41
12	Köniz	37
13	La Chaux-de-Fonds	36
14	Schaffhausen	33
15	Chur	32
16	Fribourg	32
17	Neuchâtel	30
18	Sion	28
19	Emmen	26
20	Lugano	26
21	Kriens	24
22	Yverdon	23
23	Wil	16
24	Aarau	15

MEDALS TABLE

		Overall			League			Cup			Europe			City	Stadium	Cap'ty	DoF
		G	S	B	G	S	B	G	S	B	G	S	B				
1	Grasshopper-Club	45	32	13	27	19	12	18	13				1	Zürich	Letzigrund	26 500	1886
2	Servette FC	24	28	12	17	16	12	7	12					Geneva	Stade de Genève	30 084	1890
3	FC Basel	21	12	4	12	6	4	9	6					Basel	St Jakob Park	42 500	1893
4	FC Zürich	18	9	9	11	8	7	7	1				2	Zürich	Letzigrund	26 500	1896
5	BSC Young Boys	17	20	10	11	14	9	6	6				1	Berne	Stade de Suisse Wankdorf	32 000	1898
6	Lausanne-Sport	16	15	9	7	8	8	9	7				1	Lausanne	Olympique de la Pontaise	16 000	1896
7	FC Sion	12	2	6	2	2	6	10						Sion	Stade Tourbillon	13 000	1909
8	FC La Chaux-de-Fonds	9	4	7	3	3	7	6	1					La Chaux-de-Fonds	Parc Charrière	13 000	1894
9	AC Lugano	6	9	10	3	5	10	3	4					Lugano	Stadio Cornaredo	15 000	1908
10	FC Aarau	4	3	3	3	1	3	1	2					Aarau	Brügglifeld Stadion	9 249	1902
11	Neuchâtel Xamax FC	3	8	9	3	3	9		5					Neuchâtel	Stade La Maladiere	22 100	1970
12	FC Luzern	3	4	1	1	1	1	2	3					Luzern	Stadion Allmend	18 400	1901
13	FC Winterthur	3	4	1	3	2	1		2					Wintherthur	Schützenwiese	15 000	1896
14	FC St Gallen	3	3	3	2		3	1	3					St Gallen	Espenmoos Stadion	11 300	1879
15	FC Grenchen	1	7	1		4	1	1	3					Grenchen	Bruehl Stadion		1906

RECENT LEAGUE AND CUP RECORD

	Championship						Cup		
Year	Champions	Pts	Runners-up	Pts	Third	Pts	Winners	Score	Runners-up
1995	Grasshopper-Club	37	FC Lugano	30	Neuchâtel Xamax	28	FC Sion	4-2	Grasshopper-Club
1996	Grasshopper-Club	52	FC Sion	47	Neuchâtel Xamax	43	FC Sion	3-2	Servette FC
1997	FC Sion	49	Neuchâtel Xamax	46	Grasshopper-Club	45	FC Sion	3-3 5-4p	FC Luzern
1998	Grasshopper-Club	57	Servette FC	41	Lausanne-Sports	40	Lausanne-Sports	2-2 4-3p	FC St. Gallen
1999	Servette FC	46	Grasshopper-Club	46	Lausanne-Sports	45	Lausanne-Sports	2-0	Grasshopper-Club
2000	FC St. Gallen	54	Lausanne-Sports	44	FC Basel	40	FC Zürich	2-2 3-0p	Lausanne-Sports
2001	Grasshopper-Club	46	FC Lugano	41	FC St. Gallen	40	Servette FC	3-0	Yverdon-Sports
2002	FC Basel	55	Grasshopper-Club	45	FC Lugano	42	FC Basel	2-1	Grasshopper-Club
2003	Grasshopper-Club	57	FC Basel	56	Neuchâtel Xamax	35	FC Basel	6-0	Neuchâtel Xamax
2004	FC Basel	85	BSC Young Boys	72	Servette FC	52	FC Wil	3-2	Grasshopper-Club
2005	FC Basel	70	FC Thun	60	Grasshopper-Club	50	FC Zürich	3-1	FC Luzern
2006	FC Zürich	78	FC Basel	78	BSC Young Boys	62	FC Sion	1-1 5-3p	BSC Young Boys
2007	FC Zürich	75	FC Basel	74	FC Sion	60	FC Basel	1-0	FC Luzern
2008	FC Basel	74	BSC Young Boys	70	FC Zürich	56	FC Basel	4-1	AC Bellinzona

SWITZERLAND 2007–08

AXPO SUPER LEAGUE

	Pl	W	D	L	F	A	Pts	Basel	Young Boys	Zürich	G'hoppers	Aarau	Luzern	Sion	Neuchâtel	St Gallen	Thun
FC Basel †	36	22	8	6	73	39	74		4-0 2-0	1-0 4-0	2-0 2-1	1-1 2-1	3-2 1-0	3-2 1-1	0-1 3-0	3-0 2-1	2-1 3-1
BSC Young Boys ‡	36	21	7	8	82	49	70	5-1 2-0		1-1 3-0	3-2 2-0	4-1 4-0	6-1 0-1	1-0 3-1	3-2 1-3	3-1 3-0	0-0 4-2
FC Zürich ‡	36	15	11	10	58	43	56	2-2 1-1	5-1 1-2		4-0 1-0	0-1 0-0	4-1 1-0	4-1 2-1	1-0 2-1	3-1 1-0	3-1 1-0
Grasshopper-Club	36	15	9	12	57	49	54	2-0 1-1	3-3 3-3	2-1 1-1		1-1 2-0	1-1 2-0	0-1 2-0	1-2 2-0	2-0 2-3	2-1 4-0
FC Aarau	36	11	14	11	47	48	47	0-3 2-2	1-1 0-2	1-1 0-2	2-1 2-1		0-0 2-1	2-0 2-0	3-2 2-2	2-2 2-3	1-5 0-3
FC Luzern	36	10	14	12	40	49	44	2-4 1-0	2-2 0-3	2-2 2-1	3-3 0-0	0-0 2-0		1-1 1-1	1-1 0-2	1-1 1-0	1-2 4-0
FC Sion	36	11	10	15	48	51	43	1-1 4-2	1-2 1-2	0-5 3-3	0-1 0-2	3-0 1-0	0-0 0-0		1-1 2-0	5-1 1-2	2-1 5-0
Neuchâtel Xamax	36	10	11	15	48	55	41	0-3 2-2	3-1 3-1	1-1 3-1	4-1 1-3	2-1 1-2	3-3 0-1	1-3 1-1		1-1 1-0	1-1 0-2
FC St Gallen ††	36	9	7	20	39	69	34	0-3 1-4	2-7 2-0	2-3 1-0	5-3 0-2	1-1 0-0	1-2 2-1	0-0			0-4 3-0
FC Thun	36	6	9	21	30	70	27	0-2 1-3	0-0 0-4	1-1 1-1	1-0 0-2	2-5 1-1	0-1 0-1	0-1 2-2	1-2 1-0	1-1	

18/07/2007 - 10/05/2008 • † Qualified for the UEFA Champions League • ‡ Qualified for the UEFA Cup • †† Relegation play-off
Top scorers: Hakan Yakin, Young Boys 24; Thomas Häberli, Young Boys 18; Raúl Bobadilla, Grasshoppers 18; Alvaro Saborío, Sion 17
Relegation play-off: **Bellinzona** 3-2 2-0 St Gallen

SWITZERLAND 2007–08

CHALLENGE LEAGUE (2)

	Pl	W	D	L	F	A	Pts	Vaduz	Bellinzona	Wil	Wohlen	Winterthur	Sch'hausen	Concordia	Servette	Lugano	Yverdon	Gossau	C. de Fonds	Lausanne	Locarno	Kriens	Delémont	Chiasso	Cham
FC Vaduz	34	21	7	6	75	40	70		1-1	4-1	0-0	2-1	2-1	5-1	5-1	3-2	0-0	5-1	4-0	2-1	2-2	5-1	3-2	5-2	3-0
AC Bellinzona †	34	21	6	7	74	39	69	3-1		3-0	4-4	3-3	3-1	2-0	2-1	4-1	2-0	3-1	3-1	3-1	2-0	2-1	3-1	2-1	5-0
FC Wil 1900	34	20	8	6	63	35	68	2-0	2-0		5-1	1-0	1-1	2-0	2-0	5-2	1-0	1-0	5-2	0-0	2-0	2-1	0-1	3-1	2-2
FC Wohlen	34	16	8	10	65	46	56	2-1	2-0	1-0		6-0	2-2	0-0	4-1	2-0	2-0	0-1	1-3	1-3	2-2	2-2	4-1	0-0	5-1
FC Winterthur	34	14	9	11	59	56	51	1-3	2-2	1-2	3-0		2-1	0-1	2-2	0-3	3-1	6-4	3-1	2-1	3-1	1-0	2-0	2-1	
FC Schaffhausen	34	13	10	11	53	40	49	1-3	2-0	0-1	2-0	1-0		1-0	0-1	3-0	2-2	0-2	1-2	2-1	5-0	5-0	2-0	0-0	3-0
Concordia Basel	34	13	10	11	55	54	49	1-2	4-2	4-3	2-0	2-2	2-0		2-1	1-1	2-2	1-2	5-0	4-1	1-0	1-1	0-4	2-3	3-0
Servette FC	34	12	10	12	55	46	46	3-1	2-2	0-0	1-3	1-1	1-2	3-1		6-1	1-1	2-1	0-0	4-2	0-0	1-3	1-1	5-0	2-0
AC Lugano	34	12	10	12	61	63	46	3-0	0-4	2-3	1-1	2-3	2-0	6-3	1-1		2-1	2-2	4-2	0-0	0-1	1-0	0-0	5-1	3-1
Yverdon-Sport	34	10	13	11	39	35	43	0-2	0-3	1-1	0-1	2-2	0-3	1-1	0-1	1-1		0-0	0-1	3-0	2-2	1-0	4-0	2-0	
FC Gossau	34	11	10	13	50	54	43	2-2	0-1	1-2	1-4	2-1	0-0	2-0	2-1	1-4	1-1		3-3	1-1	4-2	0-1	5-1	2-2	3-2
La Chaux-de-Fonds	34	12	7	15	53	63	43	2-0	3-2	0-1	2-1	1-0	1-2	1-3	1-2	1-1	0-0	2-0		4-2	2-3	1-1	2-1	4-0	3-1
Lausanne-Sport	34	11	9	14	46	47	42	1-1	1-2	0-0	2-1	1-3	0-0	1-1	1-1	4-0	2-0	0-2	2-2		0-1	3-1	1-2	1-0	1-0
FC Locarno	34	12	5	17	37	61	41	0-1	0-3	1-0	2-0	4-2	4-2	1-1	1-0	1-3	1-5	0-0	1-0	2-1		1-0	0-2	1-5	2-0
SC Kriens	34	8	14	12	43	54	38	0-1	1-0	0-0	1-2	2-2	2-2	3-3	2-1	2-2	1-1	0-2	3-1	1-2	2-0		1-1	1-1	1-2
SR Delémont	34	10	7	17	42	58	37	1-4	1-0	2-2	0-3	2-3	1-1	0-0	0-3	2-5	0-1	1-1	2-0	1-2	5-2	0-1		2-1	2-0
FC Chiasso	34	8	9	17	43	68	33	0-0	1-1	2-5	3-1	1-1	1-1	1-2	2-1	1-2	0-1	0-3	0-2	2-1	2-1	1-1	4-1		0-2
SC Cham	34	4	4	26	31	85	16	1-2	0-2	2-6	2-4	0-0	3-3	0-1	0-4	0-1	0-3	3-2	1-1	1-4	2-1	1-2	0-2	3-5	

20/07/2007 - 12/05/2008 • † Promotion play-off

SWISSCOM CUP 2007–08

Round of 16		Quarter-finals		Semi-finals		Final	
FC Basel	1						
Grasshopper-Club *	0	FC Basel *	2				
Yverdon-Sport	1						
Stade Nyonnais *	2	Stade Nyonnais	0	FC Basel *	1		
FC Zürich	3			FC Thun	0		
SC Kriens *	0	FC Zürich	1				
FC Luzern *	0						
FC Thun	1	FC Thun *	2			FC Basel	4
Neuchâtel Xamax	1					AC Bellinzona ‡	1
FC Schaffhausen *	0	Neuchâtel Xamax *	3				
FC Chiasso *	0						
BSC Young Boys	1	BSC Young Boys	2	Neuchâtel Xamax	0 2p		
FC Gossau	2			AC Bellinzona *	0 4p		
Lausanne-Sport *	0	FC Gossau	1				
FC Sion	1						
AC Bellinzona *	2	AC Bellinzona *	2				

* Home team • ‡ Qualified for the UEFA Cup

CUP FINAL

St Jakob-Park, Basel, 6-04-2008, Att: 33 000, Ref: Zimmerman
Scorers - Eren Derdiyok [31], Daniel Majstorovic [62], Marco Streller [63], Benjamin Huggel [65] for Basel; Christian Pouga [56] for Bellinzona

SUR – SURINAM

NATIONAL TEAM RECORD
JULY 10TH 2006 TO JULY 12TH 2010

PL	W	D	L	F	A	%
9	5	1	3	15	13	61.1

FIFA/COCA-COLA WORLD RANKING

1993	1994	1995	1996	1997	1998	1999	2000	2001	2002	2003	2004	2005	2006	2007		High	
117	104	124	131	145	160	162	164	141	141	158	149	152	122	153		87	07/08

	2007–2008											Low	
08/07	09/07	10/07	11/07	12/07	01/08	02/08	03/08	04/08	05/08	06/08	07/08	168	04/01
123	143	144	150	153	152	153	155	143	144	145	87		

Surinam's recent rise up the FIFA/Coca-Cola World Ranking and their place in the group phase of the 2010 FIFA World Cup qualifiers in the CONCACAF region, is all the more remarkable because the government of the country forbids the national team from using any of the estimated 150 players of Surinamese origin who play their football abroad. The former Dutch colony has had to do mainly with amateurs from the local league but they had little trouble disposing of tiny Montserrat in a first preliminary round match. More impressive was their 3-1 aggregate victory over neighbours Guyana in the next round. The Guyanans were expected to stroll through to the

INTERNATIONAL HONOURS
CONCACAF Champions Cup Transvaal 1973 1981

group stage but in Clifton Sandvliet, Surinam have one of the deadliest strikers in the region. His two goals against Guyana took his tally to 79 in just 68 international matches. If coach Kenneth Jaliens was allowed to approach European based players and persuade them to play for the national team, Surinam would be potential candidates for a place in the finals in South Africa. The local players do at least have a well organised league to play in which, in May 2008, was won again by Inter Moengotapoe. In the future the challenge will be to do well in the Caribbean Club Championship which will qualify three clubs for the new CONCACAF Champions League.

THE FIFA BIG COUNT OF 2006

	Male	Female		Total
Number of players	31 950	3 300	Referees and Assistant Referees	100
Professionals	0		Admin, Coaches, Technical, Medical	275
Amateurs 18+	6 655		Number of clubs	30
Youth under 18	1 395		Number of teams	292
Unregistered	14 000		Clubs with women's teams	1
Total players	35 250		Players as % of population	8.03%

Surinaamse Voetbal Bond (SVB)
Letitia Vriesdelaan 7, PO Box 1223, Paramaribo, Surinam
Tel +597 473112   Fax +597 479718
svb@sr.net   www.svb.sr
President: GISKUS Louis   General Secretary: FELTER Harold
Vice-President: KOORNDIJK Ronald   Treasurer: GOBARDHAN Waldo   Media Officer: FELTER Harold
Men's Coach: JALIENS Kenneth   Women's Coach: BENZENSTEIN Arno
SVB formed: 1920   CONCACAF: 1964   FIFA: 1929
White shirts, Green shorts, Green socks

RECENT INTERNATIONAL MATCHES PLAYED BY SURINAM

2004	Opponents	Score		Venue	Comp	Scorers	Att	Referee
24-11	Grenada	D	2-2	Tunapuna	CCq	Modeste OG [27], Sandvliet [59]	2 000	Forde BRB
26-11	Puerto Rico	D	1-1	Marabella	CCq	Sandvliet [45]		Forde BRB
28-11	Trinidad and Tobago	L	0-1	Malabar	CCq			Forde BRB
2005								
No international matches played in 2005								
2006								
6-09	Guyana	L	0-5	Willemstad	CCq			
8-09	Grenada	W	1-0	Willemstad	CCq	Kinsaine [35]		
10-09	Netherlands Antilles	W	1-0	Willemstad	CCq	Grootfaam [5]		Suazo DOM
8-11	Martinique †	L	0-1	Fort de France	CCq			
10-11	Cuba	L	1-3	Fort de France	CCq	Aroepa [90]		
12-11	Haiti	D	1-1	Fort de France	CCq	Sastrodimedjo [75]		
2007								
No international matches played in 2007								
2008								
26-03	Montserrat	W	7-1	Macoya	WCq	Christophe 2 [36 55], Wondel [44], Valies [64], Huur [80], Schurman 2 [86 88]	100	Aguilar SLV
21-05	Netherlands Antilles	L	1-2	Willemstad	Fr	Sordano [14]		
14-06	Guyana	W	1-0	Paramaribo	WCq	Sandvliet [52]	3 000	Guerrero NCA
22-06	Guyana	W	2-1	Georgetown	WCq	Van Dijk [11], Sandvliet [37]	12 000	Campbell JAM

Fr = Friendly match • GC = CONCACAF Gold Cup • WC = FIFA World Cup • q = qualifier • † Not a full international

SURINAM NATIONAL TEAM RECORDS AND RECORD SEQUENCES

Records			Sequence records					
Victory	8-1	ARU 2004	Wins	4	1992	Clean sheets	4	1980
Defeat	1-8	MEX 1977	Defeats	5	1997	Goals scored	9	1990-1992
Player Caps	68	Clifton Sandvliet	Undefeated	9	1990-1992	Without goal	2	Six times
Player Goals	79	Clifton Sandvliet	Without win	6	Four times	Goals against	22	1994-1999

SURINAM 2007-08 HOOFDKLASSE

	Pl	W	D	L	F	A	Pts
Inter Moengotapoe	22	12	7	3	38	27	43
Robinhood	22	11	5	6	42	39	38
Boskamp	22	11	3	8	28	26	36
Walking Bout Co	22	10	5	7	42	30	35
Transvaal	22	9	6	7	25	30	33
Super Red Eagles	22	10	2	10	35	33	32
FCS Nacional	22	9	3	10	36	29	30
Leo Victor	22	8	4	10	39	40	28
Voorwarts	22	7	6	9	33	35	27
Jai Hanuman	22	7	3	12	40	39	24
Ranjiet Boys	22	6	6	10	26	37	24
Royal '95	22	4	6	12	21	40	18

17/10/2007 - 14/05/2008
Relegation play-off: Jai Hanuman 0-2 **Randjiet Boys**;
Excelsior 1-0 Randjiet Boys

SVB CUP 2007-08

Quarter-finals		Semi-finals		Final	
Transvaal	Bye				
		Transvaal			
Pechan		Inter M'gotapoe			
Inter M'gotapoe	w-o			Transvaal	0 p
Boskamp	2			Notch	0 p
Royal '95	0	Boskamp			
Walking Bout Co	l 3p	Notch		13-07-2008	
Notch	1 5p				

RECENT LEAGUE RECORD

Year	Champions	Pts	Runners-up	Pts	Third	Pts
2004	Walking Bout Co	55	Inter Moengotapoe	47	Transvaal	46
2005	Robinhood	62	Royal '95	54	Walking Bout Co	53
2006	Walking Bout Co	57	Robinhood	56	Inter Moengotapoe	48
2007	Inter Moengotapoe	55	Leo Victor	46	Walking Bout Co	46
2008	Inter Moengotapoe	43	Robinhood	38	Boskamp	36

SURINAM COUNTRY INFORMATION

Capital	Paramaribo	Independence	1975 from the Netherlands	GDP per Capita	$4 000
Population	436 935	Status	Republic	GNP Ranking	158
Area km²	163 270	Language	Dutch, English, Surinamese	Dialling code	+597
Population density	2.6 per km²	Literacy rate	93%	Internet code	.sr
% in urban areas	50%	Main religion	Christian, Hindu, Muslim,	GMT +/-	-3
Cities/Towns ('000)	Paramaribo 220; Lelydorp 17; Nieuw Nickerie 13; Moengo 7; Meerzorg 6; Nieuw Amsterdam 5				
Neighbours (km)	French Guiana 510; Brazil 597; Guyana 600; North Atlantic Ocean 386				
Main stadia	André Kamperveen Stadion – Paramaribo 18 000				

SVK – SLOVAKIA

NATIONAL TEAM RECORD
JULY 10TH 2006 TO JULY 12TH 2010

PL	W	D	L	F	A	%
22	8	3	11	45	37	43.2

FIFA/COCA-COLA WORLD RANKING

1993	1994	1995	1996	1997	1998	1999	2000	2001	2002	2003	2004	2005	2006	2007		High	
150	43	35	30	34	32	21	24	47	55	50	53	45	37	53		17	05/97

2007–2008												Low	
08/07	09/07	10/07	11/07	12/07	01/08	02/08	03/08	04/08	05/08	06/08	07/08	150	12/93
39	46	50	50	53	54	56	58	66	66	66	65		

Having achieved notoriety in 2005 by qualifying for the group stage of the Champions League, Artmedia Bratislava, suffered a slump in form which coincided with the departure of coach Vladimír Weiss to Saturn in Russia. In June 2007 he returned to the renamed Artmedia Petrzalka and once more worked his magic, leading the team to a League and Cup double in 2008. Despite losing twice to defending champions Zilina, Artmedia pulled clear of their rivals at the end of the season, winning the title with two games to spare when they beat Senec in a classic 5-4 victory. Zbynek Pospech scored a hat-trick that day and he also scored the only goal of the game in the

INTERNATIONAL HONOURS
None

Slovak Cup final - an injury-time header from a Jan Kozák cross - after coming on as a substitute. Artmedia's success meant that Weiss was a natural choice for the national team job after Jan Kocian didn't have his contract renewed following a mediocre Euro 2008 campaign. Although the Slovaks finished in fourth place, just a point behind the Republic of Ireland, they were 11 points behind second placed Germany and more to the point won just twice all season, both of which were against San Marino. Standing in the way of a first World Cup finals appearance for the Slovaks are the Czech Republic and Poland in one of the least intimidating European qualifying groups.

THE FIFA BIG COUNT OF 2006

	Male	Female		Total
Number of players	596 135	26 533	Referees and Assistant Referees	2 437
Professionals	489		Admin, Coaches, Technical, Medical	16 300
Amateurs 18+	252 435		Number of clubs	2 417
Youth under 18	169 561		Number of teams	7 353
Unregistered	68 700		Clubs with women's teams	15
Total players	622 668		Players as % of population	11.45%

Slovak Football Association (SFZ)
Slovensky futbalovy zväz, Junácka 6, Bratislava 832 80, Slovakia
Tel +421 2 49249151   Fax +421 2 49249595
international@futbalsfz.sk   www.futbalsfz.sk
President: LAURINEC Frantisek   General Secretary: TOMAS Milos
Vice-President: STRAPEK Stanislav   Treasurer: GOGA Peter   Media Officer: CSIBREI Tomas
Men's Coach: WEISS Vladimir   Women's Coach: PAKUSZA Zsolt
SFZ formed: 1993   UEFA: 1994   FIFA: 1907/1994
Blue shirts with white trimmings, Blue shorts, Blue socks or White shirts with blue trimmings, White shorts, White socks

RECENT INTERNATIONAL MATCHES PLAYED BY SLOVAKIA

2004	Opponents	Score		Venue	Comp	Scorers	Att	Referee
4-09	Russia	D	1-1	Moscow	WCq	Vittek [87]	11 500	Mejuto Gonzalez ESP
8-09	Liechtenstein	W	7-0	Bratislava	WCq	Vittek 3 [15 59 81], Karhan [42], Nemeth.S [84], Mintal [85], Zabavnik [92+]	5 620	Delevic SCG
9-10	Latvia	W	4-1	Bratislava	WCq	Nemeth.S [36], Reiter [50], Karhan 2 [55 87]	13 025	Farina ITA
17-11	Slovenia	D	0-0	Trnava	Fr		5 482	Skjerven NOR
30-11	Hungary	W	1-0	Bangkok	Fr	Porazik [47]	750	Veerapool THA
2-12	Thailand	D	1-1	Bangkok	Fr	Durica [65p]. W 5-4p	5 000	Chappanimutu MAS
2005								
9-02	Romania	D	2-2	Larnaca	Fr	Vittek [12], Karhan [44]	500	Kapitanis CYP
26-03	Estonia	W	2-1	Tallinn	WCq	Mintal [58], Reiter [65]	3 051	Frojdfeldt SWE
30-03	Portugal	D	1-1	Bratislava	WCq	Karhan [8]	21 000	Sars FRA
4-06	Portugal	L	0-2	Lisbon	WCq		64 000	Collina ITA
8-06	Luxembourg	W	4-0	Luxembourg	WCq	Nemeth [5], Mintal [15], Kisel [54], Reiter [60]	2 108	Styles ENG
17-08	Liechtenstein	D	0-0	Vaduz	WCq		1 150	Layec FRA
3-09	Germany	W	2-0	Bratislava	Fr	Karhan 2 [20p 38]	9 276	Braamahr NED
7-09	Latvia	D	1-1	Riga	WCq	Vittek [35]	8 800	Plautz AUT
8-10	Estonia	W	1-0	Bratislava	WCq	Hlinka [72]	12 800	Allaerts BEL
12-10	Russia	D	0-0	Bratislava	WCq		22 317	Rosetti ITA
12-11	Spain	L	1-5	Madrid	WCpo	Nemeth [49]	47 210	De Santis ITA
16-11	Spain	D	1-1	Bratislava	WCpo	Holosko [50]	23 587	Merk GER
2006								
1-03	France	W	2-1	Paris	Fr	Nemeth.S [62], Valachovic [82]	55 000	Thomson SCO
20-05	Belgium	D	1-1	Trnava	Fr	Holosko [64]	4 174	Kassai HUN
15-08	Malta	W	3-0	Bratislava	Fr	Sebo 3 [31 75 90]	2 437	Lajuks LVA
2-09	Cyprus	W	6-1	Bratislava	ECq	Skrtel [9], Mintal 2 [33 56], Sebo 2 [43 49], Karhan [52]	4 723	Orekhov UKR
6-09	Czech Republic	L	0-3	Bratislava	ECq		27 684	Bennett ENG
7-10	Wales	W	5-1	Cardiff	ECq	Svento [14], Mintal 2 [32 38], Karhan [51], Vittek [59]	28 415	Van Egmond NED
11-10	Germany	L	1-4	Bratislava	ECq	Varga [58]	27 580	Hauge NOR
15-11	Bulgaria	W	3-1	Zilina	Fr	Mintal [8], Sapara [53], Karhan [78]	4 823	Granat POL
10-12	UAE	W	2-1	Abu Dhabi	Fr	Jonas [50], Michalik [53]		Ibrahim QAT
2007								
7-02	Poland	D	2-2	Jerez	Fr	Jakubko [1], Skrtel [45]	200	Pacheco ESP
24-03	Cyprus	W	3-1	Nicosia	ECq	Vittek [54], Skrtel [67], Jakubko [77]	2 696	Lehner AUT
28-03	Republic of Ireland	L	0-1	Dublin	ECq		71 257	Baskakov RUS
6-06	Germany	L	1-2	Hamburg	ECq	Metzelder OG [20]	51 600	Benquerença POR
22-08	France	L	0-1	Trnava	Fr		13 064	Egorov RUS
8-09	Republic of Ireland	D	2-2	Bratislava	ECq	Klimpl [37], Cech [91+]	12 360	Farina ITA
12-09	Wales	L	2-5	Trnava	ECq	Mintál 2 [12 57]	5 846	Duhamel FRA
13-10	San Marino	W	7-0	Dubnica N. Vahom	ECq	Hamšík [24], Sešták 2 [32 57], Sapara [37], Skrtel [51], Holosko [54], Durica [76p]	2 576	Wilmes LUX
16-10	Croatia	L	0-3	Rijeka	Fr		5 000	Laperriere SUI
17-11	Czech Republic	L	1-3	Prague	ECq	Kadlec OG [79]	15 651	Asumaa FIN
21-11	San Marino	W	5-0	Serravale	ECq	Michalík [42], Holosko 2 [51 57], Hamšík [53], Cech [83]	538	Sipailo LVA
2008								
6-02	Hungary	D	1-1	Limassol	Fr	Sestak [64]	100	Trattu CYP
26-03	Iceland	L	1-2	Zilina	Fr	Mintál [86]	4 120	Lehner AUT
20-05	Turkey	L	0-1	Bielefeld	Fr		13 100	Weiner GER
24-05	Switzerland	L	0-2	Lugano	Fr		10 150	Kelly IRL

Fr = Friendly match • EC = UEFA EURO 2008 • WC = FIFA World Cup • q = qualifier • po = play-off

SLOVAKIA NATIONAL TEAM RECORDS AND RECORD SEQUENCES

Records			Sequence records				
Victory	7-0	LIE 2004, SMR 2007	Wins	3	Five times	Clean sheets	4	2000
Defeat	1-6	CRO 1942	Defeats	5	2001	Goals scored	8	1996-1997
Player Caps	84	Miroslav Karhan	Undefeated	12	2000-2001	Without goal	4	2001
Player Goals	22	Szilárd Németh	Without win	6	Four times	Goals against	11	2002-2003

MAJOR CITIES/TOWNS

Population '000

1	Bratislava	421
2	Kosice	236
3	Presov	95
4	Zilina	86
5	Nitra	85
6	Banská Bystrica	81
7	Trnava	69
8	Martin	61
9	Trencin	58
10	Poprad	58
11	Prievidza	52
12	Zvolen	44
13	Povazská Bystrica	44
14	Nové Zámky	41
15	Michalovce	40
16	Spisská Nová Ves	39
17	Humenné	35
18	Ruzomberok	31
19	Dubnica nad Váhom	26
20	Rimavská Sobota	25
21	Dunajská Streda	23
22	Púchov	18
23	Zlaté Moravce	15
24	Senec	14

SLOVAK REPUBLIC; SLOVENSKA REPUBLIKA

Capital	Bratislava	Language	Slovak, Hungarian	Independence	1993
Population	5 447 502	Area	48 845 km²	% in cities	59%
GDP per cap	$13 300	Dailling code	+421	Internet .sk	GMT +/- +1

MEDALS TABLE

		Overall G S B	League G S B	Cup G S B	Europe G S B	City	Stadium	Cap'ty	DoF
1	Slovan Bratislava	7 2 3	4 1 3	3 1		Bratislava	Tehelné Pole	30 085	1919
2	Inter Bratislava	5 2 3	2 2 3	3		Bratislava	Pasienky Stadion	13 295	1945
3	Artmedia Petrzalka	4 4	2 3	2 1		Bratislava	Petrzalka Stadion	8 000	1898
4	MSK Zilina	4 2	4 2			Zilina	Pod Dubnon	6 233	1908
5	MFK Kosice	2 5 1	2 3 1	2		Kosice	Lokomotivy v Cermeli	9 600	1952
6	MFK Ruzomberok	2 1 2	1 2	1 1		Ruzomberok	MFK Stadion	5 030	1906
7	Spartak Trnava	1 5 3	2 3	1 3		Trnava	Anton Malatinsky	18 448	1923
8	Dukla Banská Bystrica	1 2 1	1 1	1 1		Banská Bystrica	Stadion SNP	10 000	1965
9	Matador Púchov	1 2	1	1 1		Púchov	Matador	5 964	1920
10	FC Senec	1 1		1 1		Senec	NTC Stadion	3 264	2004

SLOVAK CLUBS IN CZECHOSLOVAKIAN FOOTBALL

3	Slovan Bratislava	14 16 3	8 10 3	5 6	1	
5	Spartak Trnava	9 2 2	5 1 1	4 1		1
7	Lokomotíva Kosice	2 1 2		2 2 1		
8	TJ Internacional	1 6 5	1 3 5	3		
9	1.FC Kosice	1 4 2	1 2	1 3		
14	DAC Dunajská Streda	1 1		1 1		

RECENT LEAGUE AND CUP RECORD

	Championship						Cup		
Year	Champions	Pts	Runners-up	Pts	Third	Pts	Winners	Score	Runners-up
1995	Slovan Bratislava	72	1.FC Kosice	52	Inter Bratislava	50	Inter Bratislava	1-1 3-1p	Dunajska Streda
1996	Slovan Bratislava	75	1.FC Kosice	65	Spartak Trnava	63	Chemlon Humenné	2-1	Spartak Trnava
1997	1.FC Kosice	70	Spartak Trnava	69	Slovan Bratislava	50	Slovan Bratislava	1-0	Tatran Presov
1998	1.FC Kosice	68	Spartak Trnava	66	Inter Bratislava	60	Spartak Trnava	2-0	1.FC Kosice
1999	Slovan Bratislava	70	Inter Bratislava	68	Spartak Trnava	64	Slovan Bratislava	3-0	Dukla B. Bystrica
2000	Inter Bratislava	70	1.FC Kosice	61	Slovan Bratislava	57	Inter Bratislava	1-1 4-2p	1.FC Kosice
2001	Inter Bratislava	80	Slovan Bratislava	71	SCP Ruzomberok	55	Inter Bratislava	1-0	SCP Ruzomberok
2002	MSK Zilina	69	Matador Púchov	62	Inter Bratislava	56	Koba Senec	1-1 4-2p	Matador Púchov
2003	MSK Zilina	70	Artmedia Bratislava	67	Slovan Bratislava	63	Matador Púchov	2-1	Slovan Bratislava
2004	MSK Zilina	64	Dukla B. Bystrica	64	SCP Ruzomberok	55	Artmedia Bratislava	2-0	Trans Licartovce
2005	Artmedia Bratislava	72	MSK Zilina	65	Dukla B. Bystrica	52	Dukla B. Bystrica	2-1	Artmedia Bratislava
2006	MFK Ruzomberok	80	Artmedia Bratislava	74	Spartak Trnava	68	MFK Ruzomberok	0-0 4-3p	Spartak Trnava
2007	MSK Zilina	69	Artmedia Bratislava	56	MFK Kosice	41	ViOn Zlaté Moravce	4-0	FC Senec
2008	Artmedia Petrzalka	84	MSK Zilina	73	FC Nitra	57	Artmedia Petrzalka	1-0	Spartak Trnava

SLOVAKIA 2007–08

CORGON LIGA

	Pl	W	D	L	F	A	Pts
Artmedia Petrzalka	33	27	3	3	77	30	84
MSK Zilina	33	22	7	4	75	30	73
FC Nitra	33	17	6	10	40	26	57
Spartak Trnava	33	15	7	11	52	40	52
Slovan Bratislava	33	15	6	12	46	37	51
MFK Kosice	33	13	6	14	45	44	45
MFK Ruzomberok	33	10	14	9	46	43	44
Dukla Banska Bystrica	33	10	9	14	41	37	39
ZTS Dubnica	33	7	12	14	34	53	33
FC Senec	33	6	10	17	30	51	28
ViOn Zlaté Moravce	33	6	7	20	22	66	25
AS Trencín	33	3	7	23	26	77	16

Cross-results grid (columns: Artmedia, MSK Zilina, FC Nitra, Spartak, Slovan, MFK Kosice, Ruzomberok, Dukla Banska, ZTS Dubnica, FC Senec, ViOn, AS Trencín):

```
Artmedia Petrzalka    ——    2-3   1-0   3-1 2-1  2-1 2-1-0  0-1-0  3-0  6-3 2-1  1-0  3-1  5-0 4-0 3-2 1-0
MSK Zilina            1-0-0-1  ——  0-0 1-1  2-1  3-0  4-0 3-1 4-1  1-0  4-1 5-0 2-0 1-0  4-1  7-1 4-0
FC Nitra              1-0 0-3  0-1  ——  3-2 0-1  1-0  1-0  3-0 1-0 1-0 1-0  1-1  2-0  2-0 2-0 2-0 3-0
Spartak Trnava        0-2  4-1 3-1  2-1   ——   1-1 0-1 5-1 2-0  2-2  1-0 1-0 1-1 1-1  1-0  2-0  6-0
Slovan Bratislava     1-2  2-3 0-0 2-1 3-2  2-3   ——   2-1  0-1 0-0  1-0  4-1 3-2 3-0 4-0  2-2  2-1 3-0
MFK Kosice            0-1  2-0 2-2 2-1 1-1 2-1  3-2 3-0 1-1   ——   1-0  1-3  0-0 6-2 0-0 4-0  3-0  4-0 2-1
MFK Ruzomberok        0-3 2-2  1-2  2-2  2-0 4-0  0-2  1-0 3-0   ——   2-2 0-0  2-2  1-1  3-0  2-2 4-1 0-0
Dukla Banska Bystrica 2-2  1-3 1-1  1-0  0-0  0-0 0-1 1-2 3-0  1-1   ——   0-1 3-2 2-0 2-0  1-0  1-1
ZTS Dubnica           1-3 0-2  0-2  0-2 2-1  0-1  2-1  0-1 0-0 1-1  1-0   ——   1-1 0-0 4-1 2-0  2-1
FC Senec              2-3 4-5  0-0  0-1 1-0 1-3-4-1  1-0  1-1 2-3 2-2  1-1  2-1   ——   1-1 1-0  3-0
ViOn Zlaté Moravce    1-3 1-2 1-6  0-0  0-0 0-2 1-0-0-1-2-1-2-1  1-2 3-2 0-4  0-0  1-0   ——   2-0
AS Trencín            1-4  2-2  1-2  0-2 2-1  1-2   1-2   0-3 0-3 1-3 2-2 1-1 2-1 1-0 0-4 0-0 0-0
```

14/07/2007 - 31/05/2008 • † Qualified for the UEFA Champions League • ‡ Qualified for the UEFA Cup

Top scorers: Ján Novák, Kosice 17; Juraj Halenár, Artmedia 16; Peter Styvar, Zilina 15; Mário Breska, Zilina 14; Mouhamadou Seye, Dubnica 13

SLOVAKIA 2007–08 II LIGA (2)

	Pl	W	D	L	F	A	Pts
Tatran Presov	33	23	8	2	64	14	77
Sport Podbrezova	33	15	10	7	47	31	55
LAFC Lucenec	33	15	6	12	53	45	51
Inter Bratislava	33	14	8	10	46	38	50
Rimavska Sobota	33	13	11	9	40	32	50
HFK Prievidza	33	11	10	12	46	56	43
Slovan Duslo Sala	33	11	8	14	41	46	41
MFK Kosice B	33	10	7	16	41	47	37
Zemplin Michalovce	33	11	4	18	33	43	37
HFC Humenné	33	8	12	13	30	37	36
Slavoj Trebisov	33	9	7	17	31	60	34
Goral Stará Bubovna	33	7	9	17	35	58	30

14/07/2007 - 31/05/2008

SLOVENSKY POHAR 2007–08

Round of 16

Artmedia Petrzalka	0 4p
DAC Dunajská Streda*	0 2p
ZTS Dubnica *	0
Inter Bratislava	2
FC Nitra	5
Ziar nad Hronom *	1
MFK Ruzomberok	0
MSK Zilina *	3
MFK Kosice	2
AS Trencín *	0
ViOn Zlaté Moravce *	0
Slovan Bratislava	1
Tatran Presov *	2
Spisská Nová Ves	0
HFC Humenné *	0
Spartak Trnava	1

Quarter-finals

Artmedia Petrzalka	4 2
Inter Bratislava *	0 1
FC Nitra	2 0 3p
MSK Zilina *	2 0 4p
MFK Kosice *	2 0
Slovan Bratislava	0 0
Tatran Presov *	0 0
Spartak Trnava	1 0

Semi-finals

Artmedia Petrzalka	1 1
MSK Zilina *	0 0
MFK Kosice *	0 1
Spartak Trnava	0 3

Final

| Artmedia Petrzalka | 1 |
| Spartak Trnava ‡ | 0 |

CUP FINAL

Pod Dubnom, Zilina

1-05-2008

Scorer - Zbynek Pospech 91+

* Home team/home team in the first leg • ‡ Qualified for the UEFA Cup

SVN – SLOVENIA

NATIONAL TEAM RECORD
JULY 10TH 2006 TO JULY 12TH 2010

PL	W	D	L	F	A	%
18	5	4	9	14	21	38.9

FIFA/COCA-COLA WORLD RANKING

1993	1994	1995	1996	1997	1998	1999	2000	2001	2002	2003	2004	2005	2006	2007	High	
134	81	71	77	95	88	40	35	25	36	31	42	68	77	83	**25**	12/01

2007–2008												Low	
08/07	09/07	10/07	11/07	12/07	01/08	02/08	03/08	04/08	05/08	06/08	07/08	134	02/94
94	75	76	83	83	81	79	80	74	74	76	81		

Qualification for the finals of Euro 2000 and the World Cup finals in 2002 is beginning to seem like a dim and distant memory as Slovenia stuttered to a sixth place finish in the qualifiers for Euro 2008 with only Luxembourg, whom they beat twice, below them in the standings. A lack of regular first team football would appear to be hampering a number of the foreign based players although striker Milivoje Novakovic was the top scorer in the 2.Bundesliga in Germany, winning promotion with his club 1.FC Köln. Slovenia have been drawn in one of the easier 2010 FIFA World Cup qualifying groups, an opportunity for coach Matjaz Kek to get his team back on track. At home,

INTERNATIONAL HONOURS
Qualified for the FIFA World Cup finals 2002

Domzale comfortably retained their League title, the culmination of six years great work by coach Slavisa Stojanovic, but their hopes of securing a hat-trick of titles were upset when Stojanovic left at the end of the season to join Celje. Perhaps the story of the season, however, was in Ljubljana, a footballing wasteland for a number of years, where Interblock, the team owned by the so-called 'King of Roulette' Joze Pececnik, beat Maribor 2-1 in the Cup Final. A rich benefactor combined with the transformation of the historic Bezigrad stadium into a state-of-the-art arena could see the 'Devil's Team' become a force to be reckoned with in Slovenia and beyond.

THE FIFA BIG COUNT OF 2006

	Male	Female		Total
Number of players	107 255	9 670	Referees and Assistant Referees	818
Professionals	284		Admin, Coaches, Technical, Medical	5 000
Amateurs 18+	9 410		Number of clubs	328
Youth under 18	20 831		Number of teams	1 060
Unregistered	55 200		Clubs with women's teams	12
Total players	116 925		Players as % of population	5.82%

Football Association of Slovenia (NZS)

Nogometna Zveza Slovenije, Cerinova 4, PO Box 3986, Ljubljana 1001, Slovenia
Tel +386 1 5300400   Fax +386 1 5300410
nzs@nzs.si   www.nzs.si
President: ZAVRL Rudi   General Secretary: JOST Dane
Vice-President: FRANTAR Anton   Treasurer: JOST Dane   Media Officer: STANIC Uros
Men's Coach: KEK Matjaz   Women's Coach: CIRKVENCIC Zoran
NZS formed: 1920   UEFA: 1992   FIFA: 1992

White shirts with green trimmings, White shorts, White socks or Green shirts with white trimmings, Green shorts, Green socks

RECENT INTERNATIONAL MATCHES PLAYED BY SLOVENIA

2003	Opponents	Score		Venue	Comp	Scorers	Att	Referee
15-11	Croatia	D	1-1	Zagreb	ECpo	Siljak [22]	35 000	Merk GER
19-11	Croatia	L	0-1	Ljubljana	ECpo		9 000	Meier SUI
2004								
18-02	Poland	L	0-2	Cadiz	Fr		100	Barea Lopez ESP
31-03	Latvia	L	0-1	Celje	Fr		1 500	Stredak SVK
28-04	Switzerland	L	1-2	Geneva	Fr	Zahovic [45]	7 500	Bossen NED
18-08	Serbia & Montenegro	D	1-1	Ljubljana	Fr	Ceh.N [83]	8 000	Ovrebo NOR
4-09	Moldova	W	3-0	Celje	WCq	Acimovic 3 [5 27 48]	3 620	Hyytia FIN
8-09	Scotland	D	0-0	Glasgow	WCq		38 279	Larsen DEN
9-10	Italy	W	1-0	Celje	WCq	Cesar [82]	9 262	De Bleeckere BEL
13-10	Norway	L	0-3	Oslo	WCq		24 907	Ivanov.V RUS
17-11	Slovakia	D	0-0	Trnava	Fr		5 482	Skjerven NOR
2005								
9-02	Czech Republic	L	0-3	Celje	Fr		4 000	Strahonja CRO
26-03	Germany	L	0-1	Celje	Fr		9 000	Poll ENG
30-03	Belarus	D	1-1	Celje	WCq	Rodic [44]	6 450	Al Ghamdi KSA
4-06	Belarus	D	1-1	Minsk	WCq	Ceh.N [17]	29 042	Hansson SWE
17-08	Wales	D	0-0	Swansea	Fr		10 016	Stokes IRL
3-09	Norway	L	2-3	Celje	WCq	Cimirotic [4], Zlogar [83]	10 055	Medina Cantalejo ESP
7-09	Moldova	W	2-1	Chisinau	WCq	Lavric [47], Marvic [58]	7 200	Baskakov RUS
8-10	Italy	L	0-1	Palermo	WCq		19 123	Poulat FRA
12-10	Scotland	L	0-3	Celje	WCq		9 100	Temmink NED
2006								
28-02	Cyprus	W	1-0	Larnaca	Fr	Ljubijankic [84]		
1-03	Romania	L	0-2	Larnaca	Fr		300	Vialichka BLR
31-05	Trinidad and Tobago	W	3-1	Celje	Fr	Novakovic 3 [4 16 77]	2 500	Tanovic SCG
4-06	Côte d'Ivoire	L	0-3	Evry-Bondoufle	Fr		8 000	
15-08	Israel	D	1-1	Celje	Fr	Sukalo [83]	3 000	Kralovec CZE
6-09	Bulgaria	L	0-3	Sofia	ECq		14 491	Bo Larsen DEN
7-10	Luxembourg	W	2-0	Celje	ECq	Novakovic [30], Koren [44]	3 800	Kailis CYP
11-10	Belarus	L	2-4	Minsk	ECq	Cesar [19], Lavric [43]	21 150	Kassai HUN
2007								
7-02	Estonia	W	1-0	Domzale	Fr	Lavric [34p]	3 000	Ledentu FRA
24-03	Albania	D	0-0	Shkoder	ECq		7 000	Attard MLT
28-03	Netherlands	L	0-1	Celje	ECq		10 000	Mejuto Gonzalez ESP
2-06	Romania	L	1-2	Celje	ECq	Vrsic [94+]	6 500	Dougal SCO
6-06	Romania	L	0-2	Timisoara	ECq		17 850	Yefet ISR
22-08	Montenegro	D	1-1	Podgorica	Fr	Vrsic [42]	8 000	Circhetta SUI
8-09	Luxembourg	W	3-0	Luxembourg	ECq	Lavric 2 [7 47], Novakovic [37]	2 012	Berezka UKR
12-09	Belarus	W	1-0	Celje	ECq	Lavric [3p]	3 500	Banari MDA
13-10	Albania	D	0-0	Celje	ECq		3 700	Gomes POR
17-10	Netherlands	L	0-2	Eindhoven	ECq		32 500	Rizzoli ITA
21-11	Bulgaria	L	0-2	Celje	ECq		3 700	Webb ENG
2008								
6-02	Denmark	L	1-2	Nova Gorica	Fr	Novakovic [37]	1 700	Kinhofer GER
26-03	Hungary	W	1-0	Zalaegerszeg	Fr	Sisic [59]	7 000	Messner AUT
26-05	Sweden	L	0-1	Gothenburg	Fr		21 118	Collum SCO

Fr = Friendly match • EC = UEFA EURO 2004/2008 • WC = FIFA World Cup • q = qualifier • po = play-off

SLOVENIA NATIONAL TEAM RECORDS AND RECORD SEQUENCES

Records			Sequence records					
Victory	7-0	OMA 1999	Wins	4	1998	Clean sheets	4	2002
Defeat	0-5	FRA 1999, FRA 2002	Defeats	4	1997, 1998	Goals scored	9	2001-2002
Player Caps	80	Zlatko Zahovic	Undefeated	8	2001	Without goal	4	2004-2005
Player Goals	35	Zlatko Zahovic	Without win	8	2003-04, 2004-05	Goals against	13	1997-1998

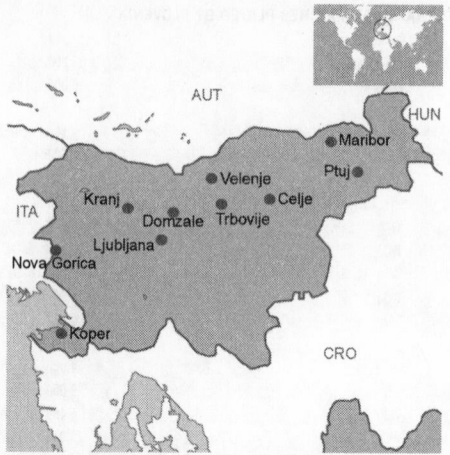

MAJOR CITIES/TOWNS

Population '000

1	Ljubljana	253
2	Maribor	86
3	Celje	36
4	Kranj	34
5	Velenje	26
6	Koper	23
7	Novo Mesto	22
8	Ptuj	18
9	Trbovlje	15
10	Kamnik	12
11	Nova Gorica	12
12	Murska Sobota	12
13	Jesenice	11
14	Skofja Loka	11
15	Domzale	11
16	Izola	10
17	Kocevje	8
18	Postojna	8
19	Ajdovscina	6
20	Crnomelj	5
21	Prevalje	4
22	Lendava	3
23	Dravograd	3
24	Kidricevo	1

REPUBLIC OF SLOVENIA; REPUBLIKA SLOVENIJA

Capital	Ljubljana	Language	Slovenian, Serbo-Croat	Independence	1991
Population	2 009 245	Area	20 273 km²	Density	99 per km²	% in cities	64%
GDP per cap	$19 000	Dailling code	+386	Internet	.si	GMT +/-	+1

MEDALS TABLE

		Overall			League			Cup			Europe			City	Stadium	Cap'ty	DoF
		G	S	B	G	S	B	G	S	G	S	B				
1	NK Maribor	12	5	3	7	3	3	5	2				Maribor	Ljudski vrt Stadion	10 210	1960
2	Olimpija Ljubljana	8	6	1	4	3	1	4	3				Ljubljana	Bezigrad Stadion	8 211	1911-2005
3	ND Gorica	6	4	4	4	3	4	2	1				Nova Gorica	Sportni Park	3 066	1947
4	NK Domzale	2	2		2	2							Domzale	Sportni Park	3 212	1921
5	FC Koper	2	1	2		1	2	2					Koper	SRC Bonifika Stadion	3 557	1955
6	NK Celje	1	5	1		1	1	1	4				Celje	Arena Petrol	12 350	1919
7	Mura Murska Sobota	1	3	2		2	2	1	1				Murska Sobota	Fazanerija Stadion	3 527	2005
8	Rudar Velenje	1		2			2	1					Velenje	Ob Jezeru	1 800	1948
9	Interblock	1						1					Ljubljana	Bezigrad		2006
10	Primorje Ajdovscina		5	1		2	1		3				Ajdovscina	Primorje Stadion	3 000	1924
11	Korotan Prevalje			1					1				Prevalje			
	Aluminij Kidricevo			1					1				Kidricevo			
	NK Dravograd			1					1				Dravograd			
14	Izola Belvedur			1			1						Izola			

RECENT LEAGUE AND CUP RECORD

	Championship						Cup		
Year	Champions	Pts	Runners-up	Pts	Third	Pts	Winners	Score	Runners-up
1995	Olimpija Ljubljana	44	NK Maribor	42	ND Gorica	41	Mura Murska Sobota	1-1 1-0	Publikum Celje
1996	ND Gorica	67	Olimpija Ljubljana	64	Mura Murska Sobota	58	Olimpija Ljubljana	1-0 1-1	Primorje Ajdovscina
1997	NK Maribor	71	Primorje Ajdovscina	66	ND Gorica	65	NK Maribor	0-0 3-0	Primorje Ajdovscina
1998	NK Maribor	67	Mura Murska Sobota	67	ND Gorica	65	Rudar Velenje	1-2 3-0	Primorje Ajdovscina
1999	NK Maribor	66	ND Gorica	62	Rudar Velenje	56	NK Maribor	3-2 2-0	Olimpija Ljubljana
2000	NK Maribor	81	ND Gorica	62	Rudar Velenje	58	Olimpija Ljubljana	1-2 2-0	Korotan Prevalje
2001	NK Maribor	62	Olimpija Ljubljana	60	Primorje Ajdovscina	56	ND Gorica	0-1 4-2	Olimpija Ljubljana
2002	NK Maribor	66	Primorje Ajdovscina	60	FC Koper	56	ND Gorica	4-0 2-1	Aluminij Kidricevo
2003	NK Maribor	62	Publikum Celje	55	Olimpija Ljubljana	54	Olimpija Ljubljana	1-1 2-2	Publikum Celje
2004	ND Gorica	56	Olimpija Ljubljana	55	NK Maribor	54	NK Maribor	4-0 3-4	Koroska Dravograd
2005	ND Gorica	65	Domzale	52	Publikum Celje	52	Publikum Celje	1-0	ND Gorica
2006	ND Gorica	73	Domzale	71	FC Koper	57	FC Koper	1-1 5-3p	Publikum Celje
2007	Domzale	76	ND Gorica	58	NK Maribor	57	FC Koper	1-0	NK Maribor
2008	Domzale	76	FC Koper	64	ND Gorica	57	Interblock Ljubljana	2-1	NK Maribor

SLOVENIA 2007–08

SIMOBIL LIGA

	Pl	W	D	L	F	A	Pts	Domzale	Koper	Gorica	Maribor	Interblock	Primorje	Nafta	Celje	Drava	Livar
Domzale †	36	22	10	4	69	28	76		0-0 1-1	2-3 1-1	4-0 0-0	2-1 1-2	2-1 3-2	5-0 2-0	2-1 4-0	4-1 2-1	2-1 1-1
FC Koper ‡	36	18	10	8	68	50	64	2-3 2-2		1-0 4-3	2-1 1-1	1-1 2-1	1-1 2-1	1-1 3-1	4-2 2-0	2-0 2-3	2-0 4-0
ND Gorica	36	16	9	11	61	50	57	1-1 2-0	2-3 2-4		3-2 2-1	1-0 2-2	1-0 1-3	3-4 4-1	0-0 0-0	1-1 1-0	1-1 6-1
NK Maribor	36	14	10	12	55	46	52	0-1 0-1	3-3 3-3	2-1 0-3		0-1 1-1	0-0 1-3	3-3 3-1	0-1 5-2	1-3 1-0	3-2 3-2
Interblock Ljubljana	36	14	8	14	49	42	50	0-2 2-3	2-2 1-2	0-1 3-0	0-1 1-0		1-0 1-2	1-0 1-1	1-1 1-1	4-1 1-2	5-1 1-0
Primorje Ajdovscina	36	14	6	16	52	41	48	0-2 0-0	2-0 4-0	1-2 1-0	0-0 1-0	2-0 0-2		1-2 2-1	0-2 5-0	2-1 1-1	4-2 3-0
Nafta Lendava	36	12	11	13	43	56	47	0-6 0-0	2-0 1-0	1-1 1-2	1-1 0-1	1-3 1-0	2-1 2-1		2-0 0-0	1-1 1-0	3-1 4-2
NK Celje	36	13	6	17	42	51	45	2-0 0-1	0-1 0-2	0-2 4-2	0-2 0-2	1-2 2-1	2-1 0-2	0-0 1-0		6-0 0-2	1-2 1-0
Drava Ptuj	36	13	5	18	45	64	44	0-0 0-6	1-0 2-1	1-0 1-3	1-3 1-2	2-0 0-2	3-2 1-0	2-2 2-1	0-2 1-2		1-3 3-1
Livar Ivanca Gorica	36	4	5	27	39	95	17	0-1 1-2	1-6 1-2	0-1 3-3	0-6 0-3	1-2 2-2	0-5 3-0	1-1 0-1	1-2 1-5	4-2 0-3	

20/07/2007 - 31/05/2008 • † Qualified for the UEFA Champions League • ‡ Qualified for the UEFA Cup
Play-off: **Drava** 2-0 0-1 Bonifika

SLOVENIA 2007–08
2.SNL (2)

	Pl	W	D	L	F	A	Pts
Rudar Velenje	27	15	5	7	70	31	50
Bonifika Koper	27	12	7	8	44	29	43
Bela Krajina	27	12	7	8	40	30	43
Aluminij Kidricevo	27	12	5	10	39	30	41
Mura Murska Sobota	27	10	7	10	31	42	37
Krsko	27	9	9	9	33	42	36
Zavrc	27	10	6	11	36	35	36
Zagorje	27	9	8	10	43	45	35
Triglav Gorenjska Kranj	27	10	5	12	36	40	35
Krka	27	4	5	18	23	71	17

11/08/2007 - 31/05/2008

POKAL HERVIS 2007–08

Round of 16

Interblock Ljubljana *	2 7p
Primorje Ajdovscina	2 6p
Krsko *	1
Nafta Lendava	3
Bela Krajina *	3
ND Gorica	1
Livar Ivanca Gorica *	1
FC Koper	4
Domzale *	7
Malecnik	1
Izola Argeta	1
NK Celje *	6
Olimpija Ljubljana	1
Drava Ptuj *	0
Dravinja Konjice	1
NK Maribor *	4

Quarter-finals

Interblock Ljubljana *	3
Nafta Lendava	1
Bela Krajina *	0
FC Koper	1
Domzale *	3
NK Celje	1
Olimpija Ljubljana	1
NK Maribor *	3

Semi-finals

Interblock Ljubljana *	2 3
FC Koper	1 2
Domzale	0 1
NK Maribor *	1 1

Final

Interblock Ljubljana ‡	2
NK Maribor	1

CUP FINAL
13-05-2008

* Home team/home team in the first leg • ‡ Qualified for the UEFA Cup

SWE – SWEDEN

NATIONAL TEAM RECORD
JULY 10TH 2006 TO JULY 12TH 2010

PL	W	D	L	F	A	%
29	13	4	12	33	32	51.7

FIFA/COCA-COLA WORLD RANKING

1993	1994	1995	1996	1997	1998	1999	2000	2001	2002	2003	2004	2005	2006	2007		High	
9	3	13	17	18	18	16	23	16	25	19	13	14	14	24		2	11/94

					2007–2008							Low	
08/07	09/07	10/07	11/07	12/07	01/08	02/08	03/08	04/08	05/08	06/08	07/08	31	08/98
19	20	24	24	24	22	24	24	24	23	30	26		

The Swedes were comfortable enough in qualifying for Euro 2008 - the fifth tournament in a row in which they have made it to the finals - but once again Lars Lagerback's ageing team failed to show any real inspiration beyond their good organisational skills. The return from international retirement of veteran striker Henrik Larsson had offered hope and the campaign began well with a 2-0 victory over defending champions Greece, but an injury-time goal by Spain's David Villa in the next match turned what would have been an excellent draw into a defeat. That left a tricky final match against Russia where a draw would have been enough, but with Zlatan Ibrahimovic not fully

INTERNATIONAL HONOURS
Olympic Games Gold 1948 Qualified for the FIFA World Cup finals 1934 1938 1950 1958 (Hosts) 1970 1974 1978 1990 1994 2002 2006
Women's European Championship 1984 Qualified for the FIFA Women's World Cup 1991 1995 1999 2003

fit, the Swedes were left chasing the game in a 2-0 defeat as yet another campaign came to a disappointing close. A home there was unmitigated joy for fans of IFK Göteborg whose team won the Allsvenskan for the first time in over a decade with a team of young players entirely from within Scandanavia. Coached by Stefan Rehn and Jonas Ohlsson, IFK finished a point ahead of Kalmar in a very tight finish also involving Djurgården, but they fell just short of the double having earlier lost to Kalmar in the Cup Final.

THE FIFA BIG COUNT OF 2006

	Male	Female		Total
Number of players	791 612	215 327	Referees and Assistant Referees	14 750
Professionals	2 001		Admin, Coaches, Technical, Medical	10 200
Amateurs 18+	231 399		Number of clubs	3 236
Youth under 18	319 599		Number of teams	31 000
Unregistered	375 000		Clubs with women's teams	1 000
Total players	1 006 939		Players as % of population	11.17%

Svenska Fotbollförbundet (SVFF)
PO Box 1216, Solna 17 123, Sweden
Tel +46 8 7350900   Fax +46 8 7350901
svff@svenskfotboll.se   www.svenskfotboll.se
President: LAGRELL Lars-Ake   General Secretary: HELLSTROMER Sune
Vice-President: LUNDQVIST Bo   Treasurer: SAHLSTROEM Kjell   Media Officer: NYSTEDT Jonas
Men's Coach: LAGERBACK Lars   Women's Coach: DENNERBY Thomas
SVFF formed: 1904   UEFA: 1954   FIFA: 1954
Yellow shirts with blue trimmings, Blue shorts, Yellow socks or Blue shirts with yellow trimmings, Blue shorts, Blue socks

RECENT INTERNATIONAL MATCHES PLAYED BY SWEDEN

2006	Opponents	Score		Venue	Comp	Scorers	Att	Referee
10-06	Trinidad and Tobago	D	0-0	Dortmund	WCr1		62 959	Maidin SIN
15-06	Paraguay	W	1-0	Berlin	WCr1	Ljungberg [89]	72 000	Michel SVK
20-06	England	D	2-2	Cologne	WCr1	Allback [51], Larsson [90]	45 000	Busacca SUI
24-06	Germany	L	0-2	Munich	WCr2		66 000	Simon BRA
16-08	Germany	L	0-3	Gelsenkirchen	Fr		53 000	Farina ITA
2-09	Latvia	W	1-0	Riga	ECq	Källström [38]	7 500	Ceferin SVN
6-09	Liechtenstein	W	3-1	Gothenburg	ECq	Allbäck 2 [2 69], Rosenberg [89]	17 735	Banari MDA
7-10	Spain	W	2-0	Stockholm	ECq	Elmander [10], Allbäck [82]	41 482	Bennett ENG
11-10	Iceland	W	2-1	Reykjavik	ECq	Källström [8], Wilhelmsson [59]	8 725	Gilewski POL
15-11	Côte d'Ivoire	L	0-1	Le Mans	Fr		3 844	Fautrel FRA
2007								
14-01	Venezuela	L	0-2	Maracaibo	Fr		14 000	Buitrago COL
18-01	Ecuador	L	1-2	Cuenca	Fr	Prica [91+]	20 000	Carrillo PER
21-01	Ecuador	D	1-1	Quito	Fr	Nannskog [69]	18 000	Garay PER
7-02	Egypt	L	0-2	Cairo	Fr		40 000	Abdalla LBY
28-03	Northern Ireland	L	1-2	Belfast	ECq	Elmander [26]	13 500	Braamhaar NED
2-06	Denmark	D	3-3	Copenhagen	ECq	Elmander 2 [7 26], Hansson [23]. Abandoned. Awarded 3-0	42 083	Fandel GER
6-06	Iceland	W	5-0	Stockholm	ECq	Allbäck 2 [11 51], Svensson.A [42], Mellberg [45], Rosenberg [50]	33 358	Hamer LUX
22-08	USA	W	1-0	Stockholm	Fr	Källström [56]	20 648	Blom NED
8-09	Denmark	D	0-0	Stockholm	ECq		33 082	De Bleeckere BEL
12-09	Montenegro	W	2-1	Podgorica	Fr	Rosenberg [71], Prica [75]	9 000	Brugger AUT
13-10	Liechtenstein	W	3-0	Vaduz	ECq	Ljungberg [19], Wilhelmsson [29], Svensson.A [56]	4 131	Dondarini ITA
17-10	Northern Ireland	D	1-1	Stockholm	ECq	Mellberg [15]	33 112	Layec FRA
17-11	Spain	L	0-3	Madrid	ECq		67 055	Rosetti ITA
21-11	Latvia	W	2-1	Stockholm	ECq	Allbäck [1], Källström [57]	26 128	Stark GER
2008								
13-01	Costa Rica	W	1-0	San Jose	Fr	Holmen [49]	7 000	Batres GUA
19-01	USA	L	0-2	Carson	Fr		14 878	Navarro CAN
6-02	Turkey	D	0-0	Istanbul	Fr		20 000	Tagliavento ITA
26-03	Brazil	L	0-1	London	Fr		60 021	Riley ENG
26-05	Slovenia	W	1-0	Gothenburg	Fr		21 118	Collum SCO
1-06	Ukraine	L	0-1	Stockholm	Fr		25 203	Einwaller AUT
10-06	Greece	W	2-0	Salzburg	ECr1	Ibrahimovic [67], Hansson [72]	31 063	Busacca SUI
14-06	Spain	L	1-2	Innsbruck	ECr1	Ibrahimovic [34]	30 772	Vink NED
18-06	Russia	L	0-2	Innsbruck	ECr1		30 772	De Bleeckere BEL

Fr = Friendly match • EC = UEFA EURO 2008 • WC = FIFA World Cup • q = qualifier • r1 = first round group • r2 = second round

SWEDEN NATIONAL TEAM PLAYERS

	Player		Ap	G	Club	Date of Birth		Player		Ap	G	Club	Date of Birth
1	Andreas Isaksson	GK	59	0	Manchester City	3 10 1981	12	Rami Shaaban	GK	16	0	Hammarby IF	30 06 1975
2	Mikael Nilsson	MF	50	3	Panathinaikos	24 06 1978	13	Johan Wiland	GK	3	0	Elfsborg IF	24 01 1981
3	Olof Mellberg	DF	85	4	Aston Villa	3 09 1977	14	Daniel Majstorovic	DF	15	1	FC Basel	5 04 1977
4	Petter Hansson	DF	35	2	Stade Rennais	14 12 1976	15	Andreas Granqvist	DF	3	0	Wigan Athletic	16 04 1985
5	Fredrik Stoor	DF	8	0	Rosenborg BK	28 02 1984	16	Kim Källström	MF	57	8	Olymp. Lyonnais	24 08 1982
6	Tobias Linderoth	MF	75	2	Galatasaray	21 04 1979	17	Henrik Larsson	FW	98	36	Helsingborgs IF	20 09 1971
7	Niclas Alexandersson	MF	109	7	IFK Göteborg	29 12 1971	18	Sebastian Larsson	MF	5	0	Birmingham City	6 06 1985
8	Anders Svensson	MF	93	15	Elfsborg IF	17 07 1976	19	Daniel Andersson	MF	65	0	Malmö FF	28 08 1977
9	Fredrik Ljungberg	MF	75	14	West Ham Utd	16 04 1977	20	Marcus Allbäck	FW	74	30	FC København	5 07 1973
10	Zlatan Ibrahimovic	FW	53	20	Internazionale	3 10 1981	21	Christian Wilhelmsson	MF	52	4	Deportivo	8 12 1979
11	Johan Elmander	FW	38	11	Toulouse FC	27 05 1981	22	Markus Rosenberg	FW	23	6	Werder Bremen	27 09 1982
							23	Mikael Dorsin	DF	12	0	CFR Cluj	6 10 1981

The Swedish squad for Euro 2008

SWEDEN NATIONAL TEAM RECORDS AND RECORD SEQUENCES

Records				Sequence records			
Victory	12-0	LVA 1927, KOR 1948		Wins	11	2001	
Defeat	1-12	ENG 1908		Defeats	6	1908-1909	
Player Caps	143	Thomas Ravelli		Undefeated	23	2000-2002	
Player Goals	49	Sven Rydell		Without win	15	1920-1921	
				Clean sheets	9	2001	
				Goals scored	28	1958-1962	
				Without goal	4	1998	
				Goals against	17	1925-1927	

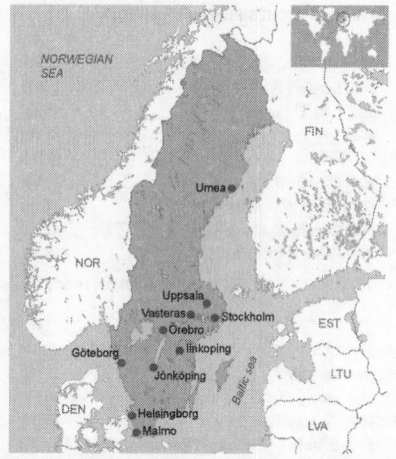

MAJOR CITIES/TOWNS
Population '000

1	Stockholm	1 721
2	Göteborg	797
3	Malmö	266
4	Uppsala	129
5	Västeras	108
6	Örebro	99
7	Linköping	97
8	Helsingborg	92
9	Jönköping	83
10	Norrköping	82
11	Lund	77
12	Umeå	75
13	Gävle	68
14	Borås	63
15	Eskilstuna	59
16	Karlstad	58
17	Halmstad	56
18	Växjö	54
19	Sundsvall	48
20	Luleå	45
21	Östersund	42
22	Borlänge	38
23	Kalmar	35
24	Landskrona	27

KINGDOM OF SWEDEN; KONUNGARIKET SVERIGE

Capital	Stockholm	Language	Swedish	Independence	1523
Population	9 031 088	Area	449 964 km²	% in cities	83%
GDP per cap	$26 800	Dailling code	+46	Internet .se	GMT +/- +1

MEDALS TABLE

		Overall			League			Cup		Europe			City	Stadium	Cap'ty	DoF
		G	S	B	G	S	B	G	S	G	S	B				
1	Malmö FF	29	19	6	15	15	6	14	3		1		Malmö	Malmö Stadion	26 500	1910
2	IFK Göteborg	24	14	13	18	9	12	4	5	2		1	Gothenburg	Ullevi	43 000	1904
3	IFK Norrköping	18	14	4	12	10	4	6	4				Norrköping	Idrottsparken	19 400	1897
4	AIK Stockholm	17	19	9	10	12	9	7	7				Solna, Stockholm	Råsunda	36 608	1896
5	Djurgårdens IF	15	14	8	11	11	8	4	3				Stockholm	Stockholms Stadion	14 500	1891
6	Örgryte IS Göteborg	15	6	5	14	5	5	1	1				Gothenburg	Valhalla IP	3 500	1887
7	Helsingborgs IF	9	11	8	6	9	8	3	2				Helsingborg	Olympia Stadion	16 673	1907
8	IF Elfsborg Borås	7	8	3	5	5	3	2	3				Borås	Borås Arena	17 800	1904
9	GAIS Göteborg	7	5	3	6	4	3	1	1				Gothenburg	Ullevi	43 000	1894
10	Östers IF Växjö	5	7	4	4	3	4	1	4				Växjö	Värendsvallen	15 000	1930
11	Halmstads BK	5	2	2	4	2	2	1					Halmstad	Orjans Vall	15 500	1914
12	Åtvidabergs FF	4	6		2	2		2	4				Atvidaberg	Kopparvallen	7 200	1907
13	Kalmar FF	3	2	2		1	2	3	1				Kalmar	Fredriksskans	8 500	1910
14	Hammarby IF	1	5	2	1	3	2		2				Stockholm	Söderstadion	16 185	1897
15	IK Sleipner Norrköping	1	4	1	1	3	1		1				Norrköping			1903
	Landskrona BoIS	1	4	1		1		1	4				Landskrona	Landskrona IP	12 000	1915

RECENT LEAGUE AND CUP RECORD

	Championship						Cup		
Year	Champions	Pts	Runners-up	Pts	Third	Pts	Winners	Score	Runners-up
1995	IFK Göteborg	46	Helsingborgs IF	42	Halmstads BK	41	Halmstads BK	3-1	AIK Stockholm
1996	IFK Göteborg	56	Malmö FF	46	Helsingborgs IF	44	AIK Stockholm	1-0	Malmö FF
1997	Halmstads BK	52	IFK Göteborg	49	Malmö FF	46	AIK Stockholm	2-1	IF Elfsborg
1998	AIK Stockholm	46	Helsingborgs IF	44	Hammarby IF	42	Helsingborgs IF	1-1 1-1 3-0p	Orgryte IS
1999	Helsingborgs IF	54	AIK Stockholm	53	Halmstads BK	48	AIK Stockholm	1-0 0-0	IFK Göteborg
2000	Halmstads BK	52	Helsingborgs IF	46	AIK Stockholm	45	Orgryte IS	2-0 0-1	IFK Göteborg
2001	Hammarby IF	48	Djurgårdens IF	47	AIK Stockholm	45	IF Elfsborg	1-1 9-8p	AIK Stockholm
2002	Djurgårdens IF	52	Malmö FF	46	Orgryte IS	44	Djurgårdens IF	1-0	AIK Stockholm
2003	Djurgårdens IF	58	Hammarby IF	51	Malmö FF	48	IF Elfsborg	2-0	Assyriska
2004	Malmö FF	52	Halmstads BK	50	IFK Göteborg	47	Djurgårdens IF	3-1	IFK Göteborg
2005	Djurgårdens IF	53	IFK Göteborg	49	Kalmar FF	43	Djurgårdens IF	2-0	Atvidabergs FF
2006	Elfsborg IF	50	AIK Stockholm	49	Hammarby IF	43	Helsingborgs IF	2-0	Gefle IF
2007	IFK Göteborg	49	Kalmar FF	48	Djurgårdens IF	46	Kalmar FF	3-0	IFK Göteborg

SWEDEN 2007

ALLSVENSKAN

	Pl	W	D	L	F	A	Pts	IFK	Kalmar	Djurgårdens	Elfsborg	AIK	Hammarby	Halmstad	Helsingborg	Malmö	Gefle	GAIS	Orebro	Trelleborg	Brom'karna
IFK Göteborg †	26	14	7	5	45	23	49		3-2	1-1	2-2	1-2	3-0	1-1	0-0	1-2	2-0	1-0	2-0	2-0	0-0
Kalmar FF ‡	26	15	3	8	43	32	48	0-5		1-0	2-1	2-0	2-0	3-0	2-0	2-0	0-1	2-2	2-0	0-1	2-2
Djurgårdens IF ‡	26	13	7	6	39	24	46	2-1	1-3		2-1	3-1	1-0	2-0	3-1	1-0	2-1	0-1	4-1	1-1	0-1
Elfsborg IF	26	10	10	6	39	30	40	3-1	2-2	2-2		2-0	1-2	1-1	0-0	1-1	1-1	5-1	0-2	2-0	3-0
AIK Stockholm	26	10	8	8	30	27	38	0-1	0-1	1-1	0-1		1-0	1-1	0-1	3-1	1-0	0-0	1-1	2-0	3-0
Hammarby IF	26	11	3	12	35	31	36	3-1	1-0	2-0	0-1	1-2		0-1	0-2	1-0	4-3	4-0	1-0	3-0	4-0
Halmstads BK	26	9	9	8	33	41	36	1-3	2-1	1-2	3-0	2-2	2-2		2-1	1-3	0-0	2-2	3-1	1-0	1-0
Helsingborgs IF	26	9	8	9	49	37	35	2-2	5-0	1-4	0-1	2-3	4-2	9-0		0-1	3-1	1-1	4-1	1-1	1-1
Malmö FF	26	9	7	10	29	28	34	0-2	1-2	1-1	1-2	4-0	1-1	1-2	1-1		1-1	1-0	0-0	0-0	2-0
Gefle IF	26	9	7	10	29	30	34	0-2	2-1	0-2	2-2	0-0	1-0	2-0	4-0	2-1		1-0	0-0	1-0	1-1
GAIS Göteborg	26	7	8	11	24	37	29	0-1	0-3	1-1	2-1	1-1	1-1	2-1	0-3	1-2	1-0		1-1	3-1	2-1
Orebro SK	26	6	7	13	28	45	25	0-4	1-3	0-0	1-1	1-4	3-1	0-3	4-3	1-1	1-2	2-1		2-0	4-0
Trelleborgs IF	26	5	8	13	22	38	23	1-1	1-3	0-3	1-2	0-0	1-0	1-1	2-3	2-1	3-2	0-1	0-0		3-3
IF Brommapojkarna	26	5	8	13	21	43	23	1-2	1-2	1-0	1-1	0-2	0-2	1-1	1-1	0-1	2-1	1-0	3-1	0-3	

6/04/2007 - 28/10/2007 • † Qualified for the UEFA Champions League • ‡ Qualified for the UEFA Cup
Top scorers: Marcus Berg, IFK Göteborg 14; Razak Omotoyossi, Helsingborgs IF 14; César Santin, Kalmar FF 12; Johan Oremo, Gefle IF 11

SWEDEN 2007 SUPERETTAN (2)

	Pl	W	D	L	F	A	Pts
IFK Norrköping	30	20	3	7	62	29	63
Ljungskile SK	30	17	4	9	42	35	55
GIF Sundsvall	30	16	6	8	48	32	54
BK Hacken Göteborg	30	17	2	11	51	30	53
Bunkeflo IF	30	14	6	10	49	49	48
Atvidabergs FF	30	14	5	11	44	35	47
IK Sirius	30	13	4	13	53	50	43
Degerfors IF	30	10	8	12	34	40	38
Mjällby AIF	30	9	9	12	39	40	36
Orgryte IS Göteborg	30	10	6	14	40	52	36
Landskrona BoIS	30	9	8	13	39	45	35
Enköpings SK	30	9	8	13	25	38	35
Jönköpings Sodra	30	9	7	14	35	47	34
Falkenbergs FF	30	9	7	14	35	52	34
Osters IF Växjö	30	8	8	14	28	35	32
IF Sylvia	30	6	9	15	36	51	27

15/04/2007 - 27/10/2007

SVENSKA CUPEN 2007

Fourth round
Kalmar FF 3 4p
Skovde AIK * 3 3p

IF Brommapojkarna * 1 4p
Osters IF Växjö 1 5p

GIF Sundsvall 2
BK Hacken Göteborg * 0

Degerfors IF 0
Väsby United * 2

Landskrona BoIS 2
Helsingborgs IF * 1

Hammarby IF * 1
IFK Norrköping 2

Mjällby AIF 1 4p
Orgryte IS Göteborg * 1 2p

Gefle IF 0
IFK Göteborg * 3

Quarter-finals
Kalmar FF 1
Osters IF Växjö * 0

GIF Sundsvall * 1
Väsby United 2

Landskrona BoIS 3
IFK Norrköping * 2

Mjällby AIF * 1
IFK Göteborg 2

Semi-finals
Kalmar FF 4
Väsby United * 1

Landskrona BoIS 0
IFK Göteborg * 4

Final
Kalmar FF ‡ 3
IFK Göteborg 0

CUP FINAL
Fredriksskans, Kalmar, 27-09-2007
Att: 6877, Ref: Ingvarsson
Scorers - Cesar Santin 2 22 88p,
Patrik Ingelsten 65 for Kalmar

* Home team • ‡ Qualified for the UEFA Cup

SWZ – SWAZILAND

NATIONAL TEAM RECORD
JULY 10TH 2006 TO JULY 12TH 2010

PL	W	D	L	F	A	%
22	5	9	8	14	33	43.2

FIFA/COCA-COLA WORLD RANKING

1993	1994	1995	1996	1997	1998	1999	2000	2001	2002	2003	2004	2005	2006	2007
99	125	148	160	165	149	127	137	132	116	114	126	134	148	148

High	
92	10/93

2007–2008											
08/07	09/07	10/07	11/07	12/07	01/08	02/08	03/08	04/08	05/08	06/08	07/08
147	149	151	151	148	148	149	153	156	154	161	123

Low	
174	10/97

Swaziland scored a famous win over Togo at the start of their 2010 FIFA World Cup qualifying campaign and continued to upset the form book in their next two matches. But the kingdom would need something of a minor miracle to advance through to the next phase of the preliminaries for the 2010 finals in neighbouring South Africa. Three points against Togo were followed by a home draw with the much-fancied Zambia. The Swazi side, 'Sihlangu', went to Zambia a week later for a return match and held out until right near the end of the game when a disputed penalty handed Zambia a hollow 1-0 win. Four points from three games means Swaziland must effectively win

INTERNATIONAL HONOURS
None

away against Togo in their last match in October 2008 to stand any chance of progress. The appointment of former South African coach Ephraim Mashaba did much to galvanise the Swazi side, which had produced relatively mediocre results over the last 18 months and seen its FIFA/Coca-Cola World Ranking hover just inside the top 150. Mashaba took over just weeks before the Togo match after the sudden departure of the Swiss-born coach Raoul Savoy. In domestic competition, the police club Royal Leopards won a third successive title but lost out on a chance of the league and cup 'double' with a shock 2-1 defeat by Malanti Chiefs in the Cup Final.

THE FIFA BIG COUNT OF 2006

	Male	Female		Total
Number of players	54 900	0	Referees and Assistant Referees	100
Professionals	0		Admin, Coaches, Technical, Medical	800
Amateurs 18+	3 300		Number of clubs	60
Youth under 18	1 700		Number of teams	220
Unregistered	3 900		Clubs with women's teams	0
Total players	54 900		Players as % of population	4.83%

National Football Association of Swaziland (NFAS)

Sigwaca House, Plot 582, Sheffield Road, PO Box 641, Mbabane H100, Swaziland
Tel +268 4046852   Fax +268 4046206
info@nfas.org.sz   www.nfas.org.sz
President: MTHETHWA Adam   General Secretary: MNGOMEZULU Frederick
Vice-President: SHONGWE Timothy   Treasurer: MNGOMEZULU Frederick   Media Officer: None
Men's Coach: MASHABA Ephraim   Women's Coach: THWALA Christian
NFAS formed: 1968   CAF: 1976   FIFA: 1978
Blue shirts, Gold shorts, Red socks

RECENT INTERNATIONAL MATCHES PLAYED BY SWAZILAND

2005	Opponents	Score	Venue	Comp	Scorers	Att	Referee
1-06	Lesotho	W 4-3	Somhlolo	Fr	Jabulani Dlamini 21, Lwazi Maziya 63, Maxwell Zikalala 78, Mfanafuthi Bhembe 93+		
11-06	Zambia	L 0-3	Lusaka	CCr1			Chidoda BOT
2006							
14-04	Lesotho	L 0-5	Maseru	Fr			
16-04	Lesotho	D 2-2	Maseru	Fr	Nkosingiphile Dlamini 5, Civil Matsebula 15		
20-05	South Africa	L 0-1	Gaborone	CCr1			Malepa BOT
21-05	Madagascar	W 2-0	Gaborone	CCr1	Zweli Msibi 54, Mzwandile Mamba 82		Malepa BOT
24-06	Mozambique	L 0-4	Maputo	Fr			
25-06	Zimbabwe	L 1-2	Maputo	Fr	Manqoba Kunene 6		
26-08	Lesotho	W 3-1	Mbabane	Fr	Mduduzi Mdluli 2 28 49, Salebona Jele 64		
3-09	Angola	L 0-2	Mbabane	CNq			Maillet SEY
7-10	Eritrea	D 0-0	Asmara	CNq			Gasingwa RWA
15-11	Botswana	L 0-1	Gaborone	Fr			
2007							
13-02	Lesotho	W 1-0	Maseru	Fr	Bheki Msimango 5		
18-03	Lesotho	L 0-1	Lobamba	Fr			
25-03	Kenya	L 0-2	Nairobi	CNq			Seechurn MRI
26-05	Mauritius	D 0-0	Mbabane	CCr1	L 5-6p		Labrosse SEY
27-05	Malawi	W 1-0	Mbabane	CCr1	Mphile Tsabedze 85		Labrosse SEY
3-06	Kenya	D 0-0	Mbabane	CNq			Katjimune NAM
17-06	Angola	L 0-3	Luanda	CNq			Marange ZIM
9-09	Eritrea	D 0-0	Manzini	CNq			Ssegonga UGA
18-11	Malawi	L 0-3	Manzini	Fr			
2008							
9-02	Botswana	L 1-4	Mbabane	Fr	Tony Tsabedze 77		
10-02	Lesotho	D 2-2	Mbabane	Fr	Barry Steenkamp 48, Baiano Kunene 58. L 1-4p		
23-05	Lesotho	D 1-1	Mbabane	Fr	Felix Badenhorst 20		
8-06	Togo	W 2-1	Mbabane	WCq	Siza Dlamini 55, Collen Salelwako 73	5 819	Niyongabo BDI
15-06	Zambia	D 0-0	Mbabane	WCq		7 462	Kotey GHA
21-06	Zambia	L 0-1	Chililabombwe	WCq		14 458	Marange ZIM
19-07	Madagascar	D 1-1	Witbank	CCr1	Phinda Dlamini 39		Nhlapo RSA
21-07	Mauritius	D 1-1	Witbank	CCr1	Gcina Mazibuko 51		Nhlapo RSA
23-07	Seychelles	W 1-0	Witbank	CCr1	Mfanzile Dlamini 89		Katjimune NAM

Fr = Friendly match • CN = CAF African Cup of Nations • CC = COSAFA Castle Cup • WC = FIFA World Cup
q = qualifier • r1 = first round group • qf = quarter-final • sf = semi-final

SWAZILAND NATIONAL TEAM RECORDS AND RECORD SEQUENCES

Records			Sequence records				
Victory	4-1	LES 1999	Wins	3	1999, 2001-2002	Clean sheets	3	2007
Defeat	1-9	ZAM 1978	Defeats	8	1969-1989	Goals scored	8	1998-1999
Player Caps	91	Mlungisi Nguban	Undefeated	9	2001-2002	Without goal	6	1993-1997
Player Goals	26	Sibusiso Dlamini	Without win	18	1969-1990	Goals against	15	1981-1990

SWAZILAND COUNTRY INFORMATION

Capital	Mbabane	Independence	1968 from the UK	GDP per Capita	$4 900
Population	1 169 241	Status	Monarchy	GNP Ranking	147
Area km²	17 363	Language	English, siSwati	Dialling code	+46
Population density	67 per km²	Literacy rate	81%	Internet code	.sz
% in urban areas	31%	Main religion	Christian 60%	GMT +/-	+1
Towns/Cities ('000)	Manzini 110; Mbabane 76; Big Bend 10; Malkerns 9; Nhlangano 9; Mhlume 8; Hluti 6				
Neighbours (km)	Mozambique 105; South Africa 430				
Main stadia	Somholo National Stadium – Mbabane 30 000				

SWAZILAND 2007-08

MTN PREMIER LEAGUE

	Pl	W	D	L	F	A	Pts	Leopards	Highlanders	Buffaloes	Green M'ba	Swallows	Wanderers	Sundowns	XI Men IF	Umbelebele	Rovers	Midas	Illovo
Royal Leopards †	22	13	5	4	39	19	44		0-1	1-1	1-0	1-0	3-0	3-1	2-0	2-1	2-1	3-1	5-0
Mbabane Highlanders	22	11	9	2	31	12	42	2-1		3-1	0-0	1-0	0-0	1-1	1-1	0-0	4-1	1-1	1-0
Young Buffaloes	22	11	7	4	30	14	40	1-1	0-0		0-1	2-0	1-1	2-0	2-0	1-0	0-2	1-0	3-0
Green Mamba	22	11	6	5	26	15	39	1-3	1-1	0-0		4-0	1-0	0-1	1-0	2-0	0-0	1-0	5-3
Mbabane Swallows	22	9	6	7	30	29	33	4-0	2-1	1-3	1-1		2-1	1-1	1-0	1-1	2-2	0-1	3-1
Manzini Wanderers	22	8	6	8	24	24	30	1-1	0-1	1-1	3-1	**1-2**		0-1	1-2	2-0	3-1	2-2	2-1
Manzini Sundowns	22	8	5	9	21	23	29	3-1	0-2	0-1	0-1	2-3	1-2		0-0	1-1	2-1	1-0	1-0
Eleven Men in Flight	22	6	7	9	15	19	25	1-1	1-3	0-1	0-0	1-0	2-0	0-1		1-0	0-1	1-0	2-0
Umbelebele	22	5	6	11	18	25	21	0-0	0-0	0-3	1-0	0-1	0-1	0-2	1-0		2-1	1-3	0-1
Mhlambanyatsi Rovers	22	4	8	10	19	30	20	0-2	0-3	1-1	1-2	1-1	1-1	1-0	0-0	0-2		0-0	0-0
Midas Mbabane City	22	5	5	12	23	41	20	0-3	1-5	2-1	0-2	3-1	0-1	2-1	1-1	2-7	0-3		4-2
Illovo	22	4	4	14	18	43	16	0-3	1-0	0-4	0-2	1-2	0-1	1-1	2-2	1-1	3-1	1-0	

29/09/2007 - 18/05/2008 • † Qualified for the CAF Champions League

SWAZI BANK CUP 2007-08

Round of 16		Quarter–finals		Semi–finals		Final	
Malanti Chiefs	2						
Moneni Pirates	0	Malanti Chiefs	1				
Arsenal	0	Mhlambanyatsi Rovers	0				
Mhlambanyatsi Rovers	2			Malanti Chiefs	1		
Zwicle	0 5p			Green Mamba	0		
Manzini Sundowns	0 4p	Zwicle	1				
Black Swallows	0	Green Mamba	2				
Green Mamba	4					Malanti Chiefs	2
Manzini Wanderers	3					Royal Leopards	1
Young Buffaloes	0	Manzini Wanderers	2				
Eleven Men in Flight	1	Mbabane Swallows	1				
Mbabane Swallows	4			Manzini Wanderers	0		
Midas Mbabane City	1			Royal Leopards	1		
Hub Sundowns	0	Midas Mbabane City	2				
Mbabane Highlanders	1	Royal Leopards	3				
Royal Leopards	3						

CUP FINAL

Somhlolo, Mbabane
6-04-2008
Scorers - Mxolisi Dlamini 36, Sabelo Hlatjwako 56 for Chiefs; Gcina Mazibuko 91+ for Leopards

RECENT LEAGUE AND CUP RECORD

	Championship							Cup		
Year	Champions	Pts	Runners-up	Pts	Third	Pts		Winners	Score	Runners-up
1996	XI Men in Flight	69	Denver Sundowns	66	C&M Eagles	56				
1997	Mbabane High'ders	54	XI Men in Flight	52	Mbabane Swallows	52		Mbabane High'ders		
1998	No championship due to season readjustment									
1999	Manzini Wanderers	48	Mbabane High'ders	45	Mbabane Swallows	44		Mbabane High'ders		
2000	Mbabane High'ders	52	Green Mamba	45	Mbabane Swallows	37		Mhlume United		
2001	Mbabane High'ders	48	Manzini Wanderers	42	Mbabane Swallows	40		XI Men in Flight	1- 4-3p	Mbabane Swallows
2002	Manzini Wanderers	46	Mhlam'yatsi Rovers	43	Mbabane Swallows	43				
2003	Manzini Wanderers	45	Mhlam'yatsi Rovers	42	Mbabane Swallows	38				
2004	Mhlam'yatsi Rovers	50	Mbabane High'ders	45	Green Mamba	37		Green Mamba	5-1	Denver Sundowns
2005	Mbabane Swallows	43	Green Mamba	43	Royal Leopards	39		Hub Sundowns	2-0	Malanti Chiefs
2006	Royal Leopards	43	Young Buffaloes	40	Mbabane High'ders	37		Mbabane Swallows	1-0	Malanti Chiefs
2007	Royal Leopards	40	Green Mamba	39	Young Buffaloes	34		Royal Leopards	1-0	Manzini Sundowns
2008	Royal Leopards	44	Mbabane High'ders	42	Young Buffaloes	40		Malanti Chiefs	2-1	Royal Leopards

SYR – SYRIA

NATIONAL TEAM RECORD
JULY 10TH 2006 TO JULY 12TH 2010

PL	W	D	L	F	A	%
34	17	5	12	56	42	57.4

FIFA/COCA-COLA WORLD RANKING

1993	1994	1995	1996	1997	1998	1999	2000	2001	2002	2003	2004	2005	2006	2007
82	105	136	115	98	84	109	100	90	91	85	85	98	112	107

High	
78	08/03

2007–2008											
08/07	09/07	10/07	11/07	12/07	01/08	02/08	03/08	04/08	05/08	06/08	07/08
112	123	126	109	107	104	103	101	98	97	97	102

Low	
145	05/96

Syria's status within Asian football has steadily improved in recent seasons, with national champions Al Karama playing a key role in increasing the nation's profile throughout the continent. The Homs-based club won the league title for a third straight season to maintain their stranglehold on the domestic scene and after beating Al Ittihad 1-0 in the Cup Final they secured the double for the second season in a row. Karama have also continued to impress in the AFC Champions League. After reaching the final of the tournament in 2006, Al Karama have continued to mix it with the leading clubs in the continent. In 2007 they again reached the quarter-finals, losing to Korean

INTERNATIONAL HONOURS
Asian Youth Championship 1994

giants Seongnam Ilhwa, and they have qualified for the last eight one more in 2008 after attracting the highest average crowd in the group stage. The national team, too, has seen a marked improvement and they narrowly missed out on qualifying for the final phase of Asia's qualifying tournament for the 2010 World Cup finals. Mohammed Kwid's team went into their clash with the United Arab Emirates favourites to progress to the final phase along with Iran, but a 3-1 loss meant the Syrians missed out by a solitary goal. As a result, Kwid - who also coaches Al Karama - stood down from his position at the helm of the national team.

THE FIFA BIG COUNT OF 2006

	Male	Female		Total
Number of players	430 800	0	Referees and Assistant Referees	700
Professionals	0		Admin, Coaches, Technical, Medical	3 600
Amateurs 18+	4 700		Number of clubs	170
Youth under 18	29 700		Number of teams	760
Unregistered	214 200		Clubs with women's teams	0
Total players	430 800		Players as % of population	2.28%

Syrian Football Association (SFA)
Al Faihaa Sports Complex, PO Box 22296, Damascus, Syria
Tel +963 11 3335866   Fax +963 11 3331511
toufiksarhan@hotmail.com   www.syrian-soccer.com
President: JAPPAN Ahmad   General Secretary: SARHAN Toufik
Vice-President: FARES Taj Addin   Treasurer: KOBEH Miadeh   Media Officer: AL LAHHAM Hisham
Men's Coach: TBD   Women's Coach: TATISH Abd Alghani
FASF formed: 1936   AFC: 1970   FIFA: 1937
Red shirts, Red shorts, Red socks

RECENT INTERNATIONAL MATCHES PLAYED BY SYRIA

2006	Opponents	Score		Venue	Comp	Scorers	Att	Referee
30-01	Bahrain	D	1-1	Manama	Fr	Zyad Chaabo [6]		
7-02	Palestine	W	3-0	Damascus	Fr			
14-02	Saudi Arabia	D	1-1	Jeddah	Fr	OG [45]		
22-02	Korea Republic	L	1-2	Aleppo	ACq	Firas Al Khatib [49]	35 000	Maidin SIN
1-03	Chinese Taipei	W	4-0	Taipei	ACq	Zyad Chaabo 2 [29 58], Jehad Al Houssain [45], Firas Al Khatib [64]	700	O Il Son PRK
2-05	United Arab Emirates	L	1-2	Dubai	Fr	Zyad Chaabo		
15-07	Iraq	L	1-3	Damascus	Fr	Zyad Chaabo [75]		
25-07	Iraq	L	1-2	Damascus	Fr	Maher Al Sayed [61]		
30-07	Jordan	L	0-3	Amman	Fr			
5-08	Libya	W	2-1	Damascus	Fr	Aatef Jenyat [23], Maher Al Sayad [35]		
16-08	Iran	D	1-1	Tehran	ACq	Zyad Chaabo [88]	40 000	Irmatov UZB
1-09	Oman	L	0-3	Muscat	Fr			
6-09	Iran	L	0-2	Damascus	ACq		10 000	Matsumura JPN
11-10	Korea Republic	D	1-1	Seoul	ACq	Maher Al Sayad [18]	24 140	Kunsuta THA
15-11	Chinese Taipei	W	3-0	Damascus	ACq	Tarek Al Jabban [50], Firas Al Khatib 2 [61 80]	1 000	Al Hilali OMA
2007								
11-01	Saudi Arabia	L	1-2	Dammam	Fr	Majed Humssi [74]		
16-06	Lebanon	W	1-0	Amman	WAr1	Zyad Chaabo [45]		
18-06	Jordan	W	1-0	Amman	WAr1	Khaled Mansour [48]		
22-06	Iraq	L	0-3	Amman	WAsf			
18-08	Bangladesh	W	2-0	New Delhi	Fr.	Maher Al Sayad [48], Zyad Chaabo [79]		
21-08	Kyrgyzstan	W	4-1	New Delhi	Fr	Maher Al Sayad [7], Zyad Chaabo [44], Mohamed Alzeno [70], Abrahiem Al Hasan [82]		
23-08	India	W	3-2	New Delhi	Fr	Khaled Mansoor Al Baba [23], Zyad Chaabo 2 [45 65]		
25-08	Cambodia	W	5-1	New Delhi	Fr	Mohamed Al Zeno [25], Zyad Chaabo [35], Maher Al Sayad 2 [51 86], Aatef Jenyat [80]		
29-08	India	L	0-1	New Delhi	Fr			
8-10	Afghanistan	W	3-0	Damascus	WCq	Mohamed Al Zeno 2 [73 87], Maher Al Sayad [81]	3 000	Al Ghamdi KSA
26-10	Afghanistan	W	2-1	Dushanbe	WCq	Aatef Jenyat [16], Feras Ismail [63]	2 000	Irmatov UZB
9-11	Indonesia	W	4-1	Jakarta	WCq	Feras Ismail [17], Mohamed Al Zeno [34], Zyad Chaabo [43], Raja Rafe [93+]	35 000	Torky IRN
18-11	Indonesia	W	7-0	Damascus	WCq	Zyad Chaabo 3 [40 44 87], Raja Rafe 3 [60 72 90], Jehad Al Houssain [81p]	5 000	Sun Baojie CHN
2008								
13-01	Qatar	D	0-0	Damascus	Fr			
23-01	Bahrain	W	2-1	Manama	Fr	Zyad Chaabo 2 [12 45]		
27-01	China PR	L	1-2	Zhongshan	Fr	Jehad Al Houssain [89]		
6-02	Iran	D	0-0	Tehran	WCq		45 000	Bashir SIN
26-03	UAE	D	1-1	Damascus	WCq	Zyad Chaabo [3]	35 000	Sun Baojie CHN
10-05	Oman	W	2-1	Damascus	Fr	Zyad Chaabo 2 [55 75]		
17-05	Iraq	W	2-1	Damascus	Fr	Mahmoud Al Amena [17], Raja Rafe [21]		
24-05	Saudi Arabia	L	0-1	Riyadh	Fr			
2-06	Kuwait	W	1-0	Damascus	WCq	Jehad Al Houssain [52]	25 000	Mujghef JOR
8-06	Kuwait	L	2-4	Kuwait City	WCq	Firas Al Khatib 2 [9 45]	10 000	Al Hilali OMA
14-06	Iran	L	0-2	Damascus	WCq		25 000	Tongkhan THA
22-06	UAE	W	3-1	Al Ain	WCq	Jehad Al Houssain 2 [34 51], Sanharib Malki [93+]	7 000	Shield AUS

Fr = Friendly match • WA = West Asian Championship • WG = West Asian Games • AC = AFC Asian Cup • WC = FIFA World Cup
q = qualifier • r1 = first round group • sf = semi-final • 3p = third place play-off • f = final

SYRIA NATIONAL TEAM RECORDS AND RECORD SEQUENCES

Records			Sequence records				
Victory	13-0	OMA 1965	Wins	4	1998, 2001, 2004	Clean sheets	5	1985
Defeat	0-8	GRE 1949, EGY 1951	Defeats	9	1977-1978	Goals scored	14	2004
Player Caps	n/a		Undefeated	10	1987-1988	Without goal	4	Three times
Player Goals	n/a		Without win	13	1981-1983	Goals against	15	1981-1983

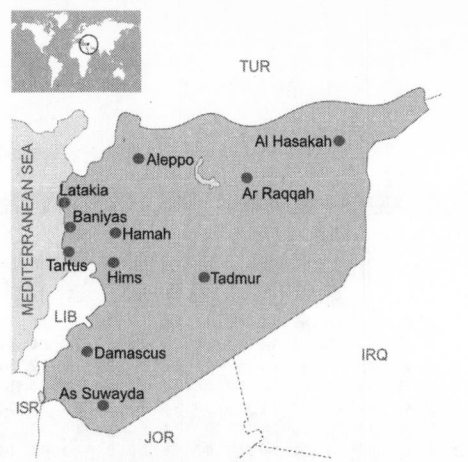

MAJOR CITIES/TOWNS

		Population '000
1	Aleppo	1 671
2	Damascus	1 603
3	Homs	845
4	Hamah	512
5	Latakia	360
6	Dayr az-Zawr	272
7	ar-Raqqah	191
8	al-Bab	152
9	Idlib	149
10	Duma	120
11	as-Safirah	111
12	Salamiyah	106
13	al-Hajar al-Aswad	100
14	Tartus	94
15	at-Tawrah	93
16	al-Qamisl	88
17	Ma'arrat-al-Numan	84
18	al-Hasakah	82
19	Darayya	76
20	Dar'a	75
21	Jabala	73
22	Manbij	73
23	Abu Kamal	66
24	A'zaz	66

SYRIAN ARAB REPUBLIC; AL JUMHURIYAH AL ARABIYAH AS SURIYAH

Capital	Damascus	Language	Arabic, Kurdish, Armenian		Independence	1946
Population	19 747 586	Area	185 180 km²	Density 97 per km²	% in cities	52%
GDP per cap	$3300	Dailling code	+963	Internet .sy	GMT + / -	+2

MEDALS TABLE

		Overall			League			Cup			Asia			City	Stadium	Cap'ty	DoF
		G	S	B	G	S	B	G	S	B	G	S	B				
1	Al Jaish	17	2		10	2		6			1			Damascus	Abbasiyyin	45 000	1947
2	Al Ittihad	14	5	12	6	5	12	8						Aleppo	International	75 000	1953
3	Al Karama	13	11	4	7	10	4	6				1		Homs	Khalid bin Walid	35 000	1928
4	Al Foutoua	6	5	3	2	5	3	4						Dayr az-Zawr	Der Ezzor		1950
5	Jabala	5	6	1	4	6	1	1						Jabala	Al Baath	10 000	
6	Al Shorta	5	4	2	1	4	2	4						Damascus	Al Jalaa	13 500	
7	Al Horriya	4	1	2	2	1	2	2						Aleppo	Hamadaniah	20 000	1952
8	Al Wahda	3	1	4	1		4	2				1		Damascus	Abbasiyyin	45 000	1928
9	Teshrin	2		3	2		3							Latakia	Al Assad	35 000	1947
10	Barada	2		2	2		2							Damascus			
11	Rmeilan	2						2									
12	Hottin	1	2	1		2	1	1						Latakia	Al Assad	35 000	1945
13	Al Majd	1	1			1		1						Damascus	Abbasiyyin	45 000	
14	Al Maghazel	1						1									

RECENT LEAGUE AND CUP RECORD

	Championship							Cup		
Year	Champions	Pts	Runners-up	Pts	Third	Pts		Winners	Score	Runners-up
1992	Al Horriya	42	Jabala	41	Al Ittihad	38		Al Horriya	1-0	Al Ittihad
1993	Al Ittihad		Al Karama		Al Horriya			Al Wahda	4-0	Hottin
1994	Al Horriya		Jabala		Al Shorta			Al Ittihad		
1995	Al Ittihad		Jabala		Al Karama			Al Karama	3-0	Hottin
1996	Al Karama	62	Hottin	51	Teshrine	45		Al Karama	3-0	Jabala
1997	Teshrine	60	Al Jaish	57	Al Karama	49		Al Jaish	2-0	Jabala
1998	Al Jaish	62	Al Karama	48	Hottine	46		Al Jaish	5-2	Al Karama
1999	Al Jaish	58	Al Karama	55	Al Wahda	44		Jabala	2-2 3-0p	Hottin
2000	Jabala	51	Hottin	50	Teshrine	50		Al Jaish	4-1	Jabala
2001	Al Jaish	60	Al Karama	51	Al Ittihad	49		Hottin	1-0	Al Jaish
2002	Al Jaish	37	Al Ittihad	35	Al Wahda	29		Al Jaish	3-0	Jabala
2003	Al Ittihad	57	Al Ittihad	54	Qardah	47		Al Wahda	5-2	Al Ittihad
2004	Al Wahda	60	Al Karama	58	Teshrine	54		Al Jaish	0-0 4-2p	Teshrine
2005	Al Ittihad	53	Al Karama	50	Al Wahda	44		Al Ittihad	3-1	Al Majd
2006	Al Karama	56	Al Jaish	53	Al Wahda	51		Al Ittihad	3-0	Teshrin
2007	Al Karama	62	Al Ittihad	55	Al Taliya	49		Al Karama	2-1	Al Taliya
2008	Al Karama	64	Al Majd	54	Al Ittihad	52		Al Karama	1-0	Al Ittihad

SYRIA 2007–08

FIRST DIVISION

	Pl	W	D	L	F	A	Pts	Karama	Majd	Ittihad	Taliya	Jaish	Foutoua	Teshrin	Hottin	Wahda	Jabala	Shorta	Nwair	Efrin	Horriya
Al Karama †	26	20	4	2	55	19	64		1-0	1-1	3-0	4-0	2-1	2-0	2-0	3-0	2-1	1-0	3-1	4-1	1-1
Al Majd	26	17	3	6	52	23	54	1-3		1-1	4-1	1-2	1-0	2-2	2-0	2-1	3-0	2-0	3-0	1-0	2-0
Al Ittihad	26	14	10	2	50	31	52	3-2	1-0		2-0	4-3	4-0	3-1	2-1	2-1	1-0	1-2	3-1	1-1	2-1
Al Taliya	26	14	4	8	39	34	46	1-3	0-5	2-2		1-0	1-0	4-1	3-1	4-0	2-0	0-0	1-0	1-0	1-0
Al Jaish	26	13	5	8	46	36	44	1-2	4-2	2-3	1-2		1-0	3-1	3-0	1-1	2-0	3-1	0-0	2-0	4-2
Al Foutoua	26	12	4	10	29	25	40	3-1	2-1	0-0	2-1	3-0		1-0	2-1	2-0	1-0	1-1	1-1	1-0	3-1
Teshrin	26	7	8	11	25	34	29	1-4	1-1	2-2	0-0	2-0	0-0		0-0	0-1	2-0	0-1	1-0	1-1	1-2
Hottin	26	7	8	11	32	42	29	3-3	0-1	2-2	2-3	4-4	1-0	2-3		1-0	1-1	2-1	2-1	1-1	1-0
Al Wahda	26	8	5	13	23	34	29	0-2	0-1	2-1	3-1	0-0	1-0	1-0	3-0		1-0	0-1	0-1	1-3	3-2
Jabala	26	8	5	13	28	41	29	0-0	1-7	2-2	1-2	1-4	1-0	0-0	1-2	2-0		3-1	0-0	4-0	3-0
Al Shorta	26	7	5	14	27	38	26	0-2	1-2	3-4	1-4	0-1	1-2	0-1	0-0	2-2	1-2		1-0	1-0	1-1
Al Nwair	26	7	5	14	20	32	26	0-2	1-2	1-1	0-2	1-2	1-0	2-0	1-0	3-2	0-1	0-2		0-0	2-0
Efrin	26	5	8	13	22	34	23	0-1	0-2	0-1	2-1	0-2	3-2	0-1	1-1	0-0	4-0	1-0	1-2		1-1
Al Horriya	26	2	8	16	28	53	14	0-1	1-3	0-0	1-1	1-1	1-2	2-4	1-4	0-0	3-4	3-5	2-1	2-2	

27/09/2007 - 5/07/2008 • † Qualified for the AFC Champions League

FASF CUP 2007–08

Round of 16			Quarter–finals			Semi–finals			Final	
Al Karama	2	3								
Al Shabab *	2	0	Al Karama *	1 0 4p						
Al Nidhal	0	2	Al Jaish	0 1 2p						
Al Jaish *	1	3				Al Karama	2 1			
Efrin *	2	1				Al Majd *	2 1			
Al Wahda	0	1	Efrin	1 0						
Al Horriya	0	1	Al Majd *	2 0						
Al Majd *	1	1							Al Karama	1
Hottin *	3	3							Al Ittihad	0
Al Nwair	0	0	Hottin *	2 4						
Al Foutoua *	1	1	Jabala	1 2						
Jabala	2	2				Hottin	1 0			
Teshrin	3	2				Al Ittihad *	2 1			
Al Qardaha *	1	3	Teshrin	0 0						
Al Taliya *	3	0	Al Ittihad *	4 0						
Al Ittihad	3	1								

* Home team in the first leg

CUP FINAL

22-07-2008

Scorer - Jehad Al Houssain [66]

TAH – TAHITI

NATIONAL TEAM RECORD
JULY 10TH 2006 TO JULY 12TH 2010

PL	W	D	L	F	A	%
3	1	0	2	1	5	33.3

FIFA/COCA-COLA WORLD RANKING

1993	1994	1995	1996	1997	1998	1999	2000	2001	2002	2003	2004	2005	2006	2007	High	
141	148	156	158	161	123	139	131	127	115	133	124	141	173	162	**111**	08/02

2007–2008												Low	
08/07	09/07	10/07	11/07	12/07	01/08	02/08	03/08	04/08	05/08	06/08	07/08	**181**	06/07
180	161	162	163	162	159	159	161	167	166	174	179		

The performance of the Tahiti national team at the football tournament of the South Pacific Games was a major disappointment for a nation that was once regarded as perhaps the strongest in the region. Indeed, Tahiti had won the tournament five times previously and only a face saving 1-0 victory in the final group match against the Cook Islands - the lowest ranked nation in the world - saved it from being an outright disaster. The tournament in Apia, which doubled up as a first round of 2010 FIFA World Cup qualifying for Oceania, was the first time that Tahiti had played a match since the last World Cup qualifiers in 2004, so perhaps the failure to progress should not be too

INTERNATIONAL HONOURS
South Pacific Games 1966 1975 1979 1983 1995   South Pacific Mini Games 1981 1985 1993

surprising. Their decline in fortunes was reflected in their descent down the world rankings from a high of 111 in August 2001 to a low of 181 in June 2007. Tahiti also lost its place in the O-League group stage when champions Manu Ura finished bottom of their group in the 2007-08 tournament although they did draw the short straw by being paired with both New Zealand clubs in the three team group. Having won the title for the third time in a row at home, Manu Ura qualified again for the O-League although they will have to play-off in order to make it to the group stage. Tefana were the other trophy winners in domestic football, after they retained the Polynesian Cup.

THE FIFA BIG COUNT OF 2006

	Male	Female		Total
Number of players	15 391	1 005	Referees and Assistant Referees	64
Professionals	0		Admin, Coaches, Technical, Medical	64
Amateurs 18+	4 429		Number of clubs	164
Youth under 18	5 367		Number of teams	650
Unregistered	4 500		Clubs with women's teams	7
Total players	16 396		Players as % of population	6.66%

Fédération Tahitienne de Football (FTF)
Rue Coppenrath, Stade de Fautaua, Case postale 50358, Pirae 98716, Tahiti, French Polynesia
Tel +689 540954   Fax +689 419629
contact@ftf.pf   www.ftf.pf
President: TEMARII Reynald   General Secretary: PERRY Vaiata
Vice-President: ARIIOTIMA Henri Thierry   Treasurer: MARTIN Jean-François   Media Officer: LATEYRON Chrystele
Men's Coach: KAUTAI Gerard   Women's Coach: APUARII Ralph
FTF formed: 1989   OFC: 1990   FIFA: 1990
Red shirts, White shorts, Red socks

RECENT INTERNATIONAL MATCHES PLAYED BY TAHITI

2002	Opponents	Score	Venue	Comp	Scorers	Att	Referee
5-07	New Zealand	L 0-4	Auckland	OCr1		1 000	Attison VAN
7-07	Solomon Islands	W 3-2	Auckland	OCr1	Booene [42], Tagawa [57], Fatupua-Lecaill [90]	1 000	Breeze AUS
9-07	Papua New Guinea	W 3-1	Auckland	OCr1	Garcia [29], Tagawa 2 [49 64]	800	Rakaroi FIJ
12-07	Australia	L 1-2	Auckland	OCsf	Zaveroni [38]	400	Rugg NZL
14-07	Vanuatu	W 1-0	Auckland	OC3p	Auraa [65]	1 000	Rakaroi FIJ
2003							
30-06	Micronesia †	W 17-0	Suva	SPr1	Tagawa 4 [8 10 19 33], OG [17], Guyon 3 [32 41 56] Bennett 4 [48 70 76 86], Tchen [69], Papaaura [71] Senechal [72], Lecaill [78], Terevaura [81]		Rakaroi FIJ
3-07	Papua New Guinea	W 3-0	Suva	SPr1	Bennett 2 [13 69], Tagawa [62]	1 000	Attison VAN
5-07	New Caledonia	L 0-4	Nadi	SPr1		3 000	Shah FIJ
7-07	Tonga	W 4-0	Lautoka	SPr1	Tagawa 2 [2 27], Bennett 2 [81 83]	3 000	Shah FIJ
9-07	Fiji	L 1-2	Lautoka	SPsf	Papura [4]	8 000	Attison VAN
11-07	Vanuatu	L 0-1	Suva	SP3p		6 000	Rakaroi FIJ
2004							
10-05	Cook Islands	W 2-0	Honiara	WCq	Temataua [2], Moretta [80]	12 000	Singh FIJ
12-05	New Caledonia	D 0-0	Honiara	WCq		14 000	Rakaroi FIJ
17-05	Tonga	W 2-0	Honiara	WCq	Wajoka [1], Temataua [78]	400	Sosongan PNG
19-05	Solomon Islands	D 1-1	Honiara	WCq	Simon [30]	18 000	Rakaroi FIJ
29-05	Fiji	D 0-0	Adelaide	WCq		3 000	Farina ITA
31-05	Australia	L 0-9	Adelaide	WCq		1 200	Attison VAN
2-06	Solomon Islands	L 0-4	Adelaide	WCq		50	Rakaroi FIJ
4-06	New Zealand	L 0-10	Adelaide	WCq		200	Shield AUS
6-06	Vanuatu	W 2-1	Adelaide	WCq	Temataua [40], Wajoka [89]	300	Rakaroi FIJ
2005							
No international matches played in 2005							
2006							
No international matches played in 2006							
2007							
25-08	New Caledonia	L 0-1	Apia	WCq		400	Hester NZL
29-08	Tuvalu †	D 1-1	Apia	WCq	Williams [45]	100	Lengeta SOL
1-09	Fiji	L 0-4	Apia	WCq		200	Fox NZL
3-09	Cook Islands	W 1-0	Apia	WCq	Tinorua [64]	100	Aimaasu SAM
2008							
No international matches played in 2008 before August							

Fr = Friendly match • OC = OFC Oceania Cup • SP = South Pacific Games • WC = FIFA World Cup
q = qualifier • r1 = first roundgroup • sf = semi-final • 3p = third place play-off • † Not a full international

TAHITI NATIONAL TEAM RECORDS AND RECORD SEQUENCES

Records		Sequence records					
Victory	30-0 COK 1971	Wins	10	1978-1980	Clean sheets	5	1995
Defeat	0-10 NZL 2004	Defeats	5	1996-1997	Goals scored	17	1981-1983
Player Caps	n/a	Undefeated	17	1981-1983	Without goal	4	2004
Player Goals	n/a	Without win	17	1959-1963	Goals against	20	1953-1963

TAHITI COUNTRY INFORMATION

Capital	Papeete	Status	French Overseas Possession, part of French Polynesia	GDP per Capita	$17 920
Population	266 339			GNP Ranking	n/a
Area km²	4 167	Language	French, Tahitian	Dialling code	+689
Population density	62 per km²	Literacy rate	98%	Internet code	.pf
% in urban areas	n/a	Main religion	Christian	GMT +/−	-10
Towns/Cities ('000)	Faaa 29; Papeete 26; Punaauia 25; Pirae 14; Mahina 14; Paea 13; Papara 10; Arue 9				
Neighbours (km)	South Pacific Ocean 2 525				
Main stadia	Stade de Fautaua – Pirae; Stade Pater – Papeete 15 000				

TAHITI 2007–08

DIVISION FEDERALE

Team	Pl	W	D	L	F	A	Pts	Manu Ura	Dragon	Tefana	Temanava	Tamarii	Jeunes T	Pirae	TAC	Central Sp.	Aorai
AS Manu Ura †	18	12	4	2	35	10	46	—	2-2	1-0	5-1	3-0	1-1	1-0	7-1	3-1	3-0
AS Dragon †	18	9	8	1	35	21	44	0-1	—	1-1	0-0	2-1	2-0	2-1	2-2	4-2	3-2
AS Tefana §1 †	18	11	4	3	39	18	43	1-2	1-1	—	1-0	2-1	3-0	3-0	4-2	5-1	5-1
AS Temanava †	18	8	4	6	24	22	38	0-0	0-1	0-4	—	4-1	1-1	2-1	3-2	0-1	3-0
AS Tamarii Faa'a	23	10	4	9	36	35	47	0-1	3-3	2-2	2-1	—	1-2		3-1	2-1 5-0	1-0 1-2
AS Jeunes Tahitiens	23	6	11	6	26	28	46	0-0	2-2	0-1	2-2	1-1 0-1	—	2-2 2-3	0-0 2-1	2-1 1-0	1-0 0-1
AS Pirae	23	9	3	11	38	39	44	2-0	1-3	2-3	0-2	0-0 2-3	2-4	—	2-1 1-1	1-2	2-5
AS Taravao AC	23	7	4	12	40	49	41	1-0	0-3	0-2	0-2	4-2 2-3	2-2	1-3	—	1-3 3-0	4-2
AS Central Sport	23	6	2	15	25	44	37	0-3	2-2	3-0	1-2	0-1	0-0	0-5 1-2	1-3	—	3-0 1-2
AS Aorai	23	4	2	17	21	53	33	0-2	0-2	1-1	0-1	1-5	0-1	1-4 0-1	1-5	1-3 0-1	—

20/09/2007 - 22/03/2008 • † Qualified for play-offs • Top four split off for a Championship round while the other play another round of fixtures against each other • Four points for a win, two points for a draw and one point for a defeat • Match in bold awarded • § = points deducted

TAHITI 2007–08
CHAMPIONSHIP PLAY-OFF

Team	Pl	W	D	L	F	A	Pts	MA	Te	Dr	Tm
AS Manu Ura †	6	4	1	1	13	3	17	—	3-0	4-1	4-0
AS Tefana	6	3	2	1	9	5	14	1-0	—	1-1	3-0
AS Dragon	6	2	3	1	11	8	13	1-1	1-1	—	5-0
AS Temanava §1	6	0	0	6	1	18	5	0-1	**0-3**	1-2	—

11/04/2008 - 16/05/2008 • † Qualified for the O-League • Man Ura had 2 bonus points for winning the first stage • Match in bold awarded • § = points deducted

COUPE DE POLYNESIE 2007–08

Round of 16

AS Tefana	3
Arue	0
AS Manu Ura	1
AS Dragon	5
AS Jeunes Tahitiens	3
Roniu	2
Tiare Hinano	1
Tiare Hinano	2
AS Temanava	2
AS Tamarii Faa'a	1
Tearaa	1
Samine Raiatea	2
Tiare Tahiti	2
AS Taravao AC	1
Vaiari Nui	0
AS Central Sport	7

Quarter–finals

AS Tefana	1 3
AS Dragon	0 1
AS Jeunes Tahitiens	1 1 3p
Tiare Hinano	1 1 4p
AS Temanava	2 2
Samine Raiatea	1 0
Tiare Tahiti	2 0
AS Central Sport	2 1

Semi–finals

AS Tefana	8 0
Tiare Hinano	0 1
AS Temanava	1 0
AS Central Sport	0 3

Final

AS Tefana	3 2
AS Central Sport	1 0

CUP FINAL

1st leg. Stade de Puurai, 23-05-2008

2nd leg. Stade Pater, 31-05-2008

RECENT LEAGUE AND CUP RECORD

	Championship	Cup			Polynesian Cup		
Year	Champions	Winners	Score	Runners-up	Winners	Score	Runners-up
2000	AS Vénus	AS Pirae		AS Vénus	AS Pirae		
2001	AS Pirae	AS Dragon	2-1	AS Vénus	AS Vénus	6-0	Central Sport
2002	AS Vénus				AS Pirae	1-0	AS Vénus
2003	AS Pirae	AS Manu-Ura	0-0 4-3p	AS Pirae			
2004	AS Manu Ura	AS Tefana	1-1 5-4p	AS Pirae	AS Dragon	1-0	AS Manu Ura
2005	AS Tefana	AS Manu-Ura	0-0 10-9p	AS Pirae	AS Pirae	2-1	AS Manu Ura
2006	AS Pirae	AS Tefana	2-0	AS Temarii	AS Temanava	2-1	AS Dragon
2007	AS Manu Ura				AS Tefana	1-1 1-1 4-3p	AS Manu Ura
2008	AS Manu Ura				AS Tefana	3-1 2-0	Central Sport

TAN – TANZANIA

NATIONAL TEAM RECORD
JULY 10TH 2006 TO JULY 12TH 2010

PL	W	D	L	F	A	%
28	11	10	7	28	24	57.1

FIFA/COCA-COLA WORLD RANKING

1993	1994	1995	1996	1997	1998	1999	2000	2001	2002	2003	2004	2005	2006	2007		High	
98	74	70	89	96	118	128	140	149	153	159	172	165	110	89		**65**	02/95

	2007–2008												Low	
08/07	09/07	10/07	11/07	12/07	01/08	02/08	03/08	04/08	05/08	06/08	07/08		**175**	11/05
102	106	106	103	89	101	101	97	94	102	101	115			

Tanzania failed at the final hurdle to qualify for the 2008 CAF Africa Cup of Nations finals, turning an advantageous position in the qualifiers on its head with defeat at home to Mozambique in the final game which was played at the new National stadium in Dar-es-Salaam. Since then it has been much the same scenario for the Taifa Stars, both in the 2010 FIFA World Cup qualifiers and the East and Central African Senior Challenge, which the country hosted in December 2007. The FIFA World Cup qualifiers started with a disappointing home draw against Mauritius and then defeat in the Cape Verde Islands. But although Tanzania secured only a point in the next two

INTERNATIONAL HONOURS
CECAFA Cup 1974 1994

matches against Cameroon they played well and as a result, their Brazilian coach Marcio Maximo was handed a contract extension. In the regional tournament, the team reached only the quarter-finals although this was a selection made up of mainland-born players as Tanzania's national team splits into the Kilimanjaro Stars (mainland) and Zanzibar for the annual East African championship. Young Africans came out best in 2008 in the perennial tussle with Simba SC for dominance of the country's club scene. Indeed, defending champions Simba dropped to third in the final standings behind runners-up Prisons.

THE FIFA BIG COUNT OF 2006

	Male	Female		Total
Number of players	225 015	1 503	Referees and Assistant Referees	475
Professionals	18		Admin, Coaches, Technical, Medical	8 300
Amateurs 18+	13 500		Number of clubs	200
Youth under 18	12 800		Number of teams	5 000
Unregistered	200 200		Clubs with women's teams	4
Total players	226 518		Players as % of population	0.60%

The Football Association of Tanzania (FAT)
Karume Memorial Stadium, Uhuru/Shaurimoyo Moyo Road, PO Box 1574, Dar-es-Salaam, Tanzania
Tel +255 745 264181   Fax +255 22 2861815
tfftz@yahoo.com   www.tfftanzania.com
President: TENGA Leodgar   General Secretary: MWAKALEBELA Frederik
Vice-President: MAGORI Crescentius   Treasurer: MWAKIBINGA Silas   Media Officer: KAIJAGE Florian
Men's Coach: MARCIO MAXIMO   Women's Coach: BONIFACE Charles
FAT formed: 1930   CAF: 1960   FIFA: 1964
Green shirts, Black shorts, Green socks

RECENT INTERNATIONAL MATCHES PLAYED BY TANZANIA

2003	Opponents	Score		Venue	Comp	Scorers	Att	Referee
11-10	Kenya	D	0-0	Dar es Salaam	WCq		8 864	Tessema ETH
11-11	Uganda	L	1-2	Kampala	Fr	Abu Masula		
15-11	Kenya	L	0-3	Nairobi	WCq		14 000	El Beltagy EGY
2004								
13-12	Zanzibar †	L	2-4	Addis Abeba	CCr1	Maxime 23, Machupa 32		
15-12	Burundi	L	0-2	Addis Abeba	CCr1			
17-12	Ethiopia	L	0-2	Addis Abeba	CCr1			
19-12	Rwanda	L	1-5	Addis Abeba	CCr1			
2005								
28-11	Burundi	W	2-1	Kigali	CCr1			
2-12	Zanzibar †	D	1-1	Kigali	CCr1			
4-12	Eritrea	W	1-0	Kigali	CCr1	Nurdin Bakari 38		
6-12	Rwanda	L	1-3	Kigali	CCr1	Sammy Kessy		
2006								
26-06	Mauritius	W	2-1	Victoria	Fr	Abdi Kassim 2 2p 19		
30-06	Seychelles	L	1-2	Victoria	Fr	Salum Ussi 15		
30-07	Rwanda	W	1-0	Dar es Salaam	Fr	Gaudence Mwaikimba 30		
2-09	Burkina Faso	W	2-1	Dar es Salaam	CNq	Bamogo OG 23, Nizar Khalfan 65		Ndinya KEN
30-09	Kenya	D	0-0	Dar es Salaam	Fr			
8-10	Mozambique	D	0-0	Maputo	CNq			Kaoma ZAM
18-11	Angola	D	1-1	Dar es Salaam	Fr	Gaudence Mwaikimba 27		
25-11	Ethiopia	W	2-1	Addis Abeba	CCr1	Amir Maftah 40, Bantu Adimin 60		
28-11	Malawi	W	2-1	Addis Abeba	CCr1	Danny Mrwanda 5, Bantu Adimin 90		
1-12	Djibouti	W	3-0	Addis Abeba	CCr1	Mrisho Ngassa 4, Hussein Swedi 44, Jerry Tegete 58		
5-12	Rwanda	L	1-2	Addis Abeba	CCqf	Jerry Tegete 30		
9-12	Congo DR	W	2-0	Dar es Salaam	Fr	Nizar Khalfan 36, Joseph Kaniki 86		
2007								
24-03	Senegal	L	0-4	Dakar	CNq			Daami TUN
26-05	Uganda	D	1-1	Kampala	Fr	Nizar Khalfan 16		
2-06	Senegal	D	1-1	Mwanza	CNq	Nizar Khalfan 17		Damon RSA
9-06	Zambia	D	1-1	Morogoro	Fr	Danny Mrwanda 51		
16-06	Burkina Faso	W	1-0	Ouagadougou	CNq	Erasto Nyoni 71		Coulibaly MLI
1-09	Uganda	W	1-0	Dar es Salaam	Fr	Abdi Kassim 55		
8-09	Mozambique	L	0-1	Dar es Salaam	CNq			Guezzaz MAR
21-11	Zambia	W	1-0	Dar es Salaam	Fr	Michael Chuma 2		
8-12	Kenya	W	2-1	Dar es Salaam	CCr1	Nizar Khalfan 16p, Danny Mrwanda 89		
12-12	Somalia	W	1-0	Dar es Salaam	CCr1	Michael Chuma 64		
15-12	Burundi	D	0-0	Dar es Salaam	CCr1			
17-12	Sudan	L	1-2	Dar es Salaam	CCqf	Danny Mrwanda 26		
2008								
4-04	Yemen	L	1-2	Sana'a	Fr	Uhuru Suleiman 20		
25-05	Malawi	D	1-1	Dar es Salaam	Fr	Salum Swedi 80		
31-05	Mauritius	D	1-1	Dar es Salaam	WCq	Danny Mrwanda 69	35 000	Marange ZIM
7-06	Cape Verde Islands	L	0-1	Praia	WCq		6 000	El Achiri MAR
14-06	Cameroon	D	0-0	Dar es Salaam	WCq		55 000	Codjia BEN
21-06	Cameroon	L	1-2	Yaounde	WCq	Danny Mrwanda 72	25 000	Mendy GAM

Fr = Friendly match • CN = CAF African Cup of Nations • CC = CECAFA Cup • WC = FIFA World Cup
q = qualifier • r1 = first round group • sf = semi-final • f = final • † Not a full international

TANZANIA NATIONAL TEAM RECORDS AND RECORD SEQUENCES

Records			Sequence records					
Victory	7-0	SOM 1995	Wins	5	1994	Clean sheets	5	1994
Defeat	0-9	KEN 1956	Defeats	6	Four times	Goals scored	11	1993-1994
Player Caps	n/a		Undefeated	9	1973-1975	Without goal	4	Four times
Player Goals	n/a		Without win	28	1984-1990	Goals against	12	2001-2002

TANZANIA COUNTRY INFORMATION

Capital	Dodoma	Independence	1964 from the UK	GDP per Capita	$600
Population	36 588 225	Status	Republic	GDP Ranking	88
Area km²	945 087	Language	Swahili, English	Dialling code	+255
Population density	38 per km²	Literacy rate	78%	Internet code	.tz
% in urban areas	24%	Main religion	Muslim 35%, Christian 30%	GMT + / –	+3
Towns/Cities ('000)	Dar es Salaam 2 698; Mwanza 436; Zanzibar 403; Arusha 341; Mbeya 291; Morogoro 250; Tanga 224; Dodoma 180; Kigoma 164; Moshi 156; Tabora 145; Songea 126, Musoma 121				
Neighbours (km)	Mozambique 756; Malawi 475; Zambia 338; Congo DR 459; Burundi 451; Rwanda 217; Uganda 396; Kenya 769; Indian Ocean 1 424				
Main stadia	National Stadium – Dar-es-Salaam 15 000; CCM Kirumba – Mwanza 30 000				

TANZANIA 2007–08

PREMIER LEAGUE (LIGI KUU TANZANIA BARA)

	Pl	W	D	L	F	A	Pts	Yanga	Prisons	Simba	Mtibwa	Kagera	JKT Ruvu	Toto Africa	Pol.Dodoma	Moro Utd	P. Morogoro	Ashanti Utd	Coastal Un	Manyema	Pan African
Young Africans	26	14	7	5	33	16	49		2-2	0-1	1-1	1-0	0-0	2-0	2-0	0-0	3-0	0-1	4-0	1-0	2-1
Prisons	26	12	9	5	35	23	45	1-2		1-0	0-0	1-2	0-0	1-0	1-1	1-0	1-2	2-0	2-0	3-1	4-2
Simba SC	26	10	12	4	34	18	42	0-0	3-1		1-1	2-1	0-0	3-0	2-2	1-1	0-0	0-0	0-2	0-0	1-1
Mtibwa Sugar	26	10	9	7	22	21	39	1-1	1-1	1-3		0-0	1-0	2-1	1-3	0-1	2-0	1-0	2-0	0-2	0-0
Kagera Sugar	26	10	8	8	26	25	38	3-1	1-0	0-1	2-1		2-1	0-0	3-2	2-3	2-1	2-2	0-0	1-1	1-0
JKT Ruvu Stars	26	9	8	9	24	23	35	0-1	1-2	0-1	1-2	2-1		1-2	2-1	2-0	1-0	1-0	2-1	1-0	1-0
Toto Africa	26	8	10	8	26	28	34	1-2	1-1	3-2	0-1	0-0	1-1		1-1	2-2	2-2	1-3	1-0	1-0	4-2
Polisi Dodoma	26	6	15	5	28	28	33	0-3	2-2	1-1	1-1	1-0	1-1	0-1		0-0	0-0	0-0	2-0	1-1	1-0
Moro United	26	7	12	7	21	21	33	1-2	1-1	1-1	1-0	3-0	2-1	1-1	0-1		1-0	0-1	0-0	0-1	1-0
Polisi Morogoro	26	9	6	11	23	24	33	1-0	0-1	0-0	0-3	0-1	0-1	1-1	0-1	1-1		2-0	3-0	2-0	1-0
Ashanti United	26	8	8	10	18	28	32	1-2	0-1	0-4	2-0	0-0	1-1	0-2	1-1	0-0	1-4		0-2	0-0	2-1
Coastal Union	26	7	7	12	18	26	28	1-0	0-0	1-0	0-1	1-0	1-0	0-0	2-3	0-0	0-0	0-1		1-1	0-1
Manyema Rangers	26	3	11	12	15	29	20	0-1	1-4	0-0	0-0	0-1	0-0	1-0	1-1	0-0	0-1	0-1	3-6		1-1
Pan African	26	4	8	14	22	35	20	0-0	0-1	1-4	0-1	1-1	2-3	0-0	1-1	2-2	0-2	0-1	2-1	2-0	

22/09/2007 - 27/04/2008 • † Qualified for the CAF Champions League • Top scorer: Michael Katende, Kagera Sugar

CLUB DIRECTORY

Club	Town/City	Stadium	Cap'ty	DoF	Lge	Cup
Mtibwa Sugar	Turiani	Jamhuri	5 000	1988	1	0
Moro United	Morogoro	Jamhuri	10 000		0	0
Pan African	Dar es Salaam	National	25 000		2	0
Polisi Dodoma	Dodoma	Jamhuri	10 000		0	0
Polisi Morogoro		Jamhuri	10 000		0	0
Prisons FC	Mbeya	Sokoine	10 000		1	0
Simba SC	Dar es Salaam	National	25 000	1936	16	3
Young Africans (Yanga)	Dar es Salaam	National	25 000		15	3

RECENT LEAGUE AND CUP RECORD

Year	Champions	Cup Winners
2000	Mtibwa Sugar	Simba SC Dar es Salaam
2001	Simba SC Dar es Salaam	Polisi Zanzibar
2002	Young Africans Dar es Salaam	Ruvu Stars
2003	Simba SC Dar es Salaam	
2004	Simba SC Dar es Salaam	
2005	Young Africans Dar es Salaam	
2007	Simba SC Dar es Salaam	
2008	Young Africans Dar es Salaam	

TCA – TURKS AND CAICOS ISLANDS

NATIONAL TEAM RECORD
JULY 10TH 2006 TO JULY 12TH 2010

PL	W	D	L	F	A	%
5	2	0	3	6	12	40

FIFA/COCA-COLA WORLD RANKING

1993	1994	1995	1996	1997	1998	1999	2000	2001	2002	2003	2004	2005	2006	2007	High	
-	-	-	-	-	-	196	200	200	202	203	203	203	169	181	**158**	02/08

2007–2008												Low	
08/07	09/07	10/07	11/07	12/07	01/08	02/08	03/08	04/08	05/08	06/08	07/08	**204**	05/06
166	181	181	181	181	179	158	160	165	164	167	166		

Tiny Turks and Caicos created their own little piece of history in February 2008 when they won a World Cup match for the first time, beating St Lucia 2-1 in Providenciales. Going into the match - the first ever to be played on home soil in Providenciales - TCI had lost all four of their previous World Cup ties, and heavily, shipping 21 goals without scoring any. A crowd over over 2,000 turned up at the new National Stadium for the match against St. Lucia - over 10 percent of the entire population of the country - drawn by the presence of Gavin Glinton, the man undeniably responsible for the upturn in fortunes. Glinton, who spent the 2007 MLS season playing alongside David

INTERNATIONAL HONOURS
None

Beckham at LA Galaxy, could have appeared for the USA or Surinam but chose the country of his birth having moved away at the age of four to America. Alongside him in the team was his USA based brother Duane but their World Cup dream came to an end in the return with a 2-0 defeat in Vieux Fort. Despite having one of the smallest populations of any member nation of FIFA, the Turks and Caicos Islands boast a well run league thanks to a well organised football association that is committed to see the game develop. Winners of the Coxco Men's League were PWC Athletic who finished two points ahead of defending champions Beaches and Provopool.

THE FIFA BIG COUNT OF 2006

	Male	Female		Total
Number of players	1 540	615	Referees and Assistant Referees	12
Professionals	0		Admin, Coaches, Technical, Medical	35
Amateurs 18+	165		Number of clubs	9
Youth under 18	450		Number of teams	9
Unregistered	1 000		Clubs with women's teams	0
Total players	2 155		Players as % of population	10.19%

Turks and Caicos Islands Football Association (TCIFA)
Tropicana Plaza, Leeward Highway, PO Box 626, Providenciales, Turks and Caicos Islands
Tel +1 649 9415532   Fax +1 649 9415554
tcifa@tciway.tc   www.football.tc
President: BRYAN Christopher   General Secretary: BIEN-AIME Sonia
Vice-President: SLATTERY James   Treasurer: DOUGLAS Jenny   Media Officer: None
Men's Coach: GREEN Matthew   Women's Coach: GREEN Matthew
TCIFA formed: 1996   CONCACAF: 1998   FIFA: 1998
White shirts, White shorts, White socks

RECENT INTERNATIONAL MATCHES PLAYED BY TURKS AND CAICOS

2004	Opponents	Score		Venue	Comp	Scorers	Att	Referee
18-02	Haiti	L	0-5	Miami †	WCq		3 000	Stott USA
21-02	Haiti	L	0-2	Hialeah †	WCq		3 000	Valenzuela USA
2005								
No international matches played in 2005								
2006								
2-09	Cuba	L	0-6	Havana	CCq			
4-09	Cayman Islands	W	2-0	Havana	CCq	Gavin Glinton [14], Maxime Fleuriot [72]	100	Stennett JAM
6-09	Bahamas	L	2-3	Havana	CCq	Gavin Glinton 2 [51 72]	120	Campbell JAM
2007								
No international matches played in 2007								
2008								
6-02	St Lucia	W	2-1	Providenciales	WCq	David Lowery [31], Gavin Glinton [74]	2 200	Whittaker CAY
26-03	St Lucia	L	0-2	Vieux Fort	WCq		1 200	Forde BRB

CC = Digicel Caribbean Cup • WC = FIFA World Cup • q = qualifier • † Both matches played in the USA

TURKS AND CAICOS ISLANDS NATIONAL TEAM RECORDS AND RECORD SEQUENCES

Records			Sequence records					
Victory	2-0	CAY 2006	Wins	1		Clean sheets	1	
Defeat	0-8	SKN 2000	Defeats	6	2000-2006	Goals scored	3	2006-2008
Player Caps	7	Errion Charles	Undefeated	1	1999, 2006	Without goal	6	2000-2006
Player Goals	4	Gavin Glinton	Without win	8	1999-2006	Goals against	8	1999-2006

TURKS AND CAICOS ISLANDS 2007–08 COXCO MEN'S LEAGUE

	Pl	W	D	L	F	A	Pts
PWC Athletic	12	8	1	3	48	24	25
Beaches	12	7	2	3	51	17	23
Provopool	12	7	2	3	54	26	23
Caribbean Concrete	12	3	2	7	22	77	11
SWA Sharks	12	1	1	10	23	54	4

RECENT LEAGUE AND CUP RECORD

	Championship						Cup		
Year	Champions	Pts	Runners-up	Pts	Third	Pts	Winners	Score	Runners-up
2000	Masters	16	Beaches	10	Sans Complex	4	Masters	2-0	Beaches
2001	Sharks	1-0	Projetech				No tournament		
2002	Beaches †	2-2	Barefoot				No tournament		
2003	Caribbean All Stars	28	Master Hammer	25	KPMG United	13	Caribbean All Stars	2-1	Master Hammer
2004	KPMG United	27	Caribbean All Stars	22	Police	14	Police	4-3	KPMG United
2005	KPMG United	30	Caribbean All Stars	25	Cost Right	14			
2006	Beaches	19	Cost Right	18	Caribbean All Stars	17	Beaches	2-1	Provopool
2007	Beaches	26	Provo Haitian Stars	19	PWC Athletic	17			
2008	PWC Athletic	25	Beaches	23	Provopool	23			

† Final abandoned at 2-2. Beaches declared champions

TURKS AND CAICOS ISLANDS COUNTRY INFORMATION

Capital	Cockburn Town	Status	Overseas territory of the UK	GDP per Capita	$9 600
Population	19 956			GNP Ranking	n/a
Area km²	430	Language	English	Dialling code	+1649
Population density	46 per km²	Literacy rate	98%	Internet code	.tc
% in urban areas	n/a	Main religion	Christian	GMT +/–	-4
Towns/Cities	Cockburn Town 5 525; Cockburn Harbour 1 744				
Neighbours (km)	North Atlantic Ocean 389				
Main stadia	National Development Facility – Providenciales 1 500				

TGA – TONGA

NATIONAL TEAM RECORD
JULY 10TH 2006 TO JULY 12TH 2010

PL	W	D	L	F	A	%
4	1	0	3	6	10	25

FIFA/COCA-COLA WORLD RANKING

1993	1994	1995	1996	1997	1998	1999	2000	2001	2002	2003	2004	2005	2006	2007	High	
-	-	-	164	174	163	178	185	173	175	180	183	185	188	170	**163**	10/98

2007–2008												Low	
08/07	09/07	10/07	11/07	12/07	01/08	02/08	03/08	04/08	05/08	06/08	07/08	**192**	07/07
192	167	168	167	170	170	173	171	175	174	180	179		

With sporting interest in Tonga centered almost exclusively on the Rugby World Cup in September 2008, the football tournament of the South Pacific Games barely registered, with the Tongan national team doing little to stir any interest. At the World Cup Tonga played the game of their lives to beat Samoa 19-15, winning plaudits around the world. It couldn't have been more different in Apia where the football team lost 2-1 to Samoa - one of three defeats at a tournament that served as a first round of qualification for the 2010 FIFA World Cup. Tonga's one victory was a 4-0 triumph over American Samoa. Anything less would have been a disaster. That victory did at least

INTERNATIONAL HONOURS
None

keep the Tongans off the bottom of the FIFA/Coca-Cola World Ranking but the fact is that the women's team made a much better job of their appearance at the tournament, where they reached the final before losing to Papua New Guinea. The country now has all of the football facilities that it needs thanks to the Goal project and it would appear that women's football is making the very best of the opportunities that it has been afforded. For the second year running there was no Tongan representation in the OFC O-League and the club game in the country is in danger of falling substantially behind its rivals in neighbouring Oceania countries.

THE FIFA BIG COUNT OF 2006

	Male	Female		Total
Number of players	4 600	400	Referees and Assistant Referees	100
Professionals	0		Admin, Coaches, Technical, Medical	100
Amateurs 18+	2 100		Number of clubs	100
Youth under 18	1 100		Number of teams	220
Unregistered	700		Clubs with women's teams	5
Total players	5 000		Players as % of population	4.36%

Tonga Football Association (FTF)
Loto Tonga Soko Center, Off Taufa'Ahau Road - 'Atele, PO Box 852, Nuku'alofa, Tonga
Tel +676 30233   Fax +676 30240
tfa@kalianet.to   www.tongafootball.com
President: VEEHALA Hon   General Secretary: FUSIMALOHI Ahongalu
Vice-President: FUSITUA Hon   Treasurer: AHO Lui   Media Officer: None
Men's Coach: UELE Kilifi   Women's Coach: UELE Kilifi
FTF formed: 1965   OFC: 1994   FIFA: 1994
Red shirts, White shorts, Red socks

RECENT INTERNATIONAL MATCHES PLAYED BY TONGA

2002	Opponents	Score		Venue	Comp	Scorers	Att	Referee
No international matches played in 2002 after June								
2003								
1-07	Papua New Guinea	D	2-2	Suva	SPr1		3 000	Singh FIJ
3-07	New Caledonia	L	0-4	Suva	SPr1		700	Shah FIJ
5-07	Micronesia †	W	7-0	Nausori	SPr1	Fonua [5], Tevi [15], Uhatahi 2 [22 36], Feao 2 [34 55], Uele [72]	1 000	Moli SOL
7-07	Tahiti	L	0-4	Lautoka	SPr1		3 000	Shah FIJ
2004								
10-05	Solomon Islands	L	0-6	Honiara	WCq		12 385	Attison VAN
15-05	Cook Islands	W	2-1	Honiara	WCq	Uhatahi [46], Vaitaki [61]	15 000	Sosongan PNG
17-05	Tahiti	L	0-2	Honiara	WCq		400	Sosongan PNG
19-05	New Caledonia	L	0-8	Honiara	WCq		14 000	Fred VAN
2005								
No international matches played in 2005								
2006								
No international matches played in 2006								
2007								
27-08	Solomon Islands	L	0-4	Apia	WCq		350	Aimaasu SAM
29-08	Samoa	L	1-2	Apia	WCq	Feao [54]	1 850	Sosongan PNG
1-09	American Samoa	W	4-0	Apia	WCq	Moala [38], Palu 2 [56 63], Uhatahi [86]	200	Minan PNG
3-09	Vanuatu	L	1-4	Apia	WCq	Savieti [50]	50	Minan PNG
2008								
No international matches played in 2008 before August								

Fr = Friendly match • SP = South Pacific Games • WC = FIFA World Cup™ • q = qualifier • r1 = first round group • † Not a full international

TONGA NATIONAL TEAM RECORDS AND RECORD SEQUENCES

Records			Sequence records					
Victory	5-0	ASA 2001	Wins	3	1994-1996	Clean sheets	2	1996
Defeat	0-22	AUS 2001	Defeats	4	1998-2000	Goals scored	4	1994-96, 2000-01
Player Caps	n/a		Undefeated	4	1994-1996	Without goal	4	1993-1994
Player Goals	n/a		Without win	6	1983-1994	Goals against	12	2001-2004

TONGA CHAMPIONS

Year	Champions
1998	SC Lotoha'apai Nuku'alofa
1999	SC Lotoha'apai Nuku'alofa
2000	SC Lotoha'apai Nuku'alofa
2001	SC Lotoha'apai Nuku'alofa
2002	SC Lotoha'apai Nuku'alofa
2003	SC Lotoha'apai Nuku'alofa
2004	SC Lotoha'apai Nuku'alofa
2005	SC Lotoha'apai Nuku'alofa
2006	SC Lotoha'apai Nuku'alofa

TONGA COUNTRY INFORMATION

Capital	Nuku'alofa	Independence	1970 from the UK	GDP per Capita	$2 200
Population	110 237	Status	Constitutional Monarchy	GNP Ranking	186
Area km²	748	Language	Tongan, English	Dialling code	+676
Population density	147 per km²	Literacy rate	98%	Internet code	.to
% in urban areas	41%	Main religion	Christian	GMT +/-	+13
Towns/Cities ('000)	Nuku'alofa 23; Mu'a 5; Neiafu 4; Haveloloto 3; Vaini 3; Tofoa-Koloua 2; Pangai 2				
Neighbours (km)	South Pacific Ocean 419				
Main stadia	Mangweni Stadium – Nuku'alofa 3 000				

THA – THAILAND

NATIONAL TEAM RECORD
JULY 10TH 2006 TO JULY 12TH 2010

PL	W	D	L	F	A	%
34	16	9	9	63	44	60.3

FIFA/COCA-COLA WORLD RANKING

1993	1994	1995	1996	1997	1998	1999	2000	2001	2002	2003	2004	2005	2006	2007	High	
69	85	77	57	54	45	60	61	61	66	60	79	111	137	121	43	09/98

					2007–2008							Low	
08/07	09/07	10/07	11/07	12/07	01/08	02/08	03/08	04/08	05/08	06/08	07/08	137	12/06
109	117	114	113	121	107	92	90	96	96	93	111		

Thailand's disappointing showing in the 2010 FIFA World Cup qualifiers ended with former Asian Coach of the Year Chanvit Polchovin standing down after the Thais finished the campaign without a win in their matches against Japan, Bahrain and Oman. His replacement was Englishman Peter Reid whose first major test will be to reclaim the ASEAN Championship from back-to-back winners Singapore as the Thais attempt to win the title for the first time since 2002. The former Sunderland and Manchester City manager will need to overhaul a squad that has lost talismanic striker Kiatisuk Senamuang while other veterans such as Therdsak Chaiman and Tawan Sripan are nearing the end

INTERNATIONAL HONOURS
SEA Games 1965 1975 1981 1983 1985 1993 1995 1997 1999 2001 2003 **Tiger Cup** 1996 2000 2002
AFC Champions League Thai Farmers Bank 1994 1995

of their careers. Reid, however, can lean on the talent in the nation's under-23 team, which won the gold medal at the South East Asian Games in 2007, as he attempts to rebuild. Chonburi FC won the league title in the first season following the merger of the Thailand Premier League and the Provincial League, and the club also made a decent impact on the 2008 AFC Champions League, missing out on qualifying for the knockout phase of the competition despite recording impressive results against Melbourne Victory, Gamba Osaka and Chunnam Dragons.

THE FIFA BIG COUNT OF 2006

	Male	Female		Total
Number of players	1 207 500	90 500	Referees and Assistant Referees	1 100
Professionals	500		Admin, Coaches, Technical, Medical	5 500
Amateurs 18+	10 700		Number of clubs	150
Youth under 18	16 500		Number of teams	1 790
Unregistered	332 400		Clubs with women's teams	0
Total players	1 298 000		Players as % of population	2.01%

The Football Association of Thailand (FAT)
National Stadium, Gate 3, Rama 1 Road, Patumwan, Bangkok 10330, Thailand
Tel +66 2 2164691   Fax +66 2 2154494
fa_thailand@yahoo.com   www.fat.org.th
President: MAKUDI Worawi   General Secretary: KOSINKAR Ong-Arj
Vice-President: JANGJANKIT Rangsarit   Treasurer: CHANAWONGSE Kasom   Media Officer: None
Men's Coach: REID Peter   Women's Coach: YODPRANG Chana
FAT formed: 1916   AFC: 1957   FIFA: 1925
Red shirts, Red shorts, Red socks

RECENT INTERNATIONAL MATCHES PLAYED BY THAILAND

2006	Opponents	Score		Venue	Comp	Scorers	Att	Referee
16-02	Iraq	W	4-3	Ayutthaya	Fr	Prat Samakrat [2], OG [10], Nirut Kumsawad [12], Apichate Puttan [55]		
26-03	Philippines	W	5-0	Chonburi	Fr	Jakkrit Bunkham [13], Teeratep Winothai 2 [20 44], Kittisak Jaiharn [58], Phaisarn Phona [90]		
10-08	China PR	L	0-4	Qinhuangdao	Fr			
24-12	Vietnam	W	2-1	Bangkok	Fr	Sarayoot Chaikamdee [36], Datsakorn Thonglao [61]		
26-12	Singapore	W	2-0	Bangkok	Fr	Kwanchai Phuangprakob [55], Kiatisuk Senamueng [63]		
28-12	Kazakhstan	D	2-2	Bangkok	Fr	Suchao Nutnum [41], Phichitpong Choeichiu [58]		
30-12	Vietnam	W	3-1	Bangkok	Fr	Sutee Suksomkit [38], Pipat Tonkanya [43], Suchao Nutnum [69]		
2007								
12-01	Myanmar	D	1-1	Bangkok	TCr1	Suchao Nutnum [94+]	15 000	Matsuo JPN
14-01	Philippines	W	4-0	Bangkok	TCr1	Sarayoot Chaikamdee 2 [15 28], Pipat Tonkanya [21], Natthaphong Samana [84]	30 000	
16-01	Malaysia	W	1-0	Bangkok	TCr1	Sarayoot Chaikamdee [48]	25 000	Matsuo JPN
24-01	Vietnam	W	2-0	Hanoi	TCsf	Datsakorn Thonglao [28], Pipat Tonkanya [81]	40 000	Napitupulu IDN
28-01	Vietnam	D	0-0	Bangkok	TCsf		35 000	Srinivasan IND
31-01	Singapore	L	1-2	Singapore	TCf	Pipat Tonkanya [50]	55 000	Ravichandran MAS
4-02	Singapore	D	1-1	Bangkok	TCf	Pipat Tonkanya [37]	30 000	Napitupulu IDN
16-05	China PR	W	1-0	Bangkok	Fr	Pipat Tonkanya [40]		
6-06	Netherlands	L	1-3	Bangkok	Fr	Tawan Sripan [65]	20 000	Ganesan SIN
2-07	Qatar	W	2-0	Bangkok	Fr	Tawan Sripan [8], Sutee Suksomkit [69p]		
7-07	Iraq	D	1-1	Bangkok	ACr1	Sutee Suksomkit [6p]	30 000	Kwon Jong Chul KOR
12-07	Oman	W	2-0	Bangkok	ACr1	Pipat Tonkanya 2 [70 78]	19 000	Lee Gi Young KOR
16-07	Australia	L	0-4	Bangkok	ACr1		46 000	Kwon Jong Chul KOR
3-10	UAE	D	1-1	Bangkok	Fr	Kiatprawut Saiwaeo [73]		
8-10	Macau	W	6-1	Bangkok	WCq	Sarayoot Chaikamdee 2 [12 49], Teerasil Dangda [21], Teeratep Winothai [55p], Patiparn Phetphun [82], Datsakorn Thonglao [91+]	11 254	Chynybekov KGZ
15-10	Macau	W	7-1	Macau	WCq	Teerasil Dangda [22], Sukha Suree [39], Nirut Surasiang [43], Datsakorn Thonglao [48], Sarayoot Chaikamdee 3 [53 57 86]	500	Recho SYR
9-11	Yemen	D	1-1	Sana'a	WCq	Sarayoot Chaikamdee [35]	12 000	Al Ghamdi KSA
18-11	Yemen	W	1-0	Bangkok	WCq	Sarayoot Chaikamdee [16]	29 000	Matsumura JPN
22-12	Uzbekistan	W	3-2	Bangkok	Fr	Sarayoot Chaikamdee 2 [5p 39], Nataporn Phanrit [89]		
26-12	Korea DPR	W	1-0	Bangkok	Fr	Narongchai Vachiraban [55]		
2008								
6-02	Japan	L	1-4	Saitama	WCq	Teeratep Winothai [22]	35 130	Al Ghamdi KSA
15-03	China PR	D	3-3	Kunming	Fr	Teeratep Winothai 2 [49 64], Tana Chanabut [81]		
26-03	Oman	L	0-1	Bangkok	WCq		40 000	Torky IRN
20-05	Nepal	W	7-0	Bangkok	Fr	Teerasil Dangda [47], Suchao Nutnum [51], Ronnachai Rangsiyo [54], Teeratep Winothai 3 [67 68 87p], Sarayoot Chaikamdee [79]		
25-05	Iraq	W	2-1	Bangkok	Fr	Teeratep Winothai [53], Teerasil Dangda [59]		
2-06	Bahrain	L	2-3	Bangkok	WCq	Sarayoot Chaikamdee [26], Teeratep Winothai [45]	15 000	Sun Baojie CHN
7-06	Bahrain	D	1-1	Manama	WCq	Datsakorn Thonglao [64]	21 000	Basma SYR
14-06	Japan	L	0-3	Bangkok	WCq		25 000	Albadwawi UAE
22-06	Oman	L	1-2	Muscat	WCq	Tawan Sripan [3p]	3 000	Mujghef JOR

Fr = Friendly match • TC = Tiger Cup/ASEAN Football Federation Championship • AC = AFC Asian Cup • WC = FIFA World Cup
q = qualifier • r1 = 1st round • sf = semi-final • f = final • † Not a full international

THAILAND NATIONAL TEAM RECORDS AND RECORD SEQUENCES

Records			Sequence records					
Victory	10-0	BRU 1970	Wins	8	1993	Clean sheets	4	Five times
Defeat	0-8	CZE 1968	Defeats	11	1959-1961	Goals scored	19	1960-1963
Player Caps	117	Kiatisuk Senamuang	Undefeated	11	1995-1996	Without goal	9	1990-1991
Player Goals	64	Kiatisuk Senamuang	Without win	23	1959-1963	Goals against	31	1959-1965

THAILAND COUNTRY INFORMATION

Capital	Bangkok	Foundation	1238	GDP per Capita	$7 400
Population	64 865 523	Status	Constitutional Monarchy	GNP Ranking	32
Area km²	514 000	Language	Thai	Dialling code	+66
Population density	126 per km²	Literacy rate	92%	Internet code	.th
% in urban areas	20%	Main religion	Buddhist	GMT + / –	+7
Towns/Cities ('000)	Bangkok 5 104; Samut Prakan 388; Nonthaburi 375; Udon Thani 247; Chon Buri 219; Nakhon Ratchasima 208; Chiang Mai 201; Hat Yai 191; Pak Kret 183; Si Racha 179				
Neighbours (km)	Laos 1 754; Cambodia 803; Malaysia 506; Myanmar 1 800; Gulf of Thailand 3 219				
Main stadia	Rajamangala – Bangkok 65 000; Suphachalasai – Bangkok 30 000				

THAILAND 2007

PROFESSIONAL LEAGUE

	Pl	W	D	L	F	A	Pts	Chonburi	KTB	BEC Tero S'na	University	Army	Tobacco	BBL	PEA	Osotspa	TOT	NakhonPathom	PAT	Suphanburi	Thai-Honda	Navy	Police
Chonburi †	30	19	6	5	50	25	63		3-2	1-3	0-1	1-1	1-2	0-0	0-1	1-0	0-0	3-1	2-0	1-0	3-2	2-1	0-1
Krung Thai Bank	30	15	9	6	40	24	54	1-1		2-1	1-2	1-0	3-0	0-0	0-1	0-0	2-0	0-3	0-1	0-0	3-2	1-1	2-1
BEC Tero Sasana	30	14	9	7	47	29	51	1-2	1-2		3-0	1-1	1-1	0-0	2-1	1-0	2-1	0-4	1-0	1-0	1-2	2-0	2-1
Bangkok University	30	14	5	11	39	36	47	3-1	2-3	0-0		1-0	1-3	1-1	0-2	1-0	1-0	2-0	1-3	0-1	3-0	1-1	3-2
Royal Thai Army	30	13	8	9	40	33	47	0-2	0-0	1-1	1-1		1-0	1-2	2-1	3-1	3-1	0-1	5-1	3-2	0-0	2-0	1-0
Thailand Tobacco	30	12	8	10	43	42	44	0-2	0-3	0-2	2-4	4-0		2-1	0-2	1-1	1-1	2-2	2-3	2-1	2-1	0-0	3-0
Bangkok Bank Ltd	30	10	14	6	28	23	44	0-2	0-1	2-1	1-0	0-1	0-1		3-1	2-2	1-0	0-0	0-0	1-1	1-0	0-0	0-0
Provincial Electrical	30	13	3	14	35	40	42	0-4	1-1	0-3	0-2	1-2	3-2	1-2		1-2	1-0	1-0	2-1	1-0	3-1	0-2	3-2
Osotspa M–150	30	10	10	10	38	36	40	0-3	2-2	2-4	2-0	0-1	0-0	1-3	3-0		1-1	0-0	2-0	1-2	1-0	2-0	2-0
Telephone – TOT	30	9	10	11	35	35	37	1-2	1-0	0-0	1-2	4-1	2-3	2-2	1-0	1-1		2-1	0-0	1-2	2-2	1-1	2-1
Nakhon Pathom	30	8	13	9	30	29	37	0-1	0-3	1-1	2-0	2-2	1-1	0-0	1-0	1-2	0-0		1-1	1-1	1-0	2-2	1-1
Port Authority	30	9	9	12	36	43	36	1-3	1-2	2-2	2-1	2-1	1-1	1-1	2-2	3-2	1-4	0-0		4-0	0-1	1-2	2-1
Suphanburi	30	9	8	13	37	45	35	2-2	0-1	1-2	1-3	2-1	1-2	3-4	1-0	2-2	1-2	4-3	1-0		2-2	1-0	1-0
Thai–Honda	30	7	8	15	26	38	29	2-4	0-1	1-0	0-0	1-1	3-2	1-0	0-2	1-2	0-1	0-0	1-1	0-0		1-0	0-1
Royal Thai Navy	30	5	12	13	21	35	27	0-1	0-0	1-1	1-0	0-4	1-2	0-1	1-1	1-1	2-1	0-1	2-1	2-2	0-2		0-0
Royal Thai Police	30	5	4	21	19	51	19	0-2	0-3	0-7	2-3	0-1	0-2	0-0	0-3	1-3	1-2	1-0	0-1	3-2	1-0	1-0	

17/03/2007 - 27/11/2007 • † Qualified for the AFC Champions League • Top scorer: Fabiano, TOT 18

THAILAND 2007 SECOND DIVISION GROUP A

	Pl	W	D	L	F	A	Pts
Customs Department	22	12	9	1	33	16	45
Coke–Bangpra	22	11	8	3	30	14	41
Rattanabundit	22	8	7	7	37	27	31
Khon Kaen	22	7	8	7	25	25	29
Rajvithi	22	7	8	7	31	34	29
Surat Thani	22	7	7	8	31	42	28
Thai Airways	22	6	10	6	19	21	28
Narathiwat	22	7	6	9	31	28	27
Air Force Training	22	6	7	9	32	33	25
Sakon Nakhon	22	4	12	6	20	32	24
Bangkok Bravo	22	5	8	9	27	35	23
Ratchaburi	22	5	4	13	31	40	19

22/04/2007 - 30/09/2007

THAILAND 2007 SECOND DIVISION GROUP B

	Pl	W	D	L	F	A	Pts
Chula–Sinthana	22	14	4	4	45	21	46
Samut Songkhram	22	13	5	4	37	22	44
Royal Thai Air Force	22	12	6	4	41	22	42
Chanthaburi	22	8	7	7	37	27	31
Phitsanulok	22	7	8	7	29	26	29
Sriracha	22	7	8	7	20	20	29
Nakhon Sawan	22	6	11	5	26	30	29
Bangkok North Central	22	9	2	11	30	35	29
Nakhon Ratchasima	22	7	7	8	27	25	28
Si Sa Ket	22	7	6	9	36	38	27
Chachoengsao	22	4	7	11	18	40	19
Royal Thai Marine C'ge	22	1	3	18	16	56	6

22/04/2007 - 30/09/2007

RECENT LEAGUE RECORD

	Championship					
Year	Champions	Pts	Runners-up	Pts	Third	Pts
2002	BEC Tero Sasana	50	Osotapa	44	Bangkok Bank	35
2003	Krung Thai Bank	36	BEC Tero Sasana	35	Port Authority	33
2004	Krung Thai Bank	38	BEC Tero Sasana	34	Osotapa	33
2005	Thailand Tobacco	34	Electical Authority	32	Osotapa	32
2006	Bangkok University	39	Osotspa	38	BEC Tero Sasana	36
2006	TOT	67	Port Authority	66	Nakhon Pathom	62
2007	Chonburi	63	Krung Thai Bank	54	BEC Tero Sasana	51

TJK – TAJIKISTAN

NATIONAL TEAM RECORD
JULY 10TH 2006 TO JULY 12TH 2010

PL	W	D	L	F	A	%
14	5	6	3	25	14	57.1

FIFA/COCA-COLA WORLD RANKING

1993	1994	1995	1996	1997	1998	1999	2000	2001	2002	2003	2004	2005	2006	2007	High	
-	155	164	163	118	120	119	134	154	168	137	136	141	124	137	**114**	07/97

	2007–2008											Low	
08/07	09/07	10/07	11/07	12/07	01/08	02/08	03/08	04/08	05/08	06/08	07/08	**180**	10/03
145	151	152	135	137	141	142	143	146	155	153	154		

Tajikistan's status as one of Asian football's weaker nations has not stopped the country from the former Soviet republic from claiming silverware at continental level. The Tajik team won the inaugural AFC Challenge Cup in 2006 and they performed well again at the 2008 tournament staged in the Indian city of Hyderabad. Having beaten the strongly fancied North Koreans in the semi-finals, they faced India in a final that had to be postponed due to severe storms in the city. Tajikistan's 2010 FIFA World Cup campaign fared less well, however. After seeing off Bangladesh in the opening round, they fell at the hands of Singapore in the second phase, losing 3-1 on

INTERNATIONAL HONOURS
AFC Challenge Cup 2006   AFC President's Cup Regar TadAZ 2005

aggregate and failing to make it through to the main group stage. Club side Regar TadAZ, AFC President's Cup champions in 2005 reached the semi-finals of the 2007 tournament in Pakistan. Wins over Pakistan Army, Bhutan side Transport United and Sri Lanka's Ratnam Sports Club took them through to the last four with a perfect record, only for them to fall at the hands of Mahendra Police Club from Nepal. Regar TadAZ did manage to defend their league title successfully while Parvoz B'jon Gafarov won the Tajikistan Cup when a solitary goal from Dzhomikhon Mukhiddinov downed Khima Dushanbe in the final.

THE FIFA BIG COUNT OF 2006

	Male	Female		Total
Number of players	123 563	9 330	Referees and Assistant Referees	56
Professionals	428		Admin, Coaches, Technical, Medical	267
Amateurs 18+	980		Number of clubs	40
Youth under 18	2 135		Number of teams	260
Unregistered	32 150		Clubs with women's teams	10
Total players	132 893		Players as % of population	1.82%

Tajikistan Football Federation (TFF)
14/ Ainy Street, Dushanbe 734 025, Tajikistan
Tel +992 372 212447   Fax +992 372 510157
tajikfootball@yahoo.com   www.none
President: QOSIMOV Suhrob   General Secretary: DAVLATOV Sherali
Vice-President: TURSUNOV Valery   Treasurer: KHOLOV Sherali   Media Officer: BURIEV Aloviddin
Men's Coach: KHABIBULLOEV Makhmadjon   Women's Coach: SATTOROV Shavkat
TFF formed: 1936   AFC: 1994   FIFA: 1994
White shirts, White shorts, White socks

RECENT INTERNATIONAL MATCHES PLAYED BY TAJIKISTAN

2004	Opponents	Score		Venue	Comp	Scorers	Att	Referee
18-02	Kyrgyzstan	W	2-1	Bishkek	WCq	Burkhanon 2 [31] [53]	14 000	Lutfullin UZB
31-03	Bahrain	D	0-0	Dushanbe	WCq		17 000	Maidin SIN
10-06	Syria	L	1-2	Homs	WCq	Kholomatov [35]	18 000	Al Fadhli KUW
8-09	Syria	L	0-1	Dushanbe	WCq		18 000	Mohd Salleh MAS
13-10	Kyrgyzstan	W	2-1	Dushanbe	WCq	Rabiev [19], Hakimov [37]	11 000	Naser Al Enezi KUW
17-11	Bahrain	L	0-4	Manama	WCq		15 000	Sun Baojie CHN
6-12	Kuwait	L	0-3	Kuwait City	Fr			
2005								
25-01	Saudi Arabia	L	0-3	Riyadh	Fr			
9-11	Afghanistan	W	4-0	Dushanbe	Fr	Hakimov 2 [28] [31], Makhmudov [45], Ashurmamadov [67]		
2006								
14-02	Qatar	L	0-2	Doha	Fr			
2-04	Macau	W	4-0	Dhaka	CCr1	Makhmudov [9], Rabiev [13], Rabimov [56], Khojaev [77]	2 000	Mombini IRN
4-04	Pakistan	W	2-0	Dhaka	CCr1	Hakimov [14], Irgashev [20]	5 000	Tan Hai CHN
6-04	Kyrgyzstan	L	0-1	Dhaka	CCr1		2 000	AK Nema IRQ
10-04	Bangladesh	W	6-1	Dhaka	CCqf	Rabimov [2], Makhmudov [20], Muhidinov [31], Hakimov [51], Rabiev [65], Nematov [81]	15 000	AK Nema IRQ
13-04	Kyrgyzstan	W	2-0	Dhaka	CCsf	Rabiev 2 [51] [92+]	2 000	Tan Hai CHN
16-04	Sri Lanka	W	4-0	Dhaka	CCf	Muhidinov 3 [1] [61] [71], Makhmudov [45]	2 000	Mombini IRN
2-07	Kazakhstan	L	1-4	Almaty	Fr	Saidov [75]		
2007								
22-08	Azerbaijan	L	2-3	Dushanbe	Fr	Barotov [18], Saidov [31]		
8-09	Kazakhstan	D	1-1	Almaty	Fr	Saidov [42]		
8-10	Bangladesh	D	1-1	Dhaka	WCq	Hakimov [58p]	700	Al Hilali OMA
28-10	Bangladesh	W	5-0	Dushanbe	WCq	Hakimov 3 [46] [47] [76p], Muhidinov [49], Vasiev [70]	10 000	Chynybekov KGZ
9-11	Singapore	L	0-2	Singapore	WCq		6 606	Kwon Jong Chul KOR
18-11	Singapore	D	1-1	Dushanbe	WCq	Ismailov [2]	21 500	Shield AUS
16-12	Oman	L	2-4	Muscat	Fr	Makhmudov [26], Shohzukhurov [47]		
2008								
13-05	Bhutan	W	3-1	Barotac	CCq	Hakimov [27p], Rabiev [60]	5 000	Ng Chiu Kok HKG
15-05	Philippines	D	0-0	Iloilo City	CCq		4 500	Albadwawi UAE
17-05	Brunei Darussalam	W	4-0	Iloilo City	CCq	Rabiev 2 [47] [87], Muhidinov [61], Hakimov [69]	450	Albadwawi UAE
30-07	Turkmenistan	D	0-0	Hyderabad	CCr1		150	Kovalenko UZB
1-08	India	D	1-1	Hyderabad	CCr1	Rabiev [11]	350	Shamsuzzaman BAN
3-08	Afghanistan	W	4-0	Hyderabad	CCr1	Rabiev 3 [14] [44] [56], Tukhtasunov [39]	150	Vo Minh Tri VIE
7-08	Korea DPR	W	1-0	Hyderabad	CCsf	Muhidinov [39]	600	Iemoto JPN
13-08	India			Delhi	CCf			

Fr = Friendly match • AC = AFC Asian Cup • CC = AFC Challenge Cup • WC = FIFA World Cup
q = qualifier • r1 = first round group • qf = quarter-final • sf = semi-final • f = final

TAJIKISTAN NATIONAL TEAM RECORDS AND RECORD SEQUENCES

Records			Sequence records				
Victory	16-0	GUM 2000	Wins	4	2003-2004	Clean sheets	3	1997, 2003, 2003
Defeat	0-5	UZB 1996, IRN 1998	Defeats	3	Three times	Goals scored	5	1997-98, 1998-99
Player Caps	n/a		Undefeated	5	2003-2004	Without goal	3	1993-94, 2004-05
Player Goals	n/a		Without win	5	1998-1999	Goals against	7	1998-1999

TAJIKISTAN COUNTRY INFORMATION

Capital	Dushanbe	Independence	1991 from the USSR	GDP per Capita	$1 000
Population	7 011 556	Status	Republic	GNP Ranking	152
Area km²	143 100	Language	Tajik, Russian	Dialling code	+992
Population density	49 per km²	Literacy rate	99%	Internet code	.tj
% in urban areas	32%	Main religion	Muslim	GMT +/–	+5
Towns/Cities ('000)	Dushanbe 543; Khujand 144; Kulob 78; Qurgonteppa 60; Uroteppa 52; Konibodom 50				
Neighbours (km)	China 414; Afghanistan 1 206; Uzbekistan 1 161 Kyrgyzstan 870;				
Main stadia	National Stadium – Dushanbe 20 000				

TAJIKISTAN 2007

PREMIER DIVISION

	Pl	W	D	L	F	A	Pts	Regar	Parvoz	Vakhsh	Tokjik	Khima	Hujand	SKA	Dinamo	Energetik	Guardia	Saroykamar
Regar TadAZ †	20	18	1	1	61	14	55		1-0	2-1	3-0	5-2	5-0	3-1	2-1	3-1	5-1	5-0
Parvoz B'jon Gafurov	20	17	0	3	52	10	51	3-1		1-0	1-0	1-0	1-0	5-0	6-0	1-0	6-1	5-0
Vakhsh Qurghonteppa	20	11	4	5	26	16	37	0-3	0-4		0-0	2-0	4-0	2-0	3-1	1-0	1-0	3-0
TojikTelecom Qur'teppa	20	11	4	5	44	23	37	0-1	3-2	2-2		2-1	3-2	3-0	5-2	3-0	2-2	6-1
Khima Dushanbe	20	9	6	5	39	27	33	0-2	2-0	0-0	0-0		4-1	3-2	2-2	5-1	2-0	1-1
FK Hujand	20	8	3	9	27	37	27	2-2	1-3	1-0	2-0	0-0		3-2	2-0	1-1	3-1	3-0
SKA Pamir Dushanbe	20	7	1	12	34	44	22	0-1	0-4	1-3	0-3	4-5	4-1		1-2	2-1	3-1	3-0
Dinamo Dushanbe	20	6	4	10	33	38	22	1-3	0-1	0-0	1-2	1-1	5-1	0-2		4-0	1-0	9-2
Energetik Dushanbe	20	5	3	12	24	40	18	0-3	1-3	1-2	3-2	0-1	2-1	2-2	0-1		1-0	2-2
Guardia Dushanbe	20	1	3	16	13	52	6	0-3	0-3	0-1	0-5	0-4	0-1	1-5	1-1	1-3		2-0
Saroykamar Panj	20	1	3	16	19	71	6	1-8	0-2	0-1	0-3	3-6	0-2	1-2	4-1	2-5	2-2	

24/03/2007 - 9/12/2007 • † Qualified for the AFC President's Cup

TAJIKISTAN CUP 2007

First round			Quarter–finals			Semi–finals		Final	
Parvoz B'jon Gafurov	4	2							
Guardia Dushanbe	0	3	Parvoz B'jon Gafurov	W-0					
Rangongaz Rudaki	0		Saroykamar Panj						
Saroykamar Panj	2					Parvoz B'jon Gafurov			
TojikTelecom	3	2				Regar TadAZ			
Hisor Gussar	2	0	TojikTelecom	0	2				
FK Hujand	1	0	Regar TadAZ	5	3				
Regar TadAZ	3	6						Parvoz B'jon Gafurov	1
Dinamo Dushanbe	3							Khima Dushanbe	0
Hylbyk Bose	0		Dinamo Dushanbe	5	5				
Vakhsh Qurghonteppa	0	2	SKA Pamir Dushanbe	2	3				
SKA Pamir Dushanbe	6	1				Dinamo Dushanbe			
Energetik Dushanbe	4	1				Khima Dushanbe			
Hair-Vahdat	2	0	Energetik Dushanbe	3					
Ravshan Kulob	1		Khima Dushanbe	4					
Khima Dushanbe	10								

CUP FINAL

17-10-2007
Scorer – Dzhomikhon Mukhiddinov [57]

* Home team in the first leg

RECENT LEAGUE AND CUP RECORD

	Championship						Cup		
Year	Champions	Pts	Runners-up	Pts	Third	Pts	Winners	Score	Runners-up
1992	Pamir Dushanbe	33	Regar TadAZ	26	Vakhsh Qur'teppa	24	Pamir Dushanbe	1-0	Regar TadAZ
1993	Sitora Dushanbe	55	Pamir Dushanbe	52	P'takor Proletarsk	42	Sitora Dushanbe	0-0 5-3p	Ravshan Kulyab
1994	Sitora Dushanbe	47	Pamir Dushanbe	45	P'takor Proletarsk	43	Ravshan Kulyab	2-1	Shodmon Ghissar
1995	Pamir Dushanbe	67	Istravshan	57	Sitora Dushanbe	52	Pakhtakor Dzh'lovsk	0-0 3-2p	Regar TadAZ
1996	Dinamo Dushanbe	73	Sitora Dushanbe	71	Khojent	64	Not played		
1997	Vakhsh Qurgonteppa	59	Ranjbar Vosse	55	Khujand	52	Vakhsh Qurgonteppa	4-0	Khujand
1998	Varzob Dushanbe	56	Khujand	44	Saddam Sarband	42	Khujand	2-1	Ranjbar Vose
1999	Varzob Dushanbe	57	Khuja Gazimalik	49	Ravshan Kulyab	46	Varzob Dushanbe	4-2p	Regar TadAZ
2000	Varzob Dushanbe	87	Regar TadAZ	77	Khujand	68	Not played		
2001	Regar TadAZ	50	Panjsher Kolk'bad	38	Pamir Dushanbe	32	Regar TadAZ	4-2	Varzob Dushanbe
2002	Regar TadAZ	58	Khujand	53	Farrukh Ghissar	44	Khujand	3-0	Vakhsh Qurgonteppa
2003	Regar TadAZ	81	Khujand	72	Aviator	71	Vakhsh Qurgonteppa		
2004	Regar TadAZ	86	Vakhsh Qurgonteppa	85	Aviator	71	Aviator B. Gafurov	5-0	Uroteppa
2005	Vakhsh Qurgonteppa	47	Regar Tursunzoda	42	Parvoz B. Gafurov	34	Regar TadAZ	1-1 4-2p	Vakhsh Qurgonteppa
2006	Regar TadAZ	55	Khima Dushanbe	54	Vakhsh Qurgonteppa	47	Regar TadAZ	2-1	Khima Dushanbe
2007	Regar TadAZ	55	Parvoz B. Gafurov	51	Vakhsh Qurgonteppa	37	Parvoz B. Gafurov	1-0	Khima Dushanbe

Tajik clubs took part in the Soviet league until the end of the 1991 season

TKM – TURKMENISTAN

NATIONAL TEAM RECORD
JULY 10TH 2006 TO JULY 12TH 2010

PL	W	D	L	F	A	%
16	4	3	9	17	20	34.4

FIFA/COCA-COLA WORLD RANKING

1993	1994	1995	1996	1997	1998	1999	2000	2001	2002	2003	2004	2005	2006	2007	High	
-	108	133	141	134	122	129	125	114	134	99	98	116	155	127	**86**	04/04

	2007–2008											Low	
08/07	09/07	10/07	11/07	12/07	01/08	02/08	03/08	04/08	05/08	06/08	07/08	**174**	09/07
172	174	158	127	127	128	135	136	147	148	150	158		

Turkmenistan comfortably saw off the challenges of Cambodia and then Hong Kong to book their place in the penultimate phase of Asia's qualifying tournament for the 2010 FIFA World Cup finals, but progressing to the final stage proved to be a step too far for the former Soviet republic. A 5-1 aggregate win over the Cambodians – with Mamedaly Karadanov scoring a goal in both Phnom Penh and Ashgabat – was followed by a scoreless draw in Hong Kong, but the Turkmens progressed to the group stage thanks to a 3-0 win at home. Drawn against South Korea, North Korea and Jordan, Turkmenistan only managed to put one point on the board in their six group games as their

INTERNATIONAL HONOURS
None

challenge for a place in South Africa fizzled out. There was also disappointment at club level when following a series of disappointing performances in the AFC Cup since the competition's inception in 2004, Turkmenistan were relegated to taking part in the AFC President's Cup, the lowest of Asia's three-tier club competitions. FK Ashgabat, who won the Turkmen league title in 2007, qualified for the finals of the 2008 tournament after seeing off the challenges of Myanmar's Kan Baw Za, Ratnam SC from Sri Lanka and Bhutan's Transport United, But unlike previous years the semi-finals and finals were not played at the same time or at the same venue as the group stage.

THE FIFA BIG COUNT OF 2006

	Male	Female		Total
Number of players	90 355	10 060	Referees and Assistant Referees	65
Professionals	280		Admin, Coaches, Technical, Medical	130
Amateurs 18+	615		Number of clubs	15
Youth under 18	310		Number of teams	98
Unregistered	23 000		Clubs with women's teams	0
Total players	100 415		Players as % of population	1.99%

Football Association of Turkmenistan (FFT)
15 A. Niyazova Street, Stadium Kopetdag, Ashgabat 744 001, Turkmenistan
Tel +993 12 477470   Fax +993 12 362355
footballtkm@mail.ru   www.none
President: YUSUPOV Aman   General Secretary: SATYLOV Meret
Vice-President: SAPAEV Allabergen   Treasurer: LEONOVA Natalya   Media Officer: IVANNIKOV Evgeniy
Men's Coach: KURBANMAMEDOV Rakhim   Women's Coach: MAMEDOV Atamyrad
FFT formed: 1992   AFC: 1994   FIFA: 1994
Green shirts, White shorts, Green socks

RECENT INTERNATIONAL MATCHES PLAYED BY TURKMENISTAN

2004	Opponents	Score		Venue	Comp	Scorers	Att	Referee
18-02	Sri Lanka	W	2-0	Ashgabat	WCq	Ovekov [40], Bayramov.N [56]	11 000	Al Bannai UAE
17-03	Yemen	W	2-1	Sana'a	Fr			
31-03	Indonesia	W	3-1	Ashgabat	WCq	Bayramov.V 2 [10 74], Kuliev [35]	5 000	Sahib Shakir IRQ
28-04	Armenia	L	0-1	Yerevan	Fr		7 500	
31-05	Qatar	L	0-5	Doha	Fr			
9-06	Saudi Arabia	L	0-3	Riyadh	WCq		1 000	Khanthama THA
18-07	Saudi Arabia	D	2-2	Chengdu	ACr1	Bayramov.N [7], Kuliev [90]	12 400	Al Qahtani KSA
22-07	Iraq	L	2-3	Chengdu	ACr1	Bayramov.V [15], Kuliev [85]	22 000	Al Fadhli KUW
26-07	Uzbekistan	L	0-1	Chongqing	ACr1		34 000	Kousa SYR
8-09	Saudi Arabia	L	0-1	Ashgabat	WCq		5 000	Kwon Jong Chul KOR
9-10	Sri Lanka	D	2-2	Colombo	WCq	Bayramov.D [20], Nazarov [70]	4 000	Al Bannai UAE
17-11	Indonesia	L	1-3	Jakarta	WCq	Durdiyev [25]	15 000	Shaban KUW
2005								
29-01	Saudi Arabia	L	0-1	Riyadh	Fr			
3-08	Bahrain	L	0-5	Manama	Fr			
2006								
No international matches played in 2006								
2007								
25-06	Qatar	L	0-1	Doha	Fr			
22-08	Lithuania	L	1-2	Kaunas	Fr	Nikitenko [90]		
11-10	Cambodia	W	1-0	Phnom Penh	WCq	Karadanov [85]	3 000	Gosh BAN
28-10	Cambodia	W	4-1	Ashgabat	WCq	Nasyrov [41], Gevorkyan 2 [50 66], Karadanov [74]	5 000	Saidov UZB
10-11	Hong Kong	D	0-0	Hong Kong	WCq		2 823	Mujghef JOR
18-11	Hong Kong	W	3-0	Ashgabat	WCq	Nasyrov [42], Bayramov [53], Mirzoev [80]	30 000	Al Hilali OMA
2008								
6-02	Korea Republic	L	0-4	Seoul	WCq		25 738	Najm LIB
26-03	Jordan	L	0-2	Ashgabat	WCq		20 000	Tongkhan THA
18-05	Oman	L	1-2	Nizwa	Fr	Saparov [53]		
2-06	Korea DPR	D	0-0	Ashgabat	WCq		20 000	Al Ghamdi KSA
7-06	Korea DPR	L	0-1	Pyongyang	WCq		25 000	Al Saeedi UAE
14-06	Korea Republic	L	1-3	Ashgabat	WCq	Ovekov [77p]	11 000	Takayama JPN
22-06	Jordan	L	0-2	Amman	WCq		150	Williams AUS
30-07	Tajikistan	D	0-0	Hyderabad	CCr1		150	Kovalenko UZB
1-08	Afghanistan	W	5-0	Hyderabad	CCr1	Ovekov 4 [1 41 77 80], Krendelev [23]	100	Saleem MDV
3-08	India	L	1-2	Hyderabad	CCr1	Orazmamedov [84]	1 000	Jasim UAE

Fr = Friendly match • AC = AFC Asian Cup • WC = FIFA World Cup • q = qualifier • r1 = first round group

TURKMENISTAN NATIONAL TEAM RECORDS AND RECORD SEQUENCES

Records			Sequence records					
Victory	11-0	AFG 2003	Wins	4	2003, 2003-2004	Clean sheets	4	2003
Defeat	1-6	KUW 2000	Defeats	5	2004-2007	Goals scored	14	2001-2004
Player Caps	n/a		Undefeated	13	2001-2004	Without goal	3	2004, 2005-2007
Player Goals	n/a		Without win	12	2004-2007	Goals against	14	2004-2007

TURKMENISTAN COUNTRY INFORMATION

Capital	Ashgabat	Independence	1991 from the USSR	GDP per Capita	$5 800
Population	4 863 169	Status	Republic	GNP Ranking	113
Area km²	488 100	Language	Turkmen, Russian, Uzbek	Dialling code	+993
Population density	10 per km²	Literacy rate	98%	Internet code	.tm
% in urban areas	45%	Main religion	Muslim	GMT +/−	+5
Cities/Towns ('000)	Ashgabat 979; Turkmenabat 234; Dasoguz 199; Mary 114; Balkanabat 87; Bayramali 75				
Neighbours (km)	Uzbekistan 1 621; Afghanistan 744; Iran 992; Kazakhstan 379; Caspian Sea 1 768				
Main stadia	Olympic Stadium – Ashgabat 30 000; Köpetdag – Ashgabat 26 000				

TURKMENISTAN 2007

FIRST DIVISION

	PI	W	D	L	F	A	Pts	FK Ashgabat	MTTU	Nebitchi	Talyp Sporty	Sagadam	Merv	Turan	Köpetdag
FK Ashgabat ‡	28	19	4	5	44	14	61		3-2 0-0	2-1 2-0	0-0 1-0	0-2 0-1	1-0 2-1	2-0 5-0	1-0 6-0
MTTU Ashgabat	28	16	8	4	66	25	56	0-0 0-0		1-2 2-1	2-3 3-0	2-1 0-0	2-0 4-1	6-0 5-0	5-3 5-0
Nebitchi Balkanabat	28	14	4	10	43	33	46	2-0 2-1	1-1 0-1		1-0 1-1	2-1 1-2	0-0 1-2	4-0 1-1	6-1 1-0
Talyp Sporty Ashgabat	28	12	5	11	41	38	41	0-2 1-3	1-1 1-2	2-0 5-1		**0-3** 0-0	2-1 1-0	2-1 3-0	0-0 0-2
Sagadam Turkmenbasy	28	10	6	12	31	32	36	2-1 0-1	0-4 3-3	0-1 1-0	3-2 0-2		1-1 0-0	2-0 0-0	1-2 **3-0**
Merv Mary	28	10	5	13	40	37	35	0-2 0-1	2-1 2-2	0-1 1-3	2-3 3-0	3-1 2-1		2-1 5-0	3-2 3-0
Turan Dasoguz	28	7	3	18	23	56	24	0-1 0-2	1-2 0-1	3-1 1-2	1-2 2-3	2-0 1-0	1-0 3-2		3-1 2-0
Köpetdag Ashgabat	28	5	3	20	21	74	18	0-2 0-3	0-3 0-6	1-5 1-2	2-1 1-6	2-0 0-3	1-1 0-3	2-0 0-0	

7/04/2007 - 28/11/2007 • ‡ Qualified for the AFC President's Cup • Match in bold awarded • Top scorer: Berdimyrat Samyradov, HTTU 16

TURKMENISTAN CUP 2007

Quarter–finals		Semi–finals		Final	
Sagadam Turkmenbasy	1 2 4p				
Talyp Sporty Ashgabat *	2 1 3p				
		Sagadam Turkmenbasy	2 2		
		Nebitchi Balkanabat *	1 0		
Turan Dasoguz *	1 1				
Nebitchi Balkanabat	3 1				
				Sagadam Turkmenbasy	1
				Merv Mary	0
MTTU Ashgabat	0 3				
FK Ashgabat *	1 0				
		MTTU Ashgabat	0 0		
		Merv Mary *	0 1		
Köpetdag Ashgabat	0 2				
Merv Mary *	1 1				

CUP FINAL

26-09-2007
Scorer - Batyr Govshakov [107]

* Home team in the first leg • ‡ Qualified for the AFC Cup

RECENT LEAGUE AND CUP RECORD

	Championship						Cup		
Year	Champions	Pts	Runners-up	Pts	Third	Pts	Winners	Score	Runners-up
1992	Köpetdag Ashgabat	54	Nebitchi Balkanabat	47	Akhal Akdashayak	46			
1993	Köpetdag Ashgabat	14	Byuzmeyin	11	Nebitchi Balkanabat	9	Köpetdag Ashgabat	4-0	Merv Mary
1994	Köpetdag Ashgabat	31	Nisa Ashgabat	24	Merv Mary	20	Köpetdag Ashgabat	2-0	Turan Dasoguz
1995	Köpetdag Ashgabat	84	Nisa Ashgabat	79	Nebitchi Balkanabat	61	Turan Dasoguz	4-3	Köpetdag Ashgabat
1996	Nisa Ashgabat	83	Köpetdag Ashgabat	74	Exkavatorshchik	60	No tournament due to season re-adjustment		
1997	No tournament due to season re-adjustment						Köpetdag Ashgabat	2-0	Nisa Ashgabat
1998	Köpetdag Ashgabat		Nisa Ashgabat				Nisa Ashgabat	3-0	Nebitchi Balkanabat
1999	Nisa Ashgabat	78	Köpetdag Ashgabat	67	Dagdan Ashgabat	60	Köpetdag Ashgabat	3-1	Nebitchi Balkanabat
2000	Köpetdag Ashgabat	56	Nebitchi Balkanabat	41	Nisa Ashgabat	37	Köpetdag Ashgabat	5-0	Nisa Ashgabat
2001	Nisa Ashgabat	77	Köpetdag Ashgabat	68	Nebitchi Balkanabat	60	Köpetdag Ashgabat	2-0	Nebitchi Balkanabat
2002	Sagadam Turk'basy	67	Nisa Ashgabat	63	Garagam Turk'abat	59	Garagam Turk'abat	0-0 4-2p	Sagadam Turk'basy
2003	Nisa Ashgabat	92	Nebitchi Balkanabat	79	Sagadam Turk'basy	76	Nebitchi Balkanabat	2-1	Nisa Ashgabat
2004	Nebitchi Balkanabat	84	Nisa Ashgabat	78	Merv Mary	67	Nebitchi Balkanabat	1-0	Asudalyk Ashgabat
2005	MTTU Ashgabat	72	Gazcy Gazojak	62	Nebitchi Balkanabat	58	Merv Mary	1-1 3-1p	Köpetdag Ashgabat
2006	MTTU Ashgabat	55	Nebitchi Balkanabat	51	FK Ashgabat	48	MTTU Ashgabat	0-0 7-6p	Köpetdag Ashgabat
2007	FK Ashgabat	61	MTTU Ashgabat	56	Nebitchi Balkanabat	46	Sagadam Turk'basy	1-0	Merv Mary

Turkmen clubs took part in the Soviet league until the end of the 1991 season

TLS – TIMOR–LESTE

NATIONAL TEAM RECORD
JULY 10TH 2006 TO JULY 12TH 2010

PL	W	D	L	F	A	%
6	0	0	6	8	28	0

FIFA/COCA-COLA WORLD RANKING

1993	1994	1995	1996	1997	1998	1999	2000	2001	2002	2003	2004	2005	2006	2007
-	-	-	-	-	-	-	-	-	-	-	-	-	198	201

High	
198	12/06

2007–2008											
08/07	09/07	10/07	11/07	12/07	01/08	02/08	03/08	04/08	05/08	06/08	07/08
199	200	200	201	201	201	202	202	202	200	199	199

Low	
202	02/08

International exposure has been hard to come by for Timor-Leste after winning their hard-earned independence from Indonesia in 2002 and the national team remains at the very bottom of the FIFA/Coca-Cola World Ranking. However, 2007 did present the nation with the opportunity to make their debut in the FIFA World Cup when they entered the Asian preliminaries for South Africa. Emilio Da Silva had the honour of scoring his country's first-ever World Cup goal after he netted twice against Hong Kong in a 3-2 loss, a match which was played in nearby Bali. Seven days later Da Silva was on target again but Hong Kong proved to be too good for the Timorese and

INTERNATIONAL HONOURS
None

they ran out 8-1 winners on the day and 11-3 victors on aggregate. The loss in Hong Kong was East Timor's 12th straight defeat since playing their first international match back in 2003 and any hopes of ending that winless streak in the qualifying phase of the 2008 AFC Challenge Cup evaporated when the national association decided not to participate in the tournament. However, the experience gained by playing in the World Cup could start to pay dividends when they attempt to qualify for 2008 ASEAN championship with Cambodia hosting a preliminary round in October 2008 before the finals in December.

THE FIFA BIG COUNT OF 2006

	Male	Female		Total
Number of players	15 500	0	Referees and Assistant Referees	0
Professionals	0		Admin, Coaches, Technical, Medical	100
Amateurs 18+	200		Number of clubs	10
Youth under 18	300		Number of teams	20
Unregistered	0		Clubs with women's teams	0
Total players	15 500		Players as % of population	1.46%

Federaçao Futebol Timor-Leste (FFTL)
Rua 12 de Novembro Sta. Cruz, PO Box 1031, Dili, Timor-Leste
Tel +670 3322231   Fax +670 3317430
federacao_futebol@yahoo.com   www.none
President: LAY Francisco Kalbuadi   General Secretary: SAMENTO Amandio
Vice-President: CABRAL FERNANDES Filomeno Pedro   Treasurer: FEREIRA Jesuina M.   Media Officer: TIMOTIO Antonio
Men's Coach: PEREIRA Joao Paulo   Women's Coach: DE ARAUJO Marcos
FFTL formed: 2002   AFC: 2002   FIFA: 2005
Red shirts, Black shorts, Red socks

RECENT INTERNATIONAL MATCHES PLAYED BY TIMOR-LESTE

2002	Opponents	Score		Venue	Comp	Scorers	Att	Referee
No international matches played before 2003								
2003								
21-03	Sri Lanka	L	2-3	Colombo	ACq			
23-03	Chinese Taipei	L	0-3	Colombo	ACq			
2004								
8-12	Malaysia	L	0-5	Kuala Lumpur	TCr1			
12-12	Thailand	L	0-8	Kuala Lumpur	TCr1			
14-12	Philippines	L	1-2	Kuala Lumpur	TCr1	Anai [14]		
16-12	Myanmar	L	1-3	Kuala Lumpur	TCr1	Simon Diamantino [15p]		
2005								
No international matches played in 2005								
2006								
12-11	Brunei	L	2-3	Bacolod	TCq	Adelio Maria Costa [33], Anatacio Belo [77]		
14-11	Philippines	L	0-7	Bacolod	TCq			
16-11	Laos	L	2-3	Bacolod	TCq	Antonio Ximenes [82], Adelio Maria Costa [89]		
20-11	Cambodia	L	1-4	Bacolod	TCq	Adelio Maria Costa [63]		
2007								
21-10	Hong Kong	L	2-3	Gianyar	WCq	Emilio Da Silva 2 [41 69]	1 500	Shaharul MAS
28-10	Hong Kong	L	1-8	Hong Kong	WCq	Emilio Da Silva	1 542	Torky IRN
2008								
No international matches played in 2008 before August								

AC = AFC Asian Cup • TC = Tiger Cup/ASEAN Football Federation Championship
q = qualifier • r1 = first round group • Matches played before September 2005 are not full internationals

TIMOR-LESTE NATIONAL TEAM RECORDS AND RECORD SEQUENCES

Records			Sequence records		
Victory	-	Never won a match	Wins	0	
Defeat	0-8	THA 2004	Defeats	12	2003-
Player Caps	n/a		Undefeated	0	
Player Goals	4	Emilio Da Silva	Without win	12	2003-

Clean sheets	0	
Goals scored	4	2006-2007
Without goal	3	2003-2004
Goals against	12	2003-

TIMOR-LESTE COUNTRY INFORMATION

Capital	Dili	Independence	2002 from Indonesia	GDP per Capita	$400
Population	1 040 880	Status	Republic	GNP Ranking	143
Area km²	15 077	Language	Tetum, Portuguese	Dialling code	+670
Population density	69 per km²	Literacy rate	58%	Internet code	.tp
% in urban areas	8%	Main religion	Christian 93%	GMT + / -	+8
Towns/Cities ('000)	Dili 159; Dare 18; Los Palos 17; Baucau 14; Ermera 12; Maliana 12				
Neighbours (km)	Indonesia 228; Timor Sea, Savu Sea and Banda Sea 706				
Main stadia	Estadio Nacional, Dili 5 000				

TOG – TOGO

NATIONAL TEAM RECORD
JULY 10TH 2006 TO JULY 12TH 2010

PL	W	D	L	F	A	%
16	6	3	7	20	21	46.9

FIFA/COCA-COLA WORLD RANKING

1993	1994	1995	1996	1997	1998	1999	2000	2001	2002	2003	2004	2005	2006	2007	High
113	86	92	87	78	68	87	81	71	86	94	89	56	60	72	**46** 08/06

2007–2008												Low
08/07	09/07	10/07	11/07	12/07	01/08	02/08	03/08	04/08	05/08	06/08	07/08	**123** 06/94
60	63	67	72	72	74	74	74	87	86	69	69	

From the heady heights of competing at the FIFA World Cup finals in Germany in 2006, Togo slumped into a crisis just over a year later after their winner-takes-all Nations Cup qualifier against Mali was disrupted by crowd violence. Togolese spectators attacked the Mali players during the 2-0 defeat in Lome in September 2007, a defeat that cost Togo a place at the finals in neighbouring Ghana and led to the imposition of a four match ban on the use of the stadium in Lome. Forced to host their opening qualifying matches for the 2010 FIFA World Cup finals in Ghana, Togo began with a win over Zambia in Accra in a disputed result, but their hopes of making it to the finals in

INTERNATIONAL HONOURS
Qualified for the FIFA World Cup finals 2006

South Arica were placed in serious jeopardy with a loss a week later at minnows Swaziland. Their failure in the 2008 CAF Africa Cup of Nations qualifiers spelt the end of the second spell in the coaching position for former Nigerian captain Stephen Keshi but it took months of negotiations before Togo finally signed a contract with his replacement, the Frenchman Henri Stambouli. ASKO Kara were crowned champions of Togo, finishing a comfortable margin ahead of US Masseda, who were playing in the top flight for the first time. Both shaded pre-competition favourite Etoile Filante into third place.

THE FIFA BIG COUNT OF 2006

	Male	Female		Total
Number of players	230 900	11 500	Referees and Assistant Referees	600
Professionals	100		Admin, Coaches, Technical, Medical	2 700
Amateurs 18+	5 200		Number of clubs	100
Youth under 18	4 500		Number of teams	620
Unregistered	15 600		Clubs with women's teams	0
Total players	242 400		Players as % of population	4.37%

Fédération Togolaise de Football (FTF)
Route Vegue, Case postale 5, Lome, Togo
Tel +228 2618657   Fax +228 2615646
ftf@ftf.tg   www.ftf.tg
President: TATA Avlessi Adaglo   General Secretary: ASSOGBAVI Komlan
Vice-President: MAWULAWOE Ameyi Komla Kuma   Treasurer: ADJETE Tino   Media Officer: KOLANI Kossi Nzonou
Men's Coach: STAMBOULI Henri   Women's Coach: MAWUENA Kodjovi
FTF formed: 1960   CAF: 1963   FIFA: 1962
Yellow shirts with green trimmings, Green shorts, White socks or Green shirts with white trimmings, Green shorts, White socks

RECENT INTERNATIONAL MATCHES PLAYED BY TOGO

2006	Opponents	Score		Venue	Comp	Scorers	Att	Referee
13-06	Korea Republic	L	1-2	Frankfurt	WCr1	Kader Coubadja [31]	48 000	Poll ENG
19-06	Switzerland	L	0-2	Dortmund	WCr1		65 000	Amarilla PAR
23-06	France	L	0-2	Cologne	WCr1		45 000	Larrionda URU
15-08	Ghana	L	0-2	London	Fr			Dean ENG
29-08	Niger	D	1-1	Lomé	Fr	Amewou [55]		
3-09	Benin	W	2-1	Lomé	CNq	Dossevi [13], Amewou [78]		Louzaya CGO
8-10	Mali	L	0-1	Bamako	CNq			Benouza ALG
15-11	Luxembourg	D	0-0	Luxembourg	Fr		1 417	Richards WAL
2007								
7-02	Cameroon	D	2-2	Lomé	Fr	Olufade [25], Adebayor [40]		
25-03	Sierra Leone	W	3-1	Lomé	CNq	Adebayor 2 [38 85], Olufade [62]		Pare BFA
3-06	Sierra Leone	W	1-0	Freetown	CNq	Junior Senaya [48]		Imiere NGA
17-06	Benin	L	1-4	Cotonou	CNq	Olufade [75]		Evehe CMR
22-08	Zambia	W	3-1	Lomé	Fr	Ayite 2 [29 41], Olufade [84]		
12-10	Mali	L	0-2	Lomé	CNq			Abdelfattah EGY
18-11	Ghana	L	0-2	Accra	Fr			
21-11	UAE	W	5-0	Accra	Fr	Moutawakilou [19], Sapol [73], OG [77], Dossevi [83], Adebayor [84]		
2008								
25-03	Guinea	L	0-2	Paris	Fr			
31-05	Zambia	W	1-0	Accra	WCq	Olufade [16]	15 000	Pare BFA
8-06	Swaziland	L	1-2	Mbabane	WCq	Olufade [88]	5 819	Niyongabo BDI

Fr = Friendly match • CN = CAF African Cup of Nations • WC = FIFA World Cup • q = qualifier • r1 = first round group

TOGO NATIONAL TEAM RECORDS AND RECORD SEQUENCES

Records			Sequence records					
Victory	5-0	UAE 2007	Wins	5	2004-2005	Clean sheets	3	Six times
Defeat	0-7	MAR 1979, TUN 2000	Defeats	5	1977-79, 1999-00	Goals scored	12	1956-1957
Player Caps	66	Jean-Paul Abalo	Undefeated	12	2004-2005	Without goal	5	2002
Player Goals	30	Emmanuel Adebayor	Without win	14	1992-94, 1999-00	Goals against	9	1983-1984

TOGO 2007 CHAMPIONNAT NATIONAL

	Pl	W	D	L	F	A	Pts
ASKO Kara	30	17	10	3	33	14	61
US Masséda	30	14	11	5	30	15	53
Etoile Filante	30	15	7	8	35	25	52
Maranatha Fiokpo	30	12	10	8	37	29	46
AS Togo-Sport	30	11	10	9	24	20	43
AS Douanes	30	10	12	8	30	25	42
US Koroki Tchamba	30	9	15	6	27	25	42
Sèmassi Sokodé	30	10	8	12	21	24	38
Kotoko Lavié	30	10	8	12	20	23	38
AC Merlan Lomé	30	7	15	8	23	20	36
Abou Ossé Anié	30	8	11	11	21	27	35
Togo Télécom	30	7	12	11	27	36	33
Tchaoudjo AC Sokodé	30	8	7	15	24	33	31
Dynamic Togolais	30	6	12	12	18	28	30
Agaza Lomé	30	6	11	13	18	32	29
Doumbé	30	5	11	14	19	31	26

23/09/2006 - 30/09/2007

RECENT LEAGUE AND CUP RECORD

Championship		Cup		
Year Champions		Winners	Score	Runners-up
2001	Dynamic Togolais	Dynamic Togolais	3-0	Sara Sport Bafilo
2002	AS Douanes	Dynamic Togolais	2-0	Doumbé
2003	No tournament	Maranatha Fiokpo		
2004	Dynamic Togolais	AS Douanes	2-1	Foadam Dapaong
2005	AS Douanes	Dynamic Togolais	1-0	Agaza Lomé
2006	Maranatha Fiokpo	AS Togo-Port	1-1 5-4p	ASKO Kara
2007	ASKO Kara			

TOGO COUNTRY INFORMATION

Capital	Lomé	Independence	1960 from France	GDP per Capita	$1 500
Population	5 556 812	Status	Republic	GNP Ranking	149
Area km²	56 785	Language	French	Dialling code	+228
Population density	97 per km²	Literacy rate	60%	Internet code	.tg
% in urban areas	31%	Main religion	Indigenous 51% Christian 29%	GMT +/–	0
Towns/Cities ('000)	Lomé 726; Kpalimé 110; Sokodé 108; Kara 94; Atakpamé 92; Bassar 55; Tsévié 55; Aného 47				
Neighbours (km)	Benin 644; Ghana 877; Burkina Faso 126; Atlantic Ocean/Bight of Benin 56				
Main stadia	Stade General Eyadema (Kegue) – Lomé 20 000				

TPE – CHINESE TAIPEI

NATIONAL TEAM RECORD
JULY 10TH 2006 TO JULY 12TH 2010

PL	W	D	L	F	A	%
17	4	3	10	28	51	32.4

FIFA/COCA-COLA WORLD RANKING

1993	1994	1995	1996	1997	1998	1999	2000	2001	2002	2003	2004	2005	2006	2007	High	
161	170	178	174	154	169	174	162	170	166	150	155	156	166	169	**144**	08/06

2007–2008												Low	
08/07	09/07	10/07	11/07	12/07	01/08	02/08	03/08	04/08	05/08	06/08	07/08	**180**	07/96
155	159	163	163	169	168	171	171	169	170	174	176		

Not much need be said about Chinese Taipei's match-up with Uzbekistan in the 2010 FIFA World Cup qualifiers - the 11-0 aggregate score says it all. Of far more interest was the national team's performance in the AFC Challenge Cup, a competition for Asia's lower-ranked nations. Originally, Taiwan had been designated hosts but, after being unable to fulfil the required criteria, had to relinquish the honour. Instead, they were forced into the qualifiers, and staged one of the four groups at the Chungshan Stadium in Taipei. In front of crowds struggling to reach four figures, they lost to Pakistan after taking an early lead, and, despite beating Guam and drawing with Sri Lanka,

INTERNATIONAL HONOURS
Asian Games 1954 1958

missed out on the finals. Of course, living on a baseball-crazy island with no real professional football the team has suffered. None of the squad plays abroad, and many are still students. Domestically, the Taiwan Power Company - Taipower - retained the title in 2008, their fifteenth in all. They are one of only two semi-pro clubs in the league. The women's national team went out in the group stages of the Asian Cup. Back in the 70s and early 80s, the famous women's 'Mulan' team was the best in Asia, and perhaps the world. Unfortunately, with the current strength of North Korea, Japan and China, the path back will be long and hard.

THE FIFA BIG COUNT OF 2006

	Male	Female		Total
Number of players	424 400	34 060	Referees and Assistant Referees	102
Professionals	0		Admin, Coaches, Technical, Medical	374
Amateurs 18+	5 960		Number of clubs	60
Youth under 18	6 600		Number of teams	600
Unregistered	75 900		Clubs with women's teams	0
Total players	458 460		Players as % of population	1.99%

Chinese Taipei Football Association (CTFA)
2F No. Yu Men St., Taipei 104, Taiwan
Tel +886 2 25961184   Fax +886 2 25951594
ctfa7155@ms59.hinet.net   www.ctfa.com.tw
President: CHIOU I-Jen   General Secretary: LIN Der Chia
Vice-President: SHI Hwei-Yow   Treasurer: LIN Shiu Yi   Media Officer: BEARE Alexander James
Men's Coach: TOSHIAKI Imai   Women's Coach: TOSHIAKI Imai
CTFA formed: 1924   AFC: 1954-75, 1990   FIFA: 1954
Blue shirts, Blue shorts, White socks

RECENT INTERNATIONAL MATCHES PLAYED BY CHINESE TAIPEI

2007	Opponents	Score	Venue	Comp	Scorers	Att	Referee
24-03	Uzbekistan	L 0-1	Taipei	Fr			
17-06	Guam	W 10-0	Macau	EAq	Lo Chih En 4 [7 28 72 88], Tsai Hui Kai [20], Feng Pao Hsing 2 [25 38], Chen Po Liang 2 [52 68], Huang Cheng Tsung [74]	10	Wan Daxue CHN
19-06	Hong Kong	D 1-1	Macau	EAq	Huang Wei Yi [51]	200	Kim Eui Soo KOR
24-06	Macau	W 7-2	Macau	EAq	Huang Wei Yi [3], Feng Pao Hsing [42], Kuo Chun Yi [52], Chen Po Liang [56], Lo Chih En 2 [57 90], Lo Chih An [71]	200	Kim Eui Soo KOR
13-10	Uzbekistan	L 0-9	Tashkent	WCq		7 000	Albadwawi UAE
28-10	Uzbekistan	L 0-2	Taipei	WCq		800	Shamsuzzaman UZB
2008							
2-04	Pakistan	L 1-2	Taipei	CCq	Lo Chi An [5]	800	Iemoto JPN
4-04	Guam	W 4-1	Taipei	CCq	Chang Han [20], Huang Wei Yi [28], Chen Po Liang [33], Chiang Shih Lu [44]	850	Win Cho MYA
6-04	Sri Lanka	D 2-2	Taipei	CCq	Chang Han [28], Tsai Hsien Tang [74]	900	Iemoto JPN
24-05	India	L 0-3	Goa	Fr			
27-05	India	D 2-2	Chennai	Fr	Chen Po Liang [4], Hsieh Meng Hsuan [48]		

Fr = Friendly match • EA = East Asian Championship • AC = AFC Asian Cup • CC = AFC Challenge Cup • WC = FIFA World Cup • q = qualifier

CHINESE TAIPEI NATIONAL TEAM RECORDS AND RECORD SEQUENCES

Records			Sequence records					
Victory	10-0	GUM 2007	Wins	8	1958-1960	Clean sheets	3	1981
Defeat	0-10	KUW 2006	Defeats	9	1988-92, 1992-96	Goals scored	15	1966-1967
Player Caps	n/a		Undefeated	11	1957-1960	Without goal	12	2000-2002
Player Goals	n/a		Without win	19	1988-1996	Goals against	15	1867-1968

CHINESE TAIPEI 2007
FUBON ENTERPRISE FOOTBALL LEAGUE

	Pl	W	D	L	F	A	Pts	TP	CK	FF	Ta
Taipower	6	3	2	1	9	11	11		1-1	0-5	2-1
Chateau Kenting	6	2	4	0	12	8	10	2-2		2-1	1-1
Fubon Financial	6	1	2	3	11	11	5	2-3	1-1		1-1
Tatung	6	1	2	3	9	11	5	0-1	2-5	4-1	

13/01/2007 - 14/04/2007 • † Qualified for the AFC President's Cup

RECENT LEAGUE RECORD

Year	Champions
2003	Taiwan Power Company Taipei
2004	Taiwan Power Company Taipei
2005	Tatung
2006	Tatung
2007	Taiwan Power Company Taipei
2008	Taiwan Power Company Taipei

CHINESE TAIPEI 2008
FUBON ENTERPRISE FOOTBALL LEAGUE

	Pl	W	D	L	F	A	Pts	Taipower	Tatung	Molten So I	E-United	Hun Sing	NSTC	Bros	Fubon F'cial
Taipower	14	11	2	1	34	6	35		1-1	1-0	6-1	1-1	2-0	4-0	1-0
Tatung	14	11	2	1	29	6	35	0-3		1-0	2-0	1-0	3-0	4-0	5-0
Molten So I	14	10	0	4	32	8	30	1-0	0-2		5-0	6-0	2-0	2-0	5-1
E-United Group	14	6	1	7	21	31	19	1-3	0-4	0-3		2-1	1-2	5-1	1-0
Hun Sing	14	4	4	6	13	20	16	0-2	1-1	1-0	1-3		1-1	1-0	0-0
NSTC	14	3	2	9	7	21	11	0-3	0-1	0-2	1-1	0-2		0-1	1-0
Bros	14	3	0	11	11	34	9	1-3	0-2	2-3	1-3	1-3	1-0		0-2
Fubon Financial	14	2	1	11	10	31	7	0-4	1-2	0-3	1-3	2-1	1-2	2-3	

5/01/2008 - 27/04/2008 • ‡ Qualified for the AFC President's Cup • Match in bold awarded

CHINESE TAIPEI COUNTRY INFORMATION

Capital	Taipei	Independence	1949	GDP per Capita	$23 400
Population	22 749 838	Status	Republic	GNP Ranking	16
Area km²	35 980	Language	Mandarin, Min	Dialling code	+886
Population density	632 per km²	Literacy rate	96%	Internet code	.tw
% in urban areas	69%	Main religion	Buddhist, Confucian, Taoist	GMT +/−	+8
Towns/Cities ('000)	Taipei 2 514; Kaoshiung 1 512; Taichung 1 083; Tainan 734; Panchiao 491; Hsinchu 413				
Neighbours (km)	Taiwan Strait, East China Sea, Philippine Sea & South China Sea 1 566				
Main stadia	Chung Shan Soccer Stadium – Taipei 25 000				

TRI – TRINIDAD AND TOBAGO

NATIONAL TEAM RECORD
JULY 10TH 2006 TO JULY 12TH 2010

PL	W	D	L	F	A	%
28	12	6	10	44	37	53.6

FIFA/COCA-COLA WORLD RANKING

1993	1994	1995	1996	1997	1998	1999	2000	2001	2002	2003	2004	2005	2006	2007		High	
88	91	57	41	56	51	44	29	32	47	70	63	50	91	81		**25**	06/01

	2007–2008											Low	
08/07	09/07	10/07	11/07	12/07	01/08	02/08	03/08	04/08	05/08	06/08	07/08	**102**	07/08
63	64	78	83	81	78	98	93	89	88	87	102		

In the wake of their appearance at the World Cup finals in Germany, Trinidad and Tobago began their quest to qualify for the 2010 finals in South Africa with what looked to be a relatively straight-forward preliminary round tie against Bermuda. However, after losing the first leg 2-1 at home in Macoya, the Soca Warriors faced the prospect of an embarrassing early exit. In January 2008 the federation had appointed the veteran Colombian Francisco Maturana as coach and his experience helped see the team through in the return in Bermuda which was won 2-0. To reach the finals in South Africa, however, Trinidad will first have to negotiate a group containing Guatemala, Cuba

INTERNATIONAL HONOURS
Qualified for the FIFA World Cup finals 2006 Caribbean Cup 1981 1989 1992 1994 1995 1996 1997 1999 2001 Champions Cup Defence Force 1978 1985

and the USA and then finish in the top three of a second group stage containing six teams. Although the Soca Warriors can count on a number of professionals abroad, the championship at home continues to be the strongest in the Caribbean with the clubs recruiting players from many of the neighbouring islands. The introduction of the CONCACAF Champions League could see it grow even stronger. The Caribbean Club Championship, in which Trinidad has a strong record, will produce three qualifiers for the Champions League and represented in the inaugural tournament will be Joe Public who finished as Caribbean runners-up in 2007.

THE FIFA BIG COUNT OF 2006

	Male	Female		Total
Number of players	71 150	13 450	Referees and Assistant Referees	250
Professionals	250		Admin, Coaches, Technical, Medical	650
Amateurs 18+	4 250		Number of clubs	95
Youth under 18	11 600		Number of teams	380
Unregistered	16 000		Clubs with women's teams	3
Total players	84 600		Players as % of population	7.94%

Trinidad and Tobago Football Federation (TTFF)
43 Dundonald Street, PO Box 400, Port of Spain, Trinidad and Tobago
Tel +1 868 6237312   Fax +1 868 6238109
richardgroden@aol.com   www.ttffonline.com
President: CAMPS Oliver   General Secretary: GRODEN Richard
Vice-President: TIM KEE Raymond   Treasurer: TBD   Media Officer: FUENTES Shaun
Men's Coach: MATURANA Francisco   Women's Coach: CHARLES Marlon
TTFF formed: 1908   CONCACAF: 1964   FIFA: 1963
Red shirts with white trimmings, Red shorts, Red socks or White shirts with red trimmings, White shorts, White socks

RECENT INTERNATIONAL MATCHES PLAYED BY TRINIDAD AND TOBAGO

2005	Opponents	Score		Venue	Comp	Scorers	Att	Referee
17-08	USA	L	0-1	Hartford	WCq		25 500	Rodriguez MEX
3-09	Guatemala	W	3-2	Port of Spain	WCq	Latapy [48], John 2 [85 86]	15 000	Archundia MEX
7-09	Costa Rica	L	0-2	San Jose	WCq		17 000	Batres GUA
8-10	Panama	W	1-0	Panama City	WCq	John [61]	1 000	Navarro CAN
12-10	Mexico	W	2-1	Port of Spain	WCq	John 2 [43 69]	23 000	Pineda HON
12-11	Bahrain	D	1-1	Port of Spain	WCpo	Birchall [76]	24 991	Shield AUS
16-11	Bahrain	W	1-0	Manama	WCpo	Lawrence [49]	35 000	Ruiz COL
2006								
28-02	Iceland	W	2-0	London	Fr	Yorke 2 [9 52p]	7 890	
10-05	Peru	D	1-1	Port of Spain	Fr	Jones [74]	20 000	Prendergast JAM
27-05	Wales	L	1-2	Graz	Fr	John [32]	8 000	Messner AUT
31-05	Slovenia	L	1-3	Celje	Fr	Birchall [26]	2 500	Tanovic SCG
3-06	Czech Republic	L	0-3	Prague	Fr		15 910	Johannesson SWE
10-06	Sweden	D	0-0	Dortmund	WCr1		62 959	Maidin SIN
15-06	England	L	0-2	Nuremberg	WCr1		41 000	Kamikawa JPN
20-06	Paraguay	L	0-2	Kaiserslautern	WCr1		46 000	Rosetti ITA
9-08	Japan	L	0-2	Tokyo	Fr		47 482	Sun Baojie CHN
7-10	St Vincent/Grenadines	W	5-0	Port of Spain	Fr	Birchall [13], John 2 [24 46], Yorke [67], Baptiste [79]	4 116	
11-10	Panama	W	2-1	Port of Spain	Fr	Jones [33], Samuel [40]		
15-11	Austria	L	1-4	Vienna	Fr	Samuel [23]	13 100	Matejek CZE
2007								
12-01	Barbados	D	1-1	Port of Spain	CCr1	Glasgow [31]		
15-01	Martinique	W	5-1	Port of Spain	CCr1	Roberts [3], Baptiste 2 [36 76], Glasgow 2 [47 83]		Moreno PAN
17-01	Haiti	W	3-1	Port of Spain	CCr1	Jemmott [15], Glasgow 2 [67 85]		Campbell JAM
20-01	Cuba	W	3-1	Port of Spain	CCsf	OG [41], Glasgow [57], Theobald [73]		
23-01	Haiti	L	1-2	Port of Spain	CCf	Daniel [66]		Moreno PAN
31-01	Panama	L	1-2	Panama City	Fr	Jack [46]	5 000	Vidal PAN
4-02	Costa Rica	L	0-4	Alajuela	Fr			Porras CRC
28-05	Haiti	W	1-0	Port of Spain	Fr			
2-06	Honduras	L	1-3	San Pedro Sula	Fr	Thomas [17]	1 907	Soriano HON
7-06	El Salvador	L	1-2	Carson	GCr1	Spann [8]	21 334	Arredondo MEX
9-06	USA	L	0-2	Carson	GCr1		27 000	Moreno PAN
12-06	Guatemala	D	1-1	Foxboro	GCr1	McFarlane [87]	26 523	Pineda HON
17-10	El Salvador	D	0-0	San Salvador	Fr		13 000	Bonilla SLV
2008								
26-01	Puerto Rico	D	2-2	Bayamon	Fr	Baptiste [57p], Power [70]		
19-03	El Salvador	W	1-0	Macoya	Fr	Daniel [57]		
26-03	Jamaica	D	2-2	Kingston	Fr	Telesford [74], Whitely [90]	20 000	Whittaker CAY
27-04	Grenada	W	2-0	Macoya	Fr	Forbes [57], Carter [68]		
11-05	Barbados	W	3-0	Macoya	Fr	Gay [41], Jorsling [87], Edwards [90]	2 500	
1-06	England	L	0-3	Port of Spain	Fr		25 001	Wijngaarde SUR
7-06	Jamaica	D	1-1	Macoya	Fr	Hyland [30]		Small BRB
15-06	Bermuda	L	1-2	Macoya	WCq	John [22]	4 585	Quesada CRC
22-06	Bermuda	W	2-0	Prospect	WCq	Roberts [9], John [66]	5 000	Batres GUA
8-07	Guyana	W	2-0	Macoya	Fr	Leon [7], Daniel [69]		
17-07	Netherlands Antilles	W	2-0	Macoya	Fr	Toussaint [53], Wolfe [91+]		

Fr = Friendly match • GC = CONCACAF Gold Cup • WC = FIFA World Cup
q = qualifier • po = play-off • r1 = first round group • sf = semi-final • f = final

TRINIDAD AND TOBAGO NATIONAL TEAM RECORDS AND RECORD SEQUENCES

Records				Sequence records					
Victory	11-0	ARU 1989		Wins	8	1996, 1999	Clean sheets	5	2000, 2004
Defeat	0-7	MEX 2000		Defeats	6	1955-1957	Goals scored	19	1998-1999
Player Caps	117	Angus Eve		Undefeated	9	1996, 1999	Without goal	5	2006
Player Goals	69	Stern John		Without win	13	1983-1985	Goals against	15	1976-1979

TRINIDAD AND TOBAGO COUNTRY INFORMATION

Capital	Port of Spain	Independence	1962 from the UK	GDP per Capita	$9 500
Population	1 096 585	Status	Republic	GNP Ranking	96
Area km²	5 128	Language	English, Hindi	Dialling code	+1 868
Population density	213 per km²	Literacy rate	98%	Internet code	.tt
% in urban areas	72%	Main religion	Christian 43%, Hindu 23%	GMT + / −	+4
Towns/Cities ('000)	Chaguanas 72; San Juan 56; San Fernando 56; Port of Spain 49; Arima 35; Marabella 26				
Neighbours (km)	Caribbean Sea & Atlantic Ocean 362				
Main stadia	Hasely Crawford Stadium – Port of Spain 27 000; Manny Ramjohn Stadium – Marabella 10 000; Marvin Lee Stadium – Tunapuna 8 000; Dr João Havelange Centre of Excellence – Macoya				

TRINIDAD AND TOBAGO 2007

PROFESSIONAL LEAGUE

	Pl	W	D	L	F	A	Pts	Jabloteh	Caledonia	Joe Public	Williams C	Defence	NE Stars	Petrotin	Rangers	Police	Tobago Utd
San Juan Jabloteh	32	18	8	6	47	31	62		2-0 2-1	1-0 0-1	1-1 0-0	1-0 0-0	2-0 2-1	2-2 1-0	1-0	1-3	5-1 3-0
Caledonia AIA	32	17	6	9	50	25	57	3-0 1-1		1-0 1-1	0-0 1-3	3-2 2-1	0-0 1-3	1-0	1-0 1-1	4-0 3-1	2-1
Joe Public	32	15	10	7	61	32	55	1-2 1-0	0-0 1-2-0		0-0 1-1	3-0 4-2	1-0 1-1	2-2 1-2	3-1	3-1 2-1	3-1
Williams Connection	32	16	7	9	47	33	55	0-0 2-1	1-2-3-1	0-2 2-1		2-1 1-1	2-3 3-0	1-2	2-2	3-1 7-0	6-0
Defence Force	32	14	9	9	45	40	51	1-1 1-2	1-0 1-0	2-0 1-0	1-4 2-0		2-1 0-3	3-0	3-3 1-1	2-0	0-0 3-2
North East Stars	32	11	11	10	42	35	44	1-1 0-2	1-1 0-0	0-0 0-2	0-0 0-0	0-0 2-2		1-1	0-1 1-0	3-2 7-1	1-0
United Petrotin	27	10	5	12	38	35	35	1-3	2-0 0-1	0-1	0-2 2-1	0-2 2-2	2-0 2-3		1-1	1-3 4-0	4-0
Superstar Rangers	27	9	5	13	48	42	32	2-3 4-0	0-1	0-3 0-3	0-2 2-4	1-2	3-1	0-1 2-1		4-1 4-0	5-0 5-0
Police	27	5	1	21	29	79	16	0-2 1-2	1-3	1-0	4-3	1-2 0-1	0-3	0-5	3-4		2-6 0-0
Tobago United	27	3	2	22	25	80	11	2-3	2-4 1-7	0-3 1-5	1-2 0-3	1-3	1-4 0-2	2-0 0-1	3-2	0-2	

14/04/2007 - 18/12/2007 • Top scorers: Peter Byers, San Juan Jabloteh 15

TRINIDAD AND TOBAGO 2007 SPORTWORLD NATIONAL SUPER LEAGUE (2)

	Pl	W	D	L	F	A	Pts
WASA	18	10	8	0	38	14	38
Defence Force	18	10	1	7	26	20	31
Joe Public FC	17	8	6	3	28	24	30
M&M Harvard	18	8	4	6	30	25	28
Harlem Strikers	17	7	5	5	25	19	26
Carnage United	16	5	4	7	15	21	19
Crab Connection	17	4	5	8	24	36	17
Angostura Phoenix	17	5	3	9	25	30	16
Caroni	18	3	6	9	22	37	15
House of Dread	16	3	4	9	17	24	13

6/06/2007 - 23/09/2007

FA TROPHY 2007

Quarter–finals		Semi–finals		Final	
Joe Public	2				
North East Stars	1	Joe Public	2		
Defence Force	0	United Petrotin	1		
United Petrotin	2			Joe Public	1
SJ Jabloteh	1			Caledonia AIA	0
W. Connection	0	SJ Jabloteh	0	Marvin Lee, Tunapuna	
Coast/Air Guard	0	Caledonia AIA	1	12-12-2007	
Caledonia AIA	4			Scorer - Roen Nelson [20]	

FIRST CITIZENS BANK CUP 2007

Quarter–finals		Semi–finals		Final	
W. Connection	0 4p				
Joe Public	0 2p	W. Connection	2		
S'star Rangers	1	SJ Jabloteh	1		
SJ Jabloteh	2			W. Connection	2
United Petrotin	2			Caledonia AIA	0
Defence Force	1	United Petrotin	0	5-10-2007	
Tobago United	0	Caledonia AIA	2	Scorer -	
Caledonia AIA	3			Jonathon Frias 2 [58 70]	

RECENT LEAGUE AND CUP RECORD

	Championship						Cup		
Year	Champions	Pts	Runners-up	Pts	Third	Pts	Winners	Score	Runners-up
2000	Williams Connection	52	Defence Force	51	San Juan Jabloteh	47	Williams Connection	1-1 5-4p	Joe Public
2001	Williams Connection	37	Joe Public	35	Defence Force	24	Joe Public	1-0	Carib
2002	San Juan Jabloteh	65	Williams Connection	62	Joe Public	48	Williams Connection	5-1	Arima Fire
2003	San Juan Jabloteh	92	Williams Connection	80	North East Stars	64	North East Stars	2-2 4-1p	Williams Connection
2004	North East Strikers	57	Williams Connection	51	San Juan Jabloteh	51		Not played	
2005	Williams Connection	54	San Juan Jabloteh	39	Caledonia AIA/Fire	34	San Juan Jabloteh	2-1	Defence Force
2006	Joe Public	65	Williams Connection	65	San Juan Jabloteh	62	WASA	3-3 4-2p	North East Stars
2007	San Juan Jabloteh	62	Caledonia AIA	57	Joe Public	55	Joe Public	1-0	Caledonia AIA

TUN – TUNISIA

NATIONAL TEAM RECORD
JULY 10TH 2006 TO JULY 12TH 2010

PL	W	D	L	F	A	%
24	13	6	5	36	17	66.7

FIFA/COCA-COLA WORLD RANKING

1993	1994	1995	1996	1997	1998	1999	2000	2001	2002	2003	2004	2005	2006	2007
32	30	22	23	23	21	31	26	28	41	45	35	28	32	47

High	
19	02/98

	2007–2008										
08/07	09/07	10/07	11/07	12/07	01/08	02/08	03/08	04/08	05/08	06/08	07/08
36	37	43	47	47	46	53	56	53	53	50	47

Low	
56	03/08

Double success in the continent's two major club competitions was a major boon for Tunisian football but the national team yet again flattered to deceive at the 2008 CAF Africa Cup of Nations finals in Ghana. Etoile du Sahel finally won the CAF Champions League title, doing so in dramatic fashion by preventing a record breaking sixth title for the Egyptian giants Al Ahly. A 3-1 away win in a thrilling second leg of the final means Etoile have now won all of Africa's club competitions. CS Sfaxien, who had been runners-up in the 2006 CAF Champions League, went on to win the 2007 Confederation Cup, beating Sudan's Al Merreikh 5-2 on aggregate in the final. But the two

INTERNATIONAL HONOURS
Qualified for the FIFA World Cup finals 1978 1998 2002 2006 CAF African Cup of Nations 2004
CAF Champions League Club Africain 1991, Esperance 1994, Etoile du Sahel 2007

were usurped by Club Africain in the Tunisian league as Etoile ceded a comfortable position to finish second and by beating Etoile 2-1 in the Cup Final, Esperance ensured all the big four won a trophy. The national side finished top of the standings in their first round group at the Nations Cup finals but then lost to Cameroon in the quarter-finals in a tournament at which they promised much more. As a result Roger Lemerre did not have his contract extended after a tenure of almost six years as national team coach and he departed with fulsome tributes at the end of June 2008.

THE FIFA BIG COUNT OF 2006

	Male	Female		Total
Number of players	500 636	24 628	Referees and Assistant Referees	998
Professionals	1 075		Admin, Coaches, Technical, Medical	6 626
Amateurs 18+	29 404		Number of clubs	250
Youth under 18	20 950		Number of teams	1 512
Unregistered	42 435		Clubs with women's teams	24
Total players	525 264		Players as % of population	5.16%

Fédération Tunisienne de Football (FTF)
Stade annexe d'El Menzah, Cité Olympique, Tunis 1003, Tunisia
Tel +216 71 793760   Fax +216 71 783843
directeur@ftf.org.tn   www.ftf.org.tn
President: SIOUD Tahar   General Secretary: KRAIEM Ridha
Vice-President: BEN AMOUR Kamel   Treasurer: HAMMAMI Mahmoud   Media Officer: CHAOUACHI Mindher
Men's Coach: COELHO Humberto   Women's Coach: LANDOULSI Samir
FTF formed: 1956   CAF: 1960   FIFA: 1960
Red shirts with white trimmings, White shorts, Red socks or White shirts with red trimmings, White shorts, White socks

RECENT INTERNATIONAL MATCHES PLAYED BY TUNISIA

2006 Opponents	Score	Venue	Comp	Scorers	Att	Referee
22-01 Zambia	W 4-1	Alexandria	CNr1	Santos 3 [35 82 90], Bouazizi [51]	16 000	Maillet SEY
26-01 South Africa	W 2-0	Alexandria	CNr1	Santos [32]	10 000	Evehe CMR
30-01 Guinea	L 0-3	Alexandria	CNr1		18 000	Maidin SIN
4-02 Nigeria	D 1-1	Port Said	CNqf	Hagui [49]	15 000	Maillet SEY
1-03 Serbia & Montenegro	L 0-1	Radès/Tunis	Fr		6 000	Haimoudi ALG
30-05 Belarus	W 3-0	Radès/Tunis	Fr	Namouchi [34p], Santos [46], Jomaa [90]	20 000	
2-06 Uruguay	D 0-0	Radès/Tunis	Fr	L 1-3p		
14-06 Saudi Arabia	D 2-2	Munich	WCr1	Jaziri [23], Jaidi [92+]	66 000	Shield AUS
19-06 Spain	L 1-3	Stuttgart	WCr1	Mnari [8]	52 000	Simon BRA
23-06 Ukraine	L 0-1	Berlin	WCr1		72 000	Amarilla PAR
16-08 Mali	L 0-1	Narbonne	Fr			
3-09 Mauritius	D 0-0	Curepipe	CNq			Ncobo RSA
7-10 Sudan	W 1-0	Radès/Tunis	CNq	Lado OG [79]		Coulibaly MLI
15-11 Libya	W 2-0	Radès/Tunis	Fr	Lachkhem [15], Zouaghi [55]		Zekrini ALG
2007						
7-02 Morocco	D 1-1	Casablanca	Fr	Jomaa [62]		
24-03 Seychelles	W 3-0	Victoria	CNq	Jomaa 3 [14 75 79]		Ssegonga UGA
2-06 Seychelles	W 4-0	Radès/Tunis	CNq	Jomaa [25], Zaiem 2 [41 66], Chermiti [83]		Diatta SEN
16-06 Mauritius	W 2-0	Radès/Tunis	CNq	Jomaa [44], Nafti [51]		Benouza ALG
22-08 Guinea	D 1-1	Radès/Tunis	Fr	Mnari [23]		
9-09 Sudan	L 2-3	Omdurman	CNq	Mugahid OG [55], Santos [81p]		Codjia BEN
17-10 UAE	W 1-0	Abu Dhabi	Fr	Belaid [29]		
17-11 Namibia	W 2-0	Radès/Tunis	Fr	Yahia [57], Jomaa [76]		
21-11 Austria	D 0-0	Vienna	Fr		13 800	Olsiak SVK
2008						
6-01 Zambia	L 1-2	Radès/Tunis	Fr	Chikhaoui [47]		
8-01 Zambia	W 1-0	Radès/Tunis	Fr	Chikhaoui [72]		
23-01 Senegal	D 2-2	Tamale	CNr1	Jomaa [9], Traoui [82]		Nichimura JPN
27-01 South Africa	W 3-1	Tamale	CNr1	Santos 2 [8 34], Ben Saada [32]		Djaoupe TOG
31-01 Angola	D 0-0	Tamale	CNr1			Codjia BEN
4-02 Cameroon	L 2-3	Tamale	CNqf	Ben Saada [35], Chikhaoui [81]		Coulibaly MLI
26-03 Côte d'Ivoire	W 2-0	Bondoufle	Fr	Belaid [58], Felhi [83]		
1-06 Burkina Faso	L 1-2	Radès/Tunis	WCq	Belaid [38]	15 000	Ambaya LBY
7-06 Seychelles	W 2-0	Victoria	WCq	Jomaa [9], Ben Saada [43]	2 033	Faduco MOZ
15-06 Burundi	W 1-0	Bujumbura	WCq	Jaidi [70]	7 000	Damon RSA
21-06 Burundi	W 2-1	Radès/Tunis	WCq	Ben Saada [21p], Jomaa [44]	6 000	Younis EGY

Fr = Friendly match • CN = CAF African Cup of Nations • CC = FIFA Confederations Cup • WC = FIFA World Cup
q = qualifier • r1 = first round group • qf = quarter-final • sf = semi-final • f = final

TUNISIA NATIONAL TEAM PLAYERS

	Player		Club	Date of Birth		Player		Club	Date of Birth
1	Hamdi Kasraoui	GK	Esperance	18 01 1983	12	Joahar Mnari	MF	Nürnberg	8 11 1976
2	Seif Ghezal	DF	Young Boys Berne	30 06 1981	13	Sabeur Ben Frej	DF	Le Mans	3 07 1979
3	Karim Hagui	DF	Bayer Leverkusen	20 01 1984	14	Chaker Zouaghi	DF	Lokomotiv Moskva	10 01 1985
4	Wissem Abdi	DF	Zamalek	2 04 1979	15	Radhi Jaidi	DF	Birmingham City	30 08 1975
5	Wissem Bekri	DF	Esperance	16 06 1984	16	Aymen Mathlouthi	GK	Etoile du Sahel	14 09 1984
6	Radhouane Felhi	DF	Etoile du Sahel	25 03 1984	17	Issam Jomaa	FW	Caen	28 01 1984
7	Chaouki Ben Saada	MF	Bastia	1 07 1989	18	Yassine Mikari	MF	Grasshoppers	9 01 1983
8	Mehdi Nafti	MF	Birmingham City	28 11 1978	19	Mehdi Meriah	DF	Etoile du Sahel	5 06 1979
9	Yassine Chikhaoui	FW	FC Zurich	22 09 1986	20	Mehdi Ben Dhifallah	FW	Etoile du Sahel	6 05 1983
10	Kamel Zaiem	MF	Esperance	25 05 1983	21	Mejdi Traoui	MF	Etoile du Sahel	13 12 1983
11	Francileudo dos Santos	FW	Toulouse	20 03 1979	22	Adel Nefzi	GK	Club Africain	16 03 1974
					23	Amine Chermiti	FW	Etoile du Sahel	26 12 1987

Tunisia's squad for the 2008 CAF Africa Cup of Nations

TUNISIA NATIONAL TEAM RECORDS AND RECORD SEQUENCES

Records			Sequence records					
Victory	7-0	TOG 2000, MWI 2005	Wins	7	1963	Clean sheets	6	1965
Defeat	1-10	HUN 1960	Defeats	5	1988	Goals scored	14	1961-1963
Player Caps	110	Sadok Sassi 'Attouga'	Undefeated	11	1975-1977	Without goal	7	2002
Player Goals	22	Francileudo Santos	Without win	14	2002	Goals against	13	1960-1962

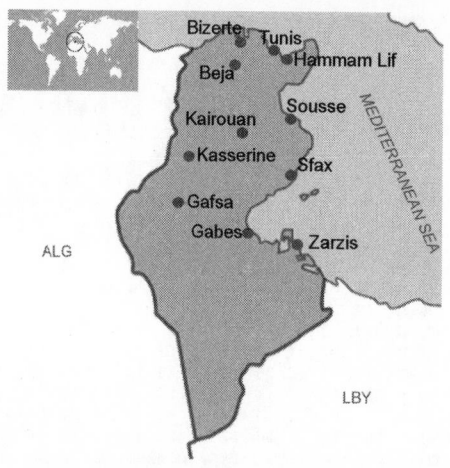

TUNISIAN REPUBLIC; AL JUMHURIYAH AT TUNISIYAH

Capital	Tunis	Language	Arabic, French	Independence	1956
Population	10 276 158	Area	163 610 km²	Density 61 per km²	% in cities	57%
GDP per cap	$6 900	Dailling code	+216	Internet .tn	GMT + / -	+1

MEDALS TABLE

			Overall			League			Cup			Africa			City	Stadium	Cap'ty	DoF
			G	S	B	G	S	B	G	S	B	G	S	B				
1	Espérance Sportive de Tunis	EST	36	19	12	20	10	9	13	6		3	3	3	Tunis	El Menzah	40 000	1919
2	Club Africain	CA	22	32	14	10	18	12	11	12		1	2	2	Tunis	El Menzah	40 000	1920
3	Etoile Sportive du Sahel	ESS	21	27	13	8	15	13	7	8		6	4		Sousse	Stade Olympique	35 000	1925
4	Club Sportif Sfaxien	CSS	12	7	6	7	1	5	3	5		2	1	1	Sfax	Stade Taïeb-Mhiri	20 000	1928
5	Stade Tunisien	ST	11	8	6	4	3	6	7	5					Tunis	Stade Zouiten	18 000	1948
6	Avenir Sportif de la Marsa	ASM	5	8	2		1	2	5	7					Marsa, Tunis	Abdellaziz Chtioui	5 000	1939
7	Club Athlétique Bizertin	CAB	4	3	2	1	2	1	2	1		1		1	Bizerte	15 octobre	8 000	1928
8	Club Sportif de Hammam Lif	CSHL	3	1	2	1	1	1	2	1				1	Hammam Lif	Maâouia Kaâbi	5 000	1944
9	Jeunesse Sportive Kairouan	JSK	1	2		1	1		1						Kairouan	Stade Zouaoui	15 000	1942
	Olympique de Béjà	OB	1	2					1	2					Béjà	Stade Olympique	5 000	1929
	Sfax Railways Sport	SRS	1	2					1	2					Sfax	Stade Taïeb-Mhiri	22 000	
12	Club Olympique Transports	COT	1	1	2		1	2	1						Tunis	Stade Zouiten	18 000	
13	Espérance Sportive de Zarzis	ESZ	1						1						Zarzis	Stade Municipal	5 000	1938
14	Stade Soussien	SS		2			1		1						Sousse	Stade Maarouf	5 000	
15	EM Mehdia	EMM	1						1						Mehdia			
	Etoile Sportive Beni Khalled	ESBK	1						1						Beni Khalled	Stade Habib Tajouri	5 000	
17	US Tunisien	UST			2			2							Tunis			

RECENT LEAGUE AND CUP RECORD

	Championship							Cup		
Year	Champions	Pts	Runners-up	Pts	Third	Pts		Winners	Score	Runners-up
1995	CS Sfaxien	38	Espérance Tunis	37	Etoile du Sahel	37		CS Sfaxien	2-1	Olympique Béja
1996	Club Africain	63	Etoile du Sahel	58	Espérance Tunis	52		Etoile du Sahel	2-1	JS Kairouan
1997	Etoile du Sahel	64	Espérance Tunis	61	CS Sfaxien	45		Espérance Tunis	1-0	CS Sfaxien
1998	Espérance Tunis	69	Cub Africain	59	Etoile du Sahel	48		Club Africain	1-1 4-2p	Olympique Béja
1999	Espérance Tunis	38	CA Bizertin	25	CS Sfaxien	24		Espérance Tunis	2-1	Club Africain
2000	Espérance Tunis	60	Etoile du Sahel	53	CS Sfaxien	35		Club Africain	0-0 4-2p	CS Sfaxien
2001	Espérance Tunis	57	Etoile du Sahel	38	Club Africain	36		CS Hammam-Lif	1-0	Etoile du Sahel
2002	Espérance Tunis	46	Etoile du Sahel	39	Club Africain	35		Tournament not finished		
2003	Espérance Tunis	57	Etoile du Sahel	38	Club Africain	35		Stade Tunisien	1-0	Club Africain
2004	Espérance Tunis	53	Etoile du Sahel	44	Club Africain	42		CS Sfaxien	2-0	Espérance Tunis
2005	CS Sfaxien	58	Etoile du Sahel	58	Club Africain	56		ES Zarzis	2-0	Espérance Tunis
2006	Espérance Tunis	56	Etoile du Sahel	55	Club Africain	47		Espérance Tunis	2-2 5-4p	Club Africain
2007	Etoile du Sahel	54	Club Africain	49	Espérance Tunis	49		Espérance Tunis	2-1	CA Bizertin
2008	Club Africain	63	Etoile du Sahel	61	Espérance Tunis			Espérance Tunis	2-1	Etoile du Sahel

TUNISIA 2007–08

LIGUE NATIONALE A

	Pl	W	D	L	F	A	Pts	Club Africain	Etoile	Espérance	Monastir	Stade	Gafsa	Marsa	Bizertin	Hammam Lif	Sfaxien	Olympique	Jendouba	St. Gabesien	Espérance Z
Club Africain †	26	19	6	1	37	12	63		0-0	1-0	1-0	2-0	1-0	1-0	2-0	2-0	1-1	1-0	0-0	3-2	2-1
Etoile du Sahel †	26	18	7	1	40	9	61	2-2		1-0	1-1	0-1	0-0	2-1	1-0	1-0	1-0	2-0	3-1	4-1	4-0
Espérance Tunis ‡	26	14	4	8	36	18	46	0-1	0-2		4-0	4-1	2-0	2-2	1-2	2-1	0-0	2-1	2-0	1-0	1-0
US Monastir ‡	26	10	6	10	27	32	36	2-1	0-0	0-0		2-0	1-0	1-2	0-0	2-1	1-0	2-1	0-0	3-2	2-0
Stade Tunisien	26	10	6	10	24	34	36	0-1	0-1	0-4	2-1		0-4	1-0	1-1	1-1	2-1	2-1	1-2	0-0	0-0
EGS Gafsa	26	11	2	13	35	31	35	2-3	0-2	0-2	2-1	0-1		2-1	4-0	1-0	1-1	0-1	4-1	3-1	2-1
AS Marsa	26	9	6	11	26	30	33	0-2	0-2	2-1	4-1	2-2	1-0		1-0	0-2	0-2	1-0	1-1	0-1	1-0
CA Bizertin	26	9	6	11	25	30	33	1-2	0-2	1-0	1-2	2-1	3-1	0-1		0-1	1-2	1-1	2-0	1-0	1-0
CS Hammam Lif	26	9	5	12	24	28	32	0-1	1-3	0-3	2-1	1-0	2-1	1-1	0-1		2-3	0-0	0-0	1-0	3-1
CS Sfaxien §2	26	7	10	9	28	29	29	0-1	0-2	0-2	4-1	2-2	0-1	1-1	2-3	1-1		1-1	2-2	2-1	1-0
Olympique Béja	26	7	7	12	21	26	28	1-1	0-2	2-0	1-2	1-2	1-3	0-1	1-0	1-0	0-1		0-0	5-2	0-0
Jendouba Sport	26	6	9	11	18	30	27	0-3	1-2	0-1	1-0	0-1	2-1	1-1	1-1	1-0	1-0	0-1		1-0	2-0
Stade Gabésien	26	5	8	13	21	34	23	0-2	0-0	0-1	1-1	0-1	2-1	2-1	2-2	0-1	0-0	0-1	3-1		0-0
Espérance Zarzis	26	2	10	14	12	31	16	0-0	0-0	1-1	0-1	1-2	1-2	2-1	1-1	1-3	1-1	1-0	0-0	0-0	

11/08/2007 - 22/05/2008 • † Qualified for the CAF Champions League • ‡ Qualified for the CAF Confederation Cup • § = points deducted

TUNISIA 2007–08
LIGUE NATIONAL B (2)

	Pl	W	D	L	F	A	Pts
ES Hammam-Sousse	26	16	6	4	43	20	54
AS Kasserine	26	17	1	8	38	22	52
CS Masakin	26	14	6	6	32	19	48
El Makarem Mahdia	26	12	5	9	30	23	41
AS Gabés	26	10	8	8	33	29	38
ES Béni Khalled	26	10	6	10	28	28	36
CS Korba	26	10	6	10	32	36	36
AS Djerba	26	8	9	9	33	33	33
SA Menzel Bougiba	26	8	7	11	26	34	31
JS Kairouan	26	8	6	12	29	40	30
Olympique Kef	26	6	11	9	29	32	29
AS Ariana	26	8	4	14	21	28	28
ES Jerba	26	7	5	14	27	40	26
EOG Kram	26	4	8	14	20	37	20

19/08/2007 - 19/04/2008

COUPE NATIONALE 2007–08

Fourth Round

Espérance Tunis	2
CA Bizertin *	1
Stade Sfaxien	1
CS Hammam Lif *	3
ES Hammam-Sousse *	2
CS Masakin	1
Espérance Zarzis	1
EGS Gafsa *	3
Stade Tunisien *	2
AS Djerba	0
Stade Gabésien	0
CS Sfaxien *	3
CO Transports *	0 4p
US Monastir	0 3p
US Zarzissienne *	0
Etoile du Sahel	2

Quarter–finals

Espérance Tunis	5
CS Hammam Lif *	2
ES Hammam-Sousse	0
EGS Gafsa *	2
Stade Tunisien *	1
CS Sfaxien	0
CO Transports	1
Etoile du Sahel *	5

Semi–finals

Espérance Tunis	3
EGS Gafsa	2
Stade Tunisien	2 5p
Etoile du Sahel	2 6p

Final

| Espérance Tunis ‡ | 2 |
| Etoile du Sahel | 1 |

* Home team • ‡ Qualified for the CAF Confederation Cup

CUP FINAL
Stade 7 Novembre, Radès
5-07-2008, Ref: Meyer (GER)
Scorers -
Hichem Aboucharouane 2 [12] [79] for
Esperance; Mehdi Meriah [17] for
Etoile

TUR – TURKEY

NATIONAL TEAM RECORD
JULY 10TH 2006 TO JULY 12TH 2010

PL	W	D	L	F	A	%
27	12	8	7	42	29	59.3

FIFA/COCA-COLA WORLD RANKING

1993	1994	1995	1996	1997	1998	1999	2000	2001	2002	2003	2004	2005	2006	2007	High	
52	48	30	31	43	57	29	30	23	9	8	14	11	26	16	**5**	06/04

	2007–2008											Low	
08/07	09/07	10/07	11/07	12/07	01/08	02/08	03/08	04/08	05/08	06/08	07/08	**67**	10/93
22	21	28	16	16	16	18	18	23	25	20	14		

Turkey's roller-coaster ride at the finals of Euro 2008 will remain one of the enduring memories of the tournament. "It ain't over 'til the fat lady sings" was given fresh meaning by the Turks who scored an injury-time winner against Switzerland, blew the Czech Republic out of the water with three goals in the last 15 minutes having trailed 2-0, and scored an equalising goal against Croatia after 122 minutes of play in the quarter-final. They almost did it again in the semi-final against Germany where a makeshift side twice came from behind only to be denied a place in the final thanks to a last minute goal by Philipp Lahm. It was the second time in a decade that the Turks

INTERNATIONAL HONOURS
Qualified for the FIFA World Cup finals 2002   UEFA European U-17 Championship 1994 2005

have fallen in the semi-finals of a major tournament but also a measure of the progress made by the national team since the dark days of the 1980s. Club football is fast improving too. Fenerbahçe have a fantastic new stadium and Galatasaray will soon follow suit as Istanbul starts to flex its muscles in European football. Fenerbahçe reached the knock-out rounds of the Champions League for the first time where they beat Sevilla in a thrilling tie on penalties before losing to Chelsea in the quarter-finals. At home, however, it was Galatasaray who were crowned champions while Kayserispor won their first trophy by beating Gencerbirligi in the Cup Final.

THE FIFA BIG COUNT OF 2006

	Male	Female		Total
Number of players	2 402 838	345 819	Referees and Assistant Referees	802
Professionals	4 491		Admin, Coaches, Technical, Medical	20 725
Amateurs 18+	59 980		Number of clubs	4 298
Youth under 18	131 916		Number of teams	9 823
Unregistered	847 000		Clubs with women's teams	152
Total players	2 748 657		Players as % of population	3.90%

Türkiye Futbol Federasyonu (TFF)
Konaklar Mah. Ihlamurlu Sok. 9, 4. Levent, Istanbul, Turkey
Tel +90 212 2827020   Fax +90 212 2827016
tff@tff.org.tr   www.tff.org
President: TBD   General Secretary: KAZANCIOGLU Metin
Vice-President: ARIBOGAN Lutfi   Treasurer: KARARTI Tuncay   Media Officer: TOZAR Turker
Men's Coach: TERIM Fatih   Women's Coach: ARSLAN Hamdi
TFF formed: 1923   UEFA: 1962   FIFA: 1923
White shirts with red trimmings, White shorts, White socks or Red shirts with white trimmings, Red shorts, Red socks

RECENT INTERNATIONAL MATCHES PLAYED BY TURKEY

2006	Opponents	Score		Venue	Comp	Scorers	Att	Referee
26-05	Ghana	D	1-1	Bochum	Fr	Nihat Kahveci [17]	9 738	Meier GER
31-05	Saudi Arabia	W	1-0	Offenbach	Fr	Necati Ates [59]	9 000	Fleischer GER
2-06	Angola	W	3-2	Arnhem	Fr	Necati Ates [53], Nihat Kahveci [71], Halil Altintop [85]	1 200	Wegereef NED
4-06	FYR Macedonia	L	0-1	Krefeld	Fr		7 000	
16-08	Luxembourg	W	1-0	Luxembourg	Fr	Fatih Tekke [26]	3 353	Weiner GER
6-09	Malta	W	2-0	Frankfurt	ECq	Nihat Kahveci [56], Tümer Metin [77]	BCD	Vázquez ESP
7-10	Hungary	W	1-0	Budapest	ECq	Tuncay Sanli [41]	6 800	Hamer LUX
11-10	Moldova	W	5-0	Frankfurt	ECq	Hakan Sükür 4 [35 37p 43 73], Tuncay Sanli [68]	BCD	Vollquartz DEN
15-11	Italy	D	1-1	Bergamo	Fr	Materazzi OG [42]	24 386	Busacca SUI
2007								
7-02	Georgia	L	0-1	Tbilisi	Fr		50 000	Lajuks LVA
24-03	Greece	W	4-1	Piraeus	ECq	Tuncay Sanli [27], Gökhan Unal [55], Tümer Metin [70], Gökdeniz [81]	31 405	Stark GER
28-03	Norway	D	2-2	Frankfurt	ECq	Hamit Altintop 2 [72 90]	BCD	Farina ITA
2-06	Bosnia-Herzegovina	L	2-3	Sarajevo	ECq	Hakan Sükür [13], Sabri [39]	13 800	Fröjdfeldt SWE
5-06	Brazil	D	0-0	Dortmund	Fr		26 700	Meyer GER
22-08	Romania	L	0-2	Bucharest	Fr		12 000	Merk GER
8-09	Malta	D	2-2	Ta'Qali	ECq	Hakan Sükür [45], Servet Cetin [78]	10 500	Messner AUT
12-09	Hungary	W	3-0	Istanbul	ECq	Gökhan Zan [68], Mehmet Aurelio [72], Halil Altintop [93+]	28 020	Dougal SCO
13-10	Moldova	D	1-1	Chisinau	ECq	Umit Karan [63]	9 815	Atkinson ENG
17-10	Greece	L	0-1	Istanbul	ECq		22 818	Mejuto Gonzalez ESP
17-11	Norway	W	2-1	Oslo	ECq	Emre Belözoglu [31], Nihat Kahveci [59]	23 783	Merk GER
21-11	Bosnia-Herzegovina	W	1-0	Istanbul	ECq	Nihat Kahveci [43]	20 106	Braamhaar NED
2008								
6-02	Sweden	D	0-0	Istanbul	Fr		20 000	Tagliavento ITA
26-03	Belarus	D	2-2	Minsk	Fr	Tuncay Sanli [38], Tümer Metin [71]	12 000	Malzinskas LTU
20-05	Slovakia	W	1-0	Bielefeld	Fr	Hakan Balta [63]	13 100	Weiner GER
25-05	Uruguay	L	2-3	Bochum	Fr	Arda Turan [13], Nihat Kahveci [51]		Meyer GER
29-05	Finland	W	2-0	Duisburg	Fr	Tuncay Sanli [15], Semih Sentürk [88]		Kinhofer GER
7-06	Portugal	L	0-2	Geneva	ECr1		29 016	Fandel GER
11-06	Switzerland	W	2-1	Basel	ECr1	Semih Sentürk [57], Arda Turan [92+]	39 730	Michel SVK
15-06	Czech Republic	W	3-2	Geneva	ECr1	Arda Turan [75], Nihat Kahveci 2 [87 89]	29 016	Fröjdfeldt SWE
20-06	Croatia	D	1-1	Vienna	ECqf	Semih Sentürk [122+]. W 3-1p	51 428	Rosetti ITA
25-06	Germany	L	2-3	Basel	ECsf	Ugur Boral [22], Semih Sentürk [86]	39 378	Busacca SUI

Fr = Friendly match • EC = UEFA EURO 2008 • WC = FIFA World Cup • q = qualifier • po = play-off

TURKEY NATIONAL TEAM PLAYERS

	Player		Ap	G	Club	Date of Birth		Player		Ap	G	Club	Date of Birth
1	Recber Rüstü	GK	118	0	Besiktas	10 05 1973	12	Tolga Zengin	GK	2	0	Trabzonspor	10 10 1983
2	Servet Cetin	DF	32	1	Galatasaray	17 03 1981	13	Emre Güngör	DF	2	0	Galatasaray	1 08 1984
3	Hakan Balta	MF	13	1	Galatasaray	23 03 1983	14	Arda Turan	MF	22	3	Galatasaray	30 01 1987
4	Gökhan Zan	DF	23	0	Besiktas	7 09 1981	15	Emre Asik	DF	31	2	Galatasaray	13 12 1973
5	Emre Belözoglu	MF	57	4	Newcastle Utd	7 09 1980	16	Ugur Boral	MF	10	1	Fenerbahçe	14 04 1982
6	Mehmet Topal	MF	9	0	Galatasaray	3 03 1986	17	Tuncay Sanli	MF	58	15	Middlesbrough	16 01 1982
7	Mehmet Aurélio	MF	23	1	Fenerbahçe	15 12 1977	18	Colin Kazım-Richards	FW	9	0	Fenerbahçe	26 08 1986
8	Nihat Kahveci	FW	59	17	Villarreal	23 11 1979	19	Ayhan Akman	MF	12	0	Galatasaray	23 02 1977
9	Semih Sentürk	FW	9	4	Fenerbahçe	29 04 1983	20	Sabri Sarıoglu	DF	19	1	Galatasaray	26 07 1984
10	Gökdeniz Karadeniz	MF	50	6	Rubin Kazan	11 01 1980	21	Mevlüt Erdinç	FW	6	0	Sochaux	25 02 1987
11	Tümer Metin	MF	26	7	Fenerbahçe	14 10 1974	22	Hamit Altintop	DF	47	2	Bayern München	8 12 1982
							23	Volkan Demirel	GK	24	0	Fenerbahçe	27 10 1981

The Turkish squad for Euro 2008

TURKEY NATIONAL TEAM RECORDS AND RECORD SEQUENCES

Records			Sequence records					
Victory	7-0	SYR, KOR, SMR	Wins	5	1995, 2002	Clean sheets	4	1958-1959
Defeat	0-8	POL, ENGx2	Defeats	8	1980-1982	Goals scored	15	1925-1931
Player Caps	118	Rustu Recber	Undefeated	15	1998-1999	Without goal	8	1980-1982
Player Goals	51	Hakan Sükür	Without win	17	1989-1992	Goals against	19	1923-1931

REPUBLIC OF TURKEY; TURKIYE CUMHURIYETI

Capital	Ankara	Language	Turkish	Formation	1923
Population	71 158 647	Area	780 580 km^2	Density 88 per km^2	% in cities 69%
GDP per cap	$6700	Dailling code	+90	Internet .tr	GMT +/- +2

MEDALS TABLE

		Overall			League			Cup			Europe			City	Stadium	Cap'ty	DoF
		G	S	B	G	S	B	G	S	B	G	S	B				
1	Galatasaray SK	32	14	16	17	9	15	14	5		1		1	Istanbul	Ali Sami Yen	23 785	1905
2	Fenerbahçe SK	21	23	6	17	16	6	4	7					Istanbul	Sükrü Saracoglu	50 509	1907
3	Besiktas JK	17	20	8	10	14	8	7	6					Istanbul	Inönü Stadi	32 750	1903
4	Trabzonspor	13	12	5	6	7	5	7	5					Trabzon	Hüseyin Avni Aker	21 700	1967
5	Altay SK	2	5	2				2	5					Izmir	Alsancak Stadi	17 500	1914
6	Gençlerbirligi SK	2	3	2			2	2	3					Ankara	19 Mayis Stadi	21 250	1923
7	MKE Ankaragücü	2	3					2	3					Ankara	19 Mayis Stadi	21 250	1910
8	Göztepe AS	2	1	2		1		2	1				1	Izmir	Alsancak Stadi	17 500	1925
9	Kocaelispor	2		1				1	2					Izmit	Ismet Pasa	15 000	1966
10	Eskisehirspor	1	5	2	3	2		1	2					Eskisehir	Atatürk Stadi	18 413	1965
11	Bursaspor	1	3					1	3					Bursa	Atatürk Stadi	19 700	1963
12	Kayserispor	1						1						Kayseri	Atatürk Stadi	26 500	1966
	Sakaryaspor	1						1						Sakarya	Atatürk Stadi	14 500	1965
14	Samsunspor		1	2		2			1					Samsun	19 Mayis Stadi	13 500	1965
15	Boluspor		1	1		1		1	1					Boluspor	Atatürk Stadi	8 000	1965
16	Adana Demirspor	1						1						Adana	5 Ocak Stadi	19 000	1940
	Adanaspor	1			1									Adana	5 Ocak Stadi	19 000	1954
	Kayseri Erciyesspor	1						1						Kayseri	Atatürk Stadi	26 500	1966
	Mersin Idman Yurdu	1						1						Mersin	Tevfik Sirri Gür	17 500	1925
	Antalyaspor	1						1						Antalya	Atatürk Stadi	12 000	1966

RECENT LEAGUE AND CUP RECORD

	Championship						Cup		
Year	Champions	Pts	Runners-up	Pts	Third	Pts	Winners	Score	Runners-up
1997	Galatasaray	82	Besiktas	74	Fenerbahçe	73	Kocaelispor	1-0 1-1	Trabzonspor
1998	Galatasaray	75	Fenerbahçe	71	Trabzonspor	66	Besiktas	1-1 1-1 4-2p	Galatasaray
1999	Galatasaray	78	Besiktas	77	Fenerbahçe	72	Galatasaray	0-0 2-0	Besiktas
2000	Galatasaray	79	Besiktas	75	Gaziantepspor	62	Galatasaray	5-3	Antalyaspor
2001	Fenerbahçe	76	Galatasaray	73	Gaziantepspor	68	Gençlerbirligi	2-2 4-1p	Fenerbahçe
2002	Galatasaray	78	Fenerbahçe	75	Besiktas	62	Kocaelispor	4-0	Besiktas
2003	Besiktas	85	Galatasaray	77	Gençlerbirligi	66	Trabzonspor	3-1	Gençlerbirligi
2004	Fenerbahçe	76	Trabzonspor	72	Besiktas	62	Trabzonspor	4-0	Gençlerbirligi
2005	Fenerbahçe	80	Trabzonspor	77	Galatasaray	76	Galatasaray	5-1	Fenerbahçe
2006	Galatasaray	83	Fenerbahçe	81	Besiktas	54	Besiktas	3-2	Fenerbahçe
2007	Fenerbahçe	70	Besiktas	61	Galatasaray	56	Besiktas	1-0	Kayseri Erciyesspor
2008	Galatasaray	79	Fenerbahçe	73	Besiktas	73	Kayserispor	0-0 11-10p	Gençlerbirligi

TURKEY 2007–08

SUPER LIG

Team	Pl	W	D	L	F	A	Pts	Galatasaray	Fenerbahçe	Besiktas	Sivasspor	Kayserispor	Trabzonspor	Denizlispor	Ankaragücü	Gaziantepspor	Ankaraspor	G'birligi Oftas	Istanbul BB	Bursaspor	Konyaspor	Gençlerbirligi	Manisaspor	Rizespor	Kasimpasa
Galatasaray †	34	24	7	3	64	23	79		1-0	2-1	2-0	2-0	1-0	2-1	1-0	0-0	0-0	2-0	2-2	1-0	6-0	3-2	6-3	4-0	0-1
Fenerbahçe †	34	22	7	5	72	37	73	2-0		2-1	1-0	2-1	3-2	4-1	2-0	2-1	4-2	3-1	2-2	0-2	4-1	3-2	4-1	1-1	3-0
Besiktas	34	23	4	7	58	32	73	1-0	1-2		1-2	0-0	3-0	3-2	3-1	3-1	3-2	0-1	0-0	3-0	1-0	1-0	5-1	1-1	4-2
Sivasspor	34	23	4	7	57	29	73	3-5	1-4	1-2		1-0	2-0	2-0	3-2	2-0	2-1	1-0	2-1	3-2	3-0	2-0	1-0	0-0	4-0
Kayserispor	34	15	10	9	50	31	55	1-1	2-1	2-0	0-1		1-0	1-1	0-2	3-1	3-1	1-1	1-2	4-1	3-0	3-0	3-1	3-0	2-0
Trabzonspor	34	14	7	13	44	39	49	0-1	2-0	2-3	**0-3**	2-1		2-0	0-0	3-2	2-1	1-2	2-1	1-1	1-0	0-0	2-2	5-1	2-1
Denizlispor	34	13	6	15	48	48	45	1-2	0-1	1-2	1-2	2-0	2-0		1-1	2-1	1-0	2-1	2-3	0-0	2-1	3-2	3-2	5-1	0-1
MKE Ankaragücü	34	11	10	13	36	44	43	0-4	0-0	0-2	2-2	1-1	0-2	3-2		1-0	1-1	2-0	1-0	0-3	2-2	1-0	1-0		2-2
Gaziantepspor	34	11	10	13	36	45	43	1-1	0-5	0-1	0-0	4-3	1-1	1-2	2-1		1-0	1-1	1-0	1-0	2-1	2-2	1-0	1-1	2-0
Ankaraspor	34	10	11	13	35	38	41	0-1	2-2	0-0	2-0	0-3	1-0	0-0	1-2	1-1		1-0	1-1	1-1	1-1	2-1	1-0	2-0	1-2
Gençlerbirligi Oftas	34	10	10	14	30	36	40	0-0	1-1	0-1	0-1	1-0	2-1	0-2	2-1	1-2	0-0		3-2	2-2	0-1	1-1	1-0	2-0	0-1
Istanbul BB	34	10	8	16	44	47	38	0-3	2-0	2-1	0-2	1-1	1-2	0-2	1-2	1-2	0-1	1-0		1-0	5-0	0-0	4-1	2-1	2-0
Bursaspor	34	9	11	14	31	40	38	0-1	1-1	0-1	0-1	0-1	1-1	1-1	2-1	1-1	0-0	1-1	2-2		1-0	2-1	1-0	2-1	1-0
Konyaspor	34	10	6	18	37	64	36	0-1	1-4	1-2	2-1	1-1	1-0	2-2	1-0	1-1	1-3	0-1	3-2	2-0		1-1	4-2	2-1	1-0
Gençlerbirligi	34	9	8	17	44	51	35	0-1	1-2	1-2	0-2	1-2	1-2	1-2	1-0	2-0	1-3	1-2	1-3	6-1			0-2	4-1	3-1
Vestel Manisaspor	34	7	8	19	42	62	29	2-2	1-1	1-2	1-1	0-1	1-1	3-2	1-2	1-0	2-1	0-2	1-1	1-1	2-0	1-2		2-1	1-2
Caykur Rizespor	34	7	8	19	32	64	29	2-5	2-4	1-2	0-2	0-0	0-4	2-0	0-0	2-1	0-1	0-0	3-1	2-0	2-2	0-2	1-4		2-0
Kasimpasa	34	8	5	21	26	56	29	0-1	1-2	1-2	0-4	0-2	0-0	1-0	2-2	0-3	1-1	0-1	3-1	1-0	0-2	2-1	0-0	2-2	

10/08/2007 - 10/05/2008 • † Qualified for the UEFA Champions League • ‡ Qualified for the UEFA Cup • Match in bold awarded
Top scorers: Semih Sentürk, Fenerbahçe 17; Filip Holosko, Besiktas 15

TURKEY 2007–08 2. LIG A

Team	Pl	W	D	L	F	A	Pts
Kocaelispor	34	19	7	8	59	37	64
Antalyaspor	34	15	16	3	56	33	61
Sakaryaspor Adapazari†	34	16	10	8	55	34	58
Eskisehirspor †	34	16	9	9	52	35	57
Diyarbakirspor †	34	16	9	9	53	37	57
Boluspor †	34	13	14	7	50	46	53
Kayseri Erciyesspor	34	14	10	10	55	42	52
Orduspor	34	12	14	8	39	44	50
Karsiyaka Izmir	34	11	14	9	44	41	47
Altay Izmir	34	13	8	13	47	47	47
Giresunspor	34	10	13	11	41	44	43
Malatyaspor	34	12	7	15	44	43	43
Kartal	34	10	12	12	52	57	42
Gaziantep BB	34	9	12	13	53	51	39
Samsunspor	34	10	8	16	45	61	38
Elazigspor	34	8	10	16	40	54	34
Istanbulspor	34	6	8	20	25	58	26
Mardinspor	34	3	5	26	26	72	14

25/08/2007 - 11/05/2008 • † Qualified for the play-offs

Play-off semi-finals: Eskisehirspor 0-0 6-5p; Sakaryaspor 2-2 1-3p Boluspor
Play-off final: Eskisehirspor 2-0 Boluspor

TURKIYE KUPASI 2007–08

Third round groups (Five teams in each group)

Group A	Pts
Caykur Rizespor	10
Besiktas	7

Group B	Pts
Gençlerbirligi	9
Adana Demirspor	9

Group C	Pts
Fenerbahçe	8
Kayserispor	8

Group D	Pts
Gençlerbirligi Oftas	9
Galatasaray	7

Quarter-finals

Kayserispor	0	3
Gençlerbirligi Oftas *	0	0
Besiktas	0	3
Caykur Rizespor *	1	2
Galatasaray	0	2
Fenerbahçe *	0	1
Adana Demirspor *	0	2
Gençlerbirligi	1	2

Semi-finals

Kayserispor	3	4
Caykur Rizespor *	0	1
Galatasaray	0	1
Gençlerbirligi *	1	1

Final

Kayserispor	0	11p
Gençlerbirligi	0	10p

CUP FINAL

Ataturk Stadi, Bursa
7-05-2008

* Home team in the first leg • ‡ Qualified for the UEFA Cup

UAE – UNITED ARAB EMIRATES

NATIONAL TEAM RECORD
JULY 10TH 2006 TO JULY 12TH 2010

PL	W	D	L	F	A	%
38	13	9	16	43	51	46.1

FIFA/COCA-COLA WORLD RANKING

1993	1994	1995	1996	1997	1998	1999	2000	2001	2002	2003	2004	2005	2006	2007
51	46	75	60	50	42	54	64	60	89	75	82	85	87	100

High	
42	11/98

2007–2008											
08/07	09/07	10/07	11/07	12/07	01/08	02/08	03/08	04/08	05/08	06/08	07/08
96	102	97	99	100	99	95	95	97	97	95	106

Low	
111	10/03

After the success of lifting the Gulf Cup at the start of 2007, there have been signs of a continued resurgence of football in the United Arab Emirates, with the national team one of the ten teams left in the 2010 FIFA World Cup qualifiers from Asia. Under the control of former Senegal coach Bruno Metsu, the Emirates squeezed into the final group stage by slenderest of margins. Having comfortably beaten Vietnam in a preliminary round, the UAE found themselves in a group with Iran, Kuwait and Syria and finished second thanks to a 3-1 win over Syria in the final game. That win was enough for Metsu's team to progress ahead of the unfortunate Syrians by virtue of a

INTERNATIONAL HONOURS
Qualified for the FIFA World Cup finals 1990   Gulf Cup 2007

better goal-difference as the UAE look to qualify for their first World Cup finals since their one-and-only appearance back in 1990. Al Shabab took the domestic league title for the first time since 1995 while Al Ahli claimed the President's Cup, but there was little success for the nation's clubs at continental level in 2008. Al Wahda had reached the semi-finals of the AFC Champions League in 2007 before being knocked out by Iranian side Sepahan, but neither 2007 league champions Al Wasl nor Al Wahda – who won the President's Cup – impressed the following season, with both sides incapable of progressing beyond the group phase.

THE FIFA BIG COUNT OF 2006

	Male	Female		Total
Number of players	82 776	0	Referees and Assistant Referees	150
Professionals	67		Admin, Coaches, Technical, Medical	836
Amateurs 18+	1 020		Number of clubs	31
Youth under 18	6 689		Number of teams	156
Unregistered	11 000		Clubs with women's teams	0
Total players	82 776		Players as % of population	3.18%

United Arab Emirates Football Association (UAEFA)
PO Box 916, Abu Dhabi, United Arab Emirates
Tel +971 2 4445600   Fax +971 2 4448558
uaefa@uae-football.org.ae   www.uaefootball.org
President: AL-RUMAITHI Mohamed   General Secretary: ABDULLAH Yousuf Mohd
Vice-President: BUJSAIM Ali   Treasurer: AL KHOURI Younes Haji   Media Officer: None
Men's Coach: MESTU Bruno   Women's Coach: None
UAEFA formed: 1971   AFC: 1974   FIFA: 1972
White shirts with red trimmings, White shorts, White socks

RECENT INTERNATIONAL MATCHES PLAYED BY THE UNITED ARAB EMIRATES

2006	Opponents	Score		Venue	Comp	Scorers	Att	Referee
18-01	Korea Republic	W	1-0	Dubai	Fr	Faisal Khalil [22]		Al Hilali OMA
22-02	Oman	W	1-0	Dubai	ACq	Ismail Matar [15]	15 000	Al Ghamdi KSA
1-03	Pakistan	W	4-1	Karachi	ACq	Subait Al Mekhaini [68], Ismail Matar [78], Salam Saad [81], Saeed Alkas [88]	10 000	Tongkhan THA
2-05	Syria	W	2-1	Dubai	Fr	Nawaf Mubarak [40], Faisal Khalil [90]		
8-08	Iran	L	0-1	Tehran	Fr		4 000	
16-08	Jordan	W	2-1	Amman	ACq	Mohammed Omar [52], Subait Khater [68]	18 000	Al Hamdan KSA
27-08	Saudi Arabia	L	0-1	Jeddah	Fr			
6-09	Jordan	D	0-0	Dubai	ACq		9 000	Al Fadhli KUW
11-10	Oman	L	1-2	Muscat	ACq	Mohammed Omar [57]	28 000	Huang Junjie CHN
15-11	Pakistan	W	3-2	Abu Dhabi	ACq	Ali Abbas [54], Mohammed Omar 2 [58 72]	6 000	Sarkar IND
6-12	Poland	L	2-5	Abu Dhabi	Fr	Subait Khater [26], Mohamed Srour [86]	1 000	Al Hilali OMA
10-12	Slovakia	L	1-2	Abu Dhabi	Fr	Ismael Matar [90]		Ibrahim QAT
2007								
12-01	Iran	L	0-2	Abu Dhabi	Fr		9 000	Omar UAE
17-01	Oman	L	1-2	Abu Dhabi	GCr1	Ismail Matar [63]		
20-01	Yemen	W	2-1	Abu Dhabi	GCr1	Mohammed Omar [2p], Basher Saeed [65]		
23-01	Kuwait	W	3-2	Abu Dhabi	GCr1	Ismael Matar 2 [1 91+], Faisal Khalil [33]		
27-01	Saudi Arabia	W	1-0	Abu Dhabi	GCsf	Ismail Matar [91+]		
30-01	Oman	W	1-0	Abu Dhabi	GCf	Ismail Matar [73]		
21-06	Malaysia	W	3-1	Kelana Jaya	Fr	Faisal Khalil [8], Ismael Matar [52], Al Shehhi [67]	2 000	Shaharul MAS
24-06	Saudi Arabia	L	0-2	Singapore	Fr			
27-06	Bahrain	D	2-2	Petaling Jaya	Fr	Al Shehi [35], Yousef Jaber [50]		
1-07	Korea DPR	W	1-0	Singapore	Fr	Yousef Jaber [52]		
8-07	Vietnam	L	0-2	Hanoi	ACr1		39 450	Najm LIB
13-07	Japan	L	1-3	Hanoi	ACr1	Saeed Alkas [66]	5 000	Tongkhan THA
16-07	Qatar	W	2-1	Ho Chi Minh City	ACr1	Saeed Alkas [59], Faisal Khalil [90]	3 000	Moradi IRN
12-09	Singapore	D	1-1	Singapore	Fr	Faisal Khalil [70]		
23-09	Lebanon	D	1-1	Dubai	Fr	Rashed Abdulrahman [90]		
3-10	Thailand	D	1-1	Bangkok	Fr	Nawaf Mubarak [89]		
8-10	Vietnam	W	1-0	Hanoi	WCq	Basher Saeed [79]	20 000	Nishimura JPN
17-10	Tunisia	L	0-1	Abu Dhabi	Fr			
28-10	Vietnam	W	5-0	Abu Dhabi	WCq	Ismael Matar [13], Ahmed Mubarak [40], Al Shehhi [53], Nawaf Mubarak [90], Saeed Al Kas [92+]	12 000	Mohd Salleh MAS
17-11	Benin	L	0-1	Accra	Fr			
21-11	Togo	L	0-5	Accra	Fr			
2008								
10-01	China PR	D	0-0	Dubai	Fr			
31-01	Iraq	L	0-1	Abu Dhabi	Fr			
6-02	Kuwait	W	2-0	Abu Dhabi	WCq	Al Shehhi [14], Faisal Khalil [53]	19 000	Irmatov UZB
19-03	Oman	D	1-1	Muscat	Fr	Abdullah Malallah [84]		
26-03	Syria	D	1-1	Damascus	WCq	Ismael Matar [54]	35 000	Sun Baojie CHN
2-06	Iran	D	0-0	Tehran	WCq		5 000	Lee Gi Young KOR
7-06	Iran	L	0-1	Al Ain	WCq		9 000	Nishimura JPN
14-06	Kuwait	W	3-2	Kuwait City	WCq	Ismael Matar 2 [23 39], Saif Mohamed [91+]	20 000	Mohd Salleh MAS
22-06	Syria	L	1-3	Al Ain	WCq	Ismael Matar [83p]	7 000	Shield AUS

Fr = Friendly match • AC = AFC Asian Cup • GC = Gulf Cup • WC = FIFA World Cup
q = qualifier • r1 = first round group • sf = semi-final • f = final

UNITED ARAB EMIRATES NATIONAL TEAM RECORDS AND RECORD SEQUENCES

Records				Sequence records				
Victory	12-0	BRU 2001	Wins	5	1993, 1998, 2007	Clean sheets	4	1985, 1993, 1996
Defeat	0-8	BRA 2005	Defeats	9	1990-1992	Goals scored	18	1999-2000
Player Caps	164	Adnan Al Talyani	Undefeated	16	1996-1997	Without goal	4	1974-1976, 1980
Player Goals	53	Adnan Al Talyani	Without win	14	1974-1979	Goals against	14	2002-2003

MAJOR CITIES/TOWNS
Population '000

1	Dubai	1 422
2	Abu Dhabi	633
3	Sharjah	584
4	Al Ain	444
5	Ajman	250
6	Ras Al Khaima	121
7	Al Fujairah	69
8	Umm al Quwain	47
9	Khor Fakkan	35

UNITED ARAB EMIRATES; AL IMARAT AL ARABIYAH AL MUTTAHIDAH

Capital	Abu Dhabi	Language	Arabic			Independence	1971
Population	4 444 011	Area	82 880 km²	Density	30 per km²	% in cities	84%
GDP per cap	$23 200	Dailling code	+971	Internet	.ae	GMT +/-	+4

MEDALS TABLE

		Overall			Lge	Cup	Asia			City	Stadium	Cap'ty	DoF
		G	S	B	G	G	G	S	B				
1	Al Ain	14	1	1	9	4	1	1	1	Al Ain	Tahnoon Bin Mohammed	10 000	1968
2	Sharjah FC	13			5	8				Sharjah	Sharjah Stadium	12 000	1966
3	Al Ahli	11			4	7				Dubai	Rashed	18 000	1970
4	Al Wasl	9	1		7	2			1	Dubai	Zabeel	18 000	1960
5	Al Shabab	7	1		3	4			1	Dubai	Al Maktoum	12 000	1958
6	Al Nasr	6			3	3				Dubai	Al Maktoum	12 000	1945
7	Al Wahda	4	1		3	1			1	Abu Dhabi	Al Nahyan	12 000	1974
8	Al Sha'ab	1	1			1		1		Sharjah	Khalid Bin Mohammed	10 000	1974
9	Ajman	1								Ajman			
10	Bani Yas	1								Abu Dhabi			
11	Emirates Club	1								Ras Al Khaima	Al Emarat	3 000	1929
	Al Fujairah									Al Fujairah			1972
	Al Jazeera									Abu Dhabi	Mohammed Bin Zayed	40 000	1974

RECENT LEAGUE AND CUP RECORD

	Championship						Cup		
Year	Champions	Pts	Runners-up	Pts	Third	Pts	Winners	Score	Runners-up
1995	Al Shabab	29	Al Ain	23	Al Wasl	18	Sharjah	0-0 5-4p	Al Ain
1996	Sharjah	39	Al Wasl	35	Al Ain	25	Al Ahli	4-1	Al Wahda
1997	Al Wasl	19	Al Nasr	16	Al Wahda	16	Al Shabab	1-1 5-4p	Al Nasr
1998	Al Ain	32	Sharjah	30	Al Wasl	23	Sharjah	3-2	Al Wasl
1999	Al Wahda	65	Al Ain	57	Al Nasr	56	Al Ain	1-0	Al Shabab
2000	Al Ain	47	Al Nasr	46	Al Wahda	45	Al Wahda	1-1 8-7p	Al Wasl
2001	Al Wahda	50	Al Ahly	42	Al Jazeera	38	Al Ain	3-2	Al Sha'ab
2002	Al Ain	47	Al Jazeera	38	Al Sha'ab	37	Al Ahli	3-1	Al Jazeera
2003	Al Ain	48	Al Wahda	43	Al Ahli	34	Sharjah	1-1 6-5p	Al Wahda
2004	Al Ain	15	Al Ahli	13	Al Shabab	7	Al Ahli	2-1	Al Sha'ab
2005	Al Wahda	62	Al Ain	57	Al Jazeera	53	Al Ain	3-1	Al Wahda
2006	Al Ahli	47	Al Wahda	47	Al Jazeera	45	Al Ain	2-1	Sharjah
2007	Al Wasl	47	Al Wahda	43	Al Jazeera	41	Al Wasl	4-1	Al Ain
2008	Al Shabab	42	Al Jazeera	39	Al Ahli	37	Al Ahli	2-0	Al Wasl

UNITED ARAB EMIRATES 2007–08

PREMIER LEAGUE

	Pl	W	D	L	F	A	Pts	Shabab	Jazeera	Ahli	Sharjah	Sha'ab	Ain	Wasl	Wahda	Nasr	Dhafra	Emirates	Hatta
Al Shabab †	22	12	6	4	44	30	42		2-1	0-4	3-0	2-2	1-0	4-0	1-1	2-1	3-1	4-3	0-1
Al Jazeera	22	11	6	5	46	31	39	0-0		1-1	4-1	1-0	1-1	2-1	2-1	4-4	1-0	4-0	3-0
Al Ahli Dubai	22	10	7	5	47	27	37	1-2	2-2		3-1	1-2	3-0	3-3	1-2	2-3	3-1	1-1	6-1
Sharjah	22	9	6	7	35	35	33	2-3	1-1	0-1		4-1	2-1	2-1	1-0	0-1	2-0	3-1	0-0
Al Sha'ab	22	9	6	7	39	44	33	2-1	2-1	1-1	0-2		2-1	0-2	2-2	2-2	0-1	3-1	2-1
Al Ain	22	9	5	8	41	36	32	3-4	4-3	1-1	3-3	1-2		3-1	2-3	2-1	4-1	1-1	3-1
Al Wasl	22	8	6	8	39	37	30	2-1	2-0	3-2	5-2	4-5	0-0		4-4	1-1	0-1	4-1	0-1
Al Wahda	22	8	6	8	42	42	30	2-2	2-1	0-1	1-1	5-2	4-3	1-2		1-0	2-3	1-3	2-1
Al Nasr	22	7	7	8	37	39	28	1-3	0-2	0-5	1-2	3-3	0-3	1-1	4-1		1-1	5-1	3-0
Dhafra	22	7	4	11	33	41	25	1-1	2-3	1-2	2-2	3-0	1-2	3-2	3-2	2-3		2-2	3-1
Emirates	22	3	7	12	36	54	16	2-2	4-5	1-2	2-2	3-3	1-2	0-1	1-1	0-1	3-1		2-5
Hatta	22	4	4	14	23	46	16	0-3	1-4	1-1	1-2	2-3	0-1	0-0	2-4	1-1	2-0	1-3	

27/09/2007 - 25/05/2008 • † Qualified for the AFC Champions League

UNITED ARAB EMIRATES 2007–08
SECOND DIVISION

	Pl	W	D	L	F	A	Pts
Al Khaleej	30	23	6	1	66	23	75
Ajman	30	18	11	1	85	40	65
Al Ittihad	30	20	2	8	67	39	62
Dibba Al Hisn	30	19	4	7	75	42	61
Al Ahli Fujeira	30	17	8	5	86	36	59
Bani-Yas	30	16	6	8	68	35	54
Al Urooba	30	15	5	10	77	53	50
Ras Al Khaima	30	11	9	10	56	56	42
Dubai	30	12	5	13	52	43	41
Dibba	30	12	3	15	42	53	39
Al Arabi	30	11	4	15	52	54	37
Thaid	30	6	6	18	45	85	24
Himriya	30	7	3	20	46	88	24
Hamra Island	30	7	2	21	34	83	23
Masafi	30	3	5	22	27	71	14
Ramms	30	1	5	24	23	100	8

27/09/2007 - 9/05/2008

PRESIDENT'S CUP 2007–08

Round of 16		Quarter-finals		Semi-finals		Final	
Al Ahli Dubai	3						
Bani-Yas *	0	Al Ahli Dubai *	3				
Ajman *	1	Al Wahda	1				
Al Wahda	3			Al Ahli Dubai	3		
Al Sha'ab *	3			Al Shabab	1		
Dibba Al Hisn	2	Al Sha'ab	1 2p				
Ras Al Khaima	1	Al Shabab *	1 4p				
Al Shabab *	3					Al Ahli Dubai	2
Sharjah *	1 8p					Al Wasl	0
Al Ain	1 7p	Sharjah *	1				
Dubai	1	Al Ahli Fujeira	0			CUP FINAL	
Al Ahli Fujeira *	3			Sharjah	4		
Dhafra *	3			Al Wasl	0		
Al Ittihad	1	Dhafra	1 3p			14-04-2008	
Thaid	2	Al Wasl *	1 4p				
Al Wasl *	3						

* Home team

UGA – UGANDA

NATIONAL TEAM RECORD
JULY 10TH 2006 TO JULY 12TH 2010

PL	W	D	L	F	A	%
28	11	11	6	38	22	58.9

FIFA/COCA-COLA WORLD RANKING

1993	1994	1995	1996	1997	1998	1999	2000	2001	2002	2003	2004	2005	2006	2007		High	
94	93	74	81	109	105	108	103	119	102	103	109	101	103	76		**66**	04/95

2007–2008												Low	
08/07	09/07	10/07	11/07	12/07	01/08	02/08	03/08	04/08	05/08	06/08	07/08	**121**	07/02
98	100	95	94	76	97	93	92	91	92	99	97		

The Cranes of Uganda looked well on course to progress to the last phase of the African qualifiers for the 2010 FIFA World Cup after some positive results in the June 2008 group games. Four points picked up in two matches against 2006 World Cup finalists Angola leaving the door wide open. That went some way to making up for Uganda's narrow failure to qualify for the 2008 CAF Africa Cup of Nations finals in Ghana. Uganda were on course to qualify as one of the three best group runners-up but their dreams were shattered at the final hurdle, losing out to Benin. The two finished in their respective groups in second place with 11 points each but Benin qualified with a

INTERNATIONAL HONOURS
CECAFA Cup 1973 1976 1977 1989 1990 1992 1996 2000 2003

marginally better goal difference. Laszlo Csaba, the youthful Hungarian coach behind the improvement, left the East African team in July 2008 to take up the manager's job at Scottish club Heart of Midlothian, taking along several players with him. In December 2007, he had led Uganda to a third place finish in the East and Central African Senior Challenge Cup. After losing to Rwanda in the semi-finals the Cranes then beat Burundi 2-0 in the third place play-off. domestic football Kampala City Council emerged as Super League winners, finishing five points ahead of SC Villa while provincial side Victor FC won the Kakungulu Cup, their first major trophy.

THE FIFA BIG COUNT OF 2006

	Male	Female		Total
Number of players	1 186 014	5 500	Referees and Assistant Referees	600
Professionals	14		Admin, Coaches, Technical, Medical	5 000
Amateurs 18+	28 000		Number of clubs	400
Youth under 18	18 500		Number of teams	2 000
Unregistered	60 000		Clubs with women's teams	2
Total players	1 191 514		Players as % of population	4.23%

Federation of Uganda Football Associations (FUFA)

FUFA House, Plot No. 879, Kyadondo Block 8, Mengo Wakaliga Road, PO Box 22518, Kampala, Uganda
Tel +256 41 272702   Fax +256 41 272702
fufaf@yahoo.com   www.fufa.co.ug
President: MULINDWA Lawrence   General Secretary: MASEMBE Charles
Vice-President: BARIGYE Richard   Treasurer: KYEYAGO Jowali   Media Officer: MULINDWA Rogers
Men's Coach: TBD   Women's Coach: None
FUFA formed: 1924   CAF: 1959   FIFA: 1959
Yellow shirts, Yellow shorts, Yellow socks

RECENT INTERNATIONAL MATCHES PLAYED BY UGANDA

2005	Opponents	Score	Venue	Comp	Scorers	Att	Referee
8-01	Egypt	L 0-3	Cairo	Fr			
26-03	South Africa	L 1-2	Johennesburg	WCq	Obua [63p]	20 000	Chukwujekwu NGA
5-06	Congo DR	L 0-4	Kinshasa	WCq		80 000	Daami TUN
18-06	Cape Verde Islands	W 1-0	Kampala	WCq	Serunkuma [36]	5 000	Kidane ERI
4-09	Ghana	L 0-2	Kumasi	WCq		45 000	Hicuburundi BDI
8-10	Burkina Faso	D 2-2	Kampala	WCq	Masaba [30], Serunkuma [71]	1 433	Benouza ALG
27-11	Ethiopia	D 0-0	Kigali	CCr1			
30-11	Djibouti	W 6-1	Kigali	CCr1	Masaba [12p], Nsereko 2 [27 29], Serunkuma [47], Mawejje [85], Muganga [89]		
1-12	Somalia	W 7-0	Kigali	CCr1	Massa 2 [15 24], Nsereko 18, Mubiru 2 [64 73], Vincent [78], Ryekwassa [88]		
3-12	Sudan	W 3-0	Kigali	CCr1	Massa [4], Serunkuma [35], Mubiru [92+]		
8-12	Rwanda	L 0-1	Kigali	CCsf			
10-12	Zanzibar †	D 0-0	Kigali	CC3p	L 4-5p		
27-12	Egypt	L 0-2	Cairo	Fr			
29-12	Ecuador	W 2-1	Cairo	Fr	Massa [47], Mwanga [54]		
2006							
26-07	Rwanda	D 1-1	Kigali	Fr	Serunkuma [88]		
5-08	Botswana	D 0-0	Kampala	Fr	W 3-1p		
16-08	Libya	L 2-3	Tripoli	Fr	Bongole [46], Serunkuma [69]		
29-08	Burkina Faso	D 0-0	Kampala	Fr			
2-09	Lesotho	W 3-0	Kampala	CNq	Massa 2 [29 42], Obua [57p]		Abdelrahman SUD
8-10	Niger	D 0-0	Niamey	CNq			Abdou Diouf SEN
27-11	Sudan	W 2-1	Addis Abeba	CCr1	Serunkuma [72], Masaba [87p]		
30-11	Rwanda	W 1-0	Addis Abeba	CCr1	Serunkuma [60]		
3-12	Somalia	W 2-0	Addis Abeba	CCr1	Wagaluka [11], Kadogo [17]		
6-12	Malawi	D 0-0	Addis Abeba	CCqf	W 4-2p		
8-12	Sudan	D 2-2	Addis Abeba	CCsf	Kayizi [15], Serunkuma [72], L 5-6p		
10-12	Rwanda	D 0-0	Addis Abeba	CC3p	L 2-4p		
2007							
24-03	Nigeria	L 0-1	Abeokuta	CNq			Diatta SEN
26-05	Tanzania	D 1-1	Kampala	Fr	Kadogo [2]		
2-06	Nigeria	W 2-1	Kampala	CNq	Obua [52p], Sekajja [65p]		Abdelfattah EGY
19-06	Lesotho	D 0-0	Maseru	CNq			Mwandike TAN
1-09	Tanzania	L 0-1	Dar es Salaam	Fr			
8-09	Niger	W 3-1	Kampala	CNq	Obua 3 [2p 76 86]		Marange ZIM
9-12	Djibouti	W 7-0	Dar es Salaam	CCr1	Kitagenda 3 [19 31 27], Wagaluka [41], Muganga [45], Odur [60], Kayizi [80]		
11-12	Rwanda	W 2-0	Dar es Salaam	CCr1	Masaba [69], Bajope [86]		
14-12	Eritrea	L 2-3	Dar es Salaam	CCr1	Muganga [54], Wagaluka [74p]		
20-12	Rwanda	L 0-1	Dar es Salaam	CCsf			
22-12	Burundi	W 2-0	Dar es Salaam	CC3p	Kitagenda 2 [60 89]		
2008							
26-03	Libya	D 1-1	Kampala	Fr	Okhuti [47]		
31-05	Niger	W 1-0	Kamapala	WCq	Sekajja [53]	25 000	Evehe CMR
8-06	Benin	L 1-4	Cotonou	WCq	Sepuya [9]	10 200	Karembe MLI
14-06	Angola	W 3-1	Kampala	WCq	Sepuya [5], Mwesigwa [18], Wagaluka [73]	20 000	Maillet SEY
23-06	Angola	D 0-0	Luanda	WCq		16 000	Mana NGA

Fr = Friendly match • CN = CAF African Cup of Nations • CC = CECAFA Cup • WC = FIFA World Cup
q = qualifier • r1 = first round group • qf = quarter-final • sf = semifinal • 3p = third place play-off • f = final • † Not a full international

UGANDA NATIONAL TEAM RECORDS AND RECORD SEQUENCES

Records			Sequence records				
Victory	13-1	KEN 1932	Wins	7	1932-1940	Clean sheets	5	1996-1998
Defeat	0-6	TUN 1999	Defeats	5	1978-1979, 2004	Goals scored	19	1931-1952
Player Caps	n/a		Undefeated	15	1996-1998	Without goal	4	1995, 1999
Player Goals	n/a		Without win	11	1995-1996	Goals against	15	1999-2000

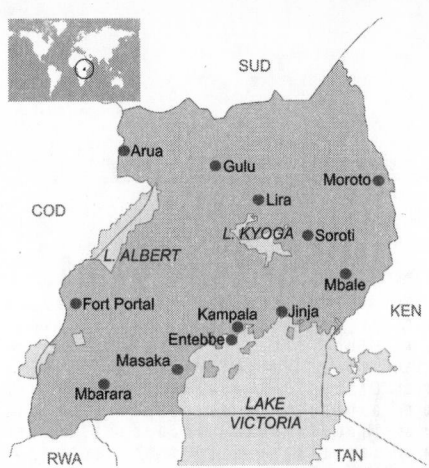

		Population '000
1	Kampala	1 455
2	Gulu	174
3	Lira	144
4	Jinja	97
5	Mbarara	86
6	Mukono	86
7	Mbale	80
8	Kasese	78
9	Kitgum	68
10	Njeru	68
11	Masaka	67
12	Entebbe	66
13	Arua	63
14	Kabale	54
15	Tororo	51
16	Iganga	50
17	Koboko	48
18	Mityana	45
19	Hoima	45
20	Busia	45
21	Soroti	44
22	Fort Portal	43
23	Lugazi	37
24	Nebbi	36

REPUBLIC OF UGANDA

Capital	Kampala	Language	English, Ganda			Independence	1962
Population	30 262 610	Area	236 040 km²	Density	111 per km²	% in cities	13%
GDP per cap	$1400	Dailling code	+256	Internet	.ug	GMT +/-	+3

MEDALS TABLE

		Overall			Lge	Cup			Africa			City	Stadium	Cap'ty	DoF
		G	S	B	G	G	S	B	G	S	B				
1	SC Villa	23	5		16	7	3		2			Kampala	Nakivubo	20 000	1975
2	Express FC	16	4	1	6	10	4			1		Kampala	Muteesa II	40 202	1957
3	Kampala City Council	16	5	1	8	8	5			1		Kampala	National Stadium	40 000	1967
4	Simba SC	3	3		2	1	2		1			Lugazi	Nakivubo	20 000	
5	Uganda Revenue Authority - URA	3			2	1						Kampala	National Stadium	40 000	
6	Coffee SC	2	2			2	2								
7	Mbale Heroes	2	1			2	1					Mbale			
8	Prisons FC	2			2							Kampala			
9	Nile Breweries	1	4		1		4					Jinja			
10	Uganda Commercial Bank	1	3		1		3					Kampala			
11	Police FC	1	1		1		1					Jinja			
	Uganda Electricity Board - Umeme	1	1			1	1					Jinja			
13	Coffee United	1			1							Kakira			
	Nsambya	1				1						Kampala			
	Victor FC	1				1						Jinja			

SC Villa were previously Nakivubo Villa • Mbale Heroes were previously Dairy Heroes and Gangama United

RECENT LEAGUE AND CUP RECORD

	Championship						Cup		
Year	Champions	Pts	Runners-up	Pts	Third	Pts	Winners	Score	Runners-up
1995	Express	74	Umeme	61	SC Villa	52	Express	2-0	Posta
1996	Express	75	Kampala CC	65	SC Villa	65	Umeme	1-0	Nile Breweries
1997	Kampala CC	76	Umeme	73	Express	72	Express	4-1	Umeme
1998	SC Villa	45	Express	44	Simba SC	39	SC Villa	2-0	Simba SC
1999	SC Villa	94	Express	92	Simba SC	76	Dairy Heroes	0-0 3-0p	Lyantonde FC
2000	SC Villa	75	Kampala CC	70	Express	65	SC Villa	1-0	Military Police
2001	SC Villa	70	Kampala CC	65	Mbale Heroes	48	Express	3-1	SC Villa
2002	SC Villa	79	Express	63	Kampala CC	61	SC Villa	2-1	Express
2003	SC Villa	72	Express	72	Kampala CC	53	Express	3-1	Police
2004	SC Villa	67	Express	57	URA Kampala	57	Kampala CC	1-1 3-2p	Express
2005	Police Jinja	3-1	SC Villa				URA Kampala	2-1	Kampala CC
2006	URA Kampala	65	Police Jinja	55	Express	54	Express	2-0	Maji FC
2007	URA Kampala	73	SC Villa	65	Police Jinja	61	Express	0-0 4-2p	Kampala CC
2008	Kampala CC	74	SC Villa	69	Police Jinja	67	Victor FC	1-0	Kinyara Sugar

UGANDA 2007–08

SUPER LEAGUE

	Pl	W	D	L	F	A	Pts	KCC	Villa	Police	URA	Victor	Express	Bunamwaya	Nalubaale	Iganga TC	Kinyara	Simba	Boroboro	Maji	Masaka LC	CRO	Ediofe	Maroons	Biharwe
Kampala City Council	34	22	8	4	61	23	74		0-0	2-0	2-1	0-1	0-1	0-0	6-1	2-1	3-1	1-0	3-2	3-0	2-2	2-0	6-0	4-1	1-0
SC Villa Kampala	34	20	9	5	52	24	69	3-2		1-3	2-1	3-1	1-1	0-0	0-1	2-0	1-0	3-2	1-1	2-1	2-0	3-2	3-0	1-0	5-0
Police Jinja	34	18	13	3	47	22	67	0-1	0-0		1-1	0-0	1-1	0-0	2-1	0-1	1-1	2-1	2-1	2-1	1-0	4-1	3-1	5-0	2-0
URA Kampala	34	13	13	8	48	34	52	2-2	0-4	1-1		1-0	3-1	1-1	2-1	3-1	2-1	0-0	6-0	1-0	1-1	4-0	3-3	5-1	1-0
Victor FC	34	12	16	6	32	22	52	0-3	**2-0**	0-0	2-0		0-0	1-0	0-0	0-0	0-0	1-2	1-0	0-0	3-0	3-0	3-0		
Express RE Kampala	34	12	15	7	30	20	51	0-0	0-1	0-0	0-0	0-0		1-1	0-0	0-0	2-0	1-1	0-1	0-2	1-0	1-1	3-0	1-0	2-0
Bunamwaya Wakiso	34	12	15	7	31	24	51	1-3	0-0	1-1	1-2	0-1	1-0		1-0	0-0	2-0	1-0	2-0	1-0	1-1	0-0	0-1	1-1	2-2
Nalubaale Buikwe	34	14	6	14	33	34	48	1-2	1-2	1-2	0-1	1-3	1-0	2-0		1-0	3-0	3-1	1-0	3-0	1-0	0-0	2-1	2-1	1-1
Iganga Town Council	34	10	12	12	29	31	42	0-1	2-1	0-1	1-1	1-1	1-2	0-1	0-0		2-0	1-1	1-2	2-1	2-0	0-0	**2-0**	2-2	1-0
Kinyara Sugar	34	10	11	13	32	39	41	1-1	0-0	2-2	1-0	3-0	0-0	2-3	1-1	1-0		0-0	2-0	2-1	2-1	2-0	1-3	2-0	2-1
SC Simba	34	10	10	14	38	37	40	0-1	1-2	1-2	1-1	2-2	0-1	1-1	0-1	2-0	1-0		2-0	1-3	1-0	0-0	3-1	5-0	1-2
Boroboro Holy Hill	34	10	9	15	29	41	39	0-1	1-0	0-1	1-1	1-1	1-2	2-2	0-1	1-0	2-0	2-0		2-1	0-0	1-0	2-1	2-0	0-0
Maji FC Kampala	34	10	8	16	35	42	38	0-1	0-2	0-2	1-0	0-0	1-3	0-0	2-0	1-1	1-0	1-1	1-1		4-0	2-2	1-0	2-2	0-1
Masaka Local Council	34	8	10	16	28	38	34	3-1	0-1	1-2	1-1	0-0	2-1	2-1	0-0	0-1	1-1	0-1	1-0	0-2		0-0	4-0	1-0	0-1
CRO Mbale	34	6	16	12	28	40	34	0-0	2-2	0-2	0-2	2-2	0-0	1-0	0-0	2-2	2-0	1-0	4-2	2-2			0-0	2-0	3-0
Ediofe Hills Arua	34	9	7	18	34	57	34	0-2	0-0	0-0	1-0	2-0	1-1	0-3	3-1	0-1	1-1	3-2	1-0	1-1	0-1	3-0		**0-2**	5-1
Maroons Kampala	34	9	5	20	25	53	32	1-1	0-2	0-1	2-0	0-2	0-2	0-1	1-0	1-2	2-0	0-2	3-0	1-0	0-1	1-0	1-0		0-0
Biharwe	34	5	9	20	26	57	24	0-2	0-2	1-1	0-0	0-1	0-2	0-1	0-1	2-2	0-1	1-3	3-3	0-1	3-3	2-1	4-2	1-2	

2/11/2007 – 22/05/2008 • † Qualified for Champions League • Matches in bold awarded
Top scorers: Bruno Olobo, Simba 15; Brian Omwony, Kampala City Council 15

KAKUNGULU CUP 2008

Round of 16

Victor FC *	2
Maji FC Kampala	1
Biharwe	0
CRO Mbale *	2
SC Villa Kampala *	5
Jogoo Youth	0
Leopards	0
URA Kampala *	2
Proline Lugogo	1
Standard High *	0
Bunamwaya Wakiso *	0 1p
Police Jinja	0 4p
Express RE Kampala	4
Boroboro Holy Hill *	0
Kampala City Council *	0 3p
Kinyara Sugar	0 5p

Quarter-finals

Victor FC *	2
CRO Mbale	0
SC Villa Kampala *	0 3p
URA Kampala	0 4p
Proline Lugogo *	0 4p
Police Jinja	0 3p
Express RE Kampala *	0
Kinyara Sugar	1

Semi-finals

Victor FC †	2
URA Kampala	0
Proline Lugogo	0
Kinyara Sugar ††	2

Final

Victor FC	1
Kinyara Sugar	0

CUP FINAL

Nakivubo, Kampala
28-05-2008
Scorer – Julius Ongude [45]

* Home team • †Played at Namboole
†† Played at Nakivubo • ‡ Qualified for the CAF Confederation Cup

UKR – UKRAINE

NATIONAL TEAM RECORD
JULY 10TH 2006 TO JULY 12TH 2010

PL	W	D	L	F	A	%
19	9	4	6	31	22	57.9

FIFA/COCA-COLA WORLD RANKING

1993	1994	1995	1996	1997	1998	1999	2000	2001	2002	2003	2004	2005	2006	2007		High	
90	77	71	59	49	47	27	34	45	45	60	57	40	13	30		11	05/07

					2007–2008								Low	
08/07	09/07	10/07	11/07	12/07	01/08	02/08	03/08	04/08	05/08	06/08	07/08		132	09/93
15	17	22	29	30	30	32	32	32	32	31	29			

The fact that Ukraine ended up in fourth place in their Euro 2008 qualifying group has to be set against the fact that they were up against both France and Italy as well as a resurgent Scotland, but the disappointment was still palpable especially when combined with the continuing uncertainty over their co-hosting of Euro 2012 with Poland. With the Poles in far better shape, especially in terms of infrastructure, there was a very real threat that hosting rights could be taken away from the Ukraine - or at least in part. Of particular concern to UEFA has been the delay in refurbishing Kyiv's Olympic Stadium, the venue for the final. One stadium nearing completion is the new

INTERNATIONAL HONOURS
Qualified for the FIFA World Cup finals 2006

US$250m Shakhtar Stadium in Donetsk, which will give the club a five star UEFA venue and they lived up to their billing by winning the League and Cup double in 2008. The championship went down to the final day of the season, a 4-1 win over neighbours Metalurh securing the title for Shakhtar. 10 days earlier, goals by Oleksandr Hladky and Oleksiy Hai had secured the Cup in a 2-0 win over rivals Dynamo, but there was disappointment at the failure to qualify from the group stage of the Champions League for the first time. Despite winning their first two games against Celtic and Benfica, they lost the next four and finished bottom.

THE FIFA BIG COUNT OF 2006

	Male	Female		Total
Number of players	2 040 756	232 261	Referees and Assistant Referees	7 530
Professionals	2 427		Admin, Coaches, Technical, Medical	8 050
Amateurs 18+	25 500		Number of clubs	68
Youth under 18	658 540		Number of teams	6 500
Unregistered	314 700		Clubs with women's teams	2
Total players	2 273 017		Players as % of population	4.87%

Football Federation of Ukraine (FFU)

Provulok Laboratornyi 7-A, PO Box 55, Kyiv 01133, Ukraine
Tel +380 44 5210521   Fax +380 44 5210550
info@ffu.org.ua   www.ffu.org.ua
President: SURKIS Grigoriy   General Secretary: BANDURKO Oleksandr
Vice-President: BANDURKO Oleksandr   Treasurer: MISCHENKO Lyudmyla   Media Officer: GOROBCHENKO Tetyana
Men's Coach: MIKHAILYCHENKO Oleksiy   Women's Coach: KUTSEV Anatoliy
FFU formed: 1991   UEFA: 1992   FIFA: 1992
Yellow shirts with blue trimmings, Yellow shorts, Yellow socks or Blue shirts with yellow trimming, Blue shorts, Blue socks

RECENT INTERNATIONAL MATCHES PLAYED BY UKRAINE

2006	Opponents		Score	Venue	Comp	Scorers	Att	Referee
28-02	Azerbaijan	D	0-0	Baku	Fr			Sipailo LVA
28-05	Costa Rica	W	4-0	Kyiv	Fr	Nazarenko 27, Vorobei 33, Kalinichenko 38, Bielik 56	25 000	Ivanov.N RUS
2-06	Italy	D	0-0	Lausanne	Fr		10 000	Nobs SUI
5-06	Libya	W	3-0	Gossau	Fr	Yezerskyi 49, Bielik 87, Vorobei 89	2 500	Wilzhaber SUI
8-06	Luxembourg	W	3-0	Luxembourg	Fr	Voronin 55, Shevchenko 83, Kalinichenko 84		Vervecken BEL
14-06	Spain	L	0-4	Leipzig	WCr1		43 000	Busacca SUI
19-06	Saudi Arabia	W	4-0	Hamburg	WCr1	Rusol 4, Rebrov 36, Shevchenko 46, Kalinichenko 84	50 000	Poll ENG
23-06	Tunisia	W	1-0	Berlin	WCr1	Shevchenko 70p	72 000	Amarilla PAR
26-06	Switzerland	D	0-0	Cologne	WCr2		45 000	Archundia MEX
30-06	Italy	L	0-3	Hamburg	WCqf		50 000	De Bleeckere BEL
15-08	Azerbaijan	W	6-0	Kyiv	Fr	Voronin 3, Nazarenko 12, Rotan 25, Husiyev 45, Vorobei 71, Bielik 91+	6 000	Sukhina RUS
6-09	Georgia	W	3-2	Kyiv	ECq	Shevchenko 31, Rotan 62, Rusol 80	35 000	Jara CZE
7-10	Italy	L	0-2	Rome	ECq		49 149	Vassaras GRE
11-10	Scotland	W	2-0	Kyiv	ECq	Kucher 60, Shevchenko 90p	50 000	Hansson SWE
2007								
7-02	Israel	D	1-1	Tel Aviv	Fr	Kalinichenko 73	12 000	Rodriguez ESP
24-03	Faroe Islands	W	2-0	Toftir	ECq	Yezerskyi 20, Gusev 57	717	Skomina SVN
28-03	Lithuania	W	1-0	Odessa	ECq	Gusev 47	33 600	Meyer GER
2-06	France	L	0-2	Paris	ECq		79 000	Medina Cantalejo ESP
22-08	Uzbekistan	W	2-1	Kyiv	Fr	Hladkiy 30, Rotan 65	4 000	Banari MDA
8-09	Georgia	D	1-1	Tbilisi	ECq	Shelayev 7	24 000	Hamer LUX
12-09	Italy	L	1-2	Kyiv	ECq	Shevchenko 71	41 500	Webb ENG
13-10	Scotland	L	1-3	Glasgow	ECq	Shevchenko 24	52 063	Vink NED
17-10	Faroe Islands	W	5-0	Kyiv	ECq	Kalynichenko 2 40 49, Gusev 2 43 45, Vorobey 64	5 000	Jakov ISR
17-11	Lithuania	L	0-2	Kaunas	ECq		3 000	Malcolm NIR
21-11	France	D	2-2	Kyiv	ECq	Voronin 14, Shevchenko 46	7 800	Ovrebø NOR
2008								
6-02	Cyprus	D	1-1	Nicosia	Fr	Milevskyi 71	500	Kasnaferis CYP
26-03	Serbia	W	2-0	Odessa	Fr	Shevchenko 54, Nazarenko 57	8 000	Lajuks LVA
24-05	Netherlands	L	0-3	Rotterdam	Fr		40 000	Circhetta SUI
1-06	Sweden	W	1-0	Stockholm	Fr	Nazarenko 82	25 203	Einwaller AUT

Fr = Friendly match • EC = UEFA EURO 2008 • WC = FIFA World Cup
q = qualifier • r1 = first round group • r2 = second round • qf = quarter-final • BCD = Behind closed doors

UKRAINE NATIONAL TEAM PLAYERS

Player		Ap	G	Club	Date of Birth	Player		Ap	G	Club	Date of Birth
Oleksandr Shovkovsky	GK	84	0	Dynamo Kyiv	2 01 1975	Anatoliy Tymoschuk	MF	77	1	Zenit St P'burg	30 03 1979
Andriy Pyatov	GK	5	0	Shakhtar D'netsk	28 06 1984	Maksym Kalynychenko	MF	36	7	Spartak Moscow	26 01 1979
Vyacheslav Kernozenko	GK	5	0	Dnipropetrovsk	4 06 1976	Serhiy Nazarenko	MF	28	5	Dnipropetrovsk	16 02 1980
Andriy Nesmachniy	DF	66	0	Dynamo Kyiv	28 02 1979	Oleksiy Hai	MF	12	0	Shakhtar D'netsk	6 11 1982
Andriy Rusol	DF	41	3	Dnipropetrovsk	16 01 1983	Yevhen Levchenko	MF	4	0	FC Groningen	2 01 1978
Volodymyr Yezerskiy	DF	39	2	Shakhtar D'netsk	15 11 1976	Denis Golaido	MF	2	0	Tav. Simferopol	3 06 1984
Dmytro Chigrinsky	DF	10	0	Shakhtar D'netsk	7 11 1986	Serhiy Kravchenko	MF	2	0	Vorskla Poltava	24 04 1983
Oleksandr Kucher	DF	9	1	Shakhtar D'netsk	22 10 1982	Andriy Shevchenko	FW	81	37	Chelsea	29 09 1976
Vyacheslav Shevchuk	DF	6	0	Shakhtar D'netsk	13 05 1979	Andriy Voronin	FW	53	6	Liverpool	21 07 1979
Vitaliy Mandzyuk	DF	4	0	Dynamo Kyiv	24 01 1986	Oleksandr Hladky	FW	8	1	Shakhtar D'netsk	24 08 1987
Hrygory Yarmash	DF	2	0	Vorskla Poltava	4 01 1985	Yevhen Seleznyov	FW	2	0	Shakhtar D'netsk	20 07 1985
The Ukraine squad for the June 2008 international against Sweden						Volodymyr Homenyuk	FW	1	0	Tav. Simferopol	19 07 1985

UKRAINE NATIONAL TEAM RECORDS AND RECORD SEQUENCES

Records			Sequence records					
Victory	6-0	AZE 2006	Wins	6	2004-2005	Clean sheets	7	2004-2005
Defeat	0-4	CRO 1995, ESP 2006	Defeats	2	Seven times	Goals scored	10	1995-1996
Player Caps	84	Oleksandr Shovkovsky	Undefeated	13	1998-1999	Without goal	3	2003
Player Goals	37	Andriy Shevchenko	Without win	11	2003-2004	Goals against	8	2004

1	Kyiv	2 469
2	Kharkiv	1 412
3	Dnipropetrovsk	1 017
4	Odessa	988
5	Donetsk	973
6	Zaporizhzhya	787
7	Lviv	710
8	Kryvyi Rih	644
9	Mykolayiv	509
10	Mariupol	477
11	Luhansk	446
12	Makiyivka	370
13	Vinnytsia	350
14	Simferopol	342
15	Sevastopol	328
16	Kherson	318
17	Poltava	318
18	Chernihiv	309
19	Cherkasy	298
20	Sumy	295
21	Zhytomyr	281
22	Horlivka	272
23	Lutsk	216
24	Uzhgorod	118

UKRAINE; UKRAYINA

Capital	Kyiv	Language	Ukrainian, Russian	Independence	1991
Population	46 299 862	Area	603 700 km²	% in cities	70%
GDP per cap	$5400	Density	79 per km²		
		Dailling code	+380	Internet .ua	GMT + / - +2

MEDALS TABLE

		Overall			League			Cup			Europe			City	Stadium	Cap'ty	DoF
		G	S	B	G	S	B	G	S	B	G	S	B				
1	Dynamo Kyiv	21	7		12	5		9	2					Kyiv	Valeriy Lobanovskyi	16 888	1927
2	Shakhtar Donetsk	10	12		4	9		6	3					Donetsk	RSK Olimpiyskiy	31 547	1936
3	Chernomorets Odessa	2	2	3		2	3	2						Odesa	Tsentralnyi	30 767	1936
4	Tavriya Simferopol	1	1		1					1				Simferopol	Lokomotiv	20 013	1958
5	Dnipro Dnipropetrovsk	4	4		1	4		3						Dnipropetrovsk	Meteor	26 345	1925
6	Karpaty Lviv	2	1			1		2						Lviv	Ukrainia	29 004	1963
7	CSCA Kyiv	2						2						Kyiv			
8	Kryvbas Kryvyi Rih	1	2			2		1						Kryvyi Rih	Metalurh	29 782	1959
	Metallist Kharkiv	1	2			2		1						Kharkiv	Metallist	28 000	1925
10	Metalurh Zaporizhya	1						1						Zaporizhya	Slavutych Arena	11 983	1935
11	Nyva Vinnytsia	1						1						Vinnytsia			

UKRAINIAN TEAMS IN SOVIET FOOTBALL

1	Dynamo Kyiv	24	13	5	13	11	3	9	2		2		2	
7	Shakhtar Donetsk	4	6	2		2	2	4	4					
9	Dnipro Dnipropetrovsk	3	2	2	2	2	2	1						
13	Zorya Luhansk	1	2		1				2					
15	Metallist Kharkiv	1	1					1	1					
16	Karpaty Lviv	1						1						

RECENT LEAGUE AND CUP RECORD

	Championship						Cup		
Year	Champions	Pts	Runners-up	Pts	Third	Pts	Winners	Score	Runners-up
1995	Dynamo Kyiv	83	Ch'morets Odesa	73	Dn. Dnipropetrovsk	65	Shakhtar Donetsk	1-1 7-6p	Dn. Dnipropetrovsk
1996	Dynamo Kyiv	79	Ch'morets Odesa	73	Dn. Dnipropetrovsk	63	Dynamo Kyiv	2-0	Nyva Vinnitsa
1997	Dynamo Kyiv	73	Shakhtar Donetsk	62	Vorskla Poltava	58	Shakhtar Donetsk	1-0	Dn. Dnipropetrovsk
1998	Dynamo Kyiv	72	Shakhtar Donetsk	67	Karpaty L'viv	57	Dynamo Kyiv	2-1	CSCA Kyiv
1999	Dynamo Kyiv	74	Shakhtar Donetsk	65	Kryvbas Kryvyi Rih	59	Dynamo Kyiv	3-0	Karpaty L'viv
2000	Dynamo Kyiv	84	Shakhtar Donetsk	66	Kryvbas Kryvyi Rih	60	Dynamo Kyiv	1-0	Kryvbas Kryvyi Rih
2001	Dynamo Kyiv	64	Shakhtar Donetsk	63	Dn. Dnipropetrovsk	55	Shakhtar Donetsk	2-1	CSCA Kyiv
2002	Shakhtar Donetsk	66	Dynamo Kyiv	65	Metalurh Donetsk	42	Shakhtar Donetsk	3-2	Dynamo Kyiv
2003	Dynamo Kyiv	73	Shakhtar Donetsk	70	Metalurh Donetsk	60	Dynamo Kyiv	2-1	Shakhtar Donetsk
2004	Dynamo Kyiv	73	Shakhtar Donetsk	70	Dn. Dnipropetrovsk	57	Shakhtar Donetsk	2-0	Dn. Dnipropetrovsk
2005	Shakhtar Donetsk	80	Dynamo Kyiv	73	Metalurh Donetsk	49	Dynamo Kyiv	1-0	Shakhtar Donetsk
2006	Shakhtar Donetsk	75	Dynamo Kyiv	75	Ch'morets Odesa	45	Dynamo Kyiv	1-0	Metalurh Zapor'hja
2007	Dynamo Kyiv	74	Shakhtar Donetsk	63	Metallist Kharkiv	61	Dynamo Kyiv	2-1	Shakhtar Donetsk
2008	Shakhtar Donetsk	74	Dynamo Kyiv	71	Metallist Kharkiv	63	Shakhtar Donetsk	2-0	Dynamo Kyiv

UKRAINE 2007–08

VYSCHA LIHA

	Pl	W	D	L	F	A	Pts	Shakhtar	Dynamo	Metalist	Dnipro	Tavriya	Arsenal	Chernomorets	Vorskla	Metalurh Z	Karpaty	Zorja	Metalurh D	Kryvbas	Kharkiv	Naftovyk	Zakarpattya
Shakhtar Donetsk †	30	24	2	4	75	24	74		1-1	4-1	4-1	2-0	4-1	0-1	2-1	4-0	3-0	3-0	4-1	1-0	2-1	1-1	5-0
Dynamo Kyiv †	30	22	5	3	65	26	71	2-1		0-1	1-3	3-0	2-2	5-2	2-1	2-1	7-3	3-0	3-3	3-0	2-0	0-1	1-0
Metalist Kharkiv ‡	30	19	6	5	51	27	63	1-3	2-2		1-0	3-0	2-4	2-0	3-0	2-1	4-0	2-1	1-1	3-2	2-0	2-0	1-0
Dnipro Dnipropetrovsk ‡	30	18	5	7	40	27	59	1-3	0-4	3-0		2-1	1-3	1-0	1-0	1-0	0-0	1-0	4-1	2-0	1-0	2-0	0-0
Tavriya Simferopol	30	13	8	9	38	40	47	3-2	1-4	0-0	0-1		1-1	3-0	1-0	2-2	2-1	2-0	3-3	4-3	1-0	1-0	4-1
Arsenal Kyiv	30	11	9	10	42	36	42	2-4	0-1	1-1	2-1	0-1		1-2	3-2	2-1	2-0	1-1	1-3	0-0	0-0	3-0	7-0
Chernomorets Odessa	30	11	5	14	27	33	38	1-2	0-0	0-1	1-2	2-0	0-1		1-0	1-1	4-0	1-0	1-1	0-1	1-1	0-1	3-1
Vorskla Poltava	30	9	9	12	28	30	36	0-1	0-1	1-1	2-1	0-0	2-1	2-0		2-1	0-0	1-1	2-0	0-3	1-1	1-1	2-0
Metalurh Zaporizhya	30	9	9	12	24	32	36	1-3	0-1	0-2	0-0	0-0	0-1	0-2	1-1		1-0	3-0	1-0	1-1	0-0	1-0	0-0
Karpaty Lviv	30	9	6	15	29	41	33	2-4	1-2	0-2	0-1	4-0	2-0	1-2	1-3			3-0	0-0	3-0	1-0	1-1	2-0
Zorja Luhansk	30	9	4	17	24	43	31	1-4	1-2	3-2	0-1	2-3	3-1	0-2	‡‡	0-1	0-1		1-1	1-2	2-1	1-0	5-0
Metalurh Donetsk	30	6	13	11	34	39	31	0-1	1-2	1-1	0-3	1-2	1-2	0-0	0-0	3-0	1-0	1-0		0-1	0-0	2-1	5-0
Kryvbas Kryvyi Rih	30	7	9	14	29	39	30	1-0	0-1	0-3	1-2	1-1	0-0	3-0	3-0	0-1	0-1	1-2	1-1		1-1	0-1	1-1
FC Kharkiv	30	6	9	15	20	32	27	0-3	0-1	0-2	1-2	1-1	0-1	1-0	0-1	0-3	0-1	1-0	0-1	1-0		1-0	0-2
Naftovyk-Ukrnafta	30	6	8	16	18	38	26	0-3	0-3	0-2	1-1	0-1	1-0	1-0	0-1	2-0	0-1	0-0	2-2	1-2	1-4		3-2
Zakarpattya Uzhgorod	30	3	9	18	17	54	18	0-1	1-4	0-1	1-1	1-0	0-0	2-0	0-0	1-1	1-2	0-2	1-1	2-3	0-3	0-0	

13/07/2007 - 17/05/2008 • † Qualified for the UEFA Champions League • ‡ Qualified for the UEFA Cup • ‡‡ Match awarded to Zorja
Top scorers: Devic, Metalist 19; Hladkiy, Shakhtar 17; Kosyrin, Metalurh Donetsk 17; Selezniov, Arsenal 17

UKRAINE 2007–08 PERSHA LIHA (2)

	Pl	W	D	L	F	A	Pts
Illychivets Mariupil	38	26	7	5	65	26	85
FK Lviv	38	23	5	10	58	29	74
Obolon Kyiv	38	22	6	10	67	42	72
Desna Chernihiv	38	20	7	11	61	44	67
Dynamo Kyiv-2	38	19	6	13	64	52	63
Dynamo-IhroServis	38	18	6	14	50	45	60
Stal Alchevsk	38	15	13	10	52	44	58
FK Oleksandrija	38	14	15	9	41	32	57
Volyn Lutsk §3	38	16	8	14	61	55	53
MFK Mykolajiv	38	13	13	12	33	27	52
Krymteplytsja	38	13	11	14	49	43	50
Dnister Ovidiopol	38	12	13	13	33	39	49
Enerhetyk Burshtyn	38	13	9	16	39	44	48
Helios Kharkiv	38	13	8	17	31	40	47
FK Sevastopol	38	12	7	19	38	55	43
Feniks-Illichovets	38	11	8	19	35	56	41
Prykarpattija I-Frank'sk	38	11	6	21	37	67	39
Dnipro Cherkasy §6	38	8	17	13	43	43	35
CSCA Kyiv	38	7	6	25	36	74	27
Stal Dniprodzerzhinsk	38	3	11	24	23	58	20

19/07/2007 - 21/06/2008 • § = points deducted

FFU CUP 2007–08

Third Round

Shakhtar Donetsk *	4	
Arsenal Kyiv	1	
Dnister Ovidiopol *	0	
Vorskla Poltava	1	
Illychivets Mariupil	2	
FK Lviv *	1	
Metalist Kharkiv	2	1p
Chernomorets Odessa *	2	4p
Metalurh Donetsk	2	
Stal Alchevsk *	1	
Desna Chernihiv *	1	2p
Naftovyk-Ukrnafta	1	4p
Tavriya Simferopol	0	6p
Nyva Ternopil *	0	5p
Dynamo-IhroServis *	1	
Dynamo Kyiv	4	

Quarter-finals

Shakhtar Donetsk	3	1
Vorskla Poltava *	0	1
Illychivets Mariupil *	2	0
Chernomorets Odessa	1	4
Metalurh Donetsk	3	1
Naftovyk-Ukrnafta *	2	0
Tavriya Simferopol *	2	0
Dynamo Kyiv	0	3

Semi-finals

Shakhtar Donetsk	2	3
Chernomorets Odessa *	1	0
Metalurh Donetsk	1	0
Dynamo Kyiv *	2	1

Final

Shakhtar Donetsk	2
Dynamo Kyiv	0

CUP FINAL

Metalist, Kharkiv, 7-05-2008
Att: 28 000, Ref: Shvetsov

Scorers - Oleksandr Hladky [44], Oleksiy Hai [78] for Shakhtar

* Home team/home team in the 1st leg

URU – URUGUAY

NATIONAL TEAM RECORD
JULY 10TH 2006 TO JULY 12TH 2010

PL	W	D	L	F	A	%
23	10	7	6	43	26	58.7

FIFA/COCA-COLA WORLD RANKING

1993	1994	1995	1996	1997	1998	1999	2000	2001	2002	2003	2004	2005	2006	2007	High	
17	37	32	43	40	76	46	32	22	28	21	16	18	29	28	**14**	08/06

				2007–2008								Low	
08/07	09/07	10/07	11/07	12/07	01/08	02/08	03/08	04/08	05/08	06/08	07/08	**76**	12/98
21	19	17	27	28	28	30	29	27	28	26	22		

Uruguay remain one of the last bastions of football in South America where the old values of one champion club a year still holds fast and in 2008 that club was Defensor Sporting. They won their first title in 17 years but there was nothing traditional about the way in which they won it. Like many others in the region Uruguay has an Apertura and Clausura stage to the championship, won in the 2007–08 season by Defensor and Peñarol respectively. The two then play each other but instead of the winner being declared the champions, a further match is required against the team with the best overall record in the season and that's where it gets bizarre because Defensor beat

INTERNATIONAL HONOURS
FIFA World Cup 1930 1950 Olympic Gold 1924 1928 Qualified for the FIFA World Cup finals 1930 (hosts) 1950 1954 1962 1966 1970 1986 1990 2002
Copa América winner 14 times Copa Libertadores Peñarol 1960 1961 1966 1982 1987 Nacional 1971 1980 1988

Peñarol in the play-off, qualifying to meet... themselves! 2008 saw the 20th anniversary of the last time a Uruguayan club won the Copa Libertadores but they came no closer to ending that run. Nacional finished runners-up in their group behind Flamengo to qualify for the first knock-out round but that's as far as they got, losing 2-0 on aggregate to São Paulo. The national team got their 2010 FIFA World Cup qualifying campaign off to a great start with a 5-0 thrashing of Bolivia and they then trounced Peru 6-0 as they look to make an increasingly rare appearance in the finals.

THE FIFA BIG COUNT OF 2006

	Male	Female		Total
Number of players	214 000	27 300	Referees and Assistant Referees	400
Professionals	1 100		Admin, Coaches, Technical, Medical	2 200
Amateurs 18+	30 000		Number of clubs	1 210
Youth under 18	8 000		Number of teams	2 200
Unregistered	94 500		Clubs with women's teams	10
Total players	241 300		Players as % of population	7.03%

Asociación Uruguaya de Fútbol (AUF)
Guayabo 1531, Montevideo 11200, Uruguay
Tel +59 82 4004814   Fax +59 82 4090550
auf@auf.org.uy   www.auf.org.uy
President: CORBO Jose Luis   General Secretary: LEIZA Adrian
Vice-President: DOMINGUEZ Jose Carlos   Treasurer: ACHE Eduardo   Media Officer: TBD
Men's Coach: TABAREZ Oscar   Women's Coach: MANZOLILLO Fabiana
AUF formed: 1900   CONMEBOL: 1916   FIFA: 1923
Sky blue with white trimmings, Black shorts, Black socks

RECENT INTERNATIONAL MATCHES PLAYED BY URUGUAY

2005	Opponents	Score		Venue	Comp	Scorers	Att	Referee
12-11	Australia	W	1-0	Montevideo	WCpo	Rodriguez.D [37]	55 000	Larsen DEN
16-11	Australia	L	0-1	Sydney	WCpo	L 2-4p	82 698	Medina Cantalejo ESP
2006								
1-03	England	L	1-2	Liverpool	Fr	Pouso [26]	40 013	Farina ITA
21-05	Northern Ireland	W	1-0	New Jersey	Fr	Estoyanoff [33]	4 152	
23-05	Romania	W	2-0	Los Angeles	Fr	Vargas 2 [46] [59]	10 000	Stott USA
27-05	Serbia & Montenegro	D	1-1	Belgrade	Fr	Godin [82]	30 000	Kos SVN
30-05	Libya	W	2-1	Radès/Tunis	Fr	Vigneri [15], Abreu [34]		
4-06	Tunisia	D	0-0	Radès/Tunis	Fr	W 3-1p		
16-08	Egypt	W	2-0	Alexandria	Fr	Godin [67], OG [83]	10 000	Benouza ALG
27-09	Venezuela	L	0-1	Maracaibo	Fr		28 000	Manzur VEN
18-10	Venezuela	W	4-0	Montevideo	Fr	Sánchez.V [12], Godin [14], Abreu [51], Blanco [88]	7 000	Silvera URU
15-11	Georgia	L	0-2	Tbilisi	Fr		12 000	Godulyan UKR
2007								
7-02	Colombia	W	3-1	Cucuta	Fr	Abreu 2 [16p] [59p], Vargas [84]	26 000	Hoyos COL
24-03	Korea Republic	W	2-0	Seoul	Fr	Bueno 2 [19] [37]	42 159	Ogiya JPN
2-06	Australia	W	2-1	Sydney	Fr	Forlán [40], Recoba [77]	61 795	Rosetti ITA
26-06	Peru	L	0-3	Merida	CAr1		23 000	Amarilla PAR
30-06	Bolivia	W	1-0	San Cristobal	CAr1	Sánchez.V [58]	18 000	Toledo USA
3-07	Venezuela	D	0-0	Merida	CAr1		42 000	Simon BRA
7-07	Venezuela	W	4-1	San Cristobal	CAqf	Forlán 2 [38] [90], Garcia.P [65], Rodriguez.C [87]	42 000	Chandia CHI
10-07	Brazil	D	2-2	Maracaibo	CAsf	Forlán [36], Abreu [70]. L 4-5p	40 000	Ruiz COL
14-07	Mexico	L	1-3	Caracas	CA3p	Abreu [22]	30 000	Reinoso ECU
12-09	South Africa	D	0-0	Johannesburg	Fr			Bwanya ZIM
13-10	Bolivia	W	5-0	Montevideo	WCq	Suarez [4], Forlan [38], Abreu [48], Sanchez [57], Bueno [82]	25 200	Selman CHI
17-10	Paraguay	L	0-1	Asuncion	WCq		23 200	Baldassi ARG
18-11	Chile	D	2-2	Montevideo	WCq	Suarez [41], Abreu [81]	35 000	Pezzotta ARG
21-11	Brazil	L	1-2	São Paulo	WCq	Abreu [8]	70 000	Baldassi ARG
2008								
6-02	Colombia	D	2-2	Montevideo	Fr	Cavani [77], Suarez [85]		
25-05	Turkey	W	3-2	Bochum	Fr	Suarez 2 [31p] [78], Rodriguez [85p]		Meyer GER
28-05	Norway	D	2-2	Oslo	Fr	Suarez [44], Eguren [69]	12 246	Buttimer IRL
14-06	Venezuela	D	1-1	Montevideo	WCq	Lugano [12]	41 831	Intriago ECU
17-06	Peru	W	6-0	Montevideo	WCq	Forlan 3 [8] [37p] [56], Bueno 2 [61] [69], Abreu [90]	20 016	Pozo CHI

Fr = Friendly match • CA = Copa América • WC = FIFA World Cup

q = qualifier • po = play-off • r1 = first round group • qf = quarter-final • sf = semi-final • 3p = third place play-off

URUGUAY NATIONAL TEAM PLAYERS

	Player		Ap	G	Club	Date of Birth		Player		Ap	G	Club	Date of Birth
1	Fabián Carini	GK	72	0	Real Murcia	26 12 1979	12	Juan Castillo	GK	2	0	Botafogo	17 04 1978
2	Diego Lugano	DF	25	1	Fenerbahçe	2 11 1980	13	Sebastián Abreu	FW	38	21	Beitar Jerusalem	17 10 1976
3	Diego Godín	DF	22	3	Villarreal	16 02 1986	14	Vicente Sánchez	FW	25	5	Schalke 04	7 12 1979
4	Martín Cáceres	DF	7	0	Barcelona	17 03 1987	15	Diego Pérez	MF			AS Monaco	18 05 1980
5	Walter Gargano	MF	16	0	Napoli	27 07 1984	16	Maximiliano Pereira	MF	40	0	Benfica	8 06 1984
6	Andrés Scotti	DF	3	0	Argentinos Jun	14 12 1975	17	Álvaro González	MF			Boca Juniors	29 10 1984
7	Bruno Silva	DF	7	0	Ajax	29 03 1980	18	Ignacio González	MF	12	0	AS Monaco	14 05 1982
8	Sebastián Eguren	MF	11	1	Villarreal	8 01 1981	19	Martín Silva	GK			Defensor	25 03 1983
9	Luis Suárez	FW	11	6	Ajax	24 01 1987	20	Carlos Adrián Valdez	DF	4	0	Reggina	2 05 1983
10	Diego Forlán	FW	48	19	Atlético Madrid	19 05 1979	21	Juan Manuel Díaz	DF			Estudiantes	28 10 1987
11	Carlos Bueno	FW	23	16	Peñarol	10 05 1980	22	Cristian Rodríguez	MF	23	3	FC Porto	30 09 1985
	Uruguay's squad for the June 2008 World Cup qualifiers						23	Sebastián Fernández	FW	2	0	Defensor	23 05 1985

URUGUAY NATIONAL TEAM RECORDS AND RECORD SEQUENCES

Records			Sequence records					
Victory	9-0	BOL 1927	Wins	7	1941-42, 1980-81	Clean sheets	6	1969-1970
Defeat	0-6	ARG 1902	Defeats	5	1916	Goals scored	20	1953-1956
Player Caps	79	Rodolfo Rodríguez	Undefeated	14	1967-1968	Without goal	4	1925, 1968. 1976
Player Goals	31	Héctor Scarone	Without win	9	1986	Goals against	18	1961-1963

ARG

BRA

Salto

Paysandu

Las Piedras

Montevideo   Ciudad de la Costa

ATLANTIC OCEAN

MAJOR CITIES/TOWNS

Population '000

1	Montevideo	1 272
2	Salto	101
3	Ciudad de la Costa	91
4	Paysandu	73
5	Las Piedras	70
6	Rivera	65
7	Maldonado	57
8	Tacuarembó	53
9	Melo	51
10	Mercedes	43
11	Artigas	42
12	Minas	38
13	San José	36
14	Durazno	34
15	Florida	32
16	Treinta y Tres	25
17	Rocha	25
18	San Carlos	25
19	Pando	24
20	Fray Bentos	23
21	Colonia	21
22	Trinidad	21
23	El Pinar	20
24	La Paz	20

ORIENTAL REPUBLIC OF URUGUAY; REPUBLICA ORIENTAL DEL URUGUAY

Capital	Montevideo	Language	Spanish			Independence	1828
Population	3 460 607	Area	176 220 km²	Density	19 per km²	% in cities	90%
GDP per cap	$12 800	Dailling code	+598	Internet	.uy	GMT + / -	-3

MEDALS TABLE

		Overall			League			Sth Am			City	Stadium	Cap'ty	DoF
		G	S	B	G	S	B	G	S	B				
1	CA Peñarol	52	44	18	47	38	5	5	6	13	Montevideo	Estadio Centenario	65 000	1891
2	Club Nacional de Football	44	44	21	41	40	12	3	4	9	Montevideo	Parque Central	20 000	1899
3	Defensor Sporting	4	5	8	4	5	8				Montevideo	Luis Franzini	18 000	1913
4	Montevideo Wanderers	4	4	14	4	6	14				Montevideo	Parque Alfredo Victor Viera	12 000	1902
5	River Plate	4	1	1	4	1	1				Montevideo			1902-20
6	Danubio	3	4	5	3	4	4			1	Montevideo	Jardines del Hipodromo	16 000	1932
7	Rampla Juniors	1	5	13	1	5	14				Montevideo	Estadio Olimpico	9 500	1914
8	Bella Vista	1	1	2	1	1	2				Montevideo	Jose Nasazzi	15 000	1920
9	Central Español	1		4	1		4				Montevideo	Parque Palermo	9 000	1905
10	Progreso	1			1						Montevideo	Parque Abraham Paladino	8 000	1917
11	Cerro		1	6		1	6				Montevideo	Luis Tróccoli	30 000	1922
12	Universal		1	4		1	4							
13	CA River Plate		1	2		1	2				Montevideo	Federico Saroldi	12 000	1932
14	Albion		1	1		1	1							
15	Rocha	1			1						Rocha	Mario Sobrero	8 000	1999
16	Fénix			3			3				Montevideo	Parque Capurro	10 000	1916
	Liverpool			3			3				Montevideo	Estadio Belvedere	9 500	1915

URUGUAY LEAGUE RECORD

Year	Winners	Score	Runners-up
1995	Peñarol	1-0 1-2 3-1	Nacional
1996	Peñarol	1-0 1-1	Nacional
1997	Peñarol	1-0 3-0	Defensor Sporting
1998	Nacional	†	
1999	Peñarol	1-1 1-1 2-1	Nacional
2000	Nacional	1-0 1-1	Peñarol
2001	Nacional	2-2 2-1	Danubio
2002	Nacional	2-1 2-1	Danubio
2003	Peñarol	1-0	Nacional
2004	Danubio	1-0	Nacional
2005	Nacional	w-o	Defensor Sporting
2006	Nacional	4-1 2-0	Rocha
2007	Danubio	†	Peñarol
2008	Defensor Sporting	†	

† Automatic champions

URUGUAY 2007–08

PRIMERA DIVISION PROFESSIONAL TABLA ANUAL

	Pl	W	D	L	F	A	Pts	Rel	Defensor	River Plate	Nacional	Peñarol	Rampla Jun	Danubio	Wanderers	Liverpool	Juventud	Cerro	Tacuarembó	Fénix	C Español	Progreso	Miramar	Bella Vista
Defensor	30	21	3	6	67	37	66	125		4-3	1-0	0-1	2-1	0-0	4-0	3-5	2-0	4-0	2-0	3-0	3-3	3-0	5-3	2-1
River Plate	30	19	4	7	85	44	61	97	5-1		3-6	2-2	7-0	1-3	5-1	3-2	2-0	0-0	5-0	1-1	3-0	6-0	2-2	2-0
Nacional	30	16	7	7	52	33	55	100	4-0	3-1		1-1	1-0	0-2	2-0	0-0	2-0	1-2	3-1	1-0	1-3	1-2	2-2	
Peñarol	30	16	6	8	61	38	54	118	0-2	3-6	4-2		5-0	2-1	0-1	4-0	3-2	3-0	1-1	2-1	2-1	0-3	1-0	6-0
Rampla Juniors	30	13	8	9	34	44	47	79	1-6	3-1	1-0	3-2		0-0	1-3	2-0	2-1	1-1	1-3	0-0	1-0	4-3	0-0	1-0
Danubio	30	13	7	10	58	47	46	112	4-3	1-5	1-3	3-1	2-2		4-1	4-3	1-2	1-2	1-3	2-2	3-1	9-1	3-0	2-2
Wanderers	30	13	5	12	44	51	44	97	1-2	1-2	1-3	1-0	1-2	2-1		2-0	1-1	1-0	1-1	1-1	2-3	2-1	2-1	0-2
Liverpool	30	12	7	11	55	45	43	85	0-0	0-2	1-1	4-3	0-1	0-0	1-1		1-1	0-1	0-0	4-0	3-0	1-2	2-0	2-2
Juventud Las Piedras	30	10	10	10	30	29	40	80	0-2	3-1	1-2	1-1	0-0	0-1	1-1	1-2		0-0	2-0	1-1	3-1	3-1	2-0	1-2
Cerro	30	9	10	11	30	38	37	74	1-2	1-4	1-1	0-0	0-1	2-0	4-3	1-5	0-0		0-2	1-1	0-0	1-0	2-0	2-3
Tacuarembó	30	9	7	14	33	50	34	70	1-0	2-3	1-4	1-2	1-0	0-2	2-0	1-4	0-1	0-1		1-1	3-1	1-3	1-0	3-2
Fénix	30	7	11	12	33	39	32	64	6-4	1-3	1-2	1-1	0-0	2-0	0-2	2-3	0-0	0-1	2-0		1-2	1-2	2-0	2-0
Central Español	30	9	5	16	38	52	32	66	1-2	3-1	1-1	0-4	1-2	2-0	0-1	1-3	2-0	2-1	1-1	2-1		3-0	1-3	2-0
Progreso	30	9	2	19	37	68	29	60	0-2	0-3	0-1	0-3	2-2	2-3	2-3	1-4	0-1	1-1	2-1	1-4	3-1		1-0	0-2
Miramar Misiones	30	8	3	19	27	47	27	61	0-2	1-3	0-1	0-2	0-2	1-4	2-4	1-0	0-1	1-1	4-0	0-1	3-1	1-0		1-0
Bella Vista	30	6	5	19	31	52	23	74	1-2	0-1	0-1	2-3	0-0	3-0	1-2	3-5	0-1	0-3	1-1	0-1	1-0	1-3	0-1	

18/08/2007 - 1/06/2008 • † Qualified for the Copa Libertadores • Relegation calculated over two seasons (promoted clubs have season total doubled)
Apertura matches are in the shaded boxes • Match in bold awarded (originally 3-2)
Top scorers: Richard Porta, River Plate 19; Cristian Stuani, Danubio 19; Bruno Fornaroli, Nacional 15

URUGUAY 2007–08 TORNEO APERTURA

	Pl	W	D	L	F	A	Pts
Defensor	15	11	2	2	26	10	35
Danubio	15	9	4	2	34	14	31
Rampla Juniors	15	9	4	2	21	12	31
River Plate	15	7	3	5	37	27	24
Nacional	15	6	6	3	19	12	24
Juventud Las Piedras	15	6	6	3	16	10	24
Cerro	15	5	8	2	16	14	23
Wanderers	15	6	3	6	24	26	21
Fénix	15	4	8	3	14	14	20
Central Español	15	5	3	7	22	28	18
Peñarol	15	4	5	6	21	23	17
Tacuarembó	15	4	5	6	15	21	17
Miramar Misiones	15	4	1	10	9	20	13
Liverpool	15	3	3	9	19	24	12
Progreso	15	3	2	10	14	38	11
Bella Vista	15	1	3	11	14	28	6

18/08/2007 - 8/12/2007

URUGUAY 2007–08 TORNEO CLAUSURA

	Pl	W	D	L	F	A	Pts
Peñarol	15	12	1	2	40	15	37
River Plate	15	12	1	2	48	17	37
Defensor	15	10	1	4	41	26	31
Liverpool	15	9	4	2	35	21	31
Nacional	15	10	1	4	33	21	31
Wanderers	15	7	2	6	20	25	23
Progreso	15	6	0	9	23	30	18
Bella Vista	15	5	2	8	17	24	17
Tacuarembó	15	5	2	8	18	29	17
Juventud Las Piedras	15	4	4	7	14	19	16
Rampla Juniors	15	4	4	7	13	32	16
Danubio	15	4	3	8	24	33	15
Central Español	15	4	2	9	16	24	14
Miramar Misiones	15	4	2	9	18	27	14
Cerro	15	4	2	9	14	25	14
Fénix	15	3	3	9	19	25	12

16/02/2008 - 1/06/2008 • Play-off: Peñarol 5-3 River Plate

CHAMPIONSHIP FINAL SERIES

1st leg. Centenario, Montevideo, 22-06-2008, Ref: Liber Prudente

Peñarol	1	Aguirregaray [43]
Defensor Sporting	2	Lamas [7], Gaglianone [20p]

Peñarol - Nicolás Ruiz - Matias Aguirregaray•, Gerardo Alcoba•, Matias Manrique•, Federico Pérez - Mario Alvarez (Omar Pérez 77), Marcel Román (José Franco 51), Antonio Pacheco•••90, Rúben Oliveira (Fernando Correa 66) - Fabián Estoyanoff, Carlos Bueno•
Defensor - Martin Silva• - Pablo Pintos, Mario Risso, Andrés Lamas, Sebastián Ariosa - Pablo Daniel Gaglianone•, Julio Marchant•, Miguel Amado• - Miguel Mercado (Diego de Souza 62), Tabaré Viudez (William Ferreira 74), Sebastián Fernández• (Regís 89)

2nd leg. Centenario, Montevideo, 22-06-2008, Att: 15 000, Ref: Liber Prudente

Defensor Sporting	0
Peñarol	0

Defensor - Martin Silva - Pablo Pintos•, Mario Risso, Andrés Lamas•, Miguel Amado - Pablo Daniel Gaglianone, Julio Marchant, Sebastián Ariosa•, Miguel Mercado (William Ferreira 69) - Tabaré Viudez (Diego de Souza 46), Sebastián Fernández (Regís 89)
Peñarol - Nicolás Ruiz - Matias Aguirregaray•, Gerardo Alcoba•, Darío Rodríguez•, Maximiliano Arias• (Fernando Correa 61•90) - Mario Alvarez (José Franco 46), Omar Pérez (Marcel Román 49), Rúben Oliveira, Diego Rodríguez• - Fabián Estoyanoff, Carlos Bueno•

The above two ties were technically the championship semi-finals - played between the winners of the Apertura and Clausura. By beating Peñarol 2-1 on aggregate, Defensor qualified to meet the winners of the Tabla Anual, which they had won, in the final. Defensor were declared champions

USA – UNITED STATES OF AMERICA

NATIONAL TEAM RECORD
JULY 10TH 2006 TO JULY 12TH 2010

PL	W	D	L	F	A	%
25	15	3	7	44	23	66

David Beckham's arrival in America may have been the story of the year for football in the country, but there was very little that he could do to revive the fortunes of his LA Galaxy team in the 2007 MLS season. They had a miserable time, failing to qualify for the play-offs, which given that eight of the 13 teams qualify, was a major disaster. Once again Houston Dynamo were the surprise team. Only admitted into the league in 2006 they met New England Revolution in the showpiece MLS Cup Final for the second year running and came from behind to win 2-1, with Dwayne Rosario scoring the winner to secure back-to-back MLS Cups for the club. Spare a thought for New England, however. It was their fourth appearance in the final and they have yet to win any of them, although six weeks before the final they had won their first trophy by winning the US Open Cup. One of Houston's most notable fans is boxing sensation Oscar de la Hoya and in February 2008 he bought a 25 percent stake in the club, promising to become actively involved when he retires in 2009. The 2007 season was the 12th in MLS history and for much of that time it has been relatively inward looking, focusing its attention on establishing its position within the United States and to

INTERNATIONAL HONOURS
FIFA Women's World Cup 1991 1999   Women's Olympic Gold 1996 2004   FIFA U-19 Women's World Championship 2002
Qualified for the FIFA World Cup 1930 1934 1950 1990 1994 1998 2002 2006
CONCACAF Gold Cup 1991 2002 2005   CONCACAF Women's Gold Cup 1991 1993 1994 2000 2002
Panamerican Games 1991   CONCACAF U-17 1983 1992
CONCACAF Champions Cup DC United 1998 Los Angeles Galaxy 2000

that end it has been a great success. In 2007 it was the 12th most attended league in the world for which figures are available with an average of 16,770 fans attending each match. CONCACAF would now like the Americans to broaden their horizons by taking a more active role in continental competition and they hope that the launch of the CONCACAF Champions League will do just that. Along with Mexico, American clubs have been allocated two spaces in the group stage of the new tournament with those slots going to the MLS Cup winner Houston and the Regular Season Winner DC United. That could increase to four if US Open Cup winner New England and the Regular Season runner-up Chivas USA make it through a preliminary round. It is hoped that with more teams playing more games that standards will rise and that the tournament will attain a status that the previous CONCACAF Champions' Cup failed to do. On offer of course is the prize of a place at the FIFA Club World Cup. The US national team had a relatively quiet year, comfortably beating Barbados in a preliminary 2010 FIFA World Cup qualifying round to set up the enticing prospect of a first visit to Havana to play Cuba in the first group stage of the qualifiers.

US Soccer Federation (USSF)
US Soccer House, 1801 S. Prairie Avenue, Chicago IL 60616, USA
Tel +1 312 8081300   Fax +1 312 8081301
communications@ussoccer.org   www.ussoccer.com
President: GULATI Sunil   General Secretary: FLYNN Dan
Vice-President: EDWARDS Mike   Treasurer: GOAZIOU Bill   Media Officer: MOORHOUSE Jim
Men's Coach: BRADLEY Bob   Women's Coach: SUNDHAGE Pia
USSF formed: 1913   CONCACAF: 1961   FIFA: 1914
White shirts with a red and blue panel on the left, Blue shorts, White socks

RECENT INTERNATIONAL MATCHES PLAYED BY THE USA

2006	Opponents	Score		Venue	Comp	Scorers	Att	Referee
23-05	Morocco	L	0-1	Nashville	Fr		26 141	Navarro CAN
26-05	Venezuela	W	2-0	Cleveland	Fr	Ching [36], Dempsey [69]	29 745	Morales MEX
28-05	Latvia	W	1-0	Hartford	Fr	McBride [43]	24 636	Dipiero CAN
12-06	Czech Republic	L	0-3	Gelsenkirchen	WCr1		52 000	Amarilla PAR
17-06	Italy	D	1-1	Kaiserslautern	WCr1	OG [27]	46 000	Larrionda URU
22-06	Ghana	L	1-2	Nuremberg	WCr1	Dempsey [43]	41 000	Merk GER
2007								
7-02	Mexico	W	2-0	Glendale	Fr	Conrad [52], Donovan [91+]	62 462	Navarro CAN
25-03	Ecuador	W	3-1	Tampa	Fr	Donovan 3 [1 66 67]	31 547	Petrescu CAN
28-03	Guatemala	D	0-0	Frisco	Fr		10 932	Archundia MEX
2-06	China PR	W	4-1	San Jose	Fr	Beasley [10p], Feilhaber [28], Dempsey [75], Onyewu [79]	20 821	Guajardo MEX
7-06	Guatemala	W	1-0	Carson	GCr1	Dempsey [26]	21 334	Pineda HON
9-06	Trinidad and Tobago	W	2-0	Carson	GCr1	Ching [29], Johnson [54]	27 000	Moreno PAN
12-06	El Salvador	W	4-0	Foxboro	GCr1	Beasley 2 [34 89], Donovan [45p], Twellman [72]	26 523	Archundia MEX
16-06	Panama	W	2-1	Foxboro	GCqf	Donovan [60p], Bocanegra [62]	22 412	Brizan TRI
21-06	Canada	W	2-1	Chicago	GCsf	Hejduk [39], Donovan [45p]	50 760	Archundia MEX
24-06	Mexico	W	2-1	Chicago	GCf	Donovan [62p], Feilhaber [73]	60 000	Batres GUA
28-06	Argentina	L	1-4	Maracaibo	CAr1	Johnson [9p]	34 500	Chandia CHI
2-07	Paraguay	L	1-3	Barinas	CAr1	Clark [40]	23 000	Rivera PER
5-07	Colombia	L	0-1	Barquisimeto	CAr1		37 000	Andarcia VEN
22-08	Sweden	L	0-1	Gothenburg	Fr		20 648	Blom NED
9-09	Brazil	L	2-4	Chicago	Fr	Bocanegra [21], Dempsey [73]	43 543	Archundia MEX
17-10	Switzerland	W	1-0	Basel	Fr	Bradley [86]	16 500	De Bleckere BEL
17-11	South Africa	W	1-0	Johannesburg	Fr	Cherundolo [27]		Maillet SEY
2008								
19-01	Sweden	W	2-0	Carson	Fr	Robinson [15], Donovan [48p]	14 878	Navarro CAN
6-02	Mexico	D	2-2	Houston	Fr	Onyewu [30], Altidore [40]	70 103	Batres GUA
26-03	Poland	W	3-0	Krakow	Fr	Bocanegra [12], Onyewu [35], Lewis [73]	21 000	Hermansen DEN
28-05	England	L	0-2	London	Fr		71 233	Vassaras GRE
4-06	Spain	L	0-1	Santander	Fr		14 232	Jareci ALB
8-06	Argentina	D	0-0	New Jersey	Fr		78 682	Aguilar SLV
15-06	Barbados	W	8-0	Carson	WCq	Dempsey 2 [1 62], Bradley [12], Ching 2 [20 88], Donovan [58], Johnson [82], Ferguson OG [85]	11 500	Rodriguez MEX
22-06	Barbados	W	1-0	Bridgetown	WCq	Lewis [21]	2 000	Moreno PAN

Fr = Friendly match • GC = CONCACAF Gold Cup • CA = Copa América • WC = FIFA World Cup
q = qualifier • r1 = first round group • qf = quarter-final • sf = semi-final • 3p = third place play-off • f = final

USA NATIONAL TEAM PLAYERS

	Player		Ap	G	Club	Date of Birth		Player		Ap	G	Club	Date of Birth
1	Chris Seitz	GK	0	0	Real Salt Lake	2 03 1987	12	John Thorrington	MF	2	0	Chicago Fire	17 10 1979
2	Dan Califf	DF	20	1	Midtjylland	17 03 1980	13	Chad Barrett	FW	1	0	Chicago Fire	30 04 1985
3	Carlos Bocanegra	DF	58	9	Rennes	25 05 1979	14	Chris Rolfe	FW	8	0	Chicago Fire	17 01 1983
4	Michael Bradley	MF	21	2	Heerenveen	31 07 1987	15	Jay DeMerit	DF	9	0	Watford	4 12 1979
5	Oguchi Onyewu	DF	34	4	Standard Liège	13 05 1982	16	Freddy Adu	FW	9	0	Benfica	2 06 1989
6	Drew Moor	DF	5	0	FC Dallas	15 01 1984	17	DaMarcus Beasley	MF	77	15	Rangers	24 05 1982
7	Eddie Lewis	MF	80	10	Derby County	17 05 1974	18	Brad Guzan	GK	9	0	Chivas USA	9 09 1984
8	Danny Szetela	MF	2	0	Brescia	17 06 1987		**Selected others**					
9	Brek Shea	FW	0	0	FC Dallas	20 02 1990		Tim Howard	GK	31	0	Everton	6 03 1979
10	Sacha Kljestan	MF	7	0	Chivas USA	9 09 1985		Frankie Hejduk	DF	78	6	Columbus Crew	5 08 1974
11	Heath Pearce	DF	16	0	Hansa Rostock	13 08 1984		Pablo Mastroeni	MF	60	0	Colorado Rapids	26 08 1976

The American squad for the June 22, 2008 World Cup qualifier
Landon Donovan   FW   101   36   LA Galaxy   4 03 1982

USA NATIONAL TEAM RECORDS AND RECORD SEQUENCES

Records			Sequence records					
Victory	8-1	CAY 1993	Wins	7	2007	Clean sheets	5	2003
Defeat	0-11	NOR 1948	Defeats	13	1973-1975	Goals scored	23	2004-2005
Player Caps	164	Cobi Jones	Undefeated	16	2004-2005	Without goal	5	1990-1991
Player Goals	36	Landon Donovan	Without win	16	1973-1976	Goals against	14	1973-1976

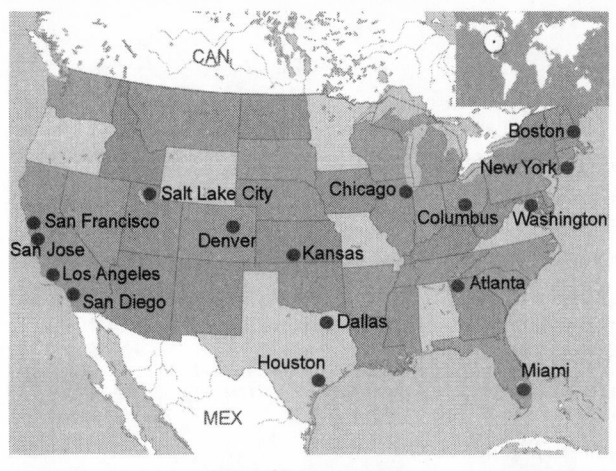

MAJOR CITIES/TOWNS
Population '000

1	New York	22 747
2	Los Angeles	17 989
3	Chicago	9 510
4	Washington	8 197
5	San Francisco	7 719
6	Philadelphia	6 268
7	Dallas	6 175
8	Boston	6 167
9	Detroit	5 925
10	Houston	5 406
11	Atlanta	4 973
12	San Diego	4 922
13	Miami	4 825
14	Phoenix	4 026
15	Seattle	3 852
16	Minneapolis	3 237
17	Cleveland	2 954
18	Denver	2 722
19	Tampa	2 653
20	Saint Louis	2 632
21	Kansas City	1 885
22	Salt Lake City	1 793
23	Columbus	1 656
24	Rochester	1 107

UNITED STATES OF AMERICA

Capital	Washington DC	Language	English, Spanish			Independence	1776
Population	301 139 947	Area	9 631 418 km²	Density	30 per km²	% in cities	76%
GDP per cap	$37 800	Dailling code	+1	Internet	.us	GMT +/-	-6/11

MEDALS TABLE

		Overall			Lge		Cup		CON'CAF			City	Stadium	Cap'ty	DoF
		G	S	B	G	S	G	S	G	S	B				
1	DC United	6	2	6	4	1	1	1	1		6	Washington	RFK Memorial	56 454	1995
2	Los Angeles Galaxy	5	6		2	3	2	2	1	1		Carson/Los Angeles	Home Depot Centre	27 000	1995
3	Chicago Fire	5	3	2	1	2	4	1			2	Chicago	Soldier Field	20 000	1997
4	Kansas City Wizards	2	1	1	1	1	1				1	Kansas City	Arrowhead	79 451	1995
5	Houston Dynamo	2		2	2						2	Houston	Robertson Stadium	33 000	2005
6	San Jose Earthquakes	2			2							San Jose	Spartan Stadium	26 000	1995-'05
7	New England Revolution	1	5		4		1	1				Foxboro/Boston	Gillette Stadium	68 756	1995
8	FC Dallas	1	2				1	2				Dallas	Pizza Hut Park	21 193	1996
9	Columbus Crew	1	1				1	1				Columbus	Crew Stadium	22 555	1994
	Rochester Raging Rhinos	1	1				1	1				Rochester	PAETEC Park	13 500	1996
11	Colorado Rapids		2		1		1					Denver	Dick's Sporting Goods Park	18 086	1995
12	Miami Fusion	1					1					Fort Lauderdale	Lockhart Stadium	20 450	1998-'01
	New York Red Bull	1										New York	Giants Stadium	80 242	1995
14	Chivas USA											Carson/Los Angeles	Home Depot Centre	27 000	2004
	Real Salt Lake											Salt Lake	Rice-Eccles	46 500	2004
	Toronto FC											Toronto	BMO Field	20 148	2006
	Tampa Bay Mutiny											Tampa	Raymond James Stadium	66 321	1996-'01

RECENT LEAGUE AND CUP RECORD

	MLS				Cup		
Year	Champions	Score	Runners-up		Winners	Score	Runners-up
1996	DC United	3-2	Los Angeles Galaxy		DC United	3-0	Rochester Rhinos
1997	DC United	2-1	Colorado Rapids		Dallas Burn	0-0 5-3p	DC United
1998	Chicago Fire	2-0	DC United		Chicago Fire	2-1	Columbus Crew
1999	DC United	2-0	Los Angeles Galaxy		Rochester Rhinos	2-0	Colorado Rapids
2000	Kansas City Wizards	1-0	Chicago Fire		Chicago Fire	2-1	Miami Fusion
2001	San Jose Earthquakes	2-1	Los Angeles Galaxy		Los Angeles Galaxy	2-1	New England Revolution
2002	Los Angeles Galaxy	1-0	New England Revolution		Columbus Crew	1-0	Los Angeles Galaxy
2003	San Jose Earthquakes	4-2	Chicago Fire		Chicago Fire	1-0	MetroStars
2004	DC United	3-2	Kansas City Wizards		Kansas City Wizards	1-0	Chicago Fire
2005	Los Angeles Galaxy	1-0	New England Revolution		Los Angeles Galaxy	1-0	FC Dallas
2006	Houston Dynamo	0-0 4-3p	New England Revolution		Chicago Fire	3-1	Los Angeles Galaxy
2007	Houston Dynamo	2-1	New England Revolution		New England Revolution	3-2	FC Dallas

USA 2007

MAJOR LEAGUE SOCCER — REGULAR SEASON

Eastern Conference	Pl	W	D	L	F	A	Pts	DC United	NE Revs	NY Red Bull	Chicago Fire	KC Wizards	C'bus Crew	Toronto	Chivas USA	H Dynamo	FC Dallas	C Rapids	LA Galaxy	Real SL
DC United †	30	16	7	7	56	34	55		1-1	4-2	3-1	3-1 0-0	2-4	2-3	4-1	2-1	2-1	3-3	4-1	1-0 2-1
New England Revs †	30	14	8	8	51	43	50	0-3		2-1	3-1	3-4 2-0 3-3 2-3 4-0 3-0	1-1	3-3	4-2	1-0	1-0	0-0		
New York Red Bulls †	30	12	7	11	47	45	43	1-0	0-1 2-2		3-0 1-0 3-3 2-1	4-0	3-0	0-2	1-0	3-0	0-1	5-4	2-2	
Chicago Fire †	30	10	10	10	31	36	40	1-1	1-0 2-1	2-2		2-1 2-0 3-2 0-0	1-1	0-1	0-4	1-2	0-0	1-0	0-0	
Kansas City Wizards †	30	11	7	12	45	45	40	0-1 1-1	0-1	3-2	3-2		1-0 3-2 3-0 1-1	3-2	0-1	1-2	2-2	0-1	1-0	
Columbus Crew	30	9	10	11	39	44	37	1-0 0-2	2-2	0-0 1-0	0-1	2-1		2-2 2-0	1-1	1-2	1-3	1-1	1-2	2-0
Toronto FC	30	6	7	17	25	49	25	1-2 0-1	2-2	1-2 2-1	3-1 0-3	0-1	1-2		0-2	1-0	4-0	2-1	0-0	0-0

Western Conference	Pl	W	D	L	F	A	Pts	DC United	NE Revs	NY Red Bull	Chicago Fire	KC Wizards	C'bus Crew	Toronto	Chivas USA	H Dynamo	FC Dallas	C Rapids	LA Galaxy	Real SL
Chivas USA †	30	15	8	7	46	28	53	2-2	2-0	3-0	1-1	2-1	2-1	2-0		0-0	2-0	2-0 1-2	1-1 3-0	4-0 1-0
Houston Dynamo †	30	15	7	8	43	23	52	1-0	0-1	4-0	0-1	1-1	1-1	0-0	1-0 4-0		2-1 1-0	2-1	0-0 1-2	4-3
FC Dallas †	30	13	5	12	37	44	44	0-4	0-1	0-1	1-1	0-2	3-2	2-0	2-0 0-0 0-3			3-1 1-0	3-1	2-1
Colorado Rapids	30	9	8	13	29	34	35	2-1	3-0	0-1	1-1	1-1	1-0	0-1	1-2		1-0 1-1		1-0 3-0	1-1 0-1
Los Angeles Galaxy	30	9	7	14	38	48	34	0-0	2-3	1-1	2-0	2-2	2-3	2-1	3-1 0-3	1-3	1-2 2-1	3-1		3-2 1-2
Real Salt Lake	30	6	9	15	31	45	27	2-1	1-2	3-3	0-2	3-1	0-0	1-2	2-3	1-0 0-1 2-2 0-1 0-2 1-0	2-2			

7/04/2007 - 21/10/2007 • † Qualified for the play-offs
Top scorers: Luciano EMILIO, DC United 20; Juan Pablo ANGEL, New York 19

MLS PLAY-OFFS 2007

Conference semi–finals			Conference finals		MLS Cup	
Houston Dynamo	0	4				
FC Dallas *	1	1	Houston Dynamo *	2		
Chivas USA	0	0	Kansas City Wizards	0		
Kansas City Wizards *	1	0			Houston Dynamo	2
Chicago Fire *	1	2			New England Revolution	1
DC United	0	2	Chicago Fire	0		
New York Red Bulls *	0	0	New England Revolution*	1		
New England Revolution	0	1	* Home team/home team in the first leg			

MLS CUP 2007

RFK Stadium, Washington, 18-11-2007, Att: 39 859, Ref: Alex Prus

Houston Dynamo 2 Ngwenya [61], De Rosario [74]
New England Revolution 1 Twellman [20]

Houston - Pat Onstad - Craig Waibel, Ryan Cochrane, Eddie Robinson, Wade Barrett, Brian Mullen, Dwayne De Rosario, Richard Mulrooney, Brad Davis, Nate Jaqua, Joseph Ngwenya (Stuart Holden 80). Tr: Dominic Kinnear
Revs - Matt Reis - Jay Heaps, Michael Parkhurst, Avery John, Wells Thompson, Shalrie Joseph, Jeff Larentowicz, Steve Ralston (Andy Dorman 78), Khano Smith, Pat Noonan, Taylor Twellman. Tr: Steve Nichol

LAMAR HUNT US OPEN CUP 2007

Second Round		Third Round		Quarter-finals		Semi-finals		Final	
		New England Revolution	4						
Western Mass Pioneers	1	Rochester Raging Rhinos *	2						
Rochester Raging Rhinos *	2			**New England Revolution** *	2				
		DC United	0	Harrisburg City Islanders	1				
Ocean City Barons *	1	**Harrisburg City Islanders** *	1			**New England Revoltion** *	2		
Harrisburg City Islanders	2					Carolina RailHawks	1		
Richmond Kickers *	2	**Richmond Kickers** *	1						
Cleveland City Stars	1	Los Angeles Galaxy	0	Richmond Kickers	0			**New England Revoltion**	3
				Carolina RailHawks *	1			FC Dallas	2
		Chicago Fire	0						
Bavarian SC	0	**Carolina RailHawks** *	1						
Carolina RailHawks *	4								
Seattle Sounders *	2	**Seattle Sounders** *	3						
Portland Timbers	1	Chivas USA	1	**Seattle Sounders** *	5				
				Colorado Rapids	0	Seattle Sounders *	1		
California Victory	1	California Victory	1			**FC Dallas**	2		
Minnesota Thunder *	0	**Colorado Rapids** *	3						
Charleston Battery *	1	**Charleston Battery** *	1	Charleston Battery *	1				
El Paso Patriots	0	Houston Dynamo	0	**FC Dallas**	2				
Atlanta Silverbacks *	1	Atlanta Silverbacks	1 3p						
Charlotte Eagles	0	**FC Dallas** *	1 4p						

* Home team

CUP FINAL

Pizza Hut Park, Frisco, Dallas
3-10-2007, Att: 10 618. Ref: Alex Prus
Scorers - Noonan 21, Twellman 41, Thompson 57
for NE Revs; Alvarez 30, Thompson 64 for Dallas

Revs - Matt REIS - Jay HEAPS, Michael PARKHURST,
James RILEY*, Andy DORMAN, Jeff LARENTOWICZ*,
Steve RALSTON, Khano SMITH, Wells THOMPSON
(Adam CRISTMAN 78), Pat NOONAN, Taylor TWELLMAN.
Tr: Steve NICOL

Dallas - Dario SALA - David WAGENFUHR
(Kenny COOPER 76), Clarence GOODSON, Adrian
SERIOUX, Drew MOOR, Dax McCARTY, Pablo RICCHETTI
(Alex YI 46) (Abe THOMPSON 63), Juan TOJA, Dominic
ODURO, Carlos RUIZ, Arturo ALVAREZ. Tr: Steve MORROW

USA 2007
USL FIRST DIVISION (2)

	Pl	W	D	L	F	A	Pts
Seattle Sounders ‡	28	16	6	6	37	23	54
Portland Timbers ‡	28	14	9	5	32	18	51
Montreal Impact ‡	28	14	8	6	32	21	50
Atlanta Silverbacks ‡	28	12	7	9	40	30	43
Rochester Rhinos ‡	28	12	6	10	39	36	42
Puerto Rico Islanders ‡	28	10	10	8	35	34	40
Vancouver Whitecaps ‡	28	9	12	7	27	24	39
Carolina RailHawks ‡	28	8	8	12	24	34	32
Miami FC Blues	28	9	4	15	31	41	31
Charleston Battery	28	8	6	14	32	39	30
Minnesota Thunder	28	5	11	12	32	35	26
California Victory	28	4	7	17	17	43	19

‡ Qualified for the play-offs

USA 2007
USL SECOND DIVISION (3)

	Pl	W	D	L	F	A	Pts
Richmond Kickers ‡	20	12	5	3	37	15	41
Cleveland City Stars ‡	20	10	9	1	31	14	39
Harrisburg City Isl's ‡	20	11	5	4	25	15	38
Charlotte Eagles ‡	20	11	2	7	40	29	35
C. Palace Baltimore	20	9	5	6	27	20	32
Western Mass Pioneers	20	7	6	7	25	26	27
Wilmington H'heads	20	4	7	9	22	30	19
Cincinnati Kings	20	4	5	11	29	41	17
N. Hampshire Ph'toms	20	3	5	12	16	34	13
Bermuda Hogges	20	3	3	14	16	45	12

‡ Qualified for the play-offs

USL FIRST DIVISION PLAY-OFFS

Quarter-finals: Montreal 3-2 0-3 **Puerto Rico**; Rochester 1-2 1-1 **Atlanta**; **Seattle** 2-0 1-0 Carolina; Vancouver 1-0 0-3 **Portland**
Semi-finals: Portland 1-1 0-0 1-3p **Atlanta**; **Seattle** 2-1 1-1 Puerto Rico
Final: **Seattle Sounders** 4-0 Atlanta Silverbacks

USL SECOND DIVISION PLAY-OFFS

Semi-finals: **Harrisburg** 1-0 Cleveland; **Richmond** 2-1 Charlotte
Final: **Harrisburg** 1-1 8-7p Richmond

CHICAGO FIRE 2007

Apr	7	NE Revs	W	1-0	Pause [4]	15 353
	15	C Rapids	D	1-1	Barrett [85]	12 110
	21	KC Wizards	W	2-1	Barrett [36], Rolfe [73p]	11 717
	29	H Dynamo	W	1-0	Rolfe [60]	13 392
May	6	NE Revs	L	1-3	Rolfe [45]	9 508
	12	Toronto FC	L	1-3	Rolfe [36]	20 000
	17	FC Dallas	L	1-2	Carr [73]	12 164
	24	NY Red Bulls	L	0-3		9 357
	27	Real SL	D	0-0		12 996
Jun	3	C'bus Crew	W	3-2	Curtin [25], Oliveira [61], Barrett [78]	10 115
	9	Chivas USA	L	0-1		20 407
	16	DC United	L	1-3	Monteiro [54]	20 161
	1	C Rapids	D	0-0		10 626
	4	LA Galaxy	L	0-2		24 333
Jul	7	Toronto FC	D	1-1	Barrett [70p]	13 080
	12	H Dynamo	L	0-4		20 034
	29	Toronto FC	W	3-0	Guerrero [37], Carr [58], Franks [75]	20 322
	4	C'bus Crew	D	0-0		20 358
Aug	18	Real SL	W	2-0	Blanco [43], Wanchope [78]	18 913
	22	KC Wizards	L	2-3	Barrett [45], Robinson [83]	12 468
	25	KC Wizards	W	2-0	Blanco [44], Carr [86]	18 453
	1	NY Red Bulls	L	0-1		13 219
	8	C'bus Crew	W	1-0	Wanchope [65]	19 983
Sept	15	NY Red Bulls	D	2-2	Blanco [54p], Segares [70]	20 586
	20	FC Dallas	D	1-1	Rolfe [56]	15 059
	23	DC United	D	1-1	Barrett [18]	20 079
	29	Chivas USA	D	1-1	Blanco [24]	27 000
Oct	6	NE Revs	W	2-1	Rolfe [45], Barrett [60]	20 014
	13	DC United	D	0-0		25 404
	21	LA Galaxy	W	1-0	Thorrington [93+]	21 374
	25	DC United	W	1-0	Rolfe [14]	17 834
Nov	1	DC United	D	2-2	Barrett [31], Rolfe [33]	19 438
	8	NE Revs	L	0-1		10 317

CHIVAS USA 2007

Apr	7	Toronto FC	W	2-0	Razov [35], Kljestan [88]	14 351
	14	H Dynamo	L	0-1		16 519
	21	Real SL	W	4-0	Galindo 2 [1 9], Razov [43], Taylor [89]	11 253
	28	LA Galaxy	L	1-3	Suarez [63]	27 000
May	6	DC United	L	1-2	Galindo [73]	14 267
	12	C'bus Crew	D	1-1	Razov [2]	12 545
	20	LA Galaxy	D	1-1	Galindo [35]	27 000
	26	FC Dallas	W	2-0	Galindo [51], Razov [92+]	8 756
Jun	9	Chicago F	W	1-0	Nagamura [79]	20 407
	16	C Rapids	W	2-0	Cooke OG [49], Galindo [63]	10 490
	21	H Dynamo	L	0-4		14 184
	30	NE Revs	W	2-0	Marsch [60], Galindo [89]	9 028
	4	FC Dallas	L	0-2		15 773
Jul	7	NE Revs	D	1-1	Suarez [5]	13 266
	14	C'bus Crew	W	2-1	Razov [19], Gaven OG [69]	10 214
	26	NY Red Bulls	W	2-0	Razov [38], Kljestan [87]	10 732
	29	KC Wizards	L	2-3	Bornstein [17], Cunliffe [55]	11 649
Aug	18	Toronto FC	W	2-0	Galindo [57], Kljestan [89]	20 178
	23	LA Galaxy	W	3-0	Galindo 2 [58 69], Mendoza [88]	27 000
	26	Real SL	W	1-0	Marsch [31]	11 217
Sept	6	DC United	D	2-2	Razov [31], Vaughn [60]	9 306
	9	NY Red Bulls	W	3-0	Galindo 2 [4 58], Razov [70p]	10 292
	13	LA Galaxy	W	3-0	Razov [23], Mendoza [88], Merlin [91+]	23 328
	16	C Rapids	D	1-1	Kljestan [13p]	14 503
	22	KC Wizards	W	2-1	Razov 2 [69 92+]	13 214
	29	Chicago F	D	1-1	Suarez [82p]	27 000
Oct	6	Real SL	W	3-2	Cunliffe 2 [22 54], Nagamura [58]	12 111
	11	FC Dallas	D	0-0		9 454
	14	C Rapids	L	1-2	Perez [78]	12 276
	20	H Dynamo	D	0-0		16 853
	27	KC Wizards	L	0-1		12 442
	3	KC Wizards	D	0-0		19 711

COLORADO RAPIDS 2007

Apr	7	DC United	W	2-1	Gomez [19], Brown [35]	18 086
	15	Chicago	D	1-1	Gomez [58]	12 110
	22	FC Dallas	L	1-3	Kirovski [34]	20 500
	30	Real SL	W	2-0	Brown [71], Beckerman [75]	14 173
May	5	Houston	L	1-3	Brown [5]	10 719
	10	Real SL	D	1-1	Stewart OG [4]	13 458
	13	NY Red Bulls	W	1-0	Hernandez [24]	7 802
	19	KC Wizards	D	1-1	Kirovski [45p]	14 577
	26	LA Galaxy	W	1-0	Gomez [71]	18 458
Jun	2	Toronto	L	1-2	Gomez [32]	20 195
	7	H Dynamo	L	1-2	Cancela [12p]	12 017
	16	Chivas USA	L	0-2		10 490
	23	FC Dallas	L	0-1		16 128
	28	DC United	L	1-4	Peterson [19]	14 982
Jul	1	Chicago F	D	0-0		10 626
	4	C'bus Crew	D	0-0		18 086
	8	NY Red Bulls	L	0-1		12 708
	22	KC Wizards	D	2-2	Kirovski [42p], Erpen [77]	7 101
Aug	4	FC Dallas	L	0-1		12 820
	11	H Dynamo	W	1-0	De Rosario OG [61]	18 024
	16	NE Revs	W	3-0	Kirovski 2 [10 41p], Cummings [76]	10 677
	26	LA Galaxy	W	3-0	Casey [26], Clark [34], Petke [43]	18 086
Sep	2	C'bus Crew	D	1-1	Casey [84]	16 036
	8	LA Galaxy	L	1-3	Ballouchy [89]	22 881
	16	Chivas USA	D	1-1	Clark [76]	14 503
	22	Real SL	L	0-1		14 089
	29	NE Revs	L	0-1		19 166
Oct	7	Toronto	W	1-0	Kirovski [44p]	10 832
	14	Chivas USA	W	2-1	Ihemelu [64], Cummings [90]	12 276
	20	Real SL	L	0-1		14 777

COLUMBUS CREW 2007

Apr	7	NY Red Bulls	D	0-0		13 782
	14	Real SL	D	0-0		16 157
	19	NE Revs	D	2-2	Grabavoy [8], Kamara [86]	13 290
	28	DC United	W	1-0	Hendrickson [28]	13 572
May	5	KC Wizards	L	0-1		7 426
	12	Chivas USA	D	1-1	Grabavoy [18]	12 545
	19	NY Red Bulls	L	0-4		10 321
	26	Toronto FC	D	2-2	Herron 2 [2 36]	11 755
Jun	3	Chicago F	L	2-3	Oughton [38], Marshall [84]	10 115
	10	H Dynamo	L	1-2	Moreno [25]	12 661
	16	NE Revs	D	3-3	Rogers [9], Schelotto [45], Moreno [85]	22 412
	20	KC Wizards	W	2-1	Gaven [56], Miglioranzi [61]	10 254
	23	LA Galaxy	W	3-2	Marshall [15], Grabavoy [58], Moreno [84]	20 109
	30	NY Red Bulls	W	1-0	Kamara [69]	11 435
Jul	4	C Rapids	D	0-0		18 086
	7	Real SL	W	2-0	Schelotto [76p], Gaven [80]	14 203
	14	Chivas USA	L	1-2	Miglioranzi [23]	10 214
	22	Toronto FC	W	2-0	Schelotto 2 [50 56]	13 479
	29	Chicago F	D	0-0		20 358
Aug	11	FC Dallas	L	2-3	Gonzalez [6], Herron [74p]	14 818
	18	DC United	L	0-2		21 639
	25	H Dynamo	D	1-1	Moreno [17]	14 351
Sept	2	C Rapids	D	1-1	Gaven [45]	16 036
	8	Chicago F	L	0-1		19 983
	15	KC Wizards	L	2-3	Moreno [65], Herron [67]	10 217
	22	Toronto FC	W	2-1	Garey [61], Thomas [83]	20 127
	30	LA Galaxy	L	1-2	Moreno [2]	
Oct	6	FC Dallas	L	1-3	Gaven [31]	19 517
	13	NE Revs	W	3-2	Gaven [61], Miglioranzi [77], Schelotto [86]	22 295
	20	DC United	W	3-2	Rogers 2 [21 91+], Moreno [66]	23 149

FC DALLAS 2007

Apr	7	Real SL	D	2-2	Cooper [19], Ruiz [94+]	18 678
	12	LA Galaxy	W	2-1	Ruiz [35p], Cooper [43]	23 596
	15	NY Red Bulls	L	0-3		8 865
	22	C Rapids	W	3-1	Nunez 2 [29 78], Oduro [93+]	20 500
	26	NY Red Bulls	L	0-1		14 087
	29	NE Revs	L	0-1		9 165
May	12	KC Wizards	W	2-1	Cooper [19], Toja [45]	10 141
	17	Chicago F	W	2-1	Cooper [24p], Toja [60]	12 164
	20	Real SL	W	2-1	Alvarez [26], Gbandi [82]	16 576
	26	Chivas USA	L	0-2		8 756
Jun	3	H Dynamo	L	1-2	Thompson [32]	13 199
	9	LA Galaxy	W	3-1	Toja [24], Thompson [54p], Moor [73]	14 640
	14	Real SL	W	1-0	Oduro [93+]	16 278
	17	Toronto	L	0-4		20 156
	23	C Rapids	W	1-0	Toja [62]	16 128
	30	H Dynamo	D	0-0		13 887
Jul	4	Chivas USA	W	2-1	Nunez [41], Oduro [86]	15 773
	14	DC United	D	3-3	Ruiz [51], Toja 2 [71 81]	20 952
	4	C Rapids	W	1-0	Moor [31]	12 820
Aug	11	C'bus Crew	W	3-2	Alvarez [60], Ruiz [80], Goodson [92+]	14 818
	19	H Dynamo	L	0-1		19 501
	1	DC United	L	0-4		15 747
	8	Toronto	W	2-0	Denilson [36p], Thompson [87p]	16 790
Sep	15	NE Revs	L	2-4	Ruiz 2 [35 84]	15 289
	20	Chicago F	D	1-1	Ruiz [93+]	15 059
	23	LA Galaxy	L	1-2	McCarty [11]	27 000
	30	H Dynamo	L	0-3		17 366
Oct	6	C'bus Crew	W	3-1	Alvarez [48], Thompson 2 [86 89]	19 517
	11	Chivas USA	D	0-0		9 454
	20	KC Wizards	L	0-2		20 500
	27	H Dynamo	W	1-0	Goodson [23]	12 537
	2	H Dynamo	L	1-4	Ruiz [14]	30 088

DC UNITED 2007

Apr	7	C Rapids	L	1-2	Emilio [80]	18 086
	14	KC Wizards	L	2-4	Emilio [11], Gomez [34]	22 358
	28	C'bus Crew	L	0-1		13 572
May	3	NE Revs	D	1-1	Moreno [50p]	12 908
	6	Chivas USA	W	2-1	Gomez [48], Moreno [65p]	14 267
	19	Toronto FC	W	2-1	Goldthwaite OG [53], Moreno [79p]	20 183
	26	H Dynamo	D	2-2	Gomez [4], Olsen [27]	18 078
Jun	2	LA Galaxy	D	0-0		21 069
	10	NY Red Bulls	W	4-2	Olsen 3 [15 72 84], Emilio [49]	18 066
	16	Chicago F	W	3-1	Dyachenko [6], Emilio 2 [25 51]	20 161
	23	Real SL	L	1-2	Emilio [87]	16 319
	28	C Rapids	W	4-1	Gomez [34p], Addlery [71], Fred [82], Emilio [87]	14 982
Jul	4	KC Wizards	W	1-0	Emilio [44]	7 872
	8	H Dynamo	L	0-1		15 033
	14	FC Dallas	D	3-3	Emilio 2 [8 47], Fred [45]	20 952
	22	NY Red Bulls	L	0-1		14 705
	5	NE Revs	W	3-0	Gros [22], Emilio 2 [31 76]	12 618
Aug	9	LA Galaxy	W	1-0	Emilio [27]	46 686
	18	C'bus Crew	W	2-0	Fred [52], Emilio [63]	21 639
	22	NY Red Bulls	W	3-1	Olsen [6], Gomez [8], Moreno [48p]	18 748
	25	Toronto FC	W	1-0	Fred [8]	20 093
	1	FC Dallas	W	4-0	Olsen 2 [4 45], Gomez [47], Fred [50]	15 747
	6	Chivas USA	D	2-2	Emilio 2 [3 26]	9 306
Sep	9	NE Revs	W	4-2	Fred [31], Moreno [59], Emilio 2 [67 83]	18 918
	12	Real SL	W	2-1	Emilio [16], Gomez [73]	14 655
	23	Chicago F	L	1-2	Moreno [84]	20 079
	29	Toronto FC	W	4-1	Burch [52], Fred [57], Moreno [66], Emilio [70]	25 174
Oct	5	KC Wizards	D	1-1	Gomez [56]	14 353
	13	Chicago F	D	0-0		25 404
	20	C'bus Crew	L	2-3	Gomez 2 [89 93+p]	23 149
	25	DC United	L	0-1		17 834
	1	Chicago F	D	2-2	Simms [69], Gomez [74]	19 438

HOUSTON DYNAMO 2007

	Date	Opponent	Res	Score	Scorers	Att
	8	LA Galaxy	D	0-0		16 404
Apr	14	Chivas USA	W	1-0	Ching 65	16 519
	21	NY Red Bulls	L	0-1		12 481
	29	Chicago F	L	0-1		13 392
	5	C Rapids	W	3-1	Ching 55, De Rosario 2 63 68	10 719
May	16	Toronto	L	0-1		19 123
	19	NE Revs	L	0-1		18 232
	26	DC United	L	1-2	De Rosario 73	18 078
	3	Dallas	W	2-1	Clark 51, Ngwenya 66	13 199
	7	C Rapids	W	2-1	Ngwenya 3, Holden 63	12 017
Jun	10	C'bus Crew	W	2-1	Ngwenya 22, Marshall OG 29	12 661
	23	Chivas USA	W	4-0	Mullan 6, Davis 3 55 70 75p	14 184
	24	KC Wizards	W	1-0	Ianni 81	8 091
	30	Dallas	D	0-0		13 887
	5	NY Red Bulls	W	4-0	Ngwenya 2 28 45, Ching 32, Holden 81	14 072
	8	DC United	W	1-0	Ching 33	15 033
Jul	12	Chicago F	W	4-0	Holden 31, Jaqua 58, Ngwenya 62, Wondolowski 91+	20 034
	15	Toronto	D	0-0		11 114
	22	NE Revs	D	3-3	De Rosario 49, Ching 2 60 61	14 606
	4	Real SL	L	0-1		13 003
Aug	11	C Rapids	L	0-1		18 024
	19	Dallas	W	1-0	Ching 42	19 501
	25	C'bus Crew	D	1-1	Jaqua 80	14 351
	1	KC Wizards	W	1-0	Ngwenya 69	13 530
Sep	8	Real SL	W	4-3	Jaqua 3 6 48 57, Robinson 28	16 104
	16	LA Galaxy	W	3-1	Cochrane 21, De Rosario 47p, Clark 73	25 217
	30	Dallas	W	3-0	De Rosario 45, Robinson 62, Holden 84	17 366
	7	LA Galaxy	L	1-2	Jaqua 21	30 588
Oct	15	Real SL	W	1-0	Holden 66	14 587
	20	Chivas USA	D	0-0		16 853
	27	Dallas	L	0-1		12 537
	2	Dallas	W	4-1	Holden 67, Ching 2 72 97, Davis 100	30 088
Nov	10	KC Wizards	W	2-0	Jaqua 35, De Rosario 81	30 972
	18	NE Revs	W	2-1	Ngwenya 61, De Rosario 74	39 859

KANSAS CITY WIZARDS 2007

	Date	Opponent	Res	Score	Scorers	Att
	14	DC United	W	4-2	Harrington 3, Victorine 8, Johnson 45, Sealy 54	22 358
Apr	21	Chicago F	L	1-2	Marinelli 90p	11 717
	25	Toronto	W	3-0	Johnson 5, Zavagnin 55, Movsisyan 70	7 438
	28	Toronto	W	1-0	Johnson 81	20 148
	5	C'bus Crew	W	1-0	Burciaga 91+	7 426
May	12	Dallas	L	1-2	Harrington 91+	10 141
	19	C Rapids	D	1-1	Arnaud 58	14 577
	26	NE Revs	W	4-3	Arnaud 25, Johnson 3 26 38 82	13 156
	2	NY Red Bulls	W	3-2	Johnson 3 46 59 85	13 875
Jun	16	NY Red Bulls	D	3-3	Zavagnin 43, Movsisyan 2 70 79	15 546
	20	C'bus Crew	L	1-2	Jewsbury 93+	10 254
	24	H Dynamo	L	0-1		8 091
	1	Toronto	D	1-1	Harrington 18	9 485
	4	DC United	L	0-1		7 872
Jul	7	LA Galaxy	D	2-2	Movsisyan 47, Arnaud 51	22 637
	14	Real SL	L	1-2	Johnson 19	11 766
	22	C Rapids	D	2-2	Johnson 2 24 43	7 101
	29	Chivas USA	W	3-2	Zavagnin 38, Arnaud 53, Movsisyan 89	11 649
	2	NE Revs	L	0-2		12 915
Aug	19	NE Revs	L	0-1		9 035
	22	Chicago F	W	3-2	Victorine 54, Sealy 68, Burciaga 82	12 468
	25	Chicago F	L	0-2		18 453
	29	Real SL	L	1-3	Johnson 59	11 721
	1	H Dynamo	D	1-1	Johnson 45	13 530
Sep	15	C'bus Crew	W	3-2	Sealy 2 31 94+, Johnson 93+p	10 217
	22	Chivas USA	L	1-2	Colombano 72	13 214
	27	LA Galaxy	L	0-1		32 867
	5	DC United	D	1-1	Sealy 44	14 353
Oct	13	NY Red Bulls	L	1-2	Jewsbury 21	20 083
	20	FC Dallas	W	2-0	Sealy 2 39 55	20 500
	27	Chivas USA	W	1-0	Arnaud 35	12 442
	3	Chivas USA	D	0-0		19 711
Nov	10	H Dynamo	L	0-2		30 972

LA GALAXY 2007

	Date	Opponent	Res	Score	Scorers	Att
	8	H Dynamo	D	0-0		16 404
Apr	12	Dallas	L	1-2	Findley 86	23 596
	28	Chivas USA	W	3-1	Donovan 8, Harmse 17, Jones 78	27 000
	12	NE Revs	L	2-3	Martino 14, Marshall 84	22 715
May	20	Chivas USA	D	1-1		27 000
	26	C Rapids	L	0-1		18 458
	2	DC United	D	0-0		21 069
	9	Dallas	L	1-3	Findley 41	14 640
Jun	17	Real SL	W	3-2	Jaqua 4, Buddle 25, Jones 65	19 225
	23	C'bus Crew	L	2-3	Glinton 66, Buddle 91+	20 109
	4	Chicago F	W	2-0	Donovan 2 16p 87p	24 333
Jul	7	KC Wizards	D	2-2	Jones 2 61 75	22 637
	5	Toronto	W	1-0		20 522
	9	DC United	L	0-1		46 686
Aug	12	NE Revs	L	0-1		35 402
	18	NY Red Bulls	L	4-5	Pavon 2 6 8, Donovan 71, Buddle 82	66 237
	23	Chivas USA	L	0-3		27 000
	26	C Rapids	L	0-3		18 086
	1	Real SL	L	1-2	Gordon 6	27 000
	8	C Rapids	W	3-1	Gordon 46, Buddle 63, Martino 70	22 881
	13	Chivas USA	L	0-3		23 328
	16	H Dynamo	L	1-3	Gordon 26	25 217
Sep	19	Real SL	D	2-2	Donovan 79p, Glinton 85	24 633
	23	Dallas	W	2-1	Donovan 25p, Klein 72	27 000
	27	KC Wizards	W	1-0	Glinton 80	32 867
	30	C'bus Crew	W	2-1	Roberts 12, Martino 16	30 588
	7	H Dynamo	W	2-1	Pavon 45, Glinton 77	30 588
Oct	13	Toronto	W	2-1	Donovan 56p, Buddle 78	27 000
	18	NY Red Bulls	D	1-1	Roberts 15	27 000
	21	Chicago F	L	0-1		21 374

NEW ENGLAND REVOLUTION 2007

	Date	Opponent	Res	Score	Scorers	Att
	7	Chicago F	L	0-1		15 353
Apr	14	Toronto	W	4-0	Twellman 2 12 18, Joseph 61p, Dorman 72	18 184
	19	C'bus Crew	D	2-2	Dorman 10, Twellman 38	13 290
	29	Dallas	W	1-0	Twellman 13	9 165
	3	DC United	D	1-1		12 908
May	6	Chicago F	W	3-1	Larentowicz 16, Ralston 68, Thompson 81	9 508
	12	LA Galaxy	W	3-2	Cristman 47, Twellman 2 52 85	22 715
	19	H Dynamos	W	1-0	Joseph 9	18 232
	26	KC Wizards	L	3-4	Ralston 11, Twellman 23, Joseph 69p	13 156
	2	Real SL	D	0-0		16 864
Jun	16	C'bus Crew	D	3-3	Cristman 2 13 32, Noonan 17	22 412
	30	Dynamo	W	3-0	Dorman 2 13 81, Noonan 33	10 114
	7	Chivas USA	L	0-2		9 028
Jul	14	NY Red Bulls	W	1-0	Dorman 38	13 819
	22	H Dynamo	D	3-3	Noonan 32, Twellman 51, Joseph 66p	14 606
	28	Real SL	W	2-1	Noonan 39, Larentowicz 82	13 193
	2	KC Wizards	W	2-0	Noonan 55, Cristman 91+	12 915
	5	DC United	L	0-3		12 618
Aug	12	LA Galaxy	W	1-0	Twellman 55	35 402
	16	C Rapids	L	0-3		10 677
	19	KC Wizards	W	1-0	Twellman 72	9 035
	25	NY Red Bulls	W	2-1	Twellman 46, Mendes OG 80	16 017
	9	DC United	L	2-4	Twellman 45, Heaps 55	18 918
Sep	15	Dallas	W	4-2	Noonan 2 29 65, Ralston 78, Smith 90	15 289
	22	NY Red Bulls	D	2-2	Twellman 2 22 70	16 823
	29	C Rapids	W	1-0	Smith 88	19 166
	6	Chicago F	L	1-2	Larentowicz 24	20 014
Oct	13	C'bus Crew	L	2-3	Twellman 26, Ralston 83	22 295
	20	Toronto	W	2-1	Parkhurst 45, Twellman 48	20 374
	27	NY Red Bulls	D	0-0		14 165
	3	NY Red Bulls	W	1-0	Twellman 64	10 166
Nov	8	Chicago	W	1-0	Twellman 38	10 317
	18	H Dynamo	L	1-2	Twellman 20	39 859

NEW YORK RED BULLS 2007

	Date	Opponent		Score	Scorers	Att.
Apr	7	C'bus Crew	D	0-0		13 782
	15	Dallas	W	3-0	Altidore [18], Mathis [34], Van den Bergh [93+]	8 865
	21	H Dynamo	W	1-0	Altidore [60]	12 481
	26	Dallas	W	1-0	Freeman [79]	14 087
May	5	Real SL	D	3-3	Richards [12], Mathis 2 [28 83]	14 789
	13	C Rapids	L	0-1		7 802
	19	C'bus Crew	W	4-0	Wolyniec [17], Mathis [51], Angel [61], Caccavale [92+]	10 321
	24	Chicago F	W	3-0	Altidore [1], Angel 2 [3 68]	9 357
Jun	2	KC Wizards	L	2-3	Angel [8], Kovalenko [88]	13 875
	6	Toronto	W	2-1	Angel 2 [69 71]	20 113
	10	DC United	L	2-4	Kovalenko [18], Angel [85]	18 066
	16	KC Wizards	D	3-3	Angel 2 [6 90p], Mathis [15]	15 546
	30	C'bus Crew	L	0-1		11 435
Jul	5	H Dynamo	L	0-4		14 072
	8	C Rapids	W	1-0	Wolyniec [19]	12 708
	14	NE Revs	L	0-1		13 819
	22	DC United	W	1-0	Wolyniec [19]	14 705
	26	Chivas USA	L	0-2		10 732
Aug	12	Toronto	W	3-0	Angel [24], Altidore 2 [50 63]	12 103
	18	LA Galaxy	W	5-4	Angel 2 [4 88], Mathis [45], Altidore 2 [49 70]	66 237
	22	DC United	L	1-3	Angel [21p]	18 748
	25	NE Revs	L	1-2	Altidore [30]	16 017
Sep	1	Chicago F	W	1-0	Angel [75]	13 219
	9	Chivas USA	L	0-3		10 292
	15	Chicago F	D	2-2	Van den Bergh [10], Angel [69p]	20 586
	22	NE Revs	D	2-2	Doe [37], Angel [84]	16 823
	29	Real SL	D	2-2	Doe [49], Angel [80p]	15 855
Oct	4	Toronto	L	1-2	Richards [75]	20 274
	13	KC Wizards	W	2-1	Angel 2 [19p 24]	20 083
	18	LA Galaxy	D	1-1	Altidore [16]	27 000
	27	NE Revs	D	0-0		14 165
	3	NE Revs	L	0-1		10 116

REAL SALT LAKE 2007

	Date	Opponent		Score	Scorers	Att.
Apr	7	Dallas	W	2-1	Cunningham 2 [29 51]	18 678
	14	C'bus Crew	D	0-0		16 157
	21	Chivas USA	L	0-4		11 253
	30	C Rapids	L	0-2		14 173
May	5	NY Red Bulls	D	3-3	Klein [61], Cunningham [90p], Brown [92+]	14 789
	10	C Rapids	D	1-1	Mastroeni OG [15]	13 458
	20	Dallas	L	1-2	Adu [68p]	16 576
	27	Chicago F	D	0-0		12 996
Jun	2	NE Revs	D	0-0		16 184
	14	Dallas	L	0-1		16 278
	17	LA Galaxy	L	2-3	Brown 2 [6 73]	19 225
	23	DC United	W	2-1	Findley 2 [41 50]	16 319
Jul	4	Toronto	L	1-2	Eskandarian [45p]	20 751
	7	C'bus Crew	L	0-2		14 203
	14	KC Wizards	L	0-1		11 766
	28	NE Revs	L	1-2	Talley [72p]	13 193
Aug	4	H Dynamo	W	1-0	Findley [84]	13 003
	18	Chicago F	L	0-2		18 913
	26	Chivas USA	L	0-1		11 217
	29	KC Wizards	W	3-1	Mantilla [1], Espindola [42], Williams [85]	11 721
Sep	1	LA Galaxy	W	2-1	Findley [67], Pope [71]	27 000
	8	H Dynamo	L	3-4	Espindola [18], Talley [69], Brown [82]	16 104
	12	DC United	L	1-2	Beckerman [32]	14 655
	15	Toronto	D	0-0		20 098
	19	LA Galaxy	D	2-2	Talley [56p], Morales [86]	24 633
	22	C Rapids	W	1-0	Brown [30]	14 089
	29	NY Red Bulls	D	2-2	Brown [22], Beckerman [75]	15 855
Oct	6	Chivas USA	L	2-3	Brown [52], Findley [63]	12 111
	15	H Dynamo	L	0-1		14 587
	20	C Rapids	W	1-0	Findley [87]	14 777

TORONTO FC 2007

	Date	Opponent		Score	Scorers	Att.
Apr	7	Chivas USA	L	0-2		14 351
	14	NE Revs	L	0-4		18 184
	25	KC Wizards	L	0-3		7 438
	28	KC Wizards	L	0-1		20 148
May	12	Chicago F	W	3-1	Dichio [24], Goldthwaite [51], Edu [75]	20 000
	16	H Dynamo	W	1-0	Welsh [25]	19 123
	19	DC United	L	1-2	Eskandarian [44]	20 183
	26	C'bus Crew	D	2-2	Dichio [27], Brennan [49]	11 755
Jun	2	C Rapids	W	2-1	Dichio [9], Boyens [28]	20 195
	6	NY Red Bulls	L	1-2	Cunningham [23]	20 113
	17	Dallas	W	4-0	Edu [22], Dichio [25], Robinson [65], Cunningham [92+]	20 156
	23	NE Revs	L	0-3		10 114
Jul	1	KC Wizards	D	1-1	Dichio [46]	9 485
	4	Real SL	W	2-1	Cunningham [19], Samuel [79p]	20 751
	7	Chicago F	D	1-1	Edu [78]	13 080
	15	H Dynamo	D	0-0		11 114
	22	C'bus Crew	L	0-2		13 479
	29	Chicago F	L	0-3		20 322
Aug	5	LA Galaxy	D	0-0		20 522
	12	NY Red Bulls	L	0-3		12 103
	18	Chivas USA	L	0-2		20 178
	25	DC United	L	0-1		20 093
Sep	8	Dallas	L	0-2		16 790
	15	Real SL	D	0-0		20 098
	22	C'bus Crew	L	1-2	Canizalez 2	20 127
	29	DC United	L	1-4	Robinson [14]	25 174
Oct	4	NY Red Bulls	W	2-1	Edu [18], Leitch [66]	20 274
	7	C Rapids	L	0-1		10 832
	13	LA Galaxy	L	1-2	Samuel [68]	27 000
	20	NE Revs	D	2-2	Samuel [59], Dichio [92+]	20 374

UZB – UZBEKISTAN

NATIONAL TEAM RECORD
JULY 10TH 2006 TO JULY 12TH 2010

PL	W	D	L	F	A	%
29	15	6	8	65	28	62.1

FIFA/COCA-COLA WORLD RANKING

1993	1994	1995	1996	1997	1998	1999	2000	2001	2002	2003	2004	2005	2006	2007		High	
-	78	97	109	79	66	55	71	62	98	81	47	59	45	64		**45**	12/06

2007–2008													Low	
08/07	09/07	10/07	11/07	12/07	01/08	02/08	03/08	04/08	05/08	06/08	07/08		**119**	11/96
58	62	63	64	64	66	68	70	60	59	58	55			

A sixth consecutive double for Pakhtakor Tashkent meant that they equalled the world record set by Dinamo Tbilisi in 1997 but it took a nerve wracking penalty shoot-out in the Cup Final to do it. Pakhtakor were unstoppable in the League, dropping just eight points all season after drawing twice with each of their closest rivals - newly promoted Kuruvchi and Mashal. The rest of the clubs in the League failed to take a single point off the champions who finished 11 points clear of Kuruvchi. Statistically it was the best-ever performance by a club in the Uzbek league as they became only the second team to go through the season unbeaten. Pakhtakor did lose a game on the

INTERNATIONAL HONOURS
Asian Games 1994

way to the Cup Final - against Neftchi in the semi-finals - and they could only draw against Kuruvchi in the final. The heroes of the shoot-out were keeper Ignatiy Nestorov who saved from Rashid Gofurov and then Temur Jorayev who kept his nerve to score the winner. There was a modicum of revenge for Kuruvchi when they topped their group in the 2008 AFC Champions League, therefore qualifying for the quarter-finals, while Pakhtakor could only manage second in theirs. In the 2010 FIFA World Cup qualifiers Uzbekistan sailed comfortably through both a preliminary round and a first group stage to make it through to the final round of Asian qualifying.

THE FIFA BIG COUNT OF 2006

	Male	Female		Total
Number of players	692 500	37 700	Referees and Assistant Referees	350
Professionals	1 580		Admin, Coaches, Technical, Medical	975
Amateurs 18+	4 460		Number of clubs	216
Youth under 18	30 500		Number of teams	24 000
Unregistered	470 300		Clubs with women's teams	0
Total players	730 200		Players as % of population	2.67%

Uzbekistan Football Federation (UFF)

O'zbekiston Futbol Federatsiyasi, Massiv Almazar, Furkat Street 15/1, Tashkent 700 003, Uzbekistan
Tel +998 71 2441684   Fax +998 71 2441683
info@the-uff.com   www.the-uff.com
President: USMANOV Mirabror   General Secretary: RAKHMATULLAEV Sardor
Vice-President: RAKHIMOV Bakhtier   Treasurer: ISKHAKOVA Zemfira   Media Officer: RIZAEV Sanjar
Men's Coach: INILEYEV Rauf   Women's Coach: YUMANGULOV Abdurahman
UFF formed: 1946   AFC: 1994   FIFA: 1994
White shirts with blue trimmings, White shorts, White socks or Blue shirts with white trimmings, Blue shorts, Blue socks

RECENT INTERNATIONAL MATCHES PLAYED BY UZBEKISTAN

2005	Opponents	Score		Venue	Comp	Scorers	Att	Referee
9-02	Saudi Arabia	D	1-1	Tashkent	WCq	Soliev 93+	45 000	Kamikawa JPN
25-03	Kuwait	L	1-2	Kuwait City	WCq	Geynrikh 77	12 000	Sun Baojie CHN
30-03	Korea Republic	L	1-2	Seoul	WCq	Geynrikh 78	62 857	Najm LIB
3-06	Korea Republic	D	1-1	Tashkent	WCq	Shatskikh 63	40 000	Moradi IRN
8-06	Saudi Arabia	L	0-3	Riyadh	WCq		72 000	Huang Junjie CHN
17-08	Kuwait	W	3-2	Tashkent	WCq	Djeparov 41p, Shatskikh 51, Soliev 76	40 000	Mohd Saleh MAS
3-09	Bahrain †	W	1-0	Tashkent	WCpo	Kasimov 12		
8-10	Bahrain	D	1-1	Tashkent	WCpo	Shatskikh 19	55 000	Busacca SUI
12-10	Bahrain	D	0-0	Manama	WCpo		25 000	Poll ENG
2006								
22-02	Bangladesh	W	5-0	Tashkent	ACq	Geynrikh 2 10 52, Djeparov 24, Shatskikh 2 34 84	12 000	Ebrahim BHR
1-03	Qatar	L	1-2	Doha	ACq	OG 20	7 000	Sun Baojie CHN
16-08	Hong Kong	D	2-2	Tashkent	ACq	Soliev 18, Shatskikh 35	15 000	Shaban KUW
6-09	Hong Kong	D	0-0	Hong Kong	ACq		7 608	Lee Gi Young KOR
11-10	Bangladesh	W	4-0	Dhaka	ACq	Zeytullaev 11, Bakaev 18, Djeparov 22, Shatskikh 39p	120	Tan Hai CHN
15-11	Qatar	W	2-0	Tashkent	ACq	Koshelev 31, Zeytullaev 52	14 000	Al Saeedi UAE
2007								
7-02	Uzbekistan	D	0-0	Karshi	Fr			
7-03	Azerbaijan	L	0-1	Shymkent	Fr			
9-03	Kyrgyzstan	W	6-0	Shymkent	Fr	Soliev 2, Bakaev 3 7p 43 89, Mandzukas 63, Shishelov 80		
11-03	Kazakhstan	D	1-1	Shymkent	Fr	Geynrikh 34		
24-03	Chinese Taipei	W	1-0	Taipei	Fr	Khoshimov 53		
27-03	China PR	L	1-3	Macau	Fr	Shishelov 76		
2-07	Iraq	W	2-0	Paju	Fr	Ibragimov 3, Bakaev 30		
5-07	Korea Republic	L	1-2	Seoul	Fr	Djeparov 59p	21 019	Prayoon THA
11-07	Iran	L	1-2	Kuala Lumpur	ACr1	Rezaei OG 16	1 863	Ghalehnoy IRN
14-07	Malaysia	W	5-0	Kuala Lumpur	ACr1	Shatskikh 2 10 89, Kapadze 30, Bakaev 45p, Ibragimov 85	7 137	Abdou QAT
18-07	China PR	W	3-0	Kuala Lumpur	ACr1	Shatskikh 72, Kapadze 86, Geynrikh 90	2 200	Al Fadhli KUW
22-07	Saudi Arabia	L	1-2	Jakarta	ACqf	Solomin 82	12 000	Kwon Jong Chul KOR
22-08	Ukraine	L	1-2	Kyiv	Fr	Geynrikh 90	4 000	Banari MDA
13-10	Chinese Taipei	W	9-0	Tashkent	WCq	Shatskikh 5 4 16 34 57 77, Kapadze 26, Karpenko 43, Bakaev 54, Salomov 68	7 000	Albadwawi UAE
28-10	Chinese Taipei	W	2-0	Taipei	WCq	Innomov 81, Suyunov 90	800	Shamsuzzaman BAN
21-11	Estonia	D	0-0	Tashkent	Fr		3 000	Irmatov UZB
22-12	Thailand	L	2-3	Bangkok	Fr	Tadjiyev 2 43 48		
24-12	Korea DPR	D	2-2	Bangkok	Fr	Solomin 53, Yafarov 65		
2008								
6-02	Lebanon	W	1-0	Beirut	WCq	Ahmedov 44	800	Al Hilali OMA
22-03	Jordan	W	4-1	Tashkent	Fr	Djeparov 4, Innomov 36, Tadjiyev 2 49 63		
26-03	Saudi Arabia	W	3-0	Tashkent	WCq	Kapadze 46, Shatskikh 66, Djeparov 68	17 000	Mohd Salleh MAS
2-06	Singapore	W	7-3	Singapore	WCq	Kapadze 10, Karpenko 21, Djeparov 2 34 44, Denisov 42, Ibragimov 62, Shatskikh 88	28 750	Albadwawi UAE
7-06	Singapore	W	1-0	Tashkent	WCq	Geynrikh 80	12 867	Kim Dong Jin KOR
14-06	Lebanon	W	3-0	Tashkent	WCq	Ahmedov 2 51 62, Djeparov 94+	7 000	Breeze AUS
22-06	Saudi Arabia	L	0-4	Riyadh	WCq		5 000	Nishimura JPN

Fr = Friendly match • AC = AFC Asian Cup • WC = FIFA World Cup • † Matched annulled due to referee error
q = qualifier • po = play-off • r1 = first round group • qf = quarter-final • po = play-off

UZBEKISTAN NATIONAL TEAM RECORDS AND RECORD SEQUENCES

Records			Sequence records					
Victory	15-0	MGL 1998	Wins	8	1994	Clean sheets	4	2004, 2006-2007
Defeat	1-8	JPN 2000	Defeats	4	2000-2001	Goals scored	18	2003-2005
Player Caps	65	Mirdzhal Kasimov	Undefeated	11	1994, 2001	Without goal	3	2000-2001
Player Goals	29	Kasimov / Shatskikh	Without win	6	1997	Goals against	9	2004-2005

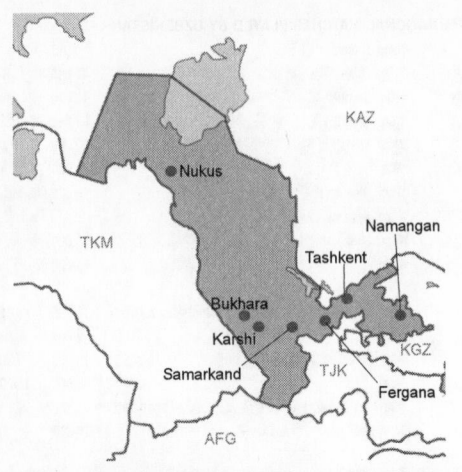

	MAJOR CITIES/TOWNS	
		Population '000
1	Tashkent	1 959
2	Namangan	446
3	Andijan	321
4	Samarkand	312
5	Bukhara	249
6	Nukus	240
7	Karshi	231
8	Kukon	187
9	Chirchik	168
10	Fergana	161
11	Jizak	159
12	Urganch	152
13	Termiz	147
14	Margilan	132
15	Navoiy	131
16	Angren	127
17	Olmalik	120
18	Bekobod	86
19	Khujayli	76
20	Denov	73
21	Shahrihan	67
22	Chust	66
23	Kagan	65
24	Zarafshon	65

REPUBLIC OF UZBEKISTAN; OZBEKISTON RESPUBLIKASI

Capital	Tashkent	Language	Uzbek, Russian			Independence	1991
Population	27 780 059	Area	447 400 km²	Density	59 per km²	% in cities	41%
GDP per cap	$1 700	Dailling code	+7	Internet	.uz	GMT + / -	+5

MEDALS TABLE

		Overall			League			Cup		Asia			City	Stadium	Cap'ty	DoF
		G	S	B	G	S	B	G	S	G	S	B				
1	Pakhtakor Tashkent	17	3	2	8	2		9	1			2	Tashkent	Pakhtakor Markaziy	55 000	1956
2	Neftchi Fergana	7	14	1	5	9		2	5			1	Fergana	Fergana	20 000	1962
3	Navbahor Namangan	4	1	8	1		8	3	1				Namangan	Markaziy	35 000	1978
4	Dustlik Tashkent	3			2			1					Tashkent			
5	MHSK Tashkent	1	2	1	1	1	1		1				Tashkent			
6	Mashal Muborak		2	1		1	1		1				Muborak	Bahrom Vafoev	10 000	1991
7	Kuruvchi Tashkent	2			1			1					Tashkent			
8	Nasah Karshi		1	4		4		1					Karshi	Markaziy	20 000	1978
	Nurafshon Bukhara	1			1								Bukhara	Markaziy	40 000	
	Samarkand Dinamo	1						1					Samarkand	Dinamo	12 500	1960
	Temirulchi Kukon	1			1								Kukon			
	Traktor Tashkent	1						1					Tashkent	Traktor	6 400	1968
13	FK Yangier	1						1					Yangier			
	Kizilgum Zarafshon			1			1						Zarafshon	Kizilgum		1994
	Sogdiana Jizak			1			1						Jizak	Markaziy	10 000	1970

RECENT LEAGUE AND CUP RECORD

	Championship						Cup		
Year	Champions	Pts	Runners-up	Pts	Third	Pts	Winners	Score	Runners-up
1995	Neftchi Fergana	76	MHSK Tashkent	74	Navbahor Nam'gan	72	Navbahor Nam'gan	1-0	MHSK Tashkent
1996	Navbahor Nam'gan	74	Neftchi Fergana	72	MHSK Tashkent	62	Neftchi Fergana	0-0 5-4p	Pkhtakor Tashkent
1997	MHSK Tashkent	90	Neftchi Fergana	81	Navbahor Nam'gan	68	Pakhtakor Tashkent	3-2	Neftchi Fergana
1998	Pakhtakor Tashkent	76	Neftchi Fergana	70	Navbahor Nam'gan	59	Navbahor Nam'gan	2-0	Neftchi Fergana
1999	Dustlik Tashkent	64	Neftchi Fergana	63	Navbahor Nam'gan	61	No tournament		
2000	Dustlik Tashkent	94	Neftchi Fergana	90	Nasaf Karshi	85	Dustlik Tashkent	4-1	Samarkand Dinamo
2001	Neftchi Fergana	84	Pakhtakor Tashkent	72	Nasaf Karshi	71	Pakhtakor Tashkent	2-1	Neftchi Fergana
2002	Pakhtakor Tashkent	74	Neftchi Fergana	69	Kizilgum Zarafshon	59	Pakhtakor Tashkent	6-3	Neftchi Fergana
2003	Pakhtakor Tashkent	77	Neftchi Fergana	71	Navbahor Nam'gan	63	Pakhtakor Tashkent	3-1	Nasaf Karshi
2004	Pakhtakor Tashkent	69	Neftchi Fergana	65	Navbahor Nam'gan	57	Pakhtakor Tashkent	3-2	Traktor Tashkent
2005	Pakhtakor Tashkent	65	Mashal Muborak	59	Nasaf Karshi	51	Pakhtakor Tashkent	1-0	Neftchi Fergana
2006	Pakhtakor Tashkent	77	Neftchi Fergana	71	Nasaf Karshi	70	Pakhtakor Tashkent	2-0	Mashal Muborak
2007	Pakhtakor Tashkent	82	Kuruvchi Tashkent	71	Mashal Muborak	70	Pakhtakor Tashkent	1-1 7-6p	Kuruvchi Tashkent

UZBEKISTAN 2007

O'ZBEKISTON CHEMPIONATI OLIY LIGA

	Pl	W	D	L	F	A	Pts	Pakhtakor	Kuruvchi	Mashal	Neftchi	Samarkand	Nasaf	Kizilgum	Navbahor	Bukhara	Andijan	Traktor	Topolon	Shurton	Lokomotiv	Metallurg	Vobkent
Pakhtakor Tashkent †	30	26	4	0	83	13	82		0-0	3-3	4-0	2-0	3-0	4-1	2-0	5-1	5-0	2-0	2-1	3-1	4-0	2-0	5-1
Kuruvchi Tashkent †	30	22	5	3	62	16	71	1-1		2-0	0-0	2-1	3-0	2-0	3-1	2-0	3-0	0-1	4-1	3-0	3-1	1-2	6-1
Mashal Muborak	30	22	4	4	62	25	70	1-1	0-1		1-0	3-1	4-1	4-0	1-0	1-0	2-1	5-2	3-0	3-0	4-1	5-1	4-1
Neftchi Fergana	30	19	4	7	53	28	61	0-3	0-2	3-1		3-1	2-1	4-2	1-1	4-0	2-1	4-1	4-0	2-1	0-1	2-1	4-0
Samarkand Dinamo	30	14	8	8	48	36	50	0-1	1-1	2-1	2-1		2-0	6-1	3-2	2-1	0-0	3-0	1-1	2-1	1-1	4-1	1-0
Nasaf Karshi	30	13	5	12	43	43	44	0-1	1-1	0-1	1-0	1-1		5-2	1-0	2-0	4-4	4-2	1-0	2-1	2-1	3-1	4-1
Kizilgum Zarafshon	30	12	3	15	42	64	39	0-11	0-2	0-0	0-0	2-1	3-1		0-1	3-1	2-0	4-2	3-0	1-2	1-0	5-1	1-0
Navbahor Namangan	30	11	4	15	37	41	37	1-2	1-4	0-1	0-1	1-0	1-1	1-2		2-1	3-0	2-0	2-1	2-1	6-2	1-1	4-1
FK Bukhara	30	11	3	16	29	43	36	0-1	1-2	0-1	0-1	1-0	1-0	3-1	1-0		2-1	5-3	1-2	1-0	1-0	2-0	1-0
FK Andijan	30	10	5	15	37	45	35	1-3	0-2	0-1	0-1	0-1	1-1	1-0	3-1	0-0		2-1	4-1	1-0	1-0	2-2	3-0
Traktor Tashkent	30	11	1	18	45	58	34	0-1	0-3	1-2	0-2	1-2	3-1	2-1	3-0	1-2	3-1		2-1	2-0	1-0	5-1	2-1
Topolon Sariosia	30	8	6	16	29	43	30	0-1	1-2	0-1	1-3	1-1	1-0	4-1	2-0	0-0	2-0	1-0		2-0	1-1	2-0	0-0
Shurton Guzor	30	8	5	17	32	51	29	0-3	0-4	2-3	0-0	4-2	0-1	1-1	1-2	2-0	2-1	3-3	1-0		1-1	2-1	2-1
Lokomotiv Tashkent	30	6	8	16	25	44	26	0-1	2-1	0-0	1-3	1-2	0-2	3-0	0-0	1-3	0-1	2-1	1-0	0-0		3-3	0-0
Metallurg Bekobod	30	6	5	19	32	62	23	0-4	0-1	0-1	1-2	1-1	2-1	0-1	1-2	2-0	1-4	1-2	2-1	4-0	0-2		0-0
FK Vobkent	30	3	6	21	23	70	15	1-3	0-1	2-4	1-4	2-2	1-2	2-4	1-0	1-1	0-4	2-1	2-2	0-4	1-0	0-1	

1/03/2007 - 6/12/2007 • † Qualified for the AFC Champions League
Top scorers: Ilhom Mominjonov, Lokomotiv/Kuruvchi 21; Farhad Tojiyev, Samarkand 20; Akmal Kholmatov, Neftchi 19; Zafar Kholmuradov, Nasaf 17
Trakor and Topolon withdrew before the start of the 2008 season. Metallurg were spared relegation while OTMK were promoted

UZBEKISTAN 2007 BIRINCHI LIGA (2)

	Pl	W	D	L	F	A	Pts
Sogdiana Jizak	38	26	7	5	79	27	85
UDJ Andijan	38	24	7	4	63	25	79
Mashal 2 Muborak	38	21	10	7	52	30	73
Akbarov Yaypan	38	20	8	10	45	31	68
Sementchi Kuvasoy	38	20	7	11	55	37	67
Kimyogar Chirchik	38	19	8	11	62	41	65
Oktepa Tashkent	38	19	8	11	67	59	65
Osiyo Tashkent	38	18	9	11	55	47	63
Kattagorgon Dinamo	38	17	9	12	58	47	60
Jaykhun Nukus	38	18	5	15	47	57	59
Gallakor Gallaorol	38	17	7	14	47	55	58
Horezm Urganch	38	16	5	17	32	59	53
Lochin Shorchi	38	13	11	14	58	58	50
OTMK Olmalik	38	13	9	16	57	49	48
Shakhontohur Tashkent	38	14	2	22	44	66	44
Lokomotiv BFK T'kent	38	12	5	21	29	46	41
Zarafshon Navai	38	10	8	20	37	69	38
FK Shahrixon	38	10	3	25	43	75	33
Kosonsoy Zakovat	38	5	3	30	20	49	18
Romiton FK	38	1	3	34	12	35	6

27/03/2007 - 6/11/2007 • OTMK promoted

UZBEKISTAN CUP 2007

Second Round
Pakhtakor Taskent	1	4
Topolon Sariosia *	1	0
FK Vobkent *	1	0
Samarkand Dinamo	1	7
Nasaf Karshi	4	7
Lochin Shorchi *	2	0
FK Bukhara *	1	0
Neftchi Fergana	1	2
Mashal Muborak	1	5
Metallurg Bekobod *	0	0
Navbahor Namangan *	4	0
Shurton Guzor	1	3
FK Andijan	3	1
UDJ Andijan *	0	2
Traktor Tashkent *	0	0
Kuruvchi Tashkent	1	4

Quarter–finals
Pakhtakor Taskent *	2	2
Samarkand Dinamo	0	2
Nasaf Karshi *	1	0
Neftchi Fergana	0	2
Mashal Muborak	3	2
Shurton Guzor *	3	0
FK Andijan	0	0
Kuruvchi Tashkent *	3	1

Semi–finals
Pakhtakor Taskent *	4	2
Neftchi Fergana	1	3
Mashal Muborak *	0	1
Kuruvchi Tashkent	0	2

Final
Pakhtakor Taskent	0	7p
Kuruvchi Tashkent	0	6p

CUP FINAL
MXSK stadium, Tashkent
9-12-2007, Att: 11 500

* Home team/home team in the first leg

VAN – VANUATU

NATIONAL TEAM RECORD
JULY 10TH 2006 TO JULY 12TH 2010

PL	W	D	L	F	A	%
12	5	1	6	33	21	45.8

FIFA/COCA-COLA WORLD RANKING

1993	1994	1995	1996	1997	1998	1999	2000	2001	2002	2003	2004	2005	2006	2007	High	
164	172	179	180	186	177	184	167	168	156	160	143	146	167	140	**131**	10/07

	2007–2008											Low	
08/07	09/07	10/07	11/07	12/07	01/08	02/08	03/08	04/08	05/08	06/08	07/08	**188**	04/00
167	133	131	141	140	139	138	141	139	142	152	155		

It proved to be a very eventual year in Vanuatu on both the domestic and international front with the national team making it through to the final round of 2010 FIFA World Cup qualifying in Oceania, while Tafea created a little piece of history by equalling Skonto Riga's record of 14 consecutive championships. A bronze medal at the football tournament of the South Pacific Games in Samoa, which doubled up as a first round of World Cup qualifying, was enough to see the national team through to the next round after they beat the Solomon Islands 2-0 in a third place play-off. In what proved to be their most successful tournament since first taking part in 1983, Vanuatu also recorded

INTERNATIONAL HONOURS
Melanesian Cup 1990

their highest ever score with the 15-0 thrashing of American Samoa. Proof of the popularity of the game came in the next stage when nearly a quarter of the population of Port Vila turned out for the visit of New Zealand, a game in which they had a first half lead but eventually lost 2-1. Vanuatu were left fighting Fiji to avoid last place in the group but once again it was a World Cup campaign to be proud of. Even more proud perhaps were Tafea who once again retained the League title and is there a player in the world who has bettered the number of championship medals won by goalkeeper David Chilla who has been with Tafea for all of their 14 championship seasons?

THE FIFA BIG COUNT OF 2006

	Male	Female		Total
Number of players	25 600	1 800	Referees and Assistant Referees	110
Professionals	0		Admin, Coaches, Technical, Medical	206
Amateurs 18+	4 050		Number of clubs	200
Youth under 18	1 250		Number of teams	400
Unregistered	21 000		Clubs with women's teams	30
Total players	27 400		Players as % of population	13.12%

Vanuatu Football Federation (VFF)
VFF House, Anabrou, PO Box 266, Port Vila, Vanuatu
Tel +678 27239   Fax +678 25236
vanua2foot@yahoo.com.vu   www.vanuafoot.com
President: MALTOCK Lambert   General Secretary: IAPSON George
Vice-President: NATONGA Saby   Treasurer: MANAROTO Albert   Media Officer: None
Men's Coach: CALVO Robert   Women's Coach: ALWIN Job
VFF formed: 1934   OFC: 1988   FIFA: 1988
Gold shirts, Black shorts, Gold socks

RECENT INTERNATIONAL MATCHES PLAYED BY VANUATU

2004	Opponents	Score		Venue	Comp	Scorers	Att	Referee
29-05	Solomon Islands	L	0-1	Adelaide	WCq		200	Shield AUS
31-05	Fiji	L	0-1	Adelaide	WCq		500	Ariiotima TAH
2-06	New Zealand	W	4-2	Adelaide	WCq	Chillia [37], Bibi [64], Maleb [72], Qoriz [88]	356	Farina ITA
4-06	Australia	L	0-3	Adelaide	WCq		4 000	Ariiotima TAH
6-06	Tahiti	L	1-2	Adelaide	WCq	Iwai [23]	300	Rakaroi FIJ
2005								
No international matches played in 2005								
2006								
No international matches played in 2006								
2007								
17-07	New Caledonia	L	3-5	Noumea	Fr	Gete [34], Masauvakalo [83], Soromon [92+]		
19-07	New Caledonia	W	2-0	Noumea	Fr	Naprapol [7], Mermer [19]		
25-08	Samoa	W	4-0	Apia	WCq	Iwai [21], Naprapol [43], Poida [66], Soromon [92+]	300	Jacques TAH
29-08	American Samoa	W	15-0	Apia	WCq	Poida [19], Mermer 4 [24 44 45 68], Sakama 3 [43 79 91+], Chichirua [56], Iwai [62], Tomake [72], Soromon 4 [81 84 86 92+]	200	Hester NZL
1-09	Solomon Islands	L	0-2	Apia	WCq		1 000	Jacques TAH
3-09	Tonga	W	4-1	Apia	WCq	Soromon 3 [24 34 41], Maleb [76]	50	Minan PNG
5-09	Fiji	L	0-3	Apia	WCq		600	Hester NZL
7-09	Solomon Islands	W	2-0	Apia	WCq	Soromon [45], Sakama [51]	200	Jacques TAH
17-11	New Zealand	L	1-2	Port Vila	WCq	Naprapol [26]	8 000	Minan PNG
21-11	New Zealand	L	1-4	Wellington	WCq	Sakama [50]	2 500	Jacques TAH
2008								
14-06	New Caledonia	D	1-1	Port Vila	WCq	Mermer [77]	4 000	Varman FIJ
21-06	New Caledonia	L	0-3	Noumea	WCq		2 700	Hester NZL

Fr = Friendly match • WC = FIFA World Cup • q = qualifierf • † Not a full international

VANUATU NATIONAL TEAM RECORDS AND RECORD SEQUENCES

Records			Sequence records					
Victory	15-0	ASA 2007	Wins	3	2004	Clean sheets	2	Five times
Defeat	0-9	NZL 1951	Defeats	6	Three times	Goals scored	13	1996-2000
Player Caps	n/a		Undefeated	6	2003	Without goal	3	1992, 2003-2004
Player Goals	n/a		Without win	9	1979-1981	Goals against	23	1951-1979

RECENT LEAGUE RECORD

Year	Port Vila Football League
1994	Tafea FC
1995	Tafea FC
1996	Tafea FC
1997	Tafea FC
1998	Tafea FC
1999	Tafea FC
2000	Tafea FC
2001	Tafea FC
2002	Tafea FC
2003	Tafea FC
2004	Tafea FC
2005	Tafea FC
2006	Tafea FC
2007	Tafea FC

VANUATU 2007 PREMIA DIVISEN

	Pl	W	D	L	F	A	Pts
Tafea	14	11	1	2	49	11	34
Tupuji Imere	14	11	1	2	47	16	34
Yatel	14	9	1	4	38	20	28
Erakor Golden Star	14	6	4	4	27	20	22
Westtan Verts	14	6	2	6	31	28	21
Amical	14	3	1	10	13	41	10
Ifira Black Bird	14	2	2	10	14	44	8
Pango Green Bird	14	1	2	11	15	54	5
to 27/10/2007							

VANUATU COUNTRY INFORMATION

Capital	Port-Vila	Independence	1980 from UK and France	GDP per Capita	$2 900
Population	202 609	Status	Republic	GNP Ranking	183
Area km²	12 200	Language	English, French, Bislama	Dialling code	+678
Population density	16 per km²	Literacy rate	53%	Internet code	.vu
% in urban areas	19%	Main religion	Christian	GMT +/–	+11
Towns/Cities ('000)	Port-Vila 35; Luganville 13; Norsup 3; Port Olry 2; Isangel ; Sola 1				
Neighbours (km)	South Pacific Ocean 2 528				
Main stadia	Korman Stadium – Port-Vila				

VEN – VENEZUELA

NATIONAL TEAM RECORD
JULY 10TH 2006 TO JULY 12TH 2010

PL	W	D	L	F	A	%
34	15	9	10	47	42	57.4

FIFA/COCA-COLA WORLD RANKING

1993	1994	1995	1996	1997	1998	1999	2000	2001	2002	2003	2004	2005	2006	2007		High
93	110	127	111	115	129	110	111	81	69	57	62	67	73	62		**48** 04/04

				2007–2008								Low
08/07	09/07	10/07	11/07	12/07	01/08	02/08	03/08	04/08	05/08	06/08	07/08	**129** 12/98
56	58	56	62	62	59	59	57	59	64	63	61	

In a telling sign that football has increased its profile dramatically in Venezuela, a fan was killed and 50 were injured as they tried to obtain tickets for the second leg of the 2008 Championship final in San Cristobal. Local team Deportivo Tachira had held defending champions Caracas FC to a 1-1 draw in the first leg and such was the demand for tickets for the return match that Tachira fans pushed over a security fence, leading to a stampede. The away goal scored by José Villafraz five minutes before the end of the first leg in the end proved decisive for Tachira after the second leg finished 0-0. It meant a first title since 2000 for Tachira and a sixth in total. A key figure in the

INTERNATIONAL HONOURS
None

growth of Venezuelan football has been national team coach Richard Paez, but after six and a half years in charge, expectations have increased dramatically and he quit following the 2010 FIFA World Cup qualifier against Bolivia, blaming fans who had insulted him and his son, national team midfielder Ricardo Paez. The Vinotinto's campaign to qualify for South Africa had started as well as could be expected with two wins in their first four games leaving his replacement Cesar Farias with a sound basis to work from, but a home defeat against Chile saw the Vinotinto slip out of the top half of the table a third of the way through qualification.

THE FIFA BIG COUNT OF 2006

	Male	Female		Total
Number of players	1 270 894	219 679	Referees and Assistant Referees	832
Professionals	546		Admin, Coaches, Technical, Medical	8 300
Amateurs 18+	9 897		Number of clubs	717
Youth under 18	28 172		Number of teams	2 449
Unregistered	516 400		Clubs with women's teams	203
Total players	1 490 573		Players as % of population	5.79%

Federación Venezolana de Fútbol (FVF)

Avda. Santos Erminy Ira, Calle las Delicias Torre Mega II, Agregar PH Quitar PH, Caracas 1050, Venezuela

Tel +58 212 7624472   Fax +58 212 7620596

sec_presidencia_fvf@cantv.net   www.federacionvenezuoladefutbol.org

President: ESQUIVEL Rafael   General Secretary: GARCIA-REGALADO Jesus

Vice-President: CABEZAS Temistocles   Treasurer: SANGLADE Luis Ignacio   Media Officer: GOUSSOT Zaiddy

Men's Coach: FARIAS Cesar   Women's Coach: BELLO Rolando

FVF formed: 1926   CONMEBOL: 1965   FIFA: 1952

Burgundy shirts with white trimmings, White shorts, White socks

RECENT INTERNATIONAL MATCHES PLAYED BY VENEZUELA

2006	Opponents	Score		Venue	Comp	Scorers	Att	Referee
2-09	Switzerland	L	0-1	Basel	Fr		12 500	Hamer LUX
6-09	Austria	W	1-0	Basel	Fr	De Ornelas [8]	1 453	Bertolini SUI
27-09	Uruguay	W	1-0	Maracaibo	Fr	Arismendi [81]	28 000	Manzur VEN
18-10	Uruguay	L	0-4	Montevideo	Fr		7 000	Silvera URU
15-11	Guatemala	W	2-1	Caracas	Fr	Villafraz [4], Rey [52]	9 000	Andarcia VEN
2007								
14-01	Sweden	W	2-0	Maracaibo	Fr	Guerra [17], Arismendi [91+]	14 000	Buitrago COL
7-02	Chile	L	0-1	Maracaibo	Fr		9 000	Buitrago COL
28-02	Mexico	L	1-3	San Diego	Fr	Arismendi [83]	63 328	Stott USA
24-03	Cuba	W	3-1	Merida	Fr	Arango [11], Torrealba [33], González.C [64]	12 000	Andarcia VEN
28-03	New Zealand	W	5-0	Maracaibo	Fr	Páez [7], De Ornelas 2 [30 75], Fedor [84p], Moran [91+]	12 000	
25-05	Honduras	W	2-1	Merida	Fr	Vielma [18], Arismendi [38]	42 000	Gomez VEN
1-06	Canada	D	2-2	Maracaibo	Fr	Cichero [22], Maldonado [25]		Lopez COL
26-06	Bolivia	D	2-2	San Cristobal	CAr1	Maldonado [21], Páez [56]	42 000	Reinoso ECU
30-06	Peru	W	2-0	San Cristobal	CAr1	Cichero [49], Arismendi [79]	42 000	Archundia MEX
3-07	Uruguay	D	0-0	Merida	CAr1		42 000	Simon BRA
7-07	Uruguay	L	1-4	San Cristobal	CAqf	Arango [41]	42 000	Chandia CHI
22-08	Paraguay	D	1-1	Ciudad del Este	Fr	Fedor [57]	5 000	Baldassi ARG
8-09	Paraguay	W	3-2	Puerto Ordaz	Fr	Arismendi [67], Maldonado [74], Guerra [90]	40 000	Lopez COL
12-09	Panama	D	1-1	Puerto La Cruz	Fr	Maldonado [90]	30 000	Buitriago COL
13-10	Ecuador	W	1-0	Quito	WCq	Rey [67]	29 644	Ortube BOL
16-10	Argentina	L	0-2	Maracaibo	WCq		10 600	Simon BRA
17-11	Colombia	L	0-1	Bogota	WCq		28 273	Selman CHI
20-11	Bolivia	W	5-3	San Cristobal	WCq	Arismendi 2 [20 40], Guerra [82], Maldonado 2 [87 89]	18 632	Fagundes BRA
2008								
3-02	Haiti	W	1-0	Maturin	Fr	Rojas [10]		Soto VEN
6-02	Haiti	D	1-1	Puerto La Cruz	Fr	Rondon.A [31]	30 000	Perluzzo VEN
23-03	El Salvador	W	1-0	Puerto Ordaz	Fr	Rondon.JS [33]	5 000	Gomez VEN
26-03	Bolivia	L	0-1	Puerto La Cruz	Fr		16 000	Buitrago COL
30-04	Colombia	L	2-5	Bucaramanga	Fr	Cichero [10], Lucena [43]	25 000	Carillo PER
30-05	Honduras	D	1-1	Fort Lauderdale	Fr	Maldonado [78p]	10 000	Wiemckowski USA
6-06	Brazil	W	2-0	Boston	Fr	Maldonado [6], Vargas [44]	68 000	Marrufo USA
9-06	Netherlands Antilles	W	1-0	Willemstad	Fr	Arismendi [74]		
14-06	Uruguay	D	1-1	Montevideo	WCq	Vargas [55]	41 831	Intriago ECU
19-06	Chile	L	2-3	Puerto La Cruz	WCq	Maldonado [59], Arango [80]	38 000	Silvera URU

Fr = Friendly match • CA = Copa América • WC = FIFA World Cup • q = qualifier • r1 = first round group • qf = quarter-final

VENEZUELA NATIONAL TEAM PLAYERS

	Player		Ap	G	Club	Date of Birth		Player		Ap	G	Club	Date of Birth
1	Renny Vega	GK	28	0	Bursaspor	4 07 1979	12	Leonardo Morales	GK			Dep. Anzoátegui	7 07 1978
2	Gerzon Chacón	DF			Dep. Tachira	21 10 1980	13	Leonel Vielma	MF	52	3	Santa Fe	30 08 1978
3	José Manuel Rey	DF	94	8	AEK Larnaca	20 05 1975	14	Luis Manuel Seijas	MF			Santa Fe	23 06 1986
4	Jonay Hernández	DF			Pontevedra	15 02 1979	15	Daniel Arismendi	FW	20	9	Atlante	4 07 1982
5	Miguel Mea Vitali	MF	74	1	FC Vaduz	19 02 1981	16	Roberto Rosales	DF			KAA Gent	20 11 1988
6	Pedro Boada	DF			Dep. Anzoátegui	26 07 1977	17	Jorge Alberto Rojas	MF	80	2	RB New York	1 10 1977
7	Jose Torrealba	FW	13	3	Dep. Tachira	13 06 1980	18	Juan Arango	FW	68	14	RCD Mallorca	16 05 1980
8	Tomás Rincón	MF	7	0	Zamora FC	13 01 1988		**Selected others**					
9	Giancarlo Maldonado	FW	33	13	Atlante	29 06 1982		Luis Vallenilla	DF	77	1	Nea Salamis	13 03 1974
10	Ronald Vargas	MF	5	2	Club Brugge	2 12 1986		Ricado Paez	MF	64	7	Veria	9 02 1979
11	Alexander Rondón	FW			Dep. Anzoátegui	30 08 1977		Héctor González	MF	53	4	AEK Larnaca	4 11 1977

The Venezuelan squad for the June 19, 2008 World Cup qualifier | Emilio Rentería | FW | 16 | 9 | Caracas FC | 9 10 1984

VENEZUELA NATIONAL TEAM RECORDS AND RECORD SEQUENCES

Records				Sequence records					
Victory	6-0	PUR 1946	Wins	4	2001	Clean sheets	4	2002	
Defeat	0-11	ARG 1975	Defeats	9	1989-1991	Goals scored	8	1946-1956	
Player Caps	79	José Manuel Tey	Undefeated	7	2007	Without goal	5	1990-1991	
Player Goals	16	Ruberth Morán	Without win	26	1989-1993	Goals against	21	1993-96, 1999-01	

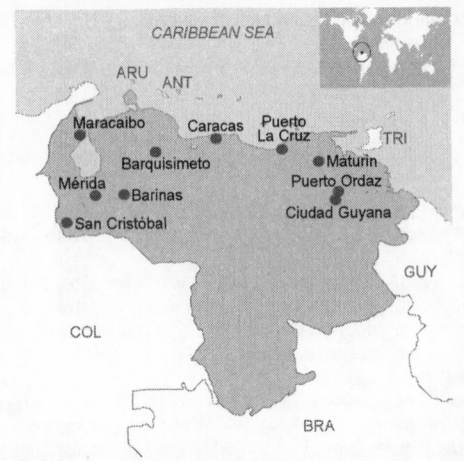

CARIBBEAN SEA

ARU ANT

Maracaibo   Caracas   Puerto La Cruz   TRI

Barquisimeto   Maturin

Mérida   Barinas   Puerto Ordaz

San Cristóbal   Ciudad Guyana

GUY

COL

BRA

MAJOR CITIES/TOWNS

Population '000

1	Maracaibo	2 054
2	Caracas	1 801
3	Valencia	1 457
4	Barquisimeto	833
5	Ciudad Guayana	792
6	Barcelona	459
7	Maturin	445
8	Maracay	399
9	Petare	386
10	Turmero	373
11	Barinas	306
12	Santa Teresa	305
13	Ciudad Bolivar	300
14	Cumaná	263
15	Baruta	252
16	San Cristóbal	249
17	Puerto la Cruz	227
18	Mérida	221
19	Guatire	208
20	Coro	205
21	Cabimas	205
22	Cúa	199
23	Acarigua	116
24	Valera	92

BOLIVARIAN REPUBLIC OF VENEZUELA; REPUBLICA BOLIVARIANA DE VENEZUELA

Capital	Caracas	Language	Spanish			Independence	1821
Population	26 023 528	Area	912 050 km²	Density	27 per km²	% in cities	93%
GDP per cap	$4 800	Dailling code	+58	Internet	.ve	GMT +/-	-4

MEDALS TABLE

		Overall			Lge			Sth Am			City	Stadium	Cap'ty	DoF
		G	S	B	G	B		G	S	B				
1	Caracas FC	9	2	1	9	2				1	Caracas	Estadio Olimpico	25 000	1967
2	Unión SC	7	3		7	3								
3	Dos Caminos SC	6	7		6	7								
	Deportivo Tachira	6	7		6	7					San Cristobal	Polideportivo de Pueblo Nuevo	30 000	1974
5	Deportivo Italia	5	6		5	6					Caracas	Brigido Iriarte	15 000	1948
6	Portuguesa FC	5	3	1	5	3		1			Acarígua	José Antonio Paez	20 000	1972
7	Centro Atlético	4	7		4	7								
8	Deportivo Galicia	4	5		4	5					Caracas	Brigido Iriarte	15 000	
	Loyola SC	4	5		4	5								
10	Deportivo Portugués	4	2		4	2								
11	CS Maritimo	4	1		4	1					Caracas			1959
12	Deportivo Venezuela	4			4									
13	Universidad Central	3	3		3	3								
14	Universidad de Los Andes	3	1	1	3	1		1			Merida	Guillermo Soto Rosas	15 000	1977
15	Estudiantes Merida	2	7		2	7					Merida	Guillermo Soto Rosas	15 000	1971

RECENT LEAGUE RECORD

	Championship						Championship Play-off		
Year	Champions	Pts	Runners-up	Pts	Third	Pts	Winners	Score	Runners-up
1995	Caracas FC	17	Minervén	16	Trullianos	14			
1996	Minervén	22	Mineros de Guayana	20	Caracas FC	19			
1997	Caracas FC						Caracas	3-1 5-0	Atlético Zulia
1998	Atlético Zulia						Atlético Zulia	1-0 4-0	Estudiantes
1999	ItalChalcao						ItalChalcao	5-1 2-1	Unión At. Táchira
2000	Deportivo Táchira	15	ItalChacao	7	Estudiantes	6			
2001	Caracas FC	35	Trujillanos	33	ItalChacao	32			
2002	Nacional Táchira						Nacional Táchira	3-3 0-0 5-3p	Estudiantes
2003	Caracas FC						Caracas FC	1-1 3-0	Unión At. Maracaibo
2004	Caracas FC	†							
2005	Unión At. Maracaibo	†							
2006	Caracas FC						Caracas FC	1-1 3-0	Unión At. Maracaibo
2007	Caracas FC						Caracas FC	1-0 0-0	Unión At. Maracaibo
2008	Deportivo Táchira						Deportivo Tachira	1-1 0-0	Caracas FC

† Automatic champions as winners of both the Apertura and Clausura

VENEZUELA 2007–08
PRIMERA DIVISION
TORNEO APERTURA 2007

	Pl	W	D	L	F	A	Pts
Caracas FC †	17	10	7	0	31	11	37
Deportivo Anzoátegui	17	10	4	3	31	12	34
Deportivo Táchira	17	7	7	3	22	10	28
Unión At. Maracaibo	17	7	7	3	26	20	28
Zamora FC	17	6	6	5	19	12	24
Portuguesa FC	17	6	6	5	15	18	24
Llaneros de Guanare	17	6	5	6	25	23	23
Mineros de Guyana	17	6	5	6	28	28	23
Aragua FC	17	6	5	6	30	30	23
Guaros de Lara	17	7	2	8	28	33	23
Trujillanos FC	17	6	5	6	22	27	23
Monagas SC	17	6	4	7	30	26	22
Deportivo Italia	17	5	7	5	17	14	22
Estudiantes Mérida	17	5	5	7	21	28	20
Atlético El Vigía	17	6	1	10	18	26	19
Carabobo FC	17	4	3	10	13	25	15
Unión Lara	17	3	5	9	25	32	14
Estrella Roja Caracas	17	3	4	10	19	45	13

4/08/2007 - 16/12/2007 • † Qualified for the final

VENEZUELA 2007–08
PRIMERA DIVISION
TORNEO CLAUSURA 2008

	Pl	W	D	L	F	A	Pts
Deportivo Táchira †	17	13	3	1	30	15	42
Caracas FC	17	10	6	1	34	18	36
Deportivo Anzoátegui	17	10	2	5	33	14	32
Deportivo Italia	17	7	7	3	23	16	28
Guaros de Lara	17	8	4	5	19	14	28
Unión At. Maracaibo	17	8	3	6	28	22	27
Zamora FC	17	8	2	7	26	25	26
Carabobo FC	17	6	6	5	19	16	24
Estrella Roja Caracas	17	7	3	7	25	31	24
Portuguesa FC	17	6	5	6	24	24	23
Atlético El Vigía	17	6	1	10	19	25	19
Estudiantes Mérida	17	4	6	7	18	26	18
Llaneros de Guanare	17	5	3	9	18	27	18
Aragua FC	17	4	5	8	18	22	17
Monagas SC	17	5	2	10	16	26	17
Mineros de Guyana	17	3	7	7	18	22	16
Unión Lara	17	3	5	9	18	30	14
Trujillanos FC	17	3	4	10	18	31	13

20/01/2008 - 25/05/2008 • † Qualified for the final

VENEZUELA 2007–08
AGGREGATE TABLE

	Pl	W	D	L	F	A	Pts	Caracas	Dep Táchira	Dep Anzoátegui	UA Maracaibo	Guaros de Lara	Deportivo Italia	Zamora	Portuguesa	Llaneros	Aragua	Mineros DG	Monagas	Carabobo	Estudiantes	Atlético El Vigía	Estrella Roja	Trujillanos	Unión Lara
Caracas FC	34	20	13	1	65	29	73		2-2	0-1	0-0	5-1	0-0	3-1	3-1	0-0	2-2	0-0	3-0	1-1	2-1	2-0	6-4	3-1	4-2
Deportivo Táchira	34	20	10	4	52	25	70	0-1		0-0	4-3	1-0	1-0	0-0	4-1	3-2	3-0	3-2	0-0	1-0	1-0	6-1	2-0	2-1	
Deportivo Anzoátegui	34	20	6	8	64	26	66	2-3	2-3		1-1	3-1	1-1	5-0	0-0	2-1	5-1	1-0	4-0	1-0	3-0	1-0	7-1	4-0	2-1
Unión At. Maracaibo	34	15	10	9	54	42	55	1-2	0-1	1-0		2-1	0-0	2-0	1-0	3-2	1-1	2-1	3-3	2-3	4-2	3-1	4-0	2-1	2-1
Guaros de Lara	34	15	6	13	47	47	51	0-0	1-0	0-1	2-1		1-1	0-3	1-0	4-3	1-0	3-1	2-2	3-1	1-1	1-0	3-1	4-1	2-1
Deportivo Italia	34	12	13	8	40	30	50	1-1	0-0	2-0	1-1	1-1		1-0	2-0	3-0	2-1	2-3	2-3	2-0	2-0	1-0	1-1	2-2	1-0
Zamora FC	34	14	8	12	45	37	50	0-2	0-0	1-1	4-0	2-1	0-2		0-0	1-1	2-0	4-1	1-2	3-2	3-1	0-1	3-0	2-0	
Portuguesa FC	34	12	11	11	39	42	47	1-1	2-2	1-0	1-1	1-0	1-0	2-1		1-0	1-0	0-3	2-1	0-0	0-0	2-3	1-2	2-1	4-0
Llaneros de Guanare	34	11	8	15	43	50	41	1-2	1-1	1-0	3-6	3-2	1-0	1-1	1-0		0-2	3-2	2-1	3-1	0-0	2-1	5-1	1-1	2-0
Aragua FC	34	10	10	14	48	52	40	1-0	1-1	1-0	1-1	3-1	1-0	2-2	2-3	3-1		1-1	1-2	1-1	5-2	2-1	3-2	2-0	1-2
Mineros de Guyana	34	9	12	13	46	50	39	1-3	2-2	1-0	2-0	0-1	2-2	0-0	3-3	3-0	0-0		1-1	2-1	2-3	1-0	6-0	1-5	3-3
Monagas SC	34	11	6	17	45	52	39	0-3	0-1	2-3	0-2	0-1	0-1	2-0	0-1	1-0	0-1	1-1		4-0	5-0	4-1	1-0	0-1	2-1
Carabobo FC	34	10	9	15	32	41	39	1-1	0-1	0-1	1-0	0-0	1-0	1-2	0-1	1-0	0-2	0-1	2-0		2-1	0-1	4-1	2-0	0-0
Estudiantes Mérida	34	9	11	14	39	53	38	1-2	0-1	1-0	0-0	2-1	2-0	2-2	2-2	1-0	1-1	1-1	2-1	2-0		1-0	1-1	1-0	2-2
Atlético El Vigía	34	12	2	20	37	51	38	0-2	1-0	1-5	0-2	0-1	1-2	0-0	0-1	3-1	3-0	0-1	1-1	2-3			1-0	2-0	2-3
Estrella Roja Caracas	34	10	7	17	44	76	37	1-1	0-1	1-3	2-1	3-2	0-0	0-1	3-3	0-1	3-2	1-0	1-1	3-2	4-1	0-1		3-2	1-4
Trujillanos FC	34	9	9	16	40	58	36	1-1	1-2	1-1	1-1	4-3	1-1	1-4	2-0	2-1	0-0	2-1	1-1	2-3	1-0	3-2	0-0		2-0
Unión Lara	34	6	10	18	43	62	28	0-2	0-0	0-3	0-1	0-1	0-0	4-0	1-1	1-1	6-4	1-1	1-3	1-1	2-1	2-3	1-2	3-0	

4/08/2007 - 25/05/2008 • † Qualified for the Copa Libertadores • ‡ Qualified for the Copa Sudamericana • Apertura matches in shaded boxes
Top scorers: Alexander Rondon, Deportivo Anzoátegui 18; Rafael Castellín, Caracas 16; Armando Maita, Monagas/UA Maracaibo 16; Johny Carneiro, Mineros 15; Wuiswel Isea, Lara/Aragua 14

CHAMPIONSHIP FINAL 2008
First leg. Olímpico, Caracas, 28-05-2008, Ref: Argote

Caracas FC 1 Valencia 80
Deportivo Tachira 1 Villafraz 85

Caracas - Vicente Rosales - Oswaldo Vizcarrondo•, Juan Valencia, Jonny Mirabal, José Mera - Juan Cominges (Jorge Casanova 71), Franklin Lucena, Ronald Vargas, Edgar Jiménez - Pablo Bastianini (Emilio Renteria 59), Rafael Castellín•
Tachira - Manuel Sanhouse - José Granados, Lucas Bovaglio, José Gonzalez•, Gerson Chacón - Mauricio Parra (Manuel Mancilla 55), Roberto Bobadilla•, José Villafraz - Jose Torrealba, Edgar Perez Greco (Habynson Escobar 59), Rolando Escobar• (Marlon Fernández 82)

CHAMPIONSHIP FINAL 2008
Second leg. Pueblo Nuevo, San Cristobal, 31-05-2008, Ref: Perluzzo

Deportivo Tachira 0
Caracas FC 0

Tachira - Manuel Sanhouse - José Granados, Lucas Bovaglio, José Gonzalez•, Gerson Chacón - Mauricio Parra (Miguel Mancilla 83), Roberto Bobadilla, Marlon Fernández• (Diego Guerrero 67), José Villafraz - Jose Torrealba, Edgar Perez Greco (Habynson Escobar 90)
Caracas - Vicente Rosales - Oswaldo Vizcarrondo, Franklin Lucena, José Mera - Luis Vera• (Alejandro Guerra• 58), Ronald Vargas, Juan Valencia, Edgar Jiménez, Guillermo Banquez - Pablo Bastianini, Emilio Renteria (Ever Espinoza 15) (Jorge Casanova 71)

VGB – BRITISH VIRGIN ISLANDS

NATIONAL TEAM RECORD
JULY 10TH 2006 TO JULY 12TH 2010

PL	W	D	L	F	A	%
4	0	4	0	4	4	50

FIFA/COCA-COLA WORLD RANKING

1993	1994	1995	1996	1997	1998	1999	2000	2001	2002	2003	2004	2005	2006	2007		High
-	-	-	-	180	187	161	172	163	161	175	165	171	190	192		**160** 03/00

2007–2008												Low
08/07	09/07	10/07	11/07	12/07	01/08	02/08	03/08	04/08	05/08	06/08	07/08	**193** 01/08
179	179	180	180	192	193	193	193	173	173	173	171	

The national team of the British Virgin Islands suffered an odd fate during the 2010 FIFA World Cup qualifiers when they became the first nation to be knocked out without having lost a game. The Nature Boyz, as the team are also known, hadn't played a match since December 2004 and in a warm up series before their World Cup tie against Bahamas, they played out two draws against neighbours US Virgin Islands. With Sherly Ground, the national stadium in Road Town not up the the required FIFA standard for international competitions, the BVIFA decided to play both matches against the Bahamas in Nassau, with the second match designated as the home match for the

INTERNATIONAL HONOURS
None

British Virgin Islands - and that's where the problem lay. Both matches were drawn, the first 1-1 and the second 2-2, but as the second match was a 'home' tie, the Bahamas qualified on away goals. The one consolation for coach Patrick Mitchell was that with four matches unbeaten, the Nature Boyz made a big leap of the FIFA/Coca-Cola World Ranking to 173rd although they are unlikely to remain there for long as they have not entered the upcoming Caribbean Cup. In the matches against Bahamas the squad was composed entirely of locally based players and of the teams in the country, Rangers remain the strongest, winning their ninth title in 10 years.

THE FIFA BIG COUNT OF 2006

	Male	Female		Total
Number of players	1 240	315	Referees and Assistant Referees	5
Professionals	0		Admin, Coaches, Technical, Medical	16
Amateurs 18+	190		Number of clubs	0
Youth under 18	245		Number of teams	14
Unregistered	120		Clubs with women's teams	0
Total players	1 555		Players as % of population	6.73%

British Virgin Islands Football Association (BVIFA)
Botanic Station Road, Road Town, PO Box 4269, Tortola, British Virgin Islands
Tel +1 284 4945655   Fax +1 284 4948968
bvifa@surfbvi.com   www.bvifa.com
President: PICKERING Franka   General Secretary: LEWIS John
Vice-President: LIBURD Aubrey   Treasurer: COOKE Martin   Media Officer: GRANT Kenrick
Men's Coach: SAMUEL Vincent   Women's Coach: SAMUEL Vincent
BVIFA formed: 1974   CONCACAF: 1996   FIFA: 1996
Gold shirts, Green shorts, Green socks

RECENT INTERNATIONAL MATCHES PLAYED BY THE BRITISH VIRGIN ISLANDS

2004	Opponents	Score		Venue	Comp	Scorers	Att	Referee
28-01	Dominica	L	0-1	Tortola	Fr			Matthew SKN
30-01	US Virgin Islands	W	5-0	Tortola	Fr	OG [18], Williams [24], Morris 2 [26 56], Ferron [88]		
1-02	Dominica	L	1-2	Tortola	Fr	Morris [28]		Charles DMA
22-02	St Lucia	L	0-1	Tortola	WCq		800	Stewart JAM
20-03	St Kitts and Nevis	L	0-4	Basseterre	Fr			
28-03	St Lucia	L	0-9	Vieux Fort	WCq		665	Corrivault CAN
25-09	US Urgin Islands	W	2-1	Tortola	Fr	Heileger [48], Ettienne [55]		
24-11	St Vincent/Grenadines	D	1-1	Kingstown	CCq	Haynes [53]	300	Prendergast JAM
26-11	Cayman Islands	L	0-1	Kingstown	CCq			
28-11	Bermuda	W	2-0	Kingstown	CCq	James 2 [12 24]	400	Matthews SKN
12-12	Trinidad and Tobago	L	0-4	Tortola	CCq		16 000	Arthur LCA
19-12	Tinidad and Tobago	L	0-2	Tunapuna	CCq			Lancaster GUY
2005								
No international matches played in 2005								
2006								
No international matches played in 2006								
2007								
No international matches played in 2007								
2008								
14-03	US Virgin Islands	D	0-0	Tortola	Fr			
15-03	US Virgin Islands	D	1-1	Tortola	Fr			
26-03	Bahamas	D	1-1	Nassau	WCq	Lennon [68]	450	Moreno PAN
30-03	Bahamas	D	2-2	Nassau	WCq	Williams 2 [72 90p]	940	Suazo DOM

Fr = Friendly match • CC = Digicel Caribbean Cup • WC = FIFA World Cup • q = qualifier

BRITISH VIRGIN ISLANDS NATIONAL TEAM RECORDS AND RECORD SEQUENCES

Records			Sequence records				
Victory	5-0	PUR, AIA, VIR	Wins	2	1999	Clean sheets	2	1999, 2001
Defeat	0-12	JAM 1994	Defeats	8	1997-1998	Goals scored	6	1999-2000
Player Caps	n/a		Undefeated	6	2000-2001	Without goal	3	Five times
Player Goals	n/a		Without win	10	1991-1997	Goals against	18	1992-1999

RECENT LEAGUE RECORD

	Tortola	Virgin Gorda
Year	Champions	Champions
2000	HBA Panthers	Rangers
2001	HBA Panthers	Rangers
2001	Future Stars United	Rangers
2002	HBA Panthers	No tournament
2003	Old Madrid	Rangers
2004	Valencia	Rangers
2005	Not finished	Hairoun
2006	No tournament	Rangers
2007	No tournament	Rangers

BRITISH VIRGIN ISLANDS COUNTRY INFORMATION

Capital	Road Town	Status	Overseas territory of the UK	GDP per Capita	$16 000
Population	22 187			GNP Ranking	n/a
Area km²	153	Language	English	Dialling code	+1284
Population density	145 per km²	Literacy rate	97%	Internet code	.vg
% in urban areas	NA	Main religion	Christian	GMT + / –	-4
Towns/Cities	Road Town 8 449; Spanish Town 355				
Neighbours (km)	Caribbean Sea & Atlantic Ocean 80				
Main stadia	Shirley Recreational Field – Road Town, Tortola 2 000				

VIE – VIETNAM

NATIONAL TEAM RECORD
JULY 10TH 2006 TO JULY 12TH 2010

PL	W	D	L	F	A	%
18	6	4	8	29	24	44.4

FIFA/COCA-COLA WORLD RANKING

1993	1994	1995	1996	1997	1998	1999	2000	2001	2002	2003	2004	2005	2006	2007	High	
135	151	122	99	104	98	102	99	105	108	98	103	120	172	142	84	09/98

2007–2008												Low	
08/07	09/07	10/07	11/07	12/07	01/08	02/08	03/08	04/08	05/08	06/08	07/08	172	12/06
124	130	139	140	142	123	116	117	115	116	112	124		

Following the excitement of their surprise run to the quarter-finals of the AFC Asian Cup in 2007, there was always likely to be a come-down for the Vietnamese and it hit hard just months later. The nation's hopes of challenging for a place at the 2010 FIFA World Cup finals came to swift end when the United Arab Emirates handed Alfred Riedl's team a 6-0 aggregate defeat to avenge their humiliating loss at the Asian Cup just three months earlier. That left the team with little to play for in 2008 and, as a result, Riedl stood down from a position that he has held on three occasions, to be replaced by Portugal's Henrique Calisto. Binh Duong cruised to the V-League title, finishing a

INTERNATIONAL HONOURS
South East Asian Games 1959

mammoth 11 points clear of second placed Dong Tham Long An while Nam Dinh - who finished fourth in the league standings - lifted the Vietnam Cup with a 1-0 win over Binh Dinh. Despite their dominance at home, Binh Duong highlighted the gap that exists between club football in Vietnam and the upper tier within the continent by falling at the first hurdle in the 2008 AFC Champions League, while Nam Dinh also finished bottom of their group in the competition's first round. In an attempt to further develop football's grassroots, the Vietnam Football Federation has signed up for the Asian Football Confederation's Vision Asia programme.

THE FIFA BIG COUNT OF 2006

	Male	Female		Total
Number of players	1 755 000	119 350	Referees and Assistant Referees	152
Professionals	100		Admin, Coaches, Technical, Medical	10 500
Amateurs 18+	20 850		Number of clubs	27
Youth under 18	2 800		Number of teams	10 000
Unregistered	793 200		Clubs with women's teams	8
Total players	1 874 350		Players as % of population	2.22%

Vietnam Football Federation (VFF)
Liên Doàn Bong Dá Viêt Nam, 18 Ly van Phuc, Dong Da District, Hanoi 844, Vietnam

Tel +84 4 8452480   Fax +84 4 8233119

vff@hn.vnn.vn   www.vff.org.vn

President: NGUYEN Trong Hy   General Secretary: TRAN Quoc Tuan

Vice-President: LE Hung Dzung   Treasurer: LE Hung Dzung   Media Officer: NGUYEN Trung Lan

Men's Coach: CALISTO Henrique   Women's Coach: TRAN Ngoc

VFF formed: 1962   AFC: 1954   FIFA: 1964

Red shirts, Red shorts, Red socks

RECENT INTERNATIONAL MATCHES PLAYED BY VIETNAM

2004 Opponents		Score	Venue	Comp	Scorers	Att	Referee
18-02 Maldives	W	4-0	Hanoi	WCq	Phan Van Tai Em 2 9 60, Nguyen Minh Hai 13, Pham Van Quyen 80p	25 000	Fong HKG
31-03 Lebanon	L	0-2	Nam Dinh	WCq		25 000	Irmatov UZB
9-06 Korea Republic	L	0-2	Daejeon	WCq		40 019	Al Mehannah KSA
20-08 Myanmar	W	5-0	Ho Chi Minh City	Fr	Le Cong Vinh 2, Thach Boa Khanh, Nguyen Minh Phuong, Pham Van Quyen		
24-08 India	W	2-1	Ho Chi Minh City	Fr	Le Cong Vinh 21, Thach Boa Khanh 57		
8-09 Korea Republic	L	1-2	Ho Chi Minh City	WCq	Phan Van Tai Em 49	25 000	Yoshida JPN
13-10 Maldives	L	0-3	Male	WCq		10 000	Haq IND
17-11 Lebanon	D	0-0	Beirut	WCq		1 000	Ebrahim BHR
7-12 Singapore	D	1-1	Ho Chi Minh City	TCr1	Thach Boa Khanh 51	20 000	Sun Baojie CHN
9-12 Cambodia	W	9-1	Ho Chi Minh City	TCr1	Thach Boa Khanh 2 8 23, Le Cong Vinh 3 58 87 89, OG 63, Dang Van Thanh 2 71 83, Nguyen Huu Thang 83	8 000	Supian MAS
11-12 Indonesia	L	0-3	Hanoi	TCr1		40 000	Sun Baojie CHN
15-12 Laos	W	3-0	Hanoi	TCr1	Le Cong Vinh 9, Nguyen Minh Phuong 41, Thach Bao Khanh 74	20 000	Rungklay THA
2005							
No international matches played in 2005							
2006							
24-12 Thailand	L	1-2	Bangkok	Fr	Phan Thanh Binh 35		
26-12 Kazakhstan	W	2-1	Bangkok	Fr	Le Hong Minh 21, Le Cong Vinh 90		
28-12 Singapore	W	3-2	Bangkok	Fr	Phan Thanh Binh 7, Nguyen Vu Phong 53, Le Cong Vinh 90		
30-12 Thailand	L	1-3	Bangkok	Fr	Phan Tan Binh 68		
2007							
13-01 Singapore	D	0-0	Singapore	TCr1		20 000	Sananwai THA
15-01 Indonesia	D	1-1	Singapore	TCr1	Supardi OG 35	4 500	Shahbuddin
17-01 Laos	W	9-0	Singapore	TCr1	Le Cong Vinh 3 1 28 58, Phan Thanh Binh 4 29 73p 81 84, Nguyen Van Bien 2 45 90	1 005	
24-01 Thailand	L	0-2	Hanoi	TCsf		40 000	Napitupulu IDN
28-01 Thailand	D	0-0	Bangkok	TCsf		35 000	Srinivasan IND
24-06 Jamaica	W	3-0	Hanoi	Fr	Le Cong Vinh 8, Tran Duc Dong 66, Nguyen Anh Duc 90		
30-06 Bahrain	W	5-3	Hanoi	Fr	Le Cong Vinh 2 11 17, Mai Tien Thanh 53, Phan Thanh Binh 77, Nguyen Anh Duc 87		
8-07 UAE	W	2-0	Hanoi	ACr1	Hyung Quang Thanh 63, Le Cong Vinh 73	39 450	Najm LIB
12-07 Qatar	D	1-1	Hanoi	ACr1	Phan Thanh Binh 32	40 000	Moradi IRN
16-07 Japan	L	1-4	Hanoi	ACr1	Suzuki OG 8	40 000	Breeze AUS
21-07 Iraq	L	0-2	Bangkok	ACqf		9 720	Nishimura JPN
8-10 UAE	L	0-1	Hanoi	WCq		20 000	Nishimura JPN
28-10 UAE	L	0-5	Abu Dhabi	WCq		12 000	Mohd Salleh MAS
2008							
11-06 Indonesia	L	0-1	Surabaya	Fr			

Fr = Friendly match • TC = Tiger Cup/ASEAN Football Federation Championship • AC = AFC Asian Cup • WC = FIFA World Cup
q = qualifier • r1 = first round group • sf = semi-final • 3p = third place play-off

VIETNAM NATIONAL TEAM RECORDS AND RECORD SEQUENCES

Records			Sequence records					
Victory	11-0	GUM 2000	Wins	6	1966	Clean sheets	6	1999
Defeat	1-9	IDN 1971	Defeats	10	1997	Goals scored	23	1949-1958
Player Caps	63	Le Huynh Duc	Undefeated	8	1954-1956	Without goal	4	1997
Player Goals	30	Le Huynh Duc	Without win	12	1974-1993	Goals against	22	1956-1959

VIETNAM COUNTRY INFORMATION

Capital	Hanoi	Independence	1954 from France	GDP per Capita	$2 500
Population	82 689 518	Status	Republic	GNP Ranking	58
Area km²	329 560	Language	Vietnamese	Dialling code	+84
Population density	251 per km²	Literacy rate	90%	Internet code	.vn
% in urban areas	21%	Main religion	Buddhist, Hoa Hao, Cao Dai	GMT + / –	+7
Towns/Cities ('000)	Ho Chi Minh City 3 467; Hanoi 1 431; Hai Phong 602; Da Nang 472; Bien Hoa 407; Hue 287				
Neighbours (km)	Cambodia 1 228; China 1 281; Laos 2 130; South China Sea & Gulf of Tonkin 3 444				
Main stadia	My Dinh – Hanoi 40 000; San Chi Lang – Da Nang 28 000; Thong Nhat – Ho Chi Minh City 25 000				

VIETNAM 2007

V-LEAGUE

	Pl	W	D	L	F	A	Pts	Binh Duong	DT Long An	HAGL	Nam Dinh	Da Nang	Binh Dinh	SLNA	TMN.CSG	Khanh Hoa	Thanh Hoa	Hanoi ACB	HP.HN	Dong Thap	Huda Hue
Binh Duong †	26	16	7	3	42	22	55		4-3	2-1	3-1	0-0	4-2	2-0	3-1	1-0	3-1	1-0	1-1	2-0	3-1
G. Dong Tam Long An	26	12	8	6	46	31	44	1-1		3-0	3-2	2-0	2-0	0-0	2-2	3-1	0-1	2-1	4-0	2-2	1-0
Hoang Anh Gia Lai	26	12	5	9	40	33	41	2-0	2-2		0-1	1-0	4-1	2-2	2-0	0-3	2-2	1-0	6-1	1-0	2-1
Nam Dinh	26	10	8	8	35	31	38	1-0	1-2	2-2		0-0	4-0	2-2	4-1	2-1	0-0	0-1	1-1	1-0	2-1
Da Nang	26	9	10	7	33	28	37	3-1	2-0	2-1	1-1		0-2	2-2	1-0	4-3	2-2	1-1	3-0	1-0	4-0
Binh Dinh	26	10	6	10	34	36	36	0-0	2-1	0-2	0-0	3-1		0-1	1-1	1-0	0-0	2-0	3-2	2-1	2-0
Song Lam Nghe An	26	8	11	7	38	35	35	1-3	2-4	3-0	1-0	1-1	3-1		2-1	0-0	0-1	3-0	1-2	1-1	2-3
TMN-Cang Saigon	26	8	10	8	41	40	34	1-1	2-2	2-2	4-3	1-2	2-2	1-0		3-1	2-0	2-1	2-0	0-0	4-1
Khatoco Khanh Hoa	26	10	4	12	30	31	34	0-1	2-1	0-1	4-0	2-1	1-0	1-2	1-1		1-1	3-2	2-1	2-1	0-0
Thanh Hoa	26	8	10	8	27	30	34	0-0	2-0	2-0	0-1	**0-3**	2-1	1-2	2-2	2-1		0-2	2-1	1-1	1-0
Hanoi ACB	26	8	7	11	30	36	31	1-2	0-0	2-1	1-1	1-1	0-2	1-1	3-1	1-0	2-2		2-2	1-0	2-1
Hoa Phat Hanoi	26	7	9	10	31	41	30	1-1	1-2	1-0	0-2	3-1	1-1	2-2	2-1	2-0	2-1	1-0		2-3	0-0
Dong Thap	26	3	11	12	21	35	20	0-1	0-0	0-2	0-1	0-0	0-4	3-3	1-3	2-1	0-0	3-1	0-0		2-2
Huda Hue	26	4	8	14	25	44	20	0-2	1-4	0-1	3-2	0-0	4-2	1-1	1-1	0-0	1-1	0-0	2-3	2-1	

3/03/2007 - 23/09/2007 • † Qualified for the AFC Champions League • Match in bold awarded • Play-off: **Hoa Phat Hanoi** 2-1 An Giang

VIETNAM CUP 2007

Round of 16		Quarter–finals		Semi–finals		Final	
Nam Dinh	4						
Quang Nam	1	**Nam Dinh**	2				
Quang Ngai	1 5p	Hoa Phat Hanoi	0				
Hoa Phat Hanoi	1 6p			**Nam Dinh**	1 4p		
Huda Hue	0 6p			Song Lam Nghe An	1 3p		
Hai Phong	0 5p	Huda Hue	0				
Da Nang	0 0p	**Song Lam Nghe An**	3				
Song Lam Nghe An	0 1p					**Nam Dinh**	1
Khatoco Khanh Hoa	1					Binh Dinh	0
Can Tho	0	**Khatoco Khanh Hoa**	1				
TMN-Cang Saigon	0	G. Dong Tam Long An	0				
G. Dong Tam Long An	2			**Khatoco Khanh Hoa**	1 6p		
Dong Thap	2			**Binh Dinh**	1 7p		
Binh Duong	1	Dong Thap	2				
Dong Nai	2 2p	**Binh Dinh**	4				
Binh Dinh	2 3p						

CUP FINAL

Ninh Binh, 30-09-2007, Att: 8000

Scorer - Tran Trong Loc [17]

RECENT LEAGUE AND CUP RECORD

	Championship						Cup		
Year	Champions	Pts	Runners-up	Pts	Third	Pts	Winners	Score	Runners-up
2001	Song Lam Nghe An	36	Nam Dinh	34	The Cong	29	Cong An HCMC	2-1	Cong An Hanoi
2002	Cang Saigon	32	Song Lam Nghe An	28	Ngan Hang Dong	26	Song Lam Nghe An	1-0	Thua Thien
2003	Hoang Anh Gia Lai	43	Gach Dong Tam	40	Nam Dinh	36	Binh Dinh	2-1	Ngan Hang Dong
2004	Hoang Anh Gia Lai	46	Nam Dinh	44	Gach Dong Tam	38	Binh Dinh	2-0	The Cong
2005	Gach Dong Tam	42	Da Nang	38	Binh Duong	38	Gach Dong Tam	5-0	Hai Phong
2006	Gach Dong Tam	40	Bin Duong	39	Binh Dinh	36	Hoa Phat Hanoi	2-0	Gach Dong Tam
2007	Bin Duong	55	Gach Dong Tam	44	Hoang Anh Gia Lai	41	Nam Dinh	1-0	Binh Dinh

Cong An = Police • The Cong = Army • Cang Saigon = Saigon Port • HCMC = Ho Chi Minh City

VIN – ST VINCENT AND THE GRENADINES

NATIONAL TEAM RECORD
JULY 10TH 2006 TO JULY 12TH 2010

PL	W	D	L	F	A	%
23	6	3	14	30	47	32.6

FIFA/COCA-COLA WORLD RANKING

1993	1994	1995	1996	1997	1998	1999	2000	2001	2002	2003	2004	2005	2006	2007	High	
129	144	95	93	122	138	141	127	125	144	169	137	130	85	101	**73**	10/07

2007–2008												Low	
08/07	09/07	10/07	11/07	12/07	01/08	02/08	03/08	04/08	05/08	06/08	07/08	**170**	02/04
104	97	73	77	101	130	139	142	144	145	147	151		

The recent good form of the St Vincent and Grenadines national team came to a grinding halt in 2008 as they equalled their worst ever run of 10 matches without a win. Going into the 2010 FIFA World Cup qualifiers, Vincy Heat faced an uphill task in qualifying for the group stage having been drawn against Canada, but in preparation the federation organised an unprecedented schedule of friendly matches. All bar one, however, were lost as were both games against the Canadians. It was certainly a setback for the team, but with a one of the strongest youth setups in the Caribbean, their goal remains to become one of the strongest Caribbean islands. There is, however, concern at the

INTERNATIONAL HONOURS
None

lack of a proper domestic league, which has forced the good footballers to look elsewhere, mainly in Trinidad. There was no better example of this than Cornelius Huggins, Vincy Heat's most capped player, and Marlon James who have both played a huge part in Kedah's extraordinary run of success in Malaysia that has seen them win five trophies in succession. James scored twice in Kedah's 2007 Malaysia Cup triumph over Perak, a team which has gone down in Kedah folklore as the 'Magnificent 11'. It was a display that helped earn James the award of most valuable foreign player in Malaysian football in 2007.

THE FIFA BIG COUNT OF 2006

	Male	Female		Total
Number of players	8 600	900	Referees and Assistant Referees	5
Professionals	0		Admin, Coaches, Technical, Medical	500
Amateurs 18+	1 100		Number of clubs	50
Youth under 18	3 300		Number of teams	300
Unregistered	1 300		Clubs with women's teams	2
Total players	9 500		Players as % of population	8.06%

Saint Vincent and the Grenadines Football Federation (SVGFF)
Murray's Road, PO Box 1278, Saint George, St Vincent and the Grenadines
Tel +1 784 4561092   Fax +1 784 4572193
svgfootball@vincysurf.com   www.svgvincyheat.com
President: DELVES Joseph   General Secretary: BENNETT Earl
Vice-President: SARDINE Ian   Treasurer: CAINE Ashley   Media Officer: BASCOMBE Lawerence
Men's Coach: TBD   Women's Coach: McCARTHY Seamus
SVGFF formed: 1979   CONCACAF: 1988   FIFA: 1988
Green shirts, Blue shorts, Green socks

RECENT INTERNATIONAL MATCHES PLAYED BY ST VINCENT AND THE GRENADINES

2004	Opponents	Score		Venue	Comp	Scorers	Att	Referee
24-11	British Virgin Islands	D	1-1	Kingstown	CCq	Forde [69]	300	Prendergast JAM
26-11	Bermuda	D	3-3	Kingstown	CCq	Pierre [7], Haynes [52], Samuel [54]		
28-11	Cayman Islands	W	4-0	Kingstown	CCq	Samuel [20], Forde [43p], Haynes [51], Gonsalves [80]	850	Prendergast JAM
12-12	Grenada	W	3-1	Kingstown	CCq	Samuel [10], Guy [23], Velox [64]		Fanus LCA
19-12	Grenada	W	1-0	St George's	CCq	Francis [6]	1 000	Small BRB
2005								
9-01	Trinidad and Tobago	L	1-3	Port of Spain	CCq	Haynes [25]	1 688	Chance ATG
16-01	Trinidad and Tobago	W	1-0	Kingstown	CCq	Forde [66p]	1 450	Pine JAM
30-01	Barbados	L	1-3	Bridgetown	Fr	Guy [14]		
2006								
27-08	Antigua and Barbuda	L	0-1	St John's	Fr			Willett ATG
10-09	Barbados	D	1-1	Bridgetown	Fr	Marshall [65]		Small BRB
27-09	Haiti	L	0-4	Kingston	CCq		3 000	Forde BRB
29-09	Jamaica	W	2-1	Kingston	CCq	John [48], Velox [70]	3 000	Brizan TRI
1-10	St Lucia	W	8-0	Kingston	CCq	Douglas [11], Samuel 5 [26 42 56 76 90], John [52], Haynes [84]	3 000	Tamayo CUB
7-10	Trinidad and Tobago	L	0-5	Port of Spain	Fr		4 116	
1-11	Grenada	W	4-1	Kingstown	Fr			
5-11	Antigua and Barbuda	D	2-2	Kingstown	Fr	Douglas [1], Francis [17]		
19-11	Bermuda	W	3-0	Bridgetown	CCq	James [58], Samuel 2 [66 77]		
21-11	Barbados	L	0-3	Bridgetown	CCq			
23-11	Bahamas	W	3-2	Bridgetown	CCq	Samuel 2 [57 61], Charles [80]		
2007								
14-01	Guyana	W	2-0	Marabella	CCr1	Samuel [4], Glynn [85]		Angela ARU
16-01	Cuba	L	0-3	Marabella	CCr1			
18-01	Guadeloupe †	L	0-1	Marabella	CCr1			Brizan TRI
30-05	Haiti	L	0-3	Port of Spain	Fr			
2008								
13-01	Guyana	L	0-1	Blairmont	Fr			
27-01	Guyana	D	2-2	Kingstown	Fr	Mannings [56], Abrams [68]		
10-02	Grenada	L	1-2	Kingstown	Fr	Rennie [13], Langaigne [61]		
13-03	Barbados	L	0-2	Kingstown	Fr			
3-06	Jamaica	L	1-5	Kingston	Fr	James [56]		
7-06	Cuba	L	0-1	Havana	Fr			
15-06	Canada	L	0-3	Kingstown	WCq			Batres GUA
20-06	Canada	L	1-4	Montreal	WCq	James [75]	11 500	Aguilar SLV

Fr = Friendly match • CC = Digicel Caribbean Cup • WC = FIFA World Cup • q = qualifier • r1 = first round group • † Not a full international

ST VINCENT AND THE GRENADINES NATIONAL TEAM RECORDS AND RECORD SEQUENCES

Records			Sequence records					
Victory	9-0	MSR 1995, VIR 2000	Wins	5	1999-2000	Clean sheets	4	1995
Defeat	0-11	MEX 1992	Defeats	7	1992-1993, 2000	Goals scored	21	1996-2000
Player Caps	145	Melvin Andrews	Undefeated	8	1995	Without goal	7	1992-1993
Player Goals	16	Shandel Samuel	Without win	10	1996	Goals against	12	1996-1998

ST VINCENT AND THE GRENADINES COUNTRY INFORMATION

Capital	Kingstown	Independence	1979 from the UK	GDP per Capita	$2 900
Population	117 193	Status	Parliamentary Democracy	GNP Ranking	176
Area km²	389	Language	English	Dialling code	+1809
Population density	301 per km²	Literacy rate	96%	Internet code	.vc
% in urban areas	46%	Main religion	Christian	GMT +/–	-4
Towns/Cities ('000)	Kingstown 17; Barroualie 2; Georgetown 2; Layou 2; Byera 1; Biabou 1				
Neighbours (km)	Caribbean Sea & Atlantic Ocean 84				
Main stadia	Arnos Vale Playing Ground – Kingstown 18 000				

VIR – US VIRGIN ISLANDS

NATIONAL TEAM RECORD
JULY 10TH 2006 TO JULY 12TH 2010

PL	W	D	L	F	A	%
5	0	2	3	2	23	20

FIFA/COCA-COLA WORLD RANKING

1993	1994	1995	1996	1997	1998	1999	2000	2001	2002	2003	2004	2005	2006	2007
-	-	-	-	-	-	194	198	198	197	199	196	196	198	201

High	
190	04/99

2007–2008											
08/07	09/07	10/07	11/07	12/07	01/08	02/08	03/08	04/08	05/08	06/08	07/08
199	200	200	201	201	201	202	202	192	192	192	193

Low	
200	09/04

The US Virgin Islands were one of just four nations, along with Anguilla, American Samoa and Tuvalu, to lose a 2010 FIFA World Cup match by a score in double figures. Two draws against close neighbours, the British Virgin Islands, actually saw the US Virgins Islands climb off the bottom of the FIFA/Coca-Cola World Ranking but that couldn't mask the weakness of the team when they faced Grenada in a preliminary round match. Without a ground that met the standards required for a World Cup match the USVI opted for a single game in Grenada rather than chose an alternative home venue in another country. A wise decision perhaps. With Grenada boasting the talents of

INTERNATIONAL HONOURS
None

Wigans's Jason Roberts and New England Revolution's Shalrie Joseph, they put their opponents to the sword with a 10-0 victory and a second leg would have only added to the misery. USVI captain Dwight Ferguson scored an own goal to take the score into double figures but he believes that progress is being made with the federation actively involved in youth development which it never bothered with in the past. In the domestic league, where all of the national team players come from, Positive Vibes won the play-off between the top two teams from St Thomas and the top two from St Croix, winning the championship over their St Thomas rivals on goal difference.

THE FIFA BIG COUNT OF 2006

	Male	Female		Total
Number of players	5 800	900	Referees and Assistant Referees	1
Professionals	0		Admin, Coaches, Technical, Medical	100
Amateurs 18+	200		Number of clubs	10
Youth under 18	700		Number of teams	20
Unregistered	1 000		Clubs with women's teams	0
Total players	6 700		Players as % of population	6.17%

U.S.V.I. Soccer Federation Inc. (USVISA)
79B-2 Peter's Rest, Christiansted, PO Box 2346, St Croix VI 00823, US Virgin Islands
Tel +1 340 7142828   Fax +1 340 7142830
usvisoccer@vipowernet.net   www.none
President: MARTIN Derrick   General Secretary: MONTICEUX Glen
Vice-President: ANTOINE Trevor   Treasurer: TBD   Media Officer: none
Men's Coach: FREEMAN Carlton   Women's Coach: WOREDE Yohannes
USVISA formed: 1992   CONCACAF: 1998   FIFA: 1998
Royal blue shirts, Royal blue shorts, Royal blue socks

RECENT INTERNATIONAL MATCHES PLAYED BY THE US VIRGIN ISLANDS

2004	Opponents	Score		Venue	Comp	Scorers	Att	Referee
30-01	British Virgin Islands	L	0-5	Road Town	Fr			
31-01	Dominica	L	0-5	Road Town	Fr			Matthew SKN
18-02	St Kitts and Nevis	L	0-4	Charlotte Amalie	WCq		225	Brizan TRI
31-03	St Kitts and Nevis	L	0-7	Basseterre	WCq		800	Recinos SLV
25-09	British Virgin Islands	L	1-2	Road Town	Fr	Challenger 65		
24-11	Haiti	L	0-11	Kingston	CCq		250	Piper TRI
26-11	Jamaica	L	1-11	Kingston	CCq	Lauro 72	4 200	Piper TRI
28-11	St Martin †	D	0-0	Kingston	CCq		200	Brizan TRI
2005								
No international matches played in 2005								
2006								
27-09	Bermuda	L	0-6	Charlotte Amalie	CCq		150	Small BRB
1-10	Dominican Republic	L	1-6	Charlotte Amalie	CCq	Pierre 7	250	Davis TRI
2007								
No international matches played in 2007 before August								
2008								
14-03	British Virgin Islands	D	0-0	Road Town	Fr			
15-03	British Virgin Islands	D	1-1	Road Town	Fr			
26-03	Grenada	L	0-10	St George's	WCq		3 000	James GUY

Fr = Friendly match • CC = Digicel Caribbean Cup • WC = FIFA World Cup • q = qualifier • † Not a full international

US VIRGIN ISLANDS NATIONAL TEAM RECORDS AND RECORD SEQUENCES

Records			Sequence records					
Victory	1-0	BVI 1998	Wins	1	1998	Clean sheets	1	1998, 1999
Defeat	1-14	LCA 2001	Defeats	19	2000-	Goals scored	3	2001-2002
Player Caps	n/a	Dwight Ferguson	Undefeated	3	1998-1999	Without goal	4	1999-2000, 2004
Player Goals	n/a		Without win	20	1999-	Goals against	18	2000-2006

US VIRGIN ISLANDS 2008
ST CROIX/ST THOMAS PLAY-OFF

	Pl	W	D	L	F	A	Pts
Positive Vibes	3	2	1	0	14	4	7
New Vibes	3	2	1	0	8	1	7
Helenites	3	1	0	2	7	14	3
Chelsea	3	0	0	3	4	14	0

17/02/2008 - 24/02/2008

RECENT LEAGUE RECORD

	Overall Championship			St Thomas/St John	St Croix
Year	Champions	Score	Runners-up	Champions	Champions
2000	United We Stand Upsetters	5-1	Helenites	United We Stand Upsetters	Helenites
2001	Not played				Not played
2002	Hatian Stars	1-0	United We Stand Upsetters	Waitikubuli United	Helenites
2003	Not played			Waitikubuli United	Helenites
2004	Not played				Helenites
2005	Positive Vibes	2-0	Helenites	Positive Vibes	Helenites
2006	New Vibes	4-2	Positive Vibes	Positive Vibes	Helenites
2007	Helenites	1-0	Positive Vibes	Positive Vibes	Helenites
2008	Positive Vibes	† (league)	New Vibes	Positive Vibes	Helenites

US VIRGIN ISLANDS COUNTRY INFORMATION

Capital	Charlottte Amalie	Status	US Unincorpoated Territory	GDP per Capita	$17 500
Population	108 775			GNP Ranking	n/a
Area km²	352	Language	English, Spanish, Creole	Dialling code	+1340
Population density	309 per km²	Literacy rate	n/a	Internet code	.vi
% in urban areas	n/a	Main religion	Christian	GMT +/–	-4
Towns/Cities ('000)	Charlotte Amalie 10; Anna's Retreat 8; Charlotte Amalie West 5; Frederiksted Southeast 3				
Neighbours (km)	Caribbean Sea & Atlantic Ocean 188				
Main stadia	Lionel Roberts – Charlotte Amalie, St Thomas 9 000				

WAL – WALES

NATIONAL TEAM RECORD
JULY 10TH 2006 TO JULY 12TH 2010

PL	W	D	L	F	A	%
22	9	6	7	31	25	54.5

FIFA/COCA-COLA WORLD RANKING

1993	1994	1995	1996	1997	1998	1999	2000	2001	2002	2003	2004	2005	2006	2007	High	
29	41	61	80	102	97	98	109	100	52	66	68	71	73	57	27	08/93

2007–2008												Low	
08/07	09/07	10/07	11/07	12/07	01/08	02/08	03/08	04/08	05/08	06/08	07/08	113	09/00
74	53	58	58	57	58	54	53	52	52	53	54		

Welsh club football had one of its best seasons for years with Cardiff City reaching the FA Cup final for the first time since winning the trophy in 1927. Against Portsmouth they more than held their own but just fell short on the day, losing 1-0 to a Kanu goal. They will be joined in the second tier of English football in 2008-09 by Swansea City, whose revival has coincided with the opening of their new Liberty Stadium. Swansea were crowned League One champions, a full ten points ahead of Nottingham Forest but perhaps the most intriguing story of the season was the success of League of Wales side Llanelli who came within a whisker of winning a unique quadruple.

INTERNATIONAL HONOURS
Qualified for the FIFA World Cup finals 1958

Llanelli is better known for its rugby team - the Scarlets - but football has secured a foothold thanks to the decision in 2005 to turn professional. Coached by the former Welsh international Peter Nicholas, Llanelli won the Welsh Premier League for the first time and added the League Cup to the trophy cabinet when they beat Rhyl in the final. They also reached the final of the FAW Premier Cup and the Welsh Cup but lost in both to miss out on the quadruple. The growing optimism in Welsh football has also started to spread to John Toshack's national team with a number of talented youngsters, like FA Cup finalist Aaron Ramsey, breaking into the squad.

THE FIFA BIG COUNT OF 2006

	Male	Female		Total
Number of players	157 550	16 000	Referees and Assistant Referees	1 120
Professionals	550		Admin, Coaches, Technical, Medical	10 200
Amateurs 18+	35 800		Number of clubs	1 900
Youth under 18	31 200		Number of teams	4 500
Unregistered	41 000		Clubs with women's teams	20
Total players	173 550		Players as % of population	5.91%

The Football Association of Wales, Ltd (FAW)
11/12 Neptune Court, Vanguard Way, Cardiff, CF24 5PJ, United Kingdom
Tel +44 29 20435830   Fax +44 29 20496953
info@faw.co.uk   www.faw.org.uk
President: REES Peter   General Secretary: COLLINS David
Vice-President: PRITCHARD Philip   Treasurer: HUGHES Trevor Lloyd   Media Officer: COLLINS David
Men's Coach: TOSHACK John MBE   Women's Coach: BEATTIE Andy
FAW formed: 1876   UEFA: 1954   FIFA: 1910-20, 1924-28, 1946
Red shirts, Red shorts, Red socks or White shirts, White shorts, White socks

RECENT INTERNATIONAL MATCHES PLAYED BY WALES

2005	Opponents	Score	Venue	Comp	Scorers	Att	Referee
17-08	Slovenia	D 0-0	Swansea	Fr		10 016	Stokes IRL
3-09	England	L 0-1	Cardiff	WCq		70 715	Ivanov.V RUS
7-09	Poland	L 0-1	Warsaw	WCq		13 500	Larsen DEN
8-10	Northern Ireland	W 3-2	Belfast	WCq	Davies [27], Robinson [37], Giggs [81]	13 451	Bossen NED
12-10	Azerbaijan	W 2-0	Cardiff	WCq	Giggs 2 [3 51]	32 628	Hansson SWE
16-11	Cyprus	L 0-1	Limassol	Fr		1 000	Jakov ISR
2006							
1-03	Paraguay	D 0-0	Cardiff	Fr		12 324	McDonald SCO
27-05	Trinidad and Tobago	W 2-1	Graz	Fr	Earnshaw 2 [38 87]	8 000	Messner AUT
15-08	Bulgaria	D 0-0	Swansea	Fr		8 200	Attard MLT
2-09	Czech Republic	L 1-2	Teplice	ECq	Jiránek OG [85]	16 200	Eriksson SWE
5-09	Brazil	L 0-2	London	Fr		22 008	Riley ENG
7-10	Slovakia	L 1-5	Cardiff	ECq	Bale [37]	28 415	Van Egmond NED
11-10	Cyprus	W 3-1	Cardiff	ECq	Koumas [33], Earnshaw [39], Bellamy [72]	20 456	Granat POL
14-11	Liechtenstein	W 4-0	Wrexham	Fr	Koumas 2 [8 14], Bellamy [76], Llewellyn [89]	8 752	Wilmes LUX
2007							
6-02	Northern Ireland	D 0-0	Belfast	Fr		13 500	Richmond SCO
24-03	Republic of Ireland	L 0-1	Dublin	ECq		72 539	Hauge NOR
28-03	San Marino	W 3-0	Cardiff	ECq	Giggs [3], Bale [20], Koumas [63p]	18 752	Tchagharyan ARM
26-05	New Zealand	D 2-2	Wrexham	Fr	Bellamy 2 [18 38]	7 819	Skjerven NOR
2-06	Czech Republic	D 0-0	Cardiff	ECq		30 174	Allaerts BEL
22-08	Bulgaria	W 1-0	Burgas	Fr	Eastwood [45]	15 000	Germanakos GRE
8-09	Germany	L 0-2	Cardiff	ECq		27 889	Mejuto Gonzalez ESP
12-09	Slovakia	W 5-2	Trnava	ECq	Eastwood [22], Bellamy 2 [34 41], OG [78], Davies.S [90]	5 846	Duhamel FRA
13-10	Cyprus	L 1-3	Nicosia	ECq	Collins [21]	2 852	Bertolini SUI
17-10	San Marino	W 2-1	Serravalle	ECq	Earnshaw [13], Ledley [36]	1 182	Zammit MLT
17-11	Republic of Ireland	D 2-2	Cardiff	ECq	Koumas 2 [23 89p]	24 619	Oriekhov UKR
21-11	Germany	D 0-0	Frankfurt	ECq		49 262	Balaj ROU
2008							
6-02	Norway	W 3-0	Wrexham	Fr	Fletcher [15], Koumas 2 [62 89]	7 553	McKeon IRE
26-03	Luxembourg	W 2-0	Luxembourg	Fr	Eastwood 2 [37 46]	3 000	Kuipers NED
28-05	Iceland	W 1-0	Reykjavik	Fr	Evans [45]	5 322	McCourt NIR
1-06	Netherlands	L 0-2	Rotterdam	Fr		48 500	Brych GER

Fr = Friendly match • EC = UEFA EURO 2008 • WC = FIFA World Cup • q = qualifier

WALES NATIONAL TEAM PLAYERS

Player		Ap	G	Club	Date of Birth	Player		Ap	G	Club	Date of Birth
Wayne Hennessey	GK	10	0	Wolverhampton	24 1 1987	Arron Davies	MF	1	0	Nottingham For	28 6 1984
Boaz Myhill	GK	1	0	Hull City	9 11 1982	David Edwards	MF	5	0	Wolverhampton	3 2 1986
Lewis Price	GK	6	0	Derby County	19 7 1984	Mark Jones	MF	2	0	Wrexham	15 8 1984
Darcy Blake	DF	0	0	Cardiff City	13 12 1988	Jason Koumas	MF	29	9	Wigan Athletic	25 9 1979
Neal Eardley	DF	7	0	Oldham Athletic	6 11 1988	Joe Ledley	MF	22	1	Cardiff City	21 1 1987
Steve Evans	DF	6	0	Wrexham	26 2 1979	Aaron Ramsey	MF	0	0	Arsenal	26 12 1990
Chris Gunter	DF	6	0	Tottenham H.	21 7 1989	Carl Robinson	MF	46	1	Toronto FC	13 10 1976
Joe Jacobson	DF	0	0	Bristol Rovers	17 11 1986	Craig Bellamy	FW	51	15	West Ham Utd	13 7 1979
Craig Morgan	DF	8	0	Peterborough U.	16 6 1985	Freddy Eastwood	FW	9	4	Wolverhampton	29 10 1983
Lewin Nyatanga	DF	21	0	Derby County	18 8 1988	Ched Evans	FW	2	1	Manchester City	28 12 1988
Sam Ricketts	DF	28	0	Hull City	11 10 1981	Daniel Nardiello	FW	3	0	Queens Park R.	22 10 1982
Ashley Williams	DF	3	0	Swansea City	23 8 1984	Sam Vokes	FW	2	0	Wolverhampton	21 10 1989
Jack Collison	MF	2	0	West Ham Utd	2 10 1988	**Selected others**					
Andrew Crofts	MF	12	0	Gillingham	20 5 1984	Simon Davies	MF	50	6	Fulham	23 10 1979

The Welsh squad for the May/June 2008 internationals

						Gareth Bale	DF	11	2	Tottenham H.	16 07 1989

WALES NATIONAL TEAM RECORDS AND RECORD SEQUENCES

Records			Sequence records					
Victory	11-0	NIR 1888	Wins	6	1980-1981	Clean sheets	4	1981, 1991
Defeat	0-9	SCO 1878	Defeats	8	1897-1900	Goals scored	16	1950-1954
Player Caps	92	Neville Southall	Undefeated	8	1980-1981	Without goal	6	1971-72, 1973-74
Player Goals	28	Ian Rush	Without win	12	1896-00, 1999-01	Goals against	28	1891-1900

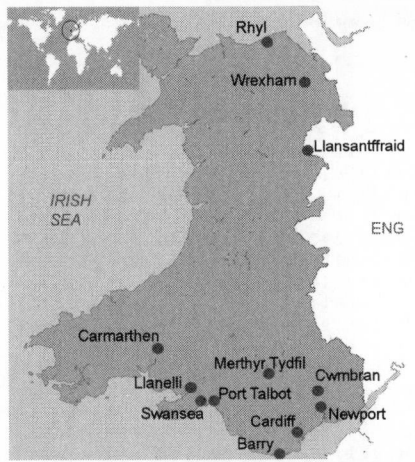

MAJOR CITIES/TOWNS

		Population '000
1	Cardiff	307
2	Swansea	171
3	Newport	117
4	Rhondda	59
5	Barry	52
6	Cwmbran	48
7	Llanelli	47
8	Neath	46
9	Wrexham	44
10	Bridgend	42
11	Port Talbot	34
12	Aberdare	33
13	Merthyr Tydfil	30
14	Rhyl	26
15	Aberystwyth	19
16	Connah's Quay	16
17	Carmarthen	15
18	Bangor	15
19	Haverfordwest	13
20	Newtown	10
21	Caernarfon	9
22	Welshpool	5
23	Porthmadog	3
24	Llansantffraid	1

WALES (PART OF THE UNITED KINGDOM)

Capital	Cardiff	Language	English, Welsh			Independence	n/a
Population	2 935 283	Area	20 798 km²	Density	141 per km²	% in cities	89%
GDP per cap	$22 160	Dailling code	+44	Internet	.uk	GMT +/-	0

MEDALS TABLE

		Overall			League			Cup			LC		PC		Europe			City	Stadium	Cap'ty	Fmd
		G	S	B	G	S	B	G	S	B	G	S	G	S	G	S	B				
1	Wrexham AFC	28	25					23	22						5	3		Wrexham	Racecourse Ground	15 500	1872
2	Cardiff City	23	12	1				22	10				1	2			1	Cardiff	Ninian Park	22 008	1899
3	Barry Town	18	3		7	1		6	1		4	1	1					Barry	Jenner Park	3 500	1912
4	Swansea City	12	10					10	8				2	2				Swansea	Liberty Stadium	20 532	1912
5	TNS Llantsantffraid	9	6		4	4		2	2		2		1					Llansantffraid	Recreation Ground	2 000	1959
6	Bangor City	8	13	3	2		3	6	8		5							Bangor	Farrar Road	2 200	1876
7	NEWI Cefn Druids	8	5					8	5									Wrexham	Plaskynaston Lane	2 500	1992
8	Rhyl	7	10	2	1	2	2	4	4		2	3		1				Rhyl	Belle Vue	4 000	1883
10	Chirk	5	1					5	1									Chirk			
12	Merthyr Tydfil	3	3					3	3									Merthyr Tydfil	Penydarren Park	10 000	1945
13	Oswestry Town	3	1					3	1									Oswestry	Park Hall		1860
	Caersws	3	1								3	1						Caersws	Recreation Ground	2 500	1887
16	Newtown	2	6			2		2	4									Newtown	Latham Park	5 000	1875
17	Llanelli AFC	2	4	1	1	1	1	2	1					1				Llanelli	Stebonheath Park	3 700	1896
19	Newport County	2	4					1	2				1	2				Newport	Newport Stadium	4 300	1912
20	Carmarthen Town	2	3	1		1		1	2		1	1						Carmarthen	Richmond Park	2 300	1948
21	Afan Lido	2	2			1			1	2								Port Talbot	The Marston's	4 200	1967

RECENT LEAGUE AND CUP RECORD

	Championship						Cup		
Year	Champions	Pts	Runners-up	Pts	Third	Pts	Winners	Score	Runners-up
1997	Barry Town	105	Inter Cardiff	84	Ebbw Vale	78	Barry Town	2-1	Cwmbran Town
1998	Barry Town	104	Newtown	78	Ebbw Vale	77	Bangor City	1-1 4-2p	Nomads
1999	Barry Town	76	Inter Cardiff	63	Cwmbran Town	57	Inter Cardiff	1-1 4-2p	Carmarthen Town
2000	TNS Llansantffraid	76	Barry Town	74	Cwmbran Town	69	Bangor City	1-0	Cwmbran Town
2001	Barry Town	77	Cwmbran Town	74	Carmarthen Town	58	Barry Town	2-0	TNS Llansantffraid
2002	Barry Town	77	TNS Llansantffraid	70	Bangor City	69	Barry Town	4-1	Bangor City
2003	Barry Town	83	TNS Llansantffraid	80	Bangor City	71	Barry Town	2-2 4-3	Cwmbran Town
2004	Rhyl	77	TNS Llansantffraid	76	Haverfordwest Cty	62	Rhyl	1-0	TNS Llansantffraid
2005	TNS Llansantffraid	78	Rhyl	74	Bangor City	67	TNS Llansantffraid	1-0	Carmarthen Town
2006	TNS Llansantffraid	86	Llanelli	68	Rhyl	64	Rhyl	2-0	Bangor City
2007	TNS Llansantffraid	76	Rhyl	69	Llanelli	63	Carmarthen Town	3-2	Afan Lido
2008	Llanelli	85	TNS Llansantffraid	78	Rhyl	69	Bangor City	4-2	Llanelli

WALES 2007–08

LEAGUE OF WALES

	Pl	W	D	L	F	A	Pts	Llanelli	New Saints	Rhyl	Port Talbot	Bangor City	Carmarthen	Neath Ath	Haverfordwest	Aberystwyth	Welshpool	Airbus UK	Cefn Druids	Newtown	Caernarfon	Connah's Quay	Porthmadog	Caersws	Llangefni
Llanelli †	34	27	4	3	99	35	85		4-0	2-1	8-0	0-2	4-1	3-3	4-2	1-0	3-0	1-1	1-0	5-0	5-1	4-0	0-1	1-1	5-0
TNS Llansantffraid ‡	34	25	3	6	85	30	78	3-0		1-0	2-1	2-1	0-3	3-1	6-2	1-0	2-0	0-0	3-0	6-0	4-0	3-1	4-1	6-0	7-1
Rhyl	34	21	6	7	60	24	69	1-2	0-1		5-0	1-2	2-1	1-0	2-0	0-0	1-1	2-1	1-0	2-1	3-1	1-0	1-0	2-1	4-1
Port Talbot Town	34	17	8	9	57	48	59	0-1	1-0	1-2		0-0	2-0	3-3	2-2	2-1	1-1	0-0	5-1	5-1	2-1	2-1	4-2	3-1	3-1
Bangor City ‡	34	15	10	9	62	31	55	1-1	1-2	1-2	0-0		1-1	1-1	2-0	1-0	1-0	5-0	5-1	2-2	5-1	3-2	2-0	1-1	2-2
Carmarthen Town	34	15	9	10	59	47	54	1-2	0-3	0-0	0-0	2-1		1-1	2-1	0-3	4-2	2-1	4-1	2-1	1-1	8-0	0-0	1-3	2-2
Neath Athletic	34	15	9	10	57	52	54	0-2	2-2	1-1	0-2	1-0	1-2		2-1	2-2	2-5	2-1	3-0	2-0	3-2	4-0	2-1	2-2	2-0
Haverfordwest County	34	14	5	15	61	59	47	1-4	0-4	1-1	2-1	0-1	2-2	1-2		3-1	1-0	4-0	3-0	3-1	1-1	6-2	3-2	1-0	5-1
Aberystwyth Town	34	13	7	14	57	45	46	1-2	5-1	0-0	2-4	2-1	0-2	1-2	2-3		2-3	0-1	0-1	2-2	4-0	6-1	2-1	2-1	3-0
Welshpool Town	34	12	10	12	49	52	46	3-3	0-3	1-0	1-3	2-0	2-2	1-2	2-1	2-3		0-1	0-1	2-1	2-4	1-1	0-3	1-1	3-0
Airbus UK	34	11	9	14	36	44	42	0-1	2-0	0-2	1-0	0-0	1-0	0-1	2-1	3-1	1-1		3-2	1-1	2-0	0-0	2-0	0-2	1-3
NEWI Cefn Druids	34	12	2	20	45	66	38	2-5	1-0	1-4	0-1	1-6	3-1	0-2	1-0	0-2	0-2	4-1		3-0	5-1	5-2	1-1	4-0	2-1
Newtown	34	9	10	15	47	66	37	3-5	0-0	0-2	0-0	2-2	0-1	3-0	1-4	1-2	1-2	1-1	1-0		3-1	4-1	4-2	2-2	2-1
Caernarfon Town	34	10	6	18	42	74	36	3-4	1-7	0-1	3-1	0-4	2-1	1-2	1-2	1-0	1-1	0-3	1-1	0-0		1-1	2-4	2-0	1-0
Connah's Quay Nomads	34	9	7	18	42	85	34	3-4	0-5	1-0	0-5	0-7	4-3	2-0	1-1	2-3	2-0	2-1	1-1	1-1	1-0		1-2	1-0	2-0
Porthmadog	34	7	6	21	48	70	27	2-4	0-1	1-0	1-2	0-0	1-2	0-0	0-2	0-2	2-6	1-1	2-2	1-2	1-3	3-3		0-1	2-4
Caersws	34	6	8	20	37	72	26	0-5	1-2	2-7	1-4	1-0	1-2	2-2	1-2	1-1	0-3	2-3	1-2	1-0	0-1	3-4	2-4		1-2
Llangefni Town	34	7	3	24	39	82	24	1-5	0-3	0-3	4-1	0-1	0-3	4-2	2-1	3-0	0-1	0-3	2-0	2-3	1-2	1-2	1-4	0-1	

17/08/2007 - 19/04/2008 • † Qualified for the UEFA Champions League • ‡ Qualified for the UEFA Cup

---

FAW PREMIER CUP 2007–08

Quarter–finals

Newport County *	1
Swansea City	0
Welshpool Town *	0
Cardiff City	1
Carmarthen Town *	3
TNS Llansantffraid	1
Wrexham	2
Llanelli *	4

Semi–finals

Newport County	1	5p
Cardiff City *	1	4p
Carmarthen Town	0	
Llanelli *	1	

Final

Newport County	1
Llanelli	0

Spytty Park, Newport
11-03-2008

* Home team

WELSH CUP 2007–08

Round of 16

Bangor City	0 3p
Aberystwyth Town *	0 2p
Caernarfon Town	0
Guilsfield Athletic *	1
Welshpool Town	2
Bryntirion Athletic *	1
Llangefni Town	1 3p
Newport YMCA *	1 4p
Rhyl	2
Haverfordwest County *	1
Caerleon	0
GAP Queens Park *	2
NEWI Cefn Druids *	0 5p
Aberaman Athletic	0 3p
Newtown *	1
Llanelli	2

Quarter–finals

Bangor City	6
Guilsfield Athletic	0
Welshpool Town	2
Newport YMCA	3
Rhyl	3
GAP Queens Park	2
NEWI Cefn Druids	3
Llanelli	6

Semi–finals

Bangor City †	3
Newport YMCA	1
Rhyl	2
Llanelli ††	5

Final

Bangor City ‡	4
Llanelli	2

CUP FINAL
Latham Park, Newtown
4-05-2008
Scorers - Ashley Stott, Chris Sargeant, Marc Limbert, Karl Noon for Bangor; Dave Swanick OG, Ryan Griffiths for Llanelli

‡ Qualified for the UEFA Cup
* Home team • † Played in Newtown • †† Played in Aberystwyth

YEM – YEMEN

NATIONAL TEAM RECORD
JULY 10TH 2006 TO JULY 12TH 2010

PL	W	D	L	F	A	%
23	6	5	12	24	32	36.9

FIFA/COCA-COLA WORLD RANKING

1993	1994	1995	1996	1997	1998	1999	2000	2001	2002	2003	2004	2005	2006	2007
91	103	123	139	128	146	158	160	135	145	132	124	139	141	144

High	
90	08/93

2007–2008											
08/07	09/07	10/07	11/07	12/07	01/08	02/08	03/08	04/08	05/08	06/08	07/08
137	141	136	144	144	143	144	138	141	140	138	143

Low	
163	07/00

As one of the lowest ranked teams in Asia, Yemen had to go through two preliminary rounds in the 2010 FIFA World Cup qualifiers. A pair of comfortable wins over the Maldives in October 2007 saw them through the first of those rounds, but the country's hopes of further progress were to end soon after. Ali Al Nono scored for the Yemenis as they recorded a 1-1 draw with Thailand in the first leg of their second round encounter in Sana'a but defeat by a solitary goal in Bangkok meant that they failed to make it through to the group stage. With their World Cup aspirations ended once again, the national side played a series of friendly matches throughout 2008. They recorded just

INTERNATIONAL HONOURS
None

one win, against Tanzania on home soil. There was little joy, either, for Yemen's club sides in continental competition with both Al Ahly Sana'a and Al Sha'ab Hadramout failing to get past the group stage of the 2008 AFC Cup. Sha'ab would have gone through to the quarter-finals had they beaten Oman's Al Nahda in the final fixture away from home but they lost 2-0. There were first time winners in both the league and the cup. Al Hilal from the city of Hudayda finished clear winners in the league in June 2008 and then claimed the double by winning the President's Cup, while Aden's Al Tilal had claimed the President's Cup for the first time the previous year.

THE FIFA BIG COUNT OF 2006

	Male	Female		Total
Number of players	355 200	28 100	Referees and Assistant Referees	252
Professionals	0		Admin, Coaches, Technical, Medical	250
Amateurs 18+	7 190		Number of clubs	110
Youth under 18	1 910		Number of teams	220
Unregistered	50 100		Clubs with women's teams	0
Total players	383 300		Players as % of population	1.79%

Yemen Football Association (YFF)
Quarter of Sport Al Jeraf, (Stadium Ali Mushen), PO Box 908, Sanaa-Yemen, Al Thawra City, Yemen
Tel +967 1 310923   Fax +967 1 310921
s.g@yemenfootball.org   www.yemenfootball.org
President: AL-EISSI Ahmed Saleh   General Secretary: SHAIBANI Hammed
Vice-President: AL AWAEJ Najeeb   Treasurer: AL TAWEL Mohamed   Media Officer: AL KHAMESE Moad
Men's Coach: SALEH Mohsen   Women's Coach: None
YFF formed: 1962   AFC: 1972   FIFA: 1980
Green shirts, Green shorts, Green socks

RECENT INTERNATIONAL MATCHES PLAYED BY YEMEN

2004	Opponents	Score		Venue	Comp	Scorers	Att	Referee
18-02	Korea DPR	D	1-1	Sana'a	WCq	Al Selwi 73	15 000	Husain BHR
17-03	Turkmenistan	L	1-2	Sana'a	Fr	Saleh Al Shekri 40p		
31-03	Thailand	L	0-3	Sana'a	WCq		25 000	Mansour LIB
9-06	United Arab Emirates	L	0-3	Al Ain	WCq		5 000	Sapaev TKM
26-08	Syria	L	1-2	Sana'a	Fr			
28-08	Syria	W	2-1	Sana'a	Fr			
8-09	United Arab Emirates	W	3-1	Sana'a	WCq	Al Nono 2 22 77, Abduljabar 49	17 000	Al Ghamdi KSA
13-10	Korea DPR	L	1-2	Pyongyang	WCq	Jaber 76	15 000	Vo Minh Tri VIE
1-11	Zambia	D	2-2	Dubai	Fr	Al Nono 83, Al Qaar 90		
17-11	Thailand	D	1-1	Bangkok	WCq	Al Shehri 69	15 000	Baskar IND
3-12	Iraq	L	1-3	Dubai	Fr	Nashwan Abdulaziz 28		
5-12	Qatar	L	0-3	Doha	Fr			
11-12	Bahrain	D	1-1	Doha	GCr1	Nasser Ghazi 47		
14-12	Saudi Arabia	L	0-2	Doha	GCr1			
17-12	Kuwait	L	0-3	Doha	GCr1			
2005								
No international matches played in 2005								
2006								
22-02	Saudi Arabia	L	0-4	Sana'a	ACq		55 000	Al Fadhli KUW
1-03	India	W	3-0	New Delhi	ACq	Salem Abdullah 6, Al Hubaishi 43, Al Nono 56p	8 000	Torky IRN
17-07	Ethiopia	L	0-1	Addis Abeba	Fr			
16-08	Japan	L	0-2	Niigata	ACq		40 913	Lee Gi Young KOR
26-08	Libya	L	0-1	Sana'a	Fr			
29-08	Libya	D	1-1	Sana'a	Fr			
6-09	Japan	L	0-1	Sana'a	ACq		7 000	Al Ghatrifi OMA
11-10	Saudi Arabia	L	0-5	Jeddah	ACq		1 500	Nema IRQ
15-11	India	W	2-1	Sana'a	ACq	Al Haggam 60, Al Nono 82	5 500	Marshoud JOR
14-12	Comoros	W	2-0	Sana'a	Fr	Al Haggam 2 73 90		
20-12	Djibouti	W	4-1	Sana'a	Fr	Al Sasi 9, Al Sahhed 50, Al Hubaishi 52, Al Tahoos 85		
2007								
7-01	Eritrea	W	4-1	Sana'a	Fr	Al Worafi 54, Al Hubaishi 71, Basuki 73, Al Haggam 79		
12-01	Bahrain	L	0-4	Dubai	Fr			
17-01	Kuwait	D	1-1	Abu Dhabi	GCr1	Al Omqy 16		
20-01	UAE	L	1-2	Abu Dhabi	GCr1	Al Sasi 90		
23-01	Oman	L	1-2	Abu Dhabi	GCr1	Mohammed Salem 9		
8-10	Maldives	W	3-0	Sana'a	WCq	Mohammed Salem 43, Al Hubaishi 66, Thabit 80	3 000	Mansour LIB
28-10	Maldives	L	0-2	Male	WCq		8 900	Sarkar IND
9-11	Thailand	D	1-1	Sana'a	WCq	Al Nono 43	12 000	Al Ghamdi KSA
18-11	Thailand	L	0-1	Bangkok	WCq		29 000	Matsumura JPN
2008								
26-01	Bahrain	L	1-2	Manama	Fr	Abdullah Yaslam 67		
4-04	Tanzania	W	2-1	Sana'a	Fr	Abdullah Yaslam 2 2 50		
25-04	Indonesia	L	0-1	Bandung	Fr			
3-05	Oman	D	0-0	Muscat	Fr			
22-05	Sudan	D	1-1	Sana'a	Fr	Muaz Assaj 47		

Fr = Friendly match • GC = Gulf Cup • AC = AFC Asian Cup • WC = FIFA World Cup • q = qualifier • r1 = first round group

YEMEN NATIONAL TEAM RECORDS AND RECORD SEQUENCES

Records			Sequence records				
Victory	11-2	BHU 2000	Wins	4	2006-2007	Clean sheets	4	1989-1990
Defeat	1-15	ALG 1973	Defeats	10	1965-1975	Goals scored	7	2001
Player Caps	n/a		Undefeated	5	2001	Without goal	5	1994-1996
Player Goals	n/a		Without win	12	1981-1989	Goals against	17	1976-1990

YEMEN COUNTRY INFORMATION

Capital	Sana'a	Unification	1990	GDP per Capita	$800
Population	20 024 867	Status	Republic	GNP Ranking	93
Area km²	527 970	Language	Arabic	Dialling code	+967
Population density	38 per km²	Literacy rate	50%	Internet code	.ye
% in urban areas	34%	Main religion	Muslim	GMT + / -	+3
Towns/Cities ('000)	Sana'a 1 937; Hudayda 617; Taizz 615; Aden 550; Mukalla 258; Ibb 234; Damar 158;				
Neighbours (km)	Oman 288; Saudi Arabia 1 458; Red Sea & Arabian Sea 1 906				
Main stadia	Ali Moshen – Sana'a 25 000				

YEMEN 2008

PREMIER LEAGUE

	Pl	W	D	L	F	A	Pts	Hilal	Ahly S	Shula	Saqr	Sha'ab H	Yarmuk	Hassan	Sha'ab I	Rasheed	Wahda A	Wahda S	Shabab	Ahli T	May 22
Al Hilal Hudayda †	26	16	3	7	36	17	51		0-0	3-0	2-0	2-1	1-2	3-0	1-0	1-0	1-0	0-1	1-0	0-1	3-0
Al Ahly Sana'a	26	11	10	5	38	23	43	1-0		5-1	4-0	3-1	1-1	1-0	0-1	1-0	1-0	2-2	4-0	1-2	0-1
Shula Aden	26	13	4	9	39	32	43	1-4	3-3		1-0	2-0	1-0	0-1	1-0	3-3	0-1	5-0	4-1	0-0	2-1
Al Saqr Taizz	26	11	8	7	33	26	41	2-3	2-0	2-0		1-1	1-0	4-0	1-0	0-1	4-1	1-1	2-1	1-1	1-1
Al Sha'ab Hadramaut	26	11	7	8	23	22	40	2-1	0-0	1-3	3-1		0-1	1-0	2-0	1-0	0-0	2-1	1-0	1-0	1-0
Al Yarmuk Sana'a	26	11	6	9	20	19	39	1-0	1-2	0-1	1-1	0-1		0-0	0-2	2-1	0-2	1-1	2-0	1-0	0-0
Hassan Abyan	26	10	7	9	31	34	37	1-1	1-2	1-1	2-1	1-0	1-0		0-2	4-1	3-4	3-2	1-1	2-1	3-0
Al Sha'ab Ibb	26	10	5	11	30	29	35	0-0	2-1	1-2	0-0	0-0	0-1	1-2		1-2	2-1	2-2	2-1	4-0	2-1
Al Rasheed Taizz	26	10	4	12	34	33	34	1-2	0-0	1-0	1-1	1-0	2-3	3-1	1-2		1-0	3-1	1-2	0-2	4-1
Al Wahda Aden	26	10	4	12	23	29	34	0-2	0-1	1-0	1-3	0-0	1-0	2-0	3-2	1-3		0-1	1-1	1-1	1-0
Al Wahda Sana'a	26	8	8	10	29	29	32	0-1	0-0	0-1	0-1	2-0	0-1	0-0	4-1	2-1	0-1		1-2	4-0	0-0
Shabab Al Jeel	26	7	8	11	28	37	29	3-1	1-1	1-2	1-2	0-0	0-1	3-3	1-1	1-1	1-0	0-1		2-1	2-1
Al Ahli Taizz	26	5	11	10	20	34	26	0-2	2-2	1-5	0-0	2-2	0-0	0-0	0-1	0-2	2-0	0-0	1-1		2-2
May 22 Sana'a	26	4	5	17	17	37	17	0-1	2-2	1-0	0-1	1-2	0-1	0-1	1-2	1-0	0-1	1-3	1-2	1-0	

28/12/2007 - 27/06/2008 • † Qualified for the AFC Cup • 2nd place play-off: Ahly Sana'a 2-0 Shula

PRESIDENTS CUP 2008

Round of 16		Quarter–finals		Semi–finals		Final
Al Hilal Hudayda	1 2					
Al Ahly Sana'a *	1 0	Al Hilal Hudayda *	1 1			
Shamshan	1 2	Shabab al Jeel	0 2			
Shabab Al Jeel *	0 3			Al Hilal Hudayda *	3 1	See page 1047 for details of the
Al Tilal Aden *	5 6			Al Ittihad Ibb	0 2	President's Cup 2007
Sabeen	0 1	Al Tilal Aden *	1 0			
Al Wahda Sana'a *	2 0	Al Ittihad Ibb	1 1			
Al Ittihad Ibb	1 1					Al Hilal Hudayda 1
Al Rasheed Taizz *	3 0					Al Sha'ab Hadramaut 0
Saioon	1 1	Al Rasheed Taizz	1 3			
Al Yarmuk Sana'a *	1 1	Al Wahda Aden *	1 0			CUP FINAL
Al Wahda Aden	1 2			Al Rasheed Taizz	0 0 1p	
Al Sha'ab Ibb *	1 2			Al Sha'ab Hadramaut *	0 0 3p	
Al Saqr Taizz	1 1	Al Sha'ab Ibb *	2 0			17-07-2008
Al Ahli Taizz *	5 2	Al Sha'ab Hadramaut	2 1			
Al Sha'ab Hadramaut	3 4					

* Home team in the first leg • † Qualified for the AFC Cup

RECENT LEAGUE AND CUP RECORD

	Championship						Cup		
Year	Champions	Pts	Runners-up	Pts	Third	Pts	Winners	Score	Runners-up
2002	Al Wahda Sana'a	63	Al Ahly Sana'a	50	Al Hilal Hudayda	39	Al Sha'ab Ibb	4-0	Al Tadamun
2003	Al Sha'ab Ibb	46	Al Tilal Aden	43	Al Hilal Hudayda	36	Al Sha'ab Ibb	2-1	Al Sha'ab Mukalla
2004	Al Sha'ab Ibb	46	Al Ahly Sana'a	44	Al Tilal Aden	39	Al Saqr Taizz	2-0	Al Sha'ab Ibb
2005	Al Tilal Aden	54	Al Saqr Taizz	47	Al Ahli Sana'a	45	Hilal Al Sahely	3-1	Al Rasheed Taizz
2006	Al Saqr Taizz	55	Al Sha'ab Ibb	48	Al Tilal Aden	43	Sha'ab Hadramaut	2-1	Al Hilal Hudayda
2007	Al Ahly Sana'a	47	Hassan Abyan	45	Al Saqr Taizz	43	Al Tilal Aden	1-0	Al Hilal Hudayda
2008	Al Hilal Hudayda	51	Al Ahly Sana'a	43	Shula Aden	43			

ZAM – ZAMBIA

NATIONAL TEAM RECORD
JULY 10TH 2006 TO JULY 12TH 2010

PL	W	D	L	F	A	%
34	15	10	9	42	29	58.8

FIFA/COCA-COLA WORLD RANKING

1993	1994	1995	1996	1997	1998	1999	2000	2001	2002	2003	2004	2005	2006	2007		High	
27	21	25	20	21	29	36	49	64	67	68	70	58	62	65		15	02/96

	2007–2008											Low	
	08/07	09/07	10/07	11/07	12/07	01/08	02/08	03/08	04/08	05/08	06/08	07/08	80	05/04
	62	61	60	68	65	67	65	67	68	67	70	73		

Zambia remains a country with a never-ending production line of young and talented footballers. Already several players from the under-20 squad that competed in Canada last year at the FIFA U-20 World Cup have made their full international debuts but Zambia failed to get past the first round at the 2008 CAF Africa Cup of Nations finals in Ghana at the start of the year and were far from impressive in the 2010 FIFA World Cup qualifiers. Elimination after picking up four points in Ghana seemed a touch harsh but the calamitous defensive errors in a 5-1 thumping by Cameroon proved costly. Coach Patrick Phiri did not have his contract renewed after the tournament and has

INTERNATIONAL HONOURS
CECAFA Cup 1984   COSAFA Castle Cup 1997 1998 2006

been replaced by 39-year-old Frenchman Herve Renard. He is a former assistant of Claude LeRoy, by whom he was recommended to the new Football Association of Zambia president, Kalusha Bwalya. There is much excitement at the prospect of Zambia's most famous footballer now taking over the reigns of the domestic game, bringing his experience from years of playing in diverse countries like Mexico and the Netherlands. Renard battled in his first competitive game as Zambia lost to Togo and then drew away at Swaziland before a controversial late penalty secured them a 1-0 win at home in the return game in the FIFA World Cup qualifiers.

THE FIFA BIG COUNT OF 2006

	Male	Female		Total
Number of players	992 786	32 031	Referees and Assistant Referees	524
Professionals	101		Admin, Coaches, Technical, Medical	11 035
Amateurs 18+	19 560		Number of clubs	470
Youth under 18	9 050		Number of teams	2 350
Unregistered	975 606		Clubs with women's teams	448
Total players	1 024 817		Players as % of population	8.91%

Football Association of Zambia (FAZ)
Football House, Alick Nkhata Road, Long Acres, PO Box 34751, 34751 Lusaka, Zambia
Tel +260 211 250940   Fax +260 211 250946
faz@zamnet.zm   www.faz.co.zm
President: KALUSHA BWALYA   General Secretary: KASENGELE M. George
Vice-President: MUNAILE Emmanuel   Treasurer: MWAMELO Boniface   Media Officer: MWANZA Erick
Men's Coach: RENARD Herve   Women's Coach: KASHIMOTO Fredrick
FAZ formed: 1929   CAF: 1964   FIFA: 1964
Green shirts, Green shorts, Green socks

RECENT INTERNATIONAL MATCHES PLAYED BY ZAMBIA

2006	Opponents	Score		Venue	Comp	Scorers	Att	Referee
21-10	Angola	W	2-0	Lusaka	CCf	Dube Phiri [76], Nsofwa [89]		Raolimanana MAD
26-11	Burundi	L	2-3	Addis Abeba	CEr1	Kalaba [61], Dube Phiri [87]		
2-12	Zanzibar †	W	4-0	Addis Abeba	CEr1	Dube Phiri 2 [34 37], Felix Katongo [69], Kalaba [73]		
5-12	Ethiopia	W	1-0	Addis Abeba	CEqf	Sakuwaha [87]		
8-12	Rwanda	W	1-0	Addis Abeba	CEsf	Lwipa [24]		
10-12	Sudan	D	0-0	Addis Abeba	CEf	W 11-10p		
2007								
25-03	Congo	D	0-0	Brazzaville	CNq			Coulibaly MLI
26-05	Namibia	W	2-1	Windhoek	Fr	Sakala 2 [25 78]		
2-06	Congo	W	3-0	Chililabombwe	CNq	Mulenga [17], Chris Katongo [60], Chalwe [72]		Rahman SUD
9-06	Tanzania	D	1-1	Morogoro	Fr	Kalaba [81]		
16-06	Chad	D	1-1	Chililabombwe	CNq	Mbesuma [57]		Ssegonga UGA
21-07	Botswana	D	0-0	Orapa	Fr	L 2-3p		
22-08	Togo	L	1-3	Lome	Fr			
9-09	South Africa	W	3-0	Cape Town	CNq	Chris Katongo 3 [9 19 20]		
29-09	Mozambique	W	3-0	Atteridgeville	CCsf	Chivuta [35], Mayuka [69], William Njovu [79]		Bennett RSA
24-10	South Africa	D	0-0	Bloemfontein	CCf	L 3-4p		Andriamiharisoa MAD
21-11	Tanzania	L	0-1	Dar es Salaam	Fr			
2008								
6-01	Tunisia	W	2-1	Radès	Fr	Felix Katongo 2 [7 10]		
8-01	Tunisia	L	0-1	Radès	Fr			
12-01	Morocco	L	0-2	Fes	Fr			
22-01	Sudan	W	3-0	Kumasi	CNr1	Chamanga [2], Mulenga [51], Felix Katonga [59]		Diatta SEN
26-01	Cameroon	L	1-5	Kumasi	CNr1	Chris Katongo [89]		Nichimura JPN
30-01	Egypt	D	1-1	Kumasi	CNr1	Chris Katongo [89]		Coulibaly MLI
22-05	Libya	D	2-2	Tripoli	Fr	Mayuka [10], Liyanga [87]		
25-05	Iran	L	2-3	Tehran	Fr	Mulenga [60], Kola [62]		
31-05	Togo	L	0-1	Accra	WCq		15 000	Pare BFA
15-06	Swaziland	D	0-0	Mbabane	WCq		7 462	Kotey GHA
21-06	Swaziland	W	1-0	Chililabombwe	WCq	Chris Katongo [86p]	14 458	Marange ZIM
27-07	Zimbabwe	D	0-0	Secunda	CCqf	W 5-4p		Nhlapo RSA
3-08	Madagascar	W	2-0	Thulamahashe	CC3p	Mayuka [56], Kombe [70]		Marange ZIM

Fr = Friendly match • CC = COSAFA Cup • CE = CECAFA Cup • CN = CAF African Cup of Nations • WC = FIFA World Cup • BCD = Behind closed doors
q = qualifier • r1 = first round group • qf = quarter-final • sf = semi-final • f = final • † Not an official international

ZAMBIA NATIONAL TEAM PLAYERS

	Player		Club	Date of Birth		Player		Club	Date of Birth
1	Mike Poto	GK	Green Buffaloes	15 01 1981	12	Dube Phiri	FW	Primeiro Agosto	16 01 1983
2	Jacob Mulenga	FW	Racing Strasbourg	12 02 1984	13	William Chinyama	DF	ZESCO United	19 04 1984
3	Kennedy Nketani	DF	ZANACO	25 11 1984	14	Emmanuel Mayuka	FW	Kabwe Warriors	21 11 1990
4	Joseph Musonda	DF	Golden Arrows RSA	30 05 1977	15	Chintu Kampamba	DF	Free State Stars RSA	28 12 1980
5	Hichani Himonde	DF	Lusaka Dynamos	1 08 1987	16	Kennedy Mweene	GK	Free State Stars RSA	11 11 1984
6	Francis Kasonde	DF	Power Dynamos	1 09 1986	17	Rainford Kalaba	MF	ZESCO United	14 08 1986
7	Clifford Mulenga	MF	Pretoria University	5 08 1987	18	Billy Mwanza	DF	Golden Arrows RSA	21 01 1983
8	Isaac Chansa	MF	Helsingborgs IF	23 03 1984	19	Clive Hachilensa	DF	IFK Marienhamm	19 07 1979
9	Felix Nsunzu	FW	Konkola Blades	2 05 1989	20	Felix Katongo	MF	Petro Atletico	18 04 1984
10	Ian Bakala	MF	Primeiro Agosto	1 11 1980	21	James Chamanga	FW	Moroka Swallows	2 02 1980
11	Chris Katongo	FW	Brøndby IF	31 07 1982	22	Kalililo Kakonje	GK	AmaZulu RSA	1 01 1985
					23	William Njovu	MF	Lusaka Dynamos	4 03 1987

Zambia's squad for the 2008 CAF Africa Cup of Nations

ZAMBIA NATIONAL TEAM RECORDS AND RECORD SEQUENCES

Records			Sequence records				
Victory	9-0	KEN 1978	Wins	8	1964-1966	Clean sheets	7	1997-1998, 2000
Defeat	1-10	COD 1969	Defeats	4	Four times	Goals scored	19	1966-1971
Player Caps	n/a	Kalusha Bwalya	Undefeated	11	Three times	Without goal	4	2001
Player Goals	n/a	Godfrey Chitalu	Without win	11	1999-2000	Goals against	10	1966-1968

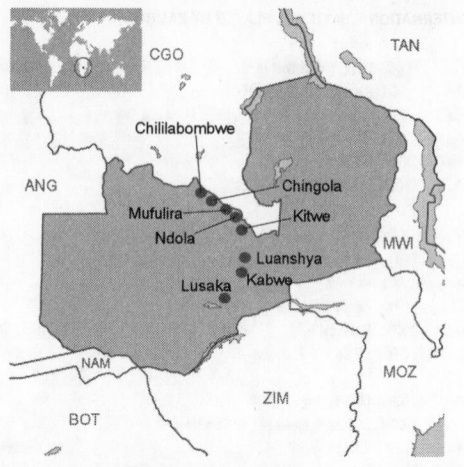

MAJOR CITIES/TOWNS

		Population '000
1	Lusaka	1 346
2	Kitwe	415
3	Ndola	401
4	Kabwe	193
5	Chingola	148
6	Mufulira	119
7	Livingstone	113
8	Luanshya	112
9	Kasama	98
10	Chipata	91
11	Kalulushi	72
12	Mazabuka	72
13	Chililabombwe	58
14	Mongu	56
15	Choma	49
16	Kafue	47
17	Kansanshi	43
18	Kapiri Mposhi	43
19	Mansa	42
20	Monze	32
21	Mpika	29
22	Nchelenge	24
23	Sesheke	23
24	Mbala	22

REPUBLIC OF ZAMBIA

Capital	Lusaka	Language	English, Bemba, Kaonda			Independence	1964
Population	11 477 447	Area	752 614 km²	Density	14 per km²	% in cities	43%
GDP per cap	$800	Dailling code	+260	Internet	.zm	GMT + / -	+2

MEDALS TABLE

		Overall			Lg	C	T8	LC	Africa			City	Stadium	Cap'ty	DoF
		G	S	B	G	G	G	G	G	S	B				
1	Mufulira Wanderers	27	3		9	9	9				3	Mufulira	Shinde	12 000	
2	Nkana	24	1	5	11	6	7			1	5	Kitwe	Scriveners	12 000	
3	Kabwe Warriors	19			5	5	8	1				Kabwe	Railways Stadium	10 000	
4	Power Dynamos	16	1		5	7	2	1	1	1		Kitwe	Arthur Davies	10 000	1977
5	Green Buffaloes	12			6	1	5					Lusaka	Independence	50 000	
6	Zanaco	10			4	1	3	2				Lusaka	Sunset Stadium	20 000	
7	Roan United	8			1	4	3					Luanshya	Kafubu	10 000	
8	Nchanga Rangers	6	1		2	1	3				1	Chingola	Nchanga Stadium	15 000	
9	City of Lusaka	5			1	2	2					Lusaka	Woodlands	10 000	
10	ZESCO United	3			1	1		1				Ndola	Dag Hammerskjold	18 000	
11	Red Arrows	3			1	1	1					Lusaka	Woodlands	10 000	

RECENT LEAGUE AND CUP RECORD

	Championship						Cup		
Year	Champions	Pts	Runners-up	Pts	Third	Pts	Winners	Score	Runners-up
2000	Power Dynamos	56	Nkana	52	Zanaco	50	Nkana	0-0 7-6p	Green Buffaloes
2001	Nkana	60	Zanaco	57	Kabwe Warriors	55	Power Dynamos	1-0	Kabwe Warriors
2002	Zanaco	61	Power Dynamos	60	Green Buffaloes	60	Zanaco	2-2 3-2p	Power Dynamos
2003	Zanaco	69	Green Buffaloes	59	Kabwe Warriors	57	Power Dynamos	1-0	Kabwe Warriors
2004	Red Arrows	62	Green Buffaloes	55	Zanaco	53	Lusaka Celtic	2-1	Kabwe Warriors
2005	Zanaco	65	Zesco United	54	Power Dynamos	52	Green Buffaloes	2-1	Red Arrows
2006	Zanaco	71	Green Buffaloes	57	Power Dynamos	51	ZESCO United	2-0	Red Arrows
2007	ZESCO United	68	Green Buffaloes	53	Power Dynamos	51	Red Arrows	2-2 3-2p	ZESCO United

BP TOP-8 CUP 2007

First Round		Semi-finals		Final	
Kabwe Warriors	1				
Power Dynamos	0	Kabwe Warriors	3		
ZESCO United	1 3p	Zanaco	2		
Zanaco	1 5p			Kabwe Warriors	3
Konkola Blades	0 4p			Nakambala Leopards	1
Forest Rangers	0 2p	Konkola Blades	1 3p	Nkoloma Stadium, Lusaka, 10-11-2007
Green Buffaloes	0 3p	Nakambala Leopards	1 4p	Scorers - Emmanuel Mayuka 3 [2 81 90]
Nakambala Leopards	0 5p			for Kabwe, Kelly Kumwenda [83] for NL

ZAMBIA 2007

KONKOLA COPPER MINES PREMIER LEAGUE

	Pl	W	D	L	F	A	Pts	ZESCO	Buffaloes	P. Dynamos	Kabwe	Y'ng Arrows	L. Dynamos	Zanaco	Konkola	Red Arrows	Nchanga	Roan Utd	City Lusaka	Zamtel	F. Rangers	Leopards	Assembly
ZESCO United	30	21	5	4	50	15	68		1-1	3-1	2-0	0-0	1-1	2-1	2-0	2-0	1-0	3-0	2-0	2-0	2-1	5-1	1-0
Green Buffaloes	30	14	11	5	39	25	53	0-3		1-3	1-0	1-2	4-0	0-0	2-1	1-0	3-1	0-0	0-0	0-0	3-3	1-0	3-0
Power Dynamos	30	14	9	7	41	25	51	1-2	1-2		1-1	0-1	1-0	2-2	2-0	1-0	1-2	3-1	0-0	1-0	5-1	3-1	0-0
Kabwe Warriors	30	14	9	7	34	22	51	0-2	2-0	0-1		1-0	1-1	1-0	2-0	3-1	1-1	1-2	0-1	2-1	2-0	2-1	1-0
Young Arrows	30	13	7	10	38	32	46	1-0	1-1	1-2	2-2		4-0	1-2	2-1	0-0	0-2	0-1	1-0	0-1	2-1	3-1	4-1
Lusaka Dynamos	30	11	13	6	25	25	46	1-1	1-1	2-1	0-0	1-0		0-0	1-0	2-1	0-0	0-1	3-0	0-0	1-0	1-0	2-1
Zanaco	30	12	9	9	38	25	45	2-3	1-2	0-0	1-3	3-2	1-2		2-0	0-1	3-0	1-0	4-1	1-0	1-0	6-1	1-1
Konkola Blades	30	11	7	12	29	26	40	1-0	0-0	0-1	1-1	4-1	3-1	1-0		2-1	0-2	1-0	4-1	0-1	0-0	4-0	0-0
Red Arrows	30	9	8	13	22	26	35	0-1	2-1	2-1	0-2	0-0	0-1	0-2	0-0		1-0	1-1	2-0	0-0	5-0	2-2	
Nchanga Rangers	30	8	10	12	25	31	34	0-0	0-1	0-1	0-1	1-2	0-0	0-0	1-2	2-0		0-0	1-0	2-2	2-2	3-3	2-1
Roan United	30	8	10	12	25	36	34	0-2	0-2	0-4	1-1	2-3	1-1	1-1	1-1	1-0	3-1		2-1	2-1	0-0	2-1	0-1
City of Lusaka	30	8	10	12	22	33	34	0-2	1-1	1-1	0-2	1-1	0-2	0-0	1-0	2-0	1-0	2-0		1-1	1-0	1-0	1-1
Zamtel	30	5	14	11	17	29	29	0-3	0-0	0-0	1-1	0-0	1-0	0-2	0-0	0-1	2-1	1-1			0-0	2-2	2-0
Forest Rangers	30	3	18	9	20	30	27	2-1	1-2	1-1	0-0	1-1	1-0	0-0	0-0	0-1	1-1	0-0	1-1			1-1	1-1
Nakambala Leopards	30	6	7	17	24	51	25	1-0	0-2	0-0	1-0	0-1	1-0	0-0	0-1	0-1	0-0	2-1	1-4	3-0	0-1		2-0
National Assembly	30	4	11	15	17	35	23	0-1	1-3	1-2	1-1	2-0	0-1	0-1	1-0	0-1	1-0	0-0	0-2	0-0	0-0	1-1	

3/03/2007 - 17/11/2007 • † Qualified for the CAF Champions League • ‡ Qualified for the CAF Confederation Cup

Top scorers: Rainford Kalaba, ZESCO 23; Enoch Sakala, ZESCO 22; Emmanuel Mayuka, Kabwe 15

COCA-COLA LEAGUE CUP 2007

First Round		Quarter-finals		Semi-finals		Final	
ZESCO United	1 3p						
Chambishi *	1 0p	ZESCO United	1				
Konkola Blades	0	Riflemen *	0				
Riflemen *	1			ZESCO United ‡	2		
Young Green Eagles *	0 3p			Nkwazi	1		
Nchanga Rangers	0 2p	Young Green Eagles	1 2p				
Zanaco	1	Nkwazi *	1 3p				
Nkwazi *	2					ZESCO United	5
Kabwe Warriors	0 5p					Nkana	0
Mining Rangers *	0 3p	Kabwe Warriors	1				
Mazabuka United *	0	Green Buffaloes *	0				
Green Buffaloes	3			Kabwe Warriors	0		
Green Eagles *	0 4p			Nkana ‡	1		
Lusaka Dynamos	0 2p	Green Eagles	0				
Young Arrows	0	Nkana *	1				
Nkana *	1						

* Home team • ‡ Held at Nkoloma, Lusaka

CUP FINAL
Nkoloma Stadium, Lusaka
29-09-2007
Scorers - Rainford Kalaba [13], Clifford Chipalo [16], Nicholas Zulu [36], Enoch Sakala [45], Yonah Mwango [57]

MOSI CUP 2007

Round of 16		Quarter-finals		Semi-finals		Final	
Red Arrows *	4						
Tazara Express	1	Red Arrows *	2				
City of Lusaka *	0	Kabwe Warriors	0				
Kabwe Warriors	1			Red Arrows ‡	4		
Forest Rangers *	2			National Assembly	1		
Green Buffaloes	1	Forest Rangers *	0				
Zamtel	2 1p	National Assembly	1				
National Assembly *	2 4p					Red Arrows	2 3p
Konkola Blades	2					ZESCO United	2 2p
Kalomo Jetters *	0	Konkola Blades	0 3p				
Lusaka Dynamos	2 5p	Nchanga Rangers *	0 1p				
Nchanga Rangers *	2 6p			Konkola Blades	0		
Young Arrows *	4			ZESCO United ‡‡	1		
Chambishi	0	Young Arrows *	3 3p				
Lusaka City Council *	1	ZESCO United	3 5p				
ZESCO United	2						

‡ Held at Nkoloma, Lusaka • ‡‡ Held at Nchanga, Chingola • * Home team

CUP FINAL
Nkoloma Stadium, Lusaka
15-12-2007
Scorers - Lawrence Pondani 2 [40][75] for Red Arrows; Nicholas Zulu [39], Enoch Sakala [76] for Zesco

ZIM – ZIMBABWE

NATIONAL TEAM RECORD
JULY 10TH 2006 TO JULY 12TH 2010

PL	W	D	L	F	A	%
19	5	9	5	15	15	50

FIFA/COCA-COLA WORLD RANKING

1993	1994	1995	1996	1997	1998	1999	2000	2001	2002	2003	2004	2005	2006	2007	High	
46	51	59	71	74	74	67	68	68	57	53	60	53	76	87	**40**	04/95

2007–2008												Low	
08/07	09/07	10/07	11/07	12/07	01/08	02/08	03/08	04/08	05/08	06/08	07/08	**101**	08/07
101	93	87	87	87	83	96	94	98	95	85	82		

Hyperinflation, economic collapse, political turmoil, violence on the streets, thousands fleeing over the border to South Africa... it's small wonder that any football was played in Zimbabwe at all. Constant changes in ticket prices, often on a daily basis, put the running of teams under massive pressure while a lack of access to foreign currency also restricted Zimbabwe's planning at national team level. But despite all of this football carried on. Perhaps spurred on by the problems there were even some notable stories, none more so than Harare club Dynamos, the best supported club in the country. In November 2007 they beat Highlanders in the ZIFA Cup Final and shortly after

INTERNATIONAL HONOURS
CECAFA Cup 1985 COSAFA Castle Cup 2000 2003

won the championship for the first time in a decade. That alone would have been enough for their supporters but then in the 2008 CAF Champions League, they sensationally eliminated holders Etoile du Sahel of Tunisia to qualify for the group stage. The national team even managed to employ a Brazilian coach for the first time, Jose Claudinei Georgini, better known as Valinhos as they prepared to take part in the 2010 FIFA World Cup qualifiers in June 2008. Amongst all the election chaos the national team kicked of its campaign to qualify for the finals in neighbouring South Africa with a draw in Guinea and a win in Harare over Namibia.

THE FIFA BIG COUNT OF 2006

	Male	Female		Total
Number of players	622 300	29 100	Referees and Assistant Referees	800
Professionals	100		Admin, Coaches, Technical, Medical	2 300
Amateurs 18+	28 600		Number of clubs	350
Youth under 18	5 900		Number of teams	1 250
Unregistered	46 800		Clubs with women's teams	0
Total players	651 400		Players as % of population	5.32%

Zimbabwe Football Association (ZIFA)

53 Livingstone Avenue, Causeway, PO Box CY 114, Harare, Zimbabwe
Tel +263 4 798631   Fax +263 4 798626
zifa@africaonline.co.zw   www.zimbabwesoccer.com
President: NYATHANGA Wellington   General Secretary: RUSHWAYA Henrietta
Vice-President: MADZORERA Tendai   Treasurer: MUZAMBI Gladmore   Media Officer: None
Men's Coach: VALINHOS   Women's Coach: GIWA Langton
ZIFA formed: 1965   CAF: 1965   FIFA: 1965
Green shirts, Yellow shorts, Green socks

RECENT INTERNATIONAL MATCHES PLAYED BY ZIMBABWE

2004	Opponents	Score	Venue	Comp	Scorers	Att	Referee
5-09	Nigeria	L 0-3	Harare	WCq		60 000	Mandzioukouta COD
10-10	Angola	L 0-1	Luanda	WCq		17 000	Lwanja MWI
24-10	Zambia	D 0-0	Harare	CCsf	L 4-5p	25 000	Simisse MRI
2005							
27-02	Malawi	L 1-2	Blantyre	Fr	Tsipa [54]		
16-03	Botswana	D 1-1	Harare	Fr	Chimedza [53]	3 000	
27-03	Angola	W 2-0	Harare	WCq	Kawondera [60], Mwaruwari [69]		Codjia BEN
16-04	Mozambique	W 3-0	Windhoek	CCr1	Chimedza 2 [66p 78], Sandaka [82]		Mufeti NAM
17-04	Botswana	W 2-0	Windhoek	CCr1	Badza [21], Sandaka [58]		Braga Mavunza ANG
5-06	Gabon	W 1-0	Harare	WCq	Ndlovu.P [52]	55 000	Ssegonga UGA
19-06	Algeria	D 2-2	Oran	WCq	Kawondera [33], Ndlovu.P [87]	15 000	Pare BFA
13-08	Angola	W 2-1	Mmabatho	CCsf	Chandida [59], Sandaka [76]		Kapanga MWI
14-08	Zambia	W 1-0	Mmabatho	CCf	Chandida [84]		Massango MOZ
28-08	Mozambique	D 0-0	Mutare	Fr			
4-09	Rwanda	W 3-1	Harare	WCq	Kawondera [4], Mwaruwari [43], Rambanapasi [78]	55 000	Ssegona UGA
8-10	Nigeria	L 1-5	Abuja	WCq	Mwaruwari [70]	45 000	Pare BFA
31-12	Zambia	D 1-1	Harare	Fr	Mbwando [63]		
2006							
5-01	Egypt	L 0-2	Alexandria	Fr			
14-01	Morocco	L 0-1	Marrakech	Fr			
23-01	Senegal	L 0-2	Port Said	CNr1		15 000	Abdel Rahman SUD
27-01	Nigeria	L 0-2	Port Said	CNr1		10 000	Coulibaly MLI
31-01	Ghana	W 2-1	Ismailia	CNr1	Chimedza [60], Mwaruwari [68]	14 000	Louzaya CGO
24-06	Malawi	D 1-1	Maputo	Fr	Gwekwerere [28p], L 1-2p		
25-06	Swaziland	W 2-1	Maputo	Fr	Gwekwerere [14], Matema [73]		
15-07	Zambia	D 0-0	Lusaka	Fr			
17-09	Angola	L 1-2	Harare	CCsf	Chandida [64]		Kaoma ZAM
7-10	Malawi	L 0-1	Blantyre	CNq			Seechun MRI
15-11	Namibia	W 3-2	Harare	Fr	Gwekwerere [11], Mushangazhike [17], Matawu [50]		
2007							
25-03	Morocco	D 1-1	Harare	CNq	Nyandoro [81]		Damon RSA
28-04	Madagascar	W 1-0	Maputo	CCr1	Nkata [8]		Faduco MOZ
29-04	Mozambique	D 0-0	Maputo	CCr1	L 4-5p		Seechun MRI
25-05	Lesotho	D 1-1	Masvingo	Fr	Antipas [57]		
29-05	Burkina Faso	D 1-1	Masvingo	Fr	Kawondera [45]		
2-06	Morocco	L 0-2	Casablanca	CNq			Daami TUN
20-08	Mozambique	D 0-0	Beira	Fr	L 1-3p		
9-09	Malawi	W 3-1	Bulawayo	CNq	Nkhata [24], Mteki [54], Mwanjili [61]		Hicuburundi BDI
2008							
11-03	South Africa	L 1-2	Johannesburg	Fr	Mushangazhike [12]		
26-03	Botswana	W 1-0	Gaborone	Fr	Malajila [48]		
1-06	Guinea	D 0-0	Conakry	WCq		12 000	Haimoudi ALG
8-06	Namibia	W 2-0	Harare	WCq	Mushangazhike 2 [26 85]	27 979	Lwanja MWI
14-06	Kenya	L 0-2	Nairobi	WCq		27 500	Diatta SEN
22-06	Kenya	D 0-0	Harare	WCq		23 000	Kotey GHA
27-07	Zambia	D 0-0	Thulamahashe	CCqf	L 4-5p		Nhlapo RSA

Fr = Friendly match • CN = CAF African Cup of Nations • CC = COSAFA Cup • WC = FIFA World Cup
q = qualifier • r1 = first round group • qf = quarter-final • sf = semi-final • f = final

ZIMBABWE NATIONAL TEAM RECORDS AND RECORD SEQUENCES

Records			Sequence records				
Victory	7-0	BOT 1990	Wins	6	2003	Clean sheets	5	2002-2003
Defeat	0-5	CIV 1989, COD 1995	Defeats	5	1997-1998	Goals scored	12	2003-2004
Player Caps	n/a		Undefeated	13	1981-1982	Without goal	4	1988, 2006
Player Goals	n/a		Without win	9	1995-96, 1997-98	Goals against	11	1995-1996

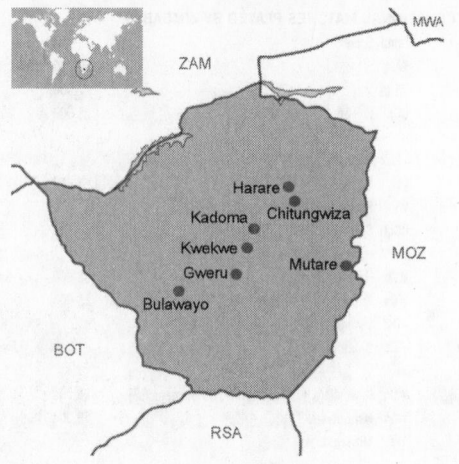

ZAM

MWA

MOZ

BOT

RSA

Harare
Kadoma　Chitungwiza
Kwekwe
Gweru
Bulawayo
Mutare

MAJOR CITIES/TOWNS		
		Population '000
1	Harare	2 919
2	Bulawayo	713
3	Mutare	193
4	Gweru	148
5	Kwekwe	103
6	Kadoma	81
7	Masvingo	80
8	Chinhoyi	65
9	Marondera	60
10	Norton	58
11	Chegutu	50
12	Bindura	40
13	Victoria Falls	38
14	Zvishavane	36
15	Redcliffe	33
16	Rusape	32
17	Hwange	31
18	Chiredzi	29
19	Beitbridge	29
20	Ruwa	29
21	Karoi	27
22	Kariba	26
23	Chipinge	19
24	Gokwe	19

REPUBLIC OF ZIMBABWE

Capital	Harare	Language	English, Shona, Sindebele	Independence	1980
Population	12 311 143	Area	390 580 km²	% in cities	32%
GDP per cap	$1 900	Dailling code	+263	Internet	.zw	GMT + / -	+2

MEDALS TABLE

		Overall			Lg	C	IT	LC	Africa			City	Stadium	Cap'ty	DoF
		G	S	B	G	G	G	G	G	S	B				
1	Dynamos	33	1		18	8	5	2			1	Harare	Rufaro	45 000	1963
2	CAPS United	21			4	8	4	5				Harare	National Stadium	60 000	1973
3	Highlanders	15			7	2	5	1				Bulawayo	Barbourfields	35 000	1926
4	Zimbabwe Saints	6			2	3	1					Bulawayo	Barbourfields	35 000	
5	Black Rhinos	5			2	1	2					Harare			1983
6	Masvingo United	5				2	3					Masvingo	Mucheke	5 000	
7	Arcadia United	3			1	2						Harare			
8	Bulawayo Rovers	3			2	1						Bulawayo			
9	Chibuku	3			1	2						Harare			
10	Sailisbury Callies	3				3						Harare			
11	Hwange (ex Wankie)	3				3						Hwange			
12	Amazulu	2			1		1					Bulawayo			
13	Black Aces	2			1			1				Harare			
14	Bulawayo Sables	2			2							Bulawayo			
15	Chapungu United	2				1	1					Gweru	Ascot	5 000	
16	Mangula	2				2						Mangula			
17	Salisbury Sables	2			2							Harare			

RECENT LEAGUE AND CUP RECORD

	Championship						Cup		
Year	Champions	Pts	Runners-up	Pts	Third	Pts	Winners	Score	Runners-up
1995	Dynamos	58	Blackpool	58	Black Aces	53	Chapungu United		
1996	CAPS United	71	Dynamos	68	Blackpool	54	Dynamos		
1997	Dynamos	68	CAPS United	57	Black Aces	50	CAPS United	3-2	Dynamos
1998	No championship due to calender reorganisation						CAPS United		
1999	Highlanders	72	Dynamos	71	Zimbabwe Saints	54	No tournament		
2000	Highlanders	78	AmaZulu	76	Dynamos	66	No tournament		
2001	Highlanders	62	AmaZulu	59	Shabanie Mine	51	Highlanders	4-1	Shabanie Mine
2002	Highlanders	72	Black Rhinos	52	AmaZulu	50	Masvingo United	2-2 4-3p	Railstars
2003	AmaZulu	51	Highlanders	50	Dynamos	48	Dynamos	2-0	Highlanders
2004	CAPS United	79	Highlanders	64	Shabanie Mine	51	CAPS United	1-0	Wankie
2005	CAPS United	58	Masvingo United	56	Highlanders	51	Masvingo United	1-1 3-1p	Highlanders
2006	Highlanders	65	Motor Action	54	Masvingo United	49	Mwana Africa	1-0	Chapungu
2007	Dynamos	64	Highlanders	55	Masvingo United	50	Dynamos	2-1	Highlanders

ZIMBABWE 2007

NATIONAL PREMIER SOCCER LEAGUE	Pl	W	D	L	F	A	Pts	Dynamos	Highlanders	Masvingo	S. Stars	Njube	Lengthens	CAPS Utd	Chapungu	Motor	L. Steel	Mono'tapa	CAPS FC	Lions	Rhinos	Hwange	Mwana
Dynamos †	30	19	7	4	41	15	64		0-0	1-0	4-1	1-0	2-1	0-0	2-0	0-0	2-0	1-0	4-1	0-0	1-3	2-1	3-0
Highlanders	30	16	7	7	44	25	55	1-2		0-0	1-4	3-0	1-0	3-0	1-0	4-0	1-0	0-1	2-1	2-0	4-0	3-1	2-1
Masvingo United	30	14	8	8	37	24	50	1-0	1-1		0-0	6-1	1-0	0-0	1-0	3-0	4-1	0-0	1-1	2-1	2-0	0-2	2-1
Shooting Stars	30	11	8	11	36	36	41	0-2	0-1	1-2		0-1	1-1	2-1	1-0	1-0	1-0	4-1	2-0	1-1	2-0	1-0	1-1
Njube Sundowns	30	12	5	13	37	45	41	0-1	2-1	0-1	1-0		2-2	2-2	4-3	1-0	5-3	3-1	0-0	2-1	4-2	3-0	0-1
Lengthens	30	11	7	12	38	36	40	0-0	1-2	1-1	0-0	3-0		1-2	3-0	1-3	4-0	1-0	1-2	1-0	1-0	3-0	3-0
CAPS United	30	8	15	7	26	25	39	0-1	1-0	1-0	1-1	2-1	1-2		3-0	1-2	0-0	0-0	1-1	3-1	0-2	0-0	0-0
Chapungu United	30	11	6	13	37	39	39	0-1	1-2	1-2	4-1	2-0	3-0	1-1		2-1	0-0	1-1	2-5	1-0	0-0	3-2	3-1
Motor Action	30	11	6	13	38	41	39	0-2	1-1	1-4	4-2	1-0	6-0	1-1	1-2		2-3	0-1	1-0	1-1	2-0	0-1	0-2
Lancashire Steel	30	10	9	11	33	40	39	1-1	1-0	2-0	1-2	1-2	2-1	0-1	1-0	1-1		3-2	0-0	3-1	1-4	0-0	2-0
Monomatapa United	30	11	5	14	33	40	38	0-2	2-3	2-0	2-0	2-1	1-3	1-2	2-1	2-3	0-2		3-1	2-1	3-1	1-1	1-0
CAPS FC Chitungwiza	30	10	7	13	36	39	37	1-2	3-1	2-0	1-3	1-0	2-3	1-0	0-2	0-1	1-1	1-0		2-1	5-0	1-0	0-0
Eastern Lions	30	7	13	10	26	31	34	1-0	0-0	2-0	2-1	0-0	0-0	1-1	1-1	1-1	0-0	2-0	1-1		1-0	1-0	3-2
Black Rhinos	30	8	10	12	32	42	34	0-2	0-0	2-1	2-2	1-1	3-1	0-0	1-2	2-1	2-0	1-1	3-1	0-0		1-1	1-1
Hwange	30	8	8	14	28	36	32	2-2	0-2	0-2	1-0	4-0	1-0	1-1	1-2	0-1	2-3	2-0	2-1	1-1	1-0		0-0
Mwana Africa	30	6	13	11	25	33	31	1-0	2-2	0-0	1-1	0-1	0-0	0-0	0-0	2-3	1-1	0-1	2-0	3-1	1-1	2-1	

3/03/2007 - 9/12/2007 • † Qualified for the CAF Champions League • Matches in bold awarded • Top scorer: Cuthbert Malajila, Chapungu 15

CBZ FA CUP 2007

Second Round		Quarter-finals		Semi-finals		Final	
Dynamos	1 2						
Hwange	1 1	Dynamos	2				
Masvingo United	0 0	Lancashire Steel	1				
Lancashire Steel	0 1			Dynamos	0 2		
Shooting Stars	2 2			Lengthens	0 0		
CAPS FC	2 0	Shooting Stars	1				
Motor Action	0	Lengthens	3				
Lengthens	2					Dynamos	2
CAPS United	0 2					Highlanders	1
Eastern Lions	0 1	CAPS United	3				
Chapungu United	1 1	Kiglon	1	CAPS United	1 1		
Kiglon	1 2			Highlanders	1 2		
Monomatapa United	1						
Border Strikers	0	Monomatapa United	1 0				
Mwana Africa	1 1	Highlanders	1 1				
Highlanders	1 3						

CUP FINAL
Barbourfields, Bulawayo
18-11-2007
Scorers - Sebastian Mutinzirwa, Murape Murape for Dynamos; Richard Choruma for Highlanders

* Home team • ‡ Qualified for the CAF Confederation Cup

PART THREE

THE
CONTINENTAL
CONFEDERATIONS

AFC

ASIAN FOOTBALL CONFEDERATION

Two years before the 2010 FIFA World Cup in South Africa, only ten of the 46 members of the Asian Football Confederation remained in the hunt for a place in the finals with the final phase of qualifying having a very familiar look to it with all five nations that took part in the 2006 finals once again in a position to qualify. The ever progressive AFC has done much to promote football in the smaller nations, but the big five of Australia, Iran, Japan, Saudi Arabia and South Korea have formed a clique that continues to dominate at both national team and club level. When a team does break through to disrupt the established order - such as Iraq winning the 2007 AFC Asian Cup - they find it hard to maintain that presence. And true enough, the Iraqis were one of the highest

THE FIFA BIG COUNT OF 2006 FOR ASIA

	Male	Female		Total
Number of players	80 075 000	5 102 000	Referees and Assistant Referees	263 000
Professionals	11 000		Admin, Coaches, Technical, Medical	410 000
Amateurs 18+	1 531 000		Number of clubs	20 000
Youth under 18	2 322		Number of teams	145 000
Unregistered	81 136 000		Clubs with women's teams	3 000
Total involved in football	85 849		Players as % of population	2.22%

profile casualties of the first two rounds of World Cup qualifying. The others were China, where football has suffered as the country concentrated on trying to top the medals table at the Beijing Olympics. Rather than trying to level the standards between Asian countries, the AFC is keen to push the development of the top nations further and having restricted entry to the Champions League in 2003, the AFC is set to expand the competition to 32 teams from 2009. Four slots will be available for the major leagues such as Japan, South Korea, China, Saudi Arabia, the UAE and Iran, while countries with big potential, such as India, will be brought into the fold. In a sign of growing Japanese enthusiam for the AFC Champions League, Urawa Reds won the 2007 tournament by beating Iran's Sepahan in the final - the first Japanese success since 1999.

Asian Football Confederation (AFC)

AFC House, Jalan 1/155B, Bukit Jalil, 57000 Kuala Lumpur, Malaysia

Tel +60 3 89943388   Fax +60 3 89946168

media@the-afc.com   www.the-afc.com

President: BIN HAMMAM Mohamed QAT   General Secretary: SAMUEL Dato' Paul Mony MAS

AFC Formed: 1954

AFC EXECUTIVE COMMITTEE

President: BIN HAMMAM Mohamed QAT	Vice-President: ZHANG Jilong CHN	Vice-President: FERNANDO V. Manilal SRI
Vice-President: TENGKU Abdullah Ahmad Shah MAS	Vice-President: AL SERKAL Yousuf UAE	Hon Treasurer: BOUZO Farouk, Gen SYR
FIFA Vice-President: CHUNG Mong Joon, Dr KOR	FIFA Executive Member: MAKUDI Worawi	FIFA Executive Member: OGURA Junji

MEMBERS OF THE EXECUTIVE COMMITTEE

RAKHIMOV BaKhtier UZB	TAHIR Dali IDN	AL MEDLEJ Hafez, Dr KSA
THAPA Ganesh NEP	HUSSAIN Mohammed Saeed IRQ	NAM SANG John Koh SIN
FARAHANI Mohsen Safai IRN	DAS MUNSHI Priya Ranjan IND	LAI Richard GUM
AL MASKERY Saif Hasil Rashid OMA		ZAW Zaw MYA

MAP OF AFC MEMBER NATIONS

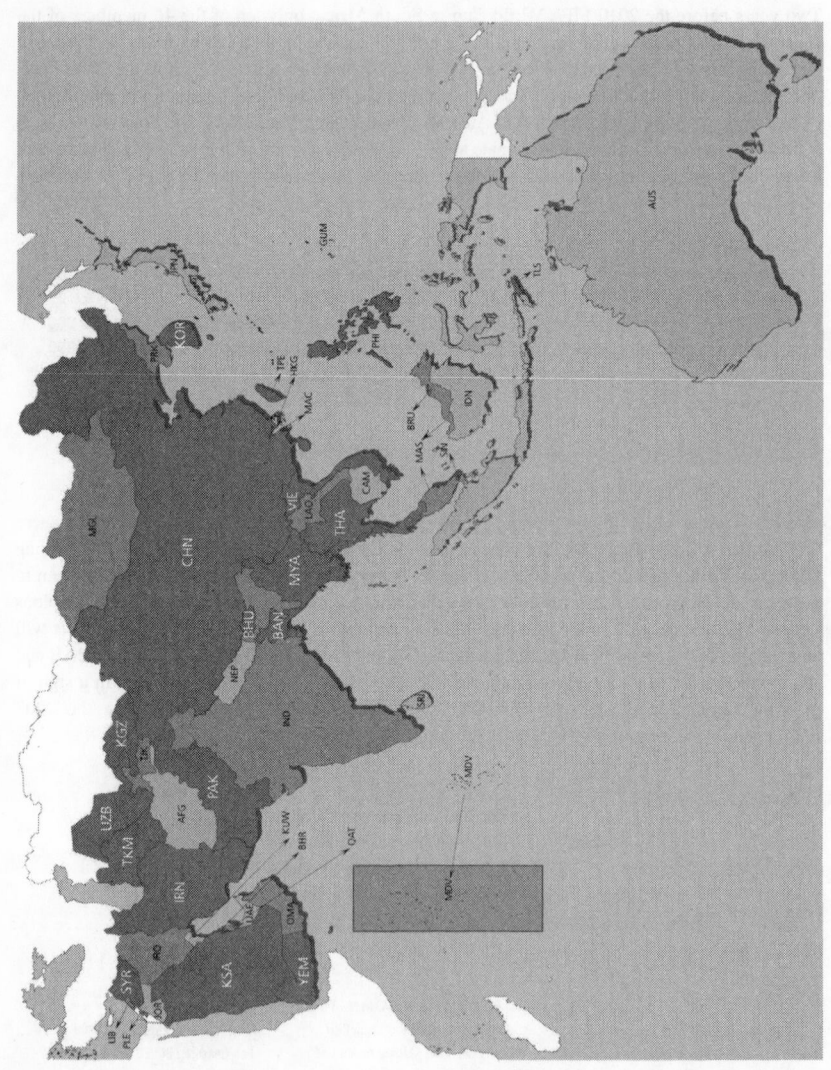

ASIAN TOURNAMENTS

AFC ASIAN CUP

Year	Host Country	Winners	Score	Runners-up	Venue
1956	Hong Kong	Korea Republic	2-1	Israel	Government Stadium, Hong Kong
1960	Korea Republic	Korea Republic	3-0	Israel	Hyochang Park, Seoul
1964	Israel	Israel	2-0	India	Bloomfield, Jaffa
1968	Iran	Iran	3-1	Burma	Amjadieh, Tehran
1972	Thailand	Iran	2-1	Korea Republic	Suphachalasai, Bangkok
1976	Iran	Iran	1-0	Kuwait	Azadi, Tehran
1980	Kuwait	Kuwait	3-0	Korea Republic	Kuwait City
1984	Singapore	Saudi Arabia	2-0	China PR	National Stadium, Singapore
1988	Qatar	Saudi Arabia	0-0 4-3p	Korea Republic	Khalifa, Doha
1992	Japan	Japan	1-0	Saudi Arabia	Main Stadium, Hiroshima
1996	UAE	Saudi Arabia	0-0 4-2p	United Arab Emirates	Zayed, Abu Dhabi
2000	Lebanon	Japan	1-0	Saudi Arabia	Camille Chamoun, Beirut
2004	China PR	Japan	3-1	China PR	Workers' Stadium, Beijing
2007	ASEAN co-hosts	Iraq	1-0	Saudi Arabia	Gelora Bung Karno, Jakarta

From 1956 to 1968 the tournament was played as a league. The result listed is that between the winners and runners-up.

AFC ASIAN CUP MEDALS TABLE

	Country	G	S	B	F	SF
1	Saudi Arabia	3	3		6	6
2	Iran	3		4	2	7
3	Japan	3			3	4
4	Korea Republic	2	3	3	3	5
5	Israel	1	2	1		
6	Kuwait	1	1	1	2	4
7	Iraq	1			1	2
8	China PR		2	2	2	6
9	Utd Arab Emirates		1		1	2
10	India			1		
	Myanmar			1		
12	Thailand			1		1
13	Chinese Taipei			1		
	Hong Kong			1		
15	Bahrain					1
	Cambodia					1
	Korea DPR					1
		14	14	14	20	40

This table represents the Gold (winners), Silver (runners-up) and
Bronze (semi-finalists) placings of countries in the AFC Asian Cup,
along with the number of appearances in the final and semi-finals

The AFC Asian Cup is the continent's premier competition for national teams. The first tournament was held in Hong Kong in 1956 and was won by South Korea who also triumphed four years later at home. Despite appearing in three more finals the Koreans have failed in their efforts to add a third title. Israel were the winners in 1964, again on home soil, but from the late 1960s to the late 1970s Iran were the undisputed kings of Asia, winning every game they played on the way to a hat-trick of titles. Kuwait were the first Arab nation to win the tournament, in 1980, and were followed by Saudi Arabia, who with three titles between 1984 and 1996, dominated for over a decade, and have appeared in six of the last seven finals. Just once since 1980 has the home nation won - in 1992 when Japan won for the first time. Coinciding with the explosion of interest in football there, the Japanese went on to win two more titles in the next four tournaments. Traditionally held every four years, the cycle was changed in 2007 to avoid clashing with other continental championships and there was another first when four nations - Indonesia, Malaysia, Thailand and Vietnam - hosted a tournament sensationally won by Iraq as civil war raged back home.

AFC WOMEN'S CHAMPIONSHIP

Year	Host Country	Winners	Score	Runners-up	Venue
1975	Hong Kong	New Zealand	3-1	Thailand	Hong Kong
1977	Chinese Tapei	Chinese Taipei	3-1	Thailand	Taipei
1979	India	Chinese Taipei	2-0	India	Calicut
1981	Hong Kong	Chinese Taipei	5-0	Thailand	Hong Kong
1983	Thailand	Thailand	3-0	India	Bangkok
1986	Hong Kong	China PR	2-0	Japan	Hong Kong
1989	Hong Kong	China PR	1-0	Chinese Taipei	Hong Kong
1991	Japan	China PR	5-0	Japan	Fukuoka
1993	Malaysia	China PR	3-0	Korea DPR	Sarawak
1995	Malaysia	China PR	2-0	Japan	Sabah
1997	China PR	China PR	2-0	Korea DPR	Guangdong
1999	Philippines	China PR	3-0	Chinese Taipei	Bacalod
2001	Chinese Taipei	Korea DPR	2-0	Japan	Taipei
2003	Thailand	Korea DPR	2-1	China PR	Bangkok
2006	Australia	China PR	2-2 4-2p	Australia	Adelaide

The AFC Women's Championship is the longest running of all the continental championships for women, though unsurprisingly it has remained the preserve of East Asia with the countries of the Middle East yet to enter a single tournament. China has emerged as the most successful nation with seven consecutive titles between 1986 and 1999. 2001 saw North Korea win the title for the first time to become the fifth different winners along with Thailand, Chinese Taipei and New Zealand. Australia look certain to present a strong challenge in the future and they reached the final in 2006 when they hosted their first AFC tournament since joining the confederation earlier in the year. Japan have made it to four finals but have yet to win.

FOOTBALL TOURNAMENT OF THE ASIAN GAMES

Year	Host Country	Winners	Score	Runners-up	Venue
1951	India	India	1-0	Iran	New Delhi
1954	Philippines	Chinese Taipei	5-2	Korea Republic	Manilla
1958	Japan	Chinese Taipei	3-2	Korea Republic	Tokyo
1962	Indonesia	India	2-1	Korea Republic	Djakarta
1966	Thailand	Burma	1-0	Iran	Bangkok
1970	Thailand	Burma	0-0 †	Korea Republic	Bangkok
1974	Iran	Iran	1-0	Israel	Tehran
1978	Thailand	Korea Republic	0-0 †	Korea DPR	Bangkok
1982	India	Iraq	1-0	Kuwait	New Delhi
1986	Korea Republic	Korea Republic	2-0	Saudi Arabia	Seoul
1990	China PR	Iran	0-0 4-1p	Korea DPR	Beijing
1994	Japan	Uzbekistan	4-2	China PR	Hiroshima
1998	Thailand	Iran	2-0	Kuwait	Bangkok
2002	Korea Republic	Iran	2-1	Japan	Busan
2006	Qatar	Qatar	1-0	Iraq	Doha

† Gold medal shared in 1970 and 1978

For many years the Football Tournament of the Asian Games rivalled the Asian Cup in importance, meaning the continent had a major championship every other year. Football was included at the very first Asiad, in New Delhi in 1951, where the matches were contested over two halves of 40 minutes. India were the first gold medalists and since then the range of winners has been more diverse than in the Asian Cup with Japan and Saudi Arabia yet to the title. Iran is the most successful nation in the tournament with four golds followed by South Korea with three. Qatar became the eighth different winners when they won the Doha games in 2006. The Asian Games operate as a regional version of the Olympics so in the amateur days this was not an issue given the lack of professional players on the continent. In 2002, as with the Olympics, the football tournament was turned into a U–23 tournament with three older players allowed.

WOMEN'S FOOTBALL TOURNAMENT OF THE ASIAN GAMES

Year	Host Country	Winners	Score	Runners-up	Venue
1990	China PR	China PR	5-0	Japan	Beijing
1994	Japan	China PR	2-0	Japan	Hiroshima
1998	Thailand	China PR	1-0	Korea DPR	Bangkok
2002	Korea Republic	Korea DPR	0-0	China PR	Busan
2006	Qatar	Korea DPR	0-0 4-2p	Japan	Doha

In 1990, 1994 and 2002 the tournament was played as a league. The result listed is that between the winners and runners-up

Given the strength of women's football in East Asia, it was a natural progression to introduce the sport to the Games when Beijing was host in 1990.

AFC CHALLENGE CUP

Year	Host Country	Winners	Score	Runners-up	Venue
2006	Bangladesh	Tajikistan	4-0	Sri Lanka	Bangabandhu, Dhaka
2008	India				Ambedkar, Delhi

The AFC Challenge Cup for national teams was launched in 2006 for the lower ranked nations on the continent in order to give these nations the realistic prospect of winning competitive honours in what is effectively the second division of Asian nations.

AFC YOUTH CHAMPIONSHIP WINNERS

Year	Host Country	Winners	Score	Runners-up	Venue
1959	Malaysia	Korea Republic	2-1	Malaysia	Kuala Lumpur
1960	Malaysia	Korea Republic	4-0	Malaysia	Kuala Lumpur
1961	Thailand	Burma	0-0†	Indonesia	Bangkok
1962	Thailand	Thailand	2-1	Korea Republic	Bangkok
1963	Malaysia	Burma	2-2†	Korea Republic	Penang
1964	Vietnam	Burma	0-0†	Israel	Saigon
1965	Japan	Israel	5-0	Burma	Tokyo
1966	Philippines	Burma	1-1	Israel	Manila
1967	Thailand	Israel	3-0	Indonesia	Bangkok
1968	Korea Republic	Burma	4-0	Malaysia	Seoul
1969	Thailand	Burma	2-2†	Thailand	Bangkok
1970	Philippines	Burma	3-0	India	Manila
1971	Japan	Israel	1-0	Korea Republic	Tokyo
1972	Thailand	Israel	1-0	Korea Republic	Bangkok
1973	Iran	Iran	2-0	Japan	Tehran
1974	Thailand	Iran	2-2†	India	Bangkok
1975	Kuwait	Iran	0-0†	Iraq	Kuwait City
1976	Thailand	Iran	0-0†	Korea DPR	Bangkok
1977	Iran	Iraq	4-3	Iran	Tehran
1978	Bangladesh	Iraq	1-1†	Korea Republic	Dhaka
1980	Thailand	Korea Republic	4-1‡	Qatar	Bangkok
1982	Thailand	Korea Republic	1-1‡	China PR	Bangkok
1984	UAE	China PR	2-2‡	Saudi Arabia	Abu Dhabi
1986	Saudi Arabia	Saudi Arabia	2-0	Bahrain	Riyadh
1988	Qatar	Iraq	1-1 5-4p	Syria	Doha
1990	Indonesia	Korea Republic	0-0 4-3p	Korea DPR	Jakarta
1992	UAE	Saudi Arabia	2-0	Korea Republic	Dubai
1994	Indonesia	Syria	2-1	Japan	Jakarta
1996	Korea Republic	Korea Republic	3-0	China PR	Suwon
1998	Thailand	Korea Republic	2-1	Japan	Chiang Mai
2000	Iran	Iraq	2-1	Japan	Tehran
2002	Qatar	Korea Republic	1-0	Japan	Doha
2004	Malaysia	Korea Republic	2-0	China PR	Kuala Lumpur
2006	India	Korea DPR	1-1 5-3p	Japan	

† Title shared between both finalists • ‡ Played on a league system so the match indicated was not a final

AFC UNDER 17 CHAMPIONSHIP WINNERS

Year	Host Country	Winners	Score	Runners-up	Venue
1984	Qatar	Saudi Arabia		Qatar	Doha
1986	Qatar	Korea Republic		Qatar	Doha
1988	Thailand	Saudi Arabia		Bahrain	Bangkok
1990	UAE	Qatar		UAE	Dubai
1992	Saudi Arabia	China PR		Qatar	Riyadh
1994	Qatar	Japan		Qatar	Doha
1996	Thailand	Oman		Thailand	Bangkok
1998	Qatar	Thailand		Qatar	Doha
2000	Vietnam SR	Oman		Iran	Danang
2002	UAE	Korea Republic		Yemen	Abu Dhabi
2004	Japan	China PR		Korea DPR	Shizuoka
2006	Singapore	Japan		Korea DPR	Singapore

AFC UNDER 19 WOMEN'S CHAMPIONSHIP WINNERS

Year	Host Country	Winners	Score	Runners-up	Venue
2002	India	Japan	2-1	Chinese Taipei	
2006	Malaysia	China PR	1-0	Korea DPR	
2007	China	Korea DPR	1-0	Japan	Sports Centre, Chongqing

AFC UNDER 16 WOMEN'S CHAMPIONSHIP WINNERS

Year	Host Country	Winners	Score	Runners-up	Venue
2005	Korea Republic	Japan	1-1 3-1p	China PR	Namhae
2007	Malaysia	Korea DPR	3-0	Japan	MPPJ Stadium, Petaling Jaya

The AFC runs tournaments at both under 17 and under 19 level for both men and women which also act as qualifiers for the FIFA tournaments held the year after.

ASEAN FOOTBALL FEDERATION CHAMPIONSHIP

Year	Host Country	Winners	Score	Runners-up	Venue
1996		Thailand	1-0	Malaysia	
1998	Vietnam	Singapore	1-0	Vietnam	Hanoi Stadium, Hanoi
2000	Thailand	Thailand	4-1	Indonesia	Bangkok
2002	Indonesia/Sin'pore	Thailand	2-2 4-2p	Indonesia	Gelora Senayan, Jakarta
2004	Malaysia/Vietnam	Singapore	3-1 2-1	Indonesia	Jakarta, Singapore
2007	Sin'pore/Thailand	Singapore	2-1 1-1	Thailand	Singapore, Bangkok

SOUTH ASIAN FOOTBALL FEDERATION CUP

Year	Host Country	Winners	Score	Runners-up	Venue
1993	Pakistan	India	2-0	Sri Lanka	Lahore
1995	Sri Lanka	Sri Lanka	1-0	India	Colombo
1997	Nepal	India	5-1	Maldives	Dasharath Rangashala, Kathmandu
1999	Goa	India	2-0	Bangladesh	Margao
2003	Bangladesh	Bangladesh	1-1 5-3p	Maldives	Bangabandu, Dhaka
2005	Pakistan	India	2-0	Bangladesh	Karachi
2008	Sri Lanka/Maldives	Maldives	1-0	India	Sugathadhasa, Colombo

EAST ASIAN CHAMPIONSHIP

Year	Host Country	Winners	Score	Runners-up	Venue
2003	Japan	Korea Republic	0-0	Japan	International, Yokohama
2005	Korea Republic	China PR	2-2	Japan	World Cup Stadium, Daejeon
2008	China PR	Korea Republic	1-1	Japan	Sports Centre, Chongqing

Tournament played as a league. The result listed is that between the winners and runners-up

WEST ASIAN FOOTBALL FEDERATION CHAMPIONSHIP

Year	Host Country	Winners	Score	Runners-up	Venue
2000	Jordan	Iran	1-0	Syria	Malek Abdullah, Amman
2002	Syria	Iraq	3-2	Jordan	Al Abbassiyyine, Damascus
2004	Iran	Iran	4-1	Syria	Tehran
2007	Jordan	Iran	2-1	Iraq	International, Amman

GULF CUP

Year	Host Country	Winners	Runners-up
1970	Bahrain	Kuwait	Bahrain
1972	Saudi Arabia	Kuwait	Saudi Arabia
1974	Kuwait	Kuwait	Saudi Arabia
1976	Qatar	Kuwait	Iraq
1979	Iraq	Iraq	Kuwait
1982	UAE	Kuwait	Bahrain
1984	Oman	Iraq	Qatar
1986	Bahrain	Kuwait	UAE
1988	Saudi Arabia	Iraq	UAE

GULF CUP

Year	Host Country	Winners	Runners-up
1990	Kuwait	Kuwait	Qatar
1992	Qatar	Qatar	Bahrain
1994	UAE	Saudi Arabia	UAE
1996	Oman	Kuwait	Qatar
1998	Bahrain	Kuwait	Saudi Arabia
2002	Saudi Arabia	Saudi Arabia	Qatar
2004	Kuwait	Saudi Arabia	Bahrain
2005	Qatar	Qatar	Oman
2007	UAE	UAE	Oman

Regional tournaments in Asia are particularly strong and they play a hugely important role given the vast size of the continent. Each of the four regional federations - ASEAN for South-East Asia, EAF for East Asia, SAFF for Southern Asia and WAFF for West Asia - runs a tournament, whilst the Gulf Cup is held for the nations bordering the Arabian Gulf.

FOOTBALL TOURNAMENT OF THE SOUTH EAST ASIAN GAMES

Year	Host Country	Winners	Score	Runners-up	Venue
1959	Thailand	Vietnam	3-1	Thailand	Bangkok
1961	Burma	Malaysia	2-0	Burma	Rangoon
1965	Malaysia	Burma	2-2†	Thailand	Kuala Lumpur
1967	Thailand	Burma	2-1	South Vietnam	Bangkok
1969	Burma	Burma	3-0	Thailand	Rangoon
1971	Malaysia	Burma	2-1	Malaysia	Kuala Lumpur
1973	Singapore	Burma	2-1	South Vietnam	Singapore
1975	Thailand	Thailand	2-1	Malaysia	Bangkok
1977	Malaysia	Malaysia	2-0	Thailand	Kuala Lumpur
1979	Indonesia	Malaysia	1-0	Indonesia	Jakarta
1981	Philippines	Thailand	2-1	Malaysia	Manila
1983	Singapore	Thailand	2-1	Singapore	Singapore
1985	Thailand	Thailand	2-0	Singpaore	Bangkok
1987	Indonesia	Indonesia	1-0	Malaysia	Jakarta
1989	Malaysia	Malaysia	3-1	Singapore	Merdeka, Kuala Lumpur
1991	Philippines	Indonesia	0-0 4-3p	Thailand	Manila
1993	Singapore	Thailand	4-3	Myanmar	Singapore
1995	Thailand	Thailand	4-0	Vietnam	Chiang Mai
1997	Indonesia	Thailand	1-1 4-2p	Indonesia	Jakarta
1999	Brunei	Thailand	2-0	Vietnam	Bandar Seri Begawan
2001	Malaysia	Thailand	1-0	Malaysia	Kuala Lumpur
2003	Vietnam	Thailand	2-1	Vietnam	Hanoi
2005	Philippines	Thailand	3-0	Vietnam	Manila
2007	Thailand	Thailand	2-0	Myanmar	Korat

† Gold medal shared • Until 2001 the SEA Games featured full national teams but is now a U-23 event

FOOTBALL TOURNAMENT OF THE EAST ASIAN GAMES

Year	Host Country	Winners	Score	Runners-up	Venue
1993	China PR	Korea Republic	1-1†	Korea DPR	Shanghai
1997	Korea Republic	Korea Republic	0-1†	Japan	Pusan
2001	Japan	Japan	2-1	Australia	Nagai, Osaka
2005	Macao	China PR	1-0	Korea DPR	Macau Stadium, Macau

† Played on a league basis. The result listed is between the top two teams, both of which occurred in the last round of games

FOOTBALL TOURNAMENT OF THE WEST ASIAN GAMES

Year	Host Country	Winners	Score	Runners-up	Venue
1997	Iran	Iran			Tehran
2002	Kuwait	Kuwait	0-0†	Iran	Al Qadisiya, Kuwait
2005	Qatar	Iraq	2-2 4-3p	Syria	Doha

† Played on a league basis. The result listed is between the top two teams which occurred in the last round of games. Syria shared second place

FOOTBALL TOURNAMENT OF THE SOUTH ASIAN GAMES

Year	Host Country	Winners	Score	Runners-up	Venue
1984	Nepal	Nepal	4-2	Bangladesh	Dasharath Rangashala, Kathmandu
1985	Bangladesh	India	1-1 4-1p	Bangladesh	Dhaka
1987	India	India	1-0	Nepal	Salt Lake, Calcutta
1989	Pakistan	Pakistan	1-0	Bangladesh	Islamabad
1991	Sri Lanka	Pakistan	2-0	Maldives	Colombo
1993	Bangladesh	Nepal	2-2 4-3p	India	Dhaka
1995	India	India	1-0	Bangladesh	Madras
1999	Nepal	Bangladesh	1-0	Nepal	Dasharath Rangashala, Kathmandu
2004	Pakistan	Pakistan	1-0	India	Jinnah Stadium, Islamabad
2006	Sri Lanka	Pakistan	1-0	Sri Lanka	Colombo

Football tournaments as part of regional games in Asia can trace their roots back to 1911 when the Far East Olympics were first held. That tournament saw the first international match ever played on Asian soil when the Philippines beat China 2-1 in Manila.

ASIAN CHAMPIONS CUP AND AFC CHAMPIONS LEAGUE FINALS

Year	Winners	Country	Score	Country	Runners-up
1967	Hapoel Tel Aviv	ISR	2-1	MAS	Selangor
1968	Maccabi Tel Aviv	ISR	1-0	KOR	Yangzee
1970	Taj Club	IRN	2-1	ISR	Hapoel Tel Aviv
1971	Maccabi Tel Aviv	ISR	W-O	IRQ	Police Club
1986	Daewoo Royals	KOR	3-1	KSA	Al Ahly
1987	Furukawa	JPN	4-3	KSA	Al Hilal
1988	Yomiuri	JPN	W-O	KSA	Al Hilal
1989	Al Saad	QAT	2-3 1-0	IRQ	Al Rasheed
1990	Liaoning	CHN	2-1 1-1	JPN	Nissan
1991	Esteghlal SC	IRN	2-1	CHN	Liaoning
1992	Al Hilal	KSA	1-1 4-3p	IRN	Esteghlal SC
1993	Pas	IRN	1-0	KSA	Al Shabab
1994	Thai Farmers Bank	THA	2-1	OMA	Omani Club
1995	Thai Farmers Bank	THA	1-0	QAT	Al Arabi
1996	Ilhwa Chunma	KOR	1-0	KSA	Al Nasr
1997	Pohang Steelers	KOR	2-1	KOR	Ilhwa Chunma
1998	Pohang Steelers	KOR	0-0 6-5p	CHN	Dalian
1999	Jubilo Iwata	JPN	2-1	IRN	Esteghlal SC
2000	Al Hilal	KSA	3-2	JPN	Jubilo Iwata
2001	Suwon Samsung Bluewings	KOR	1-0	JPN	Jubilo Iwata
2002	Suwon Samsung Bluewings	KOR	0-0 4-2p	KOR	Anyang LG Cheetahs
2003	Al Ain	UAE	2-0 0-1	THA	BEC Tero Sasana
2004	Al Ittihad	KSA	1-3 5-0	KOR	Seongnam Ilhwa Chunma
2005	Al Ittihad	KSA	1-1 4-2	UAE	Al Ain
2006	Jeonbuk Hyundai Motors	KOR	2-0 1-2	SYR	Al Karama
2007	Urawa Reds	JPN	1-1 2-0	IRN	Sepahan

AFC CUP

Year	Winners	Country	Score	Country	Runners-up
2004	Al Jaish	SYR	3-2 0-1	SYR	Al Wahda
2005	Al Faysali	JOR	1-0 3-2	LIB	Al Nejmeh
2006	Al Faysali	JOR	3-0 2-4	BHR	Muharraq
2007	Shabab Al Ordun	JOR	1-0 1-1	JOR	Al Faysali

AFC PRESIDENT'S CUP

Year	Winners	Country	Score	Country	Runners-up
2005	Regar TadAZ	TJK	3-0	KGZ	Dordoy-Dinamo
2006	Dordoy-Dinamo	KGZ	2-1	TJK	Vakhsh
2007	Dordoy-Dinamo	KGZ	2-1	NEP	Mahendra Police Club

ASIAN CUP WINNERS' CUP FINALS

Year	Winners	Country	Score	Country	Runners-up
1991	Pirouzi	IRN	0-0 1-0	BHR	Al Muharraq
1992	Nissan	JPN	1-1 5-0	KSA	Al Nasr
1993	Nissan	JPN	1-1 1-0	IRN	Pirouzi
1994	Al-Qadisiyah	KSA	4-2 2-0	HKG	South China
1995	Yokohama Flugels	JPN	2-1	UAE	Al Shaab
1996	Bellmare Hiratsuka	JPN	2-1	IRQ	Al Talaba
1997	Al Hilal	KSA	3-1	JPN	Nagoya Grampus Eight
1998	Al Nasr	KSA	1-0	KOR	Suwon Samsung Bluewings
1999	Al Ittihad	KSA	3-2	KOR	Chunnam Dragons
2000	Shimizu S-Pulse	JPN	1-0	IRQ	Al Zawra
2001	Al Shabab	KSA	4-2	CHN	Dalian Shide
2002	Al Hilal	KSA	2-1	KOR	Chonbuk Hyundai Motors

Discontinued after 2002 following the creation of the AFC Champions League

As part of his bold Vision Asia development strategy, AFC President Mohamed bin Hammam has placed the growth of club football at the heart of his plan to raise standards in the game across the continent. The launch of the AFC Champions League in 2002 was a key element and it replaced both the old Asian Champion Team's Cup and Asian Cup Winners' Cup. Entry to the AFC Champions League is restricted to the top tier of nations where club football was seen as most developed. In order to foster development in the other nations, two new competitions were also introduced - the AFC Cup and the President's Cup, with the former open to middle ranking nations and the latter for countries where football is least developed. These two tournaments aimed at increasing the competitive nature of the club game by holding out the real prospect of honours for nations unlikely ever to win the Champions League. Historically Saudi Arabian and Korean clubs have been the most successful in the Champions Teams' Cup and the AFC Champions League with 11 titles between them, while Iran, Japan and China PR have underachieved given the strength of their domestic leagues. No team has ever won the title more than twice.

AFC CHAMPIONS LEAGUE MEDALS TABLE

	Country	G	S	B	F	SF
1	Korea Republic	7	4	5	11	19
2	Saudi Arabia	4	5	1	9	10
3	Japan	4	3	2	7	10
4	Iran	3	3	5	6	13
5	Israel	3	1		4	4
6	Thailand	2	1	1	3	4
7	China PR	1	2	3	3	8
8	UAE	1	1	3	2	6
9	Qatar	1	1	1	2	3
10	Iraq		2		2	4
11	Syria		1	1	1	2
12	Malaysia		1		1	1
	Oman		1		1	1
14	Uzbekistan			3		4
15	Indonesia			1		3
16	Lebanon			1		1
	Korea DPR			1		1
	Kuwait			1		1
19	India					1
	Kazakhstan					1
	(Inclusive of 2007 tournament)	26	26	29	52	97

This table represents the Gold (winners), Silver (runners-up) and Bronze (semi-finalists) placings of clubs representing the above countries in the AFC Champions League, along with the number of appearances in the final and semi-finals

ASIAN CHAMPIONS LEAGUE MEDALS TABLE

	Country		G	S	B
1	Esteghlal SC (Taj)	IRN	2	2	3
2	Al Hilal	KSA	2	2	1
3	Thai Farmers Bank	THA	2		1
4	Al Ittihad	KSA	2		
	Maccabi Tel Aviv	ISR	2		
	Pohang Steelers	KOR	2		
	Suwon Samsung Bluewings	KOR	2		
8	Seongnam Ilhwa Chunma	KOR	1	2	1
9	Jubilo Iwata	JPN	1	2	
10	Al Ain	UAE	1	1	1
	Liaoning	CHN	1	1	1
12	Hapoel Tel Aviv	ISR	1	1	
13	Busan I'Park	KOR	1		1
	Jeonbuk Hyundai Motors	KOR	1		1
	Verdy Kawasaki (Yomiuri)	JPN	1		1
16	Al Saad	QAT	1		
	JEF United (Furukawa)	JPN	1		
	Pass	IRN	1		
	Urawa Reds	JPN	1		
20	Dalian	CHN		1	1
21	Al Ahly	KSA		1	
	Al Arabi	QAT		1	
	Al Karama	SYR		1	
	Al Nasr	KSA		1	
	Al Rasheed	IRQ		1	
	Al Shabab	KSA		1	
	Anyang LG Cheetahs	KOR		1	
	BEC Tero Sasana	THA		1	
	Omani Club	OMA		1	
	Police	IRQ		1	
	Selangor	MAS		1	
	Sepahan	IRN		1	
	Yangzee	KOR		1	
	Yokohama Marinos (Nissan)	JPN		1	
35	Pirouzi	IRN			3
36	Pakhtakor Tashkent	UZB			2
37	Al Qadisiya	KUW			1
	Al Rayyan	QAT			1
	Al Wasl	UAE			1
	April 25th	PRK			1
	Homenetmen	LIB			1
	Neftchi Fergana	UZB			1
	Sanfrecce Hiroshima (Toyo)	JPN			1
	Shenzhen	CHN			1
	Tiga Berlian	IDN			1
	Tungsten Mining	KOR			1
	Ulsan Hyundai Horang-i	KOR			1
	Al Wahda	UAE			1
			26	26	29

AFC CUP MEDALS TABLE

	Country	G	S	B	F	SF
1	Jordan	3	1	2	4	6
2	Syria	1	1		2	2
3	Lebanon		1	2	1	3
4	Bahrain		1		1	1
5	Singapore			2		2
6	Hong Kong			1		1
	Maldives			1		1
(Inclusive of 2007 tournament)		4	4	8	8	16

This table represents the Gold (winners), Silver (runners-up) and Bronze (semi-finalists) placings of clubs representing the above countries in the AFC Cup, along with the number of appearances in the final and semi-finals

AFC CUP MEDALS TABLE

	Country		G	S	B
1	Al Faysali	JOR	2	1	
2	Al Jaish	SYR	1		
	Shabab Al Ordun	JOR	1		
4	Al Nijmeh	LIB		1	2
5	Al Wahda	SYR		1	
	Muharraq	BHR		1	
7	Al Wihdat	JOR			2
8	Geylang United	SIN			1
	Home United	SIN			1
	New Radiant	MDV			1
	Sun Hei	HKG			1
			4	4	8

AFC PRESIDENT'S CUP MEDALS TABLE

	Country	G	S	B	F	SF
1	Kyrgyzstan	2	1		3	3
2	Tajikistan	1	1	1	2	3
3	Nepal		1	1	1	2
	Sri Lanka			2		2
5	Cambodia			1		1
	Chinese Taipei			1		1
(Inclusive of 2007 tournament)		3	3	2	6	12

This table represents the Gold (winners), Silver (runners-up) and Bronze (semi-finalists) placings of clubs representing the above countries in the AFC President's Cup, along with the number of appearances in the final and semi-finals

AFC PRESIDENT'S CUP MEDALS TABLE

	Country		G	S	B
1	Dordoy-Dinamo	KGZ	2	1	
2	Regar TadAZ	TJK	1		1
3	Vakhsh Qurgonteppa	TJK		1	
	Mahendra Police Club	NEP		1	
5	Blue Star Club	SRI			1
	Khmera	CAM			1
	Ratnam SC	SRI			1
	Tatung	TPE			1
	Three Star Club	NEP			1
			3	3	6

AFC CHALLENGE CUP INDIA 2008

AFC CHALLENGE CUP INDIA 2008

Qualifying groups		First round groups		Semi–finals		Final	
Group A	Pts						
Sri Lanka	7						
Pakistan	6						
Chinese Taipei	4	**Group A**	Pts				
Guam	0	India	7				
		Tajikistan	5				
Group B	Pts	Turkmenistan	4				
Tajikistan	7	Afghanistan	0	India	1		
Philippines	7			Myanmar	0		
Bhutan	1						
Brunei Darusalem	1						
						India	
Group C	Pts					Tajikistan	
Afghanistan	4						
Kyrgyzstan	3						
Bangladesh	1	**Group B**	Pts	Korea DPR	0		
		Korea DPR	9	Tajikistan	1		
		Myanmar	6				
Group D	Pts	Nepal	3				
Nepal	6	Sri Lanka	0				
Cambodia	3						
Macau	0						

India, Myanmar, Korea DPR and Tajikistan qualified automatically • Held in Hyderabad, India from 30-07-2008 to 13-08-2008 (final held in Delhi due to rain) • Full match details in next year's *Almanack of World Football*

REGIONAL TOURNAMENTS IN ASIA 2007–08

SOUTH EAST ASIAN GAMES KORAT 2007

First Round Group Stage	Pl	W	D	L	F	A	Pts	MYA	IDN	CAM	Semi–finals		Final	
Thailand	3	3	0	0	13	3	9	3-2	2-1	8-0				
Myanmar	3	1	1	1	8	5	4		0-0	6-2				
Indonesia	3	1	1	1	4	3	4			3-1	Thailand	3		
Cambodia	3	0	0	3	3	17	0				Singapore	0		
													Thailand	2
	Pl	W	D	L	F	A	Pts	SIN	MAS	LAO			Myanmar	0
Vietnam	3	2	0	1	7	5	6	2-3	3-1	2-1	Vietnam	0 1p		
Singapore	3	1	2	0	4	3	5		1-1	0-0	Myanmar	0 3p		
Malaysia	3	1	1	1	6	4	4			4-0			**3rd Place Play-off**	
Laos	3	0	1	2	1	6	1						Singapore	5

Held in Korat, Thailand from 1-12-2007 to 14-12-2007 • U-23 event

Vietnam   0

EAST ASIAN FOOTBALL CHAMPIONSHIP CHINA PR 2008

Preliminary Group Stage

Group A	Pl	W	D	L	F	A	Pts	MAC	MGL
Korea DPR	2	2	0	0	14	1	6	7-1	7-0
Macao	2	0	1	1	1	7	1		0-0
Mongolia	2	0	1	1	0	7	1		

Group B	Pl	W	D	L	F	A	Pts	TPE	GUM
Hong Kong	2	1	1	0	16	2	4	1-1	15-1
Taiwan	2	1	1	0	11	1	4	10-0	
Guam	2	0	0	2	1	25	0		

Preliminary Final

Korea DPR	1
Hong Kong	0

Final Group Stage

	Pl	W	D	L	F	A	Pts	JPN	CHN	PRK
Korea Rep	3	1	2	0	5	4	5	1-1	3-2	1-1
Japan	3	1	2	0	3	2	5		1-0	1-1
China PR	3	1	0	2	5	5	3			3-1
Korea DPR	3	0	2	1	3	5	2			

Korea DPR qualified to join China PR, Japan and Korea Republic in the final tournament • Preliminary group stage held in Taipei from 17-06-2007 to 24-06-2007 • Final group stage held in Chongqing, China PR from 17-02-2008 to 23-02-2008

Olympic Sports Centre, Chongqing
17-02-2007, 15:30, 25 000, Torky IRN

China PR   **2**
Zhou Haibin [47], Liu Jian [61]

Zong Lei - Zhang Shui, Sun Xiang•, Li Weifeng•, Xu Yunlong - Wang Dong, Qu Bo• (Lu Zheng 92+), Du Zhenyu• (Li Yan 78), Liu Jian• (Jiang Ning 78), Zhou Haibin - Zhu Ting. Tr: Vladimir Petrovic

Korea Republic   **3**
Park Chu Young 2 [43] [65], Kwak Tae Hwi [92+]

Jung Sung Ryong - Cho Yong Hyung, Kwak Hee Ju, Kwak Tae Hwi - Lee Jong Min, Cho Won Hee, Kim Nam Il, Park Won Jae - Lee Keun Ho (Ko Ki Gu 75), Park Chu Young, Yeom Ki Hun (Koo Ja Cheol 63). Tr: Huh Jung Moo

---

Olympic Sports Centre, Chongqing
17-02-2007, 18:15, 15 000, Choi MY KOR

Japan   **1**
Ryoichi Maeda [69]

Eiji Kawashima - Hiroki Mizumoto, Akira Kaji•, Yuji Nakazawa, Atsuto Uchida (Yuichi Komano 77) - Yasuhito Endo, Naotake Hanyu (Michihiro Yasuda 64), Satoru Yamagishi (Ryoichi Maeda 64), Ryuji Bando, Keita Suzuki - Yuzo Tashiro. Tr: Takeshi Okada

Korea DPR   **1**
Jong Tae Se [5]

Ri Myong Guk - Ri Jung Il, Ri Kwang Chon, Pak Chol Jin, Han Song Chol, Nam Song Chol - Pak Nam Chol• (Choe Chol Man 78), An Yong Hak, Mun In Guk, Kim Yong Jun (Kim Kun Il 68) - Jong Tae Se. Tr: Kim Jong Hun

---

Olympic Sports Centre, Chongqing
20-02-2007, 18:15, 38 000, O Tae Song PRK

China PR   **0**

Zong Lei• - Zhang Shui, Sun Xiang, Li Weifeng•, Xu Yunlong• - Wang Dong (Zhao Junzhe 53), Qu Bo, Du Zhenyu, Liu Jian (Lu Zheng 59), Zhou Haibin (Hao Junmin 76) - Zhu Ting•. Tr: Vladimir Petrovic

Japan   **1**
Koji Yamase [17]

Seigo Narazaki - Yuichi Komano (Akira Kaji 46), Michihiro Yasuda (Haotake Hanyu 58), Yuji Nakazawa, Atsuto Uchida• - Yasuyuki Konno, Yasuhito Endo, Koji Yamase (Hideo Hashimoto 90), Keita Suzuki•, Kengo Nakamura - Yuzo Tashiro. Tr: Takeshi Okada

---

Olympic Sports Centre, Chongqing
20-02-2007, 20:45, 20 000, Takayama JPN

Korea DPR   **1**
Jong Tae Se [73]

Ri Myong Guk• - Ri Jung Il, Ri Kwang Chon, Pak Chol Jin••48, Han Song Chol (Cha Jong Hyok 69), Nam Song Chol (Ji Yun Nam 46) - Pak Nam Chol (Kim Kun Il 46), An Yong Hak, Mun In Guk•, Kim Yong Jun - Jong Tae Se•. Tr: Kim Jong Hun

Korea Republic   **1**
Yeom Ki Hun [21]

Kim Yong Dae - Kang Min Soo, Kwak Hee Ju (Park Won Jae 54), Kwak Tae Hwi - Cho Won Hee, Kim Nam Il (Hwang Ji Soo 46), Lee Kwan Koo (Oh Jang Eun 60), Lee Sang Ho• - Lee Keun Ho, Yeom Ki Hun, Ko Ki Gu. Tr: Huh Jung Moo

---

Olympic Sports Centre, Chongqing
23-02-2008, 18:15, 29 000, Tan Hai CHN

Japan   **1**
Koji Yamase [68]

Yoshikatsu Kawaguchi - Akira Kaji, Yuji Nakazawa, Atsuto Uchida - Yasuyuki Konno, Yasuhito Endo, Koji Yamase (Ryuji Bando 86), Keita Suzuki, Kengo Nakamura (Michihiro Yasuda 62), Hideo Hashimoto (Kisho Yano 78) - Yuzo Tashiro. Tr: Takeshi Okada

Korea Republic   **1**
Yeom Ki Hun [15]

Kim Yong Dae - Cho Yong Hyung, Kang Min Soo, Kwak Tae Hwi - Lee Jong Min, Cho Won Hee, Kim Nam Il• (Koo Ja Cheol 58), Park Won Jae, Oh Jang Eun - Cho Jin Soo (Lee Keun Ho 66), Yeom Ki Hun. Tr: Huh Jung Moo

---

Olympic Sports Centre, Chongqing
23-02-2007, 20:45, 30 500, Torky IRN

China PR   **3**
Zhu Ting [45], Wang Dong [55], Hao Junmin [83]

Zong Lei• - Zhang Shui•, Sun Xiang, Feng Xiaoting, Wang Xiao• - Wang Dong•, Qu Bo (Xu Yunlong 69•91+), Du Zhenyu•••56, Hao Junmin•, Liu Jian• - Zhu Ting (Jiang Ning 58) (Li Yan 93+). Tr: Vladimir Petrovic

Korea DPR   **1**
Ji Yun Nam [34]

Ri Myong Guk - Cha Jong Hyok, Ri Jung Il, Ri Kwang Chon, Ji Yun Nam, Han Song Chol• (Kim Song Chol 66) - An Yong Hak (Ryang Yong Gi 83), Mun In Guk, Kim Yong Jun• - Jong Tae Se. Tr: Kim Jong Hun

---

SOUTH ASIAN GOLD CUP COLOMBO/MALE 2008

First Round Group Stage

	Pl	W	D	L	F	A	Pts	MDV	NEP	PAK
India	3	3	0	0	7	1	9	1-0	4-0	2-1
Maldives	3	2	0	1	7	2	6		4-1	3-0
Nepal	3	1	0	2	5	9	3			4-1
Pakistan	3	0	0	3	2	9	0			

	Pl	W	D	L	F	A	Pts	BHU	BAN	AFG
Sri Lanka	3	2	1	0	5	2	7	2-0	1-0	2-2
Bhutan	3	1	1	1	4	4	4		1-1	3-1
Bangladesh	3	0	2	1	3	3	2			2-2
Afghanistan	3	0	2	1	5	7	2			

Semi–finals

Maldives	1
Sri Lanka	0
Bhutan	1
India	2

Final

Maldives	1
India	0

Held in Malé, Maldives (Group A) and Colombo, Sri Lanka (Group B) from 3-06-2008 to 14-06-2008

AFC CHAMPIONS LEAGUE 2007

AFC CHAMPIONS LEAGUE 2007

Group Stage	Quarter-finals	Semi-finals	Final

Group A — Pts

Al Wahda	UAE	13
Al Zawra'a	IRQ	11
Al Arabi	KUW	7
Al Rayyan	QAT	2

Group B — Pts

Al Hilal	KSA	8
Pakhtakor Tashkent	UZB	6
Al Kuwait	KUW	2
Esteghlal	IRN	0

Quarter-final:
Urawa Reds * — 2 2
Jeonbuk Motors — 1 0

Group C — Pts

Al Karama	SYR	11
Neftchi Fergana	UZB	10
Al Najaf	IRQ	8
Al Sadd	QAT	4

Semi-final:
Urawa Reds — 2 2 5p
Seongnam Chunma* — 2 2 3p

Quarter-final:
Al Karama — 1 0
Seongnam Chunma* — 2 2

Group D — Pts

Sepahan	IRN	13
Al Shabab	KSA	10
Al Ain	UAE	6
Al Ittihad	SYR	3

Final:
Urawa Reds — 1 2
Sepahan * — 1 0

Group E — Pts

Urawa Reds	JPN	10
Sydney FC	AUS	9
Persik Kediri	IDN	7
Shanghai Shenhua	CHN	5

Quarter-final:
Al Wahda * — 0 1
Al Hilal — 0 1

Semi-final:
Al Wahda — 1 0
Sepahan * — 3 0

Group F — Pts

Kawasaki Frontale	JPN	16
Chunnam Dragons	KOR	10
Arema Malang	IDN	4
Bangkok University	THA	3

Quarter-final:
Kawasaki Frontale — 0 0 4p
Sepahan * — 0 0 5p

Group G — Pts

Seongnam Chunma	KOR	13
Shandong Luneng	CHN	13
Adelaide United	AUS	8
Dong Tam Long An	VIE	0

† Jeonbuk Hyundai Motors (KOR) given a bye to the quarter-finals as holders • * Home team in the first leg • On February 17, 2007, Esteghlal were thrown out of the tournament after failing to register their players on time

For details of group matches see *Almanack of World Football 2008*

QUARTER-FINALS

Saitama 2002, Saitama
19-09-2007, 19:30, 33 103, Mujghef JOR

Urawa Reds   **2**

Makoto Hasebe [4], Tatsuya Tanaka [58]

Ryota Tsuzuki - Keisuke Tsuboi, Marcus Tulio Tanaka, Nobuhisa Yamada, Robson Ponte (Shinji Ono 79), Keita Suzuki, Tadaaki Hirakawa, Makoto Hasebe, Yuki Abe, Yuichiro Nagai, Tatsuya Tanaka (Hideki Uchidate 90). Tr: Holger Osieck

Jeonbuk Motors   **1**

Choi Jin Cheul [90]

Sung Kyungil - Choi Chul Soon, Choi Jin Cheul, Kim Young Sun●, Chung Kyunggho - Lim Youhwan● (Kim Hyun Su 61), Jeon Kwanghwan, Kwon Jip (Kim Jae Young 84), Kim Hyeungbum (Tony Franja 56) - Ze Carlo●, Stevica Ristick. Tr: Choi Kang Hee

---

Jeonju World Cup, Jeonju
26-09-2007, 19:00, 31 000, Al Ghamdi KSA

Jeonbuk Motors   **0**

Sung Kyungil - Choi Chul Soon●, Jung Inwhan, Choi Jin Cheul●, Kim Hyun Su (Chung Jungkwan 61), Chung Kyunggho●●●23 - Kim Jae Young●, Tony Franja (Kim Hyeungbum● 50), Jeon Kwanghwan, Kwon Jip (Ze Carlo 16) - Stevica Ristick●. Tr: Choi Kang Hee

Urawa Reds   **2**

Tatsuya Tanaka [4], Ponte [66]

Ryota Tsuzuki - Keisuke Tsuboi, Marcus Tulio Tanaka, Nobuhisa Yamada, Robson Ponte (Shinji Ono 75), Keita Suzuki (Hideki Uchidate 88), Tadaaki Hirakawa, Makoto Hasebe, Yuki Abe, Yuichiro Nagai, Tatsuya Tanaka (Washington 58). Tr: Holger Osieck

---

Seongnam Sports Complex
19-09-2007, 19:00, 4103, Mombeni IRN

Seonganm Ilhwa Chunma   **2**

Kim Min Ho [74], Cho Byung Kuk [76]

Kim Yong Dae - Park Jin Sub, Cho Byung Kuk, Kim Cheol Ho (Kim Min Ho 71), Kim Young Chul, Jang Hack Yong - Kim Do Heon, Kim Sang Sik - Choi Sung Suk (Kim Dong Hun 46), Itamar (Nam Ki Il 62), Mota. Tr: Kim Hag Bum

Al Karama   **1**

Senghor Koupouleni [11]

Mosab Balhous● - Fabio Santos, Hassan Abbas●, Belal Abdulaim, Anas Al Khouja● - Jehad Al Hussein, Iyad Mando (Fahd Aodi 80), Aatef Jenyat, Firas Issmael - Ziad Chabo, Senghor Koupouleni. Tr: Mohamed Kwid

---

Khaled Ibn Al Waleed, Homs
26-09-2007, 21:30, 30 000, Al Badwawi UAE

Al Karama   **0**

Mosab Balhous - Fabio Santos, Hassan Abbas, Belal Abdulaim, Anas Al Khouja - Jehad Al Hussein, Iyad Mando (Fahd Aodi 46), Aatef Jenyat, Firas Issmael (Mohanad Ibrahim● 69) - Ziad Chabo, Senghor Koupouleni (Leandro Netto 56). Tr: Mohamed Kwid

Seonganm Ilhwa Chunma   **2**

Mota [9], Kim Dong Hun [71]

Kim Yong Dae - Park Jin Sub, Cho Byung Kuk, Kim Cheol Ho● (Kim Min Ho 89), Kim Young Chul, Jang Hack Yong● - Kim Do Heon, Kim Sang Sik - Itamar● (Cho Yong Hyung 72), Mota, Nam Ki Il (Kim Dong Hun 46). Tr: Kim Hag Bum

---

Al Nahyan, Abu Dhabi
19-09-2007, 22:00, 9000, Balideh QAT

Al Wahda   **0**

Nadir Lamyaghri - Leonardo, Basheer Saeed, Yaser Abdulla (Hamdan Ismaeel 75) - Abdulla Belal (Eisa Ahmed 79), Mohamed Othman●, Haidar Alo Ali, Mahmoud Khamis● (Yaser Matar● 75) - Ismail Matar, Ahmed Sharbini, Mohamed Saeed. Tr: Ivo Worthman

Al Hilal   **0**

Mohammed Al Daeyea - Marcelo Tavares, Khalid Al Angrie, Fahad Al Mefareg (Majed Al Marshadi 83), Abdulaziz Kahthran - Khaled Al Thaker●, Mohammed Al Shalhoub, Nawaf Al Temyat, Omar Al Ghamdi (Ahmad Al Dossary 64), Yasser Al Qahtani - Meshal Al Mouri. Tr: Olaroiu Cosmin

---

King Fahad International, Riyadh
26-09-2007, 22:15, 55 000, Kwon Jong Chul KOR

Al Hilal   **1**

Tareq El Taib [85]

Mohammed Al Daeyea - Marcelo Tavares, Ahmad Al Dossary, Saad Al Theyab (Ahmed Al Suwaileh 41), Khalid Al Angrie (Tareq El Taib 64), Fahad Al Mefareg●, Abdulaziz Kahthran● - Khaled Al Thaker, Nawaf Al Temyat● (Mohammed Al Shalhoub 76), Omar Al Ghamdi - Yasser Al Qahtani. Tr: Olaroiu Cosmin

Al Wahda   **1**

Ismail Matar [18]

Nadir Lamyaghri - Leonardo, Basheer Saeed, Yaser Abdulla● - Abdulla Belal●●●86, Mohamed Othman, Haidar Alo Ali●, Mahmoud Khamis (Tawfeeq Abdul Razzaq 45), Eisa Ahmed - Ismail Matar, Ahmed Sharbini, Mohamed Saeed. Tr: Ivo Worthman

---

Foolad Shahr, Esfahan
19-09-2007, 18:30, 25 000, Karim BHR

Sepahan   **0**

Abbas Mohammadi - Hamid Azizzadeh, Hadi Aghily, Moshen Bengar - Moharram Navidkia, Jalal Akbari (Hossein Papi 77), Hadi Jafari●, Hojatolah Zadmahmoud (Hossein Kazemi 46), Abdul Wahab Al Hail, Ehsan Hajysafi (Emad Mohammed 46) - Mahmoud Karimi. Tr: Luka Bonacic

Kawasaki Frontale   **0**

Eiji Kawashima● - Hiroki Ito, Yoshinobu Minowa, Shuhei Terada● - Magnum Tavares, Kengo Nakamura● (Masayuki Ochiai 92+), Yusuke Mori, Kazuhiro Murakami, Hiroyuki Taniguchi (Takahiro Kawamura 73) - Juninho, Jong Tae Se (Kazuki Ganaha 81). Tr: Takashi Sekizuka

---

Todoroki, Kawasaki
26-09-2007, 19:00, 13 507, Al Fadhli KUW

Kawasaki Frontale   **0 4p**

Eiji Kawashima - Hiroki Ito, Yoshinobu Minowa, Shuhei Terada - Magnum Tavares, Kengo Nakamura (Masahiro Ohashi 95), Yusuke Mori (Yusuke Igawa 74), Kazuhiro Murakami, Hiroyuki Taniguchi - Juninho, Jong Tae Se (Kazuki Ganaha 106). Tr: Takashi Sekizuka

Sepahan   **0 5p**

Abbas Mohammadi - Hamid Azizzadeh, Hadi Aghily, Moshen Bengar● - Moharram Navidkia, Jala Akbari, Hossein Kazemi (Ebrahim Lovinian 68), Abdul Wahab Al Hail●, Saeid Bayat, Ehsan Hajysafi (Farshad Bahadorani 91) - Emad Mohammed (Mohsen Hamidi 70). Tr: Luka Bonacic

SEMI-FINALS

Seongnam Sports Complex
3-10-2007, 19:00, 17 000, Abdou QAT

Seonganm Ilhwa Chunma **2**

Mota [11], Kim Do Heon [81]

Kim Yong Dae - Park Jin Sub, Cho Byung Kuk, Kim Cheol Ho (Han Dong Won 71), Kim Young Chul, Jang Hack Yong - Kim Do Heon• (Kim Min Ho 87), Kim Sang Sik• - Itamar (Kim Dong Hun 46), Mota, Nam Ki Il. Tr: Kim Hag Bum

Urawa Reds **2**

Tatsuya Tanaka [53], Ponte [66p]

Ryota Tsuzuki - Keisuke Tsuboi (Satoshi Horinouchi 67), Marcus Tulio Tanaka, Nobuhisa Yamada (Hajime Hosogai 93+), Robson Ponte, Keita Suzuki, Tadaaki Hirakawa•, Makoto Hasebe, Yuki Abe•, Tatsuya Tanaka (Yuichiro Nagai 82), Washington. Tr: Holger Osieck

Saitama 2002, Saitama
24-10-2007, 19:30, 51 651, Al Fadhli KUW

Urawa Reds **2 5p**

Washington [21], Hasebe [73]

Ryota Tsuzuki - Keisuke Tsuboi, Marcus Tulio Tanaka (Satoshi Horinouchi 91), Nobuhisa Yamada (Hajime Hosogai 103), Robson Ponte, Keita Suzuki, Tadaaki Hirakawa, Makoto Hasebe, Yuki Abe, Tatsuya Tanaka (Yuichiro Nagai 81), Washington. Tr: Holger Osieck

Seonganm Ilhwa Chunma **2 3p**

Choi Sung Kuk [56], Kim Dong Hun [68]

Kim Yong Dae - Park Jin Sub, Cho Byung Kuk, Kim Young Chul, Jang Hack Yong - Son Dae Ho (Kim Dong Hun 56), Kim Do Heon• (Kim Min Ho 84), Kim Sang Sik• - Choi Sung Kuk, Itamar, Nam Ki Il (Cho Yong Hyung 73). Tr: Kim Hag Bum

Foolad Shahr, Esfahan
3-10-2007, 20:30, 18 000, Abdul Bashir SIN

Sepahan **3**

Karimi 2 [12 58], Navidkia [85]

Abbas Mohammadi - Hadi Aghily• (Hamid Azizzadeh 67), Moshen Bengar, Jaba Mujiri - Moharram Navidkia•, Hossein Kazemi, Abdul Wahab Al Hail (Hossein Papi 81), Saeid Bayat, Ebrahim Lovinian• (Jalal Akbari 70), Ehsan Hajysafi - Mahmoud Karimi. Tr: Luka Bonacic

Al Wahda **1**

Mohamed Saeed [48]

Nadir Lamyaghri - Leonardo, Basheer Saeed, Yaser Abdulla••33 - Tawfeeq Abdul Razzaq (Mahmoud Khamis 83), Yaser Matar (Abdulla Ali 46), Mohamed Othman, Haidar Alo Ali, Eisa Ahmed - Ismael Matar, Mohamed Saeed. Tr: Ivo Worthman

Al Nahyan, Abu Dhabi
24-10-2007, 20:00, 11 000, Williams AUS

Al Wahda **0**

Nadir Lamyaghri• - Leonardo, Basheer Saeed - Tawfeeq Abdul Razzaq (Mahmoud Khamis 65), Abdulla Belal (Ahmed Sharbini 74), Mohamed Othman•, Haidar Alo Ali, Abdulraheem Jumaa, Eisa Ahmed (Saeed Salem 46) - Ismael Matar•, Mohamed Saeed. Tr: Ivo Worthman

Sepahan **0**

Abbas Mohammadi - Hadi Aghily, Moshen Bengar, Jaba Mujiri - Moharram Navidkia, Jalal Akbari (Seyed Salehi 63), Hadi Jafari• (Mohsen Hamidi 83), Abdul Wahab Al Hail, Saeid Bayat, Ehsan Hajysafi - Mahmoud Karimi• (Ebrahim Lovinian 78). Tr: Luka Bonacic

---

AFC CHAMPIONS LEAGUE FINAL FIRST LEG
Foolad Shahr, Esfahan
7-11-2007, 16:00, 25 000, Mohd Salleh MAS

SEPAHAN	1	1	URAWA REDS

Mahmoud Karimi [46]   Robson Ponte [45]

Sepahan			Urawa Reds	
1 Abbas MOHAMMADI			Ryota TSUZUKI	23
5 Hadi AGHILY			Keisuke TSUBOI	2
8 Mohsen BENGAR			NENE	5
17 Jaba MUJIRI			Satoshi HORINOUCHI	20
4 Moharram NAVIDKIA			Robson PONTE	10
6 Jalal AKBARI	46		Keita SUZUKI	13
12 Abdul Wahab AL HAIL			Tadaaki HIRAKAWA	14
2 Saeid BAYAT	46		Makoto HASEBE	17
28 Ehsan HAJYSAFI			Yuki ABE	22
13 Mahmoud KARIMI	68	73	Yuichiro NAGAI	9
20 Emad RIDHA			WASHINGTON	21
Tr: Luka BONACIC			Tr: Holger OSIECK	
Substitutes			Substitutes	
11 Hossein KAZEMI	68	73	Tatsuya TANAKA	11
18 Mohsen HAMIDI	46			
25 Ebrahim LOVINIAN	46			

AFC CHAMPIONS LEAGUE FINAL SECOND LEG
Saitama 2002, Saitama
14-11-2007, 19:25, 59 034, Irmatov UZB

URAWA REDS	2	0	SEPAHAN

Yuichiro Nagai [22], Yuki Abe [71]

Urawa Reds			Sepahan	
23 Ryota TSUZUKI			Abbas MOHAMMADI	1
2 Keisuke TSUBOI			Hadi AGHILY	5
4 Marcus Tulio TANAKA			Mohsen BENGAR	8
20 Satoshi HORINOUCHI			Jaba MUJIRI	17
10 Robson PONTE	81		Moharram NAVIDKIA	4
13 Keita SUZUKI			Abdul Wahab AL HAIL	12
14 Tadaaki HIRAKAWA		46	Mohsen HAMIDI	18
17 Makoto HASEBE		60	Saeid BAYAT	21
22 Yuki ABE			Ebrahim LOVINIAN	25
9 Yuichiro NAGAI	86		Ehsan HAJYSAFI	28
21 WASHINGTON	92	30	Emad RIDHA	20
Tr: Holger OSIECK			Tr: Luka BONACIC	
Substitutes			Substitutes	
11 Tatsuya TANAKA	86	60	Hossein KAZEMI	11
19 Hideki UCHIDATE	81	30	Mahmoud KARIMI	13
30 Masayuki OKANO	92	46	Hossein PAPI	30

AFC CHAMPIONS LEAGUE 2008

AFC CHAMPIONS LEAGUE 2008

Group Stage			Quarter–finals		Semi–finals	Final
Group A		Pts				
Kuruvchi	UZB	13				
Al Ittihad	KSA	9				
Sepahan	IRN	7				
Al Ittihad	SYR	6				
Group B		Pts				
Saipa	IRN	12				
Al Quwa Al Jawiya	IRQ	8	Urawa Reds			
Al Wasl	UAE	7	Al Qadisiya *			
Kuwait SC	KUW	5				
Group C		Pts				
Al Karama	SYR	11				
Al Wahda	UAE	9				
Al Sadd	QAT	6				
Al Ahli	KSA	4	Al Karama *			
			Gamba Osaka			
Group D		Pts				
Al Qadisiya	KUW	11				
Pakhtakor	UZB	11				
Arbil	IRQ	8				
Al Gharafa	QAT	2				
Group E		Pts	Saipa *			
Adelaide United	AUS	14	Kuruvchi			
Changchun Yatai	CHN	12				
Pohang Steelers	KOR	5				
Binh Duong	VIE	1				
Group F		Pts				
Kashima Antlers	JPN	15				
Beijing Guoan	CHN	12	Kashima Antlers *			
Krung Thai Bank	THA	7	Adelaide United			
Nam Dinh	VIE	1				
Group G		Pts				
Gamba Osaka	JPN	14				
Melbourne Victory	AUS	7				
Chunnam Dragons	KOR	6				
Chonburi	THA	5				

† Urawa Reds (JPN) given a bye to the quarter-finals as holders ● * Home team in the first leg

Remaining ties: Quarter-finals 17/09/2008 & 24/09/2008; Semi-finals 8/10/2008 & 22/10/2008; Final 5/11/2008 & 12/11/2008

GROUP A

		Pl	W	D	L	F	A	Pts	UZB	KSA	IRN	SYR
Kuruvchi	UZB	6	4	1	1	8	2	13		2-0	2-0	1-0
Al Ittihad	KSA	6	3	0	3	6	5	9	1-0		0-1	3-0
Sepahan	IRN	6	2	1	3	5	8	7	1-1	2-1		0-2
Al Ittihad	SYR	6	2	0	4	4	8	6	0-2	0-1	2-1	

Foolad Shahr, Esfahan
12-03-2008, 15:30, 15 000, Williams AUS

Sepahan 0

Abbas Mohammadi - Hadi Aghily, Mohsen Bengar - Jalal Akbari, Farshad Bahadorani (Hamed Rasouli 66) , Hossein Kazemi, Abdul Wahab Abulhail, Hossein Papi, Ehsan Hajy Safi - Emad Mohamed Ridha, Mehdi Seyed Salehi. Tr: Jorvan Viera

Al Ittihad Aleppo 2
Gomez 21, Al Agha 87

Mahmoud Karkar – Omar Hemidi, Majd Homsi, Salah Chahrour, Bakri Tarrab – Ammar Rihawi, Jesus Gomez (Obaid Al Salal 82), Jonathan Perez, Mahmoud Al Amena (Otobong Otudor 75), Yahia Al Rached (Wael Ayan 73) – Abdulfatah Al Agha. Tr: Tita

Prince Abdullah, Jeddah
12-03-2008, 18:30, 7500, Nishimura JPN

Al Ittihad Jeddah 1
Magno Alves 80

Tisir Al Antaif – Talal Assiri, Adnan Falatah, Hamad Al Montashari, Osama Al Muwalad – Tcheco, Saud Khariri, Abdullah Hidar (Manaf Aboshgair 62), Mohammed Noor – Alhassane Keita (Mohammed Abdullah 87), Magno Alves. Tr: Estevam Soares

Kuruvchi 0

Pavel Bugalo – Bakhtiyor Ashurmatov, Gochguly Gochguliyev, Alexander Khvostunov – Victor Karpenko (Shavkat Salomov 85), Azizbek Haydarov, Aleksey Nikolaev, Timur Kapadze (Sergey Lushchan 75) – Ulugbek Bakaev, Anvarjon Soliev (Rashidjon Gofurov 46), Server Djeparov. Tr: Mirdjalol Kasimov

International, Aleppo
19-03-2008, 18:00, 41 000, Balideh QAT

Al Ittihad Aleppo 0

Mahmoud Karkar – Omar Hemidi, Majd Homsi (Yousef Chikhal Eshra 81), Salah Chahrour, Bakri Tarrab – Ammar Rihawi, Jesus Gomez, Jonathan Perez, Mahmoud Al Amena (Mahmod Al Peef 80), Yahia Al Rached (Wael Ayan 70) – Abdulfatah Al Agha. Tr: Tita

Al Ittihad Jeddah 1
Magno Alves 78

Tisir Al Antaif – Redha Tukar, Adnan Falatah, Hamad Al Montashari, Osama Al Muwalad – Tcheco (Aqeal Al Qarni 92+), Saud Khariri, Abdullah Hidar, Mohammed Noor – Alhassane Keita, Magno Alves (Saleh Al Saqri 89). Tr: Estevam Soares

MHSK, Tashkent
19-03-2008, 15:00, 13 000, Al Marzouqi UAE

Kuruvchi 2
Bakaev 60, Kapadze 80

Murotjon Zukhurov – Bakhtiyor Ashurmatov, Gochguly Gochguliyev, Alexander Khvostunov – Sakhob Jurayev (Hayrulla Karimov 65) – Rashidjon Gofurov (Shavkat Salomov 50), Victor Karpenko, Azizbek Haydarov, Timur Kapadze – Ulugbek Bakaev (Anvar Rajabov 80), Server Djeparov. Tr: Mirdjalol Kasimov

Sepahan 0

Abbas Mohammadi – Hamid Azizzadeh, Hadi Aghily - Jalal Akbari, Hossein Kazemi, Abdul Wahab Abulhail (Hojatolah Mahmoud 84), Hossein Papi, Hadi Jafari (Farshad Bahadorani 89), Ehsan Hajy Safi – Emad Ridha, Mehdi Salehi (Jalalaldin Alimohammadi 82). Tr: Jorvan Viera

International, Aleppo
9-04-2008, 19:00, 20 000, Kim Dong Jin KOR

Al Ittihad Aleppo 0

Mahmoud Karkar – Omar Hemidi, Majd Homsi•81, Salah Chahrour (Yousef Chikhal Eshra 71), Bakri Tarrab – Jesus Gomez (Ayman Salal 81), Jonathan Perez, Mahmoud Al Amena (Obada Al Said 71), Ayman Habbal – Abdulfatah Al Agha, Otobong Otudor. Tr: Tita

Kuruvchi 2
Hasanov 50, Kapadze 65

Murotjon Zukhurov – Bakhtiyor Ashurmatov, Gochguly Gochguliyev, Alexander Khvostunov – Jasur Hasanov (Vyacheslav Ponomarev 69), Victor Karpenko, Azizbek Haydarov (Sergey Lushchan 87), Aleksey Nikolaev, Timur Kapadze – Ulugbek Bakaev (Anvarjon Soliev 78), Server Djeparov. Tr: Mirdjalol Kasimov

Azadi, Tehran
9-04-2008, 16:00, 6000, Sun Baojie CHN

Sepahan 2
Salehi 59, Aghily 71

Abbas Mohammadi (Masoud Hamami 84) - Hadi Aghily, Mohsen Bengar - Jalal Akbari, Farshad Bahadorani, Hossein Kazemi, Abdul Wahab Abulhail (Ebrahim Lovinian 94+), Hadi Jafari, Ehsan Hajy Safi - Mahmoud Karimi (Hossein Papi 83), Mehdi Seyed Salehi. Tr: Jorvan Viera

Al Ittihad Jeddah 1
Al Meshal 29

Tisir Al Antaif – Redha Tukar, Hamad Al Montashari, Osama Al Muwalad (Ahmed Dokhi 86) – Abdulrahman Al Qahtani (Talal Al Meshal 70), Tcheco, Abdullah Hidar, Mohammed Noor, Aqeal Al Qarni (Sultan Al Numare 80) - Alhassane Keita. Tr: Estevam Soares

MHSK, Tashkent
23-04-2008, 16:30, 10 000, Abdul Bashir SIN

Kuruvchi 1
Kapadze 30

Murotjon Zukhurov – Bakhtiyor Ashurmatov, Gochguly Gochguliyev, Alexander Khvostunov – Jasur Hasanov (Rashidjon Gofurov 65), Victor Karpenko (Anvarjon Soliev 85), Azizbek Haydarov, Aleksey Nikolaev, Timur Kapadze – Ulugbek Bakaev (Shavkat Salomov 70), Server Djeparov. Tr: Mirdjalol Kasimov

Al Ittihad Aleppo 0

Mahmoud Karkar – Omar Hemidi, Wael Ayan, Yousef Chikhal Eshra, Bakri Tarrab – Jesus Gomez (Ayman Salal 79), Jonathan Perez, Mahmoud Al Amena (Otobong Otudor 65), Yahia Al Rached (Mohammad Al Damen 90), Obada Al Said – Abdulfatah Al Agha. Tr: Tita

Prince Abdullah, Jeddah
23-04-2008, 20:45, 4000, Alfadhli KUW

Al Ittihad Jeddah 0

Mabrouk Zaid – Ahmed Dokhi, Mohammed Abdullah (Obaid Al Shamrani 67), Adnan Falatah, Hamad Al Montashari – Manaf Aboshgair, Tcheco, Saud Khariri, Mohammed Noor – Alhassane Keita (Mohammed Labieb 46), Magno Alves (Mohammed Ameen 39).

Sepahan 1
Emad Ridha 79

Masoud Hamami - Hamid Azizzadeh, Mohsen Bengar - Jalal Akbari, Farshad Bahadorani (Ebrahim Lovinian 88), Hossein Kazemi, Abdul Wahab Abulhail (Mohsen Hamidi 77), Hadi Jafari, Ehsan Hajy Safi – Emad Ridha (Hojatolah Mahmoud 85), Mehdi Salehi. Tr: Jorvan Viera

International, Aleppo
7-05-2008, 19:00, 4000, Al Ghafary JOR

Al Ittihad Aleppo 2
Perez 61, Gomez 64

Yasser Jarkas – Omar Hemidi, Salah Chahrour, Yousef Chikhal Eshra, Bakri Tarrab (Hossen Klawi 76) – Ammar Rihawi, Jesus Gomez (Ayman Salal 90), Jonathan Perez, Mahmoud Al Amena (Obada Al Said 78), Yahia Al Rached – Otobong Otudor. Tr: Tita

Sepahan 1
Aghily 46

Masoud Hamami - Hamid Azizzadeh, Hadi Aghily, Mohsen Bengar (Ebrahim Lovinian 26) - Jalal Akbari, Hossein Kazemi, Abdul Wahab Abulhail (Hojatolah Mahmoud 70), Hossein Papi, Ehsan Hajy Safi - Emad Ridha, Mehdi Salehi (Mohsen Hamidi 78). Tr: Jorvan Viera

MHSK, Tashkent
7-05-2008, 17:00, 13 000, Mohd Salleh MAS

Kuruvchi 2
Soliev 10, Djeparov 38

Murotjon Zukhurov – Bakhtiyor Ashurmatov, Gochguly Gochguliyev, Alexander Khvostunov – Jasur Hasanov (Vyacheslav Ponomarev 79), Victor Karpenko (Rashidjon Gofurov 72), Azizbek Haydarov, Aleksey Nikolaev, Timur Kapadze – Anvarjon Soliev (Anvar Rajabov 60), Server Djeparov. Tr: Mirdjalol Kasimov

Al Ittihad Jeddah 0

Tisir Al Antaif – Ahmed Dokhi (Mohammed Abdullah 78), Saleh Al Saqri, Hamad Al Montashari, Osama Al Muwalad – Mohammed Ameen (Abdulaziz Al Sibyani 46), Manaf Aboshgair, Tcheco, Saud Khariri (Ibrahim Sowed 46), Mohammed Noor - Alhassane Keita. Tr: Estevam Soares

Azadi, Tehran
21-05-2008, 17:30, 150, Al Hilali OMA

Sepahan 2
Alimohammadi 2

Mohammad Savari - Hamid Azizzadeh, Seyed Talabeh (Abolhassan Jafari 79), Jaba Mujiri - Farshad Bahadorani, Mohsen Hamidi (Amir Radi 87), Hojatolah Mahmoud (Shahryar Shirvand 80), Saeid Bayat, Ebrahim Lovinian - Hamed Rasouli, Jalalaldin Alimohammadi. Tr: Jorvan Viera

Kuruvchi 1
Gochguliyev 71

Murotjon Zukhurov – Gochguly Gochguliyev (Shavkat Raimkulov 75), Hayrulla Karimov, Alexander Khvostunov, Sakhob Jurayev – Sergey Lushchan (Azizbek Haydarov 46), Jasur Hasanov (Rashidjon Gofurov 59), Victor Karpenko, Timur Kapadze – Anvarjon Soliev, Server Djeparov. Tr: Mirdjalol Kasimov

Prince Abdullah, Jeddah
21-05-2008, 20:55, 600, Shamsuzzaman BAN

Al Ittihad Jeddah 3
Al Numare 2 30 50, Hazazi 42

Mabrouk Zaid – Mohammed Abdullah, Obaid Al Shamrani, Talal Assiri, Saleh Al Saqri – Tcheco (Ali Al Falati 82), Abdullah Hidar, Aqeal Al Qarni, Sultan Al Numare•62 – Naif Hazazi (Abdulaziz Al Sibyani 76), Talal Al Meshal (Hamad Al Montashari 73). Tr: Gabriel Calderon

Al Ittihad Aleppo 0

Mahmoud Karkar – Omar Hemidi, Wael Ayan, Salah Chahrour (Obada Al Said 68), Yousef Chikhal Eshra, Bakri Tarrab – Jesus Gomez (Ayman Salal 57), Mahmoud Al Amena, Yahia Al Rached (Ayman Habbal 84) – Abdulfatah Al Agha, Otobong Otudor. Tr: Tita

GROUP B

		Pl	W	D	L	F	A	Pts	IRN	IRQ	UAE	KUW
Saipa	IRN	6	3	3	0	7	3	12		1-1	2-0	1-0
Al Quwa Al Jawiya	IRQ	6	2	2	2	5	5	8	0-1		1-2	0-0
Al Wasl	UAE	6	2	1	3	5	7	7	1-1	0-1		1-0
Kuwait SC	KUW	6	1	2	3	4	6	5	1-1	1-2	2-1	

Al Wasl, Dubai
12-03-2008, 19:30, 7500, Al Ghamdi KSA

Al Wasl　　　　　　　　　　**0**

Majed Nasser – Sami Rubaiya (Mohammed Mubarak 82), Waheed Ismail, Ali Mahmoud (Rogerinho 70), Tariq Hassan, Abdulla Essa – Essa Ali, Khaled Darwish, Alexandre Oliveira, Tariq Darwish (Mohamed Salem Al Enazi 62) – Andre Dias. Tr: Ze Mario

Al Quwa Al Jawiya　　　　**1**
　　　　　　　　　Ali Mansour [32]

Wisam Kasid – Hussein Ali (Hader Raheem 93+), Ali Abdul Gabar, Mokhalad Ali – Haitham Kadhum, Haitham Kadhum Jasim, Ahmed Iyad, Azhar Taher, Ibrahim Kamel (Hamoodi Kadhum 68) – Ali Mansour, Yasir Abdul Muhsen (Mothna Khaled 64). Tr: Hamid Salman

---

Enghlab, Karaj
19-03-2008, 14:30, 8000, Iemoto JPN

Saipa　　　　　　　　　　**2**
　　　Issa Traore [45], Karim Ansari Fard [57]

Misagh Memarzadeh – Jalal Hosseini, Majid Ayyoubi, Kazem Bozcheloo – Omid Sharifi Nasab, Ebrahim Sadeghi, Kianoush Rahmati, Milad Zanidpour (Javad Ashtiyani 64), Mageed Gholamnejhad, Issa Traore (Amir Vaziri 71) – Karim Ansari Fard (Hamidreza Zohani 81). Tr: Ali Daei

Al Wasl　　　　　　　　　　**0**

Majed Nasser – Sami Rubaiya, Waheed Ismail, Ali Mahmoud, Abdulla Essa – Essa Ali, Khaled Darwish (Rashed Essa 73), Alexandre Oliveira, Tariq Darwish (Rogerinho 63), Faisal Ahmed – Andre Dias (Mohamed Salem Al Enazi 65). Tr: Ze Mario

---

Enghlab, Karaj
23-04-2008, 16:30, 10 000, Irmatov UZB

Saipa　　　　　　　　　　**1**
　　　　　　　Kianouah Rahmati [63p]

Rahman Ahmadi – Alou Traore, Jalal Hosseini, Majid Ayyoubi, Mohammadali Ashourizad – Omid Sharifi Nasab, Ebrahim Sadeghi, Kianoush Rahmati, Milad Zanidpour (Javad Ashtiyani 74) – Karim Ansari Fard (Roozbeh Shahalidoust 75), Amir Vaziri (Adriano Alves 60). Tr: Ali Daei

Al Quwa Al Jawiya　　　　**1**
　　　　　　　　　Ahmed Iyad [71]

Wisam Kasid – Ali Abdul Gabar, Mokhalad Ali, Jasim Swadi – Haitham Kadhum, Ahmed Iyad, Mothna Khaled, Azhar Taher, Kusay Hashim (Mohammed Hanoun 85), Ibrahim Kamel – Alaea'a Mansour (Akram Hashem 65). Tr: Hamid Salman

---

Enghlab, Karaj
7-05-2008, 16:45, 10 000, Sun Baojie CHN

Saipa　　　　　　　　　　**1**
　　　　　　　Kianouah Rahmati [24]

Rahman Ahmadi – Alou Traore, Jalal Hosseini, Majid Ayyoubi, Kazem Bozcheloo – Ebrahim Sadeghi, Kianoush Rahmati, Roozbeh Shahalidoust (Habib Houshyar 90), Milad Zanidpour (Javad Ashtiyani 70), Issa Traore – Amir Vaziri (Adriano Alves 64). Tr: Ali Daei

Kuwait SC　　　　　　　　**0**

Khalid Al Fadhli – Yaqoub Al Taher, Fahad Shaheen, Yousef Al Youha (Abdullah Al Sallal 85), Samer Al Martah – Andre Macanga, Walied Ali, Husain Al Shammari (Abdul Rhman Al Awadhi 49), Maurito (Ebrahim Shehab 66) – Ziad Jaziri, Khaled Ajab. Tr: Mohammad Ali

---

Kuwait SC, Kuwait City
12-03-2008, 19:45, 7000, Abdou QAT

Kuwait SC　　　　　　　　**1**
　　　　　　　　　Khaled Ajab [45]

Khalid Al Fadhli – Yaqoub Al Taher●81, Fahad Shaheen, Yousef Al Youha – Andre Macanga, Abdulaziz Al Marshoud (Abdul Rhman Al Awadhi 80), Walied Ali, Jarah Al Ataiqi, Maurito (Ebrahim Shehab 72) – Ziad Jaziri (Samer Al Martah 84), Khaled Ajab. Tr: Radion Gacanin

Saipa　　　　　　　　　　**1**
　　　　　　　　　Milad Zanidpour [66]

Rahman Ahmadi – Jalal Hosseini, Majid Ayyoubi, Kazem Bozcheloo – Omid Sharifi Nasab, Ebrahim Sadeghi, Kianoush Rahmati (Roozbeh Shahalidoust 61), Javad Ashtiyani (Amir Vaziri 74), Mageed Gholamnejhad, Issa Traore - Karim Ansari Fard (Milad Zanidpour 61). Tr: Ali Daei

---

Kuwait SC, Kuwait City
9-04-2008, 19:45, 1000, Mujghef JOR

Al Quwa Al Jawiya　　　　**0**

Ali Hussein – Mokhalad Ali, Hader Raheem (Kusay Hashim 82) – Haitham Kadhum, Haitham Kadhum Jasim (Mothna Khaled 46), Ahmed Iyad, Azhar Taher, Ibrahim Kamel – Ali Mansour, Alaea'a Mansour (Jasim Swadi 58), Yasir Abdul Muhsen. Tr: Hamid Salman

Saipa　　　　　　　　　　**1**
　　　　　　　　　Amir Vaziri [45]

Misagh Memarzadeh – Jalal Hosseini, Kazem Bozcheloo - Omid Nasab, Ebrahim Sadeghi, Javad Ashtiyani (Majid Ayyoubi 58), Milad Zanidpour (Kianoush Rahmati 79), Mageed Gholamnejhad●60 – Karim Fard (Issa Traore 69), Amir Vaziri. Tr: Ali Daei

---

Kuwait SC, Kuwait City
23-04-2008, 20:30, 1500, Al Ghatrifi OMA

Kuwait SC　　　　　　　　**2**
　　　Khaled Ajab [10], Abdul Rhman Al Awadhi [42]

Khalid Al Fadhli – Fahad Shaheen, Samer Al Martah, Fahad Al Reshidi – Abdulaziz Al Marshoud (Yousef Al Youha 65), Walied Ali, Jarah Al Ataiqi, Husain Al Shammari (Ebrahim Shehab 86), Maurito – Khaled Ajab (Abdulrazaq Al Buti 93+), Abdul Rhman Al Awadhi

Al Wasl　　　　　　　　　　**1**
　　　　　　　　　Essa Ali [6]

Majed Nasser – Yaser Salem, Waheed Ismail, Ali Mahmoud (Mohamed Salem Al Enazi 59), Tariq Hassan, Abdulla Essa (Khaled Darwish 74) – Essa Ali, Rogerinho, Alexandre Oliveira, Tariq Darwish - Andre Dias. Tr: Ze Mario

---

Al Wasl, Dubai
21-05-2008, 20:30, 1500, Shield AUS

Al Wasl　　　　　　　　　　**1**
　　　　　　　　　Andre Dias [92+]

Majed Nasser – Yaser Salem, Waheed Ismail, Tariq Hassan (Khalaf Ismail 71), Radhwan Saleh – Mohammed Jammal (Jassem Mubarak 82), Essa Ali, Rogerinho, Alexandre Oliveira, Tariq Darwish (Mohamed Salem Al Enazi 46) - Andre Dias. Tr: Ze Mario

Saipa　　　　　　　　　　**1**
　　　　　　　　　Issa Traore [21]

Rahman Ahmadi – Alou Traore, Majid Ayyoubi, Kazem Bozcheloo, Mohammadali Ashourizad – Omid Sharifi Nasab, Milad Zanidpour (Hossein Hosseini 56), Meisam Armian, Issa Traore (Roozbeh Shahalidoust 66) - Adriano Alves, Karim Ansari Fard (Amir Vaziri 81). Tr: Ali Daei

---

Kuwait SC, Kuwait City
19-03-2008, 19:45, 4000, Basma SYR

Al Quwa Al Jawiya　　　　**0**

Wisam Kasid – Hussein Ali (Hader Raheem 68), Ali Abdul Gabar, Mokhalad Ali – Haitham Kadhum, Haitham Kadhum Jasim (Hamoodi Kadhum 86), Ahmed Iyad, Azhar Taher, Ibrahim Kamel – Ali Mansour, Yasir Abdul Muhsen (Mothna Khaled 58). Tr: Hamid Salman

Kuwait SC　　　　　　　　**0**

Khalid Al Fadhli – Fahad Shaheen, Yousef Al Youha, Samer Al Martah (Fahad Al Reshidi 82) – Andre Macanga, Abdulaziz Al Marshoud, Walied Ali, Jarah Al Ataiqi, Maurito – Ziad Jaziri, Khaled Ajab (Abdul Rhman Al Awadhi 63). Tr: Radion Gacanin

---

Al Wasl, Dubai
9-04-2008, 19:45, 4622, Nishimura JPN

Al Wasl　　　　　　　　　　**1**
　　　　　　　　　Tariq Hassan [75]

Majed Nasser – Yaser Salem, Sami Rubaiya, Tariq Hassan, Khalaf Ismail, Radhwan Saleh – Essa Ali, Rogerinho (Khaled Darwish 75), Mohammed Mubarak (Andre Dias 63) (Jassem Mubarak 87), Alexandre Oliveira - Mohamed Salem Al Enazi. Tr: Ze Mario

Kuwait SC　　　　　　　　**0**

Khalid Al Fadhli – Yaqoub Al Taher, Yousef Al Youha (Abdul Rhman Al Awadhi 56), Abdulaziz Al Buti, Fahad Al Reshidi – Ebrahim Shehab (Abdulaziz Al Marshoud 70), Andre Macanga, Walied Ali, Jarah Al Ataiqi, Maurito - Ziad Jaziri. Tr: Radion Gacanin

---

Kuwait SC, Kuwait City
7-05-2008, 20:00, 100, Tan Hai CHN

Al Quwa Al Jawiya　　　　**1**

Wisam Kasid – Ali Abdul Gabar, Mokhalad Ali, Hader Raheem, Jasim Swadi – Haitham Kadhum Jasim, Ahmed Iyad, Azhar Taher, Ibrahim Kamel (Akram Hashem 69) – Ali Mansour, Yasir Abdul Muhsen. Tr: Hamid Salman

Al Wasl　　　　　　　　　　**2**
　　　　　　Al Enazi [49], Oliveira [64]

Majed Nasser – Yaser Salem, Waheed Ismail (Khalaf Ismail 88), Ali Mahmoud, Tariq Hassan (Sami Rubaiya 46), Radhwan Saleh – Essa Ali, Khaled Darwish, Alexandre Oliveira, Tariq Darwish – Mohamed Salem Al Enazi (Rashed Essa 72). Tr: Ze Mario

---

Kuwait SC, Kuwait City
21-05-2008, 20:30, 250, Iemoto JPN

Kuwait SC　　　　　　　　**1**
　　　　　　　　　Khaled Ajab [22]

Musab Al Kandari – Abdulaziz Al Ahmad, Samer Al Martah, Abdulrahman Al Bader (Bader Al Motairat 88), Abdulrazaq Al Buti, Fahad Al Reshidi – Ebrahim Shehab (Saud Al Otaibi 76), Abdulaziz Al Marshoud, Nawaf Al Owaisi – Abdullah Al Fadli (Abdullah Al Sallal 85), Khaled Ajab. Tr: Mohammad Ali

Al Quwa Al Jawiya　　　　**2**
　　　Haitham Jasim [17], Yasir Muhsen [48]

Ali Hussein – Ali Abdul Gabar, Mokhalad Ali, Haider Alewi – Haitham Kadhum Jasim, Hamoodi Kadhum, Mothna Khaled, Azhar Taher, Mohammed Hanoun – Ali Mansour, Yasir Abdul Muhsen (Akram Hashem 91). Tr: Hameed Al Obaid

GROUP C

Al Karama		Pl	W	D	L	F	A	Pts	SYR	UAE	QAT	KSA
Al Karama	SYR	6	3	2	1	8	3	11		4-1	1-0	0-0
Al Wahda	UAE	6	2	3	1	6	7	9	1-0		2-2	2-1
Al Sadd	QAT	6	1	3	2	6	8	6	0-2	0-0		2-1
Al Ahli	KSA	6	0	4	2	5	7	4	1-1	0-0	2-2	

Al Sadd Club, Doha
12-03-2008, 18:00, 6000, Irmatov UZB

Al Sadd 2

Marcio Emerson [3], Felipe [26]

Mohamed Saqr – Ibrahim Majed, Abdulla Koni - Wesam Riziq (Mohammed Gholam 69), Mesaad Alhamad, Magid Mohammed (Mohammed Al Yazidi 87), Felipe, Mohamed Rabia – Marcio Emerson, Carlos Tenorio, Ali Afif (Talal Al Bloushi 46). Tr: Hassan Hormatullah

Al Ahli 1

Osvaldo [74]

Yasser Al Mosailem – Leandro Bernardi, Mohammed Eid, Mohammed Massad, Walid Abdrabh, Hussain Abdul Ghani, Jufain Al Bishi (Hamoud Abbas 70) – Motaz Al Mosa (Osvaldo Felix de Souza 65), Turki Al Thagafi (Ahmed Darwish Faraj 85), Saheb Al Abdullha•45 – Malek Maaz. Tr: Nebojsa Vukovic

Al Nahyan, Abu Dhabi
19-03-2008, 20:00, 5500, Williams AUS

Al Wahda 2

Andre Luciano [22], Mohamed Al Shehhi [86]

Nadir Lamyaghri – Yaser Abdalla, Omar Ali, Eisa Ahmed, Basheer Saeed, Hamdan Al Kamali – Tawfeeq Abdul Razak (Abdulla Ali 63), Mohamed Othman (Josiel 74), Andre Luciano – Mohamed Al Shehhi, Ismail Matar (Saleh Al Menhali 80). Tr: Ahmed Abdul Halim

Al Sadd 1

Carlos Tenorio [11], Marcio Emerson [71]

Mohamed Saqr – Ibrahim Majed, Abdulla Koni – Wesam Riziq, Mesaad Alhamad (Mesaad Alhamad 93+) Magid Mohammed (Ali Afif 76), Talal Al Bloushi, Felipe, Mohamed Rabia – Marcio Emerson, Carlos Tenorio. Tr: Hassan Hormatullah

Al Nahyan, Abu Dhabi
23-04-2008, 19:45, 5000, Shield AUS

Al Wahda 2

Josiel 2 [36 86]

Nadir Lamyaghri – Yaser Abdalla, Talal Abdulla, Eisa Ahmed – Tawfeeq Albdul Razak, Mohamed Othman, Abdulla Ali (Abdulraheem Jumaa 67), Andre Luciano, Mahmoud Khamees (Haidar Alo Ali 90) – Josiel, Saleh Al Menhali (Ismail Matar 81). Tr: Ahmed Abdul Halim

Al Ahli 1

Waleed Al Gizani [82]

Abdu Al Bsisi – Mohammed Eid, Walid Abdrabh (Motaz Al Mosa 33), Hussain Abdul Ghani, Jufain Al Bishi, Ibrahim Hazzazi – Turki Al Thagafi (Waleed Al Gizani 61), Antonio Caio•83, Saheb Al Abdullha – Malek Maaz, Nasir Al Selimi (Ahmed Darwish Faraj 83). Tr: Yusuf Anbar

Al Nahyan, Abu Dhabi
7-05-2008, 20:00, 6000, Matsumura JPN

Al Wahda 1

Mohamed Al Shehhi [89]

Nadir Lamyaghri – Talal Abdulla, Basheer Saeed, Haidar Alo Ali, Hamdan Al Kamali – Tawfeeq Albdul Razak, Yaser Matar (Andre Luciano 81), Hasan Ameen – Josiel (Mohamed Al Shehhi 45), Ismail Matar, Saeed Salem (Abdulraheem Jumaa 76). Tr: Ahmed Abdul Halim

Al Karama 0

Mosab Balhous – Fabio Santos, Hassan Abbas, Belal Abduldaim, Anas Al Khouja – Jehad Al Hussein, Alaa Alshbli, Aattef Jenniat, Feras Ismail – Mohamad Al Hamwi (Mohanad Al Ibrahim 90), Ziad Chaabo (Edgard De Melo 85). Tr: Mohamed Kwid

Khaled Ibn Al Waleed, Homs
12-03-2008, 17:30, 30 000, Al Hilali OMA

Al Karama 4

Feras Ismael [4], Ziad Chabo 2 [27 49], Al Hamwi [79]

Mosab Balhous – Fabio Santos, Hassan Abbas, Belal Abduldaim, Anas Al Khouja – Jehad Al Hussein (Mohanad Al Ibrahim 88), Alaa Alshbli, Aattef Jenniat (Tamer Hajmohamed 83), Feras Ismail – Mohamad Al Hamwi, Ziad Chaabo (Edgard De Melo 76). Tr: Mohamed Kwid

Al Wahda 1

Mohamed Al Shehhi [84]

Nadir Lamyaghri – Omar Ali, Basheer Saeed, Haidar Alo Ali (Mahmoud Khamees 60), Hamdan Al Kamali – Tawfeeq Albdul Razak, Abdulla Ali (Eisa Ahmed 92+), Andre Luciano – Mohamed Al Shehhi, Josiel (Saleh Al Menhali 77), Ismail Matar. Tr: Ahmed Abdul Halim

Prince Abdullah, Jeddah
9-04-2008, 20:40, 8000, Al Fadhli KUW

Al Ahli 0

Yasser Al Mosailem – Leandro Bernardi•86, Mohammed Massad (Turki Al Thagafi 46), Hussain Abdul Ghani, Jufain Al Bishi, Ibrahim Hazzazi – Motaz Al Mosa (Osvaldo Felix de Souza 63), Saheb Al Abdullha, Hamoud Abbas (Ahmed Darwish Faraj 76) – Malek Maaz. Tr: Yusuf Anbar

Al Wahda 0

Nadir Lamyaghri – Yaser Abdalla, Omar Ali, Eisa Ahmed, Haidar Alo Ali, Hamdan Al Kamali – Tawfeeq Albdul Razak (Abdulraheem Jumaa 62), Abdulla Ali, Andre Luciano – Mohamed Al Shehhi, Josiel (Ismail Matar 58). Tr: Ahmed Abdul Halim

Khaled Ibn Al Waleed, Homs
23-04-2008, 20:30, 25 000, Breeze AUS

Al Karama 1

Aattef Jenniat [78]

Mosab Balhous – Fabio Santos, Hassan Abbas, Belal Abduldaim, Anas Al Khouja – Jehad Al Hussein, Alaa Alshbli, Aattef Jenniat (Tamer Hajmohamed 84), Feras Ismail – Mohamad Al Hamwi (Edgard De Melo 87), Ziad Chaabo (Mohanad Al Ibrahim 91+). Tr: Mohamed Kwid

Al Sadd 1

Mohamed Saqr – Ibrahim Majed (Ali Afif 80), Ali Naser (Magid Mohammed 68), Abdulla Koni – Wesam Riziq, Mesaad Alhamad, Talal Al Bloushi, Felipe, Mohamed Rabia – Marcio Emerson•65, Carlos Tenorio. Tr: Hassan Hormatullah

Al Sadd Club, Doha
21-05-2008, 20:00, 800, Lee Gi Young KOR

Al Saad 0

Mohamed Saqr – Tahir Zakaria, Sultan Al Shahwani, Hamad Al Shamari – Mesaad Alhamad, Magid Mohammed (Bakhit Al Marri 86), Mohammed Gholam, Mohammed Al Yazidi – Carlos Tenorio, Ali Afif (Hasan Al Haydos 74), Yusef Ahmed. Tr: Hassan Hormatullah

Al Wahda 0

Nadir Lamyaghri – Omar Ali, Basheer Saeed – Tawfeeq Albdul Razak, Mohamed Othman, Abdulla Ali, Andre Luciano, Abdulraheem Jumaa, Hasan Ameen – Ismail Matar, Saeed Salem (Saleh Al Menhali 65). Tr: Ahmed Abdul Halim

Prince Abdullah, Jeddah
19-03-2008, 20:35, 15 000, Sun Baojie CHN

Al Ahli 1

Turki Al Thagafi [15]

Yasser Al Mosailem – Leandro Bernardi, Mohammed Eid, Mohammed Massad, Walid Abdrabh, Hussain Abdul Ghani – Motaz Al Mosa (Ahmed Darwish Faraj 76), Turki Al Thagafi, Hamoud Abbas (Taiseer Al Jassam 46) – Malek Maaz, Osvaldo Felix de Souza (Hussain Al Absi 82). Tr: Nebojsa Vukovic

Al Karama 1

Al Hamwi [44]

Mosab Balhous – Fabio Santos, Hassan Abbas, Belal Abduldaim, Anas Al Khouja – Jehad Al Hussein, Alaa Alshbli, Aattef Jenniat (Tamer Hajmohamed 78), Feras Ismail – Mohamad Al Hamwi (Mohanad Al Ibrahim 90), Ziad Chaabo (Edgard De Melo 83). Tr: Mohamed Kwid

Al Sadd Club, Doha
9-04-2008, 18:15, 6000, Abdul Bashir SIN

Al Sadd 0

Mohamed Saqr – Ibrahim Majed – Wesam Riziq (Khalfan Ibrahim 72), Mesaad Alhamad, Magid Mohammed, Talal Al Bloushi, Mohammed Gholam (Ali Afif 80), Felipe, Mohamed Rabia – Marcio Emerson, Carlos Tenorio. Tr: Hassan Hormatullah

Al Karama 4

Al Hamwi [69], Aattef Jenniat [73]

Mosab Balhous – Fabio Santos, Hassan Abbas, Belal Abduldaim, Anas Al Khouja – Jehad Al Hussein, Alaa Alshbli, Aattef Jenniat (Tamer Hajmohamed 87), Feras Ismail – Mohamad Al Hamwi (Edgard De Melo 92+), Ziad Chaabo (Mohanad Al Ibrahim 88). Tr: Mohamed Kwid

Prince Abdullah, Jeddah
7-05-2008, 20:50, 1500, Nishimura JPN

Al Ahli 2

Tahir Zakaria OG [28], Abdul Ghani [42p]

Abdu Al Bsisi – Leandro Bernardi, Hassan Al Yamani (Ibrahim Hazzazi 66), Mohammed Massad•31, Walid Abdrabh, Hussain Abdul Ghani – Motaz Al Mosa, Saheb Al Abdullha, Ahmed Darwish Faraj – Malek Maaz (Abdelellah Hawsawi 85), Waleed Al Gizani (Hussain Al Absi 62). Tr: Yusuf Anbar

Al Sadd 2

Mohamed Gholam [33p], Yusef Ahmed [50]

Mohamed Saqr – Tahir Zakaria, Sultan Al Shahwani, Hamad Al Shamari - Magid Mohammed, Mohammed Gholam, Khalid Al Hajari (Ali Naser 46), Mohammed Al Yazidi – Hasan Al Haydos, Ali Afif, Yusef Ahmed (Meshaal Ali 80). Tr: Hassan Hormatullah

Khaled Ibn Al Waleed, Homs
21-05-2008, 20:00, 15000, Irmatov UZB

Al Karama 0

Mosab Balhous – Fabio Santos, Hassan Abbas, Belal Abduldaim, Anas Al Khouja, Tamer Hajmohamed, Safir Atasi (Fahed Oudah 67), Jehad Al Hussein, Aattef Jenniat – Mohamad Al Hamwi, Edgard De Melo (Mohanad Al Ibrahim 83). Tr: Mohamed Kwid

Al Ahli 0

Yasser Al Mosailem – Leandro Bernardi, Mohammed Eid, Mansour Al Harbi, Ali Al Abdali, Hussain Abdul Ghani, Jufain Al Bishi – Antonio Caio, Saheb Al Abdullha, Ahmed Darwish Faraj (Alaa Al Rishani 84) – Abdelellah Hawsawi (Hussain Al Absi 67). Tr: Yusuf Anbar

GROUP D

		Pl	W	D	L	F	A	Pts	KUW	UZB	IRQ	QAT
Al Qadisiya	KUW	6	3	2	1	8	7	11		2-2	1-1	1-0
Pakhtakor	UZB	6	3	2	1	13	6	11	0-1		2-0	2-0
Arbil	IRQ	6	2	2	2	8	11	8	4-2	1-5		1-1
Al Gharafa	QAT	6	0	2	4	3	8	2	0-1	2-2	0-1	

MHSK, Tashkent
12-03-2008, 15:00, 12 000, Mohd Salleh MAS

Pakhtakor 0

Ignatiy Nesterov - Asror Alikulov, Ilhomjon Suyunov - Darko Markovic (Darko Markovic 88), Akmal Holmatov (Ildar Magdeev 83), Islom Inomov, Renat Bayramov (Sadriddin Abdullaev 63), Anzur Ismailov, Odil Ahmedov - Alexander Geynrikh, Zaynitdin Tadjyiev. Tr: Ravshan Haydarov

Al Qadisiya 1
Ahmad Ajab 91+

Nawaf Al Khaldi - Ali Al Namash (Dhary Saeed 86), Mohammad Rashed, Hussain Fadhel, Nohayr Al Shamari - Ibrahima Keita, Saleh Al Sheikh, Selim Ben Achour (Ahmad Abdulla 77), Mladen Jovancic - Khalaf Al Salama (Ahmad Ajab 69), Badr Al Mutawa. Tr: Jose Garrido

---

Prince Mohammed, Zerqa
12-03-2008, 15:00, 250, Najm LIB

Arbil 1
Mouslim Mubarak 61

Dydar Hamed - Samal Saeed, Yasser Raad, Rafed Badraddin (Haider Sabbah 59), Salam Shaker - Alai Nairooz (Haydar Qaraman 46), Usama Ali, Wisam Zaki, Ahmed Abid Ali - Mouslim Mubarak, Ahmad Salah. Tr: Akram Salman

Al Gharafa 1
Araujo 13

Abdulaziz Ali - Hamed Shami, Saad Al Shammari, Ahmed Fars, Mohammed Al Haj, Mustafa Abdi - Lawrence Quaye, Otman El Assas, Soud Al Shimmeri (Saghayer Al Shammari 74) - Fahid Al Shammari (Younes Mahmoud 79), Araujo. Tr: Marcos Paqueta

---

Mohammed Al Hamed, Kuwait City
19-03-2008, 18:25, 8000, Al Ghamdi KSA

Al Qadisiya 1
Kalaf Al Salama 82

Nawaf Al Khaldi - Ali Al Namash (Dhary Saeed 53), Mohammad Rashed, Hussain Fadhel, Nohayr Al Shamari - Ibrahima Keita, Saleh Al Sheikh, Mladen Jovancic (Selim Ben Achour 53) - Khalaf Al Salama, Ahmad Ajab, Badr Al Mutawa (Hamad Al Enezi 75). Tr: Jose Garrido

Arbil 1
Ahmad Salah 28p

Dydar Hamed - Samal Saeed, Yasser Raad, Rafed Badraddin (Dara Mohammed 46), Salam Shaker - Alai Nairooz, Usama Ali, Wisam Zaki, Ahmed Abid Ali - Mouslim Mubarak (Ahmad Muhammed 89), Ahmad Salah (Haider Sabbah 60). Tr: Akram Salman

---

Al Gharafa, Al Gharafa
19-03-2008, 18:50, 2000, Lee Gi Young KOR

Al Gharafa 2
Younes Mahmoud 57, Araujo 65

Abdulaziz Ali - Hamed Shami, Saad Al Shammari, Ahmed Fars (Fahid Al Shammari 84), Mohammed Al Haj•87, Mustafa Abdi - Lawrence Quaye, Otman El Assas, Soud Al Shimmeri - Younes Mahmoud, Araujo. Tr: Marcos Paqueta

Pakhtakor 2
Alikulov 68, Farhod Tadjiyev 78

Ignatiy Nesterov - Asror Alikulov, Komoliddin Tadjiev•70, Ilhomjon Suyunov - Darko Markovic, Akmal Holmatov, Vladislav Kiryan (Ildar Magdeev 46), Islom Inomov, Anzur Ismailov (Zaynitdin Tadjiyev 60), Odil Ahmedov - Alexander Geynrikh (Farhod Tadjiyev 76). Tr: Ravshan Haydarov

---

Mohammed Al Hamed, Kuwait City
9-04-2008, 20:40, 5000, Al Ghatrifi OMA

Al Qadisiya 1
Ahmad Ajab 62

Nawaf Al Khaldi - Ali Al Namash (Ali Al Shamali 69), Hussain Fadhel, Mesaed Neda, Nohayr Al Shamari - Ibrahima Keita, Saleh Al Sheikh, Mladen Jovancic - Khalaf Al Salama (Nawaf Al Mutairi 77), Ahmad Ajab (Fayez Bandar 89), Badr Al Mutawa. Tr: Jose Garrido

Al Gharafa 0

Abdulaziz Ali - Hamed Shami, Ahmed Fars, Bilal Mohammed, Mustafa Abdi - Lawrence Quaye, Otman El Assas, Soud Al Shimmeri (Saghayer Al Shammari 88) - Fahid Al Shammari, Younes Mahmoud, Araujo. Tr: Marcos Paqueta

---

MHSK, Tashkent
9-04-2008, 16:30, 10 000, Moradi IRN

Pakhtakor 2
Suyunov 48, Geynrikh 51p

Ignatiy Nesterov - Asror Alikulov, Farhod Tadjiyev (Alexander Geynrikh 46), Ilhomjon Suyunov - Darko Markovic (Nodirbek Kuziboyev 90), Akmal Holmatov, Islom Inomov, Ildar Magdeev, Anzur Ismailov, Odil Ahmedov - Zaynitdin Tadjiyev (Renat Bayramov 68). Tr: Ravshan Haydarov

Arbil 0

Sarhank Muhsen (Dydar Hamed 56) - Samal Saeed, Yasser Raad, Rafed Badraddin, Salam Shaker - Alai Nairooz, Usama Ali (Ahmad Salah 46), Wisam Zaki, Ahmed Abid Ali - Mouslim Mubarak (Haider Sabbah 74), Luay Salah. Tr: Akram Salman

---

Al Gharafa, Al Gharafa
23-04-2008, 18:30, 1000, Takayama JPN

Al Gharafa 0

Abdulaziz Ali - Hamed Shami, Ahmed Fars, Saghayer Al Shammari (Mohammed Shaker 77), Bilal Mohammed - Abdul Aziz Wadi (Adel Jadoua 62), Lawrence Quaye, Otman El Assas, Soud Al Shimmeri - Fahid Al Shammari, Araujo. Tr: Marcos Paqueta

Al Qadisiya 1
Badr Al Mutawa 90

Nawaf Al Khaldi - Ali Al Namash, Hussain Fadhel (Mohammad Rashed 79), Mesaed Neda, Nohayr Al Shamari - Saleh Al Sheikh, Fahed Al Ebrahim (Nawaf Al Mutairi 75), Mladen Jovancic - Khalaf Al Salama (Ahmad Ajab 64), Badr Al Mutawa. Tr: Jose Garrido

---

Prince Mohammed, Zerqa
23-04-2008, 17:00, 180, Al Marzouqi UAE

Arbil 1
Haider Sabbah 18

Dydar Hamed - Samal Saeed (Rafed Badraddin 70), Yasser Raad, Salah Aldeen Siamend - Alai Nairooz, Haider Sabbah, Wisam Zaki, Ahmed Abid Ali - Mouslim Mubarak (Dara Mohammed 81), Usama Ali, Ahmad Salah (Haydar Qaraman 81). Tr: Akram Salman

Pakhtakor 5
OG 37, Kuziboyev 69, Markovic 73, Geynrikh 80, Holmatov 92+

Ignatiy Nesterov - Asror Alikulov, Ilhomjon Suyunov - Darko Markovic (Alexander Geynrikh 76), Akmal Holmatov, Vladislav Kiryan (Komoliddin Tadjiev 68), Islom Inomov, Renat Bayramov (Nodirbek Kuziboyev 58), Anzur Ismailov, Odil Ahmedov - Zaynitdin Tadjiyev. Tr: Ravshan Haydarov

---

Mohammed Al Hamed, Kuwait City
7-05-2008, 19:05, 18 000, Mujghef JOR

Al Qadisiya 2
Ahmad Ajab 21, Kalaf Al Salama 45p

Nawaf Al Khaldi - Ali Al Namash (Mohammad Rashed 83), Hussain Fadhel, Mesaed Neda, Nohayr Al Shamari - Ibrahima Keita, Saleh Al Sheikh, Nawaf Al Mutairi (Ahmad Abdulla 69), Mladen Jovancic - Khalaf Al Salama, Ahmad Ajab (Fayez Bandar 83). Tr: Jose Garrido

Pakhtakor 2
Ahmedov 37, Zaynitdin Tadjiyev 83

Ignatiy Nesterov - Asror Alikulov, Komoliddin Tadjiev (Ildar Magdeev 79), Ilhomjon Suyunov•92+ - Darko Markovic, Sadriddin Abdullaev (Farhod Tadjiyev 64), Vladislav Kiryan (Alexander Geynrikh 46), Islom Inomov, Anzur Ismailov, Odil Ahmedov - Zaynitdin Tadjiyev. Tr: Ravshan Haydarov

---

Al Gharafa, Al Gharafa
7-05-2008, 18:30, 200, Basma SYR

Al Gharafa 0

Mohammed Al Gamdi - Saghayer Al Shammari, Mohammed Al Haj, Abdulla Eyal, Naief Al Enazi, Mustafa Abdi - Abdul Aziz Wadi (Mohammed Shaker 75), Soud Al Shimmeri - Adel Jadoua (Mohammed Harees 69), Fahid Al Shammari, Fahad Al Shamari. Tr: Marcos Paqueta

Arbil 1
Ahmad Salah 28

Sarhank Muhsen - Samal Saeed, Yasser Raad, Salam Shaker - Alai Nairooz (Usama Ali 75), Haider Sabbah (Rafed Badraddin 73), Wisam Zaki (Ahmad Muhammed 91+), Ahmed Abid Ali - Mouslim Mubarak, Luay Salah, Ahmad Salah

---

MHSK, Tashkent
21-05-2008, 17:00, 3000, Tongkan THA

Pakhtakor 2
Zaynitdin Tadjiyev 19, Ahmedov 88p

Temur Juraev - Rahmatullo Berdimurodov, Alexandr Kletskov - Sadriddin Abdullaev, Nodirbek Kuziboyev, Renat Bayramov (Haydar Pirnazarov 76), Anzur Ismailov, Odil Ahmedov, Stanislav Andreev - Sanat Shikhov, Zaynitdin Tadjiyev. Tr: Ravshan Haydarov

Al Gharafa 0

Mohammed Al Gamdi - Saad Al Shammari, Saghayer Al Shammari, Mohammed Al Haj, Naief Al Enazi - Abdul Aziz Wadi (Ali Fatah 62), Mohammed Shaker, Soud Al Shimmeri - Adel Jadoua, Fahid Al Shammari, Fahad Al Shamari

---

Prince Mohammed, Zerqa
21-06-2008, 17:00, 120, Mombeni IRN

Arbil 4
Luay Salah 3 52 70 79, Ahmad Salah 89

Sarhank Muhsen - Yasser Raad, Rafed Badraddin (Salah Aldeen Siamend 68), Salam Shaker - Alai Nairooz (Usama Ali 85), Haider Sabbah (Sherzad Mohammed 93+), Wisam Zaki, Ahmed Abid Ali - Mouslim Mubarak, Luay Salah, Ahmad Salah

Al Qadisiya 2
Sadoun Hameed 23, Ali Al Kandari 34

Ali Al Eissa - Ali Al Namash, Ali Al Shamali, Sadoun Hameed, Nohayr Al Shamari - Ibrahim Keita, Fahed Al Ebrahim, Ahmad Abdulla (Tareq Al Khulaifi 75), Nawaf Al Mutairi (Dhary Saeed 71), Mladen Jovancic•54 - Ali Al Kandari. Tr: Jose Garrido

GROUP E

		Pl	W	D	L	F	A	Pts	AUS	CHN	KOR	VIE
Adelaide United	AUS	6	4	2	0	9	2	**14**		0-0	1-0	4-1
Changchun Yatai	CHN	6	3	3	0	10	3	**12**	0-0		1-0	2-1
Pohang Steelers	KOR	6	1	2	3	6	7	**5**	0-2	2-2		0-0
Binh Duong	VIE	6	0	1	5	4	17	**1**	1-2	0-5	1-4	

City Stadium, Changchun
12-03-2008, 15:30, 10 000, Al Badwawi UAE

Changchun Yatai — **2**

Du Zhenyu [4], Cui Wei [72]

Zong Lei – Wang Wanpeng, Samuel Caballero, Cui Wei – Chinwuzo Melkam, Wang Dong (Cao Tianbao 89), Jiang Pengxiang (Lu Jianjun 59), Zhang Xiaofei, Yan Feng – Du Zhenyu (Huang Jie 70), Zadi Guillaume Dah. Tr: Gao Hongbo

Binh Duong — **1**

Nguyen Ahn Duc [53]

Nguyen The Anh – Pham Minh Duc, Pham Dinh Phuoc, Nguyen Hoang Nam (Nguyen Hoang Voung 80), Huynh Quang Thanh, Vu Nhu Thanh – Nguyen Van Linh (Tran Truong Giang 49), Phung Cong Minh (Luong Trung Tuan 90) – Lancelot Kubheka, Nguyen Anh Duc, Robson. Tr: Le Thuy Hai

---

Steelyard, Pohang
12-03-2008, 19:00, 8436, Torky IRN

Pohang Steelers — **0**

Shin Hwa Yong – Kim Kwangsuk (Hwang Jinsung 62), Lee Chang Won, Cho Sung Hwan – Choi Hyojin, Kim Jaesung (Fabiano 32), Hwang Ji Soo, Kwon Jip (Kim Gi Dong 46), Park Won Jae●83 – Denilson, Namkung Do. Tr: Sergio Farias

Adelaide United — **2**

Cornthwaite [4], Djite [60]

Eugen Galekovic – Richie Alagich (Milan Susak 58), Angelo Costanzo, Cassio Oliveira, Robert Cornthwaite – Lucas Pantelis, Travis Dodd, Gyawe Salley●45, Jason Spagnuolo (Nathan Burns 63), Diego Walsh – Bruce Djite (Dezmon Giraldi 90). Tr: Aurelio Vidmar

---

Binh Duong Stadium, Binh Duong
19-03-2008, 18:00, 12 000, Mujghef JOR

Binh Duong — **1**

Lima [10p]

Tran Minh Quang – Pham Minh Duc (Tran Truong Giang 74), Pham Dinh Phuoc, Nguyen Hoang Nam (Nguyen Hoang Voung 59), Huynh Quang Thanh, Vu Nhu Thanh – Nguyen Van Linh (Giang Thanh Thong 73), Phung Cong Minh – Lancelot Kubheka, Nguyen Anh Duc, Robson. Tr: Le Thuy Hai

Pohang Steelers — **4**

Denilson 2 [49p 57p], Kim Jaesung [55], Choi Hyojin [63]

Shin Hwa Yong – Kim Kwangsuk, Lee Chang Won, Cho Sung Hwan – Choi Hyojin, Kim Gi Dong (Shin Hyungmin 67), Kim Jaesung, Hwang Jinsung (Fabiano 83), Hwang Ji Soo – Denilson, Namkung Do (Clodoaldo 88). Tr: Sergio Farias

---

Hindmarsh, Adelaide
19-03-2008, 19:30, 10 500, Takayama JPN

Adelaide United — **0**

Eugen Galekovic – Richie Alagich (Dezmon Giraldi 82), Angelo Costanzo, Cassio Oliveira, Robert Cornthwaite – Lucas Pantelis, Travis Dodd, Jason Spagnuolo (Shaun Ontong 75), Diego Walsh – Nathan Burns, Bruce Djite. Tr: Aurelio Vidmar

Changchun Yatai — **0**

An Qi – Wang Wanpeng, Samuel Caballero, Cui Wei, Lu Jianjun – Chinwuzo Melkam, Huang Jie (Tang Jing 86), Zhang Xiaofei, Yan Feng – Zadi Guillaume Dah, Cao Tianbao (Jiang Pengxiang 59) – Yang Haibo 70). Tr: Gao Hongbo

---

Binh Duong Stadium, Binh Duong
9-04-2008, 18:00, 15 000, Al Enezi KUW

Binh Duong — **1**

Kubheka [85]

Nguyen The Anh (Tran Minh Quang 14) – Pham Minh Duc, Pham Dinh Phuoc, Nguyen Hoang Nam (Nguyen Vu Phong 52), Huynh Quang Thanh, Vu Nhu Thanh – Nguyen Van Linh, Phung Cong Minh (Tran Truong Giang 84) – Lancelot Kubheka, Nguyen Anh Duc, Robson●88. Tr: Le Thuy Hai

Adelaide United — **2**

Walsh [10], Alagich [78]

Eugen Galekovic – Richie Alagich, Angelo Costanzo, Cassio Oliveira, Sasa Ognenovski – Lucas Pantelis (Shaun Ontong 90), Travis Dodd, Gyawe Salley, Jason Spagnuolo (Dezmon Giraldi 78), Diego Walsh – Nathan Burns. Tr: Aurelio Vidmar

---

City Stadium, Changchun
9-04-2008, 15:30, 18 000, Abdou QAT

Changchun Yatai — **1**

Zadi Dah [86]

Zong Lei – Tang Jing, Samuel Caballero, Cui Wei, Lu Jianjun (Wang Bo 80) – Chinwuzo Melkam, Wang Dong, Yang Haibo (Huang Jie 71), Zhang Xiaofei – Du Zhenyu, Zadi Guillaume Dah. Tr: Gao Hongbo

Pohang Steelers — **0**

Shin Hwa Yong – Kim Kwangsuk, Cho Sung Hwan, Hwang Jae Won, Shin Hyungmin – Choi Hyojin, Kim Gi Dong (Fabiano 88), Hwang Ji Soo (Kim Jaesung 44), Park Won Jae – Denilson, Clodoaldo (Lee Kwang Jae 79). Tr: Sergio Farias

---

Hindmarsh, Adelaide
23-04-2008, 19:30, 13 802, Al Hilali OMA

Adelaide United — **4**

Pantelis [56], Dodd 2 [58 61], Walsh [75]

Eugen Galekovic – Richie Alagich, Angelo Costanzo, Cassio Oliveira, Sasa Ognenovski – Lucas Pantelis (Dezmon Giraldi 80), Kristian Sarkies (Paul Agostino 65), Travis Dodd, Gyawe Salley (Fabian Barbiero 89), Diego Walsh – Nathan Burns. Tr: Aurelio Vidmar

Binh Duong — **1**

Pham Minh Duc [64]

Dang Dinh Duc – Pham Minh Duc, Pham Dinh Phuoc (Nguyen Hoang Voung 79), Nguyen Hoang Nam (Troung Van Hai 60), Huynh Quang Thanh, Vu Nhu Thanh – Nguyen Vu Phong, Tran Truong Giang, Nguyen Van Linh – Lancelot Kubheka, Nguyen Anh Duc. Tr: Le Thuy Hai

---

Steelyard, Pohang
23-04-2008, 19:00, 5468, Tongkhan THA

Pohang Steelers — **1**

Hwang Jae Won [63], Hwang Jinsung [92+]

Shin Hwa Yong – Kim Kwangsuk, Cho Sung Hwan, Hwang Jae Won – Choi Hyojin (Lee Kwang Jae 46), Kim Gi Dong (Shin Hyungmin 61), Hwang Jinsung, Hwang Ji Soo, Park Won Jae – Denilson, Namkung Do (Fabiano 72). Tr: Sergio Farias

Changchun Yatai — **2**

Wang Dong [35], Du Zhenyu [69]

Zong Lei – Tang Jing, Samuel Caballero, Lu Jianjun (Cui Wei 60), Wang Bo, Chen Lei – Wang Dong, Huang Jie (Du Zhenyu 46), Zhang Xiaofei, Yan Feng – Zadi Guillaume Dah (Liu Yulong 83). Tr: Gao Hongbo

---

Binh Duong Stadium, Binh Duong
7-05-2008, 17:00, 4000, Al Ghamdi KSA

Binh Duong — **0**

Nguyen The Anh – Nguyen Hoang Voung, Pham Minh Duc, Troung Van Hai, Vu Nhu Thanh – Nguyen Vu Phong (Bui Van Dong 70), Giang Thanh Thong, Nguyen Van Linh (Lancelot Kubheka 56), Phung Cong Minh – Nguyen Anh Duc (Tran Truong Giang 56), Robson. Tr: Le Thuy Hai

Changchun Yatai — **5**

Wang Bo [3], Zadi Dah [13], Chen Lei [37], Yan Feng [79], Caballero [90p]

Zong Lei – Samuel Caballero, Cui Wei, Wang Bo, Chen Lei – Chinwuzo Melkam, Wang Dong (Lu Jianjun 75), Zhang Xiaofei, Yan Feng – Du Zhenyu (Huang Jie 41), Zadi Guillaume Dah (Cao Tianbao 58). Tr: Gao Hongbo

---

Hindmarsh, Adelaide
7-05-2008, 19:30, 11 805, Irmatov UZB

Adelaide United — **1**

Walsh [53]

Eugen Galekovic – Richie Alagich, Robert Cornthwaite, Sasa Ognenovski – Lucas Pantelis, Kristian Sarkies (Dezmon Giraldi 84), Travis Dodd, Gyawe Salley, Diego Walsh, Fabian Barbiero (Jason Spagnuolo 92+) – Nathan Burns. Tr: Aurelio Vidmar

Pohang Steelers — **0**

Shin Hwa Yong – Kim Kwangsuk, Lee Chang Won, Jang Hyunkyu, Shin Hyungmin – Kim Jaesung, Choi Jongbum (Cho Han Bum 33), Hwang Ji Soo, Kwon Jip, Song Changho – Lee Kwang Jae. Tr: Sergio Farias

---

City Stadium, Changchun
22-05-2008, 15:30, 20 000, Mohd Salleh MAS

Changchun Yatai — **0**

Zong Lei – Samuel Caballero, Wang Bo, Chen Lei – Chinwuzo Melkam, Wang Dong, Zhang Xiaofei, Yan Feng – Du Zhenyu (Tang Jing 75), Zadi Guillaume Dah, Cao Tianbao (Huang Jie 55) (Cui Wei 83). Tr: Gao Hongbo

Adelaide United — **0**

Eugen Galekovic – Richie Alagich, Milan Susak, Angelo Costanzo, Sasa Ognenovski – Lucas Pantelis, Kristian Sarkies (Bruce Djite 57), Travis Dodd, Gyawe Salley, Fabian Barbiero (Robert Cornthwaite 91+) – Nathan Burns (Jason Spagnuolo 82). Tr: Aurelio Vidmar

---

Steelyard, Pohang
21-05-2008, 19:00, 4571, Recho SYR

Pohang Steelers — **0**

Shin Hwa Yong – Lee Chang Won, Jang Hyunkyu, Kim Sooyoun, Cho Han Bum – Choi Jongbum (Fabiano 46), Shin Kwang Hoon, Kwon Jip, Song Changho – Lee Kwang Jae (Lee Sung Jae 58), Ryu Changhyun. Tr: Sergio Farias

Binh Duong — **0**

Nguyen The Anh – Nguyen Hoang Voung, Nguyen Hoang Nam, Troung Van Hai, Huynh Quang Thanh, Vu Nhu Thanh – Tran Truong Giang, Nguyen Van Linh, Phung Cong Minh – Lancelot Kubheka, Robson. Tr: Le Thuy Hai

GROUP F

		Pl	W	D	L	F	A	Pts	JPN	CHN	THA	VIE
Kashima Antlers	JPN	6	5	0	1	28	3	15		1-0	8-1	6-0
Beijing Guoan	CHN	6	4	0	2	14	9	12	1-0		4-2	3-0
Krung Thai Bank	THA	6	2	1	3	20	27	7	1-9	5-3		9-1
Nam Dinh	VIE	6	0	1	5	4	27	1	0-4	1-3	2-2	

Chula, Bangkok
12-03-2008, 15:30, 2000, Basma SYR
Krung Thai Bank 1
Kassim Kone 64
Klisana Klunklin - Amnart Kaewkhew, Supachai Komsilp, Kraikiat Beadtaku, Suphachai Phupha (Pradit Sawangsri 81) - Anon Boonsuko, Phichitphong Choeichiu, Tanat Wongsupphalak (Yuttana Chaikaew 65), Peeraphong Pichitchotirat - Nantawat Thaensopa (Anawin Jujeen 53), Kassim Kone. Tr: Attapol Pussapakhom
Kashima Antlers 9
Tashiro 2 15 50, Iwamasa 21, Nozawa 2 34 92+, Marquinhos 3 47 69 71, Sasaki 73
Hitoshi Sogahata - Atsuto Uchida (Kenta Kasai 76), Daiki Iwamasa, Go Oiwa, Toru Araiba - Mitsuo Ogasawara, Takuya Nozawa, Masashi Motoyama, Takeshi Aoki - Yuzo Tashiro (Ryuta Sasaki 72), Araujo (Danilo 78). Tr: Oswaldo

Feng Tai, Beijing
19-03-2008, 19:00, 14 000, Al Enezi KUW
Beijing Guoan 4
Du Wenhui 2 40 74, Martinez 2 52 75
Yang Zhi - Lang Zheng, Zhou Ting (Wang Ke 80), Zhang Yonghai - Wang Changqing, Tao Wei, Stojan Ignatov (Sui Dongliang 67) - Du Wenhui, Yan Xiangchuang, Huang Bowen, Walter Martinez. Tr: Lee Jan Soo
Krung Thai Bank 2
Thaensopa 59, Pichitchotirat 65
Klisana Klunklin - Amnart Kaewkhew, Supachai Komsilp, Kraikiat Beadtaku, Pradit Sawangsri (Suphachai Phupha 78) - Anon Boonsuko, Phichitphong Choeichiu, Tanat Wongsupphalak, Peeraphong Pichitchotirat (Anawin Jujeen 86) - Nantawat Thaensopa (Sarun Promkeaw 84), Kassim Kone. Tr: Attapol Pussapakhom

Feng Tai, Beijing
23-04-2008, 20:00, 16 000, Mohd Salleh MAS
Beijing Guoan 1
Tiago 10
Yang Zhi - Zhang Shuai, Yang Pu (Wang Changqing 82), Xu Yunlong, Zhang Yonghai (Guo Hui 29) - Sui Dongliang, Tao Wei - Tiago (Yang Hao 76), Yan Xiangchuang, Huang Bowen, Walter Martinez. Tr: Lee Jan Soo
Kashima Antlers 0
Hitoshi Sogahata - Daiki Iwamasa, Go Oiwa, Toru Araiba (Naoya Ishigami 46), Masahiko Inoha - Mitsuo Ogasawara, Takuya Nozawa (Shinzoh Kohrogi 72), Masashi Motoyama (Chikashi Masuda 56), Danilo, Takeshi Aoki - Yuzo Tashiro. Tr: Oswaldo

Feng Tai, Beijing
7-05-2008, 20:00, 9000, Auda Lazm IRQ
Beijing Guoan 3
Guo Hui 15p, Wang Changqing 32, Yang Hao 78
Yang Zhi - Zhang Shuai (Xu Yunlong 46), Lu Jiang, Yu Yang - Wang Changqing, Wang Dong, Stojan Ignatov - Yan Xiangchuang (Huang Bowen 46), Yang Hao, Yang Yun (Wang Ke 66•89), Guo Hui. Tr: Lee Jan Soo
Nam Dinh 0
Bui Quang Huy - Tran Thanh Tung, Le Van Duyet, Lai Viet Huy (Nguyen Van Bien 43), Khuong Quoc Tuan (Le Ngoc Lung 88), Nguyen Quang The - Hoang Nhat Nam, Nguyen Dinh Hung (Pham Xuan Phu 76), Tran Duc Duong, Hoang Danh Ngoc - Nguyen Thanh Luan. Tr: Nguyen Ngoc Hao

My Dinh, Hanoi
12-03-2008, 17:00, 600, Kim Dong Jin KOR
Nam Dinh 1
Le Van Duyet 16
Bui Quang Huy - Tran Thanh Tung, Le Ngoc Lung (Nguyen Van Bien 86), Le Van Duyet, Nguyen Quang The, Moussa Kone - Ejike Onyeji•79, Pham Xuan Phu, Tran Duc Duong (Mai Van Hieu 79), Hoang Danh Ngoc - Obinna Ajoku (Hoang Ngoc Linh 46). Tr: Nguyen Ngoc Hao
Beijing Guoan 3
Yan Xiangchuang 2 57 92+, Du Wenhui 60
Yang Zhi - Zhang Shuai, Zhou Ting, Zhang Yonghai - Wang Changqing (Sui Dongliang 52), Tao Wei, Stojan Ignatov (Lang Zheng 83) - Tiago (Du Wenhui 39), Yan Xiangchuang, Huang Bowen, Walter Martinez. Tr: Lee Jan Soo

Chula, Bangkok
9-04-2008, 16:00, 500, Mombini IRN
Krung Thai Bank 9
Kassim Kone 4 4 44 91+ 92+, Thaensopa 3 8 46 59, Choeichiu 64, Wongsupphalak 70
Klisana Klunklin - Amnart Kaewkhew, Tada Keelalay, Supachai Komsilp, Suphachai Phupha - Anon Boonsuko, Phichitphong Choeichiu (Kumron Chinsri 68), Tanat Wongsupphalak (Mathee Pungpo 78), Peeraphong Pichitchotirat - Nantawat Thaensopa (Mongkol Tossakai 65), Kassim Kone. Tr: Attapol Pussapakhom
Nam Dinh 1
Tran Duc Duong 65
Tran Thanh Trung (Bui Quang Huy 69) - Le Ngoc Lung, Le Van Duyet, Khuong Quoc Tuan, Nguyen Quang The, Moussa Kone (Tran Thanh Tung 46) - Mai Van Hieu, Pham Xuan Phu, Tran Duc Duong - Hoang Ngoc Linh, Nguyen Thanh Luan (Nguyen Van Bien 46). Tr: Nguyen Ngoc Hao

My Dinh, Hanoi
23-04-2008, 17:00, 2000, Balideh QAT
Nam Dinh 2
Hoang Ngoc Linh 2 2 47
Bui Quang Huy - Tran Thanh Tung, Nguyen Van Bien, Lai Viet Huy, Khuong Quoc Tuan (Tran Manh Dung 57), Nguyen Quang The - Hoang Nhat Nam, Pham Xuan Phu, Tran Duc Duong, Hoang Danh Ngoc (Nguyen Viet Dung 92+) - Hoang Ngoc Linh. Tr: Nguyen Ngoc Hao
Krung Thai Bank 2
Thaensopa 20, Choeichiu 93+
Klisana Klunklin - Amnart Kaewkhew, Tada Keelalay, Supachai Komsilp, Pradit Sawangsri - Phichitphong Choeichiu, Tanat Wongsupphalak, Kumron Chinsri (Rewat Meerian 82) - Nantawat Thaensopa, Kassim Kone (Mathee Pungpo 71), Mongkol Tossakai (Wannapol Pumpakom 71). Tr: Attapol Pussapakhom

Rajamangala, Bangkok
21-05-2008, 17:00, 400, Al Marzouqi UAE
Krung Thai Bank 5
Thaensopa 4 12 45 49 69, Pichitchotirat 29
Klisana Klunklin (Sarawut Khambua 62) - Amnart Kaewkhew, Tada Keelalay (Rungroch Sawangsri 59), Supachai Komsilp, Pradit Sawangsri - Anon Boonsuko, Phichitphong Choeichiu, Tanat Wongsupphalak, Peeraphong Pichitchotirat - Nantawat Thaensopa, Kassim Kone (Yuttana Chaikaew 69). Tr: Attapol Pussapakhom
Beijing Guoan 3
Tiago 3 68 71 78
Yang Zhi - Zhang Shuai, Zhou Ting, Yang Pu (Tao Wei 46), Xu Yunlong - Sui Dongliang - Tiago, Yan Xiangchuang (Lu Jiang 73), Huang Bowen, Walter Martinez, Guo Hui (Yang Hao 46). Tr: Lee Jan Soo

Kashima, Ibaraki
19-03-2008, 19:00, 7087, Mansour LIB
Kashima Antlers 6
Motoyama 2 26 49, Marquinhos 2 59 68, Tashiro 74, Danilo 92+
Hitoshi Sogahata - Atsuto Uchida, Daiki Iwamasa, Go Oiwa, Toru Araiba - Mitsuo Ogasawara, Takuya Nozawa, Masashi Motoyama (Danilo 81), Takeshi Aoki - Yuzo Tashiro (Shinzoh Kohrogi 75), Araujo (Ryuta Sasaki 75). Tr: Oswaldo
Nam Dinh 0
Bui Quang Huy - Tran Thanh Tung, Tran Van Toan, Nguyen Van Bien (Le Van Duyet 79), Khuong Quoc Tuan, Nguyen Quang The, Moussa Kone - Nguyen Manh Tu (Pham Xuan Phu 53), Tran Duc Duong, Hoang Danh Ngoc - Hoang Ngoc Linh (Obinna Ajoku 63). Tr: Nguyen Ngoc Hao

Kashima, Ibaraki
9-04-2008, 19:00, 6487, Torky IRN
Kashima Antlers 1
Danilo 53
Hitoshi Sogahata - Atsuto Uchida (Chikashi Masuda 77), Daiki Iwamasa, Go Oiwa, Toru Araiba - Mitsuo Ogasawara, Masashi Motoyama, Danilo (Shinzoh Kohrogi 81), Takeshi Aoki - Yuzo Tashiro (Ryuta Sasaki 84), Araujo. Tr: Oswaldo
Beijing Guoan 0
Yang Zhi - Zhang Shuai, Zhou Ting•32, Xu Yunlong, Zhang Yonghai - Sui Dongliang, Tao Wei (Yan Xiangchuang 74), Wang Ke (Yang Pu 60) - Tiago (Wang Changqing 87), Huang Bowen, Walter Martinez. Tr: Lee Jan Soo

Kashima, Ibaraki
7-05-2008, 19:00, 5540, Breeze AUS
Kashima Antlers 8
Iwamasa 19, Kohrogi 21, Tashiro 45, Nozawa 2 46 66, Ogasawara 3 74 83
Hitoshi Sogahata - Daiki Iwamasa, Go Oiwa (Kenta Kasai 68), Toru Araiba, Masahiko Inoha - Mitsuo Ogasawara, Takuya Nozawa, Masashi Motoyama (Danilo 61), Shinzoh Kohrogi, Takeshi Aoki - Yuzo Tashiro (Ryuta Sasaki 77). Tr: Oswaldo
Krung Thai Bank 1
Pichitchotirat 92+
Klisana Klunklin (Sarawut Khambua 71) - Amnart Kaewkhew, Supachai Komsilp, Kraikiat Beadtaku, Suphachai Phupha - Somjate Kasarat (Kumron Chinsri 52), Anon Boonsuko, Phichitphong Choeichiu, Tanat Wongsupphalak, Peeraphong Pichitchotirat - Nantawat Thaensopa (Anawin Jujeen 76). Tr: Attapol Pussapakhom

My Dinh, Hanoi
21-05-2008, 17:00, 1200, Al Saeedi UAE
Nam Dinh 0
Tran Thanh Trung - Le Ngoc Lung (Tran Van Toan 77), Le Van Duyet, Lai Viet Huy, Khuong Quoc Tuan, Nguyen Quang The - Hoang Nhat Nam, Tran Duc Duong (Nguyen Dinh Hung 46), Nguyen Viet Dung - Nguyen Thanh Luan, Tran Manh Dung (Pham Xuan Phu 68). Tr: Nguyen Ngoc Hao
Kashima Antlers 4
Tashiro 28, Kohrogi 49, Motoyama 76, Danilo 88
Hitoshi Sogahata - Atsuto Uchida, Daiki Iwamasa, Go Oiwa, Toru Araiba - Mitsuo Ogasawara, Takuya Nozawa, Masashi Motoyama (Yasushi Endoh 83), Shinzoh Kohrogi (Ryuta Sasaki 60), Takeshi Aoki - Yuzo Tashiro (Danilo 72). Tr: Oswaldo

GROUP G

		Pl	W	D	L	F	A	Pts	JPN	AUS	KOR	THA
Gamba Osaka	JPN	6	4	2	0	14	8	14		2-0	1-1	1-1
Melbourne Victory	AUS	6	2	1	3	10	11	7	3-4		2-0	3-1
Chunnam Dragons	KOR	6	1	3	2	8	10	6	3-4	1-1		1-0
Chonburi	THA	6	1	2	3	7	10	5	0-2	3-1	2-2	

Telstra Dome, Melbourne
12-03-2008, 19:30, 23 000, Abdul Bashir SIN

Melbourne Victory 2
Muscat [28p], Vargas [66]

Serafim Theoklitos – Stilianos Pantelidis, Matthew Kemp, Rodrigo Vargas – Kevin Muscat, Claudio Caceres (Sebastian Ryall 59), Leigh Broxham, Nicholas Ward (Kaz Patatfa 74) – Daniel Allsopp, Archie Thompson, Blagoja Celeski (Daniel Vasilevski 88). Tr: Ernie Merrick

Chunnam Dragons 0

Yeom Donggyun – Jung Inwhan (Sabitovic Jasenko 66), Lee Junki – Kim Taesu, Lee Sangil, Lim Kwan Sik, Kim Seongjae, Lee Kyuro (Sandro 38), Yoo Hongyoul (Song Jung Hyun 66) – Victor Simoes, Ju Kwangyoun. Tr: Park Hang Seo

---

Supachalasai, Bangkok
19-03-2008, 19:30, 10 000, Auda Lazim IRQ

Chonburi 3
Fabiano [45], Stephane Baga 2 [79 95+]

Kosin Hathairattanakool – Nattaphong Samana, Suttinun Phukhom, Nataporn Phanrit, Surat Sukha (Kriangkrai Pimrat 64) – Arthit Suntornphit [85], Ekaphan Inthasen, Chonlatit Jantakam, Jetsadakorn Hemdaeng (Sarawut Janthapan 76) – Pipob On-mo (Stephane Baga 71), Fabiano. Tr: Jadej Meelap

Melbourne Victory 1
Allsopp [57]

Serafim Theoklitos – Stilianos Pantelidis (Daniel Vasilevski 46), Matthew Kemp (Kaz Patatfa 82), Rodrigo Vargas – Kevin Muscat, Claudio Caceres (Sebastian Ryall 46), Leigh Broxham, Nicholas Ward – Daniel Allsopp, Archie Thompson, Blagoja Celeski. Tr: Ernie Merrick

---

Supachalasai, Bangkok
23-04-2008, 19:30, 10 000, Tan Hai CHN

Chonburi 2
Pipob On-Mo [56], Phanuwat Jinta [88]

Kosin Hathairattanakool - Suttinun Phukhom, Nataporn Phanrit, Phaisan Pona, Surat Sukha - Arthit Suntornphit (Pipob On-mo 52), Jetsadakorn Hemdaeng – Stephane Baga, Fabiano (Nikorn Anuwan 87). Tr: Jadej Meelap

Chunnam Dragons 2
Lee Kyuro [5], Kim Mung Woon [48]

Yeom Donggyun – Jung Inwhan, Sabitovic Jasenko – Kim Jinhyun, Kim Taesu, Baek Seungmin, Kim Mung Woon (Hong Jongho 59), Lee Kyuro, Jeong Junyeon●25 – Andriano (Lee Yunpyo 88) Victor Simoes (Kim Ung Jin 63). Tr: Park Hang Seo

---

Supachalasai, Bangkok
7-05-2008, 19:30, 10 000, Abdou QAT

Chonburi 0

Kosin Hathairattanakool – Nattaphong Samana, Suttinun Phukhom (Kriangkrai Pimrat 73), Nataporn Phanrit, Surat Sukha – Arthit Suntornphit, Ekaphan Inthasen (Phaisan Pona 85), Chonlatit Jantakam, Jetsadakorn Hemdaeng – Pipob On-mo (Stephane Baga 67), Fabiano. Tr: Jadej Meelap

Gamba Osaka 2
Yamazaki [64], Lucas [76]

Naoki Matsuyo – Sota Nakazawa, Satoshi Yamaguchi, Akira Kaji – Takahiro Futagawa (Shu Kurata 79), Michihiro Yasuda (Takumi Shimohira 84), Tomokazu Myojin, Hideo Hashimoto – Lucas, Ryuji Bando (Masato Yamazaki 63), Jader. Tr: Akira Nishino

---

Expo '70, Osaka
12-03-2008, 19:00, 7000, Mombeni IRN

Gamba Osaka 1
Lucas [94+]

Yosuke Fujigaya – Marcelo (Ryuji Bando 72), Hiroki Mizumoto, Satoshi Yamaguchi – Yasuhito Endo, Shinichi Terada, Takahiro Futagawa (Michihiro Yasuda 83), Hayato Sasaki (Masato Yamazaki 46), Hideo Hashimoto – Lucas, Jader. Tr: Akira Nishino

Chonburi 1
Suntornphit [59]

Kosin Hathairattanakool – Nattaphong Samana, Suttinun Phukhom, Nataporn Phanrit, Surat Sukha (Kim Woon 93+) – Arthit Suntornphit (Phanuwat Jinta 68), Kriangkrai Pimrat, Ekaphan Inthasen, Chonlatit Jantakam – Pipob On-mo (Stephane Baga 55), Fabiano. Tr: Jadej Meelap

---

Gwangyang Football Stadium
9-04-2008, 19:00, 500, Al Hilali OMA

Chunnam Dragons 1
Victor Simoes [90]

Yeom Donggyun – Park Jiyong, Jung Inwhan – Kim Chiwoo, Song Jung Hyun, Lee Sangil, Kim Mung Woon (Victor Simoes 64), Kim Seongjae, Lee Kyuro (Ju Kwangyoun 68), Yoo Hongyoul (Lee Junki 92+) – Ko Kigu. Tr: Park Hang Seo

Chonburi 0

Kosin Hathairattanakool – Nattaphong Samana, Suttinun Phukhom, Nataporn Phanrit, Phaisan Pona (Phanuwat Jinta 66) – Kriangkrai Pimrat, Ekaphan Inthasen, Chonlatit Jantakam, Jetsadakorn Hemdaeng – Pipob On-mo (Stephane Baga 63), Fabiano. Tr: Jadej Meelap

---

Expo '70, Osaka
23-04-2008, 19:00, 8132, Al Badwani UAE

Gamba Osaka 2
Yamazaki 2 [31 57]

Naoki Matsuyo – Sota Nakazawa, Satoshi Yamaguchi – Yasuhito Endo, Takahiro Futagawa, Michihiro Yasuda (Hiroki Mizumoto 88), Tomokazu Myojin, Hideo Hashimoto – Lucas, Jader (Shu Kurata 82), Masato Yamazaki. Tr: Akira Nishino

Melbourne Victory 0

Serafim Theoklitos – Matthew Kemp, Rodrigo Vargas, Sebastian Ryall – Kevin Muscat, Kaz Patatfa (Tomislav Pondeljak 46), Claudio Caceres, Leigh Broxham (Stilianos Pantelidis 68), Nicholas Ward – Daniel Allsopp, Blagoja Celeski (Leandro Da Silva 75). Tr: Ernie Merrick

---

Telstra Dome, Melbourne
21-05-2008, 19:30, 9558, Mujghef JOR

Melbourne Victory 3
Muscat [56], Thompson [65], Valverde [76]

Mitchell Langerak – Steven Pace, Matthew Kemp, Rodrigo Vargas – Kevin Muscat, Carlos Valverde (Evan Berger 81), Leigh Broxham (Sebastian Ryall 77), Nicholas Ward, Tomislav Pondeljak (Archie Thompson 61) – Daniel Allsopp, Blagoja Celeski. Tr: Ernie Merrick

Chonburi 1
Fabiano [55]

Kosin Hathairattanakool – Nattaphong Samana, Phaisan Pona, Surat Sukha – Arthit Suntornphit, Kriangkrai Pimrat (Phanuwat Jinta 71), Ekaphan Inthasen (Stephane Baga 71), Chonlatit Jantakam, Jetsadakorn Hemdaeng – Pipob On-mo, Fabiano. Tr: Jadej Meelap

---

Gwangyang Football Stadium
19-03-2008, 18:30, 3000, Shamsuzzaman BAN

Chunnam Dragons 3
Victor Simoes [5], Kim Taesu 2 [29 61]

Yeom Donggyun – Sabitovic Jasenko, Lee Junki (Lee Sangil 77), Kim Ung Jin – Kim Chiwoo, Kim Taesu, Kim Mung Woon (Ju Kwangyoun 75), Lim Kwan Sik, Kim Seongjae, Lee Kyuro (Hong Jongho 81) – Victor Simoes. Tr: Park Hang Seo

Gamba Osaka 4
Futagawa [31], Bando 2 [55 76], Yasuda [59]

Yosuke Fujigaya – Sota Nakazawa, Satoshi Yamaguchi – Yasuhito Endo, Takahiro Futagawa (Masato Yamazaki 82), Michihiro Yasuda, Tomokazu Myojin, Hideo Hashimoto – Lucas, Ryuji Bando (Takuya Takei 92+), Jader (Hiroki Mizumoto 79). Tr: Akira Nishino

---

Telstra Dome, Melbourne
9-04-2008, 19:30, 23 857, Mohd Salleh MAS

Melbourne Victory 3
Allsopp 2 [4 66], Vargas [41]

Serafim Theoklitos – Steven Pace (Stilianos Pantelidis 40), Matthew Kemp, Rodrigo Vargas, Sebastian Ryall – Kevin Muscat, Claudio Caceres (Kaz Patatfa 81), Leigh Broxham, Nicholas Ward – Daniel Allsopp, Blagoja Celeski (Daniel Vasilevski 82). Tr: Ernie Merrick

Gamba Osaka 4
Futagawa [32], Jader [39], Yamaguchi [69], Lucas [89]

Yosuke Fujigaya – Sota Nakazawa, Hiroki Mizumoto (Lucas 46), Satoshi Yamaguchi – Yasuhito Endo, Takahiro Futagawa (Yohei Fukumoto 91+), Michihiro Yasuda, Tomokazu Myojin, Hideo Hashimoto – Jader, Masato Yamazaki (Shinichi Terada 62). Tr: Akira Nishino

---

Gwangyang Football Stadium
7-05-2008, 19:00, 3000, Balideh QAT

Chunnam Dragons 1
Ko Kigu [38]

Cho Min Hyuck – Park Jiyong, Sabitovic Jasenko – Kim Jinhyun (Baek Seungmin 63), Lee Sangil, Lim Kwan Sik, Lee Kyuro, Yoo Hongyoul (Kim Ung Jin 68) – Victor Simoes (Lee Sang Yong 76), Ju Kwangyoun, Ko Kigu. Tr: Park Hang Seo

Melbourne Victory 1
Pondeljak [4]

Serafim Theoklitos – Stilianos Pantelidis, Matthew Kemp, Rodrigo Vargas, Sebastian Ryall (Evan Berger 87) – Kevin Muscat, Nicholas Ward, Tomislav Pondeljak (Claudio Caceres 74) – Daniel Allsopp, Nathan Elasi (Carlos Valverde 69), Blagoja Celeski. Tr: Ernie Merrick

---

Expo '70, Osaka
21-05-2008, 19:00, 7160, Sun Baojie CHN

Gamba Osaka 1
Futagawa [75]

Naoki Matsuyo – Sota Nakazawa, Yohei Fukumoto, Takumi Shimohira, Akira Kaji – Takahiro Futagawa, Hayato Sasaki (25 83), Shu Kurata, Takuya Takei (Tomokazu Myojin 63) – Shoki Hirai (Jader 63), Masato Yamazaki. Tr: Akira Nishino

Chunnam Dragons 1
Yoo Hongyoul [85p]

Cho Min Hyuck – Sabitovic Jasenko, Lee Yunpyo, Kim Ung Jin – Lee Sangil, Kim Mung Woon (Hong Jongho 77), Lim Kwan Sik, Lee Kyuro, Jeong Junyeon (Lee Sang Yong 78), Yoo Hongyoul – Ju Kwangyoun. Tr: Park Hang Seo

AFC CUP 2007

AFC CUP 2007

Group Stage

Group A — Pts
- Al Nijmeh — LIB — 15
- Shabab Al Ordun — JOR — 13
- Muscat Club — OMA — 4
- Al Saqr — YEM — 2

Group B — Pts
- Al Wihdat — JOR — 14
- Al Muharraq — BHR — 11
- MTTU Ashgabat — TKM — 6
- Al Hilal Hudayda — YEM — 2

Group C — Pts
- Al Faysali — JOR — 11
- Dhofar Club — OMA — 10
- Al Ansar — LIB — 9
- Nebitchi Balkanabat — TKM — 2

Group D — Pts
- Sun Hei — HKG — 15
- Negeri Sembilan — MAS — 7
- Victory SC — MDV — 6
- Hoa Phat Hanoi — VIE — 3

Group E — Pts
- Sing. Armed Forces — SIN — 15
- Mahindra United — IND — 12
- Happy Valley — HKG — 9
- New Radiant — MDV — 0

Group F — Pts
- Tampines Rovers — SIN — 13
- Mohun Bagan — IND — 11
- Osotpa M-150 — THA — 10
- Pahang — MAS — 0

Quarter-finals
- Shabab Al Ordun * — 5 0
- Sing. Armed Forces — 0 3

- Mahindra United * — 1 3
- Al Nijmeh — 2 3

- Al Wihdat — 1 3
- Sun Hei * — 0 1

- Tampines Rovers * — 1 2
- Al Faysali — 2 5

Semi-finals
- Shabab Al Ordun * — 1 0
- Al Nijmeh — 0 0

- Al Wihdat — 1 1
- Al Faysali * — 1 2

Final
- Shabab Al Ordun — 1 1
- Al Faysali * — 0 1

* Home team in the first leg
For details of group matches see *Almanack of World Football 2008*

QUARTER-FINALS

Amman International, Amman
18-09-2007, 21:30, 1000, Al Saeedi UAE

Shabab Al Ordun   **5**

Bassam Khatib [19], Abo Touk [52p], Odai Alsaify [60], Mustafa Aburomeh [83], Shadi Abu-Hashhash [86]

Ahmad Nawwas - Aiad Abdulkarim, Ammar Al-Sharaydeh, Shadi Abu-Hashhash, Waseem Albzoor - Raafat Mohammad, Nour Al Takrouri (Hazem Abuhussein 86), Esam Abo Touk, Mohannad Maharmeh (Saher Adi 81) - Bassam Khatib (Mustafa Aburomeh 69), Odai Alsaify. Tr: Nizar Mahrous

Singapore Armed Forces   **0**

Shahril Jantan - Mohamed Faizal, Kenji Arai●, Mohd Razif●●68, Daniel Bennett - Therdsak Chaiman●, John Wilkinson, Mohamed Jamil Ali, Mohamed Noor Ali● - Aleksandar Duric, Ashrin Shariff (Hafiz Osman 73). Tr: Bok Kok Chuan

---

Chao Chu Kang, Singapore
25-09-2007, 1528, Yang Zhiqiang CHN

Singapore Armed Forces   **3**

OG [35], Mohamed Noor [54], Mohamed Jamil Ali [75]

Guo'an Toh - Mohamed Faizal, Kenji Arai, Daniel Bennett, Mohamad Shaiful (Faizal Abd Aziz 26) - Therdsak Chaiman, John Wilkinson (Hafiz Osman● 72), Mohamed Jamil Ali (Ashrin Shariff 78), Mustaquim Manzur, Mohamed Noor Ali - Aleksandar Duric. Tr: Bok Kok Chuan

Shabab Al Ordun   **0**

Ahmad Nawwas - Aiad Abdulkarim, Ammar Al-Sharaydeh, Saleh Taha, Shadi Abu-Hashhash●, Waseem Albzoor - Saher Adi (Nour Al Takrouri 57), Esam Abo Touk, Hazem Abuhussein (Mohannad Maharmeh 66) - Mustafa Aburomeh (Tarek Alkronz 79), Odai Alsaify. Tr: Nizar Mahrous

---

Dr Ambedkar, New Delhi
18-09-2007, 21:00, 1500, Al Mutlaq KSA

Mahindra United   **1**

Mohamed Rafi [47]

Subhasish - Pradeep, Ajayan, Harpreet Singh - Sushanth, Sukhwinder Singh●, Steven Dias, Douhou - Andrews Pomeyie, Mohamed Rafi (Edson Minga 75), Manjit Singh●. Tr: Derick Pereira

Al Nijmeh   **2**

Mohamad Ghaddar 2 [55 85]

Abdo Tafeh - Ali Wassef●, Milan Bogunovic, Khaled Hamieh, Bilal Najjarine - Yehia Hachem, Abbas Atwi, Mirko Teodorovic● - Ante Milas (Ahmad El Naamani 92+), Mohamad Ghaddar (Zakaria Charara 87), Agop Donabidian (Haitham Fattal 52). Tr: Nenad Stavric

---

Sports City, Beirut
25-09-2007, 21:00, 2000, Al Saeedi UAE

Al Nijmeh   **3**

Mohamad Ghaddar [12], Milas [24], Bogunovic [94+p]

Abdo Tafeh - Ali Wassef, Milan Bogunovic, Khaled Hamieh, Bilal Najjarine● - Yehia Hachem (Ali Nassereddine 80), Abbas Atwi, Mirko Teodorovic, Abbas Fadlallah (Zakaria Charara 67) - Ante Milas (Haitham Fattal 57), Mohamad Ghaddar●●84. Tr: Nenad Stavric

Mahindra United   **3**

Edson Minga [33], Harpreet Singh [64], Pomeyie [78]

Sandip Nandy● - Pradeep, Ajayan, Harpreet Singh● - Sushanth, Sukhwinder Singh●, Steven Dias (Manjit Singh 88), Edson Minga, Douhou - Andrews Pomeyie, Mohamed Rafi. Tr: Derick Pereira

---

Mongkok, Hong Kong
18-09-2007, 20:30, 1200, Nishimura JPN

Sun Hei   **0**

Chan Ka Ki - Chung Kin Hei Jason, Lee Wai Lun, Miguel, Cristiano Cordeiro - Lau Chi Keung Sanvel, Chu Siu Kei (Tse Man Wing 88), Lo Chi Kwan (Chan Yiu Lun 21), Lai Kai Cheuk - Fabio de Souza (Chan Ho Man 46), Giovane Da Silva. Tr: Koo Luam Khen

Al Wihdat   **1**

Ahmad Alzugheir [83]

Amer Shafi - Basem Fathi, Haitham Semrin, Hayder Jabar - Hasan Abdel-Fattah (Musab Al Rifae 85), Rafat Ali (Khalil Fetian 79), Abdallah Deeb, Faisal Ibrahim, Mohammad Jamal, Ahmad Alzugheir - Mahmoud Shelbaieh (Abdallah Ata 91+). Tr: Ismael Mohamed

---

Amman International, Amman
25-09-2007, 22:00, 9000, Mansour LIB

Al Wihdat   **3**

Mahmoud Shelbaieh [58], Amer Deeb 2 [71 78]

Amer Shafi - Basem Fathi, Haitham Semrin, Hayder Jabar - Rafat Ali●, Abdallah Deeb (Amer Deeb 59) (Musab Al Rifae 81), Faisal Ibrahim, Mohammad Jamal, Ahmad Alzugheir - Mahmoud Shelbaieh (Hasan Abdel-Fattah 64), Awad Ragheb. Tr: Ismael Mohamed

Sun Hei   **1**

Giovane Da Silva [87]

Chan Ka Ki - Chung Kin Hei Jason●, Lee Wai Lun●, Miguel, Cristiano Cordeiro● - Lau Chi Keung Sanvel●, Chu Siu Kei, Chan Liu Lun (Chan Ho Man 65), Lai Kai Cheuk - Fabio de Souza (Tse Man Wing 75), Giovane Da Silva. Tr: Koo Luam Khen

---

Tampines, Singapore
18-09-2007, 21:00, 2654, Takayama JPN

Tampines Rovers   **1**

Sead Muratovic [41p]

Mohamed Rezal - Sead Muratovic, Mohamad Nazri, Zul Zainal, Muhammad Shariff● - Suksomkit Sutee, Fahrudin Mustafic, Mohamed Rafi - Noh Alam Shah●, Mirko Grabovac (Shahdan Sulaiman 83), Peres de Oliveira● (Muhammad Ridhuan 46). Tr: Vorawan Chitavanich

Al Faysali   **2**

Moayyad Abukeshek [45], Siraj Al Tall [74]

Lo'ai Elamaireh - Moh'd Monir, Mohammed Khamis, Hatem Aqel - Haider Hussein, Baha Suleiman, Hassouneh Qasem● (Khaled Nemer 84), Qusei Alieh - Moayad Abukeshek (Haitham Al Shboul 69), Omar Abu Aqulah●●●40, Siraj Al Tall (Mohammad Zuhair 91+). Tr: Yassen Salih

---

Prince Mohammed, Zerqa
25-09-2007,

Al Faysali   **5**

Haitham Al Shaboul [35], Moayad Abukeshek [41], Siraj Al Tall 2 [45 66], Qusai Abu Alieh [70p]

Lo'ai Elamaireh● - Moh'd Monir, Mohammed Khamis●, Hatem Aqel (Mohammad Zuhair 72) - Haider Hussein, Baha Suleiman, Hassouneh Qasem, Qusei Alieh, Haitham Al Shboul (Anas Hijah 73) - Moayad Abukeshek (Abdelhadi Al Maharmeh 81), Siraj Al Tall. Tr: Yassen Salih

Tampines Rovers   **2**

Suksomkit Sutee 1, Peres De Oliveira [14]

Mohamed Rezal - Sead Muratovic, Mohamad Nazri (Mirko Grabovac 62), Zul Zainal, Muhammad Shariff● - Muhammad Ridhuan, Suksomkit Sutee, Fahrudin Mustafic●, Mohamed Rafi (Shahdan Sulaiman 67) - Noh Alam Shah●●86, Peres de Oliveira● (Aliff Safie'e 79). Tr: Vorawan Chitavanich

SEMI-FINALS

Amman International, Amman
2-10-2007, 22:00, 1500, Sun Baojie

Shabab Al Ordun	1
	Odai Alsaify [8]

Ahmad Nawwas - Aiad Abdulkarim●, Ammar Al-Sharaydeh, Shadi Abu-Hashhash, Waseem Albzoor● - Raafat Mohammad, Ahmad Aldaoud (Nour Al Takrouri 79), Esam Abo Touk (Saher Adi 87), Mohannad Maharmeh● - Bassam Khatib (Mustafa Aburomeh 63), Odai Alsaify. Tr: Nizar Mahrous

Al Nijmeh	0

Abdo Tafeh - Ahmad El Naamani (Akram Moghrabi 83), Ali Wassef, Milan Bogunovic, Khaled Hamieh, Bilal Najjarine - Yehia Hachem, Zakaria Charara (Ali Nassereddine 54), Abbas Atwi●, Mirko Teodorovic, Abbas Fadallah (Haitham Fattal 72). Tr: Nenad Stavric

---

Sports City, Beirut
23-10-2007, 19:00, 1000, Torky IRN

Al Nijmeh	0

Abdo Tafeh.- Ali Wassef, Milan Bogunovic, Khaled Hamieh, Bilal Najjarine - Yehia Hachem● (Hussein Zaher 87), Zakaria Charara (Agop Donabidian 64), Abbas Atwi, Mirko Teodorovic - Akram Moghrabi (Ahmad El Naamani● 21), Ali Nassereddine●. Tr: Nenad Stavric

Shabab Al Ordun	0

Ahmad Nawwas - Aiad Abdulkarim, Ammar Al-Sharaydeh, Saleh Taha, Shadi Abu-Hashhash, Waseem Albzoor● - Ahmad Aldaoud● (Mustafa Aburomeh● 74), Esam Abo Touk, Hazem Abuhussein (Nour Al Takrouri 92+) - Bassam Khatib● (Mohannad Maharmeh 50), Odai Alsaify●. Tr: Nizar Mahrous

---

Amman International, Amman
3-10-2007, 22:00, 15 000, Irmatov UZB

Al Faysali	1
	Siraj Al Tall [43]

Lo'ai Elamaireh - Moh'd Monir, Mohammed Khamis, Hatem Aqel - Haider Hussein, Baha Suleiman●, Hassouneh Qasem, Qusei Alieh - Moayad Abukeshek (Haitham Al Shboul 46), Omar Abu Aqulah (Khaled Nemer 64), Siraj Al Tall. Tr: Yassen Salih

Al Wihdat	1
	Mahmoud Shelbaieh [71]

Amer Shafi - Basem Fathi●, Haitham Semrin, Hayder Jabar - Hasan Abdel-Fattah (Rafat Ali 50) (Musab Al Rifae 87), Amer Deeb, Faisal Ibrahim, Mohammad Jamal (Awad Ragheb● 62), Ahmad Alzugheir, Khalil Fetian● - Mahmoud Shelbaieh●. Tr: Ismael Mohamed

---

Amman International, Amman
22-10-2007, 19:00, 17 000, Kwon Jong Chul KOR

Al Wihdat	1
	Rafat Ali [71p]

Amer Shafi - Basem Fathi, Haitham Semrin, Hayder Jabar - Hasan Abdel-Fattah (Issa Alsapah 70), Amer Deeb, Faisal Ibrahim● (Mohammad Abu Ziton 88), Mohammad Jamal (Rafat Ali 51●●72), Khalil Fetian● - Mahmoud Shelbaieh, Awad Ragheb●. Tr: Ismael Mohamed

Al Faysali	2
	Moayad Abukeshek [32], Hassouneh Qasem [60]

Lo'ai Elamaireh - Moh'd Monir, Mohammed Khamis, Hatem Aqel - Haider Hussein, Baha Suleiman, Hassouneh Qasem, Qusei Alieh, Haitham Al Shboul - Moayad Abukeshek, Siraj Al Tall. Tr: Yassen Salih

---

AFC CUP FINAL FIRST LEG
Amman International, Amman
2-11-2007, 17:00, 5500, Nishimura JPN

AL FAYSALI	0	1		SHABAB
				Odai Alsaify [52]

	Al Faysali				Shabab Al Ordun	
23	ZAPEN Alkhawaldeh				Ahmad NAWWAS	1
3	Moh'd MONIR				Aiad ABDULKARIM	5
17	HATEM Aqel				Ammar AL-SHARAYDEH	6
30	Hussein ODTALLAH				Saleh TAHA	15
4	HAIDER Hussein				Shadi ABU-HASHHASH	18
8	BAHA Suleiman				Tarek ALKRONZ	19
13	QUSAI Alieh				Esam ABO TOUK	11
14	Haitham AL SHBOUL	57			Hazem ABUHUSSEIN	16
16	ANAS Hijah	57	92		Mohannad MAHARMEH	21
19	MOAYAD Mansour	71	60		Bassam KHATIB	20
27	SIRAJ Al Tall		79		Odai ALSAIFY	24
	Tr: Yassen SALIH				Tr: Nizar MAHROUS	
	Substitutes				Substitutes	
10	Moayad ABUKESHEK	71	92		Nour AL TAKROURI	3
11	Abdelhadi ALMAHARMEH	57			Saher ADI	8
25	OMAR Abu Aqulah	57	60		Mustafa ABUROMEH	10

AFC CUP FINAL SECOND LEG
Amman International, Amman
9-11-2007, 17:00, 7500, Lee Gi Young KOR

SHABAB	1	1		AL FAYSALI
Mustafa Aburomeh [44]				Haitham Al Shboul [13]

	Shabab Al Ordun				Al Faysali	
1	Ahmad NAWWAS				LO'AI Elmaireh	1
5	Aiad ABDULKARIM				Moh'd MONIR	3
6	Ammar AL-SHARAYDEH				Mohammad KHAMEES	12
15	Saleh TAHA				HATEM Aqel	17
18	Shadi ABU-HASHHASH				HAIDER Hussein	4
23	Waseem ALBZOOR				BAHA Suleiman	8
11	Esam ABO TOUK				HASSOUNEH Qasem	12
16	Hazem ABUHUSSEIN				QUSAI Alieh	13
21	Mohannad MAHARMEH	90	55		Haitham AL SHBOUL	14
10	Mustafa ABUROMEH	85	80		Moayad ABUKESHEK	10
24	Odai ALSAIFY	92	67		SIRAJ Al Tall	27
	Tr: Nizar MAHROUS				Tr:	
	Substitutes				Substitutes	
3	Nour AL TAKROURI	85	67		Abdelhadi ALMAHARMEH	11
19	Tarek ALKRONZ	90	80		MOAYAD Mansour	19
20	Bassam KHATIB	92	55		OMAR Abu Aqulah	25

AFC CUP 2008

AFC CUP 2008					
Group Stage			**Quarter–finals**	**Semi–finals**	**Final**
Group A		Pts			
Muharraq	BHR	11	Perak *		
Dempo	IND	10	Safa		
Al Ansar	LIB	8			
Sur	OMA	4			
Group B		Pts			
Safa	LIB	10			
Al Wihdat	JOR	7			
East Bengal	IND	7	Dempo *		
Al Ahly Sana'a	YEM	6	Home United		
Group C		Pts			
Al Nahda	OMA	9			
Al Najma	BHR	7			
Shabab Al Ordun	JOR	7			
Al Sha'ab H'ramaut	YEM	6			
Group D		Pts			
Home United	SIN	15	Singapore A Forces *		
Kedah	MAS	13	Al Nahda		
South China	HKG	4			
Victory	MDV	2			
Group E		Pts			
Singapore A Forces	SIN	13			
Perak	MAS	13			
Kitchee	HKG	4	Muharraq *		
New Radiant	MDV	4	Kedah		

* Home team in the first leg
Remaining ties: Quarter-finals 16-09-2008 & 23-09-2008; Semi-finals 7-10-2007 & 21-10-2007; Final 31-10-2008 & 7-11-2008

GROUP A

Nehru, Goa, 11-03-2008, 16:00, 6000, Ng Chiu Kok HKG

| Dempo | 3 | Ranty Soleye 2 [21] [32], Chidi Edeh [62] |
| Al Ansar | 1 | Hassan Danach [89] |

National, Manama, 11-03-2008, 18:15, 2500, Iemoto JPN

| Muharraq | 3 | Leandson [24p], Jaycee Okwunwanne [45], Abdulla Al Dakeel [83] |
| Sur | 2 | Khalid Al Gheilani [35], Jose Estefane [39] |

Sports City, Beirut, 18-03-2008, 18:00, 3000, Al Yarmi YEM

| Al Ansar | 0 | |
| Muharraq | 0 | |

Nizwa, Nizwa City, 18-03-2008, 19:00, 1500, Ali Saleem MDV

| Sur | 3 | Daouda Traore [9], Mamadou Camara [69], OG [80] |
| Dempo | 2 | Ranty Soleye [26], Roberto Silva [62] |

Sports City, Beirut, 2-04-2008, 18:00, 4000, Balideh QAT

| Al Ansar | 1 | Salih Sader [28] |
| Sur | 0 | |

Nehru, Goa, 2-04-2008, 16:00, 5000, Vo Minh Tri VIE

| Dempo | 0 | |
| Muharraq | 4 | Rico 4 [8] [31] [49p] [59] |

Nizwa, Nizwa City, 16-04-2008, 19:15, 400, Al Saeedi UAE

| Sur | 0 | |
| Al Ansar | 2 | Salih Sader 2 [77] [88] |

National, Manama, 16-04-2008, 18:30, 2000, Mujghef JOR

| Muharraq | 1 | Leandson [77p] |
| Dempo | 2 | Ranty Soleye 2 [10] [62] |

Sports City, Beirut, 30-04-2008, 18:00, 1950, Tan Hai CHN

| Al Ansar | 1 | Mohamad Hammoud [84] |
| Dempo | 1 | Ranty Soleye [27] |

Nizwa, Nizwa City, 30-04-2008, 19:15, 300, Choi Myung Yong KOR

| Sur | 2 | Jose Estefane 2 [48] [62] |
| Muharraq | 2 | Leandson [45], Jaycee Okwunwanne [55] |

Nehru, Goa, 14-05-2008, 16:00, 4000, Green AUS

| Dempo | 5 | Ranty Soleye 2 [30] [38], Chidi Edeh 2 [64] [90], Climax Lawrence [72] |
| Sur | 2 | Al Sinani [75], Al Harbi [86] |

National, Manama, 21-05-2008, 18:45, 2000, Saidov UZB

| Muharraq | 4 | Mahmoud Abdulrahman [30], Leandson 2 [51] [66], Jaycee Okwunwanne [57] |
| Al Ansar | 1 | Nasrat Al Jamal [44] |

Group A	Pl	W	D	L	F	A	Pts
Muharraq	6	3	2	1	14	7	11
Dempo	6	3	1	2	13	12	10
Al Ansar	6	2	2	2	6	8	8
Sur	6	1	1	4	9	15	4

GROUP B

Ali Mohsen, Sana'a, 11-03-2008, 16:15, 13 000, Perera SRI

| Al Ahly Sana'a | 1 | Adel Al Salemi [28] |
| Al Wihdat | 1 | Hasan Abdel-Fattah [40p] |

Sports City, Beirut, 11-03-2008, 18:00, 700, Al Ghatrifi OMA

| Safa | 1 | Bernard Mbassi [17] |
| East Bengal | 0 | |

Prince Mohammad, Zerqa, 18-03-2008, 15:00, 1000, Al Saeedi UAE

| Al Wihdat | 3 | Mahmoud Shelbaieh [51], Hasan Abdel-Fattah [86], Basem Fathi [95+] |
| Safa | 3 | Prince Bobby [16], Ramez Dayoub [31], Rony Azar [83] |

Salt Lake, Kolkata, 18-03-2008, 15:00, 6000, Tojo JPN

| East Bengal | 1 | Edmilson [34] |
| Al Ahly Sana'a | 0 | |

Prince Mohammad, Zerqa, 2-04-2008, 15:30, 4000, Shahrul MAS

| Al Wihdat | 0 | |
| East Bengal | 2 | Alvito D'Cunha [58], Ikechukwu Ibe [69] |

Ali Mohsen, Sana'a, 2-04-2008, 16:15, 4000, Mahapab THA

| Al Ahly Sana'a | 0 | |
| Safa | 0 | |

Salt Lake, Kolkata, 16-04-2008, 15:00, 10 000, Vo Minh Tri VIE

| East Bengal | 2 | Syed Nabi [12], Edmilson [28] |
| Al Wihdat | 4 | Rafat Ali 2 [6] [24], Hasan Abdel-Fattah 2 [31] [34] |

Sports City, Beirut, 16-04-2008, 18:00, 1000, Shamsuzzaman BAN

| Safa | 1 | Hamze Abboud [64] |
| Al Ahly Sana'a | 0 | |

Prince Mohammad, Zerqa, 30-04-2008, 17:00, 1500, Saleem MDV

| Al Wihdat | 1 | Hasan Abdel-Fattah [30] |
| Al Ahly Sana'a | 1 | Ali Al Nono [80] |

Salt Lake, Kolkata, 30-04-2008, 15:00, 10 000, Kovalenko UZB

| East Bengal | 0 | |
| Safa | 0 | |

Ali Mohsen, Sana'a, 14-05-2008, 16:15, 1000, Orzuev TJK

| Al Ahly Sana'a | 1 | Ali Al Nono [43] |
| East Bengal | 0 | |

Sports City, Beirut, 21-05-2008, 18:00, 300,

| Safa | 3 | Rony Azar [6], Hussein Tahan [82], Amer Khan [90+] |
| Al Wihdat | 3 | Rafat Ali 2 [18] [63], Fadi Shahin [72] |

Group B	Pl	W	D	L	F	A	Pts
Safa	6	2	4	0	8	6	10
Al Wihdat	6	1	4	1	12	12	7
East Bengal	6	2	1	3	5	6	7
Al Ahly Sana'a	6	1	3	2	3	4	6

GROUP C

Nizwa, Nizwa City, 11-03-2008, 19:00, 350, Orzuev TJK

| Al Nahda | 0 | |
| Al Najma | 0 | |

Prince Mohammad, Zerqa, 11-03-2008, 15:00, 150, Tan Hai CHN

| Shabab Al Ordun | 1 | Odai Al Saify [51] |
| Sha'ab Hadramaut | 1 | Haytham Mahadi [38] |

Al Ahli, Manama, 18-03-2008, 18:45, 500, Mombeni IRN

| Al Najma | 0 | |
| Shabab Al Ordun | 0 | |

Ali Mohsen, Sana'a, 18-03-2008, 16:15, 4000, Shahrul MAS

| Sha'ab Hadramaut | 3 | Munassar Ba Haj 2 [44] [45], Murad Al Nohi [51] |
| Al Nahda | 1 | Datoma Yedibahoma [52] |

National, Manama, 2-04-2008, 18:55, 350, Perera SRI

| Al Najma | 2 | Rashed Jamal [8], Ba Karman OG [54] |
| Sha'ab Hadramaut | 1 | Alaaeldin Aly [67] |

Nizwa, Nizwa City, 2-04-2008, 19:00, 500, Al Enezi KUW

| Al Nahda | 1 | Salim Al Shamsi [26] |
| Shabab Al Ordun | 1 | Abdulhadi Al Hariri [86] |

Ali Mohsen, Sana'a, 16-04-2008, 16:15, 3000, Win Cho MYA

| Sha'ab Hadramaut | 0 | |
| Al Najma | 0 | |

Prince Mohammad, Zerqa, 16-04-2008, 17:00, 100, Saleem MDV

| Shabab Al Ordun | 0 | |
| Al Nahda | 1 | Datoma Yedibahoma [57] |

National, Manama, 30-04-2008, 19:10, 200, Abdou QAT

| Al Najma | 3 | Rashed Jamal 3 [53] [67] [77] |
| Al Nahda | 3 | Datoma Yedibahoma 2 [6] [50], Sabir Al Alawi [38] |

Ali Mohsen, Sana'a, 30-04-2008, 16:15, 4000, Al Marzouqi UAE

| Sha'ab Hadramaut | 2 | Khaled Al Arumi [5], Haytham Mahadi [88p] |
| Shabab Al Ordun | 2 | Mustafa Shehadeh [3], Mohannad Al Maharmeh [45] |

Nizwa, Nizwa City, 14-05-2008, 19:00, 300, Al Ghamdi KSA

Al Nahda 2 Mansour Al Naaimi 14, Al Mashaikhi [43]

Sha'ab Hadramaut 0

Prince Mohammad, Zerqa, 14-05-2008, 18:00, 100, Tojo JPN

Shabab Al Ordun 3 Odai Al Saifi [9], Mustafa Shehadeh [28], Esam Abou Touk [40p]

Al Najma 2 Rashed Jamal 2 [51p 69]

Group C	Pl	W	D	L	F	A	Pts
Al Nahda	6	2	3	1	8	7	9
Al Najma	6	1	4	1	7	7	7
Shabab Al Ordun	6	1	4	1	7	7	7
Al Sha'ab H'ramaut	6	1	3	2	7	8	6

GROUP D

Mongkok, Kowloon, 11-03-2008, 20:00, 3600, Win Cho MYA

South China 2 Cheng Siu Wai 2 [60 90]

Home United 3 Oliveira 2 [15 43], Shi Jiayi [77]

Darul Aman, Alor Setar, 11-03-2008, 20:45, 12 000, Al Ghafary JOR

Kedah 1 Fauzi Shaari [49]

Victory 0

Jalan Besar, Singapore, 18-03-2008, 19:45, 2693, Green AUS

Home United 5 Kengne Ludovick 2 [31 58], Sharil Ishak [36], Oliveira 2 [70 81p]

Kedah 1 Shafiq Jamal [12]

National, Male, 18-03-2008, 16:00, 6500, Kovalenko UZB

Victory 0

South China 0

Jalan Besar, Singapore, 2-04-2008, 19:45, 1223, Al Yarimi YEM

Home United 2 Indra Sahdan [37], Oliveira [50]

Victory 1 Ashad Ali [25]

Mongkok, Kowloon, 2-04-2008, 20:00, 1055, Tojo JPN

South China 1 Cristiano [59]

Kedah 3 Baddrol Bakhtiar [31], Marlon James [65], Samransak Kram [85]

National, Male, 16-04-2008, 16:00, 6000, Abdou QAT

Victory 1 Hussain Niyaz [69]

Home United 3 Sharil Ishak [56], Indra Sahdan [66], Oliveira [73]

Darul Aman, Alor Setar, 16-04-2008, 20:45, 6000, Al Yarimi YEM

Kedah 3 Marlon James [55], Nelson San Martin 2 [71 85]

South China 0

Jalan Besar, Singapore, 30-04-2008, 19:45, 1175, Mahapab THA

Home United 4 Sharil Ishak 2 [30 88], Indra Sahdan [75], Farhan Farook [87]

South China 1 Cheng Siu Wai [80]

National, Male, 30-04-2008, 16:00, 4500, Shamsuzzaman BAN

Victory 1 Jorge Rodriguez [8]

Kedah 1 Marlon James [65]

Mongkok, Kowloon, 14-05-2008, 20:00, 429, Kim Dong Jin KOR

South China 3 Tales Schutz [27], Cristiano 2 [43 68]

Victory 0

Darul Aman, Alor Setar, 14-05-2008, 20:45, 10 000, Kovalenko UZB

Kedah 4 Nelson San Martin 2 [41 59p], Mat Abu [46], Marlon James [83]

Home United 1 Kengne Ludovick [5]

Group D	Pl	W	D	L	F	A	Pts
Home United	6	5	0	1	18	10	15
Kedah	6	4	1	1	13	8	13
South China	6	1	1	4	7	13	4
Victory	6	0	2	4	3	10	2

GROUP E

National, Male, 11-03-2008, 15:45, 8000, Mahapab THA

New Radiant 1 Daniel Mbock [8]

Perak 3 Carlos Caceres 2 [9 17], Khaled Jamlus [38]

Jalan Besar, Singapore, 11-03-2008, 19:50, 2543, Vo Minh Tri VIE

Singapore AForces 4 Jamil Ali 2 [12 37], Therdsak Chaiman [25], Wang Zhenpeng OG [51]

Kitchee 0

Perak, Ipoh, 18-03-2008, 20:45, 5000, Choi Myung Yong KOR

Perak 1 Mario Berrios [45p]

Singapore AForces 6 Therdsak Chaiman [8], Duric 4 [45 49 71 74], Manzur Ahmed Khan [58]

Mongkok, Kowloon, 18-03-2008, 20:00, 1372, Al Ghatrifi OMA

Kitchee 2 Wilfred Bamnjo [11], Goran Stankovski [36]

New Radiant 0

Perak, Ipoh, 2-04-2008, 20:45, 1000, Green AUS

Perak 2 Mohamad Jaafar [11], Mario Berrios [92+]

Kitchee 1 Goran Stankovski [73]

National, Male, 2-04-2008, 15:30, 4000, Mansour LIB

New Radiant 0

Singapore AForces 3 Ashrin Shariff [7], Duric [44], Amil OG [86]

Mongkok, Kowloon, 16-04-2008, 20:00, 1138, Kovalenko UZB

Kitchee 2 Ip Chung Long [50], Wilfred Bamnjo [84]

Perak 2 Carlos Caceres 2 [17 79]

Jalan Besar, Singapore, 16-04-2008, 19:50, 1505, Auda Lazm IRQ

Singapore AForces 1 John Wilkinson [27]

New Radiant 1 Assad Abdul Gani [50]

Perak, Ipoh, 30-04-2008, 20:45, 700, Orzuev TJK

Perak 3 Jorge Munoz 2 [33 65], Razali Omar [91+]

New Radiant 0

Mongkok, Kowloon, 30-04-2008, 20:00, 813, Perera SRI

Kitchee 0

Singapore AForces 2 Ashrin Shariff [10], Duric [19]

National, Male, 14-05-2008, 15:45, 2000, Win Cho MYA

New Radiant 2 Hussein Shimaz 2 [62 66]

Kitchee 1 Ahmed Nishan OG [46]

Jalan Besar, Singapore, 14-05-2008, 19:45, 2297, Takayama JPN

Singapore AForces 0

Perak 2 Shahrul Azhar [21], Hardi Jaafar [69]

Group E	Pl	W	D	L	F	A	Pts
Singapore Armed Forces	6	4	1	1	16	4	13
Perak	6	4	1	1	13	10	13
Kitchee	6	1	1	4	6	12	4
New Radiant	6	1	1	4	4	13	4

AFC PRESIDENT'S CUP 2007

AFC PRESIDENT'S CUP PAKISTAN 2007

Group Stage	Semi–finals	Final

Group A		Pts
Regar TadAZ	TJK	9
Ratnam SC	SRI	4
Transport United	BHU	3
Pakistan Army	PAK	1

Dordoi-Dynamo	1 4p
Ratnam SC	1 3p

Dordoi-Dynamo	**2**
Mahendra Police	1

Group B		Pts
Dordoy-Dinamo	KGZ	9
Mahendra Police	NEP	4
Khemara	CAM	3
Tatung	TPE	1

Regar TadAZ	1
Mahendra Police	**2**

GROUP A

Punjab Stadium, Lahore, 20-09-2007, 20:15, 4000, Recho SYR

Pakistan Army	3	Baloch [18], Faheem [45], Shabbir [58]
Ratnam SC	3	Channa [10], Rawme [13], Kasun [43]

Punjab Stadium, Lahore, 20-09-2007, 23:00, 300, Win Cho MYA

Regar Tad AZ	13	Makhmudov 5 [18 28 45 61 76], Abdullayev 2 [35 63], Rustamov 2 [37 54], Umarbaev [66], Barotov [74],
Transport United	0	Kholbekov [80], Rabimov [87]

Punjab Stadium, Lahore, 22-09-2007, 19:30, 800, Auda Lazim IRQ

Regar TadAZ	2	Abdullayev [65], Hakimov [68]
Pakistan Army	1	Baloch [73]

Punjab Stadium, Lahore, 22-09-2007, 22:15, 300, Al Yarimi YEM

Ratnam SC	6	Rawme [13], Channa 5 [17 69 73 82 90]
Transport United	1	Gyeltshen [42]

Punjab Stadium, Lahore, 25-09-2007, 12:00, 200, Auda Lazim IRQ

Transport United	3	Wangay 2 [5 74], Jamtsho [27]
Pakistan Army	2	Shabbir [45], Faheem [92+]

Railways Stadium, Lahore, 25-09-2007, 12:00, 100, Al Ghafary JOR

Regar TadAZ	1	Abdullayev [66]
Ratnam SC	0	

Group A	Pl	W	D	L	F	A	Pts
Regar TadAZ	3	3	0	0	16	1	**9**
Ratnam SC	3	1	1	1	9	5	4
Transport United	3	1	0	2	4	21	3
Pakistan Army	3	0	1	2	6	8	1

GROUP B

Punjab Stadium, Lahore, 21-09-2007, 19:30, 500, Al Ghafary JOR

Khemara	0	
Dordoy-Dinamo	4	Ishenbaev 2 [14 36], Krasnov 2 [34p 39]

Punjab Stadium, Lahore, 21-09-2007, 22:15, 500, Vo Minh Tri VIE

Mahendra Police	0	
Tatung	0	

Punjab Stadium, Lahore, 23-09-2007, 19:30, 500, Win Cho MYA

Tatung	0	
Khemara	1	Sokumpheak [1]

Punjab Stadium, Lahore, 23-09-2007, 22:15, 500, Vo Minh Tri MYA

Dordoy-Dinamo	3	Kudrenko [23], Krasnov 2 [33 59]
Mahendra Police	0	

Punjab Stadium, Lahore, 25-09-2007, 15:30, 200 Recho SYR

Mahendra Police	6	Anant 2 [12 79], Ramesh [16], Parbat [25], Ju Manu [30], Arjun [85]
Khemara	4	Rotha [23], Bunvichet [68p], Sokumpheak 2 [70 78]

Railways Stadium, Lahore, 25-09-2007, 15:30, 300, Al Yarimi YEM

Tatung	0	
Dordoy-Dinamo	5	Muladjanov [11], Kornilov 4 [18 63 84 89]

Group A	Pl	W	D	L	F	A	Pts
Dordoy-Dinamo	3	3	0	1	12	0	**9**
Mahendra Police	3	1	1	1	6	7	4
Khemara	3	1	0	2	5	10	3
Tatung	3	0	1	2	0	6	1

SEMI-FINALS AND FINAL

Punjab Stadium, Lahore
28-09-2007, 19:30, 1000, Recho SYR

Dordoy-Dinamo	**1 4p**
	Tetteh [21]

Valerii Kashuba - Talant Samsaliev, Ruslan Sydykov, Igor Kudrenko - Sergey Kniazev, Aibek Bokoev● (Davron Askarov 49), Valery Berezovsky, Azamat Ishenbaev, Vadim Harchenko - Andrey Krasnov● (Roman Kornilov 55), David Tetteh (Artem Muladjanov 99). Tr: Boris Podkorytov

Ratnam SC	**1 3p**
	Kasun [44]

Dammika - Rizwan, Camillus, Maduranga - Tharusa, Chathura, Izzadeen, Sanjay (Shiwanka 16) - Nadeeka●, Kasun, Channa. Tr: Mohamed Nizam Packeer Ali

Punjab Stadium, Lahore
27-09-2007, 19:30, 500, Vo Minh Tri VIE

Regar TadAZ	**1**
	Rustamov [26]

Alisher Dodov - Maruf Rustamov, Farrukh Choriev, Abdullo Umarbaev (Farkhodzon Kholbekov 78), Alisher Tuhtaev, Naim Nasirov● - Khurshed Makhmudov, Alisher Hakberdiev, Rahmonali Barotov - Mansurdzhon Hakimov (Bakhtiyor Hasanov 54), Abbos Abdullayev. Tr: Makhmadjon Khabibulloev

Mahendra Police	**2**
	Ju Manu [32], Ramesh [91+]

Ritesh - Rakesh, Dipendra●, Dipak●, Rabin● - Kunjan, Arjun●, Anant, Bhola (Roshan 46) - Ramesh, Ju Manu. Tr: Birat Krishna Shrestha

Punjab Stadium, Lahore
30-09-2007, 19:30, 2000, Auda Lazim IRQ

Dordoy-Dinamo	**2**
	Ishenbaev [8p], Kornilov [74]

Valerii Kashuba - Talant Samsaliev●, Ruslan Sydykov, Igor Kudrenko - Sergey Kniazev●, Aibek Bokoev (Davron Askarov 68), Valery Berezovsky, Azamat Ishenbaev (Marlen Kasymov 81), Vadim Harchenko - Andrey Krasnov (Roman Kornilov 54), David Tetteh. Tr: Boris Podkorytov

Mahendra Police Club	**1**
	Ju Manu [92+p]

Ritesh - Rakesh, Dipendra, Dipak●, Rabin (Ganesh 68) - Parbat, Kunjan, Arjun●, Anant - Ramesh (Roshan 46), Ju Manu●. Tr: Birat Krishna Shrestha

CAF

CONFEDERATION AFRICAINE DE FOOTBALL

The biggest trend in African football over the past decade has been the ever increasing presence of footballers from south of the Sahara in the top European leagues which has, in turn, made the national teams a much more formidible presence in international competition. The Côte d'Ivoire, Nigeria, Cameroon and even the likes of Togo have seen their national teams take on a new lease of life thanks to their European pros. Nowhere has this been more evident than in Ghana, hosts and overwhelming favourites to win the 2008 Africa Cup of Nations. But football in Africa is much less predictable than in other continents, and once again it was the unheralded Egyptians who triumphed in the final in Accra to become only the third nation successfully to defend their title. North African players have made much less of an impact in Europe which has allowed the Leagues

THE FIFA BIG COUNT OF 2006 FOR AFRICA

	Male	Female		Total
Number of players	44 940 000	1 361 000	Referees and Assistant Referees	50 000
Professionals	7 000		Admin, Coaches, Technical, Medical	580 000
Amateurs 18+	926 000		Number of clubs	12 000
Youth under 18	2 156 000		Number of teams	71 000
Unregistered	43 199 000		Clubs with women's teams	1 000
Total involved in football	46 930 000		Players as % of population	5.16%

in Egypt, Tunisia and Morocco to operate at a far higher standard than in the rest of the continent. Egypt had a team based almost entirely on the outstanding Al Ahly side that has twice won the CAF Champions League in the past three seasons. It was this unity, self-belief and team spirit that won the day for the Eyptians, 1-0 winners over Cameroon in the final. Al Ahly came agonisingly close to winning an unprecedented hat-trick of Champions League titles but lost in the 2007 final to Etoile du Sahel from Tunisia. If ever a team deserved to become African champions for the first time it was Etoile, losers in both the 2004 and 2005 finals. Their record in other African competitions such as the Cup Winners Cup, CAF Cup and CAF Confederation Cup is second to none with five titles, but the big one had always eluded them.

Confédération Africaine de Football (CAF)

PO Box 23, 3 Abdel Khalek Sarwat Street, El Hay El Motamayez, 6th October City, Egypt

Tel +20 2 8371000   Fax +20 2 8370006

info@cafonline.com   www.cafonline.com

President: HAYATOU Issa CMR   General Secretary: FAHMY Mustapha EGY

CAF Formed: 1957

CAF EXECUTIVE COMMITTEE

President: HAYATOU Issa CMR	1st Vice-President: MEMENE Seyi TOG	2nd Vice-President: OLIPHANT Molefi RSA

ORDINARY MEMBERS OF THE EXECUTIVE COMMITTEE

DIAKITE Amadou MLI	DJIBRINE Adoum CHA	ADAMU Amos Dr. NGA
RAOURAOUA Mohamed ALG	BARANSANANIYE Moses BDI	PATEL Suketu SEY
REDA Hani Abu EGY	KAMACH Thierry CTA	CAMARA Almamy Kabele GUI
	MUSABYIMANA Celestin RWA	
Co-opted: ALOULOU Slim	FIFA Exco: CHIBOUB Slim TUN	General Secretary: FAHMY Mustapha EGY

MAP OF CAF MEMBER NATIONS

AFRICAN TOURNAMENTS

CAF AFRICA CUP OF NATIONS

Year	Host Country	Winners	Score	Runners-up	Venue
1957	Sudan	Egypt	4-0	Ethiopia	Municipal, Khartoum
1959	Egypt	Egypt	2-1	Sudan	Al Ahly Stadium, Cairo
1962	Ethiopia	Ethiopia	2-0	Egypt	Haile Selassie, Addis Abeba
1963	Ghana	Ghana	3-0	Sudan	Accra Stadium, Accra
1965	Tunisia	Ghana	3-2	Tunisia	Zouiten, Tunis
1968	Ethiopia	Congo Kinshasa	1-0	Ghana	Haile Selassie, Addis Abeba
1970	Sudan	Sudan	1-0	Ghana	Municipal, Khartoum
1972	Cameroon	Congo	3-2	Mali	Omnisports, Yaoundé
1974	Egypt	Zaire	2-2 2-0	Zambia	International, Cairo
1976	Ethiopia	Morocco	1-1	Guinea	Addis Abeba Stadium
1978	Ghana	Ghana	2-0	Uganda	Accra Stadium, Accra
1980	Nigeria	Nigeria	3-0	Algeria	Surulere, Lagos
1982	Libya	Ghana	1-1 7-6p	Libya	11th June Stadium, Tripoli
1984	Côte d'Ivoire	Cameroon	3-1	Nigeria	Houphouët Boigny, Abidjan
1986	Egypt	Egypt	0-0 5-4p	Cameroon	International, Cairo
1988	Morocco	Cameroon	1-0	Nigeria	Mohamed V, Casablanca
1990	Algeria	Algeria	1-0	Nigeria	Stade Olympique, Algiers
1992	Senegal	Côte d'Ivoire	0-0 11-10p	Ghana	Stade de l'Amite, Dakar
1994	Tunisia	Nigeria	2-1	Zambia	El Menzah, Tunis
1996	South Africa	South Africa	2-0	Tunisia	Soccer City, Johannesburg
1998	Burkina Faso	Egypt	2-0	South Africa	Stade du 4 Août, Ouagadougou
2000	Ghana/Nigeria	Cameroon	2-2 4-3p	Nigeria	Surulere, Lagos
2002	Mali	Cameroon	0-0 3-2p	Senegal	Stade du 26 Mars, Bamako
2004	Tunisia	Tunisia	2-1	Morocco	Rades, Tunis
2006	Egypt	Egypt	0-0 4-2p	Côte d'Ivoire	International, Cairo
2008	Ghana	Egypt	1-0	Cameroon	Ohene Djan, Accra

CAF AFRICA CUP OF NATIONS MEDALS TABLE

	Country	G	S	B	F	SF
1	Egypt	6	1	3	6	10
2	Ghana	4	3	1	7	7
3	Cameroon	4	2	1	6	8
4	Nigeria	2	4	6	6	11
5	Zaire	2		1	2	4
6	Tunisia	1	2	1	3	5
7	Sudan	1	2	1	3	2
8	Côte d'Ivoire	1	1	4	2	7
9	Algeria	1	1	2	2	5
10	South Africa	1	1		2	3
11	Morocco	1	1	1	1	4
12	Ethiopia	1	1	1		3
13	Congo	1			1	2
14	Zambia		2	3	2	5
15	Mali		1		1	4
16	Senegal		1		1	3
17	Uganda		1		1	2
18	Libya		1		1	1
19	Guinea		1			
20	Burkina Faso					1
		26	26	26	48	87

This table represents the Gold (winners), Silver (runners-up) and Bronze (semi-finalists) placings of nations in the Africa Cup of Nations, along with the number of appearances in the final and semi-finals.

Thirteen different countries have triumphed at the 25 CAF Africa Cup of Nations tournaments and this lack of domination by one country and the fact that it is played every two years means the competition gives a very good indication of the footballing prowess on the continent. The great teams from the past have all managed to inscribe their name on the trophy - Egypt team of the late 1950s; Ghana at the time of independence in the 1960s; Zaire in the early 1970s; Cameroon in the 1980s; and the Nigerians of the mid-1990s. Fifteen nations have hosted the tournament, which has grown from a three team round robin in the early years into a 16 team spectacular. For the 2006 edition the FIFA World Cup qualifiers doubled up as Nations Cup qualifiers to ease the fixture load and this remains the plan for those editions played in future FIFA World Cup years. In 2006 Egypt hosted the tournament for the fourth time and won a record fifth title. Ghana missed the opportunity to win a fifth title when they hosted the 2008 tournament and it was Egypt who triumphed - their third title in six tournaments. Remarkably the other previous joint record holders, Cameroon, have won all of their four titles away from home.

CAF AFRICAN WOMEN'S CHAMPIONSHIP

Year	Host Country	Winners	Score	Runners-up	Venue
1991		Nigeria	2-0 4-0	Cameroon	
1995		Nigeria	4-1 7-1	South Africa	
1998	Nigeria	Nigeria	2-0	Ghana	Abeokuta
2000	South Africa	Nigeria	2-0	South Africa	Johannesburg
2002	Nigeria	Nigeria	2-0	Ghana	Lagos
2004	South Africa	Nigeria	5-0	Cameroon	Johannesburg
2006	Nigeria	Nigeria	1-0	Ghana	Warri

With women's football not particulary widespread in Africa, the chance of a place in the FIFA Women's World Cup provided the spur for CAF to introduce a women's Championship. To date Nigeria has won all seven tournaments played with Ghana losing in the final three times.

AFRICAN YOUTH CHAMPIONSHIP

Year	Host Country	Winners	Score	Runners-up	Venue
1979		Algeria	2-1 2-3	Guinea	Algiers, Conakry
1981		Egypt	1-1 2-0	Cameroon	Douala, Cairo
1983		Nigeria	2-2 2-1	Côte d'Ivoire	Abidjan, Lagos
1985		Nigeria	1-1 2-1	Tunisia	Tunis, Lagos
1987		Nigeria	2-1 3-0	Togo	Lomé, Lagos
1989		Nigeria	2-1 2-0	Mali	Bamako, Lagos
1991	Egypt	Egypt	2-1	Côte d'Ivoire	Cairo
1993	Mauritius	Ghana	2-0	Cameroon	Bellevue
1995	Nigeria	Cameroon	4-0	Burundi	Lagos
1997	Morocco	Morocco	1-0	South Africa	Meknès
1999	Ghana	Ghana	1-0	Nigeria	Accra
2001	Ethiopia	Angola	2-0	Ghana	Addis Abeba
2003	Burkina Faso	Egypt	4-3	Côte d'Ivoire	Ouagadougou
2005	Benin	Nigeria	2-0	Egypt	Cotonou
2007	Congo	Congo	1-0	Nigeria	Brazzaville

AFRICAN U–17 CHAMPIONSHIP

Year	Host Country	Winners	Score	Runners-up	Venue
1995	Mali	Ghana	3-1	Nigeria	Bamako
1997	Botswana	Egypt	1-0	Mali	Gaborone
1999	Guinea	Ghana	3-1	Burkina Faso	Conakry
2001	Seychelles	Nigeria	3-0	Burkina Faso	Victoria
2003	Swaziland	Cameroon	1-0	Sierra Leone	Mbabane
2005	Gambia	Gambia	1-0	Ghana	Bakau
2007	Togo	Nigeria	1-0	Togo	Lome

AFRICAN WOMEN'S U–19 CHAMPIONSHIP

Year	Host Country	Winners	Score	Runners-up	Venue
2002		Nigeria	6-0 3-2	South Africa	
2004		Nigeria	1-0 0-0	South Africa	

FOOTBALL TOURNAMENT OF THE AFRICAN GAMES

Year	Host Country	Winners	Score	Runners-up	Venue
1965	Congo	Congo	0-0 †	Mali	Brazzaville
1973	Nigeria	Nigeria	2-0	Guinea	Lagos
1978	Algeria	Algeria	1-0	Nigeria	Algiers
1987	Kenya	Egypt	1-0	Kenya	Nairobi
1991	Egypt	Cameroon	1-0	Tunisia	Cairo
1995	Zimbabwe	Egypt	3-1	Zimbabwe	Harare
1999	South Africa	Cameroon	0-0 4-3p	Zambia	Johannesburg
2003	Nigeria	Cameroon	2-0	Nigeria	Abuja
2007	Algeria	Cameroon	1-0	Guinea	Algiers

† Decided on number of corner-kicks awarded. Congo won 7-2

WOMEN'S FOOTBALL TOURNAMENT OF THE AFRICAN GAMES

Year	Host Country	Winners	Score	Runners-up	Venue
2003	Nigeria	Nigeria	1-0	South Africa	Abuja
2007	Algeria	Nigeria	4-0	South Africa	Algiers

CECAFA CUP

Year	Host Country	Winners	Score	Runners-up	Venue
1973	Uganda	Uganda	2-1	Tanzania	
1974	Tanzania	Tanzania	1-1 5-3p	Uganda	
1975	Zambia	Kenya	0-0 5-4p	Malawi	
1976	Zanzibar	Uganda	2-0	Zambia	
1977	Somalia	Uganda	0-0 5-3p	Zambia	
1978	Malawi	Malawi	3-2	Zambia	
1979	Kenya	Malawi	3-2	Kenya	
1980	Sudan	Sudan	1-0	Tanzania	
1981	Tanzania	Kenya	1-0	Tanzania	
1982	Uganda	Kenya	1-1 5-3p	Uganda	
1983	Kenya	Kenya	1-0	Zimbabwe	
1984	Uganda	Zambia	0-0 3-0p	Malawi	Kampala
1985	Zimbabwe	Zimbabwe	2-0	Kenya	Rufaro, Harare
1986	Sudan	Not held			
1987	Ethiopia	Ethiopia	1-1 5-4p	Zimbabwe	
1988	Malawi	Malawi	3-1	Zambia	
1989	Kenya	Uganda	3-3 2-1	Malawi	Nyayo, Nairobi
1990	Zanzibar	Uganda	2-0	Sudan	
1991	Uganda	Zambia	2-0	Kenya	Kampala
1992	Tanzania	Uganda	1-0	Tanzania	Mwanza
1993	Uganda	Not held			
1994	Kenya	Tanzania	2-2 4-3p	Uganda	Nairobi
1995	Uganda	Zanzibar	1-0	Uganda	
1996	Sudan	Uganda	1-0	Sudan	
1997		Not held			
1998	Rwanda	Not held			
1999	Rwanda	Rwanda B	3-1	Kenya	Amahoro, Kigali
2000	Uganda	Uganda	2-0	Uganda B	Nakivubo, Kampala
2001	Rwanda	Ethiopia	2-1	Kenya	Amahoro, Kigali
2002	Tanzania	Kenya	3-2	Tanzania	Memorial, Arusha
2003	Sudan	Uganda	2-0	Rwanda	Khartoum
2004	Ethiopia	Ethiopia	3-0	Burundi	Addis Abeba
2005	Rwanda	Ethiopia	1-0	Rwanda	Amahoro, Kigali
2006	Ethiopia	Zambia	0-0 11-10p	Sudan	Addis Abeba
2007	Tanzania	Sudan	2-2 4-2p	Rwanda	Dar es Salaam

COSAFA CUP

Year	Host Country	Winners	Score	Runners-up	Venue
1997	Home and away	Zambia	1-1	Namibia	Windhoek
1998	Home and away	Zambia	1-0	Zimbabwe	Harare
1999	Home and away	Angola	1-0 1-1	Namibia	Luanda & Windhoek
2000	Home and away	Zimbabwe	3-0 3-0	Lesotho	Maseru & Bulawayo
2001	Home and away	Angola	0-0 1-0	Zimbabwe	Luanda & Harare
2002	Home and away	South Africa	3-1 1-0	Malawi	Blantyre & Durban
2003	Home and away	Zimbabwe	2-1 2-0	Malawi	Blantyre & Harare
2004	Home and away	Angola	0-0 5-4p	Zambia	Lusaka
2005	Home and away	Zimbabwe	1-0	Zambia	Mafikeng
2006	Home and away	Zambia	2-0	Angola	Lusaka
2007	Home and away	South Africa	0-0 4-3p	Zambia	Bloemfontein

COUPE CEMAC

Year	Host Country	Winners	Score	Runners-up	Venue
2003	Congo	Cameroon	3-2	Central African Rep.	Brazzaville
2005	Gabon	Cameroon	1-0	Chad	Libreville
2006	Equat. Guinea	Equatorial Guinea	1-1 4-2p	Cameroon	Bata
2007	Chad	Congo	1-0	Gabon	N'Djamena
2008	Cameroon	Cameroon	3-0	Congo	Yaounde

COPA AMILCAR CABRAL

Year	Host Country	Winners	Score	Runners-up	Venue
1979	Guinea-Bissau	Senegal	1-0	Mali	Bissau
1980	Gambia	Senegal	1-0	Gambia	Banjul
1981	Mali	Guinea	0-0 6-5p	Mali	Bamako
1982	Cape Verde	Guinea	3-0	Senegal	Praia
1983	Mauritania	Senegal	3-0	Guinea-Bissau	Nouakchott
1984	Sierra Leone	Senegal	0-0 5-3p	Sierra Leone	Freetown
1985	Gambia	Senegal	1-0	Gambia	Banjul
1986	Senegal	Senegal	3-1	Sierra Leone	Dakar
1987	Guinea	Guinea	1-0	Mali	Conakry
1988	Guinea-Bissau	Guinea	3-2	Mali	Bissau
1989	Mali	Mali	3-0	Guinea	Bamako
1991	Senegal	Senegal	1-0	Cape Verde Islands	Dakar
1993	Sierra Leone	Sierra Leone	2-0	Senegal	Freetown
1995	Mauritania	Sierra Leone	0-0 4-2p	Mauritania	Nouakchott
1997	Gambia	Mali	1-0	Senegal	Banjul
2000	Cape Verde	Cape Verde Islands	1-0	Senegal	Praia
2001	Mali	Senegal	3-1	Gambia	Bamako
2005	Guinea	Guinea	1-0	Senegal	Conakry
2007	Guinea-Bissau	Mali	2-1	Cape Verde Islands	Bissau

TOURNOI DE L'UEMOA

Year	Host Country	Winners	Score	Runners-up	Venue
2007	Burkina Faso	Côte d'Ivoire	2-0	Niger	Ouagadougou

There is a long and rich history of regional tournaments in Africa dating back to 1926 when William Gossage sponsored an annual competition between Kenya and Uganda. CECAFA – the Confederation of East and Central African Football Associations – organises a tournament dating back to 1973 while the Southern African nations have an annual tournament run by COSAFA - the Confederation of Southern African Football Associations. The situation in West Africa has been much more fragmented, although the Copa Amilcar Cabral has stood the test of time unlike many other tournaments in the region. The Coupe CEMAC is a recent addition. Introduced in 2003 entries come from the member states of the Communauté Economique et Monétaire de l'Afrique Central. In 2007 the first edition of the Tournoi de l'UEMOA was held with participants coming from the francophone Union Economique et Monétaire Ouest-Africaine.

CAF CHAMPIONS LEAGUE

Year	Winners	Country	Score	Country	Runners-up
1965	Oryx Douala	CMR	2-1	MLI	Stade Malien
1966	Stade Abidjan	CIV	1-3 4-1	MLI	AS Real Bamako
1967	Tout Puissant Englebert	COD	1-1 2-2	GHA	Asante Kotoko
1968	Tout Puissant Englebert	COD	5-0 1-4	TOG	Etoile Filante
1969	Al Ismaili	EGY	2-2 3-1	COD	Tout Puissant Englebert
1970	Asante Kotoko	GHA	1-1 2-1	COD	Tout Puissant Englebert
1971	Canon Yaoundé	CMR	0-3 2-0 1-0	GHA	Asante Kotoko
1972	Hafia FC Conakry	GUI	4-2 3-2	UGA	Simba FC
1973	AS Vita Kinshasa	COD	2-4 3-0	GHA	Asante Kotoko
1974	CARA Brazzaville	CGO	4-2 2-1	EGY	Mehalla Al Kubra
1975	Hafia FC Conakry	GUI	1-0 2-1	NGA	Enugu Rangers
1976	Mouloudia d'Algiers	ALG	3-0 0-3 4-1p	GUI	Hafia FC Conakry
1977	Hafia FC Conakry	GUI	1-0 3-2	GHA	Hearts of Oak
1978	Canon Yaoundé	CMR	0-0 2-0	GUI	Hafia FC Conakry
1979	Union Douala	CMR	0-1 1-0 5-3p	GHA	Hearts of Oak
1980	Canon Yaoundé	CMR	2-2 3-0	COD	AS Bilima
1981	JE Tizi-Ouzou	ALG	4-0 1-0	COD	AS Vita Kinshasa
1982	Al Ahly Cairo	EGY	3-0 1-1	GHA	Asante Kotoko
1983	Asante Kotoko	GHA	0-0 1-0	EGY	Al Ahly Cairo
1984	Zamalek	EGY	2-0 1-0	NGA	Shooting Stars
1985	FAR Rabat	MAR	5-2 1-1	COD	AS Bilima
1986	Zamalek	EGY	2-0 0-2 4-2p	CIV	Africa Sports
1987	Al Ahly Cairo	EGY	0-0 2-0	SUD	Al Hilal
1988	Entente Setif	ALG	0-1 4-0	NGA	Iwuanyanwu Owerri
1989	Raja Casablanca	MAR	1-0 0-1 4-2p	ALG	Mouloudia d'Oran
1990	JS Kabylie	ALG	1-0 0-1 5-3p	ZAM	Nkana Red Devils
1991	Club Africain	TUN	5-1 1-1	UGA	Nakivubo Villa
1992	Wydad Casablanca	MAR	2-0 0-0	SUD	Al Hilal
1993	Zamalek	EGY	0-0 0-0 7-6p	GHA	Asante Kotoko
1994	Espérance Tunis	TUN	0-0 3-1	EGY	Zamalek
1995	Orlando Pirates	RSA	2-2 1-0	CIV	ASEC Mimosas
1996	Zamalek	EGY	1-2 2-1 4-2p	NGA	Shooting Stars
1997	Raja Casablanca	MAR	0-1 1-0 5-4p	GHA	Obuasi Goldfields
1998	ASEC Mimosas	CIV	0-0 4-1	ZIM	Dynamos
1999	Raja Casablanca	MAR	0-0 0-0 4-3p	TUN	Espérance Tunis
2000	Hearts of Oak	GHA	2-1 3-1	TUN	Espérance Tunis
2001	Al Ahly Cairo	EGY	1-1 3-0	RSA	Mamelodi Sundowns
2002	Zamalek	EGY	0-0 1-0	MAR	Raja Casablanca
2003	Enyimba	NGA	2-0 0-1	EGY	Al Ismaili
2004	Enyimba	NGA	1-2 2-1 5-3p	TUN	Etoile du Sahel
2005	Al Ahly Cairo	EGY	0-0 3-0	TUN	Etoile du Sahel
2006	Al Ahly Cairo	EGY	1-1 1-0	TUN	CS Sfaxien
2007	Etoile du Sahel	TUN	0-0 3-1	EGY	Al Ahly Cairo

Previously known the African Cup of Champion Clubs, the CAF Champions League is unpredictable and never short of controversy, but it remains hugely entertaining despite the growing number of African players who will never compete in it thanks to moves to Europe at increasingly young ages. The heart of the rivalry in the tournament lies between the Arab North African countries and the sub-Saharan countries. Until the 1980s the latter held the upper hand but for 17 years between 1981 and 1997 only Ghana's Asante Kotoko and Orlando Pirates from South Africa managed to prise the Cup from the north. Since 1995 the honours have been more evenly spread. It has proved difficult for any club, however, to maintain a consistant presence in the tournament with the possible exception of the two Egyptian giants and record title holders Al Ahly and Zamalek. In 2004 Enyimba became only the second club to retain the title and the first since 1968. They were also the 19th different club from 13 different countries to have won the title. No other continent has such a range of winners. Amongst the early powers were clubs from Cameroon and Guinea, notably three times winners Canon Yaoundé and Hafia Conakry. Before the 1980s, North African clubs won the tournament just twice. Since the triumph of JS Kabylie (then called Tizi-Ouzou) it has been a very different story. Al Ahly won the cup for the first time in 1982 and had they not decided to defend their Cup Winners Cup title twice in the mid 1980s, they may well have won more than their current haul of five titles. They were clearly the best team on the continent and having suceeded in their aim of a hat trick of titles in the Cup Winners Cup, they then won the Champions Cup to make it four titles in a row and five in six seasons. Their next triumph was not until 2001, leaving the field open for rivals Zamalek. They won a record fourth title in 1996 with Ismail Youssef part of the squad in all four campaigns and then added a fifth in 2002. Raja Casablanca also made their mark, winning three titles in eleven years thanks largely to their excellent youth set up, helping to establish Morocco as the second most successful nation in the tournament after Egypt. In 1997 the tournament was rebranded as the CAF Champions League although the group stage has always been held in the closing stages of the competition rather than early on. In 2004, again following the European example, a second club from the top nations was allowed entry. The turn of the century saw Al Ahly emerge once again as the most powerful club on the continent and in 2006 they matched Zamalek's five titles.

CAF CONFEDERATION CUP

Year	Winners	Country	Score	Country	Runners-up
2004	Hearts of Oak	GHA	1-1 1-1 8-7p	GHA	Asante Kotoko
2005	FAR Rabat	MAR	0-1 3-0	NGA	Dolphin Port Harcourt
2006	Etoile du Sahel	TUN	1-1 0-0	MAR	FAR Rabat
2007	CS Sfaxien	TUN	4-2	1-0	Al Merreikh

CAF CUP WINNERS' CUP

Year	Winners	Country	Score	Country	Runners-up
1975	Tonnerre Yaoundé	CMR	1-0 4-1	CIV	Stella Abidjan
1976	Shooting Stars	NGA	4-1 0-1	CMR	Tonnerre Yaoundé
1977	Enugu Rangers	NGA	4-1 1-1	CMR	Canon Yaoundé
1978	Horoya AC Conakry	GUI	3-1 2-1	ALG	MA Hussein-Dey
1979	Canon Yaoundé	CMR	2-0 6-0	KEN	Gor Mahia
1980	TP Mazembe	COD	3-1 1-0	CIV	Africa Sports
1981	Union Douala	CMR	2-1 0-0	NGA	Stationery Stores
1982	Al Mokaoulum	EGY	2-0 2-0	ZAM	Power Dynamos
1983	Al Mokaoulum	EGY	1-0 0-0	TOG	Agaza Lomé
1984	Al Ahly Cairo	EGY	1-0 0-1 4-2p	CMR	Canon Yaoundé
1985	Al Ahly Cairo	EGY	2-0 0-1	NGA	Leventis United
1986	Al Ahly Cairo	EGY	3-0 0-2	GAB	AS Sogara
1987	Gor Mahia	KEN	2-2 1-1	TUN	Espérance Tunis
1988	CA Bizerte	TUN	0-0 1-0	NGA	Ranchers Bees
1989	Al Merreikh	SUD	1-0 0-0	NGA	Bendel United
1990	BCC Lions	NGA	3-0 1-1	TUN	Club Africain
1991	Power Dynamos	ZAM	2-3 3-1	NGA	BCC Lions
1992	Africa Sports	CIV	1-1 4-0	BDI	Vital'O
1993	Al Ahly Cairo	EGY	1-1 1-0	CIV	Africa Sports
1994	DC Motema Pembe	COD	2-2 3-0	KEN	Kenya Breweries
1995	JS Kabylie	ALG	1-1 2-1	NGA	Julius Berger
1996	Al Mokaoulum	EGY	0-0 4-0	COD	Sodigraf
1997	Etoile du Sahel	TUN	2-0 0-1	MAR	FAR Rabat
1998	Espérance Tunis	TUN	3-1 1-1	ANG	Primeiro Agosto
1999	Africa Sports	CIV	1-0 1-1	TUN	Club Africain
2000	Zamalek	EGY	4-1 0-2	CMR	Canon Yaoundé
2001	Kaiser Chiefs	RSA	1-1 1-0	ANG	Inter Luanda
2002	Wydad Casablanca	MAR	1-0 1-2	GHA	Asante Kotoko
2003	Etoile du Sahel	TUN	0-2 3-0	NGA	Julius Berger

Discontinued after the 2003 tournament and replaced by the CAF Confederation Cup

CAF CUP

Year	Winners	Country	Score	Country	Runners-up
1992	Shooting Stars	NGA	0-0 3-0	UGA	Nakivubo Villa
1993	Stella Abidjan	CIV	0-0 2-0	TAN	SC Simba
1994	Bendel Insurance	NGA	0-1 3-0	ANG	Primeiro de Maio
1995	Etoile du Sahel	TUN	0-0 2-0	GUI	Kaloum Star
1996	Kawkab Marrakech	MAR	1-3 2-0	TUN	Etoile du Sahel
1997	Esperance Tunis	TUN	0-1 2-0	ANG	Petro Atlético
1998	CS Sfaxien	TUN	1-0 3-0	SEN	ASC Jeanne d'Arc
1999	Etoile du Sahel	TUN	1-0 1-2	MAR	Wydad Casablanca
2000	JS Kabylie	ALG	1-1 0-0	EGY	Al Ismaili
2001	JS Kabylie	ALG	1-2 1-0	TUN	Etoile du Sahel
2002	JS Kabylie	ALG	4-0 0-1	CMR	Tonnerre Youndé
2003	Raja Casablanca	MAR	2-0 0-0	CMR	Cotonsport Garoua

Discontinued after the 2003 tournament and replaced by the CAF Confederation Cup

With the decision to allow more than one team from each country into the CAF Champions League, CAF decided in 2003 to discarded the Cup Winners' Cup and the CAF Cup in favour of a 'best of the rest' tournament - the CAF Confederation Cup. Teams knocked out in early rounds of the Champions League enter the Confederation Cup at the intermediate stage.

CECAFA CLUB CHAMPIONSHIP

Year	Winners	Country	Score	Country	Runners-up
1974	Simba SC	TAN	1-0 †	KEN	Abaluhya FC
1975	Young Africans	TAN	2-0	TAN	Simba SC
1976	Luo Union	KEN	2-1	TAN	Young Africans
1977	Luo Union	KEN	2-1	SOM	Horsed
1978	Kamapala City Council	UGA	0-0 3-2p	TAN	Simba SC
1979	Abaluhya FC	KEN	1-0	UGA	Kampala City Council
1980	Gor Mahia	KEN	3-2	KEN	Abaluhya FC
1981	Gor Mahia	KEN	1-0	TAN	Simba SC
1982	AFC Leopards	KEN	1-0	ZIM	Rio Tinto
1983	AFC Leopards	KEN	2-1	MWI	Admarc Tigers
1984	AFC Leopards	KEN	2-1	KEN	Gor Mahia
1985	Gor Mahia	KEN	2-0	KEN	AFC Leopards
1986	Al Merreikh	SUD	2-2 4-2p	TAN	Young Africans
1987	Nakivubo Villa	UGA	1-0	SUD	Al Merreikh
1988	Kenya Breweries	KEN	2-0	SUD	Al Merreikh
1989	Kenya Breweries	KEN	3-0	TAN	Coastal Union
1990	Not held				
1991	Simba SC	TAN	3-0	UGA	Nikivubo Villa
1992	Simba SC	TAN	1-1 5-4p	TAN	Young Africans
1993	Young Africans	TAN	2-1	UGA	Nakivubo Villa
1994	Al Merreikh	SUD	2-1	UGA	Express FC
1995	Simba SC	TAN	1-1 5-3p	UGA	Express FC
1996	Simba SC	TAN	1-0	RWA	APR FC
1997	AFC Leopards	KEN	1-0	KEN	Kenya Breweries
1998	Rayyon Sport	RWA	2-1	ZAN	Mlandege
1999	Young Africans	TAN	1-1 4-1p	UGA	SC Villa
2000	Tusker FC	KEN	3-1	RWA	APR FC
2001	Tusker FC	KEN	0-0 3-0p	KEN	Oserian
2002	Simba SC	TAN	1-0	BDI	Prince Louis
2003	SC Villa	UGA	1-0	TAN	Simba SC
2004	APR FC	RWA	3-1	KEN	Ulinzi Stars
2005	SC Villa	UGA	3-0	RWA	APR FC
2006	Police FC	UGA	2-1	TAN	Moro United
2007	APR FC	RWA	2-1	UGA	URA Kampala
2008	Tusker	KEN	2-1	UGA	URA Kampala

CAF CHAMPIONS LEAGUE MEDALS TABLE

	Country	G	S	B	F	SF
1	Egypt	11	5	8	16	24
2	Morocco	5	1	3	6	7
3	Cameroon	5		6	5	11
4	Algeria	4	1	4	5	9
5	Ghana	3	8	6	11	15
6	Congo DR	3	5	5	8	13
7	Tunisia	3	5	4	8	10
8	Guinea	3	2	3	5	8
9	Nigeria	2	4	7	6	13
10	Côte d'Ivoire	2	2	6	4	9
11	South Africa	1	1	1	2	3
12	Congo	1			1	1
13	Sudan		2	2	2	4
14	Mali		2	1	2	3
	Uganda		2	1	2	3
16	Zambia		1	6	1	7
17	Togo		1	3	1	4
18	Zimbabwe		1		1	
19	Senegal			5		5
20	Ethiopia			2		2
	Kenya			2		2
22	Angola			1		1
	Libya			1		1
	Tanzania			1		1
	(including 2007 tournament)	43	43	78	86	156

This table represents the Gold (winners), Silver (runners-up) and Bronze (semi-finalists) placings of clubs representing the above countries in the CAF Champions League, along with the number of appearances in the final and semi-finals inclusive of 2006

CAF CHAMPIONS LEAGUE MEDALS TABLE

	Country		G	S	B
1	Al Ahly Cairo	EGY	5	2	2
2	Zamalek	EGY	5	1	2
3	Hafia FC Conakry	GUI	3	2	
4	Raja Casablanca	MAR	3	1	1
5	Canon Yaoundé	CMR	3		2
6	Asante Kotoko	GHA	2	5	3
7	TP Mazembe	ZAI	2	2	2
8	Jeunesse Sportive Kabylie	ALG	2		2
9	Enyimba	NGA	2		
10	Esperance Tunis	TUN	1	2	3
11	Hearts of Oak	GHA	1	2	1
12	Etoile du Sahel	TUN	1	2	
13	ASEC Mimosas	CIV	1	1	5
14	Ismaily	EGY	1	1	3
15	AS Vita Club Kinshasa	ZAI	1	1	1
16	FAR Rabat	MAR	1		2
17	Oryx Douala	CMR	1		1
	Union Douala	CMR	1		1
19	CARA Brazzaville	CGO	1		
	Mouloudia Alger	ALG	1		
	Club Africain	TUN	1		
	Entente Setif	ALG	1		
	Orlando Pirates	RSA	1		
	Stade Abidjan	CIV	1		
	Wydad Casablanca	MAR	1		

CAF CHAMPIONS LEAGUE MEDALS TABLE

	Country		G	S	B
26	Al Hilal	SUD		2	2
27	AS Bilima	ZAI		2	
	Shooting Stars	NGR		2	
29	Nkana Red Devils	ZAM		1	5
30	Enugu Rangers	NGR		1	3
31	Iwuanyanwu Owerri	NGR		1	2
32	Ghazl Al Mehalla	EGY		1	1
	Mouloudia Oran	ALG		1	1
	CS Sfaxien	TUN		1	1
35	Africa Sports	CIV		1	
	Dynamos	ZIM		1	
	Etoile Filante	TOG		1	
	Nakivubo Villa	UGA		1	
	AS Real Bamako	MLI		1	
	Obuasi Goldfields	GHA		1	
	Mamelodi Sundowns	RSA		1	
	Simba FC	UGA		1	
	Stade Malien	MLI		1	
44	US Goree	SEN			2
	AS Kaloum Star	GUI			2
	Lomé I	TOG			2
	Jeanne d'Arc	SEN			2
48	Bendel Insurance	NGR			1
	Kenya Breweries	KEN			1
	Cotton Club	ETH			1
	ASC Diaraf	SEN			1
	Djoliba AC	MLI			1
	Express FC	UGA			1
	Great Olympics	GHA			1
	CS Imana	ZAI			1
	Al Ittihad	LBY			1
	Kakimbo FC	GUI			1
	AFC Leopards	KEN			1
	Leopard Douala	CMR			1
	FC Lupopo	ZAI			1
	Mufulira Wanderers	ZAM			1
	Petro Atlético	ANG			1
	Real Republicans	GHA			1
	St. Georges	ETH			1
	Semassi Sokode	TOG			1
	SC Simba	TAN			1
	Stationery Stores	NGR			1
	Tonnerre Yaoundé	CMR			1
	USM Alger	ALG			1
	(including 2007 tournament)		43	43	78

CAF AFRICA CUP OF NATIONS GHANA 2008 QUALIFYING TOURNAMENT

GROUP 1		PL	W	D	L	F	A	PTS		CIV	GAB	MAD
1	Côte d'Ivoire	CIV	4	3	1	0	13	0	10			5-0	5-0
2	Gabon	GAB	4	2	1	1	6	5	7		0-0		4-0
3	Madagascar	MAD	4	0	0	4	0	14	0		0-3	0-2	

GROUP 2		PL	W	D	L	F	A	PTS	EGY	MTN	BDI	BOT
1	Egypt	EGY	6	3	3	0	9	2	12		3-0	4-1	1-0
2	Mauritania	MTN	6	2	1	3	9	10	7	1-1		2-1	4-0
3	Burundi	BDI	6	2	1	3	6	8	7	0-0	3-1		1-0
4	Botswana	BOT	6	2	1	3	3	7	7	0-0	2-1	1-0	

GROUP 3		PL	W	D	L	F	A	PTS	NGA	UGA	NIG	LES
1	Nigeria	NGA	6	5	0	1	10	3	15		1-0	2-0	2-0
2	Uganda	UGA	6	3	2	1	8	3	11	2-1		3-1	3-0
3	Niger	NIG	6	1	1	4	5	11	4	1-3	0-0		2-0
4	Lesotho	LES	6	1	1	4	3	9	4	0-1	0-0	3-1	

GROUP 4		PL	W	D	L	F	A	PTS	SUD	TUN	SEY	MRI
1	Sudan	SUD	6	5	0	1	13	4	15		3-2	3-0	3-0
2	Tunisia	TUN	6	4	1	1	12	3	13	1-0		4-0	2-0
3	Seychelles	SEY	6	1	1	4	3	14	4	0-2	0-3		2-1
4	Mauritius	MRI	6	0	2	4	3	10	2	1-2	0-0	1-1	

GROUP 5		PL	W	D	L	F	A	PTS	CMR	EQG	RWA	LBR
1	Cameroon	CAM	6	5	0	1	13	4	15		3-0	2-1	3-1
2	Equatorial Guinea	EQG	6	3	1	2	6	7	10	1-0		3-1	2-1
3	Rwanda	RWA	6	2	0	4	10	11	6	0-3	2-0		4-0
4	Liberia	LBR	6	1	1	4	6	13	4	1-2	0-0	3-2	

GROUP 6		PL	W	D	L	F	A	PTS	ANG	ERI	KEN	SWZ
1	Angola	ANG	6	4	1	1	16	5	13		6-1	3-1	3-0
2	Eritrea	ERI	6	2	3	1	5	8	9	1-1		1-0	0-0
3	Kenya	KEN	6	2	1	3	6	7	7	2-1	1-2		2-0
4	Swaziland	SWZ	6	0	3	3	0	7	3	0-2	0-0	0-0	

GROUP 7		PL	W	D	L	F	A	PTS	SEN	MOZ	TAN	BFA
1	Senegal	SEN	6	3	2	1	12	3	11		2-0	4-0	5-1
2	Mozambique	MOZ	6	2	3	1	5	4	9	0-0		0-0	3-0
3	Tanzania	TAN	6	2	2	2	4	7	8	1-1	0-1		2-1
4	Burkina Faso	BFA	6	1	1	4	5	12	4	1-0	1-1	0-1	

GROUP 8		PL	W	D	L	F	A	PTS	GUI	ALG	GAM	CPV
1	Guinea	GUI	6	3	2	1	10	3	11		0-0	2-2	4-0
2	Algeria	ALG	6	2	2	2	6	6	8	0-2		1-0	2-0
3	Gambia	GAM	6	2	2	2	6	6	8	0-2	2-1		2-0
4	Cape Verde Islands	CPV	6	1	2	3	3	10	5	1-0	2-2	0-0	

GROUP 9		PL	W	D	L	F	A	PTS	MLI	BEN	TOG	SLE
1	Mali	MLI	6	3	3	0	10	1	12		1-1	1-0	6-0
2	Benin	BEN	6	3	2	1	10	4	11	0-0		4-1	2-0
3	Togo	TOG	6	3	0	3	7	9	9	0-2	2-1		3-1
4	Sierra Leone	SLE	6	0	1	5	1	14	1	0-0	0-2	0-1	

	GROUP 10		PL	W	D	L	F	A	PTS	NAM	COD	LBY	ETH
1	Namibia	NAM	6	3	1	2	9	8	10		1-1	1-0	1-0
2	Congo DR	COD	6	2	3	1	8	6	9	3-2		1-1	2-0
3	Libya	LBY	6	2	2	2	7	6	8	2-1	1-1		3-1
4	Ethiopia	ETH	6	2	0	4	5	9	6	2-3	1-0	1-0	

	GROUP 11		PL	W	D	L	F	A	PTS	ZAM	RSA	CGO	CHA
1	Zambia	ZAM	6	3	2	1	9	3	11		0-1	3-0	1-1
2	South Africa	RSA	6	3	2	1	10	4	11	1-3		0-0	4-0
3	Congo	CGO	6	1	4	1	5	6	7	0-0	1-1		3-1
4	Chad	CHA	6	0	2	4	3	14	2	0-2	0-3	1-1	

	GROUP 12		PL	W	D	L	F	A	PTS	MAR	ZIM	MWI
1	Morocco	MAR	4	3	1	0	6	1	10		2-0	2-0
2	Zimbabwe	ZIM	4	1	1	2	4	5	4	1-1		3-1
3	Malawi	MWI	4	1	0	3	2	6	3	0-1	1-0	

MATCH DETAILS

GROUP 1

Libreville
2-09-2006, Diatta SEN

Gabon   **4**
Antchouet [40], Cousin [67p], Nzigou 2 [70] [71]

Didier Ovono - Paul Kessany (Thierry Issiemou 69), Ernest Akouassaga●, Arsene do Marcolino (Rodrigue Moudounga 85), Thierry Moyouma, Georges Ambourouet●, Eric Mouloungui, Cedric Moubamba, Dieudonne Londo, Henri Antchouet (Shiva Nzigou 69), Daniel Cousin. Tr: Alain Giresse

Madagascar   **0**

Emamy David Randrianasoso - Jimmy Radafison, Valentin Mazinot●, Leonard Baraka●, Yves Xavier Ianomenzanjanahary, Guy Patrick Rene Raberanto, Damien Mahavony (Stephan Praxis Rabemananjara 72), Rija Juvence Rakotomandimby●, William Seraphin Randriamanjato (Jean Donne Rakotonirina 89), Christian Claude Isimiava (Lalaina Nomenjanahary 60'), Faneva Ima Andriatsima. Tr: Jean Francois Debon

---

Abidjan
8-10-2006, Buenkadila COD

Côte d'Ivoire   **5**
Kolo Toure [11], Arouna Kone 3 [23] [56] [68], Dindane [32]

Boubacar Barry - Steven Gohouri, Kolo Toure●, Emmanel Eboue (Bakary Kone 51), Abdoulaye Meite, Seydou Kante●, Didier Zokora, Gnegneri Yaya Toure (Didier Ya Konan 82), Arouna Kone, Aruna Dindane (Abdelkader Keita 71), Didier Drogba. Tr: Uli Stielike

Gabon   **0**

Didier Ovono - Paul Kessany, Ernest Akouassaga, Arsene do Marcolino●, Georges Ambourouet●, Eric Mouloungui, Shiva Nzigou (Roguy Meye 71), Thierry Issiemou, Cedric Moubamba, Henri Antchouet (Manga Ecuele 71), Daniel Cousin●. Tr: Alain Giresse

---

Antananarivo
25-03-2007, Maillet SEY

Madagascar   **0**

Jean Chrysostome Raharsion - Marco Randrianantoanina, Gervais Mamy Randrianarisoa, Pascal Razakanantenaina, Tsima Eddy Andriamihaja, Eric Julien Rakotondrabe, Lalaina Nomenjanahary (Claudio Randrianantoanina 82), Carlos Zozimar Dimitri, Paul Johann● (Dimby Rabeariniala 71), Faneva Ima Andriatsima (Claudio Ramiadamanana 57'), Paulin Voavy. Tr: Jean Paul Rossignol

Côte d'Ivoire   **3**
Gohouri [28], Dindane [35], Diane [81]

Boubacar Barry - Arthur Boka, Steven Gohouri, Kolo Toure● (Mamadou Doumbia 87), Gilles Yapi Yapo●, Siaka Tiene, Christian Koffi Ndri, Kanga Akale (Amara Diane 46), Salomon Kalou, Aruna Dindane (Lionel Bah 78), Didier Drogba. Tr: Uli Stielike

---

Bouaké
3-06-2007, Louzaya CGO

Côte d'Ivoire   **5**
Salomon Kalou [18], Arouna Kone 2 [37] [82], Yaya Toure [46], Drogba [87]

Boubacar Barry - Arthur Boka (Amara Diane 81), Emmanuel Eboue, Abdoulaye Meite, Didier Zokora, Gneri Yaya Toure, Siaka Tiene, Christian Koffi Ndri (Gilles Yapi Yapo 66), Salomon Kalou (Kandia Traore 74), Arouna Kone, Didier Drogba●. Tr: Uli Stielike

Madagascar   **0**

Bruno Rajaolara - Jimmy Radafison●, Marco Randrianantoanina, Aly Mohmad●, Gervais Mamy Randrianarisoa●, Pascal Razakanantenaina, Dimby Rabeariniala●, Claudio Ramiadamanana (Tahina Raharison 79), Lalaina Nomenjanahary (Thierry Rastimbazafy 85), Carlos Zozimar Dimitri (Guilliamo Randriamajaio 78'), Paulin Voavy. Tr: Herve Arsene

---

Antananarivo
17-06-2007, Mlangeni SWZ

Madagascar   **0**

Bruno Rajaozara - Jimmy Radifison●, Leonard Baraka, Gervais Mamy Randrianarisoa, Pascal Razakanantenaina, Aly Mohamed (Damien Mahavony 65), Dimby Rabeariniala●, Lalaina Nomenjanahary (Mario Miradji 55), Carlos Zozimar Dimitri, Claudio Ramiadamanana● (Milson Niasex 70), Paulin Voavy. Tr: Herve Arsene

Gabon   **2**
Akiremy [20], Meye [89]

Didier Ovono - Rodrigue Moungounga, Thibault Tchikaya, Bruno Mbanangoye●, Erwin Nguema, Remy Ndong, Dieudonne Londo, Thierry Issiemou●, Stephane Nguema (Popaul Kiende 60), Catalina Aubame● (Arsene Copa 88), Georges Akiremy (Roguy Meye 76). Tr: Alain Giresse

---

Libreville
8-09-2006, Damon RSA

Gabon   **0**

Didier Ovono - Ernest Akouassaga●, Brice Ekwele, Moise Brou, Rodrigue Moundounga●, Guy Tchingoma, Eric Mouloungui, Thierry Issiemou (Cedric Moubamba 73), Bruno Mbanangoye●, Paul Kessany (Shiva Nzigou 83), Daniel Cousin. Tr: Alain Giresse

Côte d'Ivoire   **0**

Boubacar Barry - Siaka Tiene●, Kolo Toure, Abdoulaye Meite●, Emerse Fae●, Didier Zokora, Gneri Yaya Toure, Abdelkader Keita (Salomon Kalou 62), Bakary Kone●, Aruna Dindane● (Christian Koffi Ndri 63), Arouna Kone (Amara Diane 80). Tr: Uli Stielike

GROUP 2

Cairo
2-09-2006, Haimoudi ALG

Egypt 4
Zidan [5], Hosni [29], Aboutrika [39], A Hassan [53p]

Essam Al Hadari - Ahmed Fathi, Amir Azmi Megahed•, Wael Gomaa, Ahmed Aboumosalem (Rami Adel 80), Ahmed Hassan, Mohamed Shawky, Hosni Abd Rabou, Mohamed Aboutrika (Amr Zaki 61), Mohamed Zidan, Ahmed Hossam. Tr: Hassan Shehata

Burundi 1

Aime Kitenge - Floribert Ndayisaba, Valery Nahayo, Karim Nzigiyimana, Sadiki Nsengiyumva, Selemani Ndikumana, Pablo Rulamuvyuma• (Ismael Mutambara 46), Mohsen Nzeyimana•, Saidi Ndikumana, Alain Ndizeye• (Aime Nzuhabonayo 63), Dugary Ndabashinze. Tr: Lotfi Nassem

Nouakchott
2-09-2006, Djaoupe TOG

Mauritania 4
Mbodji [3], Karamoko 2 [8] [23], Langlet [83]

Moussa Souleymane - Ahmed Sidibe, Seydou Mbodji, Mohamed Benaychou• (Mohamed Ould Mohamed Lemine 73), Bilal Sidibe, Moise Lamine Kande, Oumar Timbo (Khattry Ould Khorou 64), Pascal Gourville, Mohamed Yacouba Ba, Yohan Langlet, Moussa Karamoko (Moussa Sidi Bakayoko 87). Tr: Ali Fergani

Botswana 0

Modiri Marumo - Mompati Thuma, Khumo Mothibang•, Ernest Amos, Seabo Gbanakgosi, Ndiyapo Letsholathebe (Alex Matshameko 76), Tshepo Motlhabankwe•, Michael Mogaladi, Tshepiso Molwantwa (Malepa Bolelang 59), Moemedi Motlhaping, Joel Mogorosi. Tr: Colwyn Rowe

Gaborone
7-10-2006, Bennett RSA

Botswana 0

Modiri Marumo• - Mompati Thuma, Khumo Mothibang, Ernest Amos, Ndiyapo Letsholathebe, Tshepo Motlhabankwe, Michael Mogaladi, Dibang Moloi, Keoagile Radipotsane, Tshepiso Molwantwa (Onalethata Tshekiso 36), Moemedi Motlhaping. Tr: Colwyn Rowe

Egypt 0

Mohamed Abdel Moncef - Ahmed Fathi, Hani Said, Wael Gomaa, Sayed Moawad, Mohamed Aboutrika (Emad Moteab 57), Ahmed Fathi (Reda Shehata 80), Mohamed Shawky, Hossam Ghali•, Mohamed Zidan (Hosni Abd Rabou 66), Ahmed Hossam. Tr: Hassan Shehata

Bujumbura
8-10-2006, Abdelrahman SUD

Burundi 3
Ndikumana 2 [2] [30], Mbuzumutima [44]

Aime Kitenge - Hussein Nzeyimana, Floribert Ndayisaba, Valery Nahayo, Karim Nzigiyimana, Henry Mbazumutima•, Khalfan Kamana (Mohsin Mutambana 79), Abdallah Nduwimana•, Dugary Ndabashinze, Selemani Ndikumana (Aime Nzuhabonayo 75), Alain Ndizeye (Fidel Nimusona 61). Tr: Lotfi Nassem

Mauritania 1
Benyachou [51]

Moussa Souleymane - Ahmed Sidibe, Seydou Mbodji, Mohamed Benaychou, Bilal Sidibe•, Moise Lamine Kande, Moussa Sidi Bakayoko, Pascal Gourville, Mohamed Yacouba Ba (Mohamed Ould Mohamed Lemine 71), Yohan Langlet (Bayo Ndiaye 64), Moussa Karamoko (Brahim Bouha 15'). Tr: Ali Fergani

Cairo
25-03-2007, Benouza ALG

Egypt 3
Zidan [20], Bilal Sidibe OG [23], Ghali [66]

Essam Al Hadari (Abdelwahed El Sayed 77) - Ahmed Fathi (Omar Gamal 63), Hani Said, Shady Mohamed, Sayed Moawad, Hossam Ghali, Mohamed Shawki, Hosni Abd Rabbou, Ahmed Hassan (Ibrahim Said 77), Mohamed Zidan•, Emad Moteab•89. Tr: Hassan Shehata

Mauritania 0

Souleyman Diallo - Ahmed Sidibe, Mabrouk Ely Ould Alioune (Oumar Timbo 46), Moise Lamine Kande, Abdelaziz Camara, Bilal Sidibe•, Pascal Gourville, Mohamed Yacouba Ba•56, Bayo Ndiaye, Moussa Karamoko (Mohamed Ould Mohamed Lemine 65), Yohan Langlet (Mamadou Sidibe Diop 72). Tr: Ali Fergani

Gaborone
25-03-2007, Marange ZIM

Botswana 1
Siska [64]

Modiri Marumo - Mompati Thuma, Ernest Amos, Ndiyapo Letsholathebe, Tshepo Motlhabankwe•, Nelson Gabolwelwe, Michael Mogaladi, Mogogi Gabonamong (Keoagile Radipotsane 38), Vincent Phiri (Joel Mogorosi 61), Diphetego Selolwane, Jerome Ramatlhwakoane (Thato Siska 51). Tr: Colwyn Rowe

Burundi 0

Aime Kitenge, Hussein Nzeyimana• (Karim Nizigiyimana 66), Dugary Ndabashinze•, Valery Nahayo, Ismael Mutambara, Selemani Ndikumana, Elvis Banyihwabe (Henry Mbazumutima 81), Floribert Ndayisaba•, Selemani Musaba (Aime Nzohabonayo 70), Alain Ndizeye, Hassan Hakizimana. Tr: Lotfi Nassem

Kigali
2-06-2007, Ssegonga UGA

Burundi 1
Ndayishimiye [80]

Vladimir Niyonkuru - Hussein Nzeyimana•, Abdalaa Nduwimana, Floribert Ndayisaba, Alain Ndizeye, Ismael Mutambara, Selemani Ndikumana, Eric Ndizeye (Abdul Ndayishimiye 70), Karim Nizigiyimana (Alain Habimana 60), Elvis Banyihwabe (Divin Gateretse 60), Hassan Hakizimana. Tr: Hussein Fauzil

Botswana 0

Modiri Marumo - Mompati Thuma, Ernest Amos, Ndiyapo Letsholathebe, Keoagetse Radipotsane•, Michael Mogaladi, Nelson Gabolwelwe, Dirang Moloi (Onalethata Tshekiso 75), Jerome Ramatlhakwane (Pontsho Moloi 55), Joel Mogorosi•, Diphetego Selolwane. Tr: Colwyn Rowe

Nouakchott
3-06-2007, Sowe GAM

Mauritania 1
Langlet [70]

Souleymane Diallo - Ahmed Sidibe, Bilal Sidibe, Mohamed Ould Mohamed Lemine, Seydou Nourou Mbodi, Moise Lamine Kande, Mamadou Sidibe Diop•, Abdelaziz Camara (Bayo Ndiaye 85), Ahmed Ould Teguedi•, Dominque da Silva (Mohamed Hamoud 75). Tr: Ali Fergani

Egypt 1
Ahmed Hassan [10]

Essam Al Hadari - Wael Gomaa, Ahmed Fathi• (Omar Gamal 75), Hani Said, Sayed Moawad, Hosni Abd Rabbou, Mohamed Aboutrika, Hossam Ghali (Mahmoud Abdelrazak Shikabala 46), Mohamed Shawki, Ahmed Hassan, Amr Zaki. Tr: Hassan Shehata

Gaborone
16-06-2007, Gasingwa RWA

Botswana 2
Mafoko [19], Diphetego Selolwane [40]

Modiri Marumo, Mompati Thuma, Ernest Amos, Ndiyapo Letsholathebe, Tshepo Motlhabankwe, Michael Mogaladi•71, Boitumelo Mafoko, Onalethata Tshekiso (Dirang Moloi 80), Pontsho Moloi (Keoagetse Radipotsane 75), Joel Mogorosi, Diphetego Selolwane. Tr: Colwyn Rowe

Mauritania 1
Langlet [74]

Souleymane Diallo - Ahmed Sidibe, Bilal Sidibe, Moise Lamine Kande (Tijane Amadou Ba 65), Seydou Nourou Mbodi, Mamadou Sidibe Diop, Abdoulaziz Camara, Pascal Gourville, Ahmed Ould Teguedi (Mohamed Yacouba Ba• 46), Mohamed Ould Mohamed Lemine, Dominque da Silva (Yohan Langlet 46). Tr: Ali Fergani

Bujumbura
9-09-2007

Burundi 0

Vladimir Niyonkuru - Valery Nahayo•, Rachid Salumu (Sadiki Nsengiyumva 55), Ismael Mutambara, Dugary Ndabashinze, Alain Ndizeye, Floribert Ndayisaba, Henry Mbazumutima, Hassan Hakizimana, Aime Nzohabonayo (Sutch Ndayisuhmiye• 83), Abdalaa Nduwimana (Yamini Selemani Ndikumana 56). Tr: Adel Amrouche

Egypt 0

Essam Al Hadari - Ahmed Al Muhammadi, Hani Said, Shady Mohamed, Ibrahim Said•, Ahmed Abou Mossallem•, Ahmed Hassan•48, Hosni Abd Rabou (Hassan Mostafa), Amr Zaki (Mohamed Aboutrika), Emad Moteab (Omar Gamal), Ahmed Hossam. Tr: Hassan Shehata

Cairo
13-10-2007, Imiere NGA

Egypt 1
Mohamed Fadl [78]

Essam Al Hadari - Ahmed Al Muhammadi, Hani Said, Shady Mohamed, Sayed Moawad•, Mohamed Shawki, Hosni Abd Rabou, Mohamed Aboutrika, Amr Zaki (Ahmed Hasan Farag 79), Mohamed Zidan (Omar Gamal 70), Emad Motaeb (Mohamed Fadl 56). Tr: Hassan Shehata

Botswana 0

Modiri Marumo - Mompati Thuma, Ernest Amos•, Ndiyapo Letsholathebe, Tshepo Motlhabankwe, Mogogi Gabonamong, Khumo Motlhabankwe, Keoagetse Radipotsane (Dirang Moloi 84), Joel Mogorosi, Diphetego Selolwane (Jerome Ramatlhakwane 87), Malepa Bolelang (Nelson Gabolwelwe 84). Tr: Colwyn Rowe

Nouakchott
13-10-2007, Aboubacar CIV

Mauritania 2

Souleymane Diallo - Ahmed Sidibe, Mohamed Ould Mohamed Lemine, Bilal Sidibe, Mamadou Sidibe Diop, Abdoulaziz Camara (Boubou Ndiaye 46), Pascal Gourville•, Moise Lamine Kande, Ahmed Ould Teguedi, Dominque da Silva (Abdallahi Ould Khourou 53), Yohan Langlet. Tr: Birama Gaye

Burundi 1

Vladimir Niyonkuru - Valery Nahayo•, Ismael Mutambara, Alain Ndizeye• (Karim Nizigiyimana 70), Dugary Ndabashinze, Floribert Ndayisaba, Hussein Nzeyimana• (Abdallah Iramboa 53), Sutch Ndayisuhmiye (Emmanuel Ngama 40), Hassan Hakizimana, Aime Nzohabonayo, Henry Mbarumutima. Tr: Adel Amrouche

GROUP 3

Abuja
2-09-2006, Sowe GAM

Nigeria 2
Yakubu Aiyegbeni [27], Christian Obodo [60]

Vincent Enyeama - Joseph Yobo, Taye Taiwo, George Abbey, Obinna Nwaneri, Seyi Olofinjana (Yusuf Ayila 58), Wilson Oruma (John Obi Mikel 58), Christian Obodo, Chinedu Ogbuke (Nwankwo Kanu 75), Yakubu Aiyegbeni•, Peter Odemwingie. Tr: Austin Eguavoen

Niger 0

Saminou Rabo - Issa Aboubakar, Boukary Habibou, Abdoulkarim Oumarou, Kader Amadou, Ismael Warghalassane (Abdoulaziz Abdou Amadou 58), Modibo Sow, Abdelkarim Moussa Konate, Omar Amodu Fankele (Issaka Abdou Manzo 89), Idrissa Laouali•, Harouna Ide Loga•63. Tr: Bana Tchanille

---

Kampala
2-09-2006, Abdelrahman SUD

Uganda 3
Geoffrey Massa 2 [29 42], David Obua [57]

Dennis Onyango, Andy Mwesigwa, Nestory Kizito, Timothy Batabaire, Ibrahim Ssekagya, Noah Kasule (Simon Masaba), Johnson Bagoole (Dan Wagaluka), Vincent Kayizi, Hassan Mabiru, Godfrey Massa• (Anthony Bongole), David Obua. Tr: Laszlo Csaba

Lesotho 0

Phasumahe Kholuoe - Moitheri Ntobo, Lehlohonolo Seema•, Bokang Mothoana•, Thabo Mokhele, Refiloe Potse, Sello Muso (Lengoana Nkhethoa 62), Molefe Lekoekoe (Malefetsane Pheko• 40), Thulo Ranchobe, Moses Ramafole•, Motlatsi Shale (Bushy Moletsane 57). Tr: Motheo Mohapi

---

Maseru
8-10-2006, Marange ZIM

Lesotho 0

Phasumahe Kholuoe - Moitheri Ntobo, Lengoana Nkhethoa•, Thabo Mokhele, Thabiso Maile, Motlalepula Mofolo, Refiloe Potse (Tefo Maipato 77), Sello Muso, Bushy Moletsane• (Palekoti Mokhahlane 59), Thulo Ranchobe, Bokang Mothoana (Katleho Moleko 59). Tr: Motheo Mohapi

Nigeria 1
Yakubu Aiyegbeni [48]

Vincent Enyeama - Joseph Yobo, Taye Taiwo, George Abbey•, Obinna Nwaneri, Seyi Olofinjana, Wilson Oruma (Onyekatchi Okonkwo 84), Christian Obodo, Chinedu Ogbuke (Emmanuel Okoduwa 71), Yakubu Aiyegbeni• (Nwankwo Kanu 79), Obafemi Martins. Tr: Austin Eguavoen

---

Niamey
8-10-2006, Diouf SEN

Niger 0

Saminou Rabo - Idrissa Laouali, Abdoulkarim Oumarou, Kader Amadou, Modibo Sow, Moussa Konate, Boukari Habibou, Alhassane Issofou, Abdoulaziz Abdou Amadou (Hamidou Djibo 60), Amadou Ba (Abdourahmane Aboubakary 50), Hassayedou Idrissa (Jacques Koffi 71). Tr: Bana Tchanille

Uganda 0

Dennis Onyango, Simeon Masaba, Andy Mwesigwa•, Nestory Kizito, Timothy Batabaire•, Noah Kasule•, Johnson Bagoole, Vincent Kayizzi (Dan Wagaluka 67), Robert Ssejjemba (Hassan Mabiru 56), Godfrey Massa•, David Obua (Kadogo Alimansi 89). Tr: Laszlo Csaba

---

Abeokuta
24-03-2007, Diatta SEN

Nigeria 1
Nwankwo Kanu [73]

Austin Ejide - Joseph Yobo, Rabiu Afolabi, Taye Taiwo•, Isaac Okoronkwo (Obinna Nwaneri• 46), Seyi Olofinjana, John Obi Mikel, Christian Obodo (John Utaka 54), Nwankwo Kanu (Yusuf Ayila 85), Obafemi Martins, Peter Odemwingie. Tr: Berti Vogts

Uganda 0

Dennis Onyango - Richard Malinga, Andy Mwesigwa•, Ibrahim Sekagya, Nestory Kizito, Timothy Batabaire (Johnson Bagoole 88), Noah Kasule, Vincent Kayizzi (Dan Wagaluka 79), George Serunkuma, Hassan Mabiru (Hamis Kitagenda 80), David Obua•. Tr: Laszlo Csaba

---

Maseru
25-03-2007, Lwanja MWI

Lesotho 3
Refiloe Potse 2 [18 47], Mpitsa Marai [86]

Lerata Tsalong - Thabo Masualle, Mpitsa Marai, Thapelo Mokhehle, Moitheri Ntobo, Lehlohonolo Seema, Sello Muso, Motlalepula Mofolo (Bushy Moletsane 43), Refiloe Potse•, Thulo Ranchobe (Lire Phiri 80), Bokang Mothoana (Katleho Moleko 89). Tr: Motheo Mohapi

Niger 1
Kamilou Daouda [41]

Kassali Daouda - Modibo Sow, Moussa Konate, Kader Amadou, Abdoulkarim Oumarou, Fousseini Tounkara, Boukary Djire•57, Souleymane Cisseko• (Abdourahmane Aboubakary 87), Amadou Omar• (Mamane Laouali 77), Hamidou Djibo (Abdoulaye Mohamed 71), Kamilou Daouda•. Tr: Bana Tchanille

---

Kampala
2-06-2007, Abdelfattah EGY

Uganda 2
David Obua [52p], Ibrahim Ssekagya [65p]

Denis Onyango - Richard Malinga (Simeon Masaba 46), Nestory Kizito•, Timothy Batabaire, Ibrahim Ssekagya, Noel Kasule•73, Dan Wagaluka, Asani Bajope, David Obua (Vincent Kayazzi 57), Geoffrey Sserunkuma (Hassan Mubiru 73), Geoffrey Massa. Tr: Laszlo Csaba

Nigeria 1
John Utaka [25]

Austin Ejide• - Obinna Nwaneri (Chukwuma Akabueze 77), Taye Taiwo, Joseph Yobo, Rafiu Afolabi•, Danny Shittu, Onyekachi Okonkwo, John Utaka (Obafemi Martins 64), Sani Kaita (Stephen Makinwa 83), Nwankwo Kanu, Yakubu Aiyegbeni. Tr: Berti Vogts

---

Niamey
3-06-2007, Kotey GHA

Niger 2
Hamidou Djibo [3], Souleymane Dela Sakou [13]

Kassali Daouda - Abdoulkarim Oumarou, Kader Amadou, Moussa Konate, Idrissa Laouali, Abdou Illa Zakariyaou (Abdourahman Aboubacary 59), Harouna Ide Loga, Kamilou Daouda (Dodo Adam Hassane 75), Mahamadou Ousseini, Souleymane Dela Sakou, Hamidou Djibo (Idrissa Hasseydou 66). Tr: Amadou Hameye

Lesotho 0

Samuel Ketsekile - Thabo Masualle, Lengana Nkhethoa, Mpitsa Marai, Lehlohonolo Seema, Moitheri Ntobo, Lieta Lehloka (Sello Musa• 54), Bokang Mothoana, Refiloe Potse, Thulo Ranchobe, Thapelo Mokhehle• (Ramashalane Taeli 70). Tr: Motheo Mohapi

---

Niamey
17-06-2007, Pare BFA

Niger 1
Kamilou Daouda [68]

Kassali Daouda - Souleymane Dela Sakou, Abdoulkarim Oumarou•, Kader Amadou, Moussa Moses, Moussa Konate•, Idrissa Laouali (Idrissa Hasseydou 81), Abdou Illa Zakariyaou, Harouna Ide Loga (Ali Ousmane Amadou 85), Issoufou Alhassane (Kamilou Daouda 50), Hamidou Djibo. Tr: Amadou Hameye

Nigeria 3
Kanu [40], Taiwo [74p], Yakubu Aiyegbeni [89]

Austin Ejide - Uche Oguchi, Taye Taiwo, Danny Shittu, Rabiu Afolabi, Seyi Olofinjana, Onyekachi Okonkwo, John Utaka (Peter Odemwingie 68), Nwankwo Kanu (Yakubu Aiyegbeni 83), Stephen Makinwa, Obafemi Martins• (Sani Kaita 89). Tr: Berti Vogts

---

Maseru
19-06-2007, Mwandike TAN

Lesotho 0

Lerata Tsalong - Lehlohonolo Seema, Thapelo Mokhehle, Mpitsa Marai, Moitheri Ntobo, Ralekoti Mokhahlane•, Sello Musa (Katleho Moleko 50), Bokang Mothoana, Bushy Moletsane (Tefo Maipato 68), Thulo Ranchobe• (Lire Phiri 86), Refiloe Potse. Tr: Motheo Mohapi

Uganda 0

Denis Onyango - Simeon Masaba, Nestory Kizito, Timothy Batabaire, Andrew Mwesigwa, Dan Wagaluka, Asani Bajope, Vincent Kayazzi (Kadogo Alimansi 62), Johnson Bagoole, Geoffrey Massa (Geoffrey Sserunkuma 79), Hassan Mubiru (Eugene Sepuya 46). Tr: Laszlo Csaba

---

Kampala
8-09-2007, Marange ZIM

Uganda 3
David Obua 3 [2p 76 86]

Denis Onyango - Simeon Masaba, Nestory Kizito, Timothy Batabaire, Andrew Mwesigwa, Ibrahim Ssekaggya, Dan Wagaluka (Vincent Kayazzi 52), Noah Kasule (Asani Bajope 46), David Obua•, Geoffrey Massa, Geoffrey Sserunkuma (Hamis Kitagenda 66). Tr: Laszlo Csaba

Niger 1
Idrissa Hasseydou [44]

Kassali Daouda, Souleymane Cisseko, Kader Amadou•, Karim Paraiso•, Karim Lancina, Moussa Moses, Awally Mahaman, Pascal Anicet (Kamilou Daouda 70), Hamidou Djibo (Idrissa Laouali 69), Abdoulkarim Oumarou, Idrissa Seidou (Amadou Bouzou 87). Tr: Amadou Hameye

---

Warri
8-09-2007, Sowe GAM

Nigeria 2
Stephen Makinwa [43], Ike Uche [75]

Austin Ejide - Onyekachi Apam (Richard Eromoigbe 46), Taye Taiwo (Onyekachi Okonkwo 72), Danny Shittu, Rabiu Afolabi, Seyi Olofinjana, John Obi Mikel, John Utaka, Peter Odemwingie, Nwankwo Kanu, Stephen Makinwa (Ike Uche 64). Tr: Berti Vogts

Lesotho 0

Phasumahe Kholuoe• - Thabo Masualle, Lengana Nkhethoa, Mpitsa Marai, Motlalepula Mofolo, Tefo Maipato (Thapelo Mokhehle 46), Moli Lesesa, Makalo Mehlala, Sello Musa (Lire Phiri 83), Katleho Moleko (Bushy Moletsane 78), Refiloe Potse. Tr: Motheo Mohapi

GROUP 4

Curepipe
3-09-2006, Ncobo RSA

Mauritius 0

Orwin Castel - Jovani Jubeau•, Cyril Mourgine, Stephan L'Enfle•, Bassanio Diolle, Kervin Godon, Desire Periatambee, Sebastien Bax, Gilbert Bayaram (Jean-Noel Laboiteuse 79), Jimmy Cundasamy (Ricardo Naboth 83), Giovanni Jeannot. Tr: Sarjoo Gowreesunkur

Tunisia 0

Ali Boumnijel - Amir Haj Messaoud, Radhi Jaidi, Sabri Jabeur, Wissem El Bekri, Joahar Mnari, Mehdi Nafti (Chaker Zouaghi 77), Hocine Ragued, Hamed Namouchi, Chaouki Ben Saada (Belgacem Tonniche 85), Slama Kasdaoui (Yacine Chikhaoui 55). Tr: Roger Lemerre

---

Tunis
7-10-2006, Coulibaly MLI

Tunisia 1
Rtshard Justin Lado OG [79]

Hamdi Kasraoui, David Jemmali, Anis Ayari, Karim Hagui•, Khaled Badra, Jouhar Mnari, Kamel Zaïem, Adel Chedli, Abdelkrim Nafti• (Yacine Chikhaoui 62), Ali Zitouni. Tr: Roger Lemerre

Sudan 0

Mahjoub El Moez - Haitham Mostafa, Hassan Khalid (Ali Mohamed Khider 73), Rtshard Justin Lado, Bashir Hamuda•, Ahmed Alalezdine, Youssef Alaledin (Omar Mohamed 65), Badreldin El Dood (Ahmed Mugahid 89), Amir Damar, Musa Al Tahir, Haitham Tambal•. Tr: Mohamed Abdallah

---

Omdurman
2-06-2007, Lwanja MWI

Sudan 3
Rtshard Justin Lado 2 [26] [65], Faisal Agab [44]

Mahjoub El Moez - Ali Mohamed Khider, Rtshard Justin Lado, Gibril Alaedin, Badreldin El Dood, Ahmed Mugahid, Haitham Mostafa, Omar Bakheit, Faisal Agab (Musa Al Tahir 88), Bashir Hamuda, Haitham Tambal. Tr: Mohamed Abdallah

Mauritius 0

Yannick Mocoa - Bruno Ravinah, Henri Speville, Stephan L'Enfle•, Leroy Figaro, Tommy Sanhoboa, Stephan Pierre (Giovanny Jeannot 30), Fabrice Pithia, Guillaume Sockalingun, Andy Sophie (Colin Bell 66), Curtis Laseringue (Jerry Louis 27). Tr: Sarjoo Gowreesunkur

---

Victoria
16-06-2007, Dlamini SWZ

Seychelles 0

Ricky Rose - Denis Barbe, Godfrey Denis, Jonathan Bibi, Lorenzo Mathiot, Steve Henriette, Henny Dufresne•, Alex Nibourette, Mervyn Mathiot (Trevor Poiret 84), Colin Laporte (Achille Henriette 79), Che Dorasamy (Yelvanny Rose 58). Tr: Raoul Shungu

Sudan 2
Faisal Agab [44], Haitham Tambal [68]

Mahjoub El Moez - Ali Mohamed, Rtshard Justin Lado•, Gibril Alaedin, Omar Bakheit, Ahmed Mugahid (Musa Al Tahir 82), Haitham Mostafa, Youssef Alaledin, Haitham Tambal, Faisal Agab (Babiker Alaledin 59), Badreldin El Dood. Tr: Mohamed Abdallah

---

Khartoum
3-09-2006, Kidane ERI

Sudan 3
Badreldin El Dood [20], Haitham Tambal 2 [77p] [89]

Mahjoub El Moez - Haitham Mostafa (Bashir Hamuda 79), Hassan Khalid, Ahmed Alalezdine, Rtshard Justin Lado, Ali Mohamed, Badreldin El Dood, Omar Mohamed, Faisal Agab (Musa Al Tahir 67), Youssef Alaledin, Haitham Tambal•. Tr: Mohamed Abdallah

Seychelles 0

Nelson Sopha - Denis Barbe, Allen Larue•, Denis Belle, Verna Rose, Jonathan Bibi•, Henny Dufresne, Lorenzo Mathiot (Godrey Denis 67), Alex Nibourette (Roderick Rose 70), Don Anacoura• (Bernard St Ange• 54), Yelvanny Rose. Tr: Raoul Shungu

---

Victoria
24-03-2007, Ssegonga UGA

Seychelles 0

Nelson Sopha - Godfrey Denis, Jonathan Bibi, Denis Belle, Danny Cesar (Ted Esther 46), Allen Larue (Yelvanny Rose 60), Alex Nibourette, Denis Barbe, Philip Zialor (Mervyn Mathiot 87), Henny Dufresne, Wilnes Brutus. Tr: Raoul Shungu

Tunisia 3
Issam Jomaa 3 [14] [75] [79]

Hamdi Kasraoui - David Jemmali, Wissem Bekri, Karim Hagui, Radhi Jaidi, Houssine Ragued• (Lasaad Ouertani 46), Adel Chedli, Karim Nafti (Hamed Namouchi 64), Slim Benachour, Heykel Guemamdia (Aymen Benzekri 81), Issam Jomaa. Tr: Roger Lemerre

---

Rades
2-06-2007, Diatta SEN

Tunisia 4
Issam Jomaa [25], Zaiem 2 [41] [66], Chermiti [83]

Hamdi Kasraoui - David Jemmali, Wissem Bekri, Karim Hagui, Radhi Jaidi, Joahar Mnari (Mejdi Traoui 82), Kamel Zaiem, Slim Benachour (Abdelkarim Nafti 58), Ziad Jaziri (Amine Chermiti 70), Issam Jomaa. Tr: Roger Lemerre

Seychelles 0

Nelson Sopha - Denis Barbe, Ted Esther, Godfrey Denis, Jonathan Bibi, Steve Henriette (Denis Belle 72), Alex Nibourette, Mervyn Mathiot, Henny Dufresne, Che Dorasamy (Colin Laporte 56), Yelvanny Rose. Tr: Raoul Shungu

---

Curepipe
9-09-2007, Mwandike TAN

Mauritius 1
Christopher Perle [62]

Jean-Francois Ammomoothoo• - Jean-Noel Laboiteuse, Jean-Denis Dookhee• (Bruno Ravina 37), Kersley Levrai, Stephane L'Enfle, Bassanio Diolle, Stephane Badul (Viviadeo Boodhun 57), Colin Bell, Fabrice Pauline•, Waldo Lebreux, Christopher Perle (Andy Sophie 74). Tr: Akbar Patel

Seychelles 1
Godfrey Denis [43p]

Nelson Sopha - Lorenzo Mathiot (Fabien Cadeau 84), Godfrey Denis, Ronny Hoareau•, Steeve Henriette, Denis Barbe, Jonathan Bibi, Alex Nibourette, Colin Laporte• (Mervin Mathiot 66), Philip Zialor, Don Anacoura• (Nigel Freminot 88). Tr: Raoul Shungu

---

Victoria
7-10-2007, Raolimanana MAD

Seychelles 2
Wilnus Brutus 2 [23] [81]

Nelson Sopha - Denis Barbe, Allen Larue, Lorenzo Mathiot (Mervin Mathiot 70), Godfrey Denis, Brian Dorby (Henny Dufresne 63), Neddy Rose (Roddy Cesar 78), Denis Belle, Philip Zialor, Jonathan Bibi, Wilnes Brutus. Tr: Raoul Shungu

Mauritius 1
Kervin Gordon [53]

Orwin Castel - Cyril Mourguine, Kervin Godon, Sebastien Bax, Giovanni Naboth, Gilbert Bayaram, Jean-Noel Laboiteuse, Giovanni Jeannot (Patrick Naboth 70), Stephen L'Enflé, Jimmy Cundasamy (Kersley Appou• 58), Désiré Peeriatambee (Arassen Ragaven 74). Tr: Sarjoo Gowreesunkur

---

Curepipe
25-03-2007, Mwanza ZAM

Mauritius 1
Ricardo Naboth [61]

Yannick Macoa - Cyril Mourgine, Henri Speville, Stephan L'Enfle, Kervin Godon•, Gilbert Bayaram (Bruno Ravinah 20), Arassen Ragaven, Jimmy Cundasamy, Guillaume Sockalingum, Giovanni Jeannot (Colin Bell 84), Westley Marquette (Ricardo Naboth 30). Tr: Sarjoo Gowreesunkur

Sudan 2
Faisal Agab 2 [42] [77]

Mahjoub El Moez - Ali Mohamed Khider• (Youssef Alaledin 52), Hassan Khalid, Rtshard Justin Lado, Gibril Alaedin, Bashir Hamuda, Omar Bakheit, Ahmed Mugahid, Haitham Mostafa, Haitham Tambal (Babiker Alaledin 60), Faisal Agab•. Tr: Mohamed Abdallah

---

Rades
16-06-2006, Benouza ALG

Tunisia 2
Issam Jomaa [44], Abdelkrim Nafti [51]

Hamdi Kasraoui - David Jemmali (Amir Haj Messaoud 88), Mehdi Meriah, Radhi Jaidi, Karim Hagui, Joahar Mnari, Kamel Zaiem (Chaker Zouaghi 65), Adel Chedli, Abdelkrim Nafti, Amine Chermiti (Ali Zitouni 69), Issam Jomaa. Tr: Roger Lemerre

Mauritius 0

Yannick Mocoa - Bruno Ravinah, Fabrice Pithia (Leroy Figaro 61), Tommy Sanhoboa, Gilbert Bayaram, Henri Speville, Kervin Godon•, Giovany Jeannot, Arassen Ragaven, Guillaume Sockalingun (Ricardo Hovas 61), Fabrice Pauline (Guillaume Manvac 72). Tr: Sarjoo Gowreesunkur

---

Omdurman
9-09-2007, Codja BEN

Sudan 3
Babiker Alaledin [26], Faisal Agab [61p], Al Tahir [72]

Mahjoub El Moez (Bahaeldin Abdallah• 46) - Ali Mohamed Khider, Youssef Alaledin•, Ahmed Mugahid, Musa Al Tahir, Haitham Mostafa, Bashir Hamuda (Saifeldin Ali Idris 72), Gibril Alaedin, Badreldin El Dood, Faisal Agab (Mohamed Tahir 89), Babiker Alaledin. Tr: Mohamed Abdallah

Tunisia 2
Ahmed Mugahid OG [55], Dos Santos [81p]

Hamdi Kasraoui - David Jemmali (Sabeur Ben Frej 85), Wissem Bekri•, Wissem Abdi, Karim Hagui, Khaled Mouelhi (Amine Chermiti 66•88), Adel Chedli, Chaker Zouaghi, Abdelkrim Nafti•, Francileudo dos Santos•, Issam Jomaa (Yassine Chikhaoui 21). Tr: Roger Lemerre

GROUP 5

Kigali
3-09-2006, Ssegonga UGA

Rwanda 0

Ramadhan Nkunzingoma - Elias Ntaganda*, Abdul Sibomana (Jimmu Murisa 68), Aloua Gaseruka, Fritz Emeran, Patrick Mafisango Mutesa, Manfred Kizito, Mikey Yossam (Abedi Murenda 60), Bobo Bola, Jimmy Gatete, Olivier Karekezi. Tr: Michael Nees

Cameroon 3
Feutchine [56], Geremi Njitap [62], Nguemo [85]

Idriss Carlos Kameni - Benoit Angbwa, Rigobert Song, Geremi Fotso Njitap, Jean-Hugues Bilayi Ateba, Alioum Saidou, Jean Makoun, Salomon Olembe (Justice Wamfor 73), Landry Nguemo, Rudolph Douala (Guy Feutchine 52), Samuel Eto'o. Tr: Arie Haan

Malabo
3-09-2006, Agbenyega GHA

Equatorial Guinea 2
Juan Epitie [24], Rodolfo Bodipo [88]

Emmanuel Danilo - Lawrence Doe, Birama Diop (Damian Gregorio Enzeama 46), Silvestre Mesaka, Carolina Ronan (Alberto Edjogo 85), Luciano Mutasi*, Juvenal Edjogo, Benjamin Zarandona, Pablo Armando Essono, Juan Epitie (Justo Nguema 58), Rodolfo Bodipo. Tr: Antonio Dumas

Liberia 1
Zah Krangar [35]

Louis Crayton - Solomon Grimes, Solomon Wesseh, Gizzi Dorbor, Eric Weeks* (Jacob Toe 76), Omega Alamadine*, Zah Krangar, Prince Garwo*, George Baysah*53, Anthony Laffor, Edward Wilson (Augustine Kettor 67). Tr: Frank Jericho Nagbe

Yaounde
7-10-2006, Daami TUN

Cameroon 3
Mohamadou Idrissou 2 [72 89], Achille Webo [79]

Idriss Carlos Kameni - Jean-Hugues Bilayi Ateba, Rigobert Song, Eric Matoukou, Geremi Fotso Njitap, Landry Nguemo (Joseph Elong 89), Justice Wamfor, Jean Makoun, Guy Feutchine (Mohamadou Idrissou 50), Salomon Olembe (Stephane Mbia 79), Achille Webo*. Tr: Arie Haan

Equatorial Guinea 0

Emmanuel Danilo - Benjamin Zarandona (Luciano Mutasi 50), Jose Luis Rondo, Damian Gregorio Enzeama*, Lawrence Doe*, Carolina Ronan, Pablo Armando Essono (Ibrahima Toure 64), Ivan Zarandona (Jaime Mpanga 86), Juvenal Edjogo, Lino Makuba, Juan Epitie. Tr: Quique Setien

Monrovia
8-10-2006, Olatunde NGA

Liberia 3
Doe [27], Makor [68], Williams [76]

Louis Crayton - Solomon Grimes*, Gizzi Dorbor*, Omega Roberts, Jimmy Dixon, Kelvin Sebwe, Oliver Makor, Francis Doe, Anthony Laffor (Eric Weeks 86), Zah Krangar (Ben Martin 88), Dioh Williams. Tr: Frank Jericho Nagbe

Rwanda 2
Olivier Karekezi [70'], Abedi Mulenda [78]

Ramazan Nkunzingoma - Oliver Uwingabire (Abdul Sibomana 46), Elias Ntaganda*, Alou Gaberika, Patrick Mafisango Mutesa, Jeannot Witakenge, Manfred Kizito (Ngirinstu Mwemeriwa 64), Olivier Karekezi, Henry Munyaneza, Bola Bobo*, Jimmy Gatete (Abedi Mulenda 55). Tr: Michael Nees

Yaounde
24-03-2007, Djaoupe TOG

Cameroon 3
Achille Webo 2 [12 24], Mohamadou Idrissou [85]

Carlos Idriss Kameni - Rigobert Song, Stephane Mbia, Timothee Atouba, Eric Matoukou, Salomom Olembe (Mohamadou Idrissou 54), Geremi Fotso Njitap, Daniel Ngom Kome, Achille Webo, Achille Emana (Landry Nguemo 47), Samuel Eto'o (Justice Wamfor 60). Tr: Jules Nyongha

Liberia 1
Francis Doe [39]

Louis Crayton - Solomon Grimes*, George Gebro*61, Murphy Nagbe, Ousman Larmin, Ben Teekloh (George Baysah 66), James Lomell (Zah Krangar 71), Dulee Johnson, Francis Doe, Dioh Williams*, Anthony Laffor. Tr: Frank Jericho Nagbe

Malabo
25-03-2007, Louzaya CGO

Equatorial Guinea 3
Moreira [29], Juvenal Edjogo [75], Juan Epitie [81]

Emmanuel Danilo - Benjamin Zarandona (Silvestre Ekolo 46), Carolina Ronan, Enio de Souza Anderson (Lino Makuba 72), Fernando Alves, Jose Luis Rondo, Lawrence Doe*, Juvenal Edjogo (Ivan Zarandona 80), Juan Epitie, Andre Moreira*, Ibrahima Toure. Tr: Jordan de Freitas

Rwanda 1
Olivier Karekezi [73]

Ben Mandela - Fritz Emeran (Haruna Niyonzima 80), Mikey Yossam, Robert Ujeneza*, Jeannot Witakenge, Patrick Mafisango Mutesa, Abdul Sibomana, Manfred Kizito (Frederique Ndaka 46), Ismail Nshutiyamagara, Henry Munyaneza (Jimmy Gatete 64), Olivier Karekezi*. Tr: Michael Nees

Kigali
2-06-2007, Auda EGY

Rwanda 2
Haruna Niyonzima 2 [47 69]

Ramazani Nkunzingoma - Abdul Sibomana*, Bonaventure Hategekimana, Elias Ntaganda, Jeannot Witakenge, Ismail Nshutiyamagara, Manfred Kizito, Haruna Niyonzima (Djabil Mutarambirwa 85), Jimmy Mulisa (Mwemere Ngirinshuti 74), Said Abed Makasi (Jimmy Gatete 58), Olivier Karekezi. Tr: Michael Nees

Equatorial Guinea 0

Emmanuel Danilo - Jose Luis Rondo (Francisco Salvador Ela 77), Carolino Ronan, David Alvarez*, Fernando Alves, Silvestre Mesaka, Juvenal Edjogo (Ivan Zarandona 51), Ibrahima Toure, Javier Balboa, Enio de Souza Anderson (Juan Epitie 51), Rodolfo Bodipo*. Tr: Jordan de Freitas

Monrovia
3-06-2007, Coulibaly MLI

Liberia 1
Stephen Mennoh [65]

Sunday Seah - Murphy Nagbe, Ben Teekloh, Ousman Larmin*, Chris Gbandi (Varmah Kpoto 85), Dulee Johnson (Johnny Bleedee 46), James Lomell, Francis Doe, Zah Krangar, Frank Seator, Stephen Mennoh. Tr: Frank Jerico Nagbe

Cameroon 2
Stephane Mbia [9], Samuel Eto'o [54]

Idriss Carlos Kameni - Rigobert Song, Geremi Fotso Njitap, Timothee Atouba, Andre Bikey, Stephane Mbia (Modest Mbami 72), Jean Makoun (Guy Feutchine 83), Landry Nguemo, Achille Webo, Rudolph Douala (Idrissou Mahamadou 56), Samuel Eto'o. Tr: Jules Nyongha

Garoua
17-06-2007, Sowe GAM

Cameroon 2
Idrissou Mohamadou [34], Geremi Njitap [48]

Souleymanou Hamidou - Rigobert Song, Geremi Fotso Njitap, Andre Bikey, Stephane Mbia (Alioum Saidou 56), Jean-Hugues Bilayi Ateba, Modest Mbami (Landry Nguemo 75), Jean Makoun, Guy Feutchine, Achille Webo (Joseph-Desire Job 65), Idrissou Mahamadou. Tr: Jules Nyongha

Rwanda 1
Jimmy Gatete [77]

Ramazani Nkunzingoma - Abdul Sibomana, Bonaventure Hategekimana, Elias Ntaganda (Eric Gasana 69), Jeannot Witakenge, Ismail Nshutiyamagara, Manfred Kizito, Mwemere Ngirinshuti (Honore Kabongo 68), Haruna Niyonzima, Theoneste Muhanyimana (Jimmy Gatete 53), Said Abed Makasi. Tr: Michael Nees

Monrovia
17-06-2007, Diouf SEN

Liberia 0

Sunday Seah - Murphy Nagbe, Ousman Larmin (George Baysah 59), Dioh Williams, Zah Krangar, Solomon Grimes, Esiah Benson*, James Lomell (Tarkpor Sonkaley 54), Stephen Mennoh, Francis Doe, Anthony Laffor (Malcolm Cephas 76). Tr: Frank Jericho Nagbe

Equatorial Guinea 0

Emmanuel Danilo - Lawrence Doe, Jose Luis Rondo, David Alvarez* (Francisco Salvador Ela 75), Damian Gregorio Enzeama, Silvestre Mesaka (Domingo Akogo 88), Juvenal Edjogo (Jaime Mpanga 78), Juan Epitie, Ibrahima Toure, Lino Makuba*, Carolino Ronan*. Tr: Jordan de Freitas

Kigali
8-09-2007, Mwanza ZAM

Rwanda 4
Labama Bokota [21], Saidi Abed Makasi [29], Jeannot Witakenge [85], Olivier Karekezi [89]

Ramazani Nkunzingoma - Abdul Sibomana, Bonaventure Hategekimana*, Elias Ntaganda, Jeannot Witakenge (Jimmy Gatete 88), Ismail Nshutiyamagara, Manfred Kizito, Haruna Niyonzima (Honore Kabongo 62), Labama Bokota, Said Abed Makasi (Kase Kalisa 70), Olivier Karekezi. Tr: Michael Nees

Liberia 0

Saylee Swen - Solomon Wesseh, James Zotiah, Rashidi Williams (Arthur Jerry 72), Shleton Barlee, George Baysah, Jonny Bleedee (Vakomon Kromah 54), Frank Nagbe, Senbe Kennedy, Sunday Seah*, Anthony Laffor. Tr: Frank Jericho Nagbe

Malabo
9-09-2007, Sidibe MLI

Equatorial Guinea 1
Juvenal Edjogo [39]

Emmanuel Danilo - Lawrence Doe, Damian Gregorio Enzeama, Carolina Ronan (Alfonso Yago Yao 81), Jose Luis Rondo, Ibrahima Toure*, Benjamin Zarandona (Silvestre Mesaka 63), Javier Balboa, Juvenal Edjogo (Ivan Zarandona 70), Juan Epitie, Rodolfo Bodipo. Tr: Jordan de Freitas

Cameroon 0

Idriss Carlos Kameni - Rigobert Song*, Eric Matoukou, Geremi Fotso Njitap, Timothee Atouba, Stephane Mbia (Benoit Angbwa 81), Landry Nguemo (Modest Mbami 62), Jean Makoun, Guy Feutchine (Rudolph Douala 69), Idrissou Mahamadou, Joseph-Desire Job. Tr: Jules Nyongha

GROUP 6

Nairobi
2-09-2006, Lwanja MWI

Kenya	1
	Robert Mambo [64]

Arnold Origi - Musa Otieno, Adam Shaban, Julius Owino (Geoffrey Kokoyo 42), Wycliffe Juma, Robert Mambo (McDonald Maringa 76), Titus Mulama, Ali Mohamed, John Muiruri, Moses Odhiambo (Benjamin Maruti 53), Denis Oliech. Tr: Bernard Lama

Eritrea	2
	Origi OG [15], Shimangus Yednekatchew [65]

Simon Ghide - Efrem Bein, Elias Ali Abubeker*, Amanuel Negusse, Solomon Ogbaghabriel, Hamidy Abdelkader, Misgina Besirat (Filimon Teame 84), Tesfalidet Goitom, Yosef Michael, Suleman Mahmoud* (Berhane Aregay 89), Shimangus Yednekatchew (Temesghen Tefay 67). Tr: Dorian Marin*

Luanda
8-10-2006, Lwanja MWI

Angola	3
	Flavio 2 [37] [68], Mateus [60]

Lama - Jamba, Kali, Loco, Delgado, Andre, Mendonca (Xara 67), Miloy (Mateus 46), Ze Kalanga, Flavio, Mantorras (Love 56). Tr: Luis Oliveira Goncalves

Kenya	1
	Boniface Ambani [81]

Arnold Origi - Edwin Mukenya, Ahmed Yussuf*, Amanaka Zablon, Lyod Wahome* (Mustapha Mohamed 72), George Owino, Patrick Osiako (Abdulrakab Alwy 63), Elvis Ayany, Denis Oliech, McDonald Maringa, Hillay Echesa (Boniface Ambani 49). Tr: Tom Olaba

Asmara
2-06-2007, Marange ZIM

Eritrea	1
	Hamiday Abdelkadir [15]

Yosief Zeratsion - Ydnekachew Shimangus (Yonatan Goitom 69), Measho Berhe, Elias Debassay, Elias Ali*, Hamiday Abdelkadir, Solomon Ogbagebriel*, Tesfalidet Goitom* (Aram Negash 62), Berhane Arega, Suleiman Mohammed (Biniam Tessehaye 83), Solomon Kebede. Tr: Haile Tesfagaber

Angola	1
	Maurito [62]

Nuno - Kali, Jamba, Loco, Yamba Asha, Figueiredo (Maurito 59), Mendonca, Edson* (Marco Airosa 82), Andre, Flavio, Andre Titi Buengo (Mantorras 56). Tr: Luis Oliveira Goncalves

Luanda
17-06-2007, Marange ZIM

Angola	3
	Figueiredo [18], Love [30], Flavio [57]

Nuno - Loco, Yamba Asha, Kali, Jamba, Andre, Mendonca, Ze Kalanga* (Edson 81), Figueiredo (Andre Titi Buengo 85), Love, Flavio (Mantorras 71). Tr: Luis Oliveira Goncalves

Swaziland	0

Thokozani Mkhulisi - Absalom Dlamini*, Mxolisi Mthethwa, Mduduzi Sibya, Mphile Tsabedze, Wandile Mazibuko, Wonder Nhleko (Gcina Mazibuko* 61), Dennis Masina* (Manqoba Tsabedze 66), Mfanzile Dlamini, Siza Dlamini*, Mzwandile Mamba. Tr: Manfred Chabinga

Somhlolo
3-09-2006, Maillet SEY

Swaziland	0

Njabuliso Simelane - Mpendulo Kunene, Sipho Gumbi, Mduduzi Sibiya*, Wandile Mazibuko, Mxolisi Mthethwa*, Sibusiso Dlamini, Zweli Msibi (Manoqba Kunene 59), Siza Dlamini, Dennis Masina, Tony Tsabedze (Mduduzi Mdluli 38). Tr: Ayman El Yamani

Angola	2
	Gumbi OG [21], Loco [80]

Lama - Yamba Asha, Kali, Jamba, Loco, Ze Kalanga (Mateus 81), Figueiredo (Ze Augusto 75), Xara, Mendonca, Mantorras (Love 67), Flavio*. Tr: Luis Oliveira Gonçalves

Luanda
25-03-2007, Evehe CMR

Angola	6
	Flavio 2 [28] [69], Mantorras [36], Ze Kalanga [43], Mendonca [47], Figueiredo [84]

Lama - Jamba, Kali, Yamba Asha, Loco*, Figueiredo, Xara, Mendonca, Ze Kalanga (Edson 46), Mantorras (Andre Titi Buengo 59), Flavio (Manucho 75). Tr: Luis Oliveira Goncalves

Eritrea	1
	Misgina Besirat [73]

Simon Ghide* - Measho Berhe, Elias Ali Abubeker, Yosef Fesfazghi, Hamidy Abdelkader, Ermias Maekele*, Filimon Teame (Medhanie Aghade 49), Misgina Besirat*, Michael Yosef, Temesghen Tesfay (Yonas Negassi 74), Shimangus Yednekatchew (Berhane Aregay 63). Tr: Dorian Marin

Somhlolo
3-06-2007, Katjimune NAM

Swaziland	0

Thokozani Mkhulisi - Mpendulo Kunene, Mabandla Dlamini, Mduduzi Sibya, Wandile Mazibuko, Mphile Tsabedze*, Wonder Nhleko* (Barry Steenkamp 89), Gcina Mazibuko (Mzwandile Mamba 64), Dennis Masina, Tony Tsabedze (Siza Dlamini 47), Mfanzile Dlamini. Tr: Manfred Chabinga

Kenya	0

Arnold Origi - George Waweru*, Adam Shabani, Ibrahim Shikanda, Mulunge Ndeto, Jamal Mohammed (Patrick Oboya 69), Austine Makacha* (Andrew Oyombe 80), Titus Mulama, Robert Mambo, McDonald Maringa*, Dennis Oliech (Allan Wanga 54). Tr: Jacob Mulee

Nairobi
8-09-2007, Katjimune NAM

Kenya	2
	Patrick Oboya [18], Dennis Oliech [87]

David Okello - Ibrahim Shikanda, John Mwanji, Mulunge Ndeto, Charles Oduor (Edgar Ochieng 53), Abubakar Yusuf, Collins Ochieng (Kevin Opondo* 53), Anthony Ojiambo, Haji Mwenda (Ali Hassan 64), Patrick Oboya, Dennis Oliech. Tr: Jacob Mulee

Angola	1
	Manucho [35]

Lama - Delgado, Jamba, Kali (Joaozinho 33), Tinto, Figueiredo (Nelo 69), Andre*, Edson (Mabina 55), Mendonca, Manucho, Flavio. Tr: Luis Oliveira Goncalves

Asmara
7-10-2006, Gasingwa RWA

Eritrea	0

Yosief Zeratsion - Elias Debessay, Amanuel Negusse, Elias Ali Abubeker, Solomon Ogbaghabriel, Misgina Besirat, Tesfalidet Goitom* (Frezghi Berhe 46), Suleman Mahmoud, Yonas Fesehaye (Biniam Fesehaye 51), Shimangus Yednekatchew (Temesghen Tesfay 73). Tr: Dorian Marin

Swaziland	0

Nhlanhla Gwebu - Mpendulo Kunene, Sipho Gumbi, Mduduzi Sibiya, Wandile Mazibuko, Mxolisi Mthethwa*, Absalom Dlamini*, Zweli Msibi (Gcina Mazibuko 53), Siza Dlamini (Mzwandile Mamba 81), Dennis Masina, Tony Tsabedze. Tr: Ayman El Yamani

Nairobi
25-03-2007, Seechum MRI

Kenya	2
	MacDonald Maringa [51], Patrick Oboya [75]

Arnold Origi - Edwin Mukenya, Mulinge Ndeto, George Waweru*, Wycliffe Juma (Ibrahim Shikanda 46), Andrew Oyombe, Titus Mulama (Jamal Mohamed 69), Robert Mambo, Denis Oliech, McDonald Maringa, Michael Baraza (Patrick Oboya 50). Tr: Jacob Mulee

Swaziland	0

Njabuliso Simelane - Mpendulo Kunene, Sipho Gumbi, Mduduzi Sibiya, Wandile Mazibuko, Mabandla Dlamini, Wonder Nhleko (Salebona Jele 72), Absalom Dlamini (Nkosingiphile Tsabedze 63), Mzwandile Mamba, Dennis Masina, Tony Tsabedze (Gcina Mazibuko 81). Tr: Ayman El Yamani

Asmara
16-06-2007, Abdelrahman SUD

Eritrea	1
	Berhane Arega [80]

Yosief Zeratsion - Ydnekachew Shimangus (Filmon Teame 60), Solomon Ogbagebriel, Solomon Kebede, Dahlak Tekleab, Measho Berhe, Hamiday Abdelkadir, Berhane Arega, Aron Zekarias, Elias Debessay*, Suleiman Mohammed (Yonatan Goitom 39). Tr: Haile Tesfagaber

Kenya	0

Evans Omondi - Charles Oduor, Adam Shabani, Ibrahim Shikanda, Mulunge Ndeto, Andrew Oyombe*, Titus Mulama (Kevin Ochieng 86), Jamal Mohammed, Robert Mambo, McDonald Maringa (Allan Wanga 78), Boniface Ambani (Patrick Oboya 67). Tr: Jacob Mulee

Manzini
9-09-2007, Ssegonga UGA

Swaziland	0

Thokozani Mkhulisi - Wandile Mazibuko, Zwelithini Msibi (Dennis Fakude 57), Mxolisi Mthethwa, Mduduzi Sibya, Mphile Tsabedze (Sandile Ndlovu 57), Gcina Mazibuko, Dennis Masina, Sibusiso Dlamini, Mfanzile Dlamini (Siza Dlamini 64), Tony Tsabedze*. Tr: Manfred Chabinga

Eritrea	0

Yosief Zeratsion - Ydnekachew Shimangus (Yonatan Goitom 59), Hamiday Abdelkadir, Measho Berhe* (Ermias Maekele 63), Elias Ali Abubeker, Elias Debessay*, Solomon Kebede, Berhane Arega, Solomon Ogbagebriel, Aron Zekarias, Tesfaldet Goitom (Biniam Fessehaye 83). Tr: Haile Tesfagaber

GROUP 7

Dakar
2-09-2006, Sule NGA

Senegal 2
Dario Khan OG [35], Guirane Ndaw [61]

Tony Sylva - Guirane Ndaw, Pape Malickou Diakhate●, Lamine Diatta, Habib Beye, Frederic Mendy (Ibrahima Sidibe 82), Papa Malick Ba, Papa Bouba Diop (Abdoulaye Diagne Faye 86), Moussa Ndiaye (Ousmane Ndoye 69), El Hadj Diouf, Mamadou Niang. Tr: Henryk Kasperczak

Mozambique 0

Kampango● - Dario Khan●, Mano, Nando, Armando Sa (Miro 52), Nelinho●, Macamito● (Haji 88), Genito, Paito, Tico-Tico (Danito Parruque 69), Dario. Tr: Artur Semedo

---

Dar-es-Salaam
2-09-2006, Ndinya KEN

Tanzania 2
Harouna Bamogo OG [23], Nizar Khalfan [65]

Ivo Mapunda - Shadrack Nsajigwa, Mecky Maxime, Victor Costa, Salum Swedi, Henry Joseph, Renatus Njohola (Nizar Khalfan 46), Iddi Athumani, Gaudence Mwaikimba● (Musa Hassan Mgosi 83), Saidi Maulid, Abdi Kassim (Alfred Ulimboka 89). Tr: Marcio Maximo

Burkina Faso 1
Abdoulaye Cisse [39]

Mohamed Kabore, Mamadou Tall, Paul Koulibaly●, Harouna Bamogo, Joel Kouassi, Mahamoudou Kere, Idrissa Kabore (Georges Bonou 53), Alassane Ouedraogo (Abdoul Aziz Nikiema 84), Abdoulaye Cisse (Yahia Kebe 79), Tanguy Barro, Aristide Bance●. Tr: Idrissa Traore

---

Ouagadougou
7-10-2006, Guezzaz MAR

Burkina Faso 1
Narcisse Yameogo [59p]

Abdoulaye Soulama - Harouna Bamogo●, Bakary Kone, Mamadou Tall, Paul Koulibaly, Joel Kouassi, Charles Kabore●, Alassane Ouedraogo (Youssouf Sanou 40) Narcisse Yameogo, Jonathan Pitroipa (Aristide Bance 86), Yssouf Kone. Tr: Idrissa Traore

Senegal 0

Tony Sylva - Habib Beye●, Lamine Diatta, Pape Malickou Diakhate●59, Guirane Ndaw, Abdoulaye Diagne Faye, Pape Bouba Diop● (Moussa Ndiaye 80), Ousmane Ndoye (Pape Waigo Ndiaye 74), Diomansy Kamara (Pape Malick Ba● 63), El Hadj Diouf, Henri Camara. Tr: Henryk Kasperczak

---

Maputo
8-10-2006, Kaoma ZAM

Mozambique 0

Kampango, Nando (Campira 89), Dario Khan●, Mano, Paito, Micas●, Nelinho (Macamito 58), Genito, Miro (Mauricio 75), Domingues, Dario. Tr: Artur Semedo

Tanzania 0

Ivo Mapunda, Shadrack Nsajigwa, Mecky Maxime, Salum Swedi, Victor Costa, Henry Joseph, Saidi Maulid, Athumani Idd, Renatus Njohole (Nizar Khalfan 46), Gaudence Mwaikimba (Musa Hassan Mgosi 68), Abdi Kassim● (Hussein Swedi 81). Tr: Marcio Maximo

---

Dakar
24-03-2007, Daami TUN

Senegal 4
Mamadou Niang 3 [39] [48] [62], Diomansy Kamara [46]

Tony Sylva - Guirane Ndaw, Lamine Diatta, Abdoulaye Diagne Faye, Pascal Mendy, Moustapha Bayal Sall (Ibrahima Faye 78), Ousmane Ndoye, Frederic Mendy, Elhadj Diouf (Demba Toure 84), Diomansy Kamara, Mamadou Niang● (Henri Camara 70). Tr: Henri Kasperczak

Tanzania 0

Ivo Mapunda - Shadrack Nsajigwa, Mecky Maxime●, Victor Costa●, Yusuph Hamisi, Henry Joseph, Athumani Idd (Shabani Nditi 70), Nizar Khalfan, Gaudence Mwaikimba● (Joseph Kaniki 67), Saidi Maulid, Abdi Kassim (Amri Maftah 80). Tr: Marcio Maximo

---

Ouagadougou
24-03-2007, Imiere NGA

Burkina Faso 1
Jonathan Pitroipa [26]

Abdoulaye Soulama, Mamadou Tall, Saidou Mady Panandetiguiri, Joel Kouassi, Soumaila Tassembedo, Charles Kabore, Eric Dagbe (Alassane Ouedraogo 63), Narcisse Yameogo, Jonathan Pitroipa, Pierre Coulibaly● (Issouf Ouattara 86), Gervais Sanou (Aristides Bance 34). Tr: Idrissa Traore

Mozambique 1
Mano [2]

Kampango - Simao, Nando, Mano, Miro●, Nelinho, Carlitos, Paito, Domingues, Genito (Julinho 69●85), Tico-Tico. Tr: Mart Nooij

---

Mwanza
2-06-2007, Damon RSA

Tanzania 1
Nizar Khalfan [17]

Ivo Mapunda - Mecky Maxime, Salum Swedi, Victor Costa, Shadrack Nsajigwa, Henry Joseph, Shabani Nditi● (Juma Saidi 60), Nizar Khalfan, Abdi Kassim● (Dan Mrwanda 77), Haruna Moshi, Said Maulid. Tr: Marcio Maximo

Senegal 1
Demba Ba [75]

Tony Sylva - Habib Beye, Lamine Diatta, Pape Malickou Diakhate, Guirane Ndaw (Pascal Mendy 71), Pape Waigo Ndiaye (Pape Demba Toure 60), Pape Malick Ba, Moustapha Bayal Sall (Ousmane Ndoye 46), Frederic Mendy, Diomansy Kamara●, Demba Ba. Tr: Henryk Kasperczak

---

Maputo
3-06-2007, Raolimanana MAD

Mozambique 3
Dario [6p], Tico-Tico 2 [34] [46]

Kampango - Whiskey, Simao, Mano, Paito, Nelinho, Alvarito (Carlitos 64), Genito, Dominguez, Tico-Tico (Danito 77), Dario● (Miro 46). Tr: Mart van Nooij

Burkina Faso 1
Wilfred Sanou [38]

Abdoulaye Soulama● - Saidou Madi Panandetiguiri, Soumailla Tassembedo, Joel Kouassi, Moussa Ouattara, Charles Kabore, Bebe Kambou (Florent Rouamba 64), Wilfred Sanou (Alain Traore 75), Jonathan Pitroipa, Issouf Kone (Tanguy Barro● 58), Moumouni Dagano. Tr: Didier Notheaux

---

Ouagadougou
16-06-2007, Coulibaly MLI

Burkina Faso 0

Abdoulaye Soulama - Saidou Madi Panandetiguiri● (Charles Kabore 85), Tanguy Barro, Harouna Bamogo, Joel Kouassi, Bebe Kambou (Alain Traore 59), Wilfried Sanou, Jonathan Pitroipa (Abdoulaye Cisse 74), Moumouni Dagano. Tr: Didier Notheaux

Tanzania 1
Erasto Nyoni [71]

Ivo Mapunda - Shadrack Nsajigwa●62, Erasto Nyoni●, Salum Swedi●, Nadir Haroub●, Henry Joseph, Shaban Nditi, Nizar Khalfan, Haruna Moshi, Said Maulidi (Danny Mrwanda 78), Amir Maftah (Malegesi Mwangwa 89). Tr: Marco Maximo●65

Maputo
17-06-2007, Seechum MRI

Mozambique 0

Kampango - Dario Khan, Simao, Mano●, Paito, Nelinho, Carlitos (Alvarito 78), Genito, Miro (Mauricio 85), Dominguez, Dario (Goncalves Fumo 61). Tr: Mart van Nooij

Senegal 0

Tony Sylva - Habib Beye●, Lamine Diatta, Pape Malickou Diakhate, Guirane Ndaw, Pape Malick Ba, Pape Waigo Ndiaye (Pascal Mendy 67), Ousmane Ndoye (Adama Sene 77), Frederic Mendy, Diomansy Kamara, Pape Demba Toure (Adama Sarr 89). Tr: Henryk Kasperczak

---

Dakar
8-09-2007, Haimoudi ALG

Senegal 5
Guirane Ndaw [22], Ousmane Ndoye [72], Henri Camara 2 [74] [84], El Hadji Diouf [89]

Tony Sylva - Ferdinand Coly●, Lamine Diatta, Mohamed Adama Sarr, Guirane Ndaw, Pape Bouba Diop (Ousmane Ndoye● 60), Moustapha Bayal Sall, Diomansy Kamara (Babacar Gueye 81), Frederic Mendy, Mamadou Niang (Henri Camara 60), Elhadj Diouf. Tr: Henryk Kasperczak

Burkina Faso 1
Alain Traore [34]

Mohamed Kabore - Saidou Madi Panandetiguiri●, Arouna Bamogo● (Amadou Koulibaly 77), Paul Koulibaly●, Mamadou Tall●, Bakary Kone, Charles Kabore (Joel Kouassi 76), Jonathan Pitroipa, Sibiri Alain Traore (Aristide Bance 50), Pierre Koulibaly, Wilfried Sanou. Tr: Didier Notheaux

---

Dar-es-Salaam
8-09-2007, Guezzaz MAR

Tanzania 0

Ivo Mapunda - Mecky Maxime, Amri Mafaha, Nazir Haroub, Salum Swedi, Henry Joseph●, Nizar Khalfan, Shabani Nduti (Danny Mrwanda 46), Haruna Moshi●, Said Maulid (Joseph Kaniki 72), Abdi Kassim. Tr: Marco Maximo

Mozambique 1
Tico-Tico [2]

Kampagno - Simao, Dario Khan●, Mano, Paito, Nelinho, Genito (Danito 76), Miro● (Carlitos 83), Domingues, Tico-Tico (Rivaldo 89), Dario Monteiro. Tr: Mart van Nooij

GROUP 8

Banjul
3-09-2006, Pare BFA

Gambia 2
Jatto Ceesay [8p], Assan Jatta [89]

Pa Dembo Touray* - Simon Badjie, Mathew Mendy, Abdoulie Corr, Edrisa Sonko*, Ebrima Sillah* (Daouda Bah 88), Mustapha Kebba Jarju, Jatto Cessay* (Kemo Ceesay 78), Modou Jagne (Assan Jatta* 68), Abdou Jammeh, Lamin Conateh. Tr: Peter Bonou Johnson

Cape Verde Islands 0

Ernesto - Nelson Veiga, Ze Piguista, Pele, Nando* (Nene 76), Sandro, Lito*, Victor Moreno (Rodolfo Lima 68), Gabei, Calo (Hernani 70), Cafu. Tr: Jose Rui

---

Conakry
3-09-2006, Coulibaly MLI

Guinea 0

Kemoko Kamara - Oumar Kalabane, Kanfory Sylla, Mamadi Kabi, Camille Zayate (Daouda Jabi 78), Mohamed Alimou Diallo, Ibrahima Camara*, Mohamed Sylla, Ismael Bangoura (Kaba Diawara 60), Fode Mansare*, Ibrahima Bangoura. Tr: Patrice Neveu

Algeria 0

Lounes Gaouaoui - Mehdi Meniri*, Madjid Bougherra, Anthar Yahia, Nadir Belhadj*, Mohamed Meftah*, Abderraouf Zarabi, Chadli Amri (Ali Boulebda 89), Yazid Mansouri, Mansour Boutabout* (Hamza Yacef 88), Noureddine Daham (Brahim Mezouar 75). Tr: Jean-Michel Cavalli

---

Algiers
7-10-2006, Auda EGY

Algeria 1
Karim Ziani [75p]

Lounes Gaouaoui, Mohamed Hamdoud, Madjid Bougherra, Mehdi Meniri, Abderaouf Zarabi, Karim Ziani (Mansour Boutabout 89), Yazid Mansouri, Chadli Amri, Nadir Belhadj, Rafik Saifi (Arafat Mezouar 87), Noureddine Daham (Abdelmalek Cherrad 68). Tr: Jean-Michel Cavalli

Gambia 0

Pa Dembo Touray - Kemo Ceesay, Simon Badjie, Edrissa Sonko, Abdourahman Njie (Assan Jatta 78), Njogu Demba, Ebrima Sillah, Mustapha Kebba Jarju (Lamine Conateh 35), Momar Njie*, Abdou Jammeh*30, Mathew Mendy (Modou Jagne 86). Tr: Antoine Hey

---

Praia
7-10-2006, Diatta SEN

Cape Verde Islands 1
Lito [52]

Ernesto - Victor Moreno (Nelson Veiga 46), Ze Piguista, Pele, Nando, Sandro (Marco Soares 83), Gabei*, Nene*, Rodolfo Lima*, Hernani (Calo 70), Lito. Tr: Jose Rui

Guinea 0

Kemoko Camara - Dianbobo Balde, Daouda Jabi, Ibrahima Camara, Omar Kalabane*, Camille Zayatte (Ismael Bangoura 46), Ibrahima Bangoura, Kanfory Sylla, Mohamed Sylla, Fode Mansare, Souleymane Youla* (Kaba Diawara 58). Tr: Patrice Neveu

---

Algiers
24-03-2007, Abdelfattah EGY

Algeria 2
Noureddine Daham [60], Mehdi Meniri [89]

Lounes Gaouaoui - Ismael Bouzid*, Madjid Bougherra, Mehdi Meniri, Abderaouf Zarabi, Karim Ziani, Yazid Mansouri*, Nadir Belhadj*, Hameur Bouazza (Seiffedine Amroune 88), Rafik Saifi (Sofiane Younes 89), Noureddine Daham (Karim Matmour 73). Tr: Jean-Michel Cavalli

Cape Verde Islands 0

Ernesto - Nelson Veiga, Ze Piguista, Pele, Nando, Sandro*, Gabei* (Janicio 68), Nene* (Hernani 78), Lito, Rodolfo Lima (Cafu 83), Dady. Tr: Ricardo Rocha

---

Banjul
24-03-2007, Kotey GHA

Gambia 0

Pa Dembo Touray - Abdoulie Corr, Seyfo Soley, Pa Saikou Kujabi, Mathew Mendy (Aziz Corr Njang 63), Edrissa Sonko, Mustapha Kebba Jarju (Assan Jatta 60), Dawda Bah (Mustapha Kamal Ndaw 79), Jatto Ceesay, Njogu Demba, Lamine Conateh*. Tr: Alhagi

Guinea 2
Kaba Diawara [57], Pascal Feinduono [69]

Kemoko Camara - Daouda Jabi, Ibrahima Camara, Omar Kalabane*, Camille Zayatte, Schuman Bah, Kanfory Sylla*, Ismael Bangoura (Ibrahima Souare 80), Pascal Feindouno, Fode Mansare (Aboubacar Sylla 78), Kaba Diawara (Souleymane Youla 76). Tr: Robert Nouzaret

---

Praia
2-06-2007, Aboubacar CIV

Cape Verde Islands 2
Marco Soares [58], Hernani [89]

Ernesto - Janicio*, Pele, Ze Piguista, Vargas, Lito, Moreno* (Puma), Marco Soares, Dario (Rodolfo Lima), Calo (Hernani*). Dady. Tr: Ricardo Rocha

Algeria 2
Majid Bougherra [33], Rafik Saifi [84]

Lounes Gaouaoui*26 - Mohamed Meftah, Samir Zaoui, Madjid Bougherra, Ismael Bouzid, Abderaouf Zarabi, Karim Ziani, Chadli Amri (Karim Matmour 77), Antar Yahia, Yacine Bezzaz (Samir Hadjaoui 28), Rafik Saifi (Kamel Ghilas 89). Tr: Jean-Michel Cavalli

---

Conakry
3-06-2007, Djaoupe TOG

Guinea 2
Daouda Jabi [9], Fode Mansare [55]

Naby Diarso - Daouda Jabi, Camille Zayatte, Mamadou Alimou Diallo*, Ibrahima Camara, Ibrahima Souare*, Mohamed Sylla (Kanfory Sylla 71), Fode Mansare, Ismael Bangoura (Ibrahima Bangoura 86), Kaba Diawara (Souleymane Youla 82). Tr: Robert Nouzaret

Gambia 2
Edrissa Sonko [53], Pa Modou Jagne [85]

Musa Bajaha - Edrissa Sonko*, Abdoulie Corr, Lamin Conateh, Pa Saikou Kujabie*, Ousmane Colley, Mathew Mendy, Ebrima Sillah, Dawda Bah*, Kamala Ndaw (Modou Jagne 73), Njogu Demba (Assan Jatta 68). Tr: Jose Martinez

---

Algiers
16-06-2007, Guezzaz MAR

Algeria 0

Samir Hadjaoui - Mohamed Meftah, Mehdi Meniri, Majid Bougherra, Antar Yahia (Noureddine Daham 46), Abderraouf Zarabi (Yassine Bezzaz 8), Nadir Belhadj, Yazid Mansouri, Chadli Amri (Kamel Ghilas 64), Karim Ziani*, Rafik Saifi. Tr: Jean-Michel Cavalli

Guinea 2
Fode Mansare [44], Pascal Feindouno [85]

Naby Diarso - Daouda Jabi, Camille Zayatte (Omar Kalabane 77), Ibrahima Camara, Mohamed Alioum Diallo*, Kanfory Sylla, Mohamed Cisse, Pascal Feindouno, Ismael Bangoura (Ibrahima Bangoura 82), Souleymane Youla* (Kaba Diawara 89), Fode Mansare. Tr: Robert Nouzaret

---

Praia
16-06-2007, Aguidissou BEN

Cape Verde Islands 0

Veiga - Janicio, Pele (Loloti 70), Ze Piguista, Nando, Gabei*, Marcos Soares, Rodolfo Lima (Calo 86), Vargas (Hernani 60), Lito, Dady. Tr: Ricardo Rocha

Gambia 0

Alhagie Momodou Jobe* - Ousmane Colley, Abdou Jammeh*, Mathew Mendy, Pa Saikou Kujabie (Babucarr Sey 67), Dawda Bah*86, Mustapha Jarju*, Yankuba Cesay, Ebrima Sillah*76, Mustapha Ndaw (Modou Jagne 65), Njogu Demba (Assan Jatta 80). Tr: Jose Martinez

---

Banjul
9-09-2007, Imiere NGA

Gambia 2
Assan Jatta [71], Mathew Mendy [88]

Musa Bajaha - Edrissa Sonko (Ebrima Sillah 65), Abdoulie Carr, Mathew Mendy*, Pa Saikou Kujabi (Modou Jagne 61), Njogu Demba (Assan Jatta 57), Pa Modou Jagne, Mustapha Kebba Jargu, Ousman Jallow*76, Lamin Conateh*, Abdou Jammeh*. Tr: Jose Martinez

Algeria 1
Rafik Saifi [56]

Lounes Gaouaoui - Ismael Bouzid, Mehdi Meniri (Noureddine Daham 79), Anthar Yahia*, Abderaouf Zarabi, Karim Ziani, Madjid Bougherra*, Yazid Mansouri (Yacine Mansouri* 10), Nadir Belhadj, Rafik Saifi, Mansour Boutabout (Chadli Amri 75). Tr: Jean-Michel Cavalli

---

Conakry
9-09-2007, Trabelsi TUN

Guinea 4
Pascal Feindouno [19p], Mohamed Cisse [32], Ibrahima Camara [37], Ismael Bangoura [44]

Naby Yattara - Daouda Jabi, Ibrahima Camara, Omar Kalabane, Dianbobo Balde, Mohamed Cisse* (Samuel Johnson 56), Kanfory Sylla, Pascal Feindouno (Alhassane Keita 73), Fode Mansare*, Ismael Bangoura, Kaba Diawara (Ibrahima Yattara 71). Tr: Robert Nouzaret

Cape Verde Islands 0

Veiga - Vargas, Ricardo, Pele, Chelo (Toy Adao 46), Gabei, Lito, Marco Soares, Hernani, Rodolfo Lima* (Babanco 83), Jerry (Mateus 46). Tr: Ricardo Rocha

GROUP 9

Freetown
3-09-2006, Mbera GAB

Sierra Leone	0

Mali	0

Michael Tommy - Ibrahim Kargbo (Kemoko Kallon 89), Gibrilla Woobay•, Kewullay Conteh, Mustapha Sama•57, Umaru Bangoura, Lamine Conteh, Samuel Barley•, Benjamin Sesay, Mohamed Kallon, Sheriff Suma (Abubakar Bah 89). Tr: Jebor Sherrington

Mahamadou Sidibe - Sammy Traore, Adama Coulibaly, Souleymane Diamoutene, Djimi Traore, Alphousseiny Keita, Seydou Keita, Mamadou Diallo (Vincent Doukantie 74), Bassala Toure (Sidi Yaya Keita 89), Dramane Traore• (Sigamary Diarra 67), Frederic Kanoute•. Tr: Jean-Francois Jodar

Bamako
8-10-2006, Benouza ALG

Mali	1
	Dramane Traore 89

Togo	0

Mahamadou Sidibe - Cedric Kante, Adama Coulibaly•, Eric Sekou Chelle (Adama Tamboura 79), Souleymane Diamoutene, Drissa Diakite, Mohamed Lamine Sissoko, Bassala Toure (Dramane Traore 68), Seydou Keita, Mamadou Diallo•, Mamadi Sidibe (Harouna Diarra 87). Tr: Jean-Francois Jodar

Kossi Agassa - Jean-Paul Abalo Yaovi, Dare Nibombe•, Massamesso Tchangai•, Richmond Forson, Komlan Amevon, Alaixys Romao• (Eric Akoto 24), Salifou Moustapha•, Thomas Dossevi (Junior Senaya 79), Mohamed Kader Coubadja• (Robert Malm 71), Emmanuel Adebayor. Tr: Mawvena Kodjovi

Cotonou
3-06-2007, Guezzaz MAR

Benin	0

Rachad Chitou - Damien Chrystosome•, Abdul Adenon, Stephane Sessegnon, Silvere Tchegnon (Felicien Singbo 55), Romauld Boco, Jocelyn Ahoueya, Seidath Tchomogo, Oumar Tchomogo•, Abou Maiga (Wassiou Oladipikpo 67), Razak Omotoyossi. Tr: Waby Gomez

Mali	0

Mahamadou Sidibe - Souleymane Diamoutene, Adama Coulibaly, Boubacar Sidiki Kone•, Adama Tamboura•, Bassala Toure (Mintou Doucoure 67), Mahamadou Diarra, Alphousseiny Keita, Seydou Keita, Cheikh Oumar Dabo (Djibril Sidibe 85), Frederic Kanoute. Tr: Jean-Francois Jodar

Bamako
17-06-2007, Lemghambodj MTN

Mali	6
Djibril Sidibe 20p, Seydou Keita 2 68 88, Mamadou Diallo 76, Lassana Diallo 89, Bassala Toure 90	

Mahamadou Sidibe - Adama Coulibaly, Boubacar Sidiki Kone (Moussa Coulibaly 81), Souleymane Diamoutene, Idrissa Coulibaly• (Souleymane Dembele 69), Djibril Sidibe, Alphousseiny Keita, Seydou Keita, Bassala Toure, Mamadou Diallo, Cheikh Oumar Dabo (Lassana Diallo 76). Tr: Jean-Francois Jodar

Sierra Leone	0

Christian Coker (Habib Sesay 71) - Mustapha Sama, Ibrahim Koroma•58, Alimamy Sesay•, Jamil Kargbo (Moussa Jallow 74), Mohamed Fornah, Julius Conteh•, John Kanu, Ahmed Dian (Abdoul Din Sesay 86), Nayim Kadi, Paul Kpaka. Tr: Leroy Rosenoir

Lome
3-09-2006, Louzaya CGO

Togo	2
Thomas Dossevi 13, Komlan Amewou 78	

Abdoul Nassirou Omorou - Jean-Paul Abalo Yaovi•, Akoete Eniful, Moustapha Salifou (Ezekiel Behlow 83), Abdoul Gafar Mamah, Thomas Dossevi, Richmond Forson, Adekanmi Olufade, Komlan Amewou, Alaixys Romao (Paul Adado 61), Junior Senaya. Tr: Mawvena Kodjovi

Benin	1
	Seidath Tchomogo 86

Thomas Djilan - Damien Chrysostome, Anicet Adjamossi•, Abdul Adenon, Alain Gaspoz•, Romauld Bocco, Jocelyn Ahoueya, Muri Ogunbiyi•, Razak Omotoyossi, Stephane Sessegnon (Seidath Tchomogo 46), Nounhoum Kobena (Abou Maiga 60). Tr: Edme Codjo

Bamako
25-03-2007, Doue CIV

Mali	1
	Frederic Kanoute 53p

Mahamadou Sidibe - Adama Coulibaly, Cedric Kante, Souleymane Diamoutene, Adama Tamboura, Mahamadou Diarra, Soumaila Coulibaly (Bassala Toure 57), Mohamed Lamine Sissoko (Drissa Diakite 72), Seydou Keita, Mamadou Diallo•, Frederic Kanoute (Dramane Traore 79). Tr: Jean Francois Jodar

Benin	1
	Muri Ogunbiyi 44

Rachad Chitou - Damien Chrystosome, Abdul Adenon, Alain Gaspoz, Anicet Adjamossi•, Jocelyn Ahoueya, Seidath Tchomogo (Agnide Moustapha 87), Stephane Sessegnon, Oumar Tchomogo, Muri Ogunbiyi• (Jonas Oketola 75), Razak Omotoyossi. Tr: Waby Gomez

Freetown
3-06-2007, Imiere NGA

Sierra Leone	0

Habib Sesay - Kewullay Conteh (Julius Conteh 65), Mohamed Fornah, Mustapha Sama, Umaru Bangoura, Ahmed Dian, Albert Jarrett, Samuel Barclay, Sheriff Suma, Julius Wobay, Alimamy Sesay. Tr: Leroy Rosenoir

Togo	1
	Junior Senaya 48

Ouro Nimini Tchagnirou - Emmanuel Mathias (Kassim Guyazou 60'), Franck Atsou (Eric Akoto 86'), Abdou Djabaro Moumouni, Zanzan Atte Oudeyi, Moustapha Salifou• (Jonathan Ayite 89'), Thomas Dossevi, Souleymane Mamam, Alaixys Romao•, Abdou Nasirou Ouro Akpo, Junior Senaya. Tr: Stephen Keshi

Freetown
12-10-2007, Ambaya LBY

Sierra Leone	0

Christian Coker - Albert Foday, Mohamed Fomah, Hassan Sesay, Alimamy Sesay, Pasafa Sama•, Desmond Mansaray, Umaru Bangoura, Ismail Kamara, Julius Wobay, Sheriff Suma. Tr: Mohamed Kallon

Benin	2
	Oumar Tchomogo 2 9 65

Rachad Chitou - Damien Chrystosome, Abdul Adenon, Anicet Adjamossi, Seidath Tchomogo, Jocelyn Ahoueya, Romauld Boco, Stephane Sessegnon, Muri Ogunbiyi, Abou Maiga, Oumar Tchomogo. Tr: Waby Gomez

Cotonou
8-10-2006, Sowe GAM

Benin	2
Rachad Chitou 22p, Muri Ogunbiyi 82	

Rachad Chitou - Anicet Adjamossi, Abdul Adenon, Alain Gaspoz, Romauld Bocco, Jocelyn Ahoueya, Jonas Oketola•, Muri Ogunbiyi, Abou Maiga (Medard Zanou 82), Seidath Tchomogo, Razak Omotoyossi•. Tr: Edme Codjo

Sierra Leone	0

Michael Tommy - Ibrahim Kargbo, Kemokai Kallon (Nahim Khadi 85), Hassan Sesay•65, Umaru Bangoura, Benjamin Sesay•, Samuel Barley•, Sydney Kargbo (Sidique Mansaray 75), Paul Kpaka, Lamin Conteh (Abubakar Bah 89), Sheriff Suma. Tr: Jeboh Sherrington

Lome
25-03-2007, Pare BFA

Togo	3
Adebayor 2 38 85, Adekanmi Olufade 62	

Kossi Agassa - Dare Nibombe, Massamesso Tchangai, Zanzan Atte Oudeyi, Yao Aziawonou (Komlan Amewou 72), Abdoul Gafar Mamah, Alaixys Romao, Mohamed Kader Coubadja (Kassim Guyazou 82), Souleymane Mamam (Moustapha Salifou 55), Emmanuel Adebayor. Tr: Stephen Keshi

Sierra Leone	1
	Gibrilla Woobay 77

Michael Tommy - Ibrahim Kargbo, Kemokai Kallon• (Muwahid Sesay 77), Mohamed Fornah, Gibrilla Woobay, Alpha Suma Lansana, Pasafa Sama• (Nahim Khadi 87), Alimamy Sesay, Umaru Bangoura, Mohamed Kallon, Sheriff Suma (Brima Conteh 69). Tr: Jeboh Sherington

Cotonou
17-06-2007, Evehe CMR

Benin	4
Omotoyossi 2 44 52, Sessegnon 47, Ogunbiyi 58	

Rachad Chitou - Damien Chrystosome, Abdul Adenon, Stephane Sessegnon (Wassiou Oladipikpo 62), Alain Gaspoz•, Anicet Adjamossi, Jocelyn Ahoueya, Seidath Tchomogo, Oumar Tchomogo, Muri Ogunbiyi (Romauld Boco 75), Razak Omotoyossi• (Abou Maiga 70). Tr: Waby Gomez

Togo	1
	Adekanmi Olufade 75

Ouro Nimini Tchagnirou - Emmanuel Mathias•, Franck Atsou (Kwami Akoete Eninful 67), Yao Senaya (Floyo Ama Ayite 55), Abdou Djabaro Moumouni, Zanzan Atte Oudeyi, Komlan Amewou, Adekanmi Olufade•, Vincent Tchalla (Abdou Nasirou Ouro Akpo 60), Junior Senaya, Souleymane Mamam. Tr: Stephen Keshi

Lome
12-10-2007, Abdelfatah EGY

Togo	0

Ouro Nimini Tchagnirou - Abdoul Gafar Mamah, Dare Nibombe (Abdou Moumouni 58), Massamesso Tchangai, Zanzan Atte Oudeyi•, Alaixys Romao•, Moustapha Salifou, Junior Senaya, Adekanmi Olufade (Mohamed Kader Coubadja 51), Emmanuel Adebayor, Souleymane Maman (Thomas Dossevi• 65). Tr: Stephen Keshi

Mali	2
Frederic Kanoute 38, Mamadou Diallo 89	

Mahamadou Sidibe - Adama Tamboura•, Adama Coulibaly, Cedric Kante, Souleymane Diamoutene, Mahamadou Diarra, Seydou Keita, Mohamed Lamine Sissoko•, Bassara Toure (Mamadou Diallo 78), Dramane Traore (Mamady Sidibe 70), Frederic Kanoute. Tr: Jean-Francois Jodar

GROUP 10

Addis Abeba
3-09-2006, Abdelfattah EGY

Ethiopia	1
	Dawit Mebratu [15]

Wubshet Desalegn• - Mulualem Regassa, Degu Debebe, Tamrat Abebe, Solomon Andargachew•, Sebsebe Shegere (Yordanos Abay 82), Dawit Mebratu, Adane Girma, Mulugeta Mihret, Tafesse Tesfaye (Edilu Dereje 68), Binyam Assefa (Andualem Neguse 60). Tr: Seyoum Abate

Libya	0

Luis de Agustini - Walid Ali Ejlal (Emad Al Triki 69), Nader Shushan•, Ali El Hassay (Khaled Hussein 63), Nader Ali Abdusalam, Mohamed Abdelaziz, Tarek Tayeb (Nader Kara 55), Walid Osman, Abdelnassir Slil, Ahmed Osman, Osama Mohamed•. Tr: Mohsen Salah

Tripoli
7-10-2006, Pare BFA

Libya	1
	Khaled Hussein [75]

Muftah Ghzalla (Luis de Agustini 46), Omar Daoud (Walid Ali Ejlal 78), Nader Ali Abdusalam, Rida Milad•, Abdelnasser Slil, Mohamed Al Bashari•, Khaled Hussein, Akram Ayad (Nader Kara 46), Walid Osman, Ahmed Osman•, Ahmed Masli. Tr: Mohsen Salah

Congo DR	1
	Dikilu Bageta [37]

Robert Kidiaba - Christian Fuanda Kinkela, Dikilu Bageta, Cyrille Mubiala, Ngandu Kasongo, Tshiolola Tshinyama, Ngasanya Ilongo•, Dieudonne Kalulika (Patiyo Tambwe 71), Serge Mbala•, Tresor Mputu, Blaise Mbele (Albet Milambo 34). Tr: Henri Depireux

Addis Abeba
1-06-2006, Hicuburundi BDI

Ethiopia	1
	Salhadin Said [30]

Sadat Jemal - Degu Debebe, Yared Molla•, Yonas Gebremichael, Sebsebe Shegere (Seyoum Tesfaye• 73), Adane Girma, Lami Itana (Behailu Demeke 75), Dawit Mebratu, Fikru Teferea, Tafesse Tesfaye, Salhadin Said. Tr: Tesgaye Desta

Congo DR	0

Robert Kidiaba (Alain Kizamba 7) - Belmond Nsumbu, Dikilu Bageta, Fabrice Mvemba•, Eric Nkulukuta, Albert Milambo (Tresor Mputu 35), Tshiolola Tshinyama, Cedric Makiadi (Ibrahim Some 64), Zola Matumona, Biscotte Mbala, Dieudonne Mbokani. Tr: Henri Depireux

Tripoli
17-06-2007, Saadallah TUN

Libya	3
	Ahmed Zuwai 2 [10] [47], Salem Rewani [22]

Samir Aboud - Nader Shushan (Ashraf Al Amri 20), Walid Osman•, Nader Ali Abdusalam, Anis Eledrisi, Ali Rahuma (Ahmed Masli 61), Anis Mohamed, Salem Rewani, Mohamed Al Mugrabi, Ahmed Zuwai, Walid Ali Ejlal (Khaled Hussein 81). Tr: Mohamed El Khemsy

Ethiopia	1
	Fikru Tefera [58]

Sadat Jemal (Deyas Adugna• 37) - Degu Debebe•89, Yared Molla•, Biuzuneh Worku (Tafesse Tesfaye 34), Yonas Gebremichael (Lemi Itana 57), Seyoum Tesfaye, Behayilu Demeke, Dawit Mebratu, Adane Girma, Salhadin Said, Fikru Tefera. Tr: Tesgaye Desta

Kinshasa
3-09-2006, Evehe CMR

Congo DR	3
	Blaise Mbele [32], Kalulika [63], Kinkela [80]

Pascal Kalemba - Christian Fuanda Kinkela, Nono Lubanzadio, Dikilu Bageta, Ngandu Kasongo, Albert Milambo•, Tshiolola Tshinyama (Dieudonne Kalulika 46), Zola Matumona, Biscotte Mbala, Lieme Ebengo (Patiyo Tambwe• 64), Lelo Mbele (Nsumbu Dituabanza 73). Tr: Henri Depireux

Namibia	2
	Sydney Plaatjies 2 [34] [60]

Athiel Mbaha - Franklin April•, Hartman Toromba•, Michael Pienaar, Jeremiah Mbaisako, Sydney Plaatjies (George Hummel 75), Jamunavandu Ngatjizeko, Robert Nauseb•, Letu Shatimuene, Paulus Shipanga•60, Henrico Botes• (Rudolph Bester 85). Tr: Ben Bamfuchile

Tripoli
25-03-2007

Libya	2
	Salem Rewani [12], Tarek Tayeb [66]

Samir Aboud - Nader Shushan, Walid Ali Ejlal, Younes Hussein, Jihad Abdusalam (Walid Osman 89), Salem Rewani• (Nader Kara• 84), Ahmed Senossi, Mohamed Musa, Muataz Ali, Tarek Tayeb, Anis Mohamed• (Nader Ali Abdusalam 84). Tr: Mohamed El Khemsy

Namibia	1
	Collin Benjamin [85]

Abisai Shiningayamwe - Richard Gariseb, Michael Pienaar, George Hummel, Brian Brendell (Victor Helu 37), Robert Nauseb, Franklin April, Collin Benjamin•, Quinton Jacobs (Rudolph Bester 72), Oliver Risser, Heinrich Isaacks. Tr: Ben Bamfuchile

Windhoek
2-06-2007, Ncobo RSA

Namibia	1
	Collin Benjamin [4]

Abisai Shiningayamwe - Hartman Toromba•, Franklin April, Michael Pienaar, Letu Shatimuene, Robert Nauseb (Muna Katupose 75), Oliver Risser, Gottlieb Nakuta, Sydney Plaatjies•, Collin Benjamin, Meraai Swartbooi (Jamunovandu Ngatjizeko 87). Tr: Ben Bamfuchile

Libya	0

Luis de Agustini - Nader Shushan, Essam Rajab•, Ashraf Al Amri, Nader Ali Abdusalam•, Mohamed Al Mugrabi, Anis Eledrisi (Ahmed Shalabi 60), Wissem Abuktaef (Ahmed Zuwai 71), Walid Ali Ejlal, Ali Rahuma (Riad Lafi 60), Abdelnasser Slil. Tr: Mohamed El Khemsy

Addis Abeba
8-09-2007, Auda EGY

Ethiopia	2
	Birhanu Bogale [44], Salhadin Said [66]

Deyas Adugna - Mulugeta Mihret, Behailu Demeke (Lemi Itana 70), Birhanu Bogale (Bizuneh Worku 75), Seyoum Tesfaye, Tafesse Tesfaye•, Salhadin Seid, Fikru Tefera•, Tamirat Abebe, Adane Girma•, Berhane Aneley. Tr: Tesgaye Desta

Namibia	3
	Rudolph Bester 2 [64] [81], Muna Katupose [89]

Athiel Mbaha - Hartman Toromba•, Gottlieb Nakuta•, Michael Pienaar, Jamunovandu Ngatjizeko, Sydney Plaatjies•, Oliver Risser•, Quinton Jacobs, Brian Brendell (Muna Katupose 73), Meraai Swartbooi•, Rudolph Bester. Tr: Ben Bamfuchile

Windhoek
7-10-2006, Moeketsi LES

Namibia	1
	Quinton Jacobs [20p]

Athiel Mbaha - Richard Gariseb, Hartman Toromba, Michael Pienaar, Franklin April, Collin Benjamin, Robert Nauseb (George Hummel 61), Quinton Jacobs• (Costa Khaiseb• 74), Heinrich Isaacks (Letu Shatimuene 69), Sydney Plaatjies, Henrico Botes•87. Tr: Ben Bamfuchile

Ethiopia	0

Temesgen Chonare, Mulualem Regassa (Edilu Dereje 64), Adane Girma, Degu Debebe, Desta Gechano (Tafesse Tesfaye 46), Tamrat Abebe•, Birhanu Bogale, Dawit Mebratu, Debron Hagos (Sebsebe Shegere 46), Binyam Assefa, Andualem Negussie•. Tr: Seyoum Abate

Kinshasa
29-04-2007

Congo DR	2
	Serge Mbutu [29], Lomana LuaLua [52p]

Robert Kidiaba - Christian Fuanda Kinkela, Eric Nkulukuta, Fabrice Mvemba, Dikilu Bageta (Gladys Bokese 46), Tshiolola Tshinyama, Albert Milambo, Serge Mbutu, Tresor Mputu (Ngasanya Ilongo 62), Lelo Mbele (Alain Kaluyituka 85), Lomana LuaLua. Tr: Henri Depireux

Ethiopia	0

Sadat Jemal• - Degu Debebe, Yonas Gebremichael, Suleiman Mohamed (Birhanu Bogale 75), Bizunch Worku, Lami Itana, Alemayehu Molla, Tafesse Tesfaye, Dawit Mebratu, Salhadin Said, Fikru Tefera. Tr: Asrat Haile

Windhoek
16-06-2007, Mwanza ZAM

Namibia	1
	Michael Pienaar [38]

Abisai Shiningayamwe - Hartman Toromba, Gottlieb Nakuta•, Franklin April, Jeremia Baisako (Rudolph Bester 29), Michael Pienaar, Letu Shatimwene (Wilko Risser 82), Robert Nauseb• (Jamunovandu Ngatjizeko 72), Oliver Risser, Collin Benjamin, Meraai Swartbooi. Tr: Ben Bamfuchile

Congo DR	1
	Zola Matumona [25]

Robert Kidiaba - Eric Nkulukuta, Christian Fuanda Kinkela, Gladys Bokese, Fabrice Mvemba (Felicien Kambundi 54), Tshiolola Tshinyama, Zola Matumona (Biscotte Mbala 70), Marcel Mbayo•, Tresor Mputu, Emmanuel Mazowa Nsumbu (Ngasanya Ilongo 59), Lomana Tresor LuaLua•. Tr: Henri Depireux

Kinshasa
8-09-2007, Djaopupe TOG

Congo DR	1
	Shabani Nonda [39p]

Robert Kidiaba - Christian Fuanda Kinkela (Eric Nkulukuta 48), Dikilu Bageta, Herita Ilunga, Gladys Bokese, Tshiolola Tshinyama (Ngidi Yemweni 62), Ngasanya Ilongo, Marcel Mbayo (Zola Matumona 35), Biscotte Mbala, Shabani Nonda, Lomana LuaLua. Tr: Henri Depireux

Libya	1
	Khaled Hussein [51]

Samir Aboud - Nader Ali Abdusalam (Abdelnaser Slil 78), Walid Ali Ejlal, Younes Shibani•, Khaled Hussein, Ali Rahuma (Ahmed Wafa Abdelghadi 82), Salem Rewani (Ahmed Masli 67), Tarek Tayeb•, Mohamed Al Mugrabi, Ahmed Zuwai, Ali El Hassy•. Tr: Faouzi Benzerti

GROUP 11

Johannesburg
2-09-2006, Aboubacar CIV

South Africa   **0**

Rowen Fernandez - Vuyo Mere, Bradley Carnell• (Benedict Vilakazi 70), Aaron Mokoena, Nasief Morris, Benson Mhlongo (Siyabonga Nkosi 77), Steven Pienaar, Surprise Moriri, Dillion Sheppard, Siyabonga Nomvete, Katlego Mashego (Abram Raselemane 51). Tr: Pitso Mosimane

Congo   **0**

Barel Mouko - Camille Oponga, Fabry Makita, Christopher Samba, Christel Kimbembe, Kevin Andzouana, Gildas Ngo, Oscar Ewolo•, Denis Tsoumou, Herbie Fortune (Beaullat Sidoine 64), Armel Mamouna (Odilon Noumbemba 80). Tr: Noel Tosi

Ndjamena
3-09-2006, Shelmani LBY

Chad   **0**

Valery Ndakom - Galoum Ndilagar•, Oumar Abakar Ousmane (Lucien Teinkar 46), Alain Molengar, Armand Djerabe, Marius Mbayam, Mahamat Allacho, Gaius Doumbe (Missdongarle Betolinga 71), Oumar Francis Belongar, Saleh Mahamat, Hissein Mahamat (Ezekiel Ndouassel 62). Tr: Oumar Mahamat

Zambia   **2**
James Chamanga ⁴⁶, Dube Phiri ⁵⁹

Kennedy Mweene - Joseph Musonda, Clive Hachilensa, Billy Mwanza•, Kennedy Nketani, Mark Sinyangwe, Andrew Sinkala, Rainford Kalaba, James Chamanga (Felix Katongo 80), Chris Katongo (Ignatius Lwipa 77), Dube Phiri (Lameck Njovu 89). Tr: Patrick Phiri

Brazzaville
8-10-2006, Djaoupe TOG

Congo   **3**
Bruce ¹⁷, Malonga ³⁰, Nguessi ⁴⁶

Barel Mouko - Fabrice Nguessi (Gervais Batota 64), Camille Oponga, Destin Makita, Christopher Samba (Kevin Andzouana 85), Christel Kimbembe, Chris Malonga, Gildas Ngo, Denis Tsoumou, Armel Mamouna (Fortune Ndzi 59), Abdoulaye Bruce•. Tr: Noel Tosi

Chad   **1**
Missdongarle Betolinga ⁸⁹

Valery Ndakom• - Galoum Ndilagar•, Diondja Mbairamadji (Ahmat Brahim 59), Sitamadji Allarassem, Teinkor Nerambaye, Armand Djerabe, Hassan Diallo, Evariste Medego (Hilaire Kedigui 83), Ezekiel Ndouassel (Djimalde Dossengar 42), Oumar Francis Belongar, Missdongarle Betolinga. Tr: Okalan Natoltiga

Lusaka
8-10-2006, Maillet SEY

Zambia   **0**

Kennedy Mweene - Joseph Musonda, Clive Hachilensa, Moses Sichone (Billy Mwanza 75), Kennedy Nketani, Andrew Sinkala, Ian Bakala, Rainford Kalaba (Dube Phiri 65), Chris Katongo, Jacob Mulenga (James Chamanga 32), Collins Mbesuma. Tr: Patrick Phiri

South Africa   **1**
Aaron Mokoena ²⁸

Rowen Fernandez - Cyril Nzama, Bradley Carnell•, Aaron Mokoena, Nasief Morris, MacBeth Sibaya•, Siyabonga Nkosi, Simphiwe Tshabalala (Ricardo Katza 76), Steven Pienaar, Siyabonga Nomvete (Nathan Paulse 88), Delron Buckley (Benedict Vilakazi 71). Tr: Pitso Mosimane

Ndjamena
24-03-2007, Aguidissou BEN

Chad   **0**

Mamadou Bouba - Armand Djerabe, Djimalde Dossengar, Diondja Mbairamadji, Cesar Madalngue, Jacques Dourwe, Hassan Diallo, Marius Mbayam (Evariste Medego• 46), Ezekiel Ndouassel (Ahmat Brahim 18), Oumar Francis Belongar, Missdongarle Betolinga (Hilaire Kedigui 68). Tr: Okalan Natoltiga

South Africa   **3**
Moriri ³², Buckley ⁴⁴, Zuma ⁷⁸

Rowen Fernandez - Cyril Nzama, Lucas Thwala•, Aaron Mokoena, Nasief Morris, MacBeth Sibaya, Godfrey Sapula (Benson Mhlongo 82), Steven Pienaar•, Delron Buckley (Elrio van Heerden 66), Surprise Moriri (Siyabonga Nomvete 71), Sibusiso Zuma•. Tr: Carlos Alberto Parreira

Brazzaville
25-03-2007, Coulibaly MLI

Congo   **0**

Barel Mouko - Oscar Ewolo (Landry Djimi 74), Gildas Ngo, Kelvin Andzouana, Bienvenu Ngandzoua, Christel Kimbembe, Destin Makita, Denis Tsoumou, Lys-Bouity Mouithys• (Franchel Ibara• 46), Chris Malonga (Noel Moukila 67), Armel Mamouna. Tr: Noel Tosi

Zambia   **0**

Kennedy Mweene - Clive Hachilensa, Joseph Musonda, Billy Mwanza, Elijah Tana•, Mark Sinyangwe, Rainford Kalaba, Chris Katongo, James Chamanga (Dube Phiri 51), Felix Katongo (Ignatius Lwipa 82), Collins Mbesuma•. Tr: Patrick Phiri

Chililabombwe
2-06-2007, Rahman SUD

Zambia   **3**
Mulenga ¹⁷, Katongo ⁶⁰, Chalwe ⁷²

Kennedy Mweene - Billy Mwanza, Elijah Tana (Kennedy Nketani 32), William Chinyama, Clive Hachilensa•, Mark Sinyangwe (Lameck Njovu 87), Rainford Kalaba•, Felix Katongo (Songwe Chalwe 71), Chris Katongo•, Jacob Mulenga, Collins Mbesuma. Tr: Patrick Phiri

Congo   **0**

Barel Mouko - Brice Abdoulaye, Gildas Ngo, Cristel Kimbembe, Kelvin Andzouana, Destin Makita, Oscar Ewolo, Denis Tsoumou•, Landry Njimbi, Armel Mamouna•, Patrice Lolo. Tr: Robert Corfu

Durban
2-06-2007, Gasingwa RWA

South Africa   **4**
Morris ¹³ᵖ, Zuma 2 ²³ ³³, Nomvete ⁷⁰

Rowen Fernandez - Cyril Nzama, Bradley Carnell, Aaron Mokoena, Nasief Morris, MacBeth Sibaya, Elrio van Heerden (Teko Modise 72), Papi Zothwane (Benedict Vilakazi 63), Delron Buckley•, Surprise Moriri (Siyabonga Nomvete 63), Sibusiso Zuma. Tr: Carlos Alberto Parreira

Chad   **0**

Mamadou Bouba• - Cesar Madalngue, Sitamadji Allarassem, Teinkor Nerambaye, Armand Djerabe, Marius Mbayam, Esai Djikoloum (Doungous Mahamat 77), Abdoulaye Djideo, Hilaire Kedigui, Ahmat Brahim, Missdongarle Betolinga (Ezekiel Ndouassel 60). Tr: Okalan Natoltiga

Chililabombwe
16-06-2007, Ssegonga UGA

Zambia   **1**
Collins Mbesuma ⁵⁷

Kennedy Mweene - Clive Hachilensa, Kennedy Nketani, William Chinyama, Billy Mwanza, Rainford Kalaba, James Chamanga, Felix Katongo (Clifford Mulenga 58) (Ignatius Lwipa 84), Chris Katongo, Jacob Mulenga (Songwe Chalwe 62), Collins Mbesuma. Tr: Patrick Phiri

Chad   **1**
Hilaire Kedigui ¹⁴

Armel Koulara - Teinkor Nerambaye, Armand Djerabe, Tigaye Masrabaye, Marius Mbayam (Brahim Ahmat 63), Ezekiel Ndouassel, Esai Djikoloum (Missdongarle Betolinga 75), Hilaire Kedigui, Cesar Madalngue, Sitamadji Allarassem, Abdoulaye Djideo. Tr: Okalan Natoltiga

Pointe Noire
17-06-2007, Eyene CMR

Congo   **1**
Jean Vivien Batsimba ⁶⁵

Barel Mouko - Brice Abdoulaye, Gildas Ngo, Kelvin Andzouana, Destin Makita, Oscar Ewolo, Denis Tsoumou, Franchel Ibara (Noel Moukila• 72), Jean Vivien Batsimba• (Ulrich Longuay 89), Lys Mouitys (Armel Mamouna 59), Fabrice Ondama. Tr: Robert Corfu

South Africa   **1**
Sibusiso Zuma ⁴⁶

Rowen Fernandez - Cyril Nzama•, Bradley Carnell•, Aaron Mokoena, Nasief Morris, MacBeth Sibaya, Papi Zothwane, Delron Buckley (Siyabonga Nomvete 72), Surprise Moriri (Benson Mhlongo 88), Lerato Chabangu (Teko Modise 46), Sibusiso Zuma•. Tr: Carlos Alberto Parreira

Cape Town
9-09-2007, Evehe CMR

South Africa   **1**
Benni McCarthy ⁵⁰

Rowen Fernandez - Cyril Nzama•, Bradley Carnell, Aaron Mokoena, Nasief Morris, MacBeth Sibaya, Papi Zothwane (Teko Modise 30), Steven Pienaar (Siyabonga Nkosi 82), Delron Buckley (Thembinkosi Fanteni 69), Surprise Moriri, Benni McCarthy. Tr: Carlos Alberto Parreira

Zambia   **3**
Chris Katongo 3 ⁹ ¹⁹ ²⁰

Kennedy Mweene - Kennedy Nketani, Joseph Musonda•, Clive Hachilensa, Billy Mwanza, Isaac Chansa•78, Ian Bakala (Rainford Kalaba 64), Andrew Sinkala•, Chris Katongo•, Jacob Mulenga (Felix Katongo 89), Collins Mbesuma (Kampamba Chintu 86). Tr: Patrick Phiri

Ndjamena
9-09-2007, Pare BFA

Chad   **1**
Leger Djimenam ⁸⁸

Armel Koulara - Teinkor Nerambaye (Abakar Adoum 86), Abdoulaye Djideo, Hilaire Kedigui, Sitamadji Allarassem, Khatir Outmane (Leger Djimenam 32), Cesar Madalngue, Hassan Diallo, Armand Djerabe, Esai Djikoloum (Karl Max Barthelemy 60), Brahim Ahmat. Tr: Okalan Natoltiga

Congo   **1**
Toussaint Mayembi ⁶

Damien Massa - Destin Makita, Gildas Ngo•78, Bienvenu Ngandzoua, Jean d'Honneur Eckombe (Didas Boukaka 68), Beaulieu Sidione, Kelvin Andzouana, Landry Djinbi, Kibongui Nkounga (Bouid Itoua-Ngoua 46), Toussaint Mayembi, Patrick Lolo (Rudy Bhebey 46). Tr: Gaston Tchangana

GROUP 12

Rabat
2-09-2006, Codjia BEN

Morocco   **2**
Chamakh [50], Boussoufa [72]

Tarik Jarmouni - Walid Regragui●, Talal El Karkouri, Aziz Ben Askar, Hicham Mahdoufi, Youssef Safri (El Amine Erbate 79), Zakaria Aboub (Abdelkrim Kissi 70), Tarik Sektioui (Nourdine Boukhari 46), Mbark Boussoufa, Youssouf Hadji, Marouane Chamakh. Tr: Mohamed Fakhir

Malawi   **0**

Simeon Kapuza - James Sangala●, Moses Chavala, Clement Kafwafwa, Wisdom Ndlovu, Elvis Kafoteka (Petros Mwalweni 46), Peter Mponda, James Chilapondwa, Robert Ngambi (Dave Banda 40), Joseph Kamwendo●, Essau Kanyenda (Peter Wadabwa 85). Tr: Burkhard Ziese

Blantyre
7-10-2006, Seechum MRI

Malawi   **1**
Moses Chavula [78]

Swadi Sanudi - Peter Mponda●, Moses Chavala, James Sangala, Elvis Kafoteka, Robert Ngambi (Joel Chipofya 87), Dave Banda (Meter Wadabwa 73), James Chilapondwa●, Joseph Kamwendo, Esau Kanyenda, Russell Mwafulirwa. Tr: Kinnah Phiri

Zimbabwe   **0**

Tapuwa Kapini - Zvenyika Makonese●, James Matola, Onismor Bhasera, David Kutyaauripo, Cephas Chimedza, Esrom Nyandoro, Joel Luphahla (Clemence Matawu 86), Tinashe Nengomasha (Edzai Kasinauyo 71), Benjani Mwaruwari, Shingarayi Kawondera● (Evans Gwekwerere 84). Tr: Charles Mhlauri

Harare
25-03-2007, Damon RSA

Zimbabwe   **1**
Esrom Nyandoro [81]

Tapuwa Kapini - Noel Kaseke, Onismor Bhasera, Dickson Choto, Zvenyika Makonese, Esrom Nyandoro, Clement Matawu, Joel Luphahla (Peter Ndlovu 72), Gilbert Mushangazhike (Evans Gwekwerere 55), Cephas Chimedza (Vusi Nyoni 48), Benjani Mwaruwari. Tr: Charles Mhlauri

Morocco   **1**
Youssef Hadji [7]

Tarik Jarmouni● - Badr Kadouri (El Amine Erbate 16), Mourad Fellah●, Talal El Karkouri, Aziz Benaskar, Youssef Safri, Othmane El Assas, Noureddine Boukhari, Mohamed Yaacoubi (Adil Ramzi 54), Bouchaib El Moubarki (Jaouad Ouaddouch 84), Youssef Hadji. Tr: Mohamed Fakhir

Casablanca
2-06-2007, Daami TUN

Morocco   **2**
Chamakh [4], Youssef Hadji [26]

Tarik Jarmouni - Mikael Chretien, Talal El Karkouri, Aziz Benaskar, Hicham Mahdoufi, Abdelkrim Kissi, Houcine Kharja●, Jawad Zairi (Mohamed Yacoubi 21), Soufiane Alloudi, Youssef Hajji (El Amine Erbate 89), Marouane Chamakh (Bouchaib El Moubarki 70). Tr: Mohamed Fakhir

Zimbabwe   **0**

Tapuwa Kapini - Onismor Bhasera, Noel Kaseke, James Matola●, Zvenyika Makonese, Cephas Chimedza (Honour Gombani 71), Method Mwanjili (Vusumuzi Nyoni 46), Ronald Sibanda, Clement Matawu, Benjani Mwarwaui, Shingarayi Kawondera (Quincy Antipas 46). Tr: Charles Mhlauri

Blantyre
16-06-2007, Maillet SEY

Malawi   **0**

Semion Kapuza - James Sangala, Clement Kafwafwa, Peter Mponda●, Moses Chavula● (Emmanuel Chipatala 65), James Chilapondwa●, Tawonga Chimodzi● (Noel Mkhandawire 75), Fisher Kondowe (Rodrick Gonani 65), Joseph Kamwendo, Esau Kanyenda, Russell Mwafulirwa. Tr: Stephen Constantine

Morocco   **1**
El Moubarki [10]

Tarek Jarmouni - Mikael Chretien, Talal El Karkouri, Houssine Kharja, Aziz Benaskar, Abdelkrim Kissi, Hicham Mahdoufi, Soufiane Alloudi (El Amine Erbate 82), Youssef Hajji (Mohamed Yaacoubi 46), Marouane Chamakh, Bouchaib El Moubarki (Jawad Zairi 76). Tr: Mohamed Fakhir

Bulawayo
9-09-2007, Hicuburundi BDI

Zimbabwe   **3**
Nkhata [24], Mteki [54], Mwanjili [61]

Washington Arubi - Zephania Ngodzo, Ovidy Karuru (Admire Dzukamanja 40), Costa Nhamoinesu, Method Mwanjali, Gilbert Banda, Justice Majabvi, Mtshumayeli Moyo, Richard Mteki, Washington Pakamisa (Carrington Gomba 79), Kingstone Nkhata. Tr: Norman Mapeza

Malawi   **1**
Esau Kanyenda [43]

Swadick Sanudi - Joseph Kamwendo (Dave Banda 69), Fisher Kondowe● (Rodrick Gonani 73), Ndazviona Chilemba (Douglas Chirambo 76), James Sangala, Wisdom Ndlovu, Robert Ngambi, Elvis Kafoteka, Esau Kanyenda, Russell Mwafulirwa. Tr: Stephen Constantine

CAF AFRICA CUP OF NATIONS GHANA 2008

CAF AFRICA CUP OF NATIONS GHANA 2008

First round groups	Pts	Quarter–finals		Semi–finals		Final	
Ghana	9						
Guinea	4	Egypt	2				
Morocco	3	Angola	1				
Namibia	1						
	Pts			Egypt	4		
				Côte d'Ivoire	1		
Côte d'Ivoire	9						
Nigeria	4	Guinea	0				
Mali	4	Côte d'Ivoire	5				
Benin	1						
						Egypt	1
						Cameroon	0
	Pts						
Egypt	7						
Cameroon	6	Ghana	2				
Zambia	4	Nigeria	1				
Sudan	0						
				Ghana	0		
	Pts			Cameroon	1		
Tunisia	5						
Angola	5	Tunisia	2			3rd Place Play-off	
Senegal	2	Cameroon	3			Ghana	4
South Africa	2					Côte d'Ivoire	2

GROUP A		PL	W	D	L	F	A	PTS		GUI	MAR	NAM
1	Ghana	3	3	0	0	5	1	9		2-1	2-0	1-0
2	Guinea	3	1	1	1	5	5	4			3-2	1-1
3	Morocco	3	1	0	2	7	6	3				5-1
4	Namibia	3	0	1	2	2	7	1				

Ohene Djan, Accra
20-01-2008, 17:00, 35 000, Maillet SEY

GHA	2	1	GUI

Asamoah Gyan 55p,
Sulley Muntari 89

Oumar Kalabane 65

GHANA			GUINEA
22 Richard Kingson			Kemoko Camara 16
2 Hans Sarpei			Dianbobo Balde 5
4 John Paintsil			Alseny Camara 12
5 John Mensah (C)			Oumar Kalabane 15
18 Eric Addo			Daouda Jabi 21
8 Michael Essien			Pascal Feindouno (C) 2
7 Laryea Kingston			Mohamed Sacko 13
11 Sulley Muntari		89	Kanfory Sylla 5
3 Asamoah Gyan	85		Ismael Bangoura 10
9 Junior Agogo		62	Victor Correa 9
20 Quincy Owusu Abeyie	76	62	Souleymane Youla 11
Tr: Claude Le Roy			Tr: Robert Nouzaret
12 Dede Ayew	76	62	Naby Soumah 14
13 Baffour Gyan	85	62	Karamoko Cisse 19
		89	Mamadou Dioulde Bah 23

Ohene Djan, Accra
21-01-2008, 15:00, 2000, Evehe CMR

NAM	1	5	MAR

Brian Brendell 23

Soufiane Alloudi 3 25 28,
Tarik Sektioui 39p, Moncef Zerka 74

NAMIBIA			MOROCCO
16 Abisai Shiningayamwe			Khalid Fouhami 12
6 Franklin April	46		Michael Chretien 2
5 Richard Gariseb			Abdeslam Ouaddou 4
13 Michael Pienaar (C)			El Armine Erbate 6
19 Lazarus Kaimbi			Badr El Kaddouri 21
14 Brian Brendell			Youssef Safri 15
8 Oliver Risser			Abderrahmane Kabous 18
17 Quinton Jacobs	77	61	Soufiane Alloudi 7
22 Jamunavandu Ngatjizeko		66	Tarik Sektioui 10
7 Collin Benjamin			Maroune Chamakh 17
15 Rudolf Bester	64	70	Youssef Hadji 20
Tr: Ari Schans			Tr: Henri Michel
9 Meraai Swartbooi	77	70	Moncef Zerka 11
10 Letu Shatimuene	46	61	Youssef Mokhtari 16
20 Pineas Jacob	64	66	Hicham Aboucherouane 23

Ohene Djan, Accra
24-01-2008, 17:00, Damon RSA

GUI	3	2	MAR

Pascal Feindouno 2 11 63p,
Ismael Bangoura 60

Hicham Aboucherouane 60,
Abdeslam Ouaddou 89

GUINEA			MOROCCO
16 Kemoko Camara			Khalid Fouhami 12
3 Ibrahima Camara	81		Michael Chretien 2
21 Daouda Jabi			Badr El Kaddouri 21
15 Oumar Kalabane			El Armine Erbate 6
5 Dianbobo Balde			Abdeslam Ouaddou 4
4 Mohamed Cisse		55	Houcine Kharja 13
8 Kanfory Sylla			Abdelkrim Kissi 8
2 Pascal Feindouno (C)	67		Youssef Safri 15
10 Ismael Bangoura		67	Tarik Sektioui 10
7 Fode Mansare	79		Youssef Hadji 20
11 Souleymane Youla	77	80	Moncef Zerka 11
Tr: Robert Nouzaret			Tr: Henri Michel
6 Kamil Zayatte	81	80	Bouchaib El Moubarki 9
13 Mohamed Sacko	79	67	Maroune Chamakh 17
19 Karamoko Cisse	77	55	Hicham Aboucherouane 23

Ohene Djan, Accra
24-10-2008, 19:30, Bennaceur TUN

GHA	1	0	NAM

Junior Agogo 41

GHANA			NAMIBIA
22 Richard Kingson			Athiel Mbaha 1
2 Hans Sarpei			Hartman Toromba 3
4 John Paintsil			Richard Gariseb 5
5 John Mensah (C)			Michael Pienaar (C) 13
18 Eric Addo			Jamunavandu Ngatjizeko 22
7 Laryea Kingston	65		Oliver Risser 8
8 Michael Essien			Collin Benjamin 7
11 Sulley Muntari		83	Brian Brendell 14
20 Quincy Owusu Abeyie			Quinton Jacobs 17
3 Asamoah Gyan	65	69	Rudolf Bester 15
9 Junior Agogo		64	Sydney Plaatjies 11
Tr: Claude Le Roy			Tr: Ari Schans
12 Dede Ayew	65	83	Letu Shatimuene 10
13 Baffour Gyan	65	64	Lazarus Kaimbi 19
		69	Pineas Jacob 20

Ohene Djan, Accra
28-01-2008, 17:00, Sowe GAM

GHA	2	0	MAR

Michael Essien 26,
Sulley Muntari 44

GHANA			MOROCCO
22 Richard Kingson			Nadir Lamyaghri 1
2 Hans Sarpei			Michael Chretien 2
4 John Paintsil			El Armine Erbate 6
5 John Mensah (C)			Abdeslam Ouaddou 4
18 Eric Addo			Badr El Kaddouri 21
6 Anthony Annan		89	Abderrahmane Kabous 18
8 Michael Essien		46	Houcine Kharja 13
11 Sulley Muntari			Youssef Safri 15
20 Quincy Owusu Abeyie	89		Youssef Hadji 20
3 Asamoah Gyan	88	55	Hicham Aboucherouane 23
9 Junior Agogo	86		Maroune Chamakh 17
Tr: Claude Le Roy			Tr: Henri Michel
12 Dede Ayew	86	89	Abdelkrim Kissi 8
13 Baffour Gyan	88	46	Tarik Sektioui 10
23 Haminu Dramani	89	55	Moncef Zerka 11

Sekondi-Takoradi Stadium, Sekondi
28-01-2008, 17:00, Ssesonga UGA

GUI	1	1	NAM

Souleymane Youla 62

Brain Brendall 80

GUINEA			NAMIBIA
16 Kemoko Camara			Athiel Mbaha 1
23 Mamadou Dioulde Bah			Richard Gariseb 5
5 Dianbobo Balde			Michael Pienaar (C) 13
3 Ibrahima Camara			Hartman Toromba 3
21 Daouda Jabi			Collin Benjamin 7
15 Oumar Kalabane			Brian Brendell 14
13 Mohamed Sacko			Jamunavandu Ngatjizeko 22
14 Naby Soumah	69		Sydney Plaatjies 11
10 Ismael Bangoura			Lazarus Kaimbi 19
7 Fode Mansare	84		Muna Katupose 12
11 Souleymane Youla	75		Meraai Swartbooi 9
Tr: Robert Nouzaret			Tr: Ari Schans
8 Kanfory Sylla	69		Rudolf Bester 15
9 Victor Correa	84		Quinton Jacobs 17
19 Karamoko Cisse	75		Wycliff Kambonde 21

	GROUP B	PL	W	D	L	F	A	PTS	NGA	MLI	BEN
1	**Côte d'Ivoire**	3	3	0	0	8	1	**9**	1-0	3-0	4-1
2	**Nigeria**	3	1	1	1	2	1	**4**		0-0	2-0
3	Mali	3	1	1	1	1	3	**4**			1-0
4	Benin	3	0	0	3	1	7	**1**			

Sekondi-Takoradi Stadium, Sekondi
21-01-2008, 17:00, 20 000, Benouza MAR

NGA 0 1 CIV

Salomon Kalou 66

	NIGERIA			COTE D'IVOIRE	
12	Austin Ejide			Boubacar Barry	1
2	Joseph Yobo			Emmanuel Eboue	21
6	Danny Shittu			Kolo Toure	4
22	Onyekachi Apam			Abdoulaye Meite	12
3	Taye Taiwo			Arthur Boka	3
10	John Obi Mikel			Gneri Yaya Toure	19
14	Seyi Olofinjana			Didier Zokora	5
4	Nwankwo Kanu	55	46	Steve Gohouri	6
7	John Utaka	74	84	Didier Drogba	11
8	Yakubu Aiyegbeni			Salomon Kalou	8
9	Obafemi Martins	79		Aruna Dindane	15
	Tr: Bertie Vogts			Tr: Gerard Gili	
11	Peter Odemwingie	74	84	Bakary Kone	14
17	Stephen Makinwa	79	46	Abdelkader Keita	18
20	Onyekachi Okonkwo	55			

Sekondi-Takoradi Stadium, Sekondi
21-01-2008, 19:30, 20 000, Damon RSA

MLI 1 0 BEN

Frederic Kanoute 49p

	MALI			BENIN	
1	Mahamadou Sidibe			Rachad Chitou	1
9	Amadou Sidibe			Abdul Adenon	3
4	Adama Coulibaly			Alain Gaspoz	14
15	Cedric Kante			Damien Chrystosome	5
5	Souleymane Diamoutene			Anicet Adjamossi	15
6	Mahamadou Diarra		53	Jonas Oketola	6
18	Souleymane Dembele			Romauld Boco	7
12	Seydou Keita			Seidath Tchomogo	18
8	Bassala Toure	71	82	Jocelyn Ahoueya	19
10	Dramane Traore	55		Razak Omotoyossi	8
19	Frederic Kanoute		69	Oumar Tchomogo	10
	Tr: Jean-Francois Jodar			Tr: Reinhard Fabisch	
7	Mamady Sidibe	88 55	69	Abou Maiga	9
14	Drissa Diakite	71	53	Stephane Sessegnon	17
17	Sammy Traore	88	82	Wassiou Oladipikpo	20

Sekondi-Takoradi Stadium, Sekondi
25-01-2008, 17:00, Marange ZIM

CIV 4 1 BEN

Didier Drogba 40, Gneri Yaya Toure 44, Abdelkader Keita 52, Aruna Dindane 62

Razak Omotoyossi 89

	COTE D'IVOIRE			BENIN	
1	Boubacar Barry			Rachad Chitou	1
3	Arthur Boka			Abdul Adenon	3
21	Emmanuel Eboue			Anicet Adjamossi	15
12	Abdoulaye Meite		68	Damien Chrystosome	5
4	Kolo Toure	44	50	Alain Gaspoz	14
5	Didier Zokora			Jocelyn Ahoueya	19
19	Gneri Yaya Toure			Romauld Boco	7
15	Aruna Dindane			Stephane Sessegnon	17
18	Abdelkader Keita	76	58	Seidath Tchomogo	18
11	Didier Drogba	68		Razak Omotoyossi	8
8	Salomon Kalou			Oumar Tchomogo	10
	Tr: Gerard Gili			Tr: Reinhard Fabisch	
6	Steve Gohouri	44	58	Abou Maiga	9
10	Gervais Yao Kouassi	76	50	Mouri Ogunbiyi	11
20	Boubacar Sanogo	68	68	Noel Seka	13

Sekondi-Takoradi Stadium, Sekondi
25-01-2008, 19:30, El Arjoun MAR

NGA 0 0 MLI

	NIGERIA			MALI	
12	Austin Ejide			Mahamadou Sidibe	1
3	Taye Taiwo			Adama Tamboura	3
5	Obinna Nwaneri			Adama Coulibaly	4
6	Danny Shittu			Souleymane Diamoutene	5
2	Joseph Yobo			Cedric Kante	15
10	John Obi Mikel		87	Amadou Sidibe	9
14	Seyi Olofinjana			Mahamadou Diarra	6
18	Obinna Nsofor	85		Seydou Keita	12
8	Yakubu Aiyegbeni		83	Mohamed Sissoko	20
9	Obafemi Martins	46		Frederic Kanoute	19
11	Peter Odemwingie	57	73	Dramane Traore	10
	Tr: Bertie Vogts			Tr: Jean-Francois Jodar	
7	John Utaka	46	73	Mamadou Diallo	13
15	Ike Uche	57	83	Drissa Diakite	14
17	Stephen Makinwa	85	87	Souleymane Dembele	18

Sekondi-Takoradi Stadium, Sekondi
29-01-2008, 17:00, Bennaceur TUN

NGA 2 0 BEN

John Obi Mikel 52, Yakubu Aiyegbeni 86

	NIGERIA			BENIN	
12	Austin Ejide			Yoann Djidonou	16
2	Joseph Yobo			Abdul Adenon	3
5	Obinna Nwaneri			Damien Chrystosome	5
6	Danny Shittu			Alain Gaspoz	14
3	Taye Taiwo		46	Anicet Adjamossi	15
10	John Obi Mikel		54	Jonas Oketola	6
15	Ike Uche			Romauld Boco	7
16	Dickson Etuhu	74	84	Stephane Sessegnon	17
7	John Utaka	52		Jocelyn Ahoueya	19
8	Yakubu Aiyegbeni			Razak Omotoyossi	8
11	Peter Odemwingie	89		Oumar Tchomogo	10
	Tr: Bertie Vogts			Tr: Reinhard Fabisch	
13	Rabiu Afolabi	89	84	Abou Maiga	9
18	Obinna Nsofor	52	46	Mouri Ogunbiyi	11
21	Richard Eromoigbe	74	54	Seidath Tchomogo	18

Ohene Djan, Accra
29-01-2008, 17:00, Maillet SEY

CIV 3 0 MLI

Didier Drogba 9, Marc Zoro 54, Boubacar Sanogo 85

	COTE D'IVOIRE			MALI	
1	Boubacar Barry			Mahamadou Sidibe	1
21	Emmanuel Eboue		46	Adama Coulibaly	4
22	Marc Zoro			Cedric Kante	15
5	Didier Zokora			Adama Tamboura	3
17	Siaka Tiene			Sammy Traore	17
19	Gneri Yaya Toure			Drissa Diakite	14
7	Emerse Fae			Seydou Keita	12
13	Christian Koffi Ndri			Djibril Sidibe	11
11	Didier Drogba	75	60	Bassala Toure	8
18	Abdelkader Keita	59	46	Frederic Kanoute	19
9	Arouna Kone			Dramane Traore	10
	Tr: Gerard Gili			Tr: Jean-Francois Jodar	
14	Bakary Kone	59	46	Mamadou Diallo	13
20	Boubacar Sanogo	75	46	Mohamed Sissoko	20
			60	Mahamadou Dissa	21

	GROUP C	PL	W	D	L	F	A	PTS		CMR	ZAM	SUD
1	Egypt	3	2	1	0	8	3	7		4-2	1-1	3-0
2	Cameroon	3	2	0	1	10	5	6			5-1	3-0
3	Zambia	3	1	1	1	5	6	4				3-0
4	Sudan	3	0	0	3	0	9	0				

Baba Yara, Kumasi
22-01-2008, 17:00, Sowe GAM

EGY 4 — 2 CMR

Hosni Abd Rabou 2 14p 82, Mohamed Zidan 2 17 44
Samuel Eto'o 2 51 89p

No	EGYPT				CAMEROON			No
1	Essam Al Hadari				Idriss Carlos Kameni			1
2	Mahmoud Fathallah				Rigobert Song			4
6	Hani Said				Timothee Atouba			5
14	Sayed Moawad				Andre Bikey			23
20	Wael Gomaa				Geremi Fotso Njitap			8
8	Hosni Abd Rabou	38			Jean Makoun	38		
11	Mohamed Shawky	46			Landry Nguemo	46		13
7	Ahmed Fathi				Joel Epalle			14
9	Mohamed Zidan	69	46		Stephane Mbia	46		19
10	Emad Moteab				Samuel Eto'o			9
19	Amr Zaki	60			Mohamadou Idrissou			17
	Tr: Hasan Shehata				Tr: Otto Pfister			
3	Ahmed Al Muhammadi	69	38		Augustin Binya	38		2
22	Mohamed Aboutrika	60	46		Achille Emana	46		10
			46		Alexandre Song	46		15

Baba Yara, Kumasi
22-01-2008, 19:30, Diatta SEN

SUD 0 — 3 ZAM

James Chamanga 2, Jacob Mulenga 51, Felix Katongo 59

No	SUDAN			ZAMBIA		No
16	Mahjoub El Moez			Kennedy Mweene		16
2	Omar Bakheit			Kennedy Nketani		3
4	Mohamed Ali Khider			Joseph Musonda		4
7	Alaeldin Ahmed Gibril			Billy Mwanza		18
6	Rtshard Justin Lado			Clive Hachilensa		19
8	Haitham Mostafa			Ian Bakala		10
9	Hamouda Bashir	80		Rainford Kalaba		17
12	Badreldin El Doud			Felix Katongo		20
14	Mugahid Mohamed	24		Jacob Mulenga		2
10	Haitham Tambal		70	Dube Phiri		12
17	Faisal Agab	57	83	James Chamanga		21
	Tr: Mohamed Abdallah			Tr: Patrick Phiri		
5	Yousef Alaeldin	24	83	Clifford Mulenga		7
11	Alaeldin Babiker	57	70	Emmanuel Mayuka		14
22	Saifeldin Ali Idris	80				

Baba Yara, Kumasi
26-01-2008, 17:00, Nichimura JPN

CMR 5 — 1 ZAM

Geremi Njitap 28, Joseph Desire Job 2 31 82, Achille Emana 43, Samuel Eto'o 66p
Chris Katongo 89

No	CAMEROON			ZAMBIA		No
1	Idriss Carlos Kameni			Kennedy Mweene		16
2	Augustin Binya	63	38	Kennedy Nketani		3
3	Rigobert Song			Joseph Musonda		4
5	Timothee Atouba			Billy Mwanza		18
23	Andre Bikey			Clive Hachilensa		19
7	Modeste Mbami	67		Isaac Chansa		8
8	Geremi Fotso Njitap	81		Ian Bakala		10
15	Alexandre Song			Felix Katongo		20
10	Achille Emana	77		Chris Katongo		11
9	Samuel Eto'o			Jacob Mulenga		2
21	Joseph Desire Job	64		James Chamanga		21
	Tr: Otto Pfister			Tr: Patrick Phiri		
11	Jean Makoun	67	64	Felix Nsunzu		9
12	Alain Nkong	63	38	Chintu Kampamba		15
17	Mohamadou Idrissou	77	81	William Njovu		23

Baba Yara, Kumasi
26-01-2008, 19:30, Codjia BEN

EGY 3 — 0 SUD

Hosni Abd Rabou 29p, Mohamed Aboutrika 2 77 83

No	EGYPT			SUDAN		No
1	Essam Al Hadari			Mahjoub El Moez		16
2	Mahmoud Fathallah	56		Musa Al Tayeb		3
6	Hani Said			Mohamed Ali Khider		4
7	Ahmed Fathi		46	Alaeldin Ahmed Gibril		7
14	Sayed Moawad			Amir Damar		15
20	Wael Gomaa			Yousef Alaeldin		5
8	Hosni Abd Rabou			Rtshard Justin Lado		6
11	Mohamed Shawky			Haitham Mostafa		8
9	Mohamed Zidan	56		Badreldin El Doud		12
10	Emad Moteab		60	Haitham Tambal		10
19	Amr Zaki	80	81	Alaeldin Babiker		11
	Tr: Hasan Shehata			Tr: Mohamed Abdallah		
3	Ahmed Al Muhammadi	80	81	Faisal Agab		17
17	Ahmed Hassan	56	60	Abdelhamid Amari		20
22	Mohamed Aboutrika	56	46	Saifeldin Ali Idris		22

Baba Yara, Kumasi
30-01-2008, 17:00, Coulibaly MLI

EGY 1 — 1 ZAM

Amr Zaki 15
Chris Katongo 89

No	EGYPT			ZAMBIA		No
1	Essam Al Hadari			Kennedy Mweene		16
5	Shady Mohamed			Joseph Musonda		4
6	Hani Said			Hichani Himonde		5
14	Sayed Moawad		30	Billy Mwanza		18
20	Wael Gomaa			Clive Hachilensa		19
7	Ahmed Fathi	77		Isaac Chansa		8
8	Hosni Abd Rabou			Ian Bakala		10
11	Mohamed Shawky			Felix Katongo		20
17	Ahmed Hassan	62		Chris Katongo		11
10	Emad Moteab	77	66	Jacob Mulenga		2
19	Amr Zaki	62		James Chamanga		21
	Tr: Hasan Shehata			Tr: Patrick Phiri		
4	Ibrahim Said	77	66	Dube Phiri		12
9	Mohamed Zidan	62	30	Chintu Kampamba		15
22	Mohamed Aboutrika	62	77	Rainford Kalaba		17

Sports Stadium, Tamale
30-01-2008, 17:00, Djaoupe TOG

CMR 3 — 0 SUD

Samuel Eto'o 2 27p 89, Mohamed Ali Khider OG 33

No	CAMEROON			SUDAN		No
1	Idriss Carlos Kameni			Mahjoub El Moez		16
8	Geremi Fotso Njitap	55		Omar Bakheit		2
23	Andre Bikey			Mohamed Ali Khider		4
4	Rigobert Song			Musa Al Tayeb		3
5	Timothee Atouba	46		Amir Damar		15
7	Modeste Mbami			Yousef Alaeldin		5
10	Achille Emana	57		Rtshard Justin Lado		6
14	Joel Epalle	77		Haitham Mostafa		8
15	Alexandre Song			Hamouda Bashir		9
9	Samuel Eto'o		77	Haitham Tambal		10
21	Joseph Desire Job	62		Faisal Agab		17
	Tr: Otto Pfister			Tr: Mohamed Abdallah		
3	Bill Tchato	46	62	Alaeldin Babiker		11
18	Bertin Tomou	57	55	Mohamed Tahir		13
20	Paul Essola	77	77	Hassan Isaac Korongo		23

GROUP D	PL	W	D	L	F	A	PTS		ANG	SEN	RSA
1 Tunisia	3	1	2	0	5	3	5		0-0	2-2	3-1
2 Angola	3	1	2	0	4	2	5			3-1	1-1
3 Senegal	3	0	2	1	4	6	2				1-1
4 South Africa	3	0	2	1	3	5	2				

Sports Stadium, Tamale
23-01-2008, 17:00, Nichimura JPN

TUN 2 2 SEN

Issam Jomaa [9], Mejdi Traoui [82]

Moustapha Bayal Sall [44],
Diomansy Kamara [66]

TUNISIA			SENEGAL	
1	Hamdi Kasraoui		Tony Sylva	1
3	Radhouane Felhi		Habib Beye	21
6	Radhouane Felhi		Souleymane Diawara	5
15	Radhi Jaidi		Abdoulaye Diagne Faye	20
5	Wissem Bekri		Guirane Ndaw	3
12	Joahar Mnari	89	Diomansy Kamara	15
14	Chaker Zouaghi	80	61	Frederic Mendy	18
17	Issam Jomaa	85	63	Ousmane Ndoye	10
21	Mejdi Traoui		Moustapha Bayal Sall	12
9	Yassine Chikhaoui		El Hadji Diouf	11
11	Francileudo dos Santos	63	Mamadou Niang	8
	Tr: Roger Lemerre		Tr: Henryk Kasperczak	
10	Kamel Zaiem	63	61	Henri Camara	7
18	Yassine Mikari	85	89	Babacar Gueye	9
20	Mehdi Ben Dhifallah	80	63	Pape Bouba Diop	19

Sports Stadium, Tamale
23-01-2008, 19:30, Coulibaly MLI

RSA 1 1 ANG

Elrio van Heerden [88]

Manucho [30]

SOUTH AFRICA			ANGOLA	
16	Moeneeb Josephs		Lama	1
3	Tsepo Masilela	88	Marco Airosa	2
13	Benson Mhlongo		Kali	5
4	Aaron Mokoena		Rui Marques	15
5	Nasief Morris		Yamba Asha	6
19	Bryce Moon	71	Mendonca	14
8	Siphiwe Tshabalala	52	Figueiredo	7
9	Surprise Moriri		Andre	8
12	Teko Modise		Gilberto	11
10	Steven Pienaar		Flavio	16
15	Sibusiso Zuma		Manucho	23
	Tr: Carlos Alberto Parreira		Tr: Luis Oliveira Goncalves	
11	Elrio van Heerden	71	Edson	13
14	Lerato Chabangu	52	Ze Kalanga	17
17	Katlego Mphela	88	Loco	20

Sports Stadium, Tamale
27-01-2008, 17:00, Haimoudi ALG

SEN 1 3 ANG

Abdoulaye Faye [20]

Manucho 2 [50 67], Flavio [78]

SENEGAL			ANGOLA	
1	Tony Sylva		Lama	1
21	Habib Beye		Marco Airosa	2
5	Souleymane Diawara		Kali	5
20	Abdoulaye Diagne Faye		Yamba Asha	6
3	Guirane Ndaw	84	Rui Marques	15
18	Frederic Mendy	63	Ze Kalanga	17
19	Pape Bouba Diop		Andre	8
15	Diomansy Kamara	70	72	Maurito	10
12	Moustapha Bayal Sall	84	Gilberto	11
11	El Hadji Diouf		Flavio	16
8	Mamadou Niang	88	Manucho	23
	Tr: Henryk Kasperczak		Tr: Luis Oliveira Goncalves	
7	Henri Camara	70	84	Mateus	9
9	Babacar Gueye	63	72	Dede	19
17	Pape Modou Sougou	84	88	Loco	20

Sports Stadium, Tamale
27-01-2008, 19:30, Djaoupe TOG

TUN 3 1 RSA

Francileudo dos Santos 2 [8 34],
Chaouki Ben Saada [32]

Katlego Mphela [86]

TUNISIA			SOUTH AFRICA	
1	Hamdi Kasraoui		Moeneeb Josephs	16
3	Karim Hagui		Bryce Moon	19
13	Sabeur Ben Frej	62	Tsepo Masilela	3
15	Radhi Jaidi		Nasief Morris	5
18	Yassine Mikari		Benson Mhlongo	13
6	Mehdi Nafti		Aaron Mokoena	4
12	Joahar Mnari	75	Teko Modise	12
7	Chaouki Ben Saada		Steven Pienaar	10
21	Mejdi Traoui	46	Lerato Chabangu	14
9	Yassine Chikhaoui	81	Sibusiso Zuma	15
11	Francileudo dos Santos	67	60	Thembinkosi Fanteni	21
	Tr: Roger Lemerre		Tr: Carlos Alberto Parreira	
14	Chaker Zouaghi	75	46	Elrio van Heerden	11
17	Issam Jomaa	81	60	Katlego Mphela	17
20	Mehdi Ben Dhifallah	67	62	Brett Evans	20

Sports Stadium, Tamale
31-01-2008, 17:00, Kotey GHA

SEN 1 1 RSA

Henri Camara [37]

Elrio van Heerden [14]

SENEGAL			SOUTH AFRICA	
23	Bouna Coundoul		Moeneeb Josephs	16
13	Lamine Diatta		Tsepo Masilela	3
5	Souleymane Diawara		Aaron Mokoena	4
6	Ibrahima Faye		Nasief Morris	5
20	Abdoulaye Diagne Faye	81	Bryce Moon	19
12	Moustapha Bayal Sall		Kagisho Dikgacoi	22
15	Diomansy Kamara	82	Teko Modise	12
19	Pape Bouba Diop	50	Siphiwe Tshabalala	8
22	Pape Malick Ba	70	Surprise Moriri	9
7	Henri Camara		Elrio van Heerden	11
8	Mamadou Niang	60	89	Sibusiso Zuma	15
	Tr: Lamine Ndiaye		Tr: Carlos Alberto Parreira	
9	Babacar Gueye	50	81	Lance Davids	6
14	Pape Waigo Ndiaye	60	70	Lerato Chabangu	14
17	Pape Modou Sougou	82	89	Thembinkosi Fanteni	21

Baba Yara, Kumasi
31-01-2008, 17:00, Codjia BEN

TUN 0 0 ANG

TUNISIA			ANGOLA	
1	Hamdi Kasraoui		Lama	1
13	Sabeur Ben Frej	69	Marco Airosa	2
3	Karim Hagui		Rui Marques	15
15	Radhi Jaidi	75	Kali	5
14	Chaker Zouaghi		Yamba Asha	6
12	Joahar Mnari	83	Ze Kalanga	17
8	Mehdi Nafti		Andre	8
10	Kamel Zaiem	67	59	Maurito	10
18	Yassine Mikari		Gilberto	11
23	Amine Chermiti		Flavio	16
17	Issam Jomaa	79	Manucho	23
	Tr: Roger Lemerre		Tr: Luis Oliveira Goncalves	
6	Radhouane Felhi	75	59	Mateus	9
9	Yassine Chikhaoui	79	83	Mendonca	14
20	Mehdi Ben Dhifallah	67	69	Loco	20

QUARTER-FINALS

Baba Yara, Kumasi
4-02-2008, 17:00, Nichimura JPN

EGY 2 1 ANG

Hosni Abd Rabou 23p, Amr Zaki 38 | Manucho 27

No	EGYPT	min	min	ANGOLA	No
1	Essam Al Hadari			Lama	1
5	Shady Mohamed			Marco Airosa	2
6	Hani Said			Kali	5
20	Wael Gomaa			Yamba Asha	6
14	Sayed Moawad	66		Rui Marques	15
8	Hosni Abd Rabou			Andre	8
11	Mohamed Shawky		46	Maurito	10
7	Ahmed Fathi			Gilberto	11
22	Mohamed Aboutrika	89	73	Ze Kalanga	17
10	Emad Moteab		84	Flavio	16
19	Amr Zaki	71		Manucho	23
	Tr: Hasan Shehata			Tr: Luis Oliveira Goncalves	
2	Mahmoud Fathallah	66	73	Mateus	9
4	Ibrahim Said	89	84	Edson	13
17	Ahmed Hassan	71	46	Mendonca	14

Sekondi-Takoradi Stadium, Sekondi
3-02-2008, 20:30, Haimoudi ALG

CIV 5 0 GUI

Abdelkader Keita 25, Didier Drogba 70, Salomon Kalou 2 73 81, Bakary Kone 86

No	COTE D'IVOIRE	min	min	GUINEA	No
1	Boubacar Barry			Kemoko Camara	16
3	Arthur Boka			Mamadou Dioulde Bah	23
12	Abdoulaye Meite		82	Kamil Zayatte	6
5	Didier Zokora			Ibrahima Camara	3
21	Emmanuel Eboue			Daouda Jabi	21
13	Christian Koffi Ndri			Mohamed Alimou Diallo	17
19	Gneri Yaya Toure			Mohamed Sacko	13
18	Abdelkader Keita	74	67	Samuel Johnson	18
8	Salomon Kalou			Ismael Bangoura	10
15	Aruna Dindane	70		Fode Mansare	7
11	Didier Drogba	76	60	Souleymane Youla	11
	Tr: Gerard Gili			Tr: Robert Nouzaret	
9	Emerse Fae	74	67	Naby Soumah	14
9	Arouna Kone	70	82	Oumar Kalabane	15
14	Bakary Kone	76	60	Karamoko Cisse	19

Ohene Djan, Accra
3-02-2008, 17:00, Benouza ALG

GHA 2 1 NGA

Michael Essien 44, Junior Agogo 82 | Yakubu Aiyegbeni 35p

No	GHANA	min	min	NIGERIA	No
22	Richard Kingson			Austin Ejide	12
2	Hans Sarpei			Joseph Yobo	2
4	John Paintsil			Obinna Nwaneri	5
5	John Mensah (C)	60		Danny Shittu	6
18	Eric Addo			Taye Taiwo	3
6	Anthony Annan			Seyi Olofinjana	14
8	Michael Essien		85	John Obi Mikel	10
1	Sulley Muntari			Ike Uche	15
20	Quincy Owusu Abeyie	74	71	Dickson Etuhu	16
3	Asamoah Gyan	62		Yakubu Aiyegbeni	8
9	Junior Agogo			Peter Odemwingie	11
	Tr: Claude Le Roy			Tr: Berti Vogts	
7	Laryea Kingston	62	85	Obinna Nsofor	18
23	Haminu Dramani	74	71	Richard Eromoigbe	21

Sports Stadium, Tamale
4-02-2008, 20:30, Coulibaly MLI

TUN 2 3 CMR

Chaouki Ben Saada 35, Yassine Chikhaoui 81 | Stephane Mbia 2 18 92, Geremi Fotso Njitap 27

No	TUNISIA	min	min	CAMEROON	No
1	Hamdi Kasraoui			Idriss Carlos Kameni	1
3	Karim Hagui	38		Geremi Fotso Njitap	8
5	Wissem Bekri			Andre Bikey	23
6	Radhouane Felhi			Rigobert Song	4
15	Radhi Jaidi		109	Timothee Atouba	5
8	Mehdi Nafti	71	61	Achille Emana	10
7	Chaouki Ben Saada		65	Jean Makoun	11
12	Joahar Mnari			Alexandre Song	15
21	Mejdi Traoui			Stephane Mbia	19
9	Yassine Chikhaoui			Mohamadou Idrissou	17
11	Francileudo dos Santos	85		Samuel Eto'o	9
	Tr: Roger Lemerre			Tr: Otto Pfister	
13	Sabeur Ben Frej	38	65	Augustin Binya	2
17	Issam Jomaa	71	109	Bill Tchato	3
23	Amine Chermiti	85	61	Joel Epalle	14

SEMI-FINALS

Baba Yara, Kumasi
7-02-2008, 20:30, Maillet SEY

CIV 1 4 EGY

Abdelkader Keita 63 | Ahmed Fathi 12, Amr Zaki 2 62 67, Mohamed Aboutrika 89

No	COTE D'IVOIRE	min	min	EGYPT	No
1	Boubacar Barry	39		Essam Al Hadari	1
21	Emmanuel Eboue			Shady Mohamed	5
4	Kolo Toure			Hani Said	6
12	Abdoulaye Meite			Wael Gomaa	20
3	Arthur Boka		77	Sayed Moawad	14
13	Didier Zokora			Hosni Abd Rabou	8
19	Gneri Yaya Toure			Ahmed Hassan	17
18	Abdelkader Keita			Ahmed Fathi	7
8	Salomon Kalou	59		Mohamed Aboutrika	22
15	Aruna Dindane	78	68	Emad Moteab	10
11	Didier Drogba		86	Amr Zaki	19
	Tr: Gerard Gili			Tr: Hasan Shehata	
9	Arouna Kone	78	77	Mahmoud Fathallah	2
14	Bakary Kone	59	86	Ibrahim Said	4
16	Stephan Loboue	39	68	Mohamed Zidan	9

Ohene Djan, Accra
7-02-2008, 17:00, El Arjoun MAR

GHA 0 1 CMR

Alain Nkong 72

No	GHANA	min	min	CAMEROON	No
22	Richard Kingson			Idriss Carlos Kameni	1
2	Hans Sarpei			Geremi Fotso Njitap	8
4	John Paintsil	89		Andre Bikey	23
8	Michael Essien			Rigobert Song	4
18	Eric Addo			Timothee Atouba	5
6	Anthony Annan		77	Achille Emana	10
12	Dede Ayew	87		Alexandre Song	15
11	Sulley Muntari			Stephane Mbia	19
20	Quincy Owusu Abeyie	62	63	Joseph Desire Job	21
23	Haminu Dramani		46	Mohamadou Idrissou	17
9	Junior Agogo			Samuel Eto'o	9
	Tr: Claude Le Roy			Tr: Otto Pfister	
13	Baffour Gyan	62	77	Augustin Binya	2
15	Ahmed Barusso	87	63	Alain Nkong	12
			46	Joel Epalle	14

THIRD PLACE PLAY-OFF

Baba Yara, Kumasi
9-02-2008, 17:00, Damon RSA

GHA   4 2   CIV

Muntari [10], Owusu-Abeyie [70],
Agogo [80], Dramani [84]   Boubacar Sanogo 2 [24] [32]

GHANA					COTE D'IVOIRE
22	Richard Kingson				Tiasse Kone 23
4	John Paintsil				Siaka Tiene 17
18	Eric Addo				Marc Zoro 22
5	John Mensah (C)				Didier Zokora 5
2	Hans Sarpei				Arthur Boka 3
6	Anthony Annan				Christian Koffi Ndri 13
8	Michael Essien		83		Emerse Fae 7
11	Sulley Muntari		64		Abdelkader Keita 18
23	Haminu Dramani	89	74		Salomon Kalou 8
9	Junior Agogo	89			Didier Drogba 11
13	Baffour Gyan	20			Boubacar Sanogo 20
	Tr: Claude Le Roy				Tr: Gerard Gili
10	Kwadwo Asamoah	89	74		Gervais Yao Kouassi 10
20	Quincy Owusu Abeyie	20	83		Aruna Dindane 15
21	Harrison Afful	89	64		Gneri Yaya Toure 19

FINAL

Ohene Djan, Accra
10-02-2008, 17:00, 35 500, Coffi Codjia BEN

EGYPT   1 0   CAMEROON

Mohamed Aboutrika [77]

EGYPT						CAMEROON		
1	GK	Essam Al Hadari				Idriss Carlos Kameni	GK	1
5	DF	Shady Mohamed				Bill Tchato	DF	3
6	DF	Hani Said				Geremi Fotso Njitap	MF	8
20	DF	Wael Gomaa				Rigobert Song	DF	4
14	DF	Sayed Moawad				Timothee Atouba	DF	5
8	MF	Hosni Abd Rabou		55		Achille Emana	MF	10
7	DF	Ahmed Fathi		16		Alexandre Song	MF	15
17	MF	Ahmed Hassan				Stephane Mbia	MF	19
22	MF	Mohamed Aboutrika	89	65		Joel Epalle	MF	14
10	FW	Emad Moteab	60			Alain Nkong	MF	12
19	FW	Amr Zaki	84			Samuel Eto'o	FW	9
		Tr: Hassan Shehata				Tr: Otto Pfister		
4	DF	Ibrahim Said	89	16		Augustin Binya	DF	2
9	FW	Mohamed Zidan	60	65		Modeste Mbami	MF	7
11	MF	Mohamed Shawky	84	55		Mohamadou Idrissou	FW	17

REGIONAL TOURNAMENTS IN AFRICA 2007

TOURNOI DE L'UEMOA BURKINA FASO 2007

First Round Group Stage

Group A	Pl	W	D	L	F	A	Pts	BFA	SEN	TOG
Niger	3	2	1	0	5	3	7	0-0	3-2	2-1
Burkina Faso	3	1	2	0	2	1	5		0-0	2-1
Senegal	3	0	2	1	2	3	2			0-0
Togo	3	0	1	2	2	4	1			

Final

Cote d'Ivoire	2
Niger	0

Group B	Pl	W	D	L	F	A	Pts	MLI	BEN	GNB
Cote d'Ivoire	3	3	0	0	8	0	9	2-0	1-0	5-0
Mali	3	2	0	1	7	2	6		3-0	4-0
Benin	3	0	1	2	1	5	1			1-1
Guinea-Bissau	3	0	1	2	1	10	1			

Played in Burkina Faso from 28-10-2007 to 4-11-2007 • Tournament played with locally based players

COPA AMILCAR CABRAL GUINEA-BISSAU 2007

First Round Group Stage

Group A	Pl	W	D	L	F	A	Pts	SEN	SLE
Guinea-Bissau	2	1	1	0	3	1	4	1-1	2-0
Senegal	2	1	1	0	2	1	4		1-0
Sierra Leone	2	0	0	2	0	3	0		

Semi-finals

Mali	2
Senegal	1

Final

Mali	2
Cape Verde Islands	1

Group B	Pl	W	D	L	F	A	Pts	CPV	GAM	GUI
Mali	3	2	0	1	4	2	6	0-1	2-0	2-1
Cape Verde Islands	3	1	2	0	1	0	5		0-0	0-0
Gambia	3	1	1	1	3	2	4			3-0
Guinea	3	0	1	2	1	5	1			

Semi-finals

Guinea-Bissau	1 2p
Cape Verde Islands	1 3p

Third place play-off

Senegal	2
Guinea-Bissau	1

Played in Guinea-Bissau from 30-11-2007 to 10-12-2007 • Only Cape Verde, Gambia, Sierra Leone and Guinea-Bissau played with their full teams

CECAFA CUP TANZANIA 2007

First round groups

Group A	Pl	W	D	L	F	A	Pts	TAN	KEN	SOM
Burundi	3	2	1	0	4	0	7	0-0	1-0	3-0
Tanzania	3	2	1	0	3	1	7		2-1	1-0
Kenya	3	1	0	2	3	3	3			2-0
Somalia	3	0	0	3	0	6	0			

Quarter-finals

Sudan	2
Tanzania	1

Semi-finals

Sudan	2
Burundi	1

Final

Sudan	2 4p
Rwanda	2 2p

Group B	Pl	W	D	L	F	A	Pts	RWA	ERI	DJI
Uganda	3	2	0	1	11	3	6	2-0	2-3	7-0
Rwanda	3	2	0	1	11	3	6		2-1	9-0
Eritrea	3	2	0	1	7	6	6			3-2
Djibouti	3	0	0	3	2	19	0			

Quarter-finals

Eritrea	1
Burundi	2

Uganda	1 4p
Kenya	1 2p

Semi-finals

Uganda	0
Rwanda	1

Group C	Pl	W	D	L	F	A	Pts	SUD	ETH
Zanzibar	2	1	1	0	5	3	4	2-2	3-1
Sudan	2	0	2	0	2	2	2		0-0
Ethiopia	2	0	1	1	1	3	1		

Quarter-finals

Zanzibar	0 4p
Rwanda	0 5p

Third place play-off

Uganda	2
Burundi	0

Played in Arusha and Dar es Salaam, Tanzania from 8-12-2007 to 22-12-2007

MTN CAF CHAMPIONS LEAGUE 2007

First Round

Etoile du Sahel	TUN	Bye
Sporting da Praia	CPV	0 ‡
Fello Star Labé *	GUI	0 ‡
APR FC	RWA	2 2
St Eloi Lupopo *	COD	1 0
ASC Diaraf Dakar *	SEN	1 0
Marantha Fiokpo	TOG	0 3
TP Mazembe *	COD	3 4
Police XI	BOT	0 2
ANSE Réunion	SEY	0 0
Adema Antananarivo *	MAD	0 3
AshantiGold	GHA	1 1
Renacimiento *	EQG	0 0
FAR Rabat	MAR	Bye
Al Ittihad Tripoli *	LBY	3 1
Mogas 90	BEN	0 0
USM Alger *	ALG	3 0
AS FNIS Niamey	NIG	1 2
St George	ETH	w-o
Escom United	MWI	
Canon Yaoundé *	CMR	1 0
Etoile du Congo	CGO	0 2
Cotonsport Garoua *	CMR	3 0
URA Kampala	UGA	0 0
Mighty Barolle	LBR	1 1
Séwé Sport *	CIV	3 0
Mangasport	GAB	1 1
Primeiro de Agosto *	ANG	0 1
Os Balantas	GNB	1 1
Jeunesse Kabylie *	ALG	3 2
Al Ahly	EGY	Bye
Pamplemousse SC	MRI	0 1 8p
Highlanders *	ZIM	1 0 9p
Desportivo Maputo	MOZ	w-o
St Pierroise	REU	
Royal Leopards	SWZ	2 0
Mamelodi Sundowns *	RSA	4 2
Wydad Casablanca *	MAR	4 1
ASC Mauritel	MTN	0 2
AS Douanes Dakar ‡	SEN	2 2
Stade Malien *	MLI	1 0
FC Kallon	SLE	0 1
Ocean Boys *	NGA	0 0
ASEC Mimosas	CIV	Bye
Espérance Tunis *	TUN	4 2
Rennaisance	CHA	0 1
Likhopo Maseru *	LES	0 0
Zanaco	ZAM	0 1
Petro Atlético *	ANG	1 1
Civics	NAM	0 1
AJSM Mutsamudu	COM	1
Young Africans *	TAN	5
Nasarawa United	NGA	1 2
ASFA/Yennenga *	BFA	1 0
Asante Kotoko *	GHA	1 0 2p
Gambia Ports Authority	GAM	0 1 4p
Zamalek *	EGY	1 2
Vital'O	BDI	1 0
Polisi SC	ZAN	0 0
Al Hilal Omdurman *	SUD	4 2

Second Round

Etoile du Sahel	1 4
Fello Star Labé *	0 1
APR FC * ‡	2 0
Marantha Fiokpo	0 2
TP Mazembe	2 4
Adema Antananarivo *	2 1
AshantiGold *	2 0 6p
FAR RAbat	0 2 7p
Al Ittihad Tripoli *	4 1
AS FNIS Niamey	1 0
St George *	1 0
Etoile du Congo	0 2
Cotonsport Garoua	0 4
Séwé Sport *	1 0
Mangasport *	3 0
Jeunese Kabylie	1 3
Al Ahly	0 2
Highlanders *	0 0
Desportivo Maputo *	1 0
Mamelodi Sundowns	1 2
Wydad Casablanca	0 3
Stade Malien *	0 1
FC Kallon *	0 1
ASEC Mimosas	1 2
Espérance Tunis *	2 4
Zanaco	0 1
Petro Atlético	0 2
Young Africans *	3 0
Nasarawa United *	3 1
Gambia Ports Authority	0 2
Zamalek	0 2
Al Hilal Omdurman *	2 2

Third Round

Etoile du Sahel	0 3
Marantha Fiokpo *	0 0
TP Mazembe *	1 0
FAR Rabat	0 2
Al Ittihad Tripoli	1 2
Etoile du Congo *	3 0
Cotonsport Garoua *	1 0
Jeunesse Kabylie	0 2
Al Ahly	2 2
Mamelodi Sundowns *	2 0
Wydad Casablanca	0 0
ASEC Mimosas *	2 0
Espérance Tunis *	3 0
Young Africans	0 0
Nasarawa United *	3 0 2p
Al Hilal Omdurman	0 3 3p

‡ Sporting, Douanes & APR disqualified
* Home team in the first leg • Losing teams in the second round enter the Confederation Cup

CAF CHAMPIONS LEAGUE 2007

MTN CAF CHAMPIONS LEAGUE 2007

Champions League Stage   **Semi–finals**   **Final**

Group A		Pts	TUN	LBY	ALG	MAR
Etoile du Sahel	TUN	11		0-0	3-0	0-0
Al Ittihad Tripoli	LBY	10	2-0		1-0	2-0
JS Kabylie	ALG	7	0-2	3-1		2-0
FAR Rabat	MAR	5	0-1	1-0	1-1	

Etoile du Sahel	1	3
Al Hilal *	2	1

Etoile du Sahel *	0	3
Al Ahly	0	1

Al Ittihad *	0	0
Al Ahly	0	1

Group B		Pts	EGY	SUD	CIV	TUN
Al Ahly	EGY	12		2-0	2-0	3-0
Al Hilal	SUD	10	3-0		2-1	2-0
ASEC Mimosas	CIV	7	0-1	1-0		2-0
Espérance Tunis	TUN	5	1-0	1-1	0-0	

* Home team in the first leg • Losing teams in the second round enter the CAF Confederation Cup

GROUP A

Tripoli
22-06-2007, Sowe GAM

Al Ittihad — **1**
Alseny Camara [85]

Samir Aboud - Walid Osman (Alseny Camara 67), Osama Hamadi, Younes Shibani, Hesham Shaban, Mohamed Alsnani, Abdesalam Khamis, Abdelnasser Slil, Salem Rewani●, Ali Rahuma (Mohamed Mouldi 89), Akram Ayyad● (Mohamed Zubya 77). Tr: Branko Smiljanic

JS Kabylie — **0**

Faouzi Chaouch - Demba Barry●, Brahim Zafour●, Sofiane Bengoreine●, Mohamed Meftah, Sid Ahmed Khedis, Nabil Hamouda (Lamara Douicher 72), Cherif Abdesslam●, Tayeb Berramla (Nabil Hemani 63), Nassim Oussalah (Youcef Saibi 88), Cheikh Oumar Dabo. Tr: Azzedine Ait Djoudi

Rabat
23-06-2007, Coulibaly MLI

FAR Rabat — **0**

Tarek Jarmouni - Hafid Abdesadek, Ali Jaarafi (Mohamed Borji 74), Youssef Rabeh, Atik Chihab, Khalidi Maroufi●, Noureddine Kacemi●44, Mounir Benkassou (Jaouad Bouaouda 46), Yassine Naoum, Khalid Hirech (Idrissi Youssef Kaddioui 46●79), Jawad Ouaddouch●. Tr: Mustapha Madih

Etoile du Sahel — **1**
Sabeur Ben Frej [67p]

Aymen Mathlouthi - Mejdi Ben Mohamed, Sabeur Ben Frej●, Mehdi Meriah●, Radhouene Felhi● (Afouene Gharbi 83), Mejdi Traoui, Moussa Narry, Mohamed Ali Nafkha, Muri Ogunbiyi, Armine Chermiti● (Aymen Soltani 89), Ja. Tr: Bertrand Marchand

Tizi Ouzou
6-07-2007, Codjia BEN

JS Kabylie — **2**
Cheikh Oumar Dabo 2 [29p 43]

Faouzi Chaouchi - Mohamed Meftah, Sofiane Herkat●, Sid Ahmed Khedis, Sofiane Bengoreine (Mohamed Derrag 86), Tayeb Berramla, Lamara Douicher●, Wassiou Oladikpikpo, Youcef Saibi● (Ali Bendebka 70), Nabil Hemani (Nassim Oussalah 56), Cheikh Oumar Dabo. Tr: Kamel Mouassa

FAR Rabat — **0**

Tarek Jarmouni - Atik Chihab, Issam Erraki, Mohamed Karkouri (Tarik Marzouk 46), Youssef Rabeh, Ahmed Ajeddou●, Mohamed Lansri●, Brahim Bahri, Jaouad Bouaouda (Mohamed El Mrini 72), Hafid Abdesadek, Mohamed Borji● (Khalid Hirech 60). Tr: Mustapha Madih

Sousse
7-07-2007, Pare BFA

Etoile du Sahel — **0**

Aymen Mathlouthi - Mejdi Ben Mohamed, Sabeur Ben Frej, Radhouene Felhi, Hatem Bejaoui, Mejdi Traoui (Bassem Ben Nasr 67), Moussa Narry, Mohamed Ali Nafkha, Muri Ogunbiyi, Ja●, Aymen Soltani (Mehdi Ben Dhifallah 78). Tr: Bertrand Marchand

Al Ittihad — **0**

Samir Aboud - Naji Shushan, Osama Hamadi, Younes Shibani, Hesham Shaban●, Mahmoud Maklouf●, Mohamed Esnani, Abdelnasser Slil, Akram Omar (Abdesalam Khamis 81), Alseny Camara (Mohamed Zubya 69), Al Khalifa Rahuma (Pierre Koulibaly 88). Tr: Branko Smiljanic

Sousse
21-07-2007, Louzaya CGO

Etoile du Sahel — **3**
Amine Chermiti [1], Mejdi Ben Mohamed [48], Ja [48]

Aymen Mathlouthi - Mejdi Ben Mohamed●, Sabeur Ben Frej, Mehdi Meriah, Seif Ghezal, Khaled Melliti, Mohamed Ali Nafkha (Mejdi Traoui 79), Moussa Narry●, Muri Ogunbiyi, Amine Chermiti (Sadat Bukari 76), Ja● (Mehdi Ben Dhifallah 85). Tr: Bertrand Marchand

JS Kabylie — **0**

Faouzi Chaouch - Brahim Zafour, Mohamed Meftah●, Sofiane Bengoreine●, Demba Barry (Boubakeur Athmani 33), Sofiane Herkat, Lamara Douicher, Nassim Oussalah, Tayeb Berramla (Ali Bendebka 81), Youcef Saibi, Wassiou Oladikpikpo. Tr: Kamel Mouassa

Rabat
21-07-2007, Imiere NGA

FAR Rabat — **1**
Jawad Ouaddouch [89]

Tarek Jarmouni - Jaouad Bouaouda, Hafid Abdesadek, Youssef Rabeh●89, Youssef Basri, Mohamed Karkouri (Atik Chihab 87), Yassine Naoum (Adil Loutfi 77), Issam Erraki, Ahmed Ajeddou, Tarik Marzouk (Mohamed Borji 78), Jawad Ouaddouch. Tr: Mustapha Madih

Al Ittihad — **0**

Samir Aboud - Mahmoud Maklouf●, Naji Shushan (Alseny Camara 89), Mohamed Mouldi, Younes Shibani, Osama Hamadi, Abdelnasser Slil, Mohamed Alsnani, Walid Mhadeb● (Abdesalam Khamis 83), Ali Rahuma●, Salem Rewani (Nenad Mladenovic 64). Tr: Branko Smiljanic

Tizi Ouzou
3-08-2007, Abderrahmane SUD

JS Kabylie — **0**

Faouzi Chaouchi - Mohamed Meftah● (Tayeb Berramla 46), Demba Barry, Brahim Zafour●, Nassim Oussalah●, Lamara Douicher, Cherif Abdesslam, Wassiou Oladikpikpo, Boubakeur Athmani (Youcef Saibi 56), Issa Traore (Mohamed Derrag 77), Nabil Hemani. Tr: Kamel Mouassa

Etoile du Sahel — **2**
Muri Ogunbiyi [44], Amine Chermiti [89]

Aymen Mathlouthi - Seif Ghezal●, Sabeur Ben Frej●, Mehdi Meriah, Radhouene Felhi, Mejdi Traoui, Bassem Ben Nasr● (Hatem Bejaoui 82), Muri Ogunbiyi, Mohamed Ali Nafkha●, Afouene Gharbi (Mehdi Ben Dhifallah 78), Amine Chermiti● (Msaddek Hasnaoui 89). Tr: Bertrand Marchand

Tripoli
3-08-2007, Abdelfattah EGY

Al Ittihad — **2**
Younes Shibani [43], Salem Rewani [61]

Muftah Ghzalla - Walid Osman, Younes Shibani, Osama Hamadi, Walid Mhadeb● (Mohamed Mouldi 75), Arafa Nakua●, Yohann Langlet, Ali Rahuma●, Abdelnasser Slil●, Alseny Camara (Pierre Koulibaly 85), Salem Rewani (Nenad Mladenovic 70). Tr: Branko Smiljanic

FAR Rabat — **0**

Tarek Jarmouni, Jaouad Bouaouda, Hafid Abdesadek, Mohamed El Mrini (Adil Loutfi 58'), Youssef Basri, Mohamed Karkouri (Idrissi Youssef Kaddioui 63'), Issam Erraki, Al Jaafri, Ahmed Ajeddou (Yassine Naoum 75'), Tarik Marzouk, Jawad Ouaddouch. Tr: Mustapha Madih

Kouba
17-08-2007, Aboubacar CIV

JS Kabylie — **3**
Athmani [22], Nabil Hemani [56], Youcef Saibi [69]

Nabil Mazari - Demba Barry●, Brahim Zafour●, Sofiane Herkat●, Sofiane Bengoreine, Cherif Abdesslam, Lamara Douicher, Tayeb Berramla, Boubakeur Athmani, Nabil Hemani (Issa Traore 86), Mohamed Derrag (Youcef Saibi 67). Tr: Moussa Saib

Al Ittihad — **1**
Salem Rewani [19]

Samir Aboud - Walid Osman, Younes Shibani, Hesham Shaban, Mahmoud Maklouf, Osama Hamadi, Abdelnasser Slil, Mohamed Alsnani● (Arafa Nakua 80), Yohann Langlet (Musbah Saad 69), Nenad Mladenovic (Alseny Camara 62), Salem Rewani. Tr: Branko Smiljanic

Sousse
18-08-2007, Kotey GHA

Etoile du Sahel — **0**

Aymen Mathlouthi - Seif Ghezal, Sabeur Ben Frej, Mehdi Meriah●, Radhouene Felhi●, Mejdi Ben Mohamed, Mohamed Ali Nafkha, Moussa Narry●, Bassem Ben Nasr (Afouene Gharbi 75), Muri Ogunbiyi, Mehdi Ben Dhifallah (Aymen Soltani 75). Tr: Bertrand Marchand

FAR Rabat — **1**

Tarek Jarmouni - Mohamed El Mrini, Hafid Abdesadek, Youssef Basri, Atik Chihab (Mohamed Borji 78), Noureddine Kacemi, Tarik Marzouk (Adil Loutfi● 46), Ahmed Ajeddou●, Jawad Ouaddouch, Ali Jaarafi● (Idrissi Youssef Kaddioui 70), Yassine Naoum. Tr: Mustapha Madih

Tripoli
1-09-2007, Djaoupe TOG

Al Ittihad — **2**
Younes Shibani [12], Salem Rewani [57p]

Samir Aboud - Younes Shibani, Hesham Shaban, Mahmoud Maklouf, Osama Hamadi, Mohamed Alsnani, Walid Mhadeb, Yohann Langlet (Pierre Koulibaly 85), Ali Rahuma, Alseny Camara (Arafa Nakua 70), Salem Rewani (Musbah Saad 88). Tr: Branko Smiljanic

Etoile du Sahel — **0**

Nadim Thabet - Bessem Chouchane, Hatem Bejaoui (Ammar Jemal 68), Mahmoud Khemiri●, Mejdi Ben Mohamed (Bassem Ben Nasr 28), Mejdi Traoui, Afouene Gharbi, Msaddek Hasnaoui, Muri Ogunbiyi, Aymen Soltani, Mehdi Ben Dhifallah. Tr: Bertrand Marchand

Rabat
1-09-2007, Diouf SEN

FAR Rabat — **1**
Mounir Benkassou [22p]

Tarek Jarmouni - Noureddine Kacemi, Omar Bendriss, Hafid Abdesadek, Youssef Basri, Ali Jaarafi, Jawad Ouaddouch, Idrissi Youssef Kaddioui (Mohamed Lansri 81), Mounir Benkassou (Mohamed El Mrini 66), Issam Iraki, Adil Loutfi (Tarik Marzouk 69). Tr: Mustapha Madih

JS Kabylie — **1**
Mohamed Derrag [85]

Faouzi Chaouchi - Demba Barry, Sofiane Bengoreine, Sid Ahmed Khedis, Cherif Abdesslam, Lamara Douicher●, Nabil Hamouda, Nassim Oussalah (Mohamed Derrag 68), Boubakeur Athmani (Nabil Hemani 64), Youcef Saibi (Issa Traore 78), Tayeb Berramia. Tr: Moussa Saib

GROUP B

Tunis
23-06-2007, Maillet SEY

Espérance 0

Hamdi Kasraoui, Moyin Chaabani, Wissem Bekri, Karim Touati (Sameh Derbali 59), Zied Derbali, Ahmed Hammi (Walid Tayeb• 59), Atef Felhi, Kamel Zaiem, Hicham Aboucherouane•, Saber Khalifa•, Jerry (Salama Kasdaoui 76). Tr: Jacky Dugueperoux

ASEC Mimosas 0

Mohamed Kabore, Serges Wawa• (Arthur Kocou 89), Khaled Adenon, Dacosta Akes Goore, Ndri Alli, Hamed Diomande, Desire Maglorie Kouame, Martial Yao Kouassi (Gildas Kassiaty 72), Serges Deble (Mutiu Adegoke 84), Emmanuel Kone, Idrissu Abdul Nafiu. Tr: Patrick Liewig

Cairo
24-06-2007, Diatta SEN

Al Ahly 2
Flavio [85], Osama Hosni [89]

Essam Al Hadari - Islam El Shater, Emad Al Nahhas, Wael Gomaa•, Shady Mohamed, Mohamed Shawky, Hossam Ashour, Mohamed Barakat, Mohamed Aboutrika (Ahmed Sedik 81), Ahmed Qanawi (Flavio 46), Emad Moteab• (Osama Hosni 64). Tr: Manuel Jose

Al Hilal 0

Mahjoub El Moez• - Alaeldin Gibril, Amar Ramadan, Yusuf Mohamed, Dario Khan, Allaedin Yousef, Rtshard Justin Lado, Saif Masawi•, Haitham Mostafa, Kelechi Osunwa (Mohamed Tahir 73), Ndubuisi Eze. Tr: Ricardo Ferreira

Abidjan
8-07-2007, Marange ZIM

ASEC Mimosas 0

Vincent de Paul Angban - Khaled Adenon, Dacosta Akes Goore, Ndri Alli, Hamed Diomande, Desire Maglorie Kouame, Ali Diarra (Marc Dion Sede 58), Gildas Kassiaty (Mutiu Adegoke 67), Martial Yao Kouassi (Serges Deble 46), Emmanuel Kone, Idrissu Abdul Nafiu. Tr: Patrick Liewig

Al Ahly 1
Mohamed Aboutrika [40]

Essam Al Hadari - Ahmed Adel, Emad Al Nahhas, Ahmed El Sayed, Shady Mohamed, Mohamed Shawky, Mohamed Barakat, Gilberto (Wael Gomaa 89), Anis Boujelbene•, Mohamed Aboutrika (Osama Hosni 87), Flavio. Tr: Manuel Jose

Omdurman
8-07-2007, Ssegonga UGA

Al Hilal 2

Abubaker Sherif - Omar Bakheit, Alaeldin Ahmed Gibril•, Yusuf Mohamed (Amar Ramadan 89), Dario Khan, Yousef Allaedin, Rtshard Justin Lado, Haitham Mostafa (Saif Masawi 12), Kelechi Osunwa, Mohamed Tahir•, Ndubuisi Eze. Tr: Ricardo Ferreira

Espérance 0

Hamdi Kasraoui - Sameh Derbali, Moyin Chaabani, Wissem Bekri•, Larbi Jabeur, Ahmed Hammi, Seifallah Mahjoubi (Ahmed Ben Yahia 80), Kamel Zaiem (Zied Derbali 87), Walid Tayeb, Saber Khalifa (Naim Berbat 68), Jerry. Tr: Faouzi Benzarti

Cairo
20-07-2007, Haimoudi ALG

Al Ahly 3
Aboutrika [14], Flavio [78], Osama Hosni [85]

Essam Al Hadari - Emad Al Nahhas, Ahmed El Sayed, Shady Mohamed, Mohamed Shawky•, Mohamed Barakat (Osama Hosni 81), Anis Boujelbene• (Hossam Ashour 46), Mohamed Aboutrika, Gilberto, Emad Moteab (Islam El Shater 68), Flavio. Tr: Manuel Jose

Espérance 0

Hamdi Kasraoui - Atef Felhi, Boulbaba Saafi (Walid Tayeb 73), Karim Touati, Zied Derbali, Seifallah Mahjoubi, Ahmed Hammi•, Kamel Zaiem, Sameh Derbali, Hicham Aboucherouane, Salama Kasdaoui (Saber Khalifa 46). Tr: Larbi Zouaoui

Omdurman
22-07-2007, El Arjoune MAR

Al Hilal 2
Ndubuisi Eze [11], Yusuf Mohamed [86]

Mahjoub El Moez - Omar Bakheit, Alaeldin Ahmed Gibril (Hassan Isaac Korongo 71), Yusuf Mohamed, Dario Khan, Yousef Allaedin, Rtshard Justin Lado, Haitham Mostafa (Mutaz Kabir 62), Kelechi Osunwa (Amar Ramadan 89), Mohamed Tahir, Ndubuisi Eze. Tr: Ricardo Ferreira

ASEC Mimosas 1
Idrissu Abdul Nafiu [53]

Vincent de Paul Angban - Serges Wawa, Khaled Adenon, Dacosta Akes Goore•, Hamed Diomande•, Desire Maglorie Kouame, Ali Diarra, Serges Deble (Ndri Alli• 61), Emmanuel Umoh (Marc Dion Sede 74), Emmanuel Kone, Idrissu Abdul Nafiu• (Mutiu Adegoke 87). Tr: Patrick Liewig

Rades
4-08-2007, Ncobo RSA

Espérance 1
Salama Kasdaoui [38]

Hamdi Kasraoui - Atef Felhi, Bilel Yaken, Zied Derbali•, Boulbaba Saafi, Wissem Bekri, Ahmed Hammi, Kamel Zaiem• (Aymen Jouini Mnafeg 89), Hicham Aboucherouane (Sameh Derbali 84), Jerry (Walid Tayeb 74). Tr: Larbi Zouaoui

Al Ahly 0

Abdelhamid - Emad Al Nahhas (Ridha El Weshe 75), Ahmed El Sayed•, Ghadi Fariah, Mohamed Shawky, Hassan Mostafa (Mohamed Barakat 46), Hossam Ashour•, Gilberto•, Mohamed Aboutrika, Flavio•, Ahmed Ibrahim (Osama Hosni 67). Tr: Manuel Jose

Abidjan
5-08-2007, Evehe CMR

ASEC Mimosas 1
Antoine Ngossan [30]

Mohamed Kabore - Serges Wawa, Khaled Adenon, Dacosta Akes Goore, Hamed Diomande, Arthur Kocou, Mutiu Adegoke• (Serges Deble 66), Martial Yao Kouassi (Desire Maglorie Kouame 71), Antoine Ngossan (Gildas Kassiaty 89), Emmanuel Kone, Idrissu Abdul Nafiu. Tr: Patrick Liewig

Al Hilal 0

Mahjoub El Moez - Omar Bakheit, Alaeldin Ahmed Gibril, Yusuf Mohamed•, Dario Khan, Yousef Allaedin, Rtshard Justin Lado, Haitham Mostafa (Salih Abdellah 69), Kelechi Osunwa, Mohamed Tahir (Mutaz Kabir 76), Ndubuisi Eze (Hassan Isaac Korongo 61). Tr: Ricardo Ferreira

Abidjan
19-08-2007, Hicuburundi BDI

ASEC Mimosas 2
Bilel Yaken [OG 60], Ali Diarra [78]

Mohamed Kabore - Khaled Adenon, Dacosta Akes Goore, Ndri Alli, Hamed Diomande, Ali Diarra, Desire Maglorie Kouame, Arthur Kocou, Serge Kouakou (Gildas Kassiaty 63), Emmanuel Kone (Martial Yao Kouassi 51), Idrissu Abdul Nafiu (Emmanuel Umoh 89). Tr: Patrick Liewig

Espérance 0

Hamdi Kasraoui - Atef Felhi, Wissem Bekri, Zied Derbali•, Bilel Yaken, Karim Touati (Sameh Derbali 64), Kamel Zaiem•, Ahmed Hammi, Hicham Aboucherouane, Salama Kasdaoui (Jerry 79), Amine Ltifi (Seifallah Mahjoubi 70). Tr: Larbi Zouaoui

Omdurman
19-08-2007, Benouza ALG

Al Hilal 3
Dario Khan [59], Korongo [67], Ndubuisi Eze [87]

Mahjoub El Moez - Omar Bakheit, Yusuf Mohamed, Dario Khan, Alaeldin Gibril (Hassan Isaac Korongo 59), Allaedin Yousef•, Haitham Mostafa (Hamuda Bashir 89), Rtshard Justin Lado•, Saif Masawi, Kelechi Osunwa, Ndubuisi Eze. Tr: Ricardo Ferreira

Al Ahly 0

Essam Al Hadari - Ahmed Adel, Emad Al Nahhas, Ahmed El Sayed, Shady Mohamed, Hassan Mostafa, Hossam Ashour, Mohamed Barakat• (Wael Gomaa 77), Gilberto, Mohamed Aboutrika (Osama Hosni 65), Emad Moteab (Reda Al Weeshi 82). Tr: Manuel Jose

Cairo
2-09-2007, Guezzaz MAR

Al Ahly 2
Flavio [76], Mohamed Aboutrika [89]

Essam Al Hadari - Islam El Shater, Emad Al Nahhas, Shady Mohamed, Wael Gomaa, Hassan Mostafa (Mohamed Aboutrika 67), Hossam Ashour (Anis Boujelbene 56), Mohamed Barakat, Gilberto, Flavio, Emad Moteab (Rami Adel 79). Tr: Manuel Jose

ASEC Mimosas 0

Mohamed Kabore - Khaled Adenon, Ndri Alli, Hamed Diomande•, Dacosta Akes Goore, Ali Diarra•, Desire Maglorie Kouame•, Serge Kouakou (Gildas Kassiaty 54), Martial Yao Kouassi• (Koffi Foba Kabran Stevens 81), Antoine Ngossan (Emmanuel Umoh 80), Idrissu Abdul Nafiu. Tr: Patrick Liewig

Tunis
2-09-2007, Pare BFA

Espérance 1
Amine Ltifi [41]

Hamdi Kasraoui - Atef Felhi, Hamza Zakkar, Boulbaba Saafi, Bilel Yaken, Ahmed Hammi, Seifallah Mahjoubi•, Aymen Jouini Mnafeg (Chakib Lackhem 71), Hicham Aboucherouane, Slama Kasdaoui (Sameh Derbali 46), Amine Ltifi•. Tr: Ali ben Naji

Al Hilal 1
Ndubuisi Eze [44p]

Mahjoub El Moez - Haitham Mostafa (Mohamed Tahir 73), Rtshad Justin Lado (Hamuda Bashir• 16), Dario Khan, Yusuf Mohamed, Alaeldin Gibril, Saif Masawi, Allaedin Yousef, Hassan Isaac Korongo•, Ndubuisi Eze, Kelechi Osunwa. Tr: Ricardo Ferreira

SEMI-FINALS

Omdurman
21-09-2007, Coulibaly MLI

Al Hilal	2
	Ndubuisi Eze [61], Kelechi Osunwa [66]

Abubaker Sherif - Omar Bakheit, Yusuf Mohamed, Dario Khan, Alaeldin Gibril, Allaedin Yousef (Saif Masawi 46), Hamuda Bashir, Haitham Mostafa, Hassan Isaac Korongo, Kelechi Osunwa, Ndubuisi Eze∗. Tr: Ricardo Ferreira

Etoile du Sahel	1
	Radhouene Felhi [38]

Aymen Mathlouthi - Seif Ghezal∗, Radhouene Felhi, Hatem Bejaoui, Mahmoud Khemiri, Moussa Narry∗, Mohamed Ali Nafkha∗, Afouene Gharbi (Bassem Ben Nasr 67), Muri Ogunbiyi (Msaddek Hasnaoui 81), Ja∗, Amine Chermiti. Tr: Bertrand Marchand

Sousse
6-10-2007, Maillet SEY

Etoile du Sahel	3
	Amine Chermiti 2 [13 64], Sadat Bukari [52]

Aymen Mathlouthi - Seif Ghezal, Radhouene Felhi, Sabeur Ben Frej∗, Mehdi Meriah; Moussa Narry, Mohamed Ali Nafkha, Muri Ogunbiyi, Ja (Msaddek Hasnaoui 89), Sadat Bukari∗ (Bassem Ben Nasr 65), Amine Chermiti. Tr: Bertrand Marchand

Al Hilal	1
	Ndubuisi Eze [57]

Abubaker Sherif - Omar Bakheit, Yusuf Mohamed, Dario Khan∗, Alaeldin Gibril; Allaedin Yousef (Kelechi Osunwa 27), Hamuda Bashir (Mohamed Tahir 76), Haitham Mostafa, Seif Masawi (Hassan Isaac Korongo 67), Khalid Jolit; Ndubuisi Eze. Tr: Ricardo Ferreira

Tripoli
23-09-2007, Haimoudi ALG

Al Ittihad	0

Samir Aboud - Younes Shibani, Arafa Nakua∗ (Alseny Camara 63), Mohamed Alsnani, Mahmoud Maklouf∗, Hesham Shaban, Osama Hamadi, Yohann Langlet (Musbah Saad 80), Ali Rahuma∗, Walid Mhadeb (Mansour Bokri 89), Salem Rewani. Tr: Branko Smiljanic

Al Ahly	0

Essam Al Hadari - Ahmed Adel (Hassan Mostafa 54), Emad Al Nahhas, Ahmed El Sabed, Shady Mohamed; Hossam Ashour (Wael Gomaa 69), Anis Boujelbene, Mohamed Barakat, Gilberto, Mohamed Aboutrika (Ahmed Sedik 84); Flavio. Tr: Manuel Jose

Cairo
7-10-2007, Kotey GHA

Al Ahly	1
	Hesham Shaban OG [20]

Essam Al Hadari - Emad Al Nahhas, Ahmed El Sayed, Shady Mohamed, Hossam Ashour, Anis Boujelbene, Mohamed Barakat∗ (Hassan Mostafa 89), Gilberto, Mohamed Aboutrika (Wael Gomaa 78); Flavio (Reda Al Weeshi 90), Emad Moteab. Tr: Manuel Jose

Al Ittihad	0

Samir Aboud (Muftah Ghzalla 54) - Younes Shibani, Arafa Nakua∗, Mohamed Alsnani, Mahmoud Maklouf∗; Hesham Shaban (Pierre Coulibaly 74∗87), Osama Hamadi, Yohann Langlet, Walid Mhadeb∗ (Ali Rahuma 68), Salem Rewani, Alseny Camara. Tr: Branko Smiljanic

---

CAF CHAMPIONS LEAGUE FINAL FIRST LEG
Stade Olympique, Sousse
27-10-2007, Raphael Divine Evehe CMR

ETOILE SAHEL 0 0 AL AHLY

Etoile du Sahel			Al Ahly	
1	Aymen Mathlouthi		Essam Al Hadari	1
2	Seif Ghezal		89 Islam El Shater	2
4	Radhouene Felhi		Emad Al Nahhas	4
11	Mehdi Meriah	80	Shady Mohamed	7
13	Sabeur Ben Frej		Wael Gomaa	26
24	Moussa Narry		Hossam Ashour	25
18	Mejdi Traoui	67	Anis Boujelbene	17
19	Mohamed Ali Nafkha		Ahmed El Sayed	5
25	Muri Ogunbiyi	89	Mohamed Barakat	8
7	Ja		89 Mohamed Aboutrika	22
27	Amine Chermiti		86 Flavio	23
	Tr: Bertrand Marchand		Tr: Manuel Jose	
	Substitutes		Substitutes	
3	Sadat Bukari	67	89 Osama Hosni	18
6	Hatem Bejaoui	80	89 Ahmed Sedik	6
			86 Emad Moteab	9

CAF CHAMPIONS LEAGUE FINAL SECOND LEG
International, Cairo
9-11-2007, Abderrahim El Arjoune MAR

AL AHLY 1 3 ETOILE SAHEL

Emad Al Nahhas [50]

Afouene Gharbi [44], Amine Chermiti [89], Moussa Narry [90]

Al Ahly			Etoile du Sahel	
1	Essam Al Hadari		Aymen Mathlouthi	1
2	Islam El Shater	46	Sabeur Ben Frej	13
4	Emad Al Nahhas	61	Radhouene Felhi	4
5	Ahmed El Sayed		Ammar Jemal	5
7	Shady Mohamed		Moussa Narry	24
25	Hossam Ashour		Hatem Bejaoui	6
17	Anis Boujelbene	66	Mohamed Ali Nafkha	19
12	Gilberto	75	66 Afouene Gharbi	10
22	Mohamed Aboutrika		85 Muri Ogunbiyi	25
9	Emad Moteab		87 Ja	7
23	Flavio		Amine Chermiti	27
	Tr: Manuel Jose		Tr: Bertrand Marchand	
	Substitutes		Substitutes	
14	Hassan Mostafa	46	66 Mejdi Traoui	18
6	Ahmed Sedik	66	85 Bassem Ben Nasr	26
29	Ahmed Qanawi	75	87 Mahmoud Khemiri	15

REGIONAL CLUB TOURNAMENTS IN AFRICA 2007-08

CECAFA KAGAME INTER-CLUB CUP TANZANIA 2008

First round groups

Group A		Pl	W	D	L	F	A	Pts	KEN	BDI	SOM
Simba SC	TAN	3	2	0	1	8	3	6	2-3	1-0	5-0
Tusker	KEN	3	2	0	1	9	5	6		1-3	5-0
Vital 'O	BDI	3	1	0	2	4	4	3			1-2
BanaadirTel'com	SOM	3	1	0	2	2	11	3			

Group B		Pl	W	D	L	F	A	Pts	RWA	ETH
URA Kampala	UGA	2	1	1	0	5	2	4	4-1	1-1
Rayon Sport	RWA	2	1	0	1	3	4	3		2-0
Awassa Kenema	ETH	2	0	1	1	1	3	1		

Group C		Pl	W	D	L	F	A	Pts	ZAN	RWA
Young Africans	TAN	2	1	1	0	3	2	4	1-0	2-2
Miembeni	ZAN	2	1	0	1	2	2	3		2-1
APR FC	RWA	2	0	1	1	3	4	1		

Quarter-finals

Tusker	0 7p
Rayon Sport	0 6p

Vital 'O	0
Young Africans	2

Simba SC	2
APR FC	0

Miembeni	0
URA Kampala	2

Semi-finals

Tusker	1
Young Africans	0

Simba SC	0
URA Kampala	1

Final

Tusker	2
URA Kampala	1

Third place play-off

Simba SC	w-o
Young Africans	

The tournament took place in Morogoro and Dar es Salaam, Tanzania from 12-07-2008 to 27-07-2008

Final: New National Stadium, Dar es Salaam, 27-07-2008, Ref: Hudu Munyemana RWA

Scorers - Joseph Shikokoti 71, Oscar Kadenge 88 for Tusker; Martin Muwanga 23 for URA

Tusker - Boniface Otieno - Ibrahim Shikanda, John Njoroge, Joseph Shikokoti, Humphrey Okoti, Edward Kauka, Osborne Monday, Simon Mburu (Oscar Kadenge), Hassan Aden (John Kio), Crispin Odula (Kelvin Omondi), Justus Anene. Tr: Jacob Mulee

URA - Abbey Dhaira - Tony Mawejje, Manco Kaweesa, Joseph Owino, David Kyobe, Ismail Kogozi (Robert Okello), Dan Wagaluka, Mussa Docca (John Karangwa), Johnson Bagoole, Martin Muwanga, Samuel Mubiru

MTN CAF CHAMPIONS LEAGUE 2008

First Round

Al Ahly	EGY	Bye
Tusker *	KEN	
Al Tahrir	ERI	w-o
US Stade Tamponnaise *	REU	3 1
St Michael United	SEY	1 0
LCS Maseru	LES	0 1
Platinum Stars *	RSA	4 0
Etoile du Sahel	TUN	Bye
Commune FC	BFA	0 2
AS Douanes Dakar *	SEN	0 3
Costa do Sol *	MOZ	2 0
Ajesaia	MAD	0 1
Royal Leopards *	SWZ	0 0
Dynamos	ZIM	1 2
ASEC Mimosas	CIV	Bye
Invincible XI *	LBR	
AS Kaloum Star	GUI	w-o
ES Sétif	ALG	5 2
ASC SNIM *	MTN	1 0
Sporting Clube Bissau *	GNB	0 0
Olympique Khouribga	MAR	2 2
Inter Clube	ANG	2 2
Renacimiento *	EQG	1 1
FAR Rabat *	MAR	3 0 4p
Sporting Clube Praia	CPV	0 3 5p
Africa Sports	CIV	0 3
Tonnerre FC *	BEN	0 0
APR FC *	RWA	1 0
Zamalek	EGY	2 2
Al Hilal	SUD	Bye
URA Kampala *	UGA	0 0
Zesco United	ZAM	2 0
Curepipe Starlight *	MRI	2 0
Coin Nord	COM	0 1
Miembeni *	ZAN	0 0
Mamelodi Sundowns	RSA	1 4
JS Kabylie	ALG	Bye
Sahel SC *	NIG	1 1
AshantiGold	GHA	0 6
Gombe United	NGA	0 2 4p
DC Motema Pembe *	COD	2 0 1p
Vital'O *	BDI	0 0
Cotonsport	CMR	1 1
Enyimba *	NGA	4 3
Diables Noirs	CGO	1 2
Awassa Kenema	ETH	0 1
Simba SC *	TAN	3 1
ASKO Kara *	TOG	3 1
Union Douala	CMR	1 0
ASC Saloum *	SEN	1 0
Club Africain	TUN	2 1
Al Ittihad Tripoli	LBY	Bye
Stade Malien *	MLI	1 0
Primeiro de Agosto	ANG	2 0
FC 105 Libreville *	GAB	3 1
Hearts of Oak	GHA	0 3
Renaissance *	CHA	
TP Mazembe	COD	w-o

Second Round

Al Ahly *	w-o
Al Tahrir	
US Stade Tamponnaise	0 1
Platinum Stars *	2 1
Etoile du Sahel *	5 0
AS Douanes Dakar	0 3
Costa do Sol	0 2
Dynamos *	3 0
ASEC Mimosas *	1 1
AS Kaloum Star	1 0
ES Sétif	0 2 0p
Olympique Khouribga *	2 0 3p
Inter Clube	1 1
Sporting Clube Praia *	2 0
Africa Sports	0 2 4p
Zamalek *	2 0 5p
Al Hilal *	2 1
Zesco United	0 1
Curepipe Starlight	0 0
Mamelodi Sundowns *	3 1
JS Kabylie *	3 0
AshantiGold	0 0
Gombe United	0 2
Cotonsport *	5 1
Enyimba *	3 4
Simba SC	0 1
ASKO Kara *	2 0
Club Africain	0 4
Al Ittihad Tripoli *	1 1
Primeiro de Agosto	0 2
FC 105 Libreville	1 0
TP Mazembe *	1 1

Third Round

Al Ahly	1 2
Platinum Stars *	2 0
Etoile du Sahel	0 0
Dynamos *	1 1
ASEC Mimosas *	0 1
Olympique Khouribga	0 1
Inter Clube	0 2
Zamalek *	3 1
Al Hilal *	4 0
Mamelodi Sundowns	1 2
JS Kabylie	0 2
Cotonsport *	3 1
Enyimba *	5 1
Club Africain	1 2
Al Ittihad Tripoli *	2 0
TP Mazembe	1 2

* Home team in the first leg • Losing teams in the second round enter the Confederation Cup

CAF CHAMPIONS LEAGUE 2008

MTN CAF CHAMPIONS LEAGUE 2008

Champions League Stage   **Semi–finals**   **Final**

Group A

Team		Pts
Al Ahly	EGY	
Dynamos	ZIM	
ASEC Mimosas	CIV	
Zamalek	EGY	

Group B

Team		Pts
Al Hilal	SUD	
Cotonsport	CMR	
Enyimba	NGA	
TP Mazembe	COD	

Groups to be played from 20-07-2008 to 21-09-2008 • Semi–finals to be played on 4-10-2008 and 18-10-2008 • Final to be played on 1-11-2008 and 15-11-2008

* Home team in the first leg • Losing teams in the second round enter the CAF Confederation Cup

FIRST ROUND

Tampon, 17-02-2008, Mohamad MAD
US Stade Tamp.   3   Mamoudou Diallo [12], Farro [56], Payet [68]
St Michael Utd   1   Alex Nibourette [72]

Victoria, 1-03-2008, Roopnah
St Michael Utd   0
US Stade Tamp.   1   Mamoudou Diallo [68]

Rustenburg, 16-02-2008, Simisse
Platinum Stars   4   Mathe [14], Tshabalala [16], Mmotong [19],
LCS Maseru   0   Makgopela [89]

Maseru, 2-03-2008, Manuel ZIM
LCS Maseru   1   Makalo Mehlala [21]
Platinum Stars   0

Dakar, 16-02-2008, Attama NIG
AS Douanes   0
Commune FC   0

Ouagadougou, 1-03-2008, Lamidi BEN
Commune FC   2   Korbeogo [12], Ousmane Doumbia [52]
AS Douanes   3   Babacar Mbengue 2 [30] [84], Vito Badiane [66]

Maputo, 17-02-2008, Rafae MWI
Costa do Sol   2   Felix [31], Mambo [64p]
Ajesaia   0

Antananarivo, 4-03-2008, Hamidou ALG
Ajesaia   1   Lalaina Momenjanahary [71]
Costa do Sol   0

Mbabane, 17-02-2008, Jose
Royal Leopards   0
Dynamos   1   Lazarus Muhoni [81]

Harare, 2-03-2008, Nhlapo RSA
Dynamos   2   Justice Majabvi [49], Admire Dzukamanja [86]
Royal Leopards   0

Nouackchott, 15-02-2008, Feye CPV
ASC SNIM   1   Dina Taqillah [21p], Adiko [90]
ES Sétif   5   Touil [8], Djediat [16], Serey [84p], Ziaya [86],

Setif, 29-02-2008, Mohamed EGY
ES Sétif   2   Delhoum [5], Mecheri [15]
ASC SNIM   0

Bissau, 16-02-2008, Mendy
Sporting Bissau   0
Olymp Khouribga   2   Redouan Beklal [6], Baker Hilali [89]

Khouribga, 2-03-2008, Ragab
Olymp Khouribga   2   Amara Bangoura [41], Nizoul Abouri [75]
Sporting Bissau   0

Malabo, 17-02-2008, Solei CMR
Renacimiento   1   Lawrence Doe [37]
Inter Clube   2   Pedro Henriques 2 [1] [74]

Luanda, 29-02-2008, Mufeti NAM
Inter Clube   2   Pedro Henriques [46], Gildo [74]
Renacimiento   1   Lino Makuba [10]

Rabat, 16-02-2008, Ilboudo BFA
FAR Rabat   3   Lemnasfi [33p], El Bassel [38], Allaoui [44]
Sporting Praia   0

Praia, 1-03-2008, Lopes GAM
Sporting Praia   3   Tigana [12], Tchetcha [28], Yuri [84]
FAR Rabat   0   Sporting won 5-4p

Cotonou, 17-02-2008, Karembe MLI
Tonnerre FC   0
Africa Sports   0

Abidjan, 2-03-2008, Sowe
Africa Sports   3   Momble Dehi 2 [21] [59], Thierry Zahui [90]
Tonnerre FC   0

Kigali, 16-02-2008, Ghebremichael
APR FC   1   Akiam Jeannot [90]
Zamalek   2   Mostafa Gaafar [5], Hamza Gamal [70]

Cairo, 2-03-2008, Meddeb
Zamalek   2   Mahmoud Fatallah [52p], Sherif Ashraf [79]
APR FC   0

Kampala, 16-02-2008, Mbaga
URA Kampala   0
Zesco United   2   Elson Mkandawire [24], Nicholas Zulu [64]

Ndola, 1-03-2008, Tebogo
Zesco United   0
URA Kampala   0

Curepipe, 17-02-2008, Mnkantjo ZIM
Curepipe Starlight   2   Rodson Tojosa [41], Westley Marquette [84]
Coin Nord   0

Mitsamiouli, 1-03-2008, Boengstrong
Coin Nord   1   Issa Nazarali [38]
Curepipe Starlight   0

Zanzibar, 15-02-2008, Onyango
Miembeni   0
Sundowns   1   Moriri [83]

Pretoria, 1-03-2008, Martins
Sundowns   4   Aldave [21], Chabangu [31], Ndlovu 2 [84] [89]
Miembeni   0

Niamey, 17-02-2008, Mbengue
Sahel SC   1   Amadou Saley [27]
AshantiGold   0

Obuasi, 2-03-2008, Sanusi SLE
AshantiGold   6   Mensah [10], Asamoah [51], Wakassu [61p],
Sahel SC   1   Sacko [12].   Alhassan [73], Quaye 2 [85] [88]

Kinshasa, 17-02-2008, Dekezandji CTA
Motema Pembe   2   Mukendi Kalobo [38], Bokungu Ndjoli [43]
Gombe United   0

Gombe, 2-03-2008, Chaibou
Gombe United   2   Nura Mohamed 2 [22p] [31p]
Motema Pembe   0   Gombe won 4-2p

Bujumbura, 16-02-2008, Mufta
Vital'O   0
Cotonsport   1   Oumarou Sanda [92+]

Garoua, 9-03-2008, Diani CHA
Cotonsport   1   Ousmailia Baba [74]
Vital'O   0

Aba, 17-02-2008, Keita
Enyimba   4   Worgu 2 [19] [22], Otorogu 2 [50] [71]
Diables Noirs   1   Gandze [89]

Pointe-Noire, 2-03-2008, Atsoo TOG
Diables Noirs   2   Lepaye [84], Mafuta Mbumba [86]
Enyimba   3   Worgu 2 [50] [74], Kalu [77]

Dar es Salaam, 17-02-2008, Habonimana
Simba SC   3   Odhiambo 2 [8] [73], Mwakingwe [89]
Awassa Kenema   0

Addis Abeba, 3-02-2008, Gasingwa RWA
Awassa Kenema   1   Deribe [1]
Simba SC   1   Athumani Machupa [13]

Lome, 17-02-2008, Soussou
ASKO Kara   3   Mama Issifou [47], Liyate Kpatoumbi [61],
Union Douala   1   Masson [85]   Vincent Tchalla [88]

Yaounde, 9-03-2008, Ondo EQG
Union Douala   0
ASKO Kara   1   Vincent Tchalla [62]

Kaolack, 17-02-2008, Arthur CIV
ASC Saloum   1   Amadou Diatta [26]
Club Africain   2   Borham Ghanem [64], Oussema Sellemi [86]

Tunis, 1-03-2008, Farouk EGY
Club Africain   1   Youssef Mouihbi [28]
ASC Saloum   0

Bamako, 17-02-2008, Adigun NGA
Stade Malien   1   Issiaka Eliassou [35p]
Primeiro Agosto   2   Ze Augusto [48], Bena [74]

Luanda, 29-02-2008, Fakudze SWZ
| Primeiro Agosto | 0 | |
| Stade Malien | 0 | |

Libreville, 17-02-2008, Ebaita
| FC 105 Libreville | 3 | Lenga Basto 41, Cedric Mintsa 65, |
| Hearts of Oak | 0 | Juste Freddy Otomo 75p |

Accra, 2-03-2008, Konah
| Hearts of Oak | 3 | Asante 21, Abanga 85, Bossman 89p |
| FC 105 Libreville | 1 | Cedric Mintsa 57 |

SECOND ROUND

Rustenburg, 23-03-2008, Marange
| Platinum Stars | 2 | Lekoelea 60, Simba Marumo 75 |
| US Stade Tamp. | 0 | |

Tampon, 5-04-2008, Seechurn MRI
| US Stade Tamp. | 1 | Mamoudou Diallo 56 |
| Platinum Stars | 1 | Simba Marumo 22 |

Sousse, 22-03-2008, Khellifi
| Etoile du Sahel | 5 | Ja 30, Ben Dhifallah 2 45 72, Gharbi 70, |
| AS Douanes | 0 | Sassi 90 |

Dakar, 5-04-2008, Sidibe
| AS Douanes | 3 | Sadio Diao 2 78 88, Babacar Mbengue 86 |
| Etoile du Sahel | 0 | |

Harare, 23-03-2008, Labrosse SEY
| Dynamos | 3 | Edward Sadomba 3 9 37 83 |
| Costa do Sol | 0 | |

Maputo, 6-04-2008, Lwanja
| Costa do Sol | 2 | Josimar 36, To 42 |
| Dynamos | 0 | |

Abidjan, 23-03-2008, Tahiri
| ASEC Mimosas | 1 | Ahmed Diomande 14 |
| AS Kaloum Star | 1 | Abdul Karim Domingo 32 |

Conakry, 6-04-2008, Diouf SEN
| AS Kaloum Star | 0 | |
| ASEC Mimosas | 1 | Serges Deble 85 |

Khouribga, 22-03-2008, Serge
| Olymp Khouribga | 2 | Lemrani Alaoui 43, Zakaria Amzil 88 |
| ES Sétif | 0 | |

Setif, 6-04-2008, Manuel
| ES Sétif | 2 | Abdelmalek Ziaya 10, Lazhar Hadj Aissa 82 |
| Olymp Khouribga | 0 | Olympique won 3-0p |

Praia, 22-03-2008, Lemghaifry
| Sporting Praia | 2 | Yuri 63, Babanco 88 |
| Inter Clube | 1 | Pedro Henriques 22 |

Luanda, 6-04-2008, Kazubu
| Inter Clube | 1 | Minguito 86 |
| Sporting Praia | 0 | |

Cairo, 23-03-2008, Saadallah
| Zamalek | 2 | Amr Zaki 28, Mohamed Abou Ela 42 |
| Africa Sports | 0 | |

Abidjan, 6-04-2008, Sowe GAM
| Africa Sports | 2 | Jean-Michel Sery 2 43 67 |
| Zamalek | 0 | Zamalek won 5-4p |

Omdurman, 23-03-2008, Eyob
| Al Hilal | 2 | Kelechi Osunwa 43, Ahmed Adil 65 |
| Zesco United | 0 | |

Ndola, 5-04-2008, Chiganga
| Zesco United | 1 | Enoch Sakala 60 |
| Al Hilal | 1 | Ahmed Adil 43 |

Pretoria, 22-03-2008, Randriatsarafihavy
| Sundowns | 3 | Ndlovu 30, Moriri 52, Aldave 84 |
| Curepipe Starlight | 0 | |

Curepipe, 6-04-2008, Disang BOT
| Curepipe Starlight | 0 | |
| Sundowns | 1 | Ndlovu 32 |

Tizi-Ouzou, 21-03-2008, Ambaya
| JS Kabylie | 3 | Yacine Amaouche 3, Nabil Hemani 2 9 53 |
| AshantiGold | 0 | |

Obuasi, 6-04-2008, Rembangouet
| AshantiGold | 0 | |
| JS Kabylie | 0 | |

Garoua, 23-03-2008, Idriss
| Cotonsport | 5 | Abdoul Karim 13, Zoua Daogari 37, |
| Gombe United | 0 | Fankele Traore 3 39 49 93+ |

Gombe, 6-04-2008, Lamine
| Gombe United | 2 | Manu Bala 53, Mohammed Nura 61 |
| Cotonsport | 1 | Fankele Traore 82 |

Aba, 23-03-2008, Agbovi
| Enyimba | 3 | Worgu 3 7 37 78, Kalu 87p |
| Simba SC | 0 | |

Dar es Salaam, 26-04-2008, Infante MOZ
| Simba SC | 1 | Athumani Machupa 5 |
| Enyimba | 4 | Worgu 14, Owoeri 18, Kalu 46 |

Lome, 23-03-2008, Djaoupe
| ASKO Kara | 2 | Poupotitero Camara 58, Vincent Tchalla 78 |
| Club Africain | 0 | |

Tunis, 4-04-2008, Mamane
| Club Africain | 4 | Lassaad Ouertani 28, Oussama Sellemi 36, |
| ASKO Kara | 0 | Youssef Mouihbi 52, Ben Yahia 71 |

Tripoli, 23-03-2008, Kalyango
| Al Ittihad | 1 | Mohamed Elsani 71 |
| Primeiro Agosto | 0 | |

Luanda, 4-04-2008, Evehe CMR
| Primeiro Agosto | 2 | Harry Milanzi 2 27 56 |
| Al Ittihad | 1 | Mohamed Zubya 79 |

Lubumbashi, 23-03-2008, Fekadu
| TP Mazembe | 1 | Kabangu Matu 75 |
| FC 105 Libreville | 1 | Marcelin Gangura 82 |

Libreville, 6-04-2008, Wam
| FC 105 Libreville | 0 | |
| TP Mazembe | 1 | Luyeye Mvete 35 |

THIRD ROUND

Pretoria, 26-04-2008, Mpanisi ZAM
| Platinum Stars | 2 | Koketso Mmotong 56, Edward Williams 88 |
| Al Ahly | 1 | Emad Moteab 81 |

Cairo, 11-05-2008, Kayindi UGA
| Al Ahly | 2 | Emad Moteab 50, Flavio 69 |
| Platinum Stars | 0 | |

Harare, 27-04-2008, Mufeti NAM
| Dynamos | 1 | Desmond Maringwa 50 |
| Etoile du Sahel | 0 | |

Sousse, 10-05-2008, Keita GUI
| Etoile du Sahel | 0 | |
| Dynamos | 1 | Benjamin Marere 29 |

Abidjan, 27-04-2008, Diouf SEN
| ASEC Mimosas | 0 | |
| Olymp Khouribga | 0 | |

Khouribga, 11-05-2008, Eyene CMR
| Olymp Khouribga | 1 | Jamal Triki 68 |
| ASEC Mimosas | 1 | Ndoua Kouakou 23 |

Match details for

Zamalek v Inter Clube
Al Hilal v Sundowns
Cotonsport v JS Kabylie
Enyimba v Club Africain
Al Ittihad v TP Mazembe

are on page 907

CAF CONFEDERATION CUP 2007

First Round

Les Astres Douala	CMR	2	1	
JS Talangai *	CGO	0	0	
Tema Youth	GHA	Bye		
DC Motema Pembe	COD	Bye		
San Pedro Claver *	EQG	1	0	
Benfica Luanda	ANG	5	2	
Atraco	RWA	0	3	
Prince Louis FC *	BDI	0	0	
Notwane FC *	BOT	1	0	
Mekelakeya	ETH	1	1	
Ports Authority *	SLE	2	1	
AS Bamako	MLI	0	0	
AS Togo-Port Lomé *	TOG	1	0	
EGS Gafsa	TUN	1	2	
Mwana Africa	ZIM	3	3	
Mundu FC *	ZAN	0	1	
Inter Clube	ANG	Bye		
US Ouakam	SEN	Bye		
Sahel SC Niamey *	NIG	2	1	
Etoile Filante	BFA	2	1	
Issia Wazzi	CIV	Bye		
Delta Téléstar *	GAB	1	0	
OC Bukavu Dawa	COD	0	2	
Satelitte Conakry	GUI	3		
Benfica *	GNB	1		
CS Sfaxien	TUN	Bye		
Dolphin	NGA	Bye		
AS Denguélé	CIV	0	1	
Hawks *	GAM	0	1	
US Gorée	SEN	3	1	
NPA Anchors *	LBR	2	0	
HUS Agadir	MAR	Bye		
Green Buffaloes	ZAM	Bye		
St Michael United *	SEY	2	0	
St Pauloise	REU	1	1	
Ajesaia	MAD	0	4	
Curepipe Starlight SC *	MRI	1	0	
Ismaily	EGY	Bye		
Kwara United	NGA	1	2	
AS Dragons *	BEN	0	0	
MC Alger	ALG	Bye		
Têxtile Pungué *	MOZ	1	1	3p
Simba SC	TAN	1	1	1p
Union Douala	CMR	Bye		
ASO Chlef	ALG	1	2	
ASAC Concorde *	MTN	0	1	
ENPPI	EGY	Bye		
AS Coton Tchad	CHA	1	1	
Al Ahly Tripoli *	LBY	2	0	
Al Merreikh	SUD	Bye		

Second Round

Les Astres Douala	w-o		
Tema Youth ‡			
DC Motema Pembe	1	0	
Benfica Luanda *	4	0	
Atraco	0	2	
Mekelakeya *	1	0	
Ports Authority *	3	1	
EGS Gafsa	2	4	
Mwana Africa *	2	0	
Inter Clube	0	0	
US Ouakam	0	1	3p
Etoile Filante *	1	0	4p
Issia Wazzi	2	5	
OC Bukavu Dawa *	0	0	
Satelitte Conakry *	1	0	
CS Sfaxien	3	4	
Dolphin	0	1	
Hawks *	0	0	
US Gorée *	0	2	
HUS Agadir	0	3	
Green Buffaloes	0	2	
St Pauloise *	0	0	
Ajesaia *	2	1	
Ismaily	2	6	
Kwara United *	3	0	7p
MC Alger	0	3	6p
Têxtile Pugué *	0	0	
Union Douala	3	3	
ASO Chlef *	0	1	
ENPPI	0	0	
AS Coton Tchad *	2	0	
Al Merreikh	0	5	

Third Round

Les Astres Douala	0	1
Benfica Luanda * ‡	3	1
Atraco *	2	1
EGS Gafsa	2	1
Mwana Africa	0	3
Etoile Filante *	2	0
Issia Wazzi *	1	0
CS Sfaxien	0	2
Dolphin *	1	0 5p
HUS Agadir	0	1 3p
Green Buffaloes	1	1
Ismaily *	2	1
Kwara United	1	3
Union Douala *	1	2
ASO Chlef *	1	0
Al Merreikh	0	3

CAF CONFEDERATION CUP 2007

CAF CONFEDERATION CUP 2007

Intermediate Round				Group Stage		Final

Les Astres Douala CMR 1 2
Etoile du Congo † * CGO 2 0

EGS Gafsa TUN 1 1
Mam'di Sundowns † * RSA 2 1

Group A	Pts	TUN	COD	RSA	CMR
CS Sfaxien	13		2-0	4-0	3-0
TP Mazembe	12	2-1		3-1	2-1
Mamelodi Sundowns	6	1-2	3-2		2-1
Les Astres	4	1-1	1-2	1-0	

TP Mazembe † * COD 1 3
Mwana Africa ZIM 0 1

Cotonsport Garoua † * CMR 2 0
CS Sfaxien TUN 1 4

CS Sfaxien	4	1
Al Merreikh *	2	0

Dolphin NGA 2 2
Marantha Fiokpo † * TOG 1 0

Wydad Casablanca † * MAR 0 0
Ismaily EGY 1 2

Group B	Pts	SUD	NGA	EGY	NGA
Al Merreikh	10		6-1	1-0	4-1
Dolphin	10	3-0		2-0	2-0
Ismaily	8	1-1	1-0		1-0
Kwara United	5	2-1	0-0	1-1	

Kwara United NGA 1 1
Nasarawa United † * NGA 1 0

Young Africans † * TAN 0 0
Al Merreikh SUD 0 2

† Champions League second round losers that entered at the Intermediate round
* Home team in the first leg • ‡ Team withdrew • w-o = walk over

GROUP A

Loftus Versfeld, Pretoria, 21-07-2007, 20:10, Seechurn MRI

Sundowns	3	Ngwenya [50], Nyandoro [63], Moriri [70]
TP Mazembe	2	Tresor Mputu 2 [20 40]

Stade de la Reunification, Douala, 21-07-2007, 15:00, Agbovi GHA

Les Astres	1	Okouda [10]
CS Sfaxien	1	Nafti [38]

Taieb Mhiri, Sfax, 4-08-2007, 15:00, Banao BFA

CS Sfaxien	4	Kouassi 2 [2 28], Mbele [8], Soumah [94+]
Sundowns	0	

Kinshasa Stadium, Kinshasa, 5-08-2007, 15:00, Mwanza ZAM

TP Mazembe	2	Tresor Mputu 2 [1 61]
Les Astres	1	Ekanga [18]

Loftus Versfeld, Pretoria, 18-08-2007, 20:10, De Sousa ANG

Sundowns	2	Moriri [33], Mhlongo [61]
Les Astres	1	Ossah [31]

Kinshasa Stadium, Kinshasa , 19-08-2007, 15:00, Mathews NAM

TP Mazembe	2	Kabangu [47], Tresor Mputu [82]
CS Sfaxien	1	Mbele [36]

Stade de la Reunification, Douala, 1-09-2007, 15:00, Doue CIV

Les Astres	1	Djam
Sundowns	0	

Taieb Mhiri, Sfax, 4-08-2007, 20:00, Rassas SUD

CS Sfaxien	2	Rouid [1], Nafti [75]
TP Mazembe	0	

Taieb Mhiri, Sfax, 22-09-2007, 21:45, Sidibe MLI

CS Sfaxien	3	Mbele [43], Kouassi [55], Hamza Younes [89]
Les Astres	0	

Kinshasa Stadium, Kinshasa , 23-09-2007, 15:30, Kapanga MWI

TP Mazembe	3	Tresor Mputu [7], Kabangu [37], Kaluyituka [58p]
Sundowns	1	Ndela [85]

Loftus Versfeld, Pretoria, 6-10-2007, 20:10, Ssegonga UGA

Sundowns	1	Ndlovu [10]
CS Sfaxien	2	Chadi Hammami [82], Mbele [88]

Stade de la Reunification, Douala, 6-10-2007, 15:00, Aboubacar CIV

Les Astres	1	Ossah [6]
TP Mazembe	2	Tresor Mputu 2 [17 60]

Group A	Pl	W	D	L	F	A	Pts
CS Sfaxien	6	4	1	1	13	4	13
TP Mazembe	6	4	0	2	11	9	12
Mamelodi Sundowns	6	2	0	4	7	13	6
Les Astres	6	1	1	4	5	10	4

GROUP B

UJ Esuene, Calabar, 22-07-2007, 15:00, Eyene CMR

Dolphin	2	Olaiya [3], Bello [92+]
Kwara United	0	

Ismailya Stadium, Ismailya, 22-07-2007, 19:00, Girma ETH

Ismaily	1	Salem [81]
Al Merreikh	1	Paulinho [89]

Kwara Stadium, Kwara, 4-08-2007, 15:00, Gil GAB

Kwara United	1	Weng [32]
Ismaily	1	Fadl [75]

El Merreikh Stadium, Omdurman, 4-08-2007, 20:00, Jamel

Al Merreikh	6	Ahmed [20], Faisal Agab 2 [39 79], Alzouma [65], Idahor [77], Safari [81]
Dolphin	1	Ezeji [48]

Liberation Stadium, Port Harcourt, 18-08-2007, 16:00, Atsoo Kokou TOG

Dolphin	2	Idowu [22], Ezeji [82]
Ismaily	0	

Kwara Stadium, Kwara, 18-08-2007, 15:00, Keita GUI

Kwara United	2	Odada [47], Abidoye [80]
Al Merreikh	1	Idahor [30]

El Merreikh Stadium, Omdurman, 1-09-2007, 19:30, Jedidi TUN

Al Merreikh	4	Ahmed [13], Alsoudey [24], Safari [44], Paulino [66]
Kwara United	1	Abideye [91+]

Ismailya Stadium, Ismailya, 2-09-2007, 17:30, Mwandike TAN

Ismaily	1	Mostafa Karim [92+]
Dolphin	0	

Kwara Stadium, Kwara, 22-09-2007, 15:00, Mendy GAM

Kwara United	0	
Dolphin	0	

El Merreikh Stadium, Omdurman, 23-09-2007, 22:00, Disang BOT

Al Merreikh	1	Idahor [42]
Ismaily	0	

Liberation Stadium, Port Harcourt, 7-10-2007, 15:00, Louzaya CGO

Dolphin	3	OG [18], Uwazuoke [33p], Amaefule [63p]
Al Merreikh	0	

Ismailya Stadium, Ismailya, 7-10-2007, 17:30, Benouza ALG

Ismaily	1	Youssef Gamal [29]
Kwara United	0	

Group B	Pl	W	D	L	F	A	Pts
Al Merreikh	6	3	1	2	13	8	10
Dolphin	6	3	1	2	8	7	10
Ismaily	6	2	2	2	4	5	8
Kwara United	6	1	2	3	4	9	5

CAF CONFEDERATION CUP FINAL 1ST LEG
Al Merreikh Stadium (The Redcastle), Omdurman
3-11-2007, Kenias Marange ZIM

AL MERREIKH 2 4 CS SFAXIEN

Paulino [52], Faisal Agab [77p]

Lelo Mbele 2 [2 60],
Blaise Kouassi 2 [4 18]

Al Merreikh			CS Sfaxien
Bahaeldin Abdallah			Lotfi Saidi
Alaeldin Babiker			Amir Haj Massaoud
Jean Paul Abalo			Fateh Gharbi
Khalid Sharaf			Bechir Mechergui
Musa Al Tayeb		77	Hamdi Rouid
Elijah Tana	73		Chaker Berguagi
Mogahid Mohamed	52		Haitham Mrabet
Paulinho			Mohamed Kadri
Efosa Eguakun			Abdelkrim Nafti
Endurance Idahor		66	Lelo Mbele
Faisal Ajab			Blaise Kouassi
Tr: Otto Pfister			Tr: Michel Decastel
Substitutes			Substitutes
Amir Damar	73	77	Karim Ben Amor
Haitham Tambal	52	66	Hamza Younes

CAF CONFEDERATION CUP FINAL 2ND LEG
Taieb Mhiri, Sfax
24-11-2007, Modou Sowe GAM

CS SFAXIEN 1 0 AL MERREIKH

Amir Messaoud [86]

CS Sfaxien			Al Merreikh
Lotfi Saidi			Bahaeldin Abdallah
Amir Haj Massaoud			Mohamed Ali Kheder
Fateh Gharbi			Jean Paul Abalo
Bechir Mechergui			Badreldin El Doud
Hamdi Rouid			Ennour
Chaker Berguagi			Mogahid Mohamed
Haitham Mrabet			Paulinho
Naby Soumah			Endurance Idahor
Abdelkrim Nafti	80		Faisal Ajab
Lelo Mbele	70	85	Haitham Tambal
Blaise Kouassi			Kalak
Tr: Michel Decastel			Tr: Mohamed Abdallah
Substitutes			Substitutes
Mohamed Kadri	80	85	Abdelhamid Amari
Hamza Younes	70		

CAF CHAMPIONS LEAGUE SECOND ROUND
continued from page 903

Cairo, 26-04-2008, Lamine ALG			
Zamalek	3		Amr El Shafti [4], Abdelrazek Shikabala [10],
Inter Clube	0		Mohamed Ibrahim [26]
Luanda, 11-05-2008, Djaoupe TOG			
Inter Clube	2		Minguito 2 [50 60]
Zamalek	1		Eduardo OG [16]
Omdurman, 26-04-2008, Niyongabo BDI			
Al Hilal	4		Osunwa 2 [43 66], Tahir [52], Yusuf M'mad [63]
Sundowns	2		Dladla [27], Moriri [29]
Pretoria, 11-05-2008, Eyob ERI			
Sundowns	1		Moriri [47]
Al Hilal	0		
Garoua, 26-04-2008, Lwanja MWI			
Cotonsport	3		Zoua [20], Kamilou 2 [42 58]
JS Kabylie	0		
Tizi-Ouzou, 9-05-2008, Jedidi TUN			
JS Kabylie	2		Ben Said [6], Chaouchi [86]
Cotonsport	1		Kamilou [44]
Aba, 27-04-2008, Aguidissou BEN			
Enyimba	5		Kalu [1], Worgu [32p], Chukwudi [67], Akueme 2 [91+ 94+]
Club Africain	1		Junior Osagie [44]
Tunis 9-05-2008, Abdelfattah EGY			
Club Africain	2		Borhene Ghanem [4], Aymen Rhifi [73]
Enyimba	1		Ezenwa Otorogu [86]
Tripoli, 27-04-2008, Pare BFA			
Al Ittihad	2		Paul Koulibaly [44], Mohamed Zubya [72]
TP Mazembe	1		Bedi Mbenza [59]
Lubumbashi, 11-05-2008, Konah LBR			
TP Mazembe	2		Ngoy Bomboko [10], Mvete Luyeye [68]
Al Ittihad	0		

CAF CONFEDERATION CUP INTERMEDIATE ROUND
continued from page 911

Tizi-Ouzou, 11-07-2008, Pare BFA			
JS Kabylie	1		Adlene [92+]
Les Astres	1		Mangolo [21]
Yaounde, 27-07-2008, Doue CIV			
Les Astres	0		
JS Kabylie	1		Berramla [78]
Tripoli, 11-07-2008, Ndinya KEN			
Al Ittihad	2		Rewani [54], Shipani [87]
Asante Kotoko	1		Yaro [13]
Kumasi, 27-07-2008, Trabelsi TUN			
Asante Kotoko	3		
Al Ittihad	1		
Khouribga, 13-07-2008, Evehe CMR			
Olymp Khouribga	2		Benghoudi [1], Souari [6]
Al Merreikh	2		Faisal Agab [65], Mogahid [71]
Omdurman, 26-07-2008, Kaoma ZAM			
Al Merreikh	0		
Olymp Khouribga	0		

CAF CONFEDERATION CUP 2008

First Round

Team	Country	Result
CS Sfaxien	TUN	Bye
JSM Béjaïa	ALG	Bye
Entente Bingerville	CIV	1 3
Ports Authority *	GAM	0 0
ASC Linguère	SEN	Bye
Al Akhdar	LBY	w-o
Tourbillon	CHA	
AS Adema *	MAD	1 0
Young Africans	TAN	0 2
MC Alger	ALG	Bye
Haras Al Hedood	EGY	Bye
Mount Cameroon	CMR	1 4
JS Talangai *	CGO	2 1
Primeiro de Maio	ANG	Bye
Anse Réunion *	SEY	2 0
Petite Rivière Noire	MRI	1 0
Ajax Cape Town	RSA	Bye
Mangasport *	CMR	3 2
AS FNIS Niamey	NIG	0 0
Petro Atlético	ANG	Bye
Satellite FC	GUI	0 3
Monrovia Black Star *	LBR	0 0
Djoliba AC	MLI	Bye
Espérance Tunis	TUN	Bye
Rachad Bernoussi	MAR	Bye
Issia Wazzi	CIV	Bye
Universite National Benin	BEN	0 1
US Masséda *	TOG	2 1
AS Vita Kinshasa	COD	Bye
Inter Star	BDI	0 1 3p
Express Kampala *	UGA	1 0 4p
Maniema Union *	COD	3 0
Akonangui	EQG	0 0
Les Astres Douala	CMR	Bye
Asante Kotoko	GHA	Bye
Wikki Tourists	NGA	Bye
Casa Sports	SEN	Bye
Dolphin	NGA	Bye
Highlanders *	ZIM	3 0
Ferroviário Nampula	MOZ	0 1
Chipukizi *	ZAN	0 0
Green Buffaloes	ZAM	5 2
Rayon Sports	RWA	0 2 5p
Harar Bira *	ETH	2 0 4p
Al Merreikh	SUD	Bye

Second Round

CS Sfaxien *	1 1
JSM Béjaïa	0 1
Entente Bingerville	0 3 3p
ASC Linguère *	3 0 5p
Al Akhdar *	1 1
Young Africans	1 0
MC Alger *	0 0
Haras Al Hedood	0 1
Mount Cameroon	2 0
Primeiro de Maio *	0 1
Anse Réunion	0 1
Ajax Cape Town *	1 4
Mangasport	2 1
Petro Atlético *	1 0
Satellite FC	0 0
Djoliba AC *	2 1
Espérance Tunis	1 2
Rachad Bernoussi *	3 0
Issia Wazi *	2 1
US Masséda	0 4
AS Vita Kinshasa *	0 0 4p
Express Kampala	0 0 2p
Maniema Union	0 0
Les Astres Douala *	2 0
Asante Kotoko	2 4
Wikki Tourists *	2 1
Casa Sports *	0 1
Dolphin	0 2
Highlanders	1 1
Green Buffaloes *	1 0
Rayon Sports	0 0
Al Merreikh *	3 0

Third Round

CS Sfaxien	2 2
ASC Linguère *	3 1
Al Akhdar *	1 0
Haras Al Hedood	1 1
Mount Cameroon	1 5
Ajax Cape Town *	5 0
Mangasport	1 1
Djoliba AC *	3 2
Espérance Tunis	0 6
US Masséda *	1 1
AS Vita Kinshasa	0 1
Les Astres Douala *	0 1
Asante Kotoko	0 4
Dolphin *	2 1
Highlanders *	0 1
Al Merreikh	2 3

CAF CONFEDERATION CUP 2008

CAF CONFEDERATION CUP 2008

Intermediate Round

Group Stage

Final

CS Sfaxien	TUN	2	2
Platinum Stars † *	RSA	2	0

Mam'di Sundowns * †	RSA	1	0
Haras Al Hedood	EGY	0	2

Group A   Pts

CS Sfaxien
Haras Al Hedood
Inter Clube
Club Africain

Inter Clube † *	ANG	2	1
Mount Cameroon	CMR	1	1

Djoliba	MLI	0 0 3p
Club Africain † *	TUN	0 0 5p

Etoile du Sahel † *	TUN	2	0
Espérance Tunis	TUN	0	0

Les Astres Douala	CMR	1	0
JS Kabylie † *	ALG	1	1

Group B   Pts

Etoile du Sahel
JS Kabylie
Asante Kotoko
Al Merreikh

Asante Kotoko	GHA	1	3
Al Ittihad Tripoli † *	LBY	2	1

Olymp Khouribga † *	MAR	2	0
Al Merreikh	SUD	2	0

† Champions League second round losers that entered at the Intermediate round
* Home team in the first leg • Group matches to be played 15-08-2007 to 19-10-2008 • Final to be played on 8-11-2008 and 22-11-2008

FIRST ROUND

Banjul, 16-02-2008, Bangoura
Ports Authority	0	
ES Bingerville	1	Zeze [42]

Abidjan, 1-03-2008, Sahi
ES Bingerville	3	
Ports Authority	0	

Antananarivo, 17-02-2008, Jacques
AS Adema	1	Niasexe [72]
Young Africans	0	

Dar es Salaam, 2-03-2008, Abdel Gadir
Young Africans	2	Maurice 2 [53 69]
AS Adema	0	

Brazzaville, 17-02-2008, Biani
JS Talangai	2	Eziane [60], Ngakosso [71]
Mount Cameroon	1	Takang [79]

Yaounde, 11-03-2008, Mvibudulu
Mount Cameroon	4	Takang 2 [8 67], Francis [17], Agbor [32]
JS Talangai	1	Eziane [35]

Victoria, 16-02-2008, Ramanampamonjy
Anse Réunion	2	Rose [26], Nibourette [38]
Petite Riv. Noire	1	Laseringue [46]

Curepipe, 2-03-2008, Ncobo
Petite Riv. Noire	0	
Anse Réunion	0	

Moanda, 16-02-2008, Bodo
Mangasport	3	Djibo OG [18], Ngamana 2 [86 89]
AS FNIS Niamey	0	

Niamey, 1-03-2008, Lemahgaifry MTN
AS FNIS Niamey	0	
Mangasport	2	Dosso [19], Mabide [69]

Monrovia, 16-02-2007, Sidibe
Black Star	0	
Satellite FC	0	

Conakry, 2-03-2008, Kasse
Satellite FC	3	Koivogui [16], Bangoura [42], Camara [82]
Black Star	0	

Lome, 16-02-2008, Djaballah
US Masséda	2	Bassayi [24], Alemawo [85]
UNB	0	

Cotonou, 2-03-2008, Ramsis
UNB	1	Johnson [52]
US Masséda	1	Aloenouvou [35]

Kampala, 15-02-2008, Amwayi
Express FC	1	Bwire [23]
Inter Star	0	

Bujumbura, 2-03-2008, Kagabo
Inter Star	1	Mutabara [4]
Express FC	0	Express won 4-3p

Kinshasa, 15-02-2008, Victor
Maniema Union	3	Bokonga [37], Kalume [65], Ndarabu [85]
Akonangui	0	

Bata, 2-03-2008, Ndume
Akonangui	0	
Maniema Union	0	

Bulawayo, 17-02-2007, Mwanza
Highlanders	3	Muzokomba [18], Choruma [73], Muzingwa [87]
Ferroviário N'pula	0	

Nampula, 2-03-2008, Massango
Ferroviário N'pula	0	
Highlanders	0	

Zanzibar, 16-02-2008, Dagnew
Chipukizi	0	
Green Buffaloes	5	Mayuka [14], Tembo [21], Sebastian Mwewa [36], Newa Mwewa [61], Hanjeeme [71]

Lusaka, 1-03-2008, Niyongabo
Green Buffaloes	2	Njobvu [74], Tembo [83]
Chipukizi	0	

Addis Abeba, 17-02-2008, El Fadil
Harar Bira	2	Yared [44], Ahmed Ahmed [61]
Rayon Sports	0	

Kigali, 1-03-2008, Chiganga
Rayon Sports	2	Tuyisenge [62], Gatete [75]
Harar Bira	0	Rayon won 5-3p

SECOND ROUND

Sfax, 22-03-2008,
CS Sfaxien	1	Jabeur [56]
JSM Béjaïa	0	

Béjaïa, 4-04-2008, 4-04-2008, El Raaof
JSM Béjaïa	1	Chaouch [10]
CS Sfaxien	1	Lusadisu [23]

Saint Louis, 22-03-2008, Lemghamboji MTN
ASC Linguère	3	Tine [2], Ly Mouchid [10], Diop [13]
ES Bingerville	0	

Abidjan, 5-04-2008, Lamptey GHA
ES Bingerville	3	Takutchie 2 [42 44], Angan [59]
ASC Linguère	0	Linguère won 5-3p

Tripoli, 21-03-2008, Hama
Al Akhdar	1	Abdulhamid [47]
Young Africans	1	Hamisi [63]

Dar es Salaam, 5-04-2008, Abduillah
Young Africans	0	
Al Akhdar	1	Kamto [56]

Alger, 21-03-2008, Rouaissi
MC Alger	0	
Haras Al Hedood	0	

Alexandria, 4-04-2008, Imhamed
Haras Al Hedood	1	El Herda [17]
MC Alger	0	

Benguela, 23-03-2008, Mufeti
Primeiro de Maio	0	
Mount Cameroon	2	Akono [27], Takang [54]

Yaounde, 6-04-2008, Kouakou
Mount Cameroon	0	
Primeiro de Maio	1	Fernando [74]

Cape Town, 23-03-2008, Mpanisi
Ajax Cape Town	1	Granwald [16]
Anse Réunion	0	

Mahe, 5-04-2008, Simanga
Anse Réunion	1	Rose [35]
Ajax Cape Town	4	Paulse 2 [23 36], Evans [48], Ross OG [56]

Luanda, 23-03-2008, Nhlapo
Petro Atlético	1	David [26]
Mangasport	2	Bembagoye 2 [14 64]

Moanda, 5-04-2008, Wokoma
Mangasport	1	Dosso [17]
Petro Atlético	0	

Bamako, 23-03-2008, Soussou
Djoliba AC	2	Dembele [24], Seydou Traore [62]
Satellite FC	0	

Conakry, 5-04-2008, Ahmed Nasser
Satellite FC	0	
Djoliba AC	1	Brehima Traore [60]

Casablanca, 22-03-2008, Hamdy
Rachad Bernoussi	3	Bouraima [38], Ait Bihi [55], Hidaga [82]
Espérance	1	Bilel Yaken [47]

Tunis, 4-04-2008, Bichari
Espérance	2	Kamel Zaiem [10]
Rachad Bernoussi	0	

Abidjan, 22-03-2008, Kaba

Issia Wazi	2	Siaka 25, Kanga 80
US Masséda	0	

Lome, 6-04-2008, Jatta

US Masséda	4	Adekounle 2 25 50, Gnama 2 43 45
Issia Wazi	1	Diakite 36

Kinshasa, 3-03-2008, El Nigomi

AS Vita Kinshasa	0	
Express FC	0	

Kampala, 4-04-2008, Munyemana

Express FC	0	
AS Vita Kinshasa	0	Vita won 4-2p

Yaounde, 23-03-2008, Victor

Les Astres	2	Nya 20, Mangolo 69
Maniema Union	0	

Kinshasa, 6-04-2008, Ngbokaye

Maniema Union	0	
Les Astres	0	

Bauchi, 22-03-2008, Kagabo

Wikki Tourists	2	Rabiu 42, Abubakar 84
Asante Kotoko	2	Adjei 50, Osei Kuffour 68

Kumasi, 6-04-2008, Gabre

Asante Kotoko	4	Osei Kuffour 20, Bekoe 2 54 64, Coffie 69
Wikki Tourists	1	Auta 83

Dakar, 22-03-2008, Aguidissou

Casa Sports	0	
Dolphin	0	

Calabar, 6-04-2008, Gil

Dolphin	2	Mnake 68, Anusi 82
Casa Sports	1	Diatta 80

Lusaka, 22-03-2008, Ngosi

Green Buffaloes	1	Phiri 86
Highlanders	1	Malajila 1

Bulawayo, 6-04-2008, Phomane

Highlanders	1	Malajila 45
Green Buffaloes	0	

Omdurman, 24-03-2008, Niyongabo

Al Merreikh	3	Faisal Agab 35, El Din 54, Amare 80
Rayon Sports	0	

Kigali, 6-04-2008, Ndinya

Rayon Sports	0	
Al Merreikh	0	

THIRD ROUND

Dakar, 26-04-2008, Faial CPV

ASC Linguère	3	Iyanele, Dembele, Diop
CS Sfaxien	2	Opoku, Jaber Houcine

Tunis, 10-05-2008, Jamal LBY

CS Sfaxien	2	Basisila 17, Soumah 41
ASC Linguère	1	Ndiaye 57

Tripoli, 25-04-2008, Trabelsi TUN

Al Akhdar	1	Abdel Hamid 68
Haras Al Hedood	1	Ahmed Aid 33

Alexandria, 10-05-2008, Abdel Kader SUD

Haras Al Hedood	1	Abdel Hamid 56
Al Akhdar	0	

Cape Town, 26-04-2008, Malepa

Ajax Cape Town	5	Pualse 2, Lusself, Siwahia 2
Mount Cameroon	1	France

Yaounde, 11-05-2008, Nsue EQG

Mount Cameroon	5	Francis 3 24 32 78, Agbor 28, Ndjeyeha 89
Ajax Cape Town	0	

Bamako, 27-04-2008, Mana NGA

Djoliba AC	3	Traore , Coulibaly, Dembele
Mangasport	1	Mabedi

Moanda, 10-05-2008, Lamptey GHA

Mangasport	1	Ndjony 80
Djoliba AC	2	Traore 44, Fane 66

Lome, 27-04-2008, Mpunga COD

US Masséda	1	Gnama 40
Espérance	0	

Tunis, 10-05-2008, Pare BFA

Espérance	6	Derbali 12, Chaabni 2 51 70, Kasraoui 81,
US Masséda	1	Amegnifia 35. Aboucherouane 87

Yaounde, 27-04-2008, Moukoko CGO

Les Astres	0	
AS Vita Kinshasa	0	

Lubumbashi, 9-05-2008, Abdul Kadir SOM

AS Vita Kinshasa	1	Lofo 80
Les Astres	1	Kibong 50

Calabar, 27-04-2008, Ousmane MLI

Dolphin	2	Wobo 40, Mnake 87
Asante Kotoko	0	

Kumasi, 12-05-2008, De Sousa ANG

Asante Kotoko	4	Inkoon 45, Beloe 2 71 85, Yaro 90
Dolphin	1	Wobo 21

Harare, 26-04-2008, Ndinya KEN

Highlanders	0	
Al Merreikh	2	El Dood 56, Abelzhar 72

Omdurman, 11-05-2008, Kalyango UGA

Al Merreikh	3	Haitham Kamal 3 39 67 82
Highlanders	1	Githbert 19

INTERMEDIATE ROUND

Rustenburg, 13-07-2008, Lamptey GHA

Platinum Stars	2	Marumo 13, Masavabo 41
CS Sfaxien	2	Agyemang 52, Chaker 72

Sfax, 26-07-2008, 26-07-2008, Djaoupe TOG

CS Sfaxien	2	Kouassi 38, Ben Amor Aimen 61
Platinum Stars	0	

Pretoria, 12-07-2008, Martins ANG

Sundowns	1	Lungisane 60
Haras Al Hedood	0	

Alexandria, 26-07-2008, Jedidi TUN

Haras Al Hedood	2	Abdelghani 14, El Daly 89
Sundowns	0	

Luanda, 11-07-2008, Marange ZIM

Inter Clube	2	Iyeni 15, Ngola 24
Mount Cameroon	1	Kwedje 86

Yaounde, 25-07-2008, Diouf SEN

Mount Cameroon	1	Takang 30
Inter Clube	1	Pedro Costa 72

Tunis, 13-07-2008, Keita GUI

Club Africain	0	
Djoliba AC	0	

Bamako, 27-08-2008, Jamel LBY

Djoliba AC	0	
Club Africain	0	Club Africain won 5-3p

Sousse, 12-07-2008, Haimoudi ALG

Etoile du Sahel	2	Chermiti 17, Ogunbiyi 49
Espérance	0	

Tunis, 26-08-2008, Abdelfattah EGY

Espérance	0	
Etoile du Sahel	0	

Match details for

Les Astres v JS Kabylie
Asante Kotoko v Al Ittihad
Olympique Khouribga v Al Merreikh

are on page 907

REGIONAL TOURNAMENTS IN AFRICA 2008

COUPE DE LA CEMAC CAMEROON 2008

First Round Group Stage

Group A	Pl	W	D	L	F	A	Pts	CMR	EQG
Chad	2	1	1	0	4	3	4	2-1	2-2
Cameroon	2	1	0	1	2	2	3		1-0
Equatorial Guinea	2	0	1	1	2	3	1		

Group B	Pl	W	D	L	F	A	Pts	CGO	GAB
Central African Rep.	2	1	1	0	5	3	4	2-0	3-3
Congo	2	1	0	1	2	3	3		2-1
Gabon	2	0	1	1	4	5	1		

Played in Cameroon from 14-06-2008 to 24-06-2008 • Teams played with local players

Semi–finals

Cameroon	1
Central African Rep.	0

Chad	0
Congo	1

Final

Cameroon	3
Congo	0

Third place play-off

Central African Rep.	2
Chad	0

COSAFA CASTLE CUP SOUTH AFRICA 2008

First round groups

Group A	Pl	W	D	L	F	A	Pts	SWZ	SEY	MRI
Madagascar	3	1	2	0	4	3	5	1-1	1-1	2-1
Swaziland	3	1	2	0	3	2	5		1-0	1-1
Seychelles	3	1	1	1	8	2	4			7-0
Mauritius	3	0	1	2	2	10	1			

Group B	Pl	W	D	L	F	A	Pts	MWI	LES	COM
Namibia	3	2	1	0	5	1	7	1-0	1-1	3-0
Malawi	3	2	0	1	2	1	6		1-0	1-0
Lesotho	3	1	1	1	2	2	4			1-0
Comoros	3	0	0	3	0	5	0			

Played in South Africa from 19-07-2008 to 3-08-2008 • Angola, Botswana, Mozambique, South Africa, Zambia & Zimbabwe byes to quarter-finals

Quarter–finals

South Africa	1
Namibia	0

Zimbabwe	0 4p
Zambia	0 5p

Madagascar	1
Angola	0

Botswana	0
Mozambique	2

Semi–finals

South Africa	1
Zambia	0

Madagascar	1
Mozambique	2

Final

South Africa	2
Mozambique	1

Third place play-off

Zambia	
Madagascar	

CONCACAF

CONFEDERATION OF NORTH, CENTRAL AMERICAN AND CARIBBEAN ASSOCIATION FOOTBALL

With qualification for the 2010 FIFA World Cup in full swing in the Americas, the start of 2008 was the time when the smaller countries of the Caribbean and Central America had their time in the public eye, but alas, there were very few tales of upsets, with the usual crowd making it through the knock-out rounds to the group stage. There were some big scores - El Salvador put 12 past Anguilla, the USA scored eight against Barbados, while even within the Caribbean, Jamaica scored 13 over two legs against the Bahamas. The fundamental inequality between the nations remains the biggest headache for CONCACAF with Mexico, and latterly America, standing head and shoulders above the rest. Nowhere has this had a more debilitating effect than in club competition where the CONCACAF Champions' Cup has had less stature than every other continental competition bar the O-League in Oceania. In a bid for wider international acceptance, August 2008

THE FIFA BIG COUNT OF 2006 FOR NORTH AND CENTRAL AMERICA AND THE CARIBBEAN

	Male	Female		Total
Number of players	33 071 000	10 038 000	Referees and Assistant Referees	172 000
Professionals	9 000		Admin, Coaches, Technical, Medical	961 000
Amateurs 18+	884 000		Number of clubs	17 000
Youth under 18	5 163 000		Number of teams	490 000
Unregistered	36 988 000		Clubs with women's teams	7 000
Total involved in football	44 242 000		Players as % of population	8.53%

saw the launch of the CONCACAF Champions League, an expanded competition that will feature a four-team group stage with the top two from each group qualifying for the quarter-finals. Critical for the success of the Champions League will be the Mexican and the American clubs getting behind the new tournament. Both will have four entries with two clubs from each seeded directly into the group phase, along with one club from each of Costa Rica, El Salvador, Guatemala and Honduras. The other eight places in the groups will be determined by a single play-off round between 16 teams. The prize at the end of course is not just winning the tournament but also qualification for the FIFA Club World Cup. Pachuca were the CONCACAF representatives at the 2007 tournament in Tokyo and they will be there again for the 2008 tournament after beating Deportivo Saprissa in the final CONCACAF Champions' Cup.

Confederation of North, Central American and Caribbean Association Football (CONCACAF)

725, Fifth Avenue, Trump Tower, 17th Floor, New York, NY 1022, USA

Tel +1 212 3080 044   Fax +1 212 3081 851

mail@concacaf.net   www.concacaf.com

President: WARNER Jack A. TRI   General Secretary: BLAZER Chuck USA

CONCACAF Formed: 1961

CONCACAF EXECUTIVE COMMITTEE

President: WARNER Jack A. TRI

Vice-President: AUSTIN Lisle BRB   Vice-President: BANEGAS Alfredo Hawit HON   Vice-President: CANEDO WHITE Guillermo MEX

ORDINARY MEMBERS OF THE EXECUTIVE COMMITTEE

BURRELL Horace Capt. JAM	ALVARADO Ariel PAN	GULATI Sunil USA
FIFA Exco: SALGUERO Rafael GUA		FIFA Exco: BLAZER Chuck USA

MAP OF CONCACAF MEMBER NATIONS

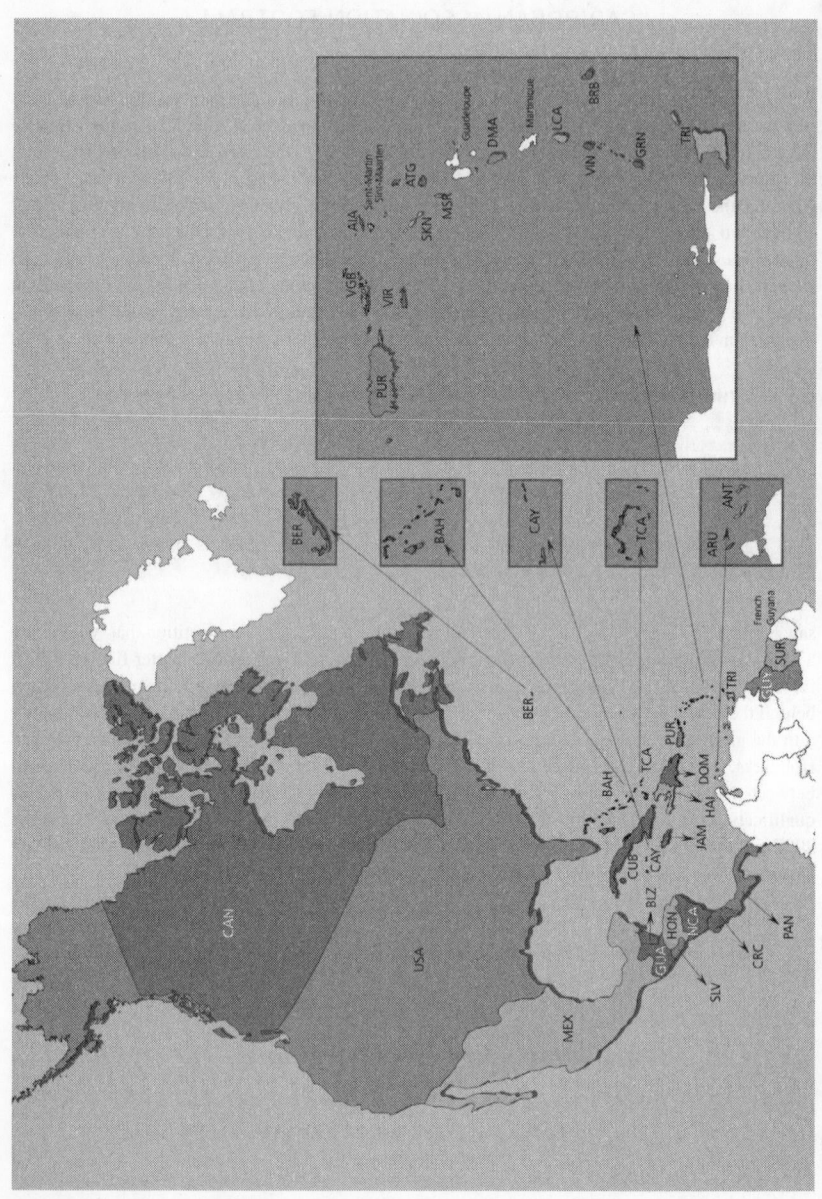

CENTRAL AMERICAN, NORTH AMERICAN AND CARIBBEAN TOURNAMENTS

CCCF CHAMPIONSHIP

Year	Host Country	Winners	Score	Runners-up	Venue
1941	Costa Rica	Costa Rica	3-1	El Salvador	San José
1943	El Salvador	El Salvador	2-1	Guatemala	San Salvador
1946	Costa Rica	Costa Rica	1-4	Guatemala	San José
1948	Guatemala	Costa Rica	2-3	Guatemala	Guatemala City
1951	Panama	Panama	2-0	Costa Rica	Panama City
1953	Costa Rica	Costa Rica	4-1	Honduras	San José
1955	Honduras	Costa Rica	2-1	Netherlands Antilles	Tegucigalpa
1957	Curaçao	Haiti	3-1	Curaçao	Willemstad
1960	Cuba	Costa Rica	4-1†	Netherlands Antilles	Havana
1961	Costa Rica	Costa Rica	4-0	El Salvador	San José

All tournaments played on a league basis. The result listed is the match played between the top two • † Play-off after both teams finished level

CONCACAF NATIONS CUP

Year	Host Country	Winners	Score	Runners-up	Venue
1963	El Salvador	Costa Rica	4-1	El Salvador	San Salvador
1965	Guatemala	Mexico	2-1	Guatemala	Guatemala City
1967	Honduras	Guatemala	1-0	Mexico	Tegucigalpa
1969	Costa Rica	Costa Rica	1-1	Guatemala	San José
1971	Trinidad & T	Mexico	0-0	Haiti	Port of Spain

All tournaments played on a league basis. The result listed is the match played between the top two

CONCACAF NATIONS CUP/FIFA WORLD CUP QUALIFIERS

Year	Host Country	Winners	Score	Runners-up	Venue
1973	Haiti	Haiti	2-1	Trinidad	Port-au-Prince
1977	Mexico	Mexico	4-1	Haiti	Mexico City
1981	Honduras	Honduras	0-0	El Salvador	Tegucigalpa
1985	Home & Away	Canada	2-1	Honduras	Saint John's
1989	Home & Away	Costa Rica	1-0	USA	San José

All tournaments played on a league basis. The result listed is the match played between the top two

CONCACAF GOLD CUP

Year	Host Country	Winners	Score	Runners-up	Venue
1991	USA	USA	0-0 4-3p	Honduras	Coliseum, Los Angeles
1993	Mexico/USA	Mexico	4-0	USA	Azteca, Mexico City
1995	USA	Mexico	2-0	Brazil	Coliseum, Los Angeles
1998	USA	Mexico	1-0	USA	Coliseum, Los Angeles
2000	USA	Canada	2-0	Colombia	Coliseum, Los Angeles
2002	USA	USA	2-0	Costa Rica	Rose Bowl, Pasadena
2003	Mexico/USA	Mexico	1-0	Brazil	Azteca, Mexico City
2005	USA	USA	0-0 3-1p	Panama	Giants Stadium, New Jersey
2007	USA	USA	2-1	Mexico	Soldier Field, Chicago

Not until the introduction of the CONCACAF Gold Cup in 1991 did Central America, North America and the Caribbean have a proper continental championship. Prior to 1963 there had been a Central American tournament with the occasional Caribbean entrant, a competition dominated by Costa Rica. 1963 saw the introduction of the CONCACAF Nations Cup, staged every other year until 1971, but the Americans and Mexicans failed to take it seriously and from 1973 until 1981 the Nations Cup was incorporated into the FIFA World Cup qualifiers. Since the creation of the CONCACAF Gold Cup in 1991, the USA has hosted every tournament (twice in conjunction with Mexico) and the two have provided the winners, with the exception of Canada in 2000.

CONCACAF WOMEN'S GOLD CUP

Year	Host Country	Winners	Score	Runners-up	Venue
1991	Haiti	USA	5-0	Canada	Port au Prince
1993	USA	USA	1-0	Canada	Long Island
1994	Canada	USA	6-0	Canada	Montreal
1998	Canada	Canada	1-0	Mexico	Toronto
2000	USA	USA	1-0	Brazil	Foxboro, Boston
2002	USA/Canada	USA	2-1	Canada	Rose Bowl, Pasadena
2006	USA	USA	2-1	Canada	Home Depot Center, Los Angeles

CONCACAF UNDER 20 WOMEN'S TOURNAMENT

Year	Host Country	Winners	Score	Runners-up	Venue
2004	Canada	Canada	2-1	USA	Frank Clair, Ottawa
2006	Mexico	USA	3-2	Canada	Veracruz

If there is one area in which CONCACAF can claim to be world beaters it is in women's football, with both the USA and Canada ranked at the highest level of the game. The Women's Gold Cup coincided with the launch of the men's competition and since then the USA have won six of the seven tournaments played, beating the only other winners, Canada, in the final of five of them.

CONCACAF UNDER 20 TOURNAMENT

Year	Host Country	Winners	Score	Runners-up	Venue
1954	Costa Rica	Costa Rica	3-1†	Panama	San José
1956	El Salvador	El Salvador	1-1†	Netherlands Antilles	San Salvador
1958	Guatemala	Guatemala	1-0†	Honduras	Guatemala City
1960	Honduras	Costa Rica	0-4†	Honduras	Tegucigalpa
1962	Panama	Mexico	1-1†	Guatemala	Panama City
1964	Guatemala	El Salvador			Guatemala City
1970	Cuba	Mexico	0-0†	Cuba	Havana
1973	Mexico	Mexico	2-0	Guatemala	Puebla
1974	Canada	Mexico	1-0	Cuba	
1976	Puerto Rico	Mexico	4-3	Honduras	
1978	Honduras	Mexico	1-0	Canada	
1980	USA	Mexico	2-0	USA	Giants Stadium, New Jersey
1982	Guatemala	Honduras	1-0	USA	Guatemala City
1984	Trinidad	Mexico	2-1	Canada	
1986	Trinidad	Canada	1-1†	USA	
1988	Guatemala	Costa Rica	3-0†	Mexico	
1990	Guatemala	Mexico	2-1†	Trinidad	Guatemala City
1992	Canada	Mexico	3-0†	USA	Victoria
1994	Honduras	Honduras	1-0†	Costa Rica	
1996	Mexico	Canada	2-2†	Mexico	Saltillo

† Final tournament played as a league. The match listed is between the top two • Played as the CCCF youth championship from 1954 to 1960

CONCACAF UNDER 17 TOURNAMENT

Year	Host Country	Winners	Score	Runners-up	Venue
1983	Trinidad	USA		Trinidad	
1985	Mexico	Mexico	1-1†	Costa Rica	
1987	Honduras	Mexico	3-1†	USA	
1988	Trinidad	Cuba	0-1†	USA	Port of Spain
1991	Trinidad	Mexico	1-1†	USA	Port of Spain
1992	Cuba	USA	3-4†	Mexico	
1994	El Salvador	Costa Rica	1-2†	USA	Flor Blanca, San Salvador
1996	Trinidad	Mexico	3-1†	USA	Port of Spain

† All final tournaments played as a league. The match listed is between the top two.

At both U-19 and U-17 levels CONCACAF tournaments have served as qualifiers for the FIFA events but since 1996, once the qualifying nations have been identified, the principle of determining the champions at each level has been abandoned.

CARIBBEAN CUP

Year	Host Country	Winners	Score	Runners-up	Venue
1989	Barbados	Trinidad & Tobago	2-1	Grenada	Bridgetown
1990	Trinidad	Not completed			
1991	Jamaica	Jamaica	2-0	Trinidad & Tobago	Kingston
1992	Trinidad	Trinidad & Tobago	3-1	Jamaica	Port of Spain
1993	Jamaica	Martinique	0-0 6-5p	Jamaica	Kingston
1994	Trinidad	Trinidad & Tobago	7-2	Martinique	Port of Spain
1995	Cayman/Jamaica	Trinidad & Tobago	5-0	St Vincent/Grenadines	George Town
1996	Trinidad	Trinidad & Tobago	2-0	Cuba	Port of Spain
1997	Antigua/St Kitts	Trinidad & Tobago	4-0	St Kitts and Nevis	St John's
1998	Jamaica/Trinidad	Jamaica	2-1	Trinidad & Tobago	Port of Spain
1999	Trinidad	Trinidad & Tobago	2-1	Cuba	Port of Spain
2001	Trinidad	Trinidad & Tobago	3-0	Haiti	Port of Spain
2005	Barbados	Jamaica	1-0†	Cuba	Waterford
2007	Trinidad	Haiti	2-1	Trinidad & Tobago	Port of Spain

† Final tournament played as a league. The match listed is between the top two.

UNCAF CUP

Year	Host Country	Winners	Score	Runners-up	Venue
1991	Costa Rica	Costa Rica	2-0†	Honduras	San José
1993	Honduras	Honduras	2-0†	Costa Rica	Tegucigalpa
1995	El Salvador	Honduras	3-0	Guatemala	San Salvador
1997	Guatemala	Costa Rica	1-1†	Guatemala	Mateo Flores, Guatemala City
1999	Costa Rica	Costa Rica	1-0†	Guatemala	San José
2001	Honduras	Guatemala	2-0†	Costa Rica	Tegucigalpa
2003	Panama	Costa Rica	1-1†	Guatemala	Rommel Fernández, Panama City
2005	Guatemala	Costa Rica	1-1 7-6p	Honduras	Mateo Flores, Guatemala City
2007	El Salvador	Costa Rica	1-1 4-1p	Panama	Cuscatlán, San Salvador

† Final tournament played as a league. The match listed is between the top two.

The UNCAF Cup, played between the nations of Central America, is a prestigious event that doubles as a qualifying competition for the Gold Cup, as does the Caribbean Cup. Trinidad and Tobago along with Jamaica have dominated the latter competition with Martinique in 1993 and Haiti in 2007 the only countries to break the duopoly while Costa Rica have won six UNCAF championships.

TORNEO INTERCLUBES DE UNCAF

Year	Winners	Country	Score	Country	Runners-up
1999	Olimpia	HON	2-0 †	CRC	LD Alajuelense
2000	Olimpia	HON	0-0 †	CRC	LD Alajuelense
2001	Municipal	GUA	1-1 †	CRC	Deportivo Saprissa
2002	LD Alajuelense	CRC	4-0 †	PAN	Arabe Unido
2003	Deportivo Saprissa	CRC	3-2	GUA	Comunicaciones
2004	Municipal	GUA	1-0 †	CRC	Deportivo Saprissa
2005	LD Alajuelense	CRC	1-0 0-1 4-2p	HON	Olimpia
2006	Puntarenas FC	CRC	3-2 0-1 3-1p	HON	Olimpia
2007	CD Motagua	HON	1-1 1-0	CRC	Deportivo Saprissa

† Played on a league system. The match listed was between the top two

CARIBBEAN CLUB TOURNAMENT

Year	Winners	Country	Score	Country	Runners-up
2003	San Juan Jabloteh	TRI	2-1 1-2 4-2p	TRI	Vibe CT Williams Connection
2004	Harbour View	JAM	1-1 2-1	JAM	Tivoli Gardens
2005	Portmore United	JAM	1-2 4-0	SUR	Robinhood
2006	Vibe CT Williams Connection	TRI	1-0	TRI	San Juan Jabloteh
2007	Harbour View	JAM	2-1	TRI	Joe Public

Not an official tournament

CONCACAF CHAMPIONS' CUP

Year	Winners	Country	Score	Country	Runners-up
1962	Guadalajara	MEX	1-0 5-0	GUA	Comunicaciones
1963	Racing Club Haïtienne	HAI	W-0	MEX	Guadalajara
1964	Not completed				
1965	Not completed				
1966	Not held				
1967	Alianza	SLV	1-2 3-0 5-3	ANT	Jong Colombia
1968	Toluca	MEX	W-0 †		
1969	Cruz Azul	MEX	0-0 1-0	GUA	Comunicaciones
1970	Cruz Azul	MEX	W-0 †		
1971	Cruz Azul	MEX	5-1	CRC	LD Alajuelense
1972	Olimpia	HON	0-0 2-0	SUR	Robinhood
1973	Transvaal	SUR	W-0 †		
1974	Municipal	GUA	2-1 2-1	SUR	Transvaal
1975	Atletico Español	MEX	3-0 2-1	SUR	Transvaal
1976	Aguila	SLV	6-1 2-1	SUR	Robinhood
1977	América	MEX	1-0 0-0	SUR	Robinhood
1978	UAG Tecos	MEX	W-0 †		
1979	Deportivo FAS	SLV	1-0 8-0	ANT	Jong Colombia
1980	UNAM Pumas	MEX	2-0 ‡	HON	Universidad de Honduras
1981	Transvaal	SUR	1-0 1-1	SLV	Atlético Marte
1982	UNAM Pumas	MEX	2-2 3-0	SUR	Robinhood
1983	Atlante	MEX	1-1 5-0	SUR	Robinhood
1984	Violette	HAI	W-0 †		
1985	Defence Force	TRI	2-0 0-1	HON	Olimpia
1986	LD Alajuelense	CRC	4-1 1-1	SUR	Transvaal
1987	América	MEX	2-0 1-1	TRI	Defence Force
1988	Olimpia	HON	2-0 2-0	TRI	Defence Force
1989	UNAM Pumas	MEX	1-1 3-1	CUB	Piñar del Rio
1990	América	MEX	2-2 6-0	CUB	Piñar del Rio
1991	Puebla	MEX	3-1 1-1	TRI	Police FC
1992	América	MEX	1-0	CRC	LD Alajuelense
1993	Deportivo Saprissa	CRC	2-2 ‡	MEX	Leon
1994	Cartagines	CRC	3-2	MEX	Atlante
1995	Deportivo Saprissa	CRC	1-0 ‡	GUA	Municipal
1996	Cruz Azul	MEX	1-1 ‡	MEX	Necaxa
1997	Cruz Azul	MEX	5-3	USA	Los Angeles Galaxy
1998	DC United	USA	1-0	MEX	Toluca
1999	Necaxa	MEX	2-1	CRC	LD Alajuelense
2000	LA Galaxy	USA	3-2	HON	Olimpia
2001	Not completed				
2002	Pachuca	MEX	1-0	MEX	Monarcas Morelia
2003	Toluca	MEX	3-3 2-1	MEX	Monarcas Morelia
2004	LD Alajuelense	CRC	1-1 4-0	CRC	Deportivo Saprissa
2005	Deportivo Saprissa	CRC	2-0 1-2	MEX	UNAM Pumas
2006	América	MEX	0-0 2-1	MEX	Toluca
2007	Pachuca	MEX	2-2 0-0 7-6p	MEX	Guadalajara

† 1968 Toluca were declared champions after Aurora GUA and Transvaal SUR were disqualified • 1970 Cruz Azul were declared champions after Deportivo Saprissa CRC and Transvaal SUR withdrew • 1973 Transvaal were declared champions after LD Alajuelense CRC and Deoprtivo Saprissa CRC withdrew • 1978 UAG Tecos were joint winners with Comunicaciones GUA and Defence Force TRI • 1984 Violette were declared champions after Guadalajara and New York Freedoms were disqualified • ‡ 1980 1993 1995 & 1996 finals played as a league with the match listed between the top two

The entry of MLS clubs in the late 1990's and, more significantly, the prospect of a place at the FIFA Club World Cup has given the CONCACAF Champions' Cup a significant boost in recent years. Without these two events, the competition was in danger of dying a death, especially given the fact that since 1998 Mexican clubs have entered South America's Copa Libertadores. First played in 1962, the CONCACAF Champions' Cup has always been dominated by Mexico. Their

CONCACAF CHAMPIONS' CUP MEDALS TABLE

	Country	G	S	B	F	SF
1	Mexico	23	10	11	33	44
2	Costa Rica	6	4	11	10	21
3	El Salvador	3	1	2	4	6
4	Surinam	2	8	3	10	13
5	Guatemala	2	3	7	5	12
6	Honduras	2	3	3	5	8
7	Trinidad and Tobago	2	3	2	5	7
8	USA	2	1	10	3	13
9	Haiti	2			2	2
10	Netherlands Antilles		2	4	2	6
11	Cuba		2		2	2
12	Martinique			3		3
13	Bermuda			1		1
		44	37	57	81	138

This table represents the Gold (winners), Silver (runners-up) and Bronze (semi-finalists) placings of clubs representing the above countries in the CONCACAF Champions' Cup, along with the number of appearances in the final and semi-finals.

22 titles is more than the number won by clubs from the rest of the clubs in the confederation combined. Had they taken the competition more seriously over the years, the number of titles won by Mexican clubs would surely have been even greater. Organising the tournament has never been easy for CONCACAF given the diverse nature of the confederation members - tiny Montserrat has a population of just 5000 whilst the USA has almost 300 million. Geographically the region has also traditionally been divided into three seperate groupings of the Caribbean, Central America and North America, the latter comprising Mexico, Canada and the USA. In the early years of the tournament all three regions held qualifying tournaments, which left an awkward numbers of teams for a final tournament and on nine ocassions over the years the competition has remained unfinished. Since the turn of the century, however, a regular format has been kept, with the winner of a Caribbean tournament and the top three from a Central American tournament joining two American and two Mexican clubs in the quarterfinals. Costa Rican clubs have provided an unexpected challenge in recent years and both Deportivo Saprissa and LD Alajuelense are in the all-time top five most successful clubs. Cruz Azul and América remain the most successful teams with five titles, but spare a thought for Suriname's Robinhood who have lost all five finals they have played in.

CONCACAF CHAMPIONS' CUP MEDALS TABLE

	Country		G	S	B
1	América	MEX	5		1
2	Cruz Azul	MEX	5		
3	Deportivo Saprissa	CRC	3	1	6
4	UNAM Pumas	MEX	3	1	
5	LD Alajuelense	CRC	2	3	4
6	Transvaal	SUR	2	3	
7	Toluca	MEX	2	2	1
8	Olimpia	HON	2	2	1
9	Defence Force	TRI	2	2	
10	Pachuca	MEX	2		1
11	Comunicaciones	GUA	1	2	3
12	Guadalajara	MEX	1	2	1
	Municipal	GUA	1	1	1
14	Necaxa	MEX	1	1	1
	Atlante	MEX	1	1	
16	Los Angeles Galaxy	USA	1	1	
17	DC United	USA	1		5
18	Alianza	SLV	1		2
19	Aguila	SLV	1		
	Atlético Español	MEX	1		
	CS Cartagines	CRC	1		
	Deportivo FAS	SLV	1		
	Puebla	MEX	1		
	Racing Club Haïtienne	HAI	1		
	UAG Tecos	MEX	1		
	Violette	HAI	1		
27	Robinhood	SUR		5	3
28	Jong Colombia	ANT		2	1
29	Piñar del Rio	CUB		2	
	Monarcas Morelia	MEX		2	
31	Leon	MEX		1	2
32	Atlético Marte	SLV		1	
	Police FC	TRI		1	
	Universidad de Honduras	HON		1	
35	Monterrey	MEX			3
36	Chicago Fire	USA			2
	SUBT	ANT			2
	Trintoc	TRI			2
39	Aurora	GUA			1
	Herediano	CRC			1
	Houston Dynamo	USA			1
	Kansas City Wizards	USA			1
	L'Aiglon	MTQ			1
	Marathon	HON			1
	Pembrooke	BER			1
	Philidelphia Ukrainians	USA			1
	Real España	HON			1
	Riviere-Pilote	MTQ			1
	US Robert	MTQ			1
	Sithoc	ANT			1
	Suchitepequez	GUA			1
	Tigres UANL	MEX			1
	Xelaju	GUA			1
			44	37	57

CONCACAF CHAMPIONS' CUP 2007–08 REGIONAL ROUNDS

TORNEO INTERCLUBES DE UNCAF

First Round

Motagua	HON	2	3
Real Esteli	NCA	0	1

Olimpia	HON	0	0
San Francisco	PAN	1	0

Xelajú	GUA	0 1 4p
Tauro FC	PAN	1 0 2p

Real Madriz	NCA	0	0
Municipal	GUA	2	6

LD Alajuelense	CRC	3	0
Isidro-Metapán	SLV	0	0

Rev Conquerors	BLZ	1 2 2p
Real España	HON	2 1 4p

Puntarenas FC	CRC	3	0
FC Belize	BLZ	0	0

Once Municipal	SLV	2	1
Deportivo Saprissa	CRC	5	0

Quarter–Finals

Motagua *	1	1
San Francisco	0	0

Xelajú *	1 1 1p
Municipal	1 1 4p

LD Alajuelense *	0 2 5p
Real España	0 2 4p

Puntarenas FC *	1	1
Deportivo Saprissa	1	2

Semi–finals

Motagua	3	3
Municipal *	1	2

LD Alajuelense	0	1
Deportivo Saprissa *	1	1

Final

Motagua	1	1
Deportivo Saprissa *	1	0

Third place play-off

Municipal ‡	3	0
LD Alajuelense	0	1

* Home team in the first leg • ‡ 1st leg abandoned at 1-2 due to pitch invasion. Awarded 3-0

CFU CARIBBEAN CHAMPIONSHIP

First Round Groups

Group A			ARU	ANT
San Juan Jabloteh	TRI	6	5-1	5-0
SV Nacional	ARU	1		1-1
Centro Barber	ANT	1		
Positive Vibes	VIR	Withdrew		

Group B			DMA	ARU
Joe Public	TRI	6	5-0	7-0
South East United	DMA	1		1-1
Racing Club Aruba	ARU	1		

Group C			JAM	SUR	ATG
Puerto Rico Is'ders	PUR	7	2-2	5-2	10-0
Harbour View	JAM	4		1-2	10-0
Inter Moengotapoe	SUR	4			3-3
Sap	ATG	1			

Group D			SUR	VIR
Portmore United	JAM	6	3-0	2-0
Leo Victor	SUR	3		4-0
Helenites	VIR	0		
Newtown United	SKN	Withdrew		

Group E			ATG	CUB	ANT
Baltimore St Marc	HAI	7	2-1	2-2	12-0
Bassa	ATG	6		2-1	4-1
Pinar del Río	CUB	4			5-1
Jong Colombia	ANT	0			

Quarter–finals

Harbour View	2
Portmore United	0

Baltimore St Marc	0
San Juan Jab'teh	1

Puerto Rico Isl	7
Leo Victor	1

Bassa	0
Joe Public	5

Semi–finals

Harbour View	0 10p
San Juan Jab'teh	0 9p

Puerto Rico Isl	0
Joe Public	1

Final

Harbour View	2
Joe Public	1

CONCACAF CHAMPIONS' CUP 2007–08

CONCACAF CHAMPIONS' CUP 2007–08

Quarter–Finals				Semi–finals			Final		
Pachuca	MEX	0	1						
Motagua *	HON	0	0						
				Pachuca *	2	1			
				DC United	0	2			
Harbour View *	JAM	1	0						
DC United	USA	1	5						
							Pachuca	1	2
							Deportivo Saprissa	1	1
Houston Dynamo	USA	0	3						
Municipal *	GUA	0	1						
				Houston Dynamo *	0	0			
				Deportivo Saprissa	0	3			
Atlante	MEX	2	0						
Deportivo Saprissa	CRC	1	3						

* Home team in the first leg
American and Mexican teams qualified directly for the quarter-finals

FIRST ROUND TORNEO INTERCLUBES DE UNCAF

1st leg. Independencia, Estelí
7-08-2007, Henry BLZ

Real Estelí **0**

Mendieta – Ruiz, Chacon, Silva (Vega 78), Calero, Mejia, Rodriguez, Lopez.S, Francisco Lopez, Molina, Martinez.S (Martinez.D 68)

Motagua **2**
Matamoros [8], Nascimiento [76]

Morales – Nacimiento (Castillo.M 82), Matamoros, Castillo.F*, Chavez, Guevara, Izaguirre, Santana (Rodas 70), Bernardez.V, Garcia, Claros* (Torlacoff 86)

2nd leg. Tiburcio Carias Andino, Tegucigalpa
16-08-2007, Bonilla SLV

Motagua **3**
Castillo.F [30], Torlacoff [45], Rodas [54]

Morales – Bryce, Torlacoff (Bernerdez.J 62), Grant, Castillo.F, Chavez, Guevara (Rivera 45), Izaguirre*, Bernardez.V, Rodas, Claros (Lopez.W)

Real Estelí **1**
Vega [86]

Mendieta – Ruiz, Chacon (Vilchez 84), Vega*, Martinez.D (Martinez.S 55), Silva, Mejia, Rodriguez.S, Franklin Lopez*, Molina, Zeledon (Francisco Lopez 45)

1st leg. Agustin Muquita Sanchez, La Chorrera
9-08-2007, Rodriguez CRC

San Francisco **0**

Negrete – Solanilla, Perez.T*, Blanco*90, Justavino*, Olivares, Ortega, Jimenez (Carrasquilla 72), Julio (Lombardo 67), Torres (Aparicio 82), De Alba. Tr: Gary Stempel

Olimpia **0**

Valladares – Figueroa, Morales*, Velasquez (Carcamo 90), Avila.N*90, Discua (Avila.E 67), Turcios*, Nuñez (Castro.M 90), Thomas, Mendoza**90, Garcia*. Tr: Nahun Espinoza

---

2nd leg. Tiburcio Carias Andino, Tegucigalpa
15-08-2007, Aguilar SLV

Olimpia **0**

Valladares – Avila.E (Navas 62), Figueroa, Morales, Carcamo (Dos Santos* 68), Tilguath, Arevalo, Turcios (Castro.M 75), Nunez, Thomas*, Garcia.O*. Tr: Nahun Espinoza

San Francisco **1**
Julio [10]

Negrete – Solanilla, Perez.T* (Carrasquilla 79), Justavino (Aparicio 67), Olivares*, Ortega* (Lombardo 73), Loo*, Jimenez, Julio, Torres, De Alba*. Tr: Gary Stempel

---

1st leg. Rommel Fernández, Panama City
8-08-2007, 950, Jimenez CRC

Tauro **1**
Palma [75]

McFarlane – Rivera, López.D, Pérez.J**90, Aguilar (Escobar 63), Skinner (Hay 28), Arosemena (Cubilla 83), Tejada*42, Palma, Melo, Dassent. Tr: Miguel Angel Mansilla

Xelajú **0**

Patterson – Girón, Contreras, Swisher, Estacuy* (Beletzuy 57), Quiñónez*, Guzmán (Jucup* 70), López.J, Piñeiro, Godoy (López.M 85), Cubero. Tr: Carlos Daniel Jurado

---

2nd leg. Mario Camposeco, Quetaltenango
14-08-2007, Duran CRC

Xelajú **1 4p**
Godoy [10]

Patterson – López.J**87, Contreras, Girón, Estacuy, Swisher (Sinay 61), Quiñónez, Sanabria (Silva 55), Piñeiro, Godoy, Cubero. Tr: Carlos Daniel Jurado

Tauro **0 2p**

McFarlane* – Rivera, López.D*, Aguilar* (Quiroz 40), Hay (Skinner 65), Arosemena, Palma, Melo, Cubilla, Escobar, Dasent. Tr: Miguel Angel Mansilla

---

1st leg. Independencia, Estelí
9-08-2007, Soriano HON

Real Madriz **0**

Irias – Barahona, Gamez*, Morales (Benavidez.J 82), Pauth, Sanchez.M, Pineda (Alfaro 46) (Suarez* 78), Sosa, Salgado, Alfaro, Crisanto

Municipal **2**
Figueroa [21], Avila [73]

Alvarez – Vides, Melgar, Thompson*63, Albizuris (Blanco* 74), Acevedo (Guevara 70), Ruano, Avila, Figueroa, Rodriguez*, Marroquin*

2nd leg. Mateo Flores, Guatemala City
16-08-2007, 2500, Rodriguez PAN

Municipal **6**
Ponciano [4], Asprilla [22], Acevedo [40], Leon [61], Marroquin [74], Papa [84]

Alvarez – Vides, Medina, Albizuris (Blanco 45), Acevedo*, Ponciano (Guevara 78), Leon*, Avila (Papa 62), Figueroa.

Real Madriz **0**

Irias – Gamez, Morales, Pauth, Sanchez, Pineda (Suarez* 45), Sosa, Salgado (Benavidez.J 69), Benavidez.E, Alfaro (Barahona 45), Crisanto.

1st leg. Alejandro Morera Soto, Alajuela
9-08-2007, Vidal PAN

LD Alajuelense **3**
Solorzano [49], Nunez 2 [60][72]

Alfaro – Wallace.H, Salazar, Nassar, Víquez, Montero, Gabas, Lara, Núñez, Parks* (Solorzano* 46), Myrie (Herrera 63), Antonio (Cunningham 74)

AD Isidro Metapán **0**

Alfaro – Avila (Martinez.J 65), Messias, Gomez.J (Aguilar 73), Gonzalez.F, Suarez, Reyes, Rodriguez.J (Mejia* 88), Iraheta, Escobar, Alvarado*

2nd leg. Jorge El Calero Suarez, Metapán
14-08-2007, Batres GUA

AD Isidro Metapán **0**

Alfaro – Avila (Martinez.J 61), Messias, Gonzalez.F, Suarez, Reyes, Rodriguez.J, Iraheta (Aguilar 61), Escobar, Mejia, Alvarado

LD Alajuelense **0**

Alfaro – Salazar, Montero*, Lara (Parks 72), Antonio, Herrera*, Myrie*, Nuñez (Gabriel* 60), Cunningham, Nassar, Solorzano (Oviedo 46)

1st leg. Francisco Morazan, San Pedro Sula
8-08-2007, Mejia SLV

Real España **2**
Valladares [21], Vallecillo.E [90]

Vallecillo.O – Fretes, Gonzales.E, Diaz.J*, Valladares (Guifarro 67), Medina (Maradiaga 56), Ferreira (Caetano* 56), Rodriguez.M, Morales, Valladares, Vallecillo.E. Tr: Magdaleno Cano

Revolutionary Conquerors **1**
Serrano [4]

West* – Nolberto, Flores, Pandy* (Cacho 74), Kuylen, Haylock (Castillo 51), Pipersburgh, Serano.D, Rowley* (Swaso 54), Serano.J, Simpson. Tr: Palmiro Salas

---

2nd leg. Carl Ramos, Dangriga
14-08-2007, Mena CRC

Revolutionary Conquerors **2 2p**
Serano [15], Kuylen [45]

West – Nolberto*, Pandy (Flores 62), Kuylen*, Haylock* (Swaso 66), Pipersburgh, Lennon, Serano.D, Serano.J, Simpson, Tasher*. Tr: Palmiro Salas

Real España **1 4p**
Diaz [27]

Vallecillo.O – Fretes, Diaz.E* (Morales 59), Caetano (Valladares 81), Medina, Palacios, Ferreira, Rodriguez.M*, Guifarro (Maradiaga 70), Vallecillo.E. Tr: Magdaleno Cano

---

1st leg. Miguel Lito Perez, Puntarenas
7-08-2007, 1600, Guerrero NCA

Puntarenas FC **3**
Bernard [26p], Sancho [72], Barbosa [81]

Orio – Gómez.E, Wong, Seravalli (Cubero 65), Espinoza, Arias, Cordero, Camacho (Guerrero 75), Bernard*, Alemán (Barbosa 68), Sancho. Tr: Luis Diego Arnáez

FC Belize **0**

Slusher* – Symms, Flowers.S*, Smith (Young 58), Nunez.E (Nunez.P 58), Leslie, McCauly, James*, Gaynair, Flowers.D (Henry 75), Thurton. Tr: Anthony Bernard

---

2nd leg. MCC Grounds, Belize City
16-08-2007, 1300, Guerra GUA

FC Belize **0**

Slusher – Flowers.S, Smith*, Leslie*, McCaulay (Gilharry 75), Nuñez.P*, Young (Zuniga 73), James, Gaynair*, Reid (Simms 58), Thurton. Tr: Anthony Bernard

Puntarenas FC **0**

Orio – Vasquez, Portuguez, Nuñez.R, Cubero (Macotelo 68), Rodriguez.R, Gomez, Guerrero (Aleman 82), Arnaez, Campos, Garro. Tr: Luis Diego Arnáez

---

1st leg. Ricardo Saprissa, San José
8-08-2007, Lopez GUA

Deportivo Municipal **5**
Arce [16], Arrieta 2 [51][69], Centeno [64], Borges [30]

Porras.J – Cordero, Badilla, Arce (Alonso* 30), Núñez.A, Brenes*, Barrantes (Borges 46), Centeno, Solís, Gómez, Alpízar (Arrieta 46). Tr: Jeaustin Campos

Once Municipal **2**
Avalos [5], Hurtado [37]

González.J – Aquino, Erazo (Artero 19), Orellana*, Troyano (Vasquez 81), Hurtado (Martinez.A 46), Quintanilla*, Ávalos, Carbajal, Guevara, Guzmán. Tr: Abel Moralejo

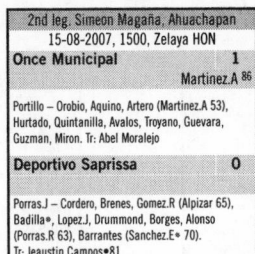

2nd leg. Simeon Magaña, Ahuachapan
15-08-2007, 1500, Zelaya HON

Once Municipal	1
	Martinez.A [86]

Portillo – Orobio, Aquino, Artero (Martinez.A 53), Hurtado, Quintanilla, Avalos, Troyano, Guevara, Guzman, Miron. Tr: Abel Moralejo

Deportivo Saprissa	0

Porras.J – Cordero, Brenes, Gomez.R (Alpizar 65), Badilla•, Lopez.J, Drummond, Borges, Alonso (Porras.R 63), Barrantes (Sanchez.E• 70). Tr: Jeaustin Campos•81

QUARTER-FINALS TORNEO INTERCLUBES DE UNCAF

1st leg. Tiburcio Carias Andino, Tegucigalpa
18-09-2007, 2515, Lopez GUA

Motagua	1
	Bryce [32]

Morales – García.O•, Bernárdez.V, Chávez, Izaguirre, Claros•, Guevara, Castillo.F, Bryce (Matamoros 67), Torlacoff (Grant 75), Rodas. Tr: Ramón Maradiaga

San Francisco	0

Negrete – Walter•, De Alba•, Loo•, Jiménez• (Carrasquilla 77), Ortega, Solís (Aparicio 63), Torres, Blanco, Justavino, Julio (Lombardo 70). Tr: Gary Stempel

2nd leg. Agustin Muquita Sanchez, La Chorrera
26-09-2007, Jimenez CRC

San Francisco	0

Negrete – Walter, Algandona, Olivares (Suárez.V), Jiménez.E, Solís• (Aparicio 75), Lombardo, Torres, Justavino, Julio (Cardales• 60), Blanco. Tr: Gary Stempel

Motagua	1
	Rodas [85]

Morales – Bernárdez.V, Chávez, García.S, Reyes•, Bryce• (Grant 82), Guzmán, Castillo.F, Guevara (Lopez.W 90), Rodas, Torlacoff (Martinez.J 60). Tr: Ramón Maradiaga

1st leg. Mario Camposeco, Quetaltenango
19-09-2007, Quesada CRC

Xelaju	1
	Quiñonez [79]

Patterson – Girón•13, Sinay, Quiñónez, Swisher, Zacarías• (Alvarez.J 78), Estacuy, Sanabria, Piñeyro (Alvarez.P), Godoy, (López.M 90), Cubero. Tr: Carlos Jurado

Municipal	1
	Ramirez [3]

Penedo – Melgar•88, Ponciano, Ruano•, Albizuris, Guevara, Thompson, Figueroa (Avila 84), García, Ramírez.G• (Vides 90), Rodríguez.M• (Asprilla 76). Tr: Victor Hugo Monzon

2nd leg. Mateo Flores, Guatemala City
25-09-2007, 6000, Aguilar SLV

Municipal	1 4p
	Ramirez.G [24]

Penedo – Ponciano•, Vides, Ruano, Albizuris•, Thompson•, Romero, García.F, Ramírez.G, Acevedo, Plata (Avila 79). Tr: Victor Hugo Monzon

Xelaju	1 1p
	Patterson [11p]

Patterson – Swisher•, Sinay, Herrera•, Estacuy, Piñeiro, López.J•, Sanabria (Antonio 59), Quiñónez, Godoy, Cubero. Tr: Carlos Jurado

1st leg. Alejandro Morera Soto, Alajuela
20-09-2007, 3000, Batres GUA

LD Alajuelense	0

Alfaro – Salazar, Montero (Wallace 56), Oviedo• (Solórzano.B 46), Gabriel (Lara• 62), Antonio•, Solórzano.J, Herrera, Myrie, Víquez, Nassar. Tr: Carlos Restrepo

Real España	0

Masías – Fretes, Valladares.M• (Andino 58), Medina, Ferreira (Lalin 86), Rodriguez.M•, Morales, Guifarro••53, Valladares.E (Palacios 68), Vallecillo.E•. Tr: Jose Cano

2nd leg. Francisco Morazán, San Pedro Sula
27-09-2007, 4973, Vidal PAN

Real España	2 4p
	Ferreira [2], Valladares.M [37]

Vallecillo.O – Vallecillo.E (Casteno 90), Valladares.E, Fretes•, Morales, Peña (Medina 83), Andino (Delgado 76), González.E•, Carlinho, Valladares.M, Ferreira•. Tr: Daniel Uberti

LD Alajuelense	2 5p
	Nuñez [7], Myrie [13]

Alfaro – Herrera (Cunningham 90), Nassar•, Salazar, Víquez, Myrie, Gabas•, Wallace•, Oviedo•, Lara, Núñez.V. Tr: Carlos Restrepo

1st leg. Miguel Lito Perez, Puntarenas
19-09-2007, 2150, Moreno PAN

Puntarenas FC	1
	Camacho [33]

Orio – Wong, Núñez.R, Gómez.E, Seravalli (Sancho 71), Cordero, Garro (Macotelo 56), Arias, Guerrero (Barbosa 60), Camacho, Alemán. Tr: Luis Diego Arnaez

Deportivo Saprissa	1
	Centeno [17]

Porras.J• – Cordero•, Drummond•, Badilla, Núñez.A•, Alonso, Gómez, Centeno• (Barrantes 54), Borges•, Solís (Bennett 76), Alpízar (Alfaro 65). Tr: Randall Row

2nd leg. Ricardo Saprissa, San José
26-09-2007, Zelaya HON

Deportivo Saprissa	2
	Solis [42], Alonso [83]

Porras.J• – Cordero•, Drummond, Badilla, Núñez.A (Borges 82), Alonso•, López.J•, Barrantes (Bennett 76), Centeno, Solís, Alpizar• (Arrieta 80). Tr: Jeaustin Campos

Puntarenas FC	1
	Gomez [69]

Orio – Wong•, Vásquez, Seravalli• (Guerrero• 52), Gómez.E, Arnáez, Cordero, Arias (Macotelo 83), Barbosa (Greaves 63), Alemán, Camacho•. Tr: Luis Diego Arnaez

SEMI-FINALS TORNEO INTERCLUBES DE UNCAF

1st leg. Mateo Flores, Guatemala City
23-10-2007, Jimenez CRC

Municipal   **1**

Ponciano [56]

Penedo – Melgar, Albizuris, Ponciano*, Ruano, Thompson (Acevedo 75), Romero, Ramírez, García (Avila 45), Rodríguez.M, Plata (Asprilla* 68). Tr: Víctor Monzon

Motagua   **3**

Guevara 2 [27 86], Nascimento [73]

Morales* – Chávez*, Izaguirre, Bernárdez.V, García.O*, Claros, Guzmán, Rodas (Reyes 88), Bryce (Grant 64), Guevara*, Nacimento (Martínez.J 86). Tr: Ramón Maradiaga

---

2nd leg. Tiburcio Carias Andino, Tegucigalpa
30-10-2007, 7000, Moreno PAN

Motagua   **3**

Nascimento [10], Chavez [41], Bernárdez.V [64]

Morales – Izaguirre, Bernárdez.V, Chávez, Matamoros (Reyes 46), Grant (Castillo.F 83), Guzmán, Claros*, Guevara, Rodas, Nacimento (Tolacoff 76). Tr: Ramón Maradiaga

Municipal   **2**

Ramirez.G [11], Romero [36]

Penedo – Vides, Melgar, Albizuris, Ruano*, Acevedo, Ramírez.G*, Guevara, Marroquín* (Garcia.F 58), Romero, Rodríguez.M* (Avila.M 76). Tr: Víctor Monzon

---

1st leg. Ricardo Saprissa, San José
25-10-2007, Lopez GUA

Deportivo Saprissa   **1**

Solís [45]

Navas – Porras.R, Bennett*, Badilla, Núñez.A, Borges, Barrantes*, Centeno*, Arrieta (Alpízar 57), Gómez.R (Alfaro 66), Solís (Brenes 73). Tr: Jeaustin Campos

LD Alajuelense   **0**

Alfaro – Nassar, Salazar*, Wallace, Herrera, Víquez (Cunningham 46), Montero, Myrie*, Pinheiro (Solórzano.B 59), Solórzano.J (Gabriel 70), Núñez.V. Tr: Carlos Restrepo

---

2nd leg. Alejandro Morera Soto, Alajuela
1-11-2007, Zelaya HON

LD Alajuelense   **1**

Martins [15]

Alfaro – Wallace, Salazar, Rodríguez.M, Víquez, Herrera (Oviedo 72), Gabas, Montero, Martins (Solórzano.J 62), Núñez.V, Cunningham (Rodriguez.E 88). Tr: Carlos Restrepo

Deportivo Saprissa   **1**

Alpizar [90]

Porras.J – Cordero, Badilla, Bennett, Alonso, Núñez.A, López.J, Barrantes, Borges (Alpízar 72), Gómez.R, Solís. Tr: Jeaustin Campos

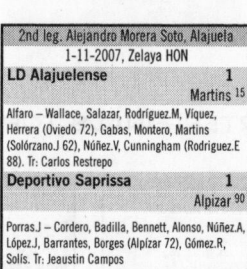

THIRD PLACE TORNEO INTERCLUBES DE UNCAF

1st leg. Alejandro Morera Soto, Alajuela
27-11-2007

LD Alajuelense   **0**

Municipal were awarded the match 3-0 after the first leg was abandoned after 81 minutes due to crowd trouble. Municipal were leading 2-1 at the time.

Municipal   **3**

2nd leg. Mateo Flores, Guatemala City
4-12-2007, 11 000, Zelaya HON

Municipal   **0**

Motta* – Vides*, Thompson, Albizuris, Romero (García.F 60), Acevedo (León 86), Ramírez.G*, Ponciano, Avila (Plata 66), Guevara*, Noriega*. Tr: Jorge José Benítez

LD Alajuelense   **1**

Myrie [53]

Alfaro – Montero*, Salazar, Oviedo, Gabriel, Gabas, Myrie, Víquez (Rodríguez.E), Cunningham*, Rodríguez.M, Solórzano.B (Pinheiro 67). Tr: Luis Diego Arnáez

FINAL TORNEO INTERCLUBES DE UNCAF

1st leg. Ricardo Saprissa, San José
28-11-2007, Batres GUA

Deportivo Saprissa   **1**

Alejandro Alpízar [8]

José Francisco Porras – Victor Cordero, Gabriel Badilla*, Jervis Drummond, Andrés Núñez, Try Bennett (Michael Barrantes 78), José Luis López*, Walter Centeno (Armando Alonso 57), Alonso Solís, Rónald Gómez (Jairo Arrieta 59), Alejandro Alpízar. Tr: Jeaustin Campos

Motagua   **1**

Oscar Garcia [49]

Donald Morales – Steven Bryce (Fernando Castillo 45), Josimar Nacimento, Luis Guzmán (Milton Reyes 83), Osman Danilo Chavez, Amado Guevara, Emilio Izaguirre, Victor Bernárdez, Oscar Samir García*, Luis Rene Rodas (Jairo Martinez* 45), Jorge Claros. Tr: Ramón Maradiaga

---

2nd leg. Tiburcio Carias Andino, Tegucigalpa
5-12-2007, 35 000, Aguilar SLV

Motagua   **1**

Josimar Nacimento [60]

Donald Morales - Josimar Nacimento (Pedro Santana 90), José Luis Grant (Jairo Martinez 44), Luis Guzmán, Osman Chavez, Amado Guevara (c), Emilio Izaguirre*, Victor Bernárdez, Óscar Samir Garcia, Luis Rodas (Milton Reyes 69), Jorge Claros*. Tr: Ramón Maradiaga

Deportivo Saprissa   **0**

Fausto González – Victor Cordero (c), Alejandro Alpízar (Jairo Arrieta 71), Alonso Solís*, Andrés Núñez, José Luis López (Ever Alfaro 80), Jervis Drummond (Ronald Gomez 65), Armando Alonso, Tray Bennett, Rándall Porras, Michael Barrantes. Tr: Jeaustin Campos

GROUP STAGE CFU CLUB CHAMPIONSHIP

Group A. Hasely Crawford, Port of Spain
4-11-2007, Forde BRB

SV Deportivo Nacional	1
	OG [72]

Giel – Leest, Tromp, Ruiz, Leocadio, Hooi (Hernandez 84), Gonzalez (Leon 66), Eckmeyer (Lampe 46), Geerman, Figora●, Romano. Tr: Cecilis Brede

Centro Barber	1
	Edgard [16p]

Pisa – Trenidad, Megija, Curtly Hooi, Sepulveda (Curly Hooi● 58), Edgard, Maria (Surandel 75), Shayron, Doran, Virginie, Molina

Group A. Hasely Crawford, Port of Spain
6-11-2007, Pinas SUR

Centro Barber	0

Pisa – Trenidad, Megija●, Curtly Hooi, Edgard●, Maria (Hansen 61) (Vincento 85), Virginie●, Shayron● (Sepulveda 71), Doran, Molina, Curly Hooi

San Juan Jabloteh	5
Guerra 2 [21 78], Gregory [24], Byers [49], Samuel [53]	

Williams – Jack, Noel, Gregory, Joseph, Guerra, Gray.I, Jamerson● (Villaroeal 45), Byers (Dummett 57), Samuel (Glen 67), Cudjoe. Tr: Terry Fenwick

Group A. Hasely Crawford, Port of Spain
8-11-2007, Peterkin JAM

San Juan Jabloteh	5
Byers [2], John.E [57], Gregory [62], Jack [70], Guerra [87]	

John.C – Jack, Murray●, Hyland, Gregory (Glen 72), Guerra, John.E, Byers (Joseph 62), Samuel (Peltier 46), Gray.C, Villaroel●. Tr: Terry Fenwick

SV Deportivo Nacional	1
	Hooi [45]

Giel – Leest●, Tromp●, Ruiz (Maria 71), Leocadio●, Marlison Hooi●, Gonzalez (Lampe 82), Eckmeyer (Geerman.J 46), Geerman.A, Figora, Romano. Tr: Cecilis Brede

Group B. Marvin Lee, Macoya
4-11-2007, Campbell JAM

Racing Club Aruba	1
	Escolana [50]

Biejen – Koek● (Paesch.R 72), Huguett●, Paesch.J, Thorde, Tromp, Ponce, Escalona, Valenton (Brison 30), Nuboer (Mayora 77), Sambo. Tr: David Douglas

Sagicor South East United	1
	Phillip.M [2]

Pascall – Graham, Cuffy.P, Charles, Phillip.W●, Cuffy.E●, Fontaine●, Joseph, McKenzie● (Cuffy.T 66), George.L● (George.S 78), Phillip.M (Sorhaindo 90). Tr: Keith Prosper

Group B. Marvin Lee, Macoya
6-11-2007, Jauregui Santillan ANT

Sagicor South East United	0

Pascall – Graham●, Charles●, George.S (Cuffy.T), Phillip.W, Cuffy.E●, Cuffy.P, Fontaine● (Challenger), Dailey, George.L (Prince), Phillip.M. Tr: Keith Prosper

Joe Public	5
Thomas [19], McAllister [24], Baptiste 2 [40 45], Richardson [43]	

Barrett – McAllister, Bacchus, Caseman, Saunders, Andrews, Gonzalez, Baptiste (Jack●), Richardson (Nelson●69), Thomas (McComie), Spann●. Tr: Michael McComie

Group B. Marvin Lee, Macoya
8-11-2007, Bonilla SLV

Joe Public	7
Baptiste 3 [18 52 78], Andrews [63], Davis 2 [65 89], Noray [82]	

Awai – Noray, Saunders, Andrews, Gonzales (Davis 35), Baptiste, Jagdeosingh, Power● (Bacchus 66), Richardson (McComie 66), Thomas●, Spann. Tr: Michael McComie

Racing Club Aruba	0

Biejen – Koek (Paesch.R 74), Huguett, Paesch.J●●34, Thorde (Grijt 76), Tromp, Ponce (Mayora 69), Escalona, Brison, Valentin, Nuboer●●37. Tr: David Douglas

Group C. Manny Ramjohn, Marabella
4-11-2007, Angela ARU

Hitachi Centre Sap	3
Mack [36], Mickel [38], Murray [72]	

Aaron – Challenger, Mack, Williams, Christian, Tonge, Parker, Limerick, McKel, Samuel (Murray 65), Luke (Thomas 71). Tr: George Warner

Inter Moengotapoe	3
Pinas 2 [16 64], Meiedjan [52]	

Damba – Jimmy, Strijder●, Adensiba, Amoeferie (Maasie 42), Jeroe.H, Bron (Lantveld 73), Meiedjan, Jeroe.F, Pinas (Brunswijk 84), Pryor. Tr: Henk Rayer

Group C. Manny Ramjohn, Marabella
4-11-2007, Bedeau GRN

Harbour View	2
Bryan [20], Taylor.F [90]	

Miller – Taylor.J, Harvey (Wright 33), Smith.O, Smith.R, Stewart, Edwards, Wolfe (Thomas.L 75), Hue (Taylor.G 78), Bryan, Taylor.F. Tr: Lenworth Hyde

Puerto Rico Islanders	2
	Delgado 2 [7 14]

Saunders – Velez●, Delgado.N, Rivera, Miranda, Villegas●, Noel (Segovia 89), Krause, Johnson (Steele 63), Atieno● (Delgado.A 59). Tr: Colin Clarke

Group C. Manny Ramjohn, Marabella
6-11-2007, Small BRB

Puerto Rico Islanders	10
Herrera [2], Noel 4 [11 44 47 48], Zapata 3 [45 51 74], Velez [72], Delgado [88]	

Behonick● – Velez, Rivera, Miranda (Avila), Ortiz, Villegas (Delgado.A 60), Noel, Atieno● (Zapata● 43), Segovia, Herrera, Steele. Tr: Colin Clarke

Hitachi Centre Sap	0

Aaron – Challenger (Brooks 57), Mack, Williams●, Christian, Tonge, Parker, Limerick, Luke (Charles 61), McKel, Samuel (Murray 54). Tr: George Warner

Group C. Manny Ramjohn, Marabella
6-11-2007, McArthur GUY

Inter Moengotapoe	2
Adensida [45], Damba [80]	

Damba – Adjoeba (Amoeferie 48) (Brunswijk 80), Jimmy●, Strijder, Maasie●, Adensiba, Jeroe.H, Bron●45, Meiedjan, Jeroe.F, Pryor●. Tr: Henk Rayer

Harbour View	1
	Hue [16]

Miller – Wright●, Smith.O●, Edwards, Bryan, Searlett, Taylor.F, Taylor.J, Stewart (Taylor.G 74), Wolfe (Thomas.L 52), Hue (Thomas.R 72). Tr: Lenworth Hyde

Group C. Ato Bolden, Couva
8-11-2007, 4000, Moreno PAN

Puerto Rico Islanders	5
Zapata [7], Delgado.N [14], Villegas [17], Noel [89], Delgado.A [90]	

Saunders – Gonzalez●42, Velez, Rivera●, Delgado.N● (Steele 88), Miranda, Villegas (Johnson 54), Noel, Krause●, Zapata (Delgado.A 62), Needham. Tr: Clarke

Inter Moengotapoe	2
	Adjoeba [36], Pinas [58]

Damba – Adjoeba (Amoeferie 65), Jimmy, Strijder, Maasie, Jeroe.H, Meiedjan●, Jeroe.F, Pinas●, Apanta (Adensiba 65), Pryor. Tr: Henk Rayer

Group C. Ato Bolden, Couva
8-11-2007, 4000, Jordan TRI

Harbour View	10
Thomas.L [11], Taylor.F 2 [35 55], Bryan 3 [31 84 90], Hue [45], Edwards [70], Peterkin [72], Kelly [82]	

Mundy – Steward, Smith.O (Wright 76), Edwards, Bryan, Smith.R, Taylor.F (Peterkin 57), Waugh, Thomas.L, Hue (Kelly 56), Taylor.J, Mundy. Tr: Lenworth Hyde

Hitachi Centre Sap	0

Aaron – Challenger, Mack, Williams●, Christian, Tonge, Parker, Limerick (Charles 74), Luke (Brooks 58), McKel●, Samuel● (Murray 38). Tr: George Warner

Group D. Larry Gomes, Malabar
4-11-2007, 100, Willet ATG

Portmore United	2
Modeste [39], Austin [46]	

Sayers – Sawyers, Swaby (Cousins 73), Williams, Modeste, Lowe, Bayliss (Davis 77), Reid, Barrett (Morrissey 65), Vernan, Austin. Tr: Linval Dixon

Helenites SC	0

Michael – Casinik (Augustin 56), George.G, St. Croix, Lesniona, Mathurin, Peter (George.A 67), St. Yille, Thomas, Joseph, Justin (Augustine 85). Tr: Nicholas Peroin

Group D. Larry Gomes, Malabar
6-11-2007, Davis TRI

Helenites SC	0

Michael – Casinik (George.G 57), George.A, St. Croix, Lesniona● (St. Yille 70), Wilton (Peter 53), Mathurin, Thomas, Joseph, Augustin, Justin●80. Tr: Nicholas Peroin

SV Leo Victor	4
Kinsaini [28], Grant [33], Sastromadjo 2 [51 81]	

Walker – Gardan, Abauna●, Sastromedjo, Sordjo (Chobin 60), Hoogrorp●, Kinsaini, Grant (Poeran 89), Mando (Lienga 65), Forster, Deolbakin. Tr: Ramak Etienne

Group D. Larry Gomes, Malabar
8-11-2007, Jauregui Santillan ANT

Portmore United	3
Morrissey [28], Lowe [41], Wolfe [75]	

Kerr – Sawyers, Swaby (Givans 75), Williams, Wolfe, Modeste (Mitchell 38), Lowe, Reid, Vernan (Powell 64), Austin, Morrissey. Tr: Linval Dixon

SV Leo Victor	0

Walker – Gardan, Abauna, Sastromedjo, Sordjo●●44, Kinsaini●, Grant, Mando (Lienga 52) (Sopennie 71), Forster, Deolbakin, Aroroman● (Dyksteel 76). Tr: Ramak Etienne

Group E. Guaracara Park, Point-a-Pierre
4-11-2007
Pinar del Rio   5
Torres 2 4 11, Alcantara 24, Morales 30, Salgado 79
Line up not available
Jong Colombia   1
Torbed 22
Line up not available

Group E. Guaracara Park, Point-a-Pierre
4-11-2007, James GUY
Baltimore St Marc   2
Junior.J 2 49 57
Junior.P – Junior (Jules 72), Baril, Luxene, Guemsly (Gabriel 83), Joseph (Tonio 84), Serge, Raymond, Vubert, Mechack, Pierre. Tr: Dorvilus Andre-Pierre
Bassa SC   1
Christian 87
Lewis – Cyrillen, Martin, Christian*, Williams*, Watts, Phillip (Braithwaite 63), Julian (Browne 57), Burton* (Hurst 83), Jeffers*, Thomas.J. Tr: Hastings

Group E. Guaracara Park, Point-a-Pierre
6-11-2007, Lancaster GUY
Bassa SC   2
Thomas.J 48, Christian 62
Lewis – Cyrillen, Browne, Christian (Martin 89), Williams, Watts, Braithwaite (Julian 72), Burton* (Rowe 87), Jeffers, Thomas.J, Carr. Tr: Hastings
Pinar del Rio   1
Alcantara 8
Hernandez – Valdes (Salgado 46), Mezquia, Monte, Martinez, Morales, Torres, Alcantara, Pita, Puente (Morejon 66), Arteaga. Tr: Louis Alberto Mijares

Group E. Guaracara Park, Point-a-Pierre
6-11-2007, Rodas GUA
Jong Colombia   0
Martina*14 – Carmelia, Clemencia* (Sanchez 46), Jansen, Caguana, Ortega (Lopez 15), Servania.F* (Martina 60), Torbed*, Servania.A**89, Felicia, Zimmerman. Tr: Erick Constancia
Baltimore St Marc   12
OG 9, Luxene 4 11 22 38 55, Raymond 19, Junior.J 31, Emerlin 2 70 76, Pierre 75, Gabriel 2 83 89
Junior.P – Vubert, Junior.J, Serge (Emerlin 63), Jean, Pierre, Luxene (Gabriel 55), Baril (Tonio 49), Raymond, Germain, Mechack. Tr: Dorvilus Andre-Pierre

Group E. Guaracara Park, Point-a-Pierre
8-11-2007, Campbell JAM
Jong Colombia   1
Clemencia 90
Martina – Carmelia, Jansen, Caguana*, Celestina, Sanchez, Servania.F (Cicilia 58), Torbed (Martina 69), Constancia, Schoop* (Clemencia 73), Felicia, Lopez. Tr: Erick Constancia
Bassa SC   4
Burton 3 44 52 58, Thomas.J 71
Lewis – Cyrillen, Browne* (Julian 73), Christian, Williams*, Watts (Romero 47), Braithwaite* (Thomas.A 71), Burton, Jeffers, Thomas.J, Carr. Tr: Hastings

Group E. Guaracara Park, Point-a-Pierre
8-11-2007, Wijngaarde SUR
Pinar del Rio   2
Martinez 67, Morales 72
Hernandez – Mezquia*, Martinez, Morales, Torres, Alcantara, Morejon (Puente 69), Cipriani, Arteaga (Salgado 88). Tr: Louis Alberto Mijares
Baltimore St Marc   2
Germain 2 48 65
Junior.P – Joseph, Vubert**90, Junior.J, Serge*, Pierre, Luxene (Gabriel 88), Baril (Jean 75), Raymond (Emerlin 86), Germain, Mechack*. Tr: Dorvilus Andre-Pierre

QUARTER-FINALS CFU CLUB CHAMPIONSHIP

Manny Ramjohn, Marabella
11-11-2007, Wijngaarde SUR
Portmore United   0
Sayers – Sawyers, Swaby (Cousins 78), Williams, Wolfe, Lowe, Mitchell, Reid, Vernan, Austin, Morrissey (Bayliss 58). Tr: Linval Dixon
Harbour View   2
Taylor.F 32, Bryan 81
Miller – Steward, Smith.O, Edwards, Bryan (Peterkin 83), Smith.R, Taylor.F, Thomas.L (Thomas.R 84), Harvey, Taylor.J, Hue (Waugh 86). Tr: Lenworth Hyde

Manny Ramjohn, Marabella
11-11-2007, Quesada CRC
San Juan Jabloteh   1
Gregory 63
Williams – Jack (Gregory 60), Murray, Peltier (Hyland 76), Noel, Joseph, Guerra (Byers 45), John.E, Gray.I, Gray.C, Cudjoe. Tr: Terry Fenwick
Baltimore St Marc   0
Junior.P – Joseph, Junior.J, Serge, Pierre, Emerlin (Gabriel 80), Luxene (Jules 84), Baril, Raymond, Germain, Mechack*. Tr: Dorvilus Andre-Pierre

Marvin Lee, Macoya
11-11-2007, 500, Brizan TRI
Puerto Rico Islanders   7
Fabrice 2 18 22, Velez 33, Zapata 57, Steele 58, Delgado.N 68, Johnson 90
Saunders* – Velez, Delgado.N, Rivera*, Miranda (Herrera 77), Noel (Delgado.A* 38), Krause, Johnson*, Steele, Zapata, Needham (Ortiz 62). Tr: Colin Clarke
SV Leo Victor   1
Gardan 43
Walker – Gardan, Abauna, Sastromedjo*, Hoogrorp, Kinsaini*, Grant (Aroman 48), Mando* (Duma 89), Forster, Deolbakin*, Chobin (Sopennie 68). Tr: Ramak Etienne

Marvin Lee, Macoya
11-11-2007, 500, Moreno PAN
Joe Public   4
Nelson 3 25 30 51, Baptiste 75
Figueroa – Noray, Saunders, Caseman, Andrews, Nelson (Awai 81), Baptiste, Jagdeosingh, Power, Thomas, Spann. Tr: Michael McComie
Bassa SC   0
Lewis – Cyrillen*, Browne, Martin, Christian*, Watts, Braithwaite (Julian 65), Burton (Romero 74), Jeffers, Thomas.J* (Pereira 86), Carr*. Tr: Hastings

SEMI-FINALS CFU CLUB CHAMPIONSHIP

Marvin Lee, Macoya	
14-11-2007, Rodas GUA	
San Juan Jabloteh	**0 10p**

Williams – Murray, Peltier (Guerra 75), Noel●, Hyland, Gregory (Glen 106), John.E, Gray.I●, Byers (Joseph 110), Gray.C, Cudjoe. Tr: Terry Fenwick

Harbour View	**0 9p**

Miller – Smith.O, Edwards, Bryan (Taylor.G 116), Smith.R●, Taylor.F, Thomas.L (Kelly 90), Harvey, Taylor.J, Steward●, Hue● (Scarlett 119). Tr: Lenworth Hyde

Marvin Lee, Macoya	
14-11-2007, Wijngaarde SUR	
Joe Public	**1**
	Richardson 80

Figueroa● – Noray, Saunders, Caseman (Richardson 33), Andrews, Nelson, Baptiste, Jagdeosingh, Power, Thomas●, Spann. Tr: Michael McComie

Puerto Rico Islanders	**0**

Saunders – Steele, Gonzalez● (Villegas 64), Velez, Delgado.N●, Rivera (Segovia 85), Miranda, Krause, Johnson, Atieno (Zapata 77), Needham. Tr: Colin Clarke

FINAL CFU CLUB CHAMPIONSHIP

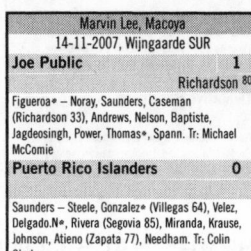

Marvin Lee, Macoya	
16-11-2007, 500, Moreno PAN	
Joe Public	**1**
	Kerry Baptiste 16

Alejandro Figueroa – Dale Saunders, Keyeno Thomas, Seon Power, Silas Spann, Lyndon Andrews (Carlos Gonzales 80), Kendall Jadgeosingh, Kerry Noray (Kendall Davis 85), Devon Caseman (Gregory Richardson● 33), Kerry Baptiste, Roen Nelson. Tr: Michael McCombie

Harbour View	**2**
	Fabian Taylor 21, Kavin Bryan 23

Dwayne Miller – Jermaine Taylor●, Christopher Harvey●●55, Oneil Smith, Ricardo Smith, Donald Stewart, Richard Edwards, Jermaine Hue● (Gregg Taylor 86), Loxley Thomas, Fabian Taylor, Kavin Bryan (Clifton Waugh 57). Tr: Lenworth Hyde

QUARTER-FINALS CONCACAF CHAMPIONS' CUP

1st leg. Tiburcio Carias Andino, Tegucigalpa	
11-03-2008, 12 000, Rodas GUA	
Motagua	**0**

Morales – Posas, Reyes (Guzman 65), Nacimento, Justavino (Torlacoff 74), Chavez, Guevara, Izaguirre●, Bernárdez.V, Rodas (Claros 80). Tr: Ramón Maradiaga

Pachuca	**0**

Calero – Manzur, Correra, Alvarez (Cabrera 79), Caballero, Salazar, Rodriguez.C, Rey, Giménez.C (Chitiva 71), Pinto, Aguilar (Montes 84). Tr: Enrique Meza

2nd leg. RFK, Washington	
18-03-2008, 12 394, Arredondo MEX	
DC United	**5**
McTavish 2 26 68, Emilio 2 63 66, Fred 88	

Wells - Peralta, Burch (Mediate 82), Fred, Gallardo (Dyachenko 72), Emilio, McTavish, Simms, Martinez, Namoff, Niell (Quaranta 64). Tr: Tom Soehn

Harbour View	**0**

Miller – Edwards●, Bryan (Blackburn 71), Amaguana, Scarlett, Taylor.F, Palmer (Kelly 72), Harvey, Taylor.J, Stewart● (Petrekin 79), Hue. Tr: Lenworth Hyde

2nd leg. Hidalgo, Pachuca	
19-03-2008, 20 000, Salazar USA	
Pachuca	**1**
	Montes 43

Calero - Manzur, Córdova, Alvarez, Caballero, Cacho (Rey 71), Salazar, Giménez.C (Cabrera 80), Pinto, Rojas, Montes (Chitiva 62). Tr: Enrique Meza

Motagua	**0**

Morales - Posas●, Reyes, Castillo●, Torlacoff (Nacimento 56), Justavino (Castillo 40), Chávez, Guevara●, Izaguirre, Bernárdez.V, Claros (Rodas 70). Tr: Ramón Maradiaga

1st leg. Mateo Flores, Guatemala City	
12-03-2008, 7000, Rodriguez CRC	
Municipal	**0**

Penedo – Romero, Guevara, Silva (Ramirez.G 66), Rodriguez.M, Garcia.F, Albizuris, Poncicano, Melgar, Thompson, Figueroa. Tr: Jorge José Benitez

Houston Dynamo	**0**

Onstad – Waibel, Boswell, Robinson, Barrett, Mulrooney, Clark, DeRosario (Mullan 83), Ashe, Ching, Wondolowski (Caraccio 83). Tr: Dominic Kinnear

1st leg. Harbour View, Kingston	
12-03-2008, 3000, Jordan TRI	
Harbour View	**1**

Miller – Edwards● (Kelly 71), Amaguana, Scarlet, Thomas.R (Bryan 77), Taylor.F, Waugh, Taylor.J●, Stewart, Wolfe (Palmer 70), Hue. Tr: Lenworth Hyde

DC United	**1**

Wells – Peralta, Burch●, Fred●, Gallardo●, Emilio, McTavish, Simms, Martinez, Namoff, Moreno (Niel 18) (Stratford 81). Tr: Tom Soehn

2nd leg. Robertson, Houston	
19-03-2008, 14 348, Morales MEX	
Houston Dynamo	**3**
DeRosario 2 46 69p, Wondolowski 72	

Onstad – Robinson, Wondolowski● (Caraccio 73), Mulrooney, Clark, DeRosario● (Mullan 77), Waibel, Barrett, Ching, Ashe, Boswell●. Tr: Dominic Kinnear

Municipal	**1**
	Ramirez 85p

Penedo – Melgar●, Thompson●, Albízures, Romero, Ramirez.G, Ponciano●, Blanco, Guevara, Rodriguez.M●, Silva (Figueroa 62). Tr: Jorge José Benitez

1st leg. Andres Quintana Roo, Cancún
13-03-2008, 4755, Batres GUA

Atlante 2
Pereyra 40, Bermudez 70

Vilar - Muñoz.J, Pererya*, Muñoz.A, Arismendi
(Romero 56), Toledo (Cardenas 34), Bermudez,
Castillo, Ovalle (Alcantar 88), Guerrero, Garcia.J*.
Tr: José Cruz

Deportivo Saprissa 1
Centeno 26

Navas – Bennett, Nuñez (Barrantes 81), Badilla,
Cordero, Drummond, Lopez.J, Alonso*, Borges*
(Solis* 60), Centeno*, Alpizar (Gomez.R 66).
Tr: Jeaustin Campos

2nd leg. Ricardo Saprissa, San José
20-03-2008, 22 000, Prus USA

Deportivo Saprissa 3
OG 2 18 66, Alonso 40

Navas - Cordero*, Núñez*, Badilla, Drummond,
Barrantes (Bennett 82), Alonso (López.J 55), Borges,
Centeno*, Gómez.R (Arrieta 87), Alpízar. Tr: Jeaustin
Campos

Atlante 0

Villar - Muñoz.J, Zamora, Pereyra (Carevic 72),
Cardenas, Muñoz.A (Cervantes 84), Bermúdez,
Castillo*, Ovalle (Romero 46), Guerrero*87,
García.J*. Tr: José Cruz

SEMI-FINALS CONCACAF CHAMPIONS' CUP

1st leg. Hidalgo, Pachuca
1-04-2008, 15 000, Moreno PAN

Pachuca 2
Montes 2 62 80

Calero - López.L, Manzur*, Correa, Caballero
(Montes 46), Chitiva, Cacho, Cabrera (Aguilar 67),
Rodríguez.G (Torres 46), Giménez.C, Pinto. Tr: Enrique
Meza

DC United 0

Wells* - Peralta, Burch, Fred, Gallardo (Dyachenko
77), Emilio, McTavish (Mediate 78), Simms, Martinez,
Namoff, Niell (Quaranta 46). Tr: Tom Soehn

2nd leg. RFK, Washington
9-04-2008, 17 329, Aguilar SLV

DC United 2
Dyachenko 85, Niell 90

Wells – Peralta, Fred, Gallardo*, Emilio*, McTavish*
(Niell 65), Simms, Martinez, Quaranta (Burch 60),
Namoff, Moreno (Dyachenko 78). Tr: Tom Soehn

Pachuca 1
Alvarez 76

Calero - López.L, Manzur, Correa, Caballero*
(Aguilar 72), Chitiva (Alvarez 58), Cacho, Cabrera,
Rodriguez.G, Gimenez.C (Torres 79), Pinto*.
Tr: Enrique Meza

1st leg. Robertson, Houston
2-04-2008, 10 260, Campbell JAM

Houston Dynamo 0

Onstad - Robinson, Ianni, Mulrooney (Cameron 75),
Caraccio (Wondolowski 80), Clark, De Rosario,
Barrett, Ching, Ashe, Boswell*. Tr: Dominic Kinnear

Deportivo Saprissa 0

Navas - Cordero, Gomez.R, Nuñez, Badilla (Jimenez 75),
Lopez.J, Drummond, Arrieta (Elizondo 63), Borges,
Alonso (Barrantes* 81), Bennett. Tr: Jeaustin Campos

2nd leg. Ricardo Saprissa, San José
9-04-2008, 20 500, Rodriguez MEX

Deportivo Saprissa 3
Alonso 35, Borges 48, Arrieta 76

Navas – Cordero, Gómez.R (Centeno 67) (Lopez.J 80),
Núñez, Badilla, Drummond, Arrieta*, Borges, Alonso,
Bennett, Barrantes (Russell 86). Tr: Jeaustin Campos

Houston Dynamo 0

Caig – Ianni, Mulrooney, Caraccio (Davis 74), Clark*,
DeRosario, Waigel (Mullan 5), Cameron, Barrett,
Ching (Wondolowski 77), Ashe. Tr: Dominic Kinnear

CONCACAF CHAMPIONS CUP FINAL 1ST LEG
Estadio Ricardo Saprissa, San José
23-04, 22 500, Carlos Batres GUA

SAPRISSA 1 1 PACHUCA

Víctor Cordero 89   Luis Gabriel Rey 47

Deportivo Saprissa				Pachuca
1	Keylor Navas			Miguel Calero 1
3	Víctor Cordero			Leobardo López 2
11	Ronald Gómez			Julio César Manzur 3
14	Andrés Núñez			Jaime Correa 6
16	Gabriel Badilla		73	Damián Alvarez 7
17	José Luis López	52		Gabriel Caballero 8
18	Jervis Drummond			Fernando Salazar 13
19	Jairo Arrieta	27		Marvin Cabrera 14
20	Celso Borges		79	Luis Gabriel Rey 18
21	Armando Alonso	76		Fausto Pinto 21
31	Michael Barrantes		62	Jose Francisco Torres 25
	Tr: Jeaustin Campos			Tr: Enrique Meza
12	Ever Alfaro	76	79	Juan Carlos Cacho 11
23	Try Bennett	52	62	Christian Giménez 19
	Cesar Elizondo Quesada	27	73	Paul Nicolas Aguilar 22

CONCACAF CHAMPIONS CUP FINAL 2ND LEG
Estadio Hidalgo, Pachuca
30-04-2008, 30 000, Mauricio Navarro CAN

PACHUCA 2 1 SAPRISSA

Christian Giménez 3,
Luis Gabriel Rey 53   Jairo Arrieta 90

Pachuca				Deportivo Saprissa
1	Miguel Calero			Keylor Navas 1
2	Leobardo López			Víctor Cordero 3
3	Julio César Manzur			Ronald Gómez 11
6	Jaime Correa			Andrés Núñez 14
7	Damián Alvarez	65	49	Gabriel Badilla 16
8	Gabriel Caballero		65	José Luis López 17
14	Marvin Cabrera			Jervis Drummond 18
16	Carlos Rodríguez			Celso Borges 20
18	Luis Gabriel Rey	82		Armando Alonso 21
19	Christian Giménez	78	56	Try Bennett 23
21	Fausto Pinto			Michael Barrantes 31
	Tr: Enrique Meza			Tr: Jeaustin Campos
10	Andrés Chitiva	78	49	Alejandro Alpizar 7
11	Juan Carlos Cacho	82	65	Pablo Brenes 9
13	Fernando Salazar	65	56	Jairo Arrieta 19

CONMEBOL

CONFEDERACION SUDAMERICANA DE FUTBOL

South America's marathon qualifying tournament for the 2010 FIFA World Cup in South Africa, which got underway almost three full years before the finals, provided the major focus of an otherwise low-key year which saw a number of notable successes for the continent's lesser-known club sides. Both of South America's major club tournaments saw first time winners with Argentina's Arsenal winning the Copa Sudamericana - their first trophy of any description - while the far more prestigious Copa Libertadores was won by LDU Quito, the first international trophy for both the club and for Ecuador. The haemorrhaging of playing talent from South America to Europe, Asia and even north Africa has undoubtedly levelled the playing field within the continent, allowing clubs like Arsenal and LDU Quito to challenge for honours. Ordinarily the hundreds of

THE FIFA BIG COUNT OF 2006 FOR SOUTH AMERICA

	Male	Female		Total
Number of players	24 703	3 074	Referees and Assistant Referees	32 000
Professionals	25 000		Admin, Coaches, Technical, Medical	136 000
Amateurs 18+	980 000		Number of clubs	47 000
Youth under 18	2 346 000		Number of teams	162 000
Unregistered	24 018 000		Clubs with women's teams	1 000
Total involved in football	27 946 000		Players as % of population	7.47%

millions of dollars earned in recent years from transfer income should have seen a boom in South American club football, but with third party ownership of young talent the order of the day, the bulk of the money has left the game with clubs unable to retain the services of even modest players. In January 2008, thanks largely to the controversy surrounding the transfer of Carlos Tevez to West Ham United in England, FIFA banned third party ownership, but it may be sometime before South American clubs benefit financially and are able to compete in the international transfer market themselves. The one tournament that has often sustained club football on the continent has been the FIFA Club World Cup along with its predecessors. South America holds the upper hand with 25 titles to Europe's 22, but Milan took a step towards restoring parity for Europe by winning the 2007 tournament, beating Boca Juniors 4-2 in the final in Japan.

Confederación Sudamericana de Fútbol (CONMEBOL)
Autopista Aeropuerto Internacional y Leonismo Luqueño, Luque, Gran Asuncion, Paraguay
Tel +595 21 645781   Fax +595 21 645791
conmebol@conmebol.com.py   www.conmebol.com
President: LEOZ Nicolás, Dr PAR   General Secretary: DELUCA Eduardo ARG
CONMEBOL Formed: 1916

CONMEBOL EXECUTIVE COMMITTEE
President: LEOZ Nicolás, Dr PAR

Vice-President: FIGUEREDO Eugenio URU	General Secretary: DELUCA Eduardo ARG	Treasurer: OSUNA Romer BOL

DIRECTORS OF THE EXECUTIVE COMMITTEE

ESQUIVEL Rafael VEN	DELFINO Nicolás PER	HARRISON Oscar PAR
CHEDID Nabí Abí BRA	CHIRIBOGA Luis ECU	FINA Alvaro COL
	ABDALAH José CHI	

MAP OF CONMEBOL MEMBER NATIONS

SOUTH AMERICAN TOURNAMENTS

COPA AMERICA

Year	Host Country	Winners	Score	Runners-up	Venue
1910	Argentina ††	Argentina	4-1	Uruguay	‡ Racing Club, Buenos Aires
1916	Argentina †	Uruguay	0-0	Argentina	‡ Racing Club, Buenos Aires
1917	Uruguay	Uruguay	1-0	Argentina	‡ Parque Pereira, Montevideo
1919	Brazil	Brazil	1-0	Uruguay	§ Laranjeiras, Rio de Janeiro
1920	Chile	Uruguay	1-1	Argentina	* Sporting Club, Vina del Mar
1921	Argentina	Argentina	1-0	Brazil	* Sportivo Barracas, Buenos Aires
1922	Brazil	Brazil	3-0	Paraguay	§ Laranjeiras, Rio de Janeiro
1923	Uruguay	Uruguay	2-0	Argentina	‡ Parque Central, Montevideo
1924	Uruguay	Uruguay	0-0	Argentina	‡ Parque Central, Montevideo
1925	Argentina	Argentina	2-2	Brazil	‡ Bombonera, Buenos Aires
1926	Chile	Uruguay	2-0	Argentina	* Sport de Nunoa, Santiago
1927	Peru	Argentina	3-2	Uruguay	* Estadio Nacional, Lima
1929	Argentina	Argentina	4-1	Paraguay	* San Lorenzo, Buenos Aires
1935	Peru †	Uruguay	3-0	Argentina	‡ Estadio Nacional, Lima
1937	Argentina	Argentina	2-0	Brazil	‡ San Lorenzo, Buenos Aires
1939	Peru	Peru	2-1	Uruguay	‡ Estadio Nacional, Lima
1941	Chile †	Argentina	1-0	Uruguay	* Estadio Nacional, Santiago
1942	Uruguay	Uruguay	1-0	Argentina	‡ Centenario, Montevideo
1945	Chile †	Argentina	3-1	Brazil	* Estadio Nacional, Santiago
1946	Argentina †	Argentina	2-0	Brazil	‡ Monumental, Buenos Aires
1947	Ecuador	Argentina	6-0	Paraguay	* Estadio Capwell, Guayaquil
1949	Brazil	Brazil	7-0	Paraguay	§ Sao Januario, Rio de Janeiro
1953	Lima	Paraguay	3-2	Brazil	§ Estadio Nacional, Lima
1955	Chile	Argentina	1-0	Chile	‡ Estadio Nacional, Santiago
1956	Uruguay †	Uruguay	1-0	Argentina	‡ Centenario, Montevideo
1957	Peru	Argentina	3-0	Brazil	‡ Estadio Nacional, Lima
1959	Argentina	Argentina	1-1	Brazil	‡ Monumental, Buenos Aires
1959	Ecuador †	Uruguay	5-0	Argentina	* Modelo, Guayaquil
1963	Bolivia	Bolivia	5-4	Brazil	‡ Felix Capriles, Cochabamba
1967	Uruguay	Uruguay	1-0	Argentina	‡ Centenario, Montevideo
1975		Peru	0-1 2-0 1-0	Colombia	Bogota, Lima, Caracas
1979		Paraguay	3-0 0-1 0-0	Chile	Asuncion, Santiago, Buenos Aires
1983		Uruguay	2-0 1-1	Brazil	Montevideo & Salvador
1987	Argentina	Uruguay	1-0	Chile	Monumental, Buenos Aires
1989	Brazil	Brazil	1-0	Uruguay	‡ Maracana, Rio de Janeiro
1991	Chile	Argentina	3-2	Brazil	* Estadio Nacional, Santiago
1993	Ecuador	Argentina	2-1	Mexico	Monumental, Guayaquil
1995	Uruguay	Uruguay	1-1 5-3p	Brazil	Centenario, Montevideo
1997	Bolivia	Brazil	3-1	Bolivia	Hernando Siles, La Paz
1999	Paraguay	Brazil	3-0	Uruguay	Defensores del Chaco, Asuncion
2001	Colombia	Colombia	1-0	Mexico	El Campin, Bogota
2004	Peru	Brazil	2-2 4-2p	Argentina	Estadio Nacional, Lima
2007	Venezuela	Brazil	3-0	Argentina	Pachencho Romero, Maracaibo

† Extraordinario tournaments are recognised as official tournaments though the teams did not compete for the Copa America • †† Unofficial tournament that is not part of the official records • ‡ Tournament played on a league system. The final game was between the top two teams
** Tournament played on a league system. The game listed between the top two teams was not the final match in the tournament • § Tournament played on a league system. The game listed was a play-off after the top two teams finished level on points.

Following the demise of the British International Championship, the Copa América is now the longest-running international competition in the world, dating back to 1916 though some historians like to point to a tournament played in 1910 that was referred to at the time as the "South American Championship". Argentina and Uruguay have always been the most enthusiastic proponents of the Copa América and each has been champions 14 times lending credence to the belief among many

South Americans that the real home of football on the continent lies around the River Plate estuary and the cities of Montevideo and Buenos Aires and not further north in Brazil. In the first 33 editions spanning 73 years the Brazilians won the title just three times and never outside of Rio de Janeiro. Aside from these three, Peru in 1939 and 1975, and Paraguay in 1953 and 1979, have been champions twice while Bolivia in 1963 and Colombia in 2001 have both won the title once. Only Venezuela, Ecuador and Chile have failed to win it. Historically the tournament has usually been played on a league system although since the 1970s a group stage followed by knock-out rounds has been the preferred format. Another innovation has been the invitation extended to Mexico to take part since 1993, along with another guest, most commonly Costa Rica or the USA. Now held every two years the Copa América has finally caught the imagination of the Brazilians and in recent years they have been the most successful nation winning three of the past four editions and their 1997 triumph in Bolivia was their first away from home. The past three FIFA World Cup qualifying campaigns in South America, in which each of the ten nations plays each other home and away, has to a certain extent cast a shadow over the Copa América. It is difficult to argue against the fact that the top team, at the end of what amounts to a three-year campaign, should be regarded as the best team on the continent rather than the Copa America champions. However, the Copa América remains an important landmark in the fixture list and it rarely fails to entertain. There are currently two club tournaments played in South America with the Copa Libertadores held in the first half of the year and the Copa Sudamericana towards the end. The Copa Libertadores is the senior of the two and has been held annually since 1960. The Copa Sudamericana is the latest in a long line of secondary tournaments following on from the Supercopa João Havelange, the Copa Mercosur and the Copa Merconorte. In the 1990s there was even a third tournament, the Copa CONMEBOL, but that lasted just eight years.

COPA AMERICA MEDALS TABLE

	Country	G	S	B	F	SF
1	Argentina	14	12	4	3	4
2	Uruguay	14	6	7	4	8
3	Brazil	8	11	7	6	8
4	Paraguay	2	5	8	1	2
5	Peru	2		4	1	4
6	Colombia	1	1	3	2	6
7	Bolivia	1	1		1	1
8	Chile		4	5	2	3
9	Mexico		2	3	2	5
10	Honduras			1		1
11	Ecuador					1
	United States					1
		42	42	42	22	42

This table represents the Gold (winners), Silver (runners-up) and Bronze (semi-finalists) placings of nation in the Copa América, along with the number of appearances in the final and semi-finals. It does not include the 1910 tournament and does not distinguish between official and extraordinario tournaments

SOUTH AMERICAN WOMEN'S CHAMPIONSHIP

Year	Host Country	Winners	Score	Runners-up	Venue
1991	Brazil	Brazil	6-1	Chile	‡ Maringá
1995	Brazil	Brazil	2-0	Argentina	Uberlândia
1998	Argentina	Brazil	7-1	Argentina	Mar del Plata
2003	Peru	Brazil	3-2	Argentina	** Lima
2006	Argentina	Argentina	2-0	Brazil	‡ Mar de Plata

‡ Tournament played on a league system. The final game was between the top two teams • ** Tournament played on a league system. The game listed between the top two teams was not the final match in the tournament.

COPA LIBERTADORES DE AMERICA

Year	Winners	Country	Score	Country	Runners-up
1960	Peñarol	URU	1-0 1-1	PAR	Olimpia
1961	Peñarol	URU	1-0 1-1	BRA	Palmeiras
1962	Santos	BRA	2-1 2-3 3-0	URU	Peñarol
1963	Santos	BRA	3-2 2-1	ARG	Boca Juniors
1964	Independiente	ARG	0-0 1-0	URU	Nacional Montevideo
1965	Independiente	ARG	1-0 1-3 4-1	URU	Peñarol
1966	Peñarol	URU	2-0 2-3 4-2	ARG	River Plate
1967	Racing Club	ARG	0-0 0-0 2-1	URU	Nacional Montevideo
1968	Estudiantes LP	ARG	2-1 1-3 2-0	BRA	Palmeiras
1969	Estudiantes LP	ARG	1-0 2-0	URU	Nacional Montevideo
1970	Estudiantes LP	ARG	1-0 0-0	URU	Peñarol
1971	Nacional Montevideo	URU	0-1 1-0 2-0	ARG	Estudiantes LP
1972	Independiente	ARG	0-0 2-1	PER	Universitario
1973	Independiente	ARG	1-1 0-0 2-1	CHI	Colo Colo
1974	Independiente	ARG	1-2 2-0 1-0	BRA	São Paulo FC
1975	Independiente	ARG	0-1 3-1 2-0	CHI	Union Española
1976	Cruzeiro	BRA	4-1 1-2 3-2	ARG	River Plate
1977	Boca Juniors	ARG	1-0 0-1 0-0 5-4p	BRA	Cruzeiro
1978	Boca Juniors	ARG	0-0 4-0	COL	Deportivo Cali
1979	Olimpia	PAR	2-0 0-0	ARG	Boca Juniors
1980	Nacional Montevideo	URU	0-0 1-0	BRA	Internacional PA
1981	Flamengo	BRA	2-1 0-1 2-0	CHI	Cobreloa
1982	Peñarol	URU	0-0 1-0	CHI	Cobreloa
1983	Grêmio	BRA	1-1 2-1	URU	Peñarol
1984	Independiente	ARG	1-0 0-0	BRA	Grêmio
1985	Argentinos Juniors	ARG	1-0 0-1 1-1 5-4p	COL	América Cali
1986	River Plate	ARG	2-1 1-0	COL	América Cali
1987	Peñarol	URU	0-2 2-1 1-0	COL	América Cali
1988	Nacional Montevideo	URU	0-1 3-0	ARG	Newell's Old Boys
1989	Atlético Nacional Medellín	COL	0-2 2-0 5-4p	PAR	Olimpia
1990	Olimpia	PAR	2-0 1-1	ECU	Barcelona
1991	Colo Colo	CHI	0-0 3-0	PAR	Olimpia
1992	São Paulo FC	BRA	1-0 0-1 3-2p	ARG	Newell's Old Boys
1993	São Paulo FC	BRA	5-1 0-2	CHI	Universidad Catolica
1994	Velez Sarsfield	ARG	1-0 0-1 5-3p	BRA	São Paulo FC
1995	Grêmio	BRA	3-1 1-1	COL	Atlético Nacional Medellín
1996	River Plate	ARG	0-1 2-0	COL	América Cali
1997	Cruzeiro	BRA	0-0 1-0	PER	Sporting Cristal
1998	Vasco da Gama	BRA	2-0 2-1	ECU	Barcelona
1999	Palmeiras	BRA	0-1 2-1 4-3p	COL	Deportivo Cali
2000	Boca Juniors	ARG	2-2 0-0 4-2p	BRA	Palmeiras
2001	Boca Juniors	ARG	1-0 0-1 3-1p	MEX	Cruz Azul
2002	Olimpia	PAR	0-1 2-1 4-2p	BRA	São Caetano
2003	Boca Juniors	ARG	2-0 3-1	BRA	Santos
2004	Once Caldas	COL	0-0 1-1 2-0p	ARG	Boca Juniors
2005	São Paulo FC	BRA	1-1 4-0	BRA	Atlético Paranaense
2006	Internacional	BRA	2-1 2-2	BRA	São Paulo FC
2007	Boca Juniors	ARG	3-0 2-0	BRA	Grêmio
2008	LDU Quito	ECU		BRA	Fluminense

COPA LIBERTADORES MEDALS TABLE

	Country	G	S	B	F	SF
1	Argentina	21	8	31	29	60
2	Brazil	13	14	20	27	47
3	Uruguay	8	7	17	15	32
4	Paraguay	3	3	13	6	19
5	Colombia	2	7	18	9	27
6	Chile	1	5	13	6	19
7	Ecuador	1	2	9	3	12
8	Peru		2	6	2	8
9	Mexico		1	5	1	6
9	Bolivia			3		3
	Venezuela			3		3
		49	49	138	98	236

This table represents the Gold (winners), Silver (runners-up) and Bronze (semi-finalists) placings of clubs representing the above countries in the Copa Libertadores, along with the number of appearances in the final and semi-finals

COPA LIBERTADORES MEDALS TABLE

	Country		G	S	B
1	Independiente	ARG	7		5
2	Boca Juniors	ARG	6	3	4
3	Peñarol	URU	5	4	10
4	Nacional Montevideo	URU	3	3	6
5	Olimpia	PAR	3	3	5
6	São Paulo FC	BRA	3	3	2
7	Estudiantes La Plata	ARG	3	1	1
8	River Plate	ARG	2	2	11
9	Grêmio	BRA	2	2	2
10	Santos FC	BRA	2	1	3
11	Cruzeiro	BRA	2	1	2
12	SE Palmeiras	BRA	1	3	2
13	Colo Colo	CHI	1	1	3
14	At. Nacional Medellín	COL	1	1	2
	Internacional PA	BRA	1	1	2
16	Flamengo	BRA	1		2
	LDU Quito	ECU	1		2
	Racing Club Avellaneda	ARG	1		2
19	Argentinos Juniors	ARG	1		1
	Vélez Sarsfield	ARG	1		1
21	Once Caldas	COL	1		
	Vasco da Gama	BRA	1		
23	América Cali	COL		4	6
24	Barcelona	ECU		2	5
25	Deportivo Cali	COL		2	2

COPA LIBERTADORES MEDALS TABLE (CONT'D)

	Country		G	S	B
26	Cobreloa	CHI		2	1
27	Newell's Old Boys	ARG		2	
28	Universidad Catolica	CHI		1	4
29	Universitario	PER		1	3
30	Union Española	CHI		1	1
31	Atlético Paranaense	BRA		1	
	Cruz Azul	MEX		1	
	Fluminense	BRA		1	
	São Caetano	BRA		1	
35	Sporting Cristal	PER		1	
36	Cerro Porteño	PAR			5
37	CF América	MEX			3
	Millonarios	COL			3
	San Lorenzo de Almagro	ARG			3
40	Alianza	PER			2
	Botafogo	BRA			2
	Chivas Guadalajara	MEX			2
	Rosario Central	ARG			2
	Universidad de Chile	CHI			2
	Libertad	PAR			2
46	Atlético Junior	COL			1
	Atlético Mineiro	BRA			1
	Atlético San Cristobal	VEN			1
	Blooming	BOL			1
	Bolivar	BOL			1
	Corinthians	BRA			1
	Cúcuta Deportiva	COL			1
	Danubio	URU			1
	Defensor Lima	PER			1
	Deportes Tolima	COL			1
	Emelec	ECU			1
	Guarani Asuncion	PAR			1
	Guarani Campinas	BRA			1
	Huracán	ARG			1
	Independiente Medellin	COL			1
	Independiente Santa Fé	COL			1
	Jorge Wilsterman	BOL			1
	Nacional Quito	ECU			1
	O'Higgins	CHI			1
	Palestino	CHI			1
	Portuguesa	VEN			1
	ULA Merida	VEN			1
			49	49	138

SUPERCOPA JOAO HAVELANGE

Year	Winners	Country	Score	Country	Runners-up
1988	Racing Club	ARG	2-1 1-1	BRA	Cruzeiro
1989	Boca Juniors	ARG	0-0 0-0 5-3p	ARG	Independiente
1990	Olimpia	PAR	3-0 3-3	URU	Nacional Montevideo
1991	Cruzeiro	BRA	0-2 3-0	ARG	River Plate
1992	Cruzeiro	BRA	4-0 0-1	ARG	Racing Club
1993	São Paulo FC	BRA	2-2 2-2 5-3p	BRA	Flamengo
1994	Independiente	ARG	1-1 1-0	ARG	Boca Juniors
1995	Independiente	ARG	2-0 0-1	BRA	Flamengo
1996	Velez Sarsfield	ARG	1-0 2-0	BRA	Cruzeiro
1997	River Plate	ARG	0-0 2-1	BRA	São Paulo FC

COPA MERCOSUR

Year	Winners	Country	Score	Country	Runners-up
1998	Palmeiras	BRA	1-2 3-1 1-0	BRA	Cruzeiro
1999	Flamengo	BRA	4-3	BRA	Palmeiras
2000	Vasco da Gama	BRA	2-0 0-1 4-3	BRA	Palmeiras
2001	San Lorenzo	ARG	0-0 1-1 4-3p	BRA	Flamengo

COPA MERCONORTE

Year	Winners	Country	Score	Country	Runners-up
1998	Atlético Nacional Medellin	COL	3-1 1-0	COL	Deportivo Cali
1999	América Cali	COL	1-2 1-0	COL	Independiente Santa Fé
2000	Atlético Nacional Medellin	COL	0-0 2-1	COL	Millonarios
2001	Millonários	COL	1-1 1-1 3-1p	ECU	Emelec

COPA CONMEBOL

Year	Winners	Country	Score	Country	Runners-up
1992	Atlético Mineiro	BRA	2-0 0-1	PAR	Olimpia
1993	Botafogo	BRA	1-1 2-2 3-1p	URU	Peñarol
1994	São Paulo FC	BRA	6-1 0-3	URU	Peñarol
1995	Rosario Central	ARG	0-4 4-0 4-3p	BRA	Atlético Mineiro
1996	Lanús	ARG	2-0 0-1	COL	Independiente Santa Fé
1997	Atlético Mineiro	BRA	4-1 1-1	ARG	Lanús
1998	Santos	BRA	1-0 0-0	ARG	Rosario Central
1999	Talleres Córdoba	ARG	2-4 3-0	BRA	CSA

COPA SUDAMERICANA

Year	Winners	Country	Score	Country	Runners-up
2002	San Lorenzo	ARG	4-0 0-0	COL	Atlético Nacional Medellin
2003	Cienciano	PER	3-3 1-0	ARG	River Plate
2004	Boca Juniors	ARG	0-1 2-0	BOL	Bolivar
2005	Boca Juniors	ARG	1-1 1-1 4-3p	MEX	Pumas UNAM
2006	Pachuca	MEX	1-1 2-1	CHI	Colo Colo
2007	Arsenal	ARG	3-2 1-2	MEX	America

COPA SUDAMERICANA MEDALS TABLE

	Country	G	S	B	F	SF
1	Argentina	4	1	2	5	7
2	Mexico	1	2	1	3	4
3	Peru	1			1	1
4	Colombia		1	2	1	3
5	Bolivia		1	1	1	2
	Chile		1	1	1	2
7	Brazil			3		3
8	Ecuador			1		1
	Uruguay			1		1
		6	6	12	12	24

This table represents the Gold (winners), Silver (runners-up) and Bronze (semi-finalists) placings of clubs representing the above countries in the Copa Merconorte, along with the number of appearances in the final and semi-finals

COPA SUDAMERICANA MEDALS TABLE

	Country		G	S	B
1	Boca Juniors	ARG	2		
2	Cienciano	PER	1		
	Pachuca	MEX	1		
	San Lorenzo	ARG	1		
	Arsenal	ARG	1		
6	Atlético Nacional Medellin	COL		1	1
	Bolivar	BOL		1	1
	River Plate	ARG		1	1
9	Colo Colo	CHI		1	
	Pumas UNAM	MEX		1	
	CF América	MEX		1	
12	Atlético Paranaense	BRA			1
	Internacional	BRA			1
	LDU Quito	ECU			1
	Millonarios	COL			1
	Nacional Montevideo	URU			1
	São Paulo FC	BRA			1
	Universidad Catolica	CHI			1
	Toluca	MEX			1
	Velez Sarsfield	ARG			1
			6	6	12

COPA SANTANDER LIBERTADORES 2008

COPA SANTANDER LIBERTADORES 2008

Preliminary Round

Cruzeiro *	BRA	3	3
Cerro Porteño	PAR	1	2
Olmedo *	ECU	1	0
Lanús	ARG	0	3
Atlas *	MEX	2	0
La Paz FC	BOL	0	1
Cienciano *	PER	1	0
Montevideo Wanderers	URU	0	0
Boyacá Chico *	COL	4	0
Audax Italiano	CHI	3	1
Arsenal *	ARG	2	1
Mineros de Guyana	VEN	0	2

Group Stage

Grupo 1		Pts	BRA	ARG	VEN	BOL
Cruzeiro	BRA	11		3-1	3-0	3-0
San Lorenzo	ARG	10	0-0		3-0	1-0
Caracas FC	VEN	7	1-1	2-0		2-1
Real Potosí	BOL	6	5-1	2-3	3-1	

Grupo 2		Pts	ARG	ARG	ECU	URU
Estudiantes La Plata	ARG	11		0-0	2-0	2-0
Lanús	ARG	10	3-3		0-0	3-1
Deportivo Cuenca	ECU	6	1-0	1-1		0-0
Danubio	URU	4	1-2	1-2	2-0	

Grupo 3		Pts	MEX	ARG	CHI	VEN
Atlas	MEX	11		3-1	3-0	3-0
Boca Juniors	ARG	10	3-0		4-3	3-0
Colo Colo	CHI	10	1-1	2-0		2-0
Unión At. Maracaibo	VEN	2	1-1	1-1	1-3	

Grupo 4		Pts	BRA	URU	PER	PER
Flamengo	BRA	13		2-0	2-1	2-0
Nacional	URU	12	3-0		3-1	1-0
Cienciano	PER	7	0-3	2-1		1-0
Coronel Bolognesi	PER	2	0-0	0-1	0-0	

Grupo 5		Pts	ARG	MEX	CHI	PER
River Plate	ARG	12		2-1	2-0	5-0
CF América	MEX	9	4-3		2-1	3-1
Universidad Catolica	CHI	9	1-2	2-0		1-0
Universidad San Martín	PER	6	2-0	1-0	0-1	

Grupo 6		Pts	COL	BRA	MEX	BOL
Cúcuta Deportivo	COL	11		0-0	1-0	0-0
Santos	BRA	10	2-1		1-0	7-0
Guadalajara	MEX	9	0-1	3-2		2-0
San José	BOL	4	2-4	2-1	0-3	

Grupo 7		Pts	BRA	COL	PAR	CHI
São Paulo FC	BRA	11		1-0	1-0	2-1
At. Nacional Medellín	COL	8	1-1		3-0	1-1
Sportivo Luqueño	PAR	7	1-1	1-3		4-1
Audax Italiano	CHI	7	1-0	1-0	1-2	

Grupo 8		Pts	BRA	ECU	ARG	PAR
Fluminense	BRA	13		1-0	6-0	2-0
LDU Quito	ECU	10	0-0		6-1	2-0
Arsenal	ARG	9	2-0	0-1		1-0
Libertad	PAR	3	1-2	3-1	1-2	

* Home team in the first leg

COPA SANTANDER LIBERTADORES 2008

Round of 16			Quarter–finals			Semi–finals			Final		
LDU Quito *	2	1									
Estudiantes LP	0	2									
			LDU Quito	1 1	5p						
			San Lorenzo *	1 1	3p						
River Plate	1	2									
San Lorenzo *	2	2									
						LDU Quito	1	0			
						CF América *	1	0			
Santos *	2	2									
Cúcuta Deportivo	0	0									
			Santos	0	1						
			CF América *	2	0						
Flamengo	4	0									
CF América *	2	3									
									LDU Quito *	4 1	3p
									Fluminense	2 3	1p
Boca Juniors *	2	2									
Cruzeiro	1	1									
			Boca Juniors *	2	3						
			Atlas	2	0						
Lanús *	0	2									
Atlas	1	2									
						Boca Juniors *	2	1			
						Fluminense	2	3			
São Paulo FC	0	2									
Nacional Mont'deo *	0	0									
			São Paulo FC *	1	1						
			Fluminense	0	3						
Atlético Nacional *	1	0									
Fluminense	2	1		* Home team in the first leg								

PRELIMINARY ROUND

Olímpico, Rio Bamba
31-01-2008, 17:00, 4036, Rivera PER

Olmedo **1**

Quiñónez [70]

Edwin Villafuerte - Omar Ledesma, Carlos Caicedo (Freddy Samaniego 45), Jose Perlaza, Juan Guerrón - Elvis Bone, Andrés Vinueza, Sebastian Vezzani (Gonzalo Chila• 65) - Lucas Godoy (Estuarto Quiñónez 45), John Tenorio•, Maximiliano Antonelli. Tr: Armando Osma

Lanús **0**

Carlos Bossio - Rodolfo Graieb, Carlos Quintana, Emir Faccioli, Maximiliano Velázquez - Sebastián Blanco (Adrián Peralta 80), Agustín Pelletieri, Matías Fritzler, Diego Valeri, Lautaro Acosta (Diego Lagos 74) - José Sand. Tr: Ramón Cabrero

---

Néstor Díaz Pérez, Buenos Aires
5-02-2008, 20:00, 8241, Lopes BRA

Lanús **2**

Fritzler [57], Biglieri [77], Velázquez [83]

Carlos Bossio - Maximiliano Velázquez, Rodolfo Graieb, Carlos Quintana, Emir Faccioli - Diego Valeri (Adrián Peralta 86), Matías Fritzler, Agustín Pelletieri, Sebastián Blanco (Sebastián Salomón 84) - José Sand, Lautaro Acosta• (Santiago Biglieri 56). Tr: Ramón Cabrero

Olmedo **0**

Edwin Villafuerte (Francisco Caicedo 27) - Juan Guerrón•, Omar Ledesma, José Perlaza, Freddy Samaniego - Elvis Bone, Gustavo Nazareno (Andrés Vinueza 60), Sebastián Vezzani - John Tenorio•92+, Maximiliano Antonelli, Cristian Badaracco (Estuardo Quiñónes 60). Tr: Armando Osma

---

Mineirão, Belo Horizonte
30-01-2008, 21:50, 38 855, Larrionda URU

Cruzeiro **3**

Ramires 2 [40] [89], Martins Moreno [55]

Fábio - Thiago Martinelli, Marquinho Paraná, Jádilson - Wagner (Fernandinho 69), Fabrício, Thiago Heleno, Ramires, Charles - Guilherme (Kerlon 60) (Marcinho 76), Marcelo Martins Moreno. Tr: Adilson Batista

Cerro Porteño **1**

Cabrera [74p]

Diego Barreto - Nelson Cabrera•, Fidel Pérez•, Jorge Nuñez - Jorge Britez, Wálter Fretes (Luis Cáceres 53), Osvaldo Hobecker (Lorgio Alvarez 46), Rodrigo Burgos - Pablo Giménez•, Marcelo Estigarribia, César Ramírez• (Victor Ferreira 67). Tr: Javier Torrente

---

Defensores del Chaco, Asunción
6-02-2008, 20:50, 12 021, Chandia CHI

Cerro Porteño **2**

Alvarez 2 [43] [64]

Diego Barreto• - Nelson Cabrera, Fidel Pérez, Alfredo Rojas (Wálter Fretes 64), Jorge Nuñez - Lorgio Alvarez, Ernesto Cristaldo• (Victor Ferreira 46), Jorge Brítez•, Luis Cáceres - Marcelo Estigarribia, César Ramírez. Tr: Javier Torrente

Cruzeiro **3**

Thiago Heleno [5], Martins Moreno [54p], Ramires [57]

Fábio - Thiago Martinelli, Marquinho Paraná, Jádilson, Thiago Heleno - Wagner, Fabrício•, Ramires•, Charles (Luis Alberto 67) - Marcelo Martins Moreno, Leandro Domingues (Fernandinho 46). Tr: Adilson Batista

---

Julio Grondona, Buenos Aires
29-01-2008, 19:30, 2431, Osses CHI

Arsenal **2**

Calderón [41], Leguizamón [78]

Mario Cuenca - Carlos Casteglione, Javier Gandolfi•, Christian Díaz, Jossimar Mosquera, Aníbal Matellán - Andrés San Martín (Cristian Pellerano 78), Martín Andrizzi•, Alejandro Gómez (Félix Leguizamón 63), Sebastián Carrera (Diego Villar 63) - José Calderón. Tr: Gustavo Alfaro

Mineros de Guyana **0**

Euro Guzmán - Atahualpa González, Jailson Dos Santos, Flavio De Jesús - Wilson Cuero, Jarrín García, Gregory Luzardo (Juan Lira• 73), Nicolás Massia (Cristian Jeandet 86), Javier Carballo (Giancarlos Cenci 85), Ederlei Pereira - Jhonny Carneiro•. Tr: Stalin Rivas

---

Polideportivo Cachamay, Puerto Ordaz
5-02-2008, 20:00, 3834, Gaciba BRA

Mineros de Guyana **2**

Pereira [45p], Dos Santos 58

Euro Guzmán - Wilson Cuero, Jarrín García•91, Atahualpa González, Jailson Dos Santos, Flavio De Jesús (Javier Caraballo• 69) - Gregory Luzardo, Nicolas Massia•, Ederlei Pereira• (Elías Leal 76) - Jhonny Carneiro•, Cristian Jeandet (Alexis Acuña 65). Tr: Stalin Rivas

Arsenal **1**

Calderón [46]

Catriel Orcellet• - Javier Gandolfi, Christian Díaz, Jossimar Mosquera, Aníbal Matellán - Andrés San Martín, Martín Andrizzi (Javier Yacuzzi 66), Carlos Castiglione, Alejandro Gómez (Leonardo Biagini 76), Sebastián Carrera (Pablo Garnier 60) - José Calderón. Tr: Gustavo Alfaro

---

Jalisco, Guadalajara
30-01-2008, 20:10, 21 595, Buckley PER

Atlas **2**

Mendivil [6], Rergis [72]

Jorge Bava - Omar Flores, Juan Medina (Luis Robles 58), Diego Colotto, Hugo Ayala - Eduardo Rergis•, Christian Valdez, Emanuel Centurión (Oscar Vera 63), Jorge Hernández - Ulises Mendivil (Flavio Santos 84), Bruno Marioni•. Tr: Miguel Brindisi

La Paz FC **0**

Mauro Machado - Rómulo Alaca, Diomedes Peña (Julio Cortéz 66), Miguel Hurtado, Juan Paz García - Edgar Olivares (Kyle Zenoni 85), Didi Torrico, Helmut Gutiérrez, Edgar Clavijo• - Regis Quaresma, Augusto Andaveris•. Tr: Sergio Apaza

---

Hernando Siles, La Paz
6-02-2008, 17:20, Arias PAR

La Paz FC **1**

Clavijo [50]

Mauro Machado - Rómulo Alaca, Diomedes Peña, Miguel Hurtado• (Juan Fierro 76), Juan Paz García•, Edgar Clavijo - Julio Cortéz, Didi Torrico, Helmut Gutiérrez• (Kyle Zenoni 89) - Regis Quaresma, Augusto Andaveris. Tr: Sergio Apaza

Atlas **0**

Jorge Bava - Luis Robles (Ricardo Jiménez 79), Hugo Ayala, Jorge Torres, Gerardo Flores, Néstor Vidrio - Eduardo Rergis, Christian Valdez, Jorge Hernández• (Jorge Achucarro 67) - Ulises Mendivil (Juan Medina 67), Bruno Marioni. Tr: Miguel Brindisi

---

Inca Garcilaso de la Vega, Cusco
31-01-2008, 19:20, 21 661, Vera ECU

Cienciano **1**

Sawa [12]

Juan Flores - Luis Marengo, Roberto Guizasola, Julio Romaña (Daniel Peláez 76), Carlos Solis• - Julio García (Aldo Olcese 70), Juan Bazalar (Edson Uribe 70), César Ccahuantico• - Gustavo Vassallo, Masakatsu Sawa, Willian Chiroque. Tr: Franco Navarro

Montevideo Wanderers **0**

Sergio Martínez• - Juan Alvez, Edgar Martínez, Emiliano Tellechea, Simón Vanderoeght (Matías Quagliotti 66), Miguel Britos• - Facundo Martínez (Diego Chavez 76), Victor Fagundez, Alvaro Fernández, Fernando Fadeuille• - Danilo Peinado (Jonathan Charquero 86). Tr: Jorge Goncalvez

---

Centenario, Montevideo
7-02-2008, 19:30, 3615, Beligoy ARG

Montevideo Wanderers **0**

Sergio Martínez - Juan Alvez, Edgar Martínez, Emiliano Tellechea (Christian Yeladian 75), Miguel Britos - Facundo Martínez, Victor Fagundez•, Alvaro Fernández, Fernando Fadeuille• (Jonathan Pérez 57) - Manuel Abreu (Manuel Abreu 74), Danilo Peinado. Tr: Jorge Goncalvez

Cienciano **0**

Juan Flores - Luis Marengo, Roberto Guizasola, Julio Romaña, Carlos Solis - Julio García• (Aldo Olcese 83), Juan Bazalar (César Ortiz 93+), César Ccahuantico, Masakatsu Sawa - Gustavo Vassallo (Victor Manique• 72), Willian Chiroque. Tr: Franco Navarro

---

El Campín, Bogotá
7-02-2008, 19:45, 1161, Soto VEN

Boyacá Chicó FC **4**

Salazar 2 [8] [90], Pacheco [37], Caneo [76]

Walter Noriega - Pedro Pino, Ever Palacios•, Jules Ntarnak (Juan Galicia 46) - Victor Pacheco, Miguel Caneo, Juna Mahecha• (Leonardo López• 46), Leoncio Alegría (Edwin Móvil 76), Oscar Díaz - Néstor Salazar, Rodrigo Saraz•••78. Tr: Alberto Gamero

Audax Italiano **3**

Ntarnak OG [1], Villanueva [21], Orellana [60]

Mario Villasanti - Boris Rieloff•, Carlos Garrido, Sebastián Rocco - Miguel Romero (Nicolás Corvetto 89), Patricio Gutiérrez, Marcelo Broli, Braulio Leal - Renato Ramos• (Renzo Yáñez 74), Carlos Villanueva, Fabián Orellana. Tr: Raúl Toro

---

Monumental, Santiago
12-02-2008, 17:00, 2327, Maldonado BOL

Audax Italiano **1**

Broli [80]

Mario Villasanti - Sebastián Rocco•, Boris Rieloff (Manuel Ibarra 72), Carlos Garrido - Miguel Romero, Patricio Gutiérrez•, Marcelo Broli, Braulio Leal• - Renato Ramos (Renzo Yáñez 72), Carlos Villanueva, Fabián Orellana. Tr: Raúl Toro

Boyacá Chicó FC **0**

Edigson Velásquez• - Juan Galicia, Pedro Pino•, Mario García (Brahaman Sinisterra 62), Ever Palacios - Víctor Pacheco, Miguel Caneo (Ferley Villamil 74), Edwin Móvil, Rubén Velásquez• (Wilmer Beltre 83), Oscar Díaz• - Néstor Salazar. Tr: Alberto Gamero

COPA LIBERTADORES 2008 939

GROUP 1

		Pl	W	D	L	F	A	Pts	BRA	ARG	VEN	BOL
Cruzeiro	BRA	6	3	2	1	11	7	11		3-1	3-0	3-0
San Lorenzo	ARG	6	3	1	2	8	7	10	0-0		3-0	1-0
Caracas FC	VEN	6	2	1	3	6	11	7	1-1	2-0		2-1
Real Potosí	BOL	6	2	0	4	11	11	6	5-1	2-3	3-1	

Olímpico, Caracas
12-02-2008, 17:50, 12 077, Duarte COL

Caracas FC 2
Vargas [39], Castellín [70]

Vicente Rosales• – Franklin Lucena, Jaime Bustamante, José Mera, Juan Valencia, Luis Vera, Édgar Jiménez (John Ocoro 86), Ronald Vargas•, Juan Cominges (Bremer Piñango 77), Rafael Castellín, Pablo Bastianini• (Emilio Rentería 80). Tr: Noel Sanvicente

San Lorenzo 0
Agustín Orión• – Cristian Tula•42, Sebastián Méndez, Jonathan Bottinelli, Diego Placente, Diego Rivero (Hernán González 46), Jorge Ortiz (Santiago Hirsig 86), Juan Torres•••89, Nicolás Torres (Bernardo Romeo 73), Andrés D'Alessandro, Néstor Silvera•. Tr: Ramón Díaz

Olímpico, Caracas
26-02-2008, 18:50, 12 426, Buitrago COL

Caracas FC 2
Rentería [3], Vargas [38]

Vicente Rosales – José Mera, Jaime Bustamante, Juan Valencia•, Emilio Rentería• (Giovanny Romero 89), Luis Vera•, Ronald Vargas•44, Franklin Lucena, Edgar Jiménez, Pablo Bastianini (Jorge Casanova• 13),Juan Cominges• (John Ocoro 77). Tr: Noel Sanvicente

Real Potosí 1
Galindo [74]

Hugo Suárez – Ronald Eguino•, Santos Amador (Marco Paz• 65), Nicolás Sartori, Percy Colque (Adrián Cuéllar 57), Nicolás Suárez•, Eduardo Ortiz•, Luis Ribeiro, Gonzalo Galindo, Alvaro Pintos, Isidro Candia. Tr: Mauricio Soria

Olímpico, Caracas
18-03-2008, 20:20, 15 837, Ruiz COL

Caracas FC 1
Valencia [30]

Vicente Rosales – Franklin Lucena•, Oswaldo Vizcarrondo•87, José Mera, Juan Valencia, Edgar Jiménez (Jorge Casanova 81), Luis Vera•, Ronald Vargas, Juan Cominges• (Gualbeto Campos• 75), Rafael Castellín, Pablo Bastianini (Emilio Rentería• 65). Tr: Noel Sanvicente

Cruzeiro 1
Martins Moreno [55p]

Fábio – Marquinho Paraná•, Giovanny Espinoza, Ramires, Wagner, Leo Fortunato, Thiago Martinelli•, Apodi, Marcelo Martins Moreno, Marcinho, Jonathan•. Tr: Adilson Batsta

Ipatingão, Ipatinga
3-04-2008, 21:00, 15 843, Chandia CHI

Cruzeiro 3
Martins Moreno 2 [11 71], Wagner [83]

Fábio• – Leo Fortunato•, Henrique (Marcinho 80), Giovanny Espinoza, Apodi, Marquinho Paraná, Ramires•, Jadilson, Wagner, Guilherme (Thiago Heleno 66), Marcelo Martins Moreno. Tr: Adilson Batista

San Lorenzo 1
Silvera [87]

Agustín Orión – Gaston Aguirre, Sebastián Méndez, Jonathan Bottinelli•, Hernán González (Daniel Bilos 51), Diego Rivero•, Pablo Alvarado, Diego Placente, Andrés D'Alessandro (Wálter Acevedo• 74), Gonzalo Bergessio, Bernardo Romeo. Tr:Ramón Díaz

Mineirão, Belo Horizonte
13-02-2008, 21:50, 33 874, Silvera URU

Cruzeiro 3
Martins Moreno [46], Ramires [52], Guilherme [67]

Fábio – Marquinho Paraná (Apodi 78), Thiago Heleno, Giovanny Espinoza, Jadilson (Fernandinho 46), Fabricio, Charles×, Ramires•, Wagner (Marcinho 65), Guilherme, Marcelo Martins Moreno. Tr: Adilson Batista

Real Potosí 0
Hugo Suárez – Luis Ribeiro, Edemir Rodríguez•, Nicolás Sartori, Marco Paz, Nicolás Suárez, Eduardo Ortiz, Miguel Loaiza (Adrián Cuéllar 59), Gonzalo Galindo• (Percy Colque 55), Alvaro Pintos, Isidro Candia (Ronald Eguino 75). Tr: Mauricio Soria

Mineirão, Belo Horizonte
4-03-2008, 19:20, 37 694, Laverni ARG

Cruzeiro 3
Guilherme [9], Ramires [28], Martins Moreno [64]

Fábio – Jonathan, Thiago Heleno•, Giovanny Espinoza×, Jadilson, Marquinho Paraná, Ramires, Charles, Wagner (Marcinho 61), Marcelo Martins Moreno (Marcel 82), Guilherme (Leandro Domingues 71). Tr: Adilson Batista

Caracas FC 0
Vicente Rosales – Franklin Lucena, José Mera, Jaime Bustamante, Juan Valencia, Luis Vera, Edgar Jiménez, Juan Cominges (Miguel Romero 84), John Ocoro (Jorge Casanova• 46), Emilio Rentería (Ever Espinoza• 69), Pablo Bastianini. Tr: Noel Sanvicente

Nuevo Gasómetro, Buenos Aires
25-03-2008, 19:00, 10 915, Lopes BRA

San Lorenzo 1
González [29p]

Agustín Orión – Hernán González•, Gaston Aguirre, Juan Torres, Sebastián Méndez•, Daniel Bilos (Román Torres 66), Diego Rivero•, Bernardo Romeo, Andrés D'Alessandro (Juan Menseguez 81), Gonzalo Bergessio (Néstor Silvera 59). Tr: Ramón Díaz

Real Potosí 1
Hugo Suárez – Luis Ribeiro, Santos Amador, Nicolás Sartori, Edemir Rodríguez, Isidro Candia, Jesús Gallegos• (Luis Sillero• 51), Marco Paz•, Percy Colque• (Adrián Cuéllar 89), Miguel Loaiza•, Alvaro Pintos. Tr: Tito Montaño

Ipatingão / Víctor Agustín Ugarte, Potosí
16-04-2008, 18:30, Intriago ECU

Real Potosí 5
Loaiza 3, Pintos 2 [12 51], Candia [66], Ribeiro [86]

Hugo Suárez – Luis Ribeiro, Marco Paz, (Eduardo Ortiz• 79), Edemir Rodríguez•, Ronald Eguino, Jesús Gallegos× (Gonzalo Galindo 76), Miguel Loaiza (Gerardo Yecerotte 81), Isidro Candia, Nicolás Suárez, Luis Sillero, Alvaro Pintos. Tr: Tito Montaño

Cruzeiro 1
Martins Moreno [29p]

Fábio – Marquinho Paraná, Giovanny Espinoza, Ramires, Wagner, Leo Fortunato, Thiago Martinelli, Henrique, Jonathan, Marcelo Martins Moreno, Charles•. Tr: Adilson Batista

Nuevo Gasómetro, Buenos Aires
21-02-2008, 20:00, 14 845, Amarilla PAR

San Lorenzo 0
Agustín Orión – Hernán González, Gaston Aguirre, Diego Placente•, Wálter Acevedo, Jonathan Bottinelli, Néstor Silvera, Santiago Hirsig (Román Aureliano 71), Daniel Bilos (Jorge Ortiz 64), Andrés D'Alessandro, Gonzalo Bergessio (Bernardo Romeo• 66). Tr: Ramón Díaz

Cruzeiro 0
Fábio – Marquinho Paraná, Thiago Martinelli, Giovanny Espinoza, Jadilson•, Charles, Fabricio, Ramires, Wagner (Fernandinho 46), Marcelo Martins Moreno• (Marcel 84), Guilherme (Marcinho 60). Tr: Adilson Batista

Víctor Agustín Ugarte, Potosí
11-03-2008, 20:10, 11 880, Larrionda URU

Real Potosí 2
Loaiza [17], Pintos [32]

Hugo Suárez – Nicolás Sartori, Edemir Rodríguez, Santos Amador, Luis Ribeiro, Nicolás Suárez•, Miguel Loaiza, Isidro Candia (Marco Paz 67), Gonzalo Galindo•50, Alvaro Pintos, Luis Sillero. Tr: Tito Montaño

San Lorenzo 3
Romeo [71], Chávez [78], Torres [88p]

Agustín Orión• – Hernán González (Cristian Chávez 70), Gaston Aguirre, Nicolás Bianchi Arce, Diego Placente, Juan Torres (Pablo Alvarado• 75), Santiago Hirsig• (Daniel Bilos 46), Diego Rivero, Bernardo Romeo, Gonzalo Bergessio, Román Torres. Tr: Ramón Díaz

Víctor Agustín Ugarte, Potosí
1-04-2008, 17:10, Buckley PER

Real Potosí 3
Candia [3], Suárez [25], Pintos [82]

Hugo Suárez – Luis Ribeiro, Nicolás Sartori, Edemir Rodríguez, Isidro Candia (Gonzalo Galindo 60), Santos Amador, Jesús Gallegos• (Eduardo Ortiz 83), Miguel Loaiza, Marco Paz•, Luis Sillero (Nicolás Suárez 71), Alvaro Pintos. Tr: Tito Montaño

Caracas FC 1
Castellín [6]

Vicente Rosales – José Mera, Jaime Bustamante•91+, Juan Valencia, Luis Vera, Rafael Castellín, Ronald Vargas, Franklin Lucena, Giovanny Romero• (Edgar Jiménez 71), Pablo Bastianini (Emilio Rentería 62), Juan Cominges (Jorge Casanova 62). Tr: Noel Sanvicente

Nuevo Gasómetro, Buenos Aires
16-04-2008, 19:30, 21 906, Roldán COL

San Lorenzo 3
Bergessio [16], Rosales OG [35], Silvera [78]

Agustín Orión – Hernán González• (Pablo Alvarado 66), Gaston Aguirre×, Sebastián Méndez, Diego Placente, Diego Rivero (Jonathan Bottinelli 46), Juan Torres, Wálter Acevedo, Andrés D'Alessandro (Román Torres 83), Néstor Silvera, Gonzalo Bergessio. Tr:Ramón Díaz

Caracas FC 0
Vicente Rosales – Franklin Lucena×, José Mera, Oswaldo Vizcarrondo, Juan Valencia•, Luis Vera, Edgar Jiménez (Pablo Bastianini 46), Ronald Vargas• (Emilio Rentería 67), Juan Cominges, Rafael Castellín, Alejandro Guerra (John Ocoro 46). Tr: Noel Sanvicente

GROUP 2

		Pl	W	D	L	F	A	Pts	ARG	ARG	ECU	URU
Estudiantes La Plata	ARG	6	3	2	1	9	5	11		0-0	2-0	2-0
Lanús	ARG	6	2	4	0	9	6	10	3-3		0-0	3-1
Deportivo Cuenca	ECU	6	1	3	2	2	5	6	1-0	1-1		0-0
Danubio	URU	6	1	1	4	5	9	4	1-2	1-2	2-0	

Alejandro Serrano Aguilar, Cuenca
12-02-2008, 19:40, 12 527, Selman CHI

Deportivo Cuenca 1
Ferradás [45]

Javier Klimowicz – Marlon Moreno*, Marcelo Fleitas, Arlin Ayoví, Marcelo Bohórquez, Jimmy Bran*, Leonardo Soledispa, German Castillo (Mariano Mina 89), Federico Barrionuevo* (Jhon García 73), Javier Toledo (Gustavo Figueroa 83), Mauricio Ferradás. Tr: Gabriel Perrone

Estudiantes LP 0

Mariano Andújar – Marcos Angeleri*, Agustín Alayes, Leandro Desabato, Juan Díaz (Enzo Pérez* 67), Juan Verón, Rodrigo Braña, Leandro Benítez, Juan Salgueiro (Pablo Lugüercio 62), Ezequiel Maggiolo (Leandro Lazzaro 62), Pablo Piatti. Tr: Roberto Sensini

Néstor Díaz Pérez, Buenos Aires
14-02-2008, 21:50, 6479, Galeano PAR

Lanús 3
Pelletieri [8], Acosta [56], Sand [88]

Carlos Bossio – Rodolfo Graieb, Carlos Quintana, Emir Faccioli, Nelson Benítez*, Sebastián Salomón (Diego González 53), Deigo Valeri (Eduardo Ledesma 81), Lautaro Acosta (Germán Cano 89), José Sand. Tr: Ramón Cabrero

Danubio 1
Abelenda [37]

Néstor Conde – Damián Malrechauffe, Daniel Lembo, Sergio Rodríguez, Leonardo Abelenda, Ribair Rodríguez, Pedro Irala*, Gabriel Alcoba (Jorge García 56), Matías Cresseri (Mateo Figoli 65), Cristian Bardaro (Deley Mena 75), Carlos Morales. Tr: Gustavo Dalto

Alejandro Serrano Aguilar, Cuenca
21-02-2008, 19:20, 8190, Buckley PER

Deportivo Cuenca 0

Javier Klimowicz – Arlin Ayoví, Marcelo Fleitas*, Marlon Moreno, Marcelo Bohórquez, Leonardo Soledispa, German Castillo, Federico Barrionuevo (Edison Preciado 70), Mauricio Ferradás, Javier Toledo (Cristin Valencia 79), Jimmy Bran. Tr: Gabriel Perrone

Danubio 0

Néstor Conde* – Damián Malrechauffe, Daniel Lembo*, Sergio Rodríguez, Matías Pérez*, Leonardo Abelenda, Ribair Rodríguez, Pedro Irala, Carlos Morales (Derlis Florentín 75), Mateo Figoli (Deley Mena 65), Cristian Bardaro (Raúl Ferro 68). Tr: Gustavo Dalto

Ciudad de La Plata, La Plata
26-02-2008, 19:00, 23 072, Favale ARG

Estudiantes LP 0

Mariano Andújar – Leandro Desabato*, Agustín Alayes, Juan Salgueiro (Pablo Lugüercio 35), Pablo Piatti, Juan Verón*, Marcos Angeleri, Leandro Benítez, Iván Moreno Y Fabianesi* (Enzo Pérez 84), Ezequiel Maggiolo (Leandro Lazzaro 65), Rodrigo Braña. Tr: Roberto Sensini

Lanús 0

Carlos Bossio – Rodolfo Graieb*, Carlos Quintana (Leonardo Sigali 88), Emir Faccioli*, Nelson Benítez, Sebastián Blanco (Sebastián Salomón* 78), Agustín Pelletieri*, Deigo González*, Diego Valeri, José Sand, Lautaro Acosta. Tr: Ramón Cabrero

Centenario, Montevideo
5-03-2008, 20:30, 19 335, Osses CHI

Danubio 1
Irala [9]

Néstor Conde - Damián Malrechauffe*, Daniel Lembo, Sergio Rodríguez*, Matías Pérez, Ribair Rodríguez*, Pedro Irala*, Gabriel Alcoba (Mateo Figoli 65), Carlos Morales (Alvaro Noble 42),Deley Mena, Cristian Bardaro (Enzo Scorza 77). Tr: Gustavo Dalto

Estudiantes LP 2
Verón [61p], Pérez [86]

Mariano Andújar – Agustín Alayes*••25, Marcos Angeleri, Leandro Desabato, Iván Fabianesi (José Basanta 46), Juan Verón*, Rodrigo Braña, Leandro Benítez, Pablo Lugüercio (Enzo Pérez* 68), Leandro Lazzaro, Pablo Piatti (Cristian Bogado 46). Tr: Roberto Sensini

Néstor Díaz Pérez, Buenos Aires
13-03-2008, 21:10, 5545, Osses CHI

Lanús 0

Carlos Bossio – Rodolfo Graieb, Carlos Quintana*, Emir Faccioli, Max Velázquez, Sebastián Blanco*, Sebastián Salomón (Diego González* 74), Agustín Pelletieri*, Diego Valeri (Adrián Peralta 53), Santiago Biglieri (Nicolás Ramírez 77), Germán Cano. Tr: Ramón Cabrero

Deportivo Cuenca 0

Javier Klimowicz – Marlon Moreno, Marcelo Fleitas*, Arlin Ayoví, Marcelo Bohórquez, Polo Wila, Leonardo Soledispa (Jhon García 81), Jimmy Bran, German Castillo (Mariano Mina 88), Mauricio Ferradás, Javier Toledo (Federico Barrionuevo 71). Tr: Gabriel Perrone

Ciudad de La Plata, La Plata
18-03-2008, 19:30, 24 617, Gaciba BRA

Estudiantes LP 2
Verón [44p], Desabato [75]

Mariano Andújar – Leandro Desabato, José Basanta, Juan Salgueiro, Pablo Piatti, Juan Verón (Diego Galván 80), Marcos Angeleri, Leandro Benítez, Iván Fabianesi (Enzo Pérez 65), Ezequiel Maggiolo (Leandro Lazzaro 65), Rodrigo Braña. Tr: Roberto Sensini

Danubio 0

Néstor Conde – Daniel Lembo, Matías Pérez, Raúl Ferro (Matías Cresseri 80), Sergio Rodríguez, Pedro Irala, Mateo Figoli, Ribair Rodríguez, Cristian Bardaro (Cristiano Gomes Machado 70), Damián Malrechauffe*, Deley Mena (Derlis Florentín 70). Tr: Gustavo Dalto

Alejandro Serrano Aguilar, Cuenca
20-03-2008, 15:00, 10 143, Fagundes BRA

Deportivo Cuenca 1
García [70]

Javier Klimowicz – Marlon Moreno, Marcelo Fleitas, Arlin Ayoví, Marcelo Bohórquez, Federico Barrionuevo (Jhon García 60), Jimmy Bran (Hólger Matamoros 60), Leonardo Soledispa, German Castillo*, Mauricio Ferradás, Javier Toledo*. Tr: Gabriel Perrone

Lanús 1
Salomón [7]

Carlos Bossio – Rodolfo Graieb*, Carlos Quintana*, Santiago Hoyos, Max Velázquez, Sebastián Salomón, Agustín Pelletieri, Deigo González, Sebastián Blanco* (Adrián Peralta 64), Santiago Biglieri (Nicolás Ramírez 28), Germán Cano (Eduardo Ledesma 80). Tr: Ramón Cabrero

Parque Central, Montevideo
27-03-2008, 18:30, Roman BRA

Danubio 2
Malrechauffe [2], Lembo [21]

Néstor Conde - Daniel Lembo, Matías Pérez*, Raúl Ferro, Sergio Rodríguez, Pedro Irala*, Mateo Figoli (Carlos Morales 63), Ribair Rodríguez, Cristian Bardaro (Jorge García 70), Damián Malrechauffe, Deley Mena (Enzo Scorza* 84). Tr: Gustavo Dalto

Deportivo Cuenca 0

Javier Klimowicz - Marlon Moreno, Marcelo Fleitas, Arlin Ayoví*, Marcelo Bohórquez, Jimmy Bran, Leonardo Soledispa* (Jhon García 46), Polo Wila*, German Castillo (Hólger Matamoros 46), Javier Toledo, Mauricio Ferradás (Federico Barrionuevo 61). Tr: Gabriel Perrone

Néstor Díaz Pérez, Buenos Aires
2-04-2008, 19:30, 10 652, Lunatti ARG

Lanús 3
Sand [10], Valeri [16], Acosta [78]

Carlos Bossio – Carlos Arce (Nicolás Ramírez 72), Carlos Quintana, Maximiliano Velázquez, Santiago Hoyos•45, Sebastián Blanco (Emir Faccioli 86), Agustín Pelletieri, Matías Fritzler, Deigo Valeri•, Lautaro Acosta, José Sand•••92+. Tr: Ramón Cabrero

Estudiantes LP 3
Desabato [21], Benítez [24], Moreno y Fabianesi [61]

Mariano Andújar• – Marcos Angeleri (Juan Díaz 65), Leandro Desabato, Agustín Alayes•••45, José Basanta, Iván Fabianesi, Rodrigo Braña•, Leandro Benítez, Juan Salgueiro, Leandro Lazzaro (Ezequiel Maggiolo 55), Pablo Piatti, (Diego Galván 35). Tr: Roberto Sensini

Parque Central, Montevideo
15-04-2008, 21:10, Lopes BRA

Danubio 1
Bardaro [87]

Néstor Conde - Damián Malrechauffe, Daniel Lembo, Sergio Rodríguez, Jorge García (Matías Pérez 65), Cristiano Gomes Machado (Mateo Figoli 54), Pedro Irala, Raúl Ferro*, Carlos Morales, Cristian Bardaro, Deley Mena (Enzo Scorza 61). Tr: Gustavo Dalto

Lanús 2
Blanco [53], Sand [63]

Carlos Bossio - Rodolfo Graieb*, Carlos Quintana, Emir Faccioli, Max Velázquez* (Carlos Arce 79), Sebastián Blanco* (Deigo González 74), Agustín Pelletieri, Matías Fritzler, Deigo Valeri, José Sand, Lautaro Acosta (Nicolás Ramírez 78. Tr: Ramón Cabrero

Ciudad de La Plata, La Plata
15-04-2008, 21:10, Amarilla PAR

Estudiantes LP 2
Lazzaro [11], Wila OG [87]

Mariano Andújar – Leonardo Sánchez*, Leandro Desabato* (Juan Díaz 85), José Basanta, Iván Fabianesi, Juan Verón, Rodrigo Braña*, Leandro Benítez, Juan Salgueiro (Deigo González 65), Leandro Lazzaro (Ezequiel Maggiolo 71), Pablo Piatti. Tr: Roberto Sensini

Deportivo Cuenca 0

Javier Klimowicz – Marlon Moreno (Hólger Matamoros 77), Marcelo Fleitas, Mariano Mina, Marcelo Bohórquez, Polo Wila, Jhon García*, Jimmy Bran•76, German Castillo, Federico Barrionuevo (Edison Preciado 46), Mauricio Ferradás*. Tr: Gabriel Perrone

GROUP 3

		Pl	W	D	L	F	A	Pts	MEX	ARG	CHI	VEN
Atlas	MEX	6	3	2	1	11	6	11		3-1	3-0	3-0
Boca Juniors	ARG	6	3	1	2	12	9	10	3-0		4-3	3-0
Colo Colo	CHI	6	3	1	2	11	9	10	1-1	2-0		2-0
Unión At. Maracaibo	VEN	6	0	2	4	3	13	2	1-1	1-1	1-3	

Pachencho, Maracaibo
20-02-2008, 19:30, 40 112, Torres PAR

Unión At. Maracaibo   **1**
       Mea Vitali [80]

Juan Henao - Pedro Fernández, Claudio Muñoz, Gregory Lancken, Juan Fuenmayor, Miguel Mea Vitali, Gabriel Urdaneta, Darío Figueroa, Jorge Rojas (Guillermo Beraza 67), Nicolás Saucedo (Heiber Díaz 89), Armando Maita (Víctor Guaza 78). Tr: Jorge Pellicer

Boca Juniors   **1**
       Battaglia [83]

Mauricio Caranta - Jonatan Maidana, Julio Cáceres, Gabriel Paletta•, Claudio Morel, Alvaro González (Fabián Vargas 70), Sebastián Battaglia•, Neri Cardozo (Jesús Datolo 70), Juan Riquelme, Martín Palermo, Rodrigo Palacio. Tr: Carlos Ischia

---

Jalisco, Guadalajara
21-02-2008, 20:40, 20 958, Beligoy ARG

Atlas   **3**
   Marioni [7], Colotto [40], Medina [68]

Jorge Bava - Diego Colotto, Ricardo Jiménez•, Néstor Vidrio, Juan Medina•, Christian Valdez•, Eduardo Rergis• (Oscar Vera 78), Emanuel Centurión• (Edgar Pacheco 82), Gerardo Flores, Jorge Achucarro (Ulises Mendivil 65), Bruno Marioni. Tr: Miguel Brindisi

Colo Colo   **0**

Cristian Muñoz - Miguel Riffo, Luis Mena, Ricardo Rojas, Gonzalo Fierro, Moisés Villarroel•, Arturo Sanhueza•, José Salcedo, Carlos Salazar (Eduardo Rubio• 53), Gustavo Biscayzacú (Jhon Castillo 67), Lucas Barrios (Cristóbal Jorquera 53). Tr: Claudio Borghi

---

Pachencho, Maracaibo
28-02-2008, 19:50, 36 215, Haro ECU

Unión At. Maracaibo   **1**
       Díaz [92+]

Juan Henao – Pedro Fernández, Gregory Lancken, Claudio Muñoz, Juan Fuenmayor•, Miguel Mea Vitali, Gabriel Urdaneta, Guillermo Beraza (Jorge Rojas 68), Darío Figueroa, Nicolás Saucedo (Heiber Díaz 55), Armando Maita (Heiber Díaz 75). Tr: Jorge Pellicer

Colo Colo   **3**
   Fierro [49], Biscayzacú [69], Lancken OG [86]

Cristian Muñoz• – Miguel Riffo, Luis Mena, Ricardo Rojas, Moisés Villarroel, Arturo Sanhueza, José Salcedo (Gonzalo Jara 60), Gonzalo Fierro, Cristóbal Jorquera, Lucas Barrios• (Carlos Salazar 70), Eduardo Rubio (Gustavo Biscayzacú• 65). Tr: Claudio Borghi

---

La Bombonera, Buenos Aires
6-03-2008, 21:20, 27 615, Silvera URU

Boca Juniors   **3**
   Palacio 2 [32 81], Palermo [82]

Mauricio Caranta - Jonatan Maidana, Julio Cáceres, Gabriel Paletta, Claudio Morel, Sebastián Battaglia, Fabián Vargas (Jesús Datolo 77), Pablo Ledesma•, Juan Riquelme (Leandro Gracián 82), Rodrigo Palacio (Lucas Castromán 84), Martín Palermo. Tr: Carlos Ischia

Atlas   **0**

Jorge Bava – Diego Colotto•, Luis Robles, Néstor Vidrio, Ricardo Flores, Eduardo Rergis•, Christian Valdez, Juan Medina (Edgar Pacheco 69), Emanuel Centurión• (Oscar Vera 60), Bruno Marioni (Ulises Mendivil 69), Jorge Achucarro•. Tr: Miguel Brindisi

---

Jalisco, Guadalajara
12-03-2008, 20:40, 15 437, Vera ECU

Atlas   **3**
   Flores [40], Achucarro [61], Marioni [66]

Jorge Bava – Diego Colotto, Luis Robles, Jorge Achucarro, Ricardo Jiménez•, Juan Medina, Emanuel Centurión (Edgar Pacheco 81), Gerardo Flores (Oscar Vera 70), Christian Valdez•, Ulises Mendivil (Bruno Marioni 26), Eduardo Rergis. Tr: Miguel Brindisi

Unión At. Maracaibo   **0**

Juan Henao• – Jorge Rojas, Claudio Muñoz, Gregory Lancken, Pedro Fernández•, Miguel Mea Vitali, Victor Villarreal (Armando Maita 61), Darío Figueroa (Nicolás Saucedo 83), Gabriel Urdaneta, Guillermo Beraza, Heiber Díaz (Victor Guaza 67). Tr: Jorge Pellicer

---

Monumental, Santiago
20-03-2008, 21:40, Vázquez URU

Colo Colo   **2**
   Jorquera [3], Biscayzacú [35]

Cristian Muñoz –Luis Mena, Jorge Carrasco, Ricardo Rojas, Gonzalo Fierro•=74, Moisés Villarroel (Gonzalo Jara 86), Arturo Sanhueza, José Salcedo•, Cristóbal Jorquera (Carlos Salazar 69), Lucas Barrios•66, Gustavo Biscayzacú (Rodolfo Moya 78). Tr: Claudio Borghi

Boca Juniors   **0**

Mauricio Caranta - Jonatan Maidana, Gabriel Paletta, Julio Cáceres, Claudio Morel•66, Pablo Ledesma• (Leandro Gracián 64), Sebastián Battaglia, Fabián Vargas• (Jesús Datolo 46), Juan Riquelme (Mauro Boselli 75), Martín Palermo, Rodrigo Palacio. Tr: Carlos Ischia

---

Pachencho, Maracaibo
25-03-2008, 19:50, 36 215, Roldán COL

Unión At. Maracaibo   **1**
       Figueroa [80p]

Juan Henao - Pedro Fernández, Gregory Lancken, Claudio Muñoz, Jorge Rojas, Miguel Mea Vitali (Víctor Villarreal 74), Gabriel Urdaneta•, Guillermo Beraza (Armando Maita 69), Darío Figueroa, Yhonatan Del Valle, Heiber Díaz (Nicolás Saucedo 81). Tr: Jorge Pellicer

Atlas   **1**
       Marioni [56p]

Jorge Bava - Diego Colotto•••66, Hugo Ayala (Néstor Vidrio 69), Omar Flores•, Gerardo Flores, Eduardo Rergis, Luis Robles, Christian Valdez•, Juan Medina•, Emanuel Centurión (Edgar Pacheco 69), Bruno Marioni. Tr: Miguel Brindisi

---

La Bombonera, Buenos Aires
27-03-2008, 21:00, Amarilla PAR

Boca Juniors   **4**
  Palermo [29], Gracián [49], Palacio [65], Cardozo [88]

Mauricio Caranta - Hugo Ibarra, Jonatan Maidana, Julio Cáceres, Luciano Monzón•66, Fabián Vargas (Neri Cardozo 64), Sebastián Battaglia• (Jesús Datolo• (Alvaro Gonzalo 82), Leandro Gracián (Facundo Roncaglia• 68), Rodrigo Palacio, Martín Palermo. Tr: Carlos Ischia

Colo Colo   **2**
   Biscayzacú 2 [25 42], Moya [92+]

Cristian Muñoz - Jorge Carrasco, Luis Mena•, Ricardo Rojas•, Gonzalo Fierro, Moisés Villarroel•, Arturo Sanhueza•, José Salcedo (Carlos Salazar 70), Cristóbal Jorquera (Rodolfo Moya 56), Jhon Castillo (José Cabión 46), Gustavo Biscayzacú. Tr: Claudio Borghi

---

Jalisco, Guadalajara
8-04-2008, 18:30, Ruiz COL

Atlas   **3**
   Flores [21], Marioni 2 [58 76]

Jorge Bava – Omar Flores•, Ricardo Jiménez, Néstor Vidrio•, Gerardo Flores, Eduardo Rergis, Juan Medina, Luis Robles, Emanuel Centurión• (Jorge Hernández 46), Jorge Achucarro (Ulises Mendivil 27) (Christian Valdez• 56), Bruno Marioni•. Tr: Miguel Brindisi

Boca Juniors   **1**
       Battaglia [30]

Mauricio Caranta – Alvaro González•, Julio Cáceres, Claudio Morel, Jonatan Maidana, Sebastián Battaglia•, Fabián Vargas•, Jesús Datolo (Neri Cardozo 73), Leandro Gracián (Cristian Chávez 73), Martín Palermo, Rodrigo Palacio. Tr: Carlos Ischia

---

Monumental, Santiago
10-04-2008, 19:10, 12 252, Ortubé BOL

Colo Colo   **2**
   Biscayzacú [47], Barrios [50]

Cristian Muñoz – Jorge Carrasco, Luis Mena, Ricardo Rojas•, Gonzalo Fierro, Moisés Villarroel, Arturo Sanhueza, José Salcedo, Daniel González (Carlos Salazar 77), Gustavo Biscayzacú, Lucas Barrios (Rodolfo Moya• 56). Tr: Fernando Astengo

Unión At. Maracaibo   **0**

Juan Henao (Tulio Hernández 54) – Pedro Fernández, Claudio Muñoz, Rafael Mea Vitali, Juan Fuenmayor (Victor Villarreal 64), Miguel Mea Vitali, Gabriel Urdaneta•, Jorge Rojas, Darío Figueroa (Nicolás Saucedo 54), Guillermo Beraza•=68, Armando Maita•. Tr: Jorge Pellicer

---

Monumental, Santiago
22-04-2008, 20:10, 16 400, Larrionda URU

Colo Colo   **1**
       Rojas [3]

Cristian Muñoz – Ricardo Rojas, Jorge Carrasco, Gonzalo Jara, Gonzalo Fierro, Arturo Sanhueza•, Luis Mena, José Salcedo (Eduardo Rubio 75), Boris Sagredo, Lucas Barrios, Gustavo Biscayzacú (Rodolfo Moya 81). Tr: Fernando Astengo

Atlas   **1**
       Colotto [65]

Jorge Bava – Jorge Torres, Néstor Vidrio, Diego Colotto, Omar Flores•, Eduardo Rergis, Luis Robles, Jorge Hernández• (Gerardo Flores 46), Juan Medina• (Christian Valdez 81), Bruno Marioni (Emanuel Centurión 84), Ulises Mendivil. Tr: Miguel Brindisi

---

La Bombonera, Buenos Aires
22-04-2008, 21:10, 38 488, Rivera PER

Boca Juniors   **3**
   Paletta [9], Datolo [20], Riquelme [73]

Mauricio Caranta – Alvaro González, Julio Cáceres, Gabriel Paletta (Jonatan Maidana 14), Luciano Monzón, Fabián Vargas (Leandro Gracián 52), Sebastián Battaglia, Jesús Datolo (Neri Cardozo 71), Juan Riquelme, Rodrigo Palacio, Martín Palermo. Tr: Carlos Ischia

Unión At. Maracaibo   **0**

Juan Henao – Gregory Lancken, Claudio Muñoz•, Julio Machado, Juan Fuenmayor, Miguel Mea Vitali, Pedro Fernández, Guillermo Beraza (Darío Figueroa 46), Gabriel Urdaneta, Jorge Rojas (Nicolás Saucedo 83), Armando Maita. Tr: Nelson Carrero

GROUP 4

		Pl	W	D	L	F	A	Pts	BRA	URU	PER	PER
Flamengo	BRA	6	4	1	1	9	4	13		2-0	2-1	2-0
Nacional	URU	6	4	0	2	9	5	12	3-0		3-1	1-0
Cienciano	PER	6	2	1	3	5	9	7	0-3	2-1		1-0
Coronel Bolognesi	PER	6	0	2	4	0	5	2	0-0	0-1	0-0	

Modelo, Tacna
13-02-2008, 18:50, 7756, Reinoso ECU

Coronel Bolognesi 0

Diego Penny – Jaime Linares, Adán Balbín, Juan Gonzales Vigil (Miguel Mostto 83), Renzo Revoredo*, Jorge Vásquez, Miguel Ostersen, Jesús Alvarez, Luis Ramírez (Enio Novoa 89), Junior Ross (Jesús Chávez 71), Eduardo Uribe. Tr: Juan Reynoso

Flamengo 0

Bruno – Léo Moura, Fabio Luciano, Ronaldo Angelim, Jonatas, Juan*, Ibson*, Toró (Kleberson 41), Souza (Marcinho 85), Diego Tardelli* (Obina 77), Jailton. Tr: Joel Santana

---

Inca Garcilaso de la Vega, Cusco
14-02-2008, 16:30, 25 038, Osses CHI

Cienciano 2
Vassallo 2 [54] [67]

Juan Flores – Manuel Marengo, Carlos Solís, Julio Romaña*, César Ccahuantico, Juan Bazalar*, Julio García (Victor Manique 75), Gustavo Vassallo* (Aldo Olcese 75), Masakatsu Sawa* (José Corcuera 90). Roberto Guizasola, Willian Chiroque. Tr: Franco Navarro

Nacional 1
Victorino [88]

Alexis Viera – Pablo Melo*, Mauricio Victorino, Diego Arismendi, Bruno Fornaroli (Juan Pereyra 70), Martín Ligüera* (Nicolás Lodeiro 88), Adrián Romero*43, Pablo Caballero, Gastón Filgueira* (Deivis Barone 30), Oscar Morales*, Richard Morales*. Tr: Gerardo Pelusso

---

Modelo, Tacna
19-02-2008, 17:00, 5790, Gasso MEX

Coronel Bolognesi 0

Diego Penny – Adrián Cortes, Jaime Linares (Enio Novoa 29), Adán Balbín, Juan Gonzales Vigil (Juan Barros 77), Jorge Vásquez*, Miguel Ostersen, Jesús Alvarez, Luis Ramírez, Junior Ross, Eduardo Uribe (Miguel Mostto 46). Tr: Juan Reynoso

Nacional 1
Fornaroli [8]

Alexis Viera – Deivis Barone, Mauricio Victorino, Diego Arismendi, Bruno Fornaroli (Nicolás Bertolo 68), Martín Ligüera* (Juan Pereyra 83), Mathías Cardaccio*, Pablo Caballero, Gastón Filgueira, Richard Morales, Oscar Morales. Tr: Gerardo Pelusso

---

Maracana, Rio de Janeiro
27-02-2008, 21:50, 27 802, Grance PAR

Flamengo 2
Souza [37], Marcinho [88]

Bruno – Léo Moura, Fabio Luciano, Ronaldo Angelim, Juan*, Ibson, Kleberson (Jonatas 84), Cristian, Toró (Obina 66), Souza, Diego Tardelli (Marcinho 66). Tr: Joel Santana

Cienciano 1
Vassallo [45]

Juan Flores* – Manuel Marengo, Carlos Solís, Julio Romaña*, Roberto Guizasola, Juan Bazalar*, Julio García*, César Ortiz, Masakatsu Sawa (José Corcuera 77), Willian Chiroque, Gustavo Vassallo. Tr: Franco Navarro

---

Parque Central, Montevideo
6-03-2008, 19:00, 13 044, Pozo CHI

Nacional 3
Morales 2 [40] [66], Fornaroli [68]

Alexis Viera – Gerardo Acosta, Mauricio Victorino, Deivis Barone, Adrián Romero, Mathías Cardaccio, Oscar Morales, Diego Arismendi* (Martín Ligüera 71), Nicolás Bertolo*, Bruno Fornaroli (Diego Perrone 84), Richard Morales (Juan Pereyra 75). Tr: Gerardo Pelusso

Flamengo 0

Bruno – Léo Moura*•51, Fabio Luciano*, Ronaldo Angelim*, Cristian, Juan, Ibson*, Kleberson (Jailton 52), Souza (Jonatas 69), Diego Tardelli (Marcinho 46), Toró•41.Tr: Joel Santana

---

Inca Garcilaso de la Vega, Cusco
11-03-2008, 16:50, 11 424, Carrillo PER

Cienciano 1
Solís [75]

Juan Flores – Manuel Marengo*, Carlos Solís, Julio Romaña, Juan Bazalar* (César Ccahuantico 81), Julio García (Cristian Guevara* 88), César Ortiz, Masakatsu Sawa* (Natalio Portillo 86), Roberto Guizasola, Gustavo Vassallo, Willian Chiroque. Tr: Franco Navarro

Coronel Bolognesi 0

Diego Penny* – Adrián Cortes*, Jaime Linares (Jesús Chávez 86), Adán Balbín, Enio Novoa, Miguel Mostto*, Renzo Revoredo, Jorge Vásquez, Miguel Ostersen, Luis Ramírez*, Eduardo Uribe (Junior Ross 80). Tr: Juan Reynoso

---

Maracana, Rio de Janeiro
19-03-2008, 21:50, 47 096, Amarilla PAR

Flamengo 2
Marcinho 2 [25] [65]

Bruno – Luizinho, Fabio Luciano, Ronaldo Angelim, Juan, Cristian, Kleberson, Ibson, Renato Augusto, Marcinho (Maximiliano Biancucchi 85), Souza* (Obina 77). Tr: Joel Santana

Nacional 0

Alexis Viera – Gerardo Acosta, Mauricio Victorino, Deivis Barone, Adrián Romero*, Mathías Cardaccio, Oscar Morales, Diego Arismendi*, Nicolás Bertolo (Martín Ligüera 65), Bruno Fornaroli* (Diego Vera 82), Richard Morales. Tr: Gerardo Pelusso

---

Modelo, Tacna
25-03-2008, 21:40, Pacheco PER

Coronel Bolognesi 0

Diego Penny – Rafael Farfán (Jorge Vásquez 77), Jaime Linares, Adán Balbín, Miguel Mostto*, Jesús Chávez (Juan Gonzales Vigil 59), Renzo Revoredo, Miguel Ostersen, Luis Ramírez, Junior Ross, Eduardo Uribe*. Tr: Juan Reynoso

Cienciano 0

Juan Flores – Manuel Marengo, Carlos Solís*, Juan Bazalar, Julio Romaña, Gustavo Vassallo, César Ortiz*, Masakatsu Sawa, Roberto Guizasola*, Willian Chiroque (José Corcuera* 59), Edson Uribe (Aldo Olcese 60). Tr: Franco Navarro

---

Parque Central, Montevideo
3-04-2008, 18:40, Oliveira BRA

Nacional 1
Barone [30]

Alexis Viera – Pablo Caballero, Mauricio Victorino, Deivis Barone, Adrián Romero, Diego Arismendi, Oscar Morales*, Martín Ligüera (Nicolás Lodeiro 89), Nicolás Bertolo (Mathías Cardaccio 60), Bruno Fornaroli* (Deigo Vera 77), Richard Morales. Tr: Gerardo Pelusso

Coronel Bolognesi 0

Alexandro Alvarez – Rafael Farfán, Adrián Cortez, Jaime Linares*, Adán Balbín, Juan Gonzales Vigil, Enio Novoa (Luis Ramírez 63•92+), Miguel Mostto, Mario Soto, Eduardo Uribe (Juan Barros 80), Jesús Alvarez*. Tr: Juan Reynoso

---

Inca Garcilaso de la Vega, Cusco
9-04-2008, 19:50, Pezzotta ARG

Cienciano 0

Juan Flores – Carlos Solís, Manuel Marengo*, Julio Romaña, Roberto Guizasola, Juan Bazalar*••63, César Ortiz*, Edson Uribe (Cristian Guevara 60), Masakatsu Sawa, Natalio Portillo (Jimmy Corrales 71), Gustavo Vassallo*. Tr: Franco Navarro

Flamengo 3
Renato Augusto [57], Toró [75], Juan [93+]

Bruno – Léo Moura, Fabio Luciano*, Ronaldo Angelim, Juan*, Kleberson, Cristian, Ibson (Jailton 92), Toró*, Renato Augusto (Obina 87), Souza (Marcinho 87). Tr: Joel Santana

---

Maracana, Rio de Janeiro
23-04-2008, 19:30, Gamboa BOL

Flamengo 2
Bruno [82], Obina [88]

Bruno – Léo Moura, Fabio Luciano, Ronaldo Angelim, Juan, Jailton, Cristian (Diego Tardelli 46), Kleberson, Toró* (Obina 68), Ibson, Marcinho*, Souza (Diego Gavilán 83). Tr: Joel Santana

Coronel Bolognesi 0

Diego Penny – Renzo Revoredo* (Rafael Farfán 85), Adán Balbín, Miguel Ostersen, Adrián Cortez, Eduardo Uribe*, Jorge Vásquez*, Jaime Linares* (Enio Novoa 62), Jesús Alvarez*, Juan Gonzales Vigil (Miguel Mostto 59), Junior Ross. Tr: Juan Reynoso

---

Parque Central, Montevideo
23-04-2008, 19:30, Chandia CHI

Nacional 3
Ligüera [39], Cardaccio [53], Vera [92+]

Alexis Viera – Mauricio Victorino, Deivis Barone, Pablo Caballero, Adrián Romero, Mathías Cardaccio*, Oscar Morales, Nicolás Bertolo, Martín Ligüera (Diego Arismendi 80), Richard Morales (Deigo Vera 65), Bruno Fornaroli Juan Pereyra 73). Tr: Gerardo Pelusso

Cienciano 1
Guevara [83]

Juan Flores – Manuel Marengo, Carlos Solís, César Ccahuantico (Cristian Guevara 7), Julio Romaña*••63, Gustavo Vassallo, César Ortiz, José Corcuera, Masakatsu Sawa (Natalio Portillo 65), Roberto Guizasola*, Aldo Olcese (Julio García 69). Tr: Franco Navarro

GROUP 5

		Pl	W	D	L	F	A	Pts	ARG	MEX	CHI	PER
River Plate	ARG	6	4	0	2	14	8	12		2-1	2-0	5-0
CF América	MEX	6	3	0	3	10	10	9	4-3		2-1	3-1
Universidad Catolica	CHI	6	3	0	3	6	6	9	1-2	2-0		1-0
Universidad San Martín	PER	6	2	0	4	4	10	6	2-0	1-0	0-1	

Monumental, Lima
13-02-2008, 16:30, 14 641, Gaciba BRA

Universidad San Martín 2
Ovelar [14], Díaz [91+]

Leao Butrón - Jorge Reyes (Bruno Bianchi 45), Jorge Huamán, Orlando Contreras, Guillermo Salas, John Hinostroza•, Edwin Pérez•, Fernando Del Solar, Pedro García (Alexander Sánchez 69), Mario Leguizamón• (José Díaz 67), Roberto Ovelar. Tr: Victor Rivera

River Plate 0

Juan Carrizo - Paulo Ferrari, Gustavo Cabral•, Eduardo Tuzzio, Cristian Villagra•, Leonardo Ponzio, Nicolás Domingo (Radamel García 46), Augusto Fernández (Matías Abelairas 77), Ariel Ortega•, Alexis Sánchez (Mauro Rosales 69), Washington Abreu. Tr: Diego Simeone

Azteca, Mexico City
20-02-2008, 21:10, 40 755, Laverni ARG

CF América 2
Cabañas [38], Higuain [90]

Armando Navarrete – Ismael Rodríguez, José Castro, Oscar Rojas, Diego Cervantes•, Salvador Cabañas, Richard Núñez (Federico Higuain 62), Carlos Infante (Jesús Sánchez• 6), Hernán López• (Juan Mosqueda 76), Germán Villa, Alejandro Argüello. Tr: Rubén Romano

Universidad Católica 1
Botinelli [70]

José Buljubasich – Rodrigo Valenzuela, Marcos González, Facundo Imboden, Eros Pérez, Gary Medel, Jorge Ormeño, Iván Vásquez, Darío Botinelli• (Rodrigo Toloza 82), Héctor Tapia (Francisco Silva 90), José Da Silva (Luis Núñez 56). Tr: Fernando Carvallo

Monumental, Lima
26-02-2008, 20:40, 12 197, Ortubé BOL

Universidad San Martín 0

Leao Butrón – Guillermo Salas, Orlando Contreras, Bruno Bianchi, Jair Céspedes, John Hinostroza•, Edwin Pérez•, Mario Leguizamón (José Díaz 60), Fernando Del Solar (Roberto Silva 71), Roberto Ovelar•, Pedro García (Alexander Sánchez 62).Tr: Víctor Rivera

Universidad Católica 1
Botinelli [29]

José Buljubasich – Rodrigo Valenzuela (Boris González 84), Marcos González, Facundo Imboden, Eros Pérez, Gary Medel•, Jorge Ormeño, Iván Vásquez, Darío Botinelli•, Luis Núñez•, José Da Silva• (Roberto Gutiérrez 74). Tr: Fernando Carvallo

Monumental, Buenos Aires
27-02-2008, 20:30, 22 597, Selman CHI

River Plate 2
García [37], Ortega [92+]

Juan Carrizo - Paulo Ferrari (Alexis Sánchez 46), Gustavo Cabral, Eduardo Tuzzio, Cristian Villagra, Matías Abelairas (Diego Buonanotte 62), Oscar Ahumada, Augusto Fernández, Ariel Ortega, Radamel García•90, Washington Abreu•. Tr: Diego Simeone

CF América 1
Cabañas [14]

Armando Navarrete - José Castro•90, Sebastián Domínguez (Jesús Sánchez 35), Diego Cervantes, Ismael Rodríguez•, Oscar Rojas, Germán Villa•, Juan Mosqueda (Richard Núñez 67), Alejandro Argüello, Hernán López• (Federico Higuain 46), Salvador Cabañas•.Tr: Rubén Romano

San Carlos de Apoquindo, Santiago
12-03-2008, 21:10, 13 654, Fagundes BRA

Universidad Católica 1
Gutiérrez [47]

José Buljubasich – Rodrigo Valenzuela, Marcos González, Facundo Imboden, Eros Pérez•, Gary Medel, Jorge Ormeño, Iván Vásquez, Darío Botinelli• (Rodrigo Toloza 82), José Da Silva (Luis Núñez 75), Roberto Gutiérrez. Tr: Fernando Carvallo

River Plate 2
Abreu [43], Rosales [87]

Juan Carrizo – Gustavo Cabral, Cristian Villagra•, Paulo Ferrari, Eduardo Tuzzio, Augusto Fernández, Ariel Ortega• (Oscar Ahumada 90), Alexis Sánchez (Mauro Rosales 66), Matías Abelairas (Diego Buonanotte• 66), Leonardo Ponzio•, Washington Abreu.Tr: Diego Simeone

Azteca, Mexico City
13-03-2008, 19:30, 28 397, Amarilla PAR

CF América 3
Márquez [39], Iñigo [48], Cabañas [70]

Armando Navarrete – Oscar Rojas•, Diego Cervantes, Richard Núñez (Juan Mosqueda 55), Jesús Sánchez, Rodrigo Iñigo (Salvador Cabañas 67), Hernán López, Alejandro Argüello•, Luis Villegas, Daniel Márquez, José Mosqueda (Carlos Sánchez 55). Tr: Norberto Scoponi

Universidad San Martín 1
Silva [7]

Leao Butrón – Jorge Huamán, Bruno Bianchi•, Orlando Contreras, Guillermo Salas•, Edwin Pérez, Victor Carrillo, Alexander Sánchez (José Díaz 59), Mario Leguizamón (Pedro García 63), Roberto Silva, Roberto Ovelar (Fernando Del Solar 68). Tr: Víctor Rivera

Monumental, Buenos Aires
26-03-2008, 21:20, Torres PAR

River Plate 2
García [1], Abreu [72]

Juan Carrizo – Paulo Ferrari, Gustavo Cabral, Eduardo Tuzzio (Danilo Gerlo 51), Cristian Villagra, Oscar Ahumada (Leonardo Ponzio• 43), Matías Abelairas•, Mauro Rosales, Radamel García (Nicolás Domingo 56), Diego Buonanotte•, Washington Abreu•. Tr: Diego Simeone

Universidad Católica 0

José Buljubasich – Rodrigo Valenzuela, Marcos González•, Facundo Imboden, Eros Pérez, Gary Medel, Jorge Ormeño, Rodrigo Toloza (Luis Núñez 66•90), Darío Botinelli•, José Da Silva, Héctor Tapia (Roberto Gutiérrez 63). Tr: Fernando Carvallo

Monumental, Lima
26-03-2008, 21:40, Soto VEN

Universidad San Martín 1
Leguizamón [36]

Leao Butrón - Jorge Huamán•, Pedro Bonilla, Orlando Contreras, Guillermo Salas•, Mario Leguizamón• (Pedro García 79), John Hinostroza, Edwin Pérez•, José Díaz (Ryan Salazar 93), Alexander Sánchez (Jair Céspedes 85), Roberto Silva. Tr: Víctor Rivera

CF América 0

Francisco Ochoa – Ismael Rodríguez•, José Castro, Oscar Rojas, Diego Cervantes, Sebastián Domínguez, Federico Higuain (Richard Núñez 66), Salvador Cabañas, Juan Mosqueda (Daniel Márquez 84), Jesús Sánchez (Enrique Esqueda 57), Alejandro Argüello. Tr: Rubén Romano

San Carlos de Apoquindo, Santiago
1-04-2008, 21:50, Arias PAR

Universidad Católica 1
Gutiérrez [88]

José Buljubasich – Rodrigo Valenzuela, Marcos González, Facundo Imboden, Eros Pérez, Gary Medel, Jorge Ormeño (Iván Vásquez 28), Rodrigo Toloza, Darío Botinelli• Héctor Tapia (Julio Gutiérrez• 69), José Da Silva. Tr: Fernando Carvallo

Universidad San Martín 0

Leao Butrón – Jorge Huamán, Bruno Bianchi•, Orlando Contreras, Guillermo Salas, José Díaz•36, John Hinostroza•, Edwin Pérez•, Mario Leguizamón (Jair Céspedes 75), Alexander Sánchez• (Josepmir Ballón 82), Roberto Silva. Tr: Víctor Rivera

Azteca, Mexico City
2-04-2008, 21:10, Silvera URU

CF América 4
Iñigo [51], Esqueda [53], Cervantes [61], Cabañas [69]

Francisco Ochoa - Rodrigo Iñigo•, Diego Cervantes, Ismael Rodríguez•, Oscar Rojas•, Germán Villa•, Alejandro Argüello, José Castro•, Juan Mosqueda (Richard Núñez 70), Federico Higuain (Salvador Cabañas 67), Enrique Esqueda (José Mosqueda 83). Tr: Ricardo Romano

River Plate 3
Archubi 2 [6 62], Cervantes OG [55]

Juan Carrizo - Paulo Ferrari (Andrés Rios 86), Nicolás Sánchez, Cristian Nasuti, Cristian Villagra, Leonardo Ponzio•, Matías Abelairas, Rodrigo Archubi• (Nicolás Domingo 75), Radamel García, Alexis Sánchez•, Washington Abreu•. Tr: Diego Simeone

San Carlos de Apoquindo, Santiago
17-04-2008, 20:30, Gaciba BRA

Universidad Católica 2
Medel [52], Botinelli [90]

José Buljubasich – Rodrigo Valenzuela, Marcos González, Facundo Imboden, Eros Pérez, Gary Medel (Nicolás Núñez 83), Iván Vásquez, Darío Botinelli•, Roberto Gutiérrez, José Da Silva. Tr: Fernando Carvallo

CF América 0

Francisco Ochoa• – Ismael Rodríguez•, José Castro, Oscar Rojas, Diego Cervantes, Salvador Cabañas, Juan Mosqueda (Federico Higuain 71), Jesús Sánchez•, Rodrigo Iñigo, Enrique Esqueda (Daniel Márquez 89), Juan Silva•. Tr: Rubén Romano

Monumental, Buenos Aires
17-04-2008, 21:30, 14 110, Ruiz COL

River Plate 5
Abreu 3 [14 51 91+], García [27], Rios [82]

Juan Carrizo – Paulo Ferrari, Gustavo Cabral, Nicolás Sánchez, Cristian Villagra, Leonardo Ponzio (Oscar Ahumada 46), Matías Abelairas (Diego Buonanotte 54), Alexis Sánchez•, Radamel García (Andrés Rios 61), Rodrigo Archubi•, Washington Abreu. Tr: Diego Simeone

Universidad San Martín 0

Leao Butrón – Jorge Huamán, Bruno Bianchi, Orlando Contreras•, Guillermo Salas, Alexander Sánchez, John Hinostroza•, Fernando Del Solar (Ronald Quinteros 46), Edwin Pérez•, Pedro García (Jair Céspedes 68), Roberto Ovelar (Roberto Silva 53). Tr: Víctor Rivera

GROUP 6

		Pl	W	D	L	F	A	Pts	COL	BRA	MEX	BOL
Cúcuta Deportivo	COL	6	3	2	1	7	4	11		0-0	1-0	0-0
Santos	BRA	6	3	1	2	13	6	10	2-1		1-0	7-0
Guadalajara	MEX	6	3	0	3	8	5	9	0-1	3-2		2-0
San José	BOL	6	1	1	4	4	17	4	2-4	2-1	0-3	

General Santander, Cúcuta
13-02-2008, 21:10, 23 269, Rivera PER

Cúcuta Deportivo   **0**

Andrés Castellanos – Elvis Rivas•, Pedro Portocarrero,
Flavio Córdoba, Elvis Gonzalez, Charles Castro,
Nelson Florez, James Castro (Edison Fonseca 66),
Macnelly Torres, Lin Henry (Eudalio Arriaga 55), Diego
Cabrera. Tr: Pedro Sarmiento

Santos   **0**

Fábio Costa – Adriano, Betão, Adailton, Domingos,
Carleto, Marcinho Guerreiro•, Rodrigo Souto, Mauricio
Molina•, Kléber Boas Pereira, Michael Quiñónez
(Wesley 46). Tr: Emerson Leão

Jalisco, Guadalajara
19-02-2008, 20:40, 5250, Intriago ECU

Guadalajara   **2**
Solís [27], Santana [53p]

Luis Michel – José Magallón, Francisco Rodríguez,
Juan Ocampo (Marco Fabián 60), Gonzalo Pineda•,
Edgar Solís (Jesús Padilla 77), Xavier Báez, Alberto
Medina, Ramón Morales, Sergio Santana (Javier
Hernández 73), Omar Bravo. Tr: Efraín Flores

San José   **0**

Daniel Vaca – Enrique Parada, Luis Palacios, Carlos
De Castro, Carlos Alvarenga, Gerson García, Sandro
Coelho Leite•, Rolando Ribera•, Darwin Peña, Alex
Da Rosa• (Martín Palavicini 89), Luis Cerutti.
Tr: Marcos Ferrufino

General Santander, Cúcuta
28-02-2008, 21:40, 12 524, Soto VEN

Cúcuta Deportivo   **0**

Andrés Castellanos – Braynner García, Flavio
Córdoba, Pedro Portocarrero, Fredy Arizala (Matías
Urbano 46), Charles Castro•86, Nelson Florez (James
Castro 8), Macnelly Torres, José Amarilla•••86,
Eudalio Arriaga (Leandro Vargas 63), Diego Cabrera.
Tr: Pedro Sarmiento

San José   **0**

Daniel Vaca• – Enrique Parada, Luis Palacios, Carlos
De Castro•, Carlos Alvarenga, Gerson García, Rolando
Ribera, Sandro Coelho Leite (Percy Pizarro 53), Darwin
Peña•, Alex Da Rosa (Mauricio Saucedo 56), Luis
Cerutti (Martín Palavicini 71). Tr: Marcos Ferrufino

Vila Belmiro, Santos
4-03-2008, 21:50, 7083, Amarilla PAR

Santos   **1**
Molina [22]

Fábio Costa – Adriano, Domingos, Betão•, Carleto,
Marcinho Guerreiro, Rodrigo Souto, Wesley (Michael
Jackson Quiñónez• 61), Mauricio Molina (Anderson
Salles 80), Mariano Tripodi (Tiago Luis• 59), Kléber
Boas Pereira. Tr: Emerson Leão

Guadalajara   **0**

Luis Michel – José Magallón, Héctor Reynoso•,
Francisco Rodríguez, Xavier Báez, Gonzalo Pineda•,
(Julio Nava 60), Edgar Solís (Javier Hernández 71),
Ramón Morales (Marco Fabián 81), Alberto Medina,
Sergio Santana, Omar Bravo. Tr: Efraín Flores

Jalisco, Guadalajara
11-03-2008, 20:30, 9487, Intriago ECU

Guadalajara   **0**

Luis Michel – José Magallón, Héctor Reynoso•,
Francisco Rodríguez, Xavier Báez (Alberto Medina 46),
Gonzalo Pineda (Omar Esparza• 60), Edgar Solís
(Javier Hernández 54), Marco Fabián•92•, Ramón
Morales, Omar Bravo, Sergio Santana. Tr: Efraín Flores

Cúcuta Deportivo   **1**
Urbano [44]

Andrés Castellanos – Braynner García•, Flavio
Córdoba, Pedro Portocarrero, Fredy Arizala, James
Castro, William Zapata, Lin Henry (Danovis
Banguero• 35), Elvis Rivas, Macnelly Torres, Matías
Urbano (Leandro Vargas 79). Tr: Pedro Sarmiento

Jesús Bermúdez, Oruro
19-03-2008, 20:50, Haro ECU

San José   **2**
Cerutti [11], García [62]

Daniel Vaca – Enrique Parada, Luis Palacios, Carlos
De Castro, Carlos Alvarenga, Gerson García (Limber
Morejón 86), Rolando Ribera, Sandro Coelho Leite,
Darwin Peña (Mauricio Saucedo 73), Alex Da Rosa
(Richard Rojas 88), Luis Cerutti. Tr: Marcos Ferrufino

Santos   **1**
Kléber Boas Pereira [23]

Fábio Costa – Adriano, Betão, Domingos•, Kléber,
Marcinho Guerreiro (Anderson Salles• 57) (Mariano
Tripodi 72), Rodrigo Souto, Wesley, Mauricio Molina,
Kléber Boas Pereira•, Sebastián Pinto (Evaldo 46).
Tr: Emerson Leão

General Santander, Cúcuta
27-03-2007, 21:30, Maldonado BOL

Cúcuta Deportivo   **1**
Urbano [62]

Andrés Castellanos – Braynner García•, Flavio
Córdoba, Pedro Portocarrero, Elvis Gonzales, Charles
Castro•, William Zapata•, James Castro, José
Amarilla (Lin Henry 84), Macnelly Torres, Matías
Urbano (Diego Cabrera 79). Tr: Pedro Sarmiento

Guadalajara   **0**

Luis Michel – José Magallón, Héctor Reynoso,
Francisco Rodríguez, Gonzalo Pineda, Sergio Avila
(Omar Arellano 62), Edgar Solís• (Sergio Santana
55), Xavier Báez•, Ramón Morales•, Alberto Medina
(Julio Nava 67), Omar Bravo. Tr: Efraín Flores

Vila Belmiro, Santos
1-04-2008, 20:30, 8340, Prudente URU

Santos   **7**
Domingos [17], Molina 4 [22 32 63 87],
Kléber Boas Pereira [79], Quiñónez [81]

Fábio Costa – Denis (Fabão 68), Domingos, Betão,
Kléber, Marcinho Guerreiro, Rodrigo Souto, Mauricio
Molina, Tabata (Michael Quiñónez 73), Wesley• (Tiago
Luis 64), Kléber Boas Pereira•. Tr: Emerson Leão

San José   **0**

Daniel Vaca – Enrique Parada, Luis Palacios•34,
Carlos De Castro, Carlos Alvarenga, Gerson García,
Rolando Ribera, Sandro Coelho Leite•, Darwin Peña
(Mauricio Saucedo 59), Alex Da Rosa• (Martín
Palavicini 61), Luis Cerutti• (Límber Morejón 83).
Tr: Marcos Ferrufino

Jesús Bermúdez, Oruro
8-04-2008, 17:00, Grance PAR

San José   **2**
Cerutti [46], Parada [77]

Daniel Vaca – Enrique Parada, René Oliva (Fernando
Batistte 44), Carlos De Castro, Carlos Alvarenga,
Gerson García (Darwin Peña 37), Rolando Ribera,
Sandro Coelho Leite•, Alex Da Rosa•, Martín Palavicini
(Mauricio Saucedo 67), Luis Cerutti. Tr: Marcos Ferrufino

Cúcuta Deportivo   **4**
Urbano 3 [35 38 79], Torres [53]

Andrés Castellanos – Braynner García•, Pedro
Portocarrero, Flavio Córdoba, Elvis Gonzales, Charles
Castro, José Amarilla (Roberto Peñaloza 87), James
Castro (Lin Henry 75), William Zapata, Macnelly
Torres•, Matías Urbano (Leandro Vargas 85).
Tr: Pedro Sarmiento

Jalisco, Guadalajara
9-04-2008, 19:50, Buitrago COL

Guadalajara   **3**
Arellano [13], Rodríguez [34], Santana [47]

Luis Michel – Edgar Solís•, José Magallón, Héctor
Reynoso•, Francisco Rodríguez, Gonzalo Pineda•,
Ramón Morales (Patricio Araujo• 70), Sergio Avila,
Alberto Medina, Omar Arellano (Omar Bravo 63),
Sergio Santana (Omar Esparza 69). Tr: Efraín Flores

Santos   **2**
Kléber Boas Pereira [39], Kléber [56]

Fábio Costa – Betão, Fabão, Domingos• (Evaldo• 39),
Denis (Michael Quiñónez 62), Marcinho Guerreiro,
Rodrigo Souto, Mauricio Molina (Tiago Luis 73),
Kléber, Wesley•, Kléber Boas Pereira. Tr: Emerson Leão

Jesús Bermúdez, Oruro
16-04-2008, 20:50, Pozo CHI

San José   **0**

Daniel Vaca• – Enrique Parada, Franklin Herrera
(Gerson García• 46), Luis Palacios, Carlos Alvarenga,
Límber Morejón, Rolando Ribera, Sandro Coelho
Leite•••55, Martín Palavicini (Mauricio Saucedo 67),
Darwin Peña (Luis Cerutti 46), Alex Da Rosa•.
Tr: Marcos Ferrufino

Guadalajara   **3**
Avila 2 [30 43], Pineda [56]

Luis Michel – Francisco Rodríguez, Héctor Reynoso•,
José Magallón• (Arturo Ledezma 66), Xavier Báez,
Gonzalo Pineda, Alberto Medina•, Sergio Avila (Jesús
Padilla 75), Marco Fabián (Julio Nava• 69), Omar
Arellano, Omar Bravo. Tr: Efraín Flores

Vila Belmiro, Santos
16-04-2008, 21:50, 9386, Larrionda URU

Santos   **2**
Kléber Boas Pereira [68], Tripodi [88]

Fábio Costa – Betão, Domingos•74, Fabão, Kléber•,
Marcinho Guerreiro•, Rodrigo Souto, Tabata (Mariano
Tripodi 46), Mauricio Molina, Wesley, Kléber Boas
Pereira.Tr: Emerson Leão

Cúcuta Deportivo   **1**
Henry [22]

Andrés Castellanos – Flavio Córdoba, Pedro Portocarrero,
Braynner García, Elvis Gonzales, Charles Castro
(Eudalio Arriaga 95), Elvis Rivas (Matías Urbano 58),
Lin Henry•74, William Zapata, Macnelly Torres,
Leandro Vargas (James Castro 58).Tr: Pedro Sarmiento

GROUP 7

		Pl	W	D	L	F	A	Pts	BRA	COL	PAR	CHI
São Paulo FC	BRA	6	3	2	1	6	4	11		1-0	1-0	2-1
At. Nacional Medellín	COL	6	2	2	2	8	5	8	1-1		3-0	1-1
Sportivo Luqueño	PAR	6	2	1	3	8	10	7	1-1	1-3		4-1
Audax Italiano	CHI	6	2	1	3	6	9	7	1-0	1-0	1-2	

Monumental, Santiago
19-02-2008, 21:20, 2428, Lopes BRA
Audax Italiano **1**

Mario Villasanti - Boris Rieloff (Mathías Vidangossy 79), Carlos Garrido, Sebastián Rocco, Patricio Gutiérrez•, Marcelo Broli, Braulio Leal, Miguel Romero, Carlos Villanueva•, Fabian Orellana, Renzo Yáñez• (Renato Ramos 71). Tr: Raúl Toro
Sportivo Luqueño **2**
Servín [8], Núñez [71]

Enrique García - Ignacio Paniagua, Rober Servín•, Diego Martínez, Reinaldo Román•, Carlos Mereles•, Víctor Quintana (Luis Núñez 39••90), Derlis Ortiz (Juan Abente 80), Charles Da Silva•, Marcos Lazaga• (Claudio Vargas• 65), Rubén Gigena. Tr: Daniel Lanata

Atanasio Girardot, Medellín
27-02-2008, 19:50, 30 918, Rivera PER
At. Nacional Medellín **1**
Córdoba [8]

David Ospina – Humberto Mendoza, Wálter Moreno, Juan Zúñiga•, Juan Vélez, Diego Toro, Luis Chará, Elkin Murillo, David Córdoba (Marlon Piedrahita 75), Sergio Galván Rey, Carmelo Valencia. Tr: Oscar Quintabani
São Paulo FC **1**
Miranda [32]

Rogério Ceni – André Dias, Miranda•, Jorge Wagner•, Eder Luis, Adriano, Joilson (Eder 73), Hernanes, Borges (Carlos Alberto 90), Richarylson•, Zé Luis. Tr: Murcy Ramalho

Morumbí, São Paulo
5-03-2008, 21:50, 29 047, Pezzotta ARG
São Paulo FC **2**
Adriano 2 [74] [84]

Rogério Ceni – Zé Luis, André Dias, Miranda, Richarylson (Júnior 61), Fábio Santos (Aloisio 70), Hernanes, Eder Luis• (Joilson 87), Jorge Wagner, Borges, Adriano•. Tr: Muricy Ramalho
Audax Italiano **1**
Villanueva [61]

Mario Villasanti – Boris Rieloff, Carlos Garrido•, Sebastián Rocco•••74, Patricio Gutiérrez, Marcelo Broli, Braulio Leal•, Miguel Romero, Carlos Villanueva (Cristián Reynero 73), Renzo Yáñez (Renato Ramos 46), Fabian Orellana. Tr: Raúl Toro

Atanasio Girardot, Medellín
6-03-2008, 21:00, 15 866, Larrionda URU
At. Nacional Medellín **3**
Galván Rey [21], Villagra [43], Valencia [81]

David Ospina – Juan Zúñiga (Marlon Piedrahita 83), Humberto Mendoza, Juan Pérez, Juan Vélez, José Amaya, Diego Toro•, Elkin Murillo (David Córdoba 74), Sergio Galván Rey, Carlos Villagra, León Muñoz (Carmelo Valencia 48). Tr: Oscar Quintabani
Sportivo Luqueño **0**

Enrique García – Celso Esquivel, Rober Servín•, Reinaldo Román, Diego Martínez, Victor Quintana, Sinecio León (Juan Hermosilla 75), Derlis Ortiz, Charles Da Silva•, Marcos Lazaga• (Adriano Duarte 48), Rubén Gigena (Claudio Vargas 53). Tr: Daniel Lanata

Monumental, Santiago
18-03-2008, 21:50, Cabrera URU
Audax Italiano **1**
Orellana [48]

Mario Villasanti – Boris Rieloff, Carlos Garrido•, César Santis, Patricio Gutiérrez, Cristián Reynero, Braulio Leal, Miguel Romero, Carlos Villanueva, Fabian Orellana, Renzo Yáñez• (Oliver Toledo• 78). Tr: Raúl Toro
At. Nacional Medellín **0**

David Ospina – Luis Chará, Juan Pérez, Humberto Mendoza, Juan Vélez, Juan Zúñiga, Juan Amaya, Diego Toro• (Carlos Villagra 58), Elkin Murillo (Marlon Piedrahita 73), Sergio Galván Rey, Carmelo Valencia (Francisco Arrué 78). Tr: Oscar Quintabani

Feliciano Cáceres, Luque
20-03-2008, 18:20, 10 111, Pezzotta ARG
Sportivo Luqueño **1**
Duarte 92+

Enrique García – Ignacio Paniagua, Rober Servín, Reinaldo Román, Diego Martínez, Víctor Quintana• (Juan Romero 71), Luis Núñez, Celso Esquivel (Juan Hermosilla 80), Juan Abente (Adriano Duarte 66), Charles Da Silva, Marcos Lazaga. Tr: Daniel Lanata
São Paulo FC **1**
Aloisio [60]

Rogério Ceni – André Dias, Miranda (Juninho 41), Jorge Wagner, Eder Luis (Carlos Alberto• 85), Adriano, Hernanes, Borges• (Aloisio 70), Richarylson, Eder, Zé Luis•. Tr: Muricy Ramalho

Morumbí, São Paulo
2-04-2008, 21:50, Vázquez URU
São Paulo FC **1**
Adriano 93+

Rogério Ceni – Zé Luis•, André Dias, Miranda•, Richarylson, Hernanes•, Fábio Santos (Dagoberto 66), Eder Luis (Carlos Alberto 72), Jorge Wagner, Borges, Adriano•. Tr: Muricy Ramalho
Sportivo Luqueño **1**

Enrique García• – Ignacio Paniagua, Rober Servín•, Diego Martínez•, Reinaldo Román•, Victor Quintana (Luis Núñez 54), Celso Esquivel, Carlos Mereles•, Claudio Vargas (Bladimiro Duarte 76), Charles Da Silva (Juan Abente 62), Marcos Lazaga. Tr: Daniel Lanata

Atanasio Girardot, Medellín
3-04-2008, 21:20, Vera ECU
At. Nacional Medellín **1**
Villagra [59]

David Ospina – Juan Zúñiga, Humberto Mendoza•, Wálter Moreno, Juan Vélez, Diego Toro, José Amaya•, Francisco Arrué (David Córdoba 74), Fernando Martel (Marlon Piedrahita 66), Sergio Galván Rey, Carlos Villagra. Tr: Oscar Quintabani
Audax Italiano **1**
Orellana [78]

Mario Villasanti – Boris Rieloff• (Oliver Toledo 62), Carlos Garrido•, Sebastián Rocco•, Patricio Gutiérrez, Cristián Reynero, Braulio Leal, Marcelo Broli•, Miguel Romero•, Fabian Orellana, Renzo Yáñez (Nicolás Ignacio 28) (Mathías Vidangossy• 76). Tr: Raúl Toro

Feliciano Cáceres, Luque
10-04-2008, 21:30, 5954, Laverni ARG
Sportivo Luqueño **1**
Lazaga [71]

Bryan López – Ignacio Paniagua•88, Rober Servín, Reinaldo Román, Diego Martínez, Celso Esquivel•, Víctor Quintana (Marcos Lazaga 46), Carlos Mereles•, Claudio Vargas (Luis Núñez 46), Charles Da Silva (Juan Hermosilla 61), Rubén Gigena. Tr: Daniel Lanata
At. Nacional Medellín **3**
Villagra [39], Galván Rey 51p, Córdoba [90]

David Ospina – Juan Zúñiga, Humberto Mendoza•88, Wálter Moreno, Harlod Martínez, Francisco Arrué• (David Córdoba 85), José Amaya, Diego Toro (Luis Chará 82), Fernando Martel (Carlos Díaz 73), Sergio Galván Rey, Carlos Villagra. Tr: Oscar Quintabani

Estadio Nacional, Santiago
10-04-2008, 21:30, 2454, Baldassi ARG
Audax Italiano **1**
Ramos [78]

Mario Villasanti – Boris Rieloff, Carlos Garrido, Sebastián Rocco, Patricio Gutiérrez, Cristián Reynero, Braulio Leal, Miguel Romero (Nicolás Corvetto 78), Marco Medel (Renato Ramos 46), Oliver Toledo (César Santis 90), Fabian Orellana. Tr: Raúl Toro
São Paulo FC **0**

Rogério Ceni – André Dias•, Miranda, Jorge Wagner, Eder Luis (Júnior 63), Adriano, Joilson, Hernanes, Borges (Dagoberto 70), Richarylson, Eder• (Hugo 82). Tr: Muricy Ramalho

Feliciano Cáceres, Luque
23-04-2008, 20:50, Silvera URU
Sportivo Luqueño **4**
Abente 2 2 [28], Gigena [8], Esquivel [44]

Enrique García – Rober Servín•, Celso Esquivel, Reinaldo Román, Diego Martínez, Carlos Mereles, Luis Núñez•, Juan Abente, Juan Hermosilla (Claudio Vargas 65), Charles Da Silva (Víctor Quintana 59), Rubén Gigena (Marcos Lazaga 60). Tr: Julio Gómez
Audax Italiano **1**
Villanueva [55]

Mario Villasanti – Boris Rieloff, Carlos Garrido, Sebastián Rocco•, Patricio Gutiérrez (César Santis• 46), Cristián Reynero, Braulio Leal•, Carlos Villanueva, Nicolás Corvetto (Renzo Yáñez 69), Fabian Orellana, Renato Ramos (Mathías Vidangosst 46). Tr: Raúl Toro

Morumbí, São Paulo
23-04-2008, 21:50, 25 902, Torres PAR
São Paulo FC **1**
Alex Silva [39]

Rogério Ceni –Miranda•, Alex Silva, André Dias (Eder 60), Zé Luis, Richarylson, Hernanes, Eder Luis (Fábio Santos 83), Jorge Wagner, Borges (Dagoberto 64), Adriano. Tr: Muricy Ramalho
At. Nacional Medellín **0**

David Ospina – Juan Zúñiga, Carlos Díaz, Wálter Moreno, Harlod Martínez, José Amaya, Luis Chará•, Juan Ramírez (Juan Vélez 71), David Córdoba (Elkin Murillo 62), Carlos Villagra (Carmelo Valencia 74), Sergio Galván Rey. Tr: Oscar Quintabani

GROUP 8

		Pl	W	D	L	F	A	Pts	BRA	ECU	ARG	PAR
Fluminense	BRA	6	4	1	1	11	3	13		1-0	6-0	2-0
LDU Quito	ECU	6	3	1	2	10	5	10	0-0		6-1	2-0
Arsenal	ARG	6	3	0	3	6	14	9	2-0	0-1		1-0
Libertad	PAR	6	1	0	5	5	10	3	1-2	3-1	1-2	

Casa Blanca, Quito
20-02-2008, 19:50, 12 144, Duarte COL

LDU Quito   0

José Cevallos• - Jairo Campos, Norberto Araujo•, Renán Calle•, Paul Ambrossi (Jaime Kaviedes 46), Enrique Vera, Patricio Urrutia, Luis Bolaños, Damián Manso, Joffre Guerrón• (Christian Suárez 74), Claudio Bieler (Agustín Delgado 68). Tr: Edgardo Bauza

Fluminense   0

Fernando Henrique - Gabriel, Thiago Silva, Luiz Alberto, Ygor•, Junior Cesar, Leandro Amaral (Darío Conca 74), Arouca, Washington, Thiago Neves (Roger• 81), Maurício• (Cícero 46). Tr: Renato Portaluppi

Maracanã, Rio de Janeiro
5-03-2008, 21:50, 32 614, Torres PAR

Fluminense   6
Thiago Neves 14, Dodô 2 25 50, Gabriel 45, Washington 72, Cícero 86

Fernando Henrique – Gabriel, Thiago Silva, Luiz Alberto, Ygor, Junior Cesar (Roger 74), Arouca (Fabinho 74), Washington, Thiago Neves (Cícero 46), Dodô, Darío Conca. Tr: Renato Portaluppi

Arsenal   0
Mario Cuenca• – Darío Espínola, Andrés San Martín (Cristian Pellerano• 18), José Calderón, Leoardo Biagini (Félix Leguizamón 62), Carlos Casteglione, Anibal Matellán, Cristian Díaz•, Jossimar Mosquera, Sebastián Carrera (Alejandro Gómez 62), Javier Yacuzzi. Tr: Gustavo Alfaro

Casa Blanca, Quito
26-03-2008, 17:00, 11 767, Archundia MEX

LDU Quito   6
Urrutia 15, Manso 20, Bolaños 2 29 43, Bieler 65, Obregón 90

José Cevallos – Jairo Campos, Norberto Araujo, Diego Calderón, Paul Ambrossi•, Enrique Vera, Patricio Urrutia, Joffre Guerrón (Alfonso Obregón 78), Luis Bolaños, Damián Manso (Edder Vaca 74), Claudio Bieler (Agustín Delgado 66). Tr: Edgardo Bauza

Arsenal   1
Leguizamón 4

Mario Cuenca - Darío Espínola, Carlos Báez, Anibal Matellán, Cristian Díaz• (Martín Andrizzi 61), Pablo Garnier•, Cristian Pellerano, Carlos Castegliones••72, Javier Yacuzzi, Leoardo Biagini (José Calderón 22), Félix Leguizamón (Sebastián Carrera 75). Tr: Gustavo Alfaro

Julio Grondona, Buenos Aires
9-04-2008, 19:30, Rivera PER

Arsenal   2
Biagini 59, Bottaro 65

Carriel Orcellet - Darío Espínola, Carlos Báez, Cristian Pellerano•, Leoardo Biagini (Alejandro Gómez 87), Alexander Corro•, Pablo Garnier•, Jossimar Mosquera•, Gustavo Toranzo•, Javier Yacuzzi (José Calderón 81), Juan Bottaro (Félix Leguizamón 74). Tr: Gustavo Alfaro

Fluminense   0

Fernando Henrique – Gabriel, Thiago Silva, Luiz Alberto, Junior Cesar, Ygor (David 73), Arouca• (Tartá 62), Maurício, Darío Conca•, Cícero• (Romeu 81), Thiago Neves•73. Tr: Renato Portaluppi

Julio Grondona, Buenos Aires
20-02-2008, 19:40, 1894, Fagundes BRA

Arsenal   1
Leguizamón 79

Mario Cuenca – Cristian Pellerano (Diego Villar• 67), José Calderón•, Félix Leguizamón, Carlos Casteglione•, Javier Gandolfi• (Darío Espínola 39), Anibal Matellán, Cristian Díaz, Jossimar Mosquera, Sebastián Carrera (Alejandro Gómez• 26), Javier Yacuzzi. Tr: Gustavo Alfaro

Libertad   0

Horacio González – Pedro Benítez, Derlis Cardozo, Edgar Balbuena, Omar Pouso•, Edgar Robles•, Vladimir Marín (Hugo Lusardi 76), Roberto Gamarra (Nelson Cuevas 76), Dante López (Nelson Romero 56), Pedro Sarabia•, Sergio Aquino. Tr: Rubén Israel

Julio Grondona, Buenos Aires
12-03-2008, 19:10, 1586, Chandia CHI

Arsenal   1

Mario Cuenca• – Carlos Báez (Cristian Díaz 46), Darío Espínola, Cristian Pellerano, José Calderón, Félix Leguizamón (Leoardo Biagini 62), Alejandro Gómez, Carlos Casteglione, Anibal Matellán•, Jossimar Mosquera•, Javier Yacuzzi (Sebastián Carrera 67). Tr: Gustavo Alfaro

LDU Quito   1
Urrutia 79p

José Cevallos – Jairo Campos, Norberto Araujo, Diego Calderón, Paul Ambrossi, Joffre Guerrón•, William Araujo• (Andrés Arrunategui 87), Patricio Urrutia•, Luis Bolaños (Pedro Larrea 73), Damián Manso (Franklin Salas 82), Claudio Bieler. Tr: Edgardo Bauza

Maracanã, Rio de Janeiro
2-04-2008, 21:50, 33 551, Selman CHI

Fluminense   2
Cícero 30, Thiago Silva 51

Fernando Henrique – Gabriel (Rafael 68), Thiago Silva, Luiz Alberto, Ygor, Junior Cesar•, Arouca, Washington, Thiago Neves (Tartá 82), Cícero (Roger 91), Darío Conca. Tr: Renato Portaluppi

Libertad   0

Horacio González• – Pedro Benítez, Derlis Cardozo, Arnaldo Vera, Edgar Balbuena, Vladimir Marín• (Wilson Pittoni 66), Roberto Gamarra (Omar Pouso• 70), Osvaldo Martínez•, Pedro Sarabia, Sergio Aquino, Victor Cáceres, Nelson Cuevas (Dante López 57). Tr: Rubén Israel

Defensores del Chaco, Asunción
16-04-2008, 20:50, 220, Maldonado BOL

Libertad   1
Cuevas 23

Victor Centurión – Derlis Cardozo•, Arnaldo Vera•, Omar Pouso•76, Edgar Robles, Wilson Pittoni (Osvaldo Martínez• 63), Adalberto Román, Hugo Lusardi (Dante López 63), Juan Olivera, Celso González•, Nelson Cuevas Nelson Romero 73). Tr: Rubén Israel

Arsenal   2
Bottaro 10, Yacuzzi 68

Mario Cuenca• – Darío Espínola (Anibal Matellán 32), Jossimar Mosquera•, Carlos Báez, Gustavo Toranzo, Pablo Garnier (Javier Yacuzzi 46), Carlos Casteglione, Sebastián Carrera, Martín Andrizzi (Alejandro Gómez 61), Leoardo Biagini, Juan Bottaro. Tr: Gustavo Alfaro

Casa Blanca, Quito
4-03-2008, 15:00, 7523, Ruiz COL

LDU Quito   2
Urrutia 71, Guerrón 82

José Cevallos – Jairo Campos, Norberto Araujo, Diego Calderón, Paul Ambrossi (Luis Bolaños 60), Joffre Guerrón, Enrique Vera•••44, Patricio Urrutia, Damián Manso (William Araujo 73), Agustín Delgado (Franklin Salas 60), Claudio Bieler. Tr: Edgardo Bauza

Libertad   0

Horacio González – Celso González, Pedro Sarabia, Pedro Benítez, Derlis Cardozo, Sergio Aquino•(Dante López 79), Victor Cáceres•, Edgar Robles, Vladimir Marín (Roberto Gamarra 72), Osvaldo Martínez (Omar Pouso• 72), Juan Samudio. Tr: Rubén Israel

Defensores del Chaco, Asunción
19-03-2008, 18:30, Baldassi ARG

Libertad   1
Samudio 30

Horacio González – Pedro Benítez, Derlis Cardozo, Edgar Balbuena• (Vladimir Marín 53), Omar Pouso, Edgar Robles•, Osvaldo Martínez, Pedro Sarabia, Sergio Aquino, Juan Samudio (Roberto Gamarra 67), Juan Olivera (Nelson Cuevas 61). Tr: Rubén Israel

Fluminense   2
Washington 2 40 50

Fernando Henrique – Gabriel•, Thiago Silva, Luiz Alberto, Ygor, Junior Cesar (Roger 80), Arouca (Maurício 67), Washington, Thiago Neves (Tartá 74), Cícero, Darío Conca•. Tr: Renato Portaluppi

Defensores del Chaco, Asunción
8-04-2008, 21:50, Larrionda URU

Libertad   3
López 10, Olivera 14, Cuevas 65

Victor Centurión - Celso González, Pedro Benítez, Adalberto Román, Arnaldo Vera, Wilson Pittoni, Sergio Aquino (Victor Cáceres 46), Edgar Robles, Hugo Lusardi (Vladimir Marín 66), Dante López, Juan Olivera (Nelson Cuevas 46). Tr: Rubén Israel

LDU Quito   1
Obregón 65

Daniel Viteri - Andrés Arrunategui•, Renán Calle, Byron Camacho•, Paul Ambrossi, Pedro Larrea (Christian Suárez 57), William Araujo, Alfonso Obregón, Edder Vaca, Claudio Bieler (Enrique Vera 57), Franklin Salas (Luis Bolaños 68). Tr: Edgardo Bauza

Maracanã, Rio de Janeiro
17-04-2008, 19:10, 19 249, Silvera URU

Fluminense   1
Cícero 30

Fernando Henrique – Gabriel•, Thiago Silva•, Luiz Alberto, Junior Cesar, Ygor, Arouca, David (Maurício 66), Darío Conca (Roger 92), Tartá (Romeu 77), Cícero. Tr: Renato Portaluppi

LDU Quito   0

Daniel Viteri – Byron Camacho•, Renán Calle, Diego Calderón, Paul Ambrossi, Pedro Larrea (Jairo Campos 71), Alfonso Obregón•, William Araujo, Christian Suárez (Joffre Guerrón 64), Edder Vaca• (Franklin Salas 73), Agustín Delgado. Tr: Edgardo Bauza

ROUND OF SIXTEEN

Casa Blanca, Quito
29-04-2008, 20:30, 17 450, Gaciba BRA

LDU Quito   **2**
Guerrón [63], Manso [77]

José Cevallos - Jairo Campos, Norberto Araujo, Paul Ambrosi•, Joffre Guerrón - Patricio Urrutia, Enrique Vera (William Araujo 91+), Luís Bolaños, Diego Calderón - Damián Manso•, Claudio Bieler (Agustín Delgado 68). Tr: Edgardo Bauza

Estudiantes LP   **0**

Mariano Andújar - Marcos Angeleri, Leandro Desábato•, José Basanta - Leandro Benítez•, Edgar González•, Juan Verón, Juan Díaz•••89 - Pablo Lugüercio (Pablo Piatti 65), Leandro Lázzaro (Ezequiel Maggiolo 83), Diego Galván (Iván Moreno y Fabianesi 73). Tr: Roberto Sensini

Ciudad de La Plata, La Plata
6-05-2008, 21:00, Ruiz COL

Estudiantes LP   **2**
Alayes [46], Maggiolo [66]

Mariano Andújar - Marcos Angeleri, Agustín Alayes, Leandro Desábato•, José Basanta (Enzo Pérez 46•90) - Leandro Benítez•, Juan Verón, Diego Galván (Ezequiel Maggiolo 62) - Juan Salgueiro, Pablo Piatti (Pablo Lugüercio 77), Leandro Lázzaro•. Tr: Roberto Sensini

LDU Quito   **1**
Bolaños [25]

José Cevallos• - Paul Ambrosi, Jairo Campos•, Norberto Araujo, Damián Manso• (Byron Camacho• 77) - Joffre Guerrón•, Patricio Urrutia•, Enrique Vera, Luís Bolaños (William Araujo 69), Diego Calderón (Renan Calle• 16) - Claudio Bieler. Tr: Edgardo Bauza

Nuevo Gasómetro, Buenos Aires
30-04-2008, 19:45, 25 337, Baldassi ARG

San Lorenzo   **2**
Silvera [27], González [87p]

Agustín Orión - Gastón Aguirre, Diego Placente•, Sebastián Méndez - Andrés D'Alessandro, Adrián González, Juan Torres, Wálter Acevedo (Santiago Hirsig 70), Diego Rivero• (Cristian Tula 90) - Gonzalo Bergessio, Néstor Silvera• (Bernardo Romeo 46). Tr: Ramón Díaz

River Plate   **1**
García [30]

Juan Carrizo - Paulo Ferrari, Gustavo Cabral, Cristian Villagra, Eduardo Tuzzio• - Oscar Ahumada, Augusto Archubi (Diego Buonanotte 62), Augusto Fernández (Alexis Sánchez 75), Matías Abelairas• - Sebastián Abreu (Ariel Ortega 81), Radamel García. Tr: Diego Simeone

Monumental, Buenos Aires
8-05-2008, 20:30, 49 983, Pezzotta ARG

River Plate   **2**
Abelairas [12], Abreu [62p]

Juan Carrizo• - Paulo Ferrari, Gustavo Cabral, Cristian Villagra•, Eduardo Tuzzio•90 - Oscar Ahumada•, Augusto Fernández• (Mauro Rosales• 64), Diego Buonanotte (Alexis Sánchez• 73), Matías Abelairas - Sebastián Abreu•, Radamel García•. Tr: Diego Simeone

San Lorenzo   **2**
Bergessio [2 69 72]

Agustín Orión• - Jonathan Bottinelli•59, Diego Placente, Sebastián Méndez (Gastón Aguirre 46) - Andrés D'Alessandro•, Adrián González, Juan Torres, Wálter Acevedo• (Pablo Alvarado 64), Diego Rivero•••42 - Gonzalo Bergessio•, Néstor Silvera (Santiago Hirsig 78). Tr: Ramón Díaz

Vila Belmiro, Santos
1-05-2008, 20:45, 17 282, Rodríguez MEX

Santos   **2**
Lima [18], Molina [71]

Fábio Costa - Kléber, Marcelo, Betão, Fabão - Maurício Molina• (Tabata 78), Marcinho Guerreiro (Adriano 64), Rodrigo Souto• - Lima (Mariano Tripodi 88), Kléber Boas Pereira•, Wesley•73. Tr: Emerson Leao

Cúcuta Deportivo   **0**

Leandro Castellanos - Pedro Portocarrero, Flavio Córdoba, Elvis González, Braynner García (Diego Cabrera 77) - Macnelly Torres, Charles Castro, William Zapata, José Amarilla (Mauricio Romero 89), James Castro (Lionard Pajoy 65) - Matías Urbano. Tr: Pedro Sarmiento

General Santander, Cúcuta
8-05-2008, 21:15, Amarilla PAR

Cúcuta Deportivo   **0**

Leandro Castellanos - Pedro Portocarrero, Flavio Córdoba, Elvis González, Elvis Rivas (Eudalio Arriaga 68) - Macnelly Torres, Charles Castro•, José Amarilla, James Castro (Lin Henry 74) - Diego Cabrera, Matías Urbano. Tr: Pedro Sarmiento

Santos   **2**
Kléber Boas Pereira [40], Lima [53]

Fábio Costa - Kléber, Marcelo, Betao, Fabao - Maurício Molina (Michael Quiñónez 68), Marcinho Guerreiro, Rodrigo Souto (Anderson Salles• 80) - Adriano•, Lima (Mariano Tripodi 74), Kleber. Tr: Emerson Leao

Azteca, Mexico City
30-04-2008, 17:45, Chandia CHI

CF América   **2**
Cervantes [45], Esqueda [72]

Francisco Ochoa - José Castro, Ismael Rodríguez, Oscar Rojas, Diego Cervantes, Sebastián Domínguez - Germán Villa•, Juan Mosqueda (Federico Higuaín 46), Juan Carlos Silva (Richard Núñez 81) - Salvador Cabañas, Enrique Esqueda•. Tr: Rubén Romano

Flamengo   **4**
Marcinho 2 [44 70], Diego Tardelli [89], Léo Moura [90]

Bruno• - Ronaldo Angelim, Juan (Léo Moura 46), Luizinho, Fabio Luciano• - Marcinho, Jailton•, Cristian (Diego Tardelli 80), Kleberson - Souza (Obina 46), Ibson. Tr: Joel Santana

Maracana, Río de Janeiro
7-05-2008, 21:50, 47 115, Intriago ECU

Flamengo   **0**

Bruno - Ronaldo Angelim, Léo Moura, Juan•84, Leonardo• - Toró, Marcinho•, Jailton (Renato Augusto 79), Kleberson (Obina 46) - Souza (Diego Tardelli 65), Ibson. Tr: Joel Santana

CF América   **3**
Cabañas 2 [20 77], Esqueda [38]

Francisco Ochoa - José Castro, Ismael Rodríguez•, Oscar Rojas•, Carlos Sanchez, Sebastián Domínguez - Germán Villa•, Alejandro Argüello (Juan Mosqueda 76), Juan Carlos Silva - Salvador Cabañas (Federico Higuaín 91+), Enrique Esqueda• (Rodrigo Iñigo 79). Tr: Rubén Romano

Mineirão, Belo Horizonte
7-05-2008, 19:10, 61 471, Chandia CHI

Cruzeiro   **1**
Wagner [56]

Fábio - Giovanny Espinoza, Marquinhos Paraná, Jonathan (Apodi 60), Thiago Heleno - Wagner, Fabrício, Ramires•••82, Charles (Henrique 71) - Guilherme (Marcinho• 46), Marcelo Martins Moreno. Tr: Adilson Batista

Boca Juniors   **2**
Palacio [36], Palermo [44]

Mauricio Caranta• - Julio Cáceres, Claudio Rodríguez, Jonathan Maidana•, Luciano Monzón• - Juan Riquelme, Sebastián Battaglia, Fabián Vargas• (Pablo Ledesma 71), Jesús Dátolo (Alvaro González 87) - Martín Palermo (Mauro Boselli 82), Rodrigo Palacio. Tr: Carlos Ischia

Néstor Díaz Pérez, Buenos Aires
29-04-2008, 20:10, 6104, Rivera PER

Lanús   **0**

Carlos Bossio - Maximiliano Velázquez (Nelson Benítez 48), Rodolfo Graieb, Carlos Quintana, Emir Faccioli - Diego Valeri, Matías Fritzler•, Agustín Pelletieri, Sebastián Blanco (Santiago Biglieri 71) - José Sand, Nicolás Ramírez (Germán Cano 59). Tr: Ramón Cabrero

Atlas   **1**
Marioni [37]

Jorge Bava• - Diego Colotto, Jorge Torres, Gerardo Flores (Jorge Hernández 59), Néstor Vidrio• - Omar Flores•, Eduardo Rergis, Juan Medina (Emanuel Centurión 72), Luis Robles - Ulises Mendivil (Danilo Gomes 53), Bruno Marioni•. Tr: Miguel Brindisi

La Bombonera, Buenos Aires
30-04-2008, 17:40, 35 137, Larrionda URU

Boca Juniors   **2**
Riquelme [6], Datolo [65]

Mauricio Caranta - Julio Cáceres, Alvaro González, Jonathan Maidana, Luciano Monzón - Juan Riquelme, Sebastián Battaglia, Fabián Vargas• (Pablo Ledesma 82), Jesús Dátolo (Christian Chávez 82) - Martín Palermo, Rodrigo Palacio. Tr: Carlos Ischia

Cruzeiro   **1**
Fabricio [78]

Fábio - Giovanny Espinoza, Marquinhos Paraná, Wagner• (Marcinho 74), Henrique• - Fabrício,Thiago Heleno, Ramires, Charles - Guilherme (Jonathan• 60), Marcelo Martins Moreno. Tr: Adilson Batista

Jalisco, Guadalajara
6-05-2008, 21:30, Torres PAR

Atlas   **2**
Marioni [29], Mendivil [78]

Jorge Bava - Omar Flores, Luis Robles•, Diego Colotto, Jorge Torres• - Gerardo Flores (Jorge Hernández 55), Néstor Vidrio, Eduardo Rergis, Juan Medina (Ricardo Giménez 80) - Ulises Mendivil• (Danilo Gomes 79), Bruno Marioni. Tr: Miguel Brindisi

Lanús   **2**
Sand [54], Acosta [90]

Carlos Bossio - Santiago Hoyos•, Maximiliano Velázquez (Adrián Peralta 74), Rodolfo Graieb, Carlos Quintana• - Diego Valeri, Matías Fritzler, Agustín Pelletieri•, Sebastián Blanco (Santiago Biglieri 70) - José Sand, Lautaro Acosta•. Tr: Ramón Cabrero

Parque Central, Montevideo
30-04-2008,22:00, Selman CHI

Nacional	0

Washington Viera - Adrián Romero•, Deivis Barone, Mauricio Victorino, Pablo Caballero• - Oscar Morales, Diego Arismendi, Mathías Cardaccio•, Martín Ligüera (Diego Vera 73) - Richard Morales (Nicolás Bertolo 66), Bruno Fornaroli. Tr: Gerardo Pelusso

São Paulo FC	0

Rogério Ceni - Zé Luis (Fábio Santos 46), Miranda, Eder, Alex Silva - Hernanes, Richarlyson•, Jorge Wagner• (Hugo 66), Éder Luís - Adriano, Borges. Tr: Muricy Ramalho

Morumbí, São Paulo
7-05-2008, 21:50, 42 050, Baldassi ARG

São Paulo FC	2
	Adriano [37], Dagoberto [88]

Rogério Ceni - Eder, Alex Silva•, Zé Luis•, Hernanes - Richarlyson, Hugo (Júnior 90), Miranda - Adriano, Borges (Fábio Santos 80), Éder Luís (Dagoberto 61). Tr: Muricy Ramalho

Nacional	0

Washington Viera - Adrián Romero, Deivis Barone, Diego Arismendi, Mauricio Victorino• - Pablo Caballero•••46, Oscar Morales, Nicolás Bertolo, Mathías Cardaccio (Martín Ligüera 70) - Richard Morales• (Diego Vera 70), Bruno Fornaroli. Tr: Gerardo Pelusso

Atanasio Girardot, Medellín
30-04-2008, 20:00, Vázquez URU

At. Nacional Medellín	1
	Arrué [53]

David Ospina•18 - Humberto Mendoza, Juan Zúñiga, Wálter Moreno• - Francisco Arrué•, José Amaya, León Muñoz (Sergio Galván Rey 46), Harold Martínez•, David Córdoba (Julián Barahona 20) - Carlos Villagra (Fernado Martel 66), Juan Vélez. Tr: Oscar Quintabani

Fluminense	2
	Thiago Neves 22p, Conca [72]

Fernando Henrique• - Thiago Silva (Roger 55), Luiz Alberto, Junior César - Arouca•, Ygor•, Gabriel, Darío Conca (Dodô 77) - Cícero•, Thiago Neves (Maurício 62), Washington•. Tr: Renato Portaluppi

Maracanã, Rio de Janeiro
6-05-2008, 18:30, 31 700, Rivera PER

Fluminense	1
	Roger [53]

Fernando Henrique - Roger, Luiz Alberto, Junior César - Ygor, Gabriel (Carlinhos• 82), Darío Conca - Cícero, Thiago Neves (Maurício 66), Washington (Tartá 72), Dodô. Tr: Renato Portaluppi

At. Nacional Medellín	0

Julián Barahona - Humberto Mendoza, Juan Zúñiga (David Córdoba 78), Walter Moreno•, Juan Vélez - Fernando Martel• (Elkin Murillo 62), Francisco Arrué, José Amaya•, León Muñoz, Harold Martínez (Diego Toro 79) - Sergio Galvan Rey. Tr: Oscar Quintabani

QUARTER-FINALS

Nuevo Gasómetro, Buenos Aires
15-05-2008, 19:00, Simon BRA

San Lorenzo	1
	González [38]

Agustín Orión – Hernán Gonzalez, Cristian Tula, Gastón Aguirre, Diego Placente• (Juan Menseguez 64), Andrés D'Alessandro•, Juan Torres•, Wálter Acevedo• (Pablo Alvarado 64), Santiago Hersig• (Germán Voboril 38), Gonzalo Bergessio•, Néstor Silvera. Tr: Ramón Díaz

LDU Quito	1
	Bieler [36]

José Cevallos• – Jairo Campos, Norberto Araujo, Renán Calle, Paul Ambrossi•, Joffre Guerrón (Alfonso Obregón 93), Enrique Vera•, Patricio Urrutia, Luis Boaños (William Araujo 79), Damián Manso (Christian Suárez 86), Claudio Bieler•. Tr: Edgardo Bauza

Casa Blanca, Quito
22-05-2008, 17:20, Rodríguez MEX

LDU Quito	1 5p
	Manso [27]

José Cevallos - Renán Calle, Jairo Campos, Norberto Araujo, Paul Ambrossi, Enrique Vera•, Patricio Urrutia, Joffre Guerrón•, Luis Bolaños• (Agustín Delgado 73), Damián Manso• (Edder Vaca 92), Claudio Bieler. Tr: Edgardo Bauza

San Lorenzo	1 3p
	Bergessio [47]

Agustín Orión• - Hernán Gonzalez, Cristian Tula, Gastón Aguirre, Diego Placente•, Diego Rivero (Pablo Alvarado 67), Santiago Hersig (Nicolás Bianchi Arce 82), Juan Torres•30, Andrés D'Alessandro, Gonzalo Bergessio, Bernardo Romeo (Román Torres• 51). Tr: Ramón Díaz

Azteca, Mexico City
15-05-2008, 19:20, Baldassi ARG

CF América	2
	Cabañas 2 [25] [62]

Francisco Ochoa - Ismael Rodríguez, Jose Castro, Óscar Rojas, Sebastián Domínguez, Salvador Cabañas, Carlos Sánchez (Rodrigo Iñigo 68), Alejandro Argüello (Jesús Sánchez 90), Enrique Esqueda (Juan Mosqueda 86), Juan Silva, Germán Villa. Tr: Juan Luna

Santos	0

Fábio Costa - Marcelo, Kléber, Betão, Rodrigo Souto, Fabão•, Marcinho Guerreiro (Adriano 80), Lima, Mauricio Molina (Tabata 46), Kléber Boas Pereira, Wesley (Mariano Trípodi 65). Tr: Emerson Leão

Vila Belmiro, Santos
22-05-2008, 21:50, Larrionda URU, 19 539

Santos	1
	Kléber Boas Pereira [62]

Fábio Costa – Betão (Michael Jackson Quiñónez 61), Marcelo, Fabão, Kléber, Marcinho Guerreiro, Rodrigo Souto, Mauricio Molina, Wesley (Mariano Trípodi 46), Lima, Kléber Boas Pereira. Tr: Emerson Leão

CF América	0

Francisco Ochoa - Jose Castro, Carlos Sánchez, Sebastián Domínguez, Ismael Rodríguez (Rodrigo Iñigo 84), Óscar Rojas, Germán Villa•, Alejandro Argüello (Jesús Sánchez 72), Juan Silva•, Salvador Cabañas•, Enrique Esqueda (Juan Mosqueda 80). Tr: Juan Luna

La Bombonera, Buenos Aires
14-05-2008, 19:20, Roldán COL

Boca Juniors	2
	Ayala OG [36], Cáceres [75]

Mauricio Caranta – Jonatan Maidana (Álvaro González 60), Julio Cáceres•, Claudio Morel, Luciano Monzón, Fabián Vargas, Sebastián Battaglia•, Jesús Datolo, Juan Riquelme, Rodrigo Palacio, Martín Palermo. Tr: Carlos Ischia

Atlas	2
	Omar Flores [5], Ayala [36]

Jorge Bava – Hugo Ayala•, Diego Colotto, Omar Flores, Jorge Torres•, Juan Medina, Christian Valdez•, Luis Robles (Gerado Flores 50), Eduardo Rergis (Ricardo Jiménez 74), Ulises Mendivil, Bruno Marioni (Jorge Hernández 90). Tr: Miguel Brindisi

Jalisco, Guadalajara
21-05-2008, 17:20, Selman CHI

Atlas	0

Jorge Bava•30 – Omar Flores, Diego Colotto•, Gerado Flores (Emanuel Centurión 46), Jorge Torres, Juan Medina, Christian Valdez•, Luis Robles (Gomes Danilo 34), Eduardo Rergis (Pedro Hernández 50), Ulises Mendivil, Bruno Marioni•. Tr: Miguel Brindisi

Boca Juniors	3
	Palermo 3 [20] [34] [38]

Pablo Migliore – Jonatan Maidana, Julio Cáceres, Gabriel Paletta• (Luciano Monzón 59), Claudio Morel, Cristian Chávez (Fabián Vargas 62), Sebastián Battaglia•, Jesús Datolo• (Pablo Ledesma 71), Juan Riquelme, Rodrigo Palacio, Martín Palermo. Tr: Carlos Ischia

Morumbí, São Paulo
14-05-2008, 21:50, 61 593, Ruiz COL

São Paulo FC 1
Adriano [19]

Rodério Ceni – Zé Luis, Miranda, Alex Silva, Jancarlos•, Fábio Santos, Hernanes•, Hugo, Richarylson, Dagoberto• (Aloisio 77), Adriano. Tr: Muricy Ramalho

Fluminense 0

Fernando Henrique – Ygor, Luiz Alberto, Roger•, Gabriel, Arouca, Cícero, Thiago Neves• (Darío Conca 60), Junior Cesar, Dodô, Washington. Tr: Renato Portaluppi

Maracanã, Rio de Janeiro
21-05-2008, 21:50, 68 191, Amarilla PAR

Fluminense 3
Washington 2 [11] [91]+, Dodô [71]

Fernando Henrique – Gabriel (Alan 88), Thiago Silva, Luiz Alberto•, Junior Cesar, Ygor (Maurício 81), Arouca (Dodô 54), Cícero, Darío Conca, Thiago Neves, Washington. Tr: Renato Portaluppi

São Paulo FC 1
Adriano [70]

Rodério Ceni – Jancarlos (Joilson 46•••84), Alex Silva, Miranda, Richarylson, Zé Luis, Fábio Santos, Hernanes, Hugo (Jorge Wagner 78), Dagoberto• (Aloisio 57), Adriano. Tr: Muricy Ramalho

SEMI-FINALS

Azteca, Mexico City
27-05-2008, 20:10, Vázquez URU

CF América 1
Esqueda [72]

Francisco Ochoa – José Castro, Carlos Sánchez, Sebastián Domínguez•74, Rodrigo Iñigo• (Hernán López 67), Óscar Rojas, Germán Villa•, Alejandro Argüello (Federico Higuaín 46), Juan Silva, Enrique Esqueda (Richard Núñez 85), Salvador Cabañas. Tr: Juan Luna

LDU Quito 2
Bolaños [62]

José Cevallos• – Renán Calle•, Norberto Araujo, Jairo Campos, Paul Ambrossi, Joffre Guerrón (Byron Camacho 92+), Patricio Urrutia, Enrique Vera, Luis Bolaños•74, Damián Manso• (William Araujo• 85), Claudio Bieler• (Agustín Delgado 53). Tr: Edgardo Bauza

Casa Blanca, Quito
3-06-2008, 20:10, 28 336, Pozo CHI

LDU Quito 0

José Cevallos – Jairo Campos, Renán Calle•, Norberto Araujo, Paul Ambrossi, Enrique Vera•, Patricio Urrutia, Joffre Guerrón, Damián Manso (William Araujo 80), Franklin Salas• (Edder Vaca 74), Claudio Bieler (Agustín Delgado 78). Tr: Edgardo Bauza

CF América 0

Francisco Ochoa – Ismael Rodríguez, José Castro, Óscar Rojas, Salvador Cabañas, Jesús Sánchez•, Hernán López (Alejandro Argüello 65•90), Germán Villa•, Carlos Sánchez•••60, Enrique Esqueda (Federico Higuaín 71), Juan Silva• (Juan Mosqueda 74). Tr: Juan Luna

El Cilindro, Buenos Aires
28-05-2008, 21:50, Silvera URU

Boca Juniors 2
Riquelme 2 [12] [65]

Pablo Migliore – Jonatan Maidana (Hugo Ibarra 61), Julio Cáceres•, Gabriel Paletta, Claudio Morel, Cristian Chávez• (Neri Cardozo 66), Sebastián Battaglia (Fabián Vargas 76), Jesús Datolo, Juan Riquelme•, Rodrigo Palacio, Martín Palermo. Tr: Carlos Ischia

Fluminense 2
Thiago Silva [16], Thiago Neves [77]

Fernando Henrique• – Gabriel, Thiago Silva, Luiz Alberto, Junior Cesar•, Maurício (Romeu• 63), Arouca•, Cícero, Thiago Neves (Roger 88), Darío Conca, Washington (Dodô 79). Tr: Renato Portaluppi

Maracanã, Rio de Janeiro
4-06-2008, 21:50, 78 856, Torres PAR

Fluminense 3
Washington [63], Ibarra OG [71], Dodô [93]+

Fernando Henrique• – Gabriel, Thiago Silva, Luiz Alberto, Junior Cesar, Ygor (Dodô• 61), Arouca•, Cícero, Darío Conca, Thiago Neves (Maurício 79), Washington• (Roger 92). Tr: Renato Portaluppi

Boca Juniors 1
Palermo [58]

Pablo Migliore – Hugo Ibarra, Julio Cáceres, Gabriel Paletta, Claudio Morel (Mauro Boselli 79), Fabián Vargas (Pablo Ledesma 46), Sebastián Battaglia, Jesús Datolo, Juan Riquelme•, Rodrigo Palacio, Martín Palermo•. Tr: Carlos Ischia

COPA LIBERTADORES FINAL 1ST LEG
Casa Blanca, Quito
25-06-2008, 19:50, 26 662, Chandia CHI

LDU QUITO 4 2 FLUMINENSE

Bieler [2], Guerrón [29], Campos [34], Urrutia [45] — Conca [12], Thiago Neves [52]

LDU QUITO			FLUMINENSE	
1	José Cevallos		Fernando Henrique	1
3	Renán Calle		Gabriel	2
2	Norberto Araujo		Thiago Silva	3
23	Jairo Campos		Luiz Alberto	4
19	Joffre Guerrón		Junior Cesar	6
20	Enrique Vera		Ygor	5
8	Patricio Urrutia	67	Arouca	8
4	Paul Ambrossi		Cícero	17
7	Luis Bolaños		Darío Conca	18
21	Damián Manso	74	90	Thiago Neves	10
16	Claudio Bieler	82	72	Washington	9
	Tr: Edgardo Bauza		Tr: Renato Portaluppi	
9	Agustín Delgado	82	72	Dodô	11
15	William Araujo	74	90	Diego	13
			67	Roger	15

COPA LIBERTADORES FINAL 2ND LEG
Maracanã, Rio de Janeiro
2-07-2008, 21:50, 78 918, Baldassi ARG

FLUMINENSE 3 1 LDU QUITO

Thiago Neves 3 [12] [28] [58] 1p 3p — Bolaños [6]

FLUMINENSE			LDU QUITO	
1	Fernando Henrique		José Cevallos	1
2	Gabriel	105	Jairo Campos	23
3	Thiago Silva		Renán Calle	3
4	Luiz Alberto	120	Norberto Araujo	2
6	Junior Cesar		Paul Ambrossi	4
5	Ygor	46	Joffre Guerrón	19
8	Arouca	110	Enrique Vera	20
17	Cícero		Patricio Urrutia	8
18	Darío Conca	105	Luis Bolaños	7
10	Thiago Neves	88	Damián Manso	21
9	Washington		Claudio Bieler	16
11	Dodô	46	105	Franklin Salas	11
13	Roger	110	88	William Araujo	15
15	Maurício	105			

COPA NISSAN SUDAMERICANA 2007

Preliminary Round				First Round				Round of 16		
				Arsenal *	ARG	1	3			
				San Lorenzo	ARG	1	0			
								Arsenal		3 1
								Goiás *		2 1
				Cruzeiro	BRA	0	1			
				Goiás *	BRA	2	0			
				DC United	USA	bye				
								DC United *		2 0
								Guadalajara		1 1
				Guadalajara	MEX	Bye				
Defensor Sporting *	URU	2	2							
Libertad	PAR	1	2	Defensor Sporting	URU	1	3			
Danubio	URU	1 1	1p	Tacuary *	PAR	1	0			
Tacuary *	PAR	1 1	4p					Defensor Sporting *		3 0
Olmedo *	ECU	1	2					El Nacional		0 2
Zamora	VEN	0	1	Olmedo	ECU	0	0			
Carabobo *	VEN	0	0	El Nacional *	ECU	2	1			
El Nacional	ECU	1	4							
				Botafogo *	BRA	3	2			
				Corinthians	BRA	1	1			
								Botafogo *		1 2
								River Plate		0 4
				River Plate	ARG	Bye				
Millonarios *	COL	0 1	5p							
Coronel Bolognesi	PER	1 0	4p	Millonarios	COL	3	0			
Universitario *	PER	0	0	At. Nacional Medellin *	COL	2	0			
At. Nacional Medellin	COL	1	1					Millonarios *		1 1 7p
Audax Italiano *	CHI	2	1					Colo Colo		1 1 6p
Jorge Wilstermann	BOL	0	1	Audax Italiano	CHI	0	1			
Real Potosi *	BOL	1	1	Colo Colo *	CHI	0	1			
Colo Colo	CHI	1	3							
				Boca Juniors	ARG	Bye				
								Boca Juniors *		2 0
								São Paulo FC		1 1
				Figueirense *	BRA	2	1			
				São Paulo FC	BRA	2	1			
				Vasco da Gama	BRA	4	2			
				Atlético Paranaense *	BRA	2	0			
								Vasco da Gama		0 3
								Lanús *		2 0
				Estudiantes LP	ARG	0	2			
				Lanús *	ARG	2	1			
				Pachuca	MEX	Bye				
								Pachuca *		1 2
								CF América		4 0
				CF América	Mex	Bye				

* Home team in the first leg

COPA NISSAN SUDAMERICANA 2007

COPA NISSAN SUDAMERICANA 2007

Quarter–finals		Semi–finals		Final	
Arsenal *	0 3				
Guadalajara	0 1				
		Arsenal *	0 0 4p		
		River Plate	0 0 2p		
Defensor Sporting *	2 0				
River Plate	2 0				
				Arsenal	3 1
				CF América *	2 2
Millonarios	1 2				
São Paulo FC *	0 0				
		Millonarios *	2 0		
		CF América	3 2		
Vasco da Gama	0 1				
CF América *	2 0				

PRELIMINARY ROUND

Centenario, Montevideo, 7-08-2007, 20:15, 2046, Gaciba BRA

Defensor Sp'ting	2	Morales 2 [17] [81]
Libertad	1	Gamarra [38]

La Olla, Asunción, 21-08-2007, 19:00, 358, Pezzotta ARG

Libertad	2	Cáceres [3], Gamarra [73]
Defensor Sp'ting	2	Morales 2 [27] [32]

La Olla, Asunción, 1-08-2007, 19:15, Laverni ARG

Tacuary	1	Fatecha [89]
Danubio	1	Noble [24]

Centenario, Montevideo, 15-08-2007, 19:30, 1863, Osses CHI

Danubio	1	Rodríguez [3]
Tacuary	1	Paniagua [24]. Tacuary won 4-1 on pens

Olímpico, Riobamba, 1-08-2007, 20:30, 3161, Buckley PER

Olmedo	1	Savoia [39]
Zamora	0	

La Carolina, Barinas, 21-08-2007, 21:30, 12 573, Lopez COL

Zamora	1	Salazar [56p]
Olmedo	2	Galván [11], Savoia [28]

Cachamay, Puerto Ordaz, 16-08-2007, 21:30, Duarte COL

Carabobo	0	
El Nacional	1	Calderon [24]

Atahualpa, Quito, 28-08-2007, 20:30, 7405, Rivera PER

El Nacional	4	Chala 2 [7] [60], Ordóñez 2 [55] [68]
Carabobo	0	

El Campín, Bogota, 2-08-2007, 20:30, 8811

Millonarios	0	
Coronel Bolognesi	1	Cominges [6]

Jorge Basadre, Tacna, 23-08-2007, 20:45, 7025, Reinoso ECU

Coronel Bolognesi	0	
Millonarios	1	Ciciliano [85]. Millonarios won 5-4 on pens

Monumental, Lima, 9-08-2007, 20:45, 21 279, Intriago ECU

Universitario	0	
At. Nacional	1	Mendoza [28]

Atanasio Girardot, Medellín, 30-08-2007, 20:30, 17 652, Ortubé BOL

At. Nacional	1	Valencia [77]
Universitario	0	

Nacional, Santiago, 31-07-2007, 20:15, 998, Vázquez URU

Audax Italiano	2	Villanueva [37], Medina [62]
J. Wilstermann	0	

Félix Capriles, Cochabamba, 7-08-2007, 21:30, 12 993, Carrillo PER

J. Wilstermann	1	Juárez [88p]
Audax Italiano	1	Medina 56

Mario Guzmán, Potosí, 2-08-2007, 19:15, 6803, Arias PAR

Real Potosí	1	Lorca OG [48]
Colo Colo	1	Jara [15]

Monumental, Santiago, 9-08-2007, 19:15, 8154, Pompei ARG

Colo Colo	3	Hernández [33], Fierro [45p], Moya [90]
Real Potosí	1	Brandan [9]

FIRST ROUND

Julio Grondona, Buenos Aires, 14-08-2007, 20:15, 4193, Laverni ARG

Arsenal	1	Casteglione [92+]
San Lorenzo	1	Silvera [22]

Nuevo Gasómetro, Buenos Aires, 6-09-2007, 20:15, 6891, Pezzotta ARG

San Lorenzo	0	
Arsenal	3	Mosquera [8], Bottinelli OG [40], Calderón [67]

Serra Dourada, Goiania, 16-08-2007, 20:15, 3629, Oliveira BRA

Goiás EC	2	Paulo Baier 2 [43p] [88p]
Cruzeiro	0	

Mineirão, Belo Horizonte, 22-08-2007, 21:45, 11 409, Tardelli BRA

Cruzeiro	1	Thiago Heleno [13]
Goiás EC	0	

La Olla, Asunción, 30-08-2007, 23:15, 883, Lopes BRA

Tacuary	1	Paniagua [13]
Defensor Sp'ting	1	Gaglianone [62]

Centenario, Montevideo, 13-09-2007, 23:15, 12 949, Favale ARG

Defensor Sp'ting	3	De Souza 2 [42p] [85], Navarro [91+]
Tacuary	0	

Atahualpa, Quito, 4-09-2007, 20:30, 3243, Vera ECU

El Nacional	2	Ordóñez [27], Kaviedes [84]
Olmedo	0	

Olímpico, Rio Bamba, 11-09-2007, 19:15, 1964, Carpio ECU

Olmedo	0	
El Nacional	1	Quiñonez [9]

Maracana, Rio de Janeiro, 21:45, 3453, Gaciba BRA

Botafogo	3	Reinaldo [1], Lúcio Flávio [35], André Lima [52]
Corinthians	1	Bruno Bonfim [82]

Pacaembú, São Paulo, 12-09-2007, 21:45, 4004, Lopes BRA

Corinthians	1	Finazzi [64]
Botafogo	2	Lúcio Flávio [58], Dodô [88]

Atanasio Girardot, Medellín, 5-09-2007, 20:45, 21 254, Hoyos COL

At. Nacional	2	Aristizábal [45p], Ramírez [86]
Millonarios	3	Estrada [48], Ciciliano 2 [54] [74p]

El Campín, Bogota, 13-09-2007, 20:45, 39 422, Duarte COL

Millonarios	0	
At. Nacional	0	

Monumental, Santiago, 28-08-2007, 19:15, 11 323, Ponce CHI

Colo Colo	0	
Audax Italiano	0	

Nacional, Santiago, 4-09-2007, 19:00, 12 931, Pozo CHI

Audax Italiano	1	Di Santo [2]
Colo Colo	1	Biscayzacú [87]

Orlando Scarpelli, Florianópolis, 15-08-2007, 7354, Beltrame BRA

Figueirense	2	Chicão [20p], Peter [42]
São Paulo FC	2	Rogério Ceni [24p], Hernanes [40]

Morumbí, São Paulo, 23-08-2007, 20:15, 4851, Lopes BRA

São Paulo FC	1	Borges [79]
Figueirense	1	Jean Carlos [57]

Kyocera Arena, Curitiba, 15-08-2007, 21:45, 5005, Seneme BRA

At. Paranaense	2	Dinei [23], Alan Bahia [82]
Vasco da Gama	4	Rubens [32], Abuda [38], Andrade [66], Conca [75]

São Januário, Rio de Janeiro, 12-09-2007, 21:45, 875, Simon BRA

Vasco da Gama	2	Marcelinho 2 [73] [77]
At. Paranaense	0	

Néstor Pérez, Buenos Aires, 8-08-2007, 21:15, 9803, Baldassi ARG

Lanús	2	Pelletieri [19], Sand [23]
Estudiantes LP	0	

Ciudad La Plata, La Plata, 5-09-2007, 20:15, 18 389, Lunati ARG

Estudiantes LP	2	Pirchio [9], Alvarez [22]
Lanús	1	Domínguez OG [60]

ROUND OF 16

Serra Dourada, Goiania, 19-09-2007, 17:15, 10 416, Amarilla PAR

Goiás EC	2	Paulo Baier 2 [25] [76]
Arsenal	3	Damonte [16], Casteglione [78], Garnier [79]

Julio Grondona, Buenos Aires, 26-09-2007, 3424, Selman CHI

Arsenal	1	Gómez [36]
Goiás EC	1	Harison [45]

Memorial, Washington, 26-09-2007, 20:45, 21 022, Baldassi ARG

DC United	2	Olsen [23], Simms [54]
Guadalajara	1	Santana [60]

Jalisco, Guadalajara, 2-10-2007, 20:15, Haro ECU

Guadalajara	1	Morales [63]
DC United	0	

Centenario, Montevideo, 20-09-2007, 21:15, 14 368, Pozo CHI

Defensor Sp'ting	3	De Souza 2 [14] [90], González [64]
El Nacional	0	

Atahualpa, Quito, 4-10-2007, 18:00, 2092, Rivera PER
El Nacional 2 Ordóñez 2 [15] [27]
Defensor Sp'ting 0

Engenhão, Rio de Janeiro, 19-09-2007, 19:30, 39 500, Ruiz COL
Botafogo 1 Joilson [44]
River Plate 0

Monumental, Buenos Aires, 27-09-2007, 20:15, 20 708, Amarilla PAR
River Plate 4 García 3 [31] [74], 92+, Ríos [80]
Botafogo 2 Lúcio Flávio [11], Dodô [65]

El Campín, Bogota, 25-09-2007, 19:00, 28 819, Rivera PER
Millonarios 1 Ciciliano [66]
Colo Colo 1 Rubio [30]

Monumental, Santiago, 4-10-2007, 21:30, 18 164, Baldassi ARG
Colo Colo 1 Biscayzacú [41]
Millonarios 1 Mosquera [37]. Millonarios won 7-6 on pens

La Bombonera, Buenos Aires, 19-09-2007, 24 790, Larrionda URU
Boca Juniors 2 Palermo 2 [26] [83]
São Paulo FC 1

Morumbí, São Paulo, 26-09-2007, 21:45, 45 906, Chandia CHI
São Paulo FC 1 Borges [53]
Boca juniors 0

Néstor Pérez, Buenos Aires, 19-09-2007, 21:45, 6112, Chandia CHI
Lanús 2 Pelletieri [32], Sand [77]
Vasco da Gama 0

São Januário, Rio de Janeiro, 26-09-2007, 21:45, 2739, Larrionda URU
Vasco da Gama 3 Leandro Amaral 2 [29] [90], Wagner Diniz [75]
Lanús 0

Hidalgo, Pachuca, 25-09-2007, 21:15, 9765, Rodríguez MEX
Pachuca 1 Giménez [39]
América 4 Insúa [33], Cabañas [47], López 2 [56] [57]

Azteca, Mexico City, 3-10-2007, 21:15, 44 477, Glower MEX
América 0
Pachuca 2 Alvarez [57], Giménez [59]

QUARTER-FINALS

Julio Grondona, Buenos Aires
10-10-2007, 19:30, 2640, Grance PAR
Arsenal	0

Mario Cuenca – Darío Espínola, Andrés San Martín, José Calderón, Santiago Raymonda (José Ulloa 76), Martín Andrizzi (Alejandro Gómez 46), Carlos Casteglione (Pablo Garnier• 46), Aníbal Matellán, Cristian Díaz, Jossimar Mosquera•, Sebastián Carrera. Tr: Gustavo Alfaro

Guadalajara	0

Luis Michelle• – José Magallón, Héctor Reynoso•, Francisco Rodríguez•90, Omar Esparza, Edgar Mejía, Sergio Ávila, Ramón Morales (Patricio Araujo 73), Gonzalo Pineda Xavier Báez 73), Sergio Santana•, Alberto Medina (Javier Hernández 89). Tr: Efraín Flores

Jalisco, Guadalajara
25-10-2007, 20:30, 19 980, Ruiz COL
Guadalajara	1
	Santana [16]

Luis Michelle - José Magallón, Héctor Reynoso•77, Edgar Mejía (Julio Nava 46), Sergio Ávila•, Gonzalo Pineda, Ramón Morales (Patricio Araujo 89), Omar Esparza• (Omar Arellano• 64), Sergio Santana, Omar Bravo, Alberto Medina. Tr: Efraín Flores

Arsenal	3
	Yacuzzi 2 [2] [27], Raymonda [78p]

Mario Cuenca – Javier Gandolfi, Jossimar Mosquera, Aníbal Matellán, Darío Espínola, Sebastián Carrera• (Pablo Garnier 56), Andrés San Martín, Carlos Casteglione•, Javier Yacuzzi, Alejandro Gómez• (Martín Andrizzi 76), José Calderón (Santiago Raymonda 71). Tr: Gustavo Alfaro

Centenario, Montevideo
25-10-2007, 21:00, 36 838, Fagundes BRA
Defensor Sporting	2
	Gaglianone [14], Valenti [84]

Martín Silva – Williams Martínez, Pablo Gaglianone•, Andrés Lamas•, Diego De Souza, Miguel Amado, Carlos Morales (Tabaré Viudez 57), Cristian González, Sergio Ariosa•, Julio Marchant (Sebastián Fernández 57), Álvaro Navarro (Sergio Valenti 72). Tr: Jorge Da Silva

River Plate	2
	Ortega [5p], García [30]

Juan Carrizo – Paulo Ferrari•, Nicolás Sánchez, Eduardo Tuzzio, Leonardo Ponzio•, Augusto Fernández, Nicolás Domingo, Fernando Belluschi•, Ariel Ortega, Mauro Rosales (Matías Abelairas 75), Radamel García•. Tr: Daniel Passarella

Monumental, Buenos Aires
30-10-2007, 21:15, 35 021, Grance PAR
River Plate	0

Juan Carrizo – Paulo Ferrari•••92+, Nicolás Sánchez (Danilo Gerlo 55), Eduardo Tuzzio, Leonardo Ponzio, Fernando Belluschi, Oscar Ahumada, Matías Abelairas, Ariel Ortega•, Mauro Rosales, Radamel García. Tr: Daniel Passarella

Defensor Sporting	0

Martín Silva• – Cristian González, Williams Martínez, Andrés Lamas•, Sergio Ariosa•, Julio Marchant•, Pablo Gaglianone (Tabaré Viudez 65), Miguel Amado, Diego De Souza (Mauro Vila 80), Sebastián Fernández, Carlos Morales (Álvaro Navarro 73). Tr: Jorge Da Silva

Morumbí, São Paulo
10-10-2007, 21:50, 6522, Pezzotta ARG
São Paulo FC	0

Bosco – Breno, André Dias, Miranda, Júnior, Hernanes, Leandro, Souza (Jorge Wagner 46), Hugo, Diego Tardelli (Aloisio 57), Richarlyson•. Tr: Muricy Ramalho

Millonarios	1
	Zapata [84]

Eduardo Blandón – Andrés Salinas, Gonzalo Martínez, Andrés Mosquera•, Alex Díaz (Luis Zapata 81), Gerardo Bedoya•, Rafael Robayo, Juan Carlos Quintero•, Johnatan Estrada, Ricardo Ciciliano (Ervin González 90), Carlos Villagra (Oscar Briceñ 92). Tr: Mario Vanemerak

El Campín, Bogota
24-10-2007, 18:50, 39 454, Vázquez URU
Millonarios	2
	Ciciliano 2 [76] [85]

Eduardo Blandón• – Andrés Salinas (Gustavo Rojas• 76), Gonzalo Martínez, Andrés Mosquera, Alex Díaz (Luis Zapata 84), Juan Carlos Quintero•, Rafael Robayo, Ervin González, Johnatan Estrada, Ricardo Ciciliano (Carlos Castillo 87), Carlos Villagra. Tr: Mario Vanemerak

São Paulo FC	0

Rogério Ceni – Breno•, André Dias, Hernanes, Souza (Diego Tardelli 68), Hugo (Jadilson 72), Aloisio, Alex Silva, Fernando• (Alex Francisco 72), Richarlyson, Dagoberto•. Tr: Muricy Ramalho

Azteca, Mexico City
10-10-2007, 19:50, 35 600, Vázquez URU
América	2
	Davino [51], López [77]

Francisco Ochoa – Ismael Rodríguez•, Óscar Rojas, Duilio Davino•, Lucas Castroman, Santiago Fernández (Enrique Esqueda 68), Juan Mosquera, Ricardo Rojas•, Hernán López, Germán Villa•, Alejandro Argüello. Tr: Daniel Brailovsky

Vasco da Gama	0

Silvio Luis – Wagner Diniz, Jorge Luiz•, Vilson•, Julio Santos•57, Rubens Junior, Roberto Lopes (Perdigão 53), Darío Conca (Enilton 69), Amaral, Alan Kardec (Andrade 67), Leandro Amaral•. Tr: Celso Roth

São Januário, Rio de Janeiro
24-10-2007, 21:50, 1312, Amarilla PAR
Vasco da Gama	1
	Leandro Amaral [10]

Cássio – Wagner Diniz, Jorge Luiz, Luizão, Rubens Junior (Enilton 77), Perdigão•, Leandro (Romario 56), Darío Conca, Alan Kardec (Marcelinho 56), Leandro Amaral•, Amaral. Tr: Romario

América	0

Francisco Ochoa – José Castro, Óscar Rojas, Duilio Davino•, Federico Insúa• (Juan Mosquerda 79), Salvador Cabañas (Lucas Castroman 55), Ricardo Rojas, Hernán López (Enrique Esqueda• 83), Germán Villa•, Alejandro Argüello•, Juan Silva. Tr: Daniel Brailovsky

SEMI-FINALS

Julio Grondona, Buenos Aires
8-11-2007, 20:45, 8929, Pezzotta ARG

Arsenal 0

Mario Cuenca - Carlos Casteglione•, Javier Gandolfi, Cristian Díaz, Jossimar Mosquera, Anibal Matellán• - Israel Damonte•, Sebastián Carrera (Alejandro Gómez 66), Diego Villar (Martín Andrizzi• 59) - José Calderon, Leonardo Biagini (Santiago Raymonda 75). Tr: Gustavo Alfaro

River Plate 0

Juan Carrizo - Eduardo Tuzzio, Cristian Nasuti (René Lima 53), Danilo Gerlo - Leonardo Ponzio•, Nicolás Domingo, Oscar Ahumada•, Fernando Bellushi - Ariel Ortega (Diego Buonanotte 81), Marco Ruben (Mauro Rosales 46), Radamel García•. Tr: Daniel Passarella

Monumental, Buenos Aires
14-11-2007, 21:15, Baldassi ARG

River Plate 0 2p

Juan Carrizo - Eduardo Tuzzio, Cristian Nasuti•, Paulo Ferrari - Leonardo Ponzio, René Lima•, Oscar Ahumada•80, Fernando Bellushi, Diego Buonanotte (Augusto Fernández 84) - Ariel Ortega (Mauro Rosales 23), Andrés Rios (Rolando Zárate 69). Tr: Daniel Passarella

Arsenal 0 4p

Mario Cuenca - Carlos Casteglione•, Javier Gandolfi, Cristian Díaz, Jossimar Mosquera, Anibal Matellán - Andrés San Martín•, Sebastián Carrera (Pablo Garnier 67) (Martín Andrizzi 90), Javier Yacuzzi - José Calderon•, Leonardo Biagini (Alejandro Gómez 70). Tr: Gustavo Alfaro

El Campín, Bogota
7-11-2007, 20:15, 40 132, Grance PAR

Millonarios 2

Bedoya [61], Estrada [67]

Eduardo Blandón - Andrés Salinas (Juan Quintero 66), Gonzalo Martínez, Andrés Mosquera•, Alex Díaz (Carlos Castillo 46), Gerardo Bedoya - Rafael Robayo, Johnatan Estrada, Ricardo Ciciliano - Carlos Villagra, Ervin González (Luis Zapata• 46). Tr: Mario Vanemerak

América 3

Villa [24], Cabañas 2 [37 85]

Francisco Ochoa - José Castro•, Oscar Rojas, Duilio Davino, Ricardo Rojas - Federico Insúa (Juan Mosqueda 75), Germán Villa•, Alejandro Argüello, Juan Silva - Hernán López, Salvador Cabañas. Tr: Daniel Brailovsky

Nemesio Diez, Toluca
13-11-2007, 20:15, Selman CHI

América 2

López 2 [6 78]

Francisco Ochoa - José Castro, Oscar Rojas, Duilio Davino, Ricardo Rojas• - Juan Mosqueda, Germán Villa, Alejandro Argüello (Jesús Sánchez 76), Juan Silva• (José Mosqueda 38) - Hernán López, Enrique Esqueda (Lucas Castroman 70). Tr: Daniel Brailovsky

Millonarios 0

Eduardo Blandón - Andrés Salinas• (Marcos Tejera 50), Gonzalo Martínez (Efraín Cortes 80), Andrés Mosquera•, Luis Zapata - Rafael Robayo, Juan Quintero, Johnatan Estrada, Ricardo Ciciliano• - Carlos Villagra•16, Carlos Castillo (Andrés Pérez 64). Tr: Mario Vanemerak

FINAL

COPA SUDAMERICANA FINAL 1ST LEG
Azteca, Mexico City
30-11-2007, 19:15, 63 455, Grance PAR

CF AMERICA 2 3 **ARSENAL**

Cabañas [5], Argüello [55]   Matellán [31], Gómez 2 [57 66]

	AMERICA			ARSENAL	
1	Francisco Ochoa			Mario Cuenca	1
3	José Antonio Castro			Javier Gandolfi	14
4	Oscar Rojas			Jossimar Mosquera	21
5	Duilio Cesar Davino			Anibal Matellán	16
16	Ricardo Rojas			Cristian Díaz	18
20	Alejandro Argüello		74	Diego Villar	25
23	Juan Carlos Silva	71		Andrés San Martín	5
18	German Villa	85	79	Carlos Casteglione	13
8	Federico Insua			Javier Yacuzzi	24
17	Hernán López		82	Alejandro Gómez	15
9	Salvador Cabanas		86	José Luis Calderón	7
	Tr: Alberto Brailovsky			Tr: Gustavo Alfaro	
13	Juan Carlos Mosqueda	71	82	Israel Damonte	8
21	Enrique Esqueda	85	74	Pablo Garnier	17
			86	Leonardo Biagini	20

COPA SUDAMERICANA FINAL 2ND LEG
Jua Domingo Peron (El Cilindro), Buenos Aires
5-12-2007, 21:30, 18 717, Ruiz COL

ARSENAL 1 2 **CF AMERICA**

Andrizzi [84]   Diaz OG [18], Silva [63]

	ARSENAL			AMERICA	
1	Mario Cuenca			Francisco Ochoa	1
14	Javier Gandolfi			José Antonio Castro	3
21	Jossimar Mosquera			Ricardo Rójas	16
16	Anibal Matellán		90	Duilio Cesar Davino	5
18	Cristian Díaz		87	Oscar Rójas	4
25	Diego Villar	68		Alejandro Argüello	20
5	Andres San Martín			Juan Carlos Silva	23
8	Israel Damonte	77		German Villa	18
24	Javier Yacuzzi	66		Federico Insua	8
15	Alejandro Gómez			Salvador Cabañas	9
7	José Luis Calderón		70	Hernán López	17
	Tr: Gustavo Alfaro			Tr: Alberto Brailovsky	
10	Santiago Raymonda	77	70	Ismael Rodríguez	2
11	Martin Andrizzi	68	90 87	Lucas Castroman	7
20	Leonardo Biagini	66			

OFC

OCEANIA FOOTBALL CONFEDERATION

It was a busy year for football in Oceania as the national teams of the region came out of hibernation to take part in the FIFA World Cup qualifiers. The sensible idea of using the football tournament of the South Pacific Games in Apia, Samoa as a preliminary round for the World Cup qualifiers saw the tournament briefly come under the international spotlight as the games played there were the first in any continent on the road to South Africa. New Caledonia captain Pierre Wajoka secured the honour of scoring the first goal of South Africa 2010. The New Caledonians went on to win the tournament, beating firstly the Solomon Islands 3-2 in an exciting semi-final, with the winner coming deep into injury-time, and then Fiji 1-0 in the final. Jose Hmae's second half goal meant a record fourth title in the South Pacific Games for New Caledonia. The consolation for Fiji was that they also progressed into the main Oceania World Cup qualifying group, along with Vanuatu, who

THE FIFA BIG COUNT OF 2006 FOR OCEANIA

	Male	Female		Total
Number of players	486 000	56 000	Referees and Assistant Referees	3 000
Professionals	n/a		Admin, Coaches, Technical, Medical	29 000
Amateurs 18+	59 000		Number of clubs	2 000
Youth under 18	175 000		Number of teams	13 000
Unregistered	301 000		Clubs with women's teams	n/a
Total involved in football	573 000		Players as % of population	4.68%

beat the Solomons in a third place play-off. New Zealand started the group as strong favourites to qualify for a play-off against the fifth placed Asian team for a place in South Africa. The group winners will also be crowned as Oceania champions and will qualify for the FIFA Confederations Cup, to be held in South Africa in 2009. Club football continued to put down stronger roots with participation in the O-League and a potential place at the FIFA Club World Cup acting as a strong incentive. Waitakere United from New Zealand, however, walked off with the cup for the second year in a row but once again they were troubled in the final, this time by Kossa from the Solomon Islands, who beat the Kiwis 3-1 at home before losing the return 5-0. In December 2007, Waitakere had taken their bow at the FIFA Club World Cup in Japan, losing a preliminary tie 3-1 against Iran's Sepahan.

Oceania Football Confederation (OFC)

Ericsson Stadium, 12 Maurice Road, Penrose, PO Box 62 586, Auckland 6, New Zealand

Tel +64 9 5258161   Fax +64 9 5258164

info@ofcfoot.org.nz   www.oceaniafootball.com

President: TEMARII Reynald TAH

General Secretary: NICHOLAS Tai COK

Vice-President: LULU Johnny VAN   Treasurer: HARMON Lee COK

OFC Formed: 1966

OFC EXECUTIVE COMMITTEE

President: TEMARII Reynald TAH

Senior Vice-President: LULU Johnny VAN   1st Vice-President: BURGESS Mark NZL   2nd Vice-President: WICKHAM Adrian SOL

3rd Vice-President: OTT Richard ASA   Treasurer: HARMON Lee COK   CHUNG David PNG

FOURNIER Claude NCL   HARERAAROA Eugene TAH   General Secretary NICHOLAS Tai COK

MAP OF OFC MEMBER NATIONS

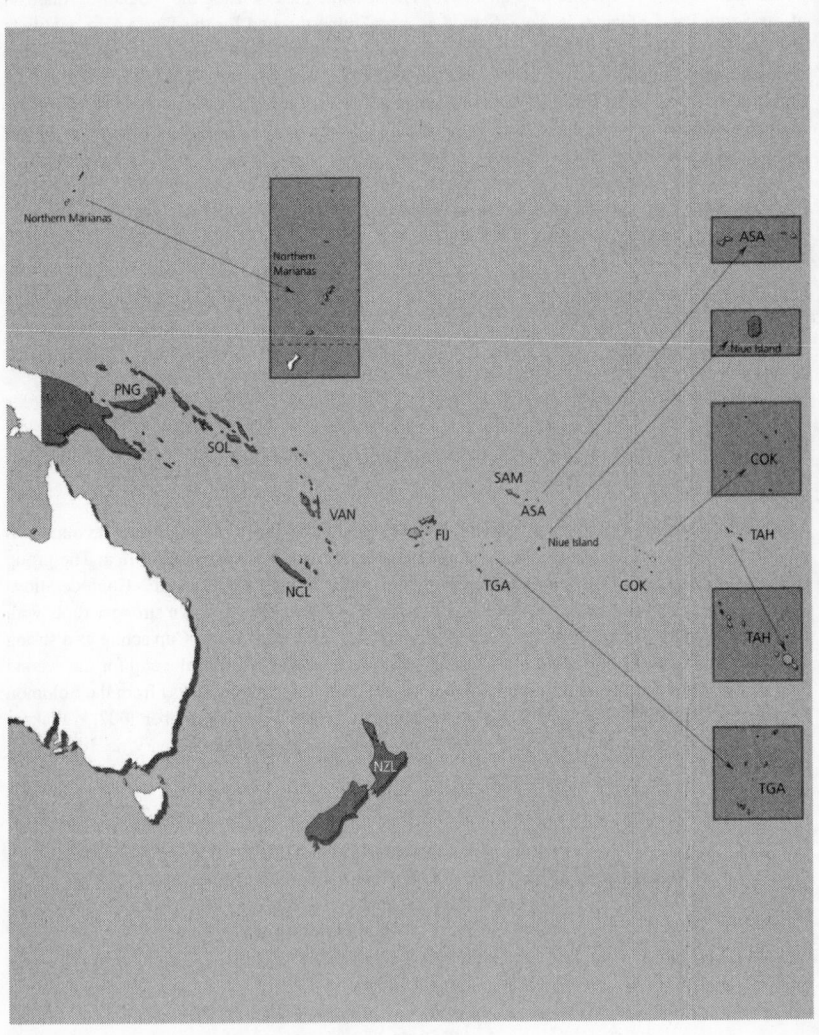

OCEANIA TOURNAMENTS

OCEANIA NATIONS CUP

Year	Host Country	Winners	Score	Runners-up	Venue
1973	New Zealand	New Zealand	2-0	Tahiti	Auckland
1980	New Caledonia	Australia	4-2	Tahiti	Nouméa
1996	Home & away	Australia	6-0 5-0	Tahiti	Papeete & Canberra
1998	Australia	New Zealand	1-0	Australia	Brisbane
2000	Tahiti	Australia	2-0	New Zealand	Stade de Pater, Papeete
2002	New Zealand	New Zealand	1-0	Australia	Ericsson Stadium, Auckland
2004	Home & away	Australia	5-1 6-0	Solomon Islands	Honaria & Sydney

OCEANIA WOMEN'S CHAMPIONSHIP

Year	Host Country	Winners	Score	Runners-up	Venue
1983	New Caledonia	New Zealand	3-2	Australia	Nouméa
1986	New Zealand	Chinese Taipei	4-1	Australia	Christchurch
1989	Australia	Chinese Taipei	1-0	New Zealand	Brisbane
1991	Australia	New Zealand	1-0 0-1 †	Australia	Sydney
1995	Papua N. Guinea	Australia	1-2 1-0 †	New Zealand	Port Moresby
1998	New Zealand	Australia	3-1	New Zealand	Mount Smart, Auckland
2003	Australia	Australia	2-0 †	New Zealand	Belconnen, Canberra
2007	Papua N. Guinea	New Zealand	7-0	Papua New Guinea	Lae

† The 1991, 1995, 2003 and 2007 tournaments were played as leagues • The results shown are those between the top two teams

OCEANIA YOUTH CHAMPIONSHIP

Year	Host Country	Winners	Score	Runners-up	Venue
1974	Tahiti	Tahiti	2-0	New Zealand	Papeete
1978	New Zealand	Australia	5-1 †	Fiji	Auckland
1980	Fiji	New Zealand	2-0	Australia	Suva
1982	Papua New Guinea	Australia	4-3	New Zealand	Port Moresby
1985	Australia	Australia	3-2 †	Israel	Sydney
1987	New Zealand	Australia	1-1 †	Israel	Auckland
1988	Fiji	Australia	1-0	New Zealand	Suva
1990	Fiji	Australia	6-0 †	New Zealand	Suva
1992	Tahiti	New Zealand	1-0 †	Tahiti	Papeete
1994	Fiji	Australia	1-0	New Zealand	Suva
1996	Tahiti	Australia	2-1	New Zealand	Papeete
1998	Samoa	Australia	2-0	Fiji	Apia
2001	New Cal/Cook Is	Australia	1-2 3-1	New Zealand	Auckland & Coffs Harbour
2003	Vanuatu/Fiji	Australia	11-0 4-0	Fiji	Melbourne & Ba
2005	Solomon Islands	Australia	3-0	Solomon Islands	Honiara
2007	New Zealand	New Zealand	3-2	Fiji	Waitakere

† The 1978, 1985, 1987, 1990, 1992 and 2007 tournaments were played as leagues • The results shown are those between the top two teams

OCEANIA U–17 CHAMPIONSHIP

Year	Host Country	Winners	Score	Runners-up	Venue
1983	New Zealand	Australia	2-1	New Zealand	Mount Smart, Auckland
1986	Chinese Taipei	Australia	0-1	New Zealand	CKF Stadium, Kaohsiung
1989	Australia	Australia	5-1	New Zealand	
1991	New Zealand	Australia	1-1 1-0	New Zealand	Napier
1993	New Zealand	Australia	3-0	Soloman Islands	
1995	Vanuatu	Australia	1-0	New Zealand	
1997	New Zealand	New Zealand	1-0	Australia	
1999	Fiji	Australia	5-0	Fiji	Churchill Park, Lautoka
2001	Samoa/Cook Isl	Australia	3-0 6-0	New Zealand	Canberra & Auckland
2003	Home & away	Australia	3-1 4-0	New Caledonia	Nouméa
2005	New Caledonia	Australia	1-0	Vanuatu	Nouméa
2007	Tahiti	New Zealand	2-1	Tahiti	Papeete

From 1983 to 1991 and in 2007 the tournaments were played as leagues • The results shown are those between the top two teams

OCEANIA WOMEN'S U-19 CHAMPIONSHIP

Year	Host Country	Winners	Score	Runners-up	Venue
2002	Tonga	Australia	6-0	New Zealand	Nuku'alofa
2004	Papua New Guinea	Australia	14-1	Papua New Guinea	Lloyd Robson Oval, Port Moresby

SOUTH PACIFIC GAMES WINNERS

Year	Host Country	Winners	Runners-up
1963	Fiji	New Caledonia	Fiji
1966	New Caledonia	Tahiti	New Caledonia
1969	Papua New Guinea	New Caledonia	Tahiti
1971	Tahiti	New Caledonia	Tahiti
1975	Guam	Tahiti	New Caledonia
1979	Fiji	Tahiti	Fiji
1983	Western Samoa	Tahiti	Fiji
1987	New Caledonia	New Caledonia	Tahiti
1991	Papua New Guinea	Fiji	Solomon Isl
1995	Tahiti	Tahiti	Solomon Isl
1999	Guam	Not played	
2003	Fiji	Fiji	New Caledonia
2007	Samoa	New Caledonia	Fiji

MELANESIAN CUP WINNERS

Year	Host Country	Winners	Runners-up
1988	Solomon Islands	Fiji	Solomon Isl
1989	Fiji	Fiji	New Caledonia
1990	Vanuatu	Vanuatu	New Caledonia
1992	Vanuatu	Fiji	New Caledonia
1994	Solomon Islands	Solomon Isl	Fiji
1996	Papua New Guinea	Papua NG	Solomon Isl
1998	Vanuatu	Fiji	Vanuatu
2000	Fiji	Fiji	Solomon Isl

SOUTH PACIFIC MINI GAMES WINNERS

Year	Host Country	Winners	Runners-up
1981	Solomon Islands	Tahiti	New Caledonia
1985	Cook Islands	Tahiti	
1989	Tonga	Papua NG	
1993	Vanuatu	Tahiti	Fiji

POLYNESIAN CUP WINNERS

Year	Host Country	Winners	Runners-up
1994	Samoa	Tahiti	Tonga
1996	Tonga	Tonga	Samoa
1998	Cook Islands	Tahiti	Cook Islands
2000	Tahiti	Tahiti	Cook Islands

O-LEAGUE

Year	Winners	Country	Score	Country	Runners-up
1987	Adelaide City	AUS	1-1 4-1p	NZL	Mount Wellington
1999	South Melbourne	AUS	5-1	FIJ	Nadi
2001	Wollongong City Wolves	AUS	1-0	VAN	Tafea FC
2005	Sydney FC	AUS	2-0	NCL	AS Magenta
2006	Auckland City	NZL	3-1	TAH	AS Piraé
2007	Waitakere United	NZL	1-2 1-0	FIJ	Ba
2008	Waitakere United	NZL	1-3 5-0	SOL	Kossa

O–LEAGUE 2007–08

PRELIMINARY ROUND

		Stade Noumea Daly, Noumea, 12-06-2007
JS Baco	2	Essien Nea [50p], Johann Mercier [73]
University	0	

		Stade Noumea Daly, Noumea, 14-06-2007
Tafea	5	Alphonse Qorig 2 [4 67], Jean Naprapol [44], Geoffrey Gete [55], Hubert Nake [86]
University	1	Richard Daniel [90]

		Stade Noumea Daly, Noumea, 16-06-2007
Tafea	5	Richard Iwai 2 [43 85], Jean Naprapol 3 [45 70 74]
JS Baco	0	

PRELIMINARY ROUND

		Pl	W	D	L	F	A	Pts		NCL	PNG
Tafea FC	VAN	2	2	0	0	10	1	6		5-0	5-1
JS Baco	NCL	2	1	0	1	2	5	3			2-0
University	PNG	2	0	0	2	1	7	0			

GROUP STAGE

GROUP A									NZL	NZL	TAH
		Pl	W	D	L	F	A	Pts	NZL	NZL	TAH
Waitakere United	NZL	4	2	2	0	5	3	8		1-1	2-1
Auckland City	NZL	4	2	1	1	8	2	7	0-1		6-0
AS Manu Ura	TAH	4	0	1	3	2	10	1	1-1	0-1	

GROUP B									SOL	VAN	FIJ
		Pl	W	D	L	F	A	Pts	SOL	VAN	FIJ
Kossa FC	SOL	4	2	2	0	8	4	8		1-1	2-0
Tafea FC	VAN	4	1	2	1	4	4	5	1-1		2-1
Ba	FIJ	4	1	0	3	4	8	3	2-4	1-0	

GROUP A

McLeod Road, Henderson, 27-10-2007		
Auckland City	6	Keryn Jordan 2 [6] [34p], Grant Young [44], Chad Coomes [52], Jeff Campbell [68], Paul Urlovic [68]
AS Manu Ura	0	

Fred Taylor Park, Auckland, 31-10-2007, Fred VAN		
Waitakere United	2	Benjamin Totori [75], Neil Emblen [79]
AS Manu Ura	1	Tamatoa Tauihara [49]

Stade Paea, Papeete, 15-02-2008		
AS Manu Ura	1	Chris Bale [63]
Waitakere United	1	Billy Mataitai [91+]

McLeod Road, Henderson, 20-02-2008		
Auckland City	0	
Waitakere United	1	Allen Pearce [57]

Stade Paea, Papeete, 28-03-2008, Zetter AUS		
AS Manu Ura	0	
Auckland City	1	George Suri [82]

Trusts Stadium, Henderson, 2-04-2008, Hauta TAH		
Waitakere United	1	Allen Pearce [30p]
Auckland City	1	Ki Hyung Lee [3]

GROUP B

Lawson Tama, Honiara, 27-10-2007		
Kossa	1	Reginald Davani [61]
Tafea	1	Alphonse Qorig [71]

Govind Park, Ba, 31-10-2007, Jacques TAH		
Ba	1	Shalen Lal [93+]
Tafea	0	

Municipal, Port Vila, 20-02-2008, Hester NZL		
Tafea	2	Jean Naprapol [14], Samson Obed [84p]
Ba	1	Avinesh Swamy [60]

Lawson Tama, Honiara, 25-02-2008		
Kossa	2	Malakai Kainihewe OG [7], James Naka [11]
Ba	0	

Municipal, Port Vila, 26-03-2008, O'Leary NZL		
Tafea	1	Francois Sakama [60]
Kossa	1	James Naka [40]

Churchill Park, Lautoka, 30-03-2008, O'Leary NZL		
Ba	2	Avinesh Suwamy [45], Josaia Bukalidi [84]
Kossa	4	Reginald Davani [12], Joe Luwi [51], James Naka [75], Paul Wale [90]

FINAL

Lawson Tama, Honiara
26-04-2008, 14:00, 20 000, Varman FIJ

Kossa — 3
Joe Luwi 2 [21] [42], James Naka [89]

Tome Faisi - Samson Takayama, Mahlon Maemania, Francis Nee, Joe Luwi, James Naka, Paul Wale (Willie Sade 89), Gideon Omokirio, Reginald Davani●, Severino Aefi. Tr: Jacob Moli

Waitakere United — 1
Jonathan Perry [48]

Richard Gillespie - Jonathan Perry, Darren Bazely, Commins Menapi● (Hoani Edwards● 78), Benjamin Totori, Allen Pearce (Graham Pearce 87), Neil Sykes, Danijel Koprivcic (Jason Hayne● 43), Chris Bale, Neil Emblen, Jake Butler. Tr: Chris Milicich

Trusts Stadium, Henderson, Auckland
11-05-2008, 14:00, Williams AUS

Waitakere United — 5
Benjamin Totori [8], Chris Bale [25], Allen Pearce 2 [72] [78], Jake Butler [85]

Richard Gillespie - Jonathan Perry, Danny Hay● (Darren Bazeley 62), Jason Hayne, Benjamin Totori (Commins Menapi 64), Allan Pearce, Neil Sykes, Danijel Koprivcic (Jason Rowley 93+), Chris Bale, Neil Emblen, Jake Butler. Tr: Chris Milicich

Kossa — 0

Severino Aefi (John Morgan 45) - Tome Faisi, Samson Takayama, Mahlon Maemania, Franco Nee, Joe Luwi, James Naka, Seni Ngava, Paul Wale (Willie Sade 74), Gideon Omokirio, Reg Davani.Tr: Jacob Moli

UEFA

UNION DES ASSOCIATIONS EUROPEENNES DE FOOTBALL

The decision by UEFA to increase the size of the European Championship from eight to sixteen teams for Euro 96 in England was doubted by some at first, but all four of the tournaments played since have produced a wonderful fiesta of football and Euro 2008 in Austria and Switzerland was no different. Indeed it may well be regarded as the best ever. The quality of football played by the likes of the Netherlands and Russia was outstanding, while for sheer entertainment the Turks kept fans on the edge of their seats until the very end of each of the five matches they played. And, have there ever been more deserving winners than Spain, who ended a 44-year trophy drought in the most spectacular of ways? In the words of UEFA president Michel Platini, "I have seen a lot of positive football from most of the teams; the one thing I can also say is that those teams who played not to lose almost

THE FIFA BIG COUNT OF 2006 FOR EUROPE

	Male	Female		Total
Number of players	55 283 000	6 364 000	Referees and Assistant Referees	322 000
Professionals	60 000		Admin, Coaches, Technical, Medical	2 100 000
Amateurs 18+	11 101 000		Number of clubs	202 000
Youth under 18	9 386 000		Number of teams	872 000
Unregistered	40 622 000		Clubs with women's teams	13 000
Total involved in football	64 069 000		Players as % of population	7.59%

always lost. It's an important lesson." It's bizarre then that Platini should wish to tinker with a winning formula by increasing the number of finalists to a largely unworkable 24 for the 2016 finals. It could prove to be the first major mistake of an otherwise progressive presidency that has seen at its heart the focus on sporting principles over business principles. The UEFA Champions League showed that there is still a way to go before Platini creates a level playing field at club level with England's Premier League providing three of the four semi-finalists and both finalists in Manchester United and Chelsea. No team represents the almost limitless wealth of the Premier League more than Roman Abramovich's Chelsea, but it still wasn't enough to overcome United after they lost on penalties in Moscow with John Terry missing a crucial kick which would have won it for the Londoners.

Union des associations européennes de football (UEFA)
Route de Genève 46, 1260 Nyon, Switzerland
Tel +41 22 9944444   Fax +41 22 9944488
info@uefa.com   www.uefa.com
President: PLATINI Michel FRA   Chief Executive: INFANTINO Gianni ITA (Interim)
UEFA Formed: 1954

UEFA EXECUTIVE COMMITTEE

President: PLATINI Michel FRA   Vice-President: ERZIK Senes TUR   Vice-President: THOMPSON Geoffrey ENG

Vice-President: VILLAR LLONA Angel Maria ESP   Vice-President: MAYER-VORFELDER Gerhard GER   Treasurer: LEFKARITIS Marios CYP

ORDINARY MEMBERS OF THE EXECUTIVE COMMITTEE

CARRARO Franco ITA

MIFSUD Joseph, Dr MLT

SPRENGERS Mathieu, Drs NED

Co-opted: STICKLER Friedrich AUT

FIFA Exco member: D'HOOGHE Michel, Dr BEL

KOLOSKOV Viacheslav, Dr RUS

OMDAL Per Ravn NOR

SURKIS Grigory UKR

Co-opted: SPIESS Giangiorgio SUI

MADAIL Gilberto, Dr POR

SANDU Mircea ROU

Chief Executive: INFANTINO Gianni ITA (Interim)

Hon President: JOHANSSON Lennart SWE

FIFA Exco member: BECKENBAUER Franz GER

MAP OF UEFA MEMBER NATIONS

EUROPEAN TOURNAMENTS

UEFA EUROPEAN CHAMPIONSHIP

Year	Host Country	Winners	Score	Runners-up	Venue
1960	France	Soviet Union	2-1	Yugoslavia	Parc des Princes, Paris
1964	Spain	Spain	2-1	Soviet Union	Bernabeu, Madrid
1968	Italy	Italy	1-1 2-0	Yugoslavia	Stadio Olimpico, Roma
1972	Belgium	Germany FR	3-0	Soviet Union	Heysel, Brussels
1976	Yugoslavia	Czechoslovakia	2-2 5-4p	Germany FR	Crvena Zvezda, Belgrade
1980	Italy	Germany FR	2-1	Belgium	Stadio Olimpico, Rome
1984	France	France	2-0	Spain	Parc des Princes, Paris
1988	Germany FR	Netherlands	2-0	Soviet Union	Olympiastadion, Munich
1992	Sweden	Denmark	2-0	Germany	Nya Ullevi, Gothenburg
1996	England	Germany	2-1	Czech Republic	Wembley, London
2000	Belgium/Netherlands	France	2-1	Italy	Feijenoord Stadion, Rotterdam
2004	Portugal	Greece	1-0	Portugal	Estadio da Luz, Lisbon
2008	Austria/Switzerland	Spain	1-0	Germany	Ernst Happel, Vienna

UEFA EUROPEAN CHAMPIONSHIP MEDALS TABLE

	Country	G	S	B	F	SF
1	Germany	3	3	1	6	7
2	Spain	2	1		3	3
3	France	2		1	2	4
4	Soviet Union	1	3		4	5
5	Czechoslovakia	1	1	2	2	3
6	Italy	1	1	1	2	3
7	Netherlands	1		4	1	5
8	Denmark	1		1	1	3
9	Greece	1			1	1
10	Yugoslavia		2		2	3
11	Portugal		1	2	1	3
12	Belgium		1	1	1	2
13	England			2		2
14	Hungary			1		2
15	Czech Republic			1	1	1
	Sweden			1		1
	Russia			1		1
	Turkey			1		1
		13	13	20	26	50

This table represents the Gold (winners), Silver (runners-up) and
Bronze (semi-finalists) placings in the UEFA European
Championship, along with the number of appearances in the final
and semi-finals

The UEFA European Championship is the second youngest of the Confederation championships after the Oceania Nations Cup. At first there was a patchy response to the tournament and it was not until the third edition that the Germans, the most succesful nation to date with three titles, bothered to enter. The French and the Spanish are the only other nations to have been European Champions more than once, and the wide range of winners has been a prominent feature and one of the major reasons for the continued success of the tournament. Only England of the traditional powers have failed to win the title but it has been the triumphs of the smaller nations such as Czechoslovakia, the Netherlands, Denmark and Greece that has caught the imagination. Only since 1980 has the European Championship had a finals tournament along the lines of the current system. From 1980 to 1992 the finals had eight teams which grew to 16 in 1996 in no small part because UEFA's membership had grown from 32, which it had been for much of the post-war period, to beyond 50 as the political boundaries of Europe were redrawn. Thirteen nations have hosted the finals but home advantage has never been a serious factor. On seven occasions the hosts have been beaten in the semi-finals, and in only three of the 12 tournaments have they actually won the title – and not since 1984 – while in 2004 Portugal became the first host nation to lose the final itself. The most recent fashion has been co-hosting - Belgium and the Netherlands in 2000, Austria and Switzerland in 2008 and Poland and the Ukraine scheduled for 2012. From 2016 the tournament is due to be increased to 24 teams.

UEFA EUROPEAN WOMEN'S CHAMPIONSHIP

Year	Host Country	Winners	Score	Runners-up	Venue
1984		Sweden	1-0 0-1 4-3p	England	Gothenburg & Luton
1987	Norway	Norway	2-1	Sweden	Ullevål, Oslo
1989	Germany FR	Germany FR	4-1	Norway	Osnabrück
1991	Denmark	Germany	3-1	Norway	Aalborg Stadion
1993	Italy	Norway	1-0	Italy	Dino Manuzzi, Cesena
1995	Germany	Germany	3-2	Sweden	Fritz Walter Stadion, Kaiserslautern
1997	Norway/Sweden	Germany	2-0	Italy	Ullevål, Oslo
2001	Germany	Germany	1-0	Sweden	Donaustadion, Ulm
2005	England	Germany	3-1	Norway	Ewood Park, Blackburn

The UEFA Women's Championship is now a flourishing event in its own right, drawing good crowds into the stadiums and earning widespread coverage in the media. An unofficial European Championship was played in Italy in 1979 but since then there have been nine official tournaments, six of which have been won by Germany. The Scandinavian countries remain strong and provided the two other winners in Norway and Sweden. The eight-team final tournament was introduced for 1997 in Norway and Sweden. Although early editions often doubled up as FIFA Women's World Cup qualifiers, these are now held separately. The 2009 edition of the tournament will take place in Finland.

UEFA EUROPEAN UNDER-17 CHAMPIONSHIP

Year	Host Country	Winners	Score	Runners-up	Venue
1982	Italy	Italy	1-0	Germany FR	Falconara
1984	Germany FR	Germany FR	2-0	Soviet Union	Ulm
1985	Hungary	Soviet Union	4-0	Greece	Budapest
1986	Greece	Spain	2-1	Italy	Athens
1987	France	Italy	1-0	Soviet Union	Paris
1988	Spain	Spain	0-0 4-2p	Portugal	Teresa Rivero, Madrid
1989	Denmark	Portugal	4-1	German DR	Vejle
1990	East Germany	Czechoslovakia	3-2	Yugoslavia	Erfurt
1991	Switzerland	Spain	2-0	Germany	Wankdorf, Berne
1992	Cyprus	Germany	2-1	Spain	Ammokostos, Larnaca
1993	Turkey	Poland	1-0	Italy	Inönü, Istanbul
1994	Rep. Ireland	Turkey	1-0	Denmark	Tolka Park, Dublin
1995	Belgium	Portugal	2-0	Spain	Brussels
1996	Austria	Portugal	1-0	France	Wien
1997	Germany	Spain	0-0 5-4p	Austria	Celle
1998	Scotland	Republic of Ireland	2-1	Italy	McDiarmid Park, Perth
1999	Czech Republic	Spain	4-1	Poland	Olomouc
2000	Israel	Portugal	2-1	Czech Republic	Ramat Gan
2001	England	Spain	1-0	France	Stadium of Light, Sunderland
2002	Denmark	Switzerland	0-0 4-2p	France	Farum Park, Farum
2003	Portugal	Portugal	2-1	Spain	Fontelo Municipal, Viseu
2004	France	France	2-1	Spain	Gaston Petit, Chateauroux
2005	Italy	Turkey	2-0	Netherlands	E. Mannucci, Pontedera
2006	Luxembourg	Russia	2-2 5-3p	Czech Republic	Josy Barthel, Luxembourg
2007	Belgium	Spain	1-0	England	RFC Tournai, Tournai
2008	Turkey	Spain	4-0	France	Mardan Sports Complex, Antalya

Played as an U-16 tournament prior to 2002

UEFA EUROPEAN UNDER-19 CHAMPIONSHIP

Year	Host Country	Winners	Score	Runners-up	Venue
1981	West Germany	Germany FR	1-0	Poland	Düsseldorf
1982	Finland	Scotland	3-1	Czechoslovakia	Helsinki
1983	England	France	1-0	Czechoslovakia	White Hart Lane, London
1984	Soviet Union	Hungary	0-0 3-2p	Soviet Union	Zentralny, Moscow
1986	Yugoslavia	German DR	3-1	Italy	Subotica
1988	Czechoslovakia	Soviet Union	3-1	Portugal	Frydek-Mistek
1990	Hungary	Soviet Union	0-0 4-2p	Portugal	Bekescsaba
1992	Germany	Turkey	2-1	Portugal	Bayreuth
1993	England	England	1-0	Turkey	City Ground, Nottingham
1994	Spain	Portugal	1-1 4-1p	Germany	Merida
1995	Greece	Spain	4-1	Italy	Katerini
1996	France/Luxemb	France	1-0	Spain	Besançon
1997	Iceland	France	1-0	Portugal	Reykjavík
1998	Cyprus	Republic of Ireland	1-1 4-3p	Germany	Larnaca
1999	Sweden	Portugal	1-0	Italy	Norrköping
2000	Germany	France	1-0	Ukraine	Nürnberg
2001	Finland	Poland	3-1	Czech Republic	Helsinki
2002	Norway	Spain	1-0	Germany	Ullevaal, Oslo
2003	Liechtenstein	Italy	2-0	Portugal	Rheinpark Stadion, Vaduz
2004	Switzerland	Spain	1-0	Turkey	Colovray, Nyon
2005	Nth. Ireland	France	3-1	England	Windsor Park, Belfast
2006	Poland	Spain	2-1	Scotland	Miejski, Poznan
2007	Austria	Spain	1-0	Greece	Linzer, Linz
2008	Czech Republic	Germany	3-1	Italy	Strelnice, Jablonec nad Nisou

Played as an U-18 tournament from 1981 to 2001

UEFA EUROPEAN UNDER-21 CHAMPIONSHIP

Year	Host Country	Winners	Score	Runners-up	Venue
1978		Yugoslavia	1-0 4-1	German DR	Halle & Mostar
1980		Soviet Union	0-0 1-0	German DR	Rostock & Moscow
1982		England	3-1 2-3	Germany FR	Sheffield & Bremen
1984		England	1-0 2-0	Spain	Seville & Sheffield
1986		Spain	1-2 2-1 3-0p	Italy	Rome & Valladolid
1988		France	0-0 3-0	Greece	Athens & Besançon
1990		Soviet Union	4-2 3-1	Yugoslavia	Sarajevo & Simferopol
1992		Italy	2-0 0-1	Sweden	Ferrara & Växjö
1994	France	Italy	1-0	Portugal	Montpellier
1996	Spain	Italy	1-1 4-2p	Spain	Barcelona
1998	Romania	Spain	1-0	Greece	Bucharest
2000	Slovakia	Italy	2-1	Czech Republic	Bratislava
2002	Switzerland	Czech Republic	0-0 3-1p	France	St Jakob Park, Basel
2004	Germany	Italy	3-0	Serbia & Montenegro	Ruhrstadion, Bochum
2006	Portugal	Netherlands	3-0	Ukraine	Bessa, Oporto
2007	Netherlands	Netherlands	4-1	Serbia	Euroborg, Groningen

Europe has a long history of youth football dating back to the launch of the International Youth Tournament by the English FA in 1948. UEFA took over the running of that event in 1956 and it remained largely unaltered until 1980 when it was replaced by two new tournaments, for players under 16 and players under 18. These have since changed to Under-17 and Under-19 Championships to tie in with the systems used by FIFA for their World Championships at these levels. In 1998 UEFA launched their Under-19 Championship for women which, like the men's events, doubles up when required as a qualifying tournament for the FIFA World Championships. UEFA has one other age-restricted event, the UEFA European Under-21 Championship which mirrors the qualifying groups of the senior men's team, with games often played the previous day. Tournaments are played over two years and since 1992 every second edition has doubled up as a qualifing tournament for the Olympic Games.

UEFA CHAMPIONS LEAGUE

Year	Winners	Country	Score	Country	Runners-up
1956	Real Madrid	ESP	4-3	FRA	Stade de Reims
1957	Real Madrid	ESP	2-0	ITA	Fiorentina
1958	Real Madrid	ESP	3-2	ITA	Milan
1959	Real Madrid	ESP	2-0	FRA	Stade de Reims
1960	Real Madrid	ESP	7-3	FRG	Eintracht Frankfurt
1961	Benfica	POR	3-2	ESP	Barcelona
1962	Benfica	POR	5-3	ESP	Real Madrid
1963	Milan	ITA	2-1	POR	Benfica
1964	Internazionale	ITA	3-1	ESP	Real Madrid
1965	Internazionale	ITA	1-0	POR	Benfica
1966	Real Madrid	ESP	2-1	YUG	Partizan Beograd
1967	Celtic	SCO	2-1	ITA	Internazionale
1968	Manchester United	ENG	4-1	POR	Benfica
1969	Milan	ITA	4-1	NED	Ajax
1970	Feyenoord	NED	2-1	SCO	Celtic
1971	Ajax	NED	2-0	GRE	Panathinaikos
1972	Ajax	NED	2-0	ITA	Internazionale
1973	Ajax	NED	1-0	ITA	Juventus
1974	Bayern München	FRG	1-1 4-0	ESP	Atlético Madrid
1975	Bayern München	FRG	2-0	ENG	Leeds United
1976	Bayern München	FRG	1-0	FRA	AS Saint-Étienne
1977	Liverpool	ENG	3-1	FRG	Borussia Mönchengladbach
1978	Liverpool	ENG	1-0	BEL	Club Brugge
1979	Nottingham Forest	ENG	1-0	SWE	Malmö FF
1980	Nottingham Forest	ENG	1-0	FRG	Hamburger SV
1981	Liverpool	ENG	1-0	ESP	Real Madrid
1982	Aston Villa	ENG	1-0	FRG	Bayern München
1983	Hamburger SV	FRG	1-0	ITA	Juventus
1984	Liverpool	ENG	1-1 4-2p	ITA	Roma
1985	Juventus	ITA	1-0	ENG	Liverpool
1986	Steaua Bucuresti	ROU	0-0 2-0p	ESP	Barcelona
1987	FC Porto	POR	2-1	FRG	Bayern München
1988	PSV Eindhoven	NED	0-0 6-5p	POR	Benfica
1989	Milan	ITA	4-0	ROU	Steaua Bucuresti
1990	Milan	ITA	1-0	POR	Benfica
1991	Crvena Zvezda Beograd	YUG	0-0 5-3p	FRA	Olympique Marseille
1992	Barcelona	ESP	1-0	ITA	Sampdoria
1993	Olympique Marseille	FRA	1-0	ITA	Milan
1994	Milan	ITA	4-0	ESP	Barcelona
1995	Ajax	NED	1-0	ITA	Milan
1996	Juventus	ITA	1-1 4-2p	NED	Ajax
1997	Borussia Dortmund	GER	3-1	ITA	Juventus
1998	Real Madrid	ESP	1-0	ITA	Juventus
1999	Manchester United	ENG	2-1	GER	Bayern München
2000	Real Madrid	ESP	3-0	ESP	Valencia
2001	Bayern München	GER	1-1 5-4p	ESP	Valencia
2002	Real Madrid	ESP	2-1	GER	Bayer Leverkusen
2003	Milan	ITA	0-0 3-2p	ITA	Juventus
2004	FC Porto	POR	3-0	FRA	Monaco
2005	Liverpool	ENG	3-3 3-2p	ITA	Milan
2006	Barcelona	ESP	2-1	ENG	Arsenal
2007	Milan	ITA	2-1	ENG	Liverpool
2008	Manchester United	ENG	1-1 6-5p	ENG	Chelsea

FAIRS CUP

Year	Winners	Country	Score	Country	Runners-up
1958	Barcelona	ESP	2-2 6-0	ENG	London Select XI
1960	Barcelona	ESP	0-0 4-1	ENG	Birmingham City
1961	Roma	ITA	2-2 2-0	ENG	Birmingham City
1962	Valencia	ESP	6-2 1-1	ESP	Barcelona
1963	Valencia	ESP	2-1 2-0	YUG	Dinamo Zagreb
1964	Real Zaragoza	ESP	2-1	ESP	Valencia
1965	Ferencváros	HUN	1-0	ITA	Juventus
1966	Barcelona	ESP	0-1 4-2	ESP	Real Zaragoza
1967	Dinamo Zagreb	YUG	2-0 0-0	ENG	Leeds United
1968	Leeds United	ENG	1-0 0-0	HUN	Ferencváros
1969	Newcastle United	ENG	3-0 3-2	HUN	Újpesti Dózsa
1970	Arsenal	ENG	1-3 3-0	BEL	RSC Anderlecht
1971	Leeds United	ENG	2-2 1-1	ITA	Juventus

UEFA CUP

Year	Winners	Country	Score	Country	Runners-up
1972	Tottenham Hotspur	ENG	2-1 1-1	ENG	Wolverhampton Wanderers
1973	Liverpool	ENG	3-0 0-2	FRG	Borussia Mönchengladbach
1974	Feyenoord	NED	2-2 2-0	ENG	Tottenham Hotspur
1975	Borussia Mönchengladbach	FRG	0-0 5-1	NED	FC Twente Enschede
1976	Liverpool	ENG	3-2 1-1	BEL	Club Brugge
1977	Juventus	ITA	1-0 1-2	ESP	Athletic Bilbao
1978	PSV Eindhoven	NED	0-0 3-0	FRA	SEC Bastia
1979	Borussia Mönchengladbach	FRG	1-1 1-0	YUG	Crvena Zvezda Beograd
1980	Eintracht Frankfurt	FRG	2-3 1-0	FRG	Borussia Mönchengladbach
1981	Ipswich Town	ENG	3-0 2-4	NED	AZ 67 Alkmaar
1982	IFK Göteborg	SWE	1-0 3-0	FRG	Hamburger SV
1983	RSC Anderlecht	BEL	1-0 1-1	POR	Benfica
1984	Tottenham Hotspur	ENG	1-1 1-1 4-3p	BEL	RSC Anderlecht
1985	Real Madrid	ESP	3-0 0-1	HUN	Videoton SC
1986	Real Madrid	ESP	5-1 0-2	FRG	1.FC Köln
1987	IFK Göteborg	SWE	1-0 1-1	SCO	Dundee United
1988	Bayer Leverkusen	FRG	0-3 3-0 3-2p	ESP	Español
1989	Napoli	ITA	2-1 3-3	FRG	VfB Stuttgart
1990	Juventus	ITA	3-1 0-0	ITA	Fiorentina
1991	Internazionale	ITA	2-0 0-1	ITA	Roma
1992	Ajax	NED	2-2 0-0	ITA	Torino
1993	Juventus	ITA	3-1 3-0	GER	Borussia Dortmund
1994	Internazionale	ITA	1-0 1-0	AUT	Austria Salzburg
1995	Parma	ITA	1-0 1-1	ITA	Juventus
1996	Bayern München	GER	2-0 3-1	FRA	Bordeaux
1997	Schalke 04	GER	1-0 0-1 4-1p	ITA	Internazionale
1998	Internazionale	ITA	3-0	ITA	Lazio
1999	Parma	ITA	3-0	FRA	Olympique Marseille
2000	Galatasaray	TUR	0-0 4-1p	ENG	Arsenal
2001	Liverpool	ENG	5-4	ESP	CD Alavés
2002	Feyenoord	NED	3-2	GER	Borussia Dortmund
2003	FC Porto	POR	3-2	SCO	Glasgow Celtic
2004	Valencia	ESP	2-0	FRA	Olympique Marseille
2005	CSKA Moskva	RUS	3-1	POR	Sporting CP
2006	Sevilla	ESP	4-0	ENG	Middlesbrough
2007	Sevilla	ESP	2-2 3-1p	ESP	Espanyol
2008	Zenit St Petersburg	RUS	2-0	SCO	Rangers

Europe's top club competition needs little introduction, although how it is referred to may need a little explanation. Launched in 1955 as the European Champion Clubs' Cup, it was often known simply as the European Cup. In 1992 it was rebranded as the UEFA Champions League, although technically speaking many of the teams taking part are not the champions of their respective leagues and half of the competition is actually run on a knock-out basis and not a league system. Traditionally played on a knock-out basis the 1991-92 season saw the first shake-up in the format with two groups of four replacing the quarter-finals, the winners of which qualified for the final. Since then the format has been tinkered with on a number of occasions, with four first round groups introduced for the 1994-95 season, six first round groups for the 1997-98 season and finally eight first round groups and four second round groups for the 1999-2000 season. Most dramatically of all perhaps was the decision taken for the 1997-98 season which allowed more than the champions from each country to take part. There was a time when winning the UEFA Cup was seen as a more challenging task than winning the European Champions Clubs' Cup. With up to three or four clubs from the top nations taking part, compared to just one in the European Cup, the depth and quality of opposition was often stronger. Rather whimsically the tournament was at first restricted to teams from cities that had staged a major international trade fair. Renamed in 1971 the UEFA Cup now finds itself in a crisis. Qualifying for the UEFA Cup and not the UEFA Champions League is now seen by the top clubs as a major disaster, hardly good for the credibility of the tournament. This decline in prestige has had one good side effect; perhaps because the pressure is not so intense or the fear of failure so great, every final in recent years has been an entertaining extravaganza.

UEFA WOMEN'S CUP

Year	Winners	Country	Score	Country	Runners-up
2002	1.FFC Frankfurt	GER	2-0	SWE	Umeå IK
2003	Umeå IK	SWE	4-1 3-0	DEN	Fortuna Hjørring
2004	Umeå IK	SWE	3-0 5-0	GER	1.FFC Frankfurt
2005	1.FFC Turbine Potsdam	GER	2-0 3-1	SWE	Djurgården/Alvsjö
2006	1.FFC Frankfurt	GER	4-0 3-2	GER	1.FFC Turbine Potsdam
2007	Arsenal	ENG	1-0 0-0	SWE	Umeå IK
2008	1.FFC Frankfurt	GER	1-1 3-2	SWE	Umeå IK

Of all of the recent additions to the UEFA calendar the UEFA Women's Cup is potentially the most interesting. Whereas women's football in the USA has had its foundations in the college system, in Europe the link with men's clubs has been stronger and could develop further if the UEFA Women's Cup fulfils its potential and prompts clubs to become more serious about funding their female sections. For the 2005 tournament 42 of UEFA's 52 members entered teams, up from 22 in the first tournament in 2001, although it is the German and Scandinavian teams that have so far been the most successful.

UEFA EUROPEAN WOMEN'S UNDER-19 CHAMPIONSHIP

Year	Host Country	Winners	Score	Runners-up	Venue
1998		Denmark	2-0 2-3	France	Aabenraa & Niederbronn-les-Bains
1999	Sweden	Sweden	1-0	Germany	Bromölla
2000	France	Germany	4-2	Spain	La Libération, Boulogne
2001	Norway	Germany	3-2	Norway	Aråsen, Lillestrom
2002	Sweden	Germany	3-1	France	Olympia, Helsingborg
2003	Germany	France	2-0	Norway	Alfred Kunze Sportpark, Leipzig
2004	Finland	Spain	2-1	Germany	Pohjola Stadion, Vantaa
2005	Hungary	Russia	2-2 6-5p	France	ZTE, Zalaegerszeg
2006	Switzerland	Germany	3-0	France	Neufeld, Berne
2007	Iceland	Germany	2-0	England	Laugardalsvöllur, Reykjavík
2008	France	Italy	1-0	Norway	Vallée du Cher, Tours

The first three tournaments were played as U-18 championships

UEFA EUROPEAN WOMEN'S UNDER-17 CHAMPIONSHIP

Year	Host Country	Winners	Score	Runners-up	Venue
2008	Switzerland	Germany	3-0	France	Colovray, Nyon

UEFA CHAMPIONS LEAGUE MEDALS TABLE

	Country	G	S	B	F	SF
1	Italy	11	14	8	25	33
2	Spain	11	9	19	20	39
3	England	11	5	16	16	32
4	Germany	6	7	10	13	23
5	Netherlands	6	2	5	8	13
6	Portugal	4	5	2	9	11
7	France	1	5	7	6	13
8	Scotland	1	1	6	2	8
9	Romania	1	1	2	2	4
	Serbia	1	1	2	2	4
11	Belgium		1	3	1	4
12	Greece		1	2	1	3
13	Sweden		1	1	1	2
14	Hungary			3		3
	Switzerland			3		3
	Ukraine			3		3
17	Austria			2		2
	Bulgaria			2		2
	Poland			2		2
20	Czech Republic			1		1
	Russia			1		1
	Slovakia			1		1
	Turkey			1		1
		53	53	102	106	208

This table represents the Gold (winners), Silver (runners-up) and Bronze (semi-finalists) placings of clubs representing the above countries in the UEFA Champions League, along with the number of appearances in the final and semi-finals

CUP WINNERS CUP MEDALS TABLE

	Country	G	S	B	F	SF
1	England	8	5	8	13	21
2	Spain	7	7	5	14	19
3	Italy	7	4	9	11	20
4	Germany	4	4	9	8	17
5	Belgium	3	4	5	7	12
6	Scotland	2	2	4	4	8
7	Ukraine	2	-	-	2	2
8	France	1	2	6	3	9
9	German DR	1	2	3	3	6
10	Netherlands	1	1	6	2	8
11	Portugal	1	1	3	2	5
12	Georgia	1		1	1	2
13	Czechoslovakia	1			1	1
14	Austria		3	1	3	4
15	Hungary		2	1	2	3
16	Russia		1	5	1	6
17	Poland		1	1	1	2
18	Czech Republic			3		3
19	Croatia			2		2
	Serbia			2		2
	Bulgaria			2		2
22	Romania			1		1
	Wales			1		1
		39	39	78	78	156

This table represents the Gold (winners), Silver (runners-up) and Bronze (semi-finalists) placings of clubs representing the above countries in the Cup Winners Cup, along with the number of appearances in the final and semi-finals

FAIRS/UEFA CUP MEDALS TABLE

	Country	G	S	B	F	SF
1	Spain	11	7	11	18	29
2	Italy	10	8	16	18	34
3	England	10	8	9	18	27
4	Germany	6	7	24	13	37
5	Netherlands	4	2	3	6	9
6	Russia	2		1	2	3
7	Sweden	2			2	2
8	Belgium	1	3	5	4	9
9	Hungary	1	3	3	4	7
10	Portugal	1	2	2	3	5
11	Croatia	1	1	1	2	3
12	Turkey	1		1	1	2
13	France		4	5	4	9
14	Scotland		3	4	3	7
15	Serbia		1	3	1	4
16	Austria		1	1	1	2
17	Czech Republic			2		2
	German DR			2		2
	Switzerland			2		2
	Romania			2		2
21	Bosnia-Herzegovina			1		1
	Denmark			1		1
	Greece			1		1
		50	50	100	100	200

This table represents the Gold (winners), Silver (runners-up) and Bronze (semi-finalists) placings of clubs representing the above countries in the UEFA Cup, along with the number of appearances in the final and semi-finals

UEFA CHAMPIONS LEAGUE MEDALS TABLE

#	Country		G	S	B
1	Real Madrid	ESP	9	3	9
2	Milan	ITA	7	4	2
3	Liverpool	ENG	5	2	3
4	Bayern München	GER	4	3	5
5	Ajax	NED	4	2	2
6	Manchester United	ENG	3		7
7	Juventus	ITA	2	5	3
8	Benfica	POR	2	5	1
9	Barcelona	ESP	2	3	5
10	Internazionale	ITA	2	2	3
11	FC Porto	POR	2		1
12	Nottingham Forest	ENG	2		
13	Glasgow Celtic	SCO	1	1	2
14	Hamburger SV	GER	1	1	1
	Olympique Marseille	FRA	1	1	1
	Steaua Bucuresti	ROU	1	1	1
17	Borussia Dortmund	GER	1		2
	Crvena Zvezda Beograd	SER	1		2
	PSV Eindhoven	NED	1		2
20	Feyenoord	NED	1		1
21	Aston Villa	ENG	1		
22	Stade de Reims	FRA		2	
	Valencia	ESP		2	
24	Chelsea	ENG		1	3
25	Atlético Madrid	ESP		1	2
	Leeds United	ENG		1	2
	AS Monaco	FRA		1	2
	Panathinaikos	GRE		1	2
29	Borussia Mönchengladbach	GER		1	1
	AS Saint-Étienne	FRA		1	1
31	Arsenal	ENG		1	
	Bayer Leverkusen	GER		1	
	Club Brugge	BEL		1	
	Eintracht Frankfurt	GER		1	
	Fiorentina	ITA		1	
	Malmö FF	SWE		1	
	Partizan Beograd	SRB		1	
	Roma	ITA		1	
	Sampdoria	ITA		1	
40	Dynamo Kyiv	UKR			3
41	RSC Anderlecht	BEL			2
	CSKA Sofia	BUL			2
	FC Zürich	SUI			2
44	FK Austria	AUT			1
	Girondins Bordeaux	FRA			1
	Deportivo La Coruna	ESP			1
	Derby County	ENG			1
	Dinamo Bucuresti	ROU			1
	Dukla Praha	CZE			1
	Dundee	SCO			1
	Dundee United	SCO			1
	Galatasaray	TUR			1
	IFK Göteborg	SWE			1
	Hibernian Edinburgh	SCO			1
	1.FC Köln	GER			1
	Legia Warszawa	POL			1

UEFA CHAMPIONS LEAGUE MEDALS TABLE (CONTD)

Country		G	S	B
FC Nantes	FRA			1
Paris Saint-Germain	FRA			1
Rába ETO Györ	HUN			1
Glasgow Rangers	SCO			1
SK Rapid Wien	AUT			1
Real Sociedad	ESP			1
Spartak Moskva	RUS			1
Spartak Trnava	SVK			1
Standard CL	BEL			1
Tottenham Hotspur	ENG			1
Ujpesti TE	HUN			1
Vasas Budapest	HUN			1
Villarreal	ESP			1
Widzew Lódz	POL			1
Young Boys Berne	SUI			1
		53	53	102

FAIRS/UEFA CUP MEDALS TABLE

	Country		G	S	B
1	Juventus	ITA	3	3	1
2	Internazionale	ITA	3	1	5
3	Barcelona	ESP	3	1	4
4	Valencia	ESP	3	1	
5	Liverpool	ENG	3		1
6	Borussia Mönchengladbach	GER	2	2	1
7	Leeds United	ENG	2	1	2
8	Tottenham Hotspur	ENG	2	1	1
9	Parma	ITA	2		1
	Real Madrid	ESP	2		1
11	Feyenoord	NED	2		
	IFK Göteborg	SWE	2		
	Sevilla	ESP	2		
14	RSC Anderlecht	BEL	1	2	
15	Ferencváros	HUN	1	1	2
16	Roma	ITA	1	1	1
17	Arsenal	ENG	1	1	
	Dinamo Zagreb	CRO	1	1	
	Real Zaragoza	ESP	1	1	
20	Bayern München	GER	1		3
21	Ajax	NED	1		1
	Bayer Leverkusen	GER	1		1
	Eintracht Frankfurt	GER	1		1
	Newcastle United	ENG	1		1
	FC Schalke 04	GER	1		1
26	CSKA Moskva	RUS	1		
	Galatasaray	TUR	1		
	Ipswich Town	ENG	1		
	Napoli	ITA	1		
	FC Porto	POR	1		
	PSV Eindhoven	NED	1		
	Zenit St Petersburg	RUS	1		
33	Birmingham City	ENG		2	1
	Borussia Dortmund	GER		2	1
35	RCD Español	ESP		2	
	Olympique Marseille	FRA		2	
37	1.FC Köln	GER		1	5
38	VfB Stuttgart	GER		1	2
39	AZ Alkmaar	NED		1	1
	Club Brugge	BEL		1	1
	Crvena Zvezda Beograd	SRB		1	1
	Fiorentina	ITA		1	1
	Glasgow Rangers	SCO		1	1
	Hamburger SV	GER		1	1
	Lazio	ITA		1	1
	Sporting CP	POR		1	1
	Twente Enschede	NED		1	1
48	Austria Salzburg	AUT		1	
	CD Alavés	ESP		1	
	Athletic Bilbao	ESP		1	
	SEC Bastia	FRA		1	
	Benfica	POR		1	
	Girondins Bordeaux	FRA		1	
	Glasgow Celtic	SCO		1	
	Dundee United	SCO		1	
	London Select XI	ENG		1	

FAIRS/UEFA CUP MEDALS TABLE

	Country		G	S	B
	Middlesbrough	ENG		1	
	Torino	ITA		1	
	Ujpesti TE	HUN		1	
	Videoton SC	HUN		1	
	Wolverhampton Wanderers	ENG		1	
62	Atlético Madrid	ESP			3
	Werder Bremen	GER			3
64	Bologna	ITA			2
	1.FC Kaiserslautern	GER			2
	Milan	ITA			2
67	AEK Athens	GRE			1
	AJ Auxerre	FRA			1
	Belgrade Select XI	SRB			1
	Boavista	POR			1
	Brondbyernes IF	DEN			1
	Cagliari	ITA			1
	Chelsea	ENG			1
	MSV Duisburg	GER			1
	Bohemians Praha	CZE			1
	Dundee	SCO			1
	1.FC Dynamo Dresden	GDR			1
	Genoa 1893	ITA			1
	Grasshopper-Club	SUI			1
	Göztepe Izmir	TUR			1
	Hibernian Edinburgh	SCO			1
	Hajduk Split	CRO			1
	Hertha BSC Berlin	GER			1
	Karlsruher SC	GER			1
	Kilmarnock	SCO			1
	RFC Liège	BEL			1
	Lausanne-Sports	SUI			1
	VfB Leipzig	GDR			1
	Racing Club Lens	FRA			1
	Manchester United	ENG			1
	AS Monaco	FRA			1
	MTK-VM Budapest	HUN			1
	RWD Molenbeek	BEL			1
	Nottingham Forest	ENG			1
	Osasuna	ESP			1
	Paris Saint-Germain	FRA			1
	Radnicki Nis	SRB			1
	Slavia Praha	CZE			1
	FC Sochaux	FRA			1
	Spartak Moskva	RUS			1
	Steaua Bucuresti	ROU			1
	Tenerife	ESP			1
	FC Tirol	AUT			1
	Universitatea Craiova	ROU			1
	Union St. Gilloise	BEL			1
	Villarreal	ESP			1
	KSV Waregem	BEL			1
	Zeljeznicar Sarajevo	BIH			1
			50	50	100

BALLON D'OR 2007

BALLON D'OR 2007

Kaká	Milan	BRA	444
Cristiano Ronaldo	Man United	POR	277
Lionel Messi	Barcelona	ARG	255
Didier Drogba	Chelsea	CIV	108
Andrea Pirlo	Milan	ITA	41
Ruud Van Nistelroij	Real Madrid	NED	39
Zlatan Ibrahimovic	Inter	SWE	31
Cesc Fabregas	Arsenal	ESP	27
Robinho	Real Madrid	BRA	24
Francesco Totti	Roma	ITA	20
Frédéric Kanouté	Sevilla	MLI	19
Ronaldinho	Barcelona	BRA	18
Steven Gerrard	Liverpool	ENG	17
Juan Román Riquelme	Boca Juniors	ARG	15
Daniel Alves	Sevilla	BRA	14

The Ballon d'Or is awarded by *France Football* magazine. From 1956 until 1994 was open only to Europeans. From 1995 until 2006 it was open to any player signed to a European club but is now open to any player in the world

RECENT BALLON D'OR AWARDS

BALLON D'OR 1998

ZIDANE Zinedine	Juventus	FRA	244
SUKER Davor	Real Madrid	CRO	68
RONALDO	Internazionale	BRA	66
OWEN Michael	Liverpool	ENG	51
RIVALDO	Barcelona	BRA	45
BATISTUTA Gabriel	Fiorentina	ARG	43
THURAM Lilian	Parma	FRA	36
BERGKAMP Dennis	Arsenal	NED	28
DAVIDS Edgar	Juventus	NED	28
DESAILLY Marcel	Chelsea	FRA	19

BALLON D'OR 1999

RIVALDO	Barcelona	BRA	219
BECKHAM David	Man United	ENG	154
SHEVCHENKO Andriy	Milan	UKR	64
BATISTUTA Gabriel	Fiorentina	ARG	48
FIGO	Barcelona	POR	38
KEANE Roy	Man United	IRL	36
VIERI Christian	Internazionale	ITA	33
VERON Juan Seb.	Lazio	ARG	30
RAUL	Real Madrid	ESP	27
MATTHAUS Lothar	Bayern	GER	16

BALLON D'OR 2000

FIGO	Real Madrid	POR	197
ZIDANE Zinedine	Juventus	FRA	181
SHEVCHENKO Andriy	Milan	UKR	85
HENRY Thierry	Arsenal	FRA	57
NESTA Alessandro	Lazio	ITA	39
RIVALDO	Barcelona	BRA	39
BATISTUTA Gabriel	Roma	ARG	26
MENDIETA Gaizka	Valencia	ESP	22
RAUL	Real Madrid	ESP	18
Two players with 10 votes			

BALLON D'OR 2001

OWEN Michael	Liverpool	ENG	176
RAUL	Real Madrid	ESP	140
KAHN Oliver	Bayern	GER	114
BECKHAM David	Man United	ENG	102
TOTTI Francesco	Roma	ITA	57
FIGO	Real Madrid	POR	56
RIVALDO	Barcelona	BRA	20
SHEVCHENKO Andriy	Milan	UKR	18
HENRY Thierry	Arsenal	FRA	14
ZIDANE Zinedine	Real Madrid	FRA	14

BALLON D'OR 2002

RONALDO	Real Madrid	BRA	171
ROBERTO CARLOS	Real Madrid	BRA	145
KAHN Oliver	Bayern	GER	114
ZIDANE Zinedine	Real Madrid	FRA	78
BALLACK Michael	Bayern	GER	67
HENRY Thierry	Arsenal	FRA	54
RAUL	Real Madrid	ESP	38
RIVALDO	Milan	BRA	29
BASTURK Yildiray	Leverkusen	TUR	13
DEL PIERO Alex	Juventus	ITA	12

BALLON D'OR 2003

NEDVED Pavel	Juventus	CZE	190
HENRY Thierry	Arsenal	FRA	128
MALDINI Paolo	Milan	ITA	123
SHEVCHENKO Andriy	Milan	UKR	67
ZIDANE Zinedine	Real Madrid	FRA	64
VAN NISTELROOIJ Ruud	Man United	NED	61
RAUL	Real Madrid	ESP	32
ROBERTO CARLOS	Real Madrid	BRA	27
BUFFON Gianluigi	Juventus	ITA	19
BECKHAM David	Real Madrid	ENG	17

BALLON D'OR 2004

SHEVCHENKO Andriy	Milan	UKR	175
DECO	Barcelona	POR	139
RONALDINHO	Barcelona	BRA	133
HENRY Thierry	Arsenal	FRA	80
ZAGORAKIS Theodoros	Bologna	GRE	44
ADRIANO	Internazionale	BRA	23
NEDVED Pavel	Juventus	CZE	23
ROONEY Wayne	Man United	ENG	22
RICARDO CARVALHO	Chelsea	POR	18
VAN NISTELROOIJ Ruud	Man United	NED	18

BALLON D'OR 2005

RONALDINHO	Barcelona	BRA	225
LAMPARD Frank	Chelsea	ENG	148
GERRARD Steven	Liverpool	ENG	142
HENRY Thierry	Arsenal	FRA	41
SHEVCHENKO Andriy	Milan	UKR	33
MALDINI Paolo	Milan	ITA	23
ADRIANO	Internazionale	BRA	22
IBRAHIMOVIC Zlatan	Juventus	SWE	21
KAKA	Milan	BRA	19
Two players with 18 votes			

BALLON D'OR 2006

CANNAVARO Fabio	Real Madrid	ITA	173
BUFFON Gianluigi	Juventus	ITA	124
HENRY Thierry	Arsenal	FRA	121
RONALDINHO	Barcelona	BRA	73
ZIDANE Zinedine	Real Madrid	FRA	71
ETO'O Samuel	Barcelona	CMR	67
KLOSE Miroslav	Werder Bremen	GER	29
DROGBA Didier	Chelsea	CIV	25
PIRLO Andrea	Milan	ITA	17
LEHMAN Jens	Arsenal	GER	13

UEFA EURO 2008 QUALIFIERS

GROUP A

GROUP A	PL	W	D	L	F	A	PTS	POL	POR	SRB	FIN	BEL	KAZ	ARM	AZE
1 Poland	14	8	4	2	24	12	28		2-1	1-1	1-3	2-0	3-1	1-0	5-0
2 Portugal	14	7	6	1	24	10	27	2-2		1-1	0-0	4-0	3-0	1-0	3-0
3 Serbia	14	6	6	2	22	11	24	2-2	1-1		0-0	1-0	1-0	3-0	1-0
4 Finland	14	6	6	2	13	7	24	0-0	1-1	0-2		2-0	2-1	1-0	2-1
5 Belgium	14	5	3	6	14	16	18	0-1	1-2	3-2	0-0		0-0	3-0	3-0
6 Kazakhstan	14	2	4	8	11	21	10	0-1	1-2	2-1	0-2	2-2		1-2	1-1
7 Armenia	12	2	3	7	4	13	9	1-0	1-1	0-0	0-0	0-1	0-1		-
8 Azerbaijan	12	1	2	9	6	28	5	1-3	0-2	1-6	1-0	0-1	1-1	-	

Poland and Portugal qualify for the finals

Ratina, Tampere
22-08-2007, 19:00, 13 047, Kassai HUN
Finland 2
Eremenko Jr 13, Tainio 61
Jussi Jääskeläinen• - Toni Kallio•, Sami Hyypiä, Hannu Tihinen, Petri Pasanen, Roman Eremenko (Daniel Sjolund 46), Markus Heikkinen•, Joonas Kolkka (Mika Nurmela 88), Teemu Tainio (Aki Riihilahti 76), Alexei Eremenko Jr, Jonatan Johansson. Tr: Roy Hodgson
Kazakhstan 1
Byakov 23
David Loria - Yegor Azovskiy, Aleksandr Kuchma, Samat Smakov, Farkhadbek Irismetov, Sergey Skorykh• (Anton Chichulin 69), Sergey Larin (Kairat Ashirbekov 78), Ruslan Baltiev•, Nurbol Zhumaskaliyev, Dmitriy Byakov, Sergey Ostapenko (Murat Suyumagambetov 70). Tr: Arno Pijpers

Republican, Yerevan
22-08-2007, 21:00, 14 935, Larsen DEN
Armenia 1
Arzumanyan 11
Roman Berezovsky - Sargis Hovsepyan, Robert Arzumanyan, Aleksandr Tadevosyan, Agvan Mkrtchyan, Levon Pachajyan, Artur Voskanyan, Ararat Arakelyan, Artavazd Karamyan (Egishe Melikyan 70), Hamlet Mkhitaryan (Gevorg Ghazaryan 59), Samvel Melkonyan (Romik Khachatryan 90). Tr: Ian Porterfield
Portugal 1
Ronaldo 37
Ricardo - Luis Miguel, Fernando Meira, Jorge Andrade• (Bruno Alves 76), Paulo Ferreira, Raul Meireles, Tiago, Deco, Cristiano Ronaldo, Hélder Postiga (Nuno Gomes 61), Simão (Ricardo Quaresma 63). Tr: Luiz Felipe Scolari

Roi Baudouin, Brussels
22-08-2007, 20:45, 19 202, Hauge NOR
Belgium 3
Dembélé 2 10 88, Mirallas 30
Stijn Stijnen - Timmy Simons, Carl Hoefkens, Thomas Vermaelen, Vincent Kompany, Gaby Mudingayi, Bart Goor•, Karel Geraerts, Kevin Mirallas (Anthony Vanden Borre 67), Moussa Dembélé (Nicolas Lombaerts 90), Steven Defour (Mbo Mpenza 86). Tr: René Vandereycken
Serbia 2
Kuzmanovic 2 73 91+
Vladimir Stojkovic - Antonio Rukavina, Nemanja Vidic•, Mladen Krstajic•, Ivica Dragutinovic, Nenad Kovacevic, Zdravko Kuzmanovic, Boško Jankovic, Ognjen Koroman (Milos Krasic 56), Danko Lazovic (Milan Smiljanic 70), Marko Pantelic (Milan Jovanovic 56). Tr: Javier Clemente

---

Crvena Zvezda, Belgrade
8-09-2007, 20:15, 10 530, Braamhaar NED
Serbia 0
Vladimir Stojkovic - Antonio Rukavina, Branislav Ivanovic, Ivica Dragutinovic, Duško Tošic• (Zoran Tosic 53), Nenad Kovacevic, Zdravko Kuzmanovic, Dejan Stankovic, Boško Jankovic• (Milan Jovanovic 54), Miloš Krasic, Danko Lazovic (Nikola Zigic 62). Tr: Javier Clemente
Finland 0
Jussi Jääskeläinen - Petri Pasanen, Sami Hyypiä, Hannu Tihinen, Toni Kuivasto, Mika Nurmela, Teemu Tainio•, Markus Heikkinen, Alexei Eremenko Jr (Mikael Forssell 74), Daniel Sjölund, Jonatan Johansson (Jarkko Wiss 78). Tr: Roy Hodgson

Estádio da Luz, Lisbon
8-09-2007, 21:00, 48 000, Rosetti ITA
Portugal 2
Maniche 50, Ronaldo 73
Ricardo - Bosingwa, Fernando Meira, Bruno Alves, Marco Caneira, Deco, Maniche, Petit, Cristiano Ronaldo, Nuno Gomes (Ricardo Quaresma 69), Simão (Joao Moutinho 81). Tr: Luiz Felipe Scolari
Poland 2
Lewandowski 44, Krzynówek 88
Artur Boruc• - Marcin Wasilewski•, Mariusz Jop, Michal Zewlakow, Grzegorz Bronowicki• (Pawel Golanski 55), Jakub Blaszczykowski, Mariusz Lewandowski, Dariusz Dudka, Euzebiusz Smolarek (Wojciech Lobodzinski 73), Jacek Krzynówek, Maciej Zurawski (Radoslaw Matusiak 56). Tr: Leo Beenhakker

José Alvalade, Lisbon
12-09-2007, 21:00, 48 000, Merk GER
Portugal 1
Simão 11
Ricardo - Paulo Ferreira, Fernando Meira, Buno Alves, Petit•, Bosingwa, Deco (Joao Moutinho 77), Maniche (Raul Meireles 83), Cristiano Ronaldo, Nuno Gomes (Ricardo Quaresma 65), Simão. Tr: Luiz Felipe Scolari
Serbia 1
Ivanovic 88
Vladimir Stojkovic• - Antonio Rukavina, Ivica Dragutinovic••92+, Nemanja Vidic•, Branislav Ivanovic, Zoran Tošic (Nikola Zigic 61), Dejan Stankovic, Nenad Kovacevic, Miloš Krasic (Marko Pantelic 61), Zdravko Kuzmanovic (Igor Duljaj 71), Milan Jovanovic. Tr: Javier Clemente

---

Tcentralny, Almaty
12-09-2007, 21:00, 18 100, Tudor ROU
Kazakhstan 2
Byakov 39, Smakov 77p
David Loria - Yegor Azovskiy (Dmitri Lyapkin 66), Samat Smakov, Farkhadbek Irismetov•, Aleksandr Kuchma, Sergey Larin (Murat Suyumagambetov 73), Sergey Skorykh, Andrei Karpovitch, Nurbol Zhumaskaliyev, Sergey Ostapenko, Dmitriy Byakov. Tr: Arno Pijpers
Belgium 2
Geraerts 13, Mirallas 24
Stijn Stijnen - Timmy Simons, Vincent Kompany, Carl Hoefkens, Thomas Vermaelen, Bart Goor (Mbo Mpenza 84), Marouane Fellaini•, Karel Geraerts (Faris Haroun 77), Steven Defour•, Kevin Mirallas (Jan Vertonghen 63), Moussa Dembélé. Tr: René Vandereycken

Olympiastadion, Helsinki
12-09-2007, 19:00, 34 088, Fandel GER
Finland 0
Jussi Jääskeläinen - Toni Kuivasto, Sami Hyypiä, Hannu Tihinen, Petri Pasanen, Daniel Sjölund, Markus Heikkinen (Jarkko Wiss 90+1), Teemu Tainio, Joonas Kolkka, Alexei Eremenko Jr•, Jonatan Johansson (Mikael Forssell 72). Tr: Roy Hodgson
Poland 0
Artur Boruc - Pawel Golanski, Mariusz Jop•, Michal Zewlakow, Jakub Blaszczykowski•, Dariusz Dudka, Radoslaw Sobolewski, Mariusz Lewandowski, Euzebiusz Smolarek (Maciej Zurawski 80), Jacek Krzynówek, Grzegorz Rasiak (Marek Saganowski 65). Tr: Leo Beenhakker

Republican, Yerevan
13-10-2007, 20:00, 7150, Johannesson SWE
Armenia 0
Roman Berezovsky - Sargis Hovsepyan, Robert Arzumanyan, Karen Dokhoyan, Aleksandr Tadevosyan, Levon Pachajyan, Artur Voskanyan (Romik Khachatryan 70), Ararat Arakelyan•, Artavazd Karamyan, Hamlet Mkhitaryan• (Aram Hakobyan 82), Samvel Melkonyan (Robert Zebelyan 62). Tr: Vardan Minasyan
Serbia 0
Vladimir Stojkovic - Antonio Rukavina•, Branislav Ivanovic, Milan Stepanov•, Duško Tošic, Nenad Kovacevic, Zdravko Kuzmanovic (Zoran Tosic 61), Dejan Stankovic•, Miloš Krasic (Bosko Jankovic 73), Marko Pantelic (Danko Lazovic 62), Nikola Zigic. Tr: Javier Clemente

Legia, Warsaw
13-10-2007, 20:30, 11 040, Berntsen NOR

Poland 3

Smolarek 3 [56] [65] [66]

Artur Boruc - Mariusz Jop, Grzegorz Bronowicki, Dariusz Dudka, Jacek Bak, Euzebiusz Smolarek, Jacek Krzynówek, Marek Saganowski (Maciej Zurawski 46), Michal Zewlakow (Marcin Wasilewski 46), Wojciech Lobodzinski (Kamil Kosowski 80), Mariusz Lewandowski. Tr: Leo Beenhakker

Kazakhstan 1

Byakov [20]

David Loria - Dmitri Lyapkin•, Aleksandr Kuchma, Samat Smakov, Kairat Nurdauletov, Sergey Skorykh (Andrei Karpovitch 81), Ruslan Baltiev, Nurbol Zhumaskaliyev, Sergey Larin (Murat Suyumagambetov 73), Sergey Ostapenko, Dmitriy Byakov (Kairat Ashirbekov 85).Tr: Arno Pijpers

Tcentralny, Almaty
17-10-2007, 20:00, 25 057, Wegereef NED

Kazakhstan 1

Byakov [93+]

David Loria - Samat Smakov•, Maksim Zhalmagambetov, Farkhadbek Irismetov•, Aleksandr Kuchma, Sergey Larin (Dmitri Lyapkin 37), Sergey Skorykh, Andrei Karpovitch• (Kairat Nurdauletov 89), Nurbol Zhumaskaliyev, Sergey Ostapenko, Dmitriy Byakov. Tr: Arno Pijpers

Portugal 2

Makukula [84], Ronaldo [91+]

Ricardo - Luis Miguel, Ricardo Carvalho, Bruno Alves, Paulo Ferreira, Maniche• (Nani 59), Deco, Miguel Veloso, Ricardo Quaresma (Joao Moutinho 85), Hugo Almeida (Ariza Makukula 63), Cristiano Ronaldo. Tr: Flávio Teixeira

Olympiastadion, Helsinki
17-11-2007, 16:00, 10 325, Hamer LUX

Finland 1

Forssell [79], Kuqi [86]

Jussi Jääskeläinen - Petri Pasanen•, Sami Hyypiä, Hannu Tihinen, Toni Kallio (Mika Vayrynen 66), Joonas Kolkka, Roman Eremenko (Shefki Kuqi 80), Teemu Tainio, Daniel Sjölund, Mikael Forssell, Jonatan Johansson (Jari Litmanen 59). Tr: Roy Hodgson

Azerbaijan 1

Gurbonov.M [63]

Farkhad Veliyev - Samir Abbasov, Usima Nduka• (Elvin Aliyev• 46), Sasha Yunisoglu•, Rashad F. Sadygov, Zaur Tagizade, Makhmud Gurbonov•, Branimir Subasic•, Zaur Ramazanov, Ramin Guliyev (Andre Ladaga 61), Jemshid Maharramov. Tr: Gjokica Hadzievski

Republican, Yerevan
21-11-2007, 19:00, 3100, Fautrel FRA

Armenia 0

Roman Berezovsky - Sargis Hovsepyan, Robert Arzumanyan, Karen Dokhoyan, Aleksandr Tadevosyan, Ararat Arakelyan (Romik Khachatryan), Artur Voskanyan (Gevorg Ghazaryan• 80), Artavazd Karamyan, Hamlet Mkhitaryan, Levon Pachajyan, Samvel Melkonyan (Edgar Manucharyan 59). Tr: Vardan Minasyan

Kazakhstan 1

Ostapenko [64]

David Loria - Kairat Nurdauletov, Aleksandr Kuchma•, Maksim Zhalmagambetov•, Farkhadbek Irismetov, Ruslan Baltiev, Sergey Larin (Dmitri Lyapkin 61), Sergey Skorykh, Nurbol Zhumaskaliyev, Sergey Ostapenko, Dmitriy Byakov. Tr: Arno Pijpers

Roi Baudouin, Brussels
13-10-2007, 20:45, 21 393, Kapitanis CYP

Belgium 0

Stijn Stijnen - Nicolas Lombaerts, Daniel Van Buyten, Vincent Kompany, Guillaume Gillet, Timmy Simons, Gaby Mudingayi, Faris Haroun (Bart Goor 67), Christophe Grégoire (Wesley Sonck 67), Kevin Mirallas• (Francois Sterchele 84), Moussa Dembélé. Tr: René Vandereycken

Finland 0

Jussi Jääskeläinen - Sami Hyypiä, Petri Pasanen, Hannu Tihinen, Toni Kallio, Alexei Eremenko Jr•, Roman Eremenko, Aki Riihilahti, Jonatan Johansson (Shefki Kuqi 90), Joonas Kolkka, Daniel Sjölund (Mika Nurmela 92+). Tr: Roy Hodgson

Roi Baudouin, Brussels
17-10-2007, 20:45, 14 812, Valgeirsson ISL

Belgium 3

Sonck [63], Dembélé [69], Geraerts [76]

Stijn Stijnen - Nicolas Lombaerts (Jan Vertonghen 83), Daniel Van Buyten (Vincent Kompany 60), Timmy Simons, Gill Swerts•, Steven Defour, Marouane Fellaini, Bart Goor, Karel Geraerts, Moussa Dembélé, Kevin Mirallas (Wesley Sonck 46). Tr: René Vandereycken

Armenia 0

Gevorg Kasparov - Aleksandr Tadevosyan (Agvan Mkrtchyan 82), Sargis Hovsepyan, Robert Arzumanyan, Karen Dokhoyan, Ararat Arakelyan, Romik Khachatryan (Aram Hakobyan 57), Levon Pachajyan, Artur Voskanyan, Samvel Melkonyan (Robert Zebelyan 70), Artavazd Karamyan. Tr: Vardan Minasyan

Slaski, Chorzow
17-11-2007, 20:30, 41 450, Larsen DEN

Poland 2

Smolarek 2 [45] [49]

Artur Boruc - Michal Zewlakow, Jacek Bak•, Marcin Wasilewski, Grzegorz Bronowicki, Wojciech Lobodzinski (Jakub Blaszczykowski• 46), Radoslaw Sobolewski, Jacek Krzynówek, Mariusz Lewandowski, Euzebiusz Smolarek (Kamil Kosowski 85), Maciej Zurawski (Rafal Murawski 82). Tr: Leo Beenhakker

Belgium 0

Stijn Stijnen - Jan Vertonghen, Daniel Van Buyten, Vincent Kompany, Guillaume Gillet, Bart Goor, Faris Haroun (Karel Geraerts 84), Marouane Fellaini, Steven Defour (Luigi Pieroni 61), Moussa Dembélé, Kevin Mirallas (Stein Huysegems 76). Tr: René Vandereycken

Estádio do Dragão, Porto
21-11-2007, 19:45, 49 000, Michel SVK

Portugal 0

Ricardo - Bosingwa, Pepe, Bruno Alves, Marco Caneira•, Fernando Meira, Miguel Veloso, Maniche (Raul Meireles 73), Cristiano Ronaldo, Nuno Gomes (Ariza Makukula• 77), Ricardo Quaresma (Nani 84). Tr: Luiz Felipe Scolari

Finland 0

Jussi Jääskeläinen - Sami Hyypiä•, Toni Kallio, Petri Pasanen•, Hannu Tihinen, Markus Heikkinen, Joonas Kolkka (Jonatan Johansson 75), Jari Litmanen (Mika Vayrynen 67), Daniel Sjölund•, Teemu Tainio (Roman Eremenko 69), Mikael Forssell•. Tr: Roy Hodgson

Tofikh Bakhramov, Baku
13-10-2007, 21:00, 25 000, Bebek CRO

Azerbaijan 0

Farkhad Veliyev - Elvin Aliyev, Samir Abbasov, Aslan Kerimov•29, Sasha Yunisoglu•, Emin Guliyev, Aleksandr Chertoganov, Emin Imamaliev (Zaur Gashimov 7), Ilgar Gurbanov (Khagani Mamedov 56), Branimir Subašic, Samir Aliyev (Alim Gurbanov 73). Tr: Shakhin Diniyev

Portugal 2

Bruno Alves [12], Hugo Almeida [45]

Ricardo• - Bruno Alves, Paulo Ferreira, Luis Miguel (Jorge Ribeiro• 75), Ricardo Carvalho, Maniche, Deco, Miguel Veloso, Cristiano Ronaldo, Ricardo Quaresma (Nani 70), Hugo Almeida. Tr: Flávio Teixeira

Tofikh Bakhramov, Baku
17-10-2007, 21:00, 3100, Einwaller UAT

Azerbaijan 1

Aliyev [26]

Farkhad Veliyev (Jahangir Hasanzade 45) - Samir Abbasov, Ramin Guliyev, Zaur Gashimov (Elmar Bakshiev• 50), Dzeykhun Sultanov• (Farrukh Ismaylov 69), Emin Guliyev, Alim Gurbanov, Aleksandr Chertoganov, Ramazan Abbasov, Samir Aliyev, Branimir Subašic. Tr: Shakhin Diniyev

Serbia 6

Tosic.D [4], Zigic 2 [17] [42], Jankovic [41], Jovanovic [75], Lazovic [81]

Vladimir Stojkovic - Milan Bisevac, Branislav Ivanovic, Antonio Rukavina, Dusko Tosic, Zoran Tosic, Igor Duljaj, Bosko Jankovic (Danko Lazovic 68), Nenad Kovacevic (Milan Jovanovic 65), Zdravko Kuzmanovic•, Nikola Zigic (Marko Pantelic 73). Tr: Javier Clemente

Dr Magalhães Pessoa, Leiria
17-11-2007, 21:00, 22 048, Riley ENG

Portugal 1

Hugo Almeida [42]

Ricardo - Bosingwa•, Fernando Meira, Bruno Alves, Marco Caneira•, Miguel Veloso, Maniche, Cristiano Ronaldo, Simão (Nani 77), Ricardo Quaresma (Manuel Fernandes 60), Hugo Almeida (Ariza Makukula 68). Tr: Flávio Teixeira

Armenia 0

Roman Berezovsky - Sargis Hovsepyan, Robert Arzumanyan•, Karen Dokhoyan, Aleksandr Tadevosyan, Ararat Arakelyan, Artur Voskanyan, Romik Khachatryan (Hamlet Mkhitaryan 59), Samvel Melkonyan (Edgar Manucharyan 63), Levon Pachajyan•, Artavazd Karamyan (Agvan Mkrtchyan 76). Tr: Vardan Minasyan

Crvena Zvezda, Belgrade
21-11-2007, 20:45, 3247, Busacca SUI

Serbia 2

Zigic [68], Lazovic [70]

Vlada Avramov - Antonio Rukavina, Branislav Ivanovic, Mladen Krstajic (Dusko Tosic 64), Ivica Dragutinovic, Zdravko Kuzmanovic, Nenad Kovacevic, Igor Duljaj (Danko Lazovic 46), Milos Krasic (Bosko Jankovic 76), Milan Jovanovic, Nikola Zigic. Tr: Javier Clemente

Poland 2

Murawski [28], Matusiak [46]

Lukasz Fabianski - Marcin Wasilewski, Jacek Bak (Michal Zewlakow 77), Mariusz Jop, Jakub Wawrzyniak, Wojciech Lobodzinski, Mariusz Lewandowski, Grzegorz Bronowicki, Rafal Murawski, Kamil Kosowski (Tomasz Zahorski 19), Grzegorz Rasiak (Radoslaw Matusiak 46). Tr: Leo Beenhakker

Tofikh Bakhramov, Baku	
21-11-2007, 21:00, 7000, Kenan ISR	
Azerbaijan	**0**

Farkhad Veliyev - Rail Melikov, Samir Abbasov, Rashad F. Sadygov, Ramin Guliyev, Makhmud Gurbonov, Aslan Kerimov (Khagani Mamedov 84), Jemshid Maharramov (Anatoli Ponomarev 77), Zaur Tagizade (Leandro Gomes 70), Zaur Ramazanov, Branimir Subasic. Tr: Gjokica Hadzievski

Belgium	**1**
	Pieroni [52]

Brian Vandenbussche - Jelle Van Damme, Daniel Van Buyten, Guillaume Gillet, Jan Vertonghen, Marouane Fellaini, Christophe Grégoire (Bart Goor 68), Gill Swerts, Karel Geraerts (Steven Defour 46), Moussa Dembélé, Luigi Pieroni (Kevin Mirallas 81). Tr: René Vandereycken

Partizan, Belgrade	
24-11-2007, 18:00, 500, Vassaras GRE	
Serbia	**1**
	Ostapenko OG [79]

Vlada Avramov• - Ivan Stevanovic, Djordje Tutoric, Branislav Ivanovic, Dusan Andjelkovic, Gojko Kacar•, Igor Duljaj, Milos Krasic• (Bosko Jankovic 24), Milan Jovanovic (Stefan Babovic 63), Nikola Zigic (Ljubomir Fejsa 80), Ranko Despotovic. Tr: Javier Clemente

Kazakhstan	**0**

David Loria - Samat Smakov, Sergey Skorykh, Maksim Zhalmagambetov•, Kairat Nurdauletov, Dmitri Lyapkin (Nurbol Zhumaskaliyev 83), Farkhadbek Irismetov, Ruslan Baltiev• (Kairat Ashirbekov 86), Andrei Karpovitch, Dmitriy Byakov•, Murat Suyumagambetov (Sergey Ostapenko 73).Tr: Arno Pijpers

GROUP B

	GROUP B	PL	W	D	L	F	A	PTS	ITA	FRA	SCO	UKR	LTU	GEO	FRO
1	Italy	12	9	2	1	22	9	29		0-0	2-0	2-0	1-1	2-0	3-1
2	France	12	8	2	2	25	5	26	3-1		0-1	2-0	2-0	1-0	5-0
3	Scotland	12	8	0	4	21	12	24	1-2	1-0		3-1	3-1	2-1	6-0
4	Ukraine	12	5	2	5	18	16	17	1-2	2-2	2-0		1-0	3-2	5-0
5	Lithuania	12	5	1	6	11	13	16	0-2	0-1	1-2	2-0		1-0	2-1
6	Georgia	12	3	1	8	16	19	10	1-3	0-3	2-0	1-1	0-2		3-1
7	Faroe Islands	12	0	0	12	4	43	0	1-2	0-6	0-2	0-2	0-1	0-6	

Italy and France qualified for the finals

Toftir, Toftir	
6-06-2007, 17:15, 4100, Kasnaferis GRE	
Faroe Islands	**0**

Jákup Mikkelsen - Atli Danielsen, Jón Jacobsen, Óli Johannesen• (Marni Djurhuus 36; Simun Samuelsen 77), Fródi Benjaminsen, Mikkjal Thomassen, Jákup Borg (Andrew Flotum 82), Súni Olsen, Rógvi Jacobsen, Christian Jacobsen, Christian Lamhauge Holst. Tr: Jógvan Martin Olsen

Scotland	**2**
	Maloney [31], O'Connor [35]

Craig Gordon - Graham Alexander, David Weir, Stephen McManus, Gary Naysmith•, Paul Hartley, Barry Ferguson•, Darren Fletcher (Gary Stewart Teale 68), Shaun Maloney (Charles Adam 77), Garry O'Connor, Kris Boyd (Steven Naismith 83). Tr: Alex Mcleish

Hampden Park, Glasgow	
8-09-2007, 15:00, 52 063, Skomina SVN	
Scotland	**3**
	Boyd [31], McManus [77], McFadden [85]

Craig Gordon - Alan Hutton•, David Weir, Stephen McManus, James McEveley, Gary Stewart Teale (James McFadden 69), Scott Brown, Darren Fletcher•, Lee McCulloch (Shaun Maloney 76), Kris Boyd, Garry O'Connor• (Craig Beattie 76). Tr: Alex Mcleish

Lithuania	**1**
	Danilevicius [61p]

Zydrunas Karcemarskas• - Marius Stankevicius• (Edgaras Jankauskas 56), Andrius Skerla, Tomas Zvirgzdauskas•, Arunas Klimavicius, Deividas Semberas, Mindaugas Kalonas, Deividas Cesnauskis, Igoris Morinas (Saulius Mikoliunas 47), Tomas Danilevicius, Andrius Velicka• (Audrius Ksanavicius• 47). Tr: Algimantas Liubinskas

Boris Paichadze, Tbilisi	
8-09-2007, 19:00, 24 000, Hamer LUX	
Georgia	**1**
	Siradze [89]

Georgi Lomaia - Mate Ghvinianidze•, Kakha Kaladze, Malkhaz Asatiani, Lasha Salukvadze, Levan Tskitishvili•, Zurab Menteshashvili (Dimitri Tatanashvili 79), Lasha Jakobia (David Siradze 62), Georgi Demetradze, 9 Aleksandr Iashvili• (Levan Kenia 62), Otar Martsvaladze. Tr: Klaus Toppmöller

Ukraine	**1**
	Shelayev [7]

Olexandr Shovkovskiy - Volodymyr Yezerskiy, Andriy Rusol, Olexandr Kucher, Anatoliy Tymoschuk, Ruslan Rotan• (Olexiy Gay 80), Serhiy Nazarenko, Oleh Gusev, Oleh Shelayev (Olexander Gladkiy 91+), Andriy Shevchenko•, Andriy Voronin (Maxym Kalynychenko 72). Tr: Oleh Blokhin

San Siro, Milan	
8-09-2007, 20:50, 81 200, Michel SVK	
Italy	**2**

Gianluigi Buffon - Massimo Oddo, Fabio Cannavaro, Andrea Barzagli, Gianluca Zambrotta, Daniele De Rossi•, Gennaro Gattuso•, Andrea Pirlo, Mauro Camoranesi (Simone Perrotta 58), Alessandro Del Piero (Antonio Di Natale 83), Filippo Inzaghi (Cristiano Lucarelli 65). Tr: Roberto Donadoni

France	**0**

Mickaël Landreau - Lassana Diarra, Lilian Thuram, Julien Escudé, Eric Abidal, Franck Ribéry (Jeremy Toulalan 86), Claude Makelele•, Patrick Vieira, Florent Malouda, Thierry Henry•, Nicolas Anelka. Tr: Raymond Domenech

S. Darius & S. Girenas, Kaunas	
12-09-2007, 20:00, 5500, Georgiev BUL	
Lithuania	**2**
	Jankauskas [8], Danilevicius [53]

Zydrunas Karcemarskas - Deividas Semberas, Arunas Klimavicius, Andrius Skerla, Vidas Alunderis, Kestutis Ivaskevicius, Saulius Mikoliunas (Andrius Velicka 32), Deividas Cesnauskis (Mindaugas Kalonas 31), Audrius Ksanavicius, Edgaras Jankauskas (Aurimas Kucys• 86), Tomas Danilevicius. Tr: Algimantas Liubinskas

Faroe Islands	**1**
	Rógvi Jacobsen [93+]

Jákup Mikkelsen - Fródi Benjaminsen, Atli Danielsen•, Christian Lamhauge Holst (Hans Samuelsen 74), Jón Jacobsen, Mikkjal Thomassen, Simun Samuelsen, Christian Jacobsen (Andrew Flotum 84), Súni Olsen• (Pauli Hansen 63), Jákup Borg, Rógvi Jacobsen. Tr: Jógvan Martin Olsen

Parc des Princes, Paris	
12-09-2007, 21:00, 43 342, Plautz AUT	
France	**0**

Mickaël Landreau - Lassana Diarra, Lilian Thuram, Julien Escudé, Eric Abidal (Karim Benzema 77), Franck Ribéry, Patrick Vieira• (Samir Nasri• 69), Claude Makelele, Florent Malouda, David Trezeguet, Nicolas Anelka. Tr: Raymond Domenech

Scotland	**1**
	McFadden [64]

Craig Gordon - Alan Hutton, Stephen McManus, David Weir, Graham Alexander, Lee McCulloch, Barry Ferguson, Darren Fletcher• (Stephen Pearson 26), Scott Brown, Paul Hartley•, James McFadden (Garry O'Connor 76).Tr: Alex Mcleish

NSC Olympiyskiy, Kyiv
12-09-2007, 21:45, 41 500, Webb ENG

Ukraine	1
	Shevchenko [71]

Olexandr Shovkovskiy - Olexandr Kucher, Volodymyr Yezerskiy, Andriy Rusol*, Oleh Shelayev, Oleh Gusev (Artem Milevskiy 88), Maxym Kalynychenko (Andriy Voronin 60), Anatoliy Tymoschuk, Olexiy Gay, Serhiy Nazarenko (Olexandr Gladkiy 69), Andriy Shevchenko. Tr: Oleh Blokhin

Italy	2
	Di Natale 2 [41] [77]

Gianluigi Buffon - Christian Panucci, Fabio Cannavaro*, Andrea Barzagli, Gianluca Zambrotta, Mauro Camoranesi (Massimo Oddo 78), Massimo Ambrosini, Andrea Pirlo, Simone Perrotta* (Alberto Aquilani* 68), Vincenzo Iaquinta (Fabio Quagliarella 85), Antonio Di Natale. Tr: Roberto Donadoni

---

Luigi Ferraris, Genoa
13-10-2006, 20:50, 23 057, Davila ESP

Italy	2
	Pirlo [44], Grosso [84]

Gianluigi Buffon - Massimo Oddo*, Christian Panucci, Andrea Barzagli, Fabio Grosso, Andrea Pirlo, Gennaro Gattuso, Massimo Ambrosini (Stefano Mauri 88), Fabio Quagliarella (Pasquale Foggia 72), Antonio Di Natale, Luca Toni. Tr: Roberto Donadoni

Georgia	0

Georgi Lomaia - Georgi Shashiashvili (David Siradze 60), Lasha Salukvadze, Malkhaz Asatiani, Zurab Khizanishvili, David Kvirkvelia*, Levan Tskitishvili, Zurab Menteshashvili, Jaba Kankava, Levan Mchedlidze (Levan Kenia 60), Georgi Demetradze* (Lasha Jakobia 85). Tr: Klaus Toppmöller

---

La Beaujoire, Nantes
17-10-2007, 21:00, 36 650, Kassai HUN

France	2
	Henry 2 [80] [81]

Mickaël Landreau - Lassana Diarra (Hatem Ben Arfa 69), Lilian Thuram, William Gallas, Eric Abidal, Jérémy Toulalan, Claude Makelele, Florent Malouda, Franck Ribéry, Thierry Henry, Karim Benzema. Tr: Raymond Domenech

Lithuania	0

Zydrunas Karcemarskas - Arunas Klimavicius, Ignas Dedura*, Andrius Skerla, Tomas Zvirgzdauskas, Aurimas Kucys* (Andrius Velicka 84), Audrius Ksanavicius* (Tadas labukas 77), Mindaugas Kalonas (Mantas Savenas 63), Igoris Morinas, Tomas Danilevicius, Edgaras Jankauskas. Tr: Algimantas Liubinskas

---

Boris Paichadze, Tbilisi
21-11-2007, 19:30, 21 300, Stavrev MKD

Georgia	0

Giorgi Makaridze - Lasha Salukvadze, Malkhaz Asatiani, Kakha Kaladze, David Kvirkvelia, Jaba Kankava, Levan Tskitishvili, Zurab Menteshashvili (Otar Marsvaladze 31), Levan Kenia, Levan Mchedlidze, David Siradze (Nickolas Gelashvili 80). Tr: Klaus Toppmöller

Lithuania	2
	Ksanavicius 2 [52] [96+]

Zydrunas Karcemarskas* - Marius Stankevicius, Tomas Zvirgzdauskas, Andrius Skerla, Gediminas Paulauskas, Ignas Dedura, Vidas Alunderis, Audrius Ksanavicius*, Mantas Savenas (Mindaugas Kalonas 67), Saulius Mikoliunas* (Igoris Morinas 76), Edgaras Jankauskas* (Andrius Velicka 52). Tr: Algimantas Liubinskas

---

Hampden Park, Glasgow
13-10-2007, 15:00, 52 063, Vink NED

Scotland	3
	Miller.K [4], McCulloch [10], McFadden [68]

Craig Gordon - Alan Hutton, David Weir, Stephen McManus, Gary Naysmith, Scott Brown (Shaun Maloney 76), Barry Ferguson*, Stephen Pearson, Lee McCulloch* (Christian Dailly 60), James McFadden (Garry O'Connor* 80), Kenny Miller*. Tr: Alex Mcleish

Ukraine	1
	Shevchenko [24]

Olexandr Shovkovskiy - Andriy Nesmachniy*, Volodymyr Yezerskiy, Dmytro Chygrynskiy, Olexandr Kucher, Oleh Gusev (Ruslan Rotan* 46), Anatoliy Tymoschuk (Oleh Shelayev 73), Olexandr Gladkiy, Andriy Vorobey* (Serhiy Nazarenko 62), Andriy Shevchenko*, Andriy Voronin. Tr: Oleh Blokhin

---

NSC Olympiyskiy, Kyiv
17-10-2007, 19:00, 5000, Jakov ISR

Ukraine	5
	Kalynychenko 2 [40] [49], Gusev 2 [43] [45],
	Vorobey [64]

Andriy Pyatov - Andriy Nesmachniy, Andriy Rusol, Dmytro Chygrynskiy, Olexiy Gai, Serhiy Nazarenko, Anatoliy Tymoschuk (Olexandr Grytsay 69), Oleh Gusev (Andriy Vorobey 62), Maxym Kalynychenko, Olexandr Gladkiy (Artem Milevskiy 46), Andriy Voronin. Tr: Oleh Blokhin

Faroe Islands	0

Jákup Mikkelsen - Atli Danielsen, Einar Hansen, Óli Hansen, Jón Jacobsen, Jóhan Davidsen, Mikkjal Thomassen (Tem Hansen 8), Christian Lamhauge Holst (Andrew Flotum 75), Christian Jacobsen (Hanus Thorleifson 89), Símun Samuelsen, Rógvi Jacobsen. Tr: Jógvan Martin Olsen

---

Hampden Park, Glasgow
17-11-2007, 17:00, 51 301, Mejuto ESP

Scotland	1
	Ferguson [65]

Craig Gordon - Alan Hutton, David Weir, Stephen McManus, Gary Naysmith*, Scott Brown (Kenny Miller 74), Darren Fletcher, Paul Hartley, Barry Ferguson, Lee McCulloch* (Kris Boyd 92+), James McFadden. Tr: Alexander Mcleish

Italy	2
	Toni [2], Panucci [91+]

Gianluigi Buffon - Christian Panucci, Fabio Cannavaro, Andrea Barzagli, Gianluca Zambrotta, Mauro Camoranesi (Giorgio Chiellini 83), Gennaro Gattuso (Daniele De Rossi 87), Andrea Pirlo, Massimo Ambrosini, Antonio Di Natale (Vincenzo Iaquinta 68), 9 Luca Toni*. Tr: Roberto Donadoni

---

Alberto Braglia, Modena
21-11-2007, 20:30, 16 142, Meyer GER

Italy	3
	Benjaminsen OG [11], Toni [36], Chiellini [41]

Marco Amelia - Massimo Oddo, Fabio Cannavaro (Daniele Bonera 53), Giorgio Chiellini, Fabio Grosso, Daniele De Rossi, Massimo Ambrosini (Fabio Quagliarella 58), Simone Perrotta, Vincenzo Iaquinta, Raffaele Palladino, Luca Toni (Alberto Gilardino 74). Tr: Roberto Donadoni

Faroe Islands	1
	Rógvi Jacobsen [83]

Jákup Mikkelsen - Jóhan Davidsen, Fródi Benjaminsen, Jón Jacobsen, Einar Hansen, Atli Danielsen, Súni Olsen, Rógvi Jacobsen, Símun Samuelsen (Hanus Thorleifson 75), Christian Jacobsen, Christian Lamhauge Holst (Andrew Flotum 86). Tr: Jógvan Martin Olsen

---

Tórsvøllur, Torshavn
13-10-2007, 16:00, 1980, Rossi SMR

Faroe Islands	0

Jákup Mikkelsen -Christian Jacobsen, Jón Jacobsen, Fródi Benjaminsen, Einar Hansen, Símun Samuelsen (Andrew Flotum 86), Súni Olsen*, Mikkjal Thomassen (Rokur Jespersen 78), Hjalgrím Elttør (Bergur Midjord 46), Rógvi Jacobsen, Christian Lamhauge Holst. Tr: Jógvan Martin Olsen

France	6
Anelka [6], Henry [8], Benzema 2 [50] [81],
Rothen [66], Ben Arfa [94+]

Mickaël Landreau - Bacary Sagna, Eric Abidal, Lilian Thuram, Patrice Evra, Jérôme Rothen, Claude Makelele (Lassana Diarra 73), Jérémy Toulalan, Franck Ribéry (Hatem Ben Arfa 64), Nicolas Anelka (Karim Benzema 46), Thierry Henry. Tr: Raymond Domenech

---

Boris Paichadze, Tbilisi
17-10-2007, 21:00, 29 377, Kircher GER

Georgia	2
	Mchedlidze [16], Siradze [64]

Giorgi Makaridze - Georgi Shashiashvili, Malkhaz Asatiani*, Lasha Salukvadze, Zurab Khizanishvili, Jaba Kankava*, Zurab Menteshashvili, Levan Kenia (Ilia Kandelaki 79), David Kvirkvelia, David Siradze (Lasha Jakobia 89), Levan Mchedlidze (Alexandre Kvakhadze 85). Tr: Klaus Toppmöller

Scotland	0

Craig Gordon - Greame Murty, Stephen McManus*, David Weir, Graham Alexander, Darren Fletcher, Barry Ferguson, Stephen Pearson (Kris Boyd 66), Shaun Maloney, Kenny Miller (Craig Beattie* 66), James McFadden. Tr: Alex Mcleish

---

S. Darius & S. Girenas, Kaunas
17-11-2007, 20:00, 3000, Malcolm NIR

Lithuania	2
	Savenas [41], Danilevicius [67]

Zydrunas Karcemarskas - Gediminas Paulauskas, Arunas Klimavicius*, Marius Stankevicius, Ignas Dedura, Andrius Skerla, Tomas Zvirgzdauskas, Tadas Papeckys (Igoris Morinas 17), Mantas Savenas, Tomas Danilevicius* (Andrius Velicka 82), Edgaras Jankauskas (Mindaugas Kalonas 90). Tr: Algimantas Liubinskas

Ukraine	0

Olexandr Shovkovskiy (Andriy Pyatov 44) - Dmytro Chygrynskiy, Vladyslav Vaschuk, Oleh Shelayev (Serhiy Nazarenko 72), Volodymyr Yezerskiy, Olexiy Gai, Anatoliy Tymoschuk, Oleh Gusev, Ruslan Rotan, Andriy Shevchenko*, Andriy Voronin (Artem Milevskiy 69). Tr:-Oleh Blokhin

---

NSC Olympiyskiy, Kyiv
21-11-2007, 21:30, 7800, Ovrebø NOR

Ukraine	2
	Voronin [14], Shevchenko [46]

Andriy Pyatov - Vladyslav Vaschuk, Olexandr Grytsay, Olexandr Romanchuk (Volodymyr Yezerskiy 81), Serhiy Fedorov, Anatoliy Tymoschuk, Oleh Gusev (Artem Milevskiy 91+), Ruslan Rotan, Olexiy Gai, Andriy Shevchenko, Andriy Voronin (Oleh Shelayev 85). Tr: Oleh Blokhin

France	2
	Henry [20], Govou [34]

Sébastien Frey - François Clerc, William Gallas, Lilian Thuram, Eric Abidal, Franck Ribéry (Hatem Ben Arfa 89), Claude Makelele, Lassana Diarra, Sidney Govou, Thierry Henry, Karim Benzema (Samir Nasri 46). Tr: Raymond Domenech

GROUP C

GROUP C	PL	W	D	L	F	A	PTS	GRE	TUR	NOR	BIH	MDA	HUN	MLT
1 Greece	12	10	1	1	25	10	31		1-4	1-0	3-2	2-1	2-0	5-0
2 Turkey	12	7	3	2	25	11	24	0-1		2-2	1-0	5-0	3-0	2-0
3 Norway	12	7	2	3	27	11	23	2-2	1-2		1-2	2-0	4-0	4-0
4 Bosnia-Herzegovina	12	4	1	7	16	22	13	0-4	3-2	0-2		0-1	1-3	1-0
5 Moldova	12	3	3	6	12	19	12	0-1	1-1	0-1	2-2		3-0	1-1
6 Hungary	12	4	0	8	11	22	12	1-2	0-1	1-4	1-0	2-0		2-0
7 Malta	12	1	2	9	10	31	5	0-1	2-2	1-4	2-5	2-3	2-1	

Greece and Turkey qualified for the finals

Sóstói, Szekesfehervar
8-09-2007, 16:00, 10 773, Trefoloni ITA
Hungary 1
Gera [39p]
Márton Fülöp - Vilmos Vanczák, Tamás Vasko•, Roland Juhász•, Zoltán Szélesi, Ádám Vass, Dániel Tozsér, Zoltán Gera, Tamás Hajnal (Csaba Csizmandia 72), Balázs Dzsudzsák (Peter Halmosi 93+), Róbert Feczesin (Attila Filkor 89). Tr: Peter Várhidi
Bosnia-Herzegovina 0

Adnan Gušo - Dzemal Berberovic, Branimir Bajic•, Ivan Radeljic, Darko Maletic (Mario Bozic 79), Elvir Rahimic•, Zvjezdan Misimovic•, Mirko Hrgovic• (Adnan Custovic 84), Zlatan Muslimovic, Vedad Ibisevic (Edin Dzeko 67), Dragan Blatnjak. Tr: Fuad Muzurovic

Ta'Qali, Ta'Qali
8-09-2007, 19:30, 10 500, Messner AUT
Malta 2
Said [41], Schembri [76]
Justin Haber - Ian Azzopardi, Brian Said•, Luke Dimech, Roderick Briffa (Kevin Sammut 88), Kenneth Scicluna, Gilbert Agius•, Jamie Pace•, Michael Mifsud, Ivan Woods (George Mallia 83), Andre Schembri• (Terence Scerri 91+). Tr: Dusan Fitzel
Turkey 2
Hakan Sükür [45], Servet Çetin [78]
Hakan Arikan - Servet Çetin, Ibrahim Toraman•, Hamit Altintop, Ibrahim Üzülmez, Sabri Sarioglu (Gokdeniz Karadeniz 52), Emre Belözoglu, Arda Turan (Ayhan Akman• 30), Tuncay Sanli (Deniz Baris 66), Halil Altintop, Hakan Sükür. Tr: Fatih Terim

Zimbru, Chisinau
8-09-2007, 21:00, 10 173, Malek POL
Moldova 0

Serghei Pascenco - Ghenadie Olexic (Serghei Rogaciov 78), Radu Rebeja, Alexandru Epureanu, Serghei Lascencov, Vitalie Bordian, Alexandru Gatcan (Alexandru Suvorov 66), Denis Zmeu, Victor Comlenoc, Igor Bugaev, Viorel Frunza•. Tr: Igor Dobrovolskiy
Norway 1
Iversen [48]
Håkon Opdal - Jarl André Storbæk, Kjetil Wæhler (Vidar Riseth 66), Brede Hangeland, John Arne Riise, Bjørn Riise, M. Andresen, Christian Grindheim, Steffen Iversen (Thorstein Helstad 68), John Carew, Morten Gamst Pedersen. Tr: Åge Hareide

---

Ullevål, Oslo
12-09-2007, 19:00, 24 080, Busacca SUI
Norway 2
Carew [15], Riise JA [39]
Håkon Opdal - Erik Hagen, Brede Hangeland, M. Andresen, John Arne Riise, Morten Gamst Pedersen, Bjørn Riise (Frode Kippe 93+), Jan Gunnar Solli (Thorstein Helstad 70), Jarl André Storbæk, John Carew•, Steffen Iversen (Vidar Riseth 80). Tr: Åge Hareide
Greece 2
Kyrgiakos 2 [7 30]
Kostas Chalkias• - Giourkas Seitaridis• (Paraskevas Antzas 64), Christos Patsatzoglou, Sotirios Kyrgiakos, Traianos Dellas•, Angelos Basinas (Georgios Samaras• 76), Georgios Karagounis, Vassilis Torossidis, Kostas Katsouranis, Dimitrios Salpingidis (Nikolaos Liberopoulos 46), Fanis Gekas•. Tr: Otto Rehhagel

Kosevo, Sarajevo
12-09-2007, 20:00, 2000, Hyytiä FIN
Bosnia-Herzegovina 0

Adnan Gušo• - Dzemal Berberovic, Branimir Bajic, Safet Nadarevic, Ivan Radelji (Vedad Ibisevic 46), Elvir Rahimic, Darko Maletic (Adnan Custovic 78), Zajko Zeba (Dario Damjanovic 47), Dragan Blatnjak, Zlatan Muslimovic, Edin Dzeko. Tr: Fuad Muzurovic
Moldova 1
Bugaev [22]
Nicolai Calancea - Alexandru Epureanu, Serghei Lascencov•, Victor Golovatenco, Radu Rebeja, Victor Comlenoc (Serghei Namasco 63), Andrei Corneencov•, Alexandru Gatcan (Nicolae Josan 85), Vitalie Bordian, Igor Bugaev•, Anatolie Doros (Serghei Rogaciov 73). Tr: Igor Dobrovolskiy

Inönü, Istanbul
12-09-2007, 20:30, 28 020, Dougal SCO
Turkey 3
Gökhan [68], Aurelio [72], Halil Altintop [93+]
Hakan Arikan - Emre Asik, Hamit Altintop•, Servet Çetin, Ibrahim Üzülmez, Mehmet Aurelio, Gökdeniz Karadeniz (Halil Altintop 61), Ayhan Akman (Serdar Ozkan 67), Tuncay Sanli, Gökhan Ünal, Nihat Kahveci (Emre Belozoglu 46). Tr: Fatih Terim
Hungary 0

Márton Fülöp (Janos Balogh 71) - Roland Juhász, Zoltán Szélesi, Vilmos Vanczák•, Csaba Csizmadia, Tamás Vasko, Ádám Vass, Zoltán Gera•••63, Balázs Dzsudzsák (Peter Halmosi 82), Tamás Hajnal•, Tamás Priskin• (Balazs Toth 66). Tr: Peter Várhidi

---

Megyeri úti, Budapest
13-10-2007, 16:20, 7633, Nalbandyan ARM
Hungary 2
Feczesin [34], Tözsér [78]
Márton Fülöp - Zoltán Szélesi, Tamás Vasko, Roland Juhász•, Béla Balogh, Ádám Vass, Dániel Tozsér, Zoltán Gera, Attila Filkor (Akos Buzsaky 75), Róbert Feczesin (Peter Rajczi 83), Balázs Dzsudzsák (Leandro 88). Tr: Peter Várhidi
Malta 0

Justin Haber - Ian Azzopardi, Brian Said, Kenneth Scicluna, Luke Dimech, Roderick Briffa, Kevin Sammut (Udochukwu Nwoko 66), George Mallia, Michael Mifsud, Ivan Woods• (Roderick Bajada 91+), Andre Schembri (Terence Scerri 83). Tr: Dusan Fitzel

Zimbru, Chisinau
13-10-2007, 21:00, 9815, Atkinson ENG
Moldova 2
Frunza [11]
Nicolai Calancea - Victor Golovatenco, Alexandru Epureanu•, Alexei Savinov, Andrei Corneencov, Vitalie Bordian, Nicolae Josan, Denis Zmeu (Serghei Namasco 87), Alexandru Gatcan (Ghenadie Olexic 89), Victor Comlenoc, Viorel Frunza (Denis Calincov 86). Tr: Igor Dobrovolskiy
Turkey 1
Umit Karan [63]
Hakan Arikan (Volkan Demirel 17) - Servet Çetin, Gökhan Zan•, Ibrahim Üzülmez, Emre Belözoglu, Mehmet Topuz, Mehmet Aurelio, Arda Turan (Tumer Metin 69), Selcuk Inan (Umit Karan 46), Tuncay Sanli, Gökhan Ünal. Tr: Fatih Terim

OACA Spyro Louis, Athens
13-10-2007, 21:30, 30 250, Gilewski POL
Greece 5
Charisteas [10], Gekas [58], Liberopoulos [73]
Antonios Nikopolidis - Traianos Dellas, Sotirios Kyrgiakos, Christos Patsatzoglou•, Vassilis Torosidis, Angelos Basinas, Georgios Karagounis, Kostas Katsouranis•, Ioannis Amanatidis (Stelios Giannakopoulos 70), Fanis Gekas (Paraskevas Antzas 81), Angelos Charisteas (Nikolaos Liberopoulos 69). Tr: Otto Rehhagel
Bosnia-Herzegovina 2
Hrgovic.M [54], Ibisevic [92+]
Adnan Gušo - Dzemal Berberovic, Branimir Bajic, Safet Nadarevic•, Branislav Krunic (Vedad Ibisevic 46), Zvjezdan Misimovic (Sejad Salihovic 82), Mirko Hrgovic•56, Admir Vladavic, Elvir Rahimic•, Dragan Blatnjak (Samir Merzic 62), Zlatan Muslimovic. Tr: Fuad Muzurovic

Ta'Qali, Ta'Qali
17-10-2007, 19:30, 7069, Ishchenko UKR

Malta	2

Scerri [71], Michael Mifsud [84p]

Justin Haber - Kenneth Scicluna• (Terence Scerri 46), Ian Azzopardi (Udochukwu Nwoko 91+), Brian Said, Luke Dimech•, Roderick Briffa, Jamie Pace, George Mallia, Ivan Woods•, Andre Schembri (Andrew Cohen 46), Michael Mifsud. Tr: Dusan Fitzel

Moldova	3

Bugaev [24p], Frunza 2 [31][35]

Serghei Pascenco77 - Victor Golovatenco•••88, Serghei Stroenco•, Serghei Lascencov, Andrei Corneencov•, Vitalie Bordian, Nicolae Josan, Alexandru Gatcan• (Denis Zmeu 77), Victor Comlenoc (Serghei Namasco 69), Viorel Frunza (Anatolie Doros 83), Igor Bugaev. Tr: Igor Dobrovolski

---

Ali Sami Yen, Istanbul
17-10-2007, 20:30, 22 818, Mejuto ESP

Turkey	0

Volkan Demirel - Servet Çetin, Gökhan Zan, Hamit Altintop, Emre Belözoglu• (Arda Turan 71), Ibrahim Uzülmez, Mehmet Aurelio, Gökdeniz Karadeniz (Hakan Sukur 65), Ümit Karan (Tumer Metin 46), Gökhan Unal, Tuncay Sanli. Tr: Fatih Terim

Greece	1

Amanatidis [79]

Kostas Chalkias - Traianos Dellas, Sotirios Kyrgiakos, Paraskevas Antzas, Giourkas Seitaridis, Vassilis Torosidis•, Georgios Karagounis, Angelos Basinas, Angelos Charisteas (Georgios Samaras 59), Ioannis Amanatidis, Fanis Gekas (Nikolaos Liberopoulos 56). Tr: Otto Rehhagel

---

Kosevo, Sarajevo
17-10-2007, 20:30, 1500, Lannoy FRA

Bosnia-Herzegovina	0

Adnan Gušo - Dzemal Berberovic, Samir Merzic, Branimir Bajic, Branislav Krunic, Dragan Blatnjak (Vedad Ibisevic 46), Zlatan Muslimovic (Edin Dzeko• 46), Zvjezdan Misimovic•, Darko Maletic (Veldin Muharemovic 78), Safet Nadarevic, Sejad Salihovic•. Tr: Fuad Muzurovic

Norway	2

Hagen [5], Riise.B [74]

Håkon Opdal - Jarl André Storbæk, Brede Hangeland, Erik Hagen•, John Arne Riise, Bjørn Riise (John Anders Bjorkoy 90+2), Martin Andresen, Christian Grindheim (Sigurd Rushfeldt• 58), Jan Gunnar Solli, Thorstein Helstad (Daniel Braaten 76), Morten Gamst Pedersen. Tr: Age Hareide

---

Zimbru, Chisinau
17-11-2007, 19:00, 6483, Královec CZE

Moldova	3

Bugaev [13], Josan [23], Alexeev [86]

Stanislav Namasco - Serghei Lascencov, Radu Rebeja, Alexandru Epureanu•, Vitalie Bordian, Serghei Namasco, Evgheni Cebotari (Semion Bulgaru 50), Denis Zmeu• (Ghenadie Olexic 93+), Nicolae Josan•, Igor Bugaev, Denis Calincov (Serghei Alexeev 64). Tr: Igor Dobrovolski

Hungary	0

Márton Fülöp• - Zoltán Szélesi, Tamás Vasko, Csaba Csizmadia, Vilmos Vanczák, Zoltán Gera•, Dániel Tozsér (Akos Buzsaky 38), Tamás Hajnal, Krisztián Vadócz (Bela Balogh 39), Balázs Dzsudzsák (Robert Feczesin 71), Tamás Priskin. Tr: Peter Várhidi

---

Ullevål, Oslo
17-11-2007, 19:00, 23 783, Merk GER

Norway	1

Hagen [12]

Håkon Opdal - Jarl André Storbæk (Sigurd Rushfeldt 88), Erik Hagen, Brede Hangeland, John Arne Riise, Bjørn Riise, Alexander Tettey, Kristofer Hæstad• (Per Ciljan Skjelbred 68), Steffen Iversen (Thorstein Helstad 84), John Carew, Morten Gamst Pedersen. Tr: Åge Hareide

Turkey	2

Emre Belözoglu [31], Nihat Kahveci [59]

Volkan Demirel• - Ibrahim Kas (Gokhan Gonul 15), Emre Asik, Servet Çetin, Hakan Balta, Hamit Altintop, Mehmet Aurelio, Emre Belözoglu, Arda Turan (Tuncay Sanli 87), Nihat Kahveci, Semih Sentürk (Yusuf Simsek• 67). Tr: Fatih Terim

---

OACA Spyro Louis, Athens
17-11-2007, 21:30, 31 332, Kaldma EST

Greece	5

Gekas 3 [32][72][74], Basinas [54], Amanatidis [61]

Antonios Nikopolidis - Christos Patsatzoglou, Traianos Dellas•, Sotirios Kyrgiakos, Vassilis Torosidis (Nikos Spiropoulos 48), Angelos Basinas, Kostas Katsouranis, Georgios Karagounis (Alexandros Tziolis 70), Stelios Giannakopoulos (Nikolaos Liberopoulos 46), Fanis Gekas, Ioannis Amanatidis. Tr: Otto Rehhagel

Malta	0

Justin Haber - Josef Mifsud, Roderick Briffa, Brian Said•, Ian Azzopardi, Luke Dimech, Jamie Pace, Kevin Sammut (Andrew Cohen 61), Udochukwu Nwoko•, Andre Schembri (Terence Scerri 68), Michael Mifsud (Gareth Sciberras 78). Tr: Dušan Fitzel

---

Ta'Qali, Ta'Qali
21-11-2007, 20:00, 7000, Baskakov RUS

Malta	1

Michael Mifsud [53]

Justin Haber - Ian Azzopardi, Luke Dimech, Stephen Wellmen•, Roderick Briffa, Udochukwu Nwoko (Andrew Cohen 86), Peter Pullicino, Ivan Woods• (Etienne Barbara 83), Jamie Pace, Andre Schembri•••68, Michael Mifsud• (Terence Scerri 87). Tr: Dusan Fitzel

Norway	4

Iversen 3 [25][27p][45], Pedersen [75]

Håkon Opdal - Jarl André Storbæk, Erik Hagen•, Brede Hangeland, John Arne Riise, Bjørn Riise (Kristofer Hæstad 75), Vidar Riseth•, Per Ciljan Skjelbred, Steffen Iversen (Sigurd Rushfeldt 84), John Carew (Thorstein Helstad 68), Morten Gamst Pedersen•. Tr: Åge Hareide

---

Ferenc Puskás, Budapest
21-11-2007, 20:15, 32 300, Styles ENG

Hungary	1

Buzsáky [7]

Márton Fülöp - Zoltán Szélesi, Tamás Vasko, Roland Juhász, Vilmos Vanczák•, Adám Vass, Dániel Tozsér• (Leandro 86), Ákos Buzsáky, Tamás Hajnal (Attila Filkor 79), Péter Halmosi (Robert Feczesin 83), Tamás Priskin. Tr: Peter Várhidi

Greece	2

Vanczák OG [22], Basinas [59p]

Kostas Chalkias (Antonios Nikopolidis 46) - Christos Patsatzoglou•, Michalis Kapsis, Loukas Vintra, Sotirios Kyrgiakos•, Angelos Basinas, Alexandros Tziolis (Georgios Samaras 46), Georgios Karagounis, Kostas Katsouranis, Fanis Gekas (Ioannis Amanatidis 84), Dimitrios Salpingidis. Tr: Otto Rehhagel

---

Ali Sami Yen, Istanbul
21-11-2007, 21:00, 20 106, Braamhaar NED

Turkey	1

Nihat Kahveci [43]

Rüstü Reçber - Gökhan Gönül, Emre Asik, Servet Çetin, Hakan Balta, Hamit Altintop, Mehmet Aurelio, Emre Belözoglu, Arda Turan (Tuncay Sanli 76), Nihat Kahveci (Gokdeniz Karadeniz 90), Semih Sentürk• (Sabri Sarioglu 61). Tr: Fatih Terim

Bosnia-Herzegovina	2

Adnan Gušo - Senidad Ibricic (Vedad Ibisevic 75), Safet Nadarevic•, Džemal Berberovic•, Samir Merzic (Veldin Muharemovic 89), Branimir Bajic, Branislav Krunic, Darko Maletic, Zvjezdan Misimovic, Elvir Rahimic, Edin Džeko (Sejad Salihovic 83). Tr: Fuad Muzurovic

---

GROUP D

	GROUP D	PL	W	D	L	F	A	PTS	CZE	GER	IRL	SVK	WAL	CYP	SMR
1	**Czech Republic**	12	9	2	1	27	5	29		1-2	1-0	3-1	2-1	1-0	7-0
2	**Germany**	12	8	3	1	35	7	27	0-3		1-0	2-1	0-0	4-0	6-0
3	Republic of Ireland	12	4	5	3	17	14	17	1-1	0-0		1-0	1-0	1-1	5-0
4	Slovakia	12	5	1	6	33	23	16	0-3	1-4	2-2		2-5	6-1	7-0
5	Wales	12	4	3	5	18	19	15	0-0	0-2	2-2	1-5		3-1	3-0
6	Cyprus	12	4	2	6	17	24	14	0-2	1-1	5-2	1-3	3-1		3-0
7	San Marino	12	0	0	12	2	57	0	0-3	0-13	1-2	0-5	1-2	0-1	

The Czech Republic and Germany qualified for the finals

Olimpico, Serravalle
22-08-2007, 21:00, 552, Janku ALB
San Marino 0

Aldo Simoncini - Carlo Valentini, Damiano Vannucci, Nicola Albani•, Alessandro Della Valle•, Gianluca Bollini (Nicola Ciacci• 77), Giovanni Bonini (Federico Nanni 84), Matteo Bugli•, Fabio Bollini• (Matteo Andreini 63), Manuel Marani, Andy Selva. Tr: Giampaolo Mazza

Cyprus 1
Okkas [54]

Antonis Georgallides - Georgos Theodotou, Paraskevas Christou, Lambros Lambrou, Christakis Marangos (Marios Nikolaou 24), Efstathios Aloneftis, Chrysostomous Michail, Alexandros Garpozis (Elias Charalambous 86), Yiasoumi Yiasoumis (Konstantinos Charalampidis 55), Yiannis Okkas, Michalis Konstantinou. Tr: Angelos Anastasiadis

Millennium Stadium, Cardiff
8-09-2007, 19:30, 27 889, Mejuto ESP
Wales 0

Wayne Hennessey - Sam Ricketts, Daniel Gabbidon•, James Collins•, Lewin Nyatanga, Joseph Ledley (Robert Earnshaw 46), Gareth Bale, Jason Koumas (Carl Fletcher 67), Carl Robinson, Simon Davies (Andrew Crofts 79), Freddy Eastwood. Tr: John Toshack

Germany 2
Klose 2 [6 60]

Jens Lehmann - Arne Friedrich, Per Mertesacker, Christoph Metzelder, Christian Pander (Piotr Trochowski 46), Roberto Hilbert, Thomas Hitzlsperger, Bastian Schweinsteiger, Marcell Jansen, Kevin Kuranyi (Lukas Podolski 72), Miroslav Klose (Patrick Helmes 87). Tr: Joachim Löw

Olimpico, Serravalle
8-09-2007, 20:15, 3412, Filipovic SRB
San Marino 0

Aldo Simoncini - Carlo Valentini, Damiano Vannucci, Davide Simoncini•, Alessandro Della Valle•••65, Gianluca Bollini (Paolo Mariotti 85), Matteo Bugli (Fabio Vitaioli 67), Fabio Bollini (Matteo Andreini 58), Manuel Marani, Andy Selva, Giovanni Bonini. Tr: Giampaolo Mazza

Czech Republic 3
Rosicky [33], Jankulovski [75], Koller [93+]

Petr Cech - Tomáš Ujfalusi, David Rozehnal, Radoslav Kováč, Marek Jankulovski, Tomáš Galásek (Jaroslav Plasil 82), Tomáš Rosicky, David Jarolím (Jan Polak 69), Marek Kulic (Stanislav Vlcek 56), Martin Fenin, Jan Koller•. Tr: Karel Brückner

Tehelné Pole, Bratislava
8-09-2007, 20:30, 12 360, Farina ITA
Slovakia 2
Klimpl [37], Cech [91+]

Stefan Senecky - Vratislav Gresko, Marek Cech, Ján Durica•, Maros Klimpl, Matej Krajcík•, Marek Mansyk, Marek Sapara (Filip Sebo 71), Marek Mintál, Filip Holosko, Stanislav Sesták (Branislav Obzera 65). Tr: Ján Kocian

Republic of Ireland 2
Ireland [7], Doyle [57]

Shay Given - John O'Shea, Stephen Kelly, Paul McShane, Richard Dunne, Lee Carsley, Aiden McGeady (Darron Gibson 61), Stephen Ireland (Jonathan Douglas 76), Kevin Kilbane, Kevin Doyle (Daryl Murphy 89), Robbie Keane. Tr: Steve Staunton

Antona Malatinského, Trnava
12-09-2007, 18:30, 5846, Duhamel FRA
Slovakia 2
Mintál 2 [12 57]

Stefan Senecky - Vratislav Gresko (Igor Zofcak 64), Maros Klimpl, Ján Durica, Marek Cech, Marek Hamšík, Peter Petrás, Marek Sapara, Marek Mintál, Stanislav Sesták (Branislav Obzera• 46), Filip Holosko. Tr: Ján Kocian

Wales 5
Eastwood [22], Bellamy 2 [34 41], Durica OG [78], Davies.S [90]

Wayne Hennessey - Sam Ricketts, Daniel Gabbidon, Craig Morgan, James Collins, Gareth Bale, Simon Davies, Carl Robinson, Joseph Ledley (David Vaughan 85), Craig Bellamy•, Freddy Eastwood (Carl Fletcher 73). Tr: John Toshack

GSP, Nicosia
12-09-2007, 20:00, 1000, Kulbakov BLR
Cyprus 3
Makridis [15], Aloneftis 2 [41 92+]

Antonis Georgallides - Elias Charalambous (Alexandros Garpozis• 65), Stelios Okkarides, Paraskevas Christou, Chrysostomous Michail, Marios Elia (Georgos Theodotou 76), Konstantinos Makridis, Marios Nikolaou•, Yiannis Okkas (Yiasoumi Yiasoumis 46), Michalis Konstantinou, Efstathios Aloneftis. Tr: Angelos Anastasiadis

San Marino 0

Federico Valentini - Carlo Valentini, Damiano Vannucci, Fabio Vitaioli, Nicola Albani (Giacomo Benedettini 81), Fabio Bollini, Matteo Andreini, Matteo Bugli, Manuel Marani (Federico Nanni 87), Andy Selva•, Giovanni Bonini (Paolo Mariotti 73). Tr: Giampaolo Mazza

Strahov, Prague
12-09-2007, 20:30, 16 648, Vassaras GRE
Czech Republic 1
Jankulovski [15]

Petr Cech - Tomáš Ujfalusi•, David Rozehnal, Radoslav Kováč, Marek Jankulovski•, Libor Sionko (Stanislav Vlcek 74), Tomáš Galásek (Tomas Sivok• 46), Tomáš Rosicky, Jan Polák•, Jaroslav Plasil, Milan Baros• (David Jarolim 89). Tr: Karel Brückner

Republic of Ireland 0

Shay Given - Stephen Kelly•, Paul McShane•, Richard Dunne, John O'Shea (Stephen Hunt 38•61), Aiden McGeady (Shane Long• 62), Lee Carsley (Andrew Keogh 82), Andy Reid, Kevin Kilbane, Kevin Doyle, Robbie Keane•. Tr: Steve Staunton

Mestsky, Dubnica nad Vahom
13-10-2007, 15:00, 2576, Wilmes LUX
Slovakia 7
Hamsík [24], Sesták 2 [32 57], Sapara [37], Skrtel [51], Holosko [54], Durica [76p]

Kamil Contofalsky - Martin Skrtel, Matej Krajcík, Ján Durica, Ottó Szabó, Marek Sapara• (Andrej Hesek 79), Marek Cech, Marek Hamšík, Ján Kozák, Stanislav Sesták (Blazej Vascak 60), Filip Holosko (Filip Sebo 71). Tr: Ján Kocian

San Marino 0

Federico Valentini - Matteo Andreini, Damiano Vannucci, Fabio Vitaioli, Nicola Albani, Alessandro Della Valle, Gianluca Bollini• (Giacomo Benedettini 57), Carlo Valentini, Matteo Bugli (Luca Bonifaci 68), Manuel Marani• (Marco De Luigi 85), Federico Nanni. Tr: Giampaolo Mazza

GSP, Nicosia
13-10-2007, 19:15, 2852, Bertolini SUI
Cyprus 3
Okkas 2 [59 68], Charalampidis [79]

Antonis Georgallides - Stelios Okkarides, Marinos Satsias (Christos Marangos• 71), Marios Elia (Konstantinos Charalampidis 63), Chrysostomous Michail (Yiasoumi Yiasoumis 46), Paraskevas Christou, Alexandros Garpozis, Konstantinos Makridis, Marios Nikolaou, Efstathios Aloneftis•, Yiannis Okkas. Tr: Angelos Anastasiadis

Wales 1
Collins [21]

Danny Coyne - Sam Ricketts (Jermaine Mauric Easter• 73), James Collins (Craig Morgan 44), Daniel Gabbidon, Gareth Bale, Lewin Nyatanga, Joseph Ledley, Carl Robinson, Simon Davies, Craig Bellamy, Freddy Eastwood• (Robert Earnshaw 58). Tr: John Toshack

Croke Park, Dublin
13-10-2007, 19:45, 67 495, Hansson SWE
Republic of Ireland 0

Shay Given - Stephen Kelly, Richard Dunne•, Joseph O'Brien, Steve Finnan, Lee Carsley•, Andy Reid, Kevin Kilbane (Daryl Murphy 92+), Andrew Keogh (Aiden McGeady 80), Kevin Doyle (Shane Long 70), Robbie Keane. Tr: Steve Staunton

Germany 0

Jens Lehmann• - Arne Friedrich•, Clemens Fritz, Marcell Jansen, Per Mertesacker, Christoph Metzelder, Torsten Frings•, Bastian Schweinsteiger (Simon Rolfes 18), Piotr Trochowski (Gonzalo Castro 90), Mario Gómez (Lukas Podolski 64), Kevin Kuranyi. Tr: Joachim Löw

Croke Park, Dublin
17-10-2007, 19:30, 54 861, Vuorela FIN
Republic of Ireland 1
Finnan [92+]

Shay Given - Steve Finnan, Kevin Kilbane, Paul McShane, John O'Shea, Joseph O'Brien (Liam Miller• 46), Andy Reid, Andrew Keogh (Aiden McGeady 63), Kevin Doyle, Robbie Keane, Stephen Hunt (Jonathan Douglas 74). Tr: Steve Staunton

Cyprus 1
Okkarides [80]

Antonis Georgallides - Marinos Satsias• (Christos Marangos 69), Stelios Okkarides, Paraskevas Christou, Konstantinos Charalampidis, Marios Elia•94+, Alexandros Garpozis, Konstantinos Makridis (Christis Theophilou 86), Marios Nikolaou, Yiannis Okkas, Yiasoumi Yiasoumi (Chrysostomous Michail 73). Tr: Angelos Anastasiadis

Olimpico, Serravalle
17-10-2007, 20:15, 1182, Zammit MLT
San Marino 0

Aldo Simoncini - Carlo Valentini•, Damiano Vannucci• (Matteo Bugli 76), Nicola Albani•••85, Alessandro Della Valle, Luca Bonifazi (Giovanni Bonini 62), Davide Simoncini, Riccardo Muccioli, Matteo Andreini, Marco De Luigi (Matteo Vitaioli• 80), Andy Selva. Tr: Giampaolo Mazza

Wales 2
Earnshaw [13], Ledley [36]

Lewis Price - Gareth Bale•, Neal Eardley, Daniel Gabbidon, Lewin Nyatanga, Carl Robinson, David Vaughan (Sam Ricketts• 62), Simon Davies, Joseph Ledley•, Robert Earnshaw, Craig Bellamy. Tr: John Toshack

Allianz Arena, Munich
17-10-2007, 20:45, 66 445, Webb ENG
Germany 0

Timo Hildebrand - Marcell Jansen, Arne Friedrich, Per Mertesacker, Christoph Metzelder (Clemens Fritz 46), Bastian Schweinsteiger (Mario Gomez 65), Torsten Frings, Piotr Trochowski (Simon Rolfes 46), David Odonkor, Kevin Kuranyi, Lukas Podolski•. Tr: Joachim Löw

Czech Republic 3
Sionko [2], Matejovsky [23], Plasil [63]

Petr Cech - Radoslav Kovác, David Rozehnal, Tomás Ujfalusi, Zdenek Pospech, Tomás Galásek, Daniel Pudil (Marek Kulic 73), Marek Matejovsky, Libor Sionko (Stanislav Vlcek 58), Jaroslav Plasil, Jan Koller (Martin Fenin 79). Tr: Karel Brückner

Millennium Stadium, Cardiff
17-11-2007, 15:00, 24 619, Oriekhov UKR
Wales 2
Koumas 2 [23 89p]

Wayne Hennessey - Neal Eardley (David Cotterill 81), James Collins, Daniel Gabbidon, Christopher Gunter, Joseph Ledley, Jason Koumas•, Carl Robinson (David Edwards 37), Carl Fletcher, Simon Davies, Freddy Eastwood (Jermaine Mauric Easter 60). Tr: John Toshack

Republic of Ireland 2
Keane [31], Doyle [60]

Shay Given - Steve Finnan, Paul McShane, John O'Shea•, Kevin Kilbane, Aiden McGeady, Lee Carsley, Liam Miller (Stephen Hunt 60), Andy Reid (Darren Potter 87), Kevin Doyle, Robbie Keane. Tr: Don Givens

AWD Arena, Hannover
17-11-2007, 20:15, 45 016, Rasmussen DEN
Germany 4
Fritz [2], Klose [20], Podolski [53], Hitzlsperger [82]

Jens Lehmann - Philipp Lahm, Christoph Metzelder, Per Mertesacker, Arne Friedrich, Piotr Trochowski (Tim Borowski 66), Thomas Hitzlsperger, Clemens Fritz (Roberto Hilbert 77), Lukas Podolski, Mario Gómez (Mike Hanke 73), Miroslav Klose. Tr: Joachim Löw

Cyprus 0

Antonis Georgallides - Lambros Lambrou, Georgos Theodotou (Marios Nikolaou 27), Paraskevas Christou, Alexandros Garpozis, Yiannis Okkas, Konstantinos Charalampidis (Christis Theophilou 46), Marinos Satsias, Efstathios Aloneftis, Konstantinos Makridis, Michalis Konstantinou (Yiasoumi Yiasoumis 68). Tr: Angelos Anastasiadis

Strahov, Prague
17-11-2007, 20:30, 15 651, Asumaa FIN
Czech Republic 3
Grygera [13], Kulic [76], Rosicky [83]

Jaromír Blazek - Zdenek Pospech, Radoslav Kovác, David Rozehnal, Zdenek Grygera (Michal Kadlec 45), Jan Polák (Marek Matejovsky 86), Tomás Galásek, Tomás Rosický, Jaroslav Plasil, Jan Koller, Milan Baros (Marek Kulic 70). Tr: Karel Brückner

Slovakia 1
Kadlec OG [79]

Kamil Contofalsky - Matej Krajcík, Martin Skrtel•, Lubomír Michalík, Marek Cech•, Zdeno Strba•, Karol Kisel (Juraj Halenar 88), Marek Sapara•, Ján Kozák, Marek Hamsík (Filip Holosko 58), Marek Mintál (Stanislav Sestak 67). Tr: Ján Kocian

GSP, Nicosia
21-11-2007, 18:30, 5866, Paniashvili GEO
Cyprus 0

Antonis Georgallides - Paraskevas Christou, Lambros Lambrou, Marios Nikolaou (Elias Charlambous• 56), Alexandros Garpozis, Konstantinos Charalampidis (Yiasoumi Yiasoumi 62), Konstantinos Makridis (Chrysostomous Michail 84), Marinos Satsias•, Efstathios Aloneftis, Yiannis Okkas, Michalis Konstantinou. Tr: Angelos Anastasiadis

Czech Republic 2
Pudil [11], Koller [74]

Daniel Zitka - Zdenek Pospech, Radoslav Kovác, David Rozehnal, Michal Kadlec•, Jaroslav Plasil (Jiri Kladrubsky 87), Tomás Galásek, Marek Matejovsky, Daniel Pudil, Marek Kulic (Milan Baros 57), Jan Koller (Martin Fenin 76). Tr: Karel Brückner

Commerzbank Arena, Frankfurt
21-11-2007, 20:30, 49 262, Balaj ROU
Germany 0

Jens Lehmann - Gonzalo Castro (Roberto Hilbert 56), Per Mertesacker, Christoph Metzelder, Philipp Lahm, Clemens Fritz, Tim Borowski, Thomas Hitzlsperger (Simon Rolfes 46), Lukas Podolski, Mario Gómez (Oliver Neuville 71), Miroslav Klose. Tr: Joachim Löw

Wales 0

Wayne Hennessey• - Sam Ricketts, Daniel Gabbidon•, James Collins•, Lewin Nyatanga, Christopher Gunter, Carl Fletcher, Simon Davies, David Edwards (Andrew Crofts 90+1), Joseph Ledley, Robert Earnshaw (Jermaine Mauric Easter 56). Tr: John Toshack

Olimpico, Serravalle
21-11-2007, 20:30, 538, Sipailo LVA
San Marino 0

Federico Valentini• - Carlo Valentini, Mauro Marani• (Matteo Andreini 84), Davide Simoncini, Alessandro Della Valle, Gianluca Bollini (Maicol Berretti 61), Michele Marani, Riccardo Muccioli•, Damiano Vannucci•, Manuel Marani, Andy Selva• (Marco De Luigi 50). Tr: Giampaolo Mazza

Slovakia 5
Michalík [42], Holosko 2 [51 57], Hamsík [53], Cech [83]

Stefan Senecky - Matej Krajcík (Peter Petras 63), Lubomír Michalík•, Tomas Hubocan•, Marek Cech, Balázs Borbély, Marek Hamsík, Karol Kisel (Otto Szabo 46), Ján Kozák, Stanislav Sesták (Juraj Halenar• 75), Filip Holosko. Tr: Ján Kocian

GROUP E

GROUP E	PL	W	D	L	F	A	PTS	CRO	RUS	ENG	ISR	MKD	EST	AND
1 Croatia	12	9	2	1	28	8	29		0-0	2-0	1-0	2-1	2-0	7-0
2 Russia	12	7	3	2	18	7	24	0-0		2-1	1-1	3-0	2-0	4-0
3 England	12	7	2	3	24	7	23	2-3	3-0		3-0	0-0	3-0	5-0
4 Israel	12	7	2	3	20	12	23	3-4	2-1	0-0		1-0	4-0	4-1
5 Macedonia FYR	12	4	2	6	12	12	14	2-0	0-2	0-1	1-2		1-1	3-0
6 Estonia	12	2	1	9	5	21	7	0-1	0-2	0-3	0-1	0-1		2-1
7 Andorra	12	0	0	12	2	42	0	0-6	0-1	0-3	0-2	0-3	0-2	

Croatia and Russia qualified for the finals

Comunal, Andorra La Vella
6-06-2007, 18:00, 680, Stokes IRL

Andorra 0

Koldo Alvarez - Ildefons Lima•, Txema García (Oscar Sonejee 61), Antoni Lima, José Manuel Ayala, Jordi Escura•, Genís García, Marcio Vieira, Marc Bernaus, Justo Ruíz, Juan Carlos Toscano Beltrán (Juli Sanchez 77≠81). Tr: David Rodrigo

Israel 2
Tamuz [37], Colautti [53]

Dudu Awat - Yoav Ziv, Arik Benado, Avi Yehiel, David Ben Dayan, Idan Tal, Yossi Benayoun, Gal Alberman (Walid Badir 71), Toto Tamuz (Yaniv Katan 77), Roberto Colautti (Omer Golan 86), Barak Itzhaki. Tr: Dror Kashtan

A Le Coq Arena, Tallinn
22-08-2007, 19:00, 7500, McCourt NIR

Estonia 2
Piiroja [34], Zelinski [92+]

Mart Poom - Enar Jääger•, Andrei Stepanov, Raio Piiroja, Dmitri Kruglov, Martin Reim, Aleksandr Dmitrijev, Ragnar Klavan•45, Joel Lindpere, Indrek Zelinski•••92+, Vladimir Voskoboinikov (Tarmo Kink 46). Tr: Viggo Jensen

Andorra 1
Silva [82]

Koldo Alvarez - Txema García, Óscar Sonejee, Antoni Lima•, Ildefons Lima•, Jordi Escura•, José Manuel Ayala (Genis Garcia 90), Marc Pujol (Juli Sanchez 80), Toni Sivera (Juan Carlos Toscano Beltran• 53), Marcio Vieira, Fernando Silva•. Tr: David Rodrigo

Wembley, London
8-09-2007, 17:00, 85 372, Vink NED

England 3
Wright-Phillips [20], Owen [50], Richards [66]

Paul Robinson - Micah Richards, Rio Ferdinand, John Terry•, Ashley Cole, Shaun Wright-Phillips (David Bentley 83), Steven Gerrard (Phil Neville 71), Gareth Barry, Joe Cole, Emile Heskey (Andrew Johnson 71), Michael Owen. Tr: Steve McClaren

Israel 0

Dudu Awat• - Yuval Shpungin, Tal Ben Haim, Shimon Gershon•, Yossi Benayoun, Walid Badir, Arik Benado• (Omwer Golan 57), Idan Tal, Yaniv Katan, Barak Itzhaki (Toto Tamuz 46). Tr: Dror Kashtan

Lokomotiv, Moscow
8-09-2007, 19:00, 23 000, Ovrebø NOR

Russia 3
Berezutski.V [6], Arshavin [83], Kerzhakov [86]

Vladimir Gabulov•70 - Vasili Berezutski, Sergei Ignashevich, Aleksei Berezutski, Vladimir Bystrov (Aleksandr Anyukov 89), Igor Semshov, Konstantin Zyrianov, Diniyar Bilyaletdinov, Andrei Arshavin, Roman Pavlyuchenko (Aleksandr Kerzhakov 66), Dmitri Sychev (Vyacheslav Malafeev 70). Tr: Guus Hiddink

Macedonia FYR 0

Petar Milosevski - Goran Popov, Vlade Lazarevski, Goce Sedloski, Igor Mitreski•≠72, Aleksandar Mitreski (Vanco Trajanov 46), Velice Sumulikoski, Darko Tasevski, Aleksandar Vasoski (Goce Toleski 88), Goran Pandev•, Aco Stojkov (Goran Maznov 46). Tr: Srecko Katanec

Maksimir, Zagreb
8-09-2007, 20:30, 15 102, Laperriere SUI

Croatia 2
Eduardo 2 [39][45]

Stipe Pletikosa - Dario Simic, Josip Simunic, Robert Kovac, Vedran Corluka, Niko Kovac, Darijo Srna•6 (Marko Babic 82), Luka Modric, Niko Kranjcar (Ivan Rakitic 60), Mladen Petric (Ivica Olic 70), Eduardo da Silva. Tr: Slaven Bilic

Estonia 0

Pavel Londak - Teet Allas•, Andrei Stepanov, Raio Piiroja, Urmas Rooba (Aivar Anniste 84), Taavi Rähn, Aleksandr Dmitrijev, Dmitri Kruglov, Joel Lindpere (Martin Reim 91+), Tarmo Kink (Kaimar Saag 80), Andres Oper. Tr: Viggo Jensen

Comunal, Andorra La Vella
12-09-2007, 18:00, 925, Thual FRA

Andorra 0

Koldo Alvarez - Antoni Lima•, Txema García, Oscar Sonejee, José Manuel Ayala,Toni Sivera• (Xavi Andorra 59), Genís García (Alex Somoza 82), Manolo Jiménez, Fernando Silva (Sergio Moreno 57), Marcio Vieira. Tr: David Rodrigo

Croatia 6
Srna [34], Petric 2 [38][44], Kranjcar [49], Eduardo [55], Rakitic [64]

Vedran Runje - Darijo Srna, Robert Kovac, Vedran Corluka, Dario Knezevic, Niko Kranjcar, Luka Modric (Bosko Balaban 46), Jerko Leko, Marko Babic, Mladen Petric (Danijel Pranjic 46), Eduardo da Silva (Ivan Rakitic 62). Tr: Slaven Bilic

Wembley, London
12-09-2007, 20:00, 86 106, Hansson SWE

England 3
Owen 2 [7][31], Ferdinand [84]

Paul Robinson - Micah Richards, Rio Ferdinand, John Terry, Ashley Cole, Shaun Wright-Phillips, Gareth Barry, Steven Gerrard, Joe Cole• (Phil Neville 88), Emile Heskey (Peter Crouch 80), Michael Owen (Stewart Downing 91+). Tr: Steve McClaren

Russia 0

Vyacheslav Malafeev - Vasili Berezutski, Sergei Ignashevich, Aleksei Berezutski, Aleksandr Anyukov (Aleksandr Kerzhakov 80), Diniyar Bilyaletdinov, Yuri Zhirkov, Igor Semshov (Vladimir Bystrov 40), Dmitri Sychev (Roman Pavlyuchenko 63), Andrei Arshavin, Konstantin Zyrianov. Tr: Guus Hiddink

Gradski, Skopje
12-09-2007, 20:30, 5000, Trattou CYP

Macedonia FYR 1
Maznov [30]

Petar Milosevski - Vlade Lazarevski, Goce Sedloski, Nikolce Noveski, Aleksandar Vasoski•, Vlatko Grozdanovski, Vanco Trajanov (Artim Polozani 46), Velice Sumulikoski, Goran Maznov•, Darko Tasevski, Aco Stojkov (Goce Toleski 81). Tr: Srecko Katanec

Estonia 1
Piiroja [17]

Pavel Londak - Enar Jääger, Andrei Stepanov, Raio Piiroja, Dmitri Kruglov, Taavi Rähn (Martin Reim 62), Aleksandr Dmitrijev, Ragnar Klavan, Joel Lindpere, Andres Oper (Aivar Anniste 90), Kaimar Saag (Tarmo Kink• 79). Tr: Viggo Jensen

Wembley, London
13-10-2007, 15:00, 86 655, Vollquartz DEN

England 3
Wright-Phillips [11], Rooney [32], Rähn OG [33]

Paul Robinson - Micah Richards, Sol Campbell, Rio Ferdinand (Jolean Lescott 46), Ashley Cole (Phil Neville 49), Shaun Wright-Phillips, Steven Gerrard, Gareth Barry, Joe Cole, Wayne Rooney, Michael Owen (Frank Lampard 70). Tr: Steve McClaren

Estonia 0

Mart Poom - Dmitri Kruglov, Andrei Stepanov, Raio Piiroja, Enar Jääger, Taavi Rähn•, Ragnar Klavan, Aleksandr Dmitrijev, Joel Lindpere•, Tarmo Kink (Kristen Viikmae 62), Kaimar Saag. Tr: Viggo Jensen

Maksimir, Zagreb
13-10-2007, 20:15, 30 084, Stark GER

Croatia 1
Eduardo [52]

Stipe Pletikosa - Dario Simic, Josip Simunic, Robert Kovac, Vedran Corluka, Darijo Srna, Luka Modric, Jerko Leko•, Ivica Olic (Ivan Rakitic 81), Niko Kranjcar (Danijel Pranjic 46), Eduardo da Silva•. Tr: Slaven Bilic

Israel 0

Nir Davidovich - Eyal Meshumar, Shimon Gershon, Tal Ben Haim•, Ygal Antebi•, Aviram Baruchya (Omer Golan 58), Gal Alberman, Yossi Benayoun, Pini Balili• (Toto Tamuz 67), Elyaniv Barda (Moshe Ohayon 75), Tamir Cohen•. Tr: Dror Kashtan

Luzhniki, Moscow
17-10-2007, 19:00, 75 000, Cantalejo ESP

Russia 2
Pavlyuchenko [69p][73]

Vladimir Gabulov - Aleksei Berezutski, Sergei Ignashevich, Vasili Berezutski• (Dmitri Torbinskiy 46), Aleksandr Anyukov, Konstantin Zyrianov, Igor Semshov, Diniyar Bilyaletdinov, Yuri Zhirkov, Andrei Arshavin (Denis Kolodin 90), Aleksandr Kerzhakov (Roman Pavlyuchenko• 58). Tr: Guus Hiddink

England 1
Rooney [29]

Paul Robinson - Micah Richards, Rio Ferdinand•, Sol Campbell, Jolean Lescott (Frank Lampard 79), Shaun Wright-Phillips (Stewart Downing 80), Steven Gerrard, Gareth Barry, Joe Cole (Peter Crouch 80), Wayne Rooney•, Michael Owen. Tr: Steve McClaren

Gradski, Skopje
17-10-2007, 20:00, 17 500, Malzinskas LTU

Macedonia FYR 3
Naumoski [30], Sedloski [44], Pandev [59]

Tome Pacovski - Vlade Lazarevski, Nikolce Noveski, Goce Sedloski, Igor Mitreski, Goran Popov, Velice Sumulikoski, Darko Tasevski (Vanco Trajanov 84), Goran Maznov (Stevica Ristic 62), Ilco Naumoski (Artim Polozani 75), Goran Pandev. Tr: Srecko Katanec

Andorra 0

Koldo Alvarez• - Oscar Sonejee•, Julià Fernández, Ildefons Lima•, José Manuel Ayala, Jordi Escura, Marc Pujol, Justo Ruíz (Xavi Andorra 63), Manolo Jiménez (Alex Somoza 78), Marcio Vieira, Juan Carlos Toscano Beltrán (Gabriel Riera 82). Tr: David Rodrigo

Comunal, Andorra La Vella
17-11-2007, 18:00, 700, Collum SCO

Andorra 0

Koldo Alvarez - Emili Garcia (Marcio Vieira• 46), Jordi Rubio, Oscar Sonejee, Antoni Lima, Ildefons Lima (Justo Ruiz 81), Manolo Jiménez, José Manuel Ayala•, Sergio Moreno (Juan Carlos Toscano Beltran• 70), Marc Pujol•, Toni Sivera. Tr: David Rodrigo

Estonia 2

Oper [31], Lindpere [60]

Pavel Londak - Enar Jääger, Dmitri Kruglov• (Konstantin Vassiljev 84), Raio Piiroja, Andrei Stepanov, Aleksandr Dmitrijev, Ragnar Klavan•, Joel Lindpere, Martin Reim• (Taijo Teniste 68), Kaimar Saag, Andres Oper (Tarmo Kink 46). Tr: Viggo Jensen

---

Gradski, Skopje
17-11-2007, 20:00, 14 500, De Bleeckere BEL

Macedonia FYR 2

Maznov [71], Naumoski [83]

Petar Milosevski - Nikolce Noveski, Igor Mitreski, Goran Popov, Goce Sedloski (Boban Grncarov 88), Vlade Lazarevski, Darko Tasevski•, Vlatko Grozdanovski, Velice Sumulikoski, Goran Maznov, Ilco Naumoski• (Artim Polozani 78). Tr: Srecko Katanec

Croatia 0

Stipe Pletikosa - Dario Simic, Josip Simunic, Robert Kovac, Vedran Corluka, Niko Kovac, Darijo Srna, Luka Modric, Niko Kranjcar (Ognjen Vukojevic 75), Mladen Petric (Marijo Mandzukic 42), Eduardo da Silva (Ivica Olic 54). Tr: Slaven Bilic

---

Ramat Gan, Tel Aviv
17-11-2007, 20:00, 29 787, Farina ITA

Israel 2

Barda [10], Golan [92+]

Dudu Awat - Yuval Shpungin, Dekel Keinan, Tal Ben Haim, Yoav Ziv, Tamir Cohen, Gal Alberman•, Barak Itzhaki (Amit Ben Shushan 62), Maor Bar Buzaglo (Moshe Ohayon 64), Elyaniv Barda, Ben Sahar• (Omer Golan 69). Tr: Dror Kashtan

Russia 1

Bilyaletdinov [61]

Vladimir Gabulov - Aleksei Berezutski, Sergei Ignashevich, Vasili Berezutski (Pavel Pogrebnyak 68), Aleksandr Anyukov•, Konstantin Zyrianov, Igor Semshov (Dmitri Torbinskiy 30), Diniyar Bilyaletdinov, Yuri Zhirkov, Andrei Arshavin, Roman Pavlyuchenko (Dmitri Sychev 52). Tr: Guus Hiddink

---

Ramat Gan, Tel Aviv
21-11-2007, 19:00, 2736, Mikulski POL

Israel 1

Barda [35]

Dudu Awat - Yuval Shpungin, Dekel Keinan, Tal Ben Haim, Yoav Ziv, Moshe Ohayon, Tamir Cohen, Maor Bar Buzaglo (Amit Ben Shushan 46), Barak Itzhaki (Aviram Baruchyan 72), Elyaniv Barda•, Roberto Colautti (Ben Sahar 55). Tr: Dror Kashtan

Macedonia FYR 0

Petar Milosevski - Nikolce Noveski, Goran Popov, Goce Sedloski, Igor Mitreski, Vlatko Grozdanovski (Slavco Georgievski 66), Velice Sumulikoski, Vlade Lazarevski, Goran Maznov (Stevica Ristic 60), Darko Tasevski (Artim Polozani 46), Aco Stojkov. Tr: Srecko Katanec

---

Wembley, London
21-11-2007, 20:00, 88 017, Fröjdfeldt SWE

England 2

Lampard [56]p, Crouch [65]

Scott Carson - Micah Richards, Sol Campbell, Jolean Lescott, Wayne Bridge, Shaun Wright-Phillips (David Beckham 46), Steven Gerrard, Gareth Barry (Jermain Defoe 46), Frank Lampard, Joe Cole (Darren Bent 80), Peter Crouch. Tr: Steve McClaren

Croatia 3

Kranjcar [8], Olic [14], Petric [77]

Stipe Pletikosa - Vedran Corluka, Dario Simic, Robert Kovac•, Josip Simunic, Darijo Srna, Luka Modric, Niko Kovac, Niko Kranjcar (Danijel Pranjic 75), Ivica Olic (Ivan Rakitic 84), Eduardo da Silva (Mladen Petric 69). Tr: Slaven Bilic

---

Comunal, Andorra La Vella
21-11-2007, 21:00, 780, Hauge NOR

Andorra 0

Koldo Alvarez• (Jose Antonio Gomes 46) - Antoni Lima•, Ildefons Lima•, Oscar Sonejee (Gabriel Riera 83), Marc Bernaus, Jordi Escura•, Manolo Jiménez, Toni Sivera, Sergio Moreno, Justo Ruíz•, Marcio Vieira (Xavi Andorra 50). Tr: David Rodrigo

Russia 1

Sychev [38]

Vladimir Gabulov - Aleksandr Anyukov, Aleksei Berezutski•, Vasili Berezutski (Dmitri Torbinskiy 38), Denis Kolodin•45, Diniyar Bilyaletdinov, Yuri Zhirkov, Konstantin Zyrianov, Andrei Arshavin•84, Aleksandr Kerzhakov, Dmitri Sychev. Tr: Guus Hiddink

---

GROUP F

GROUP F	PL	W	D	L	F	A	PTS	ESP	SWE	NIR	DEN	LVA	ISL	LIE
1 Spain	12	9	1	2	23	8	28		3-0	1-0	2-1	2-0	1-0	4-0
2 Sweden	12	8	2	2	23	9	26	2-0		1-1	0-0	2-1	5-0	3-1
3 Northern Ireland	12	6	2	4	17	14	20	3-2	2-1		2-1	1-0	0-3	3-1
4 Denmark	12	6	2	4	21	11	20	1-3	0-3	0-0		3-1	3-0	4-0
5 Latvia	12	4	0	8	15	17	12	0-2	0-1	1-0	0-2		4-0	4-1
6 Iceland	12	2	2	8	10	27	8	1-1	1-2	2-1	0-2	2-4		1-1
7 Liechtenstein	12	2	1	9	9	32	7	0-2	0-3	1-4	0-4	1-0	3-0	

Spain and Sweden qualified for the finals • Denmark v Sweden was abandoned at 89' with the score at 3-3. The match was awarded 3-0 to Sweden

---

Windsor Park, Belfast
22-08-2007, 19:45, 13 544, Matejek CZE

Northern Ireland 3

Healy 2 [5 35], Lafferty [56]

Maik Taylor - Michael Duff•, George McCartney, Christopher Baird, Stephen James Craigan, Gary Clinghan, Keith Gillespie (Stephen Jones 85), Steven Davis, Kyle Lafferty (Warren Feeney 75), David Healy, Chris Brunt (Stuart Elliott 62). Tr: Nigel Worthington

Liechtenstein 1

Frick.M [89]

Peter Jehle - Michael Stocklasa• (Yves Oehri 38), Martin Stocklasa, Martin Telser, Fabio D'Elia•, Michele Polverino, Ronny Büchel, Daniel Frick, Christoph Biedermann (Stefan Buchel 62), Raphael Rohrer (Roger Beck 74), Mario Frick. Tr: Hans-Peter Zaugg

---

Skonto, Riga
8-09-2007, 19:15, 7500, Proença POR

Latvia 1

Baird OG [69]

Andris Vanins - Dzintars Zirnis•, Kaspars Gorkss, Oskars Klava, Deniss Ivanovs, Imants Bleidelis, Jurijs Laizans, Vitalis Astafjevs, Andrejs Rubins, Maris Verpakovskis (Kristaps Blanks 90), Girts Karlsons (Vits Rimkus• 72). Tr: Aleksandrs Starkovs

Northern Ireland 0

Maik Taylor - Christopher Baird•, Michael Duff, Jonny Evans, George McCartney, Keith Gillespie•, Gary Clinghan, Steven Davis, Stuart Elliott (Chris Brunt 66), David Healy, Kyle Lafferty (Warren Feeney 72). Tr: Nigel Worthington

---

Laugardalsvöllur, Reykjavík
8-09-2007, 20:00, 9483, Stark GER

Iceland 1

Hallfredsson [40]

Arni Arason - Kristján Sigurdsson, Ragnar Sigurdsson•, Ivar Ingimarsson, Hermann Hreidarsson, Grétar Steinsson, Arnar Vidarsson (Olafur Ingi Skulason 69), Johannes Gudjonsson (Baldur Adalsteinsson 79), Emil Hallfredsson, Kari Arnason, Gunnar Heidar Thorvaldsson (Armann Bjornsson 88). Tr: Eyjólfur Sverrisson

Spain 1

Iniesta [86]

Iker Casillas - Sergio Ramos, Carlos Marchena, Juanito Gutiérrez, Mariano Pernía• (David Albelda 26), Joaquín Sánchez (Luis Garcia Fernandez 69), Xabi Alonso• 21, Xavi Hernández, David Silva, Fernando Torres (Andres Iniesta 57), David Villa. Tr: Luis Aragonés

Råsunda, Stockholm
8-09-2007, 20:30, 33 082, De Bleeckere BEL

Sweden 0

Andreas Isaksson - Mikael Nilsson, Olof Mellberg*, Petter Hansson, Erik Edman, Niclas Alexandersson, Tobias Linderoth, Anders Svensson (Kim Kallstrom 69), Christian Wilhelmsson (Kennedy Bakircioglu 57), Zlatan Ibrahimovic* (Rade Prica 89), Johan Elmander*. Tr: Lars Lagerbäck

Denmark 0

Thomas Sørensen - Leon Andreasen (Peter Lovenkrands 81), Martin Laursen, Daniel Agger*, Niclas Jensen, Thomas Helveg, Daniel Jensen*, Dennis Rommedahl, Thomas Kahlenberg (Nicklas Bendtner 54), Jon Dahl Tomasson (Michael Gravgaard 91+), Jesper Grønkjær*. Tr: Morten Olsen

Laugardalsvöllur, Reykjavík
12-09-2007, 18:05, 7727, Baskakov RUS

Iceland 2
Armann Björnsson [6], Gillespie OG [91+]

Arni Arason - Kristján Sigurdsson, Ragnar Sigurdsson, Ivar Ingimarsson, Hermann Hreidarsson*, Kari Arnason (Asgeir Asgeirsson 88), Arnar Vidarsson, Grétar Steinsson, Emil Hallfredsson, Gunnar Heidar Thorvaldsson (Olafur Ingi Skulason 79), Armann Björnsson* (Eidur Gudjohnsen 53). Tr: Eyjölfur Sverrisson

Northern Ireland 1
Healy [72p]

Maik Taylor - Christopher Baird*, Michael Duff, Jonny Evans, George McCartney, Keith Gillespie, Gary Clinghan, Steven Davis (Grant McCann 79), Chris Brunt* (Stephen Jones 83), David Healy, Warren Feeney. Tr: Nigel Worthington

NRGI Park, Aarhus
12-09-2007, 20:00, 20 005, Clattenburg ENG

Denmark 4
Nordstrand 2 [3 36], Laursen.M [12], Tomasson [18]

Thomas Sørensen - Martin Laursen, Daniel Agger (Michael Gravgaard 28), Niclas Jensen, Thomas Helveg, Leon Andreasen, Jesper Grønkjær (Thomas Kahlenberg 46), Morten Nordstrand, Jon Dahl Tomasson (Peter Lovenkrands 68), Dennis Rommedahl, Esben Hansen. Tr: Morten Olsen

Liechtenstein 0

Peter Jehle - Martin Telser, Martin Stocklasa*, Marco Ritzberger (Thomas Beck* 46), Yves Oehri (Daniel Frick 46), Ronny Büchel, Franz Burgmeier, Fabio D'Elia*, Raphael Rohrer, Michele Polverino, Mario Frick (Roger Beck 84). Tr: Hans-Peter Zaugg

Nuevo Carlos Tartiere, Oviedo
12-09-2007, 22:00, 22 560, Yefet ISR

Spain 2
Xavi [13], Torres [85]

Iker Casillas - Sergio Ramos, Carlos Marchena, Juanito Gutiérrez, Mariano Pernía, Joaquín (Miguel Angel Angulo 77), David Albelda, Xavi Hernández, David Silva (Cesc Fabregas 69), Fernando Torres, David Villa (Andres Iniesta 48). Tr: Luis Aragonés

Latvia 0

Andris Vanins - Dzintars Zirnis, Oskars Klava, Kaspars Gorkss, Deniss Ivanovs*, Imants Bleidelis (Aleksejs Visnakovs 74), Vitalis Astafjevs*, Jurijs Laizans, Andrejs Rubins, Girts Karlsons (Marians Pahars 63), Maris Verpakovskis (Kristaps Blanks 88). Tr: Aleksandrs Starkovs

Laugardalsvöllur, Reykjavík
13-10-2007, 16:00, 5865, Dean ENG

Iceland 2
Gudjohnsen 2 [4 52]

Arni Arason - Kristján Sigurdsson* (Armann Björnsson 88), Hjalmar Jonsson, Ragnar Sigurdsson, Ivar Ingimarsson, Grétar Steinsson (Kari Arnason 25), Brynjar Gunnarsson*, Johannes Gudjonsson, Emil Hallfredsson, Gunnar Heidar Thorvaldsson (Hannes Sigurdsson 65), Eidur Gudjohnsen. Tr: Eyjölfur Sverrisson

Latvia 4
Klava [27], Laizans [31], Verpakovskis 2 [37 46]

Andris Vanins - Oskars Klava, Kaspars Gorkss, Deniss Ivanovs, Dzintars Zirnis, Vitalis Astafjevs, Jurijs Laizans, Genadijs Solonicins, Aleksejs Višnakovs (Jurijs Zigajevs 92+), Girts Karlsons (Vits Rimkus 59), Maris Verpakovskis* (Marians Pahars 78). Tr: Aleksandrs Starkovs

Rheinpark, Vaduz
13-10-2007, 19:00, 4131, Dondarini ITA

Liechtenstein 0

Peter Jehle - Martin Telser*, Yves Oehri, Daniel Hasler, Franz Burgmeier (Daniel Steuble 59), Ronny Büchel, Martin Büchel (Andreas Gerster 61), Thomas Beck, Mario Frick (Roger Beck 74), Raphael Rohrer, Daniel Frick (Benjamin Fischer 60). Tr: Hans-Peter Zaugg

Sweden 3
Ljungberg [19], Wilhelmsson [29], Svensson.A [56]

Andreas Isaksson - Matias Concha, Petter Hansson, Daniel Majstorovic, Erik Edman, Christian Wilhelmsson, Tobias Linderoth (Daniel Andersson* 70), Anders Svensson, Fredrik Ljungberg (Kim Kallstrom 39), Marcus Allbäck, Johan Elmander. Tr: Lars Lagerbäck

NRGI Park, Aarhus
13-10-2007, 20:00, 19 849, Michel SVK

Denmark 1
Tomasson [87]

Thomas Sørensen - Thomas Helveg, Martin Laursen, Ulrik Laursen, Niclas Jensen (Kenneth Perez 79), Christian Poulsen, Daniel Jensen*, Leon Andreasen (Nicklas Bendtner* 46), Dennis Rommedahl, Jon Dahl Tomasson, Jesper Grønkjær (Thomas Kahlenberg 65). Tr: Morten Olsen

Spain 3
Tamudo [14], Sergio Ramos [40], Riera [89]

Iker Casillas - Carlos Marchena, Sergio Ramos, Joan Capdevila*, Raúl Albiol, David Albelda (Pablo Ibanez 64), Xavi Hernández, Andrés Iniesta, Joaquín (Albert Riera 69), Cesc Fabregas (Luis Garcia Fernandez 78), Raúl Tamudo. Tr: Luis Aragonés

Rheinpark, Vaduz
17-10-2007, 20:00, 2589, Zografos GRE

Liechtenstein 3
Frick.M [28], Beck.T 2 [80 82]

Peter Jehle - Martin Telser*, Daniel Hasler, Martin Stocklasa*, Yves Oehri, Ronny Büchel, Andreas Gerster, Franz Burgmeier, Benjamin Fischer (Thomas Beck 62), Raphael Rohrer (Roger Beck 68), Mario Frick (Fabio D'Elia 91+). Tr: Hans-Peter Zaugg

Iceland 0

Árni Arason - Hermann Hreidarsson, Kristján Sigurdsson, Ivar Ingimarsson, Ragnar Sigurdsson, Johannes Gudjonsson (Armann Bjornsson 58), Emil Hallfredsson, Arnar Vidarsson, Brynjar Gunnarsson (Asgei Asgeirsson 85), Gunnar Heidar Thorvaldsson (Helgi Sigurdsson 71), Eidur Gudjohnsen*. Tr: Eyjölfur Sverrisson

Parken, Copenhagen
17-10-2007, 20:00, 19 004, Cakir TUR

Denmark 3
Tomasson [7p], Laursen.U [27], Rommedahl [90]

Thomas Sørensen - Martin Laursen, Ulrik Laursen (Leon Andreasen 32), Chris Sørensen, Thomas Helveg, Christian Poulsen (Jesper Gronkjaer 71), Daniel Jensen*, Thomas Kahlenberg, Dennis Rommedahl, Nicklas Bendtner, Jon Dahl Tomasson. Tr: Morten Olsen

Latvia 1
Gorkss [80]

Andris Vanins - Oskars Klava, Deniss Ivanovs, Dzintars Zirnis, Kaspars Gorkss, Vitalis Astafjevs, Jurijs Laizans, Aleksejs Višnakovs (Jurijs Zigajevs 78), Genadijs Solonicins, Vits Rimkus (Andrejs Butriks 63), Marians Pahars (Deniss Kacanovs 91+). Tr: Aleksandrs Starkovs

Råsunda, Stockholm
17-10-2007, 20:30, 33 112, Layec FRA

Sweden 1
Mellberg [15]

Andreas Isaksson - Matias Concha*, Olof Mellberg, Petter Hansson*, Erik Edman, Tobias Linderoth, Anders Svensson, Christian Wilhelmsson (Mikael Nilsson 45), Kim Källström (Andreas Johansson 85), Zlatan Ibrahimovic, Johan Elmander (Marcus Allback 73). Tr: Lars Lagerbäck

Northern Ireland 1
Lafferty [72]

Maik Taylor - Gareth McAuley, Aaron Hughes, George McCartney (Tony Capaldi 87), Stephen James Craigan, Steven Davis, Gary Clinghan, Chris Brunt, David Healy, Ivan Sproule, Kyle Lafferty. Tr: Nigel Worthington

Skonto, Riga
17-11-2007, 18:00, 4800, Moen NOR

Latvia 4
Karlsons.G [14], Verpakovskis [30], Laizans [63], Visnakovs [87]

Andris Vanins - Kaspars Gorkss, Oskars Klava*, Dzintars Zirnis, Deniss Ivanovs, Imants Bleidelis (Aleksejs Visnakovs 82), Jurijs Laizans, Vitalis Astafjevs, Andrejs Rubins, Girts Karlsons* (Marians Pahars 71), Maris Verpakovskis (Vits Rimkus 77). Tr: Aleksandrs Starkovs

Liechtenstein 1
Zirnis OG [13]

Peter Jehle - Marco Ritzberger, Martin Stocklasa, Fabio D'Elia, Daniel Hasler, Ronny Büchel* (Martin Buchel 80), Andreas Gerster*, Franz Burgmeier, Raphael Rohrer (Daniel Frick* 72), Mario Frick, Benjamin Fischer (Roger Beck 71). Tr: Hans-Peter Zaugg

Windsor Park, Belfast
17-11-2007, 19:45, 12 997, Vink NED

Northern Ireland 2
Feeney [62], Healy [80]

Maik Taylor - Gareth McAuley, Jonny Evans*, Aaron Hughes, Stephen James Craigan, Gary Clinghan, Keith Gillespie* (Ivan Sproule 74), Steven Davis, Chris Brunt, David Healy, Warren Feeney (Christopher Baird 85). Tr: Nigel Worthington

Denmark 1
Bendtner [51]

Thomas Sørensen - Brian Priske (Rasmus Wurtz 72), Chris Sørensen, Martin Laursen, Per Krøldrup, Christian Poulsen, Leon Andreasen*, Thomas Kahlenberg (Dennis Sorensen 46), Dennis Rommedahl, Martin Jørgensen (Simon Poulsen 79), Nicklas Bendtner. Tr: Morten Olsen

Bernabéu, Madrid
17-11-2007, 22:00, 67 055, Rosetti ITA

Spain 3
Capdevila 14, Iniesta 39, Sergio Ramos 65

Iker Casillas - Sergio Ramos, Carles Puyol*, Carlos Marchena, Joan Capdevila, Andrés Iniesta (Joaquín 52), Cesc Fabregas, David Albelda, Xavi Hernández, David Silva (Albert Riera 66), David Villa (Raul Tamudo 52). Tr: Luis Aragonés

Sweden 0

Andreas Isaksson - Mikael Nilsson, Olof Mellberg, Petter Hansson*, Erik Edman, Christian Wilhelmsson (Kennedy Bakircioglu 79), Daniel Andersson (Kim Kallstrom 46), Anders Svensson, Fredrik Ljungberg, Zlatan Ibrahimovic, Markus Rosenberg (Markus Allback 60). Tr: Lars Lagerbäck

Gran Canaria, Las Palmas
21-11-2007, 19:00, 30 339, Fandel GER

Spain 1
Xavi 52

Pepe Reina - Sergio Ramos, Raúl Albiol, Pablo Ibáñez, Mariano Pernía, Andrés Iniesta, Xavi Hernández (David Villa 67), Cesc Fabregas (Joaquín 47), Marcos Senna, David Silva, Daniel Güiza (Raul Tamudo 57). Tr: Luis Aragonés

Northern Ireland 0

Maik Taylor - Gareth McAuley, Stephen James Craigan, Aaron Hughes, Christopher Baird, Ivan Sproule (Stephen Robinson 46), Gary Clinghan, Steven Davis, Chris Brunt (Kyle Lafferty* 59), David Healy*, Warren Feeney (Martin Paterson 72). Tr: Nigel Worthington

Parken, Copenhagen
21-11-2007, 20:00, 15 393, Benquerença POR

Denmark 3
Bendtner 34, Tomasson 44, Kahlenberg 59

Thomas Sørensen - William Kvist, Ulrik Laursen, Per Krøldrup*, Chris Sørensen, Dennis Rommedahl (Simon Poulsen 73), Daniel Jensen, Christian Poulsen, Martin Jørgensen (Thomas Kahlenberg 53), Nicklas Bendtner (Soren Larsen 84), Jon Dahl Tomasson. Tr: Morten Olsen

Iceland 0

Arni Arason - Grétar Steinsson*, Kristján Sigurdsson (Sverrir Gardarsson 7), Hermann Hreidarsson, Ragnar Sigurdsson, Theodor Bjarnason*, Brynjar Gunnarsson, Stefán Gislason*, Emil Hallfredsson (Eggert Gunnthor Jonnson 73), Veigar Páll Gunnarsson (Asgeir Asgeirsson 84), Gunnar Heidar Thorvaldsson. Tr: Olafur Johannesson

Råsunda, Stockholm
21-11-2007, 20:00, 26 128,

Sweden 2
Allbäck 1, Källström 57

Andreas Isaksson - Mikael Nilsson, Olof Mellberg, Daniel Majstorovic, Erik Edman, Christian Wilhelmsson, Kim Källström, Anders Svensson, Fredrik Ljungberg, Zlatan Ibrahimovic, Marcus Allbäck. Tr: Lars Lagerbäck

Latvia 1
Laizans 26

Aleksandrs Kolinko - Kaspars Gorkss, Igors Stepanovs, Deniss Ivanovs, Dzintars Zirnis*, Andrejs Rubins, Jurijs Laizans, Vitalis Astafjevs (Genadijs Solonicins* 49), Imants Bleidelis (Aleksejs Visnakovs 43), Girts Karlsons (Marians Pahars 62), Maris Verpakovskis. Tr: Aleksandrs Starkovs

GROUP G

GROUP G	PL	W	D	L	F	A	PTS	ROU	NED	BUL	BLR	ALB	SVN	LUX
1 Romania	12	9	2	1	26	7	29		1-0	2-2	3-1	6-1	2-0	3-0
2 Netherlands	12	8	2	2	15	5	26	0-0		2-0	3-0	2-1	2-0	1-0
3 Bulgaria	12	7	4	1	18	7	25	1-0	1-1		2-1	0-0	3-0	3-0
4 Belarus	12	4	1	7	17	23	13	1-3	2-1	0-2		2-2	4-2	0-1
5 Albania	12	2	5	5	12	18	11	0-2	0-1	1-1	2-4		0-0	2-0
6 Slovenia	12	3	2	7	9	16	11	1-2	0-1	0-2	1-0	0-0		2-0
7 Luxembourg	12	1	0	11	2	23	3	0-2	0-1	0-1	1-2	0-3	0-3	

Romania and the Netherlands qualified for the finals

Josy Barthel, Luxembourg
8-09-2007, 17:00, 2012, Berezka UKR

Luxembourg 0

Jonathan Joubert - Jérôme Bigard, Eric Hoffmann, Jeff Strasser, Jeremie Peiffer (Daniel Da Mota 52), Claudio Lombardelli (Ben Payal 46), Carlos Ferreira, Gilles Bettmer, Mario Mutsch, René Peters, Daniel Huss (Joel Kitenge 63). Tr: Guy Hellers

Slovenia 3
Lavric 2 7 47, Novakovic 37

Samir Handanovic - Miso Brecko, Mitja Mörec, Anton Zlogar (Fabijan Cipot 82), Ales Kokot, Andraz Kirm (Andrej Komac 64), Robert Koren, Dalibor Stevanovic, Dare Vrsic (Rene Mihelic* 78), Milivoje Novakovic, Klemen Lavric. Tr: Matjaz Kek

Dinamo, Minsk
8-09-2007, 19:00, 19 320, Fröjdfeldt SWE

Belarus 1
Romashchenko 20

Vasili Khomutovski* - Vladimir Korythko, Artyom Radkov, Pavel Plaskonny, Yan Tigorev, Timofei Kalachev (Aleksei Skverniuk 77), Maksim Romashchenko, Aleksandr Hleb, Igor Stasevich, Sergei Kornilenko, Vitali Rodionov (Roman Vasilyuk 61). Tr: Bernd Stange

Romania 3
Mutu 2 16 77p, Dica 42

Bogdan Lobont - Razvan Rat*, Cristian Chivu*, Dorin Goian, Petre Marin, Paul Codrea* (Eugen Trica 90), Ovidiu Petre*, Banel Nicolita, Nicolae Dica (Dorinel Munteanu 67), Adrian Mutu, Sergiu Radu (Florentin Petre 56). Tr: Victor Piturca

Amsterdam ArenA, Amsterdam
8-09-2007, 20:30, 49 500, Cantalejo ESP

Netherlands 2
Sneijder 22, Van Nistelrooy 58

Edwin van der Sar - Mario Melchiot* (Khalid Boulahrouz 57), Joris Mathijsen, Wilfred Bouma, Giovanni van Bronckhorst, Johnny Heitinga, Wesley Sneijder (Clarence Seedorf 73), Demy de Zeeuw (Nigel de Jong 81), Ryan Babel, Ruud van Nistelrooy, Robin van Persie. Tr: Marco Van Basten

Bulgaria 0

Dimitar Ivankov - Lucio Wagner* (Chavdar Yankov 78), Radostin Kishishev, Aleksandar Tunchev, Igor Tomašic, Stanislav Angelov, Georgi Peev (Ivelin Popov 60), Martin Petrov, Stilian Petrov, Dimitar Telkiyski (Velizar Dimitrov 68), Dimitar Berbatov. Tr: Dimitar Penev

Arena Petrol, Celje
12-09-2007, 19:45, 3500, Banari MDA

Slovenia	1
	Lavric [3p]

Samir Handanovic - Branko Ilic (Miso Brecko 82), Bojan Jokic, Mitja Mörec•, Fabijan Cipot, Robert Koren, Andraz Kirm, Dalibor Stevanovic (Luka Zinko 75), Valter Birsa (Dare Vrsic• 67), Milivoje Novakovic, Klemen Lavric•. Tr: Matjaz Kek

Belarus	0

Vladimir Gaev - Yan Tigorev, Artyom Radkov•••46, Pavel Plaskonny, Timofei Kalachev, Igor Stasevich, Maksim Romashchenko, Aleksandr Hleb, Sergei Kornilenko (Vitali Rodionov 46), Vladimir Korythko (Nikolai Kashevski 89), Gennadi Bliznyuk (Yegor Filipenko 74). Tr: Bernd Stange

Vasil Levski, Sofia
12-09-2007, 20:30, 4674, Demirlek TUR

Bulgaria	3
	Berbatov 2 [27] [28], Petrov.M [54p]

Georgi Petkov - Aleksandar Tunchev, Igor Tomašic, Petar Zanev•, Stanislav Angelov•, Ivelin Popov (Martin Kouchev 74), Radostin Kishishev, Stilian Petrov (Chavdar Yankov 60), Velizar Dimitrov, Dimitar Berbatov, Martin Petrov (Hristo Yovov 66). Tr: Dimitar Penev

Luxembourg	0

Jonathan Joubert - Jérôme Bigard, Kim Kinziger, Eric Hoffmann•, Jeremie Peiffer (Dan Collette 46), Jeff Strasser•, René Peters, Gilles Bettmer (Daniel Da Mota 83), Sébastien Remy•, Mario Mutsch, Daniel Huss (Ben Payal 46). Tr: Guy Hellers

Qemal Stafa, Tirana
12-09-2007, 20:45, 15 000, Riley ENG

Albania	0

Arian Beqaj - Armend Dallku•, Nevil Dede, Debatik Curri, Kristi Vangjeli, Klodian Duro• (Altin Haxhi 69), Altin Lala, Lorik Cana•87, Devis Mukaj, Erion Bogdani (Ervin Bulku 83), Edmond Kapllani• (Alban Bushaj 46). Tr: Otto Baric

Netherlands	1
	Van Nistelrooy [91+]

Edwin van der Sar - Mario Melchiot•, Joris Mathijsen, Wilfred Bouma (Urby Emanuelson 63), André Ooijer, Demy de Zeeuw, Wesley Sneijder•, Giovanni van Bronckhorst, Ryan Babel (Dirk Kuyt 75), Ruud van Nistelrooy•, Robin van Persie• (Rafael Van der Vaart 46). Tr: Marco Van Basten

Tsentralny, Gomel
13-10-2007, 18:00, 14 000, Svendsen DEN

Belarus	0

Yuri Zhevnov (Vasili Khomutovski 69) - Sergei Omelyanchuk, Igor Stasevich (Timofei Kalachev 62), Yegor Filipenko, Pavel Plaskonny, Vladimir Korythko, Aleksei Skverniuk, Maksim Romashchenko, Aleksandr Hleb, Sergei Kornilenko, Andrei Voronkov (Vitali Rodionov 80). Tr: Bernd Stange

Luxembourg	1
	Fons Leweck [95+]

Jonathan Joubert• - Benoit Lang•, Kim Kinziger, Jean Wagner, René Peters•, Ben Payal (Carlos Ferreira 79), Gilles Bettmer, Claudio Lombardelli• (Fons Leweck• 45), Sébastien Remy, Mario Mutsch, Joël Kitenge (Daniel Da Mota• 61). Tr: Guy Hellers

Farul, Constanta
13-10-2007, 20:15, 12 595, Vassaras GRE

Romania	1
	Goian [71]

Bogdan Lobont - Dorin Goian, George Ogararu•, Razvan Rat, Gabriel Tamas•, Cristian Chivu, Banel Nicolita•, Paul Codrea•, Ovidiu Petre, Ciprian Marica (Daniel Niculae 70), Adrian Mutu•. Tr: Victor Piturca

Netherlands	0

Maarten Stekelenburg - Giovanni van Bronckhorst•, Johnny Heitinga (Kew Jaliens 68), André Ooijer (Danny Koevermans 84), Joris Mathijsen•, Wilfred Bouma, Demy de Zeeuw, Rafael van der Vaart, Clarence Seedorf, Ruud van Nistelrooy•, Arjen Robben (Ryan Babel 78). Tr: Marco Van Basten

Arena Petrol, Celje
13-10-2007, 20:30, 3700, Gomes POR

Slovenia	0

Samir Handanovic - Miso Brecko•, Bojan Jokic (Branko Ilic 77), Mitja Mörec•, Fabijan Cipot, Anton Zlogar, Andraz Kirm•, Robert Koren, Valter Birsa (Rene Mihelic 82), Milivoje Novakovic (Dejan Rusic• 61), Klemen Lavric. Tr: Matjaz Kek

Albania	0

Arian Beqaj - Kristi Vangjeli, Debatik Curri•, Nevil Dede, Blerim Rrustemi, Altin Haxhi (Devis Mukaj 60), Altin Lala, Ervin Bulku, Klodian Duro (Alban Bushaj 77), Ervin Skela (Jahmir Hyka 90+1), Erion Bogdani. Tr: Otto Baric

Josy Barthel, Luxembourg
17-10-2007, 20:15, 3584, Brych GER

Luxembourg	0

Stéphane Gillet - Benoit Lang, Jean Wagner, Kim Kinziger, Eric Hoffmann, Mario Mutsch, Ben Payal (Fons Leweck 68), René Peters, Gilles Bettmer (Carlos Ferreira 49), Sébastien Remy, Joël Kitenge (Daniel Da Mota 57). Tr: Guy Hellers

Romania	2
	Petre.F [42], Marica [61]

Bogdan Lobont - George Ogararu, Gabriel Tamas, Dorin Goian, Razvan Rat, Florentin Petre•, Andrei Margaritescu, Cristian Chivu (Ovidiu Petre 87), Ciprian Marica•, Nicolae Dica (Adrian Cristea 68), Daniel Niculae (Florin Bratu 76). Tr: Victor Piturca

Philips Stadion, Eindhoven
17-10-2007, 20:30, 32 500, Rizzoli ITA

Netherlands	2
	Sneijder [14], Huntelaar [86]

Maarten Stekelenburg - Kew Jaliens, Johnny Heitinga, Wilfred Bouma, Urby Emanuelson, Wesley Sneijder, Demy de Zeeuw, Clarence Seedorf, Robin van Persie (Andre Ooijer 59), Klaas Jan Huntelaar, Rafael van der Vaart (Arjen Robben 29) (Ryan Babel 62). Tr: Marco Van Basten

Slovenia	0

Samir Handanovic - Bostjan Cesar, Robert Koren, Mitja Mörec, Mišo Brecko, Anton Zlogar, Andraz Kirm (Bojan Jokic 81), Klemen Lavric, Valter Birsa (Milivoje Novakovic 67), Branko Ilic, Andrej Komac (Zlatan Ljubijankic 85). Tr: Matjaz Kek

Qemal Stafa, Tirana
17-10-2007, 20:45, 3000, Stuchlik AUT

Albania	1
	Duro.K [25]

Arian Beqaj• - Debatik Curri, Armend Dallku•, Nevil Dede, Kristi Vangeli, Klodian Duro, Altin Haxhi (Devis Mukaj 46), Altin Lala, Ervin Skela•90, Hamdi Salihi• (Ervin Bulku 73), Erion Bogdani. Tr: Otto Baric

Bulgaria	1
	Berbatov [87]

Georgi Petkov - Radostin Kishishev, Igor Tomašic, Valentin Iliev, Lucio Wagner•, Stanislav Angelov•, Stilian Petrov (Blagoy Georgiev 46), Dimitar Telkiyski (Chavdar Yankov 46), Ivelin Popov (Hristo Yovov 72), Martin Petrov, Dimitar Berbatov. Tr: Dimitar Penev

Vasil Levski, Sofia
17-11-2007, 18:00, 6000, Plautz AUT

Bulgaria	1
	Dimitrov.V [6]

Dimitar Ivankov - Zhivko Milanov•, Igor Tomasic, Aleksandar Tunchev, Petar Zanev, Blagoy Georgiev, Stilian Petrov, Hristo Yovov (Dimitar Telkiyski 83), Velizar Dimitrov, Martin Petrov (Zdravko Lazarov 90), Dimitar Berbatov. Tr: Dimitar Penev

Romania	0

Bogdan Lobont - George Ogararu, Gabriel Tamas (Razvan Cocis 58), Dorin Goian, Razvan Rat, Paul Codrea• (Eugen Trica• 82), Ovidiu Petre, Cristian Chivu, Banel Nicolita, Ionut Mazilu (Ciprian Marica 65), Daniel Niculae. Tr: Victor Piturca

Qemal Stafa, Tirana
17-11-2007, 20:00, 2064, Demirlek TUR

Albania	2
	Bogdani [43], Kapllani [44]

Arian Beqaj - Debatik Curri, Nevil Dede, Altin Lala (Alban Bushaj 75), Blerim Rrustemi (Kristi Vangeli 38), Ervin Skela•, Lorik Cana•, Armend Dallku•, Klodian Duro, Erion Bogdani, Edmond Kapllani (Hamdi Salihi 74). Tr: Slavko Kovacic

Belarus	4
	Romashchenko 2 [32] [63p], Kutuzov 2 [45] [54]

Yuri Zhevnov - Sergei Omelyanchuk, Yegor Filipenko•, Pavel Plaskonny• (Aleksei Skverniuk 65), Roman Kirenkin•, Aleksandr Kulchiy, Timofei Kalachev• (Vladimir Korythko 75), Maksim Romashchenko, Aleksandr Hleb, Vitali Bulyga, Vitali Kutuzov• (Sergei Kornilenko 90). Tr: Bernd Stange

De Kuip, Rotterdam
17-11-2007, 20:30, 45 000, Hansson SWE

Netherlands	1
	Koevermans [43]

Edwin van der Sar - Mario Melchiot, Joris Mathijsen, Wilfred Bouma, Demy de Zeeuw, Giovanni van Bronckhorst, Rafael van der Vaart, Wesley Sneijder, Clarence Seedorf (Urby Emanuelson 77), Ruud van Nistelrooy (Dirk Kuyt 46), Danny Koevermans (Ryan Babel 84). Tr: Marco Van Basten

Luxembourg	0

Jonathan Joubert - Kim Kinziger, Eric Hoffmann, Jean Wagner, Jeff Strasser•, Mario Mutsch, René Peters, Ben Payal, Gilles Bettmer (Fons Leweck 66), Sébastien Remy, Joël Kitenge (Aurelien Joachim 50). Tr: Guy Hellers

Lia Manoliu, Bucharest
21-11-2007, 18:00, 23 427, Trivkovic CRO

Romania 6
Dica 2 [22] 71p, Tamas [53], Niculae.D 2 [62] [65], Marica [69p]

Bogdan Lobont - George Ogararu, Gabriel Tamas (Marius Constantin 78), Dorin Goian, Razvan Rat, Florentin Petre (Gheorghe Bucur 65), Andrei Margaritescu, Razvan Cocis, Daniel Niculae, Ciprian Marica• (Ionut Mazilu 73), Nicolae Dica. Tr: Victor Piturca

Albania 1
Kapllani [64]

Arian Beqaj - Debatik Curri•••61, Nevil Dede•••70, Kristi Vangjeli• (Edmond Kapllani 41), Andi Lila, Altin Haxhi, Altin Lala, Ervin Bulku, Klodian Duro (Jahmir Hyka 78), Ervin Skela, Erion Bogdani (Elis Bakaj 83). Tr: Slavko Kovacic

---

Arena Petrol, Celje
21-11-2007, 18:00, 3700, Webb ENG

Slovenia 0

Samir Handanovic - Bojan Jokic•45, Mitja Mörec, Bostjan Cesar, Miso Brecko, Anton Zlogar•, Robert Koren, Dalibor Stevanovic (Andrej Komac• 56), Andraz Kirm, Valter Birsa (Branko Ilic• 49), Klemen Lavric (Milivoje Novakovic 65). Tr: Matjaz Kek

Bulgaria 2
Georgiev [82], Berbatov [84]

Dimitar Ivankov - Zhivko Milanov (Yordan Todorov 46), Igor Tomašic, Aleksandar Tunchev, Stanislav Angelov, Blagoy Georgiev•, Stilian Petrov• (Dimitar Telkiyski 46), Hristo Yovov (Zdravko Lazarov 76), Velizar Dimitrov, Martin Petrov, Dimitar Berbatov. Tr: Dimitar Penev

---

Dinamo, Minsk
21-11-2007, 19:00. 11 900, Layec FRA

Belarus 2
Bulyga [49], Korythko [65]

Yuri Zhevnov - Sergei Omelyanchuk• (Igor Stasevich 91+), Yegor Filipenko, Roman Kirenkin, Aleksei Skverniuk, Vladimir Korythko, Aleksandr Hleb (Nikolai Kashevski 46), Aleksandr Kulchiy, Maksim Romashchenko•, Vitali Kutuzov, Vitali Bulyga (Sergei Kornilenko 86). Tr: Bernd Stange

Netherlands 1
Van der Vaart [89]

Maarten Stekelenburg - Mario Melchiot, Joris Mathijsen, André Ooijer, Wilfred Bouma, Wesley Sneijder (Dirk Kuyt 46), Rafael van der Vaart, Giovanni van Bronckhorst (Orlando Engelaar 66), Demy de Zeeuw (Nigel de Jong 69), Ryan Babel•, Danny Koevermans. Tr: Marco Van Basten

---

UEFA EURO 2008 AUSTRIA–SWITZERLAND

UEFA EURO 2008 AUSTRIA-SWITZERLAND

First round groups	Pts	Quarter–finals		Semi–finals		Final	
Portugal	6						
Turkey	6	Spain	0 4p				
Czech Republic	3	Italy	0 2p				
Switzerland	3						
				Spain	3		
	Pts			Russia	0		
Croatia	9						
Germany	6	Netherlands	1				
Austria	1	Russia	3				
Poland	1						
						Spain	1
	Pts					Germany	0
Netherlands	9						
Italy	4	Turkey	1 3p				
Romania	2	Croatia	1 1p				
France	1						
				Turkey	2		
	Pts			Germany	3		
Spain	9						
Russia	6	Portugal	2				
Sweden	3	Germany	3				
Greece	0						

	GROUP A	PL	W	D	L	F	A	PTS		TUR	CZE	SUI
1	Portugal	3	2	0	1	5	3	6		2-0	3-1	0-2
2	Turkey	3	2	0	1	5	5	6			3-2	2-1
3	Czech Republic	3	1	0	2	4	6	3				1-0
4	Switzerland	3	1	0	2	3	3	3				

(c) = Captain • † = Man of the match

St Jakob-Park, Basel
7-06-2008, 18:00, 39 730, 13°C, Rosetti ITA

SUI 0 1 CZE

Sverkos 71

#	SWITZERLAND					CZECH REPUBLIC	#
1	Diego Benaglio					Petr Cech	1
5	Stephan Lichtsteiner	75				Zdenek Grygera	2
20	Patrick Müller					† (c) Tomáš Ujfalusi	21
4	Philippe Senderos					David Rozehnal	22
3	Ludovic Magnin					Marek Jankulovski	6
19	Valon Behrami	84	83			Libor Sionko	7
8	Gökhan Inler		87			David Jarolím	14
15	Gelson Fernandes					Tomáš Galásek	4
16	Tranquillo Barnetta					Jan Polák	3
9	Alexander Frei (c)	46				Jaroslav Plasil	20
11	Marco Streller		56			Jan Koller	9
	Tr: Jakob Kuhn					Tr: Karel Brückner	
10	Hakan Yakin	46	87			Radoslav Kovác	5
12	Eren Derdiyok	84	56			Václav Sverkos	10
22	Johan Vonlanthen	75	83			Stanislav Vlcek	11

Stade de Genève, Geneva
7-06-2008, 20:45, 29 016, 14°C, Fandel GER

POR 2 0 TUR

Pepe 61, Raul Meireles 93+

#	PORTUGAL					TURKEY	#
1	Ricardo					Volkan Demirel	23
4	Bosingwa	76				Hamit Altıntop	22
15	Pepe †					Servet Cetin	2
16	Ricardo Carvalho	55				Gökhan Zan	4
2	Paulo Ferreira					Hakan Balta	3
8	Petit					Colin Kazım-Richards	18
10	João Moutinho					(c) Emre Belözoglu	5
7	Cristiano Ronaldo					Mehmet Aurélio	7
20	Deco	92+	46			Mevlüt Erdinç	21
11	Simão	83				Tuncay Sanli	17
21	Nuno Gomes (c)	69				Nihat Kahveci	8
	Tr: Luiz Felipe Scolari					Tr: Fatih Terim	
5	Fernando Meira	92+	76			Semih Sentürk	9
6	Raul Meireles	83	55			Emre Asik	15
19	Nani	69	46			Sabri Sarıoglu	20

Stade de Genève, Geneva
11-06-2008, 18:00, 29 016, 21°C, Vassaras GRE

CZE 1 3 POR

Sionko 17   Deco 8, Ronaldo 63, Quaresma 91+

#	CZECH REPUBLIC					PORTUGAL	#
1	Petr Cech					Ricardo	1
2	Zdenek Grygera					Bosingwa	4
21	Tomáš Ujfalusi (c)					Pepe	15
22	David Rozehnal					Ricardo Carvalho	16
6	Marek Jankulovski					Paulo Ferreira	2
4	Tomáš Galásek	73				Petit	8
7	Libor Sionko		75			João Moutinho	10
17	Marek Matejovsky	68				† Cristiano Ronaldo	7
3	Jan Polák					Deco	20
20	Jaroslav Plasil	85	80			Simão	11
15	David Jarolím		79			(c) Nuno Gomes	21
	Tr: Karel Brückner					Tr: Luiz Felipe Scolari	
9	Jan Koller	73	75			Fernando Meira	5
11	Stanislav Vlcek	68	79			Hugo Almeida	9
14	David Jarolím	85	80			Ricardo Quaresma	17

St Jakob-Park, Basel
11-06-2008, 20:45, 39 730, 18°C, Michel SVK

SUI 1 2 TUR

Hakan Yakin 32   Semih Sentürk 57, Arda Turan 92+

#	SWITZERLAND					TURKEY	#
1	Diego Benaglio					Volkan Demirel	23
5	Stephan Lichtsteiner					Hamit Altıntop	22
20	Patrick Müller					Emre Asik	15
4	Philippe Senderos					Servet Cetin	2
3	Ludovic Magnin (c)					Hakan Balta	3
19	Valon Behrami			46		Gökdeniz Karadeniz	10
8	Gökhan Inler			46		Tümer Metin	11
15	Gelson Fernandes	76				Mehmet Aurélio	7
16	Tranquillo Barnetta	66				† Arda Turan	14
10	Hakan Yakin	85		85		(c) Nihat Kahveci	8
12	Eren Derdiyok					Tuncay Sanli	17
	Tr: Jakob Kuhn					Tr: Fatih Terim	
7	Ricardo Cabanas	76	46			Mehmet Topal	6
14	Daniel Gygax	85	46			Semih Sentürk	9
22	Johan Vonlanthen	66	85			Colin Kazım-Richards	18

St Jakob-Park, Basel
15-06-2008, 20:45, 39 730, 12°C, Plautz AUT

SUI 2 0 POR

Hakan Yakin 2 71 83p

#	SWITZERLAND					PORTUGAL	#
18	Pascal Zuberbühler					Ricardo	1
5	Stephan Lichtsteiner	83				Miguel	13
20	Patrick Müller					Pepe	15
4	Philippe Senderos					Bruno Alves	3
3	Ludovic Magnin (c)		41			Paulo Ferreira	2
19	Valon Behrami					(c) Fernando Meira	5
15	Gelson Fernandes		71			Miguel Veloso	18
8	Gökhan Inler					Raul Meireles	6
22	Johan Vonlanthen	61				Ricardo Quaresma	17
10	Hakan Yakin †	86				Nani	19
12	Eren Derdiyok		74			Hélder Postiga	23
	Tr: Jakob Kuhn					Tr: Luiz Felipe Scolari	
7	Ricardo Cabanas	86	74			Hugo Almeida	9
13	Stéphane Grichting	83	71			João Moutinho	10
16	Tranquillo Barnetta	61	41			Jorge Ribeiro	14

Stade de Genève, Geneva
15-06-2008, 20:45, 29 016, 15°C, Fröjdfeldt SWE

TUR 3 2 CZE

Arda Turan 75,
Nihat Kahveci 2 87 89   Koller 34, Plasil 62

#	TURKEY					CZECH REPUBLIC	#
23	Volkan Demirel	95+				Petr Cech	1
22	Hamit Altıntop					Zdenek Grygera	2
13	Emre Güngör	63				(c) Tomáš Ujfalusi	21
2	Servet Cetin					David Rozehnal	22
3	Hakan Balta					Marek Jankulovski	6
7	Mehmet Topal	57				Tomáš Galásek	4
7	Mehmet Aurélio			84		Libor Sionko	7
14	Arda Turan			39		Marek Matejovsky	17
17	Tuncay Sanli					Jan Polák	3
9	Nihat Kahveci (c) †			80		Jaroslav Plasil	20
9	Semih Sentürk	46				Jan Koller	9
	Tr: Fatih Terim					Tr: Karel Brückner	
15	Emre Asik	63	84			Stanislav Vlcek	11
18	Colin Kazım-Richards	57	80			Michal Kadlec	13
20	Sabri Sarıoglu	46	39			David Jarolím	14

GROUP B	PL	W	D	L	F	A	PTS		GER	AUT	POL
1 Croatia	3	3	0	0	4	1	9		2-1	1-0	1-0
2 Germany	3	2	0	1	4	2	6			1-0	2-0
3 Austria	3	0	1	2	1	3	1				1-1
4 Poland	3	0	1	2	1	4	1				

(c) = Captain • † = Man of the match

Ernst-Happel-Stadion, Vienna
8-06-2008, 18:00, 51 428, 21°C, Vink NED

AUT 0 1 CRO

Modric [4p]

	AUSTRIA			CROATIA	
21	Jürgen Macho			† Stipe Pletikosa	1
15	Sebastian Prödl			Vedran Corluka	5
3	Martin Stranzl			Robert Kovac	4
4	Emanuel Pogatetz			Josip Simunic	3
2	Joachim Standfest			Danijel Pranjic	22
6	René Aufhauser			Darijo Srna	11
10	Andreas Ivanschitz (c)			(c) Niko Kovac	10
19	Jürgen Säumel	61		Luka Modric	14
12	Ronald Gercaliu	69	61	Niko Kranjcar	19
20	Martin Harnik		83	Ivica Olic	18
9	Roland Linz	73	72	Mladen Petric	21
	Tr: Josef Hickersberger			Tr: Slaven Bilic	
7	Ivica Vastic	61	83	Ognjen Vukojevic	8
11	Umit Korkmaz	69	61	Dario Knezevic	15
18	Roman Kienast	73	72	Igor Budan	20

Wörthersee Stadion, Klagenfurt
8-06-2008, 20:45, 30 461, 24°C, Ovrebø NOR

GER 2 0 POL

Podolski 2 [20] [72]

	GERMANY			POLAND	
1	Jens Lehmann			Artur Boruc	1
16	Philipp Lahm			Marcin Wasilewski	13
21	Christoph Metzelder			Michal Zewlakow	14
17	Per Mertesacker		75	Jacek Bak	6
2	Marcell Jansen		75	Pawel Golanski	4
4	Clemens Fritz	56	65	Wojciech Lobodzinski	17
8	Torsten Frings			Dariusz Dudka	5
13	Michael Ballack (c)		46	(c) Maciej Zurawski	9
20	Lukas Podolski †			Mariusz Lewandowski	18
9	Mario Gómez	75		Jacek Krzynówek	8
11	Miroslav Klose	91+		Euzebiusz Smolarek	7
	Tr: Joachim Löw			Tr: Leo Beenhakker	
7	Bastian Schweinsteiger	56	75	Marek Saganowski	11
15	Thomas Hitzlsperger	75	65	Lukasz Piszczek	16
22	Kevin Kuranyi	91+	46	Roger Guerreiro	20

Wörthersee Stadion, Klagenfurt
12-06-2008, 18:00, 30 461, 21°C, De Bleeckere BEL

CRO 2 1 GER

Srna [24], Olic [62]   Podolski [79]

	CROATIA			GERMANY	
1	Stipe Pletikosa			Jens Lehmann	1
5	Vedran Corluka			Philipp Lahm	16
4	Robert Kovac			Christoph Metzelder	21
3	Josip Simunic			Per Mertesacker	17
22	Danijel Pranjic		46	Marcell Jansen	2
11	Darijo Srna	80	82	Clemens Fritz	4
14	Luka Modric †			Torsten Frings	8
10	Niko Kovac (c)			(c) Michael Ballack	13
7	Ivan Rakitic			Lukas Podolski	20
19	Niko Kranjcar	85	66	Mario Gómez	9
18	Ivica Olic	72		Miroslav Klose	11
	Tr: Slaven Bilic			Tr: Joachim Löw	
15	Dario Knezevic	85	90	66 Bastian Schweinsteiger	7
16	Jerko Leko	80	46	David Odonkor	19
21	Mladen Petric	72	82	Kevin Kuranyi	22

Ernst-Happel-Stadion, Vienna
12-06-2008, 20:45, 51 428, 21°C, Webb ENG

AUT 1 1 POL

Vastic [93+p]   Guerreiro [30]

	AUSTRIA			POLAND	
21	Jürgen Macho			Artur Boruc	1
14	György Garics			Marcin Wasilewski	13
15	Sebastian Prödl		46	Mariusz Jop	2
3	Martin Stranzl			(c) Jacek Bak	6
4	Emanuel Pogatetz			Michal Zewlakow	14
8	Christoph Leitgeb			Dariusz Dudka	5
6	René Aufhauser	74		Mariusz Lewandowski	18
10	Andreas Ivanschitz (c)	64		Jacek Krzynówek	8
11	Umit Korkmaz		85	† Roger Guerreiro	20
20	Martin Harnik		83	Marek Saganowski	11
9	Roland Linz	64		Euzebiusz Smolarek	7
	Tr: Josef Hickersberger			Tr: Leo Beenhakker	
7	Ivica Vastic	64	46	Pawel Golanski	4
18	Roman Kienast	64	83	Wojciech Lobodzinski	17
19	Jürgen Säumel	74	85	Rafal Murawski	19

Wörthersee Stadion, Klagenfurt
16-06-2008, 20:45, 30 461, 22°C, Vassaras GRE

POL 0 1 CRO

Klasnic [53]

	POLAND			CROATIA	
1	Artur Boruc			Vedran Runje	23
13	Marcin Wasilewski			(c) Dario Simic	2
14	Michal Zewlakow (c)			Hrvoje Vejic	6
5	Dariusz Dudka		27	Dario Knezevic	15
3	Jakub Wawrzyniak			Danijel Pranjic	22
4	Rafal Murawski			Jerko Leko	16
18	Mariusz Lewandowski	46		Ognjen Vukojevic	8
17	Wojciech Lobodzinski	55		Nikola Pokrivac	13
20	Roger Guerreiro			Ivan Rakitic	7
8	Jacek Krzynówek		74	† Ivan Klasnic	17
11	Marek Saganowski	69	75	Mladen Petric	21
	Tr: Leo Beenhakker			Tr: Slaven Bilic	
7	Euzebiusz Smolarek	55	27	Vedran Corluka	5
21	Tomasz Zahorski	69	74	Nikola Kalinic	9
23	Adam Kokoszka	46	75	Niko Kranjcar	19

Ernst-Happel-Stadion, Vienna
16-06-2008, 20:45, 51 428, 21°C, Mejuto González ESP

AUT 0 1 GER

Ballack [49]

	AUSTRIA			GERMANY	
21	Jürgen Macho			Jens Lehmann	1
14	György Garics			Arne Friedrich	3
3	Martin Stranzl			Per Mertesacker	17
17	Martin Hiden	55		Christoph Metzelder	21
4	Emanuel Pogatetz			Philipp Lahm	16
6	René Aufhauser	63	93+	Clemens Fritz	4
10	Andreas Ivanschitz (c)			Torsten Frings	8
5	Christian Fuchs			† (c) Michael Ballack	13
20	Martin Harnik	67	83	Lukas Podolski	20
11	Umit Korkmaz		60	Mario Gómez	9
22	Erwin Hoffer			Miroslav Klose	11
	Tr: Josef Hickersberger			Tr: Joachim Löw	
8	Christoph Leitgeb	55	83	Oliver Neuville	7
18	Roman Kienast	67	60	Thomas Hitzlsperger	15
19	Jürgen Säumel	63	93+	Tim Borowski	18

GROUP C		PL	W	D	L	F	A	PTS		ITA	ROU	FRA
1	Netherlands	3	3	0	0	9	1	9		3-0	2-0	4-1
2	Italy	3	1	1	1	3	4	4			1-1	2-0
3	Romania	3	0	2	1	1	3	2				0-0
4	France	3	0	1	2	1	6	1				

(c) = Captain • † = Man of the match

Letzigrund, Zürich
9-06-2008, 18:00, 30 585, 23°C, Mejuto González ESP

ROM   0   0   FRA

ROMANIA				FRANCE	
1	Bogdan Lobont			Grégory Coupet	23
2	Cosmin Contra			Willy Sagnol	19
4	Gabriel Tamas			(c) Lilian Thuram	15
15	Dorin Goian			William Gallas	5
3	Razvan Rat			Eric Abidal	3
11	Razvan Cocis	64		Jérémy Toulalan	20
6	Mirel Radoi	93+		† Claude Makelele	6
5	Cristian Chivu (c)			Franck Ribéry	22
16	Banel Nicolita			Florent Malouda	7
21	Daniel Niculae		72	Nicolas Anelka	8
10	Adrian Mutu	78	78	Karim Benzema	9
	Tr: Victor Piturca			Tr: Raymond Domenech	
8	Paul Codrea	64	78	Samir Nasri	11
18	Marius Niculae	78	72	Bafetimbi Gomis	18
20	Nicolae Dica	93+			

Stade de Suisse (Wankdorf), Berne
9-06-2008, 20:45, 30 777, 19°C, Fröjdfeldt SWE

NED   3   0   ITA

Van Nistelrooy [26], Sneijder [31],
Van Bronckhorst [79]

NETHERLANDS				ITALY	
1	Edwin van der Sar (c)			(c) Gianluigi Buffon	1
2	André Ooijer			Christian Panucci	2
21	Khalid Boulahrouz	77		Andrea Barzagli	6
4	Joris Mathijsen		54	Marco Materazzi	23
5	Giovanni v. Bronckhorst			Gianluca Zambrotta	19
17	Nigel de Jong			Massimo Ambrosini	13
8	Orlando Engelaar			Andrea Pirlo	21
18	Dirk Kuyt	81		Gennaro Gattuso	8
23	Rafael van der Vaart		75	Mauro Camoranesi	16
10	Wesley Sneijder †			Luca Toni	9
9	Ruud van Nistelrooy	70	64	Antonio Di Natale	11
	Tr: Marco Van Basten			Tr: Roberto Donadoni	
3	John Heitinga	77	54	Fabio Grosso	3
7	Robin van Persie	70	64	Alessandro Del Piero	7
20	Ibrahim Afellay	81	75	Antonio Cassano	18

Letzigrund, Zürich
13-06-2008, 18:00, 30 585, 15°C, Ovrebø NOR

ITA   1   1   ROM

Panucci [56]

Mutu [55]

ITALY				ROMANIA	
1	Gianluigi Buffon			Bogdan Lobont	1
19	Gianluca Zambrotta			Cosmin Contra	2
2	Christian Panucci			Gabriel Tamas	4
4	Giorgio Chiellini			Dorin Goian	15
3	Fabio Grosso			Razvan Rat	3
21	Andrea Pirlo †		25	Mirel Radoi	6
10	Daniele De Rossi		60	Florentin Petre	7
16	Mauro Camoranesi	85		Paul Codrea	8
20	Simone Perrotta	57		(c) Cristian Chivu	5
7	Alessandro Del Piero (c)	77		Daniel Niculae	21
9	Luca Toni		88	Adrian Mutu	10
	Tr: Roberto Donadoni			Tr: Victor Piturca	
13	Massimo Ambrosini	85	88	Razvan Cocis	11
15	Fabio Quagliarella	77	60	Banel Nicolita	16
18	Antonio Cassano	57	25	Nicolae Dica	20

Stade de Suisse (Wankdorf), Berne
13-06-2008, 20:45, 30 777, 14°C, Fandel GER

NED   4   1   FRA

Kuyt [9], Van Persie [59], Robben [72],
Sneijder [92+]

Henry [71]

NETHERLANDS				FRANCE	
1	Edwin van der Sar (c)			Grégory Coupet	23
21	Khalid Boulahrouz			Willy Sagnol	19
2	André Ooijer			(c) Lilian Thuram	15
4	Joris Mathijsen			William Gallas	5
5	Giovanni v. Bronckhorst			Patrice Evra	13
17	Nigel de Jong			Jérémy Toulalan	20
8	Orlando Engelaar	46		Claude Makelele	6
18	Dirk Kuyt	55	75	Sidney Govou	10
23	Rafael van der Vaart	78	60	Florent Malouda	7
10	Wesley Sneijder †			Franck Ribéry	22
9	Ruud van Nistelrooy			Thierry Henry	12
	Tr: Marco Van Basten			Tr: Raymond Domenech	
7	Robin van Persie	55	75	Nicolas Anelka	8
11	Arjen Robben	46	60	Bafetimbi Gomis	18
14	Wilfred Bouma	78			

Stade de Suisse (Wankdorf), Berne
17-06-2008, 20:45, 30,777, 17°C, Busacca SUI

NED   2   0   ROM

Huntelaar [54], Van Persie [87]

NETHERLANDS				ROMANIA	
16	Maarten Stekelenburg			Bogdan Lobont	1
21	Khalid Boulahrouz	58		Cosmin Contra	2
3	John Heitinga (c)			Gabriel Tamas	4
4	Wilfred Bouma			Sorin Ghionea	14
15	Tim de Cler			Razvan Rat	3
6	Demy de Zeeuw			Razvan Cocis	11
8	Orlando Engelaar		72	Paul Codrea	8
20	Ibrahim Afellay			(c) Cristian Chivu	5
7	Robin van Persie †	82		Banel Nicolita	16
11	Arjen Robben	61	59	Marius Niculae	18
19	Klaas Jan Huntelaar	83		Adrian Mutu	10
	Tr: Marco Van Basten			Tr: Victor Piturca	
12	Mario Melchiot	58	82	Florentin Petre	7
18	Dirk Kuyt	61	72	Nicolae Dica	20
22	Jan Ven'goor of Hesselink	83	59	Daniel Niculae	21

Letzigrund, Zürich
17-06-2008, 20:45, 30 585, 16°C, Michel SVK

FRA   0   2   ITA

Pirlo [25p], De Rossi [62]

FRANCE				ITALY	
23	Grégory Coupet			(c) Gianluigi Buffon	1
14	François Clerc			Gianluca Zambrotta	19
5	William Gallas			Christian Panucci	2
3	Eric Abidal	24		Giorgio Chiellini	4
13	Patrice Evra			Fabio Grosso	3
20	Jérémy Toulalan		55	Andrea Pirlo	21
6	Claude Makelele			† Daniele De Rossi	10
10	Sidney Govou	66	82	Gennaro Gattuso	8
22	Franck Ribéry	10	64	Simone Perrotta	16
9	Karim Benzema			Luca Toni	9
12	Thierry Henry (c)			Antonio Cassano	18
	Tr: Raymond Domenech			Tr: Roberto Donadoni	
2	Jean-Alain Boumsong	26	55	Massimo Ambrosini	13
8	Nicolas Anelka	66	64	Mauro Camoranesi	16
11	Samir Nasri	26	10	82	Alberto Aquilani	22

GROUP D	PL	W	D	L	F	A	PTS
1 Spain	3	3	0	0	8	3	9
2 Russia	3	2	0	1	4	4	6
3 Sweden	3	1	0	2	3	4	3
4 Greece	3	0	0	3	1	5	0

	RUS	SWE	GRE
	4-1	2-1	2-1
		2-0	1-0
			2-0

(c) = Captain • † = Man of the match

Tivoli Neu, Innsbruck
10-06-2008, 18:00, 30 772, 28°C, Plautz AUT

ESP 4 1 RUS

Villa 3 20 44 75, Fabregas 93+   Pavlyuchenko 86

SPAIN			RUSSIA		
1 Iker Casillas (c)			Igor Akinfeev 1		
15 Sergio Ramos			Aleksandr Anyukov 22		
4 Carlos Marchena			Roman Shirokov 14		
5 Carles Puyol			Denis Kolodin 8		
11 Joan Capdevila			Yuri Zhirkov 18		
21 David Silva	77	46	Dmitri Sychev 21		
19 Marcos Senna			Konstantin Zyryanov 17		
8 Xavi Hernández			(c) Sergei Semak 11		
9 Andrés Iniesta	63	58	Igor Semshov 20		
7 David Villa †			Diniyar Bilyaletdinov 15		
9 Fernando Torres	54		Roman Pavlyuchenko 19		
Tr: Luis Aragonés			Tr: Guus Hiddink		
10 Cesc Fàbregas	54	70	Roman Adamov 6		
12 Santi Cazorla	63	58	Dmitri Torbinski 7		
14 Xabi Alonso	77	46	70 Vladimir Bystrov 23		

EM Stadion Wals-Siezenheim, Salzburg
10-06-2008, 20:45, 31 063, 24°C, Busacca SUI

GRE 0 2 SWE

     Ibrahimovic 67, Hansson 72

GREECE			SWEDEN		
1 Antonis Nikopolidis			Andreas Isaksson 1		
2 Giourkas Seitaridis			74 Niclas Alexandersson 7		
16 Sotiris Kyrgiakos			Olof Mellberg 3		
19 Paraskevas Antzas			Petter Hansson 4		
5 Traianos Dellas	70		Mikael Nilsson 2		
15 Vassilis Torosidis			78 Christian Wilhelmsson 21		
9 Angelos Charisteas			Anders Svensson 8		
6 Angelos Basinas (c)			Daniel Andersson 19		
21 Kostas Katsouranis			(c) Fredrik Ljungberg 9		
10 Giorgos Karagounis			71 † Zlatan Ibrahimovic 10		
17 Fanis Gekas	46		Henrik Larsson 17		
Tr: Otto Rehhagel			Tr: Lars Lagerbäck		
7 Giorgos Samaras	46	74	Fredrik Stoor 5		
20 Giannis Amanatidis	70	71	Johan Elmander 11		
		78	Markus Rosenberg 22		

Tivoli Neu, Innsbruck
14-06-2008, 18:00, 30 772, 19°C, Vink NED

SWE 1 2 ESP

Ibrahimovic 34   Torres 15, Villa 92+

SWEDEN			SPAIN		
1 Andreas Isaksson			(c) Iker Casillas 1		
5 Fredrik Stoor			Sergio Ramos 15		
3 Olof Mellberg			Carlos Marchena 4		
4 Petter Hansson		24	Carles Puyol 5		
2 Mikael Nilsson			Joan Capdevila 11		
11 Johan Elmander	79	59	Andrés Iniesta 6		
19 Daniel Andersson			Marcos Senna 19		
8 Anders Svensson		59	Xavi Hernández 8		
9 Fredrik Ljungberg (c)			David Silva 21		
17 Henrik Larsson	87		† David Villa 7		
10 Zlatan Ibrahimovic	46		Fernando Torres 9		
Tr: Lars Lagerbäck			Tr: Luis Aragonés		
16 Kim Källström	87	24	Raúl Albiol 2		
18 Sebastian Larsson	79	59	Cesc Fàbregas 10		
22 Markus Rosenberg	46	59	Santi Cazorla 12		

EM Stadion Wals-Siezenheim, Salzburg
14-06-2008, 20:45, 31 063, 13°C, Rosetti ITA

GRE 0 1 RUS

     Zyryanov 33

GREECE			RUSSIA		
1 Antonis Nikopolidis			Igor Akinfeev 1		
2 Giourkas Seitaridis	40		Aleksandr Anyukov 22		
5 Traianos Dellas			Denis Kolodin 8		
16 Sotiris Kyrgiakos			Sergei Ignashevich 4		
15 Vassilis Torosidis		87	Yuri Zhirkov 18		
21 Kostas Katsouranis			(c) Sergei Semak 11		
6 Angelos Basinas (c)			Dmitri Torbinski 7		
3 Christos Patsatzoglou			Konstantin Zyryanov 17		
9 Angelos Charisteas			Igor Semshov 20		
20 Giannis Amanatidis	80	70	Diniyar Bilyaletdinov 15		
23 Nikos Liberopoulos	61		† Roman Pavlyuchenko 19		
Tr: Otto Rehhagel			Tr: Guus Hiddink		
8 Stelios Giannakopoulos	80	87	Vasili Berezutski 2		
10 Giorgos Karagounis	40	70	Ivan Saenko 9		
17 Fanis Gekas	61				

EM Stadion Wals-Siezenheim, Salzburg
18-06-2008, 20:45, 30 883, 20°C, Webb ENG

GRE 1 2 ESP

Charisteas 42   De la Red 61, Güiza 88

GREECE			SPAIN		
1 Antonis Nikopolidis (c)			Pepe Reina 23		
11 Loukas Vintra			Alvaro Arbeloa 18		
16 Sotiris Kyrgiakos	62		Raúl Albiol 2		
5 Traianos Dellas			Juanito 20		
4 Nikos Spiropoulos			Fernando Navarro 3		
6 Angelos Basinas			Rubén de la Red 22		
21 Kostas Katsouranis			† (c) Xabi Alonso 14		
14 Dimitris Salpingidis	86		Sergio García 16		
10 Giorgos Karagounis	74		Cesc Fàbregas 10		
20 Giannis Amanatidis		58	Andrés Iniesta 6		
9 Angelos Charisteas			Daniel Güiza 17		
Tr: Otto Rehhagel			Tr: Luis Aragonés		
8 Stelios Giannakopoulos	86	58	Santi Cazorla 12		
19 Paraskevas Antzas	62				
22 Alexandros Tziolis	74				

Tivoli Neu, Innsbruck
18-06-2008, 20:45, 30 772, 20°C, De Bleeckere BEL

RUS 2 0 SWE

Pavlyuchenko 24, Arshavin 50

RUSSIA			SWEDEN		
1 Igor Akinfeev			Andreas Isaksson 1		
22 Aleksandr Anyukov			Fredrik Stoor 5		
4 Sergei Ignashevich			Olof Mellberg 3		
8 Denis Kolodin			Petter Hansson 4		
18 Yuri Zhirkov		79	Mikael Nilsson 2		
11 Sergei Semak (c)			Johan Elmander 11		
17 Konstantin Zyryanov		56	Daniel Andersson 19		
20 Igor Semshov			Anders Svensson 8		
15 Diniyar Bilyaletdinov	66		(c) Fredrik Ljungberg 9		
10 Andrei Arshavin †			Henrik Larsson 17		
19 Roman Pavlyuchenko	90		Zlatan Ibrahimovic 10		
Tr: Guus Hiddink			Tr: Lars Lagerbäck		
9 Ivan Saenko	66	56	Kim Källström 16		
23 Vladimir Bystrov	90	79	Marcus Allbäck 20		

QUARTER-FINALS

Ernst-Happel-Stadion, Vienna
22-06-2008, 20:45, 48 000, 31°C, Fandel GER

ESP 0 0 ITA

4 PSO 2

#	SPAIN			ITALY	#
1	Iker Casillas (c) †			(c) Gianluigi Buffon	1
15	Sergio Ramos			Gianluca Zambrotta	19
4	Carlos Marchena			Christian Panucci	2
5	Carles Puyol			Giorgio Chiellini	4
11	Joan Capdevila			Fabio Grosso	3
6	Andrés Iniesta	59	118	Alberto Aquilani	22
19	Marcos Senna			Daniele De Rossi	10
8	Xavi Hernández	60		Massimo Ambrosini	13
21	David Silva		58	Simone Perrotta	20
7	David Villa			Luca Toni	9
9	Fernando Torres	85	75	Antonio Cassano	18
	Tr: Luis Aragonés			Tr: Roberto Donadoni	
10	Cesc Fàbregas	60	118	Alessandro Del Piero	7
12	Santi Cazorla	59	75	Antonio Di Natale	11
17	Daniel Güiza	85	58	Mauro Camoranesi	16

St Jakob-Park, Basel
21-06-2008, 20:45, 38 374, 28°C, Michel SVK

NED 1 3 RUS

Van Nistelrooy 86 | Pavlyuchenko 56, Torbinski 112, Arshavin 116

#	NETHERLANDS			RUSSIA	#
1	Edwin van der Sar (c)			Igor Akinfeev	1
21	Khalid Boulahrouz	54		Aleksandr Anyukov	22
2	André Ooijer			Sergei Ignashevich	4
4	Joris Mathijsen			Denis Kolodin	8
5	Giovanni v. Bronckhorst			Yuri Zhirkov	18
17	Nigel de Jong			(c) Sergei Semak	11
8	Orlando Engelaar	62		Konstantin Zyryanov	17
18	Dirk Kuyt	46	69	Igor Semshov	20
23	Rafael van der Vaart		81	Ivan Saenko	9
10	Wesley Sneijder		105	Roman Pavlyuchenko	19
9	Ruud van Nistelrooy			† Andrei Arshavin	10
	Tr: Marco Van Basten			Tr: Guus Hiddink	
3	John Heitinga	54	81	Dmitri Torbinski	7
7	Robin van Persie	46	69	Diniyar Bilyaletdinov	15
20	Ibrahim Afellay	62	115	Dmitri Sychev	21

Ernst-Happel-Stadion, Vienna
20-06-2008, 20:45, 51 428, 31°C, Rosetti ITA

CRO 1 1 TUR

Klasnic 119 | Semih Sentürk 122+

1 PSO 3

#	CROATIA			TURKEY	#
1	Stipe Pletikosa			Recber Rüstü	1
5	Vedran Corluka			† Hamit Altintop	22
4	Robert Kovac			Gökhan Zan	4
3	Josip Simunic			Emre Asik	15
22	Danijel Pranjic			Hakan Balta	3
11	Darijo Srna		76	Mehmet Topal	6
14	Luka Modric			Sabri Sarioglu	20
10	Niko Kovac (c)			Tuncay Sanli	17
7	Ivan Rakitic			Arda Turan	14
19	Niko Kranjcar	65	61	Colin Kazim-Richards	18
18	Ivica Olic	97	117	(c) Nihat Kahveci	8
	Tr: Slaven Bilic			Tr: Fatih Terim	
17	Ivan Klasnic	97	76	Semih Sentürk	9
21	Mladen Petric	65	117	Gökdeniz Karadeniz	10
			61	Ugur Boral	16

St Jakob-Park, Basel
19-06-2008, 20:45, 39 374, 22°C, Fröjdfeldt SWE

POR 2 3 GER

Nuno Gomes 40, Hélder Postiga 87 | Schweinsteiger 22, Klose 26, Ballack 61

#	PORTUGAL			GERMANY	#
1	Ricardo			Jens Lehmann	1
4	Bosingwa			Arne Friedrich	3
15	Pepe			Per Mertesacker	17
16	Ricardo Carvalho			Christoph Metzelder	21
2	Paulo Ferreira			Philipp Lahm	16
8	Petit	73		†Bastian Schweinsteiger	7
10	João Moutinho	31		Simon Rolfes	6
7	Cristiano Ronaldo			(c) Michael Ballack	13
20	Deco			Thomas Hitzlsperger	15
11	Simão			Miroslav Klose	11
21	Nuno Gomes (c)	67		Lukas Podolski	20
	Tr: Luiz Felipe Scolari			Tr: Joachim Löw	
6	Raul Meireles	31	89	Marcell Jansen	2
19	Nani	67	83	Clemens Fritz	4
23	Hélder Postiga	73	73	Tim Borowski	18

SEMI-FINALS

Ernst-Happel-Stadion, Vienna
26-06-2008, 20:45, 51 428, 23°C, De Bleeckere BEL

RUS 0 3 ESP

Xavi 50, Güiza 73, Silva 82

#	RUSSIA			SPAIN	#
1	Igor Akinfeev			(c) Iker Casillas	1
22	Aleksandr Anyukov			Sergio Ramos	15
2	Vasili Berezutski			Carlos Marchena	4
4	Sergei Ignashevich			Carles Puyol	5
18	Yuri Zhirkov			Joan Capdevila	11
11	Sergei Semak (c)			† Andrés Iniesta	6
17	Konstantin Zyryanov			Marcos Senna	19
20	Igor Semshov	69		Xavi Hernández	8
9	Ivan Saenko			David Silva	21
19	Roman Pavlyuchenko	34		David Villa	7
10	Andrei Arshavin	69		Fernando Torres	9
	Tr: Guus Hiddink			Tr: Luis Aragonés	
15	Diniyar Bilyaletdinov	56	34	Cesc Fàbregas	10
21	Dmitri Sychev	57	69	Xabi Alonso	14
			69	Daniel Güiza	17

St Jakob-Park, Basel
25-06-2008, 20:45, 39 374, 22°C, Busacca SUI

GER 3 2 TUR

Schweinsteiger 26, Klose 79, Lahm 90 | Ugur Boral 22, Semih Sentürk 86

#	GERMANY			TURKEY	#
1	Jens Lehmann			(c) Recber Rüstü	1
3	Arne Friedrich			Sabri Sarioglu	20
17	Per Mertesacker			Mehmet Topal	6
21	Christoph Metzelder			Gökhan Zan	4
16	Philipp Lahm †			Hakan Balta	3
15	Thomas Hitzlsperger			Mehmet Aurélio	7
6	Simon Rolfes	46	92+	Colin Kazim-Richards	18
7	Bastian Schweinsteiger			Hamit Altintop	22
13	Michael Ballack (c)		81	Ayhan Akman	19
20	Lukas Podolski		84	Ugur Boral	16
11	Miroslav Klose	92+		Semih Sentürk	9
	Tr: Joachim Löw			Tr: Fatih Terim	
2	Marcell Jansen	92+	84	Gökdeniz Karadeniz	10
8	Torsten Frings	46	92+	Tümer Metin	11
			81	Mevlüt Erdinç	21

FINAL

Euro 2008 Final	Ernst-Happel-Stadion, Vienna	29-06-2008
Kick-off: 20:45	27°C Sunny	Attendance: 51 428

SPAIN   1   0   GERMANY

Fernando Torres [33]

		SPAIN		MATCH STATS					GERMANY		
1	GK	Iker Casillas (c)							Jens Lehmann	GK	1
15	DF	Sergio Ramos		12	Shots	3			Arne Friedrich	DF	3
4	DF	Carlos Marchena		7	Shots on Goal	1			Per Mertesacker	DF	17
5	DF	Carles Puyol		19	Fouls Committed	22			Christoph Metzelder	DF	21
11	DF	Joan Capdevila		7	Corner Kicks	4	46		Philipp Lahm	DF	16
19	MF	Marcos Senna		4	Offside	5			Torsten Frings	MF	8
6	MF	Andrés Iniesta		49	Possession %	51	58		Thomas Hitzlsperger	MF	15
8	MF	Xavi Hernández		(C)Captain † Man of the Match					Bastian Schweinsteiger	MF	7
10	MF	Cesc Fàbregas	63	MATCH OFFICIALS					(c) Michael Ballack	MF	13
21	MF	David Silva	66	REFEREE					Lukas Podolski	FW	20
9	FW	Fernando Torres †	78	Roberto Rosetti ITA			79		Miroslav Klose	FW	11
		Tr: Luis Aragonés		ASSISTANTS					Tr: Joachim Löw		
		Substitutes		Alessandro Griselli ITA					Substitutes		
13	GK	Andrés Palop		Paolo Calcagno ITA					Robert Enke	GK	12
23	GK	Pepe Reina		4TH OFFICIAL					René Adler	GK	23
2	DF	Raúl Albiol		Peter Fröjdfeldt SWE			46		Marcell Jansen	DF	2
3	DF	Fernando Navarro							Clemens Fritz	DF	4
7	FW	David Villa (injured)							Heiko Westermann	DF	5
12	MF	Santi Cazorla	66						Simon Rolfes	MF	6
14	MF	Xabi Alonso	63				79		Mario Gómez	FW	9
16	FW	Sergio García							Oliver Neuville	FW	10
17	FW	Daniel Güiza	78						Piotr Trochowski	MF	14
18	DF	Álvaro Arbeloa							Tim Borowski	MF	18
20	DF	Juanito							David Odonkor	FW	19
22	MF	Rubén de la Red					58		Kevin Kuranyi	FW	22

Many people will look at this Spain team because it has been a model for playing football. I think all football lovers want people to make good combinations, to get into the penalty area and to score goals. At the beginning I said that if we managed this squad well, we would be champions. I usually don't show what I feel, but I'm full inside. I don't get very emotional but there were moments out there from some of my players that filled me with emotion. We have put together a group that plays well, that keeps the ball and mixes their passes very well and that is difficult to stop.

Luis Aragonés

I'd like to congratulate Spain and their coach, because we have to recognise the high quality of their play. They played really well during the whole tournament, and today they were technically excellent and had more chances than us. They deserved to win. We're disappointed that we didn't win but I think we can be satisfied with the tournament as a whole. The team performed very well over the 45 days we've spent together, we had a lot of fun and enjoyed it, but we were very ambitious too. We're right at the top in Europe and the team in recent years has learned a lot.

Joachim Löw

PENALTY SHOOT-OUTS AT EURO 2008

CROATIA 1-3 TURKEY			
Croatia First		**Turkey Second**	
Luka Modric	✗	Arda Turan	✔
Darijo Srna	✔	Semih Sentürk	✔
Ivan Rakitic	✗	Hamit Altıntop	✔
Mladen Petric	✗		
Turkey qualified for the semi-finals 3-1 on penalties			

SPAIN 4-2 ITALY			
Spain First		**Italy Second**	
David Villa	✔	Fabio Grosso	✔
Santi Cazorla	✔	Daniele De Rossi	✗
Marcos Senna	✔	Mauro Camoranesi	✔
Daniel Güiza	✗	Antonio Di Natale	✗
Cesc Fàbregas	✔		
Spain qualified for the semi-finals 4-2 on penalties			

UEFA CHAMPIONS LEAGUE 2007–08

First Qualifying Round

Sheriff Tiraspol	MDA	2	3
Rangers FC	AND	0	0
Murata	SMR	1	0
Tampere United	FIN	2	2
Olimpi Rustavi	GEO	0	0
FK Astana	KAZ	0	3
Linfield	NIR	0	0
Elfsborg IF	SWE	0	1
Domzale	SVN	1	2
SK Tirana	ALB	0	1
Khazar Lenkoran	AZE	1	1
Dinamo Zagreb	CRO	1	3
TNS Llansantffraid	WAL	3	1
FK Ventspils	LVA	2	2
Derry City	IRL	0	0
Pyunik Yerevan	ARM	0	2
Zeta Golubovci	MNE	3	2
FBK Kaunas	LTU	1	3
Pobeda Prilep	MKD	0	0
Levadia Tallinn	EST	1	0
Marsaxlokk	MLT	0	1
Sarajevo	BIH	6	3
F91 Dudelange	LUX	1	4
MSK Zilina	SVK	2	5
FH Hafnarfjördur	ISL	4	0
HB Tórshavn	FRO	1	0
APOEL Nicosia	CYP	2	0
BATE Borisov	BLR	0	3

Second Qualifying Round

Besiktas	TUR	1	3
Sheriff Tiraspol	MDA	0	0
Tampere United	FIN	1	1
Levski Sofia	BUL	0	0
FK Astana	KAZ	1	1
Rosenborg BK	NOR	3	7
Debreceni VSC	HUN	0	0
Elfsborg IF	SWE	0	1
Domzale	SVN	1	1
Dinamo Zagreb	CRO	2	3
FC København	DEN	1	1
Beitar Jerusalem	ISR	0	1
FK Ventspils	LVA	0	0
RB Austria Salzburg	AUT	3	4
Pyunik Yerevan	ARM	0	1
Shakhtar Donetsk	UKR	2	2
Rangers	SCO	2	1
Zeta Golubovci	MNE	0	0
Crvena Zvezda	SRB	1	1
Levadia Tallinn	EST	0	2
KRC Genk	BEL	1	1
Sarajevo	BIH	2	0
MSK Zilina	SVK	0 0	3p
Slavia Praha	CZE	0 0	4p
FH Hafnarfjördur	ISL	1	1
BATE Borisov	BLR	3	1
Zaglebie Lubin	POL	0	1
Steaua Bucuresti	ROU	1	2

Third Qualifying Round

Toulouse	FRA	0	0
Liverpool	ENG	1	4
FC Zürich	SUI	1	0
Besiktas	TUR	1	2
Tampere United	FIN	0	0
Rosenborg BK	NOR	3	2
Valencia	ESP	3	2
Elfsborg IF	SWE	0	1
Werder Bremen	GER	2	3
Dinamo Zagreb	CRO	1	2
Lazio	ITA	1	3
Dinamo Bucuresti	ROU	1	1
Spartak Moskva	RUS	1 1	3p
Celtic	SCO	1 1	4p
Benfica	POR	2	1
FC København	DEN	1	0
RB Austria Salzburg	AUT	1	1
Shakhtar Donetsk	UKR	0	3
Rangers	SCO	1	0
Crvena Zvezda	SRB	0	0
Sarajevo	BIH	0	0
Dynamo Kyiv	UKR	1	3
Fenerbahçe	TUR	1	2
RSC Anderlecht	BEL	0	0
Sevilla	ESP	2	4
AEK Athens	GRE	0	1
Sparta Praha	CZE	0	0
Arsenal	ENG	2	3
Ajax	NED	0	1
Slavia Praha	CZE	1	2
BATE Borisov	BLR	2	0
Steaua Bucuresti	ROU	2	2

Group Stage

Group A		Pts
FC Porto	POR	11
Liverpool	ENG	10
Olympique Marseille	FRA	7
Besiktas	TUR	6

Group B		Pts
Chelsea	ENG	12
Schalke 04	GER	8
Rosenberg BK	NOR	7
Valencia	ESP	5

Group C		Pts
Real Madrid	ESP	11
Olympiacos	GRE	11
Werder Bremen	GER	6
Lazio	ITA	5

Group D		Pts
Milan	ITA	13
Celtic	SCO	9
Benfica	POR	7
Shakhtar Donetsk	UKR	6

Group E		Pts
Barcelona	ESP	14
Olymp. Lyonnais	FRA	10
Rangers	SCO	7
VfB Stuttgart	GER	3

Group F		Pts
Manchester United	ENG	16
Roma	ITA	11
Sporting CL	POR	7
Dynamo Kyiv	UKR	0

Group G		Pts
Internazionale	ITA	15
Fenerbahçe	TUR	11
PSV Eindhoven	NED	7
CSKA Moskva	RUS	1

Group H		Pts
Sevilla	ESP	15
Arsenal	ENG	13
Slavia Praha	CZE	5
Steaua Bucuresti	ROU	1

UEFA CHAMPIONS LEAGUE 2007–08

UEFA CHAMPIONS LEAGUE 2007–08

Round of Sixteen			Quarter–finals			Semi–finals			Final		
Manchester United	1	1									
Olympique Lyonnais *	1	0									
			Manchester United	2	1						
			Roma *	0	0						
Real Madrid	1	1									
Roma *	2	2									
						Manchester United	0	1			
						Barcelona *	0	0			
Schalke 04 *	1 0	4p									
FC Porto	0 1	1p									
			Schalke 04 *	0	0						
			Barcelona	1	1						
Celtic *	2	0									
Barcelona	3	1									
									Manchester United	1	6p
									Chelsea	1	5p
Liverpool *	2	1									
Internazionale	0	0									
			Liverpool	1	4						
			Arsenal *	1	2						
Milan	0	0									
Arsenal *	0	2									
						Liverpool *	1	2			
						Chelsea	1	3			
Fenerbahçe *	3 2	3p									
Sevilla	2 3	2p									
			Fenerbahçe *	2	0						
			Chelsea	1	2						
Olympiacos *	0	0									
Chelsea	0	3									

* Home team in the first leg • Teams placed third in the group stage qualify for the UEFA Cup as do the third qualifying round losers

FIRST QUALIFYING ROUND

Sheriff, Tiraspol
18-07-2007, 20:00, 8800, Vad HUN

Sheriff Tiraspol 2
Kuchuk [45], Gorodetchil [79]

Serghei Pascenco - Vaja Tarkhnishvili (Alexandru Suvorov 75), Wallace, Dorian Arbanas (Oleg Gumenuk• 60), Nadson Jose Ferreira, Kennedy Chinwo, Benjamin Balima (Evgheni Gorodetchil 69), Aleksei Kuchuk, Thiago Alberto Constancia, Semion Bulgaru, Andrei Corneencov. Tr: Leonid Koutchouk

FC Ranger's 0

Gregorio Rodriguez•15 - Alejandro Venturi•, Victor Moreira (Sebastian Gomez Perez 71), Jose Porta, Toni Caçador (Nicolas Martinez 90), Sergio Albanell•••86, Joao Carlos Cunha Gomes Da, Flavio Pimentel, Hernen Walker (Josep Serrano Contrer 16), Mario Pimentel•, Alex Somoza•. Tr: Jesús Lucendo Heredia

---

Estadi Comunal, Andorra La Vella
24-07-2007, 18:00, 280, Yusifov ISR

FC Ranger's 0

Ignacio Gonzalez - Alejandro Venturi, Victor Moreira (Fernando Miguel Goncalves Peire 66), Jose Porta, Toni Caçador (Nicolas Martinez 78), Justo Gonzalez•, Flavio Pimentel, Hernen Walker, Mario Pimentel, Sebastian Gomez Perez, Alex Somoza (Jose Combarros 82). Tr: Jesús Julián Lucendo Heredia

Sheriff Tiraspol 3
Balima [68], Kajkut [77], Suvorov [89]

Serghei Pascenco - Wallace• (Ben Idrissa Derme 80), Dorian Arbanas, Nadson Jose Ferreira, Kennedy Chinwo•, Benjamin Balima•, Florent Rouamba, Aleksei Kuchuk (19 Sasa Kajkut 67) Thiago Alberto Constancia (Alexandru Suvorov 72), Semion Bulgaru, Andrei Corneencov. Tr: Leonid Koutchouk

---

Olimpico, Serravaile
17-07-2007, 21:00, 2686, Stavrev MKD

Murata 1
Protti [43]

Cristiano Scalabrelli - Massimo Agostini•, Nicola Albani, Fabio Bollini (Federico Donati 72), Pasquale D'Orsi, Aldair (Brian Gasperoni 46), Cristian Protti•, Roberto Teodorani, Carlo Valentini, Fabio Vannoni (Manuel Marani 84), Fabio Vitaioli. Tr: Gian Luigi Pasquali

Tampere United 2
Niemi 2 [68] [88]

Mikko Kavén - Heikki Aho (Tomi Petrescu 52), Antti Hynynen (Sakari Saarinen 89), Toni Järvinen, Jussi Kujala, Mathias Lindström, Jari Niemi, Antti Ojanperä•, Antti Pohja, Juska Savolainen, Jarkko Wiss•. Tr: Ari Hjelm

---

Ratina, Helsinki
25-07-2007, 19:00, 5638, Wilmes LUX

Tampere United 2
Petrescu [7], Niemi [21]

Mikko Kavén - Antti Hynynen (Sakari Saarinen 46), Toni Järvinen, Jussi Kujala, Mathias Lindström (Henri Myntti 67), Jari Niemi, Antti Ojanperä, Antti Pohja, Juska Savolainen, Jarkko Wiss•, Tomi Petrescu (Chimezie Daniels Nwoke 80). Tr: Ari Hjelm

Murata 0

Cristiano Scalabrelli - Massimo Agostini, Nicola Albani, Fabio Bollini (Stefano Conti 72), Pasquale D'Orsi, Alex Gasperoni (Giulio Molinari 84), Roberto Teodorani, Carlo Valentini•, Fabio Vannoni, Fabio Vitaioli, Mohammed Zaboul (Daniele Bacciocchi 71). Tr: Gian Luigi Pasquali

---

Poladi, Rustavi
17-07-2007, 18:15, 2900, Borski POL

Olimpi Rustavi 0

Mirza Merlani - Ernest Akuassaga, David Chichveishvili, Jaba Dvali• (Bhaudry Gildas Massouanga 56), Vladimer Dvalishvili, Revaz Getsadze•, Mikheil Makhviladze, George Navalovsky, Sergi Orbeldaze, Levan Silagadze (Aleksandr Koshkadze 66), Vladan Zivkovich (Rezo Djikia 45+1). Tr: Varlam Kilasonia

FK Astana 0

Sergei Boichenko - Anton Chichulin•, Aleksandr Kuchma•, Aidar Kumisbeckov, Maksim Zhalmagambetov•, Eduard Sergienko, Kirill Kochkayev (Arsen Tlekhugov 45), Alexandr Suchkov, Emil Kenzhisariev (Zhambyl Kukeyev 73), Viktor Bulatov, Dian Todorov• (Peraly Aliyev 91+). Tr: Alexandr Irkhin

---

Centralny, Kostanay
24-07-2007, 18:30, 6000, Banari MDA

FK Astana 3
Kuchma [12], Tlekhugov [55], Zhalmagambetov [84]

Sergei Boichenko• - Anton Chichulin (Igor Aksenov 84), Aleksandr Kuchma, Aidar Kumisbeckov, Maksim Zhalmagambetov, Eduard Sergienko (Zhambyl Kukeyev 90), Murat Suyumagambetov (Arsen Tlekhugov 46), Alexandr Suchkov, Emil Kenzhisariev, Viktor Bulatov, Dian Todorov•. Tr: Aleksandr Irkhin

Olimpi Rustavi 0

Mirza Merlani - Ernest Akuassaga, David Chichveishvili (Jaba Dvali 51), Revaz Getsadze, George Navalovsky, Lasha Kebadze (Aleksandr Koshkadze 66), George Navalovsky, Sergi Orbeldaze, Levan Silagadze•, Vladan Zivkovich, Rezo Djikia•59. Tr: Varlam Kilasonia

---

Windsor Park, Belfast
17-07-2007, 19:45, 2009, Tagliavento ITA

Linfield 0

Alan Mannus - Damien Curran, Mark Dickson (Glenn Ferguson 87), Steven Douglas, Paul McAreavey (Timothy Mouncey 77), William Murphy, Aidan O'Kane, Noel Bailie, Peter Thompson (Thomas Stewart 80), Michael Gault, Jamie Mulgrew. Tr: David Jeffrey

Elfsborg IF 0

Johan Wiland - Daniel Mobaeck, Fredrik Björck, Andreas Augustsson, Anders Svensson, Stefan Ishizaki (Daniel Nils Alexandersson 89), Mathias Svensson (Denni Avdic 52), Fredrik Berglund (James Keene 68), Johan Karlsson•, Martin Andersson, Samuel Holmén. Tr: Magnus Haglund

---

Ryavallen, Boras
25-07-2007, 19:00, 1023, Brych GER

Elfsborg IF 1
Svensson.M [32]

Johan Wiland - Daniel Mobaeck, Fredrik Björck, Andreas Augustsson, Anders Svensson (Denni Avdic 60), Stefan Ishizaki, Mathias Svensson (James Keene 49), Fredrik Berglund (Daniel Nils Alexandersson 83), Johan Karlsson, Martin Andersson, Samuel Holmén. Tr: Magnus Haglund

Linfield 0

Alan Mannus - Damien Curran (Glenn Ferguson 74), Mark Dickson, Steven Douglas (Timothy Mouncey• 76), Paul McAreavey•, Aidan O'Kane, Noel Bailie, Peter Thompson, Michael Gault•, Kris Lindsam, Jamie Mulgrew (Thomas Stewart 64). Tr: David Jeffrey

---

Sportni Park, Domzale
18-07-2007, 20:15, 824, Atkinson ENG

Domzale 1
Jankovic [44]

Dejan Nemec - Janez Aljancic, Luka Elsner, Velimir Varga•, Dejan Grabic (Jaroslav Peskar 85), Juninho (Plumb Jusufi 67), Sinisa Jankovic (Slavisa Dvorancic 60), Luka Zinko, Danijel Brezic, Zlatan Ljubijankic, Andraz Kirm. Tr: Slaviša Stojanovic

SK Tirana 0

Isli Hidi - Oriaamd Abazaj, Hetlen Çapja, Nevil Dede, Klodian Duro, Indrit Fortuzi (Eldorado Merkoci 69), Gentian Hajdari (Erald Deliallisi 78), Devis Mukaj, Elvis Sina•, Erion Xhafa•, Jetmir Sefa (Ergert Bakalli 69). Tr: Sulejman Starova

---

Qemal Stafa, Tirana
25-07-2007, 20:30, 7000, Germanakos GRE

SK Tirana 1
Duro.K [74]

Isli Hidi - Oriaamd Abazaj, Ergert Bakalli, Hetlen Capja, Nevil Dede, Erald Deliallisi, Klodian Duro•, Indrit Fortuzi (Eldorado Merkoci 61), Devis Mukaj, Elvis Sina (Jetmir Sefa 70), Erion Xhafa. Tr: Sulejman Starova

Domzale 2
Ljubijankic 2 [30] [77]

Dejan Nemec - Janez Aljancic, Luka Elsner, Dejan Grabi, Juninho (Velimir Varga 13), Sinisa Jankovic (Jaroslav Peskar 73), Luka Zinko, Danijel Brezic, Dario Zahora (Tadej Apatic 88), Zlatan Ljubijankic, Andraz Kirm•. Tr: Slavisa Stojanovic

---

Tofikh Bakhramov, Baku
17-07-2007, 21:00, 16 000, Levi ISR

Khazar Lenkoran 1
Ramazanov [58]

Kamran Arhayev - Elmar Bakhshiev, Darius Zutautas, Rahid Amirguliyev, Dzeykhun Sultanov (Yacouba Bamba 84), Rashad Abdullayev (Fizuli Mamedov 79), Emin Guliyev•73, Zaur Ramazanov (Alim Gurbanov 88), Radomir Todorov, Konstantin Djambazov•, Juninho. Tr: Agasalim Mirjaradov

Dinamo Zagreb 1
Etto [63]

Georg Koch - Nikola Pokrivac (Mathias Chago 85), Josip Tadic (Marijo Mandzukic• 46), Tomislav Sokota, Hrvoje Cale, Vedran Corluka, Sammir (Etto 58), Carlos•, Dino Drpic, Luka Modric, Ognjen Vukojevic. Tr: Branko Ivankovic

---

Maksimir, Zagreb
24-07-2007, 20:15, 9240, Vazquez ESP

Dinamo Zagreb 3
Vugrinec [56], Mandzukic [99], Tadic [116]

Georg Koch - Josip Tadic, Marijo Mandzukic•, Mathias Chago (Davor Vugrinec 46) (Ante Tomic• 73), Sammir, Carlos, Etto•, Dino Drpic (Hrvoje Cale• 46), Luka Modric, Gordon Schildenfeld, Ognjen Vukojevic. Tr: Branko Ivankovic

Khazar Lenkoran 1
Juninho [16]

Kamran Arhayev - Elmar Bakhshiev, Darius Zutautas•, Rahid Amirguliyev, Edmond N'tiamoah•••79, Rashad Abdullayev (Yacouba Bamba 85), Fizuli Mamedov• (Alim Gurbanov 49), Zaur Ramazanov•, Radomir Todorov, Konstantin Djambazov•, Juninho. Tr: Agasalim Mirjaradov

Latham Park, Newtown
17-07-2007, 19:30, 649, Attard MLT

The New Saints 3

Wilde [14], Baker [54], Hogan [94+]

Paul Harrison - Phillip Baker, Steven Beck, Duane Jerome Courtney, Barry Hogan, Thomas Holmes, Chris King, Scott Ruscoe (John Leah 81), John Toner (Ronald Morgan 45), Michael Wilde, Jamie Wood (Martin Taylor 85). Tr: Kenneth Mckenna

FK Ventspils 2

Rimkus 2 [26 89]

Pavels Davidovs• - Zakhar Dubenskiy, Deniss Kacanovs, Vladimirs Kolesnicenko (Jevgenijs Kosmacovs 65), Zurab Menteshashvili•, Jean-Paul Ndeki, Vits Rimkus, Serhiy Sernetskyy, Aleksejs Soleicuks, Igor Tigirlas (Sergei Zangareev 69), Mihails Zizilevs. Tr: Roman Grygorchuk

---

Ventspils Pilsetas, Ventspils
25-07-2007, 18:00, 2000,

FK Ventspils 2

Ndeki [17], Kacanovs [53]

Pavels Davidovs - Zakhar Dubenskiy, Deniss Kacanovs, Vladimirs Kolesnicenko• (Jevgenijs Kosmacovs 70), Zurab Menteshashvili• (Alexander Mysikov 90), Jean-Paul Ndeki•, Vits Rimkus, Serhiy Sernetskyy• (Igors Slesarcuks 94+), Igor Tigirlas•, Mihails Zizilevs, Sasa Cilinsek. Tr: Roman Grygorchuk

The New Saints 1

Naylor [92+]

Paul Harrison - Phillip Baker, Steven Beck, Duane Jerome Courtney, Barry Hogan• (Martin Naylor 72), Thomas Holmes, Chris King, Carl Lamb (Alfonso Carter 57), Scott Ruscoe, Michael Wilde (Ronald Morgan 64), Jamie Wood. Tr: Kenneth Mckenna

---

Brandywell, Londonderry
18-07-2007, 19:45, 2285, Trifonos CYP

Derry City 0

Pat Jennings - Mark Farren (Peter Hynes 85), Sean Hargan, Peter Hutton, Ciaran Martyn, Edward McCallion, Pat McCourt, Gareth McGlynn (Kevin Deery 57), Barry Molloy, Samuel Morrow (Kevin McHugh 67), Ken Oman•. Tr: John Robertson

Pyunik Yerevan 0

Gevorg Kasparov - Agvan Mkrtchyan (Norayr Sahakyan 78), Rafael Nazaryan, Mauro Guevgeozian Cre (Felix Hzeina• 46), Levon Pachajyan, Robert Arzumanyan, Karen Dokhoyan, Artur Yedigaryan, Gevorg Ghazaryan (Henrik Mkhitaryan 62), Aleksandr Tadevosyan•, Sargis Hovsepyan. Tr: Armen Gyulbudaghyants

---

Republican, Yerevan
25-07-2007, 20:00, 5300, Krajnc SVN

Pyunik Yerevan 2

Avetisyan [28], Ghazaryan [67]

Gevorg Kasparov - Sargis Hovsepyan, Aleksandr Tadevosyan•, Agvan Mkrtchyan, Rafael Nazaryan (Artur Yedigaryan 59), Arsen Avetisyan• (Henrik Mkhitryan• 70), Hamlet Mkhitaryan, Levon Pachajyan, Robert Arzumanyan, Gevorg Ghazaryan (Norayr Sahakyan 81), Karen Dokhoyan. Tr: Armen Gyulbudaghyants

Derry City 0

Pat Jennings• - Killian Brennan, Kevin Deery (Ruaihdri Higgins 82), Darren Kelly•, Ciaran Martyn, Edward McCallion, Pat McCourt (Mark Farren 65), Kevin McHugh, Barry Molloy (Greg O'Halloran• 40), Samuel Morrow, Ken Oman. Tr: John Grant Robertson

---

Gradski, Podgorica
17-07-2007, 20:30, 5000, Kuipers NED

Zeta Golubovci 3

Korac [34p], Tumbasevic [36], Stjepanovic [59]

Sasa Ivanovic - Blazo Igumanovic, Marko Cetkovic, Bojan Ivanovic, Miroslav Kaludjerovic, Zarko Korac• (Zarija Pelicic 76), Darko Markovic (Vladimir Boljevic 89), Milan Radulovic, Slaven Stjepanovic (Mirko Marinkovic 89), Janko Tumbasevic, Milan Vuckovic. Tr: Slobodan Halilovic

FBK Kaunas 1

Kvaratskhelia [68]

Modestas Stonys - Mindaugas Baguzis• (Mindaugas Grigalevicius 59), Ricardas Beniusis (Marius Cinikas 76), Audrius Ksanavicius (Vygantas Zubavicius 67), Givi Kvaratskhelia, Rafael Rodrigues Ledesma, Nukri Manchkhava, Pascal Mendy•, Adrian Mrowiec, Nerijus Radzius, Ianko Valkanov•26. Tr: Arturas Ramoska

---

S.Darius & Girenas, Kaunas
24-07-2007, 20:00, 1500, Havrilla SVK

FBK Kaunas 3

Beniusis [5], Kvaratskhelia [16], Ksanavicius [20]

Marian Kello - Mindaugas Baguzis•, Ricardas Beniusis, Audrius Ksanavicius (Arkadiusz Klimek 46), Givi Kvaratskhelia•, Rafael Rodrigues Ledesma, Nukri Manchkhava•, Pascal Mendy•, Adrian Mrowiec, Edin Pehlic, Nerijus Radzius (Fernando Daniel Screpis• 69). Tr: Arturas Ramoska

Zeta Golubovci 2

Stjepanovic [34], Cetkovic [89]

Sasa Ivanovic - Blazo Igumanovic, Vladimir Boljevic (Milan Vuckovic 46), Marko Cetkovic• (Nenad Djurovic 90), Bojan Ivanovic, Miroslav Kaludjerovic, Zarko Korac, Darko Markovic•, Milan Radulovic, Slaven Stjepanovic, Janko Tumbasevic. Tr: Slobodan Halilovic

---

Goce Delcev, Prilep
18-07-2007, 17:00, 3000, Nalbandyan ARM

Pobeda Prilep 0

Darko Tofiloski - Blagojce Damevski, Goranco Georgiev (Jovica Obradovic 58), Blagoja Gesoski (Nove Aceski 16), Rock Itoua Ndinga, Miodrag Jovanovic (Ilija Nestoroski 70), Dimitar Kapinkovski, Aleksandar Krsteski, Marjan Nacev, Dusan Savik, Nebojsa Stojkovic•74. Tr: Nikolce Zdraveski

Levadia Tallinn 1

Nahk [53]

Artur Kotenko - Aleksandr Dmitrijev, Andrei Kalimullin, Tarmo Kink, Vitali Leitan, Marek Lemsalu, Tihhon Sisov, Maksim Smirnov•, Konstantin Vassiljev (Konstantin Nahk 46), Indrek Zelinski (Vitoldas Cepauskas 64), Taijo Teniste (Deniss Malov 51). Tr: Tarmo Rüütli

---

Kadriorg, Tallinn
25-07-2007, 18:30, 2297, Fabian HUN

Levadia Tallinn 0

Artur Kotenko - Nikita Andreev (Indrek Zelinski• 46), Aleksandr Dmitrijev, Andrei Kalimullin, Tarmo Kink, Vitali Leitan (Vitoldas Cepauskas 77), Marek Lemsalu, Deniss Malov, Konstantin Nahk, Tihhon Sisov•, Maksim Smirnov (Marius Dovydenas 90). Tr: Tarmo Rüütli

Pobeda Prilep 0

Darko Tofiloski - Blagojce Damevski•47, Goranco Georgiev• (Ilija Nestoroski 84), Rock Itoua Ndinga•, Miodrag Jovanovic•, Dimitar Kapinkovski, Aleksandar Krsteski, Svetozar Loncar (Martin Siskov 4), Marjan Nacev, Jovica Obradovic, Nove Aceski. Tr: Nikolce Zdraveski

---

Ta'Qali, Ta'Qali
18-07-2007, 20:00, 321, Vlk SVK

Marsaxlokk 0

Ruben Sauci, Peter Pullicino•, Shaon Bajada, Kevin Sammut, Gareth Sciberras, Shaun Tellus, Daniel Webb, Stephen Wellmen, Malcolm Licari•, Carmelo Magro, Jamie Pace. Tr: Brian Talbot

FK Sarajevo 6

Rascic 2 [5 9], Obuca 2 [20 65], Maksimovic [42], Bucan [87]

Muhamed Alaim - Sead Bucan•, Damir Hadzic, Faruk Ihtijarevic, Veldin Muharemovic, Emir Obuca, Alen Basic, Semjon Milosevic, Vladan Grujic, Marko Maksimovic, Admir Rascic. Tr: Husref Musemic

---

Kosevo, Sarajevo
24-07-2007, 20:00, 5000, Todorov BUL

FK Sarajevo 3

Mesic [42], Saraba [60], Turkovic [76]

Muhamed Alaim - Sead Bucan, Damir Hadzic, Veldin Muharemovic, Alen Basic, Semjon Milosevic•, Mirza Mesic, Vladan Grujic•, Muamer Kurto (Zdravko Saraba 46), Marko Maksimovic (Emir Janos 79), Admir Rascic (Almir Turkovic 64). Tr: Husref Musemic

Marsaxlokk 1

Ruben Debono - Shaon Bajada, Cleaven Frendo, Kevin Sammut, Gareth Sciberras (Gordon Mizzi• 81), Shaun Tellus, Stephen Wellmen•, Malcolm Licari, Carmelo Magro, Jamie Pace, Trevor Templeman. Tr: Brian Talbot

---

Jos Nosbaum, Dudelange
18-07-2007, 19:00, 1221, Gonchar RUS

F91 Dudelange 1

Di Gregorio [45p]

Jonathan Joubert - Johan Bellini, Christophe Borbiconi, Joris Di Gregorio (Gael Hug 79), Alexandre Franceschi, Thomas Gruszczynski (Emmanuel Coquelet 79), Laurent Guthleber, Nasreddine Hammami• (Walder Souto Amado 67), Thierry Joly, Loïc Mouny, Sébastien Remy. Tr: Michel Leflochmoan

MSK Zilina 2

Jez [48p], Lietava [73]

Dusan Kuciak - Mario Breska (Admir Vladavic 69), Pavel Devaty•, Tomas Hubocan, Robert Jez, Vladimir Leitner, Adam Nemec• (Ivan Lietava 59), Andrej Porazik (Peter Styvar 84), Zdeno Strba, Benjamin Vomacka•, Peter Pekarik. Tr: Pavel Vrba

---

Pod Dubnon, Zilina
25-07-2007, 20:00, 5822, Da Silva POR

MSK Zilina 5

Devaty [8], Lietava [11], Styvar 2 [29 75], Vomácka [66]

Dusan Kuciak - Mário Breska (Admir Vladavic 45), Pavel Devaty, Tomas Hubocan, Robert Jez, Vladimir Leitner, Zdeno Strba, Peter Styvar (Mario Pecalka 89), Benjamin Vomacka•, Peter Pekarik, Ivan Lietava (Adam Nemec 59). Tr: Pavel Vrba

F91 Dudelange 4

DiGregorio [40] Hammami [49] Guthleber [71], Lukic [82]

Jonathan Joubert - Walder Alves Souto Amado•, Johan Bellini (Emmanuel Coquelet 61), Jerome Bigard, Joris Di Gregorio (Lehit Zeghdane 81), Alexandre Franceschi, Thomas Gruszczynski (Zarko Lukic 73), Laurent Guthleber, Nasreddine Hammami, Loïc Mouny, Sebastien Remy. Tr: Michel Leflochmoan

Kaplakrikavöllur, Hafnarfjordur
18-07-2007, 20:00, 1422, Black NIR

FH Hafnarfjördur   4
Bjarnason [14], Vilhjalmsson 2 [16 58], Olafsson [52]

Dadi Lárusson - Freyr Bjarnason, Sverrir Gardarsson∗, Tryggvi Gudmundsson, Matthias Gudmundsson, Tommy Nielsen, Sigurvin Olafsson (Atli Gudnason 74), Gudmundur Sævarsson, Dennis Siim (Asgeir Asgeirsson 77), Davíd Vidarsson, Matthias Vilhjalmsson. Tr: Olafur Johannesson

HB Tórshavn   1
Nielsen OG [44]

Tróndur Vathnhamar - Tor-Ingar Akselsen, Jákup Borg, Mortan úr Hørg∗, Christian Jacobsen, Hans Lag, Kári Nielsen∗, Rasmus Nolsøe, Olavur Olavstovu (Pall Joensen 71), Milan Kuljic, Andrew Fløtum (Rokur Jespersen 60). Tr: Albert Ellefsen

---

Tórsvøllur, Tórshavn
25-07-2007, 19:00, 655, Kari FIN

HB Tórshavn   0

Tróndur Vathnhamar - Tor-Ingar Akselsen, Mortan úr Hørg, Rógvi Jacobsen, Rokur Jespersen (Poul Thomas Dam 82), Hans Lag∗, Kári Nielsen, Rasmus Nolsøe, Olavur Olavstovu (Pall Leivsson 82), Milan Kuljic, Andrew Fløtum∗ (Pall Joensen 76). Tr: Albert Ellefsen

FH Hafnarfjördur   0

Dadi Lárusson - Freyr Bjarnason, Sverrir Gardarsson, Tryggvi Gudmundsson (Atli Gudnason 79), Matthias Gudmundsson, Tommy Nielsen (Audjun Helgason 83), Sigurvin Ólafsson (Asgeir Asgiersson 70), Gudmundur Sævarsson, Dennis Siim∗, Davíd Vidarsson, Matthias Vilhjalmsson. Tr: Olafur Johannesson

---

GSP, Nicosia
17-07-2007, 20:00, 10 971, Thual FRA

APOEL Nicosia   2
Michail [42], Machlas [61]

Michael Morphis - Nuno Morais, Daniel Florea, Michalis Kapsis, Christos Kontis, Nikos Machlas (Manuel Francisco Barreto Sayan 91+), Konstantinos Makridis, Chrysostomous Michail, Marcos Magno Morales Tavares (Hélio Pinto 67), Ricardo Fernandes, Marinos Satsias∗ (Miltos Sapanis 74). Tr: Marinos Ouzounides

BATE Borisov   0

Aleksandr Fedorovich - Gennadi Bliznyuk (Aleksandr Vishnyakov 77), Pavel Platonov∗ (Dmitri Platonov 57), Vitali Radzionov, Artyom Radkov, Igor Stasevich (Maksim Zhavnerchik 68), Ryhor Filipenko, Vitali Kazantsev∗, Dmitri Likhtarovich, Anton Sakharov∗∗∗71, Aleksandr Ermakovich. Tr: Igor Kryushenko

---

Gradski, Borisov
24-07-2007, 19:00, 5000, Collum SCO

BATE Borisov   3
Stasevich [14], Platonov [74], Bliznyuk [104]

Aleksandr Fedorovich - Sergei Kryvets, Vitali Radzionov, Maksim Zhavnerchik∗, Artyom Radkov, Igor Stasevich (Mikhail Sivakov∗ 72), Yegor Filipenko∗, Vitali Kazantsev, Anri Khagush (Dmitri Platonov∗ 64), Dmitri Likhtarovich∗, Aleksandr Ermakovich∗ (Gennadi Bliznyuk∗ 80). Tr: Igor Kryushenko

APOEL Nicosia   0

Michael Morphis - Nuno Morais, Marios Elia, Michalis Kapsis, Christos Kontis∗, Nikos Machlas, Konstantinos Makridis, Chrysostomous Michail∗, Marcos Magno Morales Tavares (Miltos Sapanis∗ 25), Ricardo Fernandes∗, Hélio Pinto (Marios Louka 68). Tr: Marinos Ouzounides

SECOND QUALIFYING ROUND

Inönü, Istanbul
1-08-2007, 21:00, 17 871, Sippel GER

Besiktas   1
Ibrahim Toraman [73]

Rüstü Reçber - Edouard Cissé (Koray Avci 68), Deivson, Matías Delgado (Batuhan Karadeniz 46), Ibrahim Kas∗, Serdar Kurtulus, Ricardinho (Mehmet Yozgatli 86), Serdar Ozkan, Rodrigo Tello∗, Ibrahim Toraman, Ibrahim Uzülmez. Tr: Ertugrul Saglam

Sheriff Tiraspol   0

Serghei Pascenco - Dorian Arbanas, Benjamin Balima, Thiago Alberto Constancia (Sasa Kajkut 75), Andrei Corneencov (Nicolas Eduardo Demalde∗ 43), Ibrahim Gnanou, Aleksei Kuchuk, Abdul Mamah, Wallace∗, Florent Rouamba, Vaja Tarkhnishvili. Tr: Leonid Koutchouk

---

Sheriff, Tiraspol
8-08-2007, 20:00, 13 000, Brines SCO

Sheriff Tiraspol   0

Serghei Pascenco - Dorian Arbanas, Benjamin Balima, Kennedy Chinwo, Andrei Corneencov (Nicolas Eduardo Demalde 71), Ibrahim Gnanou, Aleksei Kuchuk∗, Florent Rouamba (Oleg Gumenuk 30), Vaja Tarkhnishvili, Thiago Alberto Constancia (Alexandru Suvorov 64), Abdul Mamah∗27. Tr: Leonid Koutchouk

Besiktas   3
Bobo 2 [58 69], Koray Avci [90]

Hakan Arikan - Koray Avci∗, Edouard Cissé, Bobo, Matías Delgado (Ricardinho 67), Ibrahim Kas∗ (Baki Mercimek 46), Serdar Kurtulus, Serdar Ozkan, Rodrigo Tello∗, Ibrahim Toraman, Ibrahim Uzülmez. Tr: Ertugrul Saglam

---

Ratina, Tampere
31-07-2007, 19:00, 8126, McDonald SCO

Tampere United   1
Petrescu [15]

Mikko Kavén – Antti Hynynen∗ (Heikki Aho 63), Toni Järvinen, Jussi Kujala, Mathias Lindström, Jari Niemi, Antti Ojanperä (Chimezie Daniels Nwoke 85), Antti Pohja, Juska Savolainen, Sakari Saarinen, Tomi Petrescu (Jonne Hjelm 92+). Tr: Ari Hjelm

Levski Sofia   0

Georgi Petkov - Cédric Bardon (Ekundayo Jaiyeoba 80), Valeri Domovchiyski, Richard Eromoigbe, Lucio Wagner, Zhivko Milanov, Dimitar Telkiyski, Igor Tomasic, Hristo Yovov (Nikolay Dimitrov 57), Darko Tasevski (Miroslav Ivanov 63), Chakib Benzoukane. Tr: Stanimir Stoilov

---

Vasil Levski, Sofia
7-08-2007, 20:30, 11 704, Kinhöfer GER

Levski Sofia   0

Georgi Petkov - Cédric Bardon∗ (Milan Koprivarov∗ 75), Valeri Domovchiyski, Richard Eromoigbe, Lucio Wagner, Borislav Hristov (Daniel Borimirov 42), Miroslav Ivanov, Zhivko Milanov (Ekundayo Jaiyeoba 46), Dimitar Telkiyski∗, Hristo Yovov, Chakib Benzoukane. Tr: Stanimir Stoilov

Tampere United   1
Niemi [40]

Mikko Kavén - Toni Järvinen, Jussi Kujala, Mathias Lindström, Jari Niemi (Chimezie Daniels Nwoke 64), Antti Ojanperä∗, Tomi Petrescu, Antti Pohja, Sakari Saarinen (Antti Hynynen 78), Juska Savolainen∗, Jarkko Wiss. Tr: Ari Hjelm

---

Centralny, Kostanay
1-08-2007, 19:00, 7000, Gumienny BEL

FK Astana   1
Kuchma [26]

Sergei Boichenko∗ - Peraly Aliyev (Arsen Tlekhugov 70), Viktor Bulatov, Anton Chichulin, Emil Kenzhisariev, Kirill Kochkayev∗ (Murat Suyumagambetov 50), Aleksandr Kuchma, Aidar Kumisbeckov, Eduard Sergienko (Zhambyl Kukeyev 61), Alexandr Suchkov, Mikhail Shishkin. Tr: Alexandr Irkhin

Rosenborg BK   3
Koné 2 [3 61], Iversen [56p]

Lars Hirschfeld - Christer Basma, Mikael Dorsin, Yssouf Kone∗ (Michael Kleppe Jamtfall 83), Miika Koppinen, Roar Strand (Fredrik Stoor 75), Alexander Tettey, Didier Konan Ya (Oyvind Storflor 36), Steffen Iversen, Marek Sapara, Vidar Riseth. Tr: Knut Tørum

---

Lerkendal, Trondheim
8-08-2007, 20:45, 12 827, Courtney NIR

Rosenborg BK   7
Koné 2 [1 33], Iversen [7], Traoré 3 [17 50 53], Sapara [62]

Lars Hirschfeld - Christer Basma, Mikael Dorsin, Yssouf Kone, Miika Koppinen, Roar Strand (Fredrik Stoor 46), Alexander Tettey, Steffen Iversen, Abdou Razack Traoré, Marek Sapara (Michael Kleppe Jamtfall 64), Vidar Riseth (Per Ciljan Skjelbred 46). Tr: Knut Tørum

FK Astana   1
Suchkov [22]

Yevgeniy Kuznetsov - Anton Chichulin, Emil Kenzhisariev∗, Kirill Kochkayev, Aleksandr Kuchma, Aidar Kumisbeckov, Eduard Sergienko, Alexandr Suchkov (Murat Suyumagambetov 46), Viktor Bulatov∗, Dian Todorov, Maksim Zhalmagambetov. Tr: Ivan Azovskiy

Oláh Gábor út, Debrecen
31-07-2007, 20:45, 10 000, Kaldma EST

Debreceni VSC 0

János Balogh - Csaba Bernáth, Gábor Demjén (Peter Czvitkovics 88), Tibor Dombi (Tamas Sandor 40), Adám Komlósi, Leanardo, Norbert Mészáros, Aco Stojkov (Gergely Rudolf 74), Dragan Vukmir, Balázs Dzsudzsák•, Kouemaha Dorge Rostand. Tr: Miroslav Beranek

Elfsborg IF 1
Mobäck 65

Johan Wiland - Martin Andersson•, Andreas Augustsson, Fredrik Berglund (Daniel Nils Alexandersson 59), Fredrik Björck, Samuel Holmén•, Stefan Ishizaki (Emir Bajrami 79), Johan Karlsson, James Keene, Daniel Mobäck, Anders Svensson (Denni Avdic 19). Tr: Magnus Haglund

Ryavallen, Boras
8-08-2007, 19:00, 11 952, Circhetta SUI

Elfsborg IF 0

Johan Wiland• - Martin Andersson, Andreas Augustsson, Fredrik Björck, Samuel Holmén, Stefan Ishizaki•, Johan Karlsson, James Keene (Fredrik Berglund 80), Daniel Mobäck, Anders Svensson (Denni Avdic 66) (Mathias Floren• 86), Mathias Svensson•. Tr: Magnus Haglund

Debreceni VSC 0

János Balogh - Gábor Demjén (Zsombor Kerekes• 71), Adám Komlósi•, Leanardo, Aco Stojkov (Gergely Rudolf 55), Dragan Vukmir, István Szücs, Balázs Dzsudzsák, Kouemaha Dorge Rostand•••88, Norbert Mészáros, Csaba Bernáth (Tamas Sandor• 85). Tr: Miroslav Beranek

Sportni Park, Domzale
1-08-2007, 20:30, 2787, Einwaller AUT

Domzale 1
Zezelj 87

Dejan Nemec - Janez Aljancic, Danijel Brezic, Luka Elsner, Dejan Grabic (Plump Jusufi 79), Sinisa Jankovic• (Drazen Zezelj 66), Andraz Kirm, Zlatan Ljubijankic, Velimir Varga, Dario Zahora, Luka Zinko•. Tr: Slavisa Stojanovic

Dinamo Zagreb 2
Sokota 7, Modric 50p

Georg Koch - Nikola Pokrivac (Mathias Chago 80), Etto, Tomislav Sokota (Josip Tadic 83), Hrvoje Cale, Gordon Schildenfeld, Sammir, Carlos, Franck Manga Guela (Mihael Mikic 75), Luka Modric, Ognjen Vukojevic. Tr: Branko Ivankovic

Maksimir, Zagreb
7-08-2007, 20:15, 14 550, Verbist BEL

Dinamo Zagreb 3
Vukojevic 16, Sokota 22, Sammir 60

Georg Koch - Hrvoje Cale, Etto, Luka Modric, Carlos, Mario Mandzukic•, Sammir (Mihael Mikic 82), Franck Manga Guela (Mathias Chago 46), Ognjen Vukojevic, Gordon Schildenfeld, Tomislav Sokota (Dino Drpic 64). Tr: Branko Ivankovic

Domzale 1
Zahora 27

Dejan Nemec - Janez Aljancic•, Velimir Varga, Sinisa Jankovic (Ivan Knezovic 73), Tadej Apatic (Dejan Grabic 43), Dario Zahora (Drazen Zezelj 62), Luka Zinko, Zlatan Ljubijankic, Luka Elsner•, Andraz Kirm, Danijel Brezic•. Tr: Slavisa Stojanovic

Parken, Copenhagen
31-07-2007, 20:15, 21 336, Iturralde ESP

FC København 1
Allbäck 9

Jesper Christiansen - Marcus Allbäck (Mikael Antonsson 69), Michael Gravgaard, Jesper Grønkjær, Brede Hangeland•, William Kvist, Michael Silberbauer, Hjalte Nørregaard, Niclas Jensen, Morten Nordstrand (Ailton Almeida 65), Hutchinson Afiba. Tr: Ståle Solbakken

Beitar Jersusalem 1

Tvrtko Kale - Gal Alberman, Derek Boateng•••53, Shimon Gershon•, Barak Itzhaki•, Toto Tamuz (Milovan Petar Mirosevic Albomoz 60), Michael Zandberg (Omri Afek 84), Yoav Ziv•, Arik Benado, Idan Tal, Cristian Alvarez. Tr: Itzhak Shum

Teddy Maicha, Jerusalem
7-08-2007, 21:15, 16 800, Rizzoli ITA

Beitar Jerusalem 1
Itzhaki 60

Tvrtko Kale - Gal Alberman (Hen Azriel 100), Shimon Gershon•, Barak Itzhaki, Michael Zandberg, Yoav Ziv•, Romulo Marcos Antoneli (Toto Tamuz 62), Arik Benado, Idan Tal•, Cristian Alvarez, Milovan Mirosevic (Aviram Baruchyan 46). Tr: Itzhak Shum

FC København 1
Allbäck 97

Jesper Christiansen - Marcus Allbäck• (Ailton Almeida 100), Michael Gravgaard, Jesper Grønkjær•, Brede Hangeland, William Kvist•, Michael Silberbauer, Hjalte Nørregaard, Niclas Jensen, Rasmus Würtz (Mikael Antonsson 110), Atiba Hutchinson. Tr: Ståle Solbakken

Skonto, Riga
1-08-2007, 19:00, 4000, Bossen NED

FK Ventspils 0

Pavels Davidovs - Zakhar Dubenskiy, Deniss Kacanovs, Vladimirs Kolesnicenko (Alexander Mysikov 76), Jevgenijs Kosmacovs, Jean-Paul Ndeki, Vits Rimkus, Igors Slesarcuks (Serhiy Sernetskyy 53; Kristaps Grebis 85), Igor Tigirlas, Sasa Cilinsek, Mihails Zizilevs. Tr: Roman Grygorchuk

RB Austria Salzburg 3
Aufhauser 3 20 27 83p

Timo Ochs - René Aufhauser, Ezequiel Carboni, Milan Dudic, Niko Kovac (Christoph Leitgeb 74), Karel Piták, Markus Steinhöfer, Jorge Vargas, Johan Vonlanthen (Patrik Jezek 85), Alexander Zickler (Vratislav Lokvenc 74), Ibrahim Sekagya. Tr: Giovanni Trapattoni

Wals-Siezenheim, Salzburg
8-08-2007, 20:30, 11 665, Berntsen NOR

RB Austria Salzburg 4
Aufhauser 9, Dudic 48, Ilic 77, Leitgeb 92+

Timo Ochs - René Aufhauser, Ezequiel Carboni, Milan Dudic, Patrik Jezek (Sasa Ilic 71), Vratislav Lokvenc, Markus Steinhöfer (Alex 78), Johan Vonlanthen (Vladimir Janocko 56), Tsuneyasu Miyamoto, Ibrahim Sekagya, Christoph Leitgeb. Tr: Giovanni Trapattoni

FK Ventspils 0

Andris Vanins - Zakhar Dubenskiy•, Deniss Kacanovs, Vladimirs Kolesnicenko (Jevgenijs Kosmacovs 58), Zurab Menteshashvili•, Jean-Paul Ndeki, Vits Rimkus (Andrejs Butriks 75), Igors Slesarcuks (Kristaps Grebis 46), Igor Tigirlas, Sasa Cilinsek, Mihails Zizilevs. Tr: Roman Grygorchuk

Republican, Yerevan
31-07-2007, 20:00, 8000, Messner AUT

Pyunik Yerevan 0

Gevorg Kasparov (Ignacio Lopez 44) - Robert Arzumanyan, Arsen Avetisyan• (Norayr Sahakyan 46), Karen Dokhoyan, Sargis Hovsepyan•, Hamlet Mkhitaryan•, Agvan Mkrtchyan, Rafael Nazaryan (Henrik Mkhitaryan 46), Levon Pachajyan, Gevorg Ghazaryan, Artur Yedigaryan. Tr: Armen Gyulbudaghyants

Shakhtar Donetsk 2
Gladkiy 45, Brandão 48

Andriy Pyatov - Igor Duljaj (Volodymyr Priyomov 53), Olexandr Gladkiy (Cristiano Lucarelli 52), Olexandr Kucher, Brandão (Ruslan Fomin 70), Mariusz Lewandowski, Fernandinho, Razvan Rat, Jadson Rodriguez, Darijo Srna, Dmytro Chygrynskiy•. Tr: Mircea Lucescu

RSC Olympiyskiy, Donetsk
8-08-2007, 20:00, 18 000, Ferreira POR

Shakhtar Donetsk 2
Brandão 40, Gladkiy 49

Andriy Pyatov - Igor Duljaj, Ruslan Fomin (Olexandr Gladkiy 38), Tomás Hübschman, Brandão, Mariusz Lewandowski, Luiz Adriano (Jadson Rodriguez 38), Volodymyr Priyomov, Razvan Rat, Serhiy Tkachenko (Darijo Srna 57), Volodymyr Yezerskiy. Tr: Mircea Lucescu

Pyunik Yerevan 1
Ghazaryan 31

Ignacio Lopez - Robert Arzumanyan, Karen Dokhoyan, Sargis Hovsepyan, Felix Hzeina (Norayr Sahakyan 75), Henrik Mkhitaryan, Agvan Mkrtchyan, Levon Pachajyan (Tigran Gharabaghtsyan 88), Aleksandr Tadevosyan, Gevorg Ghazaryan (Rafael Nazaryan 57), Artur Yedigaryan•52. Tr: Armen Gyulbudaghyants

Ibrox, Glasgow
31-07-2007, 20:05, 36 145, Kasnaferis GRE

Rangers 2
Weir 55, Novo 72

Allan McGregor - Kris Boyd (Kirk Broadfoot 63), Charles Adam (Nacho Novo 46), Barry Ferguson, Brahim Hemdani, David Weir, Sasa Papac, Carlos Cuéllar•, Lee McCulloch•, Alan Hutton•••59, Jean-Claude Darcheville (Filip Sebo 83). Tr: Walter Smith

Zeta Golubovci 0

Sasa Ivanovic - Marko Cetkovic (Vladimir Boljevic 83), Bojan Ivanovic, Miroslav Kaludjerovic, Zarko Korac, Darko Markovic, Milan Radulovic (Nenad Djurovic 77), Slaven Stjepanovic, Janko Tumbasevic•, Milan Vuckovic•, Blazo Igumanovic. Tr: Slobodan Halilovic

Gradski, Podgorica
7-08-2007, 20:05, 9000, Dondarini ITA

Zeta Golubovci 0

Sasa Ivanovic - Marko Cetkovic, Nenad Djurovic• (Ivan Knezevic 56), Bojan Ivanovic (Vladimir Boljevic 71), Miroslav Kaludjerovic, Zarko Korac, Darko Markovic, Milan Radulovic, Slaven Stjepanovic•, Janko Tumbasevic (Milan Vuckovic 84), Blazo Igumanovic•. Tr: Slobodan Halilovic

Rangers 1
Beasley 81

Allan McGregor - Barry Ferguson, Brahim Hemdani, Kevin Thomson (Charles Adam 87), David Weir, Kirk Broadfoot•, Sasa Papac, DaMarcus Beasley, Carlos Cuéllar, Lee McCulloch, Jean-Claude Darcheville (Nacho Novo 61). Tr: Walter Smith

Crvena Zvezda, Belgrade
1-08-2007, 20:15, 18 886, Brugger AUT

Crvena Zvezda Beograd   1

Koroman [35]

Ivan Randjelovic - Nenad Milijas, Ognjen Koroman, Hernan Barcos (Filip Djordevic 45), Joao Nuno Da Silva Lukas (Mauricio Molina Uribe 64), Ibrahima Gueye, Segundo Castillo, Dusan Andjelkovic, Djordje Tutoric, Dusan Basta* (Grzegorz Bronowicki 74), Dejan Milovanovic. Tr: Bosko Djurovski

Levadia Tallinn   0

Artur Kotenko - Vitoldas Cepauskas, Aleksandr Dmitrijev, Aleksandr Kalimullin, Tarmo Kink (Andrei Sadrin 85), Vitali Leitan (Marius Dovydenas 89), Marek Lemsalu, Deniss Malov, Tihhon Sisov, Maksim Smirnov, Indrek Zelinski (Kaimar Saag 63). Tr: Tarmo Rüütli

Kadriorg, Tallinn
8-08-2007, 18:00, 3600, Dávila ESP

Levadia Tallinn   2

Malov [33], Nahk [67]

Artur Kotenko - Aleksandr Dmitrijev, Andrei Kalimullin, Tarmo Kink (Kaimar Saag 63), Vitali Leitan, Marek Lemsalu, Deniss Malov, Konstantin Nahk, Tihhon Sisov, Maksim Smirnov (Taijo Teniste 56), Indrek Zelinski (Vitoldas Cepauskas 83). Tr: Tarmo Rüütli

Crvena Zvezda Beograd   1

Burzanovic [37]

Ivan Randjelovic - Ognjen Koroman, Hernan Barcos (Nenad Milijas 71), Igor Burzanovic* (Nikola Trajkovic 54), Joao Lukas, Ibrahima Gueye, Segundo Castillo, Dusan Andjelkovic, Djordje Tutoric, Dusan Basta* (Grzegorz Bronowicki 61), Dejan Milovanovic. Tr: Bosko Djurovski

Fenix Stadion, Genk
31-07-2007, 20:30, 11 090, Egorov RUS

KRC Genk   1

Cornelius [23]

Logan Bailly - Hans Cornelis, Faris Haroun*, Eric Matoukou (Goran Ljubojevic 74), Tomislav Mikulic*, Tom Soetaers, Ivan Bosnjak*, Jean-Philippe Caillet*, Wouter Vrancken, Alexandre Afonso Da Silv (Mohamed Dahmane 64), Balázs Tóth. Tr: Hugo Broos

FK Sarajevo   2

Rascic [15], Muharemovic [86]

Muhamed Alaim* - Milos Babic, Alen Basic, Sead Bucan (Almir Turkovic 68), Vladan Grujic, Damir Hadzic* (Muhamed Dzakmic 73), Marko Maksimovic*, Semjon Milosevic, Veldin Muharemovic, Admir Rascic* (Mirza Mesic 77), Zdravko Saraba. Tr: Husref Musemic

Kosevo II, Sarajevo
8-08-2007, 19:30, 21 000, Tudor ROU

FK Sarajevo   0

Muhamed Alaim - Alen Basic, Sead Bucan (Almir Turkovic 58), Muhamed Dzakmic, Vladan Grujic, Damir Hadzic, Marko Maksimovic (Senad Repuh 85), Semjon Milosevic, Veldin Muharemovic*, Admir Rascic (Milos Babic 78), Zdravko Saraba*. Tr: Husref Musemic

KRC Genk   1

Mikulic [58]

Logan Bailly - Hans Cornelis*, Eric Matoukou, Tomislav Mikulic*, Tom Soetaers (Gonzague Vandooren 77), Ivan Bosnjak, Elyaniv Barda, Jean-Philippe Caillet (Goran Ljubojevic 70), Wouter Vrancken, Wim De Decke (Alexandre Afonso Da Silva 38), Balázs Tóth. Tr: Hugo Broos

Pod Dubnon, Zilina
1-08-2007, 20:00, 9600, Ingvarsson

MSK Zilina   0

Dusan Kuciak - Mário Breska (Juraj Ancic 70), Pavel Devaty (Ivan Belak 93+), Robert Jez, Vladimír Leitner, Mário Pecalka*, Andrej Porázik, Zdeno Strba, Peter Styvar (Ivan Lietava 59), Peter Pekarík, Csaba Szórád. Tr: Pavel Vrba

Slavia Praha   0

Martin Vaniak - Ante Aracic***88, Petr Janda (Vladimír Smicer* 63), David Kalivoda (Marek Suchy 85), Matej Krajcik, Stanislav Vlcek, Ondrej Sourek, Mickaël Tavares, Erich Brabec, Zdenek Senkerik* (Michal Svec 46), Frantisek Drízdal. Tr: Karel Jarolim

Evzena Rosického, Prague
8-08-2007, 20:45, 11 222, Gomes POR

Slavia Praha   0 4p

Martin Vaniak - Petr Janda, David Kalivoda (Ladislav Volecak 96), Matej Krajcik, Stanislav Vlcek, Mickaël Tavares, Erich Brabec, Vladimír Smicer* (Michal Svec 78), Zdenek Senkerik (Tomas Necid* 69), Frantisek Drízdal, Marek Suchy. Tr: Karel Jarolim

MSK Zilina   0 3p

Dusan Kuciak - Mário Breska (Admir Vladavic 116), Pavel Devaty, Robert Jez, Vladimír Leitner, Ivan Lietava (Peter Styvar 54), Mário Pecalka, Andrej Porázik (Ivan Belak 73), Zdeno Strba, Benjamin Vomácka, Peter Pekarík. Tr: Pavel Vrba

PENALTIES (SLAVIA WON 4-3)

Volesák ✗; Strba ✗; Tavares ✓; Styvar ✗; Krajcik ✓; Jez ✓; Suchy ✗; Vladavic ✓; Necid ✓; Devalty ✓; Vlcek ✓; Vomácka ✗;

Kaplakrikavöllur, Hafnarfjordur
1-08-2007, 19:00, 1587, Granat POL

FH Hafnarfjördur   1

Vilhjalmsson [18]

Dadi Lárusson - Freyr Bjarnason, Sverrir Gardarsson, Tryggvi Gudmundsson, Matthias Gudmundsson (Olafur Snorrason 84), Tommy Nielsen, Sigurvin Olafsson (Arnar Gunnlaugsson 70), Gudmundur Sævarsson, Dennis Siim*, Matthias Vilhjalmsson, Petur Vidarsson (Asgeir Asgeirsson 70). Tr: Olafur Johannesson

BATE Borisov   3

Likhtarovich 3, Rodionov [50], Bliznyuk [61]

Aleksandr Fedorovich - Gennadi Bliznyuk (Maksim Zhavnerchik 65), Ryhor Filipenko, Vitali Kazantsev, Anri Khagush, Sergei Kryvets, Dmitri Likhtarovich (Mikhail Sivakov 72), Vitali Radzionov (Dmitri Platonov 73), Artyom Radkov, Igor Stasevich*, Aleksandr Ermakovich. Tr: Igor Kryushenko

Gradski, Borisov
8-08-2007, 19:00, 5300, Stuchlik AUT

BATE Borisov   1

Platonov [93+]

Aleksandr Fedorovich - Gennadi Bliznyuk (Dmitri Platonov 82), Vitali Kazantsev, Anri Khagush*, Sergei Kryvets (Pavel Platonov 63), Dmitri Likhtarovich, Vitali Rodionov*42, Artyom Radkov*, Igor Stasevich (Maksim Zhavnerchik 88), Aleksandr Ermakovich, Ryhor Filipenko. Tr: Igor Kryushenko

FH Hafnarfjördur   1

Gudmundsson.T [33]

Dadi Lárusson - Freyr Bjarnason, Sverrir Gardarsson* (Tommy Nielsen 78), Tryggvi Gudmundsson (Hjortur Valgardsson 76), Matthias Gudmundsson (Bjarki Gunnlaugsson, Audjun Helgason***42, Sigurvin Olafsson (Asgeir Asgeirsson 63), Gudmundur Sævarsson, David Vidarsson*, Matthias Vilhjalmsson. Tr: Olafur Johannesson

Górniczy Osrodek Sportu
31-07-2007, 20:45, 7300, Dereli TUR

Zaglebie Lubin   0

Michal Václavík - Manuel Arboleda, Mateusz Bartczak, Grzegorz Bartczak*, Tiago Gomes, Michal Golinski (Robert Kolendowicz 75), Macij Jwanski, Rui Miguel Melo Rodrigues (Wojciech Lobodzinski 46), Andre Nunes*, Michal Stasiak, Piotr Wlodarczyk (Michal Chalbinski 57). Tr: Cheslaw Michniewicz

Steaua Bucuresti   1

Goian [55]

Cornel Cernea* - Dorin Goian, Pawel Golanski* (Mihai Nesu 73), Mirel Radoi, Petre Marin, Ionut Rada, Adrian Neaga, Banel Nicolita* (Emanoil Badoi 77), Florin Lovin*, Marius Croitoru (Petre Ovidiu 87), Nicolae Dica. Tr: Gheorghe Hagi

Steaua, Bucharest
8-08-2007, 20:30, 16 287, Clattenburg ENG

Steaua Bucuresti   2

Nicolita [37], Zaharia [83]

Robinson Zapata - Pawel Golanski, Mirel Radoi, Petre Marin*, Ionut Rada, Petre Ovidiu, Adrian Neaga (Dorel Zaharia 80), Banel Nicolita (Eric Bicfalvi 92+), Florin Lovin, Marius Croitoru* (Valentin Badoi* 71), Nicolae Dica. Tr: Gheorghe Hagi

Zaglebie Lubin   2

Stasiak [29]

Michal Václavík - Manuel Arboleda, Mateusz Bartczak, Grzegorz Bartczak, Michal Chalbinski (Piotr Wlodarczyk 57) Rui Miguel Melo Rodrigues 72), Tiago Gomes*, Michal Golinski, Macij Jwanski*, Wojciech Lobodzinski, Michal Stasiak*, Marcin Petroń (Robert Kolendowicz 71). Tr: Cheslaw Michniewicz

THIRD QUALIFYING ROUND

Stadium Municipal, Toulouse
15-08-2007, 16:30, 30 380, Vassaras GRE

Toulouse 0

Nicolas Douchez - Paulo César (Andre-Pierre Gignac 69), Bryan Bergougnoux (Fode Mansare 46), Nicolas Dieuze, Albin Ebondo (Moussa Sissoko• 83), Johan Elmander•, Mohamed Fofana, Jérémy Mathieu, Pantxi Sirieix, Achille Emana, Mauro Cetto•. Tr: Elie Baup

Liverpool 1
Voronin 43

Pepe Reina - Álvaro Arbeloa, Jamie Carragher, Peter Crouch, Steve Finnan, Steven Gerrard (Mohamed Sissoko 64), Sami Hyypiä, Javier Mascherano, Andriy Voronin (Fernando Torres 78), Yossi Benayoun (John Arne Riise 58), Ryan Babel. Tr: Rafael Benítez

Anfield, Liverpool
28-08-2007, 19:05, 43 118, Stark GER

Liverpool 4
Crouch 19, Hyypiä 49, Kuyt 2 87 91+

Pepe Reina - Daniel Agger (Steve Finnan 81), Álvaro Arbeloa, Peter Crouch, Sami Hyypiä, Dirk Kuyt, Javier Mascherano, John Arne Riise, Mohamed Sissoko (Lucas Leiva 68), Yossi Benayoun, Sebastian Leto (Ryan Babel 75). Tr: Rafael Benítez

Toulouse 0

Nicolas Douchez - Paulo César, Nicolas Dieuze, Johan Elmander, Mohamed Fofana, Jérémy Mathieu (Moussa Sissoko 82), Pantxi Sirieix, Achille Emana (Fabinho 76), André-Pierre Gignac (Bryan Mergougnoux 54), Mauro Cetto, Nkongolo Ilunga. Tr: Elie Baup

Hardturm, Zurich
15-08-2007, 20:15, 14 000, Riley ENG

FC Zürich 1
Alphonse 97+

Johnny Leoni - Alexandre Alphonse, Clederson Cesar (Eric Hassli 83), Rafael Araujo, Florian Stahel•, Hannu Tihinen, Steve Von Bergen•, Silvan Aegerter (Tico 46), Alain Rochat•, Alem Abdi, Yassine Chikhaoui. Tr: Bernard Challandes

Besiktas 1
Delgado 3

Hakan Arikan• - Edouard Cissé, Bobo, Matías Delgado (Burak Yilmaz 78), Serdar Kurtulus, Ricardinho (Koray Avci• 62), Serdar Ozkan•, Ali Tandogan• (Ibrahim Akin 46), Ibrahim Toraman, Ibrahim Uzülmez, Gökhan Zan. Tr: Ertugrul Saglam

Inönü, Istanbul
29-08-2007, 20:15, 22 773, Fröjdfeldt SWE

Besiktas 2
Delgado 2 56 64

Hakan Arikan - Edouard Cissé•, Bobo (Batuhan Karadeniz 92+), Matías Delgado (Ali Tandogan• 74), Serdar Kurtulus, Ricardinho (Ibrahim Akin 78), Serdar Ozkan, Rodrigo Tello•, Ibrahim Toraman, Ibrahim Uzülmez, Gökhan Zan. Tr: Ertugrul Saglam

FC Zürich 0

Johnny Leoni - Heinz Barmettier•, Rafael Araujo, Marc Schneider (Sebastian Kollar 67), Florian Stahel (Marco Sconbachler 83), Hannu Tihinen, Tico, Eudi Silva de Souza (Eric Hassli 67), Yassine Chikhaoui, Alain Rochat, Alem Abdi. Tr: Bernard Challandes

Ratina, Tampere
15-08-2007, 19:00, 16 800, Proença POR

Tampere United 0

Mikko Kavén - Antti Hynynen (Chimezie Daniels Nwoke 71), Toni Järvinen, Jussi Kujala, Mathias Lindström•, Jari Niemi, Tomi Petrescu (Jonne Hjelm 86), Antti Pohja, Sakari Saarinen, Juska Savolainen, Jarkko Wiss. Tr: Ari Hjelm

Rosenborg BK 3
Koppinen 19, Koné 2 20 81

Lars Hirschfeld - Christer Basma, Mikal Dorsin (Bjorn Tore Kvarme 84), Steffen Iversen (Oyvind Storflor 25), Yssouf Kone, Miika Koppinen, Vidar Riseth, Marek Sapara, Fredrik Stoor, Alexander Tettey•, Abdou Razack Traoré (Didier Konan Ya 91+). Tr: Knut Tørum

Lerkendai, Trondheim
29-08-2007, 21:40, 14 123, Hamer LUX

Rosenborg BK 2
Sapara 45, Ya 48

Lars Hirschfeld - Christer Basma, Mikael Dorsin, Yssouf Kone, Miika Koppinen (Per Ciljan Skjelbred 45), Vidar Riseth, Marek Sapara (Steffen Iversen 76), Roar Strand (Fredrik Stoor 17), Alexander Tettey, Abdou Razack Traoré, Didier Konan Ya. Tr: Knut Tørum

Tampere United 0

Mikko Kavén - Toni Järvinen (Chimezie Daniels Nwoke 74), Jussi Kujala, Mathias Lindström, Jari Niemi, Antti Ojanperä•, Tomi Petrescu (Jonne Hjelm 85), Antti Pohja, Sakari Saarinen (Heikki Aho 46), Juska Savolainen•, Jarkko Wiss. Tr: Ari Hjelm

Mestalla, Valencia
14-08-2007, 22:00, 46 320, Malek POL

Valencia 3
Vicente 14, Silva 58, Morientes 70

Santiago Cañizares - David Albelda, Raúl Albiol, Rubén Baraja, David Silva, Carlos Marchena, Emiliano Moretti, Vicente Rodríguez (Fernando Morientes 59), Joaquín Sánchez (Miguel Angel Angulo 81), David Villa (Jaime Gavilan 78), Marco Caneira. Tr: Quique Sánchez Flores

Elfsborg IF 0

Johan Wiland - Andreas Augustsson, Fredrik Björck, Samuel Holmén, Jari Ilola (Denni Avdic 76), Stefan Ishizaki, Johan Karlsson, James Keene (Fredrik Berglund 63), Daniel Mobaeck, Anders Svensson, Mathias Svensson (Daniel Nils Alexandersson 70). Tr: Magnus Haglund

Ryavallen, Boras
29-08-2007, 20:45, 13 148, Baskakov RUS

Elfsborg IF 1
Alexandersson 31

Johan Wiland - Daniel Nils Alexandersson, Andreas Augustsson, Denni Avdic, Fredrik Berglund•, Fredrik Björck, Jari Ilola (Mathias Svensson• 64), Johan Karlsson (Martin Andersson 75), James Keene, Daniel Mobaeck (Mathias Floren 19), Anders Svensson. Tr: Magnus Haglund

Valencia 2
Helguera 4, Villa 90

Timo Hildebrand - Raúl Albiol, Jaime Gavilán, David Silva (David Villa 61), Carlos Marchena, Emiliano Moretti (Alexis Ruano Delgado 85), Fernando Morientes (Javier Arizmendi 56), Joaquín Sánchez, Iván Helguera•, Sunday Stephen Obayan, Marco Caneira. Tr: Quique Sánchez Flores

Weserstadion, Bremen
15-08-2007, 20:30, 25 474, Mallenco ESP

Werder Bremen 1
Hugo Almeida 46, Jensen.D 85

Tim Wiese - Leon Andreasen (Daniel Jensen 46), Frank Baumann, Per Mertesacker, Petri Pasanen, Diego, Naldo•, Christian Schulz, Carlos Alberto (Martin Harnik 74), Boubacar Sanogo, Kevin Schindler (Hugo Almeida 46). Tr: Thomas Schaaf

Dinamo Zagreb 1
Balaban 45

Georg Koch - Bosko Balaban• (Ivica Vrdoljak 80), Hrvoje Cale•, Sammir (Franck Manga Guela 88), Etto, Dino Drpic, Luka Modric, Nikola Pokrivac•, Gordon Schildenfeld, Tomislav Sokota (Marijo Mandzukic 37), Ognjen Vukojevic. Tr: Branko Ivankovic

Maksimir, Zagreb
29-08-2007, 20:30, 34 175, Hauge NOR

Dinamo Zagreb 2
Vukojevic 21, Modric 40

Georg Koch• - Bosko Balaban, Sammir (Mihael Mikic 76), Carlos•, Etto (Franck Manga Guela 78), Dino Drpic, Marijo Mandzukic•, Luka Modric•, Nikola Pokrivac (Davor Vugrinec 62), Gordon Schildenfeld, Ognjen Vukojevic•. Tr: Branko Ivankovic

Werder Bremen 3
Diego 2 13p 70p, Sanogo 38

Tim Wiese - Frank Baumann, Daniel Jensen, Per Mertesacker, Petri Pasanen, Hugo Almeida• (Martin Harnik 68), Diego, Naldo, Christian Schulz• (Dusko Tosic 81), Jurica Vranješ, Boubacar Sanogo (Markus Rosenberg 76). Tr: Thomas Schaaf

Stadio Olimpico, Rome
14-08-2007, 20:45, 35 172, Ovrebø NOR

Lazio 1
Mutarelli 54

Marco Ballotta - Valon Behrami•75, Cristian Ledesma, Stefano Mauri (Simone Del Nero 64), Massimo Mutarelli•••87, Goran Pandev•, Tommaso Rocchi, Emilson Cribari (Aleksandar Kolarov• 23), Lionel Scaloni, Guglielmo Stendardo (Lorenzo De Silvestri 46), Luciano Zauri. Tr: Delio Rossi

Dinamo Bucuresti 1
Danciulescu 22

Bogdan Lobont - George Blay•, Adrian Cristea•, Ionel Danciulescu, Claudiu Niculescu, Cristian Pulhac, Ianis Zicu (Daniel Oprita 7) (Florin Chiacu 74), Silviu Izvoreanu•, Vasile Nastase (Lucian Goian 32•••91+) Stefan Radu, Adrian Ropotan•. Tr: Mircea Rednic

Lia Manoliu, Bucharest
28-08-2007, 22:00, 40 164, Mejuto ESP

Dinamo Bucuresti 1
Bratu 27

Bogdan Lobont - George Blay, Adrian Cristea, Ionel Danciulescu (Catalin Munteanu 71), Andrei Margaritescu (Claudiu Niculescu 58), Cristian Pulhac•, Florin Bratu, Daniel Oprita (Hristu Chiacu 58), Vasile Nastase, Stefan Radu, Adrian Ropotan. Tr: Mircea Rednic

Lazio 3
Rocchi 2 47p 66, Pandev 53

Marco Ballotta - Lorenzo De Silvestri, Simone Del Nero (Manuel Belleri 85), Cristian Ledesma, Christian Manfredini, Gaby Mudingayi•, Goran Pandev (Igli Tare 89), Tommaso Rocchi, Emilson Cribari, Guglielmo Stendardo (Lionel Scaloni 34), Luciano Zauri. Tr: Delio Rossi

Luzhniki, Moscow
15-08-2007, 20:00, 5000, Fandel GER

Spartak Moskva 1
Pavlyuchenko 42

Stipe Pletikosa - Vladimir Bystrov (Maxym Kalynychenko 74), Radoslav Kováč, Roman Pavlyuchenko, Mozart, Florin Soava, Martin Stranzl•, Yegor Titov, Dmitri Torbinskiy, Welliton, Roman Shishkin. Tr: Stanislav Cherchesov

Celtic 1
Hartley 21

Mark Brown - John Kennedy, Stephen McManus, Shunsuke Nakamura, Lee Naylor•, Jan Vennegoor of Hesselink (Aiden McGeady 83), Mark Wilson, Massimo Donati (Evander Sno 75), Scott Brown•, Paul Hartley, Scott McDonald (Gary Caldwell 80). Tr: Gordon Strachan

---

Celtic Park, Glasgow
29-08-2007, 19:45, 57 644, Rosetti ITA

Celtic 1 4p
McDonald 27

Artur Boruc - Gary Caldwell•, Stephen McManus, Shunsuke Nakamura, Lee Naylor (Darren O'Dea 110), Jan Hesselink, Mark Wilson, Massimo Donati, Scott Brown, Scott McDonald (Maciej Zurawski 97), Aiden McGeady (Derek Riordan• 104). Tr: Gordon Strachan

Spartak Moskva 1 3p
Pavlyuchenko 45

Stipe Pletikosa - Vladimir Bystrov (Maxym Kaylynychenko 95), Radoslav Kováč, Roman Pavlyuchenko, Mozart, Florin Soava, Martin Stranzl•84, Yegor Titov, Dmitri Torbinskiy (Denis Boyarintsev 103), Welliton (Ignas Dedura 82), Roman Shishkin•. Tr: Stanislav Cherchesov

PENALTIES (CELTIC WON 4-3)

Caldwell ✓; Mozart ✓; Nakamura ✗; Titov ✗;
Hesselink ✓; Pavlyuchenko ✓; Riorden ✓;
Soáva ✓; Zurawski ✓; Kalynychenko ✗;

Estádio da Luz, Lisbon
14-08-2007, 20:15, 55 722, Kassai HUN

Benfica 2
Rui Costa 2 25 85

Quim - Nuno Assis (Nuno Gomes 74), Rui Costa•, Luisão (Freddy Adu 37), Petit•, Konstantinos Katsouranis, Léo, David Luiz•, Luís Filipe•, Óscar Cardozo, Gonzalo Bergessio (Fabio Coentrao 46). Tr: Fernando Santos

FC København 1
Hutchinson 35

Jesper Christiansen - Marcus Allbäck (Morten Nordstrand 78), Michael Gravgaard, Jesper Grønkjær•, Brede Hangeland, Atiba Hutchinson•, Niclas Jensen, William Kvist, Hjalte Nørregaard (Libor Sionko 89), Michael Silberbauer, Rasmus Würtz•. Tr: Ståle Solbakken

---

Parken, Copenhagen
29-08-2007, 20:45, 39 711, Braamhaar NED

FC København 0

Jesper Christiansen - Marcus Allbäck, Michael Gravgaard, Brede Hangeland, Atiba Hutchinson•, Niclas Jensen, William Kvist, Morten Nordstrand (Ailton Almeida 74), Hjalte Nørregaard, Michael Silberbauer, Rasmus Würtz (Libor Sionko 58). Tr: Ståle Solbakken

Benfica 1
Katsouranis 17

Quim - Rui Costa, Petit, Kostas Katsouranis•, Léo, Nuno Gomes (Gonzalo Bergessio 93+), Nélson (Nuno Assis 45), Luís Filipe, Angel Di María (Romeu Ribeiro 74), Óscar Cardozo•, Miguel Vitor•. Tr: José Antonio Camacho

---

Wals-Siezenheim, Salzburg
15-08-2007, 20:30, 23 690, Skomina SVN

RB Austria Salzburg 1
Zickler 10p

Timo Ochs - René Aufhauser•, Ezequiel Carboni, Milan Dudic•, Niko Kovac•, Christoph Leitgeb, Tsuneyasu Miyamoto, Ibrahim Sekagya, Markus Steinhöfer, Johan Vonlanthen (Karel Pitak 89), Alexander Zickler• (Vratislav Lokvenc 85). Tr: Giovanni Trapattoni

Shakhtar Donetsk 0

Andriy Pyatov - Igor Duljaj, Olexandr Gladkiy, Olexandr Kucher, Brandão (Cristiano Lucarelli 73), Fernandinho, Razvan Rat, Jadson Rodriguez (Zvonimir Vukic 69), Darijo Srna•, Dmytro Chygrynskiy, Ilsinho (Mariusz Lewandowski 81). Tr: Mircea Lucescu

---

RSC Olimpiyskiy, Donetsk
29-08-2007, 19:00, 26 000, Duhamel FRA

Shakhtar Donetsk 3
Lucarelli 9, Castillo 79p, Brandão 87

Andriy Pyatov - Olexandr Gladkiy (Brandão• 55), Olexandr Kucher, Mariusz Lewandowski• (Nery Castillo• 57), Cristiano Lucarelli•, Fernandinho, Razvan Rat, Jadson Rodriguez, Darijo Srna, Dmytro Chygrynskiy•, Ilsinho (Igor Duljaj 72). Tr: Mircea Lucescu

RB Austria Salzburg 1
Meyer 5

Timo Ochs - René Aufhauser• (Vratislav Lokvenc 89), Ezequiel Carboni, Niko Kovac, Christoph Leitgeb, Remo Meyer, Tsuneyasu Miyamoto, Ibrahim Sekagya•, Markus Steinhöfer, Johan Vonlanthen, Alexander Zickler. Tr: Giovanni Trapattoni

---

Ibrox, Glasgow
14-08-2007, 20:00, 35 364, Hansson SWE

Rangers 1
Novo 90

Allan McGregor - DaMarcus Beasley (Nacho Novo 65), Kirk Broadfoot, Carlos Cuéllar, Jean-Claude Darcheville (Daniel Cousin 65), Barry Ferguson, Brahim Hemdani, Alan Hutton, Lee McCulloch, Kevin Thomson, David Weir. Tr: Walter Smith

Crvena Zvezda Beograd 0

Ivan Randjelovic - Dusan Andjelkovic•, Grzegorz Bronowicki, Segundo Castillo•, Joao Lukas, Ibrahima Gueye, Ognjen Koroman•, Nenad Milijas, Milanko Raskovic• (Mauricio Molina• 70), Djordje Tutoric•, Filip Djordjevic• (Dejan Milovanovic 82). Tr: Milorad Kosanovic

---

Crvena Zvezda, Belgrade
28-08-2007, 20:00, 40 104, Batista POR

Crvena Zvezda 0

Ivan Randjelovic - Dusan Andjelkovic, Dusan Basta•, Igor Burzanovic• (Hernan Barcos 69), Segundo Castillo, Joao Lukas, Ibrahima Gueye•, Ognjen Koroman•, Nenad Milijas (Milanko Raskovic 73), Djordje Tutoric, Filip Djordjevic. Tr: Milorad Kosanovic

Rangers 0

Allan McGregor - Carlos Cuéllar, Jean-Claude Darcheville (Daniel Cousin 69), Barry Ferguson, Brahim Hemdani, Alan Hutton•, Lee McCulloch•, Sasa Papac, Kevin Thomson, David Weir, Steven Whittaker (DaMarcus Beasley 78). Tr: Walter Smith

---

Kosevo, Sarajevo
15-08-2007, 20:00, 21 000, Yefet ISR

FK Sarajevo 0

Muhamed Alaim - Alen Basic, Sead Buca (Almir Turkovic 57), Muhamed Dzakmic, Vladan Grujic, Damir Hadzic (Senad Repuh 46), Marko Maksimovic•, Semjon Hulosevic, Veldin Muharemovic•, Admir Rascic (Mirza Mesic 65), Zdravko Saraba. Tr: Husref Musemic

Dynamo Kyiv 1
Shatskikh 13

Olexandr Shovkovskiy - Carlos Corrêa, Goran Gavrancic, Marjan Markovic, Taras Mikhalik•, Andriy Nesmachniy, Serhiy Rebrov (Ismael Bangoura 82), Maksim Shatskikh (Kleber 67), Pape Diakhate•, Michael, Oleh Gusev (Milos Ninkovic 63). Tr: Anatoliy Demyanenko

---

Valery Lobanovskiy, Kyiv
29-08-2007, 19:00, 16 100,

Dynamo Kyiv 3
Bangoura 3, Milosevic OG 75, Rebrov 92+p

Olexandr Shovkovskiy - Carlos Corrêa (Valentin Belkevich 78), Badr El Kaddouri, Goran Gavrancic•, Marjan Markovic, Maksim Shatskikh, Tiberiu Ghioane•, Ismaël Bangoura (Serhiy Rebrov 84), Pape Diakhate•, Michael (Ruslan Rotan 82), Oleh Gusev. Tr: Anatoliy Demyanenko

FK Sarajevo 0

Muhamed Alaim (Irfan Fejzic 60) - Milos Babic, Alen Basic, Muhamed Dzakmic, Vladan Grujic, Damir Hadzic, Mirza Mesic (Haris Handzic 68), Semjon Milosevic, Admir Rascic, Senad Repuh (Emir Janos• 46), Zdravko Saraba. Tr: Husref Musemic

---

Sükrü Saracoglu, Istanbul
15-08-2007, 21:00, 37 919, Webb ENG

Fenerbahçe 1
Alex 32

Serdar Kulbilge - Edu, Mehmet Aurélio•, Deniz Baris (Selcuk Sahin 70), Deivid, Alex (Ali Bilgin 83), Mateja Kezman, Lugano, Tümer Metin (Ugur Boral 68), Önder Turaci, Roberto Carlos. Tr: Zico

RSC Anderlecht 0

Daniel Zitka - Lucas Biglia, Mbark Boussoufa (Jonathan Legear 83), Mark De Man, Olivier Deschacht, Bart Goor, Hassan Ahmed•, Roland Juhász, Mohamed Tchite (Mbo Mpenza 77), Jan Polák, Marcin Wasilewski•. Tr: Frank Vercauteren

---

Constant van den Stock, Brussels
29-08-2007, 20:30, 20 722, Busacca SUI

RSC Anderlecht 1

Daniel Zitka - Lucas Biglia•, Mbark Boussoufa (Cyril Thereau 56), Olivier Deschacht, Hassan Ahmed, Roland Juhász, Nicolas Pareja, Mohamed Tchite, Jelle Van Damme (Bart Goor 76), Jan Polák, Marcin Wasilewski (Jonathan Legear 76). Tr: Frank Vercauteren

Fenerbahçe 2
Kezman 4, Alex 73

Volkan Demirel - Edu, Mehmet Aurélio, Deniz Baris•, Deivid• (Gorcek Vederson 82), Alex (Selcuk Sahin 76), Mateja Kezman, Lugano, Tümer Metin (Colin Kazim-Richards 67), Önder Turaci•, Roberto Carlos. Tr: Zico

Sánchez-Pizjuan, Seville
15-08-2007, 20:45, 34 852, Michel SVK

Sevilla 2

Luis Fabiano [48], Kanouté [68]

Andrés Palop - Luis Fabiano (Jose Luis Marti 71), Ivica Dragutinovic, Federico Julian Fazio, Andreas Hinkel, Frédéric Kanouté, Enzo Maresca• (Seydou Keita 46), Jesús Navas, Christian Poulsen, Khalid Boulahrouz (Renato 46), Diego Capel. Tr: Juande Ramos

AEK Athens 0

Moretto - Rodolfo Arruabarrena•, Rivaldo (Panagiotis Kone 67), Júlio César, Traianos Dellas, Nikolaos Liberopoulos, Gustavo Manduca, Tamandani Wazayo Philipp Nsaliwa, Geraldo, Edson Ramos Silva (Pantelis Kafes 62), Akis Zikos• (Daniel Tozser 93+). Tr: Lorenzo Serra Ferrer

OACA Spyro Louis, Athens
3-09-2007, 21:45, 37 777, Allaerts BEL

AEK Athens 1

Rivaldo [82p]

Moretto - Rivaldo, Christos Bourbos•, Júlio César (Daniel Tozser 46), Nikolaos Liberopoulos, Gustavo Manduca, Tamandani Wazayo Philipp Nsaliwa (Charilaos Pappas 46), Sokratis Papastathopoulos•, Geraldo, Edson Ramos Silva, Akis Zikos• (Michail Pavlis 62). Tr: Lorenzo Serra Ferrer

Sevilla 4

Luis Fabiano 2 [31p 45], Keita [40], Kerzhakov [53]

Andrés Palop - Luis Fabiano (Tom De Mul 46), Ivica Dragutinovic, Federico Julian Fazio, Aleksandr Kerzhakov, Jesús Navas, Christian Poulsen (Enzo Maresca 62), Seydou Keita, Daniel Alves, Diego Capel. Tr: Juande Ramos

AXA Arena, Prague
15-08-2007, 20:45, 19 586, Cantalejo ESP

Sparta Praha 0

Tomás Postulka - Libor Dosek, Lubos Husek•, Michal Kadlec, Zdenek Pospech, Tomás Repka (Milos Brezinsky 36), Jan Rezek (Miroslav Matusovic 58), Pavel Horváth (David Limbersky 84), Jiri Kladrubsky, Marek Kulic•, Martin Abrahám. Tr: Michal Bilek

Arsenal 2

Fabregas [72], Hleb [92+]

Jens Lehmann - Gaël Clichy, Emmanuel Eboué, Mathieu Flamini•, William Gallas, Aleksandr Hleb, Tomás Rosicky (Alexandre Song 79), Kolo Touré, Robin van Persie•, Bacary Sagna, Cesc Fabregas•. Tr: Arsène Wenger

Emirates Stadium, London
29-08-2007, 20:05, 58 462, De Bleeckere BEL

Arsenal 3

Rosicky [7], Fabregas [88], Eduardo [89]

Manuel Almunia - Gaël Clichy, Gilberto, Abou Diaby (Cesc Fabregas 67), Justin Hoyte, Tomás Rosický (Denilson 73), Philippe Senderos, Kolo Touré, Robin van Persie (Emmanuel Adebayor 67), Theo Walcott•, Eduardo da Silva. Tr: Arsène Wenger

Sparta Praha 0

Tomás Postulka - Libor Dosek, Lubos Husek•, Michal Kadlec, Zdenek Pospech, Tomás Repka•, Jan Rezek (Daniel Kolar 73), Pavel Horváth, Jiri Kladrubsky (David Limbersky 77), Martin Abrahám, Marek Kulic• (Igor Zofcak 46). Tr: Michal Bilek

Amsterdam ArenA, Amsterdam
15-08-2007, 20:30, 30 000, Meyer GER

Ajax 0

Maarten Stekelenburg• - Urby Emanuelson, Gabri, Johnny Heitinga•, Klaas Jan Huntelaar, Jaap Stam, Thomas Vermaelen, Kennedy Bakircioglü, Dennis Rommedahl (Jeffrey Sarpong 82), Jürgen Colin•, Luis Suárez (Ismael Urzaiz 72). Tr: Henk Ten Cate

Slavia Praha 1

Kalivoda [75p]

Martin Vaniak - Petr Janda (Tuani Belaid 86), David Kalivoda (Ladislav Volesak 80), Matej Krajcik, Stanislav Vlcek• (Rogerio Botelho 90), Mickaël Tavares•, Erich Brabec, Michal Svec, Zdenek Senkerik•, Frantisek Drizdal, Marek Suchy. Tr: Karel Jarolim

Evzena Rosického, Prague
29-08-2007, 20:30, 17 330, Larsen DEN

Slavia Praha 2

Vlcek 2 [23 87]

Martin Vaniak - Erich Brabec, Frantisek Drizdal, Petr Janda, David Kalivoda (Ladislav Volesak• 76), Matej Krajcik, Vladimir Smicer (Milan Ivana 14) (Tomas Necid 82), Mickaël Tavares, Stanislav Vlcek, Marek Suchy, Michal Svec. Tr: Karel Jarolim

Ajax 1

Luis Suárez [34]

Maarten Stekelenburg - Urby Emanuelson• (Jan Vertonghen 58), Gabri (Ismael Urzaiz 78), Johnny Heitinga, Klaas Jan Huntelaar, Jaap Stam•, Thomas Vermaelen, Kennedy Bakircioglü (Dennis Rommedahl 65), Laurent Delorge, Jürgen Colin, Luis Suárez. Tr: Henk Ten Cate

Gradski, Borisov
15-08-2007, 20:00, 5300, Trefoloni ITA

BATE Borisov 2

Radkov [39], Bliznyuk [92+]

Aleksandr Fedorovich - Artyom Radkov, Anri Khagush•, Ryhor Filipenko, Dmitri Likhtarovich (Sergei Kryvets 53), Pavel Platonov (Mikhail Sivakov 82), Aleksandr Ermakovich (Maksim Zhavnerchik 68), Dmitri Platonov, Igor Stasevich, Gennadi Bliznyuk, Vitali Kazantsev. Tr: Igor Kryushenko

Steaua Bucuresti 2

Goian [60], Dica [85]

Robinson Zapata - Dorin Goian, Pawel Golanski•, Ionut Rada (Florin Lovin 59), Mirel Radoi•, Petre Marin, Banel Nicolita (Dorel Zaharia 73), Mihaita Plesan•, Marius Croitoru (Eric Bicfalvi 53), Nicolae Dica, Adrian Neaga. Tr: Gheorghe Hagi

Steaua, Bucharest
29-08-2007, 20:30, 24 254, Vink NED

Steaua Bucuresti 2

Zaharia [12], Neaga [54]

Robinson Zapata - Nicolae Dica•, Dorin Goian, Florin Lovin (Eric Bicfalvi 56), Petre Marin, Adrian Neaga (Marius Croitoru 69), Mihai Nesu•, Banel Nicolita, Petre Ovidiu, Ionut Rada, Dorel Zaharia (Emanoil Badoi 53). Tr: Gheorghe Hagi

BATE Borisov 0

Aleksandr Fedorovich - Gennadi Bliznyuk, Yegor Filipenko•, Vitali Kazantsev, Dmitri Likhtarovich, Dmitri Platonov, Pavel Platonov, Artyom Radkov, Anton Sakharov (Sergei Kryvets 56), Igor Stasevich• (Aleksandr Vishnyakov 84), Aleksandr Ermakovich (Valentin Radevich 77). Tr: Igor Kryushenko

GROUP A

		Pl	W	D	L	F	A	Pts	POR	ENG	FRA	TUR
FC Porto	POR	6	3	2	1	8	7	11		1-1	2-1	2-0
Liverpool	ENG	6	3	1	2	18	5	10	4-1		0-1	8-0
Olympique Marseille	FRA	6	2	1	3	6	9	7	1-1	0-4		2-0
Besiktas	TUR	6	2	0	4	4	15	6	0-1	2-1	2-1	

Estádio do Dragão, Porto
18-09-2007, 19:45, 41 208, Michel SVK

FC Porto 1
Lucho González [8p]

Nuno - Jose Bosingwa●, Joao Paulo, Bruno Alves, Paulo Assuncao, Fucile, Lucho Gonzalez, Raul Meireles (Mariano Gonzalez 64), Tarik Sektioui (Ernesto Farias 64), Ricardo Quaresma, Lisandro Lopez. Tr: Jesualdo Ferreira

Liverpool 1
Kuyt [17]

Jose Reina - Steve Finnan, Jamie Carragher, Sami Hyypia, Alvaro Arbeloa, Jermaine Pennant●●●58, Javier Mascherano●, Steven Gerrard, Ryan Babel (Fabio Aurelio 85), Dirk Kuyt●, Fernando Torres● (Andriy Voronin 76). Tr: Rafael Benitez

---

Inönü, Istanbul
3-10-2007, 21:45, 19 795, Vink NED

Besiktas 0

Hakan Arikan - Ibrahim Uzulmez, Ibrahim Toraman, Gokhan Zan, Serdar Kurtulus (Ali Tandogan● 71), Rodrigo Tello, Edouard Cisse, Matias Delgado, Serdar Ozkan, Ibrahim Akin (Federico Higuain 67), Bobo (Marcio Nobre● 27). Tr: Ertugrul Saglam

FC Porto 1
Quaresma [92+]

Helton - Fucile, Milan Stepanov, Bruno Alves●, Jose Bosingwa, Raul Meireles (Leandro Lima 88), Paulo Assuncao, Lucho Gonzalez●, Tarik Sektioui (Marek Cech 66), Lisandro Lopez (Adriano 75), Ricardo Quaresma. Tr: Jesualdo Ferreira

---

Anfield, Liverpool
6-11-2007, 19:45, 41 143, Merk GER

Liverpool 8
Crouch 2 [19 89], Benayoun 3 [32 53 56], Gerrard [69], Babel 2 [78 81]

Jose Reina - Alvaro Arbeloa, Sami Hyypia, Jamie Carragher, Fabio Aurelio (Ryan Babel 63), Yossi Benayoun, Steven Gerrard (Lucas Leiva 72), Javier Mascherano, John Arne Riise (Andriy Voronin (Harry Kewell 72), Peter Crouch. Tr: Rafael Benitez

Besiktas 0

Hakan Arikan - Serdar Kurtulus (Federico Higuain 62), Lamine Diatta, Ibrahim Toraman, Ibrahim Uzulmez, Koray Avci, Edouard Cisse, Mehmet Sedef (Ricardinho 77), Matias Delgado, Serdar Ozkan● (Ali Tandogan 46), Bobo. Tr: Ertugrul Saglam

---

Inönü, Istanbul
28-11-2007, 21:45, 19 448, M.Cantalejo ESP

Besiktas 2
Tello [27], Bobo [88]

Rustu Recber - Ali Tandogan, Baki Mercimek●, Ibrahim Toraman, Ibrahim Uzulmez, Serdar Ozkan (Marcio Nobre 75), Edouard Cisse (Koray Avci 20), Ricardinho (Ibrahim Akin● 66), Rodrigo Tello, Matias Delgado, Bobo. Tr: Ertugrul Saglam

Olympique Marseille 1
Taiwo [65]

Steve Mandanda - Ronald Zubar (Taye Taiwo 46), Gael Givet, Julien Rodriguez, Laurent Bonnart, Samir Nasri (Djibril Cisse● 26), Lorik Cana, Mathieu Valbuena, Benoit Cheyrou●, Boudewijn Zenden● (Andre Ayew● 54), Mamadou Niang●. Tr: Eric Gerets

---

Vélodrome, Marseille
18-09-2007, 20:45, 35 676, Trefoloni ITA

Olympique Marseille 2
Rodriguez [76], Cissé [91+]

Steve Mandanda - Laurent Bonnart, Jacques Faty●, Julien Rodriguez●, Taye Taiwo, Lorik Cana, Karim Ziani, Samir Nasri● (Modeste M'Bami 88), Boudewijn Zenden (Mathieu Valbuena● 76), Mamadou Niang (Vincent Gragnic 86), Djibril Cisse●. Tr: Albert Emon

Besiktas 0

Hakan Arikan - Ibrahim Uzulmez, Ibrahim Toraman, Lamine Diatta, Serdar Kurtulus (Ibrahim Kas● 25), Ricardinho (Koray Avci● 45), Edouard Cisse, Rodrigo Tello, Matias Delgado (Federico Higuain 75), Serdar Ozkan, Bobo. Tr: Ertugrul Saglam

---

Vélodrome, Marseille
24-10-2007, 20:45, 46 458, M.González ESP

Olympique Marseille 1
Niang [69]

Steve Mandanda● - Laurent Bonnart, Ronald Zubar, Jacques Faty, Gael Givet (Taye Taiwo 68), Lorik Cana, Benoit Cheyrou, Mamadou Niang●, Mathieu Valbuena, Boudewijn Zenden (Salim Arrache 55), Djibril Cisse (Andre Ayew 88). Tr: Erik Gerets

FC Porto 1
Lucho González [79p]

Helton - Jose Bosingwa, Milan Stepanov●, Bruno Alves, Fucile, Paulo Assuncao, Lucho Gonzalez, Raul Meireles (Leandro Lima 72), Ricardo Quaresma, Mariano Gonzalez (Helder Postiga 46), Lisandro Lopez. Tr: Jesualdo Ferreira

---

Estádio do Dragão, Porto
6-11-2007, 19:45, 42 217, Stark GER

FC Porto 2
Sektioui [27], Lisandro [78]

Helton● - Jose Bosingwa, Milan Stepanov, Bruno Alves, Fucile●, Paulo Assuncao, Marek Cech (Helder Postiga 59), Raul Meireles (Mario Bolatti 68), Ricardo Quaresma, Tarik Sektioui (Mariano Gonzalez 87), Lisandro Lopez. Tr: Jesualdo Ferreira

Olympique Marseille 1
Niang [47]

Steve Mandanda - Laurent Bonnart, Taye Taiwo, Julien Rodriguez, Gael Givet, Lorik Cana, Modeste M'Bami (Benoit Cheyrou 84), Mathieu Valbuena, Andre Ayew (Salim Arrache 77), Samir Nasri, Mamadou Niang (Djibril Cisse 62). Tr: Eric Gerets

---

Estádio do Dragão, Porto
11-12-2007, 19:45, 39 608, Fröjdfeldt SWE

FC Porto 2
Lucho González [44], Quaresma [62]

Helton - Jose Bosingwa, Pedro Emanuel, Bruno Alves, Fucile (Marek Cech 75), Paulo Assuncao, Raul Meireles, Lucho Gonzalez (Mario Bolatti 81), Tarik Sektioui (Helder Postiga 73), Ricardo Quaresma●, Lisandro Lopez. Tr: Jesualdo Ferreira

Besiktas 0

Rustu Recber● - Ali Tandogan, Baki Mercimek, Ibrahim Toraman, Ibrahim Uzulmez, Serdar Ozkan, Edouard Cisse, Burak Yilmaz (Ibrahim Akin● 45), Rodrigo Tello (Federico Higuain 84), Matias Delgado, Bobo●. Tr: Ertugrul Saglam

---

Anfield, Liverpool
3-10-2007, 19:45, 41 355, Plautz AUT

Liverpool 0

Jose Reina - Steve Finnan, Jamie Carragher●, Sami Hyypia, Fabio Aurelio (Andriy Voronin 70), Yossi Benayoun, Steven Gerrard●, Mohamed Sissoko●, Sebastian Leto (John Arne Riise 52), Fernando Torres, Peter Crouch (Dirk Kuyt 75). Tr: Rafael Benitez

Olympique Marseille 1
Valbuena [77]

Steve Mandanda - Laurent Bonnart, Julien Rodriguez, Gael Givet, Taye Taiwo, Lorik Cana, Benoit Cheyrou, Mathieu Valbuena (Wilson Oruma 84), Karim Ziani, Boudewijn Zenden (Salim Arrache 88), Mamadou Niang (Djibril Cisse 70). Tr: Eric Gerets

---

Inönü, Istanbul
24-10-2007, 21:45, 25 837, Larsen DEN

Besiktas 2
Hyypiä OG [13], Bobo [82]

Hakan Arikan - Ali Tandogan, Gokhan Zan, Ibrahim Toraman, Ibrahim Uzulmez, Serdar Kurtulus (Koray Avci 42), Edouard Cisse, Rodrigo Tello, Serdar Ozkan, Bobo (Lamine Diatta 86), Matias Delgado (Federico Higuain 63). Tr: Mutlu Topcu

Liverpool 1
Gerrard [85]

Jose Reina - Steve Finnan, Jamie Carragher, Sami Hyypia, (Peter Crouch 83), John Arne Riise, Jermaine Pennant (Yossi Benayoun 59), Steven Gerrard, Javier Mascherano (Lucas Leiva 76), Ryan Babel, Andriy Voronin, Dirk Kuyt. Tr: Rafael Benitez

---

Anfield, Liverpool
28-11-2007, 19:45, 41 095, Rosetti ITA

Liverpool 4
Torres 2 [19 78], Gerrard [84p], Crouch [87]

Jose Reina - Steve Finnan, Sami Hyypia●, Jamie Carragher, Alvaro Arbeloa, Yossi Benayoun (Peter Crouch 71), Steven Gerrard, Javier Mascherano, Ryan Babel (Dirk Kuyt 85), Andriy Voronin (Harry Kewell 63), Fernando Torres. Tr: Rafael Benitez

FC Porto 1
Lisandro [33]

Helton - Jose Bosingwa, Milan Stepanov●, Bruno Alves, Marek Cech, Paulo Assuncao● (Helder Postiga 81), Mariano Gonzalez (Tarik Sektioui 77), Lucho Gonzalez, Przemyslaw Kazmierczak (Raul Meireles 65), Ricardo Quaresma●, Lisandro Lopez. Tr: Jesualdo Ferreira

---

Vélodrome, Marseille
11-12-2007, 20:45, 53 097, Hauge NOR

Olympique Marseille 0

Steve Mandanda - Taye Taiwo, Julien Rodriguez, Gael Givet (Jacques Faty 45), Laurent Bonnart, Lorik Cana●, Benoit Cheyrou (Samir Nasri 34), Karim Ziani, Mathieu Valbuena, Boudewijn Zenden (Djibril Cisse 46), Mamadou Niang. Tr: Eric Gerets

Liverpool 4
Gerrard [4], Torres [11], Kuyt [48], Babel [91+]

Jose Reina - Alvaro Arbeloa, Jamie Carragher●, Sami Hyypia, John-Arne Riise, Yossi Benayoun, Steven Gerrard●4, Javier Mascherano, Harry Kewell (Fabio Aurelio● 67), Dirk Kuyt (Lucas Leiva 86), Fernando Torres (Ryan Babel 77). Tr: Rafael Benitez

GROUP B

		Pl	W	D	L	F	A	Pts	ENG	GER	NOR	ESP
Chelsea	ENG	6	3	3	0	9	2	12		2-0	1-1	0-0
Schalke 04	GER	6	2	2	2	5	4	8	0-0		3-1	0-1
Rosenborg BK	NOR	6	2	1	3	6	10	7	0-4	0-2		2-0
Valencia	ESP	6	1	2	3	2	6	5	1-2	0-0	0-2	

Stamford Bridge, London
18-09-2007, 19:45, 24 973, Duhamel FRA

Chelsea 1
Shevchenko 63

Petr Cech - Juliano Belletti, Alex, John Terry, Ashley Cole (Tal Ben Haim 74), Joe Cole (Shaun Wright-Phillips 74), Michael Essien●, Claude Makelele, Florent Malouda, Salomon Kalou, Andriy Shevchenko. Tr: Jose Mourinho

Rosenborg BK 1
Koppinen 24

Lars Hirschfeld - Roar Strand, Christer Basma (Bjorn Tore Kvarme 46), Miika Koppinen, Per Ciljan Skjelbred (Stefan Iversen), Marek Sapara (Konan Ya 69), Vidar Riseth, Alexander Tettey, Abdou Razack Traore, Yssouf Kone●. Tr: Knut Torum

Arena AufSchalke, Gelsenkirchen
18-09-2007, 20:45, 53 951, Wegereef NED

Schalke 04 0

Manuel Neuer - Rafinha (Carlos Grossmüller● 74), Heiko Westermann, Marcelo Bordon●, Christian Pander, Fabian Ernst, Ivan Rakitic, Jermaine Jones, Halil Altintop (Peter Lovenkrands 74), Gerald Asamoah (Mesut Ozil 61), Kevin Kuranyi. Tr: Oliver Reck

Valencia 1
Villa 63

Santiago Canizares - Miguel, Raul Albiol, Carlos Marchena●, Emiliano Moretti●, Miguel Angel Angulo (Joaquin 75), David Albelda●, Ivan Helguera, David Silva, David Villa (Sunny 90), Fernando Morientes (Javier Arizmendi 80). Tr: Quique Sanchez Flores

Mestalla, Valencia
3-10-2007, 20:45, 34 935, Rosetti ITA

Valencia 1
Villa 9

Timo Hildebrand - Miguel, Ivan Helguera, Raul Albiol, Emiliano Moretti, Joaquin (Angel Arizmendi 88), David Albelda (Ruben Baraja 75), Carlos Marchena●, David Silva, David Villa, Fernando Morientes (Nikola Zigic 69). Tr: Quique Sanchez Flores

Chelsea 2
Cole.J 21, Drogba 71

Petr Cech - Paulo Ferreira, Ricardo Carvalho, John Terry, Ashley Cole, Jon Obi Mikel● (Alex 89), Michael Essien (Steve Sidwell 84), Claude Makelele, Florent Malouda (Salomon Kalou 86), Joe Cole, Didier Drogba. Tr: Avram Grant

Lerkendal, Trondheim
3-10-2007, 20:45, 21 361, Gilewski POL

Rosenborg BK 0

Lars Hirschfeld - Roar Strand, Christer Basma, Miika Koppinen, Mikael Dorsin (Didier Ya Konan 79), Per Ciljan Skjelbred (Yssouf Kone 68), Marek Sapara●, Vidar Riseth●, Alexander Tettey, Abdou Razack Traore, Steffen Iversen. Tr: Knut Torum

Schalke 04 2
Jones 62, Kuranyi 89

Manuel Neuer● - Rafinha●, Heiko Westermann, Marcelo Bordon, Benedikt Howedes, Jermaine Jones● (Gustavo Varela 84), Fabian Ernst, Ivan Rakitic (Carlos Grossmüller 75), Zlatan Bajramovic, Kevin Kuranyi, Peter Lovenkrands (Gerald Asamoah 64). Tr: Mirko Slomka

Stamford Bridge, London
24-10-2007, 19:45, 40 910, Fröjdfeldt SWE

Chelsea 2
Malouda 4, Drogba 47

Petr Cech - Paulo Ferreira, Ricardo Carvalho, Alex, Wayne Bridge, Michael Essien (John Obi Mikel 70), Claude Makelele, Frank Lampard, Joe Cole (Andriy Shevchenko 89), Florent Malouda (Salomon Kalou 84), Didier Drogba. Tr: Avram Grant

Schalke 04 0

Manuel Neuer - Rafinha, Heiko Westermann, Marcelo Bordon, Dario Rodriguez ●(Zlatan Bajramovic 81), Jermaine Jones●, Fabian Ernst, Carlos Grossmüller (Mimoun Azaouagh 77), Gerald Asamoah (Ivan Rakitic 61), Peter Lovenkrands, Soren Larsen. Tr: Mirko Slomka

Lerkendal, Trondheim
24-10-2007, 20:45, 21 119, Thomson SCO

Rosenborg BK 2
Koné 53, Riseth 61

Lars Hirschfeld - Roar Strand● (Fredrik Stoor 86), Bjorn Tore Kvarme, Vidar Riseth, Mikael Dorsin, Marek Sapara, Alexander Tettey●, Per Ciljan Skjelbred, Steffen Iversen, Yssouf Kone (Oyvind Storflor 80), Abdou Razack Traore●. Tr: Knut Torum

Valencia 0

Santiago Canizares - Luis Miguel (Miguel Angel Angulo 78), Raul Albiol, Ivan Helguera, Emiliano Moretti, Joaquin, David Albelda, Carlos Marchena (Ruben Baraja 76), Jaime Gavilan (Nikola Zigic 67), Fernando Morientes, David Silva. Tr: Quique Sanchez Flores

Mestalla, Valencia
6-11-2007, 20:45, 29 725, Yefet ISR

Valencia 0

Timo Hildebrand - Miguel, Marco Caneira, Ivan Helguera, Emiliano Moretti (Miguel Angel Angulo● 63), Joaquin (Nikola Zigic 63), David Albelda, Manuel Fernandes, David Silva, David Villa, Fernando Morientes (Vicente 46). Tr: Ronald Koeman

Rosenborg 2
Iversen 2 31 58

Lars Hirschfeld - Fredrik Stoor, Bjorn Tore Kvarme, Vidar Riseth, Mikael Dorsin, Marek Sapara (Didier Konan Ya 84), Alexander Tettey, Per Ciljan Skjelbred (Oyvind Storflor 80), Steffen Iversen, Yssouf Kone, Abdou Razack Traore. Tr: Trond Henriksen

Arena AufSchalke, Gelsenkirchen
6-11-2007, 20:45, 53 951, Busacca SUI

Schalke 04 0

Manuel Neuer – Rafinha, Marcelo Bordon, Mladen Krstajic, Heiko Westermann, Jermaine Jones, Zlatan Bajramovic, Gerald Asamoah, Ivan Rakitic●, Mesut Ozil (Peter Lovenkrands 60), Soren Larsen. Tr: Mirko Slomka

Chelsea 0

Petr Cech (Carlo Cudicini 46) - Juliano Belletti (John Obi Mikel 64), Alex, Ricardo Carvalho, Wayne Bridge, Florent Malouda (Shaun Wright-Phillips 79), Frank Lampard, Claude Makelele, Michael Essien●, Joe Cole, Didier Drogba. Tr: Avram Grant

Lerkendal, Trondheim
28-11-2007, 20:45, 21 582, Benquerença POR

Rosenborg BK 0

Lars Hirschfeld - Fredrik Stoor, Bjorn Tore Kvarme, Vidar Riseth, Mikael Dorsin (Christer Basma 86), Alexander Tettey, Per Ciljan Skjelbred, Abdou Razack Traore (Roar Strand 56), Marek Sapara, Steffen Iversen, Yssouf Kone (Didier Konan Ya 63). Tr: Trond Henriksen

Chelsea 4
Drogba 2 8 20, Alex 40, Cole.J 73

Carlo Cudicini - Juliano Belletti, John Terry, Alex, Ashley Cole, Michael Essien, Claude Makelele, Frank Lampard (Claudio Pizarro 76), Shaun Wright-Phillips (Salomon Kalou 69), Joe Cole, Didier Drogba (Andriy Shevchenko 68). Tr: Avram Grant

Mestalla, Valencia
28-11-2007, 20:45, 29 232, De Bleeckere BEL

Valencia 0

Santiago Canizares - Miguel, Ivan Helguera, Carlos Marchena, Marco Caneira (Raul Albiol 42), Joaquin (David Silva 72), David Albelda●32, Edu, Joaquin, David Villa●, Fernando Morientes● (Manuel Fernandes 35). Tr: Ronald Koeman

Schalke 04 0

Manuel Neuer – Rafinha●, Marcelo Bordon, Mladen Krstajic, Heiko Westermann, Fabian Ernst, Jermaine Jones● (Zlatan Bajramovic 71), Ivan Rakitic (Carlos Grossmüller 65), Mesut Ozil●, Halil Altintop (Gerald Asamoah 80), Kevin Kuranyi. Tr: Mirko Slomka

Stamford Bridge, London
11-12-2007, 19:45, 41 139, Gilewski POL

Chelsea 0

Petr Cech - Paulo Ferreira (Juliano Belletti 71), John Terry, Tal Ben Haim, Wayne Bridge, Shaun Wright-Phillips, Michael Essien, Frank Lampard (Joe Cole 62), Salomon Kalou, Claudio Pizarro, Andriy Shevchenko (Claude Makelele 46). Tr: Avram Grant

Valencia 0

Santiago Canizares● - Miguel (Manuel Fernandes 65), Raul Albiol, Ivan Helguera, Emiliano Moretti, Sunny, Carlos Marchena, David Silva, David Villa (Javier Arizmendi 49), Fernando Morientes, Vicente (Juan Mata 75). Tr: Ronald Koeman

Arena AufSchalke, Gelsenkirchen
11-12-2007, 20:45, 53 951, Riley ENG

Schalke 04 3
Asamoah 12, Rafinha 19, Kuranyi 36

Manuel Neuer - Rafinha, Marcelo Bordon●, Dario Rodriguez, Heiko Westermann, Carlos Grossmueller, Fabian Ernst, Zlatan Bajramovic, Mesut Ozil (Levan Kobiashvili 86), Gerald Asamoah (Benedikt Hoewedes 92●), Kevin Kuranyi (Halil Altintop 88). Tr: Mirko Slomka

Rosenborg BK 1
Koné 23

Lars Hirschfeld - Fredrik Stoor, Bjorn Tore Kvarme, Vidar Riseth, Christer Basma, Marek Sapara●, Alexander Tettey, Per Ciljan Skjelbred, Roar Strand (Abdou Razack Traore 61), Steffen Iversen, Yssouf Kone (Didier Konan 77). Tr: Trond Henriksen

GROUP C

		Pl	W	D	L	F	A	Pts	ESP	GRE	GER	ITA
Real Madrid	ESP	6	3	2	1	13	9	11		4-2	2-1	3-1
Olympiacos	GRE	6	3	2	1	11	7	11	0-0		3-0	1-1
Werder Bremen	GER	6	2	0	4	8	13	6	3-2	1-3		2-1
Lazio	ITA	6	1	2	3	8	11	5	2-2	1-2	2-1	

Bernabéu, Madrid
18-09-2007, 20:45, 63 500, Webb ENG

Real Madrid 2
Raúl [16], Van Nistelrooij [74]

Iker Casillas - Marcelo, Fabio Cannavaro, Christoph Metzelder, Sergio Ramos, Wesley Sneijder, Fernando Gago, Guti (Royston Drenthe 77), Gonzalo Higuain (Robinho 69), Raul (Arjen Robben 84), Ruud van Nistelrooy•. Tr: Bernd Schuster

Werder Bremen 1
Sanogo [17]

Tim Wiese - Petri Pasanen, Per Mertesacker, Naldo, Dusko Tosic, Jurica Vranjes•, Diego•, Frank Baumann, Daniel Jensen, Boubacar Sanogo, Markus Rosenberg (Hugo Almeida 69). Tr: Thomas Schaaf

---

Karaiskakis, Piraeus
18-09-2007, 21:45, BCD, Braamhaar NED

Olympiacos 1
Galletti [55]

Antonis Nikopolidis - Christos Patsatzoglou• (Darko Kovacevic 78), Paraskevas Antzas, Michal Zewlakow, Didier Domi, Vassilis Torossidis, Luciano Galletti, Cristian Raul Ledesma, Predrag Djordjevic, Ieroklis Stoltidis, Lomana LuaLua. Tr: Panagiotis Lemonis

Lazio 1
Zauri [77]

Marco Ballotta - Lorenzo De Silvestri (Lionel Scaloni 81), Guglielmo Stendardo•, Emilson Cribari, Luciano Zauri•, Cristian Ledesma, Gaby Mudingayi, Christian Manfredini (Simone Del Nero 70), Stefano Mauri (Massimo Mutarelli• 59), Goran Pandev, Tommaso Rocchi. Tr: Delio Rossi

---

Olimpico, Rome
3-10-2007, 20:45, 52 400, De Bleeckere BEL

Lazio 2
Pandev 2 [32 75]

Marco Ballotta - Valon Behrami (Lionel Scaloni 67), Emilson Sanchez Cribari, Guglielmo Stendardo, Luciano Zauri, Gaby Mudingayi, Cristian Ledesma, Stefano Mauri (Simone Del Nero 79), Massimo Mutarelli, Goran Pandev, Tommaso Rocchi (Stephen Makinwa 66). Tr: Delio Rossi

Real Madrid 2
Van Nistelrooij 2 [8 61]

Iker Casillas - Gabriel Heinze•, Fabio Cannavaro, Sergio Ramos, Marcelo, Wesley Sneijder (Royston Drenthe 88), Mahamadou Diarra, Guti, Arjen Robben (Gonzalo Higuain 79), Raul (Javier Saviola 83), Ruud Van Nistelrooy. Tr: Bernd Schuster

---

Weserstadion, Bremen
3-10-2007, 20:45, 37 500, Larsen DEN

Werder Bremen 1
Hugo Almeida [32]

Christian Vander - Petri Pasanen, Per Mertesacker, Naldo, Dusko Tosic, Torsten Frings (Tim Borowski 63), Clemens Fritz, Daniel Jensen, Diego, Markus Rosenberg (Boubacar Sanogo• 75), Hugo Almeida. Tr: Thomas Schaaf

Olympiacos 3
Stoltidis [73], Patsatzoglou [82], Kovacevic [87]

Antonis Nikopolidis - Vassilis Torosidis, Paraskevas Antzas, Raul Bravo, Didier Domi (Julio Cesar 19), Christos Patsatzoglou, Cristian Ledesma•, Ieroklis Stoltidis (Anastasios Pantos 86), Luciano Galletti (Darko Kovacevic 72), Predrag Djordjevic, Lomana LuaLua. Tr: Panagiotis Lemonis

---

Weserstadion, Bremen
24-10-2007, 20:45, 36 587, Benquerença POR

Werder Bremen 2
Sanogo [28], Hugo Almeida [54]

Tim Wiese - Clemens Fritz, Per Mertesacker, Naldo, Petri Pasanen, Torsten Frings, Diego, Tim Borowski (Leon Andreasen 74), Boubacar Sanogo (Markus Rosenberg 64), Hugo Almeida. Tr: Thomas Schaaf

Lazio 1
Manfredini [82]

Marco Ballotta - Valon Behrami Guglielmo Stendardo, Luciano Zauri•, Aleksandar Kolarov, Gaby Mudingayi•, Mourad Meghni (Simone del Nero 51), Christian Manfredini, Massimo Mutarelli•, Goran Pandev• (Stephen Makinwa 69), Tommaso Rocchi (Igli Tare 82). Tr: Delio Rossi

---

Bernabéu, Madrid
24-10-2007, 20:45, 64 477, Ovrebø NOR

Real Madrid 4
Raúl [2], Robinho 2 [68 83], Balboa [93+]

Iker Casillas - Michel Salgado• (Gonzalo Higuain 64), Sergio Ramos, Christoph Metzelder, Marcelo, Wesley Sneijder (Javier Balboa 82), Fernando Gago, Guti, Robinho•, Raul (Miguel Torres 88), Ruud van Nistelrooy•78. Tr: Bernd Schuster

Olympiacos 2
Galletti [7], Júlio César [47]

Antonis Nikopolidis - Vassilis Torosidis•13, Paraskevas Antzas•, Julio Cesar, Raul Bravo (Michal Zewlakow 75), Luciano Galletti•, Christos Patsatzoglou•, Ieroklis Stoltidis, Cristian Raul Ledesma (Leonel Nunez 86), Predrag Djordjevic•, Lomana LuaLua (Darko Kovacevic 72). Tr: Panagiotis Lemonis

---

Olimpico, Rome
6-11-2007, 20:45, 28 236, Bebek CRO

Lazio 2
Rocchi 2 [57 68]

Marco Ballotta - Valon Behrami, Guglielmo Stendardo•, Emilson Sanchez Cribari• Lionel Zauri (Lorenzo De Silvestri• 18), Gaby Mudingayi, Cristian Ledesma, Massimo Mutarelli, Mourad Meghni (Christian Manfredini 74), Stephen Makinwa (Lionel Scaloni 88), Tommaso Rocchi•=56. Tr: Delio Rossi

Werder Bremen 1
Diego [88p]

Tim Wiese - Clemens Fritz (Martin Harnik 76), Per Mertesacker, Naldo, Petri Pasanen, Leon Andreasen•, Frank Baumann (Daniel Jensen 31), Tim Borowski, Diego•••95+, Markus Rosenberg, Hugo Almeida. Tr: Thomas Schaaf

---

Weserstadion, Bremen
28-11-2007, 20:45, 36 350, Vink NED

Werder Bremen 3
Rosenberg [5], Sanogo [40], Hunt [58]

Christian Vander - Clemens Fritz (Dusko Tosic 6), Per Mertesacker, Naldo, Petri Pasanen, Jurica Vranjes, Daniel Jensen, Frank Baumann, Aaron Hunt• (Martin Harnik 76), Markus Rosenberg, Boubacar Sanogo (Carlos Alberto 87). Tr: Thomas Schaaf

Real Madrid 2
Robinho [14], Van Nistelrooij [71]

Iker Casillas - Sergio Ramos•, Christoph Metzelder, Pepe•, Marcelo, Robinho (Arjen Robben 75), Mahamadou Diarra•, Fernando Gago (Gonzalo Higuain 61), Guti, Raul Gonzalez, Ruud van Nistelrooy. Tr: Bernd Schuster

---

Olimpico, Rome
28-11-2007, 20:45, 39 996, Webb ENG

Lazio 1
Pandev [30]

Marco Ballotta - Valon Behrami (Lionel Scaloni 77), Guglielmo Stendardo, Sebastiano Siviglia, Aleksandar Kolarov (Lorenzo De Silvestri 63), Gaby Mudingayi, Cristian Ledesma, Massimo Mutarelli (Mourad Meghni 71), Stefano Mauri, Goran Pandev, Tommaso Rocchi. Tr: Delio Rossi

Olympiacos 2
Galletti [35], Kovacevic [64]

Antonis Nikopolidis - Vassilis Torosidis•, Paraskevas Antzas, Michal Zewlakow, Anastasios Pantos, Cristian Ledesma•, Ieroklis Stoltidis, Christos Patsatzoglou (Konstantinos Mendrinos 75), Luciano Galletti, Predrag Djordjevic• (Konstantinos Mitroglou 90), Lomana LuaLua (Darko Kovacevic• 56). Tr: Panagiotis Lemonis

---

Bernabéu, Madrid
11-12-2007, 20:45, 70 559, Busacca SUI

Real Madrid 3
Baptista [13], Raúl [15], Robinho [36]

Iker Casillas - Sergio Ramos, Fabio Cannavaro, Pepe, Marcelo, Wesley Sneijder (Arjen Robben 46), Mahamadou Diarra, Julio Baptista, Robinho (Guti 46), Raul Gonzalez, Ruud van Nistelrooy (Gonzalo Higuain 73). Tr: Bernd Schuster

Lazio 1
Pandev [80]

Marco Ballotta - Lionel Scaloni, Sebastiano Siviglia, Cribari, Lorenzo De Silvestri, Gaby Mudingayi, Cristian Ledesma (Roberto Baronio 46), Massimo Mutarelli, Mourad Meghni (Christian Manfredini 63), Goran Pandev (Stephen Makinwa 82), Tommaso Rocchi•93+. Tr: Delio Rossi

---

Karaiskakis, Piraeus
11-12-2007, 21:45, 30 297, Duhamel FRA

Olympiacos 3
Stoltidis 2 [12 74], Kovacevic [70]

Antonis Nikopolidis - Anastasios Pantos, Paraskevas Antzas•, Michal Zewlakow, Vassilis Torosidis, Christos Patsatzoglou (Costas Mendrinos 24), Cristian Ledesma, Ieroklis Stoltidis, Luciano Galletti (Leonel Nunez 85), Darko Kovacevic (Costas Mitroglou• 82), Lomana LuaLua. Tr: Panagiotis Lemonis

Werder Bremen 0

Tim Wiese - Clemens Fritz, Frank Baumann (Dusko Tosic 82), Naldo, Petri Pasanen, Daniel Jensen•, Jurica Vranjes (Aaron Hunt 58), Tim Borowski, Diego, Boubacar Sanogo (Hugo Almeida 67), Markus Rosenberg•. Tr: Thomas Schaaf

GROUP D

		Pl	W	D	L	F	A	Pts	ITA	SCO	POR	UKR
Milan	ITA	6	4	1	1	12	5	13		1-0	2-1	4-1
Celtic	SCO	6	3	0	3	5	6	9	2-1		1-0	2-1
SL Benfica	POR	6	2	1	3	5	6	7	1-1	1-0		0-1
Shakhtar Donetsk	UKR	6	2	0	4	6	11	6	0-3	2-0	1-2	

San Siro, Milan
18-09-2007, 20:45, 38 358, Riley ENG

Milan — **2**

Pirlo [9], Inzaghi [24]

Dida - Massimo Oddo (Daniele Bonera 81), Alessandro Nesta, Kakha Kaladze, Marek Jankulovski, Gennaro Gattuso, Andrea Pirlo, Massimo Ambrosini, Clarence Seedorf (Emerson 75), Kaka, Filippo Inzaghi• (Alberto Gilardino 84). Tr: Carlo Ancelotti

SL Benfica — **1**

Nuno Gomes [92+]

Quim - Luis Filipe, Miguel Vitor (Augustin Binya 73), Edcarlos, Leo, Maxi Pereira, Konstantinos Katsouranis, Manuel Rui Costa (Nuno Assis 87), Angel Di Maria, Cristian Rodriguez, Oscar Cardozo• (Nuno Gomes 62). Tr: Jose Antonio Camacho

---

Estádio da Luz, Lisbon
3-10-2007, 19:45, 34 647, Stark GER

SL Benfica — **0**

Quim - Nelson (Nuno Gomes 45), Luisao, Edcarlos, Leo, Maxi Pereira, Konstantinos Katsouranis•, Manuel Rui Costa, Angel Di Maria (Augustin Binya 61), Cristian Rodriguez•, Oscar Cardozo•. Tr: Jose Antonio Camacho

Shakhtar Donetsk — **1**

Jadson [42]

Andriy Pyatov - Olexander Kucher, Darijo Srna•, Dmytro Chygrynskiy, Razvan Rat, Ilsinho (Igor Duljaj 79), Fernandinho•, Jadson (Nery Castillo• 77), Mariusz Lewandowski (Tomas Hubschman 87), Brandao, Cristiano Lucarelli. Tr: Mircea Lucescu

---

Celtic Park, Glasgow
6-11-2007, 19:45, 58 691, Hansson SWE

Celtic — **1**

McGeady [45]

Artur Boruc - Gary Caldwell, John Kennedy, Stephen McManus, Lee Naylor, Aiden McGeady, Paul Hartley, Scott Brown (Evander Sno 89), Jiri Jarosik (Massimo Donati 66), Jan Vennegoor of Hesselink (Chris Killen 66), Scott McDonald. Tr: Gordon Strachan

SL Benfica — **0**

Quim - Luis Filipe, EdCarlos, Luisao, Leo, Maxi Pereira• (Angel Di Maria 61), Konstantinos Katsouranis, Augustin Binya•85, Manuel Rui Costa (Gonzalo Bergessio 77), Cristian Rodriguez, Oscar Cardozo (Nuno Gomes 77). Tr: Jose Antonio Camacho

---

Celtic Park, Glasgow
28-11-2007, 19:45, 59 396, Layec FRA

Celtic — **2**

Jarosik [45], Donati [92+]

Artur Boruc - Gary Caldwell•, John Kennedy (Steven Pressley 42), Stephen McManus, Lee Naylor (Massimo Donati 16), Paul Hartley, Aiden McGeady, Scott Brown, Jiri Jarosik•, Jan Vennegoor of Hesselink• (Chris Killen 79), Scott McDonald. Tr: Gordon Strachan

Shakhtar Donetsk — **1**

Brandão [4]

Andriy Pyatov - Darijo Srna, Dmytro Chygrynskiy, Olexander Kucher, Razvan Rat, Tomas Hubschman, Ilsinho (Volodymyr Yezerskiy 83), Mariusz Lewandowski, Jadson, Cristiano Lucarelli (Olexandr Gladkiy 88), Brandao•. Tr: Mircea Lucescu

---

RSC Olympiyskiy, Donetsk
18-09-2007, 21:45, 25 700, Undiano ESP

Shakhter Donetsk — **2**

Brandão [6], Lucarelli [8]

Andriy Pyatov - Tomas Hubschman, Olexander Kucher, Ilsinho, Razvan Rat, Fernandinho (Igor Duljaj 86), Jadson (Nery Castillo 65), Mariusz Lewandowski, Darijo Srna•, Brandao, Cristiano Lucarelli (Olexander Gladkiy 72). Tr: Mircea Lucescu

Celtic — **0**

Artur Boruc - Lee Naylor, Gary Caldwell, Mark Wilson, Stephen McManus, Scott Brown•, Paul Hartley, Massimo Donati, Shunsuke Nakamura (Aiden McGeady 65) Jan Vennegoor of Hesselink (Maciej Zurawski 85), Scott McDonald (Chris Killen 68). Tr: Gordon Strachan

---

Estádio da Luz, Lisbon
24-10-2007, 19:45, 38 512, Busacca SUI

SL Benfica — **1**

Oscar Cardozo [87]

Quim — Luisao, Leo, Maxi Pereira, Konstantinos Katsouranis, Manuel Rui Costa, Nuno Assis (Angel Di Maria• 62), Cristian Rodriguez (Luis Filipe 84), Augustin Binya, Oscar Cardozo, Gonzalo Bergessio (Freddy Adu 62). Tr: Jose Antonio Camacho

Celtic — **0**

Artur Boruc - Gary Caldwell, John Kennedy, Stephen McManus, Lee Naylor, Jiri Jarosik, Scott Brown, Paul Hartley•, Massimo Donati (Evander Sno 65), Aiden McGeady•, Chris Killen• (Scott McDonald 74). Tr: Gordon Strachan

---

RSC Olympiyskiy, Donetsk
6-11-2007, 21:45, 25 700, Vink NED

Shakhter Donetsk — **0**

Andriy Pyatov - Darijo Srna, Volodymyr Yezerskiy, Dmytro Chygrynskiy, Razvan Rat (Willian 73), Ilsinho•, Tomas Hubschman, Fernandinho•, Jadson, Brandao (Olexandr Gladkiy 84), Cristiano Lucarelli (Nery Castillo 77). Tr: Mircea Lucescu

Milan — **3**

Inzaghi 2 [66 93+], Kaka [72]

Dida - Daniele Bonera, Kakha Kaladze, Alessandro Nesta, Serginho (Cristian Brocchi 85), Gennaro Gattuso•, Andrea Pirlo, Massimo Ambrosini•, Kaka•, Clarence Seedorf (Paolo Maldini 79), Alberto Gilardino (Filippo Inzaghi 62). Tr: Carlo Ancelotti

---

San Siro, Milan
4-12-2007, 20:45, 38 409, Ovrebø NOR

Milan — **1**

Inzaghi [70]

Zeljko Kalac - Cafu, Daniele Bonera, Dario Simic (Kakha Kaladze 30), Giuseppe Favalli, Gennaro Gattuso, Andrea Pirlo (Cristian Brocchi 74), Massimo Ambrosini, 10-Clarence Seedorf (Yoann Gourcuff 69), Filippo Inzaghi, Kaka. Tr: Carlo Ancelotti

Celtic — **0**

Artur Boruc - Gary Caldwell, Stephen McManus, Steven Pressley, Darren O'Dea, Paul Hartley, Jiri Jarosik (Maciej Zurawski 78), Aiden McGeady, Massimo Donati (Evander Sno 71), Scott Brown•, Scott McDonald (Jan Vennegoor of Hesselink 65). Tr: Gordon Strachan

---

Celtic Park, Glasgow
3-10-2007, 19:45, 58 462, Merk GER

Celtic — **2**

McManus [61], McDonald [89]

Artur Boruc - Jean-Joel Doumbe (John Kennedy 79), Stephen McManus, Gary Caldwell, Lee Naylor, Massimo Donati•, Scott Brown•, Paul Hartley, Jiri Jarosik (Chris Killen 84), Aiden McGeady (Shunsuke Nakamura 84), Scott McDonald•. Tr: Gordon Strachan

Milan — **1**

Kaká [68p]

Dida (Zeljko Kalac 90+4) - Massimo Oddo, Daniele Bonera, Alessandro Nesta•, Gennaro Gattuso, Andrea Pirlo, Massimo Ambrosini•, Kaka, Clarence Seedorf (Yoann Gourcuff 55), Filippo Inzaghi (Alberto Gilardino 77). Tr: Carlo Ancelotti

---

San Siro, Milan
24-10-207, 20:45, 36 850, M.Cantalejo ESP

Milan — **4**

Gilardino 2 [6 14], Seedorf 2 [62 69]

Zeljko Kalac - Massimo Oddo, Alessandro Nesta, Kakha Kaladze, Giuseppe Favalli (Daniele Bonera 61), Gennaro Gattuso•, Andrea Pirlo, Clarence Seedorf, Massimo Ambrosini• (Emerson 82), Kaka, Alberto Gilardino (Serginho 75). Tr: Carlo Ancelotti

Shakhtar Donetsk — **1**

Lucarelli [51]

Andriy Pyatov - Olexander Kucher (Tomas Hubschman 17), Dmytro Chygrynskiy, Razvan Rat, Ilsinho, Darijo Srna, Fernandinho•, Jadson (Nery Castillo 63), Mariusz Lewandowski, Brandao• (Olexandr Gladkiy 75), Cristiano Lucarelli•. Tr: Mircea Lucescu

---

Estádio da Luz, Lisbon
28-11-2007, 19:45, 46 034, Fandel GER

SL Benfica — **1**

Maxi Pereira [20]

Quim — Luis Filipe (Angel Di Maria 74), Luisao, David Luiz (Freddy Adu 88), Leo, Konstantinos Katsouranis, Armando Petit•, Maxi Pereira, Manuel Rui Costa, Cristian Rodriguez, Nuno Gomes (Oscar Cardozo 74). Tr: Jose Antonio Camacho

Milan — **1**

Pirlo [15]

Dida - Daniele Bonera, Kakha Kaladze•, Alessandro Nesta, Serginho• (Paolo Maldini 46), Gennaro Gattuso, Andrea Pirlo, Cristian Brocchi (Yoann Gourcuff 51), Clarence Seedorf (Massimo Oddo 73), Kaka, Alberto Gilardino. Tr: Carlo Ancelotti

---

RSC Olympiyskiy, Donetsk
4-12-2007, 21:45, 24 200, Vassaras GRE

Shakhter Donetsk — **1**

Lucarelli [30p]

Andriy Pyatov - Darijo Srna, Olexandr Kucher•, Dmytro Chygrynskiy, Razvan Rat, Ilsinho (Willian 67), Mariusz Lewandowski (Tomas Hubschman 57), Fernandinho, Jadson, Brandao• (Cristiano Lucarelli (Olexandr Gladkiy 74). Tr: Mircea Lucescu

SL Benfica — **2**

Oscar Cardozo 2 [6 22]

Quim — Nelson, Luisao, David Luiz•, Leo, Konstantinos Katsouranis, Armando Petit, Maxi Pereira (Luis Filipe• 83), Manuel Rui Costa, Angel Di Maria (Nuno Assis 62), Oscar Cardozo (Nuno Gomes 90). Tr: Jose Antonio Camacho

GROUP E

		Pl	W	D	L	F	A	Pts	ESP	FRA	SCO	GER
Barcelona	ESP	6	4	2	0	12	3	14		3-0	2-0	3-1
Olympique Lyonnais	FRA	6	3	1	2	11	10	10	2-2		0-3	4-2
Rangers	SCO	6	2	1	3	7	9	7	0-0	0-3		2-1
VfB Stuttgart	GER	6	1	0	5	7	15	3	0-2	0-2	3-2	

Ibrox, Glasgow
19-09-2007, 19:45, 49 795, Farina ITA

Rangers 2
Adam [62], Darcheville [75p]

Allan McGregor - Alan Hutton•, Carlos Cuellar, David Weir, Sasa Papac, Brahim Hemdani, Steven Whittaker (Amdy Faye• 86), Barry Ferguson, Charlie Adam (DaMarcus Beasley 67), Kevin Thomson•, Jean-Claude Darcheville (Nacho Novo 83). Tr: Walter Smith

VfB Stuttgart 1
Gómez [56]

Raphael Schafer - Ricardo Osorio, Vardar Tasci, Fernando Meira•, Arthur Boka, Pavel Pardo•, Roberto Hilbert, Sami Khedira (Yildiray Basturk 78), Antonio Da Silva (Ewerthon 70), Cacau, Mario Gomez. Tr: Armin Veh

---

Camp Nou, Barcelona
19-09-2007, 20:45, 78 698, Busacca SUI

Barcelona 3
Clerc OG [21], Messi [82], Henry [91+]

Victor Valdes - Gianluca Zambrotta, Rafael Marquez, Gabriel Milito, Eric Abidal, Gnegneri Yaya Toure•, Xavi Hernandez (Giovani dos Santos 78), Deco, Thierry Henry•, Ronaldinho (Andres Iniesta 66), Lionel Messi (Bojan Krkic 88). Tr: Frank Rijkaard

Olympique Lyonnais 0

Remy Vercoutre - Francois Clerc, Sebastien Squillaci, Mathieu Bodmer, Fabio Grosso, Nadir Belhadj (Milan Baros 62), Kim Kallstrom (Kader Keita 83), Juninho, Sidney Govou, Karim Benzema (Hatem Ben Arfa 76). Tr: Alain Perrin

---

Stade de Gerland, Lyon
2-10-2007, 20:45, 38 076, Ovrebø NOR

Olympique Lyonnais 0

Remy Vercoutre - Anthony Reveillere• (Francois Clerc 81), Sebastien Squillaci•, Cleber Anderson, Fabio Grosso, Mathieu Bodmer (Hatem Ben Arfa 60), Juninho, Kim Kallstrom, Sidney Govou, Milan Baros (Abdulkader Keita 60), Karim Benzema. Tr: Alain Perrin

Rangers 3
McCulloch [23], Cousin [48], Beasley [53]

Allan McGregor - Alan Hutton, Carlos Cuellar, David Weir, Sasa Papac, DaMarcus Beasley (Charlie Adam 90), Barry Ferguson•, Kevin Thomson•, Lee McCulloch (Nacho Novo 80), Daniel Cousin (Steven Whittaker 66). Tr: Walter Smith

---

Gottlieb-Daimler, Stuttgart
2-10-2007, 20:45, 49 725, Hansson SWE

VfB Stuttgart 0

Raphael Schafer - Ricardo Osorio (Ciprian Marica 63), Serdar Tasci, Fernando Meira, Arthur Boka, Roberto Hilbert, Pavel Pardo, Alexander Farnerud (Ludovic Magnin 76), Sami Khedira (Silvio Meissner 76), Cacau, Mario Gomez. Tr: Armin Veh

Barcelona 2
Puyol [53], Messi [67]

Victor Valdes - Oleguer, Lilian Thuram, Rafael Marquez (Carles Puyol 7) (Sylvinho 64), Eric Abidal, Xavi Hernandez, Andres Iniesta, Deco, Lionel Messi•, Thierry Henry, Ronaldinho (Bojan Krkic 82). Tr: Frank Rijkaard

---

Ibrox, Glasgow
23-10-2007, 19:45, 49 957, Plautz AUT

Rangers 0

Allan McGregor - Alan Hutton, Carlos Cuellar, David Weir•, Sasa Papac•, Nacho Novo (DaMarcus Beasley 72), Charlie Adam, Barry Ferguson, Kevin Thomson•, Lee McCulloch, Daniel Cousin. Tr: Walter Smith

Barcelona 0

Victor Valdes - Lilian Thuram, Gabriel Milito•, Carles Puyol, Eric Abidal•, Xavi Hernandez, Andres Iniesta, Eidur Gudjohnsen, Lionel Messi, Thierry Henry (Giovani dos Santos 82), Ronaldinho. Tr: Frank Rijkaard

---

Gottlieb-Daimler, Stuttgart
23-10-2007, 20:45, 51 000, Batista POR

VfB Stuttgart 0

Raphael Schafer - Roberto Hilbert•, Serdar Tasci, Fernando Meira, Ricardo Osorio, Silvio Meissner (Sami Khedira• 63), Yildiray Basturk (Ewerthon 71), Pavel Pardo, Alexander Farnerud, Mario Gomez, Cacau•. Tr: Armin Veh

Olympique Lyonnais 2
Fábio Santos [56], Benzema [79]

Remy Vercoutre• - Anthony Reveillere, Sebastien Squillaci, Cleber Anderson, Fabio Grosso, Juninho, Fabio Santos, Kim Kallstrom•, Sidney Govou (Francois Clerc 86), Karim Benzema (Mathieu Bodmer 84), Hatem Ben Arfa (Abdul Kader Keita 74). Tr: Alain Perrin

---

Stade de Gerland, Lyon
7-11-2007, 20:45, 38 215, Baskakov RUS

Olympique Lyonnais 4
Ben Arfa 2 [6 37], Kållström [15], Juninho [93+]

Remy Vercoutre - Fabio Grosso•, Cleber Anderson, Sebastien Squillaci, Anthony Reveillere•, Kim Kallstrom, Fabio Santos, Juninho, Hatem Ben Arfa (Abdulkader Keita• 70), Sidney Govou• (Francois Clerc 92+), Karim Benzema (Nadhir Belhadj 82). Tr: Alain Perrin

VfB Stuttgart 2
Gómez 2 [16 56]

Raphael Schafer - Andreas Beck (Ricardo Osorio 77), Vardar Tasci•, Ludovic Magnin (Alexander Farnerud 81), Mathieu Delpierre, Thomas Hitzlsperger•60, Yildiray Basturk•, Sami Khedira, Fernando Meira, Mario Gomez, Cacau (Ciprian Marica 58). Tr: Armin Veh

---

Camp Nou, Barcelona
7-11-2007, 20:45, 82 887, Braamhaar NED

Barcelona 2
Henry [6], Messi [43]

Victor Valdes - Carles Puyol (Oleguer 85), Lilian Thuram, Gabriel Milito, Eric Abidal, Xavi Hernandez, Yaya Toure, Andres Iniesta (Eidur Gudjohnsen 70), Lionel Messi, Ronaldinho (Bojan Krkic 77), Thierry Henry. Tr: Frank Rijkaard

Rangers 0

Allan McGregor - Alan Hutton, Carlos Cuellar, David Weir, Sasa Papac, Barry Ferguson, Brahim Hemdani, Lee McCulloch, Charles Adam (Jean-Claude Darcheville 62), DaMarcus Beasley (Nacho Novo 69), Daniel Cousin (Steven Naysmith 78). Tr: Walter Smith

---

Gottlieb-Daimler, Stuttgart
27-11-2007, 20:45, 51 000, Ceferin SVN

VfB Stuttgart 2
Cacau [45], Pardo [62], Marica [85]

Raphael Schafer - Andreas Beck, Fernando Meira, Matthieu Delpierre, Ludovic Magnin•, Pavel Pardo, Roberto Hilbert (Ewerthon 83), Thomas Hitzlsperger, Sami Khedira (Antonio da Silva 46), Ciprian Marica, Cacau (Serdar Tasci 87). Tr: Armin Veh

Rangers 2
Adam [27], Ferguson [70]

Allan McGregor - Alan Hutton•, Carlos Cuellar, David Weir, Sasa Papac, Brahim Hemdani, DaMarcus Beasley (Steven Naismith 49), Barry Ferguson, Kevin Thomson, Lee McCulloch• (Charlie Adam• 26), Jean-Claude Darcheville (Daniel Cousin 82). Tr: Walter Smith

---

Stade de Gerland, Lyon
27-11-2007, 20:45, 36 500, Farina ITA

Olympique Lyonnais 2
Juninho 2 [7 80p]

Remy Vercoutre - Anthony Reveillere, Sebastien Squillaci, Cleber Anderson, Fabio Grosso, Jeremy Toulalan, Fabio Santos• (Kim Kallstrom 68), Juninho•, Sidney Govou, Fred (Abdelkader Keita 60), Hatem Ben Arfa (Loic Remy 82). Tr: Alain Perrin

Barcelona 2
Iniesta [3], Messi [58p]

Victor Valdes - Gianluca Zambrotta (Rafael Marquez 82), Carles Puyol•, Gabriel Milito, Eric Abidal, Yaya Toure•, Xavi Hernandez•, Andres Iniesta, Lionel Messi•, Bojan Krkic, Eidur Gudjohnsen (Ronaldinho 71). Tr: Frank Rijkaard

---

Ibrox, Glasgow
12-12-2007, 19:45, 50 260, Michel SVK

Rangers 0

Allan McGregor - Alan Hutton•, Carlos Cuellar•, David Weir, Sasa Papac (Jean-Claude Darcheville 71••90), Steven Whittaker, Barry Ferguson, Brahim Hemdani (Kris Boyd 84), Kevin Thomson•, Lee McCulloch, Daniel Cousin (Steven Naismith 46). Tr: Walter Smith

Olympique Lyonnais 3
Govou [16], Benzema 2 [85 88]

•Remy Vercoutre - Francois Clerc, Anderson, Sebastien Squillaci, Fabio Grosso, Kim Kallstrom, Juninho (Milan Baros 85), Jeremy Toulalan, Sidney Govou• (Anthony Reveillere 77), Karim Benzema, Hatem Ben Arfa (Mathieu Bodmer 68). Tr: Alain Perrin

---

Camp Nou, Barcelona
12-12-2007, 20:45, 52 761, Lannoy FRA

Barcelona 3
Giovani [36], Eto'o [57], Ronaldinho [67]

Albert Jorquera - Carles Puyol, Lilian Thuram, Gabriel Milito, Silvinho, Rafael Marquez, Eidur Gudjohnsen (Bojan Krkic 52), Xavi Hernandez (Marc Crosas 69), Giovani dos Santos, Ronaldinho, Samuel Eto'o (Andres Iniesta 62). Tr: Johan Neeskens

VfB Stuttgart 1
Antonio [3]

Raphael Schafer• - Ricardo Osorio, Serdar Tasci, Matthieu Delpierre, Arthur Boka, Fernando Meira•, Yildiray Basturk (Silvio Meissner 72), Antonio da Silva, Ewerthon, Ciprian Marica (Manuel Fischer 72), Alexander Farnerud (Roberto Hilbert 58). Tr: Armin Veh

GROUP F

		Pl	W	D	L	F	A	Pts		ENG	ITA	POR	UKR
Manchester United	ENG	6	5	1	0	13	4	16			1-0	2-1	4-0
Roma	ITA	6	3	2	1	11	6	11		1-1		2-1	2-0
Sporting CP	POR	6	2	1	3	9	8	7		0-1	2-2		3-0
Dynamo Kyiv	UKR	6	0	0	6	4	19	0		2-4	1-4	1-2	

José Alvalade, Lisbon
19-09-2007, 19:45, 41 510, Fandel GER

Sporting CP 0

Vladimir Stojkovic - Abel, Tonel, Anderson Polga, Ronny (Pereirinha 74), Miguel Veloso, Marat Izmailov (Simon Vukcevic 56), Joao Moutinho, Leandro Romagnoli (Milan Purovic 68), Yannick Djalo, Liedson. Tr: Paulo Bento

Manchester United 1

Ronaldo 62

Edwin van der Sar - Wes Brown, Rio Ferdinand, Nemanja Vidic, Patrice Evra, Michael Carrick, Paul Scholes, Nani, Ryan Giggs (Anderson 76), Cristiano Ronaldo (Carlos Tevez 87), Wayne Rooney (Louis Saha 72). Tr: Alex Ferguson

---

Valery Lobanovskiy, Kyiv
2-10-2007, 21:45, 37 600, Layec FRA

Dynamo Kyiv 1

Vaschuk 28

Olexandr Shovkovsky - Vladyslav Vaschuk, Tiberiu Ghioane (Oleg Gusev 56), Taras Mikhalik●, Goran Gavrancic, Badr El Kaddouri, Ayila Yussuf, Carlos Correa●, Diogo Rincon, Maksim Shatskikh, Artem Milevskiy (Kleber● 58). Tr: Jozsef Szabo

Sporting CP 2

Tonel 14, Polga 38

Vladimir Stojkovic - Abel, Tonel, Anderson Polga●, Ronny, Miguel Veloso, Simon Vukcevic● (Marat Izmailov 68), Joao Moutinho, Leandro Romagnoli (Carlos Paredes 77), Yannick Djalo (Gladstone 90+2), Liedson. Tr: Paulo Bento

---

Old Trafford, Manchester
7-11-2007, 19:45, 75 017, Wegereef NED

Manchester United 4

Piqué 31, Tévez 37, Rooney 76, Ronaldo 88

Edwin van der Sar (Tomasz Kuszczak 80) - Daniel Simpson, Nemanja Vidic, Gerard Pique (Johnny Evans 73), Patrice Evra, Cristiano Ronaldo, Michael Carrick, Darren Fletcher, Nani, Wayne Rooney●, Carlos Tevez (Louis Saha 68). Tr: Alex Ferguson

Dynamo Kyiv 0

Olexandr Shovkovsky - Marjan Markovic, Pape Diakhate●, Serhiy Fedorov, Badr El Kaddouri, Vladyslav Vaschuk, Carlos Correa●, Tiberiu Ghioane, Oleg Gusev (Diogo Rincon 46), Ruslan Rotan (Serhiy Rebrov 46), Artem Milevskiy (Ismael Bangoura 76). Tr: Oleh Luzhny

---

Valery Lobanovskiy, Kyiv
27-11-2007, 21:45, 19 700, Stark GER

Dynamo Kyiv 1

Bangoura 63

Olexandr Rybka - Oleh Dopilka, Goran Gavrancic, Vladyslav Vaschuk●, Andriy Nesmachniy, Tiberiu Ghioane, Oleg Gusev, Milos Ninkovic (Maksim Shatskikh 55), Ruslan Rotan (Valentin Belkevich 46), Diogo Rincon (Artem Milevskiy 69), Ismael Bangoura. Tr: Oleh Luzhny

Roma 4

Panucci 4, Giuly 32, Vucinic 2 36 78

Doni - Christian Panucci, Juan, Matteo Ferrari, Max Tonetto, David Pizarro, Daniele De Rossi (Ahmed Barusso 46), Rodrigo Taddei (Mauro Esposito 46), Ludovic Giuly, Marco Cassetti●, Mirko Vucinic (Cicinho 84). Tr: Luciano Spalletti

---

Olimpico, Rome
19-09-2007, 20:45, 35 508, Hamer LUX

Roma 2

Perrotta 9, Totti 70

Doni - Marco Cassetti, Philippe Mexes, Juan (Matteo Ferrari 82), Max Tonetto●, Rodrigo Taddei, Daniele De Rossi, Simone Perrotta, Alberto Aquilani (David Pizarro 83), Mancini (Ludovic Giuly 61), Francesco Totti. Tr: Luciano Spalletti

Dynamo Kyiv 0

Olexandr Shovkovsky - Marjan Markovic, Serhiy Fedorov, Goran Gavrancic, Badr El Kaddouri, Oleh Gusev (Carlos Correa 71), Taras Mikhalik, Ayila Yussuf● (Diogo Rincon 46), Michael (Serhiy Rebrov 56), Ismael Bangoura (Diogo Rincon 46), Maksim Shatskikh. Tr: Anatoliy Demyanenko

---

Olimpico, Rome
23-10-2007, 20:45, 26 893, Hauge NOR

Roma 2

Juan 15, Vucinic 70

Doni - Christian Panucci, Philippe Mexes, Juan●, Max Tonetto, Marco Cassetti●, Daniele De Rossi, David Pizarro, Alessandro Mancini●48 (Cicinho 87), Ludovic Giuly (Matteo Brighi 73), Francesco Totti (Mirko Vucinic● 35). Tr: Luciano Spalletti

Sporting CP 1

Liedson 18

Tiago - Abel, Tonel●, Miguel Veloso, Ronny (Milan Purovic 77), Marat Izmailov (Celsinho 81), Joao Moutinho●, Simon Vukcevic (Carlos Paredes 71), Leandro Romagnoli, Liedson, Yannick Djalo. Tr: Paulo Bento

---

José Alvalade, Lisbon
7-11-2007, 19:45, 32 273, De Bleeckere BEL

Sporting CP 2

Liedson 2 22 64

Tiago - Abel●, Tonel, Anderson Polga, Ronny, Marat Izmailov (Pereirinha 89), Miguel Veloso●, Leandro Romagnoli, Joao Moutinho, Liedson, Yannick Djalo (Simon Vukcevic 63). Tr: Paulo Bento

Roma 2

Cassetti 4, Polga OG 90

Doni - Cicinho●, Philippe Mexes (Matteo Ferrari 46), Juan, Ludovic Giuly (Matteo Brighi 91+), Marco Cassetti●, Daniele De Rossi, Simone Perrotta● (Mauro Esposito 80), David Pizarro, Mancini, Mirko Vucinic●. Tr: Luciano Spalletti

---

José Alvalade, Lisbon
12-12-2007, 19:45, 19 402, Dougal SCO

Sporting CP 3

Polga 35p, João Moutinho 67, Liedson 88

Rui Patricio - Abel, Anderson Polga, Tonel, Ronny (Miguel Veloso 61), Pontus Farnerud (Simon Vukcevic 68), Joao Moutinho, Adrien Silva, Marat Izmailov, Liedson, Milan Purovic (Luis Paez 86). Tr: Paulo Bento

Dynamo Kyiv 0

Taras Lutsenko - Marjan Markovic, Oleh Dopilka, Goran Gavrancic, Andriy Nesmachniy, Tiberiu Ghioane, Oleg Gusev, Serhiy Rebrov (Valentin Belkevich 81), Maksim Shatskikh, Milos Ninkovic, Ismael Bangoura (Artem Kravets 56). Tr: Oleh Luzhny

---

Old Trafford, Manchester
2-10-2007, 19:45, 73 652, M.Gonzalez ESP

Manchester United 1

Rooney 70

Tomasz Kuszczak - John O'Shea, Nemanja Vidic, Rio Ferdinand, Patrice Evra, Cristiano Ronaldo, Michael Carrick, Paul Scholes, Nani (Ryan Giggs 80), Louis Saha (Carlos Tevez 66), Wayne Rooney (Anderson 85). Tr: Alex Ferguson

Roma 0

Gianluca Curci - Cicinho, Juan, Philippe Mexes●, Max Tonetto, Marco Cassetti●, Daniele De Rossi, David Pizarro 62), Ludovic Giuly (Mauro Esposito 80), Simone Perrotta, Mancini (Mirko Vucinic 74), Francesco Totti. Tr: Luciano Spalletti

---

Valery Lobanovskiy, Kyiv
23-10-2007, 21:45, 42 000, Kassai HUN

Dynamo Kyiv 2

Diogo Rincon 34, Bangoura 78

Olexandr Shovkovsky - Tiberiu Ghioane (Valentin Belkevich 46), Pape Diakhate●, Goran Gavrancic, Andriy Nesmachniy, Carlos Correa (Ruslan Rotan 83), Oleg Gusev, Ayila Yussuf, Ismael Bangoura, Diogo Rincon, Maksim Shatskikh (Artem Milevskiy 46). Tr: Jozsef Szabo

Manchester United 4

Ferdinand 10, Rooney 18, Ronaldo 2 41 68p

Edwin van der Sar (Tomasz Kuszczak 80) - Wes Brown, Rio Ferdinand, Nemanja Vidic, Patrice Evra, Cristiano Ronaldo, Anderson, John O'Shea, Ryan Giggs (Daniel Simpson 81), Wayne Rooney, Carlos Tevez (Nani 73). Tr: Alex Ferguson

---

Old Trafford, Manchester
27-11-2007, 19:45, 74 162, Larsen DEN

Manchester United 4

Teevez 61, Ronaldo 92+

Tomasz Kuszczak - John O'Shea, Nemanja Vidic, Rio Ferdinand, Patrice Evra●, Cristiano Ronaldo, Michael Carrick, Darren Fletcher (Carlos Tevez 46), Anderson, Nani (Ryan Giggs 46), Louis Saha (Owen Hargreaves 79). Tr: Alex Ferguson

Sporting CP 1

Abel 21

Rui Patricio - Abel, Anderson Polga●, Marian Had●, Tonel, Marat Izmailov (Bruno Pereirinha 82), Miguel Veloso, Leandro Romagnoli (Simon Vukcevic 68), Joao Moutinho, Liedson, Milan Purovic (Pontus Farnerud 82). Tr: Paulo Bento

---

Olimpico, Rome
12-12-2007, 20:45, 29 490, Hansson SWE

Roma 1

Mancini 71

Doni - Cicinho, Matteo Ferrari, Philippe Mexes, Ahmed Barusso● (Ludovic Giuly 62), Mauro Esposito (Mirko Vucinic 62), Antunes, David Pizarro, Rodrigo Taddei (Daniele De Rossi 46), Mancini, Francesco Totti. Tr: Luciano Spalletti

Manchester United 1

Piqué 34

Tomasz Kuszczak - Daniel Simpson, Gerard Pique, Johnny Evans, John O'Shea (Wes Brown 54), Chris Eagles, Darren Fletcher, Michael Carrick, Nani, Louis Saha, Wayne Rooney (Dong Fangzhuo 72)

GROUP G

		Pl	W	D	L	F	A	Pts	ITA	TUR	NED	RUS
Internazionale	ITA	6	5	0	1	12	4	15		3-0	2-0	4-2
Fenerbahçe	TUR	6	3	2	1	8	6	11	1-0		2-0	3-1
PSV Eindhoven	NED	6	2	1	3	3	6	7	0-1	0-0		2-1
CSKA Moskva	RUS	6	0	1	5	7	14	1	1-2	2-2	0-1	

Philips Stadion, Eindhoven
19-09-2007, 20:45, 30 000, Proença POR
PSV Eindhoven 2
Lazovic 59, Perez 80
Heurelho Gomes - Carlos Salcido, Manuel da Costa, Eric Addo, Alcides, Jason Culina, Timmy Simons, Ibrahim Afellay (Kenneth Perez 28), Edison Mendez (Jan Kromkamp 71), Danny Koevermans (Jefferson Farfan 75), Danko Lazovic. Tr: Ronald Koeman
CSKA Moskva 1
Vágner Love 89
Veniamin Mandrykin - Deividas Semberas, Sergei Ignashevich, Aleksei Berezutski, Vasili Berezutski, Yuri Zhirkov, Dudu•, Milos Krasic, Elvir Rahimic• (Eduardo 78), Jo, Vagner Love. Tr: Valery Gazzaev

---

Sükrü Saraçoglu, Istanbul
19-09-2007, 21:45, 44 212, M.Cantalejo ESP
Fenerbahçe 1
Deivid 43
Volkan Demirel - Onder Turaci•, Diego Lugano•, Edu, Roberto Carlos, Deniz Baris, Alex, Mehmet Aurelio, Gokcek Vederson, Mateja Kezman (Semih Senturk 67), Deivid•. Tr: Zico
Internazionale 0
Julio Cesar - Javier Zanetti, Enrique Lopez, Walter Samuel•, Andrade Maxwell, Dejan Stankovic, Olivier Dacourt (Luis Antonio Jimenez• 70), Esteban Cambiasso, Santiago Solari (Luis Figo 58), David Suazo (Hernan Crespo 72), Zlatan Ibrahimovic. Tr: Roberto Mancini

---

Lokomotiv, Moscow
2-10-2007, 20:30, 25 000, Kircher GER
CSKA Moskva 2
Krasic 50, Vágner Love 53p
Veniamin Mandrykin - Vasily Berezutsky, Sergei Ignashevich, Alexei Berezutsky, Deividas Semberas, Elvir Rahimic, Milos Krasic•, Dudu (Yevgeny Aldonin 90), Yuri Zhirkov•, Vagner Love, Jo. Tr: Valery Gazzaev
Fenerbahçe 2
Alex 9, Deivid 85
Volkan Demirel - Onder Turaci, Diego Lugano• (Gokhan Gonul), Edu• (Yasin Cakmak 71), Roberto Carlos, Alex, Mehmet Aurelio, Deniz Baris (Colin Kazim-Richards 71), Gokcek Vederson, Mateja Kezman, Deivid. Tr: Zico

---

San Siro, Milan
2-10-2007, 20:45, 34 238, Vassaras GRE
Internazionale 2
Ibrahimovic 2 15p 31
Julio Cesar - Javier Zanetti, Cristian Chivu••65, Walter Samuel•, Maxwell, Luis Figo, Esteban Cambiasso, Dejan Stankovic, Santiago Solari (Francesco Bolzoni 70), Hernan Crespo (David Suazo 61•93+), Zlatan Ibrahimovic. Tr: Roberto Mancini
PSV Eindhoven 0
Heurelho Gomes - Jan Kromkamp (Otman Bakkal 69), Eric Addo, Alcides, Carlos Salcido, Edison Mendez (Danny Koevermans 56), Kenneth Perez, Jason Culina•, Timmy Simons, Jefferson Farfan (Ismail Aissati 75), Danko Lazovic•. Tr: Ronald Koeman

---

Lokomotiv, Moscow
23-10-2007, 20:30, 24 000, Riley ENG
CSKA Moskva 1
Jô 32
Veniamin Mandrykin - Vasily Berezutsky, Sergei Ignashevich, Alexei Berezutsky (Anton Grigoryev 45), Yevgeny Aldonin, Elvir Rahimic, Milos Krasic, Dudu (Eduardo 42; Dawid Janczyk 76), Yuri Zhirkov, Daniel Carvalho, Jo. Tr: Valeri Gazzaev
Internazionale 2
Crespo 52, Samuel 80
Julio Cesar - Javier Zanetti, Ivan Cordoba, Walter Samuel, Maxwell, Luis Figo•, Patrick Vieira (Dejan Stankovic 17), Olivier Dacourt (Santiago Solari• 77), Esteban Cambiasso, Zlatan Ibrahimovic•, Hernan Crespo (Julio Cruz 62). Tr: Roberto Mancini

---

Philips Stadion, Eindhoven
23-10-2007, 20:45, 35 000, Webb ENG
PSV Eindhoven 0
Heurelho Gomes - Jan Kromkamp, Eric Addo (Mike Zonneveld 58), Dirk Marcellis•, Carlos Salcido, Kenneth Perez, Timmy Simons, Edison Mendez (Danny Koevermans 58), Otman Bakkal (Ismail Aissati 78), Jefferson Farfan•, Danko Lazovic. Tr: Ronald Koeman
Fenerbahçe 0
Volkan Demirel - Gokhan Gonul, Diego Lugano•, Edu, Roberto Carlos, Deniz Baris•, Alex (Ali Bilgin 35), Mehmet Aurelio•, Gokcek Vederson, Deivid•64, Semih Senturk (Colin Kazim-Richards 72). Tr: Zico

---

San Siro, Milan
7-11-2007, 20:45, 17 495, Allaerts BEL
Internazionale 4
Ibrahimovic 2 32 75, Cambiasso 2 34 67
Julio Cesar - Javier Zanetti, Maicon, Ivan Cordoba, Walter Samuel, Cristian Chivu, Javier Zanetti, Olivier Dacourt•, Esteban Cambiasso, Maxwell (Santiago Solari 66), Zlatan Ibrahimovic (David Suazo 84), Hernan Crespo (Julio Cruz 63). Tr: Roberto Mancini
CSKA Moskva 2
Jô 23, Vágner Love 31
Igor Akinfeev - Anton Grigoryev, Vasily Berezutsky (Eduardo 70), Alexei Berezutsky, Elvir Rahimic•, Milos Krasic, Dudu• (Ivan Taranov 83), Yuri Zhirkov•, Daniel Carvalho, Jo (Evgeni Aldonin 46), Vagner Love. Tr: Valeri Gazzaev

---

Lokomotiv, Moscow
27-11-2007, 20:30, 12 418, M.Gonzalez ESP
CSKA Moskva 0
Igor Akinfeev - Vasily Berezutsky, Sergei Ignashevich, Alexei Berezutsky•, Anton Grigoryev 86), Deividas Semberas, Yevgeny Aldonin, Dudu• (Chidi Odiah 73), Yuri Zhirkov, Ramon (Caner 61), Dawid Janczyk. Tr: Valeri Gazzaev
PSV Eindhoven 1
Farfán 39
Heurelho Gomes - Dirk Marcellis•, Carlos Salcido, Alcides, Mike Zonneveld, Edison Mendez•, Slobodan Rajkovic, Otman Bakkal (Jason Culina 77), Ibrahim Afellay, Jefferson Farfan (Danny Koevermans 81), Danko Lazovic (Kenneth Perez 84). Tr: Jan Wouters

---

San Siro, Milan
27-11-2007, 20:45, 24 736, Plautz AUT
Internazionale 3
Cruz 55, Ibrahimovic 66, Jiménez 92+
Julio Cesar - Maicon Douglas, Ivan Cordoba, Walter Samuel•, Maxwell (Luis Jimenez 73), Javier Zanetti, Cristian Chivu, Dejan Stankovic (Marco Materazzi 89), Esteban Cambiasso, Zlatan Ibrahimovic• (David Suazo 78), Julio Cruz. Tr: Roberto Mancini
Fenerbahçe 0
Volkan Demirel - Gokhan Gonul•, Diego Lugano•, Edu, Roberto Carlos, Selcuk Sahin, Alex, Mehmet Aurelio (Stephen Appiah 63), Gokcek Vederson, Deivid (Tumer Metin 83), Semih Senturk (Colin Kazim-Richards 67). Tr: Zico

---

Philips Stadion, Eindhoven
12-12-2007, 20:45, 35 000, Merk GER
PSV Eindhoven 0
Heurelho Gomes - Dirk Marcellis, Carlos Salcido, Alcides, Mike Zonneveld, Edison Mendez•28, Timmy Simons, Ibrahim Afellay (Ismail Aissati 64), Jason Culina, Jefferson Farfan (Kenneth Perez 62), Danko Lazovic (Jonathan 84). Tr: Jan Wouters
Internazionale 1
Cruz 64
Julio Cesar - Ivan Cordoba, Marco Materazzi, Rivas Lopez, Maxwell (Javier Zanetti 86), Santiago Solari, Francesco Bolzoni, Cristian Chivu (Esteban Cambiasso 68), David Suazo, Hernan Crespo, Julio Cruz (Gabriele Puccio 75). Tr: Roberto Mancini

---

Sükrü Saraçoglu, Istanbul
12-12-2007, 21:45, 45 745, Trefoloni ITA
Fenerbahçe 3
Alex 32, Ugur Boral 45 90
Volkan Demirel - Gokhan Gonul•, Diego Lugano, Edu, Roberto Carlos (Gokcek Vederson 89), Alex, Selcuk Sahin, Mehmet Aurelio, Ugur Boral (Mateja Kezman 90), Deivid, Semih Senturk (Colin Kazim-Richards 70). Tr: Zico
CSKA Moskva 1
Edu OG 30
Igor Akinfeev - Vasily Berezutsky, Alexei Berezutsky, Anton Grigoriev, Deividas Semberas•, Yevgeny Aldonin, Eduardo (Ivan Taranov 76), Yuri Zhirkov•, Ramon (Chidi Odiah 46), Caner Erkin• (Pavel Mamaev 46), Dawid Janczyk

GROUP H

		Pl	W	D	L	F	A	Pts	ESP	ENG	CZE	ROU
Sevilla	ESP	6	5	0	1	14	7	15		3-1	4-2	2-1
Arsenal	ENG	6	4	1	1	14	4	13	3-0		7-0	2-1
Slavia Praha	CZE	6	1	2	3	5	16	5	0-3	0-0		2-1
Steaua Bucuresti	ROU	6	0	1	5	4	10	1	0-2	0-1	1-1	

Emirates, London
19-09-2007, 19:45, 59 992, Fröjdfeldt SWE
Arsenal 3
Fabregas [27], Van Persie [59], Eduardo [92+]
Manuel Almunia - Bacary Sagna, Kolo Toure, Philippe Senderos, Gael Clichy, Aleksandr Hleb, Cesc Fabregas, Mathieu Flamini, Tomas Rosicky (Lassana Diabi 50), Emmanuel Adebayor• (Eduardo da Silva 83), Robin van Persie. Tr: Arsene Wenger
Sevilla 0
Andres Palop - Federico Fazio, Daniel Alves•, Julien Escude, Ivica Dragutinovic, Jesus Navas, Christian Poulsen, Diego Capel (Renato 67), Jose Luis Marti (Seydou Keita• 66), Luis Fabiano (Aleksandr Kerzhakov 46), Frederic Kanoute. Tr: Juande Ramos

Evzena Rosického, Prague
19-09-2007, 20:45, 15 723, Benquerenca POR
Slavia Praha 2
Senkerik [13], Belaid [63]
Martin Vaniak - Fratisek Drizdal, Marek Suchy, Erich Brabec (Petr Janda 42), Martin Latka (David Hubacek 45), Matej Krajcik, Tijani Belaid (Ladislav Volesak• 80), Mickael Tavares, Daniel Pudil, Zdenek Senkerik, Stanislav Vlcek. Tr: Karel Jarolim
Steaua Bucuresti 1
Goian [33]
Robinson Zapata - Valentin Badoi, Dorin Goian•, Ionut Rada, Petre Marin, Banel Nicolita, Florin Lovin• (Romeo Surdu 62), Ovidiu Petre, Vasilica Cristocea (Marius Croitoru• 53), Nicolae Dica, Victoras Iacob (Valentin Badea 71). Tr: Gheorghe Hagi

Ramón Sanchez-Pizjuan, Seville
2-10-2007, 20:45, 24 202, Baskakov RUS
Sevilla 4
Kanouté [8], Luis Fabiano [27], Escudé [58], Koné [68]
Andres Palop - Daniel Alves, Julien Escude, Khalid Boulahrouz, Ivica Dragutinovic, Jesus Navas (Duda 75), Christian Poulsen, Seydou Keita, Adriano Correia (Andreas Hinkel 81), Luis Fabiano (Arouna Kone 64), Frederic Kanoute. Tr: Juande Ramos
Slavia Praha 2
Pudil [19], Kalivoda [92+]
Martin Vaniak - Frantisek Drizdal (Milan Ivana 46), Marek Suchy, Ondrej Sourek•, David Hubacek, Matej Krajcik, Tijani Belaid (Ladislav Volesak• 73), Michal Svec, Petr Janda (David Kalivoda 64), Daniel Pudil, Stanislav Vlcek. Tr: Karel Jarolim

Steaua, Bucharest
2-10-2007, 21:45, 12 807, Hauge NOR
Steaua Bucuresti 0
Robinson Zapata - Petre Marin•, Eugen Baciu, Ionut Rada•, Iefanyi Emeghara, Banel Nicolita, Ovidiu Petre, Adrian Neaga (Dorel Zaharia 77), Romeo Surdu (Valentin Badoi 84), Nicolae Dica, Valentin Badea (Victoras Iacob 60). Tr: Massimo Pedrazzini
Arsenal 1
Van Persie [76]
Manuel Almunia - Bacary Sagna, Kolo Toure, Philippe Senderos, Gael Clichy, Emmanuel Eboue (Gilberto Silva 73), Cesc Fabregas, Mathieu Flamini, Aleksander Hleb, Emmanuel Adebayor•, Robin van Persie. Tr: Arsene Wenger

Emirates, London
23-10-2007, 19:45, 59 621, Farina ITA
Arsenal 7
Fabregas 2 [5][58], Hubácek OG [24], Walcott 2 [41][55], Hleb [51], Bendtner [89]
Manuel Almunia - Bacary Sagna, Kolo Toure, William Gallas, Gael Clichy•, Emmanuel Eboue, Cesc Fabregas, Matthieu Flamini• (Gilberto Silva 63), Aleksandr Hleb• (Tomas Rosicky 63), Theo Walcott, Emmanuel Adebayor (Nicklas Bendtner 63). Tr: Arsene Wenger
Slavia Praha 0
Martin Vaniak - Matej Jrajcik, Marek Suchy, David Hubacek, Daniel Pudil, Zdenek Senkerik, Michal Svec, Mickael Tavares (Tijani Belaid 63), David Kalivoda (Tomas Jablonsky 46), Milan Ivana (Ladislav Volesak• 56), Stanislav Vlcek. Tr: Karel Jarolim

Ramón Sanchez-Pizjuan, Seville
23-10-2007, 20:45, 28 945, Rosetti ITA
Sevilla 2
Kanouté 5, Luis Fabiano [17]
Andres Palop - Daniel Alves, Aquivaldo Mosquera, Ivica Dragutinovic, Adriano Correia•, Jesus Navas, Christian Poulsen, Seydou Keita•, Diego Capel (Jose Luis Marti 84), Luis Fabiano, Frederic Kanoute (Renato 71). Tr: Juande Ramos
Steaua Bucuresti 1
Petre [63]
Robinson Zapata - Ifeanyi Emeghara, Dorin Goian, Ionut Rada, Petre Marin•, Banel Nicolita, Marius Croitoru•, Ovidiu Petre, Romeo Surdu (Adrian Neaga 46), Nicolae Dica (Valentin Badea 46), Victoras Iacob (Dorel Zaharia• 71). Tr: Massimo Pedrazzini

Evzena Rosického, Prague
7-11-2007, 20:45, 18 000, Layec FRA
Slavia Praha 0
Michal Vorel - Matej Krajcik•, Erich Brabec, David Hubacek, Frantisek Drizdal, Vladimir Smicer (David Kalivoda 64), Marek Suchy, Michal Svec•, Mickael Tavares•, Daniel Pudil• (Tomas Jablonsky 89), Zdenek Senkerik (Milan Ivana 77). Tr: Karel Jarolim
Arsenal 0
Manuel Almunia - Lassana Diarra•, Alexandre Song, William Gallas, Gael Clichy, Theo Walcott, Gilberto, Denilson•, Abou Diaby, Eduardo da Silva (Emmanuel Eboue 81), Nicklas Bendtner (Emmanuel Adebayor 77). Tr: Arsene Wenger

Steaua, Bucharest
7-11-2007, 21:45, 7984, Fandel GER
Steaua Bucuresti 0
Robinson Zapata - Ifeanyi Emeghara•, Dorin Goian, Ionut Rada•, Mihai Nesu, Banel Nicolita, Ovidiu Petre, Florin Lovin, Marius Croitoru (Valentin Badea 46), Nicolae Dica, Victoras Iacob (Romeo Surdu 61). Tr: Marius Lacatus
Sevilla 2
Renato 2 [25][65]
Andres Palop - Daniel Alves, Aquivaldo Mosquera, Ivica Dragutinovic, Renato, Christian Poulsen, Seydou Keita, Tom De Mul (Diego Capel 63), Jesus Navas (Andreas Hinkel 89), Adriano•, Frederic Kanoute• (Luis Fabiano 68). Tr: Manuel Jimenez

Ramón Sanchez-Pizjuan, Seville
27-11-2007, 20:45, 35 529, Braamhaar NED
Sevilla 3
Keita [24], Luis Fabiano [34], Kanouté [89p]
Andres Palop• - Daniel Alves, Federico Fazio, Ivica Dragutinovic, Jose Angel Crespo• (Aquivaldo Mosquera 63), Jesus Navas, Christian Poulsen, Seydou Keita•, Adriano• (Jose Luis Marti 90), Luis Fabiano (Alexander Kerzhakov 75), Frederic Kanoute. Tr: Manuel Jimenez
Arsenal 1
Eduardo [11]
Manuel Almunia - Justin Hoyte• (Bacary Sagna 66), Kolo Toure, Philippe Senderos, Armand Traore, Emmanuel Eboue (Theo Walcott 78), Cesc Fabregas (Tomas Rosicky 56), Gilberto, Denilson•, Eduardo da Silva, Nicklas Bendtner. Tr: Arsene Wenger

Steaua, Bucharest
27-11-2007, 21:45, 8287, Hamer LUX
Steaua Bucuresti 1
Badea [12]
Robinson Zapata - Dorin Goian, Ionut Rada, Ifeanyi Emeghara, Mihai Nesu, Ovidiu Petre, Florin Lovin (Eric Bicfalvi 65), Adrian Neaga, Marius Croitoru• (Romeo Surdu 77), Valentin Badea (Vasilica Cristocea 89), Nicolae Dica. Tr: Marius Lacatus
Slavia Praha 1
Senkerik [78]
Martin Vaniak - Mickael Tavarez, Marek Suchy, Erich Brabec, Matej Krajcik•, David Hubacek•, Michal Svec (Tijani Belaid 30), Zdenek Senderik, Daniel Pudil, Ladislav Volesak (Ondrej Sourek• 59), Gaucho (Tomas Necid 77). Tr: Karel Jarolim

Emirates, London
12-12-2007, 19:45, 59 786, Baskakov RUS
Arsenal 2
Diaby [8], Bendtner [42]
Jens Lehmann - Bacary Sagna (Emmanuel Eboue 71), William Gallas, Philippe Senderos, Armand Traore, Theo Walcott, Alexandre Song, Denilson, Abou Diaby (Lassana Diarra 71), Nicklas Bendtner•, Robin van Persie (Eduardo da Silva 65). Tr: Patrick Rice
Steaua Bucuresti 1
Zaharia [68]
Robinson Zapata - Ifeanyi Emeghara, Dorin Goian, Ionut Rada, Mihai Nesu, Adrian Neaga• (Dorel Zaharia 64), Ovidiu Petre, Florin Lovin, Vasilica Cristocea (Romeo Surdu 57), Nicolae Dica, Valentin Badea (Pawel Golanski 81). Tr: Marius Lacatus

Evzena Rosického, Prague
12-12-2007, 20:45, 11 689, Kassai HUN
Slavia Praha 0
Martin Vaniak - Marek Suchy, Erich Brabec, Matej Krajcik•, David Hubacek, Vladimir Smicer (Tomas Jablonsky 46), Mickael Tavares, Tijani Belaid, Daniel Pudil (Ladislav Volesak (Tomas Necid 66), Milan Ivana. Tr: Karel Jarolim
Sevilla 3
Luis Fabiano [66], Kanouté [69], Daniel Alves [87]
Morgan De Sanctis - Daniel Alves, Lolo, Ivica Dragutinovic•, Aquivaldo Mosquera, Jesus Navas, Renato (Enzo Maresca 64), Jose Luis Marti, Diego Capel, Frederic Kanoute (Duda 70), Arouna Kone (Luis Fabiano 58). Tr: Manuel Jimenez

ROUND OF SIXTEEN

Stade de Gerland, Lyon
20-02-2008, 20:45, 39 219, Cantalejo ESP

Olympique Lyonnais 1

Benzema [54]

Gregory Coupet - Anthony Reveillere•, Jean-Alain Boumsong•, Sebastien Squillaci, Fabio Grosso, Francois Clerc (Hatem Ben Arfa 78), Kim Kallstrom•, Jeremy Toulalan, Juninho (Mathieu Bodmer 75), Sidney Govou, Karim Benzema (Fred 83). Tr: Alain Perrin

Manchester United 1

Tévez [87]

Edwin van der Sar - Wes Brown, Rio Ferdinand, Nemanja Vidic, Patrice Evra, Paul Scholes (Carlos Tevez 65), Owen Hargreaves• (Michael Carrick 78), Anderson, Cristiano Ronaldo, Wayne Rooney, Ryan Giggs (Nani 65). Tr: Alex Ferguson

---

Old Trafford, Manchester
4-03-2008, 19:45, 75 520, Rosetti ITA

Manchester United 1

Ronaldo [41]

Edwin van der Sar - Wes Brown, Rio Ferdinand, Nemanja Vidic, Patrice Evra•, Darren Fletcher•, Michael Carrick, Anderson (Carlos Tevez 70), Cristiano Ronaldo (OwenHargreaves 90+1), Wayne Rooney, Nani•. Tr: Alex Ferguson

Olympique Lyonnais 0

Gregory Coupet - Francois Clerc, Sebastien Squillaci•, Cris, Fabio Grosso•, Kim Kallstrom (Fred 79), Jeremy Toulalan, Juninho, Hatem Ben Arfa, Sidney Govou (Abdulkader Keita 68), Karim Benzema. Tr: Alain Perrin

---

Stadio Olimpico, Rome
19-02-2008, 20:45, 56 231, Fandel GER

Roma 2

Pizarro [24], Mancini [58]

Doni - Christian Panucci (Max Tonetto 67), Philippe Mexes, Juan (Matteo Ferrari 77), Marco Cassetti•, Ludovic Giuly, Daniele De Rossi•, David Pizarro (Alberto Aquilani 62), Simone Perrotta•, Mancini, Francesco Totti. Tr: Luciano Spalletti

Real Madrid 1

Raúl [8]

Iker Casillas - Sergio Ramos•, Fabio Cannavaro, Gabriel Heinze, Miguel Torres•, Guti, Mahamadou Diarra• (Royston Drenthe 79), Fernando Gago, Arjen Robben (Julio Baptista 79), Raul Gonzalez, Ruud van Nistelrooy. Tr: Bernd Schuster

---

Santiago Bernabéu, Madrid
5-03-2008, 20:45, 71 569, Vassaras GRE

Real Madrid 1

Raúl [75]

Iker Casillas - Michel Salgado (Miguel Torres 64), Fabio Cannavaro, Pepe•••71, Gabriel Heinze•, Mahamadou Diarra (Royston Drenthe 61), Fernando Gago, Julio Baptista (Roberto Soldado 85), Guti•, Robinho•, Raul Gonzalez. Tr: Bernd Schuster

Roma 2

Taddei [73], Vucinic [92+]

Doni - Cicinho• (Christian Panucci 87), Philippe Mexes, Juan, Max Tonetto•, Rodrigo Taddei•, Daniele De Rossi•, Simone Perrotta• (David Pizarro 76), Alberto Aquilani•, Mancini (Mirko Vucinic 65), Francesco Totti. Tr: Luciano Spalletti

---

Arena AufSchalke, Gelsenkirchen
19-02-2008, 20:45, 53 951, Duhamel FRA

Scalke 04 1

Kuranyi [4]

Manuel Neuer - Rafinha, Marcelo Bordo, Mladen Krstajic, Heiko Westermann, Ivan Rakitic (Carlos Grossmüller• 77), Jermaine Jones•, Fabian Ernst•, Levan Kobiashvili, Gerald Asamoah (Halil Altintop 81), Kevin Kuranyi (Vicente Sanchez 89). Tr: Mirko Slomka

FC Porto 0

Helton - Joao Paulo, Pedro Emanuel, Bruno Alves, Jorge Fucile (Mariano Gonzalez 85), Lucho Gonzalez, Paulo Assuncao, Raul Meireles, Lisandro Lopez, Ernesto Farias (Tarik Sektioui 56), Ricardo Quaresma. Tr: Jesualdo Ferreira

---

Estádio do Dragão, Porto
5-03-2008, 19:45, 45 316, Webb ENG

FC Porto 1 1p

Lisandro [86]

Helton - Jose Bosingwa (Mariano Gonzalez 54), Jorge Fucile•82, Pedro Emanuel, Bruno Alves, Lucho Gonzalez•, Paulo Assuncao, Raul Meireles (Marek Cech 99), Lisandro Lopez, Tarik Sektioui (Ernesto Farias 59), Ricardo Quaresma. Tr: Jesualdo Ferreira

Schalke 04 0 4p

Manuel Neuer - Rafinha, Marcelo Bordon (Benedikt Howedes 115), Mladen Krstajic, Heiko Westermann•, Carlos Grossmüller (Ivan Rakitic 112), Jermaine Jones•, Fabian Ernst, Levan Kobiashvili•, Halil Altintop, Kevin Kuranyi• (Gerald Asamoah 79). Tr: Mirko Slomka

---

Celtic Park, Glasgow
20-02-2008, 19:45, 58 426, Fröjdfeldt SWE

Celtic 2

Vennegoor [16], Robson [38]

Artur Boruc - Paul Caddis (Mark Wilson 61), Gary Caldwell, Stephen McManus, Lee Naylor, Shunsuke Nakamura, Barry Robson•, Paul Hartley• (Massimo Donati 66), Aiden McGeady, Jan Vennegoor of Hesselink (Georgios Samaras• 56), Scott McDonald. Tr: Gordon Strachan

Barcelona 3

Messi 2 [18][79], Henry [52]

Victor Valdes - Carles Puyol, Rafael Marquez, Gabriel Milito, Eric Abidal, Deco• (Xavi Hernandez 67), Yaya Toure, Andres Iniesta, Lionel Messi, Ronaldinho (Samuel Eto'o 73), Thierry Henry (Eidur Gudjohnsen 88). Tr: Frank Rijkaard

---

Camp Nou, Barcelona
4-03-2008, 20:45, 75 326, Vink NED

Barcelona 1

Xavi [3]

Victor Valdes - Gianluca Zambrotta, Lilian Thuram, Carles Puyol, Silvinho, Xavi Hernandez (Eidur Gudjohnsen 82), Yaya Toure (Edmilson 67), Deco, Ronaldinho, Lionel Messi (Thierry Henry 38), Samuel Eto'o. Tr: Frank Rijkaard

Celtic 0

Artur Boruc - Mark Wilson, Gary Caldwell, Stephen McManus, Lee Naylor, Shunsuke Nakamura, Scott Brown•, Paul Hartley (Scott McDonald 78), Massimo Donati (Evander Svo 46), Aiden McGeady, Jan Vennegoor of Hesselink (Georgios Samaras 54). Tr: Gordon Strachan

---

Anfield, Liverpool
19-02-2008, 19:45, 41 999, De Bleeckere BEL

Liverpool 2

Kuyt [85], Gerrard [90]

Jose Reina - Steve Finnan, Jamie Carragher, Sami Hyypia, Fabio Aurelio, Steven Gerrard, Javier Mascherano, Lucas Leiva (Peter Crouch 64), Ryan Babel (Jermaine Pennant 72), Dirk Kuyt, Fernando Torres. Tr: Rafael Benitez

Internazionale 0

Julio Cesar - Maicon Douglas, Ivan Cordoba (Nicolas Burdisso 76), Marco Materazzi•••30, Cristian Chivu•, Javier Zanetti, Esteban Cambiasso, Dejan Stankovic, Maxwell, Julio Cruz (Patrick Vieira 55), Zlatan Ibrahimovic. Tr: Roberto Mancini

---

San Siro, Milan
11-03-2008, 20:45, 78 923, Ovrebo NOR

Internazionale 0

Julio Cesar - Maicon Douglas, Nelson Rivas•, Cristian Chivu•, Nicolas Burdisso•••50, Patrick Vieira (Pele 77), Esteban Cambiasso, Dejan Stankovic• (Luis Jimenez 84), Javier Zanetti, Zlatan Ibrahimovic (David Suazo 80), Julio Cruz. Tr: Roberto Mancini

Liverpool 1

Torres [64]

Jose Reina - Jamie Carragher, Martin Skrtel, Sami Hyypia, Fabio Aurelio•, Dirk Kuyt (John Arne Riise 81), Lucas Leiva, Steven Gerrard•, Javier Mascherano (Jermaine Pennant 87), Ryan Babel• (Yossi Benayoun• 61), Fernando Torres. Tr: Rafael Benitez

---

The Emirates, London
20-02-2008, 19:45, 60 082, Larsen DEN

Arsenal 0

Jens Lehmann - Bacary Sagna, William Gallas, Kolo Toure (Philippe Senderos• 7), Gael Clichy, Emmanuel Eboue• (Theo Walcott 89), Cesc Fabregas, Mathieu Flamini, Aleksandr Hleb, Emmanuel Adebayor, Eduardo da Silva (Nicklas Bendtner 75). Tr: Arsene Wenger

Milan 0

Zeljko Kalac - Massimo Oddo, Alessandro Nesta (Marek Jankulovski 51), Kakha Kaladze, Paolo Maldini, Clarence Seedorf (Emerson 85), Gennaro Gattuso, Andrea Pirlo, Massimo Ambrosini, Kaka, Alexandre Pato• (Alberto Gilardino 77). Tr: Carlo Ancelotti

---

San Siro, Milan
4-03-2008, 20:45, 81 879, Plautz AUT

Milan 0

Zeljko Kalac - Massimo Oddo, Alessandro Nesta, Paolo Maldini, Kakha Kaladze, Gennaro Gattuso, Andrea Pirlo•, Massimo Ambrosini, Kaka•, Alexandre Pato, Filippo Inzaghi• (Alberto Gilardino 70). Tr: Carlo Ancelotti

Arsenal 2

Fàbregas [84], Adebayor [92+]

Manuel Almunia - Bacary Sagna, Philippe Senderos, William Gallas, Gael Clichy•, Emmanuel Eboue• (Theo Walcott 72), Francesc Fabregas, Abou Diaby, Mathieu Flamini, Aleksandr Hleb• (Gilberto Silva 91+), Emmanuel Adebayor. Tr: Arsene Wenger

---

Sükrü Saraçoglu, Istanbul
20-02-2008, 21:45, 46 210, Meyer GER

Fenerbahçe	3
Kezman [17], Lugano [57], Semih Sentürk [87]	

Volkan Demirel - Gokhan Gonul, Diego Lugano, Edu, Roberto Carlos• (Gokcek Vederson 68), Deivid de Souza, Selcuk Sahin•, Mehmet Aurelio, Ugur Boral• (Colin Kazim-Richards 78), Alex•, Mateja Kezman• (Semih Senturk 84). Tr: Zico

Sevilla	2
Edu OG [23], Escudé [66]	

Andres Palop• - Daniel Alves, Julien Escude, Ivica Dragutinovic, Adriano, Jesus Navas, Christian Poulsen, Seydou Keita, Duda (Diego Capel 63), Luis Fabiano, Frederic Kanoute. Tr: Manuel Jimenez

---

Ramón Sanchez-Pizjuan, Seville
4-03-2008, 20:45, 38 626, Busacca SUI

Sevilla	3 2p
Daniel Alves [5], Keita [9], Kanouté [41]	

Andres Palop - Daniel Alves•, Julien Escude, Ivica Dragutinovic, Adriano, Jesus Navas (Arouna Kone 105), Christian Poulsen (Enzo Maresca 91), Seydou Keita•, Diego Capel, Luis Fabiano (Renato 78), Frederic Kanoute. Tr: Manuel Jimenez

Fenerbahçe	2 3p
Deivid 2 [20 79]	

Volkan Demirel - Gokhan Gonul•, Diego Lugano, Edu, Gokcek Vederson•, Deivid de Souza•, Selcuk Sahin• (Semih Senturk 63), Mehmet Aurelio, Ugur Boral (Colin Kazim-Richards 111), Alex (Ali Bilgin 112), Mateja Kezman•. Tr: Zico

---

Karaiskakis, Piraeus
19-02-2008, 21:45, 31 302, Plautz AUT

Olympiacos	0

Antonis Nikopolidis - Michal Zewlakow, Julio Cesar, Paraskevas Antzas, Anastasios Pantos, Cristian Ledesma, Luciano Galletti (Leonardo 83), Vassilis Torosidis, Predrag Djordjevic (Fernando Belluschi• 76), Ieroklis Stoltidis, Darko Kovacevic (Nunez 87). Tr: Panagiotis Lemonis

Chelsea	0

Petr Cech - Juliano Belletti•, Ricardo Carvalho, Alex•, Ashley Cole•, Michael Essien, Claude Makelele•, Michael Ballack (Frank Lampard), Florent Malouda (Salomon Kalou 75), Joe Cole (Nicolas Anelka 75), Didier Drogba. Tr: Avram Grant

---

Stamford Bridge, London
5-03-2008, 19:45, 37 721, M. Gonzalez ESP

Chelsea	3
Ballack [5], Lampard [25], Kalou [48]	

Carlo Cudicini - Paulo Ferreira•, Ricardo Carvalho, John Terry•, Ashley Cole, Michael Ballack, Claude Makelele, Frank Lampard• (Michael Essien 76), Joe Cole (Shaun Wright-Phillips 79), Didier Drogba, Salomon Kalou (Florent Malouda 71). Tr: Avram Grant

Olympiacos	0

Antonis Nikopolidis - Michal Zewlakow, Julio Cesar, Paraskevas Antzas, Anastasios Pantos•, Cristian Ledesma (Fernando Belluschi 53), Vassilis Torosidis (Mirnes Sisic 76), Predrag Djordjevic (Leonardo 57), Christos Patsatzoglou, Ieroklis Stoltidis, Darko Kovacevic

---

**PENALTY SHOOT-OUT
ROUND OF 16
SCHALKE WON 4-1**

Schalke			Porto
Rafinha	✓	✓	Gonzalez
Rakitic	✓	✗	Alves
Altintop	✓	✗	Lopez
Jones	✓		

**PENALTY SHOOT-OUT
ROUND OF 16
FENERBAHÇE WON 4-1**

Sevilla			Fenerbahçe
Kanouté	✓	✓	Vederson
Escudé	✗	✗	Edu
Dragutinovic	✓	✓	Aurelio
Maresca	✗	✓	Kezman
Alves	✗		

QUARTER-FINALS

Stadio Olimpico, Rome
1-04-2008, 20:45, 60 931, De Bleeckere BEL

Roma	0

Doni - Marco Cassetti, Philippe Mexes•, Christian Panucci, Max Tonetto (Cicinho 69), Rodrigo Taddei (Ludovic Giuly 59), Daniele De Rossi, Alberto Aquilani (Mauro Esposito 76), David Pizarro•, Mancini, Mirko Vucinic. Tr: Luciano Spalletti

Manchester United	2
Ronaldo [39], Rooney [66]	

Edwin van der Sar - Wes Brown, Rio Ferdinand, Nemanja Vidic (John O'Shea 33), Patrice Evra, Michael Carrick, Paul Scholes, Anderson• (Owen Hargreaves 56), Cristiano Ronaldo, Wayne Rooney (Carlos Tevez 84), Park Ji-Sung. Tr: Alex Ferguson

---

Old Trafford, Manchester
9-04-2008, 19:45, 74 423, Ovrebo NOR

Manchester United	1
Tévez [70]	

Edwin van der Sar - Wes Brown, Gerard Pique, Rio Ferdinand, Mikael Silvestre, Park Ji-sung, Anderson (Gary Neville 81), Michael Carrick (John O'Shea 74), Owen Hargreaves, Ryan Giggs (Wayne Rooney 74), Carlos Tevez. Tr: Alex Ferguson

Roma	0

Doni - Christian Panucci, Philippe Mexes, Juan, Marco Cassetti (Max Tonetto 57), Rodrigo Taddei (Mauro Esposito 81), David Pizarro (Ludovic Giuly 69), Daniele De Rossi•30, Simone Perrotta•, Mancini, Mirko Vucinic. Tr: Luciano Spalletti

---

Arena AufSchalke, Gelsenkirchen
1-04-2008, 20:45, 53 951, Vassaras GRE

Schalke 04	0

Manuel Neuer - Rafinha, Marcelo Bordon, Mladen Krstajic•, Heiko Westermann, Gerald Asamoah (Soren Larsen• 73), Levan Kobiashvili, Fabian Ernst•, Christian Pander•, Kevin Kuranyi (Vicente Sanchez 60), Halil Altintop (Peter Lovenkrands 89). Tr: Mirko Slomka

Barcelona	1
Bojan [12]	

Victor Valdes - Gianluca Zambrotta, Carles Puyol•, Gabriel Milito•, Eric Abidal, Yaya Toure (Rafael Marquez• 73), Xavi Hernandez, Andres Iniesta, Bojan Krkic (Silvinho 86), Samuel Eto'o (Giovani dos Santos• 82), Thierry Henry. Tr: Frank Rijkaard

---

Camp Nou, Barcelona
9-04-2008, 20:45, 72 113, Rosetti ITA

Barcelona	1
Yayá Touré [43]	

Victor Valdes - Gianluca Zambrotta, Carles Puyol•, Lilian Thuram, Eric Abidal, Xavi Hernandez, Yaya Toure (Rafael Marquez 80), Andres Iniesta, Samuel Eto'o, Bojan Krkic (Giovani dos Santos 73), Thierry Henry (Eidur Gudjohnsen 91+). Tr: Frank Rijkaard

Schalke 04	0

Manuel Neuer - Rafinha•, (Soren Larsen 77), Marcelo Bordon, Mladen Krstajic, Heiko Westermann•, Gerald Asamoah (Vicente Sanchez 69), Jermaine Jones, Fabian Ernst, Levan Kobiashvili (Carlos Grossmueller 32), Kevin Kuranyi, Halil Altintop. Tr: Mirko Slomka

---

The Emirates, London
2-04-2008, 19:45, 60 041, Vink NED

Arsenal	1
Adebayor [23]	

Manuel Almunia - Kolo Toure, William Gallas, Philippe Senderos, Gael Clichy, Emmanuel Eboue (Nicklas Bendtner 67), Mathieu Flamini, Francesc Fabregas, Aleksandr Hleb, Robin van Persie (Theo Walcott 46), Emmanuel Adebayor. Tr: Arsene Wenger

Liverpool	1
Kuyt [26]	

Jose Reina - Jamie Carragher, Martin Skrtel, Sami Hyypia, Fabio Aurelio, Steven Gerrard, Javier Mascherano, Xabi Alonso (Lucas Leiva 76), Ryan Babel (Yossi Benayoun 58), Dirk Kuyt, Fernando Torres (Andriy Voronin 86). Tr: Rafael Benitez

---

Anfield, Liverpool
8-04-2008, 19:45, 41 985, Fröjdfeldt SWE

Liverpool	4
Hyypiä [30], Torres [69], Gerrard [85p], Babel [92+]	

Jose Reina - Jamie Carragher, Martin Skrtel, Sami Hyypia, Fabio Aurelio, Xabi Alonso, Steven Gerrard, Javier Mascherano, Dirk Kuyt (Alvaro Arbeloa 90), Fernando Torres (John Arne Riise 87), Peter Crouch (Ryan Babel 78). Tr: Rafael Benitez

Arsenal	2
Diaby [13], Adebayor [84]	

Manuel Almunia - Kolo Toure•, William Gallas, Philippe Senderos•, Gael Clichy, Emmanuel Eboue (Theo Walcott 72), Abou Diaby (Robin van Persie 72), Matthieu Flamini (Gilberto Silva 42), Francesc Fabregas, Aleksandr Hleb, Emmanuel Adebayor. Tr: Arsene Wenger

Şükrü Saraçoğlu, Istanbul
2-04-2008, 21:45, 49 055, Larsen DEN

Fenerbahçe	2
	Kazim-Richards 65, Deivid 81

Volkan Demirel - Onder Turaci, Diego Lugano, Edu, Gokcek Vederson, Claudio Maldonado, Mehmet Aurelio, Ugur Boral (Colin Kazim-Richards 54), Deivid de Souza, Mateja Kezman (Semih Senturk 72), Alex. Tr: Zico

Chelsea	1
	Deivid OG 13

Carlo Cudicini - Michael Essien, John Terry, Ricardo Carvalho, Ashley Cole, Michael Ballack, Claude Makelele, Frank Lampard (John Obi Mikel 76), Florent Malouda, Didier Drogba, Joe Cole (Nicolas Anelka 86). Tr: Avram Grant

Stamford Bridge, London
8-04-2008, 19:45, Fandel GER

Chelsea	2
	Ballack 4, Lampard 87

Carlo Cudicini (Henrique Hillario 26) - Michael Essien●, Ricardo Carvalho, John Terry, Ashley Cole, Michael Ballack, Claude Makelele, Frank Lampard, Joe Cole (Florent Malouda 85), Didier Drogba, Salomon Kalou (Juliano Belletti 58). Tr: Avram Grant

Fenerbahçe	0

Volkan Demirel - Gokcek Vederson (Ali Bilgin 89), Edu, Diego Lugano, Gokhan Gonul, Colin Kazim-Richards, Aurelio, Claudio Maldonado (Mateja Kezman 60), Deivid de Souza, Semih Senturk (Ugur Boral 75), Alex. Tr: Zico

SEMI-FINALS

Camp Nou, Barcelona
23-04-2008, 20:45, 95 949, Busacca SUI

Barcelona	0

Victor Valdes - Gianluca Zambrotta, Rafael Marquez●, Gabriel Milito, Eric Abidal, Xavi Hernandez, Yaya Toure, Deco (Thierry Henry 77), Lionel Messi (Bojan Krkic 62), Samuel Eto'o, Andres Iniesta. Tr: Frank Rijkaard

Manchester United	0

Edwin van der Sar - Owen Hargreaves●, Rio Ferdinand, Wes Brown, Patrice Evra, Cristiano Ronaldo=3, Michael Carrick, Paul Scholes, Park Ji-sung, Carlos Tevez (Ryan Giggs 85), Wayne Rooney (Nani 76). Tr: Alex Ferguson

Old Trafford, Manchester
29-04-2008, 20:45, 75 061, Fandel GER

Manchester United	1
	Scholes 14

Edwin van der Sar - Owen Hargreaves, Wes Brown, Rio Ferdinand, Patrice Evra (Mikael Silvestre 92+), Park Ji Sung, Michael Carrick●, Paul Scholes (Darren Fletcher 77), Nani (Ryan Giggs 77), Carlos Tevez, Cristiano Ronaldo●. Tr: Alex Ferguson

Barcelona	0

Victor Valdes - Gianluca Zambrotta●, Carles Puyol, Gabriel Milito, Eric Abidal, Xavi Hernandez, Yaya Toure● (Eidur Gudjohnsen 88), Deco●, Lionel Messi, Samuel Eto'o (Bojan Krkic 72), Andres Iniesta (Thierry Henry 61). Tr: Frank Rijkaard

Anfield, Liverpool
22-04-2008, 20:45, 42 180, PLautz AUT

Liverpool	1
	Kuyt 43

Jose Reina - Alvaro Arbeloa, Jamie Carragher, Martin Skrtel, Fabio Aurelio (John Arne Riise 62), Xabi Alonso, Javier Mascherano, Steven Gerrard, Dirk Kuyt, Ryan Babel (Yossi Benayoun 76), Fernando Torres. Tr: Rafael Benitez

Chelsea	1
	Riise OG 94+

Petr Cech - Paulo Ferreira, John Terry●, Ricardo Carvalho, Ashley Cole, Frank Lampard, Claude Makelele, Michael Ballack (Nicolas Anelka 86), Florent Malouda, Didier Drogba, Joe Cole (Salomon Kalou 63). Tr: Avram Grant

Stamford Bridge, London
30-04-2008, 20:45, 38 900, Rosetti ITA

Chelsea	3
	Drogba 2 33 105, Lampard 98

Petr Cech - Michael Essien, Ricardo Carvalho, John Terry, Ashley Cole, Claude Makelele, Michael Ballack, Frank Lampard (Andriy Schevchenko 119), Joe Cole (Nicolas Anelka 91), Didier Drogba, Salomon Kalou (Florent Malouda 70). Tr: Avram Grant

Liverpool	2
	Torres 64, Babel 117

Jose Reina - Alvaro Arbeloa●, Jamie Carragher, Martin Skrtel (Sami Hyypia 22), John Arne Riise, Xabi Alonso●, Javier Mascherano, Steven Gerrard, Dirk Kuyt, Yossi Benayoun (Jermaine Pennant 78), Fernando Torres (Ryan Babel 98). Tr: Rafael Benitez

UEFA CHAMPIONS LEAGUE FINAL 2008

Luzhniki, Moscow
21-05-2008, 20:45, 47 500, 67 310 Michel SVK

MAN UTD	1 1	CHELSEA
Ronaldo 26	6 P/S/O 5	Lampard 45

		MANCHESTER UNITED				CHELSEA		
1	GK	Edwin van der Sar				Petr Cech	GK	1
6	DF	Wes Brown	120			Michael Essien	DF	5
5	DF	Rio Ferdinand				Ricardo Carvalho	DF	6
15	DF	Nemanja Vidic				John Terry	DF	26
3	DF	Patrice Evra				Ashley Cole	DF	3
4	MF	Owen Hargreaves		99		Joe Cole	MF	10
18	MF	Paul Scholes	87			Michael Ballack	MF	13
16	MF	Michael Carrick	120			Claude Makelele	MF	4
7	MF	Cristano Ronaldo				Frank Lampard	MF	8
10	FW	Wayne Rooney	101	92		Florent Malouda	MF	15
32	FW	Carlos Tévez			116	Didier Drogba	FW	11
		Tr: Sir Alex Ferguson				Tr: Avram Grant		
8		Anderson	120	92		Salomon Kalou		21
11		Ryan Giggs	87	120		Juliano Belletti		35
17		Nani	101	99		Nicolas Anelka		39

PENALTY SHOOT-OUT FINAL MAN UTD WON 6-5		
Tévez	✓ ✓	Ballack
Carrick	✓ ✓	Belletti
Ronaldo	✗ ✓	Lampard
Hargreaves	✓ ✓	Cole.A
Nani	✓ ✗	Terry
Anderson	✓ ✓	Kalou
Giggs	✓ ✗	Anelka

MATCH STATS	
Man Utd	Chelsea
12	Shots	24
5	Shots on Goal	3
22	Fouls Committed	25
5	Corner Kicks	8
1	Offside	2
58%	Possession %	42%

UEFA CUP 2007-08

UEFA CUP 2007-08 EARLY ROUNDS FOR TEAMS IN GROUPS A TO D

First Qualifying Round

ViOn Zlaté M'vce	SVK	3	1
FK Almaty	KAZ	1	1
Lillestrøm SK	NOR	2	0
UN Käerjéng	LUX	1	1
MyPa-47	FIN	1	1
EB/Streymur	FRO	0	1
Vojvodina Novi Sad	SRB	5	2
Hibernians	MLT	1	0
Santa Coloma	AND	1	0
Maccabi Tel Aviv	ISR	0	4
MTK Budapest	HUN	2	0
Mika Ashtarak	ARM	1	1
Artmedia Petrz'ka	SVK	1	2
Zimbru Chisinau	MDA	1	2
GKS Belchatow	POL	2 0 4p	
Ameri Tbilisi	GEO	0 2 4p	
Banants Yerevan	ARM	1	0
BSC Young Boys	SUI	1	4
Rhyl	WAL	3	0
Haka Valkeakoski	FIN	1	2
Keflavik	ISL	3	1
FC Midtjylland	DEN	2	2
Bezanija NB	SRB	2	0
Besa Kavajë	ALB	2	0
Sliema Wanderers	MLT	0	0
Litex Lovech	BUL	3	4
Nistru Otaci	MDA	1 14p	
Budapest Honvéd	HUN	1 15p	
FK Aktobe	KAZ	1	2
SV Mattersburg	AUT	0	4
Carmarthen Town	WAL	0	3
Brann Bergen	NOR	8	6
Dungannon Swifts	NIR	1	0
Suduva Marij'pole	LTU	0	4

Second Qualifying Round

ViOn Zlaté M'vce	SVK	0	0
Zenit St Pet'burg	RUS	2	3
UN Käerjéng	LUX	0	0
Standard CL	BEL	3	1
MyPa-47	FIN	0	0
Blackburn Rovers	ENG	1	2
Atlético Madrid	ESP	3	2
Vojvodina Novi Sad	SRB	0	1
Maccabi Tel Aviv	ISR	1	1
Kayseri Erciy'spor	TUR	1	3
Mika Ashtarak	ARM	2	0
Artmedia Petrz'ka	SVK	1	2
Dnipro D'petrovsk	UKR	1	4
GKS Belchatow	POL	1	2
BSC Young Boys	SUI	1	1
RC Lens	FRA	1	5
Haka Valkeakoski	FIN	1	2
FC Midtjylland	DEN	2	5
Besa Kavajë	ALB	0	0
Litex Lovech	BUL	3	3
Budapest Honvéd	HUN	0	0
Hamburger SV	GER	0	4
FC Basel	SUI	2	4
SV Mattersburg	AUT	1	0
Brann Bergen	NOR	2	4
Suduva Marij'pole	LTU	1	3
Lokomotiv Sofia	BUL	3	0
Otelul Galati	ROU	1	0

First Round

Everton	ENG	1	3
Metalist Kharkiv	UKR	1	2
1.FC Nürnberg	GER	0	2
Rapid Bucuresti	ROU	0	2
Zenit St Pet'burg	RUS	3	1
Standard CL	BEL	0	1
Paços de Ferreira	POR	0	0
AZ Alkmaar	NED	1	0
Larissa	GRE	2	1
Blackburn Rovers	ENG	0	2
Atlético Madrid	ESP	4	5
Kayseri Erciy'spor	TUR	0	0
Artmedia Petrz'ka	SVK	1	0
Panathinaikos	GRE	2	3
Aberdeen	SCO	0	1
Dnipro D'petrovsk	UKR	0	1
RC Lens	FRA	1	1
FC København	DEN	1	2
FC Midtjylland	DEN	1	0
Loko'tiv Moskva	RUS	3	2
Villarreal	ESP	4	2
BATE Borisov	BLR	1	0
FC Groningen	NED	1 1 3p	
Fiorentina	ITA	1 1 4p	
AEK Athens	GRE	3	0
Austria Salzburg	AUT	0	1
Mladá Boleslav	CZE	0 1 4p	
Palermo	ITA	1 0 2p	
Dinamo Bucuresti	ROU	1	1
IF Elfsborg	SWE	2	0
Litex Lovech	BUL	0	1
Hamburger SV	GER	1	3
FK Sarajevo	BIH	1	0
FC Basel	SUI	2	6
Brann Bergen	NOR	0	2
Club Brugge	BEL	1	1
Dinamo Zagreb	CRO	0	3
Ajax	NED	1	2
Lokomotiv Sofia	BUL	1	2
Stade Rennais	FRA	3	1

Group Stage

Group A		Pts
Everton	ENG	12
1.FC Nürnberg	GER	7
Zenit St Petersburg	RUS	5
AZ Alkmaar	NED	4
Larissa	GRE	0

Group B		Pts
Atlético Madrid	ESP	10
Panathinaikos	GRE	9
Aberdeen	SCO	4
FC København	DEN	3
Lokomotiv Moskva	RUS	2

Group C		Pts
Villarreal	ESP	10
Fiorentina	ITA	8
AEK Athens	GRE	5
Mladá Boleslav	CZE	3
IF Elfsborg	SWE	1

Group D		Pts
Hamburger SV	GER	10
FC Basel	SUI	8
SK Brann Bergen	NOR	4
Dinamo Zagreb	CRO	2
Stade Rennais	FRA	2

In each preliminary and first round tie the home team in the first leg is listed above their opponent

UEFA CUP 2007–08 EARLY ROUNDS FOR TEAMS IN GROUPS E TO H

First Qualifying Round

BK Häcken	SWE	1	1
KR Reykjavik	ISL	1	0
Skonto Riga	LVA	1	0
Dinamo Minsk	BLR	1	2
St Patrick's Ath	IRL	0	0
OB Odense	DEN	0	5
Omonia Nicosia	CYP	2	2
Rudar Pljevlja	MNE	0	0
ND Gorica	SVN	1	1
Rabotnicki Skopje	MKD	2	2
Zrinjski Mostar	BIH	1	0
Partizan Beograd‡	SRB	6	5
MTK-Araz Imishli	AZE	0	0
Groclin Grodzisk	POL	0	1
Vardar Skopje	MKD	0	0
Anorthosis F'gusta	CYP	1	1
Dinamo Tbilisi	GEO	2	0
FC Vaduz	LIE	0	0
Bud'st Podgorica	MNE	1	0
Hajduk Split	CRO	1	1
HJK Helsinki	FIN	2	1
Etzella Ettelbruck	LUX	0	0
Siroki Brijeg	BIH	3	3
FC Koper	SVN	1	2
Liepajas Met'urgs	LVA	1	2
Dinamo Brest	BLR	1	1
Glentoran	NIR	0	0
AIK Stockholm	SWE	5	4
Libertas	SMR	0	0
Drogheda United	IRL	1	3
Helsingborgs IF	SWE	6	3
Trans Narva	EST	0	0
SV Ried	AUT	3	1
Neftchi Baku	AZE	1	2
Slaven Koprivnica	CRO	6	2
Teuta Durrës	ALB	2	2
B36 Tórshavn	FRO	1	2
Ekranas Pan'zys	LTU	3	3
Flora Tallinn	EST	0	0
Vålerenga IF	NOR	1	1

Second Qualifying Round

União Leiria	POR	0	1
Maccabi Netanya	ISR	0	0
BK Häcken	SWE	1	1
Dunfermline Ath.	SCO	1	0
Dinamo Minsk	BLR	1	0
OB Odense	DEN	1	4
Omonia Nicosia	CYP	1	1
CSKA Sofia	BUL	1	2
Hammarby IF	SWE	2	1
Fredrikstad FK	NOR	1	1
Rabotnicki Skopje	MKD	0	2
Zrinjski Mostar	BIH	0	1
Tobol Kostanay	KAZ	0	0
Groclin Grodzisk	POL	1	2
CFR 1907 Cluj	ROU	1	0
Anorthosis F'gusta	CYP	3	0
Dinamo Tbilisi	GEO	3	5
SK Rapid Wien	AUT	0	0
Hajduk Split	CRO	0	1
Sampdoria	ITA	1	1
HJK Helsinki	FIN	2	0
AaB Aalborg	DEN	1	3
Siroki Brijeg	BIH	0	0
Hapoel Tel Aviv	ISR	3	3
Liepajas Metalurgs	LVA	3	0
AIK Stockholm	SWE	2	2
Drogheda United	IRL	1	0
Helsingborgs IF	SWE	1	3
SV Ried	AUT	1	0
FC Sion	SUI	1	3
Slaven Koprivnica	CRO	1	1
Galatasaray	TUR	2	2
FK Austria Wien	AUT	4	1
FK Jablonec 97	CZE	3	1
Ekranas Panevezys	LTU	1	0
Vålerenga IF	NOR	1	6

First Round

Bayer Leverkusen	GER	3	2
União Leiria	POR	1	3
Spartak Moskva	RUS	5	3
BK Häcken	SWE	0	1
Empoli	ITA	2	0
FC Zürich	SUI	1	3
Sparta Praha	CZE	0 0 4p
Odense BK	DEN	0 0 3p
Toulouse FC	FRA	0	1
CSKA Sofia	BUL	0	1
Bayern München	GER	1	2
Os Belenenses	POR	0	0
Hammarby IF	SWE	2	0
Sporting Braga	POR	1	4
Rabotnicki Skopje	MKD	1	0
Bolton Wanderers	ENG	1	1
Aris Thessaloniki	GRE	1	1
Real Zaragoza	ESP	0	2
Groclin Grodzisk	POL	0	0
Crvena Zvezda	SRB	1	1
Getafe	ESP	1	2
Twente Enschede	NED	0	3
Tottenham H'spur	ENG	6	1
Anorthosis F'gusta	CYP	1	1
RSC Anderlecht	BEL	1	1
SK Rapid Wien	AUT	1	0
Sampdoria	ITA	2	0
AaB Aalborg	DEN	2	0
Hapoel Tel Aviv	ISR	0	1
AIK Stockholm	SWE	0	0
Tampere United	FIN	2	1
Girond. Bordeaux	FRA	3	1
SC Heerenveen	NED	5	1
Helsingborgs IF	SWE	3	5
FC Sion	SUI	3	1
Galatasaray	TUR	2	5
FC Sochaux	FRA	0	1
Panionios	GRE	2	0
FK Austria Wien	AUT	2	2
Vålerenga IF	NOR	0	2

Group Stage

Group E		Pts
Bayer Leverkusen	GER	9
Spartak Moskva	RUS	7
FC Zürich	SUI	6
Sparta Praha	CZE	4
Toulouse FC	FRA	3

Group F		Pts
Bayern Muenchen	GER	8
Sporting Braga	POR	6
Bolton Wanderers	ENG	6
Aris Thessaloniki	GRE	5
Crvena Zvezda Beograd	SRB	0

Group G		Pts
Getafe	ESP	9
Tottenham Hotspur	ENG	7
RSC Anderlecht	BEL	5
AaB Aalborg	DEN	4
Hapoel Tel Aviv	ISR	3

Group H		Pts
Girond. Bordeaux	FRA	12
Helsingborgs IF	SWE	7
Galatasaray	TUR	4
Panionios	GRE	4
FK Austria Wien	AUT	1

In each preliminary and first round tie the home team in the first leg is listed above their opponents • ‡ Partizan disqualified

UEFA CUP 2007-08 FINAL ROUNDS

Round of Thirty-two			Round of Sixteen			Quarter-Final			Semi-Final			Final		
Zenit St P'burg*	1	1												
Villarreal	0	2												
			Zenit St P'burg	1	2									
			Oly. Marseille *	3	0									
Spartak Moskva	0	2												
Oly. Marseille *	3	0												
						Zenit St P'burg	4	0						
						B. Leverkusen *	1	1						
Hamburger SV	3	0												
FC Zürich *	1	0												
			Hamburger SV	0	3									
			B. Leverkusen *	1	2									
Galatasaray *	0	1												
B. Leverkusen	0	5												
									Zenit St P'burg	1	4			
									Bayern M'chen*	1	0			
Getafe	1	3												
AEK Athens *	1	0												
			Getafe	2	1									
			Benfica *	1	0									
1.FC Nürnberg	0	2												
Benfica *	1	2												
						Getafe	1	3						
						Bayern M'chen*	1	3						
Anderlecht *	2	1												
Gir. Bordeaux	1	1												
			Anderlecht *	0	2									
			Bayern M'chen	5	1									
Aberdeen *	2	1												
Bayern M'chen	2	5												
												Zenit St P'burg	2	
												Rangers	0	
Fiorentina	1	2												
Rosenborg *	0	1												
			Fiorentina *	2 0	4p									
			Everton	0 2	2p									
Brann Bergen *	0	1												
Everton	2	6												
						Fiorentina *	1	2						
						PSV Eindhoven	1	0						
Tottenham H.	2	1												
Slavia Praha *	1	1												
			Tottenham H. *	0 1	5p									
			PSV Eindhoven	1 0	6p									
Helsingborgs IF	0	1												
PSV Eindhoven*	2	2												
									Fiorentina	0 0	2p			
									Rangers *	0 0	4p			
Sporting CP *	2	3												
FC Basel	0	0												
			Sporting CP	1	1									
			Bolton Wand. *	1	0									
Atlético Madrid	0	0												
Bolton Wand. *	1	0												
						Sporting CP	0	0						
						Rangers *	0	2						
Werder Bremen*	3	1												
Sporting Braga	0	0												
			Werder Bremen	0	1									
			Rangers *	2	0									
Panathinaikos	0	1												
Rangers *	0	1												

* Home team in the first leg

FIRST QUALIFYING ROUND

FC ViOn, Zlaté Moravce, 19-07-2007, 17:00, 2880, Kaasik EST

ViOn Zlaté M'vce	3	Gibala 2 [51 78], Greguska [71]
FK Almaty	1	Larin [82]

Tcentralny, Almaty, 2-08-2007, 19:30, 12 000, Stankovic SRB

FK Almaty	1	Irismetov.J [58]
ViOn Zlaté M'vce	1	Cernák [77]

Aråsen, Lillestrøm, 19-07-2007, 19:00, 1562, Whitby WAL

Lillestrøm SK	2	Occean [19], Sundgot [45p]
UN Käerjéng 97	1	Andersson OG [45]

Josy Barthel, Luxembourg, 31-07-2007, 20:00, 629, Guliyev AZE

UN Käerjéng 97	1	Boulahfari [49]
Lillestrøm SK	0	

Jalkapallokenttä, Anjalankoski, 19-07-2007, 19:00, 1481, Bede HUN

MyPa-47	1	Hyyrynen [11]
EB/Streymur	0	

Tórsvøllur, Tórshavn, 2-08-2007, 19:00, 1175, McKeon IRL

EB/Streymur	1	Potemkin [86]
MyPa-47	1	Kuparinen [70]

Vojvodina, Novi Sad, 19-07-2007, 17:30, 2000, Tsikinis GRE

Vojvodina Novi Sad	5	Despotovic 3 [21 42 89p], Duric [60], Kacar [84]
Hibernians	1	Doffo [86p]

Ta'Qali, Ta'Qali, 2-08-2007, 18:00, 150, Evans WAL

Hibernians	0	
Vojvodina Novi Sad	2	Xuereb.A OG [30], Despotovic [62]

Comunal, Andorra La Vella, 19-07-2007, 17:00, 352, Tchagharyan ARM

Santa Coloma	1	Fernández [57]
Maccabi Tel Aviv	0	

Bloomfield, Tel Aviv, 2-08-2007, 19:30, 14 272, Saliy KAZ

Maccabi Tel Aviv	4	Mesika 2 [12 25], Shivhon [63], Kamanan [71]
Santa Coloma	0	

Ullói út, Budapest, 19-07-2007, 20:30, 1050, Hinriksson ISL

MTK Budapest	2	Pintér [20], Urban [57]
Mika Ashtarak	1	Rodrigues [45]

Ashtarak Kasakh, Yerevan, 2-08-2007, 19:00, 6000, Constantin ROU

Mika Ashtarak	1	Artyom Adamyan [26]
MTK Budapest	0	

Senec Montostroj, Senec, 19-07-2007, 20:00, 2151, Strahonja CRO

Artmedia Petrzalka	1	Durica [21p]
Zimbru Chisinau	1	Zhdanov [70p]

Zimbru, Chisinau, 2-08-2007, 19:00, 6500, Burrull ESP

Zimbru Chisinau	2	Kovalchuk [34], Zhdanov [60p]
Artmedia Petrzalka	2	Guédé [73], Borbély [94+]

GKS, Belchatow, 19-07-2007, 20:45, 3000, Chapron FRA

GKS Belchatow	2	Pietrasiak 2 [51 82]
Ameri Tbilisi	0	

Mikheil Meskhi, Tbilisi, 2-08-2007, 18:45, 1009, Kister KAZ

Ameri Tbilisi	2	Tatanashvili [12], Davitashvili [46]
GKS Belchatow	0	GKS Belchatow W 4-2p

Republican, Yerevan, 19-07-2007, 19:00, 3500, Svilokos CRO

Banants Yerevan	1	Kakosyan [68]
BSC Young Boys	1	Mangane [17]

Stade de Suisse, Bern, 2-08-2007, 19:30, 5478, Sidenco MDA

BSC Young Boys	4	Daniel 2 [11 41], Calvano [21], Schneuwly [58]
Banants Yerevan	0	

Belle Vue, Rhyl, 19-07-2007, 19:30, 1778, Vervecken BEL

Rhyl	3	Moran [26], Hunt [36], Garside [47]
Haka Valkeakoski	1	Lehtinen [15]

Tehtaan Kenttä, Valkeakoski, 2-08-2007, 19:00, 1565, Nikolaev RUS

Haka Valkeakoski	2	Innanen [62], Popovich [64]
Rhyl	0	

Keflavíkurvöllur, Keflavik, 19-07-2007, 19:15, 827, Bertolini SUI

Keflavík	3	Steinarsson [27], OG [34], Samuelsen.S [57]
FC Midtjylland	2	Dadu [9], Afriyie [20]

Messecentret, Herning, 2-08-2007, 19:00, 6125, McCourt NIR

FC Midtjylland	2	Simon Poulsen [68], Dadu [75]
Keflavík	1	Sigurdsson [11]

Partizan, Belgrade, 19-07-2007, 18:00, 619, Müftüoglu TUR

Bezanija NB	2	Djalovic [37], Durovski [57p]
Besa Kavajë	2	Ishaka [49], Elokan [90]

Qemal Stafa, Tirana, 2-08-2007, 20:30, 6000, Sousa POR

Besa Kavajë	0	
Bezanija NB	0	

Ta'Qali, Ta'Qali, 19-07-2007, 19:30, 205, Mrkovic BIH

Sliema Wanderers	0	
Litx Lovech	3	Popov 2 [22 56], Beto [53]

Gradski, Lovech, 2-08-2007, 20:30, 3900, Berezka UKR

Litx Lovech	4	Boudarène [28], Beto 2 [48 60], Popov [59]
Sliema Wanderers	0	

Zimbru, Chisinau, 19-07-2007, 19:00, 1500, Demirlek TUR

Nistru Otaci	1	Malitskyy [29]
Budapest Honvéd	1	Abraham [51]

József Bozsik, Budapest, 2-08-2007, 20:30, 3023, Svendsen DEN

Budapest Honvéd	1	Abraham [14]
Nistru Otaci	1	Mekang [50]

Tcentralny, Aktobe, 19-07-2007, 21:30, 13 000, Aydinus TUR

FK Aktobe	1	Khayrullin [85]
SV Mattersburg	0	

Pappelstadion, Mattersburg, 2-08-2007, 19:30, 3700, Hermansen DEN

SV Mattersburg	4	Jancker [22], Wagner [62], Csizmadia [67], Kovrig [92+]
SV Mattersburg	2	Bogomolov [71], Kosolapov [77]

Richmond Park, Carmarthen, 19-07-2007, 19:00, 769, Godulyan UKR

Carmarthen Town	0	
SK Brann Bergen	8	Winters 3 [8 30 45], Helstad 2 [17 28], Sigurdsson.K [70], Solli [83], Björnsson [91+]

Brann, Bergen, 2-08-2007, 19:00, 4800, Schörgenhofer AUT

SK Brann Bergen	6	Moen [9], Björnsson [19], Winters 2 [27 32], Sigurdsson.K [56], Hanstveit [57]
Carmarthen Town	3	Thomas [36], Hicks 2 [47 90]

Windsor Park, Belfast, 19-07-2007, 19:45, 301, Vejlgaard DEN

Dungannon Swifts	1	McCallister [17]
Suduva Marij'pole	0	

Suduva, Marijampole, 2-08-2007, 18:00, 2500, Edvartsen NOR

Suduva Marij'pole	4	Grigas [29], Urbsys 3 [50 55 84]
Dungannon Swifts	0	

Ullevi, Gothenburg, 19-07-2007, 20:00, 7230, Malzinskas LTU

BK Häcken	1	Heden [12]
KR Reyjkavík	1	Petursson [69]

KR-völlur, Reykjavik, 2-08-2007, 18:45, 1357, Gvardis RUS

KR Reyjkavík	0	
BK Häcken	1	De Oliveira [83]

Skonto, Riga, 19-07-2007, 19:35, 3700, Zimmermann SUI

Skonto Riga	1	Pereplotkins [27]
Dinamo Minsk	1	Rák [11]

Dinamo, Minsk, 2-08-2007, 18:30, 3041, Stalhammar SWE

Dinamo Minsk	2	Rák 2 [57 74]
Skonto Riga	0	

Richmond Park, Dublin, 19-07-2007, 19:45, 1900, Fautrel FRA

St Patrick's Ath	0	
OB Odense	0	

Fionia Park, Odense, 2-08-2007, 19:00, 5306, Blom NED

OB Odense	5	Andreasen [20], Christensen 2 [29 73], Borring [45], Nymann [89]
St Patrick's Ath	0	

GSP, Nicosia, 19-07-2007, 20:00, 10 697, Deaconu ROU

Omonia Nicosia	2	Kaiafas [43], Chailis [46]
Rudar Pljevlja	0	

Gradski, Podgorica, 2-08-2007, 20:30, 1000, Casha MLT

Rudar Pljevlja	0	
Omonia Nicosia	2	Mguni [34], Ricardo Sousa [75]

Sportni Park, Nova Gorica, 19-07-2007, 20:00, 1178, Jakov ISR
ND Gorica 1 Matavz [83]
Rabotnicki Skopje 2 Suler OG [79], Velkoski [91+]

Gradski, Skopje, 2-08-2007, 20:00, 2000, Vadachkoria GEO
Rabotnicki Skopje 2 Velkoski [44], Demiri [68]
ND Gorica 1 Demirovic [85p]

Zrinjski, Mostar, 19-07-2007, 20:15, 7920, De Marco ITA
Zrinjski Mostar 1 Matko [68].   Lazetic [80]
Partizan Beograd 6 Lamina 3 [32 60 63], Maletic [40], Jovetic [48],

Partizan, Belgrade, 2-08-2007, 20:30, 10 300, Jilek CZE
Partizan Beograd 5 Maletic [4], Moreira [32], Jovetic 3 [37 51 71]
Zrinjski Mostar 0

Tofikh Bakhramov, Baku, 19-07-2007, 19:45, 3500, Vialichka BLR
MTK-Araz Imishli 0
Groclin Grodzisk 0

Groclin Dyskobolia, Grodzisk Wielkopolski, 2-08-2007, 3353, Moen NOR
Groclin Grodzisk 1 Klodawski [88]
MTK-Araz Imishli 0

Gradski, Skopje, 19-07-2007, 20:15, 1000, Coltescu ROU
Vardar Skopje 0
Anorthosis F'gusta 1 Deyanov [88]

Antonis Papadopoulos, Larnaca, 2-08-2007, 9600, Mikolajewski POL
Anorthosis F'gusta 1 Zlogar [53]
Vardar Skopje 0

Mikheil Meskhi, Tbilisi, 19-07-2007, 18:00, 1150, Sapi HUN
Dinamo Tbilisi 2 Merebashvili [66p], Akiremy Owondo [72]
FC Vaduz 0

Rheinpark, Vaduz, 2-08-2007, 19:00, 755, Simunovic CRO
FC Vaduz 0
Dinamo Tbilisi 0

Gradski, Podgorica, 19-07-2007, 20:30, 9500, Kenan ISR
Bud'st Podgorica 1 Scepanovic [59]
Hajduk Split 1 Hrgovic.M [28]

Poljud, Split, 2-08-2007, 20:15, 29 315, Zografos GRE
Hajduk Split 1 Damjanovic [46]
Bud'st Podgorica 0

Finnair, Helsinki, 19-07-2007, 19:00, 1752, Zuta LTU
HJK Helsinki 2 Bah [24], Sorsa [91+]
Etzella Ettelbrück 0

Deich, Ettelbrück, 2-08-2007, 18:30, 476, Ishchenko UKR
Etzella Ettelbrück 0
HJK Helsinki 1 Savolainen [26p]

Pecara, Siroki Brijeg, 19-07-2007, 21:00, 3489, Kulbakov BLR
Siroki Brijeg 3 Celson 2 [24 33], Ronelle [44]
FC Koper 1 Viler [8]

Arena Petrol, Celje, 2-08-2007, 20:000, 300, Hietala FIN
FC Koper 2 Volas [34], Mejac [82]
Siroki Brijeg 3 Karoglan [18], Bozig.R OG [25], Ronelle [36]

Daugava, Liepaja, 19-07-2007, 19:30, 3000, Wouters BEL
Liepajas Metalurgs 1 Ferreira De Oli [5]
Dinamo Brest 1 Sokal [77]

Brestskiy, Brest, 2-08-2007, 19:30, 10 000, Spasic SRB
Dinamo Brest 1 Sokal [47]
Liepajas Metalurgs 2 Kruglyak [40], Karlsons.G [50]

The Oval, Belfast, 19-07-2007, 19:45, 2033, Sipailo LVA
Glentoran 0   Stephenson [73], Johnson [84]
AIK Stockholm 5 Figueiredo 2 [21 62], Valdemarin [68],

Råsunda, Stockholm, 2-08-2007, 20:00, 8707, Rogalla SUI
AIK Stockholm 4 Ozkan [7], Karlsson [24], Gerndt [88], Johnson [89]
Glentoran 0

Olimpico, Serravalle, 19-07-2007, 21:00, 1080, Janku ALB
Libertas 1 Pari [77]
Drogheda United 1 Zayed [44]

Dalymount Park, Dublin, 2-08-2007, 19:45, 1850, Wouters BEL
Drogheda United 3 Keegan 2 [11 48], Byrne.S [57]
Libertas 0

Olympia, Helsingborg, 19-07-2007, 19:00, 5071, Zakharov RUS
Helsingborgs IF 6 Omotoyossi [28], Dahl [30], Larsson 2 [59 64],
Trans Narva 0   Karekesi [80], Andersson.C [84]

A Le Coq Arena, Tallinn, 2-08-2007, 18:00, 150, Van De Velde BEL
Trans Narva 0
Helsingborgs IF 3 Wahlstedt [18], Svanbäck [32], Unkari [76]

Fill Metallbau Stadion, Ried/Innkreis, 19-07-2007, 2033, Perez ESP
SV Ried 3 Drechsel [2], Brenner [87], Salihi [91+]
Neftçhi Baku 1 Aliyev [14]

Tofik Bakhramov, Baku, 2-08-2007, 25 000, Ristoskov BUL
Neftçhi Baku 2 Subasic [14], Rashad F. Sadygov [21]
SV Ried 1 Salihi [85]

Gradski, Koprivnica, 19-07-2007, 17:45, 860, Toussaint LUX
Slaven Koprivnica 6 Posavec [18p], Sehic 2 [29 47], Vrucina 2 [60 82],
Teuta Durrës 2 Xhafaj.D [10], Brahja [65].   Bosnjak.P [90]

Niko Dovana, Durrës, 2-08-2007, 16:30, 800, Kailis CYP
Teuta Durrës 2 Kuli 2 [45 74]
Slaven Koprivnica 2 Kresinger [64], Vrucina [70]

Tórsvøllur, Tórshavn, 19-07-2007, 18:00, 590, Jug SVN
B36 Tórshavn 1 Hojsted [41]
Ekranas Panevezys 3 Luksys [11], Paulauskas [45], Pogreban [67]

Aukstaitija, Panevezys, 2-08-2007, 18:00, 2800, Rossi SMR
Ekranas Panevezys 3 Sidiauskas [51], Luksys 2 [77 87]
B36 Tórshavn 2 Midjord [85], Benjaminsen [86p]

A Le Coq Arena, Tallinn, 19-07-2007, 18:45, 1200, Buttimer IRL
Flora Tallinn 0
Vålerenga IF 1 Lange [31]

Ullevål, Oslo, 2-08-2007, 19:00, 4290, Jech CZE
Vålerenga IF 1 Berre [92+]
Flora Tallinn 0

SECOND QUALIFYING ROUND

FC ViOn, Zlaté Moravce, 16-08-2007, 17:00, 3368, Rasmussen DEN
ViOn Zlaté M'vce 0
Zenit St. Pet'burg 2 Hagen [38], Ionov.A [92+]

Petrovsky, St Petersburg, 30-08-2007, 19:30, 11 992, Bossen NED
Zenit St. Pet'burg 3 Pogrebnyak [10], Maximov [61], Kim Dong Jin [71]
ViOn Zlaté M'vce 0

Josy Barthel, Luxembourg, 16-08-2007, 20:00, 7112, Valgeirsson ISL
UN Käerjéng 97 0
Standard CL 3 Mbokani Bezua [59], Witsel 2 [81 86]

Sclessin, Liege, 30-08-2007, 20:00, 8700, Mihaljevic MNE
Standard CL 1 De Camargo [89]
UN Käerjéng 97 0

Jalkapallokenttä, Anjalankoski, 16-08-2007, 19:00, 3340, Thual FRA
MyPa-47 0
Blackburn Rovers 1 Santa Cruz [6]

Ewood Park, Blackburn, 30-08-2007, 20:05, 13 490, Einwaller AUT
Blackburn Rovers 2 Bentley [48], Roberts [91+]
MyPa-47 0

Vicente Calderón, Madrid, 16-08-2007, 22:00, 33 000, Circhetta SUI
Atlético Madrid 3 Maxi Rodriguez [37], Forlán [62], Agüero [70]
Vojvodina Novi Sad 0

Vojvodina, Novi Sad, 30-08-2007, 16:30, 2200, Brych GER
Vojvodina Novi Sad 1 Buac [39]
Atlético Madrid 0 Luis Garcia [54], Seitaridis [75]

Bloomfield, Tel Aviv, 16-08-2007, 19:30, 8003, Egorov RUS
Maccabi Tel Aviv 1 Kamanan [42]
Kayseri Erciyesspor 1 Ilhan Ozbay [5]

Atatürk, Kayseri, 30-08-2007, 19:00, 11 470, Tudor ROU
Kayseri Erciyesspor 3 Ilhan Ozbay [7], Köksal [14], Oztekin [72]
Maccabi Tel Aviv 1 Haddad [40]

Republican, Yerevan, 16-08-2007, 19:00, 7500, Stankovic SRB
Mika Ashtarak 2 Shahgeldyan [8], Alex [80]
Artmedia Petrzalka 1 Fodrek [66]

Senec Montostroj, Senec, 30-08-2007, 19:00, 1400, Skjerven NOR
Artmedia Petrzalka 2 Obzera 2 [5] [72]
Mika Ashtarak 0

Meteor, Dnepropetrovsk, 16-08-2007, 20:15, 22 000, Cakir TUR
Dnipro D'petrovsk 1 Nazarenko [80]
GKS Belchatow 1 Ujek [18]

GKS, Belchatow, 30-08-2007, 20:45, 3600, Messner AUT
GKS Belchatow 2 Stolarczyk [10p], Nowak [21]. Kornilenko [40]
Dnipro D'petrovsk 4 Kravchenko [7], Shelayev [32], Smodin [33],

Stade de Suisse, Bern, 16-08-2007, 19:30, 13 411, Sandmoen NOR
BSC Young Boys 1 Calvano [71]
Racing Club Lens 1 Monterrubio [75]

Stade Félix-Bollaert, Lens, 30-08-2007, 19:00, 31 088, Clattenburg ENG
Racing Club Lens 5 Dindane 2 [13] [58], Akalé [16], Carrière [67],
BSC Young Boys 1 Varela [32]. Feindouno [89]

Tehtaan Kenttä, Valkeakoski, 16-08-2007, 19:00, 1649, Richmond SCO
Haka Valkeakoski 1 Parviainen [53]
FC Midtjylland 2 Kristensen 2 [13] [44]

Messecentret, Herning, 30-08-2007, 19:00, 4707, Stavrev MKD
FC Midtjylland 5 Flinta [16], Olsen [27], Dadu [34], Troest [67],
Haka Valkeakoski 2 Popovich [33], Kauppila [72]. Larsen [85]

Niko Dovana, Durrës, 16-08-2007, 17:00, 4000, Dondarini ITA
Besa Kavajë 0
Litex Lovech 3 Popov 2 [13] [20], Beto [32]

Gradski, Lovech, 30-08-2007, 20:30, 1210, Kenan ISR
Litex Lovech 3 Genchev [13], Beto [69], Tome [79]
Besa Kavajë 0

Megyeri úti, Budapest, 16-08-2007, 19:00, 7000, Kuipers NED
Budapest Honvéd 0
Hamburger SV 0

AOL Arena, Hamburg, 30-08-2007, 20:30, 42 090, R.Santiago ESP
Hamburger SV 4 Guerrero 2 [9] [38], OG [50], Choup-Moting [90]
Budapest Honvéd 0

St Jakob-Park, Basel, 16-08-2007, 20:15, 9203, Ingvarsson SWE
FC Basel 2 Ergic [23], Felipe Caicedo [53]
SV Mattersburg 1 Nakata.K OG [20]

Pappelstadion, Mattersburg, 30-08-2007, 18:15, 4600, Dereli TUR
SV Mattersburg 0 Carlitos [53]
FC Basel 4 Felipe Caicedo [22], Ergic [36], Streller [41],

Brann, Bergen, 16-08-2007, 19:00, 7400, Wilmes LUX
SK Brann Bergen 2 Björnsson [24], Winters [49]
Süduva Marij'pole 1 Negreiros [56p]

Süduva, Marijampole, 30-08-2007, 17:00, 2000, Banari MDA
Süduva Marij'pole 3 Urbsys [46], Maciulevicius [78], Otavio [84]
SK Brann Bergen 4 Moen [37], Björnsson [45], Solli [57], Huseklepp [63]

Balgarska Armia, Sofia, 30-08-2007, 20:30, 1500, Hyytiä FIN
Lokomotiv Sofia 3 Davtchev [19], Baldovaliev [62], Djilas [84]
Otelul Galati 1 Semeghin [74]

Otelul, Galati, 30-08-2007, 17:00, 8005, Gomes Costa POR
Otelul Galati 0
Lokomotiv Sofia 0

Dr Magalhães Pessoa, Leiria, 16-08-2007, 19:45, 1945, Collum SCO
União Leiria 0
Maccabi Netanya 0

Kiryat Eliazer, Haifa, 30-08-2007, 20:30, 7100, Corodean ROU
Maccabi Netanya 0
União Leiria 1 N'gal [84]

East End Park, Dunfermline, 16-08-2007, 19:45, 6017, Krajnc SVN
Dunfermline Ath 1 Hamilton [1]
BK Häcken 1 Henriksson [57]

Ullevi, Gothenburg, 30-08-2007, 20:00, 2712, Havrilla SVK
BK Häcken 1 Skulason [27]
Dunfermline Ath 0

Dinamo, Minsk, 16-08-2007, 19:00, 3867, Courtney NIR
Dinamo Minsk 1 Putilo [73]
OB Odense 1 Laursen [94+]

Fionia Park, Odense, 30-08-2007, 20:30, 6416, Weiner GER
OB Odense 4 Nielsen 2 [38] [55], Absolonsen 2 [77] [79]
Dinamo Minsk 0

GSP, Nicosia, 16-08-2007, 20:00, 13 140, Atkinson ENG
Omonia Nicosia 1 Kaiafas [14]
CSKA Sofia 1 Claudinei [1]

Balgarska Armia, Sofia, 30-08-2007, 20:30, 14 320, Gumienny BEL
CSKA Sofia 2 Claudinei [17], Chilikov [88]
Omonia Nicosia 1 Magno [8]

Råsunda, Stockholm, 16-08-2007, 20:00, 5500, Kelly IRL
Hammarby IF 2 Paulinho [35], Castro-Tello [49]
Fredrikstad FK 1 Kvisvik [74]

Fredrikstad, Fredrikstad, 30-08-2007, 20:00, 7548, Sukhina RUS
Fredrikstad FK 1 Bjorkoy [85]
Hammarby IF 1 Eguren [90p]

Gradski, Skopje, 16-08-2007, 20:00, 5500, Olsiak SVK
Rabotnicki Skopje 0
Zrinjski Mostar 0

Zrinjski, Mostar, 30-08-2007, 20:30, 1500, Svendsen DEN
Zrinjski Mostar 1 Ivankovic [36]
Rabotnicki Skopje 2 Milisavljevic [33], Stanisis [92+]

Tcentralny, Kostanay, 16-08-2007, 19:30, 8000, Sippel GER
Tobol Kostanay 0
Groclin Grodzisk 1 Muszalik [4]

Dyskobolia, Grodzisk Wielkopolski, 30-08-2007, 2082, Johannesson SWE
Groclin Grodzisk 2 Sikora 2 [5] [19]
Tobol Kostanay 0

CFR, Cluj-Napoca, 16-08-2007, 20:30, 7100, Bertolini SUI
CFR 1907 Cluj 1 Trica [69p]
Anorthosis F'gusta 3 Zlogar [43], Boaventura [48], Sosin [58]

Antonis Papadopoulos, Larnaca, 30-08-2007, 20:00, 9400, Dean ENG
Anorthosis F'gusta 1
CFR 1907 Cluj 0

Mikheil Meskhi, Tbilisi, 16-08-2007, 18:00, 3950, Mikulski POL
Dinamo Tbilisi 0
SK Rapid Wien 3 Fabiano [24], Hofmann [39], Bazina [53]

Gerhard Hanappi, Vienna, 30-08-2007, 20:30, 12 600, Kailis CYP
SK Rapid Wien 5 Bazina [30], Bilic [54], Hofmann 2 [59] [75p],
Dinamo Tbilisi 0 Kavlak [73]

Poljud, Split, 30-08-2007, 20:45, 28 710, Paixao POR
Hajduk Split 0
Sampdoria 1 Campagnaro [44]

Luigi Ferraris, Genoa, 30-08-2007, 20:45, 21 700, Královec CZE
Sampdoria 1 Montella [34p]
Hajduk Split 1 Hrgovic.M [83]

Finnair, Helsinki, 16-08-2007, 19:00, 4912, Matejek CZE
HJK Helsinki 2 Samura 2 [15] [56]
AaB Aalborg 1 Risgård [37]

Aalborg, Aalborg, 30-08-2007, 19:30, 3902, Malcolm NIR
AaB Aalborg 3 Enevoldsen [7], Johansson [26], Curth [43]
HJK Helsinki 0

Pecara, Siroki Brijeg, 16-08-2007, 20:00, 3000, Paniashvili GEO
Siroki Brijeg 0
Hapoel Tel Aviv 3 Abedi [14], Asulin [32], Gabriel dos Santos [74]

Bloomfield, Tel Aviv, 30-08-2007, 20:50, 5337, Szabo HUN
Hapoel Tel Aviv 3 Asulin [41], Badir [50], Natcho [75]
Siroki Brijeg 0

Daugava, Liepaja, 16-08-2007, 19:30, 2280, Georgiev BUL
Liepajas Metalurgs 3 Karlsons.G [20], Ivanovs [43], Tamosauskas [63]
AIK Stockholm 2 Ivanovs OG [49], Ivan [61]

Råsunda, Stockholm, 30-08-2007, 19:00, 7528, Richards WAL
AIK Stockholm 2 Figueiredo 2 [43] [54]
Liepajas Metalurgs 0

Dalymount Park, Dublin, 16-08-2007, 19:45, 5100, Kaldma EST
Drogheda United 1 Zayed [54]
Helsingborgs IF 1 Larsson [34]

Olympia, Helsingborg, 30-08-2007, 20:30, 4767, Godulyan UKR

Helsingborgs IF 3 Jakobsson [52], Omotoyossi [68], Karekesi [91+]

Drogheda United 0

Fill Metallbau Stadion, Ried/Innkreis, 16-08-2007, 2000, Brines SCO

SV Ried 1 Dospel [66]

FC Sion 1 Saborio [92+]

Stade de Genève, Geneva, 30-08-2007, 20:15, 4500, Asumaa FIN

FC Sion 3 Obradovic [40], Zakrzewski [44], Dominguez [47]

SV Ried 0

Gradski, Koprivnica, 16-08-2007, 18:30, 2730, Lannoy FRA

Slaven Koprivnica 1 Posavec [16]

Galatasaray 2 Ayhan Akman [42], Volkan Yaman [72]

Ali Sami Yen, Istanbul, 30-08-2007, 21:00, 2100, Rizzoli ITA

Galatasaray 2 Umit Karan [9], Hakan Sükür [37]

Slaven Koprivnica 1 Poljak [36]

Franz Horr, Vienna, 16-08-2007, 20:30, 4912, Dávila ESP

FK Austria Wien 4 Ertl [8], Kuljic 2 [20 64], Lasnik [47]

FK Jablonec 97 3 Zelenka 2 [28 36], Baranek [76]

Strelnice, Jablonec nad Nisou, 30-08-2007, 5710, Kasnaferis GRE

FK Jablonec 97 1 Rilke [83]

FK Austria Wien 1 Sariyar [39]

Aukstaitija, Panevezys, 16-08-2007, 18:00, 3300, Granat POL

Ekranas Panevezys 1 Bicka [45p]

Vålerenga IF 1 Dos Santos [76]

Ullevål, Oslo, 30-08-2007, 19:00, 2939, Vad HUN

Vålerenga IF 6 Grindheim 2 [5 45], Sørensen [42], Horn [67],

Ekranas Panevezys 0   Storbæk [81], Brix [91+]

FIRST ROUND

Goodison Park, Liverpool, 20-09-2007, 20:00, 37 120, Stuchlik AUT

Everton 1 Lescott [24]

Metalist Kharkiv 1 Edmar [78]

Metalist, Kharkiv, 4-10-2007, 21:45, 32 000, Hyytiä FIN

Metalist Kharkiv 2 Edmar [21], Mahdoufi [52]

Everton 3 Lescott [48], McFadden [72], Anichebe [88]

Frankenstadion, Nuremburg, 20-09-2007, 20:45, 40 066, Malek POL

1.FC Nürnberg 0

Rapid Bucuresti 0

Giulesti, Bucharest, 4-10-2007, 17:00, 10 340, Ingvarsson SWE

Rapid Bucuresti 2 Césinha [15], Lazar [93+]

1.FC Nürnberg 2 Kluge [22], Misimovic [56]

Petrovsky, St Petersburg, 20-09-2007, 20:00, 15 324, Vázquez ESP

Zenit St. Pet'burg 3 Arshavin 2 [36 65], Kim Dong Jin [84]

Standard CL 0

Sclessin, Liège, 4-10-2007, 20:00, 14 946, Thomson SCO

Standard CL 1 Onyewu [35]

Zenit St. Pet'burg 1 Pogrebnyak [79]

Bessa XXI, Porto, 20-09-2007, 21:00, 3452, Rasmussen DEN

Paços de Ferreira 0

AZ Alkmaar 1 Pocognoli [89]

DSB, Alkmaar, 4-10-2007, 21:30, 13 418, Tudor ROU

AZ Alkmaar 0

Paços de Ferreira 0

Panthessaliko, Volos, 20-09-2007, 18:00, 8126, Sippel GER

Larissa 2 Bakayoko [33], Cleyton [34]

Blackburn Rovers 0

Ewood Park, Blackburn, 4-10-2007, 20:00, 20 741, Circhetta SUI

Blackburn Rovers 2 Derbyshire [45p], Warnock [54]

Larissa 1 Cleyton [17]

Vicente Calderón, Madrid, 20-09-2007, 20:45, 24 431, Bossen NED

Atlético Madrid 4 Mista [13], Forlán [17], Luis García 2 [83 92+]

Kayseri Erciyesspor 0

Atatürk, Kayseri, 4-10-2007, 19:00, 3899, Messner AUT

Kayseri Erciyesspor 0   Forlán [79]

Atlético Madrid 5 Agüero 2 [6 44], Jurado [14], Maxi Rodriguez [53p],

Tehelné Pole, Bratislava, 20-09-2007, 20:15, 3951, Paixao POR

Artmedia Petrzalka 1 Urbánek [46]

Panathinaikos 2 Papadopoulos [61p], Ndoye [90]

Apostolos Nikolaidis, Athens, 2-10-2007, 18:45, 6200, Gumienny BEL

Panathinaikos 3 Papadopoulos 3 [43p 45 74p]

Artmedia Petrzalka 0

Pittodrie, Aberdeen, 20-09-2007, 20:05, 15 431, Berntsen NOR

Aberdeen 0

Dnipro D'petrovsk 0

Meteor, Dnepropetrovsk, 4-10-2007, 20:00, 18 655, Thual FRA

Dnipro D'petrovsk 1 Vorobey [76]

Aberdeen 1 Mackie [28]

Felix-Bollaert, Lens, 19-09-2007, 18:00, 24 539, Skomina SVN

Racing Club Lens 1 Dindane [70]

FC København 1 Allbäck [5]

Parken, Copenhagen, 4-10-2007, 20:15, 23 861, Gomes POR

FC København 2 Allbäck [76], Grønkjaer [112]

Racing Club Lens 1 Carriere [13]

Messecentret, Herning, 20-09-2007, 20:00, 5883, Mikulski POL

FC Midtjylland 1 Babatunde [30]

Lokomotiv Moskva 3 Samedov [61], Bilyaletdinov [69], Sychev [91+]

Lokomotiv, Moscow, 4-10-2007, 19:00, 9800, Kasnaferis GRE

Lokomotiv Moskva 2 Bilyaletdinov [11], Maminov [15]

FC Midtjylland 0

El Madrigal, Villarreal, 20-09-2007, 21:45, 10 725, Piccirillo FRA

Villarreal 4 Nihat Kahveci 2 [6 50], Senna [18], Tomasson [54]

BATE Borisov 1 Zhavnerchik [70]

Dinamo, Minsk, 4-10-2007, 20:45, 6000, Sandmoen NOR

BATE Borisov 0

Villarreal 2 Cani [24], Angel [78]

Euroborg, Groningen, 20-09-2007, 20:30, 19 486, Batista POR

FC Groningen 1 Lovre [25]

Fiorentina 1 Semioli [65]

Artemio Franchi, Florence, 4-10-2007, 21:00, 24 858, Meyer GER

Fiorentina 1 Mutu [59]. Fiorentina won 4-3 on pens

FC Groningen 1 Nevland [55]

OACA Spyro Louis, Athens, 20-09-2007, 19:00, 25 523, Dean ENG

AEK Athens 3 Geraldo [2], Rivaldo [57], Kone [88]

Austria Salzburg 0

Wals-Siezenheim, Salzburg, 4-10-2007, 20:30, 13 533, Tagliavento ITA

Austria Salzburg 1 Lokvenc [20]

AEK Athens 0

Mestsky, Mladá Boleslav, 20-09-2007, 18:15, 4110, Kinhöfer GER

Mladá Boleslav 0

Palermo 1 Jankovic [91+]

Renzo Barbera, Palermo, 4-10-2007, 20:45, 3000, I.González ESP

Palermo 0

Mladá Boleslav 0 Sedlácek [93+]. Mladá won 4-2 on pens

Dinamo, Bucharest, 20-09-2007, 20:30, 8239, Ferreira POR

Dinamo Bucuresti 1 Niculescu [8]

IF Elfsborg 2 Keene 2 [10 30]

Ryavallen, Boras, 4-10-2007, 19:00, 6827, Courtney NIR

IF Elfsborg 0

Dinamo Bucuresti 1 Danciulescu [31]

Gradski, Lovech, 18-09-2007, 19:00, 4000, Asumaa FIN

Litex Lovech 0

Hamburger SV 1 Castelen [75]

HSH Nordbank, Hamburg, 4-10-2007, 18:15, 38 212, Allaerts BEL

Hamburger SV 3 Guerrero 2 [40 52], Van der Vaart [71]

Litex Lovech 1 Popov.R [38]

Kosevo, Sarajevo, 20-09-2007, 20:00, 4000, Lajuks LVA

FK Sarajevo 1 Milosevic [93+]

FC Basel 2 Carlitos [11], Ergic [63]

St Jakob-Park, Basel, 4-10-2007, 19:30, 15 124, Gomes Costa POR

FC Basel 6 Carlitos 2 [8 9], Streller 2 [18 29], Huggel [75],

FK Sarajevo 0   Felipe Caicedo [90]

Brann, Bergen, 20-09-2007, 19:00, 10 471, Jara CZE
SK Brann Bergen 0
Club Brugge 1 Sterchele [84]

Jan Breydel, Bruges, 4-10-2007, 20:30, 14 570, Dereli TUR
Club Brugge 1 Clement [76]
SK Brann Bergen 2 Helstad [14], Winters [39]

Maksimir, Zagreb, 20-09-2007, 18:30, 25 380, Lannoy FRA
Dinamo Zagreb 0
Ajax 1 Rommedahl [61]

Amsterdam ArenA, 4-10-2007, 19:30, 44 000, Clattenburg ENG
Ajax 2 Huntelaar 2 [101] [120]
Dinamo Zagreb 3 Modric [34p], Mandzukic 2 [94] [96]

Balgarska Armia, Sofia, 20-09-2007, 20:30, 1863, Malcolm NIR
Lokomotiv Sofia 1 Davtchev [51]
Stade Rennais 3 Hansson [39], Cheyrou [74], Leroy [90]

Route de Lorient, Rennes, 4-10-2007, 20:45, 16 208, Jakobsson ISL
Stade Rennais 1 Marveaux [25]
Lokomotiv Sofia 2 Antunovic 2 [37] [40]

BayArena, Leverkusen, 20-09-2007, 17:15, 16 331, Hrinal SVK
Bayer Leverkusen 3 Kiessling 2 [19] [77], Rolfes [31]
União Leiria 1 João Paulo [29]

Dr Magalhães Pessoa, Leiria, 4-10-2007, 21:15, 1846, Kapitanis CYP
União Leiria 3 Cadu [3], João Paulo [21], Laranjeiro [90]
Bayer Leverkusen 2 Papadopoulos [10], Kiessling [87]

Luzhniki, Moscow, 20-09-2007, 18:45, 9500, Rogalla SUI
Spartak Moskva 5 Pavlyuchenko 2 [6] [13], Welliton 2 [19] [55], Titov [56]
BK Häcken 0

Ullevi, Gothenburg, 4-10-2007, 19:00, 1103, Kaldma EST
BK Häcken 1 Henriksson [84]
Spartak Moskva 3 Titov [7], Bazhenov [80], Dzyuba [91+]

Carlo Castellani, Empoli, 20-09-2007, 21:00, 5722, Yefet ISR
Empoli 2 Piccolo [44], Antonini [49p]
FC Zürich 1 Alphonse [74]

Letzigrund, Zürich, 4-10-2007, 18:30, 13 600, Ceferin SVN
FC Zürich 3 Kollar [37], Abdi [78], Alphonse [82]
Empoli 0

Strahov, Prague, 20-09-2007, 20:15, 7242, Trivkovic CRO
Sparta Praha 0
OB Odense 0

Fionia Park, Odense, 4-10-2007, 19:00, 10 565, Egorov RUS
OB Odense 0
Sparta Praha 0 Sparta won 4-3 on pens

Stade Municipal, Toulouse, 20-09-2007, 20:30, 13 341, Vollquartz DEN
Toulouse FC 0
CSKA Sofia 0

Balgarska Armia, Sofia, 4-10-2007, 20:00, 20 000, Brugger AUT
CSKA Sofia 1 Claudinei [65p]
Toulouse FC 1 Gignac [95+]

Allianz Arena, Munich, 20-09-2007, 19:00, 64 000, Johannesson SWE
Bayern München 1 Toni [34]
Os Belenenses 0

O Restelo, Lisbon, 4-10-2007, 19:30, 6603, Granat POL
Os Belenenses 0
Bayern München 2 Toni [59], Hamit Altintop [76]

Råsunda, Stockholm, 20-09-2007, 19:00, 6971, Oriekhov UKR
Hammarby IF 2 Petter Andersson 2 [50] [66]
Sporting Braga 1 Linz [59]

Municipal, Braga, 4-10-2007, 21:00, 9301, Brines SCO
Sporting Braga 4 Wender [47], Yasser 2 [69] [92+], Linz [81p]
Hammarby IF 1

Gradski, Skopje, 20-09-2007, 20:00, 8500, Szabó HUN
Rabotnicki Skopje 1 Milisavljevic [53]
Bolton Wanderers 1 Mélté [83]

Reebok, Bolton, 4-10-2007, 20:00, 17 900, Skjerven NOR
Bolton Wanderers 1 Anelka [67]
Rabotnicki Skopje 0

Kleanthis Vikelidis, Thessalonica, 20-09-2007, 18 622, Kassai HUN
Aris Thessaloniki 1 Papadopoulos.A [6]
Real Zaragoza 0

La Romareda, Zaragoza, 4-10-2007, 21:00, 24 000, Dougal SCO
Real Zaragoza 2 Oliveira [19], Sergio García [72]
Aris Thessaloniki 1 Javito [63]

Dyskobolia, Grodzisk Wielkopolski, 20-09-2007, 3107, Paniashvili GEO
Groclin Grodzisk 0
Crvena Zvezda 1 Basta [19]

Crvena Zvezda, Belgrade, 4-10-2007, 20:45, 13 364, Balaj ROU
Crvena Zvezda 1 Castillo [43]
Groclin Grodzisk 0

Coliseum, Getafe, Madrid, 20-09-2007, 21:00, 8194, Richmond SCO
Getafe 1 Uche [91+]
Twente Enschede 0

Arke, Enschede, 4-10-2007, 20:45, 13 285, Bebek CRO
Twente Enschede 3 Wielaert [30], Engelaar [117], Zomer [120]
Getafe 2 Belenguer [101], Granero [103]

White Hart Lane, London, 20-09-2007, 20:00, 35 780, Dondarini ITA
Tottenham H'spur 6 Kaboul [5], Dawson [39], Keane [42], Bent [43],
Anorthosis F'gusta 1 Zlogar [80].   Defoe 2 [65] [91+]

Antonis Papadopoulos, Larnaca, 4-10-2007, 17:45, 7800, Královec CZE
Anorthosis F'gusta 1 Pereira [54]
Tottenham H'spur 1 Keane [78]

Vanden Stock, Brussels, 20-09-2007, 20:45, 14 068, Eriksson SWE
RSC Anderlecht 1 Serhat [11]
SK Rapid Wien 1 Hofmann [82]

Gerhard Hanappi, Vienna, 4-10-2007, 20:45, 17 400, Rizzoli ITA
SK Rapid Wien 0
RSC Anderlecht 1 Hassan [22]

Luigi Ferraris, Genoa, 20-09-2007, 20:45, 16 800, Einwaller AUT
Sampdoria 2 Del Vecchio [18], Bellucci [59]
AaB Aalborg 2 Prica [19], Johansson [54]

Aalborg, Aalborg, 4-10-2007, 19:00, 10 300, Verbist BEL
AaB Aalborg 0
Sampdoria 0

Bloomfield, Tel Aviv, 20-09-2007, 20:50, 8762, Sukhina RUS
Hapoel Tel Aviv 0
AIK Stockholm 0

Råsunda, Stockholm, 4-10-2007, 20:30, 9082, Styles ENG
AIK Stockholm 0
Hapoel Tel Aviv 1 Oved [64]

Ratina, Tampere, 20-09-2007, 19:00, 5719, Richards WAL
Tampere United 2 Wiss [8], Petrescu [69]
Girond. Bordeaux 3 Cavenaghi 2 [48] [93+], Micoud [92+]

Chaban-Delmas, Bordeaux, 4-10-2007, 21:00, 8445, Ivanov RUS
Girond. Bordeaux 1 Chamakh [49]
Tampere United 1 Ojanperä [50]

Abe Lenstra, Heerenveen, 20-09-2007, 20:45, 14 500, Panic BIH
SC Heerenveen 5 Bradley 2 [20] [60], Sibon 2 [30] [35], Nielsen [59]
Helsingborgs IF 1 Larsson 2 [53] [71p], Omotoyossi [57]

Olympia, Helsingborg, 4-10-2007, 18:00, 6296, Lehner AUT
Helsingborgs IF 5 Larsson [18], Dahl [37], Omotoyossi 2 [45] [80],
SC Heerenveen 1 Sibon [89].   Makondele [51]

Stade de Genève, Geneva, 20-09-2007, 20:15, 15 000, Dávila ESP
FC Sion 3 Dominguez [6], Vanczák [9], Song OG [31]
Galatasaray 2 Lincoln [38], Linderoth [67]

Ali Sami Yen, Istanbul, 4-10-2007, 21:30, 20 719, Weiner GER
Galatasaray 5 Umit Karan 2 [22] [28], Lincoln [36], Arda Turan [68],
FC Sion 1 Nwaneri [90].   Bouzid [90]

Auguste Bonal, Montbeliard, 20-09-2007, 18:30, 9469, Corpodean ROU
FC Sochaux 0
Panionios 2 Djebbour [28], Fernandez [54]

Panionios, Athens, 4-10-2007, 21:00, 6499, Kelly IRL
Panionios 0
FC Sochaux 1 Kumordzi OG [53]

Details of FK Austria v Vålerenga IF are on page 1047

GROUP A

Petrovsky, St Petersburg, 25-10-2007, 19:30, 15 400, Kapitanis CYP
Zenit St. Pet'burg 1 Tymoschuk [43p]
AZ Alkmaar 1 Ari [20]
Goodison Park, Liverpool, 25-10-2007, 20:00, 33 777, Ingvarsson SWE
Everton 3 Cahill [14], Osman [50], Anichebe [85]
Larissa 1 Cleyton [65]
Panthessaliko, Volos, 8-11-2007, 17:30, 4753, Vollquartz DEN
Larissa 2 Alexandrou [58], Fotakis [62]
Zenit St. Pet'burg 3 Pogrebnyak [39], Zyrianov [70], Fatik Tekke [78]
Frankenstadion, Nuremburg, 8-11-2007, 21:05, 43 000, Undiano ESP
1.FC Nürnberg 0
Everton 2 Arteta [83p], Anichebe [88]
Petrovsky, St Petersburg, 29-11-2007, 19:00, 18 123, Královec CZE
Zenit St. Pet'burg 2 Pogrebnyak [76], Ionov.A [79]
1.FC Nürnberg 2 Charisteas [25], Benko [84]
DSB Stadion, Alkmaar, 29-11-2007, 20:45, 15 700, Paniashvili GEO
AZ Alkmaar 1 Dembélé [77]
Larissa 0
Goodison Park, Liverpool, 5-12-2007, 19:45, 38 407, Jakobsson ISL
Everton 1 Cahill [85]
Zenit St. Pet'burg 0
Frankenstadion, Nuremburg, 5-12-2007, 20:45, 35 020, Johannesson SWE
1.FC Nürnberg 2 Mintál 2 [83 85]
AZ Alkmaar 1 De Zeeuw [29]
DSB Stadion, Alkmaar, 20-12-2007, 20:45, 16 800, Dereli TUR
AZ Alkmaar 2 Pelle [17], Jaliens [66]
Everton 3 Johnson [2], Jagielka [44], Vaughan [80]
Panthessaliko, Volos, 20-12-2007, 21:45, 2863, Kaldma EST
Larissa 1 Kozlej [11]
1.FC Nürnberg 3 Saenko [45], Mintál [57], Charisteas [73]

Group A	Pl	W	D	L	F	A	Pts
Everton	4	4	0	0	9	3	12
1.FC Nürnberg	4	2	1	1	7	6	7
Zenit St Petersburg	4	1	2	1	6	6	5
AZ Alkmaar	4	1	1	2	6	6	4
Larissa	4	0	0	4	4	10	0

GROUP B

Apostolos Nikolaidis, Athens, 25-10-2007, 19:00, 8154, Einwaller AUT
Panathinaikos 3 Goumas [11], Papadopoulos [73], Salpingidis [77]
Aberdeen 0
Lokomotiv, Moscow, 25-10-2007, 20:45, 12 200, Clattenburg ENG
Lokomotiv Moskva 3 Bilyaletdinov [27], Odemwingie 2 [61 64]
Atlético Madrid 3 Agüero 2 [16 85], Forlán [47]
Pittodrie, Aberdeen, 8-11-2007, 20:00, 18 843, Meyer GER
Aberdeen 1 Diamond [27]
Lokomotiv Moskva 1 Ivanovic [45]
Parken, Copenhagen, 8-11-2007, 20:15, 25 142, Hrinak SVK
FC København 0
Panathinaikos 1 Ndoye [16]
Lokomotiv, Moscow, 29-11-2007, 20:30, 6500, Brugger AUT
Lokomotiv Moskva 0
FC København 1 Nordstrand [62p]
Vicente Calderón, Madrid, 29-11-2007, 20:45, 27 045, Bebek CRO
Atlético Madrid 2 Forlán [45p], Simão [61]
Aberdeen 0
Parken, Copenhagen, 5-12-2007, 20:45, 33 034, Dondarini ITA
FC København 0
Atlético Madrid 2 Simão [21], Agüero [62]

Apostolos Nikolaidis, Athens, 5-12-2007, 21:45, 7013, Circhetta SUI
Panathinaikos 2 Salpingidis 2 [70 74]
Lokomotiv Moskva 0
Pittodrie, Aberdeen, 20-12-2007, 19:45, 20 406, Batista POR
Aberdeen 4 Jamie Smith 2 [47 55], OG [71], Foster [83]
FC København 0
Vicente Calderón, Madrid, 20-12-2007, 20:45, 15 986, Kircher GER
Atlético Madrid 2 Luis Garcia [74], Simão [96+]
Panathinaikos 1 Salpingidis [34]

Group B	Pl	W	D	L	F	A	Pts
Atlético Madrid	4	3	1	0	9	4	10
Panathinaikos	4	3	0	1	7	2	9
Aberdeen	4	1	1	2	5	6	4
FC København	4	1	0	3	1	7	3
Lokomotiv Moskva	4	0	2	2	4	7	2

GROUP C

Ryavallen, Boras, 25-10-2007, 20:00, 4127, Sippel GER
IF Elfsborg 1 Mobäck [15]
AEK Athens 1 Pappas [49]
El Madrigal, Villarreal, 25-10-2007, 20:45, 12 355, Lannoy FRA
Villarreal 1 Capdevila [88]
Fiorentina 1 Vieri [48]
Mestsky, Mladá Boleslav, 8-11-2007, 20:30, 4082, Skomina SVN
Mladá Boleslav 1 Mendy [90]
Villarreal 2 Nihat Kahveci [33], Santi Cazorla [56]
Artemio Franchi, Florence, 8-11-2007, 20:45, 18 620, Dereli TUR
Fiorentina 6 Jørgensen 2 [4 78], Vieri [5], Donadel [62],.
IF Elfsborg 1 Ishizaki [41].   Krøldrup [65], Di Carmine [87]
Ryavallen, Boras, 29-11-2007, 18:15, 3632, Kelly IRL
IF Elfsborg 1 Svensson.M [31]
Mladá Boleslav 3 Táborsky [67], Mendy [79], Vorisek [95+]
OACA Spyro Louis, Athens, 29-11-2007, 21:00, 26 386, Thomson SCO
AEK Athens 1 Balzaretti OG [33]
Fiorentina 1 Osvaldo [29]
Mestsky, Mladá Boleslav, 5-12-2007, 20:45, 4670, Verbist BEL
Mladá Boleslav 0
AEK Athens 1 Nsaliwa Tamanda [46]
El Madrigal, Villarreal, 5-12-2007, 20:45, 9225, Tudor ROU
Villarreal 2 Tomasson 2 [2 51]
IF Elfsborg 0
OACA Spyro Louis, Athens, 20-12-2007, 20:45, Lehner AUT
AEK Athens 1 Rivaldo [68]
Villarreal 2 Mavuba [40], Tomasson [69]
Artemio Franchi, Florence, 20-12-2007, 20:45, 9366, Ferreira POR
Fiorentina 2 Mutu [44p], Vieri [67]
Mladá Boleslav 1 Rajnoch [60]

Group C	Pl	W	D	L	F	A	Pts
Fiorentina	4	2	2	0	10	4	8
Villarreal	4	2	1	0	5	2	7
AEK Athens	4	1	2	0	3	2	5
Mladá Boleslav	4	1	0	3	5	6	3
IF Elfsborg	4	0	1	3	3	12	1

GROUP D

Brann, Bergen, 25-10-2007, 19:00, 13 029, Kasnaferis GRE
Brann Bergen 0
Hamburger SV 1 Kompany [62]
St Jakob Park, Basel, 25-10-2007, 20:45, 11 407, Rizzoli ITA
FC Basel 1 Streller [55]
Stade Rennais 0

Route de Lorient, Rennes, 8-11-2007, 19:00, 10 108, Lehner AUT

Stade Rennais 1 Cheyrou [88p]
Brann Bergen 1 Karadas [24]

Maksimir, Zagreb, 8-11-2007, 20:15, 22 345, Gumienny BEL

Dinamo Zagreb 0
FC Basel 0

HSH Nordbank, Hamburg, 29-11-2007, 19:00, 36 472, Clattenburg ENG

Hamburger SV 3 Van der Vaart [30], Choupo-Moting [84],
Stade Rennais 0 Zidan [91+p]

Brann, Bergen, 29-11-2007, 20:15, 9962, Balaj ROU

Brann Bergen 2 Bjarnason [45], Bakke [72]
Dinamo Zagreb 1 Vukojevic [49]

Maksimir, Zagreb, 5-12-2007, 20:45, 18 870, McDonald SCO

Dinamo Zagreb 0
Hamburger SV 2 De Jong [88], Trochowski [93+p]

St Jakob Park, Basel, 5-12-2007, 20:45, 13 731, Egorov RUS

FC Basel 1 Carlitos [40]
Brann Bergen 0

HSH Nordbank, Hamburg, 20-12-2007, 20:45, 48 917, Vollquartz DEN

Hamburger SV 1 Olic [73]
FC Basel 1 Ergic [58]

Route de Lorient, Rennes, 20-12-2007, 20:45, 10 054, Courtney NIR

Stade Rennais 1 Mbia [88]
Dinamo Zagreb 1 Vukojevic [57]

Group D	Pl	W	D	L	F	A	Pts
Hamburger SV	4	3	1	0	7	1	10
FC Basel	4	2	2	0	3	1	8
SK Brann Bergen	4	1	1	2	3	4	4
Dinamo Zagreb	4	0	2	2	2	5	2
Stade Rennais	4	0	2	2	2	6	2

GROUP E

Strahov, Prague, 25-10-2007, 18:45, 6007, Dougal SCO

Sparta Praha 1 Slepicka [24]
FC Zürich 2 Kondé [38], Alphonse [62]

BayArena, Leverkusen, 25-10-2007, 19:00, 15 276, Eriksson SWE

Bayer Leverkusen 1 Kiessling [35]
Toulouse FC 0

Luzhniki, Moscow, 8-11-2007, 19:00, 25 000, Jakobsson ISL

Spartak Moskva 2 Pavlyuchenko [63p], Mozart [77p]
Bayer Leverkusen 1 Freier [91+]

Municipal, Toulouse, 8-11-2007, 20:30, 8648, I.González ESP

Toulouse FC 2 Elmander [14], Mansare [80]
Sparta Praha 3 Kisel 2 [67 88], Dosek [68]

Strahov, Prague, 29-11-2007, 18:30, 6703, Richards WAL

Sparta Praha 0
Spartak Moskva 0

Letzigrund, Zürich, 29-11-2007, 20:15, 10 600, Kasnaferis GRE

FC Zürich 2 Tihinen [42], Rafael Araujo [64p]
Toulouse FC 0

BayArena, Leverkusen, 6-12-2007, 18:15, 17 771, Atkinson ENG

Bayer Leverkusen 1 Friedrich.M [71].
Sparta Praha 0

Luzhniki, Moscow, 6-12-2007, 20:15, 18 500, Trivkovic CRO

Spartak Moskva 1 Titov [57]
FC Zürich 0

Letzigrund, Zürich, 19-12-2007, 20:45, 20 100, R.Santiago ESP

FC Zürich 0 Kiessling [80]
Bayer Leverkusen 5 Gresko [19], Bulykin 2 [23 57], Barnetta [50],

Municipal, Toulouse, 19-12-2007, 20:45, 19 428, Berntsen NOR

Toulouse FC 2 Santos 2 [41 53]
Spartak Moskva 1 Dzyuba [61p]

Group E	Pl	W	D	L	F	A	Pts
Bayer Leverkusen	4	3	0	1	8	2	9
Spartak Moskva	4	2	1	1	4	3	7
FC Zürich	4	2	0	2	4	7	6
Sparta Praha	4	1	1	2	4	5	4
Toulouse FC	4	1	0	3	4	7	3

GROUP F

Reebok, Bolton, 25-10-2007, 20:00, 10 848, Ceferin SVN

Bolton Wanderers 1 Diouf [66]
Sporting Braga 1 Jailson [87]

Crvena Zvezda, Belgrade, 25-10-2007, 21:15, 30 944, Trefoloni ITA

Crvena Zvezda 2 Koroman [16], Milijas [74]
Bayern München 3 Klose 2 [20 86], Kroos [94+]

Allianz Arena, Munich, 8-11-2007, 19:00, 66 000, Jára CZE

Bayern München 2 Podolski 2 [30 49]
Bolton Wanderers 2 Gardner [8], Davies [82]

Kleanthis Vikelidis, Thessalonica, 8-11-2007, 21:45, 14 600, Ivanov RUS

Aris Thessaloniki 3 Athanassios Papazoglou 2 [76 89], Koke [91+]
Crvena Zvezda 0

Reebok, Bolton, 29-11-2007, 20:00, 10 229, I.González ESP

Bolton Wanderers 1 Giannakopoulos [92+]
Aris Thessaloniki 1 Toni [44]

Municipal, Braga, 29-11-2007, 20:00, 8416, Eriksson SWE

Sporting Braga 1 Linz [66]
Bayern München 1 Klose [47]

Kleanthis Vikelidis, Thessalonica, 6-12-2007, 20:45, 10 854, Malek POL

Aris Thessaloniki 1 Ronaldo Guiaro [26]
Sporting Braga 1 Linz [6]

Crvena Zvezda, Belgrade, 6-12-2007, 20:45, 30 689, Allaerts BEL

Crvena Zvezda 0
Bolton Wanderers 1 McCann [45]

Municipal, Braga, 19-12-2007, 19:45, 8300, Hrinak SVK

Sporting Braga 2 Linz [11], Wender [66]
Crvena Zvezda 0

Allianz Arena, Munich, 19-12-2007, 20:45, 64 000, Yefet ISR

Bayern München 6 Toni 4 [25 38 64 66], Lell [78], Lahm [81]
Aris Thessaloniki 0

Group F	Pl	W	D	L	F	A	Pts
Bayern München	4	2	2	0	12	5	8
Sporting Braga	4	1	3	0	5	3	6
Bolton Wanderers	4	1	3	0	5	4	6
Aris Thessaloniki	4	1	2	1	5	8	5
Crvena Zvezda Beograd	4	0	0	4	2	9	0

GROUP G

White Hart Lane, London, 25-10-2007, 19:45, 26 122, Kircher GER

Tottenham H'spur 1 Defoe [19]
Getafe 2 Granero [21], Braulio [70]

Vanden Stock, Brussels, 25-10-2007, 20:45, 16 586, Tudor ROU

RSC Anderlecht 2 Frutos 2 [36 70]
Hapoel Tel Aviv 0

Bloomfield, Tel Aviv, 8-11-2007, 18:30, 9722, Gilewski POL

Hapoel Tel Aviv 0
Tottenham H'spur 2 Keane [26], Berbatov [31]

Aalborg, Aalborg, 8-11-2007, 19:15, 10 300, Duhamel FRA

AaB Aalborg 1 Lindström [86]
RSC Anderlecht 1 Jakobsen OG [59]

White Hart Lane, London, 29-11-2007, 19:45, 29 758, Proença POR
Tottenham H'spur 3 Berbatov 46, Malbranque 51, Bent.D 66
AaB Aalborg 2 Enevoldsen 2, Risgård 37

Coliseum, Getafe, Madrid, 29-11-2007, 20:45, 4025, Kapitanis CYP
Getafe 1 Pablo Hernández 91+p
Hapoel Tel Aviv 2 Badir 5, Dego 31

Aalborg, Aalborg, 6-12-2007, 20:45, 10 634, Rizzoli ITA
AaB Aalborg 1 Prica 92+
Getafe 2 Pablo Hernández 11, Granero 78

Vanden Stock, Brussels, 6-12-2007, 20:45, 19 753, Skomina SVN
RSC Anderlecht 1 Goor 68
Tottenham H'spur 1 Berbatov 71p

Coliseum, Getafe, Madrid, 19-12-2007, 20:45, 4018, Ivanov RUS
Getafe 2 Pablo Hernández 6, Celestini 50
RSC Anderlecht 1 Théréau 91+

Bloomfield, Tel Aviv, 19-12-2007, 21:45, 1692, Wegereef NED
Hapoel Tel Aviv 1 Fábio Júnior 45
AaB Aaolborg 3 Risgård 27, Jakobsen 50p, Enevoldsen 66

Group G	Pl	W	D	L	F	A	Pts
Getafe	4	3	0	1	7	5	9
Tottenham Hotspur	4	2	1	1	7	5	7
RSC Anderlecht	4	1	2	1	5	4	5
AaB Aalborg	4	1	1	2	7	7	4
Hapoel Tel Aviv	4	1	0	3	3	8	3

GROUP H

Olympia, Helsingborg, 25-10-2007, 18:00, 6451, Trivkovic CRO
Helsingborgs IF 1 Larsson 83
Panionios 1 Goundoulakis 45

Chaban-Delmas, Bordeaux, 25-10-2007, 19:00, 10 883, Malek POL
Girond. Bordeaux 2 Cavenaghi 53, Chamakh 64
Galatasaray 1 Nonda 22p

Ali Sami Yen, Istanbul, 8-11-2007, 20:00, 11 622, Dean ENG
Galatasaray 2 Nonda 2 44 91+
Helsingborgs IF 3 Larsson 30, Omotoyossi 39, Andersson.C 75

Ernst Happel, Vienna, 8-11-2007, 20:15, 20 300, Proença POR
FK Austria Wien 1 Kuljic 5
Girond. Bordeaux 2 Chamakh 45, Wendel 88p

Olympia, Helsingborg, 29-11-2007, 20:15, 8243, Genov BUL
Helsingborgs IF 3 Skúlason 47, Omotoyossi 2 66 70
FK Austria Wien 0

Panionios, Athens, 29-11-2007, 21:00, 4986, Undiano ESP
Panionios 0
Galatasaray 3 Serkan Calik 50, Song 63p, Hakan Sükür 82

Ernst Happel, Vienna, 6-12-2007, 20:45, 12 100, Granat POL
FK Austria Wien 0
Panionios 1 Majstorovic 91+

Chaban-Delmas, Bordeaux, 6-12-2007, 20:45, 9357, Meyer GER
Girond. Bordeaux 2 Chamakh 12, Jussiê 69
Helsingborgs IF 1 Larsson 17

Panionios, Athens, 19-12-2007, 21:45, 4239, Szabo HUN
Panionios 2 Djebbour 6p, Makos 20
Girond. Bordeaux 3 Cavenaghi 39, Tremoulinas 75, Moimbe 87

Ali Sami Yen, Istanbul, 19-12-2007, 21:45, 7320, Bossen NED
Galatasaray 0
FK Austria Wien 0

Group H	Pl	W	D	L	F	A	Pts
Girondins Bordeaux	4	4	0	0	9	5	12
Helsingborgs IF	4	2	1	1	8	5	7
Galatasaray	4	1	1	2	6	5	4
Panionios	4	1	1	2	4	7	4
FK Austria Wien	4	0	1	3	1	6	1

ROUND OF 32

1st leg. Petrovsky, St Petersburg
13-02-2008, 20:00, 21 750, Weiner GER
Zenit St Petersburg 1
Pogrebnyak 63

Vyacheslav Malafeev - Kim Dong Jin•, Aleksandr Anyukov•, Ivica Krizanac, Roman Shirokov, Radek Sirl, Anatoliy Tymoschuk, Konstantin Zyryanov, Viktor Fayzulin, Andrei Arshavin, Pavel Pogrebnyak•. Tr: Dick Advocaat

Villareal 0

Diego López – Gonzalo, Josemi, Diego Godin, Joan Capdevila•, Josico, Bruno (Pascal Cygan 82), Santi Cazorla (Jon Dahl Tomasson 75), Cani•, Guille Franco, Nihat (Giuseppe Rossi 66) Kahveci. Tr: Manuel Pellegrini

2nd leg. El Madrigal, Villarreal
21-02-2008, 20:45, 14 720, Messner AUT
Villarreal 2
Guille Franco 75, Tomasson 90

Diego López – Diego Godin, Gonzalo, Joan Capdevila, Angel López, Santi Cazorla, Josico (Guille Franco 46), Marcos Senna (Bruno 63), Robert Pirés, Jon Dahl Tomasson, Giuseppe Rossi (Nihat 51). Tr: Manuel Pellegrini

Zenit St Petersburg 1
Pogrebnyak 31

Vyacheslav Malafeev• - Nicolas Lombaerts (Ivica Krizanac• 34), Aleksandr Anyukov, Kim Dong Jin•, Roman Shirokov••47, Viktor Fayzulin (Lee Ho 94+), Konstantin Zyryanov•, Anatoliy Tymoschuk, Radek Sirl•••82, Andrei Arshavin (Olexandr Gorshkov 86), Pavel Pogrebnyak. Tr: Dick Advocaat

1st leg. Vélodrome, Marseille
13-02-2008, 20:45, 31 790, Proença POR
Olympique Marseille 3
Cheyrou 62, Taiwo 68, Niang 79

Steve Mandanda - Taye Taiwo, Jacques Faty (Kaboré 46), Benoît Cheyrou, Djibril Cissé, Mamadou Niang (Oruma 83), Lorik Cana•, Samir Nasri•, Laurent Bonnart, Mathieu Valbuena (Zenden 77), Gaël Givet. Tr: Erik Gerets

Spartak Moskva 0

Stipe Pletikosa - Martin Stranzl, Mozart, Aleksandr Pavlenko (Prudnikov 83), Yegor Titov, Welliton, Radoslav Kovác•, Christian Maidana (Dineev 65), Vladimir Bystrov (Pavlyuchenko 69), Sergey Parshivlyuk, Fedor Kudryashov•. Tr: Stanislav Cherchesov

2nd leg. Luzhniki, Moscow
21-02-2008, 19:30, 18 000, Einwaller AUT

Spartak Moskva 2
Pavlenko [39], Pavlyuchenko [85]

Stipe Pletikosa - Sergey Parshivlyuk (Ignas Dedura 88), Martin Stranzl, Radoslav Kovác, Fedor Kudryashov, Aleksandr Pavlenko, Mozart•, Yegor Titov (Vladimir Bystrov 76), Christian Maidana•, Roman Pavlyuchenko, Welliton (Artem Dzyuba 71). Tr: Stanislav Cherchesov

Olympique Marseille 0

Steve Mandanda• – Laurent Bonnart, Gaël Givet•, Lorik Cana•, Taye Taiwo, Mathieu Valbuena, Modeste M'Bami, Charles Kaboré (Wilson Oruma 9), Samir Nasri (Boudewijn Zenden 59), Djibril Cissé, Mamadou Niang (Karim Ziani 78). Tr: Erik Gerets

---

1st leg. Letzigrund, Zürich
14-02-2008, 20:30, 16 800, Kelly IRL

FC Zürich 1
Rochat [88]

Johnny Leoni - Florian Stahel, Heinz Barmettler (Veli Lampi 69), Hannu Tihinen, Alain Rochat•, Tico•, Silvan Aegerter, Almen Abdi (Andres Vasques 86), Dusan Djuric, Yassine Chikhaoui (Emra Tahirovic 75), Eric Hassli. Tr: Bernard Challandes

Hamburger SV 3
Jarolím [49], Olic [67], Trochowski [77]

Frank Rost - Guy Demel, Bastian Reinhardt, Joris Mathijsen, Collin Benjamin, Piotr Trochowski, Nigel de Jong•, Vincent Kompany•, Rafael van der Vaart (José Paolo Guerrero 32), David Jarolim (Miso Brecko 86), Ivica Olic (Mohamed Zidan 82). Tr: Huub Stevens

---

2nd leg. HSH Nordbank, Hamburg
21-02-2008, 17:00, 33 586, Jakobsson ISL

Hamburger SV 0

Frank Rost - Guy Demel (Jerome Boateng 78), Bastian Reinhardt, Joris Mathijsen, Collin Benjamin•, Vincent Kompany, Nigel de Jong, David Jarolim•, Piotr Trochowski (Mario Fillinger 81), Ivica Olic, José Paolo Guerrero (Eric-Maxim Choupo-Moting 63). Tr: Huub Stevens

FC Zürich 0

Johnny Leoni - Veli Lampi, Heinz Barmettler, Florian Stahel, Alain Rochat, Tico• (Oumar Kondé• 46), Silvan Aegerter, Almen Abdi (Eric Hassli 60), Yassine Chikhaoui, Dusan Djuric, Alexandre Alphonse (Emra Tahirovic 58). Tr: Bernard Challandes

---

1st leg. Ali Sami Yen, Istanbul
13-02-2008, 19:45, 20 006, Batista POR

Galatasaray 0

Orkun Usak – Servet Cetin, Emre Güngör•, Volkan Yaman (Lincoln 83), Ugur Ucar, Ayhan Akman (Hakan Balta 65), Mehmet Topal, Baris Ozbek, Arda Turan•, Hakan Sükür (Shabani Nonda 78), Ümit Karan. Tr: Karl Heinz Feldkamp

Bayer Leverkusen 0

René Adler• - Gonzalo Castro, Manuel Friedrich, Jan-Ingwer Callsen-Bracker, Simon Rolfes, Hans Sarpei, Arturo Vidal (Pirmin Schwegler 87), Bernd Schneider (Paul Freier 61), Sergej Barbarez, Tranquillo Barnetta, Stefan Kiessling. Tr: Michael Skibbe

---

2nd leg. BayArena, Leverkusen
21-02-2008, 17:00, 20 500, Skomina SVN

Bayer Leverkusen 5
Barbarez 2 [12] [22], Kiessling [13], Haggui [55], Schneider [51p]

Benedikt Fernandez, Gonzalo Castro, Manuel Friedrich, Karim Haggui, Hans Sarpei, Bernd Schneider• (Sascha Dum 75), Arturo Vidal, Simon Rolfes, Sergej Barbarez (Pirmin Schwegler 65), Tranquillo Barnetta, Stefan Kiessling• (Fanis Gekas 72). Tr: Michael Skibbe

Galatasaray 1
Barusso [87p]

Orkun Usak – Servet Cetin, Emre Güngör•, Ayhan Akman (Ahmed Apimah 68), Volkan Yaman, Mehmet Topal (Sabri Sanoglu• 46), Baris Ozbek, Arda Turan, Hakan Sükür, Umit Karan•, Serkan Calik (Lincoln 46). Tr: Karl Heinz Feldkamp

---

1st leg. OACA Spyro Louis, Athens
13-02-2008, 20:00, 13 038, Layec FRA

AEK Athens 1
Blanco [93+]

Moretto - Traianos Dellas, Sokratis Papastathopoulos, Rodolfo Arruabarrena, Nsaliwa Tamanda, Akis Zikos•, Pantelis Kafes, Charilaos Pappas (Ismael Blanco 82), Rivaldo, Gustavo Manduca (Manú 66), Nikos Liberopoulos (Mohamed Kallon 75). Tr: Nikolaus Kostenglou

Getafe 1
De la Red [86]

Pato - Cosmin Contra, Cata Díaz, Belenguer, Franck Signorino•, Fabio Celestini, Jaime Gavilán (David Cortés 61), Casquero (Rubén de la Red 68), Braulio, Ikechukwu Uche (Manu 78), Pablo Hernández•. Tr: Michael Laudrup

---

2nd leg. Coliseum, Madrid
21-02-2008, 20:45, 5728, Atkinson ENG

Getafe 3
Granero [45], Contra [82p], Braulio [84]

Oscar Ustari - Cosmin Contra, Belenguer, Mario, Fabio Celestini• (Casquero 69), Lucas Licht, Rubén de la Red, Albín (Ikechukwu Uche 59), Braulio, Esteban Granero, Pablo Hernández (David Cortés 78). Tr: Michael Laudrup

AEK Athens 0

Moretto - Nsaliwa Tamanda•, Traianos Dellas, Sokratis Papastathopoulos•, Rodolfo Arruabarrena•, Pantelis Kafes (Ismael Blanco 65), Akis Zikos, Edson Ramos Silva, Panagiotis Lagos (Gustavo Manduca 57), Rivaldo, Mohamed Kallon (Nikos Liberopoulos 72). Tr: Nikolaus Kostenglou

---

2nd leg. EasyCredit, Nuremburg
21-02-2008, 21:00, 42 890, Bebek CRO

1.FC Nürnberg 2
Charisteas [59], Saenko [66]

Jaromir Blazek - Dominik Reinhardt, Andreas Wolf, Berti Glauber, Javier Pinola•, Tomás Galásek, Jawhar Mnari (Jacques Abardonado 87), Marco Engelhardt, Angelos Charisteas, Jan Koller, Ivan Saenko. Tr: Thomas Von Heesen

Benfica 2
Oscar Cardozo [89], Di María [91+]

Quim - Luís Filipe•, Luisão, Edcarlos (Oscar Cardozo 70), Léo•, Kostas Katsouranis, Petit•, Maxi Pereira• (László Sepsi 70), Rui Costa, Nuno Assis (Angel Di María 81), Ariza Makukula•. Tr: José Antonio Camacho

---

1st leg. Vanden Stock, Brussels
13-02-2008, 20:45, 15 173, Tagliavento ITA

RSC Anderlecht 2
Polák [79], Mbo Mpenza [95+]

Daniel Zitka - Marcin Wasilewski, Nicolas Pareja, Roland Juhász•, Jelle Van Damme, Thomas Chatelle (Jonathan Legear 84), Jan Polák, Lucas Biglia, Bart Goor• (Mbo Mpenza 73), Mbark Boussoufa, Serhat Akin. Tr: Ariel Jacobs

Girondins Bordeaux 1
Jussiê [69p]

Ulrich Ramé - Matthieu Chalmé, Henrique, Souleymane Diawara, Franck Jurietti, Alou Diarra•, Alejandro Alonso• (Wendel 61), Jussiê (Johan Micoud 81), Pierre Ducasse, Gabriel Obertan, Marouane Chamakh (Fernando Cavenaghi• 61). Tr: Laurent Blanc

---

2nd leg. Chaban-Delmas, Bordeaux
21-02-2008, 20:45, 17 985, Dereli TUR

Girondins Bordeaux 1
Cavenaghi [71]

Ulrich Ramé• - Matthieu Chalmé•••87, Henrique, Souleymane Diawara, Florian Marange, Gabriel Obertan (Wendel• 77), Pierre Ducasse•, Alejandro Alonso (Johan Micoud• 52), Benoît Tremoulinas•72, David Bellion (Fernando Cavenaghi 52), Marouane Chamakh. Tr: Laurent Blanc

RSC Anderlecht 1
Chatelle [34]

Daniel Zitka• - Marcin Wasilewski, Roland Juhász• (Mark De Man 89), Nicolas Pareja, Jelle Van Damme, Thomas Chatelle (Mbo Mpenza• 60), Lucas Biglia, Jan Polák, Mbark Boussoufa•, Guillaume Gillet•, Serhat Akin (Ahmed Hassan• 69). Tr: Ariel Jacobs

---

1st leg. Pittodrie, Aberdeen
14-02-2008, 18:00,20 040, Iturralde ESP

Aberdeen 2
Walker [24], Aluko [41]

Jamie Langfield - Alan Maybury, Alexander Diamond, Andrew Considine, Lee Mair•, Barry Nicholson, Josh Walker (Karim Touzani 87), Scott Severin, Sone Aluko, Darren Mackie (Steve Lovell 68), Lee Miller. Tr: James Calderwood

Bayern München 2
Klose [29], Hamit Altintop [55]

Michael Rensing - Christian Lell (Philipp Lahm 46), Lucio, Martin Demichelis, Marcell Jansen, Hamit Altintop•55, Andreas Ottl, Zé Roberto (Lukas Podolski• 66), Bastian Schweinsteiger, Luca Toni, Miroslav Klose (Jan Schlaudraff 80). Tr: Ottmar Hitzfeld

2nd leg. Allianz Arena, Munich
21-02-2008, 18:45, 66 000, Malek POL

Bayern München **5**

Lucio [12], Van Buyten [36], Podolski 2 [71][77], Van Bommel [85]

Oliver Kahn – Willy Sagnol, Lucio, Daniel Van Buyten, Marcell Jansen, Hamit Altıntop (Bastian Schweinsteiger 75), Andreas Ottl, Mark van Bommel, Toni Kroos• (José Ernesto Sosa 69), Luca Toni (Miroslav Klose 65), Lukas Podolski. Tr: Ottmar Hitzfeld

Aberdeen **1**

Lovell [83]

Jamie Langfield - Alan Maybury•, Alexander Diamond, Andrew Considine, Richard Foster, Barry Nicholson•, Sone Aluko• (Steve Lovell 79), Scott Severin, Josh Walker• (Christopher Maguire 62), Darren Mackie• (Jeffrey De Visscher 72), Lee Miller. Tr: James Calderwood

1st leg. Lerkendal, Trondheim
14-02-2007, 20:45, 10 584, Clattenburg ENG

Rosenborg BK **0**

Rune Almenning Jarstein - Fredrik Stoor, Bjørn Tore Kvarme, Vadim Demidov, Andreas Nordvik, Per Ciljan Skjelbred, Roar Strand (Øyvind Storflor 81), Marek Sapara, Abdou Razack Traoré, Steffen Iversen (Didier Konan Ya 47), Yssouf Koné. Tr: Trond Henriksen

Fiorentina **1**

Mutu [16]

Sébastien Frey - Tomás Ujfalusi, Per Krøldrup, Alessandro Gamberini, Massimo Gobbi (Manuel Pasqual 47), Franco Semioli, Riccardo Montolivo•, Martin Jørgensen, Zdravko Kuzmanovic (Mario Alberto Santana 85), Adrian Mutu, Giampaolo Pazzini (Daniele Cacia 72). Tr: Claudio Cesare Prandelli

2nd leg. Artemio Franchi, Florence
21-02-2008, 20:45, 23 139, Ceferin SVN

Fiorentina **2**

Liverani [38], Cacia [81]

Sébastien Frey - Tomás Ujfalusi, Per Krøldrup, Dario Dainelli, Manuel Pasqual, Marco Donadel, Fabio Liverani (Zdravko Kuzmanovic 82), Riccardo Montolivo (Martin Jørgensen 64), Franco Semioli, Giampaolo Pazzini (Daniele Cacia 72), Adrian Mutu. Tr: Claudio Cesare Prandelli

Rosenborg BK **1**

Koné [88]

Rune Almenning Jarstein - Christer Basma (Alejandro Lago 54), Andreas Nordvik, Bjørn Tore Kvarme•, Vadim Demidov, Øyvind Storflor•, Alexander Tettey, Per Ciljan Skjelbred, Didier Konan Ya (Steffen Iversen 71), Yssouf Koné (John Pelu 90), Marek Sapara. Tr: Trond Henriksen

1st leg. Brann, Bergen
13-02-2008, 20:00, 16 207, Genov BUL

SK Brann Bergen **0**

Håkon Opdal - Bjørn Dahl (Michael Thwaite 89), Olafur Orn Bjarnason, Kristján Sigurdsson, Erlend Hanstveit, Jan Gunnar Solli, Eirik Bakke, Hassan El-Fakiri (Erik Huseklepp 75), Petter Vaagan Moen, Thorstein Helstad, Azar Karadas (Njogu Demba-Nyrén 69). Tr: Mons Ivar Mjelde

Everton **2**

Osman [59], Anichebe [88]

Tim Howard - Joseph Yobo, Jolean Lescott, Andrew Johnson (Victor Anichebe 76), Philip Jagielka, Tim Cahill, Phil Neville, Leon Osman, Yakubu Ayegbeni (Leighton Baines 90+3), Manuel Fernandes• (Tony Hibbert 89), Lee Carsley. Tr: David Moyes

2nd leg. Goodison Park, Liverpool
21-02-2007, 20:00, 22 843, Ivanov RUS

Everton **6**

Yakubu [36][54][72], Johnson [41][92+], Arteta [70]

Tim Howard - Phil Neville, Philip Jagielka, Jolean Lescott, Nuno Valente, Steven Pienaar, Tim Cahill (Manuel Fernandes• 46), Lee Carsley (Tony Hibbert 46), Mikel Arteta, Andrew Johnson, Yakubu Ayegbeni (Victor Anichebe 73). Tr: David Moyes

SK Brann Bergen **1**

Vaagan Moen [60]

Håkon Opdal - Bjørn Dahl, Olafur Orn Bjarnason (Azar Karadas 65), Kristján Sigurdsson, Erlend Hanstveit, Petter Vaagan Moen, Hassan El-Fakiri (Erik Huseklepp 60), Eirik Bakke•, Jan Gunnar Solli, Njogu Demba-Nyrén (Robbie Winters 72), Thorstein Helstad. Tr: Mons Ivar Mjelde

1st leg. Evzena Rosickeho, Prague
14-02-2008, 21:00, 11 134, Circhetta SUI

Slavia Praha **1**

Strihavka [69]

Martin Vaniak - Frantisek Drizdal, Martin Latka, Erich Brabec, David Hubácek•, Marek Suchy (Ladislav Volesák 83), Mickaël Tavares•, Marek Jarolim (David Kalivoda 59), Jaroslav Cerny, Daniel Pudil (Milan Ivana• 46), David Strihavka. Tr: Karel Jarolim

Tottenham Hotspur **1**

Berbatov [4], Keane [30]

Radek Cerny - Teemu Tainio• (Jamie O'Hara• 59), Jonathan Woodgate, Didier Zokora, Pascal Chimbonda, Aaron Lennon, Tom Huddlestone, Jermaine Jenas•, Steed Malbranque, Dimitar Berbatov, Robbie Keane (Darren Bent 66). Tr: Juande Ramos

2nd leg. White Hart Lane, London
21-02-2008, 19:45, 34 224, Eriksson SWE

Tottenham Hotspur **1**

O'Hara [7]

Paul Robinson - Pascal Chimbonda (Steed Malbranque 60), Didier Zokora, Teemu Tainio, Younes Kaboul, Dimitar Berbatov (Robbie Keane 46), Jamie O'Hara•, Darren Bent, Tom Huddlestone, Aaron Lennon (Jermaine Jenas 70), Jonathan Woodgate. Tr: Juande Ramos

Slavia Praha **1**

Krajcík [50]

Michal Vorel - Erich Brabec, David Hubácek, Martin Latka, Frantisek Drizdal (Ladislav Volesák 80), Daniel Pudil•, Marek Suchy, Matej Krajcík• (Tijani Belaid 87), David Kalivoda (Milan Ivana• 46), David Strihavka, Jaroslav Cerny. Tr: Karel Jarolim

1st leg. Philips Stadion, Eindhoven
13-02-2008, 20:45, 22 000, Kapitanis CYP

PSV Eindhoven **2**

Simons [7p], Lazovic [33]

Heurelho Gomes - Jan Kromkamp, Carlos Salcido, Dirk Marcellis, Mike Zonneveld, Timmy Simons, Alcides (Slobodan Rajkovic 65), Ibrahim Afellay, Otman Bakkal, Balázs Dzsudzsák•, Danko Lazovic (Danny Koevermans 71). Tr: Dwight Lodeweges

Helsingborgs IF **0**

Daniel Andersson• - Joel Ekstrand, Andreas Jakobsson, Christoffer Andersson, Andreas Landgren, Martin Kolár (Mathias Unkari 77), Marcus Lantz•, Olafur Ingi Skúlason, René Makondele, Henrik Larsson, Razak Omotoyossi (Fredrik Olsson 88). Tr: Bo Nilsson

2nd leg. Olympia, Helsingborg
21-02-2008, 20:45, 10 194, Szabo HUN

Helsingborgs IF **1**

Leandro Castan [81]

Daniel Andersson - Adama Tamboura (Andreas Landgren 46), Andreas Jakobsson, Marcus Lantz (Isaac Chansa 77), Razak Omotoyossi, Olafur Ingi Skúlason•, René Makondele, Henrik Larsson, Martin Kolár, Christoffer Andersson, Joel Ekstrand (Leandro Castan 46). Tr: Bo Nilsson

PSV Eindhoven **2**

Bakkal [47], Lazovic [65]

Heurelho Gomes• - Carlos Salcido, Mike Zonneveld, Timmy Simons, Edison Méndez, Danko Lazovic (Danny Koevermans 68), Alcides, Ibrahim Afellay (Ismail Aissati 72), Balázs Dzsudzsák (Slobodan Rajkovic 78), Dirk Marcellis, Otman Bakkal•. Tr: Dwight Lodeweges

1st leg. José Alvalade, Lisbon
13-02-2008, 20:45, 18 145, Blom NED

Sporting CP **2**

Vukcevic 2 [8][58]

Rui Patricio – Abel, Tonel, Anderson Polga, Leandro Grimi, Miguel Veloso, Marat Izmailov (Bruno Pereirinha 72), Leandro Romagnoli, Simon Vukcevic (Rodrigo Tiui 72), João Moutinho, Liedson. Tr: Paulo Bento

FC Basel **0**

Franco Costanzo (Louis Crayton 45) - Papa Malick Ba, François Marque, Daniel Majstorovic, Ronny Hodel, Benjamin Huggel, Ivan Ergic, Carlitos•, David Degen (Cabral 64), Eren Derdiyok, Eduardo. Tr: Christian Gross

2nd leg. St Jakob-Park, Basel
21-02-2008, 21:00, 16 360, Skjerven NOR

FC Basel **0**

Louis Crayton - Ronny Hodel, Daniel Majstorovic, François Marque, Reto Zanni, Benjamin Huggel (Papa Malick Ba 46), Carlitos, David Degen, Ivan Ergic (Marko Perovic 70), Eduardo (Fabian Frei 59), Eren Derdiyok. Tr: Christian Gross

Sporting CP **3**

Pereirinha [2], Liedson 2 [41][51]

Rui Patrício – Anderson Polga (Ronny 68), Tonel, Leandro Grimi (Ronny 68), Abel•, Miguel Veloso, Bruno Pereirinha, João Moutinho, Leandro Romagnoli (Pontus Farnerud 60), Rodrigo Tiui, Liedson. Tr: Paulo Bento

1st leg. Reebok, Bolton
14-02-2008, 20:00, 26 163, Rasmussen DEN

Bolton Wanderers **1**

Diouf [74]

Jussi Jääskeläinen - Nicholas Hunt, Gary Cahill, Andy O'Brien, Jlloyd Samuel, Iván Campo, El Hadji Diouf•, Daniel Guthrie (Stelios Giannakopoulos 59), Kevin Nolan, Matthew Taylor, Kevin Cyril Davies. Tr: Gary Megson

Atlético Madrid **0**

Christian Abbiati - Antonio López, Luis Perea, Pablo Ibáñez, Mariano Pernía, José Antonio Reyes• (Agüero 59), Mista (Miguel 88), Maxi Rodríguez, Cléber Santana•, Simão (Jurado 72), Diego Forlán. Tr: Javier Aguirre Onaindía

2nd leg. Vicente Calderón, Madrid
21-02-2008, 20:45, 27 590, Granat POL

Atlético Madrid 0

Christian Abbiati - Mariano Pernía, Pablo Ibáñez (Mista 67), Antonio López, Luis Perea, Jurado, Cléber Santana, Maxi Rodríguez●, Luis García (Miguel 54), José Antonio Reyes, Diego Forlán. Tr: Javier Aguirre Onaindía

Bolton Wanderers 0

Jussi Jääskeläinen - Nicholas Hunt, Andy O'Brien, Gary Cahill, Jlloyd Samuel, Stelios Giannakopoulos (El Hadji Diouf● 59), Gavin Mccann (Iván Campo 58), Kevin Nolan●, Joseph O'Brien● (Abdoulaye Méïté 85), Matthew Taylor, Kevin Davies●. Tr: Gary Megson

1st leg. Weserstadion, Bremen
13-02-2008, 20:30, 25 960, Kasnaferis GRE

Werder Bremen 3
Naldo [5], Jensen.D 27, Hugo Almeida 95+p

Tim Wiese● - Patrick Owomoyela, Naldo, Per Mertesacker, Clemens Fritz●, Daniel Jensen, Frank Baumann, Diego (Mesut Ozil 73), Aaron Hunt (Tim Borowski 59), Hugo Almeida, Markus Rosenberg. Tr: Thomas Schaaf

Sporting Braga 0

Paulo Santos - Rodriguez, Paulo Jorge●, Carlos Fernandes●, Pablo Contreras● (Stélvio Cruz● 62), Frechaut, João Pereira, Jorginho●36 (Jailson 78), Vandinho, Roland Linz●11, Matheus (Wender 67). Tr: Manuel Machado

2nd leg. Municipal, Braga
21-02-2008, 21:30, 5706, Gumienny BEL

Sporting Braga 0

Pawel Kieszek - João Pereira, Paulo Jorge●, Rodriguez, Carlos Fernandes, Stélvio Cruz● (Vandinho 61), Roberto Brum●, César Peixoto, Zé Manuel (João Tomás 47), Wender (Matheus 47), Roland Linz. Tr: Manuel Machado

Werder Bremen 1
Klasnic [78]

Tim Wiese - Clemens Fritz●, Per Mertesacker, Naldo●, Patrick Owomoyela, Daniel Jensen, Mesut Ozil (Jurica Vranjes 57), Frank Baumann, Tim Borowski (Sebastian Boenisch 79), Hugo Almeida, Markus Rosenberg (Ivan Klasnic 69). Tr: Thomas Schaaf

1st leg. Ibrox, Glasgow
13-02-2008, 20:00, 43 203, Rizzoli ITA

Rangers 0

Allan McGregor - Kirk Broadfoot, Carlos Cuéllar, David Weir, Sasa Papac, Nacho Novo (Chris Burke 81), Barry Ferguson, Steven Davis, Brahim Hemdani, Charles Adam● (Daniel Cousin 67), Lee McCulloch. Tr: Walter Smith

Panathinaikos 0

Mario Galinovic - Mikael Nilsson●, Nasief Morris, Giannis Goumas, Loukas Vintra, Dame Ndoye, Alexandros Tziolis, Marcelo Mattos, Simão●, Giorgos Karagounis, Dimitris Salpingidis (Hélder Postiga 66). Tr: José Peseiro

2nd leg. Apostolos Nikolaidis, Athens
21-02-2008, 19:00, 14 452, Brych GER

Panathinaikos 1
Goumas [12]

Mario Galinovic - Marcelo Mattos, Nasief Morris, Giannis Goumas, Hélder Postiga (Dame Ndoye 62), Dimitris Salpingidis, Giorgos Karagounis, Alexandros Tziolis (Ezequiel González 83), Loukas Vintra, Andreas Ivanschitz, Mikael Nilsson (Dimitrios Papadopoulos 86). Tr: José Peseiro

Rangers 1
Novo [81]

Allan McGregor - David Weir, Sasa Papac (Christian Dailly 66), Barry Ferguson, Brahim Hemdani (Chris Burke● 69), Kris Boyd, Nacho Novo, Charles Adam (Steven Naismith 66), Kirk Broadfoot, Carlos Cuéllar, Steven Davis. Tr: Walter Smith

ROUND OF 16

1st leg. Vélodrome, Marseille
6-03-2008, 20:45, 24 300, Kircher GER

Olympique Marseille 3
Cissé 2 37 55, Niang [48]

Sebastien Mate - Laurent Bonnart, Jacques Faty (Ronald Zubar● 44), Gael Givet, Taye Taiwo - Modeste M'Bami●, Benoit Cheyrou, Mathieu Valbuena, Samir Nasri (Charles Kabore 88) - Mamadou Niang (Boudewijn Zenden 62), Djibril Cissé. Tr: Erik Gerets

Zenit St Petersburg 1
Arshavin [82]

Vyacheslav Malafeev - Aleksandr Anyukov, Olexandr Gorshkov, Ivica Krizanac, Kim Dong Jin●, Fernando Ricksen● (Igor Denisov 70) - Anatoliy Tymoschuk, Konstantin Zyrianov, Viktor Fayzulin (Vladislav Radimov 81) - Andrei Arshavin, Pavel Pogrebnyak. Tr: Dick Advocaat

2nd leg. Petrovsky, St Petersburg
12-03-2008, 19:30, 20 400, Riley ENG

Zenit St Petersburg 2
Pogrebnyak 2 39 78

Vyacheslav Malafeev - Aleksandr Anyukov, Roman Shirokov, Ivica Krizanac, Radek Sirl - Viktor Fayzulin (Fatih Tekke 75), Konstantin Zyrianov, Igor Denisov●, Anatoliy Tymoschuk● - Andrei Arshavin●, Pavel Pogrebnyak. Tr: Dick Advocaat

Olympique Marseille 0

Steve Mandanda - Laurent Bonnart, Lorik Cana, Gael Givet (Andre Ayew 89), Taye Taiwo - Benoit Cheyrou, Modeste M'Bami●, Mathieu Valbuena, Samir Nasri - Mamadou Niang●, Djibril Cissé●. Tr: Eric Gerets

1st leg. BayArena, Leverkusen
6-03-2008, 21:05, 19 849, Thomson SCO

Bayer Leverkusen 1
Gekas [77]

Rene Adler - Gonzalo Castro, Manuel Friedrich, Karim Haggui●, Hans Sarpei - Bernd Schneider (23-Arturo Vidal 75), Simon Rolfes, Sergej Barbarez (8-Paul Freier 67), Tranquillo Barnetta - Theofanis Gekas● (Jan-Ingwer Callsen-Bracker 87), Stefan Kiessling. Tr: Michael Skibbe

Hamburger SV 0

Frank Rost - Guy Demel (Jerome Boateng 56), Bastian Reinhardt, Joris Mathijsen, Collin Benjamin - David Jarolim, Rafael van der Vaart, Nigel de Jong●, Vincent Kompany●, Ivica Olic (Piotr Trochowski 76) - Jose Guerrero● (Mohamed Zidan 79). Tr: Huub Stevens

2nd leg. HSH Nordbank, Hamburg
12-03-2008, 17:45, 38 083, Mallenco ESP

Hamburger SV 3
Trochowski 53, Guerrero 65, Van der Vaart 81

Frank Rost - Miso Brecko●, Bastian Reinhardt, Joris Mathijsen, Thimothee Atouba (Jerome Boateng 62) - Guy Demel, Vadis Odjidja-Ofoe (Piotr Trochowski 46), David Jarolim, Rafael van der Vaart● - Jose Guerrero●, Ivica Olic (Sidney Sam 76). Tr: Huub Stevens

Bayer Leverkusen 2
Barbarez 19, Gekas 55

Rene Adler - Gonzalo Castro, Manuel Friedrich, Karim Haggui, Hans Sarpei - Arturo Vidal (Dmitri Bulykin 88), Simon Rolfes, Stefan Kiessling, Sergej Barbarez● (Pirmin Schwegler● 72), Tranquillo Barnetta - Theofanis Gekas (Jan-Ingwer Callsen-Bracker 81). Tr: Michael Skibbe

1st leg. Estadio da Luz, Lisbon
6-03-2008, 20:30, 26 925, Gilewski POL

Benfica 1
Mantorras [76]

Quim - Nelson, Luisao (Marc Zoro 29), Edcarlos, Leo, Konstantinos Katsouranis, Manuel Rui Costa, Cristian Rodriguez, Angel Di Maria (Mantorras 62), Laszlo Sepsi, Oscar Cardozo●9. Tr: Jose Antonio Camacho

Getafe 2
De la Red 25, Pablo Hernández 67

Oscar Ustari - Cosmin Contra, Belenguer, Cata Diaz, Lucas Licht●, Albin, Casquero●, Pablo Hernandez●, Esteban Granero● (Mario Cotelo 46), Ruben De la Red (Fabio Celestini 73), Braulio● (Manu 61). Tr: Michael Laudrup

2nd leg. Coliseum, Madrid
12-03-2008, 21:00, 9131, Kassai HUN

Getafe 1
Albín [77]

Pato● - Cosmin Contra, Ruben De la Red, Manuel Tena, Lucas Licht●, Mario Cotelo● (David Cortes 74), Fabio Celestini, Javier Casquero, Jaime Gavilan (Juan Fortes 80), Juan Albin, Kepa Blanco (Franck Signorino 68). Tr: Michael Laudrup

Benfica 0

Quim - Nelson, Konstantinos Katsouranis●, Edcarlos● (Laszlo Sepsi 73), Leo●, Maxi Pereira● (Angel Di Maria 59), Armando Petit, Manuel Rui Costa, Cristian Rodriguez, Nuno Gomes (Mantorras 65), Ariza Makukula. Tr: Fernando Chalana

1st leg. Vanden Stock, Brussels
6-03-2008, 19:00, 21 845, Benquerença POR

RSC Anderlecht 0

Daniel Zitka - Marcin Wasilewski●●●43, Nicolas Pareja, Roland Juhasz, Jelle Van Damme - Thomas Chatelle (Ahmed Hassan 62), Lucas Biglia, Mbark Boussoufa - Guillaume Gillet●, Jan Polak, Serhat Akin (Bart Goor 70). Tr: Ariel Jacobs

Bayern München 5
Hamit Altıntop [9], Toni 45, Podolski 57, Klose 67, Ribéry 86

Michael Rensing - Willy Sagnol, Martin Demichelis, Daniel Van Buyten, Philipp Lahm - Mark van Bommel, Andreas Ottl, Hamit Altintop (Jose Ernesto Sosa● 58), Bastian Schweinsteiger (Franck Ribery 46) - Lukas Podolski, Luca Toni● (Miroslav Klose 46). Tr: Ottmar Hitzfeld

2nd leg. Allianz Arena, Munich
12-03-2008, 20:45, 63 000, Hauge NOR

Bayern München 1
Lucio [9]

Michael Rensing - Willy Sagnol, Lucio, Breno, Philipp Lahm - Jose Ernesto Sosa, Mark van Bommel, Andreas Ottl (Jan Schlaudraff 73), Toni Kroos (Franck Ribery 46) - Lukas Podolski, Miroslav Klose (Hamit Altintop 87). Tr: Ottmar Hitzfeld

RSC Anderlecht 2
Serhat 20, Yakovenko 35

Daniel Zitka (Davy Schollen 46) - Guillaume Gillet, Mark De Man, Roland Juhasz●, Olivier Deschacht● - Oleksandr Yakovenko● (Mbark Boussoufa● 66), Bakary Sare, Lucas Biglia, Ahmed Hassan, Bart Goor - Serhat Akin (Cor Gillis 90). Tr: Ariel Jacobs

1st leg. Artemio Franchi, Florence
6-03-2008, 20:45, 31 757, Allaerts BEL

Fiorentina 2
Kuzmanovic 70, Montolivo 81

Sebastien Frey - Tomas Ujfalusi●, Alessandro Gamberini, Dario Dainelli, Manuel Pasqual, Zdravko Kuzmanovic (Massimo Gobbi● 76), Marco Donadel, Riccardo Montolivo, Martin Jorgensen, Christian Vieri (Giampaolo Pazzini 67), Pablo Daniel Osvaldo (Mario Alberto Santana 74). Tr: Claudio Prandelli

Everton 0

Tim Howard● - Tony Hibbert (Andy Johnson 73), Joseph Yobo, Philip Jagielka, Jolean Lescott, Leon Osman (Mikel Arteta 56), Phil Neville, Lee Carsley, Steven Pienaar●, Tim Cahill, Yakubu Aiyegbeni●. Tr: David Moyes

2nd leg. Goodison Park, Liverpool
12-03-2007, 19:45, 38 026, Braamhaar NED

Everton 2 2p
Johnson 16, Arteta 67

Tim Howard - Phil Neville, Joleon Lescott, Joseph Yobo●, Steven Pienaar (Victor Anichebe 105), Mikel Arteta, Lee Carsley, Leon Osman, Phil Jagielka, Yakubu Ayegbeni●, Andrew Johnson (Thomas Gravesen 118). Tr: David Moyes

Fiorentina 0 4p

Sebastian Frey - Manuel Pasqual, Alessandro Gamberini●, Dario Dainelli●, Tomas Ujfalusi, Martin Jorgensen● (Mario Alberto Santana 105), Riccardo Montolivo●, Marco Donadel, Zdravko Kuzmanovic (Massimo Gobbi 90), Pablo Daniel Osvaldo, Christian Vieri (Giampaolo Pazzini● 46). Tr: Cesare Prandelli

1st leg. White Hart Lane, London
6-03-2008, 20:05, 33 259, Lannoy FRA

Tottenham Hotspur 0

Paul Robinson - Pascal Chimbonda●, Jonathan Woodgate, Ledley King (Adel Taarabt 73), Gilberto● (Jamie O'Hara 46) - Aaron Lennon, Jermaine Jenas (Tom Huddlestone 64), Didier Zokora, Steed Malbranque - Dimitar Berbatov●, Robbie Keane. Tr: Juande Ramos

PSV Eindhoven 1
Farfán 34

Heurelho Gomes - Jan Kromkamp, Dirk Marcellis, Carlos Salcido, Alcides, Jason Culina, Timmy Simons, Edison Mendez, Jefferson Farfan● (Balazs Dzsudzsak 85), Danny Koevermans (Danko Lazovic 77), Ibrahim Afellay (Otman Bakkal 90). Tr: Sef Vergoossen

2nd leg. Philips Stadion, Eindhoven
12-03-2008, 20:45, 33 050, Trefoloni ITA

PSV Eindhoven 0 6p

Heurelho Gomes - Carlos Salcido, Dirk Marcellis, Jan Kromkamp, Alcides - Ibrahim Afellay (Balazs Dzsudzsak 82), Edison Mendez (Otman Bakkal 113) - Jason Culina, Danny Koevermans (Danko Lazovic 72). Tr: Sef Vergoossen

Tottenham Hotspur 1 5p
Berbatov 81

Paul Robinson - Jonathan Woodgate, Ledley King● (Aaron Lennon 61), Lee Young Pyo (Darren Bent 46), Pascal Chimbonda - Tom Huddlestone●, Jermaine Jenas●, Steed Malbranque●, Didier Zokora● - Dimitar Berbatov, Robbie Keane (Jamie O'Hara 86). Tr: Juande Ramos

1st leg. Reebok Stadium, Bolton
6-03-2008, 20:00, 25 664, Yefet ISR

Bolton Wanderers 1
McCann 25

Ali Al-Habsi - Nicholas Hunt, Andy O'Brien, Gary Cahill, Ricardo Gardner, Ivan Campo (Andranik Teymourian 84), Kevin Davies, Joey O'Brien● (Daniel Guthrie 67), Gavin McCann●, Matthew Taylor, Heidar Helguson (Stelios Giannakopoulos 55). Tr: Gary Megson

Sporting CP 1
Vukcevic 69

Rui Patricio - Abel (Leandro Romagnoli 46), Tonel, Anderson Polga, Leandro Grimi●, Miguel Veloso, Bruno Pereirinha, Joao Moutinho, Marat Izmailov (Gladstone 85), Simon Vukcevic, Rodrigo Tiui (Adrien Silva 79). Tr: Paulo Bento

2nd leg. José Alvalade, Lisbon
13-03-2008, 20:00, 22 031, Layec FRA

Sporting CP 1
Pereirinha 85

Rui Patricio - Abel, Tonel, Anderson Polga, Leandro Grimi, Joao Moutinho●, Bruno Pereirinha, Marat Izmailov (Gladstone 87), Leandro Romagnoli (Adrien Silva 75), Liedson, Simon Vukcevic (Rodrigo Tiui 66). Tr: Paulo Bento

Bolton Wanderers 0

Ali Al-Habsi - Nicholas Hunt, Gary Cahill, Abdoulaye Meite, Jlloyd Samuel, Joey O'Brien, Daniel Guthrie●, Andranik Teymourian● (Daniel Braaten 71), Stelios Giannakopoulos, Ricardo Vaz Te, Heidar Helguson (Nathan Woolfe 76). Tr: Gary Megson

1st leg. Ibrox, Glasgow
6-03-2008, 20:00, 42 959, Hamer LUX

Rangers 2
Cousin 45, Davis 48

Allan McGregor - Kirk Broadfoot, Carlos Cuellar, David Weir, Sasa Papac, Brahim Hemdani●, Christian Dailly, Barry Ferguson, Steven Davis, Charles Adam, Daniel Cousin (Lee McCulloch 75). Tr: Walter Smith

Werder Bremen 0

Tim Wiese - Clemens Fritz, Per Mertesacker, Naldo●, Petri Pasanen (Sebastian Boenisch 64), Frank Baumann, Jurica Vranjes (Hugo Almeida● 60), Diego, Daniel Jensen, Markus Rosenberg, Aaron Hunt. Tr: Thomas Schaaf

2nd leg. Weserstadion, Bremen
13-03-2008, 20:30, 33 660, Hansson SWE

Werder Bremen 1
Diego 58

Tim Wiese - Patrick Owomoyela (Martin Harnik 78), Per Mertesacker, Naldo, Sebastian Boenisch, Daniel Jensen, Tim Borowski, Aaron Hunt, Diego, Markus Rosenberg, Hugo Almeida (Boubacar Sanogo 66). Tr: Thomas Schaaf

Rangers 0

Allan McGregor - Kirk Broadfoot, David Weir, Carlos Cuellar, Sasa Papac, Brahim Hemdani, Christian Dailly, Barry Ferguson, Steven Davis, Charles Adam● (Steven Whittaker 57), Nacho Novo (Lee McCulloch 78). Tr: Walter Smith

---

PENALTY SHOOT-OUT
ROUND OF 16
PSV EINDHOVEN V TOTTENHAM
PSV EINDHOVEN WON 6-5

Simons	✓ ✓	Berbatov
Lazovic	✗ ✓	O'Hara
Farfan	✓ ✓	Huddlestone
Salcido	✓ ✓	Bent
Dzsudzsak	✓ ✗	Jenas
Bakkal	✓ ✓	Zokora
Marcellis	✓ ✗	Chimbonda

PENALTY SHOOT-OUT
ROUND OF 16
EVERTON V FIORENTINA
FIORENTINA WON 4-2

Graveson	✓ ✓	Pazzini
Yakubu	✗ ✓	Montolivo
Arteta	✓ ✓	Osvaldo
Jagielka	✗ ✓	Santana

QUARTER-FINALS

1st leg. BayArena, Leverkusen

3-04-2008, 18:30, 19 500, Benquerença POR

Bayer Leverkusen   **1**

Kiessling [33]

Rene Adler - Gonzalo Castro, Manuel Friedrich●, Karim Haggui, Vratislav Gresko (Hans Sarpei 66) - Bernd Schneider (Sergej Barbarez 62), Arturo Vidal (Lukas Sinkiewicz 74), Simon Rolfes, Tranquillo Barnetta● - Stefan Kiessling, Theofanis Gekas. Tr: Michael Skibbe

Zenit St Petersburg   **4**

Arshavin [20], Pogrebnyak [52], Anyukov [61], Denisov [64]

Vyacheslav Malafeev - Aleksandr Anyukov, Roman Shirokov, Ivica Krizanac●, Radek Sirl - Igor Denisov, Anatoliy Tymoschuk, Konstantin Zyrianov - Andre Arshavin, Pavel Pogrebnyak, Victor Fayzulin. Tr: Dick Advocaat

2nd leg. Petrovsky, St Petersburg

10-04-2008, 20:30, 21 500, Mejuto ESP

Zenit St Petersburg   **0**

Vyacheslav Malafeev - Aleksander Anyukov, Roman Shirokov, Ivica Krizanac, Radek Sirl - Igor Denisov, Anatoliy Tymoschuk, Konstantin Zyrianov - Andrei Arshavin, Pavel Pogrebnyak, Victor Fayzulin (Vladislav Radimov 87). Tr: Dick Advocaat

Bayer Leverkusen   **1**

Bulykin [18]

Rene Adler - Gonzalo Castro●, Jan-Ingwer Callsen-Bracker, Karim Haggui, Hans Sarpei - Pirmin Schwegler (Simon Rolfes 59), Lukas Sinkiewicz● - Paul Freier● (Stefan Kiessling 68), Bernd Schneider, Sascha Dum (Theofanis Gekas 75) - Dmitri Bulykin. Tr: Michael Skibbe

1st leg. Allianz Arena, Munich

3-04-2008, 20:45, 62 000, Webb ENG

Bayern München   **1**

Toni [26]

Oliver Kahn - Philipp Lahm, Lucio, Martin Demichelis, Marcell Jansen (Christian Lell 80) - Bastian Schweinsteiger, Ze Roberto, Mark van Bommel (Andreas Ottl 86), Franck Ribery - Luca Toni● (Miroslav Klose 80), Lukas Podolski. Tr: Ottmar Hitzfeld

Getafe   **1**

Contra [90]

Oscar Ustari - David Cortes, Mario●, Manuel Tena●, Frank Signorino - Pablo Hernandez, Ruben de la Red●, Casquero (Fabio Celestini 73), Esteban Granero● (Cosmin Contra 78) - Albin, Ikechukwu Uche (Manu 68). Tr: Michael Laudrup

2nd leg. Coliseum, Madrid

10-04-2008, 20:45, 14 225, Busacca SUI

Getafe   **3**

Contra [44], Casquero [91], Braulio [93]

Roberto Abbondanzieri - David Cortes, Ruben de la Red●6, Manuel Tena, Lucas Licht - Cosmin Contra (Mario Cotelo 66), Francisco Casquero, Fabio Celestini, Jaime Gavilan, Manu del Moral (Braulio 62), Ikechukwu Uche (David Belenguer● 21). Tr: Michael Laudrup

Bayern München   **3**

Ribery [89], Toni 2 [115] [120]

Oliver Kahn - Philipp Lahm●, Martin Demichelis, Lucio, Christian Lell● (Marcell Jansen 46) - Franck Ribery, Mark van Bommel, Ze Roberto (Lukas Podolski● 75), Bastian Schweinsteiger (Jose Ernesto Sosa 64) - Miroslav Klose, Luca Toni●. Tr: Ottmar Hitzfeld

1st leg. Artemio Franchi, Florence

3-04-2008, 20:45, 34 109, Duhamel FRA

Fiorentina   **1**

Mutu [56]

Sebastien Frey - Martin Jorgensen, Alessandro Gamberini, Tomas Ujfalusi, Massimo Gobbi - Zdravko Kuzmanovic (Marco Donadel● 67), Fabio Liverani (Christian Vieri 76), Riccardo Montolivo - Mario Santana (Pablo Osvaldo 90), Giampaolo Pazzini, Adrian Mutu. Tr: Cesare Prandelli

PSV Eindhoven   **1**

Koevermans [63]

Heurelho Gomes (Bas Roorda 59) - Jan Kromkamp, Dirk Marcellis, Carlos Salcido, Slobodan Rajkovic - Edison Mendes, Timmy Simons, Ibrahim Afellay, Jason Culina - Jefferson Farfan● (Mika Vayrynen 96+), Danny Koevermans (Danko Lazovic 64). Tr: Sef Vergoossen

2nd leg. Philips Stadion, Endhoven

10-04-2008, 20:45, 35 000, Cantalejo ESP

PSV Eindhoven   **0**

Heurelho Gomes - Jan Kromkamp, Dirk Marcellis●, Carlos Salcido, Slobodan Rajkovic - Edison Mendez (Mike Zonneveld 83), Jason Culina (Mika Vayrynen 78), Timmy Simons (●80) - Otman Bakkal (Danko Lazovic 46), Danny Koevermans, Balazs Dzsudzsak. Tr: Sef Vergoossen

Fiorentina   **2**

Mutu 2 [38] [53]

Sebastien Frey - Martin Jorgensen, Alessandro Gamberini, Tomas Ujfalusi, Massimo Gobbi - Marco Donadel●, Fabio Liverani, Riccardo Montolivo - Mario Alberto Santana (Zdravko Kuzmanovic 78), Giampaolo Pazzini (Christian Vieri 73), Adrian Mutu● (Pablo Daniel Osvaldo 86). Tr: Cesare Prandelli

1st leg. Ibrox, Glasgow

3-04-2008, 10:45, 48 923, Baskakov RUS

Rangers   **0**

Allan McGregor - Kirk Broadfoot, David Weir●, Carlos Cuellar, Sasa Papac - Brahim Hemdani, Steven Davis, Barry Ferguson●, Kevin Thomson, Lee McCulloch - Jean-Claude Darcheville (Nacho Novo 72). Tr: Walter Smith

Sporting CP   **0**

Rui Patricio - Abel, Tonel, Anderson Polga, Leandro Grimi● - Miguel Veloso, Joao Moutinho, Marat Izmailov● (Bruno Pereirinha 70), Leandro Romagnoli - Liedson●, Simon Vukcevic (Yannick Djalo 75). Tr: Paulo Bento

2nd leg. José Alvalade, Lisbon

10-04-2008, 19:45, 31 500, Plautz AUT

Sporting CP   **0**

Rui Patricio - Abel, Tonel, Gladstone (Bruno Pereirinha 69), Leandro Grimi (Rodrigo Tiui 77) - Miguel Veloso, Joao Moutinho, Marat Izmailov (Yannick Djalo 62), Leandro Romagnoli - Liedson, Simon Vukcevic. Tr: Paulo Bento

Rangers   **2**

Darcheville [60], Whittaker [92+]

Allan McGregor - Kirk Broadfoot●, Christian Dailly, Carlos Cuellar, Sasa Papac● - Brahim Hemdani, Steven Davis, Barry Ferguson●, Kevin Thomson●, Lee McCulloch● (Steven Whittaker 78) - Jean-Claude Darcheville (Daniel Cousin 72). Tr: Walter Smith

SEMI-FINALS

1st leg. Allianz Arena, Munich
24-04-2008, 20:45, Michel SVK

Bayern München	1
Ribery [18]	

Oliver Kahn (Michael Rensing 67) - Philipp Lahm (Toni Kroos 80), Martin Demichelis, Lucio, Marcell Jansen - Franck Ribery, Mark van Bommel, Ze Roberto, Bastian Schweinsteiger (Christian Lell 66) - Miroslav Klose, Lukas Podolski. Tr: Ottmar Hitzfeld

Zenit St Petersburg	1
Lucio OG [60]	

Vyacheslav Malafeev - Fernando Ricksen∗, Roman Shirokov, Ivica Krizanac, Radek Sirl∗ - Igor Denisov, Anatoliy Tymoschuk, Viktor Fayzulin∗, Konstantin Zyrianov - Andrei Arshavin∗, Pavel Pogrebnyak. Tr: Dick Advocaat

2nd leg. Petrovsky, St Petersburg
1-05-2008, 20:30, Ovrebø NOR

Zenit St Petersburg	4
Pogrebnyak 2 [4 73], Zyrianov [39], Fayzulin [54]	

Vyacheslav Malafeev; Alexandr Anyukov, Roman Shirokov, Ivica Krizanac, Alexander Gorshkov - Igor Denisov (Alexei Ionov 90), Anatoly Tymoschuk, Konstantin Zyrianov, Viktor Fayzulin - Alejandro Dominguez (Lee Ho 89), Pavel Pogrebnyak∗. Tr: Dick Advocaat

Bayern München	0

Oliver Kahn - Philipp Lahm, Martin Demichelis, Lucio, Marcell Jansen (Christian Lell∗ 46) - Franck Ribery, Mark van Bommel, Ze Roberto (Lukas Podolski 46), Bastian Schweinsteiger - Miroslav Klose (Jose Sosa 62), Luca Toni∗. Tr: Ottmar Hitzfeld

1st leg. Ibrox, Glasgow
24-04-2008, 19:45, Vassaras GRE

Rangers	0

Neil Alexander - Kirk Broadfoot, David Weir, Carlos Cuellar, Sasa Papac - Steven Whittaker, Brahim Hemdani, Christian Dailly, Steven Davis, Nacho Novo (Thomas Buffel 59) - Jean-Claude Darcheville (Daniel Cousin 59). Tr: Walter Smith

Fiorentina	0

Sebastien Frey - Martin Jorgensen, Tomas Ujfalusi, Alessandro Gamberini∗, Massimo Gobbi∗ - Zdravko Kuzmanovic, Fabio Liverani, Riccardo Montolivo - Mario Alberto Santana∗, Giampaolo Pazzini (Christian Vieri 81), Adrian Mutu. Tr: Cesare Prandelli.

2nd leg. Artemio Franchi, Florence
1-05-2008, 20:45, De Bleeckere BEL

Fiorentina	0 2p

Sebastien Frey - Martin Jorgensen, Tomas Ujfalusi, Alessandro Gamberini, Massimo Gobbi - Marco Donadel (Zdravko Kuzmanovic 42), Fabio Liverani, Riccardo Montolivo - Mario Alberto Santana (Franco Semioli 94), Giampaolo Pazzini (Christian Vieri 79), Adrian Mutu. Tr: Cesare Prandelli

Rangers	0 4p

Neil Alexander - Kirk Broadfoot, Carlos Cuellar, David Weir∗, Sasa Papac - Steven Whittaker, Barry Ferguson, Brahim Hemdani, Steven Davis (Nacho Novo 81), Kevin Thomson∗ - Jean-Claude Darcheville (Daniel Cousin 65∗∗∗109). Tr: Walter Smith

PENALTIES (RANGERS WON 4-2)

Ferguson ✖; Kumanovic ✓; Whittaker ✓; Montolivo ✓; Papac ✓; Liverani ✖; Hemdani ✓; Vieri ✖; Novo ✓

FINAL

City of Manchester Stadium (Eastlands), Manchester
14-05-2008, 19:45, 47 500, Peter Fröjdfeldt SWE

ZENIT	2	0	RANGERS

Denisov [72], Zyrianov [94+]

ZENIT ST PETERSBURG					RANGERS		
16	GK	Vyacheslav Malafeev			Neil Alexander	GK	13
22	DF	Aleksandr Anyukov			Kirk Broadfoot	DF	21
4	DF	Ivica Krizanac			David Weir	DF	3
15	DF	Roman Shirokov			Carlos Cuellar	DF	24
11	MF	Radek Sirl		77	Sasa Papac	DF	5
44	MF	Anatoliy Tymoschuk		80	Brahim Hemdani	MF	7
18	MF	Konstantin Zyrianov		86	Steven Whittaker	DF	28
27	MF	Igor Denisov			Barry Ferguson	MF	6
20	MF	Viktor Fayzulin	93+		Kevin Thomson	MF	8
9	FW	Fatih Tekke			Steven Davis	MF	35
10	FW	Andrei Arshavin			Jean-Claude Darcheville	FW	19
		Tr: Dick Advocaat			Tr: Walter Smith		
1	GK	Kamil Contofalsky			Graeme Smith	GK	16
2	MF	Vladislav Radimov		86	Kris Boyd	FW	9
5	DF	Kim Dong Jin	93+	77	Nacho Novo	FW	10
7	MF	Alejandro Dominguez			Charles Adam	MF	11
25	MF	Fernando Ricksen		80	Lee McCulloch	MF	27
57	MF	Aleksei Ionov			Christian Dailly	DF	30
88	MF	Olexandr Gorshkov			Andy Faye	MF	39

UEFA WOMEN'S CUP 2007–08

SEMI-FINALS

Am Brentano Bad, Frankfurt
29-03-2008, 15:00, 5190

1.FFC Frankfurt   **4**

Pohlers 2 [5 81], Prinz 2 [19 79]

Silke Rottenberg - Gina Loren Lewandowski, Conny Pohlers, Pia Wunderlich (Karolin Thomas 27), Tina Wunderlich, Birgit Prinz, Meike Weber, Sarah Günther, Alexandra Krieger, Petra Wimbersky, Sandra Smisek (Kerstin Garefrekes 46). Tr: Jürgen Tritschoks

Bardolino Verona   **2**

Sorvillo [47], Gabbiadini [83]

Carla Brunozzi - Valeria Magrini, Maria Sorvillo, Melania Gabbiadini, Patrizia Panico, Valentina Boni, Laura Barbierato (Michela Ledri 68), Alessia Tuttino, Roberta Stefanelli, Giorgia Motta, Cristiana Girelli∗ (Rafaella Manieri 46) (Silvia Toselli 82). Tr: Renato Longega

Marc'Antonio Bentegodi, Verona
5-04-2008, 20:30, 12 000, Olander EST

Bardolino Verona   **0**

Carla Brunozzi - Maria Sorvillo (Silvia Toselli 71), Michela Ledri (Valeria Magrini 64), Melania Gabbiadini∗, Patrizia Panico, Valentina Boni, Laura Barbierato, Evelyn Vicchiarello (Cristiana Girelli 57), Alessia Tuttino∗, Roberta Stefanelli, Giorgia Motta. Tr: Renato Longega

1.FFC Frankfurt   **3**

Thomas [68], Garefrekes [80], Pohlers [81]

Silke Rottenberg - Gina Loren Lewandowski, Conny Pohlers, Tina Wunderlich, Birgit Prinz, Renate Lingor∗, Katrin Kliehm∗, Meike Weber (Kerstin Garefrekes 46), Sarah Günther (Alexandra Krieger 66), Petra Wimbersky, Karolin Thomas. Tr: Jürgen Tritschoks

Stade de Gerland, Lyon
30-03-2008, 14:30, 12 000, Schett AUT

Olympique Lyonnais   **1**

Necib [72]

Bente Nordby - Sandrine Dusang, Wendie Renard (Elodie Thomis 61), Laura Georges, Simone Gomes Jatoba, Katia Cilene Teixeira Da Sil, Camille Abily, Shirley Cruz Trana, Louisa Necib, Hoda Lattaf (Sandrine Bretigny 87), Dorte Dalum Jensen. Tr: Farid Benstiti

Umeå IK   **1**

Edlund [57]

Ulla-Karin Rönnlund - Anna Paulsson, Johanna Frisk, Karolina Westberg, Lisa Dahlkvist, Madelaine Edlund, June Pedersen (Emma Berglund 81), Johanna Rasmussen, Mami Yamaguchi (Ramona Bachmann 70), Marta, Frida Östberg∗. Tr: Andrée Jeglertz

Gammliavallen, Umeå
6-04-2008, 13:30, Ihringova ENG

Umeå IK   **0**

Ulla-Karin Rönnlund - Marta, Ramona Bachmann, Emma Berglund, Lisa Dahlkvist, Johanna Frisk, Madelaine Edlund (Sofia Jakobsson 91+), Anna Paulsson, Johanna Rasmussen, Frida Östberg, Mami Yamaguchi. Tr: Andrée Jeglertz

Olympique Lyonnais   **0**

Bente Nordby - Shirley Cruz Trana, Katia Cilene Teixeira Da Sil (Laure Lepailleur 89), Simone Gomes Jatoba, Louisa Necib, Camille Abily, Sandrine Dusang, Laura Georges∗, Hoda Lattaf (Elodie Thomis 57), Sonia Bompastor, Dorte Dalum Jensen (Sandrine Bretigny 91+∗). Tr: Farid Benstiti

Final, 1st leg, Gammliavallen, Umeå
17-05-2008, 13:00, 4130, Gyöngyi Gaal HUN

UMEA IK	1	1	FRANKFURT

Vieira da Silva [1 (12 seconds)]   Pohlers [5]

UMEA IK		1.FFC FRANKFURT	
1 Ulla-Karin Rönnlund		Silke Rottenberg	1
2 Anna Paulsson	56	Katrin Kliehm	11
3 Johanna Frisk		Gina Lewandowski	2
4 Karolina Westberg		Tina Wunderlich	8
91 Frida Östberg		Saskia Bartusiak	25
7 Lisa Dahlqvist		Kerstin Garefrekes	18
16 Mami Yamaguchi		Alexandra Krieger	14
19 Ramona Bachmann	68	Meike Weber	12
60 Marta		Petra Wimbersky	20
9 Madelaine Edlund	83	Conny Pohlers	6
13 Johanna Rasmussen		Birgit Prinz	9
Tr: Andrée Jeglertz		Tr: Hans-Jürgen Tritschoks	
21 Carola Söberg		Stephanie Ullrich	23
5 Emma Berglund		Louise Hansen	3
12 June Pedersen	56	Sarah Günther	13
15 Emmelie Konradsson	68	Anna Marciak	16
17 Emma Åberg-Zingmark		Karolin Thomas	21
18 Sofia Jakobsson		Anne Engel	26
	83	Sandra Smisek	28

Final, 2nd leg, Arena, Frankfurt
24-05-2008, 14:15, 27 640, Alexandra Ihringova ENG

FRANKFURT	3	2	UMEA IK

Pohlers 2 [7 55], Wimbersky [71]   Dahlqvist [68p], Ostberg [83]

1.FFC FRANKFURT			UMEA IK
1 Silke Rottenberg	46		Ulla-Karin Rönnlund 1
11 Katrin Kliehm	47		Anna Paulsson 2
2 Gina Lewandowski			Johanna Frisk 3
8 Tina Wunderlich			Karolina Westberg 4
25 Saskia Bartusiak			Frida Östberg 91
18 Kerstin Garefrekes			Lisa Dahlqvist 7
14 Alexandra Krieger			Mami Yamaguchi 16
12 Meike Weber		46	Emma Berglund 5
20 Petra Wimbersky	90		Marta 60
6 Conny Pohlers		63	Madelaine Edlund 9
9 Birgit Prinz			Johanna Rasmussen 13
Tr: Hans-Jürgen Tritschoks			Tr: Andrée Jeglertz
23 Stephanie Ullrich	46		Carola Söberg 21
3 Louise Hansen			June Pedersen 12
13 Sarah Günther	47		Emmelie Konradsson 15
16 Anna Marciak			Emma Åberg-Zingmark 17
21 Karolin Thomas	90	63	Sofia Jakobsson 18
26 Anne Engel		46	Ramona Bachmann 19
28 Sandra Smisek			

UEFA WOMEN'S CUP 2007-08

First round Groups

Group 1

Team		Pl	W	D	L	F	A	Pts
Everton LFC	ENG	3	3	0	0	20	0	9
FFC Zuchwil 05	SUI	3	2	0	1	11	6	6
Gintra Universitetas	LTU	3	1	0	2	2	11	3
Glentoran Belfast Utd	NIR	3	0	0	3	1	18	0

Results (SUI / LTU / NIR): Everton 5-0, 4-0, 11-0; Zuchwil 6-0, 5-1; Gintra 2-1

Group 2

Team		Pl	W	D	L	F	A	Pts
Valur Reykjavík	ISL	3	3	0	0	13	2	9
FC Honka Espoo	FIN	3	2	0	1	6	3	6
ADO Den Haag	NED	3	0	1	2	2	7	1
KÍ Klaksvík	FRO	3	0	1	2	2	11	1

Results (FIN / NED / FRO): Valur 2-1, 5-1, 6-0; Honka 1-0, 4-1; ADO 1-1

Group 3

Team		Pl	W	D	L	F	A	Pts
SV Neulengbach	AUT	3	3	0	0	15	4	9
Hibernian LFC	SCO	3	2	0	1	15	5	6
Sportowy GOL	POL	3	1	0	2	6	13	3
Mayo FC	IRL	3	0	0	3	1	15	0

Results (SCO / POL / IRL): Neulengbach 4-3, 8-1, 3-0; Hibernian 4-1, 8-0; Sportowy 4-1

Group 4

Team		Pl	W	D	L	F	A	Pts
FCL Rapid Wezemaal	BEL	3	3	0	0	5	0	9
1° Dezembro	POR	3	2	0	1	9	1	6
ZNK Osijek	CRO	3	1	0	2	2	10	3
Cardiff City LFC	WAL	3	0	0	3	1	6	0

Results (POR / CRO / WAL): Rapid 1-0, 2-0, 2-0; Dezembro 7-0, 2-0; Osijek 2-1

Group 5

Team		Pl	W	D	L	F	A	Pts
Bardolini Verona	ITA	3	3	0	0	22	0	9
Athletic Club	ESP	3	2	0	1	20	1	6
Krka Novo Mesto	SVN	3	1	0	2	5	10	3
Birkirkara FC	MLT	3	0	0	3	1	37	0

Results (ESP / SVN / MLT): Verona 1-0, 5-0, 16-0; Athletic 4-0, 16-0; Krka 5-1

Group 6

Team		Pl	W	D	L	F	A	Pts
Olympique Lyonnais	FRA	3	3	0	0	29	0	9
SFK 2000 Sarajevo	BIH	3	2	0	1	4	8	6
ZFK Skiponjat	MKD	3	1	0	2	4	13	3
Slovan Duslo Šaľa	SVK	3	0	0	3	1	17	0

Results (BIH / MKD / SVK): Lyonnais 7-0, 10-0, 12-0; Sarajevo 2-1, 2-0; Skiponjat 3-1

Group 7

Team		Pl	W	D	L	F	A	Pts
WFC Rossiyanka	RUS	3	3	0	0	28	0	9
Metalist Kharkov	UKR	3	2	0	1	18	5	6
Napredak Krusevac	SRB	3	1	0	2	8	13	3
Dinamo Tbilisi	GEO	3	0	0	3	2	38	0

Results (UKR / SRB / GEO): Rossiyanka 3-0, 7-0, 18-0; Metalist 4-2, 14-0; Napredak 6-2

Group 8

Team		Pl	W	D	L	F	A	Pts
Universitet Vitebsk	BLR	3	2	1	0	12	2	7
NSA Sofia	BUL	3	2	0	1	6	7	6
PAOK Thessaloniki	GRE	3	1	0	2	4	10	3
Pärnu FC	EST	3	0	1	2	5	8	1

Results (BUL / GRE / EST): Vitebsk 4-0, 6-0, 2-2; Sofia 3-1, 3-2; PAOK 3-1

Group 9

Team		Pl	W	D	L	F	A	Pts
Alma KTZH	KAZ	3	3	0	0	13	1	9
1.FC Femina Budapest	HUN	3	2	0	1	9	3	6
Narta Chisinau	MDA	3	1	0	2	3	8	3
Ruslan 93	AZE	3	0	0	3	1	14	0

Results (HUN / MDA / AZE): Alma 3-1, 5-0, 5-0; Femina 2-0, 6-0; Narta 3-1

Group 10

Team		Pl	W	D	L	F	A	Pts
Sparta Praha	CZE	3	2	1	0	24	4	7
CFF Clujana	ROU	3	2	1	0	15	1	7
Maccabi Holon	ISR	3	1	0	2	8	8	3
AEK Kokkinochorion	CYP	3	0	0	3	1	35	0

Results (ROU / ISR / CYP): Sparta 1-1, 4-3, 19-0; Clujana 3-0, 11-0; Holon 5-1

Second Round Groups

Group A

Team		Pl	W	D	L	F	A	Pts
Arsenal Ladies FC	ENG	3	2	1	0	14	3	7
Bardolini Verona	ITA	3	2	1	0	11	6	7
SV Neulengbach	AUT	3	1	0	2	5	10	3
Alma KTZH	KAZ	3	0	0	3	1	12	0

Results (ITA / AUT / KAZ): Arsenal 3-3, 7-0, 4-0; Verona 5-1, 3-0; Neulengbach 3-0

Group B

Team		Pl	W	D	L	F	A	Pts
Umeå IK	SWE	3	2	1	0	8	4	7
WFC Rossiyanka	RUS	3	2	1	0	5	3	7
Universitet Vitebsk	BLR	3	1	0	2	4	6	3
CFF Clujana	ROU	3	0	0	3	2	6	0

Results (RUS / BLR / ROU): Umeå 2-2, 3-1, 3-1; Rossiyanka 2-1, 1-0; Vitebsk 2-0

Group C

Team		Pl	W	D	L	F	A	Pts
1.FC Frankfurt	GER	3	2	1	0	6	3	7
FCL Rapid Wezemaal	BEL	3	1	1	1	6	3	4
Everton LFC	ENG	3	1	0	2	4	5	3
Valur Reykjavík	ISL	3	1	0	2	3	8	3

Results (BEL / ENG / ISL): Frankfurt 1-1, 2-1, 3-1; Rapid 1-2, 4-0; Everton 1-2

Group D

Team		Pl	W	D	L	F	A	Pts
Brøndby IF	DEN	3	2	1	0	4	0	7
Olympique Lyonnais	FRA	3	2	1	0	4	1	7
Kolbotn IL	NOR	3	1	0	2	3	3	3
Sparta Praha	CZE	3	0	0	3	2	9	0

Results (FRA / NOR / CZE): Brøndby 0-0, 1-0, 3-0; Lyonnais 1-0, 3-1; Kolbotn 3-1

Quarter-finals

(two legs; * = home team in the first leg)

Tie	Leg 1	Leg 2
1.FC Frankfurt * vs WFC Rossiyanka *	0	2
	0	1
Brøndby IF ‡ vs Bardolini Verona *	1	0
	0	1
Olympique Lyonnais * vs Arsenal Ladies FC	0	3
	0	2
FCL Rapid Wezemaal * vs **Umeå IK**	0	0
	4	6

Semi-finals

Tie	Leg 1	Leg 2
1.FC Frankfurt *	4	3
Bardolini Verona	2	0
Olympique Lyonnais *	1	0
Umeå IK	1	0

Final

Team	Leg 1	Leg 2
1.FC Frankfurt	1	3
Umeå IK *	1	2

Five clubs – Arsenal, Brøndby, Frankfurt, Kolbotn, Umeå – received byes to the second round • * Home team in the first leg • ‡ Brøndby won 3-2 on penalties

UEFA EUROPEAN U–17 CHAMPIONSHIP 2008

Qualifying Round Group 1

	Pl	W	D	L	F	A	Pts	GRE	LUX	KAZ
Switzerland	3	3	0	0	10	1	9	2-1	4-0	4-0
Greece	3	1	1	1	5	4	4		1-1	3-1
Luxembourg	3	1	1	1	4	7	4			3-2
Kazakhstan	3	0	0	3	3	10	0	Played in SUI		

Qualifying Round Group 2

	Pl	W	D	L	F	A	Pts	NOR	POL	MKD
Austria	3	2	0	1	7	5	6	4-2	1-0	2-3
Norway	3	1	1	1	6	4	4		0-0	4-0
Poland	3	1	1	1	4	2	4			4-1
Macedonia FYR	3	1	0	2	4	10	3	Played in POL		

Qualifying Round Group 3

	Pl	W	D	L	F	A	Pts	SCO	BLR	LIE
Slovakia	3	3	0	0	11	0	9	4-0	2-0	5-0
Scotland	3	2	0	1	13	5	6		5-1	8-0
Belarus	3	1	0	2	6	8	3			5-1
Liechtenstein	3	0	0	3	1	18	0	Played in SCO		

Qualifying Round Group 4

	Pl	W	D	L	F	A	Pts	WAL	AND	SMR
Spain	3	2	1	0	11	2	7	2-2	3-0	6-0
Wales	3	2	1	0	7	3	7		1-0	4-1
Andorra	3	1	0	2	3	4	3			3-0
San Marino	3	0	0	3	1	13	0	Played in AND		

Qualifying Round Group 5

	Pl	W	D	L	F	A	Pts	DEN	SVN	UKR
Republic of Ireland	3	3	0	0	6	1	9	2-0	1-0	3-1
Denmark	3	1	1	1	3	3	4		1-1	2-0
Slovenia	3	0	2	1	2	3	2			1-1
Ukraine	3	0	1	2	2	6	1	Played in IRL		

Qualifying Round Group 6

	Pl	W	D	L	F	A	Pts	ROU	SWE	FRO
Germany	3	1	2	0	10	2	5	1-1	1-1	8-0
Romania	3	1	2	0	2	1	5		1-0	0-0
Sweden	3	1	1	1	6	4	4			5-2
Faroe Islands	3	0	1	2	2	13	1	Played in GER		

Qualifying Round Group 7

	Pl	W	D	L	F	A	Pts	SRB	ISL	LTU
Israel	3	2	1	0	5	1	7	2-1	3-0	0-0
Serbia	3	2	0	1	4	2	6		1-0	2-0
Iceland	3	1	0	2	1	4	3			1-0
Lithuania	3	0	1	2	0	3	1	Played in SRB		

Qualifying Round Group 8

	Pl	W	D	L	F	A	Pts	HUN	GEO	BUL
Croatia	3	2	1	0	6	0	7	0-0	4-0	2-0
Hungary	3	2	1	0	4	0	7		1-0	3-0
Georgia	3	1	0	2	5	7	3			5-2
Bulgaria	3	0	0	3	2	10	0	Played in BUL		

Qualifying Round Group 9

	Pl	W	D	L	F	A	Pts	RUS	FIN	AZE
Bosnia-Herzegovina	3	2	0	1	2	2	6	0-2	1-0	1-0
Russia	3	1	2	0	4	2	5		1-1	1-1
Finland	3	0	2	1	3	4	2			2-2
Azerbaijan	3	0	2	1	3	4	2	Played in BIH		

Qualifying Round Group 10

	Pl	W	D	L	F	A	Pts	FRA	LVA	ALB
Netherlands	3	3	0	0	7	1	9	1-0	3-1	3-0
France	3	2	0	1	7	1	6		1-0	6-0
Latvia	3	0	1	2	2	5	1			1-1
Albania	3	0	1	2	1	10	1	Played in ALB		

Qualifying Round Group 11

	Pl	W	D	L	F	A	Pts	POR	EST	MLT
England	3	2	1	0	12	0	7	0-0	6-0	6-0
Portugal	3	2	1	0	8	0	7		2-0	6-0
Estonia	3	0	1	2	0	8	1			0-0
Malta	3	0	1	2	0	12	1	Played in EST		

Qualifying Round Group 12

	Pl	W	D	L	F	A	Pts	BEL	MDA	MNE
Northern Ireland	3	3	0	0	5	0	9	1-0	3-0	1-0
Belgium	3	2	0	1	5	1	6		3-0	2-0
Moldova	3	1	0	2	3	7	3			3-1
Montenegro	3	0	0	3	1	6	0	Played in BEL		

Qualifying Round Group 13

	Pl	W	D	L	F	A	Pts	CZE	CYP	ARM
Italy	3	3	0	0	11	3	9	2-1	7-1	2-1
Czech Republic	3	2	0	1	14	3	6		8-0	5-1
Cyprus	3	1	0	2	4	15	3			3-0
Armenia	3	0	0	3	2	10	0	Played in CZE		

Elite Round Group 1

	Pl	W	D	L	F	A	Pts	POR	GER	GRE
Republic of Ireland	3	1	1	1	4	3	4	2-0	1-1	1-2
Portugal	3	1	1	1	3	4	4		2-0	1-1
Germany	3	1	1	1	3	4	4			2-0
Greece	3	1	1	1	3	4	4	Played in IRL		

Elite Round Group 2

	Pl	W	D	L	F	A	Pts	CRO	BEL	DEN
Switzerland	3	2	1	0	3	1	7	1-0	1-1	1-0
Croatia	3	2	0	1	7	1	6		4-0	3-0
Belgium	3	1	1	1	6	7	4			5-2
Denmark	3	0	0	3	2	9	0	Played in CRO		

Elite Round Group 3

	Pl	W	D	L	F	A	Pts	ISR	RUS	ENG
France	3	2	1	0	7	4	7	3-2	3-1	1-1
Israel	3	1	1	1	7	6	4		3-1	2-2
Russia	3	1	0	2	5	8	3			3-2
England	3	0	2	1	5	6	2	Played in ISR		

Elite Round Group 4

	Pl	W	D	L	F	A	Pts	SWE	SVK	CZE
Serbia	3	2	1	0	6	3	7	1-1	3-1	2-1
Sweden	3	1	1	1	3	8	4		2-1	0-6
Slovakia	3	1	0	2	4	6	3			2-1
Czech Republic	3	1	0	2	8	4	3	Played in SRB		

Elite Round Group 5

	Pl	W	D	L	F	A	Pts	WAL	SVN	NIR
Scotland	3	3	0	0	5	1	9	1-0	1-0	3-1
Wales	3	1	1	1	4	3	4		1-1	3-1
Slovenia	3	1	1	1	3	2	4			2-0
Northern Ireland	3	0	0	3	2	8	0	Played in NIR		

Elite Round Group 6

	Pl	W	D	L	F	A	Pts	ROU	ITA	AUT
Spain	3	2	1	0	4	2	7	2-2	1-0	1-0
Romania	3	1	2	0	4	3	5		1-1	1-0
Italy	3	0	2	1	2	3	2			1-1
Austria	3	0	1	2	1	3	1	Played in ROU		

Elite Round Group 7

	Pl	W	D	L	F	A	Pts	NOR	BIH	HUN
Netherlands	3	2	0	1	4	1	6	2-0	0-1	2-0
Norway	3	1	1	1	3	3	4		2-0	1-1
Bosnia-Herzegovina	3	1	1	1	3	4	4			2-2
Hungary	3	0	2	1	3	5	2	Played in NED		

UEFA EUROPEAN U-17 CHAMPIONSHIP 2008

First Round Group Stage

Group A	Pl	W	D	L	F	A	Pts	NED	SRB	SCO
Turkey	3	2	1	0	4	0	7	3-0	0-0	1-0
Netherlands	3	2	0	1	3	3	6		1-0	2-0
Serbia	3	1	1	1	2	1	4			2-0
Scotland	3	0	0	3	0	5	0			

Semi-finals

Spain	2
Netherlands	1

Final

Spain	4
France	0

Group B	Pl	W	D	L	F	A	Pts	FRA	SUI	IRL
Spain	3	2	1	0	8	4	7	3-3	2-0	3-1
France	3	2	1	0	7	4	7		2-0	2-1
Switzerland	3	1	0	2	1	4	3			1-0
Republic of Ireland	3	0	0	3	2	6	0	Finals held in Turkey from 4-05-2008 to 16-05-2008		

Turkey	1 3p
France	1 4p

UEFA EUROPEAN U–19 CHAMPIONSHIP 2008

Qualifying Round Group 1

	Pl	W	D	L	F	A	Pts	BLR	IRL	AND
Portugal	3	3	0	0	5	2	9	2-1	2-1	1-0
Belarus	3	2	0	1	8	3	6		2-0	5-1
Republic of Ireland	3	1	0	2	4	4	3			3-0
Andorra	3	0	0	3	1	9	0	Played in POR		

Qualifying Round Group 2

	Pl	W	D	L	F	A	Pts	SUI	KAZ	WAL
Hungary	3	3	0	0	11	2	9	2-1	6-0	3-1
Switzerland	3	1	1	1	8	4	4		6-1	1-1
Kazakhstan	3	1	0	2	3	13	3			2-1
Wales	3	0	1	2	3	6	1	Played in HUN		

Qualifying Round Group 3

	Pl	W	D	L	F	A	Pts	ISL	BEL	ROU
England	3	3	0	0	14	2	9	5-1	3-1	6-0
Iceland	3	2	0	1	6	6	6		3-1	2-0
Belgium	3	1	0	2	6	6	3			4-0
Romania	3	0	0	3	0	12	0	Played in ENG		

Qualifying Round Group 4

	Pl	W	D	L	F	A	Pts	GRE	SVN	LUX
France	3	2	1	0	9	2	7	2-2	2-0	5-0
Greece	3	2	1	0	8	3	7		1-0	5-1
Slovenia	3	1	0	2	3	3	3			3-0
Luxembourg	3	0	0	3	1	13	0	Played in LUX		

Qualifying Round Group 5

	Pl	W	D	L	F	A	Pts	ALB	SRB	LIE
Spain	3	1	2	0	3	1	5	2-0	1-1	0-0
Albania	3	1	1	1	2	3	4		2-1	0-0
Serbia	3	1	1	1	5	3	4			3-0
Liechtenstein	3	0	2	1	0	3	2	Played in ESP		

Qualifying Round Group 6

	Pl	W	D	L	F	A	Pts	SWE	FIN	MKD
Israel	3	3	0	0	5	0	9	1-0	1-0	3-0
Sweden	3	2	0	1	5	2	6		2-0	3-1
Finland	3	1	0	2	3	3	3			3-0
Macedonia FYR	3	0	0	3	1	9	0	Played in SWE		

Qualifying Round Group 7

	Pl	W	D	L	F	A	Pts	ARM	POL	SMR
Lithuania	3	1	2	0	7	3	5	2-2	1-1	4-0
Armenia	3	1	2	0	3	2	5		0-0	1-0
Poland	3	1	2	0	6	1	5			5-0
San Marino	3	0	0	3	0	10	0	Played in LTU		

Qualifying Round Group 8

	Pl	W	D	L	F	A	Pts	NED	LVA	GEO
Norway	3	3	0	0	6	1	9	3-1	2-0	1-0
Netherlands	3	2	0	1	5	4	6		2-0	2-1
Latvia	3	1	0	2	2	4	3			2-0
Georgia	3	0	0	3	1	5	0	Played in GEO		

Qualifying Round Group 9

	Pl	W	D	L	F	A	Pts	BUL	DEN	FRO
Turkey	3	2	1	0	5	1	7	2-0	0-0	3-1
Bulgaria	3	1	1	1	2	4			1-0	0-0
Denmark	3	1	1	1	2	4				2-0
Faroe Islands	3	0	1	2	1	5	1	Played in BUL		

Qualifying Round Group 10

	Pl	W	D	L	F	A	Pts	CYP	AUT	NIR
Slovakia	3	3	0	0	9	2	9	5-1	2-0	2-1
Cyprus	3	1	1	1	4	7	4		2-1	1-1
Austria	3	1	0	2	2	4	3			1-0
Northern Ireland	3	0	1	2	2	4	1	Played in NED		

Qualifying Round Group 11

	Pl	W	D	L	F	A	Pts	MDA	AZE	SCO
Ukraine	3	3	0	0	6	1	9	2-1	3-0	1-0
Moldova	3	1	1	1	2	2	4		0-0	1-0
Azerbaijan	3	1	1	1	2	3	4			2-0
Scotland	3	0	0	3	0	4	0	Played in MDA		

Qualifying Round Group 12

	Pl	W	D	L	F	A	Pts	GER	BIH	EST
Russia	3	3	0	0	11	2	9	3-2	1-0	7-0
Germany	3	2	0	1	15	5	6		8-1	5-1
Bosnia-Herzegovina	3	0	1	2	3	11	1			2-2
Estonia	3	0	1	2	3	14	1	Played in RUS		

Qualifying Round Group 13

	Pl	W	D	L	F	A	Pts	CRO	MNE	MLT
Italy	3	3	0	0	8	2	9	3-1	3-1	2-0
Croatia	3	2	0	1	6	4	6		2-1	3-0
Montenegro	3	1	0	2	5	5	3			3-0
Malta	3	0	0	3	0	8	0	Played in ITA		

Elite Round Group 1

	Pl	W	D	L	F	A	Pts	BLR	POL	SRB
England	3	2	1	0	3	0	7	0-0	2-0	1-0
Belarus	3	1	1	1	1	4	4		1-0	0-4
Poland	3	1	0	2	1	3	3			1-0
Serbia	3	1	0	2	4	2	3	Played in BLR		

Elite Round Group 2

	Pl	W	D	L	F	A	Pts	POR	CYP	LTU
Hungary	3	2	1	0	5	3	7	1-0	2-1	2-2
Portugal	3	2	0	1	8	2	6		5-0	3-1
Cyprus	3	1	0	2	2	7	3			1-0
Lithuania	3	0	1	2	3	6	1	Played in HUN		

Elite Round Group 3

	Pl	W	D	L	F	A	Pts	ISL	NOR	ISR
Bulgaria	3	3	0	0	5	1	9	2-1	2-0	1-0
Iceland	3	2	0	1	5	4	6		3-2	1-0
Norway	3	1	0	2	4	5	3			2-0
Israel	3	0	0	3	0	4	0	Played in NOR		

Elite Round Group 4

	Pl	W	D	L	F	A	Pts	CRO	SVK	ALB
Germany	3	2	1	0	9	4	7	2-2	5-2	2-0
Croatia	3	1	2	0	5	3	5		1-1	2-0
Slovakia	3	0	2	1	5	8	2			2-2
Albania	3	0	1	2	2	6	1	Played in SVK		

Elite Round Group 5

	Pl	W	D	L	F	A	Pts	RUS	MDV	NED
Greece	3	2	0	1	6	4	6	3-1	1-2	2-1
Russia	3	1	1	1	5	6	4		2-1	2-2
Moldova	3	1	1	1	3	3	4			0-0
Netherlands	3	0	2	1	3	4	2	Played in GRE		

Elite Round Group 6

	Pl	W	D	L	F	A	Pts	FRA	SUI	SWE
Italy	3	3	0	0	6	0	9	2-0	2-0	2-0
France	3	2	0	1	5	5	6		3-2	3-0
Switzerland	3	1	0	2	6	6	3			4-1
Sweden	3	0	0	3	2	8	0	Played in SUI		

Elite Round Group 7

	Pl	W	D	L	F	A	Pts	UKR	TUR	ARM
Spain	3	3	0	0	10	3	9	3-1	3-0	4-2
Ukraine	3	2	0	1	5	3	6		3-0	1-0
Turkey	3	1	0	2	2	7	3			2-1
Armenia	3	0	0	3	3	7	0	Played in ARM		

UEFA EUROPEAN U-19 CHAMPIONSHIP 2008

First Round Group Stage

Group A	Pl	W	D	L	F	A	Pts	HUN	ESP	BUL
Germany	3	3	0	0	7	2	9	2-1	2-1	3-0
Hungary	3	2	0	1	3	2	6		1-0	1-0
Spain	3	1	0	2	5	3	3			4-0
Bulgaria	3	0	0	3	0	8	0			

Semi-finals

Germany	2
Czech Republic	1

Final

Germany	3
Italy	1

Group B	Pl	W	D	L	F	A	Pts	CZE	ENG	GRE
Italy	3	1	2	0	5	4	5	4-3	0-0	1-1
Czech Republic	3	1	1	1	5	4	4		2-0	0-0
England	3	1	1	1	3	2	4			3-0
Greece	3	0	2	1	1	4	2			

Hungary	0
Italy	1

Finals held in the Czech Republic from 14-07-2008 to 26-07-2008

UEFA WOMEN'S U-17 CHAMPIONSHIP 2008

First Qualifying Round Group 1

	Pl	W	D	L	F	A	Pts	WAL	LTU	CYP
Switzerland	3	2	1	0	11	2	7	2-2	5-0	4-0
Wales	3	1	2	0	14	4	5		2-2	10-0
Lithuania	3	1	1	1	4	7	4			2-0
Cyprus	3	0	0	3	0	16	0	Played in SUI		

First Qualifying Round Group 2

	Pl	W	D	L	F	A	Pts	POL	AZE	GRE
Netherlands	3	3	0	0	7	0	9	2-0	2-0	3-0
Poland	3	2	0	1	8	2	6		4-0	4-0
Azerbaijan	3	1	0	2	2	7	3			2-1
Greece	3	0	0	3	1	9	0	Played in POL		

First Qualifying Round Group 3

	Pl	W	D	L	F	A	Pts	BEL	FRO	EST
Finland	3	3	0	0	24	2	9	3-1	9-0	12-1
Belgium	3	2	0	1	10	4	6		5-1	4-0
Faroe Islands	3	1	0	2	2	14	3			1-0
Estonia	3	0	0	3	1	17	0	Played in EST		

First Qualifying Round Group 4

	Pl	W	D	L	F	A	Pts	SVN	UKR	LVA
Iceland	3	3	0	0	15	1	9	5-0	3-0	7-1
Slovenia	3	1	1	1	5	7	4		2-2	3-0
Ukraine	3	1	1	1	4	6	4			2-1
Latvia	3	0	0	3	2	12	0	Played in SVN		

First Qualifying Round Group 5

	Pl	W	D	L	F	A	Pts	DEN	MKD	ARM
France	3	3	0	0	31	0	9	4-0	11-0	16-0
Denmark	3	2	0	1	30	4	6		6-0	24-0
Macedonia FYR	3	1	0	2	3	18	3			3-1
Armenia	3	0	0	3	1	43	0	Played in MKD		

First Qualifying Round Group 6

	Pl	W	D	L	F	A	Pts	IRL	TUR	MDA
Sweden	3	3	0	0	17	2	9	2-1	3-1	12-0
Republic of Ireland	3	2	0	1	11	2	6		5-0	5-0
Turkey	3	1	0	2	8	8	3			7-0
Moldova	3	0	0	3	0	24	0	Played in TUR		

First Qualifying Round Group 7

	Pl	W	D	L	F	A	Pts	ESP	ITA	BLR
Czech Republic	3	2	1	0	12	3	7	1-1	3-2	8-0
Spain	3	1	2	0	14	2	5		1-1	12-0
Italy	3	1	1	1	9	6	4			6-2
Belarus	3	0	0	3	2	26	0	Played in ESP		

First Qualifying Round Group 8

	Pl	W	D	L	F	A	Pts	HUN	NIR	CRO
Scotland	3	3	0	0	13	1	9	3-1	6-0	4-0
Hungary	3	2	0	1	9	3	6		2-0	6-0
Northern Ireland	3	0	1	2	0	8	1			0-0
Croatia	3	0	1	2	0	10	1	Played in CRO		

First Qualifying Round Group 9

	Pl	W	D	L	F	A	Pts	NOR	ISR	BUL
Germany	3	3	0	0	24	1	9	6-1	8-0	10-0
Norway	3	2	0	1	22	6	6		10-0	11-0
Israel	3	1	0	2	1	18	3			1-0
Bulgaria	3	0	0	3	0	22	0	Played in NOR		

First Qualifying Round Group 10

	Pl	W	D	L	F	A	Pts	RUS	SVK	GEO
England	3	3	0	0	17	1	9	1-0	3-1	13-0
Russia	3	2	0	1	6	2	6		3-1	3-0
Slovakia	3	1	0	2	8	6	3			6-0
Georgia	3	0	0	3	0	22	0	Played in GEO		

UEFA EUROPEAN WOMEN'S U-17 CHAMPIONSHIP 2008

Second Qualifying Round

Group 1

	Pl	W	D	L	F	A	Pts	NED	CZE	BEL
England	3	2	1	0	7	1	7	0-0	4-0	3-1
Netherlands	3	1	2	0	3	1	5		2-0	1-1
Czech Republic	3	1	0	2	3	7	3			3-1
Belgium	3	0	1	2	3	7	1			

Group 2

	Pl	W	D	L	F	A	Pts	SCO	IRL	NOR
France	3	3	0	0	5	0	9	1-0	2-0	2-0
Scotland	3	2	0	1	2	1	6		1-0	1-0
Republic of Ireland	3	1	0	2	1	3	3			1-0
Norway	3	0	0	3	0	4	0			

Group 3

	Pl	W	D	L	F	A	Pts	POL	SWE	SUI
Germany	3	3	0	0	11	1	9	3-0	4-1	4-0
Poland	3	1	1	1	3	4	4		1-1	2-0
Sweden	3	0	2	1	3	6	2			1-1
Switzerland	3	0	1	2	1	7	1			

Group 4

	Pl	W	D	L	F	A	Pts	FIN	RUS	ISL
Denmark	3	2	1	0	6	2	7	0-0	2-0	4-2
Finland	3	2	1	0	5	2	7		1-0	4-2
Russia	3	1	0	2	4	6	3			4-3
Iceland	3	0	0	3	7	12	0			

Semi-finals

Germany	1
Denmark	0

England	1
France	3

Final

Germany	3
France	0

Third Place Play-off

Denmark	4
England	1

Group 1 held in the Czech Republic; Group 2 in France; Group 3 in Germany; Group 4 in Denmark
Semi-finals and final held in Nyon, Switzerland from 20-05-2008 to 23-05-2008

UEFA WOMEN'S U–19 CHAMPIONSHIP 2008

First Qualifying Round Group 1

	Pl	W	D	L	F	A	Pts	POR	ROU	GRE
Iceland	3	3	0	0	11	3	9	3-2	4-0	4-1
Portugal	3	1	0	2	6	5	3		0-2	4-0
Romania	3	1	0	2	2	5	3			0-1
Greece	3	1	0	2	2	8	3	Played in POR		

First Qualifying Round Group 2

	Pl	W	D	L	F	A	Pts	POL	TUR	BUL
Austria	3	2	1	0	8	3	7	1-1	3-2	4-0
Poland	3	1	1	1	10	5	4		7-1	2-3
Turkey	3	1	0	2	7	10	3			4-0
Bulgaria	3	1	0	2	3	10	3	Played in POL		

First Qualifying Round Group 3

	Pl	W	D	L	F	A	Pts	SWE	KAZ	GEO
Hungary	3	2	1	0	17	1	7	1-1	13-0	3-0
Sweden	3	2	1	0	16	1	7		12-0	3-0
Kazakhstan	3	1	0	2	3	25	3			3-0
Georgia (forfeit)	3	0	0	3	0	9	0	Played in SWE		

First Qualifying Round Group 4

	Pl	W	D	L	F	A	Pts	RUS	ISR	NIR
Italy	3	2	1	0	13	2	7	1-1	5-1	7-0
Russia	3	2	1	0	10	1	7		7-0	2-0
Israel	3	1	0	2	5	15	3			4-3
Northern Ireland	3	0	0	3	3	13	0	Played in RUS		

First Qualifying Round Group 5

	Pl	W	D	L	F	A	Pts	SRB	BLR	EST
Finland	3	3	0	0	12	0	9	1-0	3-0	8-0
Serbia	3	1	1	1	5	2	4		0-0	5-1
Belarus	3	1	1	1	3	3	4			3-0
Estonia	3	0	0	3	1	16	0	Played in BLR		

First Qualifying Round Group 6

	Pl	W	D	L	F	A	Pts	BEL	BIH	LVA
Denmark	3	3	0	0	14	1	9	2-1	2-0	10-0
Belgium	3	2	0	1	9	2	6		6-0	2-0
Bosnia-Herzegovina	3	1	0	2	2	9	3			2-1
Latvia	3	0	0	3	1	14	0	Played in BIH		

First Qualifying Round Group 7

	Pl	W	D	L	F	A	Pts	UKR	AZE	ARM
Scotland	3	2	1	0	18	2	7	2-2	3-0	13-0
Ukraine	3	2	1	0	7	2	7		3-0	2-0
Azerbaijan	3	0	1	2	2	8	1			2-2
Armenia	3	0	1	2	2	17	1	Played in UKR		

First Qualifying Round Group 8

	Pl	W	D	L	F	A	Pts	SUI	CRO	SVK
Republic of Ireland	3	3	0	0	13	3	9	3-2	5-1	5-0
Switzerland	3	2	0	1	11	5	6		6-2	3-0
Croatia	3	1	0	2	5	12	3			2-1
Slovakia	3	0	0	3	1	10	0	Played in SVK		

First Qualifying Round Group 9

	Pl	W	D	L	F	A	Pts	CZE	WAL	MKD
Germany	3	3	0	0	25	0	9	6-0	7-0	12-0
Czech Republic	3	2	0	1	7	9	6		3-2	4-1
Wales	3	1	0	2	4	10	3			2-0
Macedonia FYR	3	0	0	3	1	18	0	Played in MKD		

First Qualifying Round Group 10

	Pl	W	D	L	F	A	Pts	NED	SVN	MDA
Norway	3	3	0	0	19	0	9	2-0	3-0	14-0
Netherlands	3	2	0	1	18	2	6		7-0	11-0
Slovenia	3	1	0	2	5	10	3			5-0
Moldova	3	0	0	3	0	30	0	Played in SVN		

First Qualifying Round Group 11

	Pl	W	D	L	F	A	Pts	ENG	FRO	LTU
Spain	3	2	1	0	26	0	7	0-0	12-0	14-0
England	3	2	1	0	17	1	7		7-1	10-0
Faroe Islands	3	0	1	2	3	21	1			2-2
Lithuania	3	0	1	2	2	26	1	Played in LTU		

Second Qualifying Round Group 1

	Pl	W	D	L	F	A	Pts	CZE	AUT	FIN
Sweden	3	2	1	0	6	1	7	3-0	2-0	1-1
Czech Republic	3	2	0	1	3	4	6		1-0	2-1
Austria	3	1	0	2	3	3	3			3-0
Finland	3	0	1	2	2	6	1	Played in AUT		

Second Qualifying Round Group 2

	Pl	W	D	L	F	A	Pts	BEL	ISL	POL
England	3	3	0	0	12	0	9	4-0	1-0	7-0
Belgium	3	2	0	1	2	4	6		1-0	1-0
Iceland	3	0	1	2	2	4	1			2-2
Poland	3	0	1	2	2	10	1	Played in BEL		

Second Qualifying Round Group 3

	Pl	W	D	L	F	A	Pts	RUS	HUN	ROU
Germany	3	3	0	0	14	3	9	8-3	2-0	4-0
Russia	3	1	0	2	7	9	3		0-1	4-0
Hungary	3	1	0	2	3	5	3			2-3
Romania	3	1	0	2	3	10	3	Played in ROU		

Second Qualifying Round Group 4

	Pl	W	D	L	F	A	Pts	DEN	SUI	BLR
Scotland	3	2	1	0	7	4	7	2-1	2-2	3-1
Denmark	3	2	0	1	5	2	6		2-0	2-0
Switzerland	3	1	1	1	6	5	4			4-1
Belarus	3	0	0	3	2	9	0	Played in SUI		

Second Qualifying Round Group 5

	Pl	W	D	L	F	A	Pts	ITA	POR	UKR
Norway	3	3	0	0	13	3	9	2-1	5-1	6-1
Italy	3	2	0	1	9	2	6		4-0	4-0
Portugal	3	0	1	2	3	11	1			2-2
Ukraine	3	0	1	2	3	12	1	Played in POR		

Second Qualifying Round Group 6

	Pl	W	D	L	F	A	Pts	NED	IRL	SRB
Spain	3	3	0	0	11	1	9	1-0	3-1	7-0
Netherlands	3	2	0	1	9	2	6		2-0	7-1
Republic of Ireland	3	1	0	2	8	5	3			7-0
Serbia	3	0	0	3	1	21	0	Played in ESP		

UEFA EUROPEAN WOMEN'S U-19 CHAMPIONSHIP 2008

First Round Group Stage

Group A	Pl	W	D	L	F	A	Pts	NOR	FRA	ESP
Italy	3	2	0	1	4	4	6	1-0	3-1	0-3
Norway	3	1	1	1	3	3	4		1-1	2-1
France	3	1	1	1	3	4	4			1-0
Spain	3	1	0	2	4	3	3			

Semi-finals

Italy	4
Sweden	0

Final

Italy	1
Norway	0

Group B	Pl	W	D	L	F	A	Pts	SWE	ENG	SCO
Germany	3	2	1	0	10	1	7	1-1	2-0	7-0
Sweden	3	1	2	0	4	3	5		1-1	2-1
England	3	1	1	1	4	4	4			3-1
Scotland	3	0	0	3	2	12	0			

Semi-finals

Germany	1 2p
Norway	1 4p

Finals held in France from 7-07-2008 to 19-07-2008

REGIONAL CLUB TOURNAMENTS IN EUROPE

BALTIC LEAGUE 2007

First round groups

Group A		Pl	W	D	L	F	A	Pts	LTU	EST
FBK Kaunas	LTU	2	1	1	0	5	4	4		3-2
Trans Narva	EST	2	0	1	1	4	5	1	2-2	2-0
Dinaburg Daugavpils	LVA			Excluded						

Group B		Pl	W	D	L	F	A	Pts	LVA	LTU	EST
FK Ventspils	LVA	4	3	1	0	7	2	10		3-0	3-2
Ekranas Panevezys	LTU	4	1	2	1	5	7	5	0-0		2-1
TVMK Tallinn	EST	4	0	1	3	6	9	1	0-1	3-3	

Group C		Pl	W	D	L	F	A	Pts	LVA	LTU	EST
Liepajas Metalurgs	LVA	4	2	2	0	6	3	8		3-1	1-1
Zalgiris Vilnius	LTU	4	1	2	1	4	5	5	0-0		2-1
Levadia Tallin	EST	4	0	2	2	4	6	2	1-2	1-1	

Group D		Pl	W	D	L	F	A	Pts	LVA	LTU	EST
Skonto Riga	LVA	4	2	2	0	7	2	8		1-1	4-0
Vetra Vilnius	LTU	4	1	2	1	5	3	5	1-1		0-1
Flora Tallinn	EST	4	1	0	3	1	8	3	0-1	0-3	

The tournament took place from 6-03-2007 to 11-11-2007 • * Home team in the first leg

Quarter-finals

Liepajas M'lurgs*	4	1
Trans Narva	1	2
Skonto Riga *	1	0
Ekranas P'vezys	2	0
FBK Kaunas	9	1
Zalgiris Vilnius *	1	1
Vetra Vilnius *	0	2
FK Ventspils	0	4

Semi-finals

Liepajas M'lurgs*	6	2
Ekranas P'vezys	1	2
FBK Kaunas *	0	0
FK Ventspils	0	1

Final

Liepajas M'lurgs	3	5
FK Ventspils *	1	1

FINAL

1st leg. 8-11-2007
Ventspils, Att: 250
Scorers - Ferreira 3,
Karlsons 38,
Solonicins 78 for
Liepajas; Grebis 75 for
Ventspils

FINAL

2nd leg. 11-11-2007
Liepaja, Att: 1000
Scorers -
Karlssons 3 36 66 75,
Solonicins 49, Ivanovs
78 for Liepajas;
Savcenkovs 41 for
Ventspils

MISCELLANEOUS

MISCELLANEOUS

BIG COUNT AND FIFA/COCA-COLA WORLD RANKING OVERFLOW

THE FIFA BIG COUNT OF 2006 FOR ARGENTINA

	Male	Female		Total
Number of players	2 349 811	30 900	Referees and Assistant Referees	3 340
Professionals	3 530		Admin, Coaches, Technical, Medical	33 821
Amateurs 18+	88 090		Number of clubs	3 348
Youth under 18	231 196		Number of teams	23 623
Unregistered	1 225 000		Clubs with women's teams	29
Total players	2 658 811		Players as % of population	6.66%

FIFA/COCA-COLA WORLD RANKING FOR ARGENTINA

1993	1994	1995	1996	1997	1998	1999	2000	2001	2002	2003	2004	2005	2006	2007		High	
8	10	7	22	17	5	6	3	2	5	5	3	4	3	1		1	03/07

2007–2008													Low	
08/07	09/07	10/07	11/07	12/07	01/08	02/08	03/08	04/08	05/08	06/08	07/08		24	08/96
2	2	1	1	1	1	1	1	1	1	1	6			

THE FIFA BIG COUNT OF 2006 FOR AUSTRALIA

	Male	Female		Total
Number of players	781 246	189482	Referees and Assistant Referees	8 650
Professionals	200		Admin, Coaches, Technical, Medical	58 982
Amateurs 18+	107 013		Number of clubs	2 316
Youth under 18	299 775		Number of teams	20 018
Unregistered	338 000		Clubs with women's teams	1 552
Total players	970 728		Players as % of population	4.79%

FIFA/COCA-COLA WORLD RANKING FOR AUSTRALIA

1993	1994	1995	1996	1997	1998	1999	2000	2001	2002	2003	2004	2005	2006	2007		High	
49	58	51	50	35	39	89	73	48	50	82	58	48	39	48		31	07/97

2007–2008													Low	
08/07	09/07	10/07	11/07	12/07	01/08	02/08	03/08	04/08	05/08	06/08	07/08		92	06/00
49	48	52	48	48	48	38	38	43	43	35	40			

THE FIFA BIG COUNT OF 2006 FOR BRAZIL

	Male	Female		Total
Number of players	11 752 783	1 444 950	Referees and Assistant Referees	16 000
Professionals	16 200		Admin, Coaches, Technical, Medical	45 000
Amateurs 18+	472 165		Number of clubs	28 970
Youth under 18	1 347 100		Number of teams	86 910
Unregistered	6 080 000		Clubs with women's teams	238
Total players	13 197 733		Players as % of population	7.02%

FIFA/COCA-COLA WORLD RANKING FOR BRAZIL

1993	1994	1995	1996	1997	1998	1999	2000	2001	2002	2003	2004	2005	2006	2007		High	
3	1	1	1	1	1	1	1	3	1	1	1	1	1	2		1	

2007–2008													Low	
08/07	09/07	10/07	11/07	12/07	01/08	02/08	03/08	04/08	05/08	06/08	07/08		8	08/93
1	3	2	2	2	2	2	2	2	2	2	4			

THE FIFA BIG COUNT OF 2006 FOR CHINA

	Male	Female		Total
Number of players	24 266 330	1 900 000	Referees and Assistant Referees	21 657
Professionals	2 239		Admin, Coaches, Technical, Medical	107 400
Amateurs 18+	325 992		Number of clubs	1 621
Youth under 18	382 762		Number of teams	11 347
Unregistered	5 045 100		Clubs with women's teams	600
Total players	26 166 335		Players as % of population	1.99%

FIFA/COCA-COLA WORLD RANKING FOR CHINA

1993	1994	1995	1996	1997	1998	1999	2000	2001	2002	2003	2004	2005	2006	2007	High
53	40	66	76	55	37	88	75	54	63	86	54	72	84	81	**37** 12/98

2007–2008												Low
08/07	09/07	10/07	11/07	12/07	01/08	02/08	03/08	04/08	05/08	06/08	07/08	**103** 08/06
85	89	91	85	81	82	75	80	82	87	79	83	

THE FIFA BIG COUNT OF 2006 FOR EGYPT

	Male	Female		Total
Number of players	3 137 420	690	Referees and Assistant Referees	2 270
Professionals	48		Admin, Coaches, Technical, Medical	16 000
Amateurs 18+	20 135		Number of clubs	590
Youth under 18	30 777		Number of teams	6 495
Unregistered	260 000		Clubs with women's teams	18
Total players	3 138 110		Players as % of population	3.98%

FIFA/COCA-COLA WORLD RANKING FOR EGYPT

1993	1994	1995	1996	1997	1998	1999	2000	2001	2002	2003	2004	2005	2006	2007	High
26	22	23	28	32	28	38	33	41	39	32	34	32	27	39	**17** 05/98

2007–2008												Low
08/07	09/07	10/07	11/07	12/07	01/08	02/08	03/08	04/08	05/08	06/08	07/08	**44** 05/03
40	43	39	41	39	35	29	30	30	30	23	24	

THE FIFA BIG COUNT OF 2006 FOR ENGLAND

	Male	Female		Total
Number of players	3 829 000	335 110	Referees and Assistant Referees	33 186
Professionals	6 110		Admin, Coaches, Technical, Medical	135 000
Amateurs 18+	656 800		Number of clubs	40 000
Youth under 18	820 000		Number of teams	119 000
Unregistered	2 415 000		Clubs with women's teams	2 490
Total players	4 164 110		Players as % of population	8.47%

FIFA/COCA-COLA WORLD RANKING FOR ENGLAND

1993	1994	1995	1996	1997	1998	1999	2000	2001	2002	2003	2004	2005	2006	2007	High
11	18	21	12	4	9	12	17	10	7	8	8	9	5	12	**4** 09/06

2007–2008												Low
08/07	09/07	10/07	11/07	12/07	01/08	02/08	03/08	04/08	05/08	06/08	07/08	**27** 02/96
12	9	11	12	12	12	11	11	11	11	9	15	

THE FIFA BIG COUNT OF 2006 FOR FRANCE

	Male	Female		Total
Number of players	3 851 161	338 879	Referees and Assistant Referees	27 782
Professionals	1 825		Admin, Coaches, Technical, Medical	257 941
Amateurs 18+	753 244		Number of clubs	18 823
Youth under 18	1 034 046		Number of teams	111 760
Unregistered	1 233 100		Clubs with women's teams	1 239
Total players	4 190 040		Players as % of population	6.88%

FIFA/COCA-COLA WORLD RANKING FOR FRANCE

1993	1994	1995	1996	1997	1998	1999	2000	2001	2002	2003	2004	2005	2006	2007
15	19	8	3	6	2	3	2	1	2	2	2	5	4	7

High 1 05/01

2007–2008											
08/07	09/07	10/07	11/07	12/07	01/08	02/08	03/08	04/08	05/08	06/08	07/08
4	6	4	7	7	7	7	7	7	7	7	10

Low 25 04/98

THE FIFA BIG COUNT OF 2006 FOR GHANA

	Male	Female		Total
Number of players	987 500	0	Referees and Assistant Referees	800
Professionals	0		Admin, Coaches, Technical, Medical	4 400
Amateurs 18+	16 500		Number of clubs	280
Youth under 18	11 000		Number of teams	1 650
Unregistered	110 000		Clubs with women's teams	0
Total players	987 500		Players as % of population	4.41%

FIFA/COCA-COLA WORLD RANKING FOR GHANA

1993	1994	1995	1996	1997	1998	1999	2000	2001	2002	2003	2004	2005	2006	2007
37	26	29	25	57	48	48	57	59	61	78	77	50	28	43

High 14 02/08

2007–2008											
08/07	09/07	10/07	11/07	12/07	01/08	02/08	03/08	04/08	05/08	06/08	07/08
43	45	47	43	43	43	14	15	14	14	15	20

Low 89 06/04

THE FIFA BIG COUNT OF 2006 FOR GERMANY

	Male	Female		Total
Number of players	14 438 313	1 870 633	Referees and Assistant Referees	81 372
Professionals	864		Admin, Coaches, Technical, Medical	77 800
Amateurs 18+	4 221 170		Number of clubs	25 922
Youth under 18	2 081 912		Number of teams	170 480
Unregistered	10 000 000		Clubs with women's teams	915
Total players	16 308 946		Players as % of population	19.79%

FIFA/COCA-COLA WORLD RANKING FOR GERMANY

1993	1994	1995	1996	1997	1998	1999	2000	2001	2002	2003	2004	2005	2006	2007
1	5	2	2	2	3	5	11	12	4	12	19	16	6	

High 1 08/93

2007–2008											
08/07	09/07	10/07	11/07	12/07	01/08	02/08	03/08	04/08	05/08	06/08	07/08
5	5	4	5	5	5	5	5	5	5	5	3

Low 22 03/06

THE FIFA BIG COUNT OF 2006 FOR ITALY

	Male	Female		Total
Number of players	4 688 929	291 367	Referees and Assistant Referees	24 981
Professionals	3 541		Admin, Coaches, Technical, Medical	53 500
Amateurs 18+	877 602		Number of clubs	16 128
Youth under 18	557 453		Number of teams	80 864
Unregistered	3 207 700		Clubs with women's teams	569
Total players	4 980 296		Players as % of population	8.57%

FIFA/COCA-COLA WORLD RANKING FOR ITALY

1993	1994	1995	1996	1997	1998	1999	2000	2001	2002	2003	2004	2005	2006	2007
2	4	3	10	9	7	14	4	6	13	10	10	12	2	3

High 1

2007–2008											
08/07	09/07	10/07	11/07	12/07	01/08	02/08	03/08	04/08	05/08	06/08	07/08
3	1	3	3	3	3	3	3	3	3	3	2

Low 193 03/07

THE FIFA BIG COUNT OF 2006 FOR JAPAN

	Male	Female		Total
Number of players	4 500 506	304 644	Referees and Assistant Referees	189 603
Professionals	976		Admin, Coaches, Technical, Medical	60 000
Amateurs 18+	292 562		Number of clubs	1 000
Youth under 18	629 140		Number of teams	29 132
Unregistered	3 000 000		Clubs with women's teams	1 000
Total players	4 805 150		Players as % of population	3.77%

FIFA/COCA-COLA WORLD RANKING FOR JAPAN

1993	1994	1995	1996	1997	1998	1999	2000	2001	2002	2003	2004	2005	2006	2007
43	36	31	21	14	20	57	38	34	22	29	17	15	47	34

High 9 02/98

2007–2008											
08/07	09/07	10/07	11/07	12/07	01/08	02/08	03/08	04/08	05/08	06/08	07/08
41	34	30	33	34	34	35	36	36	37	38	34

Low 66 12/92

THE FIFA BIG COUNT OF 2006 FOR KOREA REPUBLIC

	Male	Female		Total
Number of players	1 021 677	72 550	Referees and Assistant Referees	948
Professionals	550		Admin, Coaches, Technical, Medical	3 700
Amateurs 18+	12 372		Number of clubs	96
Youth under 18	18 205		Number of teams	864
Unregistered	423 100		Clubs with women's teams	4
Total players	1 094 227		Players as % of population	2.24%

FIFA/COCA-COLA WORLD RANKING FOR KOREA REPUBLIC

1993	1994	1995	1996	1997	1998	1999	2000	2001	2002	2003	2004	2005	2006	2007
41	35	46	44	27	17	51	40	42	20	22	22	29	51	42

High 17 12/98

2007–2008											
08/07	09/07	10/07	11/07	12/07	01/08	02/08	03/08	04/08	05/08	06/08	07/08
50	50	46	42	42	41	41	47	50	50	45	53

Low 62 02/96

THE FIFA BIG COUNT OF 2006 FOR MEXICO

	Male	Female		Total
Number of players	7 151 688	1 327 907	Referees and Assistant Referees	4 885
Professionals	4 593		Admin, Coaches, Technical, Medical	80 904
Amateurs 18+	186 954		Number of clubs	302
Youth under 18	129 006		Number of teams	19 957
Unregistered	7 000 000		Clubs with women's teams	9
Total players	8 479 595		Players as % of population	7.89%

FIFA/COCA-COLA WORLD RANKING FOR MEXICO

1993	1994	1995	1996	1997	1998	1999	2000	2001	2002	2003	2004	2005	2006	2007		High	
16	15	12	11	5	10	10	12	9	8	7	7	5	20	15		4	02/98

2007–2008													Low	
08/07	09/07	10/07	11/07	12/07	01/08	02/08	03/08	04/08	05/08	06/08	07/08		26	06/07
11	13	15	15	15	15	16	16	16	17	14	19			

THE FIFA BIG COUNT OF 2006 FOR NIGERIA

	Male	Female		Total
Number of players	6 344 600	309 110	Referees and Assistant Referees	522
Professionals	2 440		Admin, Coaches, Technical, Medical	32 600
Amateurs 18+	26 170		Number of clubs	522
Youth under 18	30 000		Number of teams	52
Unregistered	565 000		Clubs with women's teams	1 320
Total players	6 653 710		Players as % of population	5.05%

FIFA/COCA-COLA WORLD RANKING FOR NIGERIA

1993	1994	1995	1996	1997	1998	1999	2000	2001	2002	2003	2004	2005	2006	2007		High	
18	12	27	63	71	65	76	52	40	29	35	21	24	9	20		5	04/94

2007–2008													Low	
08/07	09/07	10/07	11/07	12/07	01/08	02/08	03/08	04/08	05/08	06/08	07/08		82	11/99
26	23	19	20	20	19	45	46	39	39	34	26			

THE FIFA BIG COUNT OF 2006 FOR PORTUGAL

	Male	Female		Total
Number of players	488 787	58 947	Referees and Assistant Referees	4 471
Professionals	1 663		Admin, Coaches, Technical, Medical	34 000
Amateurs 18+	40 351		Number of clubs	2 284
Youth under 18	64 922		Number of teams	8 786
Unregistered	210 000		Clubs with women's teams	464
Total players	547 734		Players as % of population	5.16%

FIFA/COCA-COLA WORLD RANKING FOR PORTUGAL

1993	1994	1995	1996	1997	1998	1999	2000	2001	2002	2003	2004	2005	2006	2007		High	
20	20	16	13	30	36	15	6	4	11	17	9	10	8	8		4	03/01

2007–2008													Low	
08/07	09/07	10/07	11/07	12/07	01/08	02/08	03/08	04/08	05/08	06/08	07/08		43	08/98
8	10	8	8	8	8	8	8	9	9	11	9			

THE FIFA BIG COUNT OF 2006 FOR SAUDI ARABIA

	Male	Female		Total
Number of players	438 644	0	Referees and Assistant Referees	642
Professionals	488		Admin, Coaches, Technical, Medical	650
Amateurs 18+	9 390		Number of clubs	153
Youth under 18	5 266		Number of teams	780
Unregistered	92 500		Clubs with women's teams	0
Total players	438 644		Players as % of population	1.62%

FIFA/COCA-COLA WORLD RANKING FOR SAUDI ARABIA

1993	1994	1995	1996	1997	1998	1999	2000	2001	2002	2003	2004	2005	2006	2007
38	27	54	37	33	30	39	36	31	38	26	28	33	64	61

High: **21** 07/04

2007–2008											
08/07	09/07	10/07	11/07	12/07	01/08	02/08	03/08	04/08	05/08	06/08	07/08
51	51	52	57	61	57	50	50	54	54	54	49

Low: **81** 07/06

THE FIFA BIG COUNT OF 2006 FOR SOUTH AFRICA

	Male	Female		Total
Number of players	4 423 300	117 110	Referees and Assistant Referees	4 020
Professionals	1 000		Admin, Coaches, Technical, Medical	16 537
Amateurs 18+	165 560		Number of clubs	450
Youth under 18	1 300 400		Number of teams	3 200
Unregistered	2 025 000		Clubs with women's teams	450
Total players	4 540 410		Players as % of population	10.28%

FIFA/COCA-COLA WORLD RANKING FOR SOUTH AFRICA

1993	1994	1995	1996	1997	1998	1999	2000	2001	2002	2003	2004	2005	2006	2007
95	56	40	19	31	26	30	20	35	30	36	38	49	67	77

High: **16** 08/96

2007–2008											
08/07	09/07	10/07	11/07	12/07	01/08	02/08	03/08	04/08	05/08	06/08	07/08
61	73	83	77	77	78	70	71	69	69	68	67

Low: **124** 12/93

THE FIFA BIG COUNT OF 2006 FOR THE USA

	Male	Female		Total
Number of players	17 416 859	7 055 919	Referees and Assistant Referees	140 000
Professionals	1 513		Admin, Coaches, Technical, Medical	656 300
Amateurs 18+	260 928		Number of clubs	5 000
Youth under 18	3 907 065		Number of teams	400 000
Unregistered	13 466 000		Clubs with women's teams	4 000
Total players	24 472 778		Players as % of population	8.20%

FIFA/COCA-COLA WORLD RANKING FOR THE USA

1993	1994	1995	1996	1997	1998	1999	2000	2001	2002	2003	2004	2005	2006	2007
22	23	19	18	26	23	22	16	24	10	11	11	8	31	19

High: **4** 04/06

2007–2008											
08/07	09/07	10/07	11/07	12/07	01/08	02/08	03/08	04/08	05/08	06/08	07/08
17	18	18	19	19	20	26	28	21	21	21	30

Low: **35** 10/97

MOROCCO COUPE DU TRONE 2007

Round of 16		Quarter–finals		Semi–finals		Final	
FAR Rabat *	1						
Maghreb Fès	0	FAR Rabat	0 5p				
Al Mansouria	0	Mouloudia Oujda *	0 3p				
Mouloudia Oujda *	1			FAR Rabat	1 4p		
Raja Casablanca	1			Wydad Casablanca	1 3p		
Chez Ali Marrakech *	0	Raja Casablanca *	0				
Diffa El Jadida	1	Wydad Casablanca	2				
Wydad Casablanca *	2					FAR Rabat	1 5p
Kawkab Marrakech *	3					Rachad Bernoussi	1 4p
Olympique Safi	2	Kawkab Marrakech	2				
TUS Temara *	1	US Touarga *	1				
US Touarga	2			Kawkab Marrakech	1		
MA Tétouan *	2			Rachad Bernoussi	3		
AS Salé	1	MA Tétouan	1 1p				
Olympique Khouribga	0 4p	Rachad Bernoussi *	1 3p				
Rachad Bernoussi *	0 5p						

* Home team • ‡ Qualified for the CAF Confederation Cup

CUP FINAL
Complexe Sportif Olympique, Fès
25-11-2007, Ref: Rouissi

Scorers - Mostafa El Alaoui 74 for FAR;
Atik Chihab OG 27 for RBC

UEFA CUP FIRST ROUND
Continued from page 1020

Continued from page 1020

Franz Horr, Vienna, 20-09-2007, 20:45, 5100, McDonald SCO
FK Austria Wien	2	Kuljic 41, Lasnik 62
Vålerenga IF	0	

Ullevål, Oslo, 4-10-2007, 19:00, 3868, Matejek CZE
Vålerenga IF	2	Dos Santos 51, Holm.T 87
FK Austria Wien	2	Kuljic 22, Acimovic 91+

YEMEN PRESIDENTS CUP 2007

First Round		Quarter–finals		Semi–finals		Final	
Al Tilal Aden *	2 2						
Al Rasheed Taizz	0 1	Al Tilal Aden	0 7				
Al Wahda Aden	0 0	Tadamun Shabwa *	1 0				
Tadamun Shabwa *	2 2			Al Tilal Aden *	1 2		
Taawun Badan *	4 1			May 22 Sana'a	0 0		
October 14	0 0	Taawun Badan *	1 1				
Nasir Al Dalaa *	0 0	May 22 Sana'a	1 2				
May 22 Sana'a	0 3					Al Tilal Aden	1
Al Sha'ab Ibb	0 3					Al Hilal Hudayda	0
Shabab Al Baydaa *	0 1	Al Sha'ab Ibb	2 1				
Al Wahda Sana'a *	1 3	Al Ahly Sana'a *	2 0				
Al Ahly Sana'a	2 3			Al Sha'ab Ibb *	0 0		
Al Saqr Taizz *	5 3			Al Hilal Hudayda	2 1		
Al Ahli Taizz	0 1	Al Saqr Taizz	0 1				
Shabab Al Jeel *	2 0	Al Hilal Hudayda *	1 2				
Al Hilal Hudayda	0 3						

* Home team in the first leg • † Qualified for the AFC Cup

CUP FINAL
17-08-2007

ARAB CHAMPIONS LEAGUE 2007-08

First Round

Team		Leg 1	Leg 2
Entente Sétif	ALG	1	3
ASC Mauritel *	MTN	1	0
CDE Collas *	DJI	0	0
Al Wahda Mecca	KSA	8	11
Al Merreikh *	SUD	2	3
Riffa	BHR	0	1
Shabab Rafah	PLE		
Raja Casablanca	MAR	w-o	
Al Majd Damascus	SYR	2	2
Al Hilal Omdurman *	SUD	3	1
Al Ahly Sana'a *	YEM	0	4
Al Ittihad Tripoli	LBY	0	4
CA Bizertin *	TUN	1 2	4p
Al Shabab Riyadh	KSA	2 1	2p
Al Sha'ab Sharjah	UAE	0	2
Al Faysali	JOR	2	2
Al Jaish Cairo	EGY	1	2
Al Ansar *	LIB	1	1
MA Tétouan *	MAR	0	1
Al Wihdat	JOR	4	0
Al Arabi	KUW	1	2
MC Oran *	ALG	0	0
Al Talaba Baghdad *	IRQ	0	0
USM Alger	ALG	2	2
Al Taiiya Hama	SYR	1	0
Al Masry *	EGY	0	0
Chirazienne *	COM	0	0
Al Najaf	IRQ	8	1
Al Urooba Sur *	OMA	0	1
US Monastir	TUN	0	1
Kazma *	KUW	0	1
Wydad Casablanca	MAR	1	1

Second Round

Team	Leg 1	Leg 2
Entente Sétif	1	3
Al Wahda Mecca *	1	1
Al Merreikh *	2	1
Raja Casablanca	2	3
Al Majd Damascus	1	2
Al Ittihad Tripoli *	1	0
CA Bizertin *	1	2
Al Faysali	1	3
Al Jaish Cairo	0	2
Al Wihdat *	0	1
Al Arabi *	3	0
USM Alger	2	3
Al Taiiya Hama	3	0
Al Najaf *	0	0
Al Urooba Sur *	2	1
Wydad Casablanca	3	4

Group Stage

Group A

	Pl	W	D	L	F	A	Pts	ES Sétif	Al Faysali	Raja	Al Majd
Entente Sétif	6	3	2	1	10	4	11		2-1	2-0	1-1
Al Faysali	6	2	3	1	9	7	9	1-1		1-1	3-1
Raja Casablanca	6	1	4	1	3	4	7	1-0	0-0		0-0
Al Majd Damascus	6	0	3	3	5	12	3	0-4	2-3	1-1	

Group B

	Pl	W	D	L	F	A	Pts	Wydad	Al Jaish	USM Alger	Al Taliya
Wydad Casablanca	6	3	1	2	11	6	10		3-0	2-3	3-1
Al Jaish Cairo	6	2	2	2	3	5	8	0-0		0-0	1-2
USM Alger	6	2	2	2	5	5	8	2-1	0-1		0-1
Al Taliya Hama	6	2	1	3	4	7	7	0-2	0-1	0-0	

Semi-finals

Team	Leg 1	Leg 2
Entente Sétif	1	1
Al Jaish Cairo *	2	0
Al Faysali *	1	0
Wydad Casablanca	2	0

Final

Team	Leg 1	Leg 2
Entente Sétif	1	1
Wydad Casablanca *	0	0

CUP FINAL

1st leg
Stade Mohamed V. Casablanca
9-05-2008, Att: 54 000
Ref: Trabelsi TUN
Scorer - Fanid Touil [80] for ESS

2nd leg
Stade Frères Brakni, Blida
22-05-2008, Att: 40 000
Ref: Al Fadhli KUW
Scorer - Abdelmalek Ziaya [30] for ESS

* Home team in the first leg • Tournament held from 12/09/2007 - 22/05/2008

REVIEW OF WOMEN'S LEAGUE FOOTBALL

CHINA PR 2007
SUPER LEAGUE

	Pl	W	D	L	F	A	Pts
Tianjin Huisen	10	8	1/0	1	29	12	26
Dalian Shide	10	6	3/1	0	15	5	25
Shanghai SVA	10	6	2/1	1	18	13	23
Shandong Zhongqi	10	3	0/3	4	10	16	12
Hebei Ticai	10	3	1/1	5	8	13	12
Sichuan Jiannanchun	10	2	2/0	6	7	12	10
Jiangsu Huatai	10	2	0/2	6	6	15	8
Guangdong Haiyin	10	1	0/1	8	11	18	4

Cup Final: Tianjin 2-1 Dalian Shide

CZECH REPUBLIC 2007-08
FIRST DIVISION

	Pl	W	D	L	F	A	Pts
Sparta Praha	22	22	0	0	152	5	66
Slavia Praha	22	19	0	3	105	17	57
FC Slovacko Hradiste	22	19	0	3	97	18	57
FC Brno	22	9	5	8	64	44	32
Viktoria Plzen	22	10	1	11	70	43	31
FK Teplice	22	9	4	9	30	59	31
DFC Slavia Hradec Kr.	22	7	5	10	47	38	26
SK DFO Pardubice	22	7	4	11	43	53	25
DFC Hlucin	22	5	6	11	36	57	21
Slovan Liberec	22	6	3	13	24	57	21
Sokol Stara Lysa	22	3	4	15	32	53	13
DFC Rena Ivancice	22	0	0	22	6	262	0

DENMARK 2007-08
FIRST DIVISION

	Pl	W	D	L	F	A	Pts
Brøndby IF	6	5	1	0	22	0	16
Fortuna Hjørring	6	4	1	1	12	5	13
Skovlunde IF	6	0	2	4	4	15	2
Skovbakken IK	6	0	2	4	3	21	2
SønderjyskE	18	10	1	7	40	25	31
Vejle BKK	18	7	4	7	26	42	25
OB Odense	18	5	2	11	29	48	17
BK Skjold	18	3	1	14	15	53	10
Varde IF	18	3	1	14	13	83	10
Team Viborg	18	2	1	15	13	68	7

ENGLAND 2007-08
PREMIER LEAGUE

	Pl	W	D	L	F	A	Pts
Arsenal Ladies	22	20	2	0	85	15	62
Everton Ladies	22	18	3	1	69	14	57
Leeds Utd Ladies	22	12	4	6	45	33	40
Bristol Academy	22	10	4	8	45	35	34
Chelsea Ladies	22	9	5	8	40	35	32
Doncaster Rov. Belles	22	8	5	9	44	42	29
Watford Ladies	22	9	2	11	53	52	29
Blackburn Ladies	22	8	4	10	50	45	28
Birmingham Ladies	22	7	4	11	34	39	25
Liverpool Ladies	22	6	4	12	31	51	22
Cardiff Ladies	22	3	3	16	19	69	12
Charlton Women	22	0	4	18	6	91	4

Cup Final: Arsenal 4-1 Leeds Utd
League Cup: Everton 1-0 Arsenal

FINLAND 2007
FIRST DIVISION

	Pl	W	D	L	F	A	Pts
FC Honka Espoo	22	19	2	1	71	12	59
HJK Helsinki	22	18	3	1	70	23	57
PuiU Helsinki	22	9	4	9	25	25	31
Aland United	22	9	4	9	27	38	31
Ilves Tampere	22	9	0	13	22	34	27
TiPS Vantaa	22	6	8	8	25	28	26
FC Sport Vaasa	22	5	6	11	15	33	21
SC Raisio	22	6	3	13	23	43	21
KMF Kuopio	22	6	3	13	22	42	21
FC United Pietersaari	22	5	3	14	21	43	18

Cup Final: HJK Helsinki 3-1 Honka Espoo

FRANCE 2007-08
DIVISION 1

	Pl	W	D	L	F	A	Pts
Olympique Lyonnais	22	18	4	0	93	4	80
FCF Juvisy	22	15	6	1	72	13	73
Montpellier HSC	22	11	8	3	43	15	63
RC Saint-Etienne	22	10	4	8	28	22	56
Paris-SG	22	9	4	9	25	33	53
ASJ Soyaux	22	9	3	10	31	32	52
FC Vendenheim	22	8	3	11	34	60	49
Toulouse FC	22	8	2	12	26	46	48
FCF Hénin-Beaumont	22	8	0	14	29	58	46
Saint-Brieuc	22	6	3	13	28	54	43
ESOF La Roche	22	6	1	15	20	38	41
Evreux AC	22	3	4	15	11	65	35

Cup Final: Olympique Lyonnais 3-0 Paris-SG

GERMANY 2007-08
FIRST DIVISION

	Pl	W	D	L	F	A	Pts
1.FFC Frankfurt	22	17	3	2	87	22	54
FCR 2001 Duisburg	22	17	2	3	65	20	53
Turbine Potsdam	22	11	5	6	48	32	38
Bayern München	22	12	2	8	53	38	38
SC 07 Bad Neuenahr	22	12	1	9	43	33	37
VfL Wolfsburg	22	10	4	8	42	48	34
SG Essen-Schöneбеck	22	9	6	7	43	40	33
SC Freiburg	22	6	3	13	30	63	21
TSV Crailsheim	22	5	4	13	28	43	19
Hamburger SV	22	4	6	12	23	46	18
1.FC Saarbrücken	22	4	6	12	26	51	18
SG Wattenscheid 09	22	3	2	17	17	69	11

Cup Final: 1.FFC Frankfurt 5-1 1.FC Saarbrücken

ICELAND 2007
FIRST DIVISION

	Pl	W	D	L	F	A	Pts
Valur Reykjavík	16	15	1	0	88	7	46
KR Reykjavík	16	14	1	1	73	17	43
Breidablik	16	9	2	5	36	35	29
Keflavík	16	7	1	8	30	38	22
Stjarnan	16	6	3	7	28	30	21
Fylkir	16	3	4	9	21	40	13
Fjölnir	16	3	4	9	15	35	13
Thor/KA	16	4	1	11	17	52	13
IR	16	2	1	13	16	70	7

Cup Final: KR Reykjavík 3-0 Keflavík

ITALY 2007–08
FIRST DIVISION

	Pl	W	D	L	F	A	Pts
Bardolino	22	17	4	1	86	10	55
Torres Terra Sarda	22	15	3	4	48	23	48
Fiammamonza	22	10	7	5	34	22	37
Tavagnacco	22	10	6	6	38	36	36
Torino	22	11	3	8	37	23	35
Reggiana	22	8	5	9	25	33	29
Riozzese	22	8	3	11	29	39	27
Atalanta	22	8	2	12	30	39	26
Milan	22	7	5	10	24	34	26
Chiasellis	22	5	4	13	25	52	19
Trento	22	6	1	15	17	57	19
Firenze	22	4	3	15	21	46	15

Cup Final: Torres 2-3 1-0 Bardolino

JAPAN 2007
NADESHIKO LEAGUE

	Pl	W	D	L	F	A	Pts
NTV Beleza	21	17	2	2	73	12	53
TASAKI Perule FC	21	17	1	3	43	22	52
Urawa Reds Ladies	21	15	3	3	50	18	48
INAC Leonessa	21	10	1	10	37	35	31
Okayama Yunogo Belle	21	9	2	10	37	33	29
Albirex Niigata Ladies	21	3	3	15	20	50	12
Iga FC Kunoichi	21	3	2	16	18	59	11
O-hara Gakuen Ladies	21	2	2	17	14	63	8

29th All Japan Women's Football Championship Final 2008
NTV Beleza 2-0 TASAKI Perule

NORWAY 2007
FIRST DIVISION

	Pl	W	D	L	F	A	Pts
Kolbotn	18	14	2	2	64	14	44
Røa	18	14	2	2	53	18	44
Asker	18	11	5	2	54	14	38
Team Strømmen	18	10	4	4	31	19	34
Arna-Bjørnar	18	9	3	6	41	32	30
Trondheims/Ørn	18	8	2	8	33	32	26
Klepp	18	7	3	8	32	25	24
Amazon Grimstad	18	5	3	10	18	45	18
Fløya	18	4	4	10	30	48	16
Kattem	18	4	3	11	17	44	15
Sandviken	18	2	3	13	16	64	9
Grand Bodø	18	2	2	14	16	50	8

RUSSIA 2007
FIRST DIVISION

	Pl	W	D	L	F	A	Pts
Zvezda-2005 Perm	16	15	1	0	57	12	46
Rossiyanka MO	16	14	0	2	73	8	42
Nadezhda Noginsk	16	9	2	5	43	26	29
FK Khimki	16	9	0	7	30	29	27
SVSM-Izmailovo	16	6	2	8	26	31	20
FK Ryazan VDV	16	6	2	8	26	33	20
SKA Rostov-na-Donu	16	4	4	8	13	15	16
Aurora St Petersburg	16	3	1	12	12	65	10
Chertanovo Moskva	16	0	0	16	5	66	0

Cup Final: Zvezda Perm 2-1 0-0 Rossiyanka

SCOTLAND 2007–08
FIRST DIVISION

	Pl	W	D	L	F	A	Pts
Glasgow City LFC	20	19	0	1	100	14	57
Hibernian Ladies FC	20	17	1	2	95	17	52
Celtic	20	14	1	5	62	30	43
Edinburgh Ladies	20	12	2	6	67	42	38
Kilmarnock Ladies	20	9	3	8	42	47	30
Hamilton Acad'al LFC	20	8	2	10	41	59	26
Aberdeen FCL	20	7	4	9	46	41	25
Forfar Farmington LFC	20	5	4	11	32	47	19
Queens Park	20	4	3	13	42	73	15
Raith Rovers LFC	20	4	1	15	28	76	13
Vale of Clyde	20	0	1	19	11	120	1
Newburgh JFCL					Withdrew		

Cup Final: Hibernian LFC 3-1 Celtic

SPAIN 2007–08
FIRST DIVISION

	Pl	W	D	L	F	A	Pts
UD Levante	26	23	2	1	64	10	71
Rayo Femenino	26	23	2	1	82	23	71
Athletic Bilboko	26	17	2	7	72	31	53
Espanyol	26	17	1	8	62	40	52
Torrejón	26	11	4	11	44	42	37
Puebla	26	10	6	10	42	37	36
Atlético Madrid	26	11	3	12	36	42	36
Transportes Alcaine	26	10	5	11	40	47	35
UE L Estartit	26	10	4	12	39	46	34
Real Sociedad	26	7	5	14	22	47	26
Sporting de Huelva	26	6	5	15	27	43	23
Colegio Alemán	26	6	4	16	36	59	22
Oviedo Moderno	26	4	2	20	20	68	14
Sevilla FC	26	4	1	21	23	74	13

SWITZERLAND 2007–08
LIGUE NATIONALE A

	Pl	W	D	L	F	A	Pts
FC Zürich Frauen	21	14	3	4	42	32	45
FFC Zuchwil 05	21	10	6	5	45	29	36
FFC Bern	21	11	3	7	38	34	36
FC Yverdon Féminin	21	10	3	8	44	30	33
GC/Schwerzenbach	21	9	3	9	39	32	30
SK Root	21	8	4	9	46	50	28
SC LUwin.ch	21	3	5	13	28	50	14
FC Rot-Schwarz	21	3	5	13	37	62	14

Cup Final: GC Schwerzenbach 4-2 FFC Bern

SWEDEN 2007
DAMALLSVENSKAN

	Pl	W	D	L	F	A	Pts
Umeå IK	22	21	1	0	74	11	64
Djurgården/Alvsjö	22	13	4	5	61	23	43
Linköpings FC	22	12	5	5	43	25	41
Malmö FF DFF	22	11	7	4	41	23	40
Kopparbergs/Göteborg	22	10	5	7	44	36	35
KIF Orebro DFF	22	8	5	9	33	33	29
Hammarby IF DFF	22	8	5	9	34	43	29
Sunnanå SK	22	8	3	11	26	33	27
Bälinge IF	22	4	7	11	16	41	19
QBIK	22	2	9	11	18	51	15
Jitex BK Mölndal	22	2	7	13	17	59	13
Mallbackens IF Lysvik	22	3	2	17	15	44	11

Cup Final: Umeå IK 4-3 AIK Stockholm

USA 2007
W-LEAGUE

Central Conference Midwest Division

	Pl	W	D	L	F	A	Pts
FC Indiana Lionesses †	14	13	0	1	67	3	40
Chicago Gaels †	14	11	3	0	39	9	33
Minnesota Lightning	14	9	3	2	32	19	29
Cleveland Internationals	14	8	4	2	31	23	26
Michigan Hawks	14	4	9	1	12	33	13
Kalamazoo Outrage	14	2	10	2	6	36	8
Fort Wayne Fever	13	2	10	1	16	39	7
West Michigan	13	1	11	1	11	52	4

Central Conference Northern Division

	Pl	W	D	L	F	A	Pts
Ottawa Fury †	14	13	1	0	51	7	39
Toronto Lady Lynx †	14	11	2	1	40	14	34
Laval Comets †	14	9	4	1	39	17	28
Rochester Rhinos	14	6	6	2	18	33	20
Hamilton Avalanche	14	5	6	3	19	21	18
Western Mass Pioneers	14	3	9	2	18	34	11
London Gryphons	14	3	9	2	15	35	11
Vermont Lady Voltage	14	0	13	1	5	44	1

Play-off: **Laval** 2-0 Toronto
Conference play-off semi-finals: **Indiana** 5-1 Laval;
Ottawa 3-2 Chicago
Final: **Indiana** 4-3 Ottawa

Eastern Conference Atlantic Division

	Pl	W	D	L	F	A	Pts
Atlanta Silverbacks †	14	13	0	1	50	6	40
Charlotte Lady Eagles†	14	11	2	1	44	13	34
Tampa Bay Hellenic	14	8	4	2	27	16	26
Hampton Roads	14	7	6	1	28	19	22
Carolina RailHawks	14	7	6	1	22	19	22
Richmond Kickers	14	6	8	0	18	28	18
Carolina Dynamo	14	4	8	2	23	30	14
Bradenton Athletics	14	2	12	0	11	52	6
West Virginia Illusion	14	1	13	0	6	46	3

Eastern Conference Northeast Division

	Pl	W	D	L	F	A	Pts
Washington Freedom †	14	11	1	2	32	7	35
Long Island Riders †	14	9	3	2	28	13	29
Boston Renegades †	14	9	3	2	32	12	29
Jersey Sky Blue	14	8	4	2	14	10	26
Connecticut Passion	14	7	5	2	24	23	23
Nth Virginia Majestics	14	3	6	5	17	23	14
New York Magic	14	3	7	4	14	23	13
New Jersey Wildcats	14	2	10	2	17	35	8
Fredericksburg Gunners	14	0	13	1	5	37	1

Play-off: **Long Island** 1-0 Boston
Conference semi-finals: **Atlanta** 1-0 Long Island;
Washington 6-5 Charlotte
Final: **Washington** 2-1 Atlanta

Western Conference

	Pl	W	D	L	F	A	Pts
Pali Blues †	12	12	0	0	39	4	36
Vancouver Whitecaps †	12	7	2	3	21	18	24
Seattle Sounders †	12	5	3	4	19	11	19
Real Colorado Cougars	12	5	4	3	15	19	18
Fort Collins Force	12	3	6	3	15	19	12
Los Angeles Legends	12	1	9	2	11	26	5
Ventura County Fusion	12	1	10	1	9	32	4

Conference play-off: Seattle 1-0 Vancouver

Championship Finals

Semi-finals: **Pali Blues** 2-0 Washington; **Indiana** 1-0 Seattle
Third place: **Washington Freedom** 2-0 Seattle Sounders
Final: **Pali Blues** 2-1 Indiana Lionesses
Pali Blues are the 2007 W-League champions

† Qualified for the play-offs

THE (VERY) UNOFFICIAL WORLD CHAMPIONSHIP

Many Scots would tell you that the proudest moment for their national team was on April 15, 1967, the day they beat world champions England at Wembley. Working on the basis that if you beat the world champions then you must be the best in the world, this unofficial world championship builds on that theory, adopting the system boxing uses to decide its world champions. Therefore when the Scots lost to the Soviet Union in May 1967, the Soviets then became unofficial world champions and so on. The series starts in 1908 when the England amateur team, playing as Great Britain, won the first official Olympic title, at that time the world championship of football. In many cases the sequence leads naturally to the FIFA World Cup final, but where it doesn't - in 1938, 1950, 1954, 1962, 1970, 1994, 2002 and 2006 - the title is vacated and the final is used to restart the sequence.

THE (VERY) UNOFFICIAL WORLD CHAMPIONSHIP

Champions	Opponents	Score	Venue	Date
England	Denmark	2-0	London	24-10-1908
Denmark	England	2-1	Copenhagen	5-05-1910
England	Denmark	3-0	London	21-10-1911
Netherlands	England	2-1	The Hague	24-03-1913
England	Netherlands	2-1	Hull	15-11-1913
Denmark	England	3-0	Copenhagen	5-06-1914
Sweden	Denmark	4-0	Stockholm	8-10-1916
Denmark	Sweden	2-1	Stockholm	14-10-1917
Norway	Denmark	3-1	Oslo	16-06-1918
Denmark	Norway	4-0	Copenhagen	6-10-1918
Norway	Denmark	3-2	Oslo	21-09-1919
Sweden	Norway	3-0	Oslo	27-06-1920
Netherlands	Sweden	5-4	Antwerp	29-08-1920
Belgium	Netherlands	3-0	Antwerp	31-08-1920
Italy	Belgium	3-2	Antwerp	5-05-1921
Czechoslovakia	Italy	5-1	Prague	27-05-1923
Switzerland	Czechoslovakia	1-0	Paris	30-05-1924
Uruguay	Switzerland	3-0	Paris	9-06-1924
Argentina	Uruguay	3-2	Montevideo	31-08-1924
Uruguay	Argentina	1-0	Montevideo	16-11-1924
Argentina	Uruguay	1-0	Buenos Aires	5-01-1925
Uruguay	Argentina	2-0	Santiago	24-10-1926
Argentina	Uruguay	1-0	Montevideo	14-07-1927
Uruguay	Argentina	1-0	Buenos Aires	30-08-1927
Argentina	Uruguay	3-2	Lima	20-11-1927
Uruguay	Argentina	2-1	Amsterdam	13-06-1928
Paraguay	Uruguay	3-1	Asuncion	15-08-1928
Argentina	Paraguay	4-1	Buenos Aires	10-11-1929
Uruguay	Argentina	4-2	Montevideo	30-07-1930
Brazil	Uruguay	2-0	Rio de Janeiro	6-09-1931
Spain	Brazil	3-1	Genoa	27-05-1934
Italy	Spain	1-0	Florence	1-06-1934
England	Italy	3-2	London	14-11-1934
Scotland	England	2-0	Glasgow	6-04-1935
Wales	Scotland	2-1	Dundee	2-12-1936
England	Wales	2-1	Middlesbrough	17-11-1937
Scotland	England	1-0	London	9-04-1938
Vacated				
Italy	Hungary	4-2	Paris	19-06-1938
Switzerland	Italy	3-1	Zurich	12-11-1939
Hungary	Switzerland	3-0	Budapest	31-03-1940
Germany	Hungary	7-0	Cologne	6-04-1941
Switzerland	Germany	2-1	Berne	20-04-1941
Hungary	Switzerland	2-1	Zurich	16-11-1941
Germany	Hungary	5-3	Budapest	3-05-1942

THE (VERY) UNOFFICIAL WORLD CHAMPIONSHIP

Champions	Opponents	Score	Venue	Date
Sweden	Germany	3-2	Berlin	20-09-1942
Switzerland	Sweden	3-1	Zurich	15-11-1942
Hungary	Switzerland	3-1	Geneva	16-05-1943
Sweden	Hungary	7-2	Budapest	7-11-1943
Switzerland	Sweden	3-0	Geneva	25-11-1945
England	Switzerland	4-1	London	11-05-1946
France	England	2-1	Paris	19-05-1946
England	France	3-0	London	3-05-1947
Switzerland	England	1-0	Zurich	18-05-1947
France	Switzerland	2-1	Lausanne	8-06-1947
Italy	France	3-1	Paris	4-04-1948
England	Italy	4-0	Turin	16-05-1948
Scotland	England	3-1	London	9-04-1949
England	Scotland	1-0	Glasgow	15-04-1950
USA	England	1-0	Belo Horizonte	29-06-1950
Chile	USA	5-2	Recife	2-07-1950
Vacated				
Uruguay	Brazil	2-1	Rio de Janeiro	16-07-1950
Chile	Uruguay	2-0	Santiago	13-04-1952
Brazil	Chile	3-0	Santiago	20-04-1952
Peru	Brazil	1-0	Lima	19-03-1953
Uruguay	Peru	3-0	Lima	28-03-1953
Paraguay	Uruguay	4-1	Montevideo	10-04-1954
Vacated				
West Germany	Hungary	3-2	Berne	4-07-1954
Belgium	West Germany	2-0	Brussels	26-09-1954
Italy	Belgium	1-0	Bari	16-01-1955
Yugoslavia	Italy	4-0	Turin	29-05-1955
Austria	Yugoslavia	2-1	Vienna	30-10-1955
France	Austria	3-1	Paris	25-03-1956
Hungary	France	2-1	Paris	7-10-1956
Norway	Hungary	2-1	Oslo	12-06-1957
Denmark	Norway	2-0	Tammerfors	19-06-1957
Sweden	Denmark	2-1	Copenhagen	30-06-1957
West Germany	Sweden	1-0	Hamburg	20-11-1957
Czechoslovakia	West Germany	3-2	Prague	2-04-1958
Nth. Ireland	Czechoslovakia	1-0	Halmstad	8-06-1958
Argentina	Nth. Ireland	3-1	Halmstad	11-06-1958
Czechoslovakia	Argentina	6-1	Helsingborg	15-06-1958
Nth. Ireland	Czechoslovakia	2-1	Malmö	17-06-1958
France	Nth. Ireland	4-0	Norrkoping	19-06-1958
Brazil	France	5-2	Stockholm	24-06-1958
Uruguay	Brazil	3-0	Guayaquil	12-12-1959
Argentina	Uruguay	4-0	Buenos Aires	17-08-1960
Spain	Argentina	2-0	Seville	11-06-1961

THE (VERY) UNOFFICIAL WORLD CHAMPIONSHIP

Champions	Opponents	Score	Venue	Date
Czechoslovakia	Spain	1-0	Viña del Mar	31-05-1962
Mexico	Czechoslovakia	3-1	Viña del Mar	7-06-1962
Vacated				
Brazil	Czechoslovakia	3-1	Santiago	17-06-1962
Paraguay	Brazil	2-0	La Paz	17-03-1963
Bolivia	Paraguay	2-0	Cochabamba	24-03-1963
Paraguay	Bolivia	2-0	Asuncion	25-07-1965
Argentina	Paraguay	3-0	Buenos Aires	1-08-1965
Italy	Argentina	3-0	Turin	22-06-1966
Soviet Union	Italy	1-0	Sunderland	16-07-1966
West Germany	Soviet Union	2-1	Liverpool	25-07-1966
England	West Germany	4-2	London	30-07-1966
Scotland	England	3-2	London	15-04-1967
Soviet Union	Scotland	2-0	Glasgow	10-05-1967
Austria	Soviet Union	1-0	Vienna	15-10-1967
Soviet Union	Austria	3-1	Leningrad	16-06-1968
Sweden	Soviet Union		Moscow	6-08-1969
France	Sweden	3-0	Paris	1-11-1969
Switzerland	France	2-1	Basle	3-05-1970
Vacated				
Brazil	Italy	4-1	Mexico City	21-06-1970
Italy	Brazil	2-0	Rome	9-06-1973
Poland	Italy	2-1	Stuttgart	23-06-1974
West Germany	Poland	1-0	Frankfurt	3-07-1974
England	West Germany	2-0	London	12-03-1975
Czechoslovakia	England	2-1	Bratislava	30-10-1975
West Germany	Czechoslovakia	2-0	Hanover	17-11-1976
France	West Germany	1-0	Paris	23-02-1977
Rep. Ireland	France	1-0	Dublin	30-03-1977
Bulgaria	Rep. Ireland	2-0	Sofia	1-06-1977
France	Bulgaria	3-1	Paris	16-11-1977
Italy	France	2-1	Mar del Plata	2-06-1978
Netherlands	Italy	2-1	Buenos Aires	21-06-1978
Argentina	Netherlands	3-1	Buenos Aires	25-06-1978
Bolivia	Argentina	2-1	La Paz	18-07-1979
Paraguay	Bolivia	2-0	Asuncion	1-08-1979
Chile	Paraguay	1-0	Santiago	5-12-1979
Brazil	Chile	2-1	Belo Horizonte	24-06-1980
Uruguay	Brazil	2-1	Montevideo	10-01-1981
Peru	Uruguay	2-1	Montevideo	23-08-1981
Chile	Peru	2-1	Santiago	23-03-1982
Peru	Chile	1-0	Lima	30-03-1982
Poland	Peru	5-1	La Coruna	22-06-1982
Italy	Poland	2-0	Barcelona	8-07-1982
Switzerland	Italy	1-0	Rome	27-10-1982
Soviet Union	Switzerland	1-0	Lausanne	13-04-1983
Portugal	Soviet Union	1-0	Lisbon	13-11-1983
Yugoslavia	Portugal	3-2	Lisbon	2-06-1984
Belgium	Yugoslavia	2-0	Lens	13-06-1984
France	Belgium	5-0	Nantes	16-06-1984
Bulgaria	France	2-0	Sofia	2-05-1985
Netherlands	Bulgaria	1-0	Heerenveen	4-09-1985
Belgium	Netherlands	1-0	Brussels	16-10-1985
Netherlands	Belgium	2-1	Rotterdam	20-11-1985
West Germany	Netherlands	3-1	Dortmund	14-05-1986
Denmark	West Germany	2-0	Queretaro	13-06-1986
Spain	Denmark	5-1	Queretaro	18-06-1986
Belgium	Spain	1-1 5-4p	Puebla	22-06-1986
Argentina	Belgium	2-0	Mexico City	25-06-1986
Italy	Argentina	3-1	Zurich	10-06-1987
Wales	Italy	1-0	Brescia	4-06-1988
Netherlands	Wales	1-0	Amsterdam	14-09-1988
Italy	Netherlands	1-0	Rome	16-11-1988
Romania	Italy	1-0	Sibiu	29-03-1989
Poland	Romania	2-1	Warsaw	12-04-1989
England	Poland	3-0	London	3-06-1989
Uruguay	England	2-1	London	22-05-1990
Belgium	Uruguay	3-1	Verona	17-06-1990
Spain	Belgium	2-1	Verona	21-06-1990
Yugoslavia	Spain	2-1	Verona	26-06-1990
Argentina	Yugoslavia	0-0 3-2p	Florence	30-06-1990
West Germany	Argentina	1-0	Rome	8-07-1990
Wales	Germany	1-0	Cardiff	5-06-1991
Germany	Wales	4-1	Nuremberg	16-10-1991
Italy	Germany	1-0	Turin	25-03-1992
Switzerland	Italy	1-0	Berne	1-05-1993
Portugal	Switzerland	1-0	Oporto	13-10-1993
Italy	Portugal	1-0	Milan	17-11-1993
France	Italy	1-0	Naples	6-02-1994
Vacated				
Brazil	Italy	0-0 3-2p	Los Angeles	17-07-1994
Norway	Brazil	4-2	Oslo	30-05-1997
Italy	Norway	1-0	Marseille	27-06-1998
France	Italy	0-0 4-3p	Paris	3-07-1998
Russia	France	3-2	Paris	5-06-1999
Israel	Russia	4-1	Haifa	23-02-2000
Czech Republic	Israel	4-1	Prague	26-04-2000
Germany	Czech Republic	3-2	Nuremberg	3-06-2000
England	Germany	1-0	Charleroi	17-06-2000
Romania	England	3-2	Charleroi	20-06-2000
Italy	Romania	2-0	Brussels	24-06-2000
France	Italy	2-1	Rotterdam	2-07-2000
Spain	France	2-1	Valencia	28-03-2001
Netherlands	Spain	1-0	Rotterdam	27-03-2002
Vacated				
Brazil	Germany	2-0	Yokohama	30-06-2002
Paraguay	Brazil	1-0	Fortaleza	21-08-2002
Costa Rica	Paraguay	2-1	Alajuela	29-03-2003
Chile	Costa Rica	1-0	Santiago	30-04-2003
Costa Rica	Chile	1-0	San José	8-06-2003
Canada	Costa Rica	1-0	Foxboro	12-07-2003
Cuba	Canada	2-0	Foxboro	14-07-2003
Costa Rica	Cuba	3-0	Foxboro	16-07-2003
Mexico	Costa Rica	2-0	Mexico City	24-07-2003
Peru	Mexico	3-1	New Jersey	20-08-2003
Chile	Peru	2-1	Santiago	9-09-2003
Uruguay	Chile	2-1	Montevideo	15-11-2003
Jamaica	Uruguay	2-0	Kingston	18-02-2004
Nigeria	Jamaica	2-0	London	31-05-2004
Angola	Nigeria	1-0	Luanda	20-06-2004
Zimbabwe	Angola	2-0	Harare	27-03-2005
Nigeria	Zimbabwe	5-1	Abuja	8-10-2005
Romania	Nigeria	3-0	Bucharest	16-11-2005
Uruguay	Romania	2-0	Los Angeles	23-05-2006
Vacated				
Italy	France	1-1 5-3p	Berlin	9-07-2006
Croatia	Italy	2-0	Livorno	16-08-2006
Macedonia	Croatia	2-0	Skopje	17-11-2007
Israel	Macedonia	1-0	Tel Aviv	21-11-2007

APPENDIX 5 – HOW TO USE THE ALMANACK

①⇨ **Estadio Centenario, Montevideo**
7-09-2003, 16:00, 39 253, Zamora PER ⇦②

URU　　　5　0　　　BOL ⇦③

④⇨ Forlan [17], Chevanton 2 [40] [61] ⇦⑤
Abeijon [83], Bueno [88]

① Stadium and city/town where the match
was played.

② *From left to right:* Date, kick-off time,
attendance, name and nationality of
referee. Assistant referees are included for
FIFA tournaments.

③ Teams (using FIFA abbreviations) and scores.

④ Name of goal scorer and the time that the
goal was scored.

⑤ Indicates that 2 goals were scored by
Chevanton followed by the times of the
goals.

⇕

Estadio Centenario, Montevideo		
7-09-2003, 16:00, 39 253, Zamora PER		
URU	**5　0**	**BOL**
Forlan [17], Chevanton 2 [40] [61]		
Abeijon [83], Bueno [88]		

URUGUAY		BOLIVIA	
1 MUNUA Gustavo		FERNANDEZ Leonardo	21
5 SOSA Marcelo	69	PENA Juan Manuel	2
6 LOPEZ Diego		HOYOS Miguel	4
9 BUENO Carlos		SANCHEZ Oscar	5
10 LIGUERA Martin	77	ROJAS Richard	6
11 NUNEZ Richard		CRISTALDO Luis	7
14 GONZALEZ Cristian		MENDEZ Limberg	9
17 LAGO Eduardo		CASTILLO Jose	11
19 CHEVANTON Ernesto		67 RICALDI Alvaro	15
20 RECOBA Alvaro		46 RIBEIRO Luis	17
21 FORLAN Diego	76	46 MOREJON Limber	19
Tr: CARRASCO Juan Ramon		Tr: ACOSTA Nelson	
8 ABEIJON Nelson	69	46 BALDIVIESO Julio	10
15 SANCHEZ Vicente	76	46 JUSTINIANO Raul	16
16 OLIVERA Ruben	77		

	BOLIVIA	
①⇨	FERNANDEZ Leonardo 21	⇦②
	PENA Juan Manuel 2	⇦③
	HOYOS Miguel 4	
	SANCHEZ Oscar 5	
	ROJAS Richard 6	
	CRISTALDO Luis 7	
	MENDEZ Limberg 9	
	CASTILLO Jose 11	
④⇨ 67	RICALDI Alvaro 15	⇦⑤
46	RIBEIRO Luis 17	
⑥⇨ 46	MOREJON Limber 19	
	Tr: ACOSTA Nelson	⇦⑦
46	BALDIVIESO Julio 10	
46	JUSTINIANO Raul 16	⇦⑧

⇔

① Family name in capitals, followed by the
player's given name.

② Shirt number.

③ A shaded box indicates that the player
was cautioned.

④ A shaded box next to a player who has
been sent off (see below), indicates a
dismissal for two yellow cards.
A blacked-out box indicates a straight
red card.

⑤ A blacked-out box indicates the player
was dismissed at the time shown in the
centre column.

⑥ Substitution time.

⑦ Team coach/trainer.

⑧ Substitute. The time of the substitution
corresponds with the player listed in the
starting line-up.

EXPLANATION OF OTHER TERMS USED IN THE ALMANACK

In the Champions League match reports:
• indicates a booking.
•85 indicates a player was sent off (with minute).

≠90 indicates a player missed a penalty.
2✘ indicates the second penalty in a penalty
shoot-out was missed (or scored 2✓)

③ ④ ⑤

MEDALS TABLE

		Overall			League			Cup			Europe			City ②	Stadium	Cap'ty	DoF
		G	S	B	G	S	B	G	S	B	G	S	B				
1	Bayern München	39	12	14	20	7	4	13	2		6	3	10	Munich	Allianz-Arena	69 901	1900 ⇐⑦
2	1.FC Nürnberg	14	5	1	9	3		5	2				1	Nuremburg	Frankenstadion	46 780	1900
3	Schalke 04	12	16	3	7	9	1	4	7	1	↘2			Gelsenkirchen	Veltins Arena	61 524	1904

⑥

① Indicates that Bayern are the most successful team in the history of German football, above 1.FC Nürnberg in second place and Schalke in third place.
② Indicates that Bayern play in the city of Munich and use the 69,901 capacity Allianz-Arena.
③ Column G (gold) lists the total number of trophies Bayern have won – 39; Column S (silver) lists the number of times Bayern have been runners-up in the League or losing Cup Finalists - 12; Column B (bronze) lists the number of times Bayern have been finished third in the League or have been losing Cup semi-finalists.
④ This column follows the same principle as column ③ but refers only to the League.
⑤ This column follows the same principle as column ③ but refers only to the Cup.
⑥ This column follows the same principle as column ③ but refers to all three European competitions (the UEFA Champions League, the UEFA Cup and the Cup Winners Cup).
⑦ Indicates that Bayern were formed in 1900.

CHINA PR 2004

① SUPER LEAGUE	②Pl	③W	④D	⑤L	⑥F	⑦A	⑧Pts	Shenzhen	Shandong	Shanghai I	Liaoning	Dalian	Tianjin	Beijing	Shenyang	Sichuan	Shanghai S	Qingdao	Chongqing
Shenzhen Jianlibao †	22	11	9	2	30	13	42		2-1	1-0	3-0	2-2	0-1	2-0	0-0	1-1	3-1	1-0	0-0
Shandong Luneng Tai.	22	10	6	6	44	29	36	1-1		4-2	3-1	2-3	3-1	5-2	4-1	1-2	2-1	1-1	4-1
Shanghai International	22	8	8	6	39	31	32	2-2	2-1		2-1	4-0	3-0	1-1	3-1	3-2	1-1	1-0	1-2
Liaoning Zhongyu	22	10	2	10	39	40	32	1-2	2-3	2-1		1-5	1-5	1-1	1-0	0-0	5-2	3-1	3-0 ⇐⑨

15/05/2004 - 5/12/2004 • † Teams qualifying for the AFC Champions League

① Chinese champions of 2004.
All champions are listed in bold. If the club at the top of the table is not listed in bold it means that the table shown represents only part of a season. Relegated clubs are also shown in bold.
② Number of games played.
③ Number of wins.
④ Number of draws.
⑤ Number of losses.
⑥ Number of goals scored.
⑦ Number of goals conceded.
⑧ Number of points gained in the season.
⑨ This result represents the match between Liaoning Zhongyu at home and Chongqing, the away club. The home team score is listed first so Liaoning Zhongyu won 3-0 at home to Chongqing.
⑩ Dates for the season.

BRAZIL NATIONAL TEAM RECORDS AND RECORD SEQUENCES

Records			Sequence records						
Victory	10-1	BOL 1949	①	Wins	14	1997	⑤ Clean sheets	8	1989
Defeat	0-6	URU 1920	②	Defeats	4	2001	⑥ Goals scored	47	1994-1997
Player Caps	126	CAFU	③	Undefeated	43	1993-1997	⑦ Without goal	5	1990
Player Goals	77	PELE	④	Without win	7	1983-84, 1990-91	⑧ Goals against	24	1937-1944

① Number of consecutive wins.
② Number of consecutive defeats.
③ Number of consecutive games played without defeat.
④ Number of consecutive games played without a win.
⑤ Number of consecutive games played without conceding a goal.
⑥ Number of consecutive games played in which Brazil scored.
⑦ Number of consecutive games played without scoring.
⑧ Number of consecutive games played with opponent scoring.

CALENDAR OF EVENTS

FIFA AND WORLD FOOTBALL

Fixed dates for friendly internationals
20-08-2008, 19-11-2008, 11-02-2009, 12-08-2009, 3-03-2010, 11-08-2010, 17-11-2010, 9-02-2011,
10-08-2011, 29-02-2012, 15-08-2012, 14-11-2012, 6-02-2013, 14-08-2013, 5-03-2014, 13-08-2014

Fixed dates for official competitions
6/10-09-2008, 11/15-10-2008, 28-03-2009, 1-04-2009, 6/10-06-2009, 5/9-09-2009, 10/14-10-2009,
14/18-11-2009, 4/8-09-2010, 9/13-10-2010, 26/30-03-2011, 4/8-06-2011, 3/7-09-2011, 8/12-10-2011
12/16-11-2011, 8/12-09-2012, 13/17-10-2012, 23/27-03-2013, 8/12-06-2013, 7/11-09-2013,
12/16-10-2013, 16/20-11-2013, 6/10-09-2014, 11/15-11-2014

FIFA Futsal World Cup Brazil 2008
30th September to 19th October 2008

FIFA U-17 Women's World Cup New Zealand 2008
28th October to 16th November 2008

Draw for the FIFA Confederations Cup South Africa 2009
22nd November 2008 in Johannesburg

FIFA Club World Cup Japan 2008
11th to 21st December 2008

FIFA Word Player Gala 2008
12th January 2009 in Zurich

FIFA Confederations Cup South Africa 2009
14th to 29th June 2009

Draw for the 2010 FIFA World Cup South Africa
4th December 2009

2010 FIFA World Cup South Africa
11th June to 11th July 2010

THE AFC AND ASIAN FOOTBALL

AFC Asian Cup Qatar 2011
2011

CAF AND AFRICAN FOOTBALL

CAF Africa Cup of Nations Angola 2010
10th to 31st January 2010

CONCACAF

CONCACAF Gold Cup
3rd to 26th July 2009

CONMEBOL AND SOUTH AMERICAN FOOTBALL

Copa America Argentina 2011
2011

THE OFC AND FOOTBALL IN OCEANIA

OFC Nations Cup 2008
17th October 2007 to 19th November 2008

UEFA AND FOOTBALL IN EUROPE

Euro 2012 Poland/Ukraine
June 2012